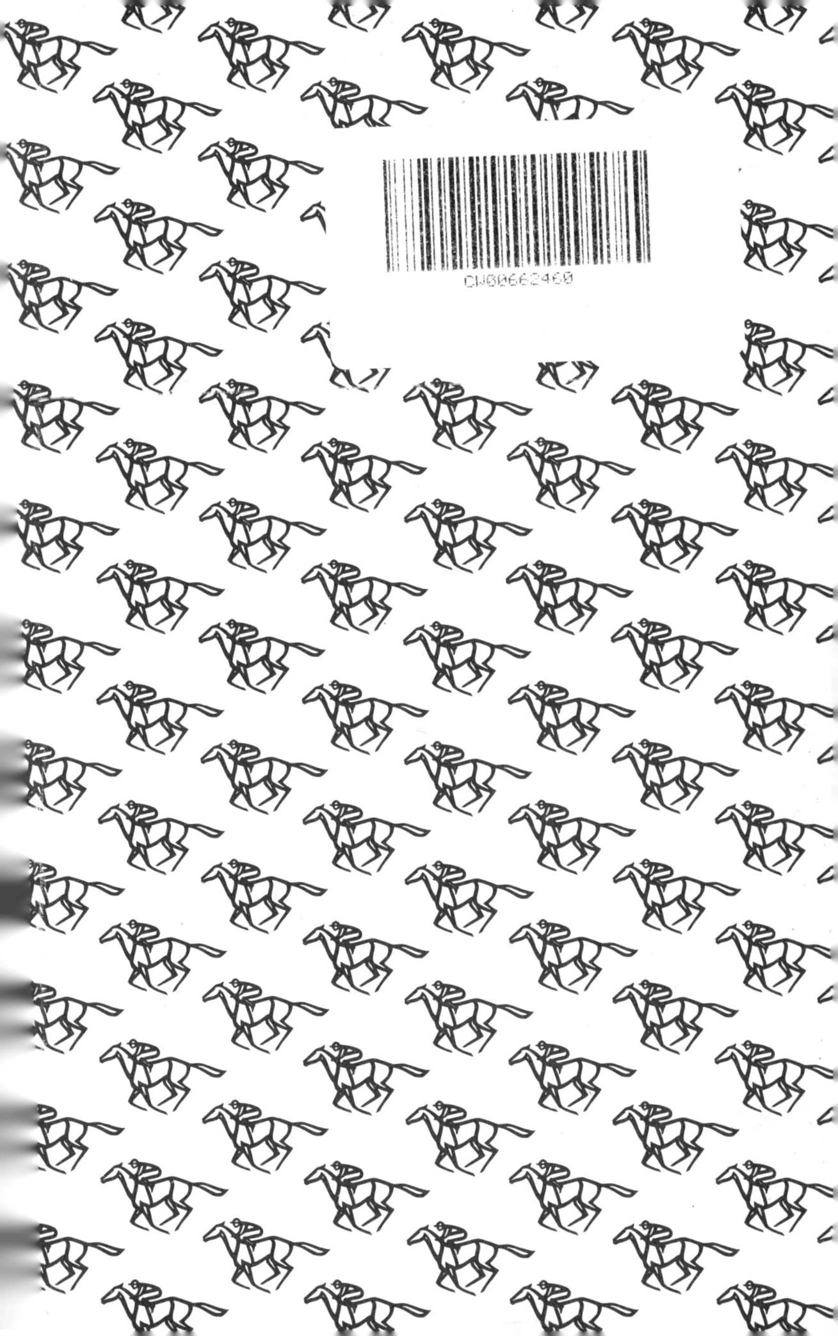
CW00662460

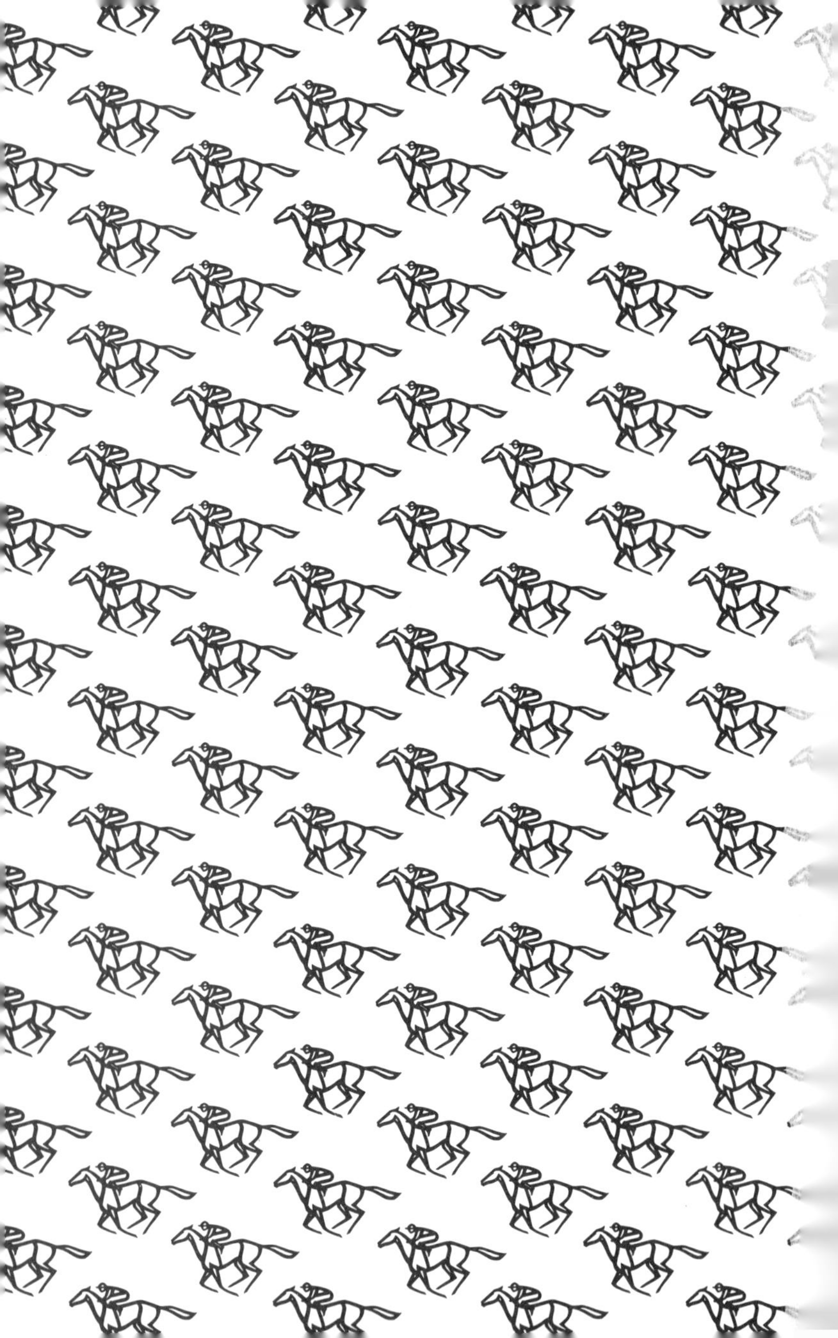

RACEHORSES OF 1995

Price £67.00

A TIMEFORM PUBLICATION

AGE, WEIGHT & DISTANCE TABLE

Timeform's scale of weight-for-age for the flat

Dist	Age	Jan		Feb		Mar		Apr		May		June	
		1-16	17-31	1-16	17-28	1-16	17-31	1-16	17-30	1-16	17-31	1-16	17-30
5f	4	10—0	10—0	10—0	10—0	10—0	10—0	10—0	10—0	10—0	10—0	10—0	10—0
	3	9—5	9—5	9—6	9—7	9—7	9—8	9—8	9—9	9—9	9-10	9-10	9-11
	2						8—0	8—1	8—3	8—4	8—5	8—6	8—7
6f	4	10—0	10—0	10—0	10—0	10—0	10—0	10—0	10—0	10—0	10—0	10—0	10—0
	3	9—2	9—3	9—4	9—5	9—5	9—6	9—7	9—7	9—8	9—8	9—9	9—9
	2									8—0	8—2	8—3	8—4
7f	4	9-13	9-13	10—0	10—0	10—0	10—0	10—0	10—0	10—0	10—0	10—0	10—0
	3	9—0	9—1	9—2	9—3	9—4	9—4	9—5	9—6	9—6	9—7	9—8	9—8
	2											7-13	8—1
1m	4	9-13	9-13	9-13	9-13	10—0	10—0	10—0	10—0	10—0	10—0	10—0	10—0
	3	8-12	8-13	9—0	9—1	9—2	9—2	9—3	9—4	9—5	9—5	9—6	9—7
	2												
9f	4	9-12	9-12	9-12	9-13	9-13	9-13	9-13	10—0	10—0	10—0	10—0	10—0
	3	8-10	8-11	8-12	8-13	9—0	9—1	9—2	9—2	9—3	9—4	9—5	9—5
	2												
1¼m	4	9-11	9-12	9-12	9-12	9-13	9-13	9-13	9-13	9-13	10—0	10—0	10—0
	3	8—8	8—9	8-10	8-11	8-12	8-13	9—0	9—1	9—2	9—2	9—3	9—4
	2												
11f	4	9-10	9-11	9-11	9-12	9-12	9-12	9-13	9-13	9-13	9-13	9-13	10—0
	3	8—6	8—7	8—8	8—9	8-10	8-11	8-12	8-13	9—0	9—1	9—2	9—2
1½m	4	9-10	9-10	9-10	9-11	9-11	9-12	9-12	9-12	9-13	9-13	9-13	9-13
	3	8—4	8—5	8—6	8—7	8—8	8—9	8-10	8-11	8-12	8-13	9—0	9—1
13f	4	9—9	9—9	9-10	9-10	9-11	9-11	9-11	9-12	9-12	9-12	9-13	9-13
	3	8—2	8—3	8—4	8—5	8—7	8—8	8—9	8-10	8-11	8-12	8-13	9—0
1¾m	4	9—8	9—8	9—9	9—9	9-10	9-10	9-11	9-11	9-12	9-12	9-12	9-13
	3	8—0	8—2	8—3	8—4	8—5	8—6	8—7	8—8	8—9	8-10	8-11	8-12
15f	4	9—7	9—8	9—8	9—9	9—9	9-10	9-10	9-11	9-11	9-11	9-12	9-12
	3	7-13	8—0	8—1	8—2	8—4	8—5	8—6	8—7	8—8	8—9	8-10	8-11
2m	4	9—6	9—7	9—7	9—8	9—9	9—9	9-10	9-10	9-11	9-11	9-11	9-12
	3	7-11	7-12	7-13	8—1	8—2	8—3	8—4	8—5	8—6	8—7	8—8	8—9
2¼m	4	9—5	9—5	9—6	9—7	9—7	9—8	9—9	9—9	9-10	9-10	9-10	9-11
	3	7—8	7—9	7-11	7-12	7-13	8—0	8—2	8—3	8—4	8—5	8—6	8—7
2½m	4	9—3	9—4	9—5	9—6	9—6	9—7	9—7	9—8	9—9	9—9	9-10	9-10
	3	7—5	7—7	7—8	7—9	7-11	7-12	7-13	8—1	8—2	8—3	8—4	8—5

For 5-y-o's and older, use 10-0 in all cases
Race distances in the above tables are shown only at 1 furlong intervals.
For races over odd distances, the nearest distance shown in the table should be used:
thus for races of 1m to 1m 109 yards, use the table weights for 1m;
for 1m 110 yards to 1m 219 yards use the 9f table

AGE, WEIGHT & DISTANCE TABLE

Timeform's scale of weight-for-age for the flat

Dist	Age	July		Aug		Sept		Oct		Nov		Dec	
		1-16	17-31	1-16	17-31	1-16	17-30	1-16	17-31	1-16	17-30	1-16	17-31
5f	4	10–0	10–0	10–0	10–0	10–0	10–0	10–0	10–0	10–0	10–0	10–0	10–0
	3	9–11	9–12	9–12	9–12	9–13	9–13	9–13	9–13	10–0	10–0	10–0	10–0
	2	8–8	8–9	8–10	8–11	8–12	8–13	9–0	9–1	9–2	9–2	9–3	9–4
6f	4	10–0	10–0	10–0	10–0	10–0	10–0	10–0	10–0	10–0	10–0	10–0	10–0
	3	9–10	9–10	9–11	9–11	9–12	9–12	9–12	9–13	9–13	9–13	9–13	10–0
	2	8–5	8–6	8–7	8–8	8–9	8–10	8–11	8–12	8–13	9–0	9–1	9–2
7f	4	10–0	10–0	10–0	10–0	10–0	10–0	10–0	10–0	10–0	10–0	10–0	10–0
	3	9–9	9–9	9–10	9–10	9–11	9–11	9–11	9–12	9–12	9–12	9–13	9–13
	2	8–2	8–3	8–4	8–5	8–6	8–7	8–9	8–10	8–11	8–12	8–13	9–0
1m	4	10–0	10–0	10–0	10–0	10–0	10–0	10–0	10–0	10–0	10–0	10–0	10–0
	3	9–7	9–8	9–8	9–9	9–9	9–10	9–10	9–11	9–11	9–12	9–12	9–12
	2			8–2	8–3	8–4	8–5	8–6	8–7	8–8	8–9	8–10	8–11
9f	4	10–0	10–0	10–0	10–0	10–0	10–0	10–0	10–0	10–0	10–0	10–0	10–0
	3	9–6	9–7	9–7	9–8	9–8	9–9	9–9	9–10	9–10	9–11	9–11	9–12
	2					8-1	8–3	8–4	8–5	8–6	8–7	8–8	8–9
1¼m	4	10–0	10–0	10–0	10–0	10–0	10–0	10–0	10–0	10–0	10–0	10–0	10–0
	3	9–5	9–5	9–6	9–7	9–7	9–8	9–8	9–9	9–9	9–10	9–10	9–11
	2							8-1	8–2	8–4	8–5	8–6	8–7
11f	4	10–0	10–0	10–0	10–0	10–0	10–0	10–0	10–0	10–0	10–0	10–0	10–0
	3	9–3	9–4	9–5	9–5	9–6	9–7	9–7	9–8	9–8	9–9	9–9	9–10
1½m	4	10–0	10–0	10–0	10–0	10–0	10–0	10–0	10–0	10–0	10–0	10–0	10–0
	3	9–2	9–2	9–3	9–4	9–5	9–5	9–6	9–7	9–7	9–8	9–9	9–9
13f	4	9–13	9–13	10–0	10–0	10–0	10–0	10–0	10–0	10–0	10–0	10–0	10–0
	3	9–0	9–1	9–2	9–3	9–4	9–4	9–5	9–6	9–6	9–7	9–8	9–8
1¾m	4	9–13	9–13	9–13	10–0	10–0	10–0	10–0	10–0	10–0	10–0	10–0	10–0
	3	8–13	9–0	9–1	9–2	9–3	9–3	9–4	9–5	9–5	9–6	9–7	9–7
15f	4	9–12	9–13	9–13	9–13	9–13	10–0	10–0	10–0	10–0	10–0	10–0	10–0
	3	8–12	8–13	9–0	9–1	9–1	9–2	9–3	9–4	9–4	9–5	9–6	9–6
2m	4	9–12	9–12	9–13	9–13	9–13	9–13	10–0	10–0	10–0	10–0	10–0	10–0
	3	8–10	8–11	8–12	8–13	9–0	9–1	9–2	9–3	9–3	9–4	9–5	9–5
2¼m	4	9–11	9–12	9–12	9–12	9–13	9–13	9–13	9–13	10–0	10–0	10–0	10–0
	3	8–8	8–9	8–10	8–11	8–12	8–13	9–0	9–1	9–2	9–2	9–3	9–4
2½m	4	9–10	9–11	9–11	9–12	9–12	9–12	9–13	9–13	9–13	9–13	10–0	10–0
	3	8–6	8–7	8–8	8–9	8–10	8–11	8–12	8–13	9–0	9–1	9–2	9–3

For 5-y-o's and older, use 10-0 in all cases
Race distances in the above tables are shown only at 1 furlong intervals.
For races over odd distances, the nearest distance shown in the table should be used:
thus for races of 1m to 1m 109 yards, use the table weights for 1m;
for 1m 110 yards to 1m 219 yards use the 9f table

CONTENTS

Compiled and produced by

G. Greetham, B.A., G. F. Walton, Dip.A.D. (Directors), J. D. Newton, B.A. (Editor-in-Chief), R. J. C. Austen, B.A. (Editor), E. K. Wilkinson (Editor), D. Cleary, B.A., S. N. Copeland, LL.B., J. Ingles, B.A., G. M. Johnstone, G. J. North, B.Sc., R. O'Brien B.A., O. C. Pennant Jones, B.A., S. D. Rowlands, B.A., R. Todd, C. S. Williams and C. Wright, B.A.

ISBN 0 900599 81 2

Racehorses of 1995

Introduction

'There's nothing like the sight of an old enemy down on his luck' (Euripides). The racing year 1995, dominated by fiscal topics, saw 'the old enemy' experiencing some of the most difficult trading conditions for many a year. With racing's finances threatened as a consequence, the bookmakers once again found themselves in the dock, accused, it seemed at times, of being the source of nearly all racing's ills. If only *all* the bookmakers' profits, some say, were to accrue directly to racing, rather than to outside shareholders, the financial problems of racing would be solved overnight. Such a view stems from the belief that the 'horseracing industry', the blanket term encompassing those involved in staging horseracing, not only has every right to a share of the money that is bet on it, but indeed that such money *belongs* to racing. Bookmakers are depicted as 'extracting huge sums of money *from* the horseracing industry' and calls are made for profits made out of betting to be 'ploughed *back* into racing.' It is nonsense, of course. What the punters bet is their own money, and the bookmakers are entitled to the money they earn for providing betting services. The 'horseracing industry' has absolutely no prior claim on it, though we daresay most off-course punters do not object strongly to supporting racing's finances through the payment of the small statutory levy on their bets—in spite of the fact that they have very little say in racing. The 'industry', and the bookmakers for that matter, have been guilty of taking the punters for granted, believing that most of them are hooked on the game, victims of their own optimism, passion and loyalty. The actions of a proportion in the latest flat season should have shaken the complacency and brought home the simple truth that horseracing has to compete with other gambling and leisure pursuits. The bookmakers' troubled year—Ladbrokes made two hundred redundancies, most at their headquarters, and Hills announced drastic cuts in their sponsorship programme—showed that the punters and the money they bet on racing cannot be taken for granted. As in any commercial activity, the customer casts the final vote, and in 1995 a disturbing number of votes swung against racing. A study by the Henley Centre, an independent research organisation, forecast in October that betting turnover on horseracing and bookmakers' profits, hit during 1995, would continue to fall. Betting, which employed around 40,000 people in 1994 when there were 9,300 betting shops in Britain, had been expected to put 6% on turnover in 1995; the Henley Centre estimated that turnover for the year would instead be down by over 9% on the projected forecast, leading, without Government help, to the *possible* closure of 2,400 betting shops and the loss of 7,400 jobs. Little wonder that the director-general of the Betting Office Licensees' Association Tom Kelly described 1995 as 'a bloody awful year for bookmaking.'

Bookmakers in search of scapegoats for their troubles didn't have far to look. The national lottery, introduced in November 1994 and drawn each Saturday, and, more importantly, the lottery's instant scratch cards, introduced in March 1995, were widely held responsible. The lottery—which plans to introduce a mid-week draw as well in 1996—absorbed cash, as it was certain to do, though betting on racing was better placed than most forms of gambling to stave off the effects. One major bingo operator, for example, reported turnover down by 15% in 1995. Winning at bingo is pure chance, like the lottery, but the major appeal of betting on racing—one that isn't used enough as a selling point—is that the element of pure chance is relatively low. The appeal of betting on the horses goes deeper for most punters than simply the hope of material reward; the vast majority base their betting on some sort of form study, and the fact that betting on racing offers the scope for winning the battle with the bookmakers through the exercise of knowledge, skill and judgement accounts largely for its popularity as an entertainment and a relaxation. But the quality of racing itself has a role in determining not just racecourse attendances but the level of betting off course as well, and here there are grounds for believing that the lottery was not the only cause of the fall in betting turnover. Evidence of disillusionment, particularly with the extensive flat-racing programme, could be found in the letters columns of the racing Press throughout the summer and the same dissatisfaction was apparent from our own research and other research conducted for articles on the subject. Ask almost anyone, it seemed, and they'd agree: there is now too much racing in the summer, which leads to an abundance of mediocre programmes; too much poor quality racing and too many races going off close together, particularly in the new crowded weekend programme (five meetings most Fridays and upwards of six on Saturdays). Punters could not take it all in and were uninspired by the poor horses, causing some to become frustrated and turn away. They won't all return. It is interesting that at least one of the major bookmakers reported just as sharp a dip in credit betting—much less likely to be attributed to the effects of the lottery—as in cash transactions in its betting shops. Bookmakers seeking to make up lost ground are likely to look increasingly at other sports, particularly those with good TV coverage, which have already generated considerable business for the new spread betting companies. The launch of William Hill Index is a pointer.

Heavy criticism from the 'great mediocre racing debate' didn't impress the British Horseracing Board, however. The BHB's chief executive Tristram Ricketts dismissed the complaints, saying in a BBC TV interview: 'There is one word to describe the shortfall in turnover—lottery!' David Oldrey, the BHB's race planning director, displayed a similarly cavalier attitude, producing a plethora of statistics to counter criticism of the racing programme. How many businesses would respond in such a way to complaints from customers? However misguided the BHB thinks its critics may be, it cannot deny that the fixture list has become the Topsy of British racing. It has 'just growed', the number of races staged on the flat in 1995 being almost 40% higher than ten years earlier (when there was no all-weather), most of the additional races inevitably catering for modest horses and arguably contributing to the loss of appetite for flat racing in 1995. The year saw an increase in evening fixtures (many of them switched from midweek afternoons despite gaps there in the fixture criteria thought ideal for 'generating' betting turnover) and all-weather fixtures, new summer fixtures over the jumps and, of course, the Sunday fixtures introduced in 1995 for the first time with betting. Unfortunately, as we said in *Racehorses of 1994*, a staple diet of low-grade handicaps and poor-quality condition races, the cornerstone of the BHB's 'competitive racing initiative', is the only way racing can service its ever-expanding fixture list on the flat. More races than ever are framed for poor horses—horses that would formerly have been rated a dash in this Annual are now given ratings in the 20's because such horses can win races—but is such a state of affairs a help or a hindrance in 'selling' the sport to the public? Weighing up some of the races nowadays boils down to trying to work out which is likely to prove the 'least worst' of a bad bunch. Some races are so unappealing that they virtually invite punters *not* to bet on them. The expanded racing programme is, of course, a further encouragement to owners—following the surprising 1993 Government concessions on VAT estimated by the BHB to be worth about £20m a year—and is also 'turnstile-friendly' in that more fixtures are staged when the public can attend, notably on evenings and Sundays. But the BHB also identifies the off-course punters as one of its 'key customer groups'. Racing as a whole is not self-sustaining, in the sense that it can be financed entirely from racecourse admission charges. The promotion of race meetings is heavily dependent on subsidy from the Levy Board, which presently takes around £50m each year from punters. Fewer punters means less money for racing and the Levy Board announced cuts for 1996, including across-the-board reductions of £3.4m in minimum prize money values, because of the declining betting turnover. Keeping existing punters in the game, as well as encouraging new ones, is a necessity.

There was a good response to the heavily promoted 'Sunday is Funday' marketing initiative in 1995 when racecourses set out to cater for families. They were rewarded with big crowds, including 20,000 for One Thousand Guineas day at Newmarket and a post-war record of 10,000 at Salisbury on the same day, British racing's first Sunday with betting. Later in the summer 38,000 attended a Sunday fixture at Chester and 16,000, another post-war record, turned up at Pontefract. Support for Sunday racing in the betting shops was lukewarm. Ladbrokes shops were closed for two racing Sundays in August, though a request, supported by the 'Big Three' bookmakers, for SIS not to broadcast pictures on those days was quite rightly turned down after protests from independent bookmakers. The BHB, worried that falling betting turnover would result in the prize-money cuts eventually announced by the Levy Board, favoured pressing the Chancellor in his November budget for a 1¾% cut in betting duty including a transfer of ¾% to the levy. The bookmakers, who campaigned for a straight 2%

'Sunday is Funday'—Chester's Sunday meeting in July attracted a crowd of 38,000

reduction in betting tax to be passed directly on to the customer in an attempt to stimulate turnover, took a dim view, saying that while they were calling for a lifeboat, the BHB was expecting the QE2! The Levy Board called for a 2¾% cut—including ½% to the levy—to bring betting duty into line with that on other forms of gambling such as the lottery and casinos. Though the BHB, the bookmakers and the Levy Board made separate submissions in July, they did make a joint presentation to the Government in October which concentrated on the *arguments* for a cut, rather than on the specific figures. The Chancellor was indeed persuaded that a reduction in betting duty was required to offset the effects on betting turnover of the introduction of the lottery—the taxation of betting on horses, in real terms, was 34% compared with the lottery at 24%—but he announced only a 1% cut in off-course betting duty, from 7¾% to 6¾%. The Chancellor told Parliament that the benefits 'should be spread between the betting industry and the horse and greyhound racing industries' and left it to the three groups to reach agreement on the division. The BHB's chairman-elect Lord Wakeham went on record as saying 'Racing must—and let there be no doubt it will—secure its fair and direct share of the funds released by the duty reduction'; the bookmakers, on the other hand, argued that racing should accept the indirect benefit arising from the anticipated increase in turnover. The Henley Centre had regarded a 2% cut in betting duty as necessary to return betting turnover to the projected position in 1995. Given a choice between a tax reduction for the punter or more prize-money for racehorse owners, it was never a serious contest. Owners may or may not have a case for a better deal, but it is impossible to justify that their lot should be rectified at the expense of punters who pay a penal rate of tax on bets placed off course. The Chancellor intimated as much some days later when making plain his intention that punters should receive a 1% deduction in betting tax. From March 1st 1996, deductions from off-course bets, which also include a payment to the levy and a sum to cover bookmakers' overheads, will come down from 10p in the pound to 9p. The Bookmakers' Committee proposed, however, in discussions with the BHB and the Levy Board, to contribute an extra 15p per £100 of horseracing turnover to the levy, bringing the levy yield at the top rate to around 1½%. If implemented, and if other bookmakers follow suit, it is estimated that an additional £4.5m could be provided for the levy.

Reproduced by kind permission of The Daily Telegraph

'I'd like to put £5 on Labour to win the next election'

Although both the BHB and the bookmakers have reaffirmed their intention to lobby for another reduction in betting duty in 1996, it would be as well if racing did more for itself in the meantime. Making the fixture list and the racing itself 'punter friendly' deserves a much higher priority.The Chancellor had transferred a ¼% cut in betting duty directly to the levy in 1992 but seemed unconvinced by the BHB's argument for a similar concession in 1995 despite concerted lobbying. Therefore, stimulating the off-course betting market and increasing turnover remains the only way to increase the yield from the levy. The bookmakers need to play their part by fostering the goodwill of their customers, rather than seeking salvation through a combination of 'turning the screw' on punters and looking towards further deregulation, such as allowing amusement machines in betting shops. Fruit machines won't contribute a penny to racing's finances and will serve only to encourage the 'lottery' mentality, reducing gambling to a question of chance rather than skill. Pointing out to punters the shocking odds offered by the lottery scratch cards—as was done on SIS screens during the year—isn't going to be enough. In a blatant stifling of competition, the Government continues to restrain bookmakers from competing on level terms with the national lottery. There is still, most obviously, a ban on radio and TV advertising. The bookmakers must therefore strive even harder to offer better value and a better service. Early prices on more races (coupled with a guarantee to lay those prices for longer), earlier first-show prices from the track, a continuation of the move towards tidy and friendly betting shops with plenty of seating (even no-smoking branches), a better service for first-time backers (a field in which innovation is largely absent)—these are among some of the ideas that might be worth pursuing. If the problems are not addressed urgently, the fatted calf will surely lose more condition!

The baking hot weather and accompanying drought did nothing to help flat racing in 1995. Firm going kept many horses off the course, while the stifling weather itself probably kept some regulars out of the betting shops in high summer. July was one of the five hottest on record and August set a new record for mean monthly temperatures in central England. The summer was one of the driest since records began in England and Wales, with less than a fifth of the normal rainfall in the three-month period from June to August. The artificial watering systems almost universally in use nowadays on Britain's racecourses played a big part in racing's battle with the elements, though they are not without problems, which are discussed in the essay on **Bahri**, whose victory in the Queen Elizabeth II Stakes owed much to a wonderful piece of opportunism by his rider Willie Carson. Bahri was one of the season's top milers but he was flattered by his six-length victory at Ascot over the top filly at the trip **Ridgewood Pearl**, subsequent winner of the Breeders' Cup Mile. **Pennekamp**, not seen out after injuring himself in the Derby, put up the best performance of the season at a mile when winning the Two Thousand Guineas in May, with Bahri back in third. Bahri went on to win the St James's Palace Stakes at Royal Ascot where he was one of five winners saddled by John Dunlop whose combined win-and-place earnings edged him in front in the 1995 official trainers' championship. One Thousand Guineas winner **Harayir** was put in her place by Ridgewood Pearl when they met in the Irish One Thousand and the Coronation Stakes at Royal Ascot, while **Miss Satamixa** (in whose essay François Boutin's career is recalled) and **Sayyedati** also showed better form among the fillies who raced at a mile. Harayir had

Sheikh Mohammed leads in Lammtarra (Walter Swinburn) after the Derby

a marvellous season nonetheless, contributing four of her owner Sheikh Hamdan's twenty British pattern-race victories during 1995, a record. As well as Bahri and Harayir, Sheikh Hamdan had a third Group 1 winner in the shape of the top two-year-old **Alhaarth** whose five successive victories included four in pattern company. His closest rival for top spot among the two-year-olds was the similarly-unbeaten Coventry, Gimcrack and Middle Park winner **Royal Applause**, owned by another member of the Al Maktoum family Sheikh Maktoum. The two leading fillies **Blue Duster** and **Bosra Sham** were also Arab-owned, the former by Sheikh Mohammed whose 'Dubai experiment' burst to fruition in 1995. The successes under the Godolphin banner were headed by the Derby, King George and Prix de l'Arc winner **Lammtarra** whose achievements deservedly earned him the Horse of the Year title, though the consistent **Pentire** ran him close at Ascot and **Freedom Cry** gave him a good race at Longchamp. The Godolphin-trained horses collected important races in six countries, which included other European classic victories from

Champion two-year-old Alhaarth cantering to the start before the Dewhurst Stakes

Vettori, **Moonshell** (in whose essay the Godolphin story is traced) and **Classic Cliche**, while **Halling** (Coral-Eclipse & Juddmonte International) and **So Factual** (Nunthorpe) also won Group 1 races in Britain. Vettori, Moonshell and Classic Cliche had all been in the care of Henry Cecil as two-year-olds. Cecil's split with Sheikh Mohammed in October, dealt with in the essay on the two-year-old **Mark of Esteem**, was one of the most dramatic news stories of the year. Classic Cliche's St Leger victory provided champion jockey Lanfranco Dettori with the thousandth winner of his career. The effervescent and popular Dettori, who went on to top the two-hundred-winner mark in a season for the second time, is a real asset to British racing.

Coincidentally, on St Leger weekend Lester Piggott, who hadn't ridden during the season, announced what should be his final retirement from the saddle. His total of 4,493 winners in Britain (including a record-breaking thirty classics) has been bettered only by Sir Gordon Richards, and the BBC Sports Review of the Year programme marked the end of an era with a special award for 'an utterly unique talent.' The fact that during his monumental career Piggott never won the main Sports Personality of the Year trophy, determined by a poll of TV viewers, puts racing's popularity in context. Racing is fortunate that most national newspapers still provide space, especially for race cards, out of all proportion to the level of reader-interest. The sports editor of *The Daily Telegraph* David Welch is among those who have warned more than once about the consequences of what he terms the 'outrageous increase in fixtures'. 'The more dross that is encouraged in the form of minor meetings, the more the opportunity diminishes for newspapers to glamorise the major occasions, and so sell the sport to the public,' says Welch. 'By sanctioning nine race meetings on Derby weekend—including three National Hunt fixtures and one on the all-weather—the BHB made it difficult for many newspapers to present the Derby in the high-profile way such a showpiece deserves. The Derby was competing for space, not just with the rest of the weekend sport, but against competition of the BHB's own making—second-rate meetings at Market Rasen, Worcester, Uttoxeter and Wolverhampton. As for the Epsom Sunday fixture, many would not have known it was on, with so little space available in national newspapers to devote to it'. Some sports editors have already responded by abbreviating or even omitting some minor cards—with barely any adverse reaction from regular readers—and it seems inevitable that others will follow.

Double Trigger (Jason Weaver)— 'number one' after victory in the Gold Cup

Vindaloo—eleven wins in 1995

With the pattern of racing laying emphasis on horses whose best distances are at a mile to a mile and a half, the top sprinters and stayers seldom receive the publicity they deserve. In 1995 we had **Lake Coniston**'s outstanding victory in the July Cup which looked, at one time, as if it might end up being the highest rated performance of the year by *any* horse and **Double Trigger**'s stayers' triple crown which gave a timely boost to the Cup races. Both horses, backed up by the likes of those tough fillies **Hever Golf Rose** and **Cherokee Rose** among the sprinters and **Further Flight** (who won the Jockey Club Cup for the fifth time) among the stayers, served as reminders of the marvellous entertainment that can be provided by good sprinters and stayers. And talking of entertainment, mention should be made of the durable three-year-old gelding **Vindaloo** who won more races than any other horse on the flat in Britain in 1995, eleven in all, and provided the headline writers with plenty of scope for a play on words as he went in 'hot pursuit' of the twentieth-century record for the most successes in handicap company in a single season (he equalled the nine victories of Star Rage, Chaplin's Club and Glencroft).

And, finally, **Celtic Swing**. The glowing tribute to him in *Racehorses of 1994* and our mistaken belief that he would win the Guineas (Pennekamp beat him a head) were born out of our interpretation of his twelve-length victory in the Racing Post Trophy. The Guineas result must have been a big disappointment to the many subscribers who backed Celtic Swing, and while he went on to win his Derby (at Chantilly though, not at Epsom), it was clear that, as a three-year-old, he was not the outstanding champion the racing world had been led to expect by huge media coverage. Timeform was roundly criticised in some quarters, John McCririck of Channel 4, for instance, castigating us and claiming that Celtic Swing's Guineas defeat was 'Timeform's blackest hour' and Monty Court of *The Sporting Life* saying that it was 'because of Timeform's exemplary reputation that the phenomenal Celtic Swing epic went out of control....once the Halifax firm had given the colt its seal of approval, half the racing media stopped thinking for themselves'. Court went on to say 'I doubt that Timeform will ever take such an indulgent view of a two-year-old again or allow such hyperbole in one of its publications'. Not everyone saw it the way McCririck and Court did. One subscriber, for example, wrote to Timeform 'It does not worry me in the least that Celtic Swing will not now win an English classic and that therefore what was written in *Racehorses of 1994* will not turn out to be quite correct. Many of your judgements are vindicated and it is no matter, and quite natural, that some turn out to be wrong. A great part of Timeform's reputation rests on your readiness to express a plain opinion and it would be far, far worse to beat about the bush in your pronouncements'. The editorial policy of Timeform has always been, and will continue to be, aimed at precision in both our thinking and in the setting out of our views. It is exceedingly rare for us to have expressed a confidence as strong as that which we did in Celtic Swing, but then again it is exceedingly rare to come across a two-year-old like him. Horses aren't machines, but Celtic Swing had certainly looked close to being one, earning a Timeform rating which hadn't been bettered by a two-year-old for more than forty years.

There is one major change to **Racehorses** this year. In line with our stated intention, we are producing, for the first time, a new 'Timeform Statistical Review' which makes statistics available covering the 1993, 1994 and 1995 flat seasons, allowing more meaningful conclusions to be drawn. To enable us to provide comprehensive and easy-to-read statistics the 'Timeform Statistical Review' (£19.95 but provided free to all Racehorses subscribers) is published in a soft bound, A4 format, which means we have discontinued the practice of providing a slip case with the Racehorses Annual.

March 1996

'Can I do this, and cannot get a crown?'—Celtic Swing in April

TIMEFORM CHAMPIONS OF 1995

HORSE OF THE YEAR
BEST THREE-YEAR-OLD COLT
BEST MIDDLE-DISTANCE HORSE
RATED AT 134

LAMMTARRA (USA)

3 ch.c. Nijinsky – Snow Bride (Blushing Groom)
Owner Saeed Maktoum Al Maktoum Trainer Saeed bin Suroor

BEST TWO-YEAR-OLD FILLY RATED AT 116p

BLUE DUSTER (USA)

2 b.f. Danzig – Blue Note (Habitat)
Owner Sheikh Mohammed Trainer D. R. Loder

BEST TWO-YEAR-OLD COLT RATED AT 126p

ALHAARTH (IRE)

2 b.c. Unfuwain – Irish Valley (Irish River)
Owner Hamdan Al Maktoum Trainer Major W. R. Hern

BEST THREE-YEAR-OLD FILLY RATED AT 125

RIDGEWOOD PEARL

3 ch.f. Indian Ridge – Ben's Pearl (Tap On Wood)
Owner Mrs Anne Coughlan Trainer J. Oxx

BEST OLDER MALE RATED AT 132

FREEDOM CRY

4 b.c. Soviet Star – Falling Star (Mount Hagen)
Owner Mr D. Wildenstein Trainer A. Fabre

BEST OLDER FEMALE RATED AT 123

HEVER GOLF ROSE

4 b.f. Efisio – Sweet Rosina (Sweet Revenge)
Owner Mr M. P. Hanson Trainer T. J. Naughton

TIMEFORM CHAMPIONS OF 1995

BEST SPRINTER RATED AT 131

LAKE CONISTON (IRE)

4 b.c. Bluebird – Persian Polly (Persian Bold)
Owner Highclere Thoroughbred Racing Ltd   Trainer G. Lewis

BEST MILER RATED AT 130

PENNEKAMP (USA)

3 b.c. Bering – Coral Dance (Green Dancer)
Owner Sheikh Mohammed   Trainer A. Fabre

BEST STAYERS RATED AT 122

DOUBLE TRIGGER (IRE)

4 ch.c Ela-Mana-Mou – Solac (Gay Lussac)
Owner Mr R. W. Huggins   Trainer M. Johnston

MOONAX (IRE)

4 ch.c. Caerleon – Moonsilk (Solinus)
Owner Godolphin   Trainer B. W. Hills

STRATEGIC CHOICE (USA)

4 b.c. Alleged – Danlu (Danzig)
Owner Mr M. Arbib   Trainer P. F. I. Cole

BEST PERFORMANCES IN HANDICAPS IN BRITAIN

Sprint Distances: **BRANSTON ABBY ran to 115**
Won Lawrence Batley Rated Stakes at York

7–9 Furlongs: **CAP JULUCA ran to 117**
Won William Hill Cambridgeshire at Newmarket

Middle Distances: **MIDNIGHT LEGEND ran to 118**
Won Schroders Glorious Rated Stakes at Goodwood

Staying Distances: **BOLD GAIT ran to 114**
Won 'Newcastle Brown Ale' Northumberland Plate at Newcastle

BEST PERFORMANCE ON ALL-WEATHER IN BRITAIN

PRINCE OF ANDROS ran to 113
Won Bass Wulfrun Stakes at Wolverhampton

THE TIMEFORM 'TOP HUNDRED'

Here are listed the 'Top 100' two-year-olds, three-year-olds and older horses in the annual.

Two-Year-Olds

126p Alhaarth
123p Royal Applause
117 Danehill Dancer
116p Blue Duster
116p Lord of Men
116 Tagula
115p Bosra Sham
114p Beauchamp King
114p Miss Tahiti
113p Loup Solitaire
113p Manninamix
113+ Titus Livius
112p Ragmar
112 Kahir Almaydan
112 Polaris Flight
111p Ashkalani
111p Eternity Range
111 Barricade
111 Go Between
111 Le Triton
111 With Fascination
110p Supreme Com'der
110? Oliviero
110 Almaty
110 Battle Dore
110 Even Top
110 Mons
110 Shake The Yoke
110 Solar Crystal
110 Woodborough
109p Polar Lights
109 Cayman Kai
109 Le Tourron
109 Lucky Lionel
108p Contare
108p Force of Will
108p Russian Revival
108 Allied Forces
108 Deed of Love
108 Mubhij
107p Lavirco
107p Occupandiste
107p South Salem
107 Dance Design
107 More Royal
107 Rio Duvida
107 Starmaniac
106p Astor Place
106p Bijou d'Inde
106p Massada
106p Spinning World
106 Committal
106 Esquive
106 My Branch
106 Tumbleweed Ridge
105p Applaud
105p Bint Shadayid
105p Cliptomania
105p Glory of Dancer
105p Mark of Esteem
105p Ruznama
105+ Winter Quarters
105? Iamus
105 Dance Sequence
105 Mawwal
104p Bint Salsabil
104p Blue Iris
104p Storm Trooper
104 Blushing Gleam
104 Inchrory
104 Like A Hawk
103p Deynawari
103p Lidanna
103p Luna Wells
103p Priory Belle
103 Catch A Glimpse
103 Mayoumbe
103 Raisonnable
103 Seattle Special
103 Shining Molly
103 Sweet Robin
103 Take A Left
103 World Premier
102p Ahkaam
102p Mick's Love
102+ Flying Squaw
102 Harghar
102 My Melody Parkes
102 Radevore
102 Ramooz
102 Resounder
101p Apple Musashi
101p Line Dancer
101p Maid For The Hills
101 Darling Flame
101 Gaitero
101 Kuantan
101 Rambling Bear
101 Tamnia
101 Wedding Gift
100P Pivotal
100p Anthelia
100p Bonarelli
100p Brave Indigo
100p Busy Flight
100p Desert Boy
100p Gentilhomme
100p Lomberto
100p Martiniquais
100p Najiya
100p Scarlet Plume
100p Sheraka
100p Wisam
100 Jedaal
100 Kafhar
100 Latin Reign
100 Prevail
100 Tarte Aux Pommes
100 Thrilling Day

Three-Year-Olds

134 Lammtarra
132 Pentire
130 Pennekamp
129 Celtic Swing
128 Swain
126 Spectrum
125 Bahri
125 Ridgewood Pearl
125 Tamure
124 Timarida
123 Miss Satamixa
123 Solon
122 Housamix
122 Montjoy
122 Riyadian
122 Shaanxi
122 Valanour
121 Definite Article
121 Desert Style
121 Flemensfirth
121 Poliglote
121 Pure Grain
121 Singspiel
121 Winged Love
120p De Quest
120 Annus Mirabilis
120 Classic Cliche
120 Diamond Mix
120 Eltish
120 Luso
120 Presenting
120 Shemaran
119 Affidavit
119 Angel In My Heart
119 Carling
119 Diffident
119 Harayir

119	Labeeb
119	Matiara
119	Oscar Schindler
119	Pipe Major
119	Posidonas
119	Tamayaz
119	Vettori
118	Adjareli
118	Atticus
118	Court of Honour
118	Fahal
118	Helmsman
118	Mind Games
118	Slicious
118	Smolensk
117p	Cap Juluca
117	Moonshell
117	Nwaamis
117	Poplar Bluff
117	Torrential
117	Valley of Gold
117	Walk On Mix
116p	All My Dreams
116p	Charnwood Forest
116p	Sebastian
116	Aqaarid
116	Balanka
116	Citadeed
116	Humbel
116	Larrocha
116	Muncie
116	Prince Arthur
116	Song of Tara
116	Tryphosa
115p	Bobinski
115	Dance A Dream
115	Dance Partner
115	Diaghilef
115	Don Corleone
115	Double Eclipse
115	Easy Option
115	Fanjica
115	Garden Rose
115	Minds Music
115	Petit Poucet
115	Solar One
114	Bishop of Cashel
114	Caramba
114	Gold And Steel
114	Ihtiram
114	Istidaad
114	Privity
114	Rifapour
114	Vadlamixa
113p	Russian Snows
113	Bin Rosie
113	Burden of Proof
113	Kalabo
113	Macanal
113	Munwar
113	Nautical Pet
113	Peckinpah's Soul
113	Royal Solo
113	Tamise
113	Tereshkova
113	Warning Shadows

Older Horses

132	Freedom Cry
131	Halling
131	Lake Coniston
129	Carnegie
128	Lando
125	Green Tune
125	Hernando
125	Pelder
124	Muhtarram
124d	Tikkanen
123	Germany
123	Hever Golf Rose
123	Missed Flight
122	Cherokee Rose
122	Double Trigger
122	Moonax
122	Sayyedati
122	Strategic Choice
122	Sunshack
121	Broadway Flyer
121	Millkom
121	Only Royale
121	Piccolo
121	Red Bishop
121	Soviet Line
120	Alderbrook
120	Always Earnest
120	Beauchamp Hero
120	Gunboat Diplomacy
120	Marildo
120	Partipral
120	So Factual
120	Sternkoenig
120	Vintage Crop
120	Young Ern
119	Balanchine
119	Flagbird
119	Monsun
119	Needle Gun
119	Nononito
119	Owington
119	Time Star
118	Branston Abby
118	Just Happy
118	Kaldounevees
118	Laroche
118	Midnight Legend
118	Royal Abjar
117	Darnay
117	Heart Lake
117	La Confederation
117	Richard of York
117	Solid Illusion
117	The Little Thief
117	Volochine
116	Alriffa
116	Cool Jazz
116	Desert Shot
116	Emperor Jones
116	Mr Martini
116	Nicolotte
116	Prince of Andros
116	Protektor
116	Sacrament
116	Tot Ou Tard
116	Ya Malak
115	Bin Ajwaad
115	Caballo
115	Concepcion
115	Dance Turn
115	Dernier Empereur
115	Further Flight
115	Hollywood Dream
115	Magical Retreat
115	Nec Plus Ultra
115	Shrewd Idea
115	Triarius
114	Agathe
114	Baron Ferdinand
114	Beat of Drums
114	Bold Gait
114	Captain Horatius
114	Eveningperformance
114	Hushang
114	Millyant
114	Overbury
114	Parthian Springs
114	Suave Tern
114	Sylvan Point
114	Tuesday's Special
114	Wind In Her Hair
114	Wizard King
113	Al Mohaajir
113	Assessor
113	Environment Friend
113	Hard To Figure
113	Ionio
113	Kornado
113	Lake Storm
113	Les Boyer
113	Linney Head
113	Morigi
113	Ridgewood Ben
113	Sand Reef
113	Shambo
113	Solidoun
113	Welsh Liberty
113	Wessam Prince
113	Zilzal Zamaan

1995 STATISTICS

The following tables show the leading owners, trainers, jockeys, and sires of winners on the flat in Britain during 1995 (Jan 1-Dec 31). The prize-money statistics, compiled by *Timeform*, relate to win-money only, which has traditionally been used to decide the trainers' championship. The jockeys' championship has traditionally been decided by the number of winners.

	OWNERS	*Horses*	*Races Won*	*Stakes £*
1	Mr Hamdan Al Maktoum	208	169	1,784,782
2	Sheikh Mohammed	191	119	993,434
3	Mr Saeed Maktoum Al Maktoum	1	2	783,260
4	Godolphin	27	14	774,288
5	Maktoum Al Maktoum	90	42	504,578
6	Mr K. Abdulla	70	41	445,402
7	Lord Weinstock & Simon Weinstock	20	18	359,609
8	Mollers Racing	5	9	268,214
9	Mr R. W. Huggins	7	8	246,412
10	Mr E. Penser	5	8	236,035
11	HRH Prince Fahd Salman	58	34	220,371
12	Cheveley Park Stud	47	29	215,179

	TRAINERS (by earnings)	*Horses*	*Individual Winners*	*Stakes £*
1	Saeed Bin Suroor	23	9	1,691,705
2	J. L. Dunlop	143	71	1,425,469
3	M. Johnston	133	57	804,045
4	M. R. Stoute	125	49	749,619
5	R. Hannon	219	83	749,506
6	B. W. Hills	115	49	701,892
7	H. R. A. Cecil	120	63	584,434
8	J. H. M. Gosden	140	62	551,172
9	P. F. I. Cole	127	56	485,113
10	C. E. Brittain	90	33	480,840
11	D. R. Loder	54	30	451,794
12	P. W. Chapple-Hyam	80	32	451,709

Note: J. L. Dunlop headed the list, taking win and place money into account.

	TRAINERS (by winners)	*Races Won*	*Runs*	*%*
1	J. L. Dunlop	126	628	20.0
2	R. Hannon	115	1055	10.9
3	M. Johnston	113	783	14.4
4	J. H. M. Gosden	86	400	21.5
5	H. R. A. Cecil	83	336	24.7
6	P. F. I. Cole	77	528	14.5
7	B. W. Hills	74	473	15.6
8	M. R. Stoute	73	415	17.5
9	J. Berry	72	706	10.1
10	M. R. Channon	71	588	12.0
11	Mrs M. Reveley	68	505	13.4
12	R. Hollinshead	59	607	9.7

JOCKEYS (by winners)	*1st*	*2nd*	*3rd*	*Unpl*	*Total Mts*	*%*
1 L. Dettori	216	164	139	485	1004	21.5
2 K. Darley	148	125	123	515	911	16.2
3 J. Weaver	144	135	127	552	958	15.0
4 W. Carson	139	91	93	393	716	19.4
5 Pat Eddery	125	79	74	368	646	19.3
6 T. Quinn	111	97	109	521	838	13.2
7 R. Cochrane	104	100	100	525	829	12.5
8 J. Reid	101	96	84	412	693	14.6
9 K. Fallon	92	107	90	368	657	14.0
10 W. Ryan	87	89	68	318	562	15.4
11 J. Carroll	76	77	64	394	611	12.4
12 M. Hills	74	57	64	333	528	14.0

JOCKEYS (by earnings)	*Wins*	*Rides*	*%*	*Stakes £*
1 L. Dettori	216	1004	21.5	1,993,610
2 W. Carson	139	716	19.4	1,708,082
3 W. R. Swinburn	60	421	14.2	1,618,311
4 Pat Eddery	125	646	19.3	1,188,224
5 J. Reid	101	693	14.6	1,159,222
6 J. Weaver	144	958	15.0	907,107
7 K. Darley	148	911	16.2	772,684
8 M. Hills	74	528	14.0	679,082
9 T. Quinn	111	838	13.2	658,222
10 R. Hughes	68	524	12.9	534,746
11 R. Cochrane	104	829	12.5	505,463
12 R. Hills	70	477	14.6	494,222

SIRES OF WINNERS	*Horses*	*Races Won*	*Stakes £*
1 Nijinsky (1967) by Northern Dancer	7	4	797,018
2 Salse (1985) by Topsider	58	36	567,653
3 Rainbow Quest (1981) by Blushing Groom	55	35	442,358
4 Sadler's Wells (1981) by Northern Dancer	71	45	436,393
5 Diesis (1980) by Sharpen Up	37	16	387,713
6 Indian Ridge (1985) by Ahonoora	49	44	369,883
7 Ela-Mana-Mou (1976) by Pitcairn	29	21	358,165
8 Riverman (1969) by Never Bend	22	10	355,600
9 Cadeaux Genereux (1985) by Young Generation	59	50	307,699
10 Green Desert (1983) by Danzig	78	49	306,429
11 Night Shift (1980) by Northern Dancer	56	40	285,587
12 Polish Precedent (1986) by Danzig	31	21	282,343

EXPLANATORY NOTES

'Racehorses of 1995' deals individually, in alphabetical sequence, with every horse that ran on the flat in Britain in 1995 (including on the all-weather tracks), plus a number of foreign-trained horses that did not race here. For each of these horses is given (1) its age, colour and sex, (2) its breeding, and, where this information has not been given in a previous Racehorses Annual, a family outline (3) a form summary giving details of all its performances during the last two seasons, together, where applicable, with the horse's rating in 1994, which appears at the start of the form summary, (4) a rating of its merit in 1995 (which appears in the margin), (5) a Timeform commentary on its racing or general characteristics as a racehorse, with some suggestions, perhaps, regarding its prospects for 1996, and (6) the name of the trainer in whose charge it was on the last occasion it ran. For each two-year-old the foaling date is also given.

The book is published with a twofold purpose. Firstly, it is intended to have permanent value as a review of the exploits and achievements of the more notable of the flat-racing thoroughbreds in 1995. Thus, while the commentaries upon the vast majority of the horses are, of necessity, in note form, the best horses are more critically examined, and the essays upon them are illustrated by half-tone portraits and photographs of some of the races in which they ran. Secondly, the book is designed to help the punter to analyse races, and the notes which follow contain instructions for using the data. The attention of foreign buyers of British bloodstock, and others who are concerned with Timeform Ratings as a measure of absolute racing class in terms of a standard scale, is particularly drawn to the section headed 'The Level of the Ratings'.

TIMEFORM RATINGS

The Timeform Rating of a horse is simply the merit of the horse expressed in pounds and is arrived at by careful examination of its running against other horses using a scale of weight for distance beaten which ranges from 3 lb a length at five furlongs and 2 lb a length at a mile and a quarter to 1 lb at two miles. Timeform maintains a 'running' handicap of all horses in training throughout the season.

THE LEVEL OF THE RATINGS

At the close of each season all the horses that have raced are re-handicapped from scratch, and each horse's rating is revised. It is also necessary to adjust the general level of the handicap, so that all the ratings are kept at the same standard level from year to year. Left to itself, the general level of the ratings, in each succeeding issue of Timeform, tends to rise steadily. For technical reasons it is desirable to allow it to do so during the season: but, in winter, when the complete re-handicap is done, the ratings must, of course, be put back on their proper level again.

This explains why, in this book, the ratings are, in general, different from those in the final issue of the 1995 Timeform Black Book.

RATINGS AND WEIGHT-FOR-AGE

The reader has, in the ratings in this book, a universal handicap embracing all the horses in training it is possible to weigh up, ranging from tip-top classic performers, with ratings from 130 to 145, down to the meanest selling platers, rated around the 20 mark. What we now have to explain is the practical use of these ratings in the business of weighing up a race.

Before doing so, it is important to mention that all ratings are at weight-for-age, so that equal ratings mean horses of equal merit: perhaps it would be clearer if we said that the universal rating handicap is really not a single handicap, but four handicaps side by side: one for two-year-olds, one for three-year-olds, one for four-year-olds and one for older horses. Thus, a three-year-old rated, for argument's sake, at 117 is deemed to be identical in point of 'merit' with a four-year-old also rated at 117: but for them to have equal chances in, say, a mile race in May, the three-year-old would need to be receiving 9 lb from the four-year-old, which is the weight difference specified by the Age, Weight and Distance Tables on pages 2 and 3.

USING THE RATINGS

In using Timeform Ratings with a view to discovering which horses in any race have the best chances at the weights, we have two distinct cases, according to whether the horses taking part are of the same age or of different ages. Here is the procedure in each case:-

A. Horses of the Same Age

If the horses all carry the same weight there are no adjustments to be made, and the horses with the highest ratings have the best chances. If the horses carry different weights, jot down their ratings, and to the rating of each horse add one point for every pound the horse is set to carry less than 10 st, or subtract one point for every pound it has to carry more than 10 st. When the ratings have been adjusted in this way the highest resultant figure indicates the horse with the best chance at the weights.

Example (any distance: any week of the season)

2 Good Girl (9-6)	....	Rating 119	....	add 8	....	127
2 Paulinus (9-4)	....	Rating 113	....	add 10	....	123
2 Abilene (8-11)	....	Rating 107	....	add 17	....	124
2 Bob's Joy (8-7)	....	Rating 108	....	add 21	....	129
2 Time Warp (8-2)	....	Rating 100	....	add 26	....	126
2 Eagle Eye (7-7)	....	Rating 92	....	add 35	....	127

Bob's Joy (129) has the best chance; Good Girl (127) and Eagle Eye (127) are the next best

B. Horses of Different Ages

Take no notice of the weight any horse receives from any other. Instead, consult the Age, Weight and Distance Tables on pages 2 and 3. Treat each horse separately, and compare the weight it has to carry with the weight prescribed for it in the tables, according to the age of the horse, the distance of the race and the month of the year. Then, add one point to the rating for each pound the horse has to carry less than the weight given in the tables:

or, subtract one point from the rating for every pound it has to carry more than the weight prescribed by the tables. The highest resultant figure indicates the horse most favoured by the weights.

Example (1½ miles on June 30th)

(Table Weights: 5-y-o 10-0; 4-y-o 9-13; 3-y-o 9-1)

6 Nimitz (10-2)	Rating 115	subtract 2	113
4 Red Devil (9-9)	Rating 114	add 4	118
6 Sweet Cindy (9-5)	Rating 115	add 9	124
3 Jailhouse (9-2)	Rating 120	subtract 1	119
4 Haakon (8-11)	Rating 101	add 16	117
3 Fine Strike (8-7)	Rating 108	add 8	116

Sweet Cindy (124) has the best chance at the weights, with 5 lb in hand of Jailhouse

TURF AND ALL-WEATHER RATINGS

When a horse has raced on turf and on all-weather and its form on one is significantly different from the other, the two ratings are given, the all-weather set out below the turf preceded by 'a'.

Thus with FREE FOR ALL 47
a55

the top figure, 47, is the rating to be used in turf races, and the one below, a55, is for use in all-weather races. Where there is only one rating, that is to be used for both turf and all-weather. Some horses that have appeared to show markedly improved form on the all-weather, and may well be better than when they last ran on turf, may be rated—in Timeform's in-season publications—in a turf race on their all-weather form, sometimes with a '?'.

NOTE ON RIDERS' ALLOWANCES

For the purposes of rating calculations it is assumed that the allowance a rider is able to claim is nullified by his or her inexperience. The adjustments to the ratings *should therefore be calculated on the weight allotted by the handicapper, or determined by the conditions of the race.* No extra 7lb should be added to the rating when a rider claims 7lb. This is the general routine procedure; but of course, after the usual adjustments have been made the quality of jockeyship is still an important factor to be considered when deciding between horses with similar chances.

WEIGHING UP A RACE

The ratings tell you which horses in a particular race are most favoured by the weights; but complete analysis demands that the racing character of each horse, as set out in the commentary upon it, is also studied carefully to see if there is any reason why the horse might be expected not to run up to its rating. It counts for little that a horse is thrown in at the weights if it has no pretensions whatever to staying the distance, or is unable to act on the prevailing going.

These two matters, suitability of distance and going, are no doubt the most important points to be considered. But there are others. For example, the ability of a horse to accommodate itself to the conformation of the track. Then there is the matter of pace versus stamina: as between two stayers of equal merit, racing over a distance suitable to both, firm going, or a small field with the prospect of a slowly-run race, would favour the one with the better pace and acceleration; whereas dead or soft going, or a big field with the prospect of a strong gallop throughout the race, would favour the sounder stayer. There is also the matter of temperament and behaviour: nobody would be in a hurry to take a short price about a horse with whom it is always an even chance whether it will give its running.

A few minutes spent checking up on these matters in the commentaries upon the horses concerned will sometimes put a very different complexion on a race from that which is put upon it by the ratings alone. We repeat, therefore, that the correct way to use Timeform, or this annual volume, in the analysis of individual races is, first to use the ratings to discover which horses are most favoured by the weights, and second, to check through the comments on the horse to discover what factors other than weight might also affect the outcome of the race.

Incidentally, in setting out the various characteristics, requirements and peculiarities of each horse in the commentary upon it, we have always expressed ourselves in as critical a manner as possible, endeavouring to say just as much, and no whit more than the facts seem to warrant. Where there are clear indications, and definite conclusions can be drawn with fair certainty, we have drawn them: if it is a matter of probability or possibility we have put it that way, being careful not to say the one when we mean the other; and where real conclusions are not to be drawn, we have been content to state the facts. Furthermore, when we say that a horse *may not* be suited by firm going, we do not expect the reader to treat it as though we had said that the horse *is not* suited by firm going. In short, both in our thinking and in the setting out of our views we have aimed at precision.

THE FORM SUMMARIES

The form summary enclosed in the brackets shows for each individual horse the distance, the state of the going and where the horse finished in each of its races on the flat during the last two seasons. Performances are in chronological sequence, the earliest being given first.

The distance of each race is given in furlongs, fractional distances being expressed in the decimal notation to the nearest tenth of a furlong. Races on an all-weather surface are prefixed by letter 'a'.

The going is symbolised as follows: h=hard or very firm; f=firm (turf) or fast (all-weather); m=on the firm side of good; g=good (turf) or standard (all-weather); d=good to soft, dead; s=soft, sticky or holding (turf) or slow (all-weather); v=heavy, very heavy or very holding.

Placings are indicated, up to sixth place, by the use of superior figures, an asterisk being used to denote a win.

Thus [1994 81: 10s* $12f^3$ 1995 11.7g $a11g^2$ Sep 7] signifies that the horse was rated 81 in 1994, when winning over 10 furlongs on soft going first time out and finishing third over twelve furlongs on firm going next time out. In 1995 he finished unplaced, not in the first six, over 11.7 furlongs on good going, and then second over eleven furlongs on standard going on an all-weather track. The date of his last run was September 7.

Included in the pedigree details are the highest Timeform Annual ratings during their racing careers of the sires, dams and sires of dams of all horses, where the information is available.

Where sale prices are given F denotes the price in guineas sold as a foal, Y the price in guineas sold as a yearling. The prefix IR denotes Irish guineas.

THE RATING SYMBOLS

The following symbols, attached to the ratings, are to be interpreted as stated:-

p likely to improve.

P capable of *much* better form.

\+ the horse may be better than we have rated it.

d the horse appears to have deteriorated, and might no longer be capable of running to the rating given.

§ unreliable (for temperamental or other reasons).

§§ so tempermentally unsatisfactory as to be not worth a rating.

? the horse's rating is suspect. If used without a rating the symbol implies that the horse can't be assessed with confidence, or, if used in the in-season Timeform publications, that the horse is out of form.

RACEHORSES OF 1995

Horse	*Commentary*	*Rating*
A-AASEM	2 ch.c. (Mar 3) Polish Precedent (USA) 131 – Janbiya (IRE) 89 (Kris 135) [1995 6m 6g^6 7m^4 Nov 3] strong, close-coupled colt: first foal: dam, winner at 7f (at 2 yrs) and 1¼m, sister to Irish 2000 Guineas winner Flash of Steel: pulled very hard first 2 starts: better form fourth of 17 to Jackson Hill in maiden at Doncaster final start, albeit giving impression most likely to prove best short of 7f. *H. Thomson Jones*	76
A BADGE TOO FAR (IRE)	5 b.m. Heraldiste (USA) 121 – Travel (Saritamer (USA) 130) [1994 NR 1995 a9.4g 10m Jun 12] lengthy, sparely-made mare: probably no longer of any account. *L. J. Barratt*	–
ABALENE	6 b.g. Forzando 122 – Riva Renald 57 (Try My Best (USA) 130) [1994 47: 13.6g^2 14.9m^6 14.1g^6 16.2f^6 12.1m^5 1995 12m 12g 12m* 13f^6 15m^3 Aug 5] small, workmanlike gelding: shows knee action: fair winning hurdler: poor handicapper on flat: won at Beverley (amateurs) in July: should stay beyond 13.6f: acts on fibresand and good to firm ground: blinkered (respectable effort) final start: inconsistent. *T. W. Donnelly*	43
ABBEY HOUSE	3 b.f. Efisio 120 – Power And Red (Skyliner 117) [1994 51, a58: 6.1m 6m^3 6d 5m^4 a5g^6 a5g* 1995 a5g^2 a5g^4 a6g* a6g^5 5.1m a6g^4 a5g^4 5.3f Jul 24] small, sturdy filly: modest performer: won apprentice claimer at Wolverhampton in March, making all: well below form afterwards: stays 6f: acts on the all-weather and on good to firm ground: blinkered/visored since fourth 2-y-o start. *R. Guest*	– a58
ABBOTT OF WHALLEY	2 b.g. (Feb 11) Marching On 101 – La Pepper 63 (Workboy 123) [1995 5g^3 6g^2 a6g* a5g^6 a5g a6g Dec 12] 5,200Y: brother to 3-y-o 5f winner Hannah's Usher and half-brother to ungenuine 6f winner Blazing Belle (by Belfort): dam, plater, won over 1m at 2 yrs: won seller at Southwell in June: soundly beaten in similar events at Wolverhampton afterwards, leaving J Berry's stable and absent over 4 months prior to penultimate outing: best form at 6f: acts on fibresand. *Martyn Wane*	56
ABDUCTION	2 ch.g. (Mar 22) Risk Me (FR) 127 – Spirit Away 54 (Dominion 123) [1995 5d 5g^4 5m^6 6g^5 5g a8.5g^6 Nov 13] 3,000Y: lengthy gelding: first foal: dam 1½m winner: poor maiden: gelded and off course 5 months before final start: should be suited by further than 5f: visored fourth start: possibly hasn't ideal attitude: sold 400 gns Doncaster November Sales. *E. Weymes*	45
ABIGAILS BOY (HOL)	6 gr.g. Superlative 118 – Heartbreaker 71 (Steel Heart 128) [1994 47, a–: 5.9v^4 a7g 6v^2 5s^4 a6g 5.2g^3 6.1s^3 6g^5 1995 5d 6s^3 6g a7g^2 a6g a7g^6 Jul 22] strong, close-coupled gelding: poor handicapper: stays 7f: acts on good to firm and heavy ground and fibresand: effective blinkered or not: none too consistent. *Dr J. D. Scargill*	44
ABINGER	3 ch.g. Absalom 128 – Western Singer (Chief Singer 131) [1994 57: 8.2g 8.2d 1995 12s^6 a14g Nov 6] neat gelding: has a round action: off course 11 months, well beaten in maiden events: stays 1½m: acts on soft ground, well beaten on fibresand: sold (Lady Herries to Miss M. Rowland) 1,500 gns Doncaster November Sales. *Lady Herries*	–
ABIR	2 ch.f. (Jan 25) Soviet Star (USA) 128 – Nafhaat (USA) 91 (Roberto (USA) 131) [1995 7m^2 Oct 30] sturdy filly: second foal: half-sister to 3-y-o 7.6f and 1¼m winner Hadeel (by Polish Precedent): dam 1½m winner: 5/2 from 5/4, 1¼ lengths second of 14 to Shemozzle in maiden at Newcastle, staying on having been held up	68 p

from wide draw: looked green beforehand: will stay at least 1m: will improve. *H. Thomson Jones*

ABLE CHOICE (IRE) 5 b.g. Taufan (USA) 119 – Great Land (USA) (Friend's Choice (USA)) [1994 –, a72: a12g* a12g^{3} a8g^{2} a9.4g^{4} 8m 11.4g a8.5g^{6} 10.1d 8g 10d 1995 a10g a12g^{2} 9.7d 11.9m 10g^{3} 8m 8m^{5} a7g* 10d 11.5s a10g Nov 8] good-topped gelding: fairly useful handicapper at his best: won at Lingfield in August: best form over 7f, has won over 1½m: acts on good to firm and soft ground, easily best form on all-weather: blinkered (out of form) final 4-y-o start: lethargic in preliminaries. *R. W. Armstrong* 49 a80

ABLE SHERIFF 3 gr.g. Doulab (USA) 115 – Rich Lass (Broxted 120) [1994 56: 6m 5m^{6} 6g a5g 5m* 5m^{6} 5s^{2} 1995 5g^{6} 5g^{3} 6g 5m 5m^{2} 5m^{5} 5f 5.1d^{6} 6g 5g^{6} Sep 28] close-coupled gelding: has a round action: poor handicapper: effective at 5f and 6f: acts on good to firm and soft ground: blinkered nowadays: inconsistent. *M. W. Easterby* 48

ABOVE THE CUT (USA) 3 ch.c. Topsider (USA) – Placer Queen (Habitat 134) [1994 91p: 7m* 7m* 1995 7.9m^{4} 8m Aug 28] close-coupled, good-bodied colt: has a quick action: off course 12 months, last in £8,900 event at York and (mulish) handicap at Ripon: should stay beyond 7f. *P. W. Harris* –

ABSALOM'S PILLAR 5 ch.g. Absalom 128 – Collapse 107 (Busted 134) [1994 57, a69: a13g^{6} a14g^{3} a14g^{2} a14g^{3} a14g^{2} 13v^{3} 14g^{6} a12g* a12g^{2} a12g^{4} a14g* a14g^{3} 1995 a14.8g^{6} a16g^{3} 14.9d^{6} a12g^{5} a12g^{6} a14g a14.8g a16g Sep 4] strong gelding: poor mover: modest handicapper: sold out of J. Hetherton's stable 13,000 gns Doncaster May Sales after fourth start: below form for new connections: stays 2m: acts on soft going and fibresand: won maiden hurdle in November. *J. Mackie* – a64 d

ABSOLUTE FOLLY 3 gr.g. Absalom 128 – Agreloui 59 (Tower Walk 130) [1994 57: 5m^{6} 5h^{3} 7m^{6} a8g a8g^{3} 1995 10g a12g* 9.9m^{3} 12m^{3} 13.8g 10.9g 11.8g a14g^{5} Dec 1] close-coupled gelding: poor performer: won seller at Wolverhampton in May: no form last 4 starts, visored final one: stays 1½m: acts on all-weather surfaces and good to firm ground: joined Mrs S. Smith. *J. Berry* 47

ABSOLUTELY FABULUS 3 gr.f. Absalom 128 – Valldemosa 81 (Music Boy 124) [1994 52: 5m^{3} 5m^{6} 5.7g^{6} 5g a5g 1995 5g^{4} 5g^{6} 5.7f 5f^{6} Jun 30] leggy filly: poor maiden handicapper: sold 480 gns Doncaster July Sales: will stay 6f: acts on good to firm ground: blinkered last 3 starts at 2 yrs: inconsistent. *J. L. Spearing* 44

ABSOLUTELY FACT (USA) 5 ch.g. Known Fact (USA) 135 – Chilly Welcome (General Assembly (USA)) [1994 56: a8g^{5} a8g^{5} a10g 8g^{6} 8.5f a7g^{2} 8g^{2} 8f^{2} 8g 8.5g^{3} 8.5v^{5} a9.3g^{5} 8g* a8.5g* a7.5g a8g 1995 a7.5g* a8g^{2} a8g^{3} a9.3g^{3} a7.5g a7.5g 8f^{6} 8f^{3} 9f^{4} 11g 8f^{4} 9f^{6} 9d* 8.5d* 9.7s 8g^{4} a8g^{4} Oct 21] smallish, stocky gelding: modest form: races mainly in Belgium nowadays: won 3 races in 1995, including 2 handicaps at Ostend in September: suited by around 1m to 1¼m: acts on firm and dead ground and all-weather surfaces. *F. Calaerts, Belgium* 39

ABSOLUTELY FAYRE 4 ch.c. Absalom 128 – June Fayre (Sagaro 133) [1994 73: 8m 6m 6g^{5} 6f^{5} 7.1m 7.5m^{6} 8m^{4} 9d 10.8s^{4} 1995 7.6m 10m^{5} 12f a10g Dec 15] smallish, leggy colt: fair performer: best effort for new stable when fifth of 11 in handicap at Sandown: stays 10.8f: acts on good to firm ground and soft, tailed off (after 5½ month break) on equitrack: looks rather one paced. *R. Akehurst* 68

ABSOLUTELYSTUNNING 2 br.f. (Feb 24) Aragon 118 – Dramatic Mood (Jalmood (USA) 126) [1995 6m 5g Sep 12] 7,700Y: sparely-made filly: first foal: dam unraced: awkward at stalls, very slow-starting sixteenth of 24 in maiden auction at Windsor, making headway from 2f out until swerving left 1f out and eased: no chance from bad draw following month: capable of better. *Mrs Barbara Waring* – p

ABSOLUTE MAGIC 5 b.g. Doulab (USA) 115 – Trickster 92 (Major Portion 129) [1994 89: 6v* 7d^{2} 8.1d^{4} 8m 7g* 7.3g^{3} 7g^{3} 7s^{2} 6d 7m 7m 1995 7m 7g^{2} 7m 7m Aug 18] sturdy gelding: usually impresses in appearance: poor mover: ran respectably in 1995 only when second in claimer at Chester in July: stays 8.1f: acts on good to firm and heavy ground: sweating (below form) twice. *W. J. Haggas* 82

ABSOLUTE MILLIONS 3 ch.f. Absalom 128 – Kinkajoo 53 (Precocious 126) [1994 –: 6g 7g^{6} 7g 8m 1995 11f Jul 12] workmanlike filly: of no account. *Martyn Wane* –

ABSOLUTE RULER (IRE) 4 ch.g. Absalom 128 – Princess Biddy 86 (Sun Prince 128) [1994 NR 1995 6.5s^3 7g 6f 6g 7.8f^5 a10g^6 a9.4g a10g Dec 18] half-brother to several winners: dam stayed 7f: fair maiden in Ireland for Neil McGrath first 5 starts: no worthwhile form here: stays 6.5f: acts on soft ground: tried blinkered, no improvement. *J. L. Harris* — 65 d

ABU DANCER (IRE) 5 b.g. Heraldiste (USA) 121 – Ottavia Abu (Octavo (USA) 115) [1994 NR 1995 a12g^5 a13g Jan 14] small gelding: of no account: dead. *K. O. Cunningham-Brown* — –

ABUNDANT 2 ch.g. (Apr 28) Rich Charlie 117 – Cabra (Red Sunset 120) [1995 6m^5 6g^4 6.1d 6.9s^3 7g^4 Sep 29] tall gelding: third foal: dam half-sister to useful middle-distance stayer Pal's Bambino: only time visored, never-nearer fourth of 6 in strongly-run listed race (could be rated 90) at Kempton: no comparable form, better rated on fourth of 11 in auction race at Goodwood final start: stayed 7f: badly drawn when blinkered third start: tended to carry head high: dead. *B. Gubby* — 70 +

ABU SIMBEL (USA) 3 ch.c. Seeking The Gold (USA) – Bold Flora (USA) (Bold Favorite (USA)) [1994 NR 1995 a8g^2 8g^2 8m* 7.9g^4 May 18] $85,000F: angular colt: half-brother to several winners, notably 1989 Grade 1 9f Demoiselle Stakes winner Rootentootenwooten (by Diesis): dam minor winner at up to 7f: progressed with every start: comfortably made all in 5-runner maiden at Newmarket in May: about 2 lengths fourth of 13 to Classicy in handicap at York 11 days later: should stay further than 1m: wears bandages. *J. H. M. Gosden* — 93

ACADEMY LIFE 3 ch.f. Royal Academy (USA) 130 – Exclusive Life (USA) (Exclusive Native (USA)) [1994 NR 1995 7m^6 10g^6 7f^4 8.5m^6 7.1s a5g^6 a7g Oct 23] rangy, unfurnished filly: fourth foal: half-sister to 3 winners, including fair 1994 1½m winner Life At Sea (by Slip Anchor) and useful 1991 2-y-o 6f winner Fair Cop (by Al Nasr): dam sprint winner in USA: best effort when fourth of 13 in maiden at Salisbury in August: disappointing afterwards: blinkered last 2 starts: sold 3,000 gns Newmarket December Sales. *P. F. I. Cole* — 72 d

ACADEMY OF DANCE (IRE) 2 b.f. (Mar 21) Royal Academy (USA) 130 – Bold Meadows 80 (Persian Bold 123) [1995 7g^2 6.9g^5 7.1s^5 Nov 2] IR 6,000Y: sister to Irish 3-y-o Boristova, 9f winner at 2 yrs, closely related to 5f (at 2 yrs) and 7f winner Field of Vision (by Vision) and half-sister to 2 winners, including useful 7f (at 2 yrs) to 1½m winner Judicial Field (by Law Society): dam, Irish 6.9f and 1½m winner, half-sister to dam of Kilijaro: second of 18 to Fairlight Down in maiden at Leicester, running on strongly: only fifth in maiden auctions at Folkestone and Edinburgh: will be well suited by middle distances. *M. Johnston* — 70

ACCESS ADVENTURER (IRE) 4 b.g. Al Hareb (USA) 123 – Olwyn 109 (Relko 136) [1994 67: 11.9m 12m^6 10.5g* 10v 1995 10m^3 11.9m 10m* 10m^4 10m* Aug 19] big gelding: won minor events at Pontefract (clearly best effort, gamely making most) and Sandown (amateurs, sweating, idled then responded to hold on) in the summer: should stay 1½m: ran once (well beaten) on heavy going, but otherwise only on good or good to firm ground: inconsistent. *R. Boss* — 78

ACCESS CARNIVAL (IRE) 4 b.g. Rousillon (USA) 133 – Flying Fairy 79 (Bustino 136) [1994 65: 8d 7s^5 7g^6 7f 10g 1995 10f^6 11.8g 7f 8g 7m a16g a10g^6 Nov 21] rangy gelding: disappointing maiden: stays 1¼m: acts on firm and dead going. *R. Boss* — 56 d

ACCESS SUN 8 b.g. Pharly (FR) 130 – Princesse du Seine (FR) (Val de Loir 133) [1994 –: 15.4v^3 1995 15.4g 17.2m 17.2m^3 17.2f^2 Jul 1] leggy gelding: unimpressive mover: poor handicapper: stays 17.2f: acts on firm ground: front runner. *J. S. King* — 42

ACCOUNTANCY JEWEL (IRE) 2 b.f. (Apr 9) Pennine Walk 120 – Polyester Girl (Ridan (USA)) [1995 7d a7g* Dec 15] IR 4,100F, IR 10,500Y: closely related to Irish 1982 2-y-o 7f winner Persian Polly (by Persian Bold), later dam of Lake Coniston, and half-sister to useful Irish 6f (at 2 yrs) to 1m winner Hazy Vision (by Vision): dam, Irish 6f winner, half-sister to top Italian 1975 2-y-o Northern Spring: ex-Irish filly: eighth in maiden at Gowran Park in July for S. J. Treacy: 7/1 from 10/1, won median auction maiden at Lingfield in December by length from Farmost (pair 7 lengths clear): will improve. *K. McAuliffe* — 71 p

ACCUSE (USA) 3 b.f. Alleged (USA) 138 – Rascal Rascal (USA) (Ack Ack (USA)) [1994 NR 1995 8m 9f^4 10.3g^4 Jul 1] $75,000Y: rather leggy filly: seventh — –

foal: sister to 7f winner Key Suspect and half-sister to 4 winners, notably smart 1992 2-y-o 7f winner Beggarman Thief (by Arctic Tern): dam minor 6f and 2-y-o 8.5f stakes winner: signs of ability in maidens: should stay 1¼m: sold 8,800 gns Newmarket December Sales. *P. F. I. Cole*

ACE CHAPEL (IRE) 3 br.g. Simply Great (FR) 122 – Sistina 76 (Charlottown 127) [1994 51: 7m 8s a7g^{6} 1995 8.3g 8f 12m^{6} 8.1m a12g^{6} Jul 22] small, angular gelding: well beaten in 1995. *C. C. Elsey* –

ACHARNE 2 ch.c. (Mar 26) Pharly (FR) 130 – Sibley 84 (Northfields (USA)) [1995 7m^{3} 7g^{5} 7m^{4} 7.1d^{2} 8d^{6} Sep 23] 18,000Y: well-made colt: has a quick action: half-brother to King Cobra (by Ardross), 1¾m listed winner in France in 1995: dam French 1¼m winner out of Oaks third Suni: fairly useful maiden: good second, despite running wide, to Masehaab at Sandown: impeded on home turn when respectable sixth of 8 to Mons in Royal Lodge Stakes at Ascot later in month: takes keen hold, but bred to stay well beyond 1m: acts on dead ground: should win a race. *C. E. Brittain* 90

ACHILLES HEEL 4 br.g. Superlative 118 – Ela-Yianni-Mou 73 (Anfield 117) [1994 –: a6g^{5} a6g^{5} a6g 1995 a7g^{6} a10g^{2} a10g^{3} 12g* 12m 12g^{6} 13g 13.9g^{6} 10g 14.9m^{5} 12m^{5} 10m 12d 12.1g^{3} 12.1g^{4} 12m^{5} 11.9m^{4} Oct 5] smallish gelding: won apprentice handicap at Doncaster in March: only poor form at best from May onwards: better at 1½m than shorter: best efforts on good ground: sometimes looks lazy. *C. N. Allen* 54 d

ACHILL PRINCESS 3 b.f. Dowsing (USA) 124 – Princess Matilda 110 (Habitat 134) [1994 47: 5g^{2} 5d^{3} 5m 5g 5f 5m^{5} 7.1m^{3} 7g^{4} 5m^{4} 7m^{3} 6s 5m^{6} 1995 8.3v^{6} 7m^{5} 8.3f 7f^{2} 5.9h* 7.1m Aug 24] close-coupled filly: poor performer: narrowly won 5-runner maiden at Carlisle in August: stays 7f: acts on hard and dead ground, possibly not very soft: blinkered (below form) twice at 2 yrs: none too consistent: sold 3,500 gns Doncaster October Sales. *W. T. Kemp* 47

ACK'S AGAIN 3 b.f. Dancing Brave (USA) 140 – Ack's Secret (USA) (Ack Ack (USA)) [1994 –: 8d 1995 12.1m 11.5g* 14.1m^{3} Aug 27] tall, quite good-topped filly: has scope: similar form when winning 5-runner maiden at Yarmouth (headed 2½f out then rallying well) and third of 4 in handicap at Redcar in the summer: should be suited by further than 14.1f (her full brother stayed 17.5f): front runner: sold 29,000 gns Newmarket December Sales. *B. W. Hills* 81

ACONITUM (USA) 7 b.g. Alleged (USA) 138 – Autumn Glory (USA) (Graustark) [1994 NR 1995 9.7m a16g^{6} Jun 8] fifth foal: half-brother to several winners in France, including smart middle-distance stayer Glorify (by Nijinsky): dam winner from 6f to 1¼m in USA: middle-distance winner in France at 3 yrs and 4 yrs: no form in claimers here. *J. M. Bradley* –

ACONORACE 3 b.c. Midyan (USA) 124 – Saint Cynthia (Welsh Saint 126) [1994 NR 1995 9.9m^{6} 10.1g 10g^{4} Jun 1] 6,200F, 6,400Y: sturdy colt: half-brother to several winners, including fairly useful 6f and 7f winner Saint Caligula (by Petorius): dam won over 1¾m and over hurdles in Ireland: no worthwhile form in maidens and seller. *R. A. Fahey* –

ACQUITTAL (IRE) 3 b.g. Danehill (USA) 126 – Perfect Alibi (Law Society (USA) 130) [1994 52: 7m 7m 1995 a8.5g^{4} 8.3v^{2} 9.7m^{3} 10m^{6} 11.1m* 11.6m^{3} 14m^{6} 10m^{4} 12.1m^{3} 12m Sep 7] unfurnished gelding: modest handicapper: won at Edinburgh (apprentices) in June: probably best at around 1½m: acts on good to firm and heavy ground: visored (ran creditably) eighth and ninth 3-y-o starts: sold (J. Fanshawe to J. Mackie) 4,800 gns Newmarket Autumn Sales. *J. R. Fanshawe* 61

ACROSS THE BAY 8 ch.g. Krayyan 117 – Siofra Beag (Steel Heart 128) [1994 57, a–: 8g^{4} 8g 8.3d^{4} 7m^{2} 8.1f* 7m^{6} 8g^{4} 8.1m^{3} 10m^{2} 10g^{4} 8m^{2} 8g^{2} 9g^{2} 8m^{2} 8.2m 8m^{4} 8f^{4} 8g^{3} a8g 8.2g^{4} a8g 1995 a8.5g a12g a8.5g 8m 8g 8f 8m Jul 10] close-coupled gelding: seems no longer of much account: sold 500 gns Doncaster August Sales. *R. W. Emery* –

ACROW LINE 10 b.g. Capricorn Line 111 – Miss Acrow (Comedy Star (USA) 121) [1994 45, a53: a14.8g^{4} a16.2g* 21.6v^{3} 15.8g a16.2g* 17.2f^{3} 1995 a14.8g^{3} 16.2m a16.2g* a16g^{2} Jun 8] stocky gelding: only poor form in 1995: won claimer at Wolverhampton (third win from 3 tries over course and distance) in May: short-headed at Southwell 17 days later: thorough stayer: acts on fibresand, good to firm ground and heavy. *D. Burchell* – a37

ACTING BRAVE 4 b.c. Dancing Brave (USA) 140 – Sarah Siddons (FR) 122 (Le Levanstell 122) [1994 96p: 10.2g^{6} 10g* 12d^{6} 12f 12m* 12m^{4} 12m* 1995 12f^{5} 12m Oct 12] robust, sturdy colt: carries condition: useful performer at 3 yrs: tailed off in rated stakes at Salisbury and Newmarket (3½ months later, moved badly to post) then sold only 6,000 gns Newmarket Autumn Sales. *G. Harwood* –

ACTION JACKSON 3 ch.g. Hadeer 118 – Water Woo (USA) 102 (Tom Rolfe) [1994 66: 6m^{6} 7m 8s^{6} 1995 7g^{5} 8m^{2} 8m^{2} 10m^{6} 9.7f^{4} a9.4g 7f a8g^{5} a8g^{5} Nov 21] close-coupled, angular gelding: fair maiden: left G. Rimmer's stable after third 3-y-o start: well below form last 4 starts: stays 9.7f: acts on firm going: wore crossed noseband (most starts) and bandages (occasionally) at 3 yrs: tried with tongue tied down: usually held up. *B. J. McMath* 66 a–

ACTUAL FACT (USA) 3 b.c. Known Fact (USA) 135 – Wistoral (USA) (Exceller (USA) 129) [1994 75p: 5.7g 5s* 1995 6m^{2} 6g^{2} 6g 7d^{5} 6.1s Oct 17] leggy colt: unimpressive mover: fairly useful handicapper: close second, staying on well, at Kempton in May and Newmarket in July: off course 2 months, disappointing afterwards: should be suited by further than 6f: acts on good to firm and soft ground. *G. Harwood* 86

ADALOALDO (USA) 3 ch.c. Arctic Tern (USA) 126 – Alicia's Lady (USA) (Al Nasr (FR) 126) [1994 70p: 7.5g^{2} 1995 12s 12g 12f^{3} 11f a10g^{5} Nov 10] leggy, close-coupled colt: modest form in claimers: stays 1½m: acts on firm ground, well beaten (in maiden) on soft: visored (stiff task) final start: sold 2,600 gns Doncaster November Sales. *P. A. Kelleway* 57

ADAMTON 3 b.g. Domynsky 110 – Berwyn (Sharpo 132) [1994 NR 1995 5d a8.5g^{4} a8.5g Nov 13] second foal: dam never ran: little promise in maidens. *Mrs J. Cecil* –

ADDAYA (IRE) 3 b.f. Persian Bold 123 – Night of Stars 89 (Sadler's Wells (USA) 132) [1994 NR 1995 8.3m May 1] IR 22,000Y: good-topped filly: has scope: second foal: dam 1m winner: backward, slow-starting fourteenth of 20 in maiden at Windsor: sold 9,800 gns Newmarket December Sales. *L. M. Cumani* –

ADDED DIMENSION (IRE) 4 b.g. Top Ville 129 – Lassalia (Sallust 134) [1994 –: a9.4g^{3} 6s 1995 a8g a12g Feb 9] smallish, well-made gelding: no worthwhile form on flat: modest hurdler for P. Winkworth. *C. T. Nash* –

ADDIE PRAY (IRE) 2 b.f. (Feb 4) Great Commotion (USA) 123 – Green Wings (General Assembly (USA)) [1995 6g^{4} 7.5d^{3} 6.9s^{6} 8f a7g a8g* Nov 24] IR 11,000F, 6,000Y: angular, quite attractive filly: fourth foal: half-sister to French 9f winner Ballymount (by Doulab) and a winner in Italy: dam won at middle distances at 4 yrs in Ireland: third of 17 in maiden auction at Beverley in September: didn't repeat that form, even when winning 16-runner seller at Southwell final start: stays 1m: looked unsuited by very soft ground. *M. A. Jarvis* 68 a60

ADILOV 3 b.g. Soviet Star (USA) 128 – Volida 105 (Posse (USA) 130) [1994 50p: 7.1d 1995 a8.5g^{5} 8f^{4} 10m May 26] rangy gelding: much his best form in maidens when never-dangerous fourth of 7 in slowly-run race at Warwick: joined R. Phillips and gelded. *J. R. Fanshawe* 67 ?

ADJACENT TOO 3 gr.f. Prince Daniel (USA) – Tula Singh 66 (Mansingh (USA) 120) [1994 –: 6v a7g 1995 10.2f a14.8g a12g^{6} 14.1f 10g Jul 19] plain, sparely-made filly: of little account. *C. C. Elsey* –

ADJARELI (IRE) 3 gr.c. Nishapour (FR) 125 – Adjriyna 82 (Top Ville 129) [1994 8d* 1995 8g* 8m^{2} 8m 7g^{4} Sep 16] medium-sized, quite attractive colt: second foal: dam, 8.5f winner, out of half-sister to dam of Blushing Groom: smart performer: won Leopardstown maiden at 2 yrs: beat Oscar Schindler by 3½ lengths in 5-runner listed event there in April, quickening to lead just inside last: improved again when length second of 9 to Spectrum in steadily-run Irish 2000 Guineas at the Curragh, staying on despite wandering: got poor run in St James's Palace Stakes at Royal Ascot: 11/10 favourite, disappointing in listed race at the Curragh 3 months later: should stay beyond 1m: yet to race on extremes of going. *J. Oxx, Ireland* 118

ADJMAL (IRE) 6 b.h. Dancing Brave (USA) 140 – Adjarida (Red God 128§) [1994 6.5s^{4} 5g^{2} 6g^{6} 6g 7m 6g^{3} 6.5s^{4} 5d^{6} 6s^{4} 1995 7s* 7d^{5} 6g* 5g* 6.5g* 6m 7m^{4} 6.5m^{6} 6d^{6} Aug 30] small, strong horse: useful performer: won minor events at Gelsenkirchen and Mulheim, listed race at Cologne then minor event at Hanover, all 96 by June: ran well in Cork And Orrery Stakes at Royal Ascot next outing, and when sixth in pattern events at Hoppegarten and Baden-Baden in August: stays 7f: acts on good to firm ground and soft. *P. Lautner, Germany*

ADLER (IRE) 2 b.g. (May 26) Warning 136 – Orangerie (FR) (Gay Mecene (USA) 128) [1995 a8.5g^5 Dec 9] 3,200Y: half-brother to 3-y-o Oleron (by Darshaan) and several winners in Italy: dam, French maiden, half-sister to Italian Oaks winner Orsa Maggiore: 33/1, around 18 lengths fifth of 13 to Kissing Gate in maiden at Wolverhampton: should do better. *M. J. Camacho* – p

ADMIRAL HOOD (USA) 4 b.g. Devil's Bag (USA) – De La Rose (USA) (Nijinsky (CAN) 138) [1994 NR 1995 a12g^6 a10g^4 Feb 28] seventh foal: brother to 2 winners, notably U.S. 2-y-o Grade 3 8.5f winner De La Devil, and half-brother to 2 winners by Conquistador Cielo, notably 2-y-o Grade 1 8.5f winner Conquistarose: dam (sister to Upper Nile) top-class filly in North America: always-prominent fourth of 10 in maiden at Lingfield: sold (Lord Huntingdon to K. Morgan) 2,800 gns Ascot May Sales. *Lord Huntingdon* 51

ADMIRAL JONES (IRE) 2 b.c. (May 12) Lycius (USA) 124 – Chelsworth 67 (Never So Bold 135) [1995 6f^6 5.1g* 5m* 5m^4 Aug 16] 8,500 2-y-o: rangy, attractive colt: impresses in appearance: first foal: dam, 5.3f winner, granddaughter of Favoletta: won maiden at Chester and nursery at Goodwood in July: never threatened when 3 lengths last of 4 to Mubhij in listed race at York: suited by 5f: taken down early last 2 starts: sold to race in USA. *M. Johnston* 94

ADMIRALS FLAME (IRE) 4 b.c. Doulab (USA) 115 – Fan The Flame 69 (Grundy 137) [1994 65: 6s* 6.1d^4 7d 8.2m 8.1m 8m^4 7.1m^2 6g 1995 a7g a10g^6 a8g 8g 8m^4 7m 10g^6 8.3m* 8f^5 8f* 8m 8m^3 8g 8f^2 Oct 12] leggy colt: fair handicapper: won at Windsor in June and Kempton in July: ran well afterwards when placed: should stay 1¼m: won on soft ground (yet to encounter such conditions again), best form on top-of-the-ground: sweating (ran poorly) eleventh 4-y-o start: wears bandages. *C. F. Wall* 79 a–

ADMIRAL'S GUEST (IRE) 3 ch.g. Be My Guest (USA) 126 – Watership (USA) (Foolish Pleasure (USA)) [1994 –p: 6d 1995 8g 8.3m 11.6m 12m^5 12f^6 15.4m Sep 7] quite attractive gelding: disappointing maiden handicapper: visored final start: sold 1,800 gns Newmarket Autumn Sales. *G. Harwood* –

ADMIRALS REALM 6 gr.g. Another Realm 118 – Bedeni 100 (Parthia 132) [1994 58: 5d 6g 5.1m^3 6m 6.1m 5m^6 5g 5f^3 6g^3 6g^6 5.1d 5.1g* 1995 5g 6m Jun 5] lengthy gelding: unimpressive mover: modest handicapper: showed nil for new stable in 1995: stays 6f: acts on firm and soft ground, ran poorly both outings on fibresand at 3 yrs: blinkered (ran well) twice at 5 yrs: inconsistent. *A. G. Newcombe* –

ADMIRALS SECRET (USA) 6 ch.g. Secreto (USA) 128 – Noble Mistress (USA) (Vaguely Noble 140) [1994 61, a70: 10.8v^2 10d 14.1d^3 14.1v^4 10d 11.4d 10.8s^5 13.8g^3 a12g* 12.4d^4 a13g^2 a13g 1995 a12g^5 12g* 12g* 12.3f^2 11.6g^5 11.6m^2 13.8m* 15.9m^6 14.4m 12g^5 12m Oct 2] good-quartered gelding: has a round action: fair handicapper: won at Pontefract and twice at Catterick: below form afterwards: stays 1¾m: acts on any turf going and on equitrack: often has tongue tied down. *C. F. Wall* 71

ADMIRAL'S WELL (IRE) 5 b.h. Sadler's Wells (USA) 132 – Exotic Bride (USA) (Blushing Groom (FR) 131) [1994 91+: 12d^2 16s* 20m^5 16.2m* 13.9m^2 18g^6 18m 1995 16.2m^6 20m^3 16f^5 16m* 18g^4 20s^5 Sep 30] good-bodied horse: usually looks very well: has a round action: useful performer: unimpressive winner of 3-runner minor event at Goodwood in August: much better form in the Cup races won by Double Trigger, 5 lengths third at Ascot, 6¾ lengths fifth at Goodwood and 5½ lengths fourth at Doncaster: stiff task, creditable though well-beaten fifth in Prix du Cadran at Longchamp final start: stays very well: acts on firm ground and soft: held up/tracks leaders: won handicap hurdle in October: genuine. *R. Akehurst* 107

ADOLESCENCE (IRE) 5 ch.m. Broken Hearted 124 – Cailin d'Oir (Roi Soleil 125) [1994 9g^3 9g^5 8g^5 7g* 8g 1995 7m 10.5g^4 10.8g^4 10m^3 11.9m 10g^2 10f^2 9m* 10m^3 9g Sep 8] angular ex-Irish mare: half-sister to several winners, including Irish 2m winner Adapt (by Smoggy) and 13f winner Romanian (by Sallust): fairly useful handicapper: won maiden at Down Royal at 4 yrs on penultimate start for J. Burns: in frame most starts in 1995, narrow winner of amateurs handicap at Goodwood in 89

August: stays 10.8f (not beaten by trip in 1½m Old Newton Cup): acts on firm ground, not tried on soft surface for long time. *K. McAuliffe*

ADONISIS 3 b.c. Emarati (USA) 74 – Kind Lady 56 (Kind of Hush 118) [1994 NR 1995 9m^3 Jul 1] third foal: half-brother to fairly useful 7f winner Amadeus Aes (by Dublin Lad) and poor 1½m winner Hush Baby (by Ballacashtal): dam 2-y-o 6f seller winner who probably stayed 1½m: 12/1, third of 4 in median auction maiden at Lingfield, never able to challenge. *T. T. Clement*
–

ADVANCE EAST 3 b.g. Polish Precedent (USA) 131 – Startino 111 (Bustino 136) [1994 68p: 7m^6 7m 7s a7g 1995 10g^6 10.3m^2 12g^2 12g^2 11.9s Oct 1] big, good-topped gelding with plenty of scope: unimpressive mover: fair maiden: second in minor event at Doncaster (short-headed, winner got first run) then 2 handicaps at Pontefract: subsequently gelded and off course nearly 4 months: weak in market, always behind on return: stays 1½m: acts on good to firm ground: held up: may be capable of better. *Mrs J. R. Ramsden*
74

AERIAL VIEW 4 br.g. Sulaafah (USA) 119 – Flying Portion 72 (Major Portion 129) [1994 34: 8f^5 16.2m^5 a12g^3 1995 a12g^4 a14.8g a16g^5 9.2g 10g^4 12.1m^4 Jun 16] tall gelding: has a quick action: poor plater: stays 1½m, not 2m: acts on fibresand, probably on firm going. *W. G. M. Turner*
–

AERLEON JANE 2 ch.f. (Mar 9) Caerleon (USA) 132 – An Empress (USA) (Affirmed (USA)) [1995 7m^2 Aug 26] sturdy filly: second live foal: half-sister to 1991 2-y-o 7f winner Alto Jane (by The Minstrel), later effective at 1¼m: dam, 8.5f graded winner and second in 9f Hollywood Oaks, out of outstanding Venezuelan filly Blondy: 6/1, unluckily beaten a head by Min Alhawa in 5-runner maiden at Goodwood, green early on, finding trouble from 2f out then finishing strongly: will be suited by middle distances: sure to improve, and win a race. *J. H. M. Gosden*
85 p

AEROKING (USA) 4 b.g. Lear Fan (USA) 130 – Blue Grass Baby (USA) (Icecapade (USA)) [1994 77: 8f^2 7.1g* 8m 1995 8.1m 10g^4 8f^4 10m 9g^5 10d 9d^6 8m^2 Oct 12] lengthy, good-topped gelding: fairly useful handicapper: ran well when second of 20 at Newmarket final start: stays 1¼m: best efforts on a sound surface, and acts on firm: races prominently: sometimes takes strong hold. *G. Harwood*
82

AETHRA (USA) 2 ch.f. (Apr 21) Trempolino (USA) 135 – All For Hope (USA) (Sensitive Prince (USA)) [1995 8f^2 Oct 25] tall, leggy filly: fourth foal: sister to 3-y-o 14.8f winner Elpida and a winner in Germany and half-sister to French 4-y-o 11f winner Sahalik (by Theatrical): dam half-sister to Prix de Diane winner Lacovia: 20/1, shaped very well when neck second of 13 to Bright Water in maiden at Yarmouth, taking good hold, challenging over 1f out and keeping on well despite running very green: will stay at least 1¼m: sure to improve and win a race. *Lady Herries*
89 p

AFFIDAVIT (USA) 3 b.c. Affirmed (USA) – Narwala 120 (Darshaan 133) [1994 NR 1995 12v* 12g* 12g 15g* 15g* 14.6d^5 Sep 9] rangy colt: first foal: dam won Princess Royal Stakes: progressed into a smart performer: won minor event at Saint-Cloud in March and listed race at Longchamp in May and (after 5 lengths seventh of 11 to Celtic Swing in Prix du Jockey-Club) landed Prix Hubert de Chaudenay at Longchamp and 4-runner Prix Berteux at Deauville (best effort, by 2 lengths from Peckinpah's Soul) in July: below form in St Leger at Doncaster (moved poorly to post, soon driven along in straight) final start: suited by further than 1½m, and stays 15f. *A. Fabre, France*
119

AFFORDABLE DORA 3 b.f. Sharrood (USA) 124 – Polly Packer 81 (Reform 132) [1994 NR 1995 11.8g Oct 10] half-sister to several winners, easily best of them being useful stayer Regal Reform (by Prince Tenderfoot): dam, second over 7f and 1m, out of very useful miler Vital Match: bandaged, signs of a little ability, keeping on steadily, in claimer at Leicester: may do better. *J. R. Fanshawe*
–

AFISIAK 2 b.f. (Feb 11) Efisio 120 – Maestrette 77 (Manado 130) [1995 5g^5 5g^2 a5g* May 4] 7,000F, IR 4,000Y: closely related to 5f (at 2 yrs) and 7f winner Formaestre (by Formidable) and half-sister to several winners, including middle-distance performer Thimbalina (by Salmon Leap): dam 1m winner: modest form in maiden auctions, making all in 5-runner race at Wolverhampton in May: will stay 6f. *M. Johnston*
60

AFRICAN CHIMES 8 b.h. Kampala 120 – Rynville (Ballymore 123) [1994 72, a76: a7g^5 a7g a6g a8g^4 7s^3 5.1m^5 a7g^4 a7g^2 5m* a6g* a7g^5 a7g^3 a6g^4 5s a7g* a5g*
76
a72

a6g^5 a7g a5g^6 1995 a6g^6 a5g^6 a6g 7g* a7g^5 a7g Nov 10] leggy, angular horse: has round action: fair handicapper: won 16-runner race at Thirsk in April: best at up to 7f, though has won at 1¼m: acts on any going: effective blinkered or not: visored once much earlier in career. *W. A. O'Gorman*

AFRICANNIGHTINGALE (IRE) 3 ch.g. Ela-Mana-Mou 132 – Glasson Lady (GER) 108 (Priamos (GER) 123) [1994 –p: 8m 1995 12f^4 12m^5 Jun 1] leggy, angular gelding: has a round action: looks a staying plater. *M. H. Tompkins* 41

AFRICAN-PARD (IRE) 3 b.g. Don't Forget Me 127 – Petite Realm 95 (Realm 129) [1994 67: 6.1s^2 6m^3 6g 1995 7.1m^6 8m^2 8.1g^3 8m^6 8.1m^3 7.1d^4 7.1g^6 Sep 23] good-topped, attractive gelding: fair maiden handicapper: will stay beyond 8.1f: acts on good to firm ground and soft. *D. Haydn Jones* 70

AFRICAN SUN (IRE) 2 b.g. (Mar 16) Mtoto 134 – Nuit d'Ete (USA) 90 (Super Concorde (USA) 128) [1995 a7g 7g Oct 10] fifth living foal: closely related to useful Irish 1m and 1¼m winner Al Guswa and a winner in Italy (both by Shernazar) and half-brother to 3-y-o Hugwity (by Cadeaux Genereux): dam 2-y-o 5f and 6f winner: backward and towards rear in maidens at Southwell (subsequently gelded) and Leicester (close up 5f) 3 months later. *B. Hanbury* –

AFSAAT 3 b.c. Efisio 120 – Blue Jane 81 (Blue Cashmere 129) [1994 NR 1995 8m^3 9m^2 8.5m^5 Sep 6] 78,000Y: good-topped, quite attractive colt: brother to fair 1m winner Eastleigh and half-brother to smart sprinter Ever Sharp (by Sharpo): dam 6f winner: demoted after narrowly winning 6-runner maiden at Redcar, leading over 1f out but edging left: ran poorly in similar event at Epsom final start, hanging left: should stay 1¼m: sent to Dubai. *M. R. Stoute* 84

AGAIN TOGETHER 2 b.f. (Apr 15) Then Again 126 – Starawak 68 (Star Appeal 133) [1995 7m 7g^2 7m 7m^3 7g^2 6m Oct 12] 9,600Y: rather leggy filly: sister to 3-y-o 7f and 1m winner Fame Again and half-sister to useful middle-distance stayer Army of Stars (by Posse): dam, 1½m winner, half-sister to Spring In Deepsea, smart winner at up to 9f: modest form placed in sellers at Newmarket and claimer at Brighton: reared stalls and left at start third outing: stays 7f: has worn bandages. *N. A. Callaghan* 58

AGATHE (USA) 4 ch.f. Manila (USA) – Albertine (FR) 117 (Irish River (FR) 131) [1994 114: 8m^4 8g^2 10.5g^3 10g* 10d^4 1995 8g^2 10.5s^2 9.3g^5 8m^3 8g^3 8m^2 8s Sep 18] tall, close-coupled filly: smart performer: ran creditably first 5 starts in 1995, placed in Prix Edmond Blanc at Saint-Cloud, Prix Corrida (set slow pace, caught post by Hollywood Dream) at Evry, Prix du Chemin de Fer du Nord (as in Edmond Blanc finishing length behind Kaldounevees) at Chantilly and Prix d'Astarte (2 lengths behind Smolensk) at Deauville: below form last 2 starts: effective at 1m to 10.5f: acts on good to firm ground and soft. *A. Fabre, France* 114

AGEEB (IRE) 2 b.c. (Apr 5) Dancing Dissident (USA) 119 – Majesty's Nurse (Indian King (USA) 128) [1995 6g 6g^5 6.9g* Oct 16] IR 8,200F, 11,000Y: third foal: half-brother to German 6f and 7f winner Marah of Sarah (by Simply Great): dam Irish firm-ground sprinter: progressive form: won 14-runner maiden auction at Folkestone in October by a short head from Al's Alibi, leading after 2f: stays 7f: sold 26,000 gns Newmarket Autumn Sales. *W. J. Haggas* 73

AGENT 2 ch.c. (Mar 16) Anshan 119 – Maria Cappuccini 70 (Siberian Express (USA) 125) [1995 6.1d 6g^5 a6g^2 Nov 20] 21,000Y: leggy colt: first foal: dam, 5f winner effective up to 7f, half-sister to Marina Park, very useful at up to 7f: sold out of W. Haggas' stable 16,000 gns Newmarket Autumn Sales after second start: ¾-length second of 15 to Kings Harmony in maiden at Southwell: will stay beyond 6f: may improve. *J. L. Eyre* 70+

AGE OF REALITY (USA) 2 b.f. (Mar 13) Alleged (USA) 138 – Isticanna (USA) 96 (Far North (CAN) 120) [1995 8m^6 7g Oct 9] tall filly: has scope: fourth foal: sister to 1993 2-y-o 7.5f winner Whatcombe and half-sister to 3-y-o 7f winner High Flown (by Lear Fan) and 8.1f (at 2 yrs) and 1¼m winner Seama (by Affirmed): dam 2-y-o 5f and 6f winner: similar form in maidens at Leicester won by Caribbean Quest and Fairlight Down, keeping on steadily: will be well suited by middle distances: will do better. *H. Candy* 63 p

AGILE 2 b.c. (Feb 3) Shareef Dancer (USA) 135 – Hence (USA) (Mr Prospector (USA)) [1995 8d Sep 27] 6,000Y, 21,000 2-y-o: lengthy, robust colt: seventh foal: 72 p half-brother to 3-y-o Be My Choice (by Be My Chief) and 3 winners, including 4-y-o 1¼m winner Ruby Heights (by Shirley Heights): dam 7f winner in USA: 33/1 and in need of race, shaped well when tenth of 18 to Mystic Knight in maiden at Salisbury, prominent to 2f out then eased good deal once beaten: sure to improve. *I. A. Balding*

AGNELLA (IRE) 2 b.f. (Mar 1) Polish Patriot (USA) 128 – Annaberta (GER) (Alpenkonig (GER)) [1995 5m^{4} 6g* 7.3m 7g^{3} Aug 25] approx £130,000Y: good-topped filly: third foal: dam won from 11f to 2m in Germany and from family of Urban Sea: impressive winner of maiden at Folkestone in June: below form in nursery before creditable third in listed race at Baden-Baden: stays 7f. *G. L. Moore* 84

AGOER 3 ch.f. Hadeer 118 – Abuzz 101 (Absalom 128) [1994 61?: 6m^{4} 6f^{3} 1995 7m^{2} 6m^{2} 7g^{4} 7m^{5} 7m^{5} 8g 7s 7f^{2} a7g a7g Dec 14] unfurnished filly: modest maiden handicapper: should stay 1m: acts on firm going, well beaten on soft ground and the all-weather: bandaged behind. *C. E. Brittain* 58

AGWA 6 b.g. Local Suitor (USA) 128 – Meissarah (USA) (Silver Hawk (USA) 123) [1994 81: a7g* a6g* a6g* a6g 6m* 6m^{5} 6m^{2} 6m^{2} 7.6m 6f 6m 1995 6m 6m^{6} 5m^{3} 5g^{2} 6m 6f^{6} 6m 6g 5s 5m a6g Nov 25] sturdy gelding: fair handicapper: creditable efforts in 1995 only in July, placed twice at Sandown and close ninth in Stewards' Cup at Goodwood: effective at 5f to 7f: acts on firm ground (probably on soft) and on equitrack: usually races prominently: sometimes taken early to start. *R. J. O'Sullivan* 81

AHAALEE (USA) 3 ch.c. Alysheba (USA) – Sans Supplement (USA) (Grey Dawn II 132) [1994 NR 1995 8d 8g^{4} 8.5m^{4} 10m^{5} 12g^{2} 14.1m 13.8g Jul 6] $140,000Y: quite attractive colt: half-brother to several winners, notably U.S. champion Turf Horse Itsallgreektome (by Sovereign Dancer): dam won 4 races: fair maiden: stayed 1½m: slipped and broke leg at Catterick: dead. *E. A. L. Dunlop* 66

AHJAY 5 br.h. Tina's Pet 121 – City Link Rose (Lochnager 132) [1994 –: 7d 7g 1995 6g^{2} 6m 7g* 7g^{4} 8m^{3} 7g 7g^{5} 7d^{6} 7f 7f* Oct 25] workmanlike horse: modest handicapper: won at Salisbury in May and Yarmouth (gambled on, one of four to race on favoured stand side, easily best effort) in October: stays 1m: acts on any ground: none too consistent. *D. A. Wilson* 60

AHKAAM (USA) 2 ch.c. (Mar 12) Riverman (USA) 131 – Rare Mint (USA) (Key To The Mint (USA)) [1995 7m^{2} 7m* 8d* Oct 14] $325,000Y: tenth foal: half-brother to several winners, notably very smart 1m (at 2 yrs) to 1½m winner Mystery Rays and 1¾m winner Dragon's Blood (both by Nijinsky) and smart 5f to 7f winner (stayed 1m) Robin des Pins (by Nureyev): dam, unplaced, out of half-sister to dams of Be My Guest and Golden Fleece: progressive Irish colt: won maiden at Fairyhouse in September and 5-runner Juddmonte Beresford Stakes at the Curragh (beat Sheraka a head) in October: will be suited by further than 1m: yet to race on extremes of going: should improve further. *D. K. Weld, Ireland* 102 p

AHLA 3 ch.f. Unfuwain (USA) 131 – Rahik 103 (Wassl 125) [1994 NR 1995 10g 14g^{3} 12m* 13.3g^{3} 11.9g^{6} 13.1g^{6} 14.6m^{2} Nov 3] rangy filly: second foal: half-sister to modest 1m winner Asalib (by Persian Bold): dam, 2-y-o 5f winner best at 7f, is daughter of smart sprinter Rambling Rose: won maiden at Kempton in June: third of 8 to Celeric in handicap at Newbury, getting run of race, but failed by some way to repeat the form: stays 1¾m: sold 36,000 gns Newmarket December Sales. *R. W. Armstrong* 90

AILESBURY HILL (USA) 2 ch.f. (Apr 18) Woodman (USA) 126 – Golden Oriole (USA) (Northern Dancer) [1995 6f^{4} 7f^{2} 8.1m^{2} 8g 8.2d^{2} 8g Oct 3] $225,000Y: good-quartered, attractive filly: good walker: unimpressive mover: sister to 3-y-o 1m winner Silvicolous and half-sister to 1m (at 2 yrs) and 1¼m winner Gold Law (by Law Society) and 1½m winner Funoon (by Kris): dam, Irish 6f winner, sister to El Gran Senor and Try My Best: fair maiden: well beaten in nursery at Warwick final start: stays 1m: acts on firm and dead ground: has been bandaged behind. *P. W. Chapple-Hyam* 77

AIN'TLIFELIKETHAT 8 gr.h. Godswalk (USA) 130 – Blue Alicia (Wolver Hollow 126) [1994 NR 1995 7m 6.9f 6f 6f 7m Aug 27] workmanlike, good-quartered horse: only poor at best since 5 yrs: stays 1m: acts on hard ground and all-weather, below best on a soft surface: visored (below form) once, usually blinkered: often slowly away. *T. J. Naughton* 39

AIRBOURNE RON (IRE) 3 b.g. Ajraas (USA) 88 – Ching A Ling (Pampapaul 121) [1994 54: 5s 5.1m^{4} 5.1g 6m 1995 a6g 7g Mar 25] strong, lengthy gelding: disappointing maiden: tried blinkered/visored. *S. G. Norton* –

AIR COMMAND (BAR) 5 br.g. Concorde Hero (USA) 101 – Hubbardair 60 (Town And Country 124) [1994 54§, a–§: a7g a6g 12.5d 8d* 7.1s 9m 12.1f 11.6m^{4} a9.4g 12m 1995 a8g 9.7g 12.5g^{5} 10m^{6} 8g^{4} 10.5d^{3} 12f^{4} 12s 12g^{6} a12g Dec 18] small, close-coupled gelding: poor handicapper: stays 11.6f: acts on good to firm and dead ground: has run poorly in blinkers and eyeshield: normally held up: ridden by Mr P. Phillips in 1995: unreliable. *C. T. Nash* — 49 § a– §

AIR COMMODORE (IRE) 4 b.g. Elegant Air 119 – Belle Enfant 87 (Beldale Flutter (USA) 130) [1994 95+: 12s 9m^{6} 7d^{3} 7d^{2} 7m 8m* 8m^{5} 8m^{2} 8d^{3} 8g* 8s^{5} 8m^{6} 1995 8.1m^{2} 8m 8m 8f* 8.1m^{6} Jul 8] strong, lengthy gelding: good walker: useful handicapper: impressive winner of 5-runner race at Bath in July: stays 1m well, and bred to stay 1¼m: acts on firm and soft ground: blinkered (well below form at Epsom) once as 3-y-o: held up/tracks leaders nowadays: consistent: reportedly suffered recurrence of off-fore injury July 17. *P. F. I. Cole* — 101

AIR OF MYSTERY 3 ch.f. Ballad Rock 122 – Keep Looking (USA) (Mr Prospector (USA)) [1994 –: 6d 6d 7g 1995 8.1d a7g Nov 8] leggy filly: no sign of ability. *N. E. Berry* — –

AIRPORT (USA) 4 b.c. Lear Fan (USA) 130 – Vague Prospect (USA) (Vaguely Noble 140) [1994 101+: 8d* 10m^{2} 10.3m^{5} 8m^{3} 10m^{2} 1995 8g* 9m^{3} 8m^{2} 10.4g 8g^{3} Sep 28] good-topped, angular colt: good mover with a long stride: useful performer: won slowly-run listed race at Doncaster in March: gave impression something amiss fourth start and off course 4½ months: looking extremely well, set lot to do when 3 lengths third of 13 to Bin Rosie in listed race at Newmarket, putting up clearly best effort: effective at 1m and 1¼m: acts on good to firm ground and dead, yet to race on extremes: tends to carry head high: often bandaged behind: has run well from front in small fields, but is usually held up: sent to Dubai. *J. H. M. Gosden* — 111

AIR WING 2 ch.c. (Apr 20) Risk Me (FR) 127 – Greenstead Lass (Double-U-Jay 120) [1995 5m^{3} 5g* Sep 12] 1,000Y, 8,800 2-y-o: unimpressive mover: brother to bad maiden Steady Risk and half-brother to several animals: dam never ran: made all and stayed on strongly on heavily favoured far rail when winning 20-runner maiden auction at Sandown by 4 lengths from Music Gold: will stay 6f: could well improve again. *M. H. Tompkins* — 83 p

AISLING'S IMAGE 3 b.f. Rambo Dancer (CAN) 107 – Mrs Cullumbine 60 (Silly Season 127) [1994 NR 1995 a8g a11g Feb 3] sixth foal: half-sister to middle-distance/staying winners Clifton Chase (by Try My Best), Our Aisling (by Blakeney) and Rakes Lane (by Pitskelly), all at least fair: dam stayed 1½m: tailed off in seller and maiden. *S. G. Norton* — –

AITCH N'BEE 12 ch.g. Northfields (USA) – Hot Case 92 (Upper Case (USA)) [1994 71, a68: 8g 8m 8f^{4} 7m^{6} 7d a8.5g^{2} a8.5g^{4} 1995 a9.4g* a8g a8g^{4} a9.4g^{2} 10.3g 8.2g 8f* 7g^{6} a9.4g^{5} Jun 10] small, strong gelding: veteran handicapper (rated 88 at his peak) who won 10 of his 66 races, including at Wolverhampton in January and Warwick (apprentices) in May: stayed 9.4f: went well on fibresand and acted on any going on turf: tried visored and blinkered early in career: dead. *Lady Herries* — 64 a70

AJDAR 4 b.g. Slip Anchor 136 – Loucoum (FR) 93 (Iron Duke (FR) 122) [1994 –: a7g a8.5g^{6} a9.4g^{5} 10m a12g 1995 a12g^{6} May 4] angular gelding: poor maiden on flat: visored (well beaten) only 4-y-o start: joined Miss G. Kelleway. *P. A. Kelleway* — –

AJKUIT (IRE) 2 b.c. (May 3) Persian Heights 129 – Hazar (IRE) 75 (Thatching 131) [1995 6.9g Oct 16] 8,000Y: first foal: dam, 7f to 8.9f winner, half-sister to smart 7f and 1m winner Llyn Gwynant: 25/1, last of 13, slowly away, in maiden auction at Folkestone. *J. J. Sheehan* — –

AKABUSI 4 gr.g. Absalom 128 – Clarandal 80 (Young Generation 129) [1994 51: a7g* a8g^{4} a7g 8g a8g a7g 1995 a6g a8g 8.2g Apr 4] seems no longer of much account: trained by M. C. Chapman first 2 starts at 4 yrs: sold 1,300 gns Doncaster May Sales. *J. Norton* — –

AKALIM 2 b.c. (Feb 15) Petong 126 – Tiszta Sharok 81 (Song 132) [1995 6.1m^{6} 6m^{5} 6m* 6g 6g^{6} 6.1m* Oct 26] 18,000Y: sturdy colt: has a quick action: fifth foal: brother to Irish 9f and 1¼m winner Petofi and half-brother to 6f winners by Indian Ridge (3-y-o Rosebud) and Absalom: dam 2-y-o 5f winner: won Newmarket maiden in July and nursery at Nottingham (by neck from Erupt) in October: stays 6f: races up with pace. *D. Morley* — 83

AKANSA (IRE) 2 ch.g. (Apr 23) Cadeaux Genereux 131 – Amerindian 84 (Commanche Run 133) [1995 7m Jul 5] second foal: dam, 1¼m winner, half-sister to smart 6f to 1m winner Capricorn Belle: second favourite, well-beaten last of 8 in maiden at Yarmouth, hanging left first 5f then allowed to coast in: subsequently gelded: clearly thought capable of better: sent to Dubai. *M. Johnston* –

AKAYID 3 b.f. Old Vic 136 – Psylla 96 (Beldale Flutter (USA) 130) [1994 –: 7.1g 1995 10g* Sep 9] workmanlike filly: 33/1, and bit backward, won 11-runner maiden at Goodwood in September by head from Fire of London, staying on strongly to lead close home: will stay 1½m: should improve again. *C. J. Benstead* 79 p

AKHIYAR (IRE) 4 gr.g. Doyoun 124 – Akishka (Nishapour (FR) 125) [1994 NR 1995 8m* 10m⁶ 10m³ 14m Jul 2] lengthy colt: first foal: dam unraced daughter of Arc winner Akiyda: useful Irish colt: 3½-length winner of 27-runner maiden at the Curragh (on heavy ground) at 2 yrs: missed 3-y-o season reportedly due to sinus problems, a virus and an operation to have one of his testicles removed: narrowly won 5-runner listed event at Leopardstown in May: gradually lost his form, 6 lengths third of 4 to Shemaran in slowly-run Gallinule Stakes at the Curragh penultimate start: probably stays 1¼m, tailed off over 1¾m: probably acts on good to firm ground and heavy. *J. Oxx, Ireland* 109

AKIL (IRE) 3 b.c. Cyrano de Bergerac 120 – Nonnita 71 (Welsh Saint 126) [1994 84p: 7g² 1995 7.1g³ 8.5m* 7.3m 8.1m* 8d* 7d 7.9m² 9d Oct 21] sturdy colt: fairly useful performer: won maiden at Beverley in July and handicaps at Sandown in August and Doncaster (rated stakes, made all) in September: stays 1m (not beaten by trip when tried at 9f): acts on good to firm ground and dead: genuine and consistent: stays in training. *R. W. Armstrong* 94

AKOLA ANGEL 3 ch.f. Indian Ridge 123 – Heavenly Note 82 (Chief Singer 131) [1994 –: 5.7g 1995 7.1m 6m a10g Sep 5] unfurnished filly: no worthwhile form. *C. R. Egerton* –

ALABANG 4 ch.g. Valiyar 129 – Seleter (Hotfoot 126) [1994 51: 8d 7g 7m⁵ 6g 5m 7.1m² 10.1d 1995 10.3m³ 8.5d 7f⁵ Oct 24] plain, quite good-topped gelding: still a maiden: twice gambled on, including at Doncaster (looked sure to win 2f out but found little) on reappearance: shaped well final start: likely to prove best at up to 1¼m: acts on firm ground, probably on dead: probably capable of better. *M. J. Camacho* 51 +

AL ABRAQ (IRE) 2 b.c. (Apr 19) Reprimand 122 – Dazzling Maid (IRE) 64 (Tate Gallery (USA) 117) [1995 7.1m* 7d⁶ Sep 26] IR 14,000F, 12,000Y: sturdy colt: first foal: dam, placed at 5f and 6f at 2 yrs, her only season to race: won median auction maiden at Sandown in August very easily by 1¼ lengths from Glenrazie: keeping-on sixth of 30 to Rio Duvida in valuable sales race at Newmarket month later: sure to improve again. *J. W. Hills* 89 p

A LA CARTE (IRE) 3 b.f. Caerleon (USA) 132 – Cheese Soup (USA) (Spectacular Bid (USA)) [1994 82: 7s² 7.9d³ 1995 7d² 8m* 8m⁶ 7f⁴ 8.1m³ 8d⁴ 8s* Oct 6] leggy filly: useful performer: successful at Ascot in £8,200 contest in May and listed race (led 2f out, beat Autumn Affair by a length) in October: stays 1m: acts on firm ground and soft: consistent: sold to race in Saudi Arabia. *J. L. Dunlop* 103

ALAKHLUKI 2 b.f. (Feb 21) Aragon 118 – Hawaiian Bloom (USA) 87 (Hawaii) [1995 6d⁶ 7.1s 6m⁵ Nov 6] third foal: half-sister to 6f winner Hawaiian Dream (by Midyan) and a winning hurdler by Formidable: dam won from 7f to 1¼m: modest form in maiden events: twice given easy time when beaten: gives impression capable of better back at 7f+. *G. Lewis* 57 p

ALAMBAR (IRE) 2 b.c. (Apr 19) Fairy King (USA) – Lightino (Bustino 136) [1995 7d 7g² 7g² Oct 23] 38,000F, IR 82,000Y: good-topped colt: third foal: dam Irish maiden half-sister to Gran Premio d'Italia and Premio Roma winner Welsh Guide: second in maidens won by Gold Disc at Leicester and Alhawa at Lingfield in October: will stay at least 1m. *P. T. Walwyn* 71

ALAMEIN (USA) 2 ch.c. (Feb 16) Roi Danzig (USA) – Pollination 100 (Pentotal) [1995 6m 7m³ 6m³ 6m⁴ Aug 29] workmanlike colt: fifth foal: half-brother to 1991 Irish 2-y-o 7f winner Nordic Beat (by Nordico): dam Irish 2-y-o 7f winner: in frame in maidens at Chester, Yarmouth and Ripon: stays 7f: joined W. Haggas. *Mrs L. Piggott* 77

ALAMI (USA) 3 br.c. Danzig (USA) – Alchaasibiyeh (USA) 85 (Seattle Slew (USA)) [1994 106: 6m* 6g* 7g^3 6m^4 1995 7m^4 a8g* Dec 31] sturdy, good sort: fluent mover: useful performer: 9/1 and looking very well, 4½ lengths fourth of 12 to Diffident in European Free Handicap at Newmarket (for H. Thomson Jones) in April: reportedly jarred a knee in race and not seen out again until winning minor event in Dubai in December: stays 1m: yet to race on a soft surface. *K. P. McLaughlin, UAE* **106**

ALANAR (USA) 3 b.c. Danzig (USA) – Classic Crown (USA) (Mr Prospector (USA)) [1994 85p: 7.1g* 7.1m* 1995 10.3g^4 10m^3 Jun 26] rangy colt: has scope: useful performer: creditable third of 4 in minor event at Windsor, running wide when in front 5f out and looking reluctant thereafter: stays 10.3f: has raced only on a sound surface: one to have reservations about: sold 32,000 gns Newmarket December Sales. *P. F. I. Cole* **93**

ALANEES 4 b.c. Cadeaux Genereux 131 – Dabaweyaa 118 (Shareef Dancer (USA) 135) [1994 110: 6m* 7.3g 6m^5 8m^2 7m^2 7m^5 1995 8g^3 8.1m^5 Apr 28] good-topped colt: has a round action: not a good walker: useful performer: respectable third in slowly-run Doncaster Mile and not discredited though last in Sandown Mile in the spring: useful form at 1m, very best efforts at 7f: acts on good to firm and dead ground: normally held up: reportedly injured a knee at Sandown and was due to undergo surgery. *C. E. Brittain* **106**

ALARABY (IRE) 3 b.f. Caerleon (USA) 132 – Circo 77 (High Top 131) [1994 66p: 8d^5 1995 10.5m 10g^4 10.2h^5 14m* 12m^3 14d^6 14m^2 Oct 13] smallish, lengthy filly: fair performer: won 4-runner maiden at Lingfield in August: improved form when second of 7 in handicap at Newmarket final start: should stay 2m: acts on good to firm ground: sold (I. Balding to Martyn Wane) 6,200 gns Newmarket December Sales. *I. A. Balding* **77**

ALARMING 3 b.f. Warning 136 – Metair 118 (Laser Light 118) [1994 61p: 7m 1995 6m^3 7.1m* 7g* 7m 7.1s^6 Sep 30] small filly: has a quick action: has been fired: fair form: won maiden at Haydock and handicap at Salisbury in July: likely to prove best at up to 1m: acts on good to firm ground, well beaten on soft: sold 13,000 gns Newmarket December Sales. *J. H. M. Gosden* **78**

AL BAHA 3 ch.f. Midyan (USA) 124 – Dafinah (USA) 89 (Graustark) [1994 59p: 6m^4 1995 6m^5 7m^2 10.1m^4 8.2d^4 Sep 19] useful-looking filly: unimpressive mover: fair maiden: may well prove best short of 1¼m: acts on good to firm ground, well below form on soft. *H. R. A. Cecil* **65**

ALBAHA (USA) 2 br.c. (Apr 25) Woodman (USA) 126 – Linda's Magic (USA) 114 (Far North (CAN) 120) [1995 6g^3 7g^6 7m^4 Oct 13] big, robust colt: fourth living foal: half-brother to useful 7f and 1m winner Mur Taasha (by Riverman) and middle-distance stayer Shujan (by Diesis): dam 6f and 7f winner: similar form in maidens at Newmarket and York first 2 starts, making most: acted as pacemaker when tailed-off last of 4 in Dewhurst Stakes at Newmarket: stays 7f. *R. W. Armstrong* **81**

ALBEIT 5 ch.m. Mandrake Major 122 – Sioux Be It (Warpath 113) [1994 43: 7.1g 8m^4 8m* 9.2f^5 8f 8f 1995 a9.4g Jun 2] neat mare: poor performer: best form at 1m: acts on firm and dead going. *M. F. Barraclough* **–**

ALBERT THE BEAR 2 b.g. (Mar 7) Puissance 110 – Florentynna Bay 61 (Aragon 118) [1995 5.1g 5m 5m^5 a6g 5f* 5.7h* 6m* 6.1m^4 6m^2 6d Sep 9] 7,800F, 21,000Y: tall, leggy, useful-looking gelding: easy mover: fourth foal: half-brother to 3-y-o 6f winner Charnwood Queen (by Cadeaux Genereux) and a winner in Hong Kong: dam 2-y-o 5f winner, half-sister to useful 1988 2-y-o Superpower: fair performer: won seller at Carlisle in June and nurseries at Bath and Catterick in August: rather disappointing final outing (dead ground), and subsequently gelded: stays 6f: acts on hard ground, showed nothing on fibresand. *J. Berry* **75**

ALBINOR (IRE) 3 b.c. Danehill (USA) 126 – Schwanensee (USA) (Mr Leader (USA)) [1994 89p: 6d^4 7m^2 8s* 8s^2 8g^2 1995 8m 8g 8f^2 8g* 8.8g^2 7.5s^4 8g^4 8m^2 Nov 12] smallish, useful-looking colt: fairly useful performer: comfortably won minor event at Milan in July: stays 8.8f: acts on firm and soft ground: to stay in Italy. *J. L. Dunlop* **94**

ALCIAN BLUE 4 b.c. Tina's Pet 121 – Rhiannon 65 (Welsh Pageant 132) [1994 53: a8.5g a12g^6 12.5v^2 16s 14.1g^2 16.1d^3 a14g 1995 17.1m 18f* Oct 16] workmanlike colt: not a good walker: modest handicapper: 25/1, won at Pontefract **47 +**

Mr E. Pick's "Alderbrook"

in October, leading over 1f out then hanging right and just holding on: stays 2¼m: acts on any going. *M. D. Hammond*

AL CORNICHE (IRE) 3 b.f. Bluebird (USA) 125 – Naxos (USA) (Big Spruce (USA)) [1994 62: 5d^3 5d^2 5.1m* 6s^3 6s^5 7m^6 8g 6.1d^6 7m 8s 1995 a7g^6 a10g^2 a10g^5 12d^3 14.1g^2 14.6m 14.1m 16.1g a16g Dec 15] small, leggy filly: poor performer: left M. Channon's stable after second 3-y-o start: stays 1¾m: acts on good to firm and soft ground and equitrack: visored (no improvement) twice at 2 yrs: none too consistent. *K. O. Cunningham-Brown* 46 a38

ALDANEH 3 ch.f. Indian Ridge 123 – Maiyaasah 75 (Kris 135) [1994 67: 6g^2 7.1g^4 7d 1995 7m* 8m 7.6m^2 7g^4 8.3m* 8.1d 8f^4 Oct 24] lengthy, rather unfurnished filly: easy mover: fair performer: won maiden at Brighton in June and handicap at Windsor in August: stays 8.3f: acts on firm ground: inconsistent: sold 38,000 gns Newmarket December Sales. *R. Hannon* 77

ALDERBROOK 6 b.h. Ardross 134 – Twine (Thatching 131) [1994 117: 10d* 10s* 10g^6 10.5m^4 10d* 9.8d* 1995 10s 10.5v^2 11s^2 May 28] rangy horse: not a good walker: very smart performer: best efforts when 3 lengths second of 10 to Pelder in Prix Ganay at Longchamp then ¾-length second of 9 to Freedom Cry in Grosser Preis der Wirtschaft at Baden-Baden later in May: should stay 1½m: suited by a soft surface: has good turn of foot, and has idled in front: had chips removed from near-fore in the summer: has rejoined K. Bailey, for whom he had won Champion Hurdle in March: game and genuine. *Mrs J. Cecil* 120

ALDEVONIE 3 b.f. Green Desert (USA) 127 – Kintail 76 (Kris 135) [1994 NR 1995 8.1g^2 May 29] second foal: dam, runner-up on debut over 1¼m, is out of smart 75 p

Sleat (winner at up to 1¼m and half-sister to St Leger winner Athens Wood): 10/3, shaped quite well in 12-runner maiden at Chepstow, staying on well from 2f out and just failing: will stay 1¼m: looked sure to improve. *H. R. A. Cecil*

ALDINGTON CHAPPLE 7 b.g. Creetown 123 – Aldington Miss (Legal Eagle 126) [1994 –: a11g^{6} a7g^{6} a8.5g 1995 a12g a11g Jan 13] leggy gelding: seems of little account on flat. *B. Preece* –

ALDWICK COLONNADE 8 ch.m. Kind of Hush 118 – Money Supply (Brigadier Gerard 144) [1994 NR 1995 a7g a8g 10f 8m 10g^{6} 8f^{3} 10g^{3} Sep 2] workmanlike mare: unimpressive walker and mover: has had foals at stud: poor performer nowadays: stays 1¼m: acts on firm and dead ground: has been bandaged: won selling hurdle in September. *M. D. I. Usher* 39

ALERTING 3 b.c. Warning 136 – Zalfa (Luthier 126) [1994 54: 7d 7d 1995 8.5m^{5} 8g 8.3m* 8.1g^{6} 8f^{6} 10f^{4} 10m 10m^{3} 8g Sep 29] small, leggy colt: modest handicapper: won at Windsor in June: probably stays 1¼m: acts on good to firm ground: visored and wore tongue strap (below form) seventh 3-y-o start: tends to hang: one to treat with caution: sold 5,500 gns Newmarket Autumn Sales. *I. A. Balding* 65 §

ALESSANDRA 2 ch.f. (Apr 5) Generous (IRE) 139 – Kiss 88 (Habitat 134) [1995 6g^{2} 7m^{5} 7.1d^{2} Oct 11] good-topped filly: closely related to fairly useful 3-y-o Alessia, 7f winner at 2 yrs, and smart middle-distance stayer Casey (both by Caerleon) and half-sister to several winners, including useful middle-distance stayer Crack (by High Line): dam sprinting half-sister to very useful stayer Meistersinger: similar form in maiden at Ascot, listed race (fifth of 8 to Mons) at Newbury and maiden at Haydock: will be well suited by middle distances: acts on good to firm and dead ground: wears bandages. *B. W. Hills* 81

ALESSIA 3 b.f. Caerleon (USA) 132 – Kiss 88 (Habitat 134) [1994 83p: 7m^{5} 7g^{3} 7d* 1995 10m^{5} 10m^{4} 12d 8s Oct 6] robust filly: fairly useful performer: contested listed races in 1995, running well at Newmarket and Newbury, then twice well beaten (sweating and edgy on first occasion) at Ascot: stays 1¼m: acts on good to firm ground and dead. *B. W. Hills* 91

ALEX 3 ch.f. Hallgate 127 – La Chiquita 84 (African Sky 124) [1994 NR 1995 7f^{6} Aug 17] first foal: dam 1m winner in Ireland later best over 5f here: 50/1, distant last of 6 in maiden at Ayr. *R. Allan* –

ALFAASELAH (GER) 3 b.f. Dancing Brave (USA) 140 – Alya (GER) (Lombard (GER) 126) [1994 84: 7m^{5} 7g* 8s^{2} 8.1s* 8s 1995 10m 8.5g* 9.5d* 10d Oct 21] lengthy filly, rather plain: fairly useful form: behind in listed race at Newmarket (final start for M.Stoute) on reappearance: won minor events at Krefeld and Frankfurt in the autumn: stays 9.5f: acts well on soft going. *U. Ostmann, Germany* 97

ALFAHAAL (IRE) 2 b.c. (Feb 10) Green Desert (USA) 127 – Fair of The Furze 112 (Ela-Mana-Mou 132) [1995 7.1d 7d Sep 27] IR 280,000Y: robust colt: brother to useful 1¼m performer Elfaslah and half-brother to top-class middle-distance performer White Muzzle (by Dancing Brave): dam Irish 1m and 1¼m winner who stayed 1½m: about 11 lengths eighth of 11 to Kings Witness in maiden at Haydock, travelling smoothly around 5f: well below that form in similar event at Salisbury 25 days later, again eased. *H. Thomson Jones* 62 +

ALFAYZA 2 b.f. (Feb 21) Danehill (USA) 126 – Dahlawise (IRE) 76 (Caerleon (USA) 132) [1995 5g^{6} 5g^{6} 5f^{5} 5m^{4} 5g^{2} 7h* 7.1m^{4} 8g Sep 15] 8,800Y: close-coupled filly: first foal: dam, 2-y-o 6f winner, should have stayed 1¼m: won nursery at Newcastle in August, making all alone on far rail: ran creditably in similar event at Edinburgh next start: best form at 7f: acts on hard ground. *J. D. Bethell* 63

ALHAARTH (IRE) 2 b.c. (Mar 7) Unfuwain (USA) 131 – Irish Valley (USA) (Irish River (FR) 131) [1995 7g* 7f* 7.1m* 7g* 7m* Oct 13] 126 p

Champion two-year-olds don't always go on to classic success, but the portents are good for Alhaarth. He looked a fine prospect the day he first set foot on a racecourse in July and he ended his first season unbeaten in five races including the Generous Dewhurst Stakes at Newmarket in October. The Dewhurst was widely accepted as the premier test for two-year-olds when it was won by Nijinsky, Mill Reef, Grundy, Wollow and The Minstrel in an eight-year period up to the mid-'seventies. Though El Gran Senor was the only other Dewhurst winner to go on

Lanson Champagne Vintage Stakes, Goodwood—Alhaarth (striped cap) is too good for Allied Forces

to classic success in the intervening period the race has enjoyed a marked revival in the 'nineties. Generous and Dr Devious, the 1990 and 1991 winners, both went on to win the Derby, while the winners in 1992 and 1994, Zafonic and Pennekamp, won the Two Thousand Guineas, and the 1993 winner Grand Lodge came very close to emulating them against Mister Baileys. Like Zafonic and Grand Lodge, Alhaarth topped the Timeform Ratings and the International Classification for two-year-olds. The latest Dewhurst field may have lacked quantity—only four runners including Alhaarth's pacemaker—but Alhaarth beat the Group 1 winners Danehill Dancer (Heinz 57 Phoenix Stakes and National Stakes) and Tagula (Prix Morny) in excellent style, pulling his way into the lead three furlongs out, having his rivals off the bit soon afterwards and running on strongly up the hill, receiving only one flick of the whip. Alhaarth's two-and-a-half-length winning margin over Danehill Dancer could have been extended had Willie Carson wished, and we have rated him accordingly.

There hasn't been a smaller field for the Dewhurst since Mill Reef beat two opponents in 1970, though how much that was a reflection of Alhaarth's reputation and how much it owed to other causes is a moot point. The long, very dry summer almost certainly kept some potentially credible opponents for Alhaarth off the course altogether, while others who made belated appearances in the autumn were understandably found easier options. In fact, Alhaarth faced only thirteen opponents in the four pattern races he contested, one fewer in total than the bunch he beat on his debut. Alhaarth fought out the finish of the Strutt & Parker Maiden at the Newmarket July meeting with another promising colt Mark of Esteem, the pair separated by a neck, pulling four lengths clear of third-placed Silver Prey, after a good tussle over the last two furlongs. Alhaarth was sent next to Goodwood for the Lanson Champagne Vintage Stakes, a race won in the previous four years by Dr Devious, Maroof, Mister Baileys and Eltish. The manner of Alhaarth's victory left little doubt that he too would go on to make an impact at the highest level. Just as he began to make his run, Alhaarth received a hefty bump from outsider Oberons Boy as that horse was squeezed by Alhaarth's main market rival Allied Forces. It looked as though Alhaarth had met trouble too near to home to be able to win, but he showed splendid acceleration once extricated and eased to the outside, and deprived Allied Forces of the lead inside the final furlong, winning in clear-cut style by a length. Though Alhaarth's trainer was keen to play down Alhaarth's prospects—'It's stupid to boost a horse up at this stage, look what happened to Celtic Swing'—it was clear that this was a horse to enthuse over. Alhaarth's post-Goodwood odds for the Two Thousand Guineas and the Derby—Ladbrokes went 25/1 for both races—underestimated his chances in those races by some way, even at such an early stage. There was, admittedly, a lot of time for others to come on the scene—and plenty of time for Alhaarth to go wrong—but it's rare to see a horse win a pattern race so decisively after overcoming serious trouble in running. Another impressive victory followed in the Solario Stakes at Sandown, Alhaarth landing the odds with ease, conceding 10 lb to the filly Staffin who had pushed the highly-regarded Bint Salsabil close in a listed event at Newmarket on her previous outing. Alhaarth had to work harder in the Laurent-Perrier Champagne Stakes at Doncaster where, setting only a steady pace in a three-horse race, he held off Rio Duvida by half a length without having to be fully extended, though he did edge left in the closing stages. Alhaarth's ante-post odds for the classics, down to 10/1 for the Guineas and 7/1 for the Derby, remained unchanged with Ladbrokes after Doncaster, though Hills pushed him out two points for the Guineas and one for the Derby. After the Dewhurst, 9/4 for the Guineas and 7/2 for the Derby were the best odds available!

Most years, the Guineas for both colts and fillies, which come barely six weeks into the turf season, are won by horses that have taken high rank as two-year-olds. Provided Alhaarth winters well, therefore, and the Dubai-founded Godolphin operation doesn't come up with a surprise packet, the Two Thousand Guineas looks his for the taking. But what of his Derby prospects? Willie Carson is on record as saying that 'there has got to be a question mark about the Derby'. 'He has a lot of speed and is out of an Irish River mare, so I just wonder about the mile and a half'. Leaving aside the by-no-means remote possibility that an unraced or lightly-raced contemporary may be able to bridge the gap by Derby time, Alhaarth was shaping as the type to do even better over middle distances in time until his last two performances once again emphasised his speed. Just because Alhaarth showed that he was capable of producing a first-class turn of speed over seven furlongs,

Laurent-Perrier Champagne Stakes, Doncaster—
more bubbly for Alhaarth; he beats Rio Duvida in a falsely-run race

Generous Dewhurst Stakes, Newmarket—the season's best two-year-old form; Alhaarth lengthens away from Danehill Dancer and Tagula

Alhaarth (IRE) (b.c. Mar 7, 1993)	Unfuwain (USA) (b 1985)	Northern Dancer (b 1961)	Nearctic
			Natalma
		Height of Fashion (b 1979)	Bustino
			Highclere
	Irish Valley (USA) (ch 1982)	Irish River (ch 1976)	Riverman
			Irish Star
		Green Valley (br 1967)	Val de Loir
			Sly Pola

however, doesn't necessarily preclude him from proving so effective at longer distances as a three-year-old. Experience shows that if a horse is bred to stay it usually does so, and if it isn't it usually doesn't. Alhaarth's pedigree is capable of different interpretations—some of the most important winners on the distaff side of his pedigree have made their mark at distances short of a mile and a half—but we're reasonably confident about his ability to stay the Derby trip. On the limited evidence available, Alhaarth's sire the impeccably-bred top-class mile-and-a-half horse Unfuwain is going to prove an influence for stamina at stud. The average distance of races won by his two crops of three-year-olds so far—his first included the Irish Oaks winner Bolas—is just over eleven furlongs. Alhaarth's dam Irish Valley was disappointing on the racecourse, failing to reach a place in six outings, on the last of them wearing blinkers. She wasn't raced after July in her three-year-old days. Alhaarth is Irish Valley's sixth foal and her second pattern winner following Green Pola (by Nijinsky) whose racing career was curtailed by an injury she suffered while being trained for the Prix Marcel Boussac; she won both her starts at two, including the Group 3 Prix du Calvados at Deauville over seven furlongs. Green Pola would have stayed a mile and a quarter at three; her full brother the useful Gaelic Myth won at up to a mile and a half on the flat and showed a similar level of ability over hurdles. Irish Valley's other winner so far Celtic Brave was still running in the States as a six-year-old; he has won eight races in his career, to the time of writing, the longest being over eight and a half furlongs. Celtic Brave is by Shadeed, much more of an influence for speed—the average distance over which his three-year-olds and upwards have won is a mile—than either Nijinsky or Unfuwain. Irish Valley herself was arguably bred to stay further than eight and a half furlongs, the longest distance she tackled. Her sire Irish River has sired winners over a wide range of distances, the average for his three-year-olds and upwards being around nine and a half furlongs, while her unraced dam Green Valley was the product of a mating between a French

Derby winner Val de Loir and a Prix de l'Abbaye winner Sly Pola. Green Valley has produced numerous winners at stud, most notably the triple Group 1 winner (Observer Gold Cup, French Guineas and Prix Lupin) Green Dancer who has made a name for himself at stud. Green Valley's other winners include the smart French middle-distance performer Ercolano and the American eleven-furlong and mile-and-a-half graded stakes winner Val Danseur. Irish Valley, by the way, was purchased by Shadwell Estates in 1990, her first Shadwell mating producing the ill-fated Finus (by Nashwan), an encouraging second to Moonshell in a Doncaster maiden on her only start. Irish Valley has no yearling, but has since produced a foal to Sadler's Wells and is in foal again to Unfuwain. The strong, well-made Alhaarth, a good mover with a powerful action and a good turn of foot, has the physical scope to grow into an even more imposing individual as a three-year-old. He has so far raced only on a sound surface. *Major W. R. Hern*

ALHAWA (USA) 2 ch.c. (Feb 8) Mt Livermore (USA) – Petrava (NZ) (Imposing (AUS)) [1995 7g* Oct 23] closely related to 1990 2-y-o 6f winner Jallad (by Blushing Groom) and half-brother to 2 winners, both at 1m: dam won from 6.5f to 9f in South Africa, where champion filly at 3 yrs: 14/1, won 9-runner maiden at Lingfield by 3 lengths from Alambar, leading 2f out and running on under hand riding: sure to improve. *C. J. Benstead* — 76 p

ALICIA (IRE) 2 b. or br.f. (Feb 27) Darshaan 133 – Tribal Rite 95 (Be My Native (USA) 122) [1995 7g Oct 23] 26,000F: fourth foal: half-sister to fair Irish 6f and 7f winner Scalp (by Thatching) and 3-y-o 12.3f winner Danesrath (by Danehill): dam 6f (at 2 yrs) to 1¼m winner: 16/1, around 14 lengths ninth of 14, never a factor, to Jezyah in maiden at Lingfield: bred to require much further than 7f. *J. L. Dunlop* — – p

A LIKELY TALE (USA) 2 b.c. (Apr 18) Alleged (USA) 138 – Thatsallshewrote (USA) (Graustark) [1995 8d[4] Sep 27] tall colt: sixth foal: half-brother to 3 minor winners in USA: dam minor winner in USA at up to 9f, sister to Prix de Royallieu winner Don't Sulk and Santa Anita Derby winner Jim French: 33/1, around 2½ lengths fourth of 18 to Mystic Knight in maiden at Salisbury: will be very well suited by middle distances: will improve. *M. Bell* — 78 p

ALILISA (USA) 7 b.m. Alydar (USA) – Balletomane (USA) (Nijinsky (CAN) 138) [1994 NR 1995 14.6g 14m Jul 7] lengthy mare: no longer of much account. *Mrs J. Jordan* — –

ALIOLI 3 br.f. Nishapour (FR) 125 – Allegra 73 (Niniski (USA) 125) [1994 –: 7g 1995 11.5g[6] 10.2m[5] 12m a11g Nov 20] smallish, workmanlike filly: no worthwhile form: sold 800 gns Newmarket December Sales. *M. J. Ryan* — –

ALI-ROYAL (IRE) 2 b.c. (Feb 9) Royal Academy (USA) 130 – Alidiva 105 (Chief Singer 131) [1995 7g[4] 7g* Oct 3] rather leggy colt: second foal: half-brother to 3-y-o Taipan (by Last Tycoon), 7f winner at 2 yrs (stays 10.5f): dam 6f to 1m winner out of smart 1982 2-y-o Alligatrix: sweating, won 17-runner maiden at Warwick by 4 lengths from Forest Robin, always prominent and clear over 1f out: will stay at least 1m: will improve further. *H. R. A. Cecil* — 87 p

ALIS PRINCESS 2 ch.f. (Mar 15) Sayf El Arab (USA) 127 – Princess Zeddera (English Prince 129) [1995 7.5m Aug 24] 3,800F: half-sister to useful 6f and 7.6f winner Hard Round (by Hard Fought): dam French 10.5f winner: 40/1, well-beaten last of 8 in maiden at Beverley. *M. P. Bielby* — –

ALISTOVER 2 b.f. (Feb 16) Zalazl (USA) 120 – Song of Gold 85 (Song 132) [1995 5d 5m 7g a8.5g[5] a7g[6] Nov 27] 750F, 2,200Y: leggy, useful-looking filly: half-sister to 4 winners here and abroad, including 6f and 7f winner Postorage (by Pyjama Hunt) and 1m and 1¼m winner Modern British (by Elegant Air): dam sprinter: well beaten in varied events. *R. Dickin* — –

ALISURA 2 br.f. (Jan 9) Lead On Time (USA) 123 – Iosifa 108 (Top Ville 129) [1995 7.1s Oct 17] fourth living foal: half-sister to winning stayers Elburg (by Ela-Mana-Mou) and Iota (by Niniski): dam 2-y-o 7f winner stayed 1½m, seemed to become temperamental: 14/1, eighth of 19 to Ski For Gold in maiden at Chepstow, never significantly better than midfield: will probably do better. *J. R. Fanshawe* — – p

ALIZARIN 6 ch.m. Noalto 120 – The Crying Game 55 (Manor Farm Boy 114) [1994 NR 1995 a11g 11.8d Apr 6] smallish, close-coupled mare: of little account: dead. *J. L. Harris* — –

ALJADEER (USA) 6 b. or br.g. Alleged (USA) 138 – Return The Roses (USA) (Carry Back) [1994 –: 10.4d 10.3s 10.1d 1995 12.3d 17.1m^6 12d^4 Jun 7] rather leggy, attractive gelding: smart as a 3-y-o, only poor nowadays: should stay at least 1¾m: blinkered last 2 starts. *M. W. Easterby* 47

ALJAWAB (USA) 4 b. or br.c. Alleged (USA) 138 – Chuckles (USA) (Riverman (USA) 131) [1994 71: 10s 11.4s^2 10.5s 12.1g 11.8d^5 10.1d 1995 11.8d 8f^4 8.3g^2 a9.4g* 8g^2 a9.4g 10m^3 10f^4 10d* 11.5s^5 10g* 10d^6 Oct 19] well-made colt: fair handicapper: won at Wolverhampton (maiden) in May, Nottingham (amateurs) in September and Leicester in October: seems best at around 1¼m: probably acts on any turf going and fibresand: blinkered (weakened tamely) final 3-y-o start: tracks leaders/held up: inconsistent: sold 21,000 gns Newmarket Autumn Sales. *J. L. Dunlop* 71

ALJAZ 5 b.g. Al Nasr (FR) 126 – Santa Linda (USA) (Sir Ivor 135) [1994 64d: 7g 5m^6 5.1m 7g a8g a8g 1995 a7g^4 a7g^3 a7g a6g^3 a7g^6 a6g^3 a6g 6v* 7m a7g 7.1d a6g^6 a6g a6g Nov 24] useful-looking gelding: modest handicapper: easy winner at Hamilton (first race on a soft surface) in March on penultimate start for D. Thom: off course nearly 5 months, no comparable form for new stable, claimed to join Miss G. Kelleway £3,000 final start: stays 7f: acts on fibresand, goes well on heavy ground: blinkered final start: inconsistent. *R. Harris* 64 d

ALJAZZAF 5 b.g. Mtoto 134 – Ibtisamm (USA) 71 (Caucasus (USA) 127) [1994 96: 10m^5 10m 10s^3 10m* 10g^6 12v^4 1995 9m 10.1f^2 10m 10g* 10.4m^6 10.1m 10d 10v Oct 7] strong gelding: useful handicapper: improved form under a fine tactical ride from J. Weaver to make all in 6-runner rated stakes at Ascot in July: below form afterwards: effective at 1¼m, and stayed 14.8f at 3 yrs: inconsistent on a soft surface, best form on a sound surface: sometimes a front runner. *R. Akehurst* 106

AL JINN 4 ch.g. Hadeer 118 – Mrs Musgrove (Jalmood (USA) 126) [1994 61d, a73?: 10m^2 12.4f^4 a10g* 11.6m 10m 10d 11.9d 10.1g 1995 10g 14.1m 16.5f Jul 27] strong, lengthy gelding: seems no longer of much account. *R. Curtis* –

ALKA INTERNATIONAL 3 b.g. Northern State (USA) 91 – Cachucha (Gay Fandango (USA) 132) [1994 50: 7m 7m 7.1d a6g^4 1995 a7g a8g^6 a10g^3 9.7m 10m 8g^5 May 30] workmanlike gelding: modest maiden: stays 1¼m: acts on equitrack: inconsistent. *J. White* 51

ALKATEB 3 ch.g. Rock City 120 – Corley Moor 97 (Habitat 134) [1994 NR 1995 9f* 10.2m^3 8.1m* 10g^2 10m^4 10g^5 Nov 12] 15,500Y: workmanlike gelding: unimpressive mover: eighth foal: half-brother to several winners, none better than himself: dam 2-y-o 5f winner: useful performer: won maiden at Goodwood and handicap at Sandown (led near line) in the summer: ran well in handicap and listed races afterwards: stays 1¼m well: acts on firm ground, yet to race on a soft surface. *Miss Gay Kelleway* 98

ALLAHRAKHA 4 ch.g. Aragon 118 – Bernigra Girl 78 (Royal Match 117) [1994 57: 8g 5.1f^4 6f^6 6m 8g^2 8m 1995 11.8d 7m May 4] leggy gelding: no worthwhile form since penultimate 3-y-o start: joined Mrs J.G. Retter. *D. R. Tucker* –

ALLEMANDE (IRE) 3 b.c. Nashwan (USA) 135 – Dance Festival 101 (Nureyev (USA) 131) [1994 NR 1995 a8.5g* 7.3g* Jul 14] lengthy, rather unfurnished colt: second foal: dam lightly-raced maiden (sixth in Irish 1000 Guineas) out of half-sister to Boldboy: won maiden at Wolverhampton (made all) in March and well-contested minor event at Newbury (waited with, leading over 1f out and staying on well to beat Indhar 1¾ lengths) in July: stays 8.5f: looked useful recruit and likely to win more races: sent to Dubai. *J. H. M. Gosden* 104 p

ALLESCA 5 b.m. Alleging (USA) 120 – Hitesca 110 (Tesco Boy 121) [1994 66: 10.8v^4 15.4v^6 11.7g 13.1g 11.8d^6 10m 10g* 10.1m^3 10m^3 10m* 10.2g^4 10m^2 11.4d* 10s^5 12s^2 11.9d^3 1995 10.3g 12m 12g 10g* 9.9d* 11.4g 11.4m Jul 8] workmanlike mare: poor mover: fair handicapper: narrowly won at Leicester in May and Beverley in June, leading close home: effective at 1¼m to 1½m: acts on good to firm and soft ground: normally held up: sometimes races lazily: normally bandaged: ridden by apprentice C. Adamson except on reappearance: tough. *M. D. I. Usher* 64

ALLEZ CYRANO (IRE) 4 b.g. Alzao (USA) 117 – Miss Bergerac (Bold Lad (IRE) 133) [1994 97: 7d 6f^5 7d* 7m 8m^3 7f* 7g 8m^5 1995 8m 8f 7.3m 10m 7g Sep 7] leggy gelding: well below form in competitive handicaps in 1995, tried visored final –

start: stays 1m: acts on firm and dead ground: usually held up: sold only 4,500 gns Newmarket Autumn Sales. *M. Bell*

ALL HONOUR 3 b.g. Kabour 80 – Tolly's Best 58 (Hittite Glory 125) [1994 NR 1995 a7g a6g a9.4g 7f Oct 3] big, strong gelding: fifth foal (all by Kabour): dam sprint maiden: no worthwhile form: sold 1,000 gns Doncaster November Sales. *D. W. Chapman* –

ALLIED FORCES (USA) 2 ch.c. (Mar 24) Miswaki (USA) 124 – Mangala (USA) (Sharpen Up 127) [1995 6g* 6m 7g* 7f² Jul 26] 108

Asked in February to nominate a horse to follow for *Timeform* readers, Henry Cecil put forward Eltish. By way of a bonus he recommended an unnamed American-bred two-year-old by Miswaki who, even at that early stage, had been really taking the eye. The youngster turned out to be Allied Forces, the stable's first two-year-old runner of the season when he readily won a maiden at York in May and one of its better inmates of that age seen in action in 1995. Allied Forces raced just three more times before he left for Dubai. He finished a disappointing eighth from a wrong-side draw in the Coventry Stakes at Royal Ascot but soon redeemed himself by becoming Cecil's tenth winner in the last fifteen runnings of the Child & Co. Superlative Stakes at Newmarket. His length-and-a-quarter defeat of the developing Mons is useful form. The performance earned him the job of defending another outstanding record of the stable's in the Lanson Champagne Vintage Stakes at Goodwood in July. That day belonged to the odds-on Alhaarth, though. It was he who impressed as a potential classic colt, while Allied Forces, giving 3 lb all round, strained to get to the front in the straight, hanging right. A length separated the pair at the finish; it could well have been three.

Allied Forces (USA) (ch.c. Mar 24, 1993)	Miswaki (USA) (ch 1978)	Mr Prospector (b 1970)	Raise A Native
			Gold Digger
		Hopespringseternal (ch 1971)	Buckpasser
			Rose Bower
	Mangala (USA) (ch 1982)	Sharpen Up (ch 1969)	Atan
			Rocchetta
		Meadow Blue (ch 1975)	Raise A Native
			Gay Hostess

Allied Forces may not be coming back from abroad. When he changed hands privately between York and Ascot (for a sum reported to be in excess of £500,000) it was said that he'd been bought with a view to racing him in Dubai. He is not part of the Godolphin operation. If he does return, the benefits of wintering there will need to have wrought abnormal improvement to take him into the top flight. Allied Forces got seven furlongs well as a two-year-old and should stay a mile at three. His dam

Child & Co. Superlative Stakes, Newmarket—Allied Forces beats Mons and Dovebrace

won over both those distances in France and his half-brother Barraq (by Crystal Glitters) won over a mile there. The dam Mangala, a daughter of an unraced sister to Majestic Prince and Crowned Prince, has also produced Shalabia (by Fast Topaze), a modest winner at seven furlongs in Britain who stays a mile. Allied Forces, a smallish, sturdy colt, is a good mover with a long stride; he acts on firm ground. *H. R. A. Cecil*

ALLIMAC NOMIS 6 b.g. Daring March 116 – Game For A Laugh 72 (Martinmas 128) [1994 NR 1995 8.3m 10g May 26] leggy, angular gelding: rated 39 at 3 yrs: backward, well beaten in 1995: fair hurdler: sold (I. (Campbell to M. Hammond) 6,500 gns Doncaster August Sales: won over fences in November. *I. Campbell*

–

ALL IN GOOD TIME 2 b.c. (Mar 18) Shadeed (USA) 135 – Good Thinking (USA) (Raja Baba (USA)) [1995 7g Sep 14] 30,000F, 11,000Y: half-brother to several winners here and in North America, including 6.9f and 1½m winner Thinking Twice (by Kris): dam, Irish 2-y-o 7f winner, half-sister to Grand Criterium winner Treizieme and Gold Cup runner-up Eastern Mystic: 50/1, last of 14 in maiden at Ayr: sold 2,000 gns Doncaster October Sales. *C. W. Thornton*

–

ALLINSON'S MATE (IRE) 7 b.g. Fayruz 116 – Piney Pass (Persian Bold 123) [1994 75: a7g^2 a8.5g^6 a8g^3 a8.5g^3 a7g* 8m^5 7g* a7g 7d^5 7.6m^6 7m^4 7m 7m 7.1m^2 7g* 7m^4 8f 7d^3 7d a8g 1995 a8g a7g^4 a7g^6 a7g^5 a7g^3 6.9m* 8m^5 7m^5 7g 7g* 7f^4 7m* 7m^2 7h^3 7.6m^3 7g 7g 7g Oct 7] small, robust gelding: carries condition: unimpressive mover: fair handicapper: won at Carlisle (claimer) in April, Doncaster in June and York in July: effective at 7f to 8.5f: acts on firm ground, dead and all-weather surfaces: blinkered since tenth 7-y-o start: usually held up: tough. *T. D. Barron*

79
a71

ALL IN THE MIND 4 b.g. Vision (USA) – No More Rosies 74 (Warpath 113) [1994 61: 12.4g* 12s^3 10.5g 15s 11.9d 1995 a12g^3 8.5d^3 15.4m a9.2g^4 7v^6 11f 11g* 9.5f 14f* 11g^6 a12g* a13.5g^3 a12g* Oct 15] unfurnished gelding: has a round action: modest performer: won handicaps at Ostend in July and August and Sterrebeek in September and claimer at Sterrebeek in October: stays 12.4f (always behind over 15.4f at Folkestone): acts on soft ground and dirt. *Alex Vanderhaeghen, Belgium*

50

ALLMOSA 6 b.m. Alleging (USA) 120 – Wimosa 92 (Mossborough 126) [1994 66: a12g^2 a14.8g^2 16m^5 13.1g^4 12d 20m^4 18f* 16.4m^3 18.7g 20f 15.4d^5 18m 16d^4 a14.8g^6 a16g^5 1995 10g 17.2m^5 14.1g^4 Jun 7] leggy, close-coupled mare: has a round action: fair handicapper: below form in 1995: stays 2½m: acts on any going, including all-weather: inconsistent. *T. J. Naughton*

–

ALL MY DREAMS (IRE) 3 b. or br.c. Assert 134 – Marie de Beaujeu (FR) 108 (Kenmare (FR) 125) [1994 NR 1995 11v^2 11d* 11g* 11d* 12m* 12m* Aug 13] 10,500Y: half-brother to winners in France (not until 4 yrs) by Deep Roots (at 1m) and Synefos (at 9.5f to 11f): dam French 2-y-o 5.5f and 6.5f winner and listed placed, did not train on: had a tremendous season, winning his last 5 races, namely maiden at Krefeld in April, minor event at Baden-Baden in May, listed race at Dresden and BMW Deutsches Derby (by 2½ lengths from Manzoni) at Hamburg, both in June, and valuable Group 2 race at Hoppegarten (beat Oxalagu by 4 lengths) in August: stays at least 1½m: acts on good to firm ground and dead: injured a tendon at Hoppegarten, was due to visit the Equine Hospital in Dubai in the winter and return to Germany in 1996: very smart performer in the making. *H. Remmert, Germany*

116 p

ALL ON 4 ch.f. Dunbeath (USA) 127 – Fresh Line 60 (High Line 125) [1994 –: 10.4m^4 1995 a12g^5 a12g* a12g^6 14.1m 9.9d^2 9.9m^3 a12g^5 a12g 10.9g 10g Sep 15] workmanlike filly: won median auction maiden at Southwell in January: no worthwhile form last 3 starts: stays 1½m: acts on dead ground and fibresand: sold 8,100 gns Doncaster October Sales. *J. Hetherton*

46

ALL SHE SURVEYS 2 b.f. (Mar 23) Mazilier (USA) 107 – Sunley Stars (Sallust 134) [1995 5m 5.3m^4 5g^5 5m* 6m Aug 14] 3,400Y: smallish filly: third foal: dam poor daughter of sister to Runnett: won maiden auction at Ripon in July: stiff task and took good hold to post, always behind in nursery at Windsor just over month later: should stay 6f: withdrawn on technicality from nursery at Lingfield in September (reluctant to go down until blinkers were removed): sold 700 gns Doncaster November Sales. *J. Akehurst*

56

ALLSTARS DANCER 2 b.f. (Mar 10) Primo Dominie 121 – Danzig Harbour – (USA) (Private Account (USA)) [1995 a7g a8g Dec 18] 15,000Y: second foal: half-sister to 1994 2-y-o 6f winner Puppet Master (by Prince Sabo): dam Irish 7f winner: behind in maidens at Wolverhampton and Lingfield. *T. J. Naughton*

ALL THE JOYS 4 b. or br.f. Adbass (USA) 102 – Joytime (John de Coombe 47 122) [1994 54: 8d^4 6g 6f 7m^3 7f 7.6g^3 10m 8g^3 9g 1995 7f 10m^6 8g^6 9.7g 12f^2 11.9f^2 14d* 15.9d 12g^3 12m^6 Oct 27] rather leggy filly: poor handicapper: did not find so much as seemed likely sixth start, but kept on well to win (first time) 19-runner race at Lingfield in September: likely to stay 2m: acts on firm and dead ground. *C. A. Cyzer*

ALL THE TIME 3 b.f. Dancing Brave (USA) 140 – Just You Wait (Nonoalco 59 (USA) 131) [1994 NR 1995 7m^4 10m 10.4m 11.9d^4 Oct 11] tall, leggy, angular filly: half-sister to several winners, including useful 4-y-o 7.6f (at 2 yrs) and 11.5f winner Waiting (by Polish Precedent) and very smart pair Reprimand (1m to 1¼m, by Mummy's Pet) and Wiorno (1¼m to 1½m, by Wassl): dam unraced daughter of very useful 1¼m winner Sleat: fourth of 19 in maiden at Newbury on debut: failed to repeat that form: should be suited by 1m+. *P. F. I. Cole*

ALLTHRUTHENIGHT (IRE) 6 ch.h. Precocious 126 – Time For Pleasure 89 (Tower Walk 130) [1994 83: 5v^2 5d^2 5f 5m* 6m 5f^3 5g^3 5m^3 5m 1995 5m^2 5.2m 5f^3 6m^4 5m Aug 28] strong, good-quartered horse: fairly useful handicapper: excellent staying-on third of 10 to Double Quick in £24,300 rated stakes at Epsom (goes well there) in June: had worst of draw final start: best at 5f: acts on any going: gets on toes and has sweated: held up. *L. J. Holt*

ALLTIME DANCER (IRE) 3 b.g. Waajib 121 – Dance On Lady (Grundy 137) 64 [1994 NR 1995 7g 5m^5 7g 6g 8m 10m 10g* 9.9m 12m^4 8.1g^2 8m* Aug 3] IR 15,000F, 7,500Y: robust gelding: impresses in appearance: third foal: dam Irish 13f winner: fair handicapper: won at Pontefract in June and (readily, showed considerable improvement) August: stays 1¼m: has raced only on a sound surface: blinkered last 3 starts: sold (Mrs J. Ramsden to O. Sherwood) 17,000 gns Doncaster August Sales: progressive winning juvenile hurdler. *Mrs J. R. Ramsden*

ALL TIME GREAT 3 b.f. Night Shift (USA) – Someone Special 105 (Habitat 96 d 134) [1994 88?: 6d* 7g^6 1995 7.3m^4 8m 8.5m 8d Sep 24] lengthy filly: useful form when about 4 lengths fourth of 8 to Aqaarid in Fred Darling Stakes at Newbury in April: failed to repeat it in 1000 Guineas at Newmarket (virtually tailed-off last) and listed events at Epsom and Ascot: should prove suited by further than 7f: wore dropped noseband and had tongue tied down penultimate start: sweating and edgy final one. *L. M. Cumani*

ALLWIGHT THEN (IRE) 4 gr.c. Dancing Dissident (USA) 119 – Abergwrle 76 (Absalom 128) [1994 80: 5.1m^2 5f 5m 5.1g 1995 5g 5m^2 5m 5m^4 5m^3 5m 5f 5.1m Aug 19] neat, good-quartered colt: has a quick action: fair handicapper on his day: soundly beaten last 3 starts: 5f performer: acts on good to firm ground: blinkered last 2 outings: races prominently. *F. H. Lee*

ALLYANA (IRE) 3 b.f. Thatching 131 – Miss Loving 89 (Northfields (USA)) 73 [1994 83p: 6d^4 1995 6m^3 6g^2 6m^3 6g^2 5d* 5g^4 5m 5f^4 Oct 16] quite attractive filly: fair handicapper: won maiden at Beverley in September: effective at 5f and 6f: acts on firm and dead going: sold 15,000 gns Newmarket December Sales. *I. A. Balding*

ALMAPA 3 ch.g. Absalom 128 – More Fun (Malicious) [1994 58: 5.1m 5f^5 6.1m^3 60 d 7m^3 a6g 8s 6.1g 6v 1995 5.1m^5 7g* 8f 7g 7f 8h^5 Aug 3] workmanlike gelding: best effort when narrowly winning 20-runner claimer at Salisbury in May, leading close home: well beaten in minor event and handicaps afterwards: should stay 1m: seemed to act on top-of-the-ground at 2 yrs. *R. J. Hodges*

ALMASI (IRE) 3 b.f. Petorius 117 – Best Niece 84 (Vaigly Great 127) [1994 65: 63 d 6.1g 6g^4 7m^3 6.1m^3 7g^5 6m* 6d 6.1d^3 6s^6 1995 6f 6m 6m^5 7m 9.7s 7f 8.2m Oct 26] sparely-made filly: modest handicapper at best, lost her form after third start: best form at 6f: acts on good to firm and soft ground. *C. F. Wall*

ALMATY (IRE) 2 b.c. (Feb 18) Dancing Dissident (USA) 119 – Almaaseh (IRE) 110 63 (Dancing Brave (USA) 140) [1995 6g^5 5g* 5g* 5m* 5f^2 5d^6 Sep 9]

The top Irish-trained two-year-old of 1995 was Almaty. He also put up the division's two best individual performances, the first in one of Ireland's rare successful forays across the Irish Sea. Glorious Goodwood was the scene of

Molecomb Stakes, Goodwood—Irish colt Almaty makes all

Almaty's bid to complete a hat-trick, his record to that date standing at two wins from three starts, fifth of ten in a maiden at the Curragh being followed by victories in a similar event at Bellewstown and the Curragh Two-Year-Old Stakes. Astonishingly in hindsight, he had been sent off 3/1 third favourite of six when a five-length winner at Bellewstown; Sweet Robin was comfortably held at bay by a length in another six-runner race when Almaty made the considerable step up in class to Group 3 level at the Curragh twelve days later. The Molecomb Stakes was not just Almaty's third win, it was his third win in July. Starting 9/2 co-second favourite in a reduced field after outsider Village Native had panicked in the stalls and injured himself and Prince Aslia, Almaty always looked to have a bit in hand over the six rivals that remained. He did not have a marked lead at any stage—and not one large enough to prevent Darley receiving a careless-riding ban after his mount drifted left in front of Cayman Kai two furlongs out—but Almaty, conceding 5 lb, made all and was a length and a half clear at the line, Cayman Kai short-heading Baize for second. That performance was clearly the best of any in victory by the latest batch of Irish two-year-olds. On a par though was Almaty in defeat on his next outing. 'Weight will stop a train', stated his trainer Con Collins after 10-3 had been enough to see Almaty beaten half a length by Sunset Reigns in the IR £16,125 European Breeders Fund Nursery at the Curragh in August. A fine effort nonetheless, and one that had him still on the course for the Flying Childers and Cornwallis. Sixth of eight, however, on good to soft ground at Doncaster in the Flying Childers, this time eleven and a quarter lengths behind Cayman Kai, was a poor show and one that saw Almaty put away until 1996. He had looked extremely well beforehand but was reported to be coughing afterwards.

Almaty (IRE) (b.c. Feb 18, 1993)	Dancing Dissident (USA) (b 1986)	Nureyev (b 1977)	Northern Dancer
			Special
		Absentia (b 1979)	Raise A Cup
			Cecelia
	Almaaseh (IRE) (b 1988)	Dancing Brave (b 1983)	Lyphard
			Navajo Princess
		Al Bahathri (ch 1982)	Blushing Groom
			Chain Store

At IR 34,000 guineas, the leggy, workmanlike Almaty was the third-highest priced yearling from the third crop of Temple Stakes winner Dancing Dissident. Trained by Michael Stoute, Dancing Dissident never raced beyond six furlongs, put up easily his best efforts on top-of-the-ground and wore blinkers for his last five

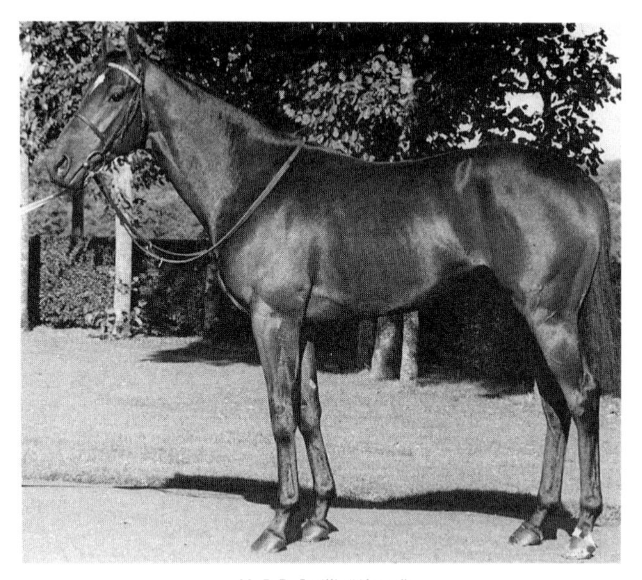

Mr P. D. Savill's "Almaty"

starts. He looks a decided influence for speed, with useful performers Miss Potter and Miss Provider in Ireland and the Francis Lee-trained Don't Worry Me and Encore M'Lady amongst those who have made an impact in Britain. The 1995 two-year-old Bonarelli showed plenty of ability for the Stoute yard. Almaty is the first foal out of Almaaseh, followed by a Royal Academy colt and Brief Truce filly. Almaaseh is from the very disappointing first crop of Dancing Brave and was hitherto as disappointing as any, managing just two undistinguished runs in maidens before she was cast out of the Al Maktoum empire for 41,000 guineas at the 1991 December Sales. Her dam Al Bahathri, contrastingly, was one of the first stars for Sheikh Hamdan, a most genuine front runner who was pipped on the post by Oh So Sharp in the One Thousand Guineas before winning her next three starts, the Irish One Thousand, Coronation Stakes and Child Stakes. Al Bahathri's first foal, the very useful miler Hasbah, is easily her best so far. Third dam Chain Store has produced three notable performers, the Grade 2 winner Geraldine's Store three years before Al Bahathri and the Cheshire Oaks winner Peplum six years after.

Almaty will surely be kept to sprint distances (he should stay six furlongs) and should win another pattern race. Most of those rated above him among the 1995 two-year-olds currently look set for greater stamina tests, though there are nearly always one or two that revert to sprinting after being tried at a mile around Guineas time. Like his sire, Almaty goes well on top-of-the-ground. His effectiveness on a soft surface is far from proven. *C. Collins, Ireland*

ALMIZAJ 3 b.f. Ballad Rock 122 – Salabella 64 (Sallust 134) [1994 62: 6s^5 6g^4 1995 8m^4 8m^4 8m^5 9h^2 8g Aug 26] tall, angular filly: good mover: fair maiden: blinkered, collapsed and died at Newcastle in August: probably stayed 9f: acted on good to firm ground. *H. Thomson Jones* 67

AL MOHAAJIR (USA) 4 ch.c. Cadeaux Genereux 131 – Lady In White 94 (Shareef Dancer (USA) 135) [1994 7g^4 9m* 10m^2 8.5m* 8m* 10d^6 1995 9m* 8.5s^2 10f^3 8m* Aug 30] first foal: dam, 1m winner, is half-sister to high-class Free Guest and smart Royal Ballerina, both middle-distance fillies: smart Irish colt: successful at 3 yrs in maiden at Tipperary and handicaps at Galway and (awarded race) Leopardstown, but reportedly had breathing problems final start: won listed events at Leopardstown (by short head from Hushang) in June and (after length third of 5 to Shemaran in Royal Whip at the Curragh) at Tralee in August: stays 1¼m: acts on firm ground and soft: consistent. *J. S. Bolger, Ireland* 113

ALMOND ROCK 3 b.g. Soviet Star (USA) 128 – Banket 120 (Glint of Gold 128) [1994 76p: 7m 7g^5 1995 8m 8m^3 8g* 8f^2 8g^3 8d* Sep 16] strong, lengthy gelding: has plenty of scope: shows a rather round action: gelded after reappearance, and progressed really well in handicaps, winning at Salisbury in July and Newbury (£18,900 event, led over 2f out, stayed on strongly to hold on) in September: will stay further than 1m, may well be suited by it: acts on firm ground and dead: hung right first 2 starts at 3 yrs: open to further improvement, and should win more races. *J. R. Fanshawe* 88 p

ALMOST A PRINCESS 7 b.m. Alleging (USA) 120 – Rabab (Thatching 131) [1994 NR 1995 a12g a14.8g Jan 25] leggy mare: no longer of much account. *W. G. M. Turner* –

AL MOULOUKI 5 b.g. Efisio 120 – Prejudice 83 (Young Generation 129) [1994 77?: 7s 8v 7s 8.1g^4 7.1g 8d 7d 1995 9.7d 8m Apr 25] good-topped gelding: has a round action: tailed-off last both starts in 1995: stays 1m: acts on soft and good to firm going: blinkered final 5-y-o start: one to be wary of: sold 5,400 gns Ascot June Sales. *J. W. Payne* –

ALMUHIMM (USA) 3 ch.g. Diesis 133 – Abeesh (USA) 77 (Nijinsky (CAN) 138) [1994 NR 1995 8.3m^4 10.1m^5 10d^3 Oct 19] rangy gelding: half-brother to several winners, including fairly useful Desert Conqueror (at up to 1¼m, by Rahy), and Moussahim (at 12.3f by Riverman): dam lightly-raced middle-distance maiden: fair form in maidens: slowly away and held up pulling hard before switched and challenging in final 1f when third of 13 at Newbury: may improve further: has been gelded. *E. A. L. Dunlop* 76

ALMUHTARAM 3 b.g. Rambo Dancer (CAN) 107 – Mrs Mainwaring (FR) 64 (Home Guard (USA) 129) [1994 73: 5d^3 6f^5 6g^5 a7g^2 7m 1995 a7g^4 a8.5g* 7.1m 7m 8.2m^6 11.4d 7g 8d^4 9f* 10f^4 9m a10g* Dec 15] strong, good-bodied gelding: good mover: fair performer at his best: won median auction maiden at Wolverhampton in January on final start for W. Haigh and (returning to form) handicaps at Redcar in October and Lingfield (amateurs) in December: stays 1¼m: acts on firm ground and all-weather: blinkered since ninth 3-y-o start. *Miss Gay Kelleway* 71

ALMUSHTARAK (IRE) 2 b.c. (May 1) Fairy King (USA) – Exciting (Mill Reef (USA) 141) [1995 5f^6 6m 6g* 6g Sep 30] 13,000 2-y-o: good-quartered colt: fifth foal: closely related to 1m (at 2 yrs) and 1¼m winner Be Exciting (by Be My Guest) and half-brother to Irish 1m winner Assuring (by Sure Blade): dam sister to very useful stayer The Miller and half-sister to very useful juveniles Magic Mirror and Treasure Trove: progressed very well, successful in minor event at Brighton in September, until running poorly in nursery at Newmarket final outing: got loose then refused to enter stalls third intended start: bred to stay further than 6f. *Miss Gay Kelleway* 85

AL NUFOOTH (IRE) 3 b.c. Green Desert (USA) 127 – Reine Maid (USA) (Mr Prospector (USA)) [1994 99p: 6m* 6g* 6m^6 6m^5 6m^5 1995 6m 6m^6 May 4] big, rangy colt: has plenty of scope: has a long stride: sweating and edgy, only fairly useful form in £8,000 event at Kempton (pulled hard and tended to hang) and minor event at Salisbury (wearing eyeshields, edged right after making most) in the spring: bred to stay beyond 6f: has raced only on a sound surface: began to look rather temperamental: stays in training. *Major W. R. Hern* 88

ALPHA CITY 3 ch.f. Unfuwain (USA) 131 – Alpha (GER) (Frontal (FR) 122) [1994 6g 8.5v* 1995 11g* 11m* 12m 10.7g* 12g* 10g^5 Oct 1] half-sister to several winners in Germany, including 4-y-o 1¼m to 1½m winner Alpha Guest (by Be My Guest): dam unraced: useful German filly: won maiden at Dusseldorf at 2 yrs: successful at 3 yrs in listed event at Mulheim in May, Group 3 Deutscher 105

Herold-Preis at Hamburg in June, conditions event at Neuss in August and Group 3 event at Hanover (made all, held Flying Dream by short head) in September: stays at least 1½m: acts on good to firm ground and heavy. *H. Jentzsch, Germany*

ALPHETON PRINCE 2 b.g. (Apr 14) Prince of Cill Dara – Batsam Lady (Battle Hymn 103) [1995 a5g^6 a6g a8.5g^6 Dec 2] first foal: dam unraced: no form in seller (debut, for R. Emery) and maidens on fibresand. *J. L. Harris* –

ALPINE 2 b.g. (Feb 26) Alzao (USA) 117 – Pine Ridge 80 (High Top 131) [1995 5m^5 6m^6 May 23] 18,000Y: well-made gelding: eighth foal: half-brother to several winners, notably In The Groove (by Night Shift): dam 1½m winner: fifth of 6 in maiden at Newmarket and sixth of 7 (blinkered) in claimer at Goodwood: subsequently gelded: sold 1,000 gns Newmarket Autumn Sales. *P. F. I. Cole* 54

ALPINE HIDEAWAY (IRE) 2 b.c. (Mar 22) Tirol 127 – Arbour (USA) 76 (Graustark) [1995 7.1g 6m Oct 13] 18,000Y: useful-looking colt: third foal: half-brother to 9f and 1½m winner in Norway: dam twice-raced 11.7f winner out of half-sister to dam of Irish St Leger winner Protection Racket: around 5 lengths eleventh of 21 to Projection in maiden at Newmarket second start, staying on never a factor: should prove suited by at least 1m. *B. Hanbury* 70

ALPINE JOHNNY 4 b.g. Salse (USA) 128 – Alpine Sunset (Auction Ring (USA) 123) [1994 60: a8g^5 a7g^2 a9.4g^2 a7g* a8g* a7g^2 a5g* a6g^3 a7g^3 7d a8.5g^2 7f^5 a6g 7.5m^3 a9.4g^4 7m 8.2g a7g a7g a6g^3 a6g a7g^2 a7g^2 1995 a8.5g^3 a7g* a7g^3 a7g^4 Jan 25] small, good-bodied gelding: has a quick action: modest performer: won seller at Southwell in January: effective at 5f to 9.4f: acts on firm ground, dead and fibresand: below form when tried visored and blinkered: refused to enter stalls Feb 3 and Feb 13. *R. Hollinshead* 60

ALPINE JOKER 2 b.g. (Feb 8) Tirol 127 – Whitstar 93 (Whitstead 125) [1995 7.1g 7.1s 6m^6 Oct 13] 16,000Y: lengthy gelding, has scope: fourth living foal: half-brother to 4-y-o Star Performer and useful 7f to 1¼m winner Two Left Feet (both by Petorius): dam, 10.2f winner at 2 yrs, half-sister to very useful 6f to 1¼m winner Homeboy: modest form in maidens at Haydock (2) and Catterick: will be suited by 1m+: pulled hard second start: has been gelded: likeable type, likely to do better. *Mrs J. R. Ramsden* – p

ALPINE SKIER (IRE) 4 b.g. Nordico (USA) – Heather Lil (Ballymore 123) [1994 71: 10.3g^4 10.5s^5 10.2g^3 10s^3 10.1m 10.2f^6 10.9g^3 9g 8m 8g 7g 8.1g 1995 10.3g 11.1g 8g^3 7.5m Jul 7] sturdy gelding: very much on the downgrade and only poor form at best in 1995: stays 11f: acts on soft going, probably not on top-of-the-ground: tried blinkered, no improvement: lacks turn of foot: sold only 700 gns Newmarket July Sales but won over 11f in Belgium in December. *Mrs M. Reveley* 38

ALPINE STORM (IRE) 3 b.f. Al Hareb (USA) 123 – Alpine Dance (USA) 62§ (Apalachee (USA) 137) [1994 –: 7g 7g 1995 8m 12.5g^5 a8.5g 10.8m 14.1m^3 10d 10g^5 9m a10g^6 a12g^3 Dec 12] workmanlike filly: poor maiden: stays 1¼m: tried blinkered, no improvement: inconsistent. *M. D. I. Usher* 37 a26

ALPINE TWIST (USA) 2 b.f. (Mar 14) Seattle Dancer (USA) 119 – Polar Bird 111 (Thatching 131) [1995 7g^5 Oct 23] first foal: dam sprinter out of sister to 1¼m Queen's Plate winner Son of Briarctic: 14/1 and ridden by claimer, under 4 lengths fifth of 13 to Tsarnista in maiden at Lingfield, always well to fore in group on unfavoured stand side: will improve. *P. W. Chapple-Hyam* 68 p

AL RAWDA (FR) 3 b.f. Green Desert (USA) 127 – Double Celt 93 (Owen Dudley 121) [1994 87: 6m* 7.5g^2 7.3v^4 1995 6m 6m^2 6m* 6g Jun 3] sturdy filly: fairly useful performer: gamely won 5-runner minor event at Goodwood in May, running on to lead inside last: never going well and tailed off in listed race at Lingfield 11 days later: effective at 6f, stays 7.5f: acts on good to firm and heavy ground: sent to Saudi Arabia. *H. R. A. Cecil* 94

ALREEH (IRE) 2 b.f. (May 10) Priolo (USA) 127 – Fleeting (USA) (Lear Fan (USA) 130) [1995 7m 6.1d 7g^5 Oct 9] good-topped filly: has a round action: second foal: dam half-sister to Taufan: blinkered and bandaged behind, easily best effort in maidens when just over 4 lengths fifth of 18 to Fairlight Down at Leicester, headed and tending to wander from 1f out: bred to stay 1m. *J. H. M. Gosden* 66

ALRIFFA 4 b.c. Danehill (USA) 126 – Sweet Soprano 80 (High Line 125) [1994 114: 8d^{2} 10d* 10m* 12d^{3} 12g^{4} 12m^{4} 12g^{5} 11.1d^{5} 11d^{2} 12g^{6} 1995 10m^{4} 12m^{5} 11.7m* 13.3g^{4} 10d* 10m^{3} 10g^{5} 12d^{6} 10m^{6} Nov 12] good-bodied colt: has a short action: smart performer: won minor event at Bath (7/4 on) and 7-runner Spillers Brigadier Gerard Stakes at Sandown (under fine tactical ride from Pat Eddery, beat Just Happy by 1¾ lengths) in May: creditable third to Desert Shot in Winter Hill Stakes at Windsor in August: ran poorly last 2 starts: suited by 1¼m to 1½m (weakened final 1f having looked likely winner of listed event over 13.3f): acts on good to firm ground and dead, yet to race on extremes: blinkered (no improvement) first 2 starts at 4 yrs: used to be held up, but made most for his 2 wins in 1995. *R. Hannon*

116

AL SAFEER (IRE) 3 b.c. Common Grounds 118 – Indian Swallow (Indian King (USA) 128) [1994 63: 6m 7.1m 7m 1995 8d^{3} 10m* 10m^{3} 12m 11.9m Jul 14] strong, lengthy colt: won maiden at Pontefract (second start for new stable) in April: ran well in steadily-run handicap at Salisbury next start, poorly (not because of trip) aftewards: better at 1¼m than shorter. *J. W. Hills*

81

ALSAHIB (USA) 2 b.c. (Feb 21) Slew O' Gold (USA) – Khwlah (USA) 99 (Best Turn (USA)) [1995 7f^{4} Oct 18] big, robust colt: has plenty of scope: sixth living foal: half-brother to 3-y-o 7f winner Khatim (by Topsider) and 1988 2-y-o 6f winner Alkariyh (by Alydar): dam, 6f winner at 2 yrs effective at 1¼m, half-sister to Saratoga Six and Dunbeath: around 3 lengths fourth of 11 to Prize Giving in steadily-run maiden at Yarmouth, flat-footed (and short of room) around 2f out then staying on well: showed a good action: will stay at least 1m: sure to improve. *H. Thomson Jones*

74 p

AL'S ALIBI 2 b.c. (Jan 19) Alzao (USA) 117 – Lady Kris (IRE) (Kris 135) [1995 5m^{6} 7d^{3} 7g 6.9g^{2} 6.9m^{5} Nov 6] 12,000Y: tall, unfurnished colt: first foal: dam, Irish 1¼m winner, half-sister to Gimcrack winner Bel Bolide, later Grade 2 winner in USA: fair form: short-headed by Ageeb in maiden auction at Folkestone: creditable fifth of 16 in nursery there following month: will stay further than 1m. *W. R. Muir*

73

AL SHAATI (FR) 5 b.m. Lead On Time (USA) 123 – With You All (Free Round (USA)) [1994 60, a50: a8g a7g a6g* 6d^{5} 6d^{2} 6m^{2} 6s^{3} 6m^{4} 6m^{6} 6g a6g 1995 a6g a5g^{6} a6g Dec 9] leggy mare: good mover: modest handicapper: below best on belated return: effective at 6f and stays 1m: acts on good to firm ground, soft and all-weather: blinkered (well beaten) second 4-y-o start. *R. J. O'Sullivan*

–
a46

AL SHADEEDAH (USA) 2 br.f. (Jan 21) Nureyev (USA) 131 – Copperama (AUS) (Comeram (FR) 127) [1995 6f^{5} 6g 7f^{3} Oct 18] IR 80,000Y: tall, unfurnished filly: looked weak: good mover: sister to 1993 2-y-o 7.6f winner Shalbourne and closely related to Irish 7f and 1m winner Stormy Exchange (by Storm Bird) and a winner in North America by El Gran Senor: dam leading performer in Australia, winner of VATC 1000 Guineas: fair form in maidens: around 1½ lengths third of 11 to Prize Giving at Yarmouth, first run for 3½ months, short of room from over 1f out and possibly unlucky: stays 7f: takes keen hold. *L. M. Cumani*

74 +

AL SHAFA 2 b.c. (Mar 26) Midyan (USA) 124 – Thundercloud 70 (Electric 126) [1995 6g^{3} 6f^{2} 6m^{2} 6f* 7.3d 7g* 7.3d Oct 21] 22,000Y: good-quartered colt: second foal: half-brother to 3-y-o Made In Heaven (by Primo Dominie), 5f and 6f winner at 2 yrs: dam, placed at 1½m from 2 starts, closely related to Julio Mariner and Juliette Marny: won 2-runner maiden at Brighton in July and nursery (one of only two to race on favoured rail) at same track in October: well beaten in nursery at Newbury final outing: stays 7f: acts on firm ground, seems unsuited by dead. *J. L. Dunlop*

84

ALTAMURA (USA) 2 b.f. (Jan 20) El Gran Senor (USA) 136 – Narwala 120 (Darshaan 133) [1995 8g^{3} 8.2m^{2} Oct 19] unfurnished filly: second foal: half-sister to smart French 3-y-o middle-distance stayer Affidavit (by Affirmed): dam won 1½m Princess Royal Stakes: placed in maidens: ¾-length second to Dushyantor at Nottingham, running on well to come 7 lengths clear of remainder despite flashing tail: will stay beyond 1m: tongue tied down both starts: last and steadily to post final outing. *J. H. M. Gosden*

82

ALTERNATION (FR) 6 ch.m. Electric 126 – Alanood 85 (Northfields (USA)) [1994 NR 1995 a16g^{5} a13g Feb 16] lengthy mare: modest winner in 1992: no form on return: acts on all-weather, below form on a soft surface: blinkered (no improvement) at 3 yrs. *J. Webber*

–

ALTOBY 4 b.g. Tobin Lad (USA) 124 – Natina-May 59 (Mandrake Major 122) [1994 48: 8.3v^4 12.5m 13.4m^2 15.8g 13.6m 1995 12m Oct 2] lengthy gelding: poor maiden handicapper: backward, tailed off only start in 1995: stays 13.4f: acts on good to firm ground: inconsistent. *E. J. Alston* –

ALUSHA 3 b.f. Soviet Star (USA) 128 – Glowing With Pride 114 (Ile de Bourbon (USA) 133) [1994 85p: 6m^2 6g* 1995 10f^4 Aug 9] well-made filly: reportedly fractured a hind leg after 2-y-o win: 8/1, 4½ lengths fourth of 9 to Ellie Ardensky in listed race at Salisbury, travelling well long way, carrying head high when one pace final 1f: not certain to stay beyond 1¼m: looked sure to improve again. *G. Wragg* 88 p

ALUTE (IRE) 3 b.f. Last Tycoon 131 – Pu Yi (Habitat 134) [1994 48: 5d^5 7.1g 1995 a8g^4 a7g^3 6.1g 8.2m May 2] lengthy filly: modest maiden: moved poorly to post and soon off bridle last 2 starts: stays 1m: acts on all-weather. *C. E. Brittain* – a58

ALWARQA 2 b.f. (Apr 2) Old Vic 136 – Ostora (USA) 83 (Blushing Groom (FR) 131) [1995 7.1s Oct 17] third foal: half-sister to 4-y-o 1½m to 2m winner Jaraab (by Sure Blade): dam maiden (stayed 1m) out of Grade 1 winner My Darling One: 10/1, around 14 lengths tenth of 19 in maiden at Chepstow, slowly into stride: should do better. *R. W. Armstrong* – p

ALWAYS ALOOF (USA) 4 b.c. Alleged (USA) 138 – Miranda (USA) 109 (Forli (ARG)) [1994 85: 8v^2 12.5m* 14g^3 12g^4 14g* 13.9m 1995 16m* 18.7m 20m 16.1m^5 15.9m^3 15.5g^2 Sep 6] tall colt: useful performer: won 20-runner Queen's Prize at Kempton in April: 3 lengths third of 6 to Double Eclipse in listed race at York (looked likely to be soundly beaten early in straight) then ½-length second of 6 to L'Ile Tudy in Prix Gladiateur (led 1½f out to close home) at Longchamp: stays well: acts on good to firm and heavy ground: held up. *M. R. Stoute* 107

ALWAYS EARNEST (USA) 7 b.g. Alleged (USA) 138 – Nettie Cometti (USA) (Giacometti 130) [1994 115: 15.5v* 15.5v* 16g^6 15.5g^2 20d^2 15.5s^2 14.5v* 1995 15s^5 15.5s* 15.5v^3 20s* Sep 30] 120

Always Earnest has come a long way since he was claimed out of Francois Boutin's stable at Saint-Cloud at three. He made further progress in the latest season, his sixth on the track, to the extent that on his win in the Prix du Cadran at Longchamp in September he is entitled to be regarded as the best stayer in France apart from Sunshack. Always Earnest and Sunshack have yet to meet. They were due to do so in October in the Prix Royal-Oak but firm ground ruled Always Earnest out.

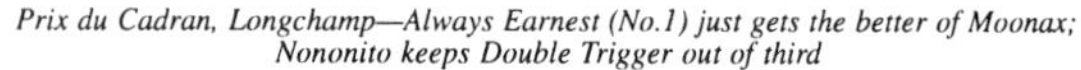

Prix du Cadran, Longchamp—Always Earnest (No.1) just gets the better of Moonax; Nononito keeps Double Trigger out of third

The two claiming races run most years at the Saint-Cloud post-Arc weekend meeting usually attract widespread interest from horse-buyers. The winner of the mile race in 1990, Sweet Glow, ended up with Martin Pipe. The following year Pipe claimed four of the first five home in the mile-and-a-half event—Val d'Authie, Slavi, First Pearl and Gold Medal—three of whom quickly made their mark over jumps in Britain. In third place that day was Always Earnest. Claimed by his present trainer for 85,898 francs, the equivalent at that time of around £8,700, he came out again at Deauville two weeks later to win a 120,000-franc handicap. In each season since, he has managed at least one victory, and by 1994 had graduated from big handicaps to listed company and was knocking on the door in the top long-distance events. That year he finished second in the Gladiateur, the Cadran and the Royal-Oak, giving almost as good as he got against the St Leger winner Moonax in the Royal-Oak. Always Earnest came up against Moonax again in the latest Prix du Cadran, following an absence of five months. He had been in decent form in the spring—winning a listed race at Evry second time up—but had not shown enough to suggest that he could improve on his previous Cadran placing even if fully fit, for this time he had Double Trigger as well as Moonax to contend with. Double Trigger started at 2/1 on in a field of six completed by Nononito, who had beaten Always Earnest in the Prix de Barbeville in the spring, Epaphos and Admiral's Well. The race produced a close finish with an unusual incident when Moonax tried to bite Always Earnest as the latter, typically, leaned into him under pressure. Always Earnest who has raced blinkered in the last two seasons, is a hard ride, genuine but lazy, usually soon off the

Mme C. Bourg's "Always Earnest"

bridle as he was here. As expected Double Trigger made the running, while Always Earnest brought up the rear. The field kept close order most of the way, the pace gradually increased from a mile out, and it was clear on the home turn that Double Trigger would not be able to shake them off. Halfway up the straight he gave way to Moonax and Always Earnest and faded into fourth, well below his best on the day. The new leaders drove on for the line, where a short head separated them. There had been a short neck between them in the Royal-Oak.

Always Earnest (USA) (b.g. 1988)	Alleged (USA) (b 1974)	Hoist The Flag (b 1968)	Tom Rolfe
			Wavy Navy
		Princess Pout (b 1966)	Prince John
			Determined Lady
	Nettie Cometti (USA) (ch 1981)	Giacometti (ch 1971)	Faberge II
			Naujwan
		Istrouma (ch 1975)	Hard Work
			Pryor C

Always Earnest's breeding is only academic now; he was gelded before he ran as a four-year-old. There is not a lot to say about it, anyway. His dam Nettie Cometti was one of the few runners of note sired by the 1974 Champion Stakes winner Giacometti in his spell at stud in the States. She won thirteen races and over half a million dollars, including the Grade 2 eleven-furlong Golden Harvest Handicap as a five-year-old. The second dam never ran, the third dam ran once unplaced. All three of Nettie Cometti's raced foals are winners, Always Earnest's younger half-sisters Symphony Lady (by Theatrical) and Cometti Slew (by Slew o'Gold) having done their winning in the States. No doubt we shall be seeing some more of Always Earnest as long as he keeps his form. A thorough stayer—he would have been a natural for the Gladiateur when it used to be run over three miles—he acts well on soft and heavy ground. *Mme M. Bollack-Badel, France*

ALWAYS GRACE 3 b.f. Never So Bold 135 – Musical Sally (USA) (The Minstrel (CAN) 135) [1994 64: 5m^3 5g^3 6f^2 6v a6g^2 a5g a7g^2 1995 a7g^4 a6g^2 6f* 5m 6m a7g Nov 13] strong filly: shows knee action: off course 6½ months, returned to best to win 5-runner median auction maiden at Folkestone in August, making most: failed by long way to repeat it: probably stays 7f: acts on all-weather surfaces and firm ground, well beaten on heavy. *Miss Gay Kelleway* 65 a56

ALWAYS GREENER (IRE) 4 gr.f. Vision (USA) – Great Meadow (Northfields (USA)) [1994 10g^6 13s^3 13g 11d^2 12g 12g 1995 a12g^3 a11g^6 a12g Sep 2] half-sister to 3 winners, including fair performer at up to 1½m Rathbrides Joy (by Kafu): dam unraced: fair maiden (rated 67) in Ireland for J. G. Burns: sold IR 2,500 gns Goffs November (1994) Sales: only modest at best here: stays at least 13f: acts on soft ground. *Mrs N. Macauley* 51

ALWAYS HAPPY 2 ch.f. (Apr 2) Sharrood (USA) 124 – Convivial 81 (Nordance (USA)) [1995 7g^4 8m^4 Nov 4] unfurnished filly: second foal: half-sister to 3-y-o Bold Revival (by Never So Bold): dam stayed 1m: kept on well when fourth in maidens won by Jezyah at Lingfield and Shaamit at Doncaster: will be suited by 1¼m+. *J. R. Fanshawe* 73

AL WIDYAN (IRE) 3 b.c. Slip Anchor 136 – Rafha 123 (Kris 135) [1994 101: 7g^3 8f* 8d* 7m 1995 10m 10d^4 9m^6 11.8f* 12m^3 Nov 4] small, sturdy colt: useful performer: off course 5½ months after reappearance: won 6-runner minor event at Leicester in October, finding gap on inner 1f out and quickening clear: best effort when 1¾ lengths third of 8 to Blushing Flame in listed event at Doncaster 12 days later: better at around 1½m than shorter: successful on dead ground, best form on top-of-the-ground: sold 44,000 gns Newmarket December Sales. *H. R. A. Cecil* 104

AL WUJUD (IRE) 4 b.c. Polish Precedent (USA) 131 – Alkariyh (USA) 79 (Alydar (USA)) [1994 37: 7d^6 8m 12.4m^3 10d 6g^2 1995 8.3g 7m^2 7g^3 6m* 7f^2 6m* 6g^2 6m* 6m Aug 15] lengthy colt: fairly useful handicapper: improved with virtually every run in 1995, winning at York, Newcastle (£15,300 event) and Newmarket (really impressive, by 5 lengths) in the summer: broke knee final start: effective at 6f (best form) and 7f: acted on firm ground: usually raced prominently: dead. *T. Dyer* 75

ALZANTI 2 b.c. (Feb 14) Alzao (USA) 117 – Mumtaz Flyer (USA) (Al Hattab (USA)) [1995 7g^6 7f* 7g* 7d^3 8m^2 Oct 20] 32,000Y: well-made colt: half-brother to several winners, including 3-y-o 5f winner Bold Frontier (by Chief Singer), stayer 88

Tailspin (by Young Generation), and 1988 2-y-o 6f winner Flight of Destiny (by Tolomeo), later 7.5f pattern winner in Italy: dam unraced half-sister to high-class American filly Wanda: won maiden at Salisbury in August and nursery at Goodwood in September: placed in nurseries afterwards, hanging when beaten neck by Crystal Falls at Doncaster: stays 1m: acts on firm and dead ground: makes running/races prominently. *P. F. I. Cole*

ALZIANAH 4 b.f. Alzao (USA) 117 – Ghassanah 73 (Pas de Seul 133) [1994 96: 7s 5.3g^{2} 6g^{6} 6m^{6} 6g* 6d^{2} 6d 5s^{5} 6v^{3} 1995 5m^{6} 6m^{2} 6m^{5} 6f^{2} 6g^{3} 6g 6g^{3} 6d^{5} Oct 19] small filly: shows knee action: useful performer: placed in Wokingham at Royal Ascot (neck second to Astrac) and Prix de Meautry at Deauville (headed inside final 1f, 2¼ lengths behind Missed Flight) in the summer: failed to repeat that form: better at 6f than 5f: acts on any going: visored (below form) once as 2-y-o. *J. D. Bethell* 102

ALZOOMO (IRE) 3 b.g. Alzao (USA) 117 – Fandangerina (USA) (Grey Dawn II 132) [1994 NR 1995 10m 11.8m 8.2d^{3} 8m a12g^{3} Dec 9] IR 60,000Y: robust gelding: closely related to 2 juvenile winners (one of them very useful) and half-brother to useful 7f (at 2 yrs) to 12.2f winner Ocean Air (by Elegant Air): dam won at up to 1m: sold out of H. Cecil's stable 9,000 gns Newmarket July Sales and gelded after debut: best efforts when third in maiden at Nottingham and handicap at Wolverhampton: stays 1½m: acts on dead ground and fibresand. *J. A. Glover* 68

ALZOTIC (IRE) 2 b.c. (Mar 26) Alzao (USA) 117 – Exotic Bride (USA) (Blushing Groom (FR) 131) [1995 8.2d 7d^{6} 7d 8f a8g^{2} a8g^{4} Nov 20] 38,000F, 23,000Y, 38,000 2-y-o: smallish, sturdy colt: seventh foal: half-brother to 3 winners, notably smart stayer Admiral's Well (by Sadler's Wells) and useful Irish middle-distance winner Yukon Gold (by Lomond): dam half-sister to Golden Fleece: much improved form when second in maiden at Southwell in November and ran creditably in nursery there later in month: bred to be suited by middle distances: easily best efforts on fibresand. *S. G. Norton* 53+ a71

AMAAM AMAAM 5 b.g. Last Tycoon 131 – What A Pity 97 (Blakeney 126) [1994 75d: 8f^{4} 7.6m 8.3m 7g 9.7g 7m 9s 1995 10m 16.1g^{6} Jun 10] leggy, angular gelding: unimpressive mover: disappointing maiden: tried blinkered. *W. J. Musson* –

AMADOUR (IRE) 2 b.c. (Mar 13) Contract Law (USA) 108 – Truly Flattering (Hard Fought 125) [1995 8g Sep 29] IR 3,000F, IR 4,300Y: workmanlike colt: third foal: dam Irish 7f winner: 40/1 and in need of race, slowly away and well beaten in maiden at Goodwood. *P. Mitchell* –

A MAGICMAN (FR) 3 br.c. The Wonder (FR) 129 – Ayanapa (FR) (Pharly (FR) 130) [1994 7g^{3} 7g* 9.5d^{3} 8s^{5} 1995 8.5s 8g^{3} 11s^{6} 12m 8m* 8d* 8g* Sep 23] half-brother to several winners, including 1½m winner Anchorman (by Un Desperado): dam unraced: useful German-trained colt: won maiden at Baden-Baden at 2 yrs: 2½ lengths third of 15 to Manzoni in Mehl-Mulhens-Rennen at Cologne, finishing well: successful in Group 3 events at Cologne and Baden-Baden then Group 2 Grosser Kaufhof Preis at Cologne: best form at 1m, though should be suited by further: acts on good to firm ground and dead. *H. Steguweit, Germany* 110

AMANAH (USA) 3 ch.f. Mr Prospector (USA) – Cheval Volant (USA) (Kris S (USA)) [1994 NR 1995 8d^{2} 7.9m* 8f^{2} 8.1m^{4} 6g Sep 29] strong, good sort: first foal: dam won from 5.5f to 8.5f in USA, twice in Grade 1 events: useful performer: won 4-runner maiden at York in June: in frame in minor event at Kempton and in listed race at Sandown next 2 starts: unimpressive in appearance, pushed along halfway and well below form in rated stakes at Newmarket final one: unlikely to have stayed beyond around 1m: acted on firm ground: visits Unfuwain. *J. H. M. Gosden* 100

AMANCIO (USA) 4 b.g. Manila (USA) – Kerry Ring (USA) (Ack Ack (USA)) [1994 84: 10d^{2} 10d^{2} 10.2g^{3} 12g* 12f 12f^{4} 1995 12f* 11.9m^{3} 12m Sep 6] big, good-bodied gelding: fairly useful performer: easily won ladies race at Epsom in June: stays 1½m: acts on firm ground and dead: front runner at 3 yrs, held up (and wore crossed noseband) in 1995: carries head awkwardly and has sometimes found little: fairly useful hurdler. *G. Harwood* 81

AMANITA 2 ch.f. (Mar 19) Lead On Time (USA) 123 – Amana River (USA) 77 (Raise A Cup (USA)) [1995 5m^{6} 6m* 7m 6g^{3} 7d^{4} Sep 26] rather unfurnished filly: second foal: half-sister to 3-y-o Bridge of Fire (by Mtoto), 6f winner at 2 yrs: dam 5f and 1m winner out of half-sister to both high-class 2-y-o filly Althea (stayed 9f) and the dam of Green Desert: won median auction maiden at Redcar in May: in frame in 72 nurseries at Ayr and Newmarket: stays 7f: acts on good to firm and dead ground: tends to sweat and get edgy. *J. W. Watts*

AMANIY (USA) 2 b.f. (Mar 27) Dayjur (USA) 137 – Muhbubh (USA) 108 (Blushing Groom (FR) 131) [1995 5g^3 5.1m* 6.1g^2 6f* 6g^3 5s^3 Oct 1] strong, good-topped filly: third foal: half-sister to 3-y-o Kayrawan (by Mr Prospector), 6f winner at 2 yrs, and 1m winner Balaabel (by Sadler's Wells): dam won Princess Margaret Stakes and is out of sister to Prix du Jockey-Club second Twig Moss: useful filly: won maiden at Chester and minor event at Thirsk in the summer: would have finished second to My Branch with a clear run in listed race at Ayr penultimate start: better at 6f than 5f: well below form on soft ground. *H. Thomson Jones* 96

AMANY (IRE) 3 b.f. Waajib 121 – Treeline 59 (High Top 131) [1994 NR 1995 7m 6g 7g^5 6f^3 6m 8g 7f^3 7g^4 Sep 13] 12,000Y: good-quartered filly: half-sister to fair 1985 2-y-o 7f winner Wryneck (by Niniski) and a winner in Norway by Sharpo: dam sprint maiden: poor maiden handicapper: should stay 1m: has raced only on a sound surface. *G. Lewis* 43

AMARETTO BAY (IRE) 2 b.c. (Jan 10) Common Grounds 118 – Harmer (IRE) 72 (Alzao (USA) 117) [1995 5.1g^6 5m* 5m^4 5d* 5m^5 6m^5 5.2g 7f 7m 6m^5 7.3d 6d^2 Oct 21] 10,000Y: sturdy, good-quartered colt: progressed well physically: unimpressive mover: first foal: dam stayed 7f: won maiden at Kempton in April and listed race at Sandown in May: excellent second of 14 in nursery at Newbury final outing: bred to stay 7f but evidently doesn't: winner on good to firm ground but best on a soft surface: blinkered last 3 outings: gets on toes: often wears a crossed noseband: sold 26,000 gns Newmarket Autumn Sales. *B. J. Meehan* 94

AMAZING BAY 2 b.f. (Feb 7) Mazilier (USA) 107 – Petriece 64 (Mummy's Pet 125) [1995 6g* 6m* 6g^5 5m^4 5.2m* 5d^5 Sep 9] 26,000Y: angular filly: second foal: half-sister to 1993 2-y-o 5f winner Smart Pet (by Petong): dam, 7f winner stayed 1m, is half-sister to dam of Lochsong: useful performer: won maiden at Newbury in May, minor event at York in June and listed race at Newbury (by 3 lengths from Maggi For Margaret, showing good turn of foot) in August: ran in pattern events otherwise: likely to prove best at up to 6f: acts on good to firm going, possibly unsuited by a soft surface: held up. *I. A. Balding* 98

AMAZING NEWS 4 ch.f. Mazilier (USA) 107 – Glint of Silver 69 (Sallust 134) [1994 47: a5g^2 a5g^4 a6g^4 a6g 5g 5f^6 1995 a5g^5 a5g Feb 9] compact filly: poor maiden: stays 6f: acts on equitrack. *Mark Campion* 43

AMBER FORT 2 gr.g. (Apr 3) Indian Ridge 123 – Lammastide 93 (Martinmas 128) [1995 7g^6 7m 8.2d 6g^2 5m a6g^3 Nov 14] 26,000Y: close-coupled gelding: half-brother to winning 5f performer Ganeshaya (by Formidable) and 1990 2-y-o 6f winner Musabiq (by Superlative): dam 2-y-o 5f winner: blinkered, creditable efforts when placed in nurseries won by King of Peru at Newmarket in September and Itsinthepost at Lingfield final start: below form without blinkers in between: best form at 6f/7f: acts on equitrack: races prominently. *P. F. I. Cole* 72

AMBER LILY 3 ch.f. Librate 91 – Just Bluffing (Green Shoon 102) [1994 –: 7f 7d 1995 10.8m 8.1m 7f 5f Aug 28] smallish filly: of little account. *J. M. Bradley* –

AMBER NECTAR 9 ch.g. Sallust 134 – Curtana (Sharp Edge 123) [1994 –: a7g 1995 6m 6m^6 8f 8.3m Jul 29] no longer of much account. *B. A. Pearce* –

AMBER VALLEY (USA) 4 ch.g. Bering 136 – Olatha (USA) (Miswaki (USA) 124) [1994 85d: 8g^4 6f 6g 12f^5 10.1f 8g 8s 7g 1995 9.7d Mar 27] close-coupled gelding: disappointing at 3 yrs: soundly beaten (for new stable) after pulling too hard only start in 1995: may prove best at up to 1m: acts on good to firm and heavy ground: bandaged off-hind: has run well when sweating: modest novice hurdler. *D. L. Williams* –

AMBIDEXTROUS (IRE) 3 b.c. Shareef Dancer (USA) 135 – Amber Fizz (USA) (Effervescing (USA)) [1994 NR 1995 10.2m 10.3m 10m^3 12m 7m a8.5g Dec 12] good-bodied colt: seventh foal: closely related to 7f winner Wasaif (by Lomond) and half-brother to 2 winners, notably smart 6f/7f performer Cool Jazz (by Lead On Time): dam ran once: modest form at best, after fourth start sold out of C. Brittain's stable 5,000 gns Newmarket September Sales: no promise for new stable: stays 10.3f: looked none too keen (hanging) third start, visored fourth. *E. J. Alston* 59

AMBOYNA BURL (IRE) 3 b.g. Cyrano de Bergerac 120 – Mind The Beat (Gulf Pearl 117) [1994 –: 5g 7.1m 7m 6d 1995 a10g 10m 7.1m 8d 6.9g 8f Oct 24] workmanlike gelding: has shown unsatisfactory temperament (refused to race last 3 starts) and little ability: blinkered once at 2 yrs: avoid. *D. A. Wilson* [§§]

AMBUSCADE (USA) 9 ch.g. Roberto (USA) 131 – Gurkhas Band (USA) (Lurullah) [1994 60: a16.2g^{4} a14.8g^{3} 18g^{6} a16.2g 16m 17.5s* 17.1s* 18s^{4} 1995 18g^{5} 16.2m 17.1m^{5} 16m^{4} 18m^{2} Jun 19] lengthy gelding: modest handicapper: did not get ideal ground conditions most of 1995, but shaped as if retaining ability: needs thorough test of stamina: probably needs give in the ground nowadays, and goes well on soft: has run well when blinkered, not tried for long time: held up. *E. J. Alston* [52]

AMEER ALFAYAAFI (IRE) 2 b.g. (Feb 24) Mujtahid (USA) 118 – Sharp Circle (IRE) 83 (Sure Blade (USA) 130) [1995 7.1g Sep 23] 66,000Y: small, sturdy gelding: first foal: dam, 1m winner better at 11.5f, half-sister to very smart sprinter Greenland Park (dam of Fitnah) and Coventry Stakes winner Red Sunset: 10/1 and burly, tenth of 16 to Polar Prince in maiden at Haydock, behind after slow start, checked when making headway 2f out and not knocked about thereafter: will improve. *A. C. Stewart* [– p]

AMEERI (USA) 3 b.c. Ogygian (USA) – Royal Suite (USA) (Herbager 136) [1994 –p: 5.2s 1995 a11g 8.2m Aug 12] lengthy colt: has plenty of scope: sold out of P. Cole's stable only 1,300 gns Newmarket July Sales, and (having been off course 16 months) well beaten in claimers for new connections: sold 850 gns Ascot August Sales. *N. P. Littmoden* [–]

AMELANCHIER 2 ch.f. (May 24) Cigar 68 – Frost In Summer (Busted 134) [1995 7g Oct 9] stocky filly: first reported foal: dam never ran: 33/1, burly and green, soundly beaten in maiden at Leicester: went freely to post. *G. B. Balding* [–]

AMERCIUS 3 ch.g. Old Vic 136 – Elarrih (USA) (Sharpen Up 127) [1994 –: a8g 1995 a8.5g^{4} 10.3g 14.1g^{3} 12.5m^{5} 14.1g 14.1m Aug 10] sparely-made gelding: poor maiden: trained until after fourth 3-y-o outing by R. Hannon: no form either start for new stable: should stay well: blinkered (only form) third and fourth 3-y-o starts. *J. E. Banks* [48]

AMIARGE 5 b.g. Reference Point 139 – Scotia Rose (Tap On Wood 130) [1994 34: 14g 16.5m 12.3m 14.6m 13.6g^{3} 16.2m^{3} 16g^{5} 16.4g^{5} 16m 17.1s^{6} 1995 14.6g 13f^{2} 14g 16m* 17.1m^{3} 16m 16d^{2} 14s^{2} 13.9g^{4} Oct 7] small, leggy gelding: modest handicapper: gained first win at Nottingham in August: appeared to run very well final outing: stays 17.1f: acts on firm and soft going: often soon off bridle: tried visored/blinkered, not in 1995. *M. Brittain* [51 ?]

A MILLION AT LAST (IRE) 2 b.g. (Mar 25) Cyrano de Bergerac 120 – Any Price (Gunner B 126) [1995 6m 6m 6m Sep 7] IR 6,500F, IR 12,000Y: half-brother to winning middle-distance performer Grog (by Auction Ring): dam half-sister to All Systems Go: well beaten, including in seller. *M. Bell* [–]

A MILLION TO ONE (IRE) 3 b.f. Common Grounds 118 – Princess Nabila (USA) (King Pellinore (USA) 127) [1994 76: 6.1m 6f^{2} 5g* 6d 5d^{4} 1995 5g 6m^{5} 7.3g^{6} 8.1g^{4} 7g* 8m^{5} Jun 26] lengthy filly: has a round action: fair performer: won claimer at Warwick in June: probably stays 1m: acts on firm and dead ground: races prominently: sold 5,000 gns Newmarket December Sales. *M. Bell* [74]

A MILLION WATTS 4 b.g. Belfort (FR) 89 – Peters Pet Girl (Norwick (USA) 125) [1994 66: 6m^{3} 7.6m^{4} 8f* 10m 10g^{3} 8s^{6} 8s 9g 1995 a8g^{2} a10g^{5} a8g* a8.5g^{2} 10m a8g^{2} 9.7m May 31] sparely-made gelding: fair handicapper on the all-weather: won at Southwell in March: well beaten on turf in 1995: stays 1¼m: acts on firm and soft ground and the all-weather: blinkered (finished last) final 2-y-o start. *Lady Herries* [– a73]

AMINGTON LASS 2 ch.f. (Mar 31) Cree Song 99 – Millfields House 70 (Record Token 128) [1995 5g 5d^{5} Sep 13] third foal: dam poor maiden appeared to stay 1¼m: better effort in maidens when fifth of 11 to First Maite at Beverley, prominent over 4f. *B. A. McMahon* [47 +]

AMIR'S BLUE (BEL) 4 br.c. Amir Albadeia (USA) – Source Bleue (FR) (Lionel 128) [1994 a8.5g* a7.5g^{2} a9.3g^{3} a8.5g* a8g a8.5g^{5} a8.5g a8.5g^{4} 1995 a9.5f^{5} 8f^{4} 9.5f^{2} 8.5g^{3} 9f^{3} 8d^{2} 8.5d 9.7s a8g^{2} Oct 21] Belgian-trained colt: third foal: half-brother to a winner in France by Solicitor: dam won 4 races at 1¼m to 1½m: modest performer: won 2 races at both 2 yrs (at 5f) and 3 yrs: made frame in [39] handicaps on several occasions in 1995: well beaten in claimer at Folkestone on eighth start on only British outing: stays 9.5f. *F. Calaerts, Belgium*

AMLAK (USA) 6 b.g. Riverman (USA) 131 – Ruwiyda (USA) 73 (In Reality) [1994 –: a8.5g 1995 a7g a12g a8g 6m 10.3m May 9] lengthy gelding: of little account nowadays. *T. Kersey* –

AMNESIA (IRE) 4 b.f. Don't Forget Me 127 – Amboselli 73 (Raga Navarro (ITY) 119) [1994 56d: a8g^3 10m^3 8.3m^2 7g 8.3g 8s 1995 8.1g^6 10g^6 9.2f^4 9.2f^3 15.1f Jun 26] lengthy filly: poor handicapper nowadays: has form at 9.2f, may prove best at around 1m: acts on firm ground: no improvement in blinkers/visor. *Mrs S. C. Bradburne* 41 ?

AMNESTY BAY 3 b.f. Thatching 131 – Sanctuary Cove (Habitat 134) [1994 NR 1995 8m 7g 8g* 8.2f^6 a8g Nov 16] light-framed filly: first foal: dam half-sister to very useful French stayer Cutting Reef: modest form: clearly best effort when winning seller at Newmarket in June: sold out of J. Fanshawe's stable 5,000 gns Newmarket September Sales after next start: off course over 4 months, tailed off in claimer at Southwell: should stay beyond 1m. *M. D. I. Usher* 63 d

AMOEBA (IRE) 2 b.f. (Mar 2) Distinctly North (USA) 115 – Lady Ingrid (Taufan (USA) 119) [1995 6g^2 5g^2 a6g^6 6g 5s^3 a6g^6 Nov 13] 9,000Y: workmanlike filly: half-sister to several animals, no winners: dam unraced: runner-up in maidens at Pontefract and Sandown in June: failed to repeat that form: stays 6f: sold 2,700 gns Doncaster November Sales. *J. Berry* 66 d

AMONG ISLANDS 4 b.f. Jupiter Island 126 – Queen of The Nile (Hittite Glory 125) [1994 NR 1995 12d^5 16m^5 Jun 26] angular filly: sixth foal: half-sister to 8.2f winner Burnditch Girl (by Raga Navarro): dam ran once: unplaced in 2 NH Flat races in the spring: never a factor in claimers at Beverley and Nottingham in June. *Mrs M. Reveley* –

AMRAK AJEEB (IRE) 3 b.c. Danehill (USA) 126 – Noble Dust (USA) (Dust Commander (USA)) [1994 52p: 7.1m 1995 7.1m^2 8m^5 7g* 8m 8g^4 10.5m* 10m^2 10m^2 10d 9g 10m^5 9d Oct 21] rather leggy colt: fairly useful performer: won maiden at Kempton in June and handicap at Haydock in August: sweating and stiff task, probably flattered when fifth of 9 to Bal Harbour in well-contested minor event at Newmarket on eleventh start: stays 10.5f: acts on good to firm ground, probably not on dead: usually bandaged: takes good hold. *B. Hanbury* 91

AMRON 8 b.g. Bold Owl 101 – Sweet Minuet (Setay 105) [1994 98: 6m* 6g 6f^6 5.6m^2 6m^4 6f 6m^4 5.6g 6d 1995 6g 6m 6m^6 6m 6f 5.6m 6g 6s 6g Oct 7] sparely-made gelding: useful sprinter at best: disappointing in 1995: stays 6f: acts on firm and dead ground (won on heavy at 2 yrs): successful 6 times at Doncaster: goes well fresh. *J. Berry* 90 d

AMY LEIGH (IRE) 2 b.f. (Apr 11) Imperial Frontier (USA) 112 – Hollyberry (IRE) (Runnett 125) [1995 a5g* 5m 5g^3 6.1m^4 5.1m^3 5g^2 5f^2 5m Oct 27] IR 2,200Y: smallish filly: first foal: dam never ran: won maiden auction at Southwell in May: best effort in minor event (second of 7 to Dwingeloo) at Catterick before well beaten in nursery at Newmarket final start: speedy, and didn't seem to stay 6f: acts on firm ground and fibresand. *Capt. J. Wilson* 78

AMY'S STAR 9 b.m. Touch Boy 109 – Keep Believing (Sweet Revenge 129) [1994 –: 7g 7.5m 1995 a11g^6 Jan 6] lengthy, lightly-made mare: little sign of ability. *P. Wigham* –

ANALOGUE (IRE) 3 b.g. Reference Point 139 – Dancing Shadow 117 (Dancer's Image (USA)) [1994 71p: 7m^4 8.1d^4 1995 10m^4 a12g Oct 23] strong, sturdy gelding: modest form at best in 1995, failing to confirm 2-y-o promise: should be well suited by middle distances: sold 6,600 gns Newmarket Autumn Sales: tried visored. *M. R. Stoute* 62

ANAM 3 b.f. Persian Bold 123 – Yaqut (USA) 77 (Northern Dancer) [1994 69: 5g^3 5.7f^3 6.9m^2 8.3g^3 1995 7m 7g^5 7m^3 7.1m* 8f 7m* 7f^4 7m 7.6d^6 7d 7f Oct 18] sturdy, quite attractive filly: fair performer: won minor events at Chepstow in July and Lingfield in August: ran poorly last 4 starts: should have stayed 1m: acted on firm going, possibly not on a soft surface: often made running: visits Cadeaux Genereux. *P. T. Walwyn* 79

ANASTINA 3 ch.f. Thatching 131 – Nikitina 106 (Nijinsky (CAN) 138) [1994 NR 1995 8d 10g Jul 12] 12,500F, 60,000Y: lengthy, good-topped filly: half-sister to 4-y-o 1¾m winner Polo Kit (by Trempolino) and several other winners, including useful Irish middle-distance stayer Excellenza (by Exceller): dam, Irish 1¼m winner, out of high-class 1969 French 2-y-o Vela: carrying plenty of condition, well beaten in maidens at Ripon and Newmarket: sold 10,000 gns Newmarket December Sales. *J. H. M. Gosden* –

ANCESTRAL JANE 2 b.f. (Feb 26) Distant Relative 128 – Antoinette Jane 86 (Ile de Bourbon (USA) 133) [1995 6f^5 6f^2 6m 7d 7f^2 8f* Oct 16] lengthy filly: second foal: half-sister to 3-y-o Hanifa (by Master Willie): dam, 2-y-o 7f winner, granddaughter of July Cup winner Parsimony, also grandam of College Chapel: much improved efforts in nurseries final 2 starts, finishing strongly to lead well inside final 1f when beating Tarry 1½ lengths at Pontefract in October (second start in 3 days): will stay at least 1¼m: will improve again. *Mrs J. R. Ramsden* 77 p

ANCHOR CLEVER 3 b.c. Slip Anchor 136 – Mountain Bluebird (USA) 79 (Clever Trick (USA)) [1994 7m^3 8v 8v^2 8.5v^3 1995 12f^4 10m^2 12m 14m* 16.2m 15g^3 14.6d^6 14s Oct 1] 20,000Y: workmanlike colt: second foal: dam, stayed 1¼m, is granddaughter of half-sister to Queen's Hussar: placed in 3 of his 4 starts at 2 yrs in Italy for L. Mariani: useful form in Britain: won minor event at Salisbury in June: best efforts when neck third of 6 to Affidavit in Prix Hubert du Chaudenay at Longchamp and staying-on sixth of 10 to Classic Cliche in St Leger at Doncaster on sixth and seventh starts: should prove better at 2m than shorter: acts on any going: carried head high second 3-y-o start and looked hard ride on fifth. *P. A. Kelleway* 106

ANCHOR CROWN 3 b.f. Slip Anchor 136 – Doumayna 79 (Kouban (FR)) [1994 NR 1995 a12g^6 9.9m a12g 11.9f Aug 22] sixth foal: sister to fairly useful 1½m winner Foil Stone and half-sister to useful middle-distance stayer Bondstone (by Millers Mate): dam, 2m winner, is half-sister to Darshaan and Darara: sold out of W. Jarvis' stable only 1,200 gns Doncaster November (1994) Sales: no sign of ability: trained first 2 starts by K. Wingrove. *J. R. Jenkins* –

ANCHORENA 3 b.f. Slip Anchor 136 – Canna (Caerleon (USA) 132) [1994 NR 1995 11.4m^2 12s^5 14.1m^5 Oct 19] tall, angular filly: first foal: dam half-sister to Oaks d'Italia and E P Taylor Stakes winner Ivor's Image: fair form when staying-on second of 13 in maiden at Sandown in August: well beaten in similar events afterwards: should be suited by further than 11.4f: edgy and sweating profusely final start: sold 4,500 gns Newmarket December Sales, to join J. A. Harris. *R. Charlton* 77 ?

ANCHOR VENTURE 2 b.c. (Mar 26) Slip Anchor 136 – Ski Michaela (USA) (Devil's Bag (USA)) [1995 8g^3 7.9g Oct 7] rangy colt: has scope: second foal: half-brother to 3-y-o 1½m winner Canton Venture (by Arctic Tern): dam twice-raced daughter of half-sister to Cannonade: remote third of 5 behind Nabhaan in maiden at Thirsk: well-beaten last of 8 in similar event at York just over a month later, leading to over 3f out: will stay middle distances. *S. P. C. Woods* 50 +

ANDRE'S AFFAIR 4 b.g. Sulaafah (USA) 119 – Andrea Dawn 47 (Run The Gantlet (USA)) [1994 NR 1995 14f 14s Sep 28] dipped-backed gelding: second foal: dam poor 1¾m winner: tailed off in maidens. *D. J. S. ffrench Davis* –

ANDSOME BOY 2 ch.g. (Apr 19) Out of Hand 84 – My Home 61 (Homing 130) [1995 a6g 6.1d^6 6f Oct 24] neat gelding: third foal: brother to 3-y-o Handson and modest 4-y-o (stays 11f) My Handy Man: dam stayed 1m: well beaten in 2 median auction maidens and an all-aged race. *C. R. Barwell* –

ANEGRE (IRE) 3 gr.g. Cyrano de Bergerac 120 – Lady Celina (FR) (Crystal Palace (FR) 132) [1994 61: 5m 5m 6g 5d 1995 6m^6 8m^6 7g^3 8g 7m^6 7f^3 7.1m a7g^5 7m^6 8h Sep 4] sturdy gelding: modest maiden: left L. J. Holt's stable after seventh 3-y-o start: stays 7f: acts on firm and dead ground: carried head awkwardly final outing: sold 3,500 gns Newmarket Autumn Sales. *S. Dow* 61

A NEW FLAME 4 gr.g. Most Welcome 131 – Couleur de Rose (Kalaglow 132) [1994 NR 1995 a12g a12g^6 a16g^6 Mar 29] 10,500Y: third foal: half-brother to 1992 2-y-o 6f winner Exclusively Yours (by Shareef Dancer): dam unraced: seems of little account: sold 1,350 gns Ascot April Sales: tried visored. *R. Guest* –

ANGAAR (IRE) 2 b.c. (Apr 26) Fairy King (USA) – Decadence (Vaigly Great 127) [1995 5s* Sep 28] IR 70,000Y: leggy colt: fifth foal: brother to useful 3-y-o 5f 77 P winner Fairy Wind and half-brother to 2 winners, notably smart sprinter Mistertopogigo (by Thatching): dam sister to Hallgate: co-favourite but bit backward, won 16-runner maiden at Lingfield by short head from Music Gold, always well there and leading close home as runner-up stumbled: almost certainly capable of considerably better. *A. C. Stewart*

ANGEL CHIMES 2 ch.f. (Apr 19) Most Welcome 131 – Bell Toll 87 (High Line 125) [1995 7m 7m^{2} 5d* 7d 8f^{3} 7m^{2} Oct 21] sturdy, workmanlike filly: has a markedly round action: third foal: half-sister to useful 3-y-o 8.1f (at 2 yrs) and 1¼m winner Warning Order (by Warrshan) and useful 1993 2-y-o 5.2f and 7f winner Prince Babar (by Fairy King): dam 2-y-o 7f and 1m winner: came from well off very strong pace to win maiden at Beverley in September: good efforts in nurseries final 2 starts, running on well though carrying head high when ¾-length second to Carburton at Doncaster: will stay beyond 1m: acts on firm and dead ground. *J. E. Banks* — 77

ANGEL FACE (USA) 2 b.f. (Jan 23) Zilzal (USA) 137 – Touching Love 109 (Touching Wood (USA) 127) [1995 7m Aug 16] rather leggy filly: fifth foal: half-sister to Irish 1m winner Layaali (by Diesis): dam, French 7f and 9f winner stayed 1½m, out of half-sister to Clever Trick: 20/1, bit backward, reluctant to post and at stalls, around 14 lengths ninth of 11 to Brilliant Red in maiden at Kempton, taking good hold: sold 2,200 gns Doncaster November Sales. *E. A. L. Dunlop* — –

ANGEL FALLS (FR) 3 b.c. Shirley Heights 130 – Waterfall (USA) (Riverman (USA) 131) [1994 9d^{2} 1995 10.5v^{4} 10s^{2} 10s* 10m* 10.5d^{2} 10.5d^{3} 10g Aug 15] 600,000 francs Y: quite attractive French colt: not a good walker: third foal: half-brother to 2 winners, including French 4-y-o 9f/9.5f winner Tumble (by Waterfall): dam, French 2-y-o 6f winner, half-sister to Prix Morny winner First Waltz: smart performer: won minor events at Saint-Cloud in March and Longchamp in April: 5 lengths second of 7 to Diamond Mix in Prix Greffulhe and 1¼ lengths third of 6 to Flemensfirth in steadily-run Prix Lupin, both at Longchamp: last of 7 in Prix Guillaume d'Ornano at Deauville around 3 months later: will stay 1½m: acts on good to firm ground and soft: sent to Dubai. *A. Fabre, France* — 110

ANGELIC BELLE 3 b.f. Komaite (USA) – Lucky Angel 68 (Lucky Wednesday 124) [1994 NR 1995 a6g a8.5g a5g Mar 20] sparely-made filly: fourth known foal: sister to 4-y-o 6f winner Angelic Dancer and half-sister to 7f winner Chickcharnie (by Stanford): dam, bred to stay 1m, was speedy as 2-y-o but didn't train on: behind in maidens and seller (blinkered) on fibresand: bolted to post second start. *N. P. Littmoden* — –

ANGELIC DANCER 4 b.f. Komaite (USA) – Lucky Angel 68 (Lucky Wednesday 124) [1994 49: a5g a5g^{4} 5m^{6} 5m^{5} 5m^{2} 5g^{6} 5m 6f* 6g^{3} 6m 5m a6g^{3} 1995 a6g a6g^{6} 6.1g^{6} 6g 6.1m a5g May 11] close-coupled filly: poor handicapper: stays 6f: acts on firm ground and fibresand: tried visored once at 2 yrs, blinkered since second 3-y-o start. *S. R. Bowring* — 47

ANGEL IN MY HEART (FR) 3 ch.f. Rainbow Quest (USA) 134 – Sweetly (FR) 88 (Lyphard (USA) 132) [1994 7.5d^{4} 8g^{4} 1995 8g^{2} 8g* 12g^{2} 10g* 10g^{4} 9.3d^{2} 10f^{2} 10f^{2} Nov 26] sparely-made French filly: half-sister to several winners, notably smart French 1987 2-y-o 6f and 7f (Salamandre) winner Common Grounds and useful 1m/9f performer Lightning Fire (both by Kris): dam won 3 races at up to 9f in USA: smart performer: won minor event at Longchamp in June and 5-runner Prix de Psyche at Deauville (by 4 lengths from Take Liberties) in August: ran very well when second in Prix de l'Opera at Longchamp (not clear run as Timarida went clear, then staying on and beaten 2½ lengths), Yellow Ribbon Invitational at Santa Anita (½ length behind Alpride) and Matriarch Stakes at Hollywood Park (length behind Duda) in the autumn: seems to stay 1½m (beaten short neck in very slowly-run Prix Minerve): acts on firm and dead ground: consistent. *J. E. Hammond, France* — 119

ANGLESEY SEA VIEW 6 gr.m. Seymour Hicks (FR) 125 – Lexham View 72 (Abwah 118) [1994 NR 1995 16.1g* 22.2m^{4} Jun 23] leggy, lengthy, angular mare: first foal: dam, placed at 7f (at 2 yrs) and 1¼m, later winning hurdler/pointer: won NH Flat race in May: fair form to win steadily-run maiden at Newmarket in June under fine ride from L. Dettori: tailed off in 5-runner Queen Alexandra Stakes at Royal Ascot 13 days later: stays 2m. *A. Bailey* — 66

ANGUS-G 3 br.g. Chief Singer 131 – Horton Line 89 (High Line 125) [1994 NR 1995 8.2d^{4} 8m^{5} Oct 2] good-quartered, useful-looking gelding: fifth living foal: — 67 p half-brother to 1m (at 2 yrs) and 1½m winner Sarsta Grai (by Blakeney): dam 1½m winner: caught the eye, never placed to challenge, in maidens at Nottingham and Pontefract in the autumn: should stay at least 1¼m: looks sure to do better. *Mrs M. Reveley*

ANGUS MCCOATUP (IRE) 2 ch.c. (Apr 21) Mac's Imp (USA) 116 – In For More (Don 128) [1995 5f^6 5g 6g 6g^5 a7g^4 a7g^2 a7g^5 Dec 12] IR 7,000Y, 10,000 2-y-o: strong, lengthy colt: has scope: carries condition: fourth foal: half-brother to fairly useful 7f winner Thunder River (by Thatching): dam unraced half-sister to Beresford Stakes winner Just A Game, later a Grade 2 winner in USA: modest form: beaten neck by Theatre Magic in nursery at Southwell in November: didn't repeat the form in similar event at Wolverhampton following month: stays 7f: acts on fibresand: races keenly. *B. A. McMahon* — 65

ANIMATION 2 ch.f. (Mar 24) Superlative 118 – What A Looker (USA) (Raise A Native) [1995 6m^6 6m Jul 2] 11,500Y: sparely-made filly: good mover: third foal: dam minor winner in North America: well beaten in median auction maiden at Leicester and maiden at Doncaster (unruly stalls). *K. McAuliffe* — –

ANISTOP 3 b.c. Nomination 125 – Pounelta 91 (Tachypous 128) [1994 55p: 7g 6s 6s 1995 7f 8.3m 10m^6 8g^2 8m 8.5s a8g* Nov 16] sparely-made colt: much improved form to win claimer at Southwell in November on first run on all-weather: stays 1m well: sometimes looks difficult ride. *R. Akehurst* — 48, a59

ANITA'S CONTESSA (IRE) 3 b.f. Anita's Prince 126 – Take More (GER) (Frontal) [1994 NR 1995 7d^6 6m 6g^6 a6g^5 a6g 7.1g 6.9g* a6g^4 a7g a6g^5 Dec 12] leggy, sparely-made filly: sister to useful sprinter/7f performer Carranita and Irish 6f and 1m winner Take More Chances and half-sister to several winners in Ireland and Germany: dam won 6 races in Germany: dropped in class, not at best when winning seller at Folkestone in October, just holding on: still below best afterwards: effective at 6f and 7f: acts on dead ground and fibresand: races prominently. *B. Palling* — 61, a68

ANJOMAJASA 3 b.f. Teenoso (USA) 135 – Captain Bonnie 60 (Captain James 123) [1994 NR 1995 6m^4 8f^5 9.7s 8f a7g Nov 8] half-sister to modest sprint winners Doesyoudoes (by Bay Express) and Check The Gate (by Blushing Scribe): dam ran only at 2 yrs, placed over 5f: well beaten (first 2 starts for Miss G. Kelleway) in varied company. *J. Ffitch-Heyes* — –

ANJOU 3 b.g. Saumarez 132 – Bourbon Topsy 108 (Ile de Bourbon (USA) 133) [1994 NR 1995 a7g^4 a10g^3 12s^5 12m* 11.8f 12m a12g^6 a16g* Dec 15] rangy gelding: second foal: dam well-bred middle-distance stayer: sold out of G. Wragg's stable 7,500 gns Newmarket July Sales and gelded after second start: fair form (easily best efforts) when winning weak apprentice maiden at Catterick in October and 14-runner handicap at Lingfield (led over 3f out, ran on well) in December: stays 2m: acts on good to firm ground and equitrack. *J. Pearce* — 72

ANLACE 6 b.m. Sure Blade (USA) – Ascot Strike (USA) 85 (Mr Prospector (USA)) [1994 57: 8m 10m 7.1s 9f^5 8.1f* 7g 7.6m^3 8f^5 1995 9g 10.8f^3 10g 8g 8g^5 10m^2 9m* 8m 10m^2 10g 11.6m^5 11.6m^6 Aug 7] rather leggy mare: modest handicapper: won amateurs race at Goodwood in June: probably stays 11.6f: acts on firm ground: blinkered (respectable second) sixth 6-y-o start: held up: sometimes looks a hard ride: won over hurdles in November. *S. Mellor* — 53

ANNABA (IRE) 2 ch.f. (Feb 9) In The Wings 128 – Anna Matrushka (Mill Reef (USA) 141) [1995 8d^3 Sep 27] workmanlike filly: fifth foal: half-sister to 3-y-o 11.5f winner Anne d'Autriche (by Rainbow Quest), smart middle-distance performer Anna of Saxony (by Ela-Mana-Mou) and fairly useful (at up to 9f) Andrassy (by Ahonoora): dam unraced daughter of champion German filly Anna Paola: 7/2, just under 2 lengths third of 18 to Mystic Knight in maiden at Salisbury, challenging over 1f out and keeping on: will be very well suited by middle distances: sure to improve. *J. H. M. Gosden* — 75 p

ANNA BANNANNA 3 b.f. Prince Sabo 123 – Top Berry 87 (High Top 131) [1994 66p: 6g 7m^3 7m* 1995 8.2g 7f 12g May 24] smallish filly: shows plenty of knee action: modest form at 2 yrs: ran badly in 1995: stays 7f: blinkered and bandaged on debut. *M. C. Pipe* — –

ANNABELLA BAGGINS (IRE) 4 b.f. Nomination 125 – Last Detail 73 (Dara Monarch 128) [1994 –: 8d^6 7m^3 8.3m 1995 a12g a8g Jan 31] sparely-made filly: no worthwhile form: tried blinkered: sold 800 gns Doncaster March Sales. *R. Boss* — –

ANNABEL'S BABY (IRE) 6 b.m. Alzao (USA) 117 – Spyglass (Double Form 130) [1994 NR 1995 12f 16.2m Aug 24] compact mare: winning plater over hurdles: poor maiden on flat. *Mrs M. McCourt* –

ANNABERG (IRE) 2 b.f. (Feb 9) Tirol 127 – Icecapped 91 (Caerleon (USA) 132) [1995 5m^{5} 5g* 6m* 8f^{3} 7g^{2} 8m Sep 6] 10,000Y: strong, lengthy filly: has plenty of scope: third foal: sister to German 3-y-o 9.5f winner Enamorata and half-sister to 4-y-o 7f and 1m winner Racing Brenda (by Faustus): dam, 1½m and 16.5f winner, out of half-sister to smart middle-distance performers Snow and Icelandic: won maiden auction at Beverley and claimer at Pontefract in July: very good second in nursery at Newcastle penultimate outing: poor effort final outing: should stay beyond 7f: yet to race on a soft surface: sold 19,000 gns Newmarket Autumn Sales. *Mrs J. R. Ramsden* 73 +

ANNAGH 2 b.f. (Apr 20) Grey Desire 115 – Tango Lady (Gorytus (USA) 132) [1995 5v^{5} 5g^{6} 6g May 20] 700F: third foal: dam unraced: of no account. *W. T. Kemp* –

ANNA-JANE 3 ch.f. Soviet Star (USA) 128 – Aloha Jane (USA) 57 (Hawaii) [1994 68p: 6m 6g^{2} 1995 7m 8m^{5} 8g 7m^{2} 8.3m^{6} 8g^{6} 7m^{2} Sep 1] leggy, lengthy filly: fair maiden handicapper: stays 1m: yet to race on a soft surface: sweating (below form) fifth and sixth 3-y-o starts: takes a keen hold. *R. Hannon* 68

ANNA OF BRUNSWICK 3 b.f. Rainbow Quest (USA) 134 – Anna Paola (GER) (Prince Ippi (GER)) [1994 NR 1995 10.1g^{2} 14d^{2} 11.5g^{2} 9.7m* Sep 7] tall, leggy, sparely-made filly: half-sister to 2 winners at 1¼m+, notably useful Atlaal (by Shareef Dancer): dam leading German filly at 2 and 3 yrs, winning 11f Preis der Diana: fair form in maidens: justified favouritism in 8-runner race at Folkestone in September, making most: stays 1¾m: acts on good to firm and dead ground: found little when odds on third start: sold 17,000 gns Newmarket December Sales. *H. R. A. Cecil* 78

ANNA SETTIC 2 b.f. (Apr 16) Pharly (FR) 130 – Gwiffina 87 (Welsh Saint 126) [1995 6m^{5} 6.9f^{2} 7f^{3} 8m^{5} 7.5d^{3} a8.5g Oct 14] 5,400F, 6,200Y: angular filly: half-sister to several winners, including fairly useful 3-y-o sprinter Tedburrow (by Dowsing) and 1¼m winner Bowcliffe (by Petoski): dam 2-y-o 6f winner stayed 7f, didn't train on: fair plater: below form on fibresand final start: stays 1m: acts on firm and dead ground: visored fourth outing (reluctant to go to post): sold 2,300 gns Newmarket Autumn Sales. *Dr J. D. Scargill* 52

ANNECY (USA) 2 b.f. (Mar 4) Mr Prospector (USA) – Lake Country (CAN) (Caucasus (USA) 127) [1995 8m^{3} Oct 20] medium-sized, good-topped filly: fourth foal: sister to 2 winners in USA and half-sister to 1¼m to 1½m winner (in France) Corrouge (by Alleged), later smart hurdler: dam won 14 races in Canada/USA at around 1m/9f and is from family of Exceller and Capote: favourite but green, 4½ lengths third of 11 to easy winner Overruled in maiden at Doncaster, soon disputing lead but one pace final 2½f: will do better. *H. R. A. Cecil* 73 p

ANNE D'AUTRICHE (IRE) 3 ch.f. Rainbow Quest (USA) 134 – Anna Matrushka (Mill Reef (USA) 141) [1994 NR 1995 10g^{3} 11.5m* 12g^{3} Sep 2] tall, lengthy, rather unfurnished filly: fourth foal: half-sister to smart middle-distance performer Anna of Saxony (by Ela-Mana-Mou) and fairly useful (at up to 9f) Andrassy (by Ahonoora): dam unraced daughter of champion German filly Anna Paola: 11/4 on, hardly off bridle to win 3-runner maiden at Yarmouth in August: looked capable of plenty of improvement, but weakened very quickly as if something amiss in 3-runner minor event at Kempton following month: sent to Dubai. *J. H. M. Gosden* 75

ANN HILL (IRE) 5 ch.m. Bob Back (USA) 124 – Yuma (USA) (Caro 133) [1994 44d: a12g^{4} a13g^{4} a13g^{3} 12m^{5} 12g^{3} 10m^{3} 10m^{4} 10.8m^{2} a13g^{2} 17.2f 10.8m^{5} 13.8g^{3} 16.2f^{6} 12f^{2} 14.1m^{6} 12g 11.8g a12g a11g a12g a13g 1995 a13g^{5} a13g^{3} a12g 12m^{4} 10m 11.9m^{4} a14g 10.8m 14.1m 10.8f a12g a14g^{3} a13g Dec 14] small mare: often sweating and unimpressive in appearance: poor plater: stays 1¾m: best turf form on a sound surface, and acts on the all-weather. *R. Hollinshead* 33

ANNIE FAY (IRE) 3 gr.f. Fayruz 116 – Angie (Prince Bee 128) [1994 61: 5m^{3} 5f* 6m^{2} 6m* 5.1g^{2} 6m^{4} 6g^{3} 6.1d^{4} 1995 6.1m^{4} 6g 5g^{3} 6g^{3} a5g 5.9f*^{dis} 7.1f^{4} 6f^{5} 6g 7g Oct 10] compact filly: poor mover: modest performer: won claimer at Carlisle in June, but disqualified after failing dope test: well below form afterwards: stays 6f: yet to race on very soft ground, acts on any other: often hangs, and has worn off-side 55 pricker: usually races prominently: sold 2,000 gns Doncaster November Sales. *J. L. Harris*

ANNIVERSARYPRESENT 3 b.c. Puissance 110 – Safidar 83 (Roan Rocket 128) [1994 93: 6g^{6} 6m^{6} 7m^{2} 7f^{2} 7m* 8d^{4} 6g^{2} 7m^{2} 1995 8g 6m^{4} 7g* 8m 7g^{3} 9f^{5} Oct 7] close-coupled colt: useful performer: won £18,800 handicap at York in May, and ran well when narrowly-beaten third in Bunbury Cup at Newmarket on final outing for G. Lewis: raced on lasix, respectable fifth of 9 in Grade 3 event at Hawthorne in October: probably stays 9f: acts on firm and dead ground: blinkered last 5 starts. *L. J. Roussel, USA* — 99

ANN'S MUSIC 2 b.f. (May 14) Clantime 101 – An-Go-Look (Don't Look 107) [1995 5g 6h 7.5m 7.5d Sep 13] angular filly: sixth foal: half-sister to 13f NH Flat race winner Anabranch (by Kind of Hush): dam winning 2m hurdler/chaser: soundly beaten in varied company: pulled hard penultimate outing. *J. M. Jefferson* — –

ANN'S PEARL (IRE) 4 br.f. Cyrano de Bergerac 120 – Pariscene 86 (Dragonara Palace (USA) 115) [1994 77: 5.7m^{2} 5m^{4} 1995 5m 5.2m 5.1m* 5g 5.7m 5.1m^{2} 5m^{6} 5g 5d 5s Oct 7] unfurnished filly: fairly useful handicapper: won at Bath in May: best at 5f: acts on good to firm and dead going, below form on equitrack: sometimes has tongue tied down: usually races prominently: none too consistent. *J. W. Hills* — 80

ANNUS MIRABILIS (FR) 3 b.c. Warning 136 – Anna Petrovna (FR) 90 (Wassl 125) [1994 112p: 7g^{4} 7s* 7m* 8s^{2} 1995 10.4g^{2} 9g^{2} 8m^{5} 12m^{3} 10.4m^{3} 10.9g* Sep 16] — 120

In the course of what was truly another auspicious year on the turf for his owner, Annus Mirabilis made into a very smart three-year-old, was consistency itself and proved effective over a wide range of distances. He went close in the Irish Derby, the Dante Stakes and the Prix Jean Prat, finished a creditable third to Halling in the Juddmonte International, and put the smart six-year-old Captain Horatius firmly in

Stakis Casinos Doonside Cup, Ayr—Annus Mirabilis makes the most of his opportunity

his place when eased in grade in the Stakis Casinos Doonside Cup on his final start of the season. In six starts he was only once unplaced—that when he got no sort of run in the St James's Palace Stakes. Annus Mirabilis has now joined the Godolphin operation and is one of those wintering in Dubai. He is a near-certainty to improve his record by winning a pattern race or two on his return.

Annus Mirabilis was very impressive in beating Captain Horatius by five lengths at Ayr in September, but the Doonside Cup has only listed status and he did start at odds on. He had been much more highly tried previously, beginning at York in May where he and Classic Cliche fought out the finish of the Dante, Classic Cliche getting the better of the argument by half a length. Neither colt went on to Epsom. Annus Mirabilis, whose stamina was in doubt, was aimed at the St James's Palace Stakes at Royal Ascot, first taking in the nine-furlong Prix Jean Prat at Chantilly. As we saw it, he could have done with more of a test in the Jean Prat. The race developed into a sprint in the straight. He was caught slightly flat-footed, then failed by a nose to pull back Torrential. Given his problems in running at Royal Ascot—he was forced back approaching the turn and had no room until the race was over—Annus Mirabilis did well to come around five lengths fifth of nine to Bahri. However, he appeared next over a mile and a half in the Irish Derby at the Curragh in July. For the third time in four races he finished within a length of the winner. He travelled best of all for a long way, held up as usual, made smooth progress once eased outside approaching the two-furlong marker, and kept on well into third place behind Winged Love and Definite Article, still gaining at the line. In the International at York six weeks later Annus Mirabilis, like the rest, found Halling much too good. He was beaten just over five lengths, having been unable to get in a blow, and finished a length and three quarters down on Bahri.

Annus Mirabilis (FR) (b.c. 1992)	Warning (b 1985)	Known Fact (b 1977)	In Reality
			Tamerett
		Slightly Dangerous (b 1979)	Roberto
			Where You Lead
	Anna Petrovna (FR) (b 1987)	Wassl (b 1980)	Mill Reef
			Hayloft
		Anna Paola (ch 1978)	Prince Ippi
			Antwerpen

The 1981 German Oaks winner Anna Paola, the grandam of Annus Mirabilis, has been in the Darley Stud since she was retired from racing. Her best runner so far is the useful middle-distance winner Atlaal, and she has been more important as the producer of Anna Petrovna and another of the stud's broodmares Anna Matrushka, the latter the dam of the 1993 Park Hill Stakes winner Anna of Saxony. Anna Petrovna had winning form in handicaps at around a mile and a quarter. Annus Mirabilis is her first foal. A tall colt, he stays a mile and a half well, acts on good to firm ground and soft, and is genuine and most consistent. *M. R. Stoute*

ANNYBAN 5 b.m. Bairn (USA) 126 – Mandrian 103 (Mandamus 120) [1994 –: a12g^4 a8g 1995 a11g^5 Aug 4] tall, lengthy mare: bad maiden. *J. Parkes* –

ANONYM (IRE) 3 b.g. Nashamaa 113 – Bonny Bertha (Capistrano 120) [1994 NR 1995 8m^3 8f 10m 9f^3 10f^4 7f* 8g* 7m^3 7m^5 7d Sep 22] 4,000 2-y-o: rather leggy, useful-looking gelding: has a quick action: half-brother to 3 minor winners: dam Irish 12.5f winner: fair handicapper: won at Doncaster (edged right) and Leicester (5/2 on, unimpressive in 3-runner event) in the summer: may prove best at around 1m: acts on firm going: often edgy: sometimes looks reluctant, and one to treat with caution: sold (J. Dunlop to D. Nicholls) 12,000 gns Newmarket Autumn Sales. *J. L. Dunlop* 71

ANORAK (USA) 5 b.g. Storm Bird (CAN) 134 – Someway Somehow (USA) (What Luck (USA)) [1994 53, a58: a7g^3 a9.4g a8.5g a7g^3 a8g^2 a9.4g* 8.3v^4 7g^3 8d 8m^6 7.6g^6 7.5m 8f^3 8m^6 a8.5g* 1995 a8g a11g a11g^6 a9.4g^5 12m^2 11.1m^3 10.9g^2 12m^4 Jul 20] leggy gelding: has a round action: poor performer: stays 1½m: acts on the all-weather: may well be unsuited by soft ground, probably acts on any other: effective in a visor: sometimes hangs left and finds little. *G. M. Moore* 46

ANOTHERANNIVERSARY 2 gr.f. (Feb 21) Emarati (USA) 74 – Final Call 79 (Town Crier 119) [1995 5m* 5m* 6m^2 5m 5m^2 Jul 7] 30,000Y: strong, well-grown filly: has scope: unimpressive mover: half-sister to 3-y-o 6f and 7f winner Jo Maximus (by Prince Sabo) and several other winners, including useful 6f winner Night Bell (by Night Shift) and 1985 2-y-o 7f winner Stage Hand (by Sagaro), later winner at 8.2f and 1½m in France: dam, 5f winner ran only at 2 yrs, half-sister to 95 good sprinter On Stage: won median auction maiden at Warwick and minor event at Windsor in spring: ran as though something amiss in Queen Mary Stakes at Ascot before best effort when second (made most) to Home Shopping in listed race at Sandown final start: a sprinter: has raced only on top-of-the-ground: bandaged behind final 3 starts: early to post on last of them. *G. Lewis*

ANOTHER BATCHWORTH 3 b.f. Beveled (USA) – Batchworth Dancer 67 (Ballacashtal (CAN)) [1994 63?: 5s 6d 1995 7g 6m 5.3f^5 5.3f^2 7m^2 6d 5.3g a5g^5 a6g* a5g a6g^3 a6g Nov 27] lengthy, unfurnished filly: modest handicapper: won at Wolverhampton in October: effective at 5f, and stays 7f: acts on firm and soft ground and the all-weather: sometimes early to post: none too consistent. *S. Mellor* — 63

ANOTHER EPISODE (IRE) 6 b.g. Drumalis 125 – Pasadena Lady (Captain James 123) [1994 79: a5g^4 a5g^5 a5g^6 a5g 5d^4 5f^2 a5g* 5g^5 5m^2 5m* a5g 5m 5g^3 5m* 5.1s^2 5s 1995 a5g^6 a5g^6 5m^5 May 8] leggy, lengthy gelding: fair front-running performer on his day in 1994: never on terms following tardy start all 3 outings in 1995: races at 5f: acts on all-weather surfaces, firm and soft ground: visored (finished last) fourth 5-y-o start: one to treat with caution. *J. Berry* — –

ANOTHER FIDDLE (IRE) 5 b.g. Waajib 121 – Elmar 87 (Lord Gayle (USA) 124) [1994 74: 6s 7m 7m* 8.1m^3 10.1m 10m^5 1995 8g 8m 8m^6 8m^5 8f^5 8f^6 8f^2 8g^2 9.7s^2 Sep 27] compact gelding: fair handicapper: put up 4 best efforts in 1995 at Goodwood: effective at 1m, shapes as if stays 9.7f: acts on firm and soft going: sometimes carries head awkwardly: has been bandaged behind: none too consistent. *R. Akehurst* — 69

ANOTHER JADE 5 ch.m. Beveled (USA) – Zamindara (Crofter (USA) 124) [1994 66d: 5d^6 6s^5 6m 5m 5g 6g 5.1m^3 6m 5m^6 6f^6 5m 6g 7d^5 5.7g 1995 a6g* 6m^4 a7g 5.3m^2 6f^3 5m^2 6m^2 6m^3 6m^2 5.2f^5 5m 5f^6 a6g Aug 11] smallish, sturdy mare: has a quick action: fair handicapper: won at Wolverhampton in April: effective at 5f, and probably stays 7f: acts on firm and soft ground and on fibresand: has won for apprentice: blinkered (well beaten) final 4-y-o start. *A. P. Jarvis* — 71

ANOTHER MONK (IRE) 4 br.g. Supreme Leader 123 – Royal Demon (Tarboosh (USA)) [1994 12g 1995 10d 6.5s^5 12m 16f 10f^6 9g 10m 10m 9d a13g^4 Dec 6] half-brother to 2 winners, including The Black Monk (1½m in Ireland, by Sexton Blake): dam Irish 5f winner: poor maiden handicapper in Ireland for T. Naughton: well beaten both outings in Britain. *R. Curtis* — 35

ANOTHER NIGHTMARE (IRE) 3 b.f. Treasure Kay 114 – Carange (Known Fact (USA) 135) [1994 59: 5g^2 5m^3 5g* 6d 6d 1995 a6g 5m 5g 5g^5 5m 5f 5f^6 5m 5m Oct 30] leggy, sparely-made filly: modest 5f performer at 2 yrs for Miss L. Perratt: no worthwhile form in 1995, trained until after eighth start by R. McKellar: may be unsuited by a soft surface: races prominently. *J. S. Goldie* — –

ANOTHERONE TO NOTE 4 ch.g. Beveled (USA) – Dame Nellie 84 (Dominion 123) [1994 61: 7f^5 6f^6 6f^3 5m^5 5.7g a6g 1995 a6g^5 a6g a6g^3 a8g 6m 6f a6g^6 a5g a7g^5 6g 8f^4 a7g a7g^5 Dec 19] leggy gelding: poor maiden handicapper: sold out of M. Heaton-Ellis' stable 1,500 gns Ascot May Sales after fifth 4-y-o start: stays 7f: acts on firm ground, well beaten on soft: no improvement in visor/blinkers: wears crossed noseband: inconsistent. *N. P. Littmoden* — 51 d

ANOTHER PICEA 2 b.g. (Apr 23) Picea 99 – Atoka 97 (March Past 124) [1995 5m 6m 8.2m Oct 26] 2,500Y: half-brother to fairly useful 1985 2-y-o 5f winner Oh Boyar (by Young Generation) and 1¼m and 10.4f winner Edge of Darkness (by Vaigly Great): dam won from 6f to 15f: well beaten in maidens: left K. Ivory's stable after second start. *N. Tinkler* — –

ANOTHER QUARTER (IRE) 2 b.f. (Apr 24) Distinctly North (USA) 115 – Numidia (Sallust 134) [1995 7g 8.2m^5 Oct 26] IR 5,600F, IR 5,000Y: leggy filly: half-sister to 3-y-o Astral Invader (by Astronef), 5f and 6f winner at 2 yrs, and 7f winner Premier Choice (by Petorius): dam, should have been suited by 1¼m+, half-sister to smart French middle-distance winner Dieter: similar form in maidens at Leicester (slowly away, green) and Nottingham (never-nearer fifth of 10 to Censor) in October: may stay beyond 1m: bandaged in front: may do better. *S. P. C. Woods* — 57

ANOTHER TIME 3 ch.g. Clantime 101 – Another Move 69 (Farm Walk 111) [1994 48: 6g 7g 6g^6 1995 6g^5 8m^5 8m^6 8g* 8g 8d* 8g^2 10f* Oct 24] neat gelding: has a quick action: left Miss S. Hall's stable after second 3-y-o start: progressive — 79 p performer, winning seller at Thirsk (landed gamble, bought in 7,000 gns) and minor events at Brighton and Redcar, all in the autumn: stays 1¼m: acts on firm and dead ground: capable of even better. *S. P. C. Woods*

ANOTHER VENTURE (IRE) 5 br.g. Tanfirion 110 – Fitz's Buck (Master Buck) [1994 NR 1995 14.1f^{5} Jun 24] good-topped gelding: half-brother to a fairly useful chaser by Monksfield: dam behind in NH Flat races: modest winning hurdler for G. M. Moore: beaten around 25 lengths in maiden at Redcar on flat debut: has joined F. Murphy. *M. Johnston* –

ANSELLMAN 5 gr.g. Absalom 128 – Grace Poole (Sallust 134) [1994 88: 6d 6s 6s^{6} 5d* 5m 6m 6f 5.2g^{5} 6g 5.6g 6d 1995 6g 5g^{5} 6d^{6} 5.1m^{2} 5m^{3} 6m 5m* 5.1h^{2} 5m^{3} 6g 5g 5m^{5} Oct 4] sturdy gelding: carries condition: has a round action: fair performer: narrowly won claimer at Catterick in August: effective at 5f and 6f: acts on hard ground, very best form with give (goes well on soft): blinkered (edgy) twice in 1993. *J. Berry* 78

ANSHAN'S DEITY 2 ch.c. (May 31) Anshan 119 – Pagan Deity 88 (Brigadier Gerard 144) [1995 5m 6g 7g^{4} 7h a7g Sep 4] 5,400Y: good-topped colt: half-brother to several winners, including 1½m to 2m winner Touching Times (by Touching Wood): dam won 3 times at around 1¼m: modest maiden: well beaten final 2 starts: should stay beyond 7f: sold 1,000 gns Doncaster October Sales. *C. W. Fairhurst* 57 ?

ANSWERS-TO-THOMAS 2 b.c. (Mar 2) Komaite (USA) – Launde Abbey 75 (Absalom 128) [1995 5g^{6} 5f^{2} 5d^{4} 6d 5m 6m^{5} Oct 30] 6,400Y: angular colt: first foal: dam 5f winner at 2 yrs: modest maiden: best efforts at 5f. *J. M. Jefferson* 62

ANTARCTICA (USA) 3 ch.f. Arctic Tern (USA) 126 – Loved Etsu (USA) (Liloy (FR) 124) [1994 NR 1995 10.3g 12g Apr 10] $11,000Y: leggy, lengthy filly: fourth foal: half-sister to a minor winner in North America by Phone Trick: dam minor winner at around 6f: well beaten in early-season maidens: sold 720 gns Doncaster November Sales. *P. A. Kelleway* –

ANTARCTIC STORM 2 b.g. (Feb 12) Emarati (USA) 74 – Katie Scarlett 70 (Lochnager 132) [1995 6m 7g Oct 23] 7,500F, 14,000Y: strong, close-coupled gelding: first foal: dam 1¼m winner also won over hurdles: backward, around 5 lengths eighth of 21 to Projection in maiden at Newmarket, never reaching leaders after making run from rear: tailed off in similar event at Lingfield 10 days later. *E. A. L. Dunlop* 72 ?

ANTARTICTERN (USA) 5 b.g. Arctic Tern (USA) 126 – False Image (USA) 79 (Danzig (USA)) [1994 84d: 10g^{2} 9g* 9.5s* 9.5d^{2} 9.5s 9f* 9s 8.9m 10.4d 10.3s 1995 12m^{5} 11f^{5} 9m^{3} 10m^{2} 10.1f^{6} 12g 10g^{2} 8.9g 14.1m Oct 26] good-bodied gelding: modest performer at best in 1995: sold out of N. Tinkler's stable 1,700 gns Doncaster May Sales after reappearance: stays 1¼m: acts on firm and soft ground: tried blinkered: ungenuine hurdler. *G. R. Oldroyd* 48

ANTHELIA 2 b.f. (May 19) Distant Relative 128 – Confection (Formidable (USA) 125) [1995 5m* 6g* 6f^{3} Oct 12] 6,500Y: quite attractive filly: progressed well physically: half-sister to 3-y-o Delicious (by Dominion) and fair 1991 2-y-o 5f and 6f winner Titch Wizard (by Bairn): dam twice-raced daughter of useful middle-distance stayer Mint: won maiden auction at Pontefract in July: improved considerably to beat Prancing a neck in minor event at Yarmouth in September, then ran a fine race when staying-on third of 26 to Blue Iris in Redcar Two-Year-Old Trophy: will show further improvement at 7f+: held up. *G. Wragg* 100 p

ANTIGUAN FLYER 6 b.g. Shirley Heights 130 – Fleet Girl (Habitat 134) [1994 –: 14m 13.9d 1995 10m 14.8m^{4} 12m 18.2g^{6} 8f Oct 18] lengthy gelding: fairly useful middle-distance stayer at 3 yrs: no form in 1995. *R. Harris* –

ANTIGUAN JANE 2 b.f. (Feb 13) Shirley Heights 130 – Dabbiana (CAN) (Fappiano (USA)) [1995 7m a7g^{3} Nov 21] good-topped filly: has scope: has a quick action: fifth foal: sister to useful middle-distance stayer Party Season and half-sister to 1990 2-y-o 7f winner Alton Bay (by Al Nasr): dam won at around 7f in USA: staying-on 6 lengths third of 11 to Banzhaf in maiden at Lingfield: will be suited by middle distances: tail flasher: will improve again. *R. W. Armstrong* 56 p

ANTONIAS MELODY 2 b.f. (Mar 4) Rambo Dancer (CAN) 107 – Ayodessa 78 (Lochnager 132) [1995 5m 5m^{2} 6m^{6} 6.1d* 6d 5m^{3} 5m^{5} Nov 3] good-topped, workmanlike filly: has scope: second foal: sister to a 2-y-o 5.5f winner in Norway at 69

2 yrs: dam sprinter: landed gamble in 22-runner nursery at Nottingham in September: ran well in similar events at Newmarket and Doncaster final 2 starts: stays 6f: acts on good to firm and dead ground: has been bandaged. *S. R. Bowring*

ANY COLOUR 2 b.f. (Feb 21) Anshan 119 – Council Rock 74 (General Assembly (USA)) [1995 6g^{6} 7m^{6} Oct 13] 5,500F: fourth foal: half-sister to 3-y-o Truly Madly Deeply (by Most Welcome): dam, maiden suited by 1¼m, daughter of Nassau Stakes winner Dancing Rocks: never-dangerous sixth in maidens won by Last Second at Redcar and Hilaala at Catterick nearly 3 weeks later. *M. J. Camacho* –

ANY MINUTE NOW (IRE) 5 b.g. Alzao (USA) 117 – Miss Siddons (Cure The Blues (USA)) [1994 –: 11.9m 1995 14.4m Jun 14] compact gelding: fair form in Ireland (successful at 1¾m) in 1993: very lightly raced and well beaten on flat since: fair winning hurdler. *J. Akehurst* –

ANY ONE LINE (IRE) 3 b.f. Contract Law (USA) 108 – North Hut (Northfields (USA)) [1994 56: 5s^{5} 6m 6g* 6m^{5} 7m 7g^{3} 6.9m^{4} 1995 8m May 4] workmanlike filly: modest form at 2 yrs for M. Channon: tailed off in handicap on only start in 1995: stays 7f: sold 4,000 gns Newmarket July Sales. *J. Akehurst* –

ANYTIME BABY 3 b.f. Bairn (USA) 126 – Cindys Gold 69 (Sonnen Gold 121) [1994 56: a6g^{5} a7g^{4} 1995 a8g a8g 7m 7f 5d^{4} 5d a5g* a6g a5g^{4} a5g^{4} Dec 6] lengthy filly: modest handicapper: trained until after second 3-y-o start by K. McAuliffe: won at Lingfield in November: best at sprint distances: acts on equitrack and dead ground: held up, and suited by strongly-run race: sometimes early or mulish to post, and refused to enter stalls in July. *P. T. Dalton* 46 a53

ANZIO (IRE) 4 b.g. Hatim (USA) 121 – Highdrive (Ballymore 123) [1994 51+: a8.5g^{4} 1995 a8g 8g 6m^{3} 6f 6g^{4} 5g* 5f^{3} 6f^{6} a5g^{2} 6m^{4} 6f 5m* 5m^{2} 5m^{4} 6g 6d* 7g 6.1s^{4} 6f^{4} a7g* a7g Dec 18] quite attractive gelding: has a round action: fairly useful performer: won seller at Folkestone in June, apprentice handicap at Windsor in August, claimer at Leicester in September and handicap at Lingfield in November: stays 7f: acts on firm and soft ground and the all-weather: sometimes bandaged: effective blinkered or not: usually races prominently. *B. A. Pearce* 79

ANZIYAN (USA) 2 b.c. (Feb 14) Danzig (USA) – Razyana (USA) 87 (His Majesty (USA)) [1995 5d* 6g^{3} Aug 1] fifth foal: brother to 2 winners, notably high-class sprinter/miler Danehill, and closely related to smart French miler Euphonic (by The Minstrel): dam, placed over 7f and 1¼m from 3 starts, is out of half-sister to Northern Dancer: won newcomers event at Chantilly in June: odds on, 3½ lengths third of 5 to With Fascination in Prix de Cabourg at Deauville nearly 2 months later: should stay beyond 6f: capable of further progress. *A. Fabre, France* 96 p

AOIFE ALAINN (IRE) 3 ch.f. Glenstal (USA) 118 – Majestic Nurse 80 (On Your Mark 125) [1994 6v 6g^{6} 7d^{3} 1995 6m^{4} 7.3g 8.1m* 8f Jul 13] workmanlike, ex-Irish filly: half-sister to several winners: dam won Irish Cambridgeshire: fair performer: won 4-runner maiden at Edinburgh in July: broke leg in minor event at Redcar: stayed 1m: acted on good to firm and good to soft ground: dead. *J. W. Hills* 64

APACHE LEN (USA) 2 br.c. (Mar 9) Rahy (USA) 115 – Shining Skin (USA) (Fappiano (USA)) [1995 7m^{6} 7f^{2} 7f^{2} Oct 31] $90,000F, 68,000Y: tall, rather leggy colt: has scope: sixth foal: half-brother to a winner in USA by Cox's Ridge: dam, 1¼m winner, half-sister to very smart 1983 Gran Criterium winner Northern Tempest: runner-up in maidens won by Dance On A Cloud at Leicester and Magic Mill at Redcar, setting pace on second occasion: will stay further than 7f. *R. Hannon* 76

APARTMENTS ABROAD 2 b.f. (Mar 2) Prince Sabo 123 – La Graciosa (Comedy Star (USA) 121) [1995 5d 6g 6f 5g^{5} 5m^{4} 6m^{5} 5g^{3} 5.3d 7f^{3} 7m^{4} a8g* Dec 18] 2,800Y: leggy filly: third foal: dam winning sprinter at 2 yrs in Scandinavia: inconsistent plater on turf though good efforts last 2 starts: showed improvement in maiden on equitrack at Lingfield in December, staying on gamely: will stay further than 1m: tried visored/blinkered. *K. McAuliffe* 54 a62

APICELLA 2 ch.c. (Mar 8) Pharly (FR) 130 – Sixslip (USA) 94 (Diesis 133) [1995 6.9s^{5} Sep 27] 2,600F, 4,200Y: second foal: half-brother to 3-y-o Huish Cross (by Absalom): dam, 1¼m and 1¾m winner, half-sister to useful 4-y-o sprinter Top Banana (by Pharly): 33/1, over 10 lengths fifth of 11 to Salmis in maiden auction at Folkestone, staying on under considerate ride after slow start: will improve. *R. Boss* 60 p

APOLLONO 3 b.g. Cyrano de Bergerac 120 – Daima (Dominion 123) [1994 61: 6g 8.1g 6d^4 7m^4 7m^6 7.3v^2 1995 7g^3 7.1m 7m^2 8f* 8.1m^2 8.5m* 8d 8m 8m Oct 28] angular gelding: fairly useful handicapper: first past post at Lingfield (reappearance, demoted for irresponsible riding) in May, Brighton (first run since being gelded, hung left) in July and Epsom in August: left R. Akehurst's stable after seventh start: stays 8.5f: acts on any going: blinkered (below form) third 2-y-o outing: possibly needs holding up. *J. R. Fanshawe* — 86

APOLLO RED 6 ch.g. Dominion 123 – Woolpack (Golden Fleece (USA) 133) [1994 50, a58: a7g* a6g^3 a8g^4 a7g^4 8d 6d* a8g^3 6m 6f^4 7f 6g^3 6m^6 a7g a7g^6 1995 a6g^5 a6g^3 a7g^6 a6g a7g a7g^3 6m^2 7f 6f 7m a7g^3 a7g a7g^2 Nov 29] smallish, sturdy gelding: modest performer: best efforts at 6f or 7f: acts on equitrack and on good to firm and dead ground: effective blinkered/visored or not: usually races prominently. *A. Moore* — 50 a58

APPEAL AGAIN (IRE) 2 br.g. (May 12) Mujtahid (USA) 118 – Diva Encore 74 (Star Appeal 133) [1995 6g 7f 6m Nov 3] IR 18,000Y: workmanlike gelding: sixth foal: half-brother to several winners, including useful sprinters Don't Worry Me and Encore M'Lady (both by Dancing Dissident): dam 1½m and 1¾m winner stayed 2m: towards rear in maidens at Pontefract, Leicester and Doncaster: burly first 2 starts: probably capable of better. *Mrs J. R. Ramsden* — –p

APPLAUD (USA) 2 ch.f. (Jan 13) Rahy (USA) 115 – Band (USA) (Northern Dancer) [1995 5g* 5f^2 6g* Jul 11] — 105 p

Nothing was seen of Applaud after the Newmarket July meeting. She was pulled out of the Lowther Stakes because of 'a slight problem' and then missed an alternative engagement in the Moyglare Stud Stakes. When last seen on the racecourse she looked like making up into a very useful filly. At that time her trainer rated her six lengths inferior to Blue Duster, with whom she had never worked. 'Of the pair', said Loder, 'Applaud would be very much the two-year-old. It will be interesting to see how she develops during the winter but .... Blue Duster has much more scope'.

Applaud was last seen out in the Hillsdown Cherry Hinton Stakes, a race she won narrowly from dead-heaters Dance Sequence, who had twice run second to Blue

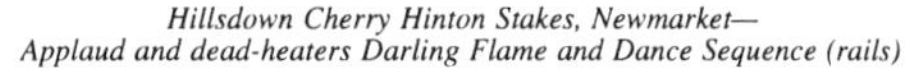

Hillsdown Cherry Hinton Stakes, Newmarket—
Applaud and dead-heaters Darling Flame and Dance Sequence (rails)

Duster, and Darling Flame. The event lost some of its value as a guide to the respective merits of the contestants through lack of a gallop; it developed into little more than a two-furlong sprint between seven of the eight starters. Applaud received an astute ride from Pat Eddery, being in prime position when the sprint began after setting the gallop with the rank outsider Beautiful Ballad; Dance Sequence, on the other hand, became short of room on the stand rails when the tempo increased. In the drive for the line Applaud held on well to the lead under firm hands-and-heels riding, with just half a length to spare when she got there. Unlike the winner, the joint-seconds were seen out again, Dance Sequence winning the Lowther (in-season Darling Flame nowhere) and performing respectably behind Blue Duster in the Cheveley Park. The Cherry Hinton was Applaud's third start. She'd been a warm order for the Windsor Castle Stakes at Royal Ascot on the strength of an impressive Leicester maiden-race win, but had been beaten on merit by Kuantan after having to wait for a run.

Applaud (USA) (ch.f. Jan 13, 1993)	Rahy (USA) (ch 1985)	Blushing Groom (ch 1974)	Red God
			Runaway Bride
		Glorious Song (b 1976)	Halo
			Ballade
	Band (USA) (b 1987)	Northern Dancer (b 1961)	Nearctic
			Natalma
		Swingtime (b 1972)	Buckpasser
			Swoon's Tune

If Applaud—a robust filly—does train on she has a sporting chance of staying further than six furlongs judging by the way she relaxed in front in the Cherry Hinton. Her sire the Middle Park second Rahy, got a mile as a three-year-old. Rahy is at stud in the USA, having been raced there at four, and Applaud, the first foal of the dam, was acquired at the Keeneland Yearling Sales for 225,000 dollars. The dam, the maiden Band, is a half-sister to the nine-furlong stakes winner Festive out of a mare who, like Rahy, raced on both sides of the Atlantic. That mare, Swingtime, was a sprinter over here, a good one, too: she won the Cork And Orrery Stakes and the Diadem Stakes in 1975. Subsequently she showed stamina in adding several Graded stakes to her tally, for the best of them were decided over further than a mile. Swingtime's dam produced another stakes filly in Bag of Tunes, a Kentucky Oaks winner. *D. R. Loder*

APPLE MUSASHI 2 b.c. (Mar 29) Never So Bold 135 – Third Movement 75 (Music Boy 124) [1995 6g^{4} 6s* 6.5g^{4} Oct 17] 22,000Y: workmanlike colt: half-brother to several winners, including useful Italian 3-y-o 5f (at 2 yrs) to 7.5f winner Bruttina (by Primo Dominie) and fair 7f/1m winner The Little Ferret (by Scottish Reel): dam (maiden) stayed 7f: progressive form: easily won maiden at Lingfield in September: 3 lengths fourth of 9 to Titus Livius in Prix Eclipse at Deauville following month: should stay 7f: likely to improve again. *J. H. M. Gosden* **101 p**

APRIL'S JOY 2 b.f. (May 11) Mazilier (USA) 107 – Ziobia 78 (Tribal Chief 125) [1995 5m^{3} 5m^{2} 5g^{4} a6g^{5} 5g^{4} a5g^{4} 5.1m^{3} 5m^{3} 5h* 5g^{2} 5g Sep 18] small, light-framed filly: half-sister to several winners, including fairly useful performers Greens Masterpiece (by Taufan), 5f winner at 2 yrs, and unreliable Qualitair Flyer (by Kampala), 6f and 8.2f winner: dam placed at up to 7f: plater: made all at Carlisle in August: best form at 5f: acts on hard ground and fibresand. *J. Norton* **56**

APRIL THE EIGHTH 2 b.c. (Mar 12) Statoblest 120 – Miami Melody (Miami Springs 121) [1995 5.2m^{3} 5f 5m* 6f* 6m^{6} Aug 13] 7,600F, 20,000Y: tall, quite good-topped colt: has scope: good mover: half-brother to several maidens: dam placed over 6f and 1½m in Ireland: successful in July in maiden at Beverley and nursery at Goodwood (in very good style by 2 lengths from Prince of Florence, running on strongly): respectable sixth of 10 behind Danehill Dancer in Heinz 57 Phoenix Stakes at Leopardstown final start: will stay beyond 6f: acts on firm going. *B. W. Hills* **95 +**

AQAARID (USA) 3 b.f. Nashwan (USA) 135 – Ashayer (USA) 118 (Lomond (USA) 128) [1994 105p: 6m* 8g* 1995 7.3m* 8m^{2} 12m^{6} Jun 9] **116**

Around fifty per cent of all racehorses are reckoned to break blood vessels to a greater or lesser degree during their racing careers, and, alas, it turned out that Aqaarid was in the vanguard. Perhaps the best-known 'bleeders' to race in Britain in recent years are the Two Thousand Guineas winner Zafonic and the King George VI

Hamdan Al Maktoum's "Aqaarid"

Chase winner Barton Bank. Victory in a classic would have put Aqaarid in the same league and she started favourite for two of them, the One Thousand Guineas and the Oaks. She was unbeaten in three starts going into the Guineas. The Virginia Water Maiden and Fillies' Mile, both at Ascot, had marked her out as classic material as a two-year-old, and every good thing said about her seemed to be confirmed in the Gainsborough Stud Fred Darling Stakes at Newbury on her reappearance. A 9/4 chance, Aqaarid faced a very mixed bag of opponents, fellow two-year-old Group 1 winners Gay Gallanta and Hoh Magic mixing it with apparent no-hopers. The Group 1 winners and no-hopers proved hard to separate where Gay Gallanta and Hoh Magic were concerned, but not with Aqaarid; pushed along to lead two furlongs out, she never looked in danger thereafter and came in two and a half lengths clear of Hoh Magic.

Sixteen days later in the Guineas, Carson chose Aqaarid in preference to Harayir. Aqaarid duly improved again, but as he rousted her along over the last three furlongs Carson had to endure the sight of Harayir breezing up to challenge; Aqaarid plugged on gamely, a clear second throughout the final furlong but never with much hope of reeling in the owner's second string who beat her by a length and a half. Still, Carson had the considerable consolation of a first-rate ride in the Oaks. It did not turn out that way. Sent off at 6/4 at Epsom, Aqaarid looked almost any price from early in straight and faded from fourth into sixth, nearly ten lengths behind the winner Moonshell. Two weeks later it was revealed that Aqaarid had a 'history of breaking blood vessels', and the following month that history caught up with her. She bled again after a half-speed gallop at Goodwood in preparation for the Irish Oaks, and at the end of the month, barely a year after making her racecourse debut, Aqaarid was retired.

Aqaarid (USA) (b.f. 1992)	Nashwan (USA) (ch 1986)	Blushing Groom (ch 1974)	Red God
			Runaway Bride
		Height of Fashion (b 1979)	Bustino
			Highclere
	Ashayer (USA) (b 1985)	Lomond (b 1980)	Northern Dancer
			My Charmer
		Good Lassie (b 1977)	Moulton
			Violetta

A sturdy, compact filly with a quick action, Aqaarid has a pedigree which backs up the strong impression given by her races that she should have been suited by middle distances. Nashwan as sire looks no bar and the dam Ashayer stayed a mile and a quarter well, adding a win in the Prix de Psyche at Deauville to those in the Virginia Water Maiden and Prix Marcel Boussac as a two-year-old. Aqaarid's fairly useful but lightly-raced brother Muwafik stayed a mile and three quarters. This, of course, is an extremely well-known family—Aqaarid is descended from Horama through both Moulton and Violetta—but Ashayer lived long enough to add only three foals to the roll call, the 1995 two-year-old being Insiyabi (by Mr Prospector) who has shown fairly useful form in maidens. Let us hope that Aqaarid the broodmare can enjoy a much longer run than Ashayer and Aqaarid the racehorse. She visits Riverman in 1996. *J. L. Dunlop*

AQUADO 6 b.g. Green Desert (USA) 127 – Meliora 73 (Crowned Prince (USA) 128) [1994 45: a6g^6 a7g^5 a6g^4 6.1m^2 a6g^3 5g^5 6g^4 5g 5.1d 6d^2 1995 a7g^5 a6g a6g a7g* a8g^2 a8g^3 a7g* a8g a8g* a7g^4 7g^2 7m^5 5g* 7g 6.9m^6 a7g^3 6m Jun 19] good-topped gelding: modest handicapper: in good form in first half of year, winning 3 times at Southwell (one an apprentice event) before end of March and in apprentice race at Hamilton in May: effective at 5f to 1m: acts on firm and dead ground and on fibresand: no improvement in blinkers/visor: sometimes bandaged: tends to hang and usually wears a brush pricker near side: joined S.R. Bowring. *A. L. Forbes* — 54

AQUA RIGIA (IRE) 3 b.f. Last Tycoon 131 – Crystal Fountain (Great Nephew 126) [1994 50: 6.1f^3 5.2m^6 6m* 7m^3 8m^4 10s 1995 9.7g 10.1m* 10.2h* 10g Sep 15] leggy, sparely-made filly: modest handicapper: successful for new stable at Yarmouth and Bath in the summer: stays 1¼m well: seems suited by top-of-the-ground and acts on hard: sold 23,000 gns Newmarket December Sales. *H. Candy* — 60

AQUILETTA 5 ch.m. Bairn (USA) 126 – Emerald Eagle 78 (Sandy Creek 123) [1994 50: 6f 6m 6m 7m^2 7m^5 6.1s^2 a6g 1995 6m 6d^5 6g 7g 7d 7m Oct 30] leggy, angular mare: well beaten in 1995: sold 750 gns Doncaster November Sales. *C. B. B. Booth* — –

ARABIAN FLIGHT 3 ch.c. Sayf El Arab (USA) 127 – Smooth Flight 78 (Sandhurst Prince 128) [1994 NR 1995 8.3m 6m 8.3m Aug 7] rather unfurnished colt: poor mover: first foal: dam miler: no sign of ability: bandaged all starts. *T. T. Clement* — –

ARABIAN HEIGHTS 2 ch.g. (Feb 11) Persian Heights 129 – Arabian Rose (USA) (Lyphard (USA) 132) [1995 6m Oct 13] 27,000Y: fourth foal: half-brother to fairly useful stayer Moonlight Quest (by Nishapour), 4-y-o 1¼m winner Pip's Dream (by Glint of Gold) and a winner in Hungary: dam ran once in France: 50/1, always behind (ran very wide on bends) in maiden at Catterick. *Mrs J. R. Ramsden* — –

ARABIAN STORY 2 gr.c. (Apr 21) Sharrood (USA) 124 – Once Upon A Time 77 (Teenoso (USA) 135) [1995 7f* Jul 20] first foal: dam won at 8.5f (at 2 yrs) and 11.7f: 10/1, won 10-runner median auction maiden at Brighton by ½ length from Mancini, running on strongly to lead line: will be well suited by 1¼m+: looked sure to improve. *Lord Huntingdon* — 78 p

ARABOYBILL 4 b.g. Aragon 118 – Floral 82 (Floribunda 136) [1994 66: 7.5m^4 7m* 7.6g^5 7m 7.3s^3 7g 9g 10g 1995 8m 10.8f 9.7f^3 9.7g* 12m 10m^6 10m^6 10f^2 10m 10d 10g 8f Oct 24] workmanlike gelding: fair handicapper at best: trained by Martyn Meade first 2 starts at 4 yrs: improved effort in first-time blinkers to win at Folkestone in July: didn't repeat the form, leaving M. Muggeridge after ninth start: stays 1¼m: acts on firm ground, appeared to run very well on heavy as 2-y-o: blinkered since fourth 4-y-o start: one to treat with caution. *R. Simpson* — 65 d

ARABRIDE 3 ch.f. Unfuwain (USA) 131 – Model Bride (USA) (Blushing Groom (FR) 131) [1994 NR 1995 8m^5 8m^2 8f* 8g^4 8g* 8g^6 Aug 26] 28,000Y: lengthy filly: second living foal: closely related to 4-y-o Mediterraneo (by Be My Guest), useful on his day at around 1m and successful over hurdles: dam unraced daughter of Mofida, dam of Zaizafon and grandam of Zafonic and Elmaamul: useful performer: made all in maiden at Ascot in June and listed race at Deauville (beat Marie de Ken a neck) in August: stumbled leaving stalls and lost a shoe when below-form sixth of 7 in Prix Quincey at Deauville final outing: should stay beyond 1m: acts on firm going but best efforts on good: sold (J. Toller to Lord Huntingdon) 145,000 gns Newmarket December Sales. *J. A. R. Toller*
104

ARAFEL 4 ch.f. Northern State (USA) 91 – Don't Loiter (Town And Country 124) [1994 –: 10d 10m 1995 a10g^4 12.5g Apr 27] lengthy, dipped-backed filly: no worthwhile form on flat. *C. James*
–

ARAGONA 6 b.m. Aragon 118 – Polly Worth 55 (Wolver Hollow 126) [1994 NR 1995 a8.5g Jan 11] leggy mare: poor performer at 4 yrs: well beaten only outing in 1995. *P. D. Cundell*
–

ARAGROVE 5 b.g. Aragon 118 – Grovehurst (Homing 130) [1994 62d: 6d 6m^6 5m^4 5g 5m 5g 6g 6g 1995 a7g a7g 6m^5 5.3m* 6f^2 5m* 6g* 6m* 5f^3 5g^2 5f* 6m^3 5m^3 5m^5 Aug 19] compact gelding: carries condition: poor mover: fairly useful handicapper: had a very good season, successful at Brighton (twice), Lingfield, Folkestone and Goodwood: effective at 5f and 6f: acts on equitrack and on firm and soft going: effective blinkered or not: usually races prominently: hung badly right fifth start: often sweats profusely: sold only 4,000 gns Newmarket Autumn Sales. *J. W. Payne*
84

ARAJAAN (USA) 2 br.c. (Feb 12) Septieme Ciel (USA) 123 – Maid's Quarters (USA) (Sauce Boat (USA)) [1995 6g^2 5.1g^3 7m^3 6m* 5g 6m 7m Oct 21] $20,000F, 40,000Y: close-coupled colt: third foal: half-brother to a winner in USA by Spend A Buck: dam won 4 races in USA: comfortable winner of nursery at Leicester in August: best efforts at 6f: didn't look at ease on bends second/third starts: has been taken early to post: sold 9,000 gns Doncaster November Sales. *B. Hanbury*
92

ARAMON 5 b.g. Aragon 118 – Princess Mona 56 (Prince Regent (FR) 129) [1994 –: 9.7m 1995 11.5m 18.2m Jul 8] good-topped gelding: poor performer on flat: modest hurdler, winner in November. *M. J. Haynes*
–

ARASONG 3 b.f. Aragon 118 – Songstead 92 (Song 132) [1994 76: 5d^5 5f* 5g^4 5m^3 6.1g^4 5m^2 6f^5 6d^6 5m^6 5.2g^4 5s^5 1995 6m^2 6m 6g 5m 5f^4 5.2m* 6f^3 5m^5 6m a5g 6.1d 6g^5 Sep 22] strong, good-quartered filly: poor mover: fair handicapper: won apprentice event at Yarmouth in July: stays 6f: acts on firm ground, bit below form on soft: sold 3,000 gns Newmarket Autumn Sales: none too consistent. *E. Weymes*
72 d

ARAWA 5 b.m. Doulab (USA) 115 – High Heather (Shirley Heights 130) [1994 44, a49: a7g^2 a7g^4 a7g a6g^2 a8g^4 a7g^3 a7g 7s^2 7d 7m a7g^3 8.5m a7g* a6g^2 7f^6 6m 10.8s 1995 a6g a6g a8g 7d a7g^6 a7g a6g a7g^6 Jun 2] leggy, plain mare: no worthwhile form in 1995: dead. *D. Marks*
–

ARCADY 2 b.f. (Apr 29) Slip Anchor 136 – Elysian 94 (Northfields (USA)) [1995 6m 7g 7m^3 a7g^6 Nov 11] leggy filly: seventh foal: sister to 2 winners, including useful 1991 2-y-o 1m winner Anchorite, later suited by 1½m, and half-sister to 1m winner Circe (by Main Reef) and useful hurdler Olympian (by High Line): dam, 2-y-o 6f winner seemed to stay 1½m, from excellent family: modest form in maidens: poor effort on fibresand final start: will stay middle distances. *P. T. Walwyn*
63

ARCATURA 3 b.g. Beveled (USA) – Bar Gold 80 (Lucky Brief 128) [1994 58: 6g^5 1995 8g 8g 8m^5 8g 8d^3 a8.5g^4 a9.4g^5 Dec 9] unfurnished gelding: fair maiden: likely to prove suited by further than 1m: acts on good to soft ground, probably on good to firm. *C. James*
67
a60

ARC BRIGHT (IRE) 5 b.h. Trempolino (USA) 135 – Brillante (FR) 118 (Green Dancer (USA) 132) [1994 44, a65: a16.2g^2 a14.8g^3 a13g* a16g* a16.2g* a16g^2 a14.8g^4 a16.2g^3 a13g^2 a14.8g 13.8d^4 14.1d 16.2m a16g^6 a16.2g^3 a14g^2 14.9m^3 16.1f^6 15.8m^5 a16.2g^2 a14.8g^5 16.1s a16g a13g^4 a16g^5 1995 a16g^2 a16g* a16g^3 a16g^2 a16g^3 a14.8g a16g^2 16.2m 14.1g^3 21.6f 14.1f* 14.9g 14.1m^5 14.1m* 14.1m^3 14.1f^4 17.2f^2 16m^5 17.2h* 15.9m^3 Aug 18] leggy, workmanlike horse: fair handicapper on the all-weather: first past post at Lingfield in January and March
50
a65

(claimer, seventh start, demoted): not so good on turf, but still won at Carlisle in May, Nottingham in June and Bath in August: stays 17.2f (seemed not to get home over 21.6f): probably acts on any going: sometimes blinkered, not in 1995: usually races prominently: very tough and genuine. *R. Hollinshead*

ARCH ANGEL (IRE) 2 ch.f. (Apr 15) Archway (IRE) 115 – Saintly Guest (What A Guest 119) [1995 6m^6 6g* 7f^2 a7g* 7f^4 6m^6 8g a8g a7g^5 a7g Dec 12] IR 4,500Y: light-framed, dipped-backed filly: half-sister to fairly useful 5-y-o sprinter Benzoe (by Taufan) and 8.5f winner King's Guest (by Tender King): dam lightly raced in France from family of Stanford Lad: narrowly won sellers at Yarmouth and Wolverhampton in the summer: stays 7f: acts on firm ground and fibresand: visored last 2 starts: very slowly away eighth outing. *D. J. S. ffrench Davis* — 55

ARC LAMP 9 b.g. Caerleon (USA) 132 – Dazzling Light 116 (Silly Season 127) [1994 51, a56: a5g a6g^6 a6g* a6g 5m a6g^4 7m^5 a5g* a5g^6 7f 6m a6g 5d a6g* a5g 1995 a6g^5 a6g a6g^6 a6g a5g 6.1m a6g^5 a6g 7f^5 5f^2 6f* 6m* 6m^4 6g Sep 1] workmanlike, angular gelding: modest handicapper: won at Redcar (claiming event) and Ripon (apprentices) in August: stays 7f: best turf form on a sound surface, acts on fibresand: blinkered (below form) once at 5 yrs: often bandaged near-hind: usually races prominently. *J. A. Glover* — 53 a47

ARC OF THE DIVER (IRE) 2 ch.c. (May 2) Archway (IRE) 115 – Inner Pearl (Gulf Pearl 117) [1995 5g^5 5f^5 6m^6 8g^2 7d Sep 27] 18,000F, 14,000Y: leggy colt: half-brother to several winners at up to 8.1f, including (by Don't Forget Me) useful pair A Smooth One (2-y-o 5f and 6f winner) and Iommelli (stays 1¼m): dam won from 4f to 9f in France: modest maiden: failed to progress from debut: seems to stay 1m. *J. Berry* — 60 d

ARCTIC CHARMER (USA) 3 ch.c. Arctic Tern (USA) 126 – Bunch of Smiles (USA) (Graustark) [1994 –: 8g 8d 1995 11.8s^2 14d^4 15.8m^4 15m^2 14f^4 a16g^3 Sep 4] quite good-topped colt: fair maiden handicapper: stays 15.8f: acts on good to firm and soft ground and on fibresand: blinkered (unruly in paddock, well beaten) second 3-y-o start: tail flasher: one to be wary of. *J. L. Dunlop* — 70

ARCTIC DIAMOND 4 b.g. Rambo Dancer (CAN) 107 – Falaka 83 (Sparkler 130) [1994 56: 10.3g^6 11.1g 8g^5 8g* 10s a8g 1995 a11g May 15] compact gelding: modest performer: no form after winning claimer at Ripon in May 1994 for Mrs J. Ramsden: blinkered only 4-y-o outing: stays 1m: acts on soft ground. *C. R. Egerton* — –

ARCTIC FANCY (USA) 2 ch.c. (Feb 5) Arctic Tern (USA) 126 – Fit And Fancy (USA) (Vaguely Noble 140) [1995 8.2d 9g^2 10m^3 Oct 2] $35,000F: big, good-topped colt: has scope: sixth foal: half-brother to 3 winners in USA, including Grade 3 1m winner Visible Gold (by Deputy Minister): dam ran once in USA: best efforts in maidens at Redcar (neck second to House of Riches) and Pontefract (still bit backward, just over 5 lengths third to Warbrook) final 2 starts, staying on well: will be suited by thorough test of stamina: likely to do better. *P. W. Harris* — 79 p

ARCTIC GUEST (IRE) 5 ch.m. Arctic Tern (USA) 126 – Sojourn 87 (Be My Guest (USA) 126) [1994 63, a65: a13g^5 a14.8g^5 a14g^2 a16g^4 a16g^3 18g 14.1d 16.2m^4 15.8g* 14.1f* 16.5m^3 17.2f^4 15.8f^4 15.8m^4 14.1g^6 18m a13g^6 1995 a16g^5 a16.2g a16g^5 Jan 24] leggy mare: fair staying handicapper at 4 yrs: no form in 1995. *C. Smith* — –

ARCTIC POPPY (USA) 3 ch.f. Arctic Tern (USA) 126 – Nether Poppleton (USA) (Deputy Minister (CAN)) [1994 67: 6d^6 7g^5 8g^5 1995 10.8m 10.2m 8g 7m^4 7g a7g 7f^6 Aug 2] leggy, workmanlike filly: fair form at 2 yrs: bandaged behind, well beaten in handicaps in 1995: should stay at least 1¼m. *I. A. Balding* — –

ARCTIC ROMANCER (IRE) 2 b.c. (Apr 4) Distinctly North (USA) 115 – Kowalski (IRE) (Cyrano de Bergerac 120) [1995 5m 5m 5g* 6f^2 5f 7.1m^6 5m^3 5m 6m^2 5g 6g^5 6d^6 5m^4 a6g^2 a6g* a8g* Dec 15] IR 19,500F, 19,000Y: rather leggy, quite attractive colt: first foal: dam ran twice as 2-y-o in Ireland: won median auction at Warwick in May and 2 nurseries (held up) at Lingfield late in year: stays 1m: acts on firm ground, goes very well on equitrack: has twice run below form in blinkers. *G. Lewis* — 76 a89

ARCTIC THUNDER (USA) 4 b.g. Far North (CAN) 120 – Flying Cloud (USA) (Roberto (USA) 131) [1994 93p: 8.3m 10g* 8.1m^4 10m^2 11.9d* 10s 1995 12m^6 11.9m* 10.4g^3 13.9m^2 11.9d^6 13.3d^2 Sep 16] leggy, workmanlike gelding: shows knee action: useful handicapper: won at York in May: good second of 23 in — 99

Autumn Cup at Newbury on final start: stays 1¾m: acts on good to firm and dead ground: usually bandaged: has run well when sweating: tongue tied down (ran poorly) fifth 4-y-o start: sold 40,000 gns Newmarket Autumn Sales. *Lady Herries*

ARCTIC ZIPPER (USA) 2 gr.g. (Apr 19) Unzipped (USA) – Arctic Fashion (USA) (The Knack 111) [1995 5d 7d^2 7d^4 6f Oct 12] $12,000Y: good-bodied gelding: closely related to a winner in USA by Naked Sky and half-brother to a winner by Northern Prospect: dam minor stakes winner at around 1m: sire probably best as sprinting 2-y-o: best effort when 9 lengths second of 8 to Hidden Oasis in maiden at Chester in September: blinkered, creditable effort (again prominent long way) in Redcar Two-Year-Old Trophy on final outing (subsequently gelded): stays 7f: acts on firm and dead ground: tailed off at Brighton third outing: wore crossed noseband and taken down steadily at Redcar: probably capable of better. *W. A. O'Gorman* 78 p

ARCTIID (USA) 2 b. or br.c. (Mar 29) Silver Hawk (USA) 123 – Arctic Eclipse (USA) (Northern Dancer) [1995 6m^4 Jun 23] $300,000Y: strong colt: fourth foal: half-brother to useful 7f (at 2 yrs) and 1¼m winner Icy South (by Alleged) and 7f winner Winter Coat (by Time For A Change): dam, 7f and 7.5f winner in France, half-sister to St Leger fourth Nemain: well-backed favourite though carrying condition, over 6 lengths fourth of 8 to Mons in maiden at Newmarket, one pace: showed a round action: looked sure to improve. *J. H. M. Gosden* 61 p

ARDLEIGH PRINCE 3 b.g. Prince Daniel (USA) – Rising Star (St Paddy 133) [1994 NR 1995 10m 10f Jun 27] 2,200Y: good-topped gelding: half-brother to several winners here and abroad, including 1¼m to 2m winner Ideal Candidate (by Celestial Storm): dam temperamental half-sister to very useful Riot Act and Laurentian Hills: 50/1, never placed to challenge towards rear of maidens at Windsor and Lingfield: sold 1,100 gns Ascot September Sales. *G. L. Moore* –

ARECIBO (FR) 3 ch.g. Dancing Spree (USA) – Anahita (FR) (Gay Mecene (USA) 128) [1994 NR 1995 6g 8.3m 7g Oct 9] 190,000 francs Y: unfurnished gelding: second foal: half-brother to winning Italian miler Alastor (by Fabulous Dancer): dam French maiden: soundly beaten in maidens: has joined J. Parkes. *G. L. Moore* –

ARGYLE CAVALIER (IRE) 5 b.g. Simply Great (FR) 122 – Fete Champetre 80 (Welsh Pageant 132) [1994 68: a12g* 11.8s^5 14g a16g* 15.8g^3 16g* 14.1m* 20m 12m^3 14.6m^3 18.7g^3 15.1m^3 16.2m 20f^6 17.5s^4 15.9s^4 17.1s^2 18m^2 1995 a16g* a14.8g* a12g^2 a16g^2 18g 16m 16m* 18.7m^5 16m^2 16m^3 13f^2 20m Jun 20] leggy, angular gelding: good walker: fair handicapper: won at Southwell and Wolverhampton in January and at Ripon (awarded race) in April: effective at 1½m to 2½m: acts on any ground and goes well on the all-weather: usually held up in touch: tough, genuine and consistent. *M. Johnston* 67 a75

ARIAN SPIRIT (IRE) 4 b.f. High Estate 127 – Astral Way (Hotfoot 126) [1994 41: 12.3d 11.1g^2 11.6g a12g^6 a12g a14g 16.4m^5 16.1s 12v 12g a16g^3 a13g a13g^2 1995 a16g* a16g^5 12.3d^4 14.1f^6 13f^4 16m^2 15.1f^5 15.1m^3 16.2g^2 15.1f* 17.1m^4 16.2m^2 16m^3 17.5g 17.1m* 18f^6 Oct 16] workmanlike filly: poor handicapper: won at Lingfield (final start for W. Musson) in January, Edinburgh in July and Pontefract in October: stays 17.1f: acts on good to firm and dead ground and on equitrack: blinkered (ran poorly) once at 3 yrs: occasional front runner: tail swisher. *J. L. Eyre* 42

ARKINDALE AMBER 3 b.g. Superpower 113 – Najat 49§ (Tender King 123) [1994 –: 5g 5m 5f 5g 1995 7.5g 5f Jul 31] close-coupled gelding: no worthwhile form: has joined R. Brotherton. *F. J. O'Mahony* –

ARLINGTON LADY 2 b.f. (Apr 25) Prince Sabo 123 – Flitcham 57 (Elegant Air 119) [1995 6g^6 6m* 5m^2 6f^6 6m^2 6m 6m^3 7.6m 7m Oct 12] 9,000Y: tall filly: first foal: dam, 13f winner at 4 yrs, stayed 15f: won seller at Brighton in June: good second in nursery at Windsor fifth start: probably stays 7.6f: yet to race on a soft surface: blinkered seventh start: wears bandages behind. *N. A. Callaghan* 65 d

ARMSTON 3 ch.g. Rock City 120 – Silka (ITY) (Lypheor 118) [1994 51: a7g 8.2d 7m 1995 a11g^5 14d^3 a12g* a14.8g^2 Jul 3] leggy gelding: shows knee action: fair handicapper, lightly-raced: easy 6-length winner of 13-runner contest at Southwell in June: stays 14.8f: acts on dead ground and fibresand: held up: possibly capable of better. *J. Wharton* 64

ARNDILLY 4 b.f. Robellino (USA) 127 – Upper Caen (High Top 131) [1994 75: 7.5d^2 8m 7m^6 8f^3 8.1m 7m^3 7g 7g a6g* a7g^4 1995 a6g a7g* a8g^3 a7g a7g^2 a7g^6 75

8.3m* 8m^4 8.3m* 8f 8m^2 8m* 9f^4 Jun 30] small, sparely-made filly: fair performer: won claimers at Wolverhampton in January and Windsor (twice) in May and handicap at Warwick in June: well below form in claimer at Goodwood (claimed £12,000) on final start: effective at 6f to 1m: acts on firm and dead going and the all-weather: blinkered since second 4-y-o start: normally held up. *B. J. Meehan*

ARNIE (IRE) 3 b.g. Double Schwartz 128 – The Moneys Gone (Precocious 126) [1994 43: 6m 6f^6 6d 6g 6g^5 8s 1995 8.1g 7m 8g 8f a10g Nov 14] good-topped gelding: poor maiden: stays 7f. *G. L. Moore* –

ARRASAS LADY 5 ch.m. Arrasas (USA) 100 – Sharelle 67 (Relko 136) [1994 39: a16g a12g^5 a10g a12g a12g a7g^6 a8g^6 a8g^3 1995 a7g^5 a8g a8g^6 a8g 9.7g 6f 8.3m 7f 7.6m Aug 12] workmanlike mare: poor maiden: trained until after third 5-y-o start by R. Flower, and for next 3 outings by J. Long: best form at 1m on fibresand: blinkered (well beaten) twice: refused to race eighth start, and not one to trust. *Jamie Poulton* – § a31 §

ARRAS ROYALE 5 ch.h. Arrasas (USA) 100 – Sheer Class (Victor Hugo) [1994 –: 6g 5d 6m 1995 a7g a16g Feb 16] angular horse: of little account: tried visored. *J. E. Long* –

ARRHYTHMIC (IRE) 2 b.f. (Mar 2) Broken Hearted 124 – Gay's Flutter 78 (Beldale Flutter (USA) 130) [1995 5m^3 5m^2 5f^2 5f^{wo} 5m^5 6g 5f^4 Oct 14] unfurnished filly: fourth foal: half-sister to a 6f to 1¼m winner in Italy by Horage: dam disappointing maiden stayed 6f: fair form: walked over in median auction at Redcar in August: creditable efforts next 2 starts in nursery at Beverley and listed race (last of 9 but prominent long way) at Ayr: will prove best at sprint distances: seemed to run too freely in blinkers final outing: sold 7,000 gns Newmarket Autumn Sales. *M. Brittain* 75

ARROGANT BOY 6 b. or br.g. Kabour 80 – Belhill 63 (Beldale Flutter (USA) 130) [1994 NR 1995 a11g a7g a7g^6 a8g a8g^5 a7g^2 a8g^6 a8g 10m a7g^6 a9.4g a8.5g a7g 8g^3 Aug 26] poor maiden handicapper: stays 1m: acts on fibresand: tried blinkered. *D. W. Chapman* 34 d

ARROGANT HEIR 2 b.c. (May 22) Henbit (USA) 130 – Quiet Arrogance (USA) 63 (Greek Sky (USA)) [1995 a7g 8.2d 10m Oct 2] strong, angular colt: first reported foal: dam, maiden, should have stayed beyond 7f: burly, no form in maidens (very slowly away on debut). *S. G. Norton* –

ART DECO LADY 4 ch.f. Master Willie 129 – Art Deco (Artaius (USA) 129) [1994 51: 10d^4 10g 12s^4 11.9f^2 13.8f^3 12.1g 1995 a12g 17.2m May 13] sturdy, lengthy filly: modest maiden for Mrs M. Reveley at 3 yrs: tailed off in 1995: resold 1,300 gns Ascot August Sales. *N. M. Babbage* –

ARTERXERXES 2 b.c. (Apr 26) Anshan 119 – Hanglands (Bustino 136) [1995 7m^6 Nov 3] 5,500Y: lengthy, quite attractive colt: half-brother to fairly useful 1992 2-y-o 5f and 6.1f winner Zuno Warrior (by Dominion): dam lightly raced: 33/1, around 8 lengths sixth of 17 to Jackson Hill in maiden at Doncaster, leading around 5f then one pace: should improve. *M. J. Heaton-Ellis* 63 p

ART FORM (USA) 8 b.g. Little Current (USA) – Christi Dawn (USA) (Grey Dawn II 132) [1994 68, a76: 14m 14.8m 15.4d^3 15.9s 17.2g^4 18m a16g* a16g* 1995 a16g* a12g* 16m 16m 17.2m 20m^2 18.2m^3 16.2g^2 16.4m Aug 18] tall, angular gelding: has a round action: fairly useful handicapper on the all-weather: won at Lingfield in January and (under 10-3) February: fair on turf: second in Ascot Stakes and £10,800 event there in mid-summer: fell on final start: finds 1½m an absolute minimum and stays 2½m well: very best turf efforts on a sound surface and goes well on all-weather surfaces: genuine. *C. A. Cyzer* 72 a84

ARTFUL DANE (IRE) 3 b.c. Danehill (USA) 126 – Art Age (Artaius (USA) 129) [1994 79: 5s^3 6g^2 5s^5 1995 8m^2 10g 8f^3 8.3m* 7.6m 8d 7s^6 Sep 28] strong, good-quartered colt: fairly useful performer: made all in maiden at Windsor in July, possibly flattered: stays 8.3f: seems to need a sound surface (acts on firm going): takes strong hold. *M. J. Heaton-Ellis* 81 ?

ARTIC COURIER 4 gr.g. Siberian Express (USA) 125 – La Reine de France (Queen's Hussar 124) [1994 78: 10m^5 11.5g^3 12m^2 12m^6 12m^2 14d^2 12g^2 14s^2 1995 12g^2 12m^6 12m^2 14m 12f^2 12.3f* 11.8g^2 11.9f^3 12m^2 12g^4 12d 12s^6 12m Nov 4] good-topped gelding: fairly useful performer: first past post in maiden at Ripon and 82 handicap at Leicester (demoted after short-heading Vindaloo) in the summer: stays 1¾m: acts on firm and soft ground: blinkered fifth 3-y-o to second 4-y-o outings: held up: consistent, but sometimes looks reluctant. *D. J. S. Cosgrove*

ART OF WAR 3 b.g. Machiavellian (USA) 123 – On The House (FR) 125 (Be My Guest (USA) 126) [1994 102p: 6g* 6d* 6m 1995 7g 6g* 6m Nov 4] compact, useful-looking gelding: created very favourable impression on first 2 career starts (won listed race) but pulled hard when in rear in Middle Park and Greenham Stakes: off course 5 months and gelded before winning minor event at Hamilton in September by 4 lengths: found little off bridle when only tenth of 12 to Carranita in listed race at Doncaster 6 weeks later: bred to stay beyond 6f: yet to race on extremes of going: sold to join M. Dickinson in USA. *R. Charlton* — 106

ART TATUM 4 b.g. Tate Gallery (USA) 117 – Rose Chanelle (Welsh Pageant 132) [1994 78d: 12.3m 12s^2 11.4g 10f 12g 14.4g 11.9g 1995 11.8d 12m^6 10m^5 May 26] small, sparely-made gelding: disappointing handicapper, poor at best in 1995: suited by 1½m+: acts on heavy ground: blinkered (well beaten) final 3-y-o start: sometimes soon off bridle: has joined Mrs M. McCourt. *R. Hannon* — 50

ARVZEES (IRE) 2 ch.c. (Mar 5) Magical Wonder (USA) 125 – Zestino (Shack (USA) 118) [1995 5g^3 5d^3 5.3m^2 5g^3 5.1g^2 5m* 5m* 5m^4 6.1m* 5m^2 7g^2 6f* 5f* 5f^4 8.2d^5 9g^4 6s^4 Oct 28] 3,600F, 3,800Y: leggy colt: fifth foal: half-brother to 11.1f winner Briggs Lad (by Be My Native): dam unraced half-sister to Oaks winner Ginevra: trained by M. Channon first 10 starts, winning sellers at Folkestone and Doncaster and claimer at Nottingham early in season: ran 4 times for Mme M. van Dijk at Ostend, winning minor event and claimer in July, before joining current stable: probably stays 7f: acts on firm and good to soft ground: sometimes swishes tail: has sweated up: seemed best held up. *P. Boudengen, Belgium* — 63

ARZANI (USA) 4 ch.c. Shahrastani (USA) 135 – Vie En Rose (USA) (Blushing Groom (FR) 131) [1994 60: 10g 1995 8.3m^3 8m 10m^5 8m^6 10d^6 Sep 14] plain colt: fair maiden at best: soundly beaten last 2 starts: stays 1¼m: acts on good to firm ground. *D. J. S. Cosgrove* — 74 d

ASAAF (USA) 12 b.g. Cutlass (USA) – Honky Chateau (USA) (Quadrangle) [1994 NR 1995 a16g a8g Mar 16] of no account. *N. P. Littmoden* — –

ASHANTI DANCER (IRE) 2 b.f. (Apr 20) Dancing Dissident (USA) 119 – Shanntabariya (IRE) (Shernazar 131) [1995 7d^6 8g^2 Sep 29] IR 7,500Y: leggy, unfurnished filly: second foal: dam, ran twice in France, 11.5f winner: 3 lengths second of 13 to Select Few in maiden at Goodwood, having gone for home over 2f out: may stay further than 1m: may improve again. *M. J. Haynes* — 71

ASHDREN 8 b.g. Lochnager 132 – Stellaris (Star Appeal 133) [1994 62: 8d a7g 8m 8m^4 8.3m^3 7.1f^6 7g* 7d^5 6.1s 7g* 8.1g a7g 1995 7.5m 7g^6 7m^5 6m 7.5m^6 7f^4 7g 8d^5 7g Oct 10] angular gelding: good walker: unimpressive mover: modest handicapper: probably needs further than 6f (stays 1m): probably acts on any going: effective visored (rarely tried) or not: swishes tail. *A. Harrison* — 56

ASHGORE 5 b.g. Efisio 120 – Fair Atlanta 73 (Tachypous 128) [1994 83: a6g* a7g* a7g^2 6m^2 6s^6 6f* 7f 6f* 6m^2 6m^3 6m 1995 a7g* 7g 6g a6g Nov 11] good-topped gelding: has reportedly had leg problems: fair performer: having first outing for well over a year, justified favouritism in claimer at Wolverhampton in August: effective at 6f and 7f: probably acts on any going on turf (best efforts on top-of-the-ground) and goes well on the all-weather: usually races prominently: genuine. *M. Johnston* — 77

ASHIK (IRE) 2 b.c. (Mar 30) Marju (IRE) 127 – Wakayi 87 (Persian Bold 123) [1995 6.1d 5.7m Sep 25] robust colt: third foal: half-brother to 3-y-o 6f winner Fata (by Machiavellian): dam, 2-y-o 5f winner, half-sister to smart sprinter Reesh out of half-sister to dam of smart sprinter Jester: no form, running as though something amiss final start: sold (P. Walwyn to L.J. Barratt) 1,400 gns Doncaster November Sales. *P. T. Walwyn* — –

ASHJAR (USA) 2 b.c. (Apr 24) Kris 135 – Jathibiyah (USA) 89 (Nureyev (USA) 131) [1995 7m^2 7d^4 7g^4 7g* Oct 23] big, lengthy colt: has scope: looked weak: has a round action: second foal: brother to 3-y-o Barriyah: dam 7f winner (at 2 yrs), stayed 1¼m, closely related to Irish 1000 Guineas winner Ensconse: fair performer: made all on favoured far side when winning 9-runner maiden at Lingfield in October by 3 lengths from Glen Parker, pair well clear: takes keen hold, and looks unlikely to stay — 81 much beyond 7f: acts on good to firm ground, below form on dead. *H. Thomson Jones*

ASHKALANI (IRE) 2 ch.c. (Mar 27) Soviet Star (USA) 128 – Ashtarka (IRE) (Dalsaan 125) [1995 8m* 8g* Nov 4] second foal: dam, French 1m winner, half-sister to Prix du Cadran winner Shafaraz: won minor event at Longchamp in October and 5-runner Prix Thomas Bryon at Saint-Cloud (held up, led inside last, beat Mayoumbe 2½ lengths) in November: will almost certainly stay beyond 1m: an interesting prospect. *A. de Royer-Dupre, France* 111 p

ASHKERNAZY (IRE) 4 ch.f. Salt Dome (USA) – Eskaroon (Artaius (USA) 129) [1994 50: 5.1g 5m 5m^6 5f^4 5.1f^3 6f 5m 5m^5 1995 5.1m^6 5g^4 5.7m 5m 5.1m^4 a5g*^{dis} 5.1m^2 5m^5 Aug 14] sparely-made filly: modest handicapper: won at Wolverhampton (only run on the all-weather) in July but later disqualified after failing dope test: stays 6f: acts on fibresand, has raced only on a sound surface on turf: visored/blinkered last 4 starts at 3 yrs: races prominently. *N. E. Berry* 48 a54

ASHOVER 5 gr.g. Petong 126 – Shiny Kay 65 (Star Appeal 133) [1994 51, a59: 10v 8.5m 8g 8m^6 10m^2 9.9m* 12f^2 12.3g^5 10m^5 10.1m 10.4d^3 12f^2 a12g^4 12s* 11.9d 1995 a11g* a12g* a11g^2 12g^4 12.3f* 12f^3 12m^5 12m* 12f^3 12f^3 12.3m 10.4g 12d* 11.9m^3 Oct 5] compact gelding: fair handicapper, better than ever in 1995: won at Southwell (twice, second a minor event) in February, Ripon in June, Thirsk in July and Beverley in September: stays 1½m: acts on firm and soft ground and goes well on all-weather surfaces: blinkered (below form) twice: often apprentice ridden: effective ridden up with pace or held up. *T. D. Barron* 64 a73

ASHTINA 10 b.g. Tina's Pet 121 – Mrewa (Runnymede 123) [1994 94: 5m 5m 5m* 5f 5.2m^3 5m 5.3f^3 5.2g* 5m* 6d 5g 5m^4 5m^2 5s^4 1995 5.2m 5.1m* 5f 5m 5.1m^4 5m 5g 5m 5m 5d 5s 5m 5m 5m 5m a6g a5g^4 Dec 6] leggy, good-topped gelding: fairly useful handicapper: reaching the veteran stage, but still won £9,200 rated stakes at Chester in May: below form afterwards, leaving R. Hodges' stable after tenth start: effective at 5f (best recent efforts) to 6f: acts on good to firm and heavy going and on equitrack, not at best on very firm ground: blinkered once at 4 yrs: sometimes taken down early: usually races prominently. *B. A. Pearce* 94 d

ASIAN ELEGANCE 3 b.f. Shareef Dancer (USA) 135 – Benazir 91 (High Top 131) [1994 45: 7g a7g^4 a8.5g^5 1995 8m Aug 14] lengthy, rather unfurnished filly: poor form in maidens as 2-y-o for M. Stoute: tailed off in handicap at Leicester on return. *H. Thomson Jones* –

ASKERN 4 gr.g. Sharrood (USA) 124 – Silk Stocking 109 (Pardao 120) [1994 78d: 10d^2 10.4m 10m 14.6f^4 12.3g 15s 11d^6 8.9d 1995 10g* 9.2f* 10f^2 11.1f^3 10.5m* 13.9m 13.1g 12m 12m Nov 4] tall, good-topped gelding: has a round action: fair performer: won sellers at Brighton (sold out of G. M. Moore's stable 7,400 gns) and Hamilton and handicap at Haydock (made all), all in the summer: effective at around 1¼m, probably stays 1¾m: acts on firm and dead ground: blinkered (out of form) final 3-y-o start. *D. Haydn Jones* 74

ASKING 3 b.g. Skyliner 117 – Ma Famille 90 (Welsh Saint 126) [1994 NR 1995 a8.5g a7g 9.9m 7m 8.2f 7m 8.2m^5 Aug 12] 3,400Y: leggy gelding: half-brother to smart sprinter Chummy's Favourite (by Song): dam won from 6f to 1m: little sign of ability on flat: tried visored: edgy and unruly in stalls on fifth start: modest form over hurdles, successful in November. *J. A. Bennett* –

ASKING FOR KINGS (IRE) 2 b.g. (Apr 11) Thatching 131 – Lady Donna 92 (Dominion 123) [1995 6m 6m^4 6m^2 7s^5 6m Oct 12] 38,000F, 8,000Y: rather unfurnished gelding: brother to 3-y-o Panama Hat and half-brother to 2 winners in Australasia: dam, 2-y-o 5f winner, half-sister to Tirol (by Thatching): modest maiden: second in seller at Yarmouth in July, final run for N. Callaghan: well beaten in nurseries after, although not well drawn first occasion: likely to stay 7f: has worn bandages behind. *S. Dow* 62

ASMAHAAN (USA) 2 br.f. (Feb 24) Dayjur (USA) 137 – Albadeeah (USA) 85 (Nashua) [1995 6f^4 Oct 23] robust, sturdy filly: sister to 3-y-o Haddeyah, 6f winner at 2 yrs, and half-sister to Irish 1988 2-y-o 1m winner Sahlee (by Lord Avie) and a winner in USA by Far North: dam 2-y-o 6f winner: 7/1 and green, just over 5 lengths fourth of 18 to Wildwood Flower in maiden at Leicester, slowly away then running on strongly from halfway: sure to improve. *H. Thomson Jones* 65 p

ASMARINA 5 b.m. Ascendant 96 – Marina Plata (Julio Mariner 127) [1994 NR 1995 a7g a12g a8g a8g^{6} a8g^{4} a9.4g* 9.9m^{6} a12g a9.4g* 8m^{3} 12m a9.4g^{4} Sep 30] leggy mare: first foal: half-sister to fairly useful 4-y-o 6f to 8.5f winner Sailormaite (by Komaite): dam 1m and 8.2f winner at 3 yrs later of no account: unraced on flat before 1995: modest form: successful at Wolverhampton in maiden handicap in April and handicap in July: may prove best at around 1¼m: acts on fibresand and good to firm ground: often claimer ridden: best efforts in blinkers (didn't wear them for first win). *S. R. Bowring* — 47 a50

ASPIRANT 7 b.g. High Top 131 – Yen (AUS) (Biscay (AUS)) [1994 NR 1995 a12g Feb 10] of no account. *J. R. Bostock* — –

ASSEMBLY DANCER 8 b.g. General Assembly (USA) – A Red Red Rose (Gulf Pearl 117) [1994 NR 1995 10d 14d 16.1g Oct 3] good-topped gelding: no longer of much account. *D. L. Williams* — –

ASSESSOR (IRE) 6 b.h. Niniski (USA) 125 – Dingle Bay (Petingo 135) [1995 16g^{2} 15.5f^{5} 14.5d* Nov 1] useful-looking horse: fluent mover: very smart performer (rated 121) at 4 yrs: subsequently sent to race in Saudi Arabia: showed he retains most of his ability when second to Further Flight in Jockey Club Cup at Newmarket, fifth to Sunshack in Prix Royal-Oak at Longchamp and winning Italian St Leger at Turin by 2¾ lengths: effective at around 1¾m and stays long distances: has form on top-of-the-ground, but goes particularly well on a soft surface: usually wears bandages: held up and ideally needs a truly-run race: genuine. *R. Hannon* — 113

ASSIGNMENT 9 b.g. Known Fact (USA) 135 – Sanctuary (Welsh Pageant 132) [1994 58: a5g^{2} a6g^{3} a6g^{3} a6g^{4} 6d 5.3g^{5} 6m^{5} 6g^{4} 6m 5m^{3} 6g a6g 1995 a6g^{4} a6g^{4} a6g 8m 9.7m^{5} 7m a6g^{4} a6g a7g Dec 14] strong, deep-girthed gelding: usually looks well: modest handicapper: well below form in 1995 after reappearance, leaving J. Ffitch-Heyes' stable after seventh start: stays 7f (at least in steadily-run race): acts on firm and dead ground and the all-weather: tried blinkered: often taken down early. *J. E. Long* — 56 d

AS SUCH (IRE) 4 b.g. Ajraas (USA) 88 – Ching A Ling (Pampapaul 121) [1994 60: a7g^{2} 10g 8.3m^{6} a5g a7g a7g^{2} 1995 a5g 6f^{6} 6g 8.2m 7m 7m^{6} 8m Aug 3] rather sparely-made gelding: soundly beaten in 1995: tried blinkered: sold 900 gns Newmarket Autumn Sales. *N. A. Callaghan* — –

ASSUMPSIT (IRE) 3 b.g. Contract Law (USA) 108 – Bridal Blush 74 (Coquelin (USA) 121) [1994 64: 5d 5f^{5} 6m^{4} 6m 1995 6g 6.1g a6g 6m^{3} 7g^{4} 6m^{3} May 25] neat gelding: has a round action: modest maiden: finds 6f a bare minimum, and should stay 1m: acts on good to firm ground: visored last 3 starts: sometimes wanders under pressure. *S. Dow* — 58

ASTERITA 3 b.f. Rainbow Quest (USA) 134 – Northshiel 85 (Northfields (USA)) [1994 78p: 7g^{2} 8.1d^{2} 1995 10m^{5} 11.5f* 12m^{5} 12g^{6} 14.6m 12d^{2} 14g^{2} Nov 26] leggy filly: fluent mover: useful performer: won listed race at Lingfield in May: good efforts afterwards in Oaks at Epsom, Irish Oaks at the Curragh, St Simon Stakes (1½ lengths second of 12 to Phantom Gold) at Newbury and Premio Roma Vecchia (fine effort, going down by a nose to Sternkoenig) at Rome: should stay beyond 1¾m: yet to race on soft going, acts on any other: led out unsold at 190,000 gns Newmarket December Sales. *R. Hannon* — 103

ASTERIX 7 ch.g. Prince Sabo 123 – Gentle Gael 97 (Celtic Ash) [1994 47: 6s 6d 6m 6.1s 7.1s 5m^{3} 8.1m^{6} 6.1m 6g^{5} 8m 8f 6g a7g 1995 6.1g^{3} 5.9m^{6} 6g 7m^{2} 7.1m^{2} 7g 6.1m^{3} 6.1m^{2} 8.1m* 9.2m^{6} 7.1m^{2} 7f 6f 6f^{5} Aug 17] smallish, lengthy gelding: unimpressive mover: modest handicapper: won amateurs event at Chepstow in July by 10 lengths: effective at 6f to 1m: acts on any going: visored all starts in 1995: good mount for inexperienced rider: won handicap hurdle in August. *J. M. Bradley* — 53

ASTON COURT 10 br.g. Tanfirion 110 – Msida (Majority Blue 126) [1994 NR 1995 16.2m Aug 10] good-topped, workmanlike gelding: winning pointer: poor maiden on flat: broke back over fences in September: dead. *B. Ellison* — –

ASTON MANOR (IRE) 3 b.g. Cyrano de Bergerac 120 – Mamie's Joy (Prince Tenderfoot (USA) 126) [1994 61: 5.7g^{5} 6d^{5} 1995 6s a6g^{2} a6g^{2} May 1] strong, compact gelding: modest maiden: should stay 7f: acts on fibresand and dead ground. *R. Hannon* — 59

ASTOR PLACE (IRE) 2 b.c. (Apr 3) Sadler's Wells (USA) 132 – Broadway Joan (USA) (Bold Arian (USA)) [1995 7g⁴ 7g* 8m⁵ Oct 15] $265,000F: rangy, attractive colt: shade unfurnished: has scope: fluent mover: seventh foal: closely related to 6 winners in USA, 5 of them by Compliance, notably Fourstardave and Irish 2000 Guineas winner Fourstarsallstar, both multiple graded stakes winners best at 1m/9f: dam unraced: progressive form: won 23-runner maiden at Newmarket in September by 2½ lengths from stable-companion Legal Right, running on really well: looking very well, beaten around 3 lengths when fifth of 7 to Loup Solitaire in Grand Criterium at Longchamp, staying on: will stay 1¼m: likely to improve further. *P. W. Chapple-Hyam* — 106 p

ASTRAC (IRE) 4 b.c. Nordico (USA) – Shirleen (Daring Display (USA) 129) [1994 93p: 7g 7.5d 7d* 7m 7.1g 7m³ 7m⁵ 7.3s² 7g³ 6d* 1995 6m⁵ 6f* 6m 6g 7g⁶ 6d³ Oct 19] sturdy colt: impresses in appearance: useful handicapper: won Wokingham Stakes at Royal Ascot: had excuses when below form next 3 starts: back to form in rated stakes at Newbury on final outing: best form at 6f: acts on firm and soft ground and on fibresand: usually races prominently. *R. Akehurst* — 96

ASTRAL INVADER (IRE) 3 ch.g. Astronef 116 – Numidia (Sallust 134) [1994 70: 5.7f⁴ 5m* 5.3f 6d* 5d² 5.2s² 6g⁵ 6m⁴ 7.3v⁶ 1995 6m⁵ 8m 7.6m³ 7g 6g 6m 5.1f⁴ 5.7h³ 5.7h⁶ 6g 6.1d⁶ 7s 7.1d Oct 10] leggy gelding: fair handicapper: consistent at 2 yrs: mostly below form after third start in 1995: effective at 5.7f, and stays 7.6f: acts on any going: no improvement in visor. *M. S. Saunders* — 68 d

ASTRAL'S CHANCE 2 ch.g. (May 11) Risk Me (FR) 127 – Astral Suite 82 (On Your Mark 125) [1995 5m⁴ a5g⁵ May 11] 6,200F, 4,800Y: compact gelding: brother to 3-y-o Pent-House Baby and half-brother to several winners, including 5f performer Valldemosa (by Music Boy) and 1m to 1½m winner Trouvere (by Free State), both fairly useful: dam 6f and 7f winner: modest form in auction events in the spring, prominent around 4f. *K. R. Burke* — 59

ASTRAL WEEKS (IRE) 4 ch.g. Astronef 116 – Doon Belle (Ardoon 124) [1994 84: 6.9s* 8s² 8v² 7d² 7d³ 7m* 8f 7m³ 7m 8g 1995 8m 7g 8m 8m 8.3m 10d 8m Oct 12] rangy gelding: poor mover: fairly useful 7f/1m handicapper at 3 yrs: well — –

Wokingham Stakes (Handicap), Royal Ascot—Astrac is clear on the far side; Alzianah, Brave Edge and Venture Capitalist lead this side home

beaten in 1995, including in blinkers: sold (R. Hannon to L. Lungo) 5,800 gns Newmarket Autumn Sales. *R. Hannon*

ASTRA MARTIN 2 ch.f. (Mar 2) Doc Marten 104 – Bertrade 75 (Homeboy 114) [1995 6g 6.1d 6f Oct 24] quite good-topped filly: fourth foal: half-sister to 4-y-o 5f (at 2 yrs) and 5.7f winner Winsome Wooster (by Primo Dominie): dam stayed 1¼m, sister to Bertie Wooster: little promise in maidens: ridden by 7-lb claimer. *P. G. Murphy* –

ASTROJOY (IRE) 3 ch.f. Astronef 116 – Pharjoy (FR) 85 (Pharly (FR) 130) [1994 49: 5d 6g 6m^5 7g 6m 8d 1995 8.1m 6g^2 6m 8h^6 10d 8m a7g a7g a6g a7g Dec 14] sparely-made filly: modest maiden: sold out of Lord Huntingdon's stable 3,300 gns Ascot July Sales after second 3-y-o start: below best afterwards: stays 1m: acts on hard ground, seemingly not on a soft surface: tried blinkered. *S. G. Knight* 50 d

ASTROLABE 3 b.g. Rainbow Quest (USA) 134 – Sextant 98 (Star Appeal 133) [1994 70: 7m 1995 10.3g^3 12f 12.3m* 14g^3 14.9m^2 14m^3 20f Jul 26] leggy, close-coupled gelding: fairly useful handicapper: made all at Chester in May: stays 14.9f: acts on good to firm ground, yet to race on a soft surface: blinkered/visored since third 3-y-o start: usually races prominently: sold 10,000 gns Newmarket Autumn Sales, and gelded. *B. W. Hills* 81

ASTUTI (IRE) 2 b.f. (Feb 19) Waajib 121 – Aunty Eileen (Ahonoora 122) [1995 6f^3 6m 6m* 6g 7d^3 7g^2 7.3d^6 8m^2 Oct 27] IR 8,500Y: workmanlike filly: fourth living foal: half-sister to 1991 2-y-o 6f winner Ambitious Venture (by Gorytus) and 5f winner Moving Image (by Nordico): dam unraced half-sister to smart sprinter Lugana Beach: made hard work of winning median auction maiden at Goodwood in August: ran much better races in defeat: stays 1m: acts on good to firm and dead ground: gave trouble at stalls some early appearances. *A. P. Jarvis* 84

A SUITABLE GIRL 4 b.f. Reprimand 122 – No Jazz 55 (Jaazeiro (USA) 127) [1994 40d: a8g^3 a8g^6 10d 10f a12g^2 a13g 8g^5 8g 1995 17.2m May 13] tall, leggy filly: no longer of much account. *D. L. Williams* –

ASWAAT (IRE) 3 b.c. Fairy King (USA) – Native Melody (Tudor Music 131) [1994 NR 1995 7g^6 a6g* a7g* Dec 29] 29,000Y: half-brother to 1989 2-y-o 7f and 1m winner Asian Pete (by Persian Bold), 5f and 1m winner Formatune (by Double Form) and a winner in Scandinavia: dam Irish 7f winner: never-nearer sixth of 10 to Dreamboat in maiden at Redcar for J. Gosden: won at Nad Al Sheba (maiden) and Jebel Ali in December: will stay 1m: should improve further. *D. Selvaratnam, UAE* 69 p

AS YOU LIKE IT (USA) 3 b.c. Nijinsky (CAN) 138 – Asiram (USA) 110 (Sharpen Up 127) [1994 –p: 8.2d 1995 10m 10m Aug 9] strong, lengthy colt: has scope: progressive maiden: still green, eighth of 18 to Polydamas at Sandown on final start, checked early in straight when towards rear and not knocked about, leaving impression might have been placed with clear run: will stay beyond 1¼m: looked sure to do better. *J. H. M. Gosden* 77 p

ATAXIA 3 b.f. Belmez (USA) 131 – Margamania (CAN) (Riverman (USA) 131) [1994 NR 1995 10m^6 May 15] 5,200Y: fifth foal: half-sister to a winner in U.S. by Titanic: dam (lightly raced in USA) half-sister to a French 1½m winner: sixth of 22 to Yoush in median auction maiden at Windsor, staying on in good style having been slowly away: sent abroad. *H. R. A. Cecil* 63

ATHENRY 2 gr.c. (Apr 7) Siberian Express (USA) 125 – Heresheis 69 (Free State 125) [1995 8d^5 10m^5 Oct 28] 6,000Y: tall, leggy colt: has a long, round action: second foal: dam stayed 2m: just over 4 lengths fifth of 20 to Helicon in maiden at Newmarket: over 6 lengths fifth of 6 to Gentilhomme in listed race at Newmarket again following month, staying on having been tapped for foot 2f out: likely to improve again. *J. Pearce* 87 p

ATHERTON GREEN (IRE) 5 ch.g. Shy Groom (USA) – Primacara 58 (Rusticaro (FR) 124) [1994 61: 10g^3 10s 1995 a11g^5 a12g^6 10f May 1] small gelding: modest performer: no worthwhile form in 1995: best at up to 10.3f: acts on good to firm and soft ground: inconsistent: fair hurdler, winner in November. *J. A. Glover* –

ATHINAR 3 b.f. Tina's Pet 121 – Highland Rossie 67 (Pablond 93) [1994 NR 1995 a7g^5 a8g^3 Feb 2] 1,350Y: half-sister to winning sprinter Diet (by Starch Reduced) and ungenuine plater The Overnight Man (by Smackover): dam won sellers at 7f and 1¼m: poor form in early-season maidens. *C. P. Wildman* 40

ATIENZA (USA) 2 ch.f. (Mar 23) Chief's Crown (USA) – Hattab Voladora (USA) (Dewan (USA)) [1995 8g 8.2m^3 Oct 26] $32,000F: 46,000Y: angular filly: half-sister to 3-y-o 16.2f winner Zuiena (by Sunshine Forever) and several winners in North America, including a Grade 2 winner over 1½m by Affirmed: dam won 18 races in USA, 4 stakes including over 5f at 6 yrs: modest form in maidens at Leicester and Nottingham in October: should stay beyond 1m. *S. C. Williams* 65

ATLAAL (USA) 3 br.c. Machiavellian (USA) 123 – Minifah (USA) 69 (Nureyev (USA) 131) [1994 73: 7d^3 7g^5 1995 7m* 8m^5 8g^2 8g 8f^5 8g^3 8.1g^4 Sep 22] tall colt: fluent mover: fair handicapper: won maiden at Kempton in April: stays 1m: acts on firm and dead ground: carries head awkwardly: sent to Dubai. *H. Thomson Jones* 76

ATLANTIC MIST 2 ch.c. (Mar 26) Elmaamul (USA) 125 – Overdue Reaction (Be My Guest (USA) 126) [1995 7g^3 7g 7f 8d Sep 30] 7,000F, 6,000Y: close-coupled colt: half-brother to German 3-y-o 1m and 9.5f winner Don't Go Crazy (by Houston) and to 2 winners in USA: dam lightly-raced half-sister to U.S. Grade 2 9f winner Wait Till Monday and smart dual-purpose horse Rare Holiday, best at 1½m on flat: easily best effort when staying-on third of 11 in maiden auction at Warwick on debut: saddle slipped in nursery final start: bred to stay beyond 7f. *B. R. Millman* 54

AT LIBERTY (IRE) 3 b.c. Danehill (USA) 126 – Music of The Night (USA) (Blushing Groom (FR) 131) [1994 82: 5d^3 5g^3 7g 7g^4 6g* 7.3s^2 7g^5 1995 7g 9m^2 10m^2 10g* 10.1m^4 12m^4 12f a12g Dec 2] sturdy colt: has a quick action: useful handicapper: won at Lingfield in June: best effort when close staying-on fourth of 20 to Diaghilef in King George V Stakes at Royal Ascot on sixth start: should stay 1¾m: acts on soft ground and good to firm. *R. Hannon* 96

ATOURS (USA) 7 b.g. Chief's Crown (USA) – Ataire (USA) (What A Pleasure (USA)) [1994 81p: 16.2d 11.5g^4 14d* 1995 16m^6 Aug 11] good-topped gelding: high-class hurdler: bandaged, in need of race and never placed to challenge in handicap at Newbury on only flat start in 1995: should stay at least 2m: acts on dead ground (effective on good to firm and heavy over hurdles): blinkered (no chance) on reappearance in 1994: remains capable of better on flat. *D. R. C. Elsworth* ?

ATRAF 2 b.c. (May 5) Clantime 101 – Flitteriss Park 62§ (Beldale Flutter (USA) 130) [1995 6g^4 5m^2 5m* 5m^2 5m^3 6m^3 6g^6 6f Oct 12] 32,000Y: small, well-made colt: fourth foal: half-brother to fairly useful 6f winners Emerging Market and Whittle Woods Girl (both by Emarati) and smart 1992 2-y-o sprinter Son Pardo (by Petong): dam untrustworthy 1m winner: fairly useful colt: won maiden at Newcastle in July: good efforts in minor event and nurseries next 4 starts: effective at 5f and 6f: acts on good to firm ground (below form in Redcar Two-Year-Old Trophy on firm, final start), yet to race on a soft surface. *D. Morley* 89 +

ATTARIKH (IRE) 2 b.c. (Mar 11) Mujtahid (USA) 118 – Silly Tune (IRE) (Coquelin (USA) 121) [1995 6m Nov 3] 38,000F: first foal: dam unraced half-sister to dam of Racing Post Trophy winner Seattle Rhyme: favourite, slowly away, ran very green and always towards rear, not knocked about, in 20-runner maiden at Doncaster: moved fluently to post: had held some good entries, and is almost certainly capable of better. *J. H. M. Gosden* – p

AT THE SAVOY (IRE) 4 gr.g. Exhibitioner 111 – Hat And Gloves (Wolver Hollow 126) [1994 51§: 7.1g 5.9v^4 6g^2 6g^3 7d 7m 6f 7d^5 6g 6.1s 6s^4 1995 a7g a7g^2 a8g^5 a7g^2 a7g^2 a6g^4 a8g* a7g^5 a6g^3 a6g^3 7.1g^4 a6g* a6g^6 7g^5 7m a7g^3 7.1m^2 8.1f^2 7.6m 7m^2 7m 8m^6 a7g^2 7m a6g a6g^3 a8g Dec 6] compact gelding: made into a fair handicapper on the all-weather in 1995, winning at Southwell in February (apprentice maiden event) and April: form on turf remains poor: effective at 6f to 1m: acts on fibresand and on any turf ground: effective blinkered or not, tried only once (well beaten) in visor: none too consistent. *T. D. Barron* 46 a64

ATTICUS (USA) 3 ch.c. Nureyev (USA) 131 – Athyka (USA) 118 (Secretariat (USA)) [1994 8v^2 6.5v* 1995 8d* 8d^2 8m^4 6.5g 8d^4 Oct 1] small, well-made colt: second foal: brother to 1m winner Athykaneyev: dam smart 9f (including at 2 yrs) to 1½m winner, won Prix de l'Opera twice: smart performer: won minor event at Evry at 2 yrs and 5-runner Prix de Fontainebleau at Longchamp (by 1½ lengths from Petit Poucet) in April: best effort when beaten a short neck by Vettori in strongly-run Poule d'Essai des Poulains again at Longchamp, making running and keeping on willingly: respectable fourth in St James's Palace Stakes at Royal Ascot and Prix du Rond-Point 118 at Longchamp afterwards: suited by around 1m: acts on good to firm and heavy ground. *Mme C. Head, France*

AUDREY GRACE 4 b.f. Infantry 122 – Fair Nic (Romancero 100) [1994 53: 8.3m 8.1g 8m 10d 7d^{2} 1995 8m 8m^{2} 9.7m 7m a8.5g^{5} 8g 8g^{3} Sep 14] lengthy filly: modest maiden handicapper: should stay beyond 1m: acts on good to firm and dead ground: visored last 3 starts: none too consistent. *B. J. Meehan* 51

AUGHFAD 9 b.h. Millfontaine 114 – Saulonika 94 (Saulingo 122) [1994 76, a65: a6g a5g^{4} a6g a5g 6.1d 5g 6s 6.1s* 5g^{2} 6m 6g^{3} a5g^{6} 5m^{3} 6g* 5.2g 6s 1995 6m 6g May 31] strong, workmanlike horse: fair sprint handicapper at 8 yrs: tailed off in 1995. *Mrs M. McCourt* –

AUGUSTAN 4 b.g. Shareef Dancer (USA) 135 – Krishnagar (Kris 135) [1994 60: 10.3g 12s 10.1m^{3} 10m 10m* a12g^{3} 11.8m^{4} 11.9m 11.9g a14g 1995 9.9m^{3} 10m a12g^{5} 12m 9.9m^{2} 10g 10g^{3} 12d 12g^{5} 11.9m* 10f^{2} 12m^{5} 10.3m^{5} 10.5m^{2} 12m^{3} 10m 11.9m 13.9g a11g Dec 1] good-topped gelding: has a markedly round action: fair handicapper: won at York (apprentices) in June: stays 1½m: acts on firm and soft going: no improvement in visor: usually held up. *S. Gollings* 68

AURIGA 2 b.f. (Mar 13) Belmez (USA) 131 – Little White Star (Mill Reef (USA) 141) [1995 6m^{2} 6m^{2} 7f^{3} 6m^{5} 7d Sep 26] unfurnished filly: unimpressive mover: half-sister to several winners, including useful sprinter Moon Drop (by Dominion) and very useful 7f and 1½m winner Beldale Star (by Beldale Flutter): dam poor maiden: refused to enter stalls on intended debut: fair maiden: well below form in nursery final outing: bred to stay beyond 7f: acts on firm ground: sent to Dubai. *I. A. Balding* 73

AUSSIE 2 b.g. (Feb 7) Sharrood (USA) 124 – Arita 78 (Never So Bold 135) [1995 5m^{2} 5g^{4} 7g 6m^{4} 7m^{2} 8.1m* 7.6m* 10d^{3} 8m^{5} Oct 20] 7,000Y: small gelding: has a round action: second foal: dam won at 5f at 2 yrs: won nurseries at Sandown (seller) in August and Lingfield in September: ran well afterwards: stays 1¼m: acts on good to firm and dead ground: sold 12,000 gns Newmarket Autumn Sales. *M. H. Tompkins* 74

AUTOBABBLE (IRE) 2 b.c. (Mar 10) Glenstal (USA) 118 – Almalat (Darshaan 133) [1995 5g^{2} 5m^{5} 6m a7g^{2} a7g a8g^{4} Dec 15] IR 8,200F, 8,400Y: useful-looking colt: first foal: dam unraced: fair maiden: will be well suited by 1¼m+: acts on equitrack: off course 5 months after second start. *R. Hannon* 68

AUTOFYR 2 br.f. (Mar 3) Autobird (FR) 71 – Fyrish 60 (Mr Fluorocarbon 126) [1995 6f^{4} 7.1g 7f 8f Oct 31] first reported foal: dam stayed 1¼m: well beaten in claimers and a nursery. *J. S. Wainwright* –

AUTUMN AFFAIR 3 b.f. Lugana Beach 116 – Miss Chalk 60 (Dominion 123) [1994 87: 5d^{3} 5m 6m^{2} 5m^{2} 6.5g^{6} 6g* 1995 7.3m^{3} 8m 7g^{6} 8d 8s^{2} 7m^{6} Oct 12] leggy filly: useful performer: third of 8 to Aqaarid in Fred Darling Stakes at Newbury and tenth of 14 in 1000 Guineas at Newmarket first 2 starts in 1995: good second of 10 to A La Carte in listed race at Ascot on penultimate outing: stays 1m: acts on good to firm ground and soft: bandaged off-hind last 2 starts. *C. E. Brittain* 100

AUTUMN COVER 3 gr.g. Nomination 125 – Respray 64 (Rusticaro (FR) 124) [1994 NR 1995 7g 8m 7f^{6} 7.1m 8m 8m^{3} 8d 8s 8g 9m 12m Nov 6] 6,200 2-y-o: strong, lengthy gelding: second foal: half-brother to 4-y-o Italian 1m to 1¼m winner Nitrito d'Amore (by Northern State): dam lightly-raced maiden: modest maiden: off course 3 months in the summer, and soundly beaten all 5 subsequent starts: should prove best at up to 1m: acts on firm ground: no improvement in blinkers: bandaged in front. *R. M. Flower* 54 d

AUTUMN (FR) 2 ch.f. (Mar 23) Rainbow Quest (USA) 134 – River Nomad 99 (Gorytus (USA) 132) [1995 7f 8f^{4} 8.2d Sep 11] leggy filly: first foal: dam 1m winner: fourth of 7 in maiden at Brighton in August: sold out of P. Cole's stable 6,000 gns Newmarket September Sales then wasn't given hard time in midfield in 20-runner maiden at Nottingham: will stay beyond 1m: joined C. Murray. *P. C. Haslam* 55 +

AUTUMN WINGS (FR) 3 b.f. In The Wings 128 – Autumn Tint (USA) (Roberto (USA) 131) [1994 64p: 7s^{3} 1995 10.5m 11.9d^{3} Oct 11] leggy, sparely-made filly: fair maiden, lightly raced: best effort when third of 19 to Richelieu at Haydock on final start: stays 1½m: carries head rather awkwardly. *B. W. Hills* 79

AVANT HUIT 3 ch.f. Clantime 101 – Apres Huit 66 (Day Is Done 115) [1994 55: 5m^{5} 5.2g^{2} 5g^{6} a5g^{2} a5g^{2} 1995 a5g^{3} a5g^{2} 5.1g Apr 4] workmanlike filly: good walker: 55

modest maiden: raced only at 5f: acts on equitrack and fibresand, has raced only on a sound surface on turf: blinkered/visored once each, running creditably: normally races prominently. *Mrs N. Macauley*

AVENUE FOCH (IRE) 6 gr.g. Saint Estephe (FR) 123 – Marie d'Irlande (FR) (Kalamoun 129) [1994 NR 1995 a9.4g Dec 9] leggy, lengthy gelding: winner in Ireland at 3 yrs, but little worthwhile form in varied company in Britain. *F. Murphy* –

AVERTI (IRE) 4 b.c. Warning 136 – Imperial Jade 105 (Lochnager 132) [1994 84+: 7m 6f 7g^5 1995 5m 6f^2 7m 5m^4 7g Sep 8] robust colt: useful performer, lightly raced: best effort when short-head second of 4 to Iltimas in minor event at Doncaster in July: effective at 5f to 7f, but very best form over 6f: acts on firm ground, yet to race on a soft surface. *W. R. Muir* 97

AVIATOR'S DREAM 5 b.g. Valiyar 129 – Maputo Princess (Raga Navarro (ITY) 119) [1994 NR 1995 a13g^5 a12g^3 a10g^4 a12g^4 a11g^3 a12g^5 11.9d* 11.9m Oct 5] robust gelding: poor performer: won novice hurdle in September and maiden handicap at Brighton (led close home) later in month: stayed 1½m: acted on fibresand and good to soft ground: no improvement in visor: dead. *J. Pearce* 39

AVIGNON (IRE) 3 gr.f. Machiavellian (USA) 123 – City Fortress (Troy 137) [1994 75p: 6m^4 1995 7m^4 8m^2 8f^6 10.2h^2 8f* 10.3m^2 8d^6 Sep 24] leggy, lightly-made filly: fairly useful performer: odds-on winner of maiden at Brighton in July: stayed 10.3f well: possibly needed a sound surface (acted on hard ground): consistent: has been retired. *P. W. Chapple-Hyam* 82

AVISHAYES (USA) 8 b.g. Al Nasr (FR) 126 – Rose Goddess (Sassafras (FR) 135) [1994 56: a11g^4 a8g^3 a9.4g^6 10m 10m^4 8h^3 9.9m^6 8m* 8.2m 8m^4 8m^5 1995 10.3g 8.2g^5 8g 8m^6 8f^6 9m 8g^4 8m 8.2m* 8f^4 9f^4 8m^3 8f^2 8m^3 8m^5 7.9g 8d 8m 10f Oct 16] big, lengthy gelding: usually impresses in appearance: modest handicapper: narrow winner at Nottingham in June: below form last 5 starts: effective at 1m to 1¼m: acts on hard ground and fibresand: effective blinkered (rarely tried nowadays) or not: has run well for lady rider: best efforts with waiting tactics. *Mrs M. Reveley* 53

AWAAMIR 2 b.f. (Apr 2) Green Desert (USA) 127 – Kadwah (USA) 80 (Mr Prospector (USA)) [1995 7f^3 7m* Oct 28] tall, unfurnished filly: second foal: closely related to 3-y-o Mutammaddin (by Polish Precedent): dam lightly-raced 1m and 1¼m winner out of high-class American turf performer Castilla: won 19-runner maiden at Newmarket in October, leading around 1f out and running on strongly to beat Chalk Dust 2 lengths: will stay further than 7f: will improve again. *J. H. M. Gosden* 85 p

AWAFEH 2 b.g. (Feb 27) Green Desert (USA) 127 – Three Piece (Jaazeiro (USA) 127) [1995 6m^5 7.1m 5g 6g 8f 5s Nov 2] 40,000Y: tall gelding: has a round action: half-brother to 3-y-o 10.5f and 11.6f winner Dance So Suite (by Shareef Dancer) and 1990 Irish 2-y-o 6f and 7f winner Treble Hook (by Ballad Rock): dam Irish maiden: modest form though ran better than finishing position suggests on occasions: may prove best at 6f/7f: keen sort, sweating profusely second outing: blinkered final 2 starts: sold 4,700 gns Doncaster November Sales. *J. W. Payne* 51

AWASHA (IRE) 3 b.f. Fairy King (USA) – Foliage (Thatching 131) [1994 NR 1995 7m^5 a7g^5 a8g^3 a7g^3 Dec 19] 7,200F, 4,600Y: smallish filly: fifth foal: half-sister to 3 winners, including (France, 9f) Tra Fiori (by Law Society): dam unraced sister to Grade 1 winner (at 9f) Fitzwilliam Place: modest maiden: should stay beyond 1m. *Miss Gay Kelleway* 57

AWAYIL (USA) 3 ch.f. Woodman (USA) 126 – Ra'a (USA) 106 (Diesis 133) [1994 62p: 5s 6g^3 1995 7.1m^6 6m* 6g^5 6f Oct 31] close-coupled filly: fairly useful performer: won handicap at Yarmouth in August: stays 6f: acts on good to firm ground: sold 17,000 gns Newmarket December Sales. *H. Thomson Jones* 82

AWESOME POWER 9 b.g. Vision (USA) – Majestic Nurse 80 (On Your Mark 125) [1994 58, a73: a10g* a10g^3 a10g* a10g^2 a10g a10g^4 a10g* a10g^3 10.5g 9.7m^5 10g^3 10g^3 8.9m^2 a10g^2 1995 a10g^2 a10g^3 a10g^2 a10g a10g 10.8m^5 10m a10g 10m^6 10m a10g a10g* a10g^2 Dec 6] strong gelding: fair performer at best on the all-weather: won seller at Lingfield in November: modest on turf: effective at 9f to 1½m: acts particularly well on equitrack: tried blinkered earlier in career. *J. W. Hills* 52 d a69 d

AWESOME VENTURE 5 b.g. Formidable (USA) 125 – Pine Ridge 80 (High Top 131) [1994 –, a70: 7g a7g^2 a6g 7g 7g 1995 7g 8f 7m^4 7m 8g 7g 6g^2 6m^6 7f^2 55 a–

5.2m^4 6m 6m^3 6m 6m^6 7g 6g a6g 7m 7f^4 Oct 25] big gelding: just a modest performer nowadays: stays 7f, not 1m: acts on firm and dead ground and on fibresand: effective visored or not, well beaten both tries in blinkers: often makes running: inconsistent. *M. C. Chapman*

AWESTRUCK 5 b.g. Primo Dominie 121 – Magic Kingdom 76 (Kings Lake (USA) 133) [1994 60d: a12g^4 a12g^2 a8.5g^3 a8.5g^2 a12g a9.4g^3 a8.5g a8.5g^6 a9.4g^6 a9.4g^2 a16.2g^4 8.5g a14.8g^4 a12g^6 a16.2g^4 a12g^4 1995 a11g a12g^3 a12g* a11g a12g* a12g^6 a12g a16.2g^4 a12g^4 a12g^4 14.1g^5 a14.8g a12g^2 a14.8g^3 10.5m^5 11.8m a12g^2 a12g a12g a12g^6 a14.8g a16g^6 Nov 29] sturdy gelding: poor mover: modest performer: won 2 handicaps at Wolverhampton (seldom raced elsewhere in 1995) in February, second an apprentice event: probably stays 1¾m: acts on fibresand and on firm and dead ground, well beaten on soft: effective blinkered/visored or not: none too consistent. *B. Preece* – a50 d

AWFULLY RISKY 4 b.f. Risk Me (FR) 127 – Gemma Kaye 91 (Cure The Blues (USA)) [1994 38: a12g^5 a9.4g^5 8.1m^2 10.3g 1995 a8g Nov 16] leggy filly: poor maiden: tried visored. *P. D. Evans* –

AXED AGAIN 3 b.f. Then Again 126 – Axe Valley 89 (Royben 125) [1994 NR 1995 7m^5 7g a8.5g Nov 13] 7,400Y: third foal: sister to 1994 Stewards' Cup winner For The Present and half-sister to 1991 2-y-o 6f winner Shalou (by Formidable): dam sprinter: no sign of ability. *N. Bycroft* –

AXEMAN (IRE) 3 b.c. Reprimand 122 – Minnie Tudor (Tudor Melody 129) [1994 97: 6m 6m* 6d 6g^6 8v^3 1995 7m^5 8.1m 7f^4 7g 7.3d 7g^5 Sep 20] leggy, good-topped colt: fairly useful handicapper: disappointing after third 3-y-o start: stays 7f: best form on a sound surface: blinkered final start: has joined D. Nicholls. *R. Hannon* 86

AXFORD (USA) 2 ch.c. (Jan 24) Woodman (USA) 126 – Timely 104 (Kings Lake (USA) 133) [1995 7g^2 8m^2 8d^6 Sep 15] rather unfurnished colt: first reported foal: dam 1m winner: useful form when second to Zelzelah in £8,100 event at Newbury and to Bijou d'Inde in Futurity Stakes at the Curragh: took keen hold and led 6f when sixth of 8 to Mick's Love in minor event at Newbury final start: stays 1m: sure to win a race. *P. W. Chapple-Hyam* 95

AYE READY 2 ch.c. (Mar 30) Music Boy 124 – Cindy's Princess (Electric 126) [1995 6g Sep 14] 8,200F, 6,400Y: second foal: dam once-raced daughter of a 15f winner: 50/1, behind in maiden auction at Ayr. *Miss L. A. Perratt* –

AYLESBURY (IRE) 2 ch.c. (Apr 3) Lycius (USA) 124 – Ayah (USA) 74 (Secreto (USA) 128) [1995 8d^6 8g* 7g* Oct 30] first foal: dam, ran 3 times, closely related to Irish Oaks dead-heater Melodist: progressive Irish colt: won minor event at Navan and 6-runner Killavullan Stakes at Leopardstown (by length from Errazuriz) within 12 days in October: stays 1m: may well improve further. *J. Oxx, Ireland* 99 p

AYUNLI 4 b.f. Chief Singer 131 – Tsungani 64 (Cure The Blues (USA)) [1994 55: 8d 8g^6 8g 7.1f^2 10m^4 8g^2 1995 10g 10m a8.5g* a8.5g a8.5g a9.4g* a9.4g^2 a9.4g^6 10g^4 12.1g* 11.9m* 12m 12m* Nov 6] tall, leggy filly: fluent mover: fair handicapper: had a good season, winning at Wolverhampton in May and August and at Hamilton in September, York (apprentices) in October and Folkestone in November: stays 1½m: acts on good to firm ground and fibresand: has been bandaged. *S. C. Williams* 71

AZDIHAAR (USA) 3 b. or br.f. Mr Prospector (USA) – Desirable 119 (Lord Gayle (USA) 124) [1994 70p: 6m^5 6g 6g^4 1995 8m^2 8m 7.6m^2 7f^2 7f^3 8f^2 7g* 7.1s* 8m Oct 12] well-made filly: fairly useful performer: won maiden at Catterick (odds on) and handicap at Haydock, both in September: stayed 1m: acted on firm and soft ground: consistent: visits Lammtarra. *J. L. Dunlop* 81

AZTEC FLYER (USA) 2 b.g. (Apr 5) Alwasmi (USA) 115 – Jetta J (USA) (Super Concorde (USA) 128) [1995 7m 7m 6g^3 7.9g^5 7d 8f 8f Oct 31] 26,000Y: tall, narrow gelding: sixth foal: half-brother to winners abroad by Manila and Verbatim: dam minor 6f (at 2 yrs) and 8.5f stakes winner: never-dangerous third of 5 in maiden at Ayr in July: well held in 4 nurseries: should stay 1m. *Mrs M. Reveley* 63 ?

AZUBAH 8 b.m. Castle Keep 121 – Louisianalightning (Music Boy 124) [1994 NR 1995 a8g a11g a13g^6 Feb 4] lengthy, rather sparely-made mare: lightly raced and no form on flat for a long time: trained on reappearance by G. M. Moore. *J. A. Harris* –

AZWAH (USA) 2 b.f. (Apr 19) Danzig (USA) – Magic Slipper 97 (Habitat 134) [1995 6m Jul 17] strong filly: sixth foal: closely related to 3-y-o Muhab (by Lyphard), useful 6f and 7f winner at 2 yrs, and 7.2f winner Wali (by Lomond), and half-sister to 6.9f winner Ahbab (by Persian Bold): dam, 1¼m and 11.5f winner, half-sister to Fairy Footsteps and Light Cavalry: 3/1, 10 lengths last of 7 to Tropical Dance in minor event at Windsor, travelling comfortably around 4f, having started slowly, then eased: looked sure to do better. *P. T. Walwyn* 65

B

BAADERAH (IRE) 3 ch.f. Cadeaux Genereux 131 – Labwa (USA) (Lyphard (USA) 132) [1994 90: 6m3 6g4 6g* 6.5g2 7m5 1995 6d* 8m2 6g2 6g* 7m 6g 6g2 Nov 19] quite attractive filly: useful performer: won minor event at Leicester and length second of 9 to Olimpia Dukakis in Premio Regina Elena at Rome in April: won listed race at Newmarket (held Branston Abby by a neck) in June: easily best subsequent effort when 4 lengths second of 10 to Beat of Drums in Premio Umbria at Rome: effective at 6f, and stayed 1m: acted on good to firm ground and dead, did not race on extremes: raced prominently: game: stud. *L. M. Cumani* 102

BABINDA 2 b.c. (Apr 15) Old Vic 136 – Babita 107 (Habitat 134) [1995 6g3 7m* Oct 14] sturdy, lengthy colt: good mover: fourth foal: brother to 3-y-o 1½m winner Bambara: dam, useful at 2 yrs, best form at 6f: won 5-runner minor event at Newmarket in October comfortably by 2 lengths from Madame Steinlen, setting pace then running on well: will stay middle distances: will improve again. *C. E. Brittain* 92 p

BABSY BABE 2 b.f. (Apr 4) Polish Patriot (USA) 128 – Welcome Break (Wollow 132) [1995 5m* 5g2 6f Oct 12] 5,000Y: tall, quite good-topped filly: has scope: half-sister to smart 6f to 1¼m winner Invited Guest (by Be My Guest) and fairly useful 3-y-o 2m winner En Vacances (by Old Vic): dam unraced half-sister to Interval and daughter of Cambridgeshire winner Intermission: withdrawn after twice unseating rider at stalls on debut: comfortable winner of maiden auction at Redcar in August: much better form when second to Oh Whataknight in minor event at Ayr and mid-division in 26-runner Redcar Two-Year-Old Trophy: stays 6f. *J. J. Quinn* 88

BABY BOB 3 b.f. Then Again 126 – Laleston 73 (Junius (USA) 124) [1994 50: 5f6 5g 7.1g 5s a6g a7g 1995 a8g a8g Jan 30] sturdy filly: has shown very little since debut: blinkered on all-weather. *J. M. P. Eustace* –

BABYLON BLUES 2 b.c. (Feb 13) Rock City 120 – Global Lady 94 (Balliol 125) [1995 5m 5m5 Apr 25] 10,000F, 4,200Y: neat colt: fourth foal: dam 6f (at 2 yrs) to 7.6f winner: well beaten in maiden at Kempton (ridden by 7-lb claimer) and seller at Folkestone 10 days later. *R. Hannon* –

BABYSHOOZ 2 b.f. (Mar 29) Efisio 120 – Payvashooz 78 (Ballacashtal (CAN)) [1995 5m 5g 6m Jun 20] 900Y: small, compact filly: second foal: dam stayed 1m: no worthwhile form in maiden auctions and a seller. *M. Brittain* –

BACK BY DAWN 2 b.c. (Jan 14) Risk Me (FR) 127 – Moonlight Princess 49 (Alias Smith (USA)) [1995 5m 5g4 6m 6m5 7f6 Aug 9] 3,000Y: leggy, close-coupled colt: has scope: unimpressive mover: fourth foal: brother to 5-y-o Lunar Risk (modest 1½m and 1¾m winner at best), and a 3-y-o 1m winner in Hungary: dam 10.8f seller winner: modest maiden: should stay 7f: wears bandages behind: flashed tail second outing, carried head high final 2 starts. *D. R. C. Elsworth* 54

BACKDROP (IRE) 2 b.c. (Apr 30) Scenic 128 – Knapping (Busted 134) [1995 7.1s4 Oct 1] IR 10,500F, 26,000Y: useful-looking colt: half-brother to several winners, including Irish 13f to 2m winner Miss Mitchell (by Sexton Blake) and Irish 1m and 9f winner Meglio Che Posso (by Try My Best): dam ran twice: 13/2, just under 4 lengths fourth of 14 to Carburton in maiden at Haydock, improving over 2f out and keeping on though green: will stay middle distances: sure to improve. *P. W. Chapple-Hyam* 74 p

BACKGAMMON 4 b.g. Midyan (USA) 124 – Messaria 68§ (Ile de Bourbon (USA) 133) [1994 91: 8d6 8m5 10.2g* 11.8m* 10f6 11.9d3 12m3 1995 12m6 Apr 15] strong, useful-looking gelding: fairly useful performer: wearing dropped noseband, respectable sixth of 17 in handicap at Kempton on first start on flat for new stable, 84 tending to wander under pressure: stays 1½m well: acts on firm and dead ground, yet to race on soft: visored (ran well) final 3-y-o start: useful form at best over hurdles, winner in December. *J. A. B. Old*

BACKHANDER (IRE) 3 b.g. Cadeaux Genereux 131 – Chevrefeuille 87 (Ile de Bourbon (USA) 133) [1994 NR 1995 7g 7.3m 7.1g 6g a7g^{6} 8m^{2} a12g^{3} Aug 5] IR 32,000Y: sturdy gelding: third foal: half-brother to 1992 2-y-o 5f winner Esthal (by Kalaglow): dam 12.2f winner out of Vielle: modest maiden: stays 1m: acts on good to firm ground, below form on all-weather: has hung under pressure and not one to trust implicitly: sold (J. Toller to Martyn Wane) 1,000 gns Newmarket Autumn Sales. *J. A. R. Toller*
56

BACK IN THE BLACK 2 br.g. (Feb 18) Petong 126 – Altara (GER) (Tarim) [1995 6m a7g Aug 4] 11,000F, 12,500Y: half-brother to winners abroad by Priamos and Never So Bold: dam lightly-raced daughter of top German filly Alaria: tailed off in sellers at Windsor and (blinkered) Southwell: sold 1,800 gns Newmarket Autumn Sales. *Mrs J. Cecil*
–

BACKSTABBER 5 ch.g. Flash of Steel 120 – Guest List 85 (Be My Guest (USA) 126) [1994 58d: a8.5g^{6} a8g a12g a12g 12.3m 7.6g a9.4g 1995 a7g^{6} a9.4g^{6} a8.5g^{3} a9.4g^{2} a9.4g 8.3g a8.5g* 12.3m^{6} a9.4g 10m Aug 21] workmanlike gelding: poor handicapper: won at Wolverhampton (amateurs) in June: well beaten afterwards: stays 9.4f: acts on fibresand: blinkered (out of form) sixth 4-y-o start: inconsistent. *Miss S. J. Wilton*
–
a40

BACKTIARI 2 b.g. (Mar 17) Backchat (USA) 98 – Tiernee Quintana (Artaius (USA) 129) [1995 7g 10m Oct 19] 1,500Y: angular, good-topped gelding: second reported foal: dam unraced: backward, tailed off in maidens at Leicester and Nottingham (median auction event). *S. Gollings*
–

BACKVIEW 3 ch.g. Backchat (USA) 98 – Book Review (Balidar 133) [1994 NR 1995 12.5m 10.2m 10.2f^{3} 8m^{4} 12.5g^{2} 14m^{6} a12g* 11.6m 12s 12.1s a10g Dec 15] short-backed gelding: second foal: dam of little account: fair form: won maiden at Wolverhampton in July, leading 4f out: well beaten afterwards: stays 12.5f (stiff task over 1¾m): acts on fibresand and firm going. *B. J. Llewellyn*
65
a68

BACKWOODS 2 ch.c. (Apr 4) In The Wings 128 – Kates Cabin 96 (Habitat 134) [1995 6m Nov 3] sturdy colt: second foal: half-brother to 3-y-o 1m winner Dunloe (by Shaadi): dam, 1m winner, out of sister to very smart soft ground stayer Old Bill: 14/1 and very green, slowly into stride and always well behind in 20-runner maiden at Doncaster: bred to need much further than 6f: sold 4,000 gns Ascot December Sales. *G. Wragg*
–

BADDI QUEST 3 b.c. Rainbow Quest (USA) 134 – Baddi Baddi (USA) (Sharpen Up 127) [1994 NR 1995 7g 10.3m 12.1g^{5} 12.5g^{4} 11.5g^{4} 10f^{2} a16g^{4} Aug 12] smallish, rather leggy colt: second foal: half-brother to French sprint (at 2yrs) and 1m winner Baddi Bird (by Storm Bird): dam 2-y-o 1m winner in France: fair maiden: stays 12.1f: acts on firm ground, yet to race on a soft surface: sold (B. Hanbury to D. Nolan) only 1,200 gns Newmarket Autumn Sales. *B. Hanbury*
71

BADGER BAY (IRE) 2 b.f. (Mar 9) Salt Dome (USA) – Legit (IRE) (Runnett 125) [1995 5m^{2} 5g^{2} 5m 5g^{2} 5g 6m^{2} Aug 10] IR 4,000Y: unfurnished filly: first foal: dam Irish maiden: trained by John Berry first 5 starts, runner-up in 3 maiden auctions: very good effort when short headed in 5-runner nursery at Yarmouth final start: better suited by 6f than 5f: sweating and edgy on third start. *C. A. Dwyer*
67

BAD NEWS 3 ch.f. Pharly (FR) 130 – Phylae (Habitat 134) [1994 56: 6m^{4} 6m 7s^{6} 6.9s^{4} 1995 7g 7m 9.9m 10m 10m a10g 7g^{4} 8f Oct 18] close-coupled filly: inconsistent maiden: trained in 1995 by G. Fierro first 5 starts, by R. Harris next 2: may prove best at up to 1m: blinkered (pulled hard, tailed off) third 3-y-o start: often wears crossed noseband: has had tongue tied down. *C. N. Allen*
53 ?

BADRI (USA) 2 b.c. (Apr 17) Topsider (USA) – Hedonic (USA) (Fappiano (USA)) [1995 7m Sep 5] $200,000F: leggy, quite good-topped colt: has scope: fourth foal: brother to a 2-y-o 1m winner in North America, and half-brother to Grade 3 1m winner Halissee (by Cozzene): dam 6f to 1m winner in USA: 11/8 favourite, tenth of 11 finishers to Caxton Star in maiden at Leicester, soon niggled along in rear and unable to challenge: will do better. *J. H. M. Gosden*
– p

BAGBY BOY 3 b.g. Puissance 110 – Miss Milton (Young Christopher 119) [1994 NR 1995 10d 12s 14g Oct 23] tall, non-thoroughbred gelding: fourth reported foal: half-brother to fairly useful sprint handicapper Poets Cove (by Bay Express): dam lightly raced on flat: no promise in maidens. *P. R. Hedger*
–

BAG OF TRICKS (IRE) 5 br.g. Chief Singer 131 – Bag Lady 86 (Be My Guest (USA) 126) [1994 55+: 13d 8g 9.7s 9g^4 10m a10g^6 1995 a10g^6 a12g^2 a10g^3 a12g^3 a12g^6 a12g* 12m^2 11.9f 12g 10m^3 12f^2 12m 12f^3 12m^6 Sep 7] strong gelding: modest handicapper: won at Lingfield in March: inconsistent afterwards: suited by middle distances: best form on a sound surface or equitrack: takes strong hold. *S. Dow*
57 a64

BAGSHOT 4 b.c. Rousillon (USA) 133 – Czar's Bride (USA) 78 (Northern Dancer) [1994 91+: 8f^5 6m^4 6m^3 7.1d* 7g* 8m^4 1995 8g^6 8m 7.3g^4 8f 8.1f^3 7.3d^6 a8g^3 a8g^3 Dec 1] good-topped colt: fairly useful handicapper: best efforts in 1995 when sixth in the Lincoln at Doncaster and third at Southwell final start: stays 1m: acts on firm and dead ground, and on fibresand, yet to race on soft: carries head high: normally held up. *R. Hannon*
84

BAHAMIAN KING (IRE) 3 b.g. Fairy King (USA) – Look of Love (General Assembly (USA)) [1994 NR 1995 10.3m Oct 21] IR 5,000Y, resold 5,000Y: first foal: dam lightly-raced maiden: 33/1, slowly away and always behind in 15-runner claimer at Doncaster: showed a round action. *S. E. Kettlewell*
–

BAHAMIAN KNIGHT (CAN) 2 b. or br.c. (Feb 7) Ascot Knight (CAN) 130 – Muskoka Command (USA) (Top Command (USA)) [1995 5m^2 6g^2 6m* 6m^3 Jun 22] $45,000Y: quite attractive colt: second foal: dam minor winner as 2-y-o in USA: won maiden at Lingfield readily by 3½ lengths from Rabican: clear of remainder when third of 8 to World Premier in Chesham Stakes at Ascot following month: will stay at least 7f. *D. R. Loder*
95

BAHAMIAN SUNSHINE (USA) 4 ch.c. Sunshine Forever (USA) – Pride of Darby (USA) (Danzig (USA)) [1994 10g* 12d 12.5g^5 10v^4 10.5v^6 1995 12.5v^3 12d^2 12.5d^5 14g^2 13.9m* 12d Oct 21] $30,000Y: tall, lengthy colt: third foal: dam, 1m winner in USA, is half-sister to Prix du Jockey-Club winner Caracolero: useful performer: trained until after third 4-y-o start by A. Fabre, winning newcomers race at 2 yrs and minor event at 3 yrs: edgy, easily won 3-runner minor event at York in October by 4 lengths from Corradini: virtually pulled up in St Simon Stakes at Newbury: unlikely to stay beyond 1¾m: acts on good to firm and heavy going. *D. R. Loder*
105

BAHITH (USA) 3 ch.c. Topsider (USA) – Alghuzaylah 90 (Habitat 134) [1994 94p: 6g* 6s^2 1995 8m 6g 6g^2 6m^2 6f^3 6g Sep 13] strong, compact colt: fairly useful performer in minor events, though tailed off final start: should stay 7f: acts on firm and soft ground: blinkered last 2 starts: has run well when sweating: sold only 12,500 gns Newmarket Autumn Sales. *H. Thomson Jones*
94

BAHRAIN QUEEN (IRE) 7 ch.m. Caerleon (USA) 132 – Bahrain Vee (CAN) (Blushing Groom (FR) 131) [1994 –: a16.2g a16g^5 21.6v 1995 16.2m^5 May 12] light-framed mare: little worthwhile form on flat: modest winning hurdler. *C. Smith*
–

BAHRI (USA) 3 b.c. Riverman (USA) 131 – Wasnah (USA) 96 (Nijinsky (CAN) 138) [1994 85+: 7g^2 8g^2 8d^2 6.1d* 1995 7g^2 8m^3 8m^3 8m* 8f^2 10.4m^2 8d* 10m^5 Oct 14]
125

Conditions for much of the British summer were among the hottest and driest encountered since records began. The artificial watering systems almost universally in use nowadays—Bath and Carlisle remain the only flat courses in Britain without one—are much more sophisticated, and the courses themselves generally better maintained, than they were when racing was affected by a similarly severe drought in 1976. Watering was by no means universal twenty years ago, but, in the interim, those who regard watering racecourses as wrong in principle have lost the argument to those who believe in it for the greater good of the sport. However, the effects of watering, coupled with the questionable accuracy of some advance going reports, still provoke plenty of controversy. An aversion to running horses on firm ground tends to encourage liberal watering during dry weather, but, as well as being one of the biggest influences on the size of fields, the state of the going is also one of the most influential factors affecting the outcome of a horserace, and therefore of crucial concern to anyone having a bet. Yet the supervision of racecourse managements in this particular area by the racing authorities leaves something to be desired. Clerks of the course are generally becoming more interventionist, often using the latitude given to them by the Jockey Club's instructions on watering to change the state of the going (until recent years watering was allowed only to promote grass growth). Both in their watering policies and their advance going reports, some clerks of the course seem to allow their judgement to be affected by wider commercial considerations. Small fields don't help attendances or betting turnover but, with a climate as changeable as Britain's, clerks of the course have to perform a delicate balancing act. It's understandable that things sometimes go wrong, but there's no excuse at all for some of the going reports that are issued. It sometimes seems that one man's 'good to firm' is another's 'good', and yet another's 'firm'. This inconsistency is damaging to racing, leaving owners, trainers, racegoers and off-course punters in a quandary. Artifical watering can change the going unevenly, depending on such things as the contours of the track and any variations in drainage and/or soil conditions, as well as on the evenness of the application of the water itself. Wind, for example, can seriously interfere with the effects of watering, while pop-up sprinklers in fixed positions sometimes bring their own problems with soft patches. Tow lines and rain guns offer better control but a newer system, in use at Haydock for the last three years, is even more flexible and is probably the most efficient installed anywhere, using a self-propelled irrigator with a boom stretching the full width of the course. The Australian-designed system, controlled by a sensor in contact with the inside running rail, directs water straight down onto the track from roughly rail height, minimising the wind effect. Ensuring that water penetrates when the ground is hard—some courses use a machine to drill the soil before watering—is also something that arguably needs more attention. The surface can easily become loose if water does not sink in, with obvious consequences for the safety of horses and jockeys, as well as for their performance. Though Jockey Club experiments with the penetrometer, which is used to assess the ground in France, are said to have proved unsatisfactory, there is a need for a more scientific approach to the analysis of the going. Further work is in progress to develop a going meter but, in the meantime, the Jockey Club—responsible for the training of clerks of the course—must strive for greater consistency.

The Jockey Club would also be well advised to have another look at the discretion given to courses in deciding how much water to put on. The days of horses always racing on a 'natural' surface may be gone but over-watering can accentuate undesirable side-effects. The effect of the draw on some racecourses can be most pronounced and, rightly or wrongly, the blame is often laid at the door of artificial watering. It is perhaps pertinent that the bias and its effect is not always predictable. At Ayr, for example, a low draw is more usually an advantage on the straight course in big fields; yet in the three sprint races with fields of twenty or more at the September meeting high numbers dominated (Cool Jazz, fifth from stall one, well clear on the far side, was probably beaten by the draw in the Ayr Gold Cup). At

St James's Palace Stakes, Royal Ascot—Bahri is most impressive

Queen Elizabeth II Stakes, Ascot—Bahri is given an inspired ride and beats Ridgewood Pearl by six lengths

Nottingham, there was a big advantage to those racing near the stand rail throughout the summer; but, at the first meeting in the autumn, it paid to be drawn on the far side. The draw played an important, often decisive, role in determining the results of races on the straight course at Newcastle in the summer when it was a big advantage to race right against the stand rail. One major race where uneven watering probably played a part in determining the outcome was the Queen Elizabeth II Stakes at the Festival of British Racing at Ascot in September. On the face of it, Bahri gave an outstanding performance to beat the subsequent Breeders' Cup Mile winner Ridgewood Pearl by six lengths. But the tactics hatched in the paddock beforehand by Bahri's connections almost certainly proved decisive. The Queen Elizabeth II Stakes is run on the round course where, in the back straight, the ground under the far rail is protected from watering and rainfall by overhanging tree branches. Bahri's rider Willie Carson assessed the going under the trees as firm—the official going on the round course was good with good to soft patches—and suggested that he should steer a wide course on Bahri in the back straight to take advantage. Bahri's intended pacemaker Muhab set off as planned on the conventional route, and, while the others followed, Bahri tacked across to race alone on the far side. Bahri had a clear lead as the runners approached the home straight where Carson steered him back across to the rest. Around three lengths clear turning for home, Bahri drew away to win virtually unchallenged by six; Ridgewood Pearl, threatening only briefly early in the straight, finished five lengths in front of third-placed Soviet Line.

Bahri's form overall is not that of a horse six lengths better than Ridgewood Pearl at weight-for-sex over a mile, and, in the circumstances, his Queen Elizabeth II Stakes performance has been passed over when considering his Timeform rating. His other achievements through the latest season, however, leave no doubt that he was a high-class performer, one of the best milers around. His only victory from four starts as a two-year-old came in a minor event at Nottingham on his final start. After Bahri had stepped up considerably on that form in the Greenham at Newbury on his reappearance—finishing a clear second to Celtic Swing—his trainer John Dunlop reported that he had 'worked like a good horse last year but was very weak'. Bahri's development over the winter was apparent from his appearance in the paddock where

Hamdan Al Maktoum's "Bahri"

he really took the eye. Carson's post-race remark that Bahri might have beaten Celtic Swing if he'd settled early on was taken by most with a pinch of salt, but there was no doubting that Bahri was worth his place in the Guineas field. He ran very well at Newmarket, keeping on for third behind Pennekamp and Celtic Swing, and with the first two set to step up in distance the way seemed open for Bahri to win a good race at a mile. The opportunity didn't come straight away, as Bahri had to settle for a close third behind Spectrum and Adjareli in the Irish Two Thousand Guineas on his next start. Starting a short-priced favourite, Bahri, who had to be reshod down at the start, didn't enjoy the clearest of runs in a muddling race in which the emphasis was very much on finishing speed. Connections felt that Bahri should have won and he went to post for the St James's Palace Stakes at Royal Ascot with Muhab to ensure a true pace. Bahri got stirred up in the preliminaries but went on to give a most impressive performance, storming clear in a matter of strides approaching the final furlong, after being poised behind Muhab and Flemensfirth early in the straight, to win by four lengths and a head from Charnwood Forest and the Poule d'Essai des Poulains winner Vettori. The fourth and fifth, Atticus and Annus Mirabilis, got no sort of run but it was stretching things to suggest that either would have made a race of it with Bahri, whose performance was one of the most striking seen in the race for years. Bahri, incidentally, was one of five winners saddled by John Dunlop at Royal Ascot; the horse also edged him past Saeed bin Suroor's combined win and place earnings for the year in Britain when fifth in the Champion Stakes at Newmarket in October on his final start. Bahri faded noticeably in the Champion and was almost certainly better at a mile than a mile and a quarter, though he put up a creditable effort at the longer trip when chasing home the runaway winner Halling in the Juddmonte

International Stakes at York in August. Bahri was also runner-up in a small field for the Sussex Stakes at Goodwood, where, except for his pacemaker Sulb, he was the only three-year-old; Sayyedati, returning to her very best, just touched off Bahri after a good battle over the last furlong.

Bahri (USA) (b.c. 1992)	Riverman (USA) (b 1969)	Never Bend (b 1960)	Nasrullah
			Lalun
		River Lady (b 1963)	Prince John
			Nile Lily
	Wasnah (USA) (b 1987)	Nijinsky (b 1967)	Northern Dancer
			Flaming Page
		Highest Trump (b 1972)	Bold Bidder
			Dear April

The well-made, handsome Bahri really looked the part as a three-year-old, though he sometimes walked stiffly behind which, coupled with a tendency to sweat and become edgy, spoiled the impression of him in the paddock. He took a good hold in his races, showing a natural inclination to get on with things, and it's not altogether surprising that Carson reportedly regarded him as far from certain to get a mile before he ran in the Guineas. Bahri was certainly bred to stay at least a mile and a quarter, being by the admirable stallion Riverman out of the Nijinsky mare Wasnah who showed more stamina than speed and would almost certainly have stayed a mile and a half. Wasnah showed useful form, including when a staying-on second in the Pretty Polly Stakes over a mile and a quarter at Newmarket, but didn't win a race. Bahri is her first foal. Bahri's grandam Highest Trump won the Queen Mary Stakes at Royal Ascot as a two-year-old and was placed in the Irish One Thousand Guineas and the Coronation Stakes at three; at stud the well-connected Highest Trump, who was one of the highest-priced American yearling fillies in her time, produced the pattern or graded winners Dance Bid (third in Shergar's Irish Derby), Northern Plain and Winglet (winner of the Grade 2 Princess Stakes in the States). Highest Trump's great-grandam Durazna was one of the leading two-year-old fillies of 1943 and herself a half-sister to the Kentucky Oaks winner Miss Dogwood, the third dam of Mr Prospector, and Crepe Myrtle, the fourth dam of Seattle Slew. Bahri takes up a career as a stallion in 1996 at Shadwell in Kentucky at a fee of 20,000 dollars, live foal. Except for the Queen Elizabeth II Stakes, Bahri did all his racing on a sound surface as a three-year-old. He was a tough and genuine racehorse. *J. L. Dunlop*

BAILEYS BRIDE (IRE) 2 ch.f. (Mar 19) Shy Groom (USA) – Lacey Brief (USA) (Roi Dagobert 128) [1995 5g^5 a5g^4 7m Jun 13] IR 8,000Y: close-coupled filly: half-sister to several winners here and abroad, including fairly useful 1983 Irish 2-y-o 7f winner Rustic Lace (by Rusticaro) and 1m winner Just Ready (by Petorius): dam Irish 9f winner: no promise, in selling company final 2 starts: sold 1,100 gns Doncaster July Sales. *M. Johnston* –

BAILEYS FIRST (IRE) 2 b.f. (Feb 26) Alzao (USA) 117 – Maiden Concert (Condorcet (FR)) [1995 6f^3 6m^3 7d^3 6m Oct 4] IR 48,000Y: sturdy filly: closely related to 1½m winner Green's Van Goyen (by Lyphard's Special) and half-sister to several winners, notably very smart 1m/1¼m performer Candy Glen (by Glenstal): dam once-raced half-sister to dam of Irish 1000 Guineas winner More So: fair form in maidens first 3 starts: soon behind in nursery at York final one: bred to stay at least 1m. *M. Johnston* 74

BAILEYS SUNSET (IRE) 3 b.g. Red Sunset 120 – Stradey Lynn 57 (Derrylin 115) [1994 72: 5d^3 5g^6 5f 6f^5 5h^2 6m^5 5m* 5m 5.2g^3 a5g^5 a5g^4 1995 a5g* a5g^6 a5g^2 a6g^2 a6g^2 6s^4 5m* 5.1g^4 5g^5 5g 5m^3 5m^5 5m^3 5f^3 5g* 5f^6 6f* 6f^6 6f^3 6g^5 6d 5g 5f Oct 16] neat gelding: fair performer: won claimers at Lingfield in January and Folkestone in April, and sellers at Ayr (handicap) and Brighton in July: below form last 4 starts, missing break on last 2: stays 6f: acts on hard going (respectable effort on soft) and equitrack (ran poorly only outing on fibresand): blinkered (below form) once at 3 yrs: has taken very strong hold to post and been awkward in paddock: sold 2,200 gns Doncaster November Sales. *M. Johnston* 72 d

BAILIWICK 2 b.g. (Mar 1) Dominion 123 – Lady Barkley (Habitat 134) [1995 6m 6.1m 6m 7.6m 8g^5 8m Oct 28] 8,500Y, 12,000 2-y-o: workmanlike gelding: third foal: half-brother to German 1m winner Lady Lucent (by Glow): dam daughter of smart sprinter Easy Landing: poor form: well beaten in seller at Newmarket final start: stays 1m. *N. A. Graham* 46

BAIRN GLEN 4 ch.f. Bairn (USA) 126 – Rage Glen 67 (Grey Mirage 128) [1994 –: 8m 8m 5g 1995 7g Apr 22] smallish filly: no sign of ability. *G. R. Oldroyd* –

BAIZE 2 ch.f. (Feb 17) Efisio 120 – Bayonne 72 (Bay Express 132) [1995 5g* 5m* 5m^{3} 6m^{5} 6f^{4} Oct 12] rather unfurnished filly: unimpressive mover: first foal: dam suited by 5f: impressive 4-length winner of maiden at Warwick and minor event at Windsor in June: ran well afterwards in Molecomb Stakes at Goodwood, Lowther Stakes at York (upset in stalls) and Redcar Two-Year-Old Trophy (fourth of 26 behind Blue Iris): stays 6f: acts on firm ground. *R. F. Johnson Houghton* 94

BAJAN AFFAIR 5 b.m. Bold Owl 101 – Silvery Moon (Lorenzaccio 130) [1994 NR 1995 13g 14.1m 16.5f 10m Aug 3] leggy mare: poor maiden handicapper: sold out of Miss L. Siddall's stable 3,400 gns Doncaster July Sales after second start: stays 1¾m: acts on good to firm ground: tried blinkered: joined K. Loads. *J. R. Bostock* –

BAJAN FRONTIER (IRE) 3 ch.f. Imperial Frontier (USA) 112 – Sajanjal (Dance In Time (CAN)) [1994 60: 5g^{5} 6.1d 1995 5m 5g^{5} 5d^{3} 6f 5m a5g a5g* Dec 2] compact filly: easily best effort since debut when making all in handicap at Wolverhampton in December: suited by 5f: bandaged behind: front runner. *F. H. Lee* 41 a54

BAJAN (IRE) 4 b.g. Taufan (USA) 119 – Thatcherite (Final Straw 127) [1994 61: 10d 10d 8.1g^{6} 8m^{3} 8g 11.1g* 11.8m^{6} 10.4d 14s 13.8g 1995 10g^{5} 10m* 12f 10.1m* Jul 6] lengthy, good-bodied gelding: fair handicapper: won at Lingfield (amateurs) in May and Yarmouth (ladies, comfortably) in July: should stay 1½m: acts on good to firm ground: visored last 5 starts (winner first occasion, failed to repeat form) at 3 yrs: races prominently: inconsistent. *Lady Herries* 66

BAJAN ROSE 3 b.f. Dashing Blade 117 – Supreme Rose 95 (Frimley Park 109) [1994 86: 5m^{3} 5m^{3} 5g* 5f^{2} 6d* 6s^{4} 5m^{6} 1995 6m 6m 6m^{6} 6m 6m^{2} 5.2m^{5} 6g^{2} 6g 5d 5g^{5} 6d^{5} 6.1s* Oct 17] leggy filly: fair handicapper: narrowly won at Chepstow in October, holding on grimly having been clear over 1f out: stays 6f: acts on firm and soft ground: usually races prominently. *M. Blanshard* 78

BAKER 2 b.g. (Apr 28) Cigar 68 – Bread 'n Honey 51 (Goldhills Pride 105) [1995 6m 6m 5g^{3} 6m 7.3d Oct 21] 1,400Y: angular gelding: half-brother to 1993 2-y-o 6f winner Storm Regent (by Prince Sabo): dam lightly-raced half-sister to smart sprinter Prince Reymo: only worthwhile form (had greatly favoured far rail) when third to Standown in claimer at Sandown: should be suited by further than 5f: sold 1,300 gns Newmarket Autumn Sales. *H. Candy* 52 ?

BAKERS DAUGHTER 3 ch.f. Bairn (USA) 126 – Tawnais 80 (Artaius (USA) 129) [1994 48: 7m 6.9m 7m 6.1d 7m 1995 a8g* a10g^{2} a8.5g^{4} a8.5g 8g* a10g^{3} 8m a10g a12g a10g^{3} Dec 18] sparely-made filly: modest performer: won sellers at Southwell in February and Leicester in July: stays 1¼m: acts on all-weather surfaces, yet to race on extremes of going on turf: inconsistent. *J. R. Arnold* 51 a57

BAKERS' GATE (USA) 3 b. or br.c. Danzig (USA) – Alydaress (USA) 124 (Alydar (USA)) [1994 NR 1995 8m^{2} 8g^{3} May 19] robust colt: has a quick action: first living foal: dam very well bred Irish Oaks and Ribblesdale winner: shaped really well when length second of 11 to Mezaan in maiden at Doncaster: 11/10, didn't improve as anticipated at Newbury 10 days later, always close up: will stay 1¼m: seemed capable of better. *J. H. M. Gosden* 79 p

BAKHETA 3 b.f. Persian Bold 123 – Vielle 123 (Ribero 126) [1994 63p: 8.1g^{2} 1995 12m 8.3m 12s 10d 9m^{4} a10g a8g Dec 1] robust filly: generally disappointing maiden for new stable: should stay 1½m: acts on good to firm ground, probably on dead. *K. T. Ivory* 46

BALA MONAAFIS (IRE) 3 b.f. In The Wings 128 – Samya's Flame 97 (Artaius (USA) 129) [1994 NR 1995 12.1m 10d Sep 13] third foal: closely-related to fairly useful 1½m winner Raneen Alwatar (by Sadler's Wells): dam, 9f and 1¼m winner, sister to Flame of Tara (dam of Salsabil and Marju) and half-sister to dam of Northern Spur: well beaten in maidens at Chepstow and Sandown 3 months later. *W. R. Muir* –

BALANCE OF POWER 3 b.g. Ballacashtal (CAN) – Moreton's Martha (Derrylin 115) [1994 75: 6g 7m^{5} 6f^{3} 6m* 6m 7d^{6} 6g^{5} 6g^{4} 6m 1995 7g^{4} 7m^{6} 6m^{5} 7.1g^{5} 6f^{5} 6m 7d^{6} 6g^{3} Oct 16] useful-looking gelding: fair handicapper: should stay 1m: acts on good to firm ground: blinkered (respectable effort) final start: has run well when sweating: inconsistent. *R. Akehurst* 72

Maktoum Al Maktoum/Godolphin's "Balanchine"

BALANCHINE (USA) 4 ch.f. Storm Bird (CAN) 134 – Morning Devotion (USA) 102 (Affirmed (USA)) [1994 131: 8m[2] 12s* 12g* 1995 10m[5] 12d[2] 12d Oct 1] 119

Balanchine's failure to recapture her best form was one of the few major disappointments in Goldolphin's season; even then she did raise hopes of an Arc victory, and at least she has made it safely to stud. Balanchine suffered a life-threatening bout of colic while in training at Newmarket in 1994 only weeks after trouncing the colts in the Irish Derby; her two previous runs had resulted in a near-miss in the One Thousand Guineas and a win in the Oaks. She had to undergo a two-hour operation on her small intestine. When well enough to make the journey, she was sent to recuperate and spend the winter in Dubai and did not reappear in public until Royal Ascot, where she started odds on for the Prince of Wales's Stakes following glowing reports from the gallops. She looked to have done well physically from three to four but faded into fifth-of-six place. Her next run, in the Prix Foy at Longchamp in September, offered considerably more encouragement, since she lost only on the nod to Carnegie in a sprint up the straight; what's more all her old battling qualities seemed to be back. However, the anticipated improvement did not materialize in the Arc. She failed to take the eye beforehand and played no real part in the race, coming tenth of sixteen to Lammtarra, sympathetically handled when clearly held. At her best she would have gone close, to say the least.

Balanchine at her best was a very good filly indeed, superior to any of the middle-distance colts of 1994 on her running in the Irish Derby. King's Theatre and Colonel Collins, who had been placed at Epsom, couldn't hold a candle to her, and she won going away by four and a half lengths. She will be remembered for that, and

Balanchine (USA) (ch.f. 1991)	Storm Bird (CAN) (b 1978)	Northern Dancer (b 1961)	Nearctic
			Natalma
		South Ocean (b 1967)	New Providence
			Shining Sun
	Morning Devotion (USA) (ch 1982)	Affirmed (ch 1975)	Exclusive Native
			Won't Tell You
		Morning Has Broken (ch 1974)	Prince John
			A Wind Is Rising

for her win in the Oaks which gave Dettori his first classic. Balanchine, a tall, attractive filly with a fluent action, acted on good to firm ground and soft. Her pedigree was examined at length and in depth in *Racehorses of 1994*. To summarize, she is out of the useful middle-distance mare Morning Devotion and, therefore, closely related to the 1992 Sun Chariot Stakes winner Red Slippers (by Nureyev). Her grandam, the lightly-raced Morning Has Broken, is a half-sister to the multiple Grade 1 winner It's In The Air. Balanchine starts her new career with a visit to Mr Prospector. *Saeed bin Suroor*

BALANKA (IRE) 3 b.f. Alzao (USA) 117 – Banana Peel (Green Dancer (USA) 132) [1994 NR 1995 10v^2 8g* 10.5m^4 9g^3 10g* 9.3d^3 10f^4 Nov 26] sturdy filly: sixth foal: half-sister to 4 winners, including fairly useful middle-distance stayer Banour (by Arctic Tern): dam, winner in USA, half-sister to dam of Bering: smart performer: won minor event at Evry in May: around a length fourth of 12 to Carling in Prix de Diane at Chantilly, not clear run for much of straight then finishing strongly: narrowly won valuable listed race at Deauville in August: bandaged, creditable third of 11 to Timarida in Prix de l'Opera at Longchamp and 1¼ lengths equal-fourth of 14 to Duda in Matriarch Stakes at Hollywood Park in the autumn: likely to prove suited by 1½m: acts on firm ground and dead. *A. de Royer Dupre, France* — 116

BALASARA (IRE) 5 ch.g. Don't Forget Me 127 – Tameen (FR) (Pharly (FR) 130) [1994 83: 10m^2 10g^2 12m^4 11.7g^3 1995 8m^2 8m^2 9m^2 9d^2 9m^3 8d^2 a10g Nov 8] stocky gelding: fair maiden handicapper: placed all starts on turf in 1995: effective at 1m to 11.7f: acts on good to firm ground and dead, well beaten on equitrack: usually blinkered: pulls hard, carries head high and has flashed tail: often a front runner: refused to enter stalls on intended 5-y-o reappearance: ungenuine. *D. R. C. Elsworth* — 79 §

BAL HARBOUR 4 b.c. Shirley Heights 130 – Balabina (USA) 110 (Nijinsky (CAN) 138) [1994 103: 10.4f^4 16.2m 1995 12f^3 12g^4 12m^4 11.6m^2 12g^2 10m* Oct 12] good-bodied colt: good walker and fluent mover: has had his problems, but is a smart performer: 6 lengths third of 6 in Hardwicke Stakes at Royal Ascot and 4 lengths fourth of 9 in Princess of Wales's Stakes at Newmarket, both behind Beauchamp Hero: contested minor events afterwards, making all to win at Newmarket in October by a length from Warning Order: effective at 1¼m and should stay further than 1½m: acts on firm ground. *H. R. A. Cecil* — 110

BALIOS (IRE) 2 b.c. (May 14) Be My Guest (USA) 126 – Clifden Bottoms (Wolver Hollow 126) [1995 8.2m a8.5g^2 Dec 2] IR 12,000Y: tall, useful-looking colt: has plenty of scope: closely related to 2 winners by Fairy King, including 7f/9f performer Hamadryad, and half-brother to a winner abroad by Dalsaan: dam, Irish 8.5f winner, half-sister to dam of Waajib: made most when 1½ lengths second of 10 to Belle's Boy in maiden at Wolverhampton: will probably improve again. *M. Johnston* — 56 p

BALI TENDER 4 ch.g. Balidar 133 – Highest Tender 56 (Prince Tenderfoot (USA) 126) [1994 NR 1995 8.5d 7.5m 12.3f^5 a8g 6m^4 6f^5 7m 5g^6 Sep 2] 3,100Y and 2-y-o: strong gelding: sixth foal: half-brother to 2 winners, notably fairly useful 5.7f (at 2 yrs) and 7f winner Chili Heights (by Chilibang): dam plater: poor maiden handicapper: best efforts at 6f: acts on firm ground: twice withdrawn after giving trouble at stalls. *M. W. Easterby* — 36

BALLAD DANCER 10 ch.g. Ballad Rock 122 – Manx Image (Dancer's Image (USA)) [1994 59d: a8g a6g^4 a6g a7s 7d 6d^3 6g 7g 6s^5 7m^6 5.9v^5 7m^6 6f 7g^6 6m^5 6m 7f^4 5m 6.9m^4 5m^2 6f 6m^6 6f 6g a8g a8g a7g^6 1995 a7g a8.5g^5 a11g^6 Jan 20] lengthy gelding: very much on the downgrade. *J. Mackie* — – §

BALLAD RULER 9 ch.g. Ballad Rock 122 – Jessamy Hall 77 (Crowned Prince (USA) 128) [1994 –: a14.8g 14.1d 1995 a14g 17.2m 14.1m Oct 19] big, rangy gelding: of little account. *P. A. Pritchard* — –

BALLADUR (USA) 2 b.c. (May 3) Nureyev (USA) 131 – Ballinderry 112 (Irish River (FR) 131) [1995 7g^3 7f^4 Oct 25] rather unfurnished colt: sixth foal: brother to smart 1¼m winner Opera Score and half-brother to Prix du Jockey-Club winner Sanglamore (by Sharpen Up): dam won Ribblesdale Stakes: in frame in maidens won by Don Micheletto at Leicester (better effort) and Mawjud at Yarmouth (took good hold in falsely-run race and rather disappointing): will stay 1m: taken down early at Yarmouth. *H. R. A. Cecil* — 83 +

BALLARD LADY (IRE) 3 ch.f. Ballad Rock 122 – First Blush (Ela-Mana-Mou 132) [1994 46: 6f 6m 7g 6m 8g 7.1d^4 7.9d 1995 7.5m 8m 10m 8.1d* 7g 8g^5 12m^2 10.5m 10.4g^6 15g 10g^6 Sep 21] big, good-topped filly: shows a round action: poor handicapper: won at Haydock in June: no form last 4 starts: stays 1½m: acts on good to firm ground and dead: visored (stiff task) final 2-y-o start: inconsistent. *J. S. Wainwright* — 49

BALLARD RING (IRE) 4 ch.f. Ballad Rock 122 – Miss Victoria (Auction Ring (USA) 123) [1994 –: 8m 7.9f 10m 8m 1995 7.5m 8g 7f^5 9g 7.5g 7.5m 7g 10m^6 10g^3 10.5g 8.9g 10f Oct 24] good-topped filly: has a round action: only modest at best nowadays: stays 1¼m: went particularly well on an easy surface as 2-y-o: tried blinkered, no improvement: inconsistent: sold 13,000 gns Newmarket December Sales. *J. S. Wainwright* — 51

BALLESTRO (IRE) 3 b.g. Astronef 116 – Balaine (GER) (Balidar 133) [1994 42: 6f 7m a7g^5 6m 8s 1995 7m^6 a9.4g 8.3m 8.3m 8.3g^5 11.6m 8m a12g 16.4m Nov 6] leggy gelding: poor mover: looks a poor maiden at best: tried blinkered/visored, no improvement. *J. Ffitch-Heyes* — – §

BALL GOWN 5 b.m. Jalmood (USA) 126 – Relatively Smart 76 (Great Nephew 126) [1994 74, a–: a7g 10m^2 10.5m^3 8.2m* 10.2g* 8d* 10m* 9g^4 8m^5 10.1g 1995 10m^2 12g* 12f^6 12m^3 10m^{*dis} 10m^4 10m^3 10d^2 9g^2 10v 8m Oct 28] small, leggy mare: fairly useful handicapper, better than ever in 1995: first past post at Doncaster in May and Newmarket (squeezed through, disqualified) in July: career-best effort in Cambridgeshire at Newmarket (carried 4 lb overweight, beaten a head by Cap Juluca, finishing strongly) in September: probably needs good test at 9f nowadays, and stays 1½m: acts on good to firm ground and dead (won a seller on soft, seemed unsuited by heavy): no form in 3 races on all-weather: usually bandaged behind: usually held up. *D. T. Thom* — 88 a–

BALLINDALLOCH 3 b.f. Damister (USA) 123 – Loch Spey (Formidable (USA) 125) [1994 NR 1995 7m^4 7f^4 Aug 17] 1,100Y: first foal: dam seemed to stay 1¼m: signs of a little ability: dead. *T. J. Etherington* — –

BALLIOL BOY 3 b.c. Nashwan (USA) 135 – Fiesta Fun 105 (Welsh Pageant 132) [1994 80p: 8.2d* 1995 10m^3 11.5f^4 12m^4 May 28] quite attractive colt: good mover: closely related to Arc winner Saumarez (by Rainbow Quest): useful form: in frame in Classic Trial at Sandown (leading until well inside final 1f when 2 lengths third to Pentire), Derby Trial at Lingfield (beaten 1¾ lengths by Munwar) and Derby Italiano (2¼ lengths behind Luso) in the spring: had leg injury afterwards but should come back into training: stays 1½m: acts on firm ground (won maiden on dead). *H. R. A. Cecil* — 109

BALLPOINT 2 ch.c. (Mar 4) Indian Ridge 123 – Ballaquine 56 (Martinmas 128) [1995 6d 7g 7g^4 Oct 23] 13,000F: sturdy colt: poor mover: half-brother to smart 7f/1m performer Swing Low (by Swing Easy) and a winner abroad: dam won 1¼m seller: modest form in maidens: first home on favoured far side when fourth of 9 to Alhawa at Lingfield on final outing: stays 7f. *R. Hannon* — 62

BALLYHAYS (IRE) 6 ch.g. Glow (USA) – Relanca (Relic) [1994 51: 6d a8g^6 10s 9f 8.3m 8m^4 8.3m^2 8m^2 8s a11g 7g a6g a8.5g* 1995 a9.4g^5 a8.5g a8g a9.4g a8g a9.4g^3 a8g a9.4g 8g* 8f 8f 8m^5 8m 8.1g 7m 8d Sep 22] lengthy gelding: won selling handicap at Yarmouth in June: no comparable form in 1995: best form at around 1m: acts on all-weather, good to firm and soft ground: blinkered (well beaten) twice: inconsistent: sold (J. Harris to N. Ayliffe) 1,000 gns Doncaster November Sales. *J. A. Harris* — 48 d

BALLYKETT NANCY (IRE) 4 b.f. Hero's Honor (USA) – Last Flair (Busted 134) [1994 107: 10d 10d* 11s* 12f^6 10g^2 12s^6 8g 10m* 12d* 12.5d 10d* 10s^2 10v* 1995 12s^2 10d 12g* 10g^3 12m^2 10m^4 12g^2 12d 11d^2 10g Oct 30] tall, leggy filly: has a markedly round action: smart performer: won listed race (sixth success in such — 110 events) at Gowran Park in June: creditable efforts afterwards when placed, in 5-runner Blandford Stakes at the Curragh (length behind Humbel) penultimate start: stayed 1½m: acted on heavy going and good to firm: edgy (below form) both starts at Ascot: genuine: cracked pelvis final start, and destroyed. *J. S. Bolger, Ireland*

BALLYKISSANGEL 2 ro.g. (Feb 27) Hadeer 118 – April Wind 91 (Windjammer (USA)) [1995 6f 7.1d 6m Oct 30] 7,600Y: tall, leggy gelding: brother to a winner in Germany and half-brother to a winner in North America by Deputy Minister: dam Irish 2-y-o 5f winner: no form in maidens, off course 3½ months after debut. *N. Bycroft* –

BALLYMAC GIRL 7 gr.m. Niniski (USA) 125 – Alruccaba 83 (Crystal Palace (FR) 132) [1994 57: 15.1g* 12s* 1995 18g 16.2m^{4} 15.4g^{2} 14.1g a16g 16g^{5} 18.2g^{5} 14s* 16.1g^{3} 15.1s a14.8g* a14g a14.8g* a12g^{5} Dec 9] leggy, sparely-made mare: modest handicapper: none too consistent, but won at Haydock (apprentices) in September by 8 lengths and twice at Wolverhampton in November: stays well: acts on good to firm and soft ground and fibresand: bandaged of late: normally held up. *J. M. Bradley* 63

BALLYMONEY (IRE) 2 b.c. (Apr 11) Fayruz 116 – Blunted (Sharpen Up 127) [1995 6m^{6} a6g^{3} a6g^{2} a7g^{3} Dec 6] IR 6,400F, 5,000Y: sturdy colt: half-brother to French sprint winner Hellisharp Run (by Runnett) and 1m winner Apatlal (by Ahonoora): dam poor maiden: beaten around 2 lengths at most when placed in maidens at Southwell and Lingfield late in year: stays 7f: acts on all-weather surfaces. *W. A. O'Gorman* 69

BALLYNAKELLY 3 ch.g. Deploy 131 – Musical Charm (USA) 78 (The Minstrel (CAN) 135) [1994 8g^{6} 7.8d* 1995 8m 8.3g 8m 12.1d a12g* a13g* Dec 6] IR 2,200Y: strong, lengthy ex-Irish gelding: third foal: closely related to useful 1993 3-y-o middle-distance stayer Sea of Rocks (by Slip Anchor) and half-brother to French 1m winner Come To Life (by Rousillon): dam 7f winner: trained by J. G. Coogan at 2 yrs, awarded claimer at Dundalk: disappointing on turf here, but won apprentice event in November (backed from 8/1 to 5/2 favourite, by 10 lengths) then handicap in December (under 7-lb claimer), both at Lingfield: stays at least 13f, should get further: acts on dead ground, goes very well on equitrack. *R. Akehurst* 73

BALLYRANTER 6 ch.g. Bold Owl 101 – Whipalash 73 (Stephen George 102) [1994 68: 8g 8m 8m^{3} 8.1m^{3} 8.3f* 8.3m^{2} 8.2m 8d^{3} 8g^{4} 10d^{3} 10.1d* a12g^{2} a12g* 1995 a10g* a10g^{4} a12g^{4} a10g^{5} Mar 25] strong, workmanlike gelding: fair performer: won minor event at Lingfield in January: stays 1½m: acts on any going except heavy: visored nowadays. *H. J. Collingridge* 68

BALLYSHEILA 3 b.f. Ayres Rock 71 – Baltana 50 (Balidar 133) [1994 NR 1995 7g 5.1h 5f 5m^{5} Sep 5] sparely-made filly: first foal: dam 2-y-o 5f seller winner: of no account. *G. F. H. Charles-Jones* –

BALLYSOKERRY (IRE) 4 b.c. Hatim (USA) 121 – Wonder Woman (Horage 124) [1994 NR 1995 12g 10.4m Oct 5] robust colt: first live foal: dam never ran: poor form in NH Flat races: tailed off in claimers. *J. Parkes* –

BALLY WONDER 3 b.f. Music Boy 124 – Salacious (Sallust 134) [1994 55: 6g^{4} 6m^{4} 7m 6m 5d a7g^{5} a7g^{6} 1995 a7g^{3} a7g^{6} Feb 17] poor maiden: stays 7f: acts on good to firm ground and equitrack: has joined Mrs. E. Heath. *D. Morris* 46

BALMAHA 4 b.f. Absalom 128 – Mo Ceri 63 (Kampala 120) [1994 60, a53: a6g^{6} a7g^{2} a8g^{2} 6.9s^{2} a8g 1995 a9.4g Mar 4] strong filly: twice raced since March, 1994, and no form: sold 4,000 gns Ascot April Sales: stays 1m: best effort on soft going. *W. J. Haggas* –

BALMORAL PRINCESS 2 b.f. (May 11) Thethingaboutitis (USA) 106 – Fair Balmoral (Hasty Word 84) [1995 a7g Nov 11] fifth reported foal: dam ran once at 2 yrs and pulled up only start over jumps: 50/1, soundly-beaten ninth of 10 in maiden at Wolverhampton. *J. H. Peacock* –

BALNIBARBI 6 b.h. Rainbow Quest (USA) 134 – Balabina (USA) 110 (Nijinsky (CAN) 138) [1994 –: 10.3g 12.4g 16s 12m 1995 12.1v Mar 31] leggy horse: seems no longer of much account. *T. Dyer* –

BALOUSTAR (USA) 2 b.f. (Feb 12) Green Forest (USA) 134 – Ballerina Star (USA) (Forli (ARG)) [1995 7g^{3} 6.1m Oct 26] lengthy, unfurnished filly: first foal: dam twice-raced half-sister to high-class 6f to 9f performer Green Line Express (by –

Green Forest): well beaten in minor events at Leicester and (unruly stalls) Nottingham. *S. P. C. Woods*

BALPARE 2 ch.f. (Mar 24) Charmer 123 – Balinese 86 (Balidar 133) [1995 6m^3 7m a7g 6m* 5.3f^4 7.3m 6m 8h^3 7g 8g^5 8m 8m^4 a6g a8g^3 Nov 30] good-topped filly: seventh foal: half-sister to several winners, including 1m winner Trembalino (by Tremblant) and 12.2f to 2m winner Sir Thomas Beecham (by Daring March): dam suited by 7f: modest form: won median auction maiden at Epsom in July: better at 7f/1m than shorter: acts on hard ground and equitrack, below form on fibresand. *N. A. Callaghan* 60 a55

BALRATH CROSS (IRE) 4 gr.g. Roi Danzig (USA) – Dawn Echo (Don (ITY) 123) [1994 NR 1995 a7g Feb 7] IR 32,000F: half-brother to 4 winners, including useful 6f and 7f winner Dawn Success (by Caerleon): dam no sign of ability: no sign of ability over hurdles or (blinkered) in maiden at Lingfield. *R. P. C. Hoad* –

BALTIC DREAM (USA) 2 b.f. (Feb 14) Danzig Connection (USA) – Ascot Princess (USA) (Vanlandingham (USA)) [1995 7g* 7.6m^3 7d Sep 26] $34,000F, IR 32,000Y: tall, lengthy filly: has scope: first foal: dam unraced half-sister to Petit Loup and Ascot Knight (both by Danzig): won median auction maiden at Leicester in August: rather disappointing afterwards in 3-runner minor event at Lingfield and 18-runner nursery at Newmarket: stays 7f: takes keen hold. *K. R. Burke* 77

BALTIC RAIDER 3 b. or br.g. Polish Precedent (USA) 131 – Sassalya (Sassafras (FR) 135) [1994 95: 5.1m^2 7g* 7m* 7m^6 1995 8g 10m^5 8g^4 Apr 22] lengthy gelding: useful form in conditions events, 3½ lengths fourth to Moments of Fortune in Thirsk Classic Trial: subsequently gelded: stays 1¼m: yet to race on a soft surface. *G. Wragg* 95

BALUTEER (IRE) 2 ch.c. (Mar 8) Ballad Rock 122 – Sweetsider (USA) (Topsider (USA)) [1995 5m^5 Apr 7] IR 13,000F: brother to 3-y-o Caddican and half-brother to several winners in Ireland and USA: dam won at around 9f at 2 yrs in USA: fifth of 8 in maiden at Lingfield: dead. *M. R. Channon* –

BALZINO (USA) 6 ch.g. Trempolino (USA) 135 – Royal Procession (USA) (Lyphard (USA) 132) [1994 59: 14g 12g^5 14.1m^4 14.6m 14.1m* 14.8f* 1995 16.1g 13.1g^5 12g^3 14.1f^6 12f^5 13.1g^4 Jul 16] sturdy, lengthy gelding: lost his way on flat: won selling hurdle in November but refused to race later in month: joined H. Alexander. *N. Tinkler* 38

BAMBARA 3 b.f. Old Vic 136 – Babita 107 (Habitat 134) [1994 51p: 7.5f 1995 a10g^5 12g* 11.4m^6 May 10] smallish filly: narrowly won maiden at Thirsk in April: easily best effort when sixth of 7 to Dance A Dream in Cheshire Oaks: stays 1½m: sold only 5,000 gns Newmarket December Sales. *C. E. Brittain* 82

BANADAM (USA) 3 ch.c. Bering 136 – Madame Alydar (USA) (Alydar (USA)) [1994 NR 1995 8d^2 7m^2 8m^4 7.1g* May 27] rather leggy colt: third foal: half-brother to a winner in North America by Palace Music: dam unplaced: fair performer: won maiden at Haydock in May, leading over 1f out and driven clear: stayed 1m: sometimes wore bandages behind: dead. *B. Hanbury* 79

BANBURY FLYER 7 b.g. Mummy's Game 120 – Haddon Anna (Dragonara Palace (USA) 115) [1994 44: a6g a5g 6m^5 6.1m 5.1f^4 5m^5 5.1m^5 5m^5 5m a6g 1995 a5g^4 a6g Feb 4] smallish gelding: poor handicapper: sold 850 gns Ascot February Sales: stays 6f: acts on firm ground, dead and equitrack: tried blinkered/visored, below form: inconsistent. *Mrs A. L. M. King* – a29

BANDAR PERAK 4 b.g. Aragon 118 – Noire Small (USA) (Elocutionist (USA)) [1994 65: 8s 10g^3 10s* 10s^3 12s* 12s^6 a12g^5 12g 16.4m 1995 14.9d 14d 11.9g Sep 20] rangy gelding: well beaten for new stable in 1995. *M. J. Haynes* –

BANDITA 4 ch.f. Chilibang 120 – La Carlotta (Ela-Mana-Mou 132) [1994 42: a6g^6 a6g 5s^3 6d 6m^4 7g 7m a5g 1995 a7g^5 a10g a12g^4 a12g^4 a12g^5 a12g 10m^6 8h^3 10.2h^6 Aug 18] smallish filly: poor maiden: trained until after sixth 4-y-o start by Miss A. Whitfield: seems effective at 1m and 1½m: acts on any going, including all-weather: blinkered (well beaten) second 3-y-o start. *D. J. S. ffrench Davis* 44

BANDIT BOY 2 gr.g. (Mar 12) Robellino (USA) 127 – Patraana (Nishapour (FR) 125) [1995 7f Jul 26] leggy, unfurnished gelding: fourth foal: brother to a winner in Hungary: dam never ran: 25/1, always behind in maiden at Doncaster: sold 1,050 gns Newmarket September Sales and gelded. *J. M. P. Eustace* –

BANDIT GIRL 2 b.f. (Mar 8) Robellino (USA) 127 – Manx Millenium 66 (Habitat 134) [1995 6s Oct 6] lengthy filly: half-sister to very useful 5f to 7f performer Blue Siren (by Bluebird), 9f winner Northern Habit (by Salmon Leap) and a winner in France: dam placed at 1m: 14/1 and very in need of race, always well behind in 11-runner maiden at Ascot: moved short to post. *I. A. Balding* –

BAND ON THE RUN 8 ch.h. Song 132 – Sylvanecte (FR) 70 (Silver Shark 129) [1994 90: 8m 7d* 7d 7.1g^4 7.9f 7g^5 8.1d 8m 7.1m 8.1m 7.3g^5 7.1g* 7g 7d 1995 7m 7m 7.1m^6 7m 7.3g^3 8.1g^3 7.1m* 8.1f^5 7.1d^3 8d* 7d 8m a9.4g Dec 2] good-topped horse: carries condition: poor mover: useful handicapper: won rated stakes at Haydock in July and £19,000 event (under 9-13, caught Scaraben close home) at Doncaster in September: below form in good company afterwards: effective at 7f to 1m: acts on firm and dead ground: has won in blinkers, but below form last 6 attempts in them: tough. *B. A. McMahon* 98

BANG IN TROUBLE (IRE) 4 b.g. Glenstal (USA) 118 – Vaguely Deesse (USA) (Vaguely Noble 140) [1994 69: 12.3d^6 12v^2 14.1m^4 15d^2 15s^2 1995 17.5g^5 14s 16m 15.1s^5 Nov 2] close-coupled gelding: good walker: staying maiden handicapper: below his best in 1995: acts on good to firm ground, best effort on soft: tried once (at 2 yrs, ran poorly) on fibresand: held up. *J. J. O'Neill* 56

BANGLES 5 ch.m. Chilibang 120 – Vague Lass 85 (Vaigly Great 127) [1994 73: 5f^3 5.1m* 5m^3 5g^6 5g^5 a5g^5 a5g 1995 5.1h^2 5m 5m* 5.1d^3 5g 6g 5m Nov 4] workmanlike mare: good mover: fair handicapper: won at Salisbury in August, making all: stays 6f: acts on hard and dead ground, yet to race on soft: visored (well beaten) final 4-y-o start: usually races prominently. *Lord Huntingdon* 73

BANNER (USA) 3 b.f. Known Fact (USA) 135 – Abeer (USA) 115 (Dewan (USA)) [1994 71p: 6m^4 6s^4 6m^3 1995 6m^4 7g^6 6m^2 7f* 7m 6g^6 Sep 1] leggy, quite attractive filly: fair performer: won 4-runner maiden at Thirsk (sweating, made all) in July: ran creditably on 4 of her other 5 outings: will prove best at up to 7f: acts on firm and soft ground: sold 14,000 gns Newmarket December Sales. *B. W. Hills* 75

BANZHAF (USA) 2 ch.c. (Mar 22) Rare Performer (USA) – Hang On For Effer (USA) (Effervescing (USA)) [1995 6g^6 a7g* a6g^4 Dec 6] $37,000Y: fifth foal: half-brother to 3 winners in USA, one minor stakes placed at 2 yrs: dam maiden in USA: sire useful sprinter: well backed all outings, winning maiden at Lingfield in November: better suited by 7f than 6f: acts on equitrack: very keen to post (not discredited) final start. *G. L. Moore* 75

BARAHIN (IRE) 6 b.g. Diesis 133 – Red Comes Up (USA) (Blushing Groom (FR) 131) [1994 60d: a10g^2 a10g^3 11.7g^2 10g 11.6d 10.2m 10m 10.1m 11.5g a10g 1995 a10g a10g^4 a10g*^{dis} 9.7f 12m Sep 7] rangy, attractive gelding: good mover: trained by M. Dixon first 2 starts in 1995: worthwhile form since April, 1994 only when disqualified winner (failed dope test) of seller at Lingfield in March: stays 11.7f: acts on good to firm ground, soft and equitrack: visored (out of form) once as 5-y-o: carries head high: not one to rely on. *J. J. Bridger* – § a56 §

BARATO 4 ch.g. Efisio 120 – Tentraco Lady 65 (Gay Fandango (USA) 132) [1994 66+: 6g* 6v^4 6d 6.9v^5 7m 8m 6m^5 6f^6 6m^4 6g^5 6f* 6g 7g 7m 1995 6g 6m^2 5g 6g* 6m^4 6m^2 6m^4 6.1m^4 5m^3 5m 6g 6g^3 6s 6d 6f Oct 23] sturdy gelding: fair handicapper: won at Ayr in June and ran creditably most other starts in July/August: claimer ridden and below form last 3 starts, meeting trouble in running on first 2 of them: effective at 5f to 7f: acts on firm going, possibly unsuited by a soft surface: sometimes bandaged near-hind/bandaged: well beaten in visor: usually held up: sometimes carries head high. *Mrs J. R. Ramsden* 76

BARBAROJA 4 ch.g. Efisio 120 – Bias 108 (Royal Prerogative 119) [1994 –: 8g^5 1995 10.4g^6 8g^5 May 29] good-topped gelding: unimpressive mover: useful performer at 2 yrs: very lightly raced and no form since, blinkered in 1995: stays 1¼m: acts on dead ground: has been gelded. *J. G. FitzGerald* –

BARBASON 3 ch.c. Polish Precedent (USA) 131 – Barada (USA) (Damascus (USA)) [1994 NR 1995 8d 10g Sep 29] compact colt: fifth foal: half-brother to 2 winners, notably fairly useful Pica (1½m, by Diesis): dam well bred but lightly raced: well beaten in maidens at Leicester and Goodwood (showed quick action) over 5½ months later: sold 3,200 gns Ascot December Sales. *J. R. Fanshawe* –

BARBEZIEUX 8 b.h. Petong 126 – Merchantmens Girl 58 (Klairon 131) [1994 48: 5d^3 6g 5v* 5f 5s 5.9m 5g 1995 5m 5m May 19] strong, workmanlike horse: poor –

sprint handicapper: never going pace in 1995: sold 1,150 gns Doncaster July Sales: acts on good to firm ground, heavy and fibresand: tried blinkered (not since 6 yrs), visored (well beaten) final 7-y-o start: often claimer ridden: often bandaged: slowly away. *M. Dods*

BARBRALLEN 3 b.f. Rambo Dancer (CAN) 107 – Barrie Baby 86 (Import 127) 38 [1994 –: 6g 7m 1995 8m 8.5m 10m 7m^5 7g a7g Nov 8] workmanlike filly: poor maiden handicapper: should stay at least 1m: early to post. *D. J. S. ffrench Davis*

BARDIA 5 b.m. Jalmood (USA) 126 – Bauhinia 70 (Sagaro 133) [1994 35: 9.9d 38 10g 10m^5 10m 10m* 10g^3 12m^5 11g^6 10m 10.1m 11.1g^6 1995 a12g 10.9m^3 12.4g 10g^2 10m 10f^4 10m^3 11f^2 10m 10m^3 11.1g^6 11f^4 10f Oct 31] small, lengthy mare: poor handicapper: effective at 1¼m, stays 1½m: acts on dead going and firm: held up: none too consistent. *Don Enrico Incisa*

BARDOLPH (USA) 8 b.g. Golden Act (USA) – Love To Barbara (USA) 79 d (Stevward) [1994 83: 18.7m^5 16s 20m^2 16m^4 20f^3 18g^3 18m 16.5v 1995 16m^3 18.7m 17.2m^6 20m 14f^3 18.2m^6 17.2f* 20f a16g^2 16.4m Aug 18] compact gelding: only a fair handicapper in 1995, best effort first outing: won at Bath in July: needs a test of stamina: acts on equitrack and firm and dead ground (has won on soft, though no form last 4 outings on it): effective blinkered or not: has run well when sweating. *P. F. I. Cole*

BARDON HILL BOY (IRE) 3 br.g. Be My Native (USA) 122 – Star With A 80 Glimer (Montekin 125) [1994 NR 1995 a10g* a10g^5 12.3m^6 a9.4g* 10m^4 10.1m a9.4g^3 11.9m^5 10m^2 10.3d^4 9.2g Sep 24] IR 2,000Y, 8,200 2-y-o: leggy, lengthy gelding: third foal: dam never ran: fairly useful handicapper: won at Lingfield (maiden) in January and Wolverhampton in May: ran well afterwards when in frame: will prove best at up to around 1¼m: acts on the all-weather, good to firm and dead ground: moved poorly to post (below form) eighth start. *B. Hanbury*

BARFORD LAD 8 b.g. Nicholas Bill 125 – Grace Poole (Sallust 134) [1994 70: 62 10d 10d^2 10.3m^2 9s^3 10m^3 10g^4 10m^3 10.1d^5 9g 1995 10.3m^5 May 9] good-topped gelding: fair handicapper: not clearest of runs only start in 1995: stays 1½m: acts on any going: not blinkered (has won in them) nor visored since 6 yrs: often sweats: often early to post nowadays: sometimes drifts and finds little under pressure: fair winning hurdler. *J. R. Fanshawe*

BARFORD SOVEREIGN 3 b.f. Unfuwain (USA) 131 – Barford Lady 93 72 (Stanford 121§) [1994 65p: 7m 8d 1995 8m^6 9.9m^2 10m^3 12m^3 11.5m^3 Jul 16] lengthy filly: has a light action: fair maiden handicapper: stays 1½m, may well stay further: all but one start on good to firm ground: has run well when sweating: consistent. *J. R. Fanshawe*

BARGASH 3 ch.g. Sharpo 132 – Anchor Inn 48 (Be My Guest (USA) 126) [1994 71 58: 7g a7g a7g a8.5g 1995 7g^2 a7g^6 6m 6m^4 6m* 6.1m 6f^2 7m 6m 7m 7m 5.1d^5 6g Sep 22] sturdy gelding: fair handicapper: won at Warwick in July: stays 7f: acts on firm and dead ground: blinkered (ran creditably, poorly) last 2 starts: inconsistent. *P. D. Evans*

BARIK (IRE) 5 b.g. Be My Guest (USA) 126 – Smoo 84 (Kris 135) [1994 a5g^5 58 a7g 1995 a6g^3 a6g^2 a8g^2 a10g^6 a7g* a5g^3 7g 6d a6g Sep 30] small, sturdy, attractive gelding: good mover: sent to UAE at 3 yrs: trained by K. McLaughlin, won handicap at Jebel Ali in March: bought 16,000 gns Newmarket July Sales: soundly beaten on return: stays 1m: acts on soft going and the sand: sold 3,300 gns Doncaster November Sales. *Mrs A. Swinbank*

BARK'N'BITE 3 b.g. Reprimand 122 – Tree Mallow 71 (Malicious) [1994 52p: 54 6f 7f 8f 10s^5 8s 8s^4 7d^6 1995 12m^3 14.6m^6 14.1m 13f^3 12.1m* 12m* 13f^4 14.1m 15g^5 Sep 14] workmanlike gelding: has a long stride: modest handicapper: successful in smallish fields at Hamilton (maiden contest) and Pontefract (made all) in July: needs at least 1½m and should be suited by test of stamina: acts on good to firm ground and soft. *Mrs M. Reveley*

BARNABY WILLOW 3 ch.g. Dominion 123 – Joli's Girl 79 (Mansingh (USA) – 120) [1994 –: 7g 8s^6 7g 1995 12m May 7] plain gelding: no form: sold (M. Ryan to B. Mactaggart) 1,050 gns Doncaster November Sales. *M. J. Ryan*

BARONESS BLIXEN 2 b.f. (Apr 11) Cyrano de Bergerac 120 – Provocation 66 56 ? (Kings Lake (USA) 133) [1995 5m^2 5g 6s 6g Oct 16] 8,500Y: quite attractive filly:

fourth foal: half-sister to modest 8.5f and 1½m winner Kings Cay (by Taufan) and winners in Macau and Italy: dam maiden best at 6f: running-on second of 5 in median auction maiden at Thirsk in August: well beaten afterwards: acts on good to firm ground. *D. J. G. Murray Smith*

BARONESS GOLD 2 ch.f. (Apr 27) Ron's Victory (USA) 129 – Baroness Gymcrak 53§ (Pharly (FR) 130) [1995 6f 7f^5 6m Aug 28] 4,100F: leggy filly: second foal: dam, ungenerous sprint maiden, half-sister to Domynsky: poor form in sellers in August: bandaged behind on final outing. *M. H. Easterby* –

BARON FERDINAND 5 ch.g. Ferdinand (USA) – In Perpetuity 90 (Great Nephew 126) [1994 109: 10g 10m^2 10m^2 10m^4 10m^3 12d^5 1995 10m* 10m* 10m^2 10g* 10.5f^4 Aug 5] strong, lengthy gelding: fine mover: has improved in each of his 4 seasons, and (gelded prior to 1995) is now a smart performer: won minor event at Newmarket (impressively) and listed race at Goodwood (always travelling best) in May and Tennents Scottish Classic at Ayr in July, last-named by a length from Captain Horatius (gave 5 lb): also good second to Marildo in La Coupe at Evry in June: should prove as effective at 1½m as 1¼m: acts on good to firm ground (below form on firm final start), raced only once on a soft surface since his 2-y-o days: wears crossed noseband and sometimes bandages: sometimes early to post: held up (settled much better in 1995) and has turn of foot. *R. Charlton* 114

BARON HRABOVSKY 2 ch.g. (Apr 4) Prince Sabo 123 – Joli's Girl 79 (Mansingh (USA) 120) [1995 6.9g 8f Oct 24] 19,000F, 12,000Y: unfurnished gelding: fourth foal: brother to useful 6f (at 2 yrs) and 1m winner Joli's Princess and half-brother to 13f and 1¾m winner Side Bar (by Mummy's Game): dam 9f winner stayed 1½m: well beaten in maiden auction at Folkestone and maiden at Leicester (bandaged behind). *P. F. I. Cole* –

BAROSKI 4 b.g. Petoski 135 – Gohar (USA) (Barachois (CAN)) [1994 –: a8g^3 a7g^5 a9.4g a12g 8.5m 1995 a12g^4 a16g a12g 16.2m^4 16.2g 12f Oct 14] smallish gelding: no worthwhile form: tried blinkered. *J. L. Harris* –

BAROSSA VALLEY (IRE) 4 b.g. Alzao (USA) 117 – Night of Wind 101 (Tumble Wind (USA)) [1994 81: 7m 6f 7.3g^6 5.6g 6g^4 6.1g 1995 5.1m^4 6g 5.2f^4 5f 6m Aug 11] robust, attractive gelding: impresses in appearance: fair handicapper: ideally suited by further than 5f, and stays 7f: has raced only on a sound surface: effective blinkered or not. *P. W. Chapple-Hyam* 77

BARRANAK (IRE) 3 b.g. Cyrano de Bergerac 120 – Saulonika 94 (Saulingo 122) [1994 NR 1995 8.1g 5g^5 6.1d a6g Nov 6] compact, deep-bodied gelding: ninth reported foal: half-brother to 3 winning sprinters by Millfontaine, notably fairly useful Aughfad: dam 2-y-o 5f winner: promising staying-on fifth of 13 in claimer at 58 ?

Tennents Scottish Classic, Ayr—Baron Ferdinand wins Scotland's only pattern race, from Captain Horatius

Sandown in September: well beaten in minor event and handicap afterwards: almost certainly a sprinter. *Mrs M. McCourt*

BARREL OF HOPE 3 b.c. Distant Relative 128 – Musianica 92 (Music Boy 124) [1994 71: 6d^{6} 6s^{4} a7g* a7g 1995 8m^{2} 7m^{3} 8m 8g^{5} a6g 7.5g 7.1g 7g^{2} 7d* 8.2m^{4} a7g Nov 24] sturdy colt: good walker: fair handicapper: blinkered and best efforts in October, winning 27-runner apprentice event at Newbury: stays 1m: acts on good to firm and soft ground and has won on fibresand: blinkered last 4 starts: often makes running. *J. L. Eyre*
79 a–

BARRICADE (USA) 2 b.c. (Feb 19) Riverman (USA) 131 – Balleta (USA) 87 (Lyphard (USA) 132) [1995 6m* 5.5g^{3} 6g^{3} 7s^{5} Sep 17] first foal: dam, won 4 races at 1m to 1¼m in USA and England, is sister to Dancing Brave and Prix de Diane/Prix Vermeille winner Jolypha: useful French colt: won newcomers event at Evry in June: neck third of 8 to Lucky Lionel in Prix Robert Papin at Maisons-Laffitte and never-nearer 1¾ lengths third of 8 to Tagula in Prix Morny at Deauville: disappointing in Prix de la Salamandre on soft ground at Longchamp, travelling well but finding little in straight: bred to be suited by much further than 6f. *A. Fabre, France*
111

BARRIYAH 3 b.f. Kris 135 – Jathibiyah (USA) 89 (Nureyev (USA) 131) [1994 NR 1995 6m 7m 7m^{4} 6d 6g Oct 16] big, angular filly: first foal: dam, 2-y-o 7f winner closely related to Irish 1000 Guineas winner Ensconse, from good family: off course 3½ months, worthwhile form only when fading fourth of 13 in maiden at Lingfield: sold 15,000 gns Newmarket December Sales. *H. Thomson Jones*
50

BARTI-DDU 4 b.g. Mister Majestic 122 – Grugiar (Red Sunset 120) [1994 63: a8g^{2} a12g^{2} a12g^{2} 10.3f a12g^{3} a7g^{4} a12g* a14.8g^{6} a9.4g^{4} a12g^{5} a12g^{5} 1995 a11g* a11g^{5} a11g^{3} 12.1v* 12.3m^{6} a12g^{4} 14.1g^{5} a12g* a12g^{3} a14g^{4} a14.8g* 12d a12g^{6} Sep 30] workmanlike gelding: good walker: modest handicapper: won at Southwell in January, Hamilton (minor event) in March and Wolverhampton in June and August: stays 14.8f: has raced almost exclusively on fibresand, but clearly acts on heavy ground: runs some poor races, but is game in a finish: sold 17,000 gns Newmarket Autumn Sales. *S. C. Williams*
61

BARTON HEIGHTS 3 b.g. Primitive Rising (USA) 113 – Changatre 76 (Malinowski (USA) 123) [1994 –: 7.1m 7s 1995 10f^{2} Aug 5] unfurnished gelding: 25/1 and ridden by 7-lb claimer, 1½ lengths second of 7 in claimer at Redcar, finishing strongly having got well behind: will be well suited by further than 1¼m: should improve. *Mrs M. Reveley*
57 p

BASHFUL BRAVE 4 ch.g. Indian Ridge 123 – Shy Dolly 74 (Cajun 120) [1994 –: 5.3m 5d 5m 1995 5m* 5m^{2} 5m* 5f^{6} 5f* 5m* 5m^{2} 5.2m 5.3f^{2} 5m 5d Sep 18] smallish gelding: fair 5f handicapper: mostly in good form in 1995 for new stable, winning 3 times at Folkestone (first of them in a minor event) and once at Warwick by early-July: acts on firm ground, possibly unsuited by a soft surface: usually races prominently. *J. W. Payne*
76

BASHTHEBOARDS 2 b.g. (Apr 1) Dancing Dissident (USA) 119 – Vilanika (FR) 81 (Top Ville 129) [1995 7.1s 7m Oct 20] 6,600Y: leggy, unfurnished gelding: first foal: dam stayed 1m: mid-divison in maidens at Haydock and (slowly away, late progress) Doncaster: will stay 1m. *J. J. Quinn*
– p

BASOOD (USA) 2 b.f. (Mar 21) Woodman (USA) 126 – Basoof (USA) 83 (Believe It (USA)) [1995 6f^{3} 7g 8m Oct 20] leggy filly: sixth foal: half-sister to 3-y-o Reaganesque (by Nijinsky) and 1993 French 2-y-o 7f winner Melting Gold (by Cadeaux Genereux) later useful at up to 1m: dam, 1m winner, half-sister to Shadeed: modest form in maidens: seems to stay 1m. *E. A. L. Dunlop*
60

BASSETLAW BELLE 6 b.m. Lucky Wednesday 124 – Delayed Action 113 (Jolly Jet 111) [1994 –: a5s 1995 a7g^{4} a8g^{6} Jan 9] leggy mare: bad maiden: should stay 1m: acts on fibresand. *N. P. Littmoden*
19

BASSMAAT (USA) 4 b.f. Cadeaux Genereux 131 – Mangayah (USA) 115 (Spectacular Bid (USA)) [1994 71+: 7g* 7g^{3} 1995 a7g 8s^{4} 7.6m 7.1d 8g 8d Sep 27] leggy filly: has a rather round action: trained until after second 4-y-o start by Mrs L. Piggott: ran creditably next outing, but well below form afterwards: will prove best at up to 1m: acts on good to firm and soft going, well beaten only start on the all-weather. *W. J. Haggas*
71 d

BATAAN (USA) 4 b.c. Manila (USA) – Comtesse de Loir (FR) 131 (Val de Loir 133) [1994 78: 10d^6 10d^3 10.4d^2 10d^4 1995 10m 8.2d Sep 19] rangy colt: carries condition: unimpressive mover: fair maiden: well below form at Nottingham in 1995, off course 4½ months in between starts: should stay 1½m: acts on dead ground: sold 4,600 gns Doncaster October Sales. *Mrs J. Cecil*

–

BATABANOO 6 ch.g. Bairn (USA) 126 – For Instance (Busted 134) [1994 79: a12g* 12m* 12.1m^6 15m* 12m 14.6d 1995 12f* 15g^4 12f^2 14.1m^2 14.1g^5 Sep 23] leggy, sparely-made gelding: has a quick action: smart hurdler: fairly useful handicapper on flat, better than ever in 1995: narrowly won Cumberland Plate (for second year running) at Carlisle in June: stays 15f: acts on firm ground and fibresand, respectable effort on dead: held up: genuine. *Mrs M. Reveley*

85

BATHILDE (IRE) 2 ch.f. (Feb 28) Generous (IRE) 139 – Bex (USA) 116 (Explodent (USA)) [1995 7m^5 Oct 28] smallish, leggy filly: second foal: dam 1m to 10.5f winner at 3 yrs: 50/1, 5½ lengths fifth of 19 to Awaamir in maiden at Newmarket, outpaced 2f out then staying on: will improve, particularly over 1m+. *M. R. Stoute*

72 p

BATH KNIGHT 2 b.g. (Apr 4) Full Extent (USA) 113 – Mybella Ann (Anfield 117) [1995 5.3m^4 5g^3 5.3f^2 5g^3 5g 5.1f 5.3f 7.1m 8m^2 a7g^5 a10g a8.5g^2 a8g Dec 15] strong, lengthy gelding: first foal: dam little sign of ability: appeared to show vast improvement when 3½ lengths second of 9 to Tart in maiden at Wolverhampton in December, making much of running: stays 8.5f: well suited by fibresand (seems only plating-class on turf/equitrack): visored (well beaten) fifth outing: has worn bandages behind: has sometimes looked a tricky ride. *D. J. S. ffrench Davis*

44 +
a65 ?

BATON BLEU 4 b.g. Music Boy 124 – Fair Eleanor (Saritamer (USA) 130) [1994 –: a5g^5 a6g 5g 5s^6 5v a5g 1995 a5g a5g^4 a5g 5d 5m May 12] sturdy gelding: poor maiden: should stay 6f: inconsistent: sold 1,200 gns Newmarket July Sales. *P. Howling*

–
a39

BATOUTOFTHEBLUE 2 br.c. (May 21) Batshoof 122 – Action Belle (Auction Ring (USA) 123) [1995 7.1d 7m Oct 20] 10,000Y: big, strong colt: poor walker: half-brother to 2 winners: dam sister to Meis-El-Reem: behind in maidens: dead. *W. W. Haigh*

–

BATTERY BOY 3 b.g. K-Battery 108 – Bonny's Pet 55 (Mummy's Pet 125) [1994 58: 6f^5 6f 7m^3 7m 7g^4 7.9d 1995 12.4g^5 10f 10.5d 8f 15.1g^5 Sep 18] useful-looking gelding: no worthwhile form in 1995: bred to stay at least 1¼m: blinkered last 3 starts. *C. W. C. Elsey*

–

BATTLE COLOURS (IRE) 6 b.g. Petorius 117 – Streamertail 81 (Shirley Heights 130) [1994 68: 7.5d 8s 8m^6 8g 7f^3 8m 7m* 8d 7g^4 7d 8s^6 a7g^5 8.2g^3 a8g* a8g^4 a8.5g^6 1995 a8g^2 a8g^4 a7g^2 a7g^4 a8g^2 a7g^2 8d^5 a8g 8.9m 8g 8m^2 8.3f^3 6.9h^2 8m^5 7d 7g 8.2m Oct 19] smallish, quite attractive gelding: poor mover: modest performer: sold out of Mrs J. Ramsden's stable 5,400 gns Doncaster May Sales after eighth start: inconsistent for new yard: stays 8.5f: acts on firm ground, soft and all-weather surfaces: tried blinkered (not for present trainer), no improvement: usually races prominently. *Don Enrico Incisa*

64 d

BATTLE DORE (USA) 2 b.c. (Feb 22) Sanglamore (USA) 126 – Nashmeel (USA) 121 (Blushing Groom (FR) 131) [1995 7g^2 8d* 9d^2 Oct 5] fourth foal: half-brother to 3 winners, including French 3-y-o 7.5f (at 2 yrs) and 1m winner Light Music (by Nijinsky): dam, French 1m winner, stayed 1¼m: useful French colt: won listed Criterium de l'Ouest at Craon in September: ¾-length second of 5 to Go Between in Prix de Conde at Longchamp last time: will stay at least 1¼m: may improve further. *A. Fabre, France*

110

BATTLESHIP BRUCE 3 b.g. Mazilier (USA) 107 – Quick Profit 78 (Formidable (USA) 125) [1994 72p: 6g 7m a7g 10s* 8.3g* a8g* 1995 a8g* a8g^2 a8.5g^4 10m 8m 8m 10g^4 11.4d 8d 9.7g^2 9m^5 Oct 27] sturdy gelding: unimpressive mover: fair performer: won minor event and should have won handicap (eased, caught post) at Lingfield in January: should stay beyond 1¼m: acts on soft ground (probably on good to firm) and on equitrack (well beaten both starts on fibresand): wears bandages behind. *N. A. Callaghan*

67
a76

BATTY'S ISLAND 6 b.g. Town And Country 124 – Just Something (Good Times (ITY)) [1994 NR 1995 16.2m^4 Aug 24] first foal: dam poor maiden: won 2

–

NH Flat races in 1993/4: fair jumper at best (has broken blood vessels): tailed-off last of 4 in maiden at Beverley on flat debut. *B. Preece*

BAWADER (USA) 3 b.f. Danzig (USA) – Michelle Mon Amour (USA) (Best Turn (USA)) [1994 6g^6 6v^2 6g* 1995 7s^3 7d^3 6m^3 6f 7g 6m^5 6d 7g^3 Oct 28] $400,000Y: rangy filly: fifth reported foal: sister to 2 winners, including smart American horse Posen, best at 1m to 1¼m: dam stakes-placed winner of 5 races: fairly useful performer: won maiden at Naas at 2 yrs: stayed 7f: acted on good to firm ground (not best of runs in Wokingham on firm), probably on heavy: blinkered from fourth 3-y-o start: consistent: visits Warning. *D. K. Weld, Ireland* 87

BAYBEEJAY 8 b.m. Buzzards Bay 128§ – Peak Condition (Mountain Call 125) [1994 –: 13.1f 1995 a16g Feb 6] lengthy, leggy mare: poor winning hurdler: bad maiden on flat: blinkered twice. *R. Brotherton* –

BAYDUR (IRE) 4 b.g. Danehill (USA) 126 – Sutton Place 105 (Tyrant (USA)) [1994 7g* 8d 1995 8v 8s 7m* 8m 9m^2 7m* 6m^3 7f^4 6g^3 7m* 8d Oct 14] IR 42,000Y: workmanlike gelding: half-brother to Desmond Stakes winner Sunstart (by Hello Gorgeous): dam won Coronation Stakes and is half-sister to Nikoli: progressed with virtually every start and is a useful performer: won maiden at Fairyhouse at 3 yrs and handicaps at Naas in May, the Curragh in July and Fairyhouse (best effort) in September: stays 9f: acts on firm ground, seemingly not on a soft surface: blinkered last 3 starts. *D. K. Weld, Ireland* 105

BAYIN (USA) 6 b.g. Caro 133 – Regatela (USA) (Dr Fager) [1994 73: 6d* 6m^4 6f^2 6f^6 6m^5 6m^4 6f^3 6g^6 6d 6d 6g^3 7d^6 7s 1995 6m 6g 7m 6g* 6g 6m^3 6m 5.1m 6g^2 6m^3 6m^5 6m Nov 4] tall, lengthy gelding: has a round action: improved again at 6 yrs, and is a fair handicapper: won at Newbury in May, leading last stride: best at 6f/7f: acts on firm and soft ground: blinkered (raced too freely) once as 4-y-o: bandaged in front: usually set plenty to do: usually ridden by R. Street: consistent. *M. D. I. Usher* 79

BAY OF ISLANDS 3 b.g. Jupiter Island 126 – Lawyer's Wave (USA) (Advocator) [1994 NR 1995 10g^4 10.1m^3 10.4g* Aug 30] close-coupled, good-bodied gelding: fourth live foal: half-brother to modest 1m winner Regent's Inlet (by It's Freezing): dam minor 8.5f stakes winner, is sister to smart American colt Kirrary: progressive form: won maiden at York in August by 2½ lengths from Harlech, left in front over 5f out and running on strongly: strong-galloping sort, will stay 1½m: capable of better still. *C. E. Brittain* 79 p

BAYOU (IRE) 4 br.c. Treasure Kay 114 – Bumpity Bump (Local Suitor (USA) 128) [1994 50: a8.5g a7g 6g^4 5d 6m^6 7m^5 8.1m^5 7g* 10m^4 8g^6 8g 9g 1995 8m^6 8.5m^2 7m 7m Aug 27] compact colt: poor performer (and inconsistent) for new stable: stays 8.5f: acts on good to firm ground and fibresand: edgy (below form) twice at 3 yrs. *J. A. Harris* 48

BAYPHIA 7 ch.g. Bay Express 132 – Sophie Avenue (Guillaume Tell (USA) 121) [1994 –: 12m^5 12.5m 11.6m 1995 a16g a12g^4 Mar 31] quite good-topped gelding: no form for 3 trainers since 4 yrs: stays 1½m well: often blinkered: sold 850 gns Ascot May Sales. *R. J. O'Sullivan* –

BAYRAK (USA) 5 b.g. Bering 136 – Phydilla (FR) 126 (Lyphard (USA) 132) [1994 78: 11.7g* 12.3m^2 1995 11.8d 12g* 12g^4 12g^5 12.1g* 12g^2 12m^4 20m 12s 12m Nov 4] compact, good-bodied gelding: fair performer: won minor event at Thirsk in April and handicap at Chepstow in May: off course 3½ months, tailed off last 2 starts: should stay beyond 12.3f, but found 2½m beyond him: acts on good to firm ground, won on soft over hurdles. *M. J. Ryan* 79

BDOORE (IRE) 7 b.m. Petoski 135 – Princess Biddy 86 (Sun Prince 128) [1994 NR 1995 11.1f^6 Aug 3] of little account. *D. A. Nolan* –

BEACONTREE 2 ch.c. (Apr 1) Lycius (USA) 124 – Beaconaire (USA) (Vaguely Noble 140) [1995 8.1s Oct 17] half-brother to several winners, including useful 4-y-o middle-distance performer Fire Worshipper (by Sadler's Wells), top-class American filly Sabin (by Lyphard) and Musidora winner Fatah Flare (by Alydar): dam, winner at up to 1¼m in France, half-sister to high-class filly Kittiwake, dam of very good American filly Miss Oceana: 5/1, well-beaten eighth of 11 in maiden at Chepstow: well bred, and likely to do better. *M. Johnston* – p

BEAN KING 9 gr.g. Ardross 134 – Meanz Beanz (High Top 131) [1994 NR 1995 15.9d5 16.2s 16d Oct 19] robust gelding: unimpressive mover: rated 101 when winning only start on flat at 5 yrs: fairly useful hurdler in 1992/3 for N. Henderson: 6 lengths fifth of 11 at Chester on return to flat, but well beaten afterwards: stays well: used to act on good to firm and dead going. *Mrs J. Cecil* 81 ?

BEARALL (IRE) 4 b.f. Al Hareb (USA) 123 – Soxoph 67 (Hotfoot 126) [1994 105: 8s 10m2 9.3v5 10g3 12d6 12g* 10f6 10s 12g 1995 10m4 12m Jun 9] small filly: useful performer: stiffish tasks and well below form in listed event at Goodwood and rated stakes at Epsom in 1995: stays 1½m: probably acts on any going except heavy. *R. Hannon* –

BEARNAISE (IRE) 2 b.f. (Jan 31) Cyrano de Bergerac 120 – Gentle Guest (IRE) (Be My Guest (USA) 126) [1995 5m4 5g5 6m2 6m3 6g6 7.3d 6m2 Nov 6] IR 4,000Y: neat, good-quartered filly: second foal: half-sister to 3-y-o Eileen's Guest (by Taufan): dam, unraced, from good family: modest maiden: should stay further than 6f: possibly unsuited by a soft surface. *R. Hannon* 64 +

BEAR TO DANCE 2 b.f. (Feb 14) Rambo Dancer (CAN) 107 – Pooh Wee 71 (Music Boy 124) [1995 5m 7m5 7d 6f Oct 24] leggy filly: first foal: dam 6f (at 2 yrs) and 1m winner out of half-sister to Irish 1000 Guineas winner Favoletta and dam of Teenoso: poor maiden: withdrawn after getting loose before fourth intended start: sweating third start. *John Berry* 46

BEAS RIVER (IRE) 2 b.c. (Apr 16) Classic Music (USA) – Simple Annie (Simply Great (FR) 122) [1995 7.6d5 7d6 6g 6g* 6f3 Oct 24] IR 13,000Y: workmanlike colt: first foal: dam lightly-raced half-sister to Annie Edge, dam of Selkirk: improved form when winning 16-runner maiden at Folkestone in good style by 3 lengths from Bells of Holland: unlucky not to have won when around 3 lengths third of 20 to Times of Times in nursery at Redcar 8 days later, running on well having been set plenty to do: has form at 7.6f but races keenly and may prove best at sprint distances. *W. R. Muir* 77

BEAT OF DRUMS 4 b.c. Warning 136 – Nyoka (USA) (Raja Baba (USA)) [1994 7.5m4 8v 7.5g* 8g 7.5g* 7.5g* 8.8v* 1995 8m4 7m* 7m2 5f5 6g2 7m* 6.5m 6g* 6g* 6g* 6d3 Dec 10] fourth foal: half-brother to 3 winners, notably useful 6f (at 2 yrs) to 1¼m performer Glacial (by Icecapade): dam unraced: smart Italian colt: successful on 10 occasions (including at 2 yrs), easily most important being 10-runner Premio Umbria at Rome in November by 4 lengths from Baaderah: stays 8.8f, but is at least as effective at 6f: acts on good to firm ground and heavy. *G. Botti, Italy* 114

BEAUCHAMP HERO 5 b.h. Midyan (USA) 124 – Buss 102 (Busted 134) [1994 104: 8s3 8m 10.4f4 10m2 8m 10m 10m* 10m6 10.4m4 11.9g 12g5 12v6 1995 12m3 14m3 12m* 12f* 12g* 12.5d3 12s5 12g Sep 24] 120

Tales of 'the one that got away' must be even more common to horserace betting than they are to angling. Such stories tend to wear quickly with repetition but, taking that risk, here is the one about a horse beaten in a handicap who went on to win two Group 2 races. The horse is Beauchamp Hero. For a lot of backers, the handicap in question will be a six-runner rated stakes at Goodwood in May—in which Beauchamp Hero started 6/4 favourite, was set too much to do and came a strong-finishing third—but there are plenty of other candidates. Prior to that Goodwood race, Beauchamp Hero had in fact had eighteen other runs in handicaps and been beaten in fifteen of them, registering two wins from five in 1993 and one from twelve in 1994. The last fifteen of his runs had been off BHB marks ranging from 94 to 103, and had been in many of the most competitive handicaps around. Commenting on his first two races of 1995 *Timeform Perspective* reported that Beauchamp Hero was 'still at the top of his form' and would 'continue to give a good account'.

This proved correct on the second count but well wide of the mark on the first. In the £21,363 Vodapage Rated Stakes Handicap at Epsom on Oaks day, Beauchamp Hero won a slowly-run race impressively. This marginal improvement was followed by a dramatic one two weeks later in the Hardwicke Stakes at Royal Ascot. The race was not a strong one numerically—with Time Star, Wind In Her Hair and Zilzal Zamaan all well below form, Beauchamp Hero was assured of a place at least—but in putting two and a half lengths between himself and Midnight Legend in the final furlong, with another three and a half back to Bal Harbour, Beauchamp

Hardwicke Stakes, Royal Ascot—
Beauchamp Hero steps up to pattern company and sees off Midnight Legend and Bal Harbour

Hero's winning performance does not look at all out of place besides those of other recent Hardwicke winners. To prove the point, it was not three weeks before he had registered another Group 2 victory, in the Princess of Wales's Stakes at Newmarket. The betting suggested this prize was a ready-made consolation for the Derby third Presenting whose challenge for the Irish Derby had recently been thwarted by an injury whilst being loaded at Cambridge airport. Two and a half furlongs out, Presenting duly moved smoothly into the lead, with 8/1-shot Beauchamp Hero pushed along last of nine. The latter had worked his way up within three lengths at the distance, however, and as Presenting found his hands full against Istidaad, Bal Harbour and In Camera, John Reid received an immediate response when he picked up the whip on Beauchamp Hero who swooped between horses in the last half furlong to win by a length. A purple patch indeed! Trainer John Dunlop had thought the Hardwicke a rather ambitious target that might nonetheless prevent Beauchamp Hero winning another handicap. The latter was certainly true, because the five-year-old's races after Newmarket were the Prix Maurice de Nieuil at Maisons-Laffitte and two Group 1 events in Germany, the Grosser Preis von Baden and Europa Preis. His third of five in a bunched finish to a steadily-run race at Maisons-Laffitte was a respectable enough effort, but he fared far less well in Germany, coming in

Princess of Wales's Stakes, Newmarket—another Group 2, from Istidaad and Presenting

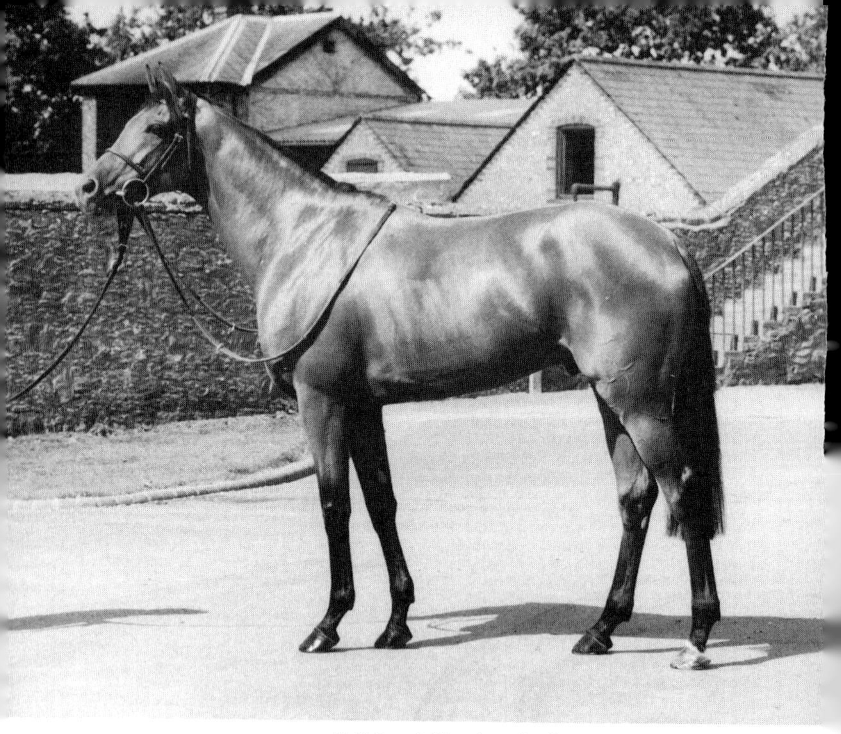

Mr E. Penser's "Beauchamp Hero"

fifth of ten to Germany at Baden-Baden and last of ten, never going well, in the Europa Preis. It seemed impossible at one stage that connections could look back on his season with any disappointment, but the news in the autumn was that Beauchamp Hero had sustained a career-ending tendon injury, probably on that final run.

Beauchamp Hero (b.h. 1990)	Midyan (USA) (b 1984)	Miswaki (ch 1978)	Mr Prospector
			Hopespringseternal
		Country Dream (b 1970)	Ribot
			Equal Venture
	Buss (ch 1969)	Busted (b 1963)	Crepello
			Sans Le Sou
		Miss Klaire II (ch 1959)	Klairon
			Miss Pink

Beauchamp Hero retires disputing top spot among the offspring of Midyan. Clearly the best of the rest is another tough individual from the Dunlop stable, the four-time Italian Group 1 winner Alhijaz, and the two of them are closely related, Beauchamp Hero's dam Buss being a sister to Alhijaz's grandam Bright Decision. A daughter of the useful sprinter Miss Klaire II and half-sister to the very useful miler Miracle, Buss began her racecourse career in unpromising fashion, withdrawn after unshipping her rider and bolting. She tried to do the same next time out but won that race and went on to have a good innings, in all winning five of her sixteen starts and showing useful form at short of a mile and a half. Genuine and consistent seem equally applicable to her stud career, with sixteen foals and thirteen winners (twelve on the flat) before she was retired in 1992. The first of those foals, Watch Out (by Blakeney), is grandam of the 1994 Caulfield Guineas winner Northwood Plume. Beauchamp Hero's owner, Mr Penser, acquired Buss when she was bought by Dunlop for 29,000 guineas in 1983 carrying her ninth foal. All of her foals since have, of course, carried the Beauchamp prefix and the four that have won—Cactus (by Niniski), Dream (by Castle Keep), Fizz (by Jalmood) and Grace (by Ardross)—all stayed at least a mile and three quarters. Beauchamp Hero though is much the best of Buss's offspring. The smart 1995 two-year-old Beauchamp King is unrelated.

Beauchamp Hero is a rangy, angular horse with a round action. Quite why he found such dramatic improvement in 1995 is hard to say, but his hat-trick of wins were all gained over one and a half miles on a sound surface; earlier efforts, however, did suggest that he stayed one and three quarter miles and acted on soft going as well. He could produce a telling late burst and was usually held up. *J. L. Dunlop*

BEAUCHAMP JADE 3 gr.f. Kalaglow 132 – Beauchamp Buzz 85 (High Top 131) [1994 72p: 7m^3 8d^6 7g^3 1995 12g^4 12.1m^3 11.8g^2 11.8f^2 12m Nov 4] unfurnished filly: fairly useful maiden handicapper: runner-up in handicap and minor event (led on home turn to inside last, ran on well) at Leicester in October: disappointing in November Handicap at Doncaster: stays 1½m, likely to stay further: acts on firm ground: held up: will win a maiden race. *H. Candy* **82**

BEAUCHAMP JAZZ 3 ch.c. Nishapour (FR) 125 – Afariya (FR) (Silver Shark 129) [1994 89: 6m^4 6m 6g^2 7m^3 8f^2 7.9d* 8s^2 1995 8d 8m* 10m^5 8m^2 8.1m^4 8f 8s^2 Oct 6] tall, leggy colt: useful performer: landed the odds in minor event at Pontefract in April: best efforts when head second to Medaille Militaire in Britannia Stakes at Royal Ascot and fourth in rated stakes at Sandown: ran poorly in Schweppes Golden Mile at Goodwood and apprentice race (7/4 on, striding out poorly) at Ascot: stays 1m well: acts on firm and soft ground: takes keen hold: stays in training. *J. L. Dunlop* **99**

BEAUCHAMP KATE 2 b.f. (Apr 26) Petoski 135 – Beauchamp Buzz 85 (High Top 131) [1995 6g^6 6d 6g Sep 30] sturdy filly: fourth foal: half-sister to 3-y-o Beauchamp Jade (by Kalaglow): dam, stayed 1m, half-sister to very smart middle-distance horse Beauchamp Hero: signs of ability in maidens, eye-catching sixth of 15 to Prima Volta after a slow start at Kempton then never placed to challenge at Newbury and Newmarket: will do better, particularly over 1m+. *H. Candy* **61 p**

BEAUCHAMP KING 2 gr.c. (May 17) Nishapour (FR) 125 – Afariya (FR) (Silver Shark 129) [1995 7f^3 7m* 8.1d* 8v* 8m* Oct 21] **114 p**

It was an unusual running of the Racing Post Trophy. Most obviously there were only the four runners (making it the smallest field for the race alongside 1990, Peter Davies' year) but scarcely less striking was the fact that here was a Group 1 race without a runner owned by any of the Al Maktoums. In the last three seasons in Britain this has happened just twice before, in the 1993 St James's Palace Stakes (in which another four-runner race included Needle Gun, owned by the Maktoum-associated Saeed Manana) and the same year's Cheveley Park Stakes. Another interesting and not unrelated statistic of the latest Racing Post Trophy was highlighted by Tony Morris. 'Who would have imagined', he wrote, 'that the line-up for a race offering nearly £140,000 in prizes would be contested by horses conceived for a total of under £15,000'.

The owners to benefit from this, in order of those the betting indicated would benefit most, were Mrs E. H. Vestey with Mons, Mr Erik Penser with Beauchamp King, Mr B. Schmidt-Bodner with Even Top and the Hesmonds Stud with Iamus. Iamus did not seem excessively priced at 33/1, but the three others all held realistic chances and were winners last time out. Mons's wide-margin success in the Royal Lodge, against his rivals' pair of listed races, earned him favouritism at 4/5. He was up against two notably progressive opponents, however, and the field had not got far up the straight before it was clear that both would press him hard. Most immediately, Even Top challenged strongly three furlongs out, but just in behind them John Reid on Beauchamp King had hardly had to move a muscle. He still hadn't a furlong and a half later, and when he gave Beauchamp King the office approaching the last they quickly went a length and a quarter up, a margin which was maintained to the line without much difficulty. Even Top just kept his head in front of Mons for second.

How do we rate Beauchamp King? Well, although he won in good style at Doncaster, his performance cannot be considered in the same class as those of fellow

Anglo African Holdings Autumn Stakes, Ascot—
the grey Beauchamp King and Storm Trooper both stay on well

Group 1 winners Alhaarth and Royal Applause. With conditions a lot less testing than at Ascot, Mons probably just failed to match his Royal Lodge form, form which had been nothing special anyway. Beauchamp King's Doncaster timefigure is unexceptional too, but we would hate this to end up a downbeat assessment—he has something still to prove in terms of class, but not much else. Good to firm ground posed no problems at Doncaster; neither had heavy going when he beat Storm Trooper one and a quarter lengths in that listed event at Ascot two weeks earlier. In the Ascot race he demonstrated tenacity and that he stayed a mile thoroughly, and at Doncaster that he was not just a thorough stayer but had a good turn of foot. With all this in his favour, it is not surprising that Beauchamp King went to Ascot having

Racing Post Trophy, Doncaster—the whole field,
with Beauchamp King the winner from Even Top (noseband), Mons (right) and Iamus

already been a clear-cut winner of a median auction maiden at Ayr in August and a well-contested conditions race at Haydock in September.

Beauchamp King's name indicates unmistakeably that his owner-breeder is Mr Penser, the Swedish banker whose British home is at Beauchamp House, Compton Beauchamp, who has three mares, and whose naming policy is reportedly determined by 'a very bad memory'! Beauchamp King's headline pedigree, however, is all about the Aga Khan. Sire Nishapour won the Aga Khan the Poule d'Essai des Poulains and saved the best for him as a stallion, siring the Prix du Jockey-Club winner Mouktar and Prix de Diane winner Shemaka. Just eight mares visited Nishapour in 1992, and he stood at 2,000 guineas in 1993, the year of his death. The dam Afariya, a daughter of the Aga Khan's high-class and versatile colt Silver Shark, had eleven races for him and won two at Fontainebleau, over seven furlongs at two years and a mile at three. By the time that the Aga Khan sold her for 10,000 guineas in 1987, Afariya had thrown six living foals and five of those turned out winners, the best being the useful Afsarjaan who was successful four times at up to nine and a half furlongs. He was by Nishapour as well. Two foals (one winner) in Sweden were followed by three return visits to Nishapour, the first resulting in Beauchamp Imperial who is reportedly 'an outstanding performer in Barbados', and the second in Beauchamp Jazz, touched off in the Britannia Handicap but a disappointment afterwards. Beauchamp King is Afariya's last foal, and she died in 1995. Although bred by the Aga Khan, Afariya does not have one of those extended pedigrees one so readily associates with him: he bought her dam Lady Millie after her racing career, a career that began amongst the top-rated fillies in France as a two-year-old, when she won the Prix Thomas Bryon, but failed to reach anything like those heights at three.

Beauchamp King (gr.c. May 17, 1993)	Nishapour (FR) (gr 1975)	Zeddaan (gr 1965)	Grey Sovereign
			Vareta
		Alama (b 1969)	Aureole
			Nucciolina
	Afariya (FR) (b 1973)	Silver Shark (gr 1963)	Buisson Ardent
			Palsaka
		Lady Millie (b 1965)	Reneged
			Milania

Looking at him in the parade ring, there is little to indicate that Beauchamp King would be much better than the mass of previous 'Beauchamps'. He is just an angular colt, and at Ascot was also sweating and edgy. A good mover, though, in his faster paces, Beauchamp King has already emphasised that it is racecourse performances which count. We will be surprised if he does not improve again. He shapes as though he will stay beyond a mile but is not at all certain to get a mile and a half. *J. L. Dunlop*

BEAUCHIEF 3 br.g. Kind of Hush 118 – Firdale Rosie 78 (Town Crier 119) – [1994 NR 1995 8.5m 10f 8m Oct 2] leggy, close-coupled gelding: eighth foal: dam, 2-y-o 5f winner, appeared not to train on: soundly beaten in maidens. *R. F. Marvin*

BEAUMAN 5 b.g. Rainbow Quest (USA) 134 – Gliding 94 (Tudor Melody 129) 66 [1994 79: 8m^5 10d^4 8d^3 8g 8.1g^3 8g^4 a8.5g 10.5g^2 10m^3 8s 11.9s^2 1995 12m 11.9m^3 10g 10.5d 10.5m^5 8.1d^6 10d 10d a8g^2 Nov 6] leggy gelding: has a round action: fair handicapper: stays 1½m: acts on good to firm ground, used to go particularly well on soft: modest form on fibresand: tried blinkered/visored, no improvement: has worn bandages behind. *P. D. Evans*

BEAU MATELOT 3 ch.g. Handsome Sailor 125 – Bellanoora 60 (Ahonoora 60 122) [1994 54: 7g 7.9d^5 1995 a8g a11g^2 a12g^3 12.3d^3 a12g^6 10f^4 10m^5 9f^5 9.9m^5 Jul 7] leggy, angular gelding: modest maiden handicapper: stays 12.3f: acts on fibresand and firm and dead ground. *J. D. Bethell*

BEAUMONT (IRE) 5 br.g. Be My Native (USA) 122 – Say Yes (Junius (USA) 63 124) [1994 72: 10d* 10v* 11.9m^5 10m 10f* 10m 10.4d^3 10d 12v 1995 9m 10.5g 10f^4 10.1g^5 10f a8g^4 a11g* Dec 1] compact gelding: modest handicapper: gelded and left J. Pearce's stable after third 5-y-o start: won at Southwell in December: should stay 1½m: acts on any ground: blinkered (raced too freely) third 5-y-o start: normally held up. *J. E. Banks*

BEAUMOOD 9 b.g. Jalmood (USA) 126 – Falcon Berry (FR) (Bustino 136) – [1994 –: 11.9m 13.1g^4 12.1g 15.1m^3 16.1s a14.8g a14g 1995 a14g Mar 3] neat gelding: no longer of much account. *E. J. Alston*

BEAU QUEST 8 b.g. Rainbow Quest (USA) 134 – Elegant Tern (USA) 102 (Sea Bird II 145) [1994 NR 1995 a12g Dec 12] small gelding: probably no longer of much account. *B. R. Cambidge* –

BEAUTETE 4 b.g. Komaite (USA) – New Central 74 (Remainder Man 126§) [1994 67: 8s 8v 8m 9.7s^5 10g 10f^3 10f* 10.1g^5 11.9f^2 11.5d 11.9g^3 12d^5 a12g^2 a12g a12g^3 a13g* 1995 a13g* a16g^6 a12g^6 11.9m^5 12m 12m 11.9m 11.5m Jun 24] strong, good-quartered gelding: won amateurs handicap at Lingfield in January: failed by long way to repeat that form: stays 13f: acts on firm ground and goes well on equitrack: carries head high, and not one to trust implicitly. *S. Dow* 70 d

BEAUTIFUL BALLAD (IRE) 2 b.f. (Feb 2) Ballad Rock 122 – Delightful Time (Manado 130) [1995 5m^4 5g* 5d^2 5m^3 6g 6g^3 6g^3 6f^5 Oct 18] IR 3,800Y: quite attractive filly: has scope: half-sister to several maidens on flat: dam maiden half-sister to Sassafras: won maiden auction at Haydock in May: fairly useful form most subsequent starts, third of 5 to Resounder in listed race at York on penultimate one: stays 6f: seems suited by an easy surface: wears bandages behind: sold (B. Hills to A. Stewart) 18,500 gns Newmarket Autumn Sales. *B. W. Hills* 84

BEAUTY DANCER (IRE) 2 b.f. (Apr 9) Alzao (USA) 117 – Dawning Beauty (IRE) (Well Decorated (USA)) [1995 5g* 5.5m^5 7.5g* 7.5g^2 7.5d* 8d^2 Oct 15] 52,000F; 25,000Y: fourth foal: half-sister to a winner in Brazil by Tate Gallery: dam, placed in Ireland, is half-sister to high-class sprinter Bluebird, out of half-sister to dam of Java Gold: useful Italian filly: won maiden at Rome in May, minor event at Naples in August, and listed race at Rome in September: 2½ lengths second of 11 to Scarlet Plume in Premio Dormello at Milan last time: stays 1m: yet to race on extremes of going. *A. Colella, Italy* 95

BEAU VENTURE (USA) 7 ch.h. Explodent (USA) – Old Westbury (USA) (Francis S) [1994 83: 5m^2 5m^2 5f 5g* 5.1g 5d 5d 5s 5v 1995 5g 5m^6 5g 5f* 5m^4 5f^2 5f^3 5m 5g 5g 5m 5m Nov 4] leggy, quite good-topped horse: unimpressive mover: fair handicapper: won at Ripon in June: well beaten last 5 starts: stays 6f, races at 5f these days: acts on firm and dead ground: blinkered twice, not since 5 yrs: held up: below form when sweating and edgy. *F. H. Lee* 82

BEBE POMME 3 b.f. Clantime 101 – Orchard Road 74 (Camden Town 125) [1994 37: 5.1m^5 6.1s a6g 1995 a5g 5.1g Apr 4] small filly: poor sprint maiden: blinkered final 3-y-o start: sold 700 gns Ascot May Sales. *Mrs N. Macauley* –

BECKY BOO 5 b.m. White Mill 76 – Aber Cothi (Dominion 123) [1994 NR 1995 10.8m^4 13.1f^2 Jul 19] leggy, sparely-made mare: seems a poor plater: stays 13.1f. *Mrs L. A. Murphy* 21

BECKYHANNAH 5 b.m. Rambling River 111 – Munequita (Marching On 101) [1994 47, a–: a6g a7g^4 6v^2 6g 6d 6g 6.1s^5 7d a7g^6 1995 a6g* a6g a6g^6 6v^5 6s Apr 12] plain mare: poor handicapper: narrowly won at Wolverhampton in January: failed to repeat the form: seems suited by 6f: acts on heavy ground and fibresand: nearly always blinkered: none too consistent. *R. Bastiman* 39

BEDAZZLE 4 b.g. Formidable (USA) 125 – Wasimah 84 (Caerleon (USA) 132) [1994 40: 6g 6m^2 8m 7.5m^5 8g 8m^6 7g 8m^3 8m^4 8s 1995 7.1d^3 a7g^6 7m^4 8.3f^3 8.2m^5 7m^4 7.1g^2 Sep 18] small, sparely-made gelding: poor maiden handicapper: stays 8.3f: acts on firm and dead ground. *M. Brittain* 38

BEDEVIL (USA) 5 b.h. Devil's Bag (USA) – Pailleron (USA) (Majestic Light (USA)) [1994 74: 12m^2 1995 16.1g^3 16.1g^4 Jun 10] tall, leggy horse: fair maiden handicapper: stays 2m: yet to race on a soft surface: front runner in 1995. *Mrs J. Cecil* 74

BEDIVERE (USA) 3 b.c. El Gran Senor (USA) 136 – Obeah 112 (Cure The Blues (USA)) [1994 83: 6m^6 7g* 7g* 7m^4 8g 8m^4 1995 8m^3 7.6m^2 8m^5 8m^3 8f 8d^2 Dec 16] neat, good-quartered colt: shows a round action: fairly useful handicapper: good efforts first 4 starts, third of 32 to Medaille Militaire in Britannia Stakes at Royal Ascot (looked in splendid shape, first home on far side) penultimate outing for P. Chapple-Hyam: will stay beyond 1m: acts on good to firm and dead ground: genuine and consistent. *G. Jones, USA* 94

BEDOUIN INVADER 3 b.c. Green Desert (USA) 127 – La Tuerta 96 (Hot Spark 126) [1994 62p: 7s 1995 6m^5 7.1m 6g^6 7.1m 6f^3 7m^6 7f* 7m^4 Sep 5] strong, deep-bodied colt: has a quick action: fair handicapper: won minor event at Brighton 75

in August: stays 7f: acts on firm ground: visored/blinkered since fifth 3-y-o start. *M. R. Stoute*

BEDSIDE MAIL 2 b.c. (Mar 8) Mazilier (USA) 107 – Lucky Flinders 77 (Free State 125) [1995 5g4 5m6 6m* 7.1m4 6m* 6m 6m5 6m3 5m* 5g 5g Sep 28] 5,000Y: sturdy colt: third foal: half-brother to 3-y-o Plucky Pet (by Petong): dam stayed 1m: fair form: won maiden auction at Kempton in June and nurseries at Lingfield in July and Ripon in August: suited by sprint distances: acts on good to firm ground: wandered badly seventh start: sold 17,000 gns Newmarket Autumn Sales. *J. M. P. Eustace* 82

BEE BEAT 7 ch.g. Bairn (USA) 126 – Thorny Rose 81 (Tap On Wood 130) [1994 53, a–: 12m4 a16.2g6 a9.4g6 12.5m2 12.1f 11.6f 11.6f 12m 11.6m* 11.5d2 14.4g3 16d3 16.2g 14s 12.1g3 16d 1995 14.9g 11.6m4 14.1m 12.1m 14g 14f 11.7h Aug 18] leggy, lightly-made gelding: unimpressive mover: untrustworthy handicapper: won over 15f in Jersey in July: stays 2m: acts on good to firm ground and dead: tried blinkered: refused to race 5 out of 7 starts here in 1995 and is one to leave alone. *A. J. Chamberlain* §§

BEECHAM 3 ch.g. Superlative 118 – Busted Harmony (Busted 134) [1994 62: 6g2 7m5 a6g6 1995 a7g2 a6g a8g6 a7g a9.4g a12g Jul 22] strong gelding: poor walker and mover: disappointing maiden: stays 7f: tried blinkered, no improvement: sold 1,300 gns Ascot September Sales. *P. C. Haslam* 52 d

BEE DEE BEST (IRE) 4 b.g. Try My Best (USA) 130 – Eloquent Charm (USA) (Private Account (USA)) [1994 44: 6s5 5f 5m6 7.1f4 7d5 11.1m5 8g5 8.3m3 9.2f 7.1m 7.1m5 a6g a7g 1995 8f 6f5 7g 8.3m5 8h5 Sep 4] leggy, quite attractive gelding: poor maiden: probably stays 11f: acts on firm going. *J. P. Smith* 37

BEE HEALTH BOY 2 b.g. (Apr 23) Superpower 113 – Rekindle 70 (Relkino 131) [1995 5m 5g6 5g5 5m2 7h6 6m 6m6 5g3 5g 6s* 5d4 7m Oct 30] 2,500F: lengthy, good-topped gelding: has scope: seventh foal: dam poor half-sister to useful 1½m to 2m winner No Bombs: best form when making all in 24-runner selling nursery at Haydock in September: raced too freely final start: best form at 6f: acts on soft ground: blinkered last 6 starts. *M. W. Easterby* 67

BEEKMAN STREET 9 b.g. Jalmood (USA) 126 – Plato's Retreat (Brigadier Gerard 144) [1994 –: 11.8g3 1995 13g May 4] leggy gelding: probably no longer of much account. *D. Haydn Jones* –

BEENY 2 b.c. (Mar 6) Lugana Beach 116 – Child Star (Precocious 126) [1995 5m 5.7h6 6m4 5.1m4 a5g* a6g a5g3 a5g Dec 1] third foal: dam little worthwhile form: off course 3 months, won nursery at Lingfield in November: unlikely to stay beyond 6f: acts on good to firm ground and equitrack (always struggling on fibresand): not particularly consistent. *A. P. Jarvis* 64 +

BEGGER'S OPERA 3 ch.c. North Briton 67 – Operelle 44 (Music Boy 124) [1994 NR 1995 8f a10g a8g Nov 21] compact colt: first foal: dam maiden sprinter: no worthwhile form. *Pat Mitchell* –

BEHAVIOUR 3 b.c. Warning 136 – Berry's Dream 101 (Darshaan 133) [1994 81p: 6d5 6d2 1995 8f* 7.9m* 8f 7.9m3 7m3 Aug 26] sturdy, compact colt: has a quick action: useful performer: won maiden at Redcar in June and handicap at York (idled) in July: well backed in good handicaps afterwards, best efforts when third to Cap Juluca at York and Tajannub at Goodwood: will prove better at 1m than shorter, and will stay further: acts on firm going, shaped well on dead at 2 yrs: held up and has turn of foot: mounted on track on final start. *Mrs J. Cecil* 96

BELANA 2 br.f. (Mar 19) Shaadi (USA) 126 – Bellagio 68 (Busted 134) [1995 7g6 7.5g4 7.5m2 8.5m* 8g Sep 15] 14,000F: tall, unfurnished filly: has scope: half-sister to several winners, including useful miler Arany (by Precocious) and 7f winner Vilany (by Never So Bold): dam 1¼m winner who stayed 1½m: won maiden at Beverley by 2 lengths from Maid For Baileys: looked to be progressing well but well below form in nursery at Ayr following month: will stay beyond 8.5f: sent to Dubai. *J. W. Watts* 78

BELDRAY PARK (IRE) 2 b. or br.c. (May 9) Superpower 113 – Ride Bold (USA) (J O Tobin (USA) 130) [1995 5f4 6m 6g6 5f4 Oct 24] 5,000Y, 14,000 2-y-o: angular colt: fifth foal: half-brother to smart Irish 3-y-o sprinter Petite Fantasy (by 58

Mansooj): dam out of sprint-winning half-sister to Jalmood: modest maiden: may prove best at 5f. *Mrs A. L. M. King*

BELFORT RULER 8 gr.g. Belfort (FR) 89 – Call Me Kate 72 (Firestreak 125) [1994 53: 8d 7.5m⁴ a6g 8m 7m 8m⁶ 7d 1995 a8g a10g⁵ Feb 21] close-coupled, workmanlike gelding: probably no longer of much account: sold 650 gns Ascot February Sales. *B. Gubby* –

BELFRY GREEN (IRE) 5 ro.g. Doulab (USA) 115 – Checkers (Habat 127) [1994 94: 8m 8g⁴ 7m* 6g² 7m* 7m 8m⁴ 7m* 7g³ 7d² 1995 7m³ 7m 7m 7m⁵ 6f 8g 7.3d 7d Sep 23] lengthy gelding: unimpressive mover: useful handicapper: best efforts in 1995 in rated stakes at Newmarket and Victoria Cup at Ascot on first 2 starts: better than position suggests on several occasions afterwards: seems ideally suited by 7f: acts on good to firm and dead ground: held up (takes good hold) and has turn of foot: genuine. *C. A. Horgan* 99

BELGRAN (USA) 6 b.g. El Gran Senor (USA) 136 – Belle of Dodge Me (USA) (Creme Dela Creme) [1994 NR 1995 11.8m 11.4g 14.9m⁶ 10.8m 14.8m 14s 12m Oct 13] strong, good-topped gelding: no longer of much account: left W. Brisbourne's stable after fifth 6-y-o outing. *P. D. Evans* –

BELIEVE ME 2 b.c. (May 14) Beveled (USA) – Pink Mex (Tickled Pink 114) [1995 6f* 7f⁵ 7m⁴ 7d⁵ 7g* 8d³ 8m* Oct 27] 9,000F, 18,000Y: smallish, good sort: fluent mover: fifth foal: half-brother to 3-y-o 1m and 1¼m winner Tragic Hero (by Tragic Role) and 1993 2-y-o 5f winner Hannah's Music (by Music Boy): dam little worthwhile form: fairly useful colt: successful in median auction maiden at Kempton in July and minor events at York (by neck from Bullfinch) and Newmarket (made all to beat Astuti 1¾ lengths) in October: stays 1m well: acts on firm and dead ground. *R. Hannon* 97

BELINDA BLUE 3 b.f. Belfort (FR) 89 – Carrula (Palm Track 122) [1994 67: 6m³ 7d⁵ 6g 1995 8g 6m⁶ Jun 20] tall, workmanlike filly: has shown little since debut. *R. A. Fahey* –

BELLACARDIA 2 b.f. (May 12) Law Society (USA) 130 – Clarista (USA) 67 (Riva Ridge (USA)) [1995 6m⁶ 8.1s Oct 17] half-sister to 3-y-o Just-Mana-Mou (by Caerleon) and several winners, including useful 4-y-o 7f winner Indhar (by Warning) and 10.8f winner Formal Invitation (by Be My Guest): dam (stayed 1¼m) half-sister to Teenoso and Topsy: favourite, around 5 lengths sixth of 10 to Balpare in median auction maiden at Epsom: remote last of 10 in maiden at Chepstow nearly 3 months later: should stay beyond 6f. *G. Lewis* 49

BELLA COOLA 3 b.f. Northern State (USA) 91 – Trigamy 112 (Tribal Chief 125) [1994 –: 6d 1995 6m 7g 6g⁴ 7m 7m Oct 20] lengthy, unfurnished filly: never-nearer fourth of 16 in handicap at Windsor in June, best effort: tends to pull hard, but should stay 7f. *C. A. Horgan* 50

BELLAPAIS (IRE) 2 b.f. (May 11) Distinctly North (USA) 115 – Mistress Vyne 63 (Prince Tenderfoot (USA) 126) [1995 6m 6m 8h⁴ 7g Sep 20] IR 1,200Y, 1,000 2-y-o: half-sister to 4 winners, including 1m seller winner Trailfinder (by Fordham): dam placed over 5f at 3 yrs: poor form, including in sellers: blinkered last 3 starts. *W. R. Muir* –

BELLA PARKES 4 b.f. Tina's Pet 121 – Summerhill Spruce 70 (Windjammer (USA)) [1994 –: 6f 6m 6g 6s 1995 a5g⁴ a6g² a6g⁵ a6g* a6g² a6g² a6g* 6g 6d 7g⁵ 6f 6g Sep 22] lengthy, workmanlike filly: fairly useful performer on the all-weather: won seller and handicap at Southwell for new stable early in year: stays 6f, probably not 7f: acts on fibresand: has won on firm ground, but best turf form on dead: effective blinkered or not: tail swisher: sold 7,200 gns Doncaster November Sales. *D. Nicholls* 60 a82

BELLAPHENTO 2 b.f. (Apr 21) Lyphento (USA) 108 – Nautical Belle 59 (Kind of Hush 118) [1995 7m Oct 28] tall, workmanlike filly: first foal: dam, maiden on flat suited by 1½m, won over hurdles: 33/1, green and in need of race, bumped leaving stalls and never a factor in 19-runner maiden at Newmarket. *R. J. R. Williams* –

BELLARA 3 b.f. Thowra (FR) – Sicilian Vespers 44 (Mummy's Game 120) [1994 –: 8.1g 1995 a10g⁶ 9.9m⁴ 12g⁴ 14.1m* 16d 17.2m 16.1g⁶ Oct 3] small filly: off course 4 months and 33/1, narrowly won strongly-run 9-runner minor event at 55

Nottingham in August, always thereabouts: no comparable form: should stay 2m: acts on good to firm ground. *N. M. Babbage*

BELLA SEDONA 3 ch.f. Belmez (USA) 131 – My Surprise (Welsh Pageant 132) [1994 –: 6g 1995 9m^{6} 7.5d 7m^{5} a9.4g Sep 30] lengthy, sturdy filly: modest form at best: should stay beyond 1m. *Lady Herries* 56

BELLAS GATE BOY 3 b.g. Doulab (USA) 115 – Celestial Air 96 (Rheingold 137) [1994 68: 6g 6m 6m^{2} 7.3g^{2} 7m^{4} 8.1g^{3} 1995 9m 8m 10m 8g^{2} 10g^{6} 8f Jul 1] leggy gelding: modest maiden handicapper: left Miss H. Knight's stable after third 3-y-o start: stays 1m: has raced only on a sound surface: blinkered (stiff task) third 3-y-o start: usually races prominently: sold 3,800 gns Doncaster October Sales to rejoin Miss Knight. *G. Lewis* 66

BELLA'S LEGACY 2 b.f. (Apr 15) Thowra (FR) – Miss Lawsuit (Neltino 97) [1995 6d Oct 19] sparely-made filly: third reported foal: sister to 3-y-o 7f winner Dancing Heart and 6f (at 2 yrs) to 1m winner Dancing Lawyer: dam, of little account on flat, winning selling hurdler: 33/1, always towards rear in 20-runner maiden at Newbury. *R. J. Hodges* –

BELLATEENA 3 b.f. Nomination 125 – Bella Travaille 82 (Workboy 123) [1994 NR 1995 a10g a8g 7m 11.6m 10f* 10.1m^{3} 10m^{5} 10d 8.2m* a10g^{2} Nov 14] sturdy, good-bodied filly: seventh foal: half-sister to 3 winners, including fair 1m winner Buzzards Bellbuoy (by Buzzards Bay): dam, best at 2 yrs, won 3 times at 5f: modest handicapper: won at Nottingham in July (maiden contest) and October: stays 1¼m well: acts on firm ground and equitrack, tailed off only start on a soft surface: races prominently. *H. J. Collingridge* 57

BELLATOR 2 b.c. (Mar 30) Simply Great (FR) 122 – Jupiter's Message (Jupiter Island 126) [1995 6d^{5} 6m^{5} 7f 8m 10d^{6} Sep 19] 6,800Y: compact, workmanlike colt: has a roundish action: first foal: dam unraced: modest maiden: will stay beyond 1¼m: pulled hard fourth start. *G. B. Balding* 61

BELLA VITESSA (IRE) 3 b.f. Thatching 131 – Burghclere 86 (Busted 134) [1994 NR 1995 10.3g^{6} 12m 11.7f 14.1g 14.1m Aug 21] small, plain filly: half-sister to several winners, including 6f (at 2 yrs) to 1¼m (Sun Chariot Stakes) winner Capo di Monte (by Final Straw), Oaks second Wind In Her Hair (by Alzao) and some stayers: dam, 1¾m winner, is daughter of Highclere: no worthwhile form: blinkered final start. *J. W. Hills* –

BELL CONTRACTORS (IRE) 3 b.g. Jareer (USA) 115 – Baghio (Ballymore 123) [1994 –: 7m 8.1g 1995 8m^{4} 10.8g^{5} 10g 12.1m 8g Jul 19] workmanlike gelding: disappointing maiden: visored final start: sold 500 gns Ascot August Sales. *C. D. Broad* 63 d

BELLE ARGENTINE (FR) 4 br.f. Fijar Tango (FR) 127 – Jarlina (Pharly (FR) 130) [1994 113: 9s^{2} 8s* 8m^{3} 8g^{3} 10.5g^{4} 8m^{5} 1995 10m^{3} May 25] leggy, workmanlike filly: smart performer at 3 yrs: wintered in Dubai: ran poorly in 4-runner listed event at Goodwood (raced freely, found little) only start in 1995: stays 10.5f: yet to race on firm going, acts on any other: held up. *Saeed bin Suroor* –

BELLEMINETTE (IRE) 4 ch.f. Simply Great (FR) 122 – Kitty's Sister (Bustino 136) [1994 65: a7g^{2} a8g* 8.2m* 8m 8.2m^{6} 8.3m 7v 7d 1995 a7g^{3} a9.4g 8s 8m^{3} 8.3g 7g* 7.1m^{4} 7f 7m^{5} 7.1m 7m a7g Oct 28] rangy filly: fair handicapper: won at Doncaster in July: effective at 7f, and stays 9.4f: acts on fibresand and good to firm ground, unsuited by a soft surface: has run well when sweating: slowly away 5 of last 6 starts: most inconsistent. *D. Haydn Jones* 59 § a65 §

BELLE OF THE BALL (IRE) 3 b.f. Fairy King (USA) – Commanche Belle 74 (Shirley Heights 130) [1994 61: 7m 7s^{5} 7d^{6} 1995 8m^{4} 7g^{6} Jun 5] good-topped, attractive filly: has scope: modest maiden: edgy and early to post, faded tamely in minor event at Thirsk (headed 2f out) final start: will be suited by further than 1m: has worn a tongue strap. *E. A. L. Dunlop* 57

BELLE'S BOY 2 b.c. (May 15) Nalchik (USA) – Ty-With-Belle 67 (Pamroy 99) [1995 10g a8g a8.5g* Dec 2] angular colt: sixth foal: half-brother to 1989 2-y-o 5f seller winner Starchy Belle (by Starch Reduced): dam fair maiden at 2 yrs: 33/1, won 10-runner maiden at Wolverhampton by 1½ lengths from Balios, always well placed and leading inside last: should stay 1¼m: acts on fibresand. *B. Palling* 59

BELLESONNETTE (IRE) 3 br.f. Damister (USA) 123 – Rocket Alert 110 (Red Alert 127) [1994 63: a7g a8.5g^{4} 6.9m^{2} 7v a7g^{4} 1995 a7g^{2} Apr 3] tall, angular filly: modest maiden: lost on the nod at Southwell only start in 1995: may well prove best at up to 7f: well beaten (sweating) on heavy ground: sent to USA. *D. Haydn Jones* — 63

BELLO GALLICO (IRE) 4 b.g. Gallic League 119 – Jeewan 82 (Touching Wood (USA) 127) [1994 75: 6s* 6d* 6g* 6f 6g 1995 6g Jul 28] rangy gelding: unimpressive mover: trained by R. Hannon at 3 yrs: off course nearly 14 months and visored, well beaten in handicap at Newmarket in July: should stay beyond 6f: acts on soft going: sold 1,700 gns Doncaster November Sales. *Lady Herries* — –

BELLS OF HOLLAND 2 b.f. (Apr 7) Belmez (USA) 131 – Annie Albright (USA) (Verbatim (USA)) [1995 7f^{5} 7m^{2} 6m^{3} 5g 6g^{2} a8g^{6} Dec 1] fourth foal: half-sister to useful 3-y-o 6f winner Shamanic (by Fairy King), 5f winner at 2 yrs: dam, Irish sprint maiden, half-sister to smart 6f and 7f winner Crystal Gazing: modest maiden: needs further than 5f and stays 7f: poor effort on fibresand final start: taken down early after proving headstrong first 2 starts: sold out of B. Hills's stable 5,500 gns Newmarket Autumn Sales prior to final outing. *W. R. Muir* — 60

BELLS OF LONGWICK 6 b.m. Myjinski (USA) – Bells of St Martin 89 (Martinmas 128) [1994 70: 5v^{3} 5d 5g* 6s^{4} 5g^{5} 5g 5m^{4} a6g 5m a5g^{4} 6f 5.2g 5g^{4} 5d^{5} 5.7g 5.2s^{3} 5d 5d^{5} 5.1g 5v 1995 5g a5g^{5} 6d a7g 6m 6.1d 5g^{6} 6d 5f a5g a6g^{5} Nov 20] leggy mare: unimpressive mover: only modest at best in 1995 for new stable: best form at 5f with give in the ground (acts on soft): below form on fibresand: effective blinkered/visored or not. *W. W. Haigh* — 54

BELMARITA (IRE) 2 ch.f. (Apr 21) Belmez (USA) 131 – Congress Lady 93 (General Assembly (USA)) [1995 7f 7m Oct 28] 46,000Y: good-bodied filly: seventh foal: half-sister to Irish 6f to 8.5f winner Sadlers Congress (by Sadler's Wells) and winners in Italy and Scandinavia: dam, 8.5f winner in France, half-sister to Ragusa out of Musidora winner Ela Marita: still backward, showed some ability in 19-runner maiden at Newmarket won by Awaamir final start, leading to halfway then weakening to finish in rear. *M. H. Tompkins* — – p

BELMEZ MELODY 3 b.f. Belmez (USA) 131 – Lypharitissima (FR) (Lightning (FR) 129) [1994 73: 7s^{4} 7.9d 1995 8.1m^{3} 7.1m Aug 25] unfurnished filly: good mover: fair maiden: tailed off as though something amiss latter start for new stable in 1995: bred to stay beyond 1m. *I. A. Balding* — 67

BELMONT PRINCESS (IRE) 5 b.m. Carmelite House (USA) 118 – Silly Song (Silly Season 127) [1994 49d: 5v 6m^{2} 5s 5.1f^{5} 5.3f^{5} 6f 6f 6m^{3} a7g 1995 a7g Jan 6] rather lightly-made mare: poor maiden: probably stays 7f: best efforts on a sound surface, tailed off on soft: hurdling with S. Mellor. *A. P. Jones* — –

BELOW THE RED LINE 2 gr.c. (May 3) Reprimand 122 – Good Try 92 (Good Bond 122) [1995 7g Oct 10] 6,700Y: small, stocky colt: half-brother to several winners, including 3-y-o 1½m winner Kalamata (by Kalaglow) and sprinter Choir Practice (by Chief Singer): dam 2-y-o 5f winner: 50/1, visored, backward and green, slow-starting last of 14 in maiden at Leicester. *Mrs N. Macauley* — –

BELZAO 2 b.c. (Mar 17) Alzao (USA) 117 – Belle Enfant 87 (Beldale Flutter (USA) 130) [1995 6g^{3} 5.2g^{3} 5.7h^{4} Jul 10] 37,000Y: sturdy, useful-looking colt: fourth foal: half-brother to 3-y-o Spanish Steps (by Danehill) and useful 1m winner Air Commodore (by Elegant Air): dam, 1½m winner, half-sister to Dewhurst winner Dashing Blade: around 2 lengths third of 6 to Dovebrace in well-contested minor event at York in May: beaten at long odds on in maidens afterwards at Newbury (reportedly returned sore) and Bath: bred to stay beyond 6f. *M. R. Channon* — 86

BE MINDFUL 3 b.c. Warning 136 – Fetlar (Pharly (FR) 130) [1994 106: 6g^{2} 6m* 7g^{3} 7m* 7m^{6} 7.3d^{3} 1995 7m 8g^{2} 8.5m^{2} 10f^{5} 8f^{3} 8.9g^{4} 8g Sep 28] smallish, leggy colt: useful performer: in frame in £11,200 contest at Thirsk, Diomed Stakes (went down by 1¼ lengths to Mr Martini) at Epsom, £13,400 event at Goodwood and listed race at York: stiff task and visored, well beaten in Newmarket listed race final start: stays 1¼m: probably acts on any going: game and genuine: sent to USA. *J. R. Fanshawe* — 102

BE MY BIRD 2 b.f. (Apr 14) Be My Chief (USA) 122 – Million Heiress (Auction Ring (USA) 123) [1995 6m 6m^{5} 7m^{3} 6.9g^{5} 7g 8g 10d 8g a8.5g^{3} Oct 14] 8,800Y: compact filly: second foal: half-sister to 1994 2-y-o 5f winner Stato One (by — 65 d

Statoblest): dam poor maiden: modest and inconsistent maiden: stays 8.5f: blinkered penultimate start (tailed off throughout). *B. J. Meehan*

BE MY CHOICE 3 ch.f. Be My Chief (USA) 122 – Hence (USA) (Mr Prospector (USA)) [1994 NR 1995 10m a11g³ a12g³ Jul 22] sixth foal: half-sister to 3 winners, notably modest 4-y-o Ruby Heights (1¼m, by Shirley Heights) and fair Trippiano (1m, by Fappiano): dam 7f winner in USA: poor form when third in claimers at Southwell: sold 8,500 gns, in foal to Rock City, Newmarket December Sales. *Mrs J. Cecil* 44

BENATOM (USA) 2 gr.c. (Mar 18) Hawkster (USA) – Dance Til Two (USA) (Sovereign Dancer (USA)) [1995 7m 10m² Oct 2] $50,000F, $75,000Y: well-made colt: has a short, quick action: first foal: dam winning miler in North America: sire high class at up to 1½m: 1¾ lengths second of 14 to Warbrook at Pontefract, making most and keeping on gamely: will stay 1½m: will improve again, and should win a race. *H. R. A. Cecil* 82 p

BEN'A'VACHEI BOY 2 gr.g. (Apr 8) Rock City 120 – Vacherin (USA) (Green Dancer (USA) 132) [1995 5m⁴ 5g 5m 6m² 6d Sep 9] 7,200F, 8,000Y: useful-looking gelding: half-brother to 4-y-o German 6.5f winner Nour El Gamra (by Formidable): dam French middle-distance winner: improved effort when staying-on length second of 8 to Willow Dale in nursery at Kempton in September: went in snatches when last of 17 in similar event at Doncaster 8 days later: will stay further than 6f: possibly unsuited by a soft surface: blinkered last 2 starts: gave trouble stalls and withdrawn once. *J. D. Bethell* 58

BEN BOWDEN 2 br.g. (Apr 19) Sharrood (USA) 124 – Elegant Rose 72 (Noalto 120) [1995 7f 7.6d 8g Sep 29] leggy, unfurnished gelding: second foal: half-brother to fairly useful 3-y-o sprinter Bowden Rose (by Dashing Blade): dam best form at 6f and 7f: seventh in maidens won by Najm Mubeen at Lingfield and Select Few at Goodwood (free to post) last 2 starts. *M. Blanshard* 62

BENCHER Q C (USA) 3 ch.c. Affirmed (USA) – Au Printemps (USA) (Dancing Champ (USA)) [1994 NR 1995 a7g* 10m⁴ 10m³ 12g² 12d³ Sep 26] $400,000Y: well-made colt: brother to multiple stakes winner Charlie Barley, Grade 3 winner at 2 yrs and 4 yrs, and half-brother to Breeders' Cup Juvenile winner Success Express (by Hold Your Peace): dam won 7 races: won maiden at Lingfield in March: improved on every start, close third of 8 to Seckar Vale in rated stakes at Newmarket final one: stays 1½m well: acts on good to firm and dead ground: made running second start, held up since: sent to J. Noseda in USA. *J. H. M. Gosden* 96

BEND WAVY (IRE) 3 ch.c. Kefaah (USA) 124 – Prosodie (FR) (Relko 136) [1994 NR 1995 8g³ 8f⁴ Oct 18] 35,000Y: good-topped colt: half-brother to several winners, including useful French 7f to 9f winner Preston (by Fabulous Dancer): dam French 10.5f winner: third of 12 in maiden at Newmarket in June, running green early on but staying on well from 3f out: seemed sure to improve, but off course 4½ months: well-backed favourite, only modest form in maiden at Yarmouth: may prove suited by forcing tactics. *L. M. Cumani* 78

BENFLEET 4 ch.c. Dominion 123 – Penultimate (Final Straw 127) [1994 76: 8.3d* 8g* 8m a12g² 9f⁴ 11.6m⁵ 10.3g⁵ 10.1g 8d 1995 a12g* a12g* a12g 10d* 10m³ 11.8m 10.3m⁶ 10m² 12f³ 12m⁴ 10m 12g² 12f 12g⁵ 16.2d² 16.2s⁵ 12m⁴ a10g² Nov 21] small, lengthy colt: improved again in 1995, and is a fairly useful handicapper: won at Lingfield (twice) in January and Leicester in April: best efforts when in frame at Ascot, Doncaster and Lingfield in the autumn: effective at 1¼m and stays 16.2f: acts on firm and dead ground (probably on soft) and on equitrack (yet to show his best in 3 tries on fibresand): often early to post: held up of late: tough and consistent. *R. W. Armstrong* 89

BEN GUNN 3 b.g. Faustus (USA) 118 – Pirate Maid (Auction Ring (USA) 123) [1994 72: 6g 6g⁴ 7m* 6d* 7v 1995 7f 6g 6m* 7f³ Jul 28] good-bodied gelding: fair performer: won handicap at Windsor in July: staying-on 2 lengths third of 16 in £19,800 handicap at Goodwood 18 days later: stays 7f: acts on firm ground and dead, well beaten on heavy. *P. T. Walwyn* 76

BENJAMINS LAW 4 b. or br.g. Mtoto 134 – Absaloute Service 96 (Absalom 128) [1994 51§: 10m 8.2s 7g⁶ 8g 9g⁶ 12s 1995 10f³ 10.3m 10g³ 10g 10m⁶ 14g 10f⁴ a7g a9.4g* a10g³ a7g² a9.4g* Dec 9] rangy, workmanlike gelding: modest handicapper: improved on the all-weather late on, winning twice at Wolverhampton: 62

stays 1¼m: acts on firm ground, goes well on fibresand (well below form both runs on equitrack): often a front runner: inconsistent. *J. A. Pickering*

BENJAROng 3 ch.f. Sharpo 132 – Rose And The Ring (Welsh Pageant 132) 41
[1994 50: 5s^3 5d 5f^6 5m* 5g^5 6m^4 5m^5 a6g 5s 1995 a8g^5 a7g^5 8.1d 6s 8.3g^4 7m 7.1m 7m a7g 8g^5 8.3g* 7d^4 7.1s^5 8m a8g Nov 16] close-coupled filly: poor at best in 1995: won claimer at Hamilton in September: stays 8.3f: acts on good to firm ground, soft and fibresand. *R. M. McKellar*

BENNY GLOW 2 b.c. (May 11) Presidium 124 – Linpac North Moor 69 86
(Moorestyle 137) [1995 5g* 5g^5 6m* 6f* Jul 27] 4,800Y: good-quartered colt: fourth foal: half-brother to 3-y-o Sharmoor (by Shardari): dam won from 7f to 8.2f: won maiden auction and nursery at Pontefract and minor event at Doncaster (well below best) in the summer: will be suited by 7f: sweating and edgy at Doncaster: sold 22,000 gns Newmarket Autumn Sales. *Mrs J. R. Ramsden*

BENTEN 3 b.f. Sharrood (USA) 124 – Lurking 69 (Formidable (USA) 125) [1994 41 §
61d: 5d^2 5g^4 5d 5m^3 5m^3 a5g^5 6g 5f^2 6m 7g^6 1995 a7g a6g^6 a5g^5 a5g^4 a5g 7.1g a6g a6g 8f^4 7.5g 10m 6m 8f^5 6g^4 8m 5.9f Jul 31] small, leggy filly: has a round action: disappointing maiden: sold out of D. Nicholls' stable 550 gns Doncaster March Sales after fifth start: stays 7f: tried blinkered/visored: usually a front runner: not one to trust. *D. W. Chapman*

BENTHAM'S ABOUT 3 b.g. Formidable (USA) 125 – Hawaiian Song 63 –
(Henbit (USA) 130) [1994 –: 6f 1995 a8.5g^5 a11g Feb 24] sturdy gelding: no form. *Dr J. D. Scargill*

BENTICO 6 b.g. Nordico (USA) – Bentinck Hotel 74 (Red God 128§) [1994 73: 74
10d 10.1m^5 10m^5 9f 10.4d 8g* 8.2g 10d a11g a9.4g* a8g* a9.4g* 1995 a9.4g^4 a9.4g^4 a9.4g^3 a9.4g^4 a8g* a9.4g^6 a10g 10m 8m^4 8g 8.2m^6 10.1f^6 a8.5g^2 a8.5g^3 a7g^2 a8.5g^2 a7g* 7g^2 8g 8g* 8.2m^6 a8g^3 a7g^5 a8g a7g^6 Dec 18] lengthy, well-made gelding: carries condition: poor mover: fair handicapper: has shown same sort of form each of last 3 seasons, winning 3 or 4 races a year: successful in 1995 at Southwell in February, Wolverhampton (claimer) in September and Leicester (20-runner minor event) in October: effective at 7f to 1¼m: acts on the all-weather, best turf form on a sound surface: effective blinkered or not: sometimes bandaged: normally held up: very tough, and consistent. *Mrs N. Macauley*

BENZOE (IRE) 5 b.g. Taufan (USA) 119 – Saintly Guest (What A Guest 119) 86
[1994 –: 6f 6m 6m^6 5f 6g 6m 6d 6d 1995 6m 6f 6m* 5g 5m^2 5m 5m^6 6m^2 6m^4 6g 6g 5m Nov 4] tall gelding: has a round action: fairly useful handicapper: re-found some form for new stable: won at Thirsk in May: effective at 5f and 6f: acts on good to firm and heavy ground: effective blinkered or not, disappointing in visor seventh 5-y-o start: sometimes gives trouble at stalls, and often slowly away: has broken blood vessels. *Mrs J. R. Ramsden*

BEQUEATH 3 ch.c. Rainbow Quest (USA) 134 – Balabina (USA) 110 (Nijinsky 89 p
(CAN) 138) [1994 NR 1995 10g^3 10g^2 Jul 12] rather unfurnished colt: fourth foal: brother to French 1½m winner Balabac and 9f/10.8f winner Balnibarbi and half-brother to useful 4-y-o 7f (at 2 yrs) to 1¼m winner Bal Harbour (by Shirley Heights): dam, 1½m winner, half-sister to Quiet Fling and Peacetime: narrowly beaten in maidens at Sandown and Newmarket (led inside last, unable to hold Royal Circle's rally, beaten a head) in the summer: will be suited by further than 1¼m: looked sure to improve again, and win races. *H. R. A. Cecil*

BERGE (IRE) 4 b.c. Most Welcome 131 – Miss Blitz 83 (Formidable (USA) 125) 68 a77
[1994 68: 6m 8.3m 8.3m 7g a6g* a7g^5 a7g^3 a6g* a6g 1995 a7g*^{dis} 6g* 7g a7g* 7f^3 a6g^3 a6g* Nov 24] lengthy, workmanlike colt: has reportedly had 4 operations on his knees: fair performer: first past post in 2 claimers at Southwell (disqualified after failing dope test first occasion) and handicap at Thirsk (off course over 5 months afterwards) in the spring, then another claimer at Southwell (barely off bridle, but finished lame) in November: best at up to 7f: acts on fibresand, best turf form on good ground: effective blinkered (usually is) or not. *W. A. O'Gorman*

BERGHOLT 3 b.g. Reprimand 122 – Kina (USA) (Bering 136) [1994 NR 1995 –
7m 8m 6m Jun 17] 4,800Y: rangy, rather unfurnished gelding: first foal: dam never ran: always behind in maidens: sold 1,350 gns Ascot September Sales. *G. L. Moore*

BERKELEY BOUNDER (USA) 3 b.c. Diesis 133 – Top Socialite (USA) 117 73
(Topsider (USA)) [1994 57: 6m^5 1995 6.9g^6 8m^3 10.3m^5 10f^2 12m^2 11.7h^3 12g^2

11.8g* 14.6m Oct 20] lengthy colt: has a round action: fair performer: trained until after sixth start by P. Cole and most consistent: won claimer at Leicester (claimed out of M. Pipe's stable £8,000) in October: tailed off in handicap at Doncaster 10 days later: stays 1½m: has raced only on a sound surface. *R. M. McKellar*

BERNARD SEVEN (IRE) 3 b.c. Taufan (USA) 119 – Madame Nureyev (USA) (Nureyev (USA) 131) [1994 80: 5d^3 5s^2 6f^3 1995 8d^3 8m^2 7.6m* 8m* 8m 10m^4 10d 7g a7g a8g^5 Dec 14] neat colt: fairly useful performer: won minor event at Lingfield (drifting left) and handicap at Ripon (third-last start for S. Woods) in May: well below form for new stable: should prove best at up to 1m (creditable 1¼m effort was in steadily-run race): acts on firm and soft ground: blinkered/visored (except once) since fourth 3-y-o start. *C. E. Brittain* — 90 d

BERNARD STAR (IRE) 3 b.f. Cyrano de Bergerac 120 – Make Your Bid 79 (Auction Ring (USA) 123) [1994 NR 1995 a7g a8.5g Feb 22] IR 1,200Y: fourth foal: half-sister to 2 minor winners: dam 1m and 9f winner: slowly away and well beaten in 2 Wolverhampton sellers. *B. J. Llewellyn* — –

BERNIE'S SISTER (IRE) 4 b.f. Jareer (USA) 115 – Amorak 85 (Wolver Hollow 126) [1994 –: a11g^4 12s^4 12.3d 8.1g 7m 10f 12g 10.1f a8.5g 7m 12s 1995 a12g a8g Feb 4] leggy, sparely-made filly: no form since 2 yrs: sold 925 gns Ascot February Sales. *C. N. Allen* — –

BE SATISFIED 2 ch.g. (Apr 24) Chilibang 120 – Gentalyn (Henbit (USA) 130) [1995 a8g a7g^4 a6g^5 Dec 14] 3,000Y: 4,200 2-y-o: sixth foal: dam unraced: plating-class form in late-year maidens on equitrack: stays 7f. *A. Moore* — 55

BESCABY BOY 9 b.g. Red Sunset 120 – Charo (Mariacci (FR) 133) [1994 66: 9.9s 12m^2 9.7s^2 10g* 9.9m^2 10.3m^4 10m* 10.3m^3 10g 8.2g^4 10.3s* 10.1d 1995 10d 10m 10m Apr 29] strong gelding: carries condition: fair performer: backward, never placed to challenge first 2 starts in 1995: gambled on and well beaten final one: stays 1½m: probably acts on any going: not tried in blinkers for long time: often bandaged: held up: sold only 600 gns Doncaster October Sales. *J. Wharton* — –

BESCABY GIRL 4 ch.f. Master Willie 129 – Thatched Grove (Thatching 131) [1994 44: 6g 6m 5.9m^4 6m 7g 6.9h^2 7g^5 7.1m 1995 a8g Jan 9] good-topped filly: unimpressive mover: poor maiden: stays 7f: acts on any going: blinkered/visored since third 3-y-o outing: sold (J. Wainwright to M. Tate) 920 gns Doncaster March Sales. *J. S. Wainwright* — –

BESSIE'S WILL 4 ch.f. Chilibang 120 – Empress Corina 74 (Free State 125) [1994 NR 1995 a6g a7g a5g a7g a6g a6g Feb 6] small, good-bodied filly: no longer of much account. *D. Haydn Jones* — –

BEST KEPT SECRET 4 b.g. Petong 126 – Glenfield Portion 86 (Mummy's Pet 125) [1994 75: 5s^4 6d^5 5f^5 a6g^3 5.9m^3 5g* 6f^3 5.9f^2 6g* 6m^4 6m* 6d^4 5f^2 6m 6.1g^6 1995 a6g^3 5.1g^2 6f 7m^2 6g^3 7.1m^3 5.9f^3 6m^5 7f^3 5h^5 6g^3 a7g^6 8.1d^6 7m Oct 30] neat gelding: has a quick action: only modest performer in 1995: stays 7f: probably acts on any going: tried blinkered/visored at 3 yrs, but seemed out of sorts at the time: tends to hang and carry head awkwardly: none too consistent: sold (J. Berry to P. D. Evans) 2,100 gns Doncaster November Sales. *J. Berry* — 64

BEST OF ALL (IRE) 3 b.f. Try My Best (USA) 130 – Skisette (Malinowski (USA) 123) [1994 69p: 6m^2 5m* 6m 1995 6m 6g 8.1s* Nov 2] rather leggy, useful-looking filly: fair performer, lightly raced: 33/1, improved form to win 14-runner handicap at Edinburgh in November, always well there: stays 8.1f: acts on good to firm ground, goes well on soft. *J. Berry* — 77

BEST OF BOLD 3 ch.g. Never So Bold 135 – I'll Try 71 (Try My Best (USA) 130) [1994 55p: 7m 1995 8m^4 8f^5 8g^4 6m 7d^6 7g 8g a7g Nov 29] compact, well-made gelding: fair maiden: fourth at Salisbury and Leicester (claimer, final start for R. Hannon) in May: below form for new yard: stays 1m: acts on good to firm ground: blinkered last 3 starts. *N. A. Graham* — 70 d

BEST OF TIMES 4 ch.f. Handsome Sailor 125 – Early Doors (Ballad Rock 122) [1994 –: 6f 1995 9.2s Apr 12] lightly-raced filly: refused to race in Hamilton claimer for new stable. *D. Moffatt* — – §

BETABETCORBETT 4 b.g. Prince Sabo 123 – Leprechaun Lady 57 (Royal Blend 117) [1994 45: 8.3v 9.9d^5 a12g^3 12m 1995 a11g a12g a14.8g Jan 25] sturdy, workmanlike gelding: seems no longer of much account. *B. P. J. Baugh* — –

BETTERGETON 3 ch.c. Rakaposhi King 119 – Celtic Tore (IRE) (Torus 117) 97 [1994 77: 7d^{5} 6v^{4} a7g^{4} a7g* 1995 8m* 7.6m^{6} 8g* 8f* 8m* 8g^{2} 7.9m 9g a12g Dec 2] workmanlike colt: progressed into a useful handicapper, winning twice at both Ripon and Doncaster: off course 6 weeks (didn't take the eye, down the field in Cambridgeshire) then 2 months (well beaten at Wolverhampton) before last 2 starts: should stay 1¼m: acts on any turf going and on fibresand: genuine. *P. J. Bevan*

BETTER OFFER (IRE) 3 b.g. Waajib 121 – Camden's Gift (Camden Town 102 125) [1994 80: 7m 7s^{2} 9.7s^{3} 1995 12m^{5} 10m^{3dis} 10m* 10m^{2} 12m* 11.9d^{2} 12d^{2} 11.9g^{2} Oct 1] big, lengthy gelding: useful handicapper: won at Lingfield and Kempton in the summer: second in rated stakes at Haydock, £46,800 event at Ascot (sweating, 1¼ lengths behind Taufan's Melody) and £11,400 contest at Brighton (beaten neck) last 3 starts: suited by good test at 1½m, and will probably get further: acts on soft ground and good to firm: carries head high. *G. Harwood*

BETTY KENWOOD 5 ch.m. Dominion 123 – Doogali 93 (Doon 124) [1994 39: – a16g^{3} a11g^{3} a13g 15.4v^{2} 15.4v 18m^{3} 17.2f^{5} 1995 a16g a12g^{6} Jan 9] angular mare: poor maiden: stays 2¼m: acts on good to firm ground, heavy and fibresand: effective in blinkers: often bandaged. *Mrs J. R. Ramsden*

BETTYKIMVIC 4 b.f. Reesh 117 – Palace Pet (Dragonara Palace (USA) 115) – [1994 –: 5g^{5} 6f a6g 1995 6m Apr 25] short-backed filly: seems no longer of much account: sold 900 gns (May) and 3,000 gns (November) at Doncaster Sales. *E. J. Alston*

BEVELED EDGE 6 ch.m. Beveled (USA) – Best Offer 96 (Crepello 136) [1994 47 60?: 5.7f^{2} 5.1m 6m 5.1m^{4} 1995 a6g^{2} a6g^{4} a6g^{4} 6m 6.1d^{4} 6d Sep 18] leggy, a58 sparely-made mare: modest handicapper: stays 6f: acts on fibresand and on firm ground, yet to race on soft: sometimes sweats: inconsistent. *B. Palling*

BEVERLY HILLS 2 b.f. (Apr 6) Shareef Dancer (USA) 135 – Debbie Harry – (USA) 70 (Alleged (USA) 138) [1995 7g a7g Nov 27] 9,000Y: neat filly: second foal: half-sister to 3-y-o Shooter (by Salse): dam stayer: refused to enter stalls on intended debut: showed little in maiden at Warwick (blinkered, swerved stalls) and maiden auction at Wolverhampton: sold 800 gns Newmarket December Sales. *J. W. Hills*

BEWARE OF AGENTS 6 b.g. Tremblant 112 – Saltation 111 (Sallust 134) 58 d [1994 74: 7f 7g a7g^{5} 8g 7f^{4} 8m 8.1m^{2} 7g^{5} 7g 1995 a7g a8.5g^{3} a8g^{5} 7d^{2} 7g^{5} 6.9f 7m a66 d 7m^{6} Jun 17] big, lengthy gelding: reportedly hobdayed: very much on the downgrade: trained by M. Hammond for fourth 6-y-o start: stays 9f: acts on any going: sold 1,800 gns (July) and 600 gns (October) Doncaster Sales. *M. Johnston*

BE WARNED 4 b.g. Warning 136 – Sagar 74 (Habitat 134) [1994 84: 8m 8g 8m^{4} 85 7m* 8g^{3} 7m^{4} 8m 6m^{2} 7g^{2} 6m^{2} 6g* 6d^{3} 5.1s^{3} 6d^{2} 6d^{5} 1995 7m 6m 6g^{6} 6m^{3} 8g 8m 6m 6g* 7d 7g 6d^{2} a7g* a7g^{4} Nov 24] good-topped gelding: unimpressive mover: fairly useful handicapper: back to form in the autumn, winning at Yarmouth in September and Southwell in November: ideally suited by 6f/7f: acts on good to firm and soft ground and on fibresand: effective blinkered or not: sometimes mounted on track: held up. *N. A. Callaghan*

BEWITCHING (USA) 2 ch.f. (Mar 20) Imp Society (USA) – Mrs Magnum 87 ? (USA) (Northjet 136) [1995 5m^{3} 5.1m^{4} 6f* 7m^{4} 6f Oct 12] 9,500F: leggy, lengthy filly: has scope: unimpressive mover: sixth foal: sister to 3 winners in USA and half-sister to another: dam unraced daughter of half-sister to Exceller: off course 3 months, won maiden at Salisbury (reluctant to post) in August: seemed to progress again when around 3 lengths fourth of 6 to Bint Shadayid in moderately-run Prestige Stakes at Goodwood nearly 3 weeks later, but down the field in Redcar Two-Year-Old Trophy in October: stays 7f. *J. A. R. Toller*

BEX BOY (IRE) 4 ch.g. Mon Tresor 113 – Calcine 75 (Roan Rocket 128) [1994 32 –: 8s 1995 10g 7.5m^{5} 8m^{3} 12.3f^{6} 8m 9.9m^{3} 8g Aug 26] plain gelding: poor performer: stays 1m: acts on good to firm ground: blinkered since third 4-y-o start. *M. W. Easterby*

BEX HILL 3 ch.f. Grey Desire 115 – Pour Moi 73 (Bay Express 132) [1994 51: – a5g 6.1m a6g^{3} a7g a7g* 10s 7g a7g 1995 a8.5g^{6} a7g a6g a7g a6g Dec 12] angular filly: no longer of much account. *D. Haydn Jones*

BEYAATEH 3 b.f. Kefaah (USA) 124 – Keswa 94 (Kings Lake (USA) 133) [1994 – NR 1995 a8g a8g a6g 12g^{6} 9.9m 12m^{6} 14.1g a12g 12m 10m Aug 12] 600 2-y-o:

good-topped filly: first foal: dam 1m (at 2 yrs) and 1½m winner out of half-sister to Celestial Storm: little sign of ability on flat. *M. C. Chapman*

BEYOND DOUBT 3 ch.f. Belmez (USA) 131 – Highbrow 112§ (Shirley Heights 130) [1994 69p: 7d^2 1995 10m* 12f* Jun 28] quite attractive filly: well-backed favourite, won 21-runner maiden event at Windsor (despite seeming green) and 4-runner handicap at Salisbury (led on bridle over 3f out, never looked in any danger), both in June: better at 1½m than shorter: looked potentially useful. *Lord Huntingdon* — 82 p

BEZIRGAN 4 b.f. Dowsing (USA) 124 – Lomond Ring (Lomond (USA) 128) [1994 44: 7g^5 7m 5.1f^4 5g^5 6f^6 7.6g^6 8m a8.5g 1995 6m 10m 8f May 26] small filly: no longer of much account: sold 625 gns Ascot June Sales. *J. Akehurst* — –

BIANCA CAPPELLO (IRE) 2 b.f. (Mar 12) Glenstal (USA) 118 – Idara 109 (Top Ville 129) [1995 7m 7.6d 7d Sep 22] IR 23,000Y: big filly: half-sister to very useful Irish 7f to 1¼m performer Idris (by Ahonoora): dam French 11f and 1½m winner: behind in maidens at Salisbury, Lingfield and Redcar: sold 4,200 gns Newmarket December Sales. *J. L. Dunlop* — –

BIANCA STELLA (USA) 2 b.c. (Apr 25) Green Dancer (USA) 132 – Sharmila (FR) (Blakeney 126) [1995 7g^6 Jul 19] IR 11,000Y: leggy, angular colt: sixth foal: half-brother to 4 winners, notably useful 3-y-o 6.1f (at 2 yrs) to 9f winner El Supremo (by Storm Bird) and 11.9f winner Severine (by Trempolino): dam once-raced half-sister to Petoski: sixth of 17 in maiden auction at Leicester: bandaged except for near-fore: dead. *M. Bell* — 58

BIASED VIEW 3 ch.g. Beveled (USA) – Scenic Villa (Top Ville 129) [1994 56: 7g^6 7m^5 7g^2 7m^2 7.5g 7g 7g 7.1g 1995 8.2m 6g 10m a10g Nov 21] quite good-topped gelding: maiden: no form for new stable in 1995. *R. Thompson* — –

BIBLIOTHEQUE (USA) 3 ch.f. Woodman (USA) 126 – Book Collector (USA) 80 (Irish River (FR) 131) [1994 NR 1995 7m^3 8m^6 8f^4 8.3m 8g* 8d* Sep 27] angular, useful-looking filly: shows a round action: first foal: dam, 1987 2-y-o 6f winner, later successful in USA: seemed disappointing after first 4 starts, but impressively justified favouritism when visored in handicaps last 2 outings: didn't get the best of runs on either occasion but produced good late burst to win at Yarmouth (maiden) and Salisbury (always travelling easily) in September: stays 1m: possibly suited by give in the ground: bandaged: very much one to keep on the right side: sent to Dubai. *J. H. M. Gosden* — 79 p

BIDE OUR TIME (USA) 3 b.c. Timeless Moment (USA) – Had To Buy (USA) (Sadair) [1994 89: 7m^3 6g* 6m 7m 1995 7m 7.3m 8.3m Aug 26] lengthy, good-topped colt: has plenty of scope: disappointing in 1995, well beaten in rated stakes: may prove best at up to 7f: blinkered final start. *J. A. R. Toller* — –

BID FOR A RAINBOW 4 b.g. Sulaafah (USA) 119 – Star Alert (Red Alert 127) [1994 –: 6.9v 7s 8.1g 7g 1995 7m Apr 17] big gelding: well beaten since 2 yrs. *Mrs M. E. Long* — –

BIG BANDS ARE BACK (USA) 3 b.g. Alleged (USA) 138 – Jetta J (USA) (Super Concorde (USA) 128) [1994 74p: 7.1m^5 7g 10g^4 1995 a7g^6 Nov 14] tall, angular gelding: fair form at 2 yrs, best effort final start: weak in betting, below form in 7f Lingfield maiden on only outing of 1995: will be suited by 1½m+: sold (B. Hills to C. Popham) 600 gns Ascot December Sales. *B. W. Hills* — 60

BIG CHANCE 6 ch.g. Sharpo 132 – Cherry Ridge 112 (Riva Ridge (USA)) [1994 46d: 8.3v 8g 10d 12.1g 7.5m^4 8m^6 7g 8m 10m 1995 a9.4g^4 8g a8g^2 a9.4g Jul 8] short-backed gelding: poor performer: stays 1m: acts on good to firm going, soft and fibresand: hurdling with J. Glover before sold to join S. Bowen 1,350 gns Ascot November Sales. *W. J. Musson* — 34

BIG PAT 6 b.g. Backchat (USA) 98 – Fallonetta 41 (Tachypous 128) [1994 76: a12g^5 12g^3 12.4g 12g* 11.8m^2 11.6m* 1995 12m^5 12g 12.1g a12g Nov 2] leggy gelding: tough and genuine at 5 yrs: shaped as if retaining ability on belated 1995 reappearance, but soundly beaten afterwards, leaving K. McAuliffe's stable after third start: effective at 11.5f to 1¾m: acts on good to firm ground and dead. *J. G. M. O'Shea* — –

BIG TICKLE (IRE) 6 b.g. Colonel Godfrey (USA) 86 – Head Scarf 59 (Tumble Wind (USA)) [1994 NR 1995 7.1m^6 Jul 2] eighth foal: half-brother to 2 minor — –

winners: dam 7f seller winner: bad hurdler: 10/1 from 33/1, almost 16 lengths last of 6 in seller at Chepstow on flat debut. *G. A. Ham*

BIG TREAT (IRE) 3 b.g. Be My Guest (USA) 126 – Cavurina 81§ (Cavo Doro 124) [1994 7g³ 7.5g 8s² 1995 11.5m⁶ 10d⁶ Sep 13] 13,500F: 14,000Y: ex-Italian gelding: half-brother to numerous winners, including useful stayer Straldi (by Elma-Mana-Mou): dam, 1¼m winner, was temperamental: fair form at best in Italy for M. Luciano at 2 yrs: weakened quickly final 2f when well beaten in maidens here: sold (P. Kelleway to P. Hiatt) 2,700 gns Doncaster November Sales. *P. A. Kelleway* –

BIJOU D'INDE 2 ch.c. (Mar 9) Cadeaux Genereux 131 – Pushkar (Northfields (USA)) [1995 6m² 6f² 7m* 8m* 8d⁵ Sep 23] 106 p

Bijou d'Inde kicked off a bad week for the Mark Johnston stable stars, his poor showing in the Royal Lodge Stakes at Ascot being followed by disappointments for Double Trigger at Longchamp, Branston Abby at Goodwood and Double Eclipse at Newmarket. In Bijou d'Inde's case at least, the set-back was not entirely a surprise. In his newspaper column that day, Johnston revealed that 'It was very difficult to decide whether to run Bijou d'Inde or not as he was out of action for most of last week due to being lame. We are quite happy that he is completely recovered but he has missed quite a bit of work and he will go into this race 9kg heavier than for his previous run.' Two days later, interviewed in the other trade paper, he revealed that the problem had recurred and Bijou d'Inde had returned lame. Bijou d'Inde is a good deal better than his nine and a half lengths fifth of eight to Mons in the Royal Lodge. That much was already apparent from his previous start when he beat Axford two and a half lengths in the Group 3 Futurity Stakes at the Curragh, another result which, taken at face value, underestimates Bijou d'Inde's ability—he could have won it by at least three lengths more. At 8/11 in an eight-runner race, followed in the betting by Chapple-Hyam's Axford with the Curragh listed winner Common Spirit considered best of the Irish, Bjiou d'Inde made the running, was the only one still on the bridle entering the straight, and won easing down. Eighteen days earlier, he had done much the same against five opponents in the £13,100 Deploy Acomb Conditions Stakes at the York Ebor meeting, the best of his chasers that day being the Maktoum-owned Hammerstein and Jarah. These two clear-cut wins followed two narrow defeats, in maidens at Newcastle and Goodwood.

Back to Bijou d'Inde after Ascot. The injury is not considered a likely problem for 1996 and given that his trainer is not one to duck a challenge, Bijou d'Inde will probably be aimed at the Guineas. He looks an interesting outsider. A big, good-topped colt with scope, he has so far shown plenty of early speed and a style of running which suggests that he will be a miler, although one cannot say categorically that he will not stay any further.

Unsurprisingly, progeny of the champion sprinter Cadeaux Genereux tend to have marked stamina limitations. He has had plenty of useful performers but the 20,000-guinea yearling Bijou d'Inde could turn out to be his best yet, an honour which currently rests with either the Sun Chariot winner Warning Shadows (one of the few Cadeaux Genereuxs who stay a mile and a quarter) or the Prix Morny winner

Futurity Stakes, the Curragh—ears pricked, Bijou d'Inde has plenty in hand of Axford

Bijou d'Inde (ch.c. Mar 9, 1993)	Cadeaux Genereux (ch 1985)	Young Generation (b 1976)	Balidar
			Brig O'Doon
		Smarten Up (ch 1975)	Sharpen Up
			L'Anguissola
	Pushkar (b 1980)	Northfields (ch 1968)	Northern Dancer
			Little Hut
		Chippings (b 1972)	Busted
			Chip

Hoh Magic. Cadeaux Genereux is easily the most prestigious sire visited by Bijou d'Inde's dam Pushkar. Nevertheless, six of her eight previous foals were winners and two of them well above average. The smart Eradicate (by Tender King) won seven races here, four (including the Magnet Cup) in a purple patch as a five-year-old that saw him sold from Peter Calver's Ripon yard to California where a short-lived career got off to a bright start with a second in the Grade 1 Oak Tree Invitational. Two years after Eradicate, Pushkar produced Hebridean (by Norwick) who developed into a high-class staying hurdler. Neither Pushkar nor her dam Chippings was raced. The third dam Chip was, but only as a two-year-old when she showed fairly useful form and won over five furlongs. Both Chippings and Chip produced noteworthy runners, however: Chippings the Irish Group 3 mile-and-a-half winner Red Chip, and Chip the smart sprinter Silver God. *M. Johnston*

BILLADDIE 2 b.g. (Feb 10) Touch of Grey 90 – Young Lady (Young Generation 129) [1995 8d 7m 6m^6 Nov 6] tall, good-topped gelding: has scope: second reported foal: dam never ran: never a factor in maidens at Newmarket and Folkestone (best effort), considerately handled after slow start each time: midfield in 27-runner seller at Newmarket in between: will stay 1m: may well be capable of better. *R. Boss* — 55 p

BILL AND WIN 4 b.g. Faustus (USA) 118 – Water Folly (Sharpo (USA) 132) [1994 –: a9.4g^3 12.1s 13.4m^6 a14.8g^5 a9.4g 10g 1995 10g Apr 24] workmanlike gelding: winning selling hurdler: no worthwhile form on flat: has joined T. Wall. *K. White* — –

BILL MOON 9 ch.g. Nicholas Bill 125 – Lunar Queen 96 (Queen's Hussar 124) [1994 36: a7g a7g^4 a7g 8m 7.6g a7g a10g a10g 1995 8g 7.1m 7m^6 6f Jul 29] leggy gelding: poor handicapper at best: mostly runs (under Miss J. Feilden) in ladies races: stays 1m: acts on firm, dead ground and equitrack, unsuited by a very soft surface. *D. T. Thom* — 28

BILLS PLOUGHGIRL 3 gr.f. Risk Me (FR) 127 – Petite Angel 30 (Burslem 123) [1994 43: 5.1m 6g 6m 5.1g^6 7g 6s a6g a5g 1995 a7g^5 8h 8f Oct 24] plain filly: no longer of any account. *J. S. Moore* — –

BILLYBACK 5 b.g. Absalom 128 – Petit Secret 64 (Petingo 135) [1994 NR 1995 9.7m Jul 12] dipped-backed gelding: modest form (rated 54) in 1993: tailed-off last in seller on return. *M. J. Ryan* — –

BILLY BUSHWACKER 4 b.g. Most Welcome 131 – Secret Valentine 71 (Wollow 132) [1994 85p: 7g* 7.5m^2 7.9m 7.1d* 7g^4 8d^3 1995 8m* 7m^6 8m^4 10m 7.9m 9g 8m^4 Oct 28] rather leggy, workmanlike gelding: useful handicapper: impressive winner at Doncaster in May: best efforts afterwards when fourth in big fields for Hunt Cup (first home on stand side) at Royal Ascot and £24,100 contest (blinkered, would have gone very close with run of race) at Newmarket: stays 1m well: acts on good to firm and dead ground, yet to race on extremes: held up. *Mrs M. Reveley* — 96

BILLY CRUNCHEON 4 b.c. Sharpo (USA) 132 – Sorayah 89 (Persian Bold 123) [1994 64: 6s* 5m^6 6m 7m 6.1s 5d^2 6d 6s 6.1g 1995 6m^4 5g May 24] small colt: disappointing handicapper, poor at best in 1995: stays 6f: acts on soft ground and good to firm: visored (out of form) final 3-y-o start. *M. C. Pipe* — 45

BILLYTOBINSLAD 4 b.g. Tobin Lad (USA) 124 – Sybilly (Nicholas Bill 125) [1994 NR 1995 12m^6 10m Aug 22] leggy, angular gelding: third foal: dam strong-pulling maiden: of no account. *Mrs V. A. Aconley* — –

BIMSEY (IRE) 5 b.h. Horage 124 – Cut It Out (Cut Above 130) [1994 NR 1995 14s^3 14.1m* Oct 19] leggy horse: first foal: dam unraced: won NH Flat race at Tralee in 1994 for Mrs E. Finn and useful 2m/2½m hurdler here, winner in November: justified favouritism in maiden at Nottingham in October by 9 lengths from Sujud, — 84 p leading over 6f out: will stay 2m: acts on good to firm and soft going: capable of better. *R. Akehurst*

BIN AJWAAD (IRE) 5 b.h. Rainbow Quest (USA) 134 – Salidar (Sallust 134) [1994 113: 8g* 10m^{5} 8m* 8g^{4} 6g^{6} 1995 8g 7d* 8v^{2} 8m* 8g^{6} 7d^{4} 7m^{2} Oct 15] tall, good-topped horse: had more than his share of injuries, including fractured hock after third start 1995: smart performer: won Sean Coughlan Gladness Stakes at the Curragh in April and listed race at Kempton in September: good short-neck second of 10 to Poplar Bluff in Prix de la Foret at Longchamp on final start: raced almost exclusively at 7f/1m (not discredited in very strongly-run Eclipse at 1¼m): acted on good to firm ground and heavy: held up: to stand at Woodditton Stud, Newmarket, fee £3,500 (no live foal, no fee). *B. Hanbury* 115

BINLABOON (IRE) 4 b. or br.c. Polish Precedent (USA) 131 – Aldhabyih 86 (General Assembly (USA)) [1994 –: 8.2s 1995 a12g^{6} a9.4g a7g 11.5g Sep 12] poor winning hurdler: little sign of ability on flat: tried blinkered. *K. G. Wingrove* –

BIN NASHWAN (USA) 3 b.c. Nashwan (USA) 135 – Dabaweyaa 118 (Shareef Dancer (USA) 135) [1994 107: 7m^{6} 6g* 7d^{3} 6m^{6} 1995 7m 7g^{5} 7g^{3} 5g^{5} Sep 28] well-made, good sort: useful performer at best: creditable seventh of 12 in European Free Handicap at Newmarket on reappearance: reportedly had wind operation in May: long way below form afterwards: stays 7f: yet to race on extremes of going: has pulled hard: hung left and flashed tail penultimate outing. *C. E. Brittain* 106 d

BIN ROSIE 3 b.g. Distant Relative 128 – Come On Rosi 77 (Valiyar 129) [1994 NR 1995 7m^{3} 7.6m^{2} 8g* 8m^{5} 8m^{2} 7.3m^{3} 7g^{2} 8g* 8m^{3} 8g Nov 12] 21,000F, IR 35,000Y: smallish, angular gelding: first foal: dam 6f winner: smart performer: won maiden in June and listed race (did nothing wrong in front, holding unlucky Red Carnival by 2 lengths) in September, both at Newmarket: effective at 7f to 1m: acts on good to firm ground, yet to race on a soft surface: visored/blinkered since fourth start: carries head awkwardly: sometimes hangs, looks difficult ride and has found little. *D. R. Loder* 113

Mr A. Merza's "Bin Ajwaad"

BINT SALSABIL (USA) 2 ch.f. (Feb 14) Nashwan (USA) 135 – Salsabil 130 (Sadler's Wells (USA) 132) [1995 6f* 7m* 8g 7m* Oct 13] 104 p

Every man and his dog seemed to know in late-spring that the unraced stable-companions Bint Salsabil and Bint Shadayid, two-year-old fillies by Nashwan out of classic-winning dams, were living up to their breeding at home. By the time Bint Salsabil made her debut in the six-furlong EBF Maiden Fillies Stakes at Ascot in June, deputising for Bint Shadayid, she was already one of the market leaders for the Guineas and Oaks. And at the time of writing she is still prominent in the ante-post betting, disputing favouritism for the Oaks with the only filly to have beaten Bint Shadayid, Bosra Sham.

Bint Salsabil's season went less smoothly than her stable-companion's. She suffered what seemed a serious reverse in the May Hill Stakes at Doncaster on her third start, coming only eighth of eleven to Bosra Sham's deputy Solar Crystal, soon bustled along and never dangerous. The first two starts had gone very well. At Ascot she looked the part in the paddock, and though just about first off the bridle when the contest developed into a two-furlong sprint she responded to win going away from the much-fancied Prancing. Six weeks later at Newmarket, up against mainly maiden and minor winners, a couple of whom had run well against Blue Duster, she won the seven-furlong Enza New Zealand Sweet Solera Stakes by a neck from Staffin. She went about her task in a pleasing fashion, once again, after being pushed along sooner than most as the speedy Tropical Dance stretched the field. Bint Salsabil took over more than a furlong out and beat off a challenge from the runner-up, holding her convincingly in the closing stages. It is not clear why Bint Salsabil, passed over by Carson at Doncaster in favour of the same owner's Ruznama who finished third, strayed so far from the script in the May Hill. The only thing we can point to is that she was less settled in the preliminaries than before. The trip didn't beat her, neither did the ground, which times suggest was good. Of course, even if she had run better, she might not have been good enough to win. In order to find out more about her before the winter, connections ran her in the Greene King Rockfel Stakes at Newmarket in October; they relied on Bint Shadayid for the harder Fillies' Mile. Bint Salsabil put Doncaster behind with a useful, front-running display (it may be significant that she was more settled beforehand than at Doncaster although she had been sweating). The main danger turned out to be her stable-companion Parrot Jungle rather than the short-priced favourite My Branch who was not seen at her best in third. Having set a very strong pace—deliberate tactics—the winner stayed on gamely to hold Parrot Jungle, who ducked to her right inside the final furlong, by three parts of a length.

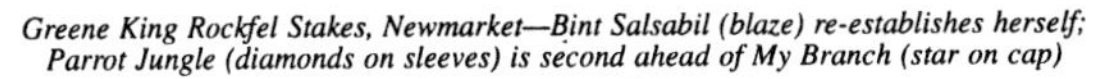
Greene King Rockfel Stakes, Newmarket—Bint Salsabil (blaze) re-establishes herself; Parrot Jungle (diamonds on sleeves) is second ahead of My Branch (star on cap)

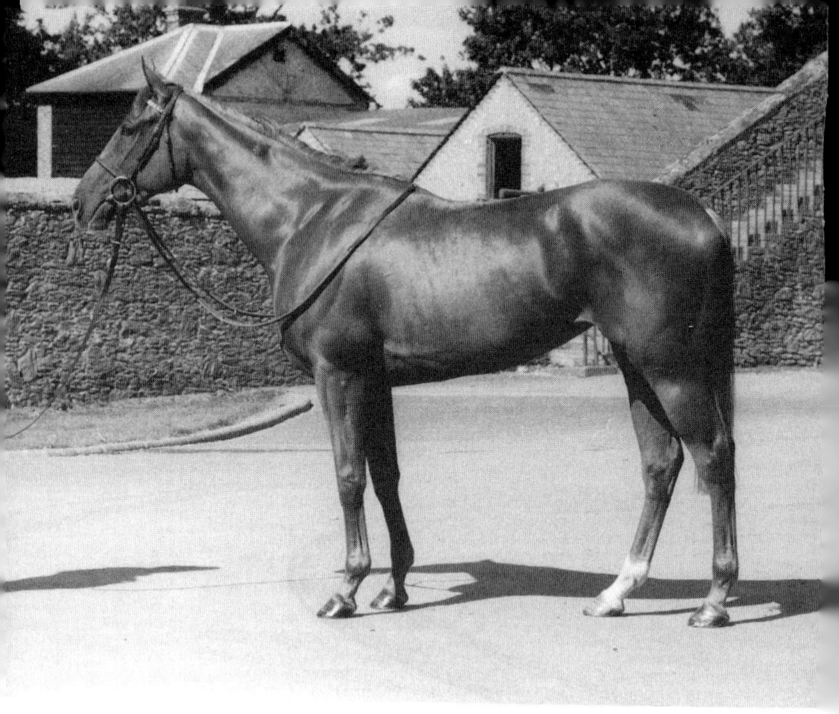

Hamdan Al Maktoum's "Bint Salsabil"

Bint Salsabil (USA) (ch.f. Feb 14, 1993)	Nashwan (USA) (ch 1986)	Blushing Groom (ch 1974)	Red God
			Runaway Bride
		Height of Fashion (b 1979)	Bustino
			Highclere
	Salsabil (b 1987)	Sadler's Wells (b 1981)	Northern Dancer
			Fairy Bridge
		Flame of Tara (b 1980)	Artaius
			Welsh Flame

The form is no more than useful. While Bint Salsabil is back on the road again she has a fair way still to go before she is good enough to take a hand in the classics. However, she has lots of physical scope—she is strongly-built and lengthy—and is a daughter of two individuals who made striking improvement from two to three. Salsabil was around 10 lb better as two-year-old than her daughter. On the last of her three starts at that age Salsabil won the Prix Marcel Boussac by two lengths. The following season she reeled off the Fred Darling Stakes, the One Thousand Guineas, the Oaks, the Irish Derby and the Prix Vermeille until the run ended in the Arc. She began her stud career in 1991 with a visit to her owner's horse Nashwan. The mating brought a filly, subsequently named Firdous, who was put into training with Dunlop as a two-year-old but has not run. Following on is a colt and then a filly by Mr Prospector. Salsabil was acquired for 440,000 guineas as a yearling, the daughter of a good racemare. Since then, the mare Flame of Tara has produced several others of note—Marju, Danse Royale, Salsabil's IR 1,500,000-guinea brother Song of Tara and the 1995 Irish two-year-old Flame of Athens. The family also hit the headlines in the States in the latest season through the Breeders' Cup Turf winner Northern Spur (by Sadler's Wells out of Flame of Tara's half-sister Fruition).

Bint Salsabil is bred to be effective at a mile to a mile and a half as a three-year-old, but if she is to win a classic it is more likely to be an Oaks than a Guineas. If she does run in the Guineas, presumably tactics will be the same as in the Rockfel. Thus far Bint Salsabil, a good mover, has shown she acts well on firm ground. Interestingly, connections seem to be of the opinion that the ground was soft, or on the soft side, at Doncaster and might have affected her performance. *J. L. Dunlop*

BINT SHADAYID (USA) 2 gr.f. (Apr 5) Nashwan (USA) 135 – Shadayid (USA) 122 (Shadeed (USA) 135) [1995 6g* 7m* 8d² Sep 24] 105 p

When the half-brothers Nashwan and Unfuwain set out on their stud careers at the Nunnery Stud in 1990, few would have expected Unfuwain to hold his own. The terms of Nashwan's syndication valued him at £18,000,000, making him the most valuable stallion to stand in Britain, and he was much the better patronised of the pair. But Unfuwain won the race to sire a classic winner, being represented by Irish Oaks winner Bolas in 1994, and has also produced a champion two-year-old in Alhaarth, whose classic prospects look distinctly rosy. Nashwan, however, has had his share of pattern winners, and seems certain to produce his first classic winner before long. The One Thousand Guineas winner Shadayid and the multiple classic-winning filly Salsabil, themselves indicative of the overall quality of the mares sent to Nashwan, both produced very promising fillies in Nashwan's third crop. Bint Salsabil and Bint Shadayid—Bint is arabic for 'daughter of'—both have classic prospects.

Bint Shadayid was well backed for the 1996 One Thousand Guineas even before she had set foot on a racecourse, Hills cutting her from 66/1 to 20/1 after a

Hamdan Al Maktoum's "Bint Shadayid"

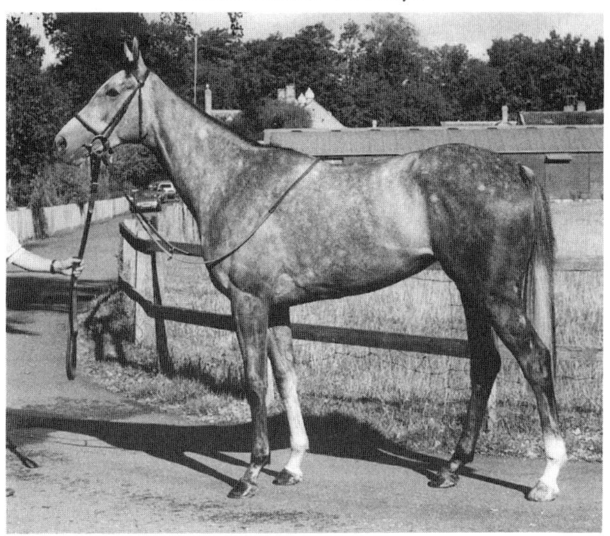

burst of interest in May. She made a pleasing winning debut at long odds on from three other unraced fillies from leading stables in a maiden at Ascot in July, before being stepped up to pattern company. Bint Shadayid still looked distinctly green in the Crowson Prestige Stakes at Goodwood at the end of August, taking time to get into top gear, after being boxed in two furlongs out, and only catching the useful Papering on the post. This was not, in itself, a performance that justified Bint Shadayid's position in the classic betting, but she looked very much the type to improve again, and ran well against the ante-post favourite for the Guineas, Bosra Sham, on her final outing of the season. Bosra Sham was well on top at the finish when beating Bint Shadayid by three and a half lengths in the Fillies' Mile at Ascot but, early in the straight, Bint Shadayid looked to be going marginally the better and she gives the impression that she'll be a stronger and better filly as a three-year-old than she was at two. She should run well in the Guineas and, however she fares at Newmarket, she looks set for a good season. There are plenty of good-class races for fillies like Bint Shadayid, and she should certainly win one or two of them.

Bint Shadayid (USA) (gr.f. Apr 5, 1993)	Nashwan (USA) (ch 1986)	Blushing Groom (ch 1974)	Red God
			Runaway Bride
		Height of Fashion (b 1979)	Bustino
			Highclere
	Shadayid (USA) (gr 1988)	Shadeed (b 1982)	Nijinsky
			Continual
		Desirable (gr 1981)	Lord Gayle
			Balidaress

Bint Shadayid, an angular and rather unfurnished filly as a two-year-old, is a fine mover. She is the first foal of Shadayid, a tough and most genuine filly who never ran a bad race and was only once out of the first three in eleven starts. A mile was undoubtedly Shadayid's best distance—lack of stamina proved her undoing in the Oaks—and we expect Bint Shadayid to follow broadly in her footsteps in that respect. Bint Shadayid's grandam Desirable won the Cheveley Park and is a half-sister to the Irish Oaks winner Alydaress and to another Cheveley Park winner Park Appeal. Bint Shadayid has so far shown that she acts on ground ranging from good to firm to dead. She has been sent to spend the winter in Dubai and will return for the One Thousand Guineas, probably under the Godolphin banner. *J. L. Dunlop*

BINT ZAMAYEM (IRE) 3 b.f. Rainbow Quest (USA) 134 – Zamayem (Sadler's Wells (USA) 132) [1994 69: 6.9m^3 8.1g 1995 11.4m^5 10g^3 12m 10g^4 13.4d 10.4m^3 10d* 10m^5 a12g Dec 2] unfurnished filly: fairly useful form when third of 8 in listed race at Newbury in May: out of her depth in the Oaks next time: some way below best afterwards, including when winning maiden at Newbury in October: should stay 1½m: best form with give in the ground: inconsistent. *B. W. Hills* — 95 d

BIRCHWOOD SUN 5 b.g. Bluebird (USA) 125 – Shapely Test (USA) (Elocutionist (USA)) [1994 65: 6d 5.9v^4 5.9v* 7.5m^6 10m 5.9m^3 6m^2 6g^2 6m^3 6g 6g 6d a7g 6g 1995 6v^3 6s 5.9m^5 7g^3 6.9f^5 7m^6 6f* 6m 5.9f* 6f 6m^5 7m^2 6f^3 6f^5 6m^3 6g^6 7d* 7.1d 6m Oct 30] compact gelding: poor mover: fair handicapper: mostly in good form in 1995, winning at Hamilton (dead heat) and Carlisle in June and at Newcastle (19-runner amateurs race) in September: effective at 6f and 7f: acts on any going: best in blinkers: often gets behind. *M. Dods* — 69

BIRD IN BLUE (IRE) 3 b.f. Bluebird (USA) 125 – Amata (USA) (Nodouble (USA)) [1994 57?: 6f^4 6g 8d 1995 10g 10.2m Jun 2] small, leggy filly: modest maiden: ran no sort of race on final start: stays 1¼m: sold 7,200 gns Newmarket July Sales. *R. Hannon* — –

BIRD ISLAND 4 gr.g. Jupiter Island 126 – Roybirdie 76 (Mansingh (USA) 120) [1994 55: 10g 8.1f* 1995 11.6m 8.3m Jun 19] leggy, workmanlike gelding: has a round action: modest performer at 3 yrs: soundly beaten here in 1995, but did win handicap in Jersey in July: should stay beyond 8.1f: acts on firm ground: often unruly in preliminaries: raced too freely on reappearance. *J. White* — –

BIREQUEST 4 ch.g. Rainbow Quest (USA) 134 – Artic Mistral (CAN) (Briartic (CAN)) [1994 66: 8m 7d^4 7.1d 8.9d 9g 1995 a10g* a10g* a10g^2 a10g^4 a10g 10.8d 8.3m Jun 19] big, workmanlike gelding: fair handicapper: improved form on the all-weather early in year, winning twice at Lingfield in January: tailed off last 3 starts, — – a77 blinkered penultimate one: stays 1¼m: easily best efforts on equitrack: front runner: sold 4,200 gns Newmarket Autumn Sales. *R. Boss*

BIRTHDAY BOY (IRE) 3 b.c. Scenic 128 – Thank You Note 73 (What A Guest 119) [1994 64p: 7m 8.2g 1995 10m 11.6m^6 11.6m 10g 10f^2 11.5m^2 10f^5 11.6m 10.1m^5 11.5g 10d^3 Sep 18] rangy, good-topped colt: fair maiden handicapper: below form last 5 starts, claimed £6,000 after final one: stays 11.6f: acts on firm ground: tried visored/blinkered, no improvement. *R. Hannon* — 69 d

BISHOP OF CASHEL 3 b.c. Warning 136 – Ballet Classique (USA) 84 (Sadler's Wells (USA) 132) [1994 111p: 7.1d^6 7s* 7.3d^2 7v* 1995 7g 8d^2 8g^2 8g* 8d^4 Sep 23] good-bodied colt: smart performer: beaten head by Nec Plus Ultra in Prix Messidor at Maisons-Laffitte and by Two O'Clock Jump in Prix Quincey at Deauville on second and third starts: won 8-runner Kiveton Park Stakes at Doncaster in September by ¾ length from Nijo, travelling smoothly to lead over 1f out: well-beaten fourth of 6 to Bahri in Queen Elizabeth II Stakes at Ascot 16 days later: stays 1m: acts on heavy going, yet to race on top-of-the-ground. *J. R. Fanshawe* — 114

BITCH 3 ch.f. Risk Me (FR) 127 – Lightning Legend 71 (Lord Gayle (USA) 124) [1994 53: 5d 6m^5 6m^5 a7g^3 6m* 6m^2 a7g^2 a6g^4 7.1g^3 8s a7g a8.5g^6 a8g 1995 7m 10m 8m^6 8.2m 6.9f^3 8m^5 Jul 21] shallow-girthed, narrow filly: poor performer: stays 1m, raced much too freely over 1¼m: acts on good to firm ground and fibresand: blinkered (ran creditably) final outing. *D. Nicholls* — 39

BITES 2 b.f. (Apr 30) Risk Me (FR) 127 – Sundaysport Splash (Lord Gayle (USA) 124) [1995 5d^6 5m^3 a5g^2 a5g^5 6g^2 6g 6m^3 6s 6f Oct 24] 1,000Y: leggy filly: fourth foal: sister to 3-y-o Nordman Lass: dam little sign of ability: plater: sold out of G. Lewis' stable 1,400 gns Ascot June Sales after fifth outing: stays 6f: no form on a soft surface. *J. A. Harris* — 46

BITE THE BULLET 4 ch.g. Ballacashtal (CAN) – Longgoe 70 (Lorenzaccio 130) [1994 NR 1995 a11g 7g 7.1m a12g Dec 18] leggy gelding: of little account. *A. J. Chamberlain* — –

BIT OF BOTHER (IRE) 2 b.c. (May 3) Millfontaine 114 – Mother White (Jukebox 120) [1995 5g^4 5g^2 5f^2 Jun 23] IR 2,400Y: half-brother to 3 winners, including 1987 2-y-o 5f and 6f winner Be My Bride (by Be My Native): dam Irish 5f winner: in frame in maiden auctions at Newcastle, Edinburgh and Ayr: will probably be suited by further than 5f. *T. D. Barron* — 58

BIT ON THE SIDE (IRE) 6 b.m. Vision (USA) – Mistress (USA) (Damascus (USA)) [1994 84: 12d* 11.9m^6 14g* 12m^6 13.9m 13.3s^5 14m 12s^2 12v 1995 12g — 82

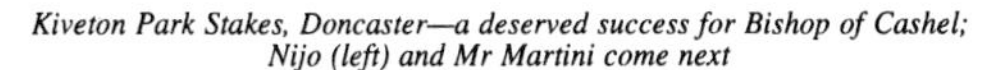

Kiveton Park Stakes, Doncaster—a deserved success for Bishop of Cashel; Nijo (left) and Mr Martini come next

12m 12m^5 13.3g^3 13.3g^4 12g* 12d^6 12s 12m Oct 21] leggy, lengthy mare: fairly useful handicapper: won at Doncaster in September, and ran very well when sixth of 18 to Taufan's Melody in £46,800 event at Ascot next time: effective at 1½m and 1¾m: has form on good to firm ground but seems suited by some give (acts on soft): tends to sweat and get on toes: held up. *W. J. Musson*

BITTER N TWISTED 3 ch.f. Jalmood (USA) 126 – Stedham 84 (Jaazeiro (USA) 127) [1994 36: 7g 8f a8g 7.1m^5 1995 a7g a8g a12g^6 11.1d^5 12f^6 May 1] small filly: poor maiden plater: tried blinkered: sold 1,100 gns Doncaster October Sales. *S. E. Kettlewell* –

BIYA (IRE) 3 ch.g. Shadeed (USA) 135 – Rosie Potts 83 (Shareef Dancer (USA) 135) [1994 NR 1995 a8.5g^2 a8g* 8m^6 9.7s Sep 27] 28,000Y: strong, useful-looking gelding: first foal: dam, 6f (at 2 yrs) and 1m winner, half-sister to very useful middle-distance performer Trakady: gelded and off course 7 months after justifying favouritism in maiden at Lingfield in January: well beaten both subsequent outings: should stay beyond 1m: acts on the all-weather. *M. Johnston* 67

BLACK BOY (IRE) 6 br.g. Auction Ring (USA) 123 – Relic Spirit (Relic) [1994 38, a40: a6g a6g^5 6f^4 6g 5m 5m a5g^4 a6g^2 a6g a5g^4 1995 a7g a5g a6g^6 5m 5.2g^5 5f Oct 14] angular, good-quartered gelding: poor mover: poor maiden: best at up to 7f: acts on fibresand, seems to need a sound surface on turf: usually blinkered or visored: usually bandaged in front: inconsistent. *R. F. Marvin* 34

BLACK ICE BOY (IRE) 4 b.g. Law Society (USA) 130 – Hogan's Sister (USA) (Speak John) [1994 –: 12d 14.1g 16.1d 1995 12m 16.5g 14.1h^6 a14g Nov 16] tall, workmanlike gelding: little worthwhile form: tried blinkered. *R. Bastiman* –

BLACKPOOL FESTIVAL (IRE) 3 b.g. Contract Law (USA) 108 – Burkina (African Sky 124) [1994 55: 5g 5f^3 5g^3 5m^6 6m^4 a7g^2 7s* a8.5g^6 1995 a8.5g a7g Jan 27] leggy, useful-looking gelding: modest performer at 2 yrs: well beaten both starts in 1995: sold 3,000 gns Doncaster February Sales. *J. Berry* –

BLACK SHADOW 3 b.f. Forzando 122 – Basenite (Mansingh (USA) 120) [1994 38: 6m 7d a6g^5 a7g 1995 a5g^6 a6g^4 a6g^3 a6g^6 6m 6f 5g 6g^5 6g^5 Jul 6] small filly: poor maiden: well below form after first 3 3-y-o starts: stays 6f: acts on equitrack: often apprentice ridden: no improvement in blinkers. *P. J. McBride* 34 a48

BLACKSPOT (IRE) 3 b.f. Contract Law (USA) 108 – Hitopah (Bustino 136) [1994 –: 6m 5m 5g 1995 7g 10m 14.1m May 30] small light-framed filly: no worthwhile form: tried blinkered. *F. H. Lee* –

BLAIR CASTLE (IRE) 4 b.g. Waajib 121 – Caimanite 62 (Tap On Wood 130) [1994 80: 8m 8g* 8m^5 8m 9g^6 8.1g^5 1995 10g^5 Sep 21] big, rather leggy gelding: fair handicapper, lightly raced: respectable fifth of 7 in rated stakes at Pontefract on only 4-y-o outing: stays 1¼m: acts on firm and dead ground. *G. B. Balding* 71 +

BLAKENMOR 2 b.g. (Jun 1) No Evil 98 – Kinz (Great Nephew 126) [1995 6m Jun 19] sixth foal: half-brother to 3-y-o 1¼m and 11f winner Fen Terrier (by Emarati) and a winner abroad by Mashhor Dancer: dam poor daughter of half-sister to Music Maestro: 50/1, soundly beaten in seller at Windsor. *R. W. Emery* –

BLANCHLAND 6 gr.g. Bellypha 130 – Premier Rose 117 (Sharp Edge 123) [1994 68: 9m* 10m^2 10.3m^6 12m 11.5d^6 10s^4 10d^4 1995 9.7m 8g 9m 10m 10.1m^5 Jul 6] tall, lengthy gelding: fair middle-distance handicapper at his best: no worthwhile form in 1995: sold (K. Ivory to P. Ritchens) 5,000 gns Ascot July Sales and gelded. *K. T. Ivory* –

BLASTED 3 ch.g. Statoblest 120 – Apprila (Bustino 136) [1994 63: 6s 6m 6.1s^4 6.9d^4 6v 1995 8.5m^3 7g 7f^5 7g 8f* 7.1m^6 8f^2 6g 7m a7g^6 Nov 8] close-coupled, unfurnished gelding: modest performer: won claimer at Salisbury in June: probably needs further than 6f (stays 8.5f): acts on firm and soft ground: has joined G. Thorner. *R. Hannon* 61

BLASTER BATES (USA) 4 b.g. Bates Motel (USA) – A Society Girl (USA) (Verbatim (USA)) [1994 42: 7m 10d 8m^5 8m 8g^4 6.9m a8.5g 8f^2 5.9h 7d^4 8m 8.3g 7.1m 1995 a8g^6 a7g Feb 27] leggy, close-coupled gelding: poor and inconsistent maiden: well beaten in 1995. *R. Brotherton* –

BLAZE AWAY (USA) 4 b.c. Polish Navy (USA) – Battle Drum (USA) (Alydar (USA)) [1994 80: 10m^5 11.5d^5 12f^4 12g 11.9d^6 10g 12m^4 14m^2 1995 16m^3 14m* 16m^5 16m^4 13.9m^5 16.1m 16.2g^3 16m* 16g^6 17.2m 18m 16.5m^6 Nov 4] tall colt: 86

usually looks very well: shows knee action: fairly useful handicapper: narrowly won at Salisbury (led close home) in May and Newbury (made all, shrewdly ridden) in August: creditable seventh of 21 in Cesarewitch at Newmarket on penultimate start, not getting clear run: should prove suited by extreme distances: goes very well on a sound surface: blinkered (took keen hold, well beaten) sixth 4-y-o start: won maiden hurdle in December. *I. A. Balding*

BLAZE OF OAK (USA) 4 ch.g. Green Forest (USA) 134 – Magic Robe (USA) (Grey Dawn II 132) [1994 71: 8m^5 8m^3 8f^6 8.2m^2 10.4g 1995 10.1m^2 10m^4 10m^5 8.9g^2 8.5d 8.2d^2 7d Sep 27] strong gelding: fair maiden: short-headed in claimer at York in August: effective at 1m and 1¼m: acts on firm and good to soft ground: takes keen hold: carries head high: often has tongue tied down: sold (W. Haggas to J. M. Bradley) 8,200 gns Newmarket Autumn Sales. *W. J. Haggas* 69

BLAZE OF SONG 3 ch.c. Jester 119 – Intellect (Frimley Park 109) [1994 62: 6g 6.1m 6m^3 8g^2 7s^5 7v^2 1995 7.5m^2 8m^5 10.3m* 8g* 8.1g* 8m Jun 20] useful-looking colt: fairly useful performer: won minor event at Doncaster (by short head, hung in front), handicap at Salisbury (by 8 lengths) and minor event at Chepstow (odds on), all in May: respectable ninth of 32 in Britannia Handicap at Royal Ascot on final start: effective at 1m, and stays 10.3f: acts on good to firm and heavy ground. *R. Hannon* 85

BLAZING MIRACLE 3 b.f. Shaab 85 – Cottage Blaze (Sunyboy 110) [1994 NR 1995 10m 8m May 13] plain filly: first foal: dam poor winning pointer out of half-sister to Tied Cottage: always behind in maidens: joined Mrs R. Henderson. *B. R. Millman* –

BLENHEIM TERRACE 2 b.g. (May 5) Rambo Dancer (CAN) 107 – Boulevard Girl 80 (Nicholas Bill 125) [1995 a7g^3 a7g 6m 7.9g Aug 31] sturdy gelding: first living foal: dam suited by test of stamina: third of 6 in median auction maiden at Southwell in July: not discredited in valuable seller at York in August: well beaten in face of stiff task (sweating) in nursery there later in month: should stay beyond 7f. *C. B. B. Booth* 49

BLESSED SPIRIT 2 ch.f. (Feb 19) Statoblest 120 – Kukri (Kris 135) [1995 6m 7m Oct 28] 8,200F, 8,200Y: unfurnished filly: third foal: half-sister to 3-y-o Toskano (by Salse) and 7f and 1m winner Sharp Rebuff (by Reprimand): dam never ran: twelfth in maidens at Newmarket won by Projection (caught eye keeping on under hands and heels) and Awaamir (still green, hampered) 15 days later. *C. F. Wall* 65

BLESSINGINDISGUISE 2 b.c. (Feb 8) Kala Shikari 125 – Blowing Bubbles 72 (Native Admiral (USA)) [1995 5m 5g* 5g^2 5d^2 5f Jun 23] 4,600Y: strong, good-topped colt: has scope: fourth reported foal: dam won 5 times between 7f and 8.3f: won maiden auction at Newcastle in May: better efforts in minor events at same course and at Beverley before (blinkered) leading 3f in Windsor Castle Stakes at Ascot final start: will stay 6f: best form on an easy surface. *M. W. Easterby* 84

BLISLAND 3 b.c. Danehill (USA) 126 – Busca (USA) 49 (Mr Prospector (USA)) [1994 59p: 8d 1995 8d^5 8.5d* 8g^3 10f^2 9g Sep 30] strong, good-bodied colt: impresses in appearance: useful performer: easy winner of maiden at Beverley (free to post) in June: improved again when placed in handicaps at Newmarket and Goodwood (½-length second of 14 to Jalfrezi in £33,600 event) in July: reportedly suffered from sore shins after Goodwood and below form in Cambridgeshire at Newmarket on only subsequent outing: stays 1¼m: acts on firm ground and dead: held up: sent to Saudi Arabia. *R. Charlton* 97

BLOCKADE (USA) 6 b.g. Imperial Falcon (CAN) – Stolen Date (USA) (Sadair) [1994 77: 7m 8s 8f 8m^4 8f^5 8f* 7m* 8m^2 1995 8d 7m* 8.1g 8g 9f* 8m* 8m^4 8f^4 7m^2 8f* 8.9g^4 Aug 30] leggy, close-coupled gelding: tubed: fair performer: successful in minor event at Newmarket in May and claimers at Goodwood, Yarmouth and Brighton in the summer: probably stays 1¼m, not raced beyond 9f since 1992: acts on firm and dead going: sometimes sweats: front runner, best when able to dictate: game in a finish. *M. Bell* 73

BLOMBERG (IRE) 3 b.c. Indian Ridge 123 – Daniella Drive (USA) (Shelter Half (USA)) [1994 92: 5s 6f 6f^5 7.5f^2 8m^4 7g^2 8m^2 1995 7g* 8m^2 7.9m 7m^2 Oct 21] smallish, sturdy colt: good mover: useful performer: easily made all in maiden at Doncaster in March: best effort when second of 10 to Two O'Clock Jump in listed race at Kempton over 3 weeks later: not seen out again for 5½ months, better effort 100 on return when second of 4 to Monaassib in minor event at Doncaster: stays 1m: acts on firm ground. *J. R. Fanshawe*

BLOSSOM DEARIE 2 b.f. (Jun 11) Landyap (USA) 112 – Jose Collins 91 (Singing Bede 122) [1995 7m Oct 30] 800Y: good-topped filly: half-sister to a winner in Italy: dam best at 5f: 50/1, burly and green, behind in maiden at Newcastle after slow start. *G. M. Moore* –

BLOTOFT 3 b.g. High Kicker (USA) – Foothold (Hotfoot 126) [1994 NR 1995 11d Sep 22] leggy gelding: seventh foal: half-brother to modest 1986 2-y-o 6f winner Connaught Lad and a winner in Norway (both by Connaught): dam ran twice at 2 yrs: 100/1 and bandaged, tailed off in Redcar seller. *Mrs S. M. Austin* –

BLOW DRY (IRE) 5 b.g. Glenstal (USA) 118 – Haco 104 (Tribal Chief 125) [1994 66: 7m 5m 6g³ 6m⁵ 6g⁴ 6m 6d 5g 1995 6s⁴ 6g 6.9f³ 7g 8.3f⁶ 7.1m⁵ 6m* 6g 7d* 6g 8g⁶ 7g 7m Oct 30] good-topped gelding: has a fluent, round action: modest handicapper: won at Hamilton (seller) in July and Lingfield (well drawn, made all) in September: effective at 6f, and probably stays 1m: acts on good to firm ground, very best efforts on an easy surface: sometimes bandaged: visored (below form) final 4-y-o start: none too consistent. *Martyn Wane* 61

BLOWEDIFIKNOW 5 b.g. Prince Rupert (FR) 121 – Ballys Princess (Salvo 129) [1994 48: a12g² a12g* a14g 14.1v 10g a11g a12g 11.5g² 14.1g* 15.1g a14g³ a14g 1995 a12g⁶ a12g⁴ a16g⁵ Feb 10] leggy, lengthy gelding: poor performer: stayed 1¾m: possibly needed some give on turf, acted on fibresand: usually visored/ blinkered last 2 seasons: inconsistent: dead. *J. Wharton* 30

BLUE ADELAIDE 2 b.f. (Apr 25) Puissance 110 – Dominion Blue 66 (Dominion 123) [1995 6.1m 6m² a5g a7g Dec 15] 7,400Y: fourth live foal: half-sister to a winner in Belgium: dam 1¼m winner: first run since mid-July when beaten head in median auction maiden at Folkestone in November: showed little afterwards: stays 6f: blinkered final outing: needs treating with caution on all-weather surfaces: sold 1,200 gns Ascot December Sales. *P. F. I. Cole* 67 a–

BLUE AND ROYAL (IRE) 3 b.g. Bluebird (USA) 125 – Cat Girl (USA) (Grey Dawn II 132) [1994 NR 1995 10g⁶ 12m 12f³ 12m 12d Oct 21] IR 15,000Y: rangy gelding: has scope: seventh foal: half-brother to fairly useful but rather temperamental 7f winner My Sister Ellen (by Lyphard) and to middle-distance winners by Kris and The Minstrel: dam good-class winner at up to 1m in USA: fair maiden: well below form last 2 starts, blinkered on final one: stays 1½m: sold (R. Hannon to Miss J. Doyle) 12,000 gns Newmarket Autumn Sales. *R. Hannon* 65 d

BLUEBEARD (IRE) 2 b.c. (Feb 19) Bluebird (USA) 125 – Shebasis (USA) (General Holme (USA) 128) [1995 7.9g 8.2m⁵ Oct 19] 26,000Y: rangy colt: has scope: third foal: dam, unraced, out of half-sister to Alysheba: visored, better effort in maidens when over 12 lengths fifth of 19 to Dushyantor at Nottingham, leading over 5f: wore crossed noseband both outings: sold 11,000 gns Newmarket Autumn Sales. *J. H. M. Gosden* 61

BLUEBERRY FIELDS 2 gr.f. (May 27) Shernazar 131 – Be Easy 110 (Be Friendly 130) [1995 6m Aug 26] leggy, quite good-topped filly: closely related to fairly useful 1¼m winner Sitting Bull (by Bustino) and half-sister to several winners, most over middle distances: dam best at up to 7f: 33/1, green and burly, always behind in maiden at Newmarket. *C. F. Wall* –

BLUE BLAZER 5 b.g. Bluebird (USA) 125 – View 88 (Shirley Heights 130) [1994 76: 10v 8s 10.3m⁵ 12m 10s⁵ 10.1m 10g* 10g⁵ 12d² 10.2s⁵ 11.9d² 13.9d 12m³ 1995 12.4g* 11.9m² 12g³ 11.9m 14m* 15g³ 14.1m⁴ 14.8m Aug 25] close-coupled, quite attractive gelding: fairly useful handicapper: won at Newcastle in May and Haydock in July: below form last 3 starts: stays 1¾m: acts on good to firm and soft ground: blinkered (well below form) once as 3-y-o: front runner when successful at 3 yrs, held up (often set plenty to do) since: often ridden by apprentice. *B. Hanbury* 82

BLUE BOMBER 4 b.g. Tina's Pet 121 – Warm Wind 84 (Tumble Wind (USA)) [1994 82: 6v⁶ 5m⁵ 6m 6m 7m 1995 8m 8g⁵ 7f⁶ 6m 7f* Oct 14] close-coupled gelding: fair handicapper: well beaten first 4 starts in 1995 (reportedly broke blood vessel on last of them) for C. Weedon, and sold only 1,650 gns Ascot August Sales: 25/1, made virtually all to win 19-runner race at Catterick on first run for new stable: stays 7f: acts on firm and dead going (tailed off on heavy). *T. D. Barron* 81

BLUE DELIGHT (IRE) 2 b.c. (May 2) Bluebird (USA) 125 – Highly Delighted (USA) (Verbatim (USA)) [1995 5.2m Apr 21] IR 8,200Y: sturdy, deep-girthed colt: has scope: half-brother to Irish 7f and 1m winner What A Pleasure (by Waajib): dam, winner of 4 races in Ireland, best at up to 1m: 50/1, backward and very green, very slowly away and behind throughout in maiden at Newbury: wore a tongue strap: joined L. Montague Hall. *G. Lewis* –

BLUE DOMAIN 4 b.g. Dominion 123 – Blue Rag 70 (Ragusa 137) [1994 –, a58: a6g a6g^2 a5g* a6g 8.2d 6g 8.2m a12g 1995 7d Sep 27] sturdy gelding: modest performer early in 1994 for R. Hollinshead: no promise only 4-y-o start: has joined R. Craggs. *M. Dods* –

BLUE DUCK (IRE) 2 ch.g. (May 31) Magical Wonder (USA) 125 – Grave Error (Northern Treat (USA)) [1995 a5g^5 Dec 19] IR 3,800Y: fifth foal: half-brother to a winner in Sweden by Anita's Prince: dam Irish 1½m winner: 8/1 from 7/2, well-beaten last of 5 in median auction maiden at Lingfield. *T. D. Barron* –

BLUE DUSTER (USA) 2 b.f. (Mar 3) Danzig (USA) – Blue Note (FR) 122 (Habitat 134) [1995 5m* 5m* 6g* 6d* Sep 26] 116 p

Though the pair are not related, comparisons between Blue Duster and the leading two-year-old filly of 1991, Marling, were being made almost from the moment Blue Duster got her career off to a winning start in a maiden at Sandown in May. Like Marling, Blue Duster justified heavy support—she was backed from odds against to 11/8-on—and showed a good turn of foot to beat another debutante Dance Sequence in good style, despite running green in front. Blue Duster's trainer David Loder, who enjoyed an exceptional ratio of winners to runners in 1995 with his two-year-olds, was assistant to Geoff Wragg when Marling was at Abington Place. Loder's post-race comments after Sandown could have left no-one in any doubt of the high regard he had for Blue Duster and she was sent next for the Queen Mary Stakes at Royal Ascot, a race Marling had won. Blue Duster was again all the rage in the betting and quickened impressively to win in the style of an above-average Queen Mary winner, Dance Sequence filling the runner-up spot a length and a half behind. The last One Thousand Guineas winner to win the Queen Mary was Waterloo back in 1971—Marling was an unlucky loser, producing a storming finish after meeting trouble in running—and talk of Blue Duster for the Guineas began in earnest after her performance. 'She reminds me so much of Marling, she's so laid back and her style of racing is much the same', said Loder. After another striking victory, readily quickening clear, in a below-par Princess Margaret Stakes at Ascot, it was intended that Blue Duster would take in the Lowther Stakes at York but a throat infection kept

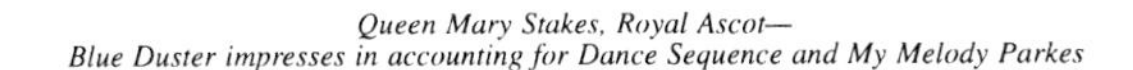

Queen Mary Stakes, Royal Ascot—
Blue Duster impresses in accounting for Dance Sequence and My Melody Parkes

her off the course until the Shadwell Stud Cheveley Park Stakes. In the meantime the Henry Cecil-trained Bosra Sham recorded an impressive win in the Fillies' Mile at Ascot, a performance that looked to mark her down as an outstanding Guineas candidate. Bosra Sham remained the ante-post favourite for the Guineas after Blue Duster had added the Cheveley Park, but, in our view, Blue Duster's own Guineas claims looked just the stronger after that performance. Blue Duster disposed of her rivals—My Branch, Najiya, Dance Sequence and Supamova—in devastating fashion, passing the post with her ears pricked after settling the issue in a matter of strides with a display of acceleration that has been the hallmark of all her races so far.

Blue Duster (USA) (b.f. Mar 3, 1993)	Danzig (USA) (b 1977)	Northern Dancer (b 1961)	Nearctic
			Natalma
		Pas de Nom (b or br 1968)	Admiral's Voyage
			Petitioner
	Blue Note (FR) (b 1985)	Habitat (b 1966)	Sir Gaylord
			Little Hut
		Balsamique (b 1973)	Tourangeau
			Bruyere

As with Marling at the end of her two-year-old days, discussion about Blue Duster's Guineas prospects centre on whether she'll get the trip. Fears that Marling wouldn't stay a mile proved unfounded and there are grounds for optimism with Blue Duster. Blue Duster's sire Danzig is regarded first and foremost as an influence for speed, but the average winning distance of races won by his three-year-olds and upwards in Europe is just over a mile. Blue Duster's dam Blue Note won over seven furlongs as a two-year-old but was clearly speedy, as she showed when a good third in the all-aged Prix du Petit Couvert over five on her final start; she improved into a smart performer at three and won the Prix de la Porte Maillot over seven furlongs and the Prix Maurice de Gheest (in which she beat Cadeaux Genereux) over six and a half. Blue Note, who is out of a dam who won at up to eleven and a half furlongs, put up a fair effort the only time she was tried beyond seven furlongs, in the Prix Perth over a mile. She produced two winners before Blue Duster and both of them were successful in useful company at a mile. Her first foal the smart Zieten, a full brother to Blue Duster, was unbeaten in four races at up to six furlongs as a two-year-old, including the Middle Park, and was returned to sprinting after landing the odds in the Group 3 Prix de Fontainebleau on his reappearance and managing only eighth in the French Guineas on his first two outings as a three-year-old; he went on to win the Challenge Stakes over seven as a four-year-old. Blue Note's second foal Slow Jazz, a

Shadwell Stud Cheveley Park Stakes, Newmarket—
Blue Duster puts My Branch, Najiya and Dance Sequence firmly in their place

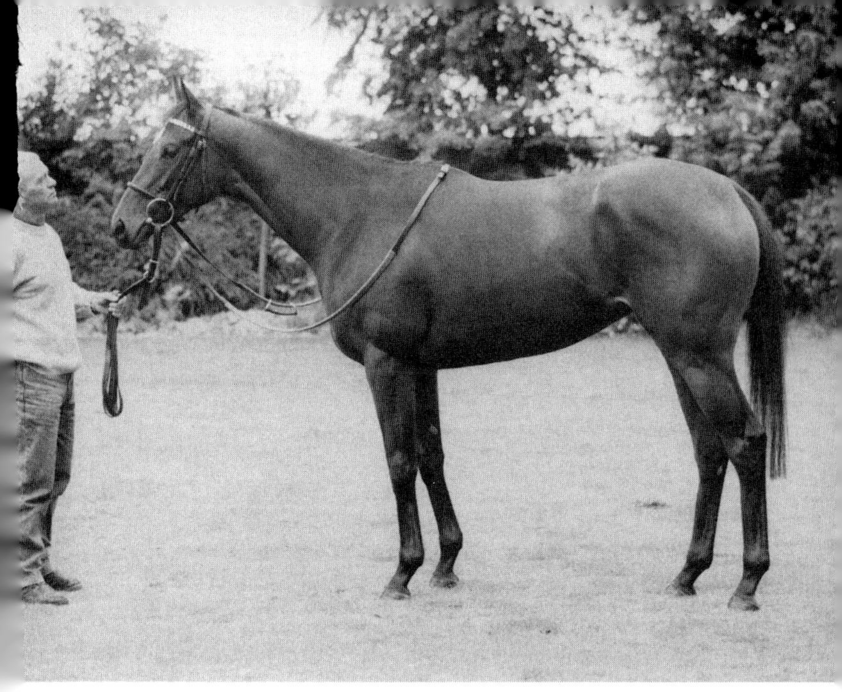

Sheikh Mohammed's "Blue Duster"

filly by Chief's Crown, a son of Danzig, was useful at her best and, after winning over six furlongs as a two-year-old, won a listed event at Maisons-Laffitte over a mile as a three-year-old. Blue Duster, herself, is amenable to restraint and settled well in her races as a two-year-old. Michael Kinane, her partner in all her races, reported after the Cheveley Park that 'she does not give me the feel of a typical sprinter, even though she has exceptional speed'. Kinane went on to say that 'seven will be no problem and if she gets the mile the others are in trouble!' Blue Duster is unlikely to stay beyond a mile and if events do show that she isn't so effective at that trip she should certainly add to her reputation over shorter distances. Blue Duster is a shade on the small side—she'll certainly be dwarfed by the imposing Bosra Sham in the Guineas preliminaries—but is a well-made, good-bodied filly who should train on. Indeed, she looks capable of even better as a three-year-old, though she'll do extremely well to match all the achievements of Marling who went on to win three Group 1 races, the Irish One Thousand Guineas, the Coronation Stakes and the Sussex Stakes. Blue Duster has so far shown her form on going ranging from good to firm to good to soft. *D. R. Loder*

BLUE ENSIGN 10 b.g. Beldale Flutter (USA) 130 – Blue Rag 70 (Ragusa 137) – [1994 37: a8g* 1995 a8g a8g Feb 25] compact gelding: only poor at end of career: stayed 1m: dead. *H. G. Rowsell*

BLUE FLYER (IRE) 2 b.g. (Mar 28) Bluebird (USA) 125 – Born To Fly (IRE) 67 57 (Last Tycoon 131) [1995 6d 6s^6 a6g^3 a7g a8g^3 Dec 15] IR 10,000F, 30,000Y: strong, lengthy gelding: has scope: has a quick action: first foal: dam suited by 6f:

sold out of I. Balding's stable 3,000 gns Newmarket Autumn Sales after second start: fair maiden: stays 1m: best efforts on equitrack (showed little on soft ground). *R. Ingram*

BLUE GRIT 9 b.g. Thatching 131 – Northern Wisdom (Northfields (USA)) [1994 62: 6g^3 6s* 6f 6m 5.9m^6 6m 7g 6g 6g* 6g 6s 7g 1995 7.1g^5 6f 8g^3 6g 6m a6g^6 6m^3 6m^4 Jul 24] good-topped gelding: modest handicapper: below form in 1995: successful at 9f in 1991, best recent form over 6f: acts on firm and soft ground: effective in visor/blinkers or not: has won when sweating: successful 5 times at Pontefract: none too consistent. *M. Dods* — 56

BLUE IRIS 2 b.f. (Feb 19) Petong 126 – Bo' Babbity 75 (Strong Gale 116) [1995 5g* 5.2g* 6f* Oct 12] — 104 p

Blue Iris became the first horse to win the Weatherbys Super Sprint and Redcar Two-Year-Old Trophy in the same season. Those efforts earned her owners in excess of £150,000 in first-place prize money, a handsome return on a filly who cost only 7,800 guineas as a yearling and whom her trainer twice failed to sell on before retaining a half-share for himself. Success in either race has usually been followed by three-year-old mediocrity but Blue Iris could do well in her second season. She has had only three races—she also won a maiden at Haydock in June on her racecourse debut. Her stable had enjoyed great success with her sire Petong in the 'eighties and will no doubt be hoping Blue Iris will be a similarly-successful standard bearer.

Unlike the Redcar Two-Year-Old Trophy, which is open to any two-year-old in training, the Super Sprint is restricted to two-year-olds which were sold or bought in as yearlings for 30,000 guineas or less. As she was acquired so cheaply Blue Iris was set to carry only 8-1 at Newbury, and she started fourth favourite at 13/2 behind the Queen Mary flop Marl, favourite at 7/2, and the unbeaten duo Ortolan and Home Shopping, the latter reappearing quickly after her victory in a listed race at Sandown eight days earlier. As things turned out Marl and Home Shopping were drawn on the slower side of the track—the seventeen-runner field split into two groups—but even granted a favourable draw it's unlikely they would have troubled Blue Iris who routed her rivals in a manner reminiscent of Lyric Fantasy in 1992. Given a good lead for three furlongs by the speedy Maggi For Margaret, Blue Iris quickened right away to come home three and a half lengths and a neck in front of Needham Star and Ortolan, both of whom stayed on strongly having found the early pace too strong. Blue Iris missed her next targets the Molecomb Stakes and Lowther Stakes,

Redcar Two-Year-Old Trophy—Blue Iris holds on well from Cayman Kai (star on cap) and Anthelia (left)

reportedly because her trainer, who'd won both races with another speedy filly, Bitty Girl, back in 1973, wasn't quite happy with her, and she wasn't seen out again until October when one of twenty-six runners that made up an ultra-competitive field for the Redcar Two-Year-Old Trophy. Blue Iris, a solid 6/1 shot despite not running for nearly three months, didn't move well to post on the unseasonably firm ground but she travelled with more fluency once the race was under way and two furlongs out could be picked out easily moving best of all at the head of the group in the centre of the track. Challenged on one side by the Flying Childers winner Cayman Kai, like Blue Iris attempting six furlongs for the first time, and on the other firstly by the 50/1-shot Red River Valley and then the unbeaten Anthelia—the favourite Meldorf, an easy winner of a maiden at Newcastle on his only previous start, finished well beaten—Blue Iris ran on strongly without coming under maximum pressure to pass the post a length and a quarter and a half a length ahead of Cayman Kai and Anthelia. Baize, a close fifth in the Lowther Stakes on her latest outing, emphasized the competitive nature of the contest by being beaten another length in fourth.

Blue Iris (b.f. Feb 19, 1993)	Petong (gr 1980)	Mansingh (b 1969)	Jaipur
			Tutasi
		Iridium (br 1969)	Linacre
			Tula Melody
	Bo' Babbity (b 1984)	Strong Gale (br 1975)	Lord Gayle
			Sterntau
		Get Ready (b 1973)	On Your Mark
			La Corsaire

The Coventry winner Petardia, the Richmond winner Son Pardo and the 1991 Super Sprint winner Paris House (a much better sprinter as a four-year-old) are also by Petong. Like them Blue Iris was purchased at Newmarket's October Yearling Sales. As her sale price indicates—she was also sold as a foal for 7,600 guineas—Blue Iris doesn't have a blue-blooded pedigree: her maternal grandsire is the top National Hunt stallion Strong Gale. There's very little stamina on the bottom line of her pedigree. Blue Iris is the third foal and second winner, following one in Jersey, of Bo' Babbity who won for the only time over five furlongs as a two-year-old and is a half-sister to the high-class Irish sprinter Anita's Prince who won the 1984 King George Stakes by four lengths. Blue Iris' second and third dams Get Ready and La Corsaire were also sprinters: Get Ready won over five furlongs on her racecourse debut while La Corsaire won three times in all at around the same distance. The unfurnished Blue Iris will most likely turn out to be a sprinter too, and probably quite a good one at that. She acts on firm going and has yet to race on a soft surface. *M. A. Jarvis*

BLUE JUDGE (IRE) 5 b.h. Rainbow Quest (USA) 134 – Water Splash (USA) 85 (Little Current (USA)) [1994 105: 14g 10s^4 12m^2 14d^4 12v^2 11d 1995 14.1g^6 14.4m^3 May 8] leggy, good-quartered ex-Irish horse: reportedly fractured off-fore cannon bone shortly after finishing second in 1993 Derby: only fairly useful form for new stable in 1995, better effort when third of 7 to Cuff Link in minor event at Kempton: should prove better at 1¾m+ than 1½m: acts on good to firm and soft ground: well beaten only try in blinkers. *R. Thompson* **90**

BLUE LUGANA 3 b.g. Lugana Beach 116 – Two Friendly 54 (Be Friendly 130) [1994 57: 5g^2 5g^6 7g 1995 6g 6g 5f^6 5f^2 5g^6 6f Aug 9] poor maiden handicapper: form only at 5f: acts on firm ground: blinkered last 4 starts. *N. Bycroft* **41**

BLUE NILE (IRE) 3 b.f. Bluebird (USA) 125 – Angelus Chimes 80 (Northfields (USA)) [1994 56: 6.1m 7m^6 8.2s^4 8s 1995 9.9m* 12g^5 10f^5 10.5g^4 10d Sep 26] unfurnished filly: fair handicapper: won at Beverley in May: should stay 1½m: acts on firm ground: held up. *A. C. Stewart* **70**

BLUE OCEAN (USA) 3 b.c. Danzig (USA) – Foreign Courier (USA) (Sir Ivor 135) [1994 79p: 6.1s^2 6g* 1995 8g 7g^5 Sep 29] strong, compact colt: has a round action: fairly useful performer: not seen until September, easily better effort when fifth of 14 to Cyrano's Lad in rated stakes at Newmarket: should stay 1m: has raced only on an easy surface. *M. R. Stoute* **83**

BLUE PENNANT 4 b.f. Jupiter Island 126 – Tudor Whisper 53 (Henry The Seventh 125) [1994 –: 7m 1995 a12g^5 a14.8g a16g a14g Apr 11] neat filly: no worthwhile form. *T. T. Bill* **–**

BLUE SIOUX 3 b.f. Indian Ridge 123 – Blues Indigo 103 (Music Boy 124) [1994 69p: 5g^5 6.1d^5 6s^3 1995 5.1g^4 6g 6g a5g^4 5g 5m a5g* a6g a5g^5 Dec 2] leggy filly: modest handicapper: won at Wolverhampton in October: best at sprint distances: acts on fibresand and soft going: blinkered last 4 starts. *J. Wharton* — 58, a63

BLUE SIREN 4 ch.f. Bluebird (USA) 125 – Manx Millenium 66 (Habitat 134) [1994 113: 7g 6m^3 6d* 5g^2 6f^5 6f^2 7m* 5m^2 1995 5m^2 5m May 6] robust, stocky filly: impresses in appearance: fluent mover: useful performer: winner on merit but demoted when first past post in Nunthorpe Stakes at York at 3 yrs: again demoted after passing post first in 12-runner listed race at Beverley on reappearance (caused slight interference to short-head runner-up El Yasaf): played up in stalls prior to Palace House Stakes at Newmarket 4 weeks later and discovered afterwards to have fractured her off-hind pedal bone: effective at 5f to 7f: acts on firm and soft ground: genuine and consistent. *I. A. Balding* — 104

BLUE SMOKE (IRE) 3 b.c. Posen (USA) – Raubritter (Levmoss 133) [1994 NR 1995 11.8s^4 12f 12m^4 14.6m 14m 16.2g^3 16m 14.1m Aug 21] IR 1,600F: strong, lengthy colt: has scope: half-brother to 3 winners over middle distances, by Pampapaul (2) and Lord Gayle: dam unraced: modest maiden: stays 16.2f: blinkered since fifth start: sold (B. McMahon to J. K. Oliver) 13,000 gns Newmarket Autumn Sales. *B. A. McMahon* — 57

BLUE SUEDE HOOFS 2 br.g. (May 8) Nomination 125 – Massive Powder (Caerleon (USA) 132) [1995 7g 6m 6f^2 Oct 24] strong, lengthy gelding: third foal: half-brother to 3-y-o Zelda Zonk (by Law Society): dam daughter of half-sister to Alydar's Best: best effort in maidens when 1½ lengths second of 19 to Thordis in median auction event at Leicester: stays 6f. *B. J. Meehan* — 73

BLUETONG 2 b.c. (Feb 27) Petong 126 – Sculpture Bleue (Claude Monet (USA) 121) [1995 5.7h 6m Aug 3] 16,000Y: second foal: half-brother to 3-y-o Jurassic Sue (by Distant Relative): dam unraced half-sister to Breeders' Cup Mile winner Steinlen: last in maidens at Bath (unseated rider beforehand) and Pontefract (blinkered, carried head awkwardly): sold 2,700 gns Newmarket Autumn Sales. *P. T. Walwyn* — –

BLUE ZULU (IRE) 3 gr.f. Don't Forget Me 127 – Aldern Stream 102 (Godswalk (USA) 130) [1994 –p: 7.1s^4 1995 8m* 10m 8f^3 8m^4 8.3m^3 Aug 26] lengthy, rather unfurnished filly: fairly useful performer: won maiden at Kempton in May: good efforts in frame in rated stakes at Newmarket and Windsor last 2 starts: effective at 1m, and stays 1¼m: acts on firm ground. *J. R. Fanshawe* — 94

BLURRED IMAGE (IRE) 4 ch.g. Exactly Sharp (USA) 121 – Bear's Affair (Gay Fandango (USA) 132) [1994 86: 7m^2 7d* 7m^6 7m 7.3g 8.1g 1995 a10g 7m 8m 6f^3 7f^3 7f^3 7f^5 5g Sep 12] leggy, good-topped gelding: good mover: fair handicapper: stays 7f: acts on firm and soft ground, ran poorly both starts on the all-weather: sweating and edgy (ran badly) final 3-y-o start: sold 6,000 gns (Doncaster October) and 2,100 gns (Ascot December) Sales. *Miss Gay Kelleway* — 74

BLUSHING FLAME (USA) 4 b.c. Blushing Groom (FR) 131 – Nearctic Flame 111 (Sadler's Wells (USA) 132) [1994 91: 10d^6 12m 10g^6 10g* 12f^6 12m^4 12m* 12v^5 1995 10m^2 12m^2 12m 13.9m 12g 12m* 12m* Nov 4] deep-bodied, lengthy colt: impresses in appearance: has a splayed action: made into a useful performer, winning 19-runner handicap (under 9-13, rallying splendidly) and 8-runner listed race (best effort, beat Capias 1¼ lengths) at Doncaster in the autumn: should stay beyond 1½m: acts on good to firm ground, below form on heavy. *M. R. Stoute* — 108

BLUSHING GLEAM 2 ch.f. (Jan 6) Caerleon (USA) 132 – Blushing Away (USA) (Blushing Groom (FR) 131) [1995 5d^2 6d* 5.5g^4 7g* 8d^5 Oct 1] close-coupled filly: has scope: second foal: half-sister to French 3-y-o 6f and 7f winner Posen Tune (by Polish Precedent): dam French 6.5f winner: useful French filly: won minor event at Chantilly in July and Prix du Calvados at Deauville (by ¾ length from Like A Hawk) in August: creditable 6½ lengths fifth of 11 in Prix Marcel Boussac at Longchamp final start, staying on steadily: will stay beyond 1m: has raced only on good or dead ground. *Mme C. Head, France* — 104

BLUSHING GRENADIER (IRE) 3 ch.g. Salt Dome (USA) – La Duse 66 (Junius (USA) 124) [1994 57: 5d 6g 6d^6 7v 1995 6.1g 6m 6m^4 7g^4 6g* 7f 8g^3 6m^4 6d^4 6.1d 7s^5 7g^4 7d Oct 19] leggy gelding: modest performer: won maiden handicap — 55 at Doncaster in July: stays 1m: acts on good to firm and soft ground: usually blinkered/visored, but has run quite well without: sold 2,800 gns Ascot November Sales. *M. J. Fetherston-Godley*

BLUSH RAMBLER (USA) 5 b.h. Blushing Groom (FR) 131 – Romanette (USA) (Alleged (USA) 138) [1994 115: 10s^5 12m^3 12f 10g^2 10s^4 12g^3 11.9s^2 1995 10m^4 11.8m^3 12m^3 Aug 11] small, attractive horse: hobdayed after final 4-y-o start: fluent mover: just a useful performer in 1995, ½-length third of 7 to Capias in listed race at Leicester on second start: stays 1½m: acts on good to firm and soft ground (ran poorly on firm): often sweats: effective from front or held up. *M. R. Stoute* — 106

BOBANLYN (IRE) 3 b.f. Dance of Life (USA) – Sheer Innocence (Shirley Heights 130) [1994 76+: 6m* 7m^6 7g* 7m^4 8s* 8g^3 7m 8s^4 1995 8m 9m 8f^4 10.1m 8.3m 10.1g^5 10g* 9f 10.3m^5 8f^6 10f Oct 31] sparely-made, angular filly: just a modest performer in 1995: won selling handicap at Redcar in September: will stay beyond 1¼m: acts on firm and soft ground: inconsistent. *D. Morris* — 60

BOBBY'S DREAM 3 b.f. Reference Point 139 – Kiralyi (FR) (Kings Lake (USA) 133) [1994 53: 7m 8m 7s 1995 11.6m 11.8g^6 14.1g^2 16m^6 15.8g^3 17.1m^5 12m Oct 27] small, sturdy, workmanlike filly: poor mover: modest maiden handicapper: thorough stayer: acts on good to firm ground. *M. H. Tompkins* — 50

BOBINSKI 3 br.c. Polish Precedent (USA) 131 – Cockade 104 (Derring-Do 131) [1994 NR 1995 10s* 9d* 9g^4 10m Jun 25] — 115 p

Bobinski, by Polish Precedent, has yet to catch the thoroughbred world's attention as his namesake did with the publication of the mammoth undertaking *Family Tables of Racehorses* back in 1953. But more will be heard of him. Andre Fabre's charge has raced only in France, won in no better than listed company, and was not seen out after June. However, he was unfortunate not to have joined his half-brother, Old Vic, as a Group 1 winner at Chantilly, and he could well make up into a leading contender for the big races in 1996.

Bobinski contested the Prix Jean Prat over nine furlongs at Chantilly in June having won a newcomers event at Longchamp in March and gained a convincing success from Suresnes in a listed race at Evry in April. Second favourite behind the Aga Khan's Prix de Guiche winner Valanour, ahead of Sheikh Mohammed's coupled entry of Torrential and Annus Mirabilis, Bobinski had to be switched three times before eventually finding daylight towards the far side then running on well behind Torrential, Annus Mirabilis and Labeeb, beaten a nose, a short neck and a neck. There is little doubt Bobinski would have won granted a clear run, and while the form does not amount to much by Group 1 standards, the race had provided less of a test of stamina and much better opponents than Bobinski had previously encountered, and his prospects seemed bright for the remainder of the season. No such luck. In June he was squeezed onto the running rail after a couple of furlongs and virtually pulled up in the Grand Prix de Paris, while in September he injured himself in his box on the Tuesday prior to the Prix Niel. And that was that.

Bobinski (br.c. 1992)	Polish Precedent (USA) (b 1986)	Danzig (b 1977)	Northern Dancer
			Pas de Nom
		Past Example (ch 1976)	Buckpasser
			Bold Example
	Cockade (b 1973)	Derring-Do (b 1961)	Darius
			Sipsey Bridge
		Camenae (b 1961)	Vimy
			Madrilene

Old Vic (by Sadler's Wells) dominates any examination of Bobinski's pedigree. He won both the Prix du Jockey-Club and Irish Derby, and when beaten narrowly by Belmez in the following year's King George VI And Queen Elizabeth Diamond Stakes, he established himself as the best older horse in Europe. The year-younger Splash of Colour (by Rainbow Quest) became Cockade's fifth winner from six live foals when he won the Prix Foy, but he injured himself in the Japan Cup and reportedly was retired to stud there. Bobinski apart, there has been nothing of note since, Cockade's only live foals being Muthhil (who never ran), the disappointing Chapka and a yearling by Unfuwain.

Bobinski is a neat colt, quite dissimilar in the early summer of his three-year-old days to both the rangy, good-bodied Old Vic and the strong Splash of Colour. Bobinski has yet to tackle a mile and a half, but there is little doubt he will get the trip, something all of Cockade's previous winners have done, for all that Bobinski's sire was a top-class miler. Polish Precedent was unbeaten in seven races including the Prix Jacques Le Marois and the Prix du Moulin, before he ran across Zilzal in the Queen Elizabeth II Stakes. Thus far, with two crops having reached the age of three, he is proving a surprisingly strong influence for stamina. His best progeny to date are Pure Grain and Riyadian. Bobinski starts his four-year-old career unpenalised for pattern-race success, and with Fabre as his trainer he could be a most interesting prospect. *A. Fabre, France*

BOB'S PLOY 3 b.g. Deploy 131 – Santa Magdalena (Hard Fought 125) [1994 77p: 7d^{4} 7g^{3} 7s^{2} 1995 9m 10.2m^{2} 10m* 10.1m^{6} 12m^{2} 12f 11g 12d Sep 24] rangy gelding: fairly useful performer: impressive winner of handicap at Kempton in May: head second of 20 to Diaghilef in strongly-run King George V Stakes at Royal Ascot two outings later: best of last 3 starts when seventh of 8 in Group 3 race at Baden-Baden on penultimate one: stays 1½m: acts on good to firm and soft going: held up: has joined M. Tompkins. *R. Akehurst* 94

BOBSWORTHATCASPERS 2 b.g. (Apr 28) Risk Me (FR) 127 – Hot Sunday Sport 42 (Star Appeal 133) [1995 5.1m^{6} 5m 6m^{2} 6m^{2} a6g 6m^{2} 7g^{3} 7f^{5} a6g^{4} 6.9f^{6} Aug 15] 2,800Y: compact gelding: second foal: brother to temperamental 3-y-o Red Hot Risk, 5f winner at 2 yrs: dam, plater, stayed 1½m: plater: well beaten last 3 starts: seems best at 6f: below form on fibresand: blinkered 4 of last 5 starts: sold 1,600 gns Ascot August Sales. *G. Lewis* 55

BODANTREE 4 b.g. Rambo Dancer (CAN) 107 – Snow Tree 86 (Welsh Pageant 132) [1994 –: a12g 10s^{6} 8.1g 1995 a12g^{4} a12g 12m 9.2f^{3} Jul 7] strong gelding: no worthwhile form on flat: trained until after second 4-y-o start by H. Oliver: tried blinkered/visored: won novice selling hurdle in July. *K. R. Burke* –

BODFARI LASS 2 b.f. (Mar 31) Tirol 127 – Sugar Loch 79 (Lochnager 132) [1995 7d 7.1s^{6} 8m^{6} Oct 20] 7,000Y: sturdy, good-quartered filly: seventh foal: half-sister to a winner in Macau by Glenstal: dam 1m winner: modest form in minor event at Newbury on debut and maiden at Doncaster on third start: may prove best at up to 7f: well below form on soft ground. *B. W. Hills* 67

BOFFY (IRE) 2 ch.c. (Apr 7) Mac's Imp (USA) 116 – No Dowry (Shy Groom (USA)) [1995 a5g^{3} 5g^{5} 5.1g^{4} 5.1m^{4} a5g^{2} 5m^{3} 5m^{5} 5m* 6g* 5g a5g^{6} 6f Oct 24] 5,600F, 6,000 2-y-o: quite attractive colt: first foal: dam Irish 2-y-o 7f winner: won seller at Leicester in August (improved form) and claimer at Haydock 9 days later: below form in nurseries last 3 starts: best form at 6f: acts on fibresand but best form on a sound surface: best held up: ridden by 7-lb claimer last 5 starts. *B. P. J. Baugh* 66

BOGART 4 gr.g. Belfort (FR) 89 – Larnem 43 (Meldrum 112) [1994 62: 7g^{5} 6m^{4} 7f^{6} 10.1f^{5} 7m^{3} 7g a7g^{6} a7g^{4} a7g* a7g^{6} 1995 a7g^{4} a7g^{3} 7.5m 5.9m 7m^{2} 7m^{3} 8f 7.1m 7m^{3} 7f^{3} a7g^{4} 7m 8.1s a7g^{2} a7g^{5} Dec 12] tall, angular gelding: modest handicapper: stays 7f: acts on the all-weather and on firm ground, possibly not on soft. *C. W. Fairhurst* 59

BOLD ACRE 5 ch.g. Never So Bold 135 – Nicola Wynn 83 (Nicholas Bill 125) [1994 56: 7.3s 10.2s^{6} 8.1m^{4} a9.4g^{4} a7g 8.3g 9.7d^{2} 8g 10d 1995 a9.4g 10f a12g Nov 11] leggy gelding: modest handicapper at 4 yrs: well beaten in 1995. *D. Burchell* –

BOLD AMUSEMENT 5 ch.g. Never So Bold 135 – Hysterical 68 (High Top 131) [1994 87: 7m^{2} 7f 7.9f 10.3m* 10m 10.3d 1995 8.9m 10.4m 8.5m* 8f^{5} 8m^{5} 10.3d 8.5d 7m Nov 3] strong gelding: fairly useful handicapper: won at Beverley in July: stays 10.3f: acts on good to firm and soft ground. *W. S. Cunningham* 84

BOLD ANGEL 8 b.g. Lochnager 132 – Lobela 77 (Lorenzaccio 130) [1994 73: 7m 7g 7.6g* 7m^{2} 7.1g 1995 7g^{5} 6m 7m^{5} 7m^{3} 7m* a7g^{5} 7.6m^{2} 7.1d 8g^{2} 8g 8.2m^{5} Oct 19] strong, close-coupled gelding: carries condition: has been fired: has a round action: fair performer: won claimer at Catterick in August: best efforts at around 7f, probably stays 1m: acts on any going: blinkered once at 3 yrs: goes well at Chester: usually held up. *M. H. Easterby* 73

BOLD APPEAL (IRE) 3 b.c. Caerleon (USA) 132 – La Bella Fontana (Lafontaine (USA) 117) [1994 NR 1995 a8.5g Jul 8] third foal: half-brother to 4-y-o 1m winner Swinging Sixties (by Fairy King): dam once-raced half-sister to useful 5f and 7f winner Abuzz: apprentice ridden, well beaten in claimer at Wolverhampton: sold 1,000 gns Newmarket July Sales. *P. W. Chapple-Hyam* –

BOLD ARISTOCRAT (IRE) 4 b.c. Bold Arrangement 127 – Wyn Mipet (Welsh Saint 126) [1994 –: 6.1v 5g^6 a6g^6 a6g^6 8m^5 6g^6 a6g 7d a6g a5g a5g 1995 a6g a6g^3 a6g^3 a7g 7d 8g a7g^4 a6g* a6g^3 a6g^5 7m 6g^5 6d^5 a7g^6 a8g a6g a6g Dec 9] quite attractive colt: modest handicapper on the all-weather: won at Southwell in July: probably only poor on turf: should stay 7f: acts on firm and dead ground and on fibresand: tried blinkered: has worn pricker near side: successful for claimer: usually held up. *R. Hollinshead* 36 a53

BOLD CHARLIE 3 ch.g. Weldnaas (USA) 112 – Flirty Lady (Never So Bold 135) [1994 NR 1995 7m 10f a12g^5 a12g Aug 5] lengthy gelding: first reported foal: dam never ran: no sign of ability. *S. Mellor* –

BOLD CYRANO (IRE) 4 b.g. Cyrano de Bergerac 120 – Court Hussar (Queen's Hussar 124) [1994 –: a6g 1995 a7g a6g a7g^5 a6g a6g^6 6.9m 6f^4 6g 6m^6 6g^3 7.1m 7m^4 6g Sep 1] workmanlike gelding: modest maiden handicapper: stays 7f: acts on firm and soft ground, no form on the all-weather. *B. Palling* 55 a–

BOLD EFFORT (FR) 3 b.g. Bold Arrangement 127 – Malham Tarn (Riverman (USA) 131) [1994 70: 6s a7g^2 a8.5g^4 a7g^2 a7g^2 a8g 1995 a7g^2 a6g* a5g^3 a6g* a6g 6m 6m* 7f^3 6g^2 6m* 6m 6g 5.6m^2 6g 5d 6g^5 6d Oct 19] good-quartered gelding: poor mover: made into a useful handicapper, winning at Lingfield in January (maiden) and February, at Salisbury (rated stakes) in May and 15-runner £39,000 William Hill Handicap (in good style) at York in June: good second of 22 to Hello Mister in Portland Handicap at Doncaster on thirteenth start: effective at 5f, and stays 7f: acts on good to firm ground (probably on dead) and the all-weather: usually makes running/races prominently: game and genuine. *K. O. Cunningham-Brown* 101

BOLD ELECT 7 b.g. Electric 126 – Famous Band (USA) (Banderilla (USA)) [1994 53: 12.3m^5 12m 12.3g^2 16.2f^3 12g 1995 9.9m 12.3f^4 Jun 21] sturdy, lengthy gelding: carries condition: modest handicapper: seemed to shape well on reappearance but distant last of four 2½ months later: stays 2m: acts on any going: usually held up: has joined E. Alston. *P. Wigham* –

William Hill Trophy (Handicap), York—Bold Effort slams a good field on Timeform Charity Day; proceeds from the Day and eve-of-meeting Dinner brought the total raised to over £2 million

BOLD ENOUGH 2 ch.f. (May 7) Bold Arrangement 127 – Sweet Enough 79 (Caerleon (USA) 132) [1995 6f 6m 5.7h^4 6d^3 7d* 7s^6 a7g Nov 24] smallish, good-topped filly: good mover: third foal: half-sister to 3-y-o Paper Cloud (by Lugana Beach): dam stayed well: modest form: won maiden at Newcastle in September despite swerving right well inside last: below form in nurseries at Ascot and Southwell last 2 starts: will stay at least 1m: may be unsuited by very soft ground/ fibresand. *B. W. Hills* 63+

BOLD FRONTIER 3 gr.g. Chief Singer 131 – Mumtaz Flyer (USA) (Al Hattab (USA)) [1994 –, a73: 6m 6m^5 a5g* a5g* 5g^6 6m 5s a5s^3 1995 a6g^2 a7g^4 a6g^4 5g^{4dis} a6g^2 a5g* Apr 15] tall, workmanlike gelding: fair handicapper: best effort when winning at Wolverhampton in April by 4 lengths, slowly away but staying on strongly: not seen out afterwards: effective at 5f to 7f: acts on fibresand, probably on equitrack: effective blinkered/visored or not: has worn bandages. *K. T. Ivory* 58 a75

BOLD FUTURE (IRE) 2 b.g. (Feb 19) Treasure Kay 114 – Mother Courage 67 (Busted 134) [1995 6m 7g 6g Sep 14] 4,500Y: tall, lengthy gelding: has scope: second foal: half-brother to Spanish 3-y-o 11f winner Antigona (by Scottish Reel): dam, maiden, stayed 2m: behind in maiden auctions at Ripon, Thirsk and Ayr. *J. W. Watts* –

BOLD GAIT 4 ch.g. Persian Bold 123 – Miller's Gait 74§ (Mill Reef (USA) 141) [1994 98p: 8v^3 10d 9d^5 10.8d* 12m^2 13.3m* 14f^2 14.6g* 12g^6 1995 16m* 13.9g^6 16.1m* 16f^4 Jul 27] 114

In 1995, the Newcastle Brown Ale Northumberland Plate had a winner who should prove worthy of the race's traditions. To win under top weight off a BHB mark of 105, giving upwards of a stone to all but two of his sixteen rivals, was praiseworthy indeed, and Bold Gait did it by four lengths. He had already dealt out similar treatment in another handicap at Newbury on his reappearance. Three furlongs out at Newcastle Bold Gait was tucked in behind the leaders, swinging along on the bridle. A furlong and a half later he had hit the front and nothing was going to stop him; those who made the best attempts were Trans Siberia, George Dillingham and Noufari. On that showing, Bold Gait looked a strong contender for pattern races. But

'Newcastle Brown Ale' Northumberland Plate (Handicap), Newcastle—Bold Gait makes light of top weight

he has yet to prove it. He has had two attempts, in the Yorkshire Cup before the Plate and the Goodwood Cup after it. In neither did he run to form, but valid excuses are not hard to find. The Yorkshire Cup was over a mile and three quarters and slowly-run—an insufficient test of stamina for Bold Gait. There was no end-to-end gallop in the Goodwood Cup either, for which he started second favourite in a good field, but his below-form fourth is more likely explained by the injury which brought his season to a premature end; having thrown down a challenge two furlongs out, Bold Gait lost his action and hung badly right, returning with a tendon injury to his near-fore.

Bold Gait (ch.g. 1991)	Persian Bold (br 1975)	Bold Lad (b 1964)	Bold River
			Barn Pride
		Relka Runner (b 1968)	Relko
			Running Blue
	Miller's Gait (b 1986)	Mill Reef (b 1968)	Never Bend
			Milan Mill
		High Gait (b 1977)	High Top
			Gay Charlotte

Bold Gait's dam Miller's Gait was seemingly ungenuine, and ended her racecourse career with Michael Stoute and Lynda Ramsden without a win or a rating but with a Timeform squiggle. She could not have made a much better start at stud, however, first foal Bold Gait being followed by the useful if not entirely trustworthy Welton Arsenal (by Statoblest). Maintaining the momentum represents something of a test—if she does then Miller's Gait would be a standard bearer for the hitherto unheralded talents of Fearless Action, sire of her foals in 1993 and 1995. Both her grandam and dam were fairly useful winners on the flat and noteworthy broodmares. Gay Charlotte produced the 1988 St Simon Stakes winner Upend, while High Gait achieved her slice of fame through the exploits of Royal Gait whose extraordinary story in three countries reached its highlights here with a victory in the 1992 Champion Hurdle, surviving a stewards inquiry, and a first-past-the-post in the Ascot Gold Cup four years earlier, when the stewards threw him out.

The angular gelding Bold Gait will almost certainly have the Gold Cup on his agenda if he recovers from injury. He still has plenty to prove before he can be considered a likely winner of that race but his record is basically progressive. An easy mover, he has a fine turn of foot for a stayer and has the potential to win another good race. He acts on firm and dead ground, not having raced on anything softer since his debut. A genuine individual, Bold Gait did however run poorly when sweating and edgy on his final start in 1994. *J. R. Fanshawe*

BOLD GEM 4 b.f. Never So Bold 135 – Precious Jade 72 (Northfields (USA)) [1994 63, a68: 6d 6d 7m 6.1f 5m^2 6f^2 6m 5v^4 a6g 5s a5g* a5g^2 1995 5g 6m 5m^6 5.1m* 6m^6 5.1h^4 5m 5m 5.7h a6g^5 5.1d a7g^5 a7g^5 a6g a7g Nov 29] lengthy filly, slightly dipped-backed: modest handicapper: dead-heated at Chepstow in July: probably stays 7f: acts on all-weather surfaces and any turf going: effective blinkered (usually is) or not: inconsistent. *B. J. Meehan* — 55

BOLD HABIT 10 ch.g. Homing 130 – Our Mother 95 (Bold Lad (IRE) 133) [1994 59: a6g^6 a7s a8.5g^2 a8g^3 7m 7v a8.5g^3 7m^2 7g^4 7.5f^4 7f a9.4g a8g^5 8g^2 1995 a8g^2 a8g^3 8m a8g 8d* a10g^5 Nov 2] sturdy, strong-quartered gelding: fair handicapper: often contests amateurs events, and put up best effort for some time when winning 29-runner affair at Redcar in September: stays 8.5f: best form on ground no softer than dead, and acts on all-weather surfaces: blinkered (below form) once at 9 yrs: held up. *J. Pearce* — 67 a57

BOLDINA BAY 3 b.f. Never So Bold 135 – Mary Martin (Be My Guest (USA) 126) [1994 70: 5m 5g^3 6f^3 7g^3 1995 7g^3 7.5d* 9g 10.1m^2 8.3m Jul 14] good-topped filly: reportedly suffered chipped sesamoid final 2-y-o start: fair performer: won maiden at Beverley in June: stayed at least 1¼m: acted on firm and good to soft ground: broke leg at Hamilton (blinkered) in July: dead. *M. Johnston* — 77

BOLD JOKER 4 b.g. Jester 119 – Bold Difference 66 (Bold Owl 101) [1994 –: 8.2m 10.8m 1995 10m 13.8f^6 11f Oct 24] lightly-made gelding: no sign of ability. *G. R. Oldroyd* — –

BOLD LOOK 4 b.g. Never So Bold 135 – Madame Bovary 82 (Ile de Bourbon (USA) 133) [1994 –: 12g 12g^5 11.5g 1995 10m* 10g 11.8g 10m 10f^2 10m^5 12m 9.7s Sep 27] rangy gelding: modest handicapper: won at Leicester in April: mostly — 61 disappointing afterwards: should stay 1½m: acts on firm going: blinkered (below form) third 4-y-o start: has run creditably for amateur: sold (P. Harris to P. Webber) 8,000 gns Newmarket Autumn Sales and gelded. *P. W. Harris*

BOLDLY SO 3 b.f. Never So Bold 135 – Baino Clinic (USA) (Sovereign Dancer (USA)) [1994 NR 1995 a6g a7g^{4} a8g 10g* 10.1g^{4} 10.5d Oct 11] 6,800Y: workmanlike filly: second foal: dam French maiden: poor performer: pulled up third start (jockey reportedly thought she'd gone lame): 7/1 from 3/1, won 19-runner selling handicap at Nottingham on turf debut in April: failed to repeat the form in non-sellers: stays 1¼m: sold 4,200 gns Newmarket Autumn Sales. *W. J. Musson* 49

BOLD MICK 4 b.c. Never So Bold 135 – Purple Fan (Dalsaan 125) [1994 60, a65: 6.9s^{3} 6v* 6d^{4} 7m 6s^{3} 7v 6.1s^{6} 7g^{5} a7g a7g^{2} 6g a8.5g^{5} 7d 1995 a7g^{4} a7g a7g 6.9d 7d 10m^{2} 10m^{4} 11.6m^{6} Jun 5] quite good-topped colt: unimpressive mover: modest performer: stays 1¼m: acts on heavy going, good to firm and fibresand: blinkered (soundly beaten) once at 2 yrs: inconsistent: sold 500 gns Ascot September Sales. *D. J. G. Murray Smith* 51

BOLD PATRIOT (IRE) 2 b.c. (Mar 25) Polish Patriot (USA) 128 – Don't Be Cruel (Persian Bold 123) [1995 6m 7d Sep 27] 20,000F, 15,000Y: useful-looking colt: second foal: dam unraced daughter of useful middle-distance filly Goody Blake: off course 3 months, ninth of 13 to Centre Stalls in maiden at Salisbury, chasing pace to 2f out: will stay 1m: may do better. *J. W. Hills* 60

BOLD PURSUIT (IRE) 6 b.g. Thatching 131 – Pursue 78 (Auction Ring (USA) 123) [1994 67: a8g^{6} a11g^{2} a12g^{4} a11g a9.4g 12g^{2} 10d* 12m* a12g*^{dis} a12g* a12g^{3} a11g^{3} a14g 1995 a14g^{3} Apr 11] tall, lengthy gelding: fair performer at 5 yrs: distant third in handicap at Southwell on only 6-y-o start: stays 1½m: acts on good to firm and dead ground and on fibresand: sometimes blinkered, not since fifth 5-y-o start: often bandaged. *J. G. FitzGerald* –

BOLD REVIVAL 3 b.f. Never So Bold 135 – Convivial 81 (Nordance (USA)) [1994 NR 1995 7.5m^{6} 6f^{2} 6m 6.1d Sep 19] 1,000F, 900Y: good-topped filly: first foal: dam 1m winner: poor maiden: tailed off last 2 starts: best effort at 6f on firm ground. *Mrs P. Sly* 56 d

BOLD SALLY 3 b.f. Bold Fox 109 – Sally Bowles 87 (Blakeney 126) [1994 NR 1995 8m 8.1g 12.1m Jun 15] close-coupled, workmanlike filly: tenth foal: dam ran twice at 2 yrs: well beaten in maidens. *Mrs S. D. Williams* –

BOLD STREET (IRE) 5 ch.g. Shy Groom (USA) – Ferry Lane (Dom Racine (FR) 121) [1994 79: a6g^{4} a7g^{4} a6g* a6g^{2} a5g^{6} 6s* 5d* 7.6m 6g^{4} 6g* 6g 6d 1995 a7g a6g^{3} 6.1m 6g 5g 6g 6s a6g^{5} a6g^{3} a6g Dec 9] workmanlike gelding: fair handicapper at best in 1995: best form at 6f or stiff 5f, but should stay 7f: acts on all-weather surfaces and soft going: usually blinkered/visored. *A. Bailey* 72

BOLD TIMES 2 br.g. (Apr 19) Timeless Times (USA) 99 – Spanish Bold 78 (Tower Walk 130) [1995 5g^{6} 5.1m* a6g^{2} 6.1m^{3} 6m^{2} 6.1m* 6m Aug 11] 1,000Y: rather leggy gelding: sixth foal: dam 7.6f and 1m winner: won seller at Nottingham and nursery at Chester in midsummer: broke leg final start: stayed 6f: acted on good to firm ground and fibresand: dead. *P. D. Evans* 79

BOLD TOP 3 ch.g. Bold Owl 101 – Whirlygigger 69 (Taufan (USA) 119) [1994 48: 7.5f 6m 7.5g 8d 1995 12m 14.1m 10m^{3} 9f 9.9m^{2} 10m^{2} 10m 10.4g 10.4m Oct 5] close-coupled gelding: poor maiden handicapper: stays 1¼m: acts on firm ground: effective in blinkers/visor or not. *B. S. Rothwell* 45

BOLLIN DOROTHY 2 b.f. (Apr 1) Rambo Dancer (CAN) 107 – Bollin Harriet (Lochnager 132) [1995 6d^{2} 5f^{3} 5m^{2} Jul 1] strong filly: second foal: half-sister to 3-y-o 5f and 6f winner Bollin Harry (by Domynsky): dam never ran: fair form when second in maidens at Haydock and Newcastle: hung right throughout on very firm ground at Ripon in between: stays 6f. *M. H. Easterby* 73

BOLLIN FRANK 3 b.c. Rambo Dancer (CAN) 107 – Bollin Emily 82 (Lochnager 132) [1994 59: 5f^{5} 6.1m^{5} 6g 6g 1995 7.1g^{4} 6m^{6} 8m^{4} 6g^{5} 7f^{3} 6g 8.1m* 7.5g^{6} 8m 7.9g^{3} 8.1g 8.1s^{2} Oct 1] good-topped colt: good walker: modest handicapper: won at Haydock in July: stays 1m: acts on good to firm ground, probably on soft: blinkered (bit below form) fourth start at 3 yrs: sometimes hangs, and has worn sliding bar bit: often a front runner. *M. H. Easterby* 62

BOLLIN HARRY 3 b.c. Domynsky 110 – Bollin Harriet (Lochnager 132) [1994 58: 6f 6m 5g 5g⁶ 6d⁵ 1995 6g* 6g⁴ 5g* 5g⁵ 6f⁴ 6m² 5m⁶ 5g 7.1g⁵ 6s Oct 1] robust, full-quartered colt: fair handicapper: won at Newcastle in May and Catterick in June: probably stays 7f: acts on good to firm ground, below form both outings on a soft surface. *M. H. Easterby* — 70

BOLLIN JOANNE 2 b.f. (Feb 27) Damister (USA) 123 – Bollin Zola 90 (Alzao (USA) 117) [1995 5g² Jun 10] strong, close-coupled filly: third foal: half-sister to 3-y-o Bollin Sophie (by Efisio): dam 5f (at 2 yrs) and 7.6f winner: well-backed 4/1-shot, 1¼ lengths second of 9 to Blue Iris in maiden at Haydock, slowly away then staying on: will stay 6f: looked sure to improve. *M. H. Easterby* — 75

BOLLIN SOPHIE 3 b.f. Efisio 120 – Bollin Zola 90 (Alzao (USA) 117) [1994 NR 1995 6g 8d 10m 8.1d 8f 8g Aug 26] strong, lengthy filly: second foal: dam 5f (at 2 yrs) and 7.6f winner: little sign of ability. *M. H. Easterby* — –

BOLOARDO 6 b.g. Persian Bold 123 – Northshiel 85 (Northfields (USA)) [1994 83d: 10f 12m 11.9m³ 13.3m⁵ 11.9m 12g 12s⁵ 1995 10.3g² 12f⁶ 11.9m 14.1g⁴ Sep 23] leggy, good-topped gelding: has a round action: fair handicapper at best in 1995, below form after reappearance: stays 1½m: acts on firm and soft going: visored (well beaten) twice: inconsistent, and sometimes looks reluctant. *C. E. Brittain* — 69 §

BOLSHOI (IRE) 3 br.c. Royal Academy (USA) 130 – Mainly Dry (The Brianstan 128) [1994 49: 7s 7g 1995 5m* 6.1g 6.1m² 5m⁴ 6g 6m Jun 17] tall, lengthy colt: fair performer: won maiden at Beverley in April: stays 6f well: acts on good to firm ground: blinkered (no improvement) last 4 starts. *J. Berry* — 74

BONARELLI (IRE) 2 b.c. (Feb 11) Dancing Dissident (USA) 119 – Sovereign Dona 117 (Sovereign Path 125) [1995 7m² 7m* 8.1m* 8g* Sep 8] IR 85,000F: sturdy, attractive colt: fluent mover: half-brother to several winners, including smart Irish middle-distance stayer Foresee (by Vision) and Breeders' Cup Mile fourth Royal Touch (by Tap On Wood): dam, half-sister to good milers Don and American Prince, won 1¼m Prix de Psyche: progressive colt, successful in maiden at Chester in July, minor event at Sandown in August and listed Bellway Homes Stardom Stakes at Goodwood in September: beat Mushahid on last 2 occasions, comfortably by ½ length in receipt of 4 lb then by head at level weights: stays 1m well: very free to post at Sandown: sometimes sweats: a likeable sort who'll probably improve again. *M. R. Stoute* — 100 p

BONITA 3 ch.f. Primo Dominie 121 – Loufagh (USA) (Bering 136) [1994 47: 6m 7m 6m³ 6.9m 7d⁴ 8g 1995 6m* 5m⁵ 6.1m 7m* 7m Jul 1] medium-sized, good-quartered filly: poor mover: reportedly in foal to Inchinor: modest handicapper: won at Folkestone (apprentices) in April and Kempton (niggled along in rear, finishing — 57

Charterhouse Conditions Stakes, Sandown—Bonarelli (right) overturns the favourite Mushahid

strongly to lead on post) in June: stayed 7f: acted on good to firm ground: bandaged: usually ridden by claimer: inconsistent. *Mrs L. Piggott*

BON LUCK (IRE) 3 ch.g. Waajib 121 – Elle Va Bon (Tanfirion 110) [1994 5v^3 5s^2 5d^2 7m 7m 5g^4 1995 7g 7.1g^2 7f^4 Jun 28] IR 8,000Y: unfurnished ex-Irish gelding: fourth foal: half-brother to modest Irish 5-y-o sprinter Elle A Ted (by Glenstal): dam Irish 7f winner at 4 yrs: trained at 2 yrs by D. Weld before sold 10,000 gns Newmarket Autumn (1994) Sales: fair form in handicaps here: should stay 1m: acts on any ground: blinkered last 2 starts at 2 yrs: bandaged near-hind in 1995. *R. Akehurst* 72

BONNE ETOILE 3 b.f. Diesis 133 – Bonne Ile 115 (Ile de Bourbon (USA) 133) [1994 61p: 8d 1995 8d^2 8f* 8f* 10.1g* Aug 28] tall, rather lightly-made filly: has scope: progressive form: won maiden at Yarmouth in June and handicaps at Doncaster in July and Newcastle (listed rated stakes) in August: justified favouritism at Newcastle by short head from Vena, getting up close home despite edging left: better at 1¼m than 1m: acts on firm and dead ground: flashes tail and carries head awkwardly: open to further improvement. *D. R. Loder* 94 p

BONNY MELODY 4 b.f. Sizzling Melody 117 – Bonny Quiver 67 (Gorytus (USA) 132) [1994 58, a50: 6.9v^2 a7g* a8g^3 a6g^3 6f^2 6g^4 a5g a7g 1995 a7g a8.5g^6 6s 6m 6.1m 6f^6 a5g* 5m^4 5.1g 5m a6g a5g* a5g 5m^6 5.1m 6g 5g a5g^6 a6g Nov 30] smallish filly: has a quick action: modest handicapper: won at Wolverhampton in May and July: disappointing last 5 starts: effective at 5f (best recent form) to 7f: acts on any going, including fibresand: blinkered/visored (below form) once each: often bandaged behind: often ridden by Amanda Sanders: usually waited with, and suited by strongly-run race: none too consistent. *P. D. Evans* 52 d a42 d

BON SECRET (IRE) 3 b.c. Classic Secret (USA) 91 – Bon Retour (Sallust 134) [1994 48, a63: 5.1m 5.7f 5.3f^3 5g 7g a6g^5 a7g^2 a6g^4 a7g^4 a5g^2 1995 a5g* a5g^3 a6g^3 a5g^4 a5g* a5g^6 a6g^2 a6g^2 a6g* a6g^5 a8g^2 a8g 7.1d a7g Nov 10] sturdy colt: fair all-weather performer: won median auction maiden (made all) in January, claimer (got up on post) in February and handicap in March, all at Lingfield: effective at 5f to 1m: has form on fibresand, but seems best on equitrack: lightly raced and poor at best on turf. *T. J. Naughton* – a71

BOOKCASE 8 b.g. Siberian Express (USA) 125 – Colourful (FR) 97 (Gay Mecene (USA) 128) [1994 59+: 11.4d 10d 12.1g^6 1995 10.3g 12m 12m* 12m^6 10g^3 10m^2 11.4g 10f^2 11.4m* 12g^4 10f* 12m^5 12m^6 10d^4 10d Sep 27] big, good-topped gelding: usually looks very well: fair handicapper: consistent in 1995, and won at Folkestone in April, Sandown in July and Salisbury in August: effective at 1¼m and probably 1¾m: possibly unsuited by very soft ground, acts on any other: blinkered once earlier in career: sometimes finds little, and is suited by extreme waiting tactics: fairly useful hurdler, winner in December. *D. R. C. Elsworth* 71

BOOST 3 b.g. Superpower 113 – Sirene Bleu Marine (USA) (Secreto (USA) 128) [1994 –: 6m 6g 5g 8s 1995 6g 7m^5 7m^4 7m^2 7f^3 8g 7f^6 7m 7m^6 Oct 30] sturdy gelding: poor maiden handicapper: should stay 1m: acts on firm ground: sold (C. Thornton to Mrs. N. Macauley) 3,600 gns Doncaster November Sales. *C. W. Thornton* 46

BORANA LODGE (USA) 2 b.g. (Mar 5) Sabona (USA) 94 – Dancing Danzig (USA) (Danzig (USA)) [1995 5m^6 5m 5f^5 7m a8g* a8s* Nov 5] $17,000Y: tall, useful-looking gelding: has scope: sixth foal: half-brother to 2 winners in North America by Well Decorated: dam won one of 25 starts and was placed in Grade 2 7f event: sire (vastly improved after leaving Europe) Grade 1 9f winner and runner-up in Breeders' Cup Mile: poor maiden (tried blinkered) for Mrs J. Ramsden before sold 3,100 gns Doncaster August Sales: successful on both outings in Sweden: stays 1m: goes well on dirt. *Helena Halling, Sweden* 48 +

BORN A LADY 2 ch.f. (May 24) Komaite (USA) – Lucky Candy 61 (Lucky Wednesday 124) [1995 a5g* 6f^6 5g^2 5g^4 6f^3 5g^5 5f^3 6.1m^4 Oct 26] 480Y: useful-looking filly: has a round action: sixth foal: half-sister to 3-y-o Noble Canonire (by Gunner B) and modest 1m winner Ace Girl (by Stanford): dam, form only at 2 yrs, out of half-sister to Gunner B: fair performer: won maiden auction at Southwell in May: mostly good efforts afterwards in nurseries and minor events: seems to stay 6f: acts on firm ground and fibresand. *N. P. Littmoden* 70

BORN TO BE WILD 3 gr.f. Pharly (FR) 130 – Carose (Caro 133) [1994 NR 1995 14d^2 12m^5 10d^2 Sep 18] tall, leggy, close-coupled filly: half-sister to several winners, including useful Italian 7f to 9f winner Rosa de Caerleon (by Caerleon) and 1¼m winner Jason's Quest (by Golden Fleece): dam half-sister to very smart French middle-distance colt Noir Et Or: poor form in sellers: claimed by M. Pipe £6,000 on final start: stays 1¾m: best efforts with give in the ground. *W. G. M. Turner* 47

BORN TO PLEASE (IRE) 3 ch.g. Waajib 121 – Gratify 65 (Grundy 137) [1994 58p: 8.1g 7s 1995 8m 8f 11.6m 11.6m^6 14m^5 12f^6 12.1m^2 11.5g^4 10.8g^4 Oct 3] useful-looking gelding: modest maiden: stays 1½m: below form on very firm ground: sold (P. Harris to P. Hobbs) 11,000 gns Newmarket Autumn Sales. *P. W. Harris* 49

BOROCAY 7 b.g. Lochnager 132 – Maybehandy 66 (Some Hand 119) [1994 –: a12g^6 1995 a12g* a12g^2 a16g^3 12.1d* 12.3d^3 Apr 5] strong, good-topped gelding: poor handicapper: won at Southwell (apprentice maiden event) in January and at Edinburgh in March: effective at 1½m to 2m: acts on heavy ground and fibresand. *M. J. Camacho* 44

BORROWBY 3 ch.c. Domynsky 110 – Close The Deal 51 (Nicholas Bill 125) [1994 53: 5g^5 5d 5m 7f 7.5g^5 7m a7g^4 a7g^3 7.5f^4 7g^2 7.9d 7g 7d 1995 7.5m 6g 8g^4 8.1m^5 8.1m^6 8g 10.5s 7m Oct 20] workmanlike colt: has a round action: poor maiden handicapper: stays 1m: acts on firm ground and fibresand, well beaten on soft: usually blinkered or visored: takes keen hold, and usually races prominently. *M. W. Easterby* 42

BOSRA SHAM (USA) 2 ch.f. (Feb 28) Woodman (USA) 126 – Korveya (USA) 116 (Riverman (USA) 131) [1995 6m* 8d* Sep 24] 115 p

The Cecil family standard, raised above Warren Place after every Group 1 victory, had remained in its box for over a year before Bosra Sham's success in the Fillies' Mile at Ascot in September. Henry Cecil has been leading trainer in Britain on ten occasions, most recently in 1993 when he just pipped Richard Hannon on first prize-money during the turf season, and he has had more pattern-race victories—passing the three-hundred mark in the latest season—than any other British trainer. But, partly for reasons discussed in the essay on Mark of Esteem, the 1995 flat-racing year won't be one he'll recall with especial satisfaction. With a filly like Bosra Sham, however, Cecil has cause to look forward to 1996 with plenty of optimism. He went on record after the Fillies' Mile as saying that 'Bosra Sham is the best two-year-old filly I have had since Oh So Sharp'. Oh So Sharp, also successful in the Fillies' Mile, went on to win the One Thousand Guineas, the Oaks and the St Leger.

Bosra Sham went into training carrying the tag of 'the highest-priced yearling in Europe'—she made 530,000 guineas at the Houghton Sales—and, even before her debut, reports of her homework suggested she might well prove special. She readily disposed of a field of maidens at Newbury in August, standing out on looks and starting odds on in a line-up of twenty-two, and had already deposed the unbeaten Blue Duster as ante-post favourite for the One Thousand Guineas before her victory in the Fillies' Mile. But for a bruised foot, Bosra Sham would have taken in the May

Fillies' Mile, Ascot—Bosra Sham lives up to her reputation, getting well on top of Bint Shadayid and Matiya

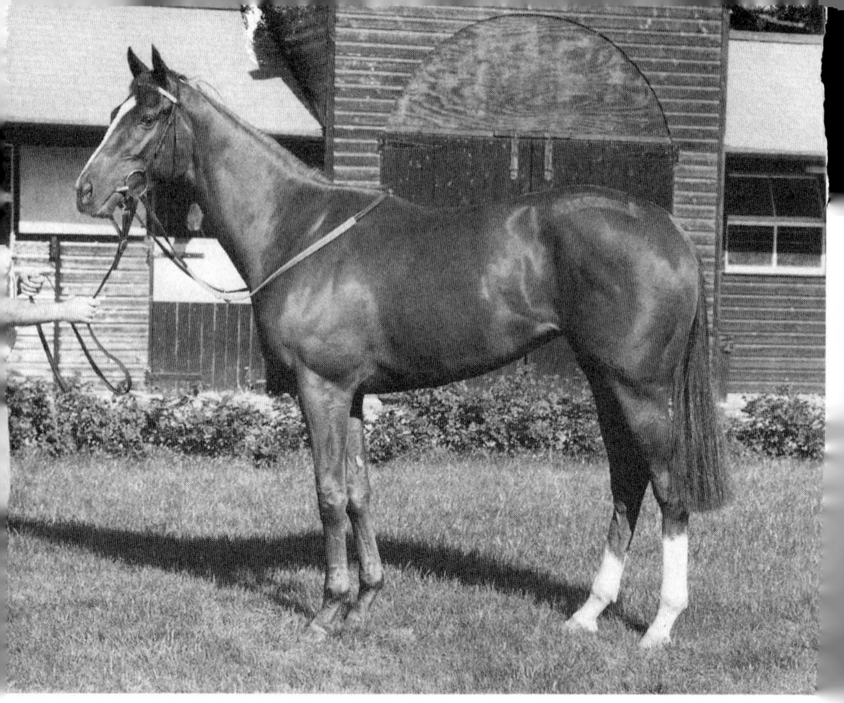

Wafic Said's "Bosra Sham"

Hill Stakes at Doncaster beforehand—won by her stand-in Solar Crystal—but the softish ground at Ascot seemed of more concern to the trainer than her lack of experience. The field for the Fillies' Mile was made up of similarly lightly-raced, well-bred and highly-regarded types, headed, in market order after the odds-on Bosra Sham, by Shawanni, who had landed some big bets when overcoming trouble in running on her debut in a Yarmouth maiden, and Bint Shadayid, who had shaped like a smart filly in the making when winning her first two starts. Bosra Sham showed some signs of inexperience, seeming to take a little time to grasp what was required when tackling Bint Shadayid for the lead early in the straight, but she was well on top at the finish. Bosra Sham strode clear in the final furlong for a three-and-a-half-length victory over Bint Shadayid, making an excellent impression; Matiya was the same distance behind Bint Shadayid in third, with Shawanni, who became stirred up at the start and ran too freely early on, dropping back to finish only fifth of six. Not even Blue Duster's splendid victory in the following week's Cheveley Park Stakes could dislodge Bosra Sham from her position as Guineas favourite, for which she went into winter quarters a top-priced 4/1.

The rangy, attractive Bosra Sham has plenty of scope and should make up into an imposing filly as a three-year-old. She looks tailor-made for the Guineas—her full brother Hector Protector and her three-parts brother Shanghai (by another Mr Prospector stallion Procida) both won the Poule d'Essai des Poulains—but whether she'll prove fully effective over the Oaks trip is another question. Bosra Sham's sire Woodman was successful over a mile as a two-year-old and, though seen out only once at three, he wasn't bred to get further. He has sired winners over a range of

		Mr Prospector (b 1970)	Raise A Native
	Woodman (USA) (ch 1983)		Gold Digger
		Playmate (ch 1975)	Buckpasser
Bosra Sham (USA) (ch.f. Feb 28, 1993)			Intriguing
		Riverman (b 1969)	Never Bend
	Korveya (USA) (ch 1982)		River Lady
		Konafa (b 1973)	Damascus
			Royal Statute

distances, his most notable over a mile and a half being the Belmont Stakes winner Hansel, but the average distance of races won by his three-year-olds and upwards in Europe is nine furlongs. Bosra Sham's dam the smart Korveya was successful at up to nine furlongs, and her grandam Konafa, also the dam of the high-class sprinter Proskona, was second in the One Thousand Guineas. This is a good family, Konafa herself being a half-sister, among others, to the good American colt Akureyri, who won in graded company at two (the Pilgrim Stakes over nine furlongs) and three (the Fountain of Youth Stakes over an extended mile), and to the Yorkshire Oaks winner Awaasif, the grandam of Lammtarra. Bosra Sham's third dam, Royal Statute, was a sister to Falafel who bred the St James's Palace Stakes winner Brief Truce and the Italian Two Thousand Guineas winner Again Tomorrow. Bosra Sham's dam, incidentally, was sold by her breeder Stavros Niarchos before Hector Protector and Shanghai, both of whom carried his colours, reached the racecourse. Niarchos bought Korveya back for 700,000 dollars at the 1989 Keeneland November Sale and sold her privately afterwards to Gerald Leigh. The Nijinsky foal Korveya was carrying turned out to be the filly Gioconda who was successful over a mile in France; Korveya's latest yearling, a colt by Nureyev, was sold to a Japanese buyer for 165,000 guineas at the Houghton Sales. Bosra Sham, incidentally, was originally named Quercifolia by her breeder but her name was changed by her present owner; she reportedly takes her name from a place in Syria. Judged on pedigree, Bosra Sham can confidently be expected to stay a mile and a quarter, and it augurs well for her Oaks prospects that she was going on strongly at the end of the Fillies' Mile. A word of warning, though—Hector Protector's stamina ran out in the last furlong or so of the Derby, in which he managed only fourth to Generous after looking likely to finish a clear third. Bosra Sham has so far raced on good to firm and good to soft going. She has the pedigree, the looks and the ability—she's sure to progress again—of a filly set to enjoy a highly successful three-year-old campaign. *H. R. A. Cecil*

BOSTON ROCK (IRE) 3 ch.c. Ballad Rock 122 – Miss Boston (FR) (River River (FR) 117) [1994 NR 1995 7.1m Jul 7] 8,200F: big, strong gelding: third foal: half-brother to fairly useful 6f (at 2 yrs) winner Bold Bostonian (by Never So Bold), who stayed 1¼m: dam, 5f winner at 2 yrs, stayed 1¼m: showed nothing in maiden at Haydock: wore a tongue strap and moved poorly to post. *P. W. Harris* –

BOSTON TEA PARTY 2 b.f. (May 13) Rambo Dancer (CAN) 107 – Tea-Pot 77 (Ragstone 128) [1995 6m 7.1m 6m^{3} 7g 6g a7g Nov 10] leggy filly: sister to 3-y-o Million Dancer and half-sister to middle-distance stayer One For The Pot (by Nicholas Bill) and Irish 1¼m winner Two Lumps (by Nomination): dam out-and-out stayer: staying-on third in claimer at Folkestone in September, final start for I. Balding and only worthwhile form. *A. Moore* 40 ?

BOUCHE BEE (USA) 3 b.f. Naevus (USA) – Miss Henderson Co (USA) (Silver Hawk (USA) 123) [1994 NR 1995 7m 6g^{2} 6m^{2} 7g* 7m* 7g* 7f^{5} 7.9m^{5} Aug 17] 33,000Y: lengthy filly: poor mover: first foal: dam, allowance winner at around 1m in USA, is half-sister to dual U.S. Grade One 8.5f winner By Land By Sea: made into a useful performer: won median auction maiden at Yarmouth and 2 handicaps at Newmarket (second a rated stakes) in the summer: good efforts in valuable handicaps at Goodwood and York last 2 starts: stays 1m: acts on firm going: sometimes bandaged behind: sold 41,000 gns Newmarket December Sales. *L. M. Cumani* 95

BOUNDARY BIRD (IRE) 2 b.g. (Apr 22) Tirol 127 – Warning Sound (Red Alert 127) [1995 5f^{4} 6m a7g^{3} 8g 7d^{5} a8g Nov 20] 10,000Y: big, leggy gelding: half-brother to several winners, including 3-y-o Loveyoumillions (by Law Society), 5f and 6f winner at 2 yrs, and 5f (at 2 yrs) and 1m winner Remthat Naser (by Sharpo): dam Irish 5f to 1¼m winner: modest maiden: gives impression should stay beyond 7f (had plenty of use made of him when well beaten facing stiff tasks in nurseries at 1m). *M. Johnston* 56

BOUNDARY EXPRESS 3 b.g. Sylvan Express 117 – Addison's Jubilee 73 (Sparkler 130) [1994 58?: 5m 6m a7g 6s 8g4 a7g 1995 a9.4g2 a8g6 a11g5 11.1g4 8m4 12m4 8.3g2 10m 9.2f5 a9.4g 12m* 14.1m3 11.9g* 15g2 14s6 14m4 Oct 13] workmanlike gelding: modest performer: claimed out of M. Johnston's stable £3,000 seventh 3-y-o start: made all in seller at Pontefract in August and amateurs handicap at Haydock in September: should stay 2m: acts on fibresand and good to firm ground, probably on soft: blinkered (looked reluctant) once, visored (below form) twice. *E. J. Alston* — 64

BOUNDLESS (IRE) 3 b.f. Cyrano de Bergerac 120 – Blink (Dike (USA)) [1994 –: 6d 7d 1995 10s a12g3 11.9m 17.2f Jul 1] workmanlike filly: poor maiden: sold 400 gns Doncaster July Sales: stays 1½m: best effort on fibresand: tried blinkered. *B. J. Meehan* — – a38

BOURSIN (IRE) 6 b.g. Taufan (USA) 119 – Cloven Dancer (USA) 86 (Hurok (USA)) [1994 75: 7m* 7m* 6d2 6m4 6m* 6f6 6g3 6g4 1995 a6g 6m 6g6 6m3 6f5 6d a6g 5.1m Oct 19] tall, leggy gelding: good mover: tubed: fair front-running performer at his best: tailed off last 3 starts, sold out of P. Calver's stable only 550 gns Ascot September Sales after first of them: effective at 6f and 7f: acts on firm and dead going: blinkered (raced too freely) final 4-y-o outing. *N. P. Littmoden* — 67 d

BOUTON D'OR 2 b.f. (Jan 11) Mazilier (USA) 107 – Cow Pastures (Homing 130) [1995 5m 5g 6g a5g5 a6g a5g2 Dec 19] 2,500Y: lengthy filly: half-sister to 1994 2-y-o 7f seller winner Petindia (by Petong) and a winner in Italy: dam unraced daughter of useful sprinter Pennycuick, a half-sister to Mummy's Pet: best effort when second of 5 in median auction maiden at Lingfield final start: well beaten (in seller) on fibresand. *P. Howling* — 53

BOWCLIFFE 4 b.g. Petoski 135 – Gwiffina 87 (Welsh Saint 126) [1994 63+: 10g 8f5 12.3m 10m* 1995 10.5d 9.7f5 14m4 14g6 Jul 27] good-topped gelding: often looks very well: modest handicapper: sold (J. Gifford to Mrs A. Naughton) 16,000 gns Doncaster August Sales: seems to stay 1¾m: acts on good to firm and dead ground: tried blinkered. *J. T. Gifford* — 58

BOWCLIFFE COURT (IRE) 3 b.g. Slip Anchor 136 – Res Nova (USA) (Blushing Groom (FR) 131) [1994 52: 7m 7m4 1995 10m 12m3 12d* 12m4 15g 14g2 14m6 Oct 13] close-coupled, rather unfurnished gelding: fair handicapper: won at Beverley in June: should stay 2m: best efforts with give in the ground: ran much too freely under 7-lb claimer on reappearance: found little on final outing. *B. W. Hills* — 68

BOWCLIFFE GRANGE (IRE) 3 b.g. Dominion Royale 112 – Cala-Vadella 110 (Mummy's Pet 125) [1994 –: 6d 1995 a8.5g 6.9f 8m 6m 5g3 Sep 2] good-topped gelding: well drawn, only worthwhile form when 8 lengths third of 16 in maiden handicap at Thirsk on final outing: a sprinter. *D. W. Chapman* — 23

BOWDEN ROSE 3 ch.f. Dashing Blade 117 – Elegant Rose 72 (Noalto 120) [1994 64: 5g3 5d3 6g 6m* 6m4 6m4 7d 6.1d 7g 1995 6.1g 8g 7g 7m4 6f* 6m* 6g* 6m2 6m6 5m6 5.7h3 5.3g* 5s 6d 6f3 Oct 25] angular, shallow-girthed filly: made into a fairly useful handicapper, winning at Salisbury (twice) and Yarmouth in the summer and at Brighton in October: effective at 5f and 6f: acts on firm and dead ground (missed break badly when well beaten on soft): blinkered since third 3-y-o start: often a front runner, but also effective held up: somewhat wayward, but successful for apprentice. *M. Blanshard* — 90

BOWLED OVER 2 b.g. (Feb 5) Batshoof 122 – Swift Linnet (Wolver Hollow 126) [1995 6s3 Sep 28] 9,500Y: workmanlike gelding: fourth foal: half-brother to a winner in Austria: dam Irish 4-y-o 13f winner: 20/1 and in need of race, over 5 lengths third of 11 to Norwegian Blue in maiden at Lingfield, staying on after slow start: showed a round action: will do better over 7f+. *C. A. Cyzer* — 67 p

BOWLERS BOY 2 ch.g. (Feb 14) Risk Me (FR) 127 – Snow Wonder (Music Boy 124) [1995 6f 6m Nov 3] 4,200Y: workmanlike gelding: has scope: first foal: dam fourth over 6f and 1m: poor form in maiden events at Pontefract (badly short of room over 1f out) and Doncaster in the autumn: will probably do better. *J. J. Quinn* — – p

BOXBOY 5 b.g. Kings Lake (USA) 133 – Majan 67 (Brigadier Gerard 144) [1994 –: a13g 11.9g 12m 12m 10.8m 11.6f 1995 a9.4g Mar 8] good-bodied gelding: no longer of much account. *G. H. Yardley* — –

BOZEMAN (IRE) 2 b.g. (Jan 11) Cyrano de Bergerac 120 – Catherine Clare 58 (Sallust 134) [1995 5.2m 5g 5g* 5m 6m 6m* 5g Sep 13] IR 9,000F, 10,000Y: smallish, sturdy, close-coupled gelding: has a quick action: half-brother to Irish 7f winner Black And Blaze and Irish 5f and 6f winner Three Musketeers (both by Taufan): dam Irish miler: won seller at Goodwood in June and claimer (apparently much improved effort) at Folkestone in September: badly drawn and hampered start in nursery at Sandown final start: stays 6f: blinkered last 2 starts: sold 5,500 gns Newmarket Autumn Sales. *R. Hannon* — 65 ?

BRACKENTHWAITE 5 ch.g. Faustus (USA) 118 – Cosset 56 (Comedy Star (USA) 121) [1994 48, a75: a9.4g a8g^5 a8.5g^6 a9.4g* a10g* 9.9s^4 10d^6 1995 a8g^4 a9.4g^5 a11g^5 a8g 10g a8.5g 10m a8.5g^2 a9.4g^5 a8.5g a8g^4 Sep 4] strong, good-quartered gelding: fair handicapper on the all-weather: below form after first two 5-y-o starts: may well be best at around 1¼m: goes well on all-weather surfaces, best turf form with some give in the ground: usually blinkered/visored: held up: won selling hurdle in December. *L. R. Lloyd-James* — – a69 d

BRADWELL (IRE) 4 b.f. Taufan (USA) 119 – Tabriya 61 (Nishapour (FR) 125) [1994 54: 6d 7f^5 5m^5 5.2g^2 5m^3 5g* 6g^5 6s 5m 5.1g a6g a6g^5 1995 a7g^3 a7g^3 a6g Jan 30] leggy filly: poor performer: probably stays 7f: acts on dead ground and fibresand: visored (well beaten) final start. *M. H. Tompkins* — 50

BRAES'O'SHIELDHILL 2 ch.f. (Mar 7) Music Maestro 119 – Dalchroy (Hotfoot 126) [1995 5d^6 5g a6g^4 a6g Aug 19] 5,000Y: leggy filly: sister to 7f and 1m winner Asithappens and half-sister to 7f winner Fuchu (by Jupiter Island) and 1989 2-y-o 5f winner Ermo Express (by Bay Express): dam, poor maiden, ran only at 2 yrs: no worthwhile form, in sellers last 2 starts: often slowly away. *A. Bailey* — –

BRAILLE (IRE) 4 br.g. Vision (USA) – Winning Feature (Red Alert 127) [1994 82: 7f 6m 8.1g 7f 8s 1995 8g 6d 10f^4 10.3m^4 11.1g 10g 10m^5 14f 11.9m* 10f* 10.3m* 10m^3 10.3d^2 10d^2 11.9g^3 10.5s^4 Oct 1] lengthy gelding: fair handicapper: won at Haydock, Ayr and Chester within a week in August, twice in apprentice events: effective at 1¼m and 1½m: acts on any going: visored (well beaten) twice: usually held up, but also effective from front. *M. G. Meagher* — 77

BRANDONHURST 5 b.g. Elegant Air 119 – Wolverina 71 (Wolver Hollow 126) [1994 69§: 10g 8.5g^6 8.9f 8m^3 9f 11.6m^2 10m^2 1995 8.2g 9g 10g 14m Jul 15] good-topped gelding: unimpressive mover: modest handicapper at best in 1995: should stay 1½m: acts on firm and dead ground: has run poorly in blinkers/visor: usually held up: often slowly away: unreliable. *Lady Herries* — 55 §

BRANDON LANE 4 b.g. Good Times (ITY) – Fauve 71 (Dominion 123) [1994 NR 1995 10m^6 8m Jul 22] quite good-topped gelding: second foal: dam, best at 2 yrs, stayed 6f: well beaten in sellers: sold 1,025 gns Ascot November Sales. *R. M. Whitaker* — –

BRANDON MAGIC 2 ch.c. (Apr 15) Primo Dominie 121 – Silk Stocking 109 (Pardao 120) [1995 6m^3 6g^2 6g* 6d* 7s* 7.3d^3 Oct 19] 36,000Y: good-topped, lengthy colt: has scope: half-brother to numerous winners, including useful 2-y-o winner Satinette (by Shirley Heights): dam (stayed 1½m) half-sister to good sprinter — 99

Hyperion Conditions Stakes, Ascot—Brandon Magic pulls back Henry The Fifth (rails) late on

Shiny Tenth: useful colt: comfortable winner of maiden at Pontefract and minor event at Salisbury in September: did well to win falsely-run 4-runner minor event at Ascot in October by neck from Henry The Fifth then ran well when under a length third of 9, to Tumbleweed Ridge in Horris Hill Stakes at Newbury final start: stays 7f: acts on soft ground. *I. A. Balding*

BRANDON PRINCE (IRE) 7 b.g. Shernazar 131 – Chanson de Paris (USA) (The Minstrel (CAN) 135) [1994 80: 16.2s^4 16s 18.7m 16.5m^6 13.9m 16.1f 16.4m 16g 14g^6 16d* 16.2g^5 16d 1995 18g 14.9d 16m 21.6f^2 17.2m May 13] close-coupled gelding: impresses in appearance: only fair handicapper nowadays: better at 2m than shorter, and stays extreme distances: acts on soft and firm ground: often used to wear blinkers, not in 1995 after reappearance: usually held up: has run well when sweating: inconsistent. *I. A. Balding* 70

BRANDONVILLE 2 b.c. (Apr 12) Never So Bold 135 – Enduring (Sadler's Wells (USA) 132) [1995 6d^6 6g^4 6.9g^4 Oct 16] 10,000Y: leggy colt: first foal: dam twice-raced half-sister to Kentucky Derby runner-up Bold Arrangement: fourth in maiden auctions at Warwick and Folkestone, better effort final outing when beaten 3 short-heads by Ageeb: finished well in all his races, and will be at least as effective at 1m as 7f: sold 16,000 gns Doncaster November Sales. *I. A. Balding* 72

BRANSTON ABBY (IRE) 6 ch.m. Risk Me (FR) 127 – Tuxford Hideaway 102 (Cawston's Clown 113) [1994 107: 7v^3 7d* 6f^4 6v^5 6f 7m 6m 6m 6d 6m 6d 6d* 6v^2 6v* 1995 5m^3 6m 7m^4 6m^2 6g^3 6d^6 6g^2 7.1g^5 6f 6m* 6m^4 7m*^{dis} 6.5g^2 7g* 6.5m^5 6g* 6d^2 7g* 6g 6d^3 7d^5 7m 6m^2 6d^2 7f Dec 10] 118

1995 saw the end of an era with the retirement of actress Julie Goodyear from her part as Bet Gilroy in the popular soap opera *Coronation Street*. It also saw a further episode in the career of another durable and much-loved northern female in the form of Branston Abby, whose racecourse appearances in recent times have been nearly as frequent as those of her human counterpart behind the bar in The Rovers Return. At the time of writing it is not clear whether Branston Abby has also earned honourable retirement or will be seen in public again in 1996. Whilst she has little left to prove in the racecourse arena, we could understand it if her connections, who are renowned for their aggressive campaigning of their racehorses, were to decide to give her another season in training. Although it might be argued that Bet Gilroy had seen better days, Branston Abby herself had never been in finer shape than she was in the latest season.

The 1995 campaign began for Branston Abby in April in the rural setting of one of her local courses, Beverley, and ended in December amid the urban sprawl of Sha Tin, Hong Kong. Between them she managed a further twenty-three runs, winning four of them, namely listed races at Newcastle in July, Gelsenkirchen-Horst in August and Doncaster in September and a rated stakes handicap at York in August.

Lawrence Batley Rated Stakes (Handicap), York—Branston Abby lands some good bets, from fast-finishing Venture Capitalist (blinkers) and Hello Mister

Kyoto Sceptre Stakes, Doncaster—busy Branston Abby is idling in front of Lovely Millie (rails) and Didina

In addition, she was disqualified after finishing first in a listed event at Dusseldorf in July when it transpired that she had been allocated an incorrect weight. There were also several creditable runs in defeat, the most notable of them third placings in the Duke of York Stakes (beaten six and a half lengths by Lake Coniston) in May and the Diadem Stakes (beaten two short heads, by Cool Jazz and Young Ern) at Ascot in September and a second in the Haydock Park Sprint Cup earlier in September. At no point was Branston Abby away from the racecourse for as much as three weeks and her busiest period (six runs between August 30th and September 30th) coincided with her best form. Were we to pick out a couple of efforts for especial mention they would be those in the Haydock Park Sprint and in victory at Doncaster. At Haydock over six furlongs Branston Abby was soon pushed along and unable to go the scorching pace set by Mind Games and Lake Coniston. But she stuck gamely to her task and came through to lead for a stride or two at around the furlong marker before the eventual one-and-a-half-length winner Cherokee Rose outpaced her. Only five days later Branston Abby made much lighter work of dismissing rather lesser opposition in the furlong-longer Kyoto Sceptre Stakes, pricking her ears and being able to idle in beating Lovely Millie by two lengths, having been produced with a furlong to go. By the season's end Branston Abby had amassed a career record of nineteen wins from a remarkable seventy-six runs.

Branston Abby (IRE) (ch.m. 1989)	Risk Me (FR) (ch 1984)	Sharpo (ch 1977)	Sharpen Up
			Moiety Bird
		Run The Risk (b 1976)	Run The Gantlet
			Siliciana
	Tuxford Hideaway (ch 1982)	Cawston's Clown (b 1974)	Comedy Star
			Cawston's Pride
		Late Idea (b 1975)	Tumble Wind
			Idylle

When the time does come for Branston Abby to be retired to the paddocks, she's got something to recommend her besides her excellent racing record. Although her sire Risk Me's record at stud is largely unexceptional, Branston Abby does hail from quite a successful distaff line. Her dam Tuxford Hideaway, a daughter of a winning miler, showed useful form over five furlongs, winning twice. Branston Abby is a second foal, following the quite useful performer at up to a mile Big Blow (by Last Tycoon). Two of the later produce have also won, namely Glowing Dancer (by Glow), a modest six-furlong winner, and Branston Jewel (by Prince Sabo). Branston Jewel was a promising two-year-old in the latest season, winning her first two starts and finishing third, promoted to second, in the Prix d'Arenberg on her only subsequent appearance. Unfortunately she suffered a serious leg injury and may well not run again.

A tall, lengthy, sparely-made mare, Branston Abby is effective at six furlongs to seven furlongs and acts on any going, except possibly firm. She is highly strung and is often mounted on the track, but is thoroughly genuine when racing. All in all, this admirable mare reflects great credit on her trainer. *M. Johnston*

BRANSTON DANNI 2 b.f. (May 1) Ron's Victory (USA) 129 – Softly Spoken 87 (Mummy's Pet 125) [1995 5.1m^{2} 5m^{5} 5f* 5m 5m^{6} 6m^{2} 6.5m 6g^{2} Sep 16] 17,000Y: close-coupled filly: third foal: half-sister to 2-y-o sprint winners Here Comes Risky (by Risk Me), and Sweet Whisper (by Petong): dam sprinter: fair performer: won median auction maiden at Edinburgh in July: good second in nurseries 2 of last 3 starts behind Arajaan at Leicester (took keen hold) and King of Peru at Ayr: stays 6f: twice slowly away, particularly so penultimate start when also jinking right: has worn bandage near-hind. *Mrs J. R. Ramsden*

73

BRANSTON JEWEL (IRE) 2 ch.f. (Mar 15) Prince Sabo 123 – Tuxford Hideaway 102 (Cawston's Clown 113) [1995 5m* 5g* 5.5g^{2} Sep 5] 21,000Y: lengthy, good-quartered, rather unfurnished filly: has plenty of scope: fifth foal: half-sister to 3-y-o Chance Me and very smart 6f/7f performer Branston Abby (both by Risk Me) and 2 winners at up to 7f: dam sprinter: won maiden at Windsor and 4-runner minor event at York in August: 4¼ lengths third of 7 to disqualified Titus Livius in Prix d'Arenberg at Chantilly following month, leading briefly 1½f out: speedy: edged left both starts in Britain, badly so at York: has reportedly suffered likely career-ending injury. *M. Johnston*

95

BRANSTON KRISTY 3 b.f. Hallgate 127 – Bare Spectacle (Welsh Pageant 132) [1994 55: 5f^{2} 6g^{2} 6g^{3} 5g^{4} 5.1m^{2} a6g^{2} a5g^{6} 5.1g a5g^{2} 5m a5g^{3} 5g^{2} 6d a5g a5g 1995 a6g a6g^{5} a5g^{3} a5g Mar 1] sparely-made filly: poor sprint maiden: acts on firm ground (yet to race on soft) and the all-weather: effective visored or not. *C. Smith*

41

BRASS TACKS 3 br.f. Prince Sabo 123 – Brassy Nell 72 (Dunbeath (USA) 127) [1994 71p: 6g^{3} 6s 1995 7f^{6} 6g^{3} 6g 8m^{3} 7f* a7g 8f^{5} Aug 22] angular filly: modest performer: won claimer at Goodwood (claimed out of R. Hannon's stable £8,000) in June, leading near finish: well below form both subsequent outings: stays 1m: acts on firm ground, ran poorly on soft and on fibresand. *R. T. Phillips*

62

BRAVEBOY 7 b.g. Never So Bold 135 – Relkina (FR) 85 (Relkino 131) [1994 63: a10g^{4} 7.6m 8.1g 7g^{3} 8d 8s^{3} 7d 8.2g 1995 a10g^{3} a9.4g^{5} a10g^{3} a11g a10g Mar 16] quite attractive gelding: modest handicapper: stays 1¼m: acts on soft going and the all-weather: tried blinkered/visored, no improvement. *C. E. Brittain*

63

BRAVE EDGE 4 b.g. Beveled (USA) – Daring Ditty (Daring March 116) [1994 84: 5g* 6.1m 5m^{4} 5.2m 1995 5.2m^{2} 5m* 5g* 5f^{4} 6f^{3} 6m 5m 5d^{3} 5m Oct 14] good-topped gelding: useful handicapper: won at Sandown in April and York (£15,300 race) in May: good third in the Wokingham at Royal Ascot on fifth start: effective at 5f and 6f: acts on firm and good to soft ground: usually held up. *R. Hannon*

102

BRAVE FIGHTER (USA) 3 b.f. Gone West (USA) – Psyched (USA) (Hagley (USA)) [1994 NR 1995 7.1m^{4} 7.6m^{6} 8f^{3} 7m^{6} Aug 10] $46,000Y, resold $65,000Y: second foal: dam Grade 3 7f winner, second in Grade 1 event at 9f: modest form in maidens, failing to progress from debut: pulled hard and well beaten when favourite for handicap at Yarmouth on final start: should stay 1m. *B. Hanbury*

61

BRAVE INDIGO 2 b.c. (Mar 24) Rainbow Quest (USA) 134 – Nyoka (USA) (Raja Baba (USA)) [1995 6g^{5} 7.5g* 7.5s^{2} 9g* 9g* Nov 19] fifth foal: half-brother to 4 winners, including useful 6f (at 2 yrs) to 1¼m performer Glacial (by Icecapade) and smart 4-y-o 6f to 8.8f winner Beat of Drums (by Warning): dam unraced: useful Italian colt: won maiden at Milan in August, minor event at Rome in October and 11-runner Premio Guido Berardelli at Rome (beat Latin Reign a nose) in November: will be well suited by 1¼m+: likely to improve further. *G. Botti, Italy*

100 p

BRAVE MAISIE (IRE) 2 b.f. (Apr 17) Mazaad 106 – London Spin 86 (Derring-Do 131) [1995 6m^{6} 7m^{4} 7f 7f 6d Sep 16] 1,800Y: leggy, unfurnished filly: half-sister to several winners on flat and over hurdles, including 7f and 1m performer Bu-Sofyan (by Runnett): dam stayed 1m: poor maiden: stays 7f: sold 500 gns Ascot September Sales. *M. McCormack*

44

BRAVE PATRIARCH (IRE) 4 gr.g. Alzao (USA) 117 – Early Rising (USA) (Grey Dawn II 132) [1994 85: 9.9d* 10.5g^{3} 12f 10g^{3} 1995 8g 8m May 8] good-topped gelding: fairly useful performer at 3 yrs: subsequently gelded, and no show in competitive handicaps in 1995: joined N. Henderson. *J. L. Dunlop*

–

BRAVE PRINCESS 3 b.f. Dancing Brave (USA) 140 – Princess Zena 96 (Habitat 134) [1994 NR 1995 7m 7g* 8.1g 8.1d a9.4g^{2} 10.5d a8g^{6} a9.4g^{5} Nov 13]

67
a70

lengthy filly: sister to a winner in Dubai and half-sister to several winners, notably very smart 1m to 1¼m winner Supreme Leader (by Bustino): dam, 2-y-o 5f winner, half-sister to dam of Pebbles: fair performer: won maiden at Warwick in May: should have stayed beyond 9.4f: acted on fibresand, well beaten both outings on a soft surface: none too consistent: stud. *M. A. Jarvis*

BRAVE REVIVAL 3 b.f. Dancing Brave (USA) 140 – Fearless Revival 102 (Cozzene (USA)) [1994 79: 7g^4 7m^2 8g* 7m^4 8m^3 1995 8m* 10m^5 8.5m^2 Jun 9] small, sturdy filly: good walker: fairly useful performer: won handicap at Newmarket on reappearance in May, making most: good efforts in Lupe Stakes at Goodwood and listed event at Epsom subsequent starts: unlikely to stay beyond 1¼m, and probably at least as good at 1m: has raced only on a sound surface: often a front runner: game. *M. R. Stoute* — 93

BRAVE SPY 4 b.g. Law Society (USA) 130 – Contralto 100 (Busted 134) [1994 70: 8d 9s^3 10g^2 10g^6 12m 12g^6 14m 1995 a10g^5 a10g^3 a11g^3 a16g^3 16g^4 a14.8g* a16g^3 a14.8g Aug 19] strong, lengthy gelding: unimpressive mover: modest handicapper: gained first success at Wolverhampton in July: stays 2m: acts on all-weather surfaces and probably on soft ground, well beaten twice on good to firm. *C. A. Cyzer* — 62

BRAYDON FOREST 3 b.c. Presidium 124 – Sleekit 78 (Blakeney 126) [1994 65: 7g^6 7g 1995 10g 10m^6 10m^5 8.3g^3 9m^2 10m^3 10g 10d^5 8d Sep 27] good-topped colt: fair maiden handicapper: worth a try over further than 1¼m: acts on good to firm and dead ground: no improvement in blinkers. *C. J. Drewe* — 65

BREAKFAST CREEK 3 b.f. Hallgate 127 – North Pine (Import 127) [1994 63: 5g^6 5m^2 5g^2 5m^3 5.1g* 5d 5g^3 1995 5.1g^4 5m 5m 5m^4 5g 5f Oct 14] sturdy filly: good mover: modest maiden: soundly beaten after reappearance: raced only at 5f: acts on good to firm and dead ground. *J. Berry* — 55

BREAK THE RULES 3 b.g. Dominion 123 – Surf Bird (Shareef Dancer (USA) 135) [1994 67p: 5d^5 5s* 6f^4 7.5f 1995 7g^4 8f^2 9.2f^3 8m* 8d Sep 9] strong gelding: fair handicapper: won at Redcar in August: looked on the upgrade but ran poorly in £19,000 event at Doncaster 13 days later: likely to stay further than 1m: acts on firm going. *Mrs M. Reveley* — 80

BRECKLAND (IRE) 5 b.h. Trojan Fen 118 – Rose Noir (Floribunda 136) [1994 42: a6g 7m 7m 8f 7d 7d a7g^5 1995 a8g a8g a7g^3 a7g^2 a7g Mar 16] leggy horse: poor maiden on balance of form, possibly flattered on penultimate start: stays 7f: acts on all-weather surfaces, and probably on good to firm and dead ground: tried blinkered. *K. O. Cunningham-Brown* — 59 ?

BRECON 2 b. or br.c. (Mar 20) High Estate 127 – No Can Tell (USA) (Clev Er Tell (USA)) [1995 6.1m^4 7m^3 6m^4 7m^5 7.3d^6 6.9m^3 Nov 6] smallish colt: fifth foal: half-brother to 1990 2-y-o 5f winner Anonoalto (by Noalto) and a winner in Hungary: dam maiden: fair form: third in maiden at Salisbury in July and nursery at Folkestone in November: will be suited by 1m+: taken down early at Folkestone: sweating penultimate start. *P. F. I. Cole* — 70

BRECONGILL LAD 3 b.g. Clantime 101 – Chikala 81 (Pitskelly 122) [1994 64: 6m^3 7d^4 6m 6g^2 6d 1995 6g 6m^3 6m 7m^3 6g* 6m^3 5m* 6g^4 7m Oct 14] leggy gelding: fairly useful handicapper: won at Newmarket (made all) in June and Thirsk in August: effective at 5f to 7f: acts on good to firm ground: blinkered since fourth 3-y-o start: tends to hang and carries head high. *Miss S. E. Hall* — 81

BREEZED WELL 9 b.g. Wolverlife 115 – Precious Baby (African Sky 124) [1994 44, a47: a11g a8.5g^4 a8.5g* 10.3g 10d^5 7v^4 8d^4 7.1s 9.9m^4 7.5f a9.4g 8.1g^5 a8g 1995 10g 7f 8g^5 7.5m^3 10f a8g 8d 11.5s^6 Sep 28] smallish, sparely-made gelding: poor mover: poor handicapper who contests amateurs/ladies events: stays 11.5f: acts on any going: blinkered (below form) once at 3 yrs. *B. R. Cambidge* — 42

BRESIL (USA) 6 ch.g. Bering 136 – Clever Bidder (USA) (Bold Bidder) [1994 –: a11g a9.4g a10g^6 a16g 11.9d 8m 1995 10g 8g 12g 10m 12m 13.1f* 14g^4 14.1m 14.1m^3 14s a14g a13g Dec 14] lengthy gelding: unimpressive mover: poor and inconsistent handicapper nowadays: won seller at Bath in July: stays 1¾m: acts on firm and soft going, no form on all-weather. *K. R. Burke* — 37 a–

BRETTON PRINCESS 3 ch.f. Handsome Sailor 125 – Cutlass Princess (USA) 41 (Cutlass (USA)) [1994 45: 5g 5g 6s a7g^5 a8.5g 1995 a8g^5 a7g^2 a7g^3 a7g^4 6s a7g^4 — 45 a7g a8.5g^{6} 9.9m 8g 6.1g^{6} Jun 8] smallish filly: poor maiden plater: stayed 7f: acted on fibresand: inconsistent: dead. *R. Hollinshead*

BRICK COURT (IRE) 3 ch.f. Bluebird (USA) 125 – Palmyra (GER) (Arratos (FR)) [1994 NR 1995 12m 10.4m 10d a12g Nov 21] 9,000Y: rather leggy, quite attractive filly: second foal: dam 2-y-o 6f winner in Germany from good German family: no worthwhile form. *R. F. Johnson Houghton* –

BRIDGE OF FIRE (FR) 3 b.g. Mtoto 134 – Amana River (USA) 77 (Raise A Cup (USA)) [1994 76: 6g^{4} 6f* 6d 1995 a8g^{5} 10d 7f 8f Oct 12] small gelding: fair form at 2 yrs for J. W. Watts before sold approx £9,100 in Dubai: last of 5 in handicap at Nad Al Sheba on only outing in Middle East: sold 7,000 gns Newmarket July Sales: soundly beaten in Redcar handicaps for new connections: should stay 1m+: possibly unsuited by a soft surface: sold 1,400 gns Doncaster October Sales. *Don Enrico Incisa* –

BRIDLINGTON BAY 2 b.g. (Mar 24) Roscoe Blake 120 – City Sound 63 (On Your Mark 125) [1995 a8.5g Dec 9] 1,500Y: half-brother to several winners, including fairly useful sprinter Ashley Rocket (by Roan Rocket): dam 6f winner: 16/1, well-beaten seventh of 13 in maiden at Wolverhampton. *J. L. Eyre* –

BRIEF GLIMPSE (IRE) 3 b. or br.f. Taufan (USA) 119 – Mini Look (FR) (In Fijar (USA) 121) [1994 91: 6g* 6m* 5.2m* 6m^{4} 6g 1995 8.5m^{3} 8m 7f* 7.3m 8g 7d Sep 30] tall, leggy, close-coupled filly: good mover: useful performer: reportedly put out her pelvis in Coronation Stakes at Royal Ascot second start: won listed race at Goodwood in July by 2 lengths from Cheyenne Spirit, leading 1f out: well below form afterwards in pattern events at Newbury, Doncaster and Goodwood: will prove best at up to around 1m: acts on firm ground: failed to settle in steadily-run race final start. *Major D. N. Chappell* 108

BRIEF RESPITE (IRE) 4 b. or br.g. Simply Great (FR) 122 – No Time To Dance (Shareef Dancer (USA) 135) [1994 73: 11v 10d 12s 11s a9.4g a8.5g^{6} 1995 a14.8g a11g a8g Feb 10] fair form on his day at 2 and 3 yrs in Ireland: no show in handicaps here. *E. J. Alston* –

BRIER CREEK (USA) 6 b.h. Blushing Groom (FR) 131 – Savannah Dancer (USA) (Northern Dancer) [1994 109: 12g 15.5g^{3} 16f^{4} 1995 10m^{3} May 6] good-topped horse: easy mover: useful performer: shaped quite well in 1¼m minor event at Newmarket on reappearance, but not seen out afterwards: stays 2m: has raced almost exclusively on a sound surface (acts on firm going): held up: genuine. *J. H. M. Gosden* 105

BRIGADORE GOLD 5 br.m. Petong 126 – Brigado 87 (Brigadier Gerard 144) [1994 33: 6g 6m 7.6g 8m^{6} 8.1m 8.1m^{4} 9.2f^{6} 8m 12.1m 1995 a11g a7g* a8g 8.1d a9.4g 8f a7g 7g a8.5g 7.1m 7.6m 5f a9.4g 8.1m 5.9h^{5} Aug 21] small mare: poor handicapper: won maiden event at Wolverhampton in March: little form afterwards, leaving A. Bailey's stable after fourth start: needs further than 5f (stays 1m): acts on hard ground and fibresand: effective blinkered or not. *F. H. Lee* 33 d

BRIGANOONE 2 b.g. (May 9) Cyrano de Bergerac 120 – Zareeta (Free State 125) [1995 5m a6g^{4} a6g 5m 7g 8f a5g Dec 1] robust gelding: fourth foal: dam little sign of ability: poor maiden: best efforts at 6f at Wolverhampton: acts on fibresand: sometimes blinkered. *S. R. Bowring* 44 a52

BRIGGS LAD (IRE) 6 ch.g. Be My Native (USA) 122 – Zestino (Shack (USA) 118) [1994 NR 1995 16.2m Apr 7] good-bodied gelding: very lightly raced and little worthwhile form both on flat and over jumps since 1993: sold 1,100 gns Doncaster October Sales. *P. T. Dalton* –

BRIGHSTONE 2 ch.c. (Feb 6) Cadeaux Genereux 131 – High Fountain 102 (High Line 125) [1995 7f* 8m* Nov 3] sturdy colt: first foal: dam 1¼m and 16.5f winner out of once-raced half-sister to Royal Palace: won maiden at Yarmouth in October readily by 1¾ lengths from Nasrudin: followed up in falsely-run 6-runner minor event at Doncaster following month, going on 2f out and not needing to be hard ridden to hold La Volta by ½ length despite racing green and hanging away from rail: will be well suited by 1¼m+: bandaged on debut: sure to improve further and win more races. *H. R. A. Cecil* 95 p

BRIGHT DIAMOND 2 b.f. (Mar 23) Never So Bold 135 – Diamond House (Habitat 134) [1995 6.1m 6d 7m^{4} 7.3d Oct 21] rather unfurnished filly: fifth foal: 58

sister to 1m winner Bold Jewel and half-sister to 7.6f (at 2 yrs) and 1½m winner Kimberley Boy (by Mtoto): dam sister to useful filly Life At The Top (stayed 1¼m): modest maiden: stays 7f. *J. R. Arnold*

BRIGHT ECLIPSE (USA) 2 br.c. (Jan 23) Sunny's Halo (CAN) – Miss Lantana (USA) (Danzig Connection (USA)) [1995 7.9m Oct 4] $50,000F, IR 43,000Y: second foal: dam unraced half-sister to Kentucky Oaks and Breeders' Cup Distaff winner Princess Rooney: 9/1 and green, behind in median auction maiden at York: should be capable of better. *J. W. Hills* – p

BRIGHTER BYFAAH (IRE) 2 ch.g. (Feb 24) Kefaah (USA) 124 – Bright Landing 78 (Sun Prince 128) [1995 10m a10g^{6} Nov 25] 5,000Y: brother to 3-y-o Carnbrea Belle, fair winner at up to 16.5f, and half-brother to 2 winners, notably useful 9f (at 2 yrs) to 2m winner Upper Strata (by Shirley Heights), the dam of 1995 Prix de la Salamandre winner Lord of Men: dam placed over 5f at 2 yrs: poor form in late-season median auction maidens at Nottingham and Lingfield. *N. A. Graham* –

BRIGHT HERITAGE (IRE) 2 b.c. (Feb 28) Ela-Mana-Mou 132 – Mother of The Wind 82 (Tumble Wind (USA)) [1995 8m^{2} 8g^{2} 8v^{3} Oct 7] strong, lengthy, attractive colt: has plenty of scope: half-brother to 3-y-o Lovely Millie (by Bluebird), useful 6f and 7f winner at 2 yrs, and several other winners, including useful 7f winner Good Sailing (by Scorpio): dam 2-y-o 7f winner: second in maidens won by Moody's Cat at Ascot and Danesman at Yarmouth: ran very well in face of stiff task when 6¼ lengths third of 5 to Beauchamp King in listed race at Ascot in October: will stay beyond 1m: acts on good to firm and heavy ground: sure to win a race. *D. R. Loder* 95

BRIGHT PARAGON (IRE) 6 b. or br.g. Treasure Kay 114 – Shining Bright (USA) (Bold Bidder) [1994 52, a–: a6g^{6} 6s^{4} 5v^{5} 5v^{2} 5.3g^{3} 5g^{4} 5d^{5} 6m^{4} 6m* 6m^{3} 6m^{5} 5m* 6m 5g^{5} 5d 5d 1995 5d 5m^{5} 5.3m 6f 6g 6d^{4} a8g Nov 20] workmanlike gelding: poor handicapper: left H. Collingridge after sixth 6-y-o start: stays 7f: acts on any going: tried visored. *M. C. Chapman* 48 d a–

BRIGHT WATER 2 b.c. (Jan 8) Caerleon (USA) 132 – Shining Water 111 (Kalaglow 132) [1995 8f* Oct 25] leggy, unfurnished colt: fifth foal: brother to Tenby and half-brother to 2 winners, including 9f/1½m performer Reflecting (by Ahonoora): dam, won Solario Stakes at 2 yrs and stayed well as 3-y-o, is daughter of Park Hill winner Idle Waters: 7/4 favourite, won 13-runner maiden at Yarmouth in October by neck from Aethra (pair 4 lengths clear) disputing lead from 3f out and keeping on well: will be very well suited by middle distances: sure to improve, and looks potentially very useful. *H. R. A. Cecil* 95 p

BRILLIANT 7 ch.m. Never So Bold 135 – Diamond Hill 82 (High Top 131) [1994 67: 8d^{5} 10.5g 9.7m* 9.9m* 10s 11.5d 10d 12s 1995 a13g Feb 16] rangy mare: fair 1m to 1¼m handicapper at best: tailed off on all-weather debut on reappearance: sold 4,500 gns Newmarket December Sales. *J. Pearce* –

BRILLIANT RED 2 b.c. (Feb 3) Royal Academy (USA) 130 – Red Comes Up (USA) (Blushing Groom (FR) 131) [1995 6g^{3} 6g^{2} 7m* 8.1d^{3} 7.3d^{5} Sep 15] tall, lengthy, unfurnished colt: looked weak: has a long stride: sixth foal: closely related to useful 1½m and 1¾m winner Kassab (by Caerleon) and half-brother to 2 winners including 1m to 10.5f winner Barahin (by Diesis): dam French maiden sister to Rainbow Quest: won maiden at Kempton in August: good third of 5 to Beauchamp King in minor event at Haydock in September and ran well off stiff mark when fifth of 15 to Ramooz in nursery at Newbury final start: will stay beyond 1m: acts on good to firm and good to soft ground. *P. F. I. Cole* 93

BRING ON THE CHOIR 3 b.f. Chief Singer 131 – Primulette 82 (Mummy's Pet 125) [1994 80: 5f^{4} 5m 5d* 1995 8m 8m 10g 7g^{5} 8f 7.1m 10m 8.1d Sep 12] leggy filly: fairly useful on most form: flattered when ninth of 14 in 1000 Guineas on second start: stays 1m: acts on good to firm and good to soft ground: visored (soundly beaten) fifth start: disappointing. *R. Boss* 87 d

BRISAS 8 ch.g. Vaigly Great 127 – Legal Sound 85 (Legal Eagle 126) [1994 51d: a5g a5g* a5g a6g^{5} a5g^{6} 5g^{6} 5f^{3} 5m 5m a6g^{5} a5g 1995 a5g a6g^{4} a6g^{6} a6g* a6g^{6} a6g 6g 5.9f^{3} 5f^{6} 5.9f^{3} 6m^{3} 5f^{4} 5m^{4} 5h^{3} 6g^{6} Sep 1] strong-quartered gelding: has a quick action: poor handicapper: held his form well in 1995: won seller at Southwell in February: suited by sprint distances: acts on fibresand and hard ground, possibly unsuited by heavy: effective blinkered/visored or not: sometimes looks none too keen. *C. W. Fairhurst* 45

BRITANNIA MILLS 4 gr.f. Nordico (USA) – May Fox 67 (Healaugh Fox) [1994 44: a7g^6 a6g^2 7m^6 7.5m 6g 6m 6f a6g 5.2g^5 6g 5m 10g* 10g 8.9m 10.1d^{4dis} 8s 7d 1995 a7g a11g^4 a11g a7g^6 a6g^5 a8g 10.3g 10m 14.1f 10.1m 9m Aug 12] small filly: unimpressive mover: poor performer: stays 1¼m: acts on fibresand, good to firm and dead ground: won over hurdles in August: inconsistent. *M. C. Chapman* 30

BROADSTAIRS BEAUTY (IRE) 5 ch.g. Dominion Royale 112 – Holy Water (Monseigneur (USA) 127) [1994 66, a80: 6.1v^3 5d^2 6.1d^3 5v^3 a5g^2 a5g* 5.1m^5 a5g* 5m^5 7g* 7d 5s* 5d^2 5d 7g^5 a5g^2 1995 5g^2 5m^2 5m* 5g* 6m 5g^5 6g 5g 6d a6g a5g* Nov 16] workmanlike gelding: has a quick action: fairly useful handicapper: gained narrow successes at Ripon in May, Newmarket (rallied splendidly to get best of five-way photo-finish) in July and Southwell (apprentices) in November: effective at 5f (best form) to 7f: acts on good to firm and heavy ground and on fibresand: best in blinkers or visor when sprinting, hasn't worn either over further: bandaged: front runner: suitable mount for claimer: tough, consistent and very game: a credit to his trainer. *S. R. Bowring* 77 a85

BROADWAY FLYER (USA) 4 b.c. Theatrical 128 – Serena (SAF) (Jan Ekels 122) [1994 119: 11s* 12.3m* 12m 12m* 11.9m^3 14.6g^2 12g 1995 12g^2 13.4m^3 12f^2 12g^5 12.5g 12g^6 Sep 24] rangy colt: very good walker: fluent mover with a round action: very smart performer: best efforts in 1995 when neck second to Strategic Choice in John Porter Stakes at Newbury on reappearance, 2¼ lengths second to Lando in Gran Premio di Milano and around 2 lengths fifth of 7 to Lammtarra in King George VI and Queen Elizabeth Diamond Stakes at Ascot: well below form in Grand Prix de Deauville and Europa Preis at Cologne (blinkered, unable to lead) last 121

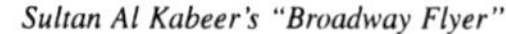

Sultan Al Kabeer's "Broadway Flyer"

2 starts: effective at 1½m and will stay 2m: acts on firm and soft ground: game front runner: to be trained by Bill Mott in USA. *J. W. Hills*

BROCKTON FLAME 3 b.f. Emarati (USA) 74 – Minne Love 67 (Homeric 133) [1994 72: 6m^{2} 6m* 6m^{4} 6m 7m 1995 6m^{3} 6m 6m 6g* 5m^{4} 6g^{2} 6m^{4} 6s^{5} 6d 6f Oct 23] well-made filly: fair handicapper: won at Windsor in June, despite flashing tail: creditable efforts most starts afterwards: should stay 7f: acts on good to firm and soft ground: has run well when sweating. *J. M. P. Eustace* — 69

BROCKTON LIGHT 3 b.f. Be My Chief (USA) 122 – Lovers Light (Grundy 137) [1994 NR 1995 8m 8m 10f^{4} 14d^{5} Jun 9] 2,000F: rather leggy filly: half-sister to 3 winners, including fair 1993 2-y-o 6f winner Glimpse (by Night Shift), and 1½m winner Eliki (by Nishapour): dam out of half-sister to Main Reef: no worthwhile form: visored third outing: twice slowly away: has joined R. Buckler. *M. R. Channon* — –

BROCKVILLE BAIRN 2 b.g. (Apr 14) Tina's Pet 121 – Snow Chief 90 (Tribal Chief 125) [1995 5m 5g 6m a5g 6m a6g Sep 4] 2,100Y: sturdy, lengthy gelding: half-brother to a 5f winner by Young Generation: dam miler: plater: acts on fibresand. *Mrs A. Swinbank* — 42

BROCTUNE BAY 6 b.g. Midyan (USA) 124 – Sweet Colleen 42 (Connaught 130) [1994 67: 12m^{5} 11.8m 11g^{3} 12.3g^{4} 13.6g^{2} 14.6d 1995 14g Sep 29] big, workmanlike gelding: fair middle-distance maiden handicapper: well beaten only start in 1995: acts on good to firm ground: fairly useful winning hurdler, including in December. *Mrs M. Reveley* — –

BROCTUNE GOLD 4 b.g. Superpower 113 – Golden Sunlight (Ile de Bourbon (USA) 133) [1994 73d: 7g^{2} 7d^{2} 8m^{4} 8f 8g 7m 8.2m 7g a8g^{4} a11g^{2} a11g 1995 7g* 6f* 7g 7f 5.9h^{3} 8g Sep 2] leggy, workmanlike gelding: easy mover: fair performer: lost his way at 3 yrs, and did the same in 1995 after winning claimers at Newcastle and Redcar in May: effective at 6f and 1m: acts on firm and soft ground: sometimes has tongue tied down: one to treat with caution. *Mrs M. Reveley* — 67 d

BRODESSA 9 gr.g. Scallywag 127 – Jeanne du Barry 74 (Dubassoff (USA)) [1994 63: 13m^{5} 14m^{3} 15.1m^{3} 15.1m* 15.1m* 12m^{2} 11.9d^{6} 12g^{3} 15.1g^{5} 1995 a16g^{2} a14.8g^{4} 16m* 14.1f* 15.1m^{2} 14.1f 16.2m* 14.1m* 15.1g^{2} 17.1m Oct 2] big, workmanlike gelding: modest performer: clear-cut winner of 2 claimers at Redcar in June and selling events at Beverley and Redcar (8/1 on) in August: stays 2m: acts on firm and dead ground and on fibresand: effective held up or from front: suitable mount for amateur. *Mrs M. Reveley* — 62

BROGANS BRUSH 2 ch.c. (Apr 11) Jendali (USA) 111 – Sweet 'n' Sharp 71 (Sharpo 132) [1995 5m^{5} a5g^{4} 6g^{6} 7m a7g 5m 7.1s Nov 2] 2,000Y: leggy colt: first reported foal: dam 2-y-o 5f winner probably stayed 6f: poor plater: visored fourth and fifth starts: sold out of C. Fairhurst's stable 500 gns Doncaster September Sales after sixth start. *J. S. Haldane* — –

BRONHALLOW 2 b.g. (Mar 17) Belmez (USA) 131 – Grey Twig 68 (Godswalk (USA) 130) [1995 8d Sep 27] 13,000Y: good-bodied gelding: half-brother to 4 winners, including 2-y-o sprint winners Mr Burfield (by Faustus) and Grey Wolf Tiger (by Rolfe): dam ran only at 2 yrs: 33/1 and bandaged near-hind, towards rear in maiden at Salisbury after slow start and taking good hold early on: taken early to post. *Mrs Barbara Waring* — –

BRONZE MAQUETTE (IRE) 5 b.m. Ahonoora 122 – Working Model 99 (Ile de Bourbon (USA) 133) [1994 46, a–: a11g 10g 9.7s a10g 11.5g 10m^{2} 10m^{2} 10.2g^{5} 10.1d 10m^{6} 10.1g a13g a12g a10g 1995 9.7m May 31] long-backed mare: good walker: poor 1¼m performer in 1994 for B. McMath: ran as if needed race on only 5-y-o start: acts on good to firm and dead going, probably not on soft: best with waiting tactics. *R. J. O'Sullivan* — –

BRONZE RUNNER 11 gr.g. Gunner B 126 – Petingalyn (Petingo 135) [1994 34, a–: 10g 10g 10m 10m^{5} 10.8f^{5} 10m 11.6f^{5} 10g^{3} 10.8m 12m^{4} 12f* 10.3g^{2} 10.8m 12g^{4} 12m 1995 10m^{6} 10m 10m* 11.5m* 9.7m 11.6m^{3} 11.6m^{4} 10.8f^{2} a10g^{6} 12d Sep 15] leggy gelding: very bad mover: veteran handicapper: capable of only poor form nowadays, but retains all his enthusiasm: won selling event at Windsor in June and apprentice race at Lingfield in July: effective at 1¼m to 1½m: acts on any going: excellent mount for inexperienced rider: has been visored, wears blinkers nowadays: tough and game. *S. Mellor* — 44 a–

BROOKE WOOD 3 b.f. Risk Me (FR) 127 – Oh My Joy 57 (Grundy 137) [1994 –: 7g^{6} 1995 a7g^{5} a8g 10m a13g Jul 1] sturdy, lengthy filly: no sign of ability. *Miss B. Sanders* –

BROOKHEAD LADY 4 b.f. Petong 126 – Lewista (Mandrake Major 122) [1994 65, a–: a6g^{6} a6g 6d 6g^{2} 5f 7m^{4} 6g 6g 1995 a6g^{5} a6g^{4} 6m* 6f 5.9f 5.9f^{6} 6m^{3} a6g^{2} 6f^{4} a7g^{4} 5.9h* 6g^{2} 6.1d 6g a7g Dec 2] leggy, angular filly: modest performer: won seller at Pontefract in April and claimer at Carlisle in August: stays 7f: acts on hard and dead ground and on fibresand: usually races prominently. *P. D. Evans* 62 a49

BROOKS MASQUERADE 4 gr.f. Absalom 128 – Miss Cindy 95 (Mansingh (USA) 120) [1994 –: 8.3d 8.2g 8.2m 1995 a12g a12g^{5} Aug 5] leggy, close-coupled filly: little sign of ability. *N. J. H. Walker* –

BROOM ISLE 7 b.m. Damister (USA) 123 – Vynz Girl 82 (Tower Walk 130) [1994 –, a58: a14.8g^{6} a12g^{3} a12g* 18.7g 12.3m^{3dis} a14.8g a11g^{5} a12g^{2} a12g^{2} 1995 a14.8g* a12g^{2} 13g^{3} May 4] lengthy, quite good-topped mare: carries condition: unimpressive mover: fair handicapper: won at Wolverhampton in March: effective at 1½m to 2m: goes particularly well on fibresand: acts on firm ground, seems unsuited by a soft surface. *D. Burchell* 46 + a68

BROTHER BARNABAS 4 ch.g. Bustino 136 – As Blessed 101 (So Blessed 130) [1994 NR 1995 8d 8g 7.5d 8f 10.9g^{5} 12f^{5} Jul 26] lengthy, sparely-made gelding: half-brother to several winners, including 1¼m and 2m winner Have Blessed (by Averof): dam 2-y-o 5f winner: no worthwhile form: sold 1,250 gns Doncaster August Sales. *C. W. Thornton* –

BROTHER ROY 2 b.c. (Feb 20) Prince Sabo 123 – Classic Heights (Shirley Heights 130) [1995 6m^{5} May 27] 21,000Y: second foal: dam unraced sister to Head For Heights: 10/1, around 9 lengths fifth of 11 to ready winner Bahamian Knight in maiden at Lingfield: looked likely to improve. *T. G. Mills* 60

BROUGHTONS BIRD (IRE) 4 b.f. Exhibitioner 111 – Mo Mhuirnin (Miner's Lamp 114) [1994 NR 1995 8.3m 8.1g 8.3m a12g Aug 5] IR 2,800Y: workmanlike filly: fourth foal: half-sister to a couple of NH horses in Ireland by Camden Town: dam, unplaced, out of smart 2-y-o 5f winner Covey: no sign of ability. *W. J. Musson* –

BROUGHTONS CHAMP 3 b.g. Dowsing (USA) 124 – Knees Up (USA) (Dancing Champ (USA)) [1994 NR 1995 8f Oct 24] 3,500Y, 1,000 2-y-o: good-topped gelding: half-brother to 1990 2-y-o 7f winner Tapatch (by Thatching), now suited by middle distances: dam unraced granddaughter of 1000 Guineas winner Glad Rags, dam of Gorytus: never-nearer 15½ lengths tenth of 19 to Tonys Gift in claimer at Leicester: looked green, and likely to do better. *W. J. Musson* – p

BROUGHTONS FORMULA 5 b.g. Night Shift (USA) – Forward Rally 84 (Formidable (USA) 125) [1994 58: a12g^{5} a12g a16.2g^{5} a14.8g* a13g^{3} a14.8g^{4} 12g* 13.8d* 14d 12m^{2} 12m 12d 11.9m^{4} a14.8g 14g 1995 11.8d 12g 14m^{6} 11.8g^{3} 11.4g^{3} 11.4m^{4} 14g 11.6m^{2} 12f* 14m* 14m^{4} 14.4m^{6} 14g 12m a13g^{4} a13g* a13g* Dec 19] compact, good-bodied gelding: poor mover: modest handicapper: had another good year, winning at Kempton (apprentices) and Sandown in the summer and at Lingfield (2 apprentices) in December: effective at 11.4f and stays 14.8f: acts on all-weather surfaces and on firm and dead ground: usually blinkered: usually held up. *W. J. Musson* 57 a66

BROUGHTON SINGER (IRE) 4 ch.f. Common Grounds 118 – Unbidden Melody (USA) (Chieftain II) [1994 61p: 7d 8.3g 7.1d 7g 8.1d^{4} 8m^{5} 9g* 1995 7g 8m 10g Oct 10] leggy filly: shows knee action: improved towards end of 1994, but well beaten on return, off course 5 months before final start: stays 9f. *W. J. Musson* –

BROUGHTON'S PORT 5 b.g. Reesh 117 – Tawnais 80 (Artaius (USA) 129) [1994 48: 6s 7v 8.1g 7g^{4} 8g a8g 8.1m 7m 1995 8g 8m 8f Oct 18] robust gelding: poor maiden: well beaten in 1995. *W. J. Musson* –

BROUGHTON'S PRIDE (IRE) 4 b.f. Superpower 113 – French Quarter (Ile de Bourbon (USA) 133) [1994 58: 8.3g 10d 8.1g 10d^{2} 12g^{6} 12g a11g^{5} a12g 1995 a12g 9.9m 10g^{2} 9.2g^{2} 10.3m 10g 9.9m^{2} 10d^{4} 8d^{3} 8g^{3} 10f Oct 16] rangy filly: modest maiden handicapper: effective at 1m to 1¼m: acts on good to firm and dead ground: visored (well beaten) first 4-y-o start, hung fire on fourth. *J. A. Glover* 55

BROUGHTONS TURMOIL 6 b.g. Petorius 117 – Rustic Stile (Rusticaro (FR) 124) [1994 NR 1995 a8g* a8g^{5} a8g* a8g 8m 7f^{2} 8.3m^{6} 7m* 7f^{5} a8.5g 7.1m* 7.3d^{4} 68 a60

7g^2 7g^4 Oct 7] workmanlike gelding: fair handicapper: unraced at 5 yrs, but had a good 1995, winning at Southwell in January, Lingfield (selling race) in February, Newmarket (apprentices) in July and Sandown in August: effective at 7f and 1m: acts on firm and dead ground and the all-weather: sometimes bandaged off-fore: has run creditably when sweating. *W. J. Musson*

BROWN CARPET 8 b. or br.g. Never So Bold 135 – Geopelia 109 (Raffingora 130) [1994 –: 8v 8.3m 1995 9.7g 11.6g^6 10m 11.6m^4 12d Oct 21] smallish, workmanlike gelding: poor handicapper: stays 11.6f: acts on firm ground, possibly not on a soft surface: usually blinkered: often bandaged behind: sold 850 gns Ascot December Sales. *C. A. Horgan* — 29

BROWN EYED GIRL 3 ch.f. Sharpo 132 – Ella Mon Amour 65 (Ela-Mana-Mou 132) [1994 66: 7m 7g^6 8.2s^4 1995 7g^2 7g^5 8.3m 9m^2 a8.5g 8.1d Sep 13] compact filly: has a quick action: fair maiden: stays 9f: well below form both outings on a soft surface, tailed off on the all-weather: inconsistent. *R. Hannon* — 70 d

BROWNLOWS 3 b.g. Prince Sabo 123 – Glockenmadel (GER) (Kaiseradler) [1994 44, a56?: 5m 5g 5g 7.1s a7g a8g a8.5g^4 1995 a10g 12m 13.8g^4 16.2g Jul 17] lengthy, dipped-backed gelding: poor maiden at 2 yrs: well beaten in 1995. *M. P. Bielby* — – §

BRUME LA VOILE 2 b.c. (May 7) Puissance 110 – Bali Lady 79 (Balidar 133) [1995 a8.5g Dec 9] first reported foal: dam thrice-raced maiden, stayed 7f well: 16/1, slow-starting eighth of 13, well beaten, in maiden at Wolverhampton. *S. C. Williams* — –

BRUMON (IRE) 4 b.g. Sadler's Wells (USA) 132 – Loveliest (USA) (Tibaldo) [1994 69: 11.9m 11.5g 12m 16g* 17.2g 13.6g 1995 13.3g 18.2m^4 16g^5 16m^3 16.4m^4 16.1f* 17.5g^6 17.1m 18m Oct 14] tall gelding: fair performer on his day: won very strongly-run handicap at Warwick in August, leading inside last: subsequently sold out of D. Arbuthnot's stable 15,000 gns Newmarket September Sales: well below form afterwards: suited by good test of stamina: acts on firm going: best efforts in blinkers/visor: has had tongue tied down. *T. Dyer* — 65

BRUNSWICK BLUE (IRE) 7 b.g. Sarab 123 – Lanata 64 (Charlottown 127) [1994 NR 1995 12m 14.1m 12g^5 14m Jul 15] small gelding: no longer of much account. *R. M. Flower* — –

BRUSQUE (USA) 11 b.g. Assert 134 – Cecelia (USA) (Royal Levee (USA)) [1994 –: a12g a14g 14.1m 13.1g^5 15.1m^5 1995 16.2m 16.2m Aug 24] compact gelding: of little account nowadays. *Don Enrico Incisa* — –

BRUZ 4 b.g. Risk Me (FR) 127 – My Croft (Crofter (USA) 124) [1994 51d: a6g^4 8m 6s^4 5v^4 6g 5d^6 a5g^3 5.9v 5m^5 6f 8f 5m 5s 1995 5m Aug 24] lengthy gelding: no worthwhile form for some time. *W. T. Kemp* — –

BRYAN ROBSON (USA) 4 b.g. Topsider (USA) – Queen's Visit (Top Command (USA)) [1994 82d: 5m* 5d^6 6d 7g 7d 7d 1995 6m^5 6m 6m 5m 5.1m Jul 20] smallish, sturdy gelding: fair handicapper at best in 1995: should stay 7f: acts on good to firm and dead ground: visored (out of form) once. *G. B. Balding* — 69 d

BUBBLE WINGS (FR) 3 b.f. In The Wings 128 – Bubble Prospector (USA) (Miswaki (USA) 124) [1994 NR 1995 a7g* Dec 19] 450,000 francs Y: third foal: half-sister to French middle-distance winners by Vernon Castle and Irish River: dam won 1m maiden in Ireland: 4/1, won 10-runner maiden at Lingfield by 3 lengths from Fresh Fruit Daily, slowly away and outpaced, hanging left but leading final 1f: will stay beyond 7f: sure to improve. *S. P. C. Woods* — 71 p

BUCKLEY BOYS 4 gr.f. Grey Desire 115 – Strip Fast 71 (Virginia Boy 106) [1994 47: a8.5g a6g^5 a7g 7m^4 6f^6 7m 7m 6.9h^3 7d^2 7m 8s^5 8d a8.5g^2 a12g^6 1995 a8.5g 7m 11.5g^2 10.1g 10.8g a11g^2 a12g Dec 12] compact filly: modest maiden: stays 1½m: acts on good to firm and soft ground and on fibresand: tried blinkered, no improvement: won over hurdles in December. *A. Bailey* — 51 a45

BUDBY 2 ch.f. (Mar 7) Rock City 120 – Lustrous 73 (Golden Act (USA)) [1995 6g Sep 30] 13,500F: neat filly: half-sister to 3-y-o Shining Edge (by Beveled), 1m winner Vanborough Lad (by Precocious), also 5f and 6.1f winner at 2 yrs, and winners abroad by Elegant Air and Sure Blade: dam 1½m winner: in need of race, caught eye in no uncertain terms when ninth of 17 in maiden at Newmarket won by Polish Spring, travelling strongly on bridle after slow start and finishing full of — 64 P running: will stay 1m: capable of considerably better and should win a race or two. *A. C. Stewart*

BUDDING ANNIE 2 b.f. (Feb 28) Lord Bud 121 – Gold Paper (FR) (Rheingold 137) [1995 6m^5 7.6d Sep 14] fifth living foal: half-sister to 10.5f winner Haroon (by Ahonoora) and Irish 8.5f winner Suir Surprise (by Rusticaro): dam daughter of half-sister to Grand Prix de Paris winner White Label: never dangerous in maidens at Lingfield: bred to stay well. *J. R. Bosley* –

BUDDY'S FRIEND (IRE) 7 ch.h. Jester 119 – Hasta (Skymaster 126) [1994 64: 7.5d^2 9d^4 8d^4 8.2f* 8g^4 8.2m^3 8.2m^4 8m 8m 8f^4 a8g* 8f a8g^2 a8g 1995 a8g^6 a8g^3 a8.5g* a8g^2 a8g^4 a8g^6 9g 7.5g^4 8.1m 8m Jun 23] workmanlike horse: poor mover: fair handicapper: won at Wolverhampton in January: effective at 7f to 1¼m: acts on the all-weather, probably on any turf ground: usually held up: goes well for Sarah Thompson: tough and genuine. *R. J. R. Williams* 56 a69

BUD'S BET (IRE) 7 b.g. Reasonable (FR) 119 – Pearl Creek (Gulf Pearl 117) [1994 NR 1995 a14g^4 a16.2g 15.8g^5 Jun 2] compact gelding: has a round action: did not run on flat at 4-6 yrs: poor at best in 1995: probably stays 15.8f: acts on good to firm and dead ground and on fibresand: blinkered final 3-y-o start. *W. W. Haigh* 29 a42

BUFF 2 b.f. (Jan 19) Persian Heights 129 – Manicure Kit (USA) (J O Tobin (USA) 130) [1995 5.2g^6 6m Jul 27] seventh foal: half-sister to 3 winners, including Shaping Up (by Storm Bird), 5.7f winner at 2 yrs: dam sprint winner at 2 yrs: last in maiden and seller at Yarmouth in July: sold 500 gns Ascot August Sales. *D. Morley* –

BUFFALO GIRL 3 b.f. Nomination 125 – Beretta (Moorestyle 137) [1994 NR 1995 8.2d Sep 19] 1,600Y, 7,200 2-y-o: lengthy filly: fourth reported foal: dam unraced half-sister to smart sprinter Abha: well beaten in maiden at Nottingham. *Lady Herries* –

BUILT FOR COMFORT (IRE) 3 b.f. Nordico (USA) – Dewan's Niece (USA) (Dewan (USA)) [1994 –: 5d 1995 8g^5 10f^2 8m 9.7g Jun 7] sturdy filly: has a quick action: fair maiden: easily best effort on reappearance: should stay 1¼m: sold (R. Hannon to N. Babbage) 1,600 gns Newmarket Autumn Sales. *R. Hannon* 64

BULLFINCH 2 ch.c. (Apr 10) Anshan 119 – Lambay 88 (Lorenzaccio 130) [1995 7.1m* 7d^6 7g^2 8m^3 Oct 27] smallish colt: has a fluent action: half-brother to several winners, including 1m to 11f performer My Lamb (by Relkino) and sprinter Bay Bay (by Bay Express), both useful: dam 2-y-o 7f winner: won median auction maiden at Sandown in August: similar form in minor events won by Believe Me at York (beaten a neck, finishing strongly) and Newmarket (took keen hold, short of room over 1f out) last 2 starts: stays 1m: may well be unsuited by a soft surface. *P. T. Walwyn* 92

BULLPEN BELLE 2 b.f. (Apr 11) Relief Pitcher 120 – Hopeful Waters 66 (Forlorn River 124) [1995 7.1s 8.2m^2 a8g^5 Nov 14] good-bodied filly: seventh foal: half-sister to 3-y-o Celestial Waters (by Monsanto): dam 6f and 7f winner: 2½ lengths second of 11 to Dance Star in maiden at Nottingham, leading until 1f out, swishing tail: never-dangerous fifth in similar event at Lingfield following month: should stay middle distances. *P. T. Walwyn* 64

BULSARA 3 b.g. Dowsing (USA) 124 – Taiga 69 (Northfields (USA)) [1994 59: 5m 7f^4 7.5f 6g 1995 7g a6g 10m* 10m 10m^2 9f* 9f^5 8d 9f Oct 3] strong gelding: modest performer: won maiden claimer at Ayr in May and handicap at Redcar in July: stays 1¼m: acts on firm and dead ground. *C. W. Fairhurst* 59

BUMBLEFOOT (IRE) 2 b.f. (Feb 27) Cyrano de Bergerac 120 – La Vosgienne (Ashmore (FR) 125) [1995 6f^4 a7g* 7.6m^3 a8.5g^2 8m a8g^6 a8g^5 Dec 1] IR 2,400Y, 2,500 2-y-o: tall, unfurnished filly: closely related to winning hurdler Ballon (by Persian Bold) and half-sister to 3 winners, including 1988 2-y-o 7f winner Shelbourne Lady (by Coquelin): dam, showed some ability in France, is half-sister to Royal Lodge winner Bengal Fire: won maiden auction at Wolverhampton in August: well beaten in sellers last 3 starts: stays 8.5f: acts on fibresand. *M. Johnston* 61 d

BUNKER (IRE) 3 b.g. Scenic 128 – Diamond Lake (Kings Lake (USA) 133) [1994 –: 6g 7s 8d 1995 12m* 12g* 12m^4 12.4h^4 11.5g 12g Sep 28] neat gelding: modest performer: got up near finish to win sellers at Pontefract (handicap) and Beverley in July: will prove suited by further than 1½m: a hard ride (soon off bridle), worth a try in blinkers/visor: suited by strong pace: sold 2,500 gns Newmarket Autumn Sales. *J. Pearce* 56

Advanced Micro Devices Sprint Stakes, Sandown—Bunty Boo and Saint Express (left) fight it out

BUNTING 3 br.f. Shaadi (USA) 126 – Warm Welcome 89 (General Assembly (USA)) [1994 87p: 8.1d^{3} 8d* 1995 9.9m* 11.5f^{2} 11d^{3} 12m Jun 9] lengthy, unfurnished filly: useful performer: won 4-runner minor event at Beverley in April: placed afterwards in listed race at Lingfield (rallying bravely, ¾ length behind Asterita) and Oaks d'Italia at Milan (headed over 1f out, 2½ lengths behind Valley of Gold) in May: well-beaten last of 10 in Oaks at Epsom on final outing: stayed 11.5f: acted on firm ground and dead: front runner: visored last 2 starts: stud. *J. H. M. Gosden* — 102

BUNTY BOO 6 b.m. Noalto 120 – Klairove 74 (Averof 123) [1994 106: 5g^{2} 5f^{3} 5g^{3} 5d^{4} 5m 6d^{2} 5g 5g^{6} 6v^{5} 1995 6g 5m 6d 6g^{6} 5m* 6g 6m^{6} 5m* 5d 6d 5f* Oct 31] leggy mare: smart performer: won 10-runner listed race at Sandown in July, 10-runner Arthur Guinness Flying Five at Leopardstown (by a length from Petite Fantasy) in September and 4-runner minor event at Redcar in October: effective at 5f (best form) and 6f: acts on firm and soft ground: usually races prominently. *R. Hannon* — 110

BURDEN OF PROOF (IRE) 3 b.c. Fairy King (USA) – Belle Passe (Be My Guest (USA) 126) [1994 102p: 7d* 8d* 1995 7d^{3} 8m^{4} 7g^{2} 6d* Oct 14] smart Irish colt: in frame in slowly-run Tetrarch Stakes and 9-runner Irish 2000 Guineas (5½ lengths behind Spectrum, keeping on never a threat, off course 4 months afterwards) at the Curragh in the spring: second run back and best effort to win 14-runner listed race there in October by 2½ lengths from Mediation: effective at 6f to 1m: acts on good to firm and dead ground, yet to race on extremes. *Charles O'Brien, Ireland* — 113

BURES (IRE) 4 b.g. Bold Arrangement 127 – Grid (FR) (Grundy 137) [1994 69: 12g^{3} 12.1s^{2} 12.1f* 13.1m^{2} 13.3g 14.8m 14m 12.1g 1995 a11g a16g a12g^{4} a16g^{4} 14.1g Jun 7] lengthy gelding: modest handicapper at best in 1995: best form at up to 13f: acts on firm and dead ground: normally visored: takes keen hold, and often a front runner: twice a winner over hurdles in October. *M. H. Tompkins* — 54

BURJ 2 b.c. (Apr 12) Aragon 118 – Aspark (Sparkler 130) [1995 5m 6m 6g 6m 6.1s Oct 17] 18,000Y: neat gelding: half-brother to fairly useful performers Amidst (from 6f at 2 yrs, to 8.1f, by Midyan) and Arturian (unreliable sprinter, by Vaigly Great): dam little form: only form when around 2½ lengths seventh of 9 behind Astuti in moderately-run median auction maiden at Goodwood on second outing: blinkered final start: sold 2,500 gns Doncaster November Sales. *N. A. Graham* — 58 ?

BURNING (USA) 3 b.c. Bering 136 – Larnica (USA) (Alydar (USA)) [1994 79p: 8g^{5} 1995 10m* 12g^{3} 12m^{6} 12f^{4} 13.9m 12d 10v 12m Oct 21] big, rangy colt with — 103 plenty of scope: useful performer: won maiden at Newmarket in April: very good efforts in King George V Stakes at Royal Ascot and £37,300 handicap at Goodwood third and fourth starts: below form afterwards: stays 1½m: acts on firm ground, seemingly not on a soft surface: held up: wears dropped noseband. *G. Harwood*

BURNT OFFERING 2 b.c. (Apr 7) Old Vic 136 – Burnt Amber (Balidar 133) [1995 7.1d 8g^4 Sep 14] 16,500Y: good-bodied colt: fifth foal: half-brother to a winner abroad by Primo Dominie: dam unraced half-sister to National Stakes winner Lockton: better run in maidens in September when under 8 lengths fourth of 8 to Danesman at Yarmouth: looks a stayer. *C. E. Brittain* 75

BURNT SIENNA (IRE) 3 b.f. Don't Forget Me 127 – Ribot Ann (Kampala 120) [1994 49p: 7g 1995 10m 7f 7g 8m 8.2m 9.7g 11.6m 8.3m^6 8.3m* 7.6m^3 8f^3 a10g^6 Dec 19] sparely-made filly: modest performer: made all in apprentice selling handicap at Windsor in July: clearly best effort when third of 19 in claimer at Leicester on eleventh start: stays 8.3f well: goes well on firm going, yet to race on a soft surface. *J. S. Moore* 54

BURNTWOOD MELODY 4 gr.g. Merdon Melody 98 – Marwick (Roan Rocket 128) [1994 –: a8.5g 1995 16.2m Apr 7] seems of little account. *J. A. Harris* –

BUROOJ 5 br.h. Danzig (USA) – Princess Sucree (USA) (Roberto (USA) 131) [1994 94: 10m* 12m* 12g^4 12m^2 1995 10m* 10m^3 10.1f* 10f^2 12m* 13.3m^4 11.1g* 12d^3 10m^3 Oct 12] big, good-topped horse: has a quick action: improved into smart performer: successful in rated stakes at Newmarket in May and Epsom in June, in 4-runner minor event at Newmarket in July and 7-runner Bonusprint September Stakes at Kempton (led early in straight, idled, held Commoner by a short head): good third to Bal Harbour in minor event at Newmarket, better subsequent effort: stays 13.3f: acts on dead going and firm: often gets on toes and sweats in preliminaries: held up: game: stays in training. *D. Morley* 111

BURSUL LADY 2 b.f. (Apr 12) Be My Chief (USA) 122 – Neverdown 50 (Never So Bold 135) [1995 7m^5 Sep 1] 3,600Y: second foal: dam 8.2f winner: 50/1, burly and green, tailed off in 5-runner minor event at Kempton: had tongue tied down. *Miss B. Sanders* –

BURY THE HATCHET 3 b.g. Be My Chief (USA) 122 – Royal Agreement (USA) (Vaguely Noble 140) [1994 55: 7g 7m 6s^5 1995 8.2g Apr 17] workmanlike –

Bonusprint September Stakes, Kempton—Burooj just holds on from Commoner (left)

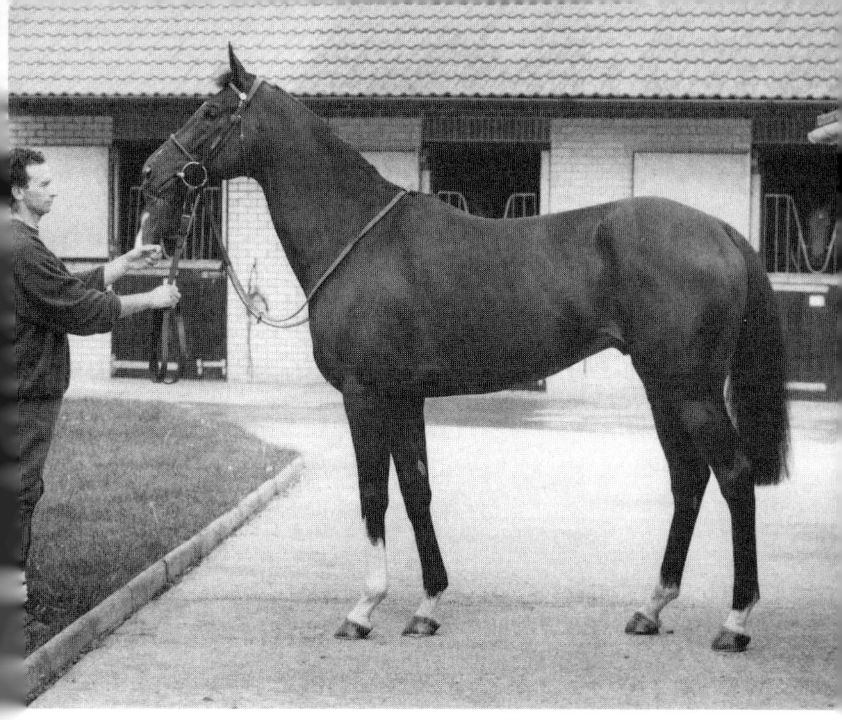

Hamdan Al Maktoum's "Burooj"

gelding: modest maiden: shaped quite well when eighth of 19 in handicap at Nottingham on reappearance, but not seen out afterwards: will be suited by 1m+. *M. H. Tompkins*

BUSHEHR (IRE) 3 b.c. Persian Bold 123 – Shejrah (USA) (Northjet 136) [1994 50: 7g 1995 8.3m 8m³ 10g* 10m⁴ 12.1m² 13.8m³ 11.8m² 15.8g Sep 16] close-coupled colt: unimpressive mover: fair performer: won claimer at Sandown in June: claimed out of J. Hills's stable £9,000 seventh start: tailed off on only flat outing for new connections: should stay beyond 1½m: has raced only on a sound surface. *S. Coathup* — 68

BUSTER 7 br.g. Macmillion 110 – Valsette (Anfield 117) [1994 –: 10m 8d 1995 8g 14.1m 10.2m Aug 28] lengthy, sparely-made gelding: no worthwhile form on flat for a long time. *Mrs Barbara Waring* — –

BUSTLE'EM (IRE) 4 b.f. Burslem 123 – Speedy Action (Horage 124) [1994 49: 7.1s³ 8.1g* 7.5m 8f 7.5f 1995 a9.4g Mar 8] workmanlike filly: poor performer: tailed off in bad seller at Wolverhampton on only 4-y-o start. *D. McCain* — –

BUSY BANANA 3 b.c. Insan (USA) 119 – Linda's Design (Persian Bold 123) [1994 69: 6f² 6m⁵ 6f* 7g⁴ 6d 1995 10.3g a10g* 8.2g* 10g² 8m* 8.5f a8.5f Dec 16] quite attractive colt: good walker and mover: fairly useful handicapper: made all at Lingfield, Nottingham and Carlisle (final start for R. Hannon) in April, impressively by 5 lengths on last 2 occasions: blinkered, well beaten in USA last 2 starts: has won over 1¼m, but best efforts around at 1m: acts on firm ground and equitrack: takes a strong hold. *D. Vienna, USA* — 82

BUSY FLIGHT 2 b.c. (Apr 2) Pharly (FR) 130 – Bustling Nelly 94 (Bustino 136) [1995 8g 8d² 7.3d² Oct 19] 26,000Y: workmanlike colt: brother to 3-y-o Silver Singer and half-brother to several winners here and abroad, including fair stayer Silk Degrees (by Dunbeath): dam middle-distance winning half-sister to Further Flight (by Pharly): ¾-length second of 8 to Mick's Love in well-contested minor event at Newbury in September, held up then staying on strongly: caught close home by ½-length winner Tumbleweed Ridge, having set steady pace, in Horris Hill Stakes at same course following month: will be well suited by 1¼m+: sure to win races. *B. W. Hills* 100 p

BUTTERWICK BELLE (IRE) 2 b.f. (Mar 5) Distinctly North (USA) 115 – Forest Berries (IRE) (Thatching 131) [1995 5m² 5m³ 6g⁴ May 26] 6,000Y: sparely-made filly: first foal: dam, never ran, half-sister to very useful middle-distance colt Pencader: similar form in auction maidens and in minor event at Pontefract: will stay beyond 6f: wears bandages. *R. A. Fahey* 64

BY ARRANGEMENT (IRE) 6 b.m. Bold Arrangement 127 – Eulalie 85 (Queen's Hussar 124) [1994 42: 11.9d 12m⁴ 11.9f⁶ 9.7m² 11.6m² 10g² 10d³ 9g 16.4s* 1995 15.4g³ 15.4m⁴ 17.2m 16.4g⁶ 16m³ Aug 26] leggy, sparely-made mare: poor handicapper: effective at 1¼m to 2m: acts on firm and soft going, well beaten on fibresand. *S. Woodman* 40

BY A WHISKER 2 ch.c. (Feb 18) Keen 116 – Razor Blade 65 (Sharp Edge 123) [1995 7m 6g 7.9m a8g⁵ a6.7s⁴ Dec 10] 4,000F, 7,200Y: lengthy, unfurnished colt: half-brother to several winners, including fair sprinter Keen Edge (by Good Times): dam 2-y-o 5f and 7f winner: best effort in maidens when seventh of 11 at Leicester: sold out of D. Arbuthnot's stable 3,500 gns Newmarket Autumn Sales before running twice in Sweden. *B. Nilsson, Sweden* 57

BY THE BAY 3 b.f. Shareef Dancer (USA) 135 – Beryl's Jewel 86 (Siliconn 121) [1994 NR 1995 7m⁴ 7m 7g³ 7m³ 7g³ 7m 8g 7s a10g⁴ a7g⁶ a7g⁶ Dec 14] rather leggy filly: half-sister to several winners, including sprinters Tylers Wood (by Homing) and Murmuring (by Kind of Hush): dam best at 5f: modest maiden: third on 3 of 5 starts for B. Hills: below form for new stable: best form at up to 7f: acts on good to firm ground, well beaten on soft: has run well when sweating. *C. C. Elsey* 64 d

C

CABALLO (GER) 4 b.c. Konigsstuhl (GER) – Carmelita (Surumu (GER)) [1994 113: 11v² 10g* 12g* 11g* 12g 12g⁶ 10g 14d* 12s 1995 11v² 10s² 12s 10g³ 12g* 11d² 12g 12s* Oct 22] smart German performer: won quite valuable event at Gelsenkirchen in August: ran very well when 2¼ lengths second of 8 to Sternkoenig in Group 3 event at Milan in September then won similar event at Dusseldorf (beat Sir King ½ length) in October: stays 1¾m: acts on heavy going, yet to race on top-of-the-ground. *H. Jentzsch, Germany* 115

CABCHARGE BLUE 3 b.f. Midyan (USA) 124 – Mashobra 75 (Vision (USA)) [1994 81: 5d³ 5d⁵ 6m³ 5.2m* 6m* 5.1m* 6m² 6.1m⁶ 6m 6d* 6.1d* 7m 6.1d³ 6.9s² a7g⁶ 1995 8d 6m 8.3g 7m a8g a6g a7g Dec 14] light-framed filly: only fair form at best in 1995: not certain to stay 1m: successful on good to firm ground, best efforts on a soft surface: below form on all-weather: tends to hang, and is a tricky ride. *T. J. Naughton* 67 d

CABCHARGE STRIKER 2 b.c. (Mar 30) Rambo Dancer (CAN) 107 – Ivory Bride 86 (Domynsky 110) [1995 5s* 5m³ 5m³ 5g⁶ 6f* 6m⁵ 7m² 7.5f* 6g 8s⁶ 8d* Nov 26] sturdy colt: has a quick action: first foal: dam 2-y-o 6f winner who stayed 1m: won median auction maiden at Leicester in March, auction event at Epsom in June and listed race (by 5¾ lengths) at Milan in July (final start for M. Channon): behind in listed events at Milan for new stable before winning minor event at Turin in November: well suited by 7f+: acts on any going: sweating and on toes when below form sixth start. *P. Ceriotti, Italy* 90

CADDICAN (IRE) 3 ch.f. Ballad Rock 122 – Sweetsider (USA) (Topsider (USA)) [1994 NR 1995 7g⁶ 8m 10.3m Oct 21] 1,100F, 4,200Y: half-sister to several –

winners in USA and Ireland: dam, won as 2-y-o in USA at around 9f, is out of half-sister to dam of Committed: well beaten in maidens and a claimer. *R. Boss*

CADDY'S FIRST 3 b.g. Petong 126 – Love Scene (Carwhite 127) [1994 50: 5.2s6 5m 5.1m5 8.1g 5.2s6 5m 1995 a8g6 7g3 a6g5 a7g3 7g 6g a7g* a7g2 7m4 a9.4g Sep 30] leggy, quite good-topped gelding: modest handicapper: won maiden event at Wolverhampton in July: best form at 7f: goes well on fibresand: acts on good to firm ground, well below form on soft: blinkered (below form) once at 2 yrs: usually races prominently. *S. Mellor* 46 a62

CADEAUX PREMIERE 4 b.g. Cadeaux Genereux 131 – Clare Island 108 (Connaught 130) [1994 –: 7m 8m 8f 8g 6f6 7g 10m 16.1d 1995 11.1g May 20] tall gelding: of little account on flat: won handicap hurdle in November. *Denys Smith* –

CADEAUX TRYST 3 b.c. Cadeaux Genereux 131 – Trystero (Shareef Dancer (USA) 135) [1994 94: 6g 6g6 6g* 7m5 1995 8m 7m2 7g* 7m 7g2 7d6 10m4 Oct 12] robust colt: shows knee action: useful handicapper: narrowly won £24,300 Ladbroke Bunbury Cup (Handicap) at Newmarket in July; best efforts when head second of 11 to Indian Fly in rated stakes at Goodwood and sixth of 27 (staying on well) to Night Dance in £52,900 event at Ascot in September: very best form at 7f, far from discredited at 1¼m: has twice run respectably on good to firm ground, but seems ideally suited by an easy surface: usually bandaged: normally held up. *E. A. L. Dunlop* 107

CA'D'ORO 2 ch.g. (Mar 3) Cadeaux Genereux 131 – Palace Street (USA) 103 (Secreto (USA) 128) [1995 5m6 6m May 21] close-coupled, rather leggy gelding: first foal: dam won at 6f and 7.2f: midfield in maidens at Sandown and Newbury in spring: subsequently gelded: looked capable of better. *G. B. Balding* 63

CAERLE LAD (IRE) 4 b.g. Caerleon (USA) 132 – Miss Zadig 102 (Thatch (USA) 136) [1994 NR 1995 10g 8.3m6 10g6 10m 9m2 10f6 10g 10d 10.8g 10f Oct 31] lengthy, robust gelding: fair maiden handicapper: sold out of G. Harwood's stable 5,200 gns Newmarket Autumn Sales after penultimate start: broke down final one: stayed 9f: acted on good to firm ground: usually fitted with net muzzle: dead. *D. Nicholls* 68

CAERPHILLY (IRE) 3 b.f. Caerleon (USA) 132 – Hooked Bid (CAN) 76 (Spectacular Bid (USA)) [1994 87: 6f5 6m* 6f4 6g2 6.5g3 7m* 7m6 1995 a7g a6g4 10v Oct 7] sturdy filly: was genuine 2-y-o for M. Johnston: ran twice in Dubai in the spring, but tailed off in rated stakes on heavy ground at Ascot on belated return: will stay at least 1m: tends to sweat and get on edge: sold 16,000 gns Newmarket December Sales. *D. Morley* –

*Ladbroke Bunbury Cup (Handicap), Newmarket—
Cadeaux Tryst bursts through to catch Sky Music (noseband);
the blinkered Anniversarypresent is a strong-finishing third*

CAFE GLACE 3 b.f. Beldale Flutter (USA) 130 – Little White Star (Mill Reef (USA) 141) [1994 –p: 6s 1995 10g 8.1g a14.8g^{6} Nov 27] sparely-made filly: well beaten. *R. Akehurst* –

CAFE SOLO 4 b. or br.f. Nomination 125 – Piney Lake 54 (Sassafras (FR) 135) [1994 51: 6d 6g^{2} 7g^{4} 8g 8m^{3} 6d* 6g 7m^{6} 5s 6d^{6} 7d 1995 8.2g 6f 7f^{3} 8g 6g 6d^{5} 6m 7g^{3} 7.1m* 7f 6g^{5} 7g 7f^{4} 7h^{4} 6m 7g 8g^{6} Sep 2] small, plain filly: poor handicapper: won at Haydock (apprentices) in July: stays 7f: acts on firm and dead ground: blinkered since sixth 4-y-o start: sometimes hangs: inconsistent. *N. Bycroft* 45

CAHERASS COURT (IRE) 4 b.f. Taufan (USA) 119 – Grass Court (Thatch (USA) 136) [1994 59, a65: 8.3m^{6} 7m^{4} 6m^{6} 7.6g 7m^{4} a7g^{3} a6g^{2} 5.1g^{6} a8.5g^{4} 1995 a6g a6g a6g a6g a8.5g a7g a6g a7g Aug 11] lengthy filly: no longer of much account. *B. Preece* –

CAHITA 3 b.f. Northern State (USA) 91 – Two Stroke (Malicious) [1994 NR 1995 9g 6f Jun 30] good-topped filly: seventh foal: half-sister to 5f winners Vivaldi (fairly useful, at 2 yrs) and Catalani (both by Music Boy): dam poor half-sister to very useful French 1¼m winner Aberdeen Park: tailed-off last in maidens. *T. J. Naughton* –

CA IRA (IRE) 4 b.f. Dancing Dissident (USA) 119 – Silver Mantle 70 (Bustino 136) [1994 –: 6f^{6} 5g 6s 1995 6g Sep 25] lengthy filly: no longer of much account. *R. C. Spicer* –

CAISSON 3 b.f. Shaadi (USA) 126 – Gibraltar Heights (High Top 131) [1994 57: 7m 7m 1995 9m^{5} 12m Jun 13] angular filly: has a rather round action: fifth of 8 in slowly-run maiden at Goodwood in May: pulled hard behind steady early pace then looked unco-ordinated and not altogether keen in handicap at Salisbury 19 days later: difficult to assess. *R. Hannon* 67 ?

CALCANDO 3 b.f. Teenoso (USA) 135 – Musical Princess 66 (Cavo Doro 124) [1994 NR 1995 12m 11.9d Oct 11] sturdy filly: has a round action: sixth foal: sister to 5-y-o Master Fiddler and half-sister to fairly useful winners Drummer Hicks (8.9f to 10.3f, by Seymour Hicks) and Oh Danny Boy (stayed 1½m, by Rabdan): dam won at up to 2m at 5 yrs: in rear in maidens at Pontefract (badly hampered) and Haydock. *E. Weymes* –

CALDER KING 4 ch.g. Rakaposhi King 119 – Name The Game 66 (Fair Season 120) [1994 69: 6g^{3} 7.1g 5.9v 8g^{4} 8m 8f^{2} 7.5m 8f* 8.3m^{3} 8m^{2} 6.9f^{5} 10m^{4} 8.3g^{2} 8.5g^{2} 10d^{3} 8s* 8g^{5} 10s 1995 a8g 10m 8m 8.5m^{3} 8g 8m 8g^{3} 10f^{6} a7g^{2} 9f a9.4g^{4} a9.4g^{5} 8g 8.1g^{2} 8g^{5} a7g^{2} 8.1s a9.4g^{3} a11g^{3} Dec 1] stocky, lengthy gelding: fair handicapper: stays 11f: acts on firm ground, soft and fibresand: nearly always visored/blinkered nowadays: has worn near-side pricker: has run creditably for amateur: held up. *J. L. Eyre* 61 a66

CALEMAN 6 b.g. Daring March 116 – Lillemor (Connaught 130) [1994 91: 8m^{5} 8m* 7f 8.5m a8.5g 7.9m^{5} 8.3m^{4} 10d^{5} 7m^{6} 1995 7m 8m 7m 8g^{5} 8f^{3} 8m 8.1m^{3} Aug 25] leggy, narrow gelding: has a round action: only a fair handicapper in 1995: effective at 7f to 8.3f: acts on firm and dead ground, no form either run on all-weather: blinkered (badly hampered) once as 4-y-o: reportedly swallowed tongue (and pulled up) penultimate 6-y-o start, and sometimes has tongue tied down: usually a front runner: sold 10,000 gns Newmarket Autumn Sales. *R. Boss* 77

CALGARY GIRL 3 ch.f. Weld 122 – Calgary 63 (Run The Gantlet (USA)) [1994 NR 1995 10d a8g^{6} a8g Dec 15] angular filly: ninth foal: half-sister to 3 winners, including fairly useful 15f winner Calicon (by Connaught): dam, middle-distance maiden, is half-sister to Cesarewitch winner Centurion: no form. *P. C. Ritchens* –

CALGARY REDEYE 8 gr.g. Kalaglow 132 – River Call (FR) (Riverman (USA) 131) [1994 NR 1995 14d Sep 27] small, dipped-backed gelding: ran twice (no form) after being fair 4-y-o: dead. *Mrs J. G. Retter* –

CALISAR 5 br.g. Mummy's Game 120 – Maycrest (Imperial Fling (USA) 116) [1994 47: a7g^{6} a7g 6.9s 6d^{6} 8.3g^{5} 8.3m 7m a8g^{6} 8m 7.6g^{5} 7m^{6} 8d a12g a8g^{5} a7g 1995 a10g^{5} a10g 8m* 9.2g 9.2g^{6} 10m 8g^{5} a8g^{4} 10m Jun 26] leggy, angular gelding: unimpressive mover: poor handicapper: won seller at Pontefract in April: stays 1¼m: acts on any going, including equitrack: blinkered (well beaten) final 4-y-o start: inconsistent: sold 4,000 gns Newmarket July Sales. *P. Howling* 41

CALLALOO 2 b.c. (Feb 21) Mtoto 134 – Catawba 98 (Mill Reef (USA) 141) [1995 7m^3 8g^6 7g Oct 10] leggy, close-coupled colt: fourth foal: half-brother to 11.9f winner Isle of Pines (by Kris) and useful middle-distance filly Licorne (by Sadler's Wells): dam, 1¼m winner stayed 1½m, daughter of Ribblesdale winner Catalpa: third of 7 to Double Leaf in minor event at Kempton in September: no comparable form in maidens at Yarmouth and Leicester: will stay well. *Mrs J. Cecil* — 70

CALLING COLLECT (USA) 6 ch.h. Phone Trick (USA) – My Little Guest (Be My Guest (USA) 126) [1994 –: 8.1d 1995 7m 8m* May 3] quite good-topped horse: reportedly fractured tibia at 5 yrs: has a quick action: lightly raced since very useful 3-y-o: mid-division in rated stakes at Newmarket then beat Airport ½ length in falsely-run 3-runner minor event at Ascot: effective at 7f to 1¼m: acts on good to firm ground and heavy: best held up. *L. M. Cumani* — 97

CALLING JAMAICA 3 b.f. Elmaamul (USA) 125 – Tolstoya (Northfields (USA)) [1994 59: 10g* 8d 1995 12.5m Apr 17] angular filly: failed by long way to repeat form (only start for P. Cole) of debut, ridden much too forcefully only start in 1995. *M. C. Pipe* — –

CALLING (USA) 4 ch.g. Phone Trick (USA) – Sweet Singer (USA) (Sing Sing (USA)) [1994 –§: 10m 11.9g 1995 6f 8g 7m 7.1m 6.9f^5 6.1m^5 a7g^6 Aug 5] good-topped gelding: no longer of any account. *W. M. Brisbourne* — –§

CALL ME ALBI (IRE) 4 ch.g. Glenstal (USA) 118 – Albeni 84 (Great Nephew 126) [1994 58: 8m 11.9m 10m 8.2m^5 9g^5 12m* 12m 11.9f^3 10m^2 11.9m* 10g^4 1995 a13g a16g^3 a16g^4 a16g^2 11.9m 17.2f 11.6m^2 12f^2 14d a16g^4 Dec 15] lengthy, good-topped gelding: only poor at best in 1995: probably stays 2m: acts on firm ground, possibly not on dead: effective blinkered/visored or not: won twice over hurdles in October. *G. L. Moore* — 49

CALL ME BLUE 5 gr.g. Kalaglow 132 – Woodfold 80 (Saritamer (USA) 130) [1994 53: 9.7g^6 10g 10.8m* a12g 1995 a10g a12g^5 a10g* a11g^6 Mar 20] leggy, angular gelding: modest performer: narrowly won minor event at Lingfield in February: seems suited by around 1¼m: acts on good to firm ground and equitrack: blinkered (well beaten) final 3-y-o outing: most inconsistent: sold 500 gns Ascot September Sales. *T. J. Naughton* — 57

CALL ME FLASH 3 ch.g. Presidium 124 – Relkisha 58 (Relkino 131) [1994 60: 7m^2 7m 8s 7s 1995 10m 8m a8g^3 Jun 16] short-backed gelding: no form since debut. *Mrs P. Sly* — –

CALL ME I'M BLUE (IRE) 5 b.g. Reasonable (FR) 119 – Bluebutton 65 (Blue Cashmere 129) [1994 104: 6m 5f^3 1995 6g 5m 5g^6 6m 5g^6 5m 5.6m^4 5d^4 5s 5m 6f Oct 31] robust, lengthy gelding: injured final 4-y-o start and only a fairly useful handicapper on return: in frame (for second time) in the Portland at Doncaster seventh start: stays 5.6f: acts on firm and dead going: well beaten only try in blinkers: tends to edge left. *N. Tinkler* — 91

CALL ME JENDIE 2 b.f. (May 7) Jendali (USA) 111 – Lady Carol 42 (Lord Gayle (USA) 124) [1995 5f 7f^5 Oct 24] half-sister to 3-y-o Carol Again (by Kind Of Hush) and fair sprinter Craigie Boy (by Crofthall): dam 1m winner: last in minor events at Catterick and Redcar. *J. P. Leigh* — –

CALLONESCY (IRE) 3 b.g. Royal Academy (USA) 130 – Take Your Mark (USA) (Round Table) [1994 NR 1995 a7g a9.4g^2 a10g 10g a7g^6 Sep 16] IR 25,000Y: closely related to a winner by Nijinsky and half-brother to several winners, notably 2000 Guineas second Charmer (won at up to 13.3f, by Be My Guest): dam lightly raced: second in Wolverhampton maiden in February: soundly beaten afterwards: had soft-palate operation: sold (C. Brittain to D. O'Brien) 1,500 gns Newmarket Autumn Sales. *C. E. Brittain* — 57

CALL TOPHORSE 3 b.g. Today And Tomorrow 78 – Sum Star 67 (Comedy Star (USA) 121) [1994 NR 1995 a7g^4 a8g 10.8m Jun 26] half-brother to 2 winners, including fair sprinter Joe Sugden (by Music Boy): dam won 5 times from 5f to 1m at 5 yrs: no worthwhile form, including in seller: joined C. Murray. *P. C. Haslam* — –

CALL TO THE BAR (IRE) 6 b.g. Kafu 120 – Papun (USA) (Mount Hagen (FR) 127) [1994 77: 5.1m^4 5d 5.7m^5 6f^5 5f^5 5.7g^4 a6g^6 1995 5m 6f^5 5m 5m 5m 6g Aug 26] leggy, sparely-made gelding: sold out of M. McCormack's stable 6,400 gns Doncaster March Sales: on the downgrade after reappearance: stays 6f: easily best — 66 d form on a sound surface: below form when blinkered (bolted) and visored once at 3 yrs. *M. Dods*

CALTHA 3 b.f. Dunbeath (USA) 127 – Rillandel (Wolver Hollow 126) [1994 42: 7m 7.5g^4 7s 1995 12m 10f 8m^4 a8g 8.2m^4 7g^4 7m* 8.1f 7m* 7.1m^2 7g Sep 16] leggy filly: poor mover: poor handicapper: won sellers at Catterick (apprentices) and Ayr in the summer: best form at around 7f: acts on firm ground, well beaten only start on soft ground and fibresand: blinkered since sixth 3-y-o start: usually front runner nowadays. *P. Calver* — 47

CALYPSO RUN 2 ch.f. (Apr 23) Lycius (USA) 124 – Sea Venture (FR) 98 (Diatome 132) [1995 6f^6 Aug 25] 32,000Y: half-sister to numerous winners, including smart middle-distance performer Sailor's Mate (by Shirley Heights) and useful 1980 French 2-y-o 6f winner Grecian Sea (by Homeric), latter dam of Yorkshire Oaks winner Hellenic: dam, from family of Reform, won over 6f at 3 yrs and stayed 1m: 11/2 and ridden by 7-lb claimer, faded into sixth of 8, around 9 lengths down on Munakeb, in maiden at Thirsk: should do better. *M. Bell* — – p

CAMDEN'S RANSOM (USA) 8 b.g. Hostage (USA) – Camden Court (USA) (Inverness Drive (USA)) [1994 –, a58: a12g^4 a7g a9.4g^5 a11g^4 a10g^6 a8g^4 1995 a10g^2 a10g^5 a11g a11g* a11g^4 a10g* a10g a11g^4 10m 10d a10g a10g^4 Dec 6] good-bodied gelding: modest handicapper: left G. Balding's stable after second start: won at Southwell and Lingfield early in year: suited by strongly-run race at 1m to 11f: acts on good to firm ground, soft and all-weather surfaces: has won for apprentice: normally held up. *H. G. Rowsell* — – a61

CAMERON HIGHLAND (IRE) 4 b.g. Night Shift (USA) – Vestal Flame 45 (Habitat 134) [1994 82: 8m^2 8.3g* 10.3m 8m 7g^4 7d^3 1995 8g 7m 7.3g a6g 7f* 8f 7m 7.1d Sep 12] big, good-topped gelding: usually impresses good deal in appearance: has a round action: 20/1, gamely won 13-runner handicap at Kempton in June: failed by very long way to repeat the form: stays 8.3f: acts on firm and dead ground: tried blinkered, no improvement: may prove best with forcing tactics. *P. F. I. Cole* — 84

CAMIONNEUR (IRE) 2 b.g. (Apr 6) Cyrano de Bergerac 120 – Fact of Time (Known Fact (USA) 135) [1995 5m^4 6m 5f^4 5m^4 5g^5 6f^4 7.9g 6g 5m^2 6f^5 5m^4 Nov 3] 5,200Y: workmanlike gelding: has scope: third foal: dam never ran: modest maiden: creditable efforts in nurseries last 3 starts: stays 6f (pulled too hard over 7.9f): seems best blinkered nowadays: consistent. *M. H. Easterby* — 57

CAMPAIGN 4 b.g. Sure Blade (USA) 130 – Just Cause (Law Society (USA) 130) [1994 87: 10m* 10m^5 1995 14.6m^5 Nov 3] well-made, attractive gelding: resold 8,200 gns Doncaster May 1995 Sales: weak in betting, well below form in minor event at Doncaster for new stable: should stay beyond 1¼m: won over hurdles in December. *M. D. Hammond* — –

CAMPASPE 3 b.f. Dominion 123 – Lady River (FR) (Sir Gaylord) [1994 NR 1995 a8.5g a8g^4 a7g 6f Jul 29] leggy filly: half-sister to numerous winners in France, including middle-distance stayer Satin River (by Satingo): dam showed a little ability in France: soundly beaten, including in seller. *J. G. FitzGerald* — –

CAMP FOLLOWER 2 b.c. (Apr 25) Warrshan (USA) 117 – House Maid 95 (Habitat 134) [1995 6g* Jul 19] 26,000Y: half-brother to 3-y-o Lynton Lad (by Superpower), 5f and 6f winner at 2 yrs, and 2 other winners, including fairly useful 8.5f winner Mona Lisa (by Henbit): dam won twice over 7f at 2 yrs: won maiden at Milan in July by a head: will stay at least 1m. *J. L. Dunlop* — ?

CANARY BLUE (IRE) 4 b.f. Bluebird (USA) 125 – Norfolk Bonnet (Morston (FR) 125) [1994 59d: 8g 10g 10d^5 14d 12.1g 14.1g 1995 a14.8g a12g Jul 22] workmanlike filly: no form on flat in 1995 for new stable: stays 1¼m: blinkered (out of form) final 3-y-o start: poor winning staying hurdler for P. Hiatt. *J. G. M. O'Shea* — –

CANARY FALCON 4 ch.g. Polish Precedent (USA) 131 – Pumpona (USA) (Sharpen Up 127) [1994 66: 7s 7.1m^3 8m^3 10.1m 8.1d 10d 1995 a10g^5 a10g^5 a7g* a7g^4 8m^6 7m^3 12m 8.1g^5 6d 7d 7m^4 a7g a9.4g^2 a9.4g Dec 9] compact gelding: good mover: fair handicapper: won maiden event at Wolverhampton in February: left R. O'Sullivan's stable after eighth outing: stays 9.4f: acts on good to firm ground and the all-weather: none too consistent. *John Berry* — 60 a66

CAN CAN CHARLIE 5 gr.g. Vaigly Great 127 – Norton Princess 76 (Wolver Hollow 126) [1994 60, a66: a8.5g a8g^2 a8g^2 a7g^5 a10g a8g^6 a7g^2 a8g* a8.5g^2 7g^3 — – a66

7.5d* 7d 8d 9.2s* a8.5g^5 9.2f 8.5g^5 8.1m^5 7g 7g a10g^4 a8.5g a10g^4 a12g^6 1995 a12g^3 a10g^2 a12g^5 a9.4g* a9.4g 9.7s^6 Sep 27] big, strong, good-topped gelding: fair handicapper: first flat start for 6 months, won at Wolverhampton (amateurs) in August: well beaten afterwards: stays 1¼m: acts on good to firm ground, soft and all-weather surfaces: blinkered (no improvement) final 4-y-o start: held up: none too consistent: won 3 times over hurdles in November. *J. Pearce*

CANDLE SMILE (USA) 3 b.c. Pleasant Colony (USA) – Silent Turn (USA) (Silent Cal (USA)) [1994 72p: 8m 1995 11m^4 13.9m^3 May 16] big, leggy colt: shows knee action: fairly useful form: in frame in maiden at Newbury (behind Tamure) and minor event at York (behind Stelvio, made most) in the spring: stays 1¾m, and may well stay 2m: has raced only on good to firm ground. *M. R. Stoute* — 93

CANDLE SMOKE (USA) 2 b. or br.g. (May 12) Woodman (USA) 126 – Light The Lights (FR) 123 (Shirley Heights 130) [1995 8m^5 Oct 27] $125,000Y: rangy, good sort: has plenty of scope: fourth foal: dam French middle-distance winner from good family: 7/1, green and short to post, remote last of 5 in minor event at Newmarket. *G. Harwood* — –

CANDRIKA 2 b.f. (Feb 12) High Estate 127 – Chevisaunce 75 (Fabulous Dancer (USA) 124) [1995 7m^2 Jun 17] sixth reported foal: half-sister to several winners in Italy: dam maiden seemed to stay 1½m: beaten a nose in maiden at Milan: will stay middle distances: seemed sure to improve. *L. M. Cumani* — 72 ?

CANDY DANCER 2 ch.g. (Mar 29) Opening Run (USA) – Poly Negative (Polyfoto 124) [1995 5m 5h^5 7f Aug 25] angular gelding: sixth reported foal: dam never ran: well beaten, in sellers last 2 starts. *C. W. Thornton* — –

CANDY'S DELIGHT 2 b.f. (Apr 24) Dunbeath (USA) 127 – Simply Candy (IRE) 42 (Simply Great (FR) 122) [1995 7.5m^6 7.5d^6 8.3g 6f Oct 24] first foal: dam, maiden, stayed 11f: poor maiden. *J. L. Eyre* — –

CANLUBANG 2 ch.f. (Feb 14) Mujtahid (USA) 118 – Snug (USA) (Lyphard (USA) 132) [1995 5m a5g^6 6g Jun 3] 2,100Y: second foal: dam never ran: no form: visored in seller final start: sold 400 gns Doncaster July Sales. *M. J. Camacho* — –

CANNIZARO (IRE) 3 b.f. Gallic League 119 – Paradise Regained 41 (North Stoke 130) [1994 NR 1995 a8g* 10g 7m 10g^5 Sep 2] angular filly: fourth live foal: half-sister to fair 5f (at 2 yrs) to modest 1½m winner Al Shany (by Burslem): dam placed at up to 15.4f: 9/2, won 12-runner median auction maiden at Lingfield in February: off course 5 months and no worthwhile form afterwards. *R. J. R. Williams* — 58 d

CANNY LAD 5 b.g. Green Ruby (USA) 104 – Young Whip (Bold Owl 101) [1994 –: a9.4g^4 8.2g 8.1m a6g 10m 7m^5 8m a7g a8g 1995 7g 8g^5 a11g 9.9m 8m 8m^4 8m^4 7.5m 8m Aug 29] workmanlike gelding: poor maiden: best form at around 1m: acts on firm ground: usually visored or blinkered: inconsistent. *M. P. Bielby* — 36

CANON CAN (USA) 2 ch.g. (Mar 31) Green Dancer (USA) 132 – Lady Argyle (USA) (Don B (USA)) [1995 9m^2 8g^5 10g Oct 9] IR 15,500Y: tall, good-topped gelding: has scope: second foal: dam unraced: second to Night Watch in maiden at Sandown in August: below that form afterwards in maiden at Yarmouth and minor event at Leicester: subsequently gelded: should stay 1¼m. *H. R. A. Cecil* — 76

CANONS PARK 2 ch.c. (Feb 8) Keen 116 – Low Line 66 (High Line 125) [1995 7.1g^3 7f* 7g^5 7g Sep 7] 27,000Y: sturdy colt: has a round action: third foal: half-brother to 1991 2-y-o 6f winner Time Lapse (by The Noble Player): dam sister to Park Hill winner Quay Line, and Shore Line, fourth in Oaks and now dam of Soviet Line: made all in maiden (beat Gentilhomme and Beauchamp King) at Kempton in June, eased several lengths close home: well beaten afterwards (none too tractable) in listed race at Newmarket (lost tooth in stalls) and minor event at Doncaster: bred to stay further than 7f: looked potentially useful at Kempton. *I. A. Balding* — 88

CANOVAS HEART 6 b.g. Balidar 133 – Worthy Venture 76 (Northfields (USA)) [1994 57+: a11g^5 a11g 8s 7g^3 5s* 1995 5d* 5m^4 5.1m^2 5g^4 a5g* a5g^2 7d^4 5g^5 Sep 23] neat gelding: has quick action: modest handicapper: won at Warwick in April and Southwell in June: effective at 5f, probably at 7f: acts on good to firm and soft ground and on fibresand: usually races prominently: consistent. *Bob Jones* — 64 a59

CAN SHE CAN CAN 3 b.f. Sulaafah (USA) 119 – Dominance (Dominion 123) [1994 49: 5m^2 5m 6f* 7m^3 1995 11.1f^6 11.1m^4 12.1f^2 14.1m^2 16m 16.2m^3 14.1m — 49

16.2m^3 15.8g^2 Sep 16] workmanlike filly: poor handicapper: stays 2m: acts on firm ground, unraced on soft surface: races prominently. *M. Johnston*

CANTE CHICO 3 b.c. Reference Point 139 – Flamenco Wave (USA) 103 (Desert Wine (USA)) [1994 NR 1995 10g 10g^6 10f^3 14.6m Oct 20] sturdy colt: third foal: half-brother to fairly useful Irish 1½m winner Father Sky (by Dancing Brave): dam won Moyglare Stud Stakes: unruly stalls but best effort in maidens when sixth of 16 at Pontefract: off course 4 months, in rear in handicap at Doncaster then sold only 1,500 gns Newmarket Autumn Sales. *T. Thomson Jones*
68

CANTON VENTURE 3 ch.g. Arctic Tern (USA) 126 – Ski Michaela (USA) (Devil's Bag (USA)) [1994 NR 1995 9g 10m^4 12m a12g* 11.8g^5 a14.8g a12g* 12m a12g Oct 14] angular gelding: first foal: dam ran twice: fair handicapper: won at Wolverhampton in July (maiden) and September: should stay further than 1½m: acts on fibresand: blinkered (ran badly) sixth 3-y-o start: inconsistent. *S. P. C. Woods*
63
a69

CAN'T SAY (IRE) 3 br.g. Gallic League 119 – Mixed Feelings (Junius (USA) 124) [1994 49: 6.1m 6m^5 7g^3 6m 1995 8.2g 7f 8.2m 8m^6 7m 6.1m 6f^6 5.3f 5f Aug 28] leggy, workmanlike gelding: of no account. *J. M. Bradley*
–

CAP AND GOWN (IRE) 3 ch.f. Royal Academy (USA) 130 – Wrapping 108§ (Kris 135) [1994 NR 1995 7d^3 8m* 7g^6 10.2m^4 8f^2 10.1m^4 8.1d Sep 12] tall, unfurnished filly: easy mover: second foal: dam, second in Italian Oaks but maiden and not one to trust, sister to Royal Lodge winner Reach: fairly useful performer: narrowly won maiden at Bath in May: in frame in handicaps before running as if something amiss final start: best form at 1m: acts on firm and dead ground: sent to Dubai. *P. F. I. Cole*
81

CAPE COLONY 3 b.g. Dominion 123 – Valiancy 87 (Grundy 137) [1994 NR 1995 a7g^6 8m^4 7g^3 7g^5 Oct 10] 15,000Y: leggy gelding: brother to modest 1m and 8.5f winner Essex Girl and half-brother to 3 winners, including modest 13.1f winner Valfleury (by Ile de Bourbon): dam 1¼m winner out of Oaks second Vals Girl: modest form: claimed £6,000 after selling handicap at Leicester final start: stays 1m: acts on fibresand and good to firm ground: twice mulish stalls. *C. F. Wall*
58

CAPE PIGEON (USA) 10 ch.g. Storm Bird (CAN) 134 – Someway Somehow (USA) (What Luck (USA)) [1994 65d: 7.6g^6 7s 7s 6.9m^4 8.3m^5 7f^6 7g^5 7.6v^4 7s^3 8.1g* a7g 1995 8.3m^4 8.3m* 8.3m^4 8.3g* Jul 3] big, strong gelding: carries plenty of condition: fair performer: has won a race or 2 in each of last 5 seasons, in 1995 winning sellers at Windsor in June and (comfortably making all) in July: stays 8.3f: acts on any going: usually blinkered or visored: formerly unreliable. *L. G. Cottrell*
65

CAPIAS (USA) 4 b.c. Alleged (USA) 138 – Smooth Bore (USA) (His Majesty (USA)) [1994 110: 10m^4 10m* 11.9m^6 12m^5 16g^2 1995 10g* 11.8m* 14m^2 12m^6 12m^2 a9.4g^5 Dec 2] lengthy colt: smart performer: won £5,000 event at Newbury in May and listed race at Leicester (under pressure 3f out, stayed on strongly to beat Totality by a neck) in June: second in Curragh Cup (rec 10 lb, beaten ½ length by Vintage Crop) and listed event at Doncaster (1¼ lengths behind Blushing Flame) afterwards: may well stay beyond 1¾m: acts on good to firm ground (respectable effort in listed race on fibresand), yet to race on a soft surface: tried blinkered/visored, no improvement: game and genuine. *J. H. M. Gosden*
110

CAPILANO PRINCESS 2 b.f. (Apr 20) Tragic Role (USA) – Lady Capilano 87 (Nebbiolo 125) [1995 5s^4 a6g^3 a6g^6 a7g^4 7.1s^3 7m* Nov 4] angular, workmanlike filly: sister to a 3-y-o in Hungary (winner at up to 8.5f) and half-sister to useful 1990 2-y-o 7f and 1m winner Gentle Aria (by Elegant Air): dam 1½m winner: won nursery at Doncaster in November, staying on strongly to beat Double Diamond 1¾ lengths: will stay 1m: acts on any ground on turf, only modest form on fibresand. *D. Haydn Jones*
75
a60

CAP JULUCA (IRE) 3 b.c. Mtoto 134 – Tabyan (USA) 68 (Topsider (USA)) [1994 NR 1995 8g^5 8.3m* 8g* 10m* 7.9m* 9g* Sep 30]
117 p

All good things come to an end, they say, but there has not been much sign of that from Cap Juluca. To date, he has had six races and won five of them, the sole defeat coming on his debut. That was in a maiden at Newbury in April when he finished fifth of twenty-four. He made no mistake in a similar event at Windsor in July and then was able to go cash-hunting, capturing prizes of £7,100, £9,878, £23,604 and £55,717. The first of that quartet brought diamonds as well for Cap

Juluca's jockey Eve Johnson Houghton after they had made virtually all in the Hortensia Diamond Conditions Stakes for lady riders at Ascot on King George day. BHB handicap marks in the nineties were shrugged off with thoroughly dominant displays of front running the following month in the Bonusprint Handicap at Newbury and the Bradford & Bingley Rated Stakes at York, in the latter stepping down from a mile and a quarter to a mile. By now the betting public had well and truly latched on to Cap Juluca: in both of those handicaps he started a well-backed favourite, and the combination of a BHB mark of 107 (a rise of 8 lb for a length-and-a-quarter victory at York) and thirty-eight opponents only just succeeded in having him headed in the betting when Cap Juluca lined up next in the William Hill Cambridgeshire Handicap at Newmarket. He was sent off 11/1 co-second favourite behind Yoush. Jason Weaver had ridden him on his previous two starts but was unavailable this time, replaced by Richard Hughes. The result was just the same. The massive field raced in two groups initially, one from halfway, and Cap Juluca was in front throughout—a magnificent sight. It was clear from a long way out that he would win, pushed along only at the two-furlong marker when the vast majority of his rivals were already backpedalling, and from there on holding an advantage of about two lengths until Ball Gown came at him in the dying strides. The neck margin between them, with Ball Gown carrying 4-lb overweight and making up about five lengths in the last two and a half furlongs, suggests that Ball Gown was unlucky, but it does not do justice to the striking impression made by Cap Juluca. That is what will be remembered.

Under top weight of 9-10, Cap Juluca was setting a new weight-carrying record for the Cambridgeshire. As we have said in a number of past essays, the conditions of this or any other of the traditional handicaps, and the circumstances surrounding them, have changed so much over the years that weight-carrying records are of much greater historical interest than real significance. As an illustration, from 1839 (its inception) to 1945, the Cambridgeshire had thirty-five winners carrying under 7-0, eight of them with less than 6-0, including Malacca in 1856 who was burdened with just 5-5. The only horses in this period to win with 9-0 or more were Foxhall in 1881 and Florence in 1884, both of whom also made the frame in the Cesarewitch in those years, Foxhall winning it. Since 1945, the weight-carrying record has been broken in 1946 (by Sayani), 1949 (Sterope), 1958 (London Cry), 1970 (Prince de Galles), 1985 (Tremblant) and now 1995. Nine others have won with 9-0 or more, six of them in the last twenty years and three in the 'nineties. The Grand Criterium, French Derby and French St Leger winner Jongleur also won the 1877 Cambridgeshire, with 8-4, while the One Thousand Guineas, Oaks and St Leger

Bradford & Bingley Rated Stakes (Handicap), York—Cap Juluca maintains the gallop to beat a strong field

William Hill Cambridgeshire Handicap, Newmarket—Cap Juluca gives Ball Gown lumps of weight

winner La Fleche took the 1892 running under 8-10. Forgive us for stating the obvious, but in assessing any horse the actual weight carried in a handicap is in itself of no relevance. What does matter is the handicap mark this weight represents, and Cap Juluca's repeated improvement to win the Cambridgeshire off 107 looks to be that of a sure-fire pattern-race winner in 1996. Few will need reminding that the 1994 Cambridgeshire winner was Halling who won off 93. Cap Juluca has done so well already that it seems foolish to try to suggest any limit to what status he might rise to in the future. His owner Mr Myers, who won the Group 2 Premio Ribot at Rome with Pater Noster in 1994, is in the enviable position of going into 1996 with another powerful string to his bow in the Newmarket listed race winner Restructure.

Cap Juluca (IRE) (b.c. 1992)	Mtoto (b 1983)	Busted (b 1963)	Crepello
			Sans Le Sou
		Amazer (b 1967)	Mincio
			Alzara
	Tabyan (USA) (b 1987)	Topsider (b 1974)	Northern Dancer
			Drumtop
		Wink (b 1979)	Forli
			Glisk

Cap Juluca's sire Mtoto had his first pattern-race winner in the latest season, the Gordon Stakes and Geoffrey Freer Stakes winner Presenting, and other noteworthy representatives of his in the last two seasons are Beau Temps, Celeric, Ptoto, Salt Lake and Sumoto. Cap Juluca's dam Tabyan was a 170,000-dollar buy as a yearling and did her racing for Sheikh Hamdan, nine times in all over two seasons and getting off the mark at the ninth attempt, in a five-runner maiden over six furlongs at Folkestone. She threw a filly by Danehill in 1993 and a colt by Selkirk in 1995. Tabyan's dam Wink also gained her victories at six furlongs. A useful filly who shaped as though she would stay beyond a mile, Wink was a half-sister to the smart American colt Glow who recently conducted stud duties in Ireland but now does so in Japan. The third dam Glisk, a winner three times at around six furlongs in North America, was a half-sister to both the million-dollar earner Royal Glint and Caerleon's dam Foreseer.

After Cap Juluca's mile-and-a-quarter win at Newbury, both his trainer and jockey said that he might well get a mile and a half as a four-year-old. It is a view with which we concur, but he clearly does not *need* to step up in trip. A good-bodied colt and fluent mover, he has so far raced only on good or good to firm ground. Front-running tactics suited him well as a three-year-old, but connections do not consider them a necessity. Unable to be put into training as a two-year-old, making up for lost time has been the order of the day so far for Cap Juluca and we fully expect him to continue in the same vein. *R. Charlton*

CAPO BAY (IRE) 2 b.g. (Mar 8) Salt Dome (USA) – Trojan Honey (Trojan Fen 118) [1995 5d a5g Apr 13] IR 1,500F, 4,300Y: leggy gelding: second foal: dam Irish maiden: soundly beaten in maiden and seller in April. *P. C. Haslam* –

CAPSTONE 2 b.f. (Mar 16) Shirley Heights 130 – Doumayna 79 (Kouban (FR)) [1995 7f 8f Oct 25] leggy filly: seventh foal: closely related to fairly useful 1½m winner Foil Stone (by Slip Anchor) and useful middle-distance stayer Bondstone (by Miller's Mate): dam, 2m winner, is half-sister to Darshaan (by Shirley Heights) and Darara: green, slowly away and well behind in maidens at Yarmouth: bandaged off-hind: will be suited by good test of stamina: will do better. *W. Jarvis* – p

CAPTAIN CARAT 4 gr.g. Handsome Sailor 125 – Gem of Gold 52 (Jellaby 124) [1994 74: a7g^2 a6g^6 a6g^3 6.1d^2 5f^6 5f^3 5m^5 7f 6m* 6m^3 6m^3 6.1g* 6m 6d 6s 5s^3 5v^2 1995 6g 6d 6.1g 6m 6m* 6m 6d 6m 6m^2 6.1m^6 6f^3 6m^2 6m^4 5g^4 6g^6 5g 5d 6m Oct 30] tall gelding: fair handicapper: won at Doncaster in May: effective at 5f, and stays 6f well: acts on any turf ground and on fibresand: has run well when sweating: best held up, ridden from front (and well below form) first 4 starts at 4 yrs: tough and consistent. *Mrs J. R. Ramsden* 69

CAPTAIN HORATIUS (IRE) 6 b.h. Taufan (USA) 119 – One Last Glimpse 73 (Relko 136) [1994 113: 10v^2 12s^5 12m* 12g^2 11d^3 11s^4 1995 10m* 12m^2 10g^2 10m^2 10.9g^2 10d Oct 3] tall, close-coupled horse: unimpressive mover: a thoroughly likeable performer who has proved very consistent (his annual rating has never been lower than 112 in 5 seasons) and took his record to 10 wins and 15 times in frame from 34 races, worth around a third of a million pounds: won strongly-contested Magnolia Stakes at Kempton (second success in race) in April under top weight by 114

Magnolia Stakes, Kempton—a second success in this race for Captain Horatius; Golden Ball and Young Buster come next

1¼ lengths from Golden Ball: second in Premio Ellington at Rome (behind Laroche) in May, Scottish Classic at Ayr (length behind Baron Ferdinand) in July, Winter Hill Stakes at Windsor (behind Desert Shot) in August and Doonside Cup at Ayr (no match for Annus Mirabilis) in September: suited by middle distances: acts on good to firm and heavy ground: has good turn of foot: game and genuine: a great credit to his trainer: stays in training. *J. L. Dunlop*

CAPTAIN MARMALADE 6 ch.g. Myjinski (USA) – Lady Seville 64 (Orange Bay 131) [1994 43, a57: a12g^3 a8.5g^4 10.3g 10.1g a8g^5 10.1m^6 8g^4 8m^3 8.1m^3 10m 8.1g 7s a8g a7g a8g a10g^2 a10g^3 a10g^5 a10g^3 1995 a13g^5 a10g^4 a10g^2 a10g^4 a10g^3 a10g^2 a10g^4 a8g^5 a10g 8.2g^2 9.7g^5 10g* 9g a8.5g^2 8g 9m a8.5g^4 10.1m 8m^5 a10g 9.7s^5 a9.4g^6 a10g Nov 2] workmanlike gelding: modest handicapper: won at Nottingham (ladies) in April: stays 1½m: acts on good to firm going, soft and all-weather surfaces: often contests ladies/amateur events: broke a blood vessel on reappearance: held up: sometimes gets well behind: none too consistent. *D. T. Thom* — 47, a54

CAPTAIN SCARLET (IRE) 4 b.g. Red Sunset 120 – Shangara (Credo 123) [1994 83: 9m 10m^4 12s* 14g* 11.1m* a12g^4 12f^3 11.9f^2 14m 1995 12g^5 Jun 9] leggy gelding: has a quick action: fairly useful handicapper at best in 1994, but retained very cheaply at sales: effective at 11f to 1¾m: acts on firm ground and soft, ran badly only start on equitrack: blinkered/visored (ran well) third to eighth 3-y-o starts and (bandaged, well below form) only start at 4 yrs: tends to wander. *B. J. Meehan* — –

CAPTAIN'S DAY 3 ch.g. Ballacashtal (CAN) – Seymour Ann (Krayyan 117) [1994 80: 6s^4 6g^4 7m 6.1m 7g* 7.6d^2 7g* 7m^5 1995 9d 8.1m 7f 8m^2 7m^3 7.1m^3 8f^5 8.1m 7.6d^5 7g Sep 30] sparely-made gelding: poor mover: fair performer: well below form last 2 outings, then gelded: should stay further than 1m: acts on firm and soft ground. *T. G. Mills* — 82

CAPTAIN SINBAD 3 b.g. Welsh Captain 113 – Lane Patrol (Hopton Lane 70) [1994 NR 1995 a6g a6g a6g 10m 5f Aug 28] tall gelding: third foal: dam of no account: no sign of ability. *K. S. Bridgwater* — –

CAPTAIN STARLIGHT (IRE) 4 b.c. Vision (USA) – Belitis 109 (Tudor Melody 129) [1994 56: 14.6f 14.1g^4 12g 12.3g 10.5g^3 10.2s 10d 1995 15.4m^6 12g 11.6m 14d^6 Jul 30] sparely-made, angular colt: seems no longer of much account: sold 900 gns Ascot July Sales. *R. Akehurst* — –

CAPTURE THE MOMENT 2 b.f. Keen 116 – Shaieef (IRE) 66 (Shareef Dancer (USA) 135) [1995 5m^4 5m^2 5g^2 5g* 5f 6m^4 6m^3 7m^6 7m a6g Nov 14] 5,600F, 7,600Y: plain, sparely-made filly: first foal: dam 1m winner stayed 1¼m: won maiden auction at Lingfield in June: below form final 3 starts: stays 6f: has been bandaged near-hind. *R. J. R. Williams* — 71

CARAMBA 3 b.f. Belmez (USA) 131 – Melodrama 102 (Busted 134) [1994 82p: 6m^3 1995 10.4m^2 10.5m 8g* 10f* 12d Sep 10] — 114

Caramba lost her maiden certificate in a Group 2 race, then for good measure followed up in another only seventeen days later. Those events were the Falmouth Stakes at Newmarket and the Vodafone Nassau Stakes at Goodwood in July, both contested by a small field, run at a dawdle and ending in a tight finish in which the winner showed herself a game filly. Caramba had Gay Gallanta and Harayir breathing down her neck at Newmarket, the post coming just too soon for Harayir who was put at a disadvantage by being last when the pace finally quickened. At Goodwood Caramba had Warning Shadows in front of her most of the way and just edged ahead after mounting a sustained challenge from two furlongs out.

Caramba was no ordinary maiden when she ran at Newmarket. Far from it. On her most recent start she had finished within two lengths of the winner, Carling, in the Prix de Diane Hermes; and in the one before that had finished a length second to the subsequent Oaks third Pure Grain in the Musidora. Arguably she was even better than the bare result both times. Inexperience seemed at the time to have cost her the race against Pure Grain at York, while she was given a lot to do by her jockey at Chantilly where she stayed on well to come seventh of twelve. Both times, particularly at Chantilly, she ran as though she was well worth trying over a mile and a half. Yet those two wins in slowly-run races, particularly the one over a mile at Newmarket, suggested she might not be so effective over a mile and a half after all. On her only subsequent outing Caramba finished last of ten behind Carling over the distance in the Prix Vermeille, beaten eight lengths, weakening in the straight having

Falmouth Stakes, Newmarket—
a close finish between, left to right, Harayir, Caramba, Gay Gallanta and Arabride

pulled hard in behind the leaders. She probably wasn't herself, but there are considerable doubts about her stamina now.

Caramba (b.f. 1992)	Belmez (USA) (b 1987)	El Gran Senor (b 1981)	Northern Dancer
			Sex Appeal
		Grace Note (b 1982)	Top Ville
			Val de Grace
	Melodrama (b 1978)	Busted (b 1963)	Crepello
			Sans Le Sou
		Matinee (gr 1971)	Zeddaan
			Harlequinade

The 1990 King George VI and Queen Elizabeth Diamond Stakes winner Belmez had his first three-year-old runners in the latest season. Some of them showed an abundance of stamina, notably Duchess of Alba and the ill-fated Pedraza. Caramba's dam, the useful Melodrama, had unusual speed for a daughter of Busted and won over six furlongs as well as a mile; but she was also a daughter of the smart

Vodafone Nassau Stakes, Goodwood—
Caramba edges out Warning Shadows (rails) for her second Group 2 inside three weeks

sprinter Matinee. Melodrama has proved an even better broodmare than racemare, and her seven runners have all made the winner's enclosure. One of them, Ritto (by Arctic Tern), finished second in the Cesarewitch as a three-year-old. The others—Lemon Souffle (by Salse), Melpomene (by Lear Fan), Quiet Week-End (by Town And Country), Kiya (by Dominion) and Aeschylus (by Troy)—were, like Caramba, much sharper individuals. Lemon Souffle was top-rated two-year-old filly in 1993. Although sustaining a nasty-looking leg injury in the Cheveley Park Stakes she was able to return in 1994 to win the Falmouth Stakes (Caramba made it three in a row in the race for her owner and trainer, following Niche and Lemon Souffle), and fetched 400,000 guineas at the December Sales the same year; Lemon Souffle was in training for part of the latest season but never ran. Caramba herself has been retained. A tall filly, she acts well on top-of-the-ground; the Vermeille is her only race on ground easier than good. *R. Hannon*

CARBURTON 2 b.c. (Feb 25) Rock City 120 – Arminda (Blakeney 126) [1995 6.1d^3 7.1s* 7m* Oct 21] strong, well-made colt: has plenty of scope: third foal: half-brother to French 6f to 7.5f winner Bold And Black (by Never So Bold): dam unraced: progressive colt: won maiden at Haydock (made all, comfortably held Crystal Falls by ½ length) and nursery at Doncaster (ridden along some way out then ran on well final 300 yds to beat Angel Chimes ¾ length) in October: will be suited by 1m+: acts on good to firm ground and soft: sure to improve again and win more races. *J. A. Glover*

91 p

CARE AND COMFORT 3 ch.f. Most Welcome 131 – Whipp's Cross 93 (Kris 135) [1994 NR 1995 6d^6 6.9g 8g 8g^4 9.7m 8d^6 8m* 7f^4 a8.5g 8m 8.2m 9m Oct 27] unfurnished filly: second foal: dam, 1¼m and 11f winner, is half-sister to very useful middle-distance stayer Glowing With Pride: modest performer: won claimer (claimed out of G. Wragg's stable £10,000) at Newmarket in July: failed to repeat that form: should prove at least as effective at 1¼m as 1m: acts on good to firm ground, tailed off on all-weather: visored (saddle slipped) tenth start. *K. McAuliffe*

64 d

CAREFUL (IRE) 2 gr.f. (Mar 6) Distinctly North (USA) 115 – Caring (Crowned Prince (USA) 128) [1995 5m 6m 7g 6g^4 7s^4 6.1s Oct 17] IR 32,000Y: tall, lengthy filly: has a quick action: has scope: eighth foal: half-sister to useful middle-distance performer Bishop's Ring (by Northfields): dam unraced half-sister to good Italian filly Godzilla, dam of 4 useful-or-better performers, notably Observation Post: modest form: best effort when over 2 lengths fourth of 13 to Lunar Mist in nursery at Haydock: should stay 7f: seems unsuited by soft ground. *B. W. Hills*

59 +

CARFAX 10 ch.g. Tachypous 128 – Montana Moss (Levmoss 133) [1994 –: a16g 16.4s^4 a16g 1995 a16.2g^3 a16g May 27] lengthy gelding: probably no longer of much account. *R. P. C. Hoad*

–

CARIAD FFOL 3 b.f. Jupiter Island 126 – Tearful Reunion (Pas de Seul 133) [1994 NR 1995 a12g Jul 17] 600F: first foal: dam poor maiden: tailed-off last in maiden at Wolverhampton. *B. J. Llewellyn*

–

CARIBBEAN DANCER 2 b.f. (Feb 14) Shareef Dancer (USA) 135 – Deposit 73 (Thatch (USA) 136) [1995 7g 8.2m^4 Oct 19] smallish, angular filly: seventh foal: half-sister to 3-y-o Dtoto (by Mtoto) and Ebor winner Deposki (by Niniski): dam, second at 6f at 2 yrs, won in West Indies: similar form in maidens won by Sil Sila at Warwick and Dushyantor at Nottingham later in month: will be suited by middle distances. *M. R. Stoute*

60

CARIBBEAN EXPRESSO (IRE) 2 b.f. (Feb 24) Soviet Lad (USA) 94 – She Is The Boss (Skyliner 117) [1995 6m Jun 23] 6,500Y: lengthy, unfurnished filly: fourth foal: dam, Irish 5f winner, sister to Blyton Lad: 33/1 and carrying condition, no promise in maiden at Newmarket: unimpressive to post. *B. Hanbury*

–

CARIBBEAN QUEST 2 b.f. (Apr 3) Rainbow Quest (USA) 134 – Jammaayil (IRE) 80 (Lomond (USA) 128) [1995 8m* 8d Oct 1] smallish, unfurnished filly: fluent mover: first foal: dam, 7f and 7.1f winner at 2 yrs, half-sister to smart 6f (at 2 yrs) to 10.5f winner Optimistic Lass, also fourth in Oaks and dam of Golden Opinion: 6/1, impressive winner of maiden at Leicester in September by 5 lengths from Fijon: slowly away and never dangerous, eased when beaten, when last of 11 in Prix Marcel Boussac at Longchamp month later: will do better. *B. Hanbury*

85 p

CARIBBEAN SURFER (USA) 6 b.g. Summing (USA) – Caribbean Surfing (USA) (Northjet 136) [1994 NR 1995 9m^6 10.9g 11.9d 15.1s Nov 2] leggy gelding: first reported foal: dam lightly-raced maiden in USA: poor winning 2m hurdler: bandaged, no promise in varied company. *J. S. Goldie* –

CARICATURE (IRE) 2 b.g. (Mar 10) Cyrano de Bergerac 120 – That's Easy (Swing Easy (USA) 126) [1995 5.2m^2 5.3f^3 6g^4 5m^2 5m^6 6m^3 6m* Sep 6] IR 9,000F, 23,000Y: sturdy gelding: half-brother to 6f (at 2 yrs) and 1½m winner Maestroso (by Mister Majestic) and two 2-y-o winners in Ireland: dam Irish 9f winner: won maiden at Epsom in September by head from The Man, making most and rallying well: stays 6f: has raced only on a sound surface: blinkered last 2 starts. *G. Lewis* 84

CARLING (FR) 3 b.f. Garde Royale 120 – Corraleja (FR) (Carvin 127) [1994 103p: 7g^3 8g* 7.5s* 8s* 1995 8d^3 8d^2 10.5m* 8g 12d* 12d 12f Nov 26] 119

Close rivalry between the three-year-old fillies Carling and Matiara, and their respective camps, enlivened the French season. Honours ended even for the year, two-all and a classic apiece, the Prix de Diane Hermes for Carling, the Dubai Poule d'Essai des Pouliches for Matiara. Both classics were well contested and their winners well up to standard. For her part, Carling was a much better filly than the results of runs against the colts in the Prix de l'Arc de Triomphe and the Japan Cup might suggest.

The Prix de Diane became something of a needle match as a result of controversy arising from the Pouliches on which the French Jockey Club met to rule on June 8th, only three days before the Diane was due to be run. Three weeks back a rough race for the Pouliches had ended in Matiara's hanging on by a nostril from a strong-finishing Carling. The Longchamp stewards had then allowed the result to stand after an inquiry, in the course of which they interviewed five of the riders involved but not the rider of Carling, Thierry Thulliez. Carling's trainer appealed against the stewards' decision to the French Jockey Club, alleging that when Matiara had been switched for a run in the straight she had indirectly caused interference to Carling. In support of the argument the trainer pointed out on a video recording of the

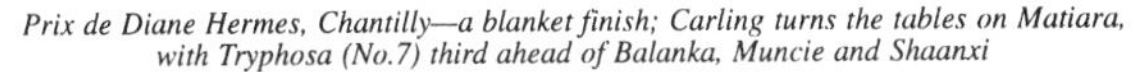

Prix de Diane Hermes, Chantilly—a blanket finish; Carling turns the tables on Matiara, with Tryphosa (No.7) third ahead of Balanka, Muncie and Shaanxi

Prix de l'Opera of 1994 what she claimed was a similar incident, the one that led to the disqualification of Erin Bird. On top of this, Carling's connections disputed the judge's interpretation of the Pouliches' photo-finish. The rulings went against Carling a second time: the appeal commission confirmed the Pouliches result. They also added four-day suspensions to Freddie Head (rider of Matiara), Olivier Peslier (on third-placed Shaanxi) and Cash Asmussen (on unplaced Piquetnol), who had all been in the thick of the action. Justice was done to Matiara: promoting Carling on anything to be seen in running would have been a travesty.

By the time the Diane was due to be decided it had become clear that there was next to nothing between the two fillies at up to a mile. They had first met in the Prix des Reservoirs at Longchamp as two-year-olds, when Carling had come out on top by a length. And they had met again on their reappearance in the spring in the Prix de la Grotte, a classic trial at Longchamp which Matiara had won by a neck and a length from Shaanxi and Carling. Carling looked more the staying type, and she started the shorter over the extra two and a half furlongs at Chantilly, second favourite to the unbeaten Prix Saint-Alary winner Muncie. Shaanxi and the unlucky Pouliches seventh Vadlamixa reopposed, while the Musidora second Caramba and the German Guineas winner Tryphosa gave the twelve-runner line-up an international flavour. The good to firm ground posed an additional question about the outcome. In the end neither distance nor ground made much difference to the two main rivals. They ran to form, Carling prevailing by a neck with Matiara the one making inroads in the closing stages. Despite a pacemaker, the field was still well bunched when Carling, attended by Matiara, was set alight from near the front halfway up the straight. Carling quickened appreciably the better and went clear before Matiara began to pull her back.

The Diane field was still bunched at the finish, right down past Tryphosa, Balanka, Muncie, Shaanxi, Caramba, Garden Rose (whose irons broke early on) and Loretta Gianni to Vadlamixa in tenth. But they were mostly goodish fillies in there, and the race had much more strength in depth than its Epsom counterpart. Most of the field continued to run well. Next port of call for some of them was Deauville in August: Carling went for the Jacques le Marois there, finishing last, while Matiara won the much easier Prix de la Nonette in a three-way photo. Carling, who had never disappointed before, was afterwards found to have some displaced vertibrae. Her rider eased up when all chance had gone. The injury can't have been too serious for Carling was out again four weeks later at Longchamp on trial for the Arc in the Prix Vermeille, back to top form, too. She produced her turn of foot to slip into the lead through a gap near the rails early in the straight, then proceeded to hold on gamely from a line of strong finishers in a steadily-run race. Matiara came fourth, beaten about a length and a half after being boxed in for much of the straight. Carling had done her Arc chances no harm, but perhaps the result provided more of a pointer to the prospects of Pure Grain who had beaten the Vermeille second and third, Valley of

Prix Vermeille, Longchamp—
Carling holds on from Sheikh Mohammed's pair Valley of Gold and Larrocha (No.2)

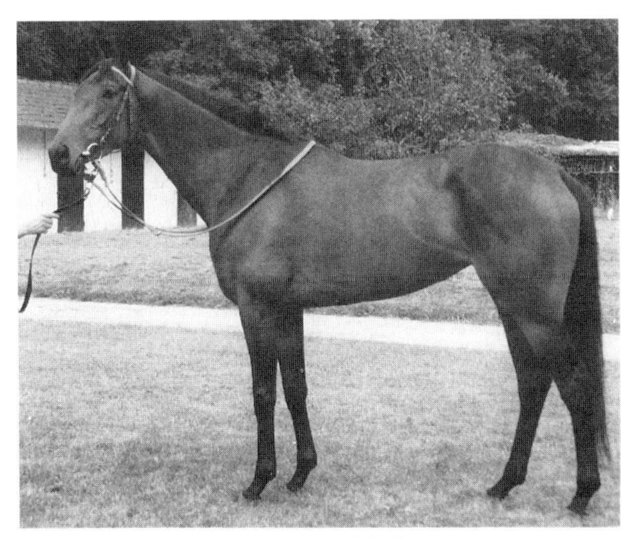

Teruya Yoshida's "Carling"

Gold and Larrocha, hollow in the Irish Oaks. Besides, Carling wasn't certain to benefit from the stiffer test of stamina the Arc seemed likely to provide.

Carling had a new owner by Arc time. She'd been sold by her breeders Ecurie Delbart for a reported 5,500,000 francs (around £700,000) to another of the stable's patrons Teruya Yoshida and carried the White Muzzle colours in the big race. She carried them without much distinction, giving the impression that the stiffer test of stamina did not suit, failing to accelerate from a good position on the home turn and finishing well held in eighth place behind Lammtarra. However, she hampered herself badly by refusing to settle early on. Carling ran a better race behind Lando in the Japan Cup at Tokyo in November but again was noticeably one-paced. Having been well placed on the inside in the straight she couldn't mount an effective challenge and dropped away from well over a furlong out, into eleventh-of-fourteen spot, around nine lengths behind the winner.

Carling (FR) (b.f. 1992)	Garde Royale (br 1980)	Mill Reef (b 1968)	Never Bend
			Milan Mill
		Royal Way (gr 1969)	Sicambre
			Right Away
	Corraleja (FR) (b 1982)	Carvin (b 1962)	Marino
			Coraline
		Darling Dale (b 1976)	Tyrant
			Treat

Matiara has the edge on Carling on pedigree although Carling's sire, the Prix Jean de Chaudenay winner Garde Royale, is a son of Mill Reef and a grandson of the Pouliches winner Right Away. The story of how Carling came to be bred was told and retold during the season. It is one of those stories that explains why hope springs eternal. In short—Carling's dam Corraleja was born with contracted tendons and such bad joints that she wasn't broken in until four years old; on her only racecourse appearance she finished down the field in a wintertime Cagnes-sur-Mer sprint at five. Given away to cereal farmer Jean Delbart, she was sent the same year on trial to a little-used stallion called Irkoust, who got her in foal. The foal was normal—as Laurielle she went on to win twice in France as a two-year-old—so Corraleja has been covered regularly since, and has three more named offspring, two of whom, the sisters Garling and Carling, have reached the racecourse. Garling, like Laurielle, was raced hard. She also won twice in France, in minor events over seven furlongs at two years and over a mile and a quarter at four. Corraleja's dam Darling Dale, Irish-bred out of the sprint handicapper Treat, was a 1,750-guinea Goffs yearling. She showed fair form in France, in winning three races at up to a mile.

Carling's emergence in this ordinary family should be a boost for her sire, whose fee at the Haras du Pin when she was conceived was only 4,000 francs plus 8,000 francs (October 1st) for thoroughbreds—a peppercorn £1,200 at 1991 exchange rates. As a racehorse Garde Royale was a late-maturing staying type who never got the chance to tackle further than a mile and a half. He has been given much of the credit for Carling, probably rightly so, but his daughter hasn't taken entirely after him. Although she is a Prix Vermeille winner there is still a slight doubt about her complete effectiveness at a mile and a half in a strongly-run race against the best. A filly with a good turn of foot, the leggy Carling acts on good to firm ground and soft. She is a genuine sort. *Mme Pat Barbe, France*

CARLITO BRIGANTE 3 b.g. Robellino (USA) 127 – Norpella 95 (Northfields (USA)) [1994 NR 1995 7.1m 8.5m 7.1m4 8m 8g4 10m3 10m5 10.3f* 9h* 11.9m 10.3d 8.1g 10.5s 8.9g2 Oct 7] 23,000Y: good-bodied gelding: has scope: fourth live foal: half-brother to 3 winners, including useful miler Ultimo Imperatore (by Cadeaux Genereux): dam 1¼m and 1½m winner who stayed 14.8f: fair performer: won handicap at Doncaster and minor event at Newcastle in the summer: form afterwards only when good staying-on second of 25 in £11,600 event at York: should stay further than 10.3f: acts on hard ground, below form on a soft surface: held up. *Mrs J. R. Ramsden* — 72

CARLOWITZ (USA) 7 b.g. Danzig (USA) – Aunt Carol (USA) (Big Spruce (USA)) [1994 49, a63: a12g* a13g4 11.9g2 a16g 12m 11.9f 11.5g6 a12g a12g5 a10g 1995 a13g* a13g5 a12g Jan 21] big gelding: modest performer: won selling handicap at Lingfield in January by 10 lengths: refused to race final start, then sold 1,250 gns Ascot February Sales: twice refused to race over hurdles for Mrs J. Sidebottom: stays 13f: acts on equitrack, possibly unsuited by soft ground: blinkered (soundly beaten) once as 6-y-o: not one to rely on. *A. Moore* — – § a63 §

CARMARTHEN BAY 2 ch.c. (Apr 12) Prionsaa 76 – Pattie's Grey 71 (Valiyar 129) [1995 6m 8.1s 6.1m3 a6g* Dec 14] neat colt: first reported foal: dam 6f winner: trained on debut by R. Emery: much improved effort when winning maiden at Lingfield in December by 8 lengths and 6 lengths: will stay beyond 6f: clearly goes very well on equitrack. *G. L. Moore* — 63 a83

CARMENTALIA 2 b.f. (Feb 4) Formidable (USA) 125 – Carmen's Joy 72 (Chief Singer 131) [1995 6g3 a7g* 8f* 8m5 8g4 8d4 8f5 Oct 16] strong, lengthy filly: has plenty of scope: first foal: dam, 2-y-o 5f winner, from family of El Gran Senor: won maiden at Southwell and nursery at Ayr in the summer: ran creditably in nurseries but well below form in listed race final start: suited by 1m: acts on firm and dead ground and fibresand: tail flasher: sold 58,000 gns Newmarket Autumn Sales to Saudi Arabia. *Sir Mark Prescott* — 81

CARMOSA (USA) 2 ch.f. (May 13) Blushing John (USA) 120 – Bobbinette (Whitstead 125) [1995 6g6 7.1s a7g4 a6g3 Dec 2] $25,000Y: lengthy filly: half-sister to 2 minor winners in USA by Polish Navy: dam, minor winner in USA, half-sister to smart 8.5f to 1¼m winner Acaroid: sixth of 14 to Rouge Rancon in maiden at Newmarket in July: failed to repeat that form, in seller final start: will stay beyond 7f: seems unsuited by soft ground, better all-weather form on equitrack: sold 7,000 gns Newmarket December Sales (has joined D. Nicholls). *W. Jarvis* — 65 a55

CARNBREA BELLE (IRE) 3 ch.f. Kefaah (USA) 124 – Bright Landing 78 (Sun Prince 128) [1994 –: 7g 7g 1995 7d 9.7m2 8.3g5 14.1m3 12g2 14.1g* 12f* 11.7h2 16.2m* 16m* 16.5f* 16.1m5 16.4f4 16d5 Sep 11] sturdy filly: unimpressive mover: fair handicapper: successful at Yarmouth, Carlisle (amateurs), Chepstow, Lingfield and Doncaster (amateurs), within about 6 weeks in mid-summer: stays 2m: — 76 acts on hard ground, probably on dead: held up: has swished tail and hung left, but seems genuine. *M. Bell*

CARNEGIE BLUE 4 b.f. Hallgate 127 – Penumbra 99 (Wolver Hollow 126) – [1994 –: a8.5g 1995 10m a5g 5.7h5 Aug 3] leggy, sparely-made filly: no form after 2 yrs: tried blinkered: dead. *A. J. Chamberlain*

CARNEGIE (IRE) 4 b.c. Sadler's Wells (USA) 132 – Detroit (FR) 131 (Riverman (USA) 131) [1994 129: 10v* 10.5v2 10.5m5 10m* 10m* 12d* 12g* 1995 12f5 12d* 12g6 12d* 12d6 12s3 Oct 28] 129

The 1994 Prix de l'Arc de Triomphe winner Carnegie has been retired to stud in Japan. The decision to keep him in training as a four-year-old was not so well rewarded as was anticipated at the time of that victory, gained on his first start in a Group 1 race, and he was not seen at his very best until on his final appearance, when third in the Breeders' Cup Turf at Belmont Park in late-October. By then he had won another of France's major races, the Grand Prix de Saint-Cloud, but had been denied his main objectives, the King George VI and Queen Elizabeth Diamond Stakes and a second Arc.

Carnegie's season got off on the wrong foot when a set-back in mid-April forced him to miss the Prix Ganay. In the circumstances it wasn't too discouraging to see him beaten in the Coronation Cup on his return, especially as the ground at Epsom rode much firmer than he had encountered before. He met three of the four who beat him that day—Sunshack, Only Royale and Tikkanen—in the Grand Prix de Saint-Cloud three weeks later, on good to soft going. And on this occasion none of them gave him as much trouble as the improving three-year-old Luso, the Chester Vase and Derby Italiano winner, astutely ridden by Ray Cochrane. Despite the presence of pacemaker Citizen Darnet, in on behalf of Tikkanen, the race was steadily run. Carnegie settled in third place behind Citizen Darnet and Luso, followed by Tot Ou Tard, Sunshack, Solid Illusion, Tikkanen and Only Royale. The last-named had moved up steadily into fourth by the home turn, where Sunshack had lost ground. Entering the short straight Luso was dashed into the lead and got first run, but Carnegie managed to pull back the four lengths or so required, quickening well under pressure to challenge inside the final furlong and get up by a short neck near the line. Only Royale kept staying on for third, ahead of Tikkanen, set plenty to do, and Sunshack. Carnegie landed the stable its fourth Grand Prix de Saint-Cloud in eight years. The same afternoon his owner and trainer won the Irish Derby with Winged Love, a son of their 1990 Grand Prix winner In The Wings.

Fabre sent both Carnegie and Winged Love on to Ascot for the King George. Winged Love acquitted himself well there but Carnegie finished only sixth of seven

Grand Prix de Saint-Cloud—Carnegie pulls back Luso near the line, with Only Royale staying on

Prix Foy, Longchamp—an Arc winner versus an Irish Derby winner, and an unusual view of the finish

behind Lammtarra, which was disappointing in view of his recent run even though he was beaten little more than three lengths. He never looked likely to play a part; when he came under pressure before the turn he couldn't quicken. However, Carnegie put himself back into the Arc reckoning with a win in the Prix Foy over the course and distance in September. Despite its shortcomings as a trial—very small field, sprint finish, slow time—there was encouragement to be had from the performances in the race of both Carnegie and Balanchine whom he held by a short head, neither ridden right out, understandably. Three weeks later Carnegie finished only sixth in the Arc, Balanchine only tenth. Carnegie was beaten over twice as far by Lammtarra as at Ascot and looked nothing like the horse that had held off Hernando, Apple Tree, Ezzoud and Bright Moon twelve months back. Although everything seemed in his favour Carnegie failed to quicken in the straight. He lost his action, reportedly finished very sore, stiff in the shoulders, and the announcement that he had run his last race came as no surprise. Happily, a change of plan allowed him to bow out on a different note in the Breeders' Cup Turf, in which he showed prominently throughout and came a clear third of thirteen, a neck and one and a half lengths behind Northern Spur and the Arc second Freedom Cry. He ran on lasix for the first time.

Carnegie (IRE) (b.c. 1991)	Sadler's Wells (USA) (b 1981)	Northern Dancer (b 1961)	Nearctic
			Natalma
		Fairy Bridge (b 1975)	Bold Reason
			Special
	Detroit (FR) (br 1977)	Riverman (b 1969)	Never Bend
			River Lady
		Derna II (b 1961)	Sunny Boy III
			Miss Barberie

Carnegie's covering fee has been announced as equivalent to 45,000 dollars. While set to be managed in Japan by the JS Company he is in the ownership of Darley Stud Management and his arrival on such terms may mark the beginning of a significant expansion in Arab interests there. The Japanese breeding industry is already a strong one, its stock upgraded in recent years by a steady intake of top-class animals from overseas, including Arc winners Dancing Brave, Carroll House and the

Sheikh Mohammed's "Carnegie"

highly successful Tony Bin. Carnegie himself could be said to have been bred to win an Arc, by Sadler's Wells out of the 1980 winner Detroit. Two of the same breeding were also seen out in Europe in the latest season and while not reaching the same heights as their brother they did pretty well, five-year-old Wayne County raising hopes of a listed-raced win and three-year-old Honfleur achieving one. Others of note out of Detroit by different sires are the 1987 St Simon Stakes winner Lake Erie (by Kings Lake) and the 1990 Prix Guillaume d'Ornano winner Antisaar (by Northern Dancer). There is a 1994 filly by Nureyev coming along.

An attractive colt of medium build, with a short, quick action, Carnegie showed his best form at a mile and a half with give in the ground; he won twice over shorter on good to firm on his way up as a three-year-old. He could produce a good turn of foot at his best. Although he didn't quite live up to the highest expectations at four he was thoroughly genuine. *A. Fabre, France*

CAROL AGAIN 3 b.f. Kind of Hush 118 – Lady Carol 42 (Lord Gayle (USA) 124) [1994 –: 6m 5f 7.1d 1995 5g[5] 6m 7m 5g 7f Oct 3] close-coupled, angular filly: failed by long way to repeat form shown on reappearance. *N. Bycroft* 40 d

CAROL'S DREAM (USA) 3 ch.c. Risen Star (USA) – Merle Halton (USA) (Rattle Dancer) [1994 66: 8s[6] 8.1g 1995 7.1m[3] 8.3m[5] 9.9m 10f[2] 10m[2] 11.5m[2] 8m[4] Aug 19] good-bodied colt: fair maiden handicapper: probably stays 11.5f: acts on firm ground. *J. W. Hills* 75

CAROMANDOO (IRE) 7 b.g. Simply Great (FR) 122 – Tanimara (Sassafras (FR) 135) [1994 NR 1995 12.5g 12.1m Jul 13] big, angular gelding: modest winning hurdler in 1992/3: of no account on flat. *A. Barrow* – §

CARONDRA 3 ch.f. Good Times (ITY) – Romany Home (Gabitat 119) [1994 –: 8d 8.3g[6] 8.1g 1995 11.1d 15m Aug 5] small filly: of no account. *R. M. McKellar* –

Keepmoat Holdings Stakes, Doncaster—Carranita has never looked in danger of defeat

CARPATHIAN 4 b.c. Danzig (USA) – Diminuendo (USA) 126 (Diesis 133) [1994 50: 10.5d^{6} 10d a8g^{6} a10g^{3} 1995 a10g^{4} a12g* 11.9f* 11.6g^{6} a12g* 12m^{2} 11.9f* 11.6m^{2} 12m a12g* Oct 14] small, good-bodied colt: fair handicapper: successful at Lingfield in January, Brighton in May, at Southwell and Brighton in the summer and at Wolverhampton in October: should stay 1¾m: goes well on the all-weather and firm ground: consistent: sold 13,000 gns Newmarket December Sales. *Lord Huntingdon* — 64 a69

CARRANITA (IRE) 5 b.m. Anita's Prince 126 – Take More (GER) (Frontal) [1994 103: 6m 6s* 6m 6d^{4} 7.1g* 6d 8g^{3} 7d* 7s^{4} 6v^{6} 1995 7.1g^{4} 7.1g^{2} 7.3g^{4} 7g 6g* 6d 6d 6m* Nov 4] leggy, angular mare: has a markedly round action: useful performer: won minor event at Yarmouth in September and listed race at Doncaster (quickened steady pace soon after halfway, held Branston Abby by 1¼ lengths) in November: stays 7.1f: acts on good to firm and soft ground: normally held up. *B. Palling* — 106

CARROLLS MARC (IRE) 7 b.g. Horage 124 – Rare Find (Rarity 129) [1994 56: a14.8g^{4} a14.8g* a14.8g* a14.8g^{2} a16.2g a12g* 12.1f^{3} a14.8g^{3} a12g* a14.8g^{4} a16.2g^{4} a12g^{4} a12g a12g 1995 a16.2g^{3} a14.8g^{4} a14.8g^{5} a12g Dec 12] angular gelding: poor mover: modest performer: left P. Haslam's stable after third start: off course 11 months, well beaten on return: stays 2m: acts on good to firm (possibly not firm) ground, dead and fibresand. *C. Murray* — 51

CARTE BLANCHE 4 b.f. Cadeaux Genereux 131 – Granny's Bank 88 (Music Boy 124) [1994 48: 7d 7s^{4} 8m 7g 8m 1995 a6g^{3} a8g* a10g^{6} 7.6m^{6} 9f a8g* a8.5g a9.4g^{6} Aug 19] good-topped, workmanlike filly: fair performer on the all-weather: won maiden at Lingfield in February and minor event at Southwell (easily best effort) in August: best form at 1m: acts on the all-weather, probably (though only poor form) on any turf going. *C. A. Cyzer* — – a67

CARWYN'S CHOICE 2 b.f. (Apr 9) Then Again 126 – Over My Head (Bay Express 132) [1995 7.1d 6g 7g 10g a5g Dec 18] tall, lengthy filly: first foal: dam well beaten: no sign of ability: usually slowly away. *P. C. Clarke* — –

CASCADIA (IRE) 2 br.f. (Mar 10) Caerleon (USA) 132 – Flood (USA) (Riverman (USA) 131) [1995 5m^{3} May 1] useful-looking filly: fourth foal: closely related to a winner in Japan by Shadeed and half-sister to 1½m winner Mr Flood (by Al Nasr): dam 6f winner from family of Generous and Triptych: 5/2 and very green, close third of 9 to Anotheranniversary in minor event at Windsor, hampered start: bred to stay at least 1m: looked sure to improve. *P. F. I. Cole* — 74+

CASHMERE LADY 3 b.f. Hubbly Bubbly (USA) – Choir (High Top 131) [1994 NR 1995 7g^2 8m^3 a8.5g* a7g* Dec 2] seventh foal: half-sister to several winners, including fairly useful 5-y-o Celestial Choir (by Celestial Storm) and Choral Sundown (at up to 10.2f, by Night Shift): dam behind in 4 races: favourite, won maiden event (made most, impressively) and handicap (came from behind, by neck), both at Wolverhampton late in year: stays 8.5f: capable of better and will win more races. *J. L. Eyre* — 75 p

CASHMIRIE 3 b.f. Domynsky 110 – Betrothed (Aglojo 119) [1994 –: 6g 7s 1995 8.1f^2 10m^2 9.2m^5 12f^4 10.5m* 10m^4 a14g^5 a12g^5 Nov 27] angular filly: bad mover: poor performer: won claimer at Haydock in August: should stay beyond 1¼m: acts on firm ground, well beaten on all-weather: saddle slipped fourth outing. *J. L. Eyre* — 46

CASHTAL LACE 2 ch.f. (Apr 22) Ballacashtal (CAN) – Chantilly Lace (FR) 69 (Carwhite 127) [1995 5f^6 6.1g May 29] smallish, close-coupled filly: first reported foal: dam 2-y-o 6f winner who stayed 3m over hurdles: tailed off in maiden and seller. *S. G. Knight* — –

CASINO CHIP 2 br.c. (Apr 12) Daring March 116 – Important Guest 53 (Be My Guest (USA) 126) [1995 7g a6g Nov 8] second foal: dam, ran 4 times, bred to stay middle distances: well beaten in maiden and claimer at Lingfield in autumn. *T. T. Clement* — –

CASK 3 br.f. Be My Chief (USA) 122 – Premiere Cuvee 109 (Formidable (USA) 125) [1994 NR 1995 7d* 8m^3 8m^4 8f* 9g^6 10f^2 10g Oct 1] 42,000Y: good-topped, well-made filly: fourth foal: half-sister to fairly useful performers Mapengo (at 1m, by Salse) and Ponsardin (at up to 7f, by Petoski): dam, sprinter, best at 4 yrs when sent to France: won maiden at Leicester in April and rated stakes (led on line) at Ascot in June: ¾-length second of 9 to Ellie Ardensky in listed race at Salisbury on final start for J. Gosden: tailed off in allowance event at Belmont final start: stays 1¼m: acts on firm and dead going. *C. Clement, USA* — 99

CASNIC (IRE) 2 b.f. (Apr 23) Petorius 117 – Romfaea (USA) (Alleged (USA) 138) [1995 a7g Sep 16] IR 3,500F, IR 1,600Y: half-sister to a winner in Italy by Posen: dam half-sister to Derby third Mashkour: 25/1, tailed off in seller at Wolverhampton. *C. A. Smith* — –

CASPER'S RISK 3 ch.g. Risk Me (FR) 127 – Trip The Daisey 53 (Touching Wood (USA) 127) [1994 54, a67: 5d 6m a7g* 7d^5 7.3s a6g a7g^6 a6g* a7g a7g 1995 7g 6s 6.1g a6g^3 a6g^2 May 4] big, lengthy gelding: modest performer: stays 7f: acts on fibresand, best turf efforts on a soft surface: blinkered: sold (D. Nicholls to T. Dyer) 1,000 gns Newmarket July Sales. *D. Nicholls* — 47 a57

CASPIAN GOLD 4 ch.g. Clantime 101 – Parijoun (Manado 130) [1994 65: a5g^5 a7g* a6g^4 a6g^4 a7g^4 1995 6m 7m May 19] good-topped gelding: modest performer at best: seems no longer of much account. *C. N. Allen* — –

CASSIMERE 3 ch.f. Clantime 101 – Poshteen 86 (Royal Smoke 113) [1994 NR 1995 6.1d^5 6m^6 Oct 28] half-sister to winning stayer/hurdler Capa (by New Member) and to dam of speedy Cape Merino: dam 2-y-o 5f winner: well beaten in minor events at Chepstow and Newmarket (ran as if something amiss) 18 days later. *Major D. N. Chappell* — –

CAST A FLY (IRE) 2 b.f. (Mar 15) Cyrano de Bergerac 120 – Leaping Salmon (Salmon Leap (USA) 131) [1995 7m Sep 5] third foal: dam, well beaten all 5 starts in Ireland, half-sister to useful 1977 Irish 2-y-o Do The Hustle: 100/1 and reluctant to post, distant last in maiden at Lingfield. *M. P. Muggeridge* — –

CASTAN (IRE) 2 b.g. (Apr 16) Persian Bold 123 – Erzsi 80 (Caerleon (USA) 132) [1995 5m^4 5m^2 6.1m 6m^3 6d 6.9m Nov 6] 32,000Y: quite attractive gelding: third reported foal: closely related to a winner in France by Persian Heights at up to 12.5f and half-brother to 1993 Irish 2-y-o 1m winner Broadmara (by Thatching): dam, Irish 1¼m winner, half-sister to Salieri: third of 5 in nursery at Lingfield in July: off course over 3 months afterwards, better effort on return when considerately-handled ninth of 16, never dangerous after very slow start, in nursery at Folkestone final start: will stay at least 1m: may be unsuited by a soft surface: hung badly right from halfway second start. *J. L. Dunlop* — 69

CASTEL ROSSELO 5 br.h. Rousillon (USA) 133 – On The House (FR) 125 (Be My Guest (USA) 126) [1994 88: 8m^4 8m^6 8g* 8m 7m^6 10m 8s^2 9g 8d 1995 a7g^2 — 88 a91

8g 7m^4 8m^3 7g^3 8g a6g a8g Dec 1] smallish, sparely-made horse: usually impresses in appearance: fairly useful handicapper: left S. Williams after second start, and B. McMath after sixth: off course 5 months: tailed off on return: stays 1m well: acts on good to firm and soft ground and on fibresand: usually held up. *R. Harris*

CASTLE COURAGEOUS 8 b.g. Castle Keep 121 – Peteona 97 (Welsh Saint 126) [1994 108: 14m^3 14s* 16.4d^5 16g* 13.9f* 16f^5 16d* 1995 14.1g^4 14.4m^4 13.3g^5 14.6m^6 14.5s Oct 15] leggy, angular gelding: good walker: at least useful performer: disappointing in 1995 after shaping quite well in 2 minor events in the spring: better at around 1¾m and 2m than shorter: acts on any going: held up: formerly thoroughly game and genuine. *Lady Herries* 104

CASTLE GOVERNOR 2 b.g. (Apr 13) Governor General 116 – Sorcha (IRE) (Shernazar 131) [1995 a6g 5d^6 7f Oct 3] 2,500F, IR 4,500Y: 2,000 2-y-o: sturdy gelding: first foal: dam tailed off in 2 NH Flat races: poor form in maidens and a claimer. *P. C. Haslam* 45

CASTLEREA LAD 6 b.h. Efisio 120 – Halo 51 (Godswalk (USA) 130) [1994 84: 6m 6f^5 6m^4 7m 6m^6 6g 6m 6m^6 6m 7.1g 1995 6g* 6d 6m^6 6f* 6m^5 6m* 6g^5 6f^6 6m 5f^6 6m 6m Aug 25] good-topped horse: fairly useful handicapper: mostly in good form, successful at Doncaster, Pontefract and Goodwood (second win in race) in the spring: effective at 6f and 7f: needs a sound surface: usually held up. *R. Hollinshead* 91

CASTLE SECRET 9 b.g. Castle Keep 121 – Baffle 87 (Petingo 135) [1994 –: 14f 17.2g a12g 1995 a16.2g^6 a16g^2 a12g a16g Nov 20] quite attractive gelding: fairly useful hurdler: no better than modest on flat nowadays: thorough stayer: acts on any going, except possibly soft: blinkered (ran well) earlier in career. *D. Burchell* 57

CASTLETOWN COUNT 3 b.g. Then Again 126 – Pepeke 78 (Mummy's Pet 125) [1994 54: 6m 7.5g 7m* 7.1m 7m 1995 10f 8m 10m 10.5d 12m 12m Jul 25] tall gelding: no worthwhile form in 1995. *K. W. Hogg, Isle of Man* –

CASTORET 9 b.g. Jalmood (USA) 126 – Blaskette 99 (Blast 125) [1994 77: 12d^6 12m 13.3s^3 13.9m^4 16.4m^6 13.3m^4 12g* 13.3s 1995 11.6g^4 a12g Jul 3] lengthy gelding: unimpressive mover: only a fair handicapper in 1994: fourth in claimer at Windsor on reappearance, but well beaten in minor event at Wolverhampton: stays 1¾m: acts on good to firm ground and soft: effective held up or from front. *J. W. Hills* 59+

CAST THE LINE 5 b.g. Pharly (FR) 130 – Off The Reel (USA) 81 (Silent Screen (USA)) [1994 72: 10m^2 11.8g^3 12m 10m^3 10m* 10m* 10m 1995 a11g Nov 20] good-topped gelding: has a round action: fair handicapper for A. Stewart at 4 yrs: modest winning hurdler in 1995/6, but well-beaten favourite in seller on return to flat: effective at 1¼m and 1½m: yet to race on a soft surface, acts on fibresand and firm going: blinkered/visored since fourth 4-y-o start: has won when sweating: often a front runner: genuine. *C. R. Egerton* –

CASUAL WATER (IRE) 4 b.g. Simply Great (FR) 122 – Top Nurse (High Top 131) [1994 51: 10d 8.3d 10m 12m^4 12f* 11.1m^6 13.6m 11.9g 1995 11.6m^5 12g* 12.1m* 14.9m* 14m^2 12m^2 11.9g* 12m^3 Oct 21] lengthy, angular gelding: poor mover: much improved handicapper for new stable, winning at Newmarket (lady amateurs), Chepstow and Warwick in the summer and £11,400 event at Brighton in October: best effort though unlucky in 19-runner event at Doncaster, not best of runs halfway up straight then finishing fastest: stays 14.9f: acts on firm and dead ground: visored/blinkered last 4 starts at 3 yrs: genuine and consistent. *A. G. Newcombe* 79+

CATAWAMPUS 4 ch.c. Beveled (USA) – Second Flower 50 (Indian Ruler (USA) 104) [1994 –: 7.1s 7.1f^5 6g 6g 8.2d 1995 10m 8.2m May 26] lightly-made colt: no worthwhile form. *C. James* –

CATCH A GLIMPSE (USA) 2 ch.f. (Jan 28) Gulch (USA) – Spring To Light (USA) 93 (Blushing Groom (FR) 131) [1995 6g^5 6g^3 6m^3 7m^2 7g 6g* Sep 25] first foal: dam ($800,000Y) Irish 6f and 7f winner: apparently her best effort by far when 1¾ lengths third of 10 to Danehill Dancer in Heinz 57 Phoenix Stakes at Leopardstown in August: blinkered last 2 starts, well beaten in Moyglare Stud Stakes then winning maiden at Listowel: should stay 7f: yet to to race on a soft surface. *D. K. Weld, Ireland* 103

CATCH THE LIGHTS 2 b.f. (Jan 12) Deploy 131 – Dream Chaser 92 (Record Token 128) [1995 6d^6 a8g* Nov 14] lengthy, angular filly: sixth foal: half-sister to winning sprinters Cradle Days (by Dance of Life) and Sister Susan (by Tate Gallery): 81 p dam suited by 6f: won 9-runner maiden at Lingfield in November readily by 2 lengths from Tissue of Lies: will stay further than 1m: will improve again. *R. Hannon*

CATCH THE PIGEON 6 b.m. Wonderful Surprise 93 – Cheeky Pigeon (Brave Invader (USA)) [1994 NR 1995 12m 13.8m4 10f4 11m6 Aug 23] first foal: dam poor half-sister to 2 winning hurdlers: modest form over hurdles: signs of only a little ability (awkward leaving stalls and unseated rider third start, remounted), on flat. *R. E. Barr* –

CATEMPO (IRE) 5 b.g. Cataldi 123 – Raise The Tempo (Relkino 131) [1994 NR 1995 10s 12g 10m May 12] good-topped gelding: no worthwhile form. *S. Dow* –

CATERCAP (IRE) 3 b.c. Royal Academy (USA) 130 – Catos Ridge (USA) (Cox's Ridge (USA)) [1994 NR 1995 8m 8m* 8.3m2 8m* 10.3d 10g Sep 29] 72,000F: rangy colt with scope: second foal: half-brother to fairly useful Irish 4-y-o 7f winner Miss Kristin (by Alzao): dam placed at 2 yrs: made all in Newmarket Challenge Whip in May and maiden at Pontefract (swishing tail, by short head) in August: well beaten afterwards: stays 1m: acts on good to firm ground: visored final start: sweating fourth and fifth starts: sent to Dubai. *J. H. M. Gosden* 80

CATHERINE'S CHOICE 2 ch.g. (May 1) Primo Dominie 121 – Bambolona 108 (Bustino 136) [1995 a8.5g5 Dec 2] 7,800F, 3,000Y: half-brother to several winners, including 6f to 8.9f winner Miss Haggis and 1¼m and 10.8f winner Scottish Bambi (both by Scottish Reel): dam 2-y-o 6f winner: 20/1, well-beaten fifth of 9 to Tart in maiden at Wolverhampton. *J. D. Bethell* –

CATICHE 3 b.f. Shavian 125 – Catalpa 115 (Reform 132) [1994 NR 1995 10m Apr 25] rather plain, unfurnished filly: poor mover: closely related to middle-distance winners Knifeboard and Kenanga (both by Kris) and half-sister to several winners, including Ribblesdale winner Strigida (by Habitat): dam and grandam won Ribblesdale Stakes: 8/1, seventh of 10 in maiden at Pontefract, bumped when beaten 2f out: sold 11,500 gns Newmarket December Sales. *Mrs J. Cecil* –

CATS BOTTOM 3 ch.f. Primo Dominie 121 – Purple Fan (Dalsaan 125) [1994 75: 5m* 5f4 6m5 6d4 5.3m6 5d2 5g 1995 6m4 5m4 6m6 6g 6g4 7m2 7m 7m5 10m4 7m6 6d Sep 18] angular filly: unimpressive mover: fair handicapper: lost her form after sixth start: stays 7f: acts on firm and dead ground: blinkered last 2 starts: sometimes slowly away: one to treat with caution. *D. J. S. Cosgrove* 73 d

CATUMBELLA (USA) 2 ch.f. (Apr 21) Diesis 133 – Benguela (USA) 76 (Little Current (USA)) [1995 8m3 Sep 5] lengthy filly: fourth reported foal: half-sister to fairly useful miler Naif (by Storm Bird) and a 1¼m winner in Italy by Taufan: dam (out of half-sister to Allez France) was placed at 6f here at 2 yrs and later won twice as 4-y-o in USA: 6/4 favourite, green and unimpressive to post, 6¼ lengths third of 11 to Caribbean Quest in maiden at Leicester, travelling well over 2f out but unable to quicken: will improve. *J. H. M. Gosden* 69 p

CATWALK GIRL 2 b.f. (Jan 22) Skyliner 117 – Pokey's Pet 56 (Uncle Pokey 116) [1995 5m5 6g2 7m3 7f2 7m* a7g Aug 4] 500Y: workmanlike filly: has a round action: fourth reported foal: half-sister to 3-y-o Hong Kong Designer (by Dunbeath): dam, plater, won at 7f and stayed 1m: plater: won at Catterick in July: stays 7f: soundly beaten on fibresand: visored last 3 starts. *S. G. Norton* 53

CAUSLEY 10 br.g. Swing Easy (USA) 126 – Four Lawns 77 (Forlorn River 124) [1994 68: a7g 8s* 7.5d 6.9s4 6.9v5 8d2 a7g2 8m2 a8g5 a7g2 8m3 1995 10.8f 8.1d 7d 8f Oct 23] good-topped, workmanlike gelding: a splendid performer up to end of 9-y-o season, but sold out of B. McMahon's stable only 1,050 gns Doncaster March Sales and no sign of retaining ability. *D. M. Hyde* –

CAVALIER ROYAL GEM 3 b.f. Cavalier Servente 67 – Springfield Match 45 (Royal Match 117) [1994 NR 1995 10f5 Jun 21] second foal: dam, maiden, best at up to 1¼m: 150/1, soon tailed off in Ripon maiden: sold 700 gns Doncaster September Sales. *P. Wigham* –

CAVATINA 5 br.m. Chief Singer 131 – Pennycuick 101 (Celtic Ash) [1994 72: 7.5g 7.5m5 7m 6m* 6m 6m 1995 7.5m 7g 7m 6.1d Sep 11] tall mare: no form in 1995. *T. W. Donnelly* –

CAVEAT EMPTOR (IRE) 2 b.c. (May 4) Distinctly North (USA) 115 – Ellebanna 69 (Tina's Pet 121) [1995 5m 5.3m6 6f2 5g 6m a6g 5.3d Sep 26] 6,600Y: 46

neat colt: first foal: dam sprinter: plater: well beaten in visor final start: stays 6f: acts on firm ground. *S. Dow*

CAVENDISH ROSE 4 ch.f. Music Boy 124 – Afef John (Monseigneur (USA) 127) [1994 NR 1995 7f^4 Jun 24] fourth foal: dam Irish 6f and 7f winner: 20/1, well-beaten last of 4 finishers in maiden at Ayr. *J. Berry* –

CAVERS YANGOUS 4 b.g. Daring March 116 – Rapid Lady 63 (Rapid River 127) [1994 70: a6g* 5s* 6d^2 6d^3 7m^4 6g 6m^5 6g 6m^6 1995 6v^6 6.9m^3 6g* a6g^2 6.9f^2 6m^2 6m 6g^6 7.6m 7g Aug 28] sturdy gelding: good walker: fair handicapper: won at Pontefract in June: well beaten last 2 starts: stays 7f: acts on firm and soft ground and on fibresand. *M. Johnston* 76

CAVIL 3 b.g. Reprimand 122 – Lagta 75 (Kris 135) [1994 NR 1995 8f^5 9m^5 11.5m^3 8m^2 8g 10d 10g Oct 10] robust gelding: fourth foal: half-brother to useful 1993 1¼m and 1½m winner (stayed 1¾m) Rudagi (by Persian Bold): dam 1½m and 1¾m winner: staying-on second of 8 in minor event at Yarmouth: soundly beaten otherwise: should stay beyond 1m: sold (C. Brittain to W. Clay) 13,500 gns Newmarket Autumn Sales and gelded. *C. E. Brittain* 65

CAVINA 5 b.m. Ardross 134 – Royal Yacht (USA) 65 (Riverman (USA) 131) [1994 38: 12m 13.4s^5 14.1g^5 1995 16.2m^6 14.9g a16g* 14d Sep 14] strong mare: won maiden at Lingfield in June, making virtually all and keeping on despite flashing tail: no comparable form: stays 2m: acts on equitrack: won maiden hurdle in October. *N. A. Graham* – a64

CAWDOR LADY 2 ch.f. (Mar 30) Clantime 101 – Moon Risk 62 (Risk Me (FR) 127) [1995 5m^2 5f^6 a6g 5f^4 6g Aug 7] first foal: dam twice-raced maiden half-sister to smart sprinter Jonacris: second of 5 in median auction maiden at Edinburgh on debut: no form afterwards in sellers, blinkered in nursery final start: seems not to stay 6f: tends to hang and looks a hard ride. *T. J. Etherington* 49 d

CAXTON STAR 2 ch.c. (Apr 28) Soviet Star (USA) 128 – Fiesta Fun 105 (Welsh Pageant 132) [1995 7m* Sep 5] 27,000Y: rather sparely-made colt: half-brother to useful 3-y-o Balliol Boy (by Nashwan), 8.2f winner at 2 yrs, and several other winners, including Arc winner Saumarez (by Rainbow Quest): dam, 1m and 1¼m winner, half-sister to smart 6f and 7f winner Derrylin: 7/2, bandaged in front and free to post, won 12-runner maiden at Leicester by 1½ lengths from Singing Patriarch, taking good hold and running on well to lead last ½f: almost certain to do very much better. *H. R. A. Cecil* 77 P

CAYMAN KAI (IRE) 2 ch.c. (May 6) Imperial Frontier (USA) 112 – Safiya (USA) (Riverman (USA) 131) [1995 5g* 5d^2 5f^3 5m^2 5m^4 5m^2 5d* 6f^2 Oct 12] 109

Two performances stand out in Cayman Kai's two-year-old career. In the Tripleprint Flying Childers Stakes at Doncaster in September, his penultimate outing, he accounted for a good-quality field led home by the subsequent Cornwallis winner Mubhij and the Norfolk Stakes and Prix Robert Papin winner Lucky Lionel; then in the Redcar Two-Year-Old Trophy in October, his first attempt at six furlongs, he beat all bar the Weatherbys Super Sprint winner Blue Iris to whom he was attempting to concede 5 lb. Cayman Kai was one of only two among the eight in the Flying Childers who had yet to win a pattern or listed race. Quickly off the bridle as Mubhij blazed the trail—a reversal of their roles in the Norfolk when Cayman Kai had finished second and Mubhij third—Cayman Kai gradually moved up to challenge, joined Mubhij at the furlong pole then finished much the stronger to win going away by three quarters of a length and a length and a quarter. A repeat of that performance, one of the best all year by a two-year-old over five furlongs, wasn't quite enough to see Cayman Kai follow up over the extra furlong at Redcar. After travelling smoothly Cayman Kai couldn't find any more in the last hundred yards, beaten not by the distance but by a better filly at the weights.

Although he took until the end of the season to show his best form, Cayman Kai had looked a useful prospect on his debut in a maiden at Lingfield in May where he beat Tarf readily by a length and a half. On that evidence Cayman Kai was the likely winner of a substandard National Stakes at Sandown later in the month but inexperience seemed to find him out there and Amaretto Bay took the initiative off him late on to win by three quarters of a length. Cayman Kai failed to act on the downhill gradients at Epsom when a disappointing third in his next race, but he bounced back with a cracking effort in the Norfolk at Ascot where he was always to

Tripleprint Flying Childers Stakes, Doncaster—
Cayman Kai heads Mubhij (striped cap) a hundred yards out

the fore in a race run at a furious gallop and hung on gamely to second, two and a half lengths behind his stable-companion Lucky Lionel. That effort suggested Cayman Kai would be winning again shortly but he was beaten twice more before the Flying Childers. He finished a neck behind Mubhij when the pair helped set the race up for Home Shopping in the Sino Group Dragon Trophy at Sandown in July, then ran a good second to the Irish raider Almaty, who was conceding 5 lb, in a well-contested Molecomb Stakes at Goodwood, hampered but not greatly inconvenienced by the length-and-a-half winner with a furlong to run.

Cayman Kai (IRE) (ch.c. May 6, 1993)	Imperial Frontier (USA) (ch 1984)	Lyphard (b 1969)	Northern Dancer
			Goofed
		Hartebeest (br 1974)	Vaguely Noble
			Sparkalark
	Safiya (USA) (b or br 1987)	Riverman (b 1969)	Never Bend
			River Lady
		Celerity (gr 1975)	Dancer's Image
			Calahorra

Cayman Kai's victory in the Flying Childers was the second in the race for his young sire following that of Imperial Bailiwick in 1993. Imperial Frontier, who is also the sire of the smart Irish miler Ivory Frontier, won the Somerville Tattersall Stakes over seven furlongs as a two-year-old and a minor event over a mile at three before ending up in the States where he ran three times without success. Cayman Kai, his best two-year-old so far, is the third foal from the unraced Riverman mare Safiya, who is a sister to the smart miler Sulaafah, a regular visitor to Germany in the 'eighties when he won the Moet & Chandon Zukunfts Rennen and the Badener Meile. Safiya's French-bred dam Celerity won two races in the States at around six furlongs and is a daughter of the smart French sprinter Calahorra whom readers might recall collapsing, exhausted by the heavy conditions, after finishing third to Swing Easy in the 1971 King's Stand Stakes. The lengthy Cayman Kai, who cost IR8,000 guineas as a foal and IR28,000 guineas as a yearling, is effective at five and six furlongs. He has yet to race on very soft ground but acts on any other. *R. Hannon*

CAYUMANQUE (CHI) 6 br.h. El Morgon (USA) – Recoleta (CHI) (Sun Sun) 96
[1994 a10g* a10g^2 1995 a12g* a12g^2 16.4m May 29] lengthy Chilean-bred horse: won Gran Premio Republica Argentina (Grade 1) over 12.5f as a 4-y-o and was placed in various other Grade 1 races in Chile and Argentina: raced 4 times in Dubai between November (1994) and February, winning a 3-runner handicap and a

5-runner conditions event: off course 3 months and 8/1, well-beaten last of 7 in Henry II Stakes at Sandown, ridden at halfway. *Saeed bin Suroor*

CD SUPER TARGETING (IRE) 2 ch.f. (May 6) Polish Patriot (USA) 128 – Hazy Bird (Ballymore 123) [1995 5.2m^{6} Apr 22] 12,000Y: strong filly: third reported foal: dam Irish middle-distance performer: well-backed favourite, sixth of 8 in maiden auction at Newbury in April, reportedly returning very sore. *M. R. Channon* 47 +

CEBWOB 2 br.f. (Feb 8) Rock City 120 – Island Ruler 79 (Ile de Bourbon (USA) 133) [1995 7m^{3} 7d* 7f^{3} Oct 23] small, sparely-made filly: first foal: dam, placed at up to 1½m, out of half-sister to Dominion: won median auction maiden at Redcar in September: much better form when 1¼ lengths third of 12 to Worldwide Elsie in nursery at Leicester month later, leading 2f out until well inside last: will stay at least 1m: bandaged behind last time. *P. F. I. Cole* 85

CEDAR DANCER 3 b.f. Rambo Dancer (CAN) 107 – Nonasalome (Absalom 128) [1994 41: 5d^{6} 5g^{5} 5.1m^{6} 5m^{3} 5g^{6} a7g^{5} 7.1g a6g^{3} 1995 6m^{3} 6.1g 6f 8.2m 5.1m 6f^{2} 8.1m^{5} 6g^{6} 6f Aug 17] unfurnished filly: poor handicapper: should stay beyond 6f: acts on firm ground and fibresand: inconsistent. *R. J. Hodges* 46

CEDAR GIRL 3 b.f. Then Again 126 – Classic Times 82 (Dominion 123) [1994 52: 5.1g^{6} 6.1s 5.1m^{3} 6m^{4} 6m* 7m^{6} 6g^{2} 6g^{4} a6g 1995 7f^{4} 5.7f 6m 6g^{4} 6m 6f Aug 15] unfurnished filly: poor handicapper: stays 7f: acts on firm ground (poor efforts on soft and fibresand): races prominently: inconsistent: joined Mrs N. Macauley. *R. J. Hodges* 44

CEDEZ LE PASSAGE (FR) 4 br.c. Warning 136 – Microcosme 100 (Golden Fleece (USA) 133) [1994 109: a8g* 8s^{5} 10.3m^{2} 12m^{4} 11.9m^{3} 10s 12g^{4} 10g^{5} 12v^{5} a8g^{4} 1995 a12g^{2} 12g 10m^{5} 10d^{4} 12d 10.1f^{5} 12m 10.4m 8g 10g^{4} 10m 10d^{3} 9.8m 10d^{6} Dec 2] leggy, close-coupled colt: only fairly useful performer on most form in 1995: stays 1½m: acts on firm ground, dead and fibresand: tried blinkered, no improvement. *C. E. Brittain* 95

CEE-JAY-AY 8 gr.g. Free State 125 – Raffinrula 75 (Raffingora 130) [1994 80, a61: a8.5g a8g^{6} 8m^{6} 7v* 7d^{2} 7.6m 7f 8.5g^{4} 7m 8.1g 8m^{2} a8.5g^{2} a8g^{4} 8f 8.1m^{2} 7.6g 10m^{6} 8g 8s^{3} 9g 1995 a7g^{6} 8g 10.8d 8g^{6} 8m^{3} 7.6m 8g 7g^{6} 8m^{4} 8m^{4} 7.6m^{5} a8.5g^{5} 7.6m^{4} 8f^{3} 7.6m 8d 8g^{4} 8.1g 7.1d^{2} 8m Oct 14] smallish, workmanlike gelding: usually looks well: only fair handicapper at best in 1995: stays 9f, but not 10.8f: acts on any going: blinkered (below form) once at 4 yrs: usually slowly away and sometimes badly so: unreliable. *J. Berry* 69 § a56 §

CEILIDH DANCER 4 ch.f. Scottish Reel 123 – Turtle Dove (Gyr (USA) 131) [1994 NR 1995 14f 11.4m Aug 30] smallish filly: half-sister to numerous winners by Warpath, including middle-distance stayer Path of Peace and out-and-out stayer Path's Sister: dam ran once: tailed-off last in maidens. *P. R. Hedger* –

CEILIDH (IRE) 2 b.g. (May 27) Classic Music (USA) – Pourboire 47 (Star Appeal 133) [1995 6m 7f 7.1m^{3} 7m Jul 19] IR 5,000F, 6,800Y: compact gelding: half-brother to 4 minor winners: dam stayed 15f: plater: sold (P. Haslam to M. Usher) 3,400 gns Newmarket September Sales. *P. C. Haslam* 41 +

CEILIDH STAR (IRE) 2 b.f. (Feb 14) Soviet Star (USA) 128 – Highland Ball 73 (Bold Lad (IRE) 133) [1995 7m 7d 8g^{5} Oct 10] 35,000Y: rangy, unfurnished filly: has scope: fourth foal: half-sister to Irish 1¼m winner Irrestible Lady (by Mtoto) and a winner in Italy by Ela-Mana-Mou: dam, middle-distance maiden, out of 1000 Guineas winner Full Dress II: similar form in maidens at Newmarket and Leicester (fifth of 17 to Forest Buck) and valuable restricted event (faced very stiff task) at Newmarket in between: will stay beyond 1m. *B. W. Hills* 63 +

CEIRSEACH (IRE) 2 br.f. Don't Forget Me 127 – Beparoejojo (Lord Gayle (USA) 124) [1995 6g^{5} 7m* 8m^{4} 7g 7d^{3} 8d^{3} 7g^{6} 9d^{2} Nov 12] closely related to very useful 7f (at 2 yrs) to 1¼m winner Project Manager (by Ahonoora) and half-sister Irish middle-distance winner Bold-E-Bee (by Persian Bold): dam tough and useful Irish middle-distance performer: fairly useful Irish filly: won maiden at Tipperary in August: ran most consistently in pattern races and a listed event last 5 starts: stays 9f: yet to race on extremes of going: blinkered since fourth start. *J. S. Bolger, Ireland* 94

CELANDINE 2 b.f. (Feb 8) Warning 136 – Silly Bold (Rousillon (USA) 133) [1995 6g^{3} 6m^{3} 5.7m* 6f^{4} Oct 18] leggy, quite attractive filly: has a quick action: first foal: dam 1m winner in France: won maiden at Bath in September by 4 lengths, 80 despite hanging right: fourth of 5 behind Tamhid in minor event at Yarmouth following month: stays 6f: sold 12,000 gns Newmarket December Sales. *R. Charlton*

CELCIUS 11 b.g. Ile de Bourbon (USA) 133 – Cistus 123 (Sun Prince 128) [1994 NR 1995 18.2m4 Jul 8] small, lengthy, lightly-made gelding: modest hurdler (sometimes finds little) nowadays: blinkered, poor form in maiden handicap at Chepstow on return to flat. *M. C. Pipe* — 31

CELEBRATION CAKE (IRE) 3 b.g. Mister Majestic 122 – My Louise 54 (Manado 130) [1994 57: 6g5 8d6 7.1s 1995 6g 8g* 7g3 8f3 8g3 8m6 7g 10.5s Sep 30] workmanlike gelding: modest handicapper: won 5-runner race at Ayr in June and creditable efforts there next 4 starts: stays 1m: acts on firm going, below form on soft: visored (below form) penultimate 3-y-o start. *Miss L. A. Perratt* — 63

CELERIC 3 b.g. Mtoto 134 – Hot Spice (Hotfoot 126) [1994 73p: 7m 7g6 8.2g4 8.2d6 1995 12.5f* 14.1m* 12m 13.3g* 16m2 13.9g* 14g3 Sep 29] tall, close-coupled gelding: has a quick action: progressed well into a useful handicapper: won at Warwick (idled) and Nottingham in May, Newbury in July and £8,100 event at York (produced storming finish to head Istabraq close home) in August: looked past best on final start: effective at 13f, should eventually prove even better at 2m: acts on firm ground, shaped well on dead: game and genuine: appeals strongly as one to continue improving in 1996, and looks sure to win more races. *D. Morley* — 100 p

CELESTIAL CHOIR 5 b.m. Celestial Storm (USA) 132 – Choir (High Top 131) [1994 88: a7g* a7g2 a8g a7g5 a8g 10.3g 7m 8f 8m2 8m* 8.1m2 7.5m2 8.3m2 8g6 8g* 7.6g4 8g5 8g* 8.1d* 8m4 8d 1995 a9.4g4 8g 9.9m 8g4 8m4 7m 7g3 8.1g 8.5m 7g4 9f 8m3 8m* 8m2 8d4 8g 9g5 8m 8m a8.5g2 a8g Dec 1] angular mare: fairly useful handicapper: first past post at Pontefract twice in August, disqualified (jockey found guilty of irresponsible riding) on first occasion: fifth of 39 to Cap Juluca in Cambridgeshire at Newmarket seventeenth start: finds 7f a bare minimum, and stays 9.4f: acts on good to firm and dead ground and on fibresand: blinkered twice, no improvement: has run well when sweating: suitable mount for apprentice: held up: tough, genuine and consistent. *J. L. Eyre* — 88 a80

CELESTIAL DOLLAR 4 b.g. Celestial Storm (USA) 132 – Pennies To Pounds 80 (Ile de Bourbon (USA) 133) [1994 NR 1995 11.7f5 8.1g 10m 10.2m a12g Sep 16] tall gelding: fifth foal: half-brother to 2 winners, including fair 7f winner Platinum Disc (by Song): dam 8.5f winner: trained by N. Babbage on debut: no worthwhile form. *O. O'Neill* — –

CELESTIAL FAITH 4 b.f. Celestial Storm (USA) 132 – All Gold Rose (Rheingold 137) [1994 –: a7g a8.5g 1995 a10g4 a12g6 a10g6 a13g Feb 2] seems of little account. *M. Johnston* — –

CELESTIAL FIRE 3 gr.g. Celestial Storm (USA) 132 – Fiery Gal (CAN) (Explodent (USA)) [1994 –: 8.5m 1995 12m 10g Jul 19] lengthy gelding: no promise in maidens and a claimer on flat: won juvenile hurdle in August. *J. White* — –

CELESTIAL KEY (USA) 5 br.g. Star de Naskra (USA) – Casa Key (USA) (Cormorant (USA)) [1994 103§: 6m 7d3 7.1g5 6v 7m4 7f 7m6 6m 6m 8g 6d 1995 6m 6m5 7m* 7g4 8.1g* 7m* 7g 7.6m 8f 7m3 7.9m 7m6 8d6 7d 9g 8m* a9.4g Dec 2] close-coupled, good-topped gelding: impresses in appearance: has a quick action: useful handicapper, and a reformed character: successful at Thirsk (£15,000 race), Haydock and Newbury (rated stakes) in May/June and, after running creditably in all but the most competitive events, in listed contest at Newmarket (squeezed through to short head First Island) in October: effective at 7f and 1m: acts on good to firm and heavy ground, and on fibresand: blinkered (soundly beaten) once as 4-y-o: led out unsold at 35,000 gns Doncaster November Sales: tough and consistent. *M. Johnston* — 106

CELESTIAL SISTER 2 ch.f. (Mar 25) Brotherly (USA) 80 – Lunaria (USA) (Twist The Axe (USA)) [1995 8.1m5 7m Sep 5] leggy, unfurnished filly: bad mover: eighth live foal: half-sister to 1½m winner Super Gunner (by Busted) and 5f and 6f winner Best Effort (by Try My Best): dam twice-raced half-sister to smart sprinter Abeer: tailed off in maidens at Sandown and Leicester. *C. D. Broad* — –

CELESTIAL WATERS 3 b.f. Monsanto (FR) 121 – Hopeful Waters 66 (Forlorn River 124) [1994 NR 1995 8.1d Oct 10] sixth foal: sister to a winning hurdler and half-sister to another: dam 6f and 7f winner: 66/1, last of 17 in seller at Chepstow. *A. P. James* — –

CELTIC CEILIDH 4 ch.f. Scottish Reel 123 – Show Home 90 (Music Boy 124) [1994 53: $5.1v^5$ 7m 8.2g 6.1s 7d $8d^2$ 10.1d 1995 $8s^2$ $10m^5$ 9.9m Apr 27] strong, good-topped filly: poor mover: poor performer: stays 1m well, should stay 1¼m: acts on firm and soft ground: inconsistent: joined Mrs M. Reveley. *J. Wharton* 47

CELTIC FRINGE 3 b.f. Shavian 125 – Highland Light 105 (Home Guard (USA) 129) [1994 NR 1995 $8.2m^2$ $9m^4$ 8m* 9f $10.2d^2$ 8m Oct 28] tall, lengthy filly with scope: closely related to fairly useful miler Gravette (by Kris) and half-sister to several winners, including 1½m and Italian St Leger winner Welsh Guide (by Caerleon): dam sprinter: fair form: comfortably made all in 6-runner maiden at Warwick in July: likely to prove best at up to 1¼m: acts on good to firm ground and dead: has looked awkward under pressure. *H. R. A. Cecil* 78

CELTIC SWING 3 br.c. Damister (USA) 123 – Celtic Ring 93 (Welsh Pageant 132) [1994 138: 7g* 7m* 8s* 1995 7g* $8m^2$ 12g* 12m Jul 2] 129

Dream's end came for Celtic Swing in the Budweiser Irish Derby in July. The sky-high hopes entertained for him after a memorable two-year-old career, temporarily resurrected when he made up for a narrow defeat in the Guineas by winning the Prix du Jockey-Club, were finally dashed when he returned lame from the Curragh. A near-fore knee injury—similar to that which ended the career of the 1994 Derby winner Erhaab—finished Celtic Swing for the season. Connections are reportedly hopeful that Celtic Swing will be in training as a four-year-old, though injuries involving severe knee ligament damage often spell the end of a flat-racer's career.

No horse's reappearance was awaited with greater anticipation than that of Celtic Swing, the winter favourite for both the Two Thousand Guineas and Derby. Such was the media interest in him—seldom can a racehorse have embarked on a classic campaign so drenched in superlatives—that his stable arranged a special gallop at Angmering Park, in front of seventy invited members of the racing media, ten days before the Tripleprint Greenham Stakes at Newbury in April. With the Dewhurst winner Pennekamp, rated as Celtic Swing's most serious rival in the Guineas, making an unconvincing reappearance over an inadequate trip in France, the expectations of what Celtic Swing might achieve in 1996 intensified. Celtic Swing came through the Greenham with his reputation undiminished. He seemed to idle after going clear but, essentially, did everything asked of him, only Bahri finishing within ten lengths in a useful field. Bahri's proximity to Celtic Swing in the

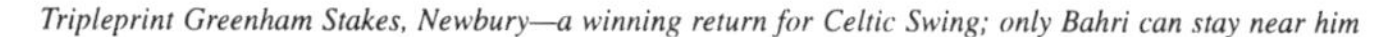

Tripleprint Greenham Stakes, Newbury—a winning return for Celtic Swing; only Bahri can stay near him

Les Emirats Arabes Unis Prix du Jockey-Club, Chantilly—
the switch to France pays off for Celtic Swing (second left, between Poliglote on the rails and Winged Love);
Classic Cliche, Flemensfirth and Diamond Mix come next

Greenham raised a question about the value of form—Bahri's subsequent third place in the Guineas confirmed that he was, as he appeared at Newbury, a much improved three-year-old—but, truth to tell, the Two Thousand Guineas looked Celtic Swing's for the taking, with the promise of even better to come when stepped up to middle distances. Celtic Swing started at 5/4-on for the Guineas, with Pennekamp and the other French-trained challenger Diffident the only others at shorter than 14/1, Bahri being one of those at that price. A narrow defeat by the confidently-ridden Pennekamp, who showed a fine burst of speed to deprive Celtic Swing of the lead inside the final furlong, destroyed the aura of invincibility that had come to surround Celtic Swing. There was, however, some unfair criticism after the Guineas. To say, or suggest, as some did, that Celtic Swing had been 'firmly put in his place by Pennekamp' was nonsense. Celtic Swing, for the first time in his career, was unable to put daylight between himself and his rivals when given the office over two furlongs out; but, to his credit, he rallied after being caught by Pennekamp and was inching back, still a head down, as the post was reached. Though the Guineas exposed a chink in Celtic Swing's armour—showing him vulnerable over a mile on top-of-the-ground to a top-class horse with a turn of foot—the margin of Pennekamp's victory was only a head and Celtic Swing gave every indication that he would leave his Guineas form behind when he got more of a test of stamina. The immediate prospect of a mouth-watering rematch in the Derby was, however, dashed by an announcement the day after the Guineas that connections were seriously considering switching Celtic Swing to Chantilly for the Prix du Jockey-Club. There had been concern about ground conditions in the week leading up to the Guineas and the owner's racing manager had been quoted as saying that 'If the ground came up firm there might have to be a rethink...his main target is the Derby'. Now, with defeat, and the fears about firm ground, the idea of Epsom seemed suddenly less appealing. There was also talk in the Celtic Swing camp of 'the hill at Epsom not being ideal for him', though jockey Kevin Darley said 'He's such a free-travelling sort of horse that he would handle coming down the hill if the ground was decent'. Owner Peter Savill, who kept his options open until the latest possible moment before supplementing him for Chantilly, shared that view, declaring 'All I can say is that if it were absolutely certain the ground would have cut in it he would be there on Derby Day'.

Condemnation of the decision to by-pass the Derby, Celtic Swing's prime target thoughout the winter, was strong. The *Racing Post* carried a simple three-line headline on its front page 'Sad, Mad, Bad' over an article by its bloodstock editor

Tony Morris. Morris conceded that 'any owner has a perfect right to do as he chooses with his own horse, and he would be foolish not to give priority to the interests of the horse when planning his campaign'. But, as Morris pointed out, the reasons cited for the switch were factors that might have been aired during the winter and 'would presumably not have been aired at all if the head verdict against Pennekamp in the Guineas had gone the other way and had kept the Triple Crown dream alive'. Declaring that the Derby was Celtic Swing's 'one natural, logical date with destiny' Morris said that the public 'who took Celtic Swing to their hearts and willed him to be a great horse...will inevitably feel dismayed, disillusioned, even cheated by this announcement'. There was, indeed, a general feeling of anti-climax—after all, Celtic Swing had run a good Derby trial in the Guineas and would have been a leading contender at Epsom—but it wasn't the end of the world. That said, Peter Savill's decision to take the unpopular course was certainly courageous, and he confessed to feeling enormous relief when Celtic Swing crossed the line first in the Prix du Jockey-Club. Celtic Swing simply had to win to provide a vindication of sorts for the decision. As Morris concluded, after comparing the relative prestige of the two Derbys, 'Celtic Swing might have run and been beaten with honour in the Derby, but there can scarcely be defeat with honour at Chantilly'. The Prix du Jockey-Club attracted eleven runners, seven of them pattern winners, and, whilst not a vintage renewal, it was certainly wrong to dismiss the field out of hand, as some did. The most significant point about the race was that it was slowly run until the home straight, placing the emphasis on speed rather than stamina. Celtic Swing was ridden in copybook style by Darley, kept close to the pace until taking up the running, travelling well, with less than two furlongs to go. As in the Guineas, however, there was no instantaneous evidence of a gulf in ability between Celtic Swing and his chasing rivals. He didn't go clear. In fact, Celtic Swing had to be firmly pushed along as he seemed to race lazily in front—a tendency reportedly also featuring in his home work—to hold off Poliglote and the strong-finishing Winged Love by half a length and a short head, with the Dante winner Classic Cliche two lengths further away in fourth after meeting trouble in running. Celtic Swing never looked like being beaten and again gave the impression he'd do better if he got into a race which brought stamina more into play. The dream that Celtic Swing would turn out to be an outstanding champion at three was still alive, though only just. Ireland beckoned next, with talk of possibly taking in the King George VI and Queen Elizabeth II Stakes and then the St Leger before the end of the season. Prevailing firm ground at the Curragh resulted in speculation once again surrounding Celtic Swing's participation in a classic. Celtic Swing's owner walked the track at least twice in the week leading up to the Irish Derby before eventually confirming the horse as a runner, with the recently-purchased Daraydan to act as a pacemaker to guarantee that there was no repeat of the Prix du Jockey-Club. With Pennekamp side-lined through an injury sustained in the Derby and the Derby winner Lammtarra also a withdrawal, Celtic Swing started a short-priced favourite at the Curragh. He was beaten in a matter of strides early in the straight, Darley reporting 'We went from the sublime to the ridiculous. It looked all over bar the shouting just before the home turn, but for some reason he would not let himself go in the straight.' Celtic Swing was clearly not right—the race went narrowly to Winged Love who finished seven places ahead—and, at the very least, it seemed improbable that he would be risked on top-of-the-ground again. Veterinary examinations carried out on his return to England confirmed severe concussion in the knee of his near-fore and torn ligaments behind the knee; specialist opinion was that the injury could have originated in the Two Thousand Guineas and possibly affected Celtic Swing in the Prix du Jockey-Club.

So Celtic Swing's season, and possibly his career, came to an abrupt end, leaving the question: how good was he? Any attempt to justify the glowing tribute to Celtic Swing in *Racehorses of 1994* runs the risk of sounding hollow to readers who backed the horse for the Guineas and Derby on the strength of what was written. But it would be wrong to overlook it. The assessment of Celtic Swing was based mainly on his performance in the Racing Post Trophy, a race he won by twelve lengths, a record winning margin in a Group 1 race for two-year-olds in Britain. Twelve months on, it's possible to argue that the performance was overrated but, if so, it wasn't by much. Second-placed Annus Mirabilis certainly didn't let the form down, running consistently in top company as a three-year-old, the cumulative total of the distances by which he was beaten in the Dante, the Prix Jean Prat, the St James's Palace (the only race in which he was out of the first three), the Irish Derby and the Juddmonte

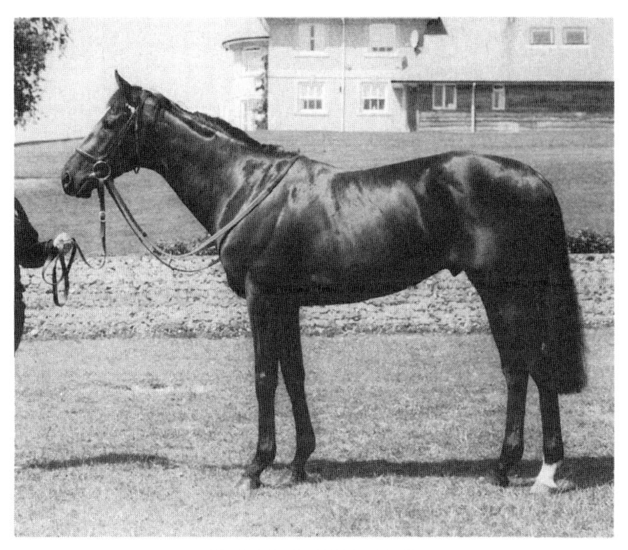

Mr P. D. Savill's "Celtic Swing"

International coming to less than the distance he was beaten by Celtic Swing at Doncaster. The Racing Post third Juyush didn't train on quite so well but confirmed himself a useful performer, while Don Corleone and Fahal were among those further down the field. There can be little doubt that Celtic Swing's performance in the Racing Post Trophy was outstanding, comparable with the best produced by a two-year-old in Timeform's experience. He didn't live up to it as a three-year-old, but by no stretch of the imagination can a horse who wins a classic and suffers a narrow defeat in another be labelled a failure. Celtic Swing was an outstanding two-year-old and a very good three-year-old. Let's hope he makes a complete recovery and is able to return to action at four.

Celtic Swing (br.c. 1992)	Damister (USA) (b 1982)	Mr Prospector (b 1970)	Raise A Native
			Gold Digger
		Batucada (b or br 1969)	Roman Line
			Whistle A Tune
	Celtic Ring (b 1984)	Welsh Pageant (b 1966)	Tudor Melody
			Picture Light
		Pencuik Jewel (b 1974)	Petingo
			Fotheringay

Celtic Swing doesn't represent the traditional ideal for a top-class performer either in appearance or pedigree. He's tall and angular, and is by the unfashionable Damister, now in Japan, out of a dam from a family best known for producing stayers. Celtic Swing's dam Celtic Ring was a fairly useful racemare, successful at a mile and a quarter and a mile and a half, and his grandam the twice-raced Pencuik Jewel was a half-sister to the Gold Cup winner Ragstone and to another good-class stayer Castle Keep, as well as to Castle Moon, the dam of St Leger winner Moon Madness, Coronation Cup winner Sheriff's Star and Goodwood Cup winner Lucky Moon. Celtic Swing may well stay beyond a mile and a half, though it's improbable that he'll be asked to do so. He acts on good to firm ground and goes extremely well on soft. *Lady Herries*

CEMAES BAY 3 b.g. Statoblest 120 – Queen And Country (Town And Country 124) [1994 63: 5m^2 7m 6m^6 5d^2 1995 5m^2 7.1m a6g^5 6m^5 6f^4 6f^4 5.1m Oct 19] small gelding: fair maiden handicapper: best at sprint distances: acts on firm and dead ground: none too consistent: sold 2,600 gns Newmarket Autumn Sales. *J. Berry* — 69

CENSOR 2 b.c. (Apr 14) Kris 135 – Mixed Applause (USA) 101 (Nijinsky (CAN) 138) [1995 8m 8.2m* Oct 26] big, lengthy colt: has plenty of scope: brother to 3-y-o Claque and 3 winners, notably high-class miler Shavian, closely related to 6f to (in Italy) 1m winner Press Gallery (by Carmelite House) and half-brother to 2 winners, notably Gold Cup winner Paean (by Bustino): dam won at up to 7f at 2 yrs: won 10-runner maiden at Nottingham by 1¾ lengths from Tasdik, leading 3f out and battling on well: will be very well suited by middle distances: should continue to progress. *H. R. A. Cecil* — 84 p

CENTAINE 3 b.f. Royal Academy (USA) 130 – Hi Lass 106 (Shirley Heights 130) [1994 6g* 8v^4 1995 8s* 8g^3 11g* 12m 10g^6 Jul 30] IR 105,000Y: first foal: dam 1½m and (easily best form) 2½m Prix Gladiateur winner: useful German filly: won maiden at Baden-Baden and fourth in Preis der Winterkonigin at 2 yrs: won listed race at Cologne in April: 1½ lengths third of 16 to Tryphosa in Arag Preis at Dusseldorf, leading briefly inside last: best effort to win 15-runner Preis der Diana at Mulheim in June by 3 lengths from Tascilla, leading over 1½f out: reportedly badly hampered in Deutsches Derby at Hamburg next start, below form in Group 1 event at Munich last time: should stay 1½m: acts on soft ground. *H. Remmert, Germany* — 109

CENTAUR EXPRESS 3 b.g. Siberian Express (USA) 125 – Gay Twenties 70 (Lord Gayle (USA) 124) [1994 37: 6g a7g^5 7g 8m 1995 a9.4g a11g a8g^5 10g a8.5g 10m^3 10m 10m Jun 21] neat gelding: poor maiden: stays 1¼m: sometimes bandaged behind: inconsistent. *A. L. Forbes* — 40

CENT NOUVELLES (USA) 3 ch.f. Storm Bird (CAN) 134 – Centavos (USA) (Scout Leader (USA)) [1994 –p: 6f 1995 7.6m 7f^3 Jul 29] useful-looking filly: quite well related, but (wearing rope-halter) worthwhile form only when length third of 4 in maiden at Thirsk, pulling very hard early then carrying head high: stays 7f: has raced only on top-of-the-ground: sent to USA. *J. H. M. Gosden* — 73

CENTRE STALLS (IRE) 2 b.c. (May 10) In The Wings 128 – Lora's Guest 99 (Be My Guest (USA) 126) [1995 7d* 7.3d Oct 19] IR 26,000Y: good-bodied colt: fourth foal: half-brother to 14.6f winner Nawahil (by Shirley Heights): dam, 7f winner stayed 1m, sister to On The House: won maiden at Salisbury by 3½ lengths from Crazy Chief: ran well when eighth of 9, beaten around 4 lengths, to Tumbleweed Ridge in Horris Hill Stakes at Newbury following month, every chance long way: will stay at least 1¼m. *R. F. Johnson Houghton* — 89

CENTURION 2 ch.c. (Apr 4) Presidium 124 – Missish (Mummy's Pet 125) [1995 5m^3 5g^3 5g^3 5m* 6f 5.3f^3 5m^3 5m^4 5m 5g^2 Sep 13] 7,800F, 28,000Y: close-coupled colt: third foal: brother to 3-y-o 6f winner Petomi, also winner over 7f at 2 yrs, and 4-y-o 5f performer Moscow Road: dam unraced: won 4-runner maiden at Epsom in July: creditable efforts afterwards when in frame in nurseries and (final start) claimer: best form at 5f: acts on firm ground. *R. Hannon* — 70

CEPHISTA 3 br.f. Shirley Heights 130 – Cephira (FR) (Abdos 134) [1994 61p: 6m 1995 11.9g^4 10f^2 10.2m^5 10.1m^4 a12g 13.1h Sep 4] angular filly: modest maiden handicapper: stays 1½m: has raced only on a sound surface: visored (tailed off on all-weather) fifth 3-y-o start. *P. T. Walwyn* — 61

CERBERA 6 b.g. Caruso 112 – Sealed Contract 76 (Runnymede 123) [1994 –: 7m 8m 5g 5.1g 1995 a6g Mar 18] plain gelding: no sign of ability: tried blinkered. *J. P. Smith* — –

CERDAN (USA) 2 ch.c. (Jun 5) Zilzal (USA) 137 – Vie En Rose (USA) (Blushing Groom (FR) 131) [1995 6m^3 Oct 27] $20,000Y: rather leggy, attractive colt: half-brother to 4-y-o Arzani (by Shahrastani) and 3 winners including 1m and 1¼m winner Marksmanship (by Sharpen Up): dam, half-sister to smart French 6f to 1m winner Vorias and good French miler Verria, placed twice from 8 starts in USA: 4/1 and keen to post, around ½-length third of 8 to Farhana in maiden at Newmarket, pulling hard early on then running on steadily from 2f out: bred to stay 1m: will improve. *M. R. Stoute* — 74 p

CERISE (IRE) 2 b.f. (Mar 3) Red Sunset 120 – Noble Nancy (Royal And Regal (USA)) [1995 6m^6 7f^4 6m 7g^4 7.5d 7.9m 8f^4 Oct 31] 3,000Y, 5,200 2-y-o: — 49

workmanlike filly: sister to 1m seller winner Dusky Nancy and a winner in Scandinavia and half-sister to fair 1993 2-y-o sprinter Vercingetorix (by Gallic League): dam Irish 1¾m winner: poor maiden: blinkered first time, creditable fourth of 16 to Daunting Destiny in nursery at Redcar on final outing: stays 1m: acts on firm ground, no form on dead. *C. W. C. Elsey*

CERTAIN WAY (IRE) 5 ch.h. Sure Blade (USA) 130 – Ruffling Point (Gorytus (USA) 132) [1994 –, a58: a11g^5 a9.4g^5 a8.5g a11g^6 a12g a8g a8g* 8.2m a9.4g a8g^6 a9.4g^2 a8g^3 a8g^4 a8.5g^4 a6g^4 a8g^5 a8g^2 a8g a9.4g^2 1995 a8g^2 a7g^4 a8g a9.4g a8.5g a7g* a8g a9.4g^6 a7g* Dec 12] neat, good-quartered horse: fair handicapper: won at Wolverhampton in November (minor event) and December: effective at 7f and stays 9.4f: acts on fibresand: usually visored at 2 yrs: blinkered (tailed off) third 4-y-o start: inconsistent. *N. P. Littmoden* – a66

CERTIFICATE-X 4 b.f. Never So Bold 135 – Screenable (USA) (Silent Screen (USA)) [1994 –: 6v^4 7.1d 5.1g 6.9m 1995 5g 5.7f May 22] leggy filly: well beaten since fair 2-y-o, backward in 1995. *Martyn Meade* –

CHADLEIGH LANE (USA) 3 ch.g. Imp Society (USA) – Beauty Hour (USA) (Bold Hour) [1994 57, a68: a6g^3 6.1m 6.1m^6 6s a6g^3 6s^4 a6g^2 a7g^3 a6g* 1995 a7g^5 a7g^5 a7g^2 a7g* 12.3m 8g^6 a8.5g a7g a7g a9.4g Nov 27] quite attractive gelding: fair performer: won 3-runner minor event at Wolverhampton in April: well beaten afterwards: stays 7f: acts on good to firm and soft ground, and on fibresand: has been gelded. *R. Hollinshead* – a68 d

CHADLEIGH WALK (IRE) 3 b. or br.c. Pennine Walk 120 – Safiya (USA) (Riverman (USA) 131) [1994 53: 5m 5g^2 5.1m^6 7g 6s 8s a8.5g a7g^4 a8g a8.5g a8.5g 1995 a8.5g^3 a9.4g^4 a12g a8.5g 8.1m 8.2m 8.1m Jul 4] sturdy colt: good walker: modest maiden plater: no form after reappearance: stays 8.5f: acts on good to firm ground and all-weather surfaces: tried visored: sold 700 gns Doncaster September Sales. *R. Hollinshead* 48 d

CHADWELL HALL 4 b.c. Kala Shikari 125 – Cherrywood Blessin (Good Times (ITY)) [1994 40: 7g 5g^4 a6g 5m^4 5m 5m^4 5m^5 6g 5d 1995 a6g^4 a6g* a6g^2 a6g^4 a6g^2 a5g^2 a5g* 5m^5 a5g^2 a5g^2 a5g^5 a6g^2 5.1d* 5d^3 5m^2 5f Oct 16] plain colt: has a round action: progressed into a fair handicapper for new stable: won at Wolverhampton in February and April and at Nottingham in September: effective at 5f and 6f: goes well on fibresand and acts on good to firm and dead ground: blinkered in 1995: usually bandaged off-hind: often has tongue tied down: often claimer ridden: races prominently: tough and game. *S. R. Bowring* 64 a69

CHAHAYA TIMOR (IRE) 3 b.g. Slip Anchor 136 – Roxy Hart (High Top 131) [1994 –p: 7g 1995 12g^6 10m^6 14.6m^3 a16g^4 a12g* a16g^2 Aug 12] sturdy, close-coupled gelding: good walker: has a rather round action: fair performer: won steadily-run maiden handicap at Wolverhampton in August, leading over 1f out: effective at 1½m to 2m: goes well on all-weather surfaces. *P. F. I. Cole* 67 a77

CHAIRMANS CHOICE 5 ch.g. Executive Man 119 – Revida Girl 63 (Habat 127) [1994 71d: a8g* a7g^2 a7g 10g 8.3f 9f 8g 1995 8.2g^4 8f^5 10m^3 8g^6 8m^2 7g^3 8m* 8f^3 7.9g* 7g a9.4g* a8g^2 Dec 1] leggy gelding: has a screw in his knee: fairly useful handicapper: won at Ripon (made all) and York (leading 2f out) in the summer and at Wolverhampton in November: seemed flattered in claimer at Goodwood eighth start, but ran almost to that form again when second at Southwell in December: stays 9.4f: acts on firm ground and fibresand: edgy sort. *A. P. Jarvis* 58 + a82

CHAKALAK 7 b.g. Damister (USA) 123 – Wig And Gown (Mandamus 120) [1994 69: 16v 16.4d 14f 13.9f* 16.1f^3 14g 20m 16.1m 16g^2 14m^5 16g^3 13.9m^3 14.6g^4 16.2g 18m 1995 16m 14.1m 13.9g 16.4g^5 17.2m^2 16.2f^5 16.2g* 16.5f^3 16.4m 15.4m^3 17.2m^3 16m^6 Oct 19] strong, compact gelding: has reportedly had tendon trouble: poor mover: only modest nowadays: first past the post under 7-lb claimer at Bath (demoted) in June and Beverley in July: effective at 1¾m, and stays very well: needs a sound surface on turf, acts on fibresand: often takes plenty of driving. *S. Dow* 51

CHALAMONT (IRE) 2 ch.f. (Apr 11) Kris 135 – Durtal 121 (Lyphard (USA) 132) [1995 6m^4 7.5d^4 6.1d^2 6f* 6.1d* Oct 10] good-quartered, unfurnished filly: good mover: half-sister to several winners, including Gold Cup winner Gildoran (by Rheingold) and ungenuine 1m winner River Defences (by Riverman): dam, winner of Cheveley Park and Fred Darling Stakes, half-sister to Detroit, dam of Carnegie: absent nearly 4 months after debut: fairly useful form when winning maiden at 88

Redcar (easing up by 10 lengths) and minor event at Chepstow (by ½ length from Trafalgar Lady) in October: bred to stay 1m+ but races keenly: acts on firm and dead ground. *P. W. Chapple-Hyam*

CHALCUCHIMA 2 gr.g. (Apr 26) Reprimand 122 – Ica (Great Nephew 126) [1995 7d^{6} 7g^{6} a8.5g^{5} Dec 2] 14,000F, 15,000Y: big, workmanlike gelding: has scope: has a fluent, round action: brother to a winner in Germany, closely related to 2 winners, notably Aragon (by Mummy's Pet), and half-brother to several winners: dam unraced half-sister to Song: sixth in maidens won by Centre Stalls at Salisbury (easily best effort) and Gold Disc at Leicester in autumn: only fifth (seemed likely to be suited by step up to 8.5f) in similar event on fibresand at Wolverhampton final start. *R. Charlton* — 65 a54

CHALDON HERRING 3 b.g. Sulaafah (USA) 119 – Langton Herring (Nearly A Hand 115) [1994 68: 5.1d^{6} 6m 6m 6.9m 7g* 7g* 7.9d^{3} 8m 7s 7d 1995 a6g a6g^{5} a7g^{4} a7g 10.3g 10d^{4} 11.1g^{2} 10g 8g May 8] quite good-topped, useful-looking gelding: has a quick action: modest handicapper: may prove ideally suited by shorter than 11f: best turf form on an easy surface: acts on fibresand: blinkered (well beaten) once at 2 yrs: weak finisher: bolted to post (withdrawn) penultimate intended start: pulled up lame final one: sold 1,500 gns Doncaster September Sales. *T. D. Barron* — 63 a50

CHALICE 2 b.f. (Mar 11) Governor General 116 – Eucharis 41 (Tickled Pink 114) [1995 6.1d 6.1d 5s^{2} 5d^{5} Oct 11] fourth foal: sister to a winning 2-y-o sprinter in Norway and half-sister to winning sprinter Barbara's Cutie (by Tina's Pet): dam, maiden, stayed 1m: much improved effort when 2 lengths second of 10 to Repatriate in maiden at Haydock in September: creditable fifth of 11 to Charterhouse Xpres in nursery there following month, again seeming to find trip on short side: should be as effective at 6f as 5f: acts on soft ground. *J. Balding* — 69

CHALK CIRCLE (IRE) 3 b.c. Sadler's Wells (USA) 132 – Grace Note (FR) 99 (Top Ville 129) [1994 NR 1995 10m Apr 18] sturdy, lengthy colt: sixth foal: closely related to top-class middle-distance colt Belmez (by El Gran Senor) and useful Irish middle-distance colt Dowland (by Sovereign Dancer) and half-brother to 4-y-o 1½m winner Dvorak (by Darshaan): dam 1¼m winner (stayed 1½m) from good family: 33/1, very green and on toes, showed nothing (hanging and looking rather uncooperative) in maiden at Newmarket: sent to Dubai. *J. H. M. Gosden* — –

CHALK DUST (USA) 2 b.f. (May 2) Unbridled (USA) – Charmie Carmie (USA) (Lyphard (USA) 132) [1995 7.1s^{6} 7m^{2} Oct 28] tall filly: has scope: eighth foal: closely related to South American Grade 1 winner Faaz (by Fappiano) and half-sister to 7f winner Himmah (by Habitat): dam maiden half-sister to Chris Evert, an excellent family: sire won Kentucky Derby and Breeders' Cup Classic: 2 lengths second of 19 to Awaamir in maiden at Newmarket, travelling strongly with pace and leading briefly around 1f out: will stay at least 1m: sure to improve again, and should win a race. *P. F. I. Cole* — 80 p

CHALKY DANCER 3 br.g. Adbass (USA) 102 – Tiny Feet (Music Maestro 119) [1994 NR 1995 10m 11.5m 9m^{4} 8g^{2} 7.5m^{2} 7.1g^{4} 7f a10g Nov 10] sturdy gelding: poor mover: seventh live foal: dam ran once at 2 yrs: poor maiden: stays 1m: acts on good to firm ground. *H. J. Collingridge* — 47

CHAMBER MUSIC 2 ch.f. (Mar 11) Music Boy 124 – Piccadilly Etta 76 (Floribunda 136) [1995 5m^{5} 5m^{6} a5g a8.5g 6m a6g Nov 13] 6,400F, 9,000Y: sturdy, close-coupled filly: sister to modest 7f/1m performer Predictable and half-sister to several winners, including fairly useful 1986 2-y-o 6f winner Einstein (by Mummy's Pet): dam won from 1½m to 2m: plater: showed little after debut: has little prospects of staying 1m: usually wears bandages behind: sold 550 gns Doncaster November Sales. *J. Berry* — –

CHAMPAGNE GOLD 8 ch.g. Bairn (USA) 126 – Halkissimo 61 (Khalkis 127) [1994 NR 1995 15.9d 16.1g 16m Oct 19] leggy gelding: fair stayer (rated 66) at 6 yrs: no worthwhile form on return: acts on good to firm and dead ground. *J. C. McConnochie* — –

CHAMPAGNE GRANDY 5 ch.m. Vaigly Great 127 – Monstrosa 70 (Monsanto (FR) 121) [1994 84: 7d* 6f 6m 7s^{5} 6d^{5} 7g^{5} 6m 6.1m 7g 6d^{3} 6d^{6} 5.7g 5s^{2} 6d 6.1d^{3} 5d^{4} 1995 6g 6m^{6} 6m 6g 7g* 6m* 6.1m 7m 6g 7.3d* 8.1g 6g 6.1s 6f Oct 31] leggy, close-coupled mare: has a quick action: fairly useful handicapper: won at Chester and Salisbury in June and at Newbury (best effort) in September: stays 7.3f: — 84 acts on good to firm ground, very best form on a soft surface: ran poorly on fibresand. *M. R. Channon*

CHAMPAGNE N DREAMS 3 b.f. Rambo Dancer (CAN) 107 – Pink Sensation 69 (Sagaro 133) [1994 50: 5f4 6g 7f6 6g 6m6 7.1m5 1995 7g 8.1g* 8g3 7g5 7.1f4 9.9g 10m4 10g 10.5s Sep 30] sturdy, close-coupled filly: modest handicapper: won at Edinburgh in May: stays 8.1f, not 1¼m: acts on firm ground, below form over 10.5f only run on a soft surface. *D. Nicholls* — 57

CHAMPAGNE PRINCE 2 b.c. (Apr 25) Prince Sabo 123 – Champagne Season (USA) 54 (Vaguely Noble 140) [1995 6g2 7m* 7m4 7.5m* 7m* 7.3d4 Sep 15] 9,000Y: smallish colt: has a roundish action: first foal: dam ran twice at 2 yrs: fairly useful colt: won maiden at Salisbury in July and nurseries at Beverley (by 4 lengths) and Chester in August: creditable fourth of 15 to Ramooz in nursery at Newbury on final outing: stays 7.5f: acts on good to firm ground and dead. *P. W. Harris* — 89

CHAMPAGNE WARRIOR (IRE) 2 b.f. (May 16) Waajib 121 – Late Swallow (My Swallow 134) [1995 6m6 7m 7m Oct 30] IR 6,500Y: good-bodied filly: sister to 5-y-o Spring Flyer, successful from 7f (at 2 yrs) to 9.4f, closely related to a winner in Italy by Try My Best and half-sister to several winners here and abroad, including smart sprinter A Prayer For Wings (by Godswalk): dam unraced: no worthwhile form in maidens: off course 3½ months after debut. *M. J. Camacho* — –

CHANCEL (USA) 4 b.f. Al Nasr (FR) 126 – Christchurch (FR) 88 (So Blessed 130) [1994 60: a10g2 11s5 a9.4g3 9.7m a10g 1995 a10g2 Feb 28] unfurnished filly: modest maiden: visored, short-headed in minor event at Lingfield, only start in 1995: should stay beyond 11f: acts on soft ground and equitrack. *Lord Huntingdon* — 52

CHANCE ME 3 ch.g. Risk Me (FR) 127 – Tuxford Hideaway 102 (Cawston's Clown 113) [1994 42: 5s 7m 7m 5m 1995 5m a5g3 5m a5g5 a5g Jul 17] leggy, lightly-made gelding: poor maiden handicapper: should stay 6f: acts on good to firm ground and on fibresand: sold 1,300 gns Doncaster October Sales. *M. Johnston* — 38

CHANCEY FELLA 4 ch.g. Sylvan Express 117 – Musical Piece 91 (Song 132) [1994 56: a8.5g a8g6 a11g6 6d2 8.2m* 8m3 8.5m6 7m2 7m6 1995 8g 8.3m 8f4 7m5 8m 7g Sep 13] compact gelding: unimpressive mover: modest handicapper: stays 8.2f well: acts on firm ground, probably on dead: usually blinkered/visored: bandaged of late: rather reluctant to race once, and not an easy ride: inconsistent: gelded. *K. T. Ivory* — 57

CHANSON D'AVRIL 4 br.f. Chief Singer 131 – Chappelle Blanche (USA) 96 (Olden Times) [1994 54: 10d 10g 7d 7m 11.9g 10.2g3 12.1g 9.7m 1995 11.9f4 13.1h 16d Sep 11] leggy filly: poor maiden handicapper for new stable: should stay 1½m. *D. A. Wilson* — 40

CHANTRY BEATH 4 ch.g. Dunbeath (USA) 127 – Sallametti (USA) 69 (Giacometti 130) [1994 68: 10.3g 12.3d6 12v3 11.8g5 11.1m2 13g2 12.1g* 12g3 11.9g* 12.1g2 12m6 1995 11.9m 14.1m6 13f3 12.3f 14f4 14m5 13.9g 12.1g* 12.1g 12m6 Oct 13] sturdy, lengthy gelding: only a modest handicapper in 1995, but won 15-runner event at Edinburgh in September in good style: well below form afterwards: stays 1¾m: acts on any ground: has won for amateur: won over hurdles in December. *C. W. Thornton* — 57

CHANTRY BELLINI 6 ch.m. Efisio 120 – Lifestyle 80 (Jimmy Reppin 131) [1994 NR 1995 a8g 8.5m* 8m3 8g* 8m 8.5m5 8.3f 8m 10.9g4 7d5 7.1s2 8g 8.1s Nov 2] small mare: poor handicapper nowadays: won at Beverley (apprentices) in May and Pontefract in June: effective at 7f, and stays 1½m: acts on good to firm and soft going: often blinkered: usually bandaged: sometimes has tongue tied down. *Mrs S. M. Austin* — 52 ?

CHAPEL ANNIE 3 ch.f. Tinoco 80 – The Suestan 71 (Ballyciptic 122) [1994 NR 1995 a7g a10g a14g4 a13g Dec 14] eighth reported foal: half-sister to winning 2m hurdler Lissahane Lass (by Daring March): dam won over 1¼m: seems of little account. *C. P. Wildman* — –

CHAPEL HAVEN (IRE) 5 ch.m. King Persian 107 – Saybya (Sallust 134) [1994 –: 11.9s 12g 1995 a12g a16g Jan 13] no sign of ability: tried blinkered. *J. Parkes* — –

CHAPEL HILL (IRE) 7 b.m. The Parson 119 – Hazy Hill (Goldhill 125) [1994 NR 1995 a12g4 a14.8g Jan 25] third foal: half-sister to a NH Flat winner by Roselier — –

and a winning jumper by The Parson: dam never ran: no worthwhile form in 2 starts on flat: modest hurdler. *B. J. Llewellyn*

CHAPTER TWO 4 ch.g. Celestial Storm (USA) 132 – Lingering 96 (Kind of Hush 118) [1994 –: a10g 1995 a10g a13g a13g Feb 2] no sign of ability. *S. Dow* –

CHARDONNAY GIRL 4 b.f. Hubbly Bubbly (USA) – Chaconia Girl (Bay Express 132) [1994 –: 5.1f 6m^{4} a7g 1995 a6g 5f 8g Sep 2] medium-sized filly: of little account. *J. M. Carr* –

CHARISSE DANCER 2 b.f. (Mar 5) Dancing Dissident (USA) 119 – Cadisa 82 (Top Ville 129) [1995 7f Oct 18] sparely-made filly: fourth foal: half-sister to winners in Ireland at 1¼m by Pharly and 1¾m by Darshaan: dam 11f winner: 33/1, didn't show much in steadily-run maiden at Yarmouth. *C. F. Wall* –

CHARITY CRUSADER 4 b.c. Rousillon (USA) 133 – Height of Folly 81 (Shirley Heights 130) [1994 96?: 12m^{4} 11.9m^{4} 16f 1995 12g^{5} 16.2m^{4} 13.9g 12f^{5} 12f^{4} Jun 28] rangy colt: unimpressive mover: fairly useful performer: effective at 1½m to around 2m: acts on firm ground, yet to race on a soft surface: blinkered last 2 starts: joined Mrs M. Reveley. *P. W. Chapple-Hyam* 88

CHARLIE BIGTIME 5 b.g. Norwick (USA) 125 – Sea Aura 89 (Roi Soleil 125) [1994 51, a54: 10d a12g^{6} 8.5m 9.7s 10m* 10m^{6} a9.4g^{5} 10g 11.5g a14.8g^{3} a12g* a16g^{4} 16s a12g 13.8g^{5} 1995 a11g^{6} a12g^{4} a16g^{6} a12g^{4} a12g* a14.8g^{4} a12g^{3} a12g 10g^{5} 12m^{2} 12g a12g^{3} 11.8m* a9.4g^{3} a12g^{4} Sep 16] sturdy gelding: unimpressive mover: modest handicapper: won at Wolverhampton (penultimate start for B. McMath) in March and Leicester (bandaged behind, first start after leaving D. Thom) in August: probably stays 2m: acts on good to firm ground and fibresand: effective visored/ blinkered or not. *R. Harris* 51

CHARLIE CHANG (IRE) 2 b.c. (Apr 4) Don't Forget Me 127 – East River (FR) (Arctic Tern (USA) 126) [1995 7m a8g* Nov 14] leggy, close-coupled colt: sixth living foal: brother to 7f (at 2 yrs) to 9f (Grade 2 event in USA) winner Eastern Memories and half-brother to 2 winners: dam French 11f winner: won 8-runner maiden at Lingfield readily by 4 lengths from Tart, quickening ahead on home bend: will stay beyond 1m: will improve again. *R. Hannon* 82 p

CHARLIE CHARLIE 4 b.g. Emarati (USA) 74 – Hound Song 84 (Jukebox 120) [1994 –: 7m 10g 1995 7g May 27] close-coupled gelding: modest maiden (rated 62) in 1993: no form for either trainer since: stays 7.6f: acts on soft ground: joined Lady Herries. *R. M. Flower* –

CHARLIE-DON'T SURF 3 b.c. Reprimand 122 – Miami Melody (Miami Springs 121) [1994 NR 1995 7g 8g 8g a10g a9.4g^{3} a7g Dec 14] 3,800Y: seventh foal: dam placed over 6f and 1½m in Ireland: poor maiden: trained until after third start by R. Thompson: form only at 9.4f. *R. Guest* 44

CHARLIES DREAM (IRE) 4 b.f. Doulab (USA) 115 – Caithness 78 (Connaught 130) [1994 –, a49: a5g a7g^{3} a8.5g* a8.5g^{4} a7g a9.4g 8.3m 8g a7g^{5} a8g^{5} a6g^{4} a7g^{4} a7g a7g^{5} a7g 1995 a8g Jan 6] smallish filly: poor performer: sold (K. Burke to K. Linton) 850 gns Doncaster February Sales: stays 8.5f: acts on all-weather, well beaten on soft ground: tried visored/blinkered, no improvement. *K. R. Burke* –

CHARLIE SILLETT 3 ch.c. Handsome Sailor 125 – Bystrouska (Gorytus (USA) 132) [1994 75: 6d 6d^{5} 6s* a7g 1995 6m^{3} 6d^{6} 6s* 6d 7m* Nov 3] tall, unfurnished colt: made into a fairly useful handicapper: won 23-runner race at Haydock in October and 21-runner event at Doncaster in November: unlucky in running in between: stays 7f: acts on good to firm ground and soft: bandaged: probably capable of further progress, and likely to win more races at 4 yrs. *B. W. Hills* 87 p

CHARLISTIONA 4 ch.f. Good Times (ITY) – Abigails Portrait 63 (Absalom 128) [1994 –: 8f 8m 7f 7d 8f^{6} a10g 1995 a7g a13g Jan 10] lengthy, angular filly: of little account. *M. Johnston* –

CHARLOTTE CORDAY 2 b.f. (Mar 9) Kris 135 – Dancing Rocks 118 (Green Dancer (USA) 132) [1995 6f^{5} Oct 23] sister to 2 winners, including 1¼m winner Gai Bulga, and half-sister to 3 winners, including 1993 2-y-o 6f and 7f winner Glatisant (by Rainbow Quest): dam won Nassau Stakes: 16/1, backward and green, shaped well when just under 6 lengths fifth of 18 to Wildwood Flower in maiden at Leicester, pushed along in rear at halfway then running on strongly under considerate handling: carried head a little high: sure to improve, particularly over 7f+. *G. Wragg* 63 p

CHARLOTTE PENNY 4 b. or br.f. High Kicker (USA) – Affluent Lady (Billion (USA) 120) [1994 –: a8s^4 a8g 9.9m a8g^6 8m 1995 a7g a8.5g^6 a8g 8.5m May 12] sparely-made filly: of little account. *N. P. Littmoden* –

CHARLTON IMP (USA) 2 b.f. (Feb 3) Imp Society (USA) – Percentage (USA) (Vaguely Noble 140) [1995 6.1d^6 Oct 10] 20,000Y: sister to 6.1f (at 2 yrs) to 8.5f winner Marabella Star and a winner in USA and half-sister to 3 winners, including champion Panamanian filly Percentile (by Silver Hawk): dam unraced half-sister to 2 stakes winners: 33/1, slowly into stride and always behind in minor event at Chepstow. *R. J. Hodges* –

CHARM DANCER 3 b.f. Rambo Dancer (CAN) 107 – Skelton 70 (Derrylin 115) [1994 NR 1995 9.9m* 10g^6 11.5f^3 10.1m^3 8g^5 8g Sep 29] leggy, lengthy filly: third foal: half-sister to sprint winner Caress (by Godswalk): dam 2-y-o 7f and 8.2f sellers winner, is half-sister to very useful stayer Brief Bay: modest form: won seller (sold out of J. Wharton's stable 9,800 gns) at Beverley in May: probably stays 11.5f: acts on good to firm ground. *M. C. Pipe* 55

CHARMED LIFE 6 b.g. Legend of France (USA) 124 – Tanagrea (Blakeney 126) [1994 39: 12.5d* 11.1d^3 11.6d 14g 1995 12m^5 16d 16.1g 14.1m 16.4m Nov 6] sturdy, good-quartered gelding: seems no longer of much account. *Mrs A. L. M. King* –

CHARMING ADMIRAL (IRE) 2 b.g. (May 19) Shareef Dancer (USA) 135 – Lilac Charm 87 (Bustino 136) [1995 8.2m Oct 19] 17,000Y: close-coupled gelding: closely related to 2 winners abroad by Fabulous Dancer and half-brother to 4 winners here and abroad, including useful German 3-y-o 1m/9f winner Ladoni (by Danehill): dam 2-y-o 6f winner: 50/1 and burly, always behind in maiden at Nottingham. *C. F. Wall* –

CHARMING BRIDE 2 b.f. (Feb 13) Charmer 123 – Loredana 64 (Grange Melody) [1995 6m^2 6m^4 Aug 5] fifth foal: half-sister to 5f (at 2 yrs) to 7f winner Nitouche (by Scottish Reel) and 1993 2-y-o 5f winner Carrie Kool (by Prince Sabo): dam 7f and 1m winner: 1¾ lengths second of 10 to Balpare in median auction maiden at Epsom: eased after reportedly striking into herself in similar event at Lingfield 10 days later. *S. C. Williams* 56

CHARNWOOD FOREST (IRE) 3 b. or br.c. Warning 136 – Dance of Leaves (Sadler's Wells (USA) 132) [1994 95p: 6m^2 1995 7m* 8m^2 7.9m* Jul 14] 116 p

When he returns from warmer climes under the Godolphin banner, this colt must be a prime candidate to rub salt in the wounds at Warren Place. His total number of races in two seasons for Henry Cecil was four, his two wins gained in contests of very limited importance, but Charnwood Forest has nonetheless looked pattern-race material virtually from the word go. Injuries have limited his achievements so far, but if those are overcome in 1996 it will be no surprise to see Charnwood Forest emerge as a leading player, whichever stable he races from. To date, Charnwood Forest has run in just one pattern race, the St James's Palace Stakes at Royal Ascot. His credentials for this Group 1 were not lengthy—a second in a valuable maiden at York the previous August and victory in a Newmarket maiden in April—yet he was sent off 6/1 co-third favourite of nine. Backers will doubtless have been encouraged by the Premio Parioli exploits of Charnwood Forest's Newmarket runner-up Prince Arthur. Reputation, however, counted for as much as anything. Charnwood Forest had stood at 16/1 for the Two Thousand Guineas even before that maiden success, a win, incidentally, which provided short-lived joy for ante-post speculators as connections immediately ruled out the Guineas because Charnwood Forest 'needed time'. At Royal Ascot, he performed in keeping both with what was known and what had been heard—inexperienced but very talented. Efforts to settle him resulted in his being anchored at the back of the field, from where he faced a troubled route forward. He had plenty of room over the last two furlongs, however, in which he set out in vain pursuit of Bahri, just getting the better of the race for second. Third was the Poule d'Essai des Poulains winner Vettori, followed by Atticus, Annus Mirabilis, Flemensfirth and Adjareli, all of whom had already been either first, second or third in Group 1 company. Contrastingly, Charnwood Forest was next seen out in the £8,865 Manchester-Singapore Stakes, a conditions race at York in mid-July. At 3/10, he was workmanlike in asserting his authority initially, but finished well on top of his three rivals, Shemaq coming second in the end but the one who made a race of it being Decorated Hero. And that was it. Charnwood Forest was not seen out again.

Sheikh Mohammed's "Charnwood Forest"

The Irish Guineas was an early-season target that went by without him, because of a pulled muscle in his near-hind quarter; he pulled a hamstring before Royal Ascot and two weeks after York he was out of the International with hamstring problems again, 'sore and a little bit short behind'.

Charnwood Forest (IRE) (b. or br.c. 1992)	Warning (b 1985)	Known Fact (b 1977)	In Reality
			Tamerett
		Slightly Dangerous (b 1979)	Roberto
			Where You Lead
	Dance of Leaves (b 1987)	Sadler's Wells (b 1981)	Northern Dancer
			Fairy Bridge
		Fall Aspen (ch 1976)	Pretense
			Change Water

Leading first-season sire in 1993 with a crop that included such as Piccolo, Prophecy and Electrify, Warning has done even better with his second crop, Charnwood Forest being joined by Annus Mirabilis, Decorated Hero, Bishop of Cashel, Inzar, Peace Envoy and Take Liberties. Charnwood Forest's dam Dance of Leaves will not have been well known before now—she never raced and Charnwood Forest is her first foal—but her dam Fall Aspen could hardly be more celebrated. Good on the racecourse as a two-year-old when she won the Grade 1 Matron Stakes, Fall Aspen has been brilliant in the paddocks, producing seven pattern winners including Group/Grade 1 winners Northern Aspen, Hamas, Fort Wood and Timber Country. Dance of Leaves is not the first of Fall Aspen's daughters to make an impact at stud; Elle Seule's third foal was the 1994 Irish One Thousand Guineas winner Mehthaaf. Dance of Leaves' next two foals are colts by Mujtahid (called Devil's Dance, and in training with Stoute) and Highest Honor, and a filly by Rainbow Quest in 1995.

Charnwood Forest should prove a hard act to follow. Physically, he will always take the eye, being very dark in colour, rangy and good-bodied in stature, and as a racehorse he looks certain to uphold the family tradition by winning a pattern race (at the very least) if those niggling injuries do not intervene once more. He shapes as if further than a mile will suit him ideally, and has yet to race on ground anything other than good to firm. Charnwood Forest's third season begins with as much expectation and speculation as the last. *H. R. A. Cecil*

CHARNWOOD NELL (USA) 2 ch.f. (May 21) Arctic Tern (USA) 126 – Aphilandra (Viceregal (CAN)) [1995 8m Sep 5] $5,500Y, 11,500 2-y-o: small filly: ninth reported foal: closely related to French 1m winner Tessancourt and French 1m (including at 2 yrs) and 9f winner Hylandra (both by Bering) and half-sister to 2 winners: dam, French 1½m winner, half-sister to high-class Soleil Noir: 11/2, little promise in maiden at Leicester. *P. A. Kelleway* –

CHARNWOOD QUEEN 3 ch.f. Cadeaux Genereux 131 – Florentynna Bay 61 (Aragon 118) [1994 –: a7g a7g 1995 a8g a6g^{6} a6g^{5} a6g^{3} a5g 6g^{3} 5f^{5} 6m^{2} 6m* 6m* 6m 6m^{2} 6.1d 6d^{3} Sep 27] modest handicapper: made virtually all to win twice at Windsor in July: needs further than 5f, and probably stays 7f: acts on good to firm ground, probably on dead: sold 4,400 gns Newmarket Autumn Sales. *R. W. Armstrong* 61

CHARTERHOUSE XPRES 2 b.c. (Feb 12) Clantime 101 – Uptown Girl 65 (Caruso 112) [1995 5m^{5} 5m a6g^{3} a6g^{2} a6g^{4} 6d 7d a5g^{3} 5d* a5g^{3} a5g^{3} Dec 18] 7,800Y: sparely-made colt: third foal: half-brother to a winner abroad by Domynsky: dam sprinter: fair form: won nursery at Haydock in October: creditable efforts afterwards: takes keen hold (has gone too fast on more than one occasion) and will prove best at sprint distances: acts on all-weather, but better form on a soft surface on turf: visored/blinkered last 5 outings. *M. McCormack* 72 a69

CHARWELTON 2 b.f. (Feb 8) Indian Ridge 123 – Bazaar Promise 58 (Native Bazaar 122) [1995 6m* Jul 29] IR 20,000Y: lengthy, workmanlike filly: third foal: sister to useful 3-y-o 6f winner Cheyenne Spirit and 8.5f and 1¼m winner Indian Express: dam temperamental sister to very useful sprinter Crofthall: 7/1, won 7-runner maiden at Goodwood by ½ length from Raed, travelling well throughout and running on well despite being carried right: looked sure to improve. *P. F. I. Cole* 78

CHASE THE MELODY 3 b.g. Sizzling Melody 117 – Odilese 82 (Mummy's Pet 125) [1994 –: a6g 1995 7g 10.2m 8f 10f^{6} Jul 24] tall, sparely-made, sprint-bred gelding: no promise: tried in visor: sold 1,800 gns Ascot July Sales. *M. J. Heaton-Ellis* –

CHASMARELLA 10 b.m. Yukon Eric (CAN) – Miss Polly Peck (March Past 124) [1994 –: 18m 1995 a16.2g^{6} 18.2m Jul 8] smallish, lengthy mare: no longer of much account. *Mrs M. E. Long* –

CHASTLETON 3 b.f. Presidium 124 – Double Stitch 74 (Wolver Hollow 126) [1994 40: 7g 7m^{6} 6d^{3} 7g^{3} 1995 a10g^{4} a8g^{2} a8g^{3} a9.4g* 8.3s^{5} 8.3g^{5} 10m 10f 8.5m^{3} 10f^{4} 10m 10.2h^{5} 8.3m 8h 10d 8.3g^{6} Sep 24] tall filly: poor performer: won seller at Wolverhampton in April: well below form last 6 starts: stays 1¼m: acts on the all-weather and on firm and dead ground, ran poorly (hanging left) on soft. *M. R. Channon* 43 d

CHATHAM ISLAND 7 ch.g. Jupiter Island 126 – Floreal 68 (Formidable (USA) 125) [1994 69, a91: 10d 10.3m^{4} 12m^{4} 12m^{4} 12d 12m^{6} a10g* 1995 a9.4g^{2} a12g^{2} 12m^{4} 10m 12g* 11.8g^{6} 12.3m 11.4m^{4} 12m^{4} Sep 6] rangy gelding: impresses in appearance: good walker: fairly useful handicapper on the all-weather, fair on turf: won at Doncaster in May: stays 1½m: yet to show his form on a soft surface: effective from front or held up: game. *C. E. Brittain* 73 a91

CHATO (USA) 3 b.c. Local Talent (USA) 122 – Quick Blush (USA) (Blushing Groom (FR) 131) [1994 5v* 5g^{4} 7d^{3} 8g* 1995 8.5s^{6} 8g 8s* 8.5m^{3} 8m^{3} 8m 8d^{3} 8g^{2} 108

10v^4 8g^5 Nov 12] $57,000Y: fourth foal: half-brother to 3 winners, notably smart German sprinter-miler Nasr Allah (by Mogambo): dam minor winner in USA: useful German colt: won maiden at Baden-Baden and Preis der Winterfavoriten (gamely) at Cologne at 2 yrs: back to form when winning 14-runner Badener Meile (by 3 lengths from Erminius) in May: placed in Diomed Stakes at Epsom, Group 2 event at Hoppegarten (1¾ lengths behind Kill The Crab) and 3 German pattern races: best form at up to 8.5f, respectable effort at 1¼m: acts on heavy going and good to firm: has had tongue tied down. *Horst Steinmetz, Germany*

CHATTAROY (IRE) 3 b.g. Persian Bold 123 – Lady Chatterley (USA) 85 (Roberto (USA) 131) [1994 83: 7g^4 7.1d^2 7m^6 1995 8m 7m^6 7g* 8m 8.1f^4 Aug 5] good-bodied gelding: has been freeze-fired on off-fore: fairly useful handicapper: sweating, came from off pace to win strongly-run event at Kempton in June: shapes as if stays at least 1m: acts on good to firm (respectable effort on firm) and dead ground: sent to Dubai. *J. H. M. Gosden* 89

CHAUVELIN (IRE) 2 ch.c. (Jan 4) Durgam (USA) – Kaliala (FR) (Pharly (FR) 130) [1995 8.1s a10g^4 Nov 25] IR 5,000F, 12,000Y: half-brother to French 1½m winner Kalaniya (by Kahyasi) and a winner in Hong Kong by Ballad Rock: dam French 1m winner: better effort in maiden events when just over 4 lengths fourth of 13 to Thorntoun Estate in median auction at Lingfield: will stay beyond 1¼m: likely to improve again. *M. Johnston* 57 p

CHAVIN POINT 2 b.f. (Feb 23) Inca Chief (USA) – To The Point 96 (Sharpen Up 127) [1995 7d 6f^6 6m Nov 3] 1,500F: sparely-made filly: half-sister to 3-y-o 6f (at 2 yrs) and 1¼m winner Kings Assembly (by Presidium) and several winners in USA: dam 2-y-o 5f winner later ran in North America: slowly away and no form in maidens. *Miss L. C. Siddall* –

CHEEKY CHAPPY 4 b.g. Sayf El Arab (USA) 127 – Guilty Guest (USA) 59 (Be My Guest (USA) 126) [1994 37: 5d a6g 5g 5m^6 5s a5g^5 1995 a5g^3 a6g^5 a6g^4 a6g^5 5g 6m a5g 6.1m^6 a5g^2 a5g^6 5g^2 a5g^5 5f 5m^4 5f^5 5h^2 5m* 5m^6 a5g* a5g* a5g^3 Dec 19] lengthy gelding: carries condition: poor mover: improved towards end of 1995, winning at Edinburgh (apprentices) in August and at Lingfield in November and (made all) December: suited by 5f: acts on hard ground and all-weather surfaces, probably unsuited by heavy: nearly always blinkered: races prominently: successful for apprentice: reliable. *D. W. Chapman* 40 + a49

CHEEKY CHARM (USA) 3 b.f. Nureyev (USA) 131 – Very Charming (USA) (Vaguely Noble 140) [1994 56p: 7g 1995 8f^5 Oct 18] leggy filly, very well bred: off course over a year, fifth of 11 in maiden at Yarmouth: may do better. *M. R. Stoute* 46 +

CHEERFUL ASPECT (IRE) 2 b.g. (Mar 9) Cadeaux Genereux 131 – Strike Home 82 (Be My Guest (USA) 126) [1995 7g^6 8g^3 8d^5 8m^4 Oct 13] big, good-bodied gelding: sixth foal: half-brother to modest 7f and 1m winner Inseyab (by Persian Bold) and 3-y-o Shining Dancer (by Rainbow Quest): dam, 11.7f winner, half-sister to Ballad Rock: fair form: fourth of 12 to Mystic Knight in nursery at Newmarket final start: will stay beyond 1m: unseated rider leaving paddock on debut (also bandaged behind). *E. A. L. Dunlop* 77

CHEERFUL GROOM (IRE) 4 ch.g. Shy Groom (USA) – Carange (Known Fact (USA) 135) [1994 56, a–: 5.9v^3 6.1f^6 6.9f* 7m 6.9m^3 7m^5 6m^5 8d 7m 6d a8g a6g a6g^4 1995 a6g^3 a6g^2 a6g^3 a6g a7g^4 a6g 6.9m 6d a5g a6g^6 a6g a7g^2 6d 7d 7m Oct 20] sturdy gelding: only poor form nowadays: should stay 1m: acts on the all-weather and any turf going: visored (out of form) once as 3-y-o: sometimes has tongue tied: wears crossed noseband: inconsistent. *J. Mackie* 41

CHELSEA CLASSIC (IRE) 2 b.f. (May 13) Classic Music (USA) – Romantic Air 62 (He Loves Me 120) [1995 5.2g^4 5d^6 Sep 13] IR 21,000Y: workmanlike filly: fifth foal: half-sister to useful 6f and 7f performer (5f winner at 2 yrs) Toocando (by Nordance): dam ran 3 times at 2 yrs, showing best form at 1m: around 8 lengths fourth of 7 to Marjaana in maiden at Newbury, soon well behind then making headway from 2f out until eased late on: well below that form in similar event at Beverley 2 months later. *M. R. Channon* 53 +

CHELSEA MY LOVE (USA) 2 ch.f. (Apr 16) Opening Verse (USA) 122 – Wewarrenju (USA) (Damascus (USA)) [1995 7m^6 Aug 15] $30,000Y, 23,000 2-y-o: unfurnished, quite attractive filly: fourth foal: half-sister to 8.5f stakes winner in –

USA by Vice Regent: dam ran 3 times in USA: 10/1 and green, tailed-off last of 6 to Bijou d'Inde in £13,100 event at York. *P. A. Kelleway*

CHEMCAST 2 ch.c. (Mar 1) Chilibang 120 – Golden October 62 (Young Generation 129) [1995 5.1m^5 a6g^5 5.1g^3 5m 5.7h^2 a5g^2 5m* 5m* 5d 5g^6 a6g a5g Dec 18] 5,000F, 5,000Y: lengthy colt: half-brother to several moderate animals: dam won at 6f: fair form: won nurseries at Goodwood in August and Folkestone in September: sold out of B. Meehan's stable 7,000 gns Newmarket Autumn Sales before final start: easily best efforts at 5f: acts on fibresand and good to firm ground (soundly beaten on dead): races prominently. *D. Nicholls* — 68 a59

CHEROKEE ROSE (IRE) 4 b.f. Dancing Brave (USA) 140 – Celtic Assembly (USA) 95 (Secretariat (USA)) [1994 7g 8g^6 8v^3 8s^4 1995 7m^3 7g* 7g* 6.5g* 6d* 5d^2 8s Oct 28] — 122

The Haydock Park Sprint Cup had an impressive winner, but not the one that had been expected. Expected may not be a strong enough word to describe Lake Coniston, four-length winner of the July Cup on his previous start who was now sent off at 3/1 on, the second odds-on shot for the Haydock Sprint since it became a Group 1 in 1988. Not even Dayjur (2/1 on) in 1990 had been considered such a good thing. Lake Coniston's attempt to do a Dayjur, however, was scuppered well before the furlong marker. Mind Games shaded him in the early stages, the pair combining to set a ferocious gallop on good to soft ground and unable to maintain it. The 1994 winner, Lavinia Fontana, soon made it clear that she would not take advantage (only three days after running in Germany) but Branston Abby and Owington put in determined bids. Branston Abby emerged the better of that duel, but even as she did so attention switched abruptly to the one remaining runner, the last and decisive arrival on the scene, the French-trained filly Cherokee Rose. Tucked in by Cash Asmussen, travelling strongly on the rails for most of the race, Cherokee Rose met with a little argy-bargy in getting free just inside the final furlong but still had time to spare; an excellent turn of foot took her to the front with fifty yards left and on to victory by a length and a half.

The Haydock Park Sprint Cup, for which she started 5/1 second favourite, was Cherokee Rose's fourth successive win in a pattern race. Prior to those, her only success had been in a minor event at Vichy in July, 1993. That had been over seven furlongs. So had six of her other ten races before the Sprint Cup, another three coming at a mile in 1994. She showed useful form in both those first two seasons, but also suffered from a virus at three. Putting that behind her, progress with age and the

Prix Maurice de Gheest, Deauville—hard-ridden Young Ern is short-headed by Cherokee Rose

adjustment in trip all combined to produce a much improved animal in the latest season. The Prix du Palais Royal at Longchamp in May kicked off her winning run, Sayyedati caught in the final strides, and a return to course and distance four weeks later for the Prix de la Porte Maillot saw her home two and a lengths clear of Bashaayeash. Poplar Bluff was third in both of those Group 3 events. The first three in the Palais Royal would all have Group 1 victories before the year was out. Cherokee Rose had two, thanks to the recent deserved upgrading of the Prix Maurice de Gheest at Deauville. Run over six and a half furlongs four weeks before Haydock, this race produced some fascinating results over the years in its old guise and lost nothing in competitiveness for its increased status and new conditions in 1995. One and a half furlongs out, seven of the ten runners were virtually in line across the track. Again, Cherokee Rose was not one of them, but another well-timed challenge in the hands of Asmussen brought her to the fore a hundred yards out, after which she had just enough in hand to hold off the renewed attentions of Young Ern. Six to seven furlongs was Cherokee Rose's trip. With five for the Abbaye she scrambled into a respectable second place, a lot better than had seemed likely at halfway or even a furlong out. One mile in the Breeders' Cup at Belmont Park and Cherokee Rose was well beaten, badly blocked on the rails entering the straight but looking well below her best anyway thereafter. She had apparently had a bad trip over. It had been reported that Sheikh Mohammed's original intention had been to retire her at the end of her three-year-old season. It was therefore a spectacularly vindicated change of heart that now sees Cherokee Rose off to stud one year later.

The delay also made a significant difference to the season's statistics of her sire Dancing Brave. Two years ago everyone was bemoaning his export to Japan after a dramatic change of fortune resulted in what now stands as eight pattern winners in his third crop, including classic winners Commander In Chief, White Muzzle and Wemyss Bight. This was an amazing figure from just forty foals. Cherokee Rose, however, was the only pattern winner from Dancing Brave's fourth or fifth crops, his

Haydock Park Sprint Cup—a four-timer for Cherokee Rose;
behind, right to left, are Branston Abby, Owington and Lake Coniston

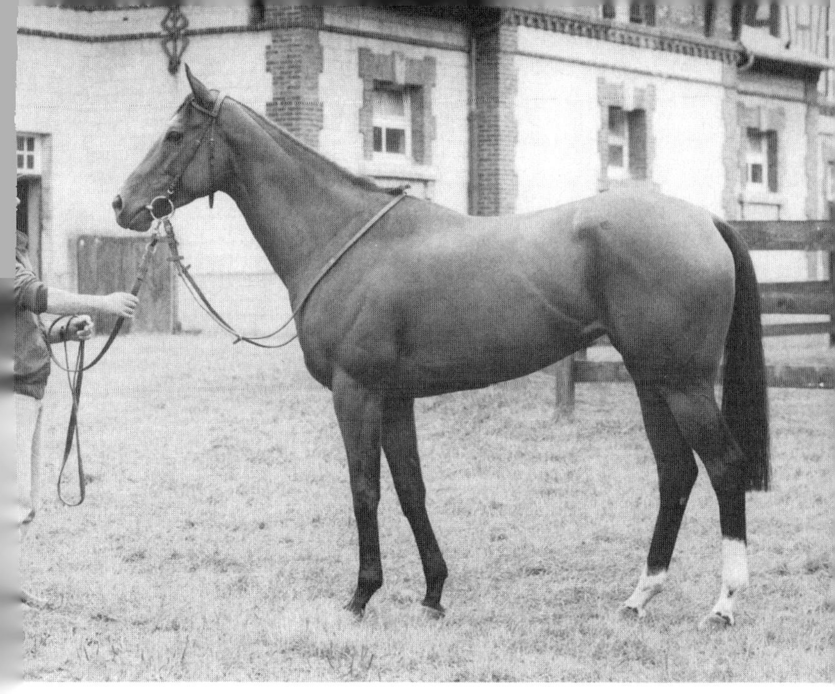

Sheikh Mohammed's "Cherokee Rose"

Cherokee Rose (IRE) (b.f. 1991)	Dancing Brave (USA) (b 1983)	Lyphard (b 1969)	Northern Dancer
			Goofed
		Navajo Princess (b 1974)	Drone
			Olmec
	Celtic Assembly (USA) (b 1981)	Secretariat (ch 1970)	Bold River
			Somethingroyal
		Welsh Garden (b 1973)	Welsh Saint
			Garden of Eden

last in Europe (the ex-British Yenda won a Grade 2 in the USA in October). She is also an oddity in her distance requirements, easily the speediest of Dancing Brave's progeny. Her dam Celtic Assembly was runner-up in the Lupe Stakes and gained her only success over an extended mile and a quarter. Three of her previous five foals were winners, including Cherokee Rose's sister Congress (over a mile at two years) and the useful but very lightly-raced six-furlong and seven-furlong winner Volksraad (by Green Desert). Next come Dail (a gelding by Shaadi), Keltoi (a colt by Soviet Star), a yearling by Arazi and a dead foal by Royal Academy. There has been plenty of cause to write about this family over the years. Fourth dam Mesopotamia and grandam Welsh Garden were both Irish-trained champion two-year-olds. They were also highly-strung individuals, Welsh Garden so much so that, no Monty Roberts on hand, she refused to have anything to do with starting stalls and had to set out her championship credentials at the minor tracks where stalls were not in operation. Notable relations in recent years are Garden of Heaven (foaled by third dam Garden of Eden when she was twenty-two), the Horris Hill winner Celtic Heir and Prix du Cadran winner Molesnes (half-brother and half-sister to Celtic Assembly),

Alderbrook (Mesopotamia is his third dam) and Halling (Mesopotamia his fourth dam). Cherokee Rose is a good-quartered, attractive filly who acted on good to soft going and ran only once on top-of-the-ground. She showed smart form at seven furlongs, even better at six. *J. E. Hammond, France*

CHERRINGTON 3 b.c. Reference Point 139 – Cherry Hinton (USA) 125 (Nijinsky (CAN) 138) [1994 67p: 7m^6 7g 8.2d^6 1995 11.8m* 12.3m^3 12m^5 14f* 13.9g^3 14g Sep 29] good-bodied, attractive colt: has a rather round action: progressed into a useful performer: won handicap at Leicester in April and rated stakes at Goodwood in July: stays 1¾m well: raced only on a sound surface at 3 yrs, shaped well on dead at 2 yrs: genuine: sent to Dubai. *G. Wragg* 96

CHERRY GARDEN (IRE) 2 b.c. (Mar 25) Treasure Kay 114 – Door To Door (USA) (Nureyev (USA) 131) [1995 6m^4 6m a7g^3 7.6m^2 8g Sep 14] IR 400F, IR 3,400Y: third foal: brother to 1m winner Collector General and half-brother to a winner in USA by Shy Groom: dam French maiden: best effort when 2½ lengths second of 11 to Aussie in nursery at Lingfield in September: tailed off in nursery at Yarmouth final start: should be suited by 1m+: acts on good to firm ground and fibresand. *T. J. Naughton* 61 a57

CHEVALIER (USA) 3 b.c. Danzig (USA) – Royal Touch 121 (Tap On Wood 130) [1994 NR 1995 8.2m^2 10.1m^2 Jul 24] first foal: dam won from 7f (at 2 yrs) to 9f (Grade 2 event in USA at 5 yrs): second in small fields in maidens at Nottingham and Newcastle (green still, never travelling fluently, again stayed on well late on) 4 weeks later: should stay 1½m: looked capable of further progress but sold 6,800 gns Ascot December Sales. *H. R. A. Cecil* 82

CHEVELEY DANCER (USA) 7 b.g. Northern Baby (CAN) 127 – Alwah (USA) (Damascus (USA)) [1994 NR 1995 9.7d^4 9.7g 10g 10g 11.6m Jun 5] big, lengthy gelding: poor handicapper on flat: should stay 1½m: tried visored: bandaged at 7 yrs: pulls hard: inconsistent. *D. A. Wilson* 42

CHEVEUX MITCHELL 8 ch.h. Dunbeath (USA) 127 – Hide Out (Habitat 134) [1994 –: 7g 7.3s 7g a7g 1995 7m May 19] sturdy horse: seems no longer of much account. *P. A. Kelleway* –

CHEWIT 3 gr.g. Beveled (USA) – Sylvan Song (Song 132) [1994 72: 7f 6.9m a7g^2 a8g 1995 a6g^2 a7g^2 a6g* 6m^2 7f^5 5.3f^5 5s a6g^3 a5g^4 Dec 14] leggy gelding: fairly useful handicapper: comfortably won at Lingfield in March: has run creditably at 7f, but may well prove best at sprint distances: acts on equitrack and firm ground: ridden by Candy Morris except final start. *A. Moore* 81 a84

CHEYENNE SPIRIT 3 ch.f. Indian Ridge 123 – Bazaar Promise 58 (Native Bazaar 122) [1994 79: 5d 5.1m* 5f^4 5s^5 5.1g* 5s 1995 6m* 5m 7f^2 6g^6 6m* 6m 6m* 7f^2 6m* 6m^3 6m* 6g^2 Sep 29] lengthy, quite attractive filly: progressed into a useful performer: successful in handicaps at Newmarket in April, York (rated stakes) in June and Haydock in July, then in minor event at Yarmouth and listed race at Newmarket (held Royale Figurine by short head) in August: beaten a neck in rated stakes at Newmarket final start: effective at 6f and 7f: acts on firm ground, not at best on soft: races prominently: game and genuine. *B. Hanbury* 107

CHEZ CATALAN 4 b.c. Niniski (USA) 125 – Miss Saint-Cloud 102 (Nonoalco (USA) 131) [1994 58: 10d^3 10d 10g 12.1m^2 13g* 15.1m* 16g^3 17.5s 1995 14.1m 14s 15.8g^3 16.2g 16.1f^2 15.4m^2 a16g^3 Dec 15] compact colt: modest handicapper: stays 16.1f: acts on equitrack and firm ground, twice well beaten on soft: best in blinkers. *R. Akehurst* 53

CHICKAWICKA (IRE) 4 b.c. Dance of Life (USA) – Shabby Doll 69 (Northfields (USA)) [1994 93: 8.1s^3 10.3m^5 12m 8m 8.1m^2 7.6m^2 8f 8.3m 10g 8m^4 1995 8g 8g 7.6m 9m 8m 7f^2 7g* 6m^5 7m 7d 6.1s Oct 17] lengthy colt: fairly useful performer on his day: made all in claimer at Chester in July: effective at 6f, and stays 1m: acts on firm and soft ground: blinkered/visored since third 4-y-o start: has worn crossed noseband: sometimes on edge: often front runner. *M. C. Pipe* 90

CHICODARI 3 b.c. Shardari 134 – Chicobin (USA) (J O Tobin (USA) 130) [1994 67p: 7s 7g 7g^4 1995 10m 10m* Jul 3] big, good-topped colt: grand sort who has plenty of scope: fair performer: sweating, far from impressive in landing the odds in 4-runner apprentice maiden at Pontefract, making all but racing lazily and looking none too keen: stays 1¼m: winner over hurdles for D. Nicholson. *Sir Mark Prescott* 51 +

Mr C. Mauritzon's "Cheyenne Spirit"

CHIEF BEE 4 b.f. Chief's Crown (USA) – Lady Be Mine (USA) 76 (Sir Ivor 135) [1994 59p: 8.2d⁴ 1995 10m⁶ 9m* 10g 12s* 14.6m* 14g⁶ Nov 26] big, good-topped filly: carries condition: lightly-raced sister to leading 1989 2-y-o Be My Chief: awarded maiden at Redcar in August then won amateurs handicap at Ascot (by 7 lengths, despite wandering under pressure) and minor event at Doncaster (barely off bridle, by 6 lengths) in the autumn: faced stiff task and beaten 10 lengths behind Sternkoenig in Premio Roma Vecchia final start: stayed 14.6f, and would have stayed further: acted on good to firm ground and soft: visits Machiavellian. *J. L. Dunlop* 89

CHIEF MINISTER (IRE) 6 br.g. Rainbow Quest (USA) 134 – Riverlily (FR) (Green Dancer (USA) 132) [1994 72: 12g 16m³ 16g³ 15.1f⁵ 16.1m³ 16.2m⁵ 16.1m 1995 16m⁴ 16.5g⁵ 16.1m Jul 1] leggy gelding: has a round action: useful hurdler: fair handicapper on flat: stays 16.5f: acts on firm and soft ground: occasionally visored/ blinkered, and has run well: reluctant stalls (ran poorly) twice. *T. Dyer* 68

CHIEF MOUSE 2 b.g. (Feb 23) Be My Chief (USA) 122 – Top Mouse (High Top 131) [1995 8d 8.2m Oct 26] sturdy gelding: good mover: half-brother to several winners, including 5f winner Idrak (by Young Generation) and 1993 2-y-o 7f winner Harvest Mouse (by Thatching), latter effective at 1½m: dam twice-raced sister to smart 5f to 10.5f winner Triple First, herself dam of Oaks-placed Maysoon and Three Tails: modest form in maidens won by Helicon at Newmarket and Censor at Nottingham following month: may do better. *R. Charlton* 61

CHIEF OF STAFF 6 ch.g. Caerleon (USA) 132 – Fanny's Cove 89 (Mill Reef (USA) 141) [1994 65, a76: a7g⁵ a11g* a12g* 10.3g 11.9f³ 6.9m⁶ 9.9g³ a7g⁵ a12g⁶ a11g³ 1995 6.9g* 7m 8.1m⁶ 10m 8.1d³ 7g⁶ 9.7s* 8g Oct 3] leggy gelding: fair 71 performer: won amateurs race and claimer at Folkestone in June and September: broke blood vessel (has done so before) and fell final start: effective at 7f to 1½m: acts on good to firm and soft ground and all-weather surfaces: sometimes looks an awkward ride: sold 3,000 gns Newmarket Autumn Sales. *J. Pearce*

CHIEF'S LADY 3 b.f. Reprimand 122 – Pussy Foot 83 (Red Sunset 120) [1994 45: a7g 6m^4 1995 5g^6 5m^6 5.3f^5 6f^6 7m^2 6d 7s 7f 7f Oct 18] modest performer: trained first 2 starts in 1995 by G. Fierro, next 5 by R. Harris: long way below form last 4 outings: stays 7f: acts on firm ground, well beaten on soft surface. *C. N. Allen* — 55 d

CHIEF'S PRINCESS 3 ch.f. Be My Chief (USA) 122 – Settlement (USA) 75 (Irish River (FR) 131) [1994 56?: 6g 8m 7s 1995 12m^4 Jun 14] good-topped, workmanlike filly: no worthwhile form since debut, for new stable in 1995: visored (swishing tail first occasion) last 2 starts. *G. Fierro* — –

CHIEF'S SONG 5 b.g. Chief Singer 131 – Tizzy 79 (Formidable (USA) 125) [1994 72: 10s 13v^4 13s 11.9d^2 12d^4 12m 1995 16m 16.4m 14m 14d^4 14g Sep 29] tall gelding: useful hurdler (won valuable event at Sandown in December), but still a maiden handicapper on flat: should stay 2m: acts on heavy ground. *S. Dow* — 58

CHIEFTAIN'S CROWN (USA) 4 ch.g. Chief's Crown (USA) – Simple Taste (USA) 93 (Sharpen Up 127) [1994 43: 8m 8.1g 9m^3 10m 8f 8m 1995 8.3m 8.3m Jul 29] strong, good-bodied gelding: poor maiden: stays 9f: tried blinkered. *J. White* — –

CHIK'S SECRET 2 ch.f. (Feb 28) Nalchik (USA) – Lana's Secret 79 (Most Secret 119) [1995 a5g^2 6.1m^4 7f 7m 10d Sep 19] lengthy filly: has a long stride: half-sister to several animals: dam 5f winner: second in seller at Southwell in May: well beaten in better races on turf: acts on fibresand. *B. Palling* — – a50

CHILDREN'S CHOICE (IRE) 4 b.f. Taufan (USA) 119 – Alice Brackloon (USA) (Melyno 130) [1994 58: 12m^5 9.7s* 10m^6 11.1m^2 11.6m 12f^2 12g 14.1m^5 12.1g^6 10s* 10m 11.9d 1995 10.3g* 12m^2 12g 10.9m 12f^5 a12g 8.2m 12m Nov 6] leggy, workmanlike filly: modest handicapper: won 27-runner ladies race at Doncaster in March: well below form last 6 outings: effective at 1¼m and 1½m: acts on firm ground and soft: bandaged off-hind first 4 starts at 4 years: races prominently. *P. J. McBride* — 63

CHILD STAR (FR) 6 gr.m. Bellypha 130 – Miss Shirley (FR) 76 (Shirley Heights 130) [1994 36, a39: a12g^3 a12g^3 a16.2g^2 a14g^6 a14.8g^2 15.4d^4 16.1s a13g^6 1995 a14.8g^3 a16.2g^2 a12g a12g^3 a16.2g* 15.4g a14.8g^5 a14.8g^5 a16.2g^5 Jul 21] angular, light-framed mare: has a round action: poor handicapper: won at Wolverhampton in April: failed to repeat that form: stays 16.2f: acts on good to firm going, soft and fibresand: apprentice/amateur ridden: won maiden hurdle in August. *D. Marks* — – a42

CHILIBANG BANG 2 b.f. (Apr 26) Chilibang 120 – Quenlyn (Welsh Pageant 132) [1995 5s* 5f^2 5m^2 5m 5f^2 a5g* a6g* 6g a7g^2 Dec 12] 4,000Y: half-sister to several winners, including sprinters Roxby Melody (by Song) and Heathyards Gem (by Governor General): dam ran 3 times at 2 yrs: modest performer: won median auction maiden at Hamilton in April and 2 sellers at Wolverhampton in August: creditable second to Honestly in nursery at Wolverhampton final outing: stays 7f: acts on firm ground though seems ideally suited by soft or fibresand: well below form (poorly drawn) when visored on fourth start. *J. Berry* — 61

CHILI HEIGHTS 5 gr.g. Chilibang 120 – Highest Tender 56 (Prince Tenderfoot (USA) 126) [1994 –: 6d^6 7d 6g 7.1d 7g 7m 1995 6m 7g 7g^5 7m^6 7g^2 6m^5 7.1m 7.3d 8d^6 7.1d^4 7d^3 Oct 19] compact gelding: modest handicapper: stays 1m: acts on good to firm and soft going: usually wears visor (has run creditably without): usually bandaged behind: sometimes needs plenty of driving: held up. *G. B. Balding* — 62

CHILI LADY 5 ch.m. Chilibang 120 – Barbary Court (Grundy 137) [1994 42: a7g^4 a6g^5 a8g^2 a8g 8d 6m a8.5g 1995 a10g^5 a8g^3 a10g^6 Jan 17] lengthy mare: poor maiden: stays 1¼m. *J. S. Moore* — 38

CHILI LASS 3 ch.f. Chilibang 120 – City Link Lass 92 (Double Jump 131) [1994 –: 6.1s 5s 5g 1995 a7g 11.5g Sep 12] strong filly: of little account. *J. Wharton* — –

CHILIOLA 4 ch.f. Chilibang 120 – Sisola (USA) (Coastal (USA)) [1994 64: 5g^3 6m^3 5g^2 6g^4 6f 1995 a6g a6g Jan 30] big, lengthy filly: good mover: modest maiden handicapper: below form in 1995: stayed 6f: acted on dead going, seemingly not on — –

top-of-the-ground or fibresand: blinkered final start: usually edgy: sold 5,000 gns, in foal to Noble Patriarch, Newmarket December Sales. *M. H. Easterby*

CHILLAM 2 ch.g. (Apr 26) Chilibang 120 – Tissue Paper 95 (Touch Paper 113) [1995 5m a5g^4 a5g^3 5f Jul 29] 3,400Y: unfurnished gelding: eighth foal: half-brother to useful 3-y-o 1m winner Hoh Express and 7f and 1m winner (stays 1¼m) Mo-Addab (both by Waajib) and winners by Lord Gayle and Yashgan: dam won 3 times over 5f at 2 yrs in Ireland: best effort when less than a length third to Jimjareer at Southwell in auction event: speedy, and likely to prove best at 5f: best form on fibresand: gelded after final start. *J. P. Leigh* – a60

CHILLINGTON 2 gr.g. (Apr 2) Chilibang 120 – Saskia's Pride (Giacometti 130) [1995 7.1s Oct 1] lengthy, rather unfurnished gelding: first reported foal: dam won NH Flat race, her only start: 50/1, tailed off in maiden at Haydock. *W. M. Brisbourne* –

CHILLY BILLY 3 b.c. Master Willie 129 – Sweet Snow (USA) (Lyphard (USA) 132) [1994 110p: 6m^5 6f^3 7g^4 6m* 1995 8m^4 8m 6g^4 8f* Jul 26] good-topped, attractive colt: has a fluent action: very useful performer: 10¾ lengths eighth of 11 to Pennekamp in 2000 Guineas at Newmarket (upset in stalls) then around 6½ lengths fourth of 7 to Lake Coniston in Duke of York Stakes for Mrs J. Ramsden: raced on Lasix and bute and won valuable event at Del Mar in July: injured afterwards and not seen out again: stays 1m: has raced only on a sound surface: headstrong (wore crossed noseband at Newmarket) and not an easy ride. *R. Frankel, USA* 110

CHILLY LAD 4 ch.g. High Kicker (USA) – Miss Poll Flinders (Swing Easy (USA) 126) [1994 58, a60: a9.4g^4 8.2v 10.3f^6 10.3f^6 a12g 10.1g* 12g 10.5g^4 10d 10.1g^5 10d^2 10.1d^2 12s^2 1995 10g Jul 28] tall gelding: has badly scarred near-fore: modest handicapper: never a threat only start in 1995: stays 1½m: acts on fibresand and heavy ground, below form on firm: blinkered/visored sixth to final 3-y-o starts. *M. J. Ryan* –

CHILLY LOOKS 2 b.f. (Mar 7) Siberian Express (USA) 125 – Exceptional Beauty 94 (Sallust 134) [1995 6g 7m 7f^3 7.5m^5 6s Sep 30] 2,600F: tall, leggy, unfurnished filly: has a round action: fifth foal: sister to 2-y-o 5f winners Winterbound (in 1994) and Good Fetch (in 1993): dam 1½m winner: plater: will probably stay beyond 7.5f: often slowly away. *M. W. Easterby* 38 +

CHILLY TIME 4 ch.f. Chilibang 120 – Leap In Time (Dance In Time (CAN)) [1994 34: 5.7m 7d 6f^4 6m a5g 6d^6 6.1s a6g^6 5d^5 6.9m 7d 1995 a6g^6 a6g 6.1g Apr 17] workmanlike filly: no form in 1995: dead. *Mrs L. A. Murphy* –

CHIMANIMANI 4 b.g. Petong 126 – La Primavera (Northfields (USA)) [1994 80: 8.5d 10m^2 11.8g* 11.7m* 12.5f* 12f* 11.9g^4 1995 14.9d 14m 11.9m^4 12.3m 14m 12m^3 11.1f^5 Aug 9] workmanlike, sparely-made gelding: progressive handicapper at 3 yrs for J. Dunlop: well beaten in 1995: should stay beyond 1½m: acts on firm ground: usually held up. *N. Tinkler* –

CHIMBORAZO 4 ch.g. Salse (USA) 128 – Pale Gold (FR) (New Chapter 106) [1994 76: 12g^2 11.9m^2 11.5g^2 13.4s^2 11.9s 1995 a12g^5 a12g 16m 14.1m a14.8g^4 May 13] sturdy gelding: still a maiden, most disappointing for new stable in 1995: should stay beyond 13.4f: acts on good to firm and soft ground. *B. J. McMath* –

CHIMING IN 3 ch.f. Niniski (USA) 125 – River Chimes 43 (Forlorn River 124) [1994 64: 5f 6g^5 6g^4 6s^5 6g^4 1995 7.5m^3 6m* 6f^2 7g^6 6g 5.9f^2 6m^4 Jul 19] angular, leggy filly: fair handicapper: won at Pontefract in April: some way below form after next start: effective at 6f, and should stay 1m: acts on firm ground, probably on soft: sold 10,000 gns Newmarket Autumn Sales. *Mrs J. R. Ramsden* 73

CHINA CASTLE 2 b.g. (Apr 17) Sayf El Arab (USA) 127 – Honey Plum 57 (Kind of Hush 118) [1995 5g 7m^6 a7g* 7.1m^6 7g a6g a7g Nov 16] 1,000Y: good-topped gelding: third foal: dam 11.5f and 1½m winner: won seller at Southwell in August: ran very wide on home bend at Edinburgh fourth outing: should stay beyond 7f: acts on fibresand. *P. C. Haslam* 51 a62

CHINA HAND (IRE) 3 ch.g. Salt Dome (USA) – China Blue (Ahonoora 122) [1994 60: 5.3d^3 5.1m^2 5f^4 6m 1995 5g 5d^4 5m^5 5f^6 5g^4 5d Sep 14] close-coupled gelding: good mover: only poor form at best in 1995 for new stable: should stay 6f: acts on firm and dead ground. *Martyn Wane* 44

CHINA MAIL (IRE) 3 b.g. Slip Anchor 136 – Fenney Mill 99 (Levmoss 133) [1994 –: 8s 1995 10.3g^6 10m 11.6m 12m^5 12m 14.1g^5 14.1f^5 14m^6 Jul 7] leggy 58 d gelding: unimpressive mover: modest maiden handicapper: looks a thorough stayer: has been gelded: sold (J. Eustace to K. Bailey) 3,000 gns Newmarket Autumn Sales. *J. M. P. Eustace*

CHINESE VIKING 3 b.g. Petorius 117 – Comhail (USA) (Nodouble (USA)) [1994 NR 1995 7f 7g 6m^6 7.1m^6 6f Jun 30] 7,400Y: workmanlike gelding: first foal: dam ran twice: has shown some signs of ability though no worthwhile form: visored final start. *G. L. Moore* –

CHING 3 b.f. Shaadi (USA) 126 – Chinese Justice (USA) (Diesis 133) [1994 74p: 6g^4 6d^6 1995 6g Mar 25] leggy filly: failed to fulfill promise of debut, hanging under pressure only start in 1995: sold 16,000 gns Newmarket July Sales. *J. H. M. Gosden* –

CHINOUR (IRE) 7 b.g. Dalsaan 125 – Chishtiya 74 (Try My Best (USA) 130) [1994 71: 8.9f 6m^4 7g^2 6g^2 6g^5 8d^4 7.1g 8g 8m* 8d^6 a6g^3 1995 a7g a7g^6 a7g^4 8g 6g* 6m^5 6m 7m^6 7g 8.3f^5 6m^5 6m* 8f^6 7m^3 7.9g 8d Sep 9] strong gelding: fair handicapper: won celebrity event at Aintree in April and amateurs contest at Newcastle in July: effective at 6f to 1m: acts on good to firm and heavy ground and on fibresand: visored (ran badly) once as 6-y-o: has run well when sweating: sometimes slowly away, usually held up: inconsistent. *E. J. Alston* 71

CHITA RIVERA 4 b.f. Chief Singer 131 – Shirley Superstar 94 (Shirley Heights 130) [1994 55: 8g 10g^4 10m^2 10m^4 10.2g 1995 a11g 10m^6 10d 14d 16.4m^2 a16g Nov 30] leggy filly: only a poor maiden nowadays: stays 16.4f: acts on good to firm and dead ground: tried visored: sold 1,000 gns Newmarket December Sales. *P. J. Makin* 40

CHLOELLA 3 b.f. Shaadi (USA) 126 – Echoing 93 (Formidable (USA) 125) [1994 46: 6g 8.2s 6s 5g^5 1995 a6g a6g^5 5g 7.1g Sep 18] leggy filly: has a round action: poor sprint maiden: headstrong, and has given trouble in preliminaries. *C. B. B. Booth* 34

CHLOES DIAMOND (IRE) 7 ch.m. Heraldiste (USA) 121 – Salique (Sallust 134) [1994 33: 8s^5 7d^5 8.5m 8g 7.1m^2 7g^6 1995 a8g 8d Apr 1] sparely-made mare: seems no longer of much account. *A. P. James* –

CHOCOLATE CHARLIE 4 b.g. Cadeaux Genereux 131 – Lady Zi (Manado 130) [1994 NR 1995 10s 12g 10m 10f^5 12d 8m 7d Oct 19] 19,000Y: tall, unfurnished gelding: half-brother to 2 winners, notably smart miler Anshan (by Persian Bold): dam minor 1½m winner in France: no worthwhile form: visored final start. *R. Charlton* –

CHOCOLATE CHIP 3 b.g. Hard Fought 125 – Roses Galore (USA) (Stage Door Johnny) [1994 45: 5d 5m^6 6d a5g 1995 a6g Nov 8] small, sturdy gelding: poor form at 2 yrs for C. James: sold 600 gns Doncaster August Sales: tailed off in bad maiden at Lingfield on belated return: tried blinkered. *B. A. Pearce* –

CHOIR MASTER (CAN) 8 b.g. Assert 134 – Choral Group (CAN) (Lord Durham (CAN)) [1994 –: 14.1g^3 16.4s^6 a13g 1995 a16g May 27] tall, lengthy gelding: no form since 4 yrs: dead. *A. Moore* –

CHORUS BOY 10 br.g. Sonnen Gold 121 – Toccata (Kythnos 126) [1994 NR 1995 a14g Nov 24] tall gelding: of no account. *Mrs S. M. Austin* –

CHOSEN MAN 3 br.g. Dowsing (USA) 124 – Town Lady 93 (Town Crier 119) [1994 –: 5m 7g 1995 6.1g 6g May 8] leggy, shallow-girthed gelding: no sign of ability. *M. W. Ellerby* –

CHOWPOR 4 b.f. Nishapour (FR) 125 – Salchow 116 (Niniski (USA) 125) [1994 56: 6m^3 6f 8m 6g 1995 12g Apr 26] quite good-topped filly: modest form at best: tailed off for new stable in 1995: sold (M. Hammond to A. Carroll) 500 gns Doncaster August Sales: should be suited by 1m+. *M. D. Hammond* –

CHRIS'S GOVERNOR 2 b.c. (Apr 28) Governor General 116 – Fara 66 (Castle Keep 121) [1995 a6g a6g Jun 24] 2,400Y: second foal: dam, 1¼m seller winner, daughter of useful 2-y-o Faridetta: better than position suggests in sellers at Wolverhampton (blinkered on debut) but is probably only poor. *R. Hollinshead* –

CHRIS'S LAD 4 b.g. Thowra (FR) – Stockline (Capricorn Line 111) [1994 70: 10g 10g 14.1g^5 14.1m* 14.1m^2 13.1f^3 a14.8g^2 16m^3 16d* 15s* 16.2g 14m 1995 14f^4 Jun 30] close-coupled gelding: fair staying handicapper at 3 yrs for B. Meehan: well beaten in 4-runner race at Goodwood on only outing in 1995: successful on good to –

firm going, better form on fibresand or with give in the ground (acts on soft): effective from front or held up. *R. J. Hodges*

CHRISTIAN FLIGHT (IRE) 6 b.m. Fayruz 116 – Opening Flight (Falcon 131) [1994 NR 1995 a8g a6g^{3} a6g^{3} a7g^{4} a6g^{4} a6g^{4} a6g a6g 6.1m* 5f^{3} May 12] workmanlike mare: poor handicapper: won at Nottingham in May: effective at 5f and 6f: acts on firm ground and fibresand: visored (stiff task) eighth 6-y-o start. *S. Gollings* 48

CHRISTIAN SPIRIT 5 gr.g. Petong 126 – Hidden Asset (Hello Gorgeous (USA) 128) [1994 –: a7g^{5} a6g a8g a12g a8g a8g 1995 a8g a7g a8g^{6} 9.7g Apr 10] leggy gelding: no worthwhile form since 2 yrs: tried blinkered. *B. A. Pearce* –

CHRISTIAN WARRIOR 6 gr.g. Primo Dominie 121 – Rashah 67 (Blakeney 126) [1994 –: a7g 8.1g a8g 1995 7g 6g 7.1m 7g^{6} 6.1m a8.5g 6f 8h Aug 8] neat gelding: no longer of much account. *R. E. Peacock* –

CHRISTMAS KISS 3 b.f. Taufan (USA) 119 – Ancestry (Persepolis (FR) 127) [1994 78: 6m^{3} 6m^{2} 6g 1995 7g^{4} 7d 6m* 7m^{4} 7g^{3} 5f* 6g^{6} 6g Sep 29] tall filly: fairly useful performer: won maiden at Salisbury in May and handicap there (claimer ridden, well backed) in June: effective at 5f to 7f: acts on firm ground, probably on dead. *R. Hannon* 82

CHUCKLESTONE 12 b.g. Chukaroo 103 – Czar's Diamond 66 (Queen's Hussar 124) [1994 61: 16.4d 17.2f^{2} 18f^{3} 17.2f^{2} 16.2m^{4} 17.2m* 16.4g 17.2g 1995 14m 17.2f 17.2h^{4} 16.4m 16.1f^{6} a16g Dec 15] sturdy gelding: veteran staying handicapper: 7 times a winner at Bath: well beaten (including at Bath) in 1995: well suited by a sound surface: visored (tailed off) earlier in career. *J. S. King* –

CICERONE 5 br.g. Tina's Pet 121 – Emma Royale 69 (Royal And Regal (USA)) [1994 43+, a56: a7g^{6} a8g a7s^{5} 7g 7.5m 7.1f 7m 7.1m^{2} 7m^{2} 7g^{2} 7g 7d a8g* 1995 a8g a8g^{4} a8g^{2} a7g^{6} a8g^{6} a9.4g 8f^{3} 8f* a9.4g^{6} a8g^{6} Nov 20] leggy, angular gelding: has a round action: modest handicapper: won apprentice claiming event at Leicester in October: stays 1m: acts on firm and soft ground and on fibresand: tried blinkered (out of form) in 1994. *J. L. Harris* 48 a51

CIM BOM BOM (IRE) 3 b.c. Dowsing (USA) 124 – Nekhbet 74 (Artaius (USA) 129) [1994 97: 5f^{4} 5d* 6m* 6m 5f* 5m^{4} 6g 1995 6m 8.1m^{4} 7.1m^{3} 8.1g May 27] strong, workmanlike colt: carries condition: good walker: fairly useful performer: ran as if something amiss in £17,700 handicap at Haydock on final outing: stays 1m: acts on firm and dead ground. *M. Bell* 93

CINDERS CHANCE 3 ch.f. Beveled (USA) – Salinas 65 (Bay Express 132) [1994 –: 5g 5s 5g^{5} 1995 5g 5g 5.9f Jun 28] small, sparely-made filly: no worthwhile form: sold 750 gns Doncaster September Sales. *M. W. Ellerby* –

CINDERS PET 4 ch.f. Aragon 118 – Salinas 65 (Bay Express 132) [1994 –: 5s a5g 1995 5g May 24] no sign of ability. *M. W. Ellerby* –

CINNAMON STICK (IRE) 2 ch.g. (Apr 28) Don't Forget Me 127 – Gothic Lady (Godswalk (USA) 130) [1995 5m^{5} a6g 6g^{4} May 30] 9,000Y: close-coupled, rather unfurnished gelding: brother to 1994 2-y-o 6f winner Unforgetableknight and half-brother to several winners including 7f/1m performer Gothic Ford (by Stanford): dam Irish 9f and 9.5f winner: poor maiden: well beaten in seller at Leicester final outing: has joined P. Felgate. *W. Jarvis* –

CIRACUSA (IRE) 3 b.g. Kahyasi 130 – Miranisa (Habitat 134) [1994 NR 1995 11.8g 14.1m^{3} Oct 19] IR 16,000Y: neat gelding: second foal: dam twice-raced close relative of Poule d'Essai des Pouliches winner Masarika: 33/1, better effort on flat when 15 lengths third of 11 to Bimsey in maiden at Nottingham, very slowly away, challenging for second 2f out then appearing to tire: won novice hurdle in November: may improve again on flat. *J. Mackie* – p

CIRCA 3 ch.f. Risk Me (FR) 127 – Dancing Belle 80 (Dance In Time (CAN)) [1994 95: 6m^{5} 6g^{6} a6g* 6m 6.5g a6g* 7s^{2} 6g 7.3v* 1995 10m May 7] good-topped filly: has a round action: made into a useful performer as 2-y-o for G. Lewis, gaining final win in listed race at Newbury: refused to settle when well-beaten last of 8 in listed race (on good to firm ground) at Newmarket on only run in 1995: stays 7.3f well, seemingly not 1¼m: acts on fibresand and heavy ground. *W. Jarvis* –

CIRCLED (USA) 2 gr.f. (Apr 2) Cozzene (USA) – Hold The Hula (USA) (Hawaii) [1995 7d 7.1d* 8s^{5} Dec 3] $37,000F, IR 12,000Y: tall, unfurnished filly: 83

has a quick action: fourth foal: half-sister to 2 winners in USA: dam minor stakes winner in USA at up to 1¼m: won 9-runner maiden at Haydock, making all and running on strongly to beat Name of Our Father 6 lengths: below that form in 9-runner listed race at Toulouse nearly 8 weeks later: should stay further than 7f: looked promising at Haydock. *B. W. Hills*

CIRCLE OF FRIENDS (IRE) 4 b.f. Taufan (USA) 119 – Pitlessie 75 (Hook Money 124) [1994 –: 7m a8g 7.3s 6.1g 1995 7m Aug 5] leggy, close-coupled filly: destroyed after breaking pelvis only start in 1995: bred to stay beyond 6f: acted on good to soft ground. *R. Akehurst* —

CIRCUS STAR 2 b.c. (Apr 18) Soviet Star (USA) 128 – Circus Act (Shirley Heights 130) [1995 7g 6m^5 6m Nov 3] 30,000Y: tall, good-topped colt: third foal: half-brother to useful 3-y-o middle-distance stayer Jellaby Askhir (by Salse): dam unraced daughter of Circus Ring: twice caught eye in no uncertain fashion in maidens, behind Ali-Royal at Warwick on debut and Miss Riviera at Doncaster on final start, on each occasion steadied in behind then running on well without coming under pressure: sure to do much better over 1m+, and is very much one to follow. *Sir Mark Prescott* 65 P

CISERANO (IRE) 2 ch.f. (Mar 22) Mujtahid (USA) 118 – Blue Persian 112 (Majority Blue 126) [1995 6g^2 6m^3 6m^4 7g^4 Jul 16] 19,000Y: sturdy, lengthy filly: has a quick action: half-sister to several winners, including smart sprinter Polykratis (by He Loves Me) and 7f winner Iranian (by Indian King): dam top-of-the-ground 5f sprinter: modest form in maidens: gives impression may prove best at 5f. *M. R. Channon* 69

CITADEED (USA) 3 b.c. Shadeed (USA) 135 – Johanna Keene (USA) (Raise A Cup (USA)) [1994 105: a6g* 6m* 6m^5 7.3d^4 7v^5 1995 7m^3 a10f a9f* a12f^3 a9f^3 a10f^6 Aug 19] lengthy, useful-looking colt: smart performer: 4¼ lengths third of 12 (mulish at stalls) to Diffident in European Free Handicap at Newmarket on reappearance: ninth of 19 in Kentucky Derby at Churchill Downs on final start for P. Chapple-Hyam: won Grade 2 Peter Pan Stakes at Belmont later in May: third in Belmont Stakes (5½ lengths behind Thunder Gulch) and Haskell Invitational (beaten 4¼ lengths by Serena's Song) at Monmouth Park: well beaten in Travers Stakes at Saratoga final start: stays 1½m: acts on good to firm and heavy ground and on dirt. *R. Violette jnr, USA* 116

CITY RHYTHM 5 b.g. Librate 91 – Star City (Royal Boxer 112) [1994 –: 8m 8m a8.5g 1995 a8.5g a12g Jan 27] sturdy gelding: of little account. *J. M. Bradley* —

CITY RUN (USA) 3 b.c. Mehmet (USA) – Sable Sham (USA) (Sham (USA)) [1994 60p: 8g 1995 7m 10m May 15] leggy, unfurnished colt: down the field in maidens. *D. J. S. Cosgrove* —

CIVIL 3 b.f. Risk Me (FR) 127 – Astrid Gilberto 75 (Runnett 125) [1994 51: 5d^3 6s^5 6g^2 5g^3 6m^6 1995 a7g Apr 11] lengthy filly: modest form at 2 yrs: tailed-off last of 12 in handicap at Southwell on only 3-y-o start. *R. Hannon* —

CIVIL LIBERTY 2 b.c. (Mar 8) Warning 136 – Libertine 114 (Hello Gorgeous (USA) 128) [1995 7f^6 7m^2 Aug 16] big, well-made colt: has plenty of scope: fourth foal: brother to useful French 3-y-o (stays 1¼m) Take Liberties, 6f winner at 2 yrs, and half-brother to French 1m winner Amandine (by Darshaan): dam 5.5f (at 2 yrs) and 1m winner also third in Pouliches and stayed 1¼m: neck second of 8 to Dublin River in minor event at Kempton, running on from rear after failing to handle bend and looking green: will stay beyond 7f: sure to improve again and should win races. *G. Lewis* 87 p

CLAIRESWAN (IRE) 3 ch.g. Rhoman Rule (USA) – Choclate Baby (Kashiwa 115) [1994 NR 1995 a8g^5 a8.5g^5 a8g^4 10.5d^4 12.3f^6 13f* a16.2g* 15m* 14.1m^2 a16g* 15g Sep 14] 1,900Y: workmanlike gelding: fourth foal: dam Irish 1¼m and 13f winner: fair handicapper: successful at Hamilton (maiden), Wolverhampton and Ayr (both amateurs) and Lingfield (by 9 lengths), all in 7 weeks in the summer: stays 16.2f: acts on firm ground and the all-weather: goes well with forcing tactics: has joined M. Tompkins. *S. C. Williams* 65

CLAN BEN (IRE) 3 ch.c. Bluebird (USA) 125 – Trina's Girl (Nonoalco (USA) 131) [1994 NR 1995 8.3m^2 8m* 8g* 9d^2 8.1s^4 8m^5 Oct 28] sturdy colt: good mover: seventh foal: half-brother to 6f and 7f winner Albyn Lady (by Be My Guest), 1¼m 101

winner My Ratbag and a 5f winner in Norway (both by Nordico): dam 2-y-o 5f winner: useful performer: won maiden at Newmarket in August and minor event at Doncaster in September: ran well all 3 subsequent outings, fifth of 7 in listed race at Newmarket on final one: stays 9f well: acts on good to firm and soft ground: stays in training. *H. R. A. Cecil*

CLAN CHIEF 2 b.c. (Apr 30) Clantime 101 – Mrs Meyrick 42 (Owen Dudley 121) [1995 5g^3 5m^3 5m^2 5.1g^2 5.1m^4 Aug 28] 3,000F, 6,000Y: second foal: dam won at up to 15f: modest maiden: below form in nursery at Chepstow final start: likely to prove best at 5f: has been bandaged behind. *J. R. Arnold* 64

CLANCY'S EXPRESS 4 b.g. Faustus (USA) 118 – Pink Pumpkin 52 (Tickled Pink 114) [1994 47?: 6m 5m 7g^5 9s^2 8s 9g 1995 a10g 6m 8.3m 10m 12g 10m^6 8.1m Jul 2] sturdy gelding: poor maiden: probably stays 1¼m: best efforts on an easy surface: blinkered last 2 starts in 1993. *G. B. Balding* 34

CLAN SCOTIA 3 ch.f. Clantime 101 – Moorhill (Vaigly Great 127) [1994 47: 5d^5 5f^5 5m^4 5m^3 5m^2 5m* 5m^6 1995 5.1m May 2] sparely made filly: poor form at 2 yrs: unruly in stalls and soundly beaten in seller on only 3-y-o start. *J. Berry* –

CLAQUE 3 ch.c. Kris 135 – Mixed Applause (USA) 101 (Nijinsky (CAN) 138) [1994 57p: 7g 7g^5 1995 12m^6 14.1f a12g a16g Nov 20] angular, useful-looking colt: good mover: modest maiden: sold out of Mrs J. Cecil's stable 7,800 gns Newmarket Autumn Sales after second 3-y-o start: well beaten afterwards: may prove best at up to 1½m. *D. W. Chapman* 63

CLARET BUMBLE 4 ch.f. Absalom 128 – Mumtaz Mayfly 64 (Tap On Wood 130) [1994 a7.5g a7.5g* 6g 5.5v^4 8d^2 8m 8g^3 7f 8.5g 8s 8g 1995 a8g^6 a8g 7v* a7.5g^2 6v^2 a7.5g* 7d* a7.5g 8v^4 6h^3 7f^3 9f 8d^5 7d a7g^5 Sep 25] leggy, sparely-made filly: rated 66 here at 2 yrs but trained since in Belgium, showing poor form at best: well beaten in claimer and apprentice handicap at Lingfield first 2 starts in 1995: won 3 times in small fields (twice at Groenendaal and once at Boitsfort) afterwards: stays 1m: acts on good to firm and heavy ground and on dirt. *Andre Hermans, Belgium* 44

CLARION CALL (IRE) 4 b.g. Don't Forget Me 127 – Hillbrow 100 (Swing Easy (USA) 126) [1994 –: 7d 5.3g 7.1d 1995 6g 8.3m a8g Nov 25] strong, lengthy gelding: no worthwhile form since 1993. *G. Thorner* –

CLARY SAGE 2 br.f. (Jan 28) Sayf El Arab (USA) 127 – Supergreen (Superlative 118) [1995 5g^4 Apr 17] 1,200Y: fourth foal: sister to 3 poor animals: dam never ran: 12/1, remote fourth in 7-runner maiden at Newcastle. *C. W. Fairhurst* –

CLASSIC AFFAIR (USA) 2 ch.f. (May 1) Trempolino (USA) 135 – Coupole (USA) 71 (Vaguely Noble 140) [1995 6s^5 7f Oct 12] 170,000 francs Y: neat filly: half-sister to 4 winners in France including 1m/9f winner Super Arianne (by Super Concorde), successful in listed race: dam 1½m winner: similar form in maidens at Lingfield won by Norwegian Blue and Redcar won by Green Charter 2 weeks later: bred to stay middle distances: bandaged near-hind and slowly away on debut. *S. C. Williams* 59

CLASSICAL STAR 6 b.h. Tout Ensemble – Spic And Span 39 (Crisp And Even 116) [1994 NR 1995 11.7m^4 9g 8m Jun 2] sturdy horse: has a free, round action: sixth reported foal: dam half-sister to good Italian performer De Hooch: fair form at best in 5 French middle-distance races in 1993 when trained by J. Lyon: poor form in novice hurdles for K. Bailey in 1993/4: tailed off on return to flat: wears bandages. *R. J. Hodges* –

CLASSIC ARTISTE (USA) 2 ch.f. (May 18) Arctic Tern (USA) 126 – Batan Gantlet (Run The Gantlet (USA)) [1995 6m^5 6m 6.1d 8.3g^5 Sep 25] $17,000F, $20,000Y: leggy, rather unfurnished filly: has a round action: half-sister to several winners in North America: dam French maiden out of sister to Derby third Pentland Firth: fifth of 8 in maiden at Newmarket for B. McMath on debut: not discredited in face of stiff task in nursery at Hamilton on final start: bred to stay middle distances: twice unruly at stalls and seems somewhat highly strung. *S. C. Williams* 56

CLASSIC BALLET (FR) 2 b.f. (Jan 24) Fabulous Dancer (USA) 124 – Tyranesque (USA) (Key To The Mint (USA)) [1995 8.1d^4 7d 8.1s^2 Nov 2] 440,000 francs Y: smallish, sturdy filly: sister to French 7f (at 2 yrs) and 1m winner Tyramisou (later winner in USA) and a winner in Spain, and half-sister to several winners in France and Spain: dam 4.5f winner at 2 yrs in France: improved effort when 1¾ 75 lengths second of 8 to Santillana in maiden at Edinburgh, battling on well having made running: stays 1m: has raced only on a soft surface. *S. C. Williams*

CLASSIC BEAUTY (IRE) 2 b.f. (Feb 25) Fairy King (USA) – Working Model 99 (Ile de Bourbon (USA) 133) [1995 6m4 7f4 Oct 31] 40,000F, 45,000Y: sturdy filly: has scope: third reported foal: half-sister to 1¼m winner Bronze Maquette (by Ahonoora): dam 1¼m winner probably ideally suited by 1½m: similar form when keeping-on fourth in October maidens won by Singing Patriarch at Catterick and Magic Mill at Redcar: will be better suited by 1m+: likely to do better. *S. C. Williams* 63 p

CLASSIC CALL (IRE) 2 b.g. (Apr 27) Classic Music (USA) – Queen of Wolves (Wolver Hollow 126) [1995 6.1m a7g Aug 5] IR 7,500F, 20,000Y: good-quartered, attractive gelding: third foal: dam Irish 6f and 9f winner stayed middle distances: weak in betting, behind in maidens at Nottingham and Wolverhampton: subsequently gelded. *M. R. Stoute* –

CLASSIC CLICHE (IRE) 3 b.c. Salse (USA) 128 – Pato 90 (High Top 131) [1994 91p: 7m* 7g2 1995 10.4g* 12g4 12f2 12m5 14.6d* Sep 9] 120

Victory for the appropriately-named Classic Cliche in the Pertemps St Leger completed a clean sweep of the five British classics for the Al Maktoums, the ruling family of Dubai. Like the Derby winner Lammtarra and the Oaks winner Moonshell, Classic Cliche was part of the phenomenally successful Godolphin operation which had around forty horses under the care of Saeed bin Suroor at Newmarket. As well as taking the stable into an unassailable lead in the trainers' table for win-money, Classic Cliche's St Leger victory also provided champion jockey Frankie Dettori with the thousandth winner of his career. In a memorable year, Dettori again went on to top the two-hundred-winner mark in Britain, becoming only the third, after Fred Archer (eight times) and Gordon Richards (twelve times), to achieve that feat more than once. And Dettori is still only twenty-five! Dettori's achievements, coupled with his infectious enthusiasm, have helped him capture the imagination of the racing public and he was given a tremendous reception at Doncaster. The victory was among the more straightforward on the Dettori conveyor belt, Classic Cliche having the St Leger in safe keeping from over two furlongs out after being sent for home soon after the field entered the home straight. Classic Cliche, who started favourite after the late withdrawal of Dettori's intended mount Presenting, won by three and a half lengths from Minds Music with Istidaad two and half further behind. By classic standards, those behind Classic Cliche were an ordinary lot, but the winner's victory couldn't have been more clear cut.

Classic Cliche ran twice for Henry Cecil as a two-year-old, winning a maiden at Newmarket on his debut and then being short-headed in a minor event at Ascot.

Homeowners Dante Stakes, York—Classic Cliche (left), Annus Mirabilis and Presenting

Pertemps St Leger Stakes, Doncaster—Classic Cliche gets the trip well; Minds Music is a clear second ahead of Istidaad (striped cap) and In Camera

Returned after wintering in Dubai and looking to have done very well physically, Classic Cliche made his mark in good company straight away, winning the Homeowners Dante Stakes over an extended mile and a quarter at York in May, gamely holding off Annus Mirabilis by half a length, the pair clear of Presenting and the Two Thousand Guineas fourth Pipe Major. Classic Cliche's pedigree cast doubts, at the time, on his likely effectiveness over longer distances—he hadn't been entered in the Derby—but he gave a good account of himself, finishing fourth after meeting plenty of trouble in running, in the Prix du Jockey-Club on his next outing. The strong-finishing Classic Cliche was only about two and a half lengths behind the winner Celtic Swing despite losing his place when hemmed in on the home turn and then having to be checked again in the straight. On the strength of this good run, Classic Cliche started favourite for the King Edward VII Stakes at Royal Ascot, only to come up against the progressive Pentire who beat him in impressive style. Classic Cliche, conceding 3 lb all round, gave another game display to take second, keeping on in a manner that suggested he'd stay further, despite his pedigree. The only race that Classic Cliche contested between Royal Ascot and the St Leger was the Irish Derby at the Curragh in July. He was a late substitute for his stable's Derby winner Lammtarra and managed only a fair fifth behind Winged Love, possibly still feeling the effects of his exertions in the King Edward VII Stakes.

Classic Cliche (IRE) (b.c. 1992)	Salse (USA) (b 1985)	Topsider (b 1974)	Northern Dancer
			Drumtop
		Carnival Princess (ch 1974)	Prince John
			Carnival Queen
	Pato (b 1982)	High Top (br 1969)	Derring-Do
			Camenae
		Patosky (b 1969)	Skymaster
			Los Patos

Doubts about Classic Cliche's stamina seemed well founded, judged on his pedigree. His sire the splendidly game Salse—whose sire and dam were both raced over sprint distances—wasn't raced beyond a mile and made his name at shorter distances, winning the Challenge Stakes and the Prix de la Foret among other races. Classic Cliche's dam Pato, a sister to the very smart sprinter Crews Hill, stayed a mile

Godolphin's "Classic Cliche"

and a quarter, at which trip she showed fairly useful form in handicaps. There is stamina further back on both sides of Classic Cliche's pedigree—Topsider, the sire of Salse, was out of Drumtop, winner of the thirteen-furlong Canadian International Championship, while Classic Cliche's great grandam the staying-bred Los Patos won at two miles. Salse has been responsible for others who stay much better than he did—he had, for example, two other runners in the St Leger, Luso and Jellaby Askhir, and at one time also looked like being represented in the race by the Ebor winner Sanmartino. Classic Cliche is the fourth foal out of Pato, whose two previous winners, the poor Cheeky Pot (by Petoski) and the useful Threatening (by Warning), stayed a mile and a half and nine furlongs respectively on the flat. Pato produced the fair staying maiden Pat Or Else (by Alzao) between Cheeky Pot and Threatening. Classic Cliche, a good-topped, attractive colt who carries condition, has yet to race on soft going but acts on any other. Like his sire, he is a genuine and consistent racehorse. *Saeed bin Suroor*

CLASSIC COLOURS (USA) 2 ch.c. (Apr 12) Blushing John (USA) 120 – All Agleam (USA) (Gleaming (USA)) [1995 7.1d^5 8f Oct 25] 40,000Y: unfurnished colt: half-brother to several winners here and abroad, including very smart miler Magic Gleam (by Danzig): dam unraced half-sister to champion American filly Davona Dale: well beaten, racing keenly, in maidens won by Circled at Haydock and Bright Water at Yarmouth. *S. C. Williams* —

CLASSIC DAISY 2 b.f. (Apr 17) Prince Sabo 123 – Bloom of Youth (IRE) (Last Tycoon 131) [1995 6m 7m^3 7.1f^3 7f 6g^6 7.1s a6g a8g Nov 24] 2,800F, IR 3,800Y, 1,900 2-y-o: second foal: sister to 3-y-o Pioneer Princess: dam unraced: plater: stays 7f: acts on firm ground and fibresand: usually blinkered/visored: sold (Miss G. Kelleway to R. Spicer) 2,100 gns Ascot December Sales. *Miss Gay Kelleway* 45 a39

CLASSIC DEFENCE (IRE) 2 b.c. (Mar 3) Cyrano de Bergerac 120 – My Alanna (Dalsaan 125) [1995 7.1m 7.5d 6d Sep 27] IR 11,000Y: unfurnished colt: 58

third foal: dam fair Irish stayer: around 7 lengths eighth of 12 to Al Abraq in auction event at Sandown (had tongue tied down) in August: failed to repeat that form: needs further than 6f. *J. W. Hills*

CLASSIC DELIGHT (USA) 2 b.f. (Jan 26) Green Forest (USA) 134 – Weather Girl (USA) (One For All (USA)) [1995 6.1m a7g^4 7.5d^5 7s Sep 28] IR 27,500Y: lengthy filly: first foal: dam, won 3 races in USA, half-sister to dam of Oaks d'Italia winner Miss Gris: some promise in maidens second and third starts: had no chance from poor draw other starts, for B. McMath on debut. *S. C. Williams* — 55

CLASSIC EAGLE 2 b.c. (Mar 18) Unfuwain (USA) 131 – La Lutine 95 (My Swallow 134) [1995 8.1s* Oct 17] half-brother to several winners here and abroad, including Middle Park winner Mon Tresor and smart 8-y-o sprinter Montendre (both by Longleat) and fairly useful stayer Mondragon (by Niniski): dam 5f and 7f winner at 2 yrs later successful at up to 10.2f: 5/1, won 11-runner maiden at Chepstow by ¾ length from Smilin N Wishin, pair 13 lengths clear, making all travelling smoothly until tiring close home: sure to improve. *S. C. Williams* — 89 p

CLASSIC EXHIBIT 6 b.g. Tate Gallery (USA) 117 – See The Tops (Cure The Blues (USA)) [1994 NR 1995 a11g a12g a12g Mar 4] leggy gelding: no longer of much account on flat: modest hurdler, formerly untrustworthy but successful 3 times in August. *A. L. Forbes* — –

CLASSIC FLYER (IRE) 2 b.f. (Feb 18) Alzao (USA) 117 – Sea Harrier (Grundy 137) [1995 6m^5 7m* 7m^5 7d Sep 26] 80,000Y: good-topped filly: has scope: fluent mover: half-sister to useful 6f and 7f winner Hill Hopper (by Danehill) and middle-distance winners Water Boatman (by Main Reef) and Glendera (by Glenstal): dam twice-raced half-sister to high-class stayer Sea Anchor: made all in falsely-run maiden at Yarmouth in July, winning readily by ½ length from Bonarelli: well beaten afterwards at Newmarket in minor event and valuable sales race (slowly away) 2 months later: will stay beyond 7f. *S. C. Williams* — 80

CLASSIC LEADER 2 b.c. (Feb 28) Thatching 131 – Tenderetta (Tender King 123) [1995 6m^2 May 21] 55,000Y: good-bodied colt: has scope: first foal: dam won at 6f and 7.9f as 2-y-o in Ireland: 7/1, neck second to Jedaal in 13-runner maiden at Ripon, soon in rear after very slow start then running on strongly final 2f despite looking green: looked sure to improve. *S. C. Williams* — 74

CLASSIC LOOK (IRE) 2 b. or br.f. (Mar 4) Classic Music (USA) – Mini Look (FR) (In Fijar (USA) 121) [1995 6m Aug 11] leggy, angular filly: second reported live foal: half-sister to smart 3-y-o 7f winner Brief Glimpse (by Taufan), also 5f and 6f winner at 2 yrs: dam French maiden: 12/1 and bit backward, towards rear in 22-runner maiden at Newbury won by Bosra Sham, making some late headway from poor draw: will probably do better. *Major D. N. Chappell* — – p

CLASSIC LOVER (IRE) 2 b.f. (Apr 14) Taufan (USA) 119 – Sound Pet (Runnett 125) [1995 6g^2 8.2d^4 9g^3 8f^6 Oct 18] IR 15,000Y: third foal: half-sister to 3-y-o Rockville Pike (by Glenstal), 5f winner at 2 yrs: dam placed in Germany: left B. McMath's stable after debut: fair form last 2 starts when third in maiden at Redcar and sixth in nursery at Yarmouth: stays 9f. *S. C. Williams* — 71

CLASSIC MODEL (IRE) 4 b.g. High Line 125 – Fast Car (FR) (Carwhite 127) [1994 63: 8.1g 10m 10m 10s^6 1995 12g Mar 23] tall, lengthy, unfurnished gelding: modest form at 3 yrs: showed little on only outing in 1995. *B. W. Hills* — –

CLASSIC PET (IRE) 3 b.f. Petorius 117 – Checkers (Habat 127) [1994 47: 6g 7g 6d 1995 6m 5m 8g 8.3m 6g 6.1m 6f 5m* 5.1d Sep 11] compact filly: modest sprint handicapper: easily best effort in 1995 when winning 18-runner race at Sandown in August, one of only 3 to race on favoured far side: acts on good to firm and dead ground: headstrong, and sometimes early to post: inconsistent. *C. A. Horgan* — 49

CLASSIC ROMANCE 2 b.f. (Feb 25) Cadeaux Genereux 131 – What A Pity 97 (Blakeney 126) [1995 7.1s* 8.1d^3 Oct 11] 38,000Y: seventh foal: half-sister to useful 1990 6f and 7f 2-y-o winner Junk Bond (by Last Tycoon) and a winner in Italy by Tap On Wood: dam, lightly-raced 7f winner, half-sister to College Chapel: won maiden at Haydock in September by 1¼ lengths from Salty Girl: eased good deal when beaten when 9¾ lengths third of 4 to Inchrory in minor event there following month: likely to stay beyond 1m. *S. C. Williams* — 79

CLASSIC SKY (IRE) 4 b.g. Jareer (USA) 115 – Nawadder 73 (Kris 135) [1994 100: 7f 6g^{2} 6m 7m^{4} 8.1m 7.3g^{4} 7g 7m^{6} 1995 7m^{2} 7m 7m^{3} 7m* 7m^{3} 8.1m 8f 7.3m^{4} 8.3m 7d Sep 23] good-topped gelding: useful handicapper: trained until after seventh 4-y-o start by B. Hanbury, winning listed event at Rome in May: would have gone close to winning but for being hampered when fourth in rated stakes at Newbury on first outing for new connections: best at around 7f: looks best on a sound surface (acts on firm going): held up. *E. A. L. Dunlop* 102

CLASSIC VICTORY 2 b.c. (Feb 4) Puissance 110 – Seattle Mama (USA) (Seattle Song (USA) 130) [1995 5m 6d 7.1m 6f* 6m^{4} 6m 6d Sep 18] 14,000F, 28,000Y: tall, quite attractive colt: has a quick action: first foal: dam unraced half-sister to Grade 1 winner Arewehavingfunyet: best effort when making all (on favoured stand rail) in maiden at Hamilton in July: contested nurseries afterwards, not discredited at Catterick first occasion: should stay 7f but races keenly: best effort on firm ground. *S. C. Williams* 72 ?

CLASSICY 3 b.c. Cadeaux Genereux 131 – Sauceboat 120 (Connaught 130) [1994 71p: 7s^{4} 7m 1995 7g* 7.6m* 7.9g* 8m 8f Jul 27] strong, good-bodied, attractive colt: fairly useful performer: justified favouritism in maiden at Catterick in April and in handicaps at Chester (£18,100 event, idled) and York in May: below form in Britannia Handicap at Royal Ascot and Schweppes Golden Mile at Goodwood (faded closing stages in very strongly-run race) afterwards: effective at 7f to 1m: acts on good to firm ground. *M. R. Stoute* 91

CLASSY CHIEF 2 b.c. (Apr 4) Be My Chief (USA) 122 – Jalopy 71 (Jalmood (USA) 126) [1995 8g 7f^{3} 8m^{2} Nov 4] big, good-bodied colt: third foal: dam, 5f winner, half-sister to useful sprinter Point of Light: fair form in maidens last 2 starts, 3½ lengths second of 23 to Shaamit in median auction event at Doncaster final one: will stay beyond 1m: took good hold to post first 2 starts. *R. Boss* 78

CLAUDIA HABIBI (IRE) 3 ch.f. Zalazl (USA) 120 – Choral Dancer (USA) (Night Shift (USA)) [1994 47: 7d 8g 1995 8m a8g 8g Jul 27] small filly: poor maiden: sold 700 gns Ascot July Sales. *C. C. Elsey* –

CLEAN EDGE (USA) 3 ch.g. Woodman (USA) 126 – Najidiya (USA) 87 (Riverman (USA) 131) [1994 –: 7m 7m 8m 1995 14.1g^{6} Apr 4] workmanlike gelding: no worthwhile form. *M. H. Tompkins* –

CLEAR ATTRACTION (USA) 3 b.f. Lear Fan (USA) 130 – Highclere 129 (Queen's Hussar 124) [1994 NR 1995 11.9d^{6} Oct 11] rangy, unfurnished filly: half-sister to several winners, including very smart 7f to 1½m winner Height of Fashion (by Bustino), later dam of Unfuwain and Nashwan, and smart middle-distance performer Milford (by Mill Reef): dam won 1000 Guineas and Prix de Diane: 10/1 and green, never-dangerous sixth of 19 to Richelieu in maiden at Haydock: should do better. *Lord Huntingdon* – p

CLEAR LOOK 5 b.m. Green Desert (USA) 127 – Avoid (USA) (Buckpasser (USA)) [1994 –§: 10d 1995 a7g^{6} a11g 9.6g^{4} 11g* 16g 12m 9f Aug 9] big, lengthy mare: ungenuine maiden here, sold out of Miss H. Knight's stable 5,600 gns Ascot February Sales after second 5-y-o start: made all in 5-runner handicap at Killarney in July: below form afterwards: stays 11f: acts on good to firm and heavy ground: blinkered 3 times in 1993, twice running creditably: finds little. *A. P. O'Brien, Ireland* 63 §

CLEARLY DEVIOUS 3 b.f. Machiavellian (USA) 123 – Shoot Clear 111 (Bay Express 132) [1994 NR 1995 8m^{2} 8f Oct 18] unfurnished filly: seventh foal: half-sister to several winners, including useful middle-distance winner Shoot Ahead (by Shirley Heights) and 1990 2-y-o 7f winner Dance Ahead (by Shareef Dancer): dam 5f to 7f winner at 2 yrs and fourth in 1000 Guineas, is half-sister to Sally Brown and Untold: favourite but in need of race, head second of 18 to Lancerette in maiden at Pontefract, looking sure to win 2f out but tiring, green and caught close home: disappointing in similar event at Yarmouth 16 days later. *J. R. Fanshawe* 71

CLEDESCHAMPS 6 b.m. Doc Marten 104 – Cape Farewell (Record Run 127) [1994 43: 5.9s^{3} 8.1g 7m^{6} a7g^{3} a7g^{3} a7g^{3} 7g^{2} a6g^{6} 1995 a7g 6s^{2} 5.9m a7g a7g Jun 8] smallish, lengthy mare: poor handicapper: effective at 6f under testing conditions, and stays 1m: best form on turf with some give in the ground, acts on fibresand. *M. W. Ellerby* 37

CLEMENTE 2 b. or br.c. (Apr 1) Robellino (USA) 127 – Gravad Lax 82 (Home Guard (USA) 129) [1995 7.1d 7d^4 8.1s^3 Oct 17] 1,900F, 17,000Y: good-bodied colt: brother to modest 1¼m winner Mighty Wrath: dam, second over 5f at 2 yrs, half-sister to 1000 Guineas winner Enstone Spark: fourth of 13 to Centre Stalls in maiden at Salisbury: remote third of 11 behind Classic Eagle in similar event at Chepstow on soft ground following month: may stay beyond 1m: took good hold second start. *R. Hannon* — 70

CLERKENWELL (USA) 2 b.c. (May 3) Sadler's Wells (USA) 132 – Forlene 108 (Forli (ARG)) [1995 8g^4 Sep 8] $230,000F: sturdy colt: ninth foal: brother to useful stayer Jungle Dancer, closely related to 1994 Irish 2-y-o 7f winner Palais Glide and French 1¼m and 10.5f winner Gloria's Dancer (both by Northern Dancer) and half-brother to useful 1¼m winner Mesleh (by Alleged): dam Irish 2-y-o 7f and 1m winner out of very smart Arkadina: 15/2, burly and green, over 8 lengths fourth of 17 to Heron Island in maiden at Doncaster, soon pushed along then staying on never a factor: will stay at least 1¼m: will improve. *M. R. Stoute* — 75 p

CLIBURNEL NEWS (IRE) 5 b.m. Horage 124 – Dublin Millennium (Dalsaan 125) [1994 59: a12g^3 a13g^6 a12g^4 15.1m* 16.2m a16g^3 13.1g* 15.1m^2 a16.2g^5 a11g^2 16.1s^6 11.5g^4 14.1g^6 1995 a13g^2 a14.8g^3 a13g^3 a12g^4 a12g^3 a13g^4 11.8d* 11.8m 13g^5 11.8m* 14.1m^4 14.1m^4 10g 13.8f^2 Oct 14] sparely-made mare: modest handicapper: trained until after sixth 5-y-o start by W. Muir: won at Leicester in April and (weak apprentice event, third-last outing for A. Forbes) May: stays 15f: acts on the all-weather and any turf going: has been bandaged behind: usually held up: none too consistent. *A. Streeter* — 61 a48

CLIFTON FOX 3 b.g. Deploy 131 – Loveskate (USA) 78 (Overskate (CAN)) [1994 79p: 7.1d^5 7.5g* 7g* 1995 10.3g 8.5m* 10.5m^3 7.9g 8m* 10.5g^5 8g^5 8d 8m^4 8m Oct 28] close-coupled gelding: fairly useful handicapper: won at Beverley in April and Leicester in May: effective at 1m to 10.5f: acts on good to firm going: usually races prominently. *J. A. Glover* — 84

CLIFTON GAME 5 b.g. Mummy's Game 120 – Brave Maiden 63 (Three Legs 128) [1994 –: 10v^6 10.2s 10.8m 1995 a12g^2 11.8d Apr 6] tall gelding: 20/1 and ridden at overweight by 7-lb claimer, only worthwhile form when neck second of 11 in handicap at Wolverhampton on reappearance: well beaten in Leicester handicap 5 weeks later: stays 1½m: acts on fibresand: has joined M. Channon. *P. G. Murphy* — – a51

CLINCHER CLUB 2 b.f. (Feb 4) Polish Patriot (USA) 128 – Merry Rous 66 (Rousillon (USA) 133) [1995 5g 5m 5m* 6m^3 6d^2 6g 6m 6.1m Oct 26] 9,000Y: leggy, close-coupled filly: second foal: half-sister to 1994 2-y-o 5f winner Bruton Stream (by Taufan): dam, 2-y-o 6f winner, half-sister to smart sprinter Tina's Pet: fair form: won maiden at Pontefract in August: best effort when second in nursery at Doncaster on fifth outing: never going well final one: stays 6f: acts on good to firm ground, best form on dead: free to post third and fourth starts. *M. Johnston* — 77

CLINT 2 b.c. (Mar 4) Colmore Row 111 – Eastwood Heiress (Known Fact (USA) 135) [1995 5g 6m^6 a6g a7g Nov 10] first foal: dam out of half-sister to 2000 Guineas winner Mon Fils: no form in varied events, in seller final start. *J. Ffitch-Heyes* — –

CLIPTOMANIA (USA) 2 b. or br.c. (Apr 10) Cryptoclearance (USA) – Mary Tavy (USA) (San Feliou (FR)) [1995 6f^2 8g* 8d* 8s^2 9.5d* Nov 19] $37,000Y: tall, leggy colt: second foal: dam winner at up to 9f in USA: sire top-class middle-distance horse: successful in minor events at Clairefontaine and Deauville in August and Bordeaux in November: 2½ lengths second of 6 to Le Triton in Prix La Rochette at Longchamp, settling well before keeping on in the straight: will stay 1¼m: may well improve further. *J-C. Rouget, France* — 105 p

CLOETTE 3 b.f. Damister (USA) 123 – Mademoiselle Chloe 106 (Night Shift (USA)) [1994 56: 6g 7g^5 1995 a7g* a7g* 6g^5 7m^6 6.9g^4 7g^6 a7g^4 Aug 4] rangy filly: fair handicapper: won at Southwell in April (median auction maiden) and May: will stay 1m: acts on fibresand: below form only try in blinkers. *W. A. O'Gorman* — 63 a69

CLOGHRAN LAD 8 ch.g. Millfontaine 114 – Lady Pitt (Pitskelly 122) [1994 NR 1995 a14g Apr 11] ran 5 times on flat in Ireland from 2 to 4 yrs without making the frame: modest hurdler, successful in seller (final outing for J. S. Smith) in March: blinkered, tailed off in poor claimer on flat following month. *Mrs M. McCourt* — –

CLOSE CONFLICT (USA) 4 b.c. High Estate 127 – Catopetl (USA) (Northern Dancer) [1994 115: 8s* 10.4f 10.2s* 12s* 12d^3 1995 12v^6 12d 12s^6 Dec 3] — –

rangy colt: shows knee action: smart performer at 3 yrs: long way below that form in pattern/listed company in 1995, off course 5½ months after reappearance: stays 1½m: goes well on soft going, moved poorly to post and well beaten on firm: wintering with J-C Rouget in France, due back in March. *P. W. Chapple-Hyam*

CLOUDED ELEGANCE 5 b.g. Elegant Air 119 – Clouded Vision 74 (So Blessed 130) [1994 76: 8m 10.8d^6 8g^5 8f* 8m 8m 8d 8f 10s* 9g 1995 10m* 10g^4 12d 10.4m Oct 4] leggy gelding: fairly useful handicapper: game winner at Nottingham in May: well below form last 2 starts: effective at 1¼m and should stay 1½m: acts on firm and soft ground: blinkered (no improvement) once, visored last 2 starts at 4 yrs: none too consistent. *Lady Herries* — 82

CLOUDS HILL (FR) 2 b.c. (Apr 10) Sarhoob (USA) 124 – Dana Dana (FR) (Pharly (FR) 130) [1995 8g^5 7d^3 Sep 27] 90,000 francs Y, resold 16,000Y: tall, quite good-topped colt: good mover: half-brother to 3 winners in France, including 3-y-o 5.5f (at 2 yrs) to 7.5f winner Eduardina (by Tagel) and 1m (at 2 yrs) and 9f winner Gage D'Amour (by Diamond Shoal): dam French 1¼m and 10.5f winner: bandaged off-hind, much better effort in maidens when close third of 12 to Final Stab at Salisbury, challenging over 1f out and running on well: will be well suited by 1m+: sure to progress again. *R. Hannon* — 84 p

CLUB ELITE 3 b.f. Salse (USA) 128 – Little Bittern (USA) 73 (Riva Ridge (USA)) [1994 42, a57: 5.2s^5 5.1m 6f^4 7m^3 a7g^2 8m 7.5g 1995 8.2m a8g^6 a8.5g^4 a8g 8f^5 10.8m a14.8g^2 14d^5 14.1m^4 16.2m^5 Aug 24] workmanlike, angular filly: poor maiden: sold out of M. Camacho's stable 420 gns Doncaster July Sales after fifth 3-y-o start: stays 14.8f: best effort on fibresand: tried visored/blinkered: sold 625 gns Ascot November Sales. *M. F. Barraclough* — 27 a34

CLUED UP 2 b.f. (Apr 10) Beveled (USA) – Scharade 74 (Lombard (GER) 126) [1995 7.5g a7g^4 7g Sep 2] 5,600Y: tall, workmanlike filly: half-sister to 3 winners in USA and one in Mexico: dam 1¼m winner from good German family: no worthwhile form in modest maiden company: slowly away all starts: sold 1,600 gns Doncaster October Sales. *M. H. Easterby* — –

CLURICAN (IRE) 6 ch.g. Dara Monarch 128 – Jane Bond 59 (Good Bond 122) [1994 NR 1995 8m 18.7m 12g May 26] close-coupled gelding: fair handicapper (rated 75) at 3 yrs: no form on return to flat, but did win selling hurdle in June. *N. Tinkler* — –

CNOCMA (IRE) 4 b.f. Tender King 123 – Peggy Dell (Sovereign Gleam 117) [1994 8v 9g 7d^5 7g 7.8m^3 10g 7g 1995 a8g 7.8f 6g 8.5g^5 7.8f* 8h Sep 4] IR 400F: IR 1,000Y: ex-Irish filly: half-sister to 2 minor winners, including 1m winner Arctic Ken: dam Irish 2-y-o 7f winner: modest performer: easily best effort in 1995 when winning handicap at Dundalk in August on final start for A. J. Martin: well beaten in selling handicap at Bath on only run here: stays 1m: acts on firm ground and dead. *W. G. M. Turner* — 45

COALISLAND 5 br.g. Kind of Hush 118 – Hit The Line 71 (Saulingo 122) [1994 –: 6v 6g 6m 6.1m 6.9g 6s 1995 a10g a10g^5 a10g a7g 5m 7m 6m 6g 9m 14m 11.6m 11.9f^4 Aug 1] good-bodied gelding: unimpressive mover: poor form at best last 2 seasons: tried blinkered/visored. *R. Ingram* — 34 d

COASTAL BLUFF 3 gr.g. Standaan (FR) 118 – Combattente (Reform 132) [1994 59p: 5g^2 1995 5d 5.1g* 5m^5 6g^4 6m^2 5d^3 5s* Oct 7] tall, leggy gelding: progressed with every run in 1995: won median auction maiden at Nottingham in April: given midsummer break after making frame in competitive events at Newmarket and York (£39,000 William Hill Trophy) fourth and fifth starts: poorly drawn, put up best effort when justifying favouritism in 24-runner £15,500 handicap at Ascot in October by neck (rated value 2 lengths) from Fire Dome, getting up well inside final 1f: stays 6f well: acts on good to firm and soft ground: usually bandaged behind: genuine: did extremely well to overcome poor draw at Ascot, and looks a very useful sprinter in the making, sure to win more races. *T. D. Barron* — 97 p

COAST ALONG (IRE) 3 b.g. Satco (FR) 112 – Golden Flats 79 (Sonnen Gold 121) [1994 41: 6f 6m 7g^5 8m^5 7.5g 10s 1995 10m 13.8g^4 16m 12m^3 13f^5 12m* a12g^6 Nov 27] sparely-made gelding: poor performer: won selling handicap at Beverley in July: sold out of C. Thornton's stable 3,600 gns Doncaster August Sales before next start: stays 1¾m: acts on good to firm ground: blinkered (swerved stalls, ran poorly) second 2-y-o start: sometimes slowly away, and often gets behind. *D. Burchell* — 39

COASTGUARDS HAVEN 3 b.g. Superpower 113 – Marton Maid 74 (Silly Season 127) [1994 NR 1995 8f 8m 10.2m 15.4g6 Jul 5] 17,000Y: close-coupled gelding: has a round action: brother to 4-y-o 6f (at 2 yrs) to 1½m winner Mr Devious and half-brother to 2 sprint winners by Sayf El Arab and a winner in Italy: dam half-sister to good sprinter Haveroid: well beaten, including in selling company. *M. J. Bolton* –

COASTGUARDS HERO 2 ch.g. (May 1) Chilibang 120 – Aldwick Colonnade 62 (Kind of Hush 118) [1995 6.1m5 6m Jul 29] lengthy gelding: first foal: dam suited by 1m: no form in median auction maidens: very unruly start and withdrawn on intended debut. *M. D. I. Usher* –

COBBLERS HILL 6 gr.g. Another Realm 118 – Morning Miss 59 (Golden Dipper 119) [1994 NR 1995 6f Oct 23] plain, workmanlike gelding: rated 56 at 4 yrs: broke leg only subsequent outing: stayed 1m: dead. *C. R. Barwell* –

COBBS CROSS 5 ch.g. Bairn (USA) 126 – Trapani (Ragusa 137) [1994 –, a53d: a8.5g2 a8g2 a7s a7g5 a7g4 7d a6g 6d a8g 7m a7g 1995 a9.4g a7g Jun 22] unfurnished gelding: of little account nowadays: tried visored/blinkered. *T. H. Caldwell* –

COBURG 3 ch.c. Old Vic 136 – Gatchina 94 (Habitat 134) [1994 NR 1995 10m 10d* Sep 13] strong, lengthy colt: good mover: fourth foal: half-brother to Irish 5f winner Desert Palace (by Green Desert): dam 1m and 9f winner, is half-sister to top-class middle-distance colt Kalaglow: 9/2 and first run for 5 months when winning 17-runner maiden at Sandown by 2½ lengths from Prickwillow, leading 2f out and running on strongly: will stay 1½m: potentially useful, and should win more races: sent to Dubai. *H. R. A. Cecil* 85 p

COCOON (IRE) 2 b.f. (May 4) Cyrano de Bergerac 120 – Arena 86 (Sallust 134) [1995 5g 5m4 6g Sep 14] 5,000Y: rather leggy, unfurnished filly: half-sister to several winners, including 1m and 9.7f winner Wakil (by Tate Gallery): dam lightly raced: easily best effort in maiden auctions when over 4 lengths fourth of 10 to Secret Voucher at Ripon in August: should be suited by further than 5f: sold 1,800 gns Doncaster October Sales. *C. W. Thornton* 51 +

CODE OF LAW (USA) 3 b.c. Woodman (USA) 126 – Eloquent Minister (USA) 109 (Deputy Minister (CAN)) [1994 NR 1995 8g* 8g5 10g Sep 29] tall colt: second foal: half-brother to fairly useful 1994 3-y-o Areciba (by Risen Star), 6f winner at 2 yrs who stayed 10.4f well: dam Irish filly best at 5f: fairly useful form: won maiden at Ayr in July, making all: very edgy, pulled hard but ran well when fifth of 8 in minor 84

Willmott Dixon Stakes (Handicap), Ascot—progressive Coastal Bluff (No. 15) defies a poor draw; Fire Dome, No Extras, Hello Mister and Lady Sheriff come next

event at Doncaster: well beaten in handicap at Newmarket on final outing: stays 1m: needs to settle: sold 5,500 gns Newmarket December Sales. *P. W. Chapple-Hyam*

CODE OF SILENCE 3 br.g. Adbass (USA) 102 – Keep Silent 83 (Balidar 133) [1994 49: 5d^3 a5g^3 6g^2 7m^6 6m^4 a7g 6m^2 8m 7g 1995 7d^5 6.1g^4 a6g 5.1m^5 7g^5 10f 8.3m^5 6g Jul 27] leggy gelding: poor mover: poor maiden: claimed out of B. Palling's stable £2,000 after fourth 3-y-o start: should stay 1m: acts on good to firm and dead ground: tried blinkered and visored. *G. F. H. Charles-Jones* — 45

COEUR FRANCAIS (FR) 3 b.g. Hero's Honor (USA) – Marie d'Anjou (FR) (Free Round (USA)) [1994 NR 1995 8d^6 8s Oct 6] 270,000 francs Y: lengthy gelding: fourth foal: dam, French 7f to 7.5f winner, is half-sister to smart French/U.S. middle-distance performer Coeur de Lion: promising sixth of 19 to Tarawa in maiden at Newbury, tiring and not knocked about: well beaten in apprentice minor event at Ascot 3 weeks later: sold (Major D. Chappell to S. Williams) 8,000 gns Newmarket Autumn Sales. *Major D. N. Chappell* — 64

COFFEE 'N CREAM 3 ch.g. Handsome Sailor 125 – Thorner Lane 86 (Tina's Pet 121) [1994 96?: 5d^5 5m* 5f^2 5m 5m 1995 6d^5 5m^5 6m^4 6f 6f* 5m^2 5f^4 6m^4 5m* 6g^4 6.1d^3 5m^2 Oct 21] strong, sprint type: useful performer: won claimer at Kempton (sweating) in July and handicap at Ascot (raced alone stands side) in August: good ½-length second of 10 to Croft Pool in rated stakes at Doncaster on final start: effective at 5f and 6f: acts on firm ground: often races prominently: sold 34,000 gns Newmarket Autumn Sales. *R. Hannon* — 101

COGGLE 3 b.f. Kind of Hush 118 – Packet 89 (Royal Palace 131) [1994 NR 1995 10m 12m 12m^5 13.8g^5 14.1g^5 11.9f* 11.9f^5 Aug 23] close-coupled filly: sister to useful 1990 2-y-o 7f and 1m winner Sea Level, closely related to smart middle-distance stayer Capstan (by Welsh Pageant), and half-sister to useful 1¼m winner Albacore (by Kris) and a winning sprinter in Hungary: dam, from family of Longboat, won at up to 1¾m: modest form: won 3-runner median auction maiden at Brighton in August, making all: tailed off in handicaps starts either side: should stay beyond 1½m: acts on firm ground, yet to race on a soft surface: blinkered last 2 starts: races prominently: edgy sort: sold 15,000 gns Newmarket December Sales. *N. A. Graham* — 60

COIGACH 4 b.f. Niniski (USA) 125 – Rynechra 102 (Blakeney 126) [1994 110p: 10m^4 12s^4 14f^2 13.9m* 14.6g* 1995 12m^5 Jul 1] leggy, angular filly: very useful middle-distance stayer at 3 yrs: well-beaten last of 5 in listed event at Newmarket in July, hanging left: stud. *H. R. A. Cecil* — –

COLD SHOULDER (IRE) 2 b.c. (Apr 21) Distinctly North (USA) 115 – Shygate (Shy Groom (USA)) [1995 6f 6m 7f^3 Aug 21] IR 12,500Y: smallish colt: second foal: half-brother to 3-y-o Sergio (by Doubletour): dam modest Irish 1½m winner: improved effort in auction events when third of 5 to Mountain Valley at Brighton final start: will stay 1m: sold 2,700 gns Ascot August Sales. *J. L. Dunlop* — 58

COLDSTREAM 2 b.c. (Feb 23) Shareef Dancer (USA) 135 – Sea Saga 91 (Dara Monarch 128) [1995 7m^3 7g* Aug 28] rangy, attractive colt: has plenty of scope: good mover: third living foal: half-brother to 3-y-o Ruddigore (by Old Vic): dam 7f winner: won 10-runner maiden at Newcastle by 1¼ lengths from Storm Trooper, travelling well behind leaders and running on strongly to lead inside final 1f: will stay 1¼m: sure to improve further, and looks a smart prospect: sent to Dubai. *L. M. Cumani* — 90 P

COLERIDGE 7 gr.g. Bellypha 130 – Quay Line 117 (High Line 125) [1994 –: a14.8g^6 18g 16.4d 16.4g 1995 16.4m 17.2m^6 14.9g^2 16.1g^6 16.4m 16g^6 a16.2g 15.4m^5 16.1g* 16m^3 16.5m a16g^3 a16g^2 a16g* a16g^6 Dec 15] tall, leggy gelding: unimpressive mover: modest handicapper: ended the year in good form, winning at Warwick (apprentices) in October and Lingfield (gamely) in November: thorough stayer: acts on the all-weather, best turf form on a sound surface: best in visor/blinkers. *J. J. Sheehan* — 53

COLLEGE DON 4 gr.g. Kalaglow 132 – Westerlake (Blakeney 126) [1994 59: 8.2m^6 7f^3 7g^4 10.3g^5 10m 8s^5 10.1d 1995 12g^4 11.8g^4 14.1m* 14.6g^4 14.6m^4 14.8m* 16.1m* 13.9m 16.1g^6 Aug 28] angular, lengthy gelding: fair handicapper: successful in the summer at Nottingham and twice at Newmarket: seems suited by test of stamina: acts on firm and soft ground. *M. P. Bielby* — 73

COLLEGE NIGHT (IRE) 3 b.f. Night Shift (USA) – Gertrude Lawrence (Ballymore 123) [1994 –: 7d 1995 9.9m^3 12g^6 10m 10.1m^5 7m 12m^6 12d 11.9d 14.1m^3 12m 12m^6 Nov 6] angular filly: unimpressive mover: poor maiden: trained first 3 starts by John Berry: stays 1¾m: acts on good to firm ground, probably on dead: has run respectably with tongue strap and when sweating. *C. A. Dwyer* — 50

COLONEL COLT 4 b.g. Saint Andrews (FR) 128§ – Vallee Des Sauges (USA) (Secretariat (USA)) [1994 –: 10.4f^5 12g 12m 10.4d 12.1g 1995 10d 10m 12.1d Oct 10] close-coupled, good-topped gelding: of little account nowadays. *R. Dickin* — –

COLORFUL AMBITION 5 b.g. Slip Anchor 136 – Reprocolor 114 (Jimmy Reppin 131) [1994 65: 9.2s^2 7d^3 9g* 10g^2 12.3g^3 10.2g 8.3g^3 1995 10.3m 9g* 9m* 10.5g^2 10.9g^2 10.3f^6 10.3d Sep 9] lengthy gelding: unimpressive walker: fair performer: won minor event at Newcastle and steadily-run handicap at Redcar (again led close home) within 6 days in May: effective at 9f and stays 1½m: acts on dead ground and good to firm. *Mrs A. Swinbank* — 76

COLOSSE 3 b.f. Reprimand 122 – French Cutie (USA) (Vaguely Noble 140) [1994 52: 7g^6 7.5m^6 6.9m 7m^4 8s 7d 1995 a7g 8m^2 10f 8m^2 8.2m^3 12.1g^2 12m a12g^6 a12g^5 a10g Dec 18] useful-looking filly: has a round action: modest maiden: claimed out of M. Jarvis' stable £3,000 fifth 3-y-o start: stays 1½m: acts on good to firm ground, no worthwhile form on all-weather: inconsistent. *J. L. Eyre* — 58 a–

COLOUR COUNSELLOR 2 gr.c. (Mar 18) Touch of Grey 90 – Bourton Downs 74 (Philip of Spain 126) [1995 a5g^3 a6g^5 7m^6 a7g a7g^5 a6g 7.1m^5 8.1m^3 a8.5d^6 10d Sep 19] half-brother to several winners, including 11f winner Just Great (by Simply Great) and 8.2f winner Neverdown (by Never So Bold): dam 2-y-o 5f winner: plater: tailed off in non-selling nursery at Nottingham final start: stays 1m: acts on good to firm ground, best form on fibresand: visored/blinkered on 5 occasions. *K. McAuliffe* — 46 a51

COLSTON-C 3 gr.g. Belfort (FR) 89 – Grand Occasion 63 (Great Nephew 126) [1994 46: 5d 6g a5g^4 a5g 1995 a8g a6g 5.1m^6 5.1m^4 5g^4 7.1m^2 8m^3 8m* 5.1f^2 5m^2 5.7h* 5.7h 7g a6g^3 a5g a7g Dec 12] angular, close-coupled gelding: fair performer on turf, modest on all-weather: won apprentice maiden at Warwick in July and handicap at Bath in August: trained by R. Hodges twelfth and thirteenth (unseated rider and bolted to post) starts only: effective at 5f to 1m: acts on equitrack, goes well on top-of-the-ground (acts on hard): visored (below form) once: usually a front runner. *C. J. Hill* — 73 a54

COLT D'OR 3 ch.g. Beldale Lark 105 – Nijinsgayle (FR) (Nice Havrais (USA) 124) [1994 –: 7g 7.6v 1995 6.9m 10m 12.5g^6 Jun 12] lengthy gelding: well beaten in maidens. *J. White* — –

COLWAY BRIDGE 2 b.c. (May 28) Colway Radial 57 – Bell Bridge Girl (Coded Scrap 90) [1995 5m^4 5f^6 a8g Nov 6] sturdy colt: first reported foal: dam tailed off in novice hurdles: fourth of 13 in claimer at Beverley: soundly beaten afterwards in minor event at Catterick and maiden at Southwell. *Mrs M. Reveley* — 55

COLWAY PRINCE (IRE) 7 b.g. Prince Tenderfoot (USA) 126 – El Cerrito (Tribal Chief 125) [1994 NR 1995 8f Jul 1] workmanlike gelding: winning selling hurdler: no form on flat. *A. P. Jones* — –

COLWAY RAKE 4 b.g. Salse (USA) 128 – Barely Hot (Bold Lad (IRE) 133) [1994 61, a73: 5d^3 5d* 6.1f^4 a6g* a7g a6g 6g 5s^6 5s 1995 6d 5g^3 6g* 6g^2 6f 5m^6 6m^2 6d 6g^2 6g Oct 7] strong, deep-bodied gelding: fair handicapper: justified favouritism in 17-runner race at Hamilton in May: ran particularly well when length second of 28 to Keston Pond in Ayr Silver Cup penultimate outing: stays 6f: acts on fibresand and on good to firm and soft ground: effective blinkered (usually is)/visored or not. *J. W. Watts* — 76

COLWAY ROCK (USA) 5 b.g. Irish River (FR) 131 – Petite Diable (USA) (Sham (USA)) [1994 –: 7.9f 8.1d^5 10.4f 8s 10.5d^6 8g 1995 10.5g 10.3m^6 8m 10.3d Sep 9] strong, compact gelding: useful performer on his day at 3 yrs: no worthwhile form in 1994 and 1995. *J. W. Watts* — –

COMANCHE COMPANION 5 b.m. Commanche Run 133 – Constant Companion 84 (Pas de Seul 133) [1994 75, a67: 6.9s^4 7.6m^4 9s^4 8v^3 7s^4 8f^4 6.9h^2 8m* 8.1m^2 7.6g 8s 8s^6 a7g^4 a8g^4 a8g 1995 7g 8.3g 7.1m^2 8.5m 8f^2 8m^5 a8g 7.1d* 8d^3 7g* 8m Oct 28] plain, close-coupled mare: has a quick action: fairly useful — 88 a–

handicapper: won at Sandown in September and York (23-runner £10,600 contest, led close home) in October: effective at 7f to 9f: acts on any turf going, has only modest form on the all-weather: has won for apprentice and when sweating: usually races prominently. *T. J. Naughton*

COMANECI (IRE) 7 b.m. Ahonoora 122 – Church Mountain 83 (Furry Glen 121) [1994 NR 1995 a16g Feb 6] lengthy, good-topped mare: modest maiden at best in 1991: well beaten in handicap at Southwell on first flat outing since. *K. S. Bridgwater* –

COME ON DANCER (IRE) 7 ch.g. Ahonoora 122 – Crimson Royale 84 (High Line 125) [1994 53: a13g^6 a7g a10g^6 a8.5g^3 a9.4g^2 10m a9.4g 10m^2 a10g 1995 a10g^4 a12g^3 a10g^6 Jul 22] modest maiden on flat: won over fences in July and August: stays 1½m: acts on all-weather surfaces: yet to race on a soft surface on flat, possibly unsuited by it over jumps. *J. White* 51

COME ON IN 2 b.c. (May 25) Most Welcome 131 – Lominda (IRE) 80 (Lomond (USA) 128) [1995 7g 10g Oct 9] 640F: first foal: dam 2-y-o 6f winner: burly, slowly away and always well behind in maiden at Warwick and seller at Leicester. *R. Dickin* –

COME ON LUCY 6 b.m. Reesh 117 – Her Excellency 36 (Dragonara Palace (USA) 115) [1994 43: 8d 8.1s 10m 6m^4 5.1g 1995 a7g Jan 21] workmanlike mare: poor maiden: has rejoined M. Eckley. *S. Coathup* –

COMEONUP 4 b.g. Most Welcome 131 – Scarlet Veil 75 (Tyrnavos 129) [1994 62: 5.7m 6d 7.1s* 6m^3 6.9m^5 8g^2 8m^6 8.2g^4 8m 1995 7g 8m 8.3g* 7.1d Oct 10] sturdy gelding: unimpressive mover: modest handicapper: 25/1-winner of 16-runner contest at Hamilton in May: well beaten otherwise in 1995: stays 8.3f: acts on good to firm and soft ground, tailed off on fibresand: often bandaged. *J. M. Bradley* 64

COME ON WINN 3 ch.f. Handsome Sailor 125 – Ragusa Girl (Morston (FR) 125) [1994 –: 6.1m 5g 1995 5m 5g a5g 5f Aug 28] leggy, sparely-made filly: unseated rider leaving stalls last 2 starts, leaving Miss S. Wilton's stable after first of them: thoroughly temperamental and best left alone. *R. Hollinshead* §§

COMFORTABLE 5 ch.g. Hard Fought 125 – Key Harvest (Deep Diver 134) [1994 –: a8g^6 12g 11.5g 1995 a11g a8g^6 a12g a7g Mar 20] workmanlike gelding: no worthwhile form: tried blinkered: sold 2,600 gns Doncaster March Sales. *S. Gollings* –

COMIC FANTASY (AUS) 2 b.f. (Jan 8) Rory's Jester (AUS) – Enchanted Dream (NZ) (Danzatore (CAN) 120) [1995 6g^4 5m^6 5.1h* 5f^3 5.1m^2 5g^2 5g^3 5m Nov 6] lengthy, unfurnished filly: fluent mover: third foal: sister to a winner and half-sister to a 5.5f winner by Last Tycoon: dam, winner in Australasia at 7f, daughter of Cheveley Park third Super Entente: sire good sprinter in Australia: made all in maiden at Bath in August: fairly useful form afterwards when runner-up in nurseries (had heavily-favoured rail for apparently best effort) but below form in minor events on last 2 starts: best at 5f: acts on hard ground: best form in blinkers: sold 6,000 gns (P. Chapple-Hyam to Martyn Wane) Newmarket December Sales. *P. W. Chapple-Hyam* 87 ?

COMMANCHE CREEK 5 b.g. Commanche Run 133 – Vice Vixen (CAN) (Vice Regent (CAN)) [1994 46§: 11.1g 15.1m^5 11.1g^3 1995 16f^5 10g Jun 12] sturdy, lengthy gelding: poor maiden: sold (J. Hellens to Miss J. du Plessis) 1,600 gns Doncaster August Sales: tried blinkered and visored and with tongue tied down: none too genuine. *J. A. Hellens* – §

COMMANCHE STORM (IRE) 3 b.g. Maelstrom Lake 118 – Commanche Maid (Commanche Run 133) [1994 –: 10g 8d 9.7s 1995 a9.4g Jan 21] small gelding: no worthwhile form including in selling company: has joined W. Mann. *K. G. Wingrove* –

COMMANDER GLEN (IRE) 3 b.g. Glenstal (USA) 118 – Une Parisienne (FR) (Bolkonski 134) [1994 52: 6d 7g 1995 10.2f 10m 12.5g 8f^6 5.9f* 7m^3 8m 6f^2 7m 7m^5 8h* 8.5s 12g Sep 28] smallish, sturdy gelding: modest handicapper: won selling events at Carlisle in July and Bath in September: stays 1m: acts on firm going: effective blinkered or not: sometimes looks none too keen: inconsistent: has joined Mrs J. Ramsden. *Martyn Meade* 61

COMMIN' UP 2 b.f. (Feb 14) Primo Dominie 121 – Ridalia 56 (Ridan (USA)) [1995 6.1d 6g 6.9g^3 Oct 16] 5,000Y: lengthy filly: has a quick action: half-sister to 4 winners, including sprinter Powder Blue (by He Loves Me) and 7.5f to 9.4f winner 67

Kelly Mac (by Precocious): dam showed a little ability: modest form in maiden races: under ½-length third of 13 to Maristax in auction event at Folkestone on final outing: better suited by 7f than 6f, and will stay 1m. *J. W. Hills*

COMMITTAL (IRE) 2 b.c. (Feb 14) Lycius (USA) 124 – Just Cause (Law Society (USA) 130) [1995 7.1m^3 8d^2 7.9g* 8m^6 Oct 15] strong, well-made colt: has a round action: third foal: half-brother to useful 3-y-o Jural (by Kris), 7f and 1m winner at 2 yrs, and 1¼m winner Campaign (by Sure Blade): dam unraced daughter of half-sister to 1000 Guineas winner Nocturnal Spree: easy winner of 8-runner maiden at York in October, pushed out to beat Silver Wing 4 lengths: ran very well in Grand Criterium at Longchamp later in month, finishing around 3 lengths sixth of 7 behind Loup Solitaire: stays 1m: strong-running type. *J. H. M. Gosden* 106

COMMON DIVINE (IRE) 2 b.f. (Apr 3) Common Grounds 118 – Day Dress (Ashmore (FR) 125) [1995 a6g^6 Dec 14] 6,400Y: fifth living foal: half-sister to Belgian 5f to 1m winner Old Hook (by Digamist) and 2 other winners abroad: dam never ran: 25/1, well-beaten sixth of 9 in maiden at Lingfield. *C. Murray* –

COMMONER (USA) 3 b.c. Far North (CAN) 120 – Searching Around (USA) (Round Table) [1994 87p: 7.1s* 7m^4 1995 10m^2 11.5f^5 12g 10m* 12m^2 11.1g^2 12g^6 12f^6 Dec 10] attractive colt: smart performer: won minor event at Newmarket in August: runner-up on next 2 starts, ridden at 2 lb overweight when keeping-on-again short-head second of 7 to Burooj in September Stakes at Kempton: creditable sixth to Lassigny in Rothmans International at Woodbine and to Partipral in Hong Kong International Vase last 2 starts: stays 1½m: probably acts on any going: effective held up or from front. *R. Hannon* 112

COMMONS WHEEL (IRE) 2 b.c. (Mar 26) Common Grounds 118 – Daisy Wheel 68 (Doulab (USA) 115) [1995 6g Oct 3] IR 6,800Y: stocky colt: first foal: dam, 2-y-o 6f winner, later won in Austria, out of half-sister to Irish Derby winner English Prince: 40/1 and backward, slowly away and always behind in maiden auction at Warwick: moved poorly to post. *D. J. S. Cosgrove* –

COMPASS POINTER 2 gr.c. (Feb 21) Mazilier (USA) 107 – Woodleys (Tyrnavos 129) [1995 7g 7.9m 8m Nov 4] 8,000Y: rather leggy, close-coupled colt: half-brother to a winner abroad by Local Suitor: dam unraced daughter of Cry of Truth: plating-class form in maiden events. *J. M. P. Eustace* –

COMPENSATE (IRE) 2 ch.f. (Jan 18) Great Commotion (USA) 123 – Clipping 76 (Kris 135) [1995 5.2m 7g 7f^5 7m Aug 4] 5,800Y: small filly: first foal: dam 1m winner: poor maiden: well beaten in seller at Newmarket final start: sold 500 gns Ascot September Sales. *M. J. Haynes* –

COMRADE CHINNERY (IRE) 2 ch.c. (Feb 22) Jareer (USA) 115 – Phar Lapa 59 (Grundy 137) [1995 5m 7d^4 7g^5 7.1m^3 8.1m^5 8m 7m Oct 21] IR 2,000F, IR 5,800Y: rather unfurnished colt: half-brother to Irish 4-y-o 9f and 1½m winner Clodaghs Fancy (by Nordance) and winning stayer Mrs Barton (by Faustus): dam staying maiden: poor maiden: third in selling nursery at Sandown in August: sold out of J. Eustace's stable 5,200 gns Newmarket September Sales and soundly beaten in face of stiff tasks both starts in Ireland: stays 1m: blinkered twice, including best effort. *A. J. Martin, Ireland* 41

COMTEC'S LEGEND 5 ch.m. Legend of France (USA) 124 – Comtec Princess 73 (Gulf Pearl 117) [1994 38, a42: a11g* a13g^6 a12g^3 a11g a11g 10g 12m^4 10m^4 9g 10g^6 9.2f^4 8.9m^6 a12g^2 11.9d 12g^5 a12g^5 a14g^5 1995 a11g^6 a12g* a12g^5 a12g^3 a11g^5 12m 12m a12g a12g* Dec 12] small mare: poor handicapper: won amateurs races at Wolverhampton in January and December: stays 1½m, apparently not 1¾m: acts on good to firm and dead ground, best recent form on the all-weather: sometimes hangs left: often bandaged near-fore: inconsistent. *J. F. Bottomley* – a45

CONCEPCION (GER) 5 b.h. Acatenango (GER) 127 – Comprida (GER) (Windwurf (GER)) [1994 115: 11s^3 10v 12s^2 12s^2 11g^3 12g^6 12g 12d^4 12s 1995 11v^4 12s^4 11s^6 11m 12g^3 12s 10d* 10d* Oct 29] smart German performer: 5 lengths third of 7 to Wind In Her Hair in Aral-Pokal at Gelsenkirchen: acted as pacemaker for Lando next outing: won 14-runner Group 3 event at Hoppegarten (by ½ length from Sylvan Point) and 6-runner Group 3 contest at Milan (by 4¾ lengths from Snowtown), both in October: stays 1½m: acts on heavy ground, not discredited on firm: ran for H. Jentzsch sixth and seventh starts. *A. Wohler, Germany* 115

CONCERT PARTY (IRE) 2 b.c. (Apr 12) Classic Music (USA) – Crown Class (USA) 53 (Chief's Crown (USA)) [1995 6g 6m 7m a6g 7.5d^4 7g 7.1g 8g Sep 21] IR 15,000Y: leggy colt: third foal: half-brother to a winner in Italy at up to 1½m by Law Society: dam ran 4 times at 2 yrs: poor maiden: sold out of J. Dunlop's stable 550 gns at Ascot August Sales after third start: stayed 7.5f: dead. *D. W. Chapman* 37

CONCER UN 3 ch.g. Lord Bud 121 – Drudwen (Sayf El Arab (USA) 127) [1994 NR 1995 a7g a7g^4 a8.5g^3 8.3v* 8f^2 9.2g^2 8.1g^3 7m^3 7g^3 7m^4 7.5g^2 8h* 8m* 8m^2 8.5m^2 8g* 8d Sep 16] 1,500F: smallish, lengthy gelding: first foal: dam ran once, winning 13f NH Flat race: fairly useful handicapper: won at Hamilton (maiden) in March, Bath and Thirsk in August and Kempton in September: bandaged near-fore, rare poor effort on final start: effective at 7f, stays 9.2f: acts on any going: tough, genuine and consistent. *S. C. Williams* 82

CONCINNITY (USA) 6 b.g. Hello Gorgeous (USA) 128 – Cincinnity (USA) (Shareef Dancer (USA) 135) [1994 NR 1995 11.6m Jul 17] rangy, good-topped gelding: modest middle-distance maiden handicapper for L. J. Holt at 4 yrs: bandaged in front, well beaten in selling company only start in 1995: inconsistent: sold (M. Madgwick to B. Scriven) 1,000 gns Ascot August Sales. *M. Madgwick* –

CONDOR RIDGE 2 b.g. (Apr 15) Inca Chief (USA) – Second Flower 50 (Indian Ruler (USA) 104) [1995 6s 6d Oct 19] leggy gelding: third foal: dam, plater, stayed 1m: tailed off in maidens at Lingfield and Newbury. *B. J. Meehan* –

CONE LANE 9 ch.g. On Your Mark 125 – Cee Beauty 74 (Ribero 126) [1994 37: a13g* a12g^3 a12g^5 a13g^4 14m^6 11.9f* 10m a13g 1995 a13g a12g^6 a13g^5 a12g a16g 12g a13g^6 a12g Nov 2] workmanlike gelding: poor handicapper: no form in 1995. *B. Gubby* –

CONEYGREE 3 b.f. Northern State (USA) 91 – Welsh Blossom 100 (Welsh Saint 126) [1994 –: 5s 6.1g^6 7f 1995 12.3d^6 12m^5 14.1m 12m^6 8m^3 8g^3 8m Aug 14] lengthy filly: poor form at best: unlikely to stay middle distances: acts on good to firm ground. *J. Wharton* 39

CONEY HILLS 4 b.f. Beverley Boy 99 – Adder Howe (Amboise 113) [1994 35: 7f 5g 5g^6 5m 5g 5g 5m^3 5g 6g 1995 5g 5g^6 6m 6g 8m 6m 7m^3 9f 5f 5g Sep 2] sparely-made filly: poor maiden: stays 7f, raced too freely when tried over 9f: acts on good to firm ground: blinkered once at 3 yrs. *N. Bycroft* 21

CONFRONTER 6 ch.g. Bluebird (USA) 125 – Grace Darling (USA) (Vaguely Noble 140) [1994 66: a10g^5 8s^4 7.5s* 8s^3 8m 8d^6 7g^2 7m^5 6.9g^2 6m^5 7.6m 7m^2 7g^2 7g^6 7m^5 7d^4 8g^3 8d^2 8m 8.2g 1995 8d* 8s^2 8g^2 8s^4 8m* 8m^3 8m 8m^2 8m^2 8m^3 7m 8f^2 8g* 8g* 7.9m^4 Oct 4] tall, angular gelding: fairly useful handicapper: held his form well in 1995, winning at Cagnes-sur-Mer (minor event) in January, Brighton in April and at Yarmouth and Brighton in September: best efforts at 7f/1m: acts on any turf going and on equitrack: has run well in blinkers/visor, but not tried at 6 yrs: effective held up or from front. *S. Dow* 84

CONIC HILL (IRE) 4 ch.g. Lomond (USA) 128 – Krisalya 98 (Kris 135) [1994 75: a8.5g 8d^3 8v^6 7m^6 8f^2 8m* 10g^5 10.1m 10g^2 9.9f* 9d 9g 1995 10.8m 8m May 29] lengthy, quite attractive gelding: fair form at 3 yrs: well beaten for new connections in 1995. *R. J. Baker* –

CONISTON LAKE (IRE) 6 ch.g. Coquelin (USA) 121 – High Lake (Quisling 117) [1994 46: a8.5g^6 a7g^5 a8g a7g 7v 7g^6 1995 a8.5g Jan 11] neat gelding: poor performer: tailed-off last in seller only outing in 1995. *G. L. Moore* –

CONQUISTAJADE (USA) 2 b. or br.f. (Apr 23) Conquistador Cielo (USA) – Uncut Jade (CAN) (Vice Regent (CAN)) [1995 6m^4 7m a8.5g^3 Dec 9] $47,000Y: tall, close-coupled filly: has a free action: closely related to a winner in North America by Geiger Counter and half-sister to useful winner at 1¼m or so Thunder Regent (by Thunder Puddles): dam unplaced all 10 starts: in frame in maidens at Goodwood in June (best effort) and Wolverhampton in December (remote third under 7-lb claimer): likely to stay 1¼m. *S. P. C. Woods* 54

CONSIDERABLE CHARM 3 ch.f. Charmer 123 – Leap In Time (Dance In Time (CAN)) [1994 NR 1995 a7g^4 a7g^2 a7g^4 8m a7g Dec 19] fourth foal: half-sister to useful 6f to 8.5f winner Neither Nor (by Norwick) and 1m and 1¼m winner Legendary Leap (by Legend of France): dam ran twice at 2 yrs: modest maiden: well 51 beaten (after 6½-month absence) last 2 starts: stays 7f: acts on equitrack. *Lord Huntingdon*

CONSORDINO 2 b.f. (Apr 19) Alzao (USA) 117 – Consolation 95 (Troy 137) [1995 7m 6m^5 7m^4 7g* 7d^2 8m^6 Oct 13] 26,000F: stocky filly: seventh foal: half-sister to 3-y-o Solatium (by Rainbow Quest) and useful 1m and 1¼m winner Claret (by Rousillon): dam, 2-y-o 7f winner stayed 1½m, half-sister to high-class middle-distance performer Morcon: improved form when winning nursery at Yarmouth in September: good ¾-length second of 15 under 7-lb claimer to Samim in similar event at Redcar 10 days later but rather disappointing in Newmarket nursery on final start: will stay middle distances: best form on an easy surface. *L. M. Cumani* — 88

CONSPICUOUS (IRE) 5 b.g. Alzao (USA) 117 – Mystery Lady (USA) (Vaguely Noble 140) [1994 57, a66: 6m 8g a9.4g^3 7d^6 11.5d^4 12.1g a10g^2 a10g^2 a9.4g^3 1995 a9.4g^5 a8g^6 10m^2 9f^2 10m* 10m^2 9g* 8s^2 8m Oct 28] close-coupled gelding: has a quick action: fairly useful handicapper: improved with almost every run in 1995, winning at Kempton in August and Goodwood (£12,100 event) in September: effective at 1m when conditions are testing, and stays 1¼m: acts on the all-weather and on any turf ground: held up (appeared not to go through with effort sixth start): takes good hold. *L. G. Cottrell* — 82

CONTARE 2 b.f. (Apr 1) Shirley Heights 130 – Balenare (Pharly (FR) 130) [1995 6.5g^3 7g* Aug 6] second foal: half-sister to 3-y-o Abetone (by Trempolino): dam half-sister to Park Hill runner-up Broomstick Corner: third to With Fascination in minor event at Evry in July: won similar event at Deauville following month by 5 lengths from Esquive: will stay middle distances: likely to improve further. *J. E. Pease, France* — 108 p

CONTRAC COUNTESS (IRE) 5 b.m. Thatching 131 – Crimson Sails (Lomond (USA) 128) [1994 NR 1995 10m Jun 26] smallish, plain mare: lightly raced and no form on flat since 1992. *M. P. Bielby* — –

CONTRACT BRIDGE (IRE) 2 b.f. (Jan 12) Contract Law (USA) 108 – Mystery Bid (Auction Ring (USA) 123) [1995 5g 5f^3 6m^2 7g^6 7.1s a7g Nov 24] 5,200Y: third foal: half-sister to 3-y-o 1½m winner Secret Service (by Classic Secret): dam Irish maiden, stayed 1½m: failed to progress after being placed in maiden auctions at Haydock and Ripon in August: should be suited by further than 6f. *C. W. Thornton* — 57 d

CONTRACT VENTURE (IRE) 3 b.g. Contract Law (USA) 108 – Ultra (Stanford 121§) [1994 62: 7m 7.1d^5 1995 8m 7g^5 8m 7m^6 8.2m^4 7m^4 Aug 26] leggy gelding: modest maiden: likely to prove best at up to 1m: acts on good to firm and dead ground: tried blinkered: has had tongue tied down: often bandaged near-hind: sold 5,000 gns Newmarket September Sales. *W. Jarvis* — 57

CONTRADICTORY 2 br.f. (Jan 10) Reprimand 122 – Artistic Licence (High Top 131) [1995 5m 6g^3 5m^6 7.5m^3 6f^6 7.5m 7d Sep 22] 6,200F, 4,200Y: leggy filly: fourth foal: dam, stayed 1¼m, out of half-sister to Circus Plume: plating-class maiden: will stay beyond 7.5f. *M. W. Easterby* — 48

CONTRAFIRE (IRE) 3 b.g. Contract Law (USA) 108 – Fiery Song (Ballad Rock 122) [1994 65: 5v 6.1m^2 5.9m^5 6m 6m 7g^6 1995 a8.5g* a8.5g^3 a10g* 10.3g^2 12.3d^2 12.3m^6 10g 10.5m^3 11.5m* 11.9g^2 10.9g^2 11f^4 Oct 31] unfurnished gelding: fair handicapper: won at Wolverhampton (maiden) in January and at Lingfield in February and August: stays 12.3f and likely to get further: acts on firm and dead going and the all-weather. *W. Jarvis* — 75

CONTRARIE 2 b.f. (Mar 23) Floose 99 – Chanita (Averof 123) [1995 a8g a7g a8g Nov 24] 2,200Y: half-sister to fair 7f to 1¼m performer Merseyside Man (by My Dad Tom): dam unraced: well beaten in maiden and sellers at Southwell. *M. J. Ryan* — –

CONWY 2 ch.f. (Feb 6) Rock City 120 – Degannwy 52 (Caerleon (USA) 132) [1995 7g Oct 9] smallish, workmanlike filly: first foal: dam probably stayed 15f: 33/1 and better for race, never better than mid-division when slow-starting ninth of 18 to Oleana in maiden at Leicester: should improve. *N. A. Graham* — – p

COOL CAPER 2 b.c. (May 6) Inca Chief (USA) – Rekindled Flame (IRE) (Kings Lake (USA) 133) [1995 a5g^4 a6g Sep 14] first foal: dam unraced daughter of half-sister to Motavato: sire (by Mr Prospector) won from 5f to 7f: about 3 lengths — 53 ?

fourth of 5 in median auction maiden at Wolverhampton in May: visored, never a factor in seller at Lingfield 4 months later. *A. G. Foster*

COOL EDGE (IRE) 4 ch.g. Nashamaa 113 – Mochara (Last Fandango 125) 84
[1994 68: 5d 6.1f* 6d³ 6g 6m 1995 6.1g⁵ 5g* 5m⁴ 5m⁴ 6d² 6g³ 7g² 7.1d² 8g² 7g³ 7.9m⁵ 8m Oct 28] rangy gelding: fairly useful performer: won minor event at Hamilton in May: ran well in handicaps thereafter, narrowly beaten on 5 occasions: effective at up to 1m: probably acts on any going: visored tenth and eleventh starts: often early to post: usually races prominently: consistent. *M. H. Tompkins*

COOL FIRE 2 b.c. (Apr 5) Colmore Row 111 – Into The Fire 74 (Dominion 123) 59
[1995 6m⁵ 7f Jul 26] 9,200F, 18,000Y: leggy, useful-looking colt: unimpressive mover: half-brother to 3-y-o Saatchmo (by Forzando) and fair sprinter Down The Middle (by Swing Easy): dam, stayed 1¼m, won in Guernsey: similar form in maidens won by Zuhair at Newmarket and Jack Jennings at Doncaster month later. *S. P. C. Woods*

COOL JAZZ 4 b.c. Lead On Time (USA) 123 – Amber Fizz (USA) (Effervescing (USA)) 116
[1994 104: 7s³ 8f 7g⁶ 6f⁴ 7g⁵ 6f 6g⁴ 6d⁴ 1995 6g 7m² 7m⁶ 7.1g³ 6g³ 6m* 7m 5.6m³ 6g⁵ 6d* 5d 7m 7f Dec 10]

American jockeys usually manage to make their mark on their rare visits to Britain, and in the latest season Corey Nakatani wasted no time in showing just why he is one of the leading riders in the States. On his first visit here Nakatani won the Diadem Stakes at Ascot in September on 33/1-shot Cool Jazz, a horse who often hangs and looks none too easy to handle. Nakatani made riding Cool Jazz look a straightforward task, and the horse produced a career-best performance in one of the season's most exciting races. Cool Jazz tracked the leaders, travelling well, until switched to the favoured stand rail to deliver his challenge a furlong and a half out. Nosing ahead shortly afterwards, Cool Jazz kept a straight course and ran on gamely to hold off the rallying Young Ern and strong-finishing Branston Abby by a short head and the same, with Harayir three quarters of a length away in fourth. It was Cool Jazz's third success in three seasons' racing and far and away the most important, his

*Diadem Stakes, Ascot—
a three-way photo between Cool Jazz (far side), Young Ern (No. 9) and Branston Abby*

Saeed Manana's "Cool Jazz"

other wins having been gained in a maiden at York at two years and a five-runner minor event at Haydock in July. He's run several good races in defeat, though, including on his outing immediately before the Diadem when fifth in the Ayr Gold Cup, coming out easily best of those who raced on the unfavoured far side of the course. Cool Jazz was tried over five furlongs and seven furlongs after Ascot. He ran creditably, despite hanging noticeably, when seventh of twelve in the Prix de l'Abbaye de Longchamp but finished last in his last two races, including the Hong Kong International Bowl.

Cool Jazz (b.c. 1991)	Lead On Time (USA) (b 1983)	Nureyev (b 1977)	Northern Dancer
			Special
		Alathea (b 1975)	Lorenzaccio
			Vive La Reine
	Amber Fizz (USA) (ch 1981)	Effervescing (ch 1973)	Le Fabuleux
			Sparkling
		Amber High (b 1968)	Ambiopoise
			Highness

Cool Jazz, a rangy, good-topped colt who impresses in appearance, is a half-brother to two winners, namely Tlail (by Sharpo), successful numerous times in Italy, and Wasaif (by Lomond), a fair performer over seven furlongs and a mile. Their dam is a once-raced daughter of the successful broodmare Amber High, whose nine winners include the very smart 1978 American two-year-old Groton High. Cool Jazz, a long-striding individual, is reported to have had problems with his feet, which probably explains his tendency to hang. He has shown useful form at seven furlongs and on firmish going, but is better at shorter distances and seems ideally suited by give in the ground. Cool Jazz ran creditably in blinkers on his final start in 1994, but was below form when visored on his reappearance in 1995. *C. E. Brittain*

COOL LUKE (IRE) 6 b.g. Red Sunset 120 – Watet Khet (FR) 82 (Wittgenstein (USA) 123) [1994 69: 10m 7f 7g 10g* 8.1d^3 10d* 10.4d^4 10.1d^3 1995 11.1s* 12g^5 Apr 26] lengthy gelding: fair handicapper: odds on after successful spell hurdling, won at Hamilton in April: should stay 1½m: ran creditably on top-of-the-ground in — 69

1993, goes well on a soft surface: blinkered (well beaten) once at 4 yrs: sometimes wears near-side pricker. *G. M. Moore*

COOL STEEL (IRE) 3 gr.g. Absalom 128 – Formidable Task 61 (Formidable (USA) 125) [1994 58: 5s^{4} 6f^{2} 5f^{6} 7m 6m 8s 6s^{5} 7d^{2} 1995 8.3v^{5} 7g 8m^{6} May 31] heavy-topped gelding: modest maiden: well beaten in 1995: usually visored: has joined Mrs. J. Brown. *Miss S. E. Hall* –

COOL TACTICIAN 3 gr.c. Petong 126 – Thevetia 65 (Mummy's Pet 125) [1994 53p: 6m 1995 6g a6g* 8.2m 6.1m 6g^{6} 8.1d^{3} 10m 7m^{6} 7.1m 6.9f^{4} a7g 5.1d a6g 6m 8.1d Oct 10] tall, leggy, quite attractive colt: fair form on the all-weather: won maiden at Wolverhampton in April: only modest on turf: soundly beaten last 5 starts: stays 1m: acts on fibresand and dead ground: sold (R. Hollinshead to C. Parker) 4,800 gns Newmarket Autumn Sales. *R. Hollinshead* 55 d a66 d

COPPER BRIGHT 2 b.g. (Jan 24) Mon Tresor 113 – Arabian Nymph 49 (Sayf El Arab (USA) 127) [1995 5.1m^{4} 6m 5m 6m 6m^{4} 6g^{5} 7.1g Sep 18] 5,000F, 8,400Y: strong gelding: second foal: dam sprint plater at 2 yrs: poor form, visored in selling nursery penultimate start: a sprinter. *P. C. Haslam* –

CORINA'S GLOW 3 gr.f. Sizzling Melody 117 – Pale Glow (Kalaglow 132) [1994 –: 7m a8g 1995 7d 9.9m May 13] leggy, angular filly: no sign of ability. *Miss J. F. Craze* –

CORIO 3 b.c. Sharpo (USA) 132 – Constant Delight 80 (Never So Bold 135) [1994 79: 5d 6f* a6g 6g^{2} 6m^{3} 6g* 6d^{5} 6g 1995 6m 7m Jul 15] quite good-topped colt: fair performer: shaped as though retaining ability on reappearance, but well beaten only subsequent start: should stay 7f: acts on firm and good to soft ground, below form on fibresand. *Miss S. E. Hall* –

CORK STREET GIRL (IRE) 3 b.f. Bold Arrangement 127 – Ward of Court (IRE) (Law Society (USA) 130) [1994 55: 5.7f^{3} 5g^{3} 6.1g 1995 a6g a5g^{4} 6m^{2} 6f 5.1f^{5} 6m 7.1m^{4} a8.5g 6m^{6} 6m^{4} 6f^{5} 5m^{3} 5f a5g Nov 2] small, sparely-made filly: unimpressive mover: modest maiden handicapper: left B. Meehan's stable after thirteenth start: effective at 5f and 6f: acts on fibresand and firm ground: blinkered last 6 starts: races prominently. *G. B. Balding* 53

CORKY'S GIRL 3 b.f. Today And Tomorrow 78 – Rectory Maid 74 (Tina's Pet 121) [1994 –: 5m 7.1g 1995 a7g Feb 3] no sign of ability. *R. M. McKellar* –

CORNICHE QUEST (IRE) 2 b.f. (Feb 22) Salt Dome (USA) – Angel Divine (Ahonoora 122) [1995 5g^{3} 5.1m 6g^{2} 6m^{3} 6m^{2} 5.7h^{3} 6m^{5} 5g^{4} 6g^{4} 7g^{5} 6g^{5} 5f^{3} 5s^{4} Nov 2] IR 7,000Y: leggy filly: second foal: dam unraced twin: modest maiden: best form at 6f: acts on firm ground (looked ill at ease on hard ground) and wasn't discredited on soft. *M. R. Channon* 63 d

CORNISH SNOW (USA) 2 br.c. (Mar 23) Storm Cat (USA) – Pleasantly Free (USA) (Pleasant Colony (USA)) [1995 6s^{4} Oct 6] $190,000F: small colt: first foal: dam, minor stakes winner at up to 1¼m in USA, granddaughter of Champion Stakes winner Hurry Harriet: heavily-backed favourite, 8½ lengths fourth of 11 to Midnight Blue in maiden at Ascot, racing keenly 4f then losing third late on: wore blinkers: moved well to post: sure to do better. *D. R. Loder* 70 p

CORONA GOLD 5 b.g. Chilibang 120 – Miss Alkie 58 (Noalcoholic (FR) 128) [1994 49: 7g 7m a8g 7m 8m^{3} 8f^{3} a7g 7.5m a8g^{4} a7g 7m a8g 1995 8m^{6} a7g^{3} a8g a7g^{5} a7g* 7.1m^{3} a8g 7d Sep 27] sturdy gelding: poor handicapper: won apprentice seller at Southwell in June: stays 1m: acts on fibresand and on firm and dead ground: effective blinkered, but rarely tried nowadays. *J. G. FitzGerald* 46

CORPORAL NYM (USA) 2 gr.c. (Mar 26) Cozzene (USA) – Fiji Fan (USA) (Danzig (USA)) [1995 6g^{4} 6m^{3} 8m^{3} Nov 3] $30,000Y: good-bodied colt: has scope: good mover: fifth foal: brother to French 1¼m winner Olden Lek and half-brother to winners in US by Linkage and Play Fellow: dam sprint winner: fairly useful form in well-contested minor events at York and Kempton in May and Doncaster (staying-on third to Brighstone) in November: will stay beyond 1m: sure to win a race. *P. F. I. Cole* 85 p

CORRADINI 3 b.c. Rainbow Quest (USA) 134 – Cruising Height 112 (Shirley Heights 130) [1994 NR 1995 11m 11.9m* 13.9m^{2} Oct 4] good sort: first foal: dam, stayed 1½m, half-sister to Park Hill winner Trampship out of half-sister to Prix Vermeille winner Paulista: fairly useful form: won strongly-run maiden at York in 92

June, leading inside last having been outpaced early in straight: moved poorly to post and in race when comfortably beaten by Bahamian Sunshine in 3-runner minor event there 3½ months later: should be suited by further than 1½m: has clearly had his problems. *H. R. A. Cecil*

CORRESPONDENCE (CAN) 5 br.g. Phone Trick (USA) – Chas' Lady (USA) (Key To The Kingdom (USA)) [1994 a7g^6 a7g a7g^5 a7g^5 1995 a8g a7g^5 a6g^6 a6g^3 5m^2 5m^4 6f 5g Sep 29] leggy, useful-looking gelding: has a round action: poor form in 1992 for J. Gosden, visored final start: trained by S. Seemar in Dubai in 1993/5, winning 7f maiden in 1993: sold 7,200 gns Newmarket July (1995) Sales: poor form on return here: will prove best at up to 7f: acts on good to firm ground and the sand: sometimes sweats: sold 2,000 gns Newmarket Autumn Sales. *Martyn Meade* 43

CORRIEVARKIE 3 ch.f. Dominion 123 – Mary Bankes (USA) (Northern Baby (CAN) 127) [1994 NR 1995 7g 7d a8g 7m^3 8g^5 Jul 19] lengthy filly: second foal: half-sister to 4-y-o Mild Rebuke (by Reprimand), useful 5f winner at 2 yrs: dam out of half-sister to high-class filly Treizieme and Gold Cup second Eastern Mystic: poor maiden: sold (Miss Gay Kelleway to T. McGovern) 1,100 gns Ascot July Sales: resold 675 gns Ascot October Sales. *Miss Gay Kelleway* 43

CORYANA DANCER (IRE) 3 b.f. Waajib 121 – Fettle (Relkino 131) [1994 NR 1995 7m^6 10.5g^6 8.1g 7.6m^4 10m^6 a7g 10.5d Oct 11] 45,000Y: leggy, quite attractive filly: half-sister to several winners, including Fumo di Londra (by Indian Ridge), useful 5f to 7f winner here at 2 yrs later 1m winner in U.S., and 11f winner Indian Plume (by Commanche Run): dam unraced half-sister to Circus Plume: fair maiden: inconsistent, and soundly beaten last 3 starts: should stay at least 1m: best efforts on good to firm ground: sweating (tailed off) third start. *R. Hollinshead* 67 d

COSY CORNER (IRE) 3 b.f. Cyrano de Bergerac 120 – Trysting Place (He Loves Me 120) [1994 7.5g^6 7d* 1995 8v^5 8.8g^2 8s 7s^3 9g^5 8g* 8g* 8g^5 10d^2 10g 8g^5 10g^6 8.5f a9s Dec 19] IR 3,800Y: strong ex-German-trained filly: fifth foal: half-sister to 1m winner Grondola (by Indian King): dam unraced half-sister to dam of Madam Gay: fairly useful performer: won maiden at 2 yrs and 2 minor events (awarded first one) all at Munich: out of her depth in Sun Chariot Stakes at Newmarket on final start for E. Pils: blinkered, well beaten in USA last 2 starts: stays 1¼m: acts on soft going. *J. Nazareth, jnr, USA* 91

COTTAGE PRINCE (IRE) 2 b.g. (Apr 27) Classic Secret (USA) 91 – Susan's Blues (Cure The Blues (USA)) [1995 5m 7g a8.5d Sep 16] IR 3,300F, 2,800Y, 7,800 2-y-o: smallish, good-bodied gelding: half-brother to 1992 2-y-o 7f seller winner Miss Fayruz and Italian 3-y-o 5f winner Modest Man (both by Fayruz): dam placed at 9f in Ireland: no form in claimer and later maiden events: unruly stalls second outing. *J. J. Quinn* –

COTTEIR CHIEF (IRE) 4 b.c. Chief Singer 131 – Hasty Key (USA) (Key To The Mint (USA)) [1994 108: 7d* 8f 8m^4 8.5m^3 10.2s^6 10s^2 12.5s* 11.8g* 12v^2 1995 12g^2 12g^6 7.9g 10.1f Jun 10] rangy colt: unimpressive mover: useful performer: best efforts in 1995 when short-headed by Fire Worshipper in minor event at Doncaster on reappearance and when sixth in John Porter Stakes at Newbury next time: stays 12.5f: has form on top-of-the-ground but is ideally suited by give, and acts on heavy: wears near-side pricker: held up: consistent. *M. C. Pipe* 107

COTTESLOE BEACH 2 ch.g. (May 17) Gabitat 119 – Georgian Quickstep (Dubassoff (USA)) [1995 6g 6m a7g a6g 6m^5 Aug 12] leggy gelding: first foal: dam poor novice hurdler: plater: needs further than 6f: has worn bandages. *K. T. Ivory* 41

COTYTTO 2 b. or br.f. (Mar 23) Puissance 110 – Drudwen (Sayf El Arab (USA) 127) [1995 5g 6m 6m 7.6m Sep 5] 6,000Y: workmanlike filly: poor mover: second foal: half-sister to fairly useful 3-y-o 1m winner Concer Un (by Lord Bud): dam won 13f NH Flat race: little sign of ability, in nursery final start. *M. J. Fetherston-Godley* –

COUCHANT (IRE) 4 b.g. Petoski 135 – Be Easy 110 (Be Friendly 130) [1994 67: 10m 12m^5 12g 8.9d 1995 12s^3 Sep 27] sturdy, close-coupled gelding: fair maiden: modest winning hurdler in July: creditable third of 11 in apprentice handicap at Folkestone 2 months later: stays 1½m: acts on good to firm and soft ground. *J. White* 66

COUNTRY LOVER 4 ch.g. Thatching 131 – Fair Country 89 (Town And Country 124) [1994 87: 7d^2 a8g* 8m 8m* 10f^2 9.5s^5 1995 8g 10m 10m^5 8.9m 10.4m 81

10f 8m 8d^{2} 8m^{5} 8m Oct 28] strong gelding: fairly useful handicapper: effective at 1m to 1¼m: acts on firm and soft going: visored (ran creditably) once in 1994. *Lord Huntingdon*

COUNTRY STAR (IRE) 4 b.g. Persian Bold 123 – Sugar Plum Fairy 91 (Sadler's Wells (USA) 132) [1994 71: 10m^{3} 10g 1995 10g^{4} 10m 10m* 10m^{2} 12g^{3} 10d^{4} 12s 10d Oct 19] workmanlike, good-bodied gelding: has reportedly split pastern and had wind operation: fairly useful performer: won maiden at Windsor in July: in frame in competitive handicaps next 3 starts: stays 1½m: acts on good to firm ground and dead (raced too freely on soft): very free to post and sweating (ran well) fifth 3-y-o start: has joined C. Brooks. *H. Candy* 85

COUNTRY THATCH 2 b.c. (Mar 13) Thatching 131 – Alencon (Northfields (USA)) [1995 6d 5s Sep 28] IR 20,000Y: neat colt: half-brother to several winners abroad: dam, winner twice in USA at up to 9f, sister to Oats: never-dangerous seventh of 16, late headway, behind Angaar in maiden at Lingfield second start: remains capable of better over 7f+. *C. A. Horgan* 56 p

COURAGE-MON-BRAVE 7 gr.g. Bold Owl 101 – Bri-Ette 53 (Brittany) [1994 NR 1995 a12g^{5} Jun 2] compact gelding: probably no longer of much account. *R. P. C. Hoad* –

COURAGEOUS DANCER (IRE) 3 b.f. Cadeaux Genereux 131 – Hafwah (Gorytus (USA) 132) [1994 NR 1995 7m^{3} 8.2m^{3} 6g* 7m* 7g^{5} 7m^{4} 6m^{5} 7g 8d^{2} 8s^{4} Oct 6] strong, lengthy filly: second foal: half-sister to 9f winner Rupan (by Taufan): dam unraced half-sister to dam of Sure Blade: fairly useful performer: won apprentice maiden at Pontefract and handicap at Lingfield in June: good efforts last 2 starts in listed events at Ascot won by Hiwaya (rated stakes) and A La Carte: stays 1m: winner on good to firm ground but goes well on a soft surface. *B. Hanbury* 94

COURBARIL 3 b.c. Warrshan (USA) 117 – Free On Board 73 (Free State 125) [1994 60: 6s 6f 7g a8g^{2} 10s^{2} 7.9d 1995 8.5d^{6} 10s^{5} 10s* 10s 10.3g^{6} 12m^{2} 12.5f^{4} 11.6m^{5} 12m^{3} 14m 11.9f* 11.6m^{3} 12g 12g^{6} Sep 29] neat colt: fair handicapper: won at Cagnes-sur-Mer (minor event) in February and Brighton in July: should stay beyond 1½m: acts on equitrack and on any turf going: sweating (ran respectably) twice at 3 yrs: apprentice ridden last 4 starts. *S. Dow* 65

COUREUR 6 b.g. Ajdal (USA) 130 – Nihad 76 (Alleged (USA) 138) [1994 62: 9.2d^{3} 9.9m^{3} 9f* 8g 8g^{4} 8m^{4} 9d* 10d 8.9d 8m 1995 8g^{2} 8.5d* 10f^{3} 8.5m^{3} 8.9g 10f Oct 31] big, close-coupled gelding: has a round action: fair handicapper: won at Beverley in June: burst a blood vessel at start next intended outing, and reportedly had knee operation after fourth: below form afterwards: effective at 1m and stays 1¼m: probably acts on any going: sold 7,000 gns Doncaster November Sales. *J. D. Bethell* 71

COURSE FISHING 4 ch.g. Squill (USA) 122 – Migoletty 59 (Oats 126) [1994 NR 1995 10m^{4} a8.5g 12.5g 10.8m 10.8m* 12m^{5} 10m^{5} 10m^{2} 10.2m* 10m 10.4m Oct 5] short-backed gelding: poor mover: poor handicapper: won at Warwick (maiden event) and Chepstow in the summer: stays 10.8f: acts on good to firm and dead ground: takes good hold. *B. A. McMahon* 47

COURTING DANGER 2 b.g. (May 6) Tina's Pet 121 – Court Town 60 (Camden Town 125) [1995 6d 6d^{4} Sep 27] workmanlike gelding: first reported foal: dam, suited by 1m, half-sister to very smart sprinter Broxted: around 10 lengths seventh of 25 to Sovereign's Crown in maiden at Newbury, prominent long way: never a serious factor in similar event at Folkestone 11 days later: will stay 7f. *D. R. Gandolfo* 57 +

COURTING NEWMARKET 7 b.g. Final Straw 127 – Warm Wind 84 (Tumble Wind (USA)) [1994 54: a6g a6g^{3} a7g^{2} a7g a8g^{6} 6.1s 7m^{4} 6m 7.1m 7m 7.6g^{6} 6f* 6.1s a7g^{4} 1995 a7g a7g 7m 7g 7.1m 9m^{6} 8.1m^{2} 8.3m Jul 29] leggy, good-topped gelding: unimpressive mover: poor form at best in 1995: should stay 1m: goes well on all-weather surfaces, also acts on firm and dead ground: tried blinkered, not for long time: inconsistent: has joined N. Babbage. *Mrs A. Knight* 43

COURT JOKER (IRE) 3 b.g. Fools Holme (USA) – Crimson Glen 70 (Glenstal (USA) 118) [1994 63: 6f 6m^{5} 6g^{3} 7s 1995 8m^{4} 10.3m^{5} 12.5m 9.9m^{4} 15g^{6} 14g 12d* Oct 21] lengthy gelding: modest performer: 25/1, best 3-y-o effort when winning claimer at Newbury in October: effective at 1½m, probably at 15f: acts on good to firm and dead ground: visored (pulled hard and well beaten) third 3-y-o start: sold 60

(M. Tompkins to Miss H. Knight) 16,000 gns Newmarket Autumn Sales. *M. H. Tompkins*

COURT MINSTREL 6 br.g. Hadeer 118 – Sheer Bliss 76 (St Paddy 133) [1994 63: 7.6g 8s 8.5m 7m 8f^2 8g^3 8m^6 7d 8g 1995 8m 7g^6 7m^4 7f^5 8f^4 8m^5 Aug 31] strong gelding: good walker: modest handicapper: effective at 7f to 1m: probably acts on any going: has run well when sweating: usually held up. *L. J. Holt* 57

COURT NAP (IRE) 3 ch.g. Waajib 121 – Mirhar (FR) (Sharpen Up 127) [1994 57: 6g 6m a6g^2 a7g^3 a6g^4 7s^5 6s 1995 a7g^5 8f^2 8g 8.3m^3 8.3g^2 7f 8.3m^2 8.5s^5 8d Sep 27] leggy, close-coupled gelding: modest maiden handicapper: will probably stay 1¼m: acts on fibresand and on firm and soft ground: won over hurdles in November. *S. Mellor* 54

COURT OF HONOUR (IRE) 3 b.c. Law Society (USA) 130 – Captive Island 116 (Northfields (USA)) [1994 106p: 8s^6 8m* 8v^3 10d* 1995 12.3m^2 12m^2 12f^5 12m 12d^3 15s^2 12d* Oct 15] 118

The Gran Premio del Jockey Club Italiano provided a handsome end-of-season reward for Court of Honour, one of the majority of horses in the line-up in Milan whose earnings, for one reason or another, did not adequately reflect their ability. Court of Honour had not won since a visit to Rome for the Premio Guido Berardelli eleven months back. He had, however, been very highly tried in the meantime and had finished out of the frame in only two of his six races—when a good fifth to Lammtarra in the Derby and a not-so-good ninth to Winged Love in the Irish Derby. Court of Honour was beaten only three lengths at Epsom, shaping like a stayer. That run had been preceded by tilts at the Chester Vase and the Derby Italiano which were both foiled by Luso, by a head at Chester, by a length and a half at Rome. On both these occasions he had also shaped like a stayer. An unplanned break followed his run in the Irish Derby, when slight lameness forced the abandonment of plans to fly him to South America for the Grande Premio Brasil. But he was on his travels again by September, first to Milan, where Posidonas and Slicious were able decisively to end his efforts to lead all the way in the Gran Premio d'Italia, thence to Longchamp where, although staying on, he couldn't prevent Grey Shot leading all the way in the fifteen-furlong Prix de Lutece and had to settle for second.

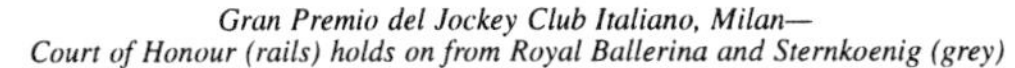

Gran Premio del Jockey Club Italiano, Milan—
Court of Honour (rails) holds on from Royal Ballerina and Sternkoenig (grey)

So back to Milan for the final call, and back to a mile and a half. First-prize money of over £180,000 for the Gran Premio del Jockey Club was enough to ensure that the locals, as usual, would be well outweighed. Their Scribano was left facing seven foreign challengers, five of whom fought out the finish, well clear of the rest of the field. The finish was one of the closest seen in a big race anywhere in Europe during the year. Court of Honour at last succeeded in leading throughout. With him on the line were the always-prominent Royal Ballerina and the strong-finishing, unlucky-in-running Sternkoenig; a neck back came the always-prominent Linney Head, another neck back the staying-on Zilzal Zamaan. Soon afterwards Court of Honour's trainer announced that the colt had been retired for the season as there was nothing left to go for. No plans for the Prix Royal-Oak or the St Leger Italiano, then. However, the Cup races are apparently under consideration for 1996.

Court of Honour (IRE) (b.c. 1992)	Law Society (USA) (br 1982)	Alleged (b 1974)	Hoist The Flag
			Princess Pout
		Bold Bikini (b 1969)	Boldnesian
			Ram-Tan
	Captive Island (ch 1982)	Northfields (ch 1968)	Northern Dancer
			Little Hut
		Icy More (ch 1975)	Ballymore
			Arctic Wave

Rightly so, the way Court of Honour has shaped for much of his career, although it is true to say that his two-and-a-half-length second to Grey Shot on his first and only attempt at a stayer's distance is a good 7 lb below the level of his Derby form. He's a very strong galloper, suited by a good pace or forcing the pace when at a mile and a half. Court of Honour is by the Irish Derby winner Law Society, a confirmed influence for stamina, out of a mare who stayed a mile and a quarter. The second dam, a daughter of the 1970 Oaks third Arctic Wave, was well suited by a mile and three quarters as a three-year-old. Court of Honour's half-brother and former stable-companion Rubhahunish (by Darshaan) was returned to Britain in December after a rather disappointing season in pattern races in Italy, in which he never got the chance he deserves to tackle further than a mile and a half. The strong, rangy Court of Honour seems to act on any going. He occasionally wears bandages. *P. W. Chapple-Hyam*

COURTOWN BOY 5 ch.g. Ballacashtal (CAN) – Palace Gossip (Tender King 123) [1994 NR 1995 10m^2 12m^3 Jul 11] first foal: dam poor maiden: won NH Flat race in 1993/4: fair and progressive hurdler (acts on firm ground), winner in April: fair form in maidens at Brighton and Pontefract in the summer: stays 1½m. *O. O'Neill* 65

COVEN MOON 5 ch.m. Crofthall 110 – Mayspark 50 (Stanford 121§) [1994 NR 1995 a8g^2 a8g^6 a8g 10.8m a9.4g 10m* a10g^6 Nov 14] lengthy mare: poor performer: gained first success in selling handicap at Nottingham in August: effective at 1m and 1¼m: acts on good to firm and soft ground and the all-weather: best recent efforts in visor. *D. Morris* 39

COVENT GARDEN GIRL 5 b.m. Sizzling Melody 117 – Azelly 77 (Pitskelly 122) [1994 64d: a5g 5s^2 5v^6 5.3g 5d 5f 6f^6 1995 5m Apr 20] lengthy mare: sprint handicapper: on the downgrade, and last of 13 on only 5-y-o start. *M. W. Easterby* –

COWBOY DREAMS (IRE) 2 b.c. (Mar 1) Nashamaa 113 – Shahrazad (Young Emperor 133) [1995 6m^5 6m 7.1d Sep 2] IR 5,500Y: rather leggy, angular colt: half-brother to Irish 7f winner Dazla (by Dublin Taxi): dam poor Irish maiden: behind in maidens at Newmarket (last of 5), Kempton (median auction event) and Haydock. *M. H. Tompkins* –

COYOTE BLUFF (IRE) 2 gr.c. (May 8) Fayruz 116 – Ikala (Lashkari 128) [1995 5d* 7g a6g^3 Oct 14] 9,000Y: leggy colt: second foal: dam fourth in Irish 2½m bumpers: fair form: won minor event at Milan in May: eighth of 11 in well-contested auction event at Goodwood nearly 5 months later then below-form third in claimer at Wolverhampton final start: stays 7f. *P. W. Chapple-Hyam* 74

COZZI (FR) 7 gr.g. Cozzene (USA) – Land Girl (USA) (Sir Ivor 135) [1994 –: 12.1m^5 12.3f^5 a12g 10.8m 9g 1995 10m 10m 12f Jun 30] big gelding: no worthwhile form. *J. M. Bradley* –

CRAB 'N LOBSTER (IRE) 5 b.m. Waajib 121 – Storm Crest 80 (Lord Gayle (USA) 124) [1994 40, a30: a8.5g a16.2g^5 a12g 11.8d^2 12g^6 16g^3 a12g^6 a14.8g^3 a12g^6 a16.2g a12g^3 15.9s^5 16.1s 1995 a16.2g a16.2g a12g Aug 5] small, leggy mare: poor maiden: tailed off in 1995, off course over 6 months after reappearance. *B. Preece* –

CRACKERNAT (IRE) 2 b.c. (Mar 29) Classic Music (USA) – Party Piece (Thatch (USA) 136) [1995 6.1m 6m* 7m^2 6m^5 8g^3 Sep 14] IR 30,000Y: compact colt: closely related to 2 winners by Glow, including 5f (at 2 yrs) and 7f winner Glowing Value, and half-brother to 7f (Ireland, 2 yrs) to 11.5f (Italy, 6 yrs) winner Magic Piece (by Magical Wonder): dam Irish maiden: won 5-runner median auction maiden at York in July: best subsequent effort when second to Dankeston in minor event at Catterick in August: probably stays 1m: looked none too keen third and fourth outings: sold 10,000 gns Newmarket Autumn Sales. *L. M. Cumani* 81 §

CRACKING PROSPECT 4 ch.g. Hubbly Bubbly (USA) – Crackerjill 37 (Sparkler 130) [1994 58: 8.1s^6 7.1g^6 8.1g 10.2m^6 1995 10m 7g 10f^6 8f^4 10.2h^4 12f Aug 15] leggy, unfurnished gelding: modest maiden handicapper: probably stays 1¼m: probably acts on any going (very best form on soft): has worn crossed noseband. *B. R. Millman* 42

CRADLE DAYS 6 b.g. Dance of Life (USA) – Dream Chaser 92 (Record Token 128) [1994 80: 5.1g^2 6m 5m 6g 5m^3 5m 6.1g^5 a6g a5g^6 1995 a6g 5m 5g 6m 7m 6g 5f^4 5m 5m^6 Aug 3] tall, lengthy, attractive gelding: fair handicapper at best in 1995: stays 6f, very best efforts at 5f: acts on good to firm and dead ground: no improvement in blinkers: sometimes early to post: tends to hang badly: one to leave alone: has joined P. Howling. *R. C. Spicer* 65 §

CRAFTY CRICKETER 4 ch.c. Clantime 101 – Ruby Shoes 46 (Day Is Done 115) [1994 –: 5d 6g 5.1g a6g a5g a7g 1995 a6g a6g a7g^5 a8g a7g^6 6m Apr 6] small colt: no worthwhile form for some time: left R. Voorspuy's stable after third 4-y-o start. *R. M. Flower* –

CRAIGIE BOY 5 b.g. Crofthall 110 – Lady Carol 42 (Lord Gayle (USA) 124) [1994 65: 5g^4 6g^4 5g^6 6d* 5v^2 6f^3 6g^6 5m^4 6g^2 6d^2 6g^6 6d^2 6d^4 5d^4 5d^2 1995 5g 6g^3 7m 5g 6f^6 6m 6m 6d 6g 6d^3 6g^2 5d^6 5m 6m Oct 30] leggy gelding: just a modest handicapper most of 1995: suited by testing conditions at 5f, and stays 6f well: probably acts on any going: usually blinkered: tough. *N. Bycroft* 65 d

CRAIGMILL 3 b.f. Slip Anchor 136 – Rynechra 102 (Blakeney 126) [1994 77p: 7m^2 7g^2 8.1g^2 7g* 1995 10g 12f Jul 26] leggy, light-framed filly: fairly useful performer: best effort when ninth of 12 in £19,400 handicap at Newmarket on reappearance: beaten long way out in similar event at Goodwood 2 weeks later, giving impression something amiss: should be suited by test of stamina: sold 8,500 gns Newmarket December Sales. *H. R. A. Cecil* 85

CRAIGMORE MAGIC (USA) 2 br.g. (Feb 12) Simply Majestic (USA) – Some Rehearsal (USA) (Halo (USA)) [1995 a6g^6 7m^5 a7g 7.1g^6 Sep 18] $16,000Y, 1,000 2-y-o: sturdy gelding: has a round action: second foal: brother to a minor 2-y-o winner in USA: dam, unplaced, closely related to Grade 1 9f winner Try Something New: poor form in varied company, including selling: reluctant stalls third start. *Miss M. K. Milligan* –

CRAIGNAIRN 2 b.c. (Mar 1) Merdon Melody 98 – Bri-Ette 53 (Brittany) [1995 5f^3 6f^3 7g^6 6h^6 7.1m^5 6g^2 6m^2 Oct 13] 8,800Y: brother to modest maiden Unison and half-brother to sprint winners Mom Sally and Miss Ellie Pea (both by Bold Owl): dam sister to useful sprinter Tinjar: much improved form in maidens last 2 starts, narrowly beaten by Diminuet at Ayr and Singing Patriarch at Catterick after making running: likely to prove best at 6f. *J. Berry* 76

CRAMONA (IRE) 5 ch.m. Carmelite House (USA) 118 – Cramond 105 (Porto Bello 118) [1994 –: a7g a8g a12g^5 a12g^6 a12g 1995 a7g Feb 13] probably of little account. *W. Storey* –

CRANBROOK KATE 3 b.f. Damister (USA) 123 – Overdraft (Bustino 136) [1994 –: 6f 5g 6d 8.2s 7g a8.5g a6g 1995 10g a12g May 4] smallish, leggy filly: no form. *J. Mackie* –

CRANFIELD CRACKER 4 b.f. Beveled (USA) – Jump To It 53 (Double Form 130) [1994 –: a5g a7g 1995 a6g a8g Feb 7] showed a little ability on only run in 1993, but none since. *D. W. P. Arbuthnot* –

CRAVEN COTTAGE 2 b.g. (Mar 27) Inca Chief (USA) – Seymour Ann (Krayyan 117) [1995 6f^6 6m 7.6d Sep 14] leggy gelding: third foal: half-brother to 2 winners, including 3-y-o Captain's Day (by Ballacashtal), 7f winner at 2 yrs: dam unraced: similar form in auction events at Kempton first 2 starts: behind in maiden at Lingfield final outing: should stay beyond 6f. *C. James* 56

CRAZY CHIEF 2 b.c. (Mar 22) Indian Ridge 123 – Bizarre Lady (Dalsaan 125) [1995 7.6d^2 7d^2 6d^3 Oct 19] lengthy, useful-looking colt: fourth foal: dam never ran: fair form placed in maidens at Lingfield, Salisbury and (length third of 20 to Fly Tip) Newbury: should stay further than 7f: races prominently. *P. F. I. Cole* 80

CRAZY PAVING (IRE) 4 b.g. Danehill (USA) 126 – Clunk Click 72 (Star Appeal 133) [1994 96: 7m* 8f 8g 7g 1995 7m Apr 19] big, good-bodied gelding: fairly useful performer: shaped quite well in rated stakes on reappearance, but not seen out again: should be well suited by further than 7f. *C. A. Cyzer* 84 +

CREATIVE ACCOUNT (USA) 2 b. or br.c. (Feb 13) Time For A Change (USA) – Stolie (USA) (Navajo (USA)) [1995 5g^5 6g^2 6f^2 6m* 6g^5 8m Oct 13] $70,000Y: third foal: brother to a minor winner in North America: dam minor stakes winner of 3 races: sire very smart 7f to 9f winner: won valuable nursery at Newmarket in August: had no luck in running in similar events at Newmarket last 2 starts: should stay further than 6f: acts on good to firm going, yet to race on a soft surface: keen sort: to be trained by T. Amos in USA. *Mrs J. R. Ramsden* 93

CREDIT CONTROLLER (IRE) 6 b.g. Dromod Hill – Fotopan (Polyfoto 124) [1994 NR 1995 14s Sep 28] fourth foal: dam winning hurdler: no promise on belated flat debut. *J. Ffitch-Heyes* –

CREDITE RISQUE 2 b.f. (Mar 15) Risk Me (FR) 127 – Lompoa (Lomond (USA) 128) [1995 5g 5.1m 5m^5 Jun 17] 5,200Y: leggy filly: second foal: sister to 3-y-o Nisya: dam ran twice: poor form in varied maiden events. *M. McCormack* 42

CREDIT SQUEEZE 5 ch.g. Superlative 118 – Money Supply (Brigadier Gerard 144) [1994 68: a12g^5 a10g^4 10.3g^6 10.3m 10m 10.5g* 9m^5 8.1f^2 10.3g^6 8m 11g* 10m^4 10m^4 12m 10s a10g^3 1995 10.3g 11.9m* 10g^3 12m* 11.9m^5 12f^4 12f^4 12g 14f Aug 5] leggy, good-topped gelding: good mover: fair handicapper: won at Brighton in April and Salisbury in May: rather disappointing afterwards: stays 1½m: acts on good to firm ground, dead and equitrack: successful for amateur: sometimes wears crossed noseband: bandaged: held up. *R. F. Johnson Houghton* 78

CREEKING 2 b.f. (Apr 29) Persian Bold 123 – Miller's Creek (USA) 62 (Star de Naskra (USA)) [1995 a6g^2 Dec 14] 26,000Y: half-sister to useful 1993 2-y-o Fast Eddy (by Sharpo), 7f winner in Germany at 4 yrs, and 6f (at 2 yrs) to 10.2f winner Stone Mill (by Caerleon): dam, suited by 1m, out of half-sister to top Canadian colt Giboulee: 11/2, 8 lengths second to Carmarthen Bay in 9-runner maiden at Lingfield, slowly away: will improve, particularly over 7f+. *Sir Mark Prescott* 59 p

CREES SQAW 3 b.f. Cree Song 99 – Elsocko 76 (Swing Easy (USA) 126) [1994 NR 1995 7g Sep 23] 400Y: third foal: half-sister to 2 winners in Hong Kong, including fair 1993 2-y-o 5f winner here Dominion King (by Dominion Royale): dam (maiden) stayed 7f: 100/1, never a threat in Redcar maiden. *B. A. McMahon* –

CRESPO (IRE) 3 b.c. Kris 135 – Fair Salinia 125 (Petingo 135) [1994 72p: 8m 8.2d^5 1995 10s^5 12.3m^4 12g* Jun 3] lengthy colt: shows a round action: progressive form: won handicap at Kempton in June: will probably be suited by further than 1½m: acts on good to firm and dead ground: looked capable of better still: sent to Dubai. *J. R. Fanshawe* 81 p

CRESTED KNIGHT (IRE) 3 gr.g. Night Shift (USA) – Casual (USA) (Caro 133) [1994 64: 6m^5 7g 7g 1995 10.3g 10.8m^4 8f^2 7.1g 8s 9.7g Oct 16] lengthy, good-topped gelding: fair maiden handicapper: very much caught the eye in £11,900 event at Ascot fifth start: well beaten at Folkestone 9 days later: should stay beyond 1m: acts on firm ground, shaped well on soft: sometimes bandaged. *C. A. Horgan* 69

CRETAN GIFT 4 ch.g. Cadeaux Genereux 131 – Caro's Niece (USA) 86 (Caro 133) [1994 54: 6m^5 a6g^4 a6g^5 6.1m^3 a6g^6 6g^5 1995 a6g^2 a6g* a6g 6m a6g^4 6.1d^2 a6g* a6g* 6f^5 7m a7g a6g^2 Dec 12] lengthy gelding: reportedly split a pastern after final start at 2 yrs: fair handicapper: won at Southwell in April and at Wolverhampton in September and October: seems to stay 7f: acts on firm and dead ground and goes well on fibresand: effective visored or not: wears crossed noseband. *N. P. Littmoden* 62 a78

CRIMINAL RECORD (USA) 5 b.g. Fighting Fit (USA) – Charlie's Angel (USA) 66 (Halo (USA)) [1994 –: a12g a12g 1995 a14g^6 a12g^6 Apr 3] good-topped gelding: modest 1½m winner at 3 yrs: no worthwhile form on flat since: won selling hurdle in June: has joined P. Bradley. *W. Clay* –

CRIMSON AND CLOVER 2 gr.f. (Apr 12) Midyan (USA) 124 – Carose (Caro 133) [1995 5.3m^3 5g^5 7g 7g* 7m^4 6.1d a7g^2 Nov 10] 5,000Y: good-topped filly: half-sister to several winners, including useful Italian 7f to 9f winner Rosa de Caerleon (by Caerleon) and 1¼m winner Jason's Quest (by Golden Fleece): dam half-sister to very smart French middle-distance colt Noir Et Or: easy winner of seller at Yarmouth (sold out of M. Bell's stable 10,000 gns) in July: best effort afterwards when short-head second of 12 in similar event at Lingfield: better suited by 7f than less: acts on equitrack: sold 6,200 gns Doncaster November Sales. *R. Akehurst* 58 a64

CRIMSON ROSELLA 2 b. or br.f. (May 27) Polar Falcon (USA) 126 – Double Finesse 97 (Double Jump 131) [1995 7f^6 Oct 18] leggy, attractive filly: fluent mover: half-sister to several winners, including smart 6f to 1m winner Larionov (by Balidar) and high-class sprinter Mr Brooks (by Blazing Saddles): dam won at up to 1m: 33/1 and bit backward, around 10 lengths sixth of 11 to Prize Giving in maiden at Yarmouth, racing keenly in steadily-run race then losing touch from 2f out: should improve. *W. J. Haggas* – p

CRIMSON SHOWER 3 b. or br.f. Dowsing (USA) 124 – Flaming Rose (USA) (Upper Nile (USA)) [1994 61p: 5d 6g^3 1995 6d^4 6g^3 7.1m^4 8.3g* 8.3m^5 8g 8m 10.3m^5 Nov 3] workmanlike filly: modest performer: won minor event at Windsor in June: stays 8.3f: acts on good to firm ground, probably on dead. *J. R. Fanshawe* 54

CRISSEM (IRE) 2 b.f. (Jan 24) Thatching 131 – Deer Emily (Alzao (USA) 117) [1995 6m^5 5f^3 5f* 7d Sep 26] 11,000Y: workmanlike filly: has scope: second foal: half-sister to useful Irish 3-y-o 7f and 9f winner Damani (by Persian Bold): dam, Irish 6f (at 2 yrs) and 1½m winner, half-sister to useful French stayer Chawn: won maiden auction at Haydock in August: ran well, though never a factor, in valuable sales race over 7f at Newmarket 7 weeks later: will probably stay 1m. *R. Hollinshead* 70

CRISTAL SPRINGS 4 b.f. Dance of Life (USA) – Cristalga 90 (High Top 131) [1994 55d: 12.3d^4 12s^5 13.1m^5 11.1f 11.5g a14g^6 a13g a13g^5 a16.2g^6 1995 a13g a13g^4 a14g 11.9m^4 21.6f^5 15.8g^4 Jun 2] angular, plain filly: poor stayer: acts on any going: visored (well beaten) fourth 3-y-o start: has run creditably when sweating: inconsistent: sold 850 gns Ascot August Sales. *B. J. McMath* 37 a–

CROCODILE ROCK 3 b.g. Sizzling Melody 117 – Sunley Sinner 93 (Try My Best (USA) 130) [1994 NR 1995 a7g a8.5g a8g 6m 8.1g 8f Jun 28] angular gelding: no worthwhile form: tried visored, blinkered and tongue tied. *M. J. Heaton-Ellis* –

CROCODILE SHOES 2 b.c. (Feb 21) Emarati (USA) 74 – Gas Only 63 (Northfields (USA)) [1995 5m^2 6m* 5.2g^5 6m Sep 2] 7,000F, 9,000Y: lengthy, attractive colt: half-brother to 1987 2-y-o 6f winner Glowing Report (by Kalaglow): dam 9f and 1¼m winner: made all in median auction event at Windsor in June despite hanging left: ran a good race when fifth of 17 (first home on heavily unfavoured far side) to Blue Iris in Super Sprint at Newbury: towards rear in valuable restricted event at the Curragh final start: stays 6f: sold 24,000 gns Newmarket Autumn Sales to Malaysia. *R. Hannon* 79 +

CROESO CYNNES 2 ch.f. (May 24) Most Welcome 131 – Miss Taleca (Pharly (FR) 130) [1995 5.1m 6g* 6m^6 6f^5 6.1d 6d 6.1s Oct 17] 700Y: compact filly: first foal: dam poor daughter of useful Irish 2-y-o Sweet Emma: won maiden auction at Warwick in June: below form in nurseries last 4 starts: stays 6f: best form on a sound surface: visored final outing: races keenly. *B. Palling* 70 d

CROESO-I-CYMRU 4 b.f. Welsh Captain 113 – Bridge of Gold 68 (Balidar 133) [1994 96: 5m* 6m^3 6m^2 6m* 6g^2 6d^5 6d^2 5.6g 1995 5.1m^5 6g 6m 5m^4 6m* 6g^3 6g^5 6g Oct 7] lengthy, workmanlike filly: good mover: fairly useful performer: trained by B. McMahon first 3 4-y-o starts: back to form in September for new stable, making all in minor event at Epsom and narrowly-beaten third of 26 (always front rank) in £16,100 handicap at Goodwood: effective at 5f and 6f: acts on good to firm ground, below form both starts on a soft surface: sometimes early to post. *R. Akehurst* 94

CROFTERS CEILIDH 3 ch.f. Scottish Reel 123 – Highland Rowena 59 (Royben 125) [1994 101: 5s^2 5.1m^6 5d^3 5d^2 5.7f^4 5f* 5m* 5.2g^4 5g^2 1995 5f^4 6g 5m –

Jun 16] leggy filly: useful and speedy juvenile: well below form all 3 starts in 1995. *B. A. McMahon*

CROFT IMPERIAL 8 ch.g. Crofthall 110 – Farinara (Dragonara Palace (USA) 115) [1994 76: a6g^3 a5g* a5g^3 a5g* a6g^3 a5g^2 a6g^3 1995 5g^5 5m 5g 5g^6 5g^2 6d 5m^4 5m^6 5m^4 5m* 5m 5.1m^4 6m* Aug 28] workmanlike, good-quartered gelding: has a quick action: fair handicapper: won at Catterick in July and Ripon (by short head) in August: effective at 5f and 6f: seems to act on any going, and went well on the all-weather at 7 yrs: effective blinkered/visored or not: tends to idle. *M. Johnston* — 72

CROFT POOL 4 b.g. Crofthall 110 – Blackpool Belle 70 (The Brianstan 128) [1994 76: a6g^4 5m^2 5m^2 5v a5g* a6g a5g* 1995 a6g* a6g^2 a6g^5 a6g^3 6m^2 5g^5 6m^2 6g^2 6m 6m 6.1m^2 6f^2 6m 6g 5g* 5m* 5m* 6m^4 a6g Nov 11] sturdy, quite attractive gelding: impresses in appearance: useful handicapper: had an excellent season, improving throughout the year and winning at Southwell in January, Haydock in September and Newmarket and Doncaster (both rated stakes) in October: soon off bridle but ran really well when fourth of 12 to Carranita in listed race at Doncaster on penultimate outing: effective at 5f and 6f: acts on firm and dead ground and the all-weather: visored (below form) once: tends to idle: tough and consistent. *J. A. Glover* — 99, a86

CROFT VALLEY 8 ch.g. Crofthall 110 – Sannavally (Sagaro 133) [1994 84+: 8.1d 7g 1995 7m^4 7.1m^2 7.6m^3 7.3m 7m^4 7g Sep 8] workmanlike gelding: useful handicapper, the winner of 9 races: in frame in 4 rated stakes in 1995: effective at 7f/1m: acted on firm and soft ground: tried visored (fair form) at 3 yrs: front runner: tough and game for most of career: broke leg on gallops: dead. *R. Akehurst* — 99

CRONK'S COURAGE 9 ch.g. Krayyan 117 – Iresine (GER) (Frontal) [1994 64d: a6g a7g 6s 6v* 6d 5d* 7.6m a5g a6g^5 a6g^6 6g^6 a6g 8s 6g 6s 1995 a7g^4 a7g 6v^4 6s a7g 5.1g^6 6g 6g Sep 25] big, strong, lengthy gelding: has a quick action: poor handicapper at best nowadays: speedy, but has won at up to 1m: acts on any going: usually visored. *M. G. Meagher* — 37

CROSS TALK (IRE) 3 b.c. Darshaan 133 – Liaison (USA) (Blushing Groom (FR) 131) [1994 NR 1995 8d 12f 8m^6 11.1f^2 13.4m^2 13.8g* 10.5s 11.8g 11.8f^5 Oct 24] close-coupled colt: second foal: dam 1¼m listed winner at 4 yrs in France: sold out of G. Harwood's stable 11,500 gns Newmarket December (1994) Sales: fair performer: won maiden at Catterick in July: below form afterwards: will stay further than 1¾m: acts on firm ground: hung badly right fourth start. *R. Hollinshead* — 70

CROSS THE BORDER 2 b.c. (Jan 18) Statoblest 120 – Brave Advance (USA) 98 (Bold Laddie (USA)) [1995 6g 5m^2 5m* 5f^2 5g^3 6g^3 Sep 20] 49,000Y: strong, attractive colt: half-brother to smart sprinter Venture Capitalist (by Never So Bold): dam, 5f winner, raced only at 2 yrs: won 5-runner median auction maiden at Thirsk — 89

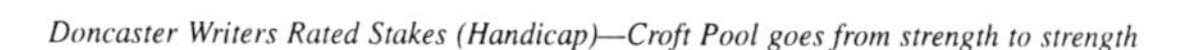
Doncaster Writers Rated Stakes (Handicap)—Croft Pool goes from strength to strength

in August: ran well placed in minor events won by Tarf at Salisbury and Oh Whataknight at Ayr next 2 starts: easily best form at 5f. *R. Hannon*

CROWDED AVENUE 3 b.g. Sizzling Melody 117 – Lady Bequick 81 (Sharpen Up 127) [1994 55: 5d 5d 5s^{6} 5.2g 1995 6m 5.1f^{6} 5g* 5m* 5m^{2} 5m* 5m^{2} 5m* 5m* 5g Sep 28] compact gelding: improved in leaps and bounds in 1995, developing into a useful handicapper: won at Ayr (maiden event, flashed tail) and Edinburgh in June, Goodwood in July, and at Epsom in August and September: didn't give his running in listed race at Newmarket on final start: raced mainly at 5f: acts on firm ground: held up, and has a good turn of foot: looks a smart sprinter in the making. *P. J. Makin* — 101 p

CROWNED GLORY (USA) 3 b.c. Chief's Crown (USA) – Cherry Jubilee (USA) (Coastal (USA)) [1994 74: 7m 8s^{2} 10g^{5} 1995 12g^{3} 11.6m 10.8g^{5} 12g* 10m^{2} 14m Jul 7] well-made colt: has reportedly had wind problems: fair performer: easy winner of 4-runner claimer at Doncaster in June: better form when staying-on second in similar event at Newmarket: upset in stalls and never going well on final start: stays 1½m: acts on good to firm and soft ground: has had tongue tied down: sold 16,000 gns Newmarket July Sales. *P. F. I. Cole* — 70

CROWNING TINO 3 b.f. Crowning Honors (CAN) – Tino Reppin 46 (Neltino 97) [1994 NR 1995 8.2d 8m 7g a7g Dec 19] sparely-made filly: second reported foal: dam suited by 7f: well beaten in maidens. *Mrs N. Macauley* — –

CROWN OF LOVE (USA) 3 b.f. Nureyev (USA) 131 – Hiaam (USA) 110 (Alydar (USA)) [1994 52p: 6g^{6} 1995 7g 7.1m^{3} 6g^{6} 6.9f^{2} 7m^{5} Aug 14] smallish, leggy filly: modest maiden: probably needs further than 6f (should stay 1m): has raced only on a sound surface: none too consistent: sent to USA. *M. R. Stoute* — 62

CROWN OF SHEBA (USA) 3 b.f. Alysheba (USA) – Belle de Jour (USA) (Speak John) [1994 NR 1995 7g^{4} 8.2m* 8g Jul 11] quite good-topped filly: twelfth reported foal: half-sister to 10 winners, including Kentucky Derby winner Spend A Buck (by Buckaroo) and 1991 2-y-o 6f winner Jode (by Danzig): dam won 6f claiming race: fair form: won maiden at Nottingham in June, leading on bit 3f out and staying on well: below form in handicap at Newmarket 15 days later: should be suited by further than 8.2f. *E. A. L. Dunlop* — 74

CROWN PROSECUTOR 5 b.g. Law Society (USA) 130 – Dance Card 69 (Be My Guest (USA) 126) [1994 NR 1995 a12g^{2} a14.8g Feb 4] half-brother to 3 useful performers, including middle-distance performer Charlo (by Chief's Crown): dam, second over 1m on second start, became disappointing: won NH Flat race in March, 1994: second in maiden at Southwell in January: broke down at Wolverhampton following month: dead. *W. R. Muir* — 62

CROWTHER HOMES 5 br.m. Neltino 97 – Fair Sara 65 (McIndoe 97) [1994 51: 13.1m^{4} 14g 12.3f^{6} 18.7g^{6} 15.1m^{2} 15.9g^{3} 13.9m 1995 12d 14g 17.1m 18f a14g a14g Nov 16] smallish mare: modest staying maiden handicapper on flat: well beaten in 1995: has joined P. Beaumont. *E. J. Alston* — –

CRUCIS (IRE) 4 gr.c. Kalaglow 132 – Brave Advance (USA) 98 (Bold Laddie (USA)) [1994 –: 8m 1995 8d 8m^{4} a8g^{3} a9.4g^{4} May 27] tall, lengthy colt: poor maiden handicapper: should stay beyond 1m: acts on fibresand: sold 1,700 gns Newmarket Autumn Sales. *B. A. McMahon* — 49

CRUMPTON HILL (IRE) 3 b.c. Thatching 131 – Senane 86 (Vitiges (FR) 132) [1994 77: 7m^{4} 7.1d^{3} 8g* 1995 8m* 8.1g^{3} 8g 8d 9g 8m Oct 14] workmanlike colt: fairly useful handicapper: won at Newbury in April in good style: failed to improve on that, but ran well when seventh of 39 to Cap Juluca in Cambridgeshire at Newmarket on penultimate start: stays 9f, should prove at least as effective back at 7f: acts on good to firm going, probably on dead: has a high head carriage: takes keen hold, and usually held up. *N. A. Graham* — 88

CRY BABY 2 b.c. (Mar 20) Bairn (USA) 126 – Estonia (Kings Lake (USA) 133) [1995 7g^{6} a7g 7f 8.3g^{6} 8f Oct 16] 3,600Y: leggy colt: first foal: dam Irish 11f winner: poor maiden: trained by K. Ivory first 3 starts: very slowly away and well beaten in nursery last time: will stay well. *N. Tinkler* — 51

CRYSTADO (FR) 6 ch.g. Crystal Glitters (USA) 127 – Kantado 93 (Saulingo 122) [1994 –: 8d 10.1d 1995 7d Sep 22] rangy gelding: lightly raced and no worthwhile form since 3 yrs, giving impression something amiss on only 6-y-o start. *J. S. Haldane* — –

CRYSTAL BLADE 3 b.c. Dashing Blade 117 – Crystal's Solo (USA) (Crystal Water (USA)) [1994 84: 7m^{2} 7f^{4} 7f^{3} 10.2g^{2} 1995 14g^{4} 11.9m^{2} 13.4m* 11.9m^{3} 13.9m^{5} 12g Sep 8] rangy colt: easy mover: fairly useful performer: won maiden at Chester in June: very good third of 8 in rated stakes at York next start: well beaten last 2 outings: winner over 13.4f, but best form at around 1½m: acts on firm ground, yet to race on a soft surface: made the running third to fifth 3-y-o starts: sold 32,000 gns Newmarket Autumn Sales. *I. A. Balding*
86

CRYSTAL CAVERN (USA) 3 ch.f. Be My Guest (USA) 126 – Krisalya 98 (Kris 135) [1994 69p: 6g^{6} 7g* 1995 8m^{5} 8m^{5} 7m 7g^{2} 8s 7f^{3} Oct 23] attractive, rather sparely-made filly: good mover: fairly useful performer: best effort when head second to Mandarina in minor event at Brighton in September: probably stays 1m: acts on good to firm ground: takes keen hold: sold 14,000 gns Newmarket December Sales. *R. Charlton*
89

CRYSTAL FALLS (IRE) 2 b.r. (Mar 7) Alzao (USA) 117 – Honourable Sheba (USA) (Roberto (USA) 131) [1995 7.5g^{6} 6m^{2} 6m^{2} 7g^{3} 8g 7.1s^{2} 8m* Oct 20] 26,000Y, 30,000 2-y-o: close-coupled rig: second foal: dam (unraced) from family of Lear Fan: fair performer: won 10-runner nursery at Doncaster on final outing by neck from Alzanti, staying on gamely having been pushed along on home turn: will stay beyond 1m: acts on good to firm and soft ground. *J. J. O'Neill*
82

CRYSTAL FAST (USA) 2 b.g. (Apr 27) Fast Play (USA) – Crystal Cave (USA) (Nearctic) [1995 a8g Nov 6] $5,200Y: half-brother to 2 winners in USA, including Ann's Bid (by Spectacular Bid), stakes winner of 11 races at up to 9f: dam, winner in USA, half-sister to Belmont Stakes winner Arts And Letters: sire probably best at 2 yrs when Grade 1 9f winner: 16/1, slowly away and always behind in maiden at Southwell. *P. A. Kelleway*
–

CRYSTAL GIFT 3 b.g. Dominion 123 – Grain Lady (USA) (Greinton 119) [1994 79: 6g^{2} a8g^{2} a6g 1995 8m^{4} a7g 6f^{3} 7m 7g 10g 8f a7g^{4} a10g^{3} a8g Nov 14] small, leggy gelding: modest maiden: left P. Cole after fourth 3-y-o start: stays 1¼m: acts on good to firm ground and equitrack: no improvement in blinkers: sold (D. Arbuthnot to A. Whillans) 2,300 gns Doncaster November Sales. *D. W. P. Arbuthnot*
63 d

CRYSTAL HEART (IRE) 4 ch.f. Broken Hearted 124 – Arachosia (Persian Bold 123) [1994 –: 10.2g 10f^{6} 11.1m 10g 1995 10m Jul 11] poor maiden: no worthwhile form: should stay beyond 1¼m. *F. J. Yardley*
–

CRYSTAL HEIGHTS (FR) 7 ch.g. Crystal Glitters (USA) 127 – Fahrenheit 69 (Mount Hagen (FR) 127) [1994 47+: a5g*^{dis} a6g 1995 a6g* a6g^{4} a6g^{2} a6g^{3} a7g^{4} a6g^{2} 7m^{6} 6f^{4} 6f^{5} 6m^{4} 7m 6.9g^{2} 7f* a7g^{4} 7m^{2} 8.5s 7g* a7g^{2} a7g Dec 15] big, strong, lengthy gelding: fair handicapper: won at Lingfield in January and at Brighton in July (claimer) and October (minor event): stays 7f: acts on firm ground and all-weather surfaces, possibly not on soft: tried blinkered/visored at 4 yrs, no improvement: bandaged in 1995: often slowly away. *R. J. O'Sullivan*
71

CRYSTAL LOOP 3 b.f. Dowsing (USA) 124 – Gipping 72 (Vision (USA)) [1994 64: 5m 7s^{5} 7.1d^{3} 5s a6g* a7g a6g^{3} a6g^{6} a6g^{2} 1995 a6g* a6g^{5} a6g^{2} a7g* a5g^{4} a6g* 5g 6m 6.1m 5g^{2} 6g^{2} 5.1g 6m^{4} 6m^{2} 5.1m* 6m^{5} 5f 5f 5m* 5.1d 5g 5g a6g a6g Dec 12] leggy, workmanlike filly: fair performer: won claimer in January and handicaps in February and March, all at Wolverhampton: inconsistent on return to turf, winning handicaps at Chester in July and Newmarket (by 2 short heads in ladies race) in August: effective at 5f to 7f: acts on all-weather surfaces and good to firm ground: races prominently: has broken blood vessels. *A. Bailey*
69
a77

CRYSTAL MAGIC 4 b.f. Mazilier (USA) 107 – Thulium (Mansingh (USA) 120) [1994 92: 5s^{6} 5f^{2} 6g 5m^{2} 5m^{5} 5m^{2} 5g^{3} 5g 1995 5.2m^{5} 5.1m^{2} 5.1m^{3} 5g Jun 3] sturdy, attractive filly: usually impresses in appearance: good mover: fairly useful handicapper: best efforts at 5f (seemed to stay 6f at 2 yrs) on a sound surface: has been bandaged behind: races prominently: blinkered (had worst of draw in listed race) final 4-y-o start: genuine. *R. Hannon*
91

CRYSTAL WARRIOR 2 b.f. (Mar 7) Warrshan (USA) 117 – Crystal's Solo (USA) (Crystal Water (USA)) [1995 7.1s^{5} Oct 17] sixth foal: half-sister to 3-y-o 13.4f winner Crystal Blade (by Dashing Blade), ungenuine 1988 2-y-o 7f winner Crystal Heights (by Wolver Heights) and a winner in Macau by Robellino: dam second once from 12 starts in USA: 20/1, around 10 lengths fifth of 19 to Ski For Gold in maiden at Chepstow, keeping on without posing any threat to leaders: will be
55 p

suited by 1¼m+: sold (I. Balding to D. Nicholls) 4,500 gns Newmarket Autumn Sales. *I. A. Balding*

CUANGO (IRE) 4 b. or br.c. Mtoto 134 – Barinia (Corvaro (USA) 124) [1994 77: 10.3m^5 12g 12g^2 12s^2 12.3m^3 13.4m^4 12m* 13.9m 10.3g^6 11d^2 12m^6 11.8g^6 12.1g* 11.8d* 1995 14.1g^3 14m^3 13.9g^3 14g^5 14g^4 16.2f 14.6g^5 14m^3 14.8m^4 14f^6 13.9g 15.9d 14s 12.1d^3 14.6m^3 14.1m* 15.1s a14.8g^2 a16g^5 Nov 20] close-coupled colt: fair handicapper: won at Nottingham in October: stays at least 14.8f: acts on good to firm and soft ground and on fibresand: normally held up: none too consistent, and not one to place maximum faith in. *R. Hollinshead* — 78 d

CUBA 3 b.g. Soviet Star (USA) 128 – Rosetta Stone 89 (Guillaume Tell (USA) 121) [1994 64p: 8m 8g 1995 8m^6 10g^6 a12g^3 10m 11.4d^6 Sep 12] big, lengthy gelding: fair maiden: well below form last 3 starts: should stay beyond 1¼m. *M. R. Stoute* — 67

CUBAN NIGHTS (USA) 3 b.g. Our Native (USA) – Havana Moon (USA) (Cox's Ridge (USA)) [1994 NR 1995 8g 6m 8m 6f 8.5g 8f^3 9m^2 10m 10m^4 12s^6 9.7g Oct 16] $27,000F: $45,000Y: sturdy ex-Irish gelding: fourth foal: half-brother to 4-y-o Sestriere (by Sir Ivor) and a winner in North America by Crafty Prospector: dam showed a little ability in USA: modest maiden at best in Ireland: sold out of D. Weld's stable 8,000 gns Doncaster September Sales after ninth start: well beaten in handicaps at Ascot (amateurs, seemed not to stay 1½m on soft ground) and Folkestone (tailed off) for new connections: stays 1¼m: acts on firm ground: blinkered last 4 starts in Ireland. *B. J. Llewellyn* — 60 d

CUBAN REEF 3 b.f. Dowsing (USA) 124 – Cox's Pippin (USA) (Cox's Ridge (USA)) [1994 54: 6.1m^5 6m^4 7.5g 6s a7g^5 1995 a10g a8g a12g 7m^3 7m* 7g 7f^3 8.2m^2 Oct 26] modest handicapper: trained until after second 3-y-o start by D. Cosgrove: in good form towards end of season, and won maiden event at Kempton in September: stays 8.2f: acts on firm ground, below form on the all-weather: has run well when sweating. *W. J. Musson* — 52

CUCKMERE VENTURE 5 br.m. King of Spain 121 – Kala Nashan 76 (Kala Shikari 125) [1994 –: 7m 6v 6.9g 7.6g 8d 1995 7f^5 a7g Nov 29] big, workmanlike mare: bad maiden. *Jamie Poulton* — –

CUFF LINK (IRE) 5 ch.g. Caerleon (USA) 132 – Corinth Canal 77 (Troy 137) [1994 109: 14.1d^2 14m* 14s 22.2f* 16.1f 15.9m^2 18g^5 20d^4 1995 14.4m* 16.4m^6 — 107

Queen Alexandra Stakes, Royal Ascot—a repeat win for Cuff Link (right); Dover Patrol is second

22.2m* 16f 15.9m^2 18g^5 16g^5 Sep 30] angular gelding: useful performer: won minor event at Kempton in May and gained a second consecutive success in Queen Alexandra Stakes (evens, comfortably beat Dover Patrol 1½ lengths) at Royal Ascot: best subsequent effort when second of 6 to Double Eclipse in listed race at York: effective at 1¾m and stays 2¾m: acts on firm ground and dead: held up/tracks leaders. *Major W. R. Hern*

CUILLIN CAPER 3 b.f. Scottish Reel 123 – That Space (Space King) [1994 NR 1995 9.9m^6 9.9m 10g Jun 12] tenth foal: dam never ran: little sign of ability on flat, but beaten only ½ length in juvenile hurdle in November. *T. R. Watson* –

CULRAIN 4 b.g. Hadeer 118 – La Vie En Primrose 104 (Henbit (USA) 130) [1994 55d: 8f^6 9.2g^2 10g 10.5g 12g 12g 10.1d 1995 a12g^5 Jan 18] smallish, sturdy gelding: modest maiden handicapper: well beaten after second 3-y-o start: should be suited by middle distances: has joined T. Caldwell. *M. G. Meagher* –

CUMBRIAN CHALLENGE (IRE) 6 ch.g. Be My Native (USA) 122 – Sixpenny (English Prince 129) [1994 NR 1995 10.4m Oct 4] leggy gelding: useful at 4 yrs: never placed to challenge in handicap at York on only flat outing since: stays 1¼m: acts on firm and dead ground, well beaten on soft and heavy: tried blinkered: useful hurdler, promising novice chaser. *M. H. Easterby* –

CUMBRIAN MAESTRO 2 b.g. (Mar 28) Puissance 110 – Flicker Toa Flame (USA) 85 (Empery (USA) 128) [1995 6d 6m^5 6m^3 6m^4 6m^4 8m 8g^3 7d^3 6m Oct 4] 5,800F, 15,000Y: tall, well-made gelding: has scope: brother to 3-y-o Last World and half-brother to 1m and 10.4f winner Quavering (by The Minstrel) and a winner in Germany: dam, stayed 1m, half-sister to Motovato, smart at up to 1m: fair maiden: good efforts, making the running, in nurseries won by Whispering Dawn at Ayr and Samim at Redcar seventh and eighth starts: needs further than 6f and stays 1m: acts on good to firm and dead ground: blinkered last 3 starts. *M. H. Easterby* 67

CUMBRIAN MINSTREL 3 b.g. Efisio 120 – Miss Nanna 56§ (Vayrann 133) [1994 63: 5m^5 5f 6f^3 5.9f^5 5h* 6m 6d^2 6d 1995 8g 8g^5 8m 10f^6 10.1m^6 10m^3 10m^6 10g Sep 23] smallish, sturdy gelding: modest handicapper: stays 1¼m: acts on hard and dead going: usually blinkered at 2 yrs, only once in 1995: well beaten when sweating profusely: sometimes none too keen: not one to trust implicitly: sold 1,400 gns Newmarket Autumn Sales. *M. H. Easterby* 49 §

CUMBRIAN RHAPSODY 5 ch.m. Sharrood (USA) 124 – Bustellina 81 (Busted 134) [1994 78: 12.4g 16d^4 12.4m 14m* 14g 12.3g^5 15m^2 13m^3 13.9m 14.6g 13.1d^4 13.9d^6 12.4d* 12v 1995 16.1g^5 14g^6 12.4m^3 11.9m^4 17.5g^3 11.9g 14s Sep 30] leggy, lengthy mare: has a round action: just a modest handicapper in 1995: at least as effective at 1½m as 15f: acts on any going: none too consistent. *M. H. Easterby* 62 §

CUMBRIAN WALTZER 10 ch.g. Stanford 121§ – Mephisto Waltz 98 (Dancer's Image (USA)) [1994 79: 6d^4 6f 7f 7m 6g^4 6m 6f^5 6f^4 6g* 6g^5 6g 1995 7g 6d^4 6g 6m^5 6d 6g^4 6g^4 6s 7g 7m a7g Nov 24] good-topped gelding: often dull in coat: good mover: fair handicapper nowadays: good fourth in Ayr Silver Cup on sixth start: probably stays 7f: acts on any going: blinkered once (finished last) at 3 yrs: held up, and often meets trouble in running. *M. H. Easterby* 78

CUPLA FOCAIL 2 b.f. (Apr 17) Inca Chief (USA) – Lizzie Bee (Kind of Hush 118) [1995 a5g 6m^6 6m a6g Sep 4] 1,000Y: second foal: half-sister to 3-y-o Honey Trader (by Beveled): dam unraced: bad plater. *W. R. Muir* –

CUPRONICKEL (IRE) 3 b.f. Distant Relative 128 – One Half Silver (CAN) (Plugged Nickle (USA)) [1994 NR 1995 7.1m 7g^6 7m 10m 8.1m Jun 16] 10,500Y: good-topped filly: third foal: half-sister to Irish 4-y-o 7f winner Opulent (by Robellino) and 7f winner Silver Standard (by Jupiter Island): dam unraced half-sister to very useful 1¼m and 1½m winner Gamberta: modest form in maidens first 2 starts: ran poorly afterwards, and sold (J. W. Watts to D. Burchell) 3,600 gns Doncaster August Sales: bred to be suited by 1m+: blinkered final outing. *J. W. Watts* 48 d

CURIE CRUSADER (IRE) 4 gr.g. Belfort (FR) 89 – Katysue 98 (King's Leap 111) [1994 54: a7g^4 a8g 8.3v* 10.1d 1995 a7g a6g* Feb 18] big, workmanlike gelding: modest performer: 25/1-winner of minor event at Wolverhampton in February: effective at 6f to 8.3f: acts on heavy and fibresand. *M. Dods* 56

CURIE EXPRESS (IRE) 3 ch.f. Fayruz 116 – Windini (Windjammer (USA)) [1994 65d: 5.1m^5 a5g^3 5f 5f* 5m^5 6d 5m 6s 6g a5g^3 a5g^6 a6g^6 1995 a5g^4 Jan 3] 45

close-coupled filly: poor performer: blinkered only outing in 1995: best efforts at 5f: acts on firm ground and the all-weather. *J. Berry*

CURRENT LEADER 2 b.c. (Feb 2) Primo Dominie 121 – Trelissick (Electric 126) [1995 5.2m 5m 7f 7f^2 7g^3 7.5d Sep 13] 3,600Y, 25,000 2-y-o: useful-looking colt: good mover: fourth foal: dam little sign of ability: modest maiden: didn't go on as anticipated and looked irresolute when heavily-backed favourite penultimate start: stays 7f: acts on firm ground, ran poorly on dead final start. *R. Hannon* — 67

CURRENT SPEECH (IRE) 4 b.g. Thatching 131 – Lady Aladdin (Persian Bold 123) [1994 71: 8m^2 7.1m 7g^2 7d^2 8s* 7s 1995 8m 8g 8g 10d^3 10.5s Oct 1] tall, close-coupled gelding: fair performer: favourite, caught the eye for third successive outing in minor event at Haydock on final start, well beaten but again looking to travel well long way, and not at all knocked about: stays 1¼m: acts on good to firm and soft ground: capable of better. *M. H. Easterby* — 71 +

CURTELACE 5 ch.g. Nishapour (FR) 125 – Khandjar 77 (Kris 135) [1994 64: 10s 12v^6 8f^6 12g^6 11.5g^4 10.2g^3 10m* 10s 1995 12m^5 10m^4 10d 10d^4 9f^2 10g^2 10f^5 Oct 16] big, plain gelding: modest handicapper: consistent in 1995, but turned it in having travelled well at Redcar fourth and fifth starts: should prove at least as effective at 1½m as 1¼m: acts on firm ground, probably on dead: blinkered (ran creditably) final outing: hung badly right on 5-y-o reappearance: carries head high: not one to trust: has joined Mrs M. Reveley. *Lady Herries* — 60 §

CUT ADRIFT 4 b.f. Nordico (USA) – Cut No Ice 97 (Great Nephew 126) [1994 67: 8g^3 8f^3 1995 a12g a8g^6 Feb 25] strong, lengthy filly: well beaten in maidens in 1995 for new stable: stayed 1m: sold 4,600 gns in foal to Forzando Newmarket December Sales. *M. R. Channon* — –

CUTPURSE MOLL 3 b.f. Green Desert (USA) 127 – Pretty Pol 102 (Final Straw 127) [1994 –p: 7s 1995 7g^5 7g^2 7m* 8m 7g 7m Nov 3] sturdy filly: fair handicapper: made all in 4-runner race at Yarmouth in July: may prove best short of 1m: acts on good to firm ground: visored last 2 starts. *J. R. Fanshawe* — 76

CUTTHROAT KID (IRE) 5 b.g. Last Tycoon 131 – Get Ahead 58 (Silly Season 127) [1994 69: a12g^5 a14.8g 13d* 15.8f^2 15.8m* 13m* 12.1g* 17.5s 13.6g 15.1g 1995 12g 13v^2 16f^5 13.1g^5 12.1g Sep 25] sturdy gelding: has a round action: fair handicapper: stays 2m: acts on any going: best when visored or blinkered. *Mrs M. Reveley* — 66

C-YER-SIMMIE (IRE) 3 b.f. Prince Rupert (FR) 121 – Battle Queen 85 (Kind of Hush 118) [1994 54, a65: a5g* 6m 6.1g^6 6.1d^6 5s^6 a5g^2 a5s^4 1995 a5g^2 a5g^2 a5g^3 5g 5s^5 5g^2 5g 5g^6 5f^3 5.1m 5f^5 5m^2 a5g^2 Sep 4] leggy filly: poor mover: modest handicapper: mostly creditable efforts in 1995: speedy, and best at around 5f: acts on firm and soft ground and the all-weather: suitable mount for 7-lb claimer. *R. Hollinshead* — 64

CYMBALO 4 ch.g. Sharpo 132 – Cynomis 82 (Shergar 140) [1994 NR 1995 10g 9.2f^6 10.9g Jul 17] second foal: brother to fairly useful but disappointing 5f winner Cynic: dam 1¼m winner: tailed off in sellers and a claimer. *J. S. Goldie* — –

CYPHELL (IRE) 3 b.f. Sadler's Wells (USA) 132 – Cipriani 102 (Habitat 134) [1994 NR 1995 8g^3 10.5m 8m^2 9.9m^3 10m^4 9.7m^2 8d^5 Sep 26] smallish, lengthy filly: third foal: dam, Irish filly suited by about 1m, out of top New Zealand filly La Mer: fair maiden: probably better suited by around 1¼m than shorter, and will be suited by 1½m: acts on good to firm ground: sweating and on toes (below form) fifth start: carried head high final outing: sold 17,000 gns Newmarket December Sales. *M. R. Stoute* — 73

CYPRESS AVENUE (IRE) 3 b.c. Law Society (USA) 130 – Flying Diva 100 (Chief Singer 131) [1994 NR 1995 11m^5 12m^3 13.9m^2 14.1f^4 14.6m^3 14.8g^5 14g^5 Oct 23] IR 7,000Y, 20,000 2-y-o: big, strong colt: first foal: dam, 2-y-o 6f and 7f winner, stayed 1m: fairly useful maiden: long way below form on 3 of last 4 starts: should stay 2m: has raced only on a sound surface: not one to trust. *R. Hannon* — 95

CYPRUS POINT 4 b.f. Unfuwain (USA) 131 – Sunshine Coast 86 (Posse (USA) 130) [1994 –: 10g 10g 8.1g 1995 a8.5g^6 a10g 7m a10g Nov 14] leggy, lengthy filly: poor maiden: soundly beaten in 1995. *S. W. Campion* — –

CYRANO'S LAD (IRE) 6 b. or br.g. Cyrano de Bergerac 120 – Patiala (Crocket 130) [1994 NR 1995 8.3m^3 6f^2 7.6g* 7m^3 8f 7m 7g 6g^2 7g* 7m^3 6d Oct 19] tall, — 96 sturdy gelding: unimpressive mover: half-brother to several winners, including useful Irish sprinter Dubel Boy (by On Your Mark), later successful in USA: dam lightly-raced maiden: made into a useful performer: trained first 5 starts by John Berry: won minor event at Lingfield in June and rated stakes at Newmarket in September: will prove best at up to 1m: acts on firm ground, well beaten on dead: usually races prominently. *C. A. Dwyer*

CYRILLIC 2 ch.f. (Feb 5) Rock City 120 – Lariston Gale 81 (Pas de Seul 133) [1995 5m² 5m 6m* 6f³ 6m⁵ 7g Oct 1] lengthy, sparely-made filly: third foal: half-sister to 3-y-o The Mestral (by Formidable): dam 2-y-o 6f winner, should have been suited by 1½m+: won 4-runner median auction maiden at Brighton in June: good fifth of 7 to Maid For The Hills in listed event at Newmarket penultimate start then off course 3 months: stays 6f: has raced only on a sound surface: sold 3,000 gns Newmarket December Sales. *P. A. Kelleway* — 73

CYRUS THE GREAT (IRE) 3 ch.g. Persian Heights 129 – Smart As Paint (USA) (Caerleon (USA) 132) [1994 76: 6m 6.9m* 7f 7m⁶ 7s 8m 1995 8d 10.5m 8g⁶ 8.1d³ 10d² 10g 8.9g Oct 7] good-topped gelding: fairly useful handicapper: stays 1¼m well: acts on firm and dead ground: sold (M. Bell to K. Bailey) 27,000 gns Newmarket Autumn Sales. *M. Bell* — 82

CZARNA (IRE) 4 b.c. Polish Precedent (USA) 131 – Noble Dust (USA) (Dust Commander (USA)) [1994 80+: 7m⁴ 7s* 8.1m⁴ 8m 1995 8g⁵ 7m 7m⁴ 8.1m² 8m 7g 6g 10m⁴ Aug 5] big, good-topped colt: fairly useful handicapper: second of 9 in Whitsun Cup at Sandown in May: below form afterwards: stays 1m (probably not 1¼m): acts on good to firm and soft going: usually races prominently. *C. E. Brittain* — 90

D

DAANIERA (IRE) 5 gr.g. Standaan (FR) 118 – Right Cash (Right Tack 131) [1994 –, a61: a5g a6g⁵ a5g a5g a7g 6d 5d 5m a5g 5.1d 5d a6g a5g a5g⁴ a5g* 1995 a5g⁵ a6g a5g a5g a5g⁶ a5g⁵ a5g a5g⁶ Dec 19] workmanlike gelding: poor mover: modest handicapper: effective at 5f to 7f: probably acts on any going: usually blinkered/visored: bandaged behind at 5 yrs: usually races prominently. *P. Howling* — – a57 ?

DAAWE (USA) 4 b.c. Danzig (USA) – Capo di Monte 118 (Final Straw 127) [1994 86: 8s⁴ 7.1g² 7d* 7.1m 7.1g 7m* 7f 1995 8g⁶ 8.9m 7m 7m 8.1s Nov 2] robust, good-bodied colt: disappointing for new stable in 1995: stays 7f: usually visored. *Mrs V. A. Aconley* — –

DABKA DANCER 2 b.c. (Feb 1) Cadeaux Genereux 131 – Lady Shipley 111 (Shirley Heights 130) [1995 7m⁵ 7g³ Sep 13] 74,000Y: strong, good sort: good walker: second foal: half-brother to a winner in Spain by Rousillon: dam, 7f (at 2 yrs) and 1¼m winner stayed 1½m, daughter of Circus Ring: prominent throughout when around 1½ lengths third of 19 to Shawanni in maiden at Yarmouth: should improve again, and win a maiden. *A. C. Stewart* — 89 p

DACHA (IRE) 3 b.c. Soviet Star (USA) 128 – Shadywood 96 (Habitat 134) [1994 76P: 8.2d³ 1995 11.8f⁴ Oct 23] tall, good sort: half-brother to very smart middle-distance stayer Madame Dubois (by Legend of France): had operation to remove bone chip in knee and off course virtually a year: looking fit and well, 5¾ lengths fourth of 6 to Al Widyan in minor event at Leicester, leading or chasing good pace, hanging right into whip in straight and eased over 1f out: looks sort to do better. *H. R. A. Cecil* — 83 p

DAFFAQ 3 b.c. Unfuwain (USA) 131 – Awayed (USA) 108 (Sir Ivor 135) [1994 76: 7g⁴ 7.9d² 1995 10.3g⁵ 8d 8.1g³ 12f Jun 10] good-topped colt: fair performer: finished lame when run as pacemaker in Derby: would have stayed middle distances: dead. *P. T. Walwyn* — 70

DAFFODIL EXPRESS (IRE) 2 b.f. (Feb 21) Skyliner 117 – Miss Henry 78 (Blue Cashmere 129) [1995 6m 5g⁴ 6.9s 6g Oct 16] 1,400Y: tall, workmanlike filly: half-sister to several winners here and abroad, including 3-y-o 5f and 6f winner One For Jeannie (by Clantime) and 1991 2-y-o 5f winner Mummys Valentine (by Mummy's Game), winner at 1m in Italy in 1995: dam, 7f winner, half-sister to very useful Rhodomantade: poor maiden: will prove best short of 7f. *M. J. Ryan* — 44

DAHIK 3 b.c. Green Desert (USA) 127 – Littlefield 100 (Bay Express 132) [1994 94+: 7f* 7m^{3} 7g^{3} 8m^{2} 1995 8m^{4} 10m^{2} 10.4m* 10.1f^{5} 10f 10m^{3} Aug 14] strong, good-bodied colt: good mover: useful performer: won rated stakes at York in May, running on to lead on line: stays 1¼m: has raced only on a sound surface: sweating first 2 starts at 3 yrs: sometimes hangs left and looks awkward ride: sent to Dubai. *Major W. R. Hern* 104

DAHIYAH (USA) 4 b.g. Ogygian (USA) – Sticky Prospect (USA) (Mr Prospector (USA)) [1994 –: 8.3g^{6} 8m 1995 a7g a8g^{4} 6m^{5} 6f* 6f 6m^{6} 6m^{6} 6f^{2} 6g Sep 14] rangy gelding: modest handicapper: won maiden event at Brighton in May: best efforts at 6f: acts on firm ground and equitrack: visored 7 of last 8 starts: races prominently: inconsistent. *G. L. Moore* 64

DAHLENBURG (IRE) 3 b. or br.g. Alzao (USA) 117 – Dahsala (Top Ville 129) [1994 NR 1995 10g 10.1g^{3} 12m 10g^{2} 10.5d 10g 8m Aug 14] 48,000F: good-topped, attractive gelding: second reported foal: half-brother to French 1¼m winner Dhaka (by Lashkari): dam French 11.5f winner: fair form in maidens: soundly beaten in handicaps last 3 starts, looking hard ride: stays 1½m: visored since fourth start: sent to Dubai. *J. H. M. Gosden* 68

DAILY CHALLENGER (USA) 3 b.g. Moment of Hope (USA) – Goodness Sakes (USA) (The Real McCoy (USA)) [1994 74: 5.1d^{4} 6f^{2} 6m 6m^{3} a7g^{5} a5g 1995 a7g^{5} a8g a11g a5g a6g 6.1g^{6} 7m^{5} 8g 5f^{4} 5.9f^{2} 5.9h^{5} Aug 21] close-coupled, quite attractive gelding: only poor form at best in 1995: should stay 7f: acts on firm ground, no form on all-weather: sold 1,000 gns Doncaster October Sales. *Ronald Thompson* 45 a–

DAILY RISK 2 ch.c. (Mar 16) Risk Me (FR) 127 – Give Me A Day (Lucky Wednesday 124) [1995 5m^{5} 5g^{6} 6m 7g^{5} 7g^{2} 7.3d^{4} Oct 21] 7,000Y: quite good-topped colt: third foal: brother to a winner in Italy: dam plater: modest maiden: creditable efforts in nurseries won by Al Shafa at Brighton and Proud Monk at Newbury on last 2 starts: stays 7f: acts on dead ground. *S. Dow* 68

DAILY SPORT GIRL 6 b.m. Risk Me (FR) 127 – Net Call 108 (Song 132) [1994 NR 1995 12.5g^{2} 11.1g^{4} May 5] lengthy mare: unimpressive mover: poor form in amateurs handicaps: stays 12.5f: acts on good to firm ground and fibresand: tried blinkered earlier in career. *B. J. Llewellyn* 40

DAILY STARLIGHT (USA) 3 br.g. Minshaanshu Amad (USA) 91§ – Appeal The Rule (USA) (Valid Appeal (USA)) [1994 55: 5g^{6} 6g 6m^{4} 7m 7.5g^{4} 8.3g^{4} 8m 1995 11.1g* 11.1f* 12.1m^{4} 13.3f* 14m^{4} 12m^{4} 12m* 13.3d 14g^{5} Sep 29] tall, useful-looking gelding: fairly useful performer: won median auction maiden at Edinburgh in May and handicaps at Hamilton and Newbury in June, and at Epsom (awarded race after slight bumping) in September: stays 1¾m: acts on firm ground, probably on dead. *Miss Gay Kelleway* 81

DAILY STARSHINE (IRE) 3 b.f. Petorius 117 – Mainly Sunset (Red Sunset 120) [1994 59: 5.1g 5m^{4} 5d^{4} 5m 5f 5.1g^{3} 5d* 5m^{5} 5s^{3} 1995 5d a5g^{3} a5g^{3} 5g^{4} 5g^{3} 5f^{5} 5m 5m 5.1d Sep 11] well-grown filly: modest sprinter on her day: long way below form last 3 starts: raced only at around 5f: acts on good to firm and soft ground and fibresand: usually blinkered nowadays: usually races prominently: sold 1,600 gns Doncaster October Sales. *J. Berry* 59 d

DAIRA 2 br.f. (May 13) Daring March 116 – Ile de Reine 64 (Ile de Bourbon (USA) 133) [1995 a7g^{5} 8.3g^{3} 7m^{5} Oct 30] tall, leggy filly: second foal: dam 14.8f winner: best effort in maidens when third of 10 to Eric's Bett in median auction at Hamilton: hampered final start: will be suited by further than 1m. *J. D. Bethell* 57

DAIRINE'S DELIGHT (IRE) 5 b.m. Fairy King (USA) – Silius (Junius (USA) 124) [1994 5s* 6g^{3} 5d* 5s* 5g* 5g* 5d^{4} 5g 1995 5g^{4} 5g* 5g^{6} 5m^{2} 5m^{3} 5g* 5d^{5} Oct 15] leggy, attractive mare: good walker: second foal: dam won Irish Cambridgeshire: smart performer: unraced at 2 yrs, successful in 2 handicaps at 3 yrs and 5 more at 4 yrs: won listed races at Tipperary in May and Newmarket (by ¾ length from Double Quick, making all in game style) in September: very speedy, and best at 5f: acts on good to firm and soft ground: blinkered (well beaten) final 4-y-o start: usually makes running: genuine and consistent: sold 80,000 gns Newmarket December Sales: reportedly to be covered then sent to Japan. *Michael Cunningham, Ireland* 109

DAKOTA BRAVE (IRE) 4 b.g. Exactly Sharp (USA) 121 – Terrama Sioux (Relkino 131) [1994 63, a68: 8g^{5} 7g 8s a12g* 9.7m^{2} 9g^{2} a12g^{2} 1995 a12g May 1] –

useful-looking gelding: fair performer: finished lame only start in 1995: effective at 9f, and stays 1½m: acts on good to firm ground, goes particularly well on fibresand: wears bandage(s). *J. Pearce*

DAKOTA GIRL 4 b.f. Northern State (USA) 91 – Marielou (FR) (Carwhite) – [1994 55: 9v 10m 10f 11.8m^4 12m^6 16.4m^3 16d^6 15.4d* 1995 15.4g Apr 10] good-topped filly: modest on flat: visored, never a threat only run on flat in 1995: stays 16.4f: acts on good to firm and dead ground: fair hurdler. *G. B. Balding*

DALCROSS 4 gr.f. Nishapour (FR) 125 – Pomade 79 (Luthier 126) [1994 57: – 8.2d^5 8g 9.7g^3 12.5f^3 10.1m 12g 15.4d 8s 8g 1995 8m 8f 8.2m 9.7m^6 7f a10g a7g Nov 29] sparely-made filly: no longer of much account. *H. J. Collingridge*

DALERIA 4 b.f. Darshaan 133 – Phaleria (USA) (Lyphard (USA) 132) [1994 12g 65 12.5g^6 12d 1995 a8.5g^4 8m 7.5m^2 a12g^2 a12g^2 a11g* Sep 4] useful-looking filly: first foal: dam, placed twice in 2 starts in France, sister to Lancashire Oaks winner Andaleeb out of Kentucky Oaks winner Bag of Tunes: unplaced at 3 yrs for Mme C. Head: trained by J. L. Eyre and Miss J. Craze first 2 starts here: won maiden handicap at Southwell in September: may well stay 1¾m. *A. Harrison*

DALESIDE 7 gr.g. Full Out (USA) – All Regal (Run The Gantlet (USA)) [1994 –: – 16.2s 10.1m^5 11.1f 10g 10m 1995 15.1m^4 15.1f Jul 28] good-topped gelding: no worthwhile form on flat since 3 yrs, but is a modest hurdler. *A. Harrison*

DALLACHIO (IRE) 4 ch.g. Shernazar 131 – Mafiosa 69 (Miami Springs 121) – [1994 8d^6 8s 10g^3 12g* 16s 1995 12m Apr 15] stocky ex-Irish gelding: third foal: dam stayed 7f at 2 yrs: fair form (rated 70) at 3 yrs, winning maiden at Clonmel: wearing tongue strap, last of 17 in face of stiff task in handicap only start here: stays 1½m (very stiff task over 2m): blinkered last 3 starts at 3 yrs: fair hurdler. *P. J. Hobbs*

DALLAI (IRE) 4 b.g. Dance of Life (USA) – Wavetree (Realm 129) [1994 –: 47 10d^6 10g 8m 8g 1995 a11g^5 a16g* a16g a16g Nov 29] leggy gelding: rallying winner of maiden at Southwell in January: no form afterwards: stays 2m: acts on good to firm and soft ground and on fibresand: blinkered (looked none too keen) final start at 3 yrs: has joined S. Harris. *Mrs N. Macauley*

DALLY BOY 3 b.g. Efisio 120 – Gay Hostess (FR) (Direct Flight) [1994 59, a70: 43 6m 7m^4 a7g^2 7m^5 7.5f 7.9d 7g^5 8d^5 1995 10m a11g 12m 8f a9.4g^4 a11g^4 Nov 20] unfurnished gelding: fair maiden at 2 yrs: poor at best on return: seems to stay 11f: best form on fibresand. *M. H. Easterby*

DALU (IRE) 4 br.f. Dancing Brave (USA) 140 – Abhaaj 91 (Kris 135) [1994 72: – 7m^2 8m* 1995 8m^6 9g May 24] unfurnished filly: reportedly knocked a joint final 3-y-o start, and well below form for new stable on return: stays 1m: yet to race on extremes of going. *M. J. Camacho*

DALWHINNIE 2 b.f. (May 23) Persian Bold 123 – Land Line (High Line 125) – [1995 8m Oct 20] 15,500Y: fourth living foal: half-sister to 4-y-o 7f winner Michellisa (by Indian Ridge): dam unraced sister to Park Hill winner Quay Line, the grandam of Pure Grain: 20/1 and backward, no significant promise in maiden at Doncaster. *J. W. Hills*

DALYSNICELITLERNER 3 gr.c. Daily Sport Soon 88 – Aphabel 72 (Belfort – (FR) 89) [1994 NR 1995 8g 11.5g Sep 12] smallish, workmanlike colt: second foal: dam 5f winner, best at 2 yrs: tailed off in seller and claimer. *J. R. Jenkins*

DAMARITA 4 ch.f. Starry Night (USA) – Sirenivo (USA) 113 (Sir Ivor 135) – [1994 –: 6s 7f 1995 11.9d Oct 11] angular filly: no promise in maidens. *Lady Herries*

DAMIER BLANC (FR) 6 b.g. Damister (USA) 123 – Roche Blanche (FR) – (Great Nephew 126) [1994 –: 14d^5 8.1g^4 1995 7m^6 Apr 17] tall gelding: fair staying handicap hurdler, but no worthwhile form in 3 runs on flat in Britain: should stay well. *M. C. Pipe*

DAMOCLES 3 b.g. Dashing Blade 117 – Madam Trilby (Grundy 137) [1994 65: – 6g 6m 7.5g 1995 7g 5.1m 7.1m^5 8.2m Jun 26] neat, quite attractive gelding: no worthwhile form since debut: sold 525 gns Ascot July Sales. *I. A. Balding*

DANAMICH (IRE) 2 b.c. (Apr 11) Fayruz 116 – Galapagos 71 (Pitskelly 122) – [1995 6m Aug 19] IR 6,200F, 14,000Y: sturdy colt: second foal: half-brother to German 3-y-o 7f winner Little Dame (by Prince Rupert): dam, placed at up to 7f, daughter of very useful Irish 2-y-o 5f winner Sweet Emma: 10/1 and burly, slowly away and always behind in maiden auction at Ripon. *J. Berry*

DANA POINT (IRE) 3 br.g. Phardante (FR) 123 – Wallpark Princess (Balidar 133) [1994 49: 6m 7m 7.5g5 1995 8m* Aug 23] stocky gelding: off course 11 months, much improved form to win apprentice handicap at Redcar, leading over 1f out: fair form at 1m and bred to stay middle distances: seemed likely to progress again. *T. D. Barron* 65 p

DANCE ACROSS (IRE) 2 b.f. (Feb 25) Nabeel Dancer (USA) 120 – Fordes Cross (Ya Zaman (USA) 122) [1995 7g 7g Oct 9] IR 11,000F, 5,000Y: sturdy filly: unimpressive mover: second foal: half-sister to Italian 1¼m winner Doulab Cross (by Doulab): dam unraced: behind in maidens at Warwick and Leicester 6 days later: sold 2,000 gns Newmarket Autumn Sales. *H. Candy* –

DANCE A DREAM 3 b.f. Sadler's Wells (USA) 132 – Exclusive Order (USA) 120 (Exclusive Native (USA)) [1994 94: 7m2 8m* 8g6 1995 11.4m* 12m2 12m4 11.9m6 Aug 16] 115

The Cheshire Oaks, demoted to listed status in 1986, has had notable winners of its last two runnings in Bolas and Dance A Dream. This, it must be said, is against the trend. If winning the Cheshire Oaks has been a pointer to anything in recent years it is a swift retirement: of its previous ten winners, only one, Braiswick, raced on here as a four-year-old; another, Chaudennay, did so in the United States. Both of those won after Chester (Chaudennnay took one minor contest from sixteen attempts in the States) but all of the other eight failed to add to their totals except Bolas. She, of course, took the Ribblesdale and Irish Oaks. As a guide to the Oaks proper, however, the 1984 to 1994 editions of the Cheshire version were of strictly limited value—only three of the winners went on to Epsom, Malaak coming ninth, Peplum eighth and Abury seventh. It was a refreshing change then when the 1995 winner Dance A Dream filled the runner-up spot in the Oaks and it was announced that she would be back in training in 1996.

Dance A Dream started second favourite at Chester behind Snowtown who had finished three places in front of her in the Fillies' Mile at Ascot the previous

Shadwell Stud Cheshire Oaks, Chester—Dance A Dream (right) outstays Yarn

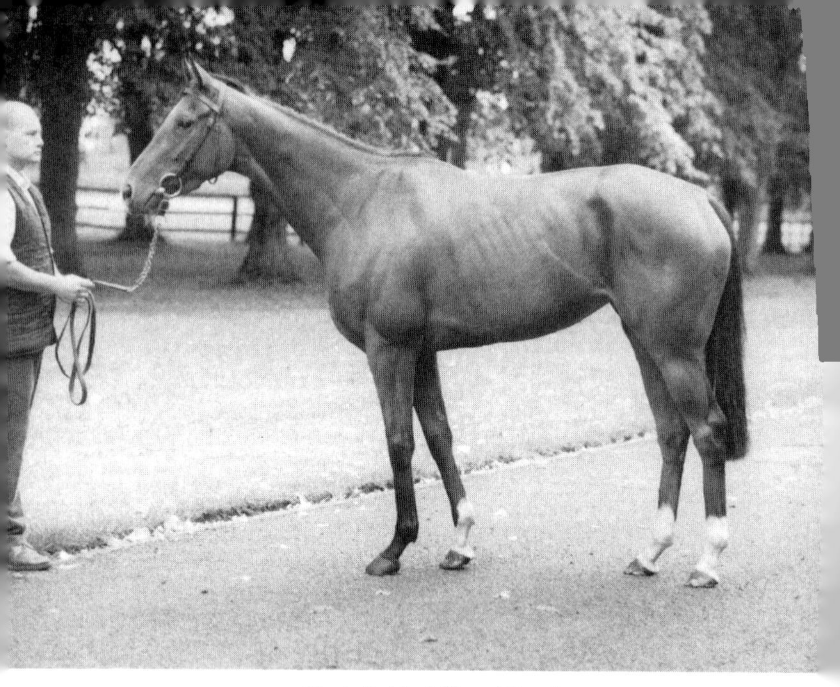

Cheveley Park Stud's "Dance A Dream"

September. All the five other Cheshire Oaks runners had last been seen out in maiden races. Only two of them had won and it was one of those, Yarn, who gave Dance A Dream most to do, going down by three quarters of a length after Dance A Dream had nosed ahead one and a half furlongs out. This performance was good enough to earn the winner a best-priced 33/1 quote for Epsom. It had shrunk to 14/1 fourth favourite by the time the race began and Dance A Dream gave a really bold showing. Trainer Michael Stoute had stated beforehand that she did not travel that well in her races and might not be suited to Epsom, adding that he expected stable-companion Pure Grain to beat her. In the race itself, however, Dance A Dream moved sweetly at the leader's quarters, being sent on with Moonshell over two furlongs out and, though always getting just the worse of that battle, she stayed on splendidly to hold off everything else. Dance A Dream was beaten a length and a quarter, with three quarters back to Pure Grain in third. At the moment, the Oaks is clearly the pinnacle of Dance A Dream's career. Her fourth of seven when an 11/10-shot in the Ribblesdale Stakes was a very flat performance, one likely explanation being the break of just thirteen days after her very hard race at Epsom, though it was also reported that she returned lame behind. After a near two-month lay-off, she did a fair bit better when four lengths sixth of eight to Pure Grain in the Yorkshire Oaks. Both of those last two races were steadily-run, which would not have favoured a horse such as Dance A Dream who stays the trip really well. She should stay a mile and three quarters. The Park Hill Stakes seemed a suitable target but by that stage she had already been put away until 1996. Our photograph of her, incidentally, was taken at the Cheveley Park Stud when she was out of training. A sturdy, lengthy filly who carries condition, Dance A Dream has done virtually all her racing on good to firm ground.

Dance A Dream (b.f. 1992)	Sadler's Wells (USA) (b 1981)	Northern Dancer (b 1961)	Nearctic
			Natalma
		Fairy Bridge (b 1975)	Bold Reason
			Special
	Exclusive Order (USA) (ch 1979)	Exclusive Native (ch 1965)	Raise A Native
			Exclusive
		Bonavista (b 1964)	Dead Ahead
			Ribotina

Moonshell and Dance A Dream provided sire Sadler's Wells with his second one-two in the Oaks in the space of three years, and Dance A Dream is the third foal of at least useful ability out of Exclusive Order to have raced in Britain in the 'nineties. The previous two are Mizaaya (by Riverman), who stayed a mile and a quarter, and the smart Sadler's Image (by Sadler's Wells), who won at up to 13.4 furlongs. The French filly Irish Order (by Irish River) was useful at up to a mile but ended up disappointing, and the 1990 foal Dancing Surpass (by Dancing Brave) was sent to Japan, at the last count winning five races and the equivalent of some £360,000. Two of Exclusive Order's remaining three previous foals were winners as well. Her next foals are a 1994 brother to Dance A Dream and a 1995 filly by Polar Falcon. Grandam Bonavista, a stakes-placed winner out of the unraced Ribotina, produced sixteen foals herself, eight of whom were winners, clearly the best of which were Exclusive Order and her brother Teddy's Courage. The latter was placed in five graded races but Exclusive Order was better, numbering the Prix de la Porte Maillot and Prix Maurice de Gheest among her four victories; she was only eighth of fifteen in On The House's One Thousand Guineas but showed that she stayed a mile when fourth in the Jacques le Marois. *M. R. Stoute*

DANCE AND SING (IRE) 5 b.g. The Noble Player (USA) 126 – Cherlinoa (FR) (Crystal Palace (FR) 132) [1994 33: 7d 10s 5s 7d a6g a6g^4 a6g a7g a6g^5 1995 a8.5g a6g 5.9f 12.1m Jul 20] workmanlike gelding: bad maiden: should stay beyond 6f: tried blinkered once. *D. L. Williams* –

DANCE BAND (USA) 3 b.c. Dixieland Band (USA) – Brief Remarks (USA) (Talc (USA)) [1994 90p: 7m* 8.1g^2 1995 9d^3 10m^4 7.6m^4 7g^2 8m 7m^3 8g^2 7m* 10m^6 Aug 11] strong, good-bodied colt: good mover: fairly useful handicapper: dead-heated at Lingfield (disputed lead throughout) in July: effective at 7f, barely stays 1¼m: acts on good to firm and dead ground: has run well when sweating: consistent. *B. Hanbury* 94

DANCE DESIGN (IRE) 2 b.f. (Feb 18) Sadler's Wells (USA) 132 – Elegance In Design 105 (Habitat 134) [1995 7s* 7m* 7g^4 8d^4 Oct 1] sturdy filly: second foal: dam, useful 6f winner, sister to high-class 7f/1m filly Chalon and closely related to very smart Irish 1m/1¼m performer Executive Perk: progressive Irish filly: won maiden at Galway and listed race at Leopardstown in August: didn't get best of runs and unlucky when 1¼ lengths fourth of 13 to Priory Belle in Moyglare Stud Stakes at the Curragh next start: 3½ lengths fourth of 11 to Miss Tahiti in strongly-run Prix Marcel Boussac at Longchamp final start, prominent long way and staying on: will stay 1¼m. *D. K. Weld, Ireland* 107

DANCE KING 3 b.g. Rambo Dancer (CAN) 107 – Northern Venture 80 (St Alphage 119) [1994 60: 6s^4 5f^5 6g^5 6d^5 7m^5 6s^2 7s 1995 a7g^3 a8g 8m^2 8m^2 10g^3 8m* 8m^2 a9.4g 8.5d 10g Sep 21] neat gelding: fair performer: left J. Banks's stable after third 3-y-o start: won 4-runner maiden at Thirsk in July: well beaten last 3 starts: effective at 1m to 1¼m: acts on any going on turf and on equitrack: blinkered (ran creditably) second 3-y-o start: races prominently: has joined R. Harris. *D. Nicholls* 70 a64

DANCE MOTION 3 b.g. Damister (USA) 123 – Tantalizing Song (CAN) (The Minstrel (CAN) 135) [1994 55: 6f a7g 6m 8s 10g^6 8d 1995 10m May 29] sturdy gelding: modest maiden: tailed off in handicap at Redcar for new stable: sold 1,000 gns Doncaster July Sales: best run at 1¼m: looked all at sea on fibresand. *T. J. Etherington* –

DANCE OF JOY 3 b.f. Shareef Dancer (USA) 135 – Lady Habitat (Habitat 134) [1994 59p: 7m^6 8.1g 8.2g^6 1995 8.2g 10.3m 10g 10f^5 Jul 24] strong, lengthy filly: no worthwhile form at 3 yrs: front runner/races prominently: joined J. Carr. *J. L. Dunlop* –

DANCE OF THE MOON 2 b.f. (Jan 29) High Estate 127 – Oh So Well (IRE) (Sadler's Wells (USA) 132) [1995 5.1g^2 5m^3 Apr 19] strong, good-bodied filly: first 72

K. Yoshida's "Dance Partner"

foal: dam daughter of Soba: well-backed favourite, placed in maidens at Nottingham and Newmarket: dead. *M. Bell*

DANCE ON A CLOUD (USA) 2 b.f. (Feb 3) Capote (USA) – Sharp Dance (USA) (Dancing Czar (USA)) [1995 7.1g6 7f* Oct 23] $110,000Y: tall, lengthy filly: has scope: first foal: dam won 10 races, including Grade 1 9f event at 5 yrs: sire champion 2-y-o colt: won 11-runner maiden at Leicester in October by 2 lengths from Apache Len, running on well despite flashing tail: will stay at least 1m: slowly away both starts: sure to improve again. *M. R. Stoute* — 76 p

DANCE ON SIXPENCE 7 b.g. Lidhame 109 – Burning Ambition (Troy 137) [1994 46: 8.5m 8f* 8m 8m2 1995 a8.5g 8m Jul 7] rangy gelding: poor handicapper: tailed off both starts for new stable: stays 1m: acts on any going: often visored earlier in career, blinkered on reappearance. *J. H. Peacock* — –

DANCE PARTNER (JPN) 3 b.f. Sunday Silence (USA) – Dancing Key (USA) (Nijinsky (CAN) 138) [1994 NR 1995 6f* 8f2 8f2 8d2 12f* 10g2 12d6 15f6 10f2 Dec 17] sixth foal: half-sister to 4 winners, notably Air Dublin (by Tony Bin), placed in Japanese equivalents of Derby and St Leger: dam unraced sister to graded stakes winner (including at 11f) Key Dancer: smart performer: contested first 5 races in Japan, notably beaten a neck in Oka Sho (1000 Guineas) before winning Yushun Himba (Oaks) in May: beaten a nose by Matiara in 4-runner Prix de la Nonette at Deauville in August: sixth in Prix Vermeille at Longchamp (not clear run) in September then sixth in Kikuka Sho (St Leger) and second in very valuable event back in Japan in November: stays 1½m: acts on firm ground and dead: has been bandaged behind: trained by Mme Pat Barbe in France. *T. Shirai, Japan* — 115

DANCE SEQUENCE (USA) 2 ch.f. (Mar 14) Mr Prospector (USA) – Dancing Tribute (USA) 115 (Nureyev (USA) 131) [1995 5m² 5m² 6g² 6m* 6d⁴ Sep 26] 105

Dance Sequence was beaten in four of her five races but that wasn't so bad: the one she won was the Lowther Stakes, and she might also have won the Cherry Hinton Stakes with better luck in running, while in the others she came up against Blue Duster. Despite being a maiden, one of only two in the line-up, Dance Sequence possessed clearly the best form and started 5/4 favourite in a field of nine for the Lowther run at York in August. She had finished a good second to Blue Duster in a maiden race at Sandown and in the Queen Mary Stakes at Royal Ascot on her first two starts, beaten no more than a length and a half on either occasion, running on strongly at Royal Ascot to come clear of the rest. Next, she had gone down narrowly to Blue Duster's stable-companion Applaud in a slowly-run Cherry Hinton at Newmarket in July, finding herself short of room when the pace suddenly increased two furlongs out, but managing to squeeze through at the distance to chase after the winner who had held prime position all the way.

Applaud had to miss the Lowther because of a late set-back. Easily the biggest danger to Dance Sequence on the day proved to be the Queen Mary third My Melody Parkes, having her first start since. Dance Sequence beat her in workmanlike style by three quarters of a length, just getting on top through the last furlong after My Melody Parkes had made the running. Our impression of Dance Sequence at this stage was that while she was useful it would be a little bit surprising if she were among the top two-year-old fillies by the end of the season. After her third tilt at Blue Duster in the Cheveley Park Stakes at Newmarket in October the firm impression was that she would not be up to beating the best of her sex. She finished a respectable fourth of five to Blue Duster, My Branch and Najiya, six lengths behind the winner, forcing the pace herself this time but joined at halfway and found wanting through the last two furlongs. However, we won't be writing her off completely. Lowther Stakes winners have generally gone on well in recent years (the last five have been Only Yours, Culture Vulture, Niche, Velvet Moon and Harayir).

If Dance Sequence takes after her dam she'll train on all right. Her dam Dancing Tribute, who finished second at odds on in the Cheveley Park for Michael

Lowther Stakes, York—Dance Sequence opens her account, at the expense of My Melody Parkes

Cheveley Park Stud's "Dance Sequence"

Dance Sequence (USA) (ch.f. Mar 14, 1993)	Mr Prospector (USA) (b 1970)	Raise A Native (ch 1961)	Native Dancer
			Raise You
		Gold Digger (ch 1961)	Nashua
			Sequence
	Dancing Tribute (USA) (b 1986)	Nureyev (b 1977)	Northern Dancer
			Special
		Sophisticated Girl (b 1980)	Stop The Music
			Close Control

Stoute in 1988, showed good form at up to a mile the following season, finishing second in the Challenge Stakes on her final appearance. Dance Sequence is her third foal, her third filly by Mr Prospector. Both the first two won as three-year-olds, Dance With Grace in a minor stakes sprint in the United States and Shake Hand in a Group 2 race over a mile in Japan. The next dam Sophisticated Girl was placed in stakes races as a three-year-old, showing her best form at around a mile, having won and shown very smart form at two. Dance Sequence cost 375,000 dollars as a yearling. Close-coupled, she was still rather unfurnished when last seen out; she tended not to impress in appearance through the season. She will almost certainly stay a mile. A fluent mover, she has run her best two races on good to firm ground (in the Lowther and Queen Mary) but there doesn't seem much wrong with her run on good to soft in the Cheveley Park. *M. R. Stoute*

DANCE SO SUITE 3 b.g. Shareef Dancer (USA) 135 – Three Piece (Jaazeiro (USA) 127) [1994 65: 6m 6.1s 6m $7g^5$ $8s^2$ $a8g^3$ 1995 11.6m* $12m^2$ $11.5m^3$ $14g^5$ 10.5s* $12.1s^5$ $a10g^3$ Nov 8] unfurnished gelding: fairly useful handicapper: won at Windsor (edgy) in June and Haydock (comfortably best effort, leading over 2f out) in September: stays 1½m, seemingly not 1¾m: acts on good to firm and soft ground and on equitrack. *P. F. I. Cole* 84 a61

DANCE STAR 2 b.f. (Apr 21) Damister (USA) 123 – Glen Dancer 102 (Furry Glen 121) [1995 7g 8.2m* Oct 26] 6,200Y: leggy, workmanlike filly: half-sister to a winner over hurdles: dam 7f winner at 2 yrs, stayed 1½m: won 11-runner maiden at Nottingham readily by 2½ lengths (rated value 5) from Bullpen Belle, smooth headway 3f out and readily asserting inside last: should stay middle distances: will improve further. *M. A. Jarvis* — 75 p

DANCES WITH HOOVES 3 b.c. Dancing Dissident (USA) 119 – Princesse Legere (USA) (Alleged (USA) 138) [1994 75p: 8.2g^{2} 1995 8d^{3} 8g Apr 22] tall, leggy colt: fair form when placed in maidens: will stay beyond 1m. *D. J. S. ffrench Davis* — 75

DANCE TO VICTORY 2 b.f. (Mar 9) Ron's Victory (USA) 129 – Nodolya 70 (Niniski (USA) 125) [1995 5d^{5} 5m^{6} Apr 7] 450Y: sparely-made filly: first foal: dam 1¼m winner, stayed 13f: behind in maiden auction and seller: sold 500 gns Doncaster May Sales. *T. D. Barron* — –

DANCE TREAT (USA) 3 ch.f. Nureyev (USA) 131 – Office Wife (USA) (Secretariat (USA)) [1994 –: 7d 1995 8.1m 10.8g* 12s^{2} 10.5v^{3} Nov 26] leggy filly: trained by M. Stoute until after reappearance: won minor event at Segre in October: probably stays 1½m. *D. Sepulchre, France* — 84

DANCE TURN 4 b.c. Damister (USA) 123 – Spin Turn (Homing 130) [1994 105p: 9d^{4} 10s 8.1m* 8.1m* 1995 8g 7.9g^{5} 8.1m* 8m^{6} 8m^{2} 10g^{2} 8f^{4} 8m^{6} 8g Sep 28] tall, good-topped colt: impresses in appearance: unimpressive mover in slower paces: smart performer: won Whitsun Cup at Sandown in May and very good second in Sea World International Stakes (length behind Darnay) at the Curragh and listed race at Newbury (worn down close home by Ihtiram) in the summer: ran poorly last 2 outings: effective at 1m to 1¼m: acts on good to firm ground and dead, respectable effort on firm: visored penultimate start: has won when sweating: races prominently: seemed thoroughly genuine prior to last 2 starts: sold 96,000 gns Newmarket Autumn Sales. *R. W. Armstrong* — 115

DANCING CAVALIER 2 b.c. (May 16) Nalchik (USA) – Miss Admington 71 (Double Jump 131) [1995 a8.5d 7.1s 7m a7g a8g a7g^{6} Dec 9] unfurnished colt: half-brother to 1¼m winner Gay Ming (by Gay Meadow): dam probably stayed 1½m: poor maiden: gives impression needs long distances. *R. Hollinshead* — –

DANCING CORMORANT 2 b.c. (Mar 25) Shareef Dancer (USA) 135 – Cormorant Creek 73 (Gorytus (USA) 132) [1995 7m^{6} 8g Sep 8] 19,000Y: smallish, strong colt: first foal: dam, 10.4f winner, half-sister to Cormorant Wood, dam of Rock Hopper (by Shareef Dancer): well beaten in maidens at York (slowly away and hung left) and Doncaster: sold 10,000 gns Doncaster November Sales. *J. D. Bethell* — –

DANCING DEBUT 2 b.f. (Jan 23) Polar Falcon (USA) 126 – Exclusive Virtue (USA) 94 (Shadeed (USA) 135) [1995 8.2m^{4} Oct 26] angular filly: first foal: dam 7f winner at 2 yrs, stayed 1½m: weak 8/1-shot, better for race and green, stayed on well when around 10 lengths fourth of 10 to Censor in maiden at Nottingham: sure to improve. *J. H. M. Gosden* — 58 p

DANCING DESTINY 3 b.f. Dancing Brave (USA) 140 – Tender Loving Care 105 (Final Straw 127) [1994 77: 7d^{2} 7.9d 1995 10g 10.8g^{2} 11f^{2} 9.9m 8g 10f 11f a8g Nov 20] quite attractive filly: fair maiden: sold out of J. Fanshawe's stable 16,000 gns Newmarket July Sales after third 3-y-o start: well beaten for new connections: stays 11f: acts on firm and dead ground. *R. Bastiman* — 70 d

DANCING DIAMOND (IRE) 5 b.m. Alzao (USA) 117 – Shay Tien 97 (Gunner B 126) [1994 49: a12g^{4} a12g^{2} a12g^{5} 9.7v a13g^{3} a13g^{5} a13g^{6} a13g^{4} 1995 a13g^{2} a12g^{3} a13g* a13g^{2} a16g* a16g Mar 2] small, sparely-made mare: modest performer: won 2 selling handicaps at Lingfield in February: needs further than 1½m (stays 2m): acts on equitrack (unraced on fibresand) and good to firm ground: has worn hood since fifth 4-y-o start: blinkered final start in 1994, visored since: normally races prominently. *Miss B. Sanders* — 56

DANCING DOT (IRE) 2 b.f. (Mar 21) Durgam (USA) – Canty's Gold 44 (Sonnen Gold 121) [1995 5f^{4} 7g 7.1g^{3} 8.3g 7f 7.1s Nov 2] 400Y: second foal: dam, poor maiden, placed twice over 7f at 2 yrs: third of 14 in claimer at Edinburgh in September: well beaten all other starts: stays 7f. *Miss L. A. Perratt* — 50 ?

DANCING HEART 3 b.g. Thowra (FR) – Miss Lawsuit (Neltino 97) [1994 69: 6m 6m^{2} 6m^{3} 6g^{6} 6g^{5} 6g 1995 7f^{4} 7g* 7m 7f^{4} 7f^{2} 6g 7s^{3} a6g^{6} 6.1s a8g^{4} a7g* a6g a8g^{3} — 72 a76

a7g Dec 18] stocky gelding: fair handicapper: successful in May (awarded race) and November (easily best effort), both at Lingfield: stays 7f, faded over 1m: acts on any going, including equitrack: races prominently: blinkered 5 times, including last 4 starts. *B. J. Meehan*

DANCING HEIGHTS (IRE) 4 b.f. High Estate 127 – Alpine Symphony (Northern Dancer) [1994 77: 8m^6 10m* 10m^3 10.2m^6 1995 8.1g^4 8.9m^5 10f 10m^6 Jul 21] sturdy filly: fairly useful handicapper: probably ideally suited by around 1¼m: acted on good to firm ground: in foal to Midyan. *I. A. Balding* 80

DANCING IMAGE 2 ch.g. (May 5) Salse (USA) 128 – Reflection 111 (Mill Reef (USA) 141) [1995 6g^3 7m^6 7d^5 Sep 27] close-coupled, attractive gelding: good mover: seventh foal: half-brother to several winners, including 7f (at 2 yrs) to 1¼m winner Empire Pool and 3-y-o 1¼m to 1½m winner Shaft of Light (both by Sharrood): dam, 2-y-o 5f to 7f winner, proved disappointing: fair form in maidens at Ascot (3 lengths third of 4 to Tamhid) and Kempton (sixth of 11 to Brilliant Red), making most: bit below par in similar event on soft surface at Salisbury last time: subsequently gelded: will stay beyond 7f. *I. A. Balding* 71

DANCING JACK 2 ch.c. (Apr 18) Clantime 101 – Sun Follower (Relkino 131) [1995 5g 5m^3 5d^5 5m^6 5m^4 5g^5 5g^6 a5g^4 a6g a5g* a6g^3 a6g^3 Dec 19] workmanlike colt: first foal: dam showed little over hurdles: modest performer: won nursery at Lingfield in November: stays 6f: acts on equitrack: takes keen hold. *J. J. Bridger* 56

DANCING JAZZTIME 4 b.f. Clantime 101 – Dance In Spain 50 (King of Spain 121) [1994 NR 1995 5d a6g Nov 24] third foal: dam disappointing 2-y-o sprint plater: of no account. *J. S. Wainwright* –

DANCING LAWYER 4 b.g. Thowra (FR) – Miss Lawsuit (Neltino 97) [1994 80: 8m 8m* 7m^2 6m^4 7m^5 7.1g^3 7m^2 7f^5 7d 8d 8g^5 7g a7g^4 a8g^2 a7g* a8g^3 1995 a7g 6m^5 7f^3 7m^4 7f^4 7m^6 8f^4 8f^3 7.1m^2 7.1d^4 a8g* a8g Dec 14] sturdy gelding: carries condition: fair handicapper: won at Lingfield in November: effective at 7f and 1m: acts on firm and dead ground and on equitrack: takes keen hold: consistent. *B. J. Meehan* 75 a80

DANCING LOTTIE (IRE) 2 b.f. (Mar 20) Dancing Dissident (USA) 119 – Charlotteen 96 (Charlottown 127) [1995 5d^2 5m 5m^6 a5g 5.2f^4 6m^4 6.1m^5 6g Aug 7] IR 2,800Y, resold IR 3,000Y: leggy, unfurnished filly: half-sister to 3 winners: dam middle-distance mare: plater: bred to stay beyond 5f, but takes keen hold and seems unlikely to do so: ran poorly only start on fibresand: sold 550 gns Doncaster November Sales. *P. A. Kelleway* 46

DANCING MAN 2 ch.c. (Apr 15) Executive Man 119 – Lyne Dancer (Be My Native (USA) 122) [1995 5g 6s 7m Oct 12] 1,050Y: big, good-topped colt: first foal: dam tailed off in a juvenile hurdle: no promise in claiming/selling company: bandaged in front last time. *Mrs M. E. Long* –

DANCING RAINBOW 2 b.f. (Feb 21) Rambo Dancer (CAN) 107 – Heemee 81 (On Your Mark 125) [1995 5m* 5g 5m^4 5g^6 6m Oct 2] compact filly: second foal: dam sprinter: won median auction maiden at Edinburgh in June: disappointing afterwards in minor event and nurseries: visored on penultimate start. *M. J. Camacho* 61

DANCING REEF 6 b.m. Miramar Reef 100§ – Facing 49 (Quiet Fling (USA) 124) [1994 NR 1995 a11g Jan 20] second foal: dam maiden plater: no sign of ability. *E. J. Alston* –

DANCING SENSATION (USA) 8 b.m. Faliraki 125 – Sweet Satina (USA) (Crimson Satan) [1994 65, a–: 7d 11.9m* 12s 12m* 12g^2 12m^3 11.8m^4 14m 10d 12m^6 12v 1995 a13g^3 a12g 12g 12g^2 12m* 13.3g^2 12f 11.4m^3 12g* 12m^5 10d Sep 13] big, good-topped mare: fluent mover: fair handicapper: won at Kempton in May and Ascot in July: unlikely to stay much beyond 13.3f: best on a sound surface: tried 9 times on all-weather (including in blinkers) and well below best: suitable mount for apprentice: has run well when sweating: held up: game. *R. Akehurst* 72 a–

DANCING SIOUX 3 b.c. Nabeel Dancer (USA) 120 – Sutosky 78 (Great Nephew 126) [1994 73p: 6v^2 1995 8g 6m^4 6f a7g 5m^4 6f^2 5d^2 5g 5.1d 8f^5 a7g^3 a9.4g^6 a7g^6 a7g Dec 14] angular colt: modest maiden: trained until after third 3-y-o outing by R. Williams: stays 7f: acts on any ground, including equitrack: blinkered (well beaten) final 3-y-o start: looked awkward ride (hung right) tenth 3-y-o start: inconsistent. *R. Guest* 61

DANCING SUNSET (IRE) 4 b.f. Red Sunset 120 – Dance Partner (USA) (Graustark) [1994 102p: 9s^3 12g* 12g^2 12m* 1995 10d* 10m^5 10g Jul 1] smart Irish filly: showed improvement when winning listed event at the Curragh in April by 8 lengths from Ozette: shade disappointing there in Tattersalls Gold Cup, decidedly so in Pretty Polly Stakes: stays 1½m: acts on good to firm ground and dead: held up. *A. P. O'Brien, Ireland* — 111

DANDE FLYER 2 b. or br.c. (Mar 27) Clantime 101 – Lyndseylee 96 (Swing Easy (USA) 126) [1995 5.1m^5 5.1m^4 5g^6 5.1f^3 5.3f^2 5.3f^4 5m^2 5d^5 5.3d 5g* 5.2f* 5m* 5m^3 Nov 3] 10,500Y: neat colt: first foal: dam best at 5f: successful in October in median auction maiden at Folkestone and clear-cut winner of nurseries (within 3 days) at Yarmouth and Newmarket: best at 5f: acts well on top-of-the-ground: best efforts ridden with restraint: sometimes used to be slowly away: sometimes hangs left: bandaged near hind last 2 starts. *D. W. P. Arbuthnot* — 77

DANEFAIR 3 b.f. Danehill (USA) 126 – Roupala (USA) 75 (Vaguely Noble 140) [1994 NR 1995 10.5d* 10g* 10m* 12g* Jul 18] second foal: half-sister to 1993 French 2-y-o 9f winner Estala (by Be My Guest): dam 1m winner (stayed 1¼m well) is half-sister to useful (at up to 7f) Ajuga and (at up to 1¼m) Devil's Rock, out of Irish 1000 Guineas and Champion Stakes winner Cairn Rouge: progressive French filly: won newcomers event at Chantilly in May, 6-runner listed events at Evry and Chantilly in June and very slowly-run 6-runner Prix Minerve at Evry (beat Angel In My Heart a short neck) in July: stays 1½m: yet to race on extremes of going: seemed a very smart filly in the making, but reportedly cracked a pastern during the Minerve and racing future is uncertain. *M. Zilber, France* — 109 p

DANEGOLD (IRE) 3 b.g. Danehill (USA) 126 – Cistus 123 (Sun Prince 128) [1994 72: 7g 7m^3 7f a8.5g^3 10s^6 1995 10.3g^3 a10g^3 a10g^5 8m* 8.1m 8g^2 8g^2 8m* 8.5m^2 10m* 8m 10.1m^4 10f 10d 8.1d* 10d 8d 10d Oct 19] sturdy, close-coupled gelding: fairly useful handicapper: won at Ripon (maiden) in April, then comfortably at Bath and Goodwood in June and at Sandown in September: well below form last 3 starts: effective at 1m, and stays 1¼m: acts on good to firm and soft ground: below form on the all-weather: visored since third 3-y-o start: inconsistent and not one to trust: has been gelded. *M. R. Channon* — 86, a58 +

DANEHILL CHIEF 3 b.g. Dunbeath (USA) 127 – Calafuria (Chief Singer 131) [1994 NR 1995 8m 6.9m May 31] 2,000Y, 7,000 2-y-o: first foal: dam of little account: tailed off in claimer and maiden: has joined G. Margarson. *M. A. Jarvis* — –

DANEHILL DANCER (IRE) 2 b.c. (Jan 30) Danehill (USA) 126 – Mira Adonde (USA) (Sharpen Up 127) [1995 6g* 6m* 7g* 7m^2 Oct 13] — 117

Some inspired purchases resulted in a remarkable year for owner Michael Tabor who collected eight Group 1 or Grade 1 races on either side of the Atlantic through Thunder Gulch (Florida Derby, Kentucky Derby, Belmont Stakes and Travers Stakes), Prince Arthur (Italian Two Thousand Guineas), Tipically Irish (Oak Leaf Stakes) and Danehill Dancer (Heinz 57 Phoenix Stakes and National Stakes). Tabor has been active in the world's sale rings in recent times. He bought Thunder Gulch as a two-year-old for 475,000 dollars. That turned out a bargain. And so, already, has Danehill Dancer at IR38,000 guineas: he has won three of his four races, and the only horse to beat him so far is the top two-year-old of 1995, Alhaarth.

Neville Callaghan had given Tabor what was then his biggest success as an owner when training Royal Derbi to win the AIG Europe Champion Hurdle at Leopardstown in 1993. Callaghan sent Danehill Dancer to the same course for his first big test in the Phoenix Stakes in August. The Phoenix Stakes has often struggled to attract a field worthy of its Group 1 status and while Danehill Dancer subsequently gave the race a boost, the fact that he started 2/1 favourite after winning just a Newmarket maiden gives some indication of the quality of the opposition. Danehill Dancer had also been a well-backed favourite when winning at the July meeting at Newmarket, accounting for Raheen by a length, and was clearly highly regarded. Phoenix Stakes rival Woodborough had beaten Raheen by a similar margin in a maiden at Goodwood while April The Eighth had also won at Goodwood, under top weight in a nursery. The British contingent was completed by the filly Flying Squaw who had pattern-race experience, having finished fourth in the Cherry Hinton prior to a narrow defeat in a listed race at Cologne. The Aidan O'Brien-trained pair of Sunset Reigns (a course-and-distance listed winner) and Ribot's Secret (runner-up to

Heinz 57 Phoenix Stakes, Leopardstown—
little between overseas challengers Danehill Dancer (right) and Woodborough

Blue Duster in the Princess Margaret Stakes) along with the Bolger-trained Deed of Love, seemed to have the best chance of keeping the prize in Ireland. Danehill Dancer was held up in touch on the outside but needed to be ridden along from about the halfway mark and still looked a little inexperienced. However, once in the lead over a furlong out, he stuck to his task well to hold Woodborough by a neck. The Irish outsider Catch A Glimpse stayed on one and a half lengths back in third ahead of Flying Squaw.

A month later Danehill Dancer was returned to Ireland for the seven-furlong National Stakes at the Curragh, this time odds in a field of seven. No significant Irish challenger had come to the fore in the meantime. Deed of Love opposed again, though Force of Will, Dermot Weld's Tralee maiden winner, was the best-supported home runner. The Chapple-Hyam stable who had fielded Woodborough at Leopardstown opposed this time with the Richmond Stakes winner Polaris Flight. The same tactics were employed on Danehill Dancer as at Leopardstown. Eddery produced him to lead on the outside a furlong out and despite tending to edge right on hitting the front, he saw out the extra furlong well, comfortably drawing one and a half lengths clear of Polaris Flight with Force of Will three quarters of a length back in third, just ahead of Deed of Love. On his final start Danehill Dancer was sent off at 2/1 behind the odds-on Alhaarth in the four-runner Dewhurst, in which the Prix Morny winner Tagula was the only other serious contender. Danehill Dancer did not impress on the way to post, but lost nothing in defeat, staying on to be beaten two and a half lengths without ever looking a threat.

Danehill Dancer's sire the Ladbroke Sprint Cup winner Danehill has enjoyed the most success of the 'shuttle stallions' who, in an increasingly popular arrangement, stand in the northern hemisphere for the first half of the year and are then flown out to Australia to cover mares in the southern-hemisphere spring. Danehill was the top sire of two-year-olds in Australia in 1993/94 and 1994/95 and top sire overall there in 1994/95. His northern hemisphere base has until now been Ireland's Coolmore Stud but after the ending of the arrangement between Coolmore and the Arrowfield Stud in Australia, Danehill is to stand in Japan in the spring of 1996. Danehill Dancer is potentially his best northern hemisphere representative to date after injuries put a halt to the progress of some of Danehill's promising performers, including Coronation Stakes winner Kissing Cousin, unbeaten French three-year-old Danefair and the ill-fated 1994 Grand Criterium favourite Indian Jones.

Danehill Dancer (IRE) (b.c. Jan 30, 1993)	Danehill (USA) (b 1986)	Danzig (b 1977)	Northern Dancer
			Pas de Nom
		Razyana (b 1981)	His Majesty
			Spring Adieu
	Mira Adonde (USA) (b or br 1986)	Sharpen Up (ch 1969)	Atan
			Rocchetta
		Lettre d'Amour (gr 1979)	Caro
			Lianga

Danehill Dancer's dam Mira Adonde ran just once, finishing seventh in a seven-furlong maiden at Newmarket on the same card that Danehill won the Free Handicap. Danehill Dancer is her third foal after two fillies by Jareer; Gift Box, who was a headstrong maiden sold for just 750 guineas at the end of her two-year-old season, and Fakhira, who won a five-furlong maiden at the Curragh on her debut as a two-year-old but was tailed off on her only start in Britain in April. Mira Adonde has since produced a sister to Danehill Dancer. Her foal by Lycius was sold for 75,000 guineas at the December Sales. The unraced grandam Lettre d'Amour has produced two winners including Swordsmith (by Diesis), successful in the seven-furlong listed John of Gaunt Stakes. Danehill Dancer's third dam is the top-class French filly Lianga. She reached her peak as a four-year-old when winning the July Cup, Prix Jacques Le Marois, Prix de l'Abbaye and Vernons Sprint Cup.

Danehill Dancer is a big, strong, lengthy individual who carries condition and has plenty of scope. He looks sure to stay a mile, and while there is no reason why he

National Stakes, the Curragh—another 1-2 for the visitors; Polaris Flight (right) pips Force of Will for second

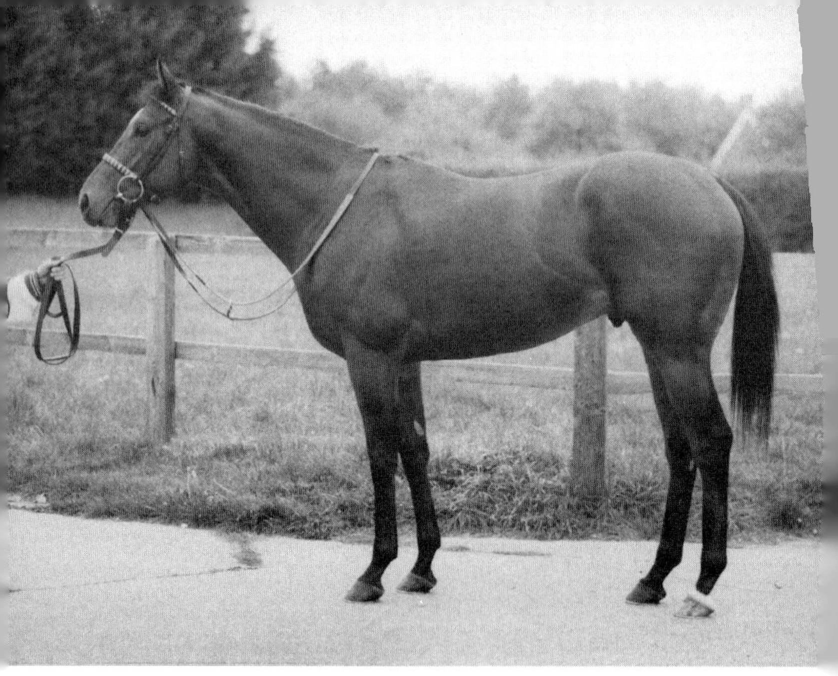

Mr M. Tabor's "Danehill Dancer"

should reverse Dewhurst placings with Alhaarth in the Two Thousand Guineas, there will be other opportunities for him. *N. A. Callaghan*

DANESMAN (IRE) 2 b.c. (Mar 5) Danehill (USA) 126 – Vernonhills (Hard Fought 125) [1995 7f4 7.1d2 8g* Sep 14] 66,000F: sturdy colt: has a quick action: has scope: third foal: brother to 7.1f winner Lantern Hill and half-brother to Italian 3-y-o 1m (at 2 yrs) and 1¼m winner Peco's Bill (by Royal Academy): dam Irish maiden half-sister to smart middle-distance performer Gulf King: progressive form in maidens, heavily-backed favourite again when decisive ½-length winner from Bright Heritage in 8-runner event at Yarmouth: stays well: will continue to improve: sent to Dubai. *J. H. M. Gosden* 96 p

DANESRATH (IRE) 3 b.f. Danehill (USA) 126 – Tribal Rite 95 (Be My Native (USA) 122) [1994 51p: 7d 1995 12.1m2 11.5m4 12.3m* 12g6 11.9g6 Sep 22] quite good-topped filly: fair handicapper: won 5-runner maiden at Chester in August, making all: should stay beyond 12.3f: acts on good to firm ground: consistent: sold 30,000 gns Newmarket December Sales. *A. C. Stewart* 78

DANGEROUS GUEST (IRE) 3 b.g. Deploy 131 – Guest List 85 (Be My Guest (USA) 126) [1994 84p: a7g* 7.1m2 1995 a9.4g3 12m 14g2 Jul 20] strong, rangy gelding: has plenty of scope: good walker: fairly useful handicapper: looking very well, keeping-on 1½ lengths second of 7 to Thaljanah at Sandown: stays 1¾m, and likely to prove suited by greater test of stamina: acts on good to firm ground and fibresand: joined J. Old and gelded. *Sir Mark Prescott* 91

DANGEROUS WATERS 2 b.f. (Feb 16) Risk Me (FR) 127 – Queen's Lake 75 (Kings Lake (USA) 133) [1995 7.1s a7g a8.5g Dec 2] 1,100Y: fourth foal: sister to –

Belgian 3-y-o 11f winner Risky Danseuse: dam stayed very well: ridden by 7-lb claimer, behind in maidens at Chepstow and Wolverhampton (2). *P. G. Murphy*

DANICO 2 ch.c. (Apr 9) Most Welcome 131 – Spica (USA) 76§ (Diesis 133) 59 [1995 7m^4 7m^6 Aug 7] 3,000Y: leggy colt: second foal: dam, 1m winner, wasn't one to trust: fourth of 11 to Too Hasty in median auction maiden at Catterick: below that form in maiden auction at Thirsk month later, failing to handle first bend and soon off bit: will stay at least 1m. *S. C. Williams*

DANIEL'S LASS 3 b.f. Prince Daniel (USA) – Haverhill Lass 67 (Music Boy – 124) [1994 NR 1995 6.1g a8g May 1] small, leggy filly: fourth reported live foal: dam sprinter: behind in seller (bandaged, taken early to post) and median auction maiden. *C. N. Allen*

DANISH CIRCUS (IRE) 2 b.c. (Feb 27) Danehill (USA) 126 – Circus Maid 74 (IRE) (High Top 131) [1995 7.1d^5 7g^3 7f^3 Oct 23] IR 24,000F, IR 32,000Y: small colt: first foal: dam, Irish maiden, out of half-sister to smart sprinter Lugana Beach: similar form in fairly useful maidens at Haydock, Warwick and Leicester: will probably stay 1m. *M. J. Heaton-Ellis*

DANJING (IRE) 3 b.g. Danehill (USA) 126 – Beijing (USA) 89 (Northjet 136) 89 [1994 81: 7g^4 8.5m^2 8s^3 10.2g^3 1995 10g* 14m^5 12f 10m 12m^4 10.1m^3 13.3d 12g* 12m^6 Oct 12] well-made gelding: fairly useful performer: won maiden at Newbury in May and claimer at Newmarket (claimed out of P. Cole's stable £20,000) in September: stays 1¾m: acts on good to firm ground and soft: blinkered last 2 starts. *S. E. Sherwood*

DANKESTON (USA) 2 b.c. (Feb 25) Elmaamul (USA) 125 – Last Request 92 96 (Dancer's Image (USA)) [1995 5s^2 5.1m* 7m^3 7m^2 7m* 7m^3 7m* 6f 8g^6 Nov 8] $45,000F, IR 37,000Y: leggy, workmanlike colt: half-brother to several winners here and abroad, including 7f winner Mawsuff (by Known Fact) and 9f and 1¼m winner Wishiah (by Persian Bold), both fairly useful: dam won over 1¼m at 2 yrs: won median auction maiden at Nottingham in May and small-field minor events at Catterick and Redcar in August: ran well when sixth of 9 to Glory of Dancer in Gran Criterium at Milan on final start: better suited by 1m than less, and will stay further: acts on good to firm ground and soft: visored last 6 starts: game and genuine. *M. Bell*

DANNISTAR 3 br.f. Puissance 110 – Loadplan Lass 63 (Nicholas Bill 125) [1994 57 NR 1995 a8.5g^5 a8.5g^2 a9.4g* a9.4g^6 Dec 9] second foal: half-sister to 4-y-o 1½m winner Hill Farm Dancer (by Gunner B): dam poor maiden, bred to stay middle distances: won claimer at Wolverhampton in November: stays 9.4f. *P. D. Evans*

DANNY'S GIFT 3 ch.f. Prince Daniel (USA) – Triple Bar 71 (Jimmy Reppin – 131) [1994 –: 6d a7g 1995 a8g a12g^4 10g 7f May 11] close-coupled, angular filly: bad maiden: stays 1½m. *Miss A. J. Whitfield*

DANSON 4 b.g. Dancing Brave (USA) 140 – Liaison (USA) (Blushing Groom – (FR) 131) [1994 NR 1995 a12g a8.5g 10.8m Jun 26] 3,800 3-y-o: first foal: dam won 1¼m listed event in France: behind in maidens (subsequently gelded) and seller. *T. H. Caldwell*

DANTEAN 3 b.g. Warning 136 – Danthonia (USA) 80 (Northern Dancer) [1994 – NR 1995 9m 14g 10g Jun 17] tall gelding: second foal: dam 2-y-o 5f winner: well beaten in maidens and (tried blinkered) claimer: sold (G. Harwood to R. O'Sullivan) 5,000 gns Newmarket July Sales and gelded. *G. Harwood*

DANTE'S RUBICON (IRE) 4 ch.g. Common Grounds 118 – Dromorehill 54 (Ballymore 123) [1994 47: a9.4g 9.9d 8.1g 6m^2 6f 6g 6g 1995 a8g a7g^5 7m^2 7g 7g 6m 7.5m* 7.5g^6 6f^2 6g 6g 7m a8g^3 Nov 16] angular gelding: has a round action: modest handicapper: won seller at Beverley in July: effective at 6f, and stays 1m: acts on any turf ground and on fibresand: usually wears a tongue strap: sometimes sweats: inconsistent: sold (J. D. Bethell to N. Ayliffe) 5,200 gns Doncaster November Sales. *J. D. Bethell*

DANUS REX (IRE) 3 b.c. Roi Danzig (USA) – Hear Me (Simply Great (FR) 59 122) [1994 52p: 7.5m 7m 7m^6 8s 8s^5 1995 10.3m 12m^6 14.1m* 12g 16m a16g Sep 4] big, lengthy colt: modest form: won strongly-run maiden handicap at Redcar in May: should have stayed 2m: acted on good to firm ground and soft: sometimes coltish: dead. *C. A. Smith*

DAPHNIS (USA) 6 b.g. Lead On Time (USA) 123 – Dancing Vaguely (USA) (Vaguely Noble 140) [1994 NR 1995 a12g^3 a12g Feb 8] third foal: half-brother to winning hurdler Reve de Valse (by Conquistador Cielo): dam French 1½m winner: NH Flat race winner: staying-on third in seller but well beaten in maiden event, both at Wolverhampton: modest winning hurdler. *W. T. Kemp* 40

DARAKAH 8 ch.m. Doulab (USA) 115 – Ladytown (English Prince 129) [1994 NR 1995 a7g a6g a10g 8d 6m^5 8m 8f^6 Jul 19] good-bodied mare: unimpressive mover: fair handicapper in 1992, then produced foals next 2 yrs: only poor form at best on return: used to be suited by 7f/1m: seemed well suited by some give in the ground at 5 yrs. *C. J. Hill* 39

DARAYDALA (IRE) 3 b.f. Royal Academy (USA) 130 – Daralinsha (USA) 116 (Empery (USA) 128) [1994 8s^3 1995 10g^3 10g^3 10g* 12g^3 12.5g^2 12g* 12.5s^2 12m 10.5d^3 Nov 17] big, lengthy filly: third foal: dam 1m (at 2 yrs, including listed race) to 1½m (Prix Minerve) winner: useful performer: won minor event at Evry in June and listed race at Chantilly in September: best efforts when 3 lengths second of 9 (staying on dourly) to Russian Snows in Prix de Royallieu at Longchamp and 1¾ lengths third of 13 to Marie de Ken in Prix Fille de L'Air at Evry: effective at 10.5f, and will stay beyond 12.5f: acts well on soft going, below form on top-of-the-ground. *A. de Royer Dupre, France* 108

DARAYDAN (IRE) 3 b.c. Kahyasi 130 – Delsy (FR) (Abdos 134) [1994 NR 1995 12g* 12g* 12g^3 12m 16d^4 12m^4 16m* Oct 27] close-coupled colt: half-brother to numerous winners, notably Prix du Jockey-Club winner Darshaan (by Shirley Heights), Prix Vermeille winner Darara (by Top Ville) and Prix de Royallieu winner Dalara (by Doyoun): dam French 1½m winner: useful performer: won maiden at Leopardstown and minor event at Gowran (third-last start for J. Oxx) in April: best effort when winning listed rated stakes at Newmarket in October, heading Kristal's Paradise near finish after protracted duel: stays 2m well: yet to race on extremes of going: blinkered (ran as pacemaker in Irish Derby) fourth start. *Lady Herries* 107

DARBY FLYER 2 ch.c. (Apr 7) Dominion Royale 112 – Shining Wood 65 (Touching Wood (USA) 127) [1995 6d a6g^3 Dec 14] 2,200F, 2,600Y: compact colt: first foal: dam maiden stayed 1¾m: better effort in maidens when remote third of 9 to Carmarthen Bay at Lingfield, late progress from well behind: will be much better suited by 1m+. *W. R. Muir* 49

DARCEY BUSSELL 3 b.f. Green Desert (USA) – Docklands (On Your Mark 125) [1994 NR 1995 8.1g 7f 8m^4 7.1s 8f^2 7f^5 Oct 25] shallow-girthed filly: half-sister to 2 winners, notably useful Port Helene (at 1½m by Troy): dam, best at up to 1m, is half-sister to 1000 Guineas winner Night Off: modest maiden: left B. Hills's stable after penultimate start: may prove suited by further than 1m: acts on firm ground: bandaged first 2 starts. *N. C. Wright* 59

DAREROCK 2 b.g. (Apr 30) Daring March 116 – Marock Morley 59 (Most Secret 119) [1995 5m 5f^5 5m^6 5g 7f Oct 3] robust gelding: half-brother to several winners, including 7f winner Vintage Type (by Import): dam won over 5f at 5 yrs: poor form in varied company, including selling. *M. Dods* –

DARING DESTINY 4 b.f. Daring March 116 – Raunchy Rita (Brigadier Gerard 144) [1994 96: 8.3d^3 7m* 8m 7.1g^2 7m^5 6m^5 6d* 6m^2 1995 6g^5 5.5s^2 7f* 6m^2 6m 7f^6 6m 6g Sep 16] workmanlike filly: has a round action: useful performer: won 5-runner listed race at Lingfield in May: subsequently fetched 87,000 gns (to dissolve a partnership) at Reading Sales: below form last 4 starts: effective at 5.5f and 7f: acts on firm and dead ground, below form on heavy: effective blinkered or not: has run well when sweating and edgy. *K. R. Burke* 104

DARING GIFT 4 b. or br.f. Never So Bold 135 – Krameria 72 (Kris 135) [1994 –: 7g 5.9m^5 6g 6m 6g 1995 6m Apr 25] leggy filly: no worthwhile form. *J. R. Bosley* –

DARING RYDE 4 b.g. Daring March 116 – Mini Myra 49 (Homing 130) [1994 –: 8m 10.5d 8d 1995 7g 8.2m^6 8g* 8.2m^5 8.1m 8m 10m 8.1d^3 8.2m Oct 19] tall gelding: poor performer: won claimer at Leicester in June: will stay beyond 1m: acts on good to firm ground: none too consistent. *J. P. Smith* 45

DARING VENTURE 2 b.f. (Apr 29) Dowsing (USA) 124 – Berberana 68 (Never So Bold 135) [1995 6m Jun 14] 3,800Y: leggy filly: first living foal: dam, –

2-y-o 6f winner, granddaughter of Sookera: 14/1, last of 13 in maiden auction at Kempton. *Martyn Meade*

DARIUS THE GREAT (IRE) 3 ch.c. Persian Heights 129 – Derring Dee 85 (Derrylin 115) [1994 NR 1995 12.5m a8g 10m^5 11.6m Jul 17] 9,000Y: angular colt: bad mover: fourth foal: half-brother to 1m (Irish 2-y-o) to 11f (in Italy) winner Sarastro (by Bob Back): dam winning 2-y-o sprinter: little sign of ability. *D. Marks* –

DARK DEED (USA) 2 ch.f. (Feb 3) Known Fact (USA) 135 – Sin Lucha (USA) (Northfields (USA)) [1995 6m^3 6m^2 6g^2 Sep 13] fifth foal: half-sister to American 3-y-o Tejano's Field (by Tejano), 4.5f winner at 2 yrs: dam unraced sister to top-class miler Northjet: placed in maiden events at Newbury, Ripon and Yarmouth, 3 lengths second of 10 to Obsessive last time: will probably stay 1m. *B. W. Hills* 81

DARK EYED LADY (IRE) 5 b.m. Exhibitioner 111 – Tribal Eye 95 (Tribal Chief 125) [1994 82: 6g* 6m 5.2m^2 6f 5.2g 5m 6d 5m a6g a6g^5 1995 a6g 6m 5.1h^5 5.3f^5 5.7h Sep 4] sturdy mare: disappointing in 1995: stays 6f: acts on firm and dead ground: blinkered (out of form) final 5-y-o start: inconsistent. *D. W. P. Arbuthnot* –

DARK MENACE 3 br.g. Beveled (USA) – Sweet And Sure (Known Fact (USA) 135) [1994 58: 6f^4 7g 5.7g 7.3v 1995 6m^3 6g^6 6f 6g 5.3f^3 7f^3 5.7h 6d Sep 27] workmanlike gelding: disappointing maiden: modest at best after reappearance: should stay 7f: best efforts on top-of-the-ground, ran poorly on heavy final 2-y-o start: blinkered (soundly beaten) last 2 starts. *S. Mellor* 71 d

DARK ROBE 2 b.f. (Mar 5) Timeless Times (USA) 99 – Harem Queen 66 (Prince Regent (FR) 129) [1995 7g Jun 17] 5,600Y: half-sister to 1989 2-y-o 6f and 7f winner Little Ripper (by Belfort) and 3 winners abroad: dam half-sister to very smart 1976 2-y-o Avgerinos: 50/1 and ridden by 7-lb claimer, tailed off in maiden auction at Warwick. *R. W. Emery* –

DARK SHOT (IRE) 3 b.c. Rock City 120 – Jeanne Avril 99 (Music Boy 124) [1994 73, a82: 6g^3 6g^3 5.2g^4 6m 6d^4 8m a7g* a6g^3 1995 a8.5g^5 a7g* a5g^3 a6g^5 a6g* 6.1g^2 a6g^5 a5g a6g Sep 16] compact colt: fluent mover: fair performer: made all in claimer at Lingfield in February and seller at Southwell in April: effective at 6f and 7f: acts on the all-weather and dead ground: effective visored or not: sold only 2,800 gns Doncaster September Sales. *J. Berry* 65

DARK TRUFFLE 2 br.f. (Feb 9) Deploy 131 – River Dove (USA) 86 (Riverman (USA) 131) [1995 6m May 19] IR 7,000Y: strong, sturdy filly: third foal: dam, 2-y-o 6f winner, out of Poule d'Essai des Pouliches second Fruhlingstag: 5/1 and in need of race, chased leaders around 4f in 9-runner maiden at Newmarket won by Paloma Bay: looked capable of better. *Mrs J. Cecil* 59

DARK WATERS (IRE) 2 b.c. (Apr 12) Darshaan 133 – Grecian Sea (FR) (Homeric 133) [1995 7m 8.2d^2 Sep 11] robust, attractive colt with scope: brother to 2 winners, notably Yorkshire Oaks winner and St Leger runner-up Hellenic, and half-brother to several winners, including useful 6f to 1½m winner Golden Wave (by Glint of Gold): dam won over 6f at 2 yrs in France: 6 lengths second of 20 to Storm Trooper in maiden at Nottingham, staying on under pressure: will be well suited by middle distances: will keep improving. *M. R. Stoute* 82 p

DARKWOOD BAY (USA) 4 b. or br.c. Green Dancer (USA) 132 – Unyielding (USA) (Never Bend) [1994 82+: 10s^5 12m 1995 10g May 31] lengthy, attractive colt: first run since 1994 Derby, bandaged and stiff task, last of 7 in minor event at Newbury: should stay beyond 1¼m. *D. R. C. Elsworth* –

DARLING CLOVER 3 ch.f. Minster Son 130 – Lady Clementine 68 (He Loves Me 120) [1994 NR 1995 a11g^4 a12g^4 a12g^2 11.6m* 11.8g 11.6m 10m^5 10.1m^2 10m^3 Aug 14] leggy, unfurnished filly: sixth foal: sister to 11.5f winner Much Too Clever and half-sister to fairly useful middle-distance stayer Much Sought After (by Adonijah): dam 5f winner: modest handicapper: won at Windsor in May: edged right and found little in claimer at Leicester final start: stays 1½m well: acts on fibresand, has raced only on a sound surface on turf. *D. Morley* 62

DARLING FLAME (USA) 2 b.f. (Apr 27) Capote (USA) – My Darling One (USA) (Exclusive Native (USA)) [1995 6g^2 6f* 6g^2 6m Aug 17] lengthy, unfurnished filly: half-sister to several winners, including 3-y-o 12.3f winner Wellsian (by Sadler's Wells) and smart 4-y-o 7f and 1m winner Heart Lake (by Nureyev): dam high-class winner at up to 9f: won maiden at Newbury in June: always to fore when 101 dead-heating for second, ½-length behind Applaud, in steadily-run Cherry Hinton Stakes at Newmarket in July: found to be in season when well below form in Lowther Stakes at York on final outing: will stay 7f. *J. H. M. Gosden*

DARNAY 4 br.c. Darshaan 133 – Flawless Image (USA) 109 (The Minstrel (CAN) 135) [1994 113: 10m^{2} 10.4f^{3} 9.3g^{2} 8m 10d 1995 8m^{2} 8m* 8f^{3} 7.3m^{3} 8m^{2} 8m Sep 3] strong, rangy colt: impresses in appearance: wintered in Dubai: smart performer: second of 32 in Royal Hunt Cup (under 9-10) at Royal Ascot on reappearance: won Sea World International at the Curragh in July by a length from Dance Turn: third in Sussex Stakes (3¾ lengths behind Sayyedati) at Goodwood and Hungerford Stakes (about a length behind Harayir) at Newbury, then ½-length second of 6 to Harayir in Celebration Mile back at Goodwood: effective at 7.3f to 1m, and probably at 1¼m: goes well on top-of-the-ground, tried only once on a soft surface: best held up (made most and well beaten in Prix du Moulin final start): thoroughly genuine and consistent. *Saeed bin Suroor* — 117

DARREN BOY (IRE) 4 ch.g. Ballad Rock 122 – Trojan Relation (Trojan Fen 118) [1994 91: 6v 6m^{3} 6g^{6} 6m* 6m 6d 1995 5.2m 6m 6f 7g Jul 13] small, sturdy gelding: fairly useful handicapper: well below form in 1995 and sold only 2,200 gns Newmarket Autumn Sales. *P. F. I. Cole* — –

DARTER (IRE) 3 b.c. Darshaan 133 – Mamouna (USA) 113 (Vaguely Noble 140) [1994 NR 1995 12.3m^{3} 13.4d^{6} 11.9d^{5} 11.8f^{3} Oct 24] good-topped colt: third foal: half-brother to middle-distance winners in Ireland by Ela-Mana-Mou and Lomond: dam (1m winner) stayed 1¼m: fair form when third in maiden at Ripon and minor event at Leicester: should be suited by test of stamina: below form on a soft surface: sold (L. Cumani to R. Akehurst) 25,000 gns Newmarket Autumn Sales. *L. M. Cumani* — 72

DASHING BLUE 2 ch.c. (May 5) Dashing Blade 117 – Blubella 86 (Balidar 133) [1995 6m^{2} 5g^{4} 5m^{2} 6m* 6d^{4} 6m* Oct 4] good-bodied colt: fourth living foal: dam sprinter: won maiden at Ripon in August: improved form (ridden with more restraint) to win 14-runner nursery at York in October by 1¼ lengths from Nilgiri Hills, quickening to lead entering final 1f: stays 6f: acts on good to firm ground and dead: bandaged near-fore last time: likely to make a very useful sprinter. *I. A. Balding* — 96 p

DASHING DANCER (IRE) 4 ch.g. Conquering Hero (USA) 116 – Santa Maria (GER) (Literat) [1994 60: 5s^{4} 5.3g 5.7m^{5} 6m 5m^{2} 5g^{4} 6m 6m^{5} 6.1s^{4} 7d^{6} 1995 6g^{5} 6f^{4} 6g^{2} 5m^{4} 6f^{3} 6m 6m^{2} 6m^{5} 6d 6f^{2} Oct 23] strong, compact gelding: modest maiden handicapper: head second of 22 at Leicester final start: stays 6f: acts on firm and soft ground: has run well when sweating: sometimes early to post. *R. Akehurst* — 65

DASHING INVADER (USA) 2 ch.c. (Feb 24) Pirate Army (USA) 118 – Cherie's Hope (USA) (Flying Paster (USA)) [1995 8d 8.2m Oct 19] $57,000F: heavy-topped colt: sixth foal: closely related to smart 1992 2-y-o 5f and 6f winner Silver Wizard (by Silver Hawk) and half-brother to 2 winners in USA: dam unraced: carrying condition, well beaten in maidens at Salisbury and Nottingham. *P. W. Harris* — –

Sea World International Stakes, the Curragh—Darnay steps up on his Hunt Cup form

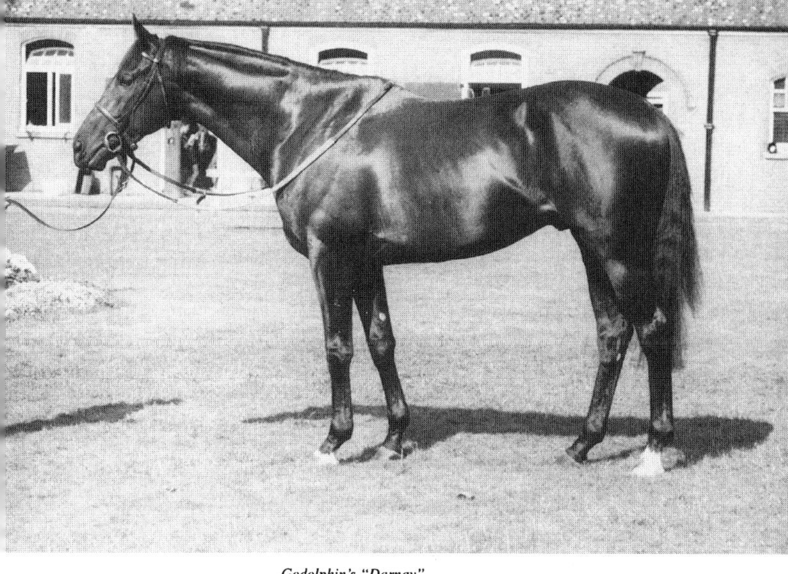

Godolphin's "Darnay"

DASHING WATER 3 b.f. Dashing Blade 117 – Peckitts Well 96 (Lochnager 132) [1994 87p: 8.1d^4 7s* 7.3v^3 1995 7m^6 7.3m^4 7g^3 7g 7f 7.3m 5m^5 Aug 24] rangy, unfurnished filly: good walker: fairly useful performer: needs further than 5f, unlikely to stay much beyond 7f: acts on good to firm ground and heavy: sometimes bandaged: takes good hold. *I. A. Balding* — 87

DAS ISLAND 3 b.c. Presidium 124 – Phamilla (IRE) (Bellypha 130) [1994 62: 5.3f^2 5m 6d^4 5m 6m a5g^2 a5g^5 a5g^2 a6g^2 a6g 1995 a6g* a6g^4 a5g^4 a7g^2 6f 6g Jun 7] leggy colt: modest performer: won median auction maiden at Lingfield in February: should stay beyond 6f: acts on firm and dead ground and on both all-weather surfaces: tends to sweat and be on toes. *J. R. Jenkins* — – a62

DASWAKI (CAN) 7 b.g. Miswaki (USA) 124 – Nice Manners (CAN) (Barachois (CAN)) [1994 NR 1995 7.1g 8.3m 9m 8g Sep 8] sturdy gelding: once fairly useful, but no longer of much account. *G. L. Moore* — –

DATO STAR (IRE) 4 br.g. Accordion – Newgate Fairy (Flair Path 122) [1994 NR 1995 16.2m^5 12m^4 13.4d^2 12m 12m^2 Nov 4] rangy gelding: good mover: second foal: dam never ran: unbeaten in 3 NH Flat races on soft or heavy ground, including at Cheltenham Festival: shaped well on his first 4 starts: much-improved form when 1½ lengths second of 18 to Snow Princess in November Handicap at Doncaster, off bridle early in straight, challenging strongly final 1f despite hanging left: effective at 1½m and will stay beyond 13.4f: acts on good to firm ground, yet to encounter soft or heavy: bandaged fourth start: sure to win races on flat. *J. M. Jefferson* — 95 p

DAUNT 3 b.c. Darshaan 133 – Minute Waltz (Sadler's Wells (USA) 132) [1994 81: 8g^4 8m 1995 8d* Apr 6] rangy colt: 7/2 second favourite, most impressive winner of 12-runner maiden at Leicester only start in 1995, leading 2f out, clearly having race sewn up before last and allowed to coast in: will stay beyond 1m: looked sure to go on and win more races. *J. H. M. Gosden* — 90 p

DAUNTING DESTINY (BEL) 2 b.c. (Apr 15) Formidable (USA) 125 – Heavy Land (FR) (Recitation (USA) 124) [1995 6m 7g 7f^2 6m 6.9g^4 7f^2 8f* Oct 31] — 77

12,000F, 4,000Y, resold 4,600Y, 6,000 2-y-o: quite good-topped colt: unimpressive mover: third reported foal: half-brother to 3-y-o 11.8f to 13.6f winner Green Land (by Hero's Honor): dam won 3 races at 2 yrs in Belgium: in good form late in year, winning 16-runner nursery at Redcar in October by head: will probably stay further than 1m: acts on firm ground. *R. Hannon*

DAUNTLESS FORT 4 gr.f. Belfort (FR) 89 – Dauntless Flight (Golden Mallard 103) [1994 –, a56: a6s* a6g^5 5d^6 6g a6g^6 a6g^6 a6g 1995 a6g a7g 7g a7g a8g 6m^5 5g 6f Oct 31] leggy filly: only a poor plater: sold out of B. Murray's stable 700 gns Doncaster March Sales after second 4-y-o start: stays 6f: acts on fibresand and good to firm ground: no improvement in visor or blinkers: tail swisher. *Mrs V. A. Aconley* — 38 a–

DAUPHIN (IRE) 2 b. or br.g. (Mar 1) Astronef 116 – Va Toujours 109 (Alzao (USA) 117) [1995 7.1m 6f Oct 24] 26,000 2-y-o: strong, lengthy gelding: has a round action: first foal: dam 6f (at 2 yrs) to 9f winner: behind in auction events at Sandown and (signs of ability, not knocked about) Leicester: may do better. *W. J. Musson* — – p

DAVID BLUE (IRE) 4 b.g. Colmore Row 111 – Royal Aunt (Martinmas 128) [1994 46: 5v 6.1d^5 6m 5s a7g 1995 a7g Jan 6] unfurnished gelding: probably no longer of much account. *J. White* — –

DAVID JAMES' GIRL 3 b.f. Faustus (USA) 118 – Eagle's Quest 62 (Legal Eagle 126) [1994 58+: 5.1m 5s* 6g a5g^2 a6g^5 a7g* 1995 a7g a6g^2 a7g a7g* a7g^4 a8.5g^6 7.6m^2 6.9f^2 a8.5g 7m a7g a6g a6g^5 a7g^3 Dec 2] leggy filly: modest performer: won handicap at Wolverhampton in March: should stay 1m: acts on good to firm and soft ground, and on fibresand. *A. Bailey* — 65 d

DAWALIB (USA) 5 ch.g. Danzig Connection (USA) – Centavos (USA) (Scout Leader (USA)) [1994 59, a81: 8g 8.1s a7g a7g^3 a8g* 7.6m^4 8f 8.3m 8.2m a6g^3 6g 8d 6s^6 7d a7g^3 a6g* a6g a8.5g^4 a6g^3 1995 a7g^5 a6g^3 a6g^4 a7g^3 a7g^3 7g* 6m^2 7.6m* 8.1g^2 7g^2 7f^2 7g^6 7m* 6d 6g Sep 16] good-topped gelding: poor mover: fair handicapper: won at Warwick in April, Chester in May and Kempton in August: effective at 6f to 1m: acts on firm and soft going and on fibresand (has run only once on equitrack): effective visored, but not tried for long time: has worn citation bridle: held up in touch of late: consistent. *D. Haydn Jones* — 71 a75

DAWAWIN (USA) 2 b.f. (Feb 26) Dixieland Band (USA) – Stalwart Moment (USA) (Stalwart (USA)) [1995 7m^3 Oct 20] $90,000F: good-topped filly: second foal: dam won both her starts at up to 1m at 3 yrs in USA: 7/1 from 4/1, burly and green, 2¾ lengths third of 21 to Germano in maiden at Doncaster, midfield after sluggish start then coming through well from over 2f out without being given at all a hard race: sure to improve, and win a race. *E. A. L. Dunlop* — 81 p

DAWLAH 3 b. or br.f. Shirley Heights 130 – Urjwan (USA) 98 (Seattle Slew (USA)) [1994 83p: 8g^2 1995 10m^2 10.4g^3 10.3g* 10.8g^3 11.9m^5 12m^5 18.2g^3 16d^5 Sep 30] lengthy filly: fairly useful form: sweating and edgy when winning maiden at Doncaster in May: seems to stay 2¼m: probably acts on good to firm ground, below form only run on soft surface: has worn tongue strap: races prominently. *H. Thomson Jones* — 91

DAWN FLIGHT 6 b.g. Precocious 126 – Sea Kestrel 82 (Sea Hawk II 131) [1994 52: 12g 12m^6 14m^4 14g 10m^3 10m 12m^3 12g^4 11.6m^3 14.1m^2 13.1g a13g a16g 1995 15.4m Sep 7] strong gelding: modest maiden handicapper: stays 1¾m: acts on good to firm and soft ground: well below form in blinkers (twice at 3 yrs) and visor (final 4-y-o start): sometimes looks reluctant: modest hurdler. *J. R. Jenkins* — –

DAWN MISSION 3 b.g. Dunbeath (USA) 127 – Bustellina 81 (Busted 134) [1994 NR 1995 12.4g^3 12m^5 12m 13.8g^3 12.4m^5 a14.8g^4 14.1m^5 11.9g^5 Sep 1] 2,600Y: rangy gelding: has scope: half-brother to 3 winners, notably fairly useful middle-distance stayer Cumbrian Rhapsody (by Sharrood): dam 1m winner: poor maiden handicapper: probably stays 14.8f: acts on good to firm ground and fibresand: blinkered (well beaten) fourth 3-y-o start: tends to pull hard: won juvenile hurdle in October. *M. H. Easterby* — 47

DAWN PALACE 4 ch.g. Dawn Johnny (USA) – Lenton Palace (Dragonara Palace (USA) 115) [1994 NR 1995 13.8m^4 Aug 1] first foal: dam poor performer: 100/1, tailed off in 5-runner seller. *T. W. Donnelly* — –

DAWN ROCK 4 b.g. Norwick (USA) 125 – Venetian Joy 80§ (Windjammer (USA)) [1994 58: a10g^2 a11g* a10g^2 12s a12g a14g^3 a11g a16g^5 1995 a16g^5 13v^6 — –

12.3d 11.1s^5 13g 15m^4 17.5g Sep 15] sparely-made gelding: sold out of P. Kelleway's stable 2,000 gns Doncaster February Sales after reappearance: no form in 1995: stays 11f: acts on all-weather surfaces (no form on turf): no improvement in blinkers/visor. *R. M. McKellar*

DAWSHA (IRE) 3 b.f. Slip Anchor 136 – Zarrara (USA) 66 (Desert Wine (USA)) [1994 59p: 7g^2 1995 8g 6m^6 10m* 10.1m^5 Jun 9] compact filly: first foal: dam 2-y-o 6f winner, is out of Argentinian Oaks winner Surera: fair form: won apprentice maiden at Lingfield in May, running on well to lead final 1f: better at 1¼m than shorter: yet to race on a soft surface: sold only 5,800 gns Newmarket Autumn Sales. *S. Dow* — 75

DAYDREAMER (USA) 2 b.c. (Feb 26) Alleged (USA) 138 – Stardusk (USA) (Stage Door Johnny) [1995 7m Nov 3] $85,000Y: strong, lengthy colt: has scope: first reported foal: dam, winner at up to 13f in US, is sister to champion turf horse Johnny D: 12/1, never-dangerous tenth of 17 to Jackson Hill in maiden at Doncaster: had blanket for entry at stalls, where rather mulish: bred to require long distances: will do better. *J. H. M. Gosden* — – p

DAYDREAM ISLAND 2 ch.f. (Feb 14) Never So Bold 135 – La Belle Vie 73 (Indian King (USA) 128) [1995 6.1d 7.1s Oct 17] unfurnished filly: first foal: dam stayed 1m: well beaten in maidens at Nottingham and Chepstow. *R. J. Baker* — –

DAYSMAN (USA) 3 b.c. Dayjur (USA) 137 – Model Village 101 (Habitat 134) [1994 NR 1995 6g 6m^4 5m^3 7g Sep 7] small, attractive colt: poor mover: first foal: dam 7f and 1m winner: fair maiden: best effort (after 4-month absence) when fourth of 9 at Newmarket: pulls hard, and probably a sprinter: sent to Dubai. *B. W. Hills* — 76

DAYS OF THUNDER 7 ch.g. Vaigly Great 127 – Silent Prayer 58 (Queen's Hussar 124) [1994 46: 10m 8m^6 9.7m 8m 1995 a11g^4 a10g^5 Mar 31] sturdy gelding: poor maiden plater nowadays: stays 11f: has raced only on a sound surface: modest winning hurdler/chaser, and won celebrity flat race in November. *J. White* — –

DAYTIME DAWN (IRE) 4 b.g. Rashar (USA) – Ard Clos (Ardoon 124) [1994 NR 1995 6.9m^5 10m May 10] fourth foal: dam poor Irish maiden: no worthwhile form: sold 1,500 gns Doncaster July Sales. *D. Moffatt* — –

DAYTONA BEACH (IRE) 5 ch.g. Bluebird (USA) 125 – Water Spirit (USA) (Riverman (USA) 131) [1994 NR 1995 a8g^2 a8g* 9g* 8m 9.7m^3 a9.4g^2 8.3m^5 a8.5g^2 8m^4 10.3m^2 7.6m 7.1m Aug 30] strong gelding: fair handicapper: trained by M. Ahern on reappearance then by P. Burgoyne next 7 starts, winning at Southwell and Kempton (apprentices) in April: stays 9.7f: acts on firm ground and fibresand: tried visored/blinkered at 3 yrs, no improvement: races prominently: won maiden hurdle in October. *D. J. S. ffrench Davis* — 66

DAY TRIPPER 2 b.g. (May 10) Forzando 122 – Solo Vacation (Pas de Seul 133) [1995 6.1m 6f^4 6m 7.6m^6 Sep 5] 2,400Y: compact gelding: fourth foal: half-brother to 11.1f winner The Lone Dancer and a winner in Italy (both by Mashhor Dancer): dam granddaughter of 1000 Guineas and Oaks second Spree, family of Juliette Marny and Julio Mariner: improved form when sixth of 11 off very stiff mark in nursery at Lingfield final start: will stay 1m: has raced only on top-of-the-ground. *G. B. Balding* — 62

DAZZLE ME 3 ch.f. Kalaglow 132 – Defy Me 75 (Bustino 136) [1994 –: 8.1d 10g 1995 7g 7m 7.1m Jun 15] sparely-made filly: no worthwhile form. *R. J. Baker* — –

DAZZLER 3 ch.g. Zalazl (USA) 120 – Mrs Danvers 87 (Balidar 133) [1994 NR 1995 10m 8.3m 8.3m 10m 14g Oct 23] 2,000Y: good-bodied gelding: fifth reported foal: half-brother to an Italian sprint winner by Rich Charlie: dam, winner at 2 yrs, best at 5f: no worthwhile form. *Mark Campion* — –

DAZZLING STAR 2 gr.f. (Mar 6) Thatching 131 – Dazzlingly Radiant 81 (Try My Best (USA) 130) [1995 6g 6g Sep 16] quite good-topped filly: second foal: sister to 3-y-o Radiance: dam 6f winner: very burly on debut: around 7 lengths seventh of 10 to The Man in maiden at Catterick last time: will improve again. *R. Hannon* — 50 p

DEADLINE TIME (IRE) 2 b.c. (Feb 23) Fayruz 116 – Cut It Fine (USA) (Big Spruce (USA)) [1995 5m^4 6.1m^5 6m 6g^5 7s^3 8g* 7.3d^3 Oct 21] IR 9,000F, 16,000Y: angular colt: has a round action: fifth reported foal: half-brother to 1991 2-y-o 7f winner Specific (by King of Spain) and 1989 Irish 2-y-o 6f winner Close The Till (by — 77

Formidable): dam stayer: won 19-runner nursery at Warwick by 3 lengths: better suited by 7f/1m than less: acts on soft ground: visored last 2 starts. *M. H. Tompkins*

DEAKEN DANCER 2 b.f. (May 4) Rambo Dancer (CAN) 107 – Une Emigree (USA) (L'Emigrant (USA) 129) [1995 5d4 5.3m5 a7g Nov 10] 550Y: leggy, sparely-made filly: second reported foal: dam unraced: poor form in auction events in spring and seller (gave some trouble at stalls) in November: withdrawn lame at start Nov 30. *K. T. Ivory* 46

DEANO'S BEENO 3 b.g. Far North (CAN) 120 – Sans Dot 92 (Busted 134) [1994 78p: 8.1g2 7.9d3 10g* 1995 12m3 12.3m2 11.9m 11.9g5 10.3d 8.5s4 Sep 19] rangy gelding: good mover: fairly useful handicapper: below form after second 3-y-o start, twice in competitive events, twice over unsuitable trips: effective at 1½m, and will be very well suited by further: acts on good to firm ground, and seemed to act on dead at 2 yrs. *M. Johnston* 85

DEARDAW 3 b.f. Tina's Pet 121 – Faw (Absalom 128) [1994 42: 5.2s4 5d5 5m 5g4 5.1g 5d 5s 1995 a6g 5.1m3 6m 5m 5g Sep 29] workmanlike filly: poor maiden: best form at 5f: visored once (below form) as 2-y-o: often slowly away: most inconsistent. *M. D. I. Usher* 42 d

DEATH BY CHOCOLATE 3 b.g. Sayf El Arab (USA) 127 – Mia Fillia 65 (Formidable (USA) 125) [1994 NR 1995 a8g5 a7g3 a8g5 a10g a8g Jun 16] 2,000Y: first foal: dam, maiden, suited by 1¼m: poor maiden plater: sold out of Dr. J. Scargill's stable 500 gns Ascot April Sales after (visored, tailed off) fourth start. *A. L. Forbes* 47

DEAUVILLE DANCER (IRE) 3 ch.g. Al Hareb (USA) 123 – Bru Ri (FR) (Sir Gaylord) [1994 48: 6m 7s 1995 10f5 9m 10m Jun 13] lengthy, sparely-made gelding: modest maiden: sold out of M. Heaton-Ellis' stable 1,550 gns Doncaster March Sales: hung left all starts in 1995, virtually unrideable last 2: looks one to steer well clear of. *D. Nicholls* – §

DEBACLE (USA) 6 b.g. Raft (USA) 125 – Kuala (USA) (Hawaii) [1994 NR 1995 a16g6 a14.8g6 Mar 18] sturdy, attractive gelding: modest winning hurdler: well beaten for new stable on only runs since fair 4-y-o: dead. *B. J. McMath* –

DEB'S BALL 9 b.m. Glenstal (USA) 118 – De'b Old Fruit (Levmoss 133) [1994 50: a12g4 12d 12g4 15.8g 15d4 12m 12.1f2 12.1g 13.8g6 1995 13g 14.1m Jun 1] quite good-topped mare: poor handicapper: never able to challenge in 1995: should stay beyond 12.2f: probably acts on any ground: tried visored, no improvement: usually gives herself lot to do: sometimes flashes tail: inconsistent. *D. Moffatt* –

DEBUTANTE DAYS 3 ch.f. Dominion 123 – Doogali 93 (Doon 124) [1994 NR 1995 10m 10m3 10m2 10m* 10g5 10.5d* Oct 11] angular filly: fifth living foal: closely related to 1m winner Daring Dove (by Daring March) and half-sister to fairly useful stayer Mount Nelson (by Morston): dam won 9 times from 1m to 1¼m: fair form: won maiden at Nottingham in August and handicap at Haydock (led over 3f out and stayed on determinedly) in October: should stay 1½m: acts on good to firm and dead ground: may well be capable of better still: sold (A. Stewart to Miss H. Knight) 29,000 gns Newmarket December Sales. *A. C. Stewart* 72 p

DECEIT THE SECOND 3 ch.g. Bairn (USA) 126 – Bushti Music 63 (Bustino 136) [1994 –: 5g 6f 7m 8s 7s 1995 6m6 8.2m6 11.8g 9.7f 8m 10.8m* 10.1m3 10f a16g3 15.8g6 16.1g5 10.3m6 a12g3 16.4m5 Nov 6] sturdy gelding: good walker: modest handicapper: won seller at Warwick in July: effective at 1¼m, and stays 2m: acts on good to firm ground and all-weather, possibly not on firm: blinkered since fourth 3-y-o start: has joined P. Rodford. *G. Lewis* 48 a55

DECEIVE 3 b.f. Machiavellian (USA) 123 – Talon d'Aiguille (USA) (Big Spruce (USA)) [1994 83p: 6g* 1995 8d May 14] sturdy filly: on toes, looking really well, had a troubled run in Poule d'Essai des Pouliches at Longchamp for new stable, hitting the rail after about 2f, plenty to do straight and never able to challenge: withdrawn from Jersey Stakes June 21 after injury in pre-parade ring: looked sure to improve further. *Saeed bin Suroor* 100 p

DECIDED (CAN) 12 b.g. Affirmed (USA) – Expediency (USA) (Vaguely Noble 140) [1994 NR 1995 16.1g Oct 3] big, strong, good-topped gelding: unimpressive mover: rated 50 at 10 yrs: bandaged and burly, no promise on return to flat: stays 2m: acts on soft ground: wears a tongue strap: modest hurdler. *R. Lee* –

DECISION MAKER (IRE) 2 b.c. (Mar 14) Taufan (USA) 119 – Vain Deb 66 (Gay Fandango (USA) 132) [1995 6g 7f^4 7f 8g^2 8d^2 Sep 27] 20,000Y: useful-looking colt: has a round action: half-brother to several winners, including Wokingham winner Red Rosein and 7.1f and 1m winner Gustavia (both by Red Sunset): dam 1m to 9f winner, stayed 1¼m: fairly useful form: best efforts when second in nursery at Yarmouth and maiden at Salisbury last 2 starts: stays 1m. *R. Hannon* — 80

DECORATED HERO 3 b.g. Warning 136 – Bequeath (USA) (Lyphard (USA) 132) [1994 NR 1995 7f* 8m* 7.9m^3 7.3m^2 7d^2 9g 8.1s^2 Oct 17] 3,900F, IR 55,000Y: small, compact gelding: has a quick action: appears to have been freeze fired on both forelegs: second foal: half-brother to fair 6f (at 2 yrs) and 7f winner Beneficiary (by Jalmood), and brother to a 2-y-o winner in Germany in 1995: dam lightly-raced 9f winner in France: smart performer: won maiden at Lingfield in May and minor event at Doncaster in July: best efforts when second in 27-runner £52,900 handicap at Ascot (1¼ lengths behind Night Dance, making virtually all) and 6-runner minor event at Chepstow (led over 1f out, headed close home by Night City) in the autumn: best at up to around 1m: winner on firm ground, very best efforts on a soft surface. *J. H. M. Gosden* — 110

DEEDEEJAY 2 b.f. (Apr 12) Cigar 68 – Miss Patdonna 62 (Starch Reduced 112) [1995 6.9f^4 6m 6m 10d a5g Nov 11] second reported foal: sister to 3-y-o Havana Miss, 6.1f seller winner at 2 yrs: dam, winning 7f plater at 2 yrs, stayed 1m: little sign of ability, mostly in sellers: visored last 2 starts. *J. M. Bradley* — –

DEED OF LOVE (USA) 2 b.c. (Feb 7) Shadeed (USA) 135 – Widaad (USA) 109 (Mr Prospector (USA)) [1995 7.5m* 7m* 6m 7g^4 Sep 16] brother to fairly useful 1992 Irish 2-y-o 5f winner Tahdeed and half-brother to a winner in USA: dam won Queen Mary Stakes: successful in minor events at Leopardstown and the Curragh in July: much better effort afterwards when around 2¼ lengths fourth of 7 to Danehill Dancer in National Stakes at the Curragh: stays 7.5f: acts on good to firm ground: blinkered (always outpaced over 6f) third start. *J. S. Bolger, Ireland* — 108

DEE-LADY 3 b.f. Deploy 131 – Bermuda Lily 78 (Dunbeath (USA) 127) [1994 91: 5m^5 5v^2 5m^2 6m^3 5f* 8g 7m^5 1995 8g^4 9.9m^2 8g^6 10g^5 8m^5 8f^5 7g 10g 8m^4 8g^4 a10g^5 a8g^4 Nov 29] small, sturdy filly: fairly useful performer: stays 1¼m: probably acts on any going (shaped well though only modest form on heavy) on turf, well below form on equitrack. *W. G. M. Turner* — 93 d

DEEP DIVIDE 3 b.f. Nashwan (USA) 135 – Miss Fancy That (USA) 99 (The Minstrel (CAN) 135) [1994 74: 8.1g^3 8g 1995 10.3g 10.2m Jun 15] big, good-topped filly: well beaten since debut: should stay at least 1¼m. *E. A. L. Dunlop* — –

DEEPLY VALE (IRE) 4 b.g. Pennine Walk 120 – Late Evening (USA) (Riverman (USA) 131) [1994 78: 6.9v^3 7s^3 6.9s* 7m 7.1d 7g^2 7d^6 a7g 1995 7m 6f 7m 6g^6 7f 7d 7g^3 a6g^2 a6g^2 a7g^3 a7g Dec 18] strong, lengthy gelding: fair handicapper: effective at 6f and 7f: acts on soft ground and fibresand, well beaten on top-of-the-ground: usually races prominently. *G. L. Moore* — 69

DEERLET 4 br.f. Darshaan 133 – Roxy Hart (High Top 131) [1994 64: 12.3g^5 11.5g 14d^4 12g^3 12g^3 a14g 1995 14.9g 16.4g Jun 7] good-bodied filly: seemed of little account for new stable and sold 4,000 gns Newmarket Autumn Sales. *K. C. Bailey* — –

DEERLY 2 b.f. (Apr 20) Hadeer 118 – Grafitti Gal (USA) (Pronto) [1995 6g* 6g^3 6m^5 6m^4 7g^3 6m^3 6m 6.1m Oct 26] quite attractive filly: half-sister to several winners including German 9.5f winner Unbelievable (by Warning): dam, won at up to 11f in USA, daughter of Grafitti, one of best fillies of her generation: won seller at Leicester in May: best effort when just under length third of 18 to Golden Pond in nursery at Pontefract in October: probably stays 7f: has raced only on a sound surface. *D. Morris* — 66

DEEVEE 6 b.h. Hallgate 127 – Lady Woodpecker 61 (Tap On Wood 130) [1994 72: 10d 8.5m^5 8g* 8m 8m^2 8m^4 10g 8s 9g 8m^5 8d^4 1995 8m* 8m 8g^2 8f^6 8g^2 8.1m 8d Sep 24] close-coupled horse: carries condition: poor mover: fairly useful handicapper: won 25-runner race at Ascot in May and twice very good second at Newmarket in the summer: best at around 1m: acts on firm and dead ground, no form only start on soft: tends to hang: has run well when sweating: usually slowly away, and held up: inconsistent. *C. J. Benstead* — 80

Timeform Futurity, Pontefract—a game performance from Defined Feature to deny Laafee

DEFINED FEATURE (IRE) 2 ch.f. (May 14) Nabeel Dancer (USA) 120 – Meissarah (USA) (Silver Hawk (USA) 123) [1995 5.1m* 5.2m^2 6m* 6m* 6g^3 Sep 2] quite attractive filly: half-sister to several winners, including 1992 2-y-o 5f winner Minshaar (by Jalmood), 6f winner Agwa (by Local Suitor) and 4-y-o 1¼m winner Tadellal (by Glint of Gold): dam never ran: fairly useful filly: won median auction maiden at Chepstow, nursery at Yarmouth and minor event at Pontefract, all small-field contests in the summer: creditable third of 6 (beaten just over length) to Rambling Bear in listed race at Kempton final start: will be at least as effective at 7f as 6f: game and genuine. *M. R. Stoute* 91

DEFINITE ARTICLE 3 b.c. Indian Ridge 123 – Summer Fashion 84 (Moorestyle 137) [1994 97p: 8.5d* 7d* 1995 10g* 12m^2 10g^4 10m^4 Sep 9] 121

The full set of Irish classics still eludes trainer Dermot Weld; but only just. He won an Irish Two Thousand Guineas with Flash of Steel, One Thousands with Prince's Polly and Trusted Partner, an Irish Oaks with Blue Wind and two Irish St Legers with Vintage Crop. Just the Irish Derby to go, then. Theatrical went close for the stable in that race in 1985, looking to have a great chance when he took over from Mouktar early in the straight and fought off Damister, but falling to Law Society in the last hundred yards. Definite Article went closer ten years on, as close as could be. On this occasion hopes of victory were raised at a later stage of the race. Definite Article turned for home lying handy with half a dozen in front of him, some of them moving equally well if not better, and was switched outside to make his run. Ridden along, he made progress to challenge two furlongs out, edged into the lead under strong driving from Winged Love and Annus Mirabilis a furlong later, and from then on held the advantage by the skin of his teeth until Winged Love snatched the prize away in the last stride.

Definite Article started joint-second favourite with the winner behind Celtic Swing at the Curragh, despite doubts about his stamina. He was the only unbeaten horse in the field of thirteen, much less highly tried than the majority but progressing well. Two starts as a two-year-old had resulted in wins in a Galway maiden and the National Stakes at the Curragh, the second a narrow one from Manashar whom he outbattled. His one appearance as a three-year-old had come in a listed race over a mile and a quarter at the Curragh in late-May. The two-length second that day, the

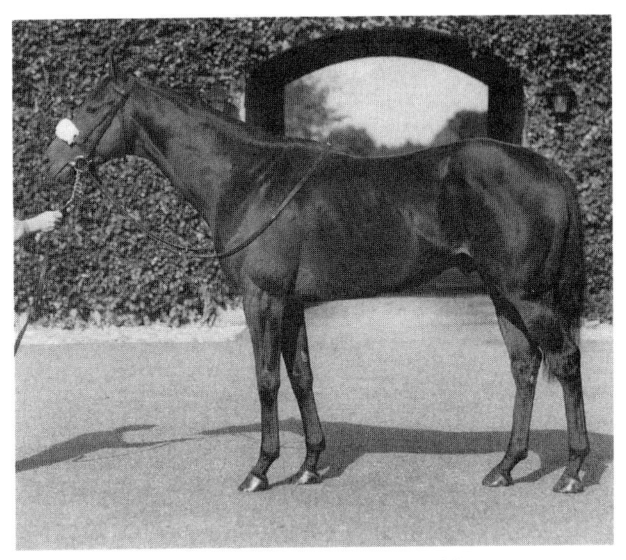

Moyglare Stud Farms Ltd's "Definite Article"

odds-on Shemaran, went on to win the Gallinule Stakes from Prince of Andros and to disappoint behind Darnay in the Sea World International before the Irish Derby came to be decided. Definite Article had a very hard race against Winged Love in the Irish Derby, possibly harder than he revealed to connections in the weeks afterwards, for when they brought him out again at the end of July in the ten-furlong Bayerisches Zuchtrennen at Munich he just wasn't himself. The trainer suspects that the very hot weather on the Continent got to the horse. Definite Article finished only fourth at Munich behind Germany, Kaldounevees and Tryphosa, three lengths behind the winner, and failed to see the race out as well as he had in the Irish Derby. Definite Article returned to form tried in blinkers in the Guinness Champion Stakes at Leopardstown in September on his only subsequent start. Whilst running well he gave the impression that he finds a mile and a quarter on the sharp side against the best. Having been held up in touch, he kept on without being able to quicken in the way that Pentire and Freedom Cry did, beaten two and a half lengths at the line and just kept out of third place by Flagbird.

Definite Article (b.c. 1992)	Indian Ridge (ch 1985)	Ahonoora (ch 1975)	Lorenzaccio
			Helen Nichols
		Hillbrow (ch 1975)	Swing Easy
			Golden City
	Summer Fashion (b 1985)	Moorestyle (b 1977)	Manade
			Guiding Star
		My Candy (b 1973)	Lorenzaccio
			Candy Gift

Definite Article is the first foal of his dam Summer Fashion, a top-of-the-ground mare who seemed barely to stay a mile and a quarter as a three-year-old but won four times over the trip later on and eventually got eleven and a half furlongs.

She was a fair handicapper and finished ninth of thirty-four in the Cambridgeshire in 1989. She and the useful middle-distance stayer Amelianne are the pick of numerous winners out of My Candy, a lightly-raced half-sister to Candy Cane, fourth in the Arc in 1969. For Definite Article to merit serious consideration for an Arc he needs to improve a little and show himself a lot better traveller. There seems no doubt he'll be given the opportunity to tackle a mile and a half again. A lengthy colt, Definite Article has yet to race on extremes of ground and hasn't raced on easier than good since he was a two-year-old; it rode good to firm in both the Irish Derby and the Leopardstown Champion Stakes. Although blinkers were tried on his on his final start he has looked nothing less than genuine in any of his races in Ireland. *D. K. Weld, Ireland*

DEGREE 2 b.f. (Feb 18) Warning 136 – Krill (Kris 135) [1995 7.5d² Sep 13] second living foal: half-sister to 3-y-o Questrill (by Rainbow Quest): dam, French 1¼m winner, out of half-sister to Robellino: 3/1, 1¼ lengths second of 12 to Wavey in maiden at Beverley, midfield after slow start then keeping on well after running green 2f out: sure to improve. *H. R. A. Cecil* — 81 p

DE LA BILLIERE (IRE) 7 b.h. King of Clubs 124 – Crazyfoot 76 (Luthier 126) [1994 NR 1995 9.7m Jul 12] tall, leggy horse: probably no longer of any account. *H. G. Rowsell* — –

DELAUNAY (IRE) 2 b.c. (Apr 29) Maelstrom Lake 118 – Artlesse (Ahonoora 122) [1995 5m⁵ 5g⁴ 6f 7m 6m³ 7.3d 6.9s 6.1s Oct 17] IR 7,500Y: leggy colt: second reported foal: brother to 3-y-o Just Dandy, 7f to 9f winner in Scandinavia: dam unraced: modest maiden: should stay beyond 6f: acts on good to firm ground (no form on a soft surface): blinkered final outing: inconsistent: sold to go to Sweden 5,600 gns Newmarket Autumn Sales. *R. Hannon* — 65

DEL DEYA (IRE) 5 br.m. Caerleon (USA) 132 – Point of Honour (Kris 135) [1994 117: 9d* 10g⁴ 10g* 10f² 10g² 10g⁴ 1995 10s² 9.3g May 28] big, plain mare: smart performer: 1½ lengths second of 10 to Flagbird in Premio Presidente della Repubblica at Rome: tailed-off last of 9 in Prix d'Ispahan at Longchamp (broke slowly, never got into race) later in May: effective at 9f and should have stayed beyond 1¼m: acted on firm ground and soft: sometimes edgy: usually raced prominently: genuine and consistent: stud. *J. H. M. Gosden* — 111

DELGARTH LADY 4 b.f. Scottish Reel 123 – Pastrana (King of Spain 121) [1994 –: 8g 8g 8.2s 1995 8.2g a9.4g⁵ a9.4g⁶ a7g⁵ a9.4g⁵ 11.9d Sep 26] leggy filly: poor maiden: stayed 9.4f: acted on fibresand: tried blinkered: inconsistent: dead. *J. L. Spearing* — 33

DELICIOUS 3 b.f. Dominion 123 – Confection (Formidable (USA) 125) [1994 –: 6m 7g 7d 1995 12f⁵ 12.1m³ 14d 14d⁵ Sep 27] leggy filly: poor maiden handicapper: stays 1¾m: acts on firm and dead ground: inconsistent. *Major D. N. Chappell* — 51

DELIFFIN 9 b.g. Wolverlife 115 – Teletype (Guillaume Tell (USA) 121) [1994 –: a16g 1995 a16g 14m Jul 15] seems no longer of much account. *R. M. Flower* — –

DELIGHTFUL DANCER (IRE) 3 b.g. Dancing Dissident (USA) 119 – Allberry (Alzao (USA) 117) [1994 65: 5m 5f⁵ 5g⁴ 7.5m 7.1d 7s⁴ 1995 8.2g⁶ 8m 6f⁵ 6m 7m 5.9h⁶ 8m⁶ 7.1g Sep 18] sturdy gelding: carries condition: modest maiden: sold out of B. Hills's stable 1,000 gns Newmarket July Sales after fifth start: seems to stay 1m: acts on firm and soft ground: tried blinkered and visored: sometimes pulls hard: most inconsistent, and one to be wary of. *J. Norton* — 56 d

DELIGHT OF DAWN 3 b.f. Never So Bold 135 – Vogos Angel 54 (Song 132) [1994 72: 6m 6m² 7g* 6m* 6m² 6m² 6g* 6.5g 7m 1995 6m 7f⁶ 8m 7.1m 7g² 7f⁶ 7m⁵ 7m* 7g* 7m* 7m⁴ 6g 6d³ 6m² 7m⁴ 7m⁵ Oct 20] angular filly: fair performer: won claimers at Newmarket (2) and Leicester in the summer: stays 7f: acts on firm ground and dead: tends to hang: usually bandaged: often slowly away, and held up. *K. T. Ivory* — 74

DELLA CASA (IRE) 2 ch.f. (Mar 20) Royal Academy (USA) 130 – Diamond Spring (USA) (Vaguely Noble 140) [1995 7m⁵ 7.1g 7f Oct 12] IR 26,000Y: angular, unfurnished filly: closely related to French middle-distance winner Didwana (by Nijinsky) and half-sister to several winners here and in France, including middle-distance performer Droiture (by Far North): dam French 1m winner from — 58 p family of Lyphard and Nobiliary: modest form in maidens, catching eye staying on under sympathetic handling when fifth to Mezzogiorno at Lingfield on debut and again when ninth of 12 to Green Charter at Redcar in October: will be well suited by 1m+: remains capable of better. *J. L. Dunlop*

DELLS DREAM (IRE) 2 b.f. (Apr 21) Classic Music (USA) – Jeewan 82 (Touching Wood (USA) 127) [1995 5.7h^5 7m^6 a6g Sep 14] third foal: half-sister to 3-y-o 7f to 1¼m winner Harry Browne (by Al Hareb) and 6f winner Bello Gallico (by Gallic League): dam 12.2f winner: no worthwhile form, including in sellers. *M. R. Channon* –

DELMOUR 4 b.g. Seymour Hicks (FR) 125 – Delbounty (Bounteous 125) [1994 –: 6m a12g 8.1m^5 1995 a9.4g 10m 8g 7.1m^6 7.6m 7m 8.1m Aug 11] small gelding: no form. *W. M. Brisbourne* –

DELPIOMBO 9 br.g. Lochnager 132 – Precious Petra 62 (Bing II) [1994 56: a8g^4 8g^5 a8g 10.3g^6 1995 8.5s Sep 19] strong gelding: probably no longer of much account. *M. R. Channon* –

DELROB 4 b.f. Reprimand 122 – Stoneydale 83 (Tickled Pink 114) [1994 48, a62: 5.1g^3 6d^6 a5g^2 a6g^3 a6g^3 6g^5 a5g* a5g* 5d a5g^6 a6g^5 1995 a5g^3 a5g^5 a6g a5g^4 a5g^3 a7g^3 a7g^5 5.1m* 5f^3 5m a5g a6g Dec 9] sparely-made filly: modest handicapper: dead-heated at Chepstow in July: very best form at up to 6f: acts on firm ground, goes well on fibresand, yet to race on equitrack: none too consistent. *D. Haydn Jones* 52 a62

DELTA ONE (IRE) 4 b.g. Danehill (USA) 126 – Seminar 113 (Don (ITY) 123) [1994 104: 7m^2 8m 7m 8f^4 8g^2 1995 a8g^4 a7g^4 a6g^2 a6g^5 a6g^4 7m^3 7g^5 7g Sep 29] smallish, sturdy gelding: useful performer: did not really take to racing in Dubai for D. Selvaratnam first 5 outings at 4 yrs: respectable efforts first 2 starts on return, but ran poorly (raced freely) last time: stays 1m well: acts on firm going, yet race on a soft surface: gelded: to be trained by U. Ostmann in Germany. *I. A. Balding* 98

DELTA SOLEIL (USA) 3 b.c. Riverman (USA) 131 – Sunny Roberta (USA) (Robellino (USA) 127) [1994 74p: 6m^4 6m^6 1995 7.9g* 10.1g 7g^4 8m^3 Oct 28] good-bodied colt: first run for over 12 months when making all in 5-runner maiden at York in August by 8 lengths: in frame in very competitive handicaps at Newmarket last 2 starts: best form at 7f and 1m (appeared not to stay 10.1f): yet to race on a soft surface: may well progress again at 4 yrs. *P. W. Harris* 96 p

DEMOKOS (FR) 10 ch.g. Dom Racine (FR) 121 – Eagletown (FR) (Dictus (FR) 126) [1994 34: 15.1f 12m^3 12f^5 12m^3 13.8g^6 14.1g 12.1m a16g 1995 12g 11.1m Jun 19] lengthy gelding: no longer of much account. *W. L. Barker* –

DEMURRER 5 b.g. Dominion 123 – Belle Enfant 87 (Beldale Flutter (USA) 130) [1994 –: 10.8m 12g 13.6g 1995 12.3d 10m^4 7.1m 8.1f^4 10m 9.2f Aug 14] tall, leggy gelding: poor maiden handicapper: probably stays 1¼m: acts on firm ground, best efforts on soft. *Mrs A. M. Naughton* 36

DENBRAE (IRE) 3 b.g. Sure Blade (USA) 130 – Fencing (Viking (USA)) [1994 66: 6m^3 a6g^4 6m^2 6g^4 1995 a6g* 6.1g* 6m^2 6m^4 6.1m^6 7g a6g 7.1d^5 Sep 13] lengthy gelding: fair performer: narrowly won maiden at Southwell in February and handicap at Nottingham in April: well below form last 4 starts: should stay 7f: acts on fibresand and good to firm ground. *D. J. G. Murray Smith* 73

DENEBOLA WAY (GR) 3 br.c. Wadood (USA) 97 – Northern Moon 76 (Ile de Bourbon (USA) 133) [1994 a5g a5g* a5g^2 a5g^2 a7g* a7g* a9g* 1995 a7g^2 a9g* 8m^5 Apr 20] leggy, close-coupled Greek-bred colt; dam, 11.5f winner, is half-sister to dam of useful French filly/US Grade 2 8.5f winner Guiza: competed in Greece on left-handed sand tracks, winning 5 of his 9 races, including that country's most prestigious race for juveniles and a Group 2 event in March: led for 6f and eased once beaten when around 13½ lengths last of 5 in Craven Stakes at Newmarket only start here: picked up a minor injury afterwards, and likely to be returned to Greece: stays 9f: difficult to assess, but probably no better than useful. *R. Charlton* ?

DENSBEN 11 b.g. Silly Prices 110 – Eliza de Rich 57 (Spanish Gold 101) [1994 68: 6m 6g^6 7.6m 6f^5 6f^3 6m^2 6f 6m^3 6f^4 6m^3 6.1g 6f^5 6m 6g 6d 7g^2 7d 8g 7s 1995 6v 6g 5.9m 5.9f^5 7g 6m^5 6.1m^2 6f^3 6m 7f 6m^6 6m^4 7m 6g* 6g* 7g 6d 5f^5 6m Oct 30] smallish, sparely-made gelding: modest handicapper: won twice at Haydock in September, ending long losing sequence in seller on first occasion: suited by 6f/7f: 59

acts on any going: below form when blinkered/visored: sometimes starts slowly, and is held up. *Denys Smith*

DENT'S DELIGHT (IRE) 3 b.f. Gallic League 119 – Sassalin (Sassafras (FR) 135) [1994 NR 1995 a8g Jan 2] IR 3,500Y: half-sister to 3 winners, including 1987 2-y-o 7f winner Lincroft Boy (by Crofter): dam won over 7.5f at 2 yrs in Ireland: tailed off in seller at Southwell. *D. W. Chapman* –

DEPRECIATE 2 ch.c. (Mar 2) Beveled (USA) – Shiny Penny 70 (Glint of Gold 128) [1995 6g* 6.1g* 6m^4 Aug 7] leggy colt: second reported live foal: dam, maiden, probably stayed 1¾m: won maiden at Goodwood in June and 5-runner minor event (made all, beat Amaniy head) at Chester in July: creditable fourth of 8 to Red Nymph in minor event at Windsor last time: stays 6f. *C. James* 84

DEPUTY TIM 12 ch.g. Crofter (USA) 124 – Kindle (Firestreak 125) [1994 46d: a9.4g^5 a9.4g 8.3v* 8.3d^3 10g 8m a8.5g 8d 1995 a9.4g a8.5g 8.3v^6 9.2s^6 Apr 12] neat gelding: probably no longer of much account. *R. Bastiman* –

DE QUEST 3 b.c. Rainbow Quest (USA) 134 – De Stael (USA) 93 (Nijinsky (CAN) 138) [1994 NR 1995 12v^2 12d^2 10.5g^2 12.5g* 12s* 12m* Oct 15] 120 p

Fabre's stable had another field-day at Longchamp on October 15th, winning all three pattern races on the card—the Grand Criterium with Loup Solitaire, the Prix de la Foret with Poplar Bluff and the Prix du Conseil de Paris with De Quest. The rapidly-improving De Quest was the easiest winner of the trio and looks a very good prospect for 1996. Making his first start in pattern company, he quickened through a gap a furlong and a half out and soon had the race in safe keeping. Neither Posidonas in fifth nor Capias in sixth ran up to his best but the form bears inspection. It is smart form to say the least. The two-length second Slicious, who couldn't land a blow, went on to win the Premio Roma back on home soil. The third horse Rainbow Dancer, a three-length fourth to Sunshack in the corresponding race in 1994, finished four lengths behind this time round, just pipping the Noailles winner Walk On Mix who was returning from a four-month break. De Quest has had little racing so far. He didn't run as a two-year-old. When he did move into action he was beaten into second place in three relatively minor events before he got off the mark, by two and a half lengths against useful animals, in a similar contest at Deauville in August. On his only other start before the Prix du Conseil de Paris he improved to win a seven-runner listed race at Maisons-Laffitte, the Prix Charles et Henry Rouher, by half a length from Homme d'Honneur.

De Quest is bred to make a four-year-old: all three of his dam's previous runners did well at that age, starting with De Quest's full brother Source of Light, the Bessborough winner of 1994 still going strong in the latest season. Next came the Fabre-trained colt Turners Hill (by Top Ville), a listed winner at both three and four and placed in better races, including a Prix du Conseil de Paris. And then the filly Wandesta (by Nashwan), one-time stable-companion of Source of Light. She has developed into a smart performer with Frankel in the United Stakes, and in 1995 won two Grade 1 Handicaps at Santa Anita—the Santa Barbara and the Santa Ana. Of the three horses, only Wandesta saw a racecourse as a two-year-old. In contrast the dam

Prix du Conseil de Paris, Longchamp—fast-improving De Quest beats Italian raider Slicious

De Stael was a two-year-old winner and a daughter of another, Peace. Peace won the Blue Seal Stakes at Ascot. She was an outstanding broodmare, the dam of ten winners, among them De Stael's brothers the good middle-distance colts Quiet Fling and Peacetime, the Cambridgeshire winner Intermission, the Bessborough winner Peaceful and the Prix Ganay runner-up Armistice Day.

De Quest (b.c. 1992)	Rainbow Quest (USA) (b 1981)	Blushing Groom (ch 1974)	Red God
			Runaway Bride
		I Will Follow (b 1975)	Herbager
			Where You Lead
	De Stael (USA) (ch 1983)	Nijinsky (b 1967)	Northern Dancer
			Flaming Page
		Peace (ch 1966)	Klairon
			Sun Rose

Source of Light, Turners Hill and Wandesta have all shown that they stay further than a mile and a half. Given the chance, De Quest will do likewise but the first priority will probably be to give him his chance in top class middle-distance company. He has a good turn of foot and will go furthest of Fabre's potentially star four-year-olds if he keeps on improving at such a rate for much longer! De Quest's best run came on good to firm ground; the best before that on soft. It's likely that he acts on any. *A. Fabre, France*

DEREK'S BO 2 b.f. (Apr 3) Rambo Dancer (CAN) 107 – Mother Hubbard (Mummy's Pet 125) [1995 5m a5g 6m^{5} 5.1m^{6} a6g 7.1s Nov 2] 1,100Y: compact filly: third foal: dam unraced: little worthwhile form. *N. Bycroft* –

DERISBAY (IRE) 7 b.g. Gorytus (USA) 132 – Current Bay (Tyrant (USA)) [1994 NR 1995 a11g Feb 3] probably no longer of much account on flat. *J. J. Bridger* –

DERNIER EMPEREUR (USA) 5 ch.h. Trempolino (USA) 135 – Dear Colleen (USA) (In Reality) [1994 125: 8m^{5} 9.3g^{5} 10g^{3} 10d* 10m* a10f 1995 8v 9.3g 10g* 10d^{2} a10f^{4} a9s Oct 28] big, good-topped horse: carries condition: impresses in appearance: has a round action: only a smart performer in 1995, and failed even to repeat the form shown when under 6 lengths seventh of 9 to Green Tune in Prix d'Ispahan at Longchamp in May: narrow winner of minor event at Vichy in August: 3 lengths second of 6 to Gunboat Diplomacy in La Coupe de Maisons-Laffitte in September: effective at 1¼m and 1½m: acts on any going on turf. *A. Fabre, France* 115

DERRICKS REFUSAL 4 b.c. Ring Bidder 88 – Hobournes Katie 39 (Starch Reduced 112) [1994 –: 7.1g a7g 8.1g 8.3m a12g 1995 a8g^{5} Jan 9] sturdy colt: no worthwhile form. *Capt. J. Wilson* –

DERRY QUEEN 3 b.f. Derrylin 115 – Emerin 85 (King Emperor (USA)) [1994 –: 5g 6m 6d 7m 1995 a5g^{6} a6g^{5} Feb 7] no worthwhile form: tried blinkered: dead. *P. D. Cundell* –

DESERT BELL (IRE) 2 b.c. (Apr 19) Green Desert (USA) 127 – Salabella 64 (Sallust 134) [1995 6m^{3} 6m^{4} 7g^{3} Sep 14] 86,000Y: small, close-coupled colt: half-brother to several winners at up to 1m, including useful pair Dedicated Lady (by Pennine Walk) and Silk Petal (by Petorius): dam (stayed 11f) half-sister to Irish St Leger winner M-Lolshan: fair form in maidens: below best final start: likely to prove best at up to 6f: sold 10,500 gns Newmarket Autumn Sales. *M. R. Stoute* 79

DESERT BOY (IRE) 2 br.c. (Mar 23) Green Desert (USA) 127 – City Fortress (Troy 137) [1995 6m* 6d^{6} Sep 16] good-bodied colt: fluent mover: fourth foal: half-brother to 3-y-o 1m winner Avignon (by Machiavellian) and very smart 1m (including at 2 yrs) to 1¼m performer Fastness (by Rousillon), Grade 1 9f winner in USA in 1995: dam French 1¼m and 12.5f winner: won 8-runner maiden at York by a short head from Leonine, disputing lead, quickening when pushed along 2f out then just holding on: heavily-backed co-favourite though sweating, tailed off in 6-runner Mill Reef Stakes at Newbury following month: will stay 7f: looked an interesting prospect at York and is well worth another chance. *P. W. Chapple-Hyam* 100 p

DESERT CAT (IRE) 2 b.c. (May 29) Green Desert (USA) 127 – Mahabba (USA) 74 (Elocutionist (USA)) [1995 7g^{5} 7.1s^{3} 8f^{4} Oct 24] strong, rangy colt: has plenty of scope: closely related to useful Irish 3-y-o 1m to 1¼m winner Radomsko and 1m (at 2 yrs) and 1¼m winner Convoy Point (both by Polish Precedent) and half-brother to several winners, including Italian Group 3 winner Ready To Dance 78 (by Wassl): dam 1½m winner: fair form in maidens: faded noticeably last 1f when fourth to Lady Carla at Leicester on final start: stays 1m, but may well prove best at up to 7f. *H. Thomson Jones*

DESERT COURIER 3 b.c. Green Desert (USA) 127 – Possessive (Posse (USA) 130) [1994 89p: 6s* 1995 7m² May 7] leggy colt: short to post, neck second of 7 to Peace Envoy in minor event at Newmarket, green then running on strongly from rear: would have improved further: dead. *M. R. Stoute* 100

DESERT FIGHTER 4 b.g. Green Desert (USA) 127 – Jungle Rose 90 (Shirley Heights 130) [1994 86: 8d 8m³ 9d⁴ a8g² 8m* 8g⁵ 10f* 10.5g* 10.4m⁶ 10d 1995 10m May 21] good-topped gelding: ran as though something amiss only start for new stable: better at around 1¼m than shorter: acts on firm ground: sold (D. Nicholson to Mrs M. Reveley) 9,000 gns Newmarket July Sales: winning hurdler but not one to trust. *D. Nicholson* –

DESERT FORCE (IRE) 6 b.g. Lomond (USA) 128 – St Padina 91 (St Paddy 133) [1994 43: 12.5d 14.1d 16.2m⁵ 1995 a16g a14g Aug 4] sturdy gelding: seems of little account on flat: fair winning hurdler at best: sold only 2,400 gns Newmarket Autumn Sales. *R. Harris* –

DESERT FROLIC (IRE) 2 b.f. (Apr 21) Persian Bold 123 – Try To Catch Me (USA) (Shareef Dancer (USA) 135) [1995 7g 7.1s⁴ Sep 30] second foal: half-sister to 1993 2-y-o 7f winner Nawafell (by Kris): dam, French miler, daughter of high-class American 6f to 1¼m winner It's In The Air: running-on 4½ lengths fourth of 7 to Classic Romance at Haydock: will stay 1¼m: slowly into stride on debut: will improve again. *M. Johnston* 62 p

DESERT GREEN (FR) 6 b.g. Green Desert (USA) 127 – Green Leaf (USA) 97 (Alydar (USA)) [1994 88: 6f⁴ 7f⁴ 6f 8m 8m* 8m² 7.9m⁴ 10s⁴ 9g 1995 7m 8m* 8.1m⁵ 8f³ 8f³ 7m⁵ 8d 8m² a9.4g Dec 2] rangy, attractive gelding: impresses in appearance: useful handicapper: won Jubilee Handicap at Kempton in May: third in Schweppes Golden Mile at Goodwood in July and ½-length second to Star of Zilzal in minor event at Bath in October: stays 1m well: acts on firm and dead ground, well beaten (in listed event over 9.4f) on fibresand: has run well when sweating: formerly looked highly strung, and goes well under tender handling: normally held up: consistent. *R. Hannon* 101

DESERT HARVEST 3 b.g. Green Desert (USA) 127 – Mill On The Floss 117 (Mill Reef (USA) 141) [1994 75p: 7d² 1995 8g⁶ 7.3m⁵ 7g 7m⁶ Aug 26] good-topped gelding: fair maiden handicapper at best: mulish at stalls and soon driven along final start: refused to enter stalls at Doncaster (blinkered) Sep 7: may do better over 1m+: temperamental, and one to treat with caution: sold (R. Charlton to C. Brooks) 13,000 gns Newmarket Autumn Sales. *R. Charlton* 76 §

DESERT INVADER (IRE) 4 br.g. Lead On Time (USA) 123 – Aljood 111 (Kris 135) [1994 88d: 6m⁵ 7f 8m a5g² 1995 a7g⁵ a8g⁶ a8g* a8g a7g³ 6d 7g 5m 6m a6g 6g⁴ 8m a6g* a6g⁶ 6g a7g⁴ a8.5g a6g³ a7g³ Dec 12] strong, lengthy gelding: good 57 a69

Winter Hill Stakes, Windsor—
Desert Shot, smart on his day, wins from Captain Horatius, Alriffa (right) and Salt Lake

Maktoum Al Maktoum's "Desert Shot"

mover: fair handicapper: won at Southwell in February and Wolverhampton in September: often pulls hard, and will prove best at up to 1m: acts on good to firm and soft ground and fibresand (below form on equitrack): tried blinkered, no improvement: not an easy ride: inconsistent. *D. W. Chapman*

DESERT LYNX (IRE) 2 b.f. (Mar 29) Green Desert (USA) 127 – Sweeping 104 (Indian King (USA) 128) [1995 6.1d^5 7d 6f Oct 23] 42,000F, 35,000Y: plain filly: third foal: half-sister to 3-y-o White Heat (by Last Tycoon): dam, 2-y-o 6f winner, is out of half-sister to Bassenthwaite, a good family: modest form in maiden at Nottingham (fifth of 23 to Thracian) on debut: poor effort on firm ground final start: stays 6f. *T. R. Watson* 65

DESERT POWER 6 b.g. Green Desert (USA) 127 – Rivers Maid 83 (Rarity 129) [1994 70: 11.7m^5 9s^6 8m 10.2m* 10.3g 1995 10.3m 10g 12.1g^4 10f 10.2m* 8g 9.9m^3 a9.4g Dec 9] smallish, good-bodied gelding: fair handicapper: trained first 3 starts at 6 yrs by Martyn Meade: won 3-finisher contest at Chepstow in July: stays 11.7f: acts on firm and heavy ground, finished last on fibresand. *D. Burchell* 67

DESERT PRESIDENT 4 ch.g. Polish Precedent (USA) 131 – Majestic Kahala (USA) (Majestic Prince) [1994 –: 10d 10.3f 10g 9s 11.8g 16.4s^3 1995 a16g^4 a12g^5 a16.2g May 22] heavy-topped gelding: carries plenty of condition: only poor at best nowadays: probably stays 2m: blinkered (set strong pace, weakened tamely) second 3-y-o start. *R. P. C. Hoad* 36

DESERT SHOT 5 b.g. Green Desert (USA) 127 – Out of Shot 116§ (Shirley Heights 130) [1994 110: 8m^3 7d 7.1g^2 7.1g^6 8.1m^4 8m* 10m* 10d^4 9m* 10g^3 1995 116

9m* 10m^5 10g 10m* 11.1g^6 Sep 2] close-coupled gelding: quite often sweating and unimpressive in appearance: has a fluent action: smart performer: won strongly-run races for Earl of Sefton Stakes at Newmarket (by a head, clear, from Overbury, nosing ahead inside last and holding on gamely) in April and Winter Hill Stakes at Windsor (by 1½ lengths from Captain Horatius) in August: ran poorly on other starts: should stay 11f: acts on dead going, very best form on a sound surface: visored (raced freely, ran creditably) third 4-y-o start: held up and has turn of foot. *M. R. Stoute*

DESERT SPRING 3 b.c. Green Desert (USA) 127 – Little Loch Broom 60 (Reform 132) [1994 –p: 7g 1995 10m^5 9m May 21] tall colt: has scope: fair form in maidens, considerately handled at Ripon last time: shapes as though he'll stay beyond 1¼m. *P. W. Harris* 69

DESERT STYLE (IRE) 3 b.c. Green Desert (USA) 127 – Organza 105 (High Top 131) [1994 96: 6v* 6m* 6g^3 7d^3 7s^2 1995 7d* 6m^2 7g* 6m* 6d 7f^2 Dec 10] 121

The best wasn't seen of the Irish colt Desert Style on his only appearance in Britain in the Diadem Stakes at Ascot in September. It's not that he couldn't travel. On his only subsequent outing he had the first three in the Diadem behind as he ran a fine race to be second in the Hong Kong International Bowl at Sha Tin, headed on the line by the Australian challenger Monopolize. The dead ground looked a possible excuse for Desert Style's somewhat disappointing seventh to Cool Jazz at Ascot, but he was blinkered for the first time at Sha Tin—where the ground was firm. Desert Style was no stranger to close finishes. He was involved in one in each of his first three races of the season in Ireland, coming out on top in two, the Lexus Tetrarch Stakes at the Curragh and the Ballycorus Stakes at Leopardstown. He beat Mistle Cat, The Puzzler and Nijo at Leopardstown but far and away his best performance at

Maktoum Al Maktoum's "Desert Style"

home came next time, when he won the Phoenix Sprint at Leopardstown pushed out by two and a half lengths and one and a half from the fillies Petite Fantasy and Cheyenne Spirit. On that run he seemed to have an excellent chance in the Diadem.

Desert Style (IRE) (b.c. 1992)	Green Desert (USA) (b 1983)	Danzig (b 1977)	Northern Dancer
			Pas de Nom
		Foreign Courier (b 1979)	Sir Ivor
			Courtly Dee
	Organza (b 1985)	High Top (b 1969)	Derring-Do
			Camanae
		Canton Silk (gr 1970)	Runnymede
			Clouded Lamp

Desert Style, a smallish, strong colt, has been retired to the Corbally Stud, co. Kildare, at a fee of IR £3,000 (October 1st). He was as effective at six furlongs as at seven. His dam the useful Organza, whose first foal he is, stayed a mile and a quarter and is a half-sister to Barathea's dam Brocade. Organza and Brocade are two of eight winners from nine runners out of the sprinter Canton Silk. We mentioned the ground at Ascot because although Desert Style won on heavy and ran well on soft as a two-year-old, and won on dead first time up as a three-year-old, he had left that form well behind since. The ground was good to firm for the Phoenix Sprint. *J. S. Bolger, Ireland*

DESERT TIGER 2 br.f. (Apr 19) Green Desert (USA) 127 – Desert Bride (USA) (Key To The Kingdom (USA)) [1995 5m^3 5g* 5m^2 5m* 6m* 6.5m^2 Sep 6] smallish, lengthy filly: first foal: dam, 7f winner at 2 yrs in France, sister to Ma Biche: won maiden at Haydock in May, and nurseries at Hamilton in July and Pontefract (by 1¼ lengths from Albert The Bear, rearing leaving stalls) in August: good second of 17 to My Branch in nursery at Doncaster on final outing, ducking left then right: stays 6.5f: highly-strung sort who usually gives trouble in preliminaries: remains open to improvement. *M. Johnston* **90 p**

DESERT TIME 5 b. or br.g. Green Desert (USA) 127 – Supper Time 71 (Shantung 132) [1994 75+: 7.1f^3 7m^5 6m* 6m 7f* 1995 8m 7.3g^6 8g* 8m 8f^5 8.1m^3 7f^5 8g 8d Sep 16] sturdy gelding: good mover: fairly useful handicapper: won at **80**

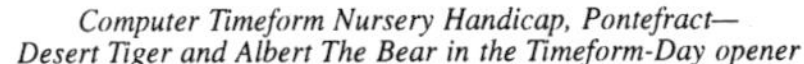
Computer Timeform Nursery Handicap, Pontefract—
Desert Tiger and Albert The Bear in the Timeform-Day opener

Goodwood in June then left C. Horgan after disappointing next 2 starts: effective at 6f to 1m: acts on firm ground (ran badly on dead): usually bandaged behind: carries head high: needs holding up: inconsistent. *M. R. Channon*

DESERT WATER (IRE) 3 b.g. Green Desert (USA) 127 – Ozone Friendly (USA) 107 (Green Forest (USA) 134) [1994 NR 1995 6d 7g 7m a7g a8g^{3} a8g a7g^{5} Dec 19] sturdy gelding: first foal: dam won Prix Robert-Papin: modest maiden: stays 1m: acts on equitrack: tried blinkered: inconsistent. *J. J. Bridger* 47

DESERT ZONE (USA) 6 ch.g. Affirmed (USA) – Deloram (CAN) (Lord Durham (CAN)) [1994 –: 8g^{6} 8m 8f 1995 8f^{5} 8.5m^{5} 8m 8g^{6} Jun 3] rangy gelding: only modest form at best in handicaps since 4 yrs: stays 1¼m, may have needed race when tried at 1½m: acts on good to firm ground, dead and fibresand. *J. L. Harris* 57

DESIDERA (IRE) 3 b.f. Shaadi (USA) 126 – Diasprina (GER) (Aspros (GER)) [1994 106: 5v^{3} 5g* 6g^{2} 8v^{5} 5.5s^{4} 1995 8g 7d* 6m^{2} 6.5m* 6d 5s Sep 30] useful German filly: easy winner of listed race at Dusseldorf in June and landed 11-runner Group 3 event at Hoppegarten in August by ½ length from Siberian Grey: no form on last 2 starts: stays 7f: acts on good to firm and dead ground, below form on very soft. *H. Blume, Germany* 102

DESIDERATA 4 b.c. Green Desert (USA) 127 – Yldizlar 77 (Star Appeal 133) [1994 –: 7d 7f^{4} 8.3m 1995 9.7d 8g^{4} 7m a7g Jun 2] modest maiden handicapper: will stay beyond 1m: inconsistent: sold 3,500 gns Newmarket July Sales. *B. W. Hills* 55

DETACHMENT (USA) 2 b.c. (Apr 27) Night Shift (USA) – Mumble Peg (General Assembly (USA)) [1995 7.1g^{2} 7f^{2} 7g^{3} Jul 16] well-made colt: sixth foal: half-brother to several winners here and abroad, including Irish 11f winner My Kerry Dancer (by Seattle Dancer) and fair 1¼m winner Halley (by Star de Naskra): dam unraced half-sister to high-class Little Bonny and smart Noelino: second to More Royal in 4-runner £8,200 event at Salisbury: long odds on, modest third in maiden at Salisbury on final outing: will stay 1m. *P. W. Chapple-Hyam* 89

DE-VEERS CURRIE (IRE) 3 b.f. Glenstal (USA) 118 – Regent Star (Prince Regent (FR) 129) [1994 –: 6g 1995 10f^{4} Jun 21] signs of a little ability in maidens. *R. F. Fisher* –

DEVILRY 5 b.g. Faustus (USA) 118 – Ancestry (Persepolis (FR) 127) [1994 NR 1995 12.1s^{4} Apr 12] good-topped gelding: has a round action: fair handicapper (rated 77) at best at 3 yrs for G. Lewis: well beaten on return: effective at 1¼m and 1½m: acts on good to firm and dead ground: blinkered last 3 starts at 3 yrs: won over hurdles in November, downed tools next time. *G. M. Moore* –

DEVON PEASANT 3 b.f. Deploy 131 – Serration (Kris 135) [1994 NR 1995 10g^{6} 10m 10g^{2} 10d^{2} Oct 19] 3,400Y: stocky filly: third live foal: half-sister to 1992 7.6f and 8.5f winner The Seer (by Robellino): dam lightly-raced maiden, fourth at 9f in France: fair form when second in maidens at Goodwood and Newbury: will stay beyond 1¼m. *L. G. Cottrell* 74

DEYNAWARI (IRE) 2 b.c. (Feb 12) Doyoun 124 – Denizliya (IRE) (Sadler's Wells (USA) 132) [1995 8g^{4} 8m* 9d* Nov 12] first foal: dam French 1½m winner: progressive Irish colt: won maiden at Navan and 17-runner listed race at Leopardstown (beat Ceirseach by 3 lengths) in the autumn: will stay beyond 9f: acts on good to firm and dead: should improve further. *J. Oxx, Ireland* 103 p

DHES-C 2 b.f. (May 12) Lochnager 132 – Keep Cool (FR) 42 (Northern Treat (USA)) [1995 a8.5g Dec 9] fourth reported foal: sister to 3-y-o Lawnswood Lady and half-sister to 4-y-o Rankaidade (by Governor General), 5f winner at 2 yrs: dam best at 1m/9f: 14/1 and ridden by 7-lb claimer, well beaten in 13-runner maiden at Wolverhampton. *R. Hollinshead* –

DHULIKHEL 2 b.f. (Mar 3) Reprimand 122 – Travel Storm 77 (Lord Gayle (USA) 124) [1995 a6g^{5} a5g^{5} 7f^{4} a6g^{3} 7f* 7g 7g a7g Dec 12] 4,300F, 750Y: third foal: sister to 3-y-o 7f and 1¼m winner Rushen Raider: dam 1¼m winner: plater: won at Brighton in August: gambled on when well beaten in non-selling nursery final start: better suited by 7f than less: acts on firm ground. *D. Marks* 54 a43

DIA GEORGY 4 b.c. Reesh 117 – Carpadia (Icecapade (USA)) [1994 58: 7.1g 10m^{4} 8.2g^{2} 10.1m 7m^{2} 8m* 8.5m 6.9f^{4} 7.6v* 8g 8.2g 1995 6.9d 8m 8m^{6} 7g a10g^{2} a8.5g* a9.4g* a8.5g 9.7g^{3} 10g a9.4g^{4} a10g^{2} a9.4g a8g a10g a10g^{5} Dec 18] leggy colt: modest handicapper: won twice at Wolverhampton in June: left R. Guest's 49 a58 stable after twelfth start: stays 1¼m: acts on any turf going, goes well on the all-weather: tail swisher: inconsistent. *Mrs N. Macauley*

DIAGHILEF (IRE) 3 b.c. Royal Academy (USA) 130 – Miss Audimar (USA) (Mr Leader (USA)) [1994 93: 6g^2 7g^2 7g^5 7.1d^3 1995 10.1g* 10.1f^4 12m* 11.9m^2 13.9m^5 Aug 16] tall, good-topped colt: good mover: progressed into a smart performer: won maiden at Newcastle in May and King George V Stakes (under top weight, producing storming run to lead close home) at Royal Ascot: neck second to Lombardic in Old Newton Cup at Haydock and excellent fifth of 21 (not getting best of runs then staying on strongly) to Sanmartino in the Ebor at York: very useful at 1½m and even better form at 1¾m: acts on good to firm ground, disappointing on dead: looked worth a place in pattern races, but not seen out again. *M. Johnston* 115

DIAMOND BANGLE 3 b.f. Chilibang 120 – My Diamond Ring 65 (Sparkling Boy 110) [1994 –: 5g 7.1g 6d 1995 a6g a8g a5g^6 Nov 30] smallish, lengthy filly: no worthwhile form. *C. C. Elsey* –

DIAMOND BEACH 2 b.c. (Apr 17) Lugana Beach 116 – Cannon Boy (USA) (Canonero II (USA)) [1995 6m 6d^5 7d^2 6f Oct 24] tall, quite attractive colt: good mover: half-brother to several winners, including 6-y-o 6f and 7f winner Maple Bay (by Bold Arrangement) and 7f winner Tender Moment (by Caerleon): dam won 9 races in USA, including Grade 3 9f event: fair maiden: best effort when 4 lengths second to Insatiable at Newcastle on penultimate start: odds on for median auction event at Leicester final start, lost all chance by stumbling badly early on: stays 7f. *B. W. Hills* 78

DIAMOND CROWN (IRE) 4 ch.g. Kris 135 – State Treasure (USA) (Secretariat (USA)) [1994 49: 8.3f 7.1f^6 8.2m^2 8f 9g 10g^3 10m* a12g 1995 10f 11.1g 10m^2 10g^3 10m 11.1m^6 12m* 12h^2 18m^3 12.1g 10.8g 13.8f^4 Oct 14] leggy gelding: modest handicapper: won seller at Beverley in August: stays at least 13.8f (creditable effort over 2¼m came in very slowly-run race): acts on firm ground, tailed off on fibresand and yet to encounter a soft surface: held up: hung left (demoted from third) final 4-y-o start: inconsistent. *Martyn Wane* 50

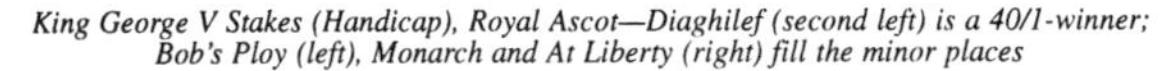
King George V Stakes (Handicap), Royal Ascot—Diaghilef (second left) is a 40/1-winner; Bob's Ploy (left), Monarch and At Liberty (right) fill the minor places

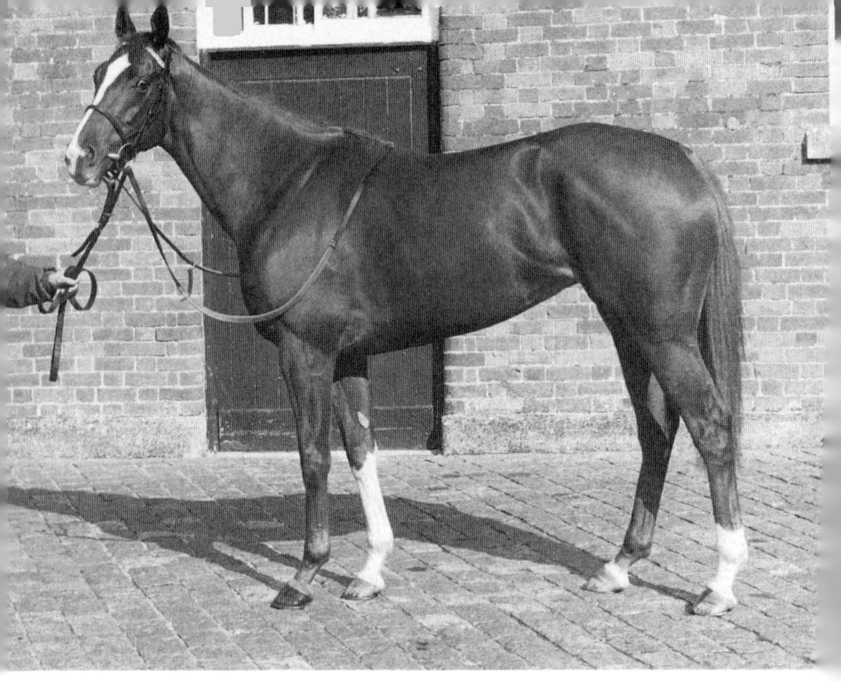

Mr K. Abdulla's "Didina"

DIAMOND CROWN (USA) 3 b.g. Gone West (USA) – Elegant Champagne (USA) (Alleged (USA) 138) [1994 NR 1995 $8m^5$ $8g^3$ Jun 3] $89,000F, $180,000Y: leggy, quite attractive gelding: first foal: dam, winner twice in USA, half-sister to high-class 1989 American 2-y-o Grand Canyon: fair form in maidens at Thirsk and Ayr: pulled hard at Ayr, and may prove best at up to 1m: joined E. Dunlop. *B. Hanbury* 66

DIAMOND HEART 2 b.f. (Apr 18) Generous (IRE) 139 – Chellita (Habitat 134) [1995 7m Aug 25] close-coupled, quite attractive filly: half-sister to several winners, including 13.4f-winner Star Master (by Rainbow Quest) and smart Tessla (by Glint of Gold), 7f and 1m winner at 2 yrs who stayed 10.5f: dam ran once: 16/1, well behind in 18-runner maiden at Newmarket: moved fluently down: sold 11,000 gns Newmarket December Sales. *H. R. A. Cecil* –

DIAMOND MARKET 3 gr.c. Absalom 128 – The Victor Girls (Crofthall 110) [1994 –: 6m 8.1g 7m 1995 $8.5d^6$ 8m $8m^4$ $a7g^2$ $a12g^4$ $9.9m^5$ $8.1s^6$ $a8.5g^2$ a11g $a8.5g^3$ Nov 13] tall, good-topped colt: modest maiden at best: stays 8.5f: acts on fibresand and good to firm ground: inconsistent. *R. Hollinshead* 50

DIAMOND MIX (IRE) 3 gr.c. Linamix (FR) 127 – Diamond Seal 93 (Persian Bold 123) [1994 107p: 8v* $8v^3$ 1995 10.5s* 10.5d* $12g^6$ $10m^3$ Jun 25] smallish, close-coupled colt: very smart performer: won listed race and 7-runner Prix Greffulhe (came away impressively in final 1f to beat Angel Falls by 5 lengths), both at Longchamp in April: unsuited by trying to come from last of 11 turning for home in steadily-run Prix du Jockey-Club at Chantilly: best effort when ¾-length third of 10 to Valanour in Grand Prix de Paris at Longchamp (always prominent) later in June: stays 1½m: acts on good to firm ground and heavy. *A. Fabre, France* 120

DIASAFINA 2 b.f. (Mar 28) Safawan 118 – Diana Dee 74 (Blakeney 126) [1995 7g a7g Nov 16] second foal: half-sister to a 1994 2-y-o 6f winner in Germany by Teenoso: dam stayed 1½m: well beaten in maiden and seller. *S. C. Williams* –

DICENTRA 2 b.f. (May 6) Rambo Dancer (CAN) 107 – Be Noble (Vaguely Noble 140) [1995 a6g a8.5g Dec 2] half-sister to several winners here and abroad: dam pulled up only start, is out of high-class 1958 2-y-o Be Careful: always behind in maidens at Southwell and Wolverhampton. *E. Weymes* –

DICK CHRISTIAN 3 ch.g. Nicholas Bill 125 – Carolynchristensen 58 (Sweet Revenge 129) [1994 NR 1995 10.2m 10g 12g 10.8f Aug 28] workmanlike gelding: fifth foal: half-brother to 2 winners, including fairly useful sprinter Maid Welcome (by Mummy's Pet): dam won from 5f to 9.4f: no sign of ability: tried blinkered: sold 3,000 gns Newmarket Autumn Sales. *B. J. Meehan* –

DICTATION (USA) 3 b.c. Dayjur (USA) 137 – Mofida 115 (Right Tack 131) [1994 NR 1995 6m^{4} 6m^{2} 7m^{3} 6f^{5} Oct 3] good-quartered colt: half-brother to several winners, including smart miler Zaizafon (by The Minstrel), dam of Zafonic: dam, very tough winner at up to 7f, grandam of Elmaamul: favourite in maidens on all 4 starts, neck second of 9 to My Cadeaux at Newmarket: well below that form in similar events at Chester and Redcar: likely to prove best at sprint distances: needs treating with some caution: sold 19,000 gns Newmarket Autumn Sales. *R. Charlton* 79

DIDINA 3 ch.f. Nashwan (USA) 135 – Didicoy (USA) 104 (Danzig (USA)) [1994 96p: 6m^{3} 6s^{2} 6d* 1995 7.1m* 7m* 7g^{3} 8.5f* 8.5s* Dec 24] good-quartered, attractive filly: smart performer, lightly raced: won 2-runner minor event at Haydock (easily) and 11-runner listed race at York (travelled well, quickened, beat Foxhound 2½ lengths) within 6 days in August: very good third of 12 to Branston Abby in listed race at Doncaster on final outing for R. Charlton: racing on lasix, won allowance race and Grade 2 event at Hollywood Park late in year: stays 8.5f: acts on firm and soft ground. *R. Frankel, USA* 111

DIEBIEDALE 3 b.f. Dominion 123 – Welwyn 92 (Welsh Saint 126) [1994 47: 6m 5.2m 1995 5g^{5} 5m^{4} 6g^{2} 5m 6.1d Sep 19] workmanlike filly: modest maiden: soundly beaten last 2 starts: stays 6f: acts on good to firm ground. *R. Boss* 58

DIEGO 2 b.c. (May 8) Belmez (USA) 131 – True Queen (USA) 79 (Silver Hawk (USA) 123) [1995 7f^{6} 9m^{3} 8.1d^{3} 10g^{4} Oct 9] 9,800Y: small, rather leggy colt: third foal: dam 1¼m winner who probably stayed 11.5f: fairly useful form: third to Inchrory in minor event at Sandown on penultimate start: only fourth of 9 to Flyfisher in minor event at Leicester month later: will stay well: best form on a soft surface. *C. E. Brittain* 89

DIET 9 b.g. Starch Reduced 112 – Highland Rossie 67 (Pablond 93) [1994 66d: 7.1g^{4} 6d^{4} 5g^{4} 5m 7.1f^{3} 6m^{6} 6g^{5} 6g^{4} 6g^{6} 6g^{3} 5m^{3} 6d^{5} 6m 5s^{5} 6g 7g^{5} 1995 6v 6g 5m 5g* 5g 6g 5g^{4} 6f^{4} 5f^{5} 5f^{2} 7.1m^{2} 6f^{2} 7.1f* 6m^{2} 6g 6f* 6m^{5} 6f^{2} 6m 5g 6g 6m 8.1s Nov 2] sturdy, good-quartered gelding: carries condition: modest handicapper: in fine form for most of year, winning at Hamilton (amateurs) in May, Edinburgh (claimer) in July and back at Hamilton (eighth course win) in August: effective at 5f to 7f: acts on any going: blinkered earlier in career, usually visored nowadays: sometimes hangs under pressure, but suitable mount for inexperienced rider: races prominently: tough. *Miss L. A. Perratt* 58

DIFFERENT TIMES (IRE) 5 b.g. Cyrano de Bergerac 120 – Centre Travel (Godswalk (USA) 130) [1994 58: a8g a8.5g a7g^{4} a7g^{3} a8.5g^{4} 8s^{2} 7.1g 7m* 8s 6.9f^{6} 7m^{2} 7f 7m 7g* 8m^{3} 8.3g^{6} 7m 7.9m 7g 8.5g 7g 7d 7d* 1995 7g Apr 21] tall, leggy gelding: modest handicapper in 1994: well below form only 5-y-o start: effective at 7f, and appeared to stay 1½m at 3 yrs: acts on good to firm ground, heavy and fibresand: effective with blinkers/visor (didn't wear either after tenth start in 1994): none too reliable. *Miss L. C. Siddall* –

DIFFIDENT (FR) 3 b.c. Nureyev (USA) 131 – Shy Princess (USA) 117 (Irish River (FR) 131) [1994 109p: 6m* 6s* 1995 7m* 8m^{6} 5g^{2} 6g* 6.5g^{4} Aug 6] 119

While the Free Handicap, latterly the European Free Handicap, has remained a feature of the Newmarket Craven meeting and was won by the subsequent Two Thousand Guineas winner Mystiko as recently as 1991, the Craven Stakes itself and the Nell Gwyn Stakes are usually much more significant classic trials nowadays. However, the general view after the latest meeting had ended seemed to be that if any

European Free Handicap, Newmarket—Diffident (right) sweeps past Harayir

future Guineas winners had been on show then they were most likely to have been seen in the Free Handicap. The hot favourite Diffident produced a spectacular turn of foot in that to snatch victory by just over a length from Harayir who finished clear of the others in a truly-run affair. The race as usual brought together horses representing a variety of the two-year-old pattern-race form lines. Diffident had won both his starts in France, including in a listed event at Evry; Harayir, top weight conceding Diffident 2lb, had won the Lowther Stakes at York.

Harayir went on to enjoy much the better season. Diffident, at least considering the impression he had made, was disappointing. He was put back to sprinting after finishing eight lengths sixth of eleven behind his shorter-priced stable-companion Pennekamp in the Guineas and made only three more appearances. He was beaten a nose by Millyant, just failing to get up, in the Prix du Gros-Chene at Chantilly in June; he won a four-runner race for the Prix de Ris-Orangis at Evry in July, starting at 2/1 on; the following month he finished fourth behind Cherokee Rose, Young Ern and Wessam Prince in the Prix Maurice de Gheest at Deauville, just under four lengths down on the winner, being unable to sustain a run from the back of the field. Diffident moved so badly to post for the Guineas that it was no great surprise his turn of foot failed to materialize, but he is probably not a miler. On results, he is not quite a top-class sprinter either. Some have been tempted to speculate that he would be a better horse back on soft going. That ignores the fact that the going was on the firm side of good both times he ran at Newmarket, not just for the Guineas.

The small, attractive Diffident is the third foal of his dam and is half-brother to two winners in France by Groom Dancer. The two won over a mile at Saint-Cloud as three-year-olds. The dam's fourth foal, Reticent (by Sadler's Wells), is in training with John Gosden. On her one attempt at a mile the dam Shy Princess came up against Miesque and Milligram in the Prix Marcel Boussac, and, in seventh, did well to limit the margin of defeat to four lengths. She won over six and seven furlongs and

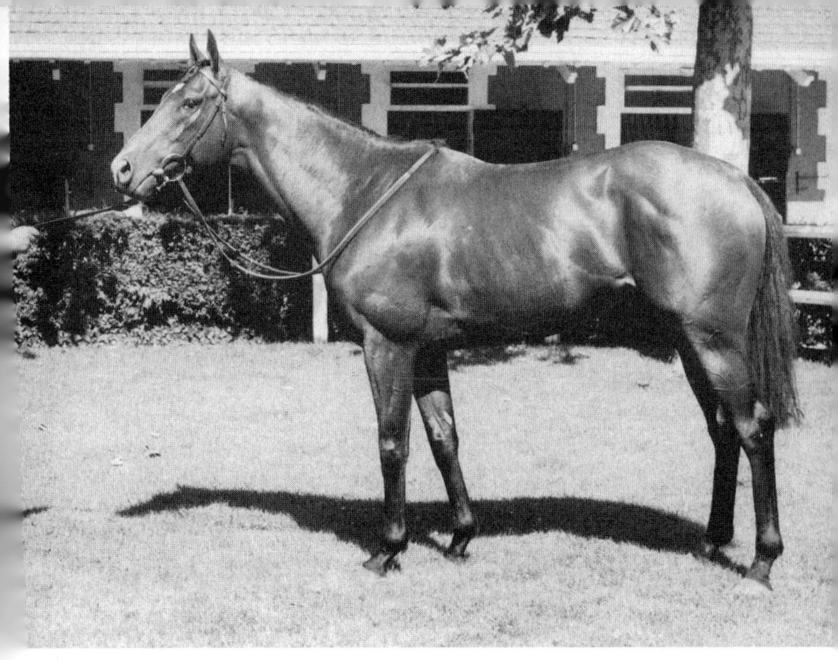

Sheikh Mohammed's "Diffident"

Diffident (FR) (b.c. 1992)	Nureyev (USA) (b 1977)	Northern Dancer (b 1961)	Nearctic
			Natalma
		Special (b 1969)	Forli
			Thong
	Shy Princess (USA) (ch 1984)	Irish River (ch 1976)	Riverman
			Irish Star
		Shy Dawn (ch 1971)	Grey Dawn II
			Shy Dancer

showed smart form in defeat in sprints, notably when second in the Prix Morny and third in the Prix de Meautry. The family hardly needs any introduction. Shy Princess' half-brother the ex-Newmarket colt Opening Verse hit the headines in 1991 by winning the Breeders' Cup Mile. Their dam Shy Dawn won nineteen of her ninety-five races over five seasons in the States, six of them Grade 3 Handicaps. Her dam's chief feat was to produce sixteen living foals of whom sixteen ran and fourteen won. Diffident was sent to Dubai for the winter and has joined the Godolphin team. *A. Fabre, France*

DIGPAST (IRE) 5 ch.g. Digamist (USA) 110 – Starlit Way 92 (Pall Mall 132) [1994 56: 8d 8g^5 8g 8f 8.3f 7m 6m^2 6m 7v a7g a7g^2 a8g^6 a7g^3 a7g* 1995 a7g^2 a7g^6 a7g^3 a7g* a7g^2 a7g* a8g^3 8.3m 7f a8g^5 a8g a7g Dec 18] lengthy, workmanlike gelding: fair handicapper: won at Lingfield in February and March: best efforts at 7f: acts on any turf going, goes very well on equitrack: usually blinkered nowadays. *R. J. O'Sullivan* – a73

DIGWANA (IRE) 2 b.g. (Apr 2) Digamist (USA) 110 – Siwana (IRE) (Dom Racine (FR) 121) [1995 5s 5g 6.1g^6 a7g Nov 10] IR 6,000F, 2,000Y: leggy, unfurnished gelding: first foal: dam winning Irish sprinter: well beaten, including in –

selling company: stumbled and unseated rider leaving stalls on final outing. *T. M. Jones*

DIL DIL 2 b.f. (Mar 27) Puissance 110 – My Croft (Crofter (USA) 124) [1995 6m 5m⁶ 5g⁴ 5g* 6m 6m⁴ 6.1d⁶ 6d Sep 18] 1,800F, 10,000Y: rather leggy, quite attractive filly: second foal: half-sister to 4-y-o Bruz (by Risk Me): dam 2-y-o 5f winner on only start: won maiden auction at Sandown in July: creditable efforts in nurseries last 3 starts: stays 6f: acts on dead ground, best form on good to firm. *R. Hannon* 67

DILLYETTA 3 ch.f. Prince Sabo 123 – Piccadilly Etta 76 (Floribunda 136) [1994 NR 1995 10m⁶ Jul 24] 500F: 2,000Y: half-sister to several winners: dam won from 1½m to 2m: 50/1, tailed off in maiden. *Ronald Thompson* –

DIMAKYA (USA) 2 b.f. (May 6) Dayjur (USA) 137 – Reloy (USA) 119 (Liloy (FR) 124) [1995 6g² 6f² 6g² 7m² Oct 5] quite attractive filly: fluent mover: fourth foal: half-sister to 3-y-o Loyalize (by Nureyev), useful 5f and 6f winner at 2 yrs, and a winner in North America by Secreto: dam won 10.5f Prix de Royaumont and Grade 1 events at 9f and 1¼m in USA: fairly useful maiden: eased once held by sole rival Thracian in minor event at York final outing: stays 7f. *D. R. Loder* 83

DIMINUET 2 b.f. (Mar 26) Dominion 123 – Primulette 82 (Mummy's Pet 125) [1995 5m 5g² 6m 6f² 6g* 7m Oct 21] 5,200Y: leggy filly: fourth foal: sister to 1992 2-y-o 6f winner Premium and half-sister to 2-y-o sprint winners Primost (by Most Welcome) and Bring On The Choir (by Chief Singer): dam 5f (at 2 yrs) and 1m winner: second of 7 to Red River Valley in nursery at Redcar (best effort) in August then won maiden auction at Ayr in September: broke blood vessel on third (pulled up) and final starts, also put back out on debut: better suited by 6f than 5f. *J. W. Watts* 71

DIMINUTIVE (USA) 2 b.c. (Apr 16) Diesis 133 – Graceful Darby (USA) (Darby Creek Road (USA)) [1995 7m⁶ 7f² 7m³ Sep 5] $24,000Y: leggy, close-coupled colt: has a round action: fourth foal: half-brother to a minor winner in USA by Forty Niner: dam Grade 3 9f winner in USA, also placed in Grade 1 9f event at 2 yrs: best effort in maidens when short-headed by Alzanti in 15-runner race at Salisbury in August: rather disappointing final start: will stay 1m. *J. W. Hills* 79

DINGO WARRIOR 3 ch.c. Roman Warrior 132 – Patsy Pennall 54 (Celtic Cone 116) [1994 –: a7g 1995 a8g a7g⁵ a10g a12g 15.4g⁴ Jul 5] poor maiden: seems suited by test of stamina. *J. Ffitch-Heyes* 33

DINO'S MISTRAL 2 b.g. (May 13) Petong 126 – Marquessa d'Howfen 93 (Pitcairn 126) [1995 6f 7.1g 7f Oct 3] rather leggy gelding: brother to poor maiden Quessong and half-brother to middle-distance winner Mardessa (by Ardross): dam 2-y-o 7f winner: well beaten in maidens and a claimer. *F. H. Lee* –

DIRAB 2 ch.c. (Apr 8) Groom Dancer (USA) 128 – Double Celt 93 (Owen Dudley 121) [1995 7.6d⁶ 8g⁴ Sep 29] sturdy colt: seventh foal: half-brother to 3-y-o 6f winner Al Rawda (by Green Desert), and several other winners: dam, suited by 1¼m, from good family: better form in maidens when staying-on fourth of 13 to Select Few at Goodwood: will stay beyond 1m: sold 14,500 gns Newmarket Autumn Sales. *H. R. A. Cecil* 67

DIRECT DIAL (USA) 3 br.c. Phone Trick (USA) – Jig Jig (USA) (Never Bend) [1994 NR 1995 7g³ 7.1g⁵ 7.1m Jul 7] $60,000Y: compact colt: ninth reported foal: half-brother to 5 winners, including a minor stakes winner by Northern Jove: dam, lightly-raced maiden, half-sister to several stakes winners: set steady pace and apparently best effort when fifth of 10 in maiden at Sandown: only seventh of 13 in similar event at Haydock 3 weeks later: has raced only at 7f on a sound surface. *J. A. R. Toller* 68

DIRTY DANCER 6 b.g. Sizzling Melody 117 – Stratch (FR) 71 (Thatch (USA) 136) [1994 NR 1995 8.3g 9m Jul 15] rangy gelding: half-brother to a winner abroad by Noalto: dam raced only at 6f: poor form at best in 3 NH Flat races: well beaten in seller at Windsor and maiden (visored) at Lingfield: sold 2,300 gns Ascot July Sales. *M. Madgwick* –

DISALLOWED (IRE) 2 b.f. (Feb 27) Distinctly North (USA) 115 – Miss Allowed (USA) (Alleged (USA) 138) [1995 5m⁶ 6.1m³ a7g⁴ 8m² 7.9g² 8g² 8d⁵ Sep 27] 16,500F, 22,000Y: useful-looking filly: has a roundish action: half-sister to several winners here and abroad, including 1½m winner Guest Right (by Be My Guest) and 1986 Irish 2-y-o 6f and 7f winner Best Try (by Try My Best): dam 76 unraced daughter of very useful middle-distance filly Miss Toshiba: fair form in nurseries when second to Traceability at Newmarket, Ramooz at York and Whispering Dawn at Ayr: looks an out-and-out stayer: below form on soft surface final start. *M. Bell*

DISCO BOY 5 b.h. Green Ruby (USA) 104 – Sweet And Shiny (Siliconn 121) [1994 59: 5d 5d^{5} 6g^{4} 5g^{5} a5g^{3} a6g^{6} 5g^{6} a5g* a6g^{6} a6g^{2} 1995 a5g^{6} a6g^{3} a6g^{6} a6g a6g a5g^{3} a6g Aug 11] neat horse: modest sprint handicapper: does most of his racing at Wolverhampton: acts on fibresand and dead ground, probably on good to firm: effective blinkered or not: usually races prominently: none too consistent. *B. A. McMahon* — 59

DISC OF GOLD (USA) 2 ch.f. (Mar 15) Silver Hawk (USA) 123 – Equal Change (USA) (Arts And Letters) [1995 7f Oct 23] small, sturdy filly: closely related to smart stakes-placed winner Make Change (by Roberto) and half-sister to several winners: dam, sprint maiden in USA, half-sister to Eclipse winner Solford: 10/1, and green, never-dangerous seventh of 11 to Dance On A Cloud in maiden at Leicester: well bred and should improve. *M. Johnston* — –p

DISCORSI 3 b.c. Machiavellian (USA) 123 – Bustara 92 (Busted 134) [1994 NR 1995 10m 10m^{4} 10m 12.3m Aug 19] leggy colt: fourth foal: half-brother to very smart middle-distance performer Young Buster (by Teenoso): dam 2-y-o 6f winner, stayed 10.2f, is out of Irish 1000 Guineas fourth Romara: signs of ability, though well beaten all starts: ran in snatches and virtually pulled up (reportedly pulled a muscle and gurgled) on final one: sold (G. Wragg to Miss Gay Kelleway) 800 gns Newmarket August Sales. *G. Wragg* — –

DISH THE DOSH 2 b.f. (Mar 29) Superpower 113 – Taxitilly (Formidable (USA) 125) [1995 5.1m 6m a6g 6m 8m 10d Sep 19] 1,000Y: tall, lengthy filly: second foal: dam unraced: little form, including in selling company: blinkered last 3 outings. *P. G. Murphy* — –

DISMISSED (USA) 2 b.c. (Apr 24) Dayjur (USA) 137 – Bemissed (USA) (Nijinsky (CAN) 138) [1995 6g* 7.1m^{3} 7d^{3} 10g^{2} Oct 9] $210,000Y: good-topped colt: seventh foal: half-brother to Oaks winner Jet Ski Lady (by Vaguely Noble) and to two 8.5f winners in USA: dam graded winner at 8.5f and 9f at 2 yrs in USA, when very smart: very green when winning maiden at Ayr in June: creditable third of 4 to Alhaarth in Solario Stakes at Sandown in July then better efforts in minor events at Leicester, short-headed by Flyfisher (rider not going for whip) on final start: stays 1¼m but may prove better at slightly shorter: acts on dead ground. *P. F. I. Cole* — 99+

DISMISSIVE (IRE) 3 ch.f. Digamist (USA) 110 – Gulf Craft (IRE) (Petorius 117) [1994 –: 6.9m a7g 1995 8m 5.3m^{6} 7f Jun 23] no worthwhile form. *Dr J. D. Scargill* — –

DISPOL CONQUEROR (IRE) 2 b.c. (Mar 7) Conquering Hero (USA) 116 – Country Niece (Great Nephew 126) [1995 5m 8.5m^{6} 7g 8f Oct 16] 3,900Y: quite attractive colt: half-brother to several winners, including useful French 10.5f winner Balibest (by Ballymore): dam ran 3 times: poor maiden: visored last 2 starts. *G. R. Oldroyd* — 38

DISPOL DANCER 4 ch.g. Salse (USA) 128 – High Quail (USA) (Blushing Groom (FR) 131) [1994 –: 8m 8d 12v^{6} 11.1f 1995 a14g Nov 16] tall, lengthy gelding: of little account. *Mrs V. A. Aconley* — –

DISPOL PRINCESS (IRE) 2 b.f. (Feb 6) Cyrano de Bergerac 120 – Tallow Hill (Dunphy 124) [1995 5m Jul 3] 1,600Y: third living foal: sister to 1991 2-y-o 5.9f and 7f winner Talberno Boy and 1992 2-y-o 5f winner Lowrianna: dam unraced half-sister to Cheveley Park winner and French 1000 Guineas second Pass The Peace: 33/1 and backward, slowly away when tailed off in maiden auction at Pontefract. *Mrs V. A. Aconley* — –

DISPOL SAPPHIRE 2 br.f. (Mar 28) Belfort (FR) 89 – Spring Rose (Blakeney 126) [1995 5m 5g^{6} 5g May 8] 650Y: small, unfurnished filly: fifth foal: sister to a winner in Holland: dam poor performer from speedy family: soundly beaten, including in seller: looked very difficult ride first 2 starts. *Mrs V. A. Aconley* — –

DISPUTED CALL (USA) 6 b.h. Alleged (USA) 138 – Tennis Partner (USA) (Northern Dancer) [1994 –: a12g a12g a12g 1995 a16g^{4} a12g a16g 14m^{2} 14f* 14m^{3} 14d 14g 12g Oct 16] big horse: modest handicapper: off course 5 months and left J. — 50

Hills after third 6-y-o start: impressive winner at Salisbury in August: well beaten last 3 starts: best efforts at up to 1¾m: acts on firm going and equitrack: blinkered (ran poorly) third 6-y-o start. *J. Ffitch-Heyes*

DISSENTOR (IRE) 3 b.g. Dancing Dissident (USA) 119 – Helen's Dynasty (Habitat 134) [1994 –: 6g 1995 7m 6.9m 7m a6g^5 a7g^5 Dec 14] compact gelding: poor form: sold out of L. Cumani's stable 3,000 gns Newmarket July Sales after second start and gelded: probably better at 7f than 6f: visored (ran well) final start. *J. A. Glover* 44

DISSIDENT DANCER 6 b.g. The Dissident 85 – Someway 53 (Dublin Taxi) [1994 –: a12g a7g^5 8s 8d 7.1s a7g 1995 a8.5g a14.8g Jan 25] no worthwhile form: tried visored. *J. H. Peacock* –

DISTANT DYNASTY 5 br.g. Another Realm 118 – Jianna 60 (Godswalk (USA) 130) [1994 57: a7g^3 a6g^2 a6g^2 a6g^5 a7g^6 6d^2 6.9v^5 7m 6m^3 6v* 6.9g a8g a6g* a6g^4 a6g a6g^6 7.6v^6 5d 5m^3 6m a7g a5g* a6g^4 a5g^5 1995 a6g^2 a5g^4 a5g^2 a5g^2 a6g a5g^2 a5g^3 5d^3 5m^2 5.3m^5 5g 5m 7m a6g 7.6m 6f a5g^2 Dec 19] lengthy, angular gelding: has a round action: modest handicapper: inconsistent in 1995: effective at 5f to 7f: acts on good to firm and heavy ground and the all-weather: rather headstrong. *B. A. Pearce* 46 a58

DISTANT KING 2 b.c. (Apr 3) Distant Relative 128 – Lindfield Belle (IRE) 78 (Fairy King (USA)) [1995 6m^5 Aug 4] 3,000F: sturdy colt: poor mover: first foal: dam 5f winner at 2 yrs: 25/1, blinkered and very burly, tailed-off last of 5 in minor event at Haydock: has joined M. W. Easterby. *S. Coathup* –

DISTANT MEMORY 6 gr.g. Don't Forget Me 127 – Canton Silk 108 (Runnymede 123) [1994 NR 1995 17.2f^6 Jul 1] sparely-made gelding: no form on flat for long time. *P. J. Hobbs* –

DISTANT PRINCESS 3 b.f. Distant Relative 128 – Sojourn 87 (Be My Guest (USA) 126) [1994 48: 6m 6g 1995 6m a8.5g 7.5g^3 7m* 8m* 7m 8g^5 a7g a7g Nov 13] workmanlike filly: shows a quick action: fair performer: won handicap and minor event at Yarmouth in August, on both occasions racing on favoured stand side: failed to reproduce the form: stays 1m: has raced only on a sound surface on turf, little form on all-weather: sold 5,400 gns Newmarket December Sales. *B. W. Hills* 69 a–

DISTANT STORM 2 ch.g. (Mar 12) Pharly (FR) 130 – Candle In The Wind 90 (Thatching 131) [1995 7g 7f* 7.3m 7f^6 7f Oct 14] 8,400F, 6,000Y: robust gelding: half-brother to several animals: dam 2-y-o 6f winner, later ran in USA: blinkered first time, came from well off strong pace when winning seller at Brighton in July: well beaten afterwards in nurseries, twice blinkered: stays 7f. *M. Bell* 63 ?

DISTINCT BEAUTY (IRE) 2 ch.f. (Jun 3) Pancho Villa (USA) – Beautiful Secret (USA) (Secreto (USA) 128) [1995 7f^6 7m a7g^2 Nov 11] workmanlike filly: third foal: half-sister to a winner in USA by Mining: dam unraced: sire good sprinter/miler: blinkered, best effort in maidens when length second of 10 to Sweet Wilhelmina at Wolverhampton: will most likely stay beyond 7f: acts on fibresand. *W. A. O'Gorman* 69

DISTINCT (IRE) 2 b.g. (Feb 27) Distinctly North (USA) 115 – Shy Jinks (Shy Groom (USA)) [1995 5g^5 May 26] IR 22,500F: second foal: dam Irish maiden: 7/2, around 11 lengths fifth of 8 in seller at Haydock: fractious stalls. *J. Berry* –

DISTINCTIVE LADY 5 ch.m. Primo Dominie 121 – Kenton's Girl 86 (Record Token 128) [1994 –: a6g a7g 8f a6g 1995 a5g a7g a6g Feb 23] no sign of ability: tried visored. *R. E. Peacock* –

DISTINCTLYFOSTER'S (IRE) 2 b.f. (May 24) Distinctly North (USA) 115 – Amata (USA) (Nodouble (USA)) [1995 6f^5 7g^5 6g^6 6g Oct 16] 3,800Y: half-sister to several winners, including very useful 7f to 8.5f winner Bluegrass Prince (by Bluebird), Grade 3 9f winner in USA in 1995: dam French middle-distance winner later successful in USA: poor maiden: seems not to stay 7f. *M. Johnston* –

DISTINCTLY RED (IRE) 2 b.c. (Apr 11) Distinctly North (USA) 115 – Persian Mistress (IRE) (Persian Bold 123) [1995 5g^6 7f Jun 24] 13,500Y: smallish, angular gelding: second foal: dam unraced half-sister to good sprinter Hallgate: tailed off in maiden at Doncaster (hampered stalls) and seller at Redcar: sold 500 gns Doncaster November Sales. *J. Berry* –

DISTINCTLY SWINGIN (IRE) 2 b.f. (Mar 6) Distinctly North (USA) 115 – Swoon Along (Dunphy 124) [1995 5m³ 5g⁵ Jul 15] IR 3,700F, IR 3,100Y: third reported foal: half-sister to a winner in Italy by Entitled: dam Irish maiden: better effort when 4½ lengths last of 5 to Martara in falsely-run minor event at Ayr: will probably stay 6f: ridden by 7-lb claimer on debut. *Miss L. A. Perratt* 60 ?

DIVERTIMIENTO 4 b.g. Night Shift (USA) – Aunt Jemima (Busted 134) [1994 62: a12g 10d 8s⁵ 1995 a11g 10.3g 10d Sep 11] good-topped gelding: modest form in 1994: well beaten at 4 yrs: sold out of J. FitzGerald's stable 5,400 gns Doncaster May Sales after reappearance: upset in stalls and unseated rider leaving them on final outing: fair hurdler, winner in November. *J. Mackie* –

DIVINA LUNA 2 b.f. (Feb 4) Dowsing (USA) 124 – Famosa (Dancing Brave (USA) 140) [1995 5g Sep 12] IR 21,000Y: smallish, workmanlike filly: first foal: dam, French 1½m winner, half-sister to Lowther winner Kingscote, the dam of very smart colt Rainbow Corner: 20/1 and carrying plenty of condition, slowly into stride and never a factor from poor draw when in 20-runner maiden auction at Sandown: should do better. *J. W. Hills* – p

DIVINA MIA 3 br.f. Dowsing (USA) 124 – Hardihostess 104 (Be My Guest (USA) 126) [1994 66: 6m* 6d 1995 8m 10m 10m³ 11m² 12m 12g Sep 29] rather unfurnished filly: fair performer: stays 11f: acts on good to firm ground: sold 11,500 gns Newmarket December Sales. *J. W. Hills* 66

DIVINE 2 b.f. (May 3) Dowsing (USA) 124 – Rectitude 99 (Runnymede 123) [1995 7d³ Sep 22] 10,000Y: unfurnished filly: closely related to 1¼m winner Rectillon (by Rousillon) and half-sister to several winners, including useful 1985 2-y-o 7f winner Normanby Lass (by Bustino): dam winner at up to 8.5f: 3/1, 4½ lengths third of 15 to Cebwob in median auction maiden at Redcar, getting into contention 3f out after slow start then one pace: will improve. *A. C. Stewart* 60 p

DIVINE PURSUIT 3 ch.f. Kris 135 – Dance Quest (FR) 117 (Green Dancer (USA) 132) [1994 64p: 7g³ 1995 8m⁴ 8.5d³ Jun 8] leggy filly: fair maiden, lightly raced: stays 8.5f: acts on good to firm and dead ground. *H. R. A. Cecil* 69

DIXIEMELODY 3 b.c. Rock City 120 – Run To The Sun (Run The Gantlet (USA)) [1994 51: 7g 1995 10f⁶ 10m 14f² 14m³ 14d 14s⁴ 14m Oct 13] close-coupled colt: fair maiden: looked a thorough stayer: acted on firm and soft ground: broke leg at Newmarket in October: dead. *R. Hannon* 73

DIXIT DOMINUS 4 b.g. Dominion 123 – So True 116 (So Blessed 130) [1994 55p: 7d⁵ 1995 7g 8.3m 10.5d Jun 9] big, lengthy gelding: no worthwhile form at 4 yrs: dead. *G. B. Balding* –

DJAIS (FR) 6 ch.g. Vacarme (USA) 121 – Dame de Carreau (FR) (Targowice (USA) 130) [1994 110: 12v³ 12m² 12g⁵ 12.5s 12d 12s⁶ 1995 14.6m⁵ 12m⁴ Jul 21] good-topped ex-French gelding: completely lost his form in 1995: stays 15f: acts on heavy going and good to firm: sold (R. Phillips to J. Jenkins) 7,200 gns Newmarket September Sales and gelded. *R. T. Phillips* –

D K REUNION 5 b.g. Welsh Captain 113 – Thetford Chase 63 (Relkino 131) [1994 –: a8.5g 1995 a12g Jan 7] no sign of ability. *R. Hollinshead* –

D'NAAN (IRE) 2 b.c. (Mar 4) Royal Academy (USA) 130 – Festive Season (USA) (Lypheor 118) [1995 7g 7.1d³ 7d 8f⁵ a8g* Nov 6] 37,000F, 36,000Y: well-made colt: has scope: second foal: dam twice-raced half-sister to Prix Marcel Boussac winner Mary Linoa: fair performer: blinkered, won maiden at Southwell in November by ½ length from Milton, pair clear: will stay beyond 1m: acts on fibresand, best turf form on a sound surface. *W. J. Haggas* 79

DOCKLANDS COURIER 3 b.g. Dominion 123 – High Quail (USA) (Blushing Groom (FR) 131) [1994 –: a8g a8.5g⁶ 1995 a7g⁴ a10g² a10g⁴ 7.9g⁵ 10m 10g a16g a12g Nov 29] smallish, robust gelding: modest maiden handicapper: will stay beyond 1¼m: acts on equitrack. *B. J. McMath* 54

DOCKLANDS LIMO 2 b.c. (Apr 26) Most Welcome 131 – Bugle Sound 96 (Bustino 136) [1995 a8g⁵ Dec 18] 9,000Y: half-brother to several winners, including 1984 Irish 1¼m winner Over The Waves (by Main Reef) and 2m seller winner Dari Sound (by Shardari): dam, stayed 1¾m, out of Melodina, dam also of Dubian and See You Then: 10/1, over 7 lengths fifth of 9 to Red Rusty in maiden at Lingfield, never a factor after slow start: will probably improve. *B. J. McMath* 56 p

DOC'S COAT 10 b.g. Tower Walk 130 – Gold Loch (Lochnager 132) [1994 NR 1995 a16g Feb 14] sturdy gelding: staying handicapper: lightly raced on flat nowadays, and well beaten only 10-y-o start. *C. P. Wildman* –

DOCTOR BRAVIOUS (IRE) 2 b.c. (Mar 25) Priolo (USA) 127 – Sharp Slipper (Sharpo 132) [1995 7.1s^6 7f^3 Oct 31] IR 46,000Y: rangy, rather unfurnished colt: second foal: dam Irish 7f and 1m winner: better effort when 4½ lengths third of 9 to Magic Mill in maiden at Redcar, staying on never a serious threat and flashing tail: will stay 1m. *M. Bell* 71

DOCTOR GREEN (FR) 2 b.c. (Mar 5) Green Desert (USA) 127 – Highbrow 112§ (Shirley Heights 130) [1995 6m Oct 13] heavy-bodied colt: third foal: half-brother to 3-y-o 1¼m and 1½m winner Beyond Doubt (by Belmez): dam, 2-y-o 1m winner later second in 1½m Ribblesdale Stakes, daughter of Highclere, dam also of good racemare and excellent broodmare Height of Fashion: 20/1, chased leaders around 5f when over 8 lengths sixteenth of 21 to Projection in maiden at Newmarket: likely to do better. *Lord Huntingdon* – p

DOCTOR ROY 7 ch.g. Electric 126 – Pushkar (Northfields (USA)) [1994 31: 10d 13s 10g^4 11.1g 10d 11.1g^4 1995 12.1d 12.3d^6 Apr 5] strong gelding: poor handicapper: stays 1½m: acts on good to firm ground and dead, possibly not on soft: has won for claimer: tends to get on edge, and sometimes pulls hard. *N. Bycroft* 29

DOCTOR'S GLORY (USA) 3 gr.f. Elmaamul (USA) 125 – Doctor Bid (USA) (Spectacular Bid (USA)) [1994 78: 5.2m* 6m^6 5.2g 6.1g^3 1995 7.1m^5 6m^6 7g^2 8m 7f^2 6g* 6m Oct 14] leggy, angular filly: has a round action: fairly useful handicapper: won rated stakes at Newmarket in September: effective at 6f and should stay 1m: has raced only on a sound surface: consistent. *R. Hannon* 91

DOCTOR'S REMEDY 9 br.g. Doc Marten 104 – Champagne Party (Amber Rama (USA) 133) [1994 –: a12g 10g^5 1995 10f^5 10f^6 12m^3 12f^5 16.2m^5 12h* 14.1m^3 12.4g^5 15.8g Sep 16] sturdy gelding: poor handicapper: narrowly won 4-runner seller at Carlisle in August: stays 1½m: acts on hard ground and dead: effective blinkered or not: inconsistent. *Mrs J. Jordan* 34

DODDINGTON FLYER 3 b.c. Distant Relative 128 – Tino-Ella 73 (Bustino 136) [1994 61: 6g^6 7g a7g 6s^3 7d 1995 a8g^5 10.3g 14.1g* 12.5m^6 14.6m* 14.1m^4 14g 12.1s 14.6m^3 a16g a16g^2 Nov 30] lengthy colt: fair handicapper: won at Nottingham and Doncaster in the spring: stays 2m: acts on good to firm and soft going and on equitrack: tends to be slowly away: often sweats: carries head high and sometimes wanders under pressure. *R. Hollinshead* 66 a59

DOLLIVER (USA) 3 b.g. Northern Baby (CAN) 127 – Mabira (Habitat 134) [1994 NR 1995 11.5m^3 12s 10g Sep 29] IR 130,000Y, only 8,600 gns 3-y-o: tall gelding: closely related to 1m winner Maridana (by Nijinsky) and half-brother to 2 winners, including 1m winner Mamouna (by Vaguely Noble): dam 1m winner in France: modest form in maidens: should prove suited by middle distances: stiff task, soundly beaten on soft ground. *S. Dow* 55

DOLLY DOLITTLE 4 ch.f. Infantry 122 – Lost Moment (Hotfoot 126) [1994 –: 8d a10g 1995 a11g^6 a12g 8f 12g 10f 14.1g^6 16.2m 11.5g Sep 12] stocky filly: no sign of ability. *H. J. Collingridge* –

DOLLY FACE 3 gr.g. Chilibang 120 – Press Corps 93 (Realm 129) [1994 65: 5m^5 5f^4 5d^4 a5g^3 5.1m^4 5m^5 a5g^2 5.3f* 5f^5 6m a6g^6 1995 a5g^4 a6g^4 a5g* a6g^3 a5g^3 a5g^2 a5g* a6g 5.3g Oct 1] sturdy gelding: fair handicapper: won at Lingfield in January and March: last of 12 (after 6-month absence) on final outing: effective at 5f (best form) and 6f: acts on firm ground (out of depth on dead) and all-weather: goes well for J. Weaver: genuine: sold 2,100 gns Doncaster November Sales. *W. R. Muir* 65

DOMAK AMAAM (IRE) 2 b.c. (Mar 5) Dominion 123 – La Courant (USA) (Little Current (USA)) [1995 7g^3 6m^2 Oct 30] 65,000Y: smallish, compact colt: third reported foal: half-brother to a winner in USA by Salt Dome: dam (showed some ability in USA) half-sister to Classic Fame: bandaged behind, 2½ lengths second to Pivotal in maiden at Newcastle, leading travelling well 2f out but no match for winner last 100 yds: will improve again. *J. H. M. Gosden* 77 p

DOMAPPEL 3 b.g. Domynsky 110 – Appelania 63 (Star Appeal 133) [1994 69: 7m 7m 7f^5 8d* 7v^3 1995 10.1g* 10d^3 10d Oct 19] lengthy gelding: fair handicapper: 33/1, awarded 19-runner race at Yarmouth in September after being beaten on merit: 73

very good third of 19 in apprentice race at Newmarket 2 weeks later: well beaten on only other 3-y-o start: should stay 1½m: acts on dead ground: won novice hurdle in December. *Mrs J. Cecil*

DOMBEY 2 b.c. (Apr 9) Dominion 123 – Arderelle (FR) 80 (Pharly (FR) 130) [1995 7g^4 7.1d^4 Oct 11] lengthy, rather sparely-made colt: has scope: brother to a winner at up to 13f in France and half-brother to several winners, including 5f and 6f winner Premier Developer (by Precocious) and smart 3-y-o 7f (at 2 yrs) to 1½m winner Spout (by Salse): dam 1¼m winner out of smart miler Arosa, dam of Arokar: stayed on well when 4¾ lengths fourth of 23 to Astor Place in maiden at Newmarket: well below that form when fourth of 9 in similar event on dead ground at Haydock 13 days later. *R. Charlton*
85

DOME PATROL 4 gr.g. Dominion 123 – Tranquility Base 112 (Roan Rocket 128) [1994 –, a55d: a6g^4 a7g^3 a7g^2 a7g* 7m^5 8g 8m a8.5g a12g a7g a8g^6 1995 a8g* a8g^4 a7g^5 a8g^4 a8g^5 a8g^4 Mar 20] poor handicapper: won at Lingfield in January: stays 1m: acts on all-weather surfaces: blinkered (ran creditably) once: sold 1,800 gns Ascot July Sales. *W. R. Muir*
– a48

DOMETTES (IRE) 2 ch.f. (Mar 1) Archway (IRE) 115 – Superetta 65 (Superlative 118) [1995 6m 6f* 6m^2 6m^5 7m* Oct 12] IR 4,000Y: sparely-made filly: first foal: dam, 1¼m winner, probably stayed 11.7f: won sellers at Lingfield in June and (off course 2½ months, improved form to win 27-runner race by short head from Sharp Shuffle) Newmarket in October: better suited by 7f than less. *R. Hannon*
65

DOMICKSKY 7 b.g. Dominion 123 – Mumruffin 101 (Mummy's Pet 125) [1994 79: a7g a6g^5 6m^4 6s^6 6v^5 6d 5m^2 5.1m^5 6s^4 6m 6s^4 6.1s 5g* 6m 5.2g^4 5m 5m^6 5m^2 5g 6m^6 5f 5m 5d^5 5m 5s^4 5v a6g 1995 5d 5m^3 5m^6 6g 5.1m^4 5m^5 5m^5 6g 6m^5 5g 5f^2 5.1m^5 5.2g^6 5.1m^5 5m^4 5f^4 5m^6 5m 5m^3 5m^2 5m 5.1d 5g 5.3g^2 5.1d^3 5f^4 5.1m^6 5m^3 Oct 30] good-topped gelding: has been hobdayed: poor mover: just a modest handicapper in 1995: best at sprint distances nowadays: acts on equitrack and on any turf going: occasionally pulls hard and flashes tail: usually held up. *M. R. Channon*
69 d

DOMINANT SERENADE 6 b.g. Dominion 123 – Sing Softly 112 (Luthier 126) [1994 NR 1995 16f^3 May 15] small, good-bodied gelding: poor mover: useful hurdler and modest chaser: maiden handicapper on flat: stays 2m: acts on any going: blinkered (well beaten) once at 3 yrs: sometimes looks none too keen, and flashed tail only 6-y-o start. *M. D. Hammond*
46 §

DOMINELLE 3 b.f. Domynsky 110 – Gymcrak Lovebird 84 (Taufan (USA) 119) [1994 59: 5d^4 5d^4 5m^2 5m 5m^5 7m^5 5g 6m* 6d 5s^4 1995 6m 5m 6g^4 6m^5 5f* 5f* 6m^3 5f^3 5m 5h^3 5f^6 a5g Oct 14] small, workmanlike filly: shows knee action: modest handicapper: won twice at Carlisle in the summer: effective at 5f, seems not to stay 7f: acts on firm and soft ground: blinkered fifth 2-y-o start: often sweating and edgy: tends to wander: usually races prominently. *M. H. Easterby*
56

DOMINION'S DREAM 3 ch.f. Dominion 123 – Sharp Jose (USA) (Sharpen Up 127) [1994 63: 5f 6d 7s^4 7s^6 1995 a7g* a7g 8f 8g^3 7.1m Jun 15] leggy filly: fair performer on the all-weather, only modest on turf: best effort to win handicap at Wolverhampton in April, rallying: claimed out of B. Smart's stable £7,000 fourth 3-y-o start: may prove best at up to 1m: acts on firm and soft ground and goes well on fibresand: winning juvenile hurdler. *M. C. Pipe*
52 a68

DOMINO FLYER 2 b.c. (Feb 5) Warrshan (USA) 117 – Great Dilemma 77 (Vaigly Great 127) [1995 5g^5 7m 5g^2 6m 6m^4 Aug 28] 6,400Y: lengthy colt: second foal: dam, suited by 1m, out of half-sister to 2000 Guineas second and Derby third Remainder Man: modest maiden: below form in sellers last 2 starts: bred to stay further than 6f: bit awkward stalls final outing. *Mrs A. Swinbank*
60 d

DOMITIA (USA) 3 ch.f. Arctic Tern (USA) 126 – Fast Trek (FR) (Trepan (FR) 133) [1994 66p: 7m 8m^5 1995 8m^5 8.2m^2 13.8g^2 10g^4 10.1m^2 8m^3 7m^4 10d^2 10g* 10.5d 10f^2 a12g^3 Nov 11] good-topped filly: fair handicapper: won ladies race at Brighton in October: similar form at 7f to 1¾m: acts on firm and dead ground: bandaged: consistent. *M. Bell*
69

DOM ONE 3 b.f. Dominion 123 – Mrs Musgrove (Jalmood (USA) 126) [1994 92: 5g* 6m^3 7.5g^3 7m* 7f* 7m^5 8g 7g^4 1995 8m May 3] lengthy, sturdy filly: fairly useful form at 2 yrs: never-dangerous ninth of 10 in £8,200 contest at Ascot only 3-y-o start: should stay 1m: has raced only on a sound surface. *J. Berry*
–

Robert Sice Memorial July Trophy Stakes, Haydock—
Don Corleone shows the best turn of foot when switched outside;
the others are, left to right, Fahal, Indian Light and Stiffelio

DOMOOR 2 b.c. (Feb 24) Dominion 123 – Corley Moor 97 (Habitat 134) [1995 5f⁴ 7m 5g 7.5d* 8.3g² a8.5g* Nov 27] 15,000Y: quite attractive colt: half-brother to several winners, including (at 6f) fairly useful 1987 2-y-o Topsy Moor (by High Top) and useful 3-y-o 8.1f and 9f winner Alkateb (by Rock City): dam 2-y-o 5f winner: made all in nurseries at Beverley (17-runner seller) in September and Wolverhampton (4 ran) in November: stays 8.5f: acts on dead ground and fibresand: flashed tail at Wolverhampton but is game and genuine. *M. Johnston* 57

DOM PENNION 4 b.f. Dominion 123 – Pennycuick 101 (Celtic Ash) [1994 64: 8g³ 7m* 7g⁶ 8.1m 1995 7m⁵ 8m⁵ 7.3g⁵ a7g⁴ a7g⁵ Jun 30] small filly: modest handicapper: creditable efforts all starts in 1995: should prove better at 1m than 7f: acts on fibresand, has raced only on a sound surface on turf: sold 7,000 gns Newmarket July Sales. *R. Guest* 59

DOMULLA 5 br.h. Dominion 123 – Ulla Laing 107 (Mummy's Pet 125) [1994 84: 6d* 6s* 6g³ 5g 6d 6d 1995 6g² 6m* 6m⁵ 6f 6m 6d* Oct 19] sparely-made horse: useful handicapper: won at Haydock in April and Newbury (16-runner rated stakes, 8 lb out of handicap, by 3 lengths) in October: stays 6f well: acts on good to firm and heavy ground: usually races prominently: free to post at Haydock: often bandaged: goes well fresh. *R. Akehurst* 105

DOMUSKY 2 ch.f. (Apr 4) Domynsky 110 – Roches Roost (Pauper) [1995 7f Oct 12] small filly: second reported foal: dam selling hurdler: 200/1 and backward, well beaten in maiden at Redcar. *F. J. O'Mahony* –

DOMYBLY 3 ch.g. Domynsky 110 – Nellie Bly 80 (Dragonara Palace (USA) 115) [1994 58: 5d⁴ 5g³ 5m⁴ 5g* 5m⁴ 5g⁵ 5f 1995 a6g Feb 27] sturdy, workmanlike gelding: modest sprinter at 2 yrs: tailed off in selling handicap on only start in 1995. *M. H. Easterby* –

DONA FILIPA 2 ch.f. (May 13) Precocious 126 – Quisissanno 76 (Be My Guest (USA) 126) [1995 7d 6d 7m Oct 20] good-topped filly: has scope: sister to useful 6f –

(at 2 yrs) and 7f winner Euro Festival and 5f (at 2 yrs) and 7f winner Willshe Gan and half-sister to several winners: dam 1½m winner: well beaten in maiden contests. *Miss L. C. Siddall*

DON CORLEONE 3 b.c. Caerleon (USA) 132 – Dance By Night 84 (Northfields (USA)) [1994 108: 7m* 7g^5 7m* 8s^4 1995 10.3g* 12f^4 11.9m* 12f^2 13.3m^3 Aug 12] neat colt: has a quick action: smart performer: won minor event at Doncaster in May and 4-runner listed race at Haydock (quickened, decisively) in July: in frame in pattern events at Royal Ascot, Goodwood and Newbury, behind Presenting in both Gordon Stakes and Geoffrey Freer Stakes last 2 starts: probably stays 13.3f: acts on firm ground, probably unsuited by soft: has worn crossed noseband: game, genuine and consistent: stays in training. *R. Charlton* 115

DONE WELL (USA) 3 b.g. Storm Bird (CAN) 134 – Suspicious Toosome (USA) (Secretariat (USA)) [1994 100: 7m^5 7g^2 7g* 7g^2 7.6d^3 8d^6 1995 7f^2 7g 8m 10.9g^5 Sep 16] big, lengthy gelding: carries plenty of condition: useful performer: only worthwhile form in 1995 when short-head second of 4 in strongly-run minor event at Salisbury: left E. Dunlop's stable after third start: should stay 1m: acts on firm ground, below form on dead: swallowed tongue second outing, wore tongue strap next time: won twice over hurdles in the autumn. *P. Monteith* 97 d

DONIA (USA) 6 ch.m. Graustark – Katrinka (USA) (Sovereign Dancer (USA)) [1994 52: a8g a12g^3 a12g* a12g a11g a12g 1995 a11g^4 a9.4g* a8g Nov 20] big, lengthy mare: modest performer: won handicap at Wolverhampton in February: stays 1½m: acts on firm and dead ground and the all-weather: blinkered 3 times, including when successful: inconsistent. *J. L. Harris* 52

DONINGTON PARK 2 ch.f. (Feb 24) Risk Me (FR) 127 – Small Double (IRE) 55 (Double Schwartz 128) [1995 5.1g^5 a5g^2 a5g^5 May 15] 1,600Y: leggy filly: first foal: dam 2-y-o 5f winner: poor form: second in 4-runner seller at Southwell in May. *J. A. Harris* 38 +

DON MICHELETTO 2 b.c. (Jan 23) Machiavellian (USA) 123 – Circe's Isle (Be My Guest (USA) 126) [1995 6d 7g* Oct 10] small colt: first foal: dam unraced half-sister to smart 7f performer Sally Rous: still green, won 14-runner maiden at Leicester in September by a neck from Winter Romance, pair 4 lengths clear, racing a little in snatches but finding plenty when driven ahead over 1f out: will stay 1m: purchased by Godolphin: coltish on debut: almost certainly capable of much better. *G. Wragg* 94 P

DONNA FUGATA (IRE) 3 br.f. Chief Singer 131 – Jumra (Thatch (USA) 136) [1994 NR 1995 a8g^6 6g 7g^5 7f Oct 3] lengthy filly: third foal: half-sister to 1990 2-y-o 1m seller winner Sharp Glow (by Reach): dam never ran: seems of little account. *C. B. B. Booth* –

DONNA VIOLA 3 b.f. Be My Chief (USA) 122 – Countess Olivia 80 (Prince Tenderfoot (USA) 126) [1994 74: 6m^5 6m^2 6m^2 7m* 7m* 7m 7s 1995 8g^3 9m^5 10g^2 10m^3 7.6m* 8m^4 8.2m* 8m^4 8.1d* 8d^5 8s^3 Oct 6] tall, workmanlike filly: made into a useful performer, winning minor event at Lingfield in July and handicaps at Nottingham in August and Sandown in September: very good third of 10 to A La Carte in listed race at Ascot on final start: effective at 7.6f, stays 1¼m: acts on good to firm ground and soft: usually held up. *C. F. Wall* 95

DO NOT DISTURB (USA) 2 ro.c. (Jan 2) Darn That Alarm (USA) – Little Emotion (USA) (Nonparrell (CAN)) [1995 6m^2 6m^2 7m^2 8.5s* 10g^3 Oct 9] light-framed colt: easy mover: second foal: dam minor 2-y-o 6f stakes winner: sire very smart at around 9f: won maiden at Epsom in September by 10 lengths (raced alone stand rail): better form when 6 lengths third of 9, eased, to Flyfisher in minor event at Leicester following month: suited by test of stamina: sold to go to Sweden 19,000 gns Newmarket Autumn Sales. *J. L. Dunlop* 92

DON PEPE 4 br.g. Dowsing (USA) 124 – Unique Treasure (Young Generation 129) [1994 64: 5m 8.1g^4 8m^6 7.1f* 7.1m^3 7f^3 7f^4 7.1m* 7d* 7d 1995 7.1g* 7g^5 7g* 7f^3 7m^6 6m 7g 8.2m Oct 19] leggy gelding: has a round action: fair handicapper: won at Edinburgh (third win there) in April and Ayr in June: effective at 7f and 1m: acts on firm and dead ground: usually a front runner: genuine. *R. Boss* 73

DONTBETALKING (IRE) 5 gr.m. Heraldiste (USA) 121 – Fine Flame (Le Prince 98) [1994 NR 1995 a11g Mar 20] workmanlike mare: poor maiden: tailed off only outing in 1995: tried blinkered/visored. *A. L. Forbes* –

DON'T CRY 7 b.m. Dominion 123 – Black Veil 53 (Blakeney 126) [1994 27: 12d^{6} 17.1d 14.1d 15.8g 12d^{3} 14.1m^{3} 14.1m^{5} 12m 15.8g^{2} 14.1m^{3} 15.8g 12.1g 13.8g 15.1g 1995 12.3d 13g^{5} 12m 14.1m^{5} 16m^{5} 18m^{5} 16m^{3} 15.8g^{4} 15.8m 15.8m^{4} 14.1h^{2} 14.1m^{2} 17.1m Oct 2] small, lengthy mare: bad staying maiden handicapper: acts on hard and soft ground: sometimes finds little. *Don Enrico Incisa* — 27

DON'T DROP BOMBS (USA) 6 ch.g. Fighting Fit (USA) – Promised Star (USA) (Star de Naskra (USA)) [1994 35, a38: a10g^{2} a12g* a12g a12g 10.1g^{3} 9.7m^{3} 10f^{5} a10g 10m 11.5m^{4} 1995 a11g^{5} a12g* a12g^{5} a13g^{2} a8g^{3} 12g 12f^{6} 9m^{5} 9.7f^{4} 8m^{2} 12m^{3} 10f* 11.5g^{5} 8d a12g a12g Nov 30] angular gelding: poor handicapper: ran mainly in amateurs/ladies events in 1995: won at Lingfield in January on penultimate start for P. Feilden and at Brighton in August: effective at 1m and stays 13f: acts on firm ground, best recent all-weather form on equitrack: usually visored nowadays: usually ridden by Miss J. Feilden: often makes running. *D. T. Thom* — 40, a34

DONT FORGET CURTIS (IRE) 3 b.g. Don't Forget Me 127 – Norse Lady (Viking (USA)) [1994 74p: 7.1s^{5} 7g^{5} 1995 a7g^{2} 8d^{5} 9m^{6} 9.9m^{3} 11.4g 10g^{2} 10f Jul 8] rangy, unfurnished gelding: fair maiden at best: stays 1¼m: acts on fibresand and good to firm and dead ground: unreliable: has joined G. M. Moore. *J. R. Fanshawe* — 79 d

DONTFORGET INSIGHT (IRE) 4 b.g. Don't Forget Me 127 – Starlust 79 (Sallust 134) [1994 82: 7d^{3} 7.6m^{4} 10v^{4} 8.5s 8.1g 1995 8m 8m^{6} 7m^{2} 7m^{6} 8.1m^{5} 8m^{5} 8f^{5} 10m^{6} 7g 7.6d^{4} Sep 14] lengthy, angular gelding: fair handicapper: effective at 7f, appears not to stay 1¼m: acts on firm and dead ground: ran respectably only try in blinkers: sometimes takes keen hold: has joined C. Brooks. *P. F. I. Cole* — 75

DON'T FORGET MIKIE (IRE) 2 b.g. (Mar 5) Don't Forget Me 127 – Sokolova 75 (Red Regent 123) [1995 5g^{3} 5d a6g^{5} 6.1f^{4} 7m^{6} 8m Sep 6] IR 6,800F, 9,600Y: close-coupled gelding: fourth foal: dam placed over 6f at 2 yrs: fair maiden: bred to stay beyond 6f: acts on firm ground: visored and bandaged when running poorly final start: sold 3,400 gns Doncaster October Sales. *M. J. Heaton-Ellis* — 67

DON'T FORGET RUBY (IRE) 3 br.f. Don't Forget Me 127 – Gaelic Jewel 89 (Scottish Rifle 127) [1994 49: 5s 6m^{4} 5.1m^{6} 6m 7.5g 6d^{4} 6.1g^{6} 1995 a8g a10g 10g^{3} 8.2m* a6g^{5} May 4] sparely-made filly: modest handicapper: won at Nottingham in May: unsuited by trip final outing: stays 8.2f well: acts on good to firm ground, has yet to show her form on the all-weather: tried visored: has been bandaged behind: hung left final outing at 2 yrs: flashes tail: racing in Yugoslavia. *D. W. P. Arbuthnot* — 50

DON'T GET CAUGHT (IRE) 3 b.f. Danehill (USA) 126 – Be Discreet (Junius (USA) 124) [1994 NR 1995 6.5v 8m^{4} 7g^{4} 7m 6f^{6} 10g^{5} 10m^{5} 7g^{5} a7g^{3} a6g a7g Dec 12] ex-Irish filly: half-sister to 1¼m winner Sarabah (by Ela-Mana-Mou): dam won at up to 7f in France: fair maiden: trained until after ninth start by Neil McGrath: well beaten in handicaps afterwards: best efforts at 7f/1m: acts on good to firm ground and equitrack: tried visored. *J. L. Harris* — 65

DON'T GIVE UP 7 b.h. Nomination 125 – Tug Along (Posse (USA) 130) [1994 33: 9g 11.6f^{6} 12m 10m a12g^{2} 1995 10m 12m a12g^{5} a16g Nov 8] workmanlike horse: poor middle-distance performer: well beaten in 1995: acts on any going: nearly always blinkered (visored early in career). *P. Burgoyne* — 33

DON'T LOOK NOW 3 ch.f. Dashing Blade 117 – Sly Wink (Song 132) [1994 63: 5m^{3} 5g^{2} 5d^{5} 5.1m^{2} 6.1g^{3} 5f 6m^{3} 6.1d^{2} 6m a6g^{2} 1995 7m^{5} 6m^{5} 6g Jul 27] sturdy filly: modest maiden at 2 yrs: well beaten in 1995: should stay 7f: acts on firm and dead ground and on equitrack: tried blinkered: sold 1,600 gns Newmarket September Sales. *Dr J. D. Scargill* — –

DON'T MEAN A THING (IRE) 3 b.c. Treasure Kay 114 – Traminer (Status Seeker) [1994 54: 7g 7m^{5} 8.1g 1995 a8g 12d 10g 12g May 24] sturdy colt: no form in 1995. *R. Hannon* — –

DONT SHOOT FAIRIES 3 ch.c. Vague Shot 108 – Fairy Fans (Petingo 135) [1994 66: 6.9d 6.9m^{6} 7s^{4} 7v 1995 a10g^{3} 10.8m^{6} 9.9m* 10.3m^{6} 9.7m^{2} 12g* 12f 10.5g* 10.3d 11.8g Oct 9] neat colt: fair handicapper: won at Beverley in April, Pontefract in June and Haydock in September: stays 1½m: acts on good to firm ground and soft: blinkered (best effort at the time) third 2-y-o start: goes well with forcing tactics: game. *C. E. Brittain* — 77

DON'T TELL ANYONE 2 gr.c. (Apr 4) Petong 126 – Glenfield Portion 86 (Mummy's Pet 125) [1995 5m^{3} 5.1m^{4} a6g^{3} 7.1m^{4} a6g^{5} 6f^{3} 6m^{4} 5m^{2} a5g* 6.1m a5g — 55

Nov 11] small colt: seventh live foal: brother to 4-y-o winning sprinter Best Kept Secret and 9-y-o 6f/7f winner Bernstein Bette and half-brother to 6f and 7.5f winner Glenfield Greta (by Gabitat): dam 2-y-o 5f winner: plater: won nursery at Wolverhampton in September: best form at 5f: acts on fibresand, has raced only on top-of-the-ground on turf: creditable effort in blinkers eighth start: sold 2,000 gns Doncaster November Sales to join P. D. Evans. *J. Berry*

DON'T TELL VICKI 2 b.f. (Apr 11) Mazilier (USA) 107 – Jans Contessa 68 (Rabdan 129) [1995 5g^{3} 5d a5g^{2} a5g^{5} 6m^{3} 6f* 7d^{2} 6m^{6} 6m^{2} 7f 6m^{5} a6g^{3} 6s a5g a6g Dec 12] smallish, workmanlike filly: has a round action: fourth foal: dam maiden (stayed 6f) out of sister to Runnett: plater: won at Brighton in May: stays 7f but better form at 6f: acts on firm and dead ground (no chance from draw on soft), and on all-weather. *J. S. Moore* — 52

DON'T WORRY ME (IRE) 3 b.f. Dancing Dissident (USA) 119 – Diva Encore 74 (Star Appeal 133) [1994 98: 5f^{2} 5m^{2} 5m^{2} 5m* 6g^{3} 5g* 5m^{2} 5s 1995 6g^{3} 5m^{3} 5f^{5} 5f^{2} 5f 5m* 5m 5m^{6} 5f^{2} Oct 31] leggy filly: has a quick action: useful performer: made all in minor event at Lingfield in August: very speedy, and best at 5f: acts on firm ground, probably unsuited by soft: often sweats: front runner: sold 31,000 gns Newmarket December Sales. *F. H. Lee* — 99

DOODIES POOL (IRE) 5 b.g. Mazaad 106 – Barncogue (Monseigneur (USA) 127) [1994 57: a8g^{6} a8g* a8g^{3} a8g^{3} a10g 10f^{5} 8g* 7f^{4} 8d 8g^{4} 8m 1995 a8g a8g^{4} a8g a10g 8.3m 7g 8.3m^{4} 7m a7g^{5} 8.5s 8g^{5} 8.2m a10g a8g Nov 20] leggy gelding: modest handicapper: left G. L. Moore's stable after ninth 5-y-o start: stays 1m, possibly not 1¼m: acts on firm ground and equitrack, below form on a soft surface: tried blinkered and visored: inconsistent. *P. Burgoyne* — 51 a41

DOO HAN (IRE) 3 ch.f. Doulab (USA) 115 – Valdora (High Hat 131) [1994 6g 6g 7v 1995 8m^{6} 7.8f^{2} 6g^{2} 7m^{4} 8g^{5} 7g 8g 8d Sep 22] rather leggy ex-Irish filly: half-sister to several winners, including useful 5f and 7f winner Lady Segrave (by Tudor Music): dam unraced half-sister to very useful Saraceno and Caprera: modest maiden handicapper in Ireland for G. M. Lyons, second at Dundalk and Ballinrobe: well beaten at Thirsk and Redcar (amateurs) for new stable: stays 7.8f: acts on firm ground. *M. D. Hammond* — 51 d

DOON RIDGE 4 ch.g. Indian Ridge 123 – Quisissanno 76 (Be My Guest (USA) 126) [1994 51: 8d^{4} 7g^{5} 7m^{4} a6g 8m^{6} 6f 1995 a9.4g 10.5s Oct 1] leggy gelding: modest winning hurdler: well beaten last 5 outings on flat. *J. J. O'Neill* — –

DOONYASHA 3 br.f. Tragic Role (USA) – Sharper Still (Sharpen Up 127) [1994 NR 1995 8.2m^{3} 10m^{5} 7.6m^{2} 10f* 8.1d Sep 2] 8,500Y: unfurnished filly: half-sister to several winners, including smart 5f to 7f performer Jimmy Barnie (by Local Suitor) and fairly useful 4-y-o 1m to 1¼m performer Samba Sharply (by Rambo Dancer): dam never ran: fair form in maiden contests, short-headed third start, workmanlike at 18/1-on when winning 3-runner median auction event at Brighton in August: stays 1¼m: acts on good to firm ground: sold 11,000 gns Newmarket Autumn Sales. *J. L. Dunlop* — 63

DOREEN'S DELIGHT 9 ch.h. Bay Express 132 – Elizabeth Howard 68 (Sharpen Up 127) [1994 –: 12g 12v^{5} a10g^{6} 1995 a12g^{5} Jan 14] strong horse: of little account. *H. J. Collingridge* — –

DORMSTON BOYO 5 b.g. Sula Bula 109 – March At Dawn (Nishapour (FR) 125) [1994 –: 10.8m a12g^{6} a12g^{2} a12g^{5} a12g^{4} a12g 1995 a12g a14.8g^{6} May 13] sparely-made gelding: no worthwhile form on flat: should stay beyond 1½m: has joined T. Wall. *K. White* — –

DORMY THREE 5 b.g. Morston (FR) 125 – Dominant 86 (Behistoun 131) [1994 83d: 14.1d^{4} 12g^{3} 22.2f 11.9f^{6} a11g^{2} 12.1g^{2} 14.1d^{4} 12g* 12s 1995 12m^{5} 12g^{4} 12f^{2} 12.1m^{2} 14g^{6} Jul 19] compact gelding: unimpressive mover: fair handicapper: consistent in 1995: should stay 2m: acts on firm and dead going: tried blinkered in France at 3 yrs, not when successful: effective from front or held up. *R. J. Hodges* — 73

DOROTHEA BROOKE (IRE) 3 b.f. Dancing Brave (USA) 140 – Connaught Bridge 124 (Connaught 130) [1994 66p: 6.9m^{3} 7g^{5} 1995 10.3g^{3} 10g 10.1m^{2} 8g^{4} 8m^{3} 8.5m* 8.1d^{5} 8.9g Oct 7] lengthy filly: has a powerful round action: fairly useful performer: won maiden at Epsom in September by 9 lengths, making all: effective at — 80

1m to 1¼m: acts on good to firm ground: below form when sweating: takes keen hold: none too consistent. *P. W. Harris*

DORSPRING (IRE) 2 b.g. (Apr 2) Jareer (USA) 115 – Daniela Samuel (USA) (No Robbery) [1995 5m a7g^5 7f 6m Nov 6] leggy gelding: closely related to 3-y-o Italian 2000 Guineas winner Prince Arthur (by Fairy King) and a winner in Macau: dam won 6 races in Italy from 5f to 1m: no worthwhile form in maiden events. *C. E. Brittain* –

DOSSES DAN (IRE) 3 b.c. Danehill (USA) 126 – Flyaway Bride (USA) 104 (Blushing Groom (FR) 131) [1994 54p: 6f 1995 7.1m^3 7m^3 7g^3 10f^5 a8.5g Aug 11] fair maiden judged on first 2 3-y-o starts: disappointing afterwards, and sold out of B. Hills's stable 6,400 gns Ascot July Sales after fourth outing: should stay at least 1m: acts on good to firm ground. *B. Preece* 73 d

DOTS DEE 6 ch.m. Librate 91 – Dejote 60 (Bay Express 132) [1994 34: 12.3d^3 12.1g 11.1f 11.1m* 10m 8.1f^4 10.1g^4 12.1f^3 11g^2 12g^4 10m^5 11.5m^3 10s^2 1995 11.1g 10m^5 10m^4 10m^5 10m 9.7f* 10.1m^3 9.9m 10f 12m^5 11.5g Sep 12] smallish, sparely-made mare: poor handicapper: won amateurs race at Folkestone in June: stays 12.3f: acts on firm and soft ground: often pulls hard. *J. M. Bradley* 31

DOUBLE AGENT 2 ch.g. (May 27) Niniski (USA) 125 – Rexana (Relko 136) [1995 7f^3 7.1m^5 9g Sep 23] 22,000Y: well-grown, rather leggy gelding: brother to 2 winners, namely smart stayers Princess Sobieska and Sergeyevich, and half-brother to 2 winners at 1½m+: dam French 1m and 1½m winner: similar form in maidens won by Myttons Mistake at Ayr and Mawwal at Sandown: absent 2½ months, gave impression something amiss in similar event at Redcar final start: subsequently gelded: looks very much an out-and-out stayer. *M. Johnston* 76

DOUBLE BLUE 6 ch.g. Town And Country 124 – Australia Fair (AUS) (Without Fear (FR) 128) [1994 104: 5d* 6f* 6m^2 6m 6f^3 5m 6f 6m^3 6m^2 5.6g^2 6d 6g* 5m 6.1g* 6d^2 6.1d* 6v* 6v^6 1995 6g^3 6m 6m 6m* 5.6m 6d 6m Oct 14] sturdy, workmanlike gelding: impresses in appearance: very useful performer: career-best effort to win 14-runner William Hill Great St Wilfrid Handicap at Ripon in August by 2½ lengths from Lennox Lewis, making all against stand rail: rather disappointing otherwise in 1995, last of 12 in listed race at Newmarket on final outing: successful at 5f, but best form over 6f: acts on any going: blinkered (ran respectably) final 4-y-o start: usually races prominently. *M. Johnston* 112

William Hill Great St Wilfrid Handicap, Ripon—Double Blue (right) excels himself; he makes all to beat Lennox Lewis and Top Banana

Coral Sprint Trophy (Handicap), York—
Double Bounce (No. 12) lands a gamble, from Highborn (No. 11) and Palo Blanco

DOUBLE BLUFF (IRE) 2 gr.g. (Feb 25) Sharrood (USA) 124 – Timely Raise (USA) (Raise A Man (USA)) [1995 7m^4 8.1g^2 Sep 1] leggy, good-topped gelding: has a round action: fourth known foal: half-brother to 3-y-o Raise The Stakes (by Forzando), useful sprinter Poker Chip (by Bluebird) and 1993 2-y-o 5f winner Double Down (by Salse): dam, miler successful 6 times in North America, sister to very useful middle-distance stayer Primitive Rising: fourth of 22 to Silver Prey in maiden at Newbury in August: beaten neck by Mick's Love in 14-runner median auction maiden at Haydock following month, worn down close home: stays 1m: refused to enter stalls at Lingfield in September. *I. A. Balding* 87

DOUBLE BOOKING (IRE) 3 b.g. Cyrano de Bergerac 120 – Holiday Regrets (Silly Season 127) [1994 –: 5d 1995 a8g Jan 5] useful-looking gelding: no sign of ability. *C. J. Hill* –

DOUBLE BOUNCE 5 b.g. Interrex (CAN) – Double Gift 68 (Cragador 110) [1994 69: 6g^5 6m^5 5.7f* 5g 6.1g^3 1995 6.1m* 6f^2 5m^4 6d* 6g^5 7g^6 6g* Oct 7] good-quartered, workmanlike gelding: fairly useful handicapper: much improved for new stable in 1995, winning at Nottingham in July, Haydock in September and (after two unlucky runs) York in October: got better of Highborn by a head when justifying favouritism in 23-runner £18,100 contest at York: stays 7f: acts on firm and dead ground: usually bandaged: successful when sweating: may be capable of better still. *P. J. Makin* 85

DOUBLE CHECK (IRE) 2 ch.f. (Apr 6) Most Welcome 131 – Marie de France (USA) 72 (Diesis 133) [1995 6.9s 7m 10m 8f Oct 31] 1,000 2-y-o: lengthy filly: first foal: dam 14.1f winner: poor form in maiden auctions and a nursery. *M. Johnston* –

DOUBLE DAGGER 4 b.c. Reference Point 139 – Tolmi 122 (Great Nephew 126) [1994 93p: 10d 10.1f^2 12.1s^2 11.9m* 12f* 1995 12.3g^2 14f^2 Jun 29] good-bodied colt: shows a quick action: useful performer: second in minor events at Chester (1¼ lengths behind Marsoom) and Salisbury (head behind Misbelief) in June: stays 1¾m: goes well on top-of-the-ground. *H. R. A. Cecil* 103

DOUBLE DASH (IRE) 2 gr.g. (Mar 25) Darshaan 133 – Safka (USA) 104 (Irish River (FR) 131) [1995 10m^6 a8g^5 Nov 6] 11,000F, IR 12,500Y: good-topped gelding: 62

not a good walker: fourth foal: half-brother to Irish 3-y-o Sannkaya (by Soviet Star), 1m winner at 2 yrs, and Irish 9f winner Safkana (by Doyoun): dam 2-y-o 5f winner out of smart French mare Safita: similar form in maidens at Pontefract and Southwell: will stay 1½m. *M. Johnston*

DOUBLE DIAMOND (IRE) 2 b.c. (Mar 26) Last Tycoon 131 – State Treasure (USA) (Secretariat (USA)) [1995 5m^4 5g^2 6.1m a7g* 7g* 8m^4 7s^5 7m^2 a7g* a8g^6 a8g^5 Dec 15] IR 9,500Y: leggy, good-topped colt: half-brother to 4-y-o 1¼m and 1½m selling winner Diamond Crown (by Kris) and 2 winners in USA: dam minor winner in USA: fairly useful form: won maiden at Wolverhampton and nurseries at Newcastle in August and at Southwell in November: stays 1m: acts on good to firm ground and fibresand, probably on equitrack: races up with pace (asked to go too fast in soft ground seventh outing). *M. Johnston* 92

DOUBLE ECHO (IRE) 7 br.g. Glow (USA) – Piculet 69 (Morston (FR) 125) [1994 68: 10v 12g^5 12.4m* 11.9m^2 12f^2 12.4f^5 12.3g 1995 11.8d 12g Apr 26] sturdy, compact gelding: fair middle-distance handicapper: well beaten in 1995. *J. D. Bethell* –

DOUBLE ECLIPSE (IRE) 3 b.c. Ela-Mana-Mou 132 – Solac (FR) (Gay Lussac (ITY) 116) [1994 103p: 10s* 10d* 10d^2 1995 12m 16.2m^2 12m 16f^2 15.9m* 16g^3 Sep 30] 115

In an age when sporting challenges are too often ducked in favour of easier options, it is good to be able to record that there are still those around who are willing to grasp the nettle. When the challenge is taken up it is of course of benefit to the sporting public, but those who would adopt a more cautious approach possibly forget that defeat need not damage reputations either. A case in point was the clash of Double Eclipse and Double Trigger in the Tiffany Goodwood Cup in July. Not only were the two horses part-owned by the same owner, they came from the same stable and were full brothers to boot. In the circumstances it would have been perfectly

Lonsdale Stakes, York—no problem for Double Eclipse

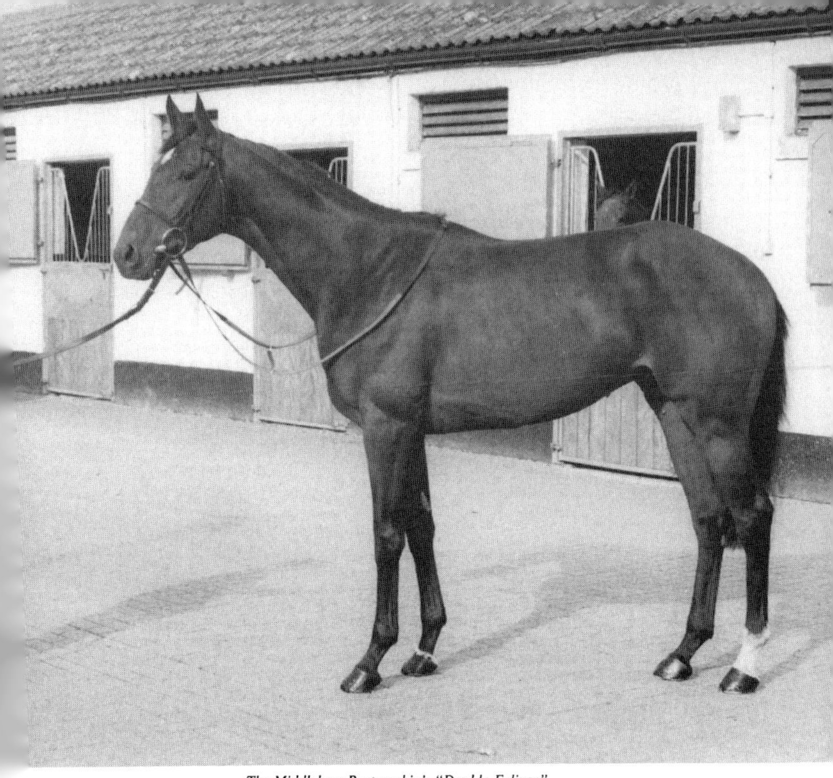

The Middleham Partnership's "Double Eclipse"

understandable had one of the horses been routed elsewhere. But, admittedly after some deliberation, both were allowed to take their chance. The result was one of the most thrilling big-race finishes in recent seasons, and few would argue that Double Eclipse and Double Trigger did anything other than enhance their respective reputations into the bargain.

Double Eclipse came into the race very much the underdog. Unlike his brother, who had already landed three prestigious races since the turn of the year, notably the Gold Cup, Double Eclipse had yet to get off the mark for the season. His three runs—a last-of-eight finishers in the Prix Hocquart at Longchamp, a second (beaten a neck by Stelvio) in the Queen's Vase at Royal Ascot and a tenth (beaten about nine lengths by Winged Love) in the Budweiser Irish Derby at the Curragh—were all useful efforts. But they did suggest that the improvement promised in his two-year-old season (when he won two of his three starts, including a listed event) might have come to an end. Sent off fourth-favourite at 15/2 at Goodwood, Double Eclipse however ran the race of his life, all but upsetting his stable-companion the favourite. In a race in which the pace steadied shortly after halfway, Double Eclipse and Double Trigger drew away in the final quarter of a mile. Throughout the closing stages there was never much in it, but, try as he might, Double Eclipse could never quite overhaul his brother (from whom he was receiving 6 lb more than weight for age) and passed the post a neck in arrears, the result in doubt right until the end. In a season that provided its share of exciting finishes, the Goodwood Cup will live much longer in the memory than most. The fact that these were two brothers fighting out the finish made it almost unique. There have been several examples in recent years of two or more brothers performing well in top races, but there are very few of those brothers actually running against each other, much less finishing first and second in the very same race. The most notable recent example is over the jumps, in which sphere Morley Street and Granville Again achieved this distinction twice during the 1992/93 season.

Both Double Eclipse and Double Trigger had a hard race at Goodwood, but they showed no permanent ill-effects for it. Double Trigger went on to complete the stayers' triple crown in the Doncaster Cup, while Double Eclipse himself won his next race, under three weeks later. The listed Lonsdale Stakes at York's Ebor meeting provided Double Eclipse with a much easier opportunity. He landed the odds comfortably by two lengths from Cuff Link, leading soon after halfway and staying on very strongly. A training set-back meant that Double Eclipse missed his intended target of the St Leger, and he was not at his best when third to Further Flight in the Jockey Club Cup at Newmarket on his only subsequent appearance.

Double Eclipse (IRE) (b.c. 1992)	Ela-Mana-Mou (b 1976)	Pitcairn (b 1971)	Petingo
			Border Bounty
		Rose Bertin (ch 1970)	High Hat
			Wide Awake
	Solac (FR) (ch 1977)	Gay Lussac (ch 1969)	Faberge II
			Green As Grass
		Soragna (b 1965)	Orvieto II
			Savigny

Details of Double Eclipse's pedigree can be found in the entry on Double Trigger, as well as under Double Eclipse's own name in *Racehorses of 1994*. Suffice it to say here that everything about Double Eclipse's breeding and racecourse performances to date suggests strongly that he'll stay well beyond two miles. Indeed, we'd have reservations about him were he to be returned to less than two miles in 1996. Double Eclipse, a tall, leggy colt with a round action who has already shown that he probably acts on any going, has plenty of scope and could well make an even better four-year-old than he was a three-year-old. All in all, he looks a good prospect for the Cup races, and further clashes with his older brother in those contests are one of the things to look forward to in the forthcoming season. *M. Johnston*

DOUBLE GLOW 3 b.f. Presidium 124 – Glow Again 78 (The Brianstan 128) [1994 63: 5d^4 5.1g^5 5d^4 a5g* a5g* a6g 5.1g* 6g^6 5g 1995 a5g^6 a6g^6 5g 6.1g 5m 6m a5g 6m 5f^6 a5g a6g a6g^6 Nov 24] leggy, angular filly: modest 5f performer at 2 yrs: soundly beaten in 1995. *N. Bycroft* –

DOUBLE JEOPARDY 4 b.g. Polish Precedent (USA) 131 – Infamy 123 (Shirley Heights 130) [1994 73p: 10g 10.1g^6 10.4g^6 1995 10m a7g^6 Dec 19] lengthy gelding: fair form in maidens as 3-y-o for L. Cumani: weak-finishing novice hurdler: no promise on return to flat: should stay 1½m. *J. White* –

DOUBLE LEAF 2 b.c. (May 4) Sadler's Wells (USA) 132 – Green Leaf (USA) 97 (Alydar (USA)) [1995 7m* 7d^2 Sep 24] tall, leggy, attractive colt: has plenty of scope: half-brother to disappointing 3-y-o Time Leader (by Lead On Time) and useful milers Desert Green (6-y-o) and Green Green Desert (4-y-o) (both by Green Desert and 6f winners at 2 yrs): dam, 2-y-o 6f winner who stayed 1¼m well, out of very smart mare Warfever: won minor event at Kempton in September by 3 lengths from Ashjar: 1¾ lengths second to Story Line in minor event at Ascot 3 weeks later, tending to hang right: will stay 1¼m: looked on the weak side, and will improve again. *M. R. Stoute* 97 p

DOUBLE MATT (IRE) 3 b.g. Double Schwartz 128 – Kasarose (Owen Dudley 121) [1994 69p: 6m^5 1995 6m^4 6m^3 6g 6m^4 6g^4 7m^3 6g* Sep 2] strong, workmanlike gelding: fair performer: won maiden at Thirsk in September: stays 7f: has raced only on a sound surface. *R. Hannon* 79

DOUBLE ON (IRE) 4 b.f. Doubletour (USA) – Nothing On (St Chad 120) [1994 7m^5 9g* 8.5m 10d^2 12g^3 12g^3 12s* 8g* 10d^3 10s* 1995 12s* 12g^2 10d^3 10m^4 12g^2 10g^6 12g^3 14g^5 9d^3 10d^4 10g^3 Oct 30] half-sister to 3 winners, including useful middle-distance performer Rivellino (by Rheingold): dam unraced half-sister to 110

1000 Guineas winner Nocturnal Spree, to Prix Saint-Alary winner Tootens and to the dam of Moonax: sire unraced half-brother to Kris and Diesis: unraced at 2 yrs: progressed well at 3 yrs, winning maiden at Gowran, handicap at Fairyhouse and listed races at Naas and Leopardstown: easy winner of minor event at Tipperary in April: 1½ lengths fourth of 7 to Prince of Andros in Tattersalls Gold Cup fourth start and under 6 lengths fifth of 7 to Strategic Choice in strongly-run Irish St Leger on eighth, both at the Curragh: respectable efforts afterwards: stays 1¾m: acts on good to firm ground and soft. *P. J. Flynn, Ireland*

DOUBLE OR BUST 2 ch.f. (Apr 25) Presidium 124 – Defy Me 75 (Bustino 136) [1995 5g5 5.1m6 6m a5g6 Dec 18] 400Y: small, light-framed filly: sixth foal: dam 2-y-o 5f winner: poor form, including in seller: left R. Baker after third start. *A. G. Newcombe* 42

DOUBLE OSCAR (IRE) 2 ch.c. (May 21) Royal Academy (USA) 130 – Broadway Rosie 101 (Absalom 128) [1995 6g* 6m3 6m4 7g 7g5 a7g4 Dec 9] 23,000F, IR 9,500Y: strong, good-bodied colt: third foal: half-brother to 3-y-o 1¼m winner Mo's Main Man (by Taufan): dam, Irish 5f to 7f winner, out of half-sister to King's Stand winner African Song: won 4-runner maiden at Ayr in June: best effort when over 2 lengths third of 4 to More Royal in minor event at Newbury 2 weeks later but finished lame: failed to show form afterwards, well beaten on fibresand final start: should stay at least 7f: yet to race on a soft surface. *M. Johnston* 88 ?

DOUBLE POINT (IRE) 2 b.g. (Feb 28) Alzao (USA) 117 – Batra (USA) 60 (Green Dancer (USA) 132) [1995 5g2 5m3 5.3f4 a6g* 6f3 6.1g3 7.5d 6m Aug 26] leggy, angular gelding: first foal: dam 2-y-o 5f winner: first past post in maidens at Brighton (demoted to fourth) and Wolverhampton in May: good third next 2 starts (to Gothenberg in listed race at Epsom on first of them) but well beaten afterwards, in valuable nursery at Newmarket final start: stays 6f: acts on firm ground and fibresand: ridden by 7-lb claimer first 3 starts: sold 13,000 gns Newmarket Autumn Sales. *M. Bell* 79

DOUBLE QUICK (IRE) 3 b.f. Superpower 113 – Haraabah (USA) 99 (Topsider (USA)) [1994 89: 5v* 5d6 6.3d 5g* 5s2 6s 1995 5g2 5s 5m* 5m* 5f* 5f2 5m5 5m4 5m2 5d6 5g2 Sep 28] good-quartered filly: useful sprinter: won handicaps at Sandown in April, Thirsk in May and Epsom (listed rated stakes) in June: creditable second of 9 in listed races at Doncaster and Newmarket (beaten ¾ length by Dairine's Delight) on 2 of last 3 starts: best at 5f: has won on heavy going, goes very well on a sound surface: early to post: usually races prominently: genuine. *M. Johnston* 107

DOUBLE RUSH (IRE) 3 b.g. Doulab (USA) 115 – Stanza Dancer (Stanford 121§) [1994 55: 5d 6g 6s5 1995 6.9d* 8.2g 7m 6.9f6 7m3 8m 8.5s2 a10g* a10g Nov 21] rangy gelding: modest performer: won maiden at Folkestone in March and minor event at Lingfield in November: stays 1¼m: acts on good to firm and soft ground and on equitrack: blinkered (out of form) fourth 3-y-o start. *T. G. Mills* 53 a61

DOUBLE SPLENDOUR (IRE) 5 b.g. Double Schwartz 128 – Princess Pamela 70 (Dragonara Palace (USA) 115) [1994 47p: a8g a7g 7g 6g 5s2 a6g* 1995 6.1g* 5m3 6m 6g* 6.1d4 6d* 6m* Oct 30] leggy, good-topped gelding: impresses in appearance: progressive handicapper: won in big fields at Nottingham in April, Yarmouth in September and Haydock and Newcastle (despite poor draw) in October: unfavoured by the draw on all 3 of his other outings in 1995: stays 6f: acts on good to firm and soft ground and on equitrack: genuine: open to still further improvement, and should make a fairly useful sprinter. *P. S. Felgate* 74 p

DOUBLE TRIGGER (IRE) 4 ch.c. Ela-Mana-Mou 132 – Solac (FR) (Gay Lussac (ITY) 116) [1994 115: 11.9m5 14.6g3 14.5v* 12g 1995 16.2m* 13.9g4 16.4m* 20m* 16f* 18g* 20s4 16s Nov 7] 122

Double Trigger has probably done more for the reputation of the Cup races than any horse since the days of those vintage stayers Sagaro, Le Moss and Ardross. The achievements of those three—who won seven Gold Cups between them in the period from 1975 to 1982—helped to bring home to the British turf authorities the tremendous interest than can be created by high-class Cup horses. Faced with increasing criticism of the bias against stayers—both in prize money for the championship races and in the overall pattern of racing—the authorities began to take their responsibilities much more seriously. From its inception, for example, the British Horseracing Board has recognised a need to 'ensure that the racing

Gold Cup, Royal Ascot—front-running Double Trigger wins most decisively from Moonax

programme maintains, and where possible, improves upon its present level of interest, and the variety that underpins that interest.' Thankfully, there has been no further erosion of opportunities for stayers in recent times. Just under one tenth of all races on the flat in Britain are nowadays run over distances in excess of a mile and a half, recognising the importance of variety in race programmes. High-class stayers remain unfashionable with breeders and there's little sign of that changing, but at least those long-distance horses that are produced are being catered for more fairly. The tremendous public interest in Double Trigger's stayers' triple crown—he won the Gold Cup, Goodwood Cup and Doncaster Cup—should serve to reinforce the BHB's long-term commitment to staying races.

The Ascot Trustees deserve a special mention for resisting the old ruling Jockey Club's wishes to reduce the distance of the Gold Cup from two and a half miles to two miles. The pressure to do so started in earnest in 1990 and even included a warning that the Gold Cup's Group 1 status might have to be reviewed if Ascot failed to comply. While Goodwood acceded to Jockey Club wishes and reduced the Goodwood Cup distance to two miles, the Ascot Trustees held out. The Doncaster Cup, sadly still very much the poor relation of the three major Cup races in terms of prize-money and prestige, remained at two and a quarter miles, partly because there

Tiffany Goodwood Cup—a family affair; Double Trigger beats his brother Double Eclipse

is no suitable place for a two-mile start at Doncaster. Ascot must take particular satisfaction from the continuing support for the Gold Cup in its traditional form. Entries for the latest edition were the highest for three years, and among them were the first three in the 1994 St Leger, in Moonax, Broadway Flyer and Double Trigger. The Gold Cup was once an automatic target for the best of the previous season's staying three-year-olds still in training, and it was encouraging that both Moonax and Double Trigger set out with the Gold Cup as their principal objective as four-year-olds. The pair met first in the Yorkshire Cup at the York spring meeting, Moonax having his first race since being returned from Dubai and Double Trigger fresh from a narrow victory in a good-quality renewal of the Insulpak Sagaro Stakes at Ascot. Moonax had Double Trigger, receiving 5 lb, back in fourth at York but the staying-on Double Trigger was clearly unsuited by the step back to a mile and three quarters and looked sure to do better at Royal Ascot. Double Trigger's most impressive runaway victory eleven days later back over two miles in the Bonusprint Henry II Stakes at Sandown confirmed as much. Moonax started 13/8 favourite for the Gold Cup with Double Trigger at 9/4 and the previous year's runner-up Vintage Crop at 3/1; none of the four other runners started at shorter than 11/1, the odds of the smart French stayer The Little Thief who sadly had to be destroyed after breaking down at halfway. The longer trip and the firmish ground undoubtedly played a part in Double Trigger's victory—Moonax wasn't the horse on top-of-the-ground at Royal Ascot that he had been on easier going in the St Leger and the Yorkshire Cup—but it was a most convincing victory nonetheless. Sent straight into the lead, Double Trigger quickened with over half a mile to run and drew right away in the home straight to beat Moonax, who was on his heels turning for home, by five lengths; Admiral's Well was only a head away third, with Vintage Crop a further two lengths back in fourth. Double Trigger's next appearance, in the Tiffany Goodwood Cup, produced one of the stories of the season as he got the better of a stirring finish with his year-younger brother Double Eclipse after again dictating the pace from the outset. This race is discussed in more detail in the essay on Double Eclipse. The long-term target for Double Trigger in the second half of the season was the Melbourne Cup, a race Vintage Crop won in 1993 and one in which Double Trigger's trainer had been represented by Quick Ransom in 1994. The tremendously game and genuine Double Trigger wasn't allowed to rest on his laurels in the meantime however. His presence frightened off some potential opponents in the East Coast Doncaster Cup and, starting at 11/4-on, he became only the fourth horse this century to land the stayers' triple crown outright. He beat Further Flight and four others with something in hand to join Alycidon, Le Moss (twice) and Longboat. Double Trigger's trip to Australia was put in some doubt when he managed only fourth, fading in the final quarter mile, to Always Earnest, Moonax and Nononito in the Prix du Cadran, form which was 7 lb or so below his best. Double Trigger was found to have a lung infection on his return to England but it cleared up in time for his Melbourne Cup challenge in November. He started 7/2 favourite, carrying top weight of 9-7, but his long journey availed him nothing as he trailed in near the back of the twenty-one runner field,

East Coast Doncaster Cup—a stayers' triple crown for Double Trigger; Further Flight is best of the rest

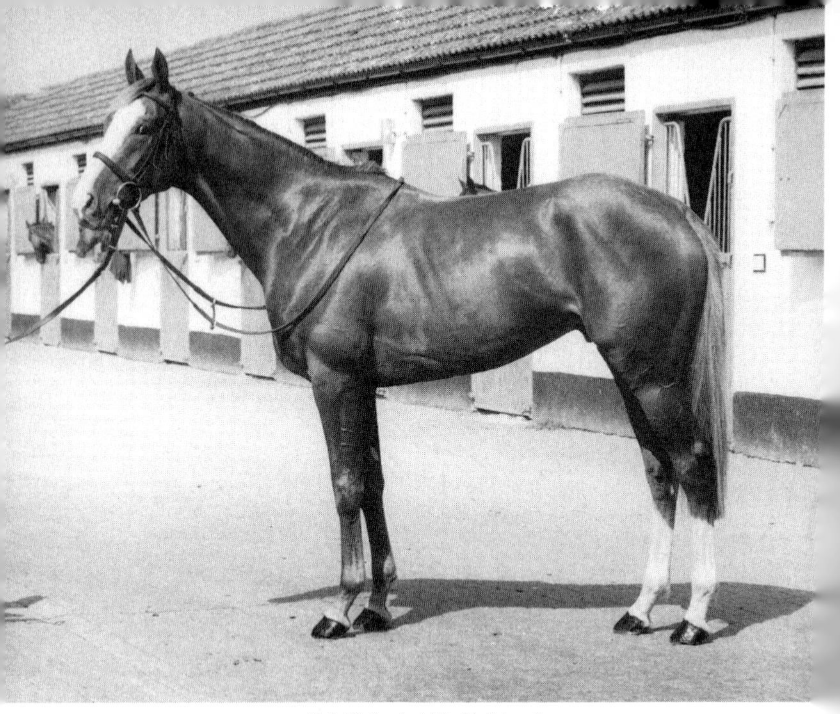

Mr R. W. Huggins' "Double Trigger"

eased right up in the closing stages. An inquiry was held before the race into an irregularity found in a blood sample but foul play was not suspected.

Double Trigger (IRE) (ch.c. 1991)	Ela-Mana-Mou (b 1976)	Pitcairn (b 1971)	Petingo
			Border Bounty
		Rose Bertin (ch 1970)	High Hat
			Wide Awake
	Solac (FR) (ch 1977)	Gay Lussac (ch 1969)	Faberge II
			Green As Grass
		Soragna (b 1965)	Orvieto II
			Savigny

The tall, leggy Double Trigger and his brother Double Eclipse were both relatively cheaply bought. Double Trigger cost only IR 7,200 guineas as a yearling, Double Eclipse IR 17,500 guineas. Their dam Solac, who ran four times in Italy without success, has bred several other winners dotted around the globe, including Farat (by Woodman) who finished third in the Cesarewitch. Double Trigger's victory in the St Leger Italiano as a three-year-old maintained the family's connection with the Italian classics. Solac is by a Derby Italiano winner Gay Lussac and is a half-sister to another, the top-class Sirlad, and to a Derby Italiano runner-up Sortingo; Soragna, the dam of Solac, Sirlad and Sortingo, won the Oaks d'Italia. Double Trigger will again be aimed at the Cup races in the next season and it will take a good horse to lower his colours at two miles to two and a half. He probably acts on any going and is effective held up or making the running. *M. Johnston*

DOUBLE UP 2 ch.f. (Feb 8) Weldnaas (USA) 112 – Bel Esprit (Sagaro 133) [1995 8d 8f Oct 25] neat filly: seventh foal: half-sister to several winners, including 6f and 7.3f winner Fille d'Esprit (by Cragador) and fairly useful 1¾m winner Wings Cove (by Elegant Air): dam showed no form on flat or over jumps: never a threat in maiden events at Salisbury (took good hold in median auction) and Yarmouth (tailed off) month later. *Lady Herries* 50

DOUBLE VINTAGE (IRE) 2 b.g. (Feb 2) Double Schwartz 128 – Great Alexandra (Runnett 125) [1995 5m 6g 5f 7m 7.5m 8m 6f Oct 16] IR 4,800Y, 4,200 2-y-o: tall, quite attractive gelding: half-brother to 1m (at 2 yrs) and 2¼m winner Non Vintage (by Shy Groom): dam 1½m winner in Ireland: soundly beaten in varied company, in blinkers final start. *M. C. Chapman* –

DOUBLEYOUBEAY 2 ch.c. (Apr 30) Beveled (USA) – Hollia 72 (Touch Boy 109) [1995 a5g* 6m^5 6m 5.1m 5h^3 5g^4 a5g^5 a7g Nov 16] 8,000Y: leggy, angular colt: half-brother to 5f winner Local Heroine (by Clantime): dam 2-y-o 5f winner: won median auction maiden at Wolverhampton in May: below that form afterwards, including in selling company on turf, but had valid excuses on all-weather last 2 starts: suited by 5f: acts on fibresand: has worn dropped noseband: sold 1,700 gns Doncaster November Sales. *J. Berry* 51 a60

DOUBLING DICE 4 b.g. Jalmood (USA) 126 – Much Too Risky 87 (Bustino 136) [1994 –: 10.1f^6 12.3f 8m 7f 8.1m^4 7.1m 1995 12.1d^2 11.1g 11.1g^5 11.1m^4 Jun 19] lengthy gelding: poor maiden handicapper: stays 1½m: acts on dead going. *R. Allan* 33

DOUCE MAISON (IRE) 4 b.f. Fools Holme (USA) – Cardomine (Dom Racine (FR) 121) [1994 60: 8.2d 7m 8g^3 8.3f^2 8.2g^2 8.2m 8.1g^2 8d* 10d^3 9g^3 1995 10m^6 a8g^2 8m 9m 10f^2 9f a8.5g^2 a9.4g^3 10m^2 12m^3 12m^6 Nov 6] lengthy filly: fair handicapper: stays 1½m: acts on firm and dead ground and goes well on fibresand: rather headstrong, and wears crossed noseband. *A. P. Jarvis* 60 a66

DOUG'S FOLLY 2 ch.f. (Apr 6) Handsome Sailor 125 – Stern Lass 79 (Bold Lad (IRE) 133) [1995 5m^3 5g^2 5m* 6m 7m 5m^4 6.1d 5m 7m Oct 21] 400Y: smallish, strong filly: third reported foal: dam, 1m winner, stayed 1¼m: made all in claimer at Beverley in June: best effort in nurseries when fourth at Ripon in August: well beaten last 3 starts: may prove suited by 6f (ridden by girl apprentice and never a factor on first attempt at trip, ran badly in blinkers on second). *M. W. Easterby* 64 ?

DOULILY 3 ch.f. French Gondolier (USA) 69 – Doulally 59 (Doulab (USA) 115) [1994 NR 1995 a7g a7g Jan 27] first foal: dam 6f winner: tailed off in sellers. *G. Holmes* –

DOVEBRACE 2 b.g. (Feb 22) Dowsing (USA) 124 – Naufrage (Main Reef 126) [1995 5m* 6g* 6m^5 7g^3 6.1m* 6m^5 5g^5 Sep 14] 1,500F, 6,200Y: leggy gelding: unimpressive mover: fourth foal: brother to 5-y-o 1¼m and 1½m winner Kismetim: dam unraced: useful performer: won maiden at Haydock in May and well-contested minor events at York (by ½ length from Lucayan Prince) in June and Chester (by short head from Mazeed) in August: ran well considering raced well away from favoured rail over inadequate trip when fifth in listed race at Ayr on final outing: will stay beyond 7f: yet to race on a soft surface: sweating and edgy fifth start. *A. Bailey* 96

DOVEDON LAD 3 ch.c. Statoblest 120 – Miss Petella (Dunphy 124) [1994 –: 7g 1995 7m a8g Nov 29] compact colt: no sign of ability. *G. C. Bravery* –

DOVER PATROL (IRE) 5 b.h. Dancing Brave (USA) 140 – Britannia's Rule 108 (Blakeney 126) [1994 97: 14.1d^3 14m^6 16.1f^6 13.9m^4 14.4g^4 16g^2 18m 16g^4 1995 14g^2 22.2m^2 Jun 23] strong, well-made horse: carries condition: impresses in appearance: fairly useful performer: second in handicap at Haydock (coltish) and 5-runner Queen Alexandra Stakes at Royal Ascot (1½ lengths behind Cuff Link), both in June: has shown his form at 1¾m and stays 2¾m: acts on firm and soft ground: bandaged in 1995: has joined Miss M. Rowland. *H. R. A. Cecil* 94

DOWDENCY 3 b.f. Dowsing (USA) 124 – Tendency 77 (Ballad Rock 122) [1994 44: 8m 8.2s 7s a8.5g^5 a8.5g^6 a7g^2 1995 a6g^5 a6g a6g^2 a7g* a8.5g^4 6s^2 7d^6 a8.5g 6.1g^5 a7g^6 7m^2 7g 8f a8g^5 a9.4g^4 a9.4g Dec 9] workmanlike filly: modest performer: won seller at Wolverhampton in February: stays 9.4f: acts on fibresand and goes well on soft going: none too consistent. *J. A. Pickering* 54 a48

DOWN THE YARD 2 b.f. (Apr 21) Batshoof 122 – Sequin Lady (Star Appeal 133) [1995 5m a5g a6g^6 6g^3 6m 5.2f^4 6m 6m* 7.5m 7.9g 7g 10d 8f Oct 16] 1,000Y, 3,200 2-y-o: workmanlike filly: half-sister to 3 winners here and abroad, two at 2 yrs, including Satin Dancer (by Rousillon), successful at 7f in 1992: dam, unraced, from family of Juliette Marny and Julio Mariner: plater: ran easily best races at Yarmouth, winning there in July: had stiff tasks in nurseries last 5 starts: should prove effective over 7f+: acts on firm ground. *M. C. Chapman* 48

DOWSONG 4 br.g. Dowsing (USA) 124 – Winsong Melody (Music Maestro 119) [1994 68: 7v^3 7d^3 6f^6 6.9s^3 8.5s 7.1m^6 7f 7d^2 7.1d 7g 1995 8g 7m 6.9f* 7f^3 7m^6 8g 8.1d^2 7m^6 Oct 20] good-topped gelding: fluent mover: fair handicapper: won at Folkestone in August: pulled up lame sixth start, and well below form both subsequent ones: stays 7f: seems to act on any going. *R. Akehurst* 73

DOYCE 6 b.m. Formidable (USA) 125 – Current Raiser 108 (Filiberto (USA) 123) [1994 75: 16v^3 18.7m* 20m^3 20f 18.2s^2 16.2g^4 18m 1995 16m^4 Apr 17] workmanlike mare: fair handicapper: creditable fifth of 20 (promoted) to Always Aloof in Queen's Prize at Kempton on only 6-y-o start: suited by test of stamina: acts on good to firm and heavy going: effective blinkered, but not tried since August 1993: consistent. *R. J. R. Williams* 67 +

DOZEN DIRHAM (USA) 3 b.g. Dayjur (USA) 137 – Capades (USA) (Overskate (CAN)) [1994 NR 1995 8d 8g Sep 2] $260,000Y: good-bodied gelding: first foal: dam, very smart Grade 1 winner, stayed 1¼m: no promise in maiden at Yarmouth and seller (reluctant at stalls) at Thirsk: sold out of E. Dunlop's stable 2,600 gns Doncaster July Sales in between. *J. Norton* –

DRAGON BOLD (IRE) 4 ch.g. Bold Arrangement 127 – Yavarro 44 (Raga Navarro (ITY) 119) [1994 –: 6f 6.9s^4 5m 6m 7.6g 7g 10v 10g^5 1995 8m a8g May 12] tall, leggy gelding: no worthwhile form since 2 yrs, including in blinkers. *L. J. Holt* –

DRAGONFLIGHT 4 b.c. Formidable (USA) 125 – Lappet (Kampala 120) [1994 –: 8d a8.5g a8.5g^5 1995 a7g^6 a8g a12g a9.4g^2 a8g 8.2m 7.6m 8g a7g a8g Nov 16] robust colt: poor maiden: only form when neck second of 8 in median auction event at Wolverhampton in March: better at 9.4f than shorter: acts on fibresand, no form on turf. *D. Haydn Jones* – a39

DRAGON GREEN 4 gr.g. Green Desert (USA) 127 – Dunoof 92 (Shirley Heights 130) [1994 10.8g^3 9.5g* 11.3g 8g* 7d 7g 1995 11.6g a7g^5 Nov 10] ex-French gelding: fourth foal: half-brother to fair middle-distance performer Folia (by Sadler's Wells) and 5-y-o German 7f to 9f winner Dunnellon (by Shareef Dancer): dam well-related 2-y-o 7f winner: trained by H. Pantall at 3 yrs, winning maiden and minor event in French Provinces: sold 5,400 gns Newmarket Autumn (1994) Sales: modest form in claimers here: stays at least 9.5f: acts on equitrack. *J. White* 61

DRAGONJOY 2 b.g. (Apr 17) Warrshan (USA) 117 – Nazakat 68 (Known Fact (USA) 135) [1995 5g 6g 6m 6m 6m 7g 8m a7g* a8g^2 a8g^6 Nov 30] 2,800Y: good-topped gelding: first foal: dam 5f winner at 2 yrs: plater: trained by L. J. Holt until after sixth start: improved effort when making all in 15-runner event at Southwell in November and ran well next start: stays 1m, but likely to prove best at up to 7f: acts on fibresand: blinkered last 3 outings: races keenly. *J. W. Payne* – a58 +

DRAGONMIST (IRE) 5 b.m. Digamist (USA) 110 – Etage (Ile de Bourbon (USA) 133) [1994 35: 8d 6m 8.2f 8.3d^5 8g 10.2m 10m^3 8.3m^5 8m 9.7m a10g^5 1995 a16g a12g 11.9m Apr 6] lengthy mare: poor maiden: no form in 1995: sold (M. Madgwick to F. Jordan) 1,000 gns Ascot April Sales *M. Madgwick* –

DRAGON ROSE 3 gr.g. Grey Desire 115 – The Shrew 92 (Relko 136) [1994 NR 1995 7.1m 7.1g May 27] good-bodied gelding: half-brother to winners in Italy by Shirley Heights and Final Straw: dam best at around 1m: always behind in 2 maidens at Haydock, running as though something amiss on second occasion. *T. P. Tate* –

DRAGON'S BACK (IRE) 2 ch.c. (Feb 7) Digamist (USA) 110 – Classic Choice (Patch 129) [1995 6m^3 6m^3 6m Sep 2] IR 9,900F, IR 14,500Y: strong, attractive colt: half-brother to 1990 2-y-o 7f seller winner Classic Ring (by Auction Ring) and 2 winners abroad: dam never ran: third in median auction maidens at Kempton and Goodwood in August: in rear in valuable restricted race at the Curragh final start: will be better suited by 7f+: should do better. *Mrs J. Cecil* 63 p

DRAMA KING 3 b.c. Tragic Role (USA) – Consistent Queen 55 (Queen's Hussar 124) [1994 44: a8g a8g^5 1995 a11g 10g Apr 4] poor form in maidens at 2 yrs: blinkered, well beaten in selling events in 1995: should prove suited by further than 1m. *S. R. Bowring* | –

DRAMATIC ACT 2 gr.f. (Apr 4) Tragic Role (USA) – Curious Feeling (Nishapour (FR) 125) [1995 8d^2 Sep 27] sparely-made, leggy filly: first foal: dam stayed 1¼m on flat and won over hurdles: 50/1, short-head second of 12 to White Sea in median auction maiden at Salisbury, switched 2f out and leading inside last until caught on line: got loose on both appearances, withdrawn on intended debut. *C. R. Barwell* | 72

DRAMATIC ENTRY (IRE) 2 b.f. (Jan 24) Persian Bold 123 – Galatrix 72 (Be My Guest (USA) 126) [1995 5f^3 5.7h^2 5.1f^2 5.2m^3 5.1h^3 5.1h^5 a6s* Dec 23] IR 13,000Y: neat filly: second foal: dam, 1m winner, out of Fillies' Mile third Alligatrix: fair form at best here: sold out of J. Toller's stable 4,000 gns Newmarket Autumn Sales after penultimate start: won maiden in Sweden in December: bred to stay 7f at least but races keenly: usually blinkered: one to treat with caution. *L. Reuterskjold, Sweden* | 68

DRAMATIC MOMENT 2 b.f. (Apr 8) Belmez (USA) 131 – Drama School 72 (Young Generation 129) [1995 7f 8.1m^6 Aug 28] 18,000Y: rangy, rather unfurnished filly: seventh foal: half-sister to several winners here and abroad, including 1¼m performer Tread The Boards (by Reprimand) and 1989 Irish 2-y-o 1m winner Annie Laurie (by Aragon): dam maiden (stayed 1m) out of half-sister to Final Straw and Achieved: modest form in maidens won by Villeggiatura at Salisbury and Waterland at Chepstow: will stay beyond 1m: should do better. *I. A. Balding* | 55 p

DR CALIGARI (IRE) 3 b.g. My Generation 111 – Mallabee 92 (Pall Mall 132) [1994 –p: 6m^3 1995 7g^2 7m^5 7g^2 7m^3 8g^5 8m^3 6.9f^3 8.3f^2 8g 8.3g^4 8f^2 7m^5 a7g^4 a8g^2 a8.5g^4 Dec 12] workmanlike gelding: fair maiden: sold out of Jack Berry's stable 7,200 gns Doncaster November Sales after penultimate start: stays 8.3f: acts on firm ground and fibresand, yet to race on a soft surface: no improvement in visor. *S. Gollings* | 68 d

DREAMBOAT (USA) 3 b.f. Mr Prospector (USA) – Gorgeous (USA) (Slew O' Gold (USA)) [1994 84p: 6g^4 6m^2 1995 7g* Sep 23] rather finely-made, attractive filly: has a quick action: off course over 11 months but well-backed 5/4-on shot, won maiden at Redcar in September by a neck, leading inside last and just holding renewed challenge of Yeast: may do better: sent to Dubai. *J. H. M. Gosden* | 76 +

DREAM CARRIER (IRE) 7 b.g. Doulab (USA) 115 – Dream Trader (Auction Ring (USA) 123) [1994 50, a73: a6g^2 a7g^2 a7g* a7g^3 a7g^5 a7g^2 7g^4 a8g^4 8m a7g a7g* 7g^4 a7g a7g* a7g^6 8.1g a7g^5 a7g^3 1995 a7g^2 a7g^5 a7g* a7g^3 a8g^4 a7g^5 a7g^4 a8.5g^6 a7g^6 a7g^6 a7g^5 7d a7g^5 a7g a7g^6 a7g a7g^4 Dec 12] strong, close-coupled gelding: carries condition: has a round action: fair performer: in good form early in year, winning claimer at Southwell in January on penultimate outing (claimed £8,000) for T. D. Barron: deteriorated over 7 starts for J. O'Shea, and just modest form for latest stable: stays 1m: acts on firm ground and goes well on fibresand: tried blinkered/visored: sometimes starts slowly, and usually held up. *R. E. Peacock* | – a73 d

DREAMER (USA) 3 ch.c. Zilzal (USA) 137 – Affection Affirmed (USA) (Affirmed (USA)) [1994 92: 5.1m* 5.1g^3 6m^3 7f^4 8.1d* 8m^4 1995 10m^4 12g^2 11s^4 12m^5 Aug 11] close-coupled colt: useful performer: hung left in front when second in minor event at Catterick in April and Group 2 event at Munich (very good head second to O'Connor but demoted) in May: got very upset in preliminaries when tailed off in minor event at Newbury on final outing: stays 1½m: acts on good to firm and dead ground: wears dropped noseband: sent to USA. *P. F. I. Cole* | 105

DREAMHILL (USA) 2 b.c. (Feb 9) Danehill (USA) 126 – Keep The Thought (USA) (Valdez (USA)) [1995 8g* Sep 9] IR 40,000Y: sixth foal: half-brother to 3 winners, all by Caerleon, including middle-distance winners Llangollen and Dreams Are Free: dam 1m winner, out of sister to dam of Seattle Slew and Lomond: co-favourite, won 6-runner maiden at Goodwood by 2 lengths from Jamaican Flight, green over 2f out but stretching clear inside last: sure to improve. *P. W. Harris* | 70 p

DREAM MISSY 4 b.f. Dreams To Reality (USA) 113 – Mrs Feathers 57 (Pyjama Hunt 126) [1994 –: 5m 6m 8m 1995 10m 9m Jun 16] good-topped filly: no worthwhile form. *J. R. Bosley* | –

DREAM OF MY LIFE (USA) 2 gr.g. (May 1) Danzatore (CAN) 120 – Sureya (Sharpen Up 127) [1995 a8.5g Dec 9] eighth foal: half-brother to winners in USA by Kings Lake and Time For A Change: dam, French 11f winner, half-sister to high-class French 1½m and 15f winner Sumayr: 20/1, slowly away and well beaten in maiden at Wolverhampton. *F. Murphy* –

DREAMS END 7 ch.h. Rainbow Quest (USA) 134 – Be Easy 110 (Be Friendly 130) [1994 87: 12d* 1995 12g4 14m 10.5g 11.9s 12.1d 10m2 12m Nov 4] sparely-made, quite attractive horse: smart hurdler: fair handicapper on flat: trained first 2 7-y-o starts by B. Llewellyn: had been failing to see out his races, and was tubed after fifth start: effective at 1¼m to 1¾m: acts on any going: sometimes bandaged: sometimes sweats: usually held up. *J. M. Bradley* 87

DREAM SWEET DREAMS (USA) 6 gr. or ro.m. Dahar (USA) 125 – Aronia (USA) (Grey Dawn II 132) [1994 NR 1995 10f3 16f4 Aug 25] good-topped mare: of little account. *F. H. Lee* –

DREAM TICKET (USA) 3 b.f. Danzig (USA) – Capo di Monte 118 (Final Straw 127) [1994 65p: 7d6 1995 7m3 7m* May 10] strong, lengthy filly: shows plenty of knee action: fair form: justified favouritism in maiden at Chester in May: should stay 1m: acts on good to firm and dead ground. *M. R. Stoute* 73

DREAM WEDDING 3 ch.f. Soviet Star (USA) 128 – Island Wedding (USA) 89 (Blushing Groom (FR) 131) [1994 NR 1995 8g6 Apr 27] quite good-topped filly: poor mover: first foal: dam, 7f and 8.5f winner, out of sister to Storm Bird: modest form when sixth of 14 to Stinging Reply in maiden at Warwick, always thereabouts: sold 4,000 gns Doncaster July Sales. *E. A. L. Dunlop* 62

DR EDGAR 3 b.g. Most Welcome 131 – African Dancer 116 (Nijinsky (CAN) 138) [1994 66: 6g 6m* 6m 1995 10.3g 10g 12.3m 11.8g5 10m* 10m 10m2 9.7g* Oct 16] strong, good-bodied gelding: fair handicapper: won at Windsor in June and Folkestone in October: stays 1¼m: has raced only on good or good to firm ground: takes a good hold, and best efforts when ridden prominently: sold (G. Wragg to M. Dods) 21,000 gns Newmarket Autumn Sales. *G. Wragg* 72

DR FRANCES (IRE) 3 b.f. Pennine Walk 120 – Pounding Beat (Ya Zaman (USA) 122) [1994 NR 1995 8g 8m 8m 10g 11.5m5 13.1h Sep 4] IR 3,200Y: good-topped filly: second foal: dam Irish 1½m winner: no worthwhile form. *C. C. Elsey* –

DRIFTHOLME 2 b.f. (Apr 28) Safawan 118 – Avahra 108 (Sahib 114) [1995 7g 7.1s 8m Nov 4] 4,000F: compact filly: half-sister to several winners, including sprinter Cumbrian Melody (by Petong) and middle-distance stayer Ruckley (by Free State): dam stayed 6f: behind in maidens. *G. L. Moore* –

DRIMARD (IRE) 4 ch.g. Ela-Mana-Mou 132 – Babilla (USA) (Raja Baba (USA)) [1994 –: 10.2g 12s 14.1m5 16g 16d 1995 11.9m5 a16g* 18m 16m a16.2g6 a14g a14g* Nov 16] big, plain gelding: poor performer: won claimer at Southwell in June and handicap there in November: stays 2m: acts on fibresand: tried visored/blinkered: inconsistent. *K. McAuliffe* 25 a41

DROMALANE (IRE) 3 b.g. Vision (USA) – Clodianus (Bay Express 132) [1994 –: 6f 5m5 1995 6g 6g3 6.5m Aug 9] workmanlike gelding: trained here by J. Carr until after reappearance, showing no worthwhile form: poor form at best in Ireland: stays 6f: best effort on good ground. *J. C. Harley, Ireland* 36

DRUM BATTLE 3 ch.c. Bold Arrangement 127 – Cannon Boy (USA) (Canonero II (USA)) [1994 NR 1995 8f4 10d5 10.5g Sep 22] workmanlike colt: unimpressive mover: brother to modest 6f and 7f winner Maple Bay and half-brother to 7f winner Tender Moment (by Caerleon) and a winner in USA by Be My Guest: dam won 9 races in USA, including Grade 3 9f event: fair form in maidens: best effort at 1m on firm ground: takes keen hold: sold 5,200 gns Doncaster November Sales. *R. Charlton* 67

DRUMDONNA (IRE) 5 b.m. Drumalis 125 – Decoy Duck 67 (Decoy Boy 129) [1994 54: 8.3v6 8d3 8.1g* 8m3 8m 8.1f3 8.1m6 8d2 8g 8m 8s 7.1s 1995 9.2m 8.3f Jul 29] rather close-coupled mare: modest 7f/1m handicapper at 4 yrs for Jack Berry: no form in 1995. *P. Beaumont* –

DRUMMER HICKS 6 b. or br.h. Seymour Hicks (FR) 125 – Musical Princess 66 (Cavo Doro 124) [1994 70: 10.4f 10m 8.9f 10.1f4 10.5g5 10g3 10.1m5 12m3 10d3 54 d

11.9s 12v^4 12.4d^5 1995 10m 10.9m^2 9g 11.1m^5 10.1m^6 a11g^6 Dec 1] workmanlike horse: impresses in appearance: has a round action: on the downgrade, modest form at best in 1995: effective at 1¼m to 1½m: probably acts on any going: sometimes gives trouble stalls: usually races prominently. *E. Weymes*

DRUMOCHTER 3 ch.g. Prince Sabo 123 – Short And Sharp 88 (Sharpen Up 127) [1994 71d: 6m^3 6f^3 7f^2 7.5m^4 7m 8s 1995 10f^2 10m^2 11.9m^3 10f 12m^6 Jul 25] unfurnished, dipped-backed gelding: still a maiden: second in handicaps at Redcar first 2 starts, unlucky when short-headed on reappearance: disappointing afterwards: stays 1¼m: acts on firm ground: tends to carry head high. *D. Morley* 55

DRUM SERGEANT 8 b.g. Elegant Air 119 – Cala-Vadella 110 (Mummy's Pet 125) [1994 –: 5m 5m 5f 6g 6d 1995 6m 7g 6g 7.5g 6m^6 Jul 5] sturdy gelding: no longer of much account. *J. Parkes* –

DRY POINT 9 ch.g. Sharpo 132 – X-Data 93 (On Your Mark 125) [1994 72: 6f 6s 6m* 6m^2 6g* 6g* 6m^4 6.1g^6 6g* 6m 6m 7g 1995 5.7f 6g 6m^2 6m 6f* 6g^5 6f^4 5.7h^6 Aug 18] strong, workmanlike gelding: has a round action: fair handicapper: won at Kempton in June: suited by 6f and a sound surface: occasionally bandaged: has worn crossed noseband: genuine. *J. A. R. Toller* 74

DR ZHIVAGO 3 b.c. Soviet Star (USA) 128 – Reltop 72 (High Top 131) [1994 69p: 8m 1995 10g^3 10d^2 12m 11.4m^3 Aug 30] big, useful-looking colt: fair maiden: should stay beyond 11.4f: acts on good to firm and dead ground. *M. A. Jarvis* 78

DTOTO 3 b.g. Mtoto 134 – Deposit 73 (Thatch (USA) 136) [1994 NR 1995 10m 10m^2 13.4d^5 11.8g Oct 9] good-topped gelding: sixth foal: half-brother to Ebor winner Deposki (by Niniski): dam second at 6f at 2 yrs, won in West Indies: fair maiden: stays 13.4f: acts on good to firm and dead ground: sold (M. Stoute to R. Baker) 10,000 gns Newmarket Autumn Sales. *M. R. Stoute* 72

DUBAI COLLEGE (IRE) 2 b.c. (Jan 25) Old Vic 136 – Murooj (USA) (Diesis 133) [1995 6g 6m^6 Aug 17] smallish colt: first foal: dam unraced half-sister to good 7f (at 2 yrs) to 1½m winner Mashkour, later Grade 1 winner at around 1¾m in USA: behind in maidens at Newmarket and Yarmouth 2½ months later. *C. E. Brittain* –

DUBAI FALCON (USA) 4 b.g. Woodman (USA) 126 – Keeper's Charm (USA) (Poker) [1994 63: 7m 8m^4 7.5m^3 8.3m 7.2g 7m^4 8.3g 1995 a9.4g a8.5g^6 a8g Mar 20] quite attractive gelding: modest maiden on flat, well beaten in 1995: fair hurdler, winner in August. *R. Dickin* –

DUBLIN INDEMNITY (USA) 6 b.g. Alphabatim (USA) 126 – Sailongal (USA) (Sail On-Sail On) [1994 –: a8g 1995 a11g Dec 1] rangy, good-topped gelding: modest 1m winner in 1992: tailed off on both flat outings since. *M. P. Bielby* –

DUBLIN RIVER (USA) 2 b.c. (Apr 24) Irish River (FR) 131 – Vivre Libre (USA) (Honest Pleasure (USA)) [1995 6m* 7m* 8.1d^5 8g^2 Sep 21] IR 23,000Y: compact colt: good mover: fifth foal: half-brother to useful 4-y-o middle-distance performer Wishing (by Lyphard's Wish) and a winner in USA: dam unraced half-sister to smart miler Vertige: won maiden at Yarmouth in July and minor event (by neck from Civil Liberty) at Kempton in August: fair second of 3 to easy winner Night Watch in minor event at Pontefract final start: should stay 1m: acts on good to firm ground, possibly unsuited by dead. *H. Thomson Jones* 94

DUCHESS OF ALBA 3 b.f. Belmez (USA) 131 – Juliette Marny 123 (Blakeney 126) [1994 NR 1995 10.1m^3 13.8m* 17.2h^2 14m^6 Aug 25] angular, light-framed filly: half-sister to several winners, including useful 4-y-o French Provincial 1½m to 2½m winner Lac Ladoga (by Sharpo), fairly useful middle-distance performer Surrey Dancer (by Shareef Dancer) and Pretty Polly winner Jolly Bay (by Mill Reef): dam won Oaks and Irish Oaks and is sister to Julio Mariner and half-sister to Scintillate: fair form: won maiden at Catterick in July: stays 17.2f. has raced only on top-of-the-ground. *R. Charlton* 75

DUCKEY FUZZ 7 b.g. Ardross 134 – Twine (Thatching 131) [1994 74: 9d 7d^3 7s^3 8g* 8m 7.9f 1995 6.9d 8d 9d Sep 30] lengthy gelding: fair 7f/1m handicapper in 1994: well beaten all 3 7-y-o starts, off course 6 months after first of them: best efforts with give in the ground (acts on soft). *R. M. Flower* –

DUCKING 3 b.f. Reprimand 122 – Gliding 94 (Tudor Melody 129) [1994 67p: 6m 7g^4 1995 7g^4 8g 8m 10f^3 a12g Nov 11] rangy filly: fair maiden on her day: stays 1¼m: acts on firm ground, yet to race on a soft surface. *J. R. Fanshawe* 71

DUELLO 4 b.g. Sure Blade (USA) 130 – Royal Loft 105 (Homing 130) [1994 56: 8s 6g 6m^{6} 7m 10g 8d 7v^{3} 6.1s 7d^{6} 7g 7d^{2} 1995 8d^{2} a8.5g^{3} a8g^{5} 8.3m^{2} 8m^{6} 8.3m 10m 7m^{5} 7.1m^{4} 8g 7.1d^{3} 8.5s* 8d^{2} 8s 8.2m Oct 19] leggy gelding: has a round action: fair handicapper: gained first success in 19-runner race at Epsom in September: stays 8.5f, probably not 1¼m: acts on good to firm and soft going and fibresand: blinkered (respectable effort) once as 3-y-o: tends to idle in front: sold 3,000 gns Newmarket Autumn Sales. *M. Blanshard* — 64 a67

DUFFERTOES 3 ch.g. High Kicker (USA) – Miss Poll Flinders (Swing Easy (USA) 126) [1994 85: 5d* 6m 6g 8s^{4} 7g* 8g 7v* 1995 8d 9m 6m 8m May 21] big, rangy gelding: fair handicapper: well below form on 3 of his 4 starts in 1995: stays 9f: acts on heavy ground and good to firm: takes keen hold. *M. J. Ryan* — 79

DUGGAN 8 b.g. Dunbeath (USA) 127 – Silka (ITY) (Lypheor 118) [1994 –: a12g^{6} a12g 12g 12.1f^{6} 14.1m 11.1m^{6} a12g 15.1g a16g 1995 11.9m* 12.1m* 12.1m^{6} 15.1f^{3} 12m^{6} a16g^{5} a12g^{6} Dec 12] lengthy, rather sparely-made gelding: poor handicapper: won at Brighton (selling event) in June and Edinburgh (apprentices) in July: stays 15f: acts on firm ground: held up: has carried head awkwardly: inconsistent. *P. D. Evans* — 35 a–

DUGORT STRAND (IRE) 4 b. or br.g. Entitled 126 – Soltina (Sun Prince 128) [1994 –, a56: a7g^{4} 8.2g 8m a7g a11g^{4} a14g* a16g 16s 1995 a16.2g a14g 14.1g Apr 17] leggy gelding: poor mover: worthwhile form only when winning amateurs maiden handicap at Southwell in August 1994: better at 1¾m than shorter: acts on fibresand: usually blinkered: runs in snatches. *J. L. Harris* — –

DUKE OF DREAMS 5 gr.g. Efisio 120 – Tame Duchess 71 (Saritamer (USA) 130) [1994 60: 8m^{5} 8m^{3} 8g^{3} 9g^{3} 8m 8g 8d 1995 10.2m 12m Jul 6] strong gelding: modest handicapper: tailed off in 1995. *R. J. Baker* — –

DUKE VALENTINO 3 br.c. Machiavellian (USA) 123 – Aldhabyih 86 (General Assembly (USA)) [1994 NR 1995 6d^{5} 7s^{2} 6d 8m^{6} 10m 8.2d^{6} 8m^{4} 8f^{6} a6g* a8g* a7g a8g^{2} a7g* Dec 18] IR 14,500Y, resold 240,000 francs Y: strong colt: sixth living foal: half-brother to fairly useful 1988 2-y-o 6f and 7f winner Alhathaf (by Tap On Wood): dam 2-y-o 5f winner who stayed 7f: had 3 outings in France for J. Hammond: sold 16,000 gns Newmarket July Sales: fairly useful form here, winning maiden and 2 handicaps at Lingfield in November/December: effective at 6f to 1m: acts on good to firm and soft ground and goes well on equitrack: has had tongue tied down. *R. Hollinshead* — 69 a81

DULFORD DOLLY 2 b.f. (Apr 11) Never So Bold 135 – High Quail (USA) (Blushing Groom (FR) 131) [1995 6.1m Jul 24] 3,800Y: seventh foal: half-sister to 3-y-o Docklands Courier (by Dominion), and a winner in USA: dam unraced: 25/1, slow-starting ninth of 11 in maiden auction at Nottingham: dead. *B. R. Millman* — –

DUNCOMBE HALL 2 b.g. (Apr 22) Salse (USA) 128 – Springs Welcome 86 (Blakeney 126) [1995 5m^{5} May 23] smallish, sturdy gelding: first foal: dam stayed 2m: 25/1 and backward, slowly away, hampered and outpaced throughout in maiden at Goodwood: subsequently gelded. *C. A. Cyzer* — –

DUNDEELIN 4 ch.f. Dunbeath (USA) 127 – Iron Lass (Thatch (USA) 136) [1994 46: a5g^{6} a6g 1995 a6g 8.1d^{4} 7.1g 8m 6.9m^{3} 11.1g 8g a6g a5g Sep 4] sparely-made filly: poor handicapper: stays 1m: acts on heavy going and on fibresand: tried visored/blinkered: looks a difficult ride: sold 500 gns Ascot November Sales. *J. L. Eyre* — 34 a43 ?

DUNE RIVER 6 b.g. Green Desert (USA) 127 – River Spey 96 (Mill Reef (USA) 141) [1994 86, a92: a8g* a8g* a8g^{3} 7.6m 8.1g^{2} 8f^{3} 7f* 7.1g 1995 a8g* 7m 8.5f Sep 21] big, robust, good-topped gelding: good walker: fairly useful handicapper on turf, useful on the all-weather: won at Lingfield in March: last in claimer at Belmont on final outing: stays 1m: acts on firm ground and the all-weather: races up with pace: game and consistent: goes well fresh. *D. R. Loder* — 79 a99

DUNGEON DANCER 3 b.c. Rambo Dancer (CAN) 107 – Falcrello 51 (Falcon 131) [1994 62: 6.1s^{2} 6m^{5} 7m* 7m^{4} 7m^{2} 7m 7.1g^{4} 8m a8g^{4} 7d^{3} 1995 8f^{3} 8m 10g^{4} 10m 10.8m* 10m^{3} Jul 10] smallish, sturdy colt: modest performer: won seller at Warwick in June: stays 10.8f: acts on firm ground and soft: usually visored: sold 7,500 gns Newmarket July Sales. *J. Akehurst* — 61

DUNGEON MASTER (IRE) 2 ch.c. (Feb 23) Polish Patriot (USA) 128 – Etty 81 (Relko 136) [1995 5g^6 5.1g* 5m* 5.5m^2 May 27] 9,800F, 14,000Y: smallish, quite attractive colt: closely related to 1993 Irish 2-y-o 8.5f winner Paugim (by Danehill) and half-brother to several winners, including Ribblesdale winner Miss Boniface (by Tap On Wood): dam, 1¼m winner, half-sister to very smart Whip It Quick: progressive youngster early in season, first past post in maiden at Nottingham, 5-runner minor event at Newmarket (final start for M. Channon, beat Night Parade ½ length) and listed race at Rome: disqualified for hanging left and causing interference after winning by 2 lengths in Italy. *L. Brogi, Italy* 92

DUNGEON PRINCESS (IRE) 2 b.f. (Jan 26) Danehill (USA) 126 – Taplow (Tap On Wood 130) [1995 6g^5 6m Oct 13] 15,000F, 15,000Y: robust filly: fifth foal: half-sister to 3-y-o Takeshi (by Cadeaux Genereux) and winning sprinter Olifantsfontein (by Thatching): dam, unraced, from family of Bassenthwaite and Hadeer: carrying condition, modest form in maidens at Redcar and Newmarket: may do better. *M. R. Channon* 56

DUNLOE (IRE) 3 b.f. Shaadi (USA) 126 – Kates Cabin 96 (Habitat 134) [1994 NR 1995 8.3m 8f* 7g Sep 13] unfurnished filly: unimpressive mover: first foal: dam 1m winner out of sister to very smart soft-ground stayer Old Bill: form only when winning maiden at Warwick in August: stays 1m: has raced only on a sound surface: sold 2,500 gns Newmarket December Sales. *G. Wragg* 54

DUNMEBRAINS (IRE) 2 ch.f. (May 7) Rich Charlie 117 – Branch Out (Star Appeal 133) [1995 6m^6 Aug 16] quite good-topped filly: fourth live foal: dam lightly-raced half-sister to useful sprinter Plain Fact: 25/1, sixth of 12 in valuable seller at York, chasing leaders and keeping on at one pace. *J. S. Moore* –

DUO MASTER 2 b.c. (Apr 7) Primo Dominie 121 – Musical Sally (USA) (The Minstrel (CAN) 135) [1995 6g 5g^3 May 25] 8,200Y, 21,000 2-y-o: good-bodied colt: brother to 1991 2-y-o 7f winner Neo-Classical and half-brother to 3-y-o 6f winner Always Grace (by Never So Bold) and 2 winners in USA by Summing: dam never ran: very promising third of 8 to Gothenberg in minor event at Newcastle in May: likeable type who looked sure to win races. *Mrs M. Reveley* 78 p

DURALOCK FENCER 2 b.g. (Mar 29) General Wade 93 – Madame Laffitte 54 (Welsh Pageant 132) [1995 5g^2 6.1m 6m 6g 6m^5 7.3d 6.9m Nov 6] 950Y: leggy gelding: half-brother to fair 6f and 7f winner By Hand (by Sayf El Arab): dam 7f winner at 2 yrs, only year to race: modest maiden: probably stays 7f: best form on a sound surface: apprentice ridden: has been bandaged near-hind. *P. G. Murphy* 58

DURANO 4 b.g. Dunbeath (USA) 127 – Norapa 91 (Ahonoora 122) [1994 59: 8d^2 8.5d^3 8m^4 a8g^3 a7g 1995 10m^5 10f* 10m^3 11f^3 12.3m^4 Aug 12] sturdy gelding: fair handicapper: won at Redcar in July: should stay 1½m: acts on dead ground, firm and fibresand: used to race prominently, held up in 1995. *M. H. Easterby* 69

DURGAMS FIRST (IRE) 3 ch.g. Durgam (USA) – Miromaid (Simply Great (FR) 122) [1994 64: 5g^5 5v^2 6f 7m^3 7.5g^2 7g^3 7.1m^2 6g^2 7g* 6m 6s^2 7d 1995 a8g* a9.4g^2 a8g* 10.3g 11.1g^3 12.5m^3 9.9m^3 10f 12m* 13.8g^3 11.9m* 10f^5 13.8g* Sep 16] small, leggy gelding: fair performer: won seller and claimer at Southwell early in year, claimers at Carlisle and Haydock (idled in front) in the summer, and seller (bought in 7,000 gns) at Catterick in September: stays 13.8f: acts on firm and soft going and on fibresand: sometimes edgy: held up: consistent. *Mrs M. Reveley* 62 a70

DURHAM 4 ch.g. Caerleon (USA) 132 – Sanctuary (Welsh Pageant 132) [1994 68: 8m^5 8s^2 10g^4 11.7f^4 1995 a11g^3 Feb 3] sparely-made gelding: fair maiden in 1994 for P. Cole: first run on all-weather and favourite, well below form in seller at Southwell only 4-y-o start: should stay 1½m: probably acts on any ground: has joined R. Simpson. *N. Tinkler* –

DURHAM DRAPES 4 b.f. Taufan (USA) 119 – Miss Bali Beach 88 (Nonoalco (USA) 131) [1994 62: 8m^3 9.9g^2 10m^4 9m^2 8f^3 10m^2 11g^4 9.9f^3 10g^4 10m^2 12g 1995 8f 9.9m^5 10m^4 12g 9f^5 8m^4 9f* 8h* 8h^6 10.4g 8g Sep 15] leggy, unfurnished filly: has a quick action: fair handicapper: won at Redcar (apprentice maiden event) and Carlisle in August: effective at 1m, probably at 11f: acts on hard ground: visored twice in 1994, running creditably first occasion: has had tongue tied down: won novice hurdle in October. *M. H. Easterby* 62

DURSHAN (USA) 6 ch.g. Shahrastani (USA) 135 – Dukayna 103 (Northfields (USA)) [1994 64d: 11.9d 14d 11.8s^6 16m^4 14.4g* 16.2m^6 14.9m^5 14m^4 14m 14.1m 54 d

16s 1995 a16g 15.4g^5 12g^3 16m^5 14.1g^3 14.4m^4 12f Jun 28] leggy, workmanlike gelding: modest handicapper at best in 1995: stays 2m: acts on good to firm and soft ground: blinkered (below best) once at 3 yrs: won over hurdles in November. *J. R. Jenkins*

DUSHYANTOR (USA) 2 b.c. (Apr 11) Sadler's Wells (USA) 132 – Slightly Dangerous (USA) 122 (Roberto (USA) 131) [1995 8.2m* Oct 19] smallish, attractive colt: half-brother to several winners, notably champion miler Warning (by Known Fact), top-class middle-distance colt Deploy (by Shirley Heights) and Derby winner Commander In Chief (by Dancing Brave): dam second in Oaks: long odds on, won 19-runner maiden at Nottingham by ¾ length from Altamura, pair 7 lengths clear, headway from position just behind leaders 3f out and running on strongly under firm hands and heels last 150 yds: sure to go on to much better things over middle distances. *H. R. A. Cecil* — 92 P

DUSK IN DAYTONA 3 b.f. Beveled (USA) – Mount of Light 61 (Sparkler 130) [1994 64: 5.7f^5 6f^4 6g 7.3s^3 1995 7g^4 10g a7g^2 7f^3 a7g^6 7f* a7g^4 a7g a7g^3 a7g Nov 29] leggy filly: has a round action: modest performer: made all in median auction maiden at Brighton in August: stays 7.3f, not 1¼m: acts on any turf going, and on all-weather surfaces: races prominently. *C. James* — 64

DUSTY POINT (IRE) 5 b.g. Reference Point 139 – Noble Dust (USA) (Dust Commander (USA)) [1994 70: 12m 13.3s^6 14g 12.4f 12f^3 12g^3 1995 12m 12g 12f a12g^6 13.1g^2 16.5f^4 14.1m^3 Aug 10] compact, good-bodied gelding: only modest handicapper in 1995: stays 2m: acts on any going: tried blinkered and visored: made winning hurdling debut (for C. Dwyer) in October. *J. Pearce* — 58

DUTCH 3 ch.c. Nicholas Bill 125 – Dutch Princess 70 (Royalty 130) [1994 NR 1995 14g Oct 23] eighth foal: brother to useful stayer Double Dutch: dam staying maiden: tailed off in maiden at Lingfield. *G. P. Enright* — –

DUTOSKY 5 b.m. Doulab (USA) 115 – Butosky 71 (Busted 134) [1994 69d: 10.3m 10m 10m^4 10.1m^2 12m 10.4f a10g^2 a10g^4 8.5m^4 a12g^3 8m a10g^3 1995 a8g^4 a10g^5 12m 10g^2 10m* 9.7g* 10f^3 Jun 23] strong, compact mare: tends to look well: unimpressive mover: fair handicapper: left R. Williams' stable after second 5-y-o start: in good form for new connections, winning at Sandown in May and Folkestone in June: suited by around 1¼m: acts on any turf ground, but seems only modest on the all-weather: blinkered (no improvement) twice at 4 yrs. *R. J. O'Sullivan* — 66 a49

DUTY SERGEANT (IRE) 6 b.g. Pennine Walk 120 – Plainsong (FR) (Amen (FR)) [1994 –: 11.9d^5 7m 7g 8.5m 6m 6m^6 1995 6m a8g^5 9.7m 11.9m^3 12m^2 Jun 14] smallish, sturdy gelding: poor handicapper: stays 1½m: acts on firm ground and dead: often used to be blinkered, not in 1995. *P. Mitchell* — 37

DUVEEN (IRE) 5 b.g. Tate Gallery (USA) 117 – Wish You Were Here (USA) 81 (Secretariat (USA)) [1994 NR 1995 a8g Dec 15] lengthy gelding: poor mover: fair middle-distances performer at 3 yrs: never a threat in claimer only start in 1995. *J. White* — –

DVORAK (IRE) 4 b.g. Darshaan 133 – Grace Note (FR) 99 (Top Ville 129) [1994 85?: 10d^4 10g^6 10.5g^4 12g a14g^4 1995 a13g^2 a12g^2 13v^3 12m* 14m^5 10f a12g a12g Dec 9] tall, good-topped gelding: fair handicapper: won at Doncaster in May on penultimate start for B. McMath: well beaten for new stable: stays 1¾m: best form on a sound surface (acts on good to firm), never travelling well on heavy. *R. Harris* — 69 d

DWINGELOO (IRE) 2 b.f. (Jan 18) Dancing Dissident (USA) 119 – Thank One's Stars (Alzao (USA) 117) [1995 6d^2 5f* Oct 14] sturdy, lengthy filly: third foal: half-sister to 6f (at 2 yrs) to 1m winner Suris and a winner in Trinidad (both by Taufan): dam unraced: 4 lengths second of 25 to Sovereign's Crown in maiden at Newbury: readily beat Amy Leigh by 1½ lengths in 7-runner minor event at Catterick following month, pair 6 lengths clear: will improve further. *Major D. N. Chappell* — 83 p

DYANKO 2 b.g. (Mar 1) Midyan (USA) 124 – Regain 86 (Relko 136) [1995 6m^4 6m Jun 14] 5,400Y: leggy, unfurnished gelding: half-brother to several winners, including stayer White River (by Pharly) and fairly useful 1m winner Wild And Loose (by Precocious): dam 1½m winner: poor form in claimer at Goodwood and maiden auction at Kempton: will be suited by 1m+: refused to enter stalls at Wolverhampton in July. *M. S. Saunders* — 49

DYNAMIS (IRE) 4 b.f. Dancing Brave (USA) 140 – Diasprina (GER) (Aspros (GER)) [1994 64: 5m 6.9s^2 7g^3 7.6g^2 6s^3 5s^4 a7g^4 a7g 1995 a8.5g^3 a7g a5g^6 a7g 10m a12g 10g a9.4g 10.2m Jul 20] compact filly: poor mover: modest performer at best in 1994: little worthwhile form here in 1995, though won in Jersey in May: stays 1¼m: acts on soft ground and fibresand. *K. O. Cunningham-Brown* 52 d

E

EAGLE CANYON (IRE) 2 b. or br.c. (May 27) Persian Bold 123 – Chrism (Baptism 119) [1995 7g 7d^5 5m^4 Oct 5] 9,000Y, 24,000 2-y-o: good-topped colt: has a round action: seventh foal: half-brother to fairly useful 1m and 10.5f winner in Italy Stremizi (by Alzao) and a winner abroad: dam Irish maiden half-sister to Shining Finish and Bright Finish from good family: best effort when over 10 lengths fifth of 8 to Story Line in minor event at Ascot penultimate start: bred to need 1m+: coltish second start. *B. Hanbury* 72

EAGLE DAY (USA) 4 b.c. Phone Trick (USA) – Ellen L (USA) (To Market) [1994 86: 6f^5 6d^3 6m^4 8m 6m 5m^2 5d^2 5m 5d 5g^2 5m^6 5m^3 1995 6g 5d 5.2m 6f^2 5.1m 5m 5g^6 a7g Nov 21] well-made colt: shows a quick action: fair maiden handicapper on balance of form: looked none too keen final start: stays 6f: acts on firm and dead ground: blinkered/visored nowadays: sold only 2,200 gns Doncaster November Sales. *D. R. C. Elsworth* 71

EARLY PEACE (IRE) 3 b.g. Bluebird (USA) 125 – Everything Nice 107 (Sovereign Path 125) [1994 NR 1995 8g 7g^3 10g^5 Jul 12] 16,000F: strong colt: half-brother to several winners, including Irish 1000 Guineas winner Nicer (by Pennine Walk): dam won from 5f (at 2 yrs) to 10.5f: stayed on well when third of 13 in maiden at Salisbury: beaten 23 lengths at Newmarket 7 weeks later, not at all knocked about final 3f: sold 11,000 gns Newmarket Autumn Sales. *R. Hannon* 73

EARLY STAR 6 b.g. Precocious 126 – Staritsa (USA) (Alleged (USA) 138) [1994 50: a8g^3 a7g^5 a9.4g a8g^5 8g^6 a8g a8g 7.1g 1995 a8g^3 a8g 7m a11g May 15] rather leggy, quite good-topped gelding: seems only poor at best nowadays: stays 1m: acts on fibresand and soft ground: tried blinkered, no improvement: inconsistent. *K. Bishop* 44

EARLY TO RISE 5 b.g. Don't Forget Me 127 – Foreno (Formidable (USA) 125) [1994 34: 12.3d 12.1g^5 12m 15.8g 1995 12.5g Jun 17] strong, close-coupled gelding: poor performer: sold 750 gns Doncaster July Sales, and joined Miss M. Bragg: stays 2m (at least in steadily-run race): acts on all-weather surfaces: blinkered (soundly beaten) 5-y-o start: inconsistent. *Miss L. C. Siddall* –

EASBY JESTER 4 b.g. Idiot's Delight 115 – Khatti Hawk (Hittite Glory 125) [1994 NR 1995 7f Aug 4] third foal: dam poor performer: behind in 2 NH Flat races and a seller: sold (S. Kettlewell to L. Barratt) 700 gns Doncaster September Sales. *S. E. Kettlewell* –

EAST BARNS (IRE) 7 gr.g. Godswalk (USA) 130 – Rocket Lass (Touch Paper 113) [1994 48, a53d: a8g^2 a8g 8.1g^2 a8g^4 7.1f^4 8m^6 a8g a8g^4 10g^3 a9.4g^3 8.2m 8.2m 10.4d 7s* a8g 7g^2 1995 6g 8.5m 10m* May 26] close-coupled gelding: has a quick action: poor handicapper: won at Nottingham in May: stays 1¼m: acts on firm and soft going and on fibresand: has worn a visor, usually blinkered: battled well for win, but is inconsistent. *S. Gollings* 50 a–

EASTER COUL (IRE) 3 br.f. Brush Aside (USA) 125 – Cree's Figurine 63 (Creetown 123) [1994 NR 1995 7m 10g 10f^3 Aug 22] workmanlike filly: fourth foal: half-sister to 2 winners, notably useful 4-y-o sprinter Royale Figurine (by Dominion Royale): dam 2-y-o 5f winner: little promise in maidens: sold 575 gns Ascot September Sales. *M. J. Fetherston-Godley* –

EASTERN PARADISE 2 b.c. (May 1) Mujtahid (USA) 118 – Bedouin Veil (USA) (Shareef Dancer (USA) 135) [1995 6.1d^4 6g* Sep 20] lengthy, workmanlike colt: has a quick action: second live foal: half-brother to 4-y-o 1¼m winner Sariyaa (by Persian Bold): dam (French 9f winner) out of Ma Biche: won 16-runner maiden at Brighton comfortably by 2½ lengths from Surtees: will stay further than 6f: tends to carry head bit high: will improve again. *M. R. Stoute* 79 p

EASTERN PROPHETS 2 b.c. (Apr 3) Emarati (USA) 74 – Four Love (Pas de Seul 133) [1995 5g^{5} 5m* 5.1f* 6g^{2} 5d* 5m 5.2g 5m^{2} 6g^{2} 5g 5s^{5} Oct 7] 4,500F, 7,000Y: good-quartered colt: first foal: dam Irish 1m winner: useful form: won maiden auction at Doncaster, minor event at Bath and £7,900 event at Beverley in first half of season: best efforts when second in nursery at Beverley and listed race at Kempton: stays 6f: sometimes on toes and sweating: tends to run a bit lazily in front. *G. Lewis* 98

EASTERN SUNRISE 2 b.g. (Apr 24) Statoblest 120 – Oriental Splendour 85 (Runnett 125) [1995 7.1g Sep 18] 12,000F, 26,000Y: second foal: half-brother to 3-y-o 5f and 6f winner Sizzling (by Sizzling Melody): dam suited by 7f: 25/1, never a factor in claimer at Edinburgh. *Mrs M. Reveley* –

EAST INDIA (IRE) 2 b.c. (Mar 7) Scenic 128 – Eastern Aura (IRE) 49 (Ahonoora 122) [1995 7f 8.1m^{2} 8.5s^{4} Sep 19] IR 12,500F, 20,000Y: strong colt: first foal: dam poor maiden: ½-length second of 8 to Ski Academy in maiden at Chepstow in August: remote fourth of 8 in maiden at Epsom following month: stays 1m: sold 15,000 gns Newmarket Autumn Sales. *R. Charlton* 75

EASTLEIGH 6 b.g. Efisio 120 – Blue Jane 81 (Blue Cashmere 129) [1994 –, a58d: a8.5g a8.5g^{2} a7g a8g a8.5g^{2} 8m a8.5g a7g^{3} a8g 7.6m a8g a8.5g^{6} a7g^{5} a7g a6g^{6} a7g^{2} 8m 7.6g a8.5g^{2} a8g a9.4g^{4} 8.1m^{6} a8.5g^{3} a8.5g a7g^{4} a8g^{3} a8.5g^{5} 8g a7g^{4} a8g^{4} a7g^{3} 1995 a8g^{5} a7g^{6} a8g^{2} a8.5g^{3} a8g^{4} a8g a8g^{2} a8g* a9.4g^{3} a8.5g^{3} a8g* a9.4g^{5} a8g^{6} a9.4g a8g^{5} a7g a8g^{4} a8g^{6} Dec 15] lengthy, workmanlike gelding: modest performer: won seller and handicap at Lingfield early on: stays 9.4f: acts on all-weather (formerly acted on good to firm ground and dead): visored twice (ran creditably) in 1994: none too consistent. *R. Hollinshead* – a58

EAST OF HEAVEN (IRE) 3 b.c. Lyphard (USA) 132 – Escaline (FR) 123 (Arctic Tern (USA) 126) [1994 8d^{2} 7.5v^{4} 6.5v^{2} 1995 8g* 9.3m^{3} 10m^{2} 10g^{4} Jul 14] half-brother to disappointing Derby fourth Kaheel (by Caro) and winners in France by Diesis and Riverman: dam won from 1m to 10.5f in France, including in Prix de Diane, and is sister to dam of Royal Abjar: smart French colt: narrowly won minor 112

Timeform Race Card Juvenile Conditions Stakes, Bath—
quite useful two-year-olds Eastern Prophets and Tadeo

event at Evry in April: ran well afterwards, 3½ lengths third to Valanour in Prix de Guiche at Longchamp, length second to Vaguely Gay in listed race on same course and ½-length fourth to Royal Solo in Prix Eugene Adam at Saint-Cloud: stays 1¼m: acts on good to firm ground and heavy. *A. Fabre, France*

EAST SHEEN 3 b.f. Salse (USA) 128 – Madam Cody (Hot Spark 126) [1994 67: 6s 7g 6d 1995 7.6m 7.1m 7f Jun 29] close-coupled filly: well beaten in 1995: should stay at least 7f: best effort on dead ground. *C. J. Benstead* –

EASY CHOICE (USA) 3 b.c. Easy Goer (USA) – Monroe (USA) 102 (Sir Ivor 135) [1994 NR 1995 8g^3 10g^4 5g^3 5g^4 6.5d^4 a8g* a8g* a8g* Dec 14] ex-French colt: half-brother to 7 winners, 4 pattern-placed, including smart miler Masterclass (by The Minstrel) and very useful 1¼m and 10.5f winner Diese (by Diesis): dam, useful Irish sprinter, is sister to Malinowski and half-sister to dam of Try My Best and El Gran Senor: fairly useful form for A. Fabre: successful here in maiden, minor event and handicap (soon outpaced and driven along, responded to strong pressure to lead last 100 yds and win going away) all at Lingfield: effective at 1m, will be well suited by return to further: acts on equitrack: capable of better still. *P. Mitchell* 81 +

EASY DOLLAR 3 ch.g. Gabitat 119 – Burglars Girl 63 (Burglar 128) [1994 63: 5g^4 6s^3 6m 1995 7m^5 6m^3 8.3m^4 8m^5 7.3m 6m^4 6f^2 6m* 7f* 7.3m^5 6m^3 8m^5 6d 7d Sep 30] tall, plain gelding: progressed very well into a useful performer: won maiden at Newmarket and £19,800 handicap at Goodwood in July: best efforts when fifth in Hungerford Stakes at Newbury then third in listed race at Newmarket: well beaten on softer ground in pattern events last 2 starts: stays 7.3f well: goes well on top-of-the-ground: nearly always visored/blinkered: tends to hang. *B. Gubby* 109

EASY D'OR 4 b.g. Glint of Gold 128 – Eastern Command (USA) 74 (Far Out East (USA)) [1994 52: 12s 12.3d^5 14.1f* 14.1m 15.4m 16g^3 16d^5 16s^5 17.1s 1995 15.8g 16m Jun 13] small, sturdy gelding: no form in 1995 for new stable: stayed 2m: acted on firm ground: fell over hurdles Jun 29: dead. *Mrs A. Swinbank* –

EASY JET (POL) 3 b.c. Robellino (USA) 127 – Etourdie (USA) (Arctic Tern (USA) 126) [1994 68: 7d 7g 8.1g 1995 7.3m^2 7.1m^2 8m^6 8d 8m Oct 14] strong colt: poor mover: fairly useful maiden handicapper: well below form last 2 outings: likely to stay beyond 1m: acts on good to firm ground, ran poorly on dead. *Lord Huntingdon* 83 d

EASY LISTENING (USA) 3 b.g. Easy Goer (USA) – Queen of Song (USA) (His Majesty (USA)) [1994 NR 1995 10.2f* May 22] rangy gelding with scope: fifth foal: half-brother to 3 winners in North America, notably minor stakes winner (at around 1m) Ladyago (by Northern Dancer): dam won 14 races including Grade 2 event at 8.5f, and is sister to smart 6f to 9f winner Cormorant: sire top class at up to 1¼m, outstanding at 1½m: 5/4 favourite though green to post and looking as if race would do him good, made a most impressive debut when winning 17-runner maiden at Bath in May by 3 lengths from Paddy's Return: injured on gallops soon after: back in full training in August, but did not reappear and gelded in the autumn: will be suited by 1½m: looked sure to improve. *R. Charlton* 79 p

EASY OPTION (IRE) 3 ch.f. Prince Sabo 123 – Brazen Faced 84 (Bold And Free 118) [1994 99: 5.1d* 5.2g* 5g 1995 5g^4 5.2d* 5d^4 Oct 1] 115

Easy Option is a very strong contender for the title 'easiest winner of 1995'. The Tony Stratton Smith Memorial Conditions Stakes at Newbury in September was not a very important contest, but it attracted six useful sprinters—or what looked to be six useful sprinters at that stage. Easy Option won turning handsprings. Walter Swinburn was able to choose at his leisure which part of the track to race on, his mount pulling double, then after half a dozen or so nudges approaching the furlong marker Easy Option took off and sauntered home clear by seven lengths, a margin which underestimated her superiority. Katya, Sharp Prod and Lennox Lewis were the others in the frame. Easy Option was somewhat better than useful on this showing. Fourth in the Prix de l'Abbaye de Longchamp sixteen days later confirmed that, but without fulfilling the sort of expectations that had looked reasonable for her after Newbury; Easy Option kept close tabs on Hever Golf Rose until fully stretched over the last two furlongs.

Until that Newbury win, Easy Option had not looked a particularly inspired acquisition for the Godolphin team. Trained by William Jarvis as a two-year-old, she had impressed in winning a median auction maiden at Nottingham and a listed race at Newbury for owner-breeders John and Susan Davis on her first two starts, before making an inauspicious debut in the Godolphin colours in the Flying Childers Stakes. After wintering in Dubai, Easy Option showed some promise when fourth, on the backward side, in a listed race at Kempton and was then put away to wait for easy ground.

Easy Option (IRE) (ch.f. 1992)	Prince Sabo (b 1982)	Young Generation (b 1976)	Balidar
			Brig O'Doon
		Jubilee Song (b 1976)	Song
			Sylvanecte
	Brazen Faced (ch 1975)	Bold And Free (ch 1969)	Bold Lad
			Free And Easy
		Maurine (b 1955)	Worden II
			Muscida

A lengthy filly who did well physically from two to three years, Easy Option is a poor walker and unimpressive mover. She remains in training. Her dam Brazen Faced was purchased by the Davises for 14,000 guineas from Lord Halifax at the 1989 December Sales. She won only one race for the earl from twelve starts, a five-furlong maiden as a two-year-old, but all of her eight foals for him were winners, the best of them being the useful 1985 two-year-old five-furlong winner Wanton (by Kris). Brazen Faced is a daughter of the useful mile and mile-and-a-quarter performer Maurine, and a half-sister to both the Musidora winner Lovers Lane and that tough and very useful middle-distance stayer, the blind-in-one-eye Belper. Brazen Faced's sire Bold And Free was a five-furlong specialist, as was Easy Option's sire Prince Sabo to whom Brazen Faced returned in 1995 after throwing fillies by Thatching in 1993 (the unraced Loose Talk) and Efisio in 1994. Easy Option is Prince Sabo's best offspring to date. The stallion looked set for a good year after the 1994 exploits of Easy Option's contemporaries Princely Hush and Maid For Walking, but that pair managed just five runs between them in 1995 and no wins. Branston Jewel looked to have the makings of a good sprinter from the latest batch of two-year-olds but suffered what is probably a career-ending injury. *Saeed bin Suroor*

EASY TO REMEMBER (IRE) 2 b.c. (Mar 26) Mujtahid (USA) 118 – In Unison (Bellypha 130) [1995 7m Aug 16] IR 16,000Y: sturdy colt: second foal: half-brother to 3-y-o 7f winner Iblis (by Danehill), 6f winner at 2 yrs: dam, 1m winner, granddaughter of top 1975 Irish 2-y-o filly Welsh Garden: 16/1, burly and green, tailed off in maiden at Kempton: sold 900 gns Newmarket Autumn Sales. *J. R. Fanshawe* –

EAU DE COLOGNE 3 b.g. Persian Bold 123 – No More Rosies 74 (Warpath 113) [1994 52p: 7d 1995 10m^5 9m^5 10g* 12m^3 12.3m^3 15g^4 13.9g 16d^4 15.1s^3 Nov 2] good-topped gelding: fair handicapper: won maiden at Ayr in June: will be suited by thorough test of stamina: acts on good to firm ground, respectable efforts on dead and soft. *C. W. Thornton* 71

EBEN AL HABEEB (IRE) 4 ch.c. Nashwan (USA) 135 – Family Style (USA) (State Dinner (USA)) [1994 79: 10m^3 10m^2 12m 1995 10m 11.8g 10g^3 11.7h^3 Sep 4] big, lengthy colt: easy mover: has had soft-palate operation and been hobdayed: fair maiden handicapper: probably stays 11.7f: probably acts on hard ground: sold 8,000 gns Newmarket Autumn Sales. *Major W. R. Hern* 74

EBEN NAAS (USA) 2 b.c. (Feb 6) Dayjur (USA) 137 – Regal State (USA) 122 (Affirmed (USA)) [1995 a8g Dec 18] 110,000Y: fourth foal: dam, 6f and 7f winner at 2 yrs in France, half-sister to Prix Morny winner Seven Springs, the dam of Distant View: sold out of M. Stoute's stable 4,000 gns Newmarket Autumn Sales: slowly away and always behind in 9-runner maiden at Lingfield. *S. C. Williams* –

EBONY BLAZE 4 b.g. Aragon 118 – Velvet Pigeon 70 (Homing 130) [1994 72d: 6g^6 6.1m^4 6s 5m^4 6m 7g 8m 7d 7d a7g a7g^5 1995 a10g 10d 8m^6 9d 7d Oct 19] workmanlike gelding: disappointing maiden: probably stayed 9f: acted on good to firm ground, probably on dead: blinkered (ran poorly) once at 3 yrs: dead. *C. P. Wildman* 50

EBONY BOY 2 bl.c. (Apr 19) Sayf El Arab (USA) 127 – Actress 73 (Known Fact (USA) 135) [1995 5s a6g^3 a5g^2 a7g^2 a7g* 5m 6m a7g^6 a7g^4 Dec 12] 11,000Y: tall, good-topped colt: second foal: half-brother to 3-y-o 5f (at 2 yrs) to 7f winner Russian Heroine (by Domynsky): dam 7f winner, stayed 1m: made all in median auction event at Southwell in July: no form on turf though had valid excuses last 2 starts: stays 7f: best form on fibresand. *J. Wharton* – a65

EBONY T-A-P-S 2 bl.f. (Apr 30) Adbass (USA) 102 – August Seventeenth 55 (Sharpo 132) [1995 7f 7g Sep 29] 500Y: small filly: has a round action: third foal: dam maiden stayed 7f: soundly beaten in claimer at Salisbury and seller at Goodwood 3 months later. *J. S. Moore* –

ECCENTRIC DANCER 2 b.f. (Mar 10) Rambo Dancer (CAN) 107 – Lady Eccentric (IRE) (Magical Wonder (USA) 125) [1995 5m^4 5m 6f^3 7f 6f Oct 24] 2,300F: lengthy filly: first foal: dam unraced: little worthwhile form: should prove better suited by 7f than shorter. *M. P. Bielby* –

ECCOLA 2 b.f. (Feb 23) Seattle Dancer (USA) 119 – Evocatrice 91 (Persepolis (FR) 127) [1995 6f 7f^5 8.1d^5 8g Oct 3] compact filly: first foal: dam French 2-y-o 7f winner (later stayed 1¼m) out of high-class French middle-distance performer Northern Trick: best effort in maidens when fifth to Papering at Goodwood on second start: behind in nursery (stiff task) final outing: bred to stay 1m: may be unsuited by soft surface. *I. A. Balding* 63

ECSTATIC MADAM (IRE) 2 b.f. (Mar 28) Statoblest 120 – Neeran (Wollow 132) [1995 6m 6g 7d^3 8f^6 Oct 12] 9,000Y: leggy filly: half-sister to several winners abroad, including Irish 4-y-o 5f winner The Barracuda (by Taufan): dam once-raced half-sister to Bustino: 5½ lengths third of 7 to Nador in maiden at Brighton: set pace and didn't repeat that form in similar event at Redcar following month: stays 7f: acts on dead ground: tail flasher: sold 6,000 gns Newmarket Autumn Sales. *B. W. Hills* 64 ?

EDAN HEIGHTS 3 b.g. Heights of Gold – Edna 92 (Shiny Tenth 120) [1994 NR 1995 7m 8m^4 8m^5 10m 10g^3 12m^2 12s* 14m^3 11.8f^2 Oct 24] sturdy, plain gelding: seventh foal: half-brother to several winners, none better than fairly useful: dam soft-ground sprinter: fair handicapper: won apprentice maiden at Folkestone in September, leading 3f out: should prove at least as good at 1¾m as 1½m: acts on firm and soft going. *S. Dow* 78

EDBAYSAAN (IRE) 5 b.h. Slip Anchor 136 – Legend of Arabia (Great Nephew 126) [1994 –: 12m^4 18g 1995 12.1m* 15.9m^6 14m^2 12m Oct 12] big, rangy horse: impresses in appearance: first run for new stable and made virtually all to beat Waiting a length in 2-runner £10,800 event at Chepstow in July: no form afterwards, and reluctant to race on second occasion: stays 2m: won on good to firm ground, best 3-y-o form on dead: blinkered final 5-y-o start: sometimes coltish: needs treating with caution. *R. Akehurst* 104 d

EDEN DANCER 3 b.g. Shareef Dancer (USA) 135 – Dash (Connaught 130) [1994 56: 5s^5 6g^6 6.1m^5 7g^5 7.9d 6s^2 1995 8.1g* 7g 8f^6 10f^5 11.1f* 9.9m Aug 9] sturdy gelding: modest performer: made all in smallish fields for maiden at Edinburgh in April and handicap at Hamilton in July: well below that form otherwise: stays 11f: acts on firm and soft ground: inconsistent. *Mrs M. Reveley* 57

EDEN'S CLOSE 6 ch.g. Green Dancer (USA) 132 – Royal Agreement (USA) (Vaguely Noble 140) [1994 –: 12g 1995 10d 10m 11.6g^4 11.5m^4 14.8m^2 Jul 22] leggy, angular gelding: fairly useful hurdler in 1994/5: only modest handicapper on flat nowadays: stays 14.8f: acts on firm and dead ground: effective when visored: sometimes sweats up. *M. H. Tompkins* 57

EDEN'S STAR (IRE) 3 b.g. Fools Holme (USA) – Flinging Star (USA) (Northern Fling (USA)) [1994 69: 6g^6 6.1m 7.5g^2 1995 10g 8.3g^3 8m 10m^4 8f* 8f^2 8.1d^2 8g Sep 20] leggy, lengthy gelding: unimpressive mover: fair handicapper: won minor event at Thirsk in August: stays 8.1f: acts on firm ground and dead: races freely and effective from front. *M. H. Tompkins* 69

EDGAR KIRBY 4 ch.g. Caerleon (USA) 132 – Martha Stevens (USA) 102 (Super Concorde (USA) 128) [1994 58: 8d 8m 7d^6 10.1m^6 10m 1995 8.1m Aug 11] sturdy gelding: modest maiden handicapper: shaped as if retaining some ability when well beaten only start in 1995: should stay 1½m: acts on good to firm and dead ground. *P. W. Harris* –

ED'S FOLLY (IRE) 2 b.c. (Feb 20) Fayruz 116 – Tabriya 61 (Nishapour (FR) 125) [1995 5m 6d 5s^3 5d^6 Oct 11] IR 8,500F, 16,000Y: good-quartered colt: half-brother to 5f winner Bradwell (by Taufan) and a winner by Tumble Wind abroad: dam lightly raced: 2½ lengths third of 16 to Angaar in maiden at Lingfield: respectable sixth of 11 in face of very stiff task in nursery at Haydock following month. *S. Dow* 59

EDUCATED PET 6 gr.g. Petong 126 – School Road 88 (Great Nephew 126) [1994 –: a6g 7f 6.1g 7f a6g 1995 a8g^{5} a7g^{6} a7g^{5} a6g a6g a9.4g 6.1g a8.5g 7m 8.1d 10m Sep 5] sturdy gelding: seems very much on the downgrade. *B. Preece* — 60 d

EELIOUS (USA) 3 b.c. Nureyev (USA) 131 – Maxencia (FR) (Tennyson (FR) 124) [1994 64p: 8m 1995 12m^{3} 14g^{5} 14.1f* 14.8g^{4} 14f^{3} 14m^{4} 13.1g Sep 16] compact colt: not a good mover: fairly useful handicapper: won maiden at Yarmouth in June, leading over 2f out: should stay beyond 14.1f (very stiff task in listed event when tried): acts on firm going, yet to race on a soft surface: sold 21,000 gns Newmarket Autumn Sales. *C. E. Brittain* — 83

EFAAD (IRE) 4 b.g. Shaadi (USA) 126 – Krismas River (Kris 135) [1994 –: 10.5d^{5} 11.9s^{5} 16.1d 1995 17.1m 14.1m May 2] tall gelding: no worthwhile form since 2 yrs. *J. Norton* — –

EFFICACIOUS (IRE) 2 ch.f. (Mar 19) Efisio 120 – Bushti Music 63 (Bustino 136) [1995 5m 6f 6f 5g 7.3d a8g^{5} Nov 30] 10,000Y, 5,000 2-y-o: lengthy, plain filly: poor walker: half-sister to several winners, including middle-distance stayer Kingsley (by Kings Lake) and 1992 2-y-o 6f winner Bourbon Jack (by Robellino) later winner in Italy at up to 1¼m: dam, stayed 9f, half-sister to very useful sprinters Hanu and Sanu: little worthwhile form on turf: fifth of 6 in nursery at Lingfield final start: stays 1m. *C. J. Benstead* — – a44

EFFICACY 4 b.f. Efisio 120 – Lady Killane 62 (Reform 132) [1994 –: 6v 6m^{6} 6f^{5} 6m 6f 1995 a7g a8g a6g^{5} a6g^{4} a5g^{5} a6g* a6g^{2} a6g^{4} a6g* a6g* a6g^{2} a6g^{5} a6g^{6} Nov 27] angular filly: bad mover: progressed into a modest performer: won claimer and 2 handicaps at Wolverhampton in first half of year: pulls hard and best at sprint distances: acts on fibresand, below form only outing on equitrack: often apprentice ridden. *A. P. Jarvis* — 57

EFIPETITE 2 ch.f. (May 20) Efisio 120 – Petite Elite 47 (Anfield 117) [1995 a5g^{5} 5m 5f^{4} a6g^{4} 6m^{5} 6f 6m a6g^{3} 7.1g 7d 7m 6f 6f a6g^{3} a8g Nov 24] good-topped filly: poor mover: second foal: half-sister to 1994 2-y-o 5f winner Little Ginger Nut (by Hallgate): dam stayed 7f: poor form in varied events: stays 6f: acts on fibresand: sweating, edgy and hung when blinkered seventh outing: sometimes looks difficult ride. *N. Bycroft* — 44

EFIZIA 5 b.m. Efisio 120 – Millie Grey 52 (Grey Ghost 98) [1994 78: 8s 8v^{2} 10m 9.9m^{4} 10.1f^{5} 10g^{2} 10m 11d^{3} 10.4d^{6} 10s 10.1d^{6} 1995 10d 10.5s^{6} 10g 10f^{6} 10f Oct 31] sturdy, workmanlike mare: fair handicapper at 4 yrs: disappointing in 1995: probably stays 11f: acts on any going: usually held up. *Mrs M. Reveley* — –

EFOSA 3 b.g. Efisio 120 – Wimosa 92 (Mossborough 126) [1994 –: 7g 1995 a12g^{6} Jul 17] leggy gelding: tailed off in maiden events. *M. P. Muggeridge* — –

EFRA 6 b.g. Efisio 120 – Ra Ra (Lord Gayle (USA) 124) [1994 70+: 6v^{3} 6d^{3} 6m 6s 6s 6m* 1995 6g^{6} 6f 6g 6m 6g^{5} Oct 16] lengthy, good-topped gelding: has a round action: fair performer: below form after reappearance: effective at 6f to 7f: acts on good to firm and heavy ground: blinkered (tailed off) once at 3 yrs. *R. Hannon* — 72

EGLWYS NEWYDD 4 ch.f. Gabitat 119 – Jalna (Free Boy 96) [1994 NR 1995 a9.4g Feb 18] 1,000 3-y-o: half-sister to NH Flat race winner Whitsun Eel (by Chukaroo): dam placed over hurdles: 33/1, well behind in seller at Wolverhampton. *K. S. Bridgwater* — –

EHTEFAAL (USA) 4 b.g. Alysheba (USA) – Bolt From The Blue (USA) (Blue Times (USA)) [1994 86: 12g^{6} 11.9m^{3} 14g* 14f^{3} 1995 a16.2g^{4} May 22] useful-looking gelding: progressed into a fairly useful performer at 3 yrs: sweating, well beaten in claimer at Wolverhampton on reappearance: stays 1¾m: acts on firm ground: visored/blinkered since third 3-y-o start: fetched 31,000 gns in 1994, but sold only 1,800 gns Ascot August Sales. *J. White* — –

EID (USA) 6 b.g. Northern Baby (CAN) 127 – Millracer (USA) 79 (Le Fabuleux 133) [1994 NR 1995 12g May 26] good-topped gelding: fair performer (rated 76) at 3 yrs for D. Morley: fair winning hurdler in 1994/5: well beaten on return to flat. *Mrs S. J. Smith* — –

EIGHTANDAHALF (IRE) 6 b.g. Be My Guest (USA) 126 – Nancy Chere (USA) (Gallant Man) [1994 67: 14.1d^{6} 18m* 14.6m 18.7g 16.5m^{4} 1995 a16g 16.2m 17.1m 21.6f May 1] good-topped, attractive gelding: carries condition: fair handicapper: well beaten in 1995: stays 2¼m: acts on firm going, below form all 4 — –

outings on a soft surface: visored (respectable effort) final 5-y-o start: normally held up/tracks leaders: inconsistent. *Mrs V. A. Aconley*

EIGHT SHARP (IRE) 3 b.g. Sure Blade (USA) 130 – Octavia Girl 104 (Octavo 72 (USA) 115) [1994 77: $6g^4$ 7m $7g^2$ 7d* $8g^3$ $8.1g^4$ 8s 1995 $10m^2$ 10.4m 10.1g Sep 13] deep-bodied gelding: fair performer: probably stays 1¼m: acts on dead ground, ran respectably (facing stiff tasks) on good to firm: sold (B. Hills to M. Hammond) 12,000 gns Newmarket Autumn Sales. *B. W. Hills*

EIGHTS HIGH (USA) 2 b.c. (Apr 3) Local Talent (USA) 122 – Vantasy Park 66 (USA) (Highland Park (USA)) [1995 5m $5m^6$ $5.1m^2$ $5.1m^2$ $6m^2$ $6m^4$ 6m 7g $7g^6$ Sep 20] $5,500F, 7,400Y: sturdy colt: has a quick action: third foal: half-brother to a winner in US by It's Freezing: dam unraced: fair maiden: well below form last 3 starts, in valuable nurseries and claimer (ran freely in blinkers): stays 6f: usually bandaged off-hind: sold 5,000 gns Newmarket Autumn Sales, to Sweden. *R. Hannon*

EILEEN'S GIRL (IRE) 2 b.f. (Feb 15) Cyrano de Bergerac 120 – Beguiled – (IRE) 54 (Be My Guest (USA) 126) [1995 $5f^6$ Jul 12] IR 2,500Y, 6,600 2-y-o: first foal: dam, disappointing maiden who should have stayed beyond 1m, sister to very useful 6f to 8.5f winner Eve's Error: 25/1, showed little in maiden auction at Redcar. *Mrs M. Reveley*

EILEEN'S GUEST (IRE) 3 b.f. Taufan (USA) 119 – Gentle Guest (IRE) (Be – My Guest (USA) 126) [1994 46: $5m^4$ $5s^5$ 1995 6.1m 7g Jun 12] sturdy, lengthy filly: poor maiden: well beaten in 1995: sold 1,400 gns Newmarket July Sales. *R. J. R. Williams*

EIRE LEATH-SCEAL 8 b.g. Legend of France (USA) 124 – Killarney Belle 63 (USA) (Irish Castle (USA)) [1994 63: 12g 12.4g 14.1d $12m^3$ 12g $12g^6$ 12g* 12m* 12.3m* $12.3m^3$ 12m* $11.8m^6$ $12.3m^6$ 12m* 14.1g $16.2f^5$ $12.3g^6$ $12.3m^5$ 13.9m $12g^6$ 14.6d* 14.1d 12.4d 15.1g 1995 $16.2m^2$ $16.2g^6$ Jul 18] small, attractive gelding: usually looks well: bad mover: really tough handicapper over the years, but not seen out again after finishing tailed off at Beverley second start in 1995: effective at 1½m to 2m: acts on firm and dead going, unsuited by heavy: visored (well beaten) second 6-y-o start: often a front runner, otherwise tracks leaders: extremely game in a finish. *M. Brittain*

EJTAAZ (USA) 4 b.g. Topsider (USA) – Summer Silence (USA) (Stop The – Music (USA)) [1994 64d: 6f $7.5g^3$ $8.5g^2$ $8f^2$ 8.2m 10m $8m^5$ 7f 10d 8.1d 12.1g 1995 14d Sep 27] compact gelding: disappointing maiden: should stay 1¼m: acts on firm ground: temperament under suspicion. *M. C. Pipe*

ELA-ARISTOKRATI (IRE) 3 b.c. Danehill (USA) 126 – Dubai Lady 78 (Kris 111 135) [1994 86: $7.1m^2$ $7.1m^2$ 8.1g* 8g 10d 1995 $8.1m^3$ 10.1f* $10.4m^2$ $10.4m^6$ $10m^5$ Aug 26] sturdy, quite attractive colt: good mover: progressed into a smart performer: won minor event at Epsom in June: neck second of 4 to Quango in listed rated stakes at York next start: best effort when 9½ lengths last of 6 to Halling in Juddmonte International at York in August: respectable 3½ lengths fifth of 9 to Desert Shot in strongly-run Winter Hill Stakes at Windsor, going on early in straight, fading inside last: stays 10.4f: acts on firm going, not disgraced only start on dead. *M. R. Stoute*

ELA MAN HOWA 4 b.g. Mtoto 134 – Top Treat (USA) 101 (Topsider (USA)) 58 [1994 61: $12g^5$ $11.9m^5$ $14g^3$ $11m^4$ 14m* $16.4g^6$ $11.9g^6$ 14m 14.1g a13g* $a12g^3$ 1995 $12g^2$ $11.9m^4$ $14g^3$ $14.1m^3$ $14g^4$ $14m^3$ $11.8m^5$ 14.4m* Sep 1] rather leggy, lightly-made gelding: fair handicapper: gamely won at Kempton in September: needs at least 1½m, and should stay beyond 14.4f: acts on good to firm ground and equitrack: effective from front (as on recent starts) or held up: consistent: sold (R. Akehurst to N. Tinkler) 9,400 gns Newmarket Autumn Sales. *R. Akehurst*

ELA-MENT (IRE) 3 b.g. Ela-Mana-Mou 132 – Dorado Llave (USA) (Well – Decorated (USA)) [1994 NR 1995 11.5s a8.5g Oct 14] IR 3,000F, IR 8,500Y resold 15,000Y: 1,000 3-y-o: first foal: dam out of sister to dam of Sure Blade: never a factor in amateurs minor event and handicap when mistakenly competing under name of Hong Kong Dollar. *B. A. Pearce*

ELA PALIKARI MOU (IRE) 4 b.g. Lomond (USA) 128 – Ionian Raja (USA) – (Raja Baba (USA)) [1994 –: $a7g^6$ 1995 $a10g^6$ $a6g^5$ 7m 10m May 12] tall gelding: no worthwhile form: joined M. Muggeridge. *R. Akehurst*

ELASHATH (USA) 2 b.c. (Mar 24) El Gran Senor (USA) 136 – Gorgeoso (USA) (Damascus (USA)) [1995 8m Oct 12] $350,000F: strong, lengthy colt: second foal: dam, maiden in USA, is out of half-sister to Al Bahathri: 14/1, burly and very green, unplaced in maiden at Newmarket won by Silver Dome, losing touch over 2f out: moved poorly to post: will do better. *J. H. M. Gosden* – p

ELATION 3 b.g. Sadler's Wells (USA) 132 – Chellita (Habitat 134) [1994 62p: 8m 8d 1995 11.8s^{5} 12m^{2} 12.5f 11.6m 13f^{6} 11.9g^{3} Sep 1] good-topped, attractive gelding: modest maiden: sold out of P. Cole's stable 9,500 gns Newmarket July Sales after fourth 3-y-o start: stays 1½m: blinkered twice, running well on first occasion: carried head awkwardly final start: inconsistent: won 3 juvenile hurdles (fair form) after final start. *G. Richards* 60

EL ATREVIDO (FR) 5 ch.g. Rainbow Quest (USA) 134 – Majestic Peck (USA) (Majestic Light (USA)) [1994 9g 12s 1995 a10g* a10g^{3} a10g* 10m a8g a10g Nov 21] third foal: half-brother to fairly useful Irish 6f to 1m winner (stayed at least 1¼m) Petronelli (by Sir Ivor): dam unplaced: ran 3 times in France for N. Clement, fairly useful form at best: won maiden in January and minor event in March, both at Lingfield: ran poorly afterwards: stays 1¼m: acts on equitrack. *N. J. H. Walker* 72

ELA-YIE-MOU (IRE) 2 ch.c. (Apr 13) Kris 135 – Green Lucia 116 (Green Dancer (USA) 132) [1995 8g^{6} 8d 8.2m^{5} Oct 26] 40,000Y: tall, rather unfurnished colt: has a round action: brother to fairly useful 3-y-o 1½m winner Korambi and half-brother to several winners, including smart 1½m/1¾m performer Luchiroverte (by Slip Anchor): dam placed in Irish Oaks and Yorkshire Oaks: progressive form in maidens: fifth of 11 to Dance Star at Nottingham, never able to challenge: will be suited by middle distances: remains capable of better. *L. M. Cumani* 63 p

EL BAILADOR (IRE) 4 b.g. Dance of Life (USA) – Sharp Ego (USA) (Sharpen Up 127) [1994 67?: 10s^{2} 10g 11.4g^{5} 11.6m 10m^{2} 10m^{5} 10.4d^{6} 10d 1995 10m^{5} 10g a8g* a10g^{5} 10m* 10m 12d^{4} 10.5s^{5} 10f^{2} Oct 24] useful-looking gelding: fair handicapper on his day: won at Lingfield (maiden event) in June and Nottingham in August: effective in strongly-run race at 1m, and stays 1½m: acts on firm ground, soft and equitrack: blinkered (well beaten) twice at 3 yrs: often a front runner. *J. D. Bethell* 68

ELBURG (IRE) 5 b.g. Ela-Mana-Mou 132 – Iosifa 108 (Top Ville 129) [1994 –: 20m 17.2f 16.1s 1995 a16g^{3} a16g^{4} a16g^{4} 18g^{4} 16m^{6} 21.6f* May 1] lengthy gelding: modest handicapper on flat nowadays: reluctant stalls, ran in snatches then (having seemed held on turn) swept through to win strongly-run event at Pontefract in May: stays extreme distances: acts on firm ground, dead and on equitrack. *R. P. C. Hoad* 65

EL DON 3 b.g. High Kicker (USA) – Madam Gerard 50 (Brigadier Gerard 144) [1994 68: 7m^{5} 8g 6v^{5} 1995 8m 7g 8.2m^{5} 10d 8m 8.2m a10g Nov 21] tall, quite good-topped gelding: disappointing in 1995. *M. J. Ryan* –

ELECTION DAY (IRE) 3 b.c. Sadler's Wells (USA) 132 – Hellenic 125 (Darshaan 133) [1994 NR 1995 10m Aug 9] sturdy colt: first foal: dam won Ribblesdale Stakes and Yorkshire Oaks: 14/1 and burly, far too green when 12¾ lengths eleventh of 18 to Polydamas in maiden at Sandown, slowly away and behind for most of race: looked sure to improve. *M. R. Stoute* – p

ELECTRIC COMMITTEE (IRE) 5 ch.g. Lancastrian 126 – Mary Black (Ardoon 124) [1994 NR 1995 15.1m^{5} Jul 4] fourth foal: dam unraced: modest winning hurdler: 25/1, made most when tailed off in claimer at Edinburgh on flat debut. *P. Monteith* –

ELECTROLYTE 5 b.g. Electric 126 – This Sensation 48 (Balidar 133) [1994 NR 1995 a16g a14.8g a16g a16g May 15] tall, good-bodied gelding: seemed of little account on first runs since fair 3-y-o. *B. Palling* –

ELEGANT FRIEND 7 ch.g. Music Boy 124 – Cardinal Palace 85 (Royal Palace 131) [1994 NR 1995 10g Sep 23] leggy, angular gelding: unimpressive mover: fair hurdler at best in 1994/5, but lost his form and sold out of M. Tompkins' stable 1,850 gns Ascot July Sales: tailed off on return (was fair performer at 4 yrs) to flat: resold 1,150 gns Doncaster October Sales. *D. W. Chapman* –

ELEGANTISSIMA 2 b.f. (Apr 19) Polish Precedent (USA) 131 – Ela Meem (USA) (Kris 135) [1995 a8g^{4} Dec 18] third foal: closely related to 3-y-o 7f to 8.5f winner Gulf Shaadi (by Shaadi): dam, lightly-raced maiden who probably stayed 59 p

1¼m, closely related to Pebbles: 14/1, 3½ lengths fourth of 9 to Red Rusty in maiden at Lingfield, always thereabouts: should improve. *S. Dow*

ELEMENTARY 12 b.g. Busted 134 – Santa Vittoria 100 (Ragusa 137) [1994 78: a12g^{3} a12g^{6} 11.9d^{3} 11.9g* a10g^{2} 12m^{3} 12.1g* 12m 11.8g* a12g^{4} 1995 a13g* a12g^{4} a12g^{2} 11.9m^{2} 12m* 12d* 15.1g* 11.8g^{2} a12g* a13g Nov 25] strong, quite attractive gelding: fair performer in claimers nowadays, the winner of 8 races since his eleventh birthday: successful in 1995 at Lingfield in January, Thirsk in May, Beverley in June (all easily), then at Edinburgh (gamely) and Lingfield (always travelling best) in the autumn: ideally suited by at least 1½m nowadays, and stays 15f: acts on any going: blinkered early in career: effective from front or held up: grand campaigner. *N. J. H. Walker* — 71

ELFIN LAUGHTER 3 b.f. Alzao (USA) 117 – Rainbow's End 83 (My Swallow 134) [1994 67: 5g^{4} 6m 5m 7.5f* 8g* 8g 1995 10g^{2} 11.4g May 30] smallish, quite attractive filly: fair performer: unlucky second of 14 in handicap at Nottingham on reappearance: never travelling particularly fluently (beaten before stamina became an issue) final start: likely to stay further than 1¼m. *R. Hannon* — 76

ELFIN QUEEN (IRE) 2 b.f. (Feb 13) Fairy King (USA) – West of Eden (Crofter (USA) 124) [1995 5g^{3} 5f^{2} 5f^{4} 5.2d Sep 16] IR 18,000Y: fourth foal: sister to fair 5f performer Cindora: dam unraced: modest form placed in maidens first 2 starts but tailed off in nursery (very early to post) at Newbury after 3-month absence: one to have reservations about. *M. Johnston* — 64 d

ELFLAND (IRE) 4 b.g. Fairy King (USA) – Ridge The Times (USA) 78 (Riva Ridge (USA)) [1994 72p: 7.1g 7.1m 6m^{4} 7f 6m^{3} 1995 6m^{4} 7g* 7g Jul 13] strong, good-bodied gelding: has a very high knee action: showed plenty of improvement in handicaps for new connections, winning in good style at Doncaster in May: raced on unfavoured side in Bunbury Cup: effective at 6f and 7f: acts on good to firm going, yet to race on a soft surface: bandaged last 2 starts: remains capable of better. *Lady Herries* — 89 p

ELITE FORCE (IRE) 2 b.g. (Feb 28) Fairy King (USA) – La Petruschka (Ballad Rock 122) [1995 7g^{5} 6d^{4} Sep 16] tall gelding: fourth foal: brother to a winner abroad: dam half-sister to good Irish sprinter Aberuschka: fifth of 8 to Mawwal in minor event at Doncaster: over 5 lengths fourth of 25 to Sovereign's Crown in maiden at Newbury week later, chasing leaders and keeping on: should stay 7f: likely to improve again. *P. W. Chapple-Hyam* — 82 p

ELITE HOPE (USA) 3 ch.f. Moment of Hope (USA) – Chervil (USA) (Greenough (USA)) [1994 83: 6m 5d^{2} 7g* 7v^{6} 1995 6g 7.1g^{2} 7m^{4} 7m^{6} 7.3d 7m^{5} Nov 3] small, sturdy filly: fairly useful handicapper: stays 7.1f: best form on a sound surface. *C. R. Egerton* — 84

ELITE JUSTICE 3 ch.g. Absalom 128 – Persian Express (Persian Bold 123) [1994 67: 7f^{4} 6.9m^{2} 7.5m* 7.3g 8m 1995 7.9g 8m^{4} 8m^{6} 10f^{3} 10f^{2} 8g^{4} Jul 27] workmanlike gelding: fair handicapper: stays 1¼m: has raced only on a sound surface: blinkered (ran poorly) third 3-y-o start. *P. F. I. Cole* — 65

ELITE NUMBER (USA) 3 ro.f. Elmaamul (USA) 125 – Comicus (USA) (Northern Jove (CAN)) [1994 56: 5.1m^{5} 7.5g 7g^{5} 8d^{4} 1995 a10g^{6} a10g a9.4g 8m 11.1f^{5} Jul 29] close-coupled filly: no form in 1995, leaving P. Cole's stable after second start and sold out of M. Camacho's 720 gns Doncaster July Sales after fourth: should stay beyond 1m: blinkered (well beaten) second 3-y-o start: best left alone. *R. M. McKellar* — –

ELITE RACING 3 b.f. Risk Me (FR) 127 – Hot Stone (Hotfoot 126) [1994 63: 5d^{2} 6m^{2} 6f^{6} 7g 6.9s^{3} 1995 8f* 9.7g 8d 8m^{4} 8.5m* 8f^{3} 8.5m^{2} 9m^{5} 8.3m^{6} 8m 8f Oct 12] leggy, quite good-topped filly: modest handicapper: won at Brighton in May and Epsom (claimer) in July: left P. Cole after ninth start: no form afterwards: stays 8.5f: acts on firm ground and soft: has been bandaged behind: tried blinkered, no improvement: found nothing under pressure eighth start: inconsistent. *N. Tinkler* — 69 d

ELLA NICO (IRE) 2 b.f. (Apr 25) Archway (IRE) 115 – Ceann-Na-Bann (Doulab (USA) 115) [1995 5d^{4} 5.5m* 5d* 6d^{4} 5g^{2} 5g^{5} 6g* 5.5g* 6d^{5} 6g Oct 23] IR 5,000Y: third foal: dam ran twice: useful French filly: won 2 claimers at Chantilly and another at Deauville in the summer: 29/1, awarded race having stayed on well from rear and snatched second near finish when 4 lengths second of 7 to Titus Livius — 96 in Prix d'Arenberg back at Chantilly in September: below form afterwards: a sprinter: acts on good to firm ground and dead: blinkered all starts. *N. Clement, France*

ELLASTYLE (IRE) 4 b.f. Waajib 121 – Grecian Hill 84 (Ela-Mana-Mou 132) [1994 –: 12m 12m5 1995 12m 12g 16m Jun 13] leggy, light-framed filly: no worthwhile form. *Miss L. C. Siddall* –

ELLE MAC 2 b.f. (Apr 11) Merdon Melody 98 – Tripolitaine (FR) (Nonoalco (USA) 131) [1995 5.1m 6m 7d Sep 22] 4,100F: good-topped filly: has a round action: half-sister to several winners, including fairly useful sprinter (at 2 yrs and 3 yrs) Walk In The Park (by Valiyar): dam won twice at around 11f in France: no form in maiden events, off course 4 months prior to final start. *M. P. Bielby* –

ELLE SHAPED (IRE) 5 b.g. Treasure Kay 114 – Mamie's Joy (Prince Tenderfoot (USA) 126) [1994 87?: 5g 5f5 5.1m3 5f 5g5 6.1m 7g2 7m* 7g* 7m 7g 7g 1995 6g 6d 6.9m2 6m3 7.6m 6m4 6m 5.1g* 6m5 5m3 6.1m5 5m 5m2 7m2 5.1m* 6m 5.1d6 5g 5m* a6g Dec 18] good-quartered gelding: fairly useful handicapper: mostly in good form in 1995 (left D. Nicholls' stable after twelth start), winning at Chester in June and August (fourth success there) and Doncaster (getting up near finish) in November: effective at 5f, and stays 7f: suited by a sound surface: sometimes bandaged: usually early to post: normally races prominently. *A. Bailey* 85

ELLIE ARDENSKY 3 b.f. Slip Anchor 136 – Circus Ring 122 (High Top 131) [1994 82p: 7d3 1995 9m* 10.8g2 12m4 10f* 10.1g3 10g5 Sep 30] unfurnished filly: useful performer: won maiden at Ripon in May and listed race (looking very well, edged right but beat Cask ¾ length) at Salisbury in August: stiff task when fifth in Sun Chariot Stakes at Newmarket in September: should prove at least as effective at 1½m as 1¼m: acts on firm going, promising effort on dead. *J. R. Fanshawe* 96

ELLY FLEETFOOT (IRE) 3 b.f. Elmaamul (USA) 125 – Fleetwood Fancy (Taufan (USA) 119) [1994 –: 5d 1995 10m 10m 11.8g 11.6g* 11.5f4 a12g a10g Nov 21] leggy, sparely-made filly: modest performer: won claimer at Windsor (claimed out of T. Mills's stable £7,000) in June: should stay at least 1½m: acts on good to firm ground, tailed off (after long break) on all-weather. *B. J. Meehan* 63

ELMER'S TUNE 3 b.c. Superpower 113 – Malindi (Mansingh (USA) 120) [1994 48: 8.2d a10g 1995 10m 8.1g 10m 10m Jun 26] small colt: seems of little account: sold 1,600 gns Ascot July Sales. *R. Hannon* –

ELMSWOOD (USA) 2 b.f. (Mar 29) Woodman (USA) 126 – Lilian Bayliss (IRE) 100 (Sadler's Wells (USA) 132) [1995 5.1m4 5m3 5g3 7.3m 6f 6.5m Sep 6] sturdy, quite attractive filly: has a rounded action: first foal: dam, 7f (at 2 yrs) and 9f winner, closely related to high-class French miler Phydilla and half-sister to smart French sprinter Ernani and very smart 1¼m/1½m performer Observation Post: progressive form in minor event and maidens first 3 starts: didn't repeat that in nurseries, harshly handicapped first 2 starts: should stay 7f: sold 34,000 gns Newmarket December Sales. *P. W. Chapple-Hyam* 68

EL NIDO 7 ch.g. Adonijah 126 – Seleter (Hotfoot 126) [1994 54, a63: a13g4 a11g2 a12g a12g* 13v4 12.4m5 a12g 12m3 a14g3 12.4d6 a14.8g4 a11g3 a14g* a12g 1995 a16g* a14g* 13v4 a14g2 a12g2 a16.2g a14g4 Nov 16] leggy, workmanlike gelding: has a round action: modest performer: won claimers at Southwell in January and March: finished lame penultimate start, well beaten final one: stays 2m: used to go well with some give in the ground, best form nowadays on the all-weather: wears crossed noseband: normally tracks leaders. *M. J. Camacho* – a63

EL OPERA (IRE) 2 b.f. (Jan 24) Sadler's Wells (USA) 132 – Ridge The Times (USA) 78 (Riva Ridge (USA)) [1995 7d4 Sep 15] 155,000Y resold 125,000Y: robust filly: has scope: closely related to very useful sprinter Pharaoh's Delight and 4-y-o 7f winner Elfland (both by Fairy King) and half-sister to 2 winners, including 1½m Oslo Cup winner Kateb (by Pennine Walk): dam 2-y-o 5f winner: 7/2 from 2/1, 7 lengths fourth of 10 to Wild Rumour in minor event at Newbury, tracking leaders then tiring final 175 yds, edging left off bridle: showed a powerful, round action: sure to improve. *P. F. I. Cole* 71 p

ELPIDA (USA) 3 b.c. Trempolino (USA) 135 – All For Hope (USA) (Sensitive Prince (USA)) [1994 65p: 7d 7g5 1995 10g 10m a14.8g* 11.5s4 a12g5 a14g a16g Nov 29] compact colt: reportedly suffered from muscle enzyme problems and off 68 d course over 4 months before (backed at long odds) winning minor event at Wolverhampton in September, going on 5f out and clear in straight: no comparable form: stays 14.8f: has worn severe noseband. *J. Pearce*

ELPIDOS 3 ch.c. Bold Arrangement 127 – Thalassa (IRE) 94 (Appiani II 128) [1994 69: 7m 7m^5 7g 8g* 1995 10.3g 12.3d^5 a12g^4 10m^3 9g^3 10.1f^2 8g^4 9f 8m* 8.1m 8g 8d^3 8m 8m Oct 14] workmanlike colt: fairly useful handicapper: won at Leicester (edged left) in August: effective at 1m and stays 1¼m: acts on firm and dead ground: blinkered final 2-y-o start (much improved form) and second 3-y-o start: inconsistent, and not one to place maximum faith in: sold (C. Brittain to M. Hammond) 26,000 gns Newmarket Autumn Sales. *C. E. Brittain* 79

ELRAAS (USA) 3 b.g. Gulch (USA) – Full Card (USA) (Damascus (USA)) [1994 –: 6m 6s 6f 6.1s 1995 6.9g Oct 16] stocky, close-coupled gelding: no worthwhile form, tailed off in seller for new stable. *John Berry* –

ELSHABIBA (USA) 2 b. or br.c. (Mar 13) Dayjur (USA) 137 – Sweet Roberta (USA) (Roberto (USA) 131) [1995 6g^2 6m* Oct 28] big, robust colt: has plenty of scope: second foal: dam, 1m (at 2 yrs) to 9f winner in USA, half-sister to high class 2-y-o Cure The Blues: ¾-length second of 4 to Tamhid in maiden at Ascot, losing action around halfway, taking plenty of time to pick up then staying on strongly close home: looking well, and heavily backed again, won mixed-age race at Newmarket over 3 months later by length from Laafee, off bridle by halfway then needing to be hard driven to get on top: will improve again, particularly over 7f+. *J. L. Dunlop* 93 p

ELSIES BAR 3 gr.f. Primo Dominie 121 – Tabeeba (Diesis 133) [1994 56: 6f^4 6m 7.5g^4 7m 1995 10g Apr 4] sturdy, lengthy filly: modest maiden: showed little in selling handicap only start in 1995. *R. M. Whitaker* –

EL SUPREMO (USA) 3 b.c. Storm Bird (CAN) 134 – Sharmila (FR) (Blakeney 126) [1994 85: 7g^2 7f^3 6.1m* 6g^6 1995 8d* 8g^5 9g* 10g^3 8g^5 Aug 3] useful-looking colt: good walker: useful performer: won 19-runner £9,300 handicap at Warwick in April and (after 3½ lengths fifth of 14 to Prince Arthur in Premio Parioli at Rome) listed event at Baden-Baden in May: creditable efforts in rated stakes at Ascot and listed event at Deauville afterwards: stays at least 1¼m (dam stoutly-bred): yet to race on soft ground, probably acts on any other: made all for 2-y-o win, held up in 1995: consistent. *D. R. Loder* 102

EL TAURUS 3 b.c. El Conquistador 109 – Meralto 60 (Noalto 120) [1994 NR 1995 a8g 6.1g Apr 24] first reported foal: dam, plater, should have stayed 1m: well beaten in claimer and seller. *K. G. Wingrove* –

ELTISH (USA) 3 b.c. Cox's Ridge (USA) – Nimble Feet (USA) 82 (Danzig (USA)) [1994 120: 7g^2 7f* 7f* 8g* 7m^3 a8.5f^2 1995 9m^3 a10f^6 10m^2 10m^5 10.4m^5 Aug 15] 120

Royal Lodge winner Eltish failed to win a race at three, but he acquitted himself with credit in the Kentucky Derby and came within a short head of winning the Prince of Wales's Stakes at Royal Ascot. Disappointing in the Eclipse and International on his last two starts, Eltish left Henry Cecil's stable, bound, as quite a few of Khalid Abdulla's horses have been, for Bobby Frankel in America. He probably has a reasonable future there as a four-year-old.

Eltish's two-length second to Timber Country in the Breeders' Cup Juvenile at Churchill Downs the previous November booked his return in May for the Kentucky Derby. He was beaten by Munwar, giving that horse 8 lb, on his reappearance in the Feilden Stakes over nine furlongs at Newmarket in April, but gave a good account of himself in the Kentucky Derby, making ground turning for home, and disputing third place inside the final furlong before fading in the last hundred yards to finish three and three quarter lengths sixth of nineteen to Thunder Gulch; Timber Country again finished in front of him, around a length and a half ahead in third. The first three in the Kentucky Derby went on to contest the Preakness at Pimlico, but Eltish's American campaign was curtailed and he was returned for the Prince of Wales's Stakes at Royal Ascot. Eltish was the sole three-year-old in a field of six, and he had a tremendous battle in the final furlong with the previous year's winner Muhtarram after both had found themselves short of room early in the straight. Eltish ran on splendidly under strong pressure but just failed to peg back Muhtarram. Eltish did not repeat the form, sweating profusely before finishing fifth of eight behind Halling in the steadily-run Coral Eclipse Stakes at Sandown, where he pulled hard in rear before being caught flat-footed, and filling the same position behind the same horse in the six-runner International at York, where Eltish was again sweating and faded disappointingly after setting a good pace to three furlongs out.

Eltish (USA) (b.c. 1992)	Cox's Ridge (USA) (b 1974)	Best Turn (b or br 1966)	Turn-To
			Sweet Clementine
		Our Martha (ch 1961)	Ballydonnell
			Corday
	Nimble Feet (USA) (b 1985)	Danzig (b 1977)	Northern Dancer
			Pas de Nom
		Nimble Folly (ch 1977)	Cyane
			Instant Sin

Eltish's pedigree was discussed in *Racehorses of 1994*. His sire Cox's Ridge did not have the best of years in 1995, though his record overall as a sire is a good one. Nimble Feet's record as a broodmare was enhanced slightly in 1995 by Eltish's half-brother Forest Gazelle winning the Grade 3 Los Angeles Handicap over six furlongs. Since Eltish, she has bred Yamuna, a once-raced Forty Niner filly also with Cecil, and a yearling filly by Riverman. The good-topped, attractive Eltish stays a mile and a quarter well and may well get a mile and a half as a four-year-old, although there'd have to be a doubt about his doing so under extremely testing conditions. Eltish is equally adept on turf and dirt and has shown his form ridden up with the pace or held up. *H. R. A. Cecil*

ELTON LEDGER (IRE) 6 b.g. Cyrano de Bergerac 120 – Princess of Nashua (Crowned Prince (USA) 128) [1994 60, a74: 5v^{2} 6m a6g* 6d^{4} a5g^{2} a6g^{5} a5g^{2} a6g* 6s 1995 a6g^{4} a7g Nov 24] good-topped gelding: fair handicapper: off course over 10 months before well beaten final start: effective at 5f and should stay 7f: acts on any going, best recent form on fibresand: often blinkered (effective without), visored last 4 outings: sometimes bandaged near-hind. *Mrs N. Macauley* – a74

ELUNED MAY 4 ch.f. Clantime 101 – Arroganza 62 (Crofthall 110) [1994 62d: 5.1g 5.1m* 5m 5.1f 5g 5.1g 1995 5g^{6} 5m Jun 26] small, sparely-made filly: no form since win at 3 yrs: should prove best at 5f: acts on firm ground: blinkered final 3-y-o start. *R. M. Whitaker* –

EL VOLADOR 8 br.g. Beldale Flutter (USA) 130 – Pharjoy (FR) 85 (Pharly (FR) 130) [1994 61d, a–: 11.9d^{5} 12d^{2} 12s^{5} 12d^{5} 12m^{4} 14g 10f^{5} 12m^{6} 1995 14d 12.1d 12m* a12g^{4} Dec 9] sturdy, workmanlike gelding: poor mover: fairly useful handicapper (successful 7 times) on equitrack, but not tried since 1993: only modest at best on turf since, winning selling handicap at Folkestone in November: should stay 1¾m: goes very well on equitrack, has form on fibresand and on firm and dead ground: successful for claimer: best held up: genuine. *R. J. O'Sullivan* 55 a72

EL YASAF (IRE) 7 b.h. Sayf El Arab (USA) 127 – Winsong Melody (Music Maestro 119) [1994 104d: 5.2s^{2} 5.1m* 5d^{5} 5.1g^{4} 5m 5m 5g^{5} 5.6g 5d^{4} 1995 5m* 5g* 5m^{5} 5m^{5} 5g^{6} 6m 6d Oct 19] small, sturdy horse: useful performer: has had 13 trainers over the years and proved none too reliable: awarded listed race at Beverley (beaten short head by Blue Siren after being slightly bumped over 1f out) and narrowly won minor event at Thirsk, both in April: fifth in Palace House Stakes at Newmarket and Temple Stakes at Sandown (final start for G. Fierro): long way below form (fifth outing only for R. Harris) afterwards: best at 5f: probably acts on any ground: tried blinkered, no improvement: has won when sweating: sold only 9,000 gns Newmarket Autumn Sales. *C. N. Allen* 105

EMBANKMENT (IRE) 5 b.g. Tate Gallery (USA) 117 – Great Leighs 87 (Vaigly Great 127) [1994 91: a10g^{4} 8m 8.1d* 8m^{4} 9s^{2} 8m 8.3m^{3} 8g^{4} 8s^{4} 10m^{3} 9v 8d 1995 8g 10m^{5} 9m^{3} 10.1f^{4} 10f 8.1m 8f 9g^{2} 8.5s^{6} Sep 19] close-coupled, good-quartered gelding: fairly useful handicapper: best form at 1m to 1¼m: acts on good to firm ground and soft: well below form only run on equitrack: held up: consistent. *R. Hannon* 89

EMBEZZLER 3 b.g. Emarati (USA) 74 – Double Touch (FR) (Nonoalco (USA) 131) [1994 56: 6m 6s 6g a7g^{4} 8g 6g^{2} 6m 1995 8.2g a6g^{6} 10f^{6} 10m 9.7m^{4} 7g 8.3m 8m^{6} 9.9m^{6} 7.5m 12m Oct 13] useful-looking gelding: poor form at best in 1995 apart from third start: sold out of G. Lewis' stable 6,400 gns Newmarket July Sales after eighth: looked temperamental last time: stays 1¼m: acts on fibresand and firm 54 d ground: effective blinkered or not: takes good hold: early to post nowadays. *S. Gollings*

EMBRACING 3 b.f. Reference Point 139 – Hug Me 96 (Shareef Dancer (USA) 135) [1994 63p: 7d^5 1995 12m^2 12.1g* 14s* 14g* 14f* 13.9m 13.9g Aug 30] unfurnished filly: fairly useful performer: won maiden at Hamilton (5/1 on) and handicaps at Sandown (2) and Goodwood, all in May/June: creditable eighth (Ebor) and tenth at York in August, though on both occasions shaped as if she'd be well suited by step up to 2m: acts on firm and soft ground. *M. R. Stoute* — 91

EMBROIDERED 2 br.f. (Feb 13) Charmer 123 – Emblazon 91 (Wolver Hollow 126) [1995 a6g a7g Nov 6] half-sister to several winners here and abroad, including 6f and 1m winner Taranga (by Music Boy) and 1989 2-y-o 6f winner Walkern Witch (by Dunbeath): dam, winner at up to 1½m, daughter of good staying 2-y-o Slip Stitch: well beaten in median auction maiden at Wolverhampton and seller at Southwell: sold 1,260 gns Ascot December Sales. *Sir Mark Prescott* — –

EMBRYONIC (IRE) 3 b.c. Prince Rupert (FR) 121 – Belle Viking (FR) (Riverman (USA) 131) [1994 75p: 7s^2 1995 12.4g* 13g* 13.1g^3 11.9s Oct 1] leggy colt: fairly useful handicapper: won at Newcastle (maiden) in April and Hamilton in May: off course 4½ months, ran well when staying-on third of 12 at Ayr in September: ran poorly on soft ground (had shaped well on it on debut) when well-backed favourite at Haydock last time: will stay beyond 13f. *R. F. Fisher* — 81

EMEI SHAN 2 br.f. (Apr 11) Inca Chief (USA) – Tricata (Electric 126) [1995 5.7m 6m 7f 8h 6s Sep 28] sparely-made filly: third foal: dam unraced: seems of little account. *P. G. Murphy* — –

EMERALD DREAM (IRE) 3 b. or br.f. Vision (USA) – Island Morn (USA) (Our Native (USA)) [1994 –: 8.2g 1995 a8g^6 a10g^5 a10g 10f^6 Jul 20] angular, rather leggy filly: poor maiden: stays 1¼m: acts on equitrack: inconsistent. *C. C. Elsey* — – a47

EMERGING MARKET 3 b.g. Emarati (USA) 74 – Flitteriss Park 62§ (Beldale Flutter (USA) 130) [1994 81: 6f* 6m^2 6m^4 1995 7m^2 6m* 6g 6m 7m^2 7f 7.3m^6 7m^3 7g^4 8.5s^5 7m^2 Oct 14] smallish, lengthy gelding: has a roundish action: fairly useful performer: won minor event at Folkestone in April: best effort when head second of 12 in steadily-run handicap at Newmarket final start: stays 7f, possibly not 8.5f: acts on firm going, below form only run on a soft surface: finds little in front, and suited by waiting tactics. *J. L. Dunlop* — 94

EMILY-MOU (IRE) 3 b.f. Cadeaux Genereux 131 – Sarajill (High Line 125) [1994 80: 6.1s 7m^3 6s a7g 1995 8m* 9f^2 8.5m^2 10g* 9f^6 10f* 11.6m^2 10m^4 10d* 10g^4 10.5d Oct 11] leggy, unfurnished filly: fair performer: mostly in good form in 1995, successful in claimer (claimed out of E. Dunlop's stable £8,000) at Newmarket, handicap at Newbury, claimer at Kempton and minor event at Nottingham: stays 11.6f: acts on firm and dead ground, ran poorly on soft and fibresand at 2 yrs: bandaged in 1995: front runner. *B. J. Meehan* — 75

EMIRATES EXPRESS 3 b.c. Shaadi (USA) 126 – Les Dancelles (Pas de Seul 133) [1994 79p: 6m 6g^3 6m^3 7g* 1995 8d 7.6m^3 7m^2 7m^2 8m 7m^3 7.6m^3 7g^6 7m^4 Oct 5] useful-looking colt: good mover: fairly useful handicapper: creditable efforts in 1995 when in frame, sweating on final start: stays 7.6f: acts on good to firm ground: races prominently: often claimer ridden: sent to Dubai. *J. W. Hills* — 88

EMMA GRIMES (IRE) 4 b.f. Nordico (USA) – Keep The Faith 86 (Furry Glen 121) [1994 –: 7d a10g 1995 8m 8.3m^5 10m^2 11.9f^4 14f^6 10d 12g^5 12m 12m Nov 6] small, leggy filly: poor maiden handicapper: stays 1¼m: acts on firm ground: blinkered (well beaten) final 3-y-o start: inconsistent. *J. S. Moore* — 42

EMNALA (IRE) 3 b.f. Contract Law (USA) 108 – African Light 65§ (Kalaglow 132) [1994 57: 6g 6.9m 8m 10s^6 10g^5 1995 a12g^5 12g 12.5m 12f^5 May 1] leggy, workmanlike filly: modest maiden at 2 yrs: no worthwhile form in 1995: stays 1¼m: acts on good to firm ground, probably on soft: well beaten on fibresand. *M. R. Channon* — –

EMPEREGRINE (USA) 2 b. or br.c. (Mar 24) Imperial Falcon (CAN) – In Spate (USA) (In Reality) [1995 6g 6g^4 6m^3 6.1m^3 7m^2 7m^6 6m^6 7g^2 7d^4 7f Oct 14] $11,000F, IR 14,500Y: workmanlike colt: fourth foal: half-brother to 2 winners in North America by Mr Prospector: dam winner at 3 yrs: fair form: creditable second — 73 of 19 in nursery at Catterick in September: won over 9.7f in France in December: tried visored: sold 16,500 gns Newmarket Autumn Sales. *C. F. Wall*

EMPEROR JONES (USA) 5 b.h. Danzig (USA) – Qui Royalty (USA) (Native Royalty (USA)) [1994 119: 8.1d^4 8m* 8m^2 8g^3 8g 8g^2 8g^4 9g^5 1995 a8g* 7f^4 8f 8m^4 7m Oct 12] strong, quite attractive horse: has a free, rather round action: smart performer: won handicap in Dubai in February before contesting 2 very valuable events (good fourth first occasion) in Tokyo in the spring: creditable fourth (hampered twice) to Harayir in Celebration Mile at Goodwood on fourth start: very useful form at 1¼m, but best efforts at 1m: possibly unsuited by soft ground, acted on any other: visored (below best) once: sometimes carried head high and wandered: reportedly sold to stand at Fares Stables, Newsells Park, Royston, fee £6,000 (Oct 1). *Saeed bin Suroor*

116

EMPHATIC CANDIDATE (IRE) 3 ch.g. Salt Dome (USA) – Humble Mission (Shack (USA) 118) [1994 75: 6s 6g 6m 7m^3 7d^2 7v 1995 6.9m^4 7f* 6m^6 7g^3 11.5m^4 a9.4g^2 a8.5g^6 10.1m Aug 28] sparely-made gelding: just a modest performer in 1995: won claimer at Brighton in May: effective at 7f to 9.4f: acts on good to firm, dead ground and fibresand, well beaten on heavy: sold 6,400 gns Newmarket September Sales. *R. Akehurst*

64

EMPOWER (IRE) 3 b.g. Tirol 127 – Trusted Maiden (Busted 134) [1994 –: 8d 1995 8d^5 10f^3 8m^3 8m^6 8m^6 Jul 21] tall, workmanlike gelding: fair maiden: finished lame final start: effective at 1m when forcing pace, stays 1¼m well: acts on firm ground. *R. Hannon*

72

EMPTY QUARTER 3 b.c. Night Shift (USA) – Infanta Real 108 (Formidable (USA) 125) [1994 NR 1995 7.1g^3 8g^2 7m 7m 8d* 7f* 8f^5 Oct 12] 36,000Y: compact, good-bodied colt: third foal: half-brother to 7f winner Tshusick (by Dancing Brave) and useful Swedish 5f to 7f winner Informant (by Kris): dam, ran only at 3 yrs, winning at 5f and 6f from 3 starts, out of half-sister to Forzando: useful performer: easily won maiden at Brighton in September, and followed up in 4-runner minor event at Redcar (easily best effort to beat Monaassib a head) following month: stays 1m: acts on firm and dead ground: wears crossed noseband: sent to Dubai. *J. H. M. Gosden*

100

ENAMEL TIGER 2 ch.g. (Feb 17) Risk Me (FR) 127 – Dancing Belle 80 (Dance In Time (CAN)) [1995 6m Oct 13] 5,000Y: big, workmanlike gelding: third foal: sister to 3-y-o Circa, useful 6f and 7.3f winner at 2 yrs, and 1993 2-y-o 5f winner Dances With Risk: dam sprinter: 33/1 and bandaged, last of 21 in maiden at Newmarket. *J. E. Banks*

–

EN ATTENDANT (FR) 7 ch.g. Bairn (USA) 126 – Vizenia (Vitiges (FR) 132) [1994 105: 7m 8m 7m* 7.6m 7m 7d 1995 7.1m^5 8.1m^6 6g^6 7m 7g 7m* 7m 7g Sep 29] attractive gelding: usually impresses in appearance: useful handicapper: has become inconsistent, clearly best effort in 1995 when winning at Chester in August: best at 7f to 1m: probably acts on any going: visored (well beaten) fifth 7-y-o start: usually bandaged: sometimes hangs: suited by strongly-run race and waiting tactics: not one to rely on. *B. Hanbury*

105 §

ENCHANTED COTTAGE 3 b.c. Governor General 116 – Mitsubishi Colour (Cut Above 130) [1994 –: 6f 6m 1995 8m 9m 7g 7g 10d 14s Sep 30] deep-bodied, lengthy colt: no worthwhile form. *M. D. Hammond*

–

ENCHANTEUR 4 b.f. Damister (USA) 123 – Brown Maid (URU) (Admirals Launch 118) [1994 NR 1995 a9.4g* a12g a9.4g^4 7g Jul 1] leggy filly: having only third outing (rated 65 on debut at 2 yrs) when winning median auction maiden at Wolverhampton in March, leading near finish: failed to repeat the form in handicaps: should stay at least 1¼m: acts on firm ground and fibresand. *T. J. Etherington*

35

ENCORE M'LADY (IRE) 4 b.f. Dancing Dissident (USA) 119 – Diva Encore 74 (Star Appeal 133) [1994 86: 5m* 5g^4 6g^2 6f* 6.1m^2 6m^6 5m 6d 1995 5.1m 6g 6f 6m 5f^4 7g 6g 5m a5g^4 a6g* Dec 9] leggy, good-topped filly: fair sprint handicapper at best in 1995: won at Wolverhampton in December: acts on fibresand and firm ground, possibly not on a soft surface: often blinkered/visored. *F. H. Lee*

71

ENDLESS FANTASY 3 b.f. Kalaglow 132 – Headrest (Habitat 134) [1994 NR 1995 a7g^5 a12g^4 10g 11.6m^5 16.4f^5 a16g^2 a16g^6 a16g^3 a16g Dec 15] 1,700Y: lengthy, sparely-made filly: has a round action: first foal: dam sister to smart 1m to 1½m

36
a51

winner One Way Street, the dam of Red Route: modest maiden: stays well: best efforts on equitrack. *C. A. Cyzer*

ENDLESS LIGHT (USA) 4 b.c. Sunshine Forever (USA) – Propositioning (USA) (Mr Prospector (USA)) [1994 90: 10.2g* 11.5d^6 10.3m 12g* 12f 1995 12m 12m 11.9m^4 14m^5 12f 10.3m^3 Jun 28] lengthy, heavy-topped colt: carries condition: impresses in appearance: fairly useful handicapper: well below form last 2 starts: stays 1½m well: acts on good to firm ground: sold 9,800 gns Ascot July Sales. *P. F. I. Cole* 86

ENDLESS WAVE 3 b.f. Indian Ridge 123 – Sound of The Sea 91 (Windjammer (USA)) [1994 78: 5d* 5.2m 5m^4 6g^5 5.2m^6 5.1g^3 5s* 6v 1995 5s 5m^3 5m 6m 5g^4 5m^6 a6g 5.1d^2 5d Sep 18] leggy filly: unimpressive mover: fair performer at 2 yrs: modest at best in 1995: stays 6f: acts on good to firm and soft going, possibly not on heavy: inconsistent: sold 4,500 gns Newmarket December Sales. *M. Bell* 64

ENDOWMENT 3 ch.c. Cadeaux Genereux 131 – Palm Springs (Top Ville 129) [1994 NR 1995 10.2m* 12g^6 10.2h^6 11.6m^4 11.7h* Aug 8] 13,000F, 31,000Y: attractive colt: first foal: dam unraced: fair form: won maiden at Bath in May and handicap there (coaxed home by W. Carson) in August: ran as though something amiss third start: stays 11.7f: has raced only on a sound surface: blinkered last 2 starts: has plenty of ability, but may not always put his best foot forward: sold 10,000 gns Newmarket Autumn Sales. *Major W. R. Hern* 75

ENERGY MAN 2 b.g. (Feb 16) Hadeer 118 – Cataclysmic 78 (Ela-Mana-Mou 132) [1995 7.1m^4 8d 7.9m^6 Oct 4] strong gelding: has a short action: fourth foal: half-brother to 4-y-o 14.1f winner Wannaplantatree (by Niniski) and a winner in Holland by Siberian Express: dam 1½m winner: modest form in maiden events: sold out of J. Fanshawe's stable 7,500 gns Newmarket Autumn Sales: has joined M. Dods. *J. R. Fanshawe* 66

ENGLISH INVADER 4 b.c. Rainbow Quest (USA) 134 – Modica 89 (Persian Bold 123) [1994 12v 12v* 12g^6 14g 12.5d 12d 10d^5 10d^3 12v* 14v 1995 14.4m^5 11.7m^2 11.5g^4 13.9m^4 Jul 15] IR 225,000Y: leggy ex-French colt: second foal: dam Irish 1m and 1¼m winner, half-sister to dam of Waajib: trained in 1994 by C. Laffon-Parias, winning minor event at Longchamp and claimer at Maisons-Laffitte: useful form facing stiff tasks here, over 10 lengths fourth of 5 to Saxon Maid in listed rated stakes at York on final outing: stays 1¾m: acts on heavy going and good to firm: blinkered seventh to tenth 3-y-o starts. *R. Akehurst* 96

EN VACANCES (IRE) 3 b.f. Old Vic 136 – Welcome Break (Wollow 132) [1994 NR 1995 8g 10m^4 12.1g^2 12.1m^5 12g a14.8g^2 a14.8g^3 16d* 15.9d 16d* Oct 19] lengthy, workmanlike filly: eighth foal: closely related to smart 6f to 1¼m winner Invited Guest (by Be My Guest), later a good winner in USA: dam unraced half-sister to Interval and daughter of Cambridgeshire winner Intermission: fair handicapper: best efforts when stepped up to 2m, winning at Nottingham in September and Newbury in October: very much a stayer: acts on fibresand and seems to go well on a soft surface. *A. G. Foster* 79 a66

ENVIRONMENTALIST (IRE) 4 b.g. Sure Blade (USA) 130 – Vielle 123 (Ribero 126) [1994 63: 8.3v 10.2g^5 10m^6 12s* 12m^6 12.1m^2 1995 a8g 12g 11.8d^5 14.1g^4 14.1m^2 a14.8g^6 a16g^4 a14.8g^4 12g^4 a12g^2 16.4m^4 a14.8g^5 a16g Nov 30] smallish, sturdy gelding: poor mover: modest handicapper: trained first 3 starts by S. Williams, next 2 by B. McMath: broke down at Lingfield final start: stayed 16.4f: acted on good to firm and soft ground and on fibresand: dead. *R. Harris* 59

ENVIRONMENT FRIEND 7 gr.h. Cozzene (USA) – Water Woo (USA) 102 (Tom Rolfe) [1994 118: 12m^2 10m^4 12m 10g^5 10m 1995 10m^3 12f 10m^4 12g 10m Oct 14] close-coupled, useful-looking horse who combined stud duties with racing and had several trainers over last 3 seasons: inconsistent and without a win after 1991 Eclipse Stakes, but still capable of smart form in 1995: length third of 7 to Prince of Andros in Tattersalls Gold Cup at the Curragh (penultimate outing for G. Rimmer) and 7¼ lengths fourth of 8 to Halling in the Eclipse at Sandown: effective at 1¼m and (at least on a sound surface) 1½m: acted on good to firm and dead ground: visored (well beaten) fifth 5-y-o start: usually held up: broke blood vessel in Champion Stakes and has been retired. *C. E. Brittain* 113

EPAGRIS 3 ch.f. Zalazl (USA) 120 – Trikymia 68 (Final Straw 127) [1994 90P: 6g* 1995 7m^2 8m^5 7m* 7m 6m^2 7f^3 7d^6 7f^2 Oct 12] quite attractive, strong-quartered 107 filly: fine, easy mover: useful performer: second of 8 to Myself in Nell Gwyn Stakes and fifth of 14 (made running) in 1000 Guineas at Newmarket first 2 3-y-o starts: edgy and sweating, landed the odds in listed event there in May, making virtually all to beat Warning Shadows by 1½ lengths: best subsequent effort third in listed race at Goodwood in July: stayed 1m: acted on firm ground: stud. *H. R. A. Cecil*

EPICA 4 b.g. Picea 99 – Aladyat § (Home Guard (USA) 129) [1994 –, a68: 10s 11s 12m4 a16.2g* 15.8g a16.2g 1995 a14.8g* a14.8g a14.8g a16.2g a16g5 May 27] sturdy, lengthy gelding: modest form at best in 1995: won seller at Wolverhampton in January: stays 16.2f: easily best form on fibresand: blinkered since fourth 3-y-o start: bandaged: often a front runner: has joined L. Barratt: unreliable. *A. Bailey* – § a49 §

EQTESAAD (USA) 4 b. or br.c. Danzig (USA) – Last Feather (USA) 120 (Vaguely Noble 140) [1994 74?: 8m2 10.1f4 a7g4 1995 a10g* a8.5g* a10g5 a8.5g* 10m 8m 10g May 30] compact colt: unimpressive mover: fair performer: won maiden at Lingfield and seller at Wolverhampton in January and handicap back at Wolverhampton in April: stays 1¼m: acts on the all-weather and on good to firm ground: has had tongue tied down: sent to USA. *S. C. Williams* 74

EQUASION (IRE) 3 b.f. Cyrano de Bergerac 120 – Konigin Kate (GER) (Authi 123) [1994 NR 1995 8m 8g 11.9f2 Aug 2] IR 10,000Y: tall, good-topped filly: half-sister to 1¼m winner Templehof and good jumper Hawthorn Blaze (both by Alzao): dam 1¼m winner in Ireland: modest form in maiden events: seems to stay 11.9f: has raced only on a sound surface: looked reluctant to race final start. *G. L. Moore* 54

EQUERRY 4 b.g. Midyan (USA) 124 – Supreme Kingdom 85 (Take A Reef 127) [1994 65: 8m a7g2 a7g2 7.2g2 8g2 8.1d2 a7g5 8.2g3 8.2d 1995 7.1d2 a8.5g2 7.1g3 8.3g6 8.5m* 8g3 a9.4g4 8m5 8.5m4 a8.5g* 8f* Jul 29] quite attractive gelding: fair handicapper: won at Beverley in May and at Wolverhampton and Thirsk in July: stays 8.5f: has modest form on fibresand, acts on firm and good to soft ground: effective in blinkers at 3 yrs, not tried since. *M. Johnston* 77 a63

EQUILIBRIUM 3 b.f. Statoblest 120 – Allander Girl (Miralgo 130) [1994 67: 6.1g* 6m5 6.1d 1995 8m5 7.1m3 a7g6 8f4 7m4 9.7s3 a9.4g Nov 27] smallish, sturdy filly: modest performer: stays 9.7f: acts on good to firm and soft ground. *J. W. Hills* 50

EQUITY'S DARLING (IRE) 3 b.f. Law Society (USA) 130 – Curie Abu (Crofter (USA) 124) [1994 –: 7.1g 1995 8d 7m6 8.3g4 12.3m a8.5g2 a8g5 a8.5g* a9.4g4 a8.5g Aug 19] lengthy filly: fair handicapper: won maiden event at Wolverhampton in July: well below form both subsequent starts: stays 8.5f: acts on good to firm ground and on fibresand: sold 5,500 gns Newmarket Autumn Sales. *M. Bell* 65

ERETAN (IRE) 4 b.g. Lashkari 128 – Eretna 87 (Golden Fleece (USA) 133) [1994 69: 11.7g 14d3 14.1g 1995 14.9g May 27] small, sturdy gelding: fair form in maidens only on second 3-y-o start: pulled up only outing on flat in 1995: dead. *T. Thomson Jones* –

ERIC'S BETT 2 gr.c. (Mar 10) Chilibang 120 – Mira Lady (Henbit (USA) 130) [1995 5m5 7m6 7.5g5 7m3 8.1g5 7g 8.3g* 8f4 7m5 Oct 30] plain colt: has a roundish action: second foal: half-brother to 1m winner Nuin-Tara (by Petoski): dam never ran: fair form: won median auction maiden at Hamilton in September: ridden by 7-lb claimer, creditable efforts afterwards in nurseries: will stay beyond 1m: acts on firm ground: twice visored: wears bandages. *Mrs S. M. Austin* 71

ERIN BIRD (FR) 4 b.f. Bluebird (USA) 125 – Maid of Erin (USA) (Irish River (FR) 131) [1994 116: 8g* 8g2 8g* 8s* 9.3g5 a9f4 1995 7f 8f 10f3 10g5 11d3 9.3d6 10g 8d2 Dec 2] big, strong, lengthy filly: smart performer: never quite recaptured her very best form in 1995: creditable third in Nassau Stakes at Goodwood and Group 3 event at Milan (3 lengths behind Sternkoenig), latter on final outing for P. Chapple-Hyam: stays 11f: acts on dirt and on any turf going. *Mme Pat Barbe, France* 111

ERIN'S LAD 4 br.c. Bold Owl 101 – Vernair (USA) 73 (Super Concorde (USA) 128) [1994 62: 8m5 8.5s5 8m 9g 1995 10m Aug 30] rather leggy colt: modest performer: raced too freely and tailed off on only 4-y-o start: stays 8.5f: acts on good to firm and soft ground. *R. Dickin* –

ERLKING (IRE) 5 b.g. Fairy King (USA) – Cape of Storms (Fordham (USA) 117) [1994 NR 1995 a8g6 a9.4g a9.4g a12g Sep 16] leggy, close-coupled gelding: –

fair 7f to 1¼m performer in 1993 for Lord Huntingdon: well beaten on flat in 1995, but won selling hurdle in December. *S. Mellor*

ERMINIUS (GER) 4 ch.c. Highest Honor (FR) 124 – Ermione (Surumu (GER)) [1994 105: 7s* 7.5d 5g^4 6g^6 8g* 7g^2 8g* 8d* 8g* 1995 8s^2 May 21] smart German colt: improved form when 3 lengths second of 14 to Chato (who received 13 lb more than weight for age) in Badener Meile, keeping on: better at 7f/1m than shorter: acted on soft going, did not race on top-of-the-ground: to stand at Gestut Rietberg. *P. Rau, Germany*
111

ERRANT 3 b.c. Last Tycoon 131 – Wayward Lass (USA) (Hail The Pirates (USA) 126) [1994 NR 1995 8g 8f a7g^4 a7g^2 Dec 19] half-brother to several winners, including 1¾m winner Syrtos (by Shareef Dancer): dam champion 3-y-o filly in USA in 1981: sold out of J. Gosden's stable 4,200 gns Newmarket July Sales after debut: form in maidens only when in frame at Lingfield last 2 starts: should stay beyond 7f. *D. J. S. Cosgrove*
65

ERTLON 5 b.g. Shareef Dancer (USA) 135 – Sharpina (Sharpen Up 127) [1994 78, a95: 7m^6 8g 7m 6.1m^4 7f^4 7g^5 7.3s 7g 7m^5 7g* a8g* 1995 a7g^2 a8.5g^2 a7g^2 a8g^3 8g 7m* 7m 7.3d 7d 7g^6 7f^4 8m^5 a9.4g Dec 2] close-coupled gelding: useful handicapper on the all-weather: in good form early in year: fairly useful on turf: made all in good style at Brighton in April, and held his form fairly well thereafter: effective at 7f and 8.5f: probably acts on any ground: blinkered (ran creditably) once as 4-y-o: sometimes bandaged behind and has tongue tied down: usually races prominently. *C. E. Brittain*
86
a99

ERUPT 2 b.g. (Mar 17) Beveled (USA) – Sparklingsovereign 53 (Sparkler 130) [1995 5m^2 6g 5.7f^4 5m^6 5m^5 5g^3 6g 6.1s* 6.1m^2 Oct 26] 3,200F, 6,200Y: leggy gelding: third foal: half-brother to 3-y-o Tilthams (by Prince Sabo): dam second over 7f at 3 yrs: fair performer: improved form last 2 starts, winning 19-runner nursery at Chepstow in October then good second in similar event at Nottingham 9 days later: stays 6f: acts on good to firm and soft ground: visored last 4 starts. *G. B. Balding*
79

ESCAPE TALK 8 gr.m. Gabitat 119 – Getaway Girl 63 (Capistrano 120) [1994 23: 12m 12g^5 13f^6 12g 1995 12g 14.1m 12m Oct 13] smallish, close-coupled mare: bad handicapper. *J. Dooler*
–

ESCARPMENT (USA) 4 ch.c. Green Dancer (USA) 132 – Revidere (USA) (Reviewer (USA)) [1994 NR 1995 12g 16.2m^5 13.3g* 14m^6 18g^6 Sep 7] rangy, rather sparely-made colt: fluent mover: useful performer: sent to Dubai after 2-y-o season, but did not race there: best effort when winning 6-runner listed event at Newbury (set steady pace, rallied, beat Sadler's Image by ¾ length) in May: well beaten in Curragh Cup and Doncaster Cup afterwards: stays 2m: acts on good to firm and dead ground, yet to race on extremes: sent to Dubai again. *P. W. Chapple-Hyam*
106

ESCOBAR (IRE) 2 br.c. (Jan 19) Cyrano de Bergerac 120 – Gale Force Seven (Strong Gale 116) [1995 6m 6g 6m Oct 13] IR 9,500F, 16,000Y: workmanlike colt: third foal: brother to a poor maiden: dam never ran: signs of ability all starts in maidens: has raced only at 6f: will do better. *P. Calver*
– p

ESKIMO KISS (IRE) 2 b.f. (Apr 29) Distinctly North (USA) 115 – Felicitas (Mr Fluorocarbon 126) [1995 6m 6m 5g 7s 7m Oct 12] IR 8,800Y: lengthy filly: half-sister to Irish 7f to 2m winner Mystical City and Italian 3-y-o Il Pugile (both by The Noble Player), winner at 7f and 1m: dam won over hurdles in Ireland after placing on flat: no worthwhile form: very stiff tasks when well beaten in nursery and seller last 2 starts. *M. J. Fetherston-Godley*
–

ESKIMO NEL (IRE) 4 ch.f. Shy Groom (USA) – North Lady (Northfields (USA)) [1994 –: a8g^5 9.7s^4 8.5m^6 10m^5 11.9f a12g 1995 10.3g Mar 24] workmanlike filly: unimpressive in appearance but caught eye keeping on late when seventh of 27 to Children's Choice in ladies handicap at Doncaster on only 4-y-o flat outing: stays 10.3f: progressed into useful hurdler. *J. L. Spearing*
34 +

ESPARTERO (IRE) 3 ch.c. Ballad Rock 122 – Elabella (Ela-Mana-Mou 132) [1994 94p: 6d* 6.1g^2 1995 6g^4 5f* 6m^4 5m^3 Sep 6] good-bodied colt: good walker: useful sprinter, lightly raced: won £13,900 handicap at Ascot in June, catching Double Quick final strides: ran an excellent race for one so inexperienced, faring best of those drawn low, when close fourth of 27 to Shikari's Son in Stewards' Cup at Goodwood: very good third of 9 to Eveningperformance in listed race at Doncaster 6
106

weeks later, staying on having been soon off bit: stays 6f: acts on firm and dead ground. *Sir Mark Prescott*

ESPERER 5 b.g. Full of Hope 125 – Priory Maid (Malinowski (USA) 123) [1994 –: a7g 1995 a10g a8g a13g a16g 8.1g May 30] good-topped gelding: of little account. *J. O'Donoghue* –

ESPERTO 2 b.g. (Apr 20) Risk Me (FR) 127 – Astrid Gilberto 75 (Runnett 125) [1995 6m^{6} 5m 7m Oct 12] 6,400Y, 5,000 2-y-o: good-topped gelding: second foal: brother to 3-y-o Civil: dam 2-y-o 5f and 6f winner: sixth of 8 to Mons in maiden at Newmarket: well beaten afterwards, in seller at Newmarket after 3-month absence last time: carried head high debut: tail swisher: has been gelded. *J. Pearce* 57 ?

ESQUIVE 2 ch.f. (Feb 4) Safawan 118 – Edraianthus 78 (Windjammer (USA)) [1995 5.5d^{3} 6d^{4} 7g^{2} 8s* 9d^{3} Oct 5] 4,600F: third foal: dam best form at 6f: useful French filly: won minor event at Longchamp in September: length third of 5 to Go Between in Prix de Conde at Longchamp last time: stays 9f: acts on soft going, yet to race on top-of-the-ground. *P. Bary, France* 106

ESSAYEFFSEE 6 b.g. Precocious 126 – Floreal 68 (Formidable (USA) 125) [1994 57: 9.9m 9.2f^{3} 9.9g^{6} 10m^{3} 10g* 12f^{4} 10.4d 10s^{5} 10s 10.1d^{5} 1995 10m^{5} 9m^{2} 9.2f^{2} 10.1m^{3} 11.1m^{3} 9f^{6} 10m* 11m^{2} 10d^{2} 9f^{5} 10f 10f^{5} Oct 31] workmanlike gelding: modest handicapper: led post to win amateurs race at Pontefract in August: effective at 9f, and stays 1½m: acts on firm and soft ground: blinkered all starts at 3 yrs: sometimes bandaged behind: consistent. *Mrs M. Reveley* 59

ESSENTIALSELECTION 2 gr.g. (Mar 24) Petong 126 – Love Scene (Carwhite 127) [1995 5g^{2} 6g^{2} 5.1m 5.7f^{3} 7f^{3} 6m^{4} Aug 16] 9,200Y: smallish gelding: second foal: brother to 3-y-o 7f winner Caddy's First: dam ran once: fair form when placed in maiden auctions: visored in valuable seller at York final start: stays 6f: sold 6,500 gns Newmarket Autumn Sales. *W. J. Haggas* 67

ESTHAL (IRE) 5 b.g. Kalaglow 132 – Chevrefeuille 87 (Ile de Bourbon (USA) 133) [1994 –: a7g 1995 8f 11.6g^{5} 10.2m 14.1f Jul 8] small gelding: won maiden at Wolverhampton at 2 yrs: no worthwhile form since. *A. Barrow* –

ESTHER LOUISE 2 b.f. (Mar 16) Governor General 116 – Cuba Libre (Rum (USA)) [1995 6g^{6} 6m 7.5m Jul 8] 3,000Y: unfurnished filly: sister to 4-y-o Natural Path and half-sister to several winners here and abroad, including (at 7f and 1m) Grey Rum (by Absalom): dam ran 3 times in Ireland: no form in sellers: seems temperamental. *M. W. Easterby* –

ESTRELA CASTANHA 3 b.f. Heights of Gold – Soleil Etoile (Roi Soleil 125) [1994 –: 7g 7d 1995 8f^{6} 9.7f 14m^{4} Aug 24] sparely-made filly: of no account. *R. M. Flower* –

ETERNALLY GRATEFUL 2 b.f. (May 14) Picea 99 – Carpadia (Icecapade (USA)) [1995 6.1d 7g a7g Nov 21] angular filly: sixth foal: half-sister to 6f (at 2 yrs) and 1m winner Tancred Grange (by Prince Sabo) and 4-y-o 7.6f to 9.4f winner Dia Georgy (by Reesh): dam placed once at 3 yrs in France: no form in maidens at Nottingham and Lingfield (2). *Mrs N. Macauley* –

ETERNITY RANGE (USA) 2 b.c. (Feb 26) Majestic Light (USA) – Northern Eternity (USA) 108 (Northern Dancer) [1995 8g* 8m^{3} Oct 15] fourth foal: brother to Grade 1 9f Hollywood Derby winner Eternity Star and half-brother to smart 6f to 9f performer Eternal Reve (by Diesis): dam 2-y-o 6f winner and second in Lowther, is half-sister to Miswaki: won minor event at Saint-Cloud in September: length third of 7 to Loup Solitaire in Grand Criterium at Longchamp, held up, outpaced early in straight then staying on: likely to stay beyond 1m: open to further progress. *P. Bary, France* 111 p

ETHBAAT (USA) 4 b. or br.c. Chief's Crown (USA) – Alchaasibiyeh (USA) 85 (Seattle Slew (USA)) [1994 93: 8m^{2} 7.1m* 7m* 8.3m 8g 1995 a7g^{5} a9g^{6} 7m 8m Oct 28] big, rangy colt: impresses in appearance: has a free, round action: fairly useful form as 3-y-o for H. Thomson Jones: unplaced twice in Dubai early in 1995 before being sold 22,000 gns Doncaster August Sales: no worthwhile form in handicaps at Newmarket on return: should prove best at up to 1m. *W. R. Muir* –

ETOILE DU NORD 3 b. or br.g. Tragic Role (USA) – Daisy Topper (Top Ville 129) [1994 49p: 7g 1995 8f Oct 18] sparely-made gelding: tailed-off last in maiden at Yarmouth on only 3-y-o start. *H. J. Collingridge* –

ETTERBY PARK (USA) 2 b.g. (May 14) Silver Hawk (USA) 123 – Bonita Francita (USA) (Devil's Bag (USA)) [1995 5m 6g5 7f 7d Sep 26] $55,000Y: quite attractive gelding: second foal: dam, winner at up to 9f, closely related to Coup de Folie, dam of Machiavellian and Exit To Nowhere: signs of ability: should stay beyond 6f: has joined Mrs J. R. Ramsden: may well improve. *M. D. I. Usher* – p

EUCHAN FALLS (IRE) 3 b.g. Durgam (USA) – Glen Maddie (Reasonable (FR) 119) [1994 65d: 5v3 5f a6g* 6.1s a5g6 a7g4 a6g3 a6g3 a6g6 a5g6 1995 a12g Sep 2] angular gelding: became disappointing in 1994: tailed off in seller on only 3-y-o start. *P. D. Evans* –

EULOGY (FR) 8 b. or br.g. Esprit du Nord (USA) 126 – Louange (Green Dancer (USA) 132) [1994 NR 1995 a14g a12g3 Apr 3] 300,000 francs Y: first foal: dam 13f winner in France: won 1¼m maiden at Saint-Cloud at 2 yrs: modest novice hurdler: signs of retaining a little ability on return to flat when third of 6 in apprentice seller at Southwell: visored (well beaten) on reappearance. *K. R. Burke* 36

EUPHYLLIA 3 b.f. Superpower 113 – Anse Chastanet (Cavo Doro 124) [1994 54: 5m 7g6 7s2 7g3 7v 1995 8m 6m a7g 7g 7m* 7m 7m a8g Dec 15] rather sparely-made filly: has a round action: fair performer: 33/1, clearly best effort to win 19-runner claimer at Doncaster in October: should stay 1m: acts on good to firm ground: ran respectably only try in visor: inconsistent. *Bob Jones* 70 a–

EUROBOX BOY 2 ch.g. (Apr 4) Savahra Sound 111 – Princess Poquito (Hard Fought 125) [1995 6.9s4 7m3 7g3 6.9m Nov 6] 3,000Y: second foal: half-brother to German 7f winner Miss Poquito (by Dunbeath): dam unraced half-sister to smart middle-distance filly Senorita Poquito: fair maiden: ran well in nursery at Folkestone final start: will stay 1m. *A. P. Jarvis* 69

EURO EXPRESS 2 ch.g. (Apr 6) Domynsky 110 – Teresa Deevey 50 (Runnett 125) [1995 5d 6m 7.5m 7m4 7m2 7m 7f2 7g 7f Oct 3] smallish, strong, close-coupled gelding: third foal: half-brother to 3-y-o Euro Rebel (by Roi Danzig), 6f winner at 2 yrs, and 1992 2-y-o 7f winner Yeveed (by Wassl): dam twice-raced 6f winner: modest performer: best efforts when second in sellers at Catterick and Thirsk in August: stays 7f: below best all 3 starts in blinkers. *M. H. Easterby* 54

EURO FORUM 3 ch.g. Deploy 131 – Unique Treasure (Young Generation 129) [1994 59: 7.1m 6m 7m 8g4 8g4 8m 1995 10.3g5 12m 11.6m 14.6m2 14s3 14.4m6 14.9m5 16m2 a16g4 12s3 12s Oct 6] workmanlike gelding: has a round action: modest maiden handicapper: stays 2m: acts on good to firm ground and soft: visored (well beaten) second 3-y-o start. *G. L. Moore* 59

EUROLINK MISCHIEF 3 b.f. Be My Chief (USA) 122 – Lady Eurolink 55 (Kala Shikari 125) [1994 NR 1995 8.2m4 10g3 9m2 12m* 13.3f2 11.9g3 12g4 11f2 Oct 31] leggy, good-topped filly: third foal: half-sister to useful middle-distance performer Duke of Eurolink (by Jupiter Island): dam 1m winner: fairly useful handicapper: won at Salisbury in June, leading post after a sustained battle last 3f: in frame all 4 subsequent starts, blinkered and unlucky on final one: stayed 13.3f: raced only on a sound surface: usually bandaged behind: stud. *L. M. Cumani* 84

EUROLINK SHADOW 3 b.c. Be My Chief (USA) 122 – Miss Top Ville (FR) (Top Ville 129) [1994 NR 1995 12m5 10d4 12m4 14.1m Oct 19] 17,000Y: robust, heavy-bodied colt: third foal: half-brother to fairly useful 1m winner Wilcuma (by Most Welcome) and a winner in Germany by Petong: dam French middle-distance winner: fair form in maidens first 2 starts: well beaten both subsequent outings, looking none too keen on final one: stays 1½m: acts on good to firm and dead ground: one to treat with caution: sold 22,000 gns Newmarket Autumn Sales. *L. M. Cumani* 70 §

EUROLINK THE REBEL (USA) 3 ch.g. Timeless Native (USA) – Seeing Stars (USA) (Unconscious (USA)) [1994 62p: 7g4 7m3 1995 7g6 8m* 8m2 8f 10.3m 10g4 8s 10.3m* Oct 21] lengthy gelding: fairly useful performer: won claimers at Goodwood in June and Doncaster (claimed by M. Hammond £12,000) in October: stays 10.3f: acts on good to firm ground, possibly not on soft: blinkered final start. *R. Akehurst* 80

EUROPEX 2 bl.g. (Mar 8) Dunbeath (USA) 127 – Afrabela 76 (African Sky 124) [1995 5m6 6m 5m3 7h4 Aug 2] 2,600Y: workmanlike gelding: third foal: half-brother to 4-y-o Waterloo Belle (by Kind of Hush): dam 6f winner: seems only poor on 45

balance of form: fourth of 8 in nursery at Newcastle final start: stays 7f. *M. H. Easterby*

EUROPHARM LASSIE 4 b.f. Tate Gallery (USA) 117 – Panama Princess 64 (Indian King (USA) 128) [1994 46: 6.9s^{5} 7m 7f 6m 6m a6g^{5} a7g^{5} a7g^{2} 1995 a6g a7g a7g^{3} a8g 5g May 20] close-coupled filly: poor maiden: below form in 1995, collapsing after line in selling handicap at Lingfield in May: stayed 7f: acted on good to firm and soft ground and on equitrack: tried visored: dead. *G. L. Moore* –

EURO REBEL 3 ch.g. Roi Danzig (USA) – Teresa Deevey 50 (Runnett 125) [1994 59: 7m 7.5g^{6} 6g 6g* 7d^{4} 1995 7.5m^{4} 7g 6m 6m^{6} Jun 13] lengthy, good-topped gelding: turned near-fore in: modest handicapper: stayed 7.5f: acted on good to firm ground and good to soft: tried blinkered: dead. *M. H. Easterby* 53

EURO SCEPTIC (IRE) 3 ch.g. Classic Secret (USA) 91 – Very Seldom (Rarity 129) [1994 53: 5d 5m^{5} 6f^{6} 6m^{4} 6m^{5} 7g^{6} 7.5g^{3} 1995 10d 7g^{6} 7.5m* 8.1g^{2} 7.5g* 7.5m^{3} 8f^{2} 7.5g 8f^{6} 7f 8f Oct 24] sturdy gelding: poor mover: poor handicapper: won at Beverley in May and June: stays 1m well: acts on firm and dead ground: usually blinkered. *M. H. Easterby* 49

EURO SINGER 3 br.g. Chief Singer 131 – Crystal Gael 79 (Sparkler 130) [1994 49: 5m 6g 6m 1995 8.2m 10m^{2} 10g^{6} 10f^{3} 12f^{5} 14d^{2} 14s^{4} Sep 30] tall gelding: modest maiden handicapper: best effort when head second of 19 at Lingfield on sixth start, clear halfway, tiring closing stages and caught near finish: stays 1¾m: acts on firm and soft ground: sold 18,000 gns Newmarket Autumn Sales. *R. Akehurst* 60

EUROTWIST 6 b.g. Viking (USA) – Orange Bowl (General Assembly (USA)) [1994 49: a13g 12g 12.1g^{4} 11.9d* 12g 1995 a11g^{6} 11.9m Oct 5] small gelding: poor handicapper at 5 yrs: fairly useful hurdler in 1994/5: well beaten on return to flat, leaving J. L. Eyre's stable after reappearance: should stay 1¾m: acts on fibresand, may well need an easy surface on turf: best held up. *S. E. Kettlewell* –

EUSKARA 2 ch.f. (Jan 30) La Grange Music 111 – Ciboure 74 (Norwick (USA) 125) [1995 a6g^{4} 6f^{5} a7g^{2} a7g^{4} a6g^{4} 6g^{6} Aug 7] smallish filly: first foal: dam 6f (at 2 yrs) and 1m winner: plater: bandaged and blinkered, well below form final start: stays 7f: best efforts on fibresand: sold 1,400 gns Ascot August Sales. *M. D. I. Usher* 40

EVA LUNA (IRE) 3 b.f. Double Schwartz 128 – Guess Again (GER) (Stradavinsky 121) [1994 106: 5d* 5g* 6g* 6g* 6g* 7d^{3} 1995 7g^{4} 5f Jun 23] well-made filly: useful performer: won Group 1 Heinz 57 Phoenix Stakes in 1994: respectable fourth in listed event at Leopardstown on reappearance but last of 10 in King's Stand Stakes at Royal Ascot over 2 months later: best form at 6f on good ground. *J. S. Bolger, Ireland* 99

EVAN CAN WAIT (IRE) 3 b.f. Phardante (FR) 123 – Brandywell (Skyliner 117) [1994 NR 1995 a8g 6.9f^{6} 8g Sep 2] 800Y: third foal: half-sister to 2 maidens by Cyrano de Bergerac: dam poor Irish maiden: soundly beaten in claimers and seller, off course 5 months after debut. *J. L. Eyre* –

EVAN 'ELP US 3 ch.g. Executive Man 119 – Recent Events (Stanford 121§) [1994 69: 6m^{2} 7.5g^{4} 7m^{2} 7m^{3} 7.5g* 8.3g^{4} 8d^{2} 1995 8.3g 7.5g^{5} 8f^{3} 8.2f^{5} 8.5g a8g^{5} 8.5d^{6} 8m^{4} 7m^{4} a9.4g^{5} Nov 13] good-topped, workmanlike gelding: fair handicapper: stays 1m: acts on firm and dead ground: visored (once) then blinkered since fourth 2-y-o start. *J. L. Eyre* 66

EVANRO (IRE) 4 ch.g. Common Grounds 118 – Opening Day (Day Is Done 115) [1994 57: 8s 7d 8m 6g* 6f^{2} 5m^{3} 6f 6f 5f 6g 6m 5m 1995 6g 7f 8f^{3} Oct 23] good-bodied gelding: poor handicapper at best in 1995, not seen out until September: stays 1m: acts on any ground: often visored in 1994. *T. D. Barron* 40

EVAPORATE 3 b.f. Insan (USA) 119 – Mona (Auction Ring (USA) 123) [1994 51?: 6m 7f 7g^{4} 7.1g 10g 7g 1995 a12g^{6} a16g Aug 24] angular filly: poor maiden: well beaten in 1995. *A. P. Jones* –

EVEN HANDED 2 b.g. (May 19) Then Again 126 – Trecauldah 69 (Treboro (USA) 114) [1995 7m 6.1m^{6} 7m^{5} 7g^{2} 7m^{5} 10d^{6} Nov 18] 9,000Y: angular gelding: second foal: dam 1¾m winner: fair form in sellers at Goodwood and Newmarket (claimed out of P. Cole's stable £8,000) before sixth of 8 in minor event at Marseilles: bred to stay beyond 1m. *Mme M. Bollack-Badel, France* 65

EVENING CHIME (USA) 2 b.g. (Mar 14) Night Shift (USA) – Brattice Cloth (USA) (L'Enjoleur (CAN)) [1995 5f^{2} 5g^{2} 5g^{3} 5f* 6m 7m* Aug 15] rather leggy, quite 83

Doncaster Bloodstock Sales Scarbrough Stakes, Doncaster—Eveningperformance beats Double Quick

attractive gelding: first foal: dam won 7 races in USA at up to around 1m: won maiden at Redcar in July and (much better form, drifted badly right) nursery at York in August: stays 7f: early to post last time: subsequently gelded. *Mrs J. R. Ramsden*

EVENING FALLS 4 ro.f. Beveled (USA) – Encore L'Amour (USA) § (Monteverdi 129) [1994 78d: 5g³ 5m 5g⁴ 6m 5d 5s⁶ 6.1g 5v 1995 5g⁵ 6m 5m a5g* a6g* 5m a6g 7g Sep 20] leggy filly: in foal to Minshaanshu Amad: modest at best in 1995: left J. Spearing's stable after second start: narrow winner of minor event and handicap at Wolverhampton in the summer: stayed 6f: acted on fibresand, possibly unsuited by a soft surface: tried blinkered: usually raced prominently. *C. James* — 56 a64

EVENINGPERFORMANCE 4 b.f. Night Shift (USA) – Classic Design (Busted 134) [1994 103p: 6d⁶ 6g³ 6g⁴ 5m⁴ 5f* 5.2s* 5m* 1995 5m 5m² 5g² 5f⁶ 5.1g 5f² 5m* 5d³ Oct 1] good-quartered filly: smart performer: won listed race at Doncaster in September by 2½ lengths from Double Quick: also ran well when second in Palace House Stakes at Newmarket and King George Stakes at Goodwood and when third of 12 to Hever Golf Rose in Prix de l'Abbaye de Longchamp on final start: very speedy, and best at 5f: acts on firm and soft ground: often sweating and edgy: front runner: stays in training. *H. Candy* — 114

EVEN TOP (IRE) 2 br.c. (Mar 12) Topanoora 118 – Skevena 57 (Niniski (USA) 125) [1995 6g⁶ 7m* 8.1d² 7g* 8m² Oct 21] — 110

Mark Tompkins has not had to wait too long before finding a potential replacement for stable star Bob's Return. It was four weeks in fact between the 1993 St Leger winner's last race and the acquisition (through the BBA) of a brown colt by Topanoora out of Skevena at the 1994 Irish National Yearling Sale. The IR 27,000 guineas paid for him (after he had fetched 3,000 as a foal) was 12,500 guineas more than that spent on Bob's Return at the same sale three years earlier, and more than twice that of the next highest-priced foal or yearling from the first crop of Topanoora. The colt is worth many times that now. Named Even Top, he had five runs as a two-year-old, improved with each of them, and has shown better form than Bob's Return at the same stage. On his final start, Even Top finished second on Town Moor in the Racing Post Trophy. That Group 1 had been his declared target as early as his second start, when he beat Murheb and seventeen others in a maiden at Newmarket in August. The route to Doncaster was a minor event at Sandown, in which he went down by a length and a quarter to Inchrory, and the listed Somerville Tattersall Stakes at Newmarket, which he won. A 12/1 chance, Even Top gained that second victory with a very game front-running performance, fighting off market leaders Tumble-

Somerville Tattersall Stakes, Newmarket—Even Top stays on from Tumbleweed Ridge (second right)

weed Ridge, Sovereign's Crown and Heron Island before he passed the post one and a half lengths to the good. Tumbleweed Ridge had looked likely to beat him at the furlong marker, and was later said to have needed the run. So to Doncaster. In a four-runner field, Even Top was clearly the pick on looks: a robust, attractive colt and a very good walker, he looked in superb condition and had more scope than the Royal Lodge winner and 4/5-shot Mons, more substance than second favourite Beauchamp King. In the race, Even Top took a narrow advantage over Mons two and a half furlongs out but Beauchamp King always had their measure and beat Even Top by a length and a quarter.

Even Top (IRE) (br.c. Mar 12, 1993)	Topanoora (b 1987)	Ahonoora (ch 1975)	Lorenzaccio
			Helen Nichols
		Topping Girl (br 1972)	Sea Hawk II
			Round Eye
	Skevena (b 1983)	Niniski (b 1976)	Nijinsky
			Virginia Hills
		Skhiza (br 1975)	Targowice
			Anticlea

Topanoora was a good-looking colt himself, and a genuine and consistent one too, out of the first two only twice in his fourteen starts. All of his races were at between a mile and a quarter and an extended mile and a half, and he won seven of them, but Topanoora is probably best remembered in defeat, when controversially demoted after passing the post by a short head in front of Rock Hopper in the Hardwicke Stakes. Even Top is the first winner and seemingly the third living foal out of the modest racehorse Skevena who won one race on the Flat—a handicap at Folkestone over an extended two miles on soft ground—and three early-season novice hurdles. She made IR 7,000 guineas when carrying her second foal early in 1989. Her dam Skhiza has had one runner of note, the useful mile-and-a-quarter winner La Vie En Primrose, but was a similar standard to Skevena on the racecourse, the winner at around a mile and a quarter of a maiden at Carlisle and handicap at Redcar. Third dam Anticlea had more to shout about, winner of both the Italian One

Thousand Guineas and Oaks. Even Top obviously has to find significant further improvement if he is to win a classic, his best chances of doing so surely being over middle distances. He should win a pattern race. *M. H. Tompkins*

EVER FRIENDS 3 ch.g. Crever 94 – Cappuccilli 111 (Lorenzaccio 130) [1994 NR 1995 a7g⁶ a10g a8g 8m a12g⁶ 14.1m⁴ Oct 19] 500 2-y-o: sparely-made gelding: half-brother to several winners, including fair middle-distance stayer Mr Copyforce (by Sharrood): dam staying 2-y-o, didn't train on: no worthwhile form: trained first 4 starts by B. McMath. *R. Harris* –

EVERGLADES (IRE) 7 b.g. Green Desert (USA) 127 – Glowing With Pride 114 (Ile de Bourbon (USA) 133) [1994 105: 6m 6d 6m 7.1m* 7.6m⁵ 7m 7.3g* 7g 7d⁵ 7g 1995 6m² 7.1g³ 6f 7.6m 7f⁴ 7m⁴ 7m⁵ Oct 5] sturdy gelding: carries condition and usually takes the eye: useful handicapper: not too consistent in 1995, and well beaten last 2 starts: probably ideally suited by further than 6f nowadays and stays 7.3f: needs a sound surface: usually held up. *R. Charlton* 105 d

EVERSET (FR) 7 b.g. Green Desert (USA) 127 – Eversince (USA) (Foolish Pleasure (USA)) [1994 66, a90: a5g⁶ a6g² a7g* a6g* 7m³ a6g³ a7g* a6g* 6g* 6m³ 6.1m² a6g* 6g 6d⁵ 6d 6g⁴ a7g* a8g³ a6g⁵ a7g* a6g³ 1995 a7g² a7g² a6g* a8g⁵ Dec 15] close-coupled gelding: unimpressive mover: useful performer, best on the all-weather: very good second in handicap at Wolverhampton on reappearance: reportedly finished lame when landing the odds in claimer at Lingfield in January: long way below best, fading closing stages over 1m, in similar event there nearly 11 months later: effective at 6f and 7f: best form on fibresand, also acts on equitrack and on firm and dead ground. *A. Bailey* – a102 d

EVER SO LYRICAL 5 b.h. Never So Bold 135 – Lyra (Blakeney 126) [1994 80: 8m² 8m* 8m⁴ 8g² 7.9m⁴ 8.1d⁴ 8.9d 1995 8m 8f³ 8s 8.2m Oct 19] strong horse: unimpressive mover: fairly useful handicapper: off course over 3 months after second outing, and well beaten both subsequent starts: should stay beyond 1m: acts on dead going and firm. *P. W. Harris* 77 d

EVERYONE CAN DREAM 2 br.c. (Apr 25) Shareef Dancer (USA) 135 – Saltation 111 (Sallust 134) [1995 5.1g 5f* 6m⁵ 5g⁵ 5g 6f Oct 24] robust, short-backed colt: half-brother to several winners here and abroad, including 6f (at 2 yrs) and 7f winner Beware of Agents (by Tremblant) and useful 7f and 1m winner Imperial Salute (by Imperial Fling): dam sprinter: won claimer at Edinburgh in June (claimed out of M. Johnston's stable £6,000): well beaten afterwards in nurseries and minor event: should stay 6f: sold 4,800 gns Doncaster November Sales. *Denys Smith* 65 d

EVEZIO RUFO 3 b.c. Blakeney 126 – Empress Corina 74 (Free State 125) [1994 81: 9v³ 9s² 9.7s* 10d 1995 11g a12g Dec 2] neat colt: unimpressive mover: stiffish task, improved on 2-y-o form when seventh of 8 in £8,600 contest at Newbury in April: sold out of J. Dunlop's stable 11,000 gns Newmarket Autumn Sales: tailed off in Wolverhampton handicap on only subsequent outing: should stay 1½m: acts on soft ground. *N. P. Littmoden* 90

EVIDENCE IN CHIEF 2 b.f. (Feb 13) Be My Chief (USA) 122 – Ominous 91 (Dominion 123) [1995 5.2m⁵ 6g⁶ 7g* 7.9g 7.6m Sep 5] 6,800Y: quite good-topped filly: half-sister to 4-y-o 6f winner Yet More Roses (by Gallic League), 1987 2-y-o 7f winner Fright (by Persian Bold) and minor winners in Italy and France: dam 7f and 1¼m winner: won maiden auction at Warwick in June: well beaten afterwards in nurseries at York (gave impression something amiss) and Lingfield (not well drawn): should be suited by 1m+. *P. F. I. Cole* 63

EWAR IMPERIAL 3 b.c. Legend of France (USA) 124 – Monaneigue Lady (Julio Mariner 127) [1994 –: 7.9d⁴ 8s 1995 10f⁴ 10m 11.5m⁶ 9.9m 8m Aug 31] small, robust colt: no worthwhile form. *C. E. Brittain* –

EWAR SUNRISE 2 ch.f. (Mar 29) Shavian 125 – Sunset Reef (Mill Reef (USA) 141) [1995 6d 7g² 7m Nov 3] 5,200F, 8,500Y: small filly: half-sister to fair 1990 2-y-o 6f winner Sunset Street (by Bellypha) and winners abroad by Caerleon and Bold Arrangement: dam, maiden, should have been suited by middle distances: raced on favoured side of track when 2 lengths second of 14 to Jezyah in maiden at Lingfield in October: well beaten on other starts: will stay at least 1m: swished tail throughout debut. *C. E. Brittain* 67

EXACTLY (IRE) 2 b.f. (Apr 1) Taufan (USA) 119 – Not Mistaken (USA) (Mill Reef (USA) 141) [1995 a5g^4 5m 5g^3 5m 7.9g^4 7.5d 10m^4 Oct 2] IR 6,500F, IR 9,000Y: leggy filly: sister to a middle-distance winner in Italy and half-sister to several winners, including fair 7f and 1m winner Dara Dee (by Dara Monarch) and useful Irish 1m and 1½m winner Bay Empress (by Empery): dam never ran: trained by M. Johnston first 4 starts: improved considerably when fourth of 14 to Warbrook in maiden at Pontefract final start: clearly very well suited by a good test of stamina. *J. L. Eyre* — 71

EXALTED (IRE) 2 b.c. (Apr 26) High Estate 127 – Heavenward (USA) (Conquistador Cielo (USA)) [1995 7m* 7m^3 8m^3 10m^6 Oct 28] IR 25,000Y: good-topped, attractive colt: type to carry condition: has scope: half-brother to 3-y-o I'm Outa Here (by Don't Forget Me) and winners in Italy by Dance of Life and Bluebird: dam ran once in USA: won 3-runner minor event at Thirsk in July: good efforts next 2 starts: should be well suited by further than 1m (gave impression something amiss when tailed off in listed race at 1¼m). *Sir Mark Prescott* — 88

EXCEEDINGLY 2 ch.f. (Mar 21) Be My Guest (USA) 126 – Kantado 93 (Saulingo 122) [1995 5g^4 5g 6m^6 Jul 6] neat filly: half-sister to several winners, notably In Excess (by Siberian Express), 6f and 7f winner here later top class in USA at 1m/1¼m: dam raced mainly at 5f: close last of 4 in maiden at Haydock in May: ran poorly afterwards, in seller at Yarmouth (bandaged) final start: should stay beyond 5f: sold 4,500 gns Newmarket September Sales. *W. Jarvis* — 55

EXCELLED (IRE) 6 gr.m. Treasure Kay 114 – Excelling Miss (USA) (Exceller (USA) 129) [1994 –: 8g 10g 8m a7g 1995 8.3g 11.6m^6 11.6m^2 11.7h* 14.4m 14d a12g Oct 23] light-framed mare: poor performer: won weak seller at Bath in August: well beaten afterwards: stays 1½m: acts on hard ground: tried blinkered. *C. J. Drewe* — 40

EXCLUSION 6 ch.g. Ballad Rock 122 – Great Exception 84 (Grundy 137) [1994 –: 10m^5 8m a12g a7g a9.4g 1995 a8g^5 a10g^6 a11g 12m^2 14.1m^5 12.1m^4 10f^3 12m^6 12.1f* 12m Aug 23] strong gelding: poor handicapper nowadays: made all in 3-runner race at Hamilton in August: stays 1½m, may get 1¾m ridden more conservatively than on fifth outing: acts on firm and soft going, below form on the all-weather: visored (out of form) final 5-y-o start: often bandaged behind: races prominently: won selling hurdle in November: subsequently changed hands 5,600 gns Doncaster November Sales. *J. Hetherton* — 43

EXCLUSIVE ASSEMBLY 3 ch.g. Weldnaas (USA) 112 – Pretty Pollyanna (General Assembly (USA)) [1994 55: 5d 5m 5g^4 5m 6g^3 6s 6m^6 1995 a7g a6g^3 a7g* a7g a8.5g^6 8.1m 6m^3 7f a7g^2 a8g a7g^3 a7g^5 a8g^5 Dec 6] lengthy gelding: modest performer: won minor event at Southwell in April: effective at 6f to 1m: goes well on the all-weather: acts on good to firm ground, possibly not on soft. *A. P. James* — 48 a60

EXECUTIVE DESIGN 3 b.g. Unfuwain (USA) 131 – Seven Seas (FR) 76 (Riverman (USA) 131) [1994 66p: 7m^4 8f 7.5g^3 1995 12.3d* 12.5m^2 12g^5 14m^2 14g^4 11.9m^6 14.1g^2 Sep 23] sturdy gelding: fairly useful handicapper: very impressive winner at Ripon in April: creditable efforts most subsequent starts: stays 1¾m well: acts on good to firm and dead ground: won juvenile hurdle in October. *Mrs M. Reveley* — 84

EXEMPTION 4 ch.g. Ballad Rock 122 – Great Exception 84 (Grundy 137) [1994 71: 10g 10d^5 10m 10.2f* 11.8m^3 10d^2 10m 12.1g^2 1995 11.8d^6 12g 12.1g^2 10.2m* 10.2m^2 10m 12d^5 10.5s^3 10d Oct 19] strong, lengthy gelding: fair handicapper: won at Chepstow in June: stays 1½m: acts on firm and soft going: occasionally makes running. *H. Candy* — 73

EXHIBIT AIR (IRE) 5 b.m. Exhibitioner 111 – Airy Queen (USA) (Sadair) [1994 65: a10g^4 a10g* a11g a10g^4 a12g^3 a12g* a10g^5 a10g a10g 10g 12g 8.3m 11.7m^4 12m* 11.9m* 14v^4 12m* 1995 12m^4 11.9f^2 11.9f^3 12g 11.9g a12g^5 a16g^4 a13g^2 Nov 25] good-quartered mare: fair handicapper: stays 2m: acts on firm and dead ground and on equitrack (below form on fibresand): effective visored/blinkered or not: inconsistent: usually races prominently. *R. Akehurst* — 67 a64

EXPANSIVE RUNNER (USA) 3 b.c. Explodent (USA) – Scissors (USA) (Blade (USA)) [1994 71p: 7s 1995 10.2m^6 11.9d Oct 11] good-bodied colt: shaped quite well on only 2-y-o start, but tailed off both outings in 1995. *P. W. Harris* — –

EXPENSIVE TASTE 2 b.f. (May 21) Cadeaux Genereux 131 – Um Lardaff (Mill Reef (USA) 141) [1995 6.9f* 8.1d^6 7d^5 Sep 26] rather unfurnished filly: third — 78 foal: dam, French 11f and 1½m winner, sister to Shirley Heights: won maiden at Folkestone in August: easily better of last 2 starts when fifth of 18 to Pacific Grove in £23,500 nursery at Newmarket: should stay 1m: tended to carry head high second start. *M. R. Stoute*

EXPLORE MONDIAL (IRE) 4 b.g. Alzao (USA) 117 – Organdy 84 (Blakeney 126) [1994 –: 10.1m 11.9f4 12g 1995 13v Mar 31] useful-looking gelding: no worthwhile form on flat since 2 yrs. *T. Dyer* –

EXPLOSIVE POWER 4 br.c. Prince Sabo 123 – Erwarton Seabreeze (Dunbeath (USA) 127) [1994 45, a52: 8v 9m4 10m a10g 10f6 7m a11g3 11.8g 11.5g5 14.1g4 a12g* 1995 a10g2 Dec 18] workmanlike colt: modest handicapper: excellent second of 13 at Lingfield on belated reappearance: should stay beyond 1½m: acts on the all-weather: blinkered (below form) sixth 3-y-o start. *G. C. Bravery* – a57

EXPORT MONDIAL 5 b.g. Night Shift (USA) – Star Face (African Sky 124) [1994 –: a8g a7g6 a8g 1995 7d 10m 8f a7g Nov 29] sturdy gelding: poor maiden at best nowadays: left P. Burgoyne after third 5-y-o start: stays 1m: acts on firm ground and dead: tried blinkered: inconsistent. *D. J. S. ffrench Davis* 40

EXPRESS GIFT 6 br.g. Bay Express 132 – Annes Gift (Ballymoss 136) [1994 68: 10m 10.4d 10d 1995 8d 12m3 14.6m6 Oct 20] angular gelding: useful hurdler: lightly raced on flat last 2 seasons, and seems just a modest handicapper nowadays: should stay 1¾m: acts on good to firm ground and goes well with plenty of give. *Mrs M. Reveley* 64

EXPRESS ROUTING 3 b.c. Aragon 118 – San Marguerite 80 (Blakeney 126) [1994 –: 5.1m 1995 5d 7f4 5g6 Jun 7] compact colt: type to carry condition: first sign of ability in maiden events when fourth of 10 to Decorated Hero at Lingfield in May: found trip too sharp on only subsequent outing: may well prove suited by further than 7f: looked capable of better. *R. Akehurst* 62 p

EXTRA HOUR (IRE) 2 b.g. (Jan 15) Cyrano de Bergerac 120 – Renzola (Dragonara Palace (USA) 115) [1995 5.2m 6m2 6m3 5.2d 5.7m4 6m Oct 12] 21,000Y: compact gelding: brother to winning sprinters Miss Nosey Parker, Rapier Point and Sober Lad: dam never ran: fair maiden: placed at Goodwood and Epsom but bit below form afterwards, twice facing very stiff tasks in nurseries: stays 6f: acts on good to firm ground. *W. R. Muir* 68

EXTREMELY FRIENDLY 2 ch.g. (Jan 19) Generous (IRE) 139 – Water Woo (USA) 102 (Tom Rolfe) [1995 7f 6m a8g6 Nov 14] neat gelding: half-brother to 3-y-o Action Jackson (by Hadeer) and half-brother to several winners here and abroad, notably high-class middle-distance performer Environment Friend (by Cozzene): dam, French 2-y-o 6f winner, daughter of Waterloo: modest form in maidens: has joined N. C. Wright. *C. E. Brittain* 60

EZEKIEL 4 ch.g. Be My Guest (USA) 126 – Judeah 69 (Great Nephew 126) [1994 –: 7v5 6.9v 8.2d 8.1f 7d 8.2d a7g a10g a9.4g 1995 a10g Jan 17] close-coupled gelding: poor maiden: well beaten since first 3-y-o start: should stay at least 1m, but pulls hard: has joined T. Clement. *J. W. Payne* –

F

FAAL MARIO (USA) 4 b.g. Gulch (USA) – Mousseline de Soie (FR) (Riverman (USA) 131) [1994 82: 7m 10.4m4 10.1m2 10m3 1995 9.9m 11.8m6 14m5 12g 12d a12g* a8s* Dec 23] leggy, close-coupled gelding: fair form: sold out of Mrs Ramsden's stable 15,000 gns Newmarket Autumn Sales after fifth start: won 2 races in Sweden later: stays 1½m: acts on good to firm ground, dead and all-weather: takes keen hold. *J. Huber, Sweden* 76

FAATEQ 2 b.c. (Mar 18) Caerleon (USA) 132 – Treble (USA) 118 (Riverman (USA) 131) [1995 7.1g3 7.5m3 8.1s4 Oct 17] good-bodied colt: good mover: first foal: dam French 9f (at 2 yrs) and 1¼m winner out of half-sister to Triptych: third in maidens won by Oblomov at Sandown and Pleasant Surprise at Beverley: ran better than remote fourth-of-11 position suggests in similar event at Chepstow on final outing: bred to stay middle distances: races keenly. *J. L. Dunlop* 73

FABILLION 3 ch.c. Deploy 131 – Kai (Kalamoun 129) [1994 NR 1995 a12g^{6} 10.2f^{5} 10g 10.8m^{6} 10d 10g 12.1s^{2} 14.1m^{2} 15.1s^{6} Nov 2] IR 1,000Y: workmanlike colt: half-brother to 2 winners by Busted, including fairly useful 1¼m winner Kaytiggy: dam never ran: fair maiden handicapper: stays 15f well, may stay further: acts on good to firm ground and soft. *C. A. Smith* — 66

FABRIANA 5 b.m. Northern State (USA) 91 – Fashion Flow (Balidar 133) [1994 55: 10v^{6} 8d 8g^{5} 7g 7m 7.6v^{2} 7.1s 1995 8s 8.3g Jun 12] sturdy mare: very much on the downgrade. *T. J. Naughton* — –

FABULOUS MTOTO 5 b.h. Mtoto 134 – El Fabulous (FR) 111 (Fabulous Dancer (USA) 124) [1994 a5g^{4} a10g^{4} a12g^{6} a11g^{5} a8g^{6} a10g^{6} a10g^{5} a8g^{5} 1995 a10g^{3} a12g* a12g^{5} a9g a9g a10g 12.1d 16m 14.1m a12g^{6} Nov 13] strong, rangy horse: had 2 seasons in Dubai, winning handicap in January for D. Selveratnam: sold 8,000 gns Newmarket July Sales: little worthwhile form on return: should stay 2m. *M. S. Saunders* — 53 d

FABULOUS PRINCESS (IRE) 4 b.f. Jareer (USA) 115 – Nora Yo Ya (Ahonoora 122) [1994 52, a42: 8m 8g^{6} a8g^{4} 7f^{6} 9.7m^{4} 10f* 11.9f^{4} 10.2m a8.5g^{4} a10g 1995 a9.4g^{5} Mar 8] leggy, shallow-girthed filly: modest form on her day: finds 8.5f a minimum, but barely stays 1½m: acts on firm ground: blinkered (well beaten) twice at 3 yrs: none too consistent: winning hurdler, finished lame in September. *C. L. Popham* — –

FACE THE FUTURE 6 ch.g. Ahonoora 122 – Chiltern Red (Red God 128§) [1994 71: 6v 6f^{4} 6m 7m^{5} 7m^{5} 7f^{2} 7g^{5} 7d^{4} 7.3s^{6} 7d^{5} 1995 6g 6m^{5} 6g 6g 6g^{3} 6f^{5} 6m^{5} 6m^{3} 6g 6g 6d a7g Nov 8] stocky gelding: has a quick action: fair handicapper: no worthwhile form after eighth outing: soundly beaten last 4 starts, leaving L. J. Holt after penultimate one: effective at 6f and 7f: acts on firm and dead ground, below form on 3 occasions on very soft: blinkered (well beaten) eleventh 6-y-o start. *S. Dow* — 66

FACE UP 8 br.h. Top Ville 129 – Pomade 79 (Luthier 126) [1994 NR 1995 7g a7g May 27] smallish, angular horse: probably no longer of much account. *B. J. Meehan* — –

FADI 4 b.g. Celestial Storm (USA) 132 – Rachael Tennessee (USA) (Matsadoon (USA)) [1994 56: 10d^{3} 12g^{6} 12m^{3} 13.6m 12m 1995 16.1g Oct 3] sturdy gelding: has a long stride: modest maiden: no promise on belated reappearance: should stay 2m. *F. Jordan* — –

FAEZ 5 b.g. Mtoto 134 – Ghanimah 98 (Caerleon (USA) 132) [1994 –: a8.5g^{6} 7d a7g a7g 1995 a6g^{4} a7g a8g^{5} 7g a7g Oct 23] sturdy, attractive gelding: no worthwhile form since 3 yrs: sold out of P. Felgate's stable 925 gns Ascot February Sales after third start: stays 1m: acts on soft going and fibresand: tried blinkered, no improvement. *R. Simpson* — –

FAG END (IRE) 2 b.f. (Jan 19) Treasure Kay 114 – Gauloise Bleue (USA) (Lyphard's Wish (FR) 124) [1995 6m^{5} 6m* 6g^{3} 7m* 7m^{2} 7m^{3} 6.5m 7g^{3} Sep 30] 6,000Y: leggy filly: unimpressive mover: third foal: sister to a 6f to 7f winner in Italy and 3-y-o Nyali Beach: dam, ran twice in France, half-sister to very useful 1m/1½m performer Grand Pavois: won maiden auction at Pontefract and 4-runner minor event at York in summer: good placed efforts afterwards, including third behind Bint Shadayid in Prestige Stakes at Goodwood and Ruznama in listed event at Newmarket: much better suited by 7f than shorter, and will stay 1m: acts on good to firm ground: genuine and consistent. *M. H. Tompkins* — 88

FAHAL (USA) 3 b.c. Silver Hawk (USA) 123 – By Land By Sea (USA) (Sauce Boat (USA)) [1994 105: 6f* 7f* 7m^{4} 7.1g^{3} 8d* 8g^{4} 8s^{6} 1995 10m^{3} 12f^{4} 11.9m^{3} 10.5f* 10g^{2} 10m^{6} Oct 14] — 118

Does he stay one and a half miles? This was a question that kept cropping up with Fahal, firstly when he showed improvement at the trip in the Derby. Fahal started a 50/1-shot at Epsom, seemingly well held on the form of his previous eight starts, but came in fourth of fifteen and at one stage threatened to do even better and cause the biggest Derby upset for twenty years. As Snow Knight had done, Fahal held the lead rounding Tattenham Corner; two lengths up on Tamure at the two-furlong pole, he was however mastered by that colt a hundred or so yards from home and then lost out to Lammtarra and Presenting as well, eventually going down by three lengths. When a horse's best form in the course of a season has been shown in a race over a mile and a half, nine times out of ten we will conclude that it stays a mile and a half. Being caught in the closing stages does not automatically label the horse in question a non-stayer. This is particularly true if it has been given an aggressive ride such as the one Richard Hills gave Fahal, enterprising tactics, incidentally, which were reminiscent of those he employed carrying the Hamdan Al-Maktoum colours on an even longer-priced contender, 250/1-shot At Talaq, when fourth on his first Derby ride in 1984. At Talaq went on to win the fifteen-furlong Grand Prix de Paris and the Melbourne Cup.

We are not suggesting that Fahal will prove a stayer. He might, of course, go on to show his best at a mile and a quarter at some future date, but what we know now is that when given three opportunities in 1995 to improve on his Derby form over significantly shorter trips, he failed to do so. Fahal had one more run at around a mile and a half, in a listed race at Haydock in July, but finished third of four at even money after pulling much too hard in a slowly-run race. The pace of the race beat him rather than the distance. At the same course four weeks later he had a strong pace over ten and a half furlongs in the Rose of Lancaster Stakes and gained a deserved first win for over a year (he had won a maiden at Yarmouth and minor event at Newcastle in June as a two-year-old). Fahal was clearly the best in at the weights in this Group 3 on his Derby form and ran to a similar level in winning by two and a half lengths, going on two furlongs out, with Young Buster getting the better of Sonic Boy for second in a race marred by the death of Wainwright and the injury to his rider Dettori. Things went less smoothly for Fahal in the Select Stakes at Goodwood the following month. This was a race run at a muddling pace and Fahal found himself boxed in at a vital stage, obtaining a clear path only when Triarius ahead of him showed much the better turn of foot. In the circumstances, Fahal's second placing there was a perfectly good effort. Position-wise, there is little to criticise in his sixth of eight in the Champion Stakes five weeks later, but, gone in his coat and sweating at one stage in the preliminaries, Fahal clearly failed to reproduce his best form on this return to Group 1 company, fading after helping to force a very strong pace.

Hamdan Al Maktoum's "Fahal"

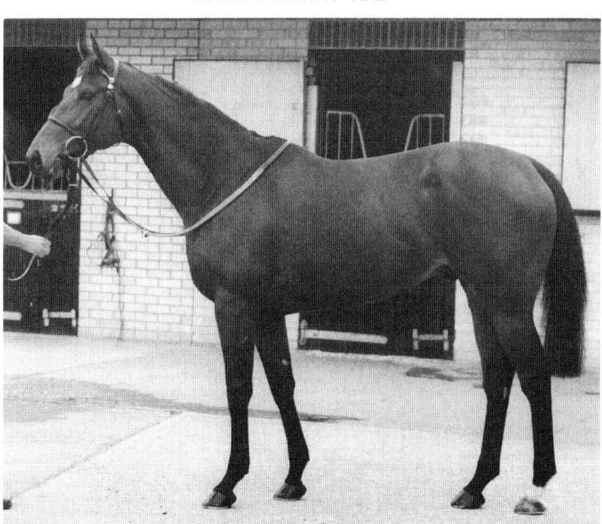

The season ended, our conclusion on Fahal's distance requirements is that he stays a mile and a half and will prove suited by a strongly-run race when at a mile and a quarter. He clearly acts on firm going, won on good to soft as a two-year-old, but was well beaten on his only start on soft (also at two years). He is a strong, rangy colt (but an unimpressive walker) whom we expect will be at least as good as a four-year-old.

Fahal (USA) (b.c. 1992)	Silver Hawk (USA) (b 1979)	Roberto (b 1969)	Hail To Reason
			Bramalea
		Gris Vitesse (gr 1966)	Amerigo
			Matchiche II
	By Land By Sea (USA) (b 1984)	Sauce Boat (ch 1975)	Key To The Mint
			Missy Baba
		Like A Train (b 1975)	Great Sun
			Boone Tavern

Fahal has always shaped like a middle-distance performer, but his year-older brother Fawran gained his last victory as a three-year-old over six furlongs in Dubai after showing fairly useful form at seven and a mile over here. Fawran made 230,000 dollars as a yearling, Fahal 160,000 and the dam's third foal, also by Silver Hawk, at 73,000 failed to reach her reserve at the 1995 Keeneland September Yearling Sale. Their dam By Land By Sea won five graded races at eight and a half furlongs as a four-year-old, two of them Grade 1 Handicaps. She is the only horse by the now-deceased Sauce Boat to have won at that level. Grandam Like A Train and third dam Boone Tavern were both minor winners. Other family runners of note in 1995 are Boone Tavern's grandson Reconnoitering, a formerly useful sprinter in the USA still going at the age of eleven, and Like A Train's two-year-old daughter Like A Hawk (by Silver Hawk) who was runner-up in two pattern events for Paul Cole. *D. Morley*

FAHEMA 3 b.f. Most Welcome 131 – Fujaiyrah 98 (In Fijar (USA) 121) [1994 64: 6.9m^4 5.2g^5 5g 7m^2 7d 7g^3 a7g 1995 a8g^5 a7g* a8g^4 a10g a8.5g a6s^2 6g* 9g^5 a6.7g a6.7g a6g^6 a6g^4 a6.7g^3 a6.7g^2 Dec 10] sturdy filly: modest performer: easily made all in seller at Lingfield in January: sold out of R. Boss's stable 3,600 gns Doncaster March Sales after fifth start: won in Sweden in June: stays 7f: acts on equitrack and dirt, best efforts on a sound surface on turf. *H. Meisel, Sweden* — 50

FAHIM 2 b.c. (Mar 19) Green Desert (USA) 127 – Mahrah (USA) 89 (Vaguely Noble 140) [1995 7g Sep 28] sturdy, attractive colt: has scope: second foal: dam 1m winner, should have stayed 1¼m: 13/2, very much caught the eye when around 9 lengths eighth of 23 to Astor Place in maiden at Newmarket, slowly away, held up well off leaders then going on well closing stages not at all knocked about: will stay 1m: sure to improve considerably, and win a race or two. *A. C. Stewart* — 74 P

FAILTE RO 3 bl.f. Macmillion 110 – Safe Passage (Charlottown 127) [1994 74: 6s 6s* a8g^2 a7g^5 1995 10g 8.2m 12m Oct 27] leggy filly: not seen out until the autumn, and disappointed: should prove well suited by 1¼m+: acts on soft ground and equitrack. *J. E. Banks* — –

FAIR AND FANCY (FR) 4 b.g. Always Fair (USA) 121 – Fancy Star (FR) (Bellypha 130) [1994 51: 8d^3 8.2d 7m 12.5m 10m^6 12g^6 8.9d 9g 10.1d 1995 12m 11.9m 14.1m^5 a14g* a14g^2 Nov 16] good-topped gelding: carries condition: has a round action: poor handicapper: won at Southwell (amateurs) in November, leading 3f out and battling on determinedly: stays 1¾m well: acts on fibresand, went well on an easy surface at 2 yrs: blinkered (finished last) third 3-y-o start: won over hurdles for Miss K. Milligan in December. *D. Nicholls* — 47

FAIR ATTRACTION 3 ch.g. Charmer 123 – Fairfields 73 (Sharpen Up 127) [1994 52: 5m 6m 6.1s 6s 6m 1995 6g 8m 10.1m^5 Jul 16] neat gelding: modest maiden at 2 yrs: soundly beaten in 1995, looking none too keen last 2 starts: stays 6f: acts on good to firm ground and soft: needs treating with caution: joined J. Toller. *A. Hide* — –

FAIRELAINE 3 b.f. Zalazl (USA) 120 – Blue And White (Busted 134) [1994 50: 6.9m 1995 a8g^3 7d a9.4g 7f^2 7.3g 10.2m^4 10g 8f^4 8.2m^3 8f^4 8.3m 10d^5 7s^2 8g^4 Oct 9] smallish, close-coupled filly: modest maiden handicapper: effective at 7f, probably at 10.2f: acts on firm ground, soft and equitrack: visored (below best) eleventh 3-y-o start. *A. P. Jarvis* — 60

FAIR ELLA (IRE) 3 ch.f. Simply Great (FR) 122 – Dance Or Burst (Try My Best (USA) 130) [1994 44, a54: 5g 6d^4 a8g 7g a6g^6 a6g a7g^3 a7g 1995 a7g^4 a10g^5 — 36

a12g 12m^5 8f^6 Jul 31] poor maiden: stays 1¼m: acts on equitrack: tried blinkered/visored, running well only on first occasion: sold 650 gns Ascot September Sales. *J. Ffitch-Heyes*

FAIREY FIREFLY 4 b.f. Hallgate 127 – Tremellick 87 (Mummy's Pet 125) [1994 59: 6g^2 6m* 5d 5s^6 1995 a6g a6g^2 a6g a6g a6g^5 Dec 9] good-topped filly: has scar on near-hindquarter: modest handicapper: below form last 3 starts: stays 6f: acts on good to firm and dead ground and on fibresand. *M. J. Camacho* — 55

FAIR FLYER (IRE) 6 b.g. Tilt Up (USA) – Fair Siobahn (Petingo 135) [1994 –: 12g^6 1995 10.3m 12d Sep 15] good-topped gelding: no form since modest 4-y-o: best form at around 1½m but has won over 15f: acts on firm and dead ground, not very soft: occasionally blinkered or visored, not since 3 yrs. *P. J. Bevan* — –

FAIRLIGHT DOWN (USA) 2 b.f. (Feb 28) Dayjur (USA) 137 – Stresa (Mill Reef (USA) 141) [1995 7g* Oct 9] $425,000Y: half-sister to several winners, including useful 3-y-o 1¼m winner Tremplin (by Trempolino), Arlington Million winner Mill Native (by Exclusive Native) and high-class 1m and 9f winner French Stress (by Sham): dam French 1¼m winner: weak 7/2-shot, comfortable winner of 18-runner maiden at Leicester by 2½ lengths from Academy of Dance: very green to post: sure to improve. *P. F. I. Cole* — 80 p

FAIRLIGHT MAGIC 3 b.f. Mandrake Major 122 – Magic Mover (Julio Mariner 127) [1994 NR 1995 a5g^6 Feb 18] 1,300 2-y-o: half-sister to a winner in Belgium by Kabour: dam poor maiden: 20/1, no promise in 6-runner Lingfield maiden. *P. C. Haslam* — –

FAIRLY SURE (IRE) 2 b.f. (Apr 12) Red Sunset 120 – Mirabiliary (USA) 74 (Crow (FR) 134) [1995 6.1m 6m a6g Sep 30] IR 5,200Y: fifth foal: sister to 3-y-o 9f and 1¼m winner Tribal Peace and half-sister to 1993 2-y-o 6f winner Midnight Magpie (by Midyan) and a winner abroad: dam 1¼m winner: never a factor in maidens: will stay well beyond 6f. *N. E. Berry* — 46

FAIR ROSE 4 b.f. Fayruz 116 – Scottish Rose 69 (Warpath 113) [1994 –: 7d 1995 a8.5g Jul 8] tailed off in claimers, at Wolverhampton for new stable on reappearance. *J. G. FitzGerald* — –

FAIR TO MIDDLING (IRE) 2 b.f. (Mar 17) Midyan (USA) 124 – Smagiada (Young Generation 129) [1995 6m 7f^5 7g 7f Oct 3] 3,100Y: seventh foal: half-sister to 1988 2-y-o 5f winner Sweet 'N' Sharp (by Sharpo): dam, winner in Italy at 7f and 7.5f, is half-sister to leading 1982 Italian 2-y-o filly Stemegna: poor form, including in selling company: sold 520 gns Doncaster November Sales. *G. L. Moore* — –

FAIRY FAY (IRE) 3 b.f. Fayruz 116 – Isa (Dance In Time (CAN)) [1994 70: 5.1m^5 a5g^2 a5g* a6g* 5m^2 a6g* 6d* 5d^5 5.2g^5 a6g* a6g^2 1995 6.1g 6m 6m^6 5g Jul 11] leggy, angular filly: fair and consistent performer at 2 yrs: soundly beaten in 1995: stays 6f well: acts on the all-weather and dead ground, probably on good to firm. *B. J. McMath* — –

FAIRY HIGHLANDS (IRE) 2 b.f. (Apr 11) Fairy King (USA) – Breyani 101 (Commanche Run 133) [1995 6g Jun 7] 15,000F, 13,000Y: first foal: dam Irish middle-distance stayer from family of Al Hareb: 8/1 from 14/1, eighth of 10 to Agnella in maiden at Folkestone, with leaders around 4f and given easy time when beaten: looked sure to improve. *S. C. Williams* — –

FAIRY KNIGHT 3 b.c. Fairy King (USA) – Vestal Flame 45 (Habitat 134) [1994 73p: 6g^6 5m 7m^2 7m 6g 1995 8m 10g* 10m^2 11.4m^2 12f 10m^4 10m 10d 8.2m 10f* 12m^2 a12g Dec 2] sturdy, close-coupled colt: has a round action: fairly useful handicapper: won at Goodwood in June and Redcar in October: stays 1½m: acts on firm ground, well beaten only runs on a soft surface and on fibresand: blinkered (respectable effort over inadequate trip) ninth 3-y-o start: sometimes bandaged behind. *R. Hannon* — 82

FAIRY PRINCE (IRE) 2 b.g. (Apr 18) Fairy King (USA) – Danger Ahead (Mill Reef (USA) 141) [1995 5m 5.1f^5 6m Aug 19] 15,000Y: small, sturdy gelding: seventh foal: brother to 3-y-o Fajjoura, fairly useful 5f winner at 2 yrs: dam unraced half-sister to very useful 1976 2-y-o 5f winner Easy Landing: no worthwhile form in minor event and maiden contests. *Mrs A. L. M. King* — –

FAIRY'S SON 3 b.g. Belmez (USA) 131 – Sea Fairy 64 (Wollow 132) [1994 51: 7.6v a6g^6 a8g a8.5g^4 1995 a8g a7g^3 a8g a11g^4 a8g^6 a9.4g 7.5m 7m May 19] small — – / a41 d gelding: sold out of W. Muir's stable 2,600 gns Doncaster March Sales after sixth 3-y-o start: no worthwhile form, pulling hard, for new stable: stays 8.5f: acts on equitrack: tried blinkered, no improvement. *D. Nicholls*

FAIRY STORY (IRE) 5 ch.m. Persian Bold 123 – Certain Story (Known Fact (USA) 135) [1994 71: 7.6m 7.1g^6 7m 6.9m^3 8.3f 7m 7g^5 7g^3 7m a8g 1995 7m* 7g^3 7m* 7.6m^5 Aug 19] angular mare: in foal to Distant Relative: fair handicapper: won at Epsom and Lingfield (shared the spoils with Dance Band) in July: stayed 7.6f: suited by a sound surface: visored (raced too freely) fifth 4-y-o start: often front runner. *R. Akehurst* — 79

FAIRY WIND (IRE) 3 b.f. Fairy King (USA) – Decadence (Vaigly Great 127) [1994 NR 1995 5.1g^5 6m 5m* 6.1m^4 5g* 5m^5 6g^6 5f^4 5m* 6g^5 5m^5 5m* Aug 16] leggy, lengthy filly: fourth foal: half-sister to smart 1994 5f winner Mistertopogigo (by Thatching) and 1993 French 2-y-o 7.5f winner Decadence (by High Estate): dam lightly-raced sister to smart sprinter Hallgate: useful handicapper: won at Beverley (maiden) in April, Salisbury in May, Newmarket in June and York (£11,200 event, showing considerable improvement) in August: best at 5f: yet to race on a soft surface: usually bandaged: has run well when sweating: sold 23,000 gns Newmarket December Sales. *N. A. Callaghan* — 95

FAIRYWINGS 2 b.f. (Mar 17) Kris 135 – Fairy Flax (IRE) 97 (Dancing Brave (USA) 140) [1995 6g 7f^6 Oct 12] 9,000F: workmanlike filly with scope: first foal: dam, 6f winner, half-sister to very useful miler Hoy out of close relative of smart 1¼m colt Elegant Air: similar form, never dangerous, in maidens at Newmarket and (blanketed for stalls entry, gave some trouble) at Redcar: will do better, particularly at 1m+. *Mrs J. R. Ramsden* — 61 p

FAITH ALONE 2 b.f. (Apr 23) Safawan 118 – Strapless 84 (Bustino 136) [1995 7f^6 7m a7g^2 a7g* Dec 6] 10,000Y: workmanlike filly: eighth foal: half-sister to 3-y-o Frontiersman (by Indian Ridge), useful 6f (at 2 yrs) and 7f winner Polish Admiral (by Roi Danzig) and a winner in Austria: dam, 6f winner, out of Cheveley Park second Dame Foolish: won 14-runner maiden auction at Lingfield by neck from Rowlandsons Charm, running on well: will be at least as effective at 1m: acts on equitrack: flashed tail third outing. *C. F. Wall* — – a69

FAITH 'N GLORY (IRE) 3 b.f. Nordico (USA) – Amalee 57 (Troy 137) [1994 61: 6m^5 5g^2 6d 1995 7g 7g^4 7m 10m Jul 10] good-quartered filly: has a long stride: modest maiden: below best in 1995: likely to prove suited by 1m+: poor effort on dead ground: sold 2,000 gns Newmarket September Sales. *R. Hannon* — –

FAJJOURA (IRE) 3 b.f. Fairy King (USA) – Danger Ahead (Mill Reef (USA) 141) [1994 84: 5d 5g* 5g* 5m 6m^4 6d^3 5m 1995 6g May 27] useful-looking filly: has a quick action: fairly useful performer at 2 yrs: last of 9 in rated stakes at Haydock on reappearance for new stable: sold 21,000 gns (July) and 12,500 gns (August), at Doncaster Sales: stays 6f: acts on good to firm and dead ground, yet to race on extremes. *J. E. Banks* — –

FAKHIRA (IRE) 3 b.f. Jareer (USA) 115 – Mira Adonde (USA) (Sharpen Up 127) [1994 5v* 5d^4 7m^3 6g^4 6m 6v 6g 1995 6d^6 Apr 6] lengthy, workmanlike filly: second foal (third is smart 2-y-o Danehill Dancer): dam once-raced granddaughter of top-class 4.5f to 1m winner Lianga: fairly useful form (rated 83) in Ireland at 2 yrs, winning maiden at the Curragh and twice fourth in listed events: sold out of K. Prendergast's stable 2,600 gns Newmarket Autumn (1994) Sales: tailed off in minor event on reappearance: stays 6f: sold 33,000 gns Newmarket December Sales. *J. Pearce* — –

FAKIH (USA) 3 b.c. Zilzal (USA) 137 – Barakat 93 (Bustino 136) [1994 66p: 7s^6 7s^2 1995 7f* May 13] good-topped colt: carrying condition, early to post and wearing net muzzle, best form in maidens when winning at Lingfield in May, leading just inside final 1f and running on well: out of stoutly-bred dam, and will be suited by 1m+: looked sure to improve further: stays in training. *A. C. Stewart* — 79 p

FALCONS DAWN 8 b.g. Exhibitioner 111 – African Bloom (African Sky 124) [1994 NR 1995 a12g a8g Feb 13] leggy gelding: probably no longer of much account. *M. G. Meagher* — –

FALLAL (IRE) 3 b.f. Fayruz 116 – Lady Bidder (Auction Ring (USA) 123) [1994 –p: a6g^5 1995 7g^5 8d^6 6m a6g^5 a6g Nov 20] poor maiden: stays 7f: acts on equitrack: blinkered (ran poorly) final 3-y-o start. *K. McAuliffe* — 47 ?

FALSE PRETENCES (IRE) 3 ch.g. Al Hareb (USA) 123 – Christle Mill (Pas de Seul 133) [1994 57d: 5d 6g^6 7m^5 6m 7m 8s a8.5g 1995 a6g^6 7m 8.3m 6g 7f 7f^5 10.8f 7g 10g Oct 1] leggy gelding: poor maiden plater: tried blinkered. *B. A. Pearce* –

FAME AGAIN 3 b.f. Then Again 126 – Starawak 68 (Star Appeal 133) [1994 83p: 5m^4 5m^4 6f^4 7m^2 8g^3 8d* 7.9d 7s* 1995 10.3g 8.5m 7m 8m^2 7g^5 7g^5 8m^2 7.1g* 7g^2 8g^3 7d^4 Sep 23] compact, workmanlike filly: fairly useful handicapper: won at Sandown in July: particularly good efforts in frame behind Knobbleeneeze at Doncaster, Scaraben at Ayr (£22,300 event) and Night Dance at Ascot (£52,900 contest) last 3 starts: suited by 7f/1m: acts on good to firm ground and soft: held up: consistent. *Mrs J. R. Ramsden* 86

FAMILY ROSE 6 gr.g. Absalom 128 – Greenhill Lass (Upper Case (USA)) [1994 NR 1995 a8g Aug 4] close-coupled gelding: tailed off in minor event at Southwell on first run since rated 49 at 4 yrs. *R. Harris* –

FANCY CLANCY 2 b.f. (Mar 19) Clantime 101 – Bold Sophie (Bold Owl 101) [1995 5m^3 5f^3 5m 5g 5g 7.1s 5s^5 Nov 2] 1,000Y: compact filly: first foal: dam never ran: poor maiden: carries head high, and sometimes hangs: has pulled hard. *Miss L. C. Siddall* 43

FANCY DESIGN (IRE) 2 b.f. (Mar 31) Cyrano de Bergerac 120 – Crimson Robes 48 (Artaius (USA) 129) [1995 7m^6 7m Sep 5] good-topped filly: sixth foal: half-sister to a couple of winners in Japan: dam maiden, stayed 1½m: well beaten in Prestige Stakes at Goodwood and maiden at Lingfield (pulled hard, looked an awkward ride) 9 days later. *P. Mitchell* –

FANCY HEIGHTS 2 b.f. (Apr 7) Shirley Heights 130 – Miss Fancy That (USA) 99 (The Minstrel (CAN) 135) [1995 7g^6 Oct 9] tall, unfurnished filly: third foal: half-sister to 3-y-o Deep Divide (by Nashwan) and 7.1f (at 2 yrs) and 10.1f winner Tajannab (by Kris): dam 2-y-o 7f winner, closely related to top-class French 1m/9f winner Thrill Show: 12/1 and very green, 11½ lengths sixth of 18 to Oleana in maiden at Leicester, slowly away, then keeping on steadily under sympathetic ride: will improve. *Lady Herries* 59 p

FANGIO 6 b.g. Nordance (USA) – Verily Jane 53 (Royben 125) [1994 82: 5.1m^2 5g^3 1995 5m^6 5m* 5g 5m* 5g^2 5f* Jun 23] workmanlike gelding: fairly useful performer, and has achieved around same level of form in each of his 4 seasons: operated on for chips on both knees after first 5-y-o start: won claimers at Ripon in April, Doncaster in May and Goodwood in June: best at 5f: has won on dead going, but best form on a sound surface: front runner: upset in stalls (well beaten) third 6-y-o start: genuine: sold for only 500 gns Ascot September Sales. *W. G. M. Turner* 84

FANJICA (IRE) 3 b.f. Law Society (USA) 130 – Florie (FR) (Gay Mecene (USA) 128) [1994 99: 8v^5 7.5v* 8g^2 9v* 8v^2 1995 10m^2 11d^4 11.9m* 13.5g^2 12d 115

Lancashire Oaks, Haydock—lone three-year-old Fanjica, by just over a length from Totality

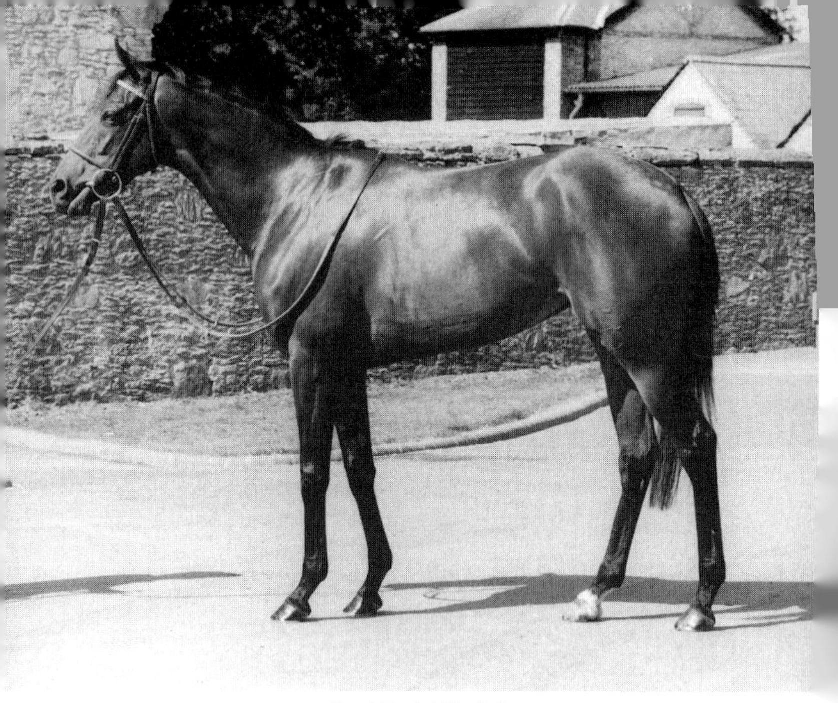

Gary A. Tanaka's "Fanjica"

10s⁵ 8.5d⁴ Dec 14] leggy filly: progressed into a smart performer: in frame in Pretty Polly Stakes and Oaks d'Italia before winning Lancashire Oaks at Haydock in July by 1¼ lengths from Totality, moving smoothly into lead 2f out then staying on strongly: ¾-length second to Sunrise Song in Prix de Pomone at Deauville, over 2 lengths seventh of 10 to Carling in Prix Vermeille at Longchamp then 3½ lengths fifth of 10 to Northern Emerald in Grade 1 Flower Bowl Handicap at Belmont on final start for J. Dunlop: below form in allowance event final start: should stay beyond 13.5f (useful half-brother Almanor stays 15f): acts on good to firm ground and heavy. *R. Rash, USA*

FANTASY FAIR 2 ch.f. (Mar 8) Salt Dome (USA) – Staiconme (USA) (Pancho Villa (USA)) [1995 5m 6s Sep 28] leggy filly: first foal: dam poor Irish maiden daughter of high-class winner at up to 1m Equanimity: behind in seller and claimer. *R. Boss* –

FANTASY RACING (IRE) 3 b.f. Tirol 127 – Highland Girl (USA) (Sir Ivor 135) [1994 79: 5d³ 5d* 5g³ 7g 7d³ 5s² 6d 6d³ 5s⁶ 1995 8d 6m⁶ 6m⁵ 7.3g 6m* 5.1m² 6.1g* 7m⁴ 7m⁵ 7f² 5.9f* 6.9f* 7m 6g⁴ 5.7h² 5.1h* 5.7h² 6f* 7m⁵ 5.7h 6g 5g 6m* 6.1s³ 6f⁵ Oct 25] lengthy, slightly hollow-backed filly: fairly useful performer: successful in claimers at Goodwood, Chester, Carlisle (twice, awarded race on first occasion) and Pontefract, minor event at Bath and handicap at Brighton: effective at 5f, and stays 7f: acts on hard going and soft: effective in visor, not tried since 2 yrs: successful for claimer: tough. *M. R. Channon* 86

FAR AHEAD 3 b.g. Soviet Star (USA) 128 – Cut Ahead 85 (Kalaglow 132) [1994 NR 1995 8.5m³ 8g² 8.2d* 8m² 7f a8.5g⁶ a10g* a12g³ Dec 2] angular, unfurnished 85 gelding: second foal: dam well-bred 1¼m winner: bought out of G. Wragg's stable 8,000 gns Newmarket Autumn (1994) Sales: trained first 2 starts by Mrs V. Aconley: improved efforts for new yard, winning maiden at Nottingham and minor event at Lingfield (seemed suited by step up in trip) in November: should stay 1½m (respectable effort when tried): acts on good to firm and dead ground, and on equitrack. *J. L. Eyre*

FARANI 3 b.f. Distant Relative 128 – Jhansi Ki Rani (USA) 94 (Far North (CAN) 120) [1994 NR 1995 7m^2 8m May 8] 15,000Y: lengthy, angular filly: has a long stride: sixth foal: half-sister to 5 winners: dam 7f and 1m winner: beaten a head, finishing strongly after having to be switched, in maiden at Newbury: broke leg at Kempton 17 days later: dead. *R. Charlton* 73

FARASTRADA 4 b.f. Midyan (USA) 124 – Dawn Redwood 63 (Mummy's Pet 125) [1994 47§, a63§: 5.1g^5 6g^6 6g 7f^3 a6g^2 5m^6 a7g 1995 a5g^2 a5g^6 a5g Jan 25] close-coupled, workmanlike filly: modest maiden: stays 6f: best effort on fibresand: tried visored/blinkered, no improvement: has looked none too keen. *B. Preece* – § a63 §

FARAWAY LASS 2 b.f. (Apr 6) Distant Relative 128 – Vague Lass 85 (Vaigly Great 127) [1995 7m 6f^6 6m^5 Nov 6] rangy filly: has scope: looked on the weak side: fluent mover: third living foal: half-sister to 4-y-o Prim Lass (by Reprimand) and winning 5-y-o sprinter Bangles (by Chilibang): dam sprinter: best effort in maidens when sixth of 18 to Wildwood Flower at Leicester on second start: took good hold over 7f on debut. *Lord Huntingdon* 63

FARAWAY WATERS 2 ch.f. (May 11) Pharly (FR) 130 – Gleaming Water 81 (Kalaglow 132) [1995 6m^2 6.1m* 8g 7d Sep 26] 15,000Y: sparely-made filly: has a quick action: second foal: half-sister to 3-y-o 7f (at 2 yrs) and 11.6f winner Paradise Waters (by Celestial Storm): dam, 2-y-o 6f winner, sister to very useful stayer Shining Water, dam of Grand Criterium winner Tenby: won maiden auction at Nottingham in August: ran well when seventh of 30 to Rio Duvida in valuable sales race at Newmarket final start, staying on strongly having had plenty to do: should stay middle distances (raced keenly and well beaten in 1m May Hill Stakes): has been bandaged behind. *D. W. P. Arbuthnot* 83

FARD (IRE) 3 gr.c. Reprimand 122 – Anneli Rose 56 (Superlative 118) [1994 118: 6m^3 6f* 5m* 6g* 6m^4 6m^2 6m* 7m^6 1995 6g^2 5f^5 6g^5 6.5g Aug 6] good-topped colt: 33/1-winner of Middle Park Stakes at 2 yrs: only useful form in 1995: best efforts when 1¼ lengths second of 9 to Roger The Butler in listed race at Lingfield and 7½ lengths fifth of 9 to Lake Coniston in July Cup at Newmarket: needed at least 6f, and should have stayed 7f: acted on firm ground: blinkered 4 times, career-best effort on first occasion: tended to wander: may well not have an ideal temperament: retired to Summerhill Stud, South Africa. *D. Morley* 108

FARFELU 8 b.h. Lyphard's Special (USA) 122 – Spring Azure 98 (Mountain Call 125) [1994 80, a86: 5.1m 6m 5m^2 a5g* 5m 5.1m^3 5g 5m* 5g^4 a5g 1995 a5g^5 a6g^4 a6g^3 a5g^6 a5g* Mar 4] robust, good-quartered horse: only fair form at best in 1995, though won 3-runner seller at Wolverhampton in March: suited by sprint distances: acted on the all-weather, hard and dead ground (unsuited by very soft): tried visored, usually blinkered: none too consistent: stud at Ridgebarn Farm (£300, Oct 1st). *W. R. Muir* – a76

FARFESTE 2 b.f. (Feb 23) Jester 119 – Our Horizon 57 (Skyliner 117) [1995 7g 7m a7g Dec 6] 1,700Y: smallish filly: second reported live foal: dam disqualified after winning 7f seller: poor form in maiden events. *D. Morris* 49

FAR FETCHED (IRE) 3 b.f. Distant Relative 128 – Gay Milly (FR) 74 (Mill Reef (USA) 141) [1994 72p: 6g* 1995 6m^3 7g^2 8.1m^3 Jul 8] leggy, quite attractive filly: half-sister to smart 1¼m winner Cocotte (by Troy): fairly useful performer: placed in minor events at Salisbury and Leicester and rated stakes (running on really well in slowly-run race, ¾ length behind Lap of Luxury) at Sandown: stays 8.1f: looked possibly capable of better. *Lord Huntingdon* 92

FARFIELDS PRINCE 3 b.g. Weldnaas (USA) 112 – Coca (Levmoss 133) [1994 55: 7s 8g 1995 7g 8g 8g 11.9m Oct 5] leggy gelding: no worthwhile form in 1995. *D. Nicholls* –

FARHANA 2 b.f. (Mar 25) Fayruz 116 – Fahrenheit 69 (Mount Hagen (FR) 127) [1995 6f^2 6m* Oct 27] rangy filly: has scope: half-sister to several winners, including 79 p fairly useful sprinter Alasib (by Siberian Express): dam ran twice at 3 yrs, placed around 7f and 1m: second of 5 to Tamhid in minor event at Yarmouth, giving winner first run but quickening well and coming clear of third: won 8-runner maiden at Newmarket 9 days later by ½ length: likely to prove best at up to 6f: bandaged off-hind: capable of better. *W. Jarvis*

FARIDA SECONDA 2 gr.f. (Feb 9) Green Ruby (USA) 104 – Faridetta 107 (Good Bond 122) [1995 a6g 5s6 Sep 30] half-sister to several winners, including sprinter Forest Fairy (by Faustus) and 1983 2-y-o 5f winner Dramatic (by Dragonara Palace): dam won four 5f races at 2 yrs: well beaten in seller at Southwell and maiden at Haydock. *J. Balding* –

FARMER JOCK 13 ch.h. Crofter (USA) 124 – Some Dame 72 (Will Somers 114§) [1994 –, a58d: a6g5 a6g6 a6g3 a6g* a6g4 a6g3 6m a6g* a7g6 a6g a6g3 a6g5 a6g a6g 6g a6g a6g a6g6 a7g 1995 a6g5 a6g a6g* a6g a6g 6m a6g5 a6g3 a7g a7g3 a6g a7g 6g Jun 14] strong, good-bodied horse: carries condition: veteran handicapper, poor nowadays: won seller at Southwell in February by a short head: stays 7f: acts on any going: effective with blinkers and visor, seldom tried since 1992: tends to hang: usually held up. *Mrs N. Macauley* 45

FARMER'S TERN (IRE) 3 ch.f. Sharrood (USA) 124 – Winter Tern (USA) (Arctic Tern (USA) 126) [1994 NR 1995 9g 10m3 8g4 8.2m a9.4g a11g Nov 20] IR 4,400Y: lengthy, unfurnished filly: first foal: dam never ran: fair form in maidens first 3 starts: behind afterwards: probably stays 1¼m: blinkered (out of form) final start: sold 1,300 gns Ascot December Sales. *W. Jarvis* 64 d

FARMOST 2 ch.g. (May 20) Pharly (FR) 130 – Dancing Meg (USA) 113 (Marshua's Dancer (USA)) [1995 6.9g a6g a7g2 Dec 15] 15,000Y: brother to useful 6f performer Flower Girl and half-brother to several winners, including 1993 2-y-o 7f winner Mytilene (by Soviet Star): dam won at 6f and 1m at 2 yrs and stayed 1½m: caught eye both starts over 7f, on final outing travelling strongly long way in median auction maiden at Lingfield then running on under hands and heels to finish length second to Accountancy Jewel: will be well suited by 1m+: refused to enter stalls third intended start: remains capable of better. *Sir Mark Prescott* 74 p

FARNDALE 8 gr.g. Vaigly Great 127 – Beloved Mistress 84 (Rarity 129) [1994 42, a59: a6g a5g a5g3 a5g2 a6g* a5g4 a6g a6g3 6.1v a6g6 6g5 5v4 a6g5 6f5 a5g a6g2 a6g a7g2 a5g* a5g3 5g5 5m 5m6 a7g a6g a6g6 a8.5g 1995 a7g a5g4 a6g2 a6g2 a6g5 a6g6 a5g3 a6g5 a5g a6g6 a5g 5g 5m 5f5 5.9h4 Aug 21] angular gelding: poor mover: modest at best: sold out of Jack Berry's stable 3,100 gns Doncaster March Sales after sixth start: stays 7f: acts on any turf ground and goes well on fibresand: blinkered (well beaten) once as 7-y-o: inconsistent: sold (R. Thompson to W. Kemp) 850 gns Doncaster October Sales. *Ronald Thompson* 36 a54 d

FARRINGDON HILL 4 b.g. Minster Son 130 – Firgrove 73 (Relkino 131) [1994 81: 12.1s5 10m3 14g4 11.8m* 13.9m6 12m 1995 11.8m3 12g May 19] rangy gelding: good mover: fair handicapper: hung and looked a tricky ride both starts in 1995: stays 1¾m: acts on good to firm and soft ground: blinkered since fourth 3-y-o start. *Major W. R. Hern* 77

FASCINATION WALTZ 8 b.m. Shy Groom (USA) – Cuckoo Weir (Double Jump 131) [1994 75: 5.7m 6m6 5m3 5g 6.1g 6g 6g 1995 6g 7g 6d5 a5g6 a6g a6g Nov 30] angular, sparely-made mare: fair form at best in 1994: disappointing on belated return in 1995: stays 6f: acts on firm and dead ground: usually held up: inconsistent. *J. J. Sheehan* 55

FASHIONABLE DANCER 5 b.g. Lomond (USA) 128 – Circulate (High Top 131) [1994 42d: 8d3 12m a11g 8f 8.3m4 8m 10m6 9s6 9.7d 11.5g 12s 1995 a8.5g Jan 11] lengthy gelding: poor maiden plater: stays 1¼m: acts on good to firm and dead ground: blinkered at 5 yrs: unreliable. *C. E. Brittain* – §

FASIH 3 b.c. Rock City 120 – Nastassia (FR) (Noble Decree (USA) 127) [1994 72p: 7s5 1995 8.1g 8m5 10m 10d* Oct 19] sturdy colt: fairly useful form: finished lame in handicap at Ripon in August: on next start won maiden at Newbury in October, leading final 1f: stays 1¼m: acts on dead ground: sold only 8,800 gns Newmarket Autumn Sales. *A. C. Stewart* 82

FAST FOOD 2 gr.g. (Apr 17) Petong 126 – Respray 64 (Rusticaro (FR) 124) [1995 7g 7g4 7f6 7f 8m Sep 5] 5,200F: leggy gelding: third foal: half-brother to 3-y-o –

Autumn Cover (by Nomination) and a 1m/1¼m winner in Italy by Northern State: dam lightly-raced maiden: well beaten in selling company: blinkered last time. *B. J. McMath*

FAST FORWARD FRED 4 gr.g. Sharrood (USA) 124 – Sun Street 73 (Ile de Bourbon (USA) 133) [1994 –: 10g 14.1g^{5} 1995 10d 14g 14g Jul 19] lengthy, workmanlike gelding: shows knee action: looked as if race would do him good on first 2 starts for new stable: no apparent excuses last time. *L. Montague Hall*

–

FASTINI GOLD 3 b.g. Weldnaas (USA) 112 – La Carlotta (Ela-Mana-Mou 132) [1994 NR 1995 9m 8.3m 8h^{2} 8f^{5} 8.1d 8m 9.7g a10g^{5} a12g Nov 21] leggy, sparely-made colt: second foal: dam unraced: modest maiden at best: should stay 9f: acts on hard ground: looks a difficult ride: inconsistent. *M. D. I. Usher*

61 d

FATAANA (USA) 3 b.f. El Gran Senor (USA) 136 – Maggie O'Brien (USA) (Quadrangle) [1994 NR 1995 8.3m 8d Sep 15] $30,000F, 240,000 francs Y: quite good-topped filly: ninth foal: half-sister to 4 minor winners in U.S: dam 1m winner: well beaten in maidens. *B. W. Hills*

–

FATA (IRE) 3 b. or br.c. Machiavellian (USA) 123 – Wakayi 87 (Persian Bold 123) [1994 76: 6g^{2} 6g^{3} 6g^{5} 6g^{4} 6v 1995 6g* 6m^{6} 6m 6g May 24] tall, quite attractive colt: has a fluent action: fair performer: coaxed home to win maiden at Doncaster on reappearance: ran poorly last 2 starts: stays 6f: acts on good to firm ground, ran poorly on heavy: effective visored or not: finds little off the bridle: sold 22,000 gns Newmarket July Sales. *P. T. Walwyn*

73

FATEHALKHAIR (IRE) 3 ch.c. Kris 135 – Midway Lady (USA) 126 (Alleged (USA) 138) [1994 NR 1995 7.9g^{4} 8d 8m Oct 2] leggy, angular colt: unimpressive mover: fifth foal: brother to UAE 1¼m winner Alasad and half-brother to useful 7f and 1m winner Umniyatee (by Green Desert): dam won 1000 Guineas and Oaks: bought unraced 1,900 gns Newmarket July 1995 Sales: bandaged, no worthwhile form in maidens. *B. Ellison*

–

FATHER DAN (IRE) 6 ch.g. Martin John – Sonia John (Main Reef 126) [1994 54: 10.8m* 12s 9.9g^{4} 9f^{4} 10.8f* 10.3g^{2} 10g^{5} 8m^{2} 10.1m 1995 a10g^{5} a10g* a10g 12m^{5} 11.9f^{4} 10g^{4} 11.8g^{2} 11.4g^{4} 11.1f^{6} 11.6m* 12m^{4} 10d^{5} 12s^{3} a11g* a12g^{2} a11g^{5} Dec 1] plain gelding: poor mover: fair handicapper: won at Lingfield (minor event) in February, Windsor (amateurs) in August and Southwell (minor event) in November: effective at 1¼m to 1½m: acts on firm and soft ground and the all-weather: visored (well beaten) final 3-y-o outing: consistent. *Miss Gay Kelleway*

59
a64

FATHER SKY 4 b.g. Dancing Brave (USA) 140 – Flamenco Wave (USA) 103 (Desert Wine (USA)) [1994 8d 12g* 12g* 1995 16m^{4} Apr 21] strong, good-bodied, ex-Irish gelding: second foal: dam won Moyglare Stud Stakes: unraced at 2 yrs: won maiden at Dundalk and minor event at Punchestown in autumn at 3 yrs (rated 82p): sold out of N. Meade's stable IR 56,000 gns Goffs October (1994) Sales: shaped quite well when fourth of 10 to Bold Gait in handicap at Newbury in April: stays 2m: won 3-runner Grade 2 novice hurdle in November: may be capable of better. *O. Sherwood*

78 +

FATHER TIM (IRE) 5 ch.g. Montekin 125 – Gentle Mulla (Sun Prince 128) [1994 NR 1995 a6g a10g 5m Apr 20] workmanlike, ex-Irish gelding: half-brother to several winners: dam never ran: behind in NH Flat race at 4 yrs for W. Mullins: no promise in claimers and seller here. *J. M. Bradley*

–

FATTASH (USA) 3 ch.g. Tejano (USA) – Green Pompadour (USA) (Green Dancer (USA) 132) [1994 52: 6f^{5} 7g 8d 1995 8g 10m 10g^{6} 12.5m^{3} 15.4g^{3} 12g 16.4m a13g Dec 14] well-made gelding: modest maiden handicapper: sold out of C. Benstead's stable 8,000 gns Newmarket July Sales after fifth start, and gelded: well beaten afterwards: stays 12.5f: acts on good to firm ground and dead: tried blinkered, no improvement. *R. P. C. Hoad*

51

FAUGERON 6 ch.g. Niniski (USA) 125 – Miss Longchamp 94 (Northfields (USA)) [1994 80: 12d 12m 14g^{2} 16.2m* 16.1m^{4} 13.9m 16d^{5} 18m 1995 12m 16m* 15.1m* 14d* 12m^{2} 13.1f^{3} 13.9g^{6} 13.9g^{6} 14.1f^{4} Oct 12] leggy, sparely-made gelding: fluent mover: only modest form in 1995, odds on when winning claimers at Nottingham (claimed out of R. Akehurst's stable £7,000) and Edinburgh and seller at Lingfield in the summer: generally below even that form afterwards: stays 2m: acts

63

on firm ground, respectable efforts at best on a soft surface: blinkered (odds on, beaten in seller) sixth 6-y-o start. *N. Tinkler*

FAUSTINO 3 b.g. Faustus (USA) 118 – Hot Case 92 (Upper Case (USA)) [1994 54: 7g 5.7g 7s 1995 a7g^{3} 8g^{6} 10m^{4} 12.5m^{6} 11.6m^{4} 11.9f^{3} 12f^{4} 11.5g Sep 12] workmanlike gelding: modest maiden handicapper: stays 12.5f: acts on fibresand and firm going, possibly not on soft: blinkered last 2 starts: sold (sold P. Cole to P. Hobbs) 8,500 gns Newmarket Autumn Sales. *P. F. I. Cole* 53

FAWJ (USA) 3 b.c. Clever Trick (USA) – Smooch (USA) (Raise A Native) [1994 60p: 7m 1995 7g^{6} 7m* 7g 7.1d Sep 12] good-topped colt: progressive form in maidens, winning at Kempton in April despite carrying head high: very long way below that form in handicaps in May (£18,800 event) and September: stays 7f: acts on good to firm ground: sold 12,000 gns Newmarket Autumn Sales. *R. W. Armstrong* 74

FAYNAZ 9 ch.h. Tumble Wind (USA) – Ceduna (FR) (Right Tack 131) [1994 33: a10g a13g a7g^{4} 9.7m a10g^{3} 7.6v a7g^{5} a7g^{6} 1995 a6g^{4} a8g^{6} 9.2g 6.9m 8.3f 6.9f Jun 29] well-made horse: poor handicapper: sold out of A. Moore's stable 825 gns Ascot February Sales after second start: well beaten on return: probably stays 9.7f: acts on equitrack and firm going: tried in blinkers/visor: inconsistent. *R. M. McKellar* – a29

FAYRE HOLLY (IRE) 2 b.f. (Mar 8) Fayruz 116 – Holly Bird (Runnett 125) [1995 5.1m^{3} 5g 6m^{4} Jul 29] IR 12,000Y: leggy filly: second live foal: dam Irish 7f and 1½m winner: modest form at best in maidens: stays 6f: slowly away second outing. *M. J. Heaton-Ellis* 57

FEARLESS DOVE 3 b.f. Nomination 125 – Stranger To Fear (Never So Bold 135) [1994 –: 6f 7.5m 7g 1995 a11g Aug 4] looks of little account. *J. Hetherton* –

FEARLESS VENTURE 3 b.c. Darshaan 133 – Push A Button (Bold Lad (IRE) 133) [1994 –: 8s 1995 12g^{4} 12m^{2} 11.4g 10.8g 14.1m^{6} Jul 5] unfurnished colt: fair maiden: well beaten last 3 starts: stays 1½m: sold 10,000 gns Newmarket July Sales. *S. P. C. Woods* 66

FEARLESS WONDER 4 b.g. Formidable (USA) 125 – Long View 68 (Persian Bold 123) [1994 65: 8.3v^{3} 10d* 12.3d 10.3f* 10g 10m 10.5g 1995 a11g^{2} 12m^{3} 14.1m a12g 12m^{6} 12f* 13.8m^{2} 12m^{4} 12.4g^{2} Aug 28] sturdy, good-bodied gelding: modest performer: won seller at Doncaster in July: stays 1¾m: acts on firm ground, dead and fibresand: blinkered at 4 yrs except (ran creditably) final start: has carried head awkwardly, gone in snatches and hung left: inconsistent: fair hurdler. *Mrs M. Reveley* 57 §

FEATHERSTONE LANE 4 b.g. Siberian Express (USA) 125 – Try Gloria (Try My Best (USA) 130) [1994 62: 5f^{6} 5f^{5} 5m 5m 5m^{5} 5f^{5} 5m^{5} 5m^{4} 5m 5.1g a6g^{2} a6g^{3} a5g^{3} a6g a5g^{2} a5g^{4} 1995 5.9m 5m^{5} 5g a5g^{3} 5.1g 5f^{2} 5f^{2} 5.2f^{3} 5m^{3} 5f^{6} a5g^{6} 5m 5m 5m 5.1d a6g^{2} a6g Sep 30] angular, workmanlike gelding: fair handicapper: effective at 5f and 6f: acts on firm and dead ground, and on all-weather surfaces: wears visor nowadays: inconsistent. *Miss L. C. Siddall* 57 a66

FEBRUARY 2 b.f. (Apr 15) Full Extent (USA) 113 – Foligno (Crofter (USA) 124) [1995 a5g^{5} 5g^{3} 5m^{3} 5f^{3} 6.1m^{5} a7g^{3} a6g^{6} 6m 6f^{3} 7f Aug 28] 3,500Y: neat filly: third foal: sister to 3-y-o Giggleswick Gossip, 6f winner at 2 yrs, and 4-y-o 5f and 6f winner Giggleswick Girl: dam won at 1½m in Ireland: poor maiden: stays 6f: not one to rely on. *M. R. Channon* 44 a–

FEELING FOOLISH (IRE) 6 ch.g. Fools Holme (USA) – Felin Geri (Silly Season 127) [1994 24: a13g^{4} a16.2g 10g 8.3m^{6} 1995 a13g^{6} Jan 10] useful-looking gelding: poor plater nowadays: stays 1½m: acts on good to firm ground, soft and all-weather surfaces: often blinkered or visored. *B. Forsey* –

FEINTE 3 b.f. Green Desert (USA) 127 – Escrime (USA) 92 (Sharpen Up 127) [1994 67p: 7g^{6} 1995 7m^{5} 8m^{2} 10f 10d 8g Oct 3] lengthy filly: modest maiden: well beaten last 3 starts: stays 1m: acts on good to firm ground: blinkered (raced freely) final start. *W. Jarvis* 62

FELINE (IRE) 4 ch.f. Pennine Walk 120 – Felin Geri (Silly Season 127) [1994 –: 8s^{6} a8g 1995 a11g^{3} a11g^{2} Feb 3] poor form: broke blood vessel on reappearance: second in seller at Southwell month later: stayed 11f: sold 4,700 gns, in foal to Emarati, Newmarket December Sales. *R. F. Johnson Houghton* 33

FELITZA (IRE) 3 b.f. Soviet Star (USA) 128 – Oh So Sharp 131 (Kris 135) [1994 77p: 7d^{4} 1995 8.3m* 7m* Jul 16] tall, useful-looking filly: shows a round action: won maiden at Windsor in June and minor event at Yarmouth (by 3 lengths 100 p from Mandarina, making all in convincing style) in July: effective at 7f, and should stay 1¼m: acts on good to firm and dead ground: looked a smart filly in the making and sure to win more races: sent to Dubai. *H. R. A. Cecil*

FENNA 2 b.f. (Apr 5) Dowsing (USA) 124 – Tasseled (USA) (Tate Gallery (USA) 117) [1995 6m^2 6m* 6m* 6m 6m^4 6m* 6.5m 6s* a6g^2 Oct 14] neat filly: has a quick action: first foal: dam, ran 3 times in North America, out of half-sister to Riverman: useful plater, successful at Yarmouth, Lingfield and Goodwood in the summer and in claimer at Lingfield in September: no comparable form in 3 nurseries: may stay 7f: acts on good to firm ground and soft (wasn't discredited on fibresand final outing): sold (S. Woods to R. Harris) 12,000 gns Newmarket Autumn Sales. *S. P. C. Woods* — 70 ?

FEN TERRIER 3 b.f. Emarati (USA) 74 – Kinz (Great Nephew 126) [1994 58: 6g^5 a6g^4 7m^4 8s^2 10s^3 8s^5 8g 1995 a11g* 11.8g 10.1g* a12g^6 a9.4g^2 a12g^2 11.1f^5 a12g 12s^4 Sep 27] sturdy filly: has a quick action: modest handicapper: won at Southwell in February and Yarmouth (making running) in June: stays 1½m, may well get further: acts on fibresand and soft ground: won juvenile hurdle in October. *W. J. Haggas* — 58

FERGAL (USA) 2 ch.c. (Mar 17) Inishpour 88 – Campus (USA) (Minnesota Mac) [1995 5f 5g^3 7.1f^5 Jul 28] half-brother to several minor winners in North America: dam won 3 races in USA at up to 7f: plater: looked likely to require further than 5f but disappointed at Edinburgh on final start: has joined Ronald Thompson. *G. M. Moore* — 48

FERNHILL BLAZE (IRE) 2 b.g. (Mar 20) High Estate 127 – Bonnie Isle 115 (Pitcairn 126) [1995 6.1m Jun 15] 9,500F, 15,000Y: half-brother to winners abroad by Irish River and Green Forest: dam, effective from 1m to 1½m, sister to Princess Royal winner Flighting: 16/1, slowly away and tailed off in median auction maiden at Chepstow: sold 450 gns Ascot July Sales and gelded. *M. C. Pipe* — –

FERN'S GOVERNOR 3 b.f. Governor General 116 – Sharp Venita 84 (Sharp Edge 123) [1994 NR 1995 7f 7.1g 8.3m 8g 9m Oct 27] big, workmanlike filly: half-sister to useful 7f and 7.6f winner Sharpalto (by Noalto) and modest 6f and 7f winner Sharp Times (by Faraway Times): dam sprinter: poor maiden handicapper: stays 9f: has raced only on a sound surface. *W. J. Musson* — 45

FERNWAY 2 ch.f. (May 26) Handsome Sailor 125 – Redgrave Design 77 (Nebbiolo 125) [1995 5g Sep 14] eighth foal: half-sister to 3-y-o Pemley (by Superpower) and 4 winners including smart sprinter Saint Express (by Clantime) and middle-distance stayer First Bid (by Crofthall): dam 2-y-o 5f winner: 11/1, slowly away and never dangerous in seller at Ayr. *R. M. Whitaker* — –

FERVENT FAN (IRE) 2 b.f. (Feb 12) Soviet Lad (USA) 94 – Shannon Lady 67 (Monsanto (FR) 121) [1995 6g 6m* 7m 6g Sep 22] 24,000Y: rather unfurnished filly: fourth foal: half-sister to 3-y-o Opera Fan (by Taufan) and 2-y-o 5f winners Area Girl (by Jareer) and Pommes Frites (by Cyrano de Bergerac): dam poor maiden: made all in median auction maiden at Lingfield in August: had stiff tasks afterwards: should stay further than 6f. *M. Bell* — 65

FESTIVE LASSIE 4 b.f. Faustus (USA) 118 – Truth Will Out 82 (Blakeney 126) [1994 NR 1995 12.3f^2 12m^2 12m^2 11m Aug 23] leggy filly: eighth foal: half-sister to 1m winner Dreyfus (by Derrylin): dam 5f winner: won NH Flat race in 1994/5: modest maiden: saddle appeared to slip in handicap final start: will stay further than 12.3f: acts on firm ground. *T. D. Barron* — 64

FFYNONE (IRE) 3 b.f. Taufan (USA) 119 – Ana Gabriella (USA) (Master Derby (USA)) [1994 80: 5.2m^4 6g* 5g^5 6m^3 5f^3 6g 1995 6m^4 7.1m^6 6m 7m 6d^2 6.1s Oct 17] good-topped filly: good walker and mover: generally disappointing in 1995, best effort penultimate start: probably stays 7f: acts on firm ground and good to soft: blinkered (well beaten) third 3-y-o start: has hung badly, and wandered under pressure: sold 1,100 gns Ascot December Sales. *R. Hannon* — 75

FIABA 7 b.m. Precocious 126 – Historia 71 (Northfields (USA)) [1994 51: 8.3g^3 8g^2 8f 8.3m^4 8.3f 7m 7g 11.5g 12g a14g 1995 a8g^3 a8g^3 a8g^4 a8.5g a8g^5 a9.4g^2 a9.4g^3 8f^2 a8.5g^5 10m 8.2m^6 a10g^6 8f 8f a6g^2 a7g^4 Dec 2] close-coupled, sparely-made mare: poor performer: stays 11.4f: acts on the all-weather and firm ground: blinkered (well beaten) once at 5 yrs: often wears bandage(s). *Mrs N. Macauley* — 44

FIDDES (IRE) 2 b.f. (Mar 28) Alzao (USA) 117 – Kashteh (IRE) 79 (Green Desert (USA) 127) [1995 6m 6g 6g^{6} 8f Oct 16] 8,000Y: 21,000 2-y-o: good-topped filly: has scope: has a quick action: first foal: dam, 7f winner at 2 yrs, out of half-sister to dam of Wemyss Bight: not given hard race when towards rear in maidens first 3 starts: seemed to finish feelingly when last of 18 in nursery at Pontefract final start: should prove suited by 1m+. *J. L. Dunlop*

51

FIDDLES DELIGHT 2 b.f. (Feb 7) Colmore Row 111 – Nutwood Emma (Henbit (USA) 130) [1995 5m^{4} a5g^{5} 6f^{4} 6f^{4} 5m 5m^{6} Aug 25] leggy, sparely-made filly: second reported foal: half-sister to poor sprinter Little Hooligan (by Rabdan): dam (poor maiden) possibly temperamental: poor form: visored in nursery final start. *M. R. Channon*

45 d

FIELD OF STARS 5 b.g. Salse (USA) 128 – Marseillaise (Artaius (USA) 129) [1994 71: 7v^{2} 8g 10.3m 9m 10.1g^{2} a9.4g^{3} 12m^{4} 11.5m^{2} 11.9g^{2} 12m^{4} 1995 a10g^{3} Jan 31] stocky, lengthy gelding: fair maiden handicapper: below form in maiden at Lingfield for new stable: stays 1½m: acts on good to firm ground, heavy and fibresand: visored last 5 starts as 4-y-o: fetched 19,000 gns in 1994, but sold only 600 gns Newmarket Autumn Sales. *N. A. Callaghan*

–

FIELD OF VISION (IRE) 5 b.g. Vision (USA) – Bold Meadows 80 (Persian Bold 123) [1994 a6g a7g a7g^{6} 1995 a6g^{5} a9g a5g^{4} a6g^{6} 7g 7f^{6} 7f^{4} 8.1s^{3} a8g^{2} a7g a7g^{3} Dec 15] neat, quite attractive gelding: has a quick action: fairly useful 3-y-o (rated 85) here: unplaced in 7 outings in Dubai and sold 8,800 gns Newmarket July (1995) Sales: fair form in handicaps on return: stays 1m: acts on any going, including equitrack: effective blinkered (was last 4 starts) or not. *M. Johnston*

68

FIELDRIDGE 6 ch.g. Rousillon (USA) 133 – Final Thought (Final Straw 127) [1994 86: 10.3m 10.1m^{4} 10m* 10.4f 10m 11.7m* 12g 1995 10m^{6} 10g 10f 10.2h^{2} 10m^{3} 10m* 9g 10.5g 11.9g Oct 1] tall, lengthy gelding: reportedly suffers from back problems: fairly useful handicapper on his day: left C. Brooks's stable after fourth 6-y-o start: won £27,900 race at Goodwood in August by 1¼ lengths from Conspicuous, always well placed: effective at 1¼m, and stays 11.7f: easily best efforts on a sound surface. *M. P. Muggeridge*

81

FIENDISH (USA) 3 ch.f. Devil's Bag (USA) – Connecting Link (USA) (Linkage (USA)) [1994 79: 6m* 7f^{2} 7.2g^{2} 1995 7.3m^{6} a8f^{4} Nov 4] leggy, quite attractive filly: good mover: 33/1 and backward in coat, much-improved form when 5¾ lengths sixth of 8 to Aqaarid in Fred Darling Stakes at Newbury on final start for P. Cole: fourth in allowance event at Delaware over 6 months later: should stay 1m: yet to race on a soft surface. *J. E. Sheppard, USA*

91

FIERY FOOTSTEPS 3 ro.f. Chilibang 120 – Dancing Daughter 79 (Dance In Time (CAN)) [1994 60: 5.1m^{3} 5m 5m 5.1m^{3} 5.1g^{4} 6m 5g a5g a7g a5g^{5} 1995 a6g^{4} a5g^{5} 5g 5.1m 5.3m^{4} a5g 5g^{4} 5.3f^{6} 6f^{4} 5.2g a6g a7g^{2} a7g Dec 14] lengthy, sparely-made filly: disappointing maiden: sold out of P. Howling's stable 620 gns Doncaster November Sales after tenth start: probably stays 7f (very best efforts at 5f): acts on good to firm ground: tried visored/blinkered, no improvement: has hung badly left: inconsistent. *S. W. Campion*

47

FIERY SUN 10 b.g. Sexton Blake 126 – Melanie Jane (Lord Gayle (USA) 124) [1994 –: 12.1m a14g a14g a16.2g 1995 a16g^{4} a13g^{2} a13g^{4} Feb 16] sturdy gelding: poor handicapper on flat: stays 13f: acts on all-weather: visored at 10 yrs: hurdling with R. Barr. *J. L. Eyre*

27

FIGHTER SQUADRON 6 ch.g. Primo Dominie 121 – Formidable Dancer 70 (Formidable (USA) 125) [1994 60, a51: 7m 5.1m^{6} 6m a7g^{5} a6g^{3} 6g 6g^{2} 6g 6g 6s* a7g 6s 8g 7s 1995 a6g^{5} a7g^{5} 8g 6.9g 7.1m 8.1m Jul 2] leggy gelding: poor handicapper for new stable: ideally suited by 6f/7f: acts on good to firm ground (has had only one run on firm since 2 yrs), soft and fibresand: wears blinkers/visor nowadays: sometimes hangs markedly left: inconsistent. *R. E. Peacock*

–
a47

FIGHTING TIMES 3 b.g. Good Times (ITY) – Duellist (Town Crier 119) [1994 NR 1995 10m 11.5m^{2} 14.6m^{6} a12g Nov 30] workmanlike gelding: fourth living foal: brother to Italian 11f to 15f winner Duel Times and half-brother to a winning middle-distance stayer in Italy by Jupiter Island: dam won twice at around 9f in Italy: ran on well when neck second of 5 in maiden at Lingfield: failed to repeat the form: should stay beyond 11.5f. *C. A. Smith*

67

FIJON (IRE) 2 b.f. (Mar 10) Doyoun 124 – Tasskeen (FR) (Lyphard (USA) 132) 71
[1995 7.5m^3 8m^2 7g^6 8m Oct 20] IR 18,000Y: leggy, sparely-made filly: unimpressive mover: ninth foal: closely related to 2 winners in France, including 9f and 11f winner Talakan (by Dalsaan), and half-sister to 2 winners in France and 1993 Irish 2-y-o 7f winner Yahthab (by Common Grounds): dam, ran once in France, granddaughter of French champion 2-y-o Texana: 5 lengths second of 11 to Caribbean Quest in maiden at Leicester in September: found trip on sharp side next time then had poor run in nursery at Doncaster: will stay 1¼m: unruly in paddock second start. *B. W. Hills*

FIKRA (USA) 2 b. or br.f. (Apr 30) Gulch (USA) – Bolt From The Blue (USA) 67
(Blue Times (USA)) [1995 6m^3 7m^6 7g^2 7g Sep 12] rangy filly: has scope: seventh foal: closely related to 3-y-o Jadwal (by Woodman), 7f winner at 2 yrs, and half-sister to several winners, including 1¾m winner Ehtefaal (by Alysheba): dam, won from 9f to 1½m in USA, half-sister to Alydar's Best: modest maiden: well beaten in Yarmouth nursery final start: should stay 1m but races keenly: free to post on second start: sold 36,000 gns Newmarket Autumn Sales. *D. Morley*

FILL THE BILL (IRE) 3 b.c. Bob Back (USA) 124 – Neat Dish (CAN) 90 106
(Stalwart (USA)) [1994 93: 7d 7v* 8d^2 8s^5 9s^2 1995 10g* 10g^5 10m^5 11m Oct 22] leggy, close-coupled colt: much improved form to win handicap at the Curragh in June: failed by some way to repeat it in Scottish Classic at Ayr, Meld Stakes at the Curragh and handicap at Naas: stays 1¼m and may stay 1½m. *J. McLoughlin, Ireland*

FILM BUFF 2 b.f. (Mar 6) Midyan (USA) 124 – Upper Circle (Shirley Heights 55
130) [1995 5.7m^6 6m 6g a8.5d^3 7d Sep 26] 31,000Y: rangy filly: second foal: half-sister to useful 3-y-o With The Fairies (by Fairy King), 7f winner at 2 yrs: dam twice-raced daughter of very useful (at up to 1¾m) Odeon: modest maiden: stiff task in nursery final start: better suited by 1m or so than less. *B. W. Hills*

FILMORE WEST 2 b.c. (Apr 13) In The Wings 128 – Sistabelle (Bellypha 130) 65 p
[1995 a8.5g^3 Dec 2] 5,000Y, 21,000 2-y-o: sixth foal: half-brother to smart 5f (at 2 yrs) to 1m winner Torch Rouge (by Warning): dam unraced sister to Bella Colora (dam of Stagecraft) and Colorspin (dam of Opera House): 6/1 from 9/2, 4 lengths third of 9 to Tart in maiden at Wolverhampton, keeping on without challenging: will stay beyond 8.5f: will improve. *P. F. I. Cole*

FINAL APPEARANCE (IRE) 3 b.c. Sadler's Wells (USA) 132 – Topping Girl 96
(Sea Hawk II 131) [1994 87p: 8m^4 8d* 1995 9d^6 12g^6 10m Oct 12] lengthy, attractive colt: improved form first 2 outings, facing stiff tasks in minor event at Newbury and listed race at Newmarket: tailed off in minor event at Newmarket final start: best effort at 1½m: yet to race on extremes of going: sold 12,000 gns Newmarket December Sales. *P. W. Chapple-Hyam*

FINAL FLING 3 b.f. Last Tycoon 131 – Lady Day (FR) (Lightning (FR) 129) 49
[1994 49p: 7d^6 1995 8d 8g^3 12.3m 10m^5 15g Sep 14] good-topped filly: unimpressive in coat: modest maiden: should prove suited by further than 1m: visored (looked none too keen under pressure) fourth 3-y-o start: joined Denys Smith. *J. W. Watts*

FINAL STAB (IRE) 2 b.c. (Feb 26) Kris 135 – Premier Rose 117 (Sharp Edge 84 p
123) [1995 7g^6 7d* Sep 27] rangy colt: shows knee action: half-brother to several winners, including fairly useful middle-distance performers George Dillingham (by Top Ville) and Opera Ghost (by Caerleon): dam stayed 1m: won maiden at Salisbury by short head from Iamus, always prominent and leading over 1f out: will stay 1m+: will do better. *P. W. Harris*

FINANCIAL STAR (IRE) 2 b.f. (Mar 30) Last Tycoon 131 – Dawn Star 94 62
(High Line 125) [1995 7f^6 7.5m Aug 24] unfurnished filly: half-sister to several winners, notably useful Dawning Street (at up to 1m, by Thatching) and Special Dawn (at up to 1¼m, by Be My Guest): dam 1¼m and 11f winner: sixth of 10 in maiden at Salisbury: broke leg at Beverley later in month: dead. *J. L. Dunlop*

FINISTERRE (IRE) 2 b.g. (Jan 29) Salt Dome (USA) – Inisfail (Persian Bold 52
123) [1995 5m^6 5g 5s^4 5d 5s a5g Nov 11] IR 7,200F, 18,000 2-y-o: leggy, rather sparely-made gelding: second foal: half-brother to a winner abroad by Al Hareb: dam Irish 1m winner: poor form in varied company, including selling final start: blinkered (below form) fourth outing. *J. J. O'Neill*

FINJAN 8 b.g. Thatching 131 – Capriconia (Try My Best (USA) 130) [1994 55, a–: a6g 5d 7m^4 6g 7.1g^5 8g^3 8d^2 a10g a8g^6 1995 a6g 8d^4 7m 7m^4 8.1g 10f Aug 2] sturdy gelding: modest performer nowadays: stays 1m: acts on firm and dead ground, no worthwhile form on all-weather: visored (ran well) at 4 yrs: has broken blood vessels: has worn tongue strap: inconsistent. *A. G. Foster* 54 a–

FINLAGGAN 3 b.f. Be My Chief (USA) 122 – Misty Halo 93 (High Top 131) [1994 64p: 7m 6.9m^6 7g^5 6.9s 1995 a16g^2 11f* 10g^2 10m^3 a16g* 16f^2 12m* 15.9d^3 15.8m^3 a12g^3 Oct 23] neat filly: good mover: fairly useful performer: won maiden at Redcar in June and minor events at Lingfield in August and Folkestone in September: best efforts at around 2m: acts on equitrack and probably on any turf going: has been bandaged behind: lacks turn of foot and goes well with forcing tactics: most consistent. *Sir Mark Prescott* 83 a77

FIONA SHANN (USA) 2 b.f. (Apr 8) Phone Trick (USA) – Aminata 98 (Glenstal (USA) 118) [1995 6g 6d 6m Nov 3] leggy, attractive filly: second foal: half-sister to 3-y-o 17.5f winner Turquoise Sea (by Shirley Heights): dam sprint pattern winner at 2 yrs in Ireland later suited by 1m: down the field in maidens but shaped encouragingly twice: will stay 1m. *J. L. Dunlop* 53+

FIONN DE COOL (IRE) 4 b.g. Mazaad 106 – Pink Fondant (Northfields (USA)) [1994 6m^4 7m^2 7d^4 8.5d^2 7g^2 7g 9g^4 7.8m^2 7d^2 8g^3 7s^5 1995 6m^3 7m 7g 7.3g^2 7m^4 8.1m^2 8g 8f* 8.1m^2 8d 8m^6 7m Nov 3] sturdy ex-Irish gelding: third foal: half-brother to 2 winners by Fayruz, notably useful 6f to 1m winner Face North: dam ran twice: trained by J. Bolger at 3 yrs: fair handicapper: made all (first win) at Salisbury in August: needs further than 6f, and stays 9f: acts on firm and dead ground. *R. Akehurst* 78

FIRBUR 2 b.c. (Mar 25) Be My Chief (USA) 122 – La Masse (High Top 131) [1995 8.2m Oct 19] 18,000Y: half-brother to 3 winners abroad, including French 11f winner North Wall (by Electric): dam French middle-distance winner: 33/1 and green, unimpressive to post then showed nothing in 19-runner maiden at Nottingham. *N. A. Graham* –

FIRE BLAST 3 b.c. Statoblest 120 – Great Aim (Great Nephew 126) [1994 67p: 6m 6g^5 1995 8g 6m 7m Jun 13] rangy colt: good walker: fair form in maidens at 2 yrs: soundly beaten in 1995: sold 4,400 gns Newmarket July Sales. *L. M. Cumani* –

FIRE DOME (IRE) 3 ch.c. Salt Dome (USA) – Penny Habit (Habitat 134) [1994 97: 5.2g* 5m^3 5g* 5m^5 1995 6m^3 6m^2 7m 6.5m 6m 6g 5s^2 5s^2 5f^6 6m^5 Nov 4] close-coupled colt: has a quick action: useful sprinter: trained until after third 3-y-o start by T. Mills: best effort neck second to Coastal Bluff in handicap at Ascot on eighth outing: effective at 5f, and stays 6.5f: acts on good to firm and soft ground: pulled hard (well below form) third 3-y-o start: often has tongue tied down. *R. Hannon* 104

FIRE OF LONDON 3 b.f. Shirley Heights 130 – Home Fire 99 (Firestreak 125) [1994 NR 1995 8.1m^6 10.4g^4 10g^2 10g Sep 29] 480,000 francs Y: unfurnished filly: has a quick action: sister to useful 7f (at 2 yrs) and 1¼m winner Spitfire and half-sister to several winners, including fair middle-distance stayer By The Fireside (by Ardross): dam sprinter: progressive form in maidens first 3 starts, leading over 1f out until post (wandering under pressure) at Goodwood: ran poorly final start: stays 1¼m: wears bandages behind: sold 12,000 gns Newmarket December Sales. *J. H. M. Gosden* 78

FIRE ON ICE (IRE) 3 b.c. Sadler's Wells (USA) 132 – Foolish Lady (USA) (Foolish Pleasure (USA)) [1994 82p: 8d^4 1995 11.4m* 12g^3 12d Sep 23] smallish, strong colt: off course 11 months, won maiden at Sandown in August, quickening to lead 2f out: best effort when third of 5 to Posidonas in minor event at Goodwood but well-beaten seventh of 8 (stiff task) in Cumberland Lodge Stakes at Ascot: stays 1½m. *M. R. Stoute* 100

FIRE THE ANVIL 3 gr.g. Chilibang 120 – Harlestone Lake 78 (Riboboy (USA) 124) [1994 NR 1995 8m 8f Oct 18] lengthy gelding: unimpressive mover: third foal: half-brother to useful stayer Harlestone Brook (by Jalmood): dam out-and-out stayer: burly, never dangerous in maidens: sold 1,600 gns Newmarket Autumn Sales. *J. L. Dunlop* –

FIRE WORSHIPPER (IRE) 4 b.c. Sadler's Wells (USA) 132 – Beaconaire (USA) (Vaguely Noble 140) [1994 89+: 10.5d* 10m 1995 12g* 12m^5 13.3d^4 Sep 16] 100 sturdy, good-bodied colt: still lightly raced, but is a useful performer: narrowly won minor event at Doncaster in March, leading over 1f out and battling on gamely: off course over 5 months, creditable fourth of 23 to Whitechapel in Autumn Cup at Newbury final start, helping force pace: stays 13.3f: yet to race on extremes of ground: wears bandages: sold only 2,500 gns Newmarket December Sales. *J. H. M. Gosden*

FIRING LINE (IRE) 6 b. or br.h. Slip Anchor 136 – Red Partridge (Solinus 130) [1994 NR 1995 10.5s* 10.5g* 10s^3 12m May 27] big, lengthy horse: very useful performer at 3 yrs for T. Stack in Ireland then sent to Italy and won 3 of 5 starts (minor events between 1¼m and 1½m) at 4 yrs: did not race in 1994: won 2 minor events at Rome in the spring: ran well when 3½ lengths third of 10 to Flagbird in Premio Presidente della Repubblica there, headed 2½f out: pulled up lame there final start: stays 1½m: acts on soft ground and good to firm: effective in blinkers/visor. *C. Marinelli, Italy* — 111

FIRLE PHANTASY 2 ch.c. (Jun 7) Pharly (FR) 130 – Shamasiya (FR) (Vayrann 133) [1995 7.1d^6 7d Sep 27] quite good-topped colt: has scope: has a round action: third foal: half-brother to 2 winners, notably useful sprinter Rock Symphony (by Ballad Rock): dam French 1½m winner: sixth of 11 to Kings Witness in maiden at Haydock: last of 11 in similar event at Newcastle over 3 weeks later: should stay 1m. *P. Calver* — 72

FIRM CONTRACT (IRE) 3 b.c. Double Schwartz 128 – Glass Goblet (USA) (Storm Bird (CAN) 134) [1994 NR 1995 6g^5 May 26] 12,500 2-y-o: first foal: dam ran 3 times in Ireland: 14/1 and in need of race, shaped quite well in 13-runner maiden at Pontefract, travelling strongly in midfield and not knocked about once clearly held: looked sure to improve. *C. N. Allen* — 56 p

FIRST AMENDMENT (IRE) 3 ch.f. Caerleon (USA) 132 – Penultimate (USA) (Roberto (USA) 131) [1994 78p: 7g^4 7d^2 1995 12m^3 May 20] tall, unfurnished, angular filly: fair form in maidens: never travelling that well, but kept on willingly at Thirsk only start in 1995: stays 1½m. *L. M. Cumani* — 77

FIRST BID 8 ch.g. Crofthall 110 – Redgrave Design 77 (Nebbiolo 125) [1994 71: 13.8d^3 12g^5 12m^5 12.3g^6 12.3m^4 12f^3 12.3g^2 11.9m^5 12.3m^3 13.9m^4 12g* 11.9d^5 14m 11.9d^5 13.9d* 13.6g* 14.6d^5 1995 12m 10f^5 12m^4 12f Jul 29] workmanlike gelding: unimpressive mover: took 24 races to get off the mark, but eventually won 9 and in frame a further 31 times in 67 races in his career, reaching his peak (rated 76) in 1993: broke down and pulled up at Thirsk final start: effective at 1½m to 1¾m: acted on any going: was very tough and reliable: dead. *R. M. Whitaker* — 68

FIRST BITE (IRE) 3 b.c. Be My Native (USA) 122 – Saga's Humour 61 (Bustino 136) [1994 64: 7g 7m 7.6v 8g* 1995 9.7m 11.8g^4 10m* 10m^4 10m 11m^3 12s Sep 27] unfurnished colt: fair handicapper: won at Nottingham in June, inconsistent afterwards: stays 11f: acts on good to firm ground, well beaten on soft and heavy: sold 13,000 gns Newmarket Autumn Sales. *J. L. Dunlop* — 70

FIRST CENTURY (IRE) 6 b.g. Petorius 117 – Parima (Pardao 120) [1994 49: a12g 18g 8.2f^6 1995 a9.4g^2 a12g Feb 18] good-quartered gelding: modest handicapper nowadays: stays 1¼m: probably acts on any ground: blinkered at 6 yrs: modest winning jumper. *M. C. Pipe* — 54

FIRST CRUSH 3 b.f. Primo Dominie 121 – Fleeting Affair 98 (Hotfoot 126) [1994 65: 5.9m^3 5.7f^2 6m* 7m* a6g^5 a6g^6 1995 a7g^2 8f* a10g^5 8f* 8.2m^2 8f^6 Aug 22] leggy filly: unimpressive mover: fair performer: beat smallish fields in minor event (first run for 5 months) at Redcar and claimer (made all) at Brighton in the summer: stays 1m: acts on equitrack, has raced only on top-of-the-ground on turf: blinkered since third 3-y-o start: races prominently. *Sir Mark Prescott* — 65

FIRST FIDDLER 2 b.c. (Jan 23) Primo Dominie 121 – Full Orchestra 83 (Shirley Heights 130) [1995 5m^3 5m^2 5m* 5m^4 6g 6d^3 Sep 9] 32,000Y: smallish, leggy colt: second foal: half-brother to 3-y-o 1m and 1¼m winner Music Maker (by Unfuwain), 8.5f winner at 2 yrs: dam 1¼m winner: won minor event at Windsor in June: seemed to run very well (could be rated 95) when close fourth of 9 to Lucky Lionel in Norfolk Stakes at Ascot, coming from well off strong pace, but didn't repeat form in July Stakes at Newmarket or minor event at Doncaster: stays 6f: blinkered fourth and fifth starts: hung left second and third outings: sold only 5,000 gns Doncaster November Sales. *W. Jarvis* — 80 +

FIRST GOLD 6 gr.g. Absalom 128 – Cindys Gold 69 (Sonnen Gold 121) [1994 67: a7g^{5} a7g^{5} a7g^{2} 6.1v^{2} 6g^{2} 6m^{2} 7g^{6} a7g^{4} 8.2m^{3} 7g^{4} 7m a8g^{4} 7m^{2} 6.1s* 7s 7.1g* 7d^{3} 7d^{5} 7s 1995 7s^{4} 6.1g^{4} 7g 6m^{3} 7g^{6} 8g a7g^{6} a8g^{2} a7g^{4} 5m^{5} 7m^{6} 8.9g^{6} 7g* 6.1d 7.1d^{5} a8g a7g^{4} Dec 12] lengthy gelding: carries condition: fair performer: won seller at Yarmouth in September: effective at 6f to 1m: probably acts on any ground: effective blinkered or not: pulls hard and not an easy ride, best held up. *J. Wharton* 66 a62

FIRST HELLO (GER) 3 b.c. Nebos (GER) 129 – First Love (GER) (Limbo (GER)) [1994 7g^{3} 8d^{5} 1995 10g* 11.8g* 11d* 11g* 11m^{3} 11g^{4} 14s* Oct 1] third foal: half-brother to 7f (at 2 yrs) to 10.8f winner First Class (by Bustino), second in Group 2 event at 1½m: dam German 9f to 11f winner: has progressed into a smart performer: won maiden at Leipzig, minor events at Krefeld and Bremen and listed race at Hamburg in May/June: 4¾ lengths fourth of 8 to Solon in Group 3 event at Baden-Baden in August: best effort when winning 13-runner BMW St Leger at Dortmund in September by 1¾ lengths from Tascilla, prominent, leading 2f out and running on: stays 1¾m: goes well on soft ground, below form on good to firm. *P. Rau, Germany* 111

FIRST ISLAND (IRE) 3 ch.c. Dominion 123 – Caymana (FR) (Bellypha 130) [1994 57p: 7m 1995 8m* 8g* 7m^{3} 8f^{2} 9d^{4} 10d^{5} 8m^{2} Oct 28] rather leggy colt: useful performer: won maiden (at 33/1) at Goodwood and minor event at Doncaster in May: best efforts when placed in Jersey Stakes (third of 16 to Sergeyev) at Royal Ascot, minor event at Goodwood (to Tamayaz) and listed race (edged left when challenging over 1f out, short-headed by Celestial Key) at Newmarket: should stay beyond 1m: acts on firm ground, possibly not on a soft surface: moved short to post final start. *G. Wragg* 106

FIRST MAITE 2 b.c. (Apr 16) Komaite (USA) – Marina Plata (Julio Mariner 127) [1995 6m a7g 5d* 6m 5d Oct 11] tall, lengthy, angular colt: has scope: has a round action: third foal: brother to useful 4-y-o Sailormaite, successful at 8.5f but best at up to 7f, and half-brother to 9.4f winner Asmarina (by Ascendant): dam won twice at around 1m: won maiden at Beverley in September: behind in nurseries last 2 starts: should stay 6f: acts on good to soft ground: blinkered. *S. R. Bowring* 65

FIRST OPTION 5 ch.g. Primo Dominie 121 – Merrywren (Julio Mariner 127) [1994 65: 5f 5g^{2} 6m^{2} 5m 5m^{3} 5m^{2} 6g^{4} 5f* 5g^{4} a5g 5d 6s^{6} 5.1g^{3} a5g^{6} a5g^{5} 1995 5g 5f 6g Sep 1] close-coupled gelding: often looks dull in coat: modest performer: no form (hampered and unseated rider final start) in selling company in 1995: effective at 5f and 6f: acts on any going and on equitrack (ran poorly sole outing on fibresand): often bandaged near-hind: has twice (not in 1995) refused to enter stalls. *R. Bastiman* –

FIRST POINT (IRE) 3 b.g. Ajraas (USA) 88 – Fifty Grand (Ballad Rock 122) [1994 46: 5m 7m a7g^{5} 5f^{6} 6d a5g 1995 a6g a7g^{6} a10g Feb 14] leggy gelding: poor mover: no form in 1995: wears bandages. *C. N. Allen* –

FIRST SHOT 4 b.c. Emarati (USA) 74 – First Time Over (Derrylin 115) [1994 NR 1995 8d Sep 26] quite lengthy colt: tailed-off last in maiden on first run since modest 2-y-o for P. Hedger. *R. Curtis* –

FIRST VEIL 5 b.m. Primo Dominie 121 – Valika 75 (Valiyar 129) [1994 –: 6g 6m 7.3g 6d 1995 7m^{3} 6m* 7m 7m 6g^{3} 6s^{3} 6d 6f^{4} Oct 25] lengthy, quite attractive mare: carries condition: fair performer: won apprentice minor event at Goodwood in July: stays 7f: acts on good to firm and soft ground: inconsistent. *J. R. Fanshawe* 75

FISHY AFFAIR 3 ch.g. Risk Me (FR) 127 – Always On A Sunday 101 (Star Appeal 133) [1994 51: 5d 5f^{2} 5m^{4} 6d^{6} 7.5g^{3} a6g 6m 6d^{6} 5g^{5} 5g a5g^{5} a6g a5s^{5} 1995 8.3g^{2} 8f^{3} 8g^{5} 7g 5d Jun 8] smallish, rather sparely-made gelding: poor maiden: sold 1,050 gns Doncaster July Sales: stays 1m: acts on firm going: tried blinkered: pulls hard: inconsistent. *T. Dyer* 41

FISIOSTAR 2 b.g. (Mar 23) Efisio 120 – Sweet Colleen 42 (Connaught 130) [1995 7.5d 7f Oct 3] 4,900Y: rather leggy gelding: poor walker: brother to 4-y-o 7f/1m winner King Chestnut and bumpers and hurdles winner Broctune Bay (by Midyan): dam suited by test of stamina on flat and won over hurdles: towards rear in maiden auction and claimer. *M. Dods* –

FIT TO SKI 2 b.f. (May 15) Niniski (USA) 125 – Baino Fit (USA) (Fit To Fight (USA)) [1995 7f 7m 7g Sep 20] 19,000Y: leggy, unfurnished filly: fourth foal: half-sister to 3-y-o Share The Secret (by Dowsing) and a winner in Germany at up to –

9.5f by Diamond Shoal: dam ran several times in France and USA: behind in maiden at Kempton and Newmarket before showing some promise in claimer at Brighton won by Times of Times: sold 5,000 gns Newmarket Autumn Sales: looked capable of better at 1m+. *M. H. Tompkins*

FITZROVIAN (IRE) 4 b.g. Miller's Mate 116 – Nuravia 91 (Nureyev (USA) 131) [1994 95: 12g* 13.9m3 14g2 16.2m 11.9m4 12f6 1995 9m5 Apr 19] leggy, close-coupled gelding: fine mover: useful performer: reportedly bit jarred up final (July) 3-y-o start: did a good pacemaking job in 7-runner Earl of Sefton Stakes at Newmarket, yet held on well to be beaten under 8 lengths by Desert Shot: has shown his form between 9f and (though weakening markedly final 1½f in Queen's Vase) 2m: has raced only on a sound surface: usually makes the running: sold only 9,000 gns Newmarket July Sales. *D. R. Loder* 95

FITZROY LAD 5 b.g. Grey Desire 115 – My-Elane 65 (Welsh Saint 126) [1994 –: 8.3g 10m 8.3f 1995 a8.5g a7g4 7.1m Jun 15] tall gelding: of little account. *R. J. Baker* –

FIVEADAY 3 ch.g. Komaite (USA) – Silently Yours (USA) 53 (Silent Screen (USA)) [1994 59: 5m6 5m 1995 a5g4 a6g6 a7g 5f 6m 6g 8m Aug 3] angular, unfurnished gelding: failed by long way to repeat reappearance form: wears a tongue strap: sold 1,800 gns Newmarket September Sales. *B. Hanbury* 59 d

FIVE TO SEVEN (USA) 6 br.g. Little Missouri (USA) – French Galaxy (USA) (Majestic Light (USA)) [1994 71: 16s2 1995 12d 17.1m 18m 15.1s a14g5 a14g6 Nov 16] good-topped gelding: has a round action: modest handicapper at best in 1995: stays 2m: acts on fibresand, best turf efforts on a soft surface: often bandaged: normally a front runner. *C. W. Thornton* 59

FLAGBIRD (USA) 4 b.f. Nureyev (USA) 131 – Up The Flagpole (USA) (Hoist The Flag (USA)) [1994 114: 8m* 8g5 8d3 1995 a7g* a8g4 10s* 9.3g6 10g* 10m3 10g2 10f4 10f Nov 26] well-made, attractive filly: pedigree details in *Racehorses of 1993*, but also half-sister to 1995 3-y-o Grade 2 7f winner Top Account (by Private Account): smart performer: trained at 2 and 3 yrs by A. Fabre: won handicap in Dubai in January, 10-runner Premio Presidente della Repubblica at Rome (beat Del Deya by 1½ lengths) in May and 10-runner Independent Pretty Polly Stakes at the Curragh (by a neck from Russian Snows) in July: 2 lengths third of 8 to Pentire in Champion Stakes at Leopardstown and went down by a head to Warning Shadows in Sun Chariot Stakes at Newmarket (final start for Saeed bin Suroor), both in September: much her better effort (on lasix and bute) in USA when under 2 lengths fourth of 12 to Alpride in Yellow Ribbon Invitational at Santa Anita: stays 1¼m: acts on firm and soft ground: consistent. *J. Noseda, USA* 119

Independent Pretty Polly Stakes, the Curragh—Flagbird (rails) rallies to beat Russian Snows

Miss P. F. O'Kelly's "Flame of Athens"

FLAG FEN (USA) 4 b. or br.g. Riverman (USA) 131 – Damascus Flag (USA) (Damascus (USA)) [1994 10g* 10d* 11d² 1995 a10g⁵ a11g⁵ 8m 8s 12d Oct 21] $38,000Y: sixth foal: half-brother to 4 minor winners in USA: dam unraced: rated 99 after winning maiden at Roscommon and handicap at the Curragh at 3 yrs for J. Oxx: well beaten in 1995, in Dubai (subsequently sold 28,000 gns Newmarket July Sales) first 2 starts: stays 11f: acts on dead ground. *Martyn Meade* –

FLAGSTAFF (USA) 2 b.c. (Mar 30) Personal Flag (USA) – Shuffle Up (USA) (Raja Baba (USA)) [1995 7m 6g a7g a7g Dec 15] $23,000F, 18,000Y: close-coupled colt: fourth foal: half-brother to a minor winner in USA by Mining: dam won 2 of her 8 starts in USA: sire (by Private Account) good class at middle distances: trained by R. Hannon first 2 starts: no worthwhile form: visored final outing. *G. L. Moore* –

FLAHUIL 2 b.f. (Mar 10) Generous (IRE) 139 – Sipsi Fach 100 (Prince Sabo 123) [1995 8m 8.2d⁴ 7g 7m a6g⁶ Dec 6] 45,000F: angular filly: first foal: dam 6f (at 2 yrs) to 10.4f winner: modest form in maidens first 3 starts: well beaten afterwards in nurseries: will stay beyond 1m. *R. Hannon* 62

FLAIR LADY 4 gr.f. Chilibang 120 – Flair Park 66 (Frimley Park 109) [1994 55: 8g³ 7f⁵ 10.8m 8.1f² 8m* a8g 8f² 7f 1995 8.5m 8.1g² 8f³ 8g 8.3g² 8.1g⁶ 8m⁵ a7g⁵ a9.4g Dec 9] lengthy filly: has a quick action: modest performer at best: stays 8.3f: acts on firm and dead ground: blinkered (ran respectably) final 2-y-o start. *W. G. M. Turner* 51 d

FLAMANDS (IRE) 2 b.f. (May 9) Sadler's Wells (USA) 132 – Fleur Royale 111 (Mill Reef (USA) 141) [1995 7g Sep 28] IR 165,000Y: fifth foal: sister to fairly useful Irish 3-y-o 11f winner Heavens Gable and closely related to 1992 Irish 2-y-o 7f winner Oiseau de Feu (by Nijinsky): dam, won 1¼m Pretty Polly Stakes and second in Irish Oaks, from family of Levmoss and Le Moss: 9/1, always behind in – p

23-runner maiden at Newmarket won by Astor Place: very likely to do better. *L. M. Cumani*

FLAMBORO 3 ch.g. Handsome Sailor 125 – Scottish Legend (Legend of France (USA) 124) [1994 65, a?: 5m^4 6f^3 6f a6g 6g* 6m^5 6d 7g^2 6d 7d* a7g 1995 7.6m 6g 7f^4 7g^5 a7g Dec 12] leggy, workmanlike gelding: fair on his day at 2 yrs: below form in 1995: stays 7f well: acts on firm ground and dead, well below form on fibresand: inconsistent. *J. D. Bethell* — 49 a–

FLAME OF ATHENS (IRE) 2 b.c. (Mar 20) Royal Academy (USA) 130 – Flame of Tara 124 (Artaius (USA) 129) [1995 6g^3 6m* Jul 2] IR 125,000Y: tall, good sort: has plenty of scope: closely related to very useful 7f (at 2 yrs) to 1¼m winner Danse Royale (by Caerleon) and half-brother to several winners, including Salsabil (by Sadler's Wells) and Marju (by Last Tycoon): dam best at 3 yrs, winning Pretty Polly Stakes and Coronation Stakes: won 7-runner P. V. Doyle Memorial Railway Stakes at the Curragh by a short head from Sweet Robin, bursting through to lead inside last: will stay at least 1m: looked sure to improve further. *M. J. Grassick, Ireland* — 98 p

FLAME OF HOPE 2 b.f. (Mar 23) Marju (IRE) 127 – Tweedling (USA) (Sir Ivor 135) [1995 7d 7m Nov 3] smallish, sturdy filly: seventh foal: half-sister to 3-y-o Portscatho (by Common Grounds) and several winners here and abroad, including 6f to 1m winner Scots Law (by Law Society) and 11f winner Lovely Lagoon (by Mill Reef): dam won at around 1m in USA: little worthwhile form in minor event at Newbury and maiden at Doncaster: will stay 1¼m+. *J. L. Dunlop* — –

FLAME VALLEY (USA) 2 b.f. (Jan 28) Gulch (USA) – Lightning Fire 105 (Kris 135) [1995 7m^4 7m^3 Sep 1] $190,000Y: leggy filly: third foal: sister to a minor winner in USA and half-sister to useful French 3-y-o 1m winner Beyrouth (by Alleged): dam, French 7f/1m winner who probably stayed 9.2f, sister to Prix de la Salamandre winner Common Grounds: beaten around 4½ lengths in minor events at Yarmouth (last of 4 to Key To A Million) and Kempton (made most in race won by Sea Spray): should stay further than 7f. *M. R. Stoute* — 72

FLAME WAR (USA) 3 ch.f. Diesis 133 – Pocketfulof Posies (USA) (Lyphard (USA) 132) [1994 71p: 6g 7d^3 1995 10m^2 12m^2 10f* 11.8g^3 10.5m^4 Aug 4] quite attractive filly: fair form: won maiden at Lingfield in June: good third of 10 in handicap at Leicester next start: stays 1½m: acts on firm going: races prominently. *H. R. A. Cecil* — 79

FLAMING JUNE (USA) 2 ch.f. (Feb 6) Storm Bird (CAN) 134 – Affirmative Fable (USA) (Affirmed (USA)) [1995 7f^3 8f^6 Oct 24] $250,000Y: leggy filly: half-sister to 3 winners, notably Majmu (by Al Nasr), successful in May Hill Stakes: dam minor winner at around 1m: similar form in maidens at Redcar and Leicester: likely to stay beyond 1m: will do better. *H. R. A. Cecil* — 69 p

FLAMINGO PARADISE 4 ch.c. Rainbow Quest (USA) 134 – Fabula Dancer (USA) (Northern Dancer) [1994 10v* 10g^2 11g^5 11g 1995 10.5v* 11s* 16g^2 16v* 16m^3 16d^6 Aug 30] first foal: dam unraced half-sister to 2 Graded Stakes winners in USA: useful German colt: won maiden at 3 yrs, minor events at Mulheim and Cologne in April and, showing improved form, 12-runner Oleander-Rennen at Baden-Baden (by a length from Ballet Prince) in May: suited by a test of stamina: acts on heavy ground. *H. Blume, Germany* — 108

FLAMMANT ROSE (IRE) 3 gr.f. Cyrano de Bergerac 120 – Sweet Class (Rusticaro (FR) 124) [1994 NR 1995 8m 8f May 22] 5,200Y: leggy, unfurnished filly: second foal: sister to Belgian 7f winner Silver Glory: dam unraced: well beaten in maidens at Bath. *Martyn Meade* — –

FLASH APPEAL 4 b.f. Tate Gallery (USA) 117 – Camomilla (Targowice (USA) 130) [1994 –: a7g a7g 1995 8.3m Jun 5] leggy filly: no worthwhile form: sold 1,500 gns Newmarket July Sales. *R. Guest* — –

FLASH ARROW 5 ch.g. Jalmood (USA) 126 – The Firebird (Busted 134) [1994 ?: 7g^3 7.5g^3 8g^3 8.2g 1995 8g Jun 5] successful in Austria at 3 yrs: well beaten both starts here: sold 600 gns Doncaster August Sales. *J. Parkes* — –

FLASHFEET 5 b.g. Rousillon (USA) 133 – Miellita 98 (King Emperor (USA)) [1994 59, a53: a10g^6 a7g^3 7v^2 8d^3 7.1s a8.5g^4 a7g^3 a7g^5 7g 7v 1995 a8.5g a9.4g^2 a8g^4 a8g^3 a7g* a7g^3 a8.5g^5 8g Jul 22] close-coupled gelding: unimpressive mover: — 59

modest handicapper: won at Wolverhampton in June: stays 9.4f: acts on heavy going and fibresand: has run well for lady: usually held up: sometimes finds little. *K. Bishop*

FLASHING SABRE 3 b.g. Statoblest 120 – Placid Pet 65 (Mummy's Pet 125) [1994 54p: 6s 6.1m 6g^6 5g 1995 a5g^3 5f 5g 5m^6 5f* 5g 5m 5m^3 5m a5g a5g Dec 19] lengthy gelding: modest handicapper: won at Edinburgh in July: will prove best at sprint distances: acts on firm ground and on fibresand: usually races prominently: none too consistent. *J. Berry* — 52 a56

FLASH IN THE PAN (IRE) 2 ch.f. (Mar 12) Bluebird (USA) 125 – Tomona (Linacre 133) [1995 6m 6m 6.1d 8f Oct 18] IR 22,000Y: angular filly: half-sister to useful 1990 2-y-o 7f winner Full of Pluck (by Try My Best), Irish 1¼m winner Hegemonic (by Godswalk) and a winner abroad: dam won at 11f and 1½m and over hurdles in Ireland: well beaten in maidens and nursery. *M. Bell* — –

FLASHMAN 5 b.g. Flash of Steel 120 – Proper Madam 93 (Mummy's Pet 125) [1994 32: 9.2f 11.1m^4 10g^4 14.6m a8g^6 11.1m^4 9g^4 8m^4 9.2f 1995 a16g* 18g 17.2m^3 16.5g^3 18m* 18.2m^2 a16.2g^2 16.1g 18f Oct 16] strong gelding: carries condition: poor handicapper: won at Southwell (amateurs race, first success) in February and Pontefract in June: stays 2¼m: probably acts on any going: effective blinkered, not tried in 1995: sometimes sweats. *B. J. Llewellyn* — 45

FLASH OF REALM (FR) 9 b.g. Super Moment (USA) – Light of Realm 116 (Realm 129) [1994 52: 13.1g^3 12.4m^2 1995 10.9g^4 13.1g^4 Sep 16] good-bodied gelding: modest performer, lightly raced, on flat: stays 13f: fair hurdler/chaser, winner as both after final start. *P. Monteith* — 59

FLASHY'S SON 7 b. or br.g. Balidar 133 – Flashy Looker 92 (Good Bond 122) [1994 68: 7m^3 7g^4 6m* 6m^2 1995 6f^3 5g^2 6g^3 6m 6m 5f* 6g* 6m^6 6m 7g^5 7g^3 6g 8f Oct 12] sturdy gelding: fair handicapper: won weak seller at Hamilton, and followed up in stronger race at Ayr later in July: effective at 5f, and stays 7f: best form on a sound surface (acts on firm going): often bandaged. *G. M. Moore* — 71

FLASS VALE 7 b.g. Final Straw 127 – Emblazon 91 (Wolver Hollow 126) [1994 –: 18g 1995 a16.2g a16g Feb 6] good-topped gelding: no form on flat for a long time. *C. W. Fairhurst* — –

FLATFORD PRINCESS 3 b.f. Prince Daniel (USA) – Printafoil (Habat 127) [1994 47: 7g 6.9m^5 7m^3 8m a7g 1995 11.9f^6 Jul 20] leggy filly: poor maiden: well beaten only 3-y-o start: should be suited by further than 7f. *G. L. Moore* — –

FLEET CADET 4 ch.c. Bairn (USA) 126 – Pirogue 99 (Reliance II 137) [1994 –: a10g 1995 a11g a8.5g^6 a7g^6 7g^6 7m* 8f 7m 7m Aug 17] sparely-made colt: poor mover: modest handicapper: won at Doncaster in May: below form afterwards: bred to be suited by middle distances, but seems best at up to 1m: acts on good to firm ground and on fibresand: blinkered from fifth 4-y-o start. *N. A. Graham* — 50

FLEET HILL (IRE) 3 b.f. Warrshan (USA) 117 – Mirkan Honey 83 (Ballymore 123) [1994 92: 6m* 7f^3 7m* 7f^6 7.5v^2 7m^3 1995 8m^4 8m 10g^2 8g^6 12m 10g^5 Jul 25] compact filly: has a quick action: useful performer: in frame in listed races at Kempton and Newbury in the spring: creditable sixth of 10 to Ridgewood Pearl in Irish 1000 Guineas at the Curragh: stays 1¼m well: probably acts on any going: sold 48,000 gns Doncaster November Sales. *M. R. Channon* — 99

FLEET PETITE (IRE) 3 b.f. Posen (USA) – Reet Petite (Thatching 131) [1994 7s 7d 7v^3 6d* 1995 7v^5 7s^3 6.5v^3 6m 7s^4 7g* 7g 7g 5m* 6m^2 5g^6 6g^4 6m Oct 21] IR 3,400Y: strong filly: third foal: half-sister to a winner in Germany by Persian Bold: dam fairly useful sprinter: fairly useful performer: won nursery at Naas at 2 yrs: successful in 1995 in handicaps at Gowran and Tralee in the summer: good fourth of 12 (despite hanging right and carrying head awkwardly) in rated stakes at Newmarket on penultimate outing: effective at 5f to 7f: acts on good to firm and heavy ground: blinkered last 5 starts: consistent. *A. Leahy, Ireland* — 87

FLEMENSFIRTH (USA) 3 b.c. Alleged (USA) 138 – Etheldreda (USA) 64 (Diesis 133) [1994 88P: 8.2d* 1995 9m^2 10.5d* 12g^5 8m^6 9.8s* Sep 30] — 121

Flemensfirth ran his best races in France, but it wasn't the air there that suited him so much as the ground. It looks very much as if he is suited by plenty of give, and his best effort to date has been on soft. On his final outing of the season, his first for three months, Flemensfirth put up a very smart performance, his best to date, in the

Prix Lupin, Longchamp—easy pickings for Flemensfirth

Prix Dollar at Longchamp in September. He had to give weight all round and seemed to be at a grave disadvantage at the weights with his elders Triarius, Just Happy, Marildo and Volochine, particularly with Triarius who had recently beaten Fahal in the Select Stakes at Goodwood. Nevertheless he was soon in front at a strong gallop, and was able to kick three lengths clear early in the straight and then find plenty under pressure. Volochine, second to Alderbrook in the race as a three-year-old in 1994, filled second place again, on this occasion half a length behind Flemensfirth and three lengths clear of Triarius who was unable to quicken. Flemensfirth had his penalty in the Prix Dollar as a result of winning the Group 1 Prix Lupin at the same course in May, a far-from-vintage Lupin in which the French colt Solar One started at odds on in a field of six. Flemensfirth turned for home in second in a steadily-run affair and was well on top of Solar One and the Greffulhe second Angel Falls by the finish. Three weeks after the Lupin he was returned to France for the Prix du Jockey-Club and finished a good fifth of eleven to Celtic Swing, just caught for

Prix Dollar, Longchamp—a very smart performance under a penalty;
Flemensfirth wins from Volochine, with Triarius (rails) third and blinkered Marildo fifth

fourth by Classic Cliche. Both he and Classic Cliche met trouble in running. Flemensfirth had to be snatched up early on and also found himself short of room entering the straight. Although Classic Cliche finished the better, Flemensfirth came within three lengths of the winner in an admittedly slowly-run affair.

The Lupin, the Jockey-Club and the Dollar were the sum of Flemensfirth's appearances in France. He made just two in Britain in 1995, both on top-of-the-ground. While the form does not compare with what followed, his dividing Munwar and Eltish in the Feilden Stakes at Newmarket in April (bandaged behind) was at the time rightly taken as very encouraging. His only previous racing experience had been in a back-end two-year-old maiden at Nottingham, which he won smoothly. The St James's Palace Stakes at Royal Ascot seemed an odd choice of race for Flemensfirth after Chantilly. Presumably the fact that he had picked up that Group 1 penalty for some of the lesser pattern events influenced the choice, but sent off the outsider bar pacemaker Muhab, he made no impression behind Bahri and was steadily outpaced in the straight.

Flemensfirth was bought as a yearling for 290,000 dollars at the Keeneland Sales. He could be described as American bred with strong European connections. His great-grandam Nato and his dam Etheldreda both made appearances on the British turf. Nato, who was a half-sister to the Irish One Thousand Guineas winner Even Star, won the New Ham Foal Stakes at Goodwood for Paddy Prendergast way back in 1955. She made into a successful broodmare in the States, producing the stakes winner Royal Bund and the dams of the stallions It's Freezing and Quack. Royal Bund's daughter Etheldreda was no great shakes on the racecourse: she reached the frame in maidens at Warwick and Catterick for Guy Hardwood, in failing

Sheikh Mohammed's "Flemensfirth"

to win proving a rare exception among her dam's numerous runners who are headed by the good American fillies Bundler and Picture Tube. One of Etheldreda's previous two foals has managed to win races in the States—by It's Freezing, he is called Daggett Peak.

Flemensfirth (USA) (b.c. 1992)	Alleged (USA) (b 1974)	Hoist The Flag (b 1968)	Tom Rolfe
			Wavy Navy
		Princess Pout (b 1966)	Prince John
			Determined Lady
	Etheldreda (USA) (ch 1985)	Diesis (ch 1980)	Sharpen Up
			Doubly Sure
		Royal Bund (ch 1961)	Royal Coinage
			Nato

Flemensfirth does not fit the general perception of his sire's stock, and he may well be ideally suited by around a mile and a quarter. It may well also be that the best has still to be seen of him. He hasn't had much racing so far. A rangy colt, rather unfurnished with scope for physical development, he should win more good races. *J. H. M. Gosden*

FLETCHER'S BOUNTY (IRE) 6 b.g. Glenstal (USA) 118 – Maimiti (Goldhill 125) [1994 50: 8m^3 8m^4 8.3g^2 8f^3 1995 a8g^3 a7g a10g a8g Mar 20] angular gelding: poor handicapper: left Mrs M. Reveley's stable after final 5-y-o start: only form in 1995 on reappearance: effective at 7f and probably stays 10.8f: acts on fibresand and any turf going: tried blinkered and visored. *W. S. Cunningham* — 46

FLEUR DE TAL 4 b.f. Primitive Rising (USA) 113 – Penset (Red Sunset 120) [1994 –: 8.2d 10d 10m 1995 a16g^5 Nov 30] leggy filly: no worthwhile form on flat for some time: tried blinkered/visored at 3 yrs: fair hurdler, successful in December. *W. G. M. Turner* — –

FLIGHT LIEUTENANT (USA) 6 b.g. Marfa (USA) – Lt Golden Girl (USA) (Lt Stevens) [1994 89: 14m^4 13.9f^2 16s 13.9m* 16.1f 13.9m 14.6g 16.2g^6 1995 12m 16.4m 13.9g 14m^6 12f 12m* 14g 13.9m 12m^3 13.3d Sep 16] tall, lengthy gelding: unimpressive mover: only fair handicapper at best in 1995: possibly fortunate (allowed to set up long lead) to win claimer at Goodwood in June: stays 2m: has won on soft going but best efforts on a sounder surface (acts on firm): blinkered (finished last) fourth 6-y-o start: has run creditably when sweating and unimpressive in appearance: usually set plenty to do: none too consistent: won maiden hurdle in November for T. Casey. *R. Hannon* — 79

FLIGHT MASTER 3 ch.c. Master Willie 129 – Mumtaz Mayfly 64 (Tap On Wood 130) [1994 64p: 7s 6.9m* 1995 9.7m^4 11.4g^3 12m^6 Jun 15] angular colt: fair handicapper: beaten only 2 short heads at Sandown on second start despite saddle slipping: tailed off at Newbury 2 weeks later: should stay 1½m. *P. J. Makin* — 65

FLIGHT SOUNDLY (IRE) 3 ch.f. Caerleon (USA) 132 – Night of Wind 101 (Tumble Wind (USA)) [1994 78: 6m^6 6f* 6d 7m 1995 7.5m 6.1m 8m^6 7f Oct 18] rather leggy filly: good mover: fair winner at 2 yrs: well below form in handicaps in 1995: should stay 7f: acts on firm ground. *M. R. Stoute* — –

FLIGHTY 2 b.f. (Feb 1) Reprimand 122 – Flight of Pleasure (USA) 74 (Roberto (USA) 131) [1995 6.1d 7f Oct 12] small, light-framed filly: first foal: dam, 6f and 7f winner at 2 yrs, stayed 1¾m: better effort in maidens, though never on terms, when seventh of 12 to Green Charter at Redcar, second start: should stay 1m: sold 6,600 gns Newmarket Autumn Sales. *L. M. Cumani* — 60

FLIM FLAM ALY (USA) 6 br.h. Tim Tam Aly (USA) – Okala Lass (USA) (Florida State) [1994 33: a8.5g a7g^6 10g^5 10.5g a8g^2 8m^4 a9.4g^4 10.8m^2 12.1g^3 10g a12g 1995 a16.2g Jan 7] leggy horse: poor handicapper: stayed 1½m: acted on firm ground and fibresand: often blinkered: dead. *L. J. Barratt* — –

FLINT AND STEEL 2 b.g. (Mar 3) Rock City 120 – Brassy Nell 72 (Dunbeath (USA) 127) [1995 7.1m 8d Sep 27] 13,500Y: useful-looking gelding: has plenty of scope: third foal: half-brother to 3-y-o 7f winner Brass Tacks (by Prince Sabo) and 1993 2-y-o 5.2f winner Dance Focus (by Aragon): dam 7.6f winner: bit backward, similar form in maiden events at Sandown and Salisbury, never-dangerous twelfth of 18 to Mystic Knight last time: should improve. *R. Hannon* — 58 p

FLIRTY GERTIE 3 ch.f. Prince Sabo 123 – Red Tapsi (Tap On Wood 130) [1994 NR 1995 5g^3 5m^2 6g^3 7g^2 8m Oct 12] big, lengthy filly: third foal: half-sister — 69

to 2 poor animals: dam, maiden second over 1½m in Ireland, is out of sister to Bustino: fair maiden: stays 7f, seemingly not 1m: has raced only on a sound surface. *R. Boss*

FLOATING LINE 7 ch.g. Bairn (USA) 126 – County Line 75 (High Line 125) [1994 71: 9.9m^{3} 10g^{4} 9.9g^{2} 12m^{2} 9.9m^{2} 12m^{2} 12.3g* 12.3m^{2} 13.9m^{6} 10d* 1995 10f^{5} 12m^{6} 12m^{5} 10g* 10.5m^{6} 13.9g^{4} 12d^{5} 11.9g^{2} 14g* 13.9g^{2} 14.6m Oct 20] lengthy gelding: has a round action: fair handicapper: won at Newmarket in July and September: effective at 1¼m and stays 1¾m: acts on firm and dead ground: has run well when sweating: usually races prominently: trained by P. Wigham first 3 starts. *E. J. Alston* — 76

FLOCHECK (USA) 2 ch.c. (May 18) Hansel (USA) – Eurobird 118 (Ela-Mana-Mou 132) [1995 8m 8.2m Oct 26] angular, unfurnished colt: looked weak: fourth foal: half-brother to useful Irish 7f (at 2 yrs) to 1¼m winner Eurostorm (by Storm Bird) and smart juvenile hurdler Tervel (by Chief's Crown): dam, very useful Irish middle-distance stayer, is half-sister to Prix du Jockey-Club winners Assert and Bikala: sire graded stakes winner at 2 yrs, and champion as 3-y-o: better form in autumn maidens behind Silver Dome at Newmarket (slowly away, never a threat) on debut: likely to stay middle distances. *J. L. Dunlop* — 67 ?

FLOOD'S FANCY 2 b. or gr.f. (Apr 4) Then Again 126 – Port Na Blath (On Your Mark 125) [1995 5m 6m 5.1m 6m* 7m 6g a6g^{5} a6g^{5} Dec 12] 8,600Y: tall, lengthy, rather dipped-backed filly: fifth foal: sister to 3-y-o Port Hedland and half-sister to fairly useful 1991 2-y-o 6f winner Combination (by Primo Dominie): dam Irish 6f winner: heavily backed when winning 9-runner seller at Haydock in July (sold out of Mrs J. R. Ramsden's stable 7,000 gns): stays 6f: acts on good to firm ground and fibresand: blinkered last 2 starts, creditable effort on first occasion. *A. Bailey* — 54

FLORAC (IRE) 5 b.m. Sayf El Arab (USA) 127 – Marton Maid 74 (Silly Season 127) [1994 44d: 5f^{4} 5m^{5} 5m^{3} 5m^{6} 5.2g^{5} 6g 5.1d a6g 1995 a5g^{6} 5g Jun 5] smallish mare: modest 5f performer at best: very much on the downgrade. *J. Balding* — –

FLORA'S TEMPLE (USA) 4 b. or br.f. Halo (USA) – Kendra Road (USA) (Kennedy Road (CAN)) [1994 NR 1995 10m Aug 9] $100,000Y: sturdy filly: seventh foal: half-sister to 3 winners, notably Grade 3 9f winner Intrusion (by Top Command): dam showed a little ability in USA at 3 yrs: burly and green, tailed off in maiden at Sandown: sold only 1,800 gns Newmarket December Sales. *J. A. R. Toller* — –

FLORENTINO (IRE) 2 b. or br.c. (Apr 22) Machiavellian (USA) 123 – Helens Dreamgirl 95 (Caerleon (USA) 132) [1995 6d Sep 16] 30,000Y: tall, close-coupled colt: has scope: second foal: half-brother to 3-y-o House of Dreams (by Darshaan): dam 1¼m winner: 33/1, carrying condition and green, never a factor in 25-runner maiden at Newbury. *B. W. Hills* — –

FLORIDANTE (USA) 3 b.c. Eastern Echo (USA) – La Belle Fleur (USA) (Vaguely Noble 140) [1994 74p: 7f^{4} 7g^{3} 1995 7m^{5} 7.6m 8m^{2} 8m^{6} 8g* 8m^{5} Jul 1] robust colt: fair handicapper: won at Doncaster in June: would have stayed beyond 1m: raced only on a sound surface: dead. *P. F. I. Cole* — 76

FLORID (USA) 4 ch.c. The Minstrel (CAN) 135 – Kenanga 105 (Kris 135) [1994 105: 10m^{4} 12g^{4} 12m^{3} 12m^{4} 11.9s* 1995 10m^{6} 10m* 10m^{2} 10g^{2} 10f^{4} 12f^{6} Jul 28] tall, good-topped colt: good walker: has a fluent action: useful form: dominated 4-runner minor event at Pontefract in April: runner-up in similar contests at Newmarket (readily outpaced by Baron Ferdinand) and Goodwood (worn down close home by Capias) next 2 starts: stays 1½m: acts on firm and soft ground: front runner/races prominently: genuine: stays in training. *H. R. A. Cecil* — 108

FLORISMART 3 b.c. Never So Bold 135 – Spoilt Again 91 (Mummy's Pet 125) [1994 70p: 7f^{5} 1995 8.3m^{4} 8.1g 10m 8m a8.5g Dec 12] sparely-made colt: modest maiden at best in 1995: sold out of J. Toller's stable 4,500 gns Newmarket Autumn Sales after penultimate start: should stay 1¼m: has raced only on a sound surface on turf. *B. P. J. Baugh* — 58

FLORRIE'M 2 ch.f. (Mar 12) Tina's Pet 121 – Rosie Dickins 59 (Blue Cashmere 129) [1995 6f 7m Oct 30] big, workmanlike filly: third foal: sister to 4-y-o Rosina's Folly: dam sprinter: burly, no worthwhile form in maidens. *J. L. Harris* — –

FLOWER MILLER 2 b.g. (Mar 22) Formidable (USA) 125 – Sunflower Seed 70 (Mummy's Pet 125) [1995 6f Jun 14] 8,500Y: first foal: dam, stayed 1½m, granddaughter of Highclere: well-backed 9/4 shot, last of 7 in maiden auction at Hamilton, slowly away, beaten and eased 1f out: subsequently gelded. *J. Hanson* –

FLOWING OCEAN 5 ch.h. Forzando 122 – Boswellia 109 (Frankincense 120) [1994 NR 1995 a7g* 8g a7g Aug 24] good-topped horse: won 1m maiden at Newcastle on last of 3 runs at 3 yrs for J. Gosden, but reportedly had knee problems afterwards: ran in handicaps in 1995, making an impressive winning return at Southwell in February: well beaten subsequently at Doncaster (£15,900 contest) in March and Lingfield 5 months later: effective at 7f and should stay beyond 1m: acts on fibresand, may well require a soft surface on turf. *Miss Gay Kelleway* 79

FLUTTER WITH LIFE 4 b.f. Hubbly Bubbly (USA) – Bet Oliver (Kala Shikari 125) [1994 –: 5g⁶ 6g 8g⁵ 1995 a6g 6m Apr 6] unfurnished filly: of little account. *Mrs A. E. Jermy* –

FLYAWAY BLUES 3 b.g. Bluebird (USA) 125 – Voltigeuse (USA) (Filiberto (USA) 123) [1994 60p: 8d 8g 7g⁶ 7d 1995 7g 10d 12.3m⁴ 13g 6m² 7g² 8m³ 8f³ 8.3f⁴ 8.3f² 7m² 7g Sep 13] tall, angular gelding: good walker: modest maiden handicapper: shaped like a stayer first 4 3-y-o starts: blinkered or visored over shorter trips last 8 outings, often running with credit but not always impressing with finishing effort: effective at 7f, and seems to stay 1½m: acts on firm ground: tends to hang: carries head high and isn't one to trust implicitly. *Mrs M. Reveley* 60

FLYFISHER (IRE) 2 b.c. (Feb 22) Batshoof 122 – Inveraven 53 (Alias Smith (USA)) [1995 8m⁶ 7.1d⁵ 10.2m² 10g* Oct 9] 24,000Y: rangy, unfurnished colt: has scope: fluent mover: fifth foal: half-brother to 3-y-o Mu-Tadil (by Be My Chief), 1993 2-y-o 7f and 7.5f winner Demi-Plie (by Squill) and a winner abroad by Celestial Storm: dam ran 3 times: progressed well, winning 9-runner minor event at Leicester in October by short head from Dismissed: suited by good test of stamina: has an awkward head carriage but races genuinely. *G. Lewis* 95

FLY FISHING (USA) 2 ch.c. (Feb 11) Miswaki (USA) 124 – Sharp Flick (USA) (Sharpen Up 127) [1995 7g 8.2m³ 8.1s³ Nov 2] third foal: dam, fourth in 5f maiden from 8 starts, half-sister to Racing Post Trophy winner Peter Davies: never able to reach leaders when third in maiden won by Dushyantor at Nottingham (came home in really good style after slow start and well behind) and Santillana at Edinburgh following month: will be well suited by middle distances: bandaged at Nottingham: remains capable of better. *Mrs J. Cecil* 74 p

FLYING FLOWERS 2 ch.f. (Mar 5) Thatching 131 – Flying Fairy 79 (Bustino 136) [1995 6m⁶ 7g Oct 23] tall, useful-looking filly: sixth foal: half-sister to 4-y-o Access Carnival (by Rousillon): dam twice-raced daughter of 1000 Guineas winner Fairy Footsteps: over 4 lengths sixth of 21 to Projection in maiden at Newmarket, running on in eye-catching style last 200 yds: disappointing in similar event at Lingfield 10 days later: should stay beyond 6f. *R. Hannon* 70

FLYING GREEN (FR) 2 ch.g. (Mar 30) Persian Bold 123 – Flying Sauce 107 (Sauce Boat (USA)) [1995 7m⁴ 7f² 7d Sep 26] 28,000Y: unfurnished gelding: brother to very useful miler Flying Brave and half-brother to several winners: dam useful French 2-y-o 6f and 1m winner: in frame in maidens at Salisbury and Kempton and ran well in face of stiff task in mid-division of 30-runner valuable sales race won by Rio Duvida at Newmarket final start: subsequently gelded: will stay further than 7f. *R. Charlton* 80

FLYING HAROLD 2 b.c. (Apr 12) Gildoran 123 – Anytime Anywhere 77 (Daring March 116) [1995 6d 7m Nov 3] close-coupled colt: first foal: dam best over sharp 5f: similar form when beaten around 8 lengths in maidens won by Fly Tip at Newbury and Wahiba Sands at Doncaster late in year. *M. R. Channon* 58

FLYING IMP 4 b.g. Faustus (USA) 118 – Quenlyn (Welsh Pageant 132) [1994 –: a11g a8g 1995 a12g a16g Jan 30] of no account. *R. Hollinshead* –

FLYING NORTH (IRE) 2 b.g. (Mar 5) Distinctly North (USA) 115 – North Kildare (USA) (Northjet 136) [1995 6f² 5.9f* 6m³ 6m 6f Oct 12] IR 12,500F, 8,000Y, 16,000 2-y-o: leggy gelding: good mover: first foal: dam, never ran, half-sister to smart miler Fanmore out of speedy Irish filly Lady Blackfoot: won maiden at Carlisle in June: good third of 11 to Rabican in strongly-run valuable nursery at Newmarket 75 in July: not discredited in similar event following month and Redcar Two-Year-Old Trophy in October: will stay beyond 6f: acts on firm ground, yet to race on a soft surface. *Mrs M. Reveley*

FLYING PENNANT (IRE) 2 ch.c. (Feb 24) Waajib 121 – Flying Beckee (IRE) 60 (Godswalk (USA) 130) [1995 7.1g Jun 16] IR 16,000Y: rangy colt: first foal: dam lightly-raced sister to very useful sprinter A Prayer For Wings: 25/1 and bit backward, never better than midfield when ninth of 11 in maiden at Sandown: looked likely to improve. *R. Hannon* 59 p

FLYING SQUAW 2 b.f. (Jan 27) Be My Chief (USA) 122 – Sea Fret 96 (Habat 127) [1995 5m* 6m* 6g^4 6m^2 6m^4 6d* Sep 1] 8,200F, IR 12,500Y: robust filly: has scope: half-sister to Irish 2m winner Top Wave (by High Top), 1989 2-y-o 5.1f winner Wave Master (by Chief Singer) and a winner in Holland: dam, 2-y-o 6f winner, out of smart Fluke, a half-sister to Buoy and Bireme: useful form: won median auction maiden at Sandown in April, minor event at Goodwood in May and 11-runner Moet & Chandon-Rennen at Baden-Baden: 2½ lengths fourth to Danehill Dancer in Heinz 57 Phoenix Stakes at Leopardstown on fifth outing: bred to stay beyond 6f: acts on good to firm and dead ground. *M. R. Channon* 102 +

FLY THE EAGLE 3 b.g. Rock City 120 – Tittlemouse 86 (Castle Keep 121) [1994 –: 6.9d 7m 6d 1995 10g 7f 12.1m 13.1h Sep 4] lengthy gelding: has been tubed: no worthwhile form: blinkered (final outing for D. ffrench Davis) second 3-y-o start. *M. P. Muggeridge* –

FLY TIP (IRE) 2 b.f. (Apr 19) Bluebird (USA) 125 – Sharp Deposit (Sharpo 132) [1995 6d* Oct 19] IR 7,000Y: unfurnished filly: first foal: dam unraced half-sister to Ebor winner Deposki: 11/1 from 6/1, won 20-runner maiden at Newbury by ½ length from Herodian, chasing leaders then quickening to lead around 1½f out: will improve. *B. W. Hills* 79 p

FOG CITY 2 b.c. (Jan 22) Damister (USA) 123 – Front Line Romance 89 (Caerleon (USA) 132) [1995 7.1m^4 7.1d^3 a6g* Oct 28] smallish colt: second foal: half-brother to 3-y-o My First Romance: dam stayed 1¼m: won 12-runner median auction maiden at Wolverhampton by length from Indian Relative, overcoming some interference to lead close home: bred to stay beyond 7f: acts on fibresand: will improve further. *W. Jarvis* 71 + a83 p

FOIST 3 b.g. Efisio 120 – When The Saints (Bay Express 132) [1994 –: 5f 6m 6m 1995 a7g 7.5m 7g 9.9m Jul 7] small, good-topped gelding: little sign of ability. *M. W. Easterby* –

FOLLOWMEGIRLS 6 b.m. Sparkling Boy 110 – Haddon Anna (Dragonara Palace (USA) 115) [1994 64: 5d^3 6m 5g^4 6m^6 6.1m 5g^4 5m* 5m^2 5m^2 5g^3 5m^4 5d^2 5d^6 1995 5d 5m^6 5f^4 5m^6 6m 5f^4 5f 5m 5m 6.1d 5d* 5m^5 Oct 30] leggy, lengthy mare: modest handicapper: consistent at 5 yrs, the opposite in 1995: won 23-runner contest at Leicester in September: effective at 5f and 6f: acts on firm and soft going: blinkered last 2 starts: often gives trouble to post, and usually goes down early: usually held up nowadays. *Mrs A. L. M. King* 54

FOLLY FINNESSE 4 b.f. Joligeneration 111 – Magic Milly 60 (Simply Great (FR) 122) [1994 80: 8.1s^2 8.1g^4 8.1m^3 8m 10.8s* 12v^6 12v 1995 a9.4g^2 a8.5g^3 a7g 10.8d 10m 7.6m 9m 8g Jun 3] lengthy filly: has a round action: fair handicapper on her day: well below form last 6 starts: stays 10.8f: acts on good to firm and soft ground and on fibresand. *B. R. Millman* 76 d

FOND EMBRACE 2 b.f. (Mar 31) Emarati (USA) 74 – Detente 87 (Dominion 123) [1995 5m^3 6f^3 5g^6 5.2d^3 Sep 16] 4,800Y: leggy filly: second foal: dam 1½m winner: fair form in maidens then nursery (around a length third of 12 to Willow Dale, doing very well as only one to race on unfavoured part of track) at Newbury: bred to be as effective at 6f as 5f but races keenly (pulled too hard second start): acts on good to firm and dead ground. *H. Candy* 75 +

FOOLS HAVEN (IRE) 3 b.g. Fools Holme (USA) – Oak Queen (King of Clubs 124) [1994 40: 5m 5v^2 5g 5v a8g 1995 8.3v Mar 31] sparely-made gelding: poor maiden: well beaten only 3-y-o start: should stay at least 1m: best efforts on heavy ground. *B. S. Rothwell* –

FOOLS MILLYONS (IRE) 3 ch.c. Fools Holme (USA) – Eloquent Charm (USA) (Private Account (USA)) [1994 48: 5m 6d^5 6m^4 5.9f 6g 6g 8f 7.5g a8g a8g 42

a8g 1995 a8g a9.4g^{4} a8g^{6} Jan 30] sturdy colt: poor maiden: sold 1,300 gns Doncaster February Sales: stays 9.4f: acts on fibresand: visored last 2 starts: has worn special tongue strap. *W. Bentley*

FOOLS OF PRIDE (IRE) 3 ch.f. Al Hareb (USA) 123 – I'll Take Paris (USA) (Vaguely Noble 140) [1994 59: 7m^{3} 7g^{3} 7g a6g^{5} 1995 a8.5g^{6} a9.4g^{4} a8g^{5} a9.4g^{5} a11g^{3} a11g^{5} a12g^{5} a9.4g^{5} 12m 16m^{3} 12m^{5} 16.2g^{6} a14.8g* 16.2m^{2} 16.2m^{6} 13.8g 17.1m a14.8g^{4} a16g Dec 15] sparely-made filly: half-sister to winners abroad by Lyphard's Wish and Youth: dam French 2-y-o 1m winner: modest form in Ireland in 1994 for R. Jennings: poor at best here: won claimer at Wolverhampton in July: stays 2m: acts on good to firm ground and fibresand. *R. Hollinshead* 39

FORBIDDEN GEM 4 b.g. Formidable (USA) 125 – Emerald Ring 74 (Auction Ring (USA) 123) [1994 –: 8s 8g 9g 6g a8g 1995 a6g^{6} a6g 8m 8f Jun 28] sparely-made gelding: no worthwhile form: sold 700 gns Ascot July Sales. *S. Woodman* –

FORCE OF WILL (USA) 2 ch.c. Diesis 133 – Clear Issue (USA) (Riverman (USA) 131) [1995 8m* 7g^{3} Sep 16] second foal: half-brother to useful Irish miler (won over 7f as 2-y-o) Union Decree (by Polish Precedent): dam, Irish 7f winner, half-sister to high-class American performer Twilight Agenda and the dam of Belmont winner Go And Go: 3/1 on, won 5-runner maiden at Tralee in August by 5 lengths: much better form when 2¼ lengths third of 7 to Danehill Dancer in National Stakes at the Curragh, keeping on: should stay beyond 1m: may well improve again. *D. K. Weld, Ireland* 108 p

FORECAST 2 b.c. (Mar 12) Formidable (USA) 125 – Princess Matilda 110 (Habitat 134) [1995 a5g Aug 11] 13,500Y: half-brother to several winners, including 3-y-o 6f winner Achill Princess (by Dowsing) and 1988 2-y-o 1m winner Mired (by Mill Reef): dam, 7f winner, half-sister to Bruni: 25/1, slowly away and never dangerous in seller at Wolverhampton. *J. Wharton* –

FOREIGN JUDGEMENT (USA) 2 b.c. (Apr 19) El Gran Senor (USA) 136 – Numeral (USA) (Alleged (USA) 138) [1995 8d^{6} 7m Oct 20] rather unfurnished colt: has a round action: third foal: brother to a minor winner in USA: dam, minor winner in USA, half-sister to Grade 2 winners Luminaire and Wistful: just under 4 lengths sixth of 18 to Mystic Knight in maiden at Salisbury: green still, found drop to 7f on good to firm ground against him in similar event at Doncaster following month: will be suited by middle distances: sold 13,500 gns Newmarket Autumn Sales. *P. W. Chapple-Hyam* 75

FOREMAN 2 b.c. (Jan 7) Timeless Times (USA) 99 – Skiddaw Bird (Bold Owl 101) [1995 5m 5m* 5m^{4} 5g 6m^{6} 5m 6d 6m a5g^{3} a6g a7g^{4} a6g^{6} Nov 29] 2,200F, 3,800Y: robust colt: first foal: dam unraced: modest form: won maiden auction at Newmarket in May: none too consistent in nurseries last 8 starts: probably stays 7f: acts on good to firm ground and all-weather surfaces: tried blinkered (creditable effort first time), visored last 4 outings. *W. A. O'Gorman* 57

FOREMMA 4 b.f. Formidable (USA) 125 – Great Dilemma 77 (Vaigly Great 127) [1994 –: 11.6f 10m^{6} 14d 1995 12g 16.4g 11.9m^{4} 10m Jun 26] lengthy filly: no worthwhile form: tried visored. *P. R. Hedger* –

FORENTIA 2 b.f. (Feb 28) Formidable (USA) 125 – Clarentia 111 (Ballad Rock 122) [1995 5g* 6g^{2} 6m^{2} 6m^{6} 6g^{5} Sep 15] good-quartered filly: third foal: half-sister to 3-y-o Larentia (by Salse): dam sprinter from family of Stilvi: fairly useful form: won maiden at Sandown in June: good second next 2 starts (to Rabican in nursery at Newmarket on second of them) then ran creditably in Lowther Stakes at York (sweating) and respectably in listed race at Ayr: stays 6f: hung badly left second outing. *J. R. Fanshawe* 89

FORESHORE (IRE) 5 b.m. Don't Forget Me 127 – Krismas River (Kris 135) [1994 59: 6d^{2} 6.1d 8v^{4} 7.3s^{4} 7g 8g a8.5g 1995 a7g a7g Feb 28] sturdy mare: modest maiden: no form for 3 different trainers last 5 starts: stays 1m: acts on heavy ground. *R. Ingram* –

FOREST BOY 2 b.g. (Jan 26) Komaite (USA) – Khadine 79 (Astec 128) [1995 a6g^{2} 6.1d a6g^{4} Sep 30] 6,200Y: strong, sturdy colt: brother to 3-y-o Kildrummy Castle and half-brother to a winner abroad by Night Shift: dam required good test of stamina: similar form in auction events at Wolverhampton, visored on final start: not well drawn in maiden at Nottingham in between: bred to stay 6f. *K. McAuliffe* 65

FOREST BUCK (USA) 2 ch.c. (Mar 4) Green Forest (USA) 134 – Perlee (FR) 122 (Margouillat (FR) 133) [1995 8g* Oct 10] close-coupled, angular colt: seventh foal: brother to 7f winner Forest Tiger and half-brother to 3 winners, notably twice-raced Poule d'Essai des Pouliches winner Pearl Bracelet (by Lyphard): dam French 1m to 1½m winner: 4/1 favourite, won 17-runner maiden at Leicester comfortably by 1¼ lengths from Jiyush, green before leading over 1f out: moved fluently to post: sure to improve, and win another race or two. *H. R. A. Cecil*
87 p

FOREST CAT (IRE) 3 b.f. Petorius 117 – Forest of Arden (Tap On Wood 130) [1994 79p: 5g^4 6d* 1995 7.3g* 7.1m* 7g^3 Jul 11] workmanlike filly: fairly useful performer, lightly raced: won handicaps at Newbury and Sandown (£10,400 event) in May: good third of 7 in rated stakes at Newmarket on final start: will stay 1m: acts on good to firm and dead ground: usually bandaged. *Mrs J. Cecil*
91

FOREST FANTASY 2 b.f. (Feb 26) Rambo Dancer (CAN) 107 – Another Treat 92 (Derring-Do 131) [1995 5g^4 5m^4 7d Sep 22] workmanlike filly: half-sister to several winners, including 5f (at 2 yrs) to 1¼m winner Stride Home (by Absalom) and 1½m winner Another Thrill (by Morston): dam middle-distance winner: poor form in claimer and maiden at Beverley and maiden auction at Redcar: needs further than 5f. *J. Wharton*
47

FOREST MILL 3 ch.f. Aragon 118 – Forest Blossom (USA) 56 (Green Forest (USA) 134) [1994 NR 1995 9m^4 10m^3 7.6m^3 11.5m a11g 10d 14d 11.8g^6 10.3m Oct 21] 7,800Y: sparely-made filly: second foal: half-sister to 1½m seller winner Flora Belle (by Glint of Gold): dam, half-sister to Yorkshire Oaks winner Magnificent Star, won in Holland: modest maiden at best: well beaten last 6 starts: should prove suited by middle distances: acts on good to firm ground, tailed off on fibresand and dead: tried visored: sold (D. Arbuthnot to J. Spearing) 3,500 gns Newmarket Autumn Sales. *D. W. P. Arbuthnot*
58 d

FOREST ROBIN 2 ch.c. (Apr 4) Formidable (USA) 125 – Blush Rambler (IRE) (Blushing Groom (FR) 131) [1995 5m^3 5m^4 6g^3 6g^4 7g^2 7m^6 Oct 20] good-quartered colt: first foal: dam, Irish 1½m winner, half-sister to useful Irish stayer Excellenza: fair maiden: stays 7f: consistent. *R. F. Johnson Houghton*
79

FOREST STAR (USA) 6 b.g. Green Forest (USA) 134 – Al Madina (USA) (Round Table) [1994 NR 1995 a13g Dec 19] well-made gelding: modest form (rated 51) at 4 yrs for Miss G. Kelleway: ridden by 5-lb claimer and 9/1 from 5/1, no immediate promise on return in handicap at Lingfield: suited by middle distances: acts on good to firm ground, well beaten on soft: visored/blinkered last 4 starts: sometimes finds little. *R. Akehurst*
–

FORESWORN (USA) 3 b.c. Alleged (USA) 138 – Sybilline (FR) (Satingo 129) [1994 NR 1995 12f^5 Apr 18] $35,000F: strong, close-coupled colt: half-brother to several winners in North America: dam, placed once from 7 starts in France, from family of Le Fabuleux: burly and green, kept on steadily when fifth of 12 to Sebastian in maiden at Newmarket in April: looked sure to improve, but sold only 2,500 gns Doncaster October Sales. *Mrs J. Cecil*
76

FOREVER BLUSHING 4 b.f. Blushing Scribe (USA) 107 – Rheinza 66 (Rheingold 137) [1994 –: 12s 10g 12s 11.9f 15.4m 1995 a12g^6 Jan 24] leggy filly: poor 7f winner at 2 yrs: no form since then. *P. Butler*
–

FOREVER DIAMONDS 8 ch.g. Good Times (ITY) – Mel Mira 68 (Roi Soleil 125) [1994 88: 8d^6 8m 8.5g* 8.1g* 8.1g^6 8m 1995 8m 8.1g^5 8.9m 8m 8.5m^3 8g^6 Aug 26] leggy, rather sparely-made gelding: fairly useful handicapper: game and consistent at his peak, but well below form last 4 starts: ideally suited by 1m to 1¼m: acts on any going: twice blinkered (below form) earlier in career. *M. H. Easterby*
86 d

FOREVER NOBLE (IRE) 2 b.c. (Apr 18) Forzando 122 – Pagan Queen 83 (Vaguely Noble 140) [1995 5m Apr 29] 12,500F, 20,000Y: sturdy, lengthy colt: brother to a winner in Czech Republic, closely related to bumpers/useful hurdles winner Arcot (by Formidable) and half-brother to several winners, including (at 1½m) La Gracile (by Nijinsky): dam won at 1½m and 1¾m: 10/1, around 11 lengths ninth of 12 to Mubhij in maiden at Sandown: looked likely to do better. *M. R. Channon*
–

FOREVER ROSES 3 b.f. Forzando 122 – Red Rose Bowl (Dragonara Palace (USA) 115) [1994 NR 1995 5.2g^3 Sep 12] half-sister to several winners, including
70 p

good sprinter Gallic League (by Welsh Saint) and 7f winner Bandol (by Blakeney): dam, Irish 2-y-o 7f winner, half-sister to Cesarewitch winner Private Audition: 1¾ lengths third of 9 to Unfuwaanah in maiden at Yarmouth on only start, keeping on well from rear: should improve. *P. F. I. Cole*

FORGETFUL 6 b.m. Don't Forget Me 127 – Peak Squaw (USA) (Icecapade (USA)) [1994 35: a12g^{3} a14.8g^{6} a12g 1995 8s^{3} 8f a12g Dec 12] leggy, workmanlike mare: poor handicapper on flat nowadays: stays 1½m: acts on firm ground, soft and probably on fibresand: blinkered (raced too freely) once at 2 yrs: sometimes carries head high. *D. Burchell* — 40

FORGIE (IRE) 2 b.g. (May 20) Don't Forget Me 127 – Damia (Vision (USA)) [1995 6m 8.2d 8.2m Oct 19] 10,000F, 11,000Y: lengthy gelding: has a round action: third foal: dam unraced half-sister to useful 1m/1¼m performer Toca Madera: well beaten in maiden auction at Ripon and maidens at Nottingham: swished tail second start. *P. Calver* — –

FORGOTTEN DANCER (IRE) 4 ch.c. Don't Forget Me 127 – Dancing Diana 82 (Raga Navarro (ITY) 119) [1994 70d: 6s 8d 8g^{5} 6m 6d 6g^{4} 5d^{3} 6m a6g^{2} a6g 1995 a6g^{4} a8g^{6} a6g a7g Feb 18] small colt: modest at best at 3 yrs: little form in 1995: stays 1m: acts on heavy going and equitrack, possibly not top-of-the-ground: tried blinkered. *R. Ingram* — –

FORGOTTEN EMPRESS 3 b.f. Dowsing (USA) 124 – Vynz Girl 82 (Tower Walk 130) [1994 71: 7.9d^{2} 7d^{6} a8.5g^{2} 1995 a8.5g* 10g Sep 21] leggy filly: modest performer: best effort on debut: won median auction maiden at Wolverhampton in February on second and final start for J. L. Eyre: in need of race, tailed off in apprentice minor event at Pontefract 7½ months later: should stay beyond 8.5f: acts on dead ground and fibresand. *A. Harrison* — 60 +

FORLIANDO 2 b.g. (May 26) Forzando 122 – Lucky Orphan 73 (Derrylin 115) [1995 6m 7.1d 8g^{5} 10g 8.1s Oct 17] 5,000Y, 9,700 2-y-o: sturdy, lengthy gelding: sixth foal: half-brother to 2 winners in Ireland by Faustus, one over hurdles: dam stayed 1¼m: well beaten, including in seller: blinkered final outing. *M. S. Saunders* — 41

FORMAESTRE (IRE) 5 b.m. Formidable (USA) 125 – Maestrette 77 (Manado 130) [1994 –: a8.5g 1995 10m 8.1m^{5} 13.1f^{3} Jul 19] small mare: poor handicapper: stays 13f: acts on firm and soft ground and on fibresand: bandaged in 1995. *R. Lee* — 26

FORMIDABLE LASS 4 ch.f. Formidable (USA) 125 – Stock Hill Lass 87 (Air Trooper 115) [1994 –: 8m 10d 1995 8.3m 11.6m 8m Aug 27] sturdy filly: of little account. *L. G. Cottrell* — –

FORMIDABLE LIZ 5 ch.m. Formidable (USA) 125 – Areej (Rusticaro (FR) 124) [1994 66, a54: 6f 6m 6m^{2} 6m^{5} 6.1m* 6m 6m 6d a7g^{3} a6g^{4} a6g^{5} a6g^{4} 1995 6g^{6} 6m 6m^{4} 6m* 6m^{4} 6m 6m 8g^{3} 7g^{5} Sep 16] sturdy, lengthy mare: unimpressive mover: modest handicapper: won at Catterick in July: probably stays 7f: acts on any turf going and on fibresand: usually races prominently: no improvement in blinkers. *M. D. Hammond* — 66 a–

FORMIDABLE PARTNER 2 b.c. (Apr 12) Formidable (USA) 125 – Brush Away (Ahonoora 122) [1995 7m^{5} Nov 3] 51,000Y: strong, good-bodied colt: seventh foal: half-brother to 4 winners, including 6f and 1m winner Mr Vincent (by Nishapour) and useful Irish performer (at up to 7f) Takwim (by Taufan): dam unraced half-sister to useful stayer Princess Genista: 7/1 and green, over 5 lengths fifth of 17 to Jackson Hill in maiden at Doncaster, chasing leaders then keeping on despite wandering and carrying head slightly awkwardly: will improve. *R. W. Armstrong* — 70 p

FORT DE FRANCE (USA) 2 b.c. (Mar 31) Alleged (USA) 138 – Fabrina (USA) 81 (Storm Bird (CAN) 134) [1995 7.1d^{6} 10.2m^{5} Sep 25] good-topped colt: has scope: fifth foal: half-brother to 3 minor winners in USA: dam stayed 1½m: signs of ability in maidens won by Masehaab at Sandown and Gentilhomme at Bath: looks a long-term prospect. *M. R. Stoute* — – p

FOR THE PRESENT 5 b.g. Then Again 126 – Axe Valley 89 (Royben 125) [1994 93: 5m^{3} 6f 5g^{4} 5f^{2} 6.1m^{3} 6f* 6m^{3} 5.6g 1995 5m May 21] strong, useful-looking gelding: fairly useful handicapper: won Stewards' Cup at Goodwood in 1994: shaped encouragingly when eighth of 14 at Ripon on reappearance, but wasn't seen again: suited by sprint distances and a sound surface: held up. *T. D. Barron* — 82 +

FORTIS PAVIOR (IRE) 5 b.g. Salt Dome (USA) – Heather Lil (Ballymore 123) [1994 NR 1995 a7g Nov 24] sturdy gelding: modest form for R. Whitaker in 1993, rated 61: well beaten in Southwell handicap on return. *C. W. C. Elsey* –

FORT KNOX (IRE) 4 b.g. Treasure Kay 114 – Single Viking (Viking (USA)) [1994 62: a6g^5 7d 6f 7g^3 7g 7.6m 7.1m 7f* 7.6g* 7m^4 7g^3 7s 7g 7d 1995 8f^5 7.6m 8m* 8.1m 7.6m 8m a7g* a10g^5 a7g^3 a7g^5 Dec 15] quite attractive gelding: shows knee action: modest handicapper: won at Newmarket (ladies race, sweating and edgy) in August and at Lingfield (apprentice contest after 2½-month absence) in November: stays 1m well: acts on all-weather tracks and on firm going, possibly not on soft: blinkered 3 times (ran poorly first 2 occasions): inconsistent. *R. M. Flower* 54 a56

FORTUITIOUS (IRE) 2 b.f. (Jan 28) Polish Patriot (USA) 128 – Echo Cove (Slip Anchor 136) [1995 5m^5 5g 6.1m 5f^3 5g^5 5m^6 6f 8.1m^4 10d Sep 19] 5,500Y: sturdy filly: first foal: dam French 11f winner: plater: stays 1m: visored third start: occasionally swishes tail. *J. R. Jenkins* 42

FORTUNES COURSE (IRE) 6 b.m. Crash Course 128 – Night Rose (Sovereign Gleam 117) [1994 40+: 14.1g^4 1995 14.1m Oct 19] smallish mare: fair hurdler, winner in November: poor form in maidens on only flat outings: will need thorough test of stamina. *J. S. King* –

FORTUNES LEAP 3 br.g. Puissance 110 – Lucky Starkist 57 (Lucky Wednesday 124) [1994 51: 5g 6g^4 6d^6 7m 1995 6.1g 5.1m a6g^6 a7g Aug 5] angular gelding: poor maiden: stays 7f: acts on good to firm ground. *Mrs L. A. Murphy* 40

FORTUNES ROSE (IRE) 3 b.f. Tremblant 112 – Night Rose (Sovereign Gleam 117) [1994 NR 1995 14f 14s 14g Oct 23] unfurnished filly: sixth foal: half-sister to 3 winning jumpers: dam unraced: no promise in maidens. *J. S. King* –

FORT VALLY 5 gr.m. Belfort (FR) 89 – Hivally (High Line 125) [1994 52: 10g^5 10.1f^6 9g^6 8f 9g* 10.1m 10.4d^6 12g^6 10.1d 1995 10g 12d 8m 9.9m^4 9f 9.9m 8m* Aug 7] leggy, lightly-made mare: in foal to Timeless Times: poor handicapper nowadays: won seller at Thirsk in August: stayed 10.4f: acted on firm and soft going: tended to wander under pressure: effective blinkered/visored (best efforts in 1995) or not. *B. W. Murray* 39

FORZAIR 3 b.g. Forzando 122 – Persian Air (Persian Bold 123) [1994 81: 5s^4 6g^3 5.2m 7g 1995 6g^2 7m^4 7m^4 6m 6g a6g^6 a7g^3 6m^5 a6g 8m 8.2m a8.5g^2 Dec 12] sturdy, sprint type: fair maiden handicapper: trained until after seventh 3-y-o start by M. McCormack: stays 8.5f: acts on good to firm ground and fibresand: effective blinkered or not. *S. R. Bowring* 73

FORZARA 2 ch.f. (Apr 30) Risk Me (FR) 127 – Valldemosa 81 (Music Boy 124) [1995 6m 5s Sep 28] rather leggy filly: third foal: half-sister to 3-y-o Absolutely Fabulus (by Absalom): dam best at 5f: well beaten in maidens. *J. Berry* –

FOSTERS TOP 3 ch.g. Pharly (FR) 130 – More Sparkle (Morston (FR) 125) [1994 –: a7g 1995 a8g 10m 8.5m^6 8g 6f^5 Jul 31] leggy gelding: little sign of ability: sold 750 gns Ascot September Sales. *J. Ffitch-Heyes* –

FOUNDRY LANE 4 b.g. Mtoto 134 – Eider 80 (Niniski (USA) 125) [1994 84p: 12g 12s^3 10.1m^2 13.1m* 12m^3 14m^3 12f 11.9m^2 11.9d* 1995 13.9g^2 12m 11.9m^6 14f* 13.9m^3 16.1g^4 12m^5 Nov 4] rangy gelding: usually looks well: has a fluent, round action: fairly useful handicapper: won at Haydock in August: in frame in Ebor at York and £13,700 event at Newcastle next 2 starts: dropped in trip, creditable fifth in November Handicap at Doncaster final outing: stays 2m: acts on any going: game and consistent. *Mrs M. Reveley* 86

FOURDANED (IRE) 2 b.c. (May 5) Danehill (USA) 126 – Pro Patria 86 (Petingo 135) [1995 7g^4 7m^4 Oct 20] IR 31,000Y: rather unfurnished colt: eighth foal: half-brother to 4 winners, including dual Oaks winner Unite (by Kris) and 1m winner Wahem (by Lomond): dam, sister to smart miler Patris, won over 5f and 6f at 2 yrs from 4 starts: promising fourth, nearest finish, in maidens won by Ali-Royal at Warwick and Germano at Doncaster in October: will stay at least 1m: sure to improve. *P. W. Harris* 81 p

FOUR LANE FLYER 3 b.f. Sayf El Arab (USA) 127 – Collegian 90 (Stanford 121§) [1994 NR 1995 7.1m 5g^6 7f^3 7.1s Sep 30] 560F: lengthy filly: sixth foal (fifth by Sayf El Arab): sister to 5f to 7f winner Unveiled and 6f (at 2 yrs) to 1½m winner –

South Sands: dam 6f and 1m winner: well beaten in maidens and handicap. *E. J. Alston*

FOUR OF SPADES 4 ch.g. Faustus (USA) 118 – Fall To Pieces (USA) 101 (Forli (ARG)) [1994 49+, a71: a5g* a5g3 a5g5 6g 6f 5m 7g 5m 7.1m3 6g6 7g6 7d4 a5g6 a6g5 a7g* a6g* 1995 a6g a6g4 a6g2 7.1g a7g2 7m* 7.1m* 7.1m2 7.6m6 7m4 a7g6 6m6 a6g* a6g2 5g 6s a5g a7g2 a6g3 a7g* Dec 15] tall, lengthy gelding: fair performer: successful in seller at Lingfield, claimer (2 days later, claimed out of W. S. Cunningham's stable £4,000) at Edinburgh and handicap at Wolverhampton, all in the summer, and in handicap at Lingfield in December: stays 7f: acts on good to firm and dead ground and goes well on the all-weather: effective blinkered or not: below form in visor: has run well when sweating: successful for apprentice: normally races prominently. *P. D. Evans* — 62 a75

FOUR WEDDINGS (USA) 2 b.g. (Feb 9) Runaway Groom (CAN) – Kitty's Best (USA) (Amen (FR)) [1995 a6g 6m5 6m Jul 20] $25,000Y: sturdy gelding: has a round action: half-brother to numerous minor winners in North America: dam unraced: sire champion 3-y-o in Canada: fifth of 9 in median auction maiden at Leicester on second start: well beaten otherwise: will stay 1m. *M. Bell* — 56 ?

FOXHILL BLUE 3 b.f. Domynsky 110 – Cornflower Blue (Tyrnavos 129) [1994 46: a6g 6f 6m6 6s a6g5 a5g 1995 a5g Jan 28] angular filly: poor maiden: sold 600 gns Ascot February Sales: stays 6f: acts on good to firm ground and all-weather surfaces: tried visored. *M. D. I. Usher* — –

FOXHOUND (USA) 4 b.c. Danzig (USA) – Lassie Dear (USA) (Buckpasser) [1994 7m4 7d3 7m4 1995 a6g* 7m2 6d Sep 24] rangy, good-looking colt: twelfth foal (all to have run have won): brother to minor winner in USA at up to 1¼m Deerhound, closely related to 2 winners, including Group 1 6f and 7f winner Wolfhound (by Nureyev), and half-brother to several winners, notably dual Grade 3 winner (placed in 5 Grade 1 events) Weekend Surprise (by Secretariat), later dam of A P Indy and Summer Squall: dam stakes winner at 2 yrs from fine family: useful performer in France for A. Fabre, winner of minor event at Chantilly and listed race at Evry at 2 yrs: in frame at 3 yrs in listed event, Prix du Palais-Royal and Prix de la Porte Maillot, all at Longchamp: trained by H. Ibrahim, won 4-runner handicap at Nad Al Sheba in February: heavily-backed favourite, good second of 11 to Didina in listed race at York on return: stiff task and not disgraced in Diadem Stakes at Ascot 5½ weeks later: stayed 7f: acted on firm ground and dead: retired to Coolmore Stud, IR 4,000 gns (Oct 1st). *Saeed bin Suroor* — 103

FOX SPARROW 5 b.g. Sharpo 132 – Wryneck 89 (Niniski (USA) 125) [1994 80: 10.8s* 10v3 11.9g3 10s3 10.5d 10.4d2 10d 1995 a11g 10.8d 12g2 Apr 22] quite attractive gelding: fairly useful handicapper at 4 yrs for R. Charlton: modest at best in 1995: stays 1½m: revels in the mud (yet to race on flat on top-of-the-ground): fair hurdler, winner in December. *N. Tinkler* — 64

FRAAM 6 b.h. Lead On Time (USA) 123 – Majestic Kahala (USA) (Majestic Prince (USA)) [1994 114: 7.3m2 8f* 7.3g 7m3 8.9d3 8g6 8m* 1995 8g2 8s2 7.1g2 8m2 8m4 8f4 7.3m4 Aug 11] good-topped horse: impresses in appearance: had screws inserted in near-fore cannon bone and similar operation on near-hind: smart performer: did not win in 1995, but became far more consistent and finished in frame on all 7 starts: ¾-length second in Group 3 events at Rome and Chantilly on second and fourth starts: topweight, led briefly over 1f out when fourth of 21 to Khayrapour when bidding for second successive Schweppes Golden Mile at Goodwood on penultimate outing: fourth of 9 to Harayir in Hungerford Stakes at Newbury 15 days later: effective at 7f and 1m: acted on any going: won when sweating: wore bandages: held up: game and genuine: injured his near-fore again in September and was retired to Holly Bush Farm Stud, near Badminton, Gloucs for £1,250, Oct 1. *E. A. L. Dunlop* — 112

FRAGARIA 3 ch.f. Be My Chief (USA) 122 – Strawberry Song 87 (Final Straw 127) [1994 NR 1995 8m 8.1m4 8f3 8m 11.9d 10.3m Oct 21] 13,500Y: angular filly: third foal: dam 1¼m winner out of half-sister to smart stayer Celtic Cone: fair form in frame in maidens at Sandown and Warwick in August: soundly beaten afterwards, including in blinkers: should stay beyond 1m: acts on firm ground: sold 6,000 gns Newmarket December Sales. *I. A. Balding* — 66 d

FRAGRANT BELLE (USA) 4 b.f. Al Nasr (FR) 126 – Zolinana (FR) 108 (Sallust 134) [1994 90: 8.1d4 10m4 12s 1995 10g6 10m5 10d Sep 16] good-topped — –

filly: good mover: fairly useful form at 3 yrs for D. Elsworth: beat only one horse in 3 races in 1995: stays 1¼m: acts on good to firm and soft ground: wore net muzzle final start. *L. G. Cottrell*

FRAISE DU ROI (IRE) 3 b.f. Roi Danzig (USA) – Stolen Fruit (Bold Lad (IRE) 133) [1994 NR 1995 a8.5g Mar 8] second living foal: dam unraced half-sister to very useful 6f to 8.5f winner Eve's Error: always behind in maiden at Wolverhampton. *Lord Huntingdon* –

FRAMED (IRE) 5 b.g. Tate Gallery (USA) 117 – Golden Thread (Glint of Gold 128) [1994 NR 1995 7f^5 a6g Nov 24] lengthy gelding: second foal: dam never ran: bandaged off-fore, never-nearer fifth of 14 in claimer at Yarmouth, not knocked about: soundly beaten in Southwell claimer following month. *S. C. Williams* 62

FRAMLEY GARTH 3 ch.f. Belmez (USA) 131 – Heavenly Abode (FR) (Habitat 134) [1994 46: a8g^5 a8g^6 a9.4g^4 1995 a10g 10g Jun 10] poor form in maidens at 2 yrs: well beaten in handicap at Lingfield in February before sold out of Sir Mark Prescott's stable 9,400 gns Ascot Sales later in month: stayed 1m: broke leg on Irish debut. *A. P. O'Brien, Ireland* –

FRANCES MARY 2 ch.f. (Mar 15) Sylvan Express 117 – Maydrum 50 (Meldrum 112) [1995 7.5m^4 7m a6g^3 a6g^4 a5g^2 5m 5s^2 a5g^2 a6g* Nov 13] fifth foal: dam lightly raced: modest performer: won 13-runner seller at Wolverhampton in November (second start in 3 days) by 2½ lengths: best form at sprint distances on fibresand/soft ground: blinkered last 2 starts: has flashed tail. *C. W. Fairhurst* 53 +

FRANCFURTER 3 b.f. Legend of France (USA) 124 – A Priori (GER) (Prince Ippi (GER)) [1994 75p: 7d^5 9.7s^2 1995 7m^4 10m* 10.5g^3 10m^5 10m* 10m Aug 27] lengthy, rather unfurnished filly: keen walker: fairly useful handicapper: won at Salisbury in May and Sandown in August: well beaten at Goodwood on final start: will stay beyond 10.5f: acts on good to firm and soft ground: blinkered last 2 starts. *R. Charlton* 89

FRAN GODFREY 2 b.f. (Feb 11) Taufan (USA) 119 – One Last Glimpse 73 (Relko 136) [1995 6m 7m a8g^2 Nov 8] 9,500Y: leggy, close-coupled filly: easy mover: sister to smart middle-distance horse Captain Horatius and half-sister to 3 winners here and abroad, including fair sprinter Running Glimpse (by Runnett): dam second from 8.2f to 10.6f: 4 lengths second of 11 to Roman Gold in maiden at Lingfield: will stay further than 1m. *P. T. Walwyn* 70

FRANKLY FRAN 3 b.f. Petorius 117 – Sunita (Owen Dudley 121) [1994 NR 1995 6g 8d Sep 15] 7,000Y: workmanlike filly: fourth foal: half-sister to fairly useful 6f to 1m performer Sagebrush Roller (by Sharpo): dam unraced half-sister to Oaks-placed Suni and Media Luna: never a threat in maidens at Lingfield in May and Newbury in September: should stay beyond 1m. *D. W. P. Arbuthnot* –

FRANK THE SWANK 4 b.g. Dunbeath (USA) 127 – Dark Amber 68 (Formidable (USA) 125) [1994 –: 10m 1995 12.3f^4 11.7f 12.1m^6 Jul 14] small, sturdy gelding: no sign of ability. *P. D. Evans* –

FRANS LAD 3 ch.g. Music Boy 124 – Moberry 54 (Mossberry 97) [1994 57: 5m^5 6g 8.1g 1995 a6g^2 a7g 6g 5m* 5f^5 a5g^4 6f^6 6.9h^4 7g a8g Nov 16] workmanlike gelding: modest performer: won maiden at Edinburgh in June: mostly disappointing afterwards: effective at 5f, and stays 7f: acts on hard ground and fibresand: effective visored/blinkered or not: usually races prominently: sold (J. Berry to W. Clay) 2,300 gns Doncaster November Sales. *J. Berry* 60

FRECKLES KELLY 3 b.f. Shavian 125 – Choke Cherry (Connaught 130) [1994 43: 6m 1995 10.1g 7m^4 7.5m^2 5f* a5g^2 5g 7f Oct 3] unfurnished filly: bad mover: modest handicapper: won selling event (bought in 5,800 gns) at Redcar in July: clearly best efforts at 5f: acts on fibresand, has raced only on a sound surface on turf: races prominently. *M. H. Easterby* 50

FRED BONGUSTO (IRE) 4 b.c. Danehill (USA) 126 – Hi Bettina 96 (Henbit (USA) 130) [1994 109: 7g* 7.5m^3 8v 8m^5 6f* 6m^5 6g 8v 6d^4 7d^3 1995 8s^6 6g* 6g^5 6f^2 6s^2 7m^6 5f 6d^3 6d 6g^3 6d^4 Dec 10] useful Italian performer: won minor event at Rome in March: ran very well when 1½ lengths second of 14 to Hever Golf Rose in Premio Melton-Memorial Tudini at Rome in May, always thereabouts: generally some way below that form afterwards: has form at 1m, but is ideally suited by 6f: acts on firm and soft ground: inconsistent. *R. Brogi, Italy* 109 d

FREDDIE BALOO 3 b.g. Satin Wood 117 – Mrs Bizz (Status Seeker) [1994 –: 6.9d 8.1g 1995 $9m^6$ a9.4g Aug 5] workmanlike gelding: no form: dead. *R. T. Phillips* –

FRED SAID RIGHT (IRE) 3 gr.g. Standaan (FR) 118 – Sleeping Car (Scorpio (FR) 127) [1994 NR 1995 7.1m 5d 6f Oct 3] IR 32,000Y: rather leggy gelding: fifth foal: brother to Irish 7f winner Track Twenty Nine: dam unraced: well beaten in maidens, weakening on each occasion: sold 1,400 gns Doncaster October Sales. *M. J. Heaton-Ellis* –

FRED'S DELIGHT (IRE) 4 b.g. Law Society (USA) 130 – Madame Nureyev (USA) (Nureyev (USA) 131) [1994 60d: 10.3g $8.2v^4$ 8v 8.2d 10m 10.5s 1995 a12g 12m Oct 2] smallish, angular gelding: no form since second 3-y-o start: sold out of M. Heaton-Ellis' stable 2,000 gns Doncaster July Sales after reappearance: should stay beyond 1m: acts on heavy going: tried blinkered/visored: not one to trust. *Mrs V. A. Aconley* –

FREEDOM CRY 4 b.c. Soviet Star (USA) 128 – Falling Star (FR) 120 (Mount Hagen (FR) 127) [1994 119: $8g^2$ $8g^4$ 8s* 8d* 1995 10s* $10.5v^4$ 11s* $10g^2$ $10m^2$ $12d^2$ $12s^2$ Oct 28] 132

Keeping Freedom Cry in training as a four-year-old paid off handsomely when he improved into the best flat racehorse of any age in France. By the end of the season there can have been very few his superior over middle distances anywhere, none by more than a pound or two on his form in the autumn when, on successive outings, he finished second to Pentire in the Irish Champion Stakes, to Lammtarra in the Prix de l'Arc de Triomphe and to Northern Spur in the Breeders' Cup Turf. He lost the three showpieces by an aggregate of a length. Towards the end his form levelled out, but connections seem to think that he will show to even better advantage at a mile and a half granted conditions which put less of an emphasis on stamina than they did in the Arc and the Breeders' Cup.

The Arc was Freedom Cry's first race over a distance as long as a mile and a half. He'd been restricted to mile races as a three-year-old, twice running creditably against Green Tune, fourth in the Poulains on the second occasion, and narrowly winning his two other starts. They were in Group 3 events, the Prix de la Jonchere at

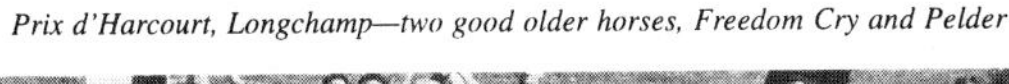
Prix d'Harcourt, Longchamp—two good older horses, Freedom Cry and Pelder

Grosser Preis der Wirtschaft, Baden-Baden—an international field; Freedom Cry beats Alderbrook (right) and Lando (left)

Maisons-Laffitte in June and the Prix Perth at Saint-Cloud in November. He put up a smart performance to get up close home from Scandinavian in the latter but, while worth more than his end-of-season rating of 111 in the International Classification, he still had some way to go to catch up with the leaders of his generation. As a four-year-old Freedom Cry had three races in the spring and three in the autumn, being prepared for the autumn campaign with a run at Deauville in August. The spring campaign went well. In hindsight it might have gone even better had he been ridden with restraint, as he usually is, instead of making the running in very testing ground in the Prix Ganay at Longchamp, in which, once headed, he held on for a creditable fourth place behind Pelder. Freedom Cry had beaten Pelder a neck when winning the Prix d'Harcourt at the same venue earlier in April. Four weeks after the Ganay he was stepped up to eleven furlongs in the Grosser Preis der Wirtschaft at Baden-Baden rather than down to nine-plus in the same day's Prix d'Ispahan. Both races attracted good fields despite catering for similar types. The Grosser Preis attracted the Ganay runner-up Alderbrook and most of the best local middle-distance talent around, Germany being a notable late-withdrawal. Freedom Cry got the trip very well in the soft ground. Waited with, he began a move around three furlongs out, quickened into the lead inside the final furlong and went on to win by three quarters of a length and a half a length from Alderbrook and Lando at weight-for-age.

Penalties and allowances came into play in the Prix Gontaut-Biron at Deauville in August, Freedom Cry facing a very stiff task indeed on his return from his short break. He had to concede the previous year's winner Hernando 9 lb and was conceding weight to all the others apart from Marildo. Hernando duly won the race again, but in finishing one and a half lengths second of nine Freedom Cry showed the best form of his life thus far. Better followed. Although Pentire came from behind him in the Guinness Champion Stakes there was no mistaking Freedom Cry possesses a top-class turn of foot. He quickened to lead entering the final furlong and was caught only on the line. Freedom Cry held a good chance in the Arc if he could reproduce the form over a mile and a half. In fact, looking wonderfully well, he excelled himself again only to find Lammtarra also still improving and just that bit too strong on the day. If connections were hoping for a steady pace for him, they must have been disappointed to see Luso force it from the start. Freedom Cry was held up in midfield before making ground early in the straight to launch a strong challenge that took him briefly into a narrow lead just inside the final furlong. Our reading of the end of the race was that Freedom Cry saw the trip out well, just as well as proven stayer Swain in third. Lammtarra needed very strong driving to prevail by three quarters of a length. At least one Arc runner, usually more, has gone on to contest the Breeders' Cup Turf each year since the series began in 1984 with All Along and Strawberry Road making the frame at Hollywood Park. On the whole the Arc runners' record is not a bad one, though a major disappointment has been that not one among winners Dancing Brave, Trempolino, Saumarez and Subotica was able to follow up in the States. Lammtarra never got his chance. In his absence Freedom Cry and Carnegie upheld the Arc form at Belmont Park while Lando finished well beaten. Freedom Cry came out decisively the better of the Fabre pair in a well-run race on ground even more testing than that for the Arc. He took up a handy position right away and comfortably maintained it round to the entrance to the short straight where he accelerated in pursuit of former stable-companion Northern Spur. At that point there was daylight between them, a gap of at least half a length. Freedom Cry closed gradually on the leader under pressure, shaking off Carnegie, but couldn't quite draw level and was being held at a neck in the last few strides.

Freedom Cry had an alternative Belmont Park engagement, second preference, in the Breeders' Cup Classic. It would have been very interesting to have seen him take on Cigar. Had he run on the dirt we might well know more about his prospects in his next major objective at the time of writing, the World Cup in Dubai, a race due to be decided over a mile and a quarter on sand. Looking further ahead, Freedom Cry, a tall colt who has shown he acts on good to firm and heavy on turf, has a bright future in European middle-distance racing as long as he retains his form and enthusiasm; middle distance includes, very definitely, a mile and a half.

		Nureyev	Northern Dancer
	Soviet Star (USA)	(b 1977)	Special
	(b 1984)	Veruschka	Venture VII
Freedom Cry		(b 1967)	Marie d'Anjou
(b.c. 1991)		Mount Hagen	Bold Bidder
	Falling Star (FR)	(ch 1971)	Moonmadness
	(ch 1980)	Free French	Northern Dancer
		(ch 1974)	Forward Gal

Freedom Cry's sire Soviet Star was a top-class sprinter-miler, the only colt to beat Miesque. He was retired to stud in Britain at the end of the 1988 season but was sent to Japan after six crops. Freedom Cry, Soviet Line and Volochine are the pick of his runners to date. The dam Falling Star, who had produced French middle-distance winners to Be My Guest and Lomond from five previous foals, raced only as a three-year-old and only at a mile. A Saint-Cloud maiden winner, she put up her best performance, a very smart one at that, in finishing third in the Prix d'Astarte. Freedom Cry's grandam Free French, bred in the purple, by Northern Dancer out of the leading American two-year-old filly of 1970, never made the racecourse. Sad to tell, none of Forward Gal's six offspring did. *A. Fabre, France*

FREEDOM FLAME 2 b.f. (Apr 7) Darshaan 133 – Fire And Shade (USA) 91 (Shadeed (USA) 135) [1995 $7g^{2}$ $7f^{2}$ Jul 26] close-coupled, quite attractive filly: not the best of walkers: fluent mover: first foal: dam, 2-y-o 6f winner, daughter of Fatah Flare: neck second of 7 to Royal Mark in maiden at Ayr, behind running green then finishing in excellent fashion: very uneasy favourite when beaten 1¼ lengths by Jack Jennings in maiden at Doncaster 10 days later, not clear run most of last 2f: will stay at least 1m: looked well worth another chance. *M. Johnston* — 79 p

FREELOADER 2 ch.c. (Apr 6) Be My Guest (USA) 126 – Andy's Find (USA) (Buckfinder (USA)) [1995 5m 6m 7f Jun 29] close-coupled colt: good mover: fifth foal: closely related to useful 1991 2-y-o 7f winner, later minor stakes winner in USA, Artic Tracker (by Eskimo) and half-brother to a winner in North America by Derby Wish: dam unraced: little sign of ability in maiden and claimers: sold 600 gns Ascot July Sales. *J. W. Hills* — –

FRENCH GINGER 4 ch.f. Most Welcome 131 – French Plait (Thatching 131) [1994 NR 1995 $8f^{5}$ $6g^{5}$ $8m^{3}$ $7.5d^{4}$ $7f^{4}$ 8g 7m Oct 20] lengthy filly: poor mover: half-sister to modest 7f/1m performer Rural Lad (by Town And Country): dam (out — 66

of 2m winner) seemingly of little account: fair maiden: likely to prove well suited by further than 1m: acts on good to firm and dead ground. *I. A. Balding*

FRENCH GRIT (IRE) 3 b.c. Common Grounds 118 – Charbatte (FR) 93 (In Fijar (USA) 121) [1994 90: 5f^{2} 5m* 6g 5g^{6} 1995 5g^{4} 6m^{2} 6m* 6g^{3} 6m^{4} 6g^{6} 7m^{5} 7g 6g 5d 7g 6f^{6} Oct 31] leggy, workmanlike colt: fairly useful handicapper: won minor event at Doncaster in May: well below form last 4 starts: effective at 6f and 7f: acts on firm ground: wears a crossed noseband. *M. Dods* — 88

FRENCH IVY (USA) 8 ch.g. Nodouble (USA) – Lierre (USA) (Gummo (USA) 117) [1994 NR 1995 17.2m^{2} 17.2m^{2} 16.2f* 16m^{4} 15.9d^{2} 16.2s^{3} Oct 6] leggy gelding: fair handicapper: won at Ascot in June: made frame on all his other outings in 1995: stays well: acts on firm and soft ground: no improvement when visored twice earlier in career: usually bandaged: held up: consistent. *F. Murphy* — 71

FREQUENT 2 ch.c. (Mar 6) Rainbow Quest (USA) 134 – Free Guest 125 (Be My Guest (USA) 126) [1995 7.5d^{2} Nov 5] fifth live foal: half-brother to 2 winners, notably Oaks runner-up Shamshir (by Kris): dam, high-class 7f to 1½m winner, won 9 of 15 starts: ½-length second in maiden at Milan in November: will do better over middle distances. *L. M. Cumani* — 78 p

FRESH FRUIT DAILY 3 b.f. Reprimand 122 – Dalmally 89 (Sharpen Up 127) [1994 92?: 7g^{5} 1995 7m^{5} 10m 7f^{2} 7m^{2} 7g^{4} 8g a7g^{2} Dec 19] tall, angular filly: fair maiden: should stay 1m+ (out of depth in Lupe Stakes over 1¼m): has raced only on a sound surface on turf: carries head awkwardly: has run well when sweating. *P. A. Kelleway* — 76

FRESH LOOK (IRE) 3 b.f. Alzao (USA) 117 – Bag Lady 86 (Be My Guest (USA) 126) [1994 64: 6m 6g^{3} 6m^{5} 7m 1995 7g^{6} 12.5g^{3} 9m 10.8m 10.1m^{3} 11.5m^{4} 11.5g* 12.1g^{6} 11.9m 12m a12g a12g Dec 9] angular, unfurnished filly: modest performer: won claimer at Yarmouth (claimed out of R. F. J. Houghton's stable £5,000) in September: well beaten afterwards: stays 12.5f: acts on good to firm ground, yet to race on a soft surface. *R. C. Spicer* — 59 d

FRET (USA) 5 b.g. Storm Bird (CAN) 134 – Windy And Mild (USA) (Best Turn (USA)) [1994 NR 1995 12g^{2} 14.1f^{5} 11m Aug 23] tall, leggy gelding: useful performer in the spring at 3 yrs for P. Cole: modest and unreliable hurdler: poor at best on return to flat: stays 1½m: acts on firm and soft going. *J. S. Wainwright* — 44

FREZELIERE 2 b.f. (Mar 17) Be My Chief (USA) 122 – Anna Karietta 82 (Precocious 126) [1995 6g^{3} 7g^{3} 7g^{4} 6m^{3} 7g^{6} 7d 7s^{2} Oct 6] leggy filly: has scope: has a roundish action: second foal: dam 6f and 7f winner from useful family: ran some good races in nurseries but is by no means a straightforward ride and remains a maiden: stays 7f: acts on good to firm and soft ground: blinkered last 2 starts. *J. L. Dunlop* — 84

FRIAR'S OAK 3 b.g. Absalom 128 – Sunset Ray 74 (Hotfoot 126) [1994 –: 7m 7s 9.7s 1995 a8g a11g Feb 17] smallish, lengthy gelding: no worthwhile form. *M. H. Tompkins* — –

FRIAR STREET (IRE) 5 b.g. Carmelite House (USA) 118 – Madam Slaney 92 (Prince Tenderfoot (USA) 126) [1994 NR 1995 9.2g^{6} 13g a8g^{4} a8g^{5} 7.1g* Sep 18] IR 5,000F: workmanlike ex-Irish gelding: fourth foal: half-brother to Cesarewitch winner Aahsaylad (by Ardross): dam 7.9f to 1¼m winner: rated 62 at 3 yrs over sprint trips for N. Meade: modest form here, best effort when making all in maiden handicap at Edinburgh in September: probably best short of 1m: blinkered (below form) once as 3-y-o: sold (E. Alston to C. Mann) 7,000 gns Doncaster October Sales. *E. J. Alston* — 51

FRIDAY NIGHT (USA) 2 b. or br.f. (Feb 19) Trempolino (USA) 135 – Assez Cuite (USA) 114 (Graustark) [1995 6m Aug 11] lengthy filly: half-sister to several winners, including Prix Royal-Oak winner El Cuite (by Vaguely Noble) and dam of Michelozzo and Micheletti: dam smart French 2-y-o: 66/1 and bit backward, soon in rear in 22-runner maiden at Newbury: will need further than 6f: sold 9,700 gns Newmarket Autumn Sales. *I. A. Balding* — –

FRIENDLY BRAVE (USA) 5 b.g. Well Decorated (USA) – Companionship (USA) (Princely Native (USA)) [1994 72: 6.9s* 7d^{4} 7d^{6} 8m 7s^{6} 8.5g 6m^{2} 6m^{4} a7g^{4} 1995 a8g a7g a10g 10d 8m 6m^{6} 7.6m^{3} 6g^{2} 6m 6m^{2} 6g 5g 5.1d 5.1m^{4} 6f a5g* a5g* Nov 10] good-quartered gelding: impresses in appearance: fairly useful handicapper: — 72 a80 claimed out of T. Mills's stable £6,500 eighth start: better than ever when winning twice at Lingfield in November: effective at 5f (best form), and stays 7f: acts on equitrack and any turf going: sometimes blinkered, hooded twice in 1994: sometimes swishes tail: often claimer ridden: usually waited with. *Miss Gay Kelleway*

FRIENDLY DREAMS (IRE) 2 gr.f. (Mar 9) Midyan (USA) 124 – Friendly Thoughts (USA) (Al Hattab (USA)) [1995 7.5d Sep 13] 4,400 2-y-o: half-sister to 3-y-o Freeze (by Be My Chief), winner at 1¼m and 10.5f in Switzerland, and 2 other winners, including fair 6f (at 2 yrs) to 11.5f winner Fancy Me (by Dunbeath): dam unraced: 25/1, last of 17 in maiden auction at Beverley. *P. T. Dalton* –

FRIENDLY FORESTER (USA) 2 b.c. (Jan 15) Woodman (USA) 126 – Cameo Performance (USA) 104 (Be My Guest (USA) 126) [1995 5m^4 5.2m^4 5m^5 5.7h^3 7m* 8h^2 Sep 4] $85,000Y: neat colt: first foal: dam 1¼m to 1½m winner later successful in USA: fairly useful performer: won nursery at Epsom in August by short head from Vola Via: good second to Pacific Grove in nursery at Bath week later: stays 1m: has raced only on top-of-the-ground: blinkered last 2 starts. *R. Charlton* 83

FRIENDLY KNIGHT 5 b.g. Horage 124 – Be A Dancer (Be Friendly 130) [1994 –: 11.1g 1995 12.1v^6 Mar 31] strong gelding: of little account. *J. S. Haldane* –

FRIENDLY LADY (USA) 3 b.f. Imp Society (USA) – Icy Friend (USA) (It's Freezing (USA) 122) [1994 62: 5m^6 5f^6 5m^3 6m^5 5d a6g^3 a6g^6 a7g 1995 a6g^4 Jan 17] small, leggy filly: modest sprint maiden at 2 yrs: well beaten only start in 1995. *W. A. O'Gorman* –

FRISKY MISS (IRE) 4 b.f. Fayruz 116 – Moira My Girl (Henbit (USA) 130) [1994 70, a67: 6d^3 a7g^3 6s^6 6g^6 7.1f^2 5.9m* 7f^2 5f^2 7m^3 6g^2 5m* a5g^6 6g 6s* a6g^2 a7g a6g* 1995 a6g^3 a7g a7g a6g^4 a6g a6g^5 7m 6.1g a6g^6 7m a6g 6f^5 6g a7g^2 6f Jul 20] close-coupled filly: unimpressive mover: fair handicapper at best: left Jack Berry's stable after reappearance: inconsistent and mostly below form afterwards: effective at 5f to 7f: acts on fibresand and probably on any turf ground. *K. O. Cunningham-Brown* 67 d

FRO 2 b.f. (Apr 1) Salse (USA) 128 – Silent Sun 90 (Blakeney 126) [1995 5.7m^5 6m Jun 16] good-topped filly: half-sister to fair 5.7f to 1m winner Silent Expression (by Siberian Express) and 1989 2-y-o 6f to 1m winner Closed Shop (by Auction Ring): dam won over 1¼m here and 1m in France: poor form in maidens at Bath and Goodwood. *J. Ffitch-Heyes* –

FROG 2 b.f. (Feb 24) Akarad (FR) 130 – Best Girl Friend (Sharrood (USA) 124) [1995 6f^5 6m 6f a6g Nov 14] 16,000Y: strong filly: first foal: dam unraced daughter of good French sprinter/miler Girl Friend, also dam of Comrade In Arms: signs of ability in maidens and an all-weather nursery late in year: bred to be suited by 7f+: looks capable of better. *Sir Mark Prescott* – p

FROGMARCH (USA) 5 ch.g. Diesis 133 – La Francaise (USA) (Jim French (USA)) [1994 NR 1995 9d 8s Oct 7] quite attractive gelding: fairly useful form (rated 92) at 3 yrs, winner over 1m: well beaten in minor event at Newbury and handicap at Ascot on belated return: sold (R. Hern to R. Phillips) 6,200 gns Newmarket Autumn Sales. *Major W. R. Hern* –

FROME LAD 3 ch.g. Buzzards Bay 128§ – Groundsel 72 (Reform 132) [1994 61: a8g^3 a8g^6 a8.5g^3 1995 a8g^4 a12g^4 12.5f^5 10.2f a14.8g* a14.8g Jul 3] compact gelding: carries condition: modest performer: made all in handicap at Wolverhampton in June: stays 14.8f well: acts on equitrack and fibresand, no form on turf. *W. G. M. Turner* – a61

FRONTIERSMAN 3 b.g. Indian Ridge 123 – Strapless 84 (Bustino 136) [1994 NR 1995 6g 5m 5m 8.1d^2 10.1m^3 8.1s Nov 2] 8,200F, IR 22,000Y: rather leggy gelding: seventh foal: half-brother to useful 6f (at 2 yrs) and 7f winner Polish Admiral (by Roi Danzig) and a winner in Austria: dam 6f winner: modest maiden handicapper: stays 1¼m: acts on good to firm and dead ground: blinkered (worst effort) final outing: sent to Dubai. *J. W. Watts* 52

FRONTMAN (IRE) 2 ch.c. (Mar 1) Imperial Frontier (USA) 112 – Countess Kildare (Dominion 123) [1995 a5g^3 Nov 24] IR 5,000F, 11,500Y: fourth foal: dam, lightly raced in Ireland, half-sister to good Italian sprinter Swing Fire: 16/1, 5½ lengths third of 16 to Galine in maiden at Southwell, keeping on well: will stay 6f: will improve. *T. D. Barron* 67 p

FROZEN SEA (USA) 4 ch.c. Diesis 133 – Ocean Ballad 104 (Grundy 137) [1994 50: 7.1g^3 1995 10m^3 10m^5 12m^3 12m^4 Sep 7] strong colt: fair maiden: stays 1½m: yet to race on a soft surface: has worn crossed noseband. *G. P. Enright* — 69

FRUITFUL AFFAIR (IRE) 6 b.m. Taufan (USA) 119 – Lucky Engagement (USA) 75 (What Luck (USA)) [1994 47: 11.8v^5 11.6d 16.4g^3 16.1f^4 16m^5 16g^2 16.4g^2 15.4d^2 16s^3 16g 1995 15.4g a16.2g 16.5g^2 12g* 14.1m^6 10m 14.4m 12d 11.5s 16m Oct 19] lengthy mare: bad mover: modest handicapper: below form after winning at Newmarket (ladies) in July: tailed off from halfway on final start: stays 2m: possibly needs an easy surface nowadays (acts on soft going). *T. Thomson Jones* — 50 d

FRUSTRATION 4 b.f. Salse (USA) 128 – Baffle 87 (Petingo 135) [1994 108: 10s^5 10m* 10g* 10g* 10f* 11.9m^3 12g^3 1995 10f^6 10.2m* Jul 20] leggy filly: unimpressive mover: useful performer: won 4 handicaps at 3 yrs: much her better effort in listed races in 1995 when winning 7-runner contest at Chepstow in July by 2 lengths from Najmat Alshemaal, leading over 1f out: stays 1½m: acts on firm ground. *Lady Herries* — 102

FRYUP SATELLITE 4 br.g. Leading Star 110 – Comedy Imp (Import 127) [1994 –: 11.1g 8s 14.1g 1995 16.2m a12g^6 9.2g 12g May 26] leggy gelding: no worthwhile form: tried blinkered: has joined Mrs. J. Brown. *L. R. Lloyd-James* — –

FUJIYAMA CREST (IRE) 3 b.g. Roi Danzig (USA) – Snoozy Time 65 (Cavo Doro 124) [1994 65p: 7m 8m 8d 1995 9.7m* 11.6m* 12.3m^4 16.2f 16.4m 15.9m* 14m* 16.2d* Sep 23] tall gelding: has an unimpressive, quick action: made into a fairly useful handicapper, winning at Folkestone and Windsor in the spring, at Chester and Sandown in August and at Ascot (£14,500 event, comfortably from Benfleet) in September: stays 16.2f well: acts on good to firm and dead ground: visored second to fifth 3-y-o starts: bandaged behind/near-hind most outings, not at — 92 p

Gordon Carter Stakes (Handicap), Ascot—Fujiyama Crest makes all, unchallenged

Ascot: sometimes wanders closing stages: front runner last 3 starts: may well be capable of better still. *M. R. Stoute*

FULL COVER (IRE) 3 b.g. Thatching 131 – Dead Certain 123§ (Absalom 128) [1994 67: 5m 7g 6g5 7m 1995 a7g6 a7g 8d Apr 6] small, quite attractive gelding: fair maiden at 2 yrs: well below form in 1995: probably stays 7f: acts on good to firm ground: visored/blinkered last 4 starts: sold 600 gns Ascot May Sales. *D. R. C. Elsworth* –

FULL GLOSS 3 ro.g. Prince Sabo 123 – Cawstons Prejudice 53 (Cawston's Clown 113) [1994 56: 5g5 5g5 7g 1995 7m 8m 7.1m 7f3 7g 8m Aug 23] tall, lengthy gelding: poor maiden: stayed 7f: raced only on a sound surface: dead. *Mrs M. Reveley* 46

FULL QUIVER 10 br.g. Gorytus (USA) 132 – Much Pleasure (Morston (FR) 125) [1994 45: 12m 11.6f2 12m3 1995 16d 14d4 Sep 27] leggy gelding: unimpressive mover: poor handicapper: stays 14.1f: acts on any going: blinkered (below form) once, often visored: sometimes bandaged: wears tongue strap: sometimes finds little. *Mrs Barbara Waring* 45

FUNKY 2 ch.f. (Mar 11) Classic Music (USA) – Foreno (Formidable (USA) 125) [1995 7m6 8.2d3 Sep 19] 12,000F: leggy, quite attractive filly: half-sister to 1½m winner Early To Rise (by Don't Forget Me) and a winner in Italy: dam sister to smart French sprinter Reasonable: 8 lengths third of 11 to Pine Needle in maiden at Nottingham, staying on steadily not knocked about: sure to improve again. *L. M. Cumani* 69 p

FUNNY ROSE 5 b.m. Belfort (FR) 89 – Scottish Rose 69 (Warpath 113) [1994 26: 13.1m6 12.1m3 15.1m 13.1g6 12.1m2 13.1g 15.1m5 1995 12.1d3 7.1g5 10m 8.1g4 7.1m6 8f4 11.1f* 10.9g3 Jul 17] bad performer: poor mover: won selling handicap at Edinburgh in July: stays 1½m: acts on firm ground and dead. *P. Monteith* 28

FUNNY WORRY 6 b.g. Jester 119 – Concern 63 (Brigadier Gerard 144) [1994 NR 1995 9.2s Apr 12] eighth foal: half-brother to several winners, including (at 14.7f) Prince Henry (by Whitstead): dam 9.4f winner: well beaten in bumpers, and always behind in claimer at Hamilton on flat debut: sold 2,700 gns Doncaster May Sales. *P. Monteith* –

FURSAN (USA) 2 b.c. (Mar 12) Fred Astaire (USA) – Ancient Art (USA) (Tell (USA)) [1995 7m 7g Sep 13] $38,000F, 16,000Y: strong, lengthy, attractive colt: closely related to a winner in USA by Nijinsky and half-brother to several winners: dam, won 4 races in USA and third in Del Mar Oaks, half-sister to Ferdinand: sire, third in Breeders' Cup Mile, had good win at 11f: eleventh of 19 in maidens won by Even Top at Newmarket and Shawanni at Yarmouth (prominent to 2f out) 3 weeks later: should improve. *N. A. Graham* 65 p

FURTHER FLIGHT 9 gr.g. Pharly (FR) 130 – Flying Nelly 107 (Nelcius 133) [1994 110: 13.9f 16.4d3 16.1f 16f 15.9m3 18g3 16g* 16g* 1995 16.2m* 16.2m 13.9g5 16.4m5 14.6m* 16f 18g2 16g* 12d Oct 21] 115

Age has done little to wither that grand campaigner Further Flight. His immensely popular victory in the Jockey Club Cup at Newmarket in October made him the first horse since the introduction of pattern races in 1971 to win the same one five times. The only other horse to win the same pattern race more than three times is the French sprinter Cricket Ball, successful in four consecutive runnings of the Prix de Meautry in the 'eighties. Further Flight has now won nine pattern events in his career which puts him third in Britain behind Brigadier Gerard (thirteen) and Ardross (eleven). As well as monopolising the Jockey Club Cup, Further Flight has also won the Goodwood Cup twice and the Doncaster Cup and St Simon Stakes. All three of those races again featured on his programme as a nine-year-old, his best effort in them coming when runner-up to Double Trigger in the Doncaster Cup. Further Flight won the Jockey Club Cup on his next start, responding gamely, after being held up as usual, to go clear in the last furlong for a two-and-a-half-length victory over Assessor, with the favourite, Goodwood Cup runner-up Double Eclipse, third in a field of eight. Some of Further Flight's earlier Jockey Club Cup victories had been achieved against weak opposition but that certainly couldn't be said about the 1995 edition in which Further Flight raced with tremendous enthusiasm. He was taken on a well-deserved lap of honour in the paddock afterwards and was applauded all the way. The Newmarket executive announced that a race was to be named after him to

Jockey Club Cup, Newmarket—1991 *Jockey Club Cup, Newmarket—1992*

Jockey Club Cup, Newmarket—1993 *Jockey Club Cup, Newmarket—1994 ...*

... and 1995, a record five-timer for Further Flight and Michael Hills

mark his achievements. The Jockey Club Cup was one of three victories during the season for Further Flight; he also won conditions events at Haydock in April, on his reappearance, and at Doncaster in July.

Further Flight (gr.g. 1986)	Pharly (FR) (ch 1974)	Lyphard (b 1969)	Northern Dancer
			Goofed
		Comely (ch 1966)	Boran
			Princesse Comnene
	Flying Nelly (gr 1970)	Nelcius (br 1963)	Tenareze
			Namagua
		Flying By (gr 1964)	Bleep-Bleep
			Japhette

It is perhaps appropriate that Further Flight has made his reputation in a race run on Cambridgeshire day: his dam Flying Nelly won the Cambridgeshire in 1974. Further Flight is leggy and angular and has a round action. He wears small bandages behind. It goes almost without saying that he is a very tough, game and genuine stayer who is a credit to his trainer. Further Flight, who remains in training, acts on firm and dead going, but not on soft. *B. W. Hills*

FURTHER FUTURE (IRE) 2 br.c. (Mar 6) Doubletour (USA) – Tamara's Reef (Main Reef 126) [1995 5.3d 6g 7m Oct 12] IR 500F, 2,400Y resold 2,300Y: rangy colt: fifth foal: brother to a poor Irish maiden and half-brother to Italian 3-y-o 6.7f (at 2 yrs) and 1m winner Anticomoro (by Mazaad): dam Irish maiden: no worthwhile form: ridden by 7-lb claimer first 2 starts. *John Berry* –

FUTURE ACT (USA) 3 b.f. Known Fact (USA) 135 – Gamberta (USA) 111 (Roberto (USA) 131) [1994 67p: 7m^{3} 1995 8d^{4} 10.1m* 10m* 10f^{6} Aug 9] quite attractive filly: useful performer: won maiden at Epsom and handicap at Ripon (led on bridle 3f out, coasted clear) in July: favourite, well below Ripon form when sixth of 9 in listed race at Salisbury on final start: stays 1¼m well: acts on good to firm ground: wears dropped/crossed noseband: sent to USA. *H. R. A. Cecil* 94

FUTURE OPTIONS 4 ch.f. Lomond (USA) 128 – Hemline 77 (Sharpo 132) [1994 71: 8.5m^{6} 8f 7d^{2} 7d^{4} 7.1d^{5} 8g^{6} 7d 1995 7f^{5} 7.1m^{4} a8.5g 6.9f 8f^{5} Aug 17] small, quite attractive filly: fair maiden at 3 yrs for J. Hills: modest at best in 1995: stays 1m: acts on firm and dead ground. *M. S. Saunders* 52

FUTURE'S TRADER 2 b.c. (Feb 24) Alzao (USA) 117 – Awatef (Ela-Mana-Mou 132) [1995 8.1s^{5} Oct 17] 25,000Y: fifth foal: brother to useful 3-y-o stayer Wot-If-We, 6f winner at 2 yrs, and half-brother to 2 winners, notably fairly useful Daja (at 7f at 2 yrs, then up to 1¼m in Italy, by Doulab): dam poor French maiden from good family: 16/1, remote fifth of 10 to Latin Reign in maiden at Chepstow, prominent around 5f then losing ground quite quickly: should do better. *R. Hannon* – p

FUZZY 3 b.c. Petong 126 – Jaydeeglen 73 (Bay Express 132) [1994 NR 1995 6.1g 8.3g 6m 5m 5.9f Jun 28] angular colt: first foal: dam, maiden, half-sister to chaser Armagret: no sign of ability: tried blinkered. *S. E. Kettlewell* –

FYNE SONG 3 b.f. Chief Singer 131 – La Reine de France (Queen's Hussar 124) [1994 48: 6g 7m 6g 6s 1995 6g a7g 7m a8.5g^{4} a7g^{4} 8m* 8.2m 7m Aug 25] rather sparely-made filly: poor handicapper: won seller at Yarmouth in August: well beaten afterwards: stays 1m: acts on fibresand and good to firm ground, well beaten on soft: sold 3,000 gns Newmarket Autumn Sales. *W. J. Musson* 41

FYORS GIFT (IRE) 2 b.f. (Feb 27) Cadeaux Genereux 131 – Miss Fyor (USA) (Danzig (USA)) [1995 5.2g^{4} 5m^{3} 7.5d Sep 13] first foal: dam unraced daughter of Ma Biche: 7½ lengths third of 8 to Soviet Style in minor event at Lingfield: always behind in maiden at Beverley final outing. *B. Hanbury* 65 ?

G

GABRIEL'S LADY 4 b.f. Valiyar 129 – Autumn Harvest (Martinmas 128) [1994 NR 1995 9f 8m^{6} 6g 6f Aug 11] half-sister to 1984 2-y-o 5f winner Jackie Blair (by Rupert Bear): dam of no account: no sign of ability: has joined H. Roswell. *Mark Campion* –

GADGE 4 br.g. Nomination 125 – Queenstyle 58 (Moorestyle 137) [1994 79: 5d 6g6 7.1d2 6g4 7.1g 7m 7.6g3 7m 7.1d5 8s* 8m 1995 8g3 7s6 8g3 8m5 8.1g5 a8.5g 7g6 8d 9g 8s 7m Nov 3] sturdy, lengthy gelding: failed to take the eye in appearance in 1995: shows knee action: fair handicapper: consistent first 5 starts, one respectable effort and 5 poor ones afterwards: better at 1m than shorter: acts on good to firm ground, goes well on soft: has been bandaged behind: tail swisher: held up/tracks leaders. *D. Morris* — 73 d

GAGAJULU 2 b.f. (Apr 7) Al Hareb (USA) 123 – Rion River (IRE) (Taufan (USA) 119) [1995 5s2 5m6 5f2 6g5 6g a5g* 5g4 5.1f* 5g* 5.3f* 5m4 5m 5.1m* 6.1d 5m6 5.2f2 5m Nov 3] 1,200Y: leggy, unfurnished filly: first foal: dam Irish 1¼m winner: fair performer: successful in summer in median auction maiden at Southwell, claimer at Nottingham and nurseries at Leicester, Brighton and Chepstow: clearly regarded as a sprinter, though bred to stay beyond 6f: acts on fibresand and any turf going: sometimes on toes. *P. D. Evans* — 75

GAITERO (FR) 2 b.c. (Apr 10) Groom Dancer (USA) 128 – First Waltz (FR) 117 (Green Dancer (USA) 132) [1995 7g4 8d* 8s4 8g3 9s6 Nov 22] 335,000 francs Y: close-coupled, quite attractive colt: fourth foal: half-brother to 2 winners, including 1m and 9f winner Waltzer (by Highest Honor): dam won Prix Morny: useful French colt: won minor event at Longchamp in September: 5 lengths fourth of 6 to Le Triton in Prix La Rochette at Longchamp (carried head awkwardly), 3¼ lengths third of 5 to Ashkalani in Prix Thomas Bryon at Saint-Cloud and under 3 lengths sixth of 7 to Spinning World in steadily-run Prix Saint-Roman at Evry afterwards: stays 9f: yet to race on top-of-the-ground. *C. Laffon-Parias, France* — 101

GALACIA (IRE) 3 br.f. Gallic League 119 – Little Wild Duck 78 (Great Heron (USA) 127) [1994 52: 5s3 5g4 5.1m2 6s3 5m 1995 6f3 Jun 30] leggy filly: modest maiden: off course over 12 months, creditable effort at Folkestone only start in 1995: stays 6f: acts on firm ground and soft. *W. G. M. Turner* — 52

GALAFRON 3 ch.c. Nashwan (USA) 135 – Gayane 125 (Nureyev (USA) 131) [1994 NR 1995 8m4 8m Aug 3] lengthy colt: fine mover with a long stride: third foal: half-brother to 4-y-o Anisimova (by Kris): dam, 6f and 7f winner is half-sister to Sun Chariot winner Ristna, out of Nassau winner Roussalka, a half-sister to Oh So Sharp: hung badly right when last in maidens at Ripon and (blinkered) Pontefract: sold 1,200 gns Newmarket Autumn Sales. *J. H. M. Gosden* — –

GALAKA 2 b.f. (Apr 17) Slip Anchor 136 – Golden Glint (Vitiges (FR) 132) [1995 8m Sep 5] quite good-topped filly: has scope: has a powerful, roundish action: sixth foal: half-sister to 2 winners in Italy, including 8.5f to 1½m winner Gopuram (by Sharpo): dam lightly-raced half-sister to Main Reef and smart middle-distance filly Moonlight Night: 16/1 and better for race, never-dangerous ninth of 11 to Caribbean Quest in maiden at Leicester: should be capable of better. *L. M. Cumani* — – p

GALAPINO 2 b.c. (Apr 6) Charmer 123 – Carousella 62 (Rousillon (USA) 133) [1995 5m4 6g3 7g4 7m6 6.1d 6f 7m 6.9m Nov 6] smallish, leggy colt: first foal: dam 8.1f winner: disappointing after making frame in maidens first 2 starts: should stay 7f: sweating fifth outing. *C. E. Brittain* — 77 d

GALINE 2 b.f. (Mar 10) Most Welcome 131 – Tarasova (USA) (Green Forest (USA) 134) [1995 6g4 6g6 a5g* Nov 24] second foal: half-sister to 3-y-o 8.2f winner Wild Palm (by Darshaan): dam twice-raced half-sister to top-class French middle-distance colt Le Marmot: fair form: won 16-runner maiden at Southwell by 2 lengths from Mask Flower: stays 6f: acts on fibresand. *W. A. O'Gorman* — 78

GALLANTE 2 b.c. (Feb 8) Rainbow Quest (USA) 134 – Mary Sunley 62 (Known Fact (USA) 135) [1995 7f4 7m5 8f Aug 22] fifth foal: half-brother to several winners here and abroad, including 1½m winner Storm Dust (by Celestial Storm): dam, maiden suited by 1¼m, half-sister to Roseate Tern and Ibn Bey: modest form in £8,200 event at Salisbury, minor event at Lingfield and maiden at Brighton: bred to stay at least 1m: wore crossed noseband on debut: sold 6,500 gns Newmarket September Sales. *P. F. I. Cole* — 62 ?

GALLANT SPIRIT (IRE) 4 br.g. Gallic League 119 – So Valiant 80 (So Blessed 130) [1994 64: 7s 5v3 6d2 8.3g 7m5 6s5 5g* 6m 6m3 a5g4 1995 6m a6g 6m 6f Aug 11] leggy gelding: has a quick action: disappointing in 1995, but never encountered a soft surface: should stay 7f: goes well on a soft surface, probably — –

unsuited by top-of-the-ground: blinkered (out of form) fifth 3-y-o start: inconsistent: sold 500 gns Doncaster October Sales. *R. J. Hodges*

GALLARDINI (IRE) 6 b.g. Nordico (USA) – Sweet (Pitskelly 122) [1994 84d: 10g* 10d* 10s^{4} 11g 8g 8.5g 9g 8d 10.4d 1995 10.3g 10g 11.9m 10m^{2} 9.9m^{4} Jul 25] leggy ex-Irish gelding: only modest handicapper at best here: probably stays 11f: best form in Ireland on soft ground: fair hurdler. *B. S. Rothwell* — 55

GALLERY ARTIST (IRE) 7 ch.h. Tate Gallery (USA) 117 – Avec L'Amour 75 (Realm 129) [1994 52, a62: a7g^{6} a8g^{2} a8.5g* a8g a8g^{6} 7.1g^{2} a8g* a8.5g^{3} a8g^{2} a8g a8g a7g^{2} a8g a7g 1995 a8g^{3} a8g^{6} a9.4g* a8g^{4} Mar 20] small horse: poor mover: modest performer on his day: won seller at Wolverhampton in March: stays 9.4f: acts on soft going and all-weather surfaces: has won for claimer: tried blinkered earlier in career: inconsistent. *R. Guest* — – a55

GALLIC VICTORY (IRE) 4 b.g. Gallic League 119 – Sally St Clair (Sallust 134) [1994 7.8f 8m* 8m 8g^{3} 9g* 12g 8d 1995 10m 9.5g^{4} 9m 9m 7g a8g^{5} Dec 15] sixth foal: half-brother to 3 minor sprint winners: dam won in Canada: fair ex-Irish handicapper: won at Naas and Ballinrobe at 3 yrs: creditable effort second start in 1995, well below form afterwards: stays 9.5f: acts on good to firm ground: blinkered (well beaten) final 2-y-o start: sold out of D. Hanley's stable 5,000 gns Newmarket Autumn Sales after fifth start. *John Berry* — 70 d

GALLOP TO GLORY 5 b.g. Petong 126 – Merchantmens Girl 58 (Klairon 131) [1994 40: a12g a10g^{3} a10g a7g^{4} a7g a7g^{2} a9.4g^{3} 10d a8g a8.5g a8g^{6} a8.5g^{5} 1995 a8g a7g^{5} a8.5g Apr 1] good-topped gelding: poor maiden: no form in 1995: effective at 7f and 1¼m: acts on good to firm ground, dead and the all-weather: below form in blinkers/visor: inconsistent. *A. L. Forbes* — –

GALLOWS CORNER (IRE) 3 b.f. Nordico (USA) – Donnarella (Dom Racine (FR) 121) [1994 83: 5s^{3} 5.3d^{3} 5.1g^{3} 5g 6m* 6g 6g^{2} 7d 6.1d* 1995 6m 6m 6g^{3} 7.1g^{6} 7m^{6} 6d Sep 18] angular, light-framed filly: fairly useful handicapper: well below form last 3 starts: should prove well suited by further than 6f: acts on good to firm and dead ground: sold 8,000 gns Newmarket Autumn Sales. *R. Hannon* — 85

GALWAY BLADE 2 b.c. (Feb 3) Faustus (USA) 118 – Slipperose 72 (Persepolis (FR) 127) [1995 8g^{4} 8d 8g^{5} 8f Oct 12] 7,400Y: tall, close-coupled colt: second foal: dam 11.5f winner: best effort in maidens when fifth of 13 to Select Few at Goodwood in September: will stay beyond 1m: poor effort on firm ground final outing. *A. P. Jarvis* — 66 ?

GAME PLOY (POL) 3 b.g. Deploy 131 – Guestimate (FR) (Be My Guest (USA) 126) [1994 72p: 8d^{3} 8d 6v^{3} 1995 9m^{3} 13.4m^{3} 10m 10d 12.1s Oct 17] tall gelding: has a round action: best effort when third of 8 in maiden at Goodwood on reappearance: well below form afterwards: should stay beyond 9f: acts on good to firm and heavy ground. *F. Murphy* — 76 d

GAMZATTI 4 gr.f. Midyan (USA) 124 – Kenmara (FR) (Kenmare (FR) 125) [1994 –: 10.3m 7g 10g 1995 a7g 10m a9.4g 10g 8m 9f Aug 5] leggy plain filly: of no account. *C. B. B. Booth* — –

GANADOR 3 gr.f. Weldnaas (USA) 112 – Shakana 91 (Grundy 137) [1994 67: 6.1g^{4} 6m^{2} 5m^{5} 1995 5.1g a7g^{3} 8.3g^{6} 7g^{2} 7.1m a7g 6.9g Oct 16] leggy filly: disappointing maiden: well beaten last 3 starts: nervy sort. *J. Berry* — 49 d

GANT BLEU (FR) 8 ch.g. Crystal Glitters (USA) 127 – Gold Honey (Artaius (USA) 129) [1994 57d: 7g^{2} 8m^{2} 7.5m 7m^{5} 7g 7g 7g 7d 8d 1995 8f 8m 7m^{3} 7m 8g 7m^{5} 8f^{5} Jun 22] rather sparely-made gelding: unimpressive looker and mover: seems poor nowadays: stays 1m: acts on hard and dead ground: visored (well below form) once at 3 yrs: inconsistent. *R. M. Whitaker* — 46 d

GARBONI (USA) 6 ch.g. Theatrical 128 – Royal Strait Flush (USA) (Seattle Slew (USA)) [1994 12d^{4} 12m 1995 a12g^{4} Feb 20] fourth foal: half-brother to 2 minor winners by Danzig and smart American 4-y-o filly Jade Flush (by Jade Hunter): dam unraced: fairly useful performer at his best in Ireland (winner 3 times at 3 yrs, once at 4 yrs) and rated 82 on reappearance at 5 yrs: sold out of D. Weld's stable 4,000 gns Doncaster October (1994) Sales: well beaten here: stays 13f: acts on heavy going. *D. Moffatt* — –

GARDEN OF HEAVEN (USA) 6 ch.g. Arctic Tern (USA) 126 – Garden of Eden 63 (Exbury 138) [1994 109: 10v 10s^{6} 10g^{3} 8m 10d 10g^{6} 10m* 10v^{5} 1995 9m — 99

12m^6 10.4g 10d^6 12m 12m^4 10g^5 Jul 22] sturdy, attractive gelding: unimpressive mover: never realised the potential shown when winning Prix du Conseil de Paris at Longchamp (rated 117p) in 1992: towards rear in pattern races, rated stakes events and a listed contest in 1995: best efforts at 1¼m/1½m: acted on good to firm and heavy going: held up: died following an operation in August. *C. E. Brittain*

GARDEN ROSE (IRE) 3 ch.f. Caerleon (USA) 132 – Gironde (USA) (Raise A 115 Native) [1994 8g^3 8s* 8g^4 8s^6 1995 8g* 10.5m 9g* 10g^3 9.3d^4 Oct 1] good-topped, attractive filly: fifth foal: sister to 1988 Queen Mary winner Gloriella, half-sister to a minor winner by Antheus and closely related to French 5-y-o miler Gaio (by Caerwent): dam second over 1m from 3 starts at 3 yrs in France: smart performer: won minor event at Deauville then around ½-length fourth of 6 to Macoumba in Prix Marcel Boussac at Longchamp at 2 yrs: won listed event at Saint-Cloud in May and 7-runner Prix Chloe at Evry (by a head from Take Liberties) in July: beaten 2 short heads by Matiara in 4-runner Prix de la Nonette at Deauville in August, creditable fourth of 11 to Timarida in Prix de l'Opera at Longchamp in October: stays 10.5f: acts on good to firm ground and soft. *P. Bary, France*

GARLANDE D'OR 3 b.f. Belfort (FR) 89 – Torville Gold (Aragon 118) [1994 50 d 53: 5f^3 5d^6 5m 5d^4 5s 1995 6.1g^6 a7g^6 6m 7.5m 7.1m Jul 13] leggy filly: poor maiden: well below form after reappearance: should stay 7f: acts on good to firm and dead ground, stiff task on soft: hurdling with P. Hiatt. *J. L. Spearing*

GARNOCK VALLEY 5 b.g. Dowsing (USA) 124 – Sunley Sinner 93 (Try My 74 d Best (USA) 130) [1994 88d: 6m^3 6s^3 6m 6m 6s^4 a6g^4 7m 7m^2 7g^2 6d 6d^6 7s^6 1995 8g^4 7m 6g 6g 7f Oct 14] neat gelding: regressed with every start in 1995: best efforts at 6f: probably acts on any going on turf, not discredited on fibresand: sometimes forces pace: seems best fresh. *J. Berry*

GATE OF HEAVEN 5 b.m. Starry Night (USA) – Halatch (Habat 127) [1994 –: 21 a12g a7g 1995 6.1g a6g^6 a6g^5 a5g 6m^4 a6g 6f 8m Aug 27] leggy mare: poor maiden a24 handicapper: trained until after fifth start by John Berry: stays 7.5f: acts on fibresand and good to firm ground: tried blinkered/visored: joined R. Spicer. *C. A. Dwyer*

GAY GALLANTA (USA) 3 ch.f. Woodman (USA) 126 – Gallanta (FR) 106 (Nureyev (USA) 131) [1994 112: 5d^5 5m* 6m^2 6s^3 6m* 1995 7.3m^5 8m 8m^5 8g^2 7f Jul 25] compact, attractive filly: best European 2-y-o filly in 1994: only useful form in 1995, best effort when short-head second of 5 to Caramba in slowly-run Falmouth Stakes at Newmarket: stays 1m: acts on good to firm ground: visored (no improvement) third 3-y-o start: ridden for a turn of foot. *M. R. Stoute*

GEE GEE TEE 2 ch.c. (Apr 30) Superlative 118 – Glorietta (USA) (Shadeed – (USA) 135) [1995 7d 6.9s 7g 6.9m Nov 6] 2,200F, 3,100Y: angular, workmanlike colt: second foal: dam unraced daughter of speedy Bitty Girl, a sister to Hot Spark: well beaten in varied events, including a nursery: has worn bandages. *J. Akehurst*

GEISWAY (CAN) 5 br.g. Geiger Counter (USA) – Broadway Beauty (USA) – (Chompion (USA)) [1994 97: 11.7m 10s 10s^5 10g^2 10m^3 10m 10.4f^4 10m 1995 8g 10m 12d 12m Jun 21] leggy, lengthy gelding: most disappointing in 1995: stays 11.1f: acts on any going: tried visored, no form: held up: needs treating with caution: has been gelded. *N. J. H. Walker*

GELSEMINE 2 b.f. (Feb 26) Mtoto 134 – Gelatine (Bold Lad (IRE) 133) [1995 73 6g 7f^3 6g Sep 1] angular filly: sixth foal: closely related to Italian 5-y-o 7f (at 2 yrs) to 15f winner Gianani (by Bustino) and half-sister to a winner there: dam ran once: third of 10 to Villeggiatura in maiden at Salisbury in August: hung left throughout when last of 14 in claimer at Haydock following month: headstrong: sold 1,600 gns Newmarket Autumn Sales. *H. Candy*

GEMOLLY (IRE) 2 b.f. (Mar 2) Be My Native (USA) 122 – Hayhurst – (Sandhurst Prince 128) [1995 6m 8d Sep 27] angular filly: second foal: dam staying maiden on flat in Ireland won over hurdles: little promise in median auction events at Windsor (not well drawn) and Salisbury (bit backward) 3 months later. *Martyn Meade*

GENERAL ASSEMBLY (IRE) 3 b.c. Pharly (FR) 130 – Hastening (Shirley 92 p Heights 130) [1994 NR 1995 12f^3 14g^2 14m^4 13.4d* Sep 20] IR 26,000Y: good-bodied colt: poor mover: third foal: closely related to 11f winner Alacrity (by Alzao): dam, unraced, from family of Kris and Diesis: off course over 3 months and

6/5 on, won 12-runner maiden at Chester in September by 7 lengths from Dato Star, leading over 2f out: likely to benefit from test of stamina: acts on firm and dead ground: bandaged off-hind second and third starts: stays in training and is useful prospect. *H. R. A. Cecil*

GENERAL CHAOS (IRE) 5 b.g. Taufan (USA) 119 – Isa (Dance In Time (CAN)) [1994 8s* 8v³ 8v 7g⁴ 8s⁵ 12g 8g* 8.5m 8m⁵ 8d³ 1995 8g 7f 7g Jul 17] IR 17,000Y: workmanlike, ex-Irish gelding: half-brother to several winners: dam never ran: fairly useful performer (rated 88) in Ireland for C. Collins, successful in maiden at 3 yrs and 2 handicaps at 4 yrs: below his best here: suited by 1m: probably acts on any going: won maiden hurdle in July. *J. J. O'Neill* –

GENERAL CHASE 5 ch.m. Scottish Reel 123 – Make A Signal 76 (Royal Gunner (USA)) [1994 –: 10m a12g⁶ 1995 a10g⁴ a10g³ a12g 12m May 9] sturdy mare: rated 63 at best at 3 yrs: failed to come on for reappearance: should stay beyond 1¼m: acts on good to firm and dead ground: visored (tailed off) final start. *I. Campbell* 47

GENERAL EQUATION 2 b.g. (Apr 27) Governor General 116 – Logarithm (King of Spain 121) [1995 5m a5g 5d a5g Sep 30] 2,400Y: first foal: dam poor half-sister to smart sprinter Northern Goddess: no worthwhile form, including in sellers. *J. Balding* –

GENERAL GLOW 2 b.c. (Feb 10) Presidium 124 – Glow Again 78 (The Brianstan 128) [1995 7g 7g 10m Oct 19] 5,400Y: tall colt: fourth foal: brother to 3-y-o Double Glow, 5f winner at 2 yrs: dam 2-y-o 5f and 6f winner: signs of ability in maiden events. *N. Bycroft* –

GENERAL GUBBINS 4 b.g. Mashhor Dancer (USA) – Crag Hall 81 (Sharpo 132) [1994 62: 5g⁵ 5m 6g* 7m 7m⁶ 6g⁶ 9.9f 8.1d 1995 6f⁴ 6m 8m 5m 7d Sep 27] sturdy gelding: good mover: modest handicapper: well below form after reappearance: should have stayed beyond 6f: acted on firm going: dead. *J. Hetherton* 61 d

GENERAL HAVEN 2 ch.c. (Mar 6) Hadeer 118 – Verchinina 99 (Star Appeal 133) [1995 a10g a7g Dec 6] 3,400Y: brother to 3-y-o Platinum Plus, winner in Czech Republic in 1995, and 1½m winner Golden Hadeer and half-brother to 9.9f winner Romola Nijinsky (by Bustino): dam 1m winner: no worthwhile form in late-season maidens at Lingfield. *T. J. Naughton* –

GENERAL HENRY 2 b.g. (Feb 28) Belmez (USA) 131 – Western Star 107 (Alcide 136) [1995 a8g a7g Dec 14] 2,000 2-y-o: half-brother to several winners, including 1m and 1½m winner Startino (by Bustino) and 1982 2-y-o 5f winner Star of Taurus (by Mansingh), both useful: dam 7f and 1¼m winner: slowly away and always behind in maiden and claimer at Lingfield late in year. *A. Moore* –

GENERAL MACARTHUR 2 b.c. (Apr 13) Alzao (USA) 117 – Royal Climber (Kings Lake (USA) 133) [1995 6g 7f 8.2d 8g 8f² Oct 24] 30,000Y: compact colt: second foal: half-brother to 3-y-o 1¼m winner Heboob Alshemaal (by Nordico): dam, Irish 7f (at 2 yrs) and 13f winner, half-sister to Oaks d'Italia winner Ivyanna: much improved effort when 4 lengths second of 12 to Lady Carla in maiden at Leicester: will be suited by further than 1m: acts on firm ground. *J. L. Dunlop* 83

GENERAL MONASH (USA) 3 b.c. Thorn Dance (USA) 107 – Zummerudd (Habitat 134) [1994 107: 5.2s* 5f³ 5.5g* 6g 1995 8d⁶ 6.5g Aug 6] strong, good-quartered colt: useful form: never-dangerous 8½ lengths sixth of 8 to Vettori in Poule d'Essai des Poulains at Longchamp in May and last of 10 in Prix Maurice de Gheest at Deauville: creditable effort at 1m, but should prove best at sprint distances: best form on an easy surface (reported to have had ulcers in throat when tried on firm) and goes well on soft. *P. W. Chapple-Hyam* 101

GENERAL MOUKTAR 5 ch.g. Hadeer 118 – Fly The Coop (Kris 135) [1994 NR 1995 12g 12m 12.3m³ 14s⁴ 14f³ 11.8g 12f⁵ 12d 14.1m Oct 26] compact, good-quartered gelding: has fluent, round action: rated 85 at 3 yrs, but only fair form in the spring at 5 yrs, and well beaten last 5 starts: probably effective at 1¼m to 1¾m: acts on good to firm and soft ground: blinkered/visored since third 5-y-o start: has joined B. Meehan. *M. C. Pipe* 74 d

GENERAL ROSE 2 b.c. (May 4) Governor General 116 – Aleda Rose 56 (Charlottown 127) [1995 5.3m* 5m⁵ 6f 7g³ 6f 7f² 7m³ 7g³ 7m⁴ Nov 4] 4,000F, 5,000Y: rather leggy, unfurnished colt: brother to 7f winner Knyaz and half-brother 73

Asko Appliances Zetland Stakes, Newmarket—a fine staying performance from the youngster Gentilhomme

to a winner abroad: dam won from 7f to 1¼m: won median auction maiden at Brighton in April: creditable efforts in frame in well-contested auction event at Goodwood and nursery at Doncaster on last 2 starts: stays 7f: acts on firm ground: sold 12,000 gns Newmarket Autumn Sales. *R. Hannon*

GENERAL SHIRLEY (IRE) 4 b.g. Shirley Heights 130 – Adjala 89 (Northfields (USA)) [1994 68d: 8v⁵ 7.1g² 10m² 10g 11.5m⁴ 8g 10.8s 1995 a10g⁵ 8.3m May 15] smallish, close-coupled gelding: disappointing maiden: stays 1¼m: acts on good to firm ground, respectable effort on equitrack: tried blinkered/visored, no form: one to be wary of. *P. R. Hedger* – §

GENERAL SIR PETER (IRE) 3 br.g. Last Tycoon 131 – Nashya (Rousillon (USA) 133) [1994 NR 1995 5d* 7.3g 5f* 5m⁶ 5g* Sep 8] big, lengthy, unfurnished gelding: first foal: dam never ran: successful in maiden at Warwick (dead heat) in April, and handicaps at Doncaster in July and (led post having been soon off bridle) September: should stay at least 6f: acts on firm and dead ground: sold only 9,000 gns Newmarket Autumn Sales. *P. F. I. Cole* 78

GENEREUX 2 ch.g. (Apr 9) Generous (IRE) 139 – Flo Russell (USA) (Round Table) [1995 8.1m Aug 28] 145,000Y: half-brother to several winners, including very useful Irish sprinter Flowing (by El Gran Senor) and useful 1m winner Crockadore (by Nijinsky), later stayed 1½m: dam placed in USA: tailed off in maiden at Chepstow: sold only 4,200 gns Newmarket Autumn Sales. *P. F. I. Cole* –

GENEROSA 2 b.f. (Apr 25) Generous (IRE) 139 – Hotel Street (USA) 93 (Alleged (USA) 138) [1995 7m² Aug 31] tall, rather unfurnished filly: sixth foal: half-sister to 7f (at 2 yrs) and 11f winner Widyan (by Fappiano) and 1991 2-y-o 7f winner Providence (by Diesis): dam, lightly-raced 1½m winner, half-sister to Royal And Regal and Regal And Royal: weak 12/1-shot, 2½ lengths second of 10 to comfortable winner More Than You Know in maiden at Salisbury, staying on from rear: sure to improve, particularly over middle distances. *H. Candy* 80 p

GENEROUS PRESENT 2 ch.g. (Feb 21) Cadeaux Genereux 131 – Dance Move (Shareef Dancer (USA) 135) [1995 6m 7m 6g Sep 21] 19,000Y: tall gelding: has a round action: second foal: dam once-raced daughter of half-sister to smart French middle-distance filly Joli Vert: burly, well beaten in maidens. *J. W. Payne* –

GENESIS FOUR 5 b.g. Dreams To Reality (USA) 113 – Relma (Relko 136) [1994 37: 6d³ 7g 6.1s 8g 8d a8g 1995 a7g² a8g* a8g a8g a12g⁴ a11g⁶ a7g² a8g a8g² a9.4g 8m 8m a8g 8m³ 6m Aug 22] neat gelding: unimpressive mover: poor handicapper: won at Southwell (apprentices) in January: effective at 7f, barely stays 1½m: acts on good to firm and dead ground and goes well on all-weather surfaces: wears blinkers: inconsistent. *S. R. Bowring* 37 a46

GENOVEFA (USA) 3 b.f. Woodman (USA) 126 – Reigning Countess (USA) (Far North (CAN) 120) [1994 8.5g³ 8v² 1995 10d⁴ 10g* 12g* 12m³ 13.5g⁴ 12.5s³ Sep 30] $140,000F: well-made filly: fourth foal: half-sister to useful Grade 3 8.5f winning filly Miss Turkana (by Turkoman) and smart 1994 3-y-o 1m and 1¼m winner Grafin (by Miswaki): dam smart 7f/1m performer in USA: useful French filly: won minor event in May and Prix de Royaumont (led near finish, beat Enquiry a short head) in June, both at Saint-Cloud: creditable efforts in frame in Prix de 107

Malleret at Longchamp, Prix de Pomone at Deauville and Prix de Royallieu (3¾ lengths third of 9 to Russian Snows) at Longchamp afterwards: stayed 13.5f: acted on good to firm ground and soft: consistent: stud. *A. Fabre, France*

GENTILHOMME 2 ch.c. (Jan 23) Generous (IRE) 139 – Bold Flawless (USA) 73 (Bold Bidder) [1995 6m 7f² 7m³ 10.2m* 10m* Oct 28] 90,000Y: tall, good-topped colt: good mover: half-brother to 3 winners, including useful 1988 2-y-o 6f and 7f winner Life At The Top (by Habitat): dam 1½m winner: progressive form: won maiden at Bath in September and (ridden much more enterprisingly) listed Asko Appliances Zetland Stakes at Newmarket in October in good style by 5 lengths from Weet-A-Minute: out-and-out galloper who requires a good test of stamina: sweating third start: will progress further. *P. F. I. Cole* — 100 p

GENTLE FRIEND 2 b.f. (May 14) Dominion 123 – Burnished (Formidable (USA) 125) [1995 6g 6m Jun 26] 16,500Y: half-sister to several winners, including fair sprinters Chain Shot (by Pas de Seul) and The Kings Daughter (by Indian King): dam unraced half-sister to smart miler Hadeer: poor form in maiden at Folkestone and median auction maiden at Windsor: sold 2,000 gns Newmarket Autumn Sales. *J. L. Dunlop* — –

GENTLE IRONY 3 b.f. Mazilier (USA) 107 – Irenic 64 (Mummy's Pet 125) [1994 63: 6g 6g 7.6v* 7s 7m 1995 a7g 9.9m⁴ 9.9m² 10.8g* 13.8g⁶ 10.1g⁵ 10g⁵ 10m³ 10g⁵ 8.5m* 8f⁵ 8.2m* 9m⁶ 10.1m² 8g 8g a7g² a8.5g⁶ 8.2m* 8f⁴ a7g⁵ a8.5g Dec 12] small filly: modest performer: well placed, and won claimers at Warwick (claimed out of P. Makin's stable £5,000) in May, Epsom in July, Nottingham in August and Nottingham (awarded race) in October: effective at 7f to 10.8f: acts on fibresand and on good to firm and heavy ground: blinkered nowadays: tough but none too consistent. *B. J. Meehan* — 60

GENTLEMAN SID 5 b.g. Brotherly (USA) 80 – Eugenes Chance (Flashback 102) [1994 –: 11.8d 14g 1995 12m 16.4g 16.1g³ 18.2m* 16.2g⁴ 16.4m* Aug 18] strong, attractive gelding: progressive (gelded and given soft palate operation) for new stable in 1995: won maiden handicap at Chepstow (leading early in straight and eased) in July and handicap at Sandown (led over 3f out) in August: suited by test of stamina: acts on good to firm ground: looked sure to continue to run well. *P. G. Murphy* — 52

GEOLLY (IRE) 3 b.g. Formidable (USA) 125 – Four-Legged Friend 101 (Aragon 118) [1994 –: 5m 1995 a8.5g⁶ a7g Nov 14] sturdy, workmanlike gelding: no form in maidens. *Dr J. D. Scargill* — –

GEORGE BULL 3 b.g. Petoski 135 – Firgrove 73 (Relkino 131) [1994 NR 1995 10m⁶ 10m 10m 13.3f 11.4d³ 11.8g Oct 9] tall, unfurnished gelding: third foal: closely related to fairly useful 1994 3-y-o 11.8f winner (stays 1¾m) Farringdon Hill (by Minster Son): dam 1¼m winner: caught the eye third start, ran too badly to be true on fourth: fair form in big fields in handicaps at Sandown and Leicester last 2 starts: looks a stayer: probably acts on good to firm and dead ground: capable of better granted test of stamina. *Major W. R. Hern* — 68 +

GEORGE DILLINGHAM 5 b.g. Top Ville 129 – Premier Rose 117 (Sharp Edge 123) [1994 89: 12v² 12d 12.4m 14g² 14m* 14m² 13.9m⁶ 13.3s 12m 1995 12g² 11.9m 13.1g⁴ 13.9m³ 16.1m³ Jul 1] workmanlike gelding: has a round action: fairly useful handicapper: ran creditably for new stable in 1995 when in frame, leading briefly over 2f out when 4¾ lengths third of 17 to Bold Gait in Northumberland Plate at Newcastle last time: subsequently gelded: stays 2m: acts on good to firm ground and heavy: visored (well below form) second 5-y-o outing: genuine. *Denys Smith* — 84

GERMANE 3 b.f. Distant Relative 128 – Fraulein Tobin (USA) 71 (J O Tobin (USA) 130) [1994 100p: 6g³ 6g³ 6s³ 7g² 7m* 1995 7m⁴ 10m⁶ 10.4m⁵ 7f 7g Sep 7] leggy filly: useful performer at best: 5 lengths fourth of 8 to Myself in steadily-run Nell Gwyn Stakes at Newmarket on reappearance: well below form afterwards, often failing to take the eye: seems not to stay 1¼m. *M. Bell* — 100 d

GERMANO 2 b.c. (Apr 3) Generous (IRE) 139 – Gay Fantastic (Ela-Mana-Mou 132) [1995 7g 7m* Oct 20] 220,000Y: tall, close-coupled colt: half-brother to several winners including 1m and 1¼m winner Potentate (by Capote): dam unraced sister to very useful middle-distance filly Gay Hellene: won 21-runner maiden at Doncaster by length from Tarneem, leading well over 1f out and running on well despite looking — 89 P green: will be very well suited by middle distances: sure to do better again, and looks a good prospect. *G. Wragg*

GERMANY (USA) 4 b.c. Trempolino (USA) 135 – Inca Princess (USA) (Big Spruce (USA)) [1994 11d* 1995 11v* 10s* 12s^3 11m^2 10g* 12s* 12g^4 10m Oct 14] 123

For the third year in a row the Germans kept five of their six Group 1 races at home, the most successful of the defenders in 1995 being the appropriately-named four-year-old Germany, winner of the Bayerisches Zuchtrennen and the Grosser Preis von Baden. Germany fractured his off-fore after a promising two-year-old season and had only one race as a three-year-old, winning a minor event in the autumn. He enjoyed a full campaign as a four-year-old, starting off by winning a listed race at Cologne in March by nine lengths from three established smart performers in Caballo, Embarcadero and Concepcion. Another defeat of Caballo in a Group 3 contest at Gelsenkirchen was followed by two races against the high-class Monsun. Germany came off worse both times, going down by two lengths in the Gerling Preis at Cologne at the end of April, and losing the Idee Hansa-Preis at Hamburg in June in the stewards' room after passing the post three quarters of a length ahead, hanging and hampering his rival at the furlong pole. Then came Germany's two important victories. He won the Dr Poth Bayerisches Zuchtrennen at Munich in July smoothly by a length and a half from Kaldounevees, with Tryphosa and odds-on Definite Article beaten a further length and half a length, but it was Germany's performance in the Grosser Preis von Baden that really stood out. While Lando and Strategic Choice failed to give their running, Germany turned the race into a procession, drawing right away to beat Lecroix by a long-looking five lengths with the remainder strung out. Talk of supplementing Germany for the Arc came to nothing, with the Al Maktoum family already well represented, and Germany went instead for the Europa Preis at Cologne where he managed only fourth to Solon, after reportedly getting very worked up in the paddock beforehand. On his only subsequent outing, he failed by a long way to give his running in the Champion Stakes at Newmarket in October, dropping right out.

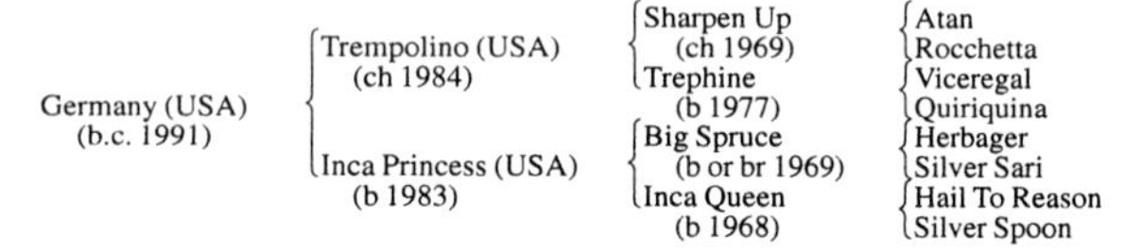

Germany (USA)
(b.c. 1991)
Trempolino (USA)
(ch 1984)
Sharpen Up
(ch 1969)
Atan
Rocchetta
Trephine
(b 1977)
Viceregal
Quiriquina
Inca Princess (USA)
(b 1983)
Big Spruce
(b or br 1969)
Herbager
Silver Sari
Inca Queen
(b 1968)
Hail To Reason
Silver Spoon

Germany has earned his fame and fortune in Germany, but his family is American, his third dam Silver Spoon being the Santa Anita Derby winner and joint-champion three-year-old filly in 1959 and her best produce, Germany's grandam Inca Queen, being one of the best older fillies of 1972. Germany's dam Inca Princess was the only one of Inca Queen's foals to race in the British Isles, and she showed modest form in winning a six-furlong maiden in Ireland. She clearly had a future at stud, however, given that she was a half-sister to Grade 2 winners Exile King and Hail Bold King. Since Inca Princess, the best offspring has been Metfield, winner of a Grade 3 event over a mile as a three-year-old and a prominent first-season stallion in 1995. Inca Princess produced foals every year from 1988 until 1994. After fetching $160,000 while carrying her second foal, she was resold, while carrying her sixth, for a mere $17,000. She looks a bargain now with all four of her offspring to reach the track having won, but her new owners have not yet reaped the benefit given that her 1993 foal died, and she was barren in 1995. Germany's sire Trempolino has yet to get a horse anywhere near so good as himself, though with Germany, Champion Stakes winner Dernier Empereur, the very smart but wayward Talloires and plenty of smart performers to represent him he is certainly a well-above-average sire. The good-topped, attractive Germany stayed a mile and a half and acted on good to firm and heavy going and was effective making the running or tracking the pace. He has been retired to Gestut Rietberg, fee on application. *Bruno Schutz, Germany*

GET TOUGH 2 b.c. (Feb 26) Petong 126 – Mrs Waddilove 79 (Bustino 136) [1995 6m 6g^6 6g 8d^6 6.9m Nov 6] 4,600F, 6,000Y, resold 5,600Y: leggy colt: fourth living foal: dam maiden stayed 7f: modest maiden: seems to stay 1m. *S. Dow* 58

GHALAYAN 3 ch.c. Nashwan (USA) 135 – Al Sylah 118 (Nureyev (USA) 131) [1994 NR 1995 8m^{4} Jul 28] big colt: fourth foal: half-brother to 7f winner Yaqthan (by Kris): dam sprinter: weak 9/4-shot and green, always outpaced in 4-runner maiden at Thirsk: sold 24,000 gns Newmarket Autumn Sales. *H. Thomson Jones* –

GHEDI (POL) 4 b.g. Vilnius (POL) – Ghaza (POL) (Pawiment (POL) 118) [1994 7g^{5} 8g^{4} 9g^{5} 9g^{2} 9g^{2} 9g* 9g^{3} 11g 8g 9g^{2} 9g^{3} 9g^{6} 1995 12.3m a8.5g Jul 21] Polish-bred gelding: recorded 1 win (over 5f) from 4 runs at 2 yrs and 1 win (over 9f) at 3 yrs in Poland: no form in claimers on flat here. *Miss Gay Kelleway* –

GHOSTLY APPARITION 2 gr.g. (Feb 28) Gods Solution 70 – Tawny 81 (Grey Ghost 98) [1995 5m^{3} 5m 5m 5m^{4} 6.1m^{4} a6g a6g^{2} 6s Sep 30] 1,250Y: tall, leggy gelding: first living foal: dam 2-y-o 5f and 6f winner: plater: good effort penultimate outing (ridden by 7-lb claimer): stays 6f: acts on equitrack and good to firm ground, ran poorly on soft. *John R. Upson* 53

GHOSTLY (IRE) 3 b.f. Fairy King (USA) – Gold Quest (FR) (Rainbow Quest (USA) 134) [1994 103: 7f^{5} 8s* 7g* 8d* 7v 1995 8d^{4} 8d^{6} 8g^{4} 8g^{4} 6g Aug 22] small filly: smart French performer: ran well in Prix de la Grotte and Poule d'Essai des Pouliches (5¾ lengths sixth to Matiara) at Longchamp, in Irish 1000 Guineas (6½ lengths behind Ridgewood Pearl) at the Curragh and Prix d'Astarte (2¾ lengths behind Smolensk) at Deauville: dropped down to 6f for Prix de Meautry at Deauville, below form never able to challenge: will be suited by further than 1m: acts on soft ground. *P. Bary, France* 110

GIDDY 2 b. or br.f. (Apr 20) Polar Falcon (USA) 126 – Spin Turn (Homing 130) [1995 7g Sep 28] sparely-made filly: sixth foal: half-sister to 3-y-o Swivel (by Salse) and 3 winners, including smart 7f (at 2 yrs) and 8.1f winner Dance Turn (by Damister) and 10.5f winner Whirl (by Bellypha): dam unraced daughter of Oaks third The Dancer: 50/1, slowly away then kept on when in mid-division of 23-runner maiden at Newmarket won by Astor Place: should do better. *D. Morley* – p

GIFTED 3 b.f. Shareef Dancer (USA) 135 – Rexana (Relko 136) [1994 –: 5f a7g 1995 a8g 9.9m 12m^{4} Jul 28] workmanlike filly: of little account. *Don Enrico Incisa* –

GIGFY 3 b.g. Warrshan (USA) 117 – Empty Purse (Pennine Walk 120) [1994 44, a60: 7m a6g^{5} a7g 6d^{5} a8g* 7g 10g 1995 a7g a7g^{6} a8g^{5} a7g^{5} a8.5g^{5} a7g 8.1m 12m 12.1m Jul 20] sturdy gelding: only poor form at best for new stable: stays 1m: acts on all-weather surfaces: tried blinkered, no improvement: poor (winning) form over hurdles. *B. J. Llewellyn* – a41 d

GIGGLESWICK GIRL 4 b.f. Full Extent (USA) 113 – Foligno (Crofter (USA) 124) [1994 59: 5v 6.1f^{5} 5s 7d^{5} a6g^{3} 1995 a7g a7g a6g^{5} 8s^{5} a7g 6.1g^{2} 6g 5.3m^{4} 5f* 5g 6f^{3} 5m* 5g^{3} 5f 5m* 5m^{4} 5m^{6} 5.9f^{3} 5.1m^{3} 5g^{4} 5f^{3} 5.1h^{5} 5f 5.1h^{3} 5.1h^{4} 5m^{4} 5.7h^{2} 5g 5d 5f 5.1m 6m Oct 30] leggy, sparely-made filly: fair handicapper: won at Carlisle (2 minor events) and Edinburgh in space of 5 weeks in May/June: held her form long time, but below form last 5 starts: effective at 5f, and should stay 7f: acts on hard and soft ground and on all-weather surfaces: often slowly away: tough. *M. R. Channon* 66 a–

GIGGLESWICK GOSSIP 3 b.f. Full Extent (USA) 113 – Foligno (Crofter (USA) 124) [1994 50: 5v^{3} 5d 6g^{6} 6f^{3} 7m^{3} a7g^{3} 6m* 6m a6g 6g^{3} 6g^{6} 5d 1995 5.3m 6m 8f Jul 1] small, sparely-made filly: no form in 1995: stays 7f: acts on good to firm ground, poor efforts on fibresand and a soft surface: inconsistent and not one to trust. *M. R. Channon* –

GI LA HIGH 2 gr.f. (Mar 26) Rich Charlie 117 – Gem of Gold 52 (Jellaby 124) [1995 a5g^{3} a5g* a5g^{2} a5g* 5.1f^{2} 5g^{5} a6g^{4} a5g^{5} a5g* Dec 18] 2,200Y: compact filly: poor mover: fourth foal: half-sister to fair sprinter Captain Carat (by Handsome Sailor): dam sprinter: won sellers at Wolverhampton and Southwell in the spring, and claimer at Lingfield in December: best form at 5f: acts on firm ground and fibresand: below form blinkered/visored. *J. Berry* 61

GILDORAN SOUND 2 b.f. (May 9) Gildoran 123 – Sound of Laughter (Hasty Word 84) [1995 7m Oct 30] 1,250Y: workmanlike filly: fifth reported foal: dam won 3 times over hurdles: 33/1 and bandaged behind, showed up 4f then faded into last in 14-runner maiden at Newcastle. *M. H. Easterby* –

GILLING DANCER (IRE) 2 b.c. (Feb 23) Dancing Dissident (USA) 119 – Rahwah 73 (Northern Baby (CAN) 127) [1995 6.1d 6d^{5} 6m^{4} Oct 30] IR 21,000Y: strong, angular colt: fourth live foal: half-brother to 1992 2-y-o 5f winner Caps 58 p

Ninety-Two (by Magicial Wonder) and fairly useful 4-y-o 1¼m and 11f winner Locorotondo (by Broken Hearted): dam, 1½m winner, out of sister to Prix Robert Papin winner Maelstrom Lake: modest form in maidens at Nottingham and Newcastle (2): sweating and on toes, never-dangerous 11 lengths fourth of 12, not knocked about, behind Pivotal on final outing: will stay 7f: remains capable of better. *P. Calver*

GILPA BLISS 4 b.f. Kabour 80 – Wind And Reign 55 (Tumble Wind (USA)) [1994 NR 1995 a5g Sep 4] fourth foal (all by Kabour): sister to fair 6-y-o sprinter Kalar: dam, plater, seemed to stay 1m: tailed off in Southwell claimer. *D. W. Chapman* –

GILPA TRINKETS 3 b.g. Full Extent (USA) 113 – Delightful Diane 49 (Kalaglow 132) [1994 41: a5g5 5g a5g6 5m6 a5g 6m 6g 7g 1995 a6g 8.1g 8.2m 6g 5f 6m 5g Sep 2] compact gelding: poor maiden handicapper: well beaten in 1995: blinkered last 3 starts. *D. W. Chapman* –

GILT THRONE 8 b.g. Thatching 131 – Nikara (FR) (Emerson) [1994 80: 7d 6.9s3 5.9v* 6.9v4 6g* 5g2 6f 5g6 6d6 6s 5m5 6.1g 5v 1995 6m May 27] leggy, workmanlike gelding: has a round action: formerly a fairly useful performer: changed hands only 2,000 gns Newmarket Autumn (1994) Sales and well beaten both starts since: probably stays 7f: below form on firm ground but acts on any other: tongue tied down nowadays: inconsistent: has joined G. Margarson. *M. H. Tompkins* –

GINAS GIRL 2 gr.f. (Jan 1) Risk Me (FR) 127 – Grey Cree 64 (Creetown 123) [1995 a5g Nov 24] 1,600Y: fourth reported live foal: dam 2-y-o 5f and 6f winner: 20/1, always behind in 16-runner maiden at Southwell. *S. R. Bowring* –

GINGER GLINT 2 ch.c. (Feb 9) Hadeer 118 – Sorayah 89 (Persian Bold 123) [1995 a6g6 6m5 6m5 7m2 7m4 7f* 7g 7g Sep 29] 6,200Y: good-topped colt: fourth foal: half-brother to 6f winner Billy Cruncheon (by Sharpo) and to a winner in Austria by Vaguely Noble: dam sprinter here, later won at up to 11f in USA: plater: won at Thirsk in August: better suited by 7f than less and will stay 1m: acts on firm ground: sold 6,200 gns Newmarket Autumn Sales. *M. J. Heaton-Ellis* 54

GINGER HODGERS 2 ch.f. (May 6) Crofthall 110 – Jarrettelle (All Systems Go 119) [1995 6m 6f5 5f 7g Sep 16] first foal: dam unraced: signs of ability in varied events. *R. M. Whitaker* –

GINGERILLO 4 ch.g. Aragon 118 – Titian Beauty (Auction Ring (USA) 123) [1994 35: 10.8v6 10.2g 8.3d 8.1s4 7f3 7m 5.1g a7g6 1995 a7g4 a7g a6g a6g Feb 7] angular gelding: poor maiden plater: stays 1m: acts on any going: normally blinkered, also wore hood final 4-y-o start: none too consistent. *T. G. Mills* 33

GINGER JIM 4 ch.g. Jalmood (USA) 126 – Stratch (FR) 71 (Thatch (USA) 136) [1994 53: 10m 9.7m 11.6f 7d 11.5d3 11.8d 1995 a12g3 a10g6 a12g3 10g3 12g3 12m3 14m3 12m 11.9d4 14.1m4 Oct 19] workmanlike gelding: shows knee action: still a maiden: long way below form last 3 starts: stays 1¾m: acts on dead ground and good to firm: tried visored, no improvement: fair hurdler, winner twice in the autumn. *P. R. Hedger* 66

GINGER TREE (USA) 3 b.f. Dayjur (USA) 137 – Carotene (CAN) (Great Nephew 126) [1994 84p: 6m* 6d3 1995 5m5 5g4 Sep 28] quite attractive filly: good mover: fairly useful form: reportedly finished distressed on reappearance: 40/1, best effort when 4 lengths fourth of 9 to Dairine's Delight in listed race at Newmarket 4½ months later, keeping on well having been soon niggled along: really needs further than 5f, and should stay 7f: yet to race on extremes of going: sent to Dubai. *P. W. Chapple-Hyam* 86

GINKA 4 b.f. Petoski 135 – Pine (Supreme Sovereign 119) [1994 57: 10m 11.7f2 12m4 11.9g5 18s 1995 a12g6 a14.8g5 11.7m 12d 10.8m Jul 7] leggy, light-bodied filly: disappointing maiden handicapper: well behind for new stable in 1995, looking reluctant last time: sold 1,050 gns Doncaster August Sales: tried blinkered/visored, no improvement. *P. J. Bevan* –

GINZA LIGHTS (IRE) 4 b.g. Tate Gallery (USA) 117 – Parkeen Princess (He Loves Me 120) [1994 67d: 6m 7g3 7m 8m5 6m5 7g4 7.1d 1995 6f May 11] sturdy gelding: still a maiden: tailed off only outing for new stable: should stay 1m: blinkered final 3-y-o start. *K. C. Bailey* –

GIRL FROM IPANEMA 4 b.f. Salse (USA) 128 – Honey Pot 111 (Hotfoot 126) [1994 106: 8g^6 8.1d* 8g^2 8m^2 8d^3 7m 8v^3 10.5v^3 1995 10m 10.5s^6 7.6g^2 8.5m^6 Jun 9] lengthy, good-topped filly: useful performer: ran creditably, though only sixth of 8 to Hollywood Dream, in slowly-run Prix Corrida at Evry in April, beaten around 2½ lengths: failed by quite some way to repeat that form in minor event at Lingfield (beaten neck) and listed event at Epsom, both in June: stays 10.5f: acts on good to firm and heavy ground. *P. F. I. Cole* — 100

GIVE IN 8 gr.g. Harlow (USA) 111 – Moment of Weakness 76 (Pieces of Eight 128) [1994 39, a48: a7g 9.7d^3 11.8g a8g a10g^5 a8g^4 1995 a8g^4 a10g^5 a10g Feb 7] leggy, narrow gelding: poor performer nowadays: stays 1¼m: acts on dead ground and equitrack, and won on fibresand in 1989: tried blinkered and visored, no improvement. *Miss Gay Kelleway* — – a38

GIVE ME A RING (IRE) 2 b.c. (Apr 1) Be My Guest (USA) 126 – Annsfield Lady (Red Sunset 120) [1995 6d 6g^4 6m^5 Aug 29] 30,000Y: useful-looking colt: has scope: fourth foal: half-brother to smart 3-y-o 7f winner and 2000 Guineas fourth Pipe Major (by Tirol), 6f and 1m winner at 2 yrs, and 2 other winners, including fairly useful 7f winner Bitter's End (by Waajib): dam, Irish 9f/1¼m performer, closely related to very useful middle-distance colt Beeshi: progressive form in maidens: caught the eye staying on well under considerate handling, having been slowly away, when over 8 lengths fifth of 16 to Dashing Blue at Ripon final outing: will improve again over 7f+. *C. W. Thornton* — 66 p

GLADYS ALTHORPE (IRE) 2 b.f. (Mar 16) Posen (USA) – Gortadoo (USA) (Sharpen Up 127) [1995 6g^5 7m^4 6m* 7m 7g 6.1d 6m 7f Oct 14] IR 2,200F: leggy filly: second foal: dam, ran once at 3 yrs in Ireland, daughter of very useful 5f to 7f winner Fenny Rough, also successful in USA: rather fortunate to win maiden at Catterick in July (runner-up eased prematurely): failed to reach frame in nurseries, but left impression on more than one occasion retained all her ability: stays 7f: acts on good to firm and dead ground. *J. L. Eyre* — 71

GLENLIVET (SWE) 7 ch.g. Grant's (DEN) – Skyline (SWE) (Jimmy Reppin 131) [1994 a6g^2 a6g^6 a6g^6 a5g^4 6f^5 6m^5 7g^2 6.5g^3 a6g^3 6d^3 6s^4 6.5g^3 6g 1995 a6g^3 a6g^5 6d^2 6g 6m^6 a8g^5 6.5m^3 6g^4 6d^3 6.5d^4 a6g^5 Oct 21] successful on 11 occasions between 3 yrs and 5 yrs, and demoted after winning a 7f listed event at Baden-Baden in 1994: ½-length second of 11 to Wessam Prince in Group 3 event there in May then third in Group 3 events at Hoppegarten (won by Desidera) and Chantilly (won by Hever Golf Rose) in September: stays 7f: acts on good to firm and soft ground: not entirely reliable. *L. Kelp, Sweden* — 110

GLEN MILLER 5 b.g. Music Boy 124 – Blakeney Sound (Blakeney 126) [1994 58d: 7s 7g^2 6s 7.6g 7.1f 7m 7g^5 7g 7f^3 7m^5 7m 7d 1995 7d 7g 7m 7m^3 7f^6 Jun 27] close-coupled, workmanlike gelding: poor mover: poor handicapper nowadays: best form at 7f: acts on firm and dead ground: tried blinkered/visored, no improvement: inconsistent. *J. W. Payne* — 32

GLEN PARKER (IRE) 2 ch.c. (Apr 30) Bluebird (USA) 125 – Trina's Girl (Nonoalco (USA) 131) [1995 7g^2 Oct 23] eighth foal: brother to useful 3-y-o 1m winner Clan Ben and half-brother to several winners, including 6f and 7f winner Albyn Lady (by Be My Guest) and 1¼m winner My Ratbag (by Nordico): dam 2-y-o 5f winner: 3/1, 3 lengths second of 9 to Ashjar in maiden at Lingfield, finishing well clear of those on unfavoured stand side despite tending to hang left late on: sure to improve. *H. R. A. Cecil* — 79 p

GLENRAZIE (IRE) 2 ch.c. (Jan 23) Kefaah (USA) 124 – Glendera 81 (Glenstal (USA) 118) [1995 7.1m^2 7.6d^2 8.3g^2 Sep 25] workmanlike colt: looked rather weak: third foal: dam, 1¼m winner who stayed 1½m, half-sister to very useful middle-distance winner Water Boatman out of half-sister to high-class stayer Sea Anchor: fair form in maiden events at Sandown, Lingfield and (caught last strides) Hamilton: stays 1m: sent to Dubai. *P. W. Chapple-Hyam* — 71

GLENROCK DANCER (IRE) 3 b.f. Glenstal (USA) 118 – Fourp'ny Rock (Ahonoora 122) [1994 NR 1995 12.1g^5 12.1f^3 11.1m^6 Jul 14] IR 1,000Y: first foal: dam lightly-raced Irish maiden: no promise in maidens and claimer: blinkered final start. *W. T. Kemp* — –

GLENUGIE 4 b.g. Insan (USA) 119 – Excavator Lady 65 (Most Secret 119) [1994 57: 8.5d^4 8.3d^5 11.1f 9m^5 10g^6 9.9f* 10m^5 1995 9.9m Apr 8] sturdy gelding: — –

modest handicapper: showed little only start in 1995: stays 1¼m: acts on any going: tried visored/blinkered, below form. *G. M. Moore*

GLENVALLY 4 gr.f. Belfort (FR) 89 – Hivally (High Line 125) [1994 51: 10m 12g 8m 12g^{4} 16.1d a14g 1995 a8g^{2} a8g a8g* a8g Mar 20] angular, workmanlike filly: carries condition: has a round action: poor performer: won apprentice maiden handicap at Southwell in February: pulled up lame final start: stays 1½m: acts on dead ground and fibresand: blinkered since final 3-y-o start. *B. W. Murray*

46

GLIDE PATH (USA) 6 ch.h. Stalwart (USA) – Jolly Polka (USA) (Nice Dancer (CAN)) [1994 102: 10d 12m^{2} 12m 11.9m* 12.3m* 12f^{5} 13.4g 11.9g* 12m 12m^{6} 1995 12m^{3} 12m 11.9m 11.9m^{2} 12f 12g* 11.9g 12m Oct 12] close-coupled horse: usually looks well: has a round action: useful handicapper: rather inconsistent in 1995, but won 12-runner Group 3 Stockholm Cup at Taby in August by short head from Theatrician: effective at 1½m (ran as if all might not have been well over 13.4f) and should stay further: probably needs a sound surface: held up. *J. W. Hills*

99

GLITTERAZZI 4 b.g. Midyan (USA) 124 – Burnt Amber (Balidar 133) [1994 NR 1995 8g^{6} a8g a10g 8.5s 14d Sep 27] sturdy, close-coupled gelding: fair maiden (rated 69) at best as 2-y-o for D. Elsworth: no promise on return: tried blinkered. *L. Montague Hall*

–

GLITTER BAY 4 b.f. Glint of Gold 128 – Town Lady 93 (Town Crier 119) [1994 –: 10s 8.3g 8m 8.1s a6g^{6} 7m 1995 a6g Jan 7] tall, unfurnished filly: no sign of ability. *C. D. Broad*

–

GLITTER OF GOLD 4 b.f. Glint of Gold 128 – Kochia 54 (Firestreak 125) [1994 68: 8m^{2} 10g^{3} 8.1g^{5} 10.4d 8.2d 1995 a11g 10m 8.3g a8.5g Jul 3] angular filly: disappointing maiden. *S. C. Williams*

–

GLOBAL DANCER 4 b.g. Night Shift (USA) – Early Call 102 (Kind of Hush 118) [1994 79: 10m a10g a11g^{4} a13g* a11g^{6} 1995 a10g^{3} a12g^{4} a10g^{6} a10g^{6} a12g^{5} 9g 12f* 14f^{2} 12g^{6} 12f^{5} 12m^{2} 11.9g^{6} a12g^{6} a16g^{6} Nov 14] useful-looking gelding: fair handicapper: trained by W. O'Gorman until after sixth 4-y-o start: won at Epsom (apprentices) in June: stays 1¾m: acts on the all-weather and goes well on firm going: tried blinkered (below form) for former stable: races prominently. *S. Dow*

75
a71

GLOBE RUNNER 2 b.c. (Mar 14) Adbass (USA) 102 – Scenic Villa (Top Ville 129) [1995 6g^{5} 6f^{4} 5f^{5} 6m Oct 2] 400Y, 5,500 2-y-o: smallish colt: fourth foal: half-brother to 3-y-o Biased View (by Beveled): dam poor maiden here and in France: modest form in auction events first 3 starts: well beaten in nursery (faced very stiff task) final start: will be suited by further than 6f. *J. J. O'Neill*

60

GLORIANA 3 b.f. Formidable (USA) 125 – Tudor Pilgrim 58 (Welsh Pageant 132) [1994 70: 7m^{3} 7g^{6} 7d 1995 10g^{2} 10.5g 11.5f^{6} 10f^{2} 9d* 10f^{4} 11.5m^{3} 10.3m 12g^{3} 12.1d Oct 10] rangy, angular filly: fair handicapper: easily won 5-runner maiden at Lingfield in July: likely to stay 1¾m: acts on firm ground and dead: visored (took keen hold, soon beaten when ridden) final start: went well with forcing tactics fourth to sixth 3-y-o starts. *Lady Herries*

78

GLORIOUS ARAGON 3 b.f. Aragon 118 – Gloria Maremmana (King Emperor (USA)) [1994 NR 1995 6m^{5} 6m^{2} 5.1g^{2} 5.2g^{4} 5g Sep 23] sturdy filly: half-sister to several winners, including 7f to 1¼m performer Emperor Hotfoot (by Hotfoot) and 1½m winner Hot Girl (by Hot Grove): dam won at 2 yrs in Italy: fair maiden on balance of form: possibly flattered when beaten a neck in £15,500 contest at Chester third start: looks a sprinter: has raced only on a sound surface. *R. F. Johnson Houghton*

86 ?

GLORIOUS BID (IRE) 3 gr.f. Horage 124 – Eclipse Bid 77 (Rusticaro (FR) 124) [1994 NR 1995 8f May 22] small filly: third foal: dam won at 1m at 4 yrs in Ireland: 100/1 and apprentice ridden, signs of ability in maiden at Bath, some late headway after slow start. *Martyn Meade*

–

GLORIOUS SOUND 2 b.c. (Feb 12) Music Boy 124 – Carlton Glory (Blakeney 126) [1995 6m 6g Sep 21] 12,500F, 15,000Y: compact colt: fourth foal: half-brother to successful stayer/hurdler Reach For Glory (by Reach): dam poor half-sister to smart French miler Gosport: well beaten in maidens at Ripon (pulled hard) and Pontefract (bandaged off-hind): sold to Norway 1,400 gns Doncaster October Sales. *J. Hanson*

–

GLORY OF DANCER 2 b.c. (May 11) Shareef Dancer (USA) 135 – Glory of Hera 99 (Formidable (USA) 125) [1995 6d* 8g^2 8g^2 8g* Nov 8] sixth live foal: half brother to minor middle-distance winners by Slip Anchor and Shirley Heights: dam best as 2-y-o sprinter: progressive Italian colt: won maiden at Rome in September and 9-runner Gran Criterium (by 2¼ lengths from Line Dancer) at Milan in November: should be suited by middle distances: may well improve further. *F. Brogi, Italy* 105 p

GLOW FORUM 4 b.f. Kalaglow 132 – Beau's Delight (USA) (Lypheor 118) [1994 42: 8m 9v 8.5m 11.6m a12g^3 a13g^5 16d a12g^4 a16g^5 a12g^3 a13g^4 a13g^3 a13g 1995 a12g a16g^5 14.1g 12m a16g a13g* 11.9f* 11.8g 12m^3 a12g^5 a13g^2 Dec 14] leggy, angular filly: poor handicapper: won sellers at Lingfield and Brighton in the summer: stays 13f: acts on firm ground and equitrack, yet to race on fibresand. *G. L. Moore* 43

GLOWING ACCOUNT (IRE) 4 b.g. Glow (USA) – Redeem Herself (General Assembly (USA)) [1994 6v 5g^6 5s^6 5d 5m^6 5g^3 5g^6 1995 a6g a8g^4 7g 8.3m 6.1m Jun 26] workmanlike ex-Irish gelding: third foal: half-brother to 7f winner Kindness Itself (by Ahonoora) and smart 6f to 1m winner Meditation (by Caerleon): dam useful 6f to 7f winner in Ireland: fair maiden (rated 71) for G. Stack in Ireland in 1994: well beaten in Britain, best form at sprint distances: acts on good to firm ground: effective blinkered or not: sold 825 gns Ascot July Sales: joined D. Hyde. *J. W. Mullins* –

GLOWING JADE 5 b.m. Kalaglow 132 – Precious Jade 72 (Northfields (USA)) [1994 71: a8g^6 8m* 8d 8m^3 8m* 8g^5 8f^3 8f^5 8m^6 9.9m 8g 7g 1995 7g* 7g^4 8m^6 8m 8g 7f Oct 24] tall, long-backed mare: fair handicapper: won apprentice race at Doncaster in May, idling and hanging after leading on bit over 2f out: left Miss Gay Kelleway's stable after fourth start, and well beaten for new connections: best form at 7f to 9f: acts on firm and dead ground, probably not on soft: ideally suited by strong pace and waiting tactics. *J. A. Glover* 75

GLOWING PATH 5 b.g. Kalaglow 132 – Top Tina (High Top 131) [1994 –: a6g a12g^5 8m 8.3m 7.6v 10.8s 1995 a12g^5 a13g Feb 2] angular gelding: no worthwhile form on flat since 3 yrs: has worn blinkers/visor. *R. J. Hodges* –

GLOWING REEDS 2 ch.f. (Apr 22) Kalaglow 132 – No Jazz 55 (Jaazeiro (USA) 127) [1995 8m Oct 28] 2,000Y, 550 2-y-o: plain filly: fourth foal: dam, best at around 1m, is half-sister to Noiritza, dam of smart sprinter Al Sylah: 40/1 and in need of race, slowly away and always behind in seller at Newmarket. *P. J. McBride* –

GLOW OF HOPE 5 b.m. Prince Sabo 123 – Impailand (Imperial Fling (USA) 116) [1994 31: a6g^4 a6g 8d 6.9s 8s 1995 5m^4 5g^4 5f 6f^4 5f Aug 9] lengthy, sparely-made mare: poor maiden handicapper: stays 6f: acts on firm and dead ground. *R. M. McKellar* 32

GOALWAH 3 b.f. Sadler's Wells (USA) 132 – Al Bahathri (USA) 123 (Blushing Groom (FR) 131) [1994 NR 1995 8f^2 8.1g^2 8.1m* 10.1g^3 8s Oct 6] leggy, angular filly: good mover: fifth foal: sister to fair 1m winner (stayed 1¼m) Alyakkh and half-sister to very useful 7f/1m performer Hasbah (by Kris): dam won Lowther Stakes and Irish 1000 Guineas: won maiden at Sandown in August: contested listed races afterwards, useful form when 1¾ lengths third of 12 to Poppy Carew at Yarmouth: stayed 10.1f: acted on firm ground, possibly unsuited by soft: visits Gulch. *H. Thomson Jones* 99

GO BETWEEN (FR) 2 b.c. (Mar 9) Highest Honor (FR) 124 – Ruffle (FR) (High Line 125) [1995 8m^3 8g^4 9d* 10g^4 Oct 29] 330,000 francs Y: fourth foal: brother to 3-y-o 5.5f (at 2 yrs) and 1m winner Tousle and half-brother to a French 11f winner by Darshaan: dam, Group 3 winner at 1m and placed at 1½m, out of sister to Mtoto: smart French colt: won 5-runner Prix de Conde at Longchamp by ¾ length from Battle Dore: around a length fourth of 5 to Polaris Flight in slowly-run Criterium de Saint-Cloud final start: should stay beyond 1¼m. *A. Spanu, France* 111

GODMERSHAM PARK 3 b.g. Warrshan (USA) 117 – Brown Velvet 68 (Mansingh (USA) 120) [1994 –: 7s 1995 7m^3 7g^2 7m^2 7g^2 7m Nov 3] leggy, lengthy gelding: fair maiden, best efforts first 2 starts: well beaten, hanging left, in 21-runner handicap at Doncaster last time: should stay 1m: refused to enter stalls second intended 3-y-o start. *M. J. Heaton-Ellis* 73

GODWIN (USA) 4 ch.f. Diesis 133 – Goodbye Shelley (FR) 116 (Home Guard (USA) 129) [1994 74p: 10d^2 1995 10m^2 10m* 11.9m^3 12f^2 10m^3 Aug 4] sturdy, lengthy filly: fairly useful performer: won maiden at Leicester in April: placed afterwards in handicap at York, rated stakes at Salisbury and minor event at Newmarket: may well stay further than 1½m: acts on firm ground and dead: races prominently: consistent: sold 22,000 gns Newmarket December Sales. *H. R. A. Cecil* — 88

GO-GO-POWER-RANGER 2 ch.g. (Mar 7) Golden Lahab (USA) – Nibelunga (Miami Springs 121) [1995 5g 7f 6.1d Sep 11] sixth foal: half-brother to 6f winner African Dash (by African Sky): dam well-bred winner at around 1m: signs of a little ability from poor draw in maiden at Nottingham on final start. *B. Ellison* — –

GO HEVER GOLF 3 ch.g. Efisio 120 – Sweet Rosina 61 (Sweet Revenge 129) [1994 63, a99+: 5s^6 5s^2 6f^2 5.1m^2 5m^3 6m 6g^2 5s a6g* a6g* a5s* 1995 a6g* 6m 6.1m* 7g 6m 5.1m^3 a6g 5m Aug 28] quite good-topped gelding: poor walker: useful handicapper: put up the best performance seen on the all-weather in winter of 1994/5 when winning well-contested race at Wolverhampton in February: emphatically justified favouritism in £10,700 event at Chester in May, making all: mostly well below form afterwards: very best form at 6f: acts on any turf going, goes well on the all-weather: blinkered (ran poorly) seventh 2-y-o start: usually bandaged behind. *T. J. Naughton* — 96, a109

GOLD AND STEEL (FR) 3 b.c. Shining Steel (FR) 123 – Horphaly (Pharly (FR) 130) [1994 7g* 7.5s* 1995 8g* 8s^2 8g* 8g* 10m^6 9.5g* 10f^5 Aug 27] ex-French colt: third foal: half-brother to French 13f winner Wapiti (by Miller's Mate) and smart 4-y-o 5.5f (at 2 yrs) to 1¼m winner Befuto (by Saint Andrews): dam ran once: smart performer: won newcomers event and minor race in the provinces at 2 yrs: successful in 1995 in minor event in February and listed race in April both at Toulouse, Prix de la Jonchere at Longchamp (last into straight, ran on to lead inside last and beat Bashaayeash by 1½ lengths) in June and American Derby at Arlington (made virtually all to beat Torrential (gave 6 lb) by 1¼ lengths final start for J. C. Rouget) in July: good fifth of 10 to Hawk Attack in Secretariat Stakes at Arlington: stays 1¼m: acts on soft ground and firm. *R. Rash, USA* — 114

GOLD BLADE 6 ch.g. Rousillon (USA) 133 – Sharp Girl (FR) 114 (Sharpman) [1994 47, a58: a10g a10g^3 a10g^3 a10g^5 10m^4 9g^6 10.8m^4 a9.4g^6 a12g^4 1995 a11g^2 a12g* 10.3g 10.5d^2 12.3f 11.1f* 9.2m^3 9.9m^2 12g^3 12d Sep 15] big, good-topped gelding: poor mover: modest performer: won amateurs handicap at Wolverhampton in January and ladies handicap at Hamilton in July: suited by middle distances: acts on any turf ground and the all-weather: sometimes bandaged near-fore: seemed effective with blinkers, but doesn't wear them nowadays: held up: ridden by Mrs L. Pearce at 6 yrs. *J. Pearce* — 51, a66

GOLD DESIRE 5 b.g. Grey Desire 115 – Glory Gold 59 (Hittite Glory 125) [1994 43: 8g 8.3d 9.2d a9.4g^5 8m^2 9g* 10g* 10g^4 11g 8.2m 10.1m^2 10.4d^5 10d^5 11.9d 1995 a11g 12.1d^5 9.2g^4 9.2g^5 11.1g^4 11.1g 12.3f^4 10.1f* 10.4g^3 Aug 31] sparely-made, plain gelding: has a round action: poor handicapper: won at Newcastle in August: stays 11f: acts on dead going and firm: visored (ran poorly) once at 3 yrs: held up/tracks leaders. *M. Brittain* — 34

GOLD DISC (USA) 2 ch.c. (Apr 19) Slew O' Gold (USA) – Singing (USA) 91 (The Minstrel (CAN) 135) [1995 7g* Oct 10] well-made, attractive colt: first foal: dam, 7f winner, half-sister to very smart 1¼m winner Two Timing out of half-sister to champion American mare Chris Evert: 13/8 favourite but green, comfortable winner of 12-runner maiden at Leicester by 2½ lengths from Alambar, pulling hard in steadily-run race then improving to lead over 1f out and running on well: moved fluently to post: sure to improve. *B. W. Hills* — 81 p

GOLDEN ARROW (IRE) 4 ch.g. Glint of Gold 128 – Sheer Luck 72 (Shergar 140) [1994 85: 10g^2 10d^2 10m^4 14g 10g 12d* 13.3s^4 11.8g^2 1995 12m 13.3d 12s Oct 6] workmanlike gelding: fluent mover: fairly useful handicapper at 3 yrs: fairly useful but unreliable hurdler: towards rear on return to flat: stays 13.3f well: acts on good to firm ground and soft. *I. A. Balding* — –

GOLDEN BALL (IRE) 4 b.c. Sadler's Wells (USA) 132 – Sun Princess 130 (English Prince 129) [1994 107: 10.3m^2 12m 12m 10m^3 12m* 14g^3 12m^6 11.8g^2 1995 10m^2 13.9g 11.5g^3 10m^2 9f^5 10f^5 a8f^2 Dec 31] strong, useful-looking colt: fluent mover: useful performer: placed in listed race at Kempton, minor events — 103 (below best) at Lingfield and Windsor (outbattled by Stiffelio, final start for M. Stoute) and allowance race at Santa Anita: stays 1¾m: acts on good to firm ground and dirt: not one to trust implicitly. *Kathy Walsh, USA*

GOLDENBERRY 4 ch.f. Sharrood (USA) 124 – Moberry 54 (Mossberry 97) [1994 –: 8s 8.3m 8d a7g 12g^5 a12g 1995 a11g a12g^4 a16g^6 a12g^5 a14g 12m 10m 9.9d 10.1d^5 15.1f a14.8g 10f Aug 23] lengthy filly: looks a bad maiden nowadays: sold out of J. Parkes' stable 500 gns Doncaster July Sales after tenth start: most inconsistent. *K. G. Wingrove* – a27

GOLDEN CHIP (IRE) 7 ch.g. M Double M (USA) – Kimangao (Garda's Revenge (USA) 119) [1994 68: 8g^5 8.1g 7m^2 8m^3 a8g^3 10.5g^4 1995 7g^4 7.5g 8.1d Sep 2] strong gelding: sometimes dull in coat: poor mover: signs of retaining his ability on reappearance but well below form afterwards: effective at 7f to 1¼m: probably acts on any going: usually races prominently. *J. L. Eyre* –

GOLDEN DIGGER (USA) 3 ch.f. Mr Prospector (USA) – Carduel (USA) (Buckpasser) [1994 66p: 6g^4 1995 10m 8m^4 8f^4 Jun 24] leggy, quite attractive filly: failed to repeat form shown on debut, on toes and edgy final start. *M. R. Stoute* –

GOLDEN ENVOY (USA) 3 b.f. Dayjur (USA) 137 – Ambassador of Luck (USA) (What Luck (USA)) [1994 –p: 6g 1995 6m 7f^2 7m Aug 27] rather leggy filly: fair maiden: 11/10, best effort when short-head second of 4 at Redcar, collared on line having dictated pace: taken down early and rider reported filly got worked up before handicap at Goodwood (tailed off) final start: should stay 1m. *J. H. M. Gosden* 68

GOLDEN FISH 3 b.g. Efisio 120 – Fishpond 71 (Homing 130) [1994 47: 5s 6s^6 8d a7g 1995 7.5m 8m^2 9.2f 10m^5 8g^3 8f Oct 23] leggy gelding: maiden plater: should stay beyond 1m: acts on good to firm and soft ground: blinkered (well beaten) final start: joined Miss K. Whitehouse. *J. L. Eyre* 52 d

GOLDEN HADEER 4 ch.c. Hadeer 118 – Verchinina 99 (Star Appeal 133) [1994 52: a10g^6 a10g 12s* 1995 a10g^6 a12g^6 Jan 27] modest performer: below form for new stable in 1995: stays 1½m: acts on soft ground. *M. J. Ryan* –

GOLDEN HELLO 4 b.g. Glint of Gold 128 – Waltz 75 (Jimmy Reppin 131) [1994 82: 12g^4 10m^4 13.1g* 12.3m^3 12m* 11.9m^6 13.9m 1995 12g Sep 8] close-coupled, workmanlike gelding: fairly useful handicapper: useful juvenile hurdler in 1994/5: burly, well beaten on belated reappearance: suited by 1½m+: acts on any going: visored (ran creditably) fourth 3-y-o start. *M. H. Easterby* –

GOLDEN LADY (IRE) 3 b.f. Danehill (USA) 126 – Gold Runner 62 (Runnett 125) [1994 73p: 6g 6g* 1995 6m* 6m^5 5.1m^2 6m 5f Jun 24] close-coupled filly: fairly useful handicapper: won at Brighton in April: blinkered, hung off bridle when running poorly in £12,900 event at Ascot final outing: stays 6f: has raced only on a sound surface: usually races prominently: sold 19,000 gns Newmarket September Sales. *R. Hannon* 82

GOLDEN MEMORIES (IRE) 4 ch.g. Shernazar 131 – Buz Kashi 123 (Bold Lad (IRE) 133) [1994 –: 8.5g^6 12.1g 8.2d 1995 a8.5g Mar 18] sturdy gelding: probably no longer of much account: sold 1,200 gns Doncaster March Sales. *M. J. Heaton-Ellis* –

GOLDEN ORB (IRE) 3 ch.g. Woodman (USA) 126 – Katie May 103 (Busted 134) [1994 8d 1995 11m* 12f* 12m* 12m* Jul 22] most progressive Irish gelding: half-brother to 3 winners, notably very smart fillies Kostroma (by Caerleon) and Grise Mine (by Crystal Palace), both effective at up to around 1¼m: dam, useful miler, is half-sister to top class sprinter Solinus: successful in 1995 in maiden at Killarney, minor events at Dundalk and Leopardstown and listed race (beat Ballykett Nancy 1½ lengths) at Leopardstown, all by July: suited by 1½m: raced only on top-of-the-ground at 3 yrs: seemed sort to improve further. *Charles O'Brien, Ireland* 111 p

GOLDEN POND (IRE) 2 b.f. (Mar 12) Don't Forget Me 127 – Golden Bloom (Main Reef 126) [1995 6.1m^6 7f^3 7m 6m 7d^4 6m* 7f^3 Oct 14] tall filly: third living foal: half-sister to Irish 9f/1¼m winner Mayfield Prince (by Thatching): dam unraced daughter of half-sister to Connaught: fair form: won 18-runner nursery at Pontefract in October: good third in similar event at Catterick 12 days later: likely to stay further than 7f: acts on firm ground and dead: tongue tied down fourth start: takes good hold. *R. F. Johnson Houghton* 72

GOLDEN POUND (USA) 3 b.c. Seeking The Gold (USA) – Coesse Express (USA) (Dewan (USA)) [1994 NR 1995 8.1g 8.3m^3 8m^2 10.5g 8f Oct 12] $200,000Y: lengthy, useful-looking colt: impresses in appearance: has had soft palate operation: good mover: third foal: half-brother to 2 winners in North America, notably 4-y-o Fly' N J Bryan (by Ogygian), Grade 3 7f winner at 3 yrs: dam won 8 races, including a minor stakes event: fair maiden: well beaten last 2 starts, sweating on final one: takes good hold and likely to prove best at up to 1m: sold (E. Dunlop to Miss Gay Kelleway) 11,000 gns Newmarket Autumn Sales. *E. A. L. Dunlop* 78

GOLDEN PUNCH (USA) 4 b.g. Seattle Song (USA) 130 – Pagan Winter (USA) (Pago Pago) [1994 NR 1995 a7g Dec 19] brother to a winner in USA and half-brother to winners in USA and France: dam won in USA: poor form in 2 NH Flat races then always behind in maiden at Lingfield. *C. A. Cyzer* –

GOLDEN RULER (USA) see Golden Touch (USA)

GOLDEN SILVER 2 b.f. (Apr 28) Precious Metal 106 – Severals Princess 44 (Formidable (USA) 125) [1995 5g 6m^3 6f^6 5g^6 5g^4 7m Oct 12] 460Y: narrow filly: has a round action: first foal: dam placed over 5f at 2 yrs: plater: sweating, below-par effort at Newmarket last time: stays 6f. *J. S. Moore* 46

GOLDEN STAR (IRE) 4 ch.g. Salse (USA) 128 – Tight Spin (High Top 131) [1994 56d: 7d 10m^5 9g^4 10m^5 9g a9.4g^4 10.1m 17.5s^5 15.8g^6 a14g 1995 10f May 1] good-bodied gelding: disappointing maiden: stays 1¼m: acts on good to firm going, dead and fibresand: blinkered twice (no improvement) at 3 yrs: inconsistent. *M. W. Easterby* –

GOLDEN TONGUE (USA) 3 ch.g. Nureyev (USA) 131 – Prayers'n Promises (USA) (Foolish Pleasure (USA)) [1994 NR 1995 7.5m^5 8g^4 8f^2 8m Jul 10] leggy gelding: brother to useful sprinter Anjiz and closely related to very smart sprinter Nabeel Dancer (by Northern Dancer): dam Grade 1 winner at 6f and 7f at 2 yrs: fair maiden: best form at 1m, but should do at least as well over shorter: has carried head awkwardly, and is one to be wary of: sold 6,400 gns Newmarket July Sales. *E. A. L. Dunlop* 63

GOLDEN TORQUE 8 br.g. Taufan (USA) 119 – Brightelmstone 105 (Prince Regent (FR) 129) [1994 65: a12g* 10d^5 1995 a12g a9.4g 13v^5 a9.4g a14.8g 10.8g^2 a12g Nov 13] strong, close-coupled gelding: modest handicapper: well below form in 1995 except (3/1 from 20/1) second under very hard ride at Warwick: suited by middle distances: acts on good to firm and heavy ground and on fibresand: effective visored earlier in career: usually ridden by claimer: best held up. *R. Bastiman* 55 a–

GOLDEN TOUCH (USA) 3 ch.c. Elmaamul (USA) 125 – Tour d'Argent (USA) (Halo (USA)) [1994 6f 1995 7m 8.2d^3 8m Oct 12] 1,000Y: compact colt: sixth foal: half-brother to 3 minor winners in U.S: dam winning sprinter: trained by J. Banks, raced as Golden Ruler only start at 2 yrs: form only when third of 12 in maiden at Nottingham: has joined N. Callaghan. *R. Champion* 66

GOLDEN TYKE (IRE) 2 b.c. (Mar 15) Soviet Lad (USA) 94 – Golden Room (African Sky 124) [1995 5m 5f Jul 29] IR 6,100Y, 21,000 2-y-o: close-coupled colt: fourth foal: dam Irish maiden: ninth of 11 in maidens at Ripon and Thirsk in July: joined M. Johnston. *M. D. Hammond* –

GOLDEN WEDDING 2 b.g. (Feb 23) Today And Tomorrow 78 – Too Familiar 52 (Oats 126) [1995 a5g 6m a6g Sep 14] leggy, good-topped gelding: fifth foal: dam won over hurdles: plater: no show when visored final outing. *D. C. O'Brien* –

GOLD KICKER 2 b.c. (May 7) High Kicker (USA) – Ship of Gold 78 (Glint of Gold 128) [1995 6.1m^4 a8g a8g Nov 14] first foal: dam, disappointing maiden, stayed 1½m: 2 lengths fourth of 8 to Sava River in maiden at Nottingham in August: tailed off in similar events at Southwell and Lingfield 3 months later. *M. J. Ryan* 61 ?

GOLDMART (IRE) 2 ch.g. (May 8) Waajib 121 – Une Parisienne (FR) (Bolkonski 134) [1995 7m 7.1s Nov 2] IR 4,600Y: sturdy gelding: sixth foal: half-brother to 3-y-o 5.9f and 1m selling winner Commander Glen (by Glenstal): dam, ran once in France, half-sister to 1¼m Prix Eugene Adam winner Un Desperado: tailed off in maiden auctions at Thirsk in August and Edinburgh in November. *T. J. Etherington* –

GOLDRILL 2 ch.g. (Mar 29) Never So Bold 135 – Irish Impulse (USA) 50 (Irish River (FR) 131) [1995 6g Sep 14] 10,500F, 8,200Y: second foal: dam poor maiden –

daughter of smart staying 2-y-o Exclusively Raised: 33/1, behind in maiden auction at Ayr. *Miss S. E. Hall*

GOLD SAND 3 b.c. Green Desert (USA) 127 – Golden Opinion (USA) 127 (Slew O' Gold (USA)) [1994 NR 1995 7.1g^{6} May 27] big, deep-bodied colt: second foal: half-brother to 1993 French 2-y-o 1m winner Sun Music (by Sadler's Wells): dam, Coronation Stakes winner (beaten head in July Cup), out of Nassau Stakes winner Optimistic Lass: 2/1 favourite, bandaged in front and green, beaten over 20 lengths in maiden at Haydock: sold 1,550 gns Ascot August Sales. *J. H. M. Gosden* –

GOLDSEARCH (IRE) 2 ch.f. (Apr 13) Fayruz 116 – Win For Me (Bonne Noel 115) [1995 6s 6m 5g^{5} a6g^{3} a5g^{5} Nov 25] IR 7,000F, 6,000Y: small, strong filly: half-sister to winners in Belgium and Hong Kong: dam unraced: modest form in varied events: third of 9 in claimer at Lingfield in November: best form at 6f: acts on equitrack: blinkered final start. *W. A. O'Gorman* 58 +

GOLD SURPRISE (IRE) 6 b. or br.g. Petorius 117 – Gold Piece (Golden Fleece (USA) 133) [1994 56: a11g^{3} a11g^{5} a11g^{2} a12s^{5} a12g^{5} 10.5g 11.1g 10g^{6} 11.1g^{2} 10.9g* 11.1m* 10g 12g^{5} 14.1m^{2} a12g* 15.1m^{2} 11.1g^{3} a12g^{3} 11.8g^{4} 16.5d^{6} 1995 a12g* a16g^{5} 11.5g a14.8g 11.1g^{4} Sep 25] smallish, workmanlike gelding: unimpressive mover: modest performer: won seller at Wolverhampton in January: stays 15f: acts on good to firm ground, soft and fibresand: usually races prominently: has run well for lady and when sweating: game. *S. E. Kettlewell* 50

GO LIKECRAZY 3 br.f. Dowsing (USA) 124 – Thessaloniki 94 (Julio Mariner 127) [1994 51: 5s^{4} 5d* 5.3g^{3} a5g^{6} 6s 6g* 7m^{2} 7m^{4} 5.1g^{6} 6d^{5} 8s 1995 a8g a8g Jan 16] leggy, sparely-made filly: winning plater at 2 yrs: well beaten in 1995: sold 1,950 gns Ascot April Sales. *K. T. Ivory* –

GO LIKE WEST 2 b.c. (Mar 15) Absalom 128 – Wyns Vision (Vision (USA)) [1995 5g 5d Mar 30] 8,400F, 6,000Y: neat colt: second foal: dam thrice-raced half-sister to smart 5f and 7f winner Glenturret: soundly beaten in maiden auctions. *J. Hetherton* –

GOLINA (IRE) 2 b.f. (Feb 10) Polish Patriot (USA) 128 – Las Bela 75 (Welsh Pageant 132) [1995 5m 5.1h Aug 8] IR 17,500Y: third reported foal: half-sister to French 1m to 9.5f winner Magical Dust (by Magical Wonder): dam, suited by 1m, is out of half-sister to very smart animals Western Jewel and Mr Fluorocarbon: well beaten in maidens at Windsor and Bath: sold 1,600 gns Newmarket Autumn Sales. *B. W. Hills* –

GONDO 8 br.g. Mansingh (USA) 120 – Secret Valentine 71 (Wollow 132) [1994 73: 5.9v^{5} 5m 6g 5m^{2} 5m^{6} 5.2g 5m^{6} 6.1m 5m^{2} 5g^{2} 6m 5.1g* 6g 5s 5.1s 5d 5d 5g 1995 a5g^{6} a6g a5g 5m 5g^{6} 5g^{6} 5g 5.1g 6m 5m 5f 5.1m 5m^{3} 6g 6d 8g 5.1d^{3} 6f Oct 23] compact gelding: poor mover: modest sprint handicapper nowadays: probably acts on any turf going, no form for a long time on fibresand: often visored, has form with blinkers (not tried for long time): tends to hang: none too consistent. *E. J. Alston* 50

GONE FOR A BURTON (IRE) 5 ch.g. Bustino 136 – Crimbourne 83 (Mummy's Pet 125) [1994 93: 12s^{2} 12m 10.4f 10.9s* 12m 12s 12v 1995 10.8d* 12g^{2} 10.4m^{5} 10.3d 10d Sep 16] workmanlike, rather sparely-made gelding: fairly useful handicapper: tends to go well fresh, and won at Warwick in April (idled) on reappearance: good efforts at Newbury and York (Magnet Cup) next 2 starts: effective at 1¼m and 1½m: acts on good to firm ground and soft: blinkered final 4-y-o start. *P. J. Makin* 90

GONE SAVAGE 7 b.g. Nomination 125 – Trwyn Cilan 89 (Import 127) [1994 66: 6m 6v^{6} 5d 6m 5d 6g 5s 5d 5s 5v 1995 6m* 6m 6g 6f 6m^{2} 5g^{5} 5g^{5} 6m 5m^{4} 6g 6g 6d^{6} 6f Oct 23] strong, good-bodied gelding: carries condition: fair sprint handicapper: more consistent in 1995 than in the past: 25/1-winner at Kempton in April on reappearance: acts on good to firm and soft ground and on equitrack: blinkered (below form) twice: sometimes bandaged behind. *W. J. Musson* 67

GOODBYE MILLIE 5 b. or br.m. Sayf El Arab (USA) 127 – Leprechaun Lady 57 (Royal Blend 117) [1994 54, a–: a12g 12m* 12g^{2} 12.1m* a12g^{6} 11.9m^{2} 12.3g^{4} 12g 12g^{6} a11g^{6} a14g 1995 a12g 12.4g 12d^{2} 12.1m* 14.1f 11.1m* 12m^{5} a11g^{6} 12.1g 11.1g^{3} 12f^{2} 11f^{3} Oct 24] angular mare: modest performer: won claimers at Edinburgh (for second year running) in June and Hamilton in July: stays 1¾m: acts on fibresand 50 a–

and any turf going: usually wears visor: blinkered (well beaten) final 4-y-o start: has worn near-side pricker: often claimer ridden. *J. L. Eyre*

GOOD FETCH 4 b.f. Siberian Express (USA) 125 – Exceptional Beauty 94 (Sallust 134) [1994 –: 5.1g 7m 6.9h^6 5d 1995 12m Aug 27] leggy, sparely-made filly: fair form at 2 yrs: no worthwhile form for several trainers since. *J. A. Bennett* –

GOOD HAND (USA) 9 ch.g. Northjet 136 – Ribonette (USA) (Ribot 142) [1994 82: 16d 16m^4 16.1f* 16.5m^5 20m 15m^4 16.2f 16.1m 17.5s^2 16g^4 16.5v 1995 16m 16f^2 16.1g* 16m 14.6g^2 16f^4 14f^5 16.1g^2 17.5g^2 13.9g 14.6m^4 16.5m^5 Nov 4] close-coupled, sparely-made gelding: fair handicapper: won at Newcastle in May for second year running: dyed-in-the-wool stayer: acts on firm and soft ground: below form when blinkered and visored earlier in career: sometimes bandaged: held up: often hangs. *J. W. Watts* 79

GOOD (IRE) 3 b.g. Persian Heights 129 – Tres Bien (Pitskelly 122) [1994 49: 7m 7g^4 7g a7g 6s^6 1995 8m 10g 14.1g 11.4m 8d 12s Sep 27] angular, workmanlike gelding: poor maiden handicapper: tried visored and blinkered. *D. T. Thom* –

GOOD MATCH (IRE) 3 br.g. Tirol 127 – Vain Deb 66 (Gay Fandango (USA) 132) [1994 –: 6m 1995 7.1m^6 5m 8m 6g^4 7g^5 7.1m^6 Jun 19] workmanlike gelding: modest maiden: should stay beyond 7f: has raced only on a sound surface. *N. Tinkler* 53

GOOD SO FA (IRE) 3 b.g. Taufan (USA) 119 – Future Shock (Full Out (USA)) [1994 52: 6f 7g^4 6g^3 8m 8s 7g^6 7s^3 1995 a8g* a8g^3 a8g^2 a10g a10g^6 8m a12g a9.4g a10g^4 Nov 25] rather leggy gelding: modest performer: won claimer at Lingfield in January on third-last start for M. Tompkins: below form for new yard: should stay beyond 1m: best form on equitrack. *C. N. Allen* – a62 d

GOOD TO TALK 2 b.g. (May 13) Weldnaas (USA) 112 – Kimble Blue 56 (Blue Refrain 121) [1995 5g 5f 5m^4 6m^6 7g 7g 6s Sep 30] 2,000Y: close-coupled gelding: fifth foal: dam 2-y-o 5f winner: poor maiden: well beaten in selling nursery final start: best form at 5f. *M. H. Easterby* 48

GOODWOOD ROCKET 2 ch.c. (Mar 28) Midyan (USA) 124 – Feather-In-Her-Cap (Primo Dominie 121) [1995 6m^3 6g^5 7m^6 6m^5 7g^3 8d^2 Sep 30] 21,000Y: sturdy, lengthy colt: second foal: half-brother to Irish 3-y-o 1½m winner Flame of Sion (by Be My Chief): dam unraced close relative of smart sprinter Governor General: fair form: unlucky in running in nurseries at Goodwood last 2 outings, particularly final start: will stay beyond 1m: acts on good to firm and dead ground. *J. L. Dunlop* 75

GOODY FOUR SHOES 7 gr.m. Blazing Saddles (AUS) – Bronzamer 86 (Saritamer (USA) 130) [1994 44: a8.5g a7g 6.1s 5d 7g^4 7d 1995 7g 7g^6 6g 7m Jun 13] leggy, close-coupled mare: poor handicapper: well beaten in 1995. *A. G. Newcombe* –

GOOGLY 6 ch.m. Sunley Builds 102 – Cheri Berry 87 (Air Trooper 115) [1994 78: 13.3s 16g^3 16d^6 12v 1995 18g^6 Mar 24] leggy mare: unimpressive mover: fair handicapper: blinkered first time and bandaged, ran respectably only 6-y-o start: probably stays 2¼m: acts on good to firm ground, goes particularly well on soft: sometimes hangs and carries head awkwardly, but is genuine: fairly useful jumper: sold 13,500 gns Doncaster July Sales. *J. White* 71 +

GOONDA 3 b.f. Darshaan 133 – Grimpola (GER) (Windwurf (GER)) [1994 72: 7m^6 8.1d^5 1995 10m* 10g^2 10g Sep 29] rangy filly: fair performer: won maiden at Newmarket in June despite hanging left: good staying-on second in handicap at Newbury following month: should stay 1½m+: took good hold to post second 3-y-o start, taken down steadily on final one: sold 21,000 gns Newmarket December Sales. *H. R. A. Cecil* 75

GORAM'S GIRL (IRE) 3 b.f. Taufan (USA) 119 – Blue Bell Lady 75 (Dunphy 124) [1994 –: 5m 6g 8d 1995 7m^6 10g 9.2f Jun 14] leggy, sparely-made filly: no worthwhile form: tried blinkered. *Mrs A. Swinbank* –

GORETSKI (IRE) 2 b.c. (Apr 9) Polish Patriot (USA) 128 – Celestial Path 101 (Godswalk (USA) 130) [1995 5d 5m 6f* 6m^4 5m^5 5g 5m Oct 13] IR 15,500Y: tall colt: unimpressive mover: half-brother to several winners, including Karazan (by Nishapour), fairly useful at up to 1¼m: dam Irish 5f to 7f winner: won seller at Redcar in August: mostly creditable efforts afterwards in non-selling nurseries, but below form at Catterick last time: stays 6f. *N. Tinkler* 55

GORINSKY (IRE) 7 ch.g. Gorytus (USA) 132 – Grapette (Nebbiolo 125) [1994 101: 5.2s 5g^2 5m^6 5m^6 6.1m^4 6f^5 5g^5 5g^2 5.6g 5g* 5m 5s^3 1995 5m^3 5g 5g^5 5m^2 5m^4 5m^3 5f Aug 5] sturdy gelding: has a quick action: useful sprint handicapper in 1994: fair at best at 7 yrs: acts on any ground, including all-weather surfaces: formerly effective in blinkers (not tried since 1992): often a front runner. *J. Berry*

79

GORODENKA BOY 5 ch.g. Then Again 126 – Simply Jane (Sharpen Up 127) [1994 34: 6g 5g 5g a5g^5 a5g^4 7g 5g 1995 a5g 8f Aug 5] tall, leggy gelding: poor maiden: well beaten in 1995. *Mrs J. Jordan*

–

GO SOUTH 11 b.g. Thatching 131 – Run To The Sun (Run The Gantlet (USA)) [1994 NR 1995 16.4m Apr 28] sturdy gelding: unreliable stayer: still capable of fair form (rated 65) in 1993: failed to complete in 2 points early in year: tailed off in handicap at Sandown on return to flat. *J. R. Jenkins*

– §

GOSPEL SONG 3 ch.c. King Among Kings 60 – Market Blues (Porto Bello 118) [1994 62: 5d 5d^3 5g^2 6f* 6m 7f^5 7f^6 a6g 6m^6 6f^3 7.1m^3 7.9d^5 7.5g^4 1995 9.2s^5 8.3g 8g^3 9.2g* 8m* 9g^4 11.1m^3 8.1m^5 10g^6 9.2f 9h^3 13f^5 Aug 9] neat colt: fair performer: won minor event at Hamilton and handicap at Thirsk in May: stays 11f: acts on hard ground: effective blinkered or not: sold (W. Kemp to A. Whillans) 11,000 gns Doncaster September Sales. *W. T. Kemp*

66

GOTHENBERG (IRE) 2 b.c. (Apr 28) Polish Patriot (USA) 128 – Be Discreet (Junius (USA) 124) [1995 5g^3 5g* 5g* 6f* 6m 6m^4 6f Oct 12] 5,700Y: tall colt: has scope: powerful mover with long stride: closely related to 3-y-o Don't Get Caught (by Danehill) and half-brother to 1¼m winner Sarabah (by Ela-Mana-Mou): dam won at up to 7f in France: won maiden auction at Hamilton and minor event at Newcastle in May and Vodata Woodcote Stakes (beat World Premier readily by 2½ lengths) at Epsom in June: creditable efforts last 2 starts, just over 4 lengths fourth of 5 to Royal Applause in Gimcrack Stakes at York in August and eleventh of 26 to Blue Iris in Redcar Two-Year-Old Trophy: stays 6f: acts on firm ground: bandaged off-hind on debut: edgy type who often sweats. *M. Johnston*

96

GOTLA BIRD 2 b.f. (Apr 2) Petong 126 – Addison's Jubilee 73 (Sparkler 130) [1995 5d^4 5s a6g Nov 20] sparely-made filly: half-sister to several winners, including 9f winner Ci Siamo (by Formidable) and 3-y-o 1½m winner Boundary Express (by Sylvan Express): dam 1m and 1¼m winner: fourth of 11 to First Maite in maiden at Beverley: fell after 1f at Southwell in November: dead. *M. Johnston*

48

GO TOO MOOR (IRE) 2 b.g. (Apr 4) Posen (USA) – Gulistan (Sharpen Up 127) [1995 7f Oct 25] 5,200Y: good-topped gelding: half-brother to untrustworthy 7.6f winner Are You Guilty (by Runnett): dam poor daughter of smart stayer Turf: 50/1, green and bit backward, tended to carry head high when last of 10 in maiden at Yarmouth. *G. C. Bravery*

–

GOVERNOR GEORGE (USA) 4 b.c. Secreto (USA) 128 – Sheena Native (USA) (Qui Native (USA)) [1994 101: 7.5d* 7g^5 8g^6 7d^6 7m^2 7d^2 1995 7m* 8m a8g^6 a6g 5.7g^6 a6g^3 a8s^3 Oct 5] compact colt: has a quick action: useful performer: has won first time out every season: won 21-runner rated stakes at Newmarket in April: ran as though something amiss in Royal Hunt Cup at Royal Ascot (2 months later) final start for J. Dunlop: stays 1m: acts on good to firm and dead ground: sometimes starts slowly: pulls hard. *L. Reuterskjold, Sweden*

105

GOVERNORS DREAM 2 b.f. (Apr 11) Governor General 116 – Friendly Miss (Be Friendly 130) [1995 5m 6s 5m 5.2f^5 a5g Nov 24] 1,000Y: robust filly: has scope: sister to 5f winner Three of Hearts and half-sister to 1985 2-y-o 6f winner Tawafan (by London Bells) and a multiple winner in Hong Kong by Noalto: dam 6f winner in Ireland: little worthwhile form: edged right into rail and fell 2f out third outing: visored fourth start. *Mrs N. Macauley*

–

GOVERNORS FORTUNE 3 b.g. Governor General 116 – Fortune's Fancy 48 (Workboy 123) [1994 NR 1995 8d 10.2m 6.1d Oct 10] stocky gelding: half-brother to fair sprint winner Ballafort (by Ballacashtal): dam poor sprint maiden: no sign of ability: sold 500 gns Ascot October Sales. *A. J. Chamberlain*

–

GOVERNOR'S LASS 3 b.f. Governor General 116 – Belle Tower 69 (Tower Walk 130) [1994 47: a7g a5g^6 1995 a7g 6s 5m^6 6.1g Apr 24] good-topped filly: no worthwhile form at 3 yrs: dead. *S. Dow*

–

GO WITH THE WIND 2 b.c. (Mar 19) Unfuwain (USA) 131 – Cominna (Dominion 123) [1995 8g 8d Sep 26] robust colt: second foal: brother to fairly useful 3-y-o Prima Cominna, 6f winner at 2 yrs: dam unraced sister to Primo Dominie: always towards rear in maidens at Doncaster and Newmarket: probably capable of better. *M. Bell* – p

GRACE CARD 9 b.g. Ela-Mana-Mou 132 – Val de Grace (FR) (Val de Loir 133) [1994 NR 1995 21.6f^{4} May 1] lengthy, workmanlike gelding: modest handicapper in 1993: fourth of 14 at Pontefract in May: suited by a thorough test of stamina: acts on firm ground, best effort on dead: joined R. Woodhouse. *Mrs M. Reveley* 44

GRACEFUL LADY 5 br.m. Bold Arrangement 127 – Northern Lady 95 (The Brianstan 128) [1994 NR 1995 8m^{4} 8f^{6} 5d Sep 13] strong, compact mare: half-sister to fairly useful 7.6f and 1m winner De Rigueur (by Derrylin): dam won 3 sprint races at 2 yrs: no worthwhile form in maidens. *E. J. Alston* –

GRACIOUS GRETCLO 2 gr.f. (Apr 1) Common Grounds 118 – Gratclo 65 (Belfort (FR) 89) [1995 5m^{3} 5m 5.1h^{5} 5g^{2} a7g^{6} a5g^{4} a6g^{2} a7g a5g^{5} Dec 18] leggy filly: second foal: half-sister to 3-y-o Pink Petal (by Northern Game): dam seemed suited by 7f: modest maiden: in frame 4 times, including in nurseries: may prove ideally suited by 6f: takes keen hold. *C. J. Hill* 54

GRANBY BELL 4 b.g. Ballacashtal (CAN) – Betbellof 65 (Averof 123) [1994 57+: 7g 10g^{5} 11.7g^{6} 11.9g* 12.1g* 12.1g^{4} 1995 11.9m 12g 12.1d^{2} 12m Nov 6] tall, angular gelding: good walker and mover: modest handicapper: form in 1995 only on third start: stays 1½m well: acts on good to soft ground: tried blinkered at 2 yrs: has won when sweating. *P. Hayward* 55

GRAND APPLAUSE (IRE) 5 gr.g. Mazaad 106 – Standing Ovation (Godswalk (USA) 130) [1994 58: 10.8m 10g^{4} a12g^{4} 16.5m 1995 a12g 10m 16.2g 13.1h^{4} 12d^{3} 14g 12s^{4} Oct 6] leggy, angular gelding: poor mover: modest maiden handicapper: stays 1¾m: acts on fibresand and on hard ground, very best form with some give: tried blinkered: has been bandaged: held up. *M. P. Muggeridge* 51

GRAND CHAPEAU (IRE) 3 b.c. Ballad Rock 122 – All Hat (Double Form 130) [1994 66: 5m 6g 6m 1995 6m 6g 6m^{4} 5.1m^{2} 5.1f^{2} 5m* 7g 5.1d 5.1m Oct 19] quite good-topped colt: modest handicapper: led final strides at Windsor in July: effective at 5f and 6f: acts on firm ground: sold (R. Hannon to D. Nicholls) 5,400 gns Newmarket Autumn Sales. *R. Hannon* 61

GRAND DU LAC (USA) 3 ch.c. Lac Ouimet (USA) – Vast Domain (CAN) (Vice Regent (CAN)) [1994 NR 1995 8f^{2} 8.1g* Jul 20] well-made colt: fifth foal: half-brother to 4 winners, including 9f stakes winner St Elias (by Temperence Hill): dam, graded-placed stakes at 2 yrs, won at up to 1¼m: sire, good-class 9f/1¼m performer, brother to St Jovite: 6/4 favourite, short to post, confirmed promise of debut by winning 15-runner maiden at Sandown in July by head from Goalwah, battling on well: will be suited by further than 1m: looked sure to do better. *D. R. Loder* 83 p

GRANDEE 4 b.c. Aragon 118 – Bourbon Queen 77 (Ile de Bourbon (USA) 133) [1994 –, a45: 6.1s a6g* a6g a6g^{6} a6g a7g 1995 a7g^{6} a7g Jan 25] small, sturdy colt: poor peformer: well beaten in 1995: sold 1,500 gns Doncaster March Sales: resold 800 gns Doncaster May Sales. *B. A. McMahon* –

GRANDES OREILLES (IRE) 3 b.f. Nordico (USA) – Top Knot (High Top 131) [1994 59: 6g^{6} 7m^{5} 6.9m^{5} 1995 10g 13.1f^{5} 12m a12g^{4} Jul 22] sturdy filly: modest maiden handicapper: stays 13f: acts on firm ground, yet to race on a soft surface: visored (took keen hold, ran poorly) final start. *N. J. H. Walker* 54

GRANDINARE (USA) 3 b. or br.c. El Gran Senor (USA) 136 – Hail The Lady (USA) (Hail The Pirates (USA) 126) [1994 81p: 7s* 1995 10m^{4} 7.3g 10m Aug 11] big colt: shows knee action: fairly useful performer: appeared to improve on debut form when last of 4 in minor event at Windsor on reappearance: well beaten afterwards: stays 1¼m: acts on good to firm and soft ground: has joined J. J. O'Neill. *P. W. Chapple-Hyam* 86

GRAND SALT (IRE) 4 b.c. Salt Dome (USA) – Fifty Grand (Ballad Rock 122) [1994 55: 6s^{6} 7s 6m^{5} 7g 6m 7m 7.6g^{5} 7d 11.5d^{6} 1995 9.7d^{6} 11.9m 8g^{6} 9m 10.8m 8.3m 8h Sep 4] close-coupled colt: modest maiden at best: well beaten last 4 starts, sold out of M. Haynes's stable 500 gns Ascot August Sales after penultimate one: 48 d stays 1¼m: acts on good to firm and dead ground: sometimes has tongue tied down. *C. L. Popham*

GRAND SELECTION (IRE) 3 b.g. Cricket Ball (USA) 124 – Sine Labe (USA) (Vaguely Noble 140) [1994 59: 6m^6 6.1s 6g 1995 a8.5g* a8g^2 a8g* a10g* a8.5g* a9.4g^3 10m* 10g^2 10.1m^2 10.1m* 12f^3 10m^2 12m^3 10.1g Sep 13] useful-looking gelding: has a round action: fairly useful handicapper: had an excellent season, winning at Wolverhampton (twice), Southwell and Lingfield early in year and at Lingfield in May and Newcastle in June: stays 1½m: acts on all-weather surfaces and on firm ground: thoroughly genuine and consistent. *M. Bell*

84

GRAND TIME 6 ch.g. Clantime 101 – Panay 77 (Arch Sculptor 123) [1994 37, a46: a6g a6g a5g^4 5v^3 5.1g 5.7g^5 6d^4 5m* 5.1f^3 5.1m^4 5m 5m a6g 1995 a5g 5d^6 5m^2 5.3m^6 5.7f^6 5g a5g 5m Aug 13] neat gelding: carries condition: poor handicapper: stays 6f: acts on the all-weather and any turf going: often wears blinkers/visor, but has run creditably without: often slowly away. *C. J. Hill*

37 a–

GRANIQUE (BEL) 3 b.g. Rabbi (BEL) – Gall (BEL) (Sea Bomb) [1994 7f^4 7f^5 7g a6.5g^5 a7g^5 a6g a7.5g^5 1995 8g^3 9d^3 a8g* a7g a8g^3 a10g* Nov 25] Belgian-bred gelding: won minor event at Sterrebeek in October and seller at Lingfield (gamely, sold Paul Smith to W. Turner £4,000) in November: stays 1¼m: acts on the all-weather. *Paul Smith, Belgium*

58

GRANMAS DELIGHT 4 b.f. Hadeer 118 – Miss Caro Star 76§ (Rusticaro (FR) 124) [1994 –, a56: a6g^3 a5g^2 a5g^3 a6g^5 5s 5.2m a5g a5g a5g^5 a5g^3 a5s^5 1995 5.3f^4 6g 5d^5 Sep 14] neat filly: modest maiden: no form in 1995: stayed 6f: dead. *M. McCormack*

–

GRANNY'S LEGACY 3 b.f. Most Welcome 131 – Historical Fact 78 (Reform 132) [1994 –: 7d 6s 7.1g 1995 9.9m a12g 12.4g 13.8g Jun 9] angular filly: of little account: sold 650 gns Doncaster July Sales. *J. D. Bethell*

–

GRATE BRITISH (IRE) 3 b.g. Astronef 116 – Stapelea (FR) (Faraway Son (USA) 130) [1994 65: 6g^4 6f^4 7g 6s^4 6g^6 8s* 7d 1995 10d 9.9m 8m^4 8g^6 11.9g^6 10d 10.5s Sep 30] good-topped gelding: poor mover: modest performer: disappointing in 1995: stays 1m: acts on firm and soft ground: inconsistent: sold 12,000 gns Doncaster November Sales and joined J. Fowler in Ireland. *E. Weymes*

62 d

GREAT BEAR 3 ch.g. Dominion 123 – Bay Bay 101 (Bay Express 132) [1994 92: 5g* 5f^4 7g^5 6s^5 6d^5 6s^4 1995 6g^6 7g^4 7f^5 8f 6d a5g a6g a6g Dec 12] compact gelding: fairly useful performer at best: ran well in minor event at Newbury on reappearance but deteriorated badly: sold out of R. Johnson Houghton's stable 6,200 gns Ascot August Sales after fourth start: tailed off for new connections: probably stays 7f: acts on firm and soft going: no improvement in blinkers: one to avoid. *D. W. Chapman*

92 d

GREAT BOND 4 b.g. Cree Song 99 – May Bond 69 (Good Bond 122) [1994 –: a8.5g 1995 a7g Jan 16] of little account. *B. A. McMahon*

–

GREAT CRUSADER 3 ch.g. Deploy 131 – Shannon Princess (Connaught 130) [1994 104?: 7f 7m^5 8g^5 10.2g* 10g^2 10s 1995 11g 12m^3 13.9m^5 16.2m^5 14.8g^3 12m^3 13.9m^4 16.2d Sep 23] smallish, strong gelding: useful performer: reluctant to jump off, pulled very hard and eventually downed tools in handicap at Ascot on final start: stays 16.2f: acts on soft ground and good to firm: blinkered last 2 starts: usually wears dropped noseband: early to post since second 3-y-o start: sometimes hangs markedly, and is a difficult ride: one to be wary of. *C. A. Cyzer*

98 §

GREAT DEEDS 4 b.f. Forzando 122 – Deed 86 (Derring-Do 131) [1994 107: 5s* 6d^5 5g* 5m 5g^6 5g^5 5d^5 6v^3 1995 5g 5m Jul 8] small, leggy filly: useful sprinter at 2 and 3 yrs: no worthwhile form in Prix du Gros-Chene at Chantilly and listed race at Sandown in 1995: probably needs give in the ground. *M. R. Channon*

–

GREAT EASEBY (IRE) 5 ch.g. Caerleon (USA) 132 – Kasala (USA) (Blushing Groom (FR) 131) [1994 NR 1995 14d 12.3f^3 14.1f^3 14s Sep 30] sturdy, good-bodied gelding: fifth reported foal: half-brother to a winner in Belgium by Chief Singer: dam unraced sister to dam of Kahyasi: fair winning staying hurdler, including in December: modest form in flat maidens: should be well suited by a thorough test of stamina. *W. Storey*

58

GREATEST 4 b.g. Superlative 118 – Pillowing 69 (Good Times (ITY)) [1994 –: 7m 7d 7m 8m 6.9m^6 10f 8.1d a7g 16.4s 1995 a7g^5 a7g^6 a7g^3 a7g* 6.9d 7m^2 8m* 7g^2

73

8f² 10.3d 8.5s 8g 8.2m Oct 19] leggy gelding: poor mover: fair performer: won claimer at Lingfield in March and handicap at Brighton in June: well below form last 4 starts: stays 1m: acts on all-weather surfaces and firm ground, no form on a soft surface: blinkered (out of form) twice as 3-y-o: races prominently. *R. Akehurst*

GREATEST HOPES 4 ch.g. Aragon 118 – Singora (Blue Cashmere 129) [1994 43: 5m 7m⁴ 7f⁴ 8d a7g² a7g a8g 1995 a7g a10g a10g⁴ a10g Feb 23] leggy, sparely-made gelding: poor maiden: probably stays 1¼m: acts on good to firm ground and equitrack: somewhat wayward. *C. J. Benstead* 32

GREAT EXPECTATIONS (FR) 4 ch.g. Village Star (FR) 131 – Balnica (FR) (Nice Havrais (USA) 124) [1994 10.5m⁵ 1995 10g 10g⁴ 13.1g⁵ 14.4m 12.5g Aug 12] nall, workmanlike gelding: fourth reported foal: dam never ran: trained by A. Fabre at 2 yrs: modest form at best in maidens and minor events here: stays 1¼m. *K. O. Cunningham-Brown* 59

GREAT HALL 6 gr.g. Hallgate 127 – Lily of France 81 (Monsanto (FR) 121) [1994 66: 6m 6d 7g 6f 6m 6g³ 6m 6m⁶ 7g⁵ 6m⁴ 6m* 6m³ 6g⁵ 6d⁵ 7m 6m 6s⁵ 6d 8g 7d 1995 a8g 6.9d⁵ 7s² 6g⁴ 6m 6f⁶ 7f 6m 7g⁶ 7m⁵ 6m⁴ 7m³ 6g* 5g 6.1m 6m 6m* 7f² 6m 7m 7.1d⁶ 6d 6d 7.1d Oct 10] compact gelding: carries condition: unimpressive mover: fair handicapper: won at Windsor in July and Newbury in August: below form last 6 starts: effective at 6f and 7f: acts on firm and soft going and on equitrack: best 6-y-o form in blinkers, visored once at 2 yrs: often bandaged behind: usually gets behind early on: successful for apprentice. *P. D. Cundell* 65

GREAT INQUEST 3 b.f. Shernazar 131 – Old Domesday Book 93 (High Top 131) [1994 NR 1995 7.3m* 8.5m 7.1m Jul 7] well-made filly: fourth foal: half-sister to very smart sprinter Owington (by Green Desert) and 7f (at 2 yrs) to 1½m winner Common Council (by Siberian Express): dam 10.4f winner better at 1½m: fairly useful form: won 16-runner maiden at Newbury in May: failed to improve on that in listed event at Epsom and handicap at Sandown (twice hampered early on): will stay 1¼m. *J. H. M. Gosden* 80

GREAT INTENT 2 gr.f. (Mar 14) Aragon 118 – Silver Berry (Lorenzaccio 130) [1995 5g⁶ Jun 17] 30,000Y: leggy filly: sister to 1992 2-y-o 5f winner Chatterberry and good sprinter Argentum and half-sister to several winners, including fair miler Eurodollar (by Sparkler): dam poor half-sister to very smart 1¼m filly Cranberry Sauce: 12/1 and bit backward, last of 6 in maiden at Sandown. *S. P. C. Woods* –

GREAT MARQUESS 8 b.h. Touching Wood (USA) 127 – Fruition 89 (Rheingold 137) [1994 a12g* a12g⁴ a12g⁵ a16s 1995 22.2m³ Jun 23] close-coupled horse: carries plenty of condition: has a quick action: smart stayer at best: won handicap at Nad Al Sheba in January 1994: eased right down entering final furlong in Queen Alexandra Stakes at Royal Ascot on only 8-y-o start: stays 2¼m: probably acts on any going: sometimes blinkered: fairly useful hurdler. *N. A. Twiston-Davies* –

GREAT ORATION (IRE) 6 b. or br.g. Simply Great (FR) 122 – Spun Gold 106 (Thatch (USA) 136) [1994 46: 12.3d 15.1m* 15.8f* 16g² 15.1m² 15.1m³ 16m⁴ 15.8g 15.1g 1995 14.1m⁶ 15.8m³ 15.1f² 17.1m* 16m⁴ 15.1s a16g⁶ Nov 20] rather leggy gelding: has a round action: poor handicapper: won at Pontefract in August, idling: stays 17.1f: acts on firm going and fibresand: effective visored or not: usually held up. *F. Watson* 46

GREAT SIMPLICITY 8 ch.g. Simply Great (FR) 122 – Affaire d'Amour (Tudor Music 131) [1994 NR 1995 11.5s Sep 28] half-brother to 2 Group 1 winners: dam unraced: fair handicapper for D. Weld at 3 yrs, winner at Leopardstown: modest hurdler here for next 2 years, but off course very long time before no show in 1995/6: bandaged, tailed off in Lingfield minor event on return to flat. *A. J. Chamberlain* –

GREAT TERN 3 b.f. Simply Great (FR) 122 – La Neva (FR) (Arctic Tern (USA) 126) [1994 NR 1995 8m⁶ 8m⁴ 12f⁶ Jul 26] 1,700Y: lengthy, workmanlike filly: fourth foal: dam French 12.5f winner: no worthwhile form. *N. M. Babbage* –

GRECIAN GARDEN 4 b.f. Sharrood (USA) 124 – Greek Goddess 82 (Young Generation 129) [1994 –: a5g 6s 8.3d⁶ a7g 10.1d 6s 1995 6m a5g May 11] small, sparely-made filly: rated 58 at 2 yrs: no worthwhile form since. *R. C. Spicer* –

GRECIAN LADY (IRE) 6 b.m. Be My Guest (USA) 126 – Grecian Sky (African Sky 124) [1994 41: 14g⁵ 10m 12m a13g 1995 a12g 14g Oct 30] winning –

hurdler in Ireland: poor maiden on flat: well beaten in 1995, trained for reappearance only by K. Burke. *S. Gannon, Ireland*

GREEK GOLD (IRE) 6 b.g. Rainbow Quest (USA) 134 – Gay Hellene 111 (Ela-Mana-Mou 132) [1994 59: a8.5g^2 a8.5g^3 a7g a9.4g a8g a8g 10m^2 10.1f^3 10d a11g* a8.5g^3 10.3s^4 a11g 1995 a11g* a11g a11g^3 a10g^2 a10g^2 a9.4g a12g^5 a8g 9.9m 8m 8.5m 8m^4 10m 10g 12f^4 10.3m a11g a8g^6 a10g Dec 18] leggy gelding: has quick action: modest performer at best: sold out of Mrs J. Ramsden's stable 5,000 gns after winning seller at Southwell in January: left G. Kelly's stable after tenth start: stays 1½m: acts on firm ground and all-weather surfaces: visored (out of form) twice as 5-y-o: has had tongue tied down: takes keen hold: often a front runner: none too consistent. *D. Nicholls* — 61 d

GREEK ICON 2 b.f. (Apr 25) Thatching 131 – Rosie Potts 83 (Shareef Dancer (USA) 135) [1995 5g^3 6m* 6m* 7g^4 6m^3 6g^4 Nov 8] IR 12,000Y: smallish, well-made filly: second foal: half-sister to 3-y-o 1m winner Biya (by Shadeed): dam, 6f (at 2 yrs) and 1m winner, half-sister to very useful middle-distance performer Trakady: fairly useful performer: won maiden auction at Ripon in August and minor event at Milan (by 8½ lengths) in September: twice ran creditably in listed races afterwards: stays 7f: yet to race on a soft surface. *J. L. Dunlop* — 87

GREEK NIGHT OUT (IRE) 4 b.f. Ela-Mana-Mou 132 – Ce Soir (Northern Baby (CAN) 127) [1994 45: a8.5g^5 a11g a12g^3 a9.4g^2 a8.5g^4 12s^3 10f* 10d a8.5g^2 a8.5g a9.4g 1995 a11g^2 a11g a10g^6 8.2g 8m 12m^5 a12g 8g 10g^6 a8.5g a12g^3 15.8g* 17.1m^3 18f^3 a14g^3 a14.8g^3 Nov 11] leggy filly: poor handicapper: trained until after fifth 4-y-o start by J. A. Harris, then until after tenth by Mrs V. Aconley: won at Catterick in September: stays 2¼m: acts on firm ground and fibresand, probably on soft: occasionally blinkered/visored, no improvement: sometimes bandaged near hind/behind. *J. L. Eyre* — 41

GREENACRES LADY 5 b.m. Seymour Hicks (FR) 125 – Moon Lady 78 (Cash And Courage 116) [1994 NR 1995 a11g^6 Aug 4] fifth foal: half-sister to fairly useful 7f/1m plater Moon Lad (by Virginia Boy) and winning hurdler Greenacres Lad (by Billion): dam won over 1m and 1¼m: well beaten in claimer at Southwell. *B. A. McMahon* — –

GREENACRES STAR 5 ch.m. Seymour Hicks (FR) 125 – Greenacres Girl (Tycoon II) [1994 35: a12g 10g 10m 8.2s a11g^5 14.1g^6 a14g^2 a14g^6 a14g^5 1995 a16g^6 a16g^2 a14.8g^3 Feb 15] sparely-made mare: poor maiden: stays 2m: acts on fibresand. *B. A. McMahon* — 41

GREEN APACHE 3 b.g. Green Desert (USA) 127 – Can Can Girl 69 (Gay Fandango (USA) 132) [1994 –: 6g 7s 1995 8.3m 5g 6g 7f^2 Aug 2] lengthy gelding: only worthwhile form when second of 13 in maiden handicap at Brighton: stays 7f: acts on firm ground: probably ungenuine: sold (T. J. Naughton to K. Wingrove) 880 gns Doncaster October Sales. *T. J. Naughton* — 26

GREENBACK (BEL) 4 b.c. Absalom 128 – Batalya (BEL) (Boulou) [1994 56, a62: a7g a9.4g^5 a8g* 8s a8g* 8m 7.5m^3 8m^5 a10g^4 8.1m 8.1f* 8m^5 1995 12f Jun 28] sturdy, lengthy colt: modest performer at 3 yrs for S. Williams: tough and genuine juvenile hurdler, winner 8 times in 1994/5: tailed off on return to flat: should stay beyond 1m: acts on equitrack and firm ground, well beaten on soft (has form on any surface over hurdles): tried visored. *P. J. Hobbs* — –

GREEN BARRIES 2 b.c. (Feb 23) Green Desert (USA) 127 – Barari (USA) (Blushing Groom (FR) 131) [1995 5d 5f^2 6m^2 Nov 3] compact colt: third living foal: half-brother to a winner in Belgium by Jareer: dam unraced half-sister to very smart French 1m/1¼m performer Colour Chart and Canadian champion Rainbows For Life: progressive colt: ½-length second of 20 to Miss Riviera in maiden at Doncaster on final start, always in front rank but hanging left near finish: better form at 6f than 5f: races keenly: unruly in paddock on debut: taken early to post on second start. *M. Johnston* — 84

GREEN BENTLEY (IRE) 2 b.f. (Apr 24) Green Desert (USA) 127 – Lady Bentley 109 (Bellypha 130) [1995 5m 6g^3 5.1f^4 7m^2 7.3m^2 7g^2 6g^6 Sep 30] angular filly: fourth foal: half-sister to Irish 1m (at 2 yrs) and 1½m winner Lord Bentley (by Rousillon): dam 1m (at 2 yrs) to 11f (Italian Oaks) winner who stayed 1½m, out of half-sister to smart stayer Yawa: fair maiden: good second in 3 nurseries (to Consordino at Yarmouth on last occasion) before looking unsuited by drop back to 6f — 76 +

in maiden at Newmarket on final start: will prove best at 7f+: acts on good to firm going. *R. Hannon*

GREEN BOPPER (USA) 2 b.c. (Apr 12) Green Dancer (USA) 132 – Wayage (USA) (Mr Prospector (USA)) [1995 7g Sep 28] $80,000Y: neat colt: fifth foal: half-brother to useful French 3-y-o Nicosie (by Northern Baby), placed at 15f, useful miler Secrage (by Secreto) and 1991 2-y-o 7f winner Minstrel's Age (by The Minstrel): dam French maiden daughter of top-class middle-distance mare Waya: 50/1, around 10 lengths tenth of 23 to Astor Place in maiden at Newmarket, keeping on steadily: will be suited by middle distances: will improve. *M. Bell* — 71 p

GREEN CHARTER 2 b.f. (May 5) Green Desert (USA) 127 – By Charter 104 (Shirley Heights 130) [1995 7m^4 6.1d 7f* Oct 12] 56,000Y: smallish, quite attractive filly: good mover: second foal: half-sister to 3-y-o Magna Carta, 7f winner at 2 yrs: dam, seemed to stay 1¼m, daughter of Time Charter: won 12-runner maiden at Redcar by a short head: will stay 1m: acts on firm ground, disappointing effort on dead: probably capable of further improvement. *H. R. A. Cecil* — 77 p

GREEN CITY 3 br.f. Rock City 120 – Pea Green 98 (Try My Best (USA) 130) [1994 74: 6m 6m* 7m^6 1995 7m 6.1g 6m 7.6m 8s a7g Oct 23] small filly: good mover: fair handicapper: disappointing in 1995: left R. Hannon's stable after fourth start: stays 7f: acts on good to firm ground. *J. Akehurst* — –

GREEN CRUSADER 4 b.g. Green Desert (USA) 127 – Hysterical 68 (High Top 131) [1994 95: 8d* 8.1s^5 7.9f^4 8m 10g^3 10g^2 10.3d^2 10s* 9g 1995 9m^6 10g^5 10m 10.3d 10d 10v Oct 7] good-topped gelding: carries condition: fairly useful handicapper: became rather disappointing, and well beaten last 4 starts: stays 10.3f: acts on any going: visored since sixth 3-y-o start: has gone early to post: sold (M. Stoute to Mrs V. Ward) 20,000 gns Newmarket Autumn Sales. *M. R. Stoute* — 88

GREEN DIVOT 4 b.f. Green Desert (USA) 127 – Cut Ahead 85 (Kalaglow 132) [1994 NR 1995 8.2d 8s^6 10m Oct 26] leggy filly: first foal: dam, 1¼m winner, is out of smart sister to Cut Above and half-sister to Irish 2000 Guineas winner Sharp Edge: no worthwhile form. *G. Wragg* — –

GREEN DOLLAR 12 b.g. Tickled Pink 114 – Burglars Girl 63 (Burglar 128) [1994 66d: 6d 5.7m^6 6m^3 6m 6m 6m 6f^6 1995 6m 6g 6d Sep 18] smallish, strong gelding: veteran sprint handicapper: soundly beaten in 1995. *P. Howling* — –

GREENFINCH (CAN) 4 gr.g. Green Dancer (USA) 132 – Princess Verna (USA) (Al Hattab (USA)) [1994 –: 8.3v 12s 8g 1995 12g^6 15.8g Jul 6] strong gelding: no form since 1993. *Mrs A. M. Naughton* — –

GREEN GEM (BEL) 2 b.f. (Mar 29) Pharly (FR) 130 – Batalya (BEL) (Boulou) [1995 7f^6 a6g^4 a7g^6 Dec 15] smallish filly: half-sister to 1m winner/useful hurdler Greenback (by Absalom), 6f to 1¼m winner Bassio (by Efisio) and a winner in Belgium by Mummy's Pet: dam won 6 races in Belgium: short of room much of straight when around length fourth of 10 to Mask Flower in slowly-run maiden at Lingfield: dropped away after helping set strong pace in median auction event there following month: should stay beyond 6f. *S. C. Williams* — 62 ?

GREEN GOLIGHTLY (USA) 4 b.c. Green Dancer (USA) 132 – Polly Daniels (USA) 110 (Clever Trick (USA)) [1994 71: 8d^5 7m 6m* 6g 7g 6s 1995 6g 6f 5f^5 5m 5g 6m 6m 6m 5m^5 6g 7d 6d 8g 7g a7g a10g a10g a6g a8g Dec 15] useful-looking colt: fair handicapper in 1994 for M. Jarvis: no form at 4 yrs. *D. A. Wilson* — –

GREEN GREEN DESERT (FR) 4 b.g. Green Desert (USA) 127 – Green Leaf (USA) 97 (Alydar (USA)) [1994 103: 8d 7m^5 8f^2 7m 9s^2 10m^2 1995 8.1m^4 10g^4 10.2m^2 8g^3 10m^2 11.6m^3 10.1s^3 Sep 19] rangy, attractive gelding: superb mover with a fluent, light action: useful performer: made frame all starts in 1995 (mainly in minor events), but again failed to add to sole (2-y-o) success, best effort when 3 lengths fourth of 5 to Missed Flight in Sandown Mile on first outing: probably stays 11.6f: acts on firm and soft ground: wears a net muzzle: lacks turn of foot: irresolute and one to treat with caution: sold (M. Stoute to Lady Herries) 36,000 gns Newmarket Autumn Sales. *M. R. Stoute* — 109 d

GREEN GREEN RUBY 3 b.g. Green Ruby (USA) 104 – Celtic Bird 77 (Celtic Cone 116) [1994 46: 6g^4 6g 7m^2 a7g^3 7f^6 7.1g^5 a8g 7g 1995 a10g 10g 7f^5 8.1g^6 10m 10m 11.9f^5 Jul 20] good-topped gelding: poor maiden: probably stays 1¼m: acts on firm ground and fibresand: tried visored, no improvement. *G. L. Moore* — 42 d

GREEN LAND (BEL) 3 b.f. Hero's Honor (USA) – Heavy Land (FR) (Recitation (USA) 124) [1994 59: 7.5g^6 6.9m^5 7d 1995 10d 8.3g^2 12m* 11.8g* 12d^3 11.4d 13.6f* 14.6m 12.1s^2 Nov 2] close-coupled filly: fair handicapper: won at Beverley and Leicester in May and at Redcar in October: should stay beyond 13.6f: acts on firm and soft ground: bandaged in 1995. *S. C. Williams* 72

GREEN PERFUME (USA) 3 b.c. Naevus (USA) – Pretty Is (USA) (Doonesbury (USA)) [1994 121: 5m^2 7g^2 6m* 6g* 6m^2 7m^2 1995 8m 7f^2 7m^6 7.3m^6 6g 7g 6d^4 Oct 19] strong, lengthy, good-looking colt: very smart juvenile: headstrong and far from an easy ride in 1995, failing by long chalk to reproduce his best: may do best as a sprinter: acts on good to firm ground: often early to post: sometimes finds little. *P. F. I. Cole* 101 §

GREEN'S BID 5 gr.g. Siberian Express (USA) 125 – Arianna Aldini (Habitat 134) [1994 65: a7g a5g^3 5d^6 5.1d^3 a5g^3 5m 6m a5g^5 6m a6g^2 6f 6g^3 5g 5m 6g 6g a5g^4 a6g a5s^3 1995 a6g^6 a6g^6 a6g a6g a6g^3 a8g* a8g^6 8m a8g 6m a5g a6g^2 6m 7m^2 6.9f* 7f a8g a7g a8g a6g^4 a5g a7g Dec 12] lengthy gelding: modest handicapper: won amateurs events at Lingfield in March and Carlisle (rallied) in June: stays 1m: acts on firm and dead ground and goes well on all-weather surfaces: below form in blinkers: none too consistent. *D. W. Chapman* 62 d

GREEN SEED (IRE) 3 b.f. Lead On Time (USA) 123 – Lady In Green (Shareef Dancer (USA) 135) [1994 78: 6f* 7.2g^3 1995 7.3g^5 7.1m^3 8m^2 8m^6 10.3m^3 Sep 6] leggy, lengthy filly: fair performer: stays 10.3f: has raced only on a sound surface: consistent. *J. R. Fanshawe* 78

GREENSPAN (IRE) 3 b.c. Be My Guest (USA) 126 – Prima Ballerina (FR) (Nonoalco (USA) 131) [1994 7d^3 8d^4 7.8s* 1995 10.4m^6 10g 12g 13.3d 10.5g 10.5s^5 Sep 30] IR 14,500Y: useful-looking ex-Irish colt: seventh foal: half-brother to 3 winners, including fairly useful Irish miler Basie Noble (by Law Society): dam unraced: fairly useful form (rated 81p) at 2 yrs for J. Bolger, winning maiden at Dundalk in November by 9 lengths: fair form in handicaps here, creditable fifth of 17 at Haydock on final outing: stays 10.5f: acts on soft going, probably on good to firm: blinkered (fell) third 3-y-o start: won juvenile hurdle in November. *W. R. Muir* 74

GREEN'S SEAGO (USA) 7 ch.g. Fighting Fit (USA) – Ornamental (USA) (Triple Crown (USA)) [1994 –: a11g a12g^6 12.5d 1995 14.1f 16.1h Aug 2] lengthy gelding: soundly beaten on flat last 3 seasons: won selling hurdles in August and October. *J. A. Harris* –

GREEN TUNE (USA) 4 ch.c. Green Dancer (USA) 132 – Soundings (USA) (Mr Prospector (USA)) [1994 123: 8g* 8g* 8m^4 8g^3 8g^2 1995 10s^4 8v* 9.3g* 8g^5 8m Sep 3] 125

How disappointing that the Prix d'Ispahan at the end of May proved to be the end, to all intents and purposes, of the racing careers of Green Tune and Pelder. Green

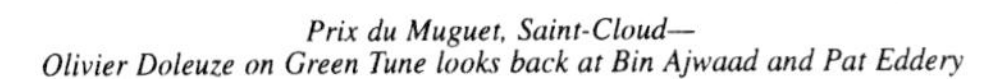

Prix du Muguet, Saint-Cloud—
Olivier Doleuze on Green Tune looks back at Bin Ajwaad and Pat Eddery

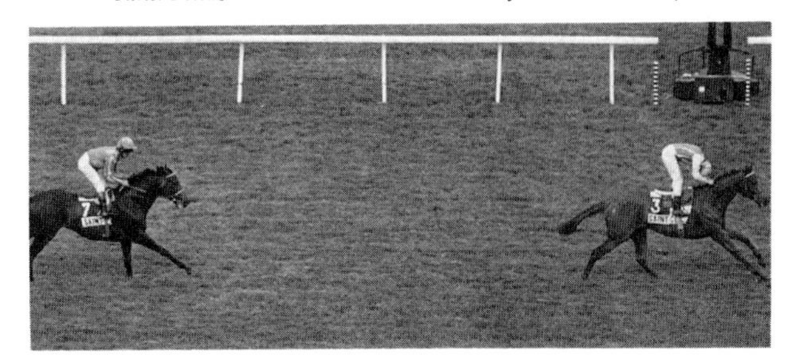

Prix d'Ispahan, Longchamp—Doleuze and Eddery (Pelder) again; Marildo finishes third

Tune did at least return to the track in late-summer, but he brought with him little of the zest that characterised his best performances. Run at Longchamp in May, the Prix d'Ispahan looked a good race on paper with five of the nine runners being previous Group 1 winners and Green Tune was made favourite partly on the strength of having given 7 lb and an impressive three-length beating to Bin Ajwaad in the Prix du Muguet at Saint-Cloud earlier in the month. Disputing favouritism with Green Tune was the revitalised Pelder, who had finished ahead of him in the Prix d'Harcourt at Longchamp in April before winning the Prix Ganay there impressively from Alderbrook and Richard of York. None of the rest started at less than 6/1, though they included the previous year's winners of the Prix Ganay (Marildo) and Champion Stakes (Dernier Empereur), as well as the first two from the recent Premio Presidente della Repubblica, Flagbird and Del Deya. Green Tune's pacemaker, Simply Tricky, set a sound pace to the straight then was brought off the rail, allowing Green Tune through into the lead about two furlongs from home. Pelder quickened impressively to join issue soon after, and the pair battled under strong pressure to the line. At first it seemed Pelder would prevail, but Green Tune fought back tenaciously to regain the advantage in the last two strides and win by a short head, the pair drawing two and a half lengths clear of the field, headed by Marildo. Post-race excuses for Pelder included the ground and the draw, but none was necessary. Green Tune returned after a planned eleven-week absence for the Prix Jacques Le Marois at Deauville, the fifth choice in a field of nine. In the event he had every chance before fading in the final three hundred yàrds to finish a respectable four lengths fifth to Miss Satamixa. He failed to come on for the run though, and beat only one home in the Prix du Moulin de Longchamp.

Green Tune (USA) (ch.c. 1991)	Green Dancer (USA) (b 1972)	Nijinsky (b 1967)	Northern Dancer
			Flaming Page
		Green Valley (br 1967)	Val de Loir
			Sly Pola
	Soundings (USA) (b 1983)	Mr Prospector (b 1970)	Raise A Native
			Gold Digger
		Ocean's Answer (b 1976)	Northern Answer
			South Ocean

There are better sire lines around than the Green Dancer branch of the Northern Dancer dynasty, though the first foals of comfortably his best son, Suave Dancer, do not reach the racecourse until 1996. Green Dancer does have a champion sire among his progeny, but it's as a jumps stallion in France that Cadoudal has made his name. On the flat there has been little else to enthuse over apart from No Attention in Japan. The distaff side of Green Tune's family was discussed in *Racehorses of 1994*. He is Soundings' third foal, preceded a year earlier by Prix Robert Papin winner Didyme (by Dixieland Band) and followed by the two-year-old Ecoute (by

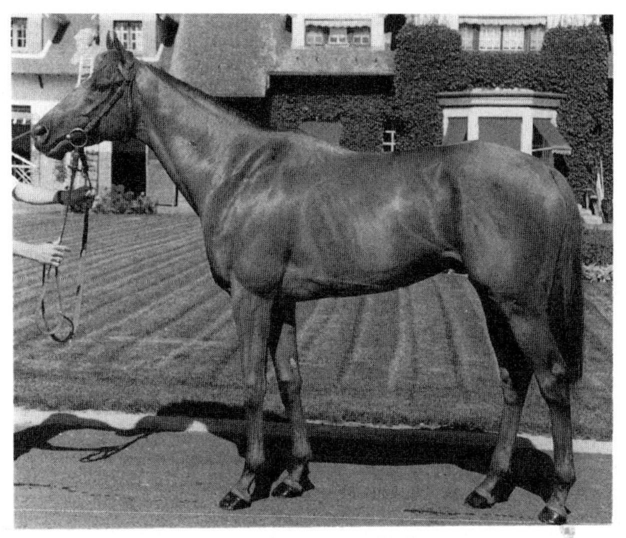

Mr J. Wertheimer's "Green Tune"

Manila) and the yearling Pas de Reponse (by Danzig). Green Tune is a tall, long-striding colt with a fluent action. He acted on good to firm and heavy ground and was effective from a mile to at least an extended nine furlongs, and probably over a mile and a quarter. For all that the game and genuine Green Tune won a classic, the Poule d'Essai des Poulains, the duel against Pelder is probably his best race. He has been retired to the Haras d'Etreham at a fee of 50,000 francs (October 1st). *Mme C. Head, France*

GREENWAY LADY 3 ch.f. Prince Daniel (USA) – Lady Ector (USA) (King Pellinore (USA) 127) [1994 NR 1995 10.1m^5 11.4m 11.5g 14g Sep 23] angular filly: half-sister to a winning middle-distance stayer in Italy by Stormy Fighter: dam never ran: no worthwhile form on flat, but won selling hurdle in November: joined Miss A. Embiricos. *C. N. Allen* –

GREENWICH AGAIN 3 b.g. Exodal (USA) – What A Challenge 70 (Sallust 134) [1994 69: 5m 5s^2 7m* 7m^6 7g^2 6.9m*^{dis} 8m^5 7.3s^6 1995 a7g^3 a8g* 9m 7.6m* 7g^5 8m 7.6m^3 8f^6 8g a8g a8g^4 Dec 15] leggy gelding: poor walker: fair performer at best: won handicap at Lingfield (on all-weather) in February and minor event there (on turf) in May: mostly below form afterwards: stays 1m: acts on good to firm and soft ground and on equitrack. *T. G. Mills* 72 d a75 d

GRESHAM FLYER 2 b.c. (Feb 24) Clantime 101 – Eleanor Cross (Kala Shikari 125) [1995 5m 6.1m 6m 6.1m a5g Nov 24] sparely-made colt: first reported foal: dam maiden, probably stayed 1m: well beaten in maidens and a minor event. *B. Richmond* –

GREY AGAIN 3 gr.f. Unfuwain (USA) 131 – Grey Goddess 117 (Godswalk (USA) 130) [1994 63?: 7m a7g* 6g 7m a6g 1995 a8.5g^3 a7g^2 8g 7.5m^3 9.9m^6 a7g^4 7g^2 7m^2 8f^5 8m a7g 7m Sep 5] leggy filly: modest handicapper: stays 8.5f: acts on good to firm ground and fibresand: usually blinkered. *S. R. Bowring* 54

GREY BLADE 3 gr.f. Dashing Blade 117 – High Matinee (Shirley Heights 130) [1994 –: 8d 1995 10m 10g 10.2m^{6} 12.5m Jun 26] big, unfurnished filly: no worthwhile form: sold (I. Balding to Mrs P. M. Pile) 2,000 gns Ascot July Sales. *I. A. Balding* –

GREY CHARMER (IRE) 6 gr.h. Alzao (USA) 117 – Sashi Woo (Rusticaro (FR) 124) [1994 57: 7d 6m 6v^{3} 6s^{5} 6g 6m^{4} 6m^{2} 6f^{3} 6g 7g 6s 8d 1995 5d^{2} 5m^{4} 6m 6g^{6} 6m^{6} 6m a6g^{4} a6g^{2} a7g a6g Dec 9] close-coupled horse: unimpressive mover: modest handicapper: stays 6f: acts on fibresand and any turf going: blinkered (below form) twice at 3 yrs: sometimes slowly away. *C. James* 57

GREYCOAT BOY 3 gr.g. Pragmatic 115 – Sirdar Girl 69 (Milford 119) [1994 –: 7g 7m 1995 10m 10.2m 14.6m^{4} 14.1m^{2} 14.1m 16.2m^{3} 14.4m^{3} 15g 17.2m* 16.2s^{2} 16d^{6} Oct 19] tall, angular gelding: fair handicapper: blinkered first time, won at Bath in September: will stay extreme distances: acts on good to firm and soft ground: blinkered last 3 starts. *B. J. Meehan* 74

GREY GALAVA 2 gr.f. (Mar 31) Generous (IRE) 139 – Galava (CAN) (Graustark) [1995 7g^{4} 7g^{5} Jul 16] lengthy filly: second foal: dam French maiden, placed at 7f and 1m: fourth of 8 to Staffin in maiden at Doncaster: well beaten in similar event at Ayr 15 days later. *B. W. Hills* 64

GREY KINGDOM 4 gr.g. Grey Desire 115 – Miss Realm 86 (Realm 129) [1994 –: 7.5m^{5} 7g^{5} 5m^{6} 1995 a7g 7.5g Jul 17] angular, leggy gelding: no worthwhile form. *M. Brittain* –

GREY LEGEND 2 gr.c. (Apr 17) Touch of Grey 90 – Northwold Star (USA) 71 (Monteverdi 129) [1995 5m^{5} 6f^{3} 6m^{3} 5m 6d Sep 18] compact colt: first reported foal: dam thorough stayer: modest form: will probably stay beyond 6f: reportedly finished lame when blinkered fourth start: edgy last 2 outings. *R. M. Flower* 63

GREY SHOT 3 gr.g. Sharrood (USA) 124 – Optaria 83 (Song 132) [1994 86p: 7d* 1995 9d^{4} 11g^{6} 12g^{3} 14g^{2} 14m^{2} 16.2m^{6} 14.8g* 13.9m^{2} 14.6m* 15s* Sep 30] leggy, unfurnished gelding: fine, easy mover: smart performer: won 5-runner listed event at Newmarket in July and 6-runner £12,900 handicap at Doncaster and 7-runner Prix de Lutece at Longchamp (beat Court of Honour 2½ lengths) in September, making virtually all on each occasion: will stay beyond 2m: acts on good to firm and soft ground: front runner: thoroughly game and genuine. *I. A. Balding* 111

GREY TOPPA 4 gr.f. Belfort (FR) 89 – Gallic Law 91 (Galivanter 131) [1994 66: 6m 7m 5g^{2} 5m* 6f 6g^{6} 5g* 5m^{4} 6m^{2} 5g 5s 6s^{6} a5g a6g 1995 a7g a6g^{5} a6g a6g 6g 5.1g a5g^{4} 5f^{6} a6g 6g a5g^{3} 6.1m a6g^{4} 5.1m^{6} a5g 6f a7g^{6} 7m Aug 25] leggy filly: poor sprint handicapper at best in 1995: sold out of Mrs J. Ramsden's stable 3,800 gns Doncaster March Sales after fourth start: acts on fibresand and probably on any turf going: sold 3,000 gns Newmarket September Sales. *N. P. Littmoden* 40

Prix de Lutece, Longchamp—Grey Shot gallops his rivals into the ground; Court of Honour (rails) just beats Periple for second, with Sanmartino fourth

Mr J. C. Smith's "Grey Shot"

GRIFFIN'S GIRL 3 ch.f. Bairn (USA) 126 – All That Crack (Stanford 121§) [1994 –: 10g 8d 1995 a7g⁶ a6g⁶ 10g⁴ Apr 4] lengthy filly: poor maiden: stays 1¼m. *R. P. C. Hoad* 32

GRIMSTONE GIRL 2 b.f. (May 18) Lochnager 132 – Estefan 58 (Taufan (USA) 119) [1995 5m³ 6g⁴ 6g 5g 5g a5g 5f³ Jul 28] close-coupled, workmanlike filly: second foal: dam stayed 6f: poor plater: lost her form after second start: stays 6f: blinkered twice: has worn bandages behind. *M. W. Easterby* 44 d

GROOMS GOLD (IRE) 3 ch.c. Groom Dancer (USA) 128 – Gortynia (FR) (My Swallow 134) [1994 61p: 7f⁵ 6g⁵ 1995 8d 10g 10f* 12.1m 10m 11.8g Oct 9] lengthy colt: fair handicapper: best effort when winning at Redcar in July: should stay beyond 1¼m: acts on firm ground: sold (P. Harris to P. Hobbs) 23,000 gns Newmarket Autumn Sales. *P. W. Harris* 66

GROUND GAME 2 b.f. (Mar 26) Gildoran 123 – Running Game 81 (Run The Gantlet (USA)) [1995 7m³ a8g* Nov 6] 600Y: seventh live foal: half-sister to a middle-distance winner in Italy by Welsh Pageant: dam 2m winner: bandaged behind, won maiden at Southwell in November by neck: will stay well: probably capable of more improvement. *D. R. Loder* 67 p

GRYADA 2 b.f. (Mar 23) Shirley Heights 130 – Grimpola (GER) (Windwurf (GER)) [1995 6.1m² 6.9g* 7m² 8g⁶ 8.3g* 8d³ Oct 15] good-topped filly: has scope: sister to 2 winners, including middle-distance performer Golan Heights, and closely related to 3-y-o 1¼m winner Goonda (by Darshaan) and out-and-out stayer Gondolier (by Slip Anchor): dam won at 6f and 1m in Germany and stayed 1½m: 93

fairly useful performer: won maiden at Folkestone in July and 3-runner minor event at Hamilton in September: creditable third of 11 to Scarlet Plume in Premio Dormello at Milan last time: will be suited by middle distances: acts on good to firm ground and dead. *W. Jarvis*

GUADO D'ANNIBALE (IRE) 6 ch.h. Glint of Gold 128 – When Lit (Northfields (USA)) [1994 10v* 10.5g^3 10g* 1995 10g* 10d^3 10g 12m^3 12f 10m* 10s^6 Sep 17] strong horse: smart performer: won 2 minor events in 1994 and another (at Naples) in February before (as in 1992) landing Gran Premio Citta di Napoli, by 3 lengths from Sugarland Express in July: stays 1½m: acts on good to firm ground and heavy. *A. Renzoni, Italy* 109

GUARDS BRIGADE 4 b.g. Bustino 136 – Light Duty 113 (Queen's Hussar 124) [1994 61§: a11g^2 a12g* 12g^6 14.1g a12g^3 a12g 11.5d a12g 1995 a11g 18g 16.2m^5 14m 13g^6 13g^3 13g^6 10g^6 Jun 2] lengthy gelding: poor performer: very best form at 1½m, but probably stays 2m: acts on good to firm ground and fibresand: visored (no form) once at 3 yrs: often makes running: has high head carriage: none too genuine. *J. Hetherton* 49 §

GUARDSMAN (IRE) 3 ch.g. Pennine Walk 120 – Peace Princess (On Your Mark 125) [1994 46: 6f 6g 5g^6 1995 a8.5g Oct 28] compact gelding: poor form at 2 yrs for C. W. C. Elsey: tailed off in maiden only 3-y-o start: sold 700 gns Doncaster November Sales. *T. H. Caldwell* –

GUESSTIMATION (USA) 6 b.g. Known Fact (USA) 135 – Best Guess (USA) (Apalachee (USA) 137) [1994 61, a54: 8d 8.2m^2 8m^5 8.3f^3 8.1m^4 8.2m^6 8d^6 8d 7m* 9.7d* 7g^2 a8.5g^2 8.1g^6 a12g a8.5g^3 a8g a8g^2 1995 7.1g^3 8m^5 9.7m* 8.3m^3 8f* 8g^4 a10g^4 9m* 8.9g^3 7g^2 8.5s^4 10d* 8.9g^5 8m 10f^4 10f^3 Oct 31] good-topped gelding: fair performer: won claimer at Folkestone in May, apprentice selling handicap at Ripon in June, seller at Kempton in August and apprentice handicap at Newmarket in September: effective at 7f to 1¼m: acts on firm and soft ground, has only modest form on the all-weather: below form most tries in blinkers: genuine and consistent. *J. Pearce* 71 a52

GUEST ALLIANCE (IRE) 3 ch.g. Zaffaran (USA) 117 – Alhargah (Be My Guest (USA) 126) [1994 55: 7f 5g 6m^6 6g^4 7m^4 a8g^6 7.6v^4 6.9d^6 7s 1995 10f^5 6.9g a8g^5 10f^3 11.9f^2 10f 11.9d^6 10g^3 a12g a16g* a16g Dec 15] modest performer: kept on dourly to win minor event at Lingfield in November: stays 2m well: acts on equitrack and any turf ground. *A. Moore* 59

GULF BAY 3 b.f. Reprimand 122 – Miss Butterfield (Cure The Blues (USA)) [1994 –: 7m 8g 8d 1995 a8g^4 10.8m 10f 10m 10.1d^2 10f^2 11.5m^6 11f^2 a12g^3 10m Aug 12] unfurnished filly: poor mover: poor maiden handicapper: stays 11f: acts on firm and dead ground and on fibresand: visored (no improvement) twice. *M. Bell* 35

GULF OF SIAM 2 ch.g. (Feb 26) Prince Sabo 123 – Jussoli (Don 128) [1995 6m^4 6g^3 6m^5 Oct 4] 10,000Y: strong, lengthy gelding: has scope: third reported foal: half-brother to 3-y-o So Amazing (by Hallgate): dam, Irish 7f (at 2 yrs) to 1¼m winner, best at middle distances: slowly away when third of 12 to Diminuet in maiden auction at Ayr: headstrong: has been gelded. *Miss S. E. Hall* 62 +

GULF SHAADI 3 b.c. Shaadi (USA) 126 – Ela Meem (USA) (Kris 135) [1994 75, a82: 6m^5 7f^4 8.1g^6 7m^5 7s a6g^6 a7g* a7g^3 1995 a7g* a7g* a8g^3 a10g^3 a8g* a7g* 7m^6 8.3m^6 a8g^2 a8.5g* 10.1m 8m^4 a8.5g^4 7.1g 7f 8f a8g Dec 14] lengthy, attractive colt: has a quick action: fairly useful performer at best: won claimer at Lingfield and handicap at Wolverhampton in January, 2 claimers at Lingfield (claimed out of C. Brittain's stable £12,000 after first of them) in March and claimer at Wolverhampton in May: well below form afterwards, leaving G. Lewis' stable after thirteenth start: effective at 7f to 1¼m: acts on the all-weather and probably on any turf ground: held up and sometimes pulls hard: slowly away last 3 starts: has had tongue tied down. *E. J. Alston* 78 d a85 d

GULF WATER (USA) 5 br.g. Al Nasr (FR) 126 – Paddle (FR) 120 (Jim French (USA)) [1994 8s^2 1995 10d Nov 13] half-brother to several winners, notably listed winners by Pharly and Gay Mecene and 1984 2-y-o 6f winner Bellwater (by Bellypha), later fourth in Prix du Jockey-Club: dam best at up to 1¼m (listed winner, fourth in Prix de Diane) is half-sister to Dunette: trained by A. Fabre to win 3 races over 7f at 2 yrs (notably in listed company) and finish in frame in all 3 starts at 3/4 yrs, showing useful form: sold 19,000 gns Newmarket Autumn (1994) Sales and –

gelded: last in listed race at Fontainebleau only outing for new stable: stays 1m: acts on heavy going. *Lady Herries*

GUMAIR (USA) 2 ch.c. (Mar 19) Summer Squall (USA) – Finisterre (AUS) (Biscay (AUS)) [1995 7g 7m^5 8m^5 8m^6 Sep 6] $85,000Y: good-bodied colt: good mover: sixth foal: half-brother to top Australasian performer (effective at 6f and stayed 1½m) Our Poetic Prince (by Yeats): dam winner in Australia: sire, very well bred, Grade 1 winner at 2 yrs and (Preakness) 3 yrs: fair form: around 6 lengths fifth to Moody's Cat in maiden at Ascot third start: ran creditably (raced on unfavoured stand side) when sixth of 17 in nursery at Doncaster on final outing: very much an out-and-out stayer. *R. Hannon* 76

GUNBOAT DIPLOMACY (FR) 4 b.c. Dominion 123 – Singapore Girl (FR) 117 (Lyphard (USA) 132) [1994 112: 11v* 10.5g^4 1995 10d* 12d Oct 1] medium-sized, rather light-bodied colt: reportedly suffers from arthritic joints and off course 16 months prior to winning 6-runner La Coupe de Maisons-Laffitte in September impressively by 3 lengths from Dernier Empereur, quickening to lead 1f out: not discredited in finishing eighth of 16 in Prix de l'Arc de Triomphe (well clear of remainder), tiring in straight: should prove fully effective at 1½m: seems to need the mud. *E. Lellouche, France* 120

GUNMAKER 6 ch.g. Gunner B 126 – Lucky Starkist 57 (Lucky Wednesday 124) [1994 –: 12.1f a12g^6 12.1g^4 16.1s 1995 a16g a12g a16.2g^2 a16g^4 12.5m a14.8g^5 Jul 17] smallish gelding: poor stayer: tried blinkered, no improvement: won over hurdles in September: inconsistent. *B. J. Llewellyn* – a32

GUNNER B SPECIAL 2 ch.g. (Feb 20) Gunner B 126 – Sola Mia 78 (Tolomeo 127) [1995 8.1g 8.2d a7g a8g Nov 24] plain, good-topped gelding: has scope: first foal: dam best at up to 1m: little sign of ability. *S. R. Bowring* –

GUNNERDALE 3 b.f. Gunner B 126 – Melody Moon 87 (Philip of Spain 126) [1994 NR 1995 10f 8m^5 7m Jun 20] angular, plain filly: poor mover: fifth reported foal: dam 7f to 1m winner: no promise in maidens. *Denys Smith* –

GUSHY 9 ch.g. Hard Fought 125 – Be Gustful (Ballymore 123) [1994 NR 1995 14g 17.2h^6 Aug 8] smallish, workmanlike gelding: no longer of any account on flat. *R. J. Baker* –

GUYMICHELLE (IRE) 3 b.f. Midyan (USA) 124 – Hemline 77 (Sharpo 132) [1994 –: 8.1g 1995 a8g a9.4g Mar 18] no sign of ability. *R. Ingram* –

GUY'S GAMBLE 2 ch.g. (Feb 14) Mazilier (USA) 107 – Deep Blue Sea (Gulf Pearl 117) [1995 a6g Dec 12] 8,000F, 10,000Y: half-brother to 3 winners, including 6f winner Blue Mischief (by Precocious) and 1½m winner Colonel Chinstrap (by Milford): dam poor sister to Coronation Cup winner Sea Chimes: 20/1, soundly beaten in seller at Wolverhampton. *J. Wharton* –

GWERNYMYNYDD 4 b.f. Dreams To Reality (USA) 113 – My Valentine Card (USA) 57§ (Forli (ARG)) [1994 41: 8d^5 10d^3 11.1f^4 12f^5 10m 10.3m^6 8f^4 a7g* 7g^3 7.1m 7g a7g 7d a6g 1995 a8.5g May 22] unfurnished filly: poor performer: sold out of S. Norton's stable 430 gns Doncaster February (1995) Sales: tailed off on only 4-y-o start: effective at 7f, and has form over as far as 11f: acts on fibresand and on firm and dead ground: front runner. *F. Jordan* –

GWESPYR 2 ch.g. (Apr 7) Sharpo 132 – Boozy 111 (Absalom 128) [1995 5g^5 5m* 5m^4 5f^5 5g^3 Jul 17] 46,000Y: leggy, close-coupled gelding: first foal: dam suited by 5f: won maiden at Lingfield in April: below form last 2 starts, subsequently gelded. *J. Berry* 72

GYMCRAK DIAMOND (IRE) 5 b.g. Taufan (USA) 119 – Down The Line 74 (Brigadier Gerard 144) [1994 41: 8.2g a6g^4 a7g^4 a7g^2 12.1m^2 1995 a12g 12m^3 15.8m^2 Aug 11] close-coupled, good-topped gelding: poor maiden: effective at 2m, in slowly-run race at least: acts on good to firm ground and fibresand: found little fourth 4-y-o start. *G. Holmes* 37

GYMCRAK FLYER 4 b.f. Aragon 118 – Intellect (Frimley Park 109) [1994 71: 5m^5 7g^3 6m* a7g^6 7f^2 7.5m^3 8m* 8f 8.5g 1995 8m 8g 8f 7f^5 7h* 7m^2 8m^4 8.1d* 7.1d^2 8d Sep 24] small filly: fair performer: won handicap at Newcastle in August and minor event at Haydock in September: stays 8.1f: acts on hard ground and dead, below form only run on fibresand: usually bandaged behind. *G. Holmes* 65

GYMCRAK GEM (IRE) 2 b.f. (May 1) Don't Forget Me 127 – Santa Patricia (IRE) (Taufan (USA) 119) [1995 6m 5d² Sep 13] IR 3,500F, 7,200Y: quite attractive filly: first foal: dam unraced: length second of 11 to First Maite in maiden at Beverley: bred to stay beyond 5f: should improve again. *G. Holmes* 57 p

GYMCRAK HERO (IRE) 3 b.g. Taufan (USA) 119 – Jamie's Girl (Captain James 123) [1994 49p: 6s⁴ 1995 10m 8.2d⁵ 9f a8g Nov 20] workmanlike, close-coupled gelding: modest maiden: stays 1m: best efforts on a soft surface: wears bandages. *G. Holmes* –

GYMCRAK JAREER (IRE) 3 b.g. Jareer (USA) 115 – Katzarah (IRE) (Pharly (FR) 130) [1994 NR 1995 7.5m³ 8.5m⁴ 7f⁴ 8g Aug 26] 7,200 2-y-o: first foal: dam never ran: no worthwhile form. *G. Holmes* –

GYMCRAK PREMIERE 7 ch.g. Primo Dominie 121 – Oraston 115 (Morston (FR) 125) [1994 94: 7d⁴ 7.9f⁶ 8.5g² 8m 10m 7.6m* 7f⁴ 8.3m⁵ 8g 7m 1995 7m⁵ 7m 8.1g⁶ 8m 7.1m⁴ 7m³ 7m⁶ 7.3m* 7g 7d⁵ 7g³ Sep 29] lengthy, workmanlike gelding: fairly useful handicapper: overcame trouble in running to win rated stakes at Newbury in August by short head: effective at 7f to 9f: probably acts on any going: tried blinkered/visored earlier in career: sometimes swerves markedly: usually bandaged behind: normally held up. *G. Holmes* 95

GYMCRAK TIGER (IRE) 5 b.g. Colmore Row 111 – Gossip (Sharp Edge 123) [1994 NR 1995 8.5m Jul 7] tall gelding: modest hurdler, winner in November: lightly raced and no worthwhile form on flat since 1992. *G. Holmes* –

GYMCRAK TYCOON 6 b.g. Last Tycoon 131 – Brazen Faced 84 (Bold And Free 118) [1994 57: a6g 7d⁵ 7.5d⁶ 6.9s 7.5m³ 5f* 5m⁴ 5.9m 5g 5m⁴ a6g 6d 1995 5.9f 5m 5.9f 5m 5g⁵ 5m 6m² 5m Aug 30] leggy, close-coupled gelding: modest handicapper: stays 7.5f, raced only at sprint distances in 1995: acts on firm ground, dead and fibresand: visored last 2 starts: may prove suited by strong handling: often bandaged. *G. Holmes* 51

GYMPIE 2 b.c. (Mar 20) Rainbow Quest (USA) 134 – Sunshine Coast 86 (Posse (USA) 130) [1995 6g 7m Oct 20] smallish, close-coupled colt: fourth foal: half-brother to German 3-y-o 9f winner Sandy Hollow (by Unfuwain): dam suited by 7f: behind in maidens won by Tagula at Newmarket and (prominent almost 5f) Germano at Doncaster 4½ months later: sold 5,800 gns Newmarket Autumn Sales. *J. H. M. Gosden* –

GYPSY LOVE (USA) 3 b.f. Woodman (USA) 126 – Pixie Erin 110 (Golden Fleece (USA) 133) [1994 61: 6m 5.1m⁴ 7s 1995 7.3g⁴ 8g 9f⁶ Jul 27] small, leggy filly: has a round action: fair maiden handicappper: should stay 1¼m: acts on firm ground: sold to USA. *P. W. Chapple-Hyam* 66

H

HABETA (USA) 9 ch.h. Habitat 134 – Prise (Busted 134) [1994 56d: 8.5m⁴ 8g² 8.5g³ 8m⁵ 8.1m⁴ 8g 8.1g 8g 8m 10.1d 1995 8m 9.2g⁴ 11.1g⁵ 8.3f* 8.1m 9f² 8.3f² Aug 9] quite good-topped horse: carries plenty of condition: only poor performer nowadays: won at Hamilton in June: effective at 1m to 1¼m: acts on any going: effective blinkered or not: held up: rather temperamental, and one to be wary of. *J. W. Watts* 45 §

HACKETTS CROSS (IRE) 7 b.g. Rusticaro (FR) 124 – Anglesea Market (Sea Hawk II 131) [1994 NR 1995 17.2f 14f⁴ 14.4m Sep 1] ex-Irish gelding: half-brother to several winners: dam poor Irish maiden: won 2 NH Flat races at 4 yrs: fair performer (rated 75) in Ireland at 5 yrs, winning maiden and amateurs race: well beaten in 1995 (carried head high second start): stays 2m: acts on firm ground: fair hurdler: not one to trust implicitly. *Noel T. Chance* –

HADABET 3 b.g. Hadeer 118 – Betsy Bay (FR) 107 (Bellypha 130) [1994 65: 8s 8.1g 1995 10m 11.8g 11.7m⁴ 11.6g² 10f* 11.7h³ 10m⁵ 10g³ 10m* 10m 10g⁶ 11.4d Sep 12] sturdy, close-coupled gelding: poor mover: fair performer: won minor event at Nottingham and apprentice handicap at Windsor (made all) in the summer: ran 68 poorly afterwards: effective at 1¼m, and stays 1½m: acts on hard ground: races prominently. *Miss Jacqueline S. Doyle*

HADADABBLE 2 ch.f. (Apr 8) Hadeer 118 – Magnifica (Sandy Creek 123) [1995 6m 6f 6m a7g Nov 24] 2,000Y: angular filly: good mover: fourth reported foal: dam, placed in France, half-sister to very useful performer (at up to 1m) Milk of The Barley: poor maiden: off course 5 months after debut: has been bandaged behind. *Pat Mitchell*

–

HADDEYAH (USA) 3 b. or br.f. Dayjur (USA) 137 – Albadeeah (USA) 85 (Nashua) [1994 68p: 6d* 1995 7m^6 6f Aug 10] quite good-topped filly: promising only start at 2 yrs, but tailed off in minor event (stumbled leaving stalls) and handicap on belated return. *H. Thomson Jones*

–

HADEEL 3 ch.f. Polish Precedent (USA) 131 – Nafhaat (USA) 91 (Roberto (USA) 131) [1994 63p: 6g^5 1995 7.6m* 10.1m* 8.5m^3 Aug 28] neat filly: fairly useful form: won maiden at Chester and handicap at Yarmouth in the summer: stays 1¼m: yet to race on a soft surface: may be capable of better. *H. Thomson Jones*

80

HADEYYA RAMZEYAH 3 b.g. Reference Point 139 – Token Gift (USA) (Lyphard (USA) 132) [1994 NR 1995 10.5g^2 10g* Jun 16] good-bodied gelding: has a round action: second foal: dam 1m and 8.5f winner in North America: narrowly won maiden at Sandown in June, held up taking keen hold, leading final 1f: likely to stay beyond 10.5f: wears bandages: looked sure to improve: sent to Dubai. *A. C. Stewart*

80 p

HADI (IRE) 4 b.g. Robellino (USA) 127 – Java Jive 63 (Hotfoot 126) [1994 –: 8s 11.6g 10g 12f^6 8.3g 8g 1995 7.1g Sep 18] good-topped gelding: of little account. *W. Storey*

–

HAGWAH (USA) 3 b.f. Dancing Brave (USA) 140 – Saraa Ree (USA) (Caro 133) [1994 74p: 7m^5 7f^2 7f 1995 10m^2 7.3g^2 9g^2 12f* 12m* 12d^6 12d Oct 21] lengthy filly: unimpressive walker: useful performer: won maiden at Kempton and 5-runner listed race at Newmarket (easily best effort, by 2½ lengths from Tinashaan, again dictating pace) in July: well below form last 2 starts, both on a soft surface: gained 1½m wins in falsely-run races, and shapes as if will prove at least as effective at 1¼m: acts on firm ground, possibly not on a soft surface: sold 160,000 gns Newmarket December Sales. *B. Hanbury*

104

HAIDO'HART 3 b.g. Pharly (FR) 130 – Try Vickers (USA) 72 (Fuzzbuster (USA)) [1994 8d 7s 6d 7s 1995 7s 5g^5 7.8f^3 8.5g^4 7m 11d Sep 22] 7,000Y, 37,000 2-y-o: leggy gelding: second foal: half-brother to fair 4-y-o sprinter Nordico Princess (by Nordico): dam, maiden, stayed 1¼m: fair maiden in Ireland: left P. Hughes's stable after fifth outing: wearing crossed noseband, well beaten in 11f seller on British debut: stays 8.5f: acts on firm and soft ground. *B. S. Rothwell*

70

HAKIKA (USA) 3 b.f. Elmaamul (USA) 125 – Balastra (USA) (Fappiano (USA)) [1994 60p: 7g^4 1995 10f^2 10m^2 9.9m* 8.5m* 8m^3 8g 10.1g 8f^3 Oct 12] tall, leggy filly: has a round action: fairly useful handicapper: won at Beverley in June and July: has won over 1¼m, but probably best at around 1m: acts on firm ground, yet to race on a soft surface: edgy sort and takes keen hold: effective from front or held up: consistent. *D. Morley*

87

HAKIKI (IRE) 3 b.c. Ballad Rock 122 – Salvationist (Mill Reef (USA) 141) [1994 88: 6s^4 7d^2 6d^3 1995 7g^3 6.9g* 6m^2 6g 6g^3 6g^6 6s Oct 1] lengthy colt: fairly useful performer: won maiden at Folkestone in April, making most and rallying well: ran creditably in handicaps next 4 starts: effective at 6f and 7f: acts on good to firm ground and dead: broke out of stalls on 3-y-o reappearance: takes keen hold: sold 26,000 gns Newmarket Autumn Sales, to Norway. *P. T. Walwyn*

86

HALA HALINA 3 gr.f. Old Vic 136 – Integrity 108 (Reform 132) [1994 NR 1995 10g 8d 10m Jul 29] 30,000Y: well-made filly: half-sister to several winners, notably very useful (at up to 1m) Radwell (by Dunbeath): dam, ideally suited by 6f, is daughter of Cry of Truth: well beaten in maidens. *J. E. Banks*

–

HALBERT 6 b.g. Song 132 – Stoneydale 83 (Tickled Pink 114) [1994 –: a7g a8g^5 1995 a7g^6 a8g a6g 5.3m 6m 6f 5g^5 5m^5 5d^3 5f* 5f^2 5f^3 5m* 5m^3 5m^5 5g 5.3f* 5m^5 5g^2 5d 5g^2 5g 5.3g a6g^6 a5g^5 Dec 19] sturdy gelding: fair handicapper on turf: won at Hamilton, Edinburgh (both selling events) and Brighton in the summer: left M. Channon after twenty-third start: best form at 5f: acts on firm and dead going, poor

70
a43

form at best on the all-weather: blinkered (ran creditably) in 1993, visored since tenth 6-y-o start: often claimer ridden: races prominently. *P. Burgoyne*

HALEBID 2 b.c. (Feb 11) Dowsing (USA) 124 – Pink Robber (USA) 85 (No Robbery) [1995 8g^6 8f^6 Oct 25] big, angular colt: fifth foal: dam 6f winner at 2 yrs: bit backward, similar form when sixth in maidens won by Forest Buck at Leicester and Bright Water at Yarmouth: sort to do better at 3 yrs. *S. P. C. Woods* — 69 p

HALFABOB (IRE) 3 ch.g. Broken Hearted 124 – Hasten (Northfields (USA)) [1994 NR 1995 a8g^5 a8g^6 7f^3 a8.5g a8.5g a10g^6 Nov 10] IR 5,400Y: half-brother to 9f to 1½m winner Fast Chick (by Henbit) and several winners abroad: dam never ran: seems of little account. *D. Haydn Jones* — –

HALF AN INCH (IRE) 2 gr.g. (Apr 16) Petoski 135 – Inch (English Prince 129) [1995 6m 6f^4 7f^2 7f^3 6d^5 7d^2 7s Oct 6] 2,000Y: sturdy gelding: half-brother to several winners, including Irish 7f and 11f winner Incharder (by Slip Anchor): dam won twice at 2 yrs in Ireland and was second in Moyglare Stud Stakes: fair maiden: best effort when length second in nursery at Brighton penultimate start: tailed off (asked to set very strong pace) in similar event at Ascot following month: needs further than 6f and will stay 1m: acts on firm ground, best form on dead: blinkered last 2 starts. *B. J. Meehan* — 71

HALF TONE 3 gr.c. Touch of Grey 90 – Demilinga (Nishapour (FR) 125) [1994 53: 6d 7s 7g a8g a5g^3 a5s^2 1995 a5g* 6m^4 a5g^2 6m^3 5m^5 5.7f^2 5m^3 6g^3 6m^5 6f 6f^5 6f^5 5m 5g^3 a5g* a5g* a6g^6 Dec 18] leggy colt: fair handicapper on the all-weather: won at Wolverhampton (maiden event) in January and at Lingfield in November and December: only poor on turf: best efforts at around 5f: acts on firm ground and goes well on the all-weather: normally blinkered: often claimer ridden. *R. M. Flower* — 46 a69

HAL HOO YAROOM 2 b.c. (Feb 18) Belmez (USA) 131 – Princess Nawaal (USA) 86 (Seattle Slew (USA)) [1995 7m 7g 8f Oct 24] tall, angular colt: good mover: third living foal: half-brother to winners in Belgium and Sweden: dam 8.5f and 9f winner: shaped well (plenty to do 2f out, nearest finish) when tenth of 22 to Silver Prey in maiden at Newbury in August: similar form when seventh in similar events at Warwick and Leicester in October: will be suited by middle distances. *Major W. R. Hern* — 71

HALKOPOUS 9 b.g. Beldale Flutter (USA) 130 – Salamina 106 (Welsh Pageant 132) [1994 89: 11.5v^3 11.9m* 11.9m 13.9f^5 15.9m* 13.9m 18.2s^4 18m 1995 13.9g^5 16.5g^5 May 27] good-bodied, workmanlike gelding: carries plenty of condition: unimpressive mover: high-class hurdler on his day: fairly useful handicapper at his best on flat: stays 2¼m: acts on any going: effective visored or not. *M. H. Tompkins* — 83

HALLELUJA TIME 3 b.g. Risk Me (FR) 127 – Warm Wind 84 (Tumble Wind (USA)) [1994 –p: 6.1d 1995 6m 5g Jun 7] strong gelding: no worthwhile form, in seller last time: sold 3,000 gns Ascot July Sales. *R. Hannon* — –

HALLIARD 4 b.g. Hallgate 127 – Princess Blanco 81 (Prince Regent (FR) 129) [1994 56: a5g^6 5s^3 5.1v^2 5.7m^2 5.1g^6 5.1m^3 5m 7g 5s^3 1995 a5g a5g* 5d 5m^5 5m* 5.3m^3 5g^5 5g 6m 5m^4 5m^5 5.1d^5 a5g a5g^4 a5g Dec 2] tall, workmanlike gelding: modest performer: won maiden at Lingfield in February and handicap at Warwick in April: below form after next start: stays 5.7f: acts on equitrack and on good to firm and heavy ground: well beaten in blinkers/visor: often races prominently. *T. M. Jones* — 65 d

HALLIKELD 2 ch.f. (Apr 27) Bustino 136 – Spring Sparkle 95 (Lord Gayle (USA) 124) [1995 9g 7m Oct 30] 850Y: workmanlike filly: third foal: dam, disappointing maiden best at 6f and 7.3f, out of half-sister to Annie Edge, dam of Selkirk: well beaten in maidens at Redcar and Newcastle. *T. J. Etherington* — –

HALLING (USA) 4 ch.c. Diesis 133 – Dance Machine 111 (Green Dancer (USA) 132) [1994 106p: 7m 8f^4 8.3m^6 10m* 10.3d* 9g* a9g* 1995 a8g* a10g* 10m* 10.4m* a10s Oct 28] — 131

Halling has come a long way since winning the Cambridgeshire on his final start in Britain as a three-year-old. That victory, his third in a row, represented useful form and he looked just the lightly-raced, progressive sort to train on. But few outside those closely connected with him could have envisaged his meteoric rise. He was returned to Britain after extending his winning sequence by three more races in Dubai, where he was trained by Hilal Ibrahim, and was pitched straight in at the deep end carrying the Godolphin colours. The Coral-Eclipse Stakes at Sandown in early-July represented a huge step up and saw Halling—fifth best in the betting at 7/1—taking on such as the bang-in-form Muhtarram and Eltish, who had fought out a close finish to the Prince of Wales's Stakes at Royal Ascot, and Singspiel, beaten a neck in the Grand Prix de Paris on his latest start. In addition, the Godolphin stable saddled the globe-trotting Red Bishop who also started at shorter odds than Halling. Walter Swinburn dictated the pace from the outset on Halling who always looked like holding on after quickening clear rounding the home turn. Singspiel got closest, rallying strongly inside the final furlong to reduce Halling's margin of victory to a neck, after Swinburn dropped his whip; Red Bishop came three lengths further back in third. Halling raced with tremendous zest at Sandown and made an even greater impression in his next race, the Juddmonte International Stakes at York in August. Starting favourite this time, he quickly sprinted clear, after cruising up and leading on the bridle over two furlongs out, to trounce the St James's Palace winner Bahri and the Irish Derby third Annus Mirabilis by three and a half lengths and one and a quarter. Halling was eased in the closing stages, but for which the winning margin would have been nearer five, and there was no doubting he had put up a tip-top performance, one which, at the time, made it difficult to envisage his being beaten. Swinburn, who has ridden plenty of champions in his time, including Shergar and the latest Derby winner Lammtarra, described Halling afterwards as 'the complete racehorse—the most versatile I have ever sat on'. Jockeys naturally tend to exaggerate in the moment of triumph but there was no mistaking that Swinburn meant every word. 'It's hard to compare different generations, but I cannot recall a more willing partner than Halling,' he said. 'I felt after the Eclipse that he'd have won by four lengths that day if I hadn't dropped my whip'.

The Breeders' Cup Classic at Belmont Park in late-October became the main target for Halling after York, with talk of his reverting to a mile for the Queen Elizabeth II Stakes at Ascot in the meantime or possibly going for the Dubai Champion Stakes at Newmarket. Unfortunately, a minor injury to an off-fore joint kept him off the course between York and Belmont Park where his clash with America's outstanding middle-distance performer Cigar was built up in the British media. The Breeders' Cup Classic, run over a mile and a quarter on dirt, is the most valuable of the seven races on Breeders' Cup day and has resulted in some memorable battles—Ferdinand and Alysheba in 1987 and Sunday Silence and Easy Goer in 1989 readily spring to mind—and another great race seemed in prospect between Cigar and Halling. Halling's winning run now stretched to eight while Cigar, likewise unbeaten for over a year, had won eleven in succession, eight of those Grade

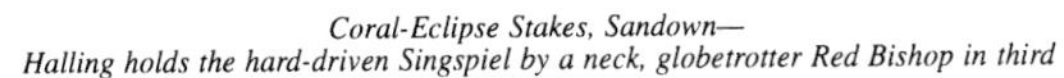

Coral-Eclipse Stakes, Sandown—
Halling holds the hard-driven Singspiel by a neck, globetrotter Red Bishop in third

1 events. Most Americans, however, regarded the Breeders' Cup Classic as a formality for the odds-on Cigar and Halling didn't even start second favourite, that position going to Unaccounted For who had run Cigar to a length in the Jockey Club Gold Cup on their latest start. Halling ran too badly to be true, looking ill at ease from a long way out and trailing in last. Whether anything was amiss hasn't been revealed but it was interesting that Halling ran on lasix. Lasix, a diuretic drug that drains the body fluids, including those in the lungs, can be given by injection to horses that are known to 'bleed' internally or 'break blood vessels' under the stress of racing. Though not a performance-enhancing drug in its own right, the use of lasix is illegal for racing in all major countries except America where each individual state racing commission makes some of its own rules. Under the local New York rules in force for the latest Breeders' Cup, veterinary evidence had to be produced to show that a horse had bled in the past before it could race on lasix. Connections of Halling confirmed that he had broken blood vessels before, though they would not specify a race or races in which it had occurred. Like the widely-used anti-inflammatory pain-killing drug bute, lasix is sometimes employed in the course of training in Britain but it is almost universally accepted here that horses should not be allowed to race on any unnatural substance. Lasix proved of no use to Halling in the Classic in which second-placed L'Carriere was the only one of the eleven runners not on the drug, but, in Europe at any rate, the argument will go on about whether horses who need medication to run to form, or to suppress infirmity, should be acknowledged as 'world champions'. The Breeders' Cup certainly deserves its billing as 'Racing's Greatest Day' but the permitted use of drugs detracts from its success. Cynics argue that so many American racehorses are now dependent on drugs that a ban would bring racing there to a standstill. Attempts to impose a 'medication-free' regime would, in any case, almost certainly be overruled by the courts in some American states as a infringement of the rights to use a legal substance. There's little chance of movement on a compromise suggested to the Breeders' Cup organisers in the past that the use of drugs should be banned, if possible, in the two Breeders' Cup races on grass, those which attract most European challengers.

Halling (USA) (ch.c. 1991)	Diesis (ch 1980)	Sharpen Up (ch 1969)	Atan
			Rocchetta
		Doubly Sure (b 1971)	Reliance II
			Soft Angels
	Dance Machine (b 1982)	Green Dancer (b 1972)	Nijinsky
			Green Valley
		Never A Lady (ch 1974)	Pontifex
			Camogie

Though successful on sand in Dubai, the leggy, attractive Halling has put up far and away his best performances on grass, in common with most of the best offspring of the Middle Park and Dewhurst winner Diesis who has spent his stud career in Kentucky. Group 1 winners such as Diminuendo, Elmaamul, Keen Hunter and Knifebox have put Diesis on the map in Europe, while he has made most impact in America through his turf performers, the Demoiselle Stakes winner Rootentootenwooten being his only important winner on dirt. Halling's dam Dance Machine was a smart racemare, winner on her only start as a two-year-old of the

Juddmonte International, York—a stunning sight; Bahri, Annus Mirabilis and Needle Gun are left trailing

Godolphin's "Halling"

Sweet Solera Stakes at Newmarket (producing a storming run after being well last two furlongs out) and successful over a mile and a quarter as a three-year-old. Dance Machine was sent to continue her career in the United States with John Gosden (Halling's trainer until after the Cambridgeshire) but she never reached the racecourse. She spent her first few years at stud in the United States where her 1990 mating with Diesis produced Halling. Halling, himself, hadn't raced when Dance Machine came up for sale at the Newmarket December Sales in 1993 in foal to Kris. Her first three foals had all been successful in France (one of them over jumps) but none of them had created much of a stir, and there was little interest in Dance Machine who was bought in by her owner-breeder Cyril Humphris for only 15,000 guineas. Since Halling, she has bred the fair staying maiden filly Torreglia (by Elmaamul) and had fillies by Kris (the foal she was carrying in 1993) and Sharpo. Halling's grandam Never A Lady was a useful and genuine performer who was effective at sprint distances and stayed a mile. According to an interview in *The Sporting Life* with Halling's breeder, Dance Machine was the result of a free nomination to Green Dancer that he won in a ballot for breeders who had patronised certain Haras du Quesnay stallions the previous year. Never A Lady, the first horse Humphris had in training, was out of an unraced daughter of the leading two-year-old filly of 1963 Mesopotamia who has turned out to be an influential broodmare, one of her daughters Garden of Eden producing the high-class American turf performer Galaxy Libra, the Prix du Conseil de Paris winner Garden of Heaven and the leading Irish two-year-old filly Welsh Garden, the last-named also the dam of Prix du Cadran winner Molesnes and grandam of Haydock Park Sprint Cup winner Cherokee Rose; another of Mesopotamia's daughters House Tie is the grandam of Champion Hurdler

Alderbrook and American Grade 1 winner Danish. Halling, who remains in training, will probably always be best at around a mile and a quarter. He acts on good to firm and good to soft going and is a genuine racehorse with a fine turn of foot. *Saeed bin Suroor*

HALLS BURN 7 b.g. Beverley Boy 99 – Wintersgame (Game Warden) [1994 NR 1995 7m 9.2f⁵ 8f⁶ 11.1f 12.1m⁵ 8.1f Jul 28] big, lengthy gelding: first foal: dam maiden pointer: of no account: tried visored. *J. S. Goldie* –

HALMANERROR 5 gr.g. Lochnager 132 – Counter Coup (Busted 134) [1994 68: 7m³ 8f⁴ 8m 7.9m 7g* 7d* 7s⁴ 1995 7s 8m 8g 6m² 6m 6m* 7m⁵ 6m* 7g³ 7g 7g 7m Nov 3] leggy, lengthy gelding: fair handicapper: twice got up close home at Pontefract in the summer: creditable third in £11,100 event at Newcastle next start but below form afterwards: effective at 6f, and stays 1m: acts on firm and soft ground: sometimes gives trouble at stalls: held up. *Mrs J. R. Ramsden* 74

HAL'S PAL 2 br.c. (Feb 6) Caerleon (USA) 132 – Refinancing (USA) (Forli (ARG)) [1995 7m⁴ 7g² Sep 13] 280,000Y: close-coupled, quite attractive colt: third known foal: half-brother to fairly useful 6f winner Minstrel's Gift (by The Minstrel) and a winner in Italy by Storm Bird: dam once-raced sister to useful Italian 1m to 1¼m performer Lonely Bird out of half-sister to Posse: 1¼ lengths second of 19 to Shawanni, prominent throughout, in maiden at Yarmouth: will stay at least 1m: likely to improve further and win a maiden. *D. R. Loder* 89 p

HAMILTON GOLD 2 ch.f. (Mar 8) Safawan 118 – Golden Della (Glint of Gold 128) [1995 5f⁵ Jun 15] 400Y: first foal: dam 8.2f winner stayed 1½m: 66/1, tailed off in maiden at Hamilton. *Martyn Wane* –

HAMILTON SILK 3 b.g. K-Battery 108 – Silver's Girl 58 (Sweet Monday 122) [1994 49?: 5d⁶ 5s 6f⁵ 8.3g⁵ 7.1s 1995 8.3v⁴ 8.3s* 9.9m 9.2g 12.1g⁴ 10.5s Sep 30] close-coupled, angular gelding: modest form at best for new stable: won seller at Hamilton in April: inconsistent facing stiffish tasks in handicaps afterwards: probably stays 12.1f: acts on soft ground: races prominently: bought by M. Pipe 10,500 gns after winning novice selling hurdle in December. *M. G. Meagher* 52

HAMLET (IRE) 2 b.c. (Apr 3) Danehill (USA) 126 – Blasted Heath 105 (Thatching 131) [1995 7m 7g 7d Sep 26] 55,000F: big, angular colt: has plenty of scope: unimpressive mover: third foal: half-brother to 3-y-o Heath Robinson (by In The Wings) and 1993 Irish 2-y-o 5f winner Wave The Wand (by Fairy King): dam Irish 5f (at 2 yrs) and 1m winner, half-sister to Middle Park winner Balla Cove: seventh of 19 in maidens at Newmarket (to Even Top) and Yarmouth (to Shawanni): creditable effort when mid-division in 30-runner valuable sales race at Newmarket, prominent to 2f out: type to do better. *M. Bell* 78 p

HAMMERSTEIN 2 b.c. (Apr 6) Kris 135 – Musical Bliss (USA) 117 (The Minstrel (CAN) 135) [1995 7g⁴ 7m² 8d⁴ Sep 23] sturdy, good-topped, attractive colt: good mover: second living foal: half-brother to 3-y-o Maquina (by Machiavellian): dam won 1000 Guineas and is half-sister to Grade 1 winner Safe Play, dam of Defensive Play: useful maiden who has kept good company, on last 2 outings 3½ lengths second to Bijou d'Inde in Acomb Stakes at York then around 10 lengths fourth of 8 to Mons in Royal Lodge Stakes at Ascot: will stay 1¼m: sure to win a race. *M. R. Stoute* 95

HAM N'EGGS 4 b.g. Robellino (USA) 127 – Rose And The Ring (Welsh Pageant 132) [1994 91: 7.9f* 8.1m 8m 8m 7d⁶ 7g 7g 8d 1995 9m² 8m 8g⁶ 7.3m 8.1m⁶ Aug 25] good-topped, attractive gelding: impresses in appearance: good walker: has a quick action: fairly useful handicapper on his day: for second year running failed to reproduce a good reappearance effort: stays 9f: easily best efforts on top-of-the-ground, appeared to act on dead at 2 yrs: sold 9,800 gns Newmarket Autumn Sales. *R. Hannon* 90

HAMPI (USA) 2 b.f. (May 10) Runaway Groom (CAN) – Foresighted Lady (USA) (Vent du Nord) [1995 a8g Dec 18] $14,000Y: half-sister to Irish 1984 2-y-o 5f winner Jaccuzi Lady (by Miami Springs), 1994 2-y-o 7f winner Pierre Bosco (by Fortunate Moment) and several minor winners in USA: dam won 3 sprints in USA: 16/1, slow-starting eighth of 9 in maiden at Lingfield. *S. P. C. Woods* –

HAMSAAT (IRE) 3 b.f. Sadler's Wells (USA) 132 – Steel Habit (Habitat 134) [1994 NR 1995 8.1g* Jun 10] 180,000Y: useful-looking filly: sister to very smart 7f 80

to 10.5f winner Batshoof and useful 1¼m winner Dress Parade and closely related to a winner by Be My Guest: dam, winner twice in Italy, is closely related to high-class sprinter Steel Heart: well-backed favourite, won maiden at Haydock, smooth headway to lead under 2f out and well on top at finish, beating Sparrowhawk 2½ lengths: wore small bandages in front: would have stayed 1¼m: visits Marju. *B. Hanbury*

HANBITOOH (USA) 2 b.c. (Jan 19) Hansel (USA) – Bitooh 117 (Seattle Slew (USA)) [1995 7f Oct 25] tall, useful-looking colt: first foal: dam, French 7f performer, won Criterium de Maisons-Laffitte at 2 yrs: 20/1, green and better for race, slowly away and well beaten in maiden at Yarmouth. *E. A. L. Dunlop* –

HANCOCK 3 b.g. Jester 119 – Fresh Line 60 (High Line 125) [1994 –: 7d 1995 13.8g Jun 9] workmanlike gelding: well beaten in maiden (at 2 yrs) and claimer. *J. Hetherton* –

HAND CRAFT (IRE) 3 b.g. Dancing Dissident (USA) 119 – Fair Flutter (Beldale Flutter (USA) 130) [1994 NR 1995 a7g* 7.1m^{3} 8.2m* 9m* Aug 12] 7,400Y: tall, good sort: fourth foal: half-brother to useful 1994 3-y-o middle-distance stayer Silence In Court (by Law Society): dam (unraced) out of sister to Master Willie: off course 4½ months after winning median auction maiden at Wolverhampton in February: successful in handicaps at Nottingham and Ripon (leading over 2f out and idling) in the summer: will stay beyond 9f: looked sure to improve again. *W. J. Haggas* 85 p

HANDMAIDEN 5 gr.m. Shardari 134 – Flyaway Bride (USA) 104 (Blushing Groom (FR) 131) [1994 NR 1995 a12g^{3} a12g* 14.1m a14.8g a14g a14g Nov 24] lengthy, angular mare: half-sister to a winner in Italy: dam useful sprinter as 2-y-o: won 2 NH Flat races at Southwell in 1993/4 for M. Camacho: won maiden event at Southwell in February for J. L. Eyre: off course 4 months and well beaten in handicaps afterwards: should stay beyond 1½m. *A. Harrison* 56 d

HAND OF STRAW (IRE) 3 b.g. Thatching 131 – Call Me Miss (Hello Gorgeous (USA) 128) [1994 NR 1995 7.1g^{5} 7.5d^{6} 8f^{4} 7.5g^{2} 8.1d 8g 7f Oct 3] IR 8,000Y: dipped-backed lengthy gelding: has a round action: third foal: half-brother to a Spanish 7f and 1m winner by Last Tycoon: dam Irish 1¼m winner: modest maiden at best: well beaten last 3 starts: will stay beyond 1m: tried blinkered, no improvement: often sweating/on toes: subject of friendly claim (£6,000) fourth start, but sold 1,500 gns Newmarket Autumn Sales. *J. W. Watts* 62

HANDSOME SQUAW 3 ch.f. Handsome Sailor 125 – Brave Squaw (High Top 131) [1994 NR 1995 6g 7m 11f a8g Nov 16] 2,500Y: leggy filly: second foal: dam showed little: little sign of ability. *B. W. Murray* –

HANDSON 3 ch.g. Out of Hand 84 – My Home 61 (Homing 130) [1994 NR 1995 a9.4g^{4} a8.5g^{6} 10.2m^{5} 12.1m Jul 20] second foal: dam poor handicapper at up to 1m: no form. *B. R. Millman* –

HAND WOVEN 3 b.g. Rambo Dancer (CAN) 107 – Lifestyle 80 (Jimmy Reppin 131) [1994 59p: 7.6v^{4} 1995 a8.5g^{2} 9m* 9.2f^{2} 9f^{3} 10.5g 12d^{2} 12g 11f* Oct 31] quite good-topped, slightly unfurnished gelding: fairly useful form: won median auction event at Ripon in July and handicap at Redcar (by neck from unlucky Eurolink Mischief) in October: stays 1½m: acts on firm and dead going: sold (W. Haggas to N. Twiston-Davies) 23,000 gns Ascot November Sales. *W. J. Haggas* 81

H'ANI 3 b.f. Woodman (USA) 126 – African Dance (USA) (El Gran Senor (USA) 136) [1994 –p: 6m 1995 7f 7g^{4} 8g 8d^{2} 8g a11g^{4} a12g^{2} a12g^{3} Nov 29] unfurnished filly: modest maiden: trained by Mrs L. Piggott until after second 3-y-o start: stays 1½m: acts on dead ground and equitrack: sold 20,000 gns Newmarket December Sales. *W. J. Haggas* 56

HANIFA 3 ch.f. Master Willie 129 – Antoinette Jane 86 (Ile de Bourbon (USA) 133) [1994 NR 1995 12m 10m 12.1f^{2} 12f^{2} 11.9f^{3} Aug 2] 2,500Y: smallish filly: first foal: dam, 2-y-o 7f winner, granddaughter of July Cup winner Parsimony, also grandam of College Chapel: signs of only a little ability in maiden events, in very small fields last 3 starts. *Miss Gay Kelleway* –

HANIYA (IRE) 3 ch.f. Caerleon (USA) 132 – Harmless Albatross 115 (Pas de Seul 133) [1994 49p: 7g 1995 10m^{3} 12m* 12f^{2} 14g^{3} 11.9g^{4} 13.9g Oct 7] small, close-coupled filly: good mover: fairly useful form: won maiden at Thirsk in May: 92

progressed well in handicaps next 3 starts: tailed off at York (quickly beaten early in straight) final one: stayed 1¾m: acted on firm ground: visits Woodman. *J. L. Dunlop*

HANK-A-CHIEF 2 b.c. (Mar 14) Inca Chief (USA) – Be Sharp 85 (Sharpen Up 127) [1995 6m^{6} 7d 7g Oct 3] neat colt: unimpressive mover: seventh reported living foal: half-brother to 1m seller winner Lilly Camilly (by Electric): dam 5f winner: well beaten in maidens: absent 3 months after debut. *M. McCormack* –

HANNAHS BAY 2 b.f. (Jan 30) Buzzards Bay 128§ – Hi-Hannah 59 (Red Sunset 120) [1995 6g 7f a7g a8g^{3} Dec 1] 1,700F: smallish filly: third reported foal: dam 1m winner: plater: blinkered, remote third to People Direct at Southwell: seems to stay 1m. *M. G. Meagher* 40

HANNAH'S USHER 3 b.g. Marching On 101 – La Pepper 63 (Workboy 123) [1994 69, a77: 5g* 5v^{4} 5f* 6g^{4} 5m* 5g^{3} 6m 5.1g 5m^{2} 5m* 5m* a5g* 1995 a5g^{2} a6g^{2} a5g* 5g 6f^{6} 5m^{3} 5.1d a5g^{5} Dec 14] sturdy gelding: fairly useful handicapper on the all-weather: won at Wolverhampton in February: only modest on turf: left P. Haslam's stable after seventh start: best at sprint distances: acts on any going: blinkered (pulled hard, worst effort) eighth 2-y-o start: takes a good hold and sometimes early to post. *C. Murray* 62 a83

HAPPY BRAVE 3 b.g. Daring March 116 – Fille de Phaeton (Sun Prince 128) [1994 48: 6g 6s^{5} 6s 1995 a7g a8g a8g^{3} a8.5g^{6} a6g 6m 7g^{4} 6f Aug 17] leggy gelding: poor maiden handicapper: stays 8.5f: best efforts on soft ground: blinkered (no improvement) fifth 3-y-o start. *P. D. Cundell* 33

HAPPY HOSTAGE 4 b.g. Beveled (USA) – Run Amber Run (Run The Gantlet (USA)) [1994 70: 7.1g^{4} 7.1g^{4} 11.1g^{3} 8.1f^{3} 8.5s 8.3m^{3} 8g^{2} 9.2g^{3} 8.3m* 8m* 9.9f^{4} 8.3f^{3} 8s^{2} 8d* 1995 9.7s 11.8g Oct 10] close-coupled gelding: poor mover: fair form in 1994: well beaten in claimers for new stable on belated return: stays 1¼m: probably acts on any ground: won selling hurdle in December. *J. White* –

HAPPY PARTNER (IRE) 2 b.c. (May 27) Nabeel Dancer (USA) 120 – Dublah (USA) (Private Account (USA)) [1995 5f^{3} 5m^{2} Aug 23] IR 2,400Y: second foal: dam never ran: better effort in maiden auctions at Redcar when beaten ¾ length by Babsy Babe in 4-runner contest in August: will be at least as effective at 6f: joined C. Murray. *P. C. Haslam* 66

HAPPY TAIPAN (IRE) 2 b.g. (Apr 20) Keen 116 – Eastern View (IRE) (Persian Bold 123) [1995 8f^{6} Aug 22] IR 8,200F, IR 10,000Y: first foal: dam unraced daughter of Clear Picture, very smart filly in France at 2 yrs: 25/1, around 7 lengths sixth of 7 to Munketh in maiden at Brighton, leading to over 2f out: should do better. *M. J. Heaton-Ellis* 58 p

HAPPY TRAVELLER (IRE) 2 b.c. (Apr 6) Treasure Kay 114 – Elegant Owl (Tumble Wind (USA)) [1995 a7g^{5} Dec 15] IR 2,900Y: third foal: brother to a bad maiden: dam poor Irish maiden daughter of French 1000 Guineas third Tawny Owl: 4/1, ran better than position suggests when over 11 lengths fifth of 9 to Accountancy Jewel in median auction maiden at Lingfield, coming out best of front runners and weakening only last 300 yds: will improve. *C. Murray* 54 p

HAPPY TYCOON (IRE) 2 br.c. (Apr 16) Polish Patriot (USA) 128 – Art Age (Artaius (USA) 129) [1995 5g* 5f 5.2g Jul 15] IR 7,500Y: close-coupled colt: fourth reported foal: closely related to 3-y-o 8.3f winner Artful Dane (by Danehill): dam never ran: won maiden auction at Edinburgh in May: outclassed in Windsor Castle Stakes at Ascot and Super Sprint (visored, raced freely) at Newbury: found to have fractured a sesamoid bone after Newbury: joined C. Murray. *M. J. Heaton-Ellis* 67

HARAYIR (USA) 3 b.f. Gulch (USA) – Saffaanh (USA) 87 (Shareef Dancer (USA) 135) [1994 108p: 6g* 6m^{2} 6m* 6m^{3} 1995 7m^{2} 8m* 8g^{5} 8m^{3} 8g^{3} 7.3m* 8m* 6d^{4} 7m* Oct 12] 119

There were some tough fillies around in Europe in 1995 when, for the second year running, one of the so-called 'weaker sex' recorded the highest number of wins by any horse in pattern company. Hever Golf Rose, whose six pattern victories were spread round four countries, followed in the footsteps of Lochsong. Not far behind Hever Golf Rose came two other very reliable, good-class fillies in the French sprinter Cherokee Rose and the Madagans One Thousand Guineas winner Harayir, both of whom recorded four victories in pattern company during the year. Harayir had a busy season for a classic filly and held her form admirably, enhancing her

Madagans One Thousand Guineas, Newmarket—Richard Hills comes in for the winning ride on Harayir; Carson is second on Aqaarid (striped cap) with Moonshell third

reputation with victories in the Hungerford Stakes, the Tripleprint Celebration Mile and the Challenge Stakes in the second half of the season.

More often than not, the One Thousand Guineas, like its colts' counterpart, goes to an animal that has been a good two-year-old, and there weren't many two-year-old fillies better than Harayir. After being narrowly beaten in the Cherry Hinton, she was an impressive winner of the Lowther before finishing third in the Cheveley Park. That last performance was widely taken as signalling the end of Harayir's improvement but, as readers of *Racehorses of 1994* will know, there was more to her performance than met the eye. 'The Harayir we saw in the autumn certainly didn't look the same filly who ran away with the Lowther in the summer...and she certainly shouldn't be ruled out of a wide-open One Thousand Guineas just yet,' was how *Racehorses* put it. Harayir had gone in her coat by the time she ran in the Cheveley Park and didn't travel with the fluency so evident in the Lowther. A good-topped, well-made filly with the scope to train on, Harayir looked an attractive each-way proposition for the Guineas for which she was around 20/1 in the ante-post market when *Racehorses* was published. She ran a first-rate Guineas

Tripleprint Celebration Mile, Goodwood—Harayir carries the first colours to victory against Darnay (second right), Realities (right) and Emperor Jones (rails)

trial, despite looking backward in her coat, when clear second under joint-top weight to the French-trained Diffident in the European Free Handicap at Newmarket, a performance that left Willie Carson in a quandary about whether to ride her or the same owner's Fillies' Mile winner Aqaarid in the Guineas, which, incidentally, was run on a Sunday for the first time. Aqaarid's clear-cut success in the Fred Darling at Newbury two days later maintained her unbeaten record (though it didn't shake our confidence in Harayir) and, with Carson choosing to ride her, she started favourite at Newmarket at 3/1. Harayir started at 5/1, joint-second favourite with Moonshell who had been wintered in Dubai after winning impressively on her only start at two. The first three in the betting filled the first three places in a field that looked well up to standard, Harayir quickening readily approaching the final furlong to win by a length and a half and three quarters from Aqaarid and Moonshell, both of whom were already being pushed along as Harayir cruised into a challenging position. Both Aqaarid and Moonshell impressed as Oaks candidates in the Guineas but it was soon apparent that connections had no plans to run Harayir at Epsom. She was to be kept at around a mile with the Irish One Thousand Guineas and the Coronation Stakes next on the agenda. Harayir failed to win either, finishing only fifth on rain-softened going at the Curragh and a creditable third at Royal Ascot, both times behind Ridgewood Pearl. The arrival on the scene of the impressive Ridgewood Pearl contributed to Harayir's generally becoming regarded as a fairly ordinary One Thousand Guineas winner, an impression strengthened when she was a beaten favourite for the third race in succession in the slowly-run Falmouth Stakes at Newmarket in July. But anyone who wrote off Harayir was in for a rude awakening. She resumed winning ways in the Hungerford Stakes at Newbury in August, beating the four-year-olds Nijo and Darnay by three quarters of a length and a head with plenty in hand, and followed up in the Tripleprint Celebration Mile a fortnight later. By now, Harayir was looking as well as at any time of the year and she produced another fine performance at Goodwood, making smooth progress to take the lead inside the final furlong and then holding off Darnay, who got to within half a length this time. Facing a stiff task under her Group 1 penalty, Harayir managed a creditable fourth when dropped back to sprinting in the Diadem Stakes at Ascot in September, and she was back in the winner's circle two and a half weeks later in the Challenge Stakes over seven furlongs at Newmarket. With conditions putting the emphasis on speed, Harayir was in her element and, after quickening ahead, she had only to be pushed out with hands and heels to hold off Soviet Line by half a length. This turned out to be Harayir's swansong. She was sent to America for the Breeders' Cup Mile in late-October but had to be withdrawn after injuring a tendon the day before the race, and she has now been retired. She visits Nashwan in 1996.

Challenge Stakes, Newmarket—Harayir is still in good form;
Soviet Line (left), Red Carnival and the grey Mistle Cat give her a run

Hamdan Al Maktoum's "Harayir"

Harayir (USA) (b.f. 1992)	Gulch (USA) (b 1984)	Mr Prospector (b 1970)	Raise A Native
			Gold Digger
		Jameela (b or br 1976)	Rambunctious
			Asbury Mary
	Saffaanh (USA) (b 1986)	Shareef Dancer (b 1980)	Northern Dancer
			Sweet Alliance
		Give Thanks (b 1980)	Relko
			Parthica

Harayir's speed as a two-year-old suggested that she'd prove best at up to a mile, even though there is plenty of stamina on the distaff side of her pedigree. Her dam Saffaanh, whose third foal Min Alhawa (by Riverman) won the last race on the card on Celebration Mile day, won at a mile and a half and is by an Irish Derby winner Shareef Dancer out of an Irish Oaks winner Give Thanks. Harayir is the latest in a long line of notable winners descended from her fourth dam the extraordinary Violetta III, whose name has cropped up very many times in *Racehorses* over the years. Harayir's great grandam Parthica was one of ten fillies produced by Violetta III, most of whom have bred good winners, including also Little Miss (dam of Italian Derby and Prix Royal-Oak winner Old Country), Irish One Thousand Guineas winner Favoletta (dam of Queen Mary winner Amaranda and Irish One Thousand Guineas runner-up Favoridge), Oaks runner-up Furioso (dam of Derby winner Teenoso and of Topsy, the dam of Derby runner-up Most Welcome), Laughing Girl (dam of pattern winners Braiswick and Percy's Lass), Nicolette (dam of the 1995 Queen Anne Stakes winner Nicolotte) and Good Lassie (dam of Prix Marcel Boussac winner Ashayer, herself the dam of Aqaarid). Though each of the first three dams in the bottom line of her pedigree was sired by a Derby winner (Parthica was by Parthia), Harayir clearly inherited the speed of her sire the Breeders' Cup Sprint winner Gulch. She takes after him in toughness too, Gulch having had thirty-two races in three seasons. Though Gulch contested all three legs of the American triple crown—also taking on and beating older horses in the Metropolitan Mile in the same thirty-six-day period—he made his name as a high-class, durable sprinter/miler. He's doing well as a stallion and was also responsible in the latest season for the Kentucky Derby winner Thunder Gulch, winner of seven of his ten races as a three-year-old. The game and genuine Harayir, a good mover in all her paces, was effective at six furlongs to a mile and acted on good to firm and good to soft going. She was usually held up in her races to make the best use of her good turn of foot. *Major W. R. Hern*

HARBOUR DUES 2 b.c. (Mar 15) Slip Anchor 136 – Quillotern (USA) (Arctic Tern (USA) 126) [1995 7.1d^4 7f^4 Oct 23] tall colt: has plenty of scope: third foal: half-brother to 3-y-o 7f winner Quilling (by Thatching) and 6f/7f winner Quinsigimond (by Formidable): dam half-sister to Leap Lively, dam of Forest Flower: similar form in maidens when fourth to Polar Eclipse at Haydock and Dance On A Cloud at Leicester, keeping on steadily: will be suited by at least 1¼m: tended to carry head high last time: will do better. *Lady Herries* — 65 p

HARBOUR ISLAND 3 b.c. Rainbow Quest (USA) 134 – Quay Line 117 (High Line 125) [1994 NR 1995 10g 14s* 16.5m^2 Oct 20] good-topped colt: half-brother to several winners, including stayer Coleridge (by Bellypha): won maiden at Lingfield in September, always thereabouts and staying on strongly: ran well against odds-on Old Rouvel in 3-runner minor event at Doncaster 3 weeks later: will be suited by test of stamina: blinkered last 2 starts: likely to improve further. *M. R. Stoute* — 89 p

HARDENFAST 2 ch.f. (May 13) Clantime 101 – Croft Original (Crofthall 110) [1995 5f^5 Aug 3] 750Y: third reported foal: dam, probably ungenuine, ran 4 times: 15/2, hung badly right when distant last of 5 in seller at Hamilton. *D. Nicholls* — –

HARDING 4 b.g. Dowsing (USA) 124 – Orange Hill 75 (High Top 131) [1994 69: 8v^3 10g^5 11.4g^6 8.2m 8.1d^3 8.1d^2 8.9d 1995 10f Oct 24] good-bodied gelding: easy mover: fair maiden handicapper: backward and raced freely for new stable on belated reappearance: should stay 1½m: acts on good to firm ground and heavy. *S. Mellor* — –

HARDING BROWN (USA) 3 ch.g. Strawberry Road (AUS) 128 – Chrysilia (USA) (Tilt Up (USA)) [1994 –: 7g 1995 10.2m 12m 11.4g 11.9m 11.5m^2 12m^6 11.9f^2 16.4f* 14.1m^6 10d 10d a8f a8.5f^6 Dec 17] strong gelding: modest performer: made all in apprentice handicap at Folkestone in August on penultimate start for G. Harwood: well beaten in USA: stays 16.4f: acts on firm ground: visored/blinkered since fifth 3-y-o start. *A. J. Bizella, USA* — 58

HARD LOVE 3 b.f. Rambo Dancer (CAN) 107 – Djimbaran Bay (Le Levanstell 122) [1994 66: 6m^5 6g^2 7m^3 6.9m^2 8m^6 7m 1995 7d 7g^4 10.2m* 10.1m^4 10.1m^2 a12g^3 12h^4 10.1g^2 a9.4g^4 a10g^5 Dec 19] leggy filly: fair handicapper: won maiden at Bath in June: sold out of S. Woods's stable 4,000 gns Doncaster Autumn Sales after eighth start: effective at 1¼m and 1½m: acts on good to firm ground and fibresand, saddle appeared to slip when tried on dead: takes good hold. *J. L. Eyre* — 67

HARD NEWS (USA) 2 b.c. (May 6) Lyphard (USA) 132 – Social Column (USA) (Swoon's Son) [1995 7d Sep 27] compact colt: brother to Mondanite, 6f to 1m winner in USA, and half-brother to 3 winners, including very smart 1¼m winner Two Timing (by Blushing Groom): dam, placed at 6f, is half-sister to champion US filly Chris Evert: 12/1 and free to post, never-dangerous seventh of 12 to Final Stab in maiden at Salisbury, keeping on after slow start: will stay further than 7f: sold only 1,400 gns Newmarket December Sales. *R. Charlton* — –

HARD TO FIGURE 9 gr.g. Telsmoss 91 – Count On Me 77 (No Mercy 126) [1994 113: 5.1m^2 6v* 7m 5.6g 6d^3 6g 6m^2 6d^5 6v 1995 6g^4 6m^5 7m 6m 6g* 6m 6m^5 5.6m 6g^6 Sep 16] rather leggy, workmanlike gelding: smart and durable performer, as good as he's ever been: 25/1, strong run to lead close home and beat Inzar a head in listed event at Newbury in July: faced stiffish tasks in tip-top sprint handicaps on 3 of his 4 starts afterwards and, despite finishing no better than sixth in any of them, emerged as the best horse (taking into account the weights carried) in the Stewards' Cup at Goodwood, the Portland at Doncaster and (for the third year running, despite being hampered) the Ayr Gold Cup: effective at up to 7f: acts on any going: usually held up: tough and genuine. *R. J. Hodges* — 113

HARD TO GET 8 b.g. Rousillon (USA) 133 – Elusive 94 (Little Current (USA)) [1994 NR 1995 17.2f Jul 1] close-coupled, angular gelding: no form on flat since 2 yrs. *M. F. Barraclough* — –

HARD TRY 3 ro.g. Sharrood (USA) 124 – Trynova 66 (Tyrnavos 129) [1994 56: a8g4 a8.5g3 1995 a8.5g3 11.1d3 a11g2 12m4 a12g a12g Aug 5] modest maiden: well beaten last 2 starts: sold (M. Camacho to Mrs S. Smith) 5,000 gns Doncaster August Sales: probably stays 1½m: won over hurdles in August. *M. J. Camacho* 56

HARDY DANCER 3 ch.c. Pharly (FR) 130 – Handy Dancer 87 (Green God 128) [1994 70p: 6m 6g3 6f 6g* 1995 8m* 9m* 12g5 10.1m3 8m 8.1f2 8.1m4 8g5 9d Oct 21] quite attractive, close-coupled colt: fairly useful handicapper: won at Leicester in April and Kempton in May: creditable efforts afterwards when in frame: effective at 1m and stays 1¼m well (not discredited at 1½m, and may well ultimately prove effective at it): acts on good to firm going: has run well when sweating. *G. L. Moore* 90

HARGHAR (USA) 2 gr.c. (Mar 10) El Gran Senor (USA) 136 – Harouniya (Siberian Express (USA) 125) [1995 6m* 6.3m3 7g5 Sep 16] second foal: dam, Irish 1m winner, from family of winners, notably high-class sprinter Hittite Glory: useful performer: won maiden at Leopardstown in August: much better form both when 3½ lengths third of 5 to Woodborough in Anglesey Stakes then (held up in rear and kept on never a threat) when 4¾ lengths fifth of 7 to Danehill Dancer in National Stakes, both at the Curragh: should stay 1m. *J. Oxx, Ireland* 102

HARLECH (IRE) 3 br.c. Caerleon (USA) 132 – Noble Lily (USA) (Vaguely Noble 140) [1994 NR 1995 8g6 10.4g2 10m4 12g Sep 29] smallish, sturdy colt: unimpressive mover: second foal: brother to very useful 4-y-o middle-distance stayer Noble Rose: dam, second at 11f from 4 starts in France, half-sister to Grade 1 9f winner Talinum: fair maiden: pushed along good way from home on all starts, looking less than genuine final one: should stay 1½m: blinkered since second start: sent to Dubai. *J. H. M. Gosden* 74

HARLEQUIN WALK (IRE) 4 ch.f. Pennine Walk 120 – Taniokey (Grundy 137) [1994 –, a54: a7g6 a10g2 a10g3 12g a12g2 11.9d a12g 1995 a12g* a12g* 15.4m Apr 25] sturdy filly: modest performer: won median auction maiden at Wolverhampton and claimer at Lingfield (claimed £7,000) in February only 2 starts for A. Hide: below form in handicap at Folkestone 2 months later: stays 1½m: acts on all-weather surfaces: blinkered first 2 starts in 1995: front runner: won over hurdles in May. *R. J. O'Sullivan* – a54

HARLESTONE BROOK 5 ch.g. Jalmood (USA) 126 – Harlestone Lake 78 (Riboboy (USA) 124) [1994 93: 14d 16d2 17.2m* 17.2f* 16.4m2 20f* 20g* 16.1m6 93

Ascot Stakes (Handicap), Royal Ascot—
Harlestone Brook beats Art Form (right) and twenty-five others in this marathon

18m 1995 16m 18.7m^2 20m* 20f^4 Jul 26] small gelding: fairly useful handicapper: runner-up to Top Cees in Chester Cup in May: became first since Atlantic Traveller in 1981/2 to win Goodwood Stakes and Ascot Stakes when successful at Royal Ascot by 1¼ lengths from Art Form, staying on strongly to lead inside last: good fourth to Imad in Goodwood Stakes despite being unsuited by steady pace, shuffled back towards rear approaching straight then making laboured progress: ideally suited by extreme distances: acts on any going: normally races prominently: genuine. *J. L. Dunlop*

HAROLDON (IRE) 6 ch.g. Heraldiste (USA) 121 – Cordon 89 (Morston (FR) 125) [1994 –: a9.4g 1995 a8g a12g^6 a11g 11.8d 10g^4 10.8f* 10.8g^2 10.8g^2 10.2m^6 11.6g* 10m^5 10g^4 12m^5 10.5g* 11.9s^4 12m Oct 21] leggy, close-coupled gelding: unimpressive mover: fairly useful handicapper: won at Warwick in May, Windsor in July and Haydock (best effort, held up in very strongly-run affair) in September: stays 1½m, at least in a steadily-run race: acts on firm ground and dead: visored (below form) twice: sometimes bandaged. *B. Palling* — 81

HARPOON LOUIE (USA) 5 b.g. Eskimo (USA) – Twelfth Pleasure (USA) (Fappiano (USA)) [1994 79: 10.3g 8d^5 8m* 10m 8.9f 8f 8.5m* 1995 8g a8.5g* a7g* a8g^4 Dec 14] big, lengthy, well-made gelding: fluent mover: fair handicapper: sold out of M. H. Easterby's stable only 2,000 gns Newmarket July Sales after reappearance: won 2 minor events at Sterrebeek in the autumn: stays 8.5f: acts on good to firm ground (very likely on firm) and soft and the all-weather. *Alex Vanderhaeghen, Belgium* — 79

HARRIET'S BEAU 2 b.c. (Apr 4) Superpower 113 – Pour Moi 73 (Bay Express 132) [1995 5m^5 5m^5 5g^4 6h^5 5m 5g Sep 23] 6,600Y: leggy colt: half-brother to 3-y-o Bex Hill (by Grey Desire), 7f winner at 2 yrs, and 7f winner Spanish Express (by King of Spain): dam placed over 5f and 6f: modest form in claimer and maiden events at Beverley first 3 starts: well below form afterwards, blinkered final start: should stay 6f. *M. W. Easterby* — 58 d

HARRKEN HEIGHTS (IRE) 3 b.f. Belmez (USA) 131 – In High Spirits (Head For Heights 125) [1994 –: 5g 1995 8f^3 8g 12.1s Nov 2] small, stocky filly: no form. *J. S. Goldie* — –

HARRY BROWNE (IRE) 3 b.g. Al Hareb (USA) 123 – Jeewan 82 (Touching Wood (USA) 127) [1994 48: 7g 5m^4 6m 6g 6s 8s 1995 a7g* a8g* a10g^3 a8g^2 7g^6 8.2g^2 9.9m^6 10f^5 10m^2 8m^6 14.1m a12g^3 10m* 9.9m* 9.9m* 10.1f^2 10.5g^3 10d 11.9m^2 14m^5 Oct 13] compact gelding: fair handicapper: won at Southwell (twice) in January, at Pontefract and Beverley (both ladies races) in July and at Beverley in August: effective at 1¼m and 1½m, twice below form over 1¾m: acts on fibresand and firm ground: held up. *Mrs J. R. Ramsden* — 75

HARRY'S COMING 11 b.g. Marching On 101 – Elegant Star 86 (Star Moss 122) [1994 53: 6.1v 6.1d^5 6m 6s 5d^5 7g^3 6m^3 6.1m^4 7g^5 6m^4 8.3m 6g^4 6f^4 5d 6s 1995 5d^2 5m^3 5.1g* 5.1m^5 5g^2 6g 6g* 5m^5 6.1m^4 5.1h^6 6f 5f Aug 28] leggy, good-topped gelding: veteran handicapper: still capable of modest form: won claimers at Nottingham in April and Warwick (apprentices) in June: below form last 5 starts: effective at 5f, and stays 7f: acts on equitrack and on firm and dead ground, unsuited by soft: tried blinkered and visored at 3 yrs. *R. J. Hodges* — 60 d

HARRY'S TREAT 3 b.f. Lochnager 132 – Megara (USA) (Thatching 131) [1994 NR 1995 7g^3 6g 7.5d 7.1f^3 Jun 26] 1,200Y: good-topped filly: fourth foal: half-sister to a French jumps winner: dam, unraced, out of close relation to Oaks winner Intrepidity: modest form when third in maiden at Catterick and handicap at Edinburgh: should stay beyond 7f. *J. L. Eyre* — 56

HARRY WELSH (IRE) 3 gr.g. Treasure Kay 114 – Excelling Miss (USA) (Exceller (USA) 129) [1994 69p: 5g^4 5d^4 7.5g^2 6.9d^3 8m^5 1995 10.2m^3 12f* a12g^4 11.8g^3 16.4f^3 16.1f^5 14d^3 17.1m 14.1m^4 a14.8g Nov 11] leggy gelding: has a quick action: modest handicapper: 6/1 on, won 2-runner median auction maiden at Carlisle in July: stays 16.4f: acts on firm and dead ground, tailed off both starts on all-weather: visored/blinkered since fifth 3-y-o start. *K. McAuliffe* — 64 a–

HARSH TIMES 2 ch.f. (Apr 3) Efisio 120 – Larnem 43 (Meldrum 112) [1995 5g^6 5m 6m^6 7m a7g^2 a6g* 7g^4 7f^6 a6g Oct 14] 3,000Y: leggy filly: fourth reported foal: half-sister to 3-y-o Rubislaw (by Dunbeath) and 6f to 10.3f winner Larn Fort and 7f winner Bogart (both by Belfort): dam 7f to 11.5f winner, probably stayed 13f: — 53 won selling nursery at Southwell in September: below form in claimers last 2 starts: stays 7f: acts on fibresand: blinkered (below form) twice, looking ungenerous first occasion: carried head high when winning. *M. H. Easterby*

HARTFIELDS BOY 2 b.g. (Apr 28) Shavian 125 – Fallen Angel 88 (Quiet Fling (USA) 124) [1995 6m 5m5 6m Aug 16] 8,600Y: small, compact gelding: half-brother to 1987 Irish 2-y-o 6f winner Nations Spirit (by Thatching) and 11.7f winner Silvie (by Kind of Hush): dam stayer: poor form in median auction maidens: should be suited by further than 6f. *B. J. Meehan* –

HARVEST DREAM 4 b.f. Primo Dominie 121 – New Pastures (Formidable (USA) 125) [1994 –: 7s 1995 8f Jun 28] tailed off in maiden and claimer: sold 500 gns Ascot November Sales. *B. J. Meehan* –

HARVEST REAPER 3 gr.g. Bairn (USA) 126 – Real Silver 85 (Silly Season 127) [1994 61: 5.1m 6g 6f6 6m4 5d2 5d3 6g 5.3g5 6s5 6m4 7.1g5 a7g 1995 7g 8g 6.9g3 a6g4 a7g a9.4g Dec 9] leggy gelding: modest maiden plater: should prove best at up to 7f: acts on good to firm ground and dead: tried visored, no improvement: takes keen hold: inconsistent. *J. L. Harris* 54 a43

HARVEST ROSE 6 b.m. Bairn (USA) 126 – Ragtime Rose (Ragstone 128) [1994 52: a7g a8.5g5 a8.5g4 a8g 8f4dis 1995 8f 8m 8m 8.1g Jul 19] angular mare: poor handicapper: well beaten in 1995: stays 1m: acts on equitrack, firm ground and dead: inconsistent. *O. O'Neill* –

HARVEY WHITE (IRE) 3 b. or br.g. Petorius 117 – Walkyria (Lord Gayle (USA) 124) [1994 67: 6d 6g 6.9m3 7v 1995 8m5 10m6 10m5 12.1m3 9.7f2 10.1m* 9.7s 9m6 a12g Nov 10] rather leggy gelding: modest handicapper: won claimer at Epsom in August, making most: stays 1½m: acts on firm going, well beaten on soft. *J. Pearce* 57

HASAID LADY (IRE) 3 b.f. Shaadi (USA) 126 – Lady Ellen 67 (Horage 124) [1994 6g4 6g4 7g2 6g 1995 7m 7m6 7f6 Aug 10] unfurnished ex-Irish filly: first foal: dam, placed over 5f at 2 yrs, half-sister to Indian Ridge: modest maiden: trained at 2 yrs by K. Prendergast: should stay 1m: has raced only on a sound surface. *R. Hannon* 58

HASTA LA VISTA 5 b.g. Superlative 118 – Falcon Berry (FR) (Bustino 136) [1994 61: a12g* a16s* a12g 12g3 12.3m3 12g a12g4 11.9m2 12.3m 16.2m6 12.3m 16m6 15.8g6 1995 a14g5 a12g a12g 12.3m3 12.3m* 12g 12g3 11.9m5 12m3 a14g Nov 6] compact gelding: has a round action: modest handicapper: won at Ripon in August: effective at 1½m to 2m: acts on good to firm ground, dead and fibresand: blinkered nowadays: usually ridden up with pace: game. *M. W. Easterby* 53

HATTAAFEH (IRE) 4 b.f. Mtoto 134 – Monongelia 98 (Welsh Pageant 132) [1994 –: 10d a12g4 1995 a13g* a13g2 a16g a11g3 11.9m3 a12g3 10g 12m a12g Nov 13] workmanlike, angular filly: modest handicapper: narrowly won maiden at Lingfield in January: off course 5½ months, below form last 3 starts: should stay further than 13f, forced to race wide when down the field over 2m: acts on good to firm ground and the all-weather: normally held up: sold (M. Jarvis to Miss B. Sanders) 10,000 gns Newmarket December Sales. *M. A. Jarvis* 60

HATTA BREEZE 3 b.f. Night Shift (USA) – Jouvencelle 68 (Rusticaro (FR) 124) [1994 53p: 6m 1995 10.5m3 10.3g5 10f3 12m 11.8g4 a8.5g* 8g3 8g* 8.2m a8g Nov 14] close-coupled, good-topped filly: fair handicapper: won at Wolverhampton (maiden event) and Leicester in the autumn: effective at 1m (best form) and stays 10.5f: acts on good to firm ground and fibresand: blinkered since fifth 3-y-o start: sweating and edgy (ran badly) second 3-y-o outing: races prominently: sold 19,000 gns Newmarket December Sales. *M. A. Jarvis* 68

HATTA RIVER (USA) 5 b.h. Irish River (FR) 131 – Fallacieuse (Habitat 134) [1994 a12g* a11g a10g3 a11g6 a12g3 a12g a10g4 1995 a9g6 a12g4 11.8m6 11m4 11m5 12d a14.8g 11.8g5 10.3m Oct 21] good-topped horse: has a long stride: spent 18 months or so in UAE with D. Selvaratnam, winning a handicap in January, 1994: bought 3,800 gns Newmarket July Sales: only modest at best on return: stays 12.5f well: best form on top-of-the-ground: tried blinkered, including when successful: formerly suited by forcing tactics: inconsistent. *J. A. Harris* 58

HATTA SUNSHINE (USA) 5 b.g. Dixieland Band (USA) – Mountain Sunshine (USA) (Vaguely Noble 140) [1994 44, a48: a12g3 a10g* a8g5 a8g4 a10g5 11.6d a10g2 9f2 8.3f6 a10g6 9f6 a10g a10g2 a10g 1995 a8g2 a8g4 a8g* 9g6 a8g3 8.3g5 46 a55

9m^4 10g^5 9f^4 a10g 8f^5 Aug 21] lengthy gelding: modest handicapper on the all-weather: won at Lingfield in March: only poor on turf: stays 1¼m: acts on equitrack and firm ground, yet to race on fibresand: inconsistent. *A. Moore*

HAUTE CUISINE 2 b.g. (Mar 21) Petong 126 – Nevis 61 (Connaught 130) [1995 5.1m^5 5m^6 Jun 16] 15,500F, 20,000Y: strong gelding: has scope: first foal: dam lightly-raced half-sister to Paris House (by Petong): behind in maidens at Chester and Sandown (stumbled stalls) month later: subsequently gelded. *J. Berry* –

HAVANA HEIGHTS (IRE) 2 ch.f. (Apr 26) Persian Heights 129 – Havana Blade (USA) (Blade (USA)) [1995 a5g 5g^6 a7g^5 Nov 27] IR 1,700Y, 1,100 2-y-o: second reported foal: dam won from 7f to 8.5f in France: trained by R. Emery first 2 starts: no worthwhile form in maiden auctions (off course 6 months before final start) and a seller. *J. L. Eyre* –

HAVANA MISS 3 b.f. Cigar 68 – Miss Patdonna 62 (Starch Reduced 112) [1994 54d: 6.1s* 7m 6.1f^6 6s 6.1g a7g 1995 a8g a6g^4 a6g^6 a6g a7g^6 a5g 5.7f 6g^4 5.1h 6d 6m 6.9g^4 8f Oct 24] leggy, sparely-made filly: poor form in 1995: probably stays 7f: acts on soft ground: tried visored and blinkered: inconsistent. *B. Palling* 46 a38

HAVE A NIGHTCAP 6 ch.g. Night Shift (USA) – Final Orders (USA) (Prince John) [1994 NR 1995 a16g a14g Mar 3] close-coupled gelding: inconsistent plater (rated 47) at 3 yrs, but no form since: fair but unreliable winning hurdler. *N. P. Littmoden* –

HAWA AL NASAMAAT (USA) 3 b.g. Houston (USA) – Barrera Miss (USA) (Barrera (USA)) [1994 73: 7f 6d^4 5.7g^2 1995 7g^3 7.1m^2 7m 7f* 7.1m^4 7f^6 7g 7d^4 Sep 30] well-made gelding: fairly useful handicapper: won at Redcar in June: will prove at least as effective at 6f as 7f: acts on good to firm and dead ground: runs the odd poor race: has been gelded. *E. A. L. Dunlop* 84

HAWAASH (IRE) 3 b.c. Royal Academy (USA) 130 – Imperial Jade 105 (Lochnager 132) [1994 NR 1995 7.1g* 7g^3 8g 7m^3 Oct 14] 68,000Y: sturdy, deep-bodied colt: fifth foal: closely related to a fairly useful winner in Germany by Kings Lake and half-brother to 3 winners, notably useful 4-y-o Averti (by Warning): dam sprinting sister to smart sprinter Reesh: fairly useful form: led on line in maiden at Sandown in June: good third of 12 in handicap at Newmarket final start: stays 7f (last of 13 in listed race over 1m): sold 23,000 gns Doncaster October Sales: sent to Norway. *J. R. Fanshawe* 94

HAWAII STORM (FR) 7 b.g. Plugged Nickle (USA) – Slewvindaloo (USA) (Seattle Slew (USA)) [1994 –, a59: a8.5g^4 a7g^4 a7g a7g a9.4g a8g a8g^5 8d a7g^3 7s 7g a7g^3 a7g^3 a7g^2 a8g* a7g 1995 a8g^4 a8g^4 a8g^2 a8g^3 a8.5g a8g a8g^2 a10g a8g^3 a8g^6 a7g* Dec 14] leggy gelding: fair handicapper, campaigned mainly on the all-weather: left Miss A. J. Whitfield after fifth start: won at Lingfield (best effort for 3 years) in December: effective at 7f and 1m (should stay further): blinkered (below form) 3 times in 1994. *D. J. S. ffrench Davis* – a70

HAWANAFA 2 b.f. (Feb 22) Tirol 127 – Woodland View (Precipice Wood 123) [1995 6f^6 7m Jul 21] tall, rather unfurnished filly: second reported foal: dam winning jumper: showed promise in maidens won by Darling Flame at Newbury (green) and Matiya at Newmarket (took good hold) under considerate ride: should stay beyond 6f. *R. Hannon* 60+

HAWKER'S NEWS (IRE) 4 b.c. Sadler's Wells (USA) 132 – High Hawk 124 (Shirley Heights 130) [1994 105: 10v* 11.5d* 12d 10m 1995 12g^5 Sep 29] quite good-topped colt: unimpressive mover with a short action: wintered in Dubai: looked extremely well but only 8½ lengths fifth of 7 in listed race at Newmarket on belated return: should stay 1½m: goes well on a soft surface: sent to France. *M. R. Stoute* 96+

HAWKISH (USA) 6 b.g. Silver Hawk (USA) 123 – Dive Royal (USA) (Inverness Drive (USA)) [1994 48: 8.5m^3 8.2f^3 10g 10.1f^4 a12g^6 10d* 11.4d^5 10.1g 10.1d 1995 9.9m^4 10g^2 10.1g^3 10m* 9f^4 10f^2 Oct 16] sturdy gelding: poor mover: modest handicapper: off course 3 months, won strongly-run 17-runner apprentice event at Leicester in September: raced mainly at around 1¼m, should stay 1½m: acts on firm ground and dead: consistent at 6 yrs. *D. Morley* 58

HAWKSLEY HILL (IRE) 2 ch.c. (Apr 17) Rahy (USA) 115 – Gaijin 97 (Caerleon (USA) 132) [1995 7m 6m a5g Nov 24] 60,000F, 40,000Y: big, workmanlike colt: has plenty of scope: third foal: dam, 6f winner at 2 yrs, best at 7f: – p withdrawn lame at start on intended debut: always towards rear in large-field maidens at Doncaster (2) and Southwell: needs further than 5f: will probably do better. *Mrs J. R. Ramsden*

HAWWAM 9 b.g. Glenstal (USA) 118 – Hone 79 (Sharpen Up 127) [1994 57: 8g6 7d2 a7g2 a8g4 a9.4g3 1995 a7g3 a8g* a8g* a8g2 a8.5g5 a8g* a8g4 8.3v3 8g2 8m 8g6 a7g4 8.1m3 8g a8g2 a8g a9.4g Dec 9] good-topped, quite attractive gelding: fair performer on the all-weather, successful in minor event and 2 handicaps at Southwell in January/February: modest on turf: effective at 7f to 1¼m: goes well on fibresand, and probably acts on any ground on turf: best with waiting tactics: sometimes early to post: sometimes swishes tail: has won for apprentice. *E. J. Alston* — 55 a73

HAYAAIN 2 b.c. (Mar 17) Shirley Heights 130 – Littlefield 100 (Bay Express 132) [1995 7g 8m5 8f Oct 24] sturdy, good-bodied colt: fifth foal: brother to fair maiden Moalem and half-brother to useful 3-y-o 7f (at 2 yrs) and 10.4f winner Dahik and 1991 2-y-o 5f winner Ebraaz (both by Green Desert): dam won from 5.8f (at 2 yrs) to 1m: fifth of 14 to Silver Dome in maiden at Newmarket: towards rear in similar event at Leicester 12 days later: likely to need middle distances. *Major W. R. Hern* — 76

HAYA YA KEFAAH 3 b.g. Kefaah (USA) 124 – Hayat (IRE) (Sadler's Wells (USA) 132) [1994 NR 1995 a9.4g a7g a8.5g a11g Feb 17] first foal: dam unraced: no sign of ability: sold (Sir Mark Prescott to N. Babbage) 2,100 gns Ascot February Sales and gelded. *Sir Mark Prescott* — –

HAY DANCE 4 b.g. Shareef Dancer (USA) 135 – Hay Reef 72 (Mill Reef (USA) 141) [1994 –: a12g4 8f 8m a8.5g a8g 1995 a12g a7g a11g6 Feb 3] close-coupled gelding: shows knee action: no worthwhile form here: sold 1,500 gns Doncaster March Sales and hurdling in Ireland. *J. P. Leigh* — –

HAYDON HILL 4 ch.f. Hadeer 118 – Coppice (Pardao 120) [1994 40: 7m4 8m4 10.2f 12m 8.5m4 9g 10g 10g 1995 a12g6 a12g Jan 16] angular filly: poor maiden: well beaten in 1995: should stay 1¼m: has raced only on a sound surface on turf: inconsistent. *P. D. Evans* — –

HAYSONG (IRE) 2 ch.f. (May 5) Ballad Rock 122 – Hay Knot (Main Reef 126) [1995 5g5 May 29] neat filly: sixth foal: half-sister to useful 7f (at 2 yrs) to 1m winner Cazzuto (by Kefaah) and 5-y-o 6f and 7f winner Walnut Burl (by Taufan): dam, unraced, from family of Wassl: 20/1, swerved leaving stalls when well-beaten fifth of 6 in maiden at Doncaster: awkward before start. *J. P. Leigh* — –

HAZARD A GUESS (IRE) 5 ch.g. Digamist (USA) 110 – Guess Who 76 (Be My Guest (USA) 126) [1994 74: 10.3g* 12d 9.9m 10m5 10g* 11.9m3 1995 10.3g 10.8d4 10f* 9.9m* 12g 12d3 12m 10m5 10m3 9.9m6 11.9g5 11.9s Oct 1] tall, leggy gelding: has improved every season, and is now a fairly useful handicapper: won at Pontefract and Beverley in May: very good fifth at Sandown (£45,900 event won by Yoush) and Haydock: suited by middle distances: acts on any ground: usually held up. *Mrs J. R. Ramsden* — 80

HAZEL 3 ro.f. Risk Me (FR) 127 – Sir Tangs Gift (Runnett 125) [1994 NR 1995 8m 7g May 24] 1,000Y: good-topped filly: third foal: sister to a 7f winner in Germany: dam, maiden, stayed 1m: modest form in maidens at Salisbury: should stay 1m. *Miss Gay Kelleway* — 57

HEAD FOR HEAVEN 5 b.g. Persian Heights 129 – Believer 112 (Blakeney 126) [1994 NR 1995 8.3m 10m6 9.7m3 9.2f2 12f 9.7m4 9m a10g Sep 5] good-topped gelding: sixth foal: half-brother to fairly useful 1989 2-y-o 5f winner Please Believe Me (by Try My Best): dam won Princess Royal Stakes: poor maiden plater: should stay 1¼m: has raced only on top-of-the-ground on turf, well beaten on equitrack: inconsistent: won 2 selling hurdles after final start. *R. P. C. Hoad* — 47

HEAD TURNER 7 b.m. My Dad Tom (USA) 109 – Top Tina (High Top 131) [1994 51: a13g2 a12g3 a12g* a13g4 a16g2 12.3m 13.1g2 14g3 20m 12.5f5 14g2 16.2m2 16.1m6 14m 1995 a12g6 a13g3 a12g* a13g* a12g2 a12g5 a16g6 a16g* 11.9m4 14m 15.4m3 16.4m6 14m 16.2g6 16.1g4 16.2s 16m Oct 19] sparely-made mare: modest handicapper: best form on all-weather, and won 3 times (once a minor event) at Lingfield by March: inconsistent afterwards, and ran as if something amiss final start: finds 1½m a bare minimum and probably stays 2½m: acts on equitrack and probably on any turf going: held up: tough. *C. P. Wildman* — 61 d

HEART BROKEN 5 b.m. Bustino 136 – Touch My Heart 61 (Steel Heart 128) [1994 51, a74: 6s a7g a6g* 6m a6g^{5} 5.9m^{2} a6g*^{dis} 6m 6m a7g* 6m 7g 6.1s 1995 6m^{6} 5m^{4} 6g* 6m 5.9f^{2} 6m a7g* Aug 4] sturdy mare: carries condition: in foal to Local Suitor: fair handicapper, easily best on all-weather: won at Catterick in June and (career-best effort on final start) at Southwell in August: best at up to 7f: went well on fibresand, acted on firm and dead ground: effective blinkered (was at Southwell) or not. *J. G. FitzGerald*
60
a78

HEAR THE MUSIC (IRE) 2 ch.f. (Mar 10) Common Grounds 118 – Tap The Line (Tap On Wood 130) [1995 5m^{2} 5m^{2} 5.2g^{4} 5f* 5.2m^{3} 5g^{6} 5s* 5d^{3} 6m^{4} 7f^{6} Nov 18] 26,000Y: tall filly: has plenty of scope: good mover: fifth foal: half-sister to 4-y-o Southern Power (by Midyan), 7f winner at 2 yrs, and 1991 2-y-o 6f winner Cut The Line (by Sharpo): dam French middle-distance winner: won maiden at Thirsk in July and minor event at Haydock (seemed to be only one to handle conditions) in October: sold out of B. Hills's stable 26,000 gns Newmarket Autumn Sales after penultimate start: soundly beaten in 100,000-dollar event at Hollywood Park final one: should stay 6f: acts on firm ground but best form on soft: tends to sweat and get on edge: blinkered (not discredited) sixth outing. *I. Jory, USA*
87

HEART LAKE 4 ch.c. Nureyev (USA) 131 – My Darling One (USA) (Exclusive Native (USA)) [1994 117: 7s* 7g^{2} 8m* 7g^{4} 7g* 8m*^{dis} 7g^{3} 1995 a8g* 7f^{5} 8f* 6g Jul 13] good-topped, attractive colt with scope: smart ex-Irish performer: won 2-runner minor event in Dubai in January and very valuable 18-runner Japanese Group 1 Yasuda Kinen (by a nose) at Tokyo in May: well-backed ante-post but ran as if something amiss in July Cup at Newmarket: stays 1m: acts on firm and soft ground: genuine: sent back to Dubai, stays in training. *Saeed bin Suroor*
117

HEATH ROBINSON (IRE) 3 b.c. In The Wings 128 – Blasted Heath 105 (Thatching 131) [1994 NR 1995 11m 10.3m^{6} 10g^{5} 10m^{3} 10m Jun 16] 105,000F: smallish, strong colt: has a round action: second foal: closely related to 1993 Irish 2-y-o 5f winner Wave The Wand (by Fairy King): dam Irish 5f (at 2 yrs) and 1m winner: fair maiden: will be well suited by 1½m+: yet to race on a soft surface: wears bandages: sent to Dubai. *J. H. M. Gosden*
80

HEATHYARDS CRUSADE (IRE) 4 ch.g. Digamist (USA) 110 – Theda 61 (Mummy's Pet 125) [1994 42: 10d^{6} 10.3f a8g^{4} a8.5g^{3} a12g^{6} a12g^{5} a14g^{4} 15s^{5} 1995 a13g Jan 12] close-coupled gelding: poor performer: well beaten only start 1995: probably stayed 1¾m: acted on fibresand and dead ground: fair form over hurdles: dead. *R. Hollinshead*
–

HEATHYARDS LADY (USA) 4 b.f. Mining (USA) – Dubiously (USA) (Jolie Jo (USA)) [1994 57, a54: 7m^{4} 7d 6d 8f* 8.5g^{5} 8m^{5} 8m^{3} 6.9f^{6} 7m 7.1d^{6} 8s 8g a6g* a8g a6g^{3} 1995 a7g^{4} a6g^{3} a6g^{3} a6g a6g^{3} a6g^{2} a7g^{4} a7g* a8.5g^{2} 7m^{3} 7g* a9.4g^{3} 8g a8.5g* a7g* a8.5g^{5} a7g^{6} Nov 24] leggy filly: fair handicapper: held her form well in 1995, winning at Wolverhampton in April, Catterick in September and twice at Wolverhampton (under 7-lb claimer) in October: effective at 6f to 9.4f: acts on any turf ground and goes well on fibresand. *R. Hollinshead*
61
a74

HEATHYARDS MAGIC (IRE) 3 b.g. Magical Strike (USA) 114 – Idle Gossip (Runnett 125) [1994 58: 6d 6v^{6} 1995 a6g* 7.6m 8f^{2} 7g^{3} a8.5g^{4} 8f^{3} 10m 8f Aug 28] tall, close-coupled gelding: fair form at best: won 3-runner maiden at Wolverhampton in April: tailed-off last on last 2 starts: stays 1m: acts on fibresand and firm ground: tends to carry head high: one to treat with caution: sold (R. Hollinshead to M. Dods) 2,400 gns Newmarket Autumn Sales. *R. Hollinshead*
68 d

HEATHYARDS ROCK 3 br.g. Rock City 120 – Prudence 68 (Grundy 137) [1994 66: 5d^{3} 6f^{3} 6m^{6} a7g^{5} 1995 a8.5g* 8g^{2} 9d^{2} 9m^{6} 10.3m^{5} a9.4g^{2} 10.5g 10.3m^{3} a9.4g^{5} 10m^{6} 10.3g^{4} 12d 10g 11.9d^{5} a12g^{6} Dec 2] tall, unfurnished gelding: useful performer at his best: won maiden at Wolverhampton in March: ran well (including in listed company) second to fifth 3-y-o starts: some way below form afterwards: stays 10.3f: acts on good to firm and dead ground and on fibresand: tried blinkered/ visored, no improvement: refused to race over hurdles in October: one to treat with caution. *R. Hollinshead*
96 d

HEAVENS ABOVE 3 br.g. Celestial Storm (USA) 132 – Regal Wonder 74 (Stupendous) [1994 47: 7.5m^{5} 7m^{5} 7m^{4} 8d 1995 12m 8g 15.8m Aug 11] good-topped gelding: looked of little account in 1995, leaving M. H. Easterby after second start, joining Mrs J. Brown after final one. *Mrs J. R. Ramsden*
–

HEAVEN SENT (IRE) 2 b.f. (Apr 15) Fayruz 116 – Folle Remont (Prince Tenderfoot (USA) 126) [1995 5m 5m^4 6m 5m 5m^6 Sep 7] half-sister to several winners here and abroad, including smart 6f/7f performer Sylvan Express and several modest animals: dam never ran: modest maiden: good sixth of 13 from poor draw to Chemcast in nursery at Folkestone final outing: best form at 5f. *P. Mitchell* 52 +

HEBOOB ALSHEMAAL (IRE) 3 b.f. Nordico (USA) – Royal Climber (Kings Lake (USA) 133) [1994 NR 1995 8d^4 10m^2 10m^2 10.5s^3 10.5d^5 a10g* a10g^3 a12g Dec 2] 33,000Y: leggy, workmanlike filly: first foal: dam fairly useful Irish middle-distance stayer, also 7f winner at 2 yrs: fair performer: won maiden at Lingfield in November easing down by 13 lengths: pulled up and dismounted final start: stays 10.5f: acts on good to firm and soft ground and on equitrack: visored/blinkered last 3 starts: sent to Dubai. *J. H. M. Gosden* 76

HEDERA (USA) 3 ch.f. Woodman (USA) 126 – Ivrea 109 (Sadler's Wells (USA) 132) [1994 78p: 7d* 1995 7m^3 7.6m^2 10m 8.2m^3 8d^3 Sep 24] leggy, unfurnished filly: fairly useful performer: respectable third of 9 in listed rated stakes at Ascot final start: stays 1m: acts on good to firm and dead ground: sent to Dubai. *M. R. Stoute* 90

HEDGEHOG 5 b.m. Electric 126 – Demderise 80 (Vaigly Great 127) [1994 –: 8g 11.5d a12g 1995 6.9g 9.7f Jun 30] lengthy mare: of no account. *J. O'Donoghue* –

HEE'S A DANCER 3 b.g. Rambo Dancer (CAN) 107 – Heemee 81 (On Your Mark 125) [1994 49: 5d 5g 5m 7f 7m 7g 7g 1995 8m^5 10m 8g Aug 26] small, leggy gelding: poor maiden: stays 1m: acts on good to firm ground: won over hurdles in September and November. *M. J. Camacho* 41

HEIGHTH OF FAME 4 b.g. Shirley Heights 130 – Land of Ivory (USA) 109 (The Minstrel (CAN) 135) [1994 –: 10m 10.2g 1995 8g^3 10.8m^6 a12g^2 Nov 13] modest maiden: sold out of S. Christian's stable 1,750 gns Ascot August Sales after second 4-y-o start: improved form when second of 12 in apprentice handicap at Wolverhampton: joined A. Wilson. *D. Burchell* 47

HEIGHTS OF LOVE 2 b.f. (Mar 4) Persian Heights 129 – Lets Fall In Love (USA) (Northern Baby (CAN) 127) [1995 5m 5m^5 5.1m^4 5.7m 5s Sep 28] neat filly: poor walker: fourth foal: half-sister to a winner in Italy: dam minor winner in USA: modest maiden: off course over 2 months after third start and no form on return: looked headstrong first 3 starts. *M. S. Saunders* 51 ?

HE KNOWS THE RULES 3 b.g. Tirol 127 – Falls of Lora 107 (Scottish Rifle 127) [1994 NR 1995 10s^4 11m Apr 21] leggy, close-coupled gelding: half-brother to useful 1m and 1¼m winner You Know The Rules (by Castle Keep) and 2m winner She Knew The Rules (by Jamesmead): dam won from 6f to 1½m: modest form in maidens at Leicester and Newbury: should prove suited by middle distances: joined R. Buckler. *M. R. Channon* 62

HELICON (IRE) 2 b.c. (Mar 19) Nashwan (USA) 135 – Hebba (USA) 80 (Nureyev (USA) 131) [1995 8d* Sep 26] angular, rather unfurnished colt: second foal: dam, 2-y-o 6f winner who stayed 1m, half-sister to top-class middle-distance performer Creme Fraiche: 7/1, won 20-runner maiden at Newmarket by length from Committal, behind after slow start then improving in good style under hands and heels from 2f out to lead inside last, running on strongly: will stay middle distances: sure to improve considerably: sent to Dubai. *H. R. A. Cecil* 96 P

HELIOS 7 br.g. Blazing Saddles (AUS) – Mary Sunley 62 (Known Fact (USA) 135) [1994 79: 8v 8g 7.1g^3 7m^2 7m^2 7f* 7g^5 7d* 7m 1995 7f 7m^3 8g^3 7m^5 7g 8.1m^5 7.1d 8s Oct 7] leggy, angular gelding: unimpressive mover: fair handicapper: creditable efforts in 1995 only when third at Goodwood: best form at 7f to 1m: acts on firm and dead going: blinkered (ran creditably) once as 5-y-o: has worn tongue strap. *N. J. H. Walker* 79 d

HELLO HOBSON'S (IRE) 5 b.m. Fayruz 116 – Castleforbes (Thatching 131) [1994 NR 1995 a6g 5.9f 6g^2 6.1m* 6m 6m^5 6g^3 6g^4 7f a6g^5 a6g Dec 9] compact, workmanlike mare: modest handicapper: won at Nottingham in June: stays 6f: acts on good to firm ground: blinkered (out of form) once in 1993. *R. Bastiman* 55 a–

HELLO MISTER 4 b.c. Efisio 120 – Ginnies Petong (Petong 126) [1994 102, a77+: 6g^5 6g^5 5.3m*^{dis} 6g^4 5.3g* 7m 6f 5m^5 5m* 6m^5 a6g^2 5.2g^6 5m^2 5g^6 6g* 5.6g* 6d^3 5g^6 7m 6d 1995 7m 5g 6g 5g 6f 5.1m^3 5m 5m^4 6m 6g^3 5.6m* 6d 7d 5s^4 6m^2 Oct 14] sturdy, good-quartered colt: useful performer: took a long time to find his form, 106

Tote-Portland Handicap, Doncaster—Hello Mister wins it again; this-side runners Bold Effort (checked cap) and Cool Jazz (striped cap) also make the frame

but better than ever in the autumn: won Tote-Portland Handicap at Doncaster in September for second year running, beating Bold Effort by 3½ lengths: good efforts in £15,500 handicap at Ascot and listed race at Newmarket (usual rider unable to claim, staying-on second of 12 to Royale Figurine) last 2 starts: effective at 5f and 6f: acts on good to firm and soft ground: often sweating and edgy: suited by waiting tactics, and well ridden by P. McCabe: tough. *J. O'Donoghue*

HELLO PETER (IRE) 3 b.g. Taufan (USA) 119 – Apple Rings 97 (Godswalk (USA) 130) [1994 –: 7m 1995 8d 8.5m4 11.5g5 Sep 12] unfurnished gelding: modest maiden: will probably prove best at up to 1¼m. *M. H. Tompkins* 49

HELMSLEY PALACE 6 b.m. Dominion 123 – Queen Midas 119 (Glint of Gold 128) [1994 NR 1995 a8g a8g Feb 4] seems of little account. *M. P. Muggeridge* –

HELMSMAN (USA) 3 b.c. El Gran Senor (USA) 136 – Sacred Journey (USA) (King's Bishop (USA)) [1994 99: 6m* 6f2 6g2 6g3 1995 7m 8f* 9f2 9f* 9f2 Nov 26] lengthy, attractive colt: has a round action: smart performer here, 7¾ lengths eighth of 12 to Diffident in European Free Handicap at Newmarket in April on final race for P. Chapple-Hyam: won allowance race at Del Mar in September by 6 lengths and Grade 3 event at Santa Anita in November by 2 lengths: ran very well when ½-length second of 13 to Labeeb in Hollywood Derby final start: stays 9f: acts on firm going: blinkered (and raced on lasix and bute) all starts in USA. *W. Dollase, USA* 118

HENCARLAM (IRE) 2 b.c. (May 8) Astronef 116 – War Ballad (FR) (Green Dancer (USA) 132) [1995 9m 8.1d Sep 12] IR 36,000Y: lengthy colt: half-brother to Irish 1¼m to 12.3f winner Sense of Value and 1989 2-y-o 5f and 7f winner Trojan Excel (both by Trojan Fen): dam placed over 10.5f in France: green and always towards rear when seventh of 8 in maiden at Sandown: tailed off in minor event there following month. *M. R. Channon* –

HENRY COOPER 2 b.g. (Apr 2) Distant Relative 128 – Miss Echo (GB) § (Chief Singer 131) [1995 7.6d a8g Nov 14] first foal: dam ungenuine maiden, should have stayed 1¼m: beaten long way in autumn maidens at Lingfield. *Dr J. D. Scargill* –

HENRY ISLAND (IRE) 2 ch.c. (Apr 13) Sharp Victor (USA) 114 – Monterana 99 (Sallust 134) [1995 a8.5g4 Dec 9] fourth foal: half-brother to 1992 2-y-o 7f winner Ginger Flower (by Niniski): dam, 6f and 7f winner at 2 yrs, out of half-sister to Italian Derby winner Ruysdael II: 7/2 from 2/1, over 15 lengths fourth of 13, slowly away, never a factor, to Kissing Gate in maiden at Wolverhampton: should do better. *G. Wragg* – p

HENRY KOEHLER 3 b.g. Hadeer 118 – William's Bird (USA) 104 (Master Willie 129) [1994 NR 1995 7g5 8m6 7g6 11.5f 8d3 8m Jun 20] smallish, sturdy gelding: has a powerful, round action: second foal: dam 5f and 7f winner at 2 yrs, ran only once at 3 yrs: fairly useful form when sixth in listed race at Kempton and Greenham Stakes at Newbury in April: beaten 2 heads in maiden at Yarmouth in June, collared near finish: well beaten in Britannia Handicap at Royal Ascot 5 days later: sent to Malaysia. *C. E. Brittain* 91

HENRY THE FIFTH 2 b.c. (Mar 24) Village Star (FR) 131 – Microcosme 100 (Golden Fleece (USA) 133) [1995 7m^4 7g 7.6d^2 7s^2 8d* 8m^4 6d^5 Dec 1] rather leggy, quite attractive colt: poor mover: fourth reported foal: half-brother to 1m winner Cedez Le Passage (by Warning), now stays 1½m, and middle-distance winner Persian Fleece (by Bold Arrangement): dam French 2-y-o 6.5f winner: fairly useful performer: won minor event at Newbury in October, battling on gamely: not discredited in similar event at Doncaster and listed race at Evry afterwards: will stay beyond 1m: acts on good to firm and soft ground: had rope halter for stalls entry. *C. E. Brittain* 92

HENRY THE HAWK 4 b.g. Doulab (USA) 115 – Plum Blossom (USA) (Gallant Romeo (USA)) [1994 50: a5g^4 5d^4 5g a5g a6g 1995 a6g a5g a6g 5d^5 5m 6g 6m^3 5g^3 5d* 5f^3 6m^2 5f^4 5g 6m^3 5h 6g Sep 1] small gelding: modest handicapper: won apprentice maiden event at Beverley in June: stays 6f: acts on all-weather surfaces and on firm and dead ground: effective visored or not: inconsistent. *M. Dods* 51

HENRY WESTON 3 b.c. Statoblest 120 – Young Tearaway 90 (Young Generation 129) [1994 –: 6.1s 6g 1995 6g 6m a6g a7g Dec 14] strong colt: no sign of ability. *P. Howling* –

HENRY WILL 11 b.g. Nicholas Bill 125 – Silver Cygnet 71 (My Swanee 122) [1994 39: 7g 7.1g^3 8.1g 7.5g* 8.1m 7.5m 7g 8m 7g 1995 7.5m 8f 7.5g 7m 8m Aug 7] workmanlike, angular gelding: probably no longer of much account. *W. L. Barker* –

HERALD ANGEL (IRE) 2 b.f. (Mar 28) Double Schwartz 128 – Gazettalong 80 (Taufan (USA) 119) [1995 6m a6g^6 6m 8m 7m^6 a6s Dec 23] workmanlike filly: second foal: dam 2-y-o 7f winner later won at 1m: ridden by 7-lb claimer, only worthwhile form when sixth of 27 in seller at Newmarket: sold out of M. Tompkins' stable 5,000 gns Newmarket Autumn Sales: behind only start in Sweden: should stay beyond 7f. *E. Henriksson, Sweden* 55 ?

HERE COMES A STAR 7 b.g. Night Shift (USA) – Rapidus (Sharpen Up 127) [1994 82: 5g^5 5m^6 5f^6 5m^3 5m^2 5m^2 5f 5m* 5g^3 6f* 5f^4 6.1g 5f^3 6m 6g 5g 5g 6g^3 1995 5m 5m^3 6d 6m^5 6f^4 6m 6m 6m^4 5m* 6m^3 5m^4 5h* 6m 5g 5d 5d^2 5m^3 5f Oct 14] sturdy, lengthy gelding: has a round action: fair performer: won claimer at Beverley (carried head rather high) in July and handicap at Carlisle in August: effective at 5f and 6f: acts on hard and dead ground: blinkered (well below form) earlier in career: best with waiting tactics. *J. M. Carr* 78

HERE COMES HERBIE 3 ch.g. Golden Lahab (USA) – Megan's Move 36 (Move Off 112) [1994 –: 9d a7g 1995 8m 12f 11f Oct 24] no worthwhile form. *W. Storey* –

HERE COMES RISKY 3 b.g. Risk Me (FR) 127 – Softly Spoken 87 (Mummy's Pet 125) [1994 83: 5s* 5d^2 6m^5 5m^3 6g^4 6d* 6g 1995 6m 6m a7g 6d 7g^4 6g 6g 6.9g^2 Oct 16] leggy, useful-looking gelding: has a round action: fair performer at best in 1995: should stay 1m: acts on good to firm and soft ground: sold 6,500 gns Newmarket Autumn Sales: sent to Belgium. *M. Johnston* 71

HERNANDO (FR) 5 b.h. Niniski (USA) 125 – Whakilyric (USA) 113 (Miswaki (USA) 124) [1994 127: 10s* 12d^4 12g^2 12f^6 12f^4 1995 10.5v^5 10g* 10m 12s^2 12s^5 12f^3 Nov 26] 125

Hernando will take over from his sire Niniski at the Lanwades Stud near Newmarket in 1996, at a fee of 8,000 guineas with the October 1st concession. He has plenty to recommend him. An attractive individual with a fluent action and a fine turn of foot, he was an even better racehorse than his sire and held a place among the best at middle distances in Europe at the ages of three, four and five. He is advertised as the winner of seven races and £1,317,124 in stakes. Most of those wins came as a three-year-old. They included one in the Prix du Jockey-Club; that same season he finished a three-quarter-length second to the Derby winner Commander In Chief in the Irish Derby. Place money in major events made up the bulk of his earnings afterwards, as his remaining two victories were gained in consecutive runnings of the Group 3 Prix Gontaut-Biron at Deauville.

Hernando's best performances as a four-year-old were to finish second in the Prix de l'Arc de Triomphe and fourth in the Japan Cup. He lost only narrowly to Carnegie at Longchamp and was unlucky in running at Tokyo, and there seemed every chance that keeping him in training in 1995 would meet with the reward such enterprise deserved. However, the year began with a potentially-disruptive change of stable on the death of trainer Francois Boutin. There followed two defeats in three starts, the second a very disappointing one in the Irish Champion Stakes when all had looked set fair for another crack at the Arc. Hernando trailed in seventh of eight at Leopardstown; the vet found him 'clinically abnormal' afterwards. All was not lost. The same week as Arc week Hernando bounced back to form in the Turf Classic Invitational at Belmont Park, finishing second of eight to the American horse Turk Passer (who had the run of the race), well clear of the rest and beaten less than a length. And he kept on song as his career began to draw to a close, returning to Belmont to gain his best placing in three starts in the Breeders' Cup Turf and then on to Tokyo to improve on his previous year's placing in the Japan Cup. Hernando finished fifth of thirteen to Northern Spur in the Breeders' Cup Turf, third of fourteen to Lando in the Japan Cup, on both occasions, typically, seeming faced with a lot to do in the straight even for one with his turn of foot. At Belmont, where he failed by a neck to catch Tamure for fourth and was beaten four and a half lengths by the winner, he had trouble getting through. At Tokyo he was beaten less than two lengths.

Hernando (FR) (b.h. 1990)	Niniski (USA) (b 1976)	Nijinsky (b 1967)	Northern Dancer
			Flaming Page
		Virginia Hills (b 1971)	Tom Rolfe
			Ridin' Easy
	Whakilyric (USA) (b 1984)	Miswaki (ch 1978)	Mr Prospector
			Hopespringseternal
		Lyrism (b 1979)	Lyphard
			Pass A Glance

Hernando has the pedigree to back up his racing record. His dam Whakilyric made such a start as a broodmare that the smart French middle-distance stayer Walter Willy (by Sadler's Wells) is the least of her first three foals, behind Hernando and Walter Willy's brother, the Breeders' Cup Mile runner-up Johann Quatz. Whakilyric won in France at up to seven furlongs, and as a two-year-old gained a place in the Prix de la Salamandre and the Prix de la Foret. The family is that of Palace Music, sire of the all-conquering Cigar. Palace Music is out of a half-sister to Hernando's great-grandam Pass A Glance, the last-named one of twelve winners, notably the Hollywood Oaks winner Prize Spot, out of her dam.

Niniski has been a strong influence for stamina as a sire but Hernando was just as effective at a mile and a quarter as a mile and a half. Although regarded by connections as ideally suited by a sound surface Hernando acted on any going. He

Prix Gontaut-Biron, Deauville—Hernando, Freedom Cry (gave 9lb) and Millkom

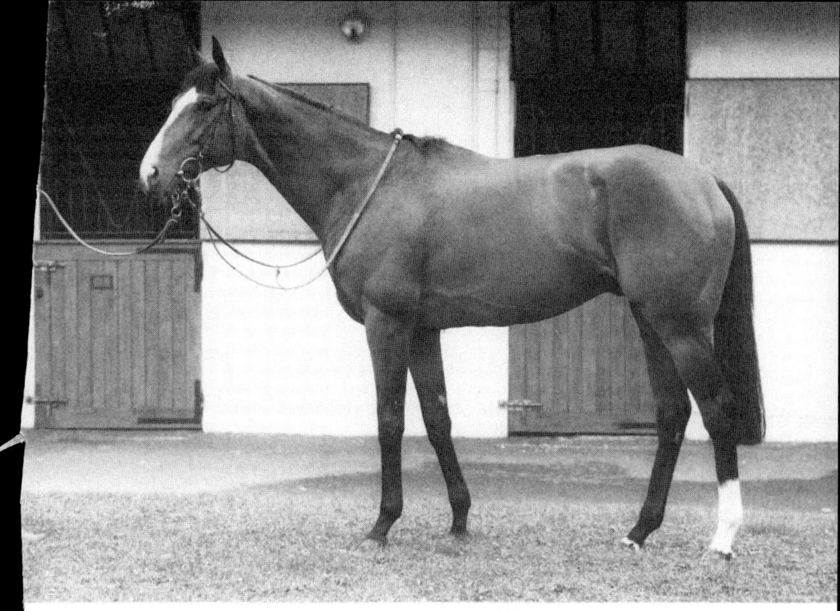

Mr S. S. Niarchos' "Hernando"

was invariably held up. A genuine sort, he sometimes sweated up. *J. E. Hammond, France*

HERODIAN (USA) 2 b. or br.c. (May 3) Housebuster (USA) – Try Something New (USA) (Hail The Pirates (USA) 126) [1995 6d² Oct 19] $95,000Y good-topped colt: fourth reported foal: half-brother to smart 1989 2-y-o 5f to 1m winner Somethingdifferent (by Green Forest), later successful in USA, and a winner by Damascus: dam good-class winner at up to 1¼m: 6/1, ½-length second of 19 to Fly Tip in maiden at Newbury, chasing leading bunch then coming through in good style from over 1f out: will improve, particularly at 7f+. *J. H. M. Gosden* — 81 p

HERON ISLAND (IRE) 2 b.c. (Jan 26) Shirley Heights 130 – Dalawara (IRE) (Top Ville 129) [1995 8g* 7g⁴ Sep 29] tall, leggy colt: first foal: dam French maiden half-sister to Darshaan (by Shirley Heights): won 17-runner maiden at Doncaster by head from Skillington, pair clear: stayed on when over 2 lengths fourth of 8 to Even Top in listed race at Newmarket later in month: will be very well suited by middle distances: wore a bandage near-hind on debut: will improve again. *P. W. Chapple-Hyam* — 99 p

HERR TRIGGER 4 gr.g. Sharrood (USA) 124 – Four-Legged Friend 101 (Aragon 118) [1994 –, a75: a8g* a8g* a10g² a8g³ a10g 1995 a10g⁴ a10g² a10g² 10m* 10f* 10m* 10m⁴ Aug 27] good-bodied gelding: has a markedly round action: fair handicapper: won at Newmarket in May and Ripon and Newmarket (sweating and edgy, stormed clear by 5 lengths) in June: ran well in £27,900 contest at Goodwood on only subsequent outing: stays 1¼m well: acts on firm ground and on equitrack: blinkered nowadays: carries head high: consistent. *Dr J. D. Scargill* — 77 +

HERSHEBAR 5 ch.h. Stanford 121§ – Sugar Token 66 (Record Token 128) [1994 55: a6g⁶ a7g⁶ a7g⁶ a6g² a5g² a5g⁵ a5g⁵ 1995 a6g Jan 21] sturdy horse: modest handicapper at 4 yrs for S. R. Bowring: no promise on reappearance after 11-month absence. *G. Fierro* — –

HE'S GOT WINGS (IRE) 2 b.c. (Apr 16) In The Wings 128 – Mariella 123 (Sir Gaylord) [1995 8.1s 8f Oct 24] 13,500F: rather unfurnished colt: half-brother to 3 winners abroad, including 1989 Prix d'Aumale winner Mackla (by Caerleon): dam, French 1½m to 1¾m winner, sister to very smart 1½m performer Scorpio and half-sister to Sagaro: always behind in maidens at Chepstow (slowly away) and Leicester. *C. D. Broad* –

HE'S SPECIAL 3 b.g. Reprimand 122 – Berylou (IRE) (Gorytus (USA) 132) [1994 NR 1995 a8g a10g a7g 12f May 1] leggy gelding: first foal: dam unraced: no form, including in selling company: sold 525 gns Ascot May Sales. *C. A. Cyzer* –

HETHERS FOOTSTEPS 3 ch.g. Tout Ensemble – Hethermai 57 (Pee Mai 107) [1994 NR 1995 10.2m May 2] third reported living foal: dam won 1m seller at 4 yrs: no promise in maiden at Bath. *P. G. Murphy* –

HEVER GOLF DIAMOND 2 b.g. (Mar 31) Nomination 125 – Cadi Ha 109 (Welsh Pageant 132) [1995 a7g Dec 6] 2,200F, 7,000Y: half-brother to French 1m and 9f winner Book of Verse (by Lypheor): dam, 7f and 1m winner who stayed 1¼m, from family of Blakeney and Morston: 25/1, no promise in maiden auction at Wolverhampton. *T. J. Naughton* –

HEVER GOLF EAGLE 2 b.c. (Apr 30) Aragon 118 – Elkie Brooks 82 (Relkino 131) [1995 7m 7m Sep 6] 25,000Y: good-bodied colt: half-brother to 3-y-o Karaar and several winners, including smart sprinter Pips Pride and fairly useful 6f to 1m winner Sunday's Hill (all 3 by Efisio): dam second over 6f at 2 yrs, didn't train on: always towards rear in maidens at Newmarket and Epsom 12 days later. *T. J. Naughton* –

HEVER GOLF EXPRESS 2 b.g. (Mar 23) Primo Dominie 121 – Everdene (Bustino 136) [1995 5m 5m^4 5m* 6f^5 5m^6 Aug 5] 13,500Y: lengthy gelding: second foal: dam French 1¼m winner: won maiden auction at Folkestone in May: disappointing afterwards in listed race at Epsom and minor event at Lingfield: subsequently gelded: should stay 6f: bandaged off-hind fourth start. *T. J. Naughton* 72

HEVER GOLF HERO 2 b.c. (Mar 23) Robellino (USA) 127 – Sweet Rosina 61 (Sweet Revenge 129) [1995 6m^4 8m 7d Sep 26] 22,000Y: tall, useful-looking colt: half-brother to several winners, including high-class 4-y-o 5f to 7f performer Hever Golf Rose (by Efisio): dam in frame at 5f and 6f: fourth of 9 in maiden at Lingfield in July under considerate ride: tailed off afterwards in maiden at Ascot and valuable sales race at Newmarket. *T. J. Naughton* 52

HEVER GOLF LADY 3 b.f. Dominion 123 – High Run (HOL) (Runnymede 123) [1994 44: 6g 6.1f^4 7m 8g a8.5g a7g^3 a7g^5 a8g 1995 a9.4g^3 a11g^2 a11g^6 a12g^3 a10g* a12g^5 12.5m^5 a16g* 16d* 15.4g^2 16.1h^2 11.8m^3 a16g^6 a16g a16g^4 a16g Dec 15] lengthy filly: modest performer: won selling handicaps at Lingfield in March and May and claimer at Yarmouth in June: stays 2m: acts on hard ground, dead and the all-weather. *T. J. Naughton* 59 a50

HEVER GOLF QUEEN 2 b.f. (Apr 4) Efisio 120 – Blue Jane 81 (Blue Cashmere 129) [1995 6m 6v 7.5g* 7.5d a7g^5 Dec 9] 11,000Y: lengthy, good-quartered filly: has scope: sister to 3-y-o Afsaat and 1m winner Eastleigh and half-sister to smart sprinter Ever Sharp (by Sharpo): dam 6f winner: won minor event in Sweden in September: no other worthwhile form: stays 7.5f: difficult to assess. *T. J. Naughton* ?

HEVER GOLF ROSE 4 b.f. Efisio 120 – Sweet Rosina 61 (Sweet Revenge 129) [1994 111: 8s 6d 6.1m^2 6g 5m 6f^2 5m^4 7m* 8f^4 7g* 6m^2 6m* 7g 6m^6 1995 7m^3 6s* 6d^4 6g^3 6s* 6m* 5f* 5m^3 6g* 6d* 6d* 5d* a6s Oct 28] 123

Hever Golf Rose—it is hard to know where to begin. She has had thirty-one starts in all and won thirteen of them, eight in 1995 including six pattern races: the epitome of toughness, Hever Golf Rose keeps coming back for more. This has taken her from handicapper to the best five-furlong performer in Europe, most of which she now seems to have visited. It is a 'rags to riches story', one whose final chapter in 1995 saw Hever Golf Rose racing round the turn at Belmont Park for a share of the million-dollar purse on offer in the Breeders' Cup Sprint. A little over three years earlier she was going round the Doncaster Sales ring and led out at 6,000 guineas, unsold.

Holsten Trophy, Hamburg—Hever Golf Rose (left) drops in on Germany

That same year, his second with a licence, Epsom trainer Joe Naughton sent out nine winners for £24,805 in win prize money. Twelve months later Naughton had twenty-two wins for £100,312. The best horse to have run for the stable looked to be the useful sprinter El Yasaf, but there was nothing very exclusive in that (although they had charge of this peripatetic individual for longer than most of his trainers). Play Hever Golf (by Alleging) had emerged as a fairly useful sprinter and his two-year-old half-sister Hever Golf Rose had won two of her four starts, a maiden auction at Doncaster and the £20,225 Colman's of Norwich Nursery at Newmarket. One year to the day, however, after Hever Golf Rose had failed to find a buyer, she made a second abortive visit to Doncaster, withdrawn lame at the start with what turned out to be a hairline fracture of the tibia. These early trials are easily forgotten because from this point on a race-by-race narrative of Hever Golf Rose's career becomes rather drawn-out. Soundness does not appear to have been much of a problem over the last two seasons. By the end of 1994 she had won a rated stakes at Newmarket, a listed race at Gelsenkirchen-Horst and the £12,800 Lawrence Batley Rated Stakes at York. She had been touched off in two valuable and prestigious

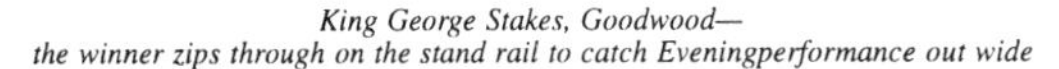

King George Stakes, Goodwood—
the winner zips through on the stand rail to catch Eveningperformance out wide

handicaps, the William Hill Trophy at York and Great St Wilfrid at Ripon. Hever Golf Rose's rating in *Racehorses of 1994* was 111.

In cricket, this figure has become famous for the somewhat eccentric suspicion with which it is treated by one international umpire. In racing, such a rating can also be regarded with wariness by trainers as it falls just within 'the twilight zone', a level of ability at which horses are too good to be campaigned extensively in handicaps but not considered good enough to have much future in British pattern races. A popular solution to this problem, one which Hever Golf Rose's connections embraced with relish, is to go in search of less competitive pattern races on the Continent. Hever Golf Rose's own answer was to improve again so that she became well worth her place in sprint races of even the highest quality. British racegoers will consequently be seeing a lot more of her in 1996. In the latest season, though, ten of her thirteen races were abroad. A reappearance at Leicester put her right for the Group 2 Premio Melton-Memorial Tudini at Rome in May which she won by a length and a half from one of the top Italian sprinters, Fred Bongusto. Four more trips abroad added victories in a listed race at Bremen in June and the Group 3 Holsten Trophy at Hamburg in July before she was seen out for a second time in Britain, at Goodwood in the King George Stakes. This was a highly-competitive Group 3 in which the penalised Hever Golf Rose had to give weight all round, her improved performances on the Continent apparently escaping the notice of many as she drifted in the betting to 10/1. Spectators were treated to a thrilling contest as Palacegate Episode then Eveningperformance set a terrific pace that led to a new course record, but for most of the way Hever Golf Rose looked unlikely to play any part in it. Towards the rear after two furlongs, she was right at the back after being impeded at halfway and had only marginally improved her position by the furlong pole. From there, however, Hever Golf Rose summoned up a storming run on the rails that took her past eight rivals and half a length clear in the last few strides from a bunched finish for second. Three pattern victories in 1995 and three to go.

First, though, there was something of a disappointment. Hever Golf Rose's debut at Group 1 level was just a fair effort compared to her Goodwood form when she came in third to So Factual and Ya Malak in the Nunthorpe Stakes at York; sweating beforehand, she led for three and a half furlongs. Time for a mid-season break, perhaps. Or for a trip to Sweden. Ten days after the Nunthorpe, Hever Golf Rose was landing odds of 7/10 in the valuable Taby Open Sprint Championship, a race with listed status, by a length and a half from the ex-British Cajun Cadet. Three days after that, and after a twenty-six-hour trip in the horsebox, she popped up at Baden-Baden for the Group 2 Jacobs Goldene Peitsche, and won again, this time beating Lavinia Fontana by two lengths with five back to the third horse Wessam Prince. Sweden, Germany...next stop, twelve days later, was France and Chantilly for the Prix de Seine-Et-Oise: an 11/10 favourite, she beat Tereshkova by a neck. 'This race', reported Naughton, 'was a bit of an afterthought'. It had been his first runner in France, but they were back just under three weeks later for the Prix de l'Abbaye de Longchamp. This was undoubtedly the crowning moment of Hever Golf Rose's

Prix de l'Abbaye de Longchamp—Hever Golf Rose crowns her magnificent season with a clear-cut win from Cherokee Rose, Eveningperformance (rails) and Easy Option

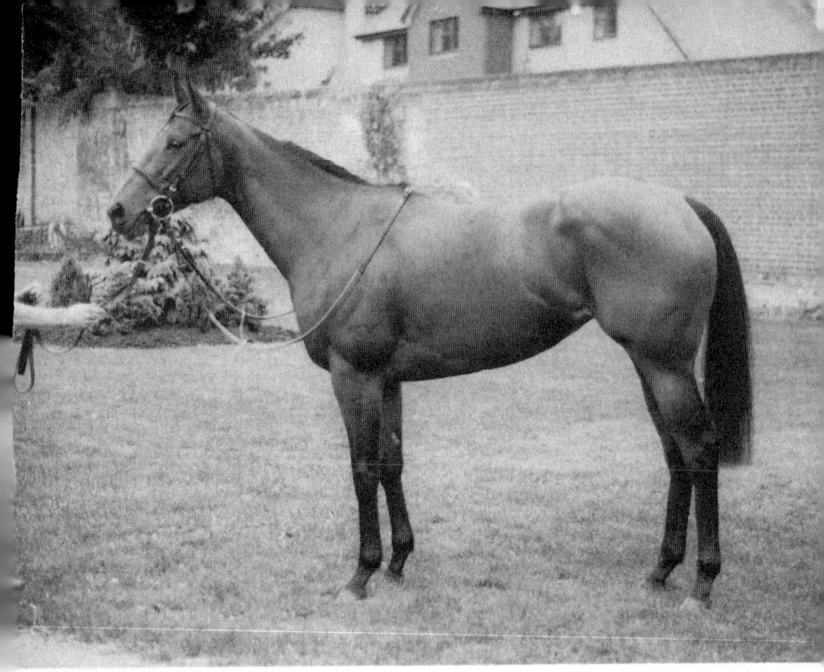

Mr M. P. Hanson's "Hever Golf Rose"

Grand Tour. British victories in the Group 1 Abbaye are commonplace nowadays—the French have not won it since 1978. Another was no surprise and neither was the strong pace set by Eveningperformance, but one thing that was not so predictable was the ease with which Hever Golf Rose kept at her quarters; she went on two furlongs out and was then driven clear of eleven rivals, two and a half lengths clear at the line. It was not a vintage renewal of the race but six of the runners had won last time out and those included the impressive Haydock Sprint Cup winner Cherokee Rose. On this occasion Cherokee Rose could only just scramble into second. Hever Golf Rose had gone in her coat but that had not stopped her recording another career-best effort. Her six pattern wins were more than those for any other horse in 1995, and her total of eight wins in one season was more than that of any other older filly trained in Britain since the war. Her career earnings now stood at over £360,000, those for the season at £312,000. Not even Hever Golf Rose's travel expenses can make much of a dent in that, and we do not suppose that connections will be smarting too much over her fruitless trip to New York for the Breeders' Cup later in October. On the muddy dirt track, she was the only European who ever held a chance of winning in the Sprint, chasing the two all-the-way leaders until the final furlong but fading into eighth. There will be plenty more opportunities for her in 1996 and all of the top sprints are now feasible targets.

Hever Golf Rose is now the best offspring of her sire Efisio and a better racehorse than he was. Temperament problems in the preliminaries threatened to sabotage Efisio's racing career at one stage, but he stuck it out for four seasons and won a pattern race in each of them. Young Ern, Pips Pride and Casteddu are his best other progeny. Not that far behind them is Hever Golf Rose's year-younger brother Go Hever Golf, another decidedly speedy individual at his best and the eighth consecutive winner for his dam Sweet Rosina. She has had nine winners in total from twelve foals of racing age, none to a fashionable sire. Her latest representative, Hever Golf Hero (by Robellino), is considered a colt with plenty of potential but has shown only modest form so far. Sweet Rosina's own racing form was a lot closer to that of Hever Golf Hero than Hever Golf Rose: an unimpressive individual in physique who made 420 guineas as a yearling, she reached the frame in two sprint maidens but rounded off her career well beaten in a selling handicap. Her parents Sweet Revenge and Welsh Bede were strikingly similar to Hever Golf Rose though. Both notably tough and genuine, Sweet Revenge was in fact another winner of the Abbaye as a four-year-old. He was even better at five years, taking the King's Stand Stakes, and Welsh Bede also reached her peak at that age, a useful five-furlong performer who retired with eight career victories. Welsh Bede's half-brother Singing Bede was a revelation as a five-year-old when he was awarded the Palace House and made all in the King George Stakes. This is a very speedy family (third dam, the useful B And D, was yet another five-furlong performer) but, ironically, until Hever Golf Rose came along, its chief claim to fame in recent years was B And D's position as third dam to the chasers Coulton and Fragrant Dawn.

Hever Golf Rose (b.f. 1991)	Efisio (b 1982)	Formidable (b 1975)	Forli
			Native Partner
		Eldoret (b 1976)	High Top
			Bamburi
	Sweet Rosina (ch 1975)	Sweet Revenge (ch 1967)	Compensation
			Too Much Honey
		Welsh Bede (ch 1964)	Welsh Abbot
			B And D

Her trainer believes that Hever Golf Rose, like some of her better relatives, will improve again as a five-year-old. Even if things go less well, of course, she owes him nothing. With Barry Hills for seven and a half years, Naughton was a contemporary of Peter Chapple-Hyam's as assistant at Manton, took out his licence the same year but, with a string that could be counted on two hands, he did not start with quite the same ammunition. In 1996 the horses in his care will number fifty-five to sixty. Hever Golf Rose is a small, strong, good-topped filly with a quick action. She showed useful form in winning twice at seven furlongs as a three-year-old but is now better over five and six. Wins in 1995 came on ground ranging from firm to soft, her best effort (in the Abbaye) coming on dead going though that fact could prove misleading given that the filly's overall record is so progressive. She is often bandaged behind. Hever Golf Rose's success story could not have come about if she were not game and genuine—the good attitude in her races seems to be matched only by that shown during hours in the horsebox. *T. J. Naughton*

HEVER GOLF STAR 3 b.g. Efisio 120 – Truly Bold 76 (Bold Lad (IRE) 133) [1994 –p: 6g 6m 1995 7g 5.3f* 6f^{5} 5m^{2} 5m^{4} a5g^{2} Nov 16] sturdy, workmanlike gelding: fair handicapper: won maiden event at Brighton in August: ran very well at Southwell on final start: best at around 5f: acts on fibresand and firm ground, yet to race on a soft surface: races prominently: may have further improvement in him. *T. J. Naughton* — 78

HEY UP DOLLY (IRE) 3 b.f. Puissance 110 – I Don't Mind 97 (Swing Easy (USA) 126) [1994 63: 5f^{6} 5m^{6} 5.9m 6f^{4} a7g^{5} 7g^{4} 6s^{2} 1995 6g 7m^{4} 7g* 7m 7.6m^{4} 7g 7.1g 8.1s Nov 2] compact filly: fair performer: won minor event at Thirsk in June: stays 7f: acts on any going: tried blinkered: none too consistent: joined J. J. O' Neill. *J. Berry* — 68 d

HI-AUD 3 b.f. Ilium 121 – Seragsbee (Sagaro 133) [1994 66: 7g 7d 7.6v 7m* 7.3v^{3} 6.9s 1995 9m 9.7m 12.5f^{3} 11.6m^{4} 11.6m* 12m* 11.7m^{3} 12m^{5} 14m Aug 25] good-bodied filly: fair handicapper: won at Windsor and Kempton in June: pulled up lame final start: would have stayed long distances: acted on good to firm ground and heavy: held up: dead. *J. Akehurst* — 69

HICKLETON LADY (IRE) 4 br.f. Kala Shikari 125 – Honest Opinion 68 (Free State 125) [1994 64: 7.1g^{6} 7m* 10m^{2} 8m^{4} 8.3g^{3} 8s* 11.1g^{5} 8.2g^{6} 1995 a8g Apr 3] small, leggy filly: modest performer in 1994 for Mrs M. Reveley: soundly beaten (first all-weather outing) on reappearance: stays 1¼m: acts on good to firm and soft ground. *Capt. J. Wilson* — –

HICKLETON MISS 2 ch.f. (Mar 22) Timeless Times (USA) 99 – Honest Opinion 68 (Free State 125) [1995 5m^{6} 5f^{2} 5f* 5g^{3} 5g^{2} 5g 5m 6f Oct 24] 1,000Y: — 58

small, sparely-made filly: half-sister to 2 winners by Daring March, one at 1¼m and the other at 5f at 2 yrs, and 7f and 1m winner Hickleton Lady (by Kala Shikari): dam 5f winner at 2 yrs: won 5-runner seller at Hamilton in August: should be as effective at 6f as 5f: slowly away last 3 starts. *Mrs M. Reveley*

HICKORY BLUE 5 ch.g. Clantime 101 – Blueit (FR) 101 (Bold Lad (IRE) 133) [1994 68, a54+: 5.1g^3 5g^2 6m^3 5.2m^2 5.1d^2 5d^2 a5g^5 1995 5m* 5m 5g 5m^6 5m^5 5g^5 5m 5.1m^3 7f^3 a6g Nov 6] leggy gelding: fair handicapper: won at Lingfield in May: effective at 5f, and stays 7f: acts on firm and dead going (probably on soft), has only modest form on fibresand: usually blinkered/visored: wears net muzzle: consistent. *Mrs N. Macauley* — 72 a–

HIDDEN OASIS 2 b.c. (Feb 3) Green Desert (USA) 127 – Secret Seeker (USA) (Mr Prospector (USA)) [1995 6g^4 7m^2 7d* Sep 20] quite attractive, rather unfurnished colt: first living foal: dam, 6f winner in USA, sister to Gone West and Lion Cavern, same family as Known Fact: progressive colt: won maiden at Chester in September (bandaged) by 9 lengths from Arctic Zipper, wandering around when sent clear but running on strongly: will stay 1m: acts on good to firm and dead ground: tended to carry head high second start, but is genuine: will improve again: sent to Dubai. *M. R. Stoute* — 96 p

HIGDEN 2 b.c. (Mar 14) Taufan (USA) 119 – Hafhafhah 74 (Shirley Heights 130) [1995 7.5d^3 10d^2 9d Dec 15] 10,500Y: first foal: dam won twice at 1m or so, including at 2 yrs: placed in maiden at Milan and minor event at Naples late in year: stays 1¼m: trained first start by N. A. Graham. *R. Tibiletti, Italy* — 68

HIGHBANK 3 b.g. Puissance 110 – Highland Daisy (He Loves Me 120) [1994 53: 6.1m 5.9f^4 7m^5 1995 8.2m 8m 10m^4 11.1f^4 11d Sep 22] tall, leggy gelding: has knee action: modest maiden: stays 1¼m: acts on firm ground: sometimes hangs: none too consistent: won selling hurdle in December: one to treat with caution. *Mrs M. Reveley* — 52

HIGHBORN (IRE) 6 b. or br.g. Double Schwartz 128 – High State 72 (Free State 125) [1994 88p: 6.1v^4 6.1d^2 a6g a7g^3 a6g* a6g* 7g* 6m* 6d^3 1995 a7g a7g^5 6g 6m^3 7.6m^4 6m^5 6.1m 6m^5 7m 6g 7d^3 6g^2 6f* Oct 31] sturdy gelding: fairly useful performer: gained a deserved success in minor event at Redcar in October: effective at 6f to 7.6f: acts on fibresand (yet to race on equitrack) and on firm and dead ground: sometimes slowly away: has run well when sweating: genuine and consistent. *P. S. Felgate* — 88

HIGHBROOK (USA) 7 b.m. Alphabatim (USA) 126 – Tellspot (USA) (Tell (USA)) [1994 NR 1995 12m 11.9m^6 14g^3 13.1g* Jun 3] lengthy mare: useful hurdler: still a fair handicapper on Flat, and won 4-runner event at Ayr in June: stays 1¾m: acts on good to firm and soft ground: usually held up. *M. H. Tompkins* — 76

HIGH COMMOTION (IRE) 3 b.f. Taufan (USA) 119 – Bumble-Bee (High Line 125) [1994 NR 1995 8g 12m^5 May 7] IR 3,000F, IR 6,000Y: lengthy filly: half-sister to 1985 Irish 2-y-o 6f and 7f winner New Beginning (by Persian Bold) and a winner in Hong Kong by Northern Date: dam, winner twice in Australia, sister to Master Willie: shaped quite well in maidens at Newbury and Salisbury (travelled well to 3f out) in the spring, but not seen out afterwards. *D. R. C. Elsworth* — 70

HIGH CUT 2 b.f. (Mar 26) Dashing Blade 117 – High Habit 79 (Slip Anchor 136) [1995 5m^2 May 16] leggy, unfurnished filly: first foal: dam, second over 11.5f, half-sister to smart sprinter Blue Siren: 11/2, length second of 8 to Tropical Dance in maiden at York, chasing leaders, running green at halfway but keeping on: looked sure to improve. *I. A. Balding* — 84 p

HIGH DESIRE (IRE) 2 b.f. (May 11) High Estate 127 – Sweet Adelaide (USA) 98 (The Minstrel (CAN) 135) [1995 7g 7f 8.1m a8g Nov 10] 8,500 2-y-o: neat filly: sister to 1m winner Sweet Trentino and half-sister to 3-y-o 5f winner Port Augusta (by Tirol) and Irish middle-distance winner Mick's Delight (by Sir Ivor): dam 2-y-o 6f winner out of half-sister to Boldboy: behind in maidens and a nursery. *J. R. Arnold* — –

HIGH DOMAIN (IRE) 4 b.c. Dominion Royale 112 – Recline 70 (Wollow 132) [1994 –: 5f 5g 5m a6g a5g 1995 5m 5m 5g^6 5f^5 5m^5 6m 5m^3 6m^2 6m 5m^6 5.1d 5g 5.1m Oct 19] sturdy, strong-quartered colt: good mover: sold out of M. McCormack's stable 3,800 gns Doncaster March Sales before reappearance: fair handicapper: sold out of T. D. Barron's stable 2,200 gns Doncaster September Sales after penultimate — 68 outing: stays 6f: acts on firm and dead ground: effective blinkered or not: edgy sort. *J. L. Spearing*

HIGHFIELD FIZZ 3 b.f. Efisio 120 – Jendor 82 (Condorcet (FR)) [1994 NR 1995 7g 7m^{6} 10f^{3} 10m 10f^{3} 11.1f^{4} 11f^{4} 10.4g 11d* 10.5s^{2} 14.1f^{6} 12.1s Nov 2] good-topped filly: has a round action: fourth reported foal: half-sister to 1993 2-y-o 7f winner Highfield Lad (by Hard Fought): dam 5f (at 2 yrs) and 1m winner who stayed 1½m: modest performer on her day: won maiden seller at Redcar in September by 5 lengths: should stay 1½m: acts on firm and soft ground: bandaged off-hind: carried head awkwardly third start. *C. W. Fairhurst* 60

HIGHFIELD PET 2 b.c. (Apr 16) Efisio 120 – Jendor 82 (Condorcet (FR)) [1995 7m 6m Oct 30] lengthy colt: has scope: fifth reported foal: brother to 3-y-o 11f winner Highfield Fizz and half-brother to 1993 2-y-o 7f winner Highfield Lad (by Hard Fought): dam 5f (at 2 yrs) and 1m winner who stayed 1½m: never a threat in maidens won by Germano at Doncaster and Pivotal at Newcastle. *M. Johnston* –

HIGH FIVE (IRE) 5 b.g. High Line 125 – Finger Lake (Kings Lake (USA) 133) [1994 62: 11.7m^{6} 13.3m^{4} 12.1s 14.1m^{4} 14.4g* 16s^{6} 1995 12g 16.4m 14m 13.3g 11.4g 20m 14g 15.4m Sep 7] angular gelding: unimpressive mover: modest staying handicapper at 4 yrs for H. Candy: long way below form for new connections. *D. A. Wilson* –

HIGH FLOWN (USA) 3 b.g. Lear Fan (USA) 130 – Isticanna (USA) 96 (Far North (CAN) 120) [1994 63, a69: 6.1m a7g^{2} a8g^{6} 7g 8g^{2} a6g a8g^{4} a7g^{6} 1995 a7g* a8g^{4} a8g 12f^{2} 9.9m^{5} 12m^{4} 16m^{6} 12m^{2} 11f^{6} 12g^{3} 12m^{2} 12.4h^{3} 10m^{5} a12g Sep 2] sturdy gelding: modest performer: easily best effort in 1995 when winning seller at Southwell (sold out of Mrs J. Ramsden's stable 4,200 gns) in January: stays 1½m: acts on hard ground and on fibresand: effective visored or not: has worn crossed noseband. *Ronald Thompson* 53 d a63 d

HIGHFLYING 9 br.g. Shirley Heights 130 – Nomadic Pleasure 91 (Habitat 134) [1994 87d: 16.5m 11.9m^{5} 16.1f 11.9g 14.1d 14.1g^{4} 12s 1995 16m^{6} 16.1g^{2} 16m* 11.9m^{2} 16.1m^{6} 15g* 16.2g* 16.1m^{3} 11.9m^{5} 16.1g Aug 28] strong, good-bodied gelding: usually impresses in appearance: poor mover: fairly useful handicapper: retains plenty of enthusiasm, and won at Ripon in May and at Ayr and Ascot (£10,800 event by 5 lengths from Art Form) within 5 days in July: effective at 1½m to 2m, and should stay 2¼m: acts on firm and dead going (unsuited by very soft): sometimes bandaged: goes well with forcing tactics: genuine. *G. M. Moore* 92

HIGH FLYING ADORED (IRE) 3 b.f. In The Wings 128 – Countess Candy 106 (Great Nephew 126) [1994 77: 7g^{4} 7s 7m 7.1g^{2} 1995 10g^{3} 11.5f* 12m* 14f^{6} Jul 27] leggy, attractive filly: has a quick action: fairly useful handicapper: won at Lingfield (in good style) in June and Epsom (cosily) in July: disappointing in rated stakes at Goodwood (jockey reported she had become upset in stalls and wouldn't give her running as a result) on final start: should stay 1¾m: acts on firm ground: sold 18,000 gns Newmarket December Sales. *J. L. Dunlop* 85

HIGH HOLME 4 ch.g. Fools Holme (USA) – Corn Seed 72 (Nicholas Bill 125) [1994 64d: 5g^{6} 5m 5m^{6} 5m 5.1d 5.1g a5g a8g 1995 a5g 6g 5g 5.1m 7m Oct 30] lengthy, sturdy gelding: no worthwhile form in 1995: tried visored: sold 950 gns Ascot December Sales. *D. T. Thom* –

HIGH HOPE HENRY (USA) 2 b.c. (Apr 19) Known Fact (USA) 135 – Parquill (USA) (One For All (USA)) [1995 5g* 8.1d Sep 12] $50,000Y: close-coupled colt: fifth foal: half-brother to 2 minor winners in USA: dam won 3 races, including 1m Grade 3 event at 2 yrs: won maiden at Kempton in April by 2½ lengths from Sonic Mail: gave impression something amiss in minor event at Sandown 4½ months later: subsequently joined D. R. Loder. *P. F. I. Cole* 80

HIGHLAND FLAME 6 ch.g. Dunbeath (USA) 127 – Blakesware Saint 74 (Welsh Saint 126) [1994 NR 1995 a13g a16g Feb 16] plain, good-topped gelding: no form on flat since 3 yrs: tried visored/blinkered: has joined A. Blackmore. *K. T. Ivory* –

HIGHLAND MAGIC (IRE) 7 b.g. Stalker 121 – Magic Picture (Deep Diver 134) [1994 79: 8s 7g^{3} 7m^{3} 7.3s 7g 7d 1995 8g 8m 7.3d 8g Oct 9] deep-girthed gelding: fair handicapper at best at 6 yrs: tailed off in 1995. *M. J. Fetherston-Godley* –

HIGH MELODY 3 b.g. Sizzling Melody 117 – Calling High (USA) 88 (Mountain Call 125) [1994 –: 6m^{6} 5.2m^{5} 7g^{6} 1995 a12g Oct 23] leggy gelding: no worthwhile form. *G. C. Bravery* –

HIGH NOTE 2 b.f. (Mar 20) Shirley Heights 130 – Soprano 112 (Kris 135) [1995 7m 7m^6 7g^4 Oct 9] lengthy, rather unfurnished filly: fluent mover: seventh foal: sister to fairly useful 1992 2-y-o 8.5f winner Zenith and half-sister to 1½m winner Trumpet (by Dominion): dam, 7.6f and 1m winner, closely related to smart 1m/1¼m performer Enharmonic: progressive form in maidens, around 2½ lengths fourth of 18 to Fairlight Down at Leicester last time, staying on after being bumped and switched 2f out: will be suited by further than 7f. *R. Charlton* — 70 p

HIGH PATRIARCH (IRE) 3 b.g. Alzao (USA) 117 – Freesia 78 (Shirley Heights 130) [1994 –: 7g 1995 10m^6 10m 10m^4 12g^3 10.5g^3 14.1f^3 14g* Oct 23] strong, stocky gelding: fair performer: won maiden at Lingfield in October: should stay beyond 1¾m: acts on firm ground, yet to race on a soft surface: blinkered/ visored since fifth 3-y-o start: sold (J. Dunlop to N. Walker) 38,000 gns Newmarket Autumn Sales. *J. L. Dunlop* — 79

HIGH PREMIUM 7 b.g. Forzando 122 – High Halo 64 (High Top 131) [1994 a6g* a6g^4 a6g^2 a8g^3 a7g^4 a7g* a6g^2 a5g* a7g^3 1995 a6g^3 a7g^3 8g* 10d^6 10.4m^4 8.2m^3 Oct 19] sturdy, good topped gelding: won 3 handicaps in Dubai in 1994 for K. McLaughlin before sold 5,500 gns Newmarket July Sales after 7-y-o reappearance: fair form for new stable, winning claimer at Ayr in September: stays 1¼m: acts on firm and dead ground: bandaged in 1995. *R. A. Fahey* — 76

HIGH PRIEST 3 b.c. Statoblest 120 – Intoxication 73 (Great Nephew 126) [1994 56p: 6m^6 6g 1995 6m^2 5m^3 5g 5m^3 6f^4 Aug 21] sturdy, compact colt: fair maiden: some way below form last 3 starts: looks a sprinter: has raced only on a sound surface: sold 7,000 gns Newmarket September Sales. *L. M. Cumani* — 67

HIGH PRIORITY (IRE) 2 b.c. (Mar 23) Marju (IRE) 127 – Blinding (IRE) (High Top 131) [1995 6g^4 5.1m* 6g 5.5g 6m^2 5m^3 6m^2 Aug 28] IR 74,900F, IR 80,000Y: strong, lengthy colt: has plenty of scope: first foal: dam ran twice at 3 yrs: half-sister to 4 winners, including smart 7f and 1m performer Hadeer, from a very successful family: won 5-runner minor event at Bath in June: faced stiff tasks in pattern races 2 of next 3 starts but good efforts in listed races last 2 outings, beaten ½ length by Mubhij at York then 9 lengths by Kahir Almaydan at Ripon (where finished well clear of remainder): bred to stay beyond 6f: very edgy and then reared leaving stalls fifth start. *M. R. Channon* — 92 +

HIGH PYRENEES 3 b.c. Shirley Heights 130 – Twyla 101 (Habitat 134) [1994 NR 1995 10.1g^3 13.1g* Jun 2] fourth foal: half-brother to smart 7f (at 2 yrs) to 12.3f winner Twist And Turn (by Groom Dancer): dam 2-y-o 6f winner, is sister to smart sprinter Defecting Dancer: sold out of L. Cumani's stable 11,000 gns Newmarket Autumn (1994) Sales: fair form: confirmed debut promise by winning maiden at Ayr in June by ½ length from Wurlitzer: will stay beyond 13f: should improve further. *R. Allan* — 72 p

HIGH RANKING 3 b.g. Governor General 116 – Lismore 61 (Relkino 131) [1994 77: 5g^4 5m* 5f^4 6m^6 5f^5 6.1m^4 5m* 5m^4 6g^4 1995 5g 5m 5m 5m 6m 5m^4 6m Aug 23] leggy, close-coupled gelding: fair sprinter at 2 yrs: well beaten in handicaps in 1995: sold 1,900 gns Newmarket Autumn Sales: sent to Italy. *M. H. Easterby* — –

HIGHSPEED (IRE) 3 ch.g. Double Schwartz 128 – High State 72 (Free State 125) [1994 NR 1995 7.1m^5 8g 7f* 7g Sep 13] small, leggy, lightly-made gelding: brother to fairly useful 6f and 7f performer Highborn and half-brother to fairly useful sprinter Macs Maharanee (by Indian King), both prolific winners: dam 9f seller winner: modest performer: won median auction maiden at Ayr in August: well beaten on only subsequent outing: stays 7f: acts on firm ground. *S. E. Kettlewell* — 53

HIGH STANDARD 3 ch.f. Kris 135 – Durrah (USA) 93 (Nijinsky (CAN) 138) [1994 77p: 6.9m 8.2s* 8g^4 1995 12g^2 12m Oct 21] leggy, shallow-girthed filly: fairly useful performer: staying-on second of 7 in rated stakes at Newbury in May: tried to break out of stalls and withdrawn at York in July: well beaten in handicap at Doncaster on only subsequent outing: stays 1½m: acts on soft ground. *M. R. Stoute* — 83

HIGH TARGET (IRE) 2 b.c. (Apr 21) High Estate 127 – Nice Point (Sharpen Up 127) [1995 5d* 6g^2 7d Sep 26] 40,000Y: half-brother to useful Irish sprinter Sharp Point (by Royal Academy) and to 2-y-o sprint winners Martanda Light (by Nishapour, later winner in Italy at up to 1m) and Northern Alert (by Northern Tempest): dam unraced half-sister to Tirol: won maiden at the Curragh in April then ¾-length second of 6 to Thrilling Day in listed race there 5 months later: respectable — 93 staying-on eleventh of 30 to Rio Duvida in valuable sales race at Newmarket final start: will stay beyond 7f. *D. K. Weld, Ireland*

HIGH TYPHA 4 b.f. Dowsing (USA) 124 – Zepha 88 (Great Nephew 126) [1994 61: 7m 7g^{4} 7m^{4} 8.1m^{5} 8.5m^{2} 8m^{3} 7f* 8g 8m 8g 1995 7g 8f 7m 7m 8m^{4} 8f^{3} 7.5m^{3} 10.9g 11.6m 9m Aug 13] lengthy filly: poor performer: stays 8.5f: acts on firm ground: best efforts in 1995 when visored: blinkered (ran creditably) fifth 3-y-o start: none too consistent: sold 18,500 gns Newmarket December Sales. *M. R. Channon* 49 d

HI HOH (IRE) 2 ch.f. (Mar 1) Fayruz 116 – Late Date (Goldhill 125) [1995 5m 5g^{5} 5f a6g Dec 2] IR 15,000Y: strong, good-topped filly: poor mover: half-sister to 3 winners in Europe, including French 7f winner Moon Grey (by Fairy King): dam lightly-raced half-sister to smart 6f and 7f performer Private Line: poor maiden: behind in seller final outing: sold out of M. Bell's stable 2,500 gns Newmarket Autumn Sales after third start. *N. P. Littmoden* –

HI KIKI 4 b.f. Rambo Dancer (CAN) 107 – Hachimitsu 39 (Vaigly Great 127) [1994 55: 7s^{3} 6m^{5} 7.1f^{4} 6m^{4} 8m 6g^{3} 7g 1995 6g 5g 5g Sep 29] small, angular filly: modest maiden at best: well beaten first 2 starts in 1995 for Mrs M. McCourt, blinkered on second of them: never-nearer eleventh of 25 in handicap at Goodwood (after 4-month absence) on final outing: ideally needs further than 5f, and should stay 1m: acts on soft ground and good to firm. *Martyn Meade* 38

HILAALA (USA) 2 ch.f. (Mar 18) Elmaamul (USA) 125 – Halholah (USA) 65 (Secreto (USA) 128) [1995 6f^{4} 7m^{3} 7g^{2} 7m* Oct 13] workmanlike filly: third foal: half-sister to useful 3-y-o 1¼m and 10.5f winner Murajja, 6.1f and 7f winner at 2 yrs, and 1993 2-y-o 6f winner Tablah (both by Silver Hawk): dam out of half-sister to Alydar: progressive form in maidens: won 14-runner median auction event at Catterick by ½ length from Indian Relative: should stay further than 7f: races keenly. *P. T. Walwyn* 78

HILL CLIMBER 2 b.c. (Apr 12) Danehill (USA) 126 – Swift Pursuit 57 (Posse (USA) 130) [1995 7g 8m Oct 28] 16,500 2-y-o: angular colt: third foal: half-brother to 3-y-o Singing Rock (by Ballad Rock), 5f winner at 2 yrs: dam second over 1m at 4 yrs: well beaten in maiden at Leicester and seller (pulled hard in blinkers) at Newmarket: coltish beforehand and wore near-side pricker final start: sold 1,200 gns Doncaster November Sales: sent to Austria. *M. Bell* –

HILL FARM DANCER 4 ch.f. Gunner B 126 – Loadplan Lass 63 (Nicholas Bill 125) [1994 48: 8.2v a8.5g^{3} 12f* 14g^{5} a12g* 12m 1995 a12g a11g^{6} a12g^{3} a12g^{2} 10.8m^{2} 11.7m* 12m^{4} 10.8g^{4} 13f 12f^{6} 11.9m^{3} a12g^{3} a12g^{4} Dec 12] sparely-made filly: fluent mover: modest handicapper: won at Bath in May: stays 1½m: acts on firm ground and fibresand: normally held up. *W. M. Brisbourne* 55

HILL FARM KATIE 4 b.f. Derrylin 115 – Kate Brook (Nicholas Bill 125) [1994 –: 7g 5m 10m 6g 6.1s 7g 1995 a9.4g^{4} a8g a6g 7g 8m a12g^{5} Dec 12] lengthy filly: poor handicapper: stays 1½m: acts on the all-weather: blinkered (below form) third 4-y-o start: inconsistent. *W. M. Brisbourne* 38

HILL HOPPER (IRE) 4 b.f. Danehill (USA) 126 – Sea Harrier (Grundy 137) [1994 106p: 6d* 6m* 6s^{2} 6m^{2} 7g* 7g* 1995 6d Sep 24] good-topped filly: useful performer at 3 yrs: well beaten in Diadem Stakes at Ascot on belated return: should stay 1m: acts on good to firm and soft ground: edgy and bandaged last 3 starts at 3 yrs. *J. H. M. Gosden* –

HILLSDOWN BOY (IRE) 5 ch.g. Dominion Royale 112 – Lady Mary (Sallust 134) [1994 –, a66: 10d a10g* a10g^{2} a10g* 1995 a10g^{4} a10g a10g^{5} a10g Feb 23] strong, stocky gelding: has a round action: fair form late in 1994: well beaten in 1995: stays 1¼m: acts on all-weather surfaces and soft ground: tried visored and blinkered (no improvement), not since 1993. *S. Dow* –

HILLSWICK 4 ch.g. Norwick (USA) 125 – Quite Lucky 69 (Precipice Wood 123) [1994 –: 7d 11.6g 10.2g 1995 11.9m 12.5g 14.9g May 27] leggy, angular gelding: no form since 2 yrs. *J. S. King* –

HILLZAH (USA) 7 ch.g. Blushing Groom (FR) 131 – Glamour Girl (ARG) (Mysolo 120) [1994 69, a80: a12g* a11g* a12g* a12g^{4} 12g 11.8v^{3} 10m 12g 12.1g^{5} 11.9d^{4} 12g^{2} 10s* 12v a12g a11g^{2} a9.4g^{6} 1995 a11g a12g* a12g^{4} a12g^{5} 11.1s^{2} 10m^{3} 10f 14.1m* 14.1m^{2} 10.5m* 16.2g^{5} Jul 21] workmanlike gelding: poor mover: fairly useful handicapper on the all-weather, fair on turf: won at Wolverhampton in 79 a82

January, Carlisle in June and Haydock (3-runner apprentice race) in July: stays 16.2f: acts on fibresand (unraced on equitrack) and any turf going: sometimes hangs markedly, but goes well for apprentice: occasionally slowly away: genuine. *R. Bastiman*

HILTONS TRAVEL (IRE) 4 b.g. Red Sunset 120 – Free Rein (Sagaro 133) – [1994 58: 5d^{4} 8g 6f^{2} 7m^{3} 7g^{2} 6f^{3} 7.1d 7g 6g a6g^{6} 1995 a6g a8g 6v Mar 31] big, workmanlike gelding: modest 6f/7f handicapper at 3 yrs: well beaten in 1995. *E. J. Alston*

HIMALAYAN BLUE 3 b.g. Hallgate 127 – Orange Parade (Dara Monarch 128) 68 [1994 64: 8d 5.7g^{5} 7s^{3} 6.9m^{2} 6d^{4} 1995 a8g^{4} a7g^{5} 10g* 10.2m 8m 10f Oct 31] tall, leggy gelding: well below form after winning at Nottingham in April: left M. Channon's stable after fifth start: stays 1¼m: acts on good to firm and soft going and on equitrack. *J. E. Banks*

HINARI VIDEO 10 b.g. Sallust 134 – Little Cynthia 76 (Wolver Hollow 126) – [1994 37, a54: a6g^{5} a5g^{3} a5g* a6g^{3} a5g a5g a5g a5g* a5g^{4} 5s^{4} 5v^{6} 5g 1995 a6g a5g a43 a5g a6g^{6} a6g a6g^{6} Feb 27] smallish, workmanlike gelding: unimpressive mover: poor handicapper nowadays: sold 950 gns Doncaster March Sales: best at sprint distances: acts on good to firm and heavy ground, but best on all-weather surfaces: tried blinkered (not since 1992). *M. Johnston*

HINDAAWEE (USA) 3 ch.g. Zilzal (USA) 137 – Sedulous 107 (Tap On Wood 87 130) [1994 85: 6f^{2} 6m* 5f^{3} 6g 1995 6m^{3} 7f^{3} 8.2m^{4} Aug 21] strong, attractive gelding: fairly useful performer: contested minor events in 1995: stays 1m: has raced only on a sound surface: wore crossed noseband last 2 starts at 2 yrs: sometimes gives trouble stalls: very slowly away final outing: takes keen hold. *E. A. L. Dunlop*

HI NOD 5 b.h. Valiyar 129 – Vikris (Viking (USA)) [1994 90: 7f* 7m^{3} 7f 8f 7.6g 99 8m^{6} 8g 7s^{4} 8m 1995 7m 7g^{4} 7f* 8m^{2} 7m^{2} 7m* 7m^{2} 7.9m 7m* Oct 5] leggy horse: impresses good deal in appearance: useful handicapper: won at Ayr in June, Newcastle (rated stakes) in July and York (another rated stakes, responded to pressure in typically gallant style to beat Western Fame by ½ length in 6-runner race) in October: effective at 7f (best form) and 1m: acts on any going: has run well when sweating: usually tracks leaders: game and genuine. *M. J. Camacho*

HINTON ROCK (IRE) 3 ch.g. Ballad Rock 122 – May Hinton 82 (Main Reef 86 126) [1994 82p: 5m^{3} 5d^{2} 5.3m* 5m^{5} 1995 5m^{4} 5m^{2} 6g 5g^{5} 5g^{5} 6g 5m^{5} 5m 5f^{2} Aug 28] strong, compact gelding: fairly useful performer: reportedly sustained an injury final 2-y-o start (June): often faced stiff tasks in 1995, mostly creditable efforts until well below form last 2 starts: claimed £7,000 after claimer at Warwick final outing: seems not to stay 6f: acts on good to firm and dead ground: no improvement in blinkers: often sweats. *M. Bell*

HI PENNY 4 b.f. Faustus (USA) 118 – High Voltage 82 (Electrify) [1994 63d: 46 d 5.1g 6d^{4} 6m a7g^{6} 6f 10.1m^{4} 8.3m 7m 6s a6g a7g 1995 a8g^{3} a10g a8g^{2} a9.4g a8g^{5} 8m 11.1g 6.9g 11.5m a8.5g Jun 30] sparely-made filly: poor handicapper nowadays: broke blood vessel and pulled up sixth start: stays 1m: acts on dead ground and the all-weather: often blinkered. *K. T. Ivory*

HIPPY 2 b.f. (Mar 3) Damister (USA) 123 – Breakaway 98 (Song 132) [1995 7m^{4} 68 p Nov 3] 8,500Y: angular filly: half-sister to a winner in Switzerland by Superlative: dam 5f winner: 14/1 and green, 3¾ lengths fourth of 18 to Wahiba Sands in maiden at Doncaster, leading briefly 2f out and keeping on: will improve. *C. E. Brittain*

HI ROCK 3 ch.f. Hard Fought 125 – Miss Racine (Dom Racine (FR) 121) [1994 55 49: a5g^{4} a6g a5g^{3} 6m^{2} 1995 a6g^{4} 7.1g^{2} 6.1m* 6m 6.1d 6m^{3} 6m^{5} a6g^{6} Dec 9] neat filly: modest performer: won seller at Nottingham in May: stays 7f well: acts on good to firm ground and fibresand. *M. J. Camacho*

HIS EXCELLENCE (USA) 2 b.c. (Feb 14) El Gran Senor (USA) 136 – Hail 84 The Lady (USA) (Hail The Pirates (USA) 126) [1995 7m^{2} 7m* 7d Sep 26] 45,000Y: good-topped colt: brother to 3-y-o Grandinare, 7f winner at 2 yrs, and half-brother to 2m winner La Menorquina (by Woodman): dam (stayed 1¼m) 8.5f stakes winner: won maiden at Leopardstown in August: creditable effort when mid-division in 30-runner valuable sales race at Newmarket 7 weeks later: will stay 1¼m. *A. P. O'Brien, Ireland*

HIT THE CANVAS (USA) 4 ch.g. At The Threshold (USA) – Also Royal (USA) (Native Royalty (USA)) [1994 69: a9.4g^2 a12g* 12.3m^6 1995 12g 14.1m^3 13.1g^3 15f* 15.1m^2 16.5f^5 16.1h^3 Aug 2] leggy gelding: fluent mover: fair performer: landed the odds in 3-runner minor event at Ayr in June: stays 2m: acts on hard ground, dead and fibresand: effective blinkered/visored or not: successful over hurdles in August (twice), September and October. *Mrs M. Reveley* 68

HIWAYA 3 b.f. Doyoun 124 – Himmah (USA) 85 (Habitat 134) [1994 101: 6g* 7g* 8s* 7g* 7.3v^2 1995 8m 8.5m^5 7g^6 8d^4 8d* Sep 24] lengthy filly: useful performer: gradually found her form in 1995, and beat Courageous Dancer by 3½ lengths in 9-runner listed rated stakes at Ascot in September on final start: should have stayed beyond 1m: suited by an easy surface (acted on heavy going): visits Unfuwain. *H. Thomson Jones* 106

HOBBS CHOICE 2 b.f. (Jan 20) Superpower 113 – Excavator Lady 65 (Most Secret 119) [1995 5d a7g 7.5m^6 6g^5 7.5d Sep 13] quite good-topped, rather plain filly: has a round action: half-sister to fairly useful 5f winner Tuscan Dawn (by Clantime) and 9.9f winner Glenugie (by Insan): dam stayed 1¾m: poor maiden: visored last 3 starts: joined G. M. Moore. *Miss J. F. Craze* –

HOD-MOD (IRE) 5 b.g. Digamist (USA) 110 – Sallymiss (Tanfirion 110) [1994 NR 1995 8.3f 9.2f Aug 14] compact gelding: no form for a long time. *Miss Z. A. Green* –

HOH EXPRESS 3 b.c. Waajib 121 – Tissue Paper 95 (Touch Paper 113) [1994 90p: 8.1g^2 8m^2 1995 10.3m 8g* 8g^2 8m 8m^3 10.4m^4 8g* 8d^3 9g 10v^3 Oct 7] unfurnished colt: useful performer: won 21-runner maiden at Newbury in May and 8-runner listed race at Baden-Baden in August: stays 10.4f: acts on good to firm and heavy ground: consistent. *I. A. Balding* 101

HOH MAGIC 3 ch.f. Cadeaux Genereux 131 – Gunner's Belle 69 (Gunner B 126) [1994 111: 5.1f* 5m^3 5m* 5f* 6d* 6m^4 1995 7.3m^2 8m^4 8d 5f 6g^3 6.5g^5 6d 7g^5 Sep 7] rangy filly: useful performer: 4¼ lengths fourth of 14 to Harayir in 1000 Guineas at Newmarket in May: back to form in July Cup at Newmarket (6½ lengths third of 9 to Lake Coniston) and Prix Maurice de Gheest at Deauville (3¾ lengths fifth of 10 to Cherokee Rose) in the summer: below form in Group 2 event at Baden-Baden and listed race at Doncaster last 2 starts: stays 1m: acts on firm and dead ground, yet to race on anything softer: normally held up in touch. *M. Bell* 108

HOH MAJESTIC (IRE) 2 b.g. (Mar 11) Soviet Lad (USA) 94 – Sevens Are Wild 40 (Petorius 117) [1995 5m* 5g 5.1m^4 5m^4 6f 5.1m^2 5m^2 5.3f^2 5g* 8m 6g Sep 22] IR 10,000Y: quite attractive gelding: second foal: dam, lightly raced, placed at 1m: won median auction maiden at Thirsk in May and nursery at Newcastle in August: best form at 5f, not discredited over 1m: usually blinkered or visored: races keenly: sometimes early to post: sold (M. Bell to Martyn Wane) 6,000 gns Newmarket Autumn Sales. *M. Bell* 69

HOH RETURNS (IRE) 2 b.c. (Mar 14) Fairy King (USA) – Cipriani 102 (Habitat 134) [1995 5.2m 6m^5 6g^3 6d^2 6m Oct 13] 36,000F, 72,000Y: good-topped colt: has scope: unimpressive mover: fourth foal: closely related to 3-y-o Cyphell (by Sadler's Wells): dam, Irish mare best at 7f/1m, daughter of champion New Zealand mare La Mer: fair form in maidens: best efforts when placed behind Obsessive at Yarmouth and Meldorf at Newcastle: stays 6f. *M. Bell* 80

HOIST (IRE) 4 ch.f. Bluebird (USA) 125 – Elevate 98 (Ela-Mana-Mou 132) [1994 75: 7.1m^5 7.6g^2 8f^3 8g^3 1995 a6g* a7g^6 Jan 31] lengthy filly: fair performer: easily landed the odds in maiden at Lingfield in January: well below form in minor event there on only subsequent start: should stay 1¼m: acts on firm ground and equitrack. *Sir Mark Prescott* 56 +

HO-JOE (IRE) 5 b.g. Burslem 123 – Walkyria (Lord Gayle (USA) 124) [1994 46: 12m a12g^6 a14.8g 13.6g^6 1995 a11g 9.9m 12m* 14.1m^2 12.3f^4 12.1m^4 Jul 2] rather sparely-made gelding: modest handicapper: won at Beverley in May: left J. Carr's stable after next outing: should stay beyond 1¾m: acts on firm ground, tailed off all 3 starts on fibresand: wears bandages: held up: won selling hurdle in November. *G. H. Yardley* 50

HOLD YOUR HAT ON 6 ch.g. Celestial Storm (USA) 132 – Thatched Grove (Thatching 131) [1994 –: 13.1m^5 1995 a16g Jan 30] no form on flat: sold 2,600 gns Doncaster August Sales. *C. W. Thornton* –

HOLIDAY ISLAND 6 ch.g. Good Times (ITY) – Green Island 89 (St Paddy 133) [1994 –: 11.4d^4 12g 1995 a13g 11.9m Apr 24] workmanlike gelding: one-time fair middle-distance performer: ran poorly in 1995: sold (R. Akehurst to P. Butler) 2,300 gns Ascot June Sales. *R. Akehurst* –

HOLLOWAY MELODY 2 ch.f. (Feb 23) Cree Song 99 – Holloway Wonder 93 (Swing Easy (USA) 126) [1995 5m^5 6.1d 8.2m a7g^6 a8g^4 Nov 24] workmanlike filly: fifth foal: sister to 4-y-o Rocky Two and half-sister to Rock Breaker (by Green Ruby) and Stoneythorpewonder (by Smackover), all 5f performers: dam effective at 5f and stayed 1m: poor form in maidens and sellers. *B. A. McMahon* 38

HOLLYWOOD DREAM (GER) 4 b.f. Master Willie 129 – Holly (GER) (Cortez (GER)) [1994 115: 8v^2 10.5g^2 11g^5 11g* 12g^4 10.5g^4 12g^4 14d^3 10.5v* 1995 10.5s* 10m^2 12f Dec 10] smart German performer: returned as good as ever, getting up on the line to win slowly-run Prix Corrida at Evry in April by a short head from Agathe in a blanket finish: respectable 1½ lengths second of 10 to Slicious in Premio Roma in November: behind in Grade 1 Hollywood Turf Cup following month: stays 1¾m: acts on heavy going, probably on good to firm. *U. Ostmann, Germany* 115

HOLTYE (IRE) 3 b.c. Danehill (USA) 126 – Sacristy 54 (Godswalk (USA) 130) [1994 94p: 7g^6 7m* 7d^2 1995 8.1m* 9m* 8m^6 8d 8g Sep 28] compact, well-made colt: useful handicapper: justified favouritism in £12,800 race at Sandown (rallied) in April and rated stakes at Newbury (idled) in May: below form in rated stakes at Doncaster and listed race at Newmarket (soon off bridle) last 2 starts: effective at 1m/9f: yet to race on extremes of going: sent to Saudi Arabia. *H. R. A. Cecil* 105

HOMEBEFOREMIDNIGHT 4 ch.f. Fools Holme (USA) – Mothers Girl (Huntercombe 133) [1994 NR 1995 a12g a12g Feb 8] 10,000Y: half-sister to several winners, including fairly useful sprinter Roman Prose (by Sallust) and French 1¼m and 11.7f winner Wolver Knight (by Wolver Hollow): dam unraced half-sister to North Stoke and Anfield: tailed off in all-weather maidens. *R. Hollinshead* –

HOME COOKIN' 2 b.f. (May 2) Salse (USA) 128 – Home Fire 99 (Firestreak 125) [1995 8m 7d 8m Nov 4] sturdy filly: has scope: half-sister to 3-y-o Fire of London (by Shirley Heights) and several winners, including fair middle-distance stayer By The Fireside (by Ardross) and useful 7f (at 2 yrs) and 1¼m winner Spitfire (by Shirley Heights): dam sprinter: towards rear in maiden at Leicester, minor event at Newbury (possibly flattered) and median auction maiden at Doncaster. *Dr J. D. Scargill* 64 ?

HOME COUNTIES (IRE) 6 ch.g. Ela-Mana-Mou 132 – Safe Home 94 (Home Guard (USA) 129) [1994 73: 10m* 8m 10.3g 11.9g 8.3g^4 10.5d 1995 10.5g^3 10m^6 Oct 26] lengthy gelding: poor mover: useful hurdler: fair handicapper on flat: should stay beyond 10.5f: acts on good to firm and dead ground: usually visored in 1994, not at all in 1995. *D. Moffatt* 74

HOMECREST 3 b.g. Petoski 135 – Homing Hill (Homing 130) [1994 NR 1995 10.3g 10.1g 8g^4 10.9g 10g a8.5g Nov 13] sturdy gelding: fourth foal: half-brother to a bumpers winner: dam bumpers winner: no worthwhile form: trained for debut by B. Ellison: tried visored. *Mrs A. M. Naughton* –

HO MEI SURPRISE 3 ch.c. Hadeer 118 – By Surprise 68 (Young Generation 129) [1994 44: 6.1s 5.1m^6 a6g^5 a6g a5g^2 a6g 1995 a7g a6g a5g^6 a5g a6g^3 a6g^4 a5g a6g^5 Jul 3] plain colt: poor walker: poor maiden handicapper: raced only at Wolverhampton in 1995: stays 6f: acts on fibresand: tried blinkered. *B. Preece* 41

HOMELAND 2 b.g. (Feb 21) Midyan (USA) 124 – Little Loch Broom 60 (Reform 132) [1995 5g^5 6g^3 6m^4 7h^2 7.5m^3 7.1m* 10d^5 8.3g* 8m a8.5g^3 a7g^5 a8g^2 a8g Dec 15] 4,200Y: smallish, angular colt: has a round action: half-brother to 3-y-o Desert Spring (by Green Desert) and several winners, including very useful 1983 2-y-o 6f winner Fawzi (by Young Generation), smart French miler Soft Currency (by Music Boy) and 8.2f (at 2 yrs) and 1¼m winner Paris of Troy (by Trojan Fen): dam placed over 1m and 1¼m: won nurseries at Sandown in August (seller, sold out of C. Thornton's stable 6,800 gns) and Hamilton in September: stays 1¼m: acts on hard and dead ground and all-weather surfaces: game and genuine. *T. J. Naughton* 69

HOMEMAKER 5 b.m. Homeboy 114 – Ganadora (Good Times (ITY)) [1994 NR 1995 a12g^4 a9.4g 11.9m 11.7m May 2] compact, workmanlike mare: poor – a41 performer at best nowadays: stays 1½m: acts on any going: below form when visored. *P. G. Murphy*

HOME SHOPPING 2 b.f. (Apr 22) Superpower 113 – Shiny Kay 65 (Star Appeal 133) [1995 5.7m* 5m* 5.2g 6g^4 6m 6g^2 7g^5 7m^4 Oct 13] 6,600Y: lengthy, angular filly: fifth foal: sister to German 3-y-o 7f and 7.5f winner Moneypower and half-sister to 3 winners, including 5-y-o 9.9f to 1½m winner Ashover (by Petong) and 1991 2-y-o 6f and 1m winner Lady Linnet (by Nomination): dam (1½m winner) half-sister to K-Battery: useful filly: won maiden at Bath in June and listed event at Sandown (by a neck from Anotheranniversary) in July: none too consistent afterwards in pattern/listed company but ran well when 2 lengths second to My Branch in listed race at Ayr in September: should stay beyond 6f: acts on good to firm ground: sold 56,000 gns Newmarket December Sales and sent to Norway. *K. McAuliffe* 97

HOMILE 7 b.g. Homing 130 – Rocas 48 (Ile de Bourbon (USA) 133) [1994 NR 1995 a14g^5 Apr 11] leggy, lengthy gelding: well beaten in claimer only 7-y-o start: best form at up to 9f: acted on good to firm and dead ground: tried blinkered: dead. *G. Fierro* –

HONDERO (GER) 5 br.h. Damister (USA) 123 – Hone 79 (Sharpen Up 127) [1994 7s* 10v* 11s^6 10g^4 10.5g* 11g* 10g 11s^6 10v^2 14d 1995 10s 10d^3 11s^2 10.5g^3 10g^4 11g^2 10g^5 10g* 10g^4 10d^4 Oct 3] half-brother to several winners, notably smart German middle-distance performer Hondo Mondo (by Caerleon): dam 2-y-o 5f winner, later did well in Belgium: smart performer: unraced at 2 yrs and ran only once at 3 yrs, but successful on 4 occasions in 1994: kept good company in 1995, best effort when 3½ lengths fifth of 9 to Germany in Bayerisches Zuchtrennen at Munich: won Group 3 Spreti-Rennen at Baden-Baden in August by a length from Upper Heights: stays 11f: acts on heavy going. *Boerje Olsson, Germany* 111

HONEST ACHIEVER (IRE) 4 gr.f. Tina's Pet 121 – Rykneld (Warpath 113) [1994 NR 1995 a8.5g a6g 8.3m 8g May 26] leggy, sparely-made filly: sixth reported foal: half-sister to fair winners It's Me (miler, by Good Times) and Derwent Valley (sprinter, by Frimley Park): dam never ran: seems of little account: tried blinkered. *A. P. James* –

HONEST DAVE 5 b.g. Derring Rose 97 – Fille de Soleil (Sunyboy 110) [1994 NR 1995 a12g^5 Jan 7] fourth foal: dam unraced half-sister to a couple of fairly useful jumpers: poor novice hurdler: tailed off on flat debut. *B. A. Pearce* –

HONEST GUEST (IRE) 2 b.f. (Jan 30) Be My Guest (USA) 126 – Good Policy (IRE) 80 (Thatching 131) [1995 6.1m^2 7.1m* 7m^4 7d^3 Sep 26] 32,000Y: leggy, workmanlike filly: first foal: dam 8.2f winner at 2 yrs: won 8-runner minor event at Sandown in July: ran well at Newmarket in listed event (fourth to Bint Salsabil) and valuable sales race (third of 30 to Rio Duvida) afterwards: effective at 7f and will stay at least 1m. *M. H. Tompkins* 91

HONESTLY 2 ch.f. (Apr 28) Weldnaas (USA) 112 – Shadha 57 (Shirley Heights 130) [1995 6m 7f^6 7d a6g^3 a7g^3 a8.5g^4 a7g* Dec 12] leggy filly: sister to 3-y-o 1½m winner Last Corner and half-sister to several winners, including fair 1990 2-y-o 5f winner Super Heights (by Superlative), subsequently poor form at up to 1½m: dam ran twice at 2 yrs: won 12-runner nursery at Wolverhampton by 4 lengths from Chilibang Bang: pulled hard over 8.5f but should prove effective at trip: easily best form on fibresand. *B. Smart* – a73

HONEST WOMAN 4 b.f. Petoski 135 – Bold Polly 67 (Bold Lad (IRE) 133) [1994 –: 7.1g^6 10f 8.1s 1995 8f 8.2m a7g a8.5g Jul 3] leggy filly: no longer of any account: sold 750 gns Ascot July Sales. *N. E. Berry* –

HONEY MOUNT 4 b.g. Shirley Heights 130 – Honeybeta 105 (Habitat 134) [1994 80: 10g 10s^3 13.3g* 14g^2 16.1m^5 14.1m* 14.6g^6 14m 1995 16g 17.2m Sep 25] leggy, angular gelding: fairly useful staying handicapper at 3 yrs for A. Stewart: well beaten in 1995. *N. J. H. Walker* –

HONEY TRADER 3 b.g. Beveled (USA) – Lizzie Bee (Kind of Hush 118) [1994 48: 5v^4 5f^3 5.1m 5m^4 5f^5 6g 1995 5d^3 5.1g 5g^6 5g 5f^5 Jul 7] leggy, angular gelding: has a round action: modest sprint maiden: easily best effort when close third of 17 at Warwick on reappearance: ran badly last 2 starts: probably acts on any ground: sold 1,200 gns Doncaster September Sales. *J. Berry* 65 d

HONFLEUR (IRE) 3 b.f. Sadler's Wells (USA) 132 – Detroit (FR) 131 (Riverman (USA) 131) [1994 NR 1995 11.9m3 10g* 12.5g6 13.5g* 14.6m6 12.5s6 Sep 30] sturdy filly: sister to Arc winner Carnegie and to useful 5-y-o middle-distance winner Wayne County, closely related to good French middle-distance performer Antisaar (by Northern Dancer) and half-sister to good middle-distance performer Lake Erie (by King's Lake): dam also won Arc: useful performer: won 4-runner maiden at Ayr (3/1 on) in July and 6-runner listed race at Deauville in August: respectable sixth in Park Hill Stakes at Doncaster and Prix de Royallieu at Longchamp last 2 starts: stayed 14.6f: acted on good to firm and soft ground: stud. *P. W. Chapple-Hyam* 100

HONG KONG DESIGNER 3 br.g. Dunbeath (USA) 127 – Pokey's Pet 56 (Uncle Pokey 116) [1994 59: 7g6 a7g6 7d 7s 1995 10d 12m 14.1m 14m3 16.2g4 13.8m3 16d 15.1g4 Sep 18] smallish gelding: has a round action: modest maiden: looks a thorough stayer: acts on good to firm and dead ground: visored (geed up, well beaten) third 3-y-o start: sold (S. Norton to A. P. James) 1,750 gns Doncaster October Sales. *S. G. Norton* 54

HONG KONG DOLLAR 3 b.g. Superpower 113 – Daleside Ladybird 66 (Tolomeo 127) [1994 62: 6f5 5m4 6d 6s 1995 5d 7g 8m4 a8.5g2 7g a6g2 5.3f4 6f4 a5g a8g a7g Nov 29] lengthy gelding: good mover: modest maiden: sold out of B. Meehan's stable 1,200 gns Newmarket September Sales after eighth 3-y-o start: well beaten all 3 actual outings for current trainer (stablemate Ela-Ment ran in Hong Kong Dollar's name on 2 other occasions): effective at 6f, and stays 8.5f: acts on fibresand and good to firm ground, possibly unsuited by soft: blinkered third to eighth 3-y-o starts: often makes running. *B. A. Pearce* 54 d

HONORABLE ESTATE (IRE) 2 b.f. (Feb 10) High Estate 127 – Holy Devotion (Commanche Run 133) [1995 5m6 5.1m3 6g3 6m* Jun 13] IR 9,000Y: good-bodied, quite attractive filly: has scope: first foal: dam stayed 1½m in Ireland: improved form when winning 10-runner maiden auction at Salisbury by a short head from Singoalla: didn't look at ease on track at Chester on second outing: bred to be very well suited by middle distances. *R. Hannon* 72 p

HOODOO (IRE) 2 b.c. (May 23) Danehill (USA) 126 – Cassina 91 (Habitat 134) [1995 5m Jun 16] 33,000Y: lengthy, quite attractive colt: closely related to temperamental 6f winner Desert Maiden (by Green Desert) and half-brother to several winners, notably very smart middle-distance performer Top Class (by High Top): dam 7f winner: 12/1, bit backward and green, well-beaten last of 7 in maiden at Sandown: coltish beforehand: sold 6,000 gns Newmarket Autumn Sales: sent to Sweden. *R. Hannon* –

HOOFPRINTS (IRE) 2 b.c. (Apr 12) Distinctly North (USA) 115 – Sweet Reprieve (Shirley Heights 130) [1995 8m Nov 4] IR 23,000F, 28,000Y: big, strong, rangy colt: has scope: half-brother to 5f and 6f winner Guns And Roses (by Ballad Rock) and a winner in Belgium: dam, placed over middle distances in Ireland, half-sister to William Hill Futurity winner Sandy Creek: 20/1, around 14 lengths tenth of 23 to Shaamit in median auction maiden at Doncaster, no impression on leaders under hands and heels last 2f: wore crossed noseband: should improve. *G. Harwood* 61 p

HOPEFUL SIGN 3 b.f. Warning 136 – Infra Green 121 (Laser Light 118) [1994 NR 1995 8d Sep 15] tall, long-backed filly: has scope: half-sister to several winners, including Queen's Vase winner Infrasonic (by Dancing Brave), smart 7f and 1m performer Greensmith (by Known Fact) and the dam of Toulon: dam won from 6f to 1½m, including Prix Ganay: well beaten in maiden at Newbury: sold 26,000 gns Newmarket December Sales. *B. W. Hills* –

HORESTI 3 b.c. Nijinsky (CAN) 138 – Sushila (Petingo 135) [1994 NR 1995 8m5 10m2 10m6 May 23] IR 625,000Y: lengthy, good-topped colt: closely related to top-class middle-distance performer Petoski (by Niniski) and another winner, and half-brother to several winners: dam, winner twice at around 1m in France, is out of sister to Val de Loir: fair form in newcomers race at Newmarket and maiden at Leicester, both in April: out of depth in Predominate Stakes at Goodwood on final outing: will be suited by further than 1¼m. *C. E. Brittain* 78

HORNPIPE 3 b.g. Handsome Sailor 125 – Snake Song 94 (Mansingh (USA) 120) [1994 55: a5g2 a6g2 a5g3 a6g5 1995 a8.5g Sep 2] quite good-topped, workmanlike –

gelding: modest form at 2 yrs: well beaten in maiden handicap at Wolverhampton on belated return: stays 6f: has raced only on fibresand. *J. Wharton*

HORSETRADER 3 b.g. Aragon 118 – Grovette (Derring-Do 131) [1994 NR 1995 8.3m 7f 7g 11.9m^6 a13g 10f a12g Nov 27] 7,400F, 14,000Y, 600 2-y-o: leggy, angular gelding: half-brother to 2 minor winners at around 1m: dam never ran: poor maiden: sold out of R. Hannon's stable 2,000 gns Ascot July Sales after fifth start: bandaged, showed nil on return: tried visored. *B. P. J. Baugh* 40

HOSWINONAME 3 ch.g. Dunbeath (USA) 127 – Miss Chrissy 91 (Ballacashtal (CAN)) [1994 –: 6v a6g a8g 1995 6f Jul 29] angular gelding: no form: tried blinkered: sold 1,000 gns Doncaster October Sales. *D. Nicholls* –

HOT BREEZE 3 br.g. Hotfoot 126 – Gunnard 62 (Gunner B 126) [1994 –: a6g 1995 a9.4g^5 Feb 15] tailed off in claimer and maiden at Wolverhampton: has joined Miss K. Whitehouse. *L. J. Barratt* –

HOT DOGGING 2 b.f. (Apr 21) Petoski 135 – Mehtab 68§ (Touching Wood (USA) 127) [1995 8.2d Sep 19] big, lengthy filly: second foal: dam, 1m winner who also won over hurdles, daughter of half-sister to Zeddaan: 50/1, backward and green, well beaten in maiden at Nottingham. *Mrs P. Sly* –

HOTLIPS HOULIHAN 2 b.f. (Apr 13) Risk Me (FR) 127 – Lana's Pet 70 (Tina's Pet 121) [1995 5g* 5.1m^3 5d^6 5m 7m* 7m 7.6m a7g Nov 24] 1,400F, 2,800Y: unfurnished filly: second reported foal: dam placed at 5f and 7f at 2 yrs: won maiden auction at Warwick in April and claimer (made all) at Thirsk in July: poor effort in nursery on fibresand final start: stays 7f: acts on good to firm ground: unruly stalls on fourth outing: flashed tail and found little on penultimate start. *R. J. R. Williams* 63

HOT SNAP 3 gr.g. Chilibang 120 – Brittle Grove 79 (Bustino 136) [1994 NR 1995 6g 6m 7g 6m 5m 6m 6f^6 7g Sep 13] 7,500F, 20,000Y: strong gelding: fourth foal: brother to a winner in Germany and half-brother to 2 winners in Germany and Italy: dam ran twice over 6f at 2 yrs: modest maiden at best: behind in handicaps last 5 starts: best effort at 6f: sold 1,800 gns Newmarket Autumn Sales: sent to Germany. *C. F. Wall* 52

HOTSPUR STREET 3 b.g. Cadeaux Genereux 131 – Excellent Alibi (USA) (Exceller (USA) 129) [1994 73: 6g 6s^2 6g^2 6.1d 1995 7g^6 a9.4g^5 10m^4 11.5m^5 8m^3 a11g^6 15g^3 14g Sep 29] tall, workmanlike gelding: has a round action: fair maiden handicapper: will stay 2m: acts on good to firm and soft ground: has joined M. W. Easterby. *M. Johnston* 67

HOUGHTON VENTURE (USA) 3 ch.c. Groom Dancer (USA) 128 – Perle Fine (USA) (Devil's Bag (USA)) [1994 NR 1995 7.1m^4 7.1m^3 8g^3 8m Aug 26] 62,000Y: quite attractive colt: good mover: first foal: dam, French maiden, half-sister to Baiser Vole, Squill and Tenue de Soiree: fair form in maidens at Haydock first 2 starts: last of 7 in similar event at Newmarket on final one: should be suited by further than 7f. *S. P. C. Woods* 73

HOUSAMIX (FR) 3 gr.c. Linamix (FR) 127 – Housatonic (USA) 59 (Riverman (USA) 131) [1994 111: 7g^5 8d* 9d^4 8s* 1995 9.3m^2 12d* Sep 10] 122

Two things strike you about the first-crop runners of French stallion Linamix: first, that an excessive number have the letters M I X in their names; second, that they have been extremely successful. The man largely responsible on both counts is Jean-Luc Lagardere. Head of the Lagardere Group (1994 profit a reported 2.6 billion francs) and in 1995 elected French racing supremo as first president of France-Galop (equivalent of the BHB), M. Lagardere also has a reported sixty-five broodmares and no fewer than twenty-two of them produced foals by his sire Linamix in 1992. The total number of foals in that first crop was thirty-two. While open to criticism on his naming policy on aesthetic grounds, M. Lagardere cannot be faulted on grounds of faith in and support for his unproven stallion. Linamix is related to a few good horses (notably his half-brother, the very smart Long Mick) but hardly bred in the purple. He was a high-class racehorse in the Lagardere colours, winner of the Poule d'Essai des Poulains in what is still race-record time and second afterwards in the Jacques le Marois, Moulin and Champion Stakes. Ninth of eighteen in the Derby was his only try at a mile and a half and one of his few disappointments. To the small number of breeders other than his owner who used him in 1991, Linamix stood at 100,000 francs (around £10,000). The fee will be 150,000 (around £19,600) in 1996 and by

Prix Niel, Longchamp—Housamix (right), Poliglote (rails) and Winged Love return from their summer break

the end of the latest season sixteen of the thirty-two in his first crop had won in France; Diamond Mix, Housamix, Miss Satamixa and Walk On Mix did so in Group 1 or Group 2 events.

Housamix had only two starts in 1995. Winner of the Prix Thomas Bryon on his final race the previous season, he reappeared in the Prix de Guiche at Longchamp in May, performed well to run Valanour to a length, but pulled up lame with a hairline fracture of a pastern. It was over four months until Housamix was seen out again, in the Prix Niel up against three colts who had all significantly improved their records while Housamix was nursing his injury: the reputations of Poliglote and Winged Love now rested on fine efforts in the French and Irish Derbys respectively; late arrival Song of Tara had begun to live up to his illustrious pedigree by winning a listed race at Maisons-Laffitte. Housamix started narrowly the outsider of four. Entering the straight, he was last of four and slightly boxed in, and that after a slow pace through the early stages (the Niel's was the slowest time of the three Longchamp 'Arc trials' that Sunday). Not perfectly positioned then, but Thierry Jarnet got a fine response from Housamix who made up about two and a half lengths in the final furlong to collar Poliglote and Winged Love in the final strides, winning by a head. The Niel's status as an Arc trial is a justified one, but none of the Niel runners went on to the Arc in the latest season. After a gallop in Arc week, M. Lagardere reported that Housamix 'went well but is probably a little tender for the Arc at this stage in his career'.

Housamix (FR) (gr.c. 1992)	Linamix (FR) (gr 1987)	Mendez (gr 1981)	Bellypha
			Miss Carina
		Lunadix (gr 1972)	Breton
			Lutine
	Housatonic (USA) (b 1987)	Riverman (b 1969)	Never Bend
			River Lady
		Hippodamia (br 1971)	Hail To Reason
			White Lie

Dam Housatonic, like sire Linamix, was totally unproven as a parent before Housamix was conceived. A contemporary of Linamix's, Housatonic had not shown much as a racehorse, her one victory in four starts for John Gosden as a three-year-old coming in a maiden over seven furlongs on the Southwell fibresand. She therefore recouped just £2,060 on the racecourse of the 135,000 dollars it had taken to buy her as a yearling. However, 56,000 guineas more came back from the December Sales. Her dam Hippodamia had had four previous winners (there has also been one since) including the Secretariat colt Globe who won the graded Excelsior and Grey Lag Handicaps over a mile and a quarter and nine furlongs as a five-year-old. Globe was nonetheless some way below the standard shown by Hippodamia, a long way judged by her six-length win in the Criterium des Pouliches. Hippodamia never matched that oustanding effort but was runner-up in the Poule d'Essai des Pouliches and Prix Saint-Alary before being switched to a pacemaking job for Dahlia. Third dam White Lie, who ran twice without success, also produced the 1986 Prix de Guiche winner Bad Conduct.

Housamix stays a mile and a half. He has yet to race on firm ground, but the evidence before his injury was that he acted on both good to firm and soft. It is to be hoped that he will get considerably more opportunities in 1996. At the moment, the result of the Prix Niel is taken at face value for our assessment of his ability. Poliglote and Winged Love may well have been suited by a much stronger pace, but who is to say that Housamix would not as well. From what we know of slowly-run races in general, he was already at a disadvantage in having to come from the rear. *A. Fabre, France*

HOUSE OF DREAMS 3 b.c. Darshaan 133 – Helens Dreamgirl 95 (Caerleon (USA) 132) [1994 –p: 7m 1995 10g^{6} 10.5g 12m^{3} 11.8f^{6} Oct 24] small colt: shows traces of stringhalt: very poor mover: fair maiden: stays 1½m: has raced only on a sound surface: sold (B. Hills to G. M. Moore) 4,800 gns Newmarket Autumn Sales. *B. W. Hills* — 64

HOUSE OF RICHES 2 b.c. (May 1) Shirley Heights 130 – Pelf (USA) 79 (Al Nasr (FR) 126) [1995 6m^{2} 7m^{2} 9g* Sep 23] lengthy colt: has scope: fifth foal: closely related to 13.8f winner Referential and a winner in UAE (both by Reference Point) and half-brother to 3-y-o Kreef (by Kris): dam, maiden here at 2 yrs later 7f winner in Italy, from good family: won 13-runner maiden at Redcar after near 3-month absence, making all and staying on well to beat Arctic Fancy by a neck: will stay middle distances. *L. M. Cumani* — 80 p

HOW COULD-I (IRE) 2 br.f. (Apr 25) Don't Forget Me 127 – Shikari Rose (Kala Shikari 125) [1995 6m 6g^{4} 7m^{4} 8m^{6} 7.5d Sep 13] IR 4,400Y: sparely-made filly: fifth live foal: half-sister to Irish 2m winner Coopers Spot-On (by Glenstal): dam, placed 8 times in Ireland, half-sister to multiple Grade 1 winning middle-distance stayer Noble Dancer: poor form in varied events: sold 800 gns Doncaster October Sales. *M. H. Easterby* — 43

HOWQUA RIVER 3 b.g. Petong 126 – Deep Blue Sea (Gulf Pearl 117) [1994 60: 6v^{5} 7m^{5} 7f 8d 7g^{6} a8g^{2} a7g 1995 a8.5g^{3} a9.4g^{5} 10.8m 7g^{5} 8m 8m Sep 25] quite good-topped gelding: easy mover: modest maiden: well below form in 1995 after reappearance: stays 8.5f: blinkered (sweating, ran poor race) second 2-y-o start. *P. W. Chapple-Hyam* — 53 d

HOW'S IT GOIN (IRE) 4 ch.g. Kefaah (USA) 124 – Cuirie (Main Reef 126) [1994 8s^{4} 12.5v^{3} 9s^{3} 11g* 11v^{6} 12g^{5} 12g^{4} 11m^{6} 16s^{6} 1995 a12g^{4} a14.8g^{2} a12g^{6} a14g^{3} 18g a16.2g 12.1m Jul 20] angular ex-Irish gelding: second foal: dam unraced: fair handicapper (rated 77) at 3 yrs for P. J. Flynn, successful at Naas in April: modest form here, best effort when second in claimer at Wolverhampton on second start: stays 14.8f: acts on heavy ground and fibresand: blinkered (pulled hard for amateur, well beaten) third 4-y-o start. *W. R. Muir* — 62 d

HOW'S YER FATHER 9 b.g. Daring March 116 – Dawn Ditty 100 (Song 132) [1994 92: 6s^{4} 7d 6m^{4} 6g^{2} 6m^{2} 6m 6f 6m 6f 6g 6m^{4} 6g 6d 6d 6.1g* 1995 6m 6m 5.1m 6m^{6} 6g^{2} 6m^{6} 6f^{4} 6m^{3} 6m 6m^{2} 6m 6g 7g 6g 6.1s Oct 17] leggy gelding: fairly useful handicapper: stays 6f: acts on any going: tried blinkered, but not for long time: has run creditably when sweating and edgy: held up: tough. *R. J. Hodges* — 88

HUGWITY 3 ch.c. Cadeaux Genereux 131 – Nuit d'Ete (USA) 90 (Super Concorde (USA) 128) [1994 NR 1995 7.3m 8g^{4} 6m Jul 21] good-bodied colt: fourth living foal: half-brother to useful Irish 1m and 1¼m winner Al Guswa and a winner in Italy from 1m to 1½m, both by Shernazar: dam 2-y-o 5f and 6f winner: fair form in maidens: unsuited by drop to 6f and not at all knocked about when below form at Newmarket on final outing: stays 1m well: has raced only on a sound surface: bandaged first 2 starts: looked capable of better. *B. Hanbury* — 73 p

HUISH CROSS 3 ch.f. Absalom 128 – Sixslip (USA) 94 (Diesis 133) [1994 63: 9d^{6} 10s 8.2d 1995 8m 12f^{6} 12d a12g Dec 18] leggy filly: modest maiden: no worthwhile form in 1995, sold out of D. Morley's stable 5,500 gns Newmarket July Sales after reappearance. *S. G. Knight* — –

HUJJAB (USA) 3 b.f. Woodman (USA) 126 – Winters' Love (USA) (Danzig (USA)) [1994 76: 6s^{3} 6g^{2} 7g^{3} 7m^{6} 7s^{3} 8d^{3} 7d^{2} 1995 8m^{3} 8m* 8m^{3} 10m^{5} 12.3m^{6} 8.5m^{5} 8.1d^{6} Sep 12] strong filly: carries condition: fairly useful handicapper: won at Salisbury in May: below form last 4 starts, blinkered on final one: stays 1m: acts on — 82 good to firm ground and soft: edgy sort, and sometimes sweats: carries head high and looks a difficult ride: sold 64,000 gns Newmarket December Sales. *J. L. Dunlop*

HULLBANK 5 b.g. Uncle Pokey 116 – Dubavarna 72 (Dubassoff (USA)) [1994 66: 14.1m³ 12m⁴ 13.8m² 14.1g² 1995 16.2m³ 14.1f* 14.6g 12m² 12d⁶ Sep 13] tall gelding: shows knee action: fair performer: won maiden at Redcar in June: stays 2m: acts on firm going: bandaged in 1995: usually held up. *W. W. Haigh* 67

HULM (IRE) 2 ch.f. (Feb 9) Mujtahid (USA) 118 – Sunley Princess 69 (Ballad Rock 122) [1995 6f² 7g³ Oct 23] IR 30,000Y: strong, lengthy filly: second foal: dam, maiden suited by 7f, half-sister to very smart middle-distance stayer Almaarad: similar form in maidens won by Chalamont at Redcar (beaten 9 lengths) and Jezyah at Lingfield (just under 3 lengths third, first home on unfavoured stand side) 3 weeks later: stays 7f. *H. Thomson Jones* 71

HUMBEL (USA) 3 b.c. Theatrical 128 – Claxton's Slew (USA) 100 (Seattle Slew (USA)) [1994 94p: 8d* 9s* 1995 10g* 10m* 12f 12m 10f⁵ 12d⁴ 11d* 11s Nov 18] quite attractive colt: good walker: powerful round-actioned galloper: smart performer: won listed event and Derrinstown Stud Derby Trial (beat Shemaran a neck) at Leopardstown in the spring and 5-runner Blandford Stakes at the Curragh (made all, beat Ballykett Nancy a length) in October: tailed off in Grade 2 event at Aqueduct final start: stays 1½m (respectable 6½ lengths eighth of 15 in the Derby): probably acts on any going. *D. K. Weld, Ireland* 116

HUMBERT'S LANDING (IRE) 4 b.c. Cyrano de Bergerac 120 – Bilander 78 (High Line 125) [1994 89: 6d⁵ 6g* 5m* 6f³ 1995 5.2m⁴ 6m* 6f Jun 23] strong, close-coupled colt: unimpressive mover: fairly useful handicapper, lightly raced: best effort when narrowly winning at Kempton in May: finished lame when heavily-backed favourite (looked in magnificent shape) for the Wokingham at Royal Ascot on final start: stays 6f: acts on firm going: usually held up: sold only 10,000 gns Newmarket Autumn Sales. *P. F. I. Cole* 96

Dr Michael Smurfit's "Humbel"

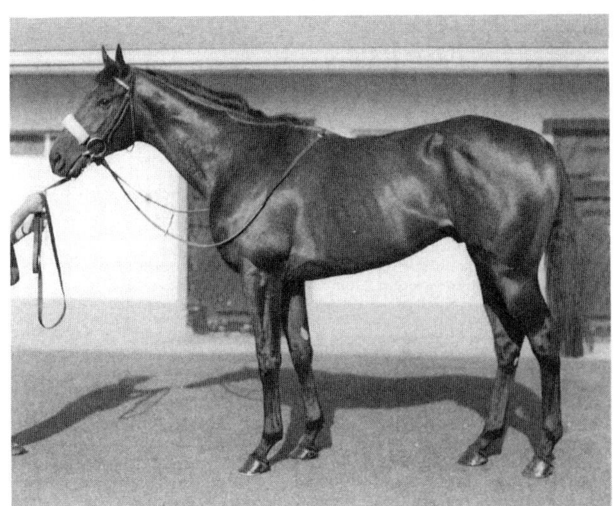

HUMOURLESS 2 ch.c. (Feb 17) Nashwan (USA) 135 – Sans Blague (USA) 108 (The Minstrel (CAN) 135) [1995 7m 8g^6 8g^4 Oct 10] good-topped colt: good walker and mover: half-brother to several winners, including very useful 1986 2-y-o 6f and 7.3f winner Nettle (by Kris) and middle-distance winner Quip (by High Line): dam suited by 1½m: progressive form in maidens at Newmarket, Doncaster and Leicester: just over 4 lengths fourth of 17 to Forest Buck last time, disputing lead over 5f: will stay middle distances: will continue to progress. *L. M. Cumani* 77 p

HUNTERS' HEAVEN (USA) 4 b.g. Seeking The Gold (USA) – Rose of Virginia (USA) (Northern Dancer) [1994 65: 8s 8m 8s^5 8.2m 8.1m^4 10.2m^2 8m 10g* 10d^4 10.4d 9.7m 1995 10m 10m 10d 8g Oct 3] strong, good-bodied gelding: fair 1¼m performer at best: well beaten in 1995. *J. Mackie* –

HUNTERS OF BRORA (IRE) 5 b.m. Sharpo 132 – Nihad 76 (Alleged (USA) 138) [1994 89: 8f^5 7m 8f 8d 7.6g^2 8m* 8g 9g^2 8m 1995 8m^2 8.5m* 8m 10f^2 10.4m 10.1g 9g^3 9d^3 Oct 21] sturdy, lengthy mare: useful handicapper: won rated stakes at Beverley in May: ran well when fast-finishing second to Silver Groom in William Hill Cup at Goodwood and when staying-on third of 39 to Cap Juluca in Cambridgeshire at Newmarket on penultimate start: stays 1¼m: probably acts on any going: held up. *J. D. Bethell* 97

HUNZA STORY 3 b.f. Rakaposhi King 119 – Sense of Occasion (Artaius (USA) 129) [1994 –: 6d 7m 1995 a8g a9.4g^2 a12g a8g 8.2m 10m^2 8m 10.8m^6 a12g 8m^5 10m* 10m 10m 8.1d 8.2m^6 11f^2 10f a9.4g^6 a12g a13g Dec 19] small filly: poor handicapper: won seller at Ripon in August: unlikely to stay much beyond 11f: acts on firm ground: has worn bandages, crossed noseband and tongue strap: none too consistent. *N. P. Littmoden* 45 a33

HURRICANE DANCER (IRE) 2 ch.f. (Feb 2) Nabeel Dancer (USA) 120 – Raging Storm (Horage 124) [1995 5g^3 5m^2 6m^4 6.1f^2 7m* 7.6m^4 7g 7s^2 7m Oct 12] IR 5,800F, 5,200Y: small, sparely-made filly: fourth foal: half-sister to two 2-y-o winners, including 1992 6f winner Rich Midas (by Salt Dome): dam Irish 2-y-o 8.5f winner: modest performer: won auction event at Yarmouth in July: poor effort in seller final outing: stays 7.6f: acts on good to firm and soft ground: has run creditably for 7-lb claimer: sold 7,000 gns Newmarket Autumn Sales. *S. P. C. Woods* 58

HURRICANE HORN (IRE) 2 ch.c. (Feb 11) Kefaah (USA) 124 – Musical Horn (Music Boy 124) [1995 5m 6m 7.1m 6m a8.5g a7g^5 a7g a10g^5 Nov 25] IR 19,000Y: lengthy, good-bodied colt: fourth foal: brother to modest Irish 3-y-o Paula's Choice: dam unraced half-sister to dam of useful Irish 2-y-o winners Cois Na Tine and Eva Luna: poor maiden: not discredited over 1¼m but gives impression will prove best at up to 1m: blinkered/visored last 3 starts, twice running respectably: sold 900 gns Ascot December Sales. *W. R. Muir* 48

HURTLEBERRY (IRE) 2 b.f. (Apr 22) Tirol 127 – Allberry (Alzao (USA) 117) [1995 5m 6f* Aug 10] IR 15,500F, 6,000Y: unfurnished filly: third foal: half-sister to 3-y-o Delightful Dancer (by Dancing Dissident): dam unraced: won 10-runner maiden auction at Salisbury by head from Lucky Revenge, always prominent and leading inside last: will stay beyond 6f: should improve again. *Lord Huntingdon* 68 p

HUSHANG (IRE) 5 b.h. Shernazar 131 – Highest Hopes 129 (Hethersett 134) [1994 8v^2 10v^2 1995 12g^2 9m^2 9.6g* 8g^3 8g* 10m^2 10g* Sep 17] half-brother to a minor winner by Crepello: dam, won Prix Vermeille, is half-sister to top-class sprinter Gratitude: smart performer: successful at 3 yrs in maiden and listed event, both at the Curragh, and runner-up in Group 2 Gallinule Stakes: won handicap at Gowran in June, listed race at the Curragh (made all, held on well by head from Ivory Frontier) in July and Group 2 event at Frankfurt (made virtually all, beat Sylvan Point a head) in September: best form at up to 1¼m, should prove as effective at 1½m: acts on good to firm and heavy ground: sold to join K. Klein in Switzerland. *J. Oxx, Ireland* 114

HUTCHIES LADY 3 b.f. Efisio 120 – Keep Mum 63 (Mummy's Pet 125) [1994 NR 1995 8d 9.2s 7g 8m 7.1m^5 10.9g^6 6f 11.1g Sep 25] small, sparely-made filly: third foal: half-sister to 1¼m and 11f winner Keep Battling (by Hard Fought): dam sprinting maiden, best at 2 yrs: no worthwhile form: tried blinkered. *R. M. McKellar* –

HYDROFOIL 3 gr.f. Sharrood (USA) 124 – Pirogue 99 (Reliance II 137) [1994 56: 5.1d^3 6m^6 6m^4 7.3g^4 8m 1995 10.3m^3 9.9m^3 12g* 11.7m* 14.1f 11.7h* a14.8g^3 12g Oct 16] leggy, lightly-made filly: modest performer: won maiden at Catterick 61

and 2 minor events (under 5-lb claimer) at Bath in the summer: better suited by 1½m than shorter, and stays 14.8f: acts on hard ground and fibresand: has run well when sweating: effective from front or held up. *B. W. Hills*

HYLTERS GIRL 3 b.f. Dominion 123 – Jolimo 92 (Fortissimo 111) [1994 –: 7s 7s a6g 1995 7m^5 7g 7f a10g Nov 10] small, sparely-made filly: no worthwhile form. *M. J. Ryan* –

HYPERTENSION 3 ch.c. Roi Danzig (USA) – Sayulita 67 (Habitat 134) [1994 NR 1995 10g 8d 10d Oct 19] 14,000Y: strong, lengthy colt: first foal: dam maiden (stayed 1½m) out of half-sister to Gift Wrapped, dam of Royal Lodge winner Reach: little form in maidens at Goodwood (moved short to post) and Newbury: may do better. *R. Hannon* –

I

IAMUS 2 ch.c. (Feb 24) Most Welcome 131 – Icefern 88 (Moorestyle 137) [1995 7.1d 7d^2 7.9m^2 8m^4 Oct 21] leggy colt: unimpressive walker: third foal: half-brother to winning sprinter Kensworth Lady (by Formidable): dam sprinter: runner-up in maidens won by Final Stab at Salisbury and Prince of My Heart (median auction event) at York (worth a rating of 84 both occasions): seemed to excel himself when 3½ lengths last of 4 to Beauchamp King in falsely-run Racing Post Trophy at Doncaster, restrained in rear and keeping on, never a danger: stays 1m. *P. T. Walwyn* 105 ?

IBERIAN DANCER (CAN) 2 b.f. (May 12) El Gran Senor (USA) – Cutty (USA) (Smart) [1995 6f^5 7m^3 Aug 16] $47,000F, 19,000Y: lengthy, unfurnished filly: closely related to smart 7f to 1¼m performer Sharp Singer (by The Minstrel), and half-sister to numerous winners abroad: dam won 9 times from 3 yrs to 5 yrs in USA, including 8.5f stakes: around 3½ lengths third of 11 to Brilliant Red in maiden at Kempton, chasing leaders and staying on: will stay further than 7f: likely to improve again. *J. W. Hills* 70 p

IBLIS (IRE) 3 b.c. Danehill (USA) 126 – In Unison (Bellypha 130) [1994 85: 6m^4 6g^2 6d* 6s 7d^3 1995 7m* 8g 7g^6 7m^5 Jul 16] close-coupled, good-quartered colt: improved considerably to win handicap at Newmarket on reappearance in tremendous style, shooting clear in the Dip: well beaten in Mehl-Mulhens-Rennen at Cologne, minor event at Leicester and rated stakes at Yarmouth (moved poorly to post) afterwards: will eventually prove effective at 1m: acts on good to firm and dead ground, probably on soft. *G. Wragg* 95 d

IBSEN 7 b.g. Gorytus (USA) 132 – State of Mind (Mill Reef (USA) 141) [1994 72: a10g^4 a16g^3 a16.2g a16g* 14.9m* 14g^3 14m^4 16s* 16g^2 1995 a16.2g^6 a16g 14.9m^4 16.2g 14m Aug 19] leggy, lengthy gelding: poor mover: fair handicapper: stays 2m: acts on equitrack, good to firm and soft going, below form on fibresand: has worn bandages: carries head high: inconsistent at 7 yrs. *R. Akehurst* 66

ICANSPELL 4 b.g. Petoski 135 – Bewitched 63 (African Sky 124) [1994 47, a54: a7g a8s^5 8f a7g* 7d 7g^6 7.1m a8g a8.5g 1995 8m 11.1g May 20] leggy gelding: soundly beaten for new stable in 1995: should stay 1m: acts on fibresand: visored/ blinkered at 4 yrs: none too consistent. *W. Storey* –

ICE MAGIC 8 ch.g. Red Sunset 120 – Free Rein (Sagaro 133) [1994 32: 10.5g 12.3m 12m^6 10.1g^5 12.1f^5 13.1g^3 15d^2 14.1d^2 12m 14s^6 1995 10.5d 12.3f^5 11.1f^5 12.1m^4 16.5f^6 14.1m^5 16.2m Aug 24] sparely-made gelding: poor performer: stays 15f: acts on firm and dead going: usually visored nowadays, tried in blinkers. *F. J. Yardley* 26

ICENI (IRE) 2 b. or br.f. (Apr 17) Distinctly North (USA) 115 – Princess Galicia 82 (Welsh Pageant 132) [1995 6.1m^4 Aug 21] 7,800Y: half-sister to 7f and 1m winner Broughton Blues (by Tender King) and 1986 Irish 2-y-o 6f winner Pageant's Pride (by Sallust): dam, maiden, stayed 1m: 7/1, 10 lengths fourth of 11 to Faraway Waters in maiden auction at Nottingham, very green and well behind then staying on under considerate ride: sold (A. Stewart to H. Candy) stable 12,500 gns Newmarket Autumn Sales: will probably improve. *A. C. Stewart* – p

ICE PICK (IRE) 2 b.c. (May 9) Distinctly North (USA) 115 – Avril's Choice (Montelimar (USA) 122) [1995 5m^{2} 5.1f^{3} 7f^{3} 7.1m^{5} 6g 7m^{6} Oct 21] 12,500Y: good-topped, attractive colt: good walker: first foal: dam lightly-raced half-sister to Trevita, a good winner at up to 1¼m: fair form: placed in minor events first 3 starts: not discredited in visor when sixth of 11 in nursery at Doncaster final start after stumbling leaving stalls: stays 7f: sold 12,000 gns Newmarket Autumn Sales: sent to Malaysia. *R. Hannon*
67

ICHOR 2 b.f. (Apr 11) Primo Dominie 121 – Adeebah (USA) 94 (Damascus (USA)) [1995 5g 5m^{3} 5.2g^{5} 5m 5g Aug 28] smallish, sparely-made filly: half-sister to several winners here and abroad, including 7f winner Junuh (by Jalmood): dam 2-y-o 5f winner: easily best form when third of 4 to Centurion in maiden at Epsom on second start: unruly at stalls last 2 outings. *H. Thomson Jones*
52 ?

IDLE FANCY 2 b.f. (Apr 27) Mujtahid (USA) 118 – Pizziri (Artaius (USA) 129) [1995 7f Aug 17] 48,000Y: leggy filly: half-sister to useful 9.2f to 1½m winner Jandeel (by Last Tycoon) and several winners in France, including useful 1989 2-y-o Femme Grise (by Auction Ring): dam won at 6f and 1m in Italy and is out of good Italian 7f and 1m filly Croda Alta: 25/1, not knocked about when tenth of 15 to Alzanti in maiden at Salisbury: will probably do better. *Lord Huntingdon*
– p

IDRIS (IRE) 5 b.h. Ahonoora 122 – Idara 109 (Top Ville 129) [1994 111: 7v^{3} 1995 9m* 8f^{2} 9d^{2} 11d^{3} 10d* Nov 7] sturdy horse: smart Irish performer: off course 15½ months, won handicap at Leopardstown in July: placed in listed events and 5-runner Group 2 Blandford Stakes at the Curragh (3 lengths behind Humbel) next 3 starts then narrowly landed minor event at the Curragh in November: stays 11f: acts on heavy going and firm: most consistent. *J. S. Bolger, Ireland*
111

I FEAR NOTHING 4 gr.f. Kalaglow 132 – Noirmont Girl 95 (Skymaster 126) [1994 –: 9.9s a7g a11g 1995 a11g Jan 2] leggy filly: no worthwhile form since 2 yrs: sold 4,800 gns Doncaster March Sales. *S. C. Williams*
–

IHTIMAAM (FR) 3 b.g. Polish Precedent (USA) 131 – Haebeh (USA) 88 (Alydar (USA)) [1994 NR 1995 8g^{5} 8m^{3} 8g^{3} 9.2f 8m 8f Oct 24] compact gelding: first known foal: dam 1¼m winner: bought out of M. Stoute's stable 16,000 gns Newmarket Autumn (1994) Sales: some promise in maidens first 3 starts: well beaten afterwards: likely to stay beyond 1m: usually gives trouble at stalls. *Mrs A. Swinbank*
69 d

IHTIRAM (IRE) 3 b.c. Royal Academy (USA) 130 – Welsh Love (Ela-Mana-Mou 132) [1994 93: 7m 7f^{3} 7.1d* 8s^{6} 7.9d^{2} 8d* 10d^{5} 1995 8m^{2} 8.1m^{2} 8m* 8m^{2} 10f^{3} 10g* 11.9m^{4} 11.1g^{5} a10g^{4} Dec 29] tall, good sort: has scope: smart performer: won 5-runner £8,800 event at Thirsk in May and 5-runner listed race at Newbury (stayed on well to wear down Dance Turn close home) in July: respectable last of 4 to Pentire in Great Voltigeur Stakes at York then soundly beaten in September Stakes at Kempton, final start for J. Dunlop: probably stays 1½m: acts on firm ground and dead, may be unsuited by very soft: tends to wander: sent to Dubai, and tailed off only outing there. *K. P. McLaughlin, UAE*
114

IJAB (CAN) 5 b.g. Ascot Knight (CAN) 130 – Renounce (USA) (Buckpasser) [1994 28: 10d 9g 10m 12.1m^{5} 1995 a11g a11g^{2} 12.1d a11g* a12g^{2} a12g^{2} 14.1f^{3} 10m a14g* a16g^{2} 15.8g 13.6f^{5} a14g^{2} a14g^{2} a14g^{2} Nov 24] good-topped gelding: modest handicapper: led final 1f to win at Southwell in April (maiden contest) and August: stays 2m: acts on good to firm going and goes well on fibresand: sometimes sweats: usually blinkered nowadays. *J. Parkes*
28
a54

IKAAB (USA) 3 b.g. Danzig (USA) – Dazzling Concorde (USA) (Super Concorde (USA) 128) [1994 99: 5m^{2} 6m* 6m* 5m 6g^{4} a8g* 1995 6g 6m^{5} 5m a8g* Dec 29] good-topped gelding: has a quick action: disappointing for R. Hern here in 1995, best effort second start: won handicap at Jebel Ali in December: stays 1m: usually blinkered or visored: usually unsavoury in preliminaries: not an easy ride: has far from ideal temperament. *K. P. McLaughlin, UAE*
85 §

IKHTIRAA (USA) 5 b.g. Imperial Falcon (CAN) – True Native (USA) (Raise A Native) [1994 54, a61: a8g* a8g^{4} a10g^{2} a8g 9.7m 8.3f 10.1m^{2} a10g^{5} 11.5d 10.1m 7.6v 9s* 9.7d a12g^{2} a12g* 1995 a16g^{4} a12g^{2} a12g^{3} a12g 12m^{3} 11.5m 12g^{4} 10m^{4} 10f^{3} a12g^{3} a16g^{2} Dec 15] lengthy, angular gelding: modest handicapper on all-weather: poor at best on turf: stays 2m: acts on any turf going, best form on all-weather surfaces: tried blinkered/visored, no improvement: normally races prominently: winning hurdler. *R. J. O'Sullivan*
43
a64

IKIS GIRL 4 ch.f. Silver Hawk (USA) 123 – Jealous One (USA) (Raise A Native) [1994 68d: 12g 8.3m² 8f² 10g⁶ 8.2m 10m³ 11.9g 1995 8s⁶ 7.5m 10g 9.9m 8.5d 18m⁶ 10.1f 7g 8.1m Jul 8] leggy, workmanlike filly: disappointing maiden. *S. Gollings* –

IKTAMAL (USA) 3 ch.c. Danzig Connection (USA) – Crystal Cup (USA) (Nijinsky (CAN) 138) [1994 –p: 7g 1995 8m² 7.1m⁶ 7m² 7f* 6m⁴ 6m* 6g* 6g* 6m⁴ Oct 14] big, strong colt: has plenty of scope: most progressive form: won maiden (carried head high) and handicap at Redcar in August and minor event at Haydock and 26-runner £16,100 handicap at Goodwood (edged ahead inside final 1f and just held on) in September: looking very well, best effort when fourth of 12 to Royale Figurine in listed race at Newmarket final start, unable to quicken from over 1f out: best at sprint distances: acts on firm ground: takes strong hold. *E. A. L. Dunlop* 104

IKTASAB 3 ch.g. Cadeaux Genereux 131 – Loucoum (FR) 93 (Iron Duke (FR) 122) [1994 –: 7g 1995 8m* 8m⁴ 7g⁶ 7m⁶ 8.1m 10d Sep 26] strong, lengthy gelding: has a round action: fairly useful handicapper: won maiden at Thirsk in May: good efforts at Doncaster (minor event) and Ayr (hampered when staying on) next 2 starts: not certain to stay beyond 1m: acts on good to firm ground: sold (E. Dunlop to P. Nicholls) 20,000 gns Newmarket Autumn Sales. *E. A. L. Dunlop* 86

IL DORIA (IRE) 2 ch.f. (Apr 28) Mac's Imp (USA) 116 – Pasadena Lady (Captain James 123) [1995 5.1m² 5f Oct 14] IR 25,000F, IR 30,000Y: leggy, light-bodied, angular filly: half-sister to 4 winners, including useful sprinters Another Episode, Palacegate Episode (both by Drumalis) and Palacegate Jack (by Neshad): dam never ran: second to 3½-length winner What Fun in minor event at Chester, slowly away, then running on well after being forced to switch: soundly beaten in maiden at Catterick 5 months later. *J. Berry* 66

IL FRATELLO 4 ch.g. Caerleon (USA) 132 – Miss Silca Key 102 (Welsh Saint 126) [1994 NR 1995 a12g a10g a6g a7g 12g⁶ 10m² May 29] workmanlike gelding: sixth foal: brother to useful 7f and 1m winner Consigliere and half-brother to 3 useful winners: dam won Jersey Stakes: best effort when second of 19 in selling handicap at Leicester final start: claimed to join N. Berry £6,500: dead. *N. A. Callaghan* 39

IL FURETTO 3 b.g. Emarati (USA) 74 – Irresistable (Siliconn 121) [1994 NR 1995 5m 6.1m 5.1m 9.7f 8.3m 6f a6g a5g Nov 30] sparely-made gelding: eighth live foal: half-brother to 1m seller winner Resister (by Monsanto): dam ran twice: of no account. *J. S. King* –

ILIUM BOURBON 3 b.f. Ilium 121 – Little Missile (Ile de Bourbon (USA) 133) [1994 NR 1995 9m 7f Aug 10] sparely-made filly: third foal: half-sister to fairly useful 4-y-o 6f winner La Petite Fusee (by Cigar) and poor 5-y-o 1m and 1¼m winner Little Miss Ribot (by Lighter): dam (stoutly bred) of little account: last in maidens. *R. J. O'Sullivan* –

ILLEGALLY YOURS 2 br.f. (Jan 12) Be My Chief (USA) 122 – Legal Precedent (Star Appeal 133) [1995 5g⁶ 6m 7m 10g a7g Dec 6] 6,000Y: leggy filly: first foal: dam unraced sister to smart miler Star Way: well behind in maidens and a seller. *L. Montague Hall* –

ILLUMINATE 2 b.c. (Apr 15) Marju (IRE) 127 – Light Bee (USA) 86 (Majestic Light (USA)) [1995 7m⁴ Sep 5] IR 16,500Y: leggy, quite attractive colt: fourth foal: half-brother to a 1995 3-y-o winner in Serbia: dam 2-y-o 5.1f and 7f winner: 20/1, burly and very green, 2½ lengths fourth of 11 finishers to Caxton Star in maiden at Leicester, slowly away and taking good hold, then staying on strongly from rear: sure to improve. *J. A. R. Toller* 70 p

ILTIMAS (USA) 3 b.f. Dayjur (USA) 137 – Tadwin 109 (Never So Bold 135) [1994 84p: 6g* 6d² 7d² 1995 7m 7.1m 6m² 6f* 5f* 6m⁶ 5.6m Sep 6] neat, strong filly: fairly useful performer: won small-field minor events at Doncaster (by short head) and Salisbury (checked slightly by short-head winner Lucky Parkes, awarded race) in the summer: stiffish tasks, ran well in listed race at Newmarket but last in Portland Handicap at Doncaster: effective at 5f, and stayed 7f: acted on firm and dead ground: sometimes gave trouble in preliminaries: tended to sweat: visits Warning. *P. T. Walwyn* 95

IL TRASTEVERE (FR) 3 b.c. L'Emigrant (USA) 129 – Ideas At Work (Persepolis (FR) 127) [1994 NR 1995 10g⁶ 10d 8d* 8m 8g 7g⁴ 9d 7f⁴ Oct 3] rather leggy colt: second foal: half-brother to La Colombina (by Houston), twice winner at 87 ?

around 11f in French Provinces: dam French 8.2f winner: trained first 5 starts by P. Bary in France, winning maiden at Saint-Cloud in May: contested minor events here, finishing last on last 2 starts: stays 1m: acts on dead ground: difficult to assess but probably fairly useful at best: sold 25,000 gns Newmarket Autumn Sales. *J. L. Dunlop*

ILUSTRE (IRE) 3 ch.g. Al Hareb (USA) 123 – Time For Pleasure (Tower Walk 130) [1994 53: 5g 5g 6m 5d 1995 6m^5 7f 6f 7m Sep 1] strong gelding: poor maiden: seems to stay 7f: acts on firm and dead ground: joined G. Fierro. *L. J. Holt* 50

ILYAZIA 4 b.f. Governor General 116 – Tina's Beauty 41 (Tina's Pet 121) [1994 a7g a8g^5 a8g^3 1995 a8g^4 a10g^4 a7g Nov 10] first living foal: dam, plater, stayed 1¼m: poor maiden in Dubai for P. Rudkin: sold 2,000 gns Newmarket July Sales: tailed off in claimer at Lingfield, first start here: stays 1m. *D. Morris* –

I'M A DREAMER (IRE) 5 b.g. Mister Majestic 122 – Lady Wise (Lord Gayle (USA) 124) [1994 65: 10.1g* 9.9s^3 9.9m^6 10g^5 10.5g 10.5d^3 10.4d 1995 a11g^4 Mar 20] good-topped gelding: fair handicapper: below best only start in 1995: stays 11f: acts on fibresand and on good to firm and soft ground. *W. W. Haigh* 51 +

IMAD (USA) 5 b. or br.g. Al Nasr (FR) 126 – Blue Grass Field 81 (Top Ville 129) [1994 NR 1995 20m 20f* 16.4m 18m Oct 14] close-coupled gelding: second foal: half-brother to fairly useful 1991 2-y-o 5f and 6f winner (later won in USA) Baltra (by Known Fact): dam maiden, stayed 8.5f: won minor event at Tipperary (rated 87) at 3 yrs: sold out of K. Prendergast's stable 13,500 gns Newmarket Autumn (1993) Sales: fair staying hurdler in 1994/5: won Country Club Hotels Goodwood Stakes in July by 1½ lengths from Upper Mount Clair, staying on strongly: below form at Sandown and Newmarket (Cesarewitch) afterwards: thorough stayer: acts on firm ground: wears a tongue strap. *J. White* 69

IMAGE MAKER (IRE) 2 gr.f. (Apr 16) Nordico (USA) – Dream Trader (Auction Ring (USA) 123) [1995 6m^5 6m^3 7f^4 a6g^2 6.1d a6g a8.5g* a8.5g^4 a8.5g^4 a8.5g^4 a8g^4 a6g Dec 12] IR 11,000Y: sturdy filly: half-sister to fair 7f/1m performer Dream Carrier (by Doulab) and a middle-distance winner in Italy: dam unraced: sold out of D. Arbuthnot's stable 5,400 gns after winning seller at Wolverhampton in October: poor efforts last 4 starts: stays 8.5f: acts on fibresand (only poor form on turf): blinkered last 2 starts. *B. Preece* 44 a58

IMLAK (IRE) 3 ch.c. Ela-Mana-Mou 132 – Mashteen (USA) (Majestic Prince (USA)) [1994 68p: 8.2d 8m 8.2d 1995 10g^4 9.9m^4 12s 10g 10f Oct 31] big, good-topped colt: has been hobdayed: has a quick action: fair performer: sold out of D. Morley's stable 5,000 gns Newmarket Autumn Sales after penultimate start: broke a blood vessel (for second time) next time, careering across track before collapsing: will probably stay further than 1¼m: yet to race on extremes of going: not one to rely on. *J. L. Harris* 66 §

I'M OUTA HERE (IRE) 3 b. or br.g. Don't Forget Me 127 – Heavenward (USA) (Conquistador Cielo (USA)) [1994 66: 7d^5 7d 1995 6.9m^6 9g 10m 7f^2 8g 7.6d^2 8f 7d Sep 14] tall, workmanlike gelding: has scope: fair maiden handicapper: effective at 7f, stays at least 1m: acts on firm and dead ground: none too consistent: sold 5,400 gns Newmarket Autumn Sales: sent to Italy. *R. Hannon* 66

IMPECCABLE 2 ch.f. (Mar 12) Mac's Imp (USA) 116 – Ethel Knight (Thatch (USA) 136) [1995 6.1m 6g 6g^4 6m 6.1s Oct 17] 12,500F, 10,000Y: compact filly: has a quick action: fifth live foal: half-sister to 3 winners, all at up to 1m, including fair 1993 2-y-o 5f winner Battling Blue (by Primo Dominie): dam lightly raced: best effort when around 11 lengths fourth of 11 to Sketchbook in maiden at Pontefract: faced stiff tasks in nurseries afterwards: has raced only at 6f: looked all at sea on soft ground: sold 1,700 gns Newmarket Autumn Sales: sent to Holland. *J. L. Dunlop* 59 +

IMPENDING DANGER 2 ch.g. (Feb 27) Fearless Action (USA) 116 – Crimson Sol (Crimson Beau 124) [1995 7m^4 a7g a7g^5 6f Aug 28] workmanlike gelding: third reported foal: half-brother to 3-y-o Phils Fortune (by Kinglet): dam poor novice hurdler: little sign of ability. *K. S. Bridgwater* –

IMPERIAL BAILIWICK (IRE) 4 b.f. Imperial Frontier (USA) 112 – Syndikos (USA) (Nashua) [1994 104: 7.3s^5 5f 6f 6d^3 5g^5 5m 6f^6 5g^3 6g 5d^4 5s^3 6v 1995 5.5g^4 5v^4 5m^6 Jun 5] small filly: poor mover: useful performer: bit below best when fourth of 9 in listed race at Evry on reappearance, decidedly so in listed race at 96

Milan and Group 3 event at Leopardstown afterwards: effective at 5f and 6f: won on firm going at 2 yrs, but seems ideally suited by give in the ground (acts on soft): sweating (lack-lustre effort) ninth 3-y-o start. *M. D. I. Usher*

IMPERIAL BID (FR) 7 b.g. No Pass No Sale 120 – Tzaritsa (USA) 113 (Young Emperor 133) [1994 63: 12g^6 12.4g 10d 10m^2 11.1m* 10.1f^4 12.1m^4 11.1m^5 10m^2 10g^6 10d 1995 a11g a11g^3 a11g^3 10.9m^4 11.1g* 10g^5 10g 11.1f^3 11.1m^4 11.1f^4 10.1m* 11.1f^4 10f^5 10f 10.1f^3 10.9g^5 12m Oct 13] leggy, close-coupled gelding: modest handicapper: won at Edinburgh in May and Newcastle in July: rather in and out afterwards: stays 1½m: acts on hard and dead ground, and on fibresand: visored (below form) final start. *Denys Smith* 59

IMPETUOUS LADY (USA) 2 b.f. (Apr 18) Imp Society (USA) – Urakawa (USA) (Roberto (USA) 131) [1995 6.1f^5 6s 6g 7f Oct 23] 7,200F, 7,600Y: good-topped, leggy filly: has a round action: tenth foal: sister to a winner in USA and half-sister to several winners in USA: dam ran 6 times in USA: under 3 lengths fifth of 9 in maiden auction at Nottingham: absent 2½ months, then no form remaining 3 starts. *W. J. Musson* 55 d

IMP EXPRESS (IRE) 2 b.c. (Mar 27) Mac's Imp (USA) 116 – Fair Chance (Young Emperor 133) [1995 5m^6 5m^5 5m* 5f^2 5g* 5m^6 5m 5m^3 6g 5m^4 Oct 13] IR 6,200Y, 7,200 2-y-o: good-topped colt: half-brother to several winners, including fairly useful 1990 2-y-o 5f winner Gold Futures (by Fayruz): dam Irish 2-y-o 5f and 7f winner: won seller at Edinburgh in June and 3-runner nursery at Ayr in July: good efforts afterwards when in frame in nurseries at Goodwood and Catterick (poorly drawn): speedy, and likely to prove best at 5f: acts on firm ground but looked well suited by an easy surface at Ayr: sold 16,500 gns Newmarket Autumn Sales. *G. M. Moore* 77

IMPINGTON (IRE) 2 b.f. (Mar 2) Mac's Imp (USA) 116 – Ultra (Stanford 121§) [1995 5.1f^4 6.1m^3 5g a6g a5g^4 a6g^4 a5g^3 Dec 19] 10,000Y: angular filly: sixth foal: half-sister to 3-y-o Contract Venture (by Contract Law) and 6f to 1m winner Sure Victory (by Stalker): dam maiden: modest maiden: sold out of M. Jarvis' stable 4,000 gns Newmarket Autumn Sales after fourth start: stays 6f: acts on good to firm ground and equitrack, below best both starts on fibresand. *W. R. Muir* 52 +

I'M PLAYING 3 br.f. Primo Dominie 121 – Play The Game 70 (Mummy's Game 120) [1994 –: 6m^6 5g^4 5m 1995 a5g^5 5f Jul 31] unfurnished filly: no worthwhile form: sold 550 gns Doncaster September Sales. *M. Johnston* –

IMPREVEDIBILE (IRE) 5 b.h. Bluebird (USA) 125 – Corozal (Corvaro (USA) 124) [1994 6g^6 6g^2 5g^3 6f^5 6g* 5m^3 7.5m* 8g* 8v* 6g^2 6d* 5d^4 7v^4 8d 1995 6g* 6m* 5v* 6s^4 5f* 6g^5 6d* 5d^6 7d^2 6d^6 Dec 10] third foal: half-brother to useful Il Corsair (by Horage) prolific winner in Italy at up to 11f, and Italian 6f to 1m winner (including in listed company) Without Delay (by Try My Best): dam 9.5f winner in Ireland: useful Italian horse: successful on 3 of his 4 starts (at 6f and 7f) at 2 yrs when trained by L. D'Auria, on 5 of his 9 starts (at 5f and 6f, including a listed race) at 3 yrs, and on 5 of his 14 starts at 4 yrs: had another fine season in 1995, successful in 2 minor events and a listed race in the spring, a valuable handicap in June and a minor race in September, all at Milan: ½-length second of 10 to Lavinia Fontana, finishing well, in Group 3 event there penultimate start: has won at 1m, probably best at up to 7f: acts on any going: wears blinkers: has worn bandages. *P. Ceriotti, Italy* 108

IMPRIMIS (IRE) 2 b.f. (Apr 16) Mac's Imp (USA) 116 – Reasonably French (Reasonable (FR) 119) [1995 5m^6 5m^3 6g^2 6f^3 6g 6g^4 5.2f^6 7m Aug 4] IR 2,000Y: small filly: second foal: dam Irish 2-y-o 7f winner: plater: best form at 6f: poor effort in visor: often claimer ridden: twice slowly away: sold 1,250 gns Doncaster October Sales. *C. N. Allen* 46

IMPROMPTU MELODY (IRE) 2 b.f. (Mar 9) Mac's Imp (USA) 116 – Greek Music (Tachypous 128) [1995 6m^6 5g 5f Jun 22] IR 9,000Y: leggy filly: third foal: half-sister to 1993 2-y-o 5f and 6f winner Leap of Faith (by Northiam) and 1991 2-y-o 5f winner Angels Answer (by Stalker): dam ran twice: well beaten in maiden events: wore crossed noseband final start. *B. S. Rothwell* –

IMPULSIVE AIR (IRE) 3 b.g. Try My Best (USA) 130 – Tracy's Sundown (Red Sunset 120) [1994 87: 5d^2 5g* 5f^3 6g^2 6d^5 1995 8g^5 7m^6 7g 8.1g 7g 8.5d 7.1g 6s 8f Oct 12] strong, useful-looking gelding: carries condition: unimpressive mover: fairly useful form when sixth of 9 in handicap at Newmarket in May: most 88 d disappointing afterwards, reluctant to race on seventh start: should stay beyond 1m: acts on good to firm ground, probably on dead: visored last 3 starts: one to be wary of: has been gelded. *E. Weymes*

I'M SUPPOSIN (IRE) 3 b.c. Posen (USA) – Robinia (USA) 90 (Roberto (USA) 131) [1994 7d^{3} 7v* 1995 7s* 10g^{4} 12g^{2} 10m 8m 9.6g^{3} 12m 10m^{6} 12m 10m^{6} 8d* 11m* Oct 22] IR 6,500Y: second foal: half-brother to useful 7f and 1m winner Paonic (by Exactly Sharp): dam 2-y-o 7f winner: smart performer: won maiden at Tipperary at 2 yrs and handicap at the Curragh in April: 400/1, 7 lengths seventh of 13 to Winged Love in strongly-run Irish Derby at the Curragh seventh start: best efforts when winning handicaps at the Curragh and Naas in October: effective at 1m and stays 1½m: acts on heavy going and good to firm. *K. Prendergast, Ireland* 112

I'M YOUR LADY 4 ch.f. Risk Me (FR) 127 – Impala Lass 81 (Kampala 120) [1994 77: 5.1m^{3} 7g 6m^{5} 6f* 5.1s^{4} 5s^{3} 7s 5v^{3} 1995 5g^{3} 6g 6.1m^{6} 6m 6m 5g 5m^{3} a5g Nov 16] plain filly: fair handicapper: not nearly so consistent as at 3 yrs: has run well at 7f, but best as a sprinter: acts on any going. *B. A. McMahon* 75

INAMINIT 2 gr.g. (Apr 10) Timeless Times (USA) 99 – Dolly Bevan 53 (Another Realm 118) [1995 5s 6m Nov 6] small gelding: third foal: half-brother to 3-y-o Pengamon and 4-y-o Oggi, both 6f winners by Efisio: dam, 2-y-o 6f winner, half-sister to smart sprinter Pip's Pride: slowly away and always behind in maidens at Lingfield and Folkestone. *H. J. Collingridge* –

IN A MOMENT (USA) 4 ch.g. Moment of Hope (USA) – Teenage Fling (USA) (Laomedonte (USA) 116) [1994 56: 7m 8g 8.2f 9.9g 10.1f^{5} 9g^{2} 8m^{6} 10.3g^{3} 11.9g^{3} 10d a9.4g^{5} 1995 a11g^{4} a11g 16.2m 14.1g Apr 17] good-topped gelding: only modest form nowadays: stays 11.9f, not 1¾m+: acts on fibresand, probably on good to firm ground and heavy: effective visored or not. *T. D. Barron* – a58

IN A TIZZY 2 b.f. (Mar 28) Sizzling Melody 117 – Tizzy 79 (Formidable (USA) 125) [1995 5d^{4} a6g a7g^{5} 7.1g^{4} 8.3g^{4} Sep 25] 2,400Y: half-sister to fairly useful 1989 2-y-o 5f winner La Galerie (by Glenstal): dam 9f and 1¼m winner: poor maiden: stays 1m: visored (soundly beaten in seller) third start. *P. C. Haslam* 42 a–

IN BEHIND (IRE) 4 b.f. Entitled 126 – Murroe Star (Glenstal (USA) 118) [1994 52: 10m^{6} 9d 10g^{6} a12g* a14.8g* 16m* a16g^{5} 16.4m^{4} 16d 1995 a12g^{6} a16g a16g a16g a16g Mar 2] sturdy, plain filly: has a round action: modest handicapper: well beaten in 1995: stays 2m: acts on good to firm ground and all-weather. *G. L. Moore* –

INCA BIRD 2 b.f. (Apr 14) Inca Chief (USA) – Polly Oligant (Prince Tenderfoot (USA) 126) [1995 7g 7.1s Oct 17] smallish, close-coupled filly: half-sister to 1989 2-y-o 6f winner Friendship Renewed (by Vaigly Great) and fair 5f to 1m winner Shift's Pal (by Record Token): dam fair 5f winner at 2 yrs in Ireland: eighth of 18 in maiden at Leicester, taking good hold after very slow start: behind in similar event at Chepstow 8 days later: sold 500 gns Doncaster November Sales. *M. McCormack* –

IN CAMERA (IRE) 3 b.c. Sadler's Wells (USA) 132 – Clandestina (USA) 98 (Secretariat (USA)) [1994 72p: 7m^{3} 7.1d^{5} 8m 1995 10m^{2} 10m* 11.5f^{3} 12f^{6} 12g^{5} 12f^{4} 14.6d^{4} 15s^{6} Sep 30] sturdy, attractive colt: good mover: smart performer: won maiden at Leicester in April: contested pattern events afterwards, in frame in Lingfield Derby Trial, Gordon Stakes at Goodwood and St Leger (6½ lengths fourth of 10 to Classic Cliche) at Doncaster: stays 14.6f: acts on firm ground and dead, well below form (in Prix Lutece) on soft: visored (edgy, ran well) seventh 3-y-o start: sometimes sweats: saddle slipped badly fourth 3-y-o outing: stays in training. *M. R. Stoute* 110

INCAPOL 2 b.c. (Apr 22) Inca Chief (USA) – Miss Poll Flinders (Swing Easy (USA) 126) [1995 5m 6g 5.1m* 5m^{3} 5g 6d 6m^{6} a6g Oct 14] 3,500Y: strong colt: fifth reported foal: half-brother to 3-y-o Duffertoes, fair 5f and 7f winner at 2 yrs, and 4-y-o 1m (at 2 yrs) and 1¼m winner Chilly Lad (both by High Kicker): dam unraced: won maiden auction at Nottingham in June: inconsistent afterwards: stays 6f: acts on good to firm ground (soundly beaten on fibresand). *M. J. Ryan* 62

INCA QUEEN 2 b.f. (Apr 24) Inca Chief (USA) – Albion Polka (Dance In Time (CAN)) [1995 a6g 5g Jul 5] fifth foal: dam never ran: well beaten in sellers. *A. G. Foster* –

INCARVILLEA (USA) 2 b.f. (Apr 20) Mr Prospector (USA) – In The Groove 127 (Night Shift (USA)) [1995 5m* 6g* May 26] neat, attractive filly: first foal: 87

dam won Irish 1000 Guineas, Champion Stakes and Coronation Cup: won maiden at Newmarket in April by neck from Hear The Music and minor event at Pontefract in May by 3 lengths from Kunucu: dead. *D. R. Loder*

INCATINKA 2 gr.f. (Apr 23) Inca Chief (USA) – Encore L'Amour (USA) § (Monteverdi 129) [1995 5.7m^{3} 6f^{4} Oct 24] sparely-made filly: fourth live foal: half-sister to 4-y-o 5f and 6f winner Evening Falls (by Beveled): dam no form and was temperamental: similar form in frame in maiden at Bath and median auction event at Leicester (stayed on despite wandering): should stay 7f. *J. L. Spearing* 63

INCHA 3 b.f. Nashwan (USA) 135 – Idle Gossip (USA) (Lyphard (USA) 132) [1994 NR 1995 8g^{2} 10.5g^{3} 8d 8m^{3} 8g Oct 3] leggy, sparely-made filly: fourth foal: half-sister to a winner abroad by Sharpen Up: dam, won from 6f to 9f in USA, from good family: fair form in 2 maidens in the spring: disappointing afterwards, soon off bridle final start: unlikely to stay beyond 1¼m. *H. Thomson Jones* 69 d

INCHCAILLOCH (IRE) 6 b.g. Lomond (USA) 128 – Glowing With Pride 114 (Ile de Bourbon (USA) 133) [1994 52: 14v 12.1g 12m 14.1d^{4} 12s^{5} 1995 16.4m^{2} 17.2m* 16m 17.2m* 17.1m 18m^{4} 16.5m Nov 4] big, strong, lengthy gelding: improved over hurdles in 1994/5 (and won over fences in November): still a fair handicapper on flat: won at Bath in May and June: good staying-on fourth of 21 in Cesarewitch: will stay extreme distances: probably acts on any going: held up. *J. S. King* 68

INCHKEITH 3 b.f. Reference Point 139 – Inchmurrin 114 (Lomond (USA) 128) [1994 NR 1995 a7g a8g^{2} a9.4g* 12d a10g^{4} 12g^{3} 10.1g^{2} 10.2m* 9.9g^{3} Jul 17] smallish filly: poor mover: third foal: half-sister to fairly useful 7f and 1m winner Ingozi (by Warning) and smart 6f and 7f winner Inchinor (by Ahonoora): dam 5f (at 2 yrs) and 1m winner: fair performer: won Wolverhampton maiden in February and handicap at Chepstow in July: stays 1½m well: acts on all-weather and good to firm ground: races prominently: consistent: sold 17,000 gns Newmarket December Sales. *G. Wragg* 72

INCHRORY 2 b.c. (Feb 1) Midyan (USA) 124 – Applecross 117 (Glint of Gold 128) [1995 6g^{5} 6.1m^{3} 7.5g* 7m^{5} 8.1d* 8.1d* Oct 11] smallish, workmanlike colt: second foal: half-brother to 3-y-o 1m winner Pennycairn (by Last Tycoon): dam, 1¼m to 13.3f winner, second in Park Hill: useful colt: won maiden at Beverley in July, and minor events at Sandown (beat Even Top 1¾ lengths) and Haydock (comfortably, giving upwards of 10 lb away) in the autumn: will stay beyond 1m: best form on an easy surface: bandaged near-hind at Beverley: reportedly sent to Norway. *H. R. A. Cecil* 104

INCHYRE 2 b.f. (Feb 4) Shirley Heights 130 – Inchmurrin 114 (Lomond (USA) 128) [1995 7m^{6} 8.1d^{2} Sep 12] angular, rather sparely-made filly: fourth foal: closely related to 3-y-o 9.4f and 10.2f winner Inchkeith (by Reference Point) and half-sister to fairly useful 7f and 1m winner Ingozi (by Warning) and smart 6f and 7f winner Inchinor (by Ahonoora): dam, 5f (at 2 yrs) and 1m winner, half-sister to very useful 1989 2-y-o Welney: odds on, tended to hang final 2f when 2 lengths second to comfortable winner Scarlet Plume in maiden event at Sandown: equipped with rope halter on debut: will stay middle distances. *R. Charlton* 81

INDEFENCE (IRE) 4 b.g. Conquering Hero (USA) 116 – Cathryn's Song (Prince Tenderfoot (USA) 126) [1994 NR 1995 9g 7m 7g^{5} 9g^{3} 8m^{6} 8m^{5} 8f^{3} Jun 29] angular gelding: shows knee action: only modest nowadays: well below form last 3 outings, folding tamely final one: joined Mrs J. Pitman and gelded: stays 9f: acts on firm ground and all-weather surfaces, below best (sweating) on dead: visored last 2 starts. *M. R. Channon* 65 d

INDERAPUTERI 5 b.m. Bold Fort 100 – Hello Cuddles 99 (He Loves Me 120) [1994 65: 8m a8g^{4} 8g^{3} 8.1g 8m* 7g 8.5m a8g 8g 7d 1995 10m 7f 8f* 8.1m^{4} 8f* 7.1m Aug 30] smallish, angular mare: unimpressive mover: fair handicapper: reportedly covered by Shareef Dancer in May after second start: won at Brighton in July (apprentices) and August: stays 1m: acts on firm ground, dead and equitrack: often bandaged: tried visored/blinkered, no improvement: apprentice ridden last 4 starts: normally held up. *Miss Gay Kelleway* 67

INDESCENT BLUE 3 b.f. Bluebird (USA) 125 – Miss Display 47 (Touch Paper 113) [1994 NR 1995 7m 8m^{4} 8.3m 8.3m 8.2m a9.4g a8g 8.5s Sep 19] 5,000Y, 16,000 2-y-o: strong filly: fourth foal: half-sister to fair 5f and 6f winner Ned's Bonanza (by 63 d

Green Ruby): dam, maiden, best at 5f: modest and inconsistent maiden: sold 1,600 gns Doncaster October Sales. *D. W. P. Arbuthnot*

INDHAR 4 b.c. Warning 136 – Clarista (USA) 67 (Riva Ridge (USA)) [1994 103: 8s^4 8f 8v^6 1995 7.3g^2 7f* 10m 8g 8g 6m^3 Oct 14] leggy, useful-looking colt: unimpressive mover: useful performer: short-head winner of minor event at Doncaster in July: back-to-form third of 12 to Royale Figurine in listed race at Newmarket final start, never able to land a blow: finds 6f a bare minimum, and should stay 1m: best efforts on a sound surface: sent to USA. *J. E. Banks* — 104

INDIAHRA 4 b.f. Indian Ridge 123 – Mavahra 93 (Mummy's Pet 125) [1994 60: 7m 5.9f^4 6f 5m^3 5.1g 6g 6d 6g^6 7s 1995 7.6m 6f^5 6m 6m a7g^4 a7g^3 a8.5g 7f 6m 6d 6.1d 5.1d^2 5f 6f a6g^2 a6g Nov 27] leggy filly: modest handicapper: stays 7f: acts on fibresand, very best efforts with some give: tried visored, no improvement. *R. Hollinshead* — 52

INDIAN BLUFF 2 b.c. (Apr 11) Indian Ridge 123 – Hannie Caulder (Workboy 123) [1995 5m^6 May 6] 18,000F, IR 26,000Y: tall colt: has scope: half-brother to 1¾m winner Trecauldah (by Treboro) and 5f winner Sister Hannah (by Monseigneur): dam unraced half-sister to 1000 Guineas winner Mrs McArdy: heavily-backed favourite, refused to settle and hung right from 2f out when last of 6 in maiden at Newmarket: sold (C. Williams to R. Harris) 2,700 gns Newmarket Autumn Sales. *C. N. Williams* — –

INDIAN COLOURS 4 b.g. Indian Forest (USA) 117 – Running Rainbow 56 (Runnett 125) [1994 NR 1995 10m^5 a7g Aug 11] third live foal: dam placed over 5f at 2 yrs: well beaten in seller and claimer. *J. Norton* — –

INDIAN CRYSTAL 4 gr.f. Petong 126 – Gentle Gypsy 94 (Junius (USA) 124) [1994 49§, a51§: 6g 5f 5d^3 5m 6f^5 a5g* 5f^3 a5g 5m^2 5g^5 5f 7g 5g^6 a5g 1995 5f^5 5.9f 6f a5g 5f^3 5m 5h^6 5f Aug 25] leggy, shallow-girthed filly: good mover: only poor form at best in 1995: best at 5f: acts on firm ground, dead, and fibresand: often blinkered or visored: sometimes slowly away: inconsistent and sometimes looks none too keen. *Mrs M. Reveley* — 35 § a– §

INDIAN FIRE 5 ch.g. Indian Forest (USA) 117 – Saintly Game (Welsh Saint 126) [1994 NR 1995 a10g a8.5g a8g 8.3m 6f May 11] little sign of ability: sold 800 gns Ascot November Sales. *K. O. Cunningham-Brown* — –

INDIAN FLY 4 b.c. Indian Ridge 123 – Tinas Image (He Loves Me 120) [1994 98: 6m* 7v 8m 7.1m^4 8m^2 7.1g* 7f^2 8d* 7g^4 7d^4 8s^2 7g^5 1995 8g 8g 7m^6 8m^3 8f^6 7.9m^2 7m^2 7g* 6m^6 8m^4 Oct 28] tall, leggy colt: good walker: useful handicapper: third in Royal Hunt Cup at Royal Ascot: won rated stakes at Goodwood in September: creditable efforts sixth of 12 to Royale Figurine then fourth of 7 (badly bumped over 1f out) to Celestial Key in listed races at Newmarket in October: effective at 6f to 1m: acts on firm and soft ground, tailed off on heavy: normally held up: tough and most consistent. *R. Hannon* — 104

INDIAN JOCKEY 3 b.g. Indian Ridge 123 – Number Eleven 69 (Local Suitor (USA) 128) [1994 54?: 6m 6g 5s 1995 10m* 10.3g* 10.2m^4 10.5m^3 10f 7.1g Sep 23] smallish, leggy gelding: won handicaps at Nottingham (sweating, seller, sold out of P. McBride's stable 7,500 gns) in May and Chester in June: below form afterwards: stays 10.3f: acts on good to firm ground: tends to pull hard: tongue tied down final start. *M. C. Pipe* — 69

INDIAN LAMENT 4 b.f. Indian Ridge 123 – Miss Swansong 61 (Young Generation 129) [1994 –§: 8s 6m 1995 5g 7.1m^5 7g^5 8m Aug 31] rather leggy filly: one to avoid. *R. J. Hodges* — – §

INDIAN LIGHT 3 ch.c. Be My Chief (USA) 122 – Beacon (High Top 131) [1994 86p: 6m^2 7g* 8.1g* 1995 9m^4 12g 11.9m^2 12f^6 10.3g^3 12d Oct 21] strong, useful-looking colt: has scope: useful performer: tenth in Prix du Jockey-Club at Chantilly: best efforts when 1¼ lengths second of 4 to Don Corleone in listed race at Haydock then 8 lengths last of 6 to Presenting in Gordon Stakes at Goodwood: well beaten in minor event (blinkered, very quietly to post) at Doncaster and St Simon Stakes (looking extremely well, tailed off) at Newbury afterwards: stays 1½m: acts on firm going, possibly not on a soft surface: sold 50,000 gns Newmarket Autumn Sales to Saudi Arabia. *J. L. Dunlop* — 105

INDIAN NECTAR 2 b.f. (Apr 1) Indian Ridge 123 – Sheer Nectar 72 (Piaffer (USA) 113) [1995 7d^6 Sep 27] sparely-made filly: third live foal: dam miler on flat and fair hurdler: 33/1 and better for race, over 10 lengths sixth of 12 to Final Stab in maiden at Salisbury, keeping on steadily final 2f: likely to do better. *G. B. Balding* – p

INDIAN RELATIVE 2 b.f. (Apr 10) Distant Relative 128 – Elegant Tern (USA) 102 (Sea Bird II 145) [1995 6g^5 7m^2 a6g^2 Oct 28] 8,000Y: smallish filly: closely related to fairly useful performer at around 1m Roseate Lodge (by Habitat) and half sister to several winners, including smart 7f (at 2 yrs) to 1¼m winner Elegant Air (by Shirley Heights) and smart 10.2f and 13.4f winner Nemesia (by Mill Reef): dam won 3 times at around 1m and stayed 1½m: fair form in maidens: will stay 1m. *R. Guest* 77

INDIAN RHAPSODY 3 b.f. Rock City 120 – Indian Love Song 68 (Be My Guest (USA) 126) [1994 58: 6g 1995 7g 6s 8.1g^4 8f* 8g^2 8.1d^4 8d* 8f^5 9.9m^6 8f^5 10m^3 7m* 7g Sep 16] unfurnished filly: modest handicapper: won at Carlisle (only time visored) in May, Yarmouth (fourth-last start for M. Channon) in June and Newmarket (seller, sold out of M. Johnston's stable 6,500 gns) in August: effective at 7f to 1¼m: acts on firm and dead ground. *A. Bailey* 56

INDIAN SERENADE 4 ch.c. Mansingh (USA) 120 – La Melodie 77 (Silly Season 127) [1994 50: 6g 8f^6 7m a7g^5 a6g^2 a6g^3 1995 a7g^3 a6g^4 a7g^2 a7g^2 a8g* a8g a7g^2 a8g a8g^2 8g 8.2m^2 Jun 12] tall colt: modest handicapper: won at Lingfield (amateurs) in March: stays 8.2f: acts on good to firm ground and goes well on all-weather surfaces: sold 2,800 gns Ascot November Sales. *P. W. Harris* 52 a60

INDIAN SPICE 3 b.f. Indian Ridge 123 – Moonlight Serenade 66 (Crooner 119) [1994 52: 5f^6 5.7f 1995 8d Sep 15] modest form on debut: soundly beaten in maiden at Newbury only start in 1995. *D. J. G. Murray Smith* –

INDIAN SUNSET 2 ch.c. (Apr 11) Indian Ridge 123 – Alanood 85 (Northfields (USA)) [1995 7m 6d Sep 16] 30,000F, 36,000Y: compact, good-bodied colt: ninth foal: half-brother to numerous winners, including 3-y-o 6f (at 2 yrs) to 9.2f winner Three Arch Bridge (by Sayf El Arab) and Norsk Oaks winner Alhayat (by Godswalk): dam 1½m winner: backward, well beaten in maidens at Leicester and Newbury (poorly drawn). *C. R. Egerton* –

INDIAN TEMPLE 4 ch.g. Minster Son 130 – Indian Flower 87 (Mansingh (USA) 120) [1994 –: 8.3f 12s 1995 8m^6 7m 8m 10f 10.8m Jul 7] big, good-topped gelding: no form since 2 yrs: visored final 3-y-o start. *M. S. Saunders* –

INDIAN TREASURE (IRE) 3 b.f. Treasure Kay 114 – Arminiya (Roan Rocket 128) [1994 NR 1995 8.3m 8.3m 8g a14g Nov 16] IR 5,600Y: workmanlike filly: sister to winning sprinter Charity Express and half-sister to several winners, including fair 1984 2-y-o 6f winner Armorad (by Red Alert): dam French 10.5f winner: no sign of ability. *D. J. S. Cosgrove* –

INDICATOR 3 b.g. Reference Point 139 – Comic Talent 105 (Pharly (FR) 130) [1994 NR 1995 10g^6 12.1g 9f^3 Jun 23] good-bodied gelding: second foal: dam 7f to 9f winner: best effort in maidens when 6½ lengths third of 10 at Goodwood final start, headed over 2f out: sold (R. Hannon to J. J. Quinn) 16,500 gns Newmarket July Sales. *R. Hannon* 70

INDIGO TIME (IRE) 3 b.c. Ela-Mana-Mou 132 – Majestic's Gold (Rheingold 137) [1994 79p: 7m 8.1g* 1995 10g^6 12s* 12m Nov 4] tall, rather unfurnished colt: off course nearly a year before reappearance: won handicap at Ascot in October, always travelling well and quickening clear from over 1f out: well beaten in November Handicap at Doncaster: probably better at 1½m than shorter: acts well on soft ground, possibly not on good to firm: effective from front or held up: looked a useful prospect at Ascot: sent to Dubai. *P. F. I. Cole* 93 +

INDIRA 2 b.f. (Mar 12) Indian Ridge 123 – Princess Rosananti (IRE) (Shareef Dancer (USA) 135) [1995 5.7h^5 6m 6s 7.3d Oct 21] 5,500Y, 9,200 2-y-o: smallish filly: second foal: half-sister to 3-y-o 12.4f seller winner Khan (by Be My Chief): dam unraced daughter of Italian 1000 Guineas winner and Irish Oaks third Rosananti: poor form in maiden events: stiff task in nursery at Newbury final outing: bred to stay beyond 6f. *H. Candy* 49

INDISCRETION (IRE) 3 b.f. Kris 135 – Foolish Dame (USA) (Foolish Pleasure (USA)) [1994 NR 1995 12g Apr 21] 17,000F: big, rangy filly: has a round action: second foal: dam, French 1½m winner, is half-sister to Poule d'Essai des –

Poulains winner Red Lord: 6/1 and bit backward, tailed-off last of 8 in maiden at Thirsk, racing freely until weakening over 2f out. *Mrs J. Cecil*

INDONESIAN (IRE) 3 b. or br.g. Alzao (USA) 117 – Miss Garuda 94 (Persian Bold 123) [1994 73p: 6f 6m^3 6m^2 1995 10m* 10g 10f 12m^4 10g^5 12g 10g 10.4m Oct 4] compact colt: unimpressive mover: fairly useful handicapper at his best: won at Newmarket in April: visored, below form last 3 starts: stays 1½m: acts on good to firm going (yet to race on a soft surface): sold (M. Bell to C. Brooks) 15,000 gns Newmarket Autumn Sales. *M. Bell* — 87 d

INDRAPURA (IRE) 3 b.g. Gallic League 119 – Stella Ann (Ahonoora 122) [1994 72: 6.1s^6 7m 7.1s^6 5s^5 1995 a8g* 7f^3 7g 7g a7g Dec 15] tall, rather leggy gelding: good mover with a long stride: fair performer: won median auction maiden at Lingfield in March, making all: no blinkers, well beaten last 3 starts: stays 1m: acts on firm ground and on equitrack: blinkered first 2 starts at 3 yrs: races prominently. *P. F. I. Cole* — 64 a67

INFAMOUS (USA) 2 ch.c. (Feb 20) Diesis 133 – Name And Fame (USA) (Arts And Letters) [1995 7g^6 Oct 3] IR 100,000Y: angular colt: half-brother to several winners in USA: dam, winner of 3 races in USA, half-sister to dam of Oh So Sharp and Roussalka: 14/1 and bit backward, over 8 lengths sixth of 17 to Ali-Royal in maiden at Warwick, keeping on without threatening: will improve. *P. F. I. Cole* — 68 p

INFANTRY DANCER 2 ch.f. (Apr 29) Infantry 122 – Electropet (Remainder Man 126§) [1995 7g^5 7g^5 7f^5 Aug 2] 450Y: second foal: sister to a winner in Germany: dam 10.1f winner: modest in maiden auctions: will be suited by further than 7f. *G. C. Bravery* — 55

INFANTRY GLEN 5 gr.g. Infantry 122 – Rage Glen 67 (Grey Mirage 128) [1994 45: a8.5g^6 a11g 9.2d^6 7m^3 1995 7d a8g Apr 26] angular gelding: poor performer: well beaten in 1995. *P. D. Cundell* — –

INFLUENCE PEDLER 2 b.g. (Feb 20) Keen 116 – La Vie En Primrose 104 (Henbit (USA) 130) [1995 7.1g 7g^6 10m 8.2m 8f a8g Nov 20] sturdy gelding: poor mover: third foal: dam 1¼m winner: modest form in varied company: stays 1m: tailed off on fibresand: sometimes sweating: trained by G. Rimmer on debut: sold 7,200 gns Newmarket Autumn Sales. *C. E. Brittain* — 53

IN GOOD FAITH 3 b.g. Beveled (USA) – Dulcidene 71 (Behistoun 131) [1994 83p: 5g 5m* 5m^3 6m 7.5f^3 7m 8s* 7.9d* 6g 1995 8m 7.9g 8.1g 11.9g 11.9s Oct 1] neat gelding: shows knee action: fairly useful performer at 2 yrs: disappointing in handicaps in 1995: may yet prove effective over middle distances: best efforts on an easy surface. *J. J. Quinn* — –

INHERENT MAGIC (IRE) 6 ch.m. Magical Wonder (USA) 125 – Flo Kelly (Florescence 120) [1994 95: 6g^2 5f^2 5m 5g^6 5g 5.2s^2 6m^4 5s* 5d a6g^2 1995 5m^6 5.6m 5g 5s* 5s a6g^5 a5g^2 Dec 14] smallish, angular mare: fairly useful performer: sold out of M. McCormack's stable 11,000 gns Doncaster March Sales before reappearance: won minor event at Haydock in September: stays 6f: acts on any going, including all-weather surfaces: bandaged: suited by strongly-run race. *W. R. Muir* — 95

IN LOVE AGAIN (IRE) 3 b.f. Prince Rupert (FR) 121 – Beloved Mistress 84 (Rarity 129) [1994 86: 5v^6 5g^2 5.1m^3 5g* 5m^3 5g^4 5m* 5m 5.3f^4 5f^4 5g* 6d^5 5.2s* 5g^5 5s^6 5g 1995 5m^6 5f 6m 5.1f^6 Jul 19] good-topped filly: good walker and mover: fairly useful performer at 2 yrs: not disgraced in handicap at Windsor on reappearance, but soundly beaten in similar events all 3 subsequent starts: stays 6f: has won on top-of-the-ground, but clearly best effort on soft. *M. R. Channon* — 76 d

INN AT THE TOP 3 b.g. Top Ville 129 – Woolpack (Golden Fleece (USA) 133) [1994 59: 8.2d a8g^6 a8g^2 1995 a8g^2 a8g^6 a10g^2 12g^5 14.1m^2 a14g 16m^2 16d^6 14g^5 Sep 23] tall gelding: modest maiden handicapper: sold out of M. Johnston's stable 19,500 gns Doncaster February Sales after third start: stays 2m: acts on good to firm ground (probably on dead) and the all-weather: visored (never going well) sixth 3-y-o start. *J. Norton* — 63

INNER CIRCLE (USA) 2 ch.f. (Feb 6) El Gran Senor (USA) 136 – Conquistress (USA) (Conquistador Cielo (USA)) [1995 6f^3 Oct 18] leggy filly: first reported foal: dam, won at up to 7f in USA, half-sister to smart French 7f/1m performer African Joy: favourite, over 4 lengths third of 5 behind Tamhid in minor — 76 p event at Yarmouth, chasing leaders over 4f: will stay 1m: will improve and should be able to win a small race. *P. W. Chapple-Hyam*

INNOCENCE 3 b.f. Unfuwain (USA) 131 – Youthful (FR) (Green Dancer (USA) 132) [1994 73: 6s^2 a6g 1995 10m 12g^6 11.9m^2 14.1g^3 11.5m^2 11.9g Sep 20] leggy filly: fair maiden handicapper: stays 1½m: acts on good to firm ground and soft. *G. Wragg* 67

INOVAR 5 b.g. Midyan (USA) 124 – Princess Cinders 61 (King of Spain 121) [1994 –: 10.4d 1995 a7g 10.1d^3 Jun 15] big, workmanlike gelding: bad maiden: stays 1¼m: acts on dead ground, probably on good to firm: edgy type. *C. B. B. Booth* 26

IN PARADISUM (USA) 2 b.g. (May 11) Opening Verse (USA) 122 – Nice Noble (USA) (Vaguely Noble 140) [1995 5m 7g 7m^6 8m* 8g^5 7.9m^6 Oct 5] 11,000Y: strong, quite attractive gelding: half-brother to several winners abroad, including French 15f winner Queen Picea (by Big Spruce): dam won at 5f and 7.5f in Italy: won selling nursery at Leicester in September by 1¾ lengths: creditable efforts afterwards in non-selling nurseries: stays 1m: sweating and took keen hold in visor second start: carried head high last time: sent to Macau. *Mrs J. R. Ramsden* 56 +

INQUISITOR (USA) 3 b.c. Alleged (USA) 138 – Imperturbable Lady (CAN) (Northern Dancer) [1994 85p: 8m 8g^2 8d^2 1995 10.3g* 12f 10g^6 11.9d* 12d^5 Sep 24] strong, good sort: impresses in appearance: has a powerful, round action: useful handicapper: impressive winner of 18-runner race at Doncaster (gambled on, off course 3 months afterwards) in March and rated stakes at Haydock (cruised to front 3f out, always in command thereafter) in September: creditable fifth of 18 in valuable event at Ascot on final outing: best form at around 1½m, but likely to prove at least as effective back at 1¼m: acts on dead ground, possibly unsuited by firm: has been bandaged: effective from front or held up: game. *J. H. M. Gosden* 109

INSATIABLE (IRE) 2 b.c. (Apr 15) Don't Forget Me 127 – Petit Eclair 94 (Major Portion 129) [1995 7g^5 7d* Sep 27] 25,000Y: half-brother to several winners in Ireland/Italy, including 9f/1¼m performer Annsfield Lady (by Red Sunset), dam of 3-y-o Pipe Major: dam 7f (at 2 yrs) and 10.8f winner: odds on, smooth 4-length winner over Diamond Beach in maiden at Newcastle, probably value for another 3 lengths: will stay 1m: sure to improve again. *M. R. Stoute* 93 p

INSIDEOUT 2 b.c. (Mar 8) Macmillion 110 – Parijoun (Manado 130) [1995 6m Oct 30] 1,550F: good-bodied colt: has scope: half-brother to 7f winner Caspian Gold (by Clantime): dam of little account: 50/1, slowly away and always behind in maiden at Newcastle. *F. Watson* –

INSIDER TRADER 4 b.g. Dowsing (USA) 124 – Careless Whisper 94 (Homing 130) [1994 82: a5g^2 5.1g 5d* 5f^2 5m^3 5.1g* 5g^6 5f^3 5m* 5m^4 5m 5m 5g* 1995 5.1m 5g 5g 5f^5 6m 5.1m 5m^2 5m^6 5d 5m^6 5f* 5m a5g Nov 16] lengthy, workmanlike gelding: poor walker and mover: fairly useful 5f handicapper: trained until after fourth 4-y-o start by R. Williams: won at Catterick in October for second year running: acts on firm and soft going and on fibresand: blinkered/visored since sixth 3-y-o outing: usually bandaged in front: usually races prominently: sold (R. Guest to Mrs J. Ramsden) 11,000 gns Doncaster November Sales. *R. Guest* 82

INSIYABI (USA) 2 b.c. (Jan 15) Mr Prospector (USA) – Ashayer (USA) 118 (Lomond (USA) 128) [1995 6s^3 7m^5 Oct 20] tall, good sort: has plenty of scope: third foal: half-brother to 3-y-o Aqaarid, second in 1000 Guineas (should have been suited by middle distances), and 1¼m and 1½m winner Muwafik (both by Nashwan): dam won from 6f (at 2 yrs) to 1¼m, including in Prix Marcel Boussac, from very good family: stayed on well when third to Midnight Blue in maiden at Ascot and when 4 lengths fifth of 21 to Germano in similar event at Doncaster: will be suited by at least 1m: had rope halter and blanket for stalls entry after refusing to enter them on intended debut: will improve again. *J. L. Dunlop* 81 p

INSPIRATION POINT 4 ch.f. Indian Ridge 123 – Low Line 66 (High Line 125) [1994 62: 7d^2 7g 7g^3 7m^2 7g 7v a7g a12g 1995 a8g^6 Feb 4] small, light-framed filly: modest maiden at best: lost her form in 1994, and well beaten only 4-y-o start. *Miss B. Sanders* –

INSTANTANEOUS 3 b.f. Rock City 120 – Mainmast 63 (Bustino 136) [1994 60: 5f 5m 7m^6 a7g* 1995 9.9m 10m^5 12m^3 14.1f^3 12m^2 12m* a12g* 14.1m^3 12g^6 a12g^5 12m^4 10.5d a11g^2 a12g Nov 13] leggy, sparely-made filly: good mover: 52 a60

modest handicapper: won at Thirsk and Wolverhampton (by 7 lengths) in the summer: effective at 11f to 1¾m: acts on firm ground and goes well on fibresand: consistent. *M. H. Easterby*

INSTANT SUCCESS (USA) 3 ch.f. Secreto (USA) 128 – Oath of Allegiance (USA) (Olden Times) [1994 58: 6m^5 7g^5 6g a5g^6 a8g 1995 a7g^5 Apr 4] smallish filly: has not repeated form shown on debut: tried blinkered. *W. A. O'Gorman* –

INTENDANT 3 b.g. Distant Relative 128 – Bunduq 67 (Scottish Rifle 127) [1994 54, a67: 6m a7g^2 a7g^3 7.9d 8s 8.1g^6 1995 8.3g^6 8m^3 8m* 8g^4 8.5g 10d 9f a7g^6 Dec 15] sturdy, lengthy gelding: modest performer: won claimer at Ripon in May: stays 1m: acts on good to firm ground and fibresand, no form on a soft surface. *J. G. FitzGerald* 59 a–

INTENTION (USA) 5 b.g. Shahrastani (USA) 135 – Mimi Baker (USA) (What Luck (USA)) [1994 63, a67: 12v^2 a16g^2 14.9d a16g^2 a14.8g^5 a14g^3 1995 a13g^4 a16g^3 a16g^4 a13g Feb 11] big, good-topped gelding: modest maiden: disappointing in 1995: stays 2m: acts on heavy ground and all-weather surfaces: tried visored: has joined P. Hedger. *I. Campbell* – a53

IN THE BAND 2 b.f. (May 3) Sharrood (USA) 124 – Upper Caen (High Top 131) [1995 8m Nov 4] 8,000Y: fifth live foal: sister to 3-y-o Upper Torrish and useful 1991 German 2-y-o Kilphedir and half-sister to 6f to 8.3f winner Arndilly (by Robellino): dam unraced sister to very useful miler Miner's Lamp: 20/1, around 8 lengths eighth of 23 to Shaamit in median auction maiden at Doncaster, held up after slow start then keeping on well: likely to improve. *Lord Huntingdon* 64 p

IN THE MONEY (IRE) 6 b.h. Top Ville 129 – Rensaler (USA) (Stop The Music (USA)) [1994 69§, a64§: 12g^2 12g 11.9m* 12m 11.9m 12m 12f^5 11.9m 12f 12g 10s^3 12.4d^3 a11g a12g^2 a13g^5 1995 a12g^2 a13g^3 a12g^2 a12g^4 a12g^3 a12g* a12g^4 12g 11.8d 12g a12g 12.3m a12g Dec 18] leggy horse: modest handicapper: won at Wolverhampton in March: stays 1½m: acts on good to firm and soft ground and the all-weather: inconsistent. *R. Hollinshead* 62 §

IN THE ZIM 3 b.f. Mtoto 134 – Monashee (USA) (Sovereign Dancer (USA)) [1994 NR 1995 7m^5 10m^6 Jun 30] 2,600Y, 7,200 2-y-o: lengthy filly: poor mover: first foal: dam unraced granddaughter of top 1964 American 2-y-o filly Queen Empress: modest form in median auction maiden at Newbury (slowly away and green) and claimer at Newmarket, both in June: should stay 1¼m: apprentice ridden both starts. *R. Hannon* 52

INTIAASH (IRE) 3 br.f. Shaadi (USA) 126 – Funun (USA) 84 (Fappiano (USA)) [1994 73p: 6g 7s^5 1995 6m^2 6m^5 6g^3 6g^4 5m^4 6d^4 5.2g^2 6f* 6.1s Oct 17] tall, lengthy, angular filly: fair performer: followed a number of creditable efforts by winning maiden at Redcar (hung left) in October: stays 6f: acts on firm and soft ground: visored (far from disgraced over 5f) fifth 3-y-o outing: consistent: sold only 2,800 gns Newmarket Autumn Sales. *P. T. Walwyn* 73

INTIDAB (USA) 2 b.c. (Mar 20) Phone Trick (USA) – Alqwani (USA) 83 (Mr Prospector (USA)) [1995 6m^4 7g^3 Aug 30] close-coupled colt: first foal: dam, 2-y-o 6f winner, out of half-sister to Bellotto: off course 10 weeks, better effort in maidens at York when staying-on third (beaten about ½ length) of 9 to Red Robbo: will stay 1m: sure to improve again and win a race. *J. H. M. Gosden* 90 p

INTISAB 2 b.f. (Apr 30) Green Desert (USA) 127 – Ardassine (Ahonoora 122) [1995 5m May 29] compact filly: seventh foal: sister to smart 7f and 1m winner Gabr and half-sister to useful 3-y-o 1¼m winner Kutta (by Old Vic) and 1991 2-y-o 6f winner Enaya (by Caerleon): dam 1½m winner from family of Slip Anchor: 8/1 and bit backward, always behind, not knocked about, in maiden at Sandown: threw jockey twice in paddock: looked sure to do better. *R. W. Armstrong* –

INTREPID FORT 6 br.g. Belfort (FR) 89 – Dauntless Flight (Golden Mallard 103) [1994 29: 8f 7.5m 10m^2 9g 1995 a8g^4 a8g 8f^6 10m Jul 11] workmanlike gelding: poor maiden handicapper: stays 1¼m: acts on good to firm ground and fibresand: usually blinkered/visored. *B. W. Murray* 29

INTRODUCING 2 b.f. (Mar 1) Mtoto 134 – D'Azy 91 (Persian Bold 123) [1995 8.1m^2 7g^2 8f^3 Oct 25] smallish, sparely-made filly: has a fluent action: third foal: sister to very smart middle-distance 3-y-o Presenting and half-sister to 1992 2-y-o 7f winner Azilian (by Top Ville): dam, 2-y-o 7f winner, half-sister to smart middle- 78 +

distance performer Sirk: fair form in maidens won by Pricket at Sandown, Oleana at Leicester and Bright Water at Yarmouth: fitted with rope halter and on last 2 starts blanketed for stalls entry (reluctant to enter them at Leicester after unseating rider and getting loose): will stay middle distances. *J. H. M. Gosden*

INVERLOCHY 2 gr.c. (Feb 20) Petong 126 – Real Princess 78 (Aragon 118) 76
[1995 6m^6 6d^4 6m^3 Oct 13] rangy colt: unimpressive mover: third foal: dam 7f winner out of very speedy 2-y-o Mange Tout: off course 4 months and blinkered, improved form when 4 lengths third of 21 to Projection in maiden at Newmarket: will stay 7f: sold 23,000 gns Newmarket Autumn Sales: sent to USA. *J. L. Dunlop*

INVEST WISELY 3 ch.g. Dashing Blade 117 – Saniette (Crystal Palace (FR) 89
132) [1994 NR 1995 8d 10m^3 9.9m^5 13.3g^5 13.3f^4 14.1g* 14.1m* 14.1m* 18.2g* Sep 14] leggy, unfurnished gelding: sixth foal: half-brother to 4 winners, none better than modest: dam ran once in France: made into a fairly useful handicapper, winning 3 times at Yarmouth and once at Redcar in second half of year, all in smallish fields: effective at 1¾m and stays 2¼m: acts on firm ground: game and genuine. *J. M. P. Eustace*

INVIGILATE 6 ch.g. Viking (USA) – Maria Da Gloria (St Chad 120) [1994 57: 58
6f^4 6d^5 6m 5.9m^4 5m^3 5m^6 5m^3 6g^6 6m* 6m* 6s^2 1995 6m 6m 6f 6f^5 5m^2 5h 5f^2 6g 5.1d 6.1d Sep 19] workmanlike gelding: unimpressive mover: modest handicapper: effective at 5f to 7f: acts on firm and soft going and the all-weather: effective visored (wasn't tried in 1995) or not. *Martyn Wane*

INVIGORATING 2 ch.f. (Feb 14) Polar Falcon (USA) 126 – Vitality 98 (Young 66
Generation 129) [1995 5.7m^2 5m^6 6f^4 7.5d^3 8g 8g Nov 7] workmanlike filly: has a long stride: first foal: dam, 6f winner at 2 yrs, stayed 9f, out of sister to 1000 Guineas and Prix de Diane winner Highclere, dam of excellent broodmare Height of Fashion: modest form here in maidens for R. Hannon first 3 starts: midfield in claimer at Evry final start: stays 7.5f. *Mme M. Bollack-Badel, France*

INVOCATION 8 ch.g. Kris 135 – Royal Saint (USA) (Crimson Satan) [1994 69, 69
a80d: a8g^2 a10g^3 a8g^6 a7g a6g^6 a6g^6 7v^5 7s^2 6m* 6m^2 a7g^5 7f^5 7m 6g^3 a8g^3 a6g^4 a71
1995 a7g^3 a7g a7g^6 a6g^4 a6g* a6g^5 6g^2 6m 6m 6f^6 6m 5.3g^6 6g a8g a7g^4 a7g^4 a7g^4 a7g Dec 15] big, strong gelding: bad mover: fair handicapper: won at Lingfield in March: effective at 6f to 1m: acts on equitrack and on good to firm and soft ground: often bandaged: blinkered/visored once each: often a front runner: tough. *A. Moore*

INZAR 4 b.g. Warning 136 – Star Face (African Sky 124) [1994 –: a10g 1995 –
a12g^6 Jan 14] smallish, lengthy gelding: modest maiden: tried blinkered: dead. *Pat Mitchell*

INZAR (USA) 3 b.c. Warning 136 – Czar's Bride (USA) 78 (Northern Dancer) 112
[1994 96p: 5.3d* 6s^4 6d* 1995 7m^5 7.3m* 7.1g^4 7m^4 6m^2 6g^2 6m 6m^2 7m* 7g* 7d* 7m^3 Oct 15] quite attractive colt: smart performer: won minor events at Newbury and Goodwood (2) before Charlton Hunt Supreme Stakes (set steady pace, beat Mutakddim a short head) at Goodwood: good third of 10 to Poplar Bluff in Prix de la Foret at Longchamp on final start: effective at 6f, and should stay 1m: acts on good to firm ground and soft: blinkered (ran creditably in Stewards' Cup) seventh start: tough and most consistent. *P. F. I. Cole*

IONIO (USA) 4 ch.c. Silver Hawk (USA) 123 – Private View (USA) 113 (Mr 113
Prospector (USA)) [1994 117: 10m^6 12m 12g^6 12m* 11.9m^2 14.6g^5 1995 a10g* 11d^6 10m^3 10m^2 12f^6 10m^6 10g^3 12f^2 12g 12g^4 12d 12d Oct 21] close-coupled colt: good mover: smart performer: idling winner of minor event at Lingfield in March: best subsequent efforts when third in 5-runner Gordon Richards Stakes at Sandown and second in 7-runner £27,500 rated stakes at Goodwood on third and eighth outings: well below form last 4 starts: stays 1½m: acts on firm ground, possibly not on a soft surface: below form blinkered/visored: normally tracks leaders, but can make the running. *C. E. Brittain*

IOTA 6 b. or br.m. Niniski (USA) 125 – Iosifa 108 (Top Ville 129) [1994 57, a62: –
a16.2g^3 a14g^4 a14.8g^3 a14.8g* a16s^6 18g 14g 14.1f^2 14g^6 14.6m 14.1m* 14.6g a69
15.9s* 18m 14.1d 1995 a14.8g^2 a14.8g^2 a14.8g^3 a12g Mar 1] smallish, sparely-made mare: fluent mover: fair handicapper: first poor effort in 1995 on final start: suited by test of stamina: acts on any turf ground and on fibresand. *J. L. Harris*

IRCHESTER LASS 3 ch.f. Presidium 124 – Fool's Errand (Milford 119) [1994 49
49: 6.1g 5m 6m^4 6.1g* 6d^6 6m 6g 1995 a8.5g^6 a7g 5m 8.2m^5 7.5m 7m 6f^3 6m^3 6m*

6.1d[6] a6g a6g[2] a7g[2] Dec 2] leggy, unfurnished filly: poor handicapper: led well inside final 1f to win 17-runner contest at Leicester in August: stays 7f: acts on fibresand and firm ground, probably on dead: tried blinkered. *S. R. Bowring*

I RECALL (IRE) 4 b.g. Don't Forget Me 127 – Sable Lake (Thatching 131) [1994 70: 8.3m 8.1s[2] 1995 10g 10m a10g[4] Jul 14] workmanlike gelding: no worthwhile form in 1995: should stay beyond 1m: possibly needs soft ground. *P. Hayward* –

I REMEMBER IT WELL (IRE) 3 ch.f. Don't Forget Me 127 – Star Cream (Star Appeal 133) [1994 –: 7d 7s 7g 1995 8f 14.1h[3] a16g Aug 24] workmanlike filly: worthwhile form only when third of 6 in maiden handicap at Carlisle: stays 1¾m: has joined M. Hourigan in Ireland. *Sir Mark Prescott* 44

IRIDAL 3 ch.g. Rainbow Quest (USA) 134 – Khandjar 77 (Kris 135) [1994 NR 1995 12g[4] 12m[2] 11.5m[3] 12m[2] 12.3m* 12g[6] Sep 16] quite attractive gelding: fifth live foal: half-brother to 4-y-o Knife Boy (by Mtoto) and 14.8f winner Shelegai (by Shernazar): dam 9f winner, is sister to Shavian and half-sister to Paean: fairly useful form: won maiden at Ripon (idled) in August: below form in handicap at Catterick on only subsequent outing: will stay beyond 1½m: yet to race on a soft surface: sold 30,000 gns Newmarket Autumn Sales. *H. R. A. Cecil* 86

IRIE MON (IRE) 3 b.g. Waajib 121 – Achafalaya (USA) (Apalachee (USA) 137) [1994 55: 8g 7g a7g[5] 1995 a8g[2] a8g[2] a7g* 7f 7g 8.1m[3] 8m[3] 8.1m[2] 8g[4] Jul 19] good-bodied gelding: modest performer: won claimer at Lingfield in February: stays 1m well: acts on equitrack and on firm ground: has had tongue tied down: sold (J. Hills to M. Bielby) 2,000 gns Newmarket Autumn Sales and gelded. *J. W. Hills* 59

IRISH ANGEL (IRE) 3 b.f. Cyrano de Bergerac 120 – Sweet Finale (Sallust 134) [1994 47: 6f a5g[5] 5.1m 6g[6] 5m[3] 5d 1995 6g 5m 6m Jul 5] angular filly: poor maiden: no form in 1995, including in blinkers and in selling company: stays 6f: sold 1,800 gns Ascot July Sales. *C. Smith* –

IRISH DOMINION 5 b.g. Dominion 123 – Irish Cookie 80 (Try My Best (USA) 130) [1994 –: a7g a9.4g 1995 8h 6f Aug 17] compact gelding: of little account nowadays: sold 650 gns Ascot November Sales. *A. Barrow* –

IRISH EMERALD 8 b.g. Taufan (USA) 119 – Gaelic Jewel 89 (Scottish Rifle 127) [1994 NR 1995 a10g[4] a10g Mar 16] close-coupled, workmanlike gelding: lightly raced and no form on flat for a long time. *G. C. Bravery* –

IRISH GROOM 8 b.g. Shy Groom (USA) – Romany Pageant (Welsh Pageant 132) [1994 –: a12g[2] a12g[6] a8.5g 1995 10.8f[3] Aug 28] angular gelding: poor handicapper: ran creditably only 8-y-o start: probably stays 1½m: acts on firm ground and fibresand, probably on heavy: often blinkered in the past. *A. Streeter* 40

IRISH KINSMAN 2 b.g. (May 4) Distant Relative 128 – Inesdela (Wolver Hollow 126) [1995 7m a6g Dec 14] rangy gelding: has scope: fifth foal: half-brother to fairly useful Irish 1990 2-y-o 5f and 6f winner Seneca Reef (by Simply Great): dam unraced: well beaten in maidens at Doncaster and Lingfield. *P. T. Walwyn* –

IRISH OASIS (IRE) 2 b.c. (May 12) Mazaad 106 – Alpenwind (Tumble Wind (USA)) [1995 a7g a7g 9g Sep 23] fifth reported foal: dam Irish 9f and 1½m winner: well beaten in seller and maidens. *B. S. Rothwell* –

IRISH SENOR (IRE) 4 ch.g. Al Hareb (USA) 123 – Rivulet (USA) (Irish River (FR) 131) [1994 79d: 10s[6] 10d* 12f[6] 14g[4] 12f 10m 10.1m 10d 1995 12m[3] 12.1m[3] Jun 16] sturdy, close-coupled gelding: modest form at best in 1995: barely stays 1¾m: acts on firm and dead ground: has found little: tried visored (when out of form) at 3 yrs. *J. L. Spearing* 56

IRKUTSK (USA) 4 b.g. Nureyev (USA) 131 – Herb Wine (USA) (Full Pocket (USA)) [1994 72: 7d 10g[3] 10m[6] 1995 10m[4] 12g[2] 12m[4] 8.1m[3] Jul 4] leggy gelding: fair maiden: stays 1½m: acts on good to firm ground: fair hurdler, winner in July. *M. C. Pipe* 68

IRON AND STEEL 2 ch.g. (Feb 18) Dominion 123 – Fairy Fortune 78 (Rainbow Quest (USA) 134) [1995 5g a6g[5] 6f[6] 6m 6.9g Oct 16] 8,600F, 11,000Y: first foal: dam, 7.6f winner, out of useful close relative of smart 1¼m colt Elegant Air: seems of little account: left G. Lewis's stable after second start: visored penultimate outing. *A. Moore* –

IRON GENT (USA) 4 b.g. Greinton 119 – Carrot Top 112 (High Hat 131) [1994 78: 10g^6 10s^6 13.3g^2 14m* 14m^5 1995 14m 15.1m^3 Aug 24] good-bodied gelding: fair handicapper at 3 yrs for J. Dunlop: not disgraced at Salisbury in May: sold out of P. Hobbs' stable 5,400 gns Doncaster May Sales: clear chance on form but last of 3 in claimer at Edinburgh 3½ months later: should stay beyond 1¾m: acts on good to firm and dead ground. *S. E. Kettlewell* –

IRONHEART 2 b.c. (Feb 17) Lycius (USA) 124 – Inshirah (USA) 90 (Caro 133) [1995 7g^4 7g Oct 10] 52,000F: close-coupled colt: fifth foal: half-brother to French 1¼m and 1½m winner Inchbracken (by Mtoto) and a winner in Belgium by Bustino: dam 2-y-o 5f and 7f winner out of half-sister to Grand Criterium winner Femme Elite: over 5 lengths fourth of 16, keeping on, to Alhaarth in maiden at Newmarket: gave impression something amiss in maiden at Leicester 2 months later: should stay 1m. *J. H. M. Gosden* 83

IRONIC (IRE) 3 b.g. Tirol 127 – Allegheny River (USA) (Lear Fan (USA) 130) [1994 NR 1995 7m 8m 8m 8.3m 8g 8g Sep 14] 15,000Y: workmanlike gelding: first foal: dam Irish 7f winner: modest maiden: should stay beyond 1m: has raced only on a sound surface: sold 1,000 gns Newmarket Autumn Sales: sent to Holland. *R. Hannon* 55

IRON MAN (IRE) 3 b.c. Conquering Hero (USA) 116 – Doppio Filo (Vision (USA)) [1994 64: 5f^3 7f^4 6m a6g a7g^4 a7g* a8g 1995 a7g^2 a8g* a7g^2 Feb 8] leggy colt: modest form: won seller at Lingfield (sold out of J. White's stable 5,000 gns) in January: ran well in handicap at Wolverhampton (slowly away) on only outing for new stable: stays 1m well: acts on firm ground and the all-weather: visored/blinkered since fifth 2-y-o start: sent to Barbados. *M. Johnston* 63

IRON N GOLD 3 b.g. Heights of Gold – Southern Dynasty 81 (Gunner B 126) [1994 –: a8g 7g 8g 1995 12d* 11.6m^5 a16g 15.4m^4 14d a13g^2 Dec 19] tall, angular gelding: has a round action: modest handicapper: won at Folkestone in March on first of only 2 starts for S. Dow before returning to 2-y-o trainer: stays 15.4f: acts on good to firm ground and dead. *A. Moore* 53

IRREPRESSIBLE (IRE) 4 b.g. Don't Forget Me 127 – Lady of Shalott 61 (Kings Lake (USA) 133) [1994 –: 7m 7m 6.1f 9.7g 10m 7g 10d 1995 10.8g 12.1d Oct 10] lengthy gelding: no longer of much account. *K. Bishop* –

IRSHAD 3 ch.c. Soviet Star (USA) 128 – Nahilah 78 (Habitat 134) [1994 63p: 7.1d^6 8.1g 1995 10.5g 8.1d Jun 9] strong colt: modest maiden: no form in 1995: stays 1m: sold 6,000 gns Newmarket July Sales. *P. T. Walwyn* –

ISITOFF 2 b.c. (Mar 19) Vague Shot 108 – Plum Blossom (USA) (Gallant Romeo (USA)) [1995 7m Oct 12] 1,400Y: lengthy colt: half-brother to several winners, including fairly useful 1986 2-y-o 5f winner Plum Drop (by Take By Storm) and 4-y-o 5f winner Henry The Hawk (by Doulab): dam never ran: 25/1 and backward, behind in 27-runner seller at Newmarket. *C. A. Dwyer* –

ISLA GLEN 2 b.f. (Apr 12) Be My Chief (USA) 122 – Serration (Kris 135) [1995 5g Apr 26] 13,000Y: quite attractive filly, rather unfurnished: fourth live foal: half-sister to 1992 2-y-o 7.6f and 8.5f winner The Seer (by Robellino): dam fourth at 9f in France: 16/1, seventh of 9 in maiden at Kempton, soon well off strong pace then late progress: looked likely to improve over 6f+. *M. McCormack* –

ISLAND BLADE (IRE) 6 b.g. Sure Blade (USA) 130 – Queen's Eyot 79 (Grundy 137) [1994 66: a16g^3 a13g^5 14.9s 14g^2 16.2m^2 16.4m* 16.1m 16.2g 16.1s^5 14.6d 1995 14m^6 14m^3 May 19] angular gelding: poor mover: modest handicapper: creditable efforts at Newmarket both 6-y-o starts: stays well: below form on very firm going, acts on any other, including equitrack: normally held up: sold 1,600 gns Newmarket July Sales. *R. Akehurst* 61

ISLAND CASCADE 3 b.f. Hadeer 118 – Island Mill 79 (Mill Reef (USA) 141) [1994 NR 1995 8g^6 10m 10m^2 10m 10g^4 10m 14.1m^6 15g 11d^5 13.6f Oct 12] close-coupled filly: fifth foal: half-sister to 1¾m winner Arrastra (by Bustino), French middle-distance winner Demasiado (by Petong) and Italian 7f to 11f winner Sharp Island (by Beveled): dam suited by a test of stamina: poor maiden: should be suited by further than 1¼m. *Don Enrico Incisa* 39

ISLAND VICTORY 2 ch.g. (Mar 6) Ron's Victory (USA) 129 – Island Mead 86 (Pharly (FR) 130) [1995 7m 7f 7f^5 8m 6g Oct 16] 3,500Y: leggy gelding: third foal: –

half-brother to 3-y-o Jobber's Fiddle (by Sizzling Melody), 7f winner at 2 yrs: dam 7f winner: no worthwhile form: visored last 2 starts: sold 3,000 gns Newmarket Autumn Sales: sent to Holland. *I. A. Balding*

ISLAY BROWN (IRE) 2 b.f. (Apr 11) Petorius 117 – Speedy Action (Horage 124) [1995 5g 7g^5 7g^3 7.1g Sep 23] IR 5,500Y: workmanlike filly: fourth foal: half-sister to 8.1f winner Bustle 'Em (by Burslem): dam Irish middle-distance winner: best effort in maidens when third of 5 behind Longing in falsely-run event at Newcastle: well beaten at Haydock month later: stays 7f. *C. W. C. Elsey* — 67 ?

ISM 3 b.g. Petong 126 – Brigado 87 (Brigadier Gerard 144) [1994 61: 6.1s 6g^5 a6g 1995 7g a11g a8g* 8.3g^6 a7g a7g* a6g^3 6d^5 7s Sep 28] good-topped gelding: fair handicapper on the all-weather, modest on turf: won at Southwell in June and July: effective at 6f, and stays 1m: acts on fibresand, has raced only on an easy surface on turf: effective blinkered or not. *Major W. R. Hern* — 56 a73

ISMENO 4 b.g. Ela-Mana-Mou 132 – Seattle Siren (USA) 101 (Seattle Slew (USA)) [1994 76: 10g^4 1995 10s 12g 11.8m 14m 12.5g^2 12f 12g^2 12.1m^3 a16g Nov 8] strong gelding: unimpressive mover: modest handicapper for new stable in 1995: stays 12.5f: front runner: won novice hurdle in December. *S. Dow* — 59

ISSHEREAL (IRE) 3 br.f. Durgam (USA) – Park Vision (Vision (USA)) [1994 NR 1995 8f 10.2h^3 10f^5 10m^6 Aug 14] small filly: first reported foal: dam never ran: no worthwhile form in claimers and maiden: tubed final start. *B. Palling* — –

ISTABRAQ (IRE) 3 b.c. Sadler's Wells (USA) 132 – Betty's Secret (USA) (Secretariat (USA)) [1994 70p: 7s 1995 10g 10.3m 12m^2 14f* 13.9g^2 15g* 16.2d 16d^2 16.5m Nov 4] useful-looking colt: has a markedly round action: fairly useful performer: won maiden at Salisbury in August and handicap at Ayr in September: easily best of last 3 starts when excellent neck second of 11 to En Vacances in handicap at Newbury on penultimate one: suited by good test of stamina: successful on firm ground, but probably ideally suited by an easy surface: bandaged last 4 starts: front runner: stays in training. *J. H. M. Gosden* — 90

ISTIDAAD (USA) 3 b.c. Chief's Crown (USA) – Mazzei Mood (USA) (Roberto (USA) 131) [1994 105p: 7m^2 7m^2 8s^2 1995 10m^2 12m* 10m^2 12f^5 12g^2 12f^3 11.6m* 14.6d^3 Sep 9] good-bodied colt: carries condition: has a round action: smart performer: won maiden at Salisbury in May and 3-runner minor event at Windsor (odds on, made all) in August: placed in Princess of Wales's Stakes at Newmarket (length second to Beauchamp King), Gordon Stakes at Goodwood (2 lengths third to Presenting) and St Leger (edgy, 6 lengths third of 10 to Classic Cliche) at Doncaster on 3 of last 4 starts: stays 14.6f well: acts on firm and dead ground, possibly unsuited by soft: has run well when sweating profusely: effective from front or held up: consistent: to join P. Hayes in Australia. *A. C. Stewart* — 114

ISTIWA 3 b.c. Statoblest 120 – Raintree Venture (Good Times (ITY)) [1994 NR 1995 8.3m 8.3m 7m^4 Aug 28] 9,600F, 52,000Y: well-made colt: fourth foal: half-brother to a winner in Italy: dam lightly-raced half-sister to very useful middle-distance filly Seventh Bride, dam of Oaks winner Polygamy: no worthwhile form in maidens. *C. J. Benstead* — –

ITAB (USA) 3 b.f. Dayjur (USA) 137 – Madame Secretary (USA) (Secretariat (USA)) [1994 69p: 6m^4 1995 8m^2 7m* 7m^5 7g^6 Jul 27] strong, compact filly: fair form: 12/1 on, comfortably made all in maiden at Brighton in June: ran poorly in handicaps afterwards: stays 1m: yet to race on a soft surface: sent to USA. *E. A. L. Dunlop* — 71

ITHKURNI (USA) 6 b.m. Green Forest (USA) 134 – Queen's Visit (Top Command (USA)) [1994 –: a5g a8g a6g 1995 6.1g May 29] sturdy, workmanlike mare: no form since 1991: dead. *P. Hayward* — –

IT IS NOW 3 ch.g. Blow The Whistle 72 – Final Game 83 (Pardao 120) [1994 –: 6v a7g a8g 1995 6f 7g 7m a5g Nov 10] smallish gelding: no worthwhile form. *S. Gollings* — –

IT'S ACADEMIC 3 b.f. Royal Academy (USA) 130 – It's Terrific (Vaguely Noble 140) [1994 –: 6m 1995 6m^5 7.1m 9.9m^4 9g^6 7g* 7.5m^5 6m 7f^3 7m^2 7f* 7m^2 6.1d* 7.1g^2 6s^4 7m^6 Oct 14] strong filly: fair handicapper: justified favouritism at Catterick (apprentice maiden) in June, Ayr in August and Nottingham in September: effective at 6f and 7f: acts on firm and soft going: held up. *Mrs J. R. Ramsden* — 73

IT'S A RIPPER 2 ch.c. (Apr 23) Weldnaas (USA) 112 – Atlantic Air (Air Trooper 115) [1995 5.1m⁵ 6m 5m³ 7m⁴ 7g 6g⁴ 7f⁶ Oct 23] 4,100F: workmanlike colt: half-brother to fair 7f and 1m winner Mullitover (by Interrex), 1990 2-y-o 5f winner Domino Dancing (by Lidhame) and a winner in Belgium: dam won over 1¼m in Italy: modest form: will stay beyond 7f: has sweated and got edgy: sold 3,500 gns Newmarket Autumn Sales: sent to Hungary. *G. Lewis* 57+

ITSINTHEPOST 2 b.f. (Feb 8) Risk Me (FR) 127 – Where's The Money 87 (Lochnager 132) [1995 5s³ 5m 6m⁴ a6g* 7g 6.1s² a6g* a6g³ a7g Dec 12] 7,400Y: leggy filly: has a very round action: first foal: dam 5f winner at 2 yrs: won maiden auction at Wolverhampton in July and nursery at Lingfield in November: stays 6f: seems ideally suited by soft ground/all-weather surfaces. *M. Johnston* 64 a77

IT'S SO EASY 4 b.f. Shaadi (USA) 126 – Carmelina 98 (Habitat 134) [1994 56, a63: 7f² a7g* 7g 8g 7d* 7.1m 7m a7g⁵ a7g a7g a6g 1995 a7g a7g⁶ a7g 7m 7f a7g⁶ 7m 6f a7g a7g³ Dec 14] unfurnished filly: poor mover: modest performer in 1994: disappointing at 4 yrs, leaving M. Johnston's stable after second start: likely to prove best at distances short of 1m: probably acts on any ground: inconsistent. *A. P. James* – a37

IT'STHEBUSINESS 3 b.g. Most Welcome 131 – Douceur (USA) (Shadeed (USA) 135) [1994 63: 6g⁵ 6d 6g⁵ 1995 6m 7f 10f⁴ 10.2m² 8.5s 10d² 9.7g Oct 16] workmanlike gelding: modest maiden handicapper: stays 1¼m: acts on good to firm going and dead, probably on soft: rather headstrong, and tends to carry head high: none too consistent: has been gelded. *S. Dow* 58

IVANHOE 4 b.g. Bairn (USA) 126 – Ural Dancer (Corvaro (USA) 124) [1994 –: 10m 8f 1995 11.9m 10.3m 8g Jun 3] lengthy, workmanlike gelding: no form since 2 yrs: has joined C. Mann. *J. R. Arnold* –

IVAN THE TERRIBLE (IRE) 7 ch.g. Siberian Express (USA) 125 – Chrisanthy 81 (So Blessed 130) [1994 –, a53: a8.5g a8.5g* a9.4g a8g² a8g a8.5g³ 8m 62 a53

Hamdan Al Maktoum's "Istidaad"

a7g a8.5g* a8.5g* a9.4g 1995 a8g^6 a8.5g^2 a8g^3 a8.5g 9.2s* 9.2g* a8g^6 a9.4g 8.9g Aug 30] lengthy, workmanlike gelding: modest performer: won claimer at Hamilton in April and minor event there in May: below form last 3 starts: effective at 1m, stays 1½m: acts on fibresand and on good to firm and soft ground: blinkered once at 2 yrs: often a front runner. *B. Ellison*

IVOR'S DEED 2 b.c. Shadeed (USA) 135 – Gena Ivor (USA) (Sir Ivor 135) 54 [1995 a8g a7g^5 a7g Dec 6] 525Y: first foal: dam won 3 races in USA: improved effort (ridden with more restraint) in maiden events when 7 lengths seventh of 14 to Faith Alone in auction race at Lingfield final start: will stay beyond 7f: stays 7f. *C. F. Wall*

IVOR'S FLUTTER 6 b.g. Beldale Flutter (USA) 130 – Rich Line (High Line – 125) [1994 81: 13.3s 17.2g* 18m^4 1995 14g 16.1m Jul 1] leggy, workmanlike gelding: fairly useful handicapper in 1994: bandaged, never dangerous in 1995: suited by good test of stamina: acts on good to firm and soft ground: needs driving, and not an easy ride. *D. R. C. Elsworth*

IVORY FRONTIER (IRE) 5 ch.h. Imperial Frontier (USA) 112 – Ivory Home 109 (FR) (Home Guard (USA) 129) [1994 8g^2 9g 8m* 7g^3 7d^5 1995 8m^2 9m 8m^6 8g^2 8f^2 7g^5 Sep 16] good-topped Irish horse: smart performer: won minor event at 4 yrs: back to form when second in listed events at Leopardstown and the Curragh stays behind Hushang) then when demoted (had drifted left under pressure) after beating Timarida a head in 5-runner Desmond Stakes at the Curragh: stays 1m: acts on firm and dead ground: sent to USA. *J. S. Bolger, Ireland*

IVORY'S GRAB HIRE 2 b.g. (Jun 3) Shavian 125 – Knees Up (USA) (Dancing 55 + Champ (USA)) [1995 5.1m 6.1m^2 5g^5 5g^6 6g^2 5.2f^3 6m^5 6m^2 6g^4 6.9f^3 8.1m^6 Aug 25] 2,400Y: quite attractive gelding: half-brother to 3-y-o Broughton's Champ (by Dowsing) and 1990 2-y-o 7f winner Tapatch (by Thatching), now suited by middle distances: dam unraced: fair plater: stays 7f: acts on firm ground, yet to race on a soft surface: blinkered seventh outing (ran poorly): has worn bandages. *K. T. Ivory*

IVY LILIAN (IRE) 3 b.f. Cyrano de Bergerac 120 – Catherine Clare 58 (Sallust 41 134) [1994 46: 5g a5g^2 6m^3 5f a8.5g a5g 1995 a5g^5 a6g^6 a5g^2 a6g^6 a5g^3 5d^4 a5g^4 a5g 5.1m 5f a5g 5.3m 8.1m 5.9f Jun 29] small filly: unimpressive mover: poor maiden handicapper: stays 6f: acts on fibresand and good to firm and dead ground: visored twice (ran well first occasion) at 2 yrs: blinkered (below form) second 3-y-o start. *W. M. Brisbourne*

IZZA 4 b.f. Unfuwain (USA) 131 – Wantage Park 104 (Pas de Seul 133) [1994 NR 41 1995 11.1s 8m 7g 8f 5g 8g 8f 15.8g^2 16f^6 15.8m* 16.1h^6 16m 15.8g Sep 16] leggy, quite attractive filly: good mover: poor handicapper: narrowly won at Catterick in July, leading post: suited by test of stamina: acts on firm ground: effective visored or not: often ridden by claimer P. Fessey: sometimes takes strong hold: won over hurdles in November. *W. Storey*

J

JAAZIM 5 ch.h. Night Shift (USA) – Mesmerize (Mill Reef (USA) 141) [1994 72 d a6g^5 a7g^3 a8g a6g^6 a7g* a6g a7g a6g a8g^5 a6g^3 1995 a7g^3 a7g* a7g a6g* a7g^6 7f 6m 8g Sep 8] strong horse: fair performer at 3 yrs: raced in Dubai in 1993/5: won handicaps at Nad Al Sheba and Abu Dhabi early in 1995 for E. Charpy: sold 30,000 gns Newmarket July Sales: well beaten for new connections: effective at 6f and 7f: acts on the sand and on firm going, yet to race on a soft surface: blinkered fifth (ran creditably) to seventh 3-y-o starts. *M. Madgwick*

JABAROOT (IRE) 4 b.g. Sadler's Wells (USA) 132 – Arctic Heroine (USA) – (Arctic Tern (USA) 126) [1994 70+: 10d 12.3m* 12m 1995 12d Jun 8] sparely-made gelding: has a quick action: fair form: off course over a year, never-dangerous ninth of 11 in handicap at Beverley: better at around 1½m than shorter: acts on good to firm ground: tongue tied down (tailed off) on 3-y-o reappearance: sold (M. Stoute to D. Nolan) only 3,000 gns Newmarket Autumn Sales. *M. R. Stoute*

JACKATACK (IRE) 3 b.g. Astronef 116 – Redwood Hut (Habitat 134) [1994 46 a63 61: 5d^4 6m^4 6m 7m 6m^6 6g^5 7.3s^4 7g^4 7s^5 8g^3 7.3v 8d 1995 a8.5g^6 a8g* a8.5g 9.7m 8.3g^5 12g 8.3g^2 8.1d^5 8f a8g a7g Dec 14] useful-looking gelding: modest performer on all-weather: won minor event at Lingfield in April: poor on turf: stays 8.3f: acts on good to firm and soft ground and goes well on equitrack: visored (never dangerous) final 3-y-o start: inconsistent. *M. R. Channon*

JACK BUTTON (IRE) 6 b.g. Kings Lake (USA) 133 – Tallantire (USA) (Icecapade (USA)) [1994 92: 16.2s^{3} 18.7m 16s^{6} 13.9m^{6} 22.2f^{5} 16.1m 14.8f^{4} 20f^{2} 16.1m* 18g^{2} 16.1m^{2} 14m 18m 16d^{3} 16.5v^{5} 1995 18.7m^{6} May 10] good-topped gelding: unimpressive mover: fairly useful handicapper: progressed into a useful hurdler in 1994/5: joint top weight and ran well when sixth of 18 to Top Cees in Chester Cup, though never a threat: suited by a thorough test of stamina: acts on any going: tried in blinkers/visor on 4 occasions (but not since 1992): occasional front runner: tough and genuine. *Bob Jones* 92

JACK JENNINGS 2 ch.c. (Feb 9) Deploy 131 – Lareyna 98 (Welsh Pageant 132) [1995 a7g^{2} 7f* 7m^{6} 8.1d^{4} 8d^{3} Sep 23] 15,000Y: strong, good-bodied colt: has scope: half-brother to numerous winners here and abroad, including 13.1f and 1¾m winner Sure Ground (by Grundy): dam 5f and 6f winner at 2 yrs: won maiden at Doncaster in July: ran excellent race in Royal Lodge Stakes at Ascot on final start when over 5 lengths third of 8 to Mons: clearly suited by a good test of stamina at 2 yrs: acts on firm ground, best effort on good to soft: often slowly away (though broke smartly at Ascot after giving trouble stalls). *B. A. McMahon* 94

JACKMANII 3 b.g. Most Welcome 131 – Blue Flower (FR) (Carwhite 127) [1994 –: 7g 8f 8d 1995 11.1g^{5} 12.4g^{4} 12.1g^{3} 11.1g 12m^{2} 11.1f^{2} 12.1m 11.1m* 11.1f^{3} 11f^{4} 11.1f^{3} 15g Sep 14] good-topped gelding: modest handicapper: got up close home in minor event at Edinburgh in July: stays 12.4f (beaten before stamina became a factor when tried at 15f): acts on firm ground: blinkered sixth to eleventh 3-y-o starts. *W. T. Kemp* 51

JACKSON HILL 2 b.c. (Mar 24) Priolo (USA) 127 – Orange Hill 75 (High Top 131) [1995 7g^{6} 7m* Nov 3] 55,000Y: heavy-topped colt: type to carry condition: has a fluent action: fifth foal: half-brother to 5-y-o Old Provence, winner at up to 1½m, and Nemir, 1½m winner in UAE (both by Rainbow Quest): dam, won Cesarewitch, half-sister to top Canadian filly Carotene: favourite and looking really well, won 17-runner maiden at Doncaster by 1¼ lengths from Kerry Ring, chasing leaders, going on 1f out and not unduly threatened: will be better suited by 1m+: sure to win more races and looks likely to make a useful colt at least. *R. Charlton* 85 p

JACKSON PARK 2 gr.g. (Feb 3) Domynsky 110 – Hysteria (Prince Bee 128) [1995 5m 7m 7f^{4} 7.9g^{3} 10d^{2} Sep 19] good-bodied gelding: fourth foal: dam unraced daughter of German 7f to 9f winner Kallista, dam of German 1000 Guineas winner Kazoo and daughter of good German mare Kandia: improved form in nurseries last 2 starts, short-headed in 20-finisher event at Nottingham last time, making most and rallying: suited by test of stamina. *M. H. Easterby* 51

JACKS TO OPEN (USA) 4 ch.g. The Minstrel (CAN) 135 – Sublime Mime (USA) (His Majesty (USA)) [1994 NR 1995 10.2h 10m 7m Aug 25] sparely-made gelding: no longer of much account. *M. J. Heaton-Ellis* – §

JACQUES POINT 3 b.f. Jester 119 – Hill of Fare (Brigadier Gerard 144) [1994 40: 5f^{5} a5g 5m 5f 1995 5m^{6} 5g Sep 2] leggy filly: poor maiden: tailed off in 1995. *A. Smith* –

JADE CITY 5 gr.g. Belfort (FR) 89 – Dear Glenda 66 (Gold Song 112) [1994 69: 8.5g 6g 7.1m 7g^{3} 7.6g 7g 6g 1995 5g^{4} 6f^{5} 8f* 7f^{5} 8f^{2} 8g^{3} a6g^{5} Sep 23] tall gelding: has a round action: fair performer at 4 yrs for J. FitzGerald: respectable fourth in seller on only outing here since: won handicap at Ostend in July: stays 1m: acts on any going: blinkered (ran well) once as 3-y-o. *Alex Vanderhaeghen, Belgium* 64

JADE PET 4 b. or br.f. Petong 126 – Pea Green 98 (Try My Best (USA) 130) [1994 90: 5f^{2} 6g^{3} 6f 5f^{5} 6g^{2} 5g 6d^{5} 6d 6m 1995 5.7m 5m* 6m 6m Aug 11] lengthy, quite good-topped filly: fairly useful handicapper: won at Lingfield in July: respectable efforts in Stewards' Cup at Goodwood and apprentice contest at Newbury afterwards: effective at 5f, and stays 6f well: acts on firm ground, probably on dead: tends to sweat and get on edge: takes keen hold. *R. Hannon* 85

JADIDH 7 b.m. Touching Wood (USA) 127 – Petrol 73 (Troy 137) [1994 NR 1995 a12g Feb 9] leggy, plain mare: fair handicap hurdler: modest maiden at best in 1993 –

(sometimes reluctant) for Mrs J. C. Dawe: tailed off on return: tried blinkered. *C. P. Wildman*

JADWAL (USA) 3 br.f. Woodman (USA) 126 – Bolt From The Blue (USA) (Blue Times (USA)) [1994 81: 7.5m^{4} 7.5f^{4} 7m* 8.1d^{2} 7m^{4} 1995 10.4g^{5} 11.8m^{4} 12.4m^{6} 11.8g^{6} 10m^{3} 11.8m^{2} 12g^{4} 12g 14.1f^{2} 14.6m^{5} Oct 20] leggy, shallow-girthed filly: fairly useful performer: neck second of 7 in falsely-run handicap at Redcar in October, swerving right and bumping winner entering final 1f: stays 1¾m: acts on firm and dead ground: often bandaged near-hind. *D. Morley* 82

JAFEICA (IRE) 4 b.c. Dance of Life (USA) – Moretta (Artaius (USA) 129) [1994 102: 7g* 7m 7.9f^{5} 8g^{2} 8g 9s^{3} 8g^{2} 9m^{5} 7g* 1995 8g 9m^{6} 7.6g^{3} 7.1g^{6} 7g 7.3m Aug 11] good-quartered colt: has a quick action: useful performer: faced stiff tasks most starts, in Bunbury Cup (sweating) at Newmarket and Hungerford Stakes (last of 9) at Newbury last 2 outings: effective at 7f, and should stay beyond 1m: acts on good to firm ground, probably on soft: normally races prominently: sold to race in USA and should more than cover his expenses there. *R. Hannon* 96

JAGELLON (USA) 4 b.c. Danzig Connection (USA) – Heavenlyspun (USA) (His Majesty (USA)) [1994 69p: 10g^{4} 1995 10g 10.1s^{4} 12s^{2} 12.1d* 10d* 10m^{2} 10d Nov 13] good-topped colt: has had interrupted career: in fine form in the autumn, winning competitive handicaps at Chepstow and Newbury in good style and showing useful form when 6 lengths second of 4 to Quandary in listed race at Newmarket (looked in tremendous shape, stayed on determinedly) penultimate start: in rear in listed race at Fontainebleau final start: effective at 1¼m and may stay beyond 1½m: acts on good to firm and soft ground: has had tongue tied down. *W. R. Muir* 99

JAHANGIR (IRE) 6 ch.g. Ballad Rock 122 – Marsh Benham (Dragonara Palace (USA) 115) [1994 NR 1995 7m a7g a10g Dec 6] leggy, workmanlike gelding: fair handicapper (rated 72) at 4 yrs, mainly for B. Hanbury: well beaten on return: stays 8.5f: acts on good to firm ground and (though below best last 6 tries on it) has form on very soft: blinkered once at 3 yrs. *Pat Mitchell* –

JAIRZINHO (USA) 6 b.g. Robellino (USA) 127 – B F'S Sailingal (USA) (Sail On-Sail On) [1994 NR 1995 10m 10m 8f a7g a8g a10g Aug 5] of little account: dead. *P. Hayward* –

JALCANTO 5 ch.g. Jalmood (USA) 126 – Bella Canto 82 (Crooner 119) [1994 55: 9m 12.4f a12g 13.6g^{6} 11g^{3} 1995 14.1f^{2} 16.2m^{3} 16m^{4} 16d Sep 11] angular, workmanlike gelding: easy mover: modest handicapper at best on flat: stays 2m: acts on good to firm and dead going: often bandaged: sometimes unruly stalls: fairly useful hurdler, impressive winner in October. *Mrs M. Reveley* 62

JALEEL 2 b.c. (Feb 26) Jareer (USA) 115 – Forest of Arden (Tap On Wood 130) [1995 5.1m^{5} 5.1m* 7f^{6} 6m 6g 6.1s^{6} Oct 17] 8,800Y: sturdy colt: fifth foal: half-brother to 3-y-o 6f (at 2 yrs) and 7f winner Forest Cat (by Petorius) and 1¼m to 1½m winner Annacurragh (by Shardari): dam Irish 7f winner out of half-sister to Sarah Siddons: won maiden auction at Bath in June: best effort when when sixth of 9 in nursery at Goodwood next time: barely stays 7f: acts on firm ground, probably on soft: fair effort when blinkered. *R. Hannon* 70

JALFREZI 3 b.f. Jalmood (USA) 126 – Annabrianna 88 (Night Shift (USA)) [1994 NR 1995 8m^{2} 8f* 9g^{2} 10g^{3} 10f* 10f^{5} 9f^{5} 9f^{2} 9.5f^{4} Dec 10] smallish, sturdy filly: fluent mover: first foal: dam 1¼m winner who stayed 1½m: fairly useful performer here: won maiden at Bath in May and strongly-run £33,600 handicap at Goodwood (by ½ length from Blisland, producing storming late challenge) in July: sold out of J. Toller's stable after sixth start: improved form when beaten a nose in valuable handicap at Bay Meadows, best of 3 starts (raced on lasix and bute) in USA: effective at 9f and should stay 1½m: acts on firm ground. *D. Vienna, USA* 103

JALMAID 3 ch.f. Jalmood (USA) 126 – Misowni (Niniski (USA) 125) [1994 66: 8.2g 7s^{6} a8g a8.5g^{5} 1995 a7g^{3} a6g^{2} a6g^{4} a6g^{5} a8g 10m^{5} 10m^{5} a7g* 10.8g a8.5g a6g a8g* a9.4g^{3} Dec 9] good-bodied filly: modest handicapper: won maiden at Wolverhampton in September and minor event at Southwell in November: stays 1¼m: acts on good to firm and soft ground, and on fibresand. *B. A. McMahon* 45 a60

JALORE 6 gr.g. Jalmood (USA) 126 – Lorelene (FR) 97 (Lorenzaccio 130) [1994 NR 1995 a14.8g 16.2m 12.1s 12.5g 21.6f 15.8g^{3} 15.1f^{4} Jun 26] lengthy, angular gelding: has a round action: only poor at best for new stable in 1995: stays 2m: used 36 to go well with give in the ground, though has won on good to firm and acts on fibresand. *S. Coathup*

JALWA (USA) 3 b.f. Northern Jove (CAN) – Outofthebluebell (USA) (Red Ryder (USA)) [1994 67: 6g 6m4 6g6 7m4 7m 1995 6g 7m a8.5g Aug 11] big, good-topped filly: well beaten in 1995 for new stable: sold 26,000 gns Newmarket September Sales. *K. T. Ivory* –

JAMAICA BRIDGE 5 b.g. Doulab (USA) 115 – Mill Hill (USA) (Riva Ridge (USA)) [1994 48: a7g6 a8g4 a8g* a8.5g a7g 8.2f a8g5 a8g a8g3 a8g4 1995 a7g5 a7g2 a6g* a6g5 a6g2 a7g2 7.1g 7m a7g4 a6g a7g a8g a6g a7g4 a6g6 Oct 28] tall, leggy gelding: modest performer on the all-weather: won seller at Southwell in January: successful at 1m, but best efforts at 6f and 7f: acts on fibresand, no form in 4 starts on turf: inconsistent. *S. G. Norton* – a63 d

JAMAICAN FLIGHT (USA) 2 b.c. (Apr 10) Sunshine Forever (USA) – Kalamona (USA) (Hawaii) [1995 8g2 8g Oct 1] $37,000Y: rather leggy colt: third foal: dam minor winner in USA: 2 lengths second of 6 to Dreamhill in maiden at Goodwood: eased right up when last in similar event at Brighton following month: will stay beyond 1m. *J. W. Hills* 66

JAMBIA 3 b.f. Sadler's Wells (USA) 132 – Ala Mahlik 116 (Ahonoora 122) [1994 69p: 8m6 1995 10.3g4 12m4 Aug 5] rangy filly: showed promise in maidens at Doncaster and Newmarket (fading after looking likely to take some catching 2f out) over 2 months later: probably stays 1½m but won't be inconvenienced by a return to shorter: looked sort to improve: sold 18,000 gns Newmarket December Sales. *H. R. A. Cecil* 68

JAMBO 2 b.f. (Mar 31) Rambo Dancer (CAN) 107 – Nicholess (Nicholas Bill 125) [1995 5m4 6g2 6g6 6m4 6f2 7.1m* Jul 4] leggy filly: first foal: dam stayed 1m: plater: won 4-runner claimer at Edinburgh by short head in July: will stay 1m: has raced only on a sound surface. *M. R. Channon* 54

JAMEEL ASMAR 3 br.c. Rock City 120 – Barsham 94 (Be My Guest (USA) 126) [1994 62p: 6d 6g3 1995 7g 10m* 10.3g* 10g5 11.9m2 13.3d 12d2 Sep 26] compact, close-coupled colt: generally progressive, and is a fairly useful handicapper: won at Pontefract and Chester in the summer: best effort when neck second of 8 to Seckar Vale in rated stakes at Newmarket final start, ridden closer to pace than usual: stays 1½m: acts on good to firm and dead ground: normally held up. *C. R. Egerton* 88

JAM N SHADEED (USA) 3 b.c. Shadeed (USA) 135 – Jamra (USA) 82 (Icecapade (USA)) [1994 73p: 7g4 1995 7.1m5 8.3m2 8f* 7m3 8m 7.1m6 Jul 7] rangy colt: good mover: fair performer: made all in maiden at Warwick in May: ran well in two 7f handicaps, best effort at Sandown last time: effective at 7f to 8.3f: acts on firm ground, yet to race on a soft surface: effective ridden from front or held up: unruly stalls (raced freely, well beaten in Britannia Stakes) fifth 3-y-o start: sent to Hong Kong. *P. F. I. Cole* 80

Volvo Truck Finance Spitfire Stakes (Handicap), Goodwood—
a very strongly-contested event, won by Jalfrezi (right) from Blisland (blaze)

JAMRAT JUMAIRAH (IRE) 2 b.f. (May 10) Polar Falcon (USA) 126 – Coryana 104 (Sassafras (FR) 135) [1995 7f^2 Oct 12] 28,000Y: lengthy filly: half-sister to several winners, notably very smart miler Waajib (by Try My Best): dam Irish middle-distance performer: 8/1 and bit backward, short-head second of 12 to Green Charter in maiden at Redcar, challenging from 2f out but running green: will stay beyond 7f: sure to improve. *E. A. L. Dunlop* — 77 p

JANDEEL (IRE) 3 b.c. Last Tycoon 131 – Pizziri (Artaius (USA) 129) [1994 NR 1995 8m^3 10.1g* 9.2f* 10g 12m* 13.3d a9d* a10g^3 Dec 31] 120,000Y: tall, good sort: half-brother to several winners in France, including 1m to 1½m winner Ianomami (by Green Desert) and 1995 4-y-o 1¼m and 10.5f winner Danish Field (by Danehill): dam 6f and 1m winner in Italy, out of leading Italian filly Croda Alta: won maiden at Newcastle in May, amateurs race at Hamilton in June and 5-runner handicap at Goodwood in August for A. Stewart: won handicap at Jebel Ali in December: stays 1½m: acts on firm ground, possibly not dead: wears bandages. *D. Selvaratnam, UAE* — 96

JANE'S SUPER TOP 3 ch.g. Superlative 118 – Top Debutante (USA) 77 (Monteverdi 129) [1994 NR 1995 11.5m^5 11d Sep 22] compact gelding: fifth foal: dam, 1m winner, stayed 9f well: well beaten in maiden and seller. *J. Pearce* — –

JANIES GIRL (IRE) 2 ch.f. (Apr 1) Persian Heights 129 – Lovat Spring (USA) (Storm Bird (CAN) 134) [1995 6m^3 6f^5 7g Oct 3] IR 11,500Y: smallish filly: first foal: dam, lightly raced Irish maiden, is out of Ivor's Image: third of 10 in median auction maiden at Epsom: ran as if something amiss second start: sweated and pulled hard final one. *K. R. Burke* — 51

JARAAB 4 b.g. Sure Blade (USA) 130 – Ostora (USA) 83 (Blushing Groom (FR) 131) [1994 40: 8d 10d 11.8g 10g 9g 1995 a12g* a16g* 15.4g 14.1g a14.8g* a14.8g* a16g^2 15.8g^5 16.4g^3 14g a16g^5 a14.8g a16g a14.8g a12g^3 a16g* a16g* a13g^5 Nov 25] stocky gelding: fair handicapper on the all-weather: won twice each at Lingfield and Wolverhampton by May and, after mid-year lull, twice more at Lingfield in November: stays 2m: acts on the all-weather: visored since fifth 4-y-o start: blinkered (gave temperamental display) third 3-y-o start: has worn tongue strap: fair hurdler. *G. Lewis* — 51 a78

JARAH (USA) 2 b.c. (Feb 25) Forty Niner (USA) – Umniyatee 104 (Green Desert (USA) 127) [1995 7g* 7m^3 Aug 15] strong, compact colt: good mover: first foal: dam (winner at 7f and 1m) daughter of 1000 Guineas and Oaks winner Midway Lady: won maiden at Ascot by head from Skillington: ran well but didn't progress quite as anticipated when 4 lengths third of 6 to Bijou d'Inde in £13,100 event at York 25 days later, again running lazily early on but nearest finish: will be well suited by 1m+: bandaged off-hind last time: strong-galloping type: will improve further: sent to Dubai. *B. Hanbury* — 98 p

JAREER DO (IRE) 3 b.f. Jareer (USA) 115 – Shining Bright (USA) (Bold Bidder) [1994 NR 1995 8.3m^6 7.1m^3 7.1m^5 7s a6g Oct 14] 1,500F: lengthy, unfurnished filly: half-sister to several winners, including 6-y-o sprinter Bright Paragon (by Treasure Kay) and 5f and 8.2f winner Shawiniga (by Lyphard's Wish): dam never ran: third of 7 in maiden at Chepstow in July: failed by long way to repeat the form: should prove at least as effective at 1m as 7f. *B. Palling* — 69 d

JARI (USA) 4 b.g. Dixieland Band (USA) – Dusty Heart (USA) (Run Dusty Run (USA)) [1994 66: 8g 8.5g* 8.2m 8.2m^4 a10g^2 1995 a9g^5 a7g* a7g a7g a12g a8g Dec 1] good-topped gelding: poor mover: fair performer on his day: trained by P. Rudkin, won handicap in Dubai in February but refused to race both subsequent starts there: sold 1,200 gns Newmarket Autumn Sales: reluctant to race both outings after return: probably stays 1¼m: acts on good to firm ground, yet to race on a soft surface: looked best in blinkers here in 1994 but also wore them last 2 starts: sometimes reluctant at stalls: one to avoid. *M. J. Polglase* — 73 §

JARROW 4 ch.g. Jalmood (USA) 126 – Invite 79 (Be My Guest (USA) 126) [1994 49: 8d 10d^3 12.1s^6 12g^5 12.1m 1995 11.8d 13g^4 13g a14.8g^6 15.8g a14.8g^6 a12g Dec 9] lengthy gelding: poor maiden: should stay beyond 13f: best effort on dead ground: visored (no improvement) second to fifth 3-y-o starts. *Mrs A. M. Naughton* — 40 d

JARZON DANCER 7 br.g. Lidhame 109 – Long Valley 71 (Ribero 126) [1994 NR 1995 10g 12g 12m 11.5m^3 18.2m 14m a10g^3 12m^4 8.3m 11.6m a14.8g^5 Aug — 37 d

11] leggy gelding: poor maiden handicapper: stays 1½m: blinkered once in 1992: inconsistent. *D. A. Wilson*

JATO 6 b.g. Pharly (FR) 130 – Minsden's Image (Dancer's Image (USA)) [1994 78: a8g 6.9s^2 7g* 6m* 6f^2 7s^5 6f 6m* 6m^3 6.1g 6f 6m 6m^4 6d^3 7g 1995 6f^3 7m^2 7g 7m^6 6m^6 7g 6g 7g Sep 30] small, sturdy gelding: good mover with a long stride: fair handicapper: failed to repeat form shown on first 2 starts, though most times ran respectably: effective at 6f and 7f: acts on firm ground and dead: blinkered twice in 1992, running well first occasion. *S. C. Williams* 78

JAVA RED (IRE) 3 b.g. Red Sunset 120 – Coffee Bean (Doulab (USA) 115) [1994 NR 1995 10m^5 a8g^3 8m* 10m Jun 19] IR 6,400F, IR 8,000Y: leggy gelding: first foal: dam poor Irish maiden: won seller at Ripon in May, strong late burst having looked held: well below form in handicap at Pontefract month later: will ultimately prove effective at 1¼m. *J. G. FitzGerald* 56

JAWAAL 5 ch.g. Soviet Star (USA) 128 – Pencil Sharpener (USA) 93 (Sharpen Up 127) [1994 92: 6g^5 8g^2 8f* 8m* 8f^3 9g 7m 1995 8g^2 7m* 7.9g* 7.1g 8m Jun 21] strong gelding: unimpressive walker: has a quick action: useful handicapper: won 25-runner Insulpak Victoria Cup at Ascot idling by a neck from Royal Hill and listed Hambleton Rated Stakes at York in tremendous style by 3 lengths from Kayvee in the spring: ran badly in listed race at Haydock (rather upset in stalls) and Royal Hunt Cup at Royal Ascot afterwards: effective at 7f and 1m: acts on firm going, yet to race on a soft surface: has tongue tied down nowadays. *Lady Herries* 103

JAWANI (IRE) 7 b.g. Last Tycoon 131 – Fabled Lady (Bold Lad (IRE) 133) [1994 51: a16g^3 1995 a16g^2 Jan 19] big, rather leggy gelding: modest handicapper: out-and-out stayer: acts on good to firm ground and all-weather surfaces: seems effective visored (was last 4 starts) or not: fairly useful hurdler, winner in October. *Dr J. D. Scargill* 47

JAWLAAT (USA) 3 b. or br.f. Dayjur (USA) 137 – Elle Seule (USA) 122 (Exclusive Native (USA)) [1994 80: 6s* 6m^2 6s 1995 7m^4 6m^3 6g^2 6m* 6m* 6g^5 6g 6g^3 5m^4 Oct 14] lengthy, strong-quartered filly: good mover: fairly useful sprinter: won handicaps at Haydock and York in July: best efforts in frame in rated stakes at Newmarket last 2 starts: stayed 6f: acted on good to firm and soft ground: was able to run well when sweating: front runner: visits Bahri. *J. L. Dunlop* 91

JAYANNPEE 4 ch.g. Doulab (USA) 115 – Amina 80 (Brigadier Gerard 144) [1994 97: 6s 5.7m* 5.1g* 6.1s 5m^6 6m^2 5.1f* 5f* 6g 5g* 5.6g^6 5g 1995 5.1m^3 5.1m^2 5f^6 6m^5 5g^3 6m^3 5m^6 6g^4 5.6m 5d 5s Oct 7] good-topped gelding: useful handicapper: again best between May and August, particularly good efforts when in frame, notably in Stewards' Cup at Goodwood sixth outing: stays 6f: acts on firm and dead ground, no form on soft: wears tongue strap. *I. A. Balding* 100

J C GREY 3 gr.g. Grey Desire 115 – Mazurkanova 63 (Song 132) [1994 43: 5f 5f^5 6m^6 6d 5f^4 5m 1995 8.3g^4 6f 6m 10m 8.1f^5 Jun 26] leggy gelding: poor maiden: best 43

Insulpak Victoria Cup, Ascot—the high-draws have it; Jawaal beats Royal Hill (left) a neck

at up to 1m: acts on firm ground: hung throughout for 7-lb claimer third 2-y-o outing and blinkered next 2 starts: sold 1,750 gns Doncaster November Sales. *Denys Smith*

JEAN DE FLORETTE (USA) 4 b.g. Our Native (USA) – The Branks (USA) 41 (Hold Your Peace (USA)) [1994 45: 8s 12m^6 12m^2 13g^4 11.6m 12m^6 1995 a14.8g a12g 11.8g^5 12.1m 11.5m^4 12m^2 11.6m^3 12m^3 a14g^6 12f^3 12m 13.1h^6 11.5g 12.1d Oct 10] lengthy gelding: has a long stride: poor maiden handicapper: trained by R. Emery first 2 outings, by John Berry next 6 at 4 yrs: stays 13.1f: acts on hard ground, below form on a soft surface and all-weather: no improvement when visored or blinkered: inconsistent: joined R. Spicer. *C. A. Dwyer*

JEAN PIERRE 2 b.c. (Apr 20) Anshan 119 – Astolat (Rusticaro (FR) 124) [1995 – 6m^4 7g 8f Oct 24] 16,000F, 8,000Y, 20,000 2-y-o: third reported foal: half-brother to 3-y-o 6.9f and 8.3f winner Ma Petite Anglaise (by Reprimand): dam Irish maiden: always behind in maidens. *J. Pearce*

JEDAAL 2 b.c. (Mar 25) Soviet Star (USA) 128 – Donya 74 (Mill Reef (USA) 100 141) [1995 6m* 6f* Jun 21] smallish, sturdy colt: fourth foal: dam twice-raced (at 1¼m and 1½m) daughter of Dunette: won 13-runner maiden (full of running at finish) then hacked up by 9 lengths in 4-runner minor event at Ripon: looked a most interesting prospect but suffered a spiral fracture to off-hind cannon bone: dead. *L. M. Cumani*

JEHOL 9 b.g. Teenoso (USA) 135 – Buz Kashi 123 (Bold Lad (IRE) 133) [1994 – NR 1995 10.8m^4 10.8m 11.6m Aug 7] lengthy gelding: fairly useful middle-distance winner in his prime: no worthwhile form in selling events on first starts since 1991. *N. M. Babbage*

JELALI (IRE) 2 b.c. (Apr 4) Last Tycoon 131 – Lautreamont (Auction Ring 68 p (USA) 123) [1995 7d 7g^4 Oct 10] IR 8,500F, 18,000Y: big, leggy colt: fifth foal: half-brother to 3-y-o Yaverland (by Astronef) and a winner in Japan by Posen: dam French 9f and 10.5f winner: under 4 lengths fourth of 12 to Gold Disc in maiden at Leicester, nearest finish after slow start: sure to improve again. *D. J. G. Murray Smith*

JELLABY ASKHIR 3 b.c. Salse (USA) 128 – Circus Act (Shirley Heights 130) 105 [1994 NR 1995 12m^4 12m* 14m* 14.6d 12g^4 12m Nov 4] 36,000Y: strong, lengthy colt: easy mover: second foal: dam unraced sister to Lupe Stakes winner Lady Shipley: left H. Cecil's stable after debut: won maiden at Newmarket and 2-runner listed race at Goodwood in August: about 12 lengths ninth of 10 to Classic Cliche in St Leger at Doncaster: contested listed races at Newmarket (ran creditably when fourth to Minds Music) and Doncaster (well beaten) afterwards: will be suited by a thorough test of stamina: reluctant at stalls, and wears rope halter and blanket. *R. Akehurst*

JEMIMA PUDDLEDUCK 4 ch.f. Tate Gallery (USA) 117 – Tittlemouse 86 59 (Castle Keep 121) [1994 62: 10.8v^4 9.7v* 9m 10d 9.7g* 10m 10g 9.9m a12g^3 10d 1995 a12g^4 9.7d^2 11.8d^3 12m^5 10.8g 9.7g^5 10.8g 12g 12m a11g* Nov 20] close-coupled filly: modest handicapper: blinkered, won seller at Southwell in November: stays 1½m: acts on heavy ground and fibresand, respectable effort on good to firm: usually races prominently: sold (D. Arbuthnot to A. Streeter) 6,100 gns Doncaster November Sales. *D. W. P. Arbuthnot*

JEMSILVERTHORN (IRE) 2 b.c. (Feb 7) Maelstrom Lake 118 – Fairy Don 46 + (Don 128) [1995 5.3f^6 5g 5g 5g 6m^6 5f^5 6g 7g^6 a8.5g a6g^6 a10g a7g^6 a7g a8g Dec 18] IR 6,000Y: 2,800 2-y-o: workmanlike colt: first foal: dam won from 7f to 9f in Ireland: poor form in varied company: stays 7f: acts on equitrack: tried visored/ blinkered, no improvement. *J. J. Bridger*

JEMTHORN BISHOP 3 b.g. Chief Singer 131 – Ravens Peak (High Top 131) – [1994 50: 5g 5d^6 5v 7m 6m^4 a7g^6 6m 1995 a8g a5g^5 a5g^6 Jan 14] leggy gelding: poor maiden: well beaten in 1995: sold 775 gns Ascot February Sales: stays 7f: acts on good to firm ground and fibresand: tried blinkered, no improvement: inconsistent. *J. J. Bridger*

JENAXA 2 ch.f. (Mar 31) Jendali (USA) 111 – Laxay 69 (Laxton 105) [1995 6.1m – Aug 2] 1,700Y: half-sister to several animals, no winners: dam 7f seller winner: 33/1, tailed off in seller at Nottingham. *M. R. Leach*

JENNY'S CHARMER 2 ch.c. (Apr 23) Charmer 123 – Jenny Wyllie 66 – (Nishapour (FR) 125) [1995 5m 5m^3 a7g 6s 5m Oct 13] second reported foal: dam maiden, stayed 2m: plater: behind in non-selling nursery last time: should stay beyond 5f. *S. E. Kettlewell*

JENOPIS 2 b.f. (Mar 20) Jendali (USA) 111 – Asoness 62 (Laxton 105) [1995 5.1m Aug 2] 1,000Y: second living foal: dam 2-y-o 6f winner: 33/1, tailed off in claimer at Nottingham. *M. R. Leach* –

JEREED'S TUT (IRE) 2 b.f. (Feb 14) Mac's Imp (USA) 116 – Jereed (IRE) (Kings Lake (USA) 133) [1995 a7g a6g Aug 19] first foal: dam, ran twice at 2 yrs in Ireland, from good family: well beaten in sellers. *J. Wharton* –

JERMYN STREET (USA) 4 b.c. Alleged (USA) 138 – My Mother Mary (USA) (Boldnesian) [1994 74: 10g3 10g* 12f 10g6 1995 12m Apr 19] medium-sized, quite attractive colt: poor mover: fair form: stiff tasks in handicaps since win in maiden, burly and always in rear only start in 1995: should stay 1½m. *Mrs J. Cecil* –

JERRY CUTRONA (IRE) 2 br.g. (Mar 21) Distinctly North (USA) 115 – Foulkesmills (Tanfirion 110) [1995 6m 7f4 7m 10d 8f3 8f2 6.9m* a8g3 Nov 10] IR 4,000F, 3,000Y, resold 3,800Y: strong gelding: has a round action: first reported foal: dam unraced: fair form: won nursery at Folkestone in November: good third in similar event final outing: will prove best at up to 1m: acts on firm and dead ground, also on equitrack. *N. A. Callaghan* 73

JERSEY BELLE 3 b.f. Distant Relative 128 – Hong Kong Girl 94 (Petong 126) [1994 53: 5.7g4 a6g a6g a8g 1995 a6g2 a7g6 6s a6g6 a6g2 6g 8.1m a6g* a6g3 a7g4 a7g a7g4 Dec 2] poor handicapper: won at Wolverhampton in July: best form at around 6f: acts on all-weather. *P. J. Makin* – a47

JESSICA'S SECRET (IRE) 3 ch.f. Classic Secret (USA) 91 – Ferry Lane (Dom Racine (FR) 121) [1994 40: 5s 5g 6d a5g 1995 a5g5 a6g 7m 5g4 5f 5m 5.9f4 5f5 Jul 13] sparely-made filly: poor maiden: sold 1,400 gns Doncaster August Sales: seems to stay 7f: acts on firm and soft ground: no improvement in blinkers. *A. Bailey* 35

JESSICA'S SONG 2 b.f. (Apr 15) Colmore Row 111 – Sideloader Special 66 (Song 132) [1995 a5g5 a6g5 6f3 5.1h* 6s Sep 28] 2,000Y: sturdy filly: third foal: half-sister to 3-y-o 12.4f winner Trumble (by Tragic Role) and 1993 2-y-o 6f winner Harpo's Special (by Superlative): dam 6f winner: made all in 6-runner maiden auction at Bath in September: had no chance on unfavoured stand side in claimer at Lingfield later in month: best at 5f: acts on hard ground. *W. G. M. Turner* 55

JESS REBEC 7 br.m. Kala Shikari 125 – Laleston 73 (Junius (USA) 124) [1994 NR 1995 5g May 24] smallish, workmanlike mare: unimpressive mover: modest and consistent handicapper (rated 59) at 5 yrs for J. Banks: never going pace at Salisbury on return: effective at 5f and 6f: acts on firm and dead ground: blinkered (ran poorly) once at 3 yrs. *D. J. S. ffrench Davis* –

JET CLASSIC 3 b.f. Risk Me (FR) 127 – Sophisticated Lady (FR) (Habitat 134) [1994 48: 5d5 5s 6s 1995 a6g 5g 6.1m 5m 8m 5m Aug 1] stocky filly: no worthwhile form in 1995: trained on reappearance by R. Emery: visored (no form) final start: sold 500 gns Doncaster September Sales. *Miss J. F. Craze* –

JEUX INTERDITS 3 ch.c. Master Willie 129 – Priors Dean 61 (Monsanto (FR) 121) [1994 a6g2 7.5v4 1995 7.5d2 6.5h3 a7.5g 5f5 5f2 6f5 Aug 15] 2,600F: Belgian-trained colt: seventh foal: half-brother to a winner abroad: dam ran only at 2 yrs, when best at 6f: poor maiden: last of 5 in median auction maiden at Folkestone final start: stays 7.5f: acts on dirt and on any turf going: visored (finished last) sixth 3-y-o start. *Paul Smith, Belgium* 43

JEWEL THIEF 5 b.g. Green Ruby (USA) 104 – Miss Display 47 (Touch Paper 113) [1994 35: a7g 7m 8g 6m 6.1m5 7.1f6 a7g 8m4 6m6 8g 1995 7g 7.1m5 8.1m5 Jul 2] strong, compact gelding: poor maiden handicapper: stays 1m: acts on good to firm going: often visored, blinkered (ran poorly) sixth 4-y-o start: poor winning hurdler. *G. B. Balding* 30

JEWEL TRADER 3 b.c. Green Ruby (USA) 104 – Maiden Bidder 66 (Shack (USA) 118) [1994 55: 6m 6m 6g 7.3v5 7v 1995 7g 8.3m 10m5 10f4 10.8m4 8g5 9.7f5 13.1h Sep 4] leggy colt: poor mover: poor maiden: should stay further than 1¼m: blinkered last 3 starts: inconsistent: hurdling with Mrs L. Jewell. *C. J. Benstead* 47

JEZYAH (USA) 2 ch.f. (Jan 30) Chief's Crown (USA) – Empress Jackie (USA) (Mount Hagen (FR) 127) [1995 6g 7m2 6g3 7g* Oct 23] $85,000Y: stocky filly: fluent mover: fourth foal: half-sister to useful 3-y-o 6f and 7f winner Tajannub (by 78

Dixieland Band) and winners in North America by Buckaroo and Tri Jet: dam, won 8 races, including minor stakes, half-sister to Irish 2000 Guineas second and Derby third Star of Gdansk: made all on favoured far side when winning maiden at Lingfield (gave plenty of trouble stalls): will stay 1m. *R. W. Armstrong*

JHAN JEON 3 b.f. Aragon 118 – Hala 57 (Persian Bold 123) [1994 49: 5v 5g^6 6g^3 6g 1995 7m a7g Jun 10] leggy, sparely-made filly: shows knee action: no worthwhile form at 3 yrs: should stay 7f. *R. A. Fahey* –

JIBEREEN 3 b.g. Lugana Beach 116 – Fashion Lover 70 (Shiny Tenth 120) [1994 91p: 7f^6 6d* 8.1g^4 6g^2 6g* 1995 6m 7m 7.1g 8m 8.1m 7g 7.1d* Oct 10] strong gelding: only a fair performer nowadays: easily best effort at 3 yrs when winning jockeys challenge handicap at Chepstow in October, allowed to dictate pace: subsequently gelded: probably stays 1m: best efforts on an easy surface. *G. Lewis* 78

JIGADEE CREEK 3 ch.c. Sharpo 132 – River's Rising (FR) 88 (Mendez (FR) 128) [1994 57: 7d 7s 1995 7g 7g 8.1d 8g Sep 29] smallish colt: modest maiden at best: below form last 3 starts: unlikely to be suited by much beyond 1m: visored (no form) final start: sold 3,600 gns Newmarket Autumn Sales: sent to Hungary. *G. Harwood* –

JIGSAW BOY 6 ch.g. Homeboy 114 – Chiparia 82 (Song 132) [1994 75d: 6s^5 6s^3 6m 6s^3 6.1s 6g^6 6m 7m^6 7f^5 7g 5s 6d 6s^2 6g 7s 5v 1995 6g^4 6g^5 6m^6 6g^6 6m^3 6d^2 7m a6g^5 6g a6g^4 a6g^2 a6g a7g^2 a6g* a6g^4 a7g^6 Dec 12] good-topped gelding: fair handicapper: won at Wolverhampton in November: stays 7f: acts on fibresand and any turf going: tried visored (not at 6 yrs), no improvement: usually held up. *P. G. Murphy* 65 a68

JIHAAD (USA) 5 b.g. Chief's Crown (USA) – Desirable 119 (Lord Gayle (USA) 124) [1994 –: a8g 10s 1995 a12g a12g Jan 20] compact, good-bodied gelding: seems no longer of much account on flat, but won handicap hurdle in December. *J. Norton* –

JILLY BEVELED 3 b.f. Beveled (USA) – Karens Valentine (Daring March 116) [1994 NR 1995 7f 8.1m 10d 8.2m Oct 26] leggy filly: first foal: dam never ran: well beaten in maidens and (sweating) handicap. *R. Hannon* –

JILLY JAFFA CAKE (IRE) 3 ch.f. Waajib 121 – Lady Fandet (Gay Fandango (USA) 132) [1994 53: 7m 6m 6d 7d a7g^4 a8g^6 1995 a8g^2 a8g^4 a11g Feb 17] only poor maiden at 3 yrs: sold 425 gns Ascot February Sales: stays 1m: acts on fibresand. *D. W. P. Arbuthnot* 42

JIMBO 4 b.c. Salse (USA) 128 – Darnelle 83 (Shirley Heights 130) [1994 NR 1995 10s 7m 7f a8g Jun 8] 17,000Y: angular, plain colt: first foal: dam, 7.6f (at 2 yrs) and 9f winner, is half-sister to Oaks runner-up Bourbon Girl: no worthwhile form on flat. *J. R. Jenkins* –

JIMJAREER (IRE) 2 br.c. (Jan 17) Jareer (USA) 115 – Onthecomet (Chief Singer 131) [1995 a5g* 6f^2 6m^4 7g^5 8g 8f Oct 31] IR 5,000Y: leggy colt: blind in off eye: fourth foal: dam unraced half-sister to Monde Bleu and Sayf El Arab: won maiden auction at Southwell in June: below form last 2 outings: stays 7f. *Capt. J. Wilson* 61

JIVE BABY 2 b.g. (Apr 21) Crowning Honors (CAN) – Jive Music 32 (Music Boy 124) [1995 5m 5f 5f Oct 24] 400Y: sturdy gelding: first foal: dam 5f winner: tailed off in maiden events: blinkered final start. *N. Bycroft* –

JIYUSH 2 b.c. (Apr 17) Generous (IRE) 139 – Urjwan (USA) 98 (Seattle Slew (USA)) [1995 8g^2 8f^4 Oct 25] big, good-topped colt: has plenty of scope: fourth living foal: half-brother to fairly useful 3-y-o 10.3f winner (seems to stay 2¼m) Dawlah (by Shirley Heights): dam, 1m winner from 2 starts, out of Kentucky Oaks winner White Star Line: similar form in maidens won by Forest Buck at Leicester and Bright Water at Yarmouth (hampered) 15 days later: bred to stay middle distances, quite a keen sort though. *H. Thomson Jones* 83 +

JOBBER'S FIDDLE 3 b.f. Sizzling Melody 117 – Island Mead 86 (Pharly (FR) 130) [1994 75d: 5m 6m 6g^5 7m^2 7f* 7.1g^6 7m 6m 8g 1995 8m a7g 8.3g 10m 8m^4 8.3m^6 8f^4 10d^6 Sep 19] strong, workmanlike filly: poor handicapper: sold out of D. ffrench Davis' stable 3,200 gns Newmarket September Sales after seventh start: stays 1m: acts on firm ground: often visored: blinkered (below form) second 3-y-o start: none too consistent. *D. L. Williams* 49

JOBIE 5 b.g. Precocious 126 – Lingering 96 (Kind of Hush 118) [1994 71+: 5g^3 5f 5m^3 1995 5m^5 6m 6g^5 7.3g 5.7f^3 5m 5m^2 6g^4 6g Oct 16] sturdy gelding: fair sprint handicapper: acts on firm and dead ground. *B. W. Hills* 70

JOE JAGGER (IRE) 4 b.g. Petorius 117 – Seapoint (Major Point) [1994 53: 9.9d 12.1s^3 11.1f^6 11.1m^4 14.1m^6 1995 a16.2g Jan 7] sparely-made gelding: modest middle-distance maiden: lost his form at 3 yrs, and tailed off only start in 1995: acts on soft ground, probably on good to firm. *Miss M. K. Milligan* –

JOE SHAW 2 ch.g. (Apr 30) Interrex (CAN) – Super Lady (Averof 123) [1995 7.1g Sep 23] 2,200F: leggy colt: brother to 3-y-o Super Sonata, 5f winner at 2 yrs, and half-brother to several winners, including 6f (at 2 yrs) to 10.8f winner Super Morning (by Martinmas): dam ran 4 times at 2 yrs: 33/1, green and in need of race, in rear in maiden at Haydock. *Mrs M. Reveley* –

JOHAYRO 2 ch.g. (Feb 4) Clantime 101 – Arroganza 62 (Crofthall 110) [1995 5g^2 5m^2 5m^2 5g 5g 5.7m^5 5f* Oct 14] 22,000Y: close-coupled gelding: has a quick action: second foal: brother to 4-y-o 5f performer Eluned May: dam 2-y-o 5f winner: fair performer: ridden by 7-lb claimer, comfortable winner of 15-runner maiden at Catterick in October by 3½ lengths: very speedy: blinkered last 2 starts, setting too fast a pace in them first time. *W. G. M. Turner* 84

JOHN LEE HOOKER 3 b.g. Superlative 118 – Aunt Jemima (Busted 134) [1994 72: 6.1s^4 7m* 7m^2 8.1g^5 7.3s 1995 9m 12.5f 11.4g^6 14.4m^3 13.3f^3 14m* 16.2m^2 16m^3 14m^5 Aug 25] workmanlike gelding: fair performer: won claimer at Sandown in July: suited by test of stamina: acts on firm ground: sometimes wears bandages: often wears crossed noseband: effective from front or held up: sold only 1,800 gns Ascot December Sales. *D. W. P. Arbuthnot* 72

JOHNNIE THE JOKER 4 gr.g. Absalom 128 – Magic Tower 76 (Tower Walk 130) [1994 60, a81: 8.2d 7.5m^5 6g 8.2m^6 a7g* a6g^2 a7g* a7g^2 a6g* a6g^2 6g 8g^2 7g 1995 7g 8f^6 7g^4 7g^4 9.9m^4 7m 8d 7f 10f a7g^6 a7g^5 a8g Dec 1] good-topped gelding: has a round action: fair handicapper on the all-weather: only modest on turf: stays 1m, probably 1¼m: acts on fibresand, firm and dead ground: usually visored/blinkered: usually races prominently. *J. P. Leigh* 52 a78

JOHNNY JONES (USA) 2 b.c. (Mar 19) Mr Prospector (USA) – Fantastic Look (USA) (Green Dancer (USA) 132) [1995 7m^5 6g^3 Sep 24] $350,000Y: lengthy, attractive colt: first foal: dam Grade 1 8.5f winner of 7 races in USA: one-paced ¾ lengths third of 4 to Marcomir in maiden at Hamilton: will prove suited by further than 6f: sold 26,000 gns Newmarket December Sales. *P. W. Chapple-Hyam* 66

JOHN O'DREAMS 10 b.g. Indian King (USA) 128 – Mississipi Shuffle 78 (Steel Heart 128) [1994 61: 5v 6.1d^6 5.1g^4 5.7g 5m* 5.7m* 5.2g* 5m 5f^3 6.1g^5 5m^3 6g 5.7g 5.1d 1995 5m 5.1m 5.1m 5m^6 5.2g^5 5.1m^6 5m 5f^5 5.7h^4 5g^3 5d^4 5.1m Oct 19] good-topped gelding: poor walker: unimpressive mover: modest handicapper: stays 6f: acts on any going: tried blinkered (below form) and visored (has run creditably) earlier in career: often bandaged: held up. *Mrs A. L. M. King* 52

JOHNS ACT (USA) 5 b.g. Late Act (USA) – Deluxe Type (USA) (Singh (USA)) [1994 83: 10m^3 12m 11.9g^5 13.4g 12d^4 10s^5 12m 12v 1995 a12g^4 a12g^3 a12g^3 a12g* 12g 13.3g* 14g^5 11.9d^5 13.3d 12m^6 Nov 4] good-topped gelding: good mover: fair handicapper: won at Wolverhampton in March and Newbury in May: stays 1¾m: acts on good to firm and soft ground and on fibresand: effective visored or not: races prominently: edgy (ran poorly) penultimate 4-y-o start. *D. Haydn Jones* 74

JOHNS JOY 10 b.g. Martin John – Saybya (Sallust 134) [1994 52: a10g 9m^2 10m^2 8.3m^3 1995 10.8g Oct 3] angular gelding: modest form at 9 yrs: bandaged and backward, no encouragement on only outing in 1995. *J. J. Bridger* –

JOHN'S LAW (IRE) 2 b.g. (Feb 15) Contract Law (USA) 108 – Vieux Carre (Pas de Seul 133) [1995 a7g Aug 5] 12,000Y: third foal: dam poor maiden, sometimes appeared reluctant: 25/1, tailed off in maiden at Wolverhampton. *M. J. Heaton-Ellis* –

JOHN-T 2 b.c. (Apr 3) Thatching 131 – Ower (IRE) 71 (Lomond (USA) 128) [1995 7f Aug 2] 21,000F, 22,000Y: sturdy, quite attractive colt: first foal: dam 7f winner who stayed 1m, half-sister to smart 1994 middle-distance 3-y-o Weigh Anchor: 25/1, looking very well but green to post, last of 15 in maiden at Kempton. *J. L. Dunlop* –

JOINT EFFORT (IRE) 4 b.f. Last Tycoon 131 – Monterana 99 (Sallust 134) [1994 48: 6g 8.3m 7m 7g^4 8s 8g^5 a6g^3 a7g^4 a6g^3 a7g a7g^3 a8g^5 1995 a7g^3 a6g^3 a7g^6 a9.4g^6 a7g^5 Mar 16] close-coupled filly: poor maiden: effective at 6f to 1m: acts on equitrack, no form only run on soft ground. *A. Moore* — 39

JOIN THE CLAN 6 ch.m. Clantime 101 – Joint Reward (Netherkelly 112) [1994 85: 6m^5 6m^3 6.1m* 6m^2 6m* 6m^3 6m^4 5g* 6g 5g* 6m 1995 6m* 6f 6f 5m* 5m^3 5g 5f^6 5m 6g 5.6m^6 6g 6g^5 Sep 13] angular mare: fairly useful handicapper: won at Leicester in May and Doncaster in July: stays 6f: acts on good to firm ground, probably on firm: has not raced on a soft surface since 1992: usually held up, and ideally suited by strongly-run race: successful for apprentice: consistent. *Mrs N. Macauley* — 95

JOINT PROSPECT 3 b.g. Midyan (USA) 124 – Freely Given 69 (Petingo 135) [1994 –: 5d 5d 8.1g 7d 1995 a8g a7g a10g Jan 31] small, compact gelding: bad maiden: sold 675 gns Ascot February Sales: tried blinkered. *C. C. Elsey* — –

JOLIS ABSENT 5 b.m. Primo Dominie 121 – Jolimo 92 (Fortissimo 111) [1994 57: 11.8s* 14g* 13.9f 11.8d* 14g 14.4g 16.2g 14m 1995 a16g 16d Sep 11] robust mare: modest middle-distance staying handicapper early in 1994: went with little sparkle both 5-y-o starts. *M. J. Ryan* — –

JOLIS PRESENT 2 b.c. (Apr 17) Prince Sabo 123 – Jolimo 92 (Fortissimo 111) [1995 5m 5m* 6f^6 6f^6 6m^5 5g^5 6.1m Oct 26] good-topped colt: half-brother to several winners, including Joli's Absent (modest at up to 15.4f, by Primo Dominie) and Osric (fairly useful at up to 1½m, by Radetzky): dam won from 1½m to 2¼m: won maiden at Windsor in June: failed to repeat that form, in nurseries last 4 starts: should be as effective at 6f as 5f: blinkered last 2 outings. *M. J. Ryan* — 70 d

JOLLY HOKEY 3 b.g. Dominion 123 – Judy's Dowry 80 (Dragonara Palace (USA) 115) [1994 –: a5g^4 a5g^4 1995 7g 6m Oct 2] workmanlike gelding: no worthwhile form. *J. Wharton* — –

JOLLY SWAGMAN 4 b.g. Governor General 116 – Armour of Light (Hot Spark 126) [1994 –: a7g^4 a8g^4 a9.4g a8g 1995 a12g^6 a13g Feb 11] bad maiden: sold 1,800 gns Ascot May Sales. *Lord Huntingdon* — –

JOLTO 6 b.g. Noalto 120 – Joytime (John de Coombe 122) [1994 71+: 7g* 7m^2 8.3f 7f^2 7.6v^3 7g^6 7s^2 7d* 7s* 1995 7m^4 7.6m^6 7m^6 7m* 7m 6m^6 7f* 7m 7g^3 7d 7m Nov 3] leggy gelding: has a round action: fair handicapper: has a very good record at Salisbury, and won there in June and August: best at up to 7.6f: acts on any going: visored (ran creditably) on equitrack once at 3 yrs: goes well with forcing tactics: has run well when sweating: genuine. *K. O. Cunningham-Brown* — 79

JO MAXIMUS 3 b.g. Prince Sabo 123 – Final Call 79 (Town Crier 119) [1994 69: 5g^5 5d^4 6g^5 5f^2 5m^3 5.2m 6g^5 1995 5s^6 5.1g^3 6m^2 6m 6m* 6m^3 6m^2 5g^3 6m^5 6m 5m 7g* 7g^4 Oct 1] workmanlike, leggy gelding: fair performer: in good form for most of 1995, and made most to win auction maiden at Brighton in June and handicap there in September: stays 7f: acts on firm and soft ground: races prominently. *S. Dow* — 79

JO MELL 2 b.g. (Mar 1) Efisio 120 – Militia Girl (Rarity 129) [1995 6f^4 7g^4 7g* 7.9m^3 Oct 5] 17,000Y: leggy, lengthy, rather unfurnished gelding: has a round action: half-brother to 11f winner Tasmim (by Be My Guest) and a winner in Italy: dam once-raced half-sister to Grade 1 middle-distance winner King's Island: made all in maiden at Ayr in September: good third of 11 to Weet-A-Minute in nursery at York 3 weeks later: stays 1m: races keenly. *M. H. Easterby* — 83 +

JONA HOLLEY 2 b.g. (Mar 25) Sharpo 132 – Spurned (USA) 91 (Robellino (USA) 127) [1995 7d 6d Oct 19] leggy gelding: has scope: second foal: half-brother to useful 3-y-o sprinter Overbrook (by Storm Cat): dam stayed 1¼m: better effort in maidens (though never threatened to reach leaders) when fourteenth of 20 to Fly Tip at Newbury. *I. A. Balding* — 54

JONBEL 7 b.g. Norwick (USA) 125 – Two Shots (Dom Racine (FR) 121) [1994 NR 1995 a11g a9.4g^5 a9.4g 9.7g Apr 10] rather dipped-backed gelding: poor maiden handicapper: stays 9.4f: acts on soft ground and fibresand: tried in blinkers and hood (twice) at 2 yrs: usually bandaged. *T. T. Clement* — 26

JO N JACK (IRE) 7 ch.g. Gorytus (USA) 132 – Dancing Song 87 (Ridan (USA)) [1994 NR 1995 a10g Aug 12] tall gelding: very lightly raced on flat since winning 1¼m Lingfield seller in 1992: tailed off only outing in 1995. *R. Ingram* — –

JONJAS CHUDLEIGH 8 ch.g. Aragon 118 – Lizabeth Chudleigh (Imperial Fling (USA) 116) [1994 NR 1995 a9.4g 14m May 7] angular gelding: useful Irish handicapper in 1991: soundly beaten on return to flat. *W. G. Turner* –

JON'S CHOICE 7 b.g. Andy Rew 103 – Whangarei 59 (Gold Rod 129) [1994 70: a7g* a6g4 a5g3 a7g* a5g3 6s a6g* a7g4 6m2 a6g2 a7g5 a5g4 a7g2 a6g5 a7g a6g 1995 a5g a5g5 a7g a6g5 a6g a6g a5g a5g4 a7g a6g6 6m a9.4g4 7m a7g a7g a7g Dec 12] compact gelding: almost always races at Wolverhampton these days: modest form at best in 1995: stays 9.4f: acts on good to firm ground, best efforts on fibresand: no improvement in blinkers: inconsistent. *B. Preece* – a55 d

JOSEPH'S WINE (IRE) 6 b.g. Smile (USA) – Femme Gendarme (USA) (Policeman (FR) 124) [1994 80+: 10d 9.2d4 10g* 9.9g* 10m* 10g* 11.6m6 8f 10.3d 10.3s 10.1d a11g* a12g3 a11g* a10g* 1995 a11g* a12g5 10.3g2 Mar 24] lengthy gelding: fairly useful handicapper, won at Southwell in January: should stay 1½m: goes well on the all-weather and probably acts on any turf going: best in blinkers: has run well when sweating: held up, and has good turn of foot. *D. Nicholls* 67 + a80

JOVALE 3 ch.c. Clantime 101 – Cutler Heights 62 (Galivanter 131) [1994 45: 5g 5g a6g a5g 1995 a8g Jan 16] unfurnished colt: poor form in maidens as 2-y-o: tailed off in seller only 3-y-o outing: has been bandaged near-hind. *S. G. Norton* –

JOVIE KING (IRE) 3 ch.c. Salt Dome (USA) – Jovial Josie (USA) (Sea Bird II 145) [1994 7s 1995 6.9g 7g 7m3 8f 10f 10m 12s 11.9d Sep 26] leggy, workmanlike ex-Irish colt: half-brother to several winners abroad and to fairly useful 1m to 13.3f winner Talos (by Taufan): dam poor sister to high-class filly and good broodmare Kittiwake: modest maiden: trained only start in 1994 by D. Hanley: left P. Mitchell's stable after sixth 3-y-o start: soundly beaten in handicaps both since: best efforts at 7f, should stay 1m: acts on good to firm ground: inconsistent. *S. Dow* 57 d

JOYCE E JACKSON 5 ch.m. Mansingh (USA) 120 – Economy Pep 69 (Jimmy Reppin 131) [1994 –: 12d 1995 a10g5 a16g a12g Feb 23] no worthwhile form: tried blinkered. *R. Ingram* –

JOYFUL (IRE) 3 b.f. Green Desert (USA) 127 – Optimistic Lass (USA) 117 (Mr Prospector (USA)) [1994 NR 1995 7.1m5 a7g* Nov 2] eighth foal: half-sister to high-class sprinter/miler Golden Opinion (by Slew O'Gold): dam won Musidora and Nassau Stakes: stepped up on debut form to win 11-runner maiden at Lingfield in November by short head from Sombreffe, getting up on line: will stay 1m: capable of better still: sent to J. Rouget in France. *J. H. M. Gosden* 71 p

JOYFUL TIMES 3 br.f. Doc Marten 104 – Time For Joy 42 (Good Times (ITY)) [1994 –: 6g 8.2s 7g a5g a7g 1995 a7g3 a8g6 a7g a6g* a6g4 a7g4 a7g4 8g6 a7g 7g Jul 1] compact filly: poor performer: got up on post to win seller at Southwell in February: below form afterwards: finds 6f a bare minimum, and stays 1m: acts on fibresand: best form without blinkers/visor: usually gets behind: often ridden by Amanda Sanders. *Mrs N. Macauley* – a47

JOYRIDER 4 b.g. Risk Me (FR) 127 – Villajoyosa (FR) (Satingo 129) [1994 –, a52: 10m a8g* a8g2 8.1g 7f a8g 7m 1995 a11g 12.1s 11.8g Oct 10] smallish gelding: modest performer at 3 yrs: no form in 1995 for new stable: stays 1m: goes well on fibresand: won selling hurdle in December. *Miss M. K. Milligan* –

JOYS FIRST 4 ch.c. Tina's Pet 121 – Greenhills Joy 90 (Radetzky 123) [1994 51: 10d 7s6 8.1g 10m6 10g 8s 9.7d 14.1g3 14.1d 1995 12m 16.1g5 a12g6 11.5m Aug 17] tall, lengthy colt: poor maiden: well beaten in 1995. *H. J. Collingridge* –

JUBA 3 b.f. Dowsing (USA) 124 – Try The Duchess 99 (Try My Best (USA) 130) [1994 NR 1995 a7g5 Nov 14] 2,000F: 4,000Y: third foal: half-sister to 1¼m winner Uncharted Waters (by Celestial Storm) and a 6f and 7f winner in UAE by Primo Dominie: dam 2-y-o 6f winner: 66/1, 5 lengths fifth of 11 to Sombreffe in maiden at Lingfield, never dangerous: should improve. *Dr J. D. Scargill* 59 p

JUBILEE LINE 5 ch.m. High Line 125 – Consistent Queen 55 (Queen's Hussar 124) [1994 –: 10m6 10g 14d6 16g 1995 11.7m a16g 10.8m2 12f 10.2m 10g Sep 2] sturdy mare: poor maiden: trained by D. Arbuthnot until after second 5-y-o start. *N. E. Berry* 33

JUBILEE PLACE (IRE) 2 br.f. (Mar 28) Prince Sabo 123 – Labelon Lady 87 (Touching Wood (USA) 127) [1995 5.1m2 5m3 6.1m* 6m* Aug 7] 3,200Y: unfurnished filly: third foal: dam 2-y-o 7f winner, stayed 1m: improved form last 2 76

starts, making all in maiden auction at Chepstow and nursery at Windsor: stays 6f. *T. Thomson Jones*

JUBRAN (USA) 9 b.g. Vaguely Noble 140 – La Vue (USA) (Reviewer (USA)) [1994 75: 10m 8.9f^{6} 10.1f^{2} 12.1m^{3} 12.3g^{3} 11.1m* 12.4f^{6} 12f^{4} 12.3g^{5} 10.1m^{6} 10m* 10.3d 8s 10m 1995 8m 10.3g^{4} 12.1m^{5} 10f^{2} 12.3m^{3} 8.1m^{4} 10.3g 10f^{4} 9.9m^{5} 10m^{4} 10m 10.9g 12.1g Sep 18] close-coupled gelding: carries condition: has a round action: fair handicapper at best: stays 12.3f: probably acts on any ground: usually makes running: has joined J. Dodds. *M. Johnston* — 72 d

JUCEA 6 b.m. Bluebird (USA) 125 – Appleby Park 98 (Bay Express 132) [1994 65: 5g^{2} 5.1m* 5f* 5m 5m 5m^{5} 5m^{2} 5g 5.1d 5m^{6} 5.1g 5g^{6} 1995 5.1m* 5m^{4} 5g^{5} 5g^{4} 5.7m^{6} 5m 5m 5.1d 5g^{3} 5m 5f^{6} 5.1m^{5} 5m^{2} Oct 30] sturdy mare: poor mover: fair handicapper: tends to go well fresh, and won at Bath in May on reappearance: races at around 5f: acts on firm ground and equitrack, seemingly not on a soft surface: no improvement in blinkers/visor. *J. L. Spearing* — 69

JUDGE ADVOCATE (IRE) 3 b.c. Contract Law (USA) 108 – Brigadina (Brigadier Gerard 144) [1994 77: 7g* 8v^{5} 1995 12m 10m Aug 19] lengthy colt: won valuable maiden auction event at Goodwood at 2 yrs: lightly raced and well below form since: should stay beyond 7f: bandaged behind in 1994. *Major D. N. Chappell* — –

JUDGE AND JURY 6 br.g. Law Society (USA) 130 – Full of Reason (USA) 105 (Bold Reason) [1994 16g 12s 1995 12.1d Mar 30] compact gelding: modest and inconsistent handicapper here in 1992: winning hurdler in Ireland for T. J. Taaffe: tailed-off last of 9 in handicap at Edinburgh on only flat outing on return to Britain: probably ungenuine: has gone back to Ireland. *L. Lungo* — – §

JUDGEMENT CALL 8 b.g. Alzao (USA) 117 – Syllabub (Silly Season 127) [1994 56: 6d^{5} 6m^{4} 5m 6g^{2} 5g^{2} 5m^{2} 5.2g* 5m 5.1d 5m 1995 5m^{6} 6m 5m^{6} 5g^{5} 6m 5.2m^{5} 5g^{4} 5.2m* 5m^{3} 5m^{3} 5m 6g^{5} Sep 14] close-coupled, good-quartered gelding: modest handicapper: won at Yarmouth in August: effective at 5f to 7f: acts on any going: blinkered (no form) once earlier in career: sometimes bandaged. *P. Howling* — 52

JUICE PLUS 4 ch.g. Kris 135 – Highland Light 105 (Home Guard (USA) 129) [1994 –: 8m 10g 8m 10g 8g 1995 12.1s^{6} 8m 8.5m 8m^{6} 10m 8m^{6} 8m 11.1g Sep 25] big, leggy gelding: poor maiden: best efforts at around 1m on top-of-the-ground: sold 750 gns Doncaster October Sales. *J. Parkes* — 26

JUICY 2 b.c. (Feb 20) Marju (IRE) 127 – Seductress 94 (Known Fact (USA) 135) [1995 5m^{3} 6f^{2} 8g^{6} 7d^{5} 7f^{4} Oct 14] 36,000Y: good-topped colt: first foal: dam sprinter: fair maiden: stays 1m: blinkered (below form) fourth start: sold 12,000 gns Newmarket Autumn Sales. *W. J. Haggas* — 72

JU JU'S GIRL (IRE) 5 br.m. Fools Holme (USA) – Arctic Ford (FR) 85 (Arctic Tern (USA) 126) [1994 9f 8g^{6} 8g 1995 a9.4g^{4} a9.4g Apr 29] ex-Irish mare: third living foal: half-sister to fair 8.5f to 1¼m winner Cold Shower (by Kings Lake): dam 7f winner: fair maiden (rated 65) at 3 yrs for A. Maxwell, but no form in 1994: poor form at best at Wolverhampton in 1995: seems to stay 9.4f: acts on soft ground, probably on fibresand: blinkered final 4-y-o start. *B. Smart* — 25

JULGARANT (IRE) 2 ch.g. (Feb 10) Jareer (USA) 115 – Naval Artiste (Captain's Gig (USA)) [1995 5m^{4} 5f^{3} 5g 5m^{4} 6f^{3} 5h^{6} a8d^{4} a8s^{5} Dec 23] 6,000Y: unfurnished gelding: half-brother to several winners, including sprinters Naval Fan (by Taufan) and Karla's Star (by Kampala): dam Irish 2-y-o 5f winner: plater: failed to progress from his first 2 runs and sold out of M. Dods's stable 500 gns Doncaster September Sales before penultimate start: tried visored. *H. Doria, Sweden* — 46

JULIA'S FREEBEE 4 b.f. Interrex (CAN) – Canadian Charisma (Supreme Sovereign 119) [1994 NR 1995 8.1g 8.3m 7.1m^{3} 6m 7f 7m Aug 25] sturdy filly: sixth foal: dam, ran twice, half-sister to smart racemare and broodmare My Therape: sold 1,200 gns Ascot April 1995 Sales before debut: no worthwhile form: tried visored: sold 1,600 gns Ascot August Sales. *T. M. Jones* — –

JUMAIRAH SUN (IRE) 3 b.f. Scenic 128 – Sun On The Spey (Glint of Gold 128) [1994 83p: 7g^{2} 7d^{2} 1995 10m^{3} 10.1m* 12g^{2} 10.1g Sep 12] lengthy filly: won maiden at Yarmouth in August: easily best effort when 2½ lengths second of 3 to Singspiel (who wasn't at his best) in slowly-run listed race at Doncaster next time: ran poorly in similar event final outing: stayed 1½m: acted on good to firm and dead ground: stud. *L. M. Cumani* — 98

JUMILLA (USA) 3 b.f. El Gran Senor (USA) 136 – Refill 88 (Mill Reef (USA) 141) [1994 82: 6g^3 6m* 6f^2 7m 7g^2 1995 8.1m^3 10m^3 10.1g^2 Sep 12] compact filly: useful performer: not seen out in 1995 until August: blinkered, best effort when second of 12 to Poppy Carew in listed race at Yarmouth on final start, every chance final 1f: stays 1¼m well: has raced only on a sound surface: has looked tricky ride, including on reappearance: to race in Dubai. *G. Wragg* 100

JUMP THE LIGHTS 2 b.g. (Mar 11) Siberian Express (USA) 125 – Turtle Dove (Gyr (USA) 131) [1995 a7g 10m^6 8.2m Oct 26] neat gelding: half-brother to numerous winners (mostly by Warpath), including useful middle-distance stayer Path of Peace and fair out-and-out stayer Path's Sister: dam ran once: modest form in maiden events at Southwell and Nottingham (2): pulled hard third start: stays 1¼m. *S. P. C. Woods* 53

JUNGLE RITES (IRE) 7 b.g. Indian King (USA) 128 – Spring Step (Tepukei 116) [1994 NR 1995 12d^6 16m Jun 26] tall gelding: half-brother to a NH Flat race winner by Rusticaro: dam never ran: won NH Flat race in 1993/4 and novice hurdle in May: in rear in claimers on only flat outings: sold (J. FitzGerald to Miss Z. Green) 6,000 gns Doncaster August Sales. *J. G. FitzGerald* –

JUNIOR BEN (IRE) 3 b.c. Tirol 127 – Piney Pass (Persian Bold 123) [1994 70: 5g 6f^2 6g^3 6m^5 6d^6 1995 10m^4 13.1g^3 14.1f^4 11.6m^5 a11g 11.9d Sep 26] quite attractive colt: fair maiden: trained by Jack Berry until after third 3-y-o start: below form last 2 starts: stays 13f: yet to race on soft going, acts on any other. *P. Howling* 68 d

JURAL 3 ch.f. Kris 135 – Just Cause (Law Society (USA) 130) [1994 104p: 7g* 7m* 8d* 8g^2 1995 11g^2 14.6d Sep 9] leggy filly, rather raw boned: has scope: most progressive at 2 yrs but reportedly slow to come to herself in 1995: ran well when ¾-length second of 8 to Solon in Furstenberg-Rennen at Baden-Baden on reappearance, making most: led 1¼m before fading when last of 10 in St Leger at Doncaster 13 days later: should stay 1½m: acts on good to firm ground and dead: twice sweating and edgy, including at Doncaster: sent to Dubai. *M. Johnston* 108

JURASSIC SUE 3 b.f. Distant Relative 128 – Sculpture Bleue (Claude Monet (USA) 121) [1994 58p: 6g 6m^4 1995 7m 8m^5 7m 8.5d^2 7f^5 8m^3 7m Aug 10] sturdy, angular filly: modest maiden: sold out of B. Hills's stable 6,200 gns Newmarket July Sales before final outing: stayed 8.5f: acted on good to firm and dead ground: blinkered/visored last 4 starts: was not one to trust: dead. *P. Howling* 63 §

JUST ANOTHER HIGH (IRE) 2 b.f. (Mar 19) High Estate 127 – Footway 97 (Sovereign Path 125) [1995 6m 7g 8g 10g Oct 9] IR 10,000Y: smallish, sturdy filly: half-sister to fair stayer Hareek (by Tap On Wood) and 1¼m seller winner Footstool (by Artaius): dam, sister to 1000 Guineas winner Humble Duty, won from 6f to 1m in Ireland: poor maiden: sold 500 gns Doncaster November Sales: sent to Austria. *Dr J. D. Scargill* –

JUST A SINGLE (IRE) 4 b.g. Adbass (USA) 102 – Sniggy 46 (Belfort (FR) 89) [1994 –: 8.3m 7m a7g^6 a7g 1995 a7g a12g Nov 21] sparely-made gelding: no form since fair 2-y-o: tried blinkered. *J. Ffitch-Heyes* –

JUST BOB 6 b.g. Alleging (USA) 120 – Diami 81 (Swing Easy (USA) 126) [1994 85, a–: 5g^6 5g 5d 5d^4 5f^4 5f* 5m^2 5m* 5m* 5m 5f 5m^4 5g 5f* 5m^4 6d 5d 5s^2 a5g 1995 6d 5g 6m 5m 5m 5m 5f^4 5m^2 5m^5 5f^2 5m^5 5g^3 5g^5 5m Oct 4] smallish, leggy gelding: unimpressive mover: only fair handicapper at best in 1995, gambled on on several occasions: successful over 6f but seems suited by 5f nowadays: acts on any turf ground, no form in 4 tries on the all-weather: often blinkered at 3 yrs, rarely nowadays: nearly always slowly away: has won for apprentice and amateur: sometimes bandaged behind. *S. E. Kettlewell* 71

JUST BY CHANCE 3 b.g. Teenoso (USA) 135 – Skerryvore 66 (Kalaglow 132) [1994 –: 7g 1995 11.7h^5 a12g Nov 27] no form on flat: has refused to race once over hurdles. *A. Barrow* –

JUST DISSIDENT (IRE) 3 b.g. Dancing Dissident (USA) 119 – Betty Bun (St Chad 120) [1994 69: 6m 6m 5m^3 5m^3 5m 1995 6g 5m 5m^3 5g^2 5g^2 6m^4 6f* 5.1m 6m 5g 5g 6g 7g 5.1m Oct 19] leggy gelding: fair sprinter: made all in 4-runner maiden at Redcar in June: below form last 5 starts: barely stays 6f: has raced only on a sound surface: usually races prominently. *R. M. Whitaker* 67

JUST FIZZY 3 b.f. Efisio 120 – Redcross Miss 64 (Tower Walk 130) [1994 47: 5m^4 5g^4 a5g^2 5g 6g* 5.1m^5 6.1d a6g 1995 8.2g 10.8m^3 9.9m^2 12.5f^6 8g^2 8.1m* 8.2m^6 8.1m* 8m^2 8m^2 8m^2 8.2m^5 Aug 2] smallish, leggy filly: unimpressive mover: modest performer: claimed out of J. Wharton's stable £4,000 fifth start: subsequently won sellers at Chepstow in June (handicap) and July (sold out of M. Pipe's stable 6,200 gns): best form at 1m: acts on firm ground, tailed off on fibresand: tail swisher: tends to sweat: races prominently. *J. Hetherton* — 61

JUST FLAMENCO 4 ch.g. Scorpio (FR) 127 – Suzannah's Song (Song 132) [1994 62d: 8.2v 8.2d^5 7.6g^4 8g^4 8g 7.5m 8m 6g^6 7g 1995 7.1g 8g a7g^5 7f^5 10m* 10m^6 10m* 10m 10.1g 10.8g 10g a11g a8g^5 a9.4g^5 a10g Dec 18] strong, lengthy gelding: good mover: modest handicapper: won twice at Windsor in July: ran as if something amiss eighth start and below form afterwards: stays 1¼m: acts on good to firm and soft ground, probably on fibresand. *M. J. Ryan* — 56 a47

JUST FOR A REASON 3 b.g. Siberian Express (USA) 125 – Artaius Rose (FR) (Artaius (USA) 129) [1994 –: 7d 6.9m 1995 8m^6 11.1g^5 10m^6 Jun 19] sturdy gelding: no worthwhile form. *D. J. G. Murray Smith* — –

JUSTFORTHERECORD 3 br.f. Forzando 122 – Classical Vintage 80 (Stradavinsky 121) [1994 NR 1995 8d 10d a10g Nov 10] 3,000Y: sparely-made filly: sixth foal: half-sister to 6f and 7f winner Abso and 1992 2-y-o 5f winner Simply Sooty (both by Absalom) and a winner in Belgium: dam 2-y-o 5f winner: no worthwhile form in maidens: moved poorly to post on debut. *B. R. Millman* — –

JUST HAPPY (USA) 4 b.c. Night Shift (USA) – Mesmerize (Mill Reef (USA) 141) [1994 113: 8g* 8f 12m 10f* 10g* 1995 10m^2 10d^2 10m^4 9.8s^6 Sep 30] rangy colt: easy mover: smart performer: best efforts when second in Tattersalls Gold Cup at the Curragh (rallied, short-headed by Prince of Andros) and Brigadier Gerard Stakes at Sandown, both in May: respectable fourth in Prince of Wales's Stakes at Royal Ascot, but below form in 7-runner Prix Dollar at Longchamp (on soft ground) over 3 months later: effective at 1¼m and should stay 1½m: acts on firm and dead ground: tends to sweat. *M. R. Stoute* — 118

JUST HARRY 4 ch.c. High Kicker (USA) – Dorame 55 (Music Boy 124) [1994 62+, a76: a8g* a8g* a7g^4 a10g^3 a8g^5 10m 9.7g 8.2m^6 7m 8m 6.9g 6m 6s 6.9m* 8.2d* 8.1g^2 a8.5g a7g^5 a7g^2 1995 a8g* a7g* a7g a9.4g^6 6.9d^2 8m^2 8g^3 8g^2 8g^2 8.2m^2 8.5m^5 8f^2 7.6m^6 8.3m 10d 8.5d^5 8d 8d^4 8s 8.2m Oct 19] good-topped colt: fairly useful handicapper on the all-weather, fair on turf: won at Southwell and Wolverhampton (for 7-lb claimer) in January: effective at 7f and 1m: goes well on all-weather surfaces, acts on firm and dead ground: blinkered (below form) once as 3-y-o: usually held up. *M. J. Ryan* — 71 a86

JUST ICE 2 b.f. (Apr 13) Polar Falcon (USA) 126 – Justine (GER) (Luciano) [1995 5g^4 5f* 5m^4 5m^2 6f* 6m^2 6s* 6g Sep 15] 20,000Y: shallow-girthed filly: has a round action: half-sister to numerous winners, including, by Star Appeal, useful 1¼m winner Always On A Sunday and 9f winner (stayed 1½m) Sunday Sport Star: dam won 4 races in Germany: won maiden at Hamilton in June and nursery at Kempton and listed race at Bordeaux (by 1½ lengths) in August: respectable effort in listed race won by My Branch at Ayr on final outing: better form at 6f than 5f: acts on any going. *Sir Mark Prescott* — 90

JUST JESTING 3 ch.g. Jester 119 – Echo Chamber 89 (Music Boy 124) [1994 56: 5s 5m^3 5g^3 5m^6 5.3f^5 6g^4 5.3m^5 6m 5.3g^4 5m^5 a6g a5g a5g^4 1995 a7g^6 a6g^5 a5g^5 a5g^6 Feb 25] good-topped gelding: poor maiden at best in 1995: best form at 5f: acts on good to firm ground and equitrack: blinkered (ran creditably) once, visored (below form) thrice: races prominently. *G. L. Moore* — 40

JUST LADY 2 b.f. (Apr 13) Emarati (USA) 74 – Just Run (IRE) 45 (Runnett 125) [1995 5d^6 5g* 5.1m 5m^2 5m^2 5m^4 5m Sep 7] leggy, lengthy filly: first foal: dam showed only a little ability: won claimer at Thirsk in April: best effort when second to Baize in minor event at Windsor on fifth start: has tremendous early pace, and will prove best at 5f: best form on good to firm ground: active type: tends to hang and is none too easy a ride. *W. G. M. Turner* — 72

JUST LIKE ME 3 b.f. Primo Dominie 121 – Amina 80 (Brigadier Gerard 144) [1994 59p: 5m^4 1995 6m^3 5g^4 6m^4 6f^5 5m^3 5d^2 6g Sep 22] angular filly: poor mover: fair maiden: stays 6f: acts on good to firm and dead ground: sold 800 gns Newmarket December Sales. *R. Guest* — 64

JUST LUCKY (IRE) 3 b.g. Fools Holme (USA) – Miss Victoria (Auction Ring (USA) 123) [1994 73p: a8g* 1995 a8g^6 a10g^5 8m a6g 8g 7.6d^5 6.9f 8f a8g a12g^4 Nov 27] sparely-made gelding: fair form when winning maiden at Southwell on only 2-y-o start: disappointing in 1995, leaving R. Armstrong's stable after eighth start: seems to stay 1½m. *Mrs N. Macauley* 41

JUST-MANA-MOU (IRE) 3 b.g. Caerleon (USA) 132 – Clarista (USA) 67 (Riva Ridge (USA)) [1994 58: 7s 7s a8g^4 1995 8.3m 7m^3 8.2f^4 8h^4 a11g 10g 12d^5 a10g^3 a12g^2 a13g^5 a13g^3 Dec 19] quite attractive gelding: modest maiden handicapper: sold out of G. Lewis' stable 10,000 gns Newmarket Autumn Sales after ninth start: stays 13f: acts on firm ground, dead and equitrack: blinkered 4 of last 5 starts. *J. J. Bridger* 49 a63

JUST MILLIE (USA) 2 ch.f. (Apr 3) Elmaamul (USA) 125 – La Plus Belle (USA) (Robellino (USA) 127) [1995 7f* 6g^5 7g^3 Sep 29] 1,800Y: workmanlike filly: fifth foal: half-sister to 2 winners abroad: dam unraced: won maiden auction at Warwick in August: similar form afterwards in minor race at Yarmouth and in seller at Goodwood: will stay further than 7f: bandaged last time. *J. E. Banks* 67

JUST NUISANCE 2 b.f. (Feb 19) Hadeer 118 – Pacific Gull (USA) 67 (Storm Bird (CAN) 134) [1995 7m^4 8m 8d 8f Oct 18] leggy filly: third foal: sister to 3-y-o Vaslav Nijinsky (1m winner in Belgium) and half-sister to miler Northern Chief (by Chief Singer): dam 8.5f winner: fourth of 7 to Matiya in maiden (could be rated 71) at Newmarket: failed to repeat that form in similar events and nursery: should stay 1m: sold 4,500 gns Newmarket Autumn Sales. *C. E. Brittain* 61 +

JUST ONE BID (IRE) 2 ch.c. (Feb 25) Jareer (USA) 115 – Roberts Pride 62 (Roberto (USA) 131) [1995 6m Jun 15] 1,600Y: tall, workmanlike colt: third foal: half-brother to very smart American 4-y-o at up to 1¼m Alpride (by Alzao): dam, maiden from 1m to 2m, out of Park Hill runner-up Glowing With Pride: 50/1 and in need of race, raced keenly to halfway in 13-runner maiden at Newbury, finishing last but one. *B. J. Meehan* –

JUST RORY 2 b.g. (Feb 23) Skyliner 117 – Judys Girl (IRE) (Simply Great (FR) 122) [1995 5v^4 5.1m^4 5g^6 a6g^4 a5g 7m^6 5h Aug 21] 1,050Y: leggy, workmanlike gelding: first foal: dam of little account: poor plater: sold out of E. Alston's stable 700 gns Doncaster August Sales after sixth start: blinkered 3 times: withdrawn once after giving trouble stalls. *Miss Z. A. Green* –

JUST WHISTLE 3 gr.f. Absalom 128 – Aunt Blue 75 (Blue Refrain 121) [1994 NR 1995 6m 7m 7.1g^4 8.1d 7g a7g 8.3f^2 Jul 29] 4,000Y: stocky filly: dam lightly-raced maiden, third twice over 7f at 2 yrs, is half-sister to very smart Sauceboat: poor maiden: better at 1m than 7f, and worth a try over further: acts on firm and dead ground: sold 6,000 gns Doncaster October Sales. *C. W. Thornton* 42

JUWEILLA 3 b.f. Pharly (FR) 130 – National Dress 64 (Welsh Pageant 132) [1994 66: 6.1m^2 7m^2 7m^2 7m* 1995 8g^3 8d^5 9f^4 9.9m 10f^4 Aug 21] good-topped filly: has a round action: fair performer on her day: refused to race last 2 starts (eventually completing tailed off on final one): should stay at least 1¼m: takes keen hold: made heavy weather of apparently simple task final 2-y-o start: one to avoid: sold 2,600 gns Newmarket Autumn Sales: sent to Germany. *J. W. Payne* 66 §

JUYUSH (USA) 3 b.c. Silver Hawk (USA) 123 – Silken Doll (USA) (Chieftain II) [1994 109: 7g^6 7f^2 7m* 8g^3 8s^3 1995 8g* 10.4g^5 8g^3 12f* 14.8g^2 16f Jul 27] compact colt: impresses in appearance: good walker and very good mover: useful performer: won minor events at Doncaster (raced rather lazily) in March and Ascot (quite valuable 4-runner race, by 4 lengths from Warning Order) in June: probably stays 14.8f: acts on firm and soft ground: hung left second 3-y-o start, sweating (below form) next time: often a front runner: stays in training. *B. W. Hills* 104

K

KAAFIH HOMM (IRE) 4 b.g. Kefaah (USA) 124 – Shereeka 76 (Shergar 140) [1994 61: 10g a7g* 1995 a10g^2 a10g* a10g* a9.4g* a10g^4 12m 10m 10.8g^3 8.5d^2 8.3m^3 8m* 7f^3 12m* 10d* 11.9g^5 a8g^2 a10g^2 Dec 19] good-topped gelding: fair handicapper: had a very good year, winning at Lingfield (twice) and Wolverhampton 65 a77 in January, at Newmarket (apprentices, dead heat) in June and at Folkestone (apprentices) and Lingfield in September: needs further than 7f, and stays 1½m: acts on firm and dead ground and all-weather-surfaces: often bandaged behind: goes well with waiting tactics. *N. A. Callaghan*

KABCAST 10 b.g. Kabour 80 – Final Cast 50 (Saulingo 122) [1994 58: 5f 5m* 5m² 5m³ 5m⁴ 5m⁴ 5g 1995 5g a5g 5f 5m 5m⁵ 5f 5m³ 5m 5h⁴ 5f 5.1d Sep 11] good-bodied gelding: modest handicapper: best at 5f: needs a sound surface on turf, no form on the all-weather: wears blinkers: often sweats: races prominently. *D. W. Chapman* 51

KABIL 3 b.c. Doyoun 124 – Alkariyh (USA) 79 (Alydar (USA)) [1994 85p: 6f⁴ 7m 6g⁴ 6g* 6g⁶ 6m² a8g³ a8g³ 1995 6m² 6m³ 7m⁵ 7m⁴ 7m⁴ 7m³ 7.1d 7g² a8g³ a8g³ Dec 29] strong, lengthy, quite attractive colt: unimpressive mover: fairly useful handicapper: first past post in £11,600 race at Newcastle (demoted for interference) in July: best efforts when placed in rated stakes at Chester and Newmarket (reluctant stalls) 2 of last 3 starts for H. Thomson Jones: stays 7f: acts on good to firm ground, below best only start on a soft surface: consistent: sent to Dubai and placed in handicaps there. *P. Rudkin, UAE* 91

KADIRI (IRE) 4 b.g. Darshaan 133 – Kadissya (USA) (Blushing Groom (FR) 131) [1994 14g³ 12.5g 10d 13s⁶ 1995 a13g³ a16g* 16.2m 17.1m³ 21.6f³ 14.9g⁴ 16.5g⁴ 20m a14g⁴ a16g a14g⁴ Nov 24] lengthy ex-Irish gelding: sixth foal: half-brother to Kahyasi (by Ile de Bourbon): dam French 1¼m listed winner: fair performer: trained prior to 4-y-o season by J. Oxx: 5-length winner of amateurs handicap at Lingfield in January: a stayer: acts on firm ground and the all-weather: blinkered last 3 starts 1994. *J. R. Bosley* 63 a68

KAF 3 ch.c. Polish Precedent (USA) 131 – Usaylah 98 (Siberian Express (USA) 125) [1994 62p: 7g 8.1g 1995 8d 10g³ 8f* 8.1m Jul 2] lengthy, rather sparely-made colt: much improved form when winning lady amateurs maiden handicap at Redcar (moved short to post) in June by 5 lengths: saddle slipped final start: stayed 1m: acted on firm ground: has been retired. *J. L. Dunlop* 77

KAFANI AL WIDD (FR) 3 b.c. Royal Academy (USA) 130 – Belle Arrivee 87 (Bustino 136) [1994 –: 8s 1995 9g 7m* 7g Jul 6] leggy colt: fair form: made all in maiden at Thirsk in June, holding on well when challenged: stiffish task, held up and never threatened in handicap at Catterick 16 days later: stays 7f, may well (dam 1¼m winner) stay further: sold 11,500 gns Newmarket Autumn Sales: sent to Malaysia. *M. R. Stoute* 71

KAFHAR 2 b.c. (Feb 18) In The Wings 128 – Ittisaal 64 (Caerleon (USA) 132) [1995 8g* 9g² 9g³ Nov 19] 220,000 Francs Y: second foal: dam, sprint maiden, half-sister to 5 winners, including listed winner Tea House, later dam of Grade 1 9f winner Danish: won maiden at Rome in October: placed behind Brave Indigo both starts afterwards, beaten 2 noses in Premio Guido Berardelli at Rome on final one: will probably stay beyond 9f: has raced only on good ground. *L. Brogi, Italy* 100

KAHIR ALMAYDAN (IRE) 2 b.c. (Apr 12) Distinctly North (USA) 115 – Kilfenora (Tribal Chief 125) [1995 6m² 6m* 6g² 6m³ 6m* 6d* 6g³ Sep 28] 112

Kahir Almaydan was sent off at odds on for the Middle Park Stakes on the strength of his successive wide-margin victories, gained from the front, in the Bonusprint Champion Two Yrs Old Trophy at Ripon in August and the Bonusprint Mill Reef Stakes at Newbury in September. He faced only four opponents and, a grand stamp of individual, was beginning to look potentially high class. However, he met his match in the Gimcrack winner Royal Applause who took him on for the lead early, got on top by halfway and showed everything a clear pair of heels up the hill. Once headed, Kahir Almaydan seemed ill-at-ease off the bridle and he also proved one-paced under the whip, Woodborough finishing much the stronger to leave him in third, nearly six lengths behind Royal Applause.

While Kahir Almaydan is better than he showed at Newmarket he is probably no better than good second division, a sprinter at that. Easily his best efforts of the season came at Ripon and Newbury. He'd won one of four previous races, barely off the bridle in a minor event at York, and on another occasion finished third to Polaris Flight and Mubhij in the Richmond Stakes at Goodwood. It was his performance at Ripon that earned him another shot at a pattern race. He won by nine lengths from High Priority in a fast time, dominating the small field over the last two furlongs.

Bonusprint Mill Reef Stakes, Newbury—Kahir Almaydan leads throughout again; Kuantan (right), Warning Time (rails) and Resounder finish almost in line

There was also a small field for the Mill Reef Stakes, lightweight too with joint-favourite Desert Boy well below par. Kahir Almaydan forced the pace again and won in a similar fashion, galloping on strongly—in sharp contrast to Newmarket—to beat Kuantan by six lengths.

The way he finished at Newbury, another furlong might be within Kahir Almaydan's compass. He strikes us most as a sprinter, though, like his sire and his maternal grandsire. The Flying Childers winner Distinctly North enjoyed a good first season as a sire, with Rabican as well as Kahir Almaydan in a large crop. The dam, the Irish two-year-old five-furlong winner Kilfenora, seemed to stay a mile at three, and her first foal, the North American winner Guy's Gold (by Tap On Wood), stayed

Mirza Al Sayegh's "Kahir Almaydan"

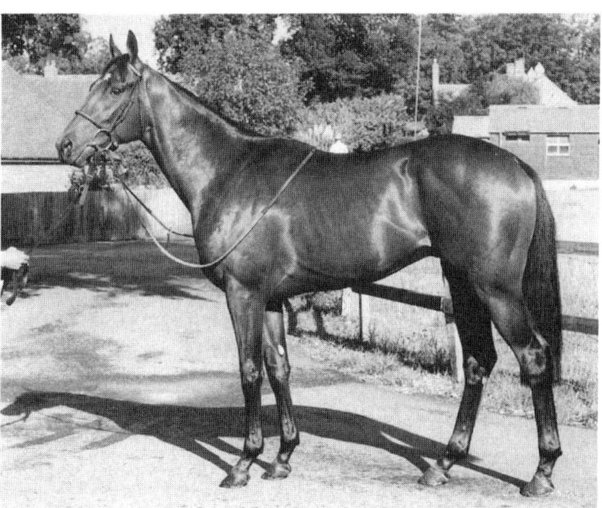

at least a mile. Her three other winning produce on the flat in Britain, African Chief (by Kafu), Herora (by Heraldiste) and Gibaltarik (by Jareer), were sprinting two-year-olds. African Chief later won over six furlongs in Hong Kong and Herora got seven. The pick of the dam's family in fairly recent times are two horses at opposite ends of the distance scale—the King's Stand, July Cup and William Hill Sprint Championship winner Never So Bold and the St Leger winner Bruni, both of them grandsons of Whimsical.

Kahir Almaydan (IRE) (b.c. Apr 12, 1993)	Distinctly North (USA) (b 1988)	Minshaanshu Amad (b or br 1979)	Northern Dancer
			Tappahannock
		Distinctiveness (b or br 1972)	Distinctive
			New Love
	Kilfenora (b 1976)	Tribal Chief (b 1967)	Princely Gift
			Mwanza
		Ribaldry (b 1971)	Ribero
			Whimsical

Kahir Almaydan was extremely well bought at the October Yearling Sales for 22,000 guineas. He is a well-made, good sort with lots of scope, and a fine mover, both at the walk and the gallop. He nearly always looked extremely well before his races, and certainly did at Newmarket, giving no hint that he might not be at his best. He won on good to firm ground at Ripon, good to soft ground at Newbury. *J. L. Dunlop*

KAI'S LADY (IRE) 2 b.f. (May 12) Jareer (USA) 115 – Rathnaleen (Scorpio (FR) 127) [1995 6g^6 May 30] 400Y: second foal: dam unraced: 25/1, tailed off in seller at Leicester. *S. W. Campion* –

KAITAK (IRE) 4 ch.g. Broken Hearted 124 – Klairelle (Klairon 131) [1994 78: 7g^3 7m^2 7f 7s 1995 8g a8.5g Apr 13] leggy, workmanlike gelding: fair handicapper: well beaten at Doncaster (£15,900 event) and Wolverhampton in 1995: should be as effective at 1m as 7f: acts on good to firm and heavy ground: fairly useful hurdler, winner in December. *J. M. Carr* –

KAJOSTAR 5 ch.m. Country Classic – Rasimareem (Golden Mallard 103) [1994 –: 6g 6s 1995 6m 7f 7f 6m Aug 22] no worthwhile form. *S. W. Campion* –

KALABO (USA) 3 b.c. Trempolino (USA) 135 – Kalikala (Darshaan 133) [1994 103p: 6g^4 7m^2 7m* 8s* 1995 12f^3 12f^5 14.6d Sep 9] strong, compact colt: smart performer: 3¾ lengths third of 8 to Pentire in King Edward VII Stakes at Royal Ascot on reappearance, staying on very strongly: around 8-lb below that form when 7½ lengths fifth of 6 in Gordon Stakes at Goodwood and 9½ lengths seventh of 10 (soon outpaced in straight) to Classic Cliche in St Leger at Doncaster: should be very well suited by further than 1½m: acts on firm and soft ground: to race in Dubai. *H. R. A. Cecil* 113

KALAKATE 10 gr.g. Kalaglow 132 – Old Kate 110 (Busted 134) [1994 NR 1995 a14g^4 12g a14.8g Jul 3] big, lengthy gelding: not even a shadow of the useful handicapper of 1988: won selling hurdle in September. *J. J. Bridger* –

KALAMATA 3 ch.c. Kalaglow 132 – Good Try 92 (Good Bond 122) [1994 NR 1995 8m^5 10.2m^2 12m^2 11f^6 a12g* Nov 11] 2,000Y: lengthy colt: half-brother to several winners, including fairly useful sprinter Choir Practice (by Chief Singer) and middle-distance performer Woodhoopoe (by Touching Wood): dam 2-y-o 5f winner: fair form: left A. Stewart's stable after fourth start: won minor event at Wolverhampton in November: should stay beyond 1½m: wandered under pressure last 2 starts. *J. A. Glover* 67 a81

KALAO TUA (IRE) 2 b.f. (Mar 30) Shaadi (USA) 126 – Lisa's Favourite (Gorytus (USA) 132) [1995 6m^2 7d Sep 26] 27,000 2-y-o: tall, angular filly: third foal: half-sister to 3-y-o Tirlie (by Tirol) and 1993 2-y-o 7f winner Majestic Heights (by High Estate): dam Irish maiden best at around 1m: short-head second of 5 to Dublin River in maiden at Yarmouth: soundly beaten in valuable sales race at Newmarket over 2 months later. *J. R. Fanshawe* 66

KALAR 6 b.g. Kabour 80 – Wind And Reign 55 (Tumble Wind (USA)) [1994 45, a65: a6g a5g a5g^2 a5g a5g^2 a5g* a5g* 5v^5 5m^5 5g 5g 6g 5g 5d a5g^3 a5g* 1995 a5g^2 a5g^2 a5g a5g^3 a5g* a5g 5d^3 6v^2 5m^4 6g^4 5m^6 5g^3 5g^5 5g^4 a6g 5m 5m^2 5m* 5m 5f* 5m^5 5g^4 5g a5g^5 a5g^2 a5g a5g^2 a5g^3 a5g Dec 14] good-bodied gelding: fair handicapper on the all-weather: won at Lingfield in March: modest at best on turf: 57 a74

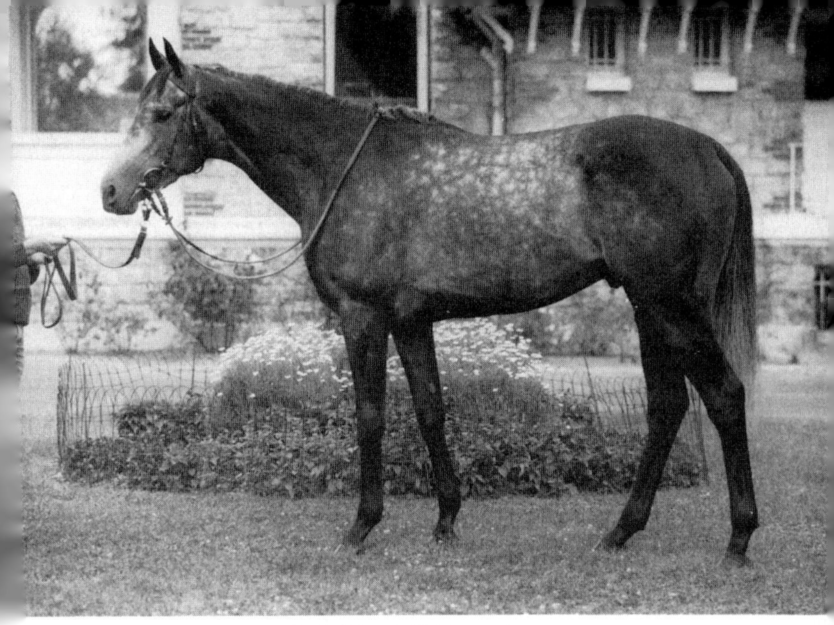

Ecurie Chalhoub's "Kaldounevees"

won at Catterick and Thirsk in August: effective at 5f and 6f: acts on the all-weather and any turf going: nearly always blinkered, has been tried visored: front runner: suitable mount for 7-lb claimer: tough. *D. W. Chapman*

KALA STAR 4 gr.f. Kalaglow 132 – Tantot 65 (Charlottown 127) [1994 –: 8.3m 10g 8.1g 11.9g^5 13.1g^6 12m 1995 12m 11.7m May 2] leggy filly: no worthwhile form: sold 725 gns Ascot September Sales. *J. Ffitch-Heyes* –

KALA SUNRISE 2 ch.c. (May 12) Kalaglow 132 – Belle of The Dawn (Bellypha 130) [1995 5.1g^4 5m* 6m 6d 7d 8f^4 Oct 16] tall, workmanlike colt: second foal: dam Irish 7f and 9f winner: won median auction maiden at Pontefract in April: apparently much improved effort when fourth of 6 to Weet-A-Minute in listed race at Pontefract final start: should stay beyond 1m: acts on firm ground. *C. Smith* 83 ?

KALDOUNEVEES (FR) 4 gr.c. Kaldoun (FR) 122 – Safaroa (FR) (Satingo 129) [1994 113: 8g 8g^2 8m* 9g^2 10s^6 10d^4 1995 8s^3 8g* 8v^3 8m* 10g^2 10f^4 11f^2 10f Oct 8] smart French colt: won Prix Edmond Blanc at Saint-Cloud (by length from Agathe) in April and Prix du Chemin de Fer du Nord at Chantilly (by ¾ length from Fraam, leading 1f out) in June: 1½ lengths second to Germany in Group 1 event at Munich in July and 1¼ lengths second of 12 to Millkom in Man o'War Stakes at Belmont in September: stays at least 11f: acts on firm and dead ground, below best on very soft: consistent granted suitable conditions, but broke blood vessel final start: has been retired to Haras du Mesnil at 15,000 francs (Oct 1). *J. E. Hammond, France* 118

KALKO 6 b.g. Kalaglow 132 – Salchow 116 (Niniski (USA) 125) [1994 46d: 8g 12.1g^6 13f^6 10g 14.1m a12g 1995 9.9m 15m^5 12.1g Sep 25] close-coupled gelding: seems of little account nowadays: trained until after reappearance by A. Harrison. *J. S. Goldie* –

KALOU 4 b.f. K-Battery 108 – Louise Moulton 90 (Moulton 128) [1994 57: 8g 7.1g^3 8g 7.5m 6f 9.9f^5 10.1m 10d^3 10.5s^3 10.3s^2 12.4d^4 1995 9.9m^5 10m^2 10.3m 10m^2 10g^3 10.1m 10.1f^4 12g* 13.1g^2 11.9s^2 12s 12.1s^3 Nov 2] small, lightly-made 71 filly: fair handicapper: won at Thirsk in September: better at 1½m than shorter and will stay 1¾m: acts on firm and soft ground: visored fourth 3-y-o to seventh 4-y-o start: tough and reliable. *C. W. C. Elsey*

KAMARI (USA) 2 ch.c. (Jan 26) Woodman (USA) 126 – Karri Valley (USA) (Storm Bird (CAN) 134) [1995 7.1s^5 Oct 1] IR 52,000Y: well-made colt: second foal: brother to useful Irish 3-y-o maiden (at 9f/1¼m) Taglioni: dam, ran once at 2 yrs in Ireland, closely related to National Stakes winner Fatherland out of Coronation Stakes winner Lisadell, an excellent family: 7/1 and green, 5 lengths fifth of 14 to Carburton in maiden at Haydock, challenging over 2f out then one pace: will do better. *A. C. Stewart* 71 p

KAMA SIMBA 3 b.g. Lear Fan (USA) 130 – Dance It (USA) (Believe It (USA)) [1994 44: 7m 7m 7s 1995 a6g^4 7g^4 8.2m* 10m^2 10f^6 8m^2 8f^4 Aug 1] compact gelding: has a round action: modest performer: won selling handicap at Nottingham (bought in 8,800 gns) in June: stays 1¼m: acts on good to firm ground: looked irresolute fifth 3-y-o start: temperament under suspicion: sold (N. Callaghan to J. White) only 2,600 gns Newmarket Autumn Sales. *N. A. Callaghan* 59

KANAT LEE (IRE) 4 b.f. Salse (USA) 128 – Badiya (USA) (Sir Ivor 135) [1994 61d: 8f 7.1m* 8m^6 8f 8m 7g 10m 12.4d 1995 10.3m 10g^4 9.9d^6 10m^3 11.9m^5 9.9g 10f^6 14.1m^4 16d 12.1g Sep 25] close-coupled filly: only poor form at best in 1995: stays 1¼m: acts on good to firm ground: inconsistent: sold (Don Enrico Incisa to Mrs V. Aconley) 1,400 gns Doncaster October Sales. *Don Enrico Incisa* 43 d

KANDAVU 2 b.f. (Mar 10) Safawan 118 – Baladee (Mummy's Pet 125) [1995 5d^2 5.2m* 5m^5 5.2g^6 6m^4 6f^3 5.2g 6f 6d Oct 21] 3,500Y: workmanlike filly: shows knee action: half-sister to a winner abroad by Dunbeath: dam unraced: won maiden auction at Newbury in April: absent 3 months before good seventh of 26 to Blue Iris in Redcar Two-Year-Old Trophy penultimate start: poor effort in nursery at Newbury 9 days later: stays 6f: acts on firm and dead ground. *M. McCormack* 87

KANDYAN 4 b.g. Shareef Dancer (USA) 135 – Kandia (GER) (Luciano) [1994 68: 8g^2 8.5d^2 10.3m^4 10.5g 10d^6 13.6g^4 14.6d 1995 12m^3 10.4g^2 10d* 12g^2 10g^2 Sep 21] close-coupled, sturdy gelding: showed knee action: fair handicapper: won at Sandown (apprentices) in September: stayed 13.6f: visored last 3 starts at 3 yrs: fell fatally over hurdles Sep 30. *M. H. Tompkins* 75

KANGRA VALLEY 4 ch.f. Indian Ridge 123 – Thorner Lane 86 (Tina's Pet 121) [1994 56: 5g 5f 5.1m a5g a5g^2 a6g 5.1d 1995 5m 5m a5g Jun 8] sturdy, plain filly: soundly beaten for new stable in 1995. *T. R. Watson* –

KANIKA 3 gr.f. Be My Chief (USA) 122 – Kalisha (Rainbow Quest (USA) 134) [1994 NR 1995 10.4g^6 Aug 30] 5,000Y: rather leggy filly: first foal: dam unraced half-sister to Kala Dancer: 16/1, mulish in preliminaries and all but refused to race in maiden at York. *B. Hanbury* §§

KARAAR 3 b.c. Efisio 120 – Elkie Brooks 82 (Relkino 131) [1994 NR 1995 7.3m 8.1g^3 9m^3 7g^6 Oct 9] 100,000Y: strong, good-bodied colt: has a markedly round action: sixth foal: brother to 3 winners, notably smart sprinter Pips Pride and fairly useful 7f/1m colt Sunday's Hill: dam, second over 6f at 2 yrs, didn't train on: third of 9 in maiden at Haydock in June: found little next start, and never going all that well (after moving badly to post) final one: bandaged behind on debut: sold only 1,600 gns Newmarket Autumn Sales. *J. H. M. Gosden* 74 ?

KARAYB (IRE) 3 b. or br.f. Last Tycoon 131 – Deira (NZ) (Sir Tristram 115) [1994 93p: 6f* 6m^4 1995 7m^3 7g* 8f 7m^5 7g^6 10g 8g^2 7f^2 Oct 23] strong, lengthy filly: carries condition: has a quick action: fairly useful form: made all in minor event at Leicester in June: below that form until second in similar events there (always close up) in October: stayed 1m: acted on firm going, did not race on a soft surface: visits Cadeaux Genereux. *D. Morley* 93

KARAYIB (USA) 3 b.f. Danzig (USA) – Aghani (USA) (Blushing Groom (FR) 131) [1994 84: 6m^5 6g^2 6f^2 7.5f^2 8.5m^3 7g* 7g* 1995 8m 7.1m 8.5m 8f Jun 24] well-made filly: fairly useful performer: best effort as 3-y-o in listed event at Epsom third start, setting strong pace: stays 8.5f: has raced only on a sound surface: visored (below form) second 3-y-o start: usually front runner: sold 48,000 gns Newmarket December Sales. *J. L. Dunlop* 81

KARAYLAR (IRE) 3 b.g. Kahyasi 130 – Karamana (Habitat 134) [1994 NR 1995 7g Sep 16] second foal: half-brother to useful Irish middle-distance performer Karikata (by Doyoun): dam unraced: 33/1, slow into stride and always well behind in maiden at Catterick. *W. Storey* –

KARDELLE 5 b.m. Kalaglow 132 – Arderelle (FR) 80 (Pharly (FR) 130) [1994 –: a12g 10d 10g 1995 10.8d Apr 1] big, workmanlike mare: no form since 3 yrs: stays 1½m: acts on good to firm and dead going: sold 46,000 gns Newmarket December Sales. *Mrs A. L. M. King* –

KARIBU (GER) 4 b.g. Dancing Brave (USA) 140 – Kaiserstadt (GER) (Dschingis Khan) [1994 NR 1995 6.9m^4 8.1g 13.1g^4 11.1g 10.4m Oct 5] rangy gelding: fourth foal: dam won 3 races and runner-up in Preis der Diana: poor maiden: trained until after second start by M. Meagher: stays 13.1f: sold (P. Monteith to J. Bennett) 800 gns Doncaster November Sales. *P. Monteith* 40

KARINA HEIGHTS (USA) 3 b.f. Irish Tower (USA) – Love Sick (USA) (Raise A Native) [1994 NR 1995 5.1g* 6g^5 5.1m^2 5m 5m 6g Sep 16] $26,000F, $22,000Y, $40,000 2-y-o: quite attractive filly: eighth foal: sister to a winner in USA and half-sister to several winners, including a 3-y-o 6f stakes winner by Pilgrim: dam unraced daughter of Grade 1 1¼m winner Coraggioso: fair form: won maiden at Nottingham in April: ran poorly in handicaps 2 of last 3 starts, folding tamely in Ayr Silver Cup final one: should stay 6f: visored (not disgraced) penultimate outing. *J. W. Watts* 78

KARINSKA 5 b.m. Master Willie 129 – Kaiserchronik (GER) (Cortez (GER)) [1994 60, a68: a6g^4 7.5d 6f 7g^4 6m^5 8f 8m 8g 8g 6g^4 7d 8g 8s 7d 8m^5 12g 1995 a8g^6 a8g^5 7.5m 8g* 8m 8.5m^6 7g* 8.3g* 8m^3 8m^3 6g^4 8m 7g 8d^3 8.1g 7.1s^3 8m Oct 14] angular, workmanlike mare: has a quick action: fair handicapper: won at Thirsk in April and at Catterick and Windsor in June: should stay beyond 1m: acts on fibresand and firm ground, probably on soft: sometimes reluctant to post and slowly away: carries head awkwardly: usually claimer ridden: held up. *M. C. Chapman* 71 a–

KARISMA (IRE) 2 b.c. (Feb 7) Tirol 127 – Avra (FR) 65 (Mendez (FR) 128) [1995 7g^4 7.9g^3 7f^3 Oct 24] 4,600F, 7,500Y: sturdy, angular colt: second foal: half-brother to Italian 3-y-o 6f winner Graphic (by Scenic): dam, second at 1¼m from 2 starts, out of half-sister to Arctic Tern: fair form in maidens won by Jo Mell at Ayr and Committal at York first 2 starts: modest third of 5 (beaten over 11 lengths) in minor event at Redcar last time: will stay beyond 1m. *Denys Smith* 73

KARLINE KA (FR) 4 ch.f. Franc Parler – Kadastra (FR) (Stradavinsky 121) [1994 –: 9v 12m 12g 1995 18m Jun 19] lengthy filly: modest winning hurdler: little worthwhile form on flat. *R. Dickin* –

KARON BEACH 4 ch.f. Handsome Sailor 125 – Winter Resort (Miami Springs 121) [1994 56: 8.1f^4 8m^3 10g^2 10.1d* a11g 11.5g a13g 1995 11.5m^6 a8.5g a12g 11.5g Sep 12] small, sparely-made filly: no form since bought out of seller at 3 yrs: stays 1¼m: acts on firm ground, dead and fibresand. *J. R. Bostock* –

KARTTIKEYA (FR) 4 br.g. Darshaan 133 – Karosa (FR) (Caro 133) [1994 81: 7d 12m^3 11.9m^2 12f 14.1g^2 14s^4 1995 10.1m^3 12m^6 14.1m^6 a11g Dec 1] strong gelding: bad mover: fair maiden: sold out of A. Stewart's stable 9,200 gns Ascot June Sales: third of 7 in minor event at Yarmouth in August: bandaged, failed to repeat that form: stays 1¾m: acts on good to firm ground, below form on soft. *Mrs N. Macauley* 74

KASS ALHAWA 2 b.c. (Feb 28) Shirley Heights 130 – Silver Braid (USA) 101 (Miswaki (USA) 124) [1995 7m^4 Aug 4] 85,000Y: good-topped colt: first foal: dam 2-y-o 7f winner later suited by 1m: 20/1, shaped well when 6¾ lengths fourth of 12 to Lord of Men in maiden at Newmarket, nearest finish under hands and heels from 2f out: will stay at least 1m: sure to do better. *M. R. Stoute* 76 p

KASSBAAN (USA) 5 b.g. Alydar (USA) – Ma Biche (USA) 125 (Key To The Kingdom (USA)) [1994 88: 8f 8g 8m 7.1m^2 7m 8m^5 a7g* 1995 a6g* a6g* a6g* 6m^3 May 23] big, good-bodied gelding: impresses in appearance: sent to Dubai after 4-y-o turf season: improved into useful performer: beat small fields in handicap (by 10 lengths) in January and conditions events (by around 8 lengths) in February and March, all at Nad Al Sheba: 5/4 on, not quite up to his Dubai standard (but best effort here) when 1¾ lengths third of 5 to Al Rawda in minor event at Goodwood, prominent, leading from halfway to inside last: effective at 6f to 1m: suited by a 104 sound surface (acts on firm going) here and goes well on sand: blinkered (below form) twice at 4 yrs: sometimes bandaged off-hind: used to be held up (taking keen hold), made running in Dubai: returned to Dubai. *Saeed bin Suroor*

KATIE KOMAITE 2 b.f. (May 12) Komaite (USA) – City To City 55 (Windjammer (USA)) [1995 5g^6 5g^4 a6g 5m^3 5f 5f 6f^6 7.1s^3 Nov 2] 3,800Y: leggy, angular filly: third foal: sister to 3-y-o 6f winner The Scythian, 5.3f winner at 2 yrs, and 7f (at 2 yrs) and 1¼m winner Komplicity: dam stayed 1m: had run of race and favoured rail when third of 14 in maiden auction at Edinburgh (could be rated 63) on final start: stays 7f: acts on good to firm and soft ground. *Capt. J. Wilson* 54+

KATIE OLIVER 3 b.f. Squill (USA) 122 – Shih Ching (USA) (Secreto (USA) 128) [1994 NR 1995 14g^5 14s^5 14.1m Oct 19] good-topped, workmanlike filly: second foal: half-sister to German 4-y-o 7.5f and 9f winner Story of Love (by Taufan): dam unraced half-sister to dual Grade 1 winner Dontstop Themusic: form in maidens only when fifth at Lingfield second start: hung badly left and eased right down (had reportedly slipped and pulled muscle) at Nottingham 3 weeks later. *B. Smart* 67

KATIE'S KID 5 br.g. Balidar 133 – Khahmens Delight (Come On Grey 96) [1994 –: 14.9s 11.7g 7d 7g 8g 6m a7g 1995 12g^2 10m* 11.5m Jun 24] leggy, angular gelding: ridden by 7-lb claimer, won handicap at Lingfield in June, always prominent: tailed off as if something amiss there week later: stays 1½m: wears bandages. *M. J. Ahern* 39

KATINIYD (IRE) 4 b.g. Kahyasi 130 – Katiyfa (Auction Ring (USA) 123) [1994 8m* 8m^3 11d^3 10d^4 12s^4 1995 11.8m Jun 17] smallish, robust gelding: second foal: half-brother to fairly useful Irish 2-y-o 7f winner Kariniyd (by Blushing Groom), who stayed 1½m: dam French 1m (listed race) and 1¼m winner: fairly useful form (rated 92) in Ireland at 3 yrs for J. Oxx, winning maiden at Naas: sold IR 10,000 gns: winning juvenile hurdler in 1994/5: 40/1, tailed off and virtually pulled up in listed event at Leicester on return to flat: stays 1½m: acts on good to firm ground and soft. *Mrs N. Macauley* –

KATYA (IRE) 3 b.f. Dancing Dissident (USA) 119 – Park Elect (Ahonoora 122) [1994 84: 5d* 5m 5f 6g^2 6d^6 5.1g^2 5s^2 5m^4 1995 7g 6m* 5m^2 6g 6g^5 6s^3 6m^3 5.1g^4 6.5g^5 5f^3 6d 6m^3 6g^2 5.2d^2 6d 5g^3 5s^4 Sep 30] lightly-made filly: has a quick action: fairly useful performer: won handicap at Kempton in April: mostly creditable efforts afterwards, keeping-on third of 9 to Dairine's Delight in listed race at Newmarket penultimate start: best at up to 6.5f: acts on firm and soft ground: tough: sold 18,000 gns Newmarket December Sales. *M. R. Channon* 93

KATY KOO 3 b.f. Presidium 124 – Francis Furness 58 (Burslem 123) [1994 NR 1995 8.1m^2 8g 10d Sep 18] 500F, 800Y: workmanlike filly: first foal: dam stayed 11f: no promise in sellers. *P. J. Bevan* –

KATY-Q (IRE) 2 b.f. (Mar 5) Taufan (USA) 119 – Swift Chorus (Music Boy 124) [1995 5g 5f^3 5f^2 6f^3 6m^6 5g* Sep 18] 13,000Y: first foal: dam, Irish 2-y-o 6f winner, half-sister to very smart middle-distance filly Talented out of daughter of good racemare and broodmare Triple First: modest form: blinkered, won 9-finisher maiden at Edinburgh in September: best form at 5f. *P. Calver* 58

KATY'S LAD 8 b.g. Camden Town 125 – Cathryn's Song (Prince Tenderfoot (USA) 126) [1994 56: 10.8v^3 9.9d 8g^2 10.3m* 12.3g^2 10.5g^5 10.8m^5 10.8s^2 a12g^5 1995 a9.4g^2 10.3m* 10.4m^5 a12g Oct 14] leggy gelding: unimpressive mover: modest performer nowadays: won claimer at Chester (for second year running) in June: below form afterwards: stays 12.3f: acts on good to firm ground and soft: effective with or without blinkers: often bandaged: mulish to post penultimate start. *B. A. McMahon* 63

KAUSAR (USA) 8 b.h. Vaguely Noble 140 – Kozana 127 (Kris 135) [1994 –: a13g 1995 a16g a12g^4 Feb 24] sturdy, lengthy horse: no longer of any account. *J. L. Eyre* –

KAYRAWAN (USA) 3 b.c. Mr Prospector (USA) – Muhbubh (USA) 108 (Blushing Groom (FR) 131) [1994 91P: 6m* 1995 6m^6 6m^5 7g^5 5.1g Jul 15] strong, lengthy colt: has plenty of scope: did not progress as anticipated in 1995, showing fairly useful form in minor events: best form at 6f: has raced only on a sound surface: sent to Dubai. *H. Thomson Jones* 90

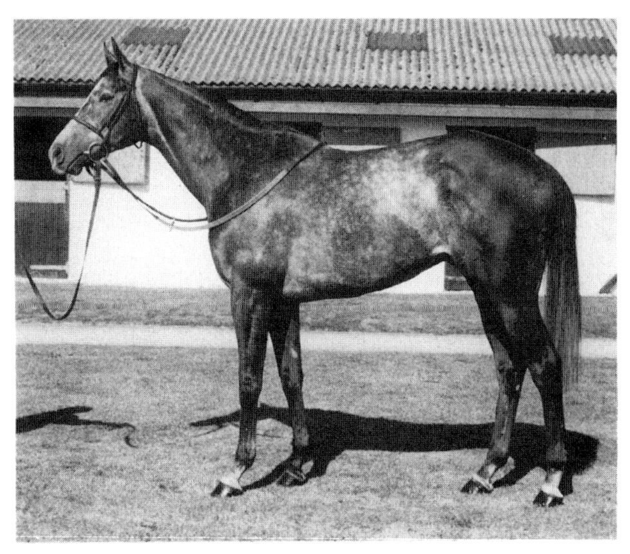

Mr J. H. Richmond-Watson's "Kayvee"

KAYVEE 6 gr.g. Kaldoun (FR) 122 – Secret Life (USA) (Elocutionist (USA)) 107
[1994 100: 7f^3 8m^5 7f^2 7m 7.6m^2 8f 7m 7g^3 9g^5 8m* 8.1g* 8d^2 1995 7m^5 7.9g^2 8m^5 8f^4 8g* 7m 7d 9g 8m Oct 28] big, close-coupled gelding: impresses in appearance: useful performer, better than ever: again ran well in some of the most prestigious handicaps without landing one, though gained deserved success in rated stakes at Ascot in July: stays 9f: acts on firm and dead ground: blinkered twice at 3 yrs, running well second occasion: sometimes wears severe noseband: held up: genuine and consistent. *G. Harwood*

KAZAKI 3 b.c. Sadler's Wells (USA) 132 – Krakow 85 (Malinowski (USA) 123) 80
[1994 NR 1995 8m^3 Apr 19] brother to useful 1¼m winner (also successful in USA) Adam Smith and smart middle-distance stayer Braashee, closely related to 7f winner Ustka (by Lomond) and half brother to Nell Gwyn winner Ghariba (by Final Straw): dam 7f winner from good family: 11/8 on and bandaged behind, 3¼ lengths third of 10 to Solar Flight in Wood Ditton Stakes at Newmarket: dead. *J. H. M. Gosden*

KAZIMIERA (IRE) 2 b.f. (May 2) Polish Patriot (USA) 128 – Cartier Bijoux 96 77 ?
(Ahonoora 122) [1995 5g^3 5g^6 5s^3 a5g^6 Dec 1] plain, leggy filly: third foal: half-sister to useful 1994 2-y-o 5f and 6f winner Fallow (by Common Grounds) and 4-y-o 5f and 6f winner Muzz (by Gallic League): dam 2-y-o 5f winner: failed to repeat debut form (when third to Some Horse in maiden at Haydock): slowly away in nursery at Southwell last time: should stay 6f: very reluctant at stalls on third outing. *M. Johnston*

KEALBRA LADY 2 b.f. (Feb 21) Petong 126 – Greensward Blaze 50 (Sagaro –
133) [1995 5.7f^6 Jul 1] 6,800Y: sister to a modest maiden and half-sister to very smart 5f (at 2 yrs) to 7f winner Prince Ferdinand (by King Of Spain) and a winner in Hong Kong by Crofter: dam won 1m seller: 50/1, virtually pulled up in maiden auction at Bath. *M. S. Saunders*

KEBILI (IRE) 2 b.f. (Mar 11) Green Desert (USA) 127 – Pebbles 135 (Sharpen Up 127) [1995 6g^{4} Jul 3] good-topped filly: sixth foal: dam won from 6f (at 2 yrs) to 1½m, showing top-class form: 9/2 and bit backward, over 8 lengths last of 4 to Tropical Dance in minor event at Windsor, slowly away and losing touch last 2f: swished tail throughout: sold 18,000 gns Newmarket December Sales. *M. R. Stoute* 66

KEDWICK (IRE) 6 b.g. Be My Guest (USA) 126 – Lady Pavlova 111 (Ballymore 123) [1994 9.6g^{2} 9.6g^{6} 9m 1995 a10g^{2} a10g^{3} a12g^{5} a8g^{2} a8g^{2} Mar 29] modest ex-Irish maiden: seventh foal: half-brother to several winners, notably smart middle-distance performer Baba Karam (by Persian Bold): dam, runner-up in Park Hill Stakes, won at up to 1¼m: trained 1994 by J. G. Burns, sold IR 3,600 gns Goffs October Sales: placed, running well, at Lingfield on 4 of 5 starts in 1995: appeared to stay 1½m in Ireland, but best efforts here over shorter: blinkered/visored at 6 yrs. *P. R. Hedger* 60

KEEN TO THE LAST (FR) 3 ch.g. Keen 116 – Derniere Danse (Gay Mecene (USA) 128) [1994 NR 1995 8.1g^{3} 10m 10m^{3} 10m 12s 12g Sep 29] strong gelding: first foal: dam well-bred French maiden: fair form in maidens first 3 starts: well beaten in handicaps afterwards: stays 1¼m: visored (out of form) final start: sold (G. Harwood to M. Hammond) 11,500 gns Newmarket Autumn Sales. *G. Harwood* 78 d

KEEP BATTLING 5 b.g. Hard Fought 125 – Keep Mum 63 (Mummy's Pet 125) [1994 –: 7.1m 7g 1995 10.9m* 10g* 8.3f^{3} 12.1m^{2} 10f^{3} 10.9g^{4} 10.1m^{5} 6m 10f^{6} 7g 12.1g^{5} 12.1g^{6} 8.9g Oct 7] unfurnished gelding: modest winning hurdler: poor handicapper on flat: won at Ayr in May and June: finds 1m a bare minimum (stays 1½m): acts on firm ground (and soft over hurdles): visored (no form) twice at 3 yrs: sweating (below form) final 5-y-o start: held up and has turn of foot. *J. S. Goldie* 44

KEEPERS DAWN (IRE) 2 b.f. (Mar 22) Alzao (USA) 117 – Keepers Lock (USA) (Sunny's Halo (CAN)) [1995 6m^{6} 6m 6.1d* 6g Sep 30] robust filly: has scope: second foal: half-sister to 3-y-o Latching (by Thatching): dam unraced: won 19-runner maiden at Nottingham in September by 3 lengths from Wee Hope, running on really well: got worked up beforehand and failed to give her running in nursery at Newmarket later in month: effective at 6f and will stay further: acts on dead ground: looked promising before Newmarket. *R. F. Johnson Houghton* 85

KEEPER'S GREY 3 gr.c. Touch of Grey 90 – Mistress Will (USA) (Master Willie 129) [1994 55: 6s a5g a7g^{2} 1995 a6g^{3} a7g^{5} a6g Apr 13] sparely-made colt: modest maiden: stayed 7f: acted on soft ground and all-weather: blinkered (below form) last 2 starts: dead. *R. Guest* 55

KEEP QUIET 3 b.f. Reprimand 122 – Silent Pool 68 (Relkino 131) [1994 54: 6.9m 8.1g^{6} a8.5g^{6} 8s 8d^{6} 8d^{6} 1995 8m 8.3m 16.4m Nov 6] neat filly: sold out of D. Arbuthnot's stable 700 gns Ascot February (1995) Sales: tailed off for new stable: bred to be suited by further than 1m: acts on good to firm and dead ground: tried blinkered, no improvement. *W. J. Musson* –

KEEP YOUR DISTANCE 5 b.g. Elegant Air 119 – Normanby Lass 100 (Bustino 136) [1994 63: a11g 12g 9.9d^{5} 12m^{2} 16m^{5} 13f* 12g^{3} 15.1m^{2} 11.1g^{6} 13.6g^{5} 12m* 12h^{2} 13m^{2} 12.1m^{3} 12f^{4} 12g 1995 11.1m^{2} 10.9g* 15.1m* 10.9g* 11.1g* 11.5s* 12m* 12m Oct 21] leggy, workmanlike gelding: fair performer: had an excellent season and won claimers at Ayr and Edinburgh in the summer, amateurs handicap at Ayr, claimer at Hamilton and amateurs minor event at Lingfield (3 days later) in September and handicap at Catterick (overcame trouble in running) in October: stiffish task (in much better race) but favourite, below form in handicap at Doncaster last time: stays 15f: acts on hard ground and soft: tough and consistent: won over hurdles in November. *Mrs M. Reveley* 77

KEIKO 2 ch.f. (Feb 10) Generous (IRE) 139 – Katsina (USA) 98 (Cox's Ridge (USA)) [1995 6m^{6} 6g^{4} 6d^{2} Sep 27] compact filly: second foal: dam, 2-y-o 7f winner, from family of Trillionaire: fair form in maidens at Newmarket, Goodwood and (equal-second to Sylva Paradise) Folkestone: will be very well suited by at least 1m: sold 9,000 gns Newmarket December Sales. *J. H. M. Gosden* 69 p

KEITH'S PRIDE (IRE) 3 gr.g. Al Hareb (USA) 123 – Zanskar (Godswalk (USA) 130) [1994 –: 6m 7m 1995 9.2s 8.3g^{5} 10m 11.1m Jun 19] leggy, close-coupled gelding: no worthwhile form. *T. Dyer* –

KELLAIRE GIRL (IRE) 3 b.f. Gallic League 119 – Frensham Manor (Le Johnstan 123) [1994 –: 5d 1995 6d^{5} 5.1g 6f^{6} 6m^{4} 8m a8g^{2} 8m^{6} 8.5m^{4} 8f 9m a8g^{2} a8g 43 a53

a7g Dec 14] tall, lengthy filly: poor maiden: stays 1m: acts on firm and dead ground and on equitrack: below form in blinkers: inconsistent. *A. Moore*

KELLY MAC 5 b.g. Precocious 126 – Ridalia 56 (Ridan (USA)) [1994 67, a70: a8g* a8g* a8g^4 a8g* 10.3g 10.1g^3 8f^4 7.5m* 8.2f^2 7g^5 8.5g* 8.3m a8.5g^5 8.1f^3 7m^4 a9.4g* 9f 8.3m^4 10m 8m^3 8d^5 9d 8g^2 8d 8.2g 1995 7.1d Oct 10] sturdy, good-quartered gelding: tough and game handicapper at 4 yrs for M. Channon: below form only start in 1995: stays 1¼m: probably acts on any going: front runner/races prominently: modest hurdler. *D. C. O'Brien* –

KELLY'S KITE 7 br.m. Buzzards Bay 128§ – Bold Kelly 83 (Pitskelly 122) [1994 –: a12g 1995 a10g a7g a8g Feb 7] compact mare: no longer of much account. *H. J. Collingridge* –

KEMO SABO 3 b.g. Prince Sabo 123 – Canoodle 66 (Warpath 113) [1994 83: 5m^3 5m^3 6f^3 6m 6s* 7.9d 7s^2 7v 1995 8d 10.5m 9.9m 8.5m^2 8g 7g^5 8m^4 8g* 7f 7.5m^2 10f^3 8g^4 8d Sep 9] lengthy gelding: good mover: fairly useful handicapper: easily best efforts when in frame, winner at Ayr (for 7-lb claimer) in July: stays 8.5f: acts on any going: has run well for amateur: sold (Mrs. J. Ramsden to C. Parker) 17,000 gns Newmarket Autumn Sales. *Mrs J. R. Ramsden* 83

KENCOL 3 b.g. Presidium 124 – Silk Lady 97 (Tribal Chief 125) [1994 71?: 6m 5s^5 6.1d 1995 5m^5 6.1g 5.1m 5g 7f^4 8f Jul 31] leggy gelding: seems just a modest maiden at best: stays 7f: probably acts on any going: blinkered (well beaten) fourth 3-y-o start: not one to rely on. *A. G. Foster* 55 ?

KENESHA (IRE) 5 br.m. Don't Forget Me 127 – Calvino (Relkino 131) [1994 NR 1995 7.1d 6s 6.9m^5 5g^3 5g 5f^2 5g 5m^3 5f^6 5g 5m^2 5f^2 6f^5 5f 5m^4 5g 5g 5f Oct 14] workmanlike mare: poor maiden handicapper: best efforts at 5f: acts on firm and dead ground: tried blinkered, no improvement: races prominently: inconsistent. *D. A. Nolan* 54 d

KENILWORTH DANCER 2 br.c. (Apr 28) Shareef Dancer (USA) 135 – Reltop 72 (High Top 131) [1995 6g^6 6d 7m 8f Oct 31] sturdy, compact colt: closely related to 1½m winner Be A Honey (by Be My Guest) and half-brother to several winners, including useful stayers Just David (by Blakeney) and Summit (by Salse): dam 1½m winner: towards rear in maidens and a nursery (tended to hang left): joined R. Woodhouse. *Mrs M. Reveley* –

KENILWORTH FORD 4 b.f. Merdon Melody 98 – Earles-Field (Wolverlife 115) [1994 –, a38: a8.5g^4 a8.5g^4 8g 8.3m a9.4g^6 a9.4g 1995 8g 7g a7g Jun 22] strong, lengthy filly: showed nil in 1995: stayed 8.5f: acted on fibresand: dead. *F. J. O'Mahony* –

KENNY DAVIS (IRE) 2 b.g. (Mar 27) Mazaad 106 – Very Seldom (Rarity 129) [1995 5s^6 5m Apr 15] 4,200Y: sparely-made gelding: half-brother to 3-y-o 7.5f winner Euro Sceptic (by Classic Secret), winning sprinter Jimmy The Skunk (by Fayruz) and 1m winner Ruby Shoes (by Day Is Done): dam ran twice on flat and placed over hurdles: well beaten in early-season auction events. *Mrs H. Parrott* –

KENSINGTON FREIGHT 3 b.f. Clantime 101 – Ascot Lass (Touching Wood (USA) 127) [1994 51: 6m 5m 6m^6 5.1g 1995 5m 5.1m 5m 7m 6m^6 6m 6m 7f^5 9m^6 Aug 13] good-topped filly: poor maiden handicapper: probably stays 7f: no improvement in visor. *J. Akehurst* 42 ?

KENTAVRUS WAY (IRE) 4 b.g. Thatching 131 – Phantom Row 37 (Adonijah 126) [1994 67d: a7g^3 7d^5 8.5m 7f^5 a7g^3 7f^5 10m* 10f^6 a10g a10g 1995 a12g a8g a10g a16g a10g Nov 14] good-bodied gelding: fair performer at best: no form in 1995: stays 1¼m: acts on firm ground, best effort on equitrack. *A. Moore* –

KENTFORD CONQUISTA 2 b.f. (Apr 12) El Conquistador 109 – Notinhand (Nearly A Hand 115) [1995 7.1s Oct 17] fourth reported foal: dam unraced: 100/1, soundly beaten in maiden at Chepstow. *J. W. Mullins* –

KENTUCKY FLYER 4 ch.f. Bairn (USA) 126 – Kentucky Air (USA) 89 (Czaravich (USA)) [1994 –: a6g^5 8d a7g a8g 1995 a12g Jan 27] neat filly: no form since 2 yrs: tried visored. *J. F. Bottomley* –

KENYATTA (USA) 6 b.g. Mogambo (USA) – Caranga (USA) (Caro 133) [1994 46d: a12g^2 a13g* a13g^2 a12g a13g^2 a12g^2 a10g a16g a13g^5 17.2f a16g^6 10m 11.5d a12g a12g^2 a16g^6 1995 a13g^4 12m a10g^5 a13g^6 a12g^3 Dec 18] leggy, quite attractive – a37

gelding: poor performer: stays 13f: acts on equitrack, no form in 6 races on turf since 1992: tried visored and blinkered, not since 1992: inconsistent. *A. Moore*

KERNOF (IRE) 2 b.g. (Apr 30) Rambo Dancer (CAN) 107 – Empress Wu 62 (High Line 125) [1995 6m 7m^{4} 6f^{4} 7g^{5} 8g Sep 14] 4,300Y, 5,200 2-y-o: leggy gelding: second foal: dam lightly raced: seems flattered by fourth of 5 to Larghetto in maiden at Hamilton third start: ran poorly in nursery at Yarmouth final one: should stay 1m. *M. D. Hammond* 60 +

KERRY RING 2 b.f. (Feb 3) Sadler's Wells (USA) 132 – Kerrera 115 (Diesis 133) [1995 7m^{2} Nov 3] third foal: half-sister to French 3-y-o 1¼m winner Kerrier (by Nashwan): dam, runner-up in 1000 Guineas then reverted to sprinting, half-sister to Rock City out of Musidora winner Rimosa's Pet: 9/2 from 5/2 and very green, 1¼ lengths second of 17 to Jackson Hill in maiden at Doncaster, losing several lengths with slow start but making good progress from 3f out, giving impression unlucky not to have won: will do a good deal better, and is sure to win races. *J. H. M. Gosden* 82 P

KESTON POND (IRE) 5 b.g. Taufan (USA) 119 – Maria Renata (Jaazeiro (USA) 127) [1994 66, a75: a7g* 8m 8s 7d a7g^{2} 8.1d 7m^{4} 8s 1995 7f* 8m^{5} 7m 7m 7m* 6g* 7g 7f Oct 18] tall, close-coupled gelding: fair handicapper: won at Yarmouth in June and at Leicester and Ayr (£12,400 Ladbroke Silver Cup, landing a gamble) in September: effective at 6f to 8.2f: acts on fibresand and firm ground: blinkered (tailed off) final 4-y-o start. *D. A. Wilson* 77

KESTREL FORBOXES (IRE) 7 b.g. Seymour Hicks (FR) 125 – Dance Mistress (Javelot 124) [1995 9m* 8.5f* 9g* 12m* 8m^{3} 10g^{4} 8g Sep 8] close-coupled gelding: unimpressive mover: fair performer (rated 79) here in 1991: has since won 11 races between 5f and 1½m in France/Jersey between 1992 and 1995, including Jersey Derby at Les Landes in August: easily best of 3 runs back here when neck third of 17 at Salisbury: finds 1m a bare minimum, and stays 1½m. *C. McCready, Jersey* 66

KETABI (USA) 4 ch.g. Alydar (USA) – Ivory Fields (USA) 110 (Sir Ivor 135) [1994 81: 10g^{3} 10.4m^{2} 10.3m 10d* 10.5d 1995 10.8d 12m Apr 19] quite attractive gelding: fluent mover: fairly useful form at 3 yrs: sweating, well beaten in handicaps at Warwick (well-backed favourite, one of only 2 to stick to inside rail) and Newmarket for new stable: subsequently gelded: stays 1¼m, should stay further: won on dead ground, better form on a sound surface. *R. Akehurst* –

KETCHICAN 3 b.g. Joligeneration 111 – Fair Melys (FR) 81 (Welsh Pageant 132) [1994 –: 6f 7d 1995 a8g^{6} 6.9d^{6} a10g Dec 18] leggy gelding: no worthwhile form. *S. G. Knight* –

KEVASINGO 3 b.g. Superpower 113 – Katharina 105 (Frankincense 120) [1994 51: 6g 6m 5m 7g^{2} a8g^{5} 1995 a8g* 8.2g^{3} 8.2m 8g^{3} 10m^{4} 10g 9m^{3} 8f* 8m^{2} 8f^{5} 8f^{6} 8m 65

Ladbroke (Ayr) Silver Cup (Handicap)—the stand side proves best, as Keston Pond wins from blinkered pair Colway Rake (noseband) and Stolen Kiss

8g Sep 29] workmanlike gelding: modest handicapper: won at Lingfield in March and Salisbury (making all in amateur riders race) in June: below form last 4 starts: best efforts at 1m: acts on equitrack and firm ground: sold (S. Dow to B. Hills) 6,000 gns Newmarket Autumn Sales. *S. Dow*

KEWAASHI (USA) 3 b.f. Storm Bird (CAN) 134 – Klarifi 91 (Habitat 134) [1994 69p: 7d^4 1995 7m 9m May 21] leggy filly: unimpressive mover: failed to confirm debut promise, badly hampered on reappearance and one-paced seventh of 10 in maiden at Ripon month later: sold 10,000 gns Newmarket December Sales. *L. M. Cumani* –

KEY PITCH (USA) 3 ch.g. Dixieland Band (USA) – Gentle Persuasion 95 (Bustino 136) [1994 65: 7m^3 7g^3 7.6d^5 a7g^3 1995 a8g 7d Oct 19] leggy gelding: modest maiden: well beaten in 1995: should stay 1m+: below best on fibresand: visored (raced freely, well beaten) final 3-y-o start. *Lord Huntingdon* –

KEYS SEMINAR 3 b.g. Pharly (FR) 130 – Mums 88 (Mummy's Pet 125) [1994 65: 6m 8.2d a6g a6g^5 a9.4g^2 1995 a10g^6 a10g^5 a8g^4 a8g^2 a9.4g^3 a7g^4 8f^4 a8g 14.1m^4 14.1g 10m 8m 8g^5 7m 7g^6 11d Sep 22] sturdy gelding: poor maiden: sold out of N. Callaghan's stable 3,100 gns Ascot April Sales after fifth start: has form between 7f and 1¾m: acts on firm and dead ground and the all-weather: tried blinkered, no improvement: often bandaged on all-weather: tends to race prominently: inconsistent. *John Berry* 49

KEY TO A MILLION (IRE) 2 b.f. (Feb 28) Treasure Kay 114 – North Lady (Northfields (USA)) [1995 5m^6 6.1m^5 7m* 7.1g^5 7m* 6m^3 7.3d Oct 21] IR 8,500Y: leggy filly: half-sister to fair 1992 2-y-o 6f winner Coy Boy (by Shy Groom) and a winner in Italy: dam poor half-sister to Lowther winner Miss Demure: made all in maiden auction at Warwick in June and 4-runner minor event at Yarmouth in August: creditable third of 29 to No Animosity in valuable restricted event at the Curragh then well beaten in listed race at Newbury on final start: stays 7f: possibly unsuited by dead ground: sold 22,000 gns Newmarket Autumn Sales. *R. Hannon* 84

KHABAR 2 b.c. (Mar 9) Forzando 122 – Ella Mon Amour 65 (Ela-Mana-Mou 132) [1995 6.1m 7m^6 7f^4 7d^5 Sep 22] 26,000F, 41,000Y: quite attractive colt: fourth foal: half-brother to 3-y-o Brown Eyed Girl (by Sharpo) and 4-y-o winning sprinter Thatcherella (by Thatching): dam stayed 9f: fair form: will stay beyond 7f: sold 12,000 gns Newmarket Autumn Sales. *D. Morley* 76

KHALIDI (IRE) 6 b.g. Shernazar 131 – Khaiyla (Mill Reef (USA) 141) [1994 NR 1995 14.1m Jun 21] close-coupled gelding: rated 66? at 4 yrs: always behind in Nottingham handicap only start in 1995: fair winning hurdler: stays 1½m: acts on good to firm ground and dead. *D. R. Gandolfo* –

KHALYANI (IRE) 5 b.g. Akarad (FR) 130 – Khaiyla (Mill Reef (USA) 141) [1994 NR 1995 9m 10d 9.7s Sep 27] ex-Irish gelding: useful middle-distance winner (rated 100) in 1993: has had only 4 outings here on flat, and no form. *R. Rowe* –

KHAMASEEN 4 b.c. Slip Anchor 136 – Tanouma (USA) 114 (Miswaki (USA) 124) [1994 114: 10v* 10s^2 12m^5 12g 12m 1995 12g^3 14.1g* 15v* 11.8m^4 14m^5 16f^3 15.9m^4 16d^5 15d^2 Oct 8] attractive colt: fluent mover: smart performer: won minor event at Nottingham (idling) and Coppa d'Oro di Milano (2/1 on, by ½ length from Michel Georges) in the spring: 4½ lengths third of 9 to Double Trigger in Goodwood Cup in July: contested listed races at Baden-Baden (rare poor effort) and Milan (ran well) last 2 starts: should stay beyond 2m: acts on any going: tends to get on edge, and sometimes sweating: races prominently: consistent: sold 38,000 gns Newmarket December Sales. *J. L. Dunlop* 110

KHAMSEH 3 b.f. Thatching 131 – Khalafiya 104 (Darshaan 133) [1994 73p: 7s^3 1995 7.1m^2 8.2m^5 6g^2 7f* 7.1m^2 7m 7m^4 7.1d^4 Sep 2] useful-looking filly: fairly useful form: won 4-finisher maiden at Ayr in June: creditable efforts on 3 of her 4 outings afterwards: stays 1m: acts on firm and soft ground: blinkered (ran creditably) final 3-y-o start: carries head high: may prove best with waiting tactics: sent to Dubai. *J. W. Watts* 85

KHAN 3 b.g. Be My Chief (USA) 122 – Princess Rosananti (IRE) (Shareef Dancer (USA) 135) [1994 58: 5d 5d^4 6f^3 6f^2 7m 1995 7.5m^4 8g^4 10g 7.5g^5 8m^3 11.1f^3 12.4h* 11.1f^2 12.3m^5 11.9g 12.1g^3 15.8m^5 Oct 13] small, sturdy gelding: modest handicapper: won 4-runner seller at Newcastle in August: below form last 3 starts: 56

stays 12.4f: acts on hard ground: sold 2,000 gns Doncaster November Sales. *C. W. Thornton*

KHATIM (USA) 3 b. or br.c. Topsider (USA) – Khwlah (USA) 99 (Best Turn (USA)) [1994 56: 6d 7g 1995 6m 7g* 7m^2 7m^2 Aug 17] quite good-topped colt: fair handicapper: much improved form to win at Yarmouth in July: stays 7f and will probably be even better suited by 1m: acts on good to firm ground: sold (H. Thomson Jones to N. Walker) 24,000 gns Newmarket Autumn Sales. *H. Thomson Jones* 70

KHAYRAPOUR (IRE) 5 b.g. Kahyasi 130 – Khayra (FR) (Zeddaan 130) [1994 68: 12m^6 10v 10d 10g^3 1995 8m 8m 8g^2 8g* 10f^6 8.1m^2 8f* Jul 27] good-bodied gelding: shows knee action: fairly useful handicapper for new stable in 1995: won at Newmarket in June by 5 lengths: unlucky penultimate start then won 21-runner £48,250 Schweppes Golden Mile at Goodwood (coming from well off strong pace to lead near finish and short-head Realities) in July: best at around 1m: acts on firm going: blinkered last 4 starts: sometimes pulls hard, and is held up. *B. J. Meehan* 92

KHAYTADA (IRE) 3 b.f. Doyoun 124 – Khaydara 103 (Indian King (USA) 128) [1994 98p: 6g* 8d^2 1995 7g* 8g^3 10g 8m* 7d Nov 12] smart Irish filly: won 6-runner listed event at Leopardstown in April by 3½ lengths from Mediation: ran well when 5 lengths third of 10 to Ridgewood Pearl in Irish 1000 Guineas at the Curragh (headed 2f out) in May: off course nearly 4 months, narrowly won slowly-run 7-runner listed race at Naas in October: stays 1m: yet to race on extremes on going: blinkered (ran badly) final 3-y-o start: seems best as front runner. *J. Oxx, Ireland* 111

KID ORY 4 ch.g. Rich Charlie 117 – Woomargama 69 (Creetown 123) [1994 71, a–: 7g 6g* 6f^4 6m^6 6m 6m a6g a7g 1995 a6g a8g 6m 7m^4 6m^3 6m^4 7f^2 7f^2 7m^2 7m^2 7g^5 7d* 7f 7f Oct 24] close-coupled gelding: fair handicapper: in fine form for most of year, and won at Redcar in September: below form afterwards: stays 7f: acts on firm and dead ground, no form in 4 outings on fibresand. *P. Calver* 71 a–

KIERCHEM (IRE) 4 b.c. Mazaad 106 – Smashing Gale (Lord Gayle (USA) 124) [1994 –: 8.3m 6.9m 6m 7m 1995 a12g^4 a14.8g Jul 17] useful-looking colt: fair form early at 2 yrs: form since only when fourth in handicap at Wolverhampton (after 12-month absence) on reappearance: stays 1½m: acts on soft going and fibresand. *R. F. Fisher* 60

KILCORAN BAY 3 b.g. Robellino (USA) 127 – Catkin (USA) (Sir Ivor 135) [1994 NR 1995 8m^3 8m^2 10d* 10m 10g 10m 12d Sep 13] 8,600Y: good-topped gelding: second foal: dam ran 3 times: won maiden at Sandown in May: failed by very long way to repeat that form in handicaps: should stay beyond 1¼m: acts on good to firm and dead going: won over hurdles in November. *I. A. Balding* 79 d

KILDEE LAD 5 b.g. Presidium 124 – National Time (USA) (Lord Avie (USA)) [1994 78: 5.1g^2 6m^3 5.7g* 5g^3 5.7m 5.7f^3 5g 6.1g 5.1m^2 5.1m^2 6f^6 5g 5d^4 5.7g^6 5m* 73

Schweppes Golden Mile (Handicap), Goodwood—
Khayrapour (No. 18) finishes very strongly to short-head Realities;
Desert Green (No. 8) is another very strong finisher and overhauls Fraam for third

5.1g* 6.1g^5 5v^6 1995 6g 6m^6 5m^3 5.1m^6 5m 6g 5.7m^4 Jun 17] leggy, close-coupled gelding: fair handicapper: effective at 5f and 6f: acts on fibresand and any turf going: held up: well ridden by J. Williams, rarely partnered by him in 1995: visored (well below form) once at 3 yrs: tough and genuine. *A. P. Jones*

KILDRUMMY CASTLE 3 b.g. Komaite (USA) – Khadine 79 (Astec 128) [1994 61: 5f^4 7m^6 7m 7m 1995 7g 8.5m^4 12m^6 12m^2 14.1m^3 15.1f 12m^2 10m Aug 3] big, strong gelding: has a powerful, round action: modest maiden handicapper: needs further than 1¼m (should stay 1¾m): acts on good to firm ground, yet to race on a soft surface: visored (inadequate trip) final 3-y-o start: inconsistent. *Mrs J. R. Ramsden*
54

KILERNAN 4 ch.g. K-Battery 108 – Lekuti (Le Coq d'Or 101) [1994 –: 8g 8g 7g 1995 6m 12d^5 12.3f^2 15.8g* 15.8m^2 16.5f^2 16.1h^4 16d^4 15.8g^4 Sep 16] leggy gelding: unimpressive mover: modest handicapper: sweating, won at Catterick in July: stays 16.5f: acts on firm and soft ground: races prominently/front runner: folded tamely seventh 4-y-o start. *T. D. Barron*
51

KILLATTY LARK (IRE) 2 ch.f. (Feb 28) Noalto 120 – Killatty Sky (IRE) (Drumalis 125) [1995 6m^4 5g 6s Sep 28] sturdy filly: unimpressive mover: first foal: dam unraced: poor form in seller and claimers: will stay beyond 6f: possibly unsuited by soft ground. *W. J. Musson*
44

KILLICK 7 b.m. Slip Anchor 136 – Enthralment (USA) 78 (Sir Ivor 135) [1994 NR 1995 a11g^2 a12g^6 a12g 9.9m^2 10.3m 12.3m* 11.1g^3 a12g 12.1m^3 12.3m^2 11.9m^3 12.3m^2 18.7g^4 12.3m^5 Jul 30] leggy, workmanlike mare: modest handicapper: won at Chester (second win in Eaton Handicap) in May, and ran well there on consecutive days in July: should prove effective at 2m+: acts on all-weather surfaces, best turf efforts on top-of-the-ground: blinkered (well beaten) once at 4 yrs: has worn tongue strap: goes well on tight tracks. *A. Bailey*
63

KILLING TIME 4 b.g. Good Times (ITY) – Kelly's Bid (Pitskelly 122) [1994 –, a62: a8.5g^2 a8.5g^2 a9.4g^3 a8.5g^2 a11g^4 a9.4g* a8.5g^2 a8.5g* a8.5g^2 a7g^5 a9.4g a12g 1995 a7g a11g* a11g* a12g* a12g^4 a12g a12g^5 May 1] compact gelding: unimpressive mover: modest performer on the all-weather: won 2 sellers and a claimer (gamely) at Southwell in January/February: sold (Mrs N. Macauley to Mrs L. Richards) 2,200 gns Ascot May Sales: stays 1½m: unraced on turf since 2 yrs: usually visored: blinkered (well beaten) once at 2 yrs: front runner most starts at 4 yrs. *Mrs N. Macauley*
–
a54

KILLMESSAN-TOWN (IRE) 2 ch.g. (Apr 24) Jareer (USA) 115 – Perfect Chance 83 (Petorius 117) [1995 7.5d^6 Sep 13] IR 5,400Y: second foal: half-brother to 3-y-o Perfect Bertie (by Cyrano de Bergerac): dam 7f winner out of half-sister to Deep Run and dam of One In A Million: 25/1, around 13 lengths sixth of 17 to Weet-A-Minute in maiden auction at Beverley, very slowly away (having given plenty of trouble at stalls) then staying on late: will improve. *J. M. Carr*
– p

KILL THE CRAB (IRE) 3 b.f. Petorius 117 – Final Decision (Tap On Wood 130) [1994 104p: 6d^2 6g^3 7m^3 7g* 8g* 8d^2 8d* 1995 8.5s^3 8g^5 8g* 8g* 8m* 10g* 12g^2 9.3d Oct 1] leggy ex-Irish filly: useful performer: successful in Norwegian 1000 Guineas and 2000 Guineas (by 8½ lengths), both at Ovrevoll, 16-runner Group 2 Berlin Brandenburg Trophy der Landesbank Berlin (narrowly beat Royal Abjar) at Hoppegarten, then quite valuable event back at Ovrevoll: beaten a head in Norwegian Derby in August: pulled hard and well beaten in Prix de l'Opera at Longchamp final start: stays 1½m: acts on soft ground and good to firm. *W. Neuroth, Norway*
106

KILLY'S FILLY 5 b.m. Lochnager 132 – May Kells (Artaius (USA) 129) [1994 52: a6g a6g a8.5g a6g^5 6.1s 1995 6.1g 9.2g May 4] rather leggy, workmanlike mare: modest performer at 4 yrs: soundly beaten in 1995. *J. M. Bradley*
–

KILNAMARTYRA GIRL 5 b.m. Arkan 78 – Star Cove 58 (Porto Bello 118) [1994 52: 8d 7.5m^4 10m 7.5m^5 6m^4 7f* 6m^3 7m 7m^2 6.1s 7g^4 8g 1995 a7g 7.5m 8g 9.9m^4 9.2g 7g^3 6.9m^2 7.5m^2 7g 8.1m 7.5g* 7m^3 8f^3 7.5m* 7.9g 7m 8.5d 8g Oct 9] lengthy mare: modest handicapper: won at Beverley in July and (amateurs) August: effective at 7f, and probably stays 1¼m: acts on firm ground: tried blinkered/visored: tends to edge left. *J. Parkes*
55

KILVINE 2 b.c. (Feb 3) Shaadi (USA) 126 – Kilavea (USA) 92 (Hawaii) [1995 6m^4 6m* 7g^4 7f^4 7m^5 Aug 15] rangy, attractive colt: half-brother to several winners,
90

notably smart middle-distance filly Kiliniski (by Niniski): dam, winner over 5f on only start, half-sister to Nureyev: won median auction at Leicester in June: good efforts afterwards in £8,100 event at Newbury and valuable nurseries at Goodwood and (looking very well) York: will stay 1m. *L. M. Cumani*

KIMBERLEY BOY 5 b.g. Mtoto 134 – Diamond House (Habitat 134) [1994 NR 1995 8d 12m* 11.9m³ 12m 12m⁴ 12m⁴ 10m⁵ 12d³ 12.1m² 10.3m⁵ 12m³ 12m⁶ Jul 7] big, lengthy gelding: modest performer: sold out of G. Charles-Jones's stable 3,000 gns Doncaster February Sales: won seller at Beverley in April: left G. Oldroyd's stable after fourth start: below form afterwards: stays 1½m: acts on good to firm ground, used to go well on soft: sometimes has tongue tied down: bandaged on reappearance: tends to pull hard: sold (M. Brittain to Mrs M. Reveley) 2,000 gns Newmarket July Sales: won selling hurdle in November. *M. Brittain* — 57 d

KIMBRIDGE KNIGHT (IRE) 3 b.c. Night Shift (USA) – Dazzling Heights 99 (Shirley Heights 130) [1994 86: 5.7f³ 7f² 7g 7m 7m 1995 9m⁵ 10.2m* 11.4g* 12m 10f⁶ 8.1m 10.3m 10g Sep 29] smallish, robust colt: fairly useful handicapper: won at Bath and Sandown in May: ran well at Royal Ascot and Goodwood (£33,600 event) next 2 starts, but well below form afterwards: stays 1½m: acts on firm ground, yet to race on a soft surface: visored (best efforts) 8 times, including since second 3-y-o outing: goes well with forcing tactics: genuine: sold 24,000 gns Newmarket Autumn Sales: sent to Malaysia. *P. T. Walwyn* — 82

KIM TATE (IRE) 3 b.f. Contract Law (USA) 108 – Keen Note 69 (Sharpo 132) [1994 NR 1995 11.5g 10.3m Oct 21] IR 3,000Y: second foal: half-sister to Italian winner Il Golpe (by Classic Secret): dam won in Belgium at 4 yrs: behind in claimers: sold 1,250 gns Newmarket Autumn Sales. *C. N. Allen* — –

KINCARDINE BRIDGE (USA) 6 b.g. Tiffany Ice (USA) – Priestess (USA) (Time To Explode (USA)) [1994 NR 1995 13.1g Jun 1] of no account. *Mrs S. C. Bradburne* — –

KINDAKOOLA 4 b. or br.g. Kind of Hush 118 – Nikoola Eve 69 (Roscoe Blake 120) [1994 –: 11.8s⁶ 10g 11.5g 1995 11.5g 8g 14g Sep 23] good-topped gelding: no worthwhile form. *M. C. Chapman* — –

KINDERGARTEN BOY (IRE) 4 b.g. Mon Tresor 113 – High Profile (High Top 131) [1994 68: a7g³ a8g² 7m* 7v⁵ 7m 10f⁵ 8.3f³ 8.2g* 8m 8s 8s 8m⁶ 1995 a7g a7g 7m⁶ 7m⁶ 8.1g 9m³ 8.3m* 7.6m⁴ 9m 8m* 7g 7f Oct 14] leggy gelding: modest handicapper: narrowly won 17-runner races at Windsor and Salisbury in the summer: stays 9f: acts on firm ground, possibly not on soft: races prominently: sold 17,000 gns Newmarket Autumn Sales. *R. Boss* — 64

KIND OF LIGHT 2 b.f. (May 6) Primo Dominie 121 – Kind Thoughts 71 (Kashmir II 125) [1995 a7g* a7g³ Dec 9] 5,000Y: half-sister to several winners here and abroad, including useful 6f (at 2 yrs) and 7f winner Kayus (by Junius), later succssful in USA, and stayer Penny Forum (by Pas De Seul): dam staying sister to Blue Cashmere: won 15-runner seller at Southwell by 7 lengths: respectable third of 7 to Le Sport in minor event at Wolverhampton following month: stays 7f: acts on fibresand. *R. Guest* — 68

KINDRED GREETING 3 b.c. Most Welcome 131 – Red Berry 115 (Great Nephew 126) [1994 –: 6m 7m 7g 1995 a10g a11g⁶ a11g 10g 9.9m⁵ 12.1g⁵ 10g⁴ 10m⁵ 10.1m² 10.1m⁴ 10m Aug 21] stocky colt: poor maiden: stays 1¼m: has raced only on a sound surface on turf: blinkered since fourth 3-y-o start. *D. Morris* — 41

KING BALANT (IRE) 3 b.g. Fairy King (USA) – Lassalia (Sallust 134) [1994 74p: 6f⁵ 6m 7.5g² 8g* 1995 8d³ 8m 10m⁴ Jun 19] sturdy, close-coupled gelding: fair handicapper: best effort, despite looking backward, at Warwick on reappearance: should prove well suited by further than 1m: best efforts on an easy surface: visored (never a threat, not knocked about) final start: sold 14,000 gns Newmarket July Sales: sent to Sweden. *M. R. Stoute* — 75

KING CHESTNUT 4 ch.g. Efisio 120 – Sweet Colleen 42 (Connaught 130) [1994 53: 8m⁶ 8m⁴ 8m 10m 7.1m* 1995 8m 7f* 7g³ 8m* 7m³ 7m 8d 9f 8f⁶ Oct 24] workmanlike gelding: modest handicapper: won at Redcar and Ayr in the summer: below form last 4 starts, blinkered on final one: stays 1m: acts on firm going. *M. Dods* — 65

KINGCHIP BOY 6 b.g. Petong 126 – Silk St James (Pas de Seul 133) [1994 80, a59+: 8d5 8d2 7.6m3 8s2 8.5m2 8.1g3 8.1m5 8.3m 8f 8m5 7m2 7m* 8.1d4 7.1d4 8g* 8m a7g a8g6 1995 a7g a8g 8m 8m* 8.5m a8g6 8f4 8.5m6 8f 8f 8.1m6 8f3 8.1m 7g 8d 8s 8.2m2 a10g Nov 2] compact gelding: unimpressive mover: fair handicapper on turf: won at Goodwood (goes well there) in May: also first past post (demoted after hanging left) in claimer at Nottingham in October: effective at 7f/1m: acts on any turf going, has only modest form on the all-weather: usually visored, blinkered twice: sometimes wanders under pressure: best held up: none too consistent. *M. J. Ryan* — 78 d a–

KING CURAN (USA) 4 b.g. Lear Fan (USA) 130 – Runaway Lady (USA) (Caucasus (USA) 127) [1994 71: 10.4m6 10m 8m 9g5 8.3g* 13.1d 10.5s 8.2g 10.1d 1995 10m 8.3g3 9.2g3 8.3g* 10g 8g* 8.3f 10f* a9.4g 8.3m4 7.6m 8.3f Aug 9] sturdy, good-bodied gelding: fair handicapper: won at Hamilton in May and Ayr (twice, gamely making all on second occasion) in June: stays 1¼m: acts on firm and dead ground (ran badly only start on the all-weather): visored (raced too freely) once at 3 yrs: usually blinkered: none too consistent. *A. Bailey* — 66

KINGDOM PRINCESS 2 br.f. (Apr 3) Forzando 122 – Song of Hope 103 (Chief Singer 131) [1995 a5g5 Nov 24] third foal: sister to 5f winner Miriam and half-sister to 3-y-o Stolen Melody (by Robellino), 6f winner at 2 yrs: dam 2-y-o 5f winner from family of Mummy's Pet: 16/1, around 12 lengths fifth of 16 to Galine in maiden at Southwell, never threatening leaders: likely to do better. *M. J. Camacho* — – p

KING ETZEL (IRE) 3 b.g. Belmez (USA) 131 – Kaiserblume (FR) (Viceregal (CAN)) [1994 NR 1995 9.7m May 31] half-brother to several middle-distance winners in Germany, including 5-y-o King's Blade (by Sure Blade): dam won 3 races in Germany and was third in German Oaks: tailed-off last of 8 in claimer at Folkestone. *J. E. Banks* — –

KINGFISHER BRAVE 2 b.c. (Mar 7) Rock City 120 – Lambada Style (IRE) 81 (Dancing Brave (USA) 140) [1995 6m5 a7g* 7m 8m3 8g6 Sep 21] 16,000F, 15,000 2-y-o: leggy colt: first foal: dam, 1m winner who stayed 1½m: won maiden at Southwell in July: good third of 17 in nursery at Doncaster: disappointing in similar event at Pontefract final start: an out-an-out galloper who'll be suited by middle distances: joined J. Dooler. *S. G. Norton* — 69

KING OF BABYLON (IRE) 3 b.g. Persian Heights 129 – My My Marie (Artaius (USA) 129) [1994 NR 1995 10m6 10d 10g Sep 29] 17,000Y: useful-looking gelding: half-brother to several winners, including 1¼m winner Don't Forget Marie (by Don't Forget Me): dam (lightly-raced) out of sister to Cheveley Park winner Pasty: sold out of R. Hannon's stable 1,100 gns Newmarket Autumn 1994 Sales and gelded: little worthwhile form: mulish at stalls second start. *Lady Herries* — –

KING OF PERU 2 br.c. (Mar 16) Inca Chief (USA) – Julie's Star (IRE) 45 (Thatching 131) [1995 6f2 6m* 6f4 6m 6g* 6g* 7.3d Oct 19] 4,200Y: close-coupled colt: has a quick action: first foal: dam maiden placed at 1m: fairly useful form: won maiden auction at Haydock in July and nurseries at Ayr and Newmarket (by 2½ lengths from Amber Fort) in September: ran respectably in Horris Hill Stakes at Newbury on final outing, seventh of 9 behind Tumbleweed Ridge: stays 7f: acts on firm and dead ground: races prominently. *A. P. Jarvis* — 94 +

KING OF SHOW (IRE) 4 b.g. Green Desert (USA) 127 – Don't Rush (USA) 93 (Alleged (USA) 138) [1994 76: 8m3 7.5g2 8f 7m 8g3 8d4 8.1s3 8.2s5 7.1d3 7d 1995 a12g a7g 8g 8m5 8.3g 9g 12.1m 9.2f4 7.1f2 7f 7m Oct 30] leggy gelding: just a modest performer at best in 1995: should stay beyond 1m: acts on firm and soft ground: no improvement in blinkers/visor. *R. Allan* — 65 d

KING OF THE EAST (IRE) 2 b.c. (Apr 28) Fairy King (USA) – Rising Tide 101 (Red Alert 127) [1995 6m4 5g5 6d* 6d5 Sep 16] 62,000F: sturdy, attractive colt: has a quick action: closely related to 2 winners by North Pole, including fairly useful Irish sprinter Northern Tide, and half-brother to a winner in Malaysia: dam 2-y-o 5f winner, didn't train on: won 8-runner minor event at Doncaster in September by ½ length from Sabot: never a serious factor when over 9 lengths fifth of 6 behind Kahir Almaydan in Mill Reef Stakes at Newbury week later: stays 6f: acts on good to soft ground. *M. R. Stoute* — 88

KING OF THE HORSE (IRE) 4 ch.g. Hatim (USA) 121 – Milly Whiteway 112 (Great White Way (USA)) [1994 –, a52: a7g5 a8g3 a8g2 a7g* 7.1m6 8m 12.4d a8g 1995 8g 16m 15.8g Sep 16] modest performer: well beaten in 1995: should stay — –

1m: acts on the all-weather, no form on turf since 2 yrs: visored second 3-y-o to first 4-y-o starts: won over hurdles in September. *W. Storey*

KING OF TUNES (FR) 3 b.c. Chief Singer 131 – Marcotte (Nebos (GER) 129) [1994 NR 1995 8s* 8.1s^5 Oct 17] 9,200Y, 5,000 2-y-o: third foal: dam, won 5 races in Belgium, is half-sister to high-class German middle-distance performer Mondrian: 33/1 on debut, won 8-runner apprentice race at Ascot in October by 7 lengths from below-form Beauchamp Jazz, moving through easily over 2f out and running on strongly: tailed off in similar event at Chepstow 11 days later. *J. J. Sheehan* — 72+

KING OPTIMIST 6 ch.g. King Persian 107 – Misoptimist 111 (Blakeney 126) [1994 NR 1995 12m Apr 8] tall, plain gelding: poor plater: tried blinkered. *A. Smith* — –

KING PARROT (IRE) 7 br.g. King of Spain 121 – Red Lory 87 (Bay Express 132) [1994 53: 8m^2 a7g 1995 a8g* a8g^5 a8g^3 a8g^6 7m 8g 7m Jun 17] leggy, workmanlike gelding: modest handicapper: won apprentice race at Southwell in January by short head: stays 1m: acts on all-weather surfaces and good to firm ground: no improvement in visor. *Lord Huntingdon* — – a54

KING RAMBO 4 b.g. Rambo Dancer (CAN) 107 – Infanta Maria 82 (King of Spain 121) [1994 62: 5s^5 5.1v^6 5g* 5.1s 1995 a5g^4 a6g^3 a5g^6 5g 5m^2 a5g* 5g 5.1g 5m^4 5m^4 a5g^2 5m^4 5m^4 6m* 5.1m a5g^2 5g 6d^4 a6g^2 a6g^3 Oct 14] sturdy, workmanlike gelding: fair handicapper: in good form nearly all year, winning at Wolverhampton in May and Haydock (claimer) in August: effective at 5f and 6f: acts on fibresand, best turf form on a sound surface: sometimes carries head awkwardly: usually held up. *R. Hollinshead* — 66 a71

KING RAT (IRE) 4 ch.g. King of Clubs 124 – Mrs Tittlemouse (Nonoalco (USA) 131) [1994 80, a92: a6g^2 a6g* a6g* 7m^5 6v a6g^2 6m^3 7.5m* 6f^3 6g^2 6m 6m^5 6g 6d 6g a7g* 6s^2 7d^4 1995 6f 6g 7g 6m 5m^6 5m^4 5m^5 5m* 5m^2 7m* 7d 6s 7g 7f^2 6f^5 a9.4g^6 Dec 2] tall, close-coupled gelding: poor walker: easy mover: fairly useful handicapper: won at Sandown and Redcar in August: effective at 5f to 7.5f: acts on the all-weather and firm ground, probably on soft (well beaten on heavy): best efforts in 1995 in blinkers/visor: often wears crossed noseband: usually races prominently. *T. J. Etherington* — 88

KINGS ASSEMBLY 3 b.c. Presidium 124 – To The Point 96 (Sharpen Up 127) [1994 65p: 6m 6s* 1995 8m^4 8m 8m^6 10g* 10d^2 Oct 19] tall, leggy colt: has scope: fair handicapper: won 19-runner race at Leicester in June: very good second of 22 to impressive Jagellon at Newbury 4½ months later on only subsequent outing: stays 1¼m: acts on good to firm and soft ground. *P. W. Harris* — 78

KINGS CAY (IRE) 4 b.g. Taufan (USA) 119 – Provocation 66 (Kings Lake (USA) 133) [1994 72: 8.5d* 10s 10m^3 12m* 1995 10.3g^6 12m^6 12.3f^3 12.3m 10.3g^5 14.6m Nov 3] useful-looking gelding: fair middle-distance performer in 1994 for D. Loder: well below form in 1995. *T. H. Caldwell* — –

KING'S CROWN 3 ch.c. Lead On Time (USA) 123 – Crystal Land (Kris 135) [1994 NR 1995 9m^3 10f* 10g^5 Jul 15] big, strong, lengthy colt: first foal: dam lightly-raced daughter of Greenland Park, dam also of Fitnah: landed the odds in maiden event at Ripon in June: tailed-off last of 5 on easier ground in listed race at Newbury on only subsequent outing: should stay beyond 1¼m: sold 18,000 gns Newmarket Autumn Sales: sent to Malaysia. *E. A. L. Dunlop* — 82

KINGSFOLD FOUNTAIN 4 b.g. Thowra (FR) – Bella Lisa (River Chanter 121) [1994 –: a10g^5 a8g 1995 a8g a12g 12m May 4] no worthwhile form: dead. *M. J. Haynes* — –

KINGSFOLD PET 6 b.g. Tina's Pet 121 – Bella Lisa (River Chanter 121) [1994 49: 15.4v* 15.4v^3 14g 1995 15.4g Apr 10] tall, rangy gelding: fairly useful hurdler: poor performer on flat: suited by a test of stamina: acts on heavy ground. *M. J. Haynes* — –

KING'S GOLD 5 b.g. King of Spain 121 – Goldyke 63 (Bustino 136) [1994 NR 1995 a10g^6 a8g^5 a8g a7g Mar 25] lengthy, workmanlike gelding: poor maiden: best form at around 1m: sold (T. M. Jones to Mrs L. Richards) 2,600 gns Ascot April Sales. *T. M. Jones* — 38

KINGS HARMONY (IRE) 2 b.c. (Feb 15) Nordico (USA) – Kingston Rose (Tudor Music 131) [1995 a7g^2 6.9s^6 6m^4 a6g* Nov 20] 10,500F, 5,500Y: half-brother to several winners, including fair 1985 2-y-o 5f winner King's Reef (by Main Reef): — 66 a72 dam Irish 5f winner: fair performer: won 15-runner maiden at Southwell by ¾ length from Agent in November: stays 7f: best form on fibresand. *P. J. Makin*

KINGS NIGHTCLUB 2 b.f. (Mar 22) Shareef Dancer (USA) 135 – Troy Moon (Troy 137) [1995 7g Oct 9] half-sister to 3-y-o Kings of Canvey Is (by Hadeer), 7f winner The Cuckoo's Nest (by Precocious) and 1991 2-y-o 7f winner Jupiter Moon (by Jupiter Island): dam maiden (stayed 1¼m) out of half-sister to Sharpen Up: 66/1 and backward, soundly beaten in maiden at Leicester. *J. White* –

KINGS OF CANVEY IS 3 ch.f. Hadeer 118 – Troy Moon (Troy 137) [1994 –: 5g 6d 1995 a5g⁶ a7g⁴ 10m⁶ a12g 12.1m Jun 15] workmanlike filly: little sign of ability on flat: won juvenile hurdle in August: sold 500 gns Ascot November Sales. *J. White* –

KING'S SHILLING (USA) 8 b.g. Fit To Fight (USA) – Pride's Crossing (USA) (Riva Ridge (USA)) [1994 54: a14g* a12g 1995 a12g 12.5g⁶ Jun 17] smallish, workmanlike gelding: fairly useful jumper at best: modest winner on flat at 7 yrs: no form in 1995, including in visor: will stay 2m: acts on any going. *H. Oliver* –

KINGS VISION 3 gr.g. Absalom 128 – Eye Sight 67 (Roscoe Blake 120) [1994 67: 6m 6m⁶ 7m³ 7.1g² 7.9d⁶ 7.5g* 7s³ 7d 7s 6g 1995 9.9m 8g 7m 7m 8m⁵ 8g 10.5d Jun 9] workmanlike gelding: ran badly in 1995: blinkered last 4 starts: runs tubed: inconsistent: sold 675 gns Ascot October Sales. *B. S. Rothwell* –

KINGS WITNESS (USA) 2 b.c. (Mar 15) Lear Fan (USA) 130 – Allison's Deeds (Sassafras (FR) 135) [1995 7.1m² 7g³ 7.1d* 7g⁵ Sep 29] $50,000Y: rangy colt: has scope: sixth foal: closely related to French 11f and 1½m winner Sium (by Silver Hawk) and half-brother to 2 minor winners in USA: dam Grade 3 winner in Canada at 1m at 2 yrs: won maiden at Haydock in September: ran very well when fifth of 8, beaten a little more than 2 lengths, to Even Top in listed race at Newmarket on final outing: will be at least as effective at 1m as 7f: active type, but became more settled latter starts: likely to improve further. *W. J. Haggas* 98 p

KINGSWOOD MANOR 3 b.g. Exodal (USA) – Angelic Appeal (Star Appeal 133) [1994 –: 6m 6m 1995 8.3m May 1] leggy gelding: no form: has joined Miss V. Williams. *M. Dixon* –

KING UBAD (USA) 6 ch.g. Trempolino (USA) 135 – Glitter (FR) 70 (Reliance II 137) [1994 NR 1995 14f⁴ 14g 12.5g⁶ 14.4m Sep 1] leggy gelding: no worthwhile form on flat in Britain. *K. O. Cunningham-Brown* –

KING WILLIAM 10 b.g. Dara Monarch 128 – Norman Delight (USA) (Val de L'Orne (FR) 133) [1994 44: 16.2m³ 16.2g³ 16.5m 1995 a16g a16g Feb 6] robust gelding: poor handicapper: soundly beaten in amateurs events in 1995. *J. L. Spearing* –

KINNEGAD KID 6 b.m. Formidable (USA) 125 – Recamier 80 (Reform 132) [1994 45: a9.4g 8s 6.9m 6g* 6m 6s a7g² 1995 a8g* a8g* a8g* a8g* a8g² a9.4g* 8s 6.1m 7.6m 7m a8g² a8.5g a8.5g* 7g⁴ 8.5s Sep 19] lengthy mare: carries condition: fair handicapper on the all-weather: successful 4 times at Lingfield and once at Wolverhampton early in year: gained sixth win of the season, putting up best effort in process, at Wolverhampton in August: only poor form on turf: stays 9.4f: best on all-weather surfaces, acts on good to firm and dead ground: visored once at 4 yrs and on last 3 starts: sold 12,000 gns Doncaster November Sales: sent to Saudi Arabia. *R. Ingram* 44 a76

KINNESCASH (IRE) 2 ch.c. (May 9) Persian Heights 129 – Gayla Orchestra (Lord Gayle (USA) 124) [1995 6m³ 6m³ a6g⁵ 5.7h* 5.1m⁵ 8h 7g⁶ 10d* 8d 10g Oct 9] IR 5,200Y, 6,000 2-y-o: leggy, unfurnished colt: fourth foal: dam, won at 2m at 4 yrs in Ireland, out of sister to Orchestra: fair form when winning seller at Bath (sold out of R. Ingram's stable 6,000 gns) in August and nursery at Nottingham in September: stays 1¼m: acts on hard and dead ground: has been bandaged. *M. S. Saunders* 66

KINOKO 7 ch.g. Bairn (USA) 126 – Octavia (Sallust 134) [1994 53: 12d* 12.4g⁴ 12g* 11.8s³ 14.1d 10m⁵ 12m 12m⁶ 12h⁴ 12.1g 1995 12g 11.8m 14.1m 15.8g 10.9g⁶ 15.8m 12m* 12.3m⁶ 15.8g 12.1g 11.9m Oct 5] lengthy gelding: poor handicapper: easily best effort in 1995 when winning at Beverley (upset in stalls) in July, idling: effective at 1¼m to 1¾m: acts on firm and dead going: tail swisher: probably best with waiting tactics: fair hurdler, winner in October. *K. W. Hogg, Isle of Man* 47

KINTAVI 5 b.g. Efisio 120 – Princess Tavi (Sea Hawk II 131) [1994 –: 11.1m 10g 1995 12d² 14.1m³ 12.5m* Jun 26] good-bodied gelding: bad mover: poor 41

handicapper: won maiden event at Warwick in June: effective at 1½m and should stay 2m: acts on firm and dead ground, effective on heavy over hurdles. *T. W. Donnelly*

KINTWYN 5 b.g. Doulab (USA) 115 – Harriet Emma (USA) (Secretariat (USA)) [1994 47, a71: a8g* a7g^5 a7g^2 a7g^4 8d^4 a10g 7m 8g a8g^5 10m a9.4g^2 8f^6 a7g^5 a8.5g^6 7g^4 a9.4g* 8g a12g^5 a10g a8g a8g^2 a10g a9.4g 1995 a8g* a9.4g* a10g^3 8m^4 a7g 8g^5 10f a10g a8g^6 Nov 25] compact gelding: has a quick action: fair performer on the all-weather: won minor event at Lingfield (made all) in February and handicap at Wolverhampton (held up) in March: poor at best on turf last 2 seasons: stays 1¼m: acts on fibresand and equitrack: tried visored/blinkered, with no improvement: often bandaged behind. *C. C. Elsey* — 47 a77

KIPINI 6 b.m. Roaring Riva 103 – Kivulini (Hotfoot 126) [1994 8v* 8.5v^2 9g* 9.3g* 8g* 7g^4 8g^5 7g 7g 8.5g^2 10v^3 9.3d* a9.3g^2 a8.5g^2 a9.3g 1995 a9.3g 9.3g^5 9.3g a9.7g^6 9.7m^6 9.3v^5 8g 11g^3 11f 9f^3 9d^4 a8g^2 8g^5 a9.3g^6 8v^4 a8g Nov 25] close-coupled, Belgian-trained mare: unimpressive mover: inconsistent maiden at 2 and 3 yrs for W. Musson: won 3 handicaps and 2 claimers at Groenendaal in 1994, showing poor form: failed to win in 1995, sixth in claimer at Folkestone fifth start on only British outing: stays 11f: acts on heavy ground and dirt. *H. Vanderdussen, Belgium* — 29

KIRA 5 b.m. Starry Night (USA) – Irish Limerick 89 (Try My Best (USA) 130) [1994 42: 7m 6m^5 7m 6f 6g 1995 6g^5 7g^3 7f^2 6f^3 6m^6 a6g a6g^2 Nov 30] leggy mare: modest maiden handicapper: stays 7f: acts on firm going and equitrack: has run creditably when sweating. *J. L. Eyre* — 56

KIRKIE CROSS 3 b.f. Efisio 120 – Balgownie 43 (Prince Tenderfoot (USA) 126) [1994 NR 1995 8g^6 9.2f^3 13.1f^3 12.1f^4 10.9g Sep 14] third foal: dam middle-distance winner: no sign of ability. *R. M. McKellar* — –

KIROV LADY (IRE) 2 b.f. (May 8) Soviet Lad (USA) 94 – Cestrefeld 94 (Capistrano 120) [1995 5.1h^2 6m* 7m^2 6.1m^5 8m^5 Nov 3] leggy filly: half-sister to several winners, including useful middle-distance performer First Victory (by Concorde Hero) and useful sprinter Troon (by Beveled): dam, 5f and 6f winner at 2 yrs, half-sister to Young Generation: fair performer: won median auction maiden at Kempton in August: best efforts afterwards in minor events when second to Sea Spray at Kempton and fifth to Brighstone in slowly-run race at Doncaster on final outing: seems suited by at least 7f: has raced only on top-of-the-ground. *R. Hannon* — 77 ?

KIROV PROTEGE (IRE) 3 b.g. Dancing Dissident (USA) 119 – Still River (Kings Lake (USA) 133) [1994 44: 6f 5f a7g 7d a7g 1995 a8g^2 a8g^5 a8g* a8.5g^2 a9.4g^2 a8g a8.5g 10m^4 10.3m^6 9.7m^2 10m 9.7g^5 10f^3 10m^4 9m a11g Nov 6] smallish, leggy gelding: modest performer: trained by R. Armstrong until after fifth start, winning selling handicap at Southwell in January: poor at best for new stable: stays 1¼m: acts on fibresand and good to firm ground: tried in blinkers and visor. *H. J. Collingridge* — 44 a57

KISMETIM 5 b.g. Dowsing (USA) 124 – Naufrage (Main Reef 126) [1994 49: 14.1d 16m 14g 12s a12g* a11g^3 14.1m^3 12.1g^3 a12g 11.8g 1995 a16g a12g 12.5g a12g^4 12g^6 11.8g a12g* Oct 28] lengthy, workmanlike gelding: poor performer: trained first 3 5-y-o starts by F. Jordan: claimed by Miss M. E. Rowland £2,000 after winning claimer at Wolverhampton in October: stays 1¾m: acts on fibresand and on good to firm and dead going: carries head high. *B. J. Meehan* — 47

KISSAVOS 9 ch.g. Cure The Blues (USA) – Hairbrush (USA) (Sir Gaylord) [1994 47: a7g a7g a7s^6 a8g a8g 8m 7m^6 7v 7.1s^6 7f 7.1m^2 7m 8.2m 8.1g* a8g^6 8m^6 a8g a8g a7g^6 1995 a8g^4 a8g a8g a8.5g 9.2g 8g 7.1m^5 7f 8m 8.1d Oct 10] small, angular gelding: poor handicapper: stays 1m: acts on any going, including all-weather surfaces: sometimes bandaged behind: no improvement in blinkers (not tried for long time) or visor: inconsistent. *C. C. Elsey* — 46 d

KISSING GATE (USA) 2 ch.f. (Mar 26) Easy Goer (USA) – Love's Reward (Nonoalco (USA) 131) [1995 8.1s^5 a8g^4 a8.5g* Dec 9] $65,000Y: fourth reported foal: half-sister to 3 winners, notably Keen Hunter (by Diesis), winner of Prix de L'Abbaye: dam lightly-raced half-sister to high-class 1984 2-y-o Bassenthwaite: won 13-runner maiden at Wolverhampton in December by neck from Red Rusty, pair 9 lengths clear: will stay beyond 8.5f: acts on fibresand: slowly away on debut. *R. Charlton* — 62

KISS KINCSEM 4 b.f. Jalmood (USA) 126 – Horns Lodge (High Line 125) [1994 62: 8.3m 10d^{3} 10.5d 10g a13g 1995 a16g a16g Jan 13] stocky filly: has a short action: no form in 1995: should prove suited by further than 1¼m: tried blinkered. *P. J. Makin* –

KISS ME AGAIN (IRE) 2 b.f. (Mar 9) Cyrano de Bergerac 120 – Now Serving (Super Concorde (USA) 128) [1995 6.1m^{4} 5g^{3} 6m* 6m* 6.5m Sep 6] IR 13,500Y: rather sparely-made filly: has a quick action: half-sister to several winners abroad, including French 9f and 1¼m winner The Boss Is Remi (by Maelstrom Lake): dam unraced: won median auction maiden then nursery (beat Just Ice a neck) at Windsor in summer: down the field in 17-runner nursery at Doncaster final outing: stays 6f: sometimes hangs left. *R. Hannon* 80

KITTY KITTY CANCAN 2 b.f. (Mar 7) Warrshan (USA) 117 – Kittycatoo Katango (USA) (Verbatim (USA)) [1995 7g Oct 3] rather unfurnished filly: fourth foal: half-sister to 6f (at 2 yrs) and 7f winner Mr Butch (by Aragon) and 6f (at 2 yrs) and 1¼m winner Miss Doody (by Gorytus): dam listed 7f winner at 2 yrs in Italy: 20/1 and bit backward, never placed to challenge when eleventh of 17 to Sil Sila in maiden at Warwick, running good deal better than position suggests: will do better. *Lady Herries* – p

KITTY WATERJET 3 ch.f. Golden Lahab (USA) – Key Harvest (Deep Diver 134) [1994 –: a6g 5g 6f^{6} a7g a8.5g 1995 a8g 7m May 29] sparely-made filly: of little account. *B. Ellison* –

KIWUD 2 ch.f. (Feb 19) Superlative 118 – Mimining 83 (Tower Walk 130) [1995 5m 5m 5g 6.1d Sep 11] strong, stocky sprint type: unimpressive mover: first foal: dam sprinter: well beaten in maidens. *G. M. Moore* –

KIYAS 4 ch.g. Nashwan (USA) 135 – Al Sylah 118 (Nureyev (USA) 131) [1994 66d: 8m^{3} 8m 8f 8d 10d 10d a8.5g a12g^{6} a16g a14g 1995 a7g^{4} a7g a6g Mar 18] close-coupled gelding: poor maiden: should stay middle distances: acts on good to firm ground: pulls hard: tends to sweat up and be edgy: not one to trust implicitly. *B. J. McMath* 37

KLIPSPINGER 2 ch.f. (Mar 5) Formidable (USA) 125 – Distant Relation (Great Nephew 126) [1995 5m^{6} 6g^{5} 5m Jun 14] 1,700F, 1,200Y: strong, lengthy filly: bad mover: second foal: sister to 4-y-o 1½m winner Ozzie Jones: dam won at 11f in France and also won over jumps in Jersey: no form, including in a seller. *B. S. Rothwell* –

KNAVE 2 b.c. (May 26) Prince Sabo 123 – Royal Agnes 71 (Royal Palace 131) [1995 7m^{6} 8.2d 7g 7f^{4} 6.9m^{6} a7g^{3} Nov 16] 5,200F: quite attractive colt: has scope: half-brother to 3-y-o Primo Panache (by Primo Dominie) and several winners, including 1m to 2m winner Dancing Days (by Glenstal) and 1991 2-y-o 5f winner She's Special (by Superlative): dam, 1¾m winner, half-sister to smart 1982 2-y-o All Systems Go: fair maiden: creditable effort in visor final start: should be at least as effective at 1m as 7f: acts on firm ground and fibresand. *R. Hannon* 66

KNAVE OF DIAMONDS 3 b.c. Bustomi 123 – Kohinoor Diamond (Roman Warrior 132) [1994 58: 8.1g a7g 1995 10g 12.1m 7m Sep 1] little worthwhile form in maidens in 1995. *R. J. Hodges* –

KNAVE'S ASH (USA) 4 ch.g. Miswaki (USA) 124 – Quiet Rendezvous (USA) (Nureyev (USA) 131) [1994 86: 7f* 8.1m^{3} 8m 8.1m 1995 8g 8m^{4} 7m 8m 10.3m* 10f^{3} 7.9m^{4} 10.1m^{4} 10g* Sep 21] compact, attractive gelding: fluent mover: useful handicapper: won £10,700 event at Doncaster in July and rated stakes (steadily-run race, well ridden by W. Swinburn) at Pontefract in September: effective in strongly-run race at 1m and stays 1¼m: acts on firm going, yet to race on a soft surface: wore net muzzle to post last 2 starts: tends to sweat: usually held up: sent to Dubai. *M. R. Stoute* 100

KNAYTON LASS 4 b.f. Presidium 124 – Sister Hannah 70 (Monseigneur (USA) 127) [1994 86d: 9d^{5} 5g^{4} 5f^{4} 6f 5m 5f 5.6g 6d 5d 5g 5v 1995 5m 5g 5f 7f 5g^{2} 5.1m^{4} 5m^{6} 5h 5g 6g* 6s 6d^{4} Oct 11] angular filly: modest handicapper at best in 1995: gained first success since debut (July 1993) in apprentice race at Redcar in September: stays 6f: acts on firm and dead going: no improvement in blinkers: wanders under pressure: inconsistent. *M. W. Easterby* 62 §

KNIGHT COMMANDER (USA) 3 b.c. Topsider (USA) – Social Registry (USA) (Raise A Native) [1994 92: 6m^3 6m* 6m^4 6m^3 6m 1995 7g 8f^4 7f* 8d Sep 9] well-made, quite attractive colt: good walker and mover: fairly useful performer: won minor event at Salisbury in August: well beaten (not because of trip) in rated stakes at Doncaster on only subsequent start: stays 7f: acts on firm ground: sold 45,000 gns Newmarket Autumn Sales to Hong Kong. *R. Hannon* — 94

KNIGHTRIDER 4 b.g. Full Extent (USA) 113 – New Street (USA) 53 (Our Native (USA)) [1994 51: 7.1s 6m^5 6f 8.3m* 8.3m 7m 8g^6 8.1g a7g^3 a7g 1995 a10g a8g a12g a9.4g 8f 8h Sep 4] neat gelding: winning plater at 3 yrs: no form in 1995. *C. D. Broad* — –

KNOBBLEENEEZE 5 ch.g. Aragon 118 – Proud Miss (USA) (Semi-Pro) [1994 78: 8s^3 8d* 7d^6 7m 7.6g* 8s^3 8v^2 7m^3 6.9g^4 8.2m^2 7g^2 7.3s* 7g 8m 7d 1995 7s^5 7m^4 8g^4 8m 7f 8.1g^2 7g 6m 7g^4 7g* 7g* 7.6d^2 8d^4 7g 7g 8m Oct 14] sturdy gelding: fairly useful performer: won handicap at Doncaster and amateurs event at Goodwood (2 days later) in September: stays 8.3f: acts on good to firm and heavy ground and on equitrack: usually wears a visor: successful for apprentice: tough and genuine. *M. R. Channon* — 78

KNOTALLY WOOD (USA) 3 b.f. Woodman (USA) 126 – Countess Tully 112 (Hotfoot 126) [1994 NR 1995 7.3m^6 8m^6 10m 10m^5 12d^3 a12g^2 a12g^6 Nov 30] angular filly: has a round action: seventh foal: half-sister to fairly useful 10.5f winner Honeychurch (by Bering) and useful 1988 French 2-y-o 1m winner Russian Countess (by Nureyev): dam useful winner at 8.5f and 1¼m in Ireland, later successful in USA: fair maiden: stays 1½m: acts on good to firm ground and the all-weather: sold 2,800 gns Newmarket December Sales. *J. W. Hills* — 70

KNOTTY SCOT 3 b.f. Scottish Reel 123 – Ballyreef (Ballymore 123) [1994 –: a7g 1995 9f a7g 10d Sep 18] of no account. *J. J. Bridger* — –

KNOWN SECRET (USA) 2 ch.c. (May 15) Known Fact (USA) 135 – Loa (USA) (Hawaii) [1995 6.1d 7.1s Oct 1] $25,000Y: workmanlike colt: third foal: half-brother to a winner in US by Crafty Prospector: dam won at up to 9f: backward, held up and always behind in maidens at Nottingham (not well drawn) and Haydock (pulled hard): will do better in due course. *Mrs J. R. Ramsden* — – p

KOATHARY (USA) 4 b.g. Capote (USA) – Jeffo (USA) (Ridan (USA)) [1994 75: 8g^6 10.5m 8.1g^4 10g 10.4g 1995 10g 10m^3 10d 10d 12.1d 10d Oct 19] big, lengthy gelding: fair handicapper: may well stay further than 1¼m: acts on good to firm ground, seemingly not on a soft surface: inconsistent. *L. G. Cottrell* — 68 d

KOMIAMAITE 3 b.g. Komaite (USA) – Mia Scintilla 54 (Blazing Saddles (AUS)) [1994 NR 1995 a6g a8g^2 a8g^5 a9.4g^2 12g a7g a7g^3 6m 8g a8g a9.4g^5 Nov 27] first foal: dam 5f performer: modest maiden: stays 9.4f: acts on fibresand, no form on turf: effective blinkered or not: pulls hard. *S. R. Bowring* — 58

KOMLUCKY 3 b.f. Komaite (USA) – Sweet And Lucky (Lucky Wednesday 124) [1994 52: 6g 6g^6 a7g^5 7g a5g a6g* 1995 a6g^4 a6g^6 a6g a5g^6 8m 5.9f^4 7g Sep 16] leggy filly: modest performer: stays 6f: acts on fibresand and firm ground: often blinkered: takes keen hold: none too consistent. *F. J. O'Mahony* — 52 d

KOMODO (USA) 3 ch.g. Ferdinand (USA) – Platonic Interest (USA) (Drone) [1994 67: 7g 7.6v^2 8.1g 8g a6g^2 1995 a10g^2 8d^6 10m 8.3m^2 8.1g^2 7g^4 a7g^6 a8g a7g a8g Dec 6] sparely-made gelding: modest maiden: left D. Elsworth's stable after sixth start: well below form afterwards: effective at 7f to 1¼m: acts on good to firm and heavy going and on equitrack. *K. O. Cunningham-Brown* — 63 d

KOMREYEV DANCER 3 b.g. Komaite (USA) – L'Ancressaan 67 (Dalsaan 125) [1994 63, a79: a7g 8d^5 7.1d^4 8d 8d^3 a8g^3 a7g^2 a8g^2 a8.5g^2 a8.5g* a7g^4 1995 a8.5g^2 a8.5g* a8.5g^4 a10g^6 a9.4g^2 10.3g^4 8d^4 9.9m^2 12.3m 12.3m a9.4g 10.3m 10m^3 10.5g^4 10g^5 Sep 29] leggy gelding: has a poor, round action: fairly useful handicapper on the all-weather, only fair on turf: won at Wolverhampton in January: stays 10.3f, probably not 1½m: acts on good to firm ground, dead and goes well on all-weather surfaces. *A. Bailey* — 72 a84

KORAMBI 3 ch.c. Kris 135 – Green Lucia 116 (Green Dancer (USA) 132) [1994 79?: 7g 8g 1995 10m^6 12m^4 12g* 12f 12m^4 10v^6 12m Nov 4] quite attractive, unfurnished colt: fairly useful performer: won rated stakes at Newbury in May: out — 93

of his depth in Derby and valuable Group 2 race at Hoppegarten next 2 starts: stays 1½m: acts on good to firm ground: usually ridden up with pace. *C. E. Brittain*

KORNADO 5 ch.h. Superlative 118 – K-Sera 95 (Lord Gayle (USA) 124) [1994 119: 10v* 10.5m 11v* 12g^5 10g^5 12g^3 12d^5 1995 10s 11s^5 11m^4 12m^3 12g^4 12s^4 12g^5 Sep 24] only a smart German horse nowadays: in frame in 4 Group 1 events in 1995 (including 5½ lengths third of 8 to Lando at Dusseldorf in July), without getting close to winning any of them: stays 1½m: has won on good to firm ground, very best efforts on good and heavy: hung under pressure (and demoted) second 4-y-o start. *A. Lowe, Germany* 113

KOSSOLIAN 2 b.f. (Mar 2) Emarati (USA) 74 – Cwm Deri (IRE) (Alzao (USA) 117) [1995 5m^2 5.1m 6.1m* 6g 6.5m 7g Sep 20] 3,600Y: lengthy filly: first foal: dam never ran: won 5-runner median auction maiden at Chepstow in July: helped set very strong pace when running poorly in claimer at Brighton on final start: stays 6.5f: far from tractable, and has twice hung badly right. *B. Palling* 72

KRALINGEN 3 ch.f. Move Off 112 – Elitist 72 (Keren 100) [1994 –: 6m 7d 7g 1995 10m 7m 8.1d 12.3f 8f 10m a12g Jul 22] sturdy filly: no worthwhile form. *N. Chamberlain* –

KRATON GARDEN (USA) 3 b.c. Sovereign Dancer (USA) – Kenanga 105 (Kris 135) [1994 –p: 7s 1995 12g 12m May 6] strong gelding: unimpressive mover: no worthwhile form in maidens: will be suited by a thorough test of stamina: sold (W. Jarvis to T. Casey) 6,500 gns Newmarket Autumn Sales. *W. Jarvis* –

KRATZ (IRE) 2 b.g. (Apr 16) Prince Rupert (FR) 121 – Some Spice (Horage 124) [1995 6g^5 7m^2 7f 7.5m^3 a7g^4 7.9g 7.5d^5 7d 7f a8g Nov 24] IR 1,800Y: leggy, unfurnished gelding: poor walker: fourth foal: dam lightly-raced maiden: plater: well below form last 3 starts: stays 7.5f: visored on 4 occasions, blinkered twice. *B. S. Rothwell* 50 d

KRAYYAN DAWN 5 ch.h. Krayyan 117 – Tana Mist 71 (Homeboy 114) [1994 47: 8s 8.3v 9d^5 7g 9.7m^3 10m^5 9.7m^6 8.3m a7g* 1995 a8g a8g^5 a10g 9.7d^3 9.7g* 10g^5 12m* 12m^6 12m^6 12s Oct 6] stocky, workmanlike horse: modest performer: won amateurs handicap in April and minor event (very cheekily by short head) in May, both at Folkestone: stays 1½m when conditions aren't testing: acts on good to firm and dead ground and on equitrack: blinkered twice at 2 yrs: held up/tracks leaders. *R. Akehurst* 54

KREEF 3 b.g. Kris 135 – Pelf (USA) 79 (Al Nasr (FR) 126) [1994 59: 7m 8g a6g^3 1995 a8g a7g^4 6m^6 a6g 6f 8.3g 7m^5 a7g^4 12s Sep 19] small, robust gelding: modest maiden: sold out of R. O'Sullivan's stable 1,850 gns Ascot July Sales after eighth start: should stay 1m: best form on equitrack: tried to refuse and unseated rider over hurdles in October, won a race in December: inconsistent. *R. Curtis* – a55

KRISCLIFFE 2 ch.c. (May 5) Kris 135 – Lady Norcliffe (USA) (Norcliffe (CAN)) [1995 6f* 6g^3 Jul 15] good-topped colt: half-brother to 1½m winner Lady St Lawrence (by Bering) and 1989 Irish 2-y-o 5f and 7f winner Shagudine (by Shadeed): dam good winner at up to 11f: won 4-runner maiden at Goodwood in June by head from Al Shafa: tailed-off last of 3 in listed race at Newbury 2 weeks later: bred to stay at least 1m: sold 10,500 gns Newmarket Autumn Sales. *P. T. Walwyn* 78

KRISHAN POWER 2 b.c. (May 3) Superpower 113 – Najat 49§ (Tender King 123) [1995 5g 5f^6 5.1m^6 Aug 2] strong, lengthy colt: good mover: second foal: brother to 3-y-o Arkindale Amber: dam 2-y-o 5f winner, became one to avoid: apparently much improved form when sixth of 10 to Tymeera in claimer at Nottingham on final start: will probably stay 6f. *M. W. Easterby* 58 ?

KRISTAL BREEZE 3 ch.f. Risk Me (FR) 127 – Mistral's Dancer (Shareef Dancer (USA) 135) [1994 47: 7f 8.2s 7g 1995 8.2g 9.7m 10.3m 10.2m^5 a12g a12g a8g 10d^4 Sep 18] lengthy, rather sparely-made filly: poor maiden: no worthwhile form in 1995: no improvement in visor. *W. R. Muir* –

KRISTAL DIVA 4 ch.f. Kris 135 – Dame Ashfield 90 (Grundy 137) [1994 60: 12f^4 1995 12d a14g Nov 16] quite good-topped filly: modest form on only outing in 1994 for M. Johnston: tailed off on return: should be suited by 1½m+. *A. G. Newcombe* –

KRISTAL'S PARADISE (IRE) 3 b.f. Bluebird (USA) 125 – Kristal's Pride (Kris 135) [1994 68: 6g 7m 8.2s^2 1995 10g^3 12g^3 14m* 16g* 16.2d^5 16d* 16m^2 99

14g[3] Nov 26] rather leggy, attractive filly: poor mover: useful handicapper: won at Haydock and Newbury in July and at Goodwood (beaten on merit by disqualified Seasonal Splendour) in September: very good efforts in listed rated stakes at Newmarket (beaten head by Daraydan) and Group 3 event at Rome (third of 11 to Sternkoenig) last 2 starts: stays 2m well: acts on good to firm and soft ground: front runner/races prominently: game and reliable: stays in training. *J. L. Dunlop*

KRISTIS GIRL 8 ch.m. Ballacashtal (CAN) – Fleur d'Amour 85 (Murrayfield 119) [1994 NR 1995 a7g a7g[4] a9.4g[2] a8.5g[5] a8.5g[3] a9.4g a12g[6] a9.4g[5] a7g[5] May 15] plain, angular mare: unimpressive mover: off course 3 years prior to reappearance: poor form on fibresand on return, mainly in sellers and claimers: stays 9.4f: acts on all-weather surfaces, used to be best with give in the ground when on turf: tried visored. *D. Haydn Jones* 41

KRIVA 3 b.f. Reference Point 139 – Kraemer (USA) (Lyphard (USA) 132) [1994 50: 8.2s 8d 1995 14.1f[5] 14.1g[4] 17.2h* a16g[3] 16.1f[3] 17.2m 14.6m Oct 20] smallish, well-made filly: fair handicapper: made all at Bath (3 runners, apprentices) in August: stays 17.2f: acts on hard ground: sold 7,500 gns Newmarket December Sales. *R. J. R. Williams* 69

KRYSTALLOS 3 b.c. Polish Precedent (USA) 131 – Dancing Crystal 76 (Kris 135) [1994 NR 1995 8m[6] 8.3m* 8g[2] 8m 10g[2] 10m Aug 11] 46,000Y: big, strong colt: has scope: fourth foal: half-brother to ungenuine 1994 3-y-o Tatjana (by Soviet Star) and winners in Germany and Japan, including 1995 German middle-distance 5-y-o Dark Canyon (by Reference Point): dam ran twice, at 6f and 7f: useful performer: won 20-runner maiden at Windsor in May: good second in £19,400 handicap at Newmarket on penultimate start, staying on: well below form in similar event at Newbury only subsequent outing: stays 1¼m well: has raced only on a sound surface: sold only 1,450 gns Ascot December Sales. *R. Hannon* 99

KRYSTAL MAX (IRE) 2 b.g. (Mar 21) Classic Music (USA) – Lake Isle (IRE) (Caerleon (USA) 132) [1995 5f* 5m[4] 5m[3] 5m[4] 5m[6] 5g[6] a5g* a6g* Dec 19] IR 6,000Y: good-topped gelding: first foal: dam lightly-raced Irish 7f winner from family of Sadler's Wells: won maiden at Redcar in June and nurseries (under 7-lb claimer) at Southwell and Lingfield in December: stays 6f: acts on firm ground and goes well on all-weather: takes keen hold. *T. D. Barron* 75 a85

KSHESSINSKAYA 3 ch.f. Hadeer 118 – Bonnie Hope (USA) (Nijinsky (CAN) 138) [1994 NR 1995 10m[6] 11.5f[3] 10m[4] 12m 12m[6] 11.9m[4] 11.5m* 16g Sep 30] leggy, quite attractive filly: blind in one eye: half-sister to several winners, including 1½m and 1¾m winner Raahin (by Super Concorde): dam ran only at 2 yrs, when successful at around 1m: trained on debut by G. Rimmer: useful form in frame in steadily-run Oaks trials at Lingfield and Goodwood in May and when last of 4 to Larrocha in listed race at York in August: 5/4 on, scrambled home in 5-runner maiden at Lingfield in September: one paced and should stay further than 1½m: has raced only on a sound surface: inconsistent, and one to treat with caution. *C. E. Brittain* 99

KUANTAN (USA) 2 b.g. (Mar 23) Gone West (USA) – Cuddly Doll (USA) (Bold Hour) [1995 5f* 6m[6] 6d[2] 7g Sep 29] $85,000Y: good-topped gelding with plenty of scope: has a long stride: freeze-fired after second start: brother to a winner in USA, closely related to Grade 1 9f Wood Memorial runner-up Burnt Hills (by Conquistador Cielo) and half-brother to several winners: dam unraced: won Windsor Castle Stakes at Ascot on debut in good style by 2½ lengths from Applaud: not discredited when 6 lengths second to Kahir Almaydan in Mill Reef Stakes at Newbury in September but below form on second and final starts and subsequently gelded: stays 6f: takes a keen hold: usually difficult at stalls (refused to enter them at Ascot in October): one to have reservations about. *P. F. I. Cole* 101

KUDOS BLUE 2 b.f. (Apr 11) Elmaamul (USA) 125 – Don't Be Shy (IRE) (Kafu 120) [1995 a7g 7f Oct 12] small, light-framed filly: first foal: dam poor half-sister to 2000 Guineas winner Tap On Wood: tailed off in maidens at Southwell and Redcar. *J. D. Bethell* –

KULSHEE MASHEE (USA) 3 ch.c. With Approval (CAN) – Princess Spook (CAN) (Majestic Prince (USA)) [1994 7g[3] 7g* 7d[2] 8g[5] 1995 11g[3] 11s[5] 11d[2] 12m 12g[3] 10d[3] 11g* 9m Oct 13] $25,000F, $75,000Y: rather leggy, angular colt: fluent mover: fifth foal: half-brother to French 7f and 7.5f winner Prospective Prince (by Woodman) and 2 winners in North America: dam 2-y-o sprint maiden winner in 96

USA: fairly useful German performer: won maiden at Hamburg at 2 yrs: generally ran with credit in 1995, winning minor event at Cologne in September: stiff task and sweating, tailed-off last of 8 in listed race at Newmarket on final start: stays 1½m: acts on soft ground, stiff task on top-of-the-ground. *Bruno Schutz, Germany*

KUMMEL KING 7 b.g. Absalom 128 – Louise 71 (Royal Palace 131) [1994 64: 6.9v^{3} 8m^{5} 8.3m^{2} 8f* 7.1m 7g^{4} 8f^{2} 8.1m^{2} 7.6g^{6} 8g^{3} 8m 1995 7m 6m^{2} 7.6m 8.1d^{5} Sep 2] compact gelding: modest performer: effective at 6f to 1m: acts on any turf going, below form on the all-weather: blinkered once earlier in career: mulish stalls (well beaten) final 6-y-o start: races prominently. *E. J. Alston* — 61

KUNG FRODE 3 ch.c. Interrex (CAN) – Harmony Heights 67 (Music Boy 124) [1994 71p: a5g 5.7g a5g* 1995 5g 5d^{5} 5.1m Oct 19] strong colt: modest performer: not seen in 1995 until September: should stay 6f: acts on fibresand and dead ground, well beaten on good to firm. *B. A. McMahon* — 63

KUNUCU (IRE) 2 ch.f. (Apr 9) Bluebird (USA) 125 – Kunuz (Ela-Mana-Mou 132) [1995 5g^{3} 5m* 5m* 6g^{2} 5d^{4} 5.2g^{4} 5.2m* 5.2m^{4} 5g^{2} 5s^{4} Oct 7] IR 11,000Y: good-quartered filly: good mover: fourth foal: sister to Irish 3-y-o 7f to 9f winner Blue Kestrel, closely related to 7.5f and 1m winner Sea-Ayr (by Magical Wonder) and half-sister to Irish 1¼m winner Yankee Singer (by Entitled): dam (ran twice) out of sister to smart Irish pair Yankee Gold and Lady Singer: won maiden auction at Ripon in April and minor events at Ayr in May and Yarmouth in July: in frame in listed race at Ayr (best effort) and Cornwallis Stakes at Ascot (hampered at stalls then seemed to make up ground too quickly) last 2 starts: stays 6f but better form at 5f: acts on good to firm and dead ground. *T. D. Barron* — 93

KURDISTAN (IRE) 5 ch.g. Persian Heights 129 – Late Sally 101 (Sallust 134) [1994 8v 7g 8g 8d* 8d 1995 8v 8g* 9m^{3} 9m^{2} 8.5s^{6} 8m^{5} 7m^{3} 8g^{3} 8d Sep 24] IR 33,000Y: third foal: brother to a winner in Ireland and half-brother to a 1m winner in Ireland by King's Lake: dam won listed sprint race: fairly useful performer: successful 4 times in Ireland, including handicap at Gowran Park in April: last of 18 (beaten when badly hampered over 1f out) in £28,900 handicap at Ascot on final outing: stays 9f: acts on good to firm and heavy ground: sometimes a front runner. *Edward Lynam, Ireland* — 86

KUSH 4 b.f. Kind of Hush 118 – Kasu 35 (Try My Best (USA) 130) [1994 –: 5.9v 8.3m a9.4g 14.1g^{6} 14.1m 1995 a11g a16g Jan 13] small, angular filly: bad staying maiden plater. *J. L. Harris* — –

Windsor Castle Stakes, Royal Ascot—a winning debut for Kuantan, at the chief expense of favourite Applaud

KUSTOM KIT (IRE) 2 ch.c. (Mar 17) Timeless Times (USA) 99 – Friendly Song 48 (Song 132) [1995 5g* 5m^3 5m 6g^6 5.2g Jul 15] 11,000Y: small, lengthy colt: first foal: dam poor maiden: won maiden auction at Doncaster in March: highly tried afterwards, appearing to run well when third in minor event at Newmarket on second outing: likely to prove best at 5f. *B. A. McMahon* — 68

KUTTA 3 b.c. Old Vic 136 – Ardassine (Ahonoora 122) [1994 NR 1995 8m 10g^3 10.4g^4 10g* 12m 10.3d^6 10d* Sep 16] quite attractive colt: good mover: sixth foal: half-brother to 3 winners, including smart 7f and 1m winner Gabr (by Green Desert) and useful 1991 2-y-o 6f winner Enaya (by Caerleon): dam 1½m winner from family of Slip Anchor: made into a useful performer: won 16-runner maiden at Pontefract in June and 20-runner £16,600 handicap at Newbury (heavily backed, beat Ball Gown by a length, not clear run early in straight but well on top at finish) in September: effective at 1¼m but will prove well suited by return to 1½m: acts on dead going, possibly not on good to firm: type to progress further in 1996, and looks sure to win more races. *R. W. Armstrong* — 101 p

KUWAM (IRE) 2 b.g. (May 23) Last Tycoon 131 – Inshad 81 (Indian King (USA) 128) [1995 6g^6 5.9f^5 Jun 28] 14,000F, 30,000Y: well-made gelding: fourth foal: half-brother to fairly useful 7f and 1m winner Mareha (by Cadeaux Genereux): dam 6f (at 2 yrs) and 7f winner from family of Bassenthwaite: faded from 2f out when last in maidens at Doncaster and Carlisle: subsequently gelded: looked capable of better. *J. Berry* — –

KYMIN (IRE) 3 b.f. Kahyasi 130 – Akila (FR) (Top Ville 129) [1994 NR 1995 12m^2 11.9f^2 12s^4 10.2g^6 Nov 10] leggy filly: half-sister to several middle-distance winners in France: dam unraced daughter of Licata, dam also of Acamas, Akarad and Akiyda: 40/1 and ridden by 7-lb claimer, 3 lengths second of 11 to Larrocha in maiden at Newmarket: disappointing afterwards in maiden (6/4 on, final start for L. Cumani) at Brighton and 2 minor events in French Provinces: bandaged behind on debut: sure to stay beyond 1½m: blinkered in France: sold 4,000 gns Newmarket December Sales. *H. Pantall, France* — 78

KYRENIA TIMES 3 b.c. Good Times (ITY) – Kyrenia Sunset (CYP) (Lucky Look (CYP)) [1994 NR 1995 12m 10m^5 May 27] tall colt: poor mover: fourth reported living foal: half-brother to 1992 2-y-o 7f winner Kyrenia Game (by Mummy's Game): dam unraced Cypriot-bred: no worthwhile form in maidens. *P. Mitchell* — –

L

LAABAS 12 br.g. Ile de Bourbon (USA) 133 – Lyric Dance 106 (Lyphard (USA) 132) [1994 53d: a14.8g^6 a16.2g^3 a16.2g^5 a16.2g^6 16v a14.8g a16.2g^5 1995 a14.8g a16.2g 14d 17.2m Sep 25] big, good-topped gelding: no longer of any account. *J. E. Long* — –

LAAFEE 2 gr.g. (Apr 5) Machiavellian (USA) 123 – Al Sylah 118 (Nureyev (USA) 131) [1995 6m^2 6m* 6m^2 6m^2 Oct 28] leggy, close-coupled gelding: has scope: fifth foal: half-brother to 3-y-o Ghalayan (by Nashwan) and 7f winner Yaqthan (by Kris): dam sprinter: fairly useful form: won maiden at Pontefract in August: beaten a length afterwards in £6,600 event at Pontefract won by Defined Feature and mixed-age event at Newmarket won by Elshabiba: will prove best at sprint distances. *H. Thomson Jones* — 93

LA ALLA WA ASA (IRE) 3 b.f. Alzao (USA) 117 – Steady The Buffs 62 (Balidar 133) [1994 NR 1995 8m^6 10d^6 Oct 19] 100,000Y: workmanlike filly: sister to useful 1993 2-y-o 1m winner Sheridan and very useful 6f (at 2 yrs) to 8.5f winner Aldbourne: dam stayed 1¼m: modest form in maidens at Pontefract (involved in bumping) and Newbury in October: likely to prove suited by further than 1¼m: sold 16,500 gns Newmarket December Sales. *J. H. M. Gosden* — 60

LAAL (USA) 3 b.g. Shirley Heights 130 – Afaff (USA) (Nijinsky (CAN) 138) [1994 63?: 7g 7g 1995 10m 10g 10.1d^6 Jun 15] strong, lengthy colt: well beaten in 1995: sold (E. Dunlop to M. Barraclough) 4,000 gns Newmarket July Sales. *E. A. L. Dunlop* — –

LAAZIM AFOOZ 2 b.c. (Apr 15) Mtoto 134 – Balwa (USA) 101 (Danzig (USA)) [1995 7f Oct 23] small, close-coupled colt: first foal: dam 5f (at 2 yrs) and 7f winner from very good family: 33/1, burly and green, little promise in maiden at Leicester. *R. T. Phillips* –

LABEEB 3 b.c. Lear Fan (USA) 130 – Lady Blackfoot 108 (Prince Tenderfoot (USA) 126) [1994 8v^4 1995 8g^3 8d^2 8d* 9g^3 10m^3 9g^5 10d^2 9f* Nov 26] 30,000F, 100,000Y: big, good-topped colt: closely related to very smart performer Fanmore (by Lear Fan) and half-brother to several winners, including 5-y-o middle-distance performer Northern Graduate (by Northrop): dam speedy Irish filly: won minor event at Longchamp in May: led 1f out to near line when short-neck third of 7 to Torrential in very slowly-run Prix Jean Prat at Chantilly next start, best effort in Europe for C. Laffon-Parias: racing on Lasix and bute and blinkered, won 13-runner Crown Royal Hollywood Derby in November by ½ length from Helmsman: stays 1¼m: acts on firm ground and dead. *N. Drysdale, USA* 119

LABEED (USA) 2 b.c. (Apr 3) Riverman (USA) 131 – Gracious Beauty (USA) 67 (Nijinsky (CAN) 138) [1995 7.1m^6 7.1g^2 7f 8m 7d^6 8f^2 Oct 12] closely-coupled, quite good-topped colt: first foal: dam, maiden who stayed 1¼m, closely related to Dayjur out of champion American sprinter Gold Beauty: fair maiden: looks an out-and-out stayer. *Major W. R. Hern* 68

LA BELLE DOMINIQUE 3 b.f. Dominion 123 – Love Street 62 (Mummy's Pet 125) [1994 76, a67: 5.7g^3 6s^5 5g^3 5s^3 a5g^2 a5g^5 1995 a5g 5.1g 5.1m 5.1m 5.1f 5g^3 5m 5.1m^3 a5g^3 5.3f^2 Jul 24] smallish, strong filly: only modest maiden handicapper at best nowadays: best form at around 5f: acts on firm and soft ground and on fibresand. *S. G. Knight* 59 a52

LA BELLE SHYANNE 4 ch.f. Shy Groom (USA) – Defy Me 75 (Bustino 136) [1994 43: 7.1s 10.2m^3 8.3m 10f^3 10m^3 11.9m^2 10d^5 11.9d 1995 a8g a12g 8.2g 11.7m^6 12g 13.1f 10m 8h^2 8h Sep 4] plain filly: usually dull in coat: bad maiden handicapper: effective at 1m to 1½m: probably acts on hard and dead going: inconsistent. *C. J. Hill* 33

LABIBEH (USA) 3 gr.f. Lyphard (USA) 132 – Asl (USA) 114 (Caro 133) [1994 70p: 7m 7m 8.1d^6 1995 11.6m 12.5g* 14.1f^4 12m* 12m* 12f* 13.4m^2 12v* 12d^4 12m^6 Nov 4] big, strong, good-bodied filly: shows a round action: won maiden at Warwick in June then handicaps at Folkestone, Catterick and Thirsk in July: showed similar form to Thirsk on 3 of last 4 starts but, 16/1, was seemingly transformed by very testing conditions when winning 5-runner Princess Royal Stakes at Ascot in October by 3½ lengths from Saxon Maid: would have stayed further than 12.5f: front runner/tracked pace: refused to enter stalls once (wore blanket at Ascot) in 1995: sometimes swished tail, but was game: visits Lahib. *J. L. Dunlop* 109

LA BOSSETTE (IRE) 3 b.f. Cyrano de Bergerac 120 – Bosquet 59 (Queen's Hussar 124) [1994 56: 5f^3 5m^2 6.1m^5 6m 6m^5 5m 1995 6.1g 6m^6 6g 6g 8m^5 7m^5 6f a5g a6g a10g Dec 18] small filly: just a poor maiden handicapper at 3 yrs: sold out of J. R. Arnold's stable 1,000 gns Ascot September Sales after seventh start: should stay 7f: has raced only on a sound surface on turf: tried in blinkers/visor, no improvement. *R. Ingram* 42 a–

Princess Royal Stakes, Ascot—the grey Labibeh and Saxon Maid in very testing conditions

LA BRIEF 3 b.f. Law Society (USA) 130 – Lady Warninglid (Ela-Mana-Mou 132) [1994 55: 7g 7g 8d 1995 12s 12m 12.1s* a16g^2 a14g* a16g* Nov 20] compact, workmanlike filly: has a round action: fair handicapper: did not reappear until late-September, then progressed well, winning at Edinburgh and twice at Southwell: stays 2m: acts on soft ground and the all-weather: should win more races. *M. J. Ryan* 73

LABUDD (USA) 5 ch.h. Deputy Minister (CAN) – Delightful Vie (USA) (Barbs Delight) [1994 a7g a8g a7g^5 a8g a7g^6 a8g^3 a6g a7g^6 1995 a7g^6 a12g^3 a12g^6 8g^4 8g 7f a10g^3 Nov 25] good-topped horse: rated 75 at 3 yrs for J. Gosden: sent to Dubai but managed only 2 places in 11 outings: sold 2,800 gns Newmarket July Sales: inconsistent on return: stays 1¼m: found little final start. *R. Ingram* 61

LAC DE GRAS (IRE) 4 gr.g. Henbit (USA) 130 – I've No Idea (Nishapour (FR) 125) [1994 –: 10d 8.3g 5.1d 5s a7g a10g 1995 a10g^5 Jan 5] leggy gelding: little sign of ability. *R. Curtis* –

LAC DESSERT (USA) 2 ch.f. (Apr 12) Lac Ouimet (USA) – Tiramisu (USA) (Roberto (USA) 131) [1995 7m* 7.5m* 7.1g^3 a8f^6 Oct 14] leggy, angular filly: second foal: dam, winner at 11f in France, half-sister to smart sprinter Al Zawbaah out of close relative of Storm Bird: sire, good-class 9f/1¼m performer, brother to St Jovite: won median auction maiden at Thirsk in June and 4-runner minor event at Beverley in July: best effort when third of 5 to Tamnia in listed event at Sandown: well beaten in $60,000 event at Belmont nearly 3 months later: should be better suited by 1m than less. *D. R. Loder* 91

LACHESIS 2 ch.f. (Feb 1) Lycius (USA) 124 – Chance All (FR) 88 (Glenstal (USA) 118) [1995 6m^3 Oct 4] compact filly: first foal: dam, 2-y-o 5f winner, should have stayed 7f, out of half-sister to Young Generation: 25/1 and bit backward, made some late progress when 12 lengths third of 9 to Victoria Regia in maiden at York: unimpressive to post then reluctant stalls: should improve. *R. Hollinshead* 55 p

LA CONFEDERATION 4 b.f. Nureyev (USA) 131 – Unite 126 (Kris 135) [1994 117: 8g* 9.3m^5 10.1m* 10g* 10m^6 1995 10d^5 11.9m^5 9.5f^4 10s Sep 23] lengthy, angular filly: smart performer: off course 2½ months, ran fairly well when about 3½ lengths fifth of 8 (never able to challenge) to Pure Grain in steadily-run Yorkshire Oaks at York: back to form when under a length fourth of 8 to Possibly Perfect in Beverly D Stakes at Arlington: should have stayed 1½m: acted on firm ground, well below form both starts on a soft surface: blanketed for stalls entry in Britain: tended to carry her head high: stud. *D. R. Loder* 117

LACRYMA CRISTI (IRE) 2 b.c. (Feb 18) Green Desert (USA) 127 – L'Anno d'Oro (Habitat 134) [1995 6m* 6g^3 Jul 27] strong, good sort: good mover: third foal: dam lightly-raced sister to Habibti: well-backed favourite though carrying condition, won 12-runner minor event at Windsor in good fashion by 4 lengths from Roses In The Snow: only third of 5 when 7/2-on shot for similar event at Salisbury later in month: looked a useful prospect at Windsor. *Mrs J. Cecil* 95 +

LA DAMA (USA) 3 ch.f. Known Fact (USA) 135 – Cypria Sacra (USA) 103 (Sharpen Up 127) [1994 70§: 6m^4 6g^6 6d 1995 6.1g 8.2m 7m Oct 30] tall filly: disappointing maiden: sold out of B. Hills's stable 2,100 gns Doncaster February Sales: well beaten (first start only for G. Oldroyd) in 1995: has worn off-side pricker: wayward (pulls hard and hangs) and is one to leave alone. *F. J. O'Mahony* – §

LADONI 3 b.c. Danehill (USA) 126 – Lilac Charm 87 (Bustino 136) [1994 8s* 1995 8v* 8.5s* 8g 9s* 8m^6 8d^2 8g^3 Sep 23] half-brother to several winners, including useful 1m (at 2 yrs) to 1¼m winner Sorceress (by Fabulous Dancer): dam, 1½m winner, out of fastest 2-y-o filly of 1971 Rose Dubarry: useful German colt: won maiden at Cologne at 2 yrs: successful at 3 yrs in listed event at Mulheim (very easily) and Group 3 event at Krefeld (leading 1½f out and hanging left) in April then (after disappointing in Mehl-Mulhens-Rennen) 11-runner Group 3 event at Dortmund (made all, by ½ length from Dream For Future) in June: placed behind A Magicman in pattern events at Baden-Baden (beaten a length) and Cologne last 2 starts: stays 9f: acts on heavy ground, respectable effort on good to firm. *H. Remmert, Germany* 108

LADY BANKES (IRE) 2 b.f. (Mar 17) Alzao (USA) 117 – Never So Fair 65 (Never So Bold 135) [1995 6g 6f^2 7.1s^6 Nov 2] 4,500Y: small filly: second foal: half-sister to 3-y-o Queen's Ransom (by Last Tycoon), 7.1f winner at 2 yrs: dam thrice-raced close relative of smart 5f performer Amaranda and half-sister to very 67 smart (at up to 1m) Favoridge: easily best effort in maiden auctions when length second of 15 to Missile at Pontefract in October: should stay 7f. *W. G. M. Turner*

LADY-BO-K 4 ch.f. Komaite (USA) – Lady Keyser 68 (Le Johnstan 123) [1994 73: 6v 6m^{3} 6f^{3} 6m* 6d 6m 6m^{6} 7g 7g 1995 5.9f^{6} 6m 6m 6.1m a5g 7m 7m 10g Sep 23] lengthy filly: disappointing in 1995: stays 6f: seems unsuited by a soft surface: blinkered (slowly away, never dangerous) sixth 4-y-o start: sold 2,200 gns Doncaster October Sales. *Capt. J. Wilson* —

LADYBOWER (IRE) 3 b.f. Pennine Walk 120 – Eimkar (Junius (USA) 124) [1994 NR 1995 a6g^{6} a6g 5.1m 8f Oct 23] 3,800Y: small filly: fourth foal: dam unraced half-sister to high-class French miler Daring Display: poor maiden: probably stays 1m. *Lord Huntingdon* 36

LADY BROKER 5 b.m. Petorius 117 – Phoenix Rose 85 (Frankincense 120) [1994 54: a7g* a7g*^{dis} a7g a7g a6g 1995 a8g Jan 9] leggy mare: modest performer: no form since winning in 1994: effective at 7f/1m: acts on fibresand. *A. Bailey* —

LADY BUNTING 8 b.m. Well Decorated (USA) – Lady's Flag (USA) (Fifth Marine (USA)) [1994 –: 7.6g 10m 1995 a12g^{5} a13g^{3} a16g Mar 2] leggy mare: capable of only bad form on flat nowadays: stays 13f: tried blinkered/visored, no improvement. *Miss B. Sanders* 26

LADY CARLA 2 b.f. (Mar 8) Caerleon (USA) 132 – Shirley Superstar 94 (Shirley Heights 130) [1995 8f* Oct 24] 220,000Y: unfurnished filly: third living foal: half-sister to 4-y-o Chita Rivera (by Chief Singer): dam lightly-raced 7f winner (at 2 yrs) out of very useful (at up to 1¾m) Odeon: 5/2, easy winner of 12-runner maiden at Leicester in October by 4 lengths from General Macarthur: sure to improve, particularly over middle distances. *H. R. A. Cecil* 90 p

LADY CAROLINE LAMB (IRE) 2 b.f. (Jan 24) Contract Law (USA) 108 – Tuft Hill 92 (Grundy 137) [1995 5m^{4} 5h* 5m^{2} 5g^{4} 5.2d^{6} 5g^{6} 6m 5m^{2} a5g^{6} Nov 2] 6,200Y: leggy, lengthy, unfurnished filly: sixth reported foal: half-sister to ungenuine 1993 2-y-o 6f winner Up The Mariners (by Classic Secret): dam, 2-y-o 6f winner, half-sister to 10.5f Prix Corrida winner Bonshamile: won 4-runner median auction maiden at Carlisle in August: several creditable efforts in nurseries afterwards: keen sort, but should stay 6f: acts on hard ground. *M. R. Channon* 64

LADY DAVENPORT (IRE) 3 b.f. Contract Law (USA) 108 – Sandhurst Goddess 103 (Sandhurst Prince 128) [1994 65: 5.1g* 5.2m^{6} 6m^{3} 6m^{4} 6g^{5} 6m^{3} 7.3g^{5} 6m^{6} 6g 7g^{4} 8d^{5} 7s 1995 a8.5g 6.1m^{2} 6f May 15] lengthy, workmanlike filly: modest performer: best at up to 7f on a sound surface: inconsistent: dead. *Ronald Thompson* 61

LADY DIGNITY (IRE) 2 b.f. (Mar 22) Nordico (USA) – Royal Respect 82 (Kings Lake (USA) 133) [1995 5g^{5} 6m^{4} a7g^{2} a7g^{4} Dec 6] 5,000F, 3,000Y: angular filly: half-sister to 1991 2-y-o 5f winner Royal Walkabout (by Pennine Walk) and a winner in Germany by Fools Holme: dam, maiden who stayed 1½m, half-sister to useful middle-distance performer Civility and smart 1976 2-y-o 5f performer Piney Ridge: best effort in maiden events when ½-length second to Victoria Venture at Wolverhampton: will be suited by further than 7f: acts on good to firm ground and fibresand. *P. J. Makin* 66

LADY ECLAT 2 b.f. (Jan 31) Nomination 125 – Romantic Saga 69 (Prince Tenderfoot (USA) 126) [1995 5m^{6} 6.1m^{6} 5m^{4} 7g 5g 5f^{6} a6g* a6g^{3} a5g^{2} Dec 18] 2,600Y: good-topped filly: second foal: sister to a bad maiden: dam placed over 5f and 6f at 2 yrs: made all in seller at Wolverhampton in December: takes keen hold, and not sure to stay 7f: acts well on all-weather: visored last 4 outings. *J. A. Glover* 54

LADY HIGHFIELD 4 br.f. High Kicker (USA) – Judy Burton (Mummy's Pet 125) [1994 51§: a8g^{6} a8s^{3} a7g^{4} 8.1g 7m a7g a8g^{5} 8.1s^{3} 7m^{2} 7m^{4} 8.2g^{5} 8s 7g 7g 7g a8g 1995 8m 9.2g a8g 10m* 10g^{2} 10m* 10m^{2} 10m^{2} 10m^{4} 10m 10d^{6} 9f 10g^{3} a11g^{5} a10g a8g Nov 20] leggy filly: modest performer: has proved inconsistent and temperamental, but in good heart in the summer and beat big fields in sellers at Leicester and Nottingham: stays 1¼m: acts on any going, including fibresand: no improvement in blinkers (not tried at 4 yrs): has been bandaged. *M. J. Ryan* 58 a–

LADY ISABELL 2 b.f. (Mar 8) Rambo Dancer (CAN) 107 – Warning Bell 88 (Bustino 136) [1995 7.6d^{6} Sep 14] 1,500F, 5,400Y: half-sister to 3-y-o Warning Shot (Dowsing), 5f winner at 2 yrs, and fairly useful 1¼m winner Virtual Reality (by Diamond Shoal): dam, 1¼m winner, daughter of half-sister to top 1981 2-y-o filly 58 p

Circus Ring: 20/1, around 7 lengths sixth of 12 to Patria in maiden at Lingfield: should improve over 1m+. *T. G. Mills*

LADY JOSHUA (IRE) 2 ch.f. (Mar 31) Royal Academy (USA) 130 – Claretta (USA) 82 (Roberto (USA) 131) [1995 7m^6 7d^2 Nov 7] sister to fairly useful Irish 3-y-o Pier House, placed at up to 1m, closely related to Sapience (by Niniski) and half-sister to several winners: dam, 2-y-o 7f winner, half-sister to Italian 1000 Guineas winner Rosananti and good English/German performer Claddagh: burly on debut: well clear of third when short-headed in 30-runner maiden at the Curragh following month: will do better over 1m+. *J. L. Dunlop* 88 p

LADY KATE (USA) 3 ch.f. Trempolino (USA) 135 – Glitter (FR) 70 (Reliance II 137) [1994 –: 8s^3 8.1g 1995 10.2m 7g 12d a7g Nov 14] close-coupled filly: of no account. *K. O. Cunningham-Brown* –

LADY KHADIJA 9 b.m. Nicholas Bill 125 – Chenkynowa 48 (Connaught 130) [1994 –: 10.3g 6g 9.2d 1995 a6g Apr 26] deep-girthed mare: no sign of ability. *G. P. Kelly* –

LADYKIRK 2 b.f. (Jan 21) Slip Anchor 136 – Lady Day (FR) (Lightning (FR) 129) [1995 8g* Sep 16] fourth living foal: half-sister to 3-y-o Final Fling (by Last Tycoon) and French 1¼m and 11f winner Fair Child (by Crystal Glitters): dam won from 9f to 12.5f in France: 25/1 from 10/1, won 11-runner maiden at Ayr by ½ length from Maid For Baileys, behind after slow start, and running on to lead well inside last: will be well suited by middle distances: will improve. *J. W. Watts* 78 p

LADY KUYNDER 3 b.f. Petoski 135 – Indian Pink (USA) (Seattle Slew (USA)) [1994 NR 1995 a12g 8.3s^6 a9.4g^6 a12g a12g^6 a12g^5 Jul 22] second foal: half-sister to 4-y-o 1½m winner Lady Tjonger (by Sharrood): dam from same family as Intrepidity and smart sprinter Acushla: no form, including in sellers: sold 1,100 gns Newmarket September Sales: sent to Pakistan. *Dr J. D. Scargill* –

LADY LACEY 8 b.m. Kampala 120 – Cecily (Prince Regent (FR) 129) [1994 62d: 8s^6 9d* 8m 8g 8v 10.8d^4 8g^2 8f^4 8g 9f 8.1g 10d^4 9d 8s 9g^3 8g^4 8g 1995 8d^6 9g 8g 8g^3 10g^5 10m^6 10m^3 10m^3 10m^6 10d^3 10d^5 9d Sep 30] rather lightly-made mare: modest handicapper: effective at 1m to 11f: seems to act on any going: has won with and without a visor: usually set plenty to do: not so good as she was, but consistent in 1995. *G. B. Balding* 50

LADY LANCER (IRE) 3 b.f. Satco (FR) 112 – Miysam 60 (Supreme Sovereign 119) [1994 NR 1995 9.9m Apr 27] leggy filly: fifth reported foal: half-sister to 1987 2-y-o 5f winner Tapestry Prints (by On Your Mark), later successful in Belgium and Norway: dam 5f winner at 2 yrs: 16/1, soon tailed off in 13-runner claimer at Beverley: sold 500 gns Ascot December Sales. *C. N. Allen* –

LADY LUCY LINNET 3 b.f. Zalazl (USA) 120 – Song Grove 61 (Song 132) [1994 –: 5d 7g^5 8d a7g 1995 a9.4g a8g Jan 30] smallish filly: of little account. *N. A. Graham* –

LADY MAGIC (IRE) 2 b.f. (Apr 24) Magical Strike (USA) 114 – Drowsy Maggie (Tumble Wind (USA)) [1995 7m^5 Jun 26] 4,000F, 5,000Y: half-sister to Irish 2-y-o 6f winners Traditional Dancer (by Krayyan) and State of The Art (by Dominion Royale): dam Irish maiden: 50/1, started slowly, went right at stalls and always behind in 5-runner maiden auction at Warwick. *C. A. Smith* –

LADY NASH 3 b.f. Nashwan (USA) 135 – Je Comprend (USA) (Caerleon (USA) 132) [1994 NR 1995 7m 7g 8f^6 8m a8g^2 Nov 20] sturdy, plain filly: first foal: dam unraced sister to very useful miler Alquoz: first worthwhile form when second of 16 in minor event at Southwell: should stay beyond 1m, but pulls hard. *C. E. Brittain* 50

LADY OF THE MIST (IRE) 2 ch.f. (Apr 28) Digamist (USA) 110 – Stradey Lynn 57 (Derrylin 115) [1995 5g 6m 8g a8.5g Oct 28] IR 4,000Y: half-sister to several winners, including 3-y-o 5f and 6f winner Baileys Sunset (by Red Sunset) and fair handicapper (at up to 1m) Northern Printer (by Baptism): dam poor maiden: poor form in maiden events and a selling nursery. *J. S. Moore* 46

LADY PLOY 3 b.f. Deploy 131 – Quisissanno 76 (Be My Guest (USA) 126) [1994 42: 7m 7.5g^5 7d 8s 7d 1995 7g Apr 22] close-coupled, sparely-made filly: shows knee action: poor maiden plater: stiff task (well beaten) only start in 1995: stays 7.5f: acts on dead ground. *Miss L. C. Siddall* –

LADY PUI 3 b.f. Puissance 110 – Kind of Shy 61 (Kind of Hush 118) [1994 66, a55: 5v* 5g^{5} 5.1g^{4} 5s^{6} 5g a5g^{4} a6g a5g* a5g 1995 a5g^{5} a5g 5m Apr 25] tall, leggy filly: well beaten in 1995: best form at 5f: acts on heavy ground and equitrack: tried visored and blinkered. *J. Berry* –

LADY QUINTA (IRE) 3 b.f. Gallic League 119 – Clogher Head (Sandford Lad 133) [1994 59: 5s^{4} 5.1d^{5} 5d 5f^{2} 5g* 5m^{3} 5.3m a5g 1995 a5g Apr 13] leggy filly: modest form: tailed off in handicap at Wolverhampton only start in 1995: speedy: may be unsuited by a soft surface: inconsistent. *J. Berry* –

LADY REEMA 4 b.f. Tragic Role (USA) – Garth Lady 79 (Jalmood (USA) 126) [1994 59d: 8g^{5} 8f^{6} 10d 11.9g 10d a10g^{2} a12g^{6} a10g^{5} 1995 a12g a10g^{2} a10g^{6} 11.9m^{6} 9g^{4} 10.8f 12g^{3} 12m 10m^{2} Jun 26] sparely-made filly: poor mover: just a poor maiden plater nowadays: effective at 1¼m, will probably stay further than 1½m: acts on equitrack and good to firm and dead ground: normally held up. *Miss A. J. Whitfield* 41 a47

LADY ROXANNE 6 br.m. Cyrano de Bergerac 120 – Red Lory 87 (Bay Express 132) [1994 56, a48: a7g a5g^{2} a5g^{4} a6g^{2} a5g^{2} a6g 6d^{3} 5d* a5g a6g 1995 a6g^{6} a6g* a6g Mar 8] leggy, sparely-made mare: has a quick action: modest handicapper: narrowly won at Southwell in February, only worthwhile form in 1995: effective at 5f to 7f: acts on dead ground and all-weather surfaces: usually visored. *Lord Huntingdon* – a50

LADY SABINA 5 ch.m. Bairn (USA) 126 – Calibina 101 (Caliban 123) [1994 43: a8g^{5} a7g 8.3m 7g 8s 8g^{4} 8m 1995 a10g a10g 8.3g^{4} 10m^{3} 10f^{3} 12f 10m^{2} 10g* 10d^{5} 9d^{2} Sep 30] workmanlike mare: modest handicapper: won apprentice handicap at Kempton in September, leading over 2f out: stays 1¼m, and should get further: acts on firm ground, heavy and on equitrack. *W. J. Musson* 52 a33

LADY SHERIFF 4 b.f. Taufan (USA) 119 – Midaan (Sallust 134) [1994 45, a40: 6d 5m 5m 6g 5m 5m 5f^{5} 5g 5d^{5} a5g^{4} a5g 1995 5m^{3} 5m* 5g* 5g^{2} 5m 5m* 5m* 5m^{2} 5f^{2} 5.1m^{5} 5g^{2} 5d^{4} 5s^{5} 5f^{2} 5m^{4} 5m^{4} a5g^{5} Nov 16] workmanklike filly: has a markedly round action: recovered from whatever was ailing her in 1994 and progressed steadily throughout 1995 into a fairly useful handicapper: won at Thirsk in May and June and at Catterick and York in July: has raced mainly at 5f: acts on firm and soft ground, yet to prove effective on all-weather: usually blinkered: sometimes bandaged behind: successful for claimer: races prominently: tough. *M. W. Easterby* 85 a60 +

LADY SILK 4 ch.f. Prince Sabo 123 – Adduce (USA) (Alleged (USA) 138) [1994 67: a7g a7g^{5} a6s^{2} a6g^{6} a6g^{6} 7g 5.9s 6.1d* 6s^{2} 7m^{4} 6f^{6} 8.1g a7g^{5} a6g* a6g* 6m* 6m 7m 6d 6g 8.2g 7d 1995 6.1m a7g a7g a6g a6g a8g^{3} a8g^{3} a7g^{6} Dec 2] leggy filly: only a modest handicapper for new stables (left J. Hetherton after third start) in 1995: stays 1m: acts on good to firm ground, soft and fibresand: tried visored (not in 1995), seems better without: sometimes early to post. *Miss J. F. Craze* 52

LADYS PROMISE 3 b.f. Rakaposhi King 119 – Acting Lady VII (Damsire Unregistered) [1994 –: a5g 1995 8.3g 12m^{6} 13.8m^{5} 5f 7g Sep 23] unfurnished, non-thoroughbred filly: trained first 2 starts at 3 yrs by Martyn Wane: no sign of ability: visored final start. *G. R. Oldroyd* –

LADY THIANG 2 gr.f. (Feb 13) Petong 126 – Good Woman 60 (Good Times (ITY)) [1995 6m 6m* Aug 26] 9,700Y: neat filly: fourth foal: sister to 1992 2-y-o 6.1f winner Gangleader and half-sister to a winner in Italy by Slip Anchor: dam (maiden, probably stayed 6f) half-sister to smart 1985 2-y-o 5f and 7f winner Moorgate Man: won 24-runner maiden auction at Windsor by a neck from Mandarella, keeping on gamely under vigorous ride: may improve again. *C. F. Wall* 70 p

LADY TJONGER 4 b.f. Sharrood (USA) 124 – Indian Pink (USA) (Seattle Slew (USA)) [1994 44, a46: a9.4g^{5} a8g^{4} 12s 10g^{3} 11.1m^{6} a12g* 12g 1995 a12g a12g^{2} a12g a12g Jul 22] leggy, angular filly: poor form at best: showed little in 1995: stays 1½m well: acts on fibresand: visored (showed little) final 3-y-o start. *Dr J. D. Scargill* 26

LADY VALENSINA (IRE) 4 ch.f. Jareer (USA) 115 – Coshlea 63 (Red Alert 127) [1994 63: 7d^{4} 8.1g^{4} 9.7d^{6} 8s^{4} 7d^{5} a8.5g^{6} 1995 a8.5g^{5} a6g^{5} a8g 17.2m 10.8g^{6} 10.8m^{5} a8.5g Jul 21] workmanlike filly: just a poor maiden at best in 1995: stays 1m: acts on soft going: tried blinkered, no improvement. *B. J. Llewellyn* 45

LADY WILLIAMS (IRE) 4 ch.f. Roi Danzig (USA) – Apple Rings 97 (Godswalk (USA) 130) [1994 65: a8g* 9m^{2} 7.9f^{3} a8g^{6} 10g^{2} 9f^{2} 8m^{5} 8.5m* 8.1d 1995 a8g^{6} a8g^{4} a10g 8g 8f^{6} 10m Aug 26] lengthy, angular filly: good mover: modest 62 d handicapper: ran creditably in 1995 only on second start: sold 4,000 gns Ascot August Sales: stays 1¼m: acts on firm ground and equitrack: visored (looked unenthusiastic under pressure) final start. *Lord Huntingdon*

LADY WOODSTOCK 3 b.f. Chilibang 120 – Vent du Soir (Main Reef 126) [1994 –§: 5d 7d 6d 6m 1995 12.1m Aug 28] lengthy filly: of little account: sold 1,150 gns Ascot September Sales. *P. G. Murphy* – §

LA FANDANGO (IRE) 2 b.f. (Feb 18) Taufan (USA) 119 – Cursory Look (USA) (Nijinsky (CAN) 138) [1995 7m 7m^3 7.5m^5 7g^5 8.3g 8f 8f Oct 31] 5,400 2-y-o: angular filly: has scope: has a round action: first foal: dam, ran once in Ireland, from family of Hernando: modest maiden: stays 1m: acts on firm ground. *M. W. Easterby* 51

LA FEMME FRANCAISE (IRE) 2 gr.f. (Apr 22) Petong 126 – Pear Drop 74 (Bustino 136) [1995 7g 7.1s Oct 17] 12,500Y: third reported foal: dam third over 1m on only start at 2 yrs but seemed not to train on: soundly beaten in claimer at Brighton (slowly away) and maiden at Chepstow: sent to Italy. *M. R. Channon* –

LA FILLE DE CIRQUE 3 ch.f. Cadeaux Genereux 131 – Lady of The Land 75 (Wollow 132) [1994 –: 6g 1995 a8g^5 a8g^4 a6g^6 8g^3 8.2m 8m* 8f^2 8m 10f^2 10m^4 Aug 28] smallish filly: modest performer: won claimer at Newmarket in July: stays 1¼m: has raced only on a sound surface on turf: sometimes bandaged: found little second 3-y-o start: sweating freely (ran poorly) on fifth: none too consistent. *R. J. R. Williams* 49

LA FINALE 2 ch.f. (Apr 10) Dunbeath (USA) 127 – Jamarj 113 (Tyrnavos 129) [1995 6m^4 5m^3 6m^6 6d 7d^2 8f^5 a7g^3 a8g^3 Nov 24] smallish, close-coupled filly: has a quick action: third foal: half-sister to 4-y-o Our Bessie (by Persian Bold): dam best at 1m or 9f: modest maiden: some way below form in sellers on fibresand last 2 starts: stays 1m: best form on a soft surface. *M. H. Easterby* 60 a45

LAGAN 2 b.g. (Mar 8) Shareef Dancer (USA) 135 – Lagta 75 (Kris 135) [1995 6.1g^5 8g^3 7g^6 a7g Nov 16] good-bodied gelding: fifth foal: half-brother to 3-y-o Cavil (by Reprimand) and useful middle-distance performer Rudagi (by Persian Bold): dam 1½m and 1¾m winner: modest form in small-field minor events and Lingfield maiden: stiff task in nursery final start: bred to stay middle distances: sold 6,800 gns Ascot December Sales. *C. E. Brittain* 55 +

LAGO DI VARANO 3 b.g. Clantime 101 – On The Record 72 (Record Token 128) [1994 97: 5g* 5f^2 6m^2 6m^5 6m^5 6g^5 5.1s* 5s* 5g^4 6g 1995 6g^2 5m^3 6m^5 5m 5m 6g^4 5s 5f^4 Oct 31] strong, useful-looking gelding: good walker: useful performer: ran well on 3 of first 4 starts: regressive form last 4 starts: stays 6f: acts on firm and soft ground: blinkered/visored since seventh 2-y-o start: usually races prominently: has been gelded. *J. Berry* 97 d

LA GRAN SENORITA (USA) 3 br.f. El Gran Senor (USA) 136 – Yanuka 111 (Pitcairn 126) [1994 66: 5m^5 7s^2 7.1g^5 7d^5 1995 7.3g 6g^2 5.7h^5 8.1d^2 8s^4 Oct 6] leggy filly: fair maiden handicapper: stays 1m: acts on hard and soft ground: carried head high penultimate 3-y-o start: sold 15,000 gns Newmarket December Sales. *P. F. I. Cole* 77

LA HAYE SAINTE 2 ch.f. (Apr 26) Rock City 120 – Billante (USA) (Graustark) [1995 a7g^2 a7g^6 a7g^6 7g 10g Oct 9] 3,000Y: half-sister to several winners, including 1¾m winners Ela Billante (by Ela-Mana-Mou) and (in Ireland) Youthful Miss (by Youth): dam unraced half-sister to 1000 Guineas winner Waterloo, grandam of Environment Friend: head second of 8 in seller at Wolverhampton: below that form afterwards in varied company, showing little both starts on turf. *D. J. S. Cosgrove* – a49·

LAHIK (IRE) 2 b.c. (Apr 9) Lycius (USA) 124 – Sangala (FR) (Jim French (USA)) [1995 6.1m 7.5m Jul 25] 19,000Y: useful-looking colt: not a good walker: half-brother to 3 winners in France from 9f to 1½m: dam unraced from family of Doyoun and Dafayna: 14/1 and burly, never a factor in maidens at Nottingham and Beverley: has joined K. Ivory. *T. Thomson Jones* –

LAID BACK LUCY 2 b. or br.f. (Feb 24) Prince Daniel (USA) – Granny's Birthday (Young Generation 129) [1995 6f a7g a8g Dec 1] 400Y: leggy, sparely-made filly: second foal: dam maiden stayed 7f: always behind in maiden auction at Pontefract and sellers at Southwell. *J. A. Harris* –

LAJADHAL (FR) 6 gr.g. Bellypha 130 – Rose d'Amour (USA) (Lines of Power (USA)) [1994 –: 11.7g 10.8m 10s 10.5g 11.1m 10m 12m^6 a12g^4 14d a12g a16g a16g a13g 1995 14.1g 17.2m 17.2m 17.2f^5 18.2m 12.1m 17.2h^5 Aug 8] leggy gelding: of little account: tried in blinkers and visor: won maiden hurdle in November. *K. Bishop* –

LAKE CONISTON (IRE) 4 b.c. Bluebird (USA) 125 – Persian Polly 99 (Persian Bold 123) [1994 119: 8d^5 6f^2 7.1m^6 6m* 6f 5m^2 6m* 5m^4 6g* 6g* 1995 6m* 6g* 6m^2 6g* 6d^4 a6s Oct 28] 131

Lake Coniston, by Bluebird. The suggestion of speed records did not seem out of place after Lake Coniston's exhilarating triumph in the July Cup. No other sprinter could get near him that day or near that performance in any other race in 1995. It was not far off being the highest-rated performance of the year full stop. Neither was the July Cup a Hamas-like flash in the pan, although the winner's aura of invincibility was shattered by the season's end. Lake Coniston's season can be treated in two halves—three races in which he looked in a class of his own, and three in which he didn't. His campaign began pretty much in full stride. Victories in the Prix de Meautry and Diadem Stakes the previous autumn gave him a favourite's chance in the Abernant Stakes at Newmarket in April but Lake Coniston simply thrashed his ten rivals, tracking the very strong pace set by the Scandinavian challenger Windmachine before bringing the game to an end two and a half furlongs out. Conceding weight all round, he beat the in-form Triple Joy by three and a half lengths with the good yardstick Montendre third. Opponents of a higher calibre were dealt with just as impressively in the Duke of York Stakes at York one month later. This time the winning margin was three lengths as Lake Coniston made all, ahead of the Godolphin five-year-old So Factual, Branston Abby, the Two Thousand Guineas runners Chilly Billy and Zeb, and two of the previous season's leading two-year-old sprinters Raah Algharb and Princely Hush. To treat this collection as he did required a performance from Lake Coniston not much less worthy than that which he produced at Newmarket two months later.

The Group 1 July Cup is nearly always a fiercely competitive event, and in the previous ten runnings it was more often than not won by under a length, four times by a head. The 1995 renewal was won by four lengths and for a longer winning distance you have to go back to Thatching's five-length triumph in 1979. Marwell and Hamas both won by three. Lake Coniston's opponents would have to have been a markedly sub-standard bunch for his not to have been a top-class performance, and they certainly weren't that. In betting order, he was up against the 1994 July Cup winner Owington; the Jersey Stakes winner Sergeyev, on a five-timer; the King's

Duke of York Stakes, York—Lake Coniston shows himself a high-class sprinter as he shrugs off So Factual

Stand winner Piccolo; the Godolphin pair Heart Lake and So Factual, both of whom had also won big races on their latest starts; Middle Park winner Fard; Prix Morny winner and One Thousand Guineas fourth Hoh Magic; and the Ballyogan Stakes winner Millstream. There is no question of the form being held down by one of these excelling themselves, as each of them ran at least as well in one other race in 1995, except for Fard, and he came very close to doing so. The winning timefigure of .98 fast was equivalent to a timerating of 125. In short, Lake Coniston's winning performance was every bit as good as it looked. Bowling along in front seemingly going well within himself, he had everything except Owington off the bridle shortly after halfway, and two furlongs out it was clear that Lake Coniston would win and win decisively; he was three lengths up at the furlong pole and made a serene progress from thereon, Pat Eddery waving the whip but applying it only the once. Piccolo finished second, clear by two and a half lengths of third-placed Hoh Magic.

Lake Coniston's starting prices were 7/4 favourite in the Abernant, 11/8 on in the Duke of York and 13/8 in the July Cup. He was also 11/8 on in the Cork And Orrery and 3/1 on in the Haydock Park Sprint Cup, but in both of these races met with defeat. There were 'no excuses' but plenty of possible explanations for these two set-backs, particularly for the Cork And Orrery at Royal Ascot. This turned out to be a bizarre contest, one in which it is difficult to pinpoint exactly where Lake Coniston lost the race; in the final strides So Factual (receiving 4 lb and the only serious rival) caught him to win by a head, but prior to that the two had effectively been in separate races, Lake Coniston setting a breakneck pace on the stand side and So Factual ridden rather more patiently on the other; two furlongs out and about three lengths up, Lake Coniston began drifting to his right and in the last seventy yards, tiring, he did so markedly. The ground was good to firm, as it had been for the Duke of York, but Lake Coniston's best efforts in 1994 had been on good going and so was his July Cup triumph which came after the Cork And Orrery. The draw, the pace of the race, the ground, perhaps some other factor (the trainer suggested that Lake Coniston had been in front for so long that he lost concentration) as well—whatever the reason, Lake Coniston was well below his best form. The ground and pace were also suggested for his Haydock reverse which came just over seven weeks after the July Cup. On this occasion was the ground too soft or, in disputing it with Mind Games up front in relatively testing conditions, was he just asked to go too fast? Was it simply an off-day that saw Lake Coniston mastered before the final furlong and finish fourth of six? A lot of questions and, of course, no definitive answer, not even in the form-book. Unfortunately, a third disappointing effort, perhaps his worst, was still to come. We will not repeat the host of mitigating circumstances for this race, those which European horses can usually fall back on for their lack of achievement at the various Breeders' Cup meetings. Suffice to say that Lake Coniston, drawn widest of all in the Sprint, managed to get into about fifth of thirteen after two furlongs but was

July Cup, Newmarket—an even better performance from Lake Consiston; a posse of Group 1 winners can't get near

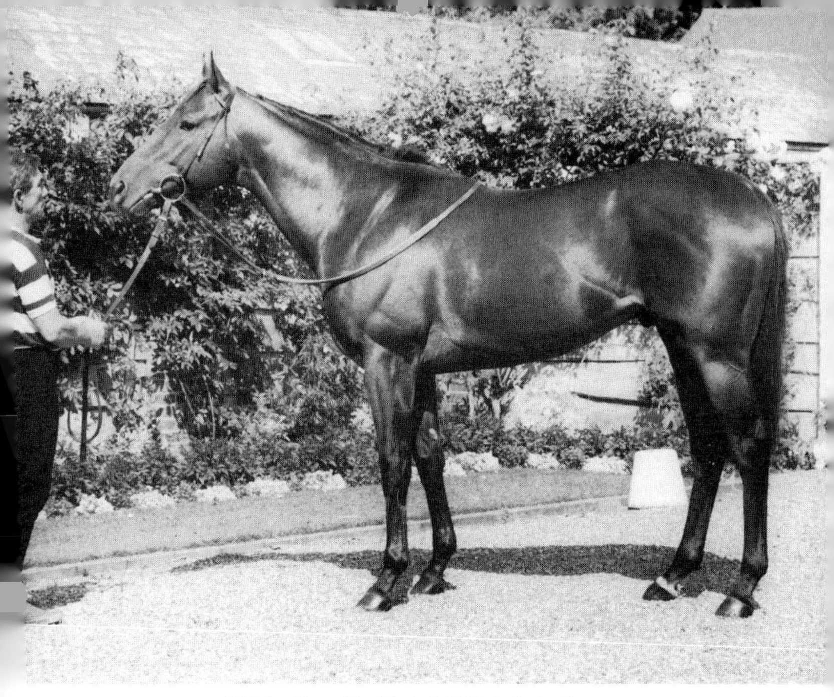

Highclere Thoroughbred Racing Ltd's "Lake Coniston"

backpedalling swiftly thereafter. His, therefore, is a by no means flawless record, but what must be remembered is exactly what Lake Coniston did achieve. Epsom had two representatives in the Breeders' Cup Sprint, Hever Golf Rose in the form of her life and Lake Coniston whose latest start had been a flop, but it was Lake Coniston who stood at consistently shorter odds in the British betting—he had even been favourite in some lists—and on his July Cup form, and for that matter his Duke of York Stakes form, that was completely justified. The Timeform Rating for Lake Coniston is higher than any given to his immediate predecessor as champion sprinter, Lochsong.

Lake Coniston (IRE) (b.c. 1991)	Bluebird (USA) (b 1984)	Storm Bird (b 1978)	Northern Dancer
			South Ocean
		Ivory Dawn (b 1978)	Sir Ivor
			Dusky Evening
	Persian Polly (ch 1980)	Persian Bold (br 1975)	Bold Lad
			Relkarunner
		Polyester Girl (b 1974)	Ridan
			Garrucha

Efforts to stand Lake Coniston in Britain proved in vain so he will be at Coolmore in 1996, standing at a fee of IR10,000 guineas (October 1st) following his sale after the July Cup and before the Haydock Park Sprint in a deal reportedly worth £2 million. He made 22,000 guineas when a yearling. Woodlands Stud's part in the acquisition means that Lake Coniston will be covering in Australia as well. His sire Bluebird has had plenty of success with his Southern Hemisphere runners and retains his popularity here if the 103 mares covered by him at IR 8,000 guineas a time in 1995 is anything to go by. Lake Coniston's dam Persian Polly has had two foals since him, the fair 1995 seven-furlong winner Nottash (by Royal Academy) and a 1995 filly foal by Case Law. Her latest covering was by Mujadil who, like Bluebird, is by Storm Bird. Her record so far is seven winners from eight foals. The only one not to have won has also had his moment of fame—making his only start that season, Merchant House (by Salmon Leap) was a faller at the first when a 250/1-shot in the 1994 Champion Hurdle. Best of the rest is Treble Eight (by Kings Lake) who ran in Quest For Fame's Derby. All three dams on the bottom line of Lake Coniston's pedigree were winners; Persian Polly was a useful two-year-old in Ireland when she won over seven furlongs, and third dam Garrucha came fourth in the Prix Morny. Persian Polly's dam is also a half-sister to the dam of the smart Geoff Lewis-trained sprinter Perion.

We now know that Lake Coniston, as Lewis maintained from an early stage in his career, was indeed a much better horse than Perion. A strong, rangy colt and a good mover, Lake Coniston did very well physically from three to four years. Often taken early to post in the latest season, his best efforts were at six furlongs on good ground. *G. Lewis*

LAKELINE LEGEND (IRE) 2 ch.c. (Apr 23) Caerleon (USA) 132 – Bottom Line 90 (Double Jump 131) [1995 8g³ Oct 10] workmanlike colt: brother to fairly useful middle-distance performers Knight Line Dancer, Courtline Jester and Front Line Romance and half-brother to fairly useful stayer Goldline Seeker (by Damister): dam won from 1m to 1½m: 5/1 from 14/1 and in need of race, 4¼ lengths third of 17 to Forest Buck in maiden at Leicester, always prominent and keeping on: sure to improve. *M. A. Jarvis* — 77 p

LAKESIDE EXPRESS 2 ch.f. (Mar 10) Siberian Express (USA) 125 – Jenny's Rocket 90 (Roan Rocket 128) [1995 7g 6f Oct 24] 2,000Y: angular filly: eighth foal: half-sister to 5f winner Sleepers (by Swing Easy) and 1m winner Precious Ballerina and a winner in Norway (both by Ballacashtal): dam 2-y-o 6f winner, also won over hurdles: well beaten in seller at Goodwood and median auction maiden at Leicester. *J. S. Moore* — –

LAKE STORM (IRE) 4 b.c. Maelstrom Lake 118 – Our Duck (The Go-Between 129) [1994 7.5d* 8g* 8g* 7.5g⁴ 8m* 8m² 1995 7.5m³ 8d³ 8g* 8s⁴ 8m⁶ 8d² 8g* 8d² 9d* 8d* 8m² 8d² Nov 29] IR 3,000Y: half-brother to 3 winners, including fairly useful sprinter One Liner (by Skyliner): dam unraced: smart Italian colt: won minor events at Varese and Milan, a handicap at Milan and a listed race at Rome at 3 yrs, not seen out after June: successful in 1995 in 3 minor events at Milan and another at Turin: much improved form and failed by only a short head to land first pattern race in Premio Ribot at Rome penultimate start, leading inside last until caught post by Welsh Liberty: stays 9f: acts on good to firm ground and soft. *G. Botti, Italy* — 113

LALINDI (IRE) 4 b.f. Cadeaux Genereux 131 – Soemba 86 (General Assembly (USA)) [1994 66, a80: 6d² 7m³ 8m⁴ 8f 7g a7g a9.4g* 10d⁵ a12g* 11.9s 1995 14.9d* 16m⁵ 16.4m³ 14m⁵ 16m³ 16m² 16.1g* 20m Jun 20] big, strong, lengthy filly: fair handicapper: improved form on turf for new stable, winning at Warwick in April and (making most and keeping on) June: stays 2m (had a rough race when tried at 2½m): acts on good to firm and dead ground, and on fibresand: blinkered (finished last) fifth 3-y-o start: usually held up/tracks leaders: consistent. *D. R. C. Elsworth* — 76

LA MENORQUINA (USA) 5 b.m. Woodman (USA) 126 – Hail The Lady (USA) (Hail The Pirates (USA) 126) [1994 35: a11g⁶ a12g 12m 12.1f 12m 11.6m 13.1g 12g⁴ 14s³ 12g a14.8g⁵ a16g⁴ 1995 a12g⁵ a16g* a14g² 14.1m a16g* 16.4g⁴ a14.8g⁴ a16g⁶ Sep 4] quite good-topped mare: modest handicapper on the all-weather: won at Southwell in February and May: poor on turf: suited by test of stamina: acts on the all-weather and on good to firm and soft going: often comes from long way off pace: won novice hurdle in November. *D. Marks* — 30 a53

L'AMI LOUIS (USA) 2 ch.c. (Feb 7) Easy Goer (USA) – Jadana (Pharly (FR) 130) [1995 5m² 5f* 6m* May 27] $225,000Y: well-made, quite attractive colt: good walker and mover: half-brother to several winners in France and USA, notably Grade 1 9f and 1¼m winner Jade Hunter (by Mr Prospector): dam, winner at up to 1m, closely related to Monteverdi: won maiden at Pontefract (easily) and minor event at Kempton (battled on well to beat Oberons Boy a head) in May: will stay beyond 1m: looked likely to continue progressing. *J. H. M. Gosden* — 93 p

LAMMTARRA (USA) 3 ch.c. Nijinsky (CAN) 138 – Snow Bride (USA) 121 (Blushing Groom (FR) 131) [1994 93p: 7g* 1995 12f* 12g* 12d* Oct 1] 134

There's more than one school of thought about what constitutes greatness in a racehorse. Lammtarra's feat of winning the Derby and the two races widely accepted as the principal tests of Europe's middle-distance horses, the King George and the Prix de l'Arc, led inevitably to comparisons with Mill Reef. Mill Reef and the unbeaten Lammtarra are the only horses to have completed that particular treble and, perhaps more significantly, they are among only five to complete the King George-Arc double in the same year. Twenty-four King George winners have gone on to attempt the double and ten of them failed even to reach the frame at Longchamp. Like the overwhelming majority of Prix de l'Arc winners, Lammtarra had to give the best performance of his career to win the race and join the select band of Ribot, Ballymoss, Mill Reef and Dancing Brave. The significance of Lammtarra's achievement wasn't lost on the Press, most of whom were unstinting in their praise. Alastair Down, racing journalist of the year, filed one of his typically evocative pieces from Longchamp for *The Sporting Life*. Down was careful to warn his readers that he was well aware that 'in the excited, adrenalin-filled aftermath of a great race, it is so easy to let the true significance of what you have witnessed slip past you.' He made it clear that his conclusions were drawn after 'taking a step back for a moment to try to take a cool, semi-detached look at Lammtarra's unprecedented achievement.' He then went on to point out that 'Mill Reef may have achieved that treble, but that great thoroughbred tasted defeat en route. Here we have the champion racehorse in its purest form—undefeated'. Down's eulogy concluded with the statement that, in the Arc, he had witnessed 'an exceptionally tough performance by a very great horse.' Others, in the modern idiom, used descriptions such as 'superhorse' and 'ultimate racing machine' to describe Lammtarra, and there was no doubt that a good section of the Press was convinced that he deserved to rank alongside Mill Reef and, therefore, the other great middle-distance champions. It could—with strong justification—also have been emphasised that Lammtarra had

Vodafone Derby Stakes, Epsom—Court of Honour (rails) and Fahal are chased into the straight by (left to right) Tamure, Riyadian and Maralinga, with Presenting (white colours) on their heels; Lammtarra is tucked in on the rails behind Presenting

Vodafone Derby Stakes, Epsom—Lammtarra storms by;
Tamure, Presenting, Fahal and Court of Honour chase him home

managed his outstanding achievements despite singular inexperience. A minor set-back at two years, and a serious lung infection contracted after being transferred to Dubai over the winter, contributed to the infrequency of Lammtarra's appearances and he became the first horse to win the Arc having previously run in only three races (no horse had previously won the King George having run before in only two). Yet there were detractors, among them those who claimed that Lammtarra lacked the characteristic which 'defines the truly great racehorse'—'a brilliant turn of foot' or 'the ability to quicken off a fast pace', depending upon which proponent of that particular theory you happened to read.

All in all, most of the appreciations of Lammtarra after the Arc relied almost entirely on subjective judgement, with little resort to traditional tools such as form-book and stop-watch. 'Races are all about beating other horses, not about winning distances or times' seems to be a supposition becoming more and more widely accepted among contemporary commentators, many of whom tend to judge horses largely on the prestige of the races they win rather than on the quality of their performances. For our part, that much overused adjective 'great' continues to be mentioned with precision in these Annuals. The reader will never find it used thoughtlessly. In fact, in nearly fifty years, only a dozen or so horses have merited the description *great* in these pages. As we have said before, the phrase 'a great horse' means to us one of such superlative merit as to make him, or her, far superior to the general run of classic winners. In our view, Mill Reef was such a horse. As a three-year-old, he won the King George by six lengths and the Arc by three and, in the course of a fourteen-race career (ended by injury), recorded other wide-margin victories, including, as a two-year-old, the Coventry by eight lengths and the Gimcrack by ten, and, on the first of two starts as a four-year-old, the Prix Ganay by ten. Mill Reef was beaten twice—once as a two-year-old and then by his great contemporary Brigadier Gerard in the Two Thousand Guineas. Compare Lammtarra's truncated big-race record: after winning the Derby by a length, he took the King George by a neck and the Arc by three quarters of a length. His rider Frankie Dettori, who, incidentally, asked after the Arc 'Can anyone beat what he has done?', claimed that Lammtarra would have won by three lengths in another fifty yards at Longchamp. That could give a misleading impression, however. Lammtarra responded with the utmost gameness to hold the very strong challenge of Freedom Cry, but it would be a mistake for anyone to assume that Lammtarra won with something to spare; Lammtarra was first and foremost a stayer and he was still running on strongly as the post was reached, but he hadn't much, if anything, in hand of Freedom Cry at the line. Unbeaten status alone doesn't betoken greatness—Morston and Golden Fleece, unbeaten in careers no longer than Lammtarra's, would also qualify among post-war Derby winners if it did—but unbeaten horses can sometimes prove difficult to assess. Lammtarra, for example, improved with each of his races and may well have had further potential. His achievements as a three-year-old were remarkable, and who is to say that such an inexperienced colt wouldn't have been capable of even better form as a four-year-old. A more thorough test of Lammtarra's ability would have helped to reveal just how good a racehorse he was. Perhaps it might have shown him conclusively to be a great one. But he must be rated strictly on the value of his performances. Our reading of the form-book ranks Lammtarra only a little better than average as recent middle-distance champions go. In the intervening eight-year period between Dancing Brave and Lammtarra, the King George winners Reference Point, Nashwan, Generous and St Jovite, and the Arc winners Trempolino and Suave Dancer, have all achieved higher Timeform Ratings than Lammtarra.

If Lammtarra had followed in the footsteps of Morston, Golden Fleece and some other post-war Derby winners and never run after Epsom, his story would nonetheless still have been extraordinary. He had made his only previous public appearance when successful in the Washington Singer Stakes at Newbury the previous August; far from fully wound up, he looked a very useful prospect in beating Myself by three quarters of a length that day but wasn't seen out again. The racing world was shocked by the murder of his trainer Alex Scott (who had backed him for the Derby at 33/1 after Newbury) in September. Transferred to Dubai for the winter, Lammtarra's Derby hopes must have seemed a pipedream as the Dubai Veterinary Hospital treated a life-threatening abscess on his lung. But he recovered well and was sent to Britain, as planned, to be trained at Newmarket by the Godolphin team. In mid-May, Godolphin's racing manager Simon Crisford reported that it was 'questionable' whether Lammtarra would make the Derby line-up. 'He's behind the other horses in terms of fitness,' he said. But Lammtarra made such progress that, by Derby Day, Crisford was saying that there wasn't much to choose between Lammtarra and Godolphin's other Derby runner, the Poule d'Essai des Poulains winner Vettori; the pair started at 14/1 and 20/1 respectively, Vettori's longer odds reflecting stamina doubts. The period leading up to the Derby had been dominated by ill-informed accusations that Epsom was watering the track 'excessively' to ensure the participation of the winter favourite Celtic Swing. As so often, however, some of the speculation—'It's like the Somme down there' and 'the groundsman's gone berserk' were remarks made on one edition of Channel 4's *Morning Line*—proved well wide of the mark. Celtic Swing was rerouted to the Prix du Jockey-Club as the Epsom going remained distinctly on the firm side. Two unbeaten classic winners, Two Thousand Guineas winner Pennekamp and Irish Guineas winner Spectrum, headed the betting on the Derby, which was sponsored for the first time by Vodafone. Pennekamp had been favourite since narrowly defeating Celtic Swing at Newmarket and, after Celtic Swing's victory in the Prix du Jockey-Club six days before the Derby, Pennekamp started at 11/8, with Spectrum at 5/1. Stamina doubts were expressed in some quarters about Pennekamp and Spectrum but both were bred to stay middle distances. In all, there were five unbeaten colts in the line-up including the 9/1-shot Tamure, who had followed a similar path to Epsom to the 1993 winner Commander In Chief, being unraced at two and concluding a three-race Derby preparation with a hard-earned victory in the Glasgow Stakes at the York May meeting, where he gave every indication he'd be all the better for a return to a mile and a half. The first two in the Dante Stakes at York, nowadays usually one of the most significant trials, were both missing but third-placed Presenting took his chance after his trainer had been among the fiercest critics of Epsom's perceived watering policy. Tamure and Presenting were sure to stay, as were Munwar and Riyadian, first and second in the Lingfield Derby Trial, and the Irish challenger Humbel who had stretched his unbeaten sequence to four in the Leopardstown Derby Trial. Lammtarra took up a handy position from the start, but dropped down the field when caught up in some scrimmaging after about two furlongs. His inexperience showed and he still had plenty to do early in the straight where the race began to take a most unexpected shape. Pennekamp and Spectrum were already well beaten as the Predominate third Fahal led from Tamure, the Chester Vase and Derby Italiano runner-up Court of Honour, Riyadian and Presenting at the two-furlong marker where the strongly-ridden Lammtarra still had about seven lengths to make up. Rather like Erhaab the previous year, Lammtarra produced a late surge—he was still only fifth a furlong out—to overhaul the leaders inside the last hundred yards. He won in good style by a length from Tamure with the strong-finishing Presenting three quarters of a length further back in third; Fahal, beaten another length and a quarter, came fourth, pipping Court of Honour, with Vettori, Riyadian and Humbel next. The stewards held an inquiry and found that Lammtarra had interfered with Munwar at around the two-furlong marker, but they were satisfied that the interference was accidental and ordered the placings to remain unaltered. Pennekamp and Spectrum both returned with injuries while Munwar's pacemaker Daffaq damaged a knee so badly that he had to be put down. Epsom now faced criticism for not having provided ground with enough resilience to prevent jarring and other injuries that so often follow a firm-ground Derby. The going—not officially changed from good to firm to firm until *after* the Derby—was undoubtedly the main factor in Lammtarra's setting a new time record of 2m 32.31sec for the Epsom mile and a half course, expunging Mahmoud's almost legendary record for the Derby by around a second and a half, and also beating by exactly a second the previous best over the course, set by Bustino in the 1975 Coronation Cup.

Sheikh Mohammed has seen his colours carried to many memorable big-race successes but not yet in the Derby (Pennekamp and Tamure represented him in the latest running). He did, however, take special satisfaction from Lammtarra's victory. Lammtarra, in the colours of Sheikh Mohammed's teenaged nephew Saeed Maktoum Al Maktoum, confirmed that Sheikh Mohammed's personal project, the 'Dubai experiment', has proved a major breakthrough in the training of racehorses. The success of the Godolphin-trained horses worldwide was one of the stories of 1995 and more can be found on it in the essay on the Oaks winner Moonshell. Lammtarra's Derby victory on his first public appearance for ten months represented a tremendous training performance for the Godolphin team; only Grand Parade in 1919 had won the Derby this century on his seasonal debut, and only two other twentieth-century Derby winners, Bois Roussel in 1938 and Morston in 1973, had been successful having run only once before in their life.

The latest Derby, the first to be run on a Saturday since 1953, failed to produce the expected significant boost to the attendance or to the television audience. The course reported that the attendance increased by three per cent. An audited 3.9 million watched the race on Channel 4, compared to the previous year's 4.3 million. The Saturday audience for 'bread-and-butter' racing on Channel 4 is around a

King George VI and Queen Elizabeth Diamond Stakes, Ascot—
Lammtarra is the first to beat Pentire in 1995; the others in view are
Strategic Choice (rails), Winged Love (No. 7), Broadway Flyer and Carnegie

Forte Prix de l'Arc de Triomphe, Longchamp—end of an unforgettable career; Lammtarra proves just too strong for Freedom Cry as Swain and Lando stay on behind

million and, though the size of the Derby audience doesn't compare with that for the Grand National (11.9 million in 1995), it's as well to bear in mind that only 1.7 million tuned in for Britain's major all-aged championship the King George VI and Queen Elizabeth Stakes at Ascot in July (the race was shown on BBC 1 and there was a 1.6 million audience at the same time on BBC 2 for the Open Golf which had been on BBC 1 before the King George coverage began). Criticism for moving the Derby from Wednesday to Saturday came, surprisingly, from the bookmakers, some of whom had, equally surprisingly, predicted only the previous year that a Saturday Derby would bring betting turnover on the Derby close to that for the Grand National. In the event, off-course turnover came nowhere near expectations, some figures showing business only marginally up on a normal Saturday. The Derby, which had the field largely to itself when it was run on a Wednesday, faced competition in 1995 from World Cup rugby (ITV) and test-match cricket (BBC 1), though the timing of the race coincided with the tea interval at Headingley. Derby Day in 1996 clashes with England's opening game at Wembley in the European football championship, though the Derby's starting time has been brought forward to avoid a direct clash. Our view is that, in the long run, the Derby will fare better on a Saturday or on a Sunday than on a Wednesday and the management of United Racecourses rightly resisted suggestions of an immediate switch back to the traditional day. Some of the targets for the first Saturday Derby may have turned out to be over-ambitious but that's no reason, in itself, for initial judgements to be revised. Let's give the idea a chance!

The atmosphere of gloom that followed the latest running of the Derby wasn't helped by the general reaction to the quality of the race itself. Those behind Lammtarra seemed a second-rate lot by Derby standards, the proximity of outsiders Fahal and Court of Honour holding down the form. Lammtarra's course record, like most course records, was a product of the prevailing conditions—firm ground and a strongly-run race—and comparisons with other times on the day showed that his time performance wasn't anything to get excited about. In short, it didn't look a good Derby at the time (though six of the first seven did eventually go on to win in pattern company before the end of the season). By the time Lammtarra, who missed the Irish Derby because of a slight hind-leg injury, lined up for the King George VI and Queen Elizabeth Diamond Stakes at Ascot six weeks later, all six of the Derby runners that had run subsequently, including Presenting, Fahal and Court of Honour, had been beaten. In the week leading up to the King George, Lammtarra wasn't even ante-post

Saeed Maktoum Al Maktoum's "Lammtarra"

favourite, that position being filled by another three-year-old, Pentire, who had run up a sequence and had been particularly impressive in the King Edward VII Stakes at Royal Ascot on his latest outing. Also in the King George line-up was the Irish Derby winner Winged Love, whose stable also saddled the previous year's Arc winner Carnegie, winner of the Grand Prix de Saint-Cloud on his latest start and, on form, easily the pick of the older horses opposing the trio of three-year-olds. With Pentire easy to back on the day, Lammtarra started favourite at 9/4, followed by Carnegie at 11/4, Pentire at 3/1, Winged Love at 9/2, and 12/1 bar. Carnegie never looking like playing a major part in the finish which was fought out by Lammtarra and Pentire. Frankie Dettori, who replaced Derby-winning jockey Walter Swinburn in a surprise move, was at work some way out on Lammtarra who also received a bump on the home turn. Lammtarra looked held as Pentire quickened to the front just inside the two-furlong marker but he maintained a persistent challenge under pressure and wore down Pentire in the last furlong, Dettori getting everything out of his mount as he edged home by a neck. Strategic Choice ran very well to finish third, a length and a half behind Pentire, with Winged Love a head away fourth and Broadway Flyer, staying on after making most, the same distance away fifth. The early pace in the King George wasn't strong by the usual standards of the race and, with Lammtarra shaping like a horse who'd be very well suited by a stiffer test of stamina, the Godolphin team left nothing to chance in the Prix de l'Arc de Triomphe. The Derby Italiano winner Luso, a close second to Carnegie in the Grand Prix de Saint-Cloud, was used as a pacemaker at Longchamp, though it was, to say the least, disappointing for backers of Luso, a 22/1-chance, that no announcement of his intended role was made before the race. Owned by Saeed Manana, a friend of Sheikh Mohammed, Luso fulfilled his duties admirably, blinkered for the first time. Lammtarra tracked Luso, travelling strongly from the start, until being sent for home in earnest rounding the final turn, with about two and a half furlongs to run. Forcefully ridden—Dettori's repeated use of the whip over the last furlong and a half would surely have been questioned by British stewards—Lammtarra kept on doggedly, stretching his field until only the four-year-old Freedom Cry still posed a threat. Lammtarra couldn't shake off Freedom Cry, who actually got his head in front just inside the final furlong, but he fought back to win by three quarters of a length. Swain, an unbeaten stable-companion of the runner-up, came third, a further two lengths away, with the high-class German middle-distance performer Lando, Irish Oaks and Yorkshire Oaks winner Pure Grain and Carnegie, winner of the Prix Foy since running in the King George, completing the first six in a field of sixteen that was well up to the usual standard for the race. The reception that met Lammtarra was one of the most enthusiastic seen for any big-race winner all season, the demonstrative Dettori's own response including an unprecedented parading of his trophy in front of the packed stands.

There was talk after the Arc of a possible finale to Lammtarra's career in the Breeders' Cup Turf. The four Arc winners who had previously attempted the double, Dancing Brave, Trempolino, Saumarez and Subotica, had all failed, but there seemed little logic in judging the unique Lammtarra's prospects on the records of his predecessors. It was, in truth, a pity that he wasn't given the opportunity to add to his already-impressive collection of records. He looked in tremendous shape at Longchamp and, as we have said, his performance suggested he was still improving. Lammtarra, the first Derby winner in four years not to have departed directly to Japan, is to stand his first season at Dalham Hall Stud, Newmarket, in 1996 at a fee of £30,000, with the October 1st concession. He is expected to cover fifty mares.

Lammtarra (USA) (ch.c. 1992)	Nijinsky (CAN) (b 1967)	Northern Dancer (b 1961)	Nearctic
			Natalma
		Flaming Page (b 1959)	Bull Page
			Flaring Top
	Snow Bride (USA) (ch 1986)	Blushing Groom (ch 1974)	Red God
			Runaway Bride
		Awaasif (b 1979)	Snow Knight
			Royal Statute

Lammtarra's victory in the Derby also earned him a place in the breeding records as the first winner of the race produced from a mating between a Derby winner and an Oaks winner. He's the best possible advertisement for that old adage of 'putting the best to the best and hoping for the best'. Lammtarra is Nijinsky's third Derby winner, following Golden Fleece and Shahrastani, and two other Derby winners, Kahyasi and Generous, have been sired by sons of Nijinsky. Lammtarra was conceived when Nijinsky was twenty-four and was one of twenty-nine live foals in his 1992 crop; Nijinsky died in April 1992, leaving a final crop of twelve live foals in 1993. Nijinsky has overtaken his own sire Northern Dancer in the number of stakes winners he has produced, his total standing at over one hundred and fifty worldwide; he has had over ninety individual pattern or graded winners in North America and the major European countries. Lammtarra's dam Snow Bride earned her status as an Oaks winner when a technicality led to the disqualification of the first-past-the-post Aliysa, whose owner the Aga Khan lost a long-drawn-out legal battle to have her reinstated and only ended his subsequent boycott of British racing in the latest season. The Oaks was one of five victories in seven starts for Snow Bride who ran in the colours of her breeder Sheikh Mohammed as a two-year-old and in those of Lammtarra's owner at three when she also won the Musidora Stakes at York and the Princess Royal Stakes at Ascot. She stayed a mile and a half well but lacked a turn of foot and would have been an interesting prospect over a mile and three quarters. Snow Bride's sire and dam, Blushing Groom and Awaasif, who finished in the frame in the Derby and Oaks respectively, were both top performers, Awaasif winning the Yorkshire Oaks and Gran Premio del Jockey Club and finishing third in the Prix de l'Arc. Awaasif, sired by Derby winner Snow Knight, is from a good family, her dam Royal Statute being a sister to Falafel who bred the St James's Palace winner Brief Truce and the Italian Two Thousand Guineas winner Again Tomorrow. Royal Statute's produce also include the One Thousand Guineas second Konafa, the dam of the high-class sprinter Proskona and of Korveya, the dam of the highly promising

Bosra Sham. Lammtarra is the second foal of Snow Bride, whose first, a Shadeed filly named Mousquet, never reached the racecourse. Snow Bride's two-year-old colt Earth Shaker (by Zilzal) was in training with Michael Stoute in the latest season but wasn't raced. Snow Bride also has a yearling colt by Zilzal and a filly foal by the same sire. In appearance, Lammtarra is made in the mould of his dam, a smallish, rather sparely-made type, rather than of his sire who was an outstanding-looking animal of ample proportions. The smallish, attractive Lammtarra, a fluent mover with a rather round action, was a shade mulish at the stalls at Ascot and decidedly reluctant in the preliminaries at Longchamp but he never showed the slightest sign of temperament once racing and was thoroughly genuine. He was effective at a mile and a half and would have been very well suited by further (he'd have been tailor-made for the St Leger), and he acted on firm and good to soft going. Lammtarra's tremendous achievements made him a worthy and predictable winner of the annual Racehorse of the Year award organised by the Racegoers Club. Sixteen of the twenty-six members of the Press panel voted for Lammtarra, nine going for Irish-trained Ridgewood Pearl and one for Pentire. *Saeed bin Suroor*

LA MODISTE 2 b.f. (Mar 28) Most Welcome 131 – Dismiss 95 (Daring March 116) [1995 5m 6m^{2} 6m^{4} 7m^{4} 6f* 8h* 7g^{6} 8v^{5} Oct 7] angular filly: second foal: dam suited by 1¼m: won median auction maiden at Brighton in August and 4-runner minor event (beat Parrot Jungle 2½ lengths) at Bath in September: stiff task in listed races last 2 starts: ideally needs further than 6f and stays 1m: acts on hard ground. *S. Dow* — 81

LAMP OF PHOEBUS (USA) 3 b. or br.f. Sunshine Forever (USA) – Siala (FR) (Sharpman) [1994 NR 1995 10m 10m Apr 28] workmanlike filly: fifth reported living foal: half-sister to 3 winners, notably very useful French 9f (at 2 yrs) and 10.5f winner Accomodating (by Akarad): dam, French middle-distance maiden, half-sister to high-class middle-distance colt Sadjiyd: bandaged all round, no promise in maidens at Kempton and Sandown: sold 1,500 gns Newmarket December Sales. *J. H. M. Gosden* — –

LANCASHIRE LEGEND 2 gr.g. (Mar 17) Belfort (FR) 89 – Peters Pet Girl (Norwick (USA) 125) [1995 6m^{4} 6m^{4} 6d Sep 30] 4,200F, 10,000Y: workmanlike gelding: second foal: brother to 4-y-o 1m winner A Million Watts: dam never ran: best effort when fourth of 8 to Caricature in maiden at Epsom penultimate start: will stay beyond 6f: seems unsuited by a soft surface. *S. Dow* — 66

LANCASHIRE LIFE (IRE) 4 b.g. Petorius 117 – Parlais 101 (Pardao 120) [1994 54: 8.1g^{2} 8.3d^{2} 8.1g 8m^{4} 8g 8.1m^{2} 8m^{6} 7g^{2} 7.1m^{4} a7g 7.1d 1995 a7g 8m 10m 8m* 7.5m^{4} 8.1m^{2} 8m^{6} 7.6m^{5} 8m 7.5m^{4} 10m 8.5d 8d Sep 22] strong gelding: modest handicapper: won (for first time) at Carlisle in June: well beaten last 3 starts: should stay beyond 1m (raced too freely when tried): acts on good to firm and dead ground: often a front runner. *E. J. Alston* — 55

LANCASTER BOMBER 3 b.f. Golden Lahab (USA) – Miami Dolphin 85 (Derrylin 115) [1994 NR 1995 7g 10g^{6} Jun 3] second reported foal: half-sister to 4-y-o sprinter Red Five (by Clantime): dam best at sprint distances: 20/1, well beaten in claimers. *D. Moffatt* — –

LANCERETTE 3 ch.f. Sharpo 132 – Corvelle (Reliance II 137) [1994 NR 1995 7g 8d^{4} 8m* 10d Oct 19] tall, angular filly: sixth live foal: sister to a winner in Hong Kong and half-sister to 3 winners, none better than fair: dam showed little form: narrowly won maiden at Pontefract in October, making up plenty of ground after a troubled run: ran as if something amiss final start: should stay beyond 1m. *N. A. Graham* — 72

LANCER (USA) 3 ch.g. Diesis 133 – Last Bird (USA) (Sea Bird II 145) [1994 88p: 7.5m* 7g^{3} 1995 9d^{5} 11.5f^{6} 12g^{6} 8m 8.5m^{4} 10.3f Jul 26] useful-looking, finely-made gelding: rather disappointing in 1995: seems to stay 11.5f: probably acts on firm and dead ground: blinkered (sweating, well beaten) fourth 3-y-o start: takes good hold: gelded: hurdling before sold (J. H. Johnson to R. Juckes) 6,000 gns Doncaster November Sales: not one to have complete faith in. *M. Bell* — 89 d

LANDLORD 3 b.g. Be My Chief (USA) 122 – Pubby 73 (Doctor Wall 107) [1994 81p: 6g^{5} 7m* 1995 6g 7f^{6} 7m^{4} 8m 7m 7m^{3} 8g a9.4g^{5} a8.5g^{2} a12g a10g* Dec 6] rather unfurnished gelding: fair form: 7/1 from 16/1, won 8-runner minor event at Lingfield — 71 a61

in December, leading well inside last: stays 1¼m: acts on good to firm going and all-weather: blinkered since fifth 3-y-o start: inconsistent. *J. A. R. Toller*

LANDO (GER) 5 b.h. Acatenango (GER) 127 – Laurea (GER) (Sharpman) [1994 123: 11v 11g* 12m⁴ 12g⁵ 12g* 12g 12d* 1995 11s³ 12f* 12m* 12s 12d⁴ 12s 12f* Nov 26] 128

'Ende gut, alles gut'. All's well that ends well, and, for Lando, his triumph at Tokyo will be remembered long after the disappointment of Baden-Baden, Longchamp and Belmont Park. In November, Lando became the first European-trained horse since Le Glorieux in 1987, and the first from Germany, to land the richly-endowed Japan Cup, which is now firmly established as a major international race and is a prime target for middle-distance horses from all over the world. Not only did Lando set a new record for money won by a European-trained horse, he greatly boosted a reputation previously best appreciated within the borders of Germany and Italy.

Already the winner of the German Derby in 1993, the Gran Premio del Jockey Club e Coppa d'Oro in 1994 and the Grosser Preis von Baden in both those years, Lando took his number of Group 1 victories in Europe to six in the summer of 1995. In a strongly-run Gran Premio di Milano (the course record was lowered) on firm ground in June, he cruised past Broadway Flyer and Strategic Choice a furlong out to win by two and a quarter lengths and three quarters of a length, with nine lengths and more back to four others. The placed horses went on to perform well in the King George in July, and it was disappointing not to see Lando at Ascot; he beat Strategic Choice and Broadway Flyer further than Lammtarra and Pentire did in the King George. Instead, Lando stayed in Germany for the Preis der Privatbankiers Merck, Finck & Co at Dusseldorf the same weekend and achieved what we already knew he could, easily beating seven other German horses, led home by his half-brother Laroche. But Lando's connections haven't shirked many challenges, even when ground conditions have been on the soft side. Indeed, Lando's last four races were in four different countries. After finishing tailed off on soft ground in the Grosser Preis von Baden, Lando ran well on good to soft in the Prix de l'Arc de Triomphe at Longchamp to finish four and a half lengths fourth of sixteen to Lammtarra, though he was never travelling all that fluently, and was scrubbed along and steered rather wide throughout. He was well below his best under very testing

Japan Cup, Tokyo—Lando wins, Hernando (striped sleeves) is third

conditions at Belmont Park for the Breeders' Cup Turf, in which he finished well beaten and returned with cuts which required stitches. He was still sent to Japan, however, where the ground came up firm.

In a strong field for the Japan Cup, Lando crowned his career with his best performance, moving keenly from the start, quickening to lead at around the furlong pole and always holding the home-trained favourite Hishi Amazon (never out of the first two in sixteen races) and Hernando; front-runner Taiki Blizzard finished fourth, Arlington Million winner Awad fifth, Japan's 1994 Horse of the Year Narita Brian sixth, 1994 Japan Cup-third Royce And Royce seventh and Arlington Million runner-up Sandpit eighth in the field of fourteen which also including Pure Grain who suffered a career-ending injury, and Carling, who was well beaten. Lando was ridden in most of his races in the latest season by Michael Roberts but it is worth recording that Peter Schiergen, successful on him at Dusseldorf, went on to retain his title of champion jockey in Germany with 271 winners, a European record.

Lando (GER) (b.c. 1990)	Acatenango (GER) (ch 1982)	Surumu (ch 1974)	Literat
			Surama
		Aggravate (b 1966)	Aggressor
			Raven Locks
	Laurea (GER) (b 1983)	Sharpman (b 1976)	Sharpen Up
			Miss Manon
		Licata (b 1973)	Dschingis Khan
			Liberty

Lando's pedigree was examined in *Racehorses of 1993*. The record of his very well bred dam Laurea needs updating as she has now bred three winners, Lando being preceded by Lunetta (by Athenagoras), who won three minor races at eight and a half furlongs, and succeeded by Laroche (by Nebos), the German Derby winner of 1994. The only subsequent offspring still alive is a filly foal by Shirley Heights. Lando's sire Acatenango was a racehorse of similar merit (he had an essay in *Racehorses of 1986*) and he has made a good start at stud, his five crops of racing age having produced other pattern winners in Protektor, Epaphos, Elacata and Concepcion. Lando, an outcross to Northern Dancer, will surely do well at stud in Germany where he retires to Gestut Ittlingen at a fee of 20,000 DM for 1996. Best at a mile and a half, the tough and genuine Lando occasionally showed very smart form on a soft surface, but was extremely well suited by top-of-the-ground, conditions which often favour horses whose most effective weapon is a turn of foot. *H. Jentzsch, Germany*

LANESRA BREEZE 3 b.g. Petoski 135 – Constant Companion 84 (Pas de Seul 133) [1994 –: a7g 1995 a8.5g^6 a8g 10m Jun 6] third foal: half-brother to 7f to 8.3f winner Comanche Companion (by Commanche Run): dam, 1m winner, stayed 1¼m: no worthwhile form. *T. J. Naughton* –

LANGTONIAN 6 br.g. Primo Dominie 121 – Yankee Special 60 (Bold Lad (IRE) 133) [1994 39§, a65§: 5d^4 7.1g^6 5m 5v 6f 5m 5g^6 6f 8m 8f^5 8m 8g^4 a8g^3 a6g^3 a8g* a8g^5 1995 a6g^3 7m 7.1m 8g^6 8.1f 8.3f^5 a8g 7d a7g^6 a8g Nov 16] sturdy gelding: carries condition: only poor at best in 1995: stays 1m: acts on fibresand, probably on any turf going: normally visored/blinkered: usually finds little under pressure. *J. L. Eyre* – § a48 §

LANGUEDOC 8 b.g. Rousillon (USA) 133 – Can Can Girl 69 (Gay Fandango (USA) 132) [1994 50§: 6v^5 6g^3 7m 6g 7f 6g^2 6m 6g^6 6d^4 7g^3 8g 8d^5 a8g 1995 8.1d Mar 30] tall, attractive gelding: poor handicapper: well beaten only outing of 1995: best form at 6f to 1m: acts on heavy going and all-weather surfaces, possibly unsuited by top-of-the-ground nowadays: blinkered (below form) once earlier in career: takes good hold: wayward and unreliable. *Martyn Wane* – §

LA PERRUCHE (IRE) 2 b.f. (Mar 31) Cyrano de Bergerac 120 – Red Lory 87 (Bay Express 132) [1995 a6g a6g Dec 14] IR 14,000Y: seventh foal: sister to 2 winners including Cyrano Storme, winning sprinter in France and (Grade 3 event in 1995) USA, and half-sister to 1m winner King Parrot (by King of Spain) and a winner in Holland: dam 2-y-o 5f winner: better effort in Lingfield maidens when close eighth of 10 to Mask Flower in slowly-run race on debut. *Lord Huntingdon* 55

LA PETITE FUSEE 4 br.f. Cigar 68 – Little Missile (Ile de Bourbon (USA) 133) [1994 64: a7g^5 8d^3 8s 7m 11.9g^4 10g 7m 6g* 6f 6f 7m 6g^3 6g* 6.1g^6 a6g^3 a7g 75 a81

1995 6m 6m^2 6f^5 6g* 6m^3 7f 6m^5 6m 6g^2 7g 6.1s a6g* a7g* a5g Nov 16] rangy, workmanlike filly: fairly useful handicapper: won at Lingfield in June and at Southwell (in tremendous style) and Wolverhampton (minor event) in November: bred to stay beyond 1m, but races freely and best efforts at up to 7f: acts on firm and dead ground and on fibresand: usually bandaged behind: front runner: game. *R. J. O'Sullivan*

LAP OF LUXURY 6 gr.m. Sharrood (USA) 124 – Lap of Honour 100 (Final Straw 127) [1994 107: 8m 8.1m 8f 8.1m^5 7.9m* 8m^5 8g* 8g^5 8m^3 8d^2 1995 8.1m 8m 8.1m* 7f 7.9m 8m^3 8g^2 8g^6 9m^2 Oct 13] sparely-made mare: unimpressive mover: useful performer, as good as ever: won rated stakes at Sandown in July: particularly good efforts when neck second of 9 to Timarida in Matron Stakes at the Curragh and short-head second of 8 to Restructure in listed race (challenged from over 1f out) at Newmarket: stays 9f: acts on good to firm ground and dead: held up: has never been seen out before the end of May, and has tended to take a run or two to return to form. *W. Jarvis* — 107

LAPU-LAPU 2 b.f. (Apr 18) Prince Sabo 123 – Seleter (Hotfoot 126) [1995 6m 6m Oct 30] lengthy filly: half-sister to fair performers Calachuchi (by Martinmas) and El Nido (by Adonijah), winners from 7.5f to 12.4f and 9f to 2m respectively: dam no form: towards rear in maidens at Catterick (some headway when hampered over 1f out) and Nottingham (under considerate ride): may do better. *M. J. Camacho* — –

LARENTIA 3 ch.f. Salse (USA) 128 – Clarentia 111 (Ballad Rock 122) [1994 58: 6g^6 7g^5 1995 10m^6 8.5m^6 9.9m Aug 24] quite attractive filly: disappointing maiden. *J. Parkes* — –

LA RESIDENCE 4 b.g. Doulab (USA) 115 – Ideal Home 104 (Home Guard (USA) 129) [1994 64d: 7s^3 10d 6m^6 8m^5 7g^5 7m^6 7m^3 6g a6g^4 a7g 1995 a7g* a7g^4 a8g a8g^2 a9.4g^5 a8g a7g Jun 2] small, sturdy gelding: modest handicapper: won maiden event at Southwell in January: soundly beaten last 2 starts: stays 1m: acts on good to firm and soft ground and the all-weather: blinkered (soon tailed off) once in 1993: has looked ungenuine: sold (Mrs N. Macauley to W. G. M. Turner) 1,050 gns Ascot July Sales. *Mrs N. Macauley* — 51 §

LARGHETTO (IRE) 2 ch.c. (Apr 17) Lycius (USA) 124 – Spoilt Again 91 (Mummy's Pet 125) [1995 5m^2 5g^2 5g 6f^2 6f* 6m^5 Aug 27] leggy colt: fourth foal: half-brother to 3-y-o Florismart (by Never So Bold) and 1¼m winner Teen Jay (by Teenoso): dam, 9f and 1¼m winner, is out of Park Hill winner Reload, a half-sister to 1000 Guineas winner Full Dress II: fair form: made all in maiden at Hamilton in August: stays 6f: blinkered third start (ran poorly): not particularly consistent: sent to Dubai. *J. Berry* — 75

LARN FORT 5 gr.g. Belfort (FR) 89 – Larnem 43 (Meldrum 112) [1994 49: a7g a7s^4 a8g a8g^6 7d 6.9s^2 11.1f^4 9m 11.1m^4 9.9g* 9.9m^5 9.9m^3 11g 10m 12g 10.1d^4 1995 a8g^3 a8g* 10.3g^4 9.9m* 10g 10.3m* 10g^2 10.8g^4 10m^4 9.9m^2 10f^4 11.5m^6 10d a9.4g 10f^4 a11g^2 a12g^6 Dec 12] tall, leggy gelding: modest handicapper: won at Southwell in January, Beverley in April and Doncaster in May: effective at 7f, and stays 11f: acts on firm ground, soft and fibresand: has won for amateur: visored (usually) or blinkered nowadays: held up. *C. W. Fairhurst* — 58

LAROCHE (GER) 4 b.c. Nebos (GER) 129 – Laurea (GER) (Sharpman (FR) 124) [1994 116: 10s* 10s^3 11g* 11g* 12g* 12g^4 12g^6 1995 12s^5 12m* 11m^3 12m^2 12.5g^4 12g Sep 24] smart German colt: won Premio Ellington at Rome in May by 1¼ lengths from Captain Horatius: ran well when 1¼ lengths third of 10 to demoted Germany in Idee Hansa Preis at Hamburg and when 2½ lengths second of 8 to Lando in Group 1 event at Dusseldorf: stays 1½m: acts on soft going and good to firm: blinkered since third 3-y-o start: front runner: best when able to dominate, and not the most consistent. *H. Jentzsch, Germany* — 118

LARROCHA (IRE) 3 b.f. Sadler's Wells (USA) 132 – Le Melody 102 (Levmoss 133) [1994 NR 1995 12m* 10m* 12g^5 11.9m* 12d^3 Sep 10] — 116

Luca Cumani took few chances in his bid to send out a sixth consecutive winner of the Galtres Stakes. He had four of the fourteen five-day declarations and three of the four top rated. In the event, Noble Rose went for the Yorkshire Oaks, Saxon Maid for the Ebor and Pumice for the Knavesmire Handicap, but Cumani still had the 11/4-on Galtres favourite when only three of the rest stood their ground against his chosen representative, best of the quartet, Larrocha. With six more against her on her previous outing, Larrocha had started 9/4 favourite in no less a contest than the Irish Oaks. She too had been a five-day entry for the Yorkshire Oaks. Something of a good thing then in a four-runner listed race, Larrocha duly added her name to those of Madiriya, Nibbs Point, Cunning, Kithanga and Noble Rose who had already monopolised the race for Cumani in the 'nineties. There was a moment of worry when Segovia kicked on over three furlongs out, but Larrocha had her at the two-furlong pole and then looked better and better, extending her advantage to nine lengths at the line.

Three months before that, Larrocha's name had still not entered the form-book. A comfortable winning debut in May when favourite for a maiden at Newmarket drew the encouraging observation from connections that 'they must be a pretty moderate bunch'. 'Elephant-like' was the description they gave to her physical appearance at Newbury four weeks later, but reactions to Larrocha's performance had to be rather more positive; dropped back to a mile and a quarter for the listed Ballymacoll Stud Stakes, she treated some useful opponents with disdain, leaving them well strung out as she made all in grand style, not having to be pushed out at all in the last half furlong to beat Poppy Carew and Spout by five lengths. Larrocha's two outings in listed races were runaway triumphs. Her two other appearances, however, both at Group 1 level, ended in defeat. In the Irish Oaks she challenged for the lead three furlongs out but was soon going nowhere and ended up just over ten lengths behind Pure Grain, well below her best. Third in the Prix Vermeille, though, beaten about a length and a half, was narrowly her best effort; again ridden up with pace, she could never get back into contention after Carling had quickened on early in the straight.

Galtres Stakes, York—Larrocha extends her trainer's outstanding run in this race

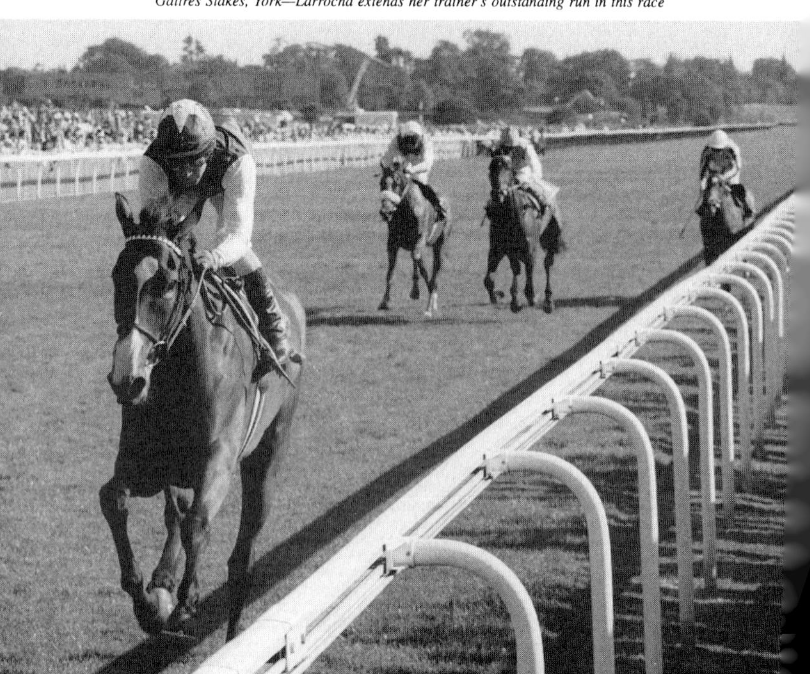

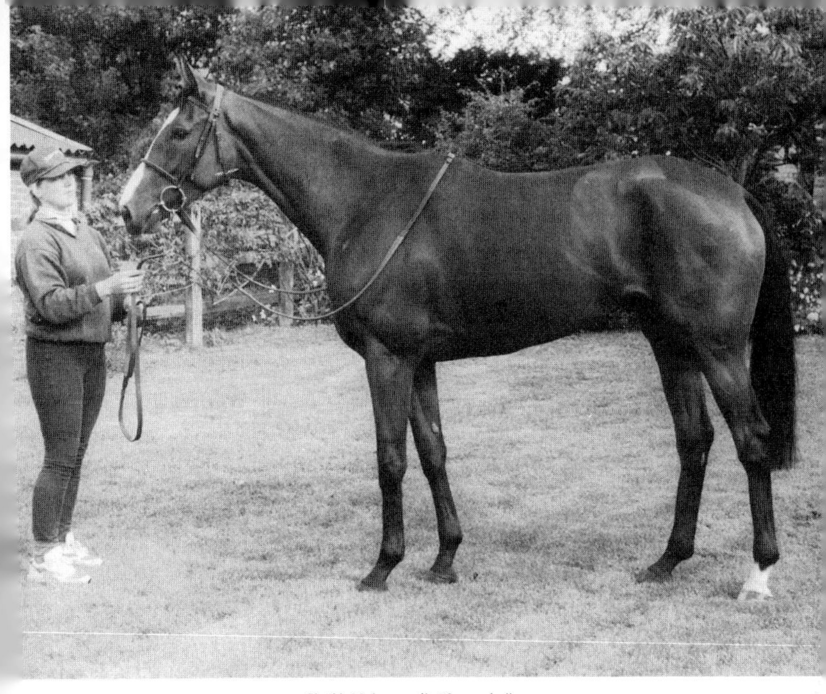

Sheikh Mohammed's "Larrocha"

Larrocha (IRE) (b.f. 1992)	Sadler's Wells (USA) (b 1981)	Northern Dancer (b 1961)	Nearctic
			Natalma
		Fairy Bridge (b 1975)	Bold Reason
			Special
	Le Melody (ch 1971)	Levmoss (b 1965)	Le Levanstell
			Feemoss
		Arctic Melody (b 1961)	Arctic Slave
			Bell Bird

So Larrocha has yet to win a pattern race. That will be temporary. She might not win one for Cumani though, because she has been sent to winter in Dubai. What conditions will prove ideal for her? Groundwise, she has not raced on anything more extreme than good to firm or good to soft, but clearly acts on both of those. As for trip, a frequently mentioned alternative to the Vermeille was a step up in distance for the St Leger or Park Hill. If reproducing her Vermeille form, she would have walked the Group 3 Park Hill and gone close with the 3 lb fillies allowance in the St Leger. Of course, Larrocha was not the finished article as a three-year-old—a tall, rather leggy filly, who is a fluent mover—but on current evidence she lacks the turn of foot ideally necessary at Group 1 level over a mile and a half. The further she goes, the better she gets. Readers will not need much more convincing that stamina is a strong suit when they see that Larrocha is a half-sister to Ardross (by Run The Gantlet). Le Melody, who at twenty-four was covered by Unblest in 1995, has had six other winners. One was in Japan and another, Adrana (by Bold Lad), ran only as a two-year-old, but the other four all won over at least a mile and a quarter. The best of them was the Sun Chariot and September Stakes runner-up Gesedeh (by Ela-Mana-Mou). Le Melody had only two races and won them both, over seven furlongs (at two years) and a mile and a quarter in Ireland. She is a half-sister to the Irish One Thousand Guineas winner Arctique Royale and a daughter of the Musidora winner Arctic Melody. Arctique Royale is one more to have made an impact at stud, with the very smart middle-distance colt Modhish and one of the top Irish middle-distance fillies of the latest season Russian Snows (both, like Larrocha, by Sadler's Wells), and Le Melody's daughter Adrana is another, with the smart miler Alflora. This is a good family and it is no wonder that Larrocha fetched 96,000 Irish guineas as a foal and 175,000 as a yearling. She still has a bright future. *L. M. Cumani*

LARRY LAMBRUSCO 2 b.g. (Feb 26) Executive Man 119 – Freudenau (Wassl 125) [1995 6m 8.1g a8.5d⁴ Sep 16] 7,600 2-y-o: leggy gelding: first reported foal: dam, ran 3 times, half-sister to champion Venezuelan performer The Iron: best effort in maiden events when fourth of 8 in falsely-run race at Wolverhampton on final start: stays 8.5f. *M. A. Jarvis* 54

LARRYLUKEATHUGH 2 b.g. (Jan 28) Prince Sabo 123 – Hidden Asset (Hello Gorgeous (USA) 128) [1995 6g⁴ 6m 6f⁵ 6g 7.5d Sep 13] 5,400F, 8,800Y, 5,200 2-y-o: lengthy, unfurnished gelding: fourth foal: half-brother to 1992 2-y-o 1m winner Christian Spirit (by Petong): dam seemed of little account: seemed to show some ability first 2 starts but well beaten after in a selling nursery final start: probably doesn't stay 7.5f: blinkered third outing. *J. J. O'Neill* 56 ?

LASER LIFE STAR 2 b.f. (Apr 27) Jester 119 – Not Alone 84 (Pas de Seul 133) [1995 6g 6f⁵ a6g Aug 19] 1,800Y: third foal: dam disappointing maiden: gambled-on favourite, raced keenly when close fifth of 11 in seller (sweating) at Lingfield in June: eased right up in similar event at Wolverhampton nearly 2 months later: sent to Bahrain. *C. N. Williams* 48

LA SPEZIA 5 b.m. Last Tycoon 131 – Helenetta 97 (Troy 137) [1994 64: 10v 10d 12m* 12g⁵ 12m³ 12m⁴ 11.9m² 11.8m² 1995 14.1g 14m⁶ 12g³ 13.3g May 31] rather sparely-made mare: modest performer at end of career: should have stayed beyond 1½m: acted on good to firm and soft going: severed tendon final start: dead. *M. Blanshard* 59

LASSEMAN 2 ch.c. Cadeaux Genereux 131 – Lillemor (Connaught 130) [1995 7m³ 7d⁶ Sep 24] robust, workmanlike colt: sort to carry condition: fourth foal: half-brother to 3-y-o 6f winner Pelleman (by Distant Relative) and 7f/1m performer Caleman and 1990 2-y-o 6f winner Danneman (both by Daring March): dam (ran twice) out of half-sister to Steel Heart: 2¼ lengths third to Caxton Star in maiden at Leicester, rather slowly away then running on: always towards rear when sixth of 8 to Story Line in minor event at Ascot 19 days later: will probably stay 1m. *R. Boss* 71

LASS OF KINLOCH 3 gr.f. Rock City 120 – Normanby Lass 100 (Bustino 136) [1994 46d: 5m³ 5m 6g⁶ 6g 7.5g 7g 1995 a8g 8m 10f⁶ 10m Aug 12] small, leggy filly: no form in 1995. *M. Brittain* –

LAST AMBITION (IRE) 3 b.f. Cadeaux Genereux 131 – Fabulous Rina (FR) (Fabulous Dancer (USA) 124) [1994 NR 1995 7g 9f 7.6m 6m Jul 24] 10,000Y: fourth foal: half-sister to 7f winner Sehailah (by Mtoto): dam, French 1¼m and 10.5f winner, is closely related to smart French middle-distance performer Lys River: no promise in 3 maidens and a handicap: sold 800 gns Newmarket December Sales. *C. R. Egerton* –

LAST BUT NOT LEAST 2 b.f. (May 10) Dominion 123 – Almadaniyah (Dunbeath (USA) 127) [1995 6d 6m³ a5g⁴ Nov 24] 1,500Y, 1,000 2-y-o: sturdy filly: third foal: half-sister to a winner in Italy by Midyan: dam unraced: modest form in maidens: stays 6f: acts on good to firm ground and fibresand. *R. F. Johnson Houghton* 63

LAST CORNER 3 b.c. Weldnaas (USA) 112 – Shadha 57 (Shirley Heights 130) [1994 59: 5s⁴ 5v⁵ 6g 7f 8s 1995 a12g* a12g² 11.6m 12.3m³ 11.8g³ 12g⁶ 14.1f⁶ a12g* a11g² 12h³ 11.5g² a14.8g² 12.1g⁵ a12g Oct 23] leggy, unfurnished colt: modest performer on turf, fair on all-weather: won median auction maiden at Wolverhampton in April and claimer at Southwell in July: stays 14.8f: acts on fibresand and good to firm ground, shaped well on soft on debut: usually held up: sold 8,000 gns Newmarket Autumn Sales: sent to Germany. *R. Hollinshead* 57 a65

LAST LAUGH (IRE) 3 b.f. Last Tycoon 131 – Little Me (Connaught 130) [1994 73: 6m* 6f³ 6m 7s 7.9d 1995 8.2g³ 8g 10m² 12g* 12m 12.1m⁵ 12.1m* 12.1s Oct 17] 59 small, leggy filly: only modest at best in 1995: won claimers at Newbury (claimed out of R. Hannon's stable £10,000) in May and Chepstow in August: will stay beyond 12.1f: acts on firm ground, no form on a soft surface. *M. C. Pipe*

LAST ROUNDUP 3 b.g. Good Times (ITY) – Washita (Valiyar 129) [1994 86p: 7s^2 7g* 6d^4 1995 8d 8g 7m 7m 10.3d 11.8g Oct 9] strong, close-coupled gelding: has a round action: disappointing in handicaps in 1995: should stay 1m: one to treat with some caution. *C. W. Thornton* –

LAST SECOND (IRE) 2 gr.f. (Mar 1) Alzao (USA) 117 – Alruccaba 83 (Crystal Palace (FR) 132) [1995 6g* 7d* Oct 7] IR 120,000Y: half-sister to 3 middle-distance winners, including Irish fillies Arrikala and Alouette (both by Darshaan), former third in Irish Oaks: dam 2-y-o 6f winner: won maiden at Redcar in September and 7-runner C L Weld Park Stakes at the Curragh (quickened in tremendous fashion last 75 yds after bad run to head Super Gift close home) in October: looks a smart middle-distance filly in the making. *Sir Mark Prescott* 97 P

LAST SPIN 3 b.f. Unfuwain (USA) 131 – Spin (High Top 131) [1994 77: 8g^2 8m 1995 10m 11.5f^5 12m 16.2g^5 a11g Sep 4] rangy, unfurnished filly: disappointing in 1995: should prove suited by middle distances: won over hurdles in December. *J. R. Jenkins* –

LAST STRAW 7 b.g. Blushing Scribe (USA) 107 – Straw Reef 64 (Final Straw 127) [1994 37: a5g a5g a5g^3 a5g 5m^5 a5g a6g^5 5m^4 a6g^4 a5g^5 a7g a6g 5.1g 1995 a6g a6g a6g 5.1g Apr 24] leggy, workmanlike gelding: seems no longer of much account. *B. Preece* –

LAST TOKEN 2 b.g. (Apr 16) Nomination 125 – Beretta (Moorestyle 137) [1995 6m* 6g^2 7g Sep 9] 2,000Y, 2,000 2-y-o: tall, workmanlike gelding: has a round action: fifth reported foal: brother to 3-y-o Buffalo Girl: dam unraced half-sister to smart sprinter Abha: won maiden auction at Salisbury in July: ran very well when 4 lengths second of 5 to Warning Time in minor event at same track later in month: last of 10 in nursery at Goodwood on final outing: stays 6f. *J. S. Moore* 77

LAST WORLD 3 b.f. Puissance 110 – Flicker Toa Flame (USA) 85 (Empery (USA) 128) [1994 –: 5.7g 5s 5g 1995 5g 5f^6 5g 5d a7g a6g a6g Dec 12] leggy filly: sold 600 gns Doncaster March Sales: 66/1, appeared to show only worthwhile form when equal-sixth of 16 in claimer at Warwick. *J. A. Pickering* 43 ?

LA SUQUET 3 b.f. Puissance 110 – Persian Case (Upper Case (USA)) [1994 54: 5m^2 5m^4 5d^3 5s^3 1995 a5g^4 6d^2 5.1g^2 5.1g^2 5m^5 5g* 5.1m May 9] sparely-made filly: fair performer: won handicap at Hamilton in May: best form at 5f: acts on good to firm and soft ground, well below form on equitrack: usually races prominently: wanders under pressure, and none too easy a ride. *M. R. Channon* 72

LATAHAAB (USA) 4 b.c. Lyphard (USA) 132 – Eye Drop (USA) 96 (Irish River (FR) 131) [1994 12v^4 12s 10g 12d* 12m^5 10g 12d^4 11d^2 1995 a10g^3 12g 16.2m^6 16m* 16.1m 15.9m^2 14.8m* 16d^6 16m^6 Oct 27] sturdy, quite attractive colt: fifth foal: dam, 6f winner at 2 yrs (only season to race), is out of Pushy: trained by Mme C. Head until end of 1994, winning handicap at Evry: fairly useful handicapper here: won at Kempton in May and Newmarket in August, both times leading some way out: stays 2m (not certain to get 2½m): acts on dead ground and good to firm: tried blinkered, not when successful: races prominently. *R. Akehurst* 92

LA TANSANI (IRE) 2 b.c. (Feb 9) High Estate 127 – Hana Marie 101§ (Formidable (USA) 125) [1995 6m 5m^6 6.1m 6f^6 Jul 26] IR 32,000Y: good-bodied colt: second foal: dam 2-y-o 5f and 6f winner: seems modest maiden on balance of form: likely to stay 7f. *R. Hannon* 60 +

LATCHING (IRE) 3 ch.f. Thatching 131 – Keepers Lock (USA) (Sunny's Halo (CAN)) [1994 75p: 6m^2 7s^3 1995 8g^6 9g^4 6m^3 6m^4 5g^3 6g 6m^3 Oct 28] tall, lengthy filly: has plenty of scope: fair maiden handicapper: probably ideally suited by 6f+, and has form over as far as 9f: acts on good to firm and soft ground: blinkered (below best) fourth 3-y-o start. *R. F. Johnson Houghton* 76

LATCH KEY LADY (USA) 3 b.f. Tejano (USA) – Key To The Heart (USA) (Arts And Letters) [1994 48: 5m^3 6m 6m 1995 a12g Sep 16] leggy filly: soundly beaten since debut: joined R. Woodhouse. *M. Johnston* –

LATE MAIL (USA) 3 b.g. Simply Majestic (USA) – Total Chic (USA) (Far North (CAN) 120) [1994 48: 7m 7m 1995 10f^4 12g 10m Jun 6] no worthwhile form in 1995. *J. M. P. Eustace* –

LA THUILE 3 b.f. Statoblest 120 – Mild Wind (Porto Bello 118) [1994 46: 6d 6g 6s 1995 5.1m 7g 6m 6m 8g a10g 5m Aug 25] leggy, narrow filly: no form in 1995: tried blinkered: sold 1,000 gns Ascot August Sales. *M. D. I. Usher* –

LATIN BEAUTY 2 b.f. (May 1) Then Again 126 – Rather Warm 103 (Tribal Chief 125) [1995 5m 5.3f^5 May 11] 7,000Y: sturdy filly: sister to a poor maiden and half-sister to several winners, including 1991 2-y-o 6f winner Prince Emilio (by Prince Sabo): dam won at up to 7.6f at 2 yrs: poor form in maiden events: dead. *R. Hannon* 49

LATIN LEADER 5 b.g. Primo Dominie 121 – Ravaro 96 (Raga Navarro (ITY) 119) [1994 62: 10d 7m^4 8m^5 1995 10m* 10.1g 9.7s^4 a8.5g^5 a9.4g Nov 13] workmanlike gelding: has a round action: modest performer: won seller at Windsor in August: failed to repeat the form: stays 1¼m: acts on firm and dead going: blinkered last 3 starts: may prove best with strong handling. *C. R. Egerton* 64 a–

LATIN REIGN (USA) 2 b. or br.c. (Apr 13) El Gran Senor (USA) 136 – Love Bunny (USA) (Exclusive Native (USA)) [1995 7g 7m^4 8.3g^2 8.1s* 9g^2 Nov 19] smallish, attractive colt: tenth foal: half-brother to 1m winner Easy Over (by Transworld) and several winners abroad: dam won over 6f at 2 yrs on only start in USA: won maiden at Chepstow in October: much improved form when beaten nose by Brave Indigo in Premio Guido Berardelli at Rome final start: will stay at least 1¼m: acts on good to firm and soft ground: sent to USA. *P. W. Chapple-Hyam* 100

L A TOUCH 2 b.f. (Apr 21) Tina's Pet 121 – Silvers Era 72 (Balidar 133) [1995 a5g a5g 5.1g^4 6.1m^6 6g^2 6m* 6m 6m^4 a6g^5 5.3d^5 6s Sep 30] strong, lengthy filly: fifth foal: half-sister to 1994 2-y-o 6f winner Silver Thatching (by Puissance): dam best at 5f: plater: won at Leicester in August: none too consistent afterwards: stays 6f: acts on good to firm ground. *C. A. Dwyer* 53

LATVIAN 8 gr.g. Rousillon (USA) 133 – Lorelene (FR) 97 (Lorenzaccio 130) [1994 72: 11.1f^3 11.1f^4 11.1m^4 15.1f^2 11.1m* 12.1m^5 11.1m^3 12h^3 13m* 11.9m^2 16.1m 12.1g^3 10.1d 1995 12.4g^3 11.1g^2 13.1g^2 13f^6 12m* 12.4m^3 12m* 12m^5 13.1g 11.1g^2 12f^6 15.1s Nov 2] lengthy gelding: fair handicapper: won at Catterick (claimer) in July and Pontefract (rallied well) in August: below that form afterwards, particularly on last 2 starts: effective at 11f to 15f: acts on hard ground, below form all 4 runs on dead: blinkered 3 times (won on first occasion), but not since 6 yrs. *R. Allan* 76

LATZIO 2 b.f. (Apr 10) Arrasas (USA) 100 – Remould 83 (Reform 132) [1995 6m 6f 6m^4 5m^3 a6g 7g a6g a6g a5g Dec 18] half-sister to middle-distance winner Deal On (by Quiet Fling) and 3 winners abroad: dam 2-y-o 5f winner: little form: runs as though likely to prove best at 5f: blinkered final outing. *B. A. Pearce* –

LAUDATION (IRE) 3 ch.g. Bold Arrangement 127 – Hooray Lady 92 (Ahonoora 122) [1994 NR 1995 8g 8m 10m 8.2f Jul 8] 11,000Y: lengthy, unfurnished gelding: first foal: dam won 5 times at 1m or so and seemed to stay 1½m: no worthwhile form: sold 800 gns Ascot November Sales. *G. B. Balding* –

LAUGHING BUCCANEER 2 ch.g. (May 16) Weldnaas (USA) 112 – Atlantic Line (Capricorn Line 111) [1995 5g^6 6m^3 7f 7.3m 6f^6 7m^2 8.5s^5 7m 7.3d^5 a8g^4 a5g a6g^4 Nov 29] 4,000F, 3,500Y: tall gelding: third foal: half-brother to 4-y-o Thrower (by Thowra): dam unraced: fair maiden (could be rated 73): established long lead when head second of 9 to Paint It Black in median auction at Epsom in September: failed to repeat that form: bred to stay beyond 7f but races keenly: normally blinkered (not last time): usually a front runner. *B. J. Meehan* 62 + a57

LAUREL CROWN (IRE) 2 b.c. (Mar 13) Thatching 131 – Laureon (Caerleon (USA) 132) [1995 5f^3 5g^4 5.1m^2 6m^3 7g Jul 19] 12,000Y: sturdy colt: second foal: half-brother to 3-y-o Poly Laureon (by Fairy King), 5f winner at 2 yrs: dam half-sister to Cheshire Oaks winner Helenetta: modest maiden: creditable third of 7 to Mazeed in maiden at Newcastle on penultimate outing: below form twice for 7-lb claimer, over 7f final outing: sold 2,200 gns Doncaster October Sales: sent to Belgium. *J. Berry* 69

LAVANDA 2 b.f. (Feb 23) Soviet Star (USA) 128 – One Life (USA) (L'Emigrant (USA) 129) [1995 6f^4 Oct 3] 42,000Y: half-sister to useful 7.5f (at 2 yrs) and 1½m winner Tenorio (by Law Society) and 2 winners in France, including 7f to 9f winner Lithuania (by Ti King): dam unraced half-sister to Miesque: well-backed favourite, 60 ?

11 lengths fourth of 7 to Chalamont in maiden at Redcar, racing freely then hanging left and not looking an easy ride: bred to stay 1m. *D. R. Loder*

LAVENDER BLOOM (IRE) 2 ch.f. (May 1) Broken Hearted 124 – African Bloom (African Sky 124) [1995 5m⁴ 7d a6g⁴ a5g⁴ Dec 19] IR 4,800Y: seventh foal: half-sister to 1988 2-y-o 5f winner Hogans Hero (by Krayyan) and 5f (at 2 yrs) to 1¼m winner Falcons Dawn (by Exhibitioner): dam Irish 7f winner: Irish filly: modest maiden: below form last 3 starts: bred to stay at least 7f. *Michael Cunningham, Ireland* 60 a43

LAVENDER DELLA (IRE) 2 gr.f. (Apr 21) Shernazar 131 – All In White (FR) (Carwhite 127) [1995 7m⁵ 7f⁶ 6g Oct 3] IR 2,800F, IR 3,700Y: neat filly: half-sister to 1990 2-y-o 6f winner Sail Past (by No Pass No Sale) and a winner in Germany: dam, French 10.5f winner, half-sister to smart middle-distance winners Praise and Hard To Sing: poor form in maiden auctions at Warwick: bred to stay long distances. *M. J. Fetherston-Godley* 47

LAVENDER (IRE) 3 ch.f. Kris 135 – Sailor's Mate 114 (Shirley Heights 130) [1994 NR 1995 10.5m⁵ 10.1g⁴ 10m⁴ Jun 19] third foal: closely related to Cutlass (by Sure Blade), fair maiden here successful over 1½m in French Provinces: dam 1½m winner: modest form in maidens first 2 starts, last of 4 at Brighton final one: below form in maiden at Brighton following month: sent to New Zealand. *L. M. Cumani* 63

LAVINIA FONTANA (IRE) 6 ch.m. Sharpo 132 – Belle Origine (USA) (Exclusive Native (USA)) [1994 119: 6d⁴ 5d² 6m 6.5g³ 6g* 5g 7g 7v* 6d 1995 8s² 6.5g⁶ 6d² 6d⁶ 5d⁵ 7d* 6g⁶ Nov 19] lengthy, angular mare: smart performer, not so good as at 5 yrs: best efforts in 1995 when 2 lengths second of 9 in Group 2 event at Baden-Baden and around 4 lengths fifth of 12 in Prix de l'Abbaye de Longchamp, both won by Hever Golf Rose: won Premio Chiusara at Milan in November (for second year running) by ½ length from Imprevedibile, leading final 1f: broke blood vessel in similar event at Rome final start: very best form at sprint distances, but won at 7f: needed give in the ground, and went well on heavy: blinkered (below form) once at 3 yrs: game: has been retired. *J. L. Dunlop* 111

Cyril Humphris' "Lavinia Fontana"

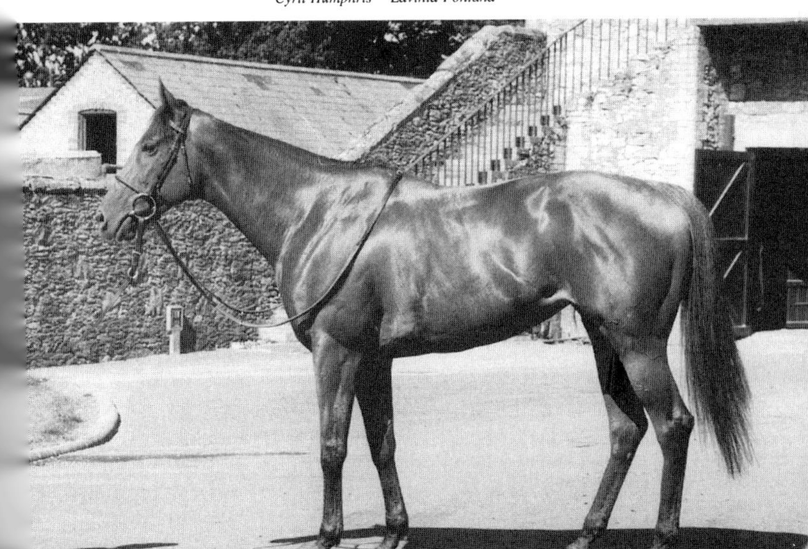

LAVIRCO (GER) 2 br.c. (Mar 19) Konigsstuhl (GER) – La Virginia (GER) (Surumu (GER)) [1995 8s* 8s* Oct 15] first foal: dam, German 1¼m winner, is sister to dam of top-class middle distance colt Lomitas from an excellent German family: promising German colt: won maiden at Mulheim in September and very valuable Preis der Winterfavoriten at Cologne (by 1½ lengths from Barlovento) in October: should prove well suited by middle distances: the leading German 2-y-o colt, and clearly a most interesting prospect. *P. Rau, Germany*

107 p

LA VOLTA 2 b.f. (Feb 22) Komaite (USA) – Khadino (Relkino 131) [1995 5g* 6d^{6} 6f 7f* 8m^{2} Nov 3] strong, lengthy filly: third foal: sister to 3-y-o Mr Teigh and 1993 2-y-o 6f winner Springhead: dam no form: fairly useful filly: successful in median auction maiden at Hamilton in the spring (off course 4 months afterwards) and minor event at Redcar (held Roses In The Snow by a head) in October: creditable ½-length second of 6 to Brighstone in slowly-run minor event at Doncaster final outing: stays 1m: acts on firm ground. *J. G. FitzGerald*

86

LAWBUSTER (IRE) 3 b.g. Contract Law (USA) 108 – Tora Tora (Home Guard (USA) 129) [1994 47: 6.1m 6g 6m 7g^{5} 7g a8.5g^{4} 1995 a8g^{2} a10g^{3} a9.4g^{3} a8g a10g^{4} a8.5g a12g^{5} 12.5m Jun 26] compact gelding: unimpressive mover: poor maiden: sold out of W. Muir's stable 2,800 gns Doncaster March Sales after seventh start: well beaten on return: stays 1¼m: acts on all-weather, yet to race on a soft surface: blinkered 4 times, on first 2 occasions putting up best efforts: sold 1,200 gns Ascot December Sales. *M. J. Wilkinson*

53 d

LAW COMMISSION 5 ch.g. Ela-Mana-Mou 132 – Adjala 89 (Northfields (USA)) [1994 85: 8m 7d 7d 6m^{2} 6f 6g 1995 7m 6g 6g 8f^{3} 6f^{6} 6f* 7.3d Sep 15] small, sturdy gelding: fairly useful handicapper: narrowly won strongly-run race at Salisbury in August: broke out of stalls and withdrawn at Ascot Sep 23: needs a stiff track when racing at 6f, but unlikely to stay beyond 1m: acts on any going: none too consistent. *D. R. C. Elsworth*

83

LAW DANCER (IRE) 2 b.c. (Feb 18) Alzao (USA) 117 – Judicial (USA) (Law Society (USA) 130) [1995 7.1d^{5} 7g^{6} Sep 29] 30,000F, 18,000Y: first foal: dam, winner from 11f to 1¾m in Ireland, out of close relation of Green Dancer: best effort when sixth of 11 behind Quakers Field in well-contested auction event at Goodwood, never far away and eased when beaten: will stay middle distances. *T. G. Mills*

76 +

LAWFUL LOVE (IRE) 5 b.g. Law Society (USA) 130 – Amata (USA) (Nodouble (USA)) [1994 NR 1995 10m 12m^{6} 12d 11.9d Oct 11] IR 14,500F: 15,500Y: leggy gelding: shows knee action: brother to Irish 1½m winner Law Chambers and half-brother to several winners, notably smart Bluegrass Prince (at up to 9f, by Bluebird): dam French (middle-distance) and USA winner: well beaten in maidens and claimers. *T. W. Donnelly*

–

LAWN ORDER 2 b.f. (Apr 30) Efisio 120 – Zebra Grass 85 (Run The Gantlet (USA)) [1995 5f 6m 5m 6.1d Sep 11] 3,400F, 6,200Y: angular, good-quartered filly: half-sister to several winners, including 1989 2-y-o 1m winner Pay The Bank (by High Top) and stayer Fedra (by Grundy): dam 2-y-o 6f and 7f winner from family of Royal Palace: around 4 lengths seventh of 10 in maiden auction at Haydock in August: raced away from favoured part of track all subsequent starts, doing well to finish eighth of 22 in nursery at Nottingham on final outing: will be suited by further than 6f: will do better. *Mrs J. R. Ramsden*

51 p

LAWNSWOOD CAPTAIN (IRE) 2 ro.c. (Jan 19) Maelstrom Lake 118 – Morgiana (Godswalk (USA) 130) [1995 a5g 5.1g 6m^{3} 5m^{6} 7.5d 6s 8f^{5} 8f Oct 31] IR 5,500Y: angular colt: half-brother to 4-y-o 5f (at 2 yrs) to 7.1f winner Ochos Rios (by Horage) and a winner in Belgium by Yashgan: dam poor maiden: poor form: stays 1m: none too consistent. *R. Hollinshead*

50

LAWNSWOOD JUNIOR 8 gr.g. Bairn (USA) 126 – Easymede 85 (Runnymede 123) [1994 NR 1995 8.2g 7g 8.3g 8.1g 8.1f 10.5m Aug 11] workmanlike gelding: unimpressive mover: fair handicapper (rated 69) at 6 yrs: behind all starts on return: stays 1¼m: probably acts on any going: tried blinkered/visored, earlier in career: modest hurdler. *J. L. Spearing*

–

LAWNSWOOD LADY 3 b.f. Lochnager 132 – Keep Cool (FR) 42 (Northern Treat (USA)) [1994 56: 5m 5d^{4} 5.1m 5.1g^{3} 5f 5m 6.1d a5g^{5} 6s 6.1g 5g^{3} a5g a6g a5g a5g^{3} a6g^{2} 1995 a7g^{6} a8g^{6} a6g^{5} a6g a6g^{3} a6g a5g^{5} a6g^{5} a6g 6.1g a6g^{4} a6g 5.9f Jul 31] neat filly: poor maiden: stays 6f: best turf form with some give in the ground, also

39

acts on fibresand: tried blinkered, no improvement: tends to sweat: hurdling with Mrs F. Owen. *R. Hollinshead*

LAXFORD BRIDGE 4 b.c. Lomond (USA) 128 – Connaught Bridge 124 (Connaught 130) [1994 84: 10m^4 10m* 11.9m 10.3d^4 10m 1995 10m 10.3m^3 10m 10m^6 10f 10f^3 9.9m^5 10m Aug 13] sturdy, lengthy colt: showed knee action: fairly useful handicapper on his day: should have stayed 1½m: acted on firm ground and good to soft: dead. *P. W. Harris* 85

LAY THE BLAME 2 b.c. (Apr 30) Reprimand 122 – Rose And The Ring (Welsh Pageant 132) [1995 7.1m^6 6.1d^6 6g* 6.1m* Oct 26] 14,500Y: good-bodied colt: half-brother to 3-y-o 5f (at 2 yrs) and 8.3f winner Benjarong (by Sharpo), fairly useful 4-y-o 7f/1m performer Ham N' Eggs (by Robellino), and several other winners: dam ran twice: progressive form: won 15-runner maiden auction at Warwick and 10-runner minor event at Nottingham (led inside final 1f and beat Mutamanni a head), in October: should prove effective at 7f: bandaged off-hind on debut: a nice type who will improve further. *W. Jarvis* 90 p

LEADING PRINCESS (IRE) 4 gr.f. Double Schwartz 128 – Jenny Diver (USA) (Hatchet Man (USA)) [1994 45: 7.1g 6g a6g 5g^4 5m^2 5m* 5m^2 5m 6g 5s 6g^4 1995 5m^3 5g 5m 5f 5f^3 5f 5g 5g 5f^5 5m^5 6m 5f 6g* 5m* a6g^4 Nov 20] leggy filly: modest handicapper: won at Hamilton (apprentices) in September and Newcastle (raced on favoured far side) in October: stays 6f: acts on firm and soft ground: visored or (at 4 yrs) blinkered since second 3-y-o start: sometimes carries head high: usually races prominently. *Miss L. A. Perratt* 55

LEADING SPIRIT (IRE) 3 b.g. Fairy King (USA) – Shopping (FR) (Sheshoon 132) [1994 –: 7g 7s 1995 7g^6 8.2m^4 11.6m^5 14.1g^2 a14g 11.4d* 12.1g* 11.8g^6 12.1s Oct 17] leggy gelding: fair handicapper: progressed steadily, winning at Sandown and Hamilton (made all) in September: effective at 11.4f, may well stay 2m: acts on good to firm ground and dead, below form on soft ground and only try on fibresand. *C. F. Wall* 77

LEAP FOR JOY 3 ch.f. Sharpo 132 – Humble Pie 92 (Known Fact (USA) 135) [1994 85: 5g^4 6d^2 6g* 6s^3 6s 1995 5g 5d^2 5d* 6m Nov 4] compact filly: useful performer: off course 6 months after reappearance: best effort when leading inside last and beating Palacegate Episode ½ length in Group 3 Premio Omenoni at Milan in October: persistently short of room from halfway in listed race at Doncaster 3 weeks later, and run best ignored: stays 6f: acts on soft ground. *J. H. M. Gosden* 109

LEAP IN THE DARK (IRE) 6 br.h. Shadeed (USA) 135 – Star Guide (FR) (Targowice (USA) 130) [1994 NR 1995 16.1g^6 14.1m 14.1f^4 14.1f^2 14.1f 12m 16m 14.1m^2 15.8g Sep 16] big, lengthy, sparely-made horse: poor performer: stays 1¾m: probably acts on firm ground: blinkered (well beaten) once in 1993. *Miss L. C. Siddall* 34

LEAP YEAR BABY (IRE) 3 b.f. Digamist (USA) 110 – Rahwah 73 (Northern Baby (CAN) 127) [1994 43: 5.1d 7m^4 6g 1995 7g 8.3g 10m 7g 5f Jun 15] leggy, shallow-girthed filly: well beaten for new stable: tried blinkered/visored. *M. D. Hammond* –

LEAR DANCER (USA) 4 b. or br.g. Lear Fan (USA) 130 – Green Gown (Green Dancer (USA) 132) [1994 66: 9m 11.1f* 14.4g^4 13.3g^5 12m^2 14m^2 12m^3 11.8m^3 14v^3 11.9g^2 1995 12m 11.5m^2 12m^6 16g* 16.2d^6 11.9g a16g^3 a16g^4 Nov 29] leggy, workmanlike gelding: fair performer: stepped up in trip when winning handicap at Goodwood in September, coming from last to first: suited by test of stamina: acts on any going, including equitrack: effective visored/blinkered or not: none too consistent. *P. Mitchell* 72

LEAR JET (USA) 2 b.c. (Apr 10) Lear Fan (USA) 130 – Lajna 88 (Be My Guest (USA) 126) [1995 8d^4 8d Sep 27] strong, rangy, good sort: has plenty of scope: fifth foal: brother to fairly useful 1991 2-y-o winner Solar Star and half-brother to 3-y-o 7.5f and 1m winner Ninia (by Affirmed) and useful 1993 2-y-o 5f and 6f winner Gold Land (by Gone West): dam twice-raced half-sister to Soviet Line out of Oaks fourth Shore Line: promising 4 lengths fourth of 8 to Mick's Love in well-contested minor event at Newbury, staying on strongly close home: looking very well, failed to reproduce that form when seventh of 18 to Mystic Knight in maiden at Salisbury: worth another chance to confirm form of debut. *P. F. I. Cole* 90

LEARNING CURVE (IRE) 2 gr.f. (Apr 26) Archway (IRE) 115 – Children's Hour (Mummy's Pet 125) [1995 6m a5g^{3} a5g Nov 24] IR 7,000Y: fourth foal: half-sister to 3-y-o Sharp Holly (by Exactly Sharp) and 6f winner Common Law (by Common Grounds): dam, Irish maiden placed at 12.8f, daughter of Portland Handicap winner Matinee, family of Lemon Souffle: keeping-on third in seller at Wolverhampton in November: probably requires further than 5f. *Sir Mark Prescott* 43

LEAR WHITE (USA) 4 b.c. Lear Fan (USA) 130 – White Water (FR) (Pharly (FR) 130) [1994 8s^{4} 7.5m* 8v^{3} 8m^{4} 9d^{3} 10d^{2} 10d^{3} 10d^{3} 8v 8d 1995 8.5g^{5} 10g^{2} 8d* 8d* 8m* 8s* 10s^{4} 8s^{5} 8m^{4} 8m^{3} 8.5g^{2} 8d 10g Oct 29] $50,000Y: third foal: brother to fairly useful French winner (at up to 1½m) Sky Run and half-brother to a minor winner in France by Saint Estephe: dam won 10 races between 6.5f to 11.5f in France and Italy, and placed in pattern company: smart Italian colt: won 2 minor events and listed race at 2 yrs, and minor event at 3 yrs: successful in 1995 in 2 minor events in March, then listed race and Group 3 event (by ¾ length from Fraam, leading well inside last) in April, all at Rome: good fourth of 10 to Flagbird in Premio Presidente della Repubblica there next start: rather inconsistent in varied company afterwards: effective at 1m to 1¼m: acts on good to firm ground and heavy. *F. Brogi, Italy* 111

LEAVE IT TO LIB 8 b.m. Tender King 123 – Nuit de Vin (Nebbiolo 125) [1994 58: 7.5g 8f 7.1m^{5} 7m^{4} 7f^{4} 8.2m^{3} 8m^{6} 8f 8.1g 1995 8g 8.1m 10m 8m 10.4g Aug 31] small, sparely-made mare: on the downgrade and one to leave alone nowadays. *P. Calver* –

LE BAL 3 b.f. Rambo Dancer (CAN) 107 – Skarberg (FR) (Noir Et Or 125) [1994 41: 6.1m 6.1m^{4} 6m^{3} 7g^{6} 6m 1995 8d 8m^{6} 6.1m^{2} 6g 6m^{6} 6m 6.1m 8.2f Jul 8] angular filly: poor performer: effective at 6f, probably at 1m: acts on good to firm ground: blinkered/visored since second 3-y-o start: inconsistent: joined Miss J. Craze. *Mrs N. Macauley* 41

LECROIX (GER) 3 b.c. Assert 134 – Las Palmas (Experte (GER)) [1994 6g^{3} 7g* 1995 11s^{2} 11s^{2} 11s* 12m 12g^{2} 12s^{2} Sep 3] half-brother to 6.5f (at 2 yrs) to 8.5f winner Le Jardin (by Gimont) and 4-y-o 1m to 16.5f winner Leconte (by Homing): dam winner in Germany: smart performer: won valuable event at Dortmund at 2 yrs and Group 2 contest at Cologne (beat Kalimnos by 2 lengths) in June: best efforts when 2 lengths second of 7 to Wind In Her Hair in Aral-Pokal at Gelsenkirchen then when 5 lengths second of 10 to impressive Germany in Grosser Preis von Baden: stays 1½m: acts on soft ground, worst effort in 1995 on good to firm. *M. Hofer, Germany* 112

LEEDONS PARK 3 br.g. Precocious 126 – Scottish Rose 69 (Warpath 113) [1994 –: 6m 9d 7s 1995 10g 14.1h^{5} Aug 16] lengthy gelding: no sign of ability. *M. W. Easterby* –

LEES PLEASE (IRE) 3 b.c. Glenstal (USA) 118 – Perfect Choice 64 (Bold Lad (IRE) 133) [1994 62: 5.1m 6g^{4} 7m^{4} 7m* 7g^{2} 8g 10s 8s* 7.3v^{4} 6.9s 1995 8.3m a8.5g 8.1d 8g a10g Nov 14] leggy, close-coupled colt: modest handicapper: disappointing at 3 yrs: stays 1m: acts on good to firm ground and heavy: sold (K. Cunningham-Brown to N. Ayliffe) 1,500 gns Ascot December Sales. *K. O. Cunningham-Brown* –

LEGAITAK 3 b.g. Rock City 120 – Bridestones 92 (Jan Ekels 122) [1994 NR 1995 10.1m 7m^{4} Aug 19] 36,000Y: half-brother to several winners, including smart 7f to 1¼m performer Lockton (by Moorestyle): dam middle distance winner: slowly away and last in minor event and maiden. *B. Hanbury* –

LEGAL BRIEF 3 b.g. Law Society (USA) 130 – Ahonita 90 (Ahonoora 122) [1994 –: 6g 7.5f 1995 10.1g 8m 8g 10d Sep 18] good-topped gelding: seems of little account: sold 650 gns Doncaster November Sales. *J. S. Wainwright* –

LEGAL FICTION 4 b.g. Shadeed (USA) 135 – Rally For Justice (Dominion 123) [1994 66: 8m^{2} 7m^{4} 10m^{5} 7.6g 12.1g^{5} 15s 8g^{6} 1995 a7g* a9.4g* a8.5g* a8g^{4} a7g^{5} a9.4g^{3} a12g 8.5m 8.3f 7m^{3} 8.1f* 10.4m 7g^{3} 7m^{4} 8m^{5} 8.3f 8m^{3} 7.1d^{5} 8g 8d 7f Oct 18] leggy gelding: fair handicapper: won at Southwell (maiden) and Wolverhampton (twice) early on, and at Edinburgh in July: effective at 7f to 9.4f: acts on firm ground and the all-weather, probably on dead: blinkered (well beaten) final start: sold only 9,000 gns Newmarket Autumn Sales. *M. Johnston* 71 a78

LEGAL ISSUE (IRE) 3 b.c. Contract Law (USA) 108 – Natuschka (Authi 123) [1994 60: a6g^{3} a7g a7g^{6} 5d^{3} 5s^{4} 1995 8.1g^{5} 7g^{3} 7g^{2} 7.1m* 8f^{2} 7g^{2} 7g^{2} 8h^{2} 8m^{4} 7.1m* 71

7g Sep 13] sturdy colt: fair performer: gradually progressed throughout the year, winning maiden and handicap at Edinburgh in the summer: effective at 7f, stays 1m: acts on fibresand and hard ground, probably on soft: sold (Sir Mark Prescott to W. Haigh) 17,000 gns Newmarket Autumn Sales. *Sir Mark Prescott*

LEGALLY DELICIOUS 3 b.f. Law Society (USA) 130 – Bold Apple (Bold Lad (IRE) 133) [1994 54p: a8g4 1995 a8g* a8.5g5 a8g* a8g* a8.5g3 a7g a11g a8g Jul 13] modest form: won seller in January and claimers in April (claimed out of J. Banks's stable £4,000) and May (claimed out of B. McMath's stable £4,000), all at Southwell: well below form afterwards: stays 1m: yet to race on turf: sold 1,000 gns Newmarket December Sales. *D. W. Chapman* — 67 d

LEGAL RIGHT (USA) 2 b.c. (Feb 27) Alleged (USA) 138 – Rose Red (USA) 92 (Northern Dancer) [1995 7g2 Sep 28] closely related to 13f winner Zind (by Law Society), useful at 2 yrs when third in Racing Post Trophy, and half-brother to a winner in USA by Seattle Slew and to the dam of very useful Irish sprinter Archway and Derby winner Dr Devious: dam, Irish 2-y-o 6f winner unraced at 3 yrs, is half-sister to high-class 1m to 1½m winner Critique: 16/1, 2½ lengths second of 23 to stable-companion Astor Place in maiden at Newmarket, leading 3f out then keeping on well once headed: moved well to post: looks a useful colt in the making, and is sure to win a race. *P. W. Chapple-Hyam* — 91 p

LEGAL TRAIN 4 ch.g. Siberian Express (USA) 125 – Pushkinia (FR) 95 (Pharly (FR) 130) [1994 56: 9m5 10d4 10.5g2 12.5m2 10m* 12g 12g2 11.5d 1995 11.9f May 11] angular, workmanlike gelding: modest handicapper: stumbled and fell 3f out at Brighton only start in 1995: effective at 1¼m to 12.5f: acted on firm and dead ground: blinkered (below form) once at 2 yrs: dead. *A. Hide* — –

LEGATEE 4 ch.f. Risk Me (FR) 127 – Legal Sound 85 (Legal Eagle 126) [1994 64: 5.3g6 7m6 6m a5g3 a6g3 1995 a6g3 6.9d6 a8.5g 6.9g6 a8.5g3 a7g2 a7g* a7g3 a8.5g 7g 6f a6g a7g a6g Dec 9] lengthy filly: fair performer: made all in handicap at Wolverhampton in August: claimed out of B. Meehan's stable £4,000 eighth start: bandaged, well below form for new stable: stays 8.5f: acts on fibresand and good to firm ground, very best form on soft: tried blinkered/visored, below form: active type, and usually races prominently. *A. Streeter* — 64 d

LEGENDARY LADY 4 b.f. Reprimand 122 – Sharp Celine (Sharpo 132) [1994 –: 6m 8m 7d 1995 10m Jul 10] leggy filly: little form. *R. T. Phillips* — –

LEGENDARY LEAP 5 b.m. Legend of France (USA) 124 – Leap In Time (Dance In Time (CAN)) [1994 69: 9d 8.3m4 7g2 8s2 10d2 1995 8f 8m* 10f* 10f6 10d 9g Sep 30] lengthy mare: fairly useful handicapper: won twice at Newbury in June: creditable sixth of 14 in £35,300 event at Goodwood in July: off course 2 months after that and ran poorly afterwards: stays 1¼m: acts on firm and dead ground, probably on soft: held up in touch at 5 yrs. *Lord Huntingdon* — 80

LEGEND DULAC (IRE) 6 b.g. Legend of France (USA) 124 – Westerlake (Blakeney 126) [1994 47: a7g 8g 8f6 7m a7g 7m4 7g* 7m6 7m 8g 8m 7g6 1995 7m2 a8g3 7f6 7f2 7m4 8d 7d 8f a8g Nov 16] small gelding: poor handicapper: sold out of J. L. Harris' stable 850 gns Ascot February Sales: effective at 7f and 1m: acts on soft going and firm and on fibresand: headstrong and sometimes wears net muzzle: races prominently: inconsistent: sold 520 gns Doncaster November Sales. *J. A. Harris* — 47 a39

LEGENDRA 5 ch.m. Legend of France (USA) 124 – Obertura (USA) 100 (Roberto (USA) 131) [1994 –: 10.8m5 10m 1995 10s 13.1f4 May 22] strong, workmanlike mare: fair form when second (including on good to firm ground and soft) in 3 NH Flat races: poor maiden at best on flat: will be suited by further than 13f: often bandaged. *P. G. Murphy* — 48

L'EGLISE BELLE 3 b.f. Minster Son 130 – Haddon Anna (Dragonara Palace (USA) 115) [1994 46: 5.1f 5.1m5 6d 6.1s5 1995 5.1g 7f6 7m 7g5 8m5 8f5 8h 8f Oct 24] tall filly: poor maiden: stays 1m: acts on firm ground: blinkered (no improvement) last 2 starts. *Mrs A. L. M. King* — 41

LEGUARD EXPRESS (IRE) 7 b.g. Double Schwartz 128 – All Moss 66 (Prince Tenderfoot (USA) 126) [1994 53: 8s4 10v2 10v 8m4 a8.5g 10.8d3 10.2s3 7m* 7.1m* 7.1m3 6m3 7s 1995 7g 5.7f a7g 7g Jun 17] good-topped gelding: carries condition: modest handicapper: well beaten in 1995: stays 10.8f: acts on good to firm ground and heavy: nearly always blinkered: sometimes sweating. *O. O'Neill* — –

LEHMANS LADY 3 ch.f. Move Off 112 – Lehmans Lot (Oats 126) [1994 46: 5g6 6m6 7f4 6g 7d 1995 8.3f Jun 15] leggy, unfurnished filly: poor maiden: well beaten only start in 1995. *Mrs M. Reveley* –

LEIF THE LUCKY (USA) 6 ch.g. Lemhi Gold (USA) 123 – Corvine (USA) (Crow (FR) 134) [1994 91: 8v* 8m3 8.1g 8f2 8d* 8g 8s2 8m 1995 8g4 8m 8.1g 8m Jun 21] rather leggy, short-backed gelding: fairly useful handicapper: creditable fourth of 23 to Roving Minstrel in the Lincoln at Doncaster: well below form 2 of 3 starts afterwards: effective at 1m and 1¼m: acts on any ground, but has gained all 5 successes on an easy surface: usually held up. *Miss S. E. Hall* 86

LEIGH CROFTER 6 ch.g. Son of Shaka 119 – Ganadora (Good Times (ITY)) [1994 83: 6s* 5v* 6d4 6s* 6m* 6s2 5.7m4 6.1m 7.3s 5d 6d 6.1g4 5v a6g a6g4 1995 a5g4 a5g* a5g3 a6g5 a5g2 a6g2 a5g6 5m 6g 6d a6g 7.3d 5d2 5.1d4 6g6 7d a6g4 a6g2 a5g6 Nov 16] workmanlike gelding: fairly useful handicapper: won at Wolverhampton in January: lost his form in the spring, but back to best in November: effective at 5f and 6f: acts on good to firm and heavy ground and on fibresand: usually blinkered/visored: usually bandaged. *P. D. Cundell* 73 a82

LEITH ACADEMY (USA) 2 b.f. (May 2) Academy Award (USA) – Uvula (USA) (His Majesty (USA)) [1995 6g5 6f* 7.5m2 7m3 Aug 23] $6,000Y: tall, unfurnished filly: half-sister to useful 7f and 9f winner Risen Moon (by Hawaiian Sound) and 2 winners in USA: dam, minor winner in USA, sister to good-class middle-distance filly Ribbon (dam of Preakness and Belmont winner Risen Star): sire (by Secretariat) Grade 2 1¼m winner: won median auction maiden at Ayr in June: hung right and never able to reach all-the-way winner Lac Dessert in minor event at Beverley following month then well-beaten last of 3 behind Dankeston in similar contest at Redcar: will stay beyond 7.5f. *B. W. Hills* 73

LELISE (IRE) 3 b.f. Milk of The Barley 115 – Frolic (Good Times (ITY)) [1994 –: 7m 6.1s 1995 8m6 6.1m 11.9m Jun 1] sparely-made filly: has finished behind all 51 of her opponents. *A. P. Jarvis* –

LENNOX LADY 2 b.f. (May 2) Dominion Royale 112 – Balgownie 43 (Prince Tenderfoot (USA) 126) [1995 8g 7.1g 8.3g Sep 25] fourth foal: half-sister to 3-y-o Kirkie Cross (by Efisio): dam middle-distance winner: tailed off in maidens and a claimer in Scotland. *R. M. McKellar* –

LENNOX LEWIS 3 b.c. Superpower 113 – Song's Best (Never So Bold 135) [1994 93: 6d 5f2 5m* 6m* 6m* 6m5 6g3 1995 6m5 6g2 6g 5m4 6g 7m 6m6 6m2 6g5 5.2d4 6d Oct 19] good-quartered colt: has a quick action: useful performer: best efforts when in frame in listed events at Haydock and Sandown, then when second of 14 to Double Blue in Great St Wilfrid Handicap at Ripon: well below form last 2 starts, as if something amiss final one: stays 6f: acts on good to firm ground, possibly not on dead: genuine. *A. P. Jarvis* 100

LEONINE (IRE) 2 gr.c. (Apr 27) Danehill (USA) 126 – Inanna 105 (Persian Bold 123) [1995 6m2 6g* Aug 31] IR 47,000Y: tall colt: has scope: easy mover: fifth foal: half-brother to 12.5f winner Mrs Snuggs (by Law Society) and fairly useful but irresolute Ivana (by Taufan): dam Irish 2-y-o 6f and 1m winner: useful form in maidens at York: short-headed by Desert Boy in 8-runner event then landed odds in 5-runner race 2 weeks later, leading on bridle entering final 1f and running on strongly to beat Musick House 1¼ lengths: will be at least as effective at 7f+ as over 6f: sure to improve again. *P. F. I. Cole* 99 p

LEONTIOS (IRE) 3 b.c. Alzao (USA) 117 – Akamantis 97 (Kris 135) [1994 72p: 6g 7f5 8.2g5 1995 10m5 Apr 20] good-bodied colt: carries condition: progressive form in maidens at 2 yrs: respectable fifth of 10 in handicap at Newmarket, only start at 3 yrs: will stay at least 1½m: sold 10,000 gns Newmarket Autumn Sales. *M. H. Tompkins* 65 +

LEPINE (IRE) 4 ch.g. Tate Gallery (USA) 117 – Riverine (FR) (Riverman (USA) 131) [1994 80: 5d* 6d 5f 6f* 6m* 6m4 6g 6m 6d 5g3 1995 5m 6g2 6f3 6g 6m3 5f2 5m3 5g6 5f Oct 14] small, sturdy gelding: fair handicapper: best effort at 4 yrs when beaten a neck in £10,800 race at Haydock: stays 6f, at least as effective at 5f: acts on firm and dead ground: visored/blinkered since fifth 4-y-o start: often sweats freely: front runner: usually early to post: sold only 7,500 gns Newmarket Autumn Sales: sent to Sweden. *J. W. Watts* 78

LER CRU (IRE) 6 b.g. Lafontaine (USA) 117 – Kirsova (Absalom 128) [1994 –: 11.6m a9.4g 10m 7d 1995 11.6m Aug 7] strong-quartered, deep-bodied gelding: no longer of much account. *J. Ffitch-Heyes* –

LES BOYER 4 b.c. Midyan (USA) 124 – Debutante 78 (Silly Season 127) [1994 113: 8.1d³ 7g 8m⁴ 8g* 8g* 7.5g² 9g² 8g* 8v² 8v* 1995 8g³ 8f⁴ 8d² 8s* 8m⁵ 8s* 8d⁴ 10d⁶ Oct 29] close-coupled, quite attractive colt: smart Italian-trained performer: ran creditably when placed in Prix Edmond Blanc at Saint-Cloud and listed event at Milan prior to winning 7-runner Premio Emilio Turati at Milan (by 4½ lengths from Lavinia Fontana) in June: easy winner of minor race and respectable fourth of 11 to Nicolotte in Group 1 event at Milan in the autumn: stays 1m: acts on heavy going. *G. Botti, Italy* 113

LESLEY'S FASHION 4 ro.f. Dominion 123 – Firelighter (Kalaglow 132) [1994 66: 10m⁴ 11.5g⁶ 10g* 10g 1995 10.3m⁵ 10g 10m 9f 10m Aug 13] leggy, sparely-made filly: fair handicapper: good efforts when in mid-division in £10,500 event at Chester on reappearance and £45,900 event at Sandown third start: effective at 1¼m, probably at 11.5f: acts on good to firm ground, unraced on soft surface since debut. *D. J. S. ffrench Davis* 67

LE SORCIER 3 ch.g. Prince Des Coeurs (USA) – Pink N' Perky 56 (Tickled Pink 114) [1994 –: 7.6v 6m 8g 1995 9m 10m Jul 10] plain, workmanlike gelding: well beaten on flat. *G. P. Enright* –

LE SPORT 2 b.g. (Mar 20) Dowsing (USA) 124 – Tendency 77 (Ballad Rock 122) [1995 5.1m⁵ 6d 8m a7g* Dec 9] 3,000F: leggy, lengthy gelding: third foal: brother to 3-y-o 7f winner Dowdency: dam 4-y-o 6f winner: trained by D. Nicholls first 2 starts: 33/1, won 7-runner minor event at Wolverhampton in December by head from Victim of Love, pair clear: stays 7f (pulled very hard over 1m): clearly goes well on fibresand. *A. Bailey* 52 + a76

LE TEMERAIRE 9 b.g. Top Ville 129 – La Mirande (FR) (Le Fabuleux 133) [1994 43: a12g³ a11g⁵ a12g⁵ 10d 12.1g⁴ 12g⁴ 12g 12f⁴ 12m⁵ 13.8g⁵ 10g⁵ 12.1m 12f⁶ 12g 1995 12.3f 12m 12f⁵ 10.3m a14g Nov 16] sturdy gelding: probably of little account nowadays. *Don Enrico Incisa* –

LE TETEU (FR) 2 b.c. (Apr 12) Saint Andrews (FR) 128§ – Nouvelle Star (USA) (Star de Naskra (USA)) [1995 6.1d Sep 11] 84,000 francs F, 9,200Y: rather leggy, close-coupled colt: third foal: dam 1m to 10.5f winner in France: 20/1, burly and green, around 11 lengths ninth of 20, never dangerous, to Ocean Grove in maiden at Nottingham, keeping on not knocked about: will improve, particularly over further than 6f. *Bob Jones* – p

LETLUCE 2 b.f. (Jan 19) Aragon 118 – Childish Prank (Teenoso (USA) 135) [1995 7g* 7m⁶ Aug 16] 10,000Y: smallish, well-made filly: second foal: dam unraced daughter of smart Joking Apart: won maiden auction at Leicester in July by 1½ lengths from White Sea: similar form when sixth of 8 in minor event at Kempton month later. *J. R. Arnold* 73

LE TOURRON (FR) 2 b.c. (Jun 2) Kaldoun (FR) 122 – Orangerie (USA) (Arctic Tern (USA) 126) [1995 7g⁴ 7.5g* 8g⁴ 8s⁵ 8m⁴ 9d³ 10g² 9s² Dec 5] third foal: half-brother to a winner in Belgium by Always Fair: dam, 11.5f winner in French provinces, half-sister to very smart French middle-distance filly Ode: useful French colt: won minor event at Deauville in August: good efforts last 2 starts, beaten neck by Polar Lights in minor event at Saint-Cloud and ½ length by Supreme Commander in listed race at Evry: will stay beyond 1¼m: acts on soft ground: blinkered twice. *E. Lellouche, France* 109

LE TRITON (USA) 2 b.c. (Feb 27) El Gran Senor (USA) 136 – La Tritona (Touching Wood (USA) 127) [1995 8g* 8s⁴ 8s* 8m⁴ Oct 15] 550,000 francs Y: quite attractive colt: first foal: dam 1¼m to 12.5f winner in France (including Group 3), half-sister to Japan Cup winner Le Glorieux: smart performer: successful in newcomers race at Deauville in August and 6-runner Prix La Rochette at Longchamp (by 2½ lengths from Cliptomania, making all) in September: fourth in pattern events otherwise, around a length behind Loup Solitaire in 8-runner Grand Criterium at Longchamp last time: will be well suited by middle distances: acts on good to firm ground and soft. *Mme C. Head, France* 111

LETSBEONESTABOUTIT 9 b.g. Petong 126 – My Bushbaby 100 (Hul A Hul 124) [1994 63d: a6g⁶ a7g⁴ a8g a7g⁴ a7g³ a8g a7g* a7g⁴ 6s a7g a7g² a7g a6g 7f 10m 56 d a7g 6g^{2} 7g a7g 1995 a6g a6g* a6g^{6} a7g a6g^{3} a7g^{3} a7g^{4} a6g a7g^{6} a8.5g a7g^{4} 8g a7g^{5} Jun 10] tall, strong gelding: bad mover: modest performer: won minor event at Wolverhampton in January: sold out of Mrs N. Macauley's stable 1,000 gns Ascot May Sales after tenth start: stays 7f: unsuited by very soft ground, acts on any other including all-weather surfaces: normally blinkered or visored: inconsistent: sent to Belgium. *Miss Gay Kelleway*

LET'S GET LOST 6 ch.g. Chief Singer 131 – Lost In France 80 (Northfields (USA)) [1994 72: 12g 10d^{3} 10d* 12.4m^{6} 12m 12m^{5} 10.5m* 11.9m^{4} 14.6g 13.1d^{3} 11.9s 1995 a11g^{6} a11g^{4} a11g^{4} a12g^{5} 9.9m 12.5g a11g^{4} Dec 1] lengthy gelding: modest handicapper at best in 1995: trained until after second start by Mrs J. Ramsden: below form afterwards: stays 13f: acts on good to firm and dead ground (never going well on soft) and on fibresand: often wears dropped/crossed noseband: has worn bandages: blinkered (below form) once: held up: won novice hurdle in October. *J. A. Harris* – a59

LET'S HANG ON (IRE) 2 b.f. (Apr 11) Petorius 117 – Madam Slaney 92 (Prince Tenderfoot (USA) 126) [1995 a7g^{5} a7g Nov 16] IR 4,000F, 6,200Y: half-sister to fairly useful stayer Aahsaylad (by Ardross) and 7f winner Friar Street (by Carmelite House): dam 7.9f to 1¼m winner: soundly beaten in median auction maiden (in July) and a seller at Southwell. *W. W. Haigh* –

LETTERLUNA 3 ch.f. Shavian 125 – Alteza Real 84 (Mansingh (USA) 120) [1994 NR 1995 8.3m^{5} Jun 26] angular filly: eighth live foal: half-sister to several winners, including useful 1987 2-y-o sprinter Infanta Real (by Formidable): dam, 5f winner, is half-sister to Forzando: always-prominent fifth of 18 to Felitza in maiden at Windsor: looked capable of better. *D. R. Gandolfo* 53

LEVEL EDGE 4 b.f. Beveled (USA) – Luaga 49 (Tyrnavos 129) [1994 55: 7d^{4} 6m^{6} 7g^{2} 7m a7g^{6} 8g^{5} 8d* a7g* a8.5g^{5} a7g 1995 a8g a8g 8m^{6} 8g 8g 8f^{6} a9.4g^{3} a9.4g^{6} 10g^{5} 11.9m Oct 5] leggy filly: modest handicapper: left M. Johnston's stable after second 4-y-o start: effective at 7f to 9.4f: acts on all-weather surfaces, best turf efforts on an easy surface: sold (M. Hammond to H. Alexander) 1,400 gns Doncaster November Sales. *M. D. Hammond* 39 a51

LEXUS (IRE) 7 b.g. Gorytus (USA) 132 – Pepi Image (USA) 111 (National) [1994 38: 8d^{2} 10.1f^{5} 11.1m^{2} 11.1f^{2} 12m^{5} 11.1m^{2} 9.7m^{6} 1995 a10g^{3} a10g^{5} a8g^{4} a10g a11g 10.8g^{3} 10f^{4} 12g Sep 28] good-bodied gelding: poor handicapper nowadays: stays 11f: acts on firm ground, soft and all-weather surfaces: seems effective blinkered or not. *R. J. R. Williams* 31 a39

LIA FAIL (IRE) 2 b.f. (May 23) Soviet Lad (USA) 94 – Sympathy 77 (Precocious 126) [1995 5m^{2} 6.1m^{6} 6m 6f 6f^{5} Oct 24] IR 3,400Y: leggy, angular filly: third foal: dam 7f winner at 3 yrs (her only start) out of half-sister to very smart middle-distance performer John French: modest form: short-head second of 7 in maiden auction at Ripon: appeared to run very well when in mid-division in valuable restricted race at the Curragh on third start: should stay 7f. *R. Hollinshead* 56 +

LIBERATRICE (FR) 2 b.f. (Jan 22) Assert 134 – Liberale (FR) (Fabulous Dancer (USA) 124) [1995 7g Oct 23] sixth reported foal: half-sister to useful French 1989 2-y-o 5.5f winner Zinarelle (by Zino), later 7f winner, and a winner in Belgium: dam won from 6f (at 2 yrs) to 1½m in France: 25/1, always towards rear on favoured far side in maiden at Lingfield: probably needs time and distance. *J. L. Dunlop* – p

LIDANNA 2 b.f. (Feb 1) Nicholas (USA) 111 – Shapely Test (USA) (Elocutionist (USA)) [1995 6g^{3} 5m* 6.3m^{2} Sep 2] 13,000Y: half-sister to several winners including fair 5-y-o Birchwood Sun (by Bluebird), winner at up to 7f: dam Irish 1m winner: progressive Irish filly: won maiden at Tipperary in August: 1½ lengths second of 5 to Woodborough in Anglesey Stakes at the Curragh 9 days later: should stay at least 7f: yet to race on a soft surface: sure to improve further. *D. Hanley, Ireland* 103 p

LIDHAMA (USA) 3 b.f. Sword Dance – Running Melody 86 (Rheingold 137) [1994 NR 1995 7m 8.3m 7f 7.1d 9.7g^{3} 12m^{2} 12m Nov 6] big, strong, good-topped filly: has a round action: fourth reported foal: half-sister to useful 7.1f and 1m winner Waikiki Beach (by Fighting Fit) and fairly useful 6f and 7f winner Rocky Waters (by Rocky Marriage): dam 1m and 1¼m winner: fair handicapper, improved form after being stepped up in trip: stays 1½m: acts on good to firm ground. *G. Lewis* 66

LIEFLING (USA) 2 b.f. (Mar 21) Alleged (USA) 138 – Mata Cara 98 (Storm Bird (CAN) 134) [1995 7m Nov 3] first foal: dam (7f winner) daughter of Fatah Flare: 10/1, sweating and bandaged behind, chased stand-side leaders around 5f when eleventh of 18 to Wahiba Sands in maiden at Doncaster in November: will do better. *J. H. M. Gosden* – p

LIFE'S A BREEZE 6 b.g. Aragon 118 – Zahira (What A Guest 119) [1994 –, a52: a6g^3 a6g^2 a6g* a6g 5v^4 a6g^5 a5g^4 a5g* a5g^3 a5g^5 a6g a6g^4 1995 a6g a6g^6 5d a7g Dec 12] close-coupled gelding: modest all-weather handicapper: no form in 1995, leaving P. Felgate after third start. *R. Lee* –

LIFE'S TOO SHORT (IRE) 4 br.f. Astronef 116 – Quality of Life (Auction Ring (USA) 123) [1994 49: 6m^3 8.1f^2 7m 8m 10f^3 10m^2 6.1s 1995 8f^2 8g 7g 9.7f Jun 30] sturdy filly: poor handicapper: well below form after reappearance: stays 1¼m: acts on firm ground: tried blinkered when out of form. *J. E. Banks* 49 d

LIFFEYSIDE LEADER (IRE) 4 ch.f. Exhibitioner 111 – Cheerleader 90 (Floribunda 136) [1994 NR 1995 a10g a10g Jan 28] half-sister to several winners here and in Italy, including modest 1990 2-y-o 5f to 7f winner Panama Pete and 1¼m winner Another Wish (both by Horage): dam 2-y-o 5.1f winner later successful in Italy, is half-sister to On Your Mark: behind in maiden and claimer at Lingfield. *H. J. Collingridge* –

LIFT BOY (USA) 6 b.g. Fighting Fit (USA) – Pressure Seat (USA) (Ginistrelli (USA) 117) [1994 –, a55: a6g a6g^2 a6g^3 a5g^3 a5g^3 5v^6 5g 5g^6 1995 a6g* a5g^3 a6g^2 a6g^4 5.3m 7f 5g* 5m^6 a5g a5g^6 a6g^5 Nov 30] small, sturdy gelding: fair performer on the all-weather: won claimer at Wolverhampton in January: lightly raced on turf since 1992, showing poor form to win selling handicap at Lingfield in May: effective at 5f to 7f: acts on all-weather surfaces and good to firm and soft ground: visored (no improvement) twice at 2 yrs. *A. Moore* 48 a66

LIGHT FANTASTIC 3 gr.f. Deploy 131 – La Nureyeva (USA) 83 (Nureyev (USA) 131) [1994 NR 1995 8m^2 a8g^5 Nov 29] fifth foal: half-sister to 1m winner Very Bold (by Never So Bold) and 4-y-o Reason To Dance (by Damister), 5.1f and 5.7f winner at 2 yrs better suited by 1m+: dam, stayed 1m, half-sister to William Hill Futurity second Cock Robin: close second of 7 in maiden at Brighton: soundly beaten in minor event at Lingfield nearly 6 months later. *R. Charlton* 66

LIGHT MOVEMENT (IRE) 5 br.g. Thatching 131 – Annie Albright (USA) (Verbatim (USA)) [1994 –: 10.4d 6.1g 5d 1995 7g 5.9m 5m 6m a5g a6g Nov 24] strong, compact, good-bodied gelding: little worthwhile form. *W. S. Cunningham* –

LIGHTNING QUEST (IRE) 4 b.g. Rainbow Quest (USA) 134 – Rare Roberta (USA) 118 (Roberto (USA) 131) [1994 42: 12.3d 12.3d 8g 9m^6 10m^3 10g 10g^6 14.1f* 13.6m^2 15.8g 1995 a12g 16.2m 14.1m 14.1f^4 13g 14.1m 12f^3 12m^4 16.2g^5 13.6f Oct 12] tall, close-coupled gelding: poor performer: should stay 2m: acts on firm and soft ground: tried blinkered: sold 5,000 gns Doncaster November Sales. *J. S. Wainwright* 34

LIGHT REFLECTIONS 2 b.c. (Mar 26) Rainbow Quest (USA) 134 – Tajfah (USA) (Shadeed (USA) 135) [1995 7m Aug 11] rangy, attractive colt: has scope: has a long stride: second foal: dam unraced half-sister to Lead On Time and Great Commotion out of half-sister to R B Chesne: 16/1, bit backward and green, given sympathetic ride when remote seventh of 8 to Mons in listed race at Newbury, held up and dropping away well over 2f out: should do better. *B. W. Hills* – p

LIGURIAN (USA) 3 b.f. Ogygian (USA) – Ida's Image (USA) (Alydar (USA)) [1994 58: 6.1m^4 7m^4 1995 7g 6g^3 7.1m Jun 19] sparely-made filly: modest maiden: tailed off final start: stays 7f: has raced only on a sound surface: blinkered last 2 outings: has run creditably when sweating: sold 9,600 gns Newmarket December Sales. *J. W. Watts* 52

LIKE A HAWK (USA) 2 b.f. (Feb 16) Silver Hawk (USA) 123 – Like A Train (USA) (Great Sun (USA)) [1995 5.1m^5 6g* 6m^2 7g^2 8g^2 8f Nov 24] $42,000Y: leggy, good-quartered filly: good mover: half-sister to several winners in North America, including dual Grade 1 8.5f handicap winner By Land By Sea (by Sauce Boat), dam of smart 3-y-o Fahal (by Silver Hawk): won maiden at Salisbury in July: beaten ¾ length by Blushing Gleam in Prix du Calvados at Deauville then 1¼ lengths by Solar Crystal in May Hill Stakes at Doncaster (sweating and rather edgy, final start for P. 104

Cole) on last 2 outings here: well beaten in Grade 3 Miesque Stakes at Hollywood Park 2½ months later: stays 1m. *W. E. Walden, USA*

LILAC RAIN 3 b.f. Petong 126 – Dame Corley (L'Enjoleur (CAN)) [1994 41: 8s 7s 7m 8d 1995 10g a7g³ 10m a8g a12g Nov 27] angular filly: poor maiden: stays 1m: acts on fibresand and dead ground: blinkered (ran creditably) final 2-y-o start. *J. R. Arnold* 38

LILA PEDIGO (IRE) 2 b.f. (Mar 1) Classic Secret (USA) 91 – Miss Goldie Locks (Dara Monarch 128) [1995 a5g³ a5g³ a6g* 6g* 5m⁴ 6.1d a6g⁵ Oct 14] IR 5,000Y: leggy filly: first foal: dam no worthwhile form: won sellers at Wolverhampton in May and Catterick in June: poor form afterwards in nurseries and (hung badly left) a claimer: better suited by 6f than 5f: acts on fibresand: sold (J. Berry to Miss J. Craze) 3,000 gns Doncaster November Sales. *J. Berry* 56+

LILBURNE (IRE) 2 b.g. (Feb 13) Lycius (USA) 124 – Hayat (IRE) (Sadler's Wells (USA) 132) [1995 7f⁶ Jun 23] second foal: half-brother to 3-y-o Haya Ya Kefaah (by Kefaah): dam unraced close relation of smart French colt (at up to 11f) Lichine: last of 6 behind Myttons Mistake in maiden at Ayr, eased when beaten: subsequently gelded: looked likely to do better: sent to Dubai. *J. Berry* – p

L'ILE TUDY (IRE) 5 b.m. Wassl 125 – Melinte (IRE) (Caerleon (USA) 132) [1994 12g 10g 12.5g³ 12m 15.5g² 16d 13g* 12.5g* 12.1g³ 12s* 10.5v² 10v 1995 12m⁴ 12v³ 12s 12.5d⁴ 13.5g³ 12.5g⁶ 15.5g* 12.5s Sep 30] tall, leggy mare: first foal: dam unraced sister to high-class racemare (won 3 Grade 1 events) Kostroma and half-sister to Prix Saint-Alary winner Grise Mine: useful French performer: did not win at 2 yrs or 3 yrs, easily most important win at 4 yrs in listed event at Maisons-Laffitte: in frame in 1995 in Prix Maurice de Nieuil at Maisons-Laffitte and in Prix de Pomone at Deauville in the summer: won 6-runner Prix Gladiateur at Longchamp in September by ½ length from Always Aloof, leading close home: ran as if something amiss final start: effective at 1½m and stays 15.5f: acts on heavy ground, probably on good to firm. *Mme M. Bollack-Badel, France* 106

LILLIBELLA 2 b.f. (Mar 13) Reprimand 122 – Clarandal 80 (Young Generation 129) [1995 5m⁶ 6g Sep 2] tall, leggy filly: good walker: seventh foal: sister to 3-y-o Lost Realm and half-sister to 7f winner Akabusi (by Absalom) and a winner in Norway: dam 1m winner: sixth of 11 to Incarvillea in maiden at Newmarket: hung badly left and virtually pulled up in similar event (mounted on track) at Kempton 4½ months later. *I. A. Balding* 62

LILLI CLAIRE 2 ch.f. (Mar 8) Beveled (USA) – Lillicara (FR) (Caracolero (USA) 131) [1995 7f³ 6.9f⁴ 6m* 6.1d 7g* Sep 29] sparely-made filly: half-sister to several winners, including 1988 2-y-o 5f winner Charm and 7f and 1m winner Rowlandsons Gems (both by Enchantment): dam never ran: won sellers at Windsor in August and Goodwood (beat Even Handed by 4 lengths in 18-runner race) in September: stays 7f. *A. G. Foster* 70

LIMERICK PRINCESS (IRE) 2 ch.f. (May 14) Polish Patriot (USA) 128 – Princess of Nashua (Crowned Prince (USA) 128) [1995 5m 5f³ 5m² 5g* 5f 5m⁵ 6.1m⁴ 5m 5m Oct 13] workmanlike filly: closely related to useful 1994 2-y-o 5f/6f winner Limerick Belle (by Roi Danzig) and half-sister to several winners, including fairly useful sprinters It's All Academic (by Mazaad) and Elton Ledger (by Cyrano de Bergerac): dam unraced: fair performer: won maiden at Catterick in June: ran creditably next 3 starts but below form in nurseries last 2 outings: will prove best at 5f: bandaged behind on debut. *J. Berry* 68

LIMOSA 4 b.f. Jalmood (USA) 126 – Larive 80 (Blakeney 126) [1994 61: 11.7m⁵ 13.8f² 15.4m* 12m³ 14.1g⁵ 14g 15.4d 13.9d³ 16g 1995 15.4m 16f⁴ 14.9g⁶ 16.4g 14.1m Aug 21] leggy filly: modest handicapper at 3 yrs, poor at best in 1995: should stay 2m: acts on firm and dead ground: no improvement in blinkers. *R. F. Johnson Houghton* –

LIMYSKI 2 b.g. (Apr 30) Petoski 135 – Hachimitsu 39 (Vaigly Great 127) [1995 7g 8.1g Sep 1] 4,200Y: fourth foal: half-brother to 4-y-o Hi Kiki (by Rambo Dancer): dam 7f and 8.3f winner: backward, soundly beaten in maiden at Ayr (slowly away) and median auction maiden at Haydock. *Mrs A. Swinbank* –

LINCOLN TREASURE (IRE) 4 ch.g. Mon Tresor 113 – Beaded Bubbles (Simply Great (FR) 122) [1994 53, a35+: a8g 9.9m 6g 7f⁴ a7g⁴ 7g* 8m 6s 1995 10m 53 a–

14.1f 8g* 7m^6 Aug 5] small gelding: modest performer: won seller at Newmarket in July: stays 1m: acts on firm and dead ground: blinkered (below form) once at 2 yrs. *M. C. Chapman*

LINCON TWENTY ONE 2 ch.f. (May 17) Sharpo 132 – Angels Are Blue 73 (Stanford 121§) [1995 5d^3 5m Apr 15] 3,600F, 3,100Y: close-coupled filly: fourth foal: half-sister to 1991 French 2-y-o 7f winner Valiant Miss (by Valiyar): dam, 5.8f winner, half-sister to smart sprinter Polykratis: poor form in maiden auction at Folkestone and maiden at Kempton. *M. J. Haynes* 39

LINCSTONE BOY (IRE) 7 b.g. Kafu 120 – Babylon (Hello Gorgeous (USA) 128) [1994 –§: a6g a6g^5 5d^6 a5g^6 1995 a5g Mar 16] tall, plain gelding: poor sprint handicapper: stumbled badly and unseated rider on only 7-y-o start: acts on good to firm and soft ground and on fibresand: normally wears blinkers or visor: ungenuine. *Miss J. F. Craze* – §

LINDAS DELIGHT 2 b.f. (May 13) Batshoof 122 – Agreloui 59 (Tower Walk 130) [1995 6m* 7f 7.1m 6d 10g^5 8m Oct 28] 1,500F, 2,700Y, 3,000 2-y-o: good-bodied filly: half-sister to 3 winners by Absalom, including 3-y-o 1½m winner Absolute Folly and 7f to 9.4f winner Abeloni: dam lightly raced: plater: won at Windsor in July: failed to repeat that form though not discredited penultimate outing: likely to prove best at up to 1m: bandaged behind final start. *J. S. Moore* 54 d

LINDISFARNE LADY 3 b.f. Jupiter Island 126 – Harifa (Local Suitor (USA) 128) [1994 50: 5m^4 5.9f 7m^2 7.5f^5 7m 8s 7d 1995 10m 12m 11f* 14.1m^5 12.4h^2 12m^4 12.4g^3 11.5g 13.6f^4 Oct 12] leggy, angular filly: poor performer: won apprentice selling handicap at Redcar in July: stays 13.6f: acts on hard ground: carried head awkwardly sixth 3-y-o start. *Mrs M. Reveley* 45

LINE DANCER 2 b.c. (Feb 5) Shareef Dancer (USA) 135 – Note Book 94 (Mummy's Pet 125) [1995 6.1m* 6m^2 7m^3 8g^2 Nov 8] IR 50,000Y: angular, useful-looking colt: fourth foal: closely related to 2 winners, notably 3-y-o The Jotter, useful sprinter at 2 yrs: dam, 6f winner, half-sister to smart miler Long Row out of Irish 1000 Guineas winner Front Row: progressive colt: won median auction maiden at Chepstow in June: third of 8 to Mons in listed race at Newbury then 2¼ lengths second of 9 to Glory of Dancer in Gran Criterium at Milan: better suited by 1m than less: has raced only on a sound surface: will improve further. *W. Jarvis* 101 p

LINGER 3 b.f. Sharrood (USA) 124 – Waitingformargaret 78 (Kris 135) [1994 67: 6m 6d* 7g 6.5g 1995 8m 7m 7m* 7g^3 7g^6 7g^3 8g^2 Oct 3] workmanlike filly: fair performer: won handicap at Warwick in July: stays 1m: acts on good to firm and good to soft ground: sold 11,000 gns Newmarket Autumn Sales. *Lord Huntingdon* 68

LINNEY HEAD (USA) 4 b.c. Lyphard (USA) 132 – Royalivor (USA) (Sir Ivor 135) [1994 109+: 9d* 10s* 12m 1995 12g^5 13.4m^4 13.3g^3 16.4m^3 12f^5 12d^4 Oct 15] good-bodied, attractive colt: impresses in appearance: has a powerful round action: smart performer: reportedly fractured a cannon bone final 3-y-o start (subsequently off course 11 months) and wrenched a front shoe off second outing in 1995: best effort when under ¾-length fourth of 8 to Court of Honour in Gran Premio del Jockey Club Italiano at Milan on final start, always chasing winner: probably stays 16.4f: has useful form on good to firm ground, but best with some give and acts on soft: normally tracks pace: sent to Dubai. *J. H. M. Gosden* 113

LINOISE (FR) 3 b.f. Caerwent 123 – Lineo (Gift Card (FR) 124) [1994 7d^3 7d^2 6s^5 1995 8g 6m* 5.5g^2 5m* 6g^2 6g 6d^4 Sep 11] fourth foal: half-sister to winners in France (between 9f and 10.5f) by Fabulous Dancer and Mille Balles: dam French 4f to 1m winner, is half-sister to smart miler Gracioso: useful French filly: successful in minor event in May and listed race (by ½ length from Ya Malak) in June, both at Evry: ran well when ½-length second of 4 to Diffident in Prix de Ris-Orangis there, leading over 1f out to close home: below form afterwards: stays 7f, best form as a sprinter: acts on good to firm ground and dead. *E. Le Guen, France* 108

LINPAC WEST 9 b.h. Posse (USA) 130 – North Page (FR) 81 (Northfields (USA)) [1994 107: 12m^2 10s* 14g 12.5s^3 10s^6 12v^6 12v^3 1995 12g^6 14.1g^2 11.9d 13.3d Sep 16] lengthy, angular horse: poor mover: just a useful performer nowadays: easily best 9-y-o start when second of 6 in steadily-run minor event at Nottingham in April: ran as if something amiss final outing: effective at 1¼m when conditions are testing and stays 1¾m: best on an easy surface and goes well in the mud: held up: sometimes edges under pressure, but is game. *C. W. C. Elsey* 100

LIONEL EDWARDS (IRE) 2 b.g. (Mar 19) Polish Patriot (USA) 128 – Western Heights (Shirley Heights 130) [1995 6g5 6.1m3 6.1m3 7.5m3 a7g3 Sep 4] 17,000Y, 33,000 2-y-o: quite attractive gelding: first foal: dam unraced half-sister to smart middle-distance filly Startino: fair form in maidens: will stay further than 7.5f: consistent. *P. F. I. Cole* 73

LION TOWER 3 b.c. Soviet Star (USA) 128 – Percy's Lass 120§ (Blakeney 126) [1994 NR 1995 9g3 10.5g2 Sep 22] smallish, deep-girthed, attractive colt: third foal: half-brother to reluctant 1994 3-y-o Morpeth (by Sadler's Wells) and very useful 1m and 1¼m winner Blue Lion (by Lomond): dam, 6f (at 2 yrs) to 11.1f winner who became temperamental, from very good family: fairly useful form in maidens won by Triquetti at Lingfield and Merry Festival at Haydock (edged left) 4 months apart: stays 10.5f: edgy and coltish at Haydock: sent to Dubai. *H. R. A. Cecil* 82

LIPIZZANER (IRE) 3 b.c. Tirol 127 – Olderfleet 59 (Steel Heart 128) [1994 80: 6g 6f2 6m3 6g* 7.1g6 1995 8m4 7m2 7g2 8m 7.6m* 7.3m 8g3 8.5s 7g Sep 29] good-topped colt: useful performer: won 4-runner minor event at Chester in July: below form in blinkers last 2 starts: stays 1m: acts on firm ground, possibly not on soft: sent to Dubai. *B. W. Hills* 95

LITERARY SOCIETY (USA) 2 ch.c. (May 1) Runaway Groom (CAN) – Dancing Gull (USA) (Northern Dancer) [1995 5g6 5d3 Sep 13] $52,000F, $67,000Y: small, sturdy colt: ninth foal: half-brother to several winners in USA, including a 2-y-o stakes winner by Rahy: dam unraced half-sister to very smart Irish middle-distance performer Nemain: sixth of 9 in minor event at Doncaster, never reaching leaders: made much of running when 4 lengths third of 11 to First Maite in maiden at Beverley over 2 months later: may do better. *J. A. R. Toller* 60

LITTLE BLACK DRESS (USA) 2 b.f. (Feb 9) Black Tie Affair – Seattle Kat (USA) (Seattle Song (USA) 130) [1995 7.6d5 7g4 Oct 9] $50,000F, $40,000Y: smallish, good-topped filly: first foal: dam won at up to 1¼m in USA: just over 7 lengths fourth of 18 to Oleana in maiden at Leicester last time, keeping on under tender handling from 2f out (should have finished third, and jockey suspended for failing to obtain best placing): will stay 1¼m. *R. Charlton* 71

LITTLE BLACKFOOT 7 b.g. Sicyos (USA) 126 – Nip In The Air (USA) 114 (Northern Dancer) [1994 –: a11g a12s a12g 1995 8g 10f3 11.9m5 14.1m Aug 12] workmanlike gelding: poor performer: stays 1¼m: acts on firm ground: tried blinkered and visored: inconsistent: won selling hurdle in November. *J. L. Harris* 34

LITTLE CONKER 7 ch.g. All Systems Go 119 – L'Irondelle (On Your Mark 125) [1994 NR 1995 16.2m6 Aug 10] workmanlike, close-coupled gelding: of no account. *A. Smith* –

LITTLE HOOLIGAN 4 b. or br.g. Rabdan 129 – Nutwood Emma (Henbit (USA) 130) [1994 47: 8.3d 8m6 8f 5m6 6m5 a5g* 5.9h2 6f2 7f4 6g5 6m4 6m4 6g 6g2 6s 5d6 5.1g 6.9m5 1995 5.3m 7m May 4] small gelding: has a round action: poor handicapper: soundly beaten in 1995: sold 675 gns Ascot June Sales: stays 6.9f: acts on hard and dead ground: usually visored: won over hurdles for G. Edwards in August and October. *J. Akehurst* –

LITTLE IBNR 4 b.g. Formidable (USA) 125 – Zalatia 97 (Music Boy 124) [1994 58, a71: a6g4 8g 7f2 a7g3 6m2 6m4 5g2 a7g2 6g2 a5g3 a5g a6g4 a6g* a6g* a6g4 a6g2 1995 a7g2 a7g* a6g* a7g* a6g a7g 6g 7g 5.1d4 6s2 6d 5.1m* 5m a6g3 a7g a6g* Dec 12] workmanlike gelding: fairly useful performer on the all-weather, successful in handicaps at Wolverhampton (twice) and Southwell in January/February and in claimer at Wolverhampton in December: fair on turf, and won 26-runner minor event at Nottingham in October: effective at 5f to 7f: acts on firm and soft ground and goes well on all-weather surfaces: has won in blinkers and run respectably in a visor, but not tried in 1995: has been bandaged and worn tongue strap: often a front runner: genuine. *P. D. Evans* 64 a91

LITTLE KENNY 2 b.f. (Mar 25) Warning 136 – Tarvie 101 (Swing Easy (USA) 126) [1995 6m6 6.1m 6m 6.1d5 7d Sep 26] 5,200Y: sister to a poor maiden, closely related to 1989 2-y-o 5f winner Regal Peace (by Known Fact) and half-sister to several winners, including very speedy 1985 2-y-o Stalker (by Kala Shikari): dam sprinter: modest maiden: gave impression something amiss when tailed off in nursery at Brighton final start: stays 6f. *M. J. Fetherston-Godley* 50

LITTLE LUCKY 2 b.f. (Apr 27) Weldnaas (USA) 112 – Classy Nancy (USA) (Cutlass (USA)) [1995 5.2m 5f3 Aug 11] 3,500F, 5,600Y: leggy filly: half-sister to useful sprinter Bold Lez (by Never So Bold): dam won at up to 6f in USA: third of 6 in maiden at Folkestone: dead. *G. Lewis* 52

LITTLE LUKE (IRE) 4 b.c. Somethingfabulous (USA) – Yours Sincerely (USA) (Stalwart (USA)) [1994 52: a10g3 a10g 12s 11.9d 12m6 11.6g* 10d3 11.4g2 14.1m 11.6m4 12m 10d 12g 12m 1995 a12g Jan 26] angular, sparely-made colt: modest middle-distance handicapper: soundly beaten in 1995. *P. Butler* –

LITTLE MILLIE 2 b.f. (Apr 24) Colmore Row 111 – Little Kraker 69 (Godswalk (USA) 130) [1995 6m 6.1d5 6d Oct 19] leggy filly: first foal: dam best at up to 1¼m: seemed to run quite well when fifth to Chalamont in minor event at Chepstow on second start but no other form: bandaged near-hind final outing. *P. Hayward* –

LITTLE MINER (IRE) 4 b. or br.f. Miner's Lamp 114 – Hot Sauce (Hot Spark 126) [1994 –: a8.5g a8g 11.9g a10g a11g 1995 a11g5 Jan 6] no form on flat since 1993: has joined I. Jones. *B. Palling* –

LITTLE MISS RIBOT 5 b.m. Lighter 111 – Little Missile (Ile de Bourbon (USA) 133) [1994 45: a10g a8g a6g a6g4 a6g4 a8g3 6m5 8g 7d5 7g2 8m* 8f3 9.7m2 10f2 10d a12g 1995 a10g a10g* a10g* a10g4 12m Aug 27] lengthy mare: poor handicapper: won at Lingfield in January and February: off course 6 months, well beaten in NH jockeys race at Goodwood on final start: stays 1¼m: acts on equitrack: best efforts on turf on a sound surface: held up. *R. J. O'Sullivan* – a37

LITTLE NOGGINS (IRE) 2 b.f. (Apr 5) Salt Dome (USA) – Calash (Indian King (USA) 128) [1995 5m* 6m* 5m 5g3 6m5 5.2f4 Oct 25] leggy filly: third reported foal: half-sister to 3-y-o 5.7f to 7f winner Master Millfield (by Prince Rupert): dam half-sister to very useful 1983 2-y-o 7f winner Knoxville: won median auction event at Beverley (only outing for John Berry) in July and claimer at Lingfield in August: carried head high when below form on firm ground final start: stays 6f: ridden by 7-lb claimer fifth start. *C. A. Dwyer* 78

LITTLE PILGRIM 2 b.c. (Apr 29) Precocious 126 – Bonny Bright Eyes 58 (Rarity 129) [1995 6s6 6f 6m Nov 6] strong, lengthy colt: has scope: sixth foal: half-brother to 1994 2-y-o 5f winner Willrack Farrier (by Lugana Beach) and a winner in France by Reach: dam poor plater: around 11 lengths sixth of 11 to Midnight Blue in maiden at Ascot, leading at good gallop 4f then fading: well beaten afterwards in auction events at Pontefract and Folkestone. *T. M. Jones* 62 ?

LITTLE REDWING 3 ch.f. Be My Chief (USA) 122 – Forward Rally 84 (Formidable (USA) 125) [1994 NR 1995 10m Apr 19] fourth foal: half-sister to 1m to 1¾m winner Broughtons Formula (by Night Shift) and French 4-y-o middle-distance winner Boniterro (by Bustino): dam 8.2f to 1¼m winner: about 20 lengths eighth of 16 in maiden at Pontefract, green and never dangerous. *Mrs J. Cecil* –

LITTLE SABOTEUR 6 ch.m. Prince Sabo 123 – Shoot To Win (FR) (Rabdan 129) [1994 65, a70: a5g 5.7f 6f6 5m* 5d3 a5g2 5.1d a5g5 a5g2 1995 a5g3 a5g* a5g4 a5g2 5m a5g4 5m4 a6g3 a7g a5g5 a5g a6g Nov 25] useful-looking mare: fair handicapper: won claimer at Lingfield in January: well beaten last 4 starts: effective at 5f and 6f: acts on good to firm and soft going and goes well on the all-weather: effective blinkered or not: ran poorly when sweating: usually bandaged near-hind. *P. J. Makin* 59 a75

LITTLE SCARLETT 3 b.f. Mazilier (USA) 107 – Scarlett Holly 81 (Red Sunset 120) [1994 54: 6g a8g2 a8.5g3 a8.5g3 a7g4 1995 a8g6 a8g2 a8.5g* a9.4g a10g5 a8.5g* Dec 12] small filly: modest performer: won seller at Wolverhampton in April and handicap there in December: stays 8.5f: acts on the all-weather. *P. J. Makin* 53

LITTLE SECRET (IRE) 3 ch.g. Waajib 121 – Talking Shop (General Assembly (USA)) [1994 –: 7f 8.5m 7s 1995 10.8m 12.5f May 8] rather leggy gelding: of no account. *T. M. Jones* –

LITTLE SERENA 5 b.m. Primitive Rising (USA) 113 – Navos (Tyrnavos 129) [1994 NR 1995 13.4d Sep 20] angular mare: first foal: dam winning hurdler: well beaten in maiden at Chester. *W. M. Brisbourne* –

LITTLE SHEFFORD 3 ch.g. Ballacashtal (CAN) – Wolstenbury (Lochnager 132) [1994 –: 7g 5.7g 1995 10.2m 10g 8m 10f Jun 29] leggy gelding: no form. *D. J. S. ffrench Davis* –

LITTLE TYSON (IRE) 3 b.g. Gale Yaka 87 – Avionne 59 (Derrylin 115) [1994 NR 1995 a6g 7f May 11] first reported foal: dam successful over 1m on Flat and in 5 selling contests at around 2m over hurdles: no sign of ability. *J. J. Bridger* –

LITTLE WILMA 3 b.f. Zalazl (USA) 120 – Miss Sanur (Mummy's Pet 125) [1994 NR 1995 a8.5g² 6.1m⁶ a7g May 15] small filly: second foal: dam, unraced, out of a 2-y-o 7f winner who stayed 1½m: poor form in sellers: tailed off in claimer final start. *A. P. Jarvis* 41

LITUUS (USA) 2 gr. or ro.c. (Feb 28) El Gran Senor (USA) 136 – Liturgism (USA) (Native Charger) [1995 7m Nov 3] $220,000F: good-topped colt: sixth foal: brother to smart 6f (at 2 yrs) to 1¼m winner Young Senor and half-brother to 3 winners here and abroad, including fairly useful middle-distance stayer Eastern Diamond (by Diamond Shoal): dam, minor stakes winner in USA at up to 9f, is half-sister to Grade 1 winner at up to 1¼m Coup de Fusil: favourite though burly and green, slowly away and never a threat in 18-runner maiden at Doncaster won by Wahiba Sands: had blanket for stalls entry: will do better. *J. H. M. Gosden* – p

LIVE PROJECT (IRE) 3 b.g. Project Manager 111 – Saturday Live (Junius (USA) 124) [1994 5s³ 5v 7d⁶ 1995 7v* 7s 7g 7m² 7s 5g 8g a7g² a7g a8g⁴ a7g a7g Dec 12] sparely-made ex-Irish gelding: first live foal: dam fairly useful Irish sprinter: fair performer: trained by J. Bolger until after fifth 3-y-o start, winning maiden at Down Royal in March: best efforts here on the all-weather at Lingfield: stays 1m: acts on good to firm and heavy ground and on equitrack. *M. Johnston* 77 d

LIVIO (USA) 4 b.g. Lyphard (USA) 132 – Make Change (USA) (Roberto (USA) 131) [1994 –: 8m 8m 1995 11.9d Oct 11] good-topped gelding: fair winning (21f) hurdler: no promise on return to flat: blinkered (signs of temperament) second 3-y-o start. *L. Lungo* –

LLIA 3 b.f. Shirley Heights 130 – Llyn Gwynant 115 (Persian Bold 123) [1994 87p: 7g⁴ 7d* 8d⁴ 1995 10m³ 12g⁵ 12m⁵ Jul 22] lengthy filly: useful performer: good staying-on third of 8 to Musetta in listed race at Newmarket in May: somewhat flattered (could be rated 101) when 2¼ lengths last of 5 in Prix de Royaumont at Saint-Cloud (making much of running) following month: dropped out long way from home in listed race at Newmarket on only subsequent start: stayed 1½m: did not race on extremes of going: stud. *J. L. Dunlop* 94

LLOC 3 b.f. Absalom 128 – Nosey 96 (Nebbiolo 125) [1994 79d: 5s* 5v³ 5g⁴ 5m 5f³ 5f⁵ 5g² 5m⁶ 5.3g³ 6m a6g 1995 5d 5g a5g⁴ 5g⁵ a5g 5m⁵ 5g⁴ a5g² 5m³ 5g 5.1d a5g 6f Oct 23] neat, good-quartered filly: seems just a modest handicapper nowadays: trained until after ninth 3-y-o outing by John Berry: speedy, and best at 5f: acts on fibresand and any turf going: no improvement in visor or blinkers: usually races prominently. *C. A. Dwyer* 52

LOBANA (IRE) 3 b.f. Fairy King (USA) – Sable Lake (Thatching 131) [1994 NR 1995 7m 8g May 19] 40,000Y: angular filly: fourth foal: closely related to a winner in Spain and half-sister to a winner in Germany/Norway: dam Irish maiden, showed some form at 2 yrs: no worthwhile form in maidens at Newbury in the spring, carrying head high on debut, hanging left under pressure next time: sent to UAE. *J. W. Hills* –

LOBILIO (USA) 6 b.g. Robellino (USA) 127 – Nabila (USA) 58 (Foolish Pleasure (USA)) [1994 66§: a12g³ a12g³ 12.5d³ 12.1g 12.1g 1995 a14.8g Jan 4] well-made gelding: fair handicapper: well beaten only run in 1995: suited by middle distances: acted on good to firm ground, soft and fibresand: normally visored or blinkered: was not one to trust: dead. *D. Burchell* – §

LOBKOV 3 ch.f. Dunbeath (USA) 127 – Lucy Manette 53 (Final Straw 127) [1994 –: 5.3g 1995 10m Aug 14] leggy, sparely-made filly: well beaten in sellers. *R. Curtis* –

LOCAL HEROINE 5 ch.m. Clantime 101 – Hollia 72 (Touch Boy 109) [1994 62: a5g⁶ 5g 5.1d⁶ 5g³ 5f* 5f² 5m⁴ 5m 5f⁵ 5m⁶ 5g⁴ 5.1g 1995 5.1d 5d 5f Oct 14] sturdy mare: modest 5f handicapper: no form in 1995: sold 1,300 gns Doncaster October Sales. *J. Berry* –

LOCH MARINER 3 b.f. Lochnager 132 – Sky Mariner 59 (Julio Mariner 127) [1994 –: 5d⁶ 5d 5m 6s 1995 5g Sep 2] workmanlike filly: seems of little account: tried –

blinkered: sold (J. L. Eyre to S. Campion) 1,500 gns Doncaster September Sales. *J. L. Eyre*

LOCHON 4 br.g. Lochnager 132 – Sky Mariner 59 (Julio Mariner 127) [1994 65: 6g^{2} 5d^{3} 6g^{6} 6d* 6f^{2} 5.9f^{6} 5m^{3} 6g^{5} 5s 6g 1995 6g 5f 5m 5m* 5m^{5} 6m^{5} 6m 5g 5f^{6} 5f a5g^{3} Dec 6] compact, workmanlike gelding: modest handicapper: left W. Barker's stable after second 4-y-o start: won at Pontefract in August: effective at 5f and 6f: acts on any going: visored (raced freely and well beaten) tenth 4-y-o start: has run well when sweating. *J. L. Eyre*
61

LOCHORE 5 b.g. Nordico (USA) – Hound Song 84 (Jukebox 120) [1994 60: a8.5g* a9.4g^{4} a8.5g^{5} a8g^{3} a10g^{6} a12g^{5} 1995 10m 10f a11g^{5} 11.1g 9.9m^{5} a9.4g Jul 8] small gelding: poor mover: modest handicapper: best form at up to 8.5f: acted on good to firm and dead ground and the all-weather: blinkered final 2-y-o start: looked temperamental on occasions: dead. *Mrs V. A. Aconley*
37
a52

LOCH PATRICK 5 b.g. Beveled (USA) – Daisy Loch (Lochnager 132) [1994 104p: 5d^{4} 5m^{4} 5.1f* 5m* 1995 5g^{6} 5g* 5m 5f 5g Sep 28] well-made, really imposing gelding: useful performer: won minor event at Sandown in June by ¾ length from Lucky Parkes: easily best run afterwards when eighth in King George Stakes at Goodwood on fourth outing: effective at 5f and 6f: acts on firm and dead going: has joined M. Madgwick. *L. J. Holt*
107

LOCH STYLE 2 b.g. (Mar 26) Lochnager 132 – Simply Style (Bairn (USA) 126) [1995 a6g^{6} a8.5g^{4} a6g^{4} Dec 12] first foal: dam unraced daughter of close relative to Stilvi: similar form when fourth in maiden and seller at Wolverhampton in December: really needs further than 6f, and stays 8.5f. *R. Hollinshead*
54

LOCOROTONDO (IRE) 4 b.f. Broken Hearted 124 – Rahwah 73 (Northern Baby (CAN) 127) [1994 83: 10m 8.2m^{3} 10m^{3} 10m* 10g^{6} 10.1d* 11d* 14m^{6} 1995 10m 10m 10m 10.1g^{2} 10m a12g^{2} a12g^{4} a10g* 11m* 10g^{2} 10d^{6} 10g Oct 10] long-backed filly: has a short, round action: fair performer, best form on turf: won minor events at Lingfield (easily) and Redcar in the summer: stays 1½m: acts on good to firm and dead ground and the all-weather: usually bandaged. *M. Bell*
71
a66

LOGIE 3 ch.g. Prince Sabo 123 – Ashdown (Pharly (FR) 130) [1994 67: 5v a6g^{2} 1995 a7g^{5} a6g a7g^{2} 8.2g a8g^{5} Apr 26] lengthy gelding: modest maiden: stays 7f: acts on the all-weather: no form on turf: blinkered (stumbled, soon no threat) second 3-y-o start: sold 3,000 gns Ascot May Sales. *M. A. Jarvis*
–
a56

LOGIE PERT LAD 3 b.g. Green Ruby (USA) 104 – Rhazya (Rousillon (USA) 133) [1994 –: a6g a6g 1995 a6g 5m 6m 6m 5g 5.1m 5f 5d 7g 6.9g Oct 16] leggy gelding: little sign of ability. *J. J. Bridger*
–

LOKI (IRE) 7 ch.g. Thatching 131 – Sigym (Lord Gayle (USA) 124) [1994 92: 10s* 10m 1995 a8.5g^{6} a10g 11.4m* 12g 12g* 10d 12s a12g^{2} a12g* a12g^{4} Nov 21] strong gelding: sometimes dull in coat: fluent mover: fairly useful handicapper: back with former trainer after a spell in Ireland with D. Weld: won at Sandown (minor event) in August, Catterick in September and Lingfield in November: seems suited by around 1½m nowadays: acts on good to firm ground and equitrack, very best form on an easy surface: occasionally blinkered/visored (not in 1995): usually bandaged: held up. *G. Lewis*
87
a75

LOMAS (IRE) 4 b.c. Ela-Mana-Mou 132 – Bold Miss (Bold Lad (IRE) 133) [1994 95: 10m^{5} 1995 8.1m 9m 10.8g 7.1g^{4} 8f Jun 29] sturdy colt: fairly useful handicapper at best in 1995: best efforts at 7f, should be suited by further: acts on good to firm and dead ground. *Mrs H. Parrott*
80

LOMBARDIC (USA) 4 b.c. Private Account (USA) – If Winter Comes (USA) (Dancing Champ (USA)) [1994 90: 10d^{4} 10.3m^{3} 10g^{2} 10m^{2} 11.7f* 12f 13.9m^{2} 12m^{6} 1995 13.9m^{4} 11.9m* 11.9m* 13.9m 12g 12d^{6} Sep 26] good-topped colt: has a round action: useful handicapper: successful within a week in July in Old Newton Cup at Haydock and 3-runner rated stakes at York, making all on each occasion: below form afterwards: best form at 1½m, but stays 13.9f: acts on firm and dead ground. *Mrs J. Cecil*
95

LOMBARD SHIPS 8 ch.m. Orchestra 118 – Tina's Star (Simbir 130) [1994 55, a51: a8.5g^{5} 8m 9d^{3} 8s^{2} 8m 8m 8.2g 10s a8.5g a8g^{6} a10g a8.5g^{4} 1995 a12g Jan 7] sparely-made mare: seems on the downgrade, and well beaten (too far out to blame lack of stamina) in seller on only 8-y-o start. *A. Bailey*
–

LOMBERTO 2 b.c. (Feb 27) Robellino (USA) 127 – Lamees (USA) (Lomond (USA) 128) [1995 6m^4 7m^2 7.1d* 7.3d^5 Oct 19] 9,500F, 22,000Y: good sort: second foal: half-brother to 1994 2-y-o 5f and 6f winner Don Alvaro (by Forzando): dam unraced daughter of useful French 1¼m and 10.5f winner Vachti: stayed on in good style when winning steadily-run maiden at Sandown in September by 3½ lengths from Sunley Secure: did well to finish under 2 lengths fifth of 9 to Tumbleweed Ridge in Horris Hill Stakes at Newbury following month, in rear when steady pace quickened around 2f out: will be well suited by 1m+: acts on dead ground: very much the sort to keep improving. *R. Hannon* — 100 p

LONELY LEADER (IRE) 2 ch.c. (Apr 18) Royal Academy (USA) 130 – Queen To Conquer (USA) 112 (King's Bishop (USA)) [1995 8g^3 Sep 8] 40,000Y: good-bodied colt: good walker: half-brother to several winners, notably very useful German performer (effective at 6f, probably stayed 11f) Quebrada and useful 1988 2-y-o 6f winner Court (both by Devil's Bag): dam very useful 1m to 11f winner here, subsequently Grade 1 1¼m winner in USA: 5/1 and green, over 5 lengths third of 17 to Heron Island in maiden at Doncaster, slowly into stride, coming clear of rest entering last then eased when no chance with first two: sure to improve, and win a race. *R. Hannon* — 86 p

LONE RISK 4 b.g. Risk Me (FR) 127 – Madam de Seul 104 (Pas de Seul 133) [1994 49: a8.5g^4 a8.5g* a8g^4 a9.4g* a9.4g^5 a9.4g^4 a9.4g* a9.4g^6 10.8v* 12s a12g^2 a12g^4 a12g^3 a12g^2 12.1g 14.1g^2 1995 a14.8g^2 a14.8g^6 12.5g^3 a12g a14.8g 15.8g a14g Nov 6] neat gelding: has a round action: modest performer: trained by M. Pipe first 2 starts at 4 yrs: well beaten after rejoining former trainer: stays 14.8f: acts on heavy ground and fibresand: blinkered once in 1993: sometimes wears tongue strap and (reportedly resented it second 4-y-o start) brush pricker: sold 1,100 gns Doncaster November Sales. *C. N. Allen* — 58 d

LONESOME TRAIN (USA) 6 ch.g. Crafty Prospector (USA) – Alaki Miss (USA) (Olden Times) [1994 –: 8g^6 1995 8g Sep 14] sturdy gelding: modest middle-distance handicapper (rated 52) at 3 yrs for J. Gosden: very lightly raced and no worthwhile form on flat since: useful hurdler, winner in November. *C. Weedon* — –

LONGCROFT 3 ch.f. Weldnaas (USA) 112 – Najariya (Northfields (USA)) [1994 35: 5g 5d 6.1g^4 1995 7g a7g 8.2m 10m 10m^4 13.1g* 12m 14.1f^6 11f^5 11.1m^4 12g^4 Jul 17] leggy, sparely-made filly: poor performer: won claimer at Ayr in June: probably stays 1¾m: acts on firm going: has been bandaged: none too consistent. *K. W. Hogg, Isle of Man* — 40

LONG FURLONG 7 b.g. Castle Keep 121 – Myrtlegrove (Scottish Rifle 127) [1994 50: a10g a13g^3 10g^6 10m 9g^2 9.7m* 10f^4 12s^3 a10g^6 1995 a12g* a12g^3 a12g a12g^5 a12g^3 a10g Sep 5] leggy gelding: poor performer: won handicap at Lingfield in January: claimed out of R. Akehurst's stable £4,000 next start: stayed 1½m: acted on the all-weather and any turf going: below form blinkered/visored: sometimes found little: dead. *J. R. Bosley* — 50

LONGHILL BOY 2 b.g. (May 9) Statoblest 120 – Summer Eve 63 (Hotfoot 126) [1995 5m 6f 5g^5 6g Sep 20] 6,600F, 7,600Y: leggy gelding: fourth foal: half-brother to a 2-y-o winner in Holland by Chilibang: dam maiden suited by 6f: apparently best effort in maiden events when equal-ninth of 16 to Eastern Paradise at Brighton final start: flashed tail penultimate outing. *B. J. Meehan* — 55 ?

LONGING (USA) 2 ch.f. (Feb 8) Lyphard's Wish (FR) 124 – Fussiness (USA) (L'Enjoleur (CAN)) [1995 7g* 8g^4 Sep 8] leggy filly: unimpressive mover: first foal: dam unraced half-sister to several winners here and abroad, including smart middle-distance performer Noelino and high-class 1m to 1½m performer Little Bonny: won maiden at Newcastle in August by 4 lengths from Fikra: one-paced 4½ lengths fourth of 5 behind Bonarelli in listed race at Goodwood following month: will stay beyond 1m: sent to USA. *D. R. Loder* — 86

LON ISA 4 ch.f. Grey Desire 115 – Stripanoora (Ahonoora 122) [1994 –: 8.2d 10.8m^6 10.2f 11.8m 10m^5 a8.5g 10d 1995 a7g a12g^2 a13g^3 a12g^2 a12g a16g^3 Mar 29] lengthy filly: modest maiden: stays 1½m: acts on dead ground and equitrack. *B. Palling* — 50

LOOKINGFORARAINBOW (IRE) 7 ch.g. Godswalk (USA) 130 – Bridget Folly (Crofter (USA) 124) [1994 84: a14g a9.4g^5 8m 11.9g^4 16m 12m^3 11.9f* 12m* 12m^2 11.9f* 13.9m 10.1d^6 14m 12v 12v 1995 14.9d 12m 12.3m^4 12g^5 12g* 12m^3 — 80

12m^2 12m^3 11.9f^4 12g^5 6m^6 10m 14.8m^6 Aug 25] close-coupled gelding: fairly useful handicapper: won at Thirsk in June: effective at 1½m and probably stays 2m: acts on any turf going (particularly effective on top-of-the-ground) and on the all-weather: takes good hold, and usually held up: has hung and found little: needs strong handling, and well ridden by M. Wigham: tough. *Bob Jones*

LORD ADVOCATE 7 br.g. Law Society (USA) 130 – Kereolle (Riverman (USA) 131) [1994 –§: a16.2g 15.1m^3 15.1m^5 10.9g 15.1m 15.1m 15.1g 1995 14.1f^3 11.1g* 14.1m^2 13f* 13f 11.1m^2 12.1m^6 11.1m^3 11.1f^6 15.1f^5 12f^4 13f^3 13f^4 12.1f^3 12.1m* 12.1g 12.1g Sep 25] workmanlike gelding: very poor mover: poor handicapper: made all at Hamilton in May (seller) and June and at Edinburgh in August: stays 2m: acts on firm ground, dead and the all-weather: usually blinkered/ visored: sometimes forces pace. *D. A. Nolan* — 42 §

LORD ALFIE 6 ch.g. Beveled (USA) – Fair Nic (Romancero 100) [1994 54: 7g^3 8.2m 7g 1995 7m 8g 8g 7m Jun 17] tall, sparely-made gelding: modest handicapper: no form since 5-y-o reappearance. *R. J. Meehan* — –

LORDAN VELVET (IRE) 3 br.g. Lord Americo – Danny's Miracle (Superlative 118) [1994 52: 6m 6d^4 5g^5 7g 6s 1995 11.1f 7m^5 5.9f^6 Jul 31] neat gelding: poor maiden here: sold 2,400 gns Doncaster August Sales: won over 11.5f in Norway in September. *L. Lungo* — 37

LORD BARNARD (IRE) 5 gr.g. Toca Madera 111 – Avital (Pitskelly 122) [1994 16g 14g 12d 10v 5g^5 7d 6s^5 1995 7g 6d^5 a6g Nov 24] ex-Irish gelding: third foal: brother to useful 1994 3-y-o maiden Little Musgrave and closely related to modest miler Zeppeki (by Taufan): dam never ran: lightly raced and poor form: first run for 6 months when fifth of 25 in apprentice handicap at the Curragh: very stiff task, behind in claimer at Southwell 17 days later: should stay 7f: has joined C. Murray. *J. E. Mulhern, Ireland* — 38

LORD CORNELIOUS 2 b.c. (May 26) Lochnager 132 – Title (Brigadier Gerard 144) [1995 5f^4 Jul 7] third foal: dam well beaten: tailed off in 4-runner median auction maiden at Hamilton. *D. A. Nolan* — –

LORD ELLANGOWAN (IRE) 2 ch.c. (May 4) Astronef 116 – Gossip (Sharp Edge 123) [1995 5s 6.9g a8g Nov 8] 5,600Y, 4,800 2-y-o: small colt: brother to 1993 2-y-o 6f winner Celestial Rumour and half-brother to 3 winners here and abroad, including 1992 2-y-o 6f winner Gymcrak Tiger (by Colmore Row): dam no sign of ability: soundly beaten in maidens and maiden auction. *R. Ingram* — –

LORD FREDERICK 3 b.g. Wonderful Surprise 93 – Romany Framboise (Amboise 113) [1994 NR 1995 a9.4g 11.9m^6 Jul 7] good-topped gelding: first reported foal: dam never ran: last in claimers at Wolverhampton and Haydock. *Miss S. J. Wilton* — –

LORD GLENVARA (IRE) 7 ch.g. Millfontaine 114 – Ishtar (Dike (USA)) [1994 46: 11.5d 7.6v 8m a13g a10g^4 1995 10.8g Oct 3] workmanlike gelding: blinkered, well beaten only flat outing in 1995: won selling hurdle in October. *T. P. McGovern* — –

LORD HASTIE (USA) 7 b.g. Affirmed (USA) – Sheika (USA) (Minnesota Mac) [1994 NR 1995 9.9m 13g a16g 14g^4 16.5g 14.6g^3 12.4m* 12.3f* 13f^2 11.9m^4 12d 12.1g^2 11.9s* 12m^6 12m^4 Nov 4] tall, rather leggy gelding: modest handicapper: won at Newcastle and Ripon in July and at Haydock in October: good fourth in November Handicap at Doncaster final start: effective at 1½m to 2m: acts on any turf going and on fibresand: blinkered (winner) once in 1992: tends to hang left and sometimes wears near-side pricker: game and consistent. *C. W. Thornton* — 63

LORD HIGH ADMIRAL (CAN) 7 b.g. Bering 136 – Baltic Sea (CAN) (Danzig (USA)) [1994 95: 6s 5.2s^3 5d^6 5m* 5m^4 5m^6 5g 5.6g 5s^2 1995 5.2m 5m^3 5g 5g* 5m* 5.6m 5g^6 5s Oct 7] tall, leggy gelding: impresses in appearance: useful performer on his day: visored first time, won 17-runner handicap at Haydock (for second year running) in May: unchallenged when landing the odds in claimer (claimed out of M. Heaton-Ellis' stable £15,000) at Sandown following month: well below form afterwards: best at 5f: acts on soft ground and good to firm: visored/ blinkered last 5 starts: has run creditably sweating: taken down alone: goes well for M. Roberts: often front runner: has returned to M. Heaton-Ellis. *C. R. Egerton* — 95 d

LORD JIM (IRE) 3 b.c. Kahyasi 130 – Sarah Georgina 79 (Persian Bold 123) [1994 75: 7f 8.1g^5 10.2g^4 8g 1995 11.8s* 12m^4 13.9m^4 14m^3 16.2m 14.6m^2 15g^6 13.3d a12g^4 Dec 2] good-bodied colt: useful performer: made all in maiden at Leicester in March: best efforts in minor events fourth and sixth outings: stays 14.6f: acts on good to firm and soft ground, probably on fibresand: none too consistent. *Miss Gay Kelleway* — 96

LORD LAMBSON 6 b.g. Today And Tomorrow 78 – Sum Star 67 (Comedy Star (USA) 121) [1994 –: 9.9d 12.4m 1995 8.9g Oct 7] tall gelding: poor maiden: lightly raced and no form since 1993. *J. Pearce* — –

LORD OBERON (IRE) 7 b.g. Fairy King (USA) – Vaguely Jade (Corvaro (USA) 124) [1994 62: 8m 8v 8g 8.1g 10.8f 8f* 8m^5 8.1g* 8.2m^3 8d^3 8s 8d^5 8m 10d^6 1995 8.1m* 8g^2 8.1m* 8f^6 8.2m^4 Aug 21] lengthy gelding: carries condition: modest handicapper: won at Chepstow in July and Haydock (made all) in August: effective at 1m to 1¼m: acts on firm and soft ground, twice below form on heavy: visored earlier in career. *J. Akehurst* — 64

LORD OF A DANCE 4 b.c. Night Shift (USA) – Toot Toot 59 (Alias Smith (USA)) [1994 60: 8g^5 10d 10.1m^6 1995 10d^6 9.2g May 4] sturdy colt: modest maiden, very lightly raced: signs of retaining a little ability for new stable in 1995: should prove suited by further than 1¼m: well beaten only start on top-of-the-ground. *W. J. Haggas* — 49

LORD OF MEN 2 ch.c. (Mar 8) Groom Dancer (USA) 128 – Upper Strata 109 (Shirley Heights 130) [1995 7g^6 7m* 7.6m* 7s* Sep 17] — 116 p

For the first time since 1970 the French won only one (the Grand Criterium) of their four Group 1 two-year-old races open to colts: the Prix Morny (won by Tagula), the Prix de la Salamandre (Lord of Men) and the Criterium de Saint-Cloud (Polaris Flight) all fell to British raiders. The French have supplied the joint or outright official champion two-year-old on seven occasions since their inclusion in the International Classification in 1978, but the form of their best colts was well below standard in 1995. Indeed, the first French runner home in both the Morny and the Salamandre was the filly With Fascination, while the first seven home the Grand Criterium, which Loup Solitaire won by a short head, were covered by little more than three lengths.

The field lined up against Lord of Men in the Salamandre at Longchamp in September was just stronger than the Grand Criterium, and certainly as good as the one Tagula had beaten in the Morny at Deauville in August. It included With

Prix de la Salamandre, Longchamp—
Lord of Men makes significant improvement to beat the French filly With Fascination

Sheikh Mohammed's "Lord of Men"

Fascination and third-placed Barricade from the Morny, the pair separated there by a fast-diminishing three quarters of a length, as well as the promising Titus Livius, a four-length winner of the five-furlong Prix d'Arenberg, and another good British challenger, Woodborough, who'd finished a length and a half behind Danehill Dancer in the Phoenix Stakes before being sent back to Ireland to win the Anglesey. Lord of Men, winner of a maiden race at Newmarket and a three-runner minor event at Lingfield in August on his last two starts, hadn't yet encountered pattern-class rivals, but he'd made considerable improvement in the short time since his debut in July and his eight-length demolition of the useful Sava River at Lingfield suggested that, at the very least, he wouldn't be outclassed. Those who supported Lord of Men on the French tote at odds of 6/1 were always on good terms with themselves for he was soon in good position and came home a length ahead of With Fascination after a ding-dong tussle from the turn into the straight. For much of that time there was a great deal less between the pair as the front-running With Fascination held the call travelling smoothly, but in the last hundred yards the filly's stamina began to give out and Lord of Men stayed on strongly to win going away. None of the five other runners threatened seriously to catch the first two: Woodborough, the very early leader, finished two lengths back in third after being slightly short of room at one stage, then came the non-staying Titus Livius and the disappointing favourite Barricade who seemed ill-at-ease on the soft ground. Lord of Men had either the Dewhurst or the Grand Criterium as his final objective of the season but apparently met with a minor set-back. Had he been sent for the Grand Criterium in the form he was in in the Salamandre he'd probably have won that as well.

Lord of Men (ch.c. Mar 8, 1993)	Groom Dancer (USA) (b 1984)	Blushing Groom (ch 1974)	Red God
			Runaway Bride
		Featherhill (b 1978)	Lyphard
			Lady Berry
	Upper Strata (b 1985)	Shirley Heights (b 1975)	Mill Reef
			Hardiemma
		Bright Landing (ch 1978)	Sun Prince
			Land Ho

Given that Lord of Men's sire Groom Dancer was sold to Japan in 1994 cynics might have seen it as inevitable that 1995 would provide him with another Group 1 winner. His first two crops include the Prix Maurice de Gheest winner Pursuit of Love, Chester Vase winner Twist And Turn and the Prix Jean Prat winner Le Balafre, but the decision to sell him abroad was made after two less fruitful crops which yielded only one pattern victory, that of the Prix des Chenes winner Coco Passion. Groom Dancer disappointed in the Derby and Arc de Triomphe but won five pattern races in all at up to ten and a half furlongs and was a high-class performer who possessed an excellent turn of foot. Lord of Men's dam Upper Strata was an altogether different type of horse, one who relished a mile and a quarter as a two-year-old and long distances and enterprising tactics as a four-year-old (she never ran at three after suffering an injury to a tendon). Lord of Men is her third foal and second winner following the 1994 Prix de Diane runner-up Her Ladyship (by Polish Precedent), a winner over ten and a half furlongs; she has since had another foal by Polish Precedent and one by Wolfhound. In racing character Upper Strata resembled her sire Shirley Heights much more than most members of her female family; Bright Landing, for instance, was placed over five furlongs as a two-year-old, Land Ho produced the very speedy two-year-old Easy Landing and Lord of Men's fourth dam Lucasland won the July Cup as did her half-brother So Blessed. Incidentally, Lucasland managed to breed a Lingfield Oaks Trial winner, Lucent, when put to the Irish Derby winner Irish Ball, but, more in the family tradition, she is also the third dam of the top-class miler Sonic Lady. Lord of Men looks a good bet both to stay a mile and a half and make further improvement as a three-year-old. His stable provided the second and third in the 1995 Derby and the genuine Lord of Men looks the type to put up a good show at Epsom, or in the Prix du Jockey-Club if connections opt for Chantilly. A robust colt who acts on good to firm ground and soft, he has worn a crossed noseband and was equipped with a blanket for stalls entry for all his races in Britain. *J. H. M. Gosden*

LORD OLIVIER (IRE) 5 b.g. The Noble Player (USA) 126 – Burkina (African Sky 124) [1994 98: 6g* 6m 6m^{5} 6m 6f^{4} 6f^{4} 6m^{2} 1995 6g^{6} 6m 6m 6f^{4} 6m^{2} 6m 5.6m 6g 6g Oct 7] strong gelding: usually looks well: bad mover: useful handicapper: none too consistent in 1995: gelded after third outing: best effort when ¾-length second of 20 to Tiler in £15,000 contest at York in August: stays 6f: very best efforts on a sound surface: no improvement in blinkers. *W. Jarvis* — 98

LORD PALMERSTON (USA) 3 b.g. Hawkster (USA) – First Minister (USA) (Deputy Minister (CAN)) [1994 70: 7g^{6} 8s^{5} 1995 10m 8.3g 12m 8h^{6} Aug 8] tall, close-coupled gelding: fair form as 2-y-o: no worthwhile form in 1995: headstrong, taken early to post and has worn dropped noseband: sold (P. Cole to K. Morgan) 6,800 gns Newmarket September Sales. *P. F. I. Cole* — –

LORD SKY 4 b.g. Emarati (USA) 74 – Summer Sky 75 (Skyliner 117) [1994 72d: 5m^{3} 5.7m* 5.1g 6g 5s 5d 1995 a5g* a6g^{2} a5g 5g 5m 5.1m 5g 5.1g a6g^{4} 5g 5.1d a5g^{4} a5g^{6} Dec 14] leggy gelding: fairly useful handicapper on the all-weather: landed gamble at Wolverhampton in February: modest form at best on turf in 1995: effective at 5f and 6f: acts on good to firm and soft ground and the all-weather: no improvement in blinkers/visor. *A. Bailey* — 61 d / a84 d

LORD VIVIENNE (IRE) 6 b.g. Don't Forget Me 127 – Lady Vivienne (Golden Fleece (USA) 133) [1994 NR 1995 a7g 6.9f 9.9m^{3} 10m^{3} 7.5g^{2} 8.5m^{4} 6f 8m 9.2f^{5} 8d^{6} Sep 22] lengthy gelding: poor performer: sold out of J. Charlton's stable 2,000 gns Doncaster May Sales after reappearance: stayed 1¼m: acted on firm and dead ground: temperamental: tried in blinkers, and various other equipment: dead. *B. S. Rothwell* — 43 §

LORD WELLINGTON (IRE) 4 b.g. Taufan (USA) 119 – Merrie Laughter (Morston (FR) 125) [1994 30: 11.6g^{6} 11.6g 11.6m 10g^{5} 12g^{3} 11.5m^{5} 1995 a12g 11.9f May 11] leggy, dipped-backed gelding: bad maiden handicapper: stays 1½m: acts on firm ground. *J. R. Jenkins* — –

LORE 3 ch.f. Bairn (USA) 126 – Lorelene (FR) 97 (Lorenzaccio 130) [1994 NR 1995 a7g 6f Jul 12] half-sister to several winners, all at 1m+, including 2m winner Thunderheart (by Celestial Storm) and (at up to 13f) Latvian (by Rousillon): dam, 1¼m to 1½m winner, second in Ebor: bought out of L. Cumani's stable 3,700 gns Newmarket Autumn (1994) Sales: well beaten in claimers. *R. Ingram* — –

LORELEI LEE (IRE) 3 ch.f. Old Vic 136 – Most Amusing (Blushing Groom (FR) 131) [1994 7g 1995 5d^5 6.9m^2 5m 7m 8.5d* 8m 10g 8.5g* 8.5m^3 8f 6.9f 9m^3 10f^3 8.9g^5 8.5d 8.3g a6g Nov 20] small, plain ex-Irish filly: first foal: dam unraced half-sister to Saratoga Six and Dunbeath: tailed off on only outing at 2 yrs for M. Kauntze: modest form here: narrowly won maiden and apprentice handicap at Beverley in the summer: well below form last 5 starts: stays 9f well: acts on good to firm and dead ground: sold 3,500 gns Newmarket December Sales. *John Berry*
64

LORETTA GIANNI (FR) 3 b.f. Classic Account 69 – Seasonal Pleasure (USA) (Graustark) [1994 8g^2 7.5d* 8d^3 8v^4 1995 10.5g^2 10.5g^2 10.5m 10m^6 8d^3 10.5g^3 10.5d^5 8d^6 Dec 2] first foal: dam unraced half-sister to several winners: useful French filly: won minor event at Evry and fourth in Prix des Chenes at 2 yrs: second in Prix Penelope (behind Muncie) and Prix Cleopatre (behind Valley of Gold), both at Saint-Cloud in the spring: comfortably best of last 5 starts when 2¾ lengths third of 7 to Tamise in Prix de Flore there: stays 10.5f: acts on good to firm ground and heavy. *D. Smaga, France*
107

LORINS GOLD 5 ch.g. Rich Charlie 117 – Woolcana 71 (Some Hand 119) [1994 48d: 5.3g^6 5g^2 5.7g 6v 5.1m 6m 5.1m 5f^5 6f 6m^6 5.1d^3 5s 5.1g^3 1995 5m 5.7f^5 6f^5 6m 6m^5 7.1m 6f 8m^3 Aug 27] well-made gelding: tends to look dull in coat: poor maiden handicapper: disappointing since 1993: stays 1m: acts on firm and dead going, below form on very soft: effective blinkered or not: usually races prominently. *Andrew Turnell*
36

LORSANGINNER (IRE) 3 b.f. Contract Law (USA) 108 – Castleforbes (Thatching 131) [1994 NR 1995 7m Apr 21] 7,000Y: half-sister to modest 5f and 6f winner Hello Hobson's (by Fayruz) and a champion in Czechoslovakia: dam a twin: unimpressive to post and tailed off in maiden at Newbury. *S. Dow*
–

LOS ALAMOS 2 b.f. (Apr 12) Keen 116 – Washita (Valiyar 129) [1995 5g^3 7.9m 8.1s^4 a8g^3 a8.5g^3 Nov 27] neat filly: second foal: half-sister to 3-y-o Last Roundup (by Good Times), 7f winner at 2 yrs: dam poor maiden: fair form last 3 starts: stays 8.5f: acts on soft ground and fibresand: one paced. *C. W. Thornton*
67

LOST LAGOON (USA) 3 ch.c. Riverman (USA) 131 – Lost Virtue (USA) (Cloudy Dawn (USA)) [1994 NR 1995 10m^4 Aug 9] leggy, close-coupled colt: brother to high-class 1m/1¼m performer All At Sea, also second in Oaks, and half-brother to numerous winners, notably Free Handicap winner Over The Ocean (by Super Concorde) and useful 4-y-o 9f/1¼m winner Quandary (by Blushing Groom): dam, unraced, from family of Damascus: weak in market and bandaged, shaped well when 2¾ lengths fourth of 18 to Polydamas in maiden at Sandown, disputing lead 2f out until inside last: moved poorly to post: looked sure to improve. *H. R. A. Cecil*
83 p

LOST REALM 3 b.g. Reprimand 122 – Clarandal 80 (Young Generation 129) [1994 NR 1995 14g Oct 23] 17,000Y, 15,000 2-y-o: sixth foal: half-brother to 7f winner Akabusi (by Absalom) and a winner in Norway: dam 1m winner: tailed off in maiden at Lingfield. *Martyn Meade*
–

LOTHLORIEN (USA) 2 ch.f. (Jan 30) Woodman (USA) 126 – Fairy Dancer (USA) 94 (Nijinsky (CAN) 138) [1995 7.1s^2 Oct 17] $250,000Y: fifth foal: half-sister to 3 winners, including 1¾m winner Wand (by Reference Point) and Irish 7f and 9f winner Adjudicate (by Law Society): dam twice-raced 6f winner, closely related to Sadler's Wells: 4/1, beaten a head by Ski For Gold in 19-runner maiden at Chepstow, losing position slightly around halfway then staying on well: should improve. *P. W. Chapple-Hyam*
76 p

LOTTIES BID 3 b.f. Ring Bidder 88 – Gleneagle 91 (Swing Easy (USA) 126) [1994 NR 1995 a7g^6 a7g^5 a6g^4 6s 5d Sep 13] big, workmanlike filly: half-sister to several winners, including 6f winner Melodic Drive (by Sizzling Melody): dam 5f and 6f winner: poor form on fibresand, including in sellers: well beaten both outings on turf: effective at 6f, and should stay 1m. *P. S. Felgate*
–
a45

LOUGH ERNE 3 b.f. Never So Bold 135 – Laugharne (Known Fact (USA) 135) [1994 –: 6g 1995 6g 6m^4 6m^3 6m^5 6g^2 6m 6g 7s Sep 28] tall, useful-looking filly: fair handicapper: should stay beyond 6f: acts on good to firm ground. *C. F. Wall*
73

LOUISIANA PURCHASE 2 b.g. (Mar 12) Macmillion 110 – My Charade 79 (Cawston's Clown 113) [1995 7m 7.1g 10.2m Sep 25] tall, unfurnished gelding:
–

brother to 4-y-o stayer Tommy Cooper and winning stayer Smilingatstrangers: dam 1¾m winner: well beaten in maidens at Salisbury, Sandown (tongue tied down) and Bath (slowly away): headstrong. *Mrs Barbara Waring*

LOUIS' QUEEN (IRE) 3 b.f. Tragic Role (USA) – Bourbon Queen 77 (Ile de Bourbon (USA) 133) [1994 91: 5m* 6m* 7g* 7s* 7.5v* 7.3v 1995 8.1m^2 8g^6 8s^5 8m^6 8g^3 Nov 8] tall, quite attractive filly: useful performer: best efforts when second of 6 in listed race at Sandown on reappearance and when close third of 7 in Group 3 event at Milan in November: stays 1m: acts on good to firm ground and heavy: stays in training. *J. L. Dunlop* — 102

LOUISVILLE BELLE (IRE) 6 ch.m. Ahonoora 122 – Lomond Fairy (Lomond (USA) 128) [1994 61d: 8s^5 7d 7.3s^5 8.1m 7.1m^5 7g 7.1g 9v 1995 8m^5 7f 6.1g^2 5.7m^5 6m* 6m^4 6m^3 6m 7.1m^3 6d 5g^4 5g 7m Oct 28] small, sturdy mare: modest handicapper: won at Windsor in June: effective at 5f to 1m: acts on good to firm and soft ground: usually bandaged: often claimer ridden: inconsistent. *M. D. I. Usher* — 59

LOUP SOLITAIRE (USA) 2 b.c. (Mar 1) Lear Fan (USA) 130 – Louveterie (USA) 123 (Nureyev (USA) 131) [1995 8m^2 8g^3 8m* Oct 15] — 113 p

After attracting a four-runner turn-out the previous season, the smallest field for well over sixty years, the Grand Criterium was restored to its traditional place in the French Calendar in 1995; it had formed part of the Arc-weekend programme since 1989. The return to the later date originally failed to attract a larger field, though, with only four engaged until they were joined by supplementary entries Astor Place and Committal from Britain and Andre Fabre's Loup Solitaire. A twice-raced maiden facing six last-time-out winners, Loup Solitaire was sent off the outsider of the field. He had chased home his stable-companion Radevore in a newcomers race at Longchamp in September and then finished third to Eternity Range (who was to renew rivalry in the Criterium) in a minor event at Saint-Cloud later in the month. Loup Solitaire's stable-companion Manninamix started a short-priced favourite for the Criterium after his win in the Prix des Chenes. The Criquette Head stable supplied the two other home runners, Le Triton, winner of the Prix La Rochette, and Dark Nile, winner of his only start. Astor Place and Committal both took a big step up after winning maidens at Newmarket and York.

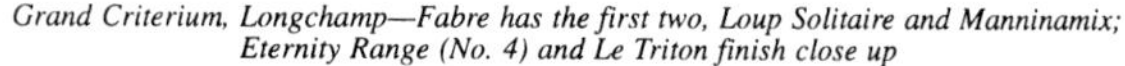

Grand Criterium, Longchamp—Fabre has the first two, Loup Solitaire and Manninamix; Eternity Range (No. 4) and Le Triton finish close up

Loup Solitaire held a good position throughout, settled off the strong pace set by Le Triton on the unseasonably-firmish going, with Manninamix tucked in behind. Le Triton maintained his lead to halfway up the straight where Loup Solitaire was asked for his effort. Meanwhile Manninamix was pulled out from behind his stable-companion, taking a while to find his stride, but, once he did, a close struggle ensued with Loup Solitaire responding gamely to hold on by a short head in a nip-and-tuck finish. Eternity Range stayed on well a length behind in third with Le Triton a nose back in fourth. The whole field was covered by just over three lengths at the line despite the race being truly run.

So for the second year running Fabre saddled the first two in the Grand Criterium; for the second year running owner Jean-Luc Lagardere saw his representative in the race beaten by a stable-companion. The previous year, Walk On Mix had suffered the same fate as Manninamix, while in 1989 their sire Linamix, also owned by Lagardere, had himself finished runner-up in the race, beaten by Jade Robbery who was also trained by Fabre. The Grand Criterium has been a happier race for Loup Solitaire's owner Daniel Wildenstein; he had won it twice before, with Yelapa in 1968 and Lost World in 1993. Fabre, Wildenstein and jockey Peslier were also completing a notable double in the top French two-year-old races, having won the Prix Marcel Boussac with Miss Tahiti a fortnight earlier.

Loup Solitaire (USA) (b.c. Mar 1, 1993)	Lear Fan (USA) (b 1981)	Roberto (b 1969)	Hail To Reason
			Bramalea
		Wac (b 1969)	Lt Stevens
			Belthazar
	Louveterie (USA) (ch 1986)	Nureyev (b 1977)	Northern Dancer
			Special
		Lupe (b 1967)	Primera
			Alcoa

For different reasons, Loup Solitaire's parents can both be considered unlucky not to have won a classic. High-class miler though he was, Loup Solitaire's

Daniel Wildenstein's "Loup Solitaire"

sire Lear Fan was foaled in the same year as El Gran Senor and Chief Singer to whom he finished third in an exceptional Two Thousand Guineas. Two of Lear Fan's best performers have run for Wildenstein, namely Criterium de Saint-Cloud winner Glaieul and Prix de l'Opera winner Verveine. Loup Solitaire's dam Louveterie was one of the worst sufferers in a rough Prix de Diane, but despite a buffeting was beaten only a short neck by Lady In Silver. She had won her only start at two, the Prix Vanteaux on her return at three and was short-headed in the Prix Saint-Alary prior to the Diane, but suffered a career-ending injury on the gallops after it. Her first foal, by Alysheba, failed by a long way in two starts to live up to her name of L'Ideale. Loup Solitaire is her second, while her yearling (a colt named Loup Sauvage) and foal are both by Riverman. The next dam Lupe won six of her seven starts, notably the Oaks and Coronation Cup, and has produced a string of pattern-class performers, including Earl of Sefton Stakes winner Legend of France, Prix Jean de Chaudenay winner Lascaux and Louve Romaine who, like Louveterie, was placed in both the Prix Saint-Alary and the Prix de Diane. The third dam Alcoa, a thorough stayer, was beaten a short head in the 1961 Cesarewitch.

Loup Solitaire's form is well below the level normally required to win the Grand Criterium and well below that of the best of his contemporaries in Britain. At present it is hard to see where a worthwhile French challenge for the Two Thousand Guineas will come from. There seems little to choose between the top French colts—those in the Grand Criterium and the likes of unbeaten pattern winners Spinning World and Ashkalani. The good-topped Loup Solitaire has plenty of scope for improvement, though. He will probably stay a mile and a quarter; he has yet to race on a soft surface. *A. Fabre, France*

LOVE BATETA (IRE) 2 b. or br.f. (Feb 25) Caerleon (USA) 132 – Marie Noelle (FR) 114 (Brigadier Gerard 144) [1995 7g^6 Oct 23] 35,000Y: closely related to useful 3-y-o 9f winner (best at 1½m) Triquetti (by Royal Academy) and half-sister to several winners, including Prix Marcel Boussac winner Mary Linoa (by L'Emigrant) and useful middle-distance performer Tapis Rouge (by Irish River): dam French 2-y-o 7.5f winner, later won at up to 1¼m in USA: 16/1, 5 lengths sixth of 13 to Tsarnista in maiden at Lingfield, third home on favoured far side: will do better, particularly at 1m+. *R. Hannon* **60 p**

LOVE BIRD (IRE) 2 b.g. (Mar 11) Bluebird (USA) 125 – Top Glad (USA) (I'm Glad (ARG)) [1995 6f^4 6m^5 6m 8g^5 a8g^4 Nov 10] IR 25,000Y: good-topped colt: first foal: dam won at up to 9f at 2 yrs in USA: fair maiden: fourth of 12 to Quality in nursery at Lingfield final start: will be suited by further than 1m. *M. Johnston* **73**

LOVE LEGEND 10 ch.g. Glint of Gold 128 – Sweet Emma 108 (Welsh Saint 126) [1994 64: a7g^6 a6g^3 a7g^2 a7g^3 a8.5g^3 a8.5g^4 a8.5g 5.7m 6m* 6f^2 6m^6 6.1m^6 7m^5 6g^3 5g 6m^4 6m^4 6s^4 6d 7s^6 a7g^6 6g a7g 1995 a8.5g^4 6f 7f^4 8m 8.3g 7.1m* 8m^6 7g 7.1m 8.3m^4 7.5m^4 7m^2 7m 8d^4 7g 8.2m^4 7f^4 a9.4g a8g^4 a8g^5 Nov 25] smallish, sparely-made gelding: often dull in coat: has a quick action: modest handicapper nowadays: won amateurs race at Chepstow in June: effective at 6f to 8.5f: acts on firm and dead ground and the all-weather: used to be visored (occasionally blinkered), not since 1993: sometimes bandaged. *D. W. P. Arbuthnot* **59 d**

LOVELY LYCA 3 ch.f. Night Shift (USA) – Turban 80 (Glint of Gold 128) [1994 NR 1995 7m 8.1g* 10m^2 11.4m^6 12f 11.4m^3 10.3m 10d 11.8f* 12.1s Nov 2] small, compact filly: third foal: sister to 1m/8.5f winner Barboukh and half-sister to fairly useful 1993 2-y-o 6.1f winner Tricorne (by Green Desert): dam, 1¼m winner who stayed 1½m, half-sister to Old Vic: fair performer: won maiden at Chepstow in May and minor event at Leicester in October: probably better at 1½m than 1¼m (may well stay further): acts on firm ground, possibly not on soft: sold 81,000 gns Newmarket December Sales. *J. W. Hills* **76**

LOVELY ME (IRE) 4 b.f. Vision (USA) – Self Satisfied 100 (Great Nephew 126) [1994 70: 7m^6 6m 7g^3 7d 6.1s^3 7g 6d^6 5v a5g 1995 a7g 7m^6 5f^3 5.7h 5d Sep 14] leggy filly: modest maiden handicapper: effective at 5f to 7f: acts on firm and soft ground: blinkered (below form) last 3 starts at 3 yrs: inconsistent. *R. F. Johnson Houghton* **62**

LOVELY MILLIE (IRE) 3 b.f. Bluebird (USA) 125 – Mother of The Wind 82 (Tumble Wind (USA)) [1994 97p: 6.1g* 6m* 6g* 6m^4 7.1g* 1995 7g^2 Sep 7] strong, lengthy filly: fine mover: useful performer: ran only once in 1995, but improved on **108**

2-y-o form when 2 lengths second of 12 to Branston Abby in listed race at Doncaster, leading briefly under 2f out: likely to prove best up to around 7f: has raced only on a sound surface: carries head high: sent to UAE. *D. R. Loder*

LOVELY MORNING 2 b.f. (May 6) Thowra (FR) – Sweet Pleasure 88 (Sweet Revenge 129) [1995 8d Sep 27] workmanlike filly: half-sister to several winners, including useful 1986 French 2-y-o sprinter Ma Columbine (by Jaazeiro) and 1½m and 1¾m winner Haddaaj (by Ela-Mana-Mou): dam 2-y-o 6f winner: 14/1 and bit backward, over 11 lengths ninth of 12 to White Sea in median auction maiden at Salisbury, green and never really a threat: should improve. *R. Hannon* – p

LOVELY PROSPECT 2 b.f. (Mar 21) Lycius (USA) 124 – Lovely Lagoon 68 (Mill Reef (USA) 141) [1995 7m 7.5d^2 6.9s* 8m Oct 13] 8,000Y: tall filly: third foal: half-sister to fairly useful 3-y-o 7.1f to 1½m winner Vindaloo (by Indian Ridge): dam twice-raced 11f winner: won maiden auction at Folkestone in September: stays 7.5f: equipped with rope halter on debut, when very nervy beforehand: races keenly. *R. Guest* 74

LOVE OF THE NORTH (IRE) 4 b.g. Nordico (USA) – Avec L'Amour 75 (Realm 129) [1994 43: a9.4g^4 a8.5g^4 a9.4g^5 8d 7m a12g^2 a9.4g^3 a11g a14g 1995 a9.4g a12g^3 a14.8g^5 Jul 22] leggy gelding: poor middle-distance performer: well beaten in 1995. *R. T. Juckes* –

LOVE THE BLUES 3 ch.f. Bluebird (USA) 125 – Love Match (USA) 73 (Affiliate (USA)) [1994 NR 1995 8g 10d^3 10g^6 11.8g Oct 9] strong, lengthy filly: half-sister to fair middle-distance winner Burgoyne (by Ardross), later a useful staying hurdler, and 1½m winner Valatch (by Valiyar): dam ran twice: fair maiden: should be suited by further than 11.8f. *D. Nicholson* 69

LOVEYOUMILLIONS (IRE) 3 b.c. Law Society (USA) 130 – Warning Sound (Red Alert 127) [1994 95: 5m^2 5m* 5m^2 5.2m 6d* 6g 1995 6m^4 6g^4 7m 6m 6g 7m^3 a6g^6 a7g^4 Nov 16] workmanlike colt: fairly useful performer: best effort in 1995 when fourth in Greenlands Stakes at the Curragh on reappearance: stays 7f: acts on good to firm and dead ground and on fibresand: blinkered last 6 starts. *M. Johnston* 95 d

LOVING LEGACY 4 ch.f. Caerleon (USA) 132 – Tender Loving Care 105 (Final Straw 127) [1994 67: 8m 10.3m 8m^4 8g 1995 a8.5g 10.1m^6 Jul 27] leggy filly: shaped well on first run at 2 yrs, but failed to confirm the promise: modest at best in 1995: should stay 1m: often bandaged near-hind: one to have reservations about. *W. J. Haggas* 57

LOWAWATHA 7 b.g. Dancing Brave (USA) 140 – Shorthouse 102 (Habitat 134) [1994 79, a83: a9.4g a10g^2 a9.4g^2 a10g^2 a9.4g^2 9.7s* 10.3m 10g^2 10m* 10.4f^6 10f^6 10.1m* 10.3d^5 10.4d 10.1g^3 1995 10m 10m^5 9m^4 10g Jun 12] good-topped gelding: fair handicapper at best in 1995: gave impression something amiss on reappearance: effective at 9f and remains worth another try at 1½m: goes very well on the all-weather, and acts on firm and soft ground: often has tongue tied down: races prominently: genuine: has joined Mrs. E. Heath. *D. Morris* 75

LOYALIZE (USA) 3 b.f. Nureyev (USA) 131 – Reloy (USA) 119 (Liloy (FR) 124) [1994 105: 6m^2 5m* 5f* 6d^2 6s* 6m 1995 7.3m 5m 6g^5 May 27] sturdy, attractive filly: useful performer: well beaten in Fred Darling Stakes at Newbury and 5f Palace House Stakes at Newmarket on first 2 3-y-o starts, but fared better when keeping-on fifth of 9 in £12,400 rated stakes at Haydock on final outing: should have stayed 1m: won on firm going, but best efforts on an easy surface: edgy in preliminaries in 1995: stud. *D. R. Loder* 98

LUCAYAN CAY (IRE) 4 ch.g. Al Hareb (USA) 123 – Flying Melody (Auction Ring (USA) 123) [1994 78: 7d 8m 8.5g* 10m^6 8m^2 8f 10m^2 10.1d^5 1995 10.8g Jun 7] angular, close-coupled gelding: fair performer in 1994: tailed off when pulled up and dismounted in Warwick handicap on only flat start for new stable: subsequently gelded: stays 1¼m: acts on good to firm and dead ground. *Mrs J. Pitman* –

LUCAYAN PRINCE (USA) 2 br.c. (Apr 2) Fast Play (USA) – Now That's Funny (USA) (Saratoga Six (USA)) [1995 5m* 6g^2 May 17] $55,000Y: leggy, close-coupled colt: second foal: half-brother to 8.5f stakes winner Akiba (by Tejano): dam, winner in USA, half-sister to French filly Tropicaro, winner of Prix Marcel Boussac: won maiden at Newmarket in April by 2 lengths: beaten ½ length by Dovebrace in well-contested 6-runner minor event at York following month, carrying 94 head high early then swerving left inside last when still every chance: stays 6f: reported in June to have injured knee. *D. R. Loder*

LUCAYAN SUNSHINE (USA) 3 b.f. Sunshine Forever (USA) – Be Bop A Lu (USA) (Mr Prospector (USA)) [1994 8g^4 10g^5 1995 11.9g^2 14.1f^2 11.5g^3 11.9m^3 10.5g^2 11.9g* 12s^2 Oct 6] $34,000Y: lengthy ex-French filly: second foal: half-sister to a minor winner in USA by Pancho Villa: dam won sprint maiden at 3 yrs: trained by A. Fabre at 2 yrs: fairly useful handicapper: initially looked an awkward ride here, but improved efforts last 3 starts: won handicap at Haydock (got up on post) in September: good second of 15, no match for Indigo Time, at Ascot 2 weeks later: should stay beyond 1½m: acts on firm going and soft: no improvement in blinkers: has run creditably when sweating and edgy. *Lady Herries* — 87

LUCIDITY 3 br.f. Vision (USA) – Boo Hoo 68 (Mummy's Pet 125) [1994 67: 6f^4 6g 5f^5 7m^4 6g^2 8s^5 8.1g* 1995 10.3g 10g^5 12.3m 12g a12g a12g^6 10m^2 10.5g 8g Oct 9] small, leggy filly: poor walker: has a round action: modest handicapper: stays 1½m: probably acts on any going on turf, no form on the all-weather. *C. W. Thornton* — 54 a–

LUCKNAM STYLE 7 b.g. Macmillion 110 – Mrs Currie 74 (He Loves Me 120) [1994 50: a10g^3 a8g^3 a8g a7g^6 a10g^3 a8g 9.7s 8g* 7.6m 8.3f^6 7m 8d 8g a7g 1995 8m 8.1g^5 7.6d^4 6.9f^3 8f^6 Aug 21] leggy, sparely-made gelding: poor performer: stays 1¼m: acts on firm ground: nearly always blinkered/visored nowadays: usually wears a tongue strap: often bandaged behind: inconsistent: joined L.J. Barratt. *Mrs Barbara Waring* — 42

LUCKY BEA 2 b.g. (May 8) Lochnager 132 – Knocksharry 58 (Palm Track 122) [1995 5d 5m 5m^2 5f^3 5f^2 7m 6m 6f 6m^5 10d 7f^5 8f Oct 16] 1,200Y: robust gelding: has a rounded action: fourth foal: dam sprinter: plating-class maiden: stays 7f: acts on firm going: often gives trouble at start and sometimes starts slowly: best later efforts when blinkered (only twice). *M. W. Easterby* — 50

LUCKY COIN 3 b.f. Hadeer 118 – Lucky Omen 99 (Queen's Hussar 124) [1994 68: 6m^5 7f 1995 7m 10.2m^3 10.4g^4 12m 10.1g^3 14.1f^3 11.9m* 11.5m^2 12m 12s Sep 27] quite attractive filly: fair handicapper: won at Haydock in July: stays 1¾m: acts on firm ground: has run well when sweating: sold 12,500 gns Ascot October Sales. *C. E. Brittain* — 73

LUCKY DI (USA) 3 b.c. Diesis 133 – Lucky Song (USA) 117 (Seattle Song (USA) 130) [1994 NR 1995 8d* 11g^2 Apr 22] tall, good sort: first reported foal: dam won Park Hill Stakes: won 18-runner maiden at Ripon in April: favourite, showed useful form when 1¼ lengths second of 8 to Posidonas in £8,600 contest at Newbury 17 days later, leading under 2f out until worn down last ½f: should stay 1½m: looked capable of better still: stays in training. *L. M. Cumani* — 103 p

LUCKY LEES (IRE) 2 b.c. (Apr 28) Treasure Kay 114 – Appiana (Prince Ippi (GER)) [1995 a7g^6 8.2d 10.2m Sep 25] IR 3,600Y, 1,100 2-y-o: leggy, unfurnished colt: half-brother to a winner in Austria: dam, winner in Germany (including at 2 yrs), sister to Anna Paola, leading filly at 2 yrs and 3 yrs in Germany, grandam of good 3-y-o Annus Mirabilis: well beaten in seller and 2 maidens: sold 500 gns Doncaster November Sales. *P. G. Murphy* — –

LUCKY LIONEL (USA) 2 ch.c. (Apr 9) Mt Livermore (USA) – Crafty Nan (USA) (Crafty Prospector (USA)) [1995 5m* 6f^4 5m* 6g^6 5.5g* 6g 5d^3 6g^4 Sep 28] — 109

The Norfolk winner Lucky Lionel struck the first of many blows for the British two-year-olds in their annual confrontation with the French by narrowly getting the better of the filly Shining Molly and the colt Barricade in the Prix Robert Papin at reopened Maisons-Laffitte in July. The victory, which preceded those by Tagula in the Prix Morny, Lord of Men in the Prix de la Salamandre and Polaris Flight in the Criterium de Saint-Cloud, was gained by the minimum margin, a nose, and demonstrated a good measure of courage on behalf of Lucky Lionel who rallied gamely to wrest back the advantage he'd lost to Shining Molly shortly before the post. Lucky Lionel was held up for as long as possible at Maisons-Laffitte and those tactics, which had also been employed in the Norfolk at Ascot in June, seem to suit him ideally. The Norfolk, in fact, couldn't have been set up better for Lucky Lionel: allowed to bide his time at the back as Eastern Prophets, Cayman Kai and Night Parade disputed the lead at a furious pace, he came through very strongly a furlong out to win decisively by two and a half lengths from his stable-companion Cayman Kai.

For all the battling qualities he exhibited at Maisons-Laffitte, Lucky Lionel isn't altogether predictable and his overall record is rather an in-and-out one. Already the winner of a Newmarket maiden in May, he can be excused his fourth in the Woodcote Stakes at Epsom in June on his second start as he failed to handle the track, and that in the Prix Morny at Deauville in August on his sixth on account of an unfavourable draw, but he ran below expectations in the July Stakes at Newmarket on his fourth start, eased down to finish sixth of nine behind Tagula, and to a certain extent also in the Middle Park Stakes at the same venue in October on his final start when he never threatened to take a hand and finished nearly eight lengths down on Royal Applause, in fourth place. In keeping with the general pattern of his performances, that display in the Middle Park followed his best of the season in the Flying Childers at Doncaster in September. Lucky Lionel faced no easy task at Doncaster, conceding weight to all except the Molecomb winner Almaty, and never seriously looked like getting his fourth win of the season, but he stayed on well in the last furlong and a half to get within three quarters of a length and a length and a quarter of Cayman Kai and Mubhij at the line.

Lucky Lionel (USA) (ch.c. Apr 9, 1993)	Mt Livermore (USA) (ch 1981)	Blushing Groom (ch 1974)	Red God
			Runaway Bride
		Flama Ardiente (ch 1972)	Crimson Satan
			Royal Rafale
	Crafty Nan (USA) (ch 1987)	Crafty Prospector (ch 1979)	Mr Prospector
			Real Crafty Lady
		Blake's Twin (br 1977)	Blakeney
			Regal Twin

Lucky Lionel is the first pattern winner in Britain sired by Mt Livermore. From the same Blushing Groom crop as Rainbow Quest, Mt Livermore really hit the heights as a four-year-old when he was among the best sprinters in America, winning the Grade 2 Carter Handicap over seven furlongs and finishing third in the Breeders' Cup Sprint. Based at Gainesway Farm, he has steadily been making a name for himself as a stallion in the States with the top-class sprinter Housebuster, the Breeders' Cup Juvenile Fillies winner Eliza and the Canadian Horse of The Year Peaks And Valleys among his best progeny. Lucky Lionel is the third foal from his

Norfolk Stakes, Royal Ascot—Lucky Lionel gets well on top near the finish

Prix Robert Papin, Maisons-Laffitte—a fine shot of the finish; Lucky Lionel scrapes home from Shining Molly and Barricade

dam Crafty Nan, an unraced sister to one minor winner and a three-part or half-sister to several more. Following Lucky Lionel, her first winner, Crafty Nan was covered by The Prime Minister (a son of Deputy Minister) and produced a colt who made 30,000 dollars at the 1995 Keeneland September Yearling Sale, 7,000 dollars less than Lucky Lionel had in the same ring twelve months earlier. Like her daughter, Lucky Lionel's grandam Blake's Twin never ran, but her own dam Regal Twin won over a mile as a three-year-old and is the antecedent of several speedy animals, among them the useful 1981 two-year-old filly Corley Moor and the useful sprinters Overbrook and Don't Worry Me. Lucky Lionel, a smallish, leggy colt and an easy mover, has been campaigned only at sprint distances so far, although he should stay seven furlongs. He acts on good to firm and dead ground. *R. Hannon*

LUCKY LUCAYA (USA) 3 b.f. Chief's Crown (USA) – Minstrelete (USA) (Round Table) [1994 72: 6m 5d^3 7m^2 7m* 7.1g^5 7f 8g 1995 7f 6m Aug 5] sturdy filly: good mover: fair performer at best at 2 yrs: no worthwhile form in 1995: should stay 1m: acts on good to firm ground: sold 20,000 gns Newmarket December Sales. *Lady Herries* –

LUCKY PARKES 5 b.m. Full Extent (USA) 113 – Summerhill Spruce 70 (Windjammer (USA)) [1994 98: 5.1g* 5d^6 5g* 5.1m^2 5.1g^2 5g^2 5d^4 5m* 5g^2 1995 5m^5 5.1m* 5.1m* 5f^3 5g^2 5.1g^3 5f^2 5m^3 5m^2 5.2d^5 5d^2 Sep 27] strong, lengthy, good-quartered mare: good walker: useful performer: prolific winner of minor events: unbeaten in 4 runs at Bath, and twice justified favouritism in small fields there in May: also passed post first (demoted for slight interference) at Salisbury in August: races at around 5f: acts on firm and dead ground: tends to edge left: forces pace: genuine and consistent. *J. Berry* 100

LUCKY PEG 3 b.f. Komaite (USA) – Lucky Grove 43 (Lucky Wednesday 124) [1994 40: 5f^4 5m 5g 5g 1995 a8g^3 a7g^3 8.1g^5 a8g 5f 5.9f 6m Jul 5] poor maiden: stays 1m: acts on fibresand, has raced on only on a sound surface on turf: tried blinkered. *F. J. O'Mahony* 40

LUCKY QUEST 3 b.g. Rainbow Quest (USA) 134 – Pretty Lucky 68 (Shirley Heights 130) [1994 NR 1995 10g 10g^5 10g a12g 11.4d 14d^6 Sep 27] lengthy, unfurnished gelding: second foal: half-brother to 4-y-o 1m and 1½m winner Tovarich (by Soviet Star): dam, lightly-raced maiden, stayed 1½m: fair form in maiden at Pontefract on second start: failed to repeat it: tried blinkered: sold 5,000 gns Newmarket Autumn Sales. *N. A. Graham* — 71 d

LUCKY RABBIT 2 b.c. (Mar 8) Last Tycoon 131 – Lady Philippa (IRE) 77 (Taufan (USA) 119) [1995 6m^2 6g^5 6f^3 6m^3 8m^5 8g Sep 15] 15,000Y: rather unfurnished colt: good walker and fluent mover: first foal: dam 1m and 1¼m winner: fair maiden: stays 1m: sweating third start: upset in stalls and ran poorly second outing: sold 21,000 gns Newmarket Autumn Sales: sent to Malaysia. *B. W. Hills* — 74

LUCKY REVENGE 2 b.f. (May 3) Komaite (USA) – Sweet And Lucky (Lucky Wednesday 124) [1995 5.1m^3 5.1m^3 a7g 6.1m 6f^2 6.1m^2 6m^2 6.5m Sep 6] 480Y: leggy, angular filly: second foal: sister to 3-y-o Komlucky, 6f winner at 2 yrs: dam never ran: modest maiden: runner-up in maiden auctions and seller: below form in nursery at Doncaster final start: not certain to stay 7f: poor effort (in seller) on fibresand. *Martyn Meade* — 62

LUCKY SOPH (USA) 3 b.f. Cozzene (USA) – Lucky Spell (USA) (Lucky Mel) [1994 50p: 6.1m^6 1995 7m^2 7.5d^3 8f* 8f 9h^4 Aug 2] small, unfurnished filly: fair performer: didn't need to show best form to make all in 3-runner maiden at Ayr in June: well below form afterwards: stays 1m: acts on firm and dead ground: usually bandaged behind. *B. W. Hills* — 66

LUCKY TUCKY 4 b.g. Alleging (USA) 120 – Romana 72 (Roman Warrior 132) [1994 64: 6.9v^4 8g^4 7m^2 8g* 8f 7m^3 8m^6 1995 9.7d 8m 8g 7f^4 8m^6 a8g^4 a8g Nov 20] leggy, close-coupled gelding: modest handicapper: best efforts at around 1m, should prove effective at 1¼m: acts on good to firm ground, probably on dead: ran poorly only try in a visor. *J. R. Jenkins* — 57

LUCY'S GOLD 4 b.f. Efisio 120 – Hinton Rose (Frimley Park 109) [1994 –: 6g^4 6f 6g 5m a5g^6 1995 5.1g a5g a5g 5g 6g 10m Jun 21] compact filly: poor and inconsistent sprint maiden: soundly beaten in 1995: tried blinkered and visored. *M. J. Ryan* — –

LUDGATE (USA) 3 b.f. Lyphard (USA) 132 – Hatton Gardens 96 (Auction Ring (USA) 123) [1994 82: 6m^4 7.6v^2 7.1d* 7m^4 7m 1995 10.4g* 10g^6 10d^6 9m^2 8g^4 8d^2 Nov 27] good-bodied filly: has rather a round action: useful performer: won minor event at York in May on penultimate start for R. Williams: good second in listed races at Longchamp and Saint-Cloud in the autumn: stays 10.4f well: acts on good to firm and dead ground, probably on heavy. *N. Clement, France* — 104

LUGANA BOY 2 b.g. (May 12) Lugana Beach 116 – Mischievous Tyke 50 (Flying Tyke 90) [1995 5m 6g 5f Oct 24] close-coupled gelding: first foal: dam stayed 7.5f: refused to race all 3 starts, blinkered for first of them: banned from racing on flat under Rules of Racing, November 30. *A. Smith* — §§

LUGANA VISION 3 b.f. Lugana Beach 116 – Regal Look (IRE) 46 (Vision (USA)) [1994 55d: 5v^5 a5g^3 5d^2 5f 5.2m^4 a5g^3 5m^4 6s a5g^4 1995 5m^6 6g^4 a5g^2 5g* 5m^3 6m^3 6.1m 6f^3 a6g 5m^2 5m^4 6.1d 5d 5g 5.1m Oct 19] leggy filly: modest handicapper: won at Catterick in June: left G. Fierro after seventh start and R. Harris after fourteenth one: stays 6f: acts on good to firm and dead ground and on fibresand: effective blinkered/visored or not: sold 3,100 gns Newmarket Autumn Sales: sent to Italy. *C. N. Allen* — 52 a40

LUKES BROTHER (IRE) 4 ch.g. Kirchner 110 – Golden Baby 52 (Sharpen Up 127) [1994 39: 7m a5g^6 5m^5 5m^5 7f 5.9h^5 5g^5 5f^6 6g 1995 a6g Apr 11] angular, unfurnished gelding: poor sprint maiden: well beaten only 4-y-o start: tried to unship rider (apprentice) leaving paddock final 3-y-o start. *R. F. Marvin* — –

LUNAR GRIS 2 gr.f. (Feb 9) Absalom 128 – Sliprail (USA) 86 (Our Native (USA)) [1995 6m a5g^6 6m 6f a8g Nov 6] 3,800F, 4,000Y, 6,600 2-y-o: leggy filly: poor mover: first foal: dam 10.2f winner: no worthwhile form in varied company, including selling on fibresand: has been bandaged. *J. E. Banks* — –

LUNAR MISSION (IRE) 4 b.g. Waajib 121 – Lunulae (Tumble Wind (USA)) [1994 83: 8v 8g 8.3d 7.1g* 8m 8m^6 8g* 10f* 10m^3 10f 8.1g 10d 1995 a8g 10.3m^2 8m 8.3m 10m^3 10m^6 10.1g* 10g^6 10g 10.3m^2 Oct 21] workmanlike gelding: carries — 62

condition: modest form at best in 1995: won seller at Yarmouth in September: better at 1¼m than shorter: acts on any going: tried visored, no improvement: sweating (soundly beaten) third 4-y-o start: sold 7,500 gns Newmarket Autumn Sales. *J. M. P. Eustace*

LUNAR MIST 2 b.f. (Jun 3) Komaite (USA) – Sugar Token 66 (Record Token 128) [1995 5g* 6m 6.1d⁴ 5g* 6g* 5g* 6m* 6d* Oct 21] smallish filly: fourth foal: half-sister to 5f and 6f winner Hershebar (by Stanford): dam won at 6f and 7f, including at 2 yrs: progressed really well: successful in seller at Haydock in May and autumn nurseries at Edinburgh, Haydock, Newmarket (2) and Newbury: beat Amaretto Bay by 1¼ lengths final start: stays 6f: acts on good to firm and dead ground: tough and genuine: held up and has good turn of foot. *Martyn Meade* 93 +

LUNAR PRINCE 5 b.g. Mansingh (USA) 120 – Lunate (Faraway Times (USA) 123) [1994 NR 1995 a5g a7g a8g 5.2m Jul 5] lengthy gelding: no sign of ability. *T. T. Clement* –

LUNAR RISK 5 b.g. Risk Me (FR) 127 – Moonlight Princess 49 (Alias Smith (USA)) [1994 54: 11.9d 16.4d⁴ 14f* 14g 16s 20m a16g⁴ 14g 1995 15.4g 16m⁶ 12f 11.4g² 12f 12.1m⁶ 12m Jul 26] good-bodied gelding: usually impresses in appearance: poor handicapper at best in 1995: effective at 1½m and probably stays 2m: acts on any going: visored (stiff task) once at 3 yrs: tricky ride: inconsistent. *Miss B. Sanders* 44

LUNA WELLS (IRE) 2 b.f. (Mar 2) Sadler's Wells (USA) 132 – Lunadix (FR) (Breton 130) [1995 10g* 9d* 9s² Nov 22] twelfth foal: half-sister to numerous winners, notably Poule d'Essai des Poulains winner and Champion Stakes second Linamix (by Mendez) and very smart middle-distance colt Long Mick (by Gay Mecene): dam 6f (at 2 yrs) and 1m winner: won newcomers event at Angers, and minor race at Evry before finishing short-neck second of 7 to Spinning World in Prix Saint-Roman at Evry: will be suited by 1½m: acts on soft ground: likely to improve further. *D. Sepulchre, France* 103 p

LUSO 3 b.c. Salse (USA) 128 – Lucayan Princess 111 (High Line 125) [1994 77p: 7g⁴ 1995 8g 10m² 10m⁴ 12.3m* 12m* 12d² 11.9m³ 14.6d 12d Oct 1] 120

Those unfortunate enough to have backed Luso for the Prix de l'Arc de Triomphe could have saved themselves the time and effort involved in placing the wager by putting their money down the nearest drain, for they had virtually no chance of collecting on the bet. Not because the Derby Italiano winner Luso was a no-hoper on form, even though he was one of the outsiders, but because he was in the race as pacemaker for the favourite Lammtarra, a fact which hadn't been revealed to the general public. With no other runner in the field in the same ownership or in the same stable, and with Asmussen booked to ride, who could have guessed Luso's role? Luso

Derby Italiano, Rome—Luso leads home the British raiders;
Court of Honour (spotted cap) gets past Precede (striped cap) by the line

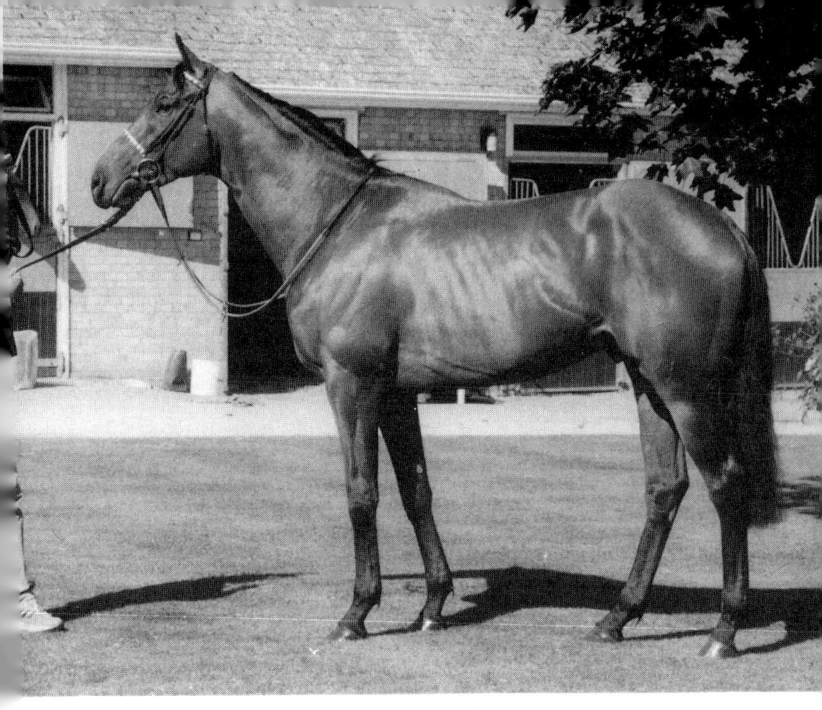

Saeed Manana's "Luso"

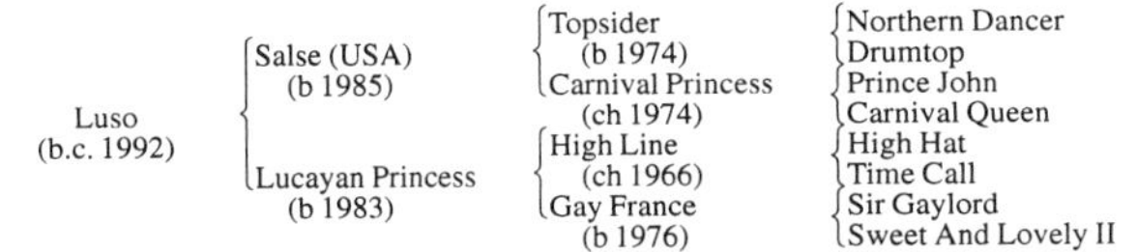

Luso (b.c. 1992)	Salse (USA) (b 1985)	Topsider (b 1974)	Northern Dancer
			Drumtop
		Carnival Princess (ch 1974)	Prince John
			Carnival Queen
	Lucayan Princess (b 1983)	High Line (ch 1966)	High Hat
			Time Call
		Gay France (b 1976)	Sir Gaylord
			Sweet And Lovely II

(blinkered for the first time) and Asmussen did their job well, setting a strong pace until approaching the straight, where Lammtarra took over. As was to be expected, Luso dropped right out of contention as his exertions took their toll. Luso had also finished down the field in his previous race, the St Leger, but on that occasion there appeared to be no excuses. It wasn't the trip, for Luso never threatened to take a hand in the finish, and he should be given another chance to show what he can do over further than one and a half miles. Luso ran well on his first four starts at that distance, winning the first two. He beat Court of Honour by a head in the Dalham Chester Vase and by one and a half lengths in the Derby Italiano in Rome, both in May. He led a furlong out in the former, and over two furlongs out in the latter after being switched to the far rail to deliver his challenge. Luso went on to show even better form in defeat on his next two outings, caught on the post by Carnegie after quickening clear early in the short straight in the Grand Prix de Saint-Cloud, then outpaced by Pentire and Singspiel, conceding weight to both, after leading until over two furlongs out in the Great Voltigeur Stakes at York.

Luso's half-brother Needle Gun (by Sure Blade) also ran in the Derby Italiano, finishing runner-up to White Muzzle in 1993. The smart Needle Gun, useful sprinter Luana (by Shaadi) and modest miler Celia Brady (by Last Tycoon) are the three other winners produced by Lucayan Princess. The very useful Lucayan Princess ran three times at two years, gaining the second of her two wins in the Sweet Solera Stakes, and once as a three-year-old, finishing third in the Cheshire Oaks. The next dam Gay France, successful over six furlongs as a two-year-old, is one of eleven winners produced by Sweet And Lovely II, who won two races in France. Luso, a rangy good sort who usually impresses in appearance, acts on good to firm ground and dead, and he has yet to race on extremes. He's thoroughly genuine. *C. E. Brittain*

LUSSURIA (IRE) 2 b.f. (Mar 25) Last Tycoon 131 – Shabbaba (USA) (Arctic Tern (USA) 126) [1995 5d4 5.2m2 5m3 5.3f* 6m6 6m5 7f2 6f* 6m5 7f2 Aug 23] IR 5,000F, 6,200Y: smallish, close-coupled filly: second foal: half-sister to Italian 3-y-o 5f winner Shappar (by Bluebird): dam unraced: fair performer: awarded maiden at Brighton in May and won seller at same course in August: below best last 2 starts: best form at 5f or 6f: acts on firm ground: sent to Sweden. *B. J. Meehan* 67

LYDHURST (USA) 2 b.c. (May 21) Runaway Groom (CAN) – Release The Lyd (USA) (Lydian (FR) 120) [1995 8d 7m Oct 12] $45,000Y: lengthy colt: fourth foal: half-brother to a minor winner in USA, by Sauce Boat: dam won 4 races in USA, including minor stakes at up to 6f at 2 yrs: eleventh of 20 to Helicon in maiden at Newmarket: favourite and visored, only eighth of 27 to Domettes in seller at same course 16 days later: sold 10,500 gns Newmarket Autumn Sales. *D. R. Loder* 63

LYFORD LAW (IRE) 3 b.c. Contract Law (USA) 108 – Kilboy Concorde (African Sky 124) [1994 75p: 6m2 1995 a7g* 8.5m2 7.6m 7.1m 7m4 a8.5g* Nov 11] compact colt: useful performer: overcame greenness to win maiden at Lingfield in March: easily best effort when winning handicap at Wolverhampton in November (after near 5-month absence), landing gamble in good style by 6 lengths: stays 8.5f well: goes well on the all-weather: usually bandaged: sent to Dubai. *J. H. M. Gosden* 82 a97

LYNTON LAD 3 b.g. Superpower 113 – House Maid 95 (Habitat 134) [1994 85: 6m2 5g* 5g3 6d6 6g* 1995 6m5 6f 7.1m 6g 6s 6g 7d2 8.2m5 Oct 26] quite attractive, good-topped gelding: fairly useful handicapper: below form in 1995 after reappearance: stays 1m: acts on good to firm and dead ground: effective blinkered or not. *C. P. E. Brooks* 88 d

LYPHARD'S HONOR (FR) 3 b.c. Highest Honor (FR) 124 – Domludge (USA) (Lyphard (USA) 132) [1994 8g2 8d2 8g2 8d* 1995 8g* 8d4 8g Jun 3] medium-sized, quite attractive colt: not a good walker: fourth reported foal: half-brother to smart ex-Irish middle-distance performer Shrewd Idea (by Alleged), winner in France at 5 yrs: dam lightly-raced half-sister to high-class 6f (at 2 yrs) to 1½m winner Mrs Penny and to dam of Hatoof: useful French performer: won minor events at Saint-Cloud in December 1994: made winning reappearance in 5-runner event at Evry in April: best effort when under 5 lengths fourth of 8 to Vettori in Poule d'Essai des Poulains at Longchamp, soon off bridle and hanging left up the straight: favourite, disappointing last of 7 in Prix de la Jonchere there on final start: effective at 1m and should eventually be suited by middle distances: yet to race on extremes of going. *A. Fabre, France* 109

LYRIKOS (USA) 3 b.c. Lyphard (USA) 132 – Full of Fable (USA) (Devil's Bag (USA)) [1994 NR 1995 8g* 8m2 8m3 May 20] leggy, quite attractive colt: good mover: third foal: half-brother to a winner in North America by Majestic Light: dam unraced half-sister to Committed: 5-length winner of 24-runner maiden at Newbury in April: staying-on neck second of 4 in steadily-run minor event at Doncaster, but failed to progress again in similar contest at Thirsk on final start, pulling hard and seeming ill-at-ease on turns: stays 1m: yet to race on a soft surface: bandaged near-fore all starts: sent to France. *H. R. A. Cecil* 98

LYZIA (IRE) 2 ch.f. (Mar 8) Lycius (USA) 124 – Zia (USA) 88 (Shareef Dancer (USA) 135) [1995 6f3 6g5 7m 7d 7m3 Oct 28] leggy, close-coupled filly: third foal: half-sister to 3-y-o Zeliba (by Doyoun): dam, 12.2f winner, closely related to smart 1m to 1¼m performer Media Starguest and from good family: fair maiden: fifth of 7 to Blue Duster in Princess Margaret Stakes at Ascot in July: creditable efforts last 2 starts: stays 7f. *C. E. Brittain* 77

M

MA BELLE POULE 2 b.f. (Apr 30) Slip Anchor 136 – The Kings Daughter 79 (Indian King (USA) 128) [1995 6.1d^3 7d Sep 26] compact filly: second foal: half-sister to 3-y-o 5f and 6f winner The Kings Ransom (by Cadeaux Genereux): dam sprinter: third of 23 to Thracian in maiden at Nottingham, keeping on strongly after being pushed along early: mid-division in 30-runner valuable sales race won by Rio Duvida at Newmarket week later, leading group on stand rail to over 2f out: will improve. *P. F. I. Cole* 73 p

MABTHUL (USA) 7 b.g. Northern Baby (CAN) 127 – Persuadable (USA) (What A Pleasure (USA)) [1994 NR 1995 a11g Jan 13] big, rangy gelding: no form on flat since 2 yrs. *R. T. Juckes* – §

MA BULSIE 2 b.f. (Apr 3) Beveled (USA) – Cool Run 87 (Deep Run 119) [1995 5m 6m 7m 7m Nov 4] small filly: first foal: dam best at 1¼m/1½m: signs of ability in maidens first 3 starts: stiff task in nursery final one: will stay beyond 7f: twice slowly away, hampered at stalls last time. *B. A. McMahon* –

MACANAL (USA) 3 b.c. Northern Flagship (USA) 96 – Magnala (ARG) (Mount Athos 118) [1994 110p: 6m* 6g* 6g* 7d* 1995 6v* 6g* 8m^5 6.5g* 6.5g^2 6.5d* Oct 8] smart German colt: won listed race at Baden-Baden in May, minor event at Hanover in June and listed races at Munich in July (beat Branston Abby 1¼ lengths) and October (by 1¼ lengths from Sharp Prod): stays 7f: acts on good to firm ground and heavy: suffered shock defeat (at 5/1 on) penultimate start, but otherwise consistent. *H. Jentzsch, Germany* 113

MACAROON LADY 4 b.f. Prince Sabo 123 – Cookie Time (Posse (USA) 130) [1994 32: a5g^5 a6g 1995 6.1d 5d Sep 18] workmanlike filly: poor maiden plater: tailed off in 1995. *N. Bycroft* –

MACEDONAS 7 b.g. Niniski (USA) 125 – Miss Saint-Cloud 102 (Nonoalco (USA) 131) [1994 NR 1995 11.5m Jun 24] tall, leggy gelding: disappointing maiden at 3 yrs: no promise on return: modest chaser/fair hurdler. *G. Thorner* –

MACFARLANE 7 br.g. Kala Shikari 125 – Tarvie 101 (Swing Easy (USA) 126) [1994 82: 6v^4 5.2s 5.1m^6 5f^6 5g 5.1g^2 5g* 6d 5m 5s^5 5v a6g 1995 5m 5g^4 5g 6g^2 5.1g^3 6m 5.2g^3 6g 5.1d* 5m 5s 6.1s 5m Nov 4] stocky, lengthy gelding: poor mover: fair handicapper: won at Chester (has a good record there) in September: effective at 5f and 6f: has form on firm going, but seems ideally suited by an easy surface: has worn tongue strap: inconsistent. *M. J. Fetherston-Godley* 72

MACKOOK (USA) 3 b. or br.c. Seeking The Gold (USA) – L'Incestueuse (USA) (Lypheor 118) [1994 64p: 7g 1995 10m^4 10.3m^4 8f^2 8.3m* 8.3m^4 10.1g Sep 13] tall, leggy colt: fairly useful performer: made all in maiden at Windsor in August: faced stiff tasks in handicaps, creditable fourth of 12 (made most) in rated stakes at Windsor: effective at 1m and 1¼m: acts on firm going, yet to race on a soft surface: sweating (below best) second 3-y-o start: sent to Dubai. *M. R. Stoute* 83

MACK THE KNIFE 6 b.g. Kris 135 – The Dancer (FR) 122 (Green Dancer (USA) 132) [1994 111: 13.4m 11.8m* 12g^2 12m^6 12m^2 12f^6 10m^2 12m^6 1995 12g^2 11.9d^2 Oct 11] strong, close-coupled gelding: has a round action: useful performer: not seen for new stable until late-September: 2½ lengths second of 7 to Minds Music in listed event at Newmarket then 4 lengths second of 5 to Sebastian in minor race at Haydock: stays 14.6f, but races over shorter distances nowadays: acts on any ground: blinkered at 4 yrs and on 5-y-o reappearance: held up nowadays: carries head awkwardly but is genuine: won over hurdles in December. *M. C. Pipe* 108

MACMORRIS (USA) 2 b.c. (Apr 8) Silver Hawk (USA) 123 – Andover Cottage (USA) (Affiliate (USA)) [1995 7f Aug 9] $40,000Y: good-bodied colt: half-brother to several winners, including useful 1987 Irish 2-y-o Saxon Cottage (by Our Native): dam winning half-sister to champion middle-distance 3-y-o Temperence Hill and to dam of champion older horse Vanlandingham: 9/1 and bandaged off-fore, remote seventh of 9 in maiden at Salisbury, leading 4f before dropping away very quickly. *P. F. I. Cole* –

MAC OATES 2 b.c. (Mar 23) Bairn (USA) 126 – Bit of A Lass 59 (Wassl 125) [1995 6g 6d^5 6f Oct 24] lengthy, unfurnished colt: second foal: dam suited by 1¼m: similar form in maidens at Goodwood first 2 starts: only eighth of 19 to Thordis in 61

median auction event at Leicester last time: will be suited by further than 6f. *D. W. P. Arbuthnot*

MACOUMBA (USA) 3 b.f. Mr Prospector (USA) – Maximova (FR) 121 (Green Dancer (USA) 132) [1994 104p: 8g* 8g* 1995 6.5g* 8m6 8m 8g Jul 30] leggy, quite attractive filly: useful performer: won very slowly-run Prix Imprudence (by a head from Smolensk) at Evry in April: got no sort of run when 6¼ lengths sixth to Harayir in 1000 Guineas at Newmarket next start: disappointing in Coronation Stakes at Royal Ascot and Prix d'Astarte at Deauville (reportedly broke bone in foot) afterwards: edgy, rather high-spirited type, and was unlikely to stay beyond 1m: raced only on a sound surface: usually held up for turn of foot: has been retired. *Mme C. Head, France* 111

MAC RAMBLER 8 b.g. Hotfoot 126 – Arkengarthdale (Sweet Story 122) [1994 31: 12d5 14.1v4 14.1d 14.1v3 11.8d4 1995 12.3d 13g3 12g5 May 26] heavy-topped gelding: poor maiden handicapper: stays 1¾m: acts on heavy ground: usually bandaged. *N. Bycroft* 31

MAC'S BOY 6 b.g. Macmillion 110 – Tender Manx (Owen Dudley 121) [1994 –: 10.2g 12.1s a14g 1995 a16g Jan 13] angular gelding: of little account. *B. Palling* –

MACS CLAN 2 ch.f. (Apr 13) Clantime 101 – Kabella (Kabour 80) [1995 5m Aug 10] sparely-made filly: first foal: dam well beaten in varied events: 25/1 and bandaged behind, showed nothing in claimer at Beverley. *N. P. Littmoden* –

MACS MAHARANEE 8 b.m. Indian King (USA) 128 – High State 72 (Free State 125) [1994 81: 6d 6s 6f 5d 6m* 6m5 6f 6.1m5 6g4 6m 5g3 5d4 1995 a7g a6g 6m5 6m6 6m5 6g3 6f2 7m4 6m2 6.1m3 5f Aug 5] good-topped mare: unimpressive mover: fairly useful handicapper: seems suited by 6f nowadays: acts on firm and dead ground: tends to take several runs to come to herself, but consistent afterwards in 1995. *P. S. Felgate* 76

MAC'S TAXI 3 b.g. Komaite (USA) – Orange Silk 68 (Moulton 128) [1994 59: 5m 6f2 a6g3 6m4 a7g6 1995 a7g2 a7g2 a7g* a7g5 7g* 8.2m2 a7g 6f4 7m4 7g6 a6g 7m4 Jul 19] compact gelding: fair handicapper: won at Lingfield (2 ran) in January and Catterick (by 8 lengths, best effort) in April: ran poorly last 2 starts: best at up to 7f: acts on equitrack and firm ground: has run well when sweating: often forces pace: none too consistent. *P. C. Haslam* 70 a60

MAD ABOUT THE GIRL (IRE) 3 b.f. Cyrano de Bergerac 120 – Makalu 79 (Godswalk (USA) 130) [1994 NR 1995 7.1m6 7m 7g 7f 7m Oct 20] 2,200F, 8,200Y: angular filly: third foal: sister to fair sprint winner Mr Bergerac: dam stayed 1¼m: no worthwhile form. *D. J. S. Cosgrove* –

MADAIYN (IRE) 3 ch.c. Shernazar 131 – Mill River (FR) (Mill Reef (USA) 141) [1994 NR 1995 12d* 12g2 14m2 Jun 16] eighth foal: half-brother to 6 winners, notably smart 1½m Prix d'Hedouville winner Malakim (by Blushing Groom), and to the unraced dam of Prix Vanteaux winner Masslama: dam, French 10.5f winner, is half-sister to top-class 1m to 1½m winner Riverqueen: lightly-raced French colt: won minor event at Saint-Cloud in April: runner-up in listed race at Longchamp (beaten neck by Affidavit) and Prix du Lys at Saint-Cloud (2½ lengths behind Swain) afterwards: stays 1¾m. *A. de Royer Dupre, France* 110

MADAM CHAIRMAN 6 ch.m. Ore 116 – Comedown (Royalty 130) [1994 NR 1995 a12g Feb 27] third foal: dam never ran: well beaten over jumps and in a maiden. *N. P. Littmoden* –

MADAME STEINLEN 2 b.f. (Apr 10) Steinlen 127 – Equadif (FR) (Abdos 134) [1995 6d6 7g5 7m2 Oct 14] 560,000 francs Y: close-coupled, good-topped filly: half-sister to 2 winners, notably top-class French middle-distance colt Epervier Bleu (by Saint Cyrien): dam won at 9f and 1½m in French provinces: improved effort when 2 lengths second of 5 to Babinda in minor event at Newmarket, staying on well: will be suited by 1m+. *B. W. Hills* 78

MADAM MARASH (IRE) 2 b.f. (May 3) Astronef 116 – Ballybannon 76 (Ballymore 123) [1995 6g 6m 7.1s5 7.3d Oct 21] IR 1,600F, IR 3,000Y: leggy filly: half-sister to Irish 1½m winner Indian Desire (by Indian King) and 2 winners abroad: dam, 1m and 1¼m winner in Ireland from 3 starts, sister to Irish Oaks third Racquette and half-sister to Arctique Royale and the dam of Ardross: modest maiden: stiff task, 51 behind in nursery final start: will be suited by further than 1m: acts on soft ground. *A. G. Foster*

MADAM PIGTAILS 2 ch.f. (Feb 28) Rich Charlie 117 – School Dinners 74 (Sharpo 132) [1995 5g a5g Nov 11] 750Y: first reported foal: dam, second at 7f, out of half-sister to smart stayer Petty Officer: well beaten in maiden auction at Catterick in June and seller at Wolverhampton in November. *P. J. McBride* –

MADAM SUNPAK 3 b.f. Rambo Dancer (CAN) 107 – Flying Hyde (Petong 126) [1994 NR 1995 a8g^6 a8g a5g Mar 20] first living foal: dam, pulled up only run over hurdles, is out of a French 1¼m winner: well beaten in 3 sellers: sold 650 gns Doncaster March Sales. *Mrs V. A. Aconley* –

MADAM ZANDO 2 ch.f. (Apr 22) Forzando 122 – Madam Trilby (Grundy 137) [1995 5.2g^3 6m^2 5g 5g^6 Sep 18] third foal: half-sister to 3-y-o Damocles (by Dashing Blade) and a winner in Scandinavia: dam out of half-sister to Circus Plume: trained by J. Eustace, placed in maiden and seller at Yarmouth in July: blinkered and ridden by 7-lb claimer, below that form in maidens at Haydock (gave impression something amiss) and Edinburgh: will stay beyond 6f. *J. Balding* 47

MADE IN HEAVEN 3 ch.f. Primo Dominie 121 – Thundercloud 70 (Electric 126) [1994 76: 5g* 5f^3 6m^3 a6g^2 6.1s* 7m 1995 7.5m 10.5g^6 8f^6 7.6m^6 Jul 14] leggy filly: fair performer at 2 yrs: disappointing in 1995: stays 7f: probably acts on any going. *J. W. Hills* –

MADLY SHARP 4 ch.g. Sharpo 132 – Madison Girl 68 (Last Fandango 125) [1994 89+: 7.1s^2 7g^4 8m^2 6m* 6d 7g^2 1995 6m 7m* 8m 7g^4 6m Aug 15] big, workmanlike gelding: has a round action: useful handicapper: easily best efforts when winning rated stakes in May in good style and fourth of 19 to Cadeaux Tryst in Bunbury Cup in July, both at Newmarket: stays 7f: acts on good to firm ground, probably on soft: normally races just off pace. *J. W. Watts* 97

MAD MILITANT (IRE) 6 b.g. Vision (USA) – Ullapool (Dominion 123) [1994 80: a12g^5 a12g^2 a12g* a12g^5 a12g 12g 11.9g^6 12.3m* a12g^5 12.3m^2 12.3g^2 15.9m^5 11.9d 11.9s 12.4d a12g a11g^4 1995 a12g* a12g^2 a12g* a12g^3 a12g^2 a12g^2 a12g* 12.5g^4 12.3m^5 a11g* a12g 10g^5 12m Oct 2] compact gelding: unimpressive mover: just fair form in 1995: won claimers at Wolverhampton and Southwell in January and February: claimed out of R. Hollinshead's stable £6,000 after sixth outing: won similar events on same courses in April and August (latter final start for A. Forbes, reportedly returned lame): no form on return: stays 1½m, probably not 2m: below form on firm ground, acts on any other turf going and on fibresand (has had only one run on equitrack): bandaged last 2 starts: sometimes looks less than keen: has been gelded. *A. Streeter* 76 d

MADONNA DA ROSSI 2 b.f. (Apr 19) Mtoto 134 – Granny's Bank 88 (Music Boy 124) [1995 7f^4 6g^5 6m^5 7.1g^2 a8.5g^4 Oct 14] 14,500Y: fifth reported foal: half-sister to 3-y-o Swiss Bank (by Robellion), 4-y-o 1m winner Carte Blanche (by Cadeaux Genereux) and a winner in West Indies: dam miler: modest form: stays 8.5f: acts on firm ground and fibresand: takes keen hold: sold (Sir Mark Prescott to M. Dods) 4,000 gns Newmarket Autumn Sales. *Sir Mark Prescott* 53

MADURAI 4 b.f. Chilibang 120 – Macarte (FR) (Gift Card (FR) 124) [1994 71: 6v^3 6f 6g 6g 6g^2 6.1s* 6s^3 1995 6m 6m Jun 5] sturdy, lengthy filly: fair handicapper: long way below form both starts in 1995: stayed 6f: acted on heavy ground: stud. *J. L. Dunlop* –

MAESTRO TIME (USA) 2 br.g. (Mar 11) Fred Astaire (USA) – Time For Muir (USA) (Sham (USA)) [1995 a8g a8.5g^6 Dec 2] $5,000Y resold 6,600Y: half-brother to a winner in North America: dam unraced: better effort in maidens when sixth at Wolverhampton: would have stayed beyond 8.5f: dead. *T. D. Barron* 52

MAETERLINCK (IRE) 3 b.c. Bluebird (USA) 125 – Entracte 109 (Henbit (USA) 130) [1994 65p: 7s 1995 7g^2 10m* 12m 10.3m^3 10.3m* 10f^5 10m Aug 11] good-topped colt: has scope: fairly useful form: won maiden at Ripon in April and 3-runner minor event at Chester (made all) in July: best of those up with pace throughout when fifth of 14 to Jalfrezi in £33,600 handicap at Goodwood: stays 10.3f: acts on firm ground: well beaten final start, and sold only 2,600 gns Newmarket Autumn Sales. *B. W. Hills* 88

MAFTUN (USA) 3 ch.c. Elmaamul (USA) 125 – Allesheny 85 (Be My Guest (USA) 126) [1994 NR 1995 10g² 10m⁶ 10d 12g⁵ Sep 29] 48,000Y: quite attractive colt: unimpressive mover: fifth reported foal: half-brother to Irish 7f winner Allegheny River (by Lear Fan): dam Irish 2-y-o 6f winner: fair form at his best: stays 1½m: worst effort on dead ground: sold (Major Hern to G. M. Moore) 10,000 gns Newmarket Autumn Sales. *Major W. R. Hern* 70

MAFUTA (IRE) 3 b.f. Mtoto 134 – Chrism (Baptism 119) [1994 NR 1995 9f⁵ 8d 10.2m⁴ 12m a13g a13g Dec 6] 9,000Y: leggy, lengthy filly: sixth foal: half-sister to 3 winners, notably fairly useful 1m and 10.5f winner Stremizi (by Alzao): dam, Irish maiden, half-sister to Shining Finish and Bright Finish from good family: bought out of L. Cumani's stable 4,000 gns Newmarket Autumn (1994) Sales: no worthwhile form: likely to prove suited by 1½m+. *J. J. Sheehan* –

MAGGI FOR MARGARET 2 b.f. (May 22) Shavian 125 – Feather Flower 74 (Relkino 131) [1995 5d* 5g³ 5g* 5.2g 5m* 5.2m² 5g* 5.5g⁶ 5d Sep 9] 5,800F, 3,500Y: sturdy filly: progressed well physically: half-sister to 3 winners by Kalaglow, including 1½m winner Meavy, and a winner in Brazil by Posse: dam placed at 1¼m here before winning at 11.8f in France: useful performer: won maiden auction at Folkestone in March, minor events at Doncaster and Newmarket in July and listed race at Deauville (beat Prince Aslia ¾ length) in August: below form in Prix d'Arenberg at Chantilly and Flying Childers Stakes at Doncaster within 4 days in September: speedy: acts on good to firm and dead ground. *M. R. Channon* 97

MAGICAL BELLE (IRE) 3 ch.f. Magical Strike (USA) 114 – Bel Ria (Gay Fandango (USA) 132) [1994 56d: a7g* 6m⁴ a7g 7s a8.5g⁴ a8g 1995 7.1m a7g⁶ Jul 3] small filly: soundly beaten in 1995: should stay 1m: tried visored: sold 875 gns Ascot July Sales: sent to Cyprus. *C. A. Smith* –

MAGICAL BID (IRE) 3 b.g. Magical Strike (USA) 114 – Fortera (FR) (Sanctus II 132) [1994 61?: 5.1m 6.1m⁴ 6m 6g⁵ 7m 8d 7s⁴ 7g 7g 1995 7g 7.1m 10.2m 8.2m 10g 8.1m⁶ 8.2m² 8m 11d⁶ Sep 22] good-topped gelding: poor walker: poor maiden: easily best effort on soft ground: tried visored, no improvement: bandaged: unreliable. *J. M. Bradley* 42

MAGICAL BLUES (IRE) 3 b.g. Magical Strike (USA) 114 – Blue Bell Girl (Blakeney 126) [1994 77: 7g 7m³ a7g³ 7s⁴ 8d⁴ 8.3g³ 1995 8m⁵ 8.3m 8g Jun 10] rangy gelding: went wrong way temperamentally for new stable, refusing to race final outing: stays 1m: well below form on fibresand: tried blinkered: has worn near-side pricker and been fitted with bells on bridle: gelded and joined W. Musson: one to avoid. *K. T. Ivory* §§

MAGICAL MANOEUVERS 3 b.c. Cree Song 99 – Orbital Manoeuvers (Space King 115) [1994 57: 5d³ 5m⁵ 5m 7.1d 7s⁶ 7g 1995 6.1g² 5.1f a5g² Jul 21] workmanlike colt: modest maiden handicapper: should stay 7f: acts on firm and dead ground and on fibresand. *B. A. McMahon* 57

MAGICAL MIDNIGHT 2 ch.f. (Mar 9) Timeless Times (USA) 99 – Mayor 86 (Laxton 105) [1995 5g 5g a5g⁵ 6.1d 6s⁵ Sep 30] 3,400Y: good-bodied filly: second reported foal: half-sister to 4-y-o 5f winner Nineacres (by Sayf El Arab): dam suited by 6f: poor form: good fifth of 24 to Bee Health Boy in selling nursery at Haydock last time: stays 6f: acts on soft ground. *N. Tinkler* 42

MAGICAL MILL 2 ch.f. (Mar 6) Prince Sabo 123 – Mimram Melody 65 (Music Boy 124) [1995 5g 6.1d a6g a7g Nov 16] 4,800Y: smallish, lengthy filly: second reported foal: half-sister to a winner in Scandinavia: dam 5f winner: soundly beaten in varied company, including selling. *R. Guest* –

MAGICAL RETREAT (USA) 5 b.m. Sir Ivor 135 – Known Charter 96 (Known Fact (USA) 135) [1994 99: 10.4f³ 10s⁴ 10g 11.9m⁴ 13.9f³ 12f⁴ 1995 12m² 11.9m³ 13.9m² 11.9m² Aug 16] small, workmanlike mare: in foal to Shirley Heights: useful on most form from 3 yrs to 5 yrs: placed in listed event at Newmarket, Lancashire Oaks at Haydock and listed rated stakes at York on first 3 starts in 1995: 33/1, excelled herself when head second of 8 to Pure Grain in Yorkshire Oaks at York final outing, setting steady pace, headed over 3f out then battling back in superb fashion: effective at 1¼m to 14.8f: probably acted on any going: game and genuine. *C. A. Cyzer* 115

MAGICATION 5 b.m. Nomination 125 – Gundreda 93 (Gunner B 126) [1994 43: a7g 7m 8g 7m 7.5m 7m⁴ 8g³ 8m⁵ 8m⁵ 7g* 7g 8g² 7.6g 7d³ 7m 8s⁴ 1995 8g 8g 7f 40

7m 7m^4 10.2h^4 8m 8g^6 7g 10.1g 9.7s^6 8.2m a11g^3 a12g Dec 12] small, sturdy mare: carries condition: poor handicapper: sold out of C. Allen's stable 1,200 gns Doncaster November Sales after thirteenth start: stays 11f: acts on any going: blinkered (below form) 3 times at 4 yrs: sometimes bandaged/has tongue tied down: tends to get behind: none too consistent. *B. Richmond*

MAGIC BIRD (IRE) 2 b.f. (May 3) Bluebird (USA) 125 – Frans Cap (Captain James 123) [1995 5d a6g^3 a6g^2 a6g^5 a7g 7f^6 Aug 25] 5,200Y: leggy, unfurnished filly: fourth foal: half-sister to 1991 2-y-o 5f winner Sara Anne (by Sarab): dam Irish maiden, seemed to stay 1¾m: poor plater: sold out of J. Spearing's stable 500 gns Doncaster July Sales after penultimate start: twice blinkered: sold 500 gns Doncaster October Sales. *J. Norton* –

MAGIC GALOP (USA) 2 b.c. (Jan 25) Seattle Dancer (USA) 119 – Jardin de Nuit (USA) (Raja Baba (USA)) [1995 6g^4 Jul 30] $22,000F: fifth foal: half-brother to smart French 1m winner Hudo (by Hero's Honour) and French 11f winner Howlin' (by Alleged): dam, minor winner in USA, half-sister to 9f Delaware Oaks winner Up The Flagpole: well-beaten last of 4 in listed newcomers race at Deauville: likely to do better. *D. R. C. Elsworth* – p

MAGIC HEIGHTS 2 gr.c. (Apr 26) Deploy 131 – Lady Regent (Wolver Hollow 126) [1995 8.2m^6 Oct 26] 2,200F, 2,800Y, 12,000 2-y-o: good-bodied colt: seventh foal: half-brother to 6f and 7f winner Trojan General (by Trojan Fen): dam, won over 7f at 3 yrs in Ireland, half-sister to very smart middle-distance performer Infamy (by Shirley Heights): weak 9/1-shot, carrying condition and green, slowly away and never a threat when sixth of 10 to Censor in maiden at Nottingham: should improve. *J. E. Banks* 57 p

MAGIC IMP (IRE) 2 b.f. (May 15) Petorius 117 – Magic Green (Magic Mirror 105) [1995 5m^4 5g^2 5g^3 5g^5 6m 5m^4 Aug 25] IR 1,150F, 2,300Y: leggy, unfurnished filly: first living foal: dam Irish maiden placed at 2 yrs: modest maiden: should stay 6f: fair effort when visored: sold 6,500 gns Newmarket Autumn Sales: sent to Barbados. *W. J. Musson* 59

MAGIC JUNCTION (USA) 4 b.c. Danzig Connection (USA) – Sleeping Beauty 87 (Mill Reef (USA) 141) [1994 82: a8.5g* a8.5g* a9.4g* a8.5g* 12f 10d^2 9v^3 1995 10.4m 12d^2 a10g^4 Nov 8] lengthy, sturdy colt: fairly useful handicapper in 1994: winning hurdler in 1994/5: not seen out on flat until October, and below form: stays 1½m well: acts on fibresand and heavy ground, ran creditably over hurdles on firm. *Lord Huntingdon* 69

MAGIC LAKE 2 b.f. (Apr 16) Primo Dominie 121 – Magic Kingdom 76 (Kings Lake (USA) 133) [1995 5m^6 5.1g^6 a6g^3 7m^3 7.1m^2 6d^4 8.3g^3 7g^2 8m^2 7m Oct 21] lengthy, quite good-topped filly: fourth foal: sister to 6f to 1½m winner Awestruck: dam, second over 1m on all 3 starts, daughter of very useful French middle-distance performer Darine: poor form for W. Haggas first 3 starts: easily best subsequent effort when length second to Mystic Knight in nursery at Newmarket penultimate start: stays 1m: acts on firm and dead ground. *E. J. Alston* 68 ?

MAGIC LEADER (IRE) 3 b. or br.g. Architect (USA) – Magic Rotation (USA) (His Majesty (USA)) [1994 48?: 5m^6 6g 6m 5d 5g^5 a6g a5g^5 a5g 1995 a5g^5 a8g 5g 8m^6 10m 8m^6 10m 7f Oct 25] small gelding: bad maiden on most form: visored (no form) final 3-y-o start: wears bandages. *T. T. Clement* –

MAGIC MAIL 2 b.c. (Feb 4) Aragon 118 – Blue Rhythm 72 (Blue Cashmere 129) [1995 5m^3 Oct 5] 11,000Y: rangy colt: has scope: second foal: dam stayed 7f: 7/1 and green, 3½ lengths third of 4 finishers to Music Gold in maiden at York: sure to improve. *J. M. P. Eustace* 71 p

MAGIC MELODY 2 b.f. (Apr 23) Petong 126 – Miss Rossi (Artaius (USA) 129) [1995 6.1d 6g^3 6d a6g Oct 28] leggy filly: fifth live foal: half-sister to 4 winning sprinters, including useful pair Dancing Music (by Music Boy) and Heather Bank (by Nordance): dam unraced: modest form in maidens at Redcar and Newbury (eighth of 20 to Fly Tip): sprint bred: well beaten on fibresand. *J. L. Spearing* 62

MAGIC MILL (IRE) 2 b.c. (Apr 15) Simply Great (FR) 122 – Rosy O'Leary (Majetta 115) [1995 7d^3 7f* Oct 31] IR 5,400F, IR 3,000Y: half-brother to several winners, including 9f to 1½m winner Gillies Prince (by Furry Glen) and 1m winner Bradman (by Don): dam never ran: won 9-runner maiden at Redcar (sweating) by 2½ 82 p lengths from Apache Len: will be well suited by 1m+: will improve again. *F. J. O'Mahony*

MAGIC ORB 5 b.m. Primo Dominie 121 – Tricky 66 (Song 132) [1994 78: 5d^5 5d 5m* 5m 1995 5g^5 6g^2 5f^4 6m^5 5m^4 5g^6 6m 5m 6d Sep 2] small, sparely-made mare: in foal to Aragon: unimpressive mover: fairly useful handicapper at best for new connections: effective at 5f and 6f: acted on good to firm and dead ground, unsuited by heavy: held up: reared over in stalls (and withdrawn) before Stewards' Cup. *J. L. Harris* 81 d

MAGIC PEARL 5 gr.m. Belfort (FR) 89 – Oyster Gray 61 (Tanfirion 110) [1994 83: 5m^2 6.1m^5 6m^4 5f 5g 5f 5.1g^4 6d 5d 7d 1995 5g 5.1m^3 5g 5m 5m 6g^6 5f Oct 16] leggy, angular mare: rather disappointing in 1995, and tailed off last 3 starts: stays an easy 6f: acts on good to firm ground and dead: has bolted to post, and often taken down alone: sold 880 gns Doncaster November Sales. *E. J. Alston* 79 d

MAGIC RON 2 b.g. (Mar 21) Ron's Victory (USA) 129 – Magical Spirit 70 (Top Ville 129) [1995 7m 8.1g 10.2m^4 Sep 25] useful-looking gelding: second foal: half-brother to 3-y-o 9f winner Sharpical (by Sharpo): dam, placed over middle distances, half-sister to good 7f to 1½m winner John French: visored, best effort in maiden events when around 8½ lengths fourth to Gentilhomme in 8-runner maiden at Bath: stays 1¼m: headstrong sort: hung left second start. *M. Bell* 77

MAGIC TIMES 4 b.g. Good Times (ITY) – Young Wilkie (Callernish) [1994 63: 8f 8m^5 a12g* 12g 12.1m 1995 a12g 12.1v Mar 31] big gelding: tailed off since last win: stays at least 1½m. *M. Johnston* –

MAGNA CARTA 3 b.c. Royal Academy (USA) 130 – By Charter 104 (Shirley Heights 130) [1994 85p: 7g a7g* 1995 8m 7g May 18] smallish, workmanlike colt: fairly useful form: weakened quickly in listed race at Kempton and £18,800 handicap at York in the spring: sold only 4,600 gns Newmarket Autumn Sales. *M. R. Stoute* 81

MAGNATE'S POINT 3 b.c. Last Tycoon 131 – Kindjal 84 (Kris 135) [1994 80p: 6m^3 6s^5 1995 8m 7m 9m 7f Oct 18] unfurnished colt: failed to progress from promising debut: should stay 1m+: edgy and carried head awkwardly second start: sometimes sweats: rather headstrong: one to treat with caution. *P. W. Harris* –

MAGNIFICENT DEVIL (USA) 3 ch.c. Devil's Bag (USA) – Magnificent Lady 74 (Nonoalco (USA) 131) [1994 56p: 6.1s^4 1995 6m* 7m^4 7m 5m^6 Jul 8] lengthy, good-topped colt with scope: has a quick action: half-brother to smart 6f and 7.2f winner Firm Landing (by J O Tobin): won maiden at Newmarket in April: faced stiff tasks last 2 starts, appearing to improve when sixth of 10 in listed race at Sandown: effective at 5f, and stays 7f: acts on good to firm ground: takes keen hold: sent to USA. *J. W. Watts* 94

MAGNUMS SECRET 3 b.f. Hubbly Bubbly (USA) – Black Veil 53 (Blakeney 126) [1994 43: 6g 6g 6g 1995 9g^5 7g 8m 10m^6 Aug 12] lengthy, unfurnished filly: poor maiden: should be suited by further than 9f: inconsistent. *J. L. Eyre* 49

MAHOOL (USA) 6 b.g. Alydar (USA) – Tax Dodge (USA) (Seattle Slew (USA)) [1994 88: a7g* 8m a8.5g^5 a7g* 7m^2 7.6m* 7f^5 7s 7m 8g* 7.1m* 8m 8.1m 9g^5 1995 a7g* 8g 7.5m Apr 7] tall gelding: impresses in appearance: fairly useful handicapper: better than ever when winning well-contested event at Wolverhampton in March: pulled up after breaking blood vessel final start: effective at 7f and 1m: goes well on fibresand: acts on firm and dead ground, well below form on soft: often wears crossed noseband: effective from front or held up. *J. L. Eyre* – a94

MAIANDROS (GR) 3 ch.c. Flash N Thunder (USA) 115 – Mous Mous (GR) (Etoile Lointaine (USA)) [1994 71: 7g^5 7m^4 a6g* 1995 a6g^4 6m 7f* 7.9g 7.1g^6 7m* 7m 8.5f 8g^2 Nov 24] leggy colt: fairly useful handicapper: led final 1f when winning at Warwick (drifted right having been ridden along at halfway) in May and Lingfield (4-runner minor event, took strong hold) on penultimate start for R. Charlton in June: racing on lasix, second in claimer at Fair Grounds, much his better effort in USA: stays 1m: acts on firm ground and the all-weather: inconsistent. *T. Amoss, USA* 91

MAID FOR BAILEYS (IRE) 2 b.f. (May 2) Marju (IRE) 127 – Island Time (USA) (Bold Hour) [1995 6g^4 7g^2 7g 7f^2 8.5m^2 8g^2 8g^2 Oct 3] 9,400F, IR 23,000Y: leggy, useful-looking filly: half-sister to several winners in Italy and Ireland, including smart Italian 9f/11f winner Sugarland Express (by Roi Danzig): dam Irish 77

1m winner: fair maiden: good second of 19 in nursery at Warwick final start: stays 8.5f. *M. Johnston*

MAID FOR THE HILLS 2 b.f. (Feb 17) Indian Ridge 123 – Stinging Nettle 90 (Sharpen Up 127) [1995 6g* 6m* Jul 1] 32,000Y: rather unfurnished filly: fifth foal: half-sister to 2-y-o 5f and 6f winners Maid For Walking and Royal Insignia (both by Prince Sabo) and a winner in Italy: dam, 6f winner on 2-y-o debut but no form after, half-sister to very smart 7f to 1¼m winner Gairloch and smart miler Whistlefield: won maiden and 7-runner listed event (gamely, hard driven to lead close home by neck from Persian Secret), both at Newmarket in midsummer: will probably stay 7f: displayed a likeable attitude and looked sure to make further progress. *D. R. Loder* — 101 p

MAID FOR WALKING 3 b. or br.f. Prince Sabo 123 – Stinging Nettle 90 (Sharpen Up 127) [1994 99: 5m² 5d* 5m 6f* 6m² 5.2g⁶ 7g⁵ 7m² 6g* 1995 6g³ 7m⁴ 7.6m⁵ 7f⁴ Jul 27] leggy, close-coupled filly: has a quick action: useful performer, but inclined to run odd poor race: best effort when fifth of 11 in listed rated stakes at Lingfield: stays 7f: acts on firm and dead ground. *D. R. Loder* — 101

MAID O'CANNIE 4 b.f. Efisio 120 – Ichnusa 83 (Bay Express 132) [1994 72: 6g⁴ 8d 5d² 6m⁵ 6g* 6f³ 6m² a6g³ 6m 6d² 7m 1995 6d 5m⁴ 5m⁶ 6m 6m 6m⁶ 6m³ 6d* 6.1d³ 6d Oct 11] strong, workmanlike filly: caught the eye in no uncertain manner on several occasions and didn't have to be at best to justify strong support in 20-runner minor event at Leicester in September: best form at around 6f: acts on firm and dead ground: best efforts visored/blinkered: often taken early to post: sometimes slowly away. *M. W. Easterby* — 62

MAID WELCOME 8 br.m. Mummy's Pet 125 – Carolynchristensen 58 (Sweet Revenge 129) [1994 61: a7g⁴ a7g⁶ a6g⁶ a7s³ a7g³ a8.5g⁵ a8g* a7g⁴ 8d⁴ 7m 8g⁶ 7f a7g⁶ 6.1s² 7s 6g a7g a7g a7g* a7g* a7g³ 1995 a7g⁴ a7g* a7g² a7g⁵ a7g⁴ a7g³ a7g* 6m a8g a7g³ a7g a7g a7g² Dec 14] sturdy mare: has a round action: modest handicapper: won apprentice event in January and minor event in March, both at Lingfield: races mainly at 7f nowadays: acts on any turf going, and goes well on all-weather surfaces: blinkered or visored: ridden by Amanda Sanders at 8 yrs: front runner/races prominently. *Mrs N. Macauley* — – a64

MAIN BRACE 4 b.g. Robellino (USA) 127 – Mystery Ship 105 (Decoy Boy 129) [1994 59d: 7.1s² 8.3m 7.1m 7m a7g 7m 7g 1995 a8g⁶ a8.5g⁴ a8g⁶ 7.1m 8.1g a7g Jul 21] workmanlike gelding: poor performer: should stay beyond 7f: blinkered (well beaten) final start: gelded: sold 600 gns Ascot November Sales. *K. R. Burke* — 38

MAIN OFFENDER 3 ch.c. Be My Chief (USA) 122 – Messaria 68§ (Ile de Bourbon (USA) 133) [1994 84p: 8g⁴ 1995 10m⁵ 10.3m³ 12.1g³ 10d² 10m* 10d Nov 24] big, good-topped colt: has plenty of scope: fairly useful form: off course nearly 5 months after third start, and bandaged behind afterwards: narrowly won minor event at Nottingham in October, rallying gamely (final outing for H. Cecil): in mid-division in minor event at Evry: stays 10.3f and should get 1½m: acts on good to firm and (probably) good to soft ground. *D. Sepulchre, France* — 87

MAI PEN RAI 7 ch.g. All Systems Go 119 – Jersey Maid 82 (On Your Mark 125) [1994 37, a–: a8.5g 9.7s³ 11.9d 11.7g⁵ 10.8m 7v 8.2m 10m⁴ 1995 10m 8g a7g 8f⁴ 8f⁶ 8.3m 8f⁶ Aug 17] sparely-made, angular gelding: poor handicapper: stays 11.7f: acts on any going on turf, no form on the all-weather: visored (ran well) 3 times at 5 yrs: inconsistent. *R. J. Hodges* — 30 a–

MAITEAMIA 2 ch.g. (May 2) Komaite (USA) – Mia Scintilla 54 (Blazing Saddles (AUS)) [1995 a7g 6.1d 6g 8g Oct 3] robust gelding: second foal: brother to 3-y-o Komiamaite: dam 5f performer: first sign of ability when eighth of 19 in nursery at Warwick on final start: likely to prove best at up to 1m: blinkered first 3 starts: will do better. *S. R. Bowring* — 45 p

MAJAL (IRE) 6 b.g. Caerleon (USA) 132 – Park Special (Relkino 131) [1994 51: a12g 12g 8g 8f⁵ 8h⁴ 1995 a12g* a12g Feb 21] good-bodied gelding: unimpressive mover: modest handicapper: won at Lingfield (leading final 1f) in February: may well stay beyond 1½m: acts on any going: none too consistent: fair hurdler. *J. S. Wainwright* — 55

MAJBOOR YAFOOZ (USA) 5 b.g. Silver Hawk (USA) 123 – Forced To Fly (USA) (Accipiter (USA)) [1994 70: 7d³ 11.9f⁴ 10m 1995 10m⁴ May 15] lengthy gelding: has a round action: fair maiden: respectable fourth of 8 in minor event at — 65

Windsor only start in 1995: effective at 7f and 1¼m (very stiff task at 11.9f): probably acts on good to firm and dead ground: takes keen hold. *J. R. Bosley*

MAJDAK JEREEB (IRE) 2 b.c. (Mar 2) Alzao (USA) 117 – Aunty (FR) 114 (Riverman (USA) 131) [1995 7m⁵ 7.1d 7.1d⁴ 7d Sep 26] 48,000Y: good-bodied colt with an easy action: seventh foal: half-brother to 2 winners by Sadler's Wells, notably useful 1988 Irish 2-y-o 5f and 6f winner Kyra: dam French 1¼m winner, is half-sister to Ebor winner Crazy out of smart French middle-distance winner Aunt Zara: fair form in maidens first 3 starts, fourth to Masehaab at Sandown on last of them: similar form though never a factor in valuable sales race at Newmarket final start: will stay at least 1m. *Major W. R. Hern* 75

MAJESTIC ROLE (FR) 4 ch.f. Theatrical 128 – Autocratic (Tyrant (USA)) [1994 107: 10g 10d⁶ 12s⁶ 16.2m 12d⁵ 1995 11.9m³ 12g⁶ Sep 12] leggy, sparely-made filly: in foal to Caerleon: capable of useful form at 3 yrs: below form when 9½ lengths third of 4 to impressive Larrocha in listed race at York on belated reappearance: ran badly in similar event at Galway following month: stayed 1½m, appeared not to get 2m in Queen's Vase: acted on soft ground. *M. Kauntze, Ireland* 94

MAJOR CHANGE 3 gr.c. Sharrood (USA) 124 – May The Fourteenth 53 (Thatching 131) [1994 71p: 6g⁴ 1995 8g⁵ 8m* 9g⁴ 10g³ 10f³ 12m³ 10g 10d⁵ Oct 19] close-coupled colt: fairly useful form: won median auction maiden at Leicester in May: good efforts next 4 starts in handicaps: stays 1½m: acts on firm ground, respectable effort on dead: sometimes front runner. *R. Hannon* 88

MAJOR DUNDEE (IRE) 2 b.c. (Mar 21) Distinctly North (USA) 115 – Indigo Blue (IRE) 56 (Bluebird (USA) 125) [1995 7m⁴ Aug 16] 30,000Y: useful-looking colt: first foal: dam sprinting half-sister to Mistertopogigo out of sister to Hallgate: 25/1, green and bit backward, around 4 lengths fourth of 11 to Brilliant Red in maiden at Kempton, running on well under hands and heels: type to improve and win races. *R. Hannon* 74 p

MAJOR MOUSE 7 ch.g. All Systems Go 119 – Tzu-Hsi (Songedor 116) [1994 57: a8.5g a8g³ 8g 8s a8g⁶ 1995 a8g a8g³ a8g² a8g² 8m a8g* 8m⁵ 8m⁵ a8g* Jun 22] strong gelding: modest on turf, fair handicapper on the all-weather: won at Southwell in May and June: got trapped in stalls and withdrawn there Aug 4: should stay beyond 1m: acts on firm going and fibresand. *W. W. Haigh* 50 a68

MAJOR QUALITY 2 b.c. (Mar 9) Sizzling Melody 117 – Bonne de Berry (Habitat 134) [1995 6m³ Nov 3] workmanlike colt: sixth foal: brother to winning sprinter Breakfast Boogie and half-brother to French 1989 2-y-o 5.5f winner Sabaya (by Vayrann): dam French 1¼m winner: 14/1, 3½ lengths third of 20 to Miss Riviera in maiden at Doncaster, improving from midfield over 2f out but no match for first two closing stages: will improve. *J. R. Fanshawe* 75 p

MAJOR SNUGFIT 3 b.g. Tina's Pet 121 – Sequoia 87 (Sassafras (FR) 135) [1994 47: a6g 5g a5g 8d 6s³ 7g 1995 8d Sep 22] workmanlike gelding: poor handicapper: stays 1m: acts on soft ground: blinkered third to final outings at 2 yrs: inconsistent. *M. W. Easterby* –

MAKASKAMINA 2 b. or br.g. (Mar 4) Mtoto 134 – Flying Flo Jo (USA) 56 (Aloma's Ruler (USA)) [1995 a7g 7f⁴ 7m⁵ 5m 8g⁴ 8m a8g Nov 8] smallish, close-coupled gelding: second foal: dam 6f winner: modest maiden plater, trained by B. Hanbury first 4 starts: fourth of 19 to Deadline Time in nursery at Warwick fifth start: will stay beyond 1m. *P. Mitchell* 53

MAKE A STAND 4 ch.g. Master Willie 129 – Make A Signal 76 (Royal Gunner (USA)) [1994 –: 10.2g 1995 8m 10g 12f 10m 11.6m 11.8m* 14g⁶ Sep 29] tall, angular gelding: well beaten until easy winner of strongly-run claimer at Leicester (claimed out of H. Candy's stable £8,000) in August, leading 2f out and idling: short of room 3f out, but below that form anyway in handicap at Newmarket following month: should stay beyond 11.8f: acts on good to firm and dead ground: blinkered (well beaten) fourth and fifth 4-y-o starts. *M. C. Pipe* 72

MAKE THE BREAK 4 b.g. Dominion 123 – Souadah (USA) (General Holme (USA) 128) [1994 68: 8d³ 7m* 7.6g³ 8v⁶ 7.1s⁴ 7f³ 7g³ 7m 6f* 7v 7d 7g⁴ a7g⁴ a6g a8.5g 1995 a7g a6g⁵ a6g a9.4g 7d 6m a6g 7m⁶ 6f 6m⁶ 8d Sep 22] compact, good-bodied gelding: well on the downgrade: left S. Coathup's stable after tenth 48 d start: stays 1m: acts on firm and soft ground and the all-weather: no improvement in blinkers. *M. W. Easterby*

MAKE TIME 3 b.f. Sayf El Arab (USA) 127 – Moment In Time 91 (Without Fear (FR) 128) [1994 79: 5d^{6} 6g* 6s* 6v^{4} 1995 6g 6m 6g^{4} 8m^{3} 7m^{2} 7.1g^{3} Sep 23] smallish filly: fair handicapper: not so good as at 2 yrs, but consistent: effective at 6f to 1m: acts on good to firm ground, went well on a soft surface at 2 yrs: suitable mount for 7-lb claimer: sold 3,200 gns Newmarket Autumn Sales: sent to Italy. *J. Pearce* 66

MAKRI 3 b.f. Night Shift (USA) – Maria Isabella (FR) (Young Generation 129) [1994 NR 1995 8.2m^{6} 8m^{3} 7m^{4} 7g^{4} 9.9g^{4} 10g^{5} 10d^{3} Aug 21] sturdy filly: half-sister to several winners, including middle-distance performers Top Royal (by High Top) and Streisand (by Unfuwain), latter useful in Italy in 1994: dam, ran 3 times in France, half-sister to useful 1986 French 2-y-o 6.5f winner Microcosme: fair maiden handicapper, trained first 3 starts by Mrs J. Cecil: stays 1¼m: races prominently: has had tongue tied down. *D. Sepulchre, France* 65

MALIBU MAN 3 ch.c. Ballacashtal (CAN) – National Time (USA) (Lord Avie (USA)) [1994 53: 6m 5m 6s 5m^{6} 1995 6m 6m a5g^{4} a6g* a5g^{3} a5g* a6g^{5} 6.1d^{5} 5g^{2} 5.1d^{6} 5.1m Oct 19] quite good-topped colt: has a round action: fair form on all-weather, winning handicaps at Wolverhampton in June and July: modest on turf: stays 6f: acts on good to firm and dead ground and goes well on fibresand: usually races prominently: has run well when sweating. *S. Mellor* 63 a75

MALICE CORNER 2 ch.c. (May 6) Savahra Sound 111 – Najd 86 (St Chad 120) [1995 5.1m 5g a6g 6g Oct 16] 4,500Y: leggy colt: closely related to 1986 2-y-o 5f winner Copper Red (by Song) and half-brother to 2 winners in France by Vitiges, one at 7f and 1m, the other over middle distances: dam 5f winner: no worthwhile form, including in a seller: sold 500 gns Ascot October Sales. *L. G. Cottrell* –

MALIHABAD (IRE) 6 ch.g. Shahrastani (USA) 135 – Mill River (FR) (Mill Reef (USA) 141) [1994 NR 1995 12.3m^{4} 10.5m^{4} 13.4d Sep 20] deep-girthed, workmanlike gelding: has a round action: half-brother to several winners, notably smart Malakim (1½m, by Blushing Groom): dam well-bred French 10.5f winner: won NH Flat race and maiden hurdle at 4 yrs in Ireland for F. Flood: sold IR 6,000 gns Goffs February Sales: modest form here in claimers and maiden: should prove suited by good pace at 1½m+. *R. Hollinshead* 55

MALINDI BAY 7 gr.g. Grey Desire 115 – Malindi (Mansingh (USA) 120) [1994 NR 1995 10f^{5} 10m^{2} 10f^{4} a10g 10m 10g 10.3m Oct 21] angular, close-coupled gelding: poor plater: stays 1¼m: acts on firm ground, probably on dead: blinkered (well beaten) twice earlier in career: inconsistent. *B. J. McMath* 33

MALINGERER 4 gr.f. Petong 126 – Crystal Gael 79 (Sparkler 130) [1994 –: 8m 7v 7m 6f 6m 8.3m 8.5m a10g^{4} a12g a10g 1995 a16g a12g^{3} a13g^{3} a11g^{4} a12g^{5} a13g a12g 8g 9.7g^{2} 12.5m 10f^{5} 9.7m 11.6m 12f 12f^{5} Aug 15] leggy filly: poor maiden handicapper: stays 1½m: acts on firm ground: inconsistent. *D. A. Wilson* 39 d

MALLIA 2 b.c. (Apr 5) Statoblest 120 – Pronetta (USA) (Mr Prospector (USA)) [1995 5d^{4} 5m^{2} 5g* May 4] 4,200Y: dipped-backed colt: half-brother to several minor winners in North America: dam minor winner in USA: won maiden auction at Hamilton in May by ¾ length from Red River Valley: looked to be progressing well but not seen out afterwards. *T. D. Barron* 76

MALSISIO 3 b.f. Efisio 120 – Moonlight Fling (Imperial Fling (USA) 116) [1994 –: 6g 1995 a7g 9.9m 8m 6m 5f 6f Jul 29] leggy filly: seems of little account: sold 520 gns Doncaster September Sales. *S. G. Norton* –

MALZOOM 3 b.c. Statoblest 120 – Plum Bold 83 (Be My Guest (USA) 126) [1994 –: 6g 1995 a8.5g^{5} a9.4g^{6} 6.1g 6s 7g 7m 7.5m^{6} 7g 8.1m^{2} 8f^{3} 7.1m 8m^{3} 8g 11.1g Sep 25] close-coupled colt: poor maiden handicapper: stays 1m: acts on good to firm ground: reared leaving stalls (unseated rider) once at 3 yrs: inconsistent. *S. E. Kettlewell* 33

MAMALAMA 7 ch.m. Nishapour (FR) 125 – Gauloise 93 (Welsh Pageant 132) [1994 25: a16g^{4} a13g^{5} 1995 a12g Jan 27] leggy, angular mare: probably no longer of much account on flat. *B. J. Llewellyn* –

MAMLAKAH (IRE) 3 ch.f. Unfuwain (USA) 131 – Narjis (USA) 87 (Blushing Groom (FR) 131) [1994 104p: 6m^{6} 7m* 7m* 8g* 1995 8m 7.3g^{3} 7f^{5} 8.1m^{5} 7g Sep 7] strong, lengthy filly: good mover with a long stride: useful performer: eighth of 10 in 100

Coronation Stakes at Royal Ascot on reappearance: creditable efforts in minor/listed events (including when edgy fourth start) except final outing: stayed 1m: did not race on a soft surface: blinkered last 2 starts: took keen hold: often front-runner: visits Gulch. *H. Thomson Jones*

MAMLOUK 3 gr.g. Distant Relative 128 – Nelly Do Da 78 (Derring-Do 131) [1994 –: 7g 1995 10g Sep 29] rangy gelding: half-brother to stayers Retouch (by Touching Wood) and Jonsalan (by Robellino), both at least fairly useful: 25/1, towards rear in maidens. *J. W. Payne* –

MAMMA'S DUE 3 ch.f. Precocious 126 – Maple Syrup 89 (Charlottown 127) [1994 NR 1995 a6g^4 a6g^2 5m^5 6m^5 a5g^3 5g 6d Oct 11] 9,000Y: quite good-topped filly: half-sister to several winners, including Irish 9f and 11f winner Fish Merchant (by Blue Cashmere) and fairly useful sprinter Mamma's Too (by Skyliner): dam, placed over 6f and 1¼m, is daughter of Sweet Solera: very unruly stalls and injured on intended debut in April 1994: modest form at best in 1995: well beaten last 2 starts: stays 6f: acts on good to firm ground and fibresand: sold 1,700 gns Doncaster October Sales. *J. Berry* 59 d

MAMNOON (USA) 4 b.g. Nijinsky (CAN) 138 – Continual (USA) (Damascus (USA)) [1994 79: 8f^5 10m^2 10g^3 1995 12.3m 10.5g 14.1m Oct 19] sturdy gelding: tailed off all starts for new stable: tried blinkered/visored. *W. Clay* –

MAM'SELLE BERGERAC (IRE) 2 b.f. (Jan 28) Cyrano de Bergerac 120 – Miss Merryweather (Sexton Blake 126) [1995 6m^6 6m 7.6d 6.9g^6 7g^4 Oct 23] IR 5,000Y: fourth foal: half-sister to 1990 2-y-o 5f winner L'Ete (by Kafu) and a winner in Spain by Be My Native: dam lightly raced in Ireland: ran well when over 3 lengths fourth of 13 to Tsarnista in maiden at Lingfield on final outing: stays 7f. *P. Mitchell* 64

MAM'ZELLE ANGOT 5 b.m. Balidar 133 – Ragirl (Ragusa 137) [1994 65: 9.2f^2 9.9m^3 10f^5 a8.5g^2 8.3g* 8h^2 8g^5 10.1d a9.4g* 1995 a8g^2 a9.4g^3 8.3v a8.5g a9.4g^3 a8.5g a8.5g^6 Aug 11] strong mare: modest handicapper: trained first 3 starts in 1995 by J. L. Eyre, fourth by Miss J. Craze: below form last 2 starts: stays 9.4f: probably acts on any going, including fibresand: often wears bandages behind. *A. Harrison* 64

MANABAR 3 b.g. Reprimand 122 – Ring of Pearl (Auction Ring (USA) 123) [1994 79p: 6m^2 1995 8f^3 8g* 9g 8g 9d Sep 30] useful-looking, rather unfurnished gelding: has been hobdayed: won maiden at Thirsk in June: off course over 3 months, behind in handicaps afterwards: will probably prove best at up to 1m: sold (D. Morley to M. Polglase) 6,500 gns Newmarket Autumn Sales. *D. Morley* 79 d

MANCINI 2 b. or br.g. (Feb 27) Nomination 125 – Roman Blue (Charlottown 127) [1995 6g^4 7f^2 7f* Aug 2] 9,000F, 10,500Y: rather unfurnished gelding: half-brother to 5f winner Color Blind (by Tromos) and several winners abroad: dam won Italian 1000 Guineas and second in Italian Oaks: fair form in maidens: won 6-runner auction event at Brighton in August by 3 lengths from Half An Inch: will stay beyond 7f. *M. Bell* 80 +

MANDALAY PRINCE 11 b.g. Nishapour (FR) 125 – Ops (Welsh Saint 126) [1994 NR 1995 17.1m 21.6f May 1] lengthy, well-made gelding: probably no longer of any account. *T. Kersey* – §

MANDAPAN 2 b.f. (Mar 16) Rolfe (USA) 77 – Aventina 83 (Averof 123) [1995 7m Oct 12] small, leggy filly: half-sister to several winners, including useful 1986 2-y-o 6f and 7f winner Monterana (by Sallust) and 7f to 1¼m plater Alvin York (by Known Fact): dam, won over 7f at 2 yrs, half-sister to Italian Derby winner Ruysdael II: 33/1 and green, mid-division in 27-runner seller at Newmarket: sold 3,200 gns Newmarket Autumn Sales. *S. P. C. Woods* –

MANDARINA (USA) 3 ch.f. El Gran Senor (USA) 136 – Oriental Mystique 97 (Kris 135) [1994 72p: 7m^3 7m* 1995 8m^6 10m^6 8f^4 7m^2 8.3m 7g* 8g^2 8d^3 Nov 27] good-topped filly with plenty of scope: good mover: useful performer: narrowly won minor event at Brighton in September, leading over 1f out and battling on well: best efforts when placed in listed races at Milan (beaten neck by Penny Drops) and Saint-Cloud (headed close home, beaten ¾ length by Passionnee) last 2 starts: effective at 7f, probably at 1¼m: acts on firm going and dead: sold 105,000 gns Newmarket December Sales. *L. M. Cumani* 105

MANDERELLA 2 b.f. (Apr 3) Clantime 101 – Ascot Lass (Touching Wood (USA) 127) [1995 6.1f^6 6m^2 6g 7d^2 6f Oct 16] 2,600Y: workmanlike filly: poor mover: second reported foal: sister to 3-y-o Kensington Freight: dam never ran: modest maiden: best efforts when second in auction events at Windsor and Redcar: stays 7f: below form both starts on firm ground: bandaged off-hind last 2 starts. *J. Akehurst* — 65

MANDY'S RISK 2 ch.g. (Apr 5) Risk Me (FR) 127 – Lightning Legend 71 (Lord Gayle (USA) 124) [1995 5m 5.3m 5g 6m a5g Aug 11] 2,600Y: leggy gelding: poor mover: fourth foal: brother to 3 platers including 3-y-o Bitch, 6f winner at 2 yrs: dam 2-y-o 7f winner: poor plater: visored final start: sold 500 gns Ascot September Sales. *T. M. Jones* — –

MANFUL 3 b.g. Efisio 120 – Mandrian 103 (Mandamus 120) [1994 86: 5s 5v 5g 6d^3 6f* 7f^2 6f* 7d^2 7m 8s^4 8.1s^3 8s^5 1995 9d^6 10.5m 12g^5 12g^4 12d^4 12m 12.4m^5 12.3m^5 13.8m^4 10.9g^6 13.1g 10f^6 11f^5 a10g^2 a12g^3 a12g a12g^2 a12g^2 Dec 18] useful-looking gelding: fair handicapper at best: stays 1½m: acts on any going: tried visored (out of form) twice at 3 yrs: has given trouble in preliminaries. *J. Hetherton* — 82 d

MANILA BAY (USA) 5 b.g. Manila (USA) – Betty Money (USA) (Our Native (USA)) [1994 –: 10.8d 12.5f^6 1995 10m 11.7h^4 12.1m^6 14d Sep 27] rangy gelding: no worthwhile form since 3 yrs. *J. S. King* — –

MANNINAMIX 2 gr.c. (Apr 23) Linamix (FR) 127 – Mrs Annie (FR) (Bolkonski 134) [1995 8g* 8s* 8m^2 Oct 15] tall, leggy colt: ninth foal: half-brother to several winners, including smart performers Mister Riv (stayed 1¾m, by River River), Mister Sicy (best at 1¼m, by Sicyos) and Mrs Arkada (stayed 1¼m, by Akarad): dam French 7f winner: progressive French colt: won minor event at Deauville in August and 6-runner Prix des Chenes at Chantilly (stayed on to lead close home and beat Winter Quarters a neck) in September: short-head second of 7 to Loup Solitaire in Grand Criterium at Longchamp final start, checked over 1f out then finishing strongly: will stay 1¼m: will improve further. *A. Fabre, France* — 113 p

MAN OF WIT (IRE) 2 b.c. (Feb 19) Fayruz 116 – Laughing Matter 56 (Lochnager 132) [1995 5.2m^6 6m^4 5g 5s Sep 28] 6,500F, 15,000Y: leggy, quite good-topped colt: half-brother to 2 winners in France by Moulin, including middle-distance performer Winged Flight: dam sprinter: off course over 4 months, ran well despite sweating, when fourth of 14 to My Mariam in maiden at Newmarket in August: behind in listed race at Ayr and maiden (ran as if something amiss) at Lingfield last 2 starts: races keenly: very much a sprinter. *A. P. Jarvis* — 74

MANOLETE 4 b.g. Hard Fought 125 – Andalucia 57 (Rheingold 137) [1994 49: 10d 11.1m a12g^3 11.1m^6 12m^2 a14g^6 14.1m 11.9g 15s 12s a12g^5 a12g^4 1995 a14.8g^5 a12g a12g^3 a12g^3 a12g^4 a12g 11.5s Sep 28] good-topped gelding: poor performer: sold out of C. W. C. Elsey's stable 2,900 gns Ascot June Sales after fifth start: tailed off afterwards: stays at least 1½m: acts on good to firm ground and fibresand: blinkered (except once) since fourth 3-y-o start: second in selling hurdle (claimed £6,000 to join Mrs Merrita Jones) in December. *J. Ffitch-Heyes* — 43

MANOLO (FR) 2 b.g. (Feb 14) Cricket Ball (USA) 124 – Malouna (FR) (General Holme (USA) 128) [1995 5m^3 Apr 19] 90,000 francs Y: lengthy gelding: first foal: dam French 8.2f winner: 4/1, over 2 lengths third of 16 to Kala Sunrise in median auction maiden at Pontefract: looked sure to improve. *J. Berry* — 66

MANOR ADVENTURE 5 ch.m. Smackover 107 – Klairove 74 (Averof 123) [1994 66d: 5m 5.1m 5m 5f 5g^2 6f 5f^6 5m 5.1g^3 5d 5d a5g^6 a6g a5g^6 a8g 1995 6m 5.7f May 22] good-bodied mare: fair handicapper at best in 1994: well beaten on return: suited by 5f: acts on good to firm and dead ground: blinkered (below form) last 2 starts at 4 yrs: inconsistent. *P. T. Dalton* — –

MANOY 2 b.g. (Apr 26) Precocious 126 – Redcross Miss 64 (Tower Walk 130) [1995 6m^6 7m 6m Oct 30] 11,000Y: useful-looking gelding: fifth living foal: half-brother to 3-y-o 6f (at 2 yrs) and 8.1f winner Just Fizzy (by Efisio), 1992 2-y-o 5f winner Ruby Cooper (by Green Ruby) and 1993 2-y-o 5f winner Valiant Man (by Valiyar): dam middle-distance maiden: well beaten in maidens. *J. Hetherton* — –

MANSAB (USA) 2 b.c. (Jan 28) Housebuster (USA) – Epitome (USA) (Summing (USA)) [1995 6d^4 6m^3 Oct 30] $400,000Y: neat colt: third foal: half-brother to a winner in UAE by Mr Prospector: dam won Breeders' Cup Juvenile — 66

Fillies: sire, twice champion sprinter, stayed 1m well: similar form in frame in maidens won by Trafalgar Lady at Goodwood and Pivotal at Newcastle, held up then one pace: will be suited by 7f+. *J. L. Dunlop*

MANS PASSION 3 gr.g. Jupiter Island 126 – Roybirdie 76 (Mansingh (USA) 120) [1994 –: 6m 7.1m 7m 1995 10m 6m Jun 19] sturdy, close-coupled gelding: no sign of ability. *J. White* –

MANSUR (IRE) 3 b.g. Be My Chief (USA) 122 – Moorish Idol 90 (Aragon 118) [1994 75p: 7.1g^{4} 7g^{3} 1995 12g^{3} 10f 14.1f^{2} 13.8m^{3} 11.9m^{4} 10d^{5} 11.9d^{5} Sep 26] compact, good-topped gelding: good walker and mover: reportedly injured a pastern at 2 yrs: disappointing in 1995 other than when second of 8 in maiden at Yarmouth in June: stays 1¾m: visored (took good hold, folded tamely) first 2 starts at 3 yrs: not one to trust: gelded. *D. R. Loder* 75 ?

MANZONI (GER) 3 b.c. Solarstern (FR) – Manege (Neckar) [1994 7g^{2} 7g* 7g^{4} 8s* 1995 8.5s 8g* 11s^{4} 12m^{2} 12m^{4} 10g* 10g^{3} Sep 17] brother to very smart 7f (at 2 yrs) to 1½m performer Martessa and half-brother to several winners: dam fairly useful 5f (at 2 yrs) and 11f winner in Germany: smart German colt: successful at 2 yrs in maiden at Hanover and quite valuable event (hampered, promoted) at Munich: won 15-runner Mehl-Mulhens-Rennen at Cologne by 2 lengths from Montjoy, leading inside final 1f: in frame in Deutsches Derby at Hamburg (2½ lengths second of 18 to All My Dreams), Group 1 event at Dusseldorf (6 lengths fourth to Lando), listed race at Hanover (comfortable winner) and Group 2 event at Frankfurt: stays 1½m: fairly useful form on soft ground, easily best efforts on a sound surface. *A. Wohler, Germany* 112

MA PETITE ANGLAISE 3 b.f. Reprimand 122 – Astolat (Rusticaro (FR) 124) [1994 66: 7m 7m^{4} 6.1m^{3} 7d^{3} 1995 6.9m* 8.3g* 8.1g^{5} 9g 8.3m* 7.6m 8d^{5} 8m 8m Oct 28] good-bodied filly: fairly useful handicapper: won at Folkestone (apprentice maiden) and Hamilton in the spring and at Windsor in July: below form last 4 starts: should stay 9f+: acts on good to firm and dead ground: held up. *W. Jarvis* 81

MAPLE BAY (IRE) 6 b.g. Bold Arrangement 127 – Cannon Boy (USA) (Canonero II (USA)) [1994 60d: a16.2g a6g* a7g* a6g^{3} a8.5g a7g^{2} a7g a8.5g^{6} a6g 7m a8.5g^{4} a7g 1995 8.1m a7g^{5} a8.5g^{5} 6g^{3} a7g^{2} a6g^{3} a7g^{3} a10g a9.4g^{4} a7g^{2} Dec 12] tall, workmanlike gelding: fair performer: mostly ran creditably in 1995: effective at 6f, and seemed at 3 yrs to stay 1½m: acts on fibresand and on dead ground: tried blinkered, not when successful. *A. Bailey* 54 + a67

MAPLE BURL 2 b.g. (Feb 24) Dominion 123 – Carn Maire 83 (Northern Prospect (USA)) [1995 6g 7g 6d 6m Nov 6] 2,000Y, 8,200Y 2-y-o: compact gelding: first foal: dam 5f winner at 2 yrs: modest form in maidens (best effort on third start, running-on seventh of 20, not knocked about, behind Fly Tip at Newbury) and well-contested auction event: should stay 7f: acts on good to soft ground, showed little on good to firm. *S. Dow* 68

MAPLESTEAD (IRE) 3 b.c. Shareef Dancer (USA) 135 – Halstead 76 (Bustino 136) [1994 –: 7s 7s 1995 10m 8m^{6} May 5] small, strong colt: no worthwhile form: sold 9,000 gns Newmarket July Sales: sent to Norway. *C. E. Brittain* –

MAQUINA 3 b.f. Machiavellian (USA) 123 – Musical Bliss (USA) 117 (The Minstrel (CAN) 135) [1994 NR 1995 7g Jun 14] smallish, sturdy filly: first living foal: dam won 1000 Guineas and is half-sister to Grade 1 winner Safe Play, dam of Defensive Play: 5/1 and bandaged behind, never a factor in maiden at Yarmouth: sent to Japan. *J. H. M. Gosden* –

MARAADY (USA) 6 b.g. Alydar (USA) – Ma Petite Jolie (USA) 80 (Northern Dancer) [1994 –: 11.9g 12m 14g 1995 12g 12g a14g^{6} 10m Aug 19] leggy gelding: of little account: dead. *G. P. Enright* –

MARADONNA (USA) 6 b.g. Alleged (USA) 138 – Kiss 88 (Habitat 134) [1994 66: 11.6m 14g^{3} 12g 14v^{5} 1995 a16g a14.8g^{2} a16g* 16m^{2} 20m 14.8m Jul 22] big, strong, lengthy gelding: fair performer: promoted after being slightly hampered in tremendous struggle with Arc Bright in claimer at Lingfield in March: broke a leg final start: stayed 2m: acted on dead going, good to firm and all-weather: dead. *J. White* 69

MARALINGA (IRE) 3 ch.c. Simply Great (FR) 122 – Bellinzona (Northfields (USA)) [1994 84p: 6s^{5} 6f 7g* 8m^{3} 1995 a10g* 12.3m^{3} 10.4m^{2} 12f 12g^{5} 9g 11s^{2} 106 a9.4g4 Dec 2] workmanlike colt: useful performer: won Kentucky Derby Trial at Lingfield in April: easily best efforts when in frame in Chester Vase (third-last outing for M. Bell) next start and in listed races in French provinces in October and at Wolverhampton in December: effective at 9.4f to 1½m: acts on firm and soft ground and on all-weather: usually races prominently: reportedly twisted a plate (finished sore in Derby, off course 3 months) fourth 3-y-o start. *Lady Herries*

MARASCHINO 2 ch.f. (Feb 18) Lycius (USA) 124 – Mystery Ship 105 (Decoy Boy 129) [1995 5m 5f5 6.1m 6d Sep 18] 13,500Y: close-coupled filly: half-sister to 3-y-o Mysterian (by Unfuwain), 1m and 8.5f winner in Sweden, and 3 other winners, including 7f and 1m winner Final Enigma (by Final Straw): dam 2-y-o 5f and 7f winner: modest form: well beaten (sweating, raced freely) in nursery final outing. *M. J. Heaton-Ellis* — 50

MARAWIS (USA) 2 b.c. (Feb 22) Danzig (USA) – Ra'a (USA) 106 (Diesis 133) [1995 6d5 6m4 Nov 3] strong, compact colt: second foal: half-brother to 3-y-o 6f winner Awayil (by Woodman): dam, sprinter, out of useful sprinter Shicklah: similar form in 20-runner maidens won by Fly Tip at Newbury and Miss Riviera at Doncaster, disputing lead around 5f: may prove suited by 5f. *H. Thomson Jones* — 75

MARBLE 4 b.f. Petong 126 – Hymettus 103 (Blakeney 126) [1994 47: a9.4g4 7d 6.9v4 8.3f5 7f4 11g3 12m 11.1m5 8.3g 11.1g* 10.5s 11.8g 1995 a11g 12.1v 10m 9.2g 11f6 Oct 24] sparely-made filly: no worthwhile form in 1995, leaving Martyn Wane's stable after fourth start: stays 11f: acts on dead going: headstrong and inconsistent. *M. G. Meagher* — –

MARBLE FALLS (IRE) 3 b.f. Tirol 127 – Majolique (USA) (Irish River (FR) 131) [1994 7.5d5 1995 10s* 10s2 10s* 9.3v2 10d2 10g4 8d 10.5d Nov 17] first foal: dam, ran 3 times, is half-sister to Dancing Maid (Pouliches and Vermeille at 3 yrs) and Mona Stella (Prix de l'Opera): useful French filly: won minor events at Evry in February and Longchamp in April: second of 5 to Secret Quest (beaten 2½ lengths) in Prix Vanteaux then to Muncie (beaten 4 lengths) in Prix Saint-Alary, both at Longchamp: below form last 3 starts: effective at around 1¼m, and may well stay 1½m: yet to race on top-of-the-ground. *E. Lellouche, France* — 107

MARCHANT MING (IRE) 3 br.g. Persian Bold 123 – Hot Curry (USA) (Sharpen Up 127) [1994 61: 7d 7s 1995 a10g4 a9.4g3 11.6m 12g3 11.7m2 10.8m 11.5m* 11.5m5 11.4d5 Sep 12] sparely-made gelding: modest performer: took time to return to form, but won maiden handicap (unchallenged) at Yarmouth in August: below form afterwards: stays 1½m: blinkered since fourth 3-y-o start: has looked none too keen (found little eighth 3-y-o start) and not one to trust implicitly: sold (M. Jarvis to M. Hammond) 7,000 gns Newmarket Autumn Sales. *M. A. Jarvis* — 64 a46 +

MARCHMAN 10 b.g. Daring March 116 – Saltation 111 (Sallust 134) [1994 NR 1995 10m4 12g 9m2 8f3 10m Jul 17] big, strong, good-topped gelding: modest performer (rated 60) at 8 yrs: poor claiming handicapper (found little final start) on return: effective at 1m and stays 1¾m: best form on a sound surface and acts on firm going. *J. S. King* — 49

MARCO MAGNIFICO (USA) 5 b. or br.g. Bering 136 – Viscosity (USA) (Sir Ivor 135) [1994 73: 13.9f 16.5m 12m 16.1f 12.3g 12m a12g6 a13g2 1995 a16g4 17.5g 12m Oct 2] leggy gelding: fair at best in 1994: sold out of B. Hills's stable 10,000 gns Doncaster February Sales after reappearance: tailed off twice in the autumn: stays 1¾m well: acts on equitrack and dead ground, probably on firm: modest hurdler, winner in December. *T. Dyer* — –

MARCOMIR (USA) 2 b.c. (Apr 9) Dayjur (USA) 137 – Mariella (USA) 106 (Roberto (USA) 131) [1995 6g* Sep 24] closely related to 11.9f winner Duke of Warsaw (by Danzig) and half-brother to a minor winner in North America: dam, middle-distance winner, out of Oaks winner Monade: heavily-backed favourite, won 4-runner maiden at Hamilton by 1¼ lengths from Ocean Stream, running green and not getting on top until well inside last: sure to improve. *M. Johnston* — 76 p

MARGARET MODES 3 b.f. Thatching 131 – Avant-Garde (Pas de Seul 133) [1994 NR 1995 a7g 7f 10.8g3 10g 8h 8.2m 11.9f Aug 22] 5,600Y: workmanlike filly: fourth foal: dam ran once at 2 yrs in Ireland: no form, including in sellers: visored/blinkered (tailed off) once each: sold (C. Cyzer to H. Manners) 1,900 gns Ascot August Sales. *C. A. Cyzer* — –

MARGARETROSE ANNA 3 b.f. Handsome Sailor 125 – Be Bold (Bustino 136) [1994 54: 6g^3 7m^6 6s^6 5s^4 1995 6f^6 Oct 3] good-topped, workmanlike filly: modest maiden at 2 yrs: needed race on belated return: stays 7f: acts on good to firm and soft ground. *E. J. Alston* –

MARGI BOO 2 ch.f. (Apr 1) Risk Me (FR) 127 – Louisianalightning (Music Boy 124) [1995 5d 5s^4 a5g 6g 7f Oct 3] 4,000Y: close-coupled filly: half-sister to winning sprinters Lightning Belle (by Belfort) and Mimining (by Tower Walk) and 7f to 1½m winner Azubah (by Castle Keep): dam ran once: well beaten in maiden events (absent 4 months prior to penultimate start) and a claimer: sold (G. Moore to R. Juckes) 500 gns Doncaster November Sales. *G. M. Moore* –

MARGUERITE BAY (IRE) 3 b.f. Darshaan 133 – Idrak 68 (Young Generation 129) [1994 NR 1995 7m* 8f^6 10.5g 8m Oct 2] sturdy, lengthy filly: good mover: third foal: half-sister to 4-y-o Recaptured Days (by Salse), 6f winner at 2 yrs: dam sprinter from family of Triple First, Maysoon and Three Tails: won maiden at Goodwood in May, staying on strongly: off course 3 months, well beaten in handicaps at Haydock and Pontefract (visored) last 2 starts: should stay beyond 1m: sold 4,600 gns Doncaster October Sales. *E. A. L. Dunlop* 73

MARHA 3 br.f. Shaadi (USA) 126 – Balqis (USA) 93 (Advocator) [1994 85: 5g^2 6g* 6g 1995 6m^4 6m* 6m^4 6m Aug 25] fairly useful performer: narrow winner of minor event at Newmarket in June, quickening to lead inside the final 1f despite tending to carry head awkwardly: well below form in listed race at Newmarket final start: may have stayed 7f, but would not have got nearly so far (1¼m+) as most of her siblings: did not race on a soft surface: early to post after debut: visits Persian Bold. *H. Thomson Jones* 95

MARIE DE KEN (FR) 3 b.f. Kendor (FR) 122 – Marie de Vez (FR) (Crystal Palace (FR) 132) [1994 110: 7d* 9d^2 10s^4 1995 8d^5 8g^2 8g^2 10d* 9.3d 10.5g^4 10.5d* Nov 17] big, workmanlike, French filly: smart performer: did not reappear until July: won listed event at Longchamp in September and Prix Fille de L'Air at Evry (by length from Restiv Star) in November: effective at 1m and stays 10.5f: acts on dead going (probably on soft), yet to race on top-of-the-ground. *A. de Royer-Dupre, France* 110

MARIGLIANO (USA) 2 b.c. (Apr 15) Riverman (USA) 131 – Mount Holyoke 93 (Golden Fleece (USA) 133) [1995 7m^3 Nov 3] rather leggy, quite attractive colt: half-brother to useful middle-distance performer Wootton Rivers (by Woodman), also 7f to 1¼m winner at 2 yrs: dam, 1m winner, is daughter of smart sprinter Amaranda: 10/1 and gone in coat, 1¾ lengths third of 18 to Wahiba Sands in maiden at Doncaster, always at head of stand-side group and keeping on well: wore bandages: sure to improve. *M. R. Stoute* 75 p

MARILDO (FR) 8 b.h. Romildo 124 – Marike (FR) (Nasram II 125) [1994 124: 10s^4 10v^3 10.5m* 9.3g^3 12g 10d^3 8g^6 10g* 10f^6 1995 10v^4 10s 10.5v 9.3g^3 10m* 10g* 10g 10d^4 9.8s^5 10m Nov 12] tall French horse: very smart performer: returned to near best when 2½ lengths third of 9 to Green Tune in Prix d'Ispahan at Longchamp in May: conceded weight all round when winning La Coupe at Evry (by a length from Baron Ferdinand) and Grand Prix de Vichy (by 3 lengths from Solidoun) in mid-summer: regressive form afterwards: has won at 13f, but best efforts at around 1¼m: suited by a sound surface, has run respectably on heavy: wears blinkers: effective from front or held up. *D. Smaga, France* 120

MARINO STREET 2 b.f. (Apr 16) Totem (USA) 118 – Demerger 61 (Dominion 123) [1995 7f^5 6m^4 5f^3 a6g^5 a6g^2 a6g^5 Dec 19] 1,800Y: fourth foal: half-sister to 3-y-o Slybird (by Precocious) and 1993 2-y-o 5f winner Bev's Folly (by Chilibang): dam, best at 2 yrs, is half-sister to dam of Tenby: in frame in maiden events at Ballinrobe and Down Royal when trained by G. Cully in Ireland: similar form in 2 of 3 runs here: should stay 7f: below form on fibresand. *P. D. Evans* 63

MARIPOSA GROVE 3 b.f. Kalaglow 132 – Feather Flower 74 (Relkino 131) [1994 47: 7m^6 6.9d^5 7g 1995 8m 11.6m 11.8g 8.2m Jun 26] leggy, unfurnished filly: poor maiden handicapper: soundly beaten last 3 starts: should stay 1½m. *R. Curtis* –

MARISTAX 2 b.f. (Feb 16) Reprimand 122 – Marista (Mansingh (USA) 120) [1995 5m^4 6.1d^4 6g^2 6.9g* Oct 16] 10,500Y: leggy, sparely-made filly: sister to 1993 2-y-o 6f winner Strapped, closely related to useful 1988 2-y-o 5f winner Four-Legged Friend (by Aragon) and half-sister to good 1991 2-y-o 6f winner 74 p

Superstrike (by Superlative), later graded winner in USA: dam lightly raced and looked temperamental: progressive form: won 13-runner maiden auction at Folkestone by a head from Trojan Risk, doing particularly well to lead on line as saddle slipped 2f out and rider rode without irons most of last 1f: better suited by 7f than less: will continue to progress. *P. J. Makin*

MARJAANA (IRE) 2 b.f. (Jan 24) Shaadi (USA) 126 – Funun (USA) 84 (Fappiano (USA)) [1995 6f^3 5.2g* 6f^2 7g^4 7d Sep 26] well-made filly: second foal: sister to 3-y-o 6f winner Intiaash: dam, winner from 5f to 7f, out of half-sister to Tasso: won 7-runner maiden at Newbury in July: not discredited when fourth of 14 to Consordino in nursery at Yarmouth on penultimate outing: probably stays 7f. *P. T. Walwyn* — 76

MARJAN (IRE) 4 ch.f. Classic Secret (USA) 91 – Powder Lass 76 (Tap On Wood 130) [1994 NR 1995 7f^6 a8g a14.8g^5 Nov 27] leggy filly: seems no longer of much account. *T. H. Caldwell* — –

MARJIMEL 4 b.f. Backchat (USA) 98 – Mary's Double (Majetta 115) [1994 –: 14d^5 14.1g 14.6s 1995 14.1m 12m^5 12d 10m^6 Jun 12] leggy, angular filly: poor mover: poor handicapper: probably needs at least 1½m: acts on good to firm ground: inconsistent. *J. L. Eyre* — 46

MARJONS BOY 8 ch.g. Enchantment 115 – Nevilles Cross (USA) 67 (Nodouble (USA)) [1994 NR 1995 a16g Mar 2] big, angular gelding: probably no longer of much account. *C. A. Horgan* — – §

MARJORIE ROSE (IRE) 2 b.f. (Apr 25) Magical Strike (USA) 114 – Arrapata (Thatching 131) [1995 5g^3 5g^2 5g^5 6m^4 Jul 8] 1,900Y: workmanlike filly: has scope: half-sister to 1993 2-y-o 5f winner Dance of The Swans (by Try My Best) and 2 other winners, including leading 1988 Scandinavian 2-y-o Henry Light (by Salmon Leap): dam unraced: strong-finishing second of 4 in maiden at Haydock in May: ran respectably final start: stays 6f. *A. Bailey* — 64

MARJORIE'S MEMORY (IRE) 4 b.f. Fairy King (USA) – Burnished Gold 74 (Breton 130) [1994 76: 7m 5.3f* 5m^6 5f 5g^4 1995 5g^5 5m 6f Jul 29] workmanlike filly: has a quick action: fair sprinter on her day at 3 yrs: well beaten in claimer (final outing for M. Heaton-Ellis) and handicaps in 1995: acts on firm ground, tailed off on dead: inconsistent: sold 7,500 gns Newmarket December Sales. *Mrs A. Swinbank* — –

MARJORIE'S ORCHID 4 gr.f. Petong 126 – Aonia 97 (Mummy's Pet 125) [1994 49: 5.7m^6 7g 8.2m 6f 1995 a7g 8.3m May 15] compact filly: well beaten since 1994 reappearance: should stay 6f+: blinkered final 3-y-o start. *M. J. Heaton-Ellis* — –

MARKETEER MAGIC 2 ch.c. (Feb 13) Clantime 101 – Mary From Dunlow 49 (Nicholas Bill 125) [1995 5m 5f^4 6.1m^6 6m 5m^5 a6g 7.5d Sep 13] 6,200Y: compact colt: first foal: dam 2-y-o 5f winner, later had form at 1m: fourth of 5 in median auction maiden at Redcar in May: failed to repeat that form, well beaten in selling nurseries on last 2 starts: sold 800 gns Doncaster October Sales. *J. Berry* — 53 d

MARKETING MAN 5 b.g. Sizzling Melody 117 – Best Offer 96 (Crepello 136) [1994 NR 1995 a13g Jan 12] tall, angular gelding: little sign of ability on flat. *Pat Mitchell* — –

MARK OF ESTEEM (IRE) 2 b.c. (Mar 26) Darshaan 133 – Homage (Ajdal (USA) 130) [1995 7g^2 7f* Jul 28] — 105 p

'Things can only get better for Henry Cecil' stated one columnist in *The Sporting Life* on Tuesday, October 3rd. Well, not quite right. The following day's front-page headline in the same paper read 'Sheikh sacks Cecil' and the Sheikh in question was Sheikh Mohammed. While millions of television viewers were tuning in each week to watch the BBC's production of Pride and Prejudice, the racing world was gripped as a rather less happy conclusion emerged in its own drama of apparently idyllic partnerships. The title of Jane Austen's novel was not inappropriate to the widely polarised comment that followed. The relationship between Henry Cecil and Sheikh Mohammed had looked as productive as any between a trainer and an owner, resulting in fifty-seven European pattern wins, beginning with Oh So Sharp's Fillies' Mile in 1984 and ending with Stelvio's Queen's Vase in 1995. The famous names in between included Indian Skimmer, Diminuendo, Salse, Reprimand, Old Vic, Belmez and King's Theatre. Trainers losing horses or breaking up with owners is hardly a new phenomenon—and we dare say that the two of them in this case are big enough to get by without each other—but, apart from sheer newsworthiness, this divorce obviously had wider implications given the scale of Sheikh Mohammed's patronage and the seemingly crucial role played by his ambitions for Godolphin. Moonshell, Classic Cliche and Vettori left Cecil as two-year-olds in 1994 and returned to win classics in the royal blue under Saeed bin Suroor in 1995. Allied Forces was purchased in the summer, by someone unconnected to the Al Maktoums, to race in Dubai. Another Cecil-trained two-year-old, Mark of Esteem, was withdrawn from the Royal Lodge Stakes and sent to Dubai, followed soon afterwards by the three-year-olds Kalabo and Marocco. Unproven individuals have so far formed the clear majority of three-year-olds in the still-small Godolphin team, but the spectre of the unproven remaining unproven to the detriment of the two-year-old pattern races was clearly a concern. A possible breakdown in relations between the ten-times champion trainer and nine-times champion owner first came to light when Cecil's wife voiced their distress at losing these horses in an interview with Jonathan Powell of the *Sunday Express* in September, a probable breakdown when the Sheikh responded with an angry and personal dressing-down of his critics in a press conference on Royal Lodge day. The language of Mrs Cecil's disappointment was more emotive but the substance very similar to some of the comments Cecil himself had made in a *Guardian* article back in June, in which he had at the same time however said that he had no complaints about Godolphin and 'I take off my hat to Sheikh Mohammed'. Three months later relations were not so cordial as the Mark of Esteem case brought matters to a head, Sheikh Mohammed's team stating that the colt would not have been able to run in the Royal Lodge anyway because he had a knee injury which the trainer had not told them about. As we have said, this affair provided a lighter to wider concerns. Among these were complaints and weariness about Al Maktoum domination (evinced most clearly in the classics but also felt at much lower levels) and domesday fears that there were plans to make Dubai the centre of thoroughbred racing. It is right, of course, for British racing to be concerned about its future—money talks and Britain no longer has the same share of it—and the same point has to be made regarding the continuing drain of some of our best bloodstock to Japan, in that case a drain that is unlikely to allow them or their progeny to appear at Ascot or any other European racecourse.

Contrastingly, there is little to write about the colt that brought these issues to the surface again, Mark of Esteem. So far, that is. From what we saw of him in two races in July he is well up to pattern company. A neck was all that separated him from Alhaarth on their debuts in a maiden at Newmarket and seventeen days later Mark of Esteem won a £7,000 maiden on the Friday of the Goodwood meeting. In the latter he started 15/8 on, travelled strongly on the heels of the leaders, quickened on two furlongs out then stretched away without having to be at all hard ridden; he was worth a good deal more than the eventual three lengths at which he led in Tawkil, Reinhardt and Night Watch, and has been rated accordingly. The knee injury—said to be a degenerative condition, resulting in acute soreness, that might require surgery—is clearly something of a worry. Without it, Mark of Esteem has a very bright future. He will stay at least a mile.

Mark of Esteem (IRE) (b.c. Mar 26, 1993)	Darshaan (br 1981)	Shirley Heights (b 1975)	Mill Reef
			Hardiemma
		Delsy (br 1972)	Abdos
			Kelty
	Homage (b 1989)	Ajdal (b 1984)	Northern Dancer
			Native Partner
		Home Love (b 1976)	Vaguely Noble
			Homespun

An attractive colt and a good mover, he is the first foal out of an unraced half-sister to Local Suitor and Local Talent. Local Suitor was himself a star two-year-old for Sheikh Mohammed back in 1984. Trained by Dick Hern, he started co-favourite with the Cecil charge Presidium in the Mill Reef Stakes and beat him by a length and a half before narrowly losing out to Kala Dancer and Law Society in the Dewhurst. However, after being beaten eleven and a half lengths in the Craven, Local Suitor met with a set-back and was retired to stud. His greatest achievement in that sphere, the very smart three-year-old Solon, has of course come since his departure to Germany. His half-brother Local Talent also merited a place at stud, in the USA; probably his best-known representatives here are the David Elsworth-trained Star Talent and the 1995 Diomed Stakes challenger from Germany, Chato. Local Talent managed only two runs as a three-year-old, but one of those was a win in the Prix

Sheikh Mohammed's "Mark of Esteem"

Jean Prat. This pair's dam Home Love never raced at all, but she is a half-sister to three colts by Nijinsky that did well, in Sportin' Life, Folk Art and Mashaallah. *H. R. A. Cecil*

MARL 2 ch.f. (Feb 4) Lycius (USA) 124 – Pamela Peach 81 (Habitat 134) [1995 5m² 5.2g* 5m⁶ 5.2g Jul 15] 20,000Y: sparely-made filly: second foal: dam maiden here (effective at 6f and 7f) who later won in USA: 6-length winner (from Satellite Star) of well-contested minor event at Newbury in May: never able to challenge in Queen Mary Stakes at Ascot following month or in Super Sprint at Newbury (where badly drawn) in July: will be better suited by 6f, particularly when ground is on firm side. *R. Akehurst* — 92

MARMY 2 b.f. (Mar 23) Midyan (USA) 124 – Usaylah 98 (Siberian Express (USA) 125) [1995 6m³ 7m a6g 6m 8m Sep 5] 2,600Y: smallish filly: second foal: half-sister to 3-y-o 1m winner Kaf (by Polish Precedent): dam 9f to 10.6f winner: plater: failed to progress after shaping quite well on debut: blinkered third start: sold 2,800 gns Newmarket Autumn Sales: sent to Holland. *M. H. Easterby* — 43 d

MAROCCO (USA) 3 ch.c. Diesis 133 – Bank On Love (USA) (Gallant Romeo (USA)) [1994 NR 1995 7.3m⁴ 8g⁵ 7.5m* 7f⁴ 7f⁶ Aug 2] $150,000F: rather leggy colt (has badly scarred shins): brother to very useful 6f and 7.2f winner Weldnaas and half-brother to several winners: dam well bred but unraced: fairly useful performer: landed the odds in maiden at Beverley in June: stays 7.5f: acts on firm going, yet to race on a soft surface: sent to Dubai. *H. R. A. Cecil* — 80

MARONETTA 3 ch.f. Kristian – Suzannah's Song (Song 132) [1994 –: 7g a7g 1995 a7g a10g 10.1m⁵ 11d² 11.9d² 16.4m³ a14g a13g Dec 19] angular filly: poor — 43 a–

maiden handicapper: stays 16.4f: acts on good to firm and dead ground, well beaten on all-weather. *M. J. Ryan*

MAROWINS 6 ch.g. Sweet Monday 122 – Top Cover (High Top 131) [1994 47, a65: a8.5g^{2} a8.5g* a9.4g* a8.5g* a9.4g^{3} a8.5g^{5} a8.5g^{4} 9.2d^{3} 9.2f^{4} a8.5g^{4} 8m^{5} 8g^{2} 8.1g 8.9d 1995 a8g a8g^{4} a9.4g^{5} a9.4g a8.5g* a8.5g* 8.3g^{4} 8.3g^{6} 8g* 8.1m a8.5g^{6} 8.1m 8g 8d Sep 9] robust gelding: has a quick action: fair handicapper on the all-weather, winning minor event and handicap at Wolverhampton in April: poor on turf, winning at Thirsk in June: stays 1¼m: probably acts on any going, goes well on fibresand: below form when visored at 2 yrs: sometimes sweats: held up, and suited by strongly-run race: tough. *E. J. Alston* — 49 a70

MARROWFAT LADY (IRE) 4 b.f. Astronef 116 – Lady Topknot (High Top 131) [1994 7s 7.8f^{4} 7m 5g^{4} 6g 8g^{5} 7g^{3} 7g^{3} 7d 7g 1995 7g^{5} 7m 6.9f* 6.9g* 8.3m^{2} 7m Jul 26] rangy, ex-Irish filly: fourth foal: half-sister to French 1¼m and hurdles winner Lady Hays (by Hays): dam unplaced: sold out of J. Coogan's stable IR 2,200 gns Goffs October 1994 Sales: fair handicapper: won at Folkestone in June and (5 days later) July: never a factor in 16-runner race at Epsom last time: stays 8.3f: probably acts on any going: tried blinkered in Ireland: sold (R. Millman to G. Fierro) only 700 gns Ascot September Sales. *B. R. Millman* — 67

MARSAYAS (IRE) 2 ch.c. (Apr 25) Classic Music (USA) – Babiana (CAN) 90 (Sharpen Up 127) [1995 7.5d 7f a8g^{6} Nov 6] IR 11,500Y, 8,000 2-y-o: third foal: half-brother to German 1994 2-y-o 7f winner Royal Moon (by Deploy) and a winner at up to 9f in Hungary by Glint of Gold: dam 2-y-o 7f winner: no worthwhile form in maiden events. *M. J. Camacho* — –

MARSH ARAB 4 b.g. Night Shift (USA) – Ophrys 90 (Nonoalco (USA) 131) [1994 54: 8.1g^{5} 7f 7g^{5} 8d a7g 1995 a8.5g^{6} a6g a7g 5d 6g Sep 22] big, workmanlike gelding: modest performer: no worthwhile form for new stable in 1995: stays 8.2f: below form on firm going: visored (no form) third 4-y-o start: inconsistent. *J. Balding* — –

MARSOOM (CAN) 4 b.c. Wild Again (USA) – Sadwester (USA) (Honest Pleasure (USA)) [1994 100: 10v^{2} 10.3m^{4} 12g* 12d^{4} 8f^{5} 10m^{2} 10m^{5} 11.9m* 11.9d 1995 12m^{4} 10.4g^{2} 11.5g^{2} 12.3g* 12m^{5} 11.9m^{5} 10g^{4} Jul 22] strong, good-topped colt: useful performer: ran to exactly the same figure first 6 starts in 1995, winning 3-runner minor event at Chester in June then fifth in Bessborough Stakes at Royal Ascot and Old Newton Cup at Haydock: sweating, ran creditably final one: should stay beyond 1½m: acts on firm ground and dead: wears bandage(s): occasionally held up, normally tracks leaders: genuine and tremendously consistent. *B. Hanbury* — 103

MARTARA (IRE) 2 b.c. (Mar 23) Marju (IRE) 127 – Alrayhah (Habitat 134) [1995 5d^{6} 5.2m^{5} 5g* 6f^{4} 6m 5.2d^{4} 5d^{2} Sep 19] IR 33,000Y: sturdy, lengthy colt: fourth foal: half-brother to 2 winners in Italy: dam poor maiden: won minor event at Ayr in July: failed to repeat that form in nurseries: should have stayed at least 6f at 2 yrs: dead. *M. R. Channon* — 76 ?

MARTHA QUEST 2 ch.f. (Jan 7) Rainbow Quest (USA) 134 – Magic Flute (USA) (The Minstrel (CAN) 135) [1995 6.9g^{4} 7m^{4} 9m^{4} 7m^{2} Oct 13] sparely-made filly: first foal: dam unraced sister to Free Handicap winner Noble Minstrel: modest form in maidens and a private sweepstakes at Newmarket: didn't give her running at Chester on second outing: stays 9f: bandaged off-hind (and free to post) third start: sold 7,500 gns Newmarket December Sales. *B. W. Hills* — 65

MARTINIQUAIS (IRE) 2 ch.c. Simply Great (FR) 122 – Majolique (USA) (Irish River (FR) 131) [1995 7g* 7g* 8s^{3} Sep 18] second foal: half-brother to useful French 3-y-o 1¼m winner Marble Falls (by Tirol): dam, ran 3 times, is half-sister to top-class (at up to 1½m) Dancing Maid: useful French form: won newcomers race and minor event in the provinces in the summer: 2¾ lengths third of 6 to Manninamix in Prix des Chenes at Chantilly in September: likely to be well suited by middle distances. *A. Fabre, France* — 100 p

MARTINOSKY 9 b.g. Martinmas 128 – Bewitched 63 (African Sky 124) [1994 NR 1995 a6g^{5} a6g 6.9d^{4} a6g 7g Apr 27] big gelding: good walker: fair handicapper (rated 67) at 7 yrs: only modest at best in 1995: suited by 6f/7f: acts on any turf going (below form all 3 all-weather starts): effective in blinkers (rarely tried) or not: none too consistent. *G. C. Bravery* — 57 a47

MARTINS FOLLY 2 ch.f. (Mar 21) Beveled (USA) – Millingdale 65 (Tumble Wind (USA)) [1995 5.1h^{6} 7m a8.5g Dec 9] half-sister to 7f winner Lady Stock (by Crofter) and 2m winner Norstock (by Norwick): dam, ran only at 2 yrs, second over 5f and 6f: soundly beaten in maidens. *J. White* –

MARWELL INDIGO 3 br.g. Interrex (CAN) – Lily of France 81 (Monsanto (FR) 121) [1994 NR 1995 6m 6f^{4} 6g 5g 7d Oct 19] fifth foal: half-brother to winning sprinter Great Hall (by Hallgate): dam sprinter: poor maiden: trained until after third start by J. Toller. *P. D. Cundell* 49

MARY MACBLAIN 6 b.m. Damister (USA) 123 – Tzarina (USA) (Gallant Romeo (USA)) [1994 35: 10d^{4} 10v^{4} 8.2f 10g 7g^{3} 7g 8m* 7g^{4} a8g 1995 8.5m^{5} 8g 8g^{2} 8f^{6} 8.1f 10.1m a7g a10g^{4} a10g Dec 18] plain, shallow-girthed mare: has a round action: poor handicapper: stays 1¼m: probably acts on any ground: blinkered (ran poorly) once at 4 yrs: has worn near-side pricker: none too consistent. *J. L. Harris* 40

MARY'S CASE (IRE) 5 b.g. Taufan (USA) 119 – Second Service (Red Regent 123) [1994 9f 7.8f 6.5g^{3} 7d^{3} 6g^{7} 7g^{7} 7d 1995 a7g^{5} a7g^{3} a7g^{3} a8g^{2} 8.1d^{3} a8g 7m 8.1g* 7.5g^{6} 8m^{2} 8.1m^{2} 8.1f^{4} 7.1m 8m^{2} 8g a8g^{2} 7g* 7g^{2} 8f^{4} Oct 18] IR 5,000Y: ex-Irish gelding: fourth foal: dam unplaced: has twice been operated on for wind problems: modest performer: trained by P. Woods in Ireland at 4 yrs: narrowly won seller at Edinburgh in May and handicap at Ayr in September: will prove best at up to 1m: acts on good to firm and dead ground and all-weather surfaces: effective blinkered (usually is) or not: tends to hang: often has tongue tied down: consistent on form but temperamental: sold (M. Johnston to Mrs J. D. Goodfellow) 6,200 gns Doncaster October Sales. *M. Johnston* 64 § a61 §

MARY'S WAY (GR) 3 b.f. Night Shift (USA) – Sally (DEN) (Faraway Times (USA) 123) [1994 NR 1995 8m* 10.4g 8g^{6} Oct 10] close-coupled filly: first foal: dam unraced half-sister to dam of In The Groove (by Night Shift): seemed particularly green when winning maiden at Salisbury, coming from last to lead inside final 1f: tailed off in minor events at York (later in May) and Leicester (sweating, in October): should stay beyond 1m: sold 12,000 gns Newmarket December Sales. *R. Charlton* 78

MARZIPAN (IRE) 3 br.f. Green Desert (USA) 127 – Lady Zi (Manado 130) [1994 74p: 6g 7g^{2} 1995 8g 10g 10.2h^{3} 10m^{2} 10.2m^{5} 11.9d Sep 26] rather unfurnished filly: just a modest maiden in 1995: should stay beyond 1¼m: acts on hard ground, possibly not on a soft surface: none too consistent: sold 10,000 gns Newmarket December Sales: sent to France. *J. W. Hills* 60

MASAAFAAT (USA) 3 b.f. Woodman (USA) 126 – Pirouette 114 (Sadler's Wells (USA) 132) [1994 NR 1995 8g 7.5d^{2} 7.6m^{5} 7m^{3} 7g^{3} Sep 16] IR 77,000Y: angular filly: first foal: dam, Irish 7f winner, half-sister to very smart sprinter Ballad Rock: fair maiden: stays 1m: acts on good to firm ground, seemed particularly suited by dead: bandaged in front: sold 28,000 gns Newmarket December Sales. *M. R. Stoute* 71

MASAFAH (USA) 3 ch.f. Cadeaux Genereux 131 – Tatwij (USA) 94 (Topsider (USA)) [1994 67: 6g^{3} 5g^{2} 6d 1995 6.1m 6g* Jun 7] unfurnished filly: fair form: easily best effort when winning handicap at Yarmouth in June, overcoming trouble in running and showing a good turn of foot: effective at 6f and will stay 7f: looked sure to win more races: sold only 7,000 gns Newmarket December Sales. *H. Thomson Jones* 81

MASAI MAN (USA) 4 ch.g. Riverman (USA) 131 – Green Oasis (FR) 108 (Green Dancer (USA) 132) [1994 –: 8m 8g 10m 1995 a14g Apr 11] big, lengthy gelding: signs of ability for L. Cumani at 3 yrs: off course 10 months and blinkered, virtually pulled up in strongly-run handicap at Southwell only start in 1995: should stay at least 1¼m. *S. R. Bowring* –

MASBRO BIRD 2 b.f. (Apr 17) Midyan (USA) 124 – Grinning (IRE) (Bellypha 130) [1995 5g 5.1m 7f 6m Sep 7] 2,200Y: leggy filly: second foal: dam unraced: poor form in maidens and a claimer. *B. R. Millman* –

MASCALLS LADY 10 b.m. Nicholas Bill 125 – Whisper Gently 91 (Pitskelly 122) [1994 NR 1995 8.1m 12m Jul 6] rather plain, leggy mare: no longer of any account. *N. B. Thomson* –

MASEHAAB (IRE) 2 b.c. (Jan 30) Mujtahid (USA) 118 – Firefly Night (Salmon Leap (USA) 131) [1995 6m^3 7.1d* 7g* Oct 10] 50,000F: strong, lengthy colt: third foal: half-brother to 1m winner Classical Rock (by Ballad Rock): dam never ran: won 9-runner maiden at Sandown in September on first run for 5 months by a neck from Acharne, getting on top close home: sweating, workmanlike when winning slowly-run 4-runner minor event at Leicester following month by 1¾ lengths from Magic Lake: will stay 1m: has scope, and is likely to do better. *J. L. Dunlop* 91 p

MASK FLOWER (USA) 2 b.f. (Apr 28) Dayjur (USA) 137 – Nom de Plume (USA) 116 (Nodouble (USA)) [1995 5g^4 5g^2 5m^2 a5g^2 a6g* Nov 30] fourth foal: half-sister to useful 7.1f winner Pen Point (by Diesis): dam, 1m to 10.5f winner, half-sister to high-class 1982 USA 2-y-o Total Departure: fair form: given good tactical ride when winning maiden at Lingfield in November: stays 6f: acts on good to firm ground and all-weather surfaces. *M. Johnston* 72

MASNAD (USA) 4 ch.c. Mt Livermore (USA) – Fateful Princess (USA) 95 (Vaguely Noble 140) [1994 101p: 8m* 7f^2 1995 7m^4 7m 7m May 19] strong, lengthy, attractive colt: has had wind operation: useful form at 3 yrs: well below best in 1995, tailed off last 2 starts: stays 1m: usually a front runner: early to post: one to treat with caution: sold only 4,000 gns Newmarket Autumn Sales: sent to Italy. *R. W. Armstrong* –

MASNUN (USA) 10 gr.g. Nureyev (USA) 131 – Careless Kitten (USA) (Caro 133) [1994 71: a8g^5 7s 6m^3 6m^2 5.7f^5 6f* 6g 6d 6m^2 a7g^4 a8g^5 a8g^2 a8g* 1995 a7g a8g* a8g^2 a10g* a10g* 8f^4 a7g 7g a7g^6 a10g^3 a7g* a8g^3 Dec 15] sturdy gelding: fair performer nowadays: first past post in 4 claimers in a row (demoted for interference on second of them) at Lingfield early in 1995, and won another in November: effective at 7f and stays 1¼m: acts on equitrack and probably on any turf going (seems particularly effective on a sound surface): often on toes: held up. *R. J. O'Sullivan* 71

MASON (IRE) 3 ch.g. Simply Great (FR) 122 – Viva Ronda 67 (Kampala 120) [1994 53p: 6d 6.1m 1995 6m^3 6m a8.5g a7g Sep 16] modest maiden: soundly beaten after reappearance: should be suited by further than 6f. *S. Mellor* 54 d

MASQUERADE 2 b.c. (Mar 18) Alzao (USA) 117 – Melpomene (USA) 103 (Lear Fan (USA) 130) [1995 7f^5 7m* 7d Sep 26] 20,000Y: compact colt: first foal: dam, miler, half-sister to Caramba and Lemon Souffle: won 11-runner maiden at Leicester in September by 1¼ lengths from Do Not Disturb: beaten long way out in valuable sales race at Newmarket final start: will stay at least 1m: sold to race in USA. *L. M. Cumani* 80

MASRAH DUBAI (USA) 4 b.g. Theatrical 128 – Roycon 100 (High Top 131) [1994 52: a8g^5 a7g^5 1995 a10g^2 a12g^5 Feb 9] lightly-raced gelding: progressive maiden: stays at least 1½m: sold (M. Jarvis to D. Burchell) 8,600 gns Ascot February Sales. *M. A. Jarvis* 62

MASRUF (IRE) 3 b.c. Taufan (USA) 119 – Queen's Share (Main Reef 126) [1994 88: 6f^3 6m* 7g^2 6m^6 1995 7f 7m 8m 6m^4 7f 7.1d Sep 13] good-bodied colt: fairly useful performer at 2 yrs: disappointing in 1995: stays 7f. *T. Thomson Jones* –

MASSADA 2 b.f. (Mar 16) Most Welcome 131 – Maracuja (USA) (Riverman (USA) 131) [1995 6g^6 7g* 7s^6 8v* Oct 3] 8,000Y: second foal (first died in training): dam, French 2-y-o 1m winner, out of half-sister to Graded Stakes winner and excellent broodmare Lassie Dear: won maiden in August and valuable Preis der Winterkonigin (around 50/1 in 14-runner event, came home 11 lengths clear), both at Mulheim: should stay 1¼m: the best German 2-y-o filly and clearly a very interesting prospect. *H. Remmert, Germany* 106 p

MASTER BEVELED 5 b.g. Beveled (USA) – Miss Anniversary §§ (Tachypous 128) [1994 90p: a8.5g^3 a9.4g^2 8m^4 a8.5g 8v* 7m* 8m^3 8.1g^2 8.3m a8.5g 8m 8m 8.1g 8.1d* 8.1d^3 10m^2 8.9d* 8m^2 8d* 1995 a7g a9.4g a10g 8g 8g 8.1m 10m 8.1g 8.1g 8m 7.9g^5 8d^5 8g^6 8d^6 9g 8m Oct 14] lengthy gelding: still a fairly useful handicapper, though not so good as at 4 yrs: has run creditably at 1¼m but is probably best at around 1m: acts on good to firm and heavy ground: tried visored/blinkered at 3 yrs: won twice over hurdles in the autumn. *P. D. Evans* 86 d

MASTER CHARTER 3 ch.g. Master Willie 129 – Irene's Charter 72 (Persian Bold 123) [1994 NR 1995 5m 11.1g^2 12m^6 7f 7m* 8.2m^6 Oct 26] 15,000Y: lengthy, 61

workmanlike gelding: poor mover: second foal: dam, probably best short of 1½m, won 4 races: modest form: game winner of apprentice handicap at Doncaster in October: stays 11.1f: acts on good to firm ground, yet to race on a soft surface. *Mrs J. R. Ramsden*

MASTER FIDDLER 5 b.g. Teenoso (USA) 135 – Musical Princess 66 (Cavo Doro 124) [1994 –: 8m^5 8d 1995 10m 10m 10g^5 12.1m^5 10f^6 9f^2 9.9m^4 Aug 24] sturdy gelding: bad maiden: stays 1¼m: probably acts on any going: inconsistent. *E. Weymes* — 29

MASTER GLEN 7 ch.g. Rabdan 129 – Rage Glen 67 (Grey Mirage 128) [1994 NR 1995 a16g Nov 20] smallish gelding: unimpressive mover: modest performer (rated 63, stayed 1¼m and unsuited by top-of-the-ground) at 3 yrs but tailed off only starts in 1993 and 1995. *G. R. Oldroyd* — –

MASTER HYDE (USA) 6 gr.g. Trempolino (USA) 135 – Sandspur (USA) (Al Hattab (USA)) [1994 57, a63: a10g^2 a9.4g^5 a10g^4 6.9f 6.9m 9.2g 7f^2 8d^6 12.1m* 12f^5 12g^3 1995 12f* 11.9m 16.1g^5 12.1g Sep 18] leggy, workmanlike gelding: modest handicapper: won 4-runner race at Carlisle in July: stays 1½m: acts on firm and soft ground and on equitrack (below form on fibresand): has worn blinkers and visor, but not for a long time: none too consistent: fair winning hurdler. *W. Storey* — 62

MASTER LYNX (USA) 2 b.c. (Apr 12) Cutlass (USA) – La Ninouchka (USA) (Bombay Duck (USA)) [1995 6m 7m^6 Jul 15] $50,000Y: close-coupled colt: brother to 1993 2-y-o 7.3f winner Plunder Bay and half-brother to several winners, including very smart middle-distance performer Silver Wisp (by Silver Hawk): dam won 2 races at up to 9f: always towards rear in maiden at Newbury and 7-runner minor event at Lingfield 2 months later: looked likely to do better. *G. Lewis* — – p

MASTER M-E-N (IRE) 3 ch.g. My Generation 111 – Secret Lightning (USA) 78 (Secretariat (USA)) [1994 67: 5g^4 5m^2 6f 5m* 5f 6.1g^4 6d 6d^2 5s a6g 6d^5 a5g 1995 7m 5.1f 8.1m^4 8f^3 8.1m 8g^2 7m^6 8h^3 Sep 4] close-coupled, quite attractive gelding: only modest performer nowadays: stays 1m: acts on firm and dead ground (well beaten on soft and fibresand): blinkered/visored since fourth 2-y-o outing. *N. M. Babbage* — 54

MASTER MILLFIELD (IRE) 3 b.g. Prince Rupert (FR) 121 – Calash (Indian King (USA) 128) [1994 78: 6.1g^2 7g 7m^6 a7g a7g* a6g* a7g* a8g^2 1995 a7g^3 a6g^4 a7g^3 a7g* a7g^4 6.1g 8f^4 8m^2 7m^5 7m^3 5.1h^4 6m^3 7f^3 5.7h* 8g^4 6g a7g a6g a8.5g^3 a7g Dec 18] tall gelding: fair handicapper: won at Lingfield in February and Bath in September: joined R. Hodges for fifteenth and sixteenth starts only: effective at sprint distances, and stays 1m: goes well on the all-weather, has raced only on a sound surface on turf: usually races prominently. *C. J. Hill* — 68 a75

MASTER OF PASSION 6 b.g. Primo Dominie 121 – Crime of Passion 115 (Dragonara Palace (USA) 115) [1994 87: 6m 5.2s^4 6m a6g 5g^6 5m^5 6f 5.2g^2 5g^3 6d* 6d^5 6v 1995 6m 6g^4 6m^4 6f^5 5m^2 6m 5.2m* 5.6m^5 6g^4 5d 6g Oct 7] lengthy, angular gelding: has a quick action: fairly useful handicapper: mostly in good form in 1995, winning at Newbury in August: creditable efforts in the Portland at Doncaster and Gold Cup at Ayr next 2 starts: below form afterwards: effective at 5f to 7f: acts on firm ground and dead (visored, soundly beaten only start on fibresand): also tried blinkered/visored at 3 yrs: usually races prominently. *J. M. P. Eustace* — 89

MASTER OFTHE HOUSE 9 b.g. Kind of Hush 118 – Miss Racine (Dom Racine (FR) 121) [1994 66: 9.9d* 10g* 10m^3 8m* 10.3g* 11.9m 8.3g 9g 1995 10g 7g^5 8.9m 8f* 10.3g 10m^4 8.3f^3 8m^3 8m^3 9.2g^6 9f^6 Oct 3] sturdy gelding: poor mover: fair handicapper: won at Carlisle (Silver Bell for second year running) in June: effective at 7f to 11f: acts on any going: has been tried in blinkers and visor, but not for some time: held up: effective for amateur/apprentice. *M. D. Hammond* — 66

MASTER OF TROY 7 b.g. Trojan Fen 118 – Gohar (USA) (Barachois (CAN)) [1994 59: 14.1v* 13f^5 1995 21.6f May 1] close-coupled gelding: has had only 6 races on flat: visored, tailed off in strongly-run handicap at Pontefract only start in 1995: stays 1¾m: fair hurdler who is best visored. *C. Parker* — –

MASTER PLANNER 6 b.g. Night Shift (USA) – Shaky Puddin (Ragstone 128) [1994 101: 6g 6m* 6m 6f^3 6m^4 6m 6f 5m 6f 6m^3 5.6g^4 5g 6m 6d 1995 6m* 6m^3 6g^5 6m^3 6f 5m^5 5m^4 6m 6m 6g Aug 30] strong, close-coupled gelding: impresses in appearance: useful handicapper: won rated stakes at Newmarket (for second year — 102 running) in May: well below form under optimum conditions at Goodwood (Stewards' Cup) and York (twice) last 3 starts: suited by 6f and a sound surface (acts on firm ground): usually races prominently: successful for claimer. *C. A. Cyzer*

MASTERPLAYER (GER) 3 b.c. Alzao (USA) 117 – Majoritat (GER) (Konigsstuhl (GER)) [1994 NR 1995 10s^3 9.5s^3 12s* 11s* 12m^3 12g^5 Jul 30] fourth foal: closely related to useful 9f to 1½m winner Majority (by Dancing Brave) and half-brother to fair 1½m winner Maji (by Shareef Dancer): dam 7f (at 2 yrs) to 11f winner, won 6 of her 9 races, notably Preis der Diana: smart German colt: won maiden at Baden-Baden in May and valuable event at Bremen in June: best effort when 2¾ lengths third of 18 to All My Dreams in Deutsches Derby at Hamburg, running on well from rear: rather disappointing favourite final start: stays 1½m: acts on good to firm ground and soft. *H. Remmert, Germany* 112

MASTER REACH 6 br.g. Reach 122 – Lady Donaro 76 (Ardoon 124) [1994 NR 1995 a16g^6 Mar 2] tall, workmanlike gelding: poor maiden: blinkered last 3 starts at 4 yrs. *B. J. Meehan* –

MASTER SHOWMAN (IRE) 4 b.g. Alzao (USA) 117 – Arctic Winter (CAN) (Briartic (CAN)) [1994 10g^3 10g^6 10d 14g^6 12s 1995 a9.4g 10m Aug 21] 44,000Y: ex-Irish gelding: fifth foal: half-brother to smart sprinter Polar Bird (by Thatching) and 7f and 1m winner Polar Storm (by Law Society): dam (sister to Queen's Plate winner Son of Briartic) won at 2 yrs in Germany: fair maiden at best (rated 77) at 3 yrs for C. O'Brien, sold only 3,300 gns Newmarket Autumn Sales: tailed-off last in handicaps here: stays 1¼m. *H. Oliver* –

MASURI KABISA (USA) 4 ch.f. Ascot Knight (CAN) 130 – Imperverse (USA) (Impressive) [1994 37: 9.9g 7g 8.3m 7g 11.5g^2 11.9m^4 12.1m^6 11.9d 12g 1995 10.8f^5 12g 12m^5 12.5m^2 14.1f^6 12m^3 12f* 11.9f* 12m^3 12.1g 12m Oct 27] smallish, workmanlike filly: poor handicapper: won at Folkestone (gambled on, maiden event) and Brighton in August: stays 1½m: acts on firm ground: has been visored, including since first win. *H. J. Collingridge* 46

MATAMOROS 3 gr.c. Kalaglow 132 – Palama (USA) (Blushing Groom (FR) 131) [1994 64p: 7m 7s 8.1g 1995 10.8m^2 12.5f 10d^6 11.9d^3 13.6f^2 16m Oct 19] sparely-made colt: fair maiden handicapper: unlucky on reappearance and ran well when placed in the autumn: should be suited by thorough test of stamina: acts on firm and dead ground, well beaten on soft: visored (raced too freely) final start: sold 11,500 gns Newmarket Autumn Sales. *J. L. Dunlop* 77

MATARUN (IRE) 7 b.h. Commanche Run 133 – Miss Mat (Matahawk 127) [1994 115: 10s* 10v^6 12m 12g^6 11v^6 10g 10d^5 12d^2 10.7s^5 12v* 10s^3 12g^4 1995 13s^2 10v^3 15.5s^5 12g 12g 11d^6 10d^6 11g^5 10.6v* 12d 12d^6 12s* Dec 3] smart French horse: ran well when third in Prix Exbury at Saint-Cloud (length behind Tuesday's Special) in March: below form afterwards except when winning listed events in the Provinces in October and (by 4 lengths from Fanion de Fete) December: stays 1½m: acts on heavy going: none too consistent. *H. Van de Poele, France* 111

MATCH THE COLOUR 2 b.g. (Apr 27) Full Extent (USA) 113 – Matching Lines 72 (Thatching 131) [1995 6m 5.7h^4 Aug 3] second foal: half-brother to 3-y-o Oneineverycolour (by Midyan), 5.1f winner at 2 yrs: dam sprinter: well beaten in median auction maiden at Windsor and seller at Bath. *M. R. Channon* –

MATIARA (USA) 3 b.f. Bering 136 – Most Precious (USA) (Nureyev (USA) 131) [1994 6.5s* 8s^2 1995 8d* 8d* 10.5m^2 10g* 12d^4 10g^2 10f Nov 26] 119

A good renewal of the Dubai Poule d'Essai des Pouliches fell to the favourite Matiara, who in accounting for one of the classic's biggest fields this century brought yet more success in the race to the Head family. The home-bred filly was trained by Criquette Head and ridden by Freddie for Ecurie Aland. Sixteen runners went to post, eight representing the form of the trial race run over the course three weeks earlier, the Prix de la Grotte in which Matiara had fought back to win narrowly from Shaanxi and Carling. That had been Matiara's first start of the season and her third in all. The previous autumn she had finished a length second to Carling in the Group 3 Prix des Reservoirs at Longchamp after winning a Saint-Cloud maiden, and she got into the International Classification at around mid-table. All told, twelve of the Pouliches field had made the International Classification, the highest-rated being British-

Dubai Poule d'Essai des Pouliches, Longchamp—
Matiara (far side) just holds on from Carling; Shaanxi is third

trained Hoh Magic who had already gone on to take fourth place behind Harayir in the One Thousand Guineas.

The Pouliches' big field contributed to a rough race, as did the steady pace on settling down. Afterwards hard-luck stories abounded, recriminations flew, and the inevitable stewards inquiry, which allowed the result to stand, was by no means an end to the matter. Our view was that the race went to the best filly on the day, even though her jockey was one of the three—the riders of third-placed Shaanxi and unplaced Piquetnol were the others—called to account by the second inquiry which finally declared the result valid in early-June. The race ended in a desperately close finish between Matiara and Carling. Matiara, having bumped her way out past Piquetnol early in the straight, showed an excellent turn of foot to go clear but she began to falter in the closing stages, holding on by a nose as Carling came with a rattle. Shaanxi and the Imprudence runner-up Smolensk also finished strongly in third and fourth, two lengths and a further two lengths behind; both had been involved in scrimmaging. Hoh Magic failed to reproduce her Guineas form under the more testing conditions, and was eventually put back to sprinting.

Matiara was beaten by Carling in their two subsequent meetings but ran very well each time. The eagerly-anticipated return match in the Prix de Diane Hermes at Chantilly in June went Carling's way by a neck. Matiara stayed much better than some predicted; in fact, on this occasion it was she who came home the stronger after Carling had shown the better pace halfway up the straight. There was clearly very little between them, a point re-emphasised over a furlong and a half further in the Prix Vermeille at Longchamp in September, where Carling enjoyed the run of the race and won while Matiara became trapped against the far rail for much of the straight yet finished no more than a length and a half down in fourth. Both fillies had been seen out at Deauville in between, Matiara scraping home by short heads from the Japanese Oaks winner Dance Partner and the Prix Chloe winner Garden Rose in a four-runner Prix de la Nonette, waited with then hard ridden to catch up just in time. Reportedly the trainer toyed for a while with the idea of trying her in blinkers in the Vermeille. Matiara ran twice in North America after the Vermeille. Her first run there, when favourite for the E. P. Taylor Stakes at Woodbine in October, measured up to her best efforts in Europe but she met trouble in running and caught a tartar in the fast-improving Timarida who beat her three and a half lengths. Her second run came in another prestigious fillies and mares event on the turf, the Matriarch Stakes

Ecurie Aland's "Matiara"

at Hollywood Park in late-November. She finished slightly closer to that race's winner Duda yet was seven places lower down the order than at Woodbine. Freddie Head claimed she had been ill-at-ease on the turns.

Matiara (USA) (b.f. 1992)	Bering (ch 1983)	Arctic Tern (ch 1973)	Sea Bird II
			Bubbling Beauty
		Beaune (ch 1974)	Lyphard
			Barbra
	Most Precious (USA) (b or br 1985)	Nureyev (b 1977)	Northern Dancer
			Special
		Miss Summer (br 1979)	Luthier
			Miss Manon

Matiara's run in the Pouliches gave her sire a classic winner on consecutive weekends, following Pennekamp at Newmarket. Bering, second to Dancing Brave in the Arc, was brought back from Kentucky to the Haras du Quesnay in 1992 and will stand at a fee of 130,000 francs in 1996. Matiara has been entirely responsible for putting her dam Most Precious on the map as a broodmare after an unplaced foal by Devil's Bag and a non-runner by Mr Prospector. Most Precious is the pick of her dam's runners so far—placed in the Grand Criterium and the Prix de la Salamandre and a winner over a mile at Deauville—although the Cecil three-year-old Private Line comes close. The family is a good one. The third dam Miss Manon finished fourth in the Prix de Diane and produced six winners, all of note. They include the classics-placed Sharpman, Most Precious' dam the French listed-race winner Miss Summer and the Ribblesdale Stakes winner Ballinderry, the dam of Sanglamore.

Matiara will presumably be at stud herself in 1996. A good-looking filly, she stayed a mile and a half and seemed to act on any going. *Mme C. Head, France*

MATISSE 4 b.f. Shareef Dancer (USA) 135 – Late Matinee 84 (Red Sunset 120) [1994 58, a–: 6d^{5} 6.1m 5m^{2} 7m^{3} 6m^{5} 7m^{4} 6g 7g 8g a7g a7g 1995 6m 6.9m 12g 8.1m^{3} 8.1m 8g^{4} 8.1f^{5} 8g^{2} 7.1g^{3} 8f^{6} 7m^{3} a8g Nov 20] strong filly: poor maiden handicapper: stays 1m: acts on firm and dead ground, no form on all-weather: blinkered (no improvement) second 4-y-o start: sometimes starts slowly. *J. D. Bethell* 43 a–

MATIYA (IRE) 2 b.f. (Apr 7) Alzao (USA) 117 – Purchasepaperchase 104 (Young Generation 129) [1995 7m* 6m^{3} 8.1d^{2} 8d^{3} Sep 24] IR 38,000Y: strong, well-made filly: has a round action: fifth foal: closely related to a winner in Germany by Lyphard and half-sister to 3-y-o 1¼m winner Never Explain (by Fairy King) and Irish 1m winner Al Naayy (by Tate Gallery): dam 1m/1¼m performer: won maiden at Newmarket in July: subsequently placed in minor events at Pontefract and Haydock and Fillies' Mile (excellent third, beaten 7 lengths by Bosra Sham after forcing strong pace) at Ascot: will stay beyond 1m: acts on good to firm and dead ground. *B. Hanbury* 98

MATTHEW DAVID 5 ch.h. Indian Forest (USA) 117 – Mazurkanova 63 (Song 132) [1994 38, a58: a6g 5g^{6} a6g^{4} a7g 5.1d^{5} a6g a5s* 1995 a6g^{2} a6g^{5} a6g^{4} a6g a8g^{3} a7g^{3} a6g^{5} a6g^{6} a6g 5d^{5} a5g a6g* a6g^{4} a5g^{2} a6g^{6} Dec 12] small, sparely-made horse: has a roundish action: poor handicapper: narrowly won at Southwell (all 4 wins there) in August: stays 6f: best form on fibresand: also acts on soft ground (has had only one run on top-of-the-ground): effective blinkered or not: usually bandaged. *S. R. Bowring* 27 + a50

MATTHIAS MYSTIQUE 2 gr.f. (Mar 19) Sharrood (USA) 124 – Sheznice (IRE) 58 (Try My Best (USA) 130) [1995 6m 6.9s a7g Nov 21] 8,200F, 4,100Y: leggy filly: first foal: dam twice-raced close relative of smart 6f and 7f performer Glen Kate and daughter of half-sister to smart stayer Midshipman: well beaten in maiden events. *Miss B. Sanders* –

MATTIMEO (IRE) 2 b.g. (Mar 18) Prince Rupert (FR) 121 – Herila (FR) (Bold Lad (USA)) [1995 7m^{5} Nov 3] 4,000Y: stocky gelding: half-brother to 4 middle-distance winners in France: dam French 11f winner: 25/1 and in need of race, 5 lengths fifth of 18 to Wahiba Sands in maiden at Doncaster, always to fore of stand-side group and keeping on well: will improve. *A. P. Jarvis* 66 p

MAURANGI 4 b.g. Warning 136 – Spin Dry (High Top 131) [1994 60: 10.3f 10g 8d* 8g^{3} 8.5m* 9.9f 10d 1995 8.2g 8.5m 8g^{5} 8g^{6} 8.9m^{4} 10.1m 10.1m^{4} Jul 26] tall, leggy gelding: modest handicapper: stays 9f: acts on good to firm and dead ground: usually held up: effective blinkered (not tried at 4 yrs) or not. *B. W. Murray* 58

MAWINGO (IRE) 2 b.c. (Mar 4) Taufan (USA) 119 – Tappen Zee (Sandhurst Prince 128) [1995 7m^{6} a7g^{5} Dec 6] IR 10,000Y: leggy colt: second foal: half-brother to 3-y-o Tappen Lady (by Doulab): dam Irish 7f winner: similar form in maiden events won by Wahiba Sands at Doncaster and Faith Alone at Lingfield following month: will stay 1m. *G. Wragg* 63

MAWJUD 2 b.c. (Jan 25) Mujtahid (USA) 118 – Elfaslah (IRE) 107 (Green Desert (USA) 127) [1995 7f* Oct 25] good-topped colt: first foal: dam, winner 3 times at around 1¼m, daughter of White Muzzle's dam Fair of The Furze: 8/1 and green, made all in 10-runner maiden at Yarmouth in October to beat Medieval Lady a neck, tending to hang left and carry head high throughout: will improve. *H. Thomson Jones* 84 p

MAWSAM 3 ch.c. Nashwan (USA) 135 – Tabdea (USA) 106 (Topsider (USA)) [1994 NR 1995 7m Jul 16] sturdy colt: first foal: dam 6f and 1m winner: tailed off in maiden at Yarmouth: dead. *E. A. L. Dunlop* –

MAWWAL (USA) 2 ch.c. (Feb 13) Elmaamul (USA) 125 – Dish Dash 118 (Bustino 136) [1995 6g^{5} 6g^{4} 7.1m* 7m* 7g* 8d Sep 23] tall, rather unfurnished colt: has scope: fluent mover: ninth foal: half-brother to several winners, including good miler Maroof (by Danzig) and useful 1986 2-y-o 7f winner Arrasas (by Irish River): dam won Ribblesdale Stakes: successful in maiden at Sandown and 5-runner minor event at Newmarket in July and 8-runner minor event at Doncaster (by 3½ lengths in good style from Tria Kemata) in September: favourite, slowly into stride and threatened only briefly 2f out when well-beaten seventh of 8 in Royal Lodge Stakes 105 at Ascot on final outing: should stay 1m: acts on good to firm ground: races keenly. *R. W. Armstrong*

MAYBANK (IRE) 3 gr.g. Contract Law (USA) 108 – Katysue 98 (King's Leap 111) [1994 NR 1995 6g 5d Apr 1] 6,600Y: big, good-topped gelding: half-brother to 4 winners, including 1986 2-y-o 5f winner Sinclair Lady (by Absalom), later temperamental, and 4-y-o 6f and 8.3f winner Curie Crusader (by Belfort): dam won 5 times over 5f at 2 yrs: 33/1, no promise in maidens: subsequently gelded. *B. A. McMahon* –

MAYBE TODAY 3 br.f. Today And Tomorrow 78 – Sonairo (Tudor Rhythm 112) [1994 65: 6.1s^3 7s^3 7g 6.9s 1995 6m 8m 8.1m^2 8.3m 10d Sep 13] smallish, leggy filly: disappointing maiden: stays 1m: acts on soft ground, probably on good to firm: inconsistent. *B. R. Millman* 54

MAYDAAN (IRE) 3 b.f. Alzao (USA) 117 – Spring Reel (Mill Reef (USA) 141) [1994 72: 5d* 6.1g^4 1995 6m^2 6.1g^4 5.7h Aug 18] neat filly: fair performer: off course around 2½ months, last of 8 in handicap at Bath final start: bred to stay 1m: sent to Dubai. *B. Hanbury* 79

MAYDAY KITTY 3 ch.f. Interrex (CAN) – T Catty (USA) 62 (Sensitive Prince (USA)) [1994 –: 5s^6 5d^6 1995 a8g a10g^6 a12g^2 a10g^2 11.1g^4 a16g^4 11.9m^3 13.8g^5 a16g^6 Jun 17] sparely-made filly: poor maiden: should stay 1¾m: usually visored when on all-weather: has hung: none too consistent. *W. G. M. Turner* 38

MAYGAIN (IRE) 2 b.g. (Mar 29) Kefaah (USA) 124 – Sistina 76 (Charlottown 127) [1995 6m 6g^5 6g 7d^6 Jun 15] IR 6,000Y: good-topped gelding: half-brother to 3-y-o Ace Chapel (by Simply Great) and several winners, including useful French middle-distance stayer Wolverist (by Wolver Hollow): dam stayer: little worthwhile form in sellers last 3 starts: bred to be suited by further than 6f. *M. R. Channon* –

MAY KING MAYHEM 2 ch.c. (May 6) Great Commotion (USA) 123 – Queen Ranavalona (Sure Blade (USA) 130) [1995 7f^5 7m Sep 5] 11,000Y, 10,500 2-y-o: close-coupled colt: has a round action: second foal: dam unraced close relative of Lowther winner Prickle: well beaten in maiden events at Brighton (auction race) and Leicester: has joined Mrs A. L. M. King. *W. R. Muir* –

MAYOUMBE (FR) 2 gr.c. (Feb 16) Kaldoun (FR) 122 – Moucha (Fabulous Dancer (USA) 124) [1995 5d^3 6m* 7g^2 6.5g^2 8s^6 8g^2 Nov 4] 240,000 francs Y: first foal: dam French 7.5f winner: useful French colt: won minor event at Chantilly in June: best effort when 2½ lengths second of 5 to Ashkalani in Prix Thomas Bryon at Saint-Cloud on final start: stays 1m: acts on good to firm ground, below form on soft. *J. E. Pease, France* 103

MAY QUEEN MEGAN 2 gr.f. (Mar 23) Petorius 117 – Siva (FR) (Bellypha 130) [1995 5g^3 6f^6 6m^3 Nov 6] 8,200 2-y-o: small filly: fourth foal: sister to French 3-y-o 1m winner Petosiva and half-sister to a winner in Austria by Persian Bold: dam French 1m to 11.2f winner: modest form when keeping-on third to Dande Flyer then Village Native in median auction maidens at Folkestone: will stay beyond 6f: well beaten on firm ground. *Mrs A. L. M. King* 63

MAYREAU 3 b.f. Slip Anchor 136 – Compton Lady (USA) 100 (Sovereign Dancer (USA)) [1994 69p: 7.1g 7d^3 1995 10m^2 11.7h^2 10g 12.1s Oct 17] lengthy filly: fairly useful maiden at best: not seen out until late-August then second in small fields at Goodwood and Bath: well below form last 2 starts: stays 1½m: acts on hard ground: sold only 7,800 gns Newmarket Autumn Sales: sent to Norway. *G. Harwood* 80 d

MAYSANN 3 br.c. Shirley Heights 130 – Tanouma (USA) 114 (Miswaki (USA) 124) [1994 –p: 7m 7m 8.2d 1995 12d 12.3d^4 14.6m a14.8g^2 14.1f^2 18.2m Jul 8] sturdy colt: has a quick action: modest maiden handicapper: stays 14.8f: acts on firm and dead ground, and on fibresand: blinkered since third 3-y-o start: sold 4,200 gns Newmarket July Sales: sent to Italy. *J. L. Dunlop* 61

MAYSIMP (IRE) 2 ch.f. (Apr 23) Mac's Imp (USA) 116 – Splendid Yankee (Yankee Gold 115) [1995 6d 5f^4 5.1g^5 5f 5g 6s Sep 30] IR 5,000Y, 4,500 2-y-o: leggy filly: unimpressive mover: fourth reported foal: half-sister to Irish 3-y-o Vail Star (by Fayruz), 5f winner at 2 yrs, and fairly useful 1990 2-y-o 5f winner Racketeer (by Stalker): dam Irish maiden on flat and over hurdles: poor maiden: has been bandaged behind. *B. P. J. Baugh* –

MAZCOBAR 2 ch.c. (Mar 23) Mazilier (USA) 107 – Barbary Court (Grundy 137) [1995 6d 8g 7g4 Oct 23] good-bodied colt: fourth foal: brother to 4-y-o Mazirah and half-brother to 7.1f winner Noble Pet (by Petong): dam poor maiden: modest form in maidens: 9¾ lengths fourth of 9 to Ashjar at Lingfield on final outing, second home of those who raced on advantageous far side. *P. J. Makin* 58

MAZEED (IRE) 2 ch.c. (Apr 9) Lycius (USA) 124 – Maraatib (IRE) 93 (Green Desert (USA) 127) [1995 6m* 6m* 6.1m2 6g6 Sep 2] neat colt: not a good walker: first foal: dam sprinter: won maiden at Newcastle in June and 5-runner minor event at Haydock (plenty in hand from The Frisky Farmer) in August: short-head second of 4 to Dovebrace in minor event at Chester on penultimate start: well below form in listed race at Kempton final start: stays 6f. *H. Thomson Jones* 95

MAZEEKA (IRE) 4 ch.f. Glow (USA) – Saluti Tutti 77 (Trojan Fen 118) [1994 71, a65: a6g5 a7g 5.1f5 7m 8m3 8.3m* 6.9h* 9f 8f* 8.5f3 7m5 a7g5 7m3 a7g2 a8g a7g6 1995 a7g6 Mar 25] neat filly: fair performer: well below form only start in 1995: stays 8.3f: acts on hard ground and the all-weather, well below form on dead. *W. A. O'Gorman* –

MAZIERE 3 ch.f. Mazilier (USA) 107 – Good Game 71 (Mummy's Game 120) [1994 45: 5m6 6m 6.1s 1995 10f5 10f Aug 2] small, angular filly: poor form: may well prove best short of 1¼m. *M. J. Heaton-Ellis* 39

MAZILLA 3 b.f. Mazilier (USA) 107 – Mo Ceri 63 (Kampala 120) [1994 59: 6s2 8d 6s3 a7g5 1995 a8g2 a8g* a7g* a7g4 a8g2 a7g3 8.2m 8g a12g a8g a9.4g2 a9.4g a8.5g Dec 12] leggy filly: modest performer: won sellers at Southwell and Wolverhampton in January: sold out of W. Haggas' stable 6,400 gns Ascot April Sales after sixth start: below form (next outing only for A. Forbes) afterwards: stays 1m: acts on soft ground and all-weather surfaces. *A. Streeter* 59 d

MAZIRAH 4 b.g. Mazilier (USA) 107 – Barbary Court (Grundy 137) [1994 61: 7s5 7g4 7f 8f5 10g 8m5 8d4 8s2 10d5 1995 a9.4g3 10m Apr 29] tall, useful-looking gelding: modest maiden handicapper: below form in 1995: subsequently gelded: likely to stay beyond 1¼m: acts on firm and soft ground and on fibresand: blinkered (ran respectably) fourth 3-y-o start. *P. J. Makin* 51

MAZOSKI 2 b.g. (May 17) Mazilier (USA) 107 – Madam Petoski 61 (Petoski 135) [1995 6.1m5 7d5 Jun 15] 3,200Y, 3,800 2-y-o: stocky gelding: unimpressive mover: first foal: dam sprint maiden: well beaten in claimer and seller: sold 3,000 gns Newmarket Autumn Sales: sent to Spain. *P. C. Haslam* –

MAZZARELLO (IRE) 5 ch.g. Hatim (USA) 121 – Royal Demon (Tarboosh (USA)) [1994 33: 5s4 7f 6m4 6m 5m5 5g 1995 5m a6g 5m* 5g* 6f4 5f 5g a5g Dec 6] lengthy, sparely-made gelding: poor handicapper: won in May (apprentices) and June (gamely), both at Goodwood: well below form afterwards: best form at 5f: acts on good to firm ground: best visored: makes running/races prominently. *R. Curtis* 45 a–

MBULWA 9 ch.g. Be My Guest (USA) 126 – Bundu (FR) 88 (Habitat 134) [1994 55, a–: 8d 7.1f* 6.9f4 8.1m2 7f5 7.5m 9g3 8m3 9.2f2 10.1m3 8f* 9d a9.4g4 a8.5g6 1995 7g2 8g 7g 8.3f 11.1m5 10.4m3 8f* 8f3 7m2 a9.4g Nov 13] smallish, sturdy gelding: modest handicapper: left S. Kettlewell and off course 3 months after fifth start: won at Redcar in October: effective at 7f to 1¼m: has gained all his 7 successes on a sound surface (acts on firm ground), below form all 3 outings on the all-weather: effective blinkered (not tried for new stable) or not: often early to post and mulish at stalls: usually races prominently. *R. A. Fahey* 60 a–

MCA BELOW THE LINE 7 ch.g. Lucky Wednesday 124 – Delayed Action 113 (Jolly Jet 111) [1994 66: 7d2 7.5d 7g3 7g3 8f2 7.5m2 8.1f2 7m4 7.5m4 8g4 7g5 8.5g 1995 8m 8.1m5 10m 8f5 8h5 12d 10d Sep 22] strong, dipped-backed gelding: poor mover: only a modest handicapper at best in 1995: trained until after second start by W. L. Barker: stays 8.5f: acts on any going, including all-weather surfaces: tried in blinkers, but usually visored: inconsistent. *J. L. Eyre* 57 d

MCKELLAR (IRE) 6 b.h. Lomond (USA) 128 – Local Belle (Ballymore 123) [1994 NR 1995 8g6 a6g Nov 27] IR 17,500 2-y-o: ex-Irish horse: second foal: dam Irish 1½m winner: lightly raced (ran twice at 3 yrs, rated 61 over 8.5f) in Ireland: well beaten in maiden at Listowel (final outing for P. Henley) and handicap at Wolverhampton (outpaced) in 1995. *T. D. Barron* –

MD THOMPSON 3 ch.f. Siberian Express (USA) 125 – Zipperti Do 70 (Precocious 126) [1994 NR 1995 8m 6.9m^3 7m^3 a7g^3 9f^5 8g^4 a8.5g^3 a7g^3 Sep 16] sturdy, plain filly: second foal: half-sister to 1¼m winner Wonderful Day (by Niniski): dam 1m winner out of Cherry Hinton runner-up Doobie Do: modest maiden handicapper: stays 9f: acts on firm ground and fibresand: consistent. *S. C. Williams* 50

MEANT TO BE 5 b.m. Morston (FR) 125 – Lady Gerardina 82 (Levmoss 133) [1994 78: 10d^6 12m^4 14g 12d^5 12m* 16f 12m^5 12d* 11d^4 12m^2 12m a12g^3 1995 a14.8g^4 11.8g 12m^3 12m^3 16.2d^4 16.2s* Oct 6] lengthy, sparely-made mare: fairly useful handicapper: narrowly won at Ascot in October, leading 4f out and battling on gamely: effective at 1½m, stays 16.2f: acts on fibresand, and on good to firm and heavy going: blinkered (below form) fourth 4-y-o start: consistent. *Lady Herries* 84

ME CHEROKEE 3 br.f. Persian Bold 123 – Siouan 78 (So Blessed 130) [1994 NR 1995 6g 7.5d 7.5m^4 Jun 14] 7,400F: leggy filly: sister to 4-y-o Taza and half-sister to several winners, including very smart middle-distance colt Apache (by Great Nephew): dam 1½m winner, is half-sister to high-class middle-distance stayer Dakota and very useful Warpath: clear signs of ability in maidens: should do better. *C. W. Thornton* – p

MEDAILLE MILITAIRE 3 gr.c. Highest Honor (FR) 124 – Lovely Noor (USA) (Fappiano (USA)) [1994 77p: 7d^6 8g^3 1995 8g* 8m* 7.6m^6 10.4m* 12d^5 Sep 23] tall, leggy colt: progressive performer: won maiden at Newcastle in April, Britannia Handicap at Royal Ascot (just got up, landed big gamble) and rated stakes at York (leading over 1f out and surging 2½ lengths clear from Taufan's Melody) in August: creditable effort on form when 10½ lengths fifth of 8 to Riyadian in Cumberland Lodge Stakes at Ascot, but was in trouble before the home turn: better at 1¼m than shorter, will probably prove fully effective at 1½m: acts on good to firm ground, possibly unsuited by good to soft: equipped with rope halter: held up: stays in training, and should win more races. *J. L. Dunlop* 103

MEDIA EXPRESS 3 b.c. Sayf El Arab (USA) 127 – Far Claim (USA) 35 (Far North (CAN) 120) [1994 59: 5f^4 5m^3 5v^3 5g* 5m^6 5.1g 5d^4 6g^4 6g^6 1995 6.9d 6.1g^3 6.1g* 6g 6d 6m^6 7m a6g 8.1d* Oct 10] small, leggy colt: fair handicapper: easily best effort to win at Nottingham in April, making all against favoured stand rail: 71

Britannia Stakes (Handicap), Royal Ascot—
heads down as Medaille Militaire (right), 4/1 favourite in a field of thirty-two, finally reels in 25/1 stable-companion Beauchamp Jazz

disappointing afterwards, leaving T. Mills's stable after fifth start, sold out of R. Hannon's stable 1,000 gns Newmarket September Sales after seventh: nowhere near best to win 19-runner seller at Chepstow (led 1f out) in October: stays 1m: acts on any ground. *M. Brittain*

MEDIA MESSENGER 6 b.g. Hadeer 118 – Willow Court (USA) (Little Current (USA)) [1994 37: a8g^2 8.2f 8.1m 10g^3 11.1g^3 10m 8.3g^4 10.9g^5 9.2f 1995 a8g a12g a12g Dec 18] close-coupled gelding: poor performer nowadays: sold (Denys Smith to N. Littmoden) 1,000 gns Doncaster March Sales after reappearance: well beaten on return: stays 11f: acts on good to firm and soft ground, probably on fibresand. *N. P. Littmoden* –

MEDIA NOX 2 ch.f. (Mar 12) Lycius (USA) 124 – Sky Love (USA) 93 (Nijinsky (CAN) 138) [1995 5d* 5m* 5.5g^5 Jul 23] fourth foal: half-sister to smart Bonash, pattern winner at 1m (at 2 yrs), 9.2f and 1½m, and French 1½m winner Rainy Sky (both by Rainbow Quest): dam, 1¼m winner, is half-sister to Raft: useful French filly: won newcomers event and 6-runner Prix du Bois (10/7 on, led well over 1f out, held Shining Molly by a nose), both at Chantilly in June: below form in Prix Robert Papin at Maisons-Laffitte and not seen out again: should stay at least 7f. *A. Fabre, France* 98 +

MEDIATE (IRE) 3 b.g. Thatching 131 – Unheard Melody (Lomond (USA) 128) [1994 61: 5s 5.1m^3 6f 5m* 5m^2 6m 7m 6d 6.1g a8g^6 a7g* a6g^3 1995 a7g^4 a7g^3 8.3m a7g* 8.5m^5 7g^2 6f^6 8m a7g^3 a8.5g Dec 12] compact gelding: has a quick action: fair form: won claimer at Lingfield in July: sold out of R. Hannon's stable 5,200 gns Newmarket September Sales after eighth start and gelded: stays 7f: acts on equitrack and good to firm ground, possibly unsuited by a soft surface: effective blinkered or not: inconsistent and not one to rely on. *A. Hide* 70 §

MEDIATION (IRE) 3 ch.f. Caerleon (USA) 132 – Redeem Herself (General Assembly (USA)) [1994 97: 7g* 7d^4 8d^3 1995 7g^2 8m* 8g 7m^6 6m 6m^5 6g* 7f^3 6d^2 8g^5 Oct 27] medium-sized, useful-looking filly: smart performer: won Derrinstown Stud 1000 Guineas Trial at Leopardstown in May, but only seventh of 10 (never got in a blow) in Irish 1000 Guineas at the Curragh: best effort when narrow winner of valuable handicap at the Curragh in September: stays 1m: acts on firm and dead ground. *J. Oxx, Ireland* 110

MEDIATOR 6 b.g. Valiyar 129 – Blushing Cousin (Great Nephew 126) [1994 43: a16g* a16g* a16g a16g a16g 11.9d^2 11.9m^2 12s^5 16.4g a16g a12g^4 1995 a16g a12g^5 11.9m Jun 1] well-made gelding: poor form on flat: sold 2,800 gns Ascot July Sales: stays 2m: acts on equitrack, good to firm ground and dead (not on heavy): tried visored/blinkered. *A. Moore* –

MEDIEVAL LADY 2 ch.f. (May 24) Efisio 120 – Ritsurin 79 (Mount Hagen (FR) 127) [1995 7g^5 7f^2 Oct 25] sturdy filly: closely related to 1987 2-y-o 6f winner Reformado (by Formidable) and half-sister to several winners, including 5.3f (at 2 yrs) to 1¼m winner Jagjet (by Vayraan): dam 2-y-o 6f winner: running-on neck second of 10 to Mawjud in maiden at Yarmouth: should stay 1m: probably open to further improvement. *Lady Herries* 78 p

MEDIEVAL MISS 3 b.f. Risk Me (FR) 127 – Dona Krista 84 (King of Spain 121) [1994 72: 5m^5 6f^3 6g^2 6.1s^2 7s^5 1995 5m 6m a6g^4 a5g 7f^3 8.5m^3 6m 6d Sep 18] sturdy filly: fair maiden at best: sold out of G. Lewis' stable 9,400 gns Newmarket July Sales after sixth start: stays 7f: acts on fibresand, firm and soft ground: tried blinkered/visored: front runner: inconsistent. *Mrs N. Macauley* 64 d

MEDITERRANEO 4 ch.g. Be My Guest (USA) 126 – Model Bride (USA) (Blushing Groom (FR) 131) [1994 100: 9d^3 8.1d^2 8m 10m^5 12d 1995 10m Apr 17] attractive gelding: shows a quick action: useful performer at 3 yrs: left J. Dunlop's stable and sent hurdling: 50/1, tailed off in face of stiff task in listed event only start on flat in 1995: subsequently gelded: should stay 1¼m: acts on good to firm and dead ground: blinkered (respectable effort) penultimate 3-y-o start. *R. Akehurst* –

MEDLAND (IRE) 5 ch.g. Imperial Frontier (USA) 112 – Miami Dancer 55 (Miami Springs 121) [1994 37, a51: a6g^5 a8g^2 a7g^2 a8.5g^4 a7s a8g^2 a8g* a8g^2 a8g* 8g a8g 6f 8f^4 10f a8g^3 1995 a11g^6 a10g* a10g^3 a7g a9.4g^5 a9.4g^3 a8g^4 a8.5g Jun 24] stocky gelding: poor mover: modest performer: won claimer at Lingfield in January: claimed out of W. G. Turner's stable £3,000 next time: stays 1¼m: acts on firm ground (no form on a soft surface), better on all-weather. *B. J. McMath* – a54

MEDWAY (IRE) 3 ch.f. Shernazar 131 – Sea Port (Averof 123) [1994 NR 1995 12m^3 13.1f^2 12.1f* 14m 17.5g 12s^2 Sep 27] IR 8,600Y: seventh foal: half-sister to 4 winners, including fairly useful miler Wassl Port (by Wassl) and Cesarewitch winner Old Red (by Ela-Mana-Mou): dam fourth on only start, is half-sister to high-class stayer Sea Anchor: modest form: easily won 4-runner maiden at Edinburgh (making all, by 13 lengths) in June: back to form when second of 18 at Folkestone (kept on no chance with winner) final start: looks a stayer. *M. H. Tompkins* 60

MEESON TIMES 7 b.m. Enchantment 115 – National Time (USA) (Lord Avie (USA)) [1994 –: a6g 1995 a6g^3 a7g^6 a7g^6 a6g^6 5d Mar 30] sturdy, compact mare: has round action: poor handicapper: stays 7f: acts on any going, goes well on the all-weather: best without a visor: none too consistent. *R. Bastiman* 45

MEETING POINT 2 b.f. (Feb 20) Common Grounds 118 – Pastrana (King of Spain 121) [1995 5m^2 5m^3 6g^3 6m^6 5f^2 6f^3 5m 6m 5g^4 7f Oct 3] 6,600F, 29,000Y: rather sparely-made filly: fourth foal: dam twice-raced daughter of close relative to Song: disappointing maiden: stays 6f: blinkered last 2 starts: sold 5,200 gns Newmarket Autumn Sales. *Mrs M. Reveley* 63 d

MEGA TID 3 b.g. Old Vic 136 – Dunoof 92 (Shirley Heights 130) [1994 NR 1995 a10g* 8g 11.9m 11.6m 10m 10g a9.4g^4 a10g^3 9m a8.5g^5 10m^3 a16g Aug 24] leggy gelding: closely related to fair middle-distance performer Folia (by Sadler's Wells) and half-brother to winners in Germany and France: dam well-bred 2-y-o 7f winner: sold out of C. Brittain's stable 4,000 gns Ascot December (1994) Sales: modest performer: landed a gamble in maiden at Lingfield in February: should stay beyond 1¼m: acts on good to firm ground and all-weather surfaces: occasionally bandaged: none too consistent and one to treat with caution. *B. A. Pearce* 45 a50

MEGHDOOT 3 b.f. Celestial Storm (USA) 132 – Greenhills Joy 90 (Radetzky 123) [1994 75: 8d^4 7s^2 a7g^5 1995 10m^4 10m^2 10m^2 10d^4 12g* 12.1s Nov 2] compact, workmanlike filly: unimpressive mover: fair performer: won handicap at Goodwood in September, always thereabouts: stays 1½m well: acts on good to firm and soft ground, below form only run on equitrack. *H. J. Collingridge* 75

MEG'S MEMORY (IRE) 2 b.f. (Jan 19) Superlative 118 – Meanz Beanz (High Top 131) [1995 5.7h^2 5.1h^2 6g 6g 6.9g Oct 16] 3,800Y: rather leggy filly: eighth live foal: half-sister to fairly useful stayer Bean King (by Ardross): dam unraced half-sister to very smart sprinter Chilibang: modest maiden: well beaten last 3 starts, in blinkers last 2: should stay beyond 6f. *John Berry* 53

MELASUS (IRE) 3 ch.g. Nashamaa 113 – Sweet Camden 62 (Camden Town 125) [1994 79: 6m* 5f 6g 7m* 1995 7g 8m Jun 20] lengthy gelding: fair form at 2 yrs: shaped quite well on reappearance but well beaten in Britannia Handicap at Royal Ascot 17 days later: should stay 1m: acts on good to firm ground: bandaged behind. *D. W. P. Arbuthnot* –

MELDORF 2 ch.c. (Mar 14) Lycius (USA) 124 – Melanoura (Imperial Fling (USA) 116) [1995 6d* 6f Oct 12] 32,000F: sturdy colt: fifth foal: half-brother to sprint winners by Absalom (2) and Alleging (fairly useful Computer Kid): dam ran twice: impressive winner of 11-runner maiden (beat Hoh Returns by 4 lengths, pair well clear) at Newcastle in September: well-backed favourite, lost place around halfway when fourteenth of 26 behind Blue Iris in Redcar Two-Year-Old Trophy at Redcar (moved unimpressively down) following month: looked potentially very useful at Newcastle, and is well worth another chance. *D. R. Loder* 93 p

MELISSA'S BABY 3 b.f. Then Again 126 – Have Form (Haveroid 122) [1994 –: 10g 8d 1995 8.3g May 4] strong, lengthy filly: well beaten, in claimer for new stable. *Miss L. A. Perratt* –

MELLING 4 b.g. Thowra (FR) – Miss Melmore (Nishapour (FR) 125) [1994 NR 1995 a7g 12g Apr 10] workmanlike gelding: fourth live foal: half-brother to 1m winner Imhotep (by Claude Monet): dam placed over 6f in Ireland: looks of no account. *R. J. Hodges* –

MELLORS (IRE) 2 b.c. (Apr 15) Common Grounds 118 – Simply Beautiful (IRE) (Simply Great (FR) 122) [1995 5.1m^5 5m^3 6m 8g^4 Sep 14] IR 14,500Y: well-made colt: has a round action: first foal: dam, Irish maiden, stayed 1½m: best effort when 6 lengths fourth of 10 to easy winner Opera in nursery at Yarmouth final 64 start, racing freely in blinkers: stays 1m: sold 10,000 gns Newmarket Autumn Sales. *J. A. R. Toller*

MELLOTTIE 10 b. or br.g. Meldrum 112 – Lottie Lehmann 69 (Goldhill 125) [1994 106: 8d⁴ 7v² 7.1g² 7.9f 7.9f 10m 7f 8g 9g 9m³ 8d 1995 8g 8g⁶ 7.9g 9.2f² 8m 8m⁵ 8f* 9.9m* 10m* 9g 10.4m* Oct 5] round-barrelled gelding: carries plenty of condition: gradually on the downgrade, but is still a useful performer: won claimer at Goodwood in July, handicaps at Beverley and Ripon in August and another claimer at York in October: effective at 1m to 1¼m: fair efforts on dead ground, but goes particularly well on a sound surface: normally held up: tough. *Mrs M. Reveley* 98

MELLOUISE 4 ch.f. Handsome Sailor 125 – Calton Colleen 60 (Sagaro 133) [1994 NR 1995 10m Apr 29] angular filly: second foal: dam 11f winner: little promise in 3 NH Flat races, and (gave trouble at stalls) a seller. *D. Eddy* –

MELMOTH (USA) 3 b.c. Nureyev (USA) 131 – Memories (USA) (Hail The Pirates (USA) 126) [1994 NR 1995 8g⁴ Jul 16] $285,000Y: second foal: dam won Grade 2 9f event at 2 yrs: 7/2 from 2/1, 5 lengths fourth of 7 to Code of Law in maiden at Ayr, in touch, pushed along 3f out: sent to Dubai. *J. H. M. Gosden* 68 p

MELODIC DRIVE 5 b. or br.g. Sizzling Melody 117 – Gleneagle 91 (Swing Easy (USA) 126) [1994 59§: 6.1v 6s a7g 6g* 6m⁵ 6g 6d 6s 6g 1995 a7g 6g³ 6m* 6f* Jun 23] lengthy, workmanlike gelding: has a round action: fair handicapper: unreliable at 4 yrs, but ran well for new stable and showed improved form to win 2 handicaps at Redcar in June: best efforts over 6f: acts on firm and dead ground: tried blinkered, including last 3 outings: usually slowly away. *J. A. Glover* 69 a–

MELODY DANCER 4 b.g. Rambo Dancer (CAN) 107 – Secret Song 83 (Tudor Melody 129) [1994 56: 8.1g³ 8.3d a8g⁴ 10g³ 12m² a12g⁴ 11g⁵ 12.1m⁶ 8s 10.3s 1995 a8g 10m 7.5g 11.1f Jul 28] compact gelding: has a sharp action: modest maiden handicapper: trained by R. Emery on 1995 reappearance: showed little in 1995: stays 1½m: acts on fibresand, good to firm ground and soft: tried blinkered/visored, below form: has been bandaged off-hind: sold (Miss J. Craze to J. Andrews) 1,150 gns Doncaster September Sales. *Miss J. F. Craze* –

Steve Nesbitt Challenge Trophy Handicap, Ripon—
Vindaloo's record attempt is foiled in the dying strides by grand old stager Mellottie

MELODY WHEEL 3 b.f. Merdon Melody 98 – Spare Wheel 67 (Track Spare 125) [1994 NR 1995 7m^5 Jul 16] 2,500Y: angular filly: sixth reported foal: half-sister to 1m (at 2 yrs) and 6f winner Pacific Rim (by Absalom): dam won 1½m seller and over hurdles: 33/1, bit backward and unimpressive to post, 6 lengths fifth of 8 in maiden at Yarmouth, held up and running green 2f out, then not knocked about unduly. *A. Hide* — 60 p

MELOS 2 b.f. (Apr 7) Emarati (USA) 74 – Double Stretch (Double-U-Jay 120) [1995 5m a6g^6 5m^5 a5g Sep 30] 1,500 2-y-o: unfurnished filly: third reported foal: dam poor maiden: no form, including in sellers. *Ronald Thompson* — –

MELS BABY (IRE) 2 br.g. (Apr 30) Contract Law (USA) 108 – Launch The Raft (Home Guard (USA) 129) [1995 5m 5m 6g^4 7m^6 7f^5 6m 7.5d 7f 6f^6 Oct 16] IR 1,800Y, 4,000 2-y-o: tall, leggy, light-bodied gelding: half-brother to a winner over hurdles by Shy Groom: dam unraced: only poor form (including in sellers) until improved effort when sixth of 15 to Missile in maiden auction at Pontefract final start: stays 7f: blinkered twice (including final outing) and visored sixth start (poor effort). *J. L. Eyre* — 53

MELT THE CLOUDS (CAN) 2 ch.c. (Jan 17) Diesis 133 – Population (General Assembly (USA)) [1995 7m Oct 20] $95,000Y: second foal: dam Irish maiden from family of Providential, Play It Safe and Hethersett: 14/1 and burly, over 6 lengths seventh of 21 to Germano in maiden at Doncaster, green after slow start then steady late progress under hand riding: will improve, particularly over 1m+. *P. W. Harris* — 73 p

MEMBERS WELCOME (IRE) 2 b.g. (Apr 15) Eve's Error 113 – Manuale Del Utente (Montekin 125) [1995 5.1m 5.1f^6 5.1m^3 6.1m^6 5g 6g 6.1s Oct 17] IR 500F, IR 2,000Y, 4,000 2-y-o: lengthy, angular gelding: first foal: dam won at 7f (in Ireland at 2 yrs) and over hurdles: modest form: stays 6f: acts on good to firm ground. *P. G. Murphy* — 54 +

MEMORABLE 4 b.g. Don't Forget Me 127 – Jhansi Ki Rani (USA) 94 (Far North (CAN) 120) [1994 71d: 10.3m 12.5v* 12s^5 14.6f^3 12f^2 13.8d* 14m 15.1m^5 15.8m 15d^4 17.5s 15.8g^5 16.1d 1995 14.1g^6 14.1g^4 15.8g^4 12.1m 17.5g Sep 15] lengthy, angular gelding: fair hurdler: disappointing on return to flat: stays 14.6f well: acts on any ground: often visored/blinkered: a hard ride, and not one to trust implicitly. *J. Hetherton* — 47 d

MEMORY'S MUSIC 3 b.c. Dance of Life (USA) – Sheer Luck 72 (Shergar 140) [1994 –: 7m 8d 1995 10m 7f^6 a10g^4 10m^6 a8.5g 7.1g Sep 18] lengthy colt: poor maiden handicapper: may well prove suited by further than 1¼m: visored (well below form) final 3-y-o start: sold (I. Balding to M. Madgwick) 4,000 gns Newmarket Autumn Sales. *I. A. Balding* — 50

MENAS GOLD 3 b.f. Heights of Gold – Tolomena 61 (Tolomeo 127) [1994 92p: 5d^6 5g^5 6s^5 6g^3 7f* 7.3g* 7.9d* 8g 1995 8m 8m 8.5m^4 8f^5 9f Jul 26] small filly: fairly useful performer: flattered by proximity when twelfth of 14 in 1000 Guineas at Newmarket second 3-y-o start: ran creditably in listed contests at Epsom and Ascot next 2 starts: below form in handicap at Goodwood (hanging right off bridle) final one: should stay 1m: acts on firm and dead ground. *S. Dow* — 88

MENDIP MIST 7 ch.m. Known Fact (USA) 135 – Silver Surprise 78 (Son of Silver 123) [1994 NR 1995 a12g Jan 27] leggy mare: probably no longer of much account. *B. R. Millman* — –

MENDIP SON 5 b.g. Hallgate 127 – Silver Surprise 78 (Son of Silver 123) [1994 48d: 10g^2 12m 11.7g 11.5d 1995 15.4m Apr 25] sturdy gelding: looked one to avoid at 4 yrs: modest hurdler in 1994/5: always in rear on return to flat: sold 2,400 gns Ascot November Sales. *J. Ffitch-Heyes* — –

MENOO HAL BATAL (USA) 2 b.c. (Mar 17) Gone West (USA) – Bank On Love (USA) (Gallant Romeo (USA)) [1995 7f^5 Oct 25] $200,000Y: leggy colt: has scope: half-brother to several winners, notably very useful 6f and 7.2f winner Weldnaas and 3-y-o 7.5f winner Marocco (both by Diesis): dam unraced sister to smart 1982 2-y-o Gallant Special out of sister to champion 2-y-o filly Numbered Account: 10/1, 3¼ lengths fifth of 10 to Mawjud in maiden at Yarmouth, pulling hard then no extra: will improve. *M. R. Stoute* — 75 p

MENSHAAR (USA) 3 b.g. Hawkster (USA) – Klassy Imp (USA) (Imp Society (USA)) [1994 NR 1995 10m 10.1g 12m May 19] $85,000Y: strong, rangy gelding: second foal: dam unraced: very burly and always behind in maidens: sold (J. Gosden to L. Lungo) 8,500 gns Newmarket July Sales. *J. H. M. Gosden* –

MENSHOOD (IRE) 3 b.c. Roi Danzig (USA) – Takhiyra (Vayrann 133) [1994 NR 1995 10.3g² Mar 23] IR 20,000Y: good-topped colt: second foal: dam unraced half-sister to Princess Royal winner Tashtiya: 10/1 and bit backward, shaped encouragingly when second of 12 in maiden at Doncaster, leading until inside final quarter-mile: should stay 1½m: sent to Dubai. *B. Hanbury* 79

MENTALASANYTHIN 6 b.g. Ballacashtal (CAN) – Lafrowda 71 (Crimson Beau 124) [1994 57, a75: a8.5g³ a8g⁴ a9.4g 13m 11.1g 8.3g⁵ 8d⁵ 10m 8s 12.1g* 11.9s⁶ 12g 10.1d⁶ a12g⁵ 1995 a9.4g a16.2g a8g* a8g⁴ a12g² a12g⁶ a12g³ 12g⁵ 10.3g 13g² 11.1g³ 13g² 13g² 10g² 10.5d* 13f* 11.1m⁴ 11.1f² 10.9g³ 11.9m² 10.9g³ 12.1g⁵ Sep 25] sturdy gelding: fair handicapper: won at Lingfield (amateurs) in January and at Haydock (amateurs) and Hamilton in June: effective at 1m and stays 13f (soundly beaten over 2m): acts on the all-weather and any turf going: has run creditably for amateur: tough. *A. Bailey* 72

MENTAL PRESSURE 2 ch.g. (Feb 4) Polar Falcon (USA) 126 – Hysterical 68 (High Top 131) [1995 7g 8g³ Sep 16] 62,000F, IR 50,000Y: rangy, useful-looking gelding: half-brother to several winners, including useful 7f to 9f winner Comic Talent (by Pharly) and useful 7f (at 2 yrs) to 1¼m winner Green Crusader (by Green Desert): dam won over 1½m at 4 yrs, only season to race: 1½ lengths third of 11, one pace, to Ladykirk in maiden at Ayr: will stay further than 1m: has joined Mrs M. Reveley: will improve again. *M. R. Channon* 75 p

MENTOR (GR) 3 b.c. Wadood (USA) 97 – Queen of The North (Northfields (USA)) [1994 82: a8g³ 7.6v* 7.6s² 8.1s⁵ 1995 a10g⁶ 8m 10g² 12f³ 12.3m⁴ Jul 14] sturdy colt: fairly useful handicapper: stays 1½m: acts on any going: sold to race in USA. *R. Charlton* 87

MERANTI 2 b.c. (Apr 13) Puissance 110 – Sorrowful (Moorestyle 137) [1995 5g 5g⁶ 5m⁴ 5m 6m⁴ 6g⁴ 6s⁵ a8g Nov 10] 10,000Y: tall, useful-looking colt: half-brother to a winner in Norway by Grey Desire: dam ran twice at 2 yrs: trained first 7 starts by L. J. Holt: fair form at best in maidens: stays 6f (took keen hold and well beaten in 1m nursery): below form on soft ground. *S. Dow* 67

MERCADIER 4 ch.g. Rainbow Quest (USA) 134 – Gerardmer (FR) (Brigadier Gerard 144) [1994 75p: 10.1g² 10.4g⁴ 1995 10m⁴ 14m* May 24] tall, lengthy gelding: has a short, rather round action: reportedly chipped a bone final 3-y-o start: improved form in 1995, winning 6-runner rated stakes at Goodwood (allowed to set up a long lead, 10 lengths clear entering straight, held Wishing by a neck) in May: stays 1¾m: reluctant stalls second 4-y-o start: subsequently gelded: sent to Dubai. *C. E. Brittain* 88

MERCHANT HOUSE (IRE) 7 ch.g. Salmon Leap (USA) 131 – Persian Polly 99 (Persian Bold 123) [1994 45: a16s a12g 10d⁴ 1995 a11g May 15] workmanlike gelding: poor maiden: off course over a year, well beaten only start on flat for new stable: will stay 1½m: acts on dead ground: sent to Sweden. *G. Fierro* –

MERGER MANIA 3 b.g. Precocious 126 – Scrummage 64 (Workboy 123) [1994 NR 1995 8.1m⁴ 8.3g Sep 24] close-coupled gelding: third reported foal: dam 7f and 1m winner at 4 yrs: tailed-off last in seller and claimer. *Miss J. F. Craze* –

MERIBEL (IRE) 2 b.f. (Apr 18) Nashwan (USA) 135 – Dark Lomond 122 (Lomond (USA) 128) [1995 7.1s³ Sep 30] fourth foal: sister to smart Irish middle-distance performer Gothic Dream, and half-sister to a winner in Japan by Kris: dam (from excellent family) won Irish St Leger: 7/4 favourite though green, 3¼ lengths third of 7 to Classic Romance in maiden at Haydock, held up then keeping on: will be suited by middle distances: sure to improve. *P. W. Chapple-Hyam* 65 p

MERIT (IRE) 3 b.c. Rainbow Quest (USA) 134 – Fur Hat (Habitat 134) [1994 63p: 8.2d 1995 8g 8m⁶ 11.8g 9.7g a12g* 15.1s* 16.5m* Nov 4] rangy colt: poor mover: off course 5 months after second 3-y-o start: successful, against quite large fields of handicappers, at Lingfield (only time blinkered), Edinburgh (most impressive) and Doncaster (heavily backed, led over 2f out and ran on strongly) 74 p within 12 days in the autumn: effective at 1½m to 15f, and will stay 2m: acts on good to firm and soft ground, and equitrack: still on the upgrade. *P. F. I. Cole*

MERLIN'S FANCY 3 b.f. Caerleon (USA) 132 – Smarten Up 119 (Sharpen Up 127) [1994 45: 6g 1995 6m 6m^{6} 5m a7g 8g 7f Oct 25] small, leggy filly: fluent mover: modest maiden: probably stays 1m: inconsistent. *W. Jarvis* — 62 d

MERLIN'S HONOUR 2 ch.f. (Mar 15) Crowning Honors (CAN) – Miss Merlin 79 (Manacle 123) [1995 5m 5g a6g^{2} 7.1g 7f Oct 3] 8,200Y: leggy filly: half-sister to 3-y-o Rubylee (by Persian Bold) and to several winners: dam won twice at 6f: only form when second in seller at Wolverhampton in May: stays 6f: sold 1,000 gns Doncaster October Sales: has joined John Berry. *P. C. Haslam* — 32

MERRIE LE BOW 3 b.f. Merdon Melody 98 – Arch Sculptress 85 (Arch Sculptor 123) [1994 51: a5g^{6} a5g^{3} 1995 a5g^{2} a6g^{3} a6g^{3} a6g^{3} a5g 7g^{6} 8m 7m^{3} 6m^{4} 5.2g 7g^{4} 7m^{5} 7f Oct 25] lengthy filly: modest maiden handicapper: stays 7f: acts the all-weather: visored (no improvement) tenth 3-y-o start: sometimes looks none too keen. *Pat Mitchell* — 44 a55

MERRILY 2 gr.f. (Feb 1) Sharrood (USA) 124 – Babycham Sparkle 80 (So Blessed 130) [1995 6m^{5} May 30] 13,500Y: unfurnished filly: sister to 5f winner Aroom and half-sister to winning sprinters Number Eleven (by Local Suitor) and Champagne Girl (by Robellino): dam, 2-y-o 5f and 6f winner, half-sister to smart French middle-distance colt El Famoso: 12/1 and carrying plenty of condition, 9¼ lengths fifth of 6 to Amanita in median auction maiden at Redcar: wore bandages behind: looked sure to do better. *Miss S. E. Hall* — 48

MERRY FESTIVAL (USA) 3 b.f. Private Account (USA) – Beat (USA) (Nijinsky (CAN) 138) [1994 NR 1995 7m 10.1m^{4} 10.5g* Sep 22] tall, rangy filly: second foal: dam, winner 4 times and placed in 2 Grade 3 handicaps (at 8.5f and 9f), is half-sister to very smart U.S. filly Too Chic: best effort in maidens when winning at Haydock in September, moving easily into lead 2f out and holding on: stays 10.5f: capable of better: sent to Dubai. *J. H. M. Gosden* — 82 p

MERRY MERMAID 5 ch.m. Bairn (USA) 126 – Manna Green (Bustino 136) [1994 50d: 11.9m 12g 12m^{2} 12m^{6} a12g^{5} 12g^{5} 12.1g 12.1g^{3} 1995 12.3d* 12g 12m^{2} 12.4g^{6} 12d Jun 7] tall, sparely-made mare: reportedly broke blood vessels in 1994: poor form: comfortable winner of seller at Ripon (bought in 5,600 gns) in April: stays 12.4f: acts on good to firm ground, very best efforts in the mud: has run well when sweating: usually held up: modest hurdler: sold (J. Bottomley to B. Mactaggart) 900 gns Doncaster November Sales. *J. F. Bottomley* — 48

MERSEYSIDE MAN 9 b.g. My Dad Tom (USA) 109 – Chanita (Averof 123) [1994 36: a12g a8.5g^{4} a10g 1995 10m a8.5g Jun 2] lengthy, workmanlike gelding: probably no longer of any account. *Dr J. D. Scargill* — –

METAL BOYS 8 b.g. Krayyan 117 – Idle Gossip (Runnett 125) [1994 76: 5g^{4} 5s 1995 5m 5g 5g 5m^{3} 5m 5g 5g 5m 5m^{3} 5m 5m Nov 4] sturdy gelding: poor mover: fair handicapper: best at 5f: probably acts on any ground: has won for apprentice: usually races prominently: inconsistent at 8 yrs. *Miss L. C. Siddall* — 67

METAL STORM (FR) 7 b.h. Kenmare (FR) 125 – Porphyrine (FR) (Habitat 134) [1994 89: 8m^{6} 10v 6g 7v^{4} 8g 8s 8s a8g* 1995 a9.4g a8g^{3} Feb 11] lengthy, good-topped horse: fairly useful performer nowadays: stays 1m: acts on heavy ground and equitrack (below form on fibresand on reappearance): sometimes bandaged at 6 yrs: normally chases pace, held up last time: sent to Australia. *K. O. Cunningham-Brown* — 85

MEXICAN DANCER 6 b.m. Dance of Life (USA) – Mexican Two Step (Gay Fandango (USA) 132) [1994 21: a11g a10g a8.5g 8d 8.3g 8f 10m 9.7m 11.9f 1995 a16g a8g a14g^{3} Apr 11] sparely-made mare: unimpressive mover: bad performer nowadays: stays 1¾m: acts on any going: blinkered (well beaten) once at 3 yrs: inconsistent. *P. Howling* — –

MEZAAN (IRE) 3 ch.c. Royal Academy (USA) 130 – Arctic Heroine (USA) (Arctic Tern (USA) 126) [1994 89p: 8g^{4} 1995 10m^{5} 8m* 8.1g^{4} 10.4m^{5} 11.9g* 12d Sep 24] rangy colt: has plenty of scope: good mover: useful performer: won maiden at Doncaster in May and rated stakes at York (storming clear) in August: creditable seventh of 18 to Taufan's Melody in £46,800 event at Ascot last time, leading 4f out — 98 to 2f out: very well suited by at least 1½m: acts on good to firm ground and dead: made running on reappearance, not afterwards. *M. R. Stoute*

MEZZOGIORNO 2 b.f. (Apr 15) Unfuwain (USA) 131 – Aigue 96 (High Top 131) [1995 7m^4 7m* 7d^2 Sep 26] 46,000Y: tall, unfurnished filly: has plenty of scope: second foal: dam stayed 1m, sister to smart middle-distance performer Torchon from family of Mystiko: comfortably made all in maiden at Lingfield in September: improved effort when length second of 30 to Rio Duvida in valuable sales race at Newmarket 3 weeks later: will stay at least 1m: looks a very useful prospect. *G. Wragg* 96 p

MEZZORAMIO 3 ch.g. Cadeaux Genereux 131 – Hopeful Search (USA) 71 (Vaguely Noble 140) [1994 51p: a7g^4 1995 a7g^4 a9.4g^3 a8g a8.5g^6 a7g^5 a11g Aug 4] poor form: trained by Sir Mark Prescott until after reappearance: stays 8.5f: has raced only on fibresand: visored/blinkered since third 3-y-o start. *K. A. Morgan* 44

MHEANMETOO 4 ch.g. Roi Danzig (USA) – Spinster 75 (Grundy 137) [1994 68: 8d 7m^3 7m^3 7f 7g 7d 6g 1995 a6g^6 a6g a7g Mar 2] workmanlike gelding: no form for new stable in 1995: stays 7f: may be unsuited by a soft surface. *D. L. Williams* –

MHEMEANLES 5 br.g. Jalmood (USA) 126 – Folle Idee (USA) (Foolish Pleasure (USA)) [1994 NR 1995 a11g 14m 11.1g 10g* 11.1f^4 12f^4 a14g 10.3m^4 10.2m 10g^3 10.8g^6 11.8g Oct 10] compact gelding: has a round action: only poor performer nowadays: sold out of M. H. Easterby's stable 1,400 gns Ascot February Sales after reappearance: won seller at Pontefract in June: probably stays 1½m: used to act on any turf ground (no form either start on all-weather): tried blinkered, no improvement: inconsistent. *Capt. J. Wilson* 46

MIAMI BANKER 9 ch.g. Miami Springs 121 – Banking Coyne 76 (Deep Diver 134) [1994 39§: 5d^4 5s^3 1995 a5g^5 a5g 5g^3 5f^2 5m^2 5.1m^2 5m* 5f* 5m^5 5m^4 5m^2 5d 5.3g Oct 1] strong, lengthy gelding: unimpressive mover: modest at best since 1992: gained narrow successes at Epsom and Kempton in the summer: probably best at 5f nowadays: acts on any going: usually blinkered: races prominently. *W. R. Muir* 60

MIASMA (USA) 3 b.f. Lear Fan (USA) 130 – Syrian Circle (USA) (Damascus (USA)) [1994 92: 6m^4 6m* 6g^4 7.1g^2 8g 8g 1995 10m 8.2m^2 7.1m^2 8m^3 Sep 25] tall, lengthy filly: good mover with long stride: fairly useful performer: placed last 3 starts in minor events at Nottingham, Chepstow and (battling on well) Bath: should stay beyond 8.2f: has raced only on a sound surface: front runner: sold 47,000 gns Newmarket December Sales. *J. A. R. Toller* 90

MICHAELMAS PARK (IRE) 4 ch.g. Common Grounds 118 – Fresh As A Daisy (Stanford 121§) [1994 57: 7f^6 7m* 8.2m 7m 7.6v 8.2g 1995 9m 7f Jul 12] neat gelding: disappointing handicapper, last on both outings for new stable: should stay 1m: acts on good to firm ground, well beaten on heavy: blinkered (looked reluctant) final 4-y-o start: taken down early in 1995: one to treat with caution. *T. M. Jones* – §

MICHELLE'S ELLA (IRE) 3 b.f. Ela-Mana-Mou 132 – Bustina (FR) (Busted 134) [1994 NR 1995 10.3g^6 Jul 1] 4,500F: angular filly: half-sister to 3 winners in Ireland, including quite useful 6f to 1m winner Miss Lillian (by Sandford Lad): dam fourth of 16 on only start at 2 yrs in France: 33/1, tailed-off sixth of 7 in maiden at Doncaster. *C. D. Broad* –

MICHELLISA 4 b.f. Indian Ridge 123 – Land Line (High Line 125) [1994 55: 7g^6 7m 8f^6 10m 7.1f 7m^6 5g^3 6m^2 6f^2 5m^2 5g^3 6.1s^6 5.1g^4 1995 5m^4 5.9m^4 6m^3 6f^3 7m* 8.2m^2 8g^2 8.5d^4 7.1s^4 8g^3 8.2m Oct 19] lengthy filly: modest handicapper: gained her first success at Catterick in August: stays 8.2f well: acts on firm and soft ground: blinkered twice in 1994: sometimes bandaged behind: pulls hard: consistent. *J. D. Bethell* 61

MICK'S LOVE (IRE) 2 b.c. (Feb 12) Law Society (USA) 130 – Flute (FR) (Luthier 126) [1995 8.1g* 8d* Sep 15] 102 p

Vettori, Moonshell, Lammtarra and Classic Cliche all won classics in Europe for the Godolphin training operation in the latest season after promising two-year-old campaigns with other trainers. Godolphin's classic plans in 1996 could well include the promising Mark of Esteem and the Coventry runner-up Russian Revival, as well as the Fillies' Mile runner-up Bint Shadayid, but it will pay to watch out also for the unexposed maiden winners Coldstream, Don Micheletto, Helicon and the filly Pricket (a full sister to Diminuendo), all of whom are rated with a large 'P' in this

Annual. All these horses mentioned were trained in British stables as two-year-olds, as was the Derby prospect Mick's Love, transferred to Godolphin after being purchased privately out of Mark Johnston's yard in late-November. Johnston describes Mick's Love, unbeaten in two starts, as 'a seriously good horse and perhaps the best-looking horse I've had.' Mick's Love made his debut in a median auction maiden—he cost IR 24,000 guineas as a yearling—at Haydock in early-September, upsetting the odds laid on Double Bluff who had finished a promising fourth in a good maiden (in which Coldstream, also making his debut, had finished third) at Newbury. Mick's Love was green and some way short of peak fitness but he got up to beat Double Bluff by a neck, looking a useful staying two-year-old in the making. It wouldn't have been a surprise to see Mick's Love aimed at the Zetland Stakes which his stable had won with the brothers Double Trigger and Double Eclipse in the two previous years. In the event Polar Eclipse, winner of a Haydock maiden in October, represented the stable in the Zetland (finishing third), Mick's Love already having concluded his campaign in the Haynes, Hanson and Clark Stakes at Newbury in mid-September. Mick's Love stayed on strongly to hold off Busy Flight and Sasuru by three quarters of a length and a length and a half, a useful and game performance in what is nearly always an informative race; Busy Flight went on to finish second in the Horris Hill Stakes on his next start. There should certainly be more improvement to come from Mick's Love when he gets the opportunity to race over middle distances as a three-year-old, and he looks just the sort for whom a winter in Dubai could do much.

Mick's Love (IRE) (b.c. Feb 12, 1993)	Law Society (USA) (br 1982)	Alleged (b 1974)	Hoist The Flag
			Princess Pout
		Bold Bikini (b 1969)	Boldnesian
			Ran-Tan
	Flute (FR) (b 1977)	Luthier (b 1965)	Klairon
			Flute Enchantee
		Perle Fine (br 1969)	Fine Top
			Seed Pearl

Mick's Love is a fine stamp of horse, good-topped and sturdy with plenty of scope, and is the fifth winner bred by his dam Flute who showed some ability and was placed three times in France. The most important of her winners before Mick's Love was the Irish Cambridgeshire winner Any Song (by Bold Lad (IRE)) who also went on to be successful in the States. Flute's three other winners are: Millford Haven (by Welsh Saint), successful in a maiden race at Limerick as a three-year-old, Sylvan Sabre (by Flash of Steel), a fairly useful but unreliable handicapper who won at up to a mile and a quarter and has also been successful over hurdles, and the fairly useful Irish three-year-old Lilting Air (by Glenstal), successful at six furlongs and nine furlongs in the latest season. Perle Fine, the once-raced grandam of Mick's Love, was a sister to the Prix de Diane winner Fine Pearl. Mick's Love has yet to race on a firm surface; the going was good at Haydock and on the easy side at Newbury. *M. Johnston*

MICROLITE (USA) 4 b.f. Lear Fan (USA) 130 – Comicus (USA) (Northern Jove (CAN)) [1994 73: 8d^5 10.5g^4 9d^3 12g^3 10g^2 10m^2 10.2m^3 12m* 12m* 13.9d 1995 14m 12m 12.4g^4 16m^5 12f^5 12m^3 12f^3 10.1f Aug 26] sturdy filly: shows traces of stringhalt: fair handicapper at best in 1995: stays at least 12.4f: acts on any ground: effective blinkered or not: effective from front or held up: none too consistent. *M. D. Hammond* 68 d

MIDAS GOLD 2 ch.c. (Mar 17) Prince Sabo 123 – So Rewarding (Never So Bold 135) [1995 6m 7m 6s^3 a6g^6 Oct 14] 5,100Y: lengthy colt: second foal: brother to 3-y-o Never Say So: dam never ran: best efforts in claimers at Lingfield and at Wolverhampton last 2 starts: stays 6f: acts on soft ground and fibresand: sold 2,600 gns Newmarket Autumn Sales: sent to Austria. *B. J. Meehan* 60

MIDDLE EAST 2 b.g. (May 31) Beveled (USA) – Godara (Bustino 136) [1995 5f* 7m^4 6m^3 6d 6m Oct 2] 2,000Y: tall, leggy gelding: third foal: dam ran 3 times on flat at 4 yrs: won maiden auction at Redcar in July: creditable third of 8 to Mybotye in nursery at Redcar third start: ran poorly (sweating) in similar event at Pontefract final outing: keen sort who'll prove best at up to 6f. *T. D. Barron* 66 +

MIDLIN 5 ch.m. Midyan (USA) 124 – Western Line (High Line 125) [1994 –: 8m 8g a8g a11g 1995 a11g^5 a11g^5 a12g^5 a11g^4 10m May 29] angular mare: poor maiden: 36

probably stays 11f: acts on fibresand: sold 1,500 gns Newmarket Autumn Sales. *J. L. Harris*

MIDNIGHT BLUE 2 br.f. (Apr 12) Be My Chief (USA) 122 – Guyum (Rousillon (USA) 133) [1995 6s* Oct 6] leggy, lengthy filly: first foal: dam half-sister to smart sprinter Enchantment: 16/1, won 11-runner maiden at Ascot in good style by 3 lengths from Mutamanni, moving smoothly behind strong pace then quickening well and running on strongly: will be at least as effective at 7f: sure to do better. *W. Jarvis* — 83 p

MIDNIGHT BREAK 3 ch.f. Night Shift (USA) – Splintering 80 (Sharpo 132) [1994 78d: 5d² 5g² 5m² 5f⁵ 5.7g⁴ 1995 6m⁵ 5.1f³ 5g* 6m* 5.7f 6m⁵ 5m² 5m⁵ 6.1d 5g Sep 28] good-bodied filly: fair handicapper: won at Warwick and Leicester in June: stays 6f: acts on firm and dead ground: visored (slowly away, below form) final start. *P. T. Walwyn* — 66

MIDNIGHT COOKIE 2 b.c. (Apr 23) Midyan (USA) 124 – Midnight's Reward 84 (Night Shift (USA)) [1995 5.1m 5.2g 6m 5s 6.1s 5g 6m⁶ 5m a5g² Nov 25] 8,400Y: sturdy, good-quartered colt: third foal: brother to 1994 2-y-o 5f winner Soca King: dam 2-y-o 5f winner: little worthwhile form for R. Hodges first 4 starts: showed more for new trainer, caught on line in nursery at Lingfield in November: stays 6f: acts on good to firm and soft ground and equitrack. *B. A. Pearce* — 54

MIDNIGHT ESCAPE 2 b.g. (Feb 20) Aragon 118 – Executive Lady 59 (Night Shift (USA)) [1995 5g⁴ 5m* 6m⁴ 5g³ Jul 19] 7,000Y: workmanlike gelding: second foal: closely related to 3-y-o Zatopek (by Reprimand): dam stayed 7f: won maiden auction at Lingfield in June: good keeping-on third to Gagajulu in nursery at Leicester on final outing: stays 6f. *C. F. Wall* — 80

MIDNIGHT JAZZ (IRE) 5 b.h. Shardari 134 – Round Midnight 64 (Star Appeal 133) [1994 81: a10g* a12g² a10g⁵ a9.4g² a8.5g² 10m 8m* 8.9f⁵ a8.5g 1995 10.8m 10m 8m³ 8g 10m⁴ 7m* 8.3m 7m⁶ 8g⁶ 7f Oct 18] rangy horse: fair handicapper: won at Yarmouth in July: below form afterwards: effective at 7f and stays easy 1½m: acts on all-weather tracks and good to firm ground: blinkered (out of form) final start: usually held up: inconsistent: sold 15,000 gns Newmarket Autumn Sales. *W. A. O'Gorman* — 75

MIDNIGHT LEGEND 4 b.c. Night Shift (USA) – Myth 89 (Troy 137) [1994 112: 8m* 7.9f 10m³ 12f* 10.4f² 12f* 14g* 14.6g 1995 10d 12f² 12g 12f* 13.3m² 11.1g Sep 2] robust, round-barrelled colt: carries condition and impresses in appearance: good mover: smart performer: forced rather close to outside rail, changed legs, stumbled and rider unseated at Sandown on reappearance: 2½ lengths second to Beauchamp Hero in Hardwicke Stakes at Royal Ascot, winner of 7-runner Schroders Glorious Rated Stakes at Goodwood by 1½ lengths from Ionio, then 3 lengths second to Presenting in Geoffrey Freer Stakes at Newbury: tailed right off, as if something amiss, final start: stays 1¾m: goes very well on top-of-the-ground: usually races prominently and with great zest: said to have got stirred up (ran poorly) third 4-y-o start: has proved thoroughly genuine in a battle: stays in training. *L. M. Cumani* — 118

Schroders Glorious Rated Stakes (Handicap), Goodwood—
Midnight Legend is well on top of Ionio to record the season's highest-rated performance in a handicap

MIDNIGHT MASS 3 b.f. Mandrake Major 122 – Kirkby 85 (Midsummer Night II 117) [1994 NR 1995 8g 7f 12g^6 Jul 17] lengthy filly: sister to 6f to 10.6f winner Majority Holding (by Mandrake Major) and half-sister to several winners, including 7f winner Train of Thought: dam won twice over 1¼m: last in maidens (for A. G. Foster, blinkered second start) and a seller. *Miss J. F. Craze* –

MIDNIGHT SPELL 3 ch.f. Night Shift (USA) – Bundled Up (USA) (Sharpen Up 127) [1994 79p: 7s^4 7m 1995 6.9g^2 6m a6g 6g^3 5.2g^6 5d Sep 27] sturdy filly: fair maiden: creditable efforts as 3-y-o when placed: stays 7f: acts on good to firm ground, probably on soft: blinkered (finished last) final start. *Mrs J. Cecil* 74

MIDNIGHT WALKER 3 b.f. Exodal (USA) – Petite Butterfly 67 (Absalom 128) [1994 NR 1995 7f 7m 8.2d Sep 19] small filly: first foal: dam 6f and 7f winner: well beaten in maidens. *Mrs S. D. Williams* –

MIDTIME (IRE) 2 b.c. (Feb 3) Formidable (USA) 125 – Between Time 75 (Elegant Air 119) [1995 7g^4 7.5m^4 a7g^6 Sep 4] sturdy colt: second foal: half-brother to 3-y-o 12.3f and 14.1f winner Outstayed Welcome (by Be My Guest): dam 6f winner best at 2 yrs: similar form in maidens won by Subterfuge at Newmarket (4 ran) and Pleasant Surprise at Beverley: below form in similar event at Southwell final start: will stay further than 7.5f: sold 4,600 gns Newmarket Autumn Sales. *M. R. Stoute* 72

MIDWICH CUCKOO 3 b.c. Midyan (USA) 124 – Portvasco 90 (Sharpo 132) [1994 82: 6f^6 6g^2 5.3m* 6d^2 6s 6g^3 1995 8m 7m^3 6f* 7.1m 7m^2 7.1d 7m Oct 14] workmanlike colt: fairly useful handicapper: won at Ripon in June: effective at 6f in a strongly-run race, and stays 1m: acts on firm and soft ground: visored (below best) final start: sold 9,000 gns Newmarket Autumn Sales: sent to Czech Republic. *P. T. Walwyn* 87

MIDYAN BLUE (IRE) 5 ch.g. Midyan (USA) 124 – Jarretiere 78 (Star Appeal 133) [1994 74: 12v^5 14d 12m^5 16.5m 14g^5 16.1f 11.9g^2 13.9m 12f 13.1d^2 11.9s^3 12v a12g 1995 11.8m^2 13.9g* 16.5g^4 14g^3 14m^2 14g* 14.8m^5 13.9m^2 13.9g^5 13.3d 13.9g^4 Oct 7] sparely-made gelding: shows plenty of knee action: fairly useful handicapper: ran well most starts in 1995, winning at York in May and Sandown in July: game short-head second of 21 to Sanmartino in Tote Ebor at York in August: stays 1¾m, seemingly not 16.5f: acts on good to firm ground and soft: has run well when sweating: has made running/chased leaders on recent starts. *J. M. P. Eustace* 86

MIGHTY KINGDOM (IRE) 4 b.f. Mister Majestic 122 – Great Land (USA) (Friend's Choice (USA)) [1994 44: 7f 8.2m^4 8s 10.3s a8g^5 a8g a12g 1995 a12g a13g^5 a12g 8.1m* 7m^4 8m* 10m^3 10m 8m 8m^6 8h^2 11.5g 8m 8f^5 8f^2 Oct 23] lengthy filly: poor handicapper: trained until after third 4-y-o start by R. Emery, next 5 (winning at Edinburgh and Warwick (seller) in the summer) by John Berry: inconsistent afterwards: stays 1¼m: acts on fibresand and hard going, well beaten on soft: effective blinkered or not: usually races prominently: sold 5,200 gns Newmarket Autumn Sales. *C. A. Dwyer* 48

MIGHTY MARSTON 3 b.g. Mazilier (USA) 107 – Thulium (Mansingh (USA) 120) [1994 –: 8m 1995 8m 7.5d 8f* 8m 7g^2 8h^4 8f Aug 17] robust, compact gelding: fair handicapper: won apprentice race at Ayr in June: should stay beyond 1m: acts on firm going: inconsistent: sold 7,800 gns Newmarket September Sales. *Lady Herries* 71

MIGHTY PHANTOM (USA) 2 b.f. (Mar 9) Lear Fan (USA) 130 – Migiyas 87 (Kings Lake (USA) 133) [1995 6g^5 7.5d Sep 13] 12,000Y: quite attractive filly: fifth foal: half-sister to 3-y-o 14.1f to 2m winner Nanton Point (by Darshaan), 1¾m winner Last Conquest (by Slip Anchor) and 1992 2-y-o 6f winner Break My Heart (by Broken Hearted): dam 5f (at 2 yrs) and 7f winner: over 4 lengths fifth of 15 to Prima Volta in maiden at Kempton in September, running on well under hands and heels: soon struggling in similar event at Beverley 11 days later: should stay beyond 6f. *J. W. Hills* 60

MIGHTY SQUAW 3 b.f. Indian Ridge 123 – Mighty Flash 81 (Rolfe (USA) 77) [1994 NR 1995 7m^5 8m^5 8m a7g 7m^6 10.1m^4 a10g^2 10.2h^6 12s^3 11.9d 12m^4 14g^4 Oct 23] 26,000Y: quite good-topped filly: half-sister to 4-y-o 7f (including at 2 yrs, here) to 8.5f (Grade 3 in USA in 1995) winner Mighty Forum (by Presidium): dam staying sister to smart miler Mighty Fly and Derby third Mighty Flutter: modest maiden: stays 1½m: best effort on soft ground: tried blinkered/visored, no improvement: inconsistent: has joined D. Elsworth. *Miss Gay Kelleway* 58

MIGNONNETTE (FR) 2 gr.f. (Feb 27) Mtoto 134 – Cut Velvet (USA) (Northern Dancer) [1995 6.9f[5] 7g Oct 9] ninth reported foal: half-sister to 4 winners abroad including Cold Breeze (by Thatching), winner in Italy at up to 9f: dam 1m winner in USA: poor form in maidens at Folkestone (slowly away) and Leicester: sent to UAE. *I. A. Balding* 47

MIGWAR 2 b.c. (Feb 12) Unfuwain (USA) 131 – Pick of The Pops 109 (High Top 131) [1995 7g 7m[5] Oct 14] 40,000Y: deep-girthed, attractive colt: third foal: dam 2-y-o 7f winner from very good family: bit backward, never better than mid-division, not given a hard race, when eleventh of 23 to Astor Place in maiden at Newmarket: 8½ lengths last of 5 to Babinda in minor event at Newmarket following month, unimpressive to post then dropping away from 1½f out after losing action. *L. M. Cumani* 68

MIHRIZ (IRE) 3 b.g. Machiavellian (USA) 123 – Ghzaalh (USA) 87 (Northern Dancer) [1994 73: 6f[5] 6g[4] 6m* 7m 1995 8m[4] 9m[2] 10g[5] 10g[6] Jun 16] sturdy, useful-looking colt: fluent mover: fairly useful handicapper: well below form last 2 starts: stays 9f: acts on good to firm ground: sold only 5,000 gns Newmarket Autumn Sales. *Major W. R. Hern* 84

MILBANK CHALLENGER 5 gr.g. Belfort (FR) 89 – Princess Sharpenup 63 (Lochnager 132) [1994 51: 5g 6g 7g 5.9v[3] 6d[6] 5m 1995 6.9m 5m 6f May 15] workmanlike gelding: no worthwhile form for new stable: stays 6f: acts on any going: effective blinkered/visored or not: inconsistent. *W. Storey* –

MILES AWAY (IRE) 3 ch.f. Ballad Rock 122 – Far From Home 73 (Habitat 134) [1994 54: 6.9m 7g[6] 1995 6m 8m[3] 8.1g May 30] leggy, angular filly: poor maiden: stays 1m: has raced only on a sound surface: inconsistent: sold 3,200 gns Newmarket July Sales. *J. R. Fanshawe* 43

MILETRIAN CITY 2 gr.c. (Apr 19) Petong 126 – Blueit (FR) 101 (Bold Lad (IRE) 133) [1995 a6g 6f 5d[5] 6g[4] Sep 24] 21,000Y: smallish, strong colt: half-brother to several winning sprinters, including useful Blues Indigo (by Music Boy): dam 2-y-o 5f winner: apparently improved effort in maidens (could be rated 59) when around 4 lengths fifth of 11 to Angel Chimes at Beverley, staying on from off very strong pace: looked worthy only of a place in sellers on other form. *J. Berry* 53 +

MILETRIAN REFURB (IRE) 2 b. or br.g. (Mar 27) Anita's Prince 126 – Lady of Man 85 (So Blessed 130) [1995 5g[5] 5.1g[5] 5m[2] 7f 6.1m[5] 6m[2] 5.3d* 5m[5] Oct 13] IR 4,200F, IR 11,000Y: compact gelding: unimpressive mover: brother to 3 winners in Ireland at up to 1m: dam 5f and 7f winner: plater: won at Brighton in September: stays 6f: acts on good to firm and dead ground. *M. R. Channon* 59

MILFORD SOUND 2 b.c. (Feb 17) Batshoof 122 – Nafis (USA) (Nodouble (USA)) [1995 7m Oct 20] 28,000Y: second foal: dam unraced: 16/1, backward and green, around 12 lengths tenth of 21 to Germano in maiden at Doncaster, in touch 5f then left behind, not given hard race: should do better. *J. R. Fanshawe* – p

MILLAZURE (USA) 3 b.f. Dayjur (USA) 137 – Milligram 130 (Mill Reef (USA) 141) [1994 NR 1995 7.1g[4] 7m[3] 6g[5] 7.1d[6] Sep 13] unfurnished filly: fourth foal: half-sister to fair 7f winner Footlight Fantasy (by Nureyev): dam top-class miler out of 1000 Guineas winner One In A Million: fair maiden: below form last 2 starts, finding little final one: should stay beyond 7f: has worn blanket for stalls entry. *R. Charlton* 71

MILL DANCER (IRE) 3 b.f. Broken Hearted 124 – Theatral (Orchestra 118) [1994 NR 1995 8g 8m[3] 8g[3] 8.1m* 8f 10d* 10.5s[6] 10.5d[6] Oct 11] IR 650Y: leggy filly: first foal: dam winning hurdler: modest form: won sellers at Haydock (odds on) and Leicester (gamely made all, retained 11,000 gns) in September: worth trying beyond 10.5f: acts on good to firm ground (ran poorly on firm), goes well on a soft surface: sometimes takes keen hold. *E. J. Alston* 49

MILLEMAY 5 br.m. Respect 95 – Ravenscraig (Impecunious) [1994 –: 13g 7g 1995 6s[5] 6g[5] 7m[6] May 10] good-topped filly: poor sprint maiden: hung left under pressure second 5-y-o start. *P. Monteith* 36 ?

MILL END LADY 2 b.f. (Feb 1) Tina's Pet 121 – Azelly 77 (Pitskelly 122) [1995 5m[6] 5g 7.5d 7d[5] 5m Oct 13] 7,200Y: unfurnished filly: has knee action: half-sister to 5f winner Covent Garden Girl (by Sizzling Melody) and 2 winners 49

abroad: dam placed over 5f at 2 yrs then failed to train on: modest maiden: very stiff task and always behind in nursery at Catterick final start: stays 7f. *M. W. Easterby*

MILLESIME (IRE) 3 ch.g. Glow (USA) – Persian Myth (Persian Bold 123) [1994 NR 1995 5m4 6g 6.9m4 6g5 6f4 6g3 5.1m* 5.1f* 5f6 5.2m2 5m 5m3 5.1d Sep 11] IR 10,000Y: unfurnished gelding: half-brother to several winners: dam ran once: fair performer: won 4-runner races for maiden at Chepstow and minor event at Bath in July: effective at 5f (best form) and 6f: acts on firm ground, soundly beaten only start on dead: tongue tied last 2 starts: races prominently: suitable mount for an inexperienced rider. *B. Hanbury* 71

MILL HOUSE BOY (IRE) 2 b.g. (Mar 7) Astronef 116 – Avantage Service (IRE) (Exactly Sharp (USA) 121) [1995 7m 6m 7m Jul 19] IR 1,600Y: leggy gelding: first foal: dam unraced half-sister to smart 1m/1¼m performer Splendid Moment out of Irish Oaks third Racquette, family of Ardross: soundly beaten in median auction maiden and sellers. *B. S. Rothwell* –

MILLION DANCER 3 b.c. Rambo Dancer (CAN) 107 – Tea-Pot 77 (Ragstone 128) [1994 71: 7m6 7m2 7g3 a7g3 8m 7g6 10g3 1995 10g 12.5f 12g3 May 31] leggy colt: good mover: form for new stable only (edging left and looking bit reluctant) in Newbury claimer final start: will probably stay beyond 1½m: has raced only on a sound surface when on turf: unreliable. *M. C. Pipe* 43 +

MILLKOM 4 b.c. Cyrano de Bergerac 120 – Good Game 71 (Mummy's Game 120) [1994 124: 8s* 9.3m* 9.3g* 10d* 10d* 12g a10f 1995 10s5 10.5v 8g* 8d2 10g3 11f* Sep 16] very smart colt: won minor event in the Provinces and respectable 2½ lengths third of 9 to Hernando in Prix Gontaut-Biron at Deauville in the summer: won 12-runner Man o'War Stakes at Belmont in September in most impressive style, barely off bridle and beating Kaldounevees by 1¼ lengths: stays 1½m: acts on any going on turf, but soundly beaten on dirt in Breeders' Cup in 1994: held up and has turn of foot: tore a sheath in off-fore tendon at Belmont and future remains in doubt. *J-C. Rouget, France* 121

MILLRIDGE (IRE) 4 ch.f. Indian Ridge 123 – African Desert 84 (African Sky 124) [1994 35§: 8g 7d 8g6 8g3 7m 8f 5.2m4 5d 7d 1995 8d a9.4g a6g6 May 4] unfurnished filly: poor maiden: no form in 1995: blinkered (ran badly) once as 3-y-o: headstrong: most inconsistent. *R. Lee* – §

MILLSOLIN (IRE) 7 b.g. Millfontaine 114 – Isolin (Saulingo 122) [1994 72: 7m 8f 7g a8g* 1995 a7g4 a8g5 Feb 17] leggy, workmanlike gelding: has a round action: fair handicapper at his best: well below best in 1995 and sold only 1,000 gns Ascot February Sales: stays 1m: acts on good to firm and dead ground and on fibresand: has hung and wandered under pressure: sometimes sweats. *R. Akehurst* –

MILLSTOCK 5 b.m. Interrex (CAN) – Millingdale 65 (Tumble Wind (USA)) [1994 NR 1995 8m 5g 7.1m5 Jul 2] half-sister to 2 winners: dam ran only at 2 yrs: –

Prix du Gros-Chene, Chantilly—the first of two French pattern races which fell to Millyant in 1995; Diffident (right) is second, Struggler (left) third and Palacegate Episode (noseband) fourth

poor hurdler: well beaten in sellers on flat: sold 1,000 gns Ascot July Sales. *A. P. Jones*

MILLSTREAM (USA) 3 b.f. Dayjur (USA) 137 – Aquaba (USA) (Damascus (USA)) [1994 107: 5m* 5f* 5m 5s* 6m^6 5g^3 5m* 1995 5m^3 5m^4 5m^2 5m* 5f^4 6g^6 5f^4 5m Aug 17] good-topped filly: useful performer: won Ballyogan Stakes at Leopardstown in June by ½ length from Mistertopogigo, making all: creditable efforts in top company most other starts, second in Temple Stakes at Sandown (to Mind Games) and fourth in King's Stand Stakes at Ascot and King George Stakes at Goodwood: below form in Nunthorpe Stakes at York final one: effective at 5f and 6f: acts on any going: early to post at 3 yrs: sweats: races prominently: sent to Dubai. *M. Johnston* 107

MILL THYME 3 b.f. Thowra (FR) – Milinetta (Milford 119) [1994 NR 1995 10m 10.1g^4 10f^6 11f^3 12m^6 Jul 29] smallish, good-bodied filly: second foal: dam won over hurdles: modest form at best in maidens and a handicap: withdrawn fourth intended start after getting loose and then refusing to enter stalls: won over hurdles in December. *Mrs M. Reveley* 56

MILLTOWN CLASSIC (IRE) 3 b.f. Classic Secret (USA) 91 – Houwara (IRE) (Darshaan 133) [1994 –: a7g 5f^5 1995 7m^4 8g^6 8f 8m^6 9.9m^6 13.8g Sep 16] leggy, sparely-made filly: poor maiden: stays 1m: inconsistent. *J. Parkes* 33

MILLYANT 5 ch.m. Primo Dominie 121 – Jubilee Song 71 (Song 132) [1994 105: 5d 5m* 5m^6 5m 5d^6 5g^3 5m^2 5s* a6f 1995 5g^4 5g* 5f 5m^5 5m^3 5d^6 5f* Oct 22] strong, long-backed mare: carries condition: tends to be unimpressive in coat: smart performer: won 11-runner Prix du Gros-Chene at Chantilly in June by nose from Diffident and 7-runner Prix du Petit Couvert (for second year running, beat disqualified Windmachine a short neck) at Longchamp in October: speedy, and has raced only at 5f in Europe: acts on firm ground and soft, below best (in America) on dirt: usually bandaged near-hind. *R. Guest* 114

Mr C. J. Mills's "Millyant"

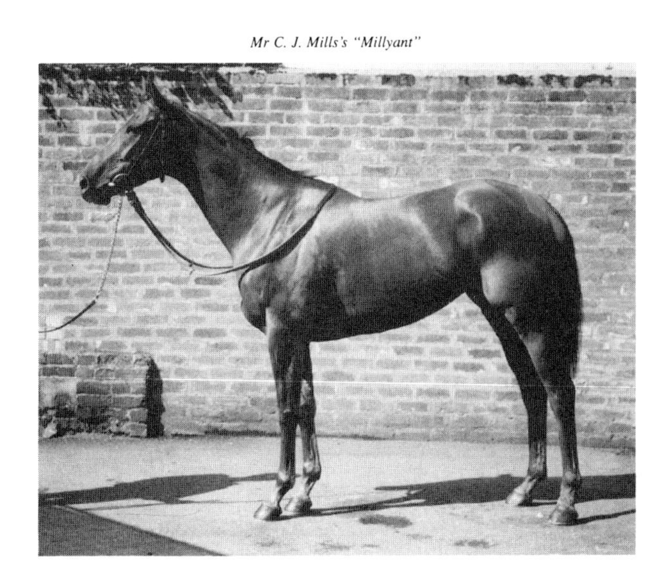

MILNGAVIE (IRE) 5 ch.g. Pharly (FR) 130 – Wig And Gown (Mandamus 120) 36 a60 d [1994 52, a69: a16.2g* a14.8g* a14g a16.2g^2 a13g^3 a16g* a14.8g^2 a16g^5 a14.8g* 14.9s 16.2s^3 14.1d^3 16d^5 13s^5 16m^6 13f^3 14.1f^2 13m^2 15.1f^3 15.1m^5 16g^5 12.1g^6 13.9d^5 16g 12.4d^2 15.1g^3 a16g^3 1995 a14.8g^5 a12g^3 a14.8g^5 a12g a12g a16g 13v 12.1s^3 21.6f 15.1f^2 15.1m^3 15.1f^6 13.8m^2 13f^2 17.1m^5 12.1m^4 15.8g 16.4m* a13g^5 a16g Dec 15] close-coupled gelding: has a round action: modest handicapper at best on all-weather, only poor on turf: won claiming handicap at Folkestone in November: effective at 1½m, and stays 16.2f: acts on firm and soft ground, best form on all-weather surfaces: blinkered (except once) since thirteenth 5-y-o start: inconsistent. *M. Johnston*

MILOS 4 b.g. Efisio 120 – Elkie Brooks 82 (Relkino 131) [1994 71: a7g^5 a7g^2 a6s* – a79 d a7g^4 a6g^4 a7g* a6g^4 a6g^2 5.7m^3 7m a6g^2 a7g* 7m* 7g^6 7.1m^5 7g 7d^2 a7g^3 a7g^2 a7g^5 a7g a7g^4 1995 a7g^3 a7g^3 5m 7.1m 7.1d a7g a7g^2 a7g^2 a7g Dec 18] big, strong gelding: shows knee action: fair handicapper: effective at 6f and 7f: acts on all-weather surfaces, good to firm and dead ground: effective from front or held up. *T. J. Naughton*

MILTAK 3 b.f. Risk Me (FR) 127 – Tralee Maiden (IRE) 63 (Persian Bold 123) 41 [1994 –: 5d 5g^6 5g 1995 5.1m 8.1m^5 8.1m^3 8m a9.4g 11.9f^4 12m^4 a11g^5 Nov 20] small, light-framed filly: poor maiden plater: stays 1½m: acts on firm ground, below form both starts on fibresand: blinkered (bad form) twice in 1994. *P. J. Makin*

MILTON 2 ch.c. (Apr 22) Groom Dancer (USA) 128 – Gold Flair 93 (Tap On 75 Wood 130) [1995 a8g^2 a8g^3 Nov 14] third foal: half-brother to 3-y-o Night Flare (by Night Shift) and 1993 2-y-o 7f winner Duball Remy (by Roi Danzig): dam, maiden who stayed 1½m, sister to good middle-distance winner Nisnas: green, similar form, raced prominently when placed in maidens won by D'Naan at Southwell and Lingfield: will stay middle distances. *P. F. I. Cole*

MIME TIME (IRE) 2 ch.c. (Mar 23) Classic Music (USA) – Beyond Words – (Ballad Rock 122) [1995 8g Sep 8] 23,000F, 17,500Y: strong, lengthy colt: fourth foal: half-brother to fairly useful 3-y-o Time For Action (by Alzao), 8.3f winner at 2 yrs: dam unraced: 20/1, tailed off in maiden at Doncaster: moved poorly to post: sold 3,600 gns Newmarket Autumn Sales. *W. Jarvis*

MIM-LOU-AND 3 b.g. Glacial Storm (USA) 127 – Tina's Melody 80 (Tina's Pet 51 121) [1994 –: 7m 7m 8.1g 1995 12d^4 14.1g^4 12m 9.7m^3 a9.4g^6 9.7g 9.7m^2 9.7f^3 10.2m^4 Aug 28] leggy, close-coupled gelding: modest maiden handicapper: stays 9.7f: acts on firm ground and dead: pulls hard: sold (R. Millman to Miss H. Knight) 12,500 gns Newmarket Autumn Sales. *B. R. Millman*

MIMOSA 2 ch.f. (Feb 12) Midyan (USA) 124 – Figini 74 (Glint of Gold 128) 66 [1995 5m 5m^5 5m 5g 6d^2 7g Oct 23] 12,500Y: good-bodied filly: fifth foal: half-sister to 3-y-o Taylord (by Cadeaux Genereux), 6f (at 2 yrs) and 8.2f winner Killy (by Dominion) and a winner in Germany: dam lightly-raced half-sister to high-class middle-distance colt Electric: fair maiden: creditable second to Trafalgar Lady at Goodwood in September, final start for L. J. Holt: below form final outing: should stay 7f: acts on good to firm and good to soft ground. *S. Dow*

MIN ALHAWA (USA) 2 b.f. (Apr 2) Riverman (USA) 131 – Saffaanh (USA) 87 87 p (Shareef Dancer (USA) 135) [1995 6f^2 7m* Aug 26] tall, rather unfurnished filly: third foal: sister to modest middle-distance maiden Waqood and half-sister to Harayir (by Gulch): dam, 12.2f winner, out of Give Thanks and from excellent family: 1¾ lengths second of 11 to Darling Flame in maiden at Newbury in June: won 5-runner maiden at Goodwood in August by a head from Aerleon Jane, taking long time to hit top speed: should stay middle distances: will improve. *Major W. R. Hern*

MIND GAMES 3 b.c. Puissance 110 – Aryaf (CAN) (Vice Regent (CAN)) [1994 118 107: 5m* 5g* 5f* 6g^5 6m 5g^2 6m 1995 5m* 5m* 5m* 5f^3 5m^6 6d^5 5d Oct 1]

Mind Games's fortunes in the second half of the season mirrored those of his stable, whose expected stream of winners didn't materialise. Like many of his stable-companions Mind Games was under a cloud, and he failed by a long way to live up to the form he had shown in the spring, when victories at Haydock, Newmarket and Sandown on his first three starts gave good reasons for thinking that he would turn out to be the season's leading five-furlong performer. Don't give up on

Tripleprint Temple Stakes, Sandown—Mind Games wins easily

him yet, though. Mind Games, on his day, is a very talented sprinter, and a game one, too. If he recaptures his sparkle he'll be a force to reckon with again in 1996.

Mind Games, who had provided Jack Berry with his first winner at Royal Ascot when taking the 1994 Norfolk Stakes, returned to the meeting in June holding a major chance in the King's Stand Stakes. He'd shown improved form each time when winning the BNFL Field Marshall Stakes at Haydock by two and a half lengths from Wavian, the Dubai Racing Club Palace House Stakes at Newmarket by a length from Eveningperformance and the Tripleprint Temple Stakes at Sandown by three lengths from Millstream. Mind Games was particularly impressive at Sandown, taking up the running at halfway and keeping on strongly, and he was sent off at 8/11 in the King's Stand. Those who laid the odds might have thought they were going to collect when Mind Games took a narrow advantage at the distance, but had been put under strong pressure to do so and had nothing left when Piccolo and Struggler, both coming from off a strong pace, went past him in the last half furlong. Mind Games was odds on again in his next race, the Nunthorpe Stakes at York, but he was no better for his two-month break and could finish only sixth to So Factual, losing a couple of lengths at the start having become restless when installed. A combination of six furlongs and good to soft ground proved too much of a test for Mind Games in the Haydock Park Sprint Cup, but he ran respectably on similar ground in the five-furlong Prix de l'Abbaye de Longchamp on his final start, finishing eighth of twelve. Mind Games has put up his best performances on good to firm.

Mind Games (b.c. 1992)	Puissance (b 1986)	Thatching (b 1975)	Thatch
			Abella
		Girton (b 1976)	Balidar
			Miss Dorothy
	Aryaf (CAN) (b 1986)	Vice Regent (ch 1967)	Northern Dancer
			Victoria Regina
		Fashion Front (b 1980)	Habitat
			Front Row

The leggy, lengthy Mind Games, bought at 18,000 guineas as a yearling, is from the first crop of Puissance, who was thought of as a possible Two Thousand Guineas contender after winning by six lengths on his only outing as a two-year-old. Trained by Vincent O'Brien, he turned out to be a sprinter and won both his starts as a three-year-old, putting up a very useful performance in the six-furlong Greenlands Stakes. Subsequently found to have fractured his near-fore knee, Puissance failed to recover his form in three runs the following season and was retired to stud. The dam, Aryaf, a granddaughter of the Irish One Thousand Guineas winner and excellent broodmare Front Row, ran three times. She ran with some promise as a two-year-old, but showed nothing in two outings at three years and was subsequently sold for 2,100 guineas. Aryaf's first foal Able Fun (by Double Schwartz) hasn't run since winning a one-mile maiden on the equitrack at Lingfield in November, 1993. *J. Berry*

MINDRACE 2 b.g. (Mar 28) Tina's Pet 121 – High Velocity 53 (Frimley Park 109) [1995 6m a7g 5g^{6} 6f^{3} Oct 24] 3,200Y: leggy gelding: third foal: dam modest 5f handicapper: vastly improved effort when under 2 lengths third of 19 to Thordis in median auction maiden at Leicester: will prove best at sprint distances: acts on firm ground. *K. T. Ivory* 73

MINDS MUSIC (USA) 3 ch.c. Silver Hawk (USA) 123 – Misinskie (USA) 84 (Nijinsky (CAN) 138) [1994 NR 1995 10m* 10.4g^{2} 10.3g^{2} 14.6d^{2} 12g* Sep 29] 115

Minds Music did not race as a two-year-old, was off the course for over three months in the middle of his three-year-old season, but still managed to finish runner-up in the St Leger. He never threatened to win the final classic, but his effort in pursuit of Classic Cliche over the last three furlongs was two and a half lengths too good for third-placed Istidaad and the seven others. One of the complete outsiders in betting the previous morning, a move in to 12/1 presaged Minds Music's good run. There were few other such indications. Nothing had been seen of him on the racecourse since late-May, nothing beyond ten furlongs and eighty-five yards, and nothing in listed, let alone pattern, races. Minds Music's latest appearance had been on Town Moor though, in the Doncaster Sunday Market Conditions Stakes in which he had been sent off at 11/8 on but been short-headed by Don Corleone. He had also been narrowly beaten earlier in the month by Tamure in another £8,300 conditions event, the Glasgow Stakes at York, and prior to that his only racecourse experience was a short-head win over Istidaad in a twenty-one-runner maiden at Kempton in April. In short, Minds Music had come up against some talented opponents and shown very useful form and a genuine attitude, but the St Leger was a step into the

Racing Post Godolphin Stakes, Newmarket—Minds Music at 2/1 on

unknown. With a St Leger second added to his curriculum vitae, however, Minds Music was a 2/1-on shot in the Racing Post Godolphin Stakes at Newmarket twenty days later. This listed race crops up fairly regularly in the programmes of St Leger also-rans despite its being run over more than two and a half furlongs less. The step down in trip did not look in Minds Music's favour judged on the length of time it took him to get on top of 20/1-shot and seasonal debutant Mack The Knife, but he was well on top eventually, drawing clear on the rising ground to win by two and a half lengths. The form he showed here was virtually on a par with his St Leger effort, but connections indicated afterwards that the Cup races might be on the agenda for Minds Music in 1996.

Minds Music (USA) (ch.c. 1992)	Silver Hawk (USA) (b 1979)	Roberto (b 1969)	Hail To Reason
			Bramalea
		Gris Vitesse (gr 1966)	Amerigo
			Matchiche II
	Misinskie (USA) (b 1980)	Nijinsky (b 1967)	Northern Dancer
			Flaming Page
		Kankakee Miss (br 1967)	Better Bee
			Golden Beach

The dam Misinskie had had two winners in Britain prior to Minds Music, the Windsor Castle Stakes winner Space Cruiser (by Foolish Pleasure) and the very useful miler Ajfan (by Woodman) who was a close third in Sayyedati's One Thousand Guineas. Neither of that pair's performances in this country hinted at any great stamina reserves, but after disappointing in the second half of his two-year-old season Space Cruiser was sent to Norway where he won their Two Thousand Guineas and was second in both the Norsk Derby and Norsk St Leger. Minds Music is the dam's seventh foal to reach racing age; the others include maiden race winners by Temperence Hill (over an extended eleven furlongs in the French Provinces) and Conquistador Cielo. Second dam Kankakee Miss will be best known for her son the high-class sprinter/miler Clever Trick, and third dam Golden Beach for the exploits of two of her other daughters in producing the high-class middle-distance performers Ascot Knight, Petit Loup and Alydeed. Kankakee Miss and Golden Beach in fact produced an aggregate of twenty-four winners. Misinskie was not one of them. She made the frame on all four of her outings as a two-year-old but accomplished very little the following season, all in all failing to live up to her 300,000-dollar yearling tag. Minds Music made 75,000 at the same age, just below average for his good sire Silver Hawk whose other winners in Britain in 1996 included the Derby fourth Fahal.

Minds Music is a strong, lengthy colt with scope. A rather lazy but genuine individual, he stayed the St Leger trip well but others make more appeal for the Cup races at this stage. He is a poor mover, and it probably is significant that he did not appear again on top-of-the-ground after his debut. *H. R. A. Cecil*

MIN ELREEH (USA) 2 b.f. (Jan 20) Danzig (USA) – Roseate Tern 123 (Blakeney 126) [1995 6m^6 Aug 11] unfurnished filly: first foal: dam, winner of Yorkshire Oaks and third in Oaks and St Leger, half-sister to high-class middle-distance performer Ibn Bey out of half-sister to Teleprompter and Chatoyant: 25/1, shaped with plenty of promise when 8¾ lengths sixth of 22 to Bosra Sham in maiden at Newbury, staying on under a sympathetic ride: will stay further than 6f: sure to improve. *Major W. R. Hern* — 68 p

MINNEOLA 3 ch.f. Midyan (USA) 124 – High Halo 64 (High Top 131) [1994 NR 1995 10m 10m Aug 23] fifth foal: half-sister to fairly useful 6f to 1m winner High Premium (by Forzando) and minor European 7f winner Corcovado (by Formidable): dam thrice-raced 1m winner, would have stayed further: well behind in maidens: sold 575 gns Ascot October Sales. *R. T. Phillips* — –

MINNESOTA VIKING 4 b.g. Northern State (USA) 91 – Miskin 58 (Star Appeal 133) [1994 70: 8.3d^5 10m^5 10f^2 13.6g* 12g* 14.1g^2 14.4g^4 12m^4 1995 11.8g 10f^5 14m^4 12g^2 14.1m 12s^2 12g* 12m^3 Nov 6] stocky gelding: modest handicapper: won at Folkestone (amateurs) in October: stays 14.4f: acts on soft ground, inconsistent on top-of-the-ground: held up. *Lady Herries* — 61

MINNISAM 2 ch.c. (May 7) Niniski (USA) 125 – Wise Speculation (USA) (Mr Prospector (USA)) [1995 7f 8.1s^4 8.2m Oct 26] 10,000Y: angular colt: half-brother to very useful middle-distance stayer Always Friendly (by High Line) and several winners in Scandinavia: dam ran 3 times: some promise in maidens at Goodwood, Chepstow and Nottingham: looks a stayer. *J. L. Dunlop* — – p

MINOLETTI 2 b.g. (May 11) Emarati (USA) 74 – French Plait (Thatching 131) 70 p
[1995 6g^5 Oct 3] 8,000F, 9,000Y: good-bodied gelding: half-brother to 4-y-o French Ginger (by Most Welcome) and 7f/1m winner Rural Lad (by Town And Country): dam (out of 2m winner) seemingly of little account: 12/1 and green, shaped well when just over 3 lengths fifth of 15 to Lay The Blame in maiden auction at Warwick, taken left over 1f out then running on not knocked about: sure to improve. *E. A. L. Dunlop*

MINSTERBEACH 2 ch.c. (Feb 2) Minster Son 130 – China Beach 55§ –
(Superlative 118) [1995 7.1g 7g 8.1m^5 8.2d 7s 8m Oct 20] workmanlike colt: easy mover: first foal: dam, 1m winner, was one to treat with caution: difficult to assess but seems only modest at best: races keenly, and may prove best short of 1m: well beaten on soft ground in visor penultimate start: sent to Sweden. *C. E. Brittain*

MINSTER GLORY 4 b.g. Minster Son 130 – Rapid Glory 75 (Hittite Glory 125) 43
[1994 NR 1995 a12g a7g a6g 9.9m^2 Apr 8] close-coupled gelding: fifth foal: dam 2-y-o 5f winner: easily best effort on flat when second of 16 in handicap at Beverley, racing keenly behind leaders and running on well: stays 1¼m: acts on good to firm ground: won novice hurdle in May. *M. W. Easterby*

MINT A MILLION (IRE) 4 b.g. Thatching 131 – Often (Ballymore 123) [1994 –
62d: 6.9v^2 6.9v^4 8m 7g 9f 8g^6 11.7f^4 a12g 7f^5 7.2g^5 7m 8g^3 8g 1995 a12g^4 15.4g a14.8g 10m 12g 15.4m 14d Sep 14] neat gelding: has a round action: seems just a poor performer nowadays: best form at up to 1m: probably acts on any going: inconsistent. *M. Blanshard*

MIRADOR 4 b.f. Town And Country 124 – Wild Jewel (Great Heron (USA) 127) –
[1994 53: 10s 10d^6 11.6g 11.9g^2 10g^4 11.7m^2 12m^4 12d 1995 11.9m Apr 6] close-coupled filly: modest maiden handicapper: probably needed race only start in 1995: should stay beyond 1½m: acts on good to firm ground, no form on a soft surface. *R. Curtis*

MIRIAM 4 br.f. Forzando 122 – Song of Hope 103 (Chief Singer 131) [1994 59, 55 a–
a–: 5.1g^3 5v^3 5.7g^4 5g 5m* 5m^3 5.1f^2 5f^4 5.1m 5m^2 5g 5.1g a6g a5g 1995 5.1m 5.1m 5m^3 5m^3 5m^5 5.1h^5 5f^2 5m 5m 5.1d 5g Sep 29] compact, good-quartered filly: modest handicapper: below form last 4 starts: best form at 5f: very best efforts on a sound surface (acts on firm going): no improvement in blinkers: usually races prominently: sometimes early to post: sold 2,200 gns Newmarket Autumn Sales. *M. J. Fetherston-Godley*

MIRONOV 2 b.c. (Mar 12) Marju (IRE) 127 – Marquina (FR) (Posse (USA) 130) 79 p
[1995 7.5d* Nov 5] 11,000Y: sixth foal: half-brother to 3 winners in France, including 1½m winner Marquinor (by Fabulous Dancer): dam French 10.5f winner: won 6-runner maiden at Milan in November by ½ length from Frequent: will stay middle distances. *M. R. Channon*

MIROSWAKI (USA) 5 br.g. Miswaki (USA) 124 – Miroswava (FR) 115 (In 71
Fijar (USA) 121) [1994 72: 9g 14.6s^3 a13g^2 a16g^2 a13g^2 1995 12g^5 14.1m^6 14.9m 16.1m 14.6m a16g^2 Nov 29] good-bodied gelding: fair maiden handicapper: well below form (on a sound surface) first 5 starts in 1995 for G. Fierro: ran well at Lingfield on first outing for new trainer: stays 2m: acts on soft ground and equitrack: has worn tongue strap and dropped noseband. *R. Akehurst*

MISBELIEF 5 b. or br.m. Shirley Heights 130 – Misguided 106 (Homing 130) 107
[1994 107: 12d^5 12f* 12m^2 11.9f^4 14m^2 13.4g^2 14.6g^3 12g^2 12m^5 1995 14.4m^2 12.3g^3 14f* 11.9m^5 13.9m 14.6m^2 Sep 6] leggy mare: easy mover: useful performer: reportedly suffered muscle problems on second 5-y-o start: narrowly won minor event at Salisbury in June: good seventh of 21 in the Ebor at York and placed (for second year running) in Park Hill Stakes at Doncaster on final start (beaten ½ length by Noble Rose): will stay beyond 14.6f: has raced mainly on a sound surface: tongue tied down last 4 starts: genuine. *J. R. Fanshawe*

MISCHIEF STAR 2 b.f. (Jan 29) Be My Chief (USA) 122 – Star Face (African 57
Sky 124) [1995 7m 7m^4 8.1d Sep 12] 13,000Y: big, good-topped filly: has scope: half-sister to 3-y-o 7.6f winner Mo's Star (by Most Welcome) and several winners, including smart 7f to 11.3f winner Lord Of The Field (by Jalmood) and 6f and 1m winner Torquemada (by Try My Best): dam French 10.5f winner: modest form: remote fourth of 5 to Sea Spray in minor event at Kempton: should stay 1m. *D. R. C. Elsworth*

MISHAWEER 2 b.f. (May 6) Primo Dominie 121 – Ideal Home 104 (Home Guard (USA) 129) [1995 6g Sep 23] 50,000Y: closely related to useful Irish 5f/7f performer Bezelle (by Dominion), later 1m winner in USA, and half-sister to 4-y-o 7f winner La Residence (by Doulab): dam 2-y-o 5f winner: 7/1, always behind when last of 9 in maiden at Redcar. *J. R. Fanshawe* –

MISKY BAY 2 b.c. (Apr 10) Shareef Dancer (USA) 135 – Rain Date (Rainbow Quest (USA) 134) [1995 8m Nov 4] stocky colt: second foal: half-brother to 3-y-o 7f winner Polar Queen (by Polish Precedent): dam daughter of Roussalka, a half-sister to Oh So Sharp: 10/1 and in need of race, around 12 lengths ninth of 23 to Shaamit in median auction maiden at Doncaster, running on not knocked about: will do better. *J. H. M. Gosden* 61 p

MISLEMANI (IRE) 5 b.g. Kris 135 – Meis El-Reem 124 (Auction Ring (USA) 123) [1994 56, a52: 10.3g 8g 8.3f^5 7f^3 7.2g^3 7g 7.1g^3 a6g a8g^3 a8g a10g 1995 6m 7g 8m^3 a7g^2 a9.4g^5 7.1m^3 7m* 8m^6 7.3d 7g^2 7g a8g^3 a7g^3 Nov 24] sturdy, close-coupled gelding: modest handicapper: won at Epsom in July: effective at 7f, and stays 9.4f: acts on firm and dead going and on fibresand, well beaten on equitrack. *A. G. Newcombe* 64

MISSAL (IRE) 6 b.m. Alzao (USA) 117 – Priors Mistress 71 (Sallust 134) [1994 NR 1995 7f Oct 25] small mare: of little account. *Pat Mitchell* –

MISS ARAGON 7 b.m. Aragon 118 – Lavenham Blue (Streetfighter 120) [1994 57: 6f^4 6m^6 5m^4 5.2g 5m 6m^2 6m^2 6.1g^4 6g^3 6m 5f 6m^3 6g 6g^6 1995 5g^2 5m 6g 6m 6m^3 6m* 6g* 6d^5 6.1d 6.1d 6g 5m Oct 4] rangy mare: good mover: modest handicapper: won twice at Newmarket in July: below form afterwards: effective at 5f and 6f: possibly unsuited by very firm ground, acts on any other. *Miss L. C. Siddall* 59

MISS BIARRITZ 3 b.f. Be My Guest (USA) 126 – Miss Bergerac (Bold Lad (IRE) 133) [1994 –: 7g 7d 1995 8d Apr 6] lengthy filly: no form in maidens, pulled up lame only 3-y-o start: sold 1,300 gns Newmarket December Sales. *M. Bell* –

MISS BIGWIG 2 b.f. (Apr 23) Distinctly North (USA) 115 – Jacqui Joy 63 (Music Boy 124) [1995 5d* 5g^4 5m^5 5f* 5m^6 5m^2 5d* 5s^4 Oct 1] 6,000Y: leggy, close-coupled filly: fourth foal: dam best at 5f: won maiden at Warwick in April, claimer at Edinburgh in July and nursery at Epsom in September: speedy: acts on firm and dead ground (below form on soft final start). *J. Berry* 84

MISS CAROTTENE 2 b.f. (Mar 31) Siberian Express (USA) 125 – Silk St James (Pas de Seul 133) [1995 6m 6g 5m 5g 6f^2 6m 6f^2 5m^3 6.1d 7d 7f a6g Dec 19] 5,000F, 11,000Y: good-topped filly: fourth reported foal: half-sister to 3 winners, including fair (at up to 7f) Prima Silk (by Primo Dominie) and 1m winner Misty Silks (by Scottish Reel): dam unraced: modest maiden at best: visored, well beaten in nurseries last 3 starts: stays 6f: acts on firm ground (efforts on dead inconclusive): has run creditably in blinkers. *M. J. Ryan* 56

MISS CHARLIE 5 ch.m. Pharly (FR) 130 – Close To You 44 (Nebbiolo 125) [1994 42: 6.9f^5 6g^5 a7g 7g a7g a8.5g^3 1995 a8.5g^2 a8.5g a9.4g a10g 7m^2 Aug 19] leggy, angular mare: poor maiden: stays 8.5f: acts on firm ground and fibresand: somewhat headstrong, and sometimes early to post: has joined T. Wall. *A. Bailey* 42

MISSED FLIGHT 5 b.h. Dominion 123 – Loveskate (USA) 78 (Overskate (CAN)) [1994 119: 8m^{3dis} 8s* 8m^3 8m 8g* 7g^2 8f 1995 8g^3 8.1m* 8m^3 6g* 8m^3 Sep 3] 123

Retired after sustaining an over-reach injury while being prepared for the Queen Elizabeth II Stakes, the very smart Missed Flight will stand at Wood Farm Stud in Shropshire in 1996 at a fee of £2,000. Missed Flight is being retained by his Austrian owner Mr Grubmuller, who has enjoyed such great success with this genuine and versatile performer in the past three seasons. During that time Missed Flight won six races worth almost £137,000, and in addition earned around £58,000 in place money; not bad for a horse who fetched just 7,000 guineas when he first passed through the sales ring as a foal. Eleven months later Missed Flight was sold on for 31,000 guineas, and his market value continued to increase as he progressed from promising two-year-old to useful handicapper then to pattern-race winner. Missed Flight's last three victories all came in pattern races, namely the Prix du Rond-Point at Longchamp in 1994 and the Sandown Mile and Prix de Meautry at Deauville in 1995. Previously thought suited by give in the ground and a winner on

Sandown Mile—Missed Flight shows much the best turn of foot; blinkered Ridgewood Ben is second

heavy, Missed Flight showed himself effective on good to firm going in the Sandown Mile in April, quickening impressively over a furlong out and beating Ridgewood Ben by one and three quarter lengths. Missed Flight who was tried over a mile and a half on his first outing as a three-year-old, has plenty of speed, so it came as no surprise that he was able to put some no more than very useful sprinters in their place in the six-furlong Meautry. On his first attempt at a distance shorter than seven furlongs, Missed Flight took the lead just inside the final furlong and won by one and a half lengths and three quarters of a length from the other British challengers, Warning Star and Alzianah. Returned to a mile in the Group 1 Prix du Moulin de Longchamp, Missed Flight ran a cracking race to finish third behind Ridgewood Pearl and Shaanxi, beaten three quarters of a length and the same. Missed Flight was clearly better than ever at this stage of his career, and it's unfortunate that injury denied him the opportunity to enhance his reputation still further in the autumn.

Missed Flight (b.h. 1990)	Dominion (b 1972)	Derring-Do (br 1961)	Darius
			Sipsey Bridge
		Picture Palace (b 1961)	Princely Gift
			Palais Glide
	Loveskate (USA) (b 1984)	Overskate (ch 1975)	Nodouble
			Overstate
		Gangster of Love (b 1972)	Round Table
			Woozem

Missed Flight, a lengthy horse, is the second foal of Loveskate, who won a maiden over an extended fifteen furlongs on the second of two starts. A close relation to the smart middle-distance colt Raft and half-sister to the dam of the very useful French filly Bonash, Lovestake is a granddaughter of Woozem, one of the leading U.S. two-year-old fillies in 1966. Loveskate was responsible for two other winners in 1995, both at around one mile, namely the fairly useful performers Perilous Plight (by Siberian Express) and Clifton Fox (by Deploy). Missed Flight sometimes idled in front and was best held up; he had a good turn of foot. *C. F. Wall*

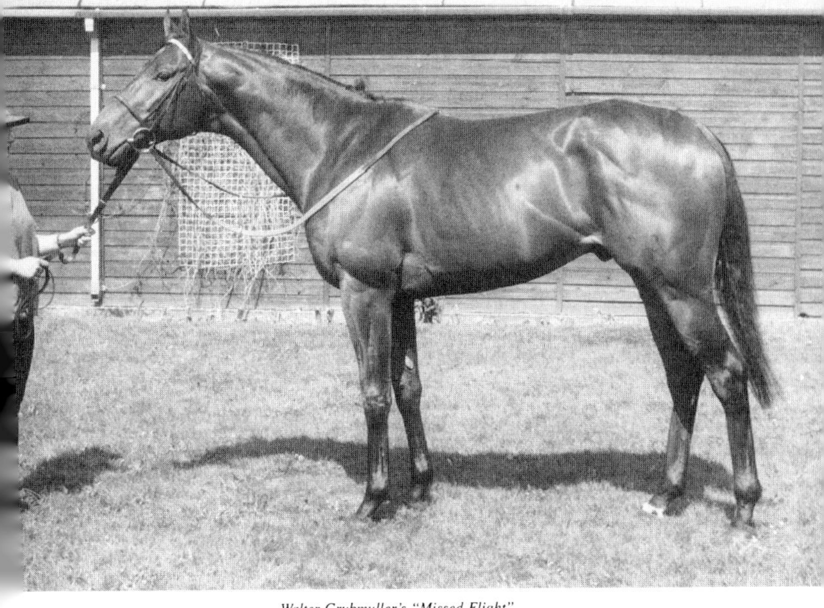

Walter Grubmuller's "Missed Flight"

MISSED THE BOAT (IRE) 5 b.g. Cyrano de Bergerac 120 – Lady Portobello (Porto Bello 118) [1994 –: a7g a12g³ a14.8g 1995 10f 13.1h* 12d a13g Dec 19] rather leggy gelding: modest handicapper: form in 1995 only when winning maiden event at Bath in September: stays 13.1f: acts on hard going, dead and fibresand: tried blinkered/visored earlier in career. *A. G. Newcombe* 46

MISSEL 3 b.c. Storm Bird (CAN) 134 – Miss Demure 106 (Shy Groom (USA)) [1994 102: 6g* 6m³ 7m⁴ 1995 8m⁵ Apr 15] quite attractive colt: has a quick action: useful form at 2 yrs: bit backward, fifth of 10 to Two O'Clock Jump in listed race at Kempton only start in 1995, making most: subsequently joined Saeed bin Suroor: should prove best at up to 1m. *P. W. Chapple-Hyam* 92 +

MISS ELECTRA 3 b.f. Superpower 113 – Apocalypse (Auction Ring (USA) 123) [1994 47: 5s⁵ 5d 6g a5g 5.1m⁴ 6g 5.1g 5d 7.5g 1995 7m 6g Sep 14] sturdy filly: poor maiden: well beaten in 1995. *M. Blanshard* –

MISS FELIXSTOWE (USA) 3 ch.f. Tejano (USA) – Sonseri 95 (Prince Tenderfoot (USA) 126) [1994 47: 6m 6.1m 6d 6.1d 5m 1995 6.1g 8.3g⁴ 9f 8g³ 9f⁴ 10m² 10m⁵ Aug 21] angular, workmanlike filly: modest maiden handicapper: better at 1¼m than shorter: acts on firm going, probably on dead: consistent: sold 2,200 gns Newmarket September Sales. *Mrs M. Reveley* 50

MISS FREEBIE (IRE) 4 b.f. Satco (FR) 112 – Masina (Current Coin 118) [1994 48: a11g² a8g² 12.5v⁴ a8g a12g 11g⁵ a12g⁵ 14.1g 10.8s 1995 a11g a14.8g Feb 15] leggy, sparely-made filly: inconsistent plater: well beaten at 4 yrs: has joined M. Brittain. *B. A. McMahon* –

MISS GREENYARDS 4 b.f. Stalker 121 – Isle Maree (Star Appeal 133) [1994 NR 1995 9.2s Apr 12] 800F: second foal: dam unraced: no sign of ability on flat or over hurdles. *J. S. Haldane* –

MISS GRUNTLED 4 b.f. Arctic Lord 114 – Sweet Move (Corvaro (USA) 124) – [1994 –: 12g a12g6 1995 14.4m 10.2m Jun 17] sparely-made filly: no form. *D. J. S. ffrench Davis*

MISS HAVERSHAM 3 b.f. Salse (USA) 128 – Rustic Stile (Rusticaro (FR) 124) 81 [1994 81p: 6g2 1995 7m 8m 8.1m2 10.2d3 Oct 10] sturdy filly: fairly useful maiden: stays 1¼m: acts on good to firm ground, probably on dead: sold 20,500 gns Ascot October Sales. *C. A. Cyzer*

MISS HOTSHOT 2 ch.f. (Feb 14) Chilibang 120 – Emma's Double (Double – Form 130) [1995 5m 5f 5g 5f6 Jul 28] 1,500F, 1,000Y: good-topped filly: third foal: dam Irish 1¼m winner: no sign of ability: sold 500 gns Ascot November Sales. *R. Bastiman*

MISSILE 2 b.g. (Feb 25) Rock City 120 – Fast Chick 93 (Henbit (USA) 130) 83 p [1995 7g 6.9s2 6f* Oct 16] 5,500Y: tall, good-topped gelding: has scope: second foal: dam 9f to 1½m winner: well clear of third when going down by 1¼ lengths to Salmis in maiden auction at Folkestone: landed odds in similar event over 6f at Pontefract 19 days later, not handling bend too well and needing to be driven to lead inside last: really needs further than 6f, and will stay at least 1m: remains capable of better. *W. J. Haggas*

MISSILE TOE (IRE) 2 b.c. (Mar 25) Exactly Sharp (USA) 121 – Debach Dust 71 64 (Indian King (USA) 128) [1995 5.1m2 a5g2 6g5 6m6 6m* 5m5 6m5 6g5 6g3 Sep 30] 3,000F, 6,000Y: good-topped colt: poor walker: third foal: dam maiden half-sister to useful sprinter Cameroun: made all in maiden auction at Newcastle in July: ran very well (held up) when just over 2½ lengths third of 16 to King of Peru in nursery at Newmarket on final start: stays 6f: acts on good to firm ground and fibresand: genuine. *J. E. Banks*

MISS IMPULSE 2 b.f. (Apr 21) Precocious 126 – Dingle Belle 72 (Dominion 43 123) [1995 6.1m3 6g3 a5g 6.1m6 Aug 2] compact filly: unimpressive mover: seventh living foal: sister to 3-y-o Presto Boy, closely related to 1987 2-y-o 6f winner Snake Eye (by Tina's Pet) and half-sister to 1990 5f winner Belle Chose (by Bairn): dam, 13.8f winner, half-sister to very smart Town And Country: poor form in claimer and sellers. *J. Wharton*

MISS IRON HEART (USA) 3 b.f. Minshaanshu Amad (USA) 91§ – Iron – Franco (USA) (Barrera (USA)) [1994 54: 5g5 6g 6g a5g a7g 1995 7g 7.1f6 a7g 7g 10.3m Nov 3] well-made, quite attractive filly: modest sprint maiden at 2 yrs: soundly beaten in 1995: blinkered, tongue tied and edgy final start. *D. J. S. Cosgrove*

MISS JEMMIMA 3 b.f. Night Shift (USA) – Jenny Mere (Brigadier Gerard 144) 60 d [1994 NR 1995 a8.5g a7g5 8g 8.2m4 10g 8g 9m a8g Nov 20] angular filly: third foal: sister to poor maiden Horizontale: dam poor maiden who stayed 1m: modest maiden: well beaten last 4 starts, showing signs of temperament: stays 8.2f: acts on good to firm ground: sometimes pulls hard: sold 1,600 gns Newmarket December Sales: sent to Holland. *Lord Huntingdon*

MISS KATIE LOUISE 4 b.f. Monsanto (FR) 121 – Shari Louise 78 (Radetzky – 123) [1994 –: a7g5 a6g5 a10g4 9.9s 8.1s 1995 a7g Mar 4] sparely-made filly: of no account. *A. P. James*

MISS LAUGHTER 3 b.f. Sulaafah (USA) 119 – Miss Comedy 56 (Comedy Star 49 (USA) 121) [1994 54: 5.7g6 6d 1995 5.1g 8f4 8m 7f 7.1m6 8f* 6.9h3 8g Sep 29] lengthy, angular filly: modest performer: won minor event at Brighton in July, making all: better at 1m than shorter: acts on hard ground. *J. W. Hills*

MISS MAH-JONG 4 b.f. Absalom 128 – Brookfield Miss 73 (Welsh Pageant 44 + 132) [1994 72: 7.5d5 7m 10.4m 8f 7m3 7m4 8.5m2 6s 8g6 a8g 1995 a8g 8.3m6 May 15] good-bodied filly: poor form at best on flat in 1995: stays 1m: acts on firm ground and good to soft: tried blinkered: unreliable winning hurdler. *J. White*

MISS MERCY (IRE) 3 b.f. Law Society (USA) 130 – Missing You 89 – (Ahonoora 122) [1994 62: 5g4 6m 5f6 6g5 6d 6s* 7m 1995 7m a7g a8g Nov 16] small, sparely-made filly: well beaten in 1995: should stay beyond 6f: acts on firm and soft going: sold 3,600 gns Doncaster November Sales. *C. N. Allen*

MISS MOVIE WORLD 6 b.m. Slim Jim 112 – Regal Artist 72 (Breakspear II) 63 [1994 63: 5m5 5m* 5g* 5g* 6m 5g 5d 1995 5g2 5m5 5m4 5m 5m 5m5 5f5 5d Sep 18] sturdy mare: modest handicapper: none too consistent in 1995: has won at 6f, but probably best at 5f: acts on all-weather surfaces, probably suited by a sound surface on turf: no improvement in blinkers: often apprentice ridden: races prominently. *M. D. Hammond*

MISS OFFSET 2 ch.f. (May 21) Timeless Times (USA) 99 – Farinara (Dragonara Palace (USA) 115) [1995 5v^2 5.3m^3 5g^6 a5g^2 a6g a6g* 7d* 7f 8f^5 8g Sep 14] 4,800Y: leggy filly: has a quick action: half-sister to fair 8-y-o sprinter Croft Imperial (by Crofthall): dam (unraced) out of useful 5f mare Faridina: won sellers at (Wolverhampton made all) and Yarmouth in June: well beaten in nurseries last 3 outings: stays 7f: best form on fibresand or an easy surface on turf: blinkered last 5 outings: looked unco-operative late on. *M. Johnston* 61

MISS PARKES 6 ch.m. Mummy's Game 120 – Bonne Baiser 88 (Most Secret 119) [1994 NR 1995 14s a12g a16g Nov 29] leggy, lengthy mare: of little account. *P. C. Clarke* –

MISS PICKPOCKET (IRE) 2 b.f. (Feb 14) Petorius 117 – Fingers (Lord Gayle (USA) 124) [1995 a6g^3 6d^5 6g^6 a7g^3 a5g* Dec 19] IR 5,600Y: leggy filly: sister to 5f (at 2 yrs) and 1m winner Premier Touch and half-sister to several winners, notably useful middle-distance stayer Hollow Hand (by Wolver Hollow): dam, Irish 1½m winner, out of sister to very smart sprinter Forlorn River: clearly flattered when 4½ lengths fifth of 8 in Blue Seal Stakes at Ascot on second start: third in seller before winning weak median auction maiden event at Lingfield in December: stays 7f. *P. A. Kelleway* 64

MISS PIGALLE 4 b.f. Good Times (ITY) – Panayr (Faraway Times (USA) 123) [1994 40: 6m 6m 8d^5 7f^4 7.1m 7m 6f 6f^2 6g 7d 5m^5 7.1m^4 1995 6g 7m^3 6m^6 8g^5 8.3f 8.1m^3 6.9f^6 7.1m* 8.1f^6 6g 6f^3 7m 7m 7f^5 7g^4 7d Sep 27] leggy filly: poor handicapper: gained first success at Edinburgh in July: stays 1m: acts on firm ground, probably on dead: usually blinkered: inconsistent. *Miss L. A. Perratt* 40

MISS PIN UP 6 gr.m. Kalaglow 132 – Allander Girl (Miralgo 130) [1994 79: 14d^4 11.9m 12.3m* 13.9m^2 14.1d^2 14m^5 13.9d 1995 12m^2 11.5m* 12g^5 11.9f^5 14m^5 12.3m Aug 19] leggy, sparely-made mare: fairly useful handicapper: won at Yarmouth in July: ran poorly last 3 starts: effective at 1½m and possibly does not stay beyond 1¾m: acts on good to firm and dead ground: below best when blinkered earlier in career: usually races on a galloping track. *W. J. Haggas* 86 d

MISS PRAVDA 2 ch.f. (Feb 17) Soviet Star (USA) 128 – Miss Paige (AUS) (Luskin Star (AUS)) [1995 6g 7m^3 Oct 13] plain filly: first foal: dam won over 5½f in Australia: bit backward, in rear in 17-runner maiden at Newmarket: 4 lengths last of 3 in Newmarket Challenge Cup 2 weeks later. *P. T. Walwyn* 62

MISS PRISM 2 b.f. (May 2) Niniski (USA) 125 – Reflected Glory (SWE) (Relko 136) [1995 7m^5 7g Oct 9] angular filly: closely related to 1993 2-y-o 7.5f winner Gloriette (by Petoski) and half-sister to 1990 2-y-o 5f winner Relpour (by Nishapour) and several winners in Sweden: dam staying maiden: well beaten in maidens at Goodwood (lost several lengths at start) and Leicester. *J. L. Dunlop* –

MISS RIVIERA 2 b.f. (Mar 26) Kris 135 – Miss Beaulieu 106 (Northfields (USA)) [1995 6m* Nov 3] sturdy, lengthy filly: half-sister to fairly useful 7f/1m winner Toujours Riviera (by Rainbow Quest) and several winners over middle distances, some also temperamental: dam 6f and 1¼m winner: 9/2 from 11/2 though burly, won 20-runner maiden at Doncaster in November by ½ length from Green Barries, pair clear, soon in touch after slow start, moving through strongly 2f out then quickening ahead near finish despite being hampered by runner-up: sure to show considerable improvement, particularly over further, and has the makings of a useful performer. *G. Wragg* 84 P

MISS ROBERTO (IRE) 2 ch.f. (Mar 13) Don Roberto (USA) – Frau Ahuyentante (ARG) (Frari (ARG)) [1995 6.1d 8g^6 6.1m^6 6.9m Nov 6] plain, good-quartered filly: half-sister to 2 winners in Spain and one in Argentina: dam Argentinian-bred: little worthwhile form in maidens, minor event and a nursery, blinkered final start. *Mrs M. McCourt* –

MISS SACHA (IRE) 4 b.f. Last Tycoon 131 – Heaven High (High Line 125) [1994 107: 7d^3 5v* 8d^5 5m^4 6d^4 1995 7.1m 6m Aug 25] rangy ex-Irish filly: useful performer for C. Collins at 3 yrs: bandaged, well beaten in listed races at Haydock (rated stakes) and Newmarket in 1995: effective at 5f with testing conditions, and –

stays 1m: acts on heavy going, possibly not on top-of-the-ground: sold 25,000 gns Newmarket December Sales. *D. R. Loder*

MISS SATAMIXA (FR) 3 gr.f. Linamix (FR) 127 – Miss Satin 113 (Satingo 129) [1994 $6g^3$ $7g^*$ $5g^4$ $8g^3$ $6s^4$ $9v^4$ 1995 $5.5g^*$ $7g^*$ $8g^*$ $8m^6$ Sep 3] 123

Trainer Francois Boutin died in February. He was barely fifty-eight but had been at the top of his profession for a long time, ever since 1968 when he sent over La Lagune for the Oaks. Other classic winners had followed down the years, many in fact: Nonoalco, Caracolero, Malacate, Lagunette, Rex Magna, Elgay, Marracci, Garrido, Zino, River Lady, L'Emigrant, Northern Trick, Lacovia, the magnificent Miesque, Resless Kara, Blushing John, Linamix, Hector Protector, Shanghai, Kingmambo, Madeleine's Dream, Hernando and finally, in 1994, East of The Moon. Except for that controversial stewards' decision at Newmarket, Nureyev would have been another. And Boutin had trained better than almost any on that roll of honour—triple Gold Cup winner Sagaro, Washington International and dual Turf Classic winner April Run and runaway Breeders' Cup Juvenile winner Arazi. In France, where he had won all the classics and almost everything else bar the Arc, Boutin had been beginning to make some of the big races almost his own. His two-year-olds had lifted the Prix de la Salamandre twelve times, the Criterium de Maisons-Laffitte nine, the Prix Morny seven; their seniors had taken seven runnings of the Prix Jacques le Marois, six of the Poule d'Essai des Poulains and the Prix Lupin. When he died, future winners of two of those races were present in the yard, though neither Miss Satamixa nor Titus Livius was easily recognizable as such.

The future Prix Jacques le Marois winner Miss Satamixa was not easily recognizable as such to many observers right up to the 'off': she was taking a very big step up in grade in the race, run at Deauville in August, and started the longest-priced in the field of nine apart from Prince Arthur, a horse who had run in two classics and won one of them. Miss Satamixa had seemed fairly exposed as a two-year-old, finishing no better than third in four listed races after winning a restricted event at Deauville. However, she won a minor race for Fabre at Chantilly on her reappearance in late-May and easily followed up against six of her age and sex in listed company at Maisons-Laffitte two months later. That was the extent of her form as she lined up for the Marois. Compare it with Sayyedati's, the winner in 1993, second to East of The Moon in 1994 and recently successful in the Sussex Stakes; or with Green Tune's, or for that matter with Nicolotte's, the other older horse in the field. Those good older horses were opposed by fillies representing current French classic form in Carling, Shaanxi and Miss Satamixa's strongly-fancied stable-companion Smolensk, and by the Godolphin colt Tamayaz who started favourite after impressing at Goodwood. Miss Satamixa took the step up in her stride, moving smoothly tucked in against the stand rail as Tamayaz set a sound gallop, quickening

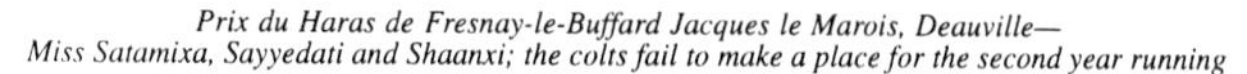
Prix du Haras de Fresnay-le-Buffard Jacques le Marois, Deauville—
Miss Satamixa, Sayyedati and Shaanxi; the colts fail to make a place for the second year running

very well to lead inside the last after Sayyedati had gone on, and running on to deny the British mare a second win by a length. Shaanxi came third ahead of Tamayaz. Apart from sixth-placed Prince Arthur the remainder disappointed in varying degrees, but Miss Satamixa's performance measures up to the high standards of the Marois. She and another four of the field went on to tackle Ridgewood Pearl in the Emirates Prix du Moulin de Longchamp, where Shaanxi did best, finishing a half-length second. Miss Satamixa couldn't reproduce her turn of foot but ran creditably on the firmer ground, finishing just under three lengths behind the winner in sixth. She wasn't seen out again, and has now been retired.

Miss Satamixa (FR) (gr.f. 1992)	Linamix (FR) (gr 1987)	Mendez (gr 1981)	Bellypha
			Miss Carina
		Lunadix (gr 1972)	Breton
			Lutine
	Miss Satin (b 1975)	Satingo (b 1970)	Petingo
			Saquebute
		Miss Skyscraper (ch 1967)	Skymaster
			Ski Maid

Miss Satamixa's emergence as a good miler in the summer paid another compliment to her very promising young sire, as, surely, did the fact that she is the best of the eight runners so far produced by her dam. However, she is not the only one of note among the eight. Five of the others have been successful in France and they include the Prix d'Arenberg third Miss Annie (by Bolkonski) and the listed race winner Miss d'Ouilly (by Bikala). The Linamix two-year-old of 1995, Massatixa, looks capable of winning as well. The dam Miss Satin appeared in Boutin's string in her day. Unlike her daughter she was better at two than three—a winner of both her starts at two, over seven furlongs at Deauville and Longchamp. Miss Satin's dam Miss Skyscraper, out of a Park Hill Stakes second, made a couple of appearances on a French track but was based at Newmarket with Ryan Jarvis, for whom she won the Kempton One Thousand Guineas Trial and finished third in the Jersey Stakes and Bunbury Cup. *A. Fabre, France*

MISS SIHAM (IRE) 6 ch.m. Green Forest (USA) 134 – Miss Derby (USA) (Master Derby (USA)) [1994 42: 6f 5m 5g 5d a5s^{6} 1995 a6g^{6} a5g 5m^{2} 5m 5g^{4} 5f 5g* 5m Aug 13] sturdy mare: unimpressive mover: modest handicapper: left J. Balding's stable after second 6-y-o start: best performance since 1991 to win 17-runner race at Beverley in July, making all against far rail: unruly stalls and well beaten only subsequent start: effective at 5f (best form) and 6f: acts on firm and dead ground and on fibresand: races prominently: sold 1,800 gns Doncaster November Sales. *D. Nicholls* — 50

MISS SPENT YOUTH 4 ch.f. Sylvan Express 117 – Cedar Lady (Telsmoss 91) [1994 –: 8m 5.7m 1995 7.1m^{6} 8h Sep 4] angular, workmanlike filly: no worthwhile form. *R. J. Hodges* — –

MISS SPRINGTIME 4 b.f. Bluebird (USA) 125 – Spring Lane 85 (Forlorn River 124) [1994 65: 7f^{4} 6.9f^{2} 7m* a8g* a8g 7m^{3} 8.9m^{5} 8s^{3} 1995 8.1d 8d a9.4g Sep 30] lengthy, good-topped filly: fair performer for Sir Mark Prescott in 1994: well beaten in 1995, looking irresolute second start: sold 1,500 gns Doncaster November Sales: one to treat with caution. *J. J. O'Neill* — –

MISS SUZY 3 br.f. Kind of Hush 118 – Pickwood Sue 74 (Right Boy 137) [1994 –: 5g 1995 a8g a8g a8g a8g^{5} a11g^{5} a11g Feb 24] leggy, sparely-made filly: no worthwhile form. *J. P. Leigh* — –

MISS SWING KING (IRE) 2 b.f. (Mar 11) Waajib 121 – Hyland Rose (Steel Heart 128) [1995 7g^{6} 8.1m^{3} 7m^{5} Aug 31] IR 2,500F, IR 14,000Y: leggy, unfurnished filly: has scope: half-sister to a winner in Macau: dam Irish maiden: fair form in maidens at Sandown and Salisbury 6 days later: will prove best at 1m+: sold 17,500 gns Newmarket Autumn Sales: sent to Norway. *R. Hannon* — 77

MISS TAHITI (IRE) 2 b.f. (May 3) Tirol 127 – Mini Luthe (FR) (Luthier 126) [1995 8g* 8d^{2} 8d* Oct 1] — 114 p

For once, France is without a strong contender for top European two-year-old. The best of that age to emerge there was a filly, the Prix Marcel Boussac winner Miss Tahiti—an appropriate name in an autumn which saw the French make more of an impact in the South Pacific than at Newmarket. Unusually, and significantly, not one French-trained two-year-old was sent to race in Britain in 1995. Competition between the two countries was confined to France where British-trained youngsters enjoyed an above-average measure of success, winning the Prix Robert Papin, Prix Morny, Prix de la Salamandre and Criterium de Saint-Cloud amongst other races.

After five wins in the previous ten runnings, the latest British challenge for the Marcel Boussac at Longchamp in October looked potentially strong, with impressive maiden-race winners Caribbean Quest and Sea Spray second and third in the betting, backed up by the May Hill winner Solar Crystal and another maiden winner Moody's Cat. Along with the improving Irish filly Dance Design, overseas runners made up nearly half the field. The French had the favourite, Shake The Yoke, an impressive two-length winner from Miss Tahiti, after getting first run, in the Prix d'Aumale at Longchamp on their previous outing. Miss Tahiti had been out once before that, in a newcomers event at Deauville in which she looked a staying prospect in narrowly beating her odds-on stable-companion Rose Bourbon.

Solar Crystal ensured a strong gallop from the start in the Boussac and, turning for home, Miss Tahiti was chased along to follow Shake The Yoke who had thrown down her challenge to the leader. After taking some time to warm to her task, Miss Tahiti nosed into the lead inside the final furlong and quickly asserted to beat Shake The Yoke two lengths with Solar Crystal a head back in third and Dance Design fourth. The other British runners occupied the last three places. The race was a good test of stamina, and the form should prove solid.

Miss Tahiti (IRE) (b.f. May 3, 1993)	Tirol (br 1987)	Thatching (b 1975)	Thatch
			Abella
		Alpine Neice (b 1972)	Great Nephew
			Fragrant Morn
	Mini Luthe (FR) (b 1982)	Luthier (br 1965)	Klairon
			Flute Enchantee
		Minifer (b 1973)	Jim French
			Valmarena

Miss Tahiti would surely be a long way down the list if her stable's inmates were arranged in order of eye-catching pedigrees but it would not be the first time that her owner-breeder Daniel Wildenstein has achieved Group 1 success with an animal from somewhat unusual origins. Miss Tahiti is from the second crop of Tirol,

Prix Marcel Boussac Criterium des Pouliches, Longchamp—
Miss Tahiti finishes well on top, from Shake The Yoke and Solar Crystal

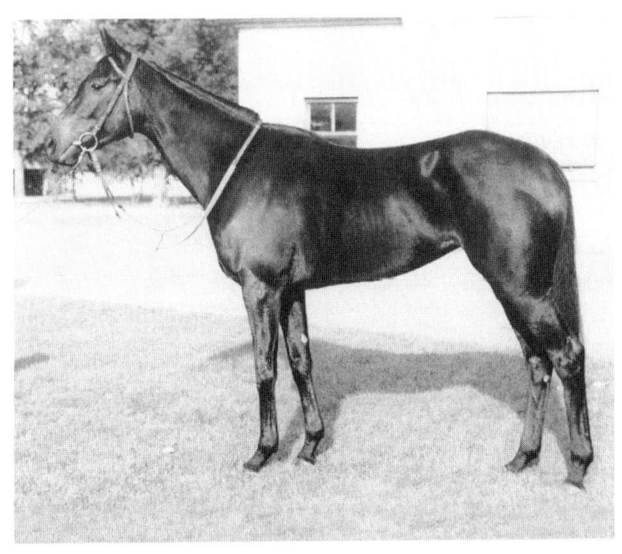

Daniel Wildenstein's "Miss Tahiti"

the dual Two Thousand Guineas winner who stands at Castle Hyde Stud at a fee of IR4,000 guineas. Game and genuine with a turn of foot, Tirol was only once asked to race beyond a mile, finishing third in the mile-and-a-quarter Grand Prix de Paris. He has already produced a smart performer for Wildenstein in Marble Falls, runner-up in the latest Prix Saint-Alary. Tirol's best performer to date is Pipe Major, fourth in the Two Thousand Guineas and winner of the Criterion Stakes, but Miss Tahiti has the potential to be better. The dam Mini Luthe was kept busy in her second season, running sixteen times with only one win in a fifteen-furlong handicap, to show for it. Her first three living foals (by No Pass No Sale, Simply Great and Commanche Run) all won over at least one and a quarter miles and the second of them was also successful over hurdles. She now has a filly foal by Fairy King. The next two dams, Minifer and Valmarena, were both winners, the latter (also third in the Prix de Malleret) in listed company. More remotely, this is the family of sire Val de Loir, winner of the Prix du Jockey-Club. Miss Tahiti, a rangy filly with plenty of scope, looks sure to progress and play a leading part in the major races for fillies, and we are confident she will stay the distance of the Prix de Diane. Wildenstein owned the only filly so far to win both the Marcel Boussac and the Prix de Diane, Allez France. *A. Fabre, France*

MISS THE BEAT 3 b.f. Music Boy 124 – Bad Start (USA) (Bold Bidder) [1994 NR 1995 a6g a9.4g a5g Sep 4] sixth foal: half-sister to several poor animals: dam, unplaced on 6 starts in France, is daughter of smart French 9f and 10.5f winner North Sea: soundly beaten in claimers: tried blinkered. *S. Mellor* –

MISS TICKLEPENNY 3 b.f. Distant Relative 128 – Aphrosina (Known Fact (USA) 135) [1994 NR 1995 7f4 a10g a8g Nov 21] 28,000Y: fourth foal: half-sister to a minor winner in USA by Night Shift: dam poor half-sister to smart sprinter Enchantment: well beaten in minor event and maidens. *Major D. N. Chappell* –

MISS TIPSY 4 b.f. Reprimand 122 – Miss Alkie 58 (Noalcoholic (FR) 128) [1994 35: 7m^5 5.9v 6m 7g 8f^5 8.2g 6m^5 a6g^3 a6g 1995 a7g a7g Feb 6] good-bodied filly: poor maiden: no form in 1995. *W. W. Haigh* –

MISS TOFFEE NOSE (IRE) 3 b.f. Cyrano de Bergerac 120 – Sweet Reprieve (Shirley Heights 130) [1994 –: 6.9m 7m 6d 7d^5 1995 a8g^6 a8g^5 Feb 20] sparely-made filly: no worthwhile form: sold 700 gns Ascot February Sales. *D. J. S. Cosgrove* –

MISS TRI COLOUR 3 b.f. Shavian 125 – Bourgeonette 81 (Mummy's Pet 125) [1994 –: 6g 6d 6m 7.1s 1995 8.1g^6 10f 7g a6g Jul 17] lengthy filly: well beaten in maidens and handicaps: headstrong, and has little chance of staying 7f: tried visored. *F. H. Lee* –

MISS UNIVERSAL (IRE) 2 ch.f. (Apr 29) Lycius (USA) 124 – Madame Nureyev (USA) (Nureyev (USA) 131) [1995 6d 7d Sep 26] 28,000Y: fifth foal: half-sister to 3-y-o 7.6f and 1m winner Bernard Seven (by Taufan) and 7f winner Fen Dance (by Trojan Fen): dam French 2-y-o 6f winner: twelfth of 25 to Sovereign's Crown in maiden at Newbury: keeping-on twelfth of 30 to Rio Duvida in valuable sales race at Newmarket 10 days later, never threatening leaders after getting behind. *C. E. Brittain* 79 ?

MISSUS MURHILL (IRE) 4 ch.f. Mon Tresor 113 – Decoy Duck 67 (Decoy Boy 129) [1994 8v^6 9d^6 8s^6 9g 7g 8d^6 1995 a11g^6 a12g^6 10.3g 9.9m^5 12d 11.1m* 10.1m 12.1f^3 12m^6 11m^5 Aug 23] IR 7,600Y: plain ex-Irish filly: fourth foal: half-sister to 1½m winner Portofino (by Coquelin) and 7f (at 2 yrs) to 1m winner Drumdonna (by Drumalis): dam 2-y-o 6f winner, only season to race: trained at 2 and 3 yrs (rated 78) by D. Weld, winning 2-y-o 7f auction event at Listowel: poor and inconsistent here: narrowly won handicap at Edinburgh in June: stays 1½m: acts on firm and soft ground: blinkered (no form) twice at 3 yrs: sold 1,250 gns Doncaster October Sales. *N. Tinkler* 41 d

MISS VAXETTE 6 b.m. Norwick (USA) 125 – Langton Herring (Nearly A Hand 115) [1994 79d: 5.2s 5.1g^4 5f 5m 6g 5m* 5g^6 6m 5d 5v 1995 5g^4 7f^4 7g 5m Jul 8] compact mare: seems on the downgrade, and only modest form at best in 1995: best at around 5f: possibly unsuited by very soft ground, acts on any other: sold 2,400 gns Newmarket December Sales. *M. Brittain* 57

MISS WATERLINE 2 br.f. (Mar 20) Rock City 120 – Final Shot 91 (Dalsaan 125) [1995 5d^5 5m^3 5m 6d* 5m^4 7.1g^3 6d Sep 27] 5,400F, 12,000Y: small, sparely-made filly: first foal: dam won Ayr Gold Cup: made all in maiden at Haydock in June: ran creditably in minor events next 2 starts: stays 6f: acts on good to firm and dead ground. *P. D. Evans* 72

MISS WHITTINGHAM (IRE) 5 b.m. Fayruz 116 – Windini (Windjammer (USA)) [1994 61, a48+: a6g a6g^5 6d^6 5m 6f^4 5m^4 5g^5 7d^3 7m^2 7f^5 8.1g 6g 6.1s 1995 6v 6g^3 5.9m^3 5g 6.9f 6m^5 6f 6f Aug 5] compact, good-bodied mare: unimpressive mover: modest handicapper on her day: well beaten last 5 starts: needs further than 5f (stays 7f): acts on good to firm ground and dead and on fibresand: tried visored/ blinkered, best form without: has won for 7-lb claimer: none too consistent. *J. Berry* 57 d a–

MISS ZANZIBAR 3 b.f. Kefaah (USA) 124 – Circe 73 (Main Reef 126) [1994 53: 5f^2 6f^4 5m^4 6m 6g^3 6g^6 1995 6m 8m* a8.5g^2 9.9m^3 7.5g^4 10g^4 a9.4g^3 8h^3 7m Aug 27] sparely-made filly: modest performer: won seller at Pontefract in June: stays 1¼m: acts on firm ground and fibresand, yet to race on a soft surface: held up. *R. A. Fahey* 60

MISTER ASPECTO (IRE) 2 b.g. (May 11) Caerleon (USA) 132 – Gironde (USA) (Raise A Native) [1995 7g 7g^6 9g 7.1s Oct 1] 24,000Y: quite good-topped gelding: has scope: sixth foal: brother to smart French 3-y-o 1m and 9f winner Garden Rose and 1988 Queen Mary winner Gloriella, closely related to French 1m winner Gaio (by Caerwent) and half-brother to a minor winner by Antheus: dam second over 1m from 3 starts at 3 yrs in France: modest form in maidens: bred to stay at least 1m: disappointing on soft ground: gelded after final start. *M. Johnston* 64

MISTER BEAT 4 b.g. Brustolon 117 – Miss May (FR) (Northern Treat (USA)) [1994 67: 9.9d 8m^6 8g^6 a8.5g 8m^4 10.5g^2 8.9m^4 10.4d^6 10s^4 1995 a11g Jan 16] leggy, workmanlike gelding: fair performer: stayed 10.5f: acted on good to firm and good to soft ground (probably on soft) and on fibresand: blinkered once: dead. *J. G. FitzGerald* –

MISTER BLAKE 5 b.g. Damister (USA) 123 – Larive 80 (Blakeney 126) [1994 NR 1995 a7g Jan 13] compact gelding: fair performer (rated 65) at 3 yrs for W. O'Gorman: well beaten only run in 1995: sold (I. Campbell to Mrs A. Hamilton-Fairley) 4,000 gns Doncaster August Sales: ungenuine selling hurdler. *I. Campbell* –

MISTER FIRE EYES (IRE) 3 b.g. Petorius 117 – Surfing 71 (Grundy 137) [1994 66+, a83+: 6m 7m 6g^4 7d 6g 8d^5 6.9s* a7g* a7g* 1995 a9.4g* 7g* 8d^2 7.5m^5 7m 7g 7g 8m 8m^4 7m^5 9f^2 10m^4 8.1d 7g 8.2m^2 7m a6g^2 a6g* Dec 1] strong gelding: shows a powerful action: useful handicapper: better on the all-weather than turf: won at Wolverhampton in February, Doncaster in March and Southwell in December: effective at 6f to 1¼m: acts on firm and soft ground and goes well on the all-weather: effective blinkered/visored or not: often races up with pace: tough. *C. E. Brittain* 86 a99

MISTER FOX 4 b.g. Latest Model 115 – Impromptu 88 (My Swanee 122) [1994 –: 6m 7m 7f 1995 7.6d 10m Aug 14] tall, leggy gelding: no sign of ability. *R. J. Hodges* –

MISTER JOEL 2 b.g. (Mar 8) Risk Me (FR) 127 – Net Call 108 (Song 132) [1995 7f 6m 6g 6s^2 7f^2 8f 5f* 5m Nov 3] 2,600Y: lengthy, good-topped gelding: brother to 1991 2-y-o 6f winner Daily Sport Girl and half-brother to fair 1m winner Dayajeer and fairly useful 6f and 7f winner Raabihah (both by Shirley Heights): dam seemed best at 6f: made all in maiden auction at Redcar in October: stiff task in nursery at Doncaster following month: likely to prove best at sprint distances: acts on any going: best form in blinkers: tail swisher. *M. W. Easterby* 62

MISTER JOLSON 6 br.g. Latest Model 115 – Impromptu 88 (My Swanee 122) [1994 90: 5.1g* 5.1m^3 6s* 6g^5 5m^3 5m* 5g^5 5m^5 6f 5g^3 5.6g 6d 5d 5m* 1995 6g 5.2m^3 6m 6m^3 6f 6f 5g^5 6m 6g 5.3g^4 6d 6.1s Oct 17] tall, lengthy gelding: impresses in appearance: fairly useful handicapper: none too consistent in 1995: effective at 5f and 6f: acts on good to firm and soft ground and on equitrack: sometimes bandaged near-fore: held up. *R. J. Hodges* 90 d

MISTER LAWSON 9 ch.g. Blushing Scribe (USA) 107 – Nonpareil (FR) 92 (Pharly (FR) 130) [1994 NR 1995 a14g Nov 16] close-coupled gelding: no longer of much account. *B. Smart* –

MISTER O'GRADY (IRE) 4 b.g. Mister Majestic 122 – Judy O'Grady (Whistler 129) [1994 45: 10s 12.5m 10m^5 a10g* a10g^3 10.1m^2 a10g a10g a10g 1995 10.8f^6 9.7m^5 10.2m^5 9m* 10m 10f* 11.5m^4 Aug 24] robust, workmanlike gelding: modest handicapper: got up closing stages to win at Lingfield in June and Brighton in August: may prove ideally suited by around 1¼m: acts on firm ground and equitrack: effective blinkered/visored or not: races prominently: carried head high final 4-y-o start. *R. Akehurst* 51

MISTER RAIDER 3 ch.g. Ballacashtal (CAN) – Martian Melody 62 (Enchantment 115) [1994 45: 5.2s 5m 5m^5 1995 a6g 5d^4 6m^2 5.1g^4 5.1m 6f 5g^4 6g^5 5m 6f^4 6f^4 a5g a5g Dec 19] slightly dipped-backed gelding: poor maiden handicapper: raced only at sprint distances: acts on firm and dead ground: effective blinkered or not. *S. Mellor* 49

MISTER RM 3 b.g. Dominion 123 – La Cabrilla 89 (Carwhite 127) [1994 –: a6g 1995 6m 8.3m 7g* 7.3d^2 7d 8s Oct 7] good-topped gelding: fair performer: won maiden at Catterick in June: effective at 7f, and should prove at least as good back at 1m: best efforts on an easy surface. *R. Guest* 79

MISTER SEAN (IRE) 2 b.c. (Apr 27) Mac's Imp (USA) 116 – Maid of Mourne (Fairy King (USA)) [1995 5g^5 6g 5f^2 5.1m^2 5m^2 5m^5 5d^6 5.3d Sep 26] IR 8,000F: compact, good-bodied colt: progressed well physically: poor mover: second foal: dam Irish 2-y-o 6f winner: modest maiden: didn't shown his form last 3 starts, twice running too freely: speedy: acts on firm ground: blinkered in seller final outing. *J. W. Payne* 65

MISTERTOPOGIGO (IRE) 5 b.h. Thatching 131 – Decadence (Vaigly Great 127) [1994 118: 5m* 5f* 5m^3 5m^2 5m^3 5g* 5g^2 1995 5g^2 5m 5m^2 5f 5f 5m Aug 17] strong, lengthy horse: poor mover: smart sprinter for B. Beasley in 1994: not so good in 1995, runner-up in minor event at Thirsk (idled in front, should have won) and Ballyogan Stakes at Leopardstown (beaten ½ length by Millstream): joined M. Johnston after last of 8 in Nunthorpe Stakes at York, but later injured tendon above 105 the hock: 5f performer: acted on firm and dead ground, not discredited on heavy: blinkered (well beaten) fourth 5-y-o start: often bandaged behind: sometimes awkward in preliminaries: needed to be held up as long as possible: tended to hang left in 1995: will stand at Beechgrove Stud, Lincolnshire, fee £1,500 (Oct 1). *W. S. Cunningham*

MISTER WESTSOUND 3 b.g. Cyrano de Bergerac 120 – Captivate 79 (Mansingh (USA) 120) [1994 61: 6m^6 5m* 5m^3 6g 5m 1995 5g^4 5g 5g 6f^5 5m^2 5f^2 5f^2 5m^3 5g^3 5f 6m* 6f* 7f^2 7.1m^6 7g 7d^4 6g^2 7f^2 7f^6 6m Oct 30] workmanlike gelding: fair handicapper: won at Ayr (hung badly left) and Hamilton in August: stays 7f: acts on firm and dead ground: usually blinkered/visored: slow starter and tends to hang. *Miss L. A. Perratt* — 66

MISTER WOODSTICK (IRE) 2 b.c. (Apr 25) Distinctly North (USA) 115 – Crannog (Habitat 134) [1995 5g 8g Sep 8] IR 15,500F, IR 12,000Y: robust, close-coupled colt: half-brother to several winners, including 1991 2-y-o 7f winner Parlemo (by Dance of Life) and useful Irish 6f/7f peformer Diligent Dodger (by Posen): dam, Irish 6f winner, sister to very smart sprinters Bitty Girl and Hot Spark: down the field in large-field maidens at Haydock and Doncaster. *M. A. Jarvis* — –

MISTINGUETT (IRE) 3 b.f. Doyoun 124 – Sidama (FR) (Top Ville 129) [1994 75p: 6.9m^4 7d^4 8g* 1995 10.5m^6 12m^6 10.5d^2 a12g^5 Dec 2] leggy, sparely-made filly: fair performer: left R. Hannon's stable after second 3-y-o start: best effort (after near 6-month absence) when 2½ lengths second of 16 in handicap at Haydock on first outing for new stable: should stay beyond 10.5f: acts on dead ground: sold (D. Loder to N. Twiston-Davies) 16,000 gns Newmarket December Sales. *D. R. Loder* — 77

MISTLE CAT (USA) 5 gr.h. Storm Cat (USA) – Mistle Toe (USA) (Maribeau) [1994 108: 7.3m^5 8m^3 8g^6 9s* 9.8d^4 9m^2 8d^6 1995 7m^2 7.1g* 7g^2 7m^4 7m^2 6.5m 7m^4 6m^6 8m^4 Nov 12] angular horse: smart performer: comfortably made all in minor event at Haydock in May: good efforts in 4 pattern events, second in Ballycorus Stakes at Leopardstown (head behind Desert Style) and Beeswing Stakes at Newcastle (length behind Shahid) then around 2½ lengths fourth in Challenge Stakes at Newmarket and Premio Ribot at Rome: effective at 7f, and stays 9.8f: acts on good to firm and soft ground: blinkered (ran respectably) final 4-y-o start: often a front runner: game. *S. P. C. Woods* — 111

MISTRESS THAMES 3 br.f. Sharpo 132 – Miss Thames 105 (Tower Walk 130) [1994 NR 1995 6g^3 7g 6f^3 6g Oct 16] good-bodied filly: has a round action: sixth foal: half-sister to 4 winners, including useful 5-y-o 7.5f winner River Board (by Dominion) and fair 1¼m and 1½m winner Caspian Beluga (by Persian Bold): dam useful at up to 1m: modest maiden: looked rather unlucky at Doncaster in March, but didn't really confirm the promise: should prove suited by 7f+: has raced only on a sound surface. *J. R. Fanshawe* — 63

MISTY MELODY 3 b.f. Digamist (USA) 110 – Broken Melody (Busted 134) [1994 57: 7f 7g 6.1g^6 6v 1995 6.9m^5 7.1m 7m^4 Jul 5] leggy, narrow filly: modest form at 2 yrs: no form in 1995: should stay at least 7f: sold 700 gns Ascot October Sales. *R. Akehurst* — –

MISTY SILKS 5 b.m. Scottish Reel 123 – Silk St James (Pas de Seul 133) [1994 78: 8s^4 8s 8d^3 8m^3 8g 8g* 8f^6 8g^6 8m 9f^4 8.1m^4 10g^3 9d^4 10.1d 10.8s^6 8.2g^2 8d* 1995 a10g 8s* 8g 8m^6 8m 8.1g 8.3m 9g 8d^6 8g 8g^2 8f Oct 24] smallish, stocky mare: fair handicapper: won at Leicester (fourth success there) in March: inconsistent afterwards: effective at 1m to 1¼m: respectable efforts on top-of-the-ground, but all 7 wins with give (goes well on soft): well beaten only start on equitrack: held up. *M. J. Ryan* — 78

MISWAKI BELLE (USA) 3 b.f. Miswaki (USA) 124 – Belle Et Deluree (USA) (The Minstrel (CAN) 135) [1994 NR 1995 7m^2 Jul 16] good-topped filly: third foal: half-sister to 2 minor winners: dam, French 1m (at 2 yrs) and 1¼m winner, is closely related to Cheveley Park second Dancing Tribute: joint favourite but green, shaped well when ½-length second of 8 to Sveltana in maiden at Yarmouth, keeping on after being slightly checked 1f out: looked sure to improve. *J. H. M. Gosden* — 73 p

MITHRAIC (IRE) 3 b.g. Kefaah (USA) 124 – Persian's Glory (Prince Tenderfoot (USA) 126) [1994 NR 1995 8g^2 8.5m 8.1g^6 8g 10f^3 Aug 5] IR 17,000Y: big, lengthy gelding: half-brother to several winners here and abroad, including 7f — 59

and 1m winner Imperial Palace (by Jaazeiro): dam 5f winner at 2 yrs in Ireland: modest maiden: stays 1¼m: has joined W. S. Cunningham. *J. W. Watts*

MITSIS 4 b.g. Picea 99 – Edith Piaf 70 (Thatch (USA) 136) [1994 39: 8m 6m 5m^4 5f^3 6m 5.2g^3 5g^4 5m^5 5g^2 5.1g^5 6m 1995 5.2m^6 7m^6 7.6m 10.8f Aug 28] compact gelding: poor maiden handicapper: left R. Harris after reappearance, rejoined him after final start: stays 7f: acts on firm going: often blinkered or visored. *G. C. Bravery* 40

MIXED MOOD 3 br.f. Jalmood (USA) 126 – Cool Combination 76 (Indian King (USA) 128) [1994 59: 5.1g^4 5m 6.1s^5 7m^4 a6g^3 6m 5.1g^5 a6g 1995 a7g^5 a6g* a7g^4 6g^5 7g a6g* a7g a6g 6.1d a7g 8.1d Oct 10] lengthy, angular filly: modest performer: won median auction maiden at Southwell in April: left B. Palling's stable after fifth outing: won apprentice handicap at Wolverhampton (in July) next time: well beaten afterwards: stays 7f: goes well on fibresand: acts on soft going, below form on top-of-the-ground: no improvement in blinkers. *B. J. Llewellyn* 40 a65

MIZAG (IRE) 3 b.c. High Estate 127 – Greatest Pleasure (Be My Guest (USA) 126) [1994 NR 1995 6m Jun 17] 20,000Y: fourth foal: half-brother to Irish 1993 2-y-o 7f winner Doherty (by Entitled): dam unraced: behind in maiden at Lingfield: sold 3,000 gns Newmarket July Sales: dead. *C. J. Benstead* –

MIZYAN (IRE) 7 b.g. Melyno 130 – Maid of Erin (USA) (Irish River (FR) 131) [1994 NR 1995 a16g^2 a12g^4 a14g* 14.1g^2 14.1m* 15.8g^6 Jun 3] tall, leggy gelding: has a round action: fair handicapper: won at Southwell in April and Nottingham in May: tailed off on final start: finds 1½m a minimum and stays well: acts on good to firm and dead ground and goes well on all-weather surfaces: blinkered (no improvement) twice at 5 yrs: held up/tracks leaders. *J. E. Banks* 64 a71

MNEMONIC 3 b.f. Mtoto 134 – Neenah 107 (Bold Lad (IRE) 133) [1994 60: 6f* 7g^6 1995 8f^6 8.3m 8g 8.2m a10g^4 Nov 21] rather unfurnished filly: modest handicapper: likely to stay further than 1¼m: acts on firm going and equitrack: sold 12,500 gns Newmarket December Sales. *H. Candy* 54

MO-ADDAB (IRE) 5 b.g. Waajib 121 – Tissue Paper 95 (Touch Paper 113) [1994 80: 7g* 8g^4 10.1m^4 8m^2 8f^2 8f 8g* 8s^6 8m^3 7d 1995 8m^3 8m 10.1f^3 8g^4 8m^2 8m* 8d 8d* 8m^2 8m Oct 28] leggy, useful-looking gelding: keen walker: fairly useful 84

Mail On Sunday Mile Final (Handicap), Ascot—
25/1-shot Mo-Addab (second right) narrowly prevails from, right to left, Second Chance, Wentbridge Lad, Comanche Companion and Toujours Riviera

handicapper: awarded race at Pontefract in August and won £28,900 contest at Ascot in September: very good neck second of 23 to Stone Ridge in £29,570 event at Newmarket on penultimate start: best efforts at 1m: acts on firm going and good to soft: sometimes flashes tail: has run well when sweating: tough and consistent. *A. C. Stewart*

MOBILE KING 2 ch.g. (Mar 28) Colmore Row 111 – Donosa (Posse (USA) 130) [1995 5.1f a5g 6m Aug 26] second foal: dam probably of little account: no form in maiden and sellers. *A. P. Jarvis* –

MOCCASIN RUN (USA) 4 b.c. Topsider (USA) – Regal Heights (USA) (Forli (ARG)) [1994 100: 6m^5 7g 7f^3 7.3m* 1995 7m^6 7m 7.1m* 7.9g 7.1g 7.6m* 7.9m 7m^2 8g^4 7d Sep 23] rather leggy, quite attractive colt: useful performer: won listed rated stakes at Haydock (made all) in May and Lingfield (held up, led close home) in July: good fourth in Kiveton Park Stakes at Doncaster on penultimate start: early to post, well below form in £52,900 handicap at Ascot on final outing: stays 1m: acts on firm ground, below form only outing on a soft surface: blinkered (raced too freely) fifth start: inconsistent: sent to USA. *I. A. Balding* 107

MOCKINGBIRD 4 ch.f. Sharpo 132 – Mountain Bluebird (USA) 79 (Clever Trick (USA)) [1994 –: 5g 8.1m^6 7f 6g 7m 7s 7g 6m 1995 a6g a7g a11g Feb 20] of little account. *B. Preece* –

MODAJJAJ 3 ch.g. Polish Precedent (USA) 131 – Upend 120 (Main Reef 126) [1994 NR 1995 10g 10.4m^4 11.9d Oct 11] 40,000Y: smallish, strong gelding: third foal: half-brother to useful 1994 middle-distance filly Shortfall (by Last Tycoon): dam, 1¼m and 1½m winner, half-sister to dam of Royal Gait: no worthwhile form in maidens but showed signs of ability: sold 2,900 gns Ascot December Sales. *M. A. Jarvis* –

MODERN DAY (USA) 2 b.c. (Mar 27) Dayjur (USA) 137 – Modena (USA) (Roberto (USA) 131) [1995 6g^3 7.5m* 7m^2 8g^5 Sep 8] neat, strong colt: fifth foal: half-brother to 3 winners, notably high-class middle-distance colt Elmaamul (by Diesis): dam unraced half-sister to smart miler Zaizafon (dam of Zafonic): beat Pleasant Surprise ½ length in maiden at Beverley in July after giving runner-up plenty of start: creditable head second of 3 to Dankeston in minor event at Redcar following month: out of his depth in listed race at Goodwood final start: best form at around 7f: swished tail in paddock and unruly stalls at Beverley: sold 16,000 gns Newmarket December Sales. *H. R. A. Cecil* 90

MODEST HOPE (USA) 8 b.g. Blushing Groom (FR) 131 – Key Dancer (USA) (Nijinsky (CAN) 138) [1994 51: a11g^6 a12g^3 a11g^3 a14g^6 a12g^3 a11g^2 a12g 10.8m^5 a11g^2 a12g^4 10g 10.5m^4 10.1m^4 10m^3 11.5m* 12g* 12s a12g^5 a14g^5 a11g^6 a14g a12g^4 1995 a12g^3 a11g^3 a12g^6 a11g^5 a11g a12g^2 a11g* a12g^2 9.9m a12g 10.3m a12g^4 10m 14.1m^4 16m 11.5g^6 a12g 12m a14g^3 a12g^3 Dec 12] big, rather angular gelding: poor mover: modest handicapper: won at Southwell in March: stays 1¾m: has won only on a sound surface (acts on good to firm) or the all-weather: sometimes bandaged behind. *B. Richmond* 51

MOGIN 2 ch.f. (Apr 5) Komaite (USA) – Misdevious (USA) (Alleged (USA) 138) [1995 6m 7g Oct 9] big, plain filly: seventh reported foal: half-sister to 3 winners abroad: dam, unraced, from family of Cheveley Park winner Sookera: slowly away and always behind in maidens at Lingfield and (swerved left start) Leicester: gave trouble at stalls both outings, particularly last time. *J. Ffitch-Heyes* –

MOGWAI (IRE) 6 b.g. Alzao (USA) 117 – Maltese Pet 74 (Dragonara Palace (USA) 115) [1994 –: a7g 12v^6 5.7m^5 6.9g 7f 6g 8.1g 1995 a10g a10g^4 a13g^4 Feb 2] smallish, strong gelding: no form since 1993: sold (Martyn Meade to R. Buckler) 1,300 gns Ascot February Sales. *Martyn Meade* –

MOHAAJIR (USA) 4 b.c. Sadler's Wells (USA) 132 – Very Charming (USA) (Vaguely Noble 140) [1994 12g* 12g* 1995 12g* 14g* 12g^2 14m^3 14m^4 Aug 30] good sort: brother to smart 1¼m winner Theatrical Charmer and half-brother to several winners, most at middle distances: dam, French 10.5f winner, is sister to Dahlia: useful Irish colt, still lightly raced: won maiden and minor event at Leopardstown at 3 yrs: successful at 4 yrs in minor event at Tipperary and listed race (by 3 lengths from Lake Kariba) at Leopardstown within 6 days in May: placed behind Vintage Crop in minor event at Leopardstown and 7-runner Curragh Cup (rec 108

10 lb, beaten 1½ lengths, wandering under pressure) next 2 starts: stays 1¾m: has raced only on good or good to firm ground. *J. S. Bolger, Ireland*

MOHANNAD (IRE) 2 b.c. (Mar 14) Royal Academy (USA) 130 – Pudibunda (Bold Lad (IRE) 133) [1995 8m Oct 12] IR 38,000F, 30,000Y: rangy, unfurnished colt: closely related to a winner in France by Caerleon and half-brother to 3 winners, including Irish 7f (at 2 yrs) and 1¼m winner Thin Ice (by Try My Best): dam unraced half-sister to John Porter winner Icelandic: 33/1 and green, under 9 lengths tenth of 14 to Silver Dome in maiden at Newmarket, keeping on steadily: probably capable of better. *J. W. Hills*
68 p

MOHAWK TRAIL 6 b.g. Midyan (USA) 124 – Indian Wells (Reliance II 137) [1994 71+: 8s 7m 10.1f* 10.1m 1995 8f 8m 8g Jun 7] big, strong gelding: easily landed gamble in apprentice handicap at Yarmouth in summer of 1994: weak in market since, tailed off in 1995. *G. Lewis*
–

MOHICAN BRAVE (IRE) 5 ch.g. Salt Dome (USA) – Mrs Tittlemouse (Nonoalco (USA) 131) [1994 –, a66: 8d a8g a8g a7g^{2} a7g* a8.5g a8g^{3} a8g 8.2m a8g 1995 a8g a6.5d Dec 13] tall, close-coupled gelding: well beaten in 1995: sold out of J. Harris' stable 1,500 gns Newmarket September Sales after reappearance: often blinkered: sometimes takes little interest. *A. C. Avilla, USA*
–

MOI CANARD 2 ch.c. (Mar 31) Bold Owl 101 – Royal Scots Greys 38 (Blazing Saddles (AUS)) [1995 a5g* a6g^{2} a6g* 6m^{3} 6.1m^{2} 6m 6m^{2} 6f* 6f^{2} 6m^{5} 6m^{4} 6s^{5} a6g* a6g^{4} a6g^{2} a6g^{5} Dec 6] 5,600Y: compact colt: second foal: dam, poor maiden, stayed 8.5f: modest form: won sellers at Southwell and Wolverhampton in May and claimers at Hamilton in August and Lingfield (claimed out of Jack Berry's stable £5,000) in November: better suited by 6f than 5f: acts on firm ground and fibresand, modest effort on soft. *B. A. Pearce*
61
a66

MOKAITE 4 b.f. Komaite (USA) – Manhunt 70 (Posse (USA) 130) [1994 40, a–: a7g a7g 7g^{2} 7g 6m 6g 1995 5m 10.5d Jun 9] unfurnished filly: poor performer at 3 yrs: winning hurdler in 1994/5 for Mrs M. Kendall: stiff tasks and well beaten in 1995: sold 600 gns Doncaster July (1995) Sales. *M. A. Barnes*
–

MOKHTAR (IRE) 4 b.c. Sadler's Wells (USA) 132 – Flame of Tara 124 (Artaius (USA) 129) [1994 87: 10d^{2} 10m^{3} 12g^{3} 1995 12g* 14m 12m* 11.9m 11.9d Sep 2] sturdy, well-made colt: good walker and mover: fairly useful performer: reportedly twisted a joint behind final outing (May) in 1994: won maiden at Folkestone in April and handicap at Newmarket in June: well beaten afterwards, giving impression something amiss final start: stays 1½m: acts on good to firm and dead ground: blinkered (hung, carried head awkwardly, well beaten) fourth 4-y-o start: sometimes flashes tail: not one to trust implicitly: sold 15,000 gns Newmarket December Sales. *J. L. Dunlop*
90 ?

MOKUTI 3 b.c. Green Desert (USA) 127 – Marie d'Argonne (FR) (Jefferson 129) [1994 NR 1995 7g^{4} 8m^{3} 8g^{3} Jun 7] 100,000Y: small colt: fourth foal: half-brother to 2 winners, notably high-class French 6f to 1m performer Polar Falcon (by Nureyev): dam, French 1¼m winner successful also at 8.5f and 9f in USA, is half-sister to very smart French middle-distance filly Marie de Litz: fair maiden: may be suited by further than 1m: looks a hard ride and may benefit from blinkers. *G. Wragg*
73

MOLED AGAIN 4 b.g. Then Again 126 – Miss Milton (Young Christopher 119) [1994 –: 10.2g 1995 11.9m a12g May 1] non-thoroughbred gelding: of no account: dead. *J. R. Bosley*
–

MOLLINSBURN (IRE) 4 br.g. Tender King 123 – Roundstone Lass (Montekin 125) [1994 –: 8d 12s 1995 a12g Feb 8] angular gelding: probably of little account nowadays. *J. A. Harris*
–

MOMENTS OF FORTUNE (USA) 3 b.c. Timeless Moment (USA) – How Fortunate (USA) (What Luck (USA)) [1994 80p: 7g^{5} 6g* 1995 8g^{3} 8g* 10f* 9m^{5} 12m Jun 22] close-coupled, good-bodied gelding: good mover: useful performer: won £11,200 contest at Thirsk (gamely made most) and listed race at Milan (got up close home) in the spring: moved short to post before well beaten in King George V Stakes at Royal Ascot on final start: stays 1¼m: has raced only on a sound surface: blinkered (edgy, respectable effort) fourth 3-y-o start: tends to sweat. *B. Hanbury*
98

MONAASSIB (IRE) 4 ch.g. Cadeaux Genereux 131 – Pluvial 90 (Habat 127) [1994 97: 6f* 6m^{4} 5.6m^{3} 5g^{5} 6m* 1995 6g^{4} 6m 7f^{2} 7m 7f^{2} 7m* Oct 21] stocky,
101

sprint type: unimpressive mover: useful performer: won minor event at Doncaster in October: stays 7f: has raced only on a sound surface: bandaged behind. *E. A. L. Dunlop*

MONACO GOLD (IRE) 3 b.g. Durgam (USA) – Monaco Ville (Rheingold 137) [1994 50: 6g 7.1s 9d 1995 15g 12.1g Sep 24] neat gelding: modest maiden at 2 yrs for L. Lungo: tailed off on return. *R. M. McKellar* –

MONARCH 3 b.c. Sadler's Wells (USA) 132 – Bint Pasha (USA) 126 (Affirmed (USA)) [1994 66: $7g^3$ 8.1g $7g^6$ 8m 1995 $a11g^3$ 12m* $12.3m^2$ 12m* $12m^3$ $11.8g^3$ Oct 9] strong, good-topped colt: has scope: progressive handicapper: won at Newbury in April and June, both in good style: best efforts when third in King George V Stakes at Royal Ascot (found plenty of trouble and beaten only ½ length by Diaghilef) and 18-runner race at Leicester (after 3½-month absence) on last 2 starts: effective at 1½m and will be suited by 1¾m+: acts on good to firm ground: open to further improvement, and should win more races in 1996. *P. F. I. Cole* 92 p

MONDRAGON 5 b.g. Niniski (USA) 125 – La Lutine 95 (My Swallow 134) [1994 82: 12g 12g 16g* $16.2m^3$ $14.1m^5$ $18m^6$ $16.5v^2$ 1995 18g $16m^3$ 18.7m 16.1m $16f^3$ $16.1m^4$ Aug 4] smallish, leggy gelding: good mover: fair handicapper: suited by thorough test of stamina: probably acts on any ground: usually held up. *Mrs M. Reveley* 76

MONEEFA 4 br.f. Darshaan 133 – Abha 117 (Thatching 131) [1994 69: $8.1g^3$ $7.9d^5$ $8g^3$ 1995 $7m^4$ $a8g^6$ 9.9g* 10.3d $8s^6$ $8f^5$ Oct 24] leggy filly: fair performer on balance: won handicap at Beverley in July: very stiff task and probably flattered when never-dangerous sixth of 10 in listed race at Ascot penultimate start: stayed 1¼m: acted on firm and soft ground: stud. *H. R. A. Cecil* 73 +

MONEGHETTI 4 ch.g. Faustus (USA) 118 – The Victor Girls (Crofthall 110) [1994 –: 8f $7.1f^6$ 1995 $10m^3$ a11g a16.2g a7g* $a8g^3$ $a8.5g^3$ a8g* a7g Aug 4] good-topped gelding: poor handicapper: won at Wolverhampton (maiden event) in June and Southwell in July: stays 8.5f: acts on fibresand: has joined M. Pipe. *R. Hollinshead* 48

MONGOL WARRIOR (USA) 2 b.c. (Apr 10) Deputy Minister (CAN) – Surely Georgie's (USA) (Alleged (USA) 138) [1995 $6g^3$ Jul 14] good-quartered colt: sixth foal: half-brother to several winners, including smart Irish middle-distance performer George Augustus (by El Gran Senor) and useful Irish 1994 2-y-o 6f winner First Eleven (by Topsider): dam Grade 3 1m winner at 2 yrs, placed in Grade 3 11f contest at 3 yrs: 16/1, 3 lengths third of 13 to Shaniko in maiden at Newbury, headway 2f out and keeping on well: looked sure to improve. *Lord Huntingdon* 79 p

MONICA MAGUIRE 3 ch.f. Prince Ragusa 96 – Mary Maguire 73 (Rapid River 127) [1994 NR 1995 $10m^6$ 12.4g Aug 28] leggy filly: second living foal: sister to 5-y-o Maguire: dam winning sprinter: tailed off in sellers. *G. M. Moore* –

MONIQUES VENTURE 2 b.f. (Mar 31) Midyan (USA) 124 – Bumpkin 108 (Free State 125) [1995 $a6g^6$ $6m^6$ 6m Sep 7] 6,500F: seventh foal: half-sister to 10.2f winner Pumpkin (by Top Ville) and a winner in Hong Kong by Never So Bold: dam sprinter: little form in sellers and a claimer. *D. J. S. Cosgrove* –

MONIS (IRE) 4 ch.g. Waajib 121 – Gratify 65 (Grundy 137) [1994 90: 7m $8.5g^3$ 7g $7.9f^2$ $7.5m^2$ $8.1m^6$ 7.9m 8m 1995 a6g $a6g^4$ a7g $a7g^4$ a6g 7.6m 5g 6d a6g $a6g^4$ Dec 12] neat gelding: fairly useful handicapper at 3 yrs for T. Thomson Jones: well beaten in 5 races in Dubai early in 1995 for S. Seemar: sold 6,200 gns Newmarket July Sales: modest at best for new connections: stays 8.5f: acts on firm and dead ground: tried visored: takes keen hold. *J. Balding* 53

MONKEY BOY (IRE) 4 b.g. Mazaad 106 – Zareeta (Free State 125) [1994 51?, a37: a8g $a11g^3$ $8.3v^2$ 12.3d 8.1g a8g 1995 a8g 10m Apr 29] sturdy gelding: poor maiden: no form in 1995, sold out of Martyn Wane's stable 480 gns Doncaster February Sales after reappearance: does not stay 12.3f, and best effort at 1m: acts on heavy ground: tried blinkered. *T. T. Bill* –

MONKEY FACE 4 gr.f. Clantime 101 – Charming View 62 (Workboy 123) [1994 –: 6m 6f 1995 7m 6g $7.5m^4$ 6m 8m $8g^5$ Sep 2] leggy, lengthy filly: poor maiden plater: probably stays 1m: yet to race on a soft surface: ran creditably only try in blinkers. *J. Hetherton* 42 d

MONKEY WENCH (IRE) 4 b.f. Taufan (USA) 119 – Northern Valkyrie (Glenstal (USA) 118) [1994 63: 6g 8.1g 8.3d4 11.1f3 10m* 9.2f4 11.1g4 11.1m3 9.2f* 13.1g2 10s 12.1g 1995 11.1s4 11.1g 10.9m5 11.1g2 13.1g3 11.1m6 15.1f5 Jun 26] tall, quite good-topped filly: poor mover: modest handicapper: trained until after fifth 4-y-o start by Jack Berry: probably stays 13f: best efforts on a sound surface (acts on firm going): blinkered once, often visored: easy winner of novice hurdle in October for Mrs J. D. Goodfellow. *P. Monteith* 51 d

MONKEY ZANTY (IRE) 2 b.f. (May 24) Distinctly North (USA) 115 – Achafalaya (USA) (Apalachee (USA) 137) [1995 a5g2 5f2 6m 5f4 5g a5g4 a6g6 a6g* a6g6 Dec 19] IR 900F, IR 4,000Y: half-sister to several winners, including 1989 2-y-o 7f winner Bolshoi Prince (by Gorytus) and 3-y-o 7f winner Irie Mon (by Waajib): dam maiden (probably stayed 1½m) half-sister to smart Le Joli, stakes winner at up to 1m: sold out of Jack Berry's stable 500 gns Doncaster November Sales after sixth outing: returned to near debut form when winning seller at Wolverhampton in December: stays 6f: acts on fibresand. *J. L. Harris* 54

MONO LADY (IRE) 2 b.f. (Feb 17) Polish Patriot (USA) 128 – Phylella (Persian Bold 123) [1995 5g 5.2m4 5m6 5.7m4 6.1s Oct 17] IR 9,000Y: unfurnished filly: third foal: half-sister to Irish 3-y-o Foravella (by Cadeaux Genereux), 6f winner at 2 yrs: dam won in France (at 1¼m) and USA: modest form in maiden auctions at Doncaster and Newbury on first 2 starts: failed to progress, off course 4 months before final outing, first for 4 months: should stay beyond 5f: very unruly going down fourth outing. *D. Haydn Jones* 61 ?

MON PERE 2 b.c. (Mar 29) Belfort (FR) 89 – Lady Ever-So-Sure 80 (Malicious) [1995 7.5m 7.1m 8.5s 7f Oct 23] leggy, quite attractive colt: sixth foal: brother to 2 poor maidens: dam won from 6f to 1½m, mostly in sellers: signs of ability but last of 12 in nursery (flashed tail) on final start. *K. McAuliffe* –

MONRUSH (IRE) 4 b.g. Shirley Heights 130 – Switched On 84 (Known Fact (USA) 135) [1994 –: 8s 1995 10d 12m Aug 27] good-topped gelding: tailed off all 3 starts since 1993: joined Miss V. Williams. *S. Dow* –

MONS 2 b.c. (Feb 21) Deploy 131 – Morina (USA) (Lyphard (USA) 132) [1995 6m* 7g2 7m* 8d* 8m3 Oct 21] 110

Mons was seen in an increasingly good light with an increasing test of stamina. With slightly less of a test, his improvement came to an end. That is one way in which Mons's performances as a two-year-old can be summarised and, although the whole story is of course rather more complicated, it captures the essence of the horse well enough. A strongly-run race over a mile on good to soft ground on Ascot's round course is a stiff test for a two-year-old. This is what faced Mons in the Royal Lodge Stakes in September and he won by a long-looking five lengths—we made it just over seven. For him there was no respite of better ground under the trees which Bahri found in the Queen Elizabeth II two races later—Mons also made most of the running, but on the inside rail almost from the stalls. Going into the turn for home he had an advantage of about half a length but could certainly not be called the winner with any confidence. Once into the straight, however, the entire field was flat out and Mons had his rivals beaten off one and a half furlongs out. Those who followed him in were, in finishing order, the three-times winner More Royal; Doncaster maiden winner Jack Jennings; Musical Bliss's son Hammerstein; injured Bijou d'Inde; maiden Acharne; Maroof's half-brother Mawwal, who was seeking his fourth win in a row; and 66/1-shot Oblomov. Mons, third favourite behind Mawwal, had taken a six-furlong maiden at Newmarket in June by three lengths then been raised to listed company over seven furlongs at Newmarket and Newbury, going down by one and a

Royal Lodge Stakes, Ascot—More Royal and Jack Jennings cannot stay with Mons

Mrs E. H. Vestey's "Mons"

quarter lengths to Allied Forces before seeing off Yarob by a length and three quarters four weeks later. Forcing tactics and an excellent attitude under pressure had seen him justify favouritism in the Washington Singer at Newbury. Repeating the dose in the Royal Lodge resulted in his being made a 4/5-shot back on good to firm ground in the four-runner Racing Post Trophy a month later, but although his battling qualities were once more very much in evidence, this time they were not enough. Beauchamp King outpaced him fairly comfortably in the closing stages while Even Top did so marginally.

Mons (b.c. Feb 21, 1993)	Deploy (b 1987)	Shirley Heights (b 1975)	Mill Reef
			Hardiemma
		Slightly Dangerous (b 1979)	Roberto
			Where You Lead
	Morina (USA) (b 1988)	Lyphard (b 1969)	Northern Dancer
			Goofed
		Arewehavingfunyet (b 1983)	Sham
			Just Jazz

At 31,000 guineas as a yearling, Mons fetched easily the highest price from the first two crops of Deploy. He also made 11,500 as a foal and his dam Morina had been carrying him when she was sold by Juddmonte Farms for 14,000. Deploy's initial fee of £5,000 has now been halved. The number of mares he covered was cut even more drastically after his first season (from fifty to twenty-two) then more than doubled (twenty-one to fifty-three) from his third to fourth. Mons, the first runner likely to boost Deploy's popularity, is in fact one of only fifteen foals from the second crop. It must have been long odds indeed against another being the Royal Lodge third Jack Jennings. Deploy had an excellent pedigree and one high-class performance (when second to Salsabil in the Irish Derby) to recommend him. The highlight of Morina's racing career appears to have been a win in an eleven-furlong maiden at Le Touquet, but she was very well bred judged on sire Lyphard and the two-year-old performances of her dam Arewehavingfunyet. With not much to distinguish her on pedigree, Arewehavingfunyet was close to the best of her sex in the United States in her first season when she won five races, including the Grade 1 Oak Leaf Stakes. She failed to win again as a three-year-old, however.

Mons's best chances of winning pattern races at that age will surely have to be over at least a mile and a half, or on a soft surface, possibly both. His dam is reportedly a small individual and Mons is a neat, compact colt, both supporting the old theory about the most likely stature of first foals, although Deploy was of course on the small side as well. Mons is an unimpressive walker but did impress in condition. He got very much on his toes when mounted at Doncaster, but has demonstrated an imperturbable attitude in his races. *L. M. Cumani*

MONSIEUR CULSYTH 2 b.g. (Apr 16) Mon Tresor 113 – Regal Salute 68 (Dara Monarch 128) [1995 5s^5 5g* 5m* 6g^4 5m^6 a6g 5g Sep 14] leggy gelding: second foal: half-brother to 3-y-o 7f winner in Denmark Culsyth Lady (by Puissance): dam, maiden, suited by 1¼m: won seller at Catterick in April and claimer at Beverley in May: well beaten in sellers last 3 outings: best form at 5f. *J. Berry* — 59 d

MONSIEUR PETONG 4 b.g. Petong 126 – Little Madam 66 (Habat 127) [1994 60d: a5g^2 a5g^3 a5g^2 a6g^2 a6g^3 a6g^4 a7g^2 a6g^2 a5g^3 a6g^5 a6g* a6g^3 a6g^3 a7g^4 7d^2 6v 6d^5 5.1g 7m 5.7m 5.1m 6f a6g 6d a6g 6s a7g^5 a7g a8g 1995 a7g^6 a8g^5 a8g^4 a8g a7g a6g a6g^2 a6g^4 a6g 8m 5m a7g May 15] good-bodied gelding: poor mover: poor performer nowadays: sold out of D. Nicholls' stable 800 gns Doncaster February Sales after fourth 4-y-o start: best at up to 1m: best recent form on the all-weather: sent to Belgium. *J. Parkes* — 41

MONSUN (GER) 5 br.h. Konigsstuhl (GER) – Mosella (GER) (Surumu (GER)) [1994 122: 12s* 12m^6 12m^3 12g^2 12g^2 12d* 12g^2 1995 12s* 11s^6 11m* 12g^5 Aug 6] big, angular horse: one of the best horses in Germany in each of the last 3 seasons: successful in 1995 in Gerling Preis at Cologne (gave 6 lb, beat Protektor 1¾ lengths) and Idee Hansa Preis (finished ¾ length behind Germany after reportedly being squeezed 1f out, awarded race) at Hamburg: below form on other starts: suited by 1½m: smart form on top-of-the-ground, but was extremely well suited by plenty of give: raced prominently: genuine: retired to Gestut Schlenderhan, fee 15,000DM. *H. Jentzsch, Germany* — 119

MONTAGNE 6 br.m. Midyan (USA) 124 – La Masse (High Top 131) [1994 NR 1995 a9.4g Apr 15] good-topped mare: poor handicapper (rated 49) at 3 yrs for H. Candy: lightly raced and no form since: has joined E. Alston. *M. W. Eckley* — –

MONTAGUE DAWSON (IRE) 3 ch.g. Doulab (USA) 115 – Annacloy (Majority Blue 126) [1994 –: 6m 6.9m 1995 a6g* a6g* a7g^4 a6g^3 6m a8.5g^5 a6g^4 a7g^3 6m a6g^6 a6g a6g a5g^4 a6g^4 a6g^6 Dec 1] angular gelding: fair performer on the all-weather: won median auction maiden at Southwell and handicap at Lingfield early in year: effective at 5f and stays 7f: acts on the all-weather: blinkered (below form) twice: sometimes bandaged. *Mrs N. Macauley* — – a66 d

MONTANELLI (FR) 3 b.g. Dowsing (USA) 124 – Honeymooning (USA) (Blushing Groom (FR) 131) [1994 68p: a7g^3 1995 a7g* a8g* a8g^2 7g 8m^6 8m a6g a9.4g^6 Jul 21] compact gelding: fairly useful performer at best on the all-weather, successful in maiden at Wolverhampton in January and minor event at Lingfield in February: well below form last 5 starts: stays 1m well: acts on the all-weather, little worthwhile form on turf: visored (ran well) third start, blinkered sixth. *K. McAuliffe* — – a84

MONT D'OR (USA) 5 b.g. Devil's Bag (USA) – Most Precious (USA) (Nureyev (USA) 131) [1994 NR 1995 10d 9f 14f^5 Jun 29] tall ex-French gelding: first foal: half-brother to 1995 Poule d'Essai des Pouliches winner Matiara (by Bering): dam, smart French filly, won twice at 1m including a listed race: well beaten in 3 starts at 3 yrs for Mme C. Head and sold cheaply at end of 1993: well beaten in maidens and minor event (bandaged) here. *J. O'Donoghue* — –

MONTE CAVO 4 b.g. Bustino 136 – Dance Festival 101 (Nureyev (USA) 131) – [1994 61: 8d^5 7.1g^2 11.1g^4 8.5g^4 12.3m^5 a12g^5 12.3g 11.5g 1995 a11g 7g Aug 31] unfurnished gelding: modest maiden: well beaten in 1995. *M. Brittain*

MONTECRISTO 2 br.g. (Apr 17) Warning 136 – Sutosky 78 (Great Nephew 126) [1995 8.1m^5 7g 7g 6.9m Nov 6] 27,000Y: useful-looking gelding: third foal: half-brother to 3-y-o Dancing Sioux (by Nabeel Dancer): dam suited by 1m to 1¼m: 3 lengths fifth of 8 to Ski Academy in maiden at Chepstow, best effort: will stay beyond 1m: has been gelded. *R. Guest* — 69

MONTEJURRA 3 b.c. Belmez (USA) 131 – Graphite (USA) 80 (Mr Prospector (USA)) [1994 NR 1995 11m^3 Apr 21] rangy colt: has scope: third foal: half-brother to fairly useful 7f winner Clovis Point (by Kris): dam, 9f winner, out of smart sprinter Stellarette, a half-sister to champion 1979 Canadian filly and good broodmare Kamar: green, shaped well when 2¾ lengths third of 15 to Tamure in maiden at Newbury: showed a quick action: will stay at least 1½m: looked sure to improve and win races: sent to Dubai. *H. R. A. Cecil* — 96 p

MONTENDRE 8 b.g. Longleat (USA) 109 – La Lutine 95 (My Swallow 134) [1994 107: 6m^2 6g 6v^2 7.1g^4 6f 6m^6 6m^3 6g 7m^5 6m^5 7s 1995 6g* 6m^3 6m^4 6g^4 6d^6 6d 6m Nov 4] leggy gelding: shows traces of stringhalt: fluent mover: smart performer: won listed race at Doncaster in March: ran his best race for nearly 2 years when close sixth of 15 to Cool Jazz in Diadem Stakes at Ascot on fifth start: probably needs at least 6f nowadays, and stays 7f: acts on good to firm and heavy ground: held up: tough. *M. McCormack* — 112

MONTJOY (USA) 3 b.c. Manila (USA) – Wendy's Ten (USA) (Tentam (USA)) [1994 108: 6g^3 6f* 7f^2 7d^2 8d^3 1995 8m^2 8g^2 7m 10.2m* 10g^2 10g* 10m^3 10m^3 Nov 12] — 122

Montjoy was in the form of his life in the autumn and looks like being yet another money-spinning four-year-old for the stable. Montjoy was highly regarded as a two-year-old but, after winning the Chesham Stakes at Royal Ascot, he found at least one too good in his three remaining races, notably Pennekamp in the Prix de la Salamandre. And his form as a three-year-old seemed to leave him with a lot to find in the Champion Stakes. Despite splint trouble he'd managed six races, winning two—a virtual non-event at Chepstow and the Group 3 Prix Guillaume d'Ornano at Deauville, the latter by a neck from Clive Brittain's filly Warning Shadows. Otherwise it had been second in the Craven Stakes, second in the Mehl-Mulhens-Rennen, eighth of sixteen in the Jersey Stakes and second in the Prix Eugene Adam, twice beaten only a neck.

Montjoy had been running as though a mile and a quarter suited him better than a mile. In the Champion Stakes he ran as though he may well stay further. A 25/1-shot, he was outpaced before finishing so strongly that he almost snatched

Prix Guillaume d'Ornano, Deauville—
British raiders Montjoy and Warning Shadows beat the favourite Silent Warrior

second place from his stable-companion Riyadian. Spectrum, who produced much the best turn of foot, had two lengths to spare. This was easily Montjoy's best run up to this point. It remains a career-best. Significantly, he followed up with his clear second-best in the Premio Roma in November in which he finished under two lengths third to the Conseil de Paris runner-up Slicious, having held the lead from two furlongs out until caught inside the last by the winner.

Montjoy (USA) (b.c. 1992)	Manila (USA) (b 1983)	Lyphard (b 1969)	Northern Dancer
			Goofed
		Dona Ysidra (b 1975)	Le Fabuleux
			Matriarch
	Wendy's Ten (USA) (b 1979)	Tentam (b or br 1969)	Intentionally
			Tamerett
		Screen Credit (b 1972)	Prince John
			Added Attraction

Montjoy's sire Manila stayed a mile and a half really well. In fact he gained two of his most important wins at that distance, in the Breeders' Cup Turf and the Turf Classic. Two of his best progeny so far are the former stable-companions of Montjoy, Great Palm and Time Star, the latter of whom also stayed a mile and a half, while his best runner Bien Bien stayed well. Montjoy's dam was useful at around seven furlongs. All in all, Montjoy is well worth a trial over a mile and a half. He has done most of his racing on a sound surface but has shown he acts on good to soft ground as well as firm. Two of his best points we've still to mention; he is an impressive individual, strong and rangy, and is a thoroughly genuine sort. *P. F. I. Cole*

MONTONE (IRE) 5 b.g. Pennine Walk 120 – Aztec Princess (Indian King (USA) 128) [1994 64: 6g^2 5.9s* 6d^3 8.2f^5 6.9m* 8m^2 8.3m^4 11g^6 7.5f* a9.4g^5 8m^2 a8g 7.1d 8g 8g 1995 8d^3 9.7g^2 9g^2 10m^2 10m^2 7g 9m 9.7f^2 8.5m 11.6m^3 10m 10f^6 a10g^4 a7g^3 a10g^5 a12g^5 a10g Dec 15] good-topped gelding: modest handicapper: contested amateur events most starts in 1995: left K. Burke after twelfth start: stays 1½m: acts on the all-weather and on any turf going: blinkered once (well beaten) at 3 yrs: effective held up or from front. *J. R. Jenkins* 60

MONTRESTAR 2 ch.g. (May 7) Mon Tresor 113 – Wing of Freedom (Troy 137) [1995 5m* 6g^4 5m^3 5m 5.3f^3 6d 6g Sep 22] strong, good-topped gelding: has scope: third foal: half-brother to 3-y-o Polli Pui (by Puissance): dam staying maiden: won maiden at Ripon in April: usually creditable efforts afterwards: stays 6f: best form on top-of-the-ground: blinkered (ran creditably) fifth start, visored (below form) sixth. *P. D. Evans* 63

MONTSERRAT 3 b.f. Aragon 118 – Follow The Stars 86 (Sparkler 130) [1994 74: 5v* 5d* 5m 5.2m 7d 5s^4 1995 5m 6g^5 7g 7f 6g^5 6g 6s^6 6.1s^5 6m^4 Oct 28] small, close-coupled filly: fair handicapper at best: stays 6f: acts on good to firm and heavy ground: usually races prominently: visored (raced freely but ran well facing stiff task) final start. *L. G. Cottrell* 78 d

MONTY 3 ch.g. Colmore Row 111 – Sussarando (Music Boy 124) [1994 NR 1995 6.1d^4 6m^5 a7g a7g Nov 29] leggy gelding: third foal: dam, maiden, barely stayed 7f: modest maiden: stays 7f: bandaged off-hind. *Major D. N. Chappell* 53

MONUMENT 3 ch.g. Cadeaux Genereux 131 – In Perpetuity 90 (Great Nephew 126) [1994 NR 1995 8.1g^4 8.1g 8m* 8.1m 10.3d Sep 9] quite good-topped gelding: fifth foal: half-brother to 4-y-o 11.7f winner Jacob Faithful (by Unfuwain), smart middle-distance performer Baron Ferdinand (by Ferdinand) and a winner in North America by Linkage: dam, 1¼m and 10.8f winner, is half-sister to Shirley Heights: fair performer: best effort when narrowly winning maiden at Kempton in August: will eventually prove fully effective beyond 1m: sold (R. Charlton to J. King) 14,500 gns Doncaster November Sales. *R. Charlton* 78

MOODY 3 ch.f. Risk Me (FR) 127 – Bocas Rose 106 (Jalmood (USA) 126) [1994 62p: 5m 6s* 1995 7.3g 7.1m 6.1m^3 5g Sep 28] sparely-made, plain filly: modest handicapper: stays 7.3f: best efforts on an easy surface, and acts on soft ground: tongue tied and bandaged (well beaten) final start: sold 2,500 gns Doncaster October Sales. *Miss Gay Kelleway* 62

MOODY'S CAT (IRE) 2 b.f. (Mar 7) Alzao (USA) 117 – Zamayem (Sadler's Wells (USA) 132) [1995 7m^2 8m* 8d Oct 1] close-coupled filly: third foal: half-sister to 3-y-o 1¼m winner Bint Zamayem (by Rainbow Quest) and smart French 6f (at 2 93 p yrs) and 1m winner Rouquette (by Rousillon): dam, unraced, from family of Full Dress II: made all in 8-runner maiden at Ascot in August, battling on well to win by 1¼ lengths from Bright Heritage: soon driven along when 12½ lengths ninth of 11 in Prix Marcel Boussac at Longchamp over 5 weeks later: probably capable of better. *B. W. Hills*

MOOFAJI 4 b.c. Night Shift (USA) – Three Piece (Jaazeiro (USA) 127) [1994 69: 8m^6 10g 8.1g^3 8.2m^2 7m^4 8.2m^5 8.3m^5 8.2m 1995 8.3g 10.9m 8.1f 8m^4 8.5m 12f 7m Oct 30] strong colt: has had soft palate operation, been hobdayed and tubed: just a modest performer in 1995: should stay beyond 1m: acts on good to firm ground: has worn tongue strap. *F. Watson* 52 d

MOONAX (IRE) 4 ch.c. Caerleon (USA) 132 – Moonsilk (Solinus 130) [1994 121: 10.3m* 12g* 12.3m^2 12m^5 12g 12g^3 14.6g* 15.5s* 1995 13.9g* 20m^2 14g^2 20s^2 Sep 30] 122

The descriptions 'fighting back', 'battling it out', 'head-to-head', etc, all had added resonance when Moonax and Always Earnest took each other on in the Prix du Cadran at Longchamp in September. Moonax had looked the likely winner early in the straight but Always Earnest came with a steady run on the outside to join Moonax in the final furlong, drifting into him in the process. Moonax's response was to have a word in his ear, more accurately to aim a bite at his opponent (who luckily was wearing blinkers) before the pair passed the post clear of the rest, the short-head verdict going to Always Earnest. Regular supporters of Moonax might well have exhibited a somewhat fractious demeanour themselves at this the close of Moonax's four-year-old season. The 1994 St Leger and Prix Royal-Oak winner had looked all set for a glorious progress through the top stayers' races when he followed up in the Yorkshire Cup on his reappearance, but, after that, things did not go quite according to plan.

Moonax's Yorkshire Cup triumph was impressive. Giving 5 lb all round in a strong field, he was the only one not to have run earlier in the season, but he had been in Dubai for the winter and looked to have done really well physically. The Godolphin team are not known for sending out runners half-cocked—they certainly were not in this particular week—and Moonax looked very much in charge when he breezed up two furlongs out, confirming it when he could still be eased close home in beating Parthian Springs by a length and a quarter, value for at least two and a half. The five other runners, in finishing order, were Shambo, Double Trigger, Further

Yorkshire Cup, York—Moonax stakes an early claim to the stayers' title; Double Trigger (left) comes fourth

Flight, Bold Gait and Golden Ball. The pace of the race was a steady one. Double Trigger for one was clearly inconvenienced, but, from what we had seen of Moonax and the sustained efforts required from his jockeys the previous season, such a race had looked most unlikely to suit him either. Moonax was sent from Saeed bin Suroor's charge back to his handler as a three-year-old, Barry Hills, on the night of the Yorkshire Cup. The Lambourn trainer should have had sweet dreams.

Four weeks later, Moonax was sent off 13/8 favourite for the Gold Cup at Royal Ascot. He had not had the chance to try two and a half miles before, but the style of his victories the previous autumn indicated that he would most likely stay. Of bigger concern was the ground: Moonax's achievements on top-of-the-ground twelve months earlier had failed to give any clues as to the extent of his ability. It is this factor which almost certainly explains why Double Trigger was able not just to turn the tables on Moonax in the Gold Cup but to beat him five lengths. Moonax got to the heels of the all-the-way leader turning for home but could not hold him back thereafter. It was three months until he was seen out again, at the Curragh bidding to be the first horse to win the St Leger and both its French and Irish equivalents. The record was denied him by just a head. It looked as if he would not come nearly so close at the two-furlong marker, which he approached feeling his rider's whip while Strategic Choice was still on the bridle, but Moonax kept on gamely, the pair drawing clear in the last hundred yards. Moonax's Yorkshire Cup win was therefore followed by three seconds, two of them in photo-finishes. An attempt to go one better in the Prix Royal-Oak had to be abandoned because of a minor injury when he knocked his off-hind. Moonax remains in training and this time has not been sent to winter in Dubai, having reportedly proved somewhat difficult the previous season.

Moonax (IRE) (ch.c. 1991)	Caerleon (USA) (b 1980)	Nijinsky (b 1967)	Northern Dancer
			Flaming Page
		Foreseer (b or br 1969)	Round Table
			Regal Gleam
	Moonsilk (b 1980)	Solinus (b 1975)	Comedy Star
			Cawston's Pride
		Night Attire (ch 1966)	Shantung
			Twilight Hour

For those good efforts on his last two starts the going was good at the Curragh, soft at Longchamp. Backers should take careful notice of ground conditions for Moonax's future races, but with conditions in his favour he remains a match for any stayer. Moonax, whose dam is a half-sister to both the One Thousand Guineas winner Nocturnal Spree and Prix Saint-Alary winner Tootens, was a far-from-obvious stayer judged on pedigree. An update of the dam's producing record is that her 1995 three-year-old and two-year-old were both seen out in Ireland: Nordic Spree (by Nordico) still has not won a race but his younger half-sister Night Spell (by Fairy King) showed fair form and took a maiden over one mile at Gowran Park. Night Spell wore blinkers for her last two starts and it has to be a possibility that Moonax will be tried in them as well. The biting incident was not a great surprise because Moonax has long held a somewhat unsavoury reputation—he was, for instance, responsible for a flagrant breach of security when breaking the arm of one of the Queen's bodyguards in the parade ring at Royal Ascot. Less of a worry to those around him, Moonax is also a tail swisher. It will be an intriguing encounter if he ever finds himself involved in a head-to-head with the old Arcadian Heights. *B. W. Hills*

MOONCUSSER 2 b.g. (Mar 30) Forzando 122 – Ragged Moon 72 (Raga Navarro (ITY) 119) [1995 5m^5 5m a6g 5.9f^4 6f^5 7d^4 Sep 27] 40,000F: smallish, sturdy gelding: has a round action: seventh foal: brother to useful 1991 2-y-o 6f winner Misterioso and half-brother to 3-y-o Pewter Lass (by Dowsing) and 3 winners: dam won 1m sellers: modest maiden: will stay further than 7f. *J. G. FitzGerald* 57

MOONEE VALLEY 3 ch.g. Superlative 118 – Superlife (USA) 64 (Super Concorde (USA) 128) [1994 67: 5d^4 5g^4 5.1m^6 7.3g 6d^3 7m^4 1995 6.9d^5 a8g^5 Apr 7] sturdy gelding: fair maiden at 2 yrs, not seen after August: well beaten in 1995. *R. Hannon* –

MOON KING (IRE) 3 ch.c. Cadeaux Genereux 131 – Moon Drop 103 (Dominion 123) [1994 102: 5.2s* 6m^2 6m^3 6s^6 6m 1995 7g^3 8g 7.3m^2 7f* 8g 7f* 7m^4 8g^6 Nov 12] good-quartered colt: useful performer: won minor events at Salisbury in 102

June and Redcar (3-runner race, shrewdly ridden) in October: creditable 6¼ lengths sixth of 10 to demoted Neverneyev in Prix Perth at Saint-Cloud final start: stays 1m: acts on firm going, impressive maiden winner on soft. *R. Hannon*

MOONLIGHT AIR 4 b.f. Bold Owl 101 – Havon Air (Celtic Cone 116) [1994 – NR 1995 7.5d 7.5m 10.8f 11.9d Sep 26] fourth foal: half-sister to winning 2m hurdler Mariner's Air (by Julio Mariner): dam winning hurdler: of little account on flat, but has shown ability over hurdles. *J. L. Spearing*

MOONLIGHT CALYPSO 4 ch.f. Jupiter Island 126 – Moonlight Bay 53 49 (Palm Track 122) [1994 –: 8s 12g 1995 a12g^5 11.1g* 12.4g^5 May 24] lengthy filly: poor handicapper: won amateurs race at Hamilton in May: finished lame after only subsequent start: stays 12.4f. *E. J. Alston*

MOONLIGHT QUEST 7 gr.g. Nishapour (FR) 125 – Arabian Rose (USA) 79 (Lyphard (USA) 132) [1994 72: 11.8s 12.3m^4 14g^3 14g^3 12.3m^6 14g 12m^5 16.2f 1995 16.2m* 16m^2 18.7m 16m^2 17.2m* 16.2f^6 16.2m^3 18.7g^2 15.9m* 16.2m^4 15.9m^5 16d^3 Sep 30] close-coupled, workmanlike gelding: carries condition: fair handicapper: won at Beverley in April, Bath (promoted) in June and Chester (5-runner rated stakes) in July: stays well: best form on ground no softer than dead: sometimes pulls hard: effective in blinkers, didn't wear them in 1995: has wandered, but is genuine. *B. Hanbury*

MOONLIGHT SAUNTER (USA) 3 ch.f. Woodman (USA) 126 – Etoile 85 d'Amore (USA) 81 (The Minstrel (CAN) 135) [1994 83p: 6d^3 6s^2 1995 7m* 7g^4 6.1m 6m 7f Aug 17] good-topped, attractive filly: has a fluent action: fairly useful performer: won maiden at Newmarket in May despite carrying head high: very good fourth of 7 in minor event at Leicester month later, but well beaten in handicaps afterwards: may prove best at up to 7f: best efforts on an easy surface. *E. A. L. Dunlop*

MOON MAGIC 3 b.f. Polish Precedent (USA) 131 – Castle Moon 79 (Kalamoun 62 p 129) [1994 NR 1995 10.4g^3 Aug 30] quite attractive filly: half-sister to several winners, notably Sheriff's Star (by Posse) and Moon Madness (by Vitiges): dam, 1m to 13f winner, is sister to Castle Keep and half-sister to Ragstone: tongue tied, 6½ lengths third of 6 finishers in maiden won by Bay of Islands at York, tending to hang and carrying tail high throughout race: should stay beyond 10.4f: should do better. *Lady Herries*

MOON MISTRESS 4 br.f. Storm Cat (USA) – Spirit of The Wind (USA) (Little – Current (USA)) [1994 82: 8.1s^2 8m* 10m 1995 10.3d 8d Sep 24] good-topped filly: fairly useful form at 3 yrs for P. Chapple-Hyam: not seen out in 1995 until September, sweating and edgy both starts and below form: stays 1¼m, but takes keen hold and may prove ideally suited by shorter: acts on good to firm ground and soft. *Lady Herries*

MOON OVER AWIR (IRE) 3 ch.f. Machiavellian (USA) 123 – Shirley Reef 73 (Shirley Heights 130) [1994 NR 1995 8g 7g 8f 11.9m^5 10g^5 9s Oct 25] 45,000Y: half-sister to Italian Oaks winner Atoll and 1½m winner Ahoy (both by Caerleon): dam useful 2-y-o in Italy: fair maiden: sold out of L. Cumani's stable 18,000 gns Newmarket July Sales after third start: best effort when fifth at Roscommon on fifth outing: stays 1¼m: below form both runs on top-of-the-ground: blinkered last 2 starts. *A. P. O'Brien, Ireland*

MOONSHELL (IRE) 3 b.f. Sadler's Wells (USA) 132 – Moon Cactus 118 (Kris 117 135) [1994 90P: 8d* 1995 8m^3 12m* Jun 9]

Sheikh Mohammed's 'Dubai experiment' took another leap forward in the latest season when the Godolphin training operation set up a permanent European base at Newmarket. Godolphin's first successes, in 1994, highlighted by the classic victories of Balanchine, had come with horses officially based in Dubai but 'Saeed bin Suroor, Newmarket' became a familiar mark of identification in 1995. Selecting around forty horses from a larger string based in Dubai over the winter (over fifty of the excess Godolphin stock appeared in the Tattersalls July Sales catalogue), Godolphin's British-based operation sent out nine individual winners of fourteen races, worth £1,691,705, in Britain alone, and collected important races in the United States, Italy, France, Japan and Ireland. 'Nothing but the best' would be an appropriate motto for Godolphin, both in selecting its horses and in the races it aims them at. Godolphin had four European classic winners, Vettori, Moonshell,

Vodafone Oaks, Epsom—the first four are Moonshell, Dance A Dream (rails), Pure Grain and Musetta

Lammtarra and Classic Cliche, all of whom had been transferred from British stables at the end of promising two-year-old careers. As Sheikh Mohammed says 'We only winter good horses. You cannot take a donkey and bring back a racehorse.' The Sheikh's idea to form a Dubai wing of the Al Maktoum family's massive racing operation came after his filly Dayflower—taken to Dubai after her two-year-old season 'to sweeten up her mind'—came a good fifth in the 1993 One Thousand Guineas (she went on to win a minor event at York before being well beaten in the Irish Guineas and the Prix de Diane on her last two starts in Europe). Balanchine and seven others, sent for the Guineas meeting, spearheaded the Godolphin challenge in 1994 and were joined later by a further half dozen who included the subsequent Guinness Champion Stakes winner Cezanne. The experiment, to see how horses would react to spending the winter in a warmer climate, has been an unqualified success. It would seem logical to conclude that such horses may enjoy an advantage in the early part of the season, but it seems equally logical that any advantage must be eroded as the season wears on. That aside, it is abundantly clear that Godolphin's extraordinary results are a great tribute to the skill of the team involved in the operation. Jeremy Noseda, closely involved with the Godolphin horses in the past two years, says there is no magic formula. 'Everything—the feeding, the veterinary help, the training facilities, the staff—is absolutely the best of the best. From Sheikh Mohammed down, the team is utterly professional,' Noseda, who is setting up on his own in America in 1996, said in an interview in the *Independent on Sunday*. 'Yes, we have nice horses. But one of our advantages is that with only forty we are able to leave no stone unturned to bring out the maximum potential in each individual.' Godolphin-trained horses won no fewer than seven Group 1 races in Britain in 1995, pushing Saeed bin Suroor to the top of the trainers' table on win-money. To find a parallel it's necessary to go back to the heyday of those legendary Irish raiders Paddy Prendergast and Vincent O'Brien. Prendergast was champion trainer in Britain in 1963, 1964 and 1965, also taking the title despite winning fewer than twenty races on each occasion, while the first of O'Brien's championships in 1966 was achieved with only seven individual winners of eight races, including the One Thousand Guineas, the Oaks, the Eclipse and the Champion Stakes. O'Brien also won the title in 1977, saddling thirteen individual winners of eighteen races.

Moonshell was raced only once as a two-year-old, looking a really good prospect when winning a maiden at Doncaster in October for Henry Cecil. She seemed certain to make her mark in pattern company, particularly over middle distances, and became one of the leading fancies in the betting on the fillies' classics over the winter. Like Balanchine the year before, Moonshell raced in Britain under the joint ownership of Maktoum Al Maktoum and Godolphin and was prepared for the One Thousand Guineas first time out. She was easily the pick of the paddock and ran very well, considering it was only her second run, staying on for third to Harayir and Aqaarid, in the process confirming that the Oaks trip would be right up her street. Moonshell and Aqaarid were the only runners in the Guineas who went on to Epsom—five of the previous ten Oaks winners had run in the Guineas—and they started first and second favourite, Aqaarid at 6/4, Moonshell at 3/1. The Musidora winner Pure Grain, at 7/2, was the only other runner to start at odds shorter than 14/1 in a domestic field that, overall was a little below the usual standard for the race. The 14/1-shot was Pure Grain's stable-companion Dance A Dream, winner of the Cheshire Oaks on her reappearance, and it was the two stable-mates who chased home Moonshell. Most of the lesser lights were in trouble a long way from home, as, surprisingly, was Aqaarid who dropped away tamely early in the straight, clearly not herself. Moonshell kept on strongly after taking it up two furlongs out to hold off Dance A Dream and Pure Grain by a length and a quarter and three quarters of a length. Moonshell looked sure to go on improving but a training set-back kept her out of the Irish Oaks and at the end of July it was announced that she would not race again as a three-year-old. Plans at the time of writing are that she will be in training again in 1996.

Moonshell (IRE) (b.f. 1992)	Sadler's Wells (USA) (b 1981)	Northern Dancer (b 1961)	Nearctic
			Natalma
		Fairy Bridge (b 1975)	Bold Reason
			Special
	Moon Cactus (b 1987)	Kris (ch 1976)	Sharpen Up
			Doubly Sure
		Lady Moon (b 1980)	Mill Reef
			Moonlight Night

The lengthy, angular Moonshell, a poor mover with a quick action, is the third Sadler's Wells filly to win the Oaks in six years (following Salsabil and Intrepidity) and is the first foal of the Lupe Stakes winner Moon Cactus who had herself been a possible for the Oaks in Salsabil's year. After much deliberation Moon Cactus ran instead in the Prix de Diane, partly because the right-handed Chantilly track was thought likely to be more suitable for her because of restricted vision in her left eye. Moon Cactus was promoted to runner-up in the Prix de Diane, behind her stable-companion Rafha, when second-past-the-post Colour Chart was demoted for causing interference. The Prix de Diane's distance, ten and a half furlongs, was the longest Moon Cactus tackled. She was a keen, strong-pulling type and may not have got the Oaks trip, though there is plenty of stamina in her pedigree. Kris, the sire of Moon Cactus, has sired two Oaks winners (Oh So Sharp and Unite) and Lady Moon, the dam of Moon Cactus, won three times at around a mile and a half and is out of the Musidora winner and Oaks third Moonlight Night. Moonlight Night, a half-sister to the Cumberland Lodge and St Simon Stakes winner Main Reef, comes from a fine family, being a daughter of Lovely Light, a half-sister, among others, to Picture Light (the dam of Welsh Pageant and Photo Flash), Chandelier (the dam of Crocket) and Crystal Palace (the dam of Royal Palace, Prince Consort and Selhurst, and the grandam of Light Cavalry and Fairy Footsteps). Lady Moon was carrying Moon Cactus when Sheikh Mohammed paid 600,000 guineas for her on the dispersal of Jim Joel's Childwick Bury bloodstock at the December Sales in 1986. Moon Cactus's second foal Moonfire, a full sister to Moonshell, was reportedly in training with David Loder in the latest season but was never entered. Moonshell, who stays a mile and a half well and would get further, has yet to race on extremes of going. She is a genuine type who will add interest to the top middle-distance races if she returns fit and well as a four-year-old. *Saeed bin Suroor*

MOONSHINE DANCER 5 b.g. Northern State (USA) 91 – Double Birthday (Cavo Doro 124) [1994 48, a50: a14.8g^3 a16s^2 a14g^5 16.2s^2 17.1d^3 16.2m 15.8g 17.1s^3 18s^3 1995 a16g a16g 15.8g^5 17.1m^6 18f^5 Oct 16] sturdy, workmanlike gelding: poor staying maiden handicapper: stays 2½m: acts on any going, including fibresand: fair hurdler, twice successful in November. *Mrs M. Reveley* — 42

MOON STRIKE (FR) 5 b. or br.g. Strike Gold (USA) – Lady Lamia (USA) (Secreto (USA) 128) [1994 74: a7g^2 6v 6f 8g 7g 7m^3 7d 1995 a7g* a8g^5 7f* 7g Jul 13] lengthy gelding: usually looks very well: fair handicapper: won at Lingfield in January (all-weather) and May (turf, second a ladies race): effective at 7f to 1m: acts on equitrack, firm and dead ground (tailed off on heavy): no improvement in blinkers: idles in front and best held up: has worn net muzzle and carried head awkwardly: sometimes bandaged behind. *W. Jarvis* — 78 a83

MORE BILLS (IRE) 3 b.g. Gallic League 119 – Lady Portobello (Porto Bello 118) [1994 47: 6d 6.9m 6s 1995 a5g a7g^4 a10g 7f a12g a12g Nov 29] leggy gelding: poor maiden: best efforts at around 7f: tried blinkered/visored. *A. Moore* 39 d

MORE ROYAL (USA) 2 ch.c. (Apr 30) Mt Livermore (USA) – Royal Run (USA) (Wavering Monarch (USA)) [1995 6m* 7f* 7f^3 7g* 8d^2 8s^5 Sep 30] $90,000Y: rather leggy, quite attractive colt: fourth foal: half-brother to very smart American 3-y-o Tejano Run (by Tejano), 4.5f to 8.5f winner at 2 yrs also third in Breeders' Cup Juvenile and second in Kentucky Derby: dam unraced: won 4-runner minor event at Newbury (by a neck from Mushahid) and 4-runner £8,200 event at Salisbury (pipped Detachment) in June and listed race at Deauville (by 1½ lengths from Starmaniac) in August: 5 lengths (looked more like 7) second to Mons in Royal Lodge Stakes at Ascot: rather unimpressive in appearance, hung left in straight and well below form in Prix La Rochette at Longchamp week later: stays 1m: acts on firm ground and dead: sent to USA. *I. A. Balding* 107

MORE THAN YOU KNOW (IRE) 2 ch.f. (Apr 11) Kefaah (USA) 124 – Foston Bridge 68 (Relkino 131) [1995 7m* 8d^2 Oct 21] IR 4,100Y: angular filly: half-sister to 3 winners, including 1990 2-y-o 5f winner Sing 'N Swing (by Chief Singer) and 1991 2-y-o 1m winner Wise Move (by Celestial Storm): dam placed at 7f at 2 yrs: 33/1, comfortable winner of maiden at Salisbury in August by 2½ lengths from Generosa: ran well when 1¼ lengths second of 5 to Henry The Fifth in minor event at Newbury nearly 2 months later: stays 1m: acts on good to firm and soft ground. *R. Hannon* 88

MORIGI 4 b.c. Rousillon (USA) 133 – Ibtidaar (USA) 90 (Danzig (USA)) [1994 7.5d* 7.5g* 7.5g* 8v 8s* 8f^3 8m^3 9s^2 1995 7.5m* 8f^2 8d^4 8f* 8m^2 8d* 8m^2 8d^3 8m^3 Nov 12] approx 16,000Y in Italy: second foal: half-brother to fair 1992 3-y-o 1½m winner Mujid (by Kalaglow): dam, 7f winner, is out of half-sister to very smart It's Freezing: won newcomers event at 2 yrs then 4 races (including a listed event) and third in a Group 2 contest at 3 yrs: successful in 1995 in 2 minor events at Milan and quite valuable limited handicap at Merano: ran well last 2 starts when third in Premio Vittorio di Capua at Milan (1¾ lengths behind Nicolotte) and Premio Ribot at Rome (beaten ¾ length by Welsh Liberty): stays 9f: acts on any going. *I. Tellini, Italy* 113

MORJINSKI 5 ch.m. Myjinski (USA) – Morley (Hotfoot 126) [1994 –: 11.9m a16.2g 1995 a7g a12g Jan 21] no sign of ability. *D. J. S. ffrench Davis* –

MORNING MASTER 3 b.g. Jupiter Island 126 – Hound Song 84 (Jukebox 120) [1994 NR 1995 10m 12m 10d 12s 6.9g a10g Nov 14] half-brother to 2 winners, including Lochore (1m, by Nordico): dam sprinter: seems of little account: tried blinkered. *R. M. Flower* –

MORNING SIR 2 b.c. (May 27) Southern Music 104 – Morning Miss 59 (Golden Dipper 119) [1995 8.1s^6 Oct 17] 1,500Y: brother to poor 3-y-o Pacific Overture and half-brother to 2 winners, including fair 1989 2-y-o 5.8f and 1m winner Conjurer (by Magic Mirror): dam 8.3f winner: 40/1, always well behind in maiden at Chepstow. *C. R. Barwell* –

MORNING SURPRISE 2 b. or br.f. (Apr 13) Tragic Role (USA) – Fleur de Foret (USA) 61§ (Green Forest (USA) 134) [1995 5g^4 a5g a5g* a6g^2 6m^6 6f^3 6.1d^3 7s Sep 28] small, leggy filly: has a quick action: third foal: half-sister to 3-y-o 7.5f and 1m winner Proud Image (by Zalazl): dam, sprint maiden, became ungenuine at 3 yrs: won seller at Southwell in July: good placed efforts in nurseries won by Times Of Times at Warwick and Antonias Melody at Nottingham: stays 6f: acts on firm and dead ground (had no chance from poor draw on soft) and fibresand: good mount for 7-lb claimer: sometimes gives trouble beforehand. *A. P. Jarvis* 58

MOROCCO (IRE) 6 b.g. Cyrano de Bergerac 120 – Lightning Laser 68 (Monseigneur (USA) 127) [1994 73d: 7g 8m 7f^6 7.3s^3 7s 7.1g 7m 7f^6 7f^6 8m* 7d 8m^3 8.1g^3 8.2g 8d 1995 8.3m 8.3g 8.3f 8.1m* 8f^5 8.3m 8f^3 7m 8h^2 6.9h* 7m^4 7.1m 7d^3 7g 7g^2 7f 7f^5 7f^6 Oct 25] small, workmanlike gelding: unimpressive mover: fair handicapper at best: won at Edinburgh in June and Carlisle (minor event) in August: stays 1m: acts on any going: blinkered/visored 4 times earlier in career: usually held up: sometimes carries head high and often finds little: none too consistent. *M. R. Channon* 73 ?

MORSKI 6 ch.g. Morston (FR) 125 – Lady Gainsborough (Sky Gipsy 117) [1994 NR 1995 11.8g Oct 10] leggy gelding: of little account. *T. T. Bill* –

MORSTOCK 5 gr.g. Beveled (USA) – Miss Melmore (Nishapour (FR) 125) [1994 54: 12v^{3} 10d^{5} 10m^{5} 7v 8.2m 9f 13.1f^{3} 12g^{4} 13.1g^{2} 14d 1995 9.7d 12.1d Oct 10] workmanlike gelding: poor maiden handicapper: should stay beyond 13.1f: acts on any ground: fairly useful hurdler. *R. J. Hodges* 44

MOSCOW MIST (IRE) 4 b.g. Soviet Star (USA) 128 – Ivory Dawn (USA) (Sir Ivor 135) [1994 7.5s 1995 10g^{6} 9g^{2} 8f^{2} Jun 24] lengthy, good-topped ex-French gelding: sixth live foal: half-brother to high-class sprinter Bluebird and 1985 2-y-o 6f winner Ivory Gull (both by Storm Bird): dam unraced: fairly useful maiden: last of 8 in minor event at Evry at 3 yrs for A. Fabre: second here at Lingfield and Redcar (sweating): should be suited by return to further than 1m: looked sure to win races. *Lady Herries* 83

MOSCOW ROAD 4 b.g. Presidium 124 – Missish (Mummy's Pet 125) [1994 76§: 5d 5.1m 5.3g 5g^{3} 5m^{4} 5m 5m^{2} 5m^{6} 5m^{5} 5d* a5g 1995 a5g^{3} a6g^{6} a5g^{5} Mar 2] small, sparely-made gelding: fair performer at best nowadays: raced mainly at 5f: acts on equitrack and probably on any turf ground (goes well on a soft surface): sometimes hangs left: usually bandaged behind: has carried head high: one to be wary of. *Miss B. Sanders* 74 §

MOSHAAJIR (USA) 5 b.h. Woodman (USA) 126 – Hidden Trail (USA) (Gleaming (USA)) [1994 75: 12m 14.1d 12f^{5} 14.6m* 14m* 14.8f^{6} 13.8g^{2} 16.2f 1995 14.1g 16f* 14g* 15.8g^{2} 14g^{6} 14.1f^{5} 16m Oct 19] rangy, good sort: unimpressive mover: fair handicapper: won at Redcar and Haydock (made virtually all) in May: off course over 3½ months, well beaten last 3 starts: stays 2m: acts on firm going and dead, possibly unsuited by soft: sometimes carries head awkwardly, but is genuine. *C. Smith* 77

MO'S MAIN MAN (IRE) 3 b.g. Taufan (USA) 119 – Broadway Rosie 101 (Absalom 128) [1994 65: 5s^{5} 6m 6m 7g 7m^{5} a8g a8g^{5} 7m^{5} 9.7s^{5} 1995 a10g^{5} 10s^{4} 10g* 10s 8d 10.8m 10g May 20] quite good-topped gelding: had a round action: improved form at Cagnes-sur-Mer early in 1995, winning minor event in January by a nose: soundly beaten last 4 starts: stayed 1¼m: acted on good to firm and soft ground: blinkered twice, running creditably on second occasion: dead. *S. Dow* 77 ?

MOSSALIER 3 b.f. Mazilier (USA) 107 – Mosso 81 (Ercolano (USA) 118) [1994 57: 6.1s 5g^{4} 6.1f^{2} 7f^{3} 6m^{6} 8m 6.1s^{5} 7m 6s^{6} 1995 5.1m 7f^{6} May 11] workmanlike filly: modest maiden as 2-y-o for R. Simpson: well beaten in 1995: stays 7f: acts on any going: below form in blinkers: not an easy ride. *Martyn Meade* –

MO'S STAR 3 b.f. Most Welcome 131 – Star Face (African Sky 124) [1994 59: 6g 7.6d^{4} 8m 8s 1995 6.9m^{3} 6.9m^{2} 6.9g^{5} 8.3m^{6} 8.3m^{3} 7.6d^{6} 7.6m* 7f 8.3m^{5} 8g 8g Sep 8] workmanlike filly: fair performer: won median auction maiden at Lingfield in August: stays 8.3f: acts on good to firm and dead ground. *S. Dow* 63

MOST BEAUTIFUL 4 ch.f. Most Welcome 131 – Sorebelle 95 (Prince Tenderfoot (USA) 126) [1994 44: 10d^{6} 8m 10g 10m 14.1m^{5} 15.4m^{2} 14.9m^{5} 12g 16.1s 1995 a16g^{5} Jan 30] strong filly: poor maiden: probably suited by test of stamina. *K. S. Bridgwater* –

MOST BECOMING 3 b.f. Most Welcome 131 – Tolomette (Tolomeo 127) [1994 NR 1995 12.1m 10d 10.5g 8.1d 8f Oct 24] 2,400Y: sturdy filly: poor mover: second foal: half-sister to a 6f winner in Spain by Aragon: dam French 1m winner: probably of little account: tried blinkered/visored: sold 600 gns Ascot December Sales. *J. R. Arnold* –

MO STOPHER 3 ch.f. Sharpo 132 – Red Gloves 83 (Red God 128§) [1994 47: 5d 6g 6m 5f 7m 7g 1995 7m Jun 14] small, close-coupled filly: poor maiden: ran as though something amiss on only 3-y-o start: has joined W. Jarvis. *R. Akehurst* –

MOST UPPITTY 3 gr.f. Absalom 128 – Hyatti 74 (Habitat 134) [1994 69: 6.1g^{6} 5m* 5f^{5} 5.1s^{5} 5.2s 1995 5d 6.1g a6g^{5} a5g^{3} a5g a5g^{2} a6g^{6} a5g^{4} 5f a5g^{3} 5g a6g* a6g^{5} Dec 1] lengthy, good-topped filly: modest at best in 1995: won claimer at Southwell in November: stays 6f: acts on fibresand and firm ground, possibly unsuited by soft: usually races prominently: no improvement in blinkers. *J. Berry* – a58

MOST WELCOME NEWS 3 b.g. Most Welcome 131 – In The Papers (Aragon 118) [1994 54: 6g 7g 7s a8g^{6} a10g^{5} 1995 10.8m 8.2m^{5} 8m 8g a8g^{6} 11.9f^{6} Aug 22] well-made gelding: poor maiden: should stay beyond 1m: acts on good to firm and soft ground and on equitrack: tried blinkered. *J. R. Jenkins* 43

MOTAKABBER (IRE) 3 b.c. Sadler's Wells (USA) 132 – High Spirited 80 (Shirley Heights 130) [1994 NR 1995 10s^2 10.4m* Oct 5] 460,000Y: attractive, good-topped colt: first foal: dam, 1¾m and 2m winner, sister to High Hawk, herself dam of In The Wings (by Sadler's Wells): second to Parthian Springs in maiden at Leicester in March: evens, won similar event (8-runner) at York over 6 months later by 1¾ lengths from Step Aloft, travelling smoothly to lead over 1f out and having plenty in hand: will stay at least 1½m: a smart performer in the making, but sent to Dubai and far from certain to return. *J. H. M. Gosden* — 92 P

MOUJEEB (USA) 5 b.h. Riverman (USA) 131 – Capricorn Belle 115 (Nonoalco (USA) 131) [1994 62: a6g* a6g 6m 6g 5m^2 5m* 6s^5 5m^2 5.1g^2 7g a5g^2 1995 6g^4 6m 6f^2 7m^4 5m^2 5g^3 a5g^5 6g 5g 6m 5m^5 5m 6m^6 5m^4 5.1d 6.1d 6d 7m 5.1m^2 6f^2 a6g a6g Nov 30] lengthy, workmanlike horse: unimpressive mover: modest handicapper: in good form in first half of 1995, inconsistent in second: stays 6f: acts on firm and soft ground and all-weather surfaces: best visored. *Pat Mitchell* — 62

MOULTAZIM (USA) 5 b.g. Diesis 133 – Maysoon 121 (Shergar 140) [1994 61d: 10m^4 8.1g^5 10m^5 10s 8g 1995 12m a8g 10d Sep 19] lengthy, good-bodied gelding: modest and unreliable maiden: well beaten in 1995. *R. J. Price* — –

MOUNA EL ARAB 2 b.f. (Feb 22) Governor General 116 – Dancing May 31 (Tina's Pet 121) [1995 5g^5 5g May 26] close-coupled filly: first foal: dam plater: fifth of 6 in median auction maiden at Hamilton: helped set very strong pace when last of 8 in seller at Haydock 3 weeks later: sold 400 gns Doncaster July Sales. *J. Berry* — –

MOUNTAIN BOY 4 b.g. Blakeney 126 – Fire Mountain 87 (Dragonara Palace (USA) 115) [1994 NR 1995 a10g^5 a12g a12g Feb 27] seventh foal: half-brother to fair sprinter Saint Systems (by Uncle Pokey): dam 2-y-o 5f winner: well beaten in maidens. *M. Johnston* — –

MOUNTAIN DREAM 2 b.c. (Mar 19) Batshoof 122 – Echoing 93 (Formidable (USA) 125) [1995 7m^5 7g a8g^5 a10g Nov 25] 20,000F, 21,000Y: fifth foal: half-brother to 3-y-o Chloella (by Shaadi), 4-y-o 1½m winner Sommersby (by Vision) and 6f winner Buckski Echo (by Petoski): dam 2-y-o 5f winner from family of Time Charter: apparently fair form on turf first 2 starts: only poor form on all-weather subsequently: seems not to stay 1¼m. *P. F. I. Cole* — 65 ? a–

MOUNTAIN HOLLY 2 b.f. (Apr 7) Shirley Heights 130 – Ela Romara 124 (Ela-Mana-Mou 132) [1995 7m Oct 28] third foal: half-sister to smart middle-distance performer Foyer (by Sadler's Wells): dam won Lowther and Nassau Stakes: 10/1 and bit backward, shaped well when 7 lengths seventh of 19 to Awaamir in maiden at Newmarket, staying on steadily from rear without being given unduly hard race: has scope and will do better, particularly over middle distances. *D. R. Loder* — 69 p

MOUNTAINS OF MIST (IRE) 3 b.f. Shirley Heights 130 – Magic of Life (USA) 118 (Seattle Slew (USA)) [1994 NR 1995 10g* 10.3m^4 10.5d Nov 17] leggy, workmanlike filly: third foal: half-sister to useful middle-distance 4-y-o From Beyond and 10.7f winner Circle of Chalk (both by Kris): dam 5f to 1m winner from excellent family: fairly useful performer, lightly raced: won maiden at Newbury in May: again short-priced favourite when only fourth of 7 in minor event at Doncaster in November: stiff task, not discredited towards rear in Group 3 event at Evry on only subsequent start: will be very well suited by further than 10.5f: sold 120,000 gns Newmarket December Sales. *R. Charlton* — 80

MOUNTAIN VALLEY 2 gr.f. (Apr 5) Midyan (USA) 124 – Glow Plug (Kalaglow 132) [1995 6g^3 6g^4 7m^4 7g^2 7f* Aug 21] 10,500Y: tall filly: third foal: half-sister to a winner in Spain by Sizzling Melody: dam unraced close relation of Kampala: fair form: won 5-runner maiden auction at Brighton final start comfortably by 1½ lengths: very edgy, easily best previous effort when short-headed by Baltic Dream in median auction at Leicester time before: stays 7f. *P. F. I. Cole* — 77

MOUNTGATE 3 b.c. Merdon Melody 98 – Young Whip (Bold Owl 101) [1994 72: 7g^5 7g^3 7d^4 1995 9m^6 7g 7.5g* 8m 8g 7.1g 8m^3 7m 7m* Oct 28] good-quartered colt: fair handicapper: won at Beverley in July and Newmarket in October: will prove best at up to 1m: acts on good to firm and dead ground: has given trouble in preliminaries, plenty of it on eighth start when also very slowly into stride: temperamental and not one to rely on. *M. P. Bielby* — 78 §

MOURNE MOUNTAINS 2 b.c. (Apr 5) Scenic 128 – Orlaith 68 (Final Straw 127) [1995 7m Sep 5] rangy colt: fourth living foal: half-brother to 4-y-o 10.1f winner Telopea (by Teenoso): dam, third over 6f on only start, is out of half-sister to Irish Oaks winner Swiftfoot: 25/1 and burly, around 12 lengths eighth of 11 to Masquerade in maiden at Leicester, never dangerous: may do better. *H. Candy* — p

MOUSEHOLE 3 b.g. Statoblest 120 – Alo Ez 100 (Alzao (USA) 117) [1994 –: 6g 1995 6m 6m 5g^3 6g^2 6m* 5m^2 6g^4 6g 6g Oct 16] strong gelding: fair handicapper: won at Thirsk in June: well beaten last 3 starts: subsequently gelded: likely to need a stiff 5f, and should stay beyond 6f: has raced only on a sound surface. *R. Guest* 71

MOVE DARLING 2 ch.f. (Feb 3) Rock City 120 – Larive 80 (Blakeney 126) [1995 6m 6m Jul 26] 5,800Y: half-sister to several winners, including 15.4f winner Limosa (by Jalmood) and 7f and 1m winner Mister Blake (by Damister): dam 1½m winner who stayed 2m: well beaten in maiden auction at Salisbury and median auction maiden at Epsom. *C. A. Cyzer* –

MOVE SMARTLY (IRE) 5 b.h. Smarten (USA) – Key Maneuver (USA) (Key To Content (USA)) [1994 59: 8.2m* 7.9f^3 8m^5 8f^4 10.5m^5 8g^2 8g^5 8m^4 8g a8g 1995 8m 10.3m 8g^5 8m^6 8.1m^2 7m 7f* 8.1m^2 7m 7.1d 8d 8g 7m Oct 30] sturdy, workmanlike horse: unimpressive mover: modest performer: won seller at Redcar in August in good style: well below form last 5 starts: effective at 7f to 9f: acts on firm and dead ground: blinkered 3 starts at 4 yrs, visored since fifth 5-y-o start. *F. H. Lee* 60

MOVE WITH EDES 3 b.g. Tragic Role (USA) – Good Time Girl 65 (Good Times (ITY)) [1994 59: 6m 7.5g* 1995 8.3g^6 8.3m^5 8m^4 7m* 7f Oct 25] leggy gelding: modest performer: best effort to win seller at Yarmouth (bought in 5,000 gns) in July, making most: ran as though needing race on only subsequent outing 3½ months later: should stay 1m: has raced only on a sound surface. *W. G. M. Turner* 65

MOVING ARROW 4 ch.g. Indian Ridge 123 – Another Move 69 (Farm Walk 111) [1994 93: 8f^5 10.4f^6 8g^2 10.4f 9g^2 8m^2 9g 1995 8g^2 8.1m^4 8.5m^3 8g 8m^6 8g 8.1f* 7.9m^6 8m 7g 7.9m* Oct 4] lengthy gelding: useful handicapper: ran well in the Lincoln (runner-up) and Royal Hunt Cup: made all in rated stakes at Haydock in August and York in October, well ridden by J. Weaver on each occasion: best at around 1m: probably acts on any ground: visored fifth (ran well) and sixth 4-y-o starts: has gone early to post: races freely: none too consistent. *Miss S. E. Hall* 96

MOVING UP (IRE) 2 ch.f. (Apr 19) Don't Forget Me 127 – Our Pet 64 (Mummy's Pet 125) [1995 5g^3 5.1m^2 6g 6m 7g^6 Sep 29] sparely-made filly: fifth foal: sister to 3-y-o Our Darling Boy, 5.3f winner at 2 yrs, and 6f and 1m winner Southern Memories: dam 2-y-o 1m winner: modest form in maidens at Sandown and Chepstow first 2 starts: failed to repeat the form, including in selling company: should stay at least 1m: bandaged near hind final start. *G. L. Moore* 61 d

MOWLAIE 4 ch.g. Nashwan (USA) 135 – Durrah (USA) 93 (Nijinsky (CAN) 138) [1994 79: 10d 10g^3 10g^5 10m 10m* 9f^5 1995 12m^6 10m 10f^4 15.8g^6 10m^3 10.3d 8.5d^3 8.2m a10g a14.8g a14g^5 a12g Dec 12] good-topped gelding: good mover: fair handicapper: sold out of J. Bethell's stable 8,500 gns Doncaster August Sales after fourth start: stays 1½m (but probably not 15f+): acts on firm and dead ground: sometimes sweats and gets on edge. *D. W. Chapman* 74 d

MOYLOUGH REBEL 2 ch.c. (May 16) Hotfoot 126 – Stellajoe 39 (Le Dauphin 73) [1995 7.1g 6f^5 10g Oct 9] workmanlike colt: first reported living foal: dam, should have stayed beyond 6f on flat, winning selling hurdler: no worthwhile form in varied company, including selling: bandaged near-fore final start. *Mrs M. E. Long* –

MR ABBOT 5 b.g. Midyan (USA) 124 – Abbotswood (Ahonoora 122) [1994 45d: a12g* a11g a14g a12g 1995 a11g Mar 20] sturdy gelding: won claimer at Southwell in April 1994 for Mrs M. Reveley: no form afterwards for 3 different trainers. *G. R. Oldroyd* –

MR BEAN 5 b.g. Salse (USA) 128 – Goody Blake 103 (Blakeney 126) [1994 –, a45: a13g^3 a12g* a11g^3 a12g^2 a12g a12g^2 11.7g a14.8g 12d a12g^3 1995 a12g^4 a12g^2 a12g* a12g^3 a11g* a11g^2 a11g* a12g^3 12f^3 a12g^5 Nov 11] good-bodied gelding: unimpressive mover: fair handicapper: won at Southwell in February (amateurs), March and May: well beaten after 5-month absence final start: stays 13f: acts on 67 fibresand, probably on firm ground: visored (below form) 3 times earlier in career: normally races up with pace, held up for final win: genuine. *K. R. Burke*

MR BERGERAC (IRE) 4 b.g. Cyrano de Bergerac 120 – Makalu 79 (Godswalk (USA) 130) [1994 76: a6g^{2} 5s^{5} 6s 5.1g^{5} 5.1f^{6} 5f 6g 7.1d^{5} 6.1g^{3} 6.1g^{2} 6g 5v 1995 5g* 5.2m^{3} 5m* 5.6m 5g^{3} 6s 5m a6g* a7g^{3} Nov 16] leggy, sparely-made gelding: fairly useful handicapper: better than ever in 1995, winning at Sandown in July and August and at Wolverhampton in November: effective at 5f and 7f: acts on good to firm and soft going and goes well on the all-weather: successful when sweating. *B. Palling* — 88 a94

MR B REASONABLE (IRE) 4 b.g. Reasonable (FR) 119 – Dunbally 57 (Dunphy 124) [1994 –: 5m 6d 6g 6m 1995 a6g^{6} a6g a6g a8g Feb 13] sparely-made gelding: of little account nowadays. *S. W. Campion* — –

MR BROWNING (USA) 4 br.g. Al Nasr (FR) 126 – Crinoline 72 (Blakeney 126) [1994 55: 8m 8.1g^{6} 8m^{4} 8.1d 10d 8.2d 1995 a8g^{4} a10g^{5} a8g 11.9m^{2} 12m^{3} 12m^{2} 12g^{2} 12f* 11.6m 12m* 12s 12m Oct 21] well-made gelding: fair handicapper: left Mark Campion's stable after third 4-y-o start: won at Folkestone (easily) and Goodwood (contest for NH jockeys) in the summer: stays 1½m, may well get further: acts on firm and dead ground: blinkered since sixth 4-y-o start: best forcing pace. *R. Akehurst* — 78

MR BUTCH 5 b.h. Aragon 118 – Kittycatoo Katango (USA) (Verbatim (USA)) [1994 59+: 7g^{6} 7g^{6} 1995 8.2m 11.6m Aug 7] smallish, good-quartered horse: modest handicapper, lightly raced: tailed off in 1995. *R. Curtis* — –

MR CHRISTIE 3 b.g. Doulab (USA) 115 – Hi There 89 (High Top 131) [1994 65: 7.5g 7g 8.2d 8.1g^{3} 1995 8.5m^{6} 8m^{3} 10.1g^{6} 8.5d^{4} 10m 8m^{6} 7.9g 10.5g 11.9m Oct 5] workmanlike gelding: modest maiden: mostly disappointing in 1995: stays 1¼m: acts on good to firm ground and dead. *Miss L. C. Siddall* — 59 d

MR CONFUSION (IRE) 7 b.h. Kafu 120 – Mrs Foodbroker (Home Guard (USA) 129) [1994 95: 10m^{6} 10.4f^{3} 10m 9g^{3} 12v 1995 10.4g^{4} 10m 10.3m^{4} 10.4m Jul 15] workmanlike horse: has a long stride: good walker: fairly useful handicapper: has had several trainers over the years: best 7-y-o efforts in rated stakes at York and Zetland Gold Cup at Redcar first 2 starts: effective at 9f and should stay 1½m: seems to act on any going (had seemed suited by some give earlier in career): usually held up, and sometimes idles in front. *Miss S. E. Hall* — 86

MR COPYFORCE 5 gr.g. Sharrood (USA) 124 – Cappuccilli 111 (Lorenzaccio 130) [1994 60d, a66d: 12d^{3} 11.9f a12g* 11.5m^{4} 12m^{3} 14m^{5} 14.4g 11.4d a12g 1995 a12g^{5} a16g^{6} 14.4m a16g Dec 15] lengthy gelding: fair middle-distance staying handicapper: on the downgrade on the flat: won novice hurdle in September. *Miss B. Sanders* — –

MR CUBE (IRE) 5 ch.h. Tate Gallery (USA) 117 – Truly Thankful (CAN) (Graustark) [1994 50§, a43§: a8.5g a7g a9.4g a9.4g a7g 7m a8g^{5} 8g 8.2m 8.1m^{4} 8m^{5} 8f 8f* 8.3m^{5} 8.1m^{5} 8.2m^{4} 8.2m 7s^{3} 8m 8g a7g 1995 8m^{2} 8f^{3} 8f 8m 8g^{3} 8.2m^{5} 7g* 8m 8f^{5} 7f* 7m* 7.6m^{3} 7m^{4} 7m 7g Sep 13] sturdy horse: fair handicapper: formerly unreliable, but in very good form in the summer, winning at Warwick, Kempton and Newcastle, first and last apprentice events: effective at 7f and 1m: acts on all-weather surfaces, firm and soft ground: tends to wander and carry head awkwardly: blinkered (well beaten) once at 2 yrs, visored every start in 1995. *J. M. Bradley* — 63 a–

MR DARCY 3 b.g. Dominion 123 – Rose Chanelle (Welsh Pageant 132) [1994 –: 7g 1995 14m^{3} Aug 24] smallish, lengthy gelding: no sign of ability: sold 2,500 gns Newmarket Autumn Sales. *C. A. Cyzer* — –

MR DEVIOUS 4 b.g. Superpower 113 – Marton Maid 74 (Silly Season 127) [1994 62, a66: a9.4g^{2} a10g^{3} a9.4g^{3} a8.5g^{6} 8s 12.5v^{4} 11.1g^{4} 8m 10m^{2} 10m^{2} 10.8d* 10m* 10m* a12g^{2} a12g* a12g^{3} 12f a9.4g 11.8g^{5} 10s^{6} 12s a12g 1995 10g 10g May 20] close-coupled gelding: unimpressive mover: fair middle-distance performer at 3 yrs: well beaten in 1995: acts on fibresand, good to firm and dead ground (probably on soft): effective blinkered/visored or not: won twice over hurdles in the summer: sold (P. Hobbs to A. Whillans) 2,600 gns Doncaster October Sales. *P. J. Hobbs* — –

MR EGLANTINE 3 ch.g. Mr Fluorocarbon 126 – Sweet Rosa (Absalom 128) [1994 –: 5m^{6} 5m^{6} 6s 1995 10m 10m 11d Sep 22] tall, workmanlike gelding: seems of little account. *A. Smith* — –

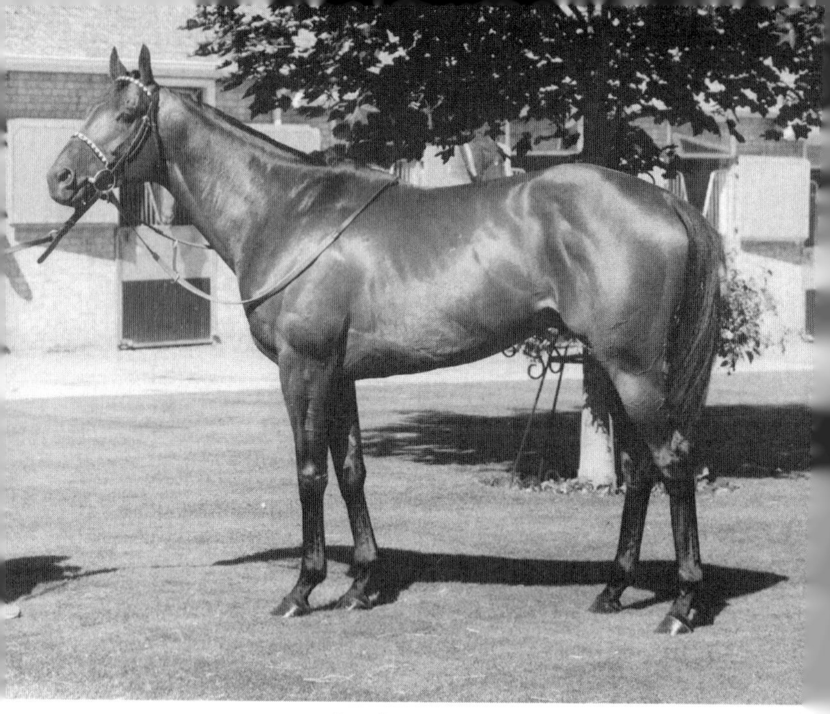

Parrot Racing's "Mr Martini"

MR FROSTY 3 b.g. Absalom 128 – Chadenshe 94 (Taufan (USA) 119) [1994 –: 6m⁶ 6g 6m 1995 a7g* a7g² 7g³ 10d 8m⁴ a7g a7g³ a8g³ Nov 14] lengthy gelding: fair performer: won maiden at Lingfield in January: stays 1m (seemed not to stay 1¼m): acts on equitrack: best turf effort on good ground. *W. Jarvis* 62 a70

MR GENEAOLOGY (USA) 5 b.g. Procida (USA) 129 – Que Mona (USA) (Ribot 142) [1994 NR 1995 17.2f³ 17.2h² 14.1m² 16m* Aug 29] leggy, angular gelding: fair hurdler/poor chaser (sometimes looks reluctant): modest form on flat in 1995, winning handicap at Ripon in August: stays 17.2f: acts on any going: best in visor or blinkers (has also worn a hood). *F. Murphy* 62

MR JASPER 3 b.g. Colmore Row 111 – Spic And Span 39 (Crisp And Even 116) [1994 –: a5g 1995 7m⁶ Jul 5] sparely-made gelding: no sign of ability. *Mrs N. Macauley* –

MR LOWRY 3 b.g. Rambo Dancer (CAN) 107 – Be Royal 97 (Royal Palm 131) [1994 50: 5d⁵ 5m⁶ 6m⁶ 7g 6.1m 6d³ 1995 a10g⁴ a7g⁴ a7g a7g May 27] leggy gelding: poor mover: modest maiden: well below form in 1995 after reappearance: sold privately 950 gns out of R. Boss's stable Doncaster March Sales after third start: likely to prove best at up to 1¼m: acts on good to firm and dead ground and on equitrack: blinkered (below form) twice. *L. J. Barratt* 50

MR MACTAVISH 3 ch.g. Salse (USA) 128 – Sharmood (USA) (Sharpen Up 127) [1994 72: 6d 8g⁶ 8.1g³ 8g 1995 a9.4g* a10g a12g³ 14.6m 14.1m⁵ May 26] sparely-made, close-coupled gelding: fair performer: won median auction maiden at Wolverhampton in January: stayed 1¾m: acted on fibresand and good to firm ground: dead. *Mrs J. Cecil* 68

MR MARTINI (IRE) 5 b.h. Pennine Walk 120 – Arab Art (Artaius (USA) 129) [1994 95: 7d^4 7d 7.9f 6m 8.1m^3 7g^6 7m^5 7d^4 9v^4 8d a6g 1995 a7g^6 8g^3 7m 8.1m* 8m^3 8.5m* 7m 8m^3 8f* 8g^3 8d^5 8m a9.4g Dec 2] smallish horse: smart performer, much improved in 1995: won rated stakes at Sandown in April, Vodafone Diomed Stakes at Epsom in June and Desmond Stakes at the Curragh (narrowly-beaten third behind Ivory Frontier and Timarida, but hampered and promoted) in August: very good ¾-length third of 8 to Bishop of Cashel in steadily-run Kiveton Park Stakes at Doncaster tenth start: below form last 3: best form at around 1m: acts on any going: tried blinkered and visored, better form without. *C. E. Brittain*

116

MR MEDLEY 3 b.g. Merdon Melody 98 – Hsian (Shantung 132) [1994 NR 1995 9d^3 8m^4 8d^2 10g^4 10d a8g^6 a8g Dec 15] 3,500F, 30,000Y: lengthy, angular gelding: half-brother to winning miler Salbyng (by Night Shift) and 7f winner Manalapan (by Superlative): dam lightly-raced half-sister to smart 6f to 1m winner Bas Bleu and very useful middle-distance performer Primerello: fair maiden at best: well below form last 4 starts: should stay 1¼m: acts on good to firm and dead ground. *R. Hannon*

75 d

MR MORIARTY (IRE) 4 ch.g. Tate Gallery (USA) 117 – Bernica (FR) 114 (Caro 133) [1994 32: a8.5g^5 a8.5g^5 a8g a8g^5 a8.5g^5 12m^6 10.8m 1995 a12g^5 a12g^2 a12g^3 a8g^5 a11g^5 a11g^5 14.1g 8.2m a8.5g^5 a8g a8g^6 a9.4g^4 10.8m 6f^4 6m 5d Sep 13] neat gelding: poor maiden handicapper: stays 1½m: acts on fibresand and firm and dead going: tried blinkered, no improvement: often bandaged behind: won over hurdles in November and December. *S. R. Bowring*

41

MR NEVERMIND (IRE) 5 b.g. The Noble Player (USA) 126 – Salacia 93 (Seaepic (USA) 100) [1994 67, a78: 8d^2 8g^3 7m^3 7.3s 7g^5 7f^4 7d^3 7d a7g* a8g^2 a8g^2 1995 a7g^5 a8g^3 a8g^4 a7g^2 6.9d 7g^2 6.9g^2 6.9f^3 7.6m^2 8.1m 7d a7g^2 a8g* a8g* Dec 15] useful-looking gelding: has a quick action: fair performer: won minor event and claimer at Lingfield late in year, both in good style: stays 1m: probably acts on any ground: effective with blinkers at 2 and 3 yrs, not tried since. *G. L. Moore*

67
a78

MR OSCAR 3 b.g. Belfort (FR) 89 – Moushka (Song 132) [1994 43: 5g^5 1995 5m* 5m* Sep 5] smallish, good-quartered gelding: made all in 7-runner maiden at Ripon (by 6 lengths) in August and 5-runner minor event at Leicester (really impressive, beat below-form Lucky Parkes by 5 lengths despite hanging right) in September: very speedy, and will prove best at 5f: has raced only on a sound surface: still lightly raced, looks sure to progress further and win more races. *M. Johnston*

95 p

MR PERSONALITY 3 ch.g. Bairn (USA) 126 – Gentle Gain 58 (Final Straw 127) [1994 NR 1995 7g 8d 10m 8.1m^3 Aug 11] 9,500Y: workmanlike gelding: first foal: dam, maiden, should have been suited by further than 7f: no worthwhile form in maidens and seller, and looks a hard ride: sold (Mrs. M. Reveley to K. Warner) 850 gns Doncaster November Sales. *Mrs M. Reveley*

–

MR POPPLETON 6 ch.g. Ballacashtal (CAN) – Greenstead Lady 67 (Great Nephew 126) [1994 –: a16.2g 1995 11.6m Aug 7] big gelding: no longer of any account. *R. Brotherton*

–

MR ROUGH 4 b.g. Fayruz 116 – Rheinbloom 66 (Rheingold 137) [1994 56: 8.2v 8v 10d^6 9.7g^4 9f^3 10g 10g 10d^6 8m* 8g^3 8d^3 1995 8m* 8.3g^3 8g^2 8.3g 8.3m^2 7.6m^6 8g^2 8.9g a8g Nov 2] sturdy, close-coupled gelding: fair handicapper: won at Brighton in April: effective at 7.6f, and stays 1¼m: acts on firm and dead ground (below form on soft). *D. Morris*

68

MRS BIZZYBODY 4 b.f. Efisio 120 – Mrs Bizz (Status Seeker) [1994 –: a10g a8g a9.4g^6 a7g^6 6m 7f 8d a7g 1995 a7g^4 a8g Feb 25] unfurnished filly: no form since 1993. *T. J. Naughton*

–

MRS JAWLEYFORD (USA) 7 b.m. Dixieland Band (USA) – Did She Agree (USA) (Restless Native) [1994 43, a58: a16g^6 a16g^3 16.1f a14g^4 16.2g^5 a16.2g* 15.1m^4 a16g^3 a14g^4 a16.2g* 1995 a16.2g^5 a16g a16g a14g a14g Nov 24] angular mare: has round action: poor handicapper: disappointing in 1995: suited by test of stamina: acts well on fibresand: often bandaged. *C. Smith*

–

MRS JOGGLEBURY 4 b.f. Chilibang 120 – Madame Bleu 44 (Bruni 132) [1994 –: a6s 1995 a11g a12g 16d^5 Jun 15] of no account. *C. Smith*

–

MRS KEEN 2 b.f. (May 29) Beveled (USA) – Haiti Mill 68 (Free State 125) [1995 6f 6m Nov 6] workmanlike filly: fifth foal: sister to 7f winner Level Up and half-sister to 6f and 7f winner Nigel's Lucky Girl (by Belfort): dam, maiden suited

–

by 1m, out of sister to Petong: always behind in median auction maidens at Leicester and Folkestone (slowly away) late in year. *Mrs M. McCourt*

MR SLICK 3 ch.g. Sharpo 132 – Taj Victory 68 (Final Straw 127) [1994 53: 6m 6m 7g a5g a6g^5 a5g 1995 8.3s^4 6g^2 6g May 8] unfurnished gelding: poor maiden: stays 7f: tried blinkered. *W. Storey* — 45

MRS MCBADGER 2 ch.f. (Jan 29) Weldnaas (USA) 112 – Scottish Lady (Dunbeath (USA) 127) [1995 5m^4 5g^4 6m 5m^6 6s^3 6.1s^3 6m^6 Nov 6] 2,200Y: rather unfurnished filly: second foal: sister to 3-y-o 6f and 7.6f winner Sharp 'n Smart: dam won 5 races in Italy, from 6f to 7.5f: fair maiden: stays 6f: has form on good to firm ground but seems very well suited by soft. *B. Smart* — 67

MRS NEVERMIND 2 b.f. (Mar 15) Sayf El Arab (USA) 127 – Mana (GER) (Windwurf (GER)) [1995 6g 6f^3 6m^4 Aug 24] 7,000F, 6,800Y: leggy, close-coupled filly: sixth reported live foal: half-sister to 1994 2-y-o 6f winner Dansu (by Superlative) and several other winners, including 1990 2-y-o 7f winner Losmanar (by Los Santos): dam won at 2 yrs in Germany: poor form in varied company, including selling: stays 6f. *G. L. Moore* — 42

MR SPEAKER (IRE) 2 ch.g. (Apr 10) Statoblest 120 – Casting Vote (USA) 54 (Monteverdi 129) [1995 5m a7g 6.1m 6d^3 6d^6 Sep 18] 13,500Y: close-coupled, workmanlike gelding: second foal: dam, suited by 1¼m on flat, won over hurdles: improved form in nurseries last 2 starts: should be well suited by 7f+: acts on dead ground. *C. F. Wall* — 62

MR SPECULATOR 2 ch.g. (Feb 22) Kefaah (USA) 124 – Humanity (Ahonoora 122) [1995 8d Sep 26] 4,500Y: strong, lengthy gelding: first foal: dam (unraced) out of half-sister to Oaks second Vielle: 33/1 and in need of race, never a threat after slow start when fourteenth of 20 to Helicon in maiden at Newmarket. *P. A. Kelleway* — –

MRS TIGGER 3 ch.f. Absalom 128 – Steffi 67 (Precocious 126) [1994 46: 6g^4 6m 7m 7m a8g^4 1995 a10g a12g a8g 8m 7m 6f Aug 11] poor maiden: well beaten in 1995: tried blinkered: sold 1,500 gns Newmarket September Sales: sent to Cyprus. *R. W. Armstrong* — –

MR TEDDY 2 gr.g. (Feb 13) Absalom 128 – Chadenshe 94 (Taufan (USA) 119) [1995 6m a7g^6 Nov 21] small, close-coupled gelding: second reported foal: brother to 3-y-o 7f winner Mr Frosty: dam suited by 7f/1m: slowly away and always behind in maidens at Newmarket and Lingfield: sold 850 gns Ascot December Sales. *W. Jarvis* — –

MR TEIGH 3 b.g. Komaite (USA) – Khadino (Relkino 131) [1994 70: 6m^2 6m^5 1995 6g^4 5g 5.1m^5 a8g^4 7m^6 Jul 1] sturdy gelding: fair maiden: well below form in 1995 after reappearance: should stay 7f: has raced only on a sound surface on turf: blinkered (looked none too keen) second start, visored (set strong pace, weakened) final one. *K. McAuliffe* — 71 d

MR TOWSER 4 b.g. Faustus (USA) 118 – Saltina (Bustino 136) [1994 70, a73: 10d^2 11.1g^2 11.1f^2 11.1m^2 a12g^2 a12g* 13.6m^4 12.1g 14s^5 11.8d^4 1995 a11g^2 a11g^4 a12g* 12g^4 12m^5 Jun 20] close-coupled gelding: fair handicapper: won at Southwell in April: stays 1½m well: acts on firm and dead ground and goes well on fibresand: has had tongue tied down and often wears a crossed noseband: usually races prominently: game. *W. W. Haigh* — 62 a78

MS JONES (IRE) 2 ch.f. (May 16) Headin' Up – Deep Joy (Deep Run 119) [1995 a8g Nov 24] fourth reported foal: dam unraced: 33/1, slow-starting last of 16 in seller at Southwell. *R. Brotherton* — –

MU-ARRIK 7 b. or br.h. Aragon 118 – Maravilla 73 (Mandrake Major 122) [1994 60, a–: 5.9s^2 6d^2 7m^5 6d^3 6m 7f 6g^5 6g 6g* 6.1s^3 5d 1995 6d 6.1g 5.9m 5g^6 6f^6 a6g 6f 6g 6g^5 7f 7f Oct 24] sparely-made horse: has a quick action: modest handicapper: effective at 6f and 7f: acts on all-weather surfaces and probably on any turf going: often blinkered/visored: has won for amateur: none too consistent. *G. R. Oldroyd* — 58 d a–

MUA-TAB 2 ch.f. (Apr 2) Polish Precedent (USA) 131 – Alsabiha 99 (Lord Gayle (USA) 124) [1995 6g^4 Sep 30] lengthy, unfurnished filly: third foal: dam, 6f and 1m winner, granddaughter of Park Hill winner Parmelia, half-sister to St Paddy: 33/1 and free to post, fourth of 17 to Polish Spring in maiden at Newmarket, going on strongly at the finish: will be suited by further than 6f: sure to improve. *P. T. Walwyn* — 76 p

MUBARIZ (IRE) 3 b.c. Royal Academy (USA) 130 – Ringtail 102 (Auction Ring (USA) 123) [1994 NR 1995 7f² May 13] IR 85,000Y: well-made, attractive colt: half-brother to 3 winners, including 7f/1m winner Waterlord (by Bob Back) and fairly useful 1990 2-y-o 6f winner Mohawk Chief (by Ahonoora): dam 2-y-o 5f winner: burly and green, 1½ lengths second of 11 to Fakih in maiden at Lingfield, leading 2f out until just inside last: looked sure to improve: stays in training. *E. A. L. Dunlop* 75 p

MUBHIJ (IRE) 2 ch.c. (Feb 3) Mujtahid (USA) 118 – Abhaaj 91 (Kris 135) [1995 5m* 5m³ 5m³ 6m² 5m* 5d² 5s* Oct 7] 108

Mubhij might have had the favoured rail and not a great deal to beat in the Cornwallis Stakes at Ascot in October, but there's no denying his victory there was deserved reward for a series of fine efforts in a seven-race season which never once saw him out of the first three. Three of those placings had been achieved in the Norfolk Stakes at Ascot, the Richmond Stakes at Goodwood and the Flying Childers Stakes at Doncaster, and made Mubhij the clear form selection against the Timeform Harry Rosebery winner Westcourt Magic and six other mostly-exposed rivals in a substandard renewal at Ascot. Mubhij had never encountered ground quite so soft as it was at Ascot but he'd looked perfectly at ease on good to soft in the Flying Childers and a plum draw on the less testing ground next to the stand rail meant he looked a fair betting proposition at odds against. He won in good style. Quickly seizing the initiative as Westcourt Magic caused some interference leaving the stalls, Mubhij seldom looked like being headed, and needed only to be pushed along with hands and heels from over a furlong out to beat Westcourt Magic readily by three and a half lengths.

Mubhij had first made a good impression on his debut at Sandown in May when he quickened clear of a good-looking field of maidens only to flag before getting home by only a head from another promising colt in Bahamian Knight. On the strength of that performance, Mubhij started co-favourite at 9/4 with the impressive Chester winner Night Parade in the Norfolk at Ascot in June, but though he had easily the better of that particular battle he went down by two and a half lengths and a neck to Lucky Lionel and Cayman Kai, beaten already when the winner drifted across him inside the last furlong. If anything, Mubhij was rather disappointing in his next race, the Sino Group Dragon Trophy at Sandown in July. He managed to beat Cayman Kai by the same distance Cayman Kai had beaten him in the Norfolk, but had little left at the end of a race in which he and the two other leaders, who included the 20/1 runner-up Anotheranniversary, possibly went too fast and didn't have enough left to hold off Home Shopping. Mubhij received a less forcing ride in the Richmond later in the month and very nearly stole the race, gradually increasing what was only a fair early gallop but finding the winning post coming a stride too late as Polaris Flight finished fast to win by a neck. Mubhij appeared next at York on Gimcrack day, not in the Gimcrack itself but back over five furlongs in the less competitive Roses Stakes. It might have appeared a straightforward task on form, but Mubhij, sweating and failing for once to take the eye beforehand, conspired to make it difficult by hanging left and having to be coaxed home to win with nothing to spare in a finish of necks with Rambling Bear and High Priority. Mubhij had his final race before the Cornwallis, and his first on anything other than good to firm ground, in the Flying Childers

Willmott Dixon Cornwallis Stakes, Ascot—Mubhij gives no cause for concern to favourite-backers

at Doncaster in September. Whether easy underfoot conditions suit Mubhij ideally remains to be seen—it must be a distinct possibility after his performance in the Cornwallis—but they brought about an immediate improvement at Doncaster on his previous five-furlong form and he ran an excellent race, leading at a strong pace for over four furlongs before going down by three quarters of a length to his old rival Cayman Kai, Rambling Bear much further behind in fourth this time.

Mubhij (IRE) (ch.c. Feb 3, 1993)	Mujtahid (USA) (ch 1988)	Woodman (ch 1983)	Mr Prospector
			Playmate
		Mesmerize (b 1982)	Mill Reef
			Jeanie Duff
	Abhaaj (b 1984)	Kris (ch 1976)	Sharpen Up
			Doubly Sure
		Ibtihaj (b 1979)	Raja Baba
			Pas de Nom

Mubhij is the best two-year-old from the first crop of the 1990 July Stakes and Gimcrack Stakes winner Mujtahid who flopped at odds on in the Dewhurst and never ran as a three-year-old after suffering a stress-fracture to a cannon-bone. Not surprisingly, Mujtahid was well supported by owner Hamdan Al Maktoum's mares when he was retired to Derrinstown Stud in Ireland and it was a mating with one of them, Abhaaj, which produced Mubhij. Like Mujtahid, Abhaaj won two of her four races as a two-year-old, a maiden at Lingfield and a minor event at Bath, but she failed to train on and was retired after finishing last on her only start at three. She has produced two other winners, the one-mile winner Dalu (by Rainbow Quest) and the 1992 Irish two-year-old seven-furlong winner Ibda (by Mtoto), and since Mubhij, her third foal, she has had a colt by Marju named Zaahir. Abhaaj is a daughter of the useful 1981 two-year-old five-furlong winner Ibtihaj, a half-sister to the brilliant sire Danzig but rather a disappointment as a broodmare with only two winners from seven foals of racing age. As a stallion Danzig is an influence for speed which isn't at all surprising given that his dam Pas de Nom was a very useful sprinter in the States in the 'seventies, winning nine races in all. Mubhij, a robust, lengthy, good-quartered colt and a good walker too, will also prove best at sprint distances, more likely better at five furlongs than six. He acts on any going. *B. W. Hills*

MUCHTARAK (IRE) 3 b.c. Try My Best (USA) 130 – Secret Hideaway (USA) (Key To The Mint (USA)) [1994 81p: 5g 5g* 6.1d^2 1995 7f^2 6g 7m^5 7m* 8.1m 8.5m Aug 28] good-topped colt: fairly useful handicapper: won at Lingfield in July: should stay 1m: yet to race on soft ground, probably acts on any other: takes strong hold: sent to Dubai. *C. J. Benstead* 88

MUCH TOO HIGH 3 b.g. Salse (USA) 128 – Hi-Li (High Top 131) [1994 52: 5v 8.1g 7.5g 1995 10.8m^5 11.6m 16.4g^2 14.1g^3 14.1f^4 14d^5 16.1g Oct 3] angular colt: modest maiden handicapper: well beaten last 3 starts: seems suited by test of stamina: best form on good ground: won juvenile hurdle in November. *T. J. Naughton* 57

MUDLARK 3 b.g. Salse (USA) 128 – Mortal Sin (USA) (Green Forest (USA) 134) [1994 55: 7s 6g^5 7d 1995 8.3g^3 10g^3 a8g^5 Jun 16] good-bodied gelding: poor maiden: sold (J. W. Watts to J. Norton) 4,100 gns Doncaster July Sales: probably stays 1¼m: blinkered all 3 starts in 1995: sometimes bandaged. *J. W. Watts* 45

MUFAREJ (USA) 3 ch.c. Riverman (USA) 131 – Azayim 111 (Be My Guest (USA) 126) [1994 82: 8.2d^2 7g^2 1995 7m* 7g Sep 29] leggy colt: fairly useful performer: justified favouritism in maiden at Lingfield in September: again favourite but facing stiffish task, creditable ninth of 14 in rated stakes at Newmarket on only subsequent outing, never able to challenge and eased: will prove suited by further than 7f, probably by 1¼m: sent to Dubai: remains capable of better. *R. W. Armstrong* 82 p

MUFERR (IRE) 3 b.c. Groom Dancer (USA) 128 – Tiavanita (USA) (J O Tobin (USA) 130) [1994 74: 6m 7m 8.2d^5 a8g^4 1995 8.2g* 9m 10m* a9d^2 a8g^4 Dec 29] quite attractive colt: unimpressive mover: fairly useful form: won handicaps at Nottingham (apprentices) in April and Ripon (by 3 lengths from Kalou, pair clear) in May for L. Cumani: narrowly beaten in handicap at Jebel Ali in December: will stay at least 1½m: acts on good to firm ground. *D. Selvaratnam, UAE* 85

MUHAB (USA) 3 b. or br.c. Lyphard (USA) 132 – Magic Slipper 97 (Habitat 134) [1994 100p: 6m 6g* 7m* 6m^2 7m^2 1995 8m^4 7m^5 8m 8d 8d^6 Sep 23] strong, good-bodied colt: useful performer: best 3-y-o effort when fourth to Sonic Boy in 100 d minor event at Doncaster on reappearance: well below form on other starts, but twice acted as pacemaker in Group 1 events: stays 1m: acts on good to firm ground: sold 12,000 gns Newmarket December Sales: sent to Norway. *P. T. Walwyn*

MUHANDAM (IRE) 2 b.c. (Feb 19) Common Grounds 118 – Unbidden Melody (USA) (Chieftain II) [1995 6m 6g⁵ 6g³ Sep 16] IR 45,000Y: compact colt: brother to 4-y-o 9f winner Broughton Singer and half-brother to several winners, including 1989 2-y-o 6f winner Ruling Passion (by Bairn): dam half-sister to Faustus: improved effort when 1¼ lengths third of 10 to The Man in maiden at Catterick: will stay further than 6f: carried head awkwardly last 2 starts. *M. R. Stoute* 70

MUHANDIS 2 b.c. (Feb 14) Persian Bold 123 – Night At Sea 107 (Night Shift (USA)) [1995 6d³ 6m Oct 13] 50,000Y: workmanlike colt: second foal: half-brother to 3-y-o South Sea Bubble (by Bustino): dam sprinter: third of 7 to Trafalgar Lady in maiden at Goodwood, bit squeezed for room over 1f out then tending to edge right: bandaged behind, mid-field in 21-runner maiden won by Projection at Newmarket following month: likely to do better. *J. H. M. Gosden* 67 p

MUHTADI (IRE) 2 br.c. (Apr 20) Marju (IRE) 127 – Moon Parade 73 (Welsh Pageant 132) [1995 7m 8m⁴ 8g 8m Oct 20] 70,000F: good-topped colt: sixth foal: half-brother to smart middle-distance stayer Rain Rider (by Fools Holme), Irish 12f and 13f winner Coronado (by Rainbow Quest) and a winner in Italy: dam 10.2f winner, is out of very smart middle-distance stayer Castle Keep and half-sister to Gold Cup winner Ragstone: stayed on well when around 6 lengths fourth of 8 to Moody's Cat in maiden at Ascot: spread 3 plates before running slightly below that form next time but well beaten in nursery at Doncaster on final outing: will stay at least 1¼m: looked a long-term prospect. *J. L. Dunlop* 76

MUHTARRAM (USA) 6 b.h. Alleged (USA) 138 – Ballet de France (USA) 101 (Northern Dancer) [1994 125: 10f* 9.3g² 10m* 12g² 10.4m² 10f³ 10g⁴ 10m³ 1995 8m⁵ 10m* 10m⁶ Jul 8] 124

Muhtarram finally takes his place at stud in 1996. He raced for five seasons, had twenty starts, won eight of them and was out of the frame in only four. Unbeaten in two races as a two-year-old, his subsequent wins included the Irish Champion Stakes as a four-year-old, Premio Presidente della Repubblica as a five-year-old, and Prince of Wales's Stakes as a five and six-year-old. He made the frame in the Derby, Prix d'Ispahan, Grand Prix de Saint-Cloud, International Stakes, Arlington Million

Prince of Wales's Stakes, Royal Ascot—
Muhtarram and Willie Carson find the gap for the second year running;
this time they deprive Eltish (near side) and Needle Gun

and Champion Stakes. In the latest season, Muhtarram joined Connaught and Mtoto as the only dual winners of the Prince of Wales's Stakes at Royal Ascot since the race was revived in 1968. Muhtarram's two victories came in very similar fashion, squeezing through the narrowest of gaps entering the final furlong and then just holding on; those denied in the photo-finish were Ezzoud and Chatoyant in 1994, Eltish in 1995. A most genuine individual, although connections were wary of him idling in front, Muhtarram was also a consistent one, something that is not apparent from his three races in the latest season. Injuries had their say almost throughout his long career and they explain his two disappointments in 1995: lame behind after the Lockinge Stakes at Newbury in May, things looked far more serious for a while when Muhtarram strained ligaments on his off-fore during the Eclipse at Sandown in July, but thankfully he has been able to take the retirement which he so richly deserved.

Muhtarram (USA) (b.h. 1989)	Alleged (USA) (b 1974)	Hoist The Flag (b 1968)	Tom Rolfe
			Wavy Navy
		Princess Pout (b 1966)	Prince John
			Determined Lady
	Ballet de France (USA) (b 1981)	Northern Dancer (b 1961)	Nearctic
			Natalma
		Fabulous Native (ch 1974)	Le Fabuleux
			Alyne Que

A sturdy, good-quartered, attractive horse who carried plenty of condition, Muhtarram has a short, quick action and was allowed to race only on a sound surface. He was effective at nine furlongs to a mile and a half. Details of his pedigree have been given in past Annuals. In summary, he is among the top half dozen racehorses by Alleged and his dam Ballet de France, a useful filly in Ireland who never raced beyond a mile, is a half-sister to the high-class middle-distance performer St Hilarion. Muhtarram will be standing at the Nunnery Stud, Norfolk, at a fee of £3,000 (live foal). *J. H. M. Gosden*

MUKABIR (USA) 2 b.c. (Mar 13) Dayjur (USA) 137 – Copper Creek 78 (Habitat 134) [1995 6m 6m Aug 26] $200,000F: well-made colt: has a round action: half-brother to 1992 2-y-o 6f and 7f winner Wathik (by Ogygian), 5f winner My Sovereign (by Sovereign Dancer) and a winner in USA: dam 6f winner from good family: well backed both starts, equipped with crossed noseband and tongue tied down when staying on steadily from mid-division behind My Mariam in maiden at Newmarket last time: headstrong: clearly thought to have ability but needs to become more tractable. *Major W. R. Hern* 71 +

MUKALLAD (IRE) 3 ch.c. Unfuwain (USA) 131 – Nouvelle Star (AUS) (Luskin Star (AUS)) [1994 NR 1995 8.1g^5 May 29] sixth foal: half-brother to 7f winner Sariah (by Kris): dam won from 5f to 8.2f in Australia and was champion older filly at 4 yrs: fifth of 12 in maiden at Chepstow: would have stayed beyond 1m: dead. *Major W. R. Hern* 62

MUKHATAB 3 b.c. Soviet Star (USA) 128 – Azyaa 101 (Kris 135) [1994 NR 1995 7.3m 8g* 8.2m^2 8m^2 8d Sep 24] strong colt: fourth foal: brother to useful 7f winner Ihtiraz and half-brother to 10.5f winner Shafi (by Reference Point): dam, 7.5f winner, is granddaughter of Milly Moss: fairly useful performer: won maiden at Yarmouth in June: good efforts in handicaps next 2 starts: stays 1m: acts on good to firm ground, possibly not on a soft surface: takes keen hold. *H. Thomson Jones* 86

MUKHLLES (USA) 2 b.c. (Feb 16) Diesis 133 – Serenely (USA) (Alydar (USA)) [1995 6g^5 Jul 14] $275,000Y: unfurnished colt: first foal: dam ran once: well-backed 9/2-shot, 6½ lengths fifth of 13 to Shaniko in maiden at Newbury, making effort 2f out then one pace not knocked about: unimpressive to post: will stay at least 7f: looked sure to improve. *Major W. R. Hern* 69 p

MUKTABAS (IRE) 3 b.c. Alzao (USA) 117 – Welsh Fantasy 104 (Welsh Pageant 132) [1994 78p: 6f* 1995 7f^2 8.2m* 7g^3 8m^5 Sep 25] lengthy colt: useful performer: won minor event at Nottingham in August: ran well next time, but never going well on final outing: stays 1m well: acts on firm ground: sent to Dubai. *J. H. M. Gosden* 97

MULCIBER 7 b.g. Head For Heights 125 – Quisissanno 76 (Be My Guest (USA) 126) [1994 61, a69+: a10g^4 10m^6 10m^3 10f^6 9g^2 a10g^6 1995 a10g^5 10g^6 10.2h^4 Jul 10] leggy gelding: modest handicapper: has form from 7.6f to 1½m: best on 64

equitrack, acts on good to firm ground, not on soft: twice blinkered (no improvement) at 4 yrs: has worn crossed noseband: usually held up: fairly useful hurdler, winner in August. *G. Harwood*

MULHOLLANDE LAD (IRE) 2 ch.g. (Feb 23) Mulhollande (USA) 107 – La Kumbha (FR) (Critique (USA) 126) [1995 5m 7g 7g^{4} a7g a8g Nov 24] IR 5,800Y, 2,000 2-y-o: small gelding: second foal: dam 1¼m and 10.5f winner in France, also winner over jumps: well beaten all starts. *M. C. Chapman* –

MULLAGH HILL LAD (IRE) 2 b.c. (Mar 15) Cyrano de Bergerac 120 – Fantasise (FR) (General Assembly (USA)) [1995 a5g^{6} 6f a6g 5m^{3} 6.1m^{4} a5g* a5g^{2} Dec 1] IR 1,600F: third foal: dipped-backed colt: half-brother to German 7f to 1m winner Key Largo Star (by Pennine Walk): dam second over 7f at 2 yrs in Ireland: ready winner of seller at Wolverhampton in November: ran very well when beaten neck in non-selling nursery at Southwell following month: has plenty of speed and best form at 5f: acts on on good to firm ground but goes particularly well on fibresand: sometimes tends to hang. *B. A. McMahon* 56 a73

MULLITOVER 5 ch.g. Interrex (CAN) – Atlantic Air (Air Trooper 115) [1994 67, a78: a8g^{5} a9.4g 7f^{5} 7d^{6} 7.1d^{6} 7g 7d 7s^{5} a7g* a8g^{6} a7g 1995 a8g^{4} a7g a7g^{2} 7f^{6} 7g^{4} 8.3m* 7m* 8.1m^{4} 7m* 7g^{5} 7m* Oct 14] close-coupled, workmanlike gelding: fairly useful handicapper: had a good year, winning at Windsor and Kempton in August, Lingfield in September and Newmarket in October: effective at 7f to 8.3f: acts on firm and soft going and the all-weather: usually races prominently. *M. J. Heaton-Ellis* 88

MULTI FRANCHISE 2 ch.g. (Mar 26) Gabitat 119 – Gabibti (IRE) 82 (Dara Monarch 128) [1995 5m 6m 6f^{3} a7g* 8m a6g a7g Dec 14] leggy gelding: first foal: dam effective from 5f to 7f: won seller at Wolverhampton in June: gelded and off course 2 months afterwards and failed to recapture form: stays 7f well: acts on firm ground and fibresand: visored third start, blinkered sixth (also blinkered when bolted third intended outing). *B. Gubby* 59 d

MUNAADEE (USA) 3 b.c. Green Dancer (USA) 132 – Aliysa 126 (Darshaan 133) [1994 60: 7m^{3} 1995 10.1g^{2} May 8] tall, good-topped colt: stepped up on debut form when 4 lengths second of 10 to Diaghilef in maiden at Newcastle: will stay 1½m: looked sure to improve again: sold 18,000 gns Doncaster October Sales. *E. A. L. Dunlop* 75

MUNAKEB (FR) 2 b.c. (Mar 7) Topsider (USA) – Antartica (FR) 124 (Arctic Tern (USA) 126) [1995 5f^{6} 6f* 6d 6m Oct 4] small, leggy colt: good walker: unimpressive mover: fourth foal: half-brother to 6f (at 2 yrs) to 1¼m winner Ribhi (by Riverman) and fair 1993 2-y-o 6f winner Kutbeya (by Diesis): dam 1m winner, stayed 1¼m: showed vastly improved form when making all on stand rail in maiden at Thirsk in August: failed to repeat that form in nurseries, tailed off at York final start: will stay beyond 6f: withdrawn at start intended debut: sold 12,500 gns Newmarket Autumn Sales. *R. W. Armstrong* 73

MUNCIE (IRE) 3 b.f. Sadler's Wells (USA) 132 – Martingale 103 (Luthier 126) [1994 NR 1995 10s* 10.5g* 10d* 10.5m^{5} 12d^{5} Sep 10] French-trained filly: tenth 116

Prix Saint-Alary, Longchamp—Muncie is clear;
Marble Falls (near side) beats Secret Quest for second

Daniel Wildenstein's "Muncie"

foal, easily best of previous 9 being smart French 1985 3-y-o 9f to 15.5f (Prix Royal-Oak) winner Mersey (by Crystal Palace): dam 1m winner: smart performer: won newcomers event and Prix Penelope (by 2 lengths from Loretta Gianni) at Saint-Cloud and 5-runner Prix Saint-Alary at Longchamp (by 4 lengths from Marble Falls), all in the spring: ran creditably when little over a length fifth to Carling in both Prix de Diane Hermes at Chantilly (reportedly sprained an ankle) in June and Prix Vermeille at Longchamp (stayed on from rear) in September: stays 1½m: acts on good to firm ground and soft. *A. Fabre, France*

MUNIF (IRE) 3 ch.c. Caerleon (USA) 132 – Forest Lair (Habitat 134) [1994 7d² 6g² 7d* 1995 7v⁴ 7v² 11m⁴ 11g* 12g* 12m⁴ 12m⁵ 14m* 12d 11m Oct 22] neat colt: 107

Tripleprint Derby Trial Stakes, Lingfield—Munwar at the peak of his season; it's early days yet for second-placed Riyadian (second right)

third foal: dam, Irish 2-y-o 1m winner who stayed 1¼m, is half-sister to Pampabird: useful handicapper: successful at the Curragh, Down Royal (IR £32,500 Ulster Harp Derby by a head) and Tralee (IR £16,400 event), all in the summer: well beaten in valuable race at Ascot on penultimate start: stays 1¾m: acts on good to firm and heavy ground: stays in training. *D. K. Weld, Ireland*

MUNKETH (USA) 2 b.c. (Apr 12) Red Ransom (USA) – Chewsy Suzy (USA) (Barachois (CAN)) [1995 6m 6.1m^{2} 7.5g^{3} 7.3m^{6} 8f* 8h 8g^{3} 8f Oct 18] $47,000F, $200,000Y: leggy, quite attractive colt: seventh reported foal: half-brother to 4 winners, including minor 6f stakes winner Fantastic Robber (by No Robbery): dam winning sprinter: comfortably won maiden at Brighton in August: good third to Vanishing Point in nursery at Pontefract penultimate start: stays 1m: acts on firm ground: headstrong, and sometimes finds little off bridle: sold 16,000 gns Newmarket Autumn Sales: sent to Norway. *J. L. Dunlop* — 80

MUNNASIB (FR) 5 ch.g. Highest Honor (FR) 124 – Parole Et Musique (USA) (Nureyev (USA) 131) [1994 NR 1995 a12g Feb 20] angular gelding: lightly raced and well beaten (for several trainers) since 1992. *P. M. McEntee* — –

MUNTAFI 4 b.g. Unfuwain (USA) 131 – Princess Sucree (USA) (Roberto (USA) 131) [1994 82?: 12g^{2} 12m* 14g^{6} 16.2m 16.1m 10g 1995 16m May 21] lengthy, angular gelding: lost his way at 3 yrs when trained by J. Dunlop: winning hurdler for new stable, but well beaten on return to flat: needs treating with caution. *G. Harwood* — –

MUNWAR 3 b.c. Kalaglow 132 – Oatfield 69 (Great Nephew 126) [1994 91P: 7g^{3} 8s* 1995 9m* 11.5f* 12f 12m 10m 9m^{5} Oct 13] tall, quite attractive colt: good mover: smart performer: won listed race at Newmarket (by 2½ lengths from Flemensfirth) and Tripleprint Derby Trial at Lingfield (by a head from Riyadian) in the spring: well below form in Derby, Irish Derby, Winter Hill Stakes at Windsor and listed race at Newmarket (visored) afterwards: stays 11.5f: acts on firm ground and soft: races prominently: to join P. Hayes in Australia. *P. T. Walwyn* — 113

MURAJJA (USA) 3 ch.c. Silver Hawk (USA) 123 – Halholah (USA) 65 (Secreto (USA) 128) [1994 94p: 6.1s* 7d* 1995 10.5m* 10m* 10.3m^{3} 12f Jun 23] rangy, good-topped colt: useful performer: won handicap at Haydock and 3-runner rated stakes at Ripon (easily made all) in April: very good third of 5 to Pentire in listed race at Chester in May, making most and rallying very well despite looking ill-at-ease on track: last of 8 in King Edward VII Stakes at Royal Ascot on only subsequent outing: should stay 1½m: has useful form on top-of-the-ground, but gave strong impression he was unsuited by firm going at Ascot: effective from front or held up: stays in training. *P. T. Walwyn* — 104

MURHEB 2 b.g. (Mar 8) Mtoto 134 – Masarrah 91 (Formidable (USA) 125) [1995 7m 7m^{2} Aug 25] good-bodied gelding: third foal: brother to poor maiden Ahsant Mtoto and half-brother to fairly useful 3-y-o 7f winner (including at 2 yrs) Shefoog (by Kefaah): dam 6f winner: sweating and edgy when 1¼ lengths second of 19 to Even Top in maiden at Newmarket, making much of running: stays 7f: will improve again, and is clearly capable of winning a race. *R. W. Armstrong* — 87 p

MURPHY'S GOLD (IRE) 4 ch.g. Salt Dome (USA) – Winter Harvest (Grundy 137) [1994 51: 10d 7.5m 6g 6m^{5} 6.9m* 9.9g^{4} 8g* 8f^{6} 8.1m 8m^{5} 7g^{5} 7s^{6} 1995 a8g 8m^{4} 8.5m^{2} 10m^{6} 8g^{4} 7.5m* 8m^{3} 8.5m* 7.9m^{2} 8.5m 7m 8.5d Sep 13] tall gelding: modest handicapper: won at Beverley in June and July: stays 8.5f well, not 1¼m: acts on firm ground, below form on soft: blinkered (well beaten) twice as 3-y-o: successful for a lady. *R. A. Fahey* — 63

MURPHYS WAY 6 br.m. Ardross 134 – Choir (High Top 131) [1994 NR 1995 a11g^{4} a12g^{2} a16g^{4} 16.2m^{6} 17.1m 21.6f^{6} 16.2m^{4} a14g Aug 4] big, lengthy mare: poor maiden handicapper: stays 16.2f: acts on dead ground, good to firm and fibresand: tried visored: has worn near-side pricker. *J. L. Eyre* — 38

MURRAY'S MAZDA (IRE) 6 ch.g. M Double M (USA) – Lamya 73 (Hittite Glory 125) [1994 65d: 6g^{5} 5d^{2} 5.9v^{2} 6f^{3} 6f^{2} 6g 5m 6g 6m 5m 5f^{2} 6f^{4} 6m 5s 6g 1995 5g^{4} 6f 5f 5m^{5} 5g^{6} 6m^{2} 6f^{4} 6m^{4} 5f 5g 7d^{2} 6m a7g^{5} Nov 13] leggy gelding: poor handicapper at best nowadays: stays 7f: seems to act on any going: well beaten in blinkers/visor: sometimes bandaged. *J. L. Eyre* — 48

MUSETTA (IRE) 3 b.f. Cadeaux Genereux 131 – Monaiya (Shareef Dancer (USA) 135) [1994 99: 7m^{5} 7m^{6} 6g^{2} 7s* 8g^{5} 1995 8m 10m* 10.4m^{3} 12m^{4} 12m^{3} 12g^{4} — 107

10.5f 12d 10g Sep 30] lengthy filly: useful performer: won listed race at Newmarket in May by ¾ length from Fanjica: in frame in Musidora Stakes at York, Oaks (5½ lengths fourth to Moonshell) at Epsom, Ribblesdale Stakes at Royal Ascot and Irish Oaks (over 10 lengths behind Pure Grain) at the Curragh: settled in preliminaries for a change but ran badly in Sun Chariot Stakes at Newmarket on final outing: stays 1½m: acts on soft ground and good to firm: tends to sweat and be rather edgy: often front runner. *C. E. Brittain*

MUSEUM (IRE) 4 b.g. Tate Gallery (USA) 117 – Go Anywhere (Grundy 137) [1994 84: 8g^2 9d^2 12.1s* 11.8m^4 12g^5 14m^4 12s 1995 12m^6 10.8g 10m 12g 9f 10f Oct 16] sparely-made gelding: fairly useful performer at 3 yrs: below his best in handicaps in 1995: sold out of H. Candy's stable 9,000 gns Newmarket July Sales after second start: stays 1¾m: acts on soft ground and good to firm. *D. Nicholls* –

MUSHAHADAH (IRE) 2 ch.f. (May 12) Ela-Mana-Mou 132 – Mashteen (USA) (Majestic Prince (USA)) [1995 7m Sep 5] lengthy filly: sister to 3-y-o Imlak and half-sister to several winners, including smart 1983 and 1984 2-y-o's Foulaad (by Raja Baba) and Cedilla (by Caro): dam smart stakes winner at 6f and 7f from excellent family: 20/1, broke near-fore in maiden at Leicester: dead. *D. Morley* –

MUSHAHID (USA) 2 b.c. (Apr 3) Wild Again (USA) – Playful Queen (USA) (Majestic Prince) [1995 6g* 6m^2 7m* 7f^4 8.1m^2 8g^2 8f^3 Oct 16] $80,000Y: big, well-made colt: has plenty of scope: good mover: half-brother to 11.7f winner Play Games (by Nijinsky): dam, 4-y-o 7f stakes winner, half-sister to several good winners, notably triple Grade 1 winner (from 1m to 1½m) Fit To Fight: useful colt: won maiden at Doncaster in May and minor event at Newcastle in June: ran well next 3 starts, 3½ lengths fourth of 6 to Alhaarth in Lanson Champagne Vintage Stakes at Goodwood then second to Bonarelli in minor event at Sandown and listed race at 99

Mr B. H. Voak's "Musetta"

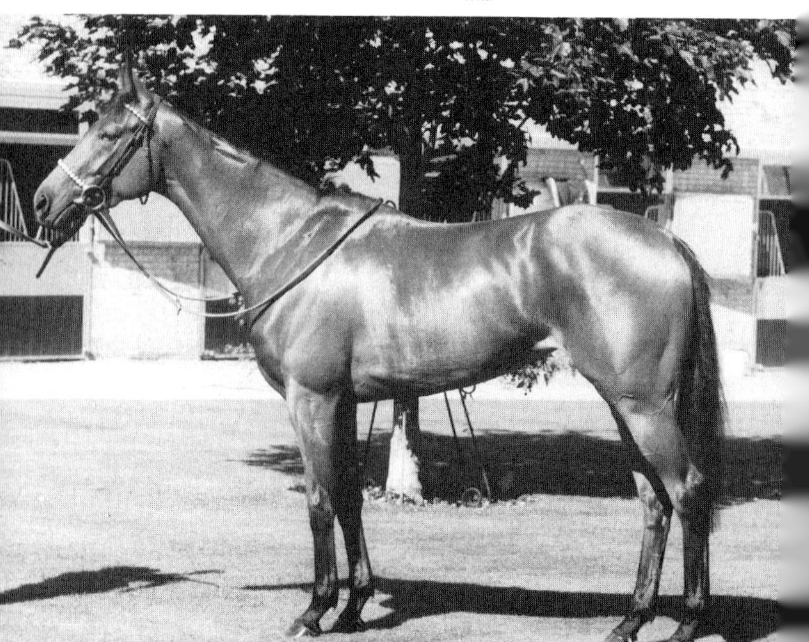

Goodwood: below form in listed race at Pontefract final outing: stays 1m: acts on firm going. *J. L. Dunlop*

MUSHTAK (USA) 2 b.c. (Feb 7) Topsider (USA) – Informatique (USA) (Quack (USA)) [1995 7m^4 8d 8.1s Oct 17] $135,000Y: smallish, sturdy colt: good mover: fifth foal: half-brother to fairly useful performers Sharp Imposter (winner at up to 15.5f in France, by Diesis) and Informatrice (1992 2-y-o 7f winner, by Trempolino): dam, second over 11f in France, half-sister to Grade 1 winners State Dinner (stayed 1½m) and Banquet Table (at 2 yrs): fourth of 11 to Masquerade in maiden at Leicester: soundly beaten afterwards in similar events at Newmarket and Chepstow (seemed all at sea on soft ground): sold only 1,800 gns Doncaster November Sales: sent to Sweden. *Major W. R. Hern* — 66 ?

MUSICA 3 ch.f. Primo Dominie 121 – Show Home 90 (Music Boy 124) [1994 67p: 5g^3 5g* 1995 5s^3 6m^6 5m^5 5m 5.3f* 5f 5f 5d^5 Sep 27] sturdy filly: fairly useful handicapper: won at Brighton in May: never going pace all 3 subsequent starts: stays 6f: acts on firm and soft going: visored fifth to seventh 3-y-o starts: sometimes early to post: none too consistent. *M. R. Channon* — 82

MUSICAL FANTASY (IRE) 3 b.f. Gallic League 119 – Trubbach (Vitiges (FR) 132) [1994 56: 6g 5.1g^4 6g 5.3g^6 a6g* a5g^3 a5g 1995 a5g^3 a6g^5 Feb 14] modest performer: tailed off on second and final 3-y-o start: sold (B. Meehan to W. G. M. Turner) 1,000 gns Ascot February Sales: stays 6f: acts on equitrack (hampered only outing on fibresand): races prominently: sold 480 gns Ascot July Sales. *B. J. Meehan* — 53

MUSICAL HEIGHTS (IRE) 2 b.f. (Mar 28) Roaring Riva 103 – Littleton Song 73 (Song 132) [1995 5g Oct 16] IR 1,400F, IR 1,200Y, 3,000 2-y-o: half-sister to several winners here and abroad, all by Elegant Air, including 13f winner Headless Heights and 1990 2-y-o 6f seller winner Shepherd's Song: dam 2-y-o 6f winner: 25/1, last of 11 in median auction maiden at Folkestone. *C. A. Dwyer* — –

MUSICAL MARCH 4 b.f. Daring March 116 – Musical Princess 66 (Cavo Doro 124) [1994 –: 7m^6 8f 6g 7.1m 1995 12f^6 8m 8f Jul 31] robust, good-bodied filly: little sign of ability. *E. Weymes* — –

MUSICAL SEASON 3 b.c. Merdon Melody 98 – Earles-Field (Wolverlife 115) [1994 91: 5d* 6m^3 5f^3 5.1g^2 5s^2 6g 5s* 1995 5m^6 6m^5 5m 6m^2 5.2m Aug 12] lengthy, quite attractive colt: keen walker: unimpressive mover: fairly useful handicapper: best efforts in 1995 when fifth of 15 in £39,000 race at York in June and second of 10 there in July: seemed to lose his action and finished tailed off on final outing: best form at 6f: acts on good to firm and soft ground. *T. D. Barron* — 92

MUSIC GOLD (IRE) 2 b. or br.c. (Apr 14) Taufan (USA) 119 – Nonnita 71 (Welsh Saint 126) [1995 5g^2 5s^2 5m* 5m^2 Nov 3] IR 16,000F, 15,000Y: leggy, close-coupled colt: brother to a winner in UAE and half-brother to 3 winners, including 3-y-o 1m and 8.5f winner Akil (by Cyrano de Bergerac): dam 6f winner: won 5-runner maiden at York in October by length from Songsheet: looking really well, excellent short-head second of 11 to Polly Golightly in nursery at Doncaster (early to post) following month: will probably stay 6f. *W. A. O'Gorman* — 91

MUSIC IN MOTION 2 b.f. (Apr 21) Batshoof 122 – Falaka 83 (Sparkler 130) [1995 6.9s Sep 27] fifth reported foal: half-sister to 7f and 1m winner Arctic Diamond (by Rambo Dancer) and 1992 2-y-o 6f winner Skullcap (by Sharrood): dam 7f and 1m winner: 33/1, showed nothing in maiden auction at Folkestone. *P. Howling* — –

MUSICK HOUSE (IRE) 2 b.c. (Feb 6) Sadler's Wells (USA) 132 – Hot Princess 101 (Hot Spark 126) [1995 6g^2 Aug 31] smallish, attractive colt: third known living foal: closely related to Rodrigo de Triano (by El Gran Senor) and half-brother to 1990 2-y-o 7f winner Cedrela (by Assert): dam Irish 5f to 7f winner, later won in USA: 5/1, beaten 1¼ lengths by Leonine in 5-runner maiden at York, soon well there after sluggish start then running on well though decisively held: will do better, particularly over 7f+, and looks a useful prospect. *P. W. Chapple-Hyam* — 96 p

MUSIC MAKER 3 b.f. Unfuwain (USA) 131 – Full Orchestra 83 (Shirley Heights 130) [1994 68p: 7m a7g^2 a8.5g* 1995 8m^3 a8g* a12g 10m* a8g 10m^2 10d^6 Sep 13] leggy filly: modest performer: won minor events at Lingfield in June and Nottingham (gamely) in July: stays 1¼m: acts on good to firm ground and the all-weather: sold 24,000 gns Newmarket Autumn Sales. *Sir Mark Prescott* — 61

MUSIC MISTRESS (IRE) 2 ch.f. (Mar 26) Classic Music (USA) – Blue Scholar 60 (Hotfoot 126) [1995 5f^5 5g^2 6m^3 5m* 5.7h^2 7.1m^4 6m^3 7d 6.1m Oct 26] IR 5,400Y, 7,000 2-y-o: smallish, rather unfurnished filly: half-sister to several maidens, including 4-y-o Irish sprinter My Trivet (by Thatching): dam won in Denmark: won seller at Lingfield in July: mostly ran creditably in nurseries and sellers after: stays 7f: acts on hard ground, possibly unsuited by dead. *R. Hannon* 55

MUSIC THEATRE 2 b.c. (Feb 11) Dancing Spree (USA) – Downshire (IRE) (Darshaan 133) [1995 a6g^3 a7g^2 Aug 5] first foal: dam ran once: sire won Breeders' Cup Sprint: placed in maidens at Wolverhampton: 4 lengths second of 11 to Double Diamond last time: should improve again: sent to Dubai. *Sir Mark Prescott* 75 p

MUSTAFFA (IRE) 2 ch.g. (Mar 23) Fayruz 116 – Crimson Sunset (Red Sunset 120) [1995 a5g^4 5m^2 a6g^3 6g^5 5.1m^6 Jun 12] IR 4,400F: leggy gelding: first foal: dam Irish 1¾m winner: plater: stays 6f: best form on top-of-the-ground. *M. R. Channon* 49 a41

MUSTANG 2 ch.c. (Jan 27) Thatching 131 – Lassoo 87 (Caerleon (USA) 132) [1995 7g 7d^4 Sep 27] first foal: dam, maiden, placed from 7f (at 2 yrs) to 11f, half-sister to very smart middle-distance colt Apache: modest form in maidens at Ayr and Newcastle, one-paced fourth of 11 to Insatiable last time, leading over 4f: will stay further than 7f. *C. W. Thornton* 62 p

MUSTN'T GRUMBLE (IRE) 5 b.g. Orchestra 118 – Gentle Heiress (Prince Tenderfoot (USA) 126) [1994 80: a7g a7g a6g* a6g^5 6g* a6g^3 6g^3 6m^2 6f^3 7m* 7.1g 7d 7g 8.1g a7g* a6g^2 a6g^2 1995 a7g 6m^5 a7g 7g^6 6g^6 a7g Sep 30] sturdy gelding: just a modest handicapper in 1995: stays 7f: probably acts on any going, including all-weather: often used to be blinkered, but is at least as effective without. *W. S. Cunningham* 64 a–

MUTABASSIM (IRE) 3 b.c. Green Desert (USA) 127 – Almarai (USA) 73 (Vaguely Noble 140) [1994 54p: 8g 7s^4 1995 6m^6 6m 7m^2 8.2m^4 7.6m^3 7m* 7m 7f^3 8g Nov 11] rangy colt: unimpressive mover: fair handicapper: won at Yarmouth in August: likely to prove best at up to 1m: acts on firm ground: has had tongue tied down: sometimes finds little and is one to have reservations about: sold out of A. Stewart's stable 18,000 gns Newmarket Autumn Sales and unplaced first outing for new connections. *R. Feligioni, Italy* 79

MUTADARRA (IRE) 2 ch.c. (Apr 2) Mujtahid (USA) 118 – Silver Echo (Caerleon (USA) 132) [1995 6m^2 Oct 13] IR 170,000Y: tall, angular, unfurnished colt: half-brother to useful Irish 1m (at 2 yrs) and 1¼m winner Artema (by Common Grounds) and 1992 2-y-o 7f winner Rapid Retreat (by Exactly Sharp), latter stayed 14.8f: dam unraced half-sister to Irish 2000 Guineas third Prince Echo: 5/2 favourite, short-head second of 21 to Projection in maiden at Newmarket, running on strongly and doing very well to come 4 lengths clear of remainder in last 200 yds: will stay beyond 6f: sure to improve, and win a race. *R. W. Armstrong* 89 p

MU-TADIL 3 gr.g. Be My Chief (USA) 122 – Inveraven 53 (Alias Smith (USA)) [1994 NR 1995 10g^5 13.4d Sep 20] 26,000Y: smallish, good-bodied gelding: fourth foal: half-brother to 4-y-o Demi-Plie (by Squill), 7f and 7.5f winner at 2 yrs, and a winner in Belgium by Celestial Storm: dam ran 3 times: fifth of 11 in maiden at Goodwood on debut, staying on strongly from rear: tailed off in similar event at Chester 11 days later: sold (W. R. Hern to R. Baker) 4,500 gns Newmarket Autumn Sales. *Major W. R. Hern* 73

MUTAHASSIN (USA) 2 b.c. (Mar 12) Dixieland Band (USA) – Katie Lynn (USA) (Star de Naskra (USA)) [1995 6.1d 6s^2 Sep 28] $120,000Y: strong, compact colt: second foal: dam minor winner at 2 yrs in USA: 5 lengths second to Norwegian Blue in 11-runner maiden at Lingfield, matching strides with winner 4f: sold 12,000 gns Newmarket Autumn Sales: sent to Sweden. *R. W. Armstrong* 68

MUTAKDDIM (USA) 4 ch.c. Seeking The Gold (USA) – Oscillate (USA) (Seattle Slew (USA)) [1994 112: 6m* 5.6m* 6f 6d^2 6m^4 7g* 7g^6 1995 8.1m^3 8m^4 7.1g* 7m 7d^2 7m^4 8g^3 Nov 12] rangy, attractive colt: has a quickish action: smart performer: won listed event at Haydock (by a neck from Carranita) in June: contested pattern events otherwise in 1995, short-headed by Inzar in steadily-run Supreme Stakes at Goodwood in September, and under a length behind demoted Neverneyev in Prix Perth at Saint-Cloud final start: effective at 6f to 1m: acts on good to firm and dead ground: held up/tracks leaders: to join J. Noseda in USA. *J. H. M. Gosden* 112

MUTAMANNI (USA) 2 b.c. (Mar 21) Caerleon (USA) 132 – Mathkurh (USA) 84 p 97 (Riverman (USA) 131) [1995 6s^2 6.1m^2 Oct 26] rather leggy colt: first foal: dam sprinting half-sister to useful 1988 6f 2-y-o winner Muhbubh: similar form when second to Midnight Blue in maiden at Ascot and Lay The Blame in minor event at Nottingham (odds on, beaten head in 10-runner race) in October: bred to stay further than 6f: acts on good to firm and soft ground: likely to do better. *H. Thomson Jones*

MUTAMMADDIN 3 b. or br.c. Polish Precedent (USA) 131 – Kadwah (USA) – 80 (Mr Prospector (USA)) [1994 NR 1995 12m Aug 5] rangy colt: first foal: dam lightly-raced 1m and 1¼m winner out of high-class American turf performer Castilla: bandaged behind and backward, very green and showed nothing in maiden at Newmarket: dead. *J. H. M. Gosden*

MUTAWALI (IRE) 5 ch.g. Exactly Sharp (USA) 121 – Ludovica (Bustino 136) – [1994 –: 11.6d 10.2s^5 10.8m^5 12.1f 1995 10m May 29] rather sparely-made gelding: disappointing middle-distance maiden: no worthwhile form on flat since 1993. *R. J. Baker*

MUTAZZ (USA) 3 b.c. Woodman (USA) 126 – Ghashtah (USA) (Nijinsky 69 (CAN) 138) [1994 62: 7.1d 7g 7s 1995 10g^4 12m^3 11.6m^2 14d^2 Jun 9] neat colt: has a round action: poor walker: fair maiden: stays 1¾m: acts on dead and good to firm ground, well beaten on soft: front runner: sold 18,500 gns Newmarket July Sales. *Major W. R. Hern*

MUTEE (IRE) 2 b.f. (Apr 22) Mujtahid (USA) 118 – Cum Laude 102 (Shareef – Dancer (USA) 135) [1995 a6g Dec 14] second foal: dam, 1¼m and 11.5f winner, half-sister to Procida (by Mr Prospector): 8/1, slowly away when tailed off in maiden at Lingfield. *M. Johnston*

MUTIARA 4 b.f. Never So Bold 135 – Hello Cuddles 99 (He Loves Me 120) – [1994 –: 5m a7g 1995 a12g Feb 9] leggy filly: showed modest ability only run at 2 yrs, none since. *Miss Gay Kelleway*

MUTINIQUE 4 br.f. General Wade 93 – Little Visitor (Tina's Pet 121) [1994 49, – a–: a7g^6 6s^2 6v^5 6d* 6m 7m^3 6m^2 6s^2 7d* 8.5m 7g^5 6g 6d^5 a8g a7g 1995 8m 7m a8.5g 8g^6 6g 6f 7f 7g^6 7d a7g a7g a10g a10g a12g Nov 30] small filly: poor performer at best: little form in 1995. *B. A. Pearce*

MUZRAK (CAN) 4 ch.c. Forty Niner (USA) – Linda North (USA) (Northern 55 Dancer) [1994 9s^6 10m^2 10m^2 12d^4 10m^4 9.6d 1995 9.9m 10m 8.5m 12g^3 13f^3 10f^5 12.1m^2 Jul 14] $225,000Y: angular ex-Irish colt: eighth foal: closely related to very smart U.S. 6f to (Grade 1 event) 9f winner Norquestor (by Conquistador Cielo) and a winner by Gone West and half-brother to 3 winners: dam minor stakes winner in Canada, half-sister to Turf Classic winner Noble Fighter: fair form (rated 76) at 3 yrs before sold out of K. Prendergast's stable 6,800 gns Newmarket Autumn (1994) Sales: modest maiden handicapper here: stays 13f: acts on firm ground: visored (carried head high) sixth start. *M. D. Hammond*

MUZZ (IRE) 4 br.g. Gallic League 119 – Cartier Bijoux 96 (Ahonoora 122) [1994 – 62, a67: a5g^4 a6g* 5g^2 5g^3 5d* 6g 5g 5d^6 5d^2 5m^3 5m 5m 5g 6d 5d a5g 1995 a5g 6g 6g 5g May 20] leggy, lengthy gelding: lost his form at 3 yrs, and showed nothing worthwhile in 1995: sold out of M. Johnston's stable 1,000 gns Doncaster February Sales after reappearance. *R. M. McKellar*

MY ABBEY 6 b.m. Hadeer 118 – Rose Barton (Pas de Seul 133) [1994 60: 5m 5f^2 60 5.1g^5 5g^4 5g^4 5g 1995 5g^6 5m* 5m 5f^6 5m^6 6m 5m 5.1m^3 5f^4 5g Sep 14] leggy, rather close-coupled mare: modest handicapper on her day: well drawn, best 6-y-o effort when winning 20-runner race at Thirsk in May: best form at 5f, should stay 6f: acts on firm ground, possibly not on a soft surface: visored (ran creditably) earlier in career: often early to post: inconsistent. *E. J. Alston*

MY ARCHIE 2 b.c. (Mar 26) Silver Arch – My Alma (IRE) 72 (Reasonable (FR) – 119) [1995 7d 8.1d^4 Oct 11] rather unfurnished colt: first foal: dam, sprinter, winner at 2 yrs: well behind throughout in maiden at Chester and 4-runner minor event at Haydock. *R. D. E. Woodhouse*

MYASHA (USA) 6 b.g. Imp Society (USA) – Mauna Loa (USA) (Hawaii) [1994 74 79: a5g* a5g^6 5m^4 5m* 5g^3 5d a6g^6 5g* 1995 a5g* 5m 6g^5 6g 5f^5 5g^3 a7.5g^6 a5g* 5v^2 a5g Dec 14] neat gelding: fair performer: won handicaps at Sterrebeek in March (amateurs) and October: best effort here in 1995 when seventh of 11 in handicap at

Shadwell Stud Firth of Clyde Stakes, Ayr—a much-improved filly in My Branch

Lingfield on second start: effective at 5f to 7f: acts on good to firm ground, dead and equitrack: below form blinkered: often bandaged behind. *Alex Vanderhaeghen, Belgium*

MY BEST VALENTINE 5 b.h. Try My Best (USA) 130 – Pas de Calais (Pas de Seul 133) [1994 89: 7d 7.6m 7f² 7m 7s 7m* 7f³ 7m 7.1g 7g⁶ 7d⁵ 1995 a8g 7m 6m⁴ 6f⁵ 6f 6m 7m 6m³ 6g Sep 16] compact horse: carries condition: fairly useful handicapper: poorly drawn, good third of 22 to No Extras in £14,900 event at Goodwood in August: effective at 6f, and stays 7.5f: acts on firm and dead ground, ran poorly on equitrack on reappearance: effective blinkered or not. *J. White* — 85

MY BONUS 5 b.m. Cyrano de Bergerac 120 – Dress In Spring 63 (Northfields (USA)) [1994 –: 7m a6g 1995 a5g Dec 19] leggy filly: fair sprint handicapper at 3 yrs: no form since. *D. J. S. Cosgrove* — –

MYBOTYE 2 br.c. (Feb 22) Rambo Dancer (CAN) 107 – Sigh 75 (Highland Melody 112) [1995 6g 5g* 6m* Aug 27] 2,000Y: sturdy, workmanlike colt: has a round action: fifth foal: half-brother to winning jumper Frankus and a winner in Hong Kong (both by Nicholas Bill): dam won at 1m: won maiden auction at Pontefract in June and nursery at Redcar (by ½ length from Shontaine, running on well after being held up in strongly-run race) 2½ months later: bred to stay 1m: likely to improve again. *G. R. Oldroyd* — 69 p

MY BOY JOSH 3 ch.g. Risk Me (FR) 127 – Merry Kate 69§ (Shirley Heights 130) [1994 NR 1995 8d 10m 10m a14.8g⁴ a12g² Jul 22] 2,200Y: sparely-made gelding: third foal: dam, maiden, best effort at 1½m: modest maiden handicapper: showed gradual improvement in 1995: probably stays 14.8f: acts on fibresand. *R. Guest* — 60

MY BRANCH 2 b.f. (May 21) Distant Relative 128 – Pay The Bank 81 (High Top 131) [1995 5.2g² 5m* 6m³ 6m² 6.5m* 6g* 6d² 7m³ Oct 13] leggy, attractive filly: second foal: dam 2-y-o 1m winner who stayed 1¼m: won maiden at Ripon in July: developed into a useful filly ridden for a turn of foot, winning 17-runner nursery at Doncaster and listed Shadwell Stud Firth of Clyde Stakes (by 2 lengths from Home Shopping) at Ayr before running Blue Duster to 2½ lengths in Cheveley Park Stakes at Newmarket: looked very well but ran lack-lustre race when 2¾ lengths third of 8 to Bint Salsabil in Rockfel Stakes at Newmarket on final outing: should stay at least 7f: acts on good to firm and dead ground. *B. W. Hills* — 106

MY BRAVE GIRL 3 b.f. Never So Bold 135 – Souadah (USA) (General Holme (USA) 128) [1994 NR 1995 7g^5 8.3m 8.3m 9.7s Sep 27] 10,500Y: tall, unfurnished filly: second foal: half-sister to 4-y-o 5f (at 2 yrs) to 7f winner Make The Break (by Dominion): dam unraced daughter of speedy Bitty Girl, dam also of smart Irish performer Beaudelaire and sister to Hot Spark: no worthwhile form: shaped as if should be suited by further than 1m: sold (H. Cecil to B. Richmond) 1,000 gns Doncaster November Sales. *H. R. A. Cecil* –

MY CADEAUX 3 ch.f. Cadeaux Genereux 131 – Jubilee Song 71 (Song 132) [1994 NR 1995 6m^2 6m* 6g Sep 1] 36,000Y: angular filly: poor mover: ninth living foal: half-sister to several winners, including very smart Prince Sabo (by Young Generation) and very useful 5-y-o Millyant (by Primo Dominie), both best at 5f: dam 5f winner: fair form: narrowly won maiden at Newmarket (wore down Dictation close home) in August: respectable seventh of 9 in minor event at Haydock 4 weeks later, tending to hang left: likely to prove best at sprint distances: has raced only on a sound surface. *R. Guest* 75

MY CHERRYWELL 5 br.m. Kirchner 110 – Cherrywood Blessin (Good Times (ITY)) [1994 52: 5g 5d 5d^2 5m 5m^2 5g^3 5m^5 5g^6 5d^2 5d^5 a5g^3 1995 a5g 5d* 5g 5g^2 a5g^2 a5g^5 5m^5 5m^3 5m a5g 5.1d a6g* a7g Dec 2] lengthy mare: modest handicapper: gained first victory at Edinburgh in March, and showed improved form to win at Southwell in November: stays 6f: acts on good to firm and dead ground and goes well on the all-weather: often bandaged behind: effective blinkered/visored or not. *L. R. Lloyd-James* 54 a60

MY DARLINGDAUGHTER 3 ch.f. Night Shift (USA) – Nicoletta 81 (Busted 134) [1994 NR 1995 10d Sep 13] 12,000F, 700,000 francs Y: useful-looking filly: sister to very smart 7f (at 2 yrs) and 1m winner 4-y-o Nicolotte, and half-sister to several winners, including fairly useful 7f (at 2 yrs) to 1½m winner Nickle Plated (by Auction Ring): dam 9f winner, is half-sister to Irish 1000 Guineas winner Favoletta and dam of Teenoso: moved well to post but showed little in race when well beaten in maiden at Sandown. *R. Charlton* –

MY DUTCH GIRL 3 b.f. Midyan (USA) 124 – Double Dutch 100 (Nicholas Bill 125) [1994 47: 6g 7.1m 7m^6 1995 12s 12s Sep 27] small filly: poor form in maidens at 2 yrs: stiff tasks, soundly beaten in 1995: should stay at least 1¼m. *Miss B. Sanders* –

MY EMMA 2 b.f. (Mar 19) Marju (IRE) 127 – Pato 90 (High Top 131) [1995 7g Oct 9] workmanlike filly: fifth foal: half-sister to several winners, notably St Leger winner Classic Cliche (by Salse): dam, 7f (at 2 yrs) and 1¼m winner, sister to smart sprinter Crews Hill: 14/1 and bit backward, just over 7 lengths seventh of 18, slowly away, to Fairlight Down in maiden at Leicester: moved fluently to post: will do better. *R. Guest* 63 p

MY FIORE 4 b.f. Midyan (USA) 124 – My Tootsie 88 (Tap On Wood 130) [1994 –: a12g^5 9.9g 1995 10m May 26] angular, close-coupled filly: no sign of ability: has joined A. Forte. *P. J. Bevan* –

MY FIRST ROMANCE 3 b.f. Danehill (USA) 126 – Front Line Romance 89 (Caerleon (USA) 132) [1994 –: 6g 1995 7m^6 May 5] unfurnished filly: 33/1 and burly, better effort in maidens when close sixth of 8 at Newmarket on only 3-y-o start, leading until about 2f out: sold 20,000 gns Newmarket July Sales. *M. A. Jarvis* 61

MYFONTAINE 8 b.h. Persepolis (FR) 127 – Mortefontaine (FR) (Polic 126) [1994 60: 10.8v* 8d* 8d 11.6d 10.1f^3 8.3m^5 10m^2 10f^2 10m^4 9d^6 10.8s 1995 10.8d 10m 9.2g^5 10.8g* 10.8g* 10.8g* 10g^4 12.3m^5 11.6m^6 10g^2 10.1g^2 10d Sep 26] leggy horse: fair handicapper: won 3 times in space of 16 days at Warwick in the spring, taking tally of course successes there to seven: effective at 1m to 10.8f: acts on any going: has hung left. *K. T. Ivory* 68

MY FOXY LADY 5 b.m. Jalmood (USA) 126 – La Petite Noblesse 105 (Thatching 131) [1994 –: 5.7g a5s 1995 a5g a6g a8g^6 Feb 3] leggy mare: has stringhalt: poor handicapper: no form for a long time. *J. A. Harris* –

MY GALLERY (IRE) 4 ch.f. Tate Gallery (USA) 117 – Sententious (Kautokeino (FR)) [1994 56: 6g 5m 7g^4 7.1d 7.1s^3 7g 8.2d a8g 1995 9g a8.5g^3 a7g^5 a6g^3 8f^2 a7g* a7g* 6m 7.6m a7g^5 a6g 7g^5 a7g a6g^6 Nov 20] angular filly: fair performer on the all-weather: won claimer and minor event at Wolverhampton in July: modest on turf: effective at 6f, and stays 8.5f: acts on firm and soft ground and 57 d a68 d on fibresand: tried blinkered: has run well when sweating: sold 7,200 gns Newmarket December Sales. *A. Bailey*

MY GINA 3 ch.f. Be My Chief (USA) 122 – Ginny Binny 113 (Ahonoora 122) [1994 NR 1995 8.1g^{4} 8g^{2} 8f* 8m 8g^{5} 8g^{4} 9.2g* Sep 24] 6,800F: workmanlike filly: third foal: dam Italian 6f winner at 2 and 3 yrs: fairly useful performer: won maiden at Ripon in June and handicap at Hamilton in September: should stay 1¼m: has raced only on a sound surface. *M. R. Stoute* — 83

MY GODSON 5 br.g. Valiyar 129 – Blessit 79 (So Blessed 130) [1994 51, a–: 6g^{5} 5d 5m 5m 6d^{5} 6d^{3} 7f^{2} a6g 8m^{5} 8m 8f^{2} a7g 8.1g 8d 1995 7.1g 6g^{6} 6.9f^{4} 7m 8g^{5} 7m 8m 8g^{2} 7d a8g Nov 20] sturdy gelding: has a round action: poor performer: stays 1m: acts on firm and soft ground, below form on fibresand: effective blinkered/visored or not: sweating profusely (finished last) on reappearance: usually races prominently. *F. J. O'Mahony* — 45 a–

MY HANDSOME PRINCE 3 b.g. Handsome Sailor 125 – My Serenade (USA) 45 (Sensitive Prince (USA)) [1994 –: 5m a7g 5.1g 6m 8m 10g 1995 8m^{3} 8m^{2} 8.2m^{5} 8f 8.5g 8m^{5} Aug 19] useful-looking gelding: poor maiden: well beaten last 3 starts, mulish to post on final one: stays 1m: acts on good to firm ground: blinkered (no form) once at 2 yrs. *P. J. Bevan* — 40

MY HANDY MAN 4 ch.g. Out of Hand 84 – My Home 61 (Homing 130) [1994 58: 7g 8.2m^{3} 8m 8s 8m 9g 1995 a11g^{2} a12g 8m 9.2g^{2} 8g 8g 8.3f 8.3f^{2} 8.1f^{5} 12m 8f Oct 24] lengthy gelding: poor mover: modest maiden handicapper: stays 11f: acts on firm ground and fibresand: sold 3,000 gns Doncaster November Sales. *R. Allan* — 56

MY IRISH 5 b.h. Assert 134 – Cremets 94 (Mummy's Pet 125) [1994 11g^{6} 11s^{4} 10.5g 10s^{2} 15m 11g^{2} 12g^{6} 10v* 11d^{5} 11v* 10v^{6} 9v^{2} 11.3s* 11.3s^{3} 1995 12m^{3} 10d 12d* 12s^{2} 12f* 11d^{6} 12s* 15d* 14.5d^{3} 14g^{5} 10.2d^{5} Dec 26] first foal to race: dam 6f (at 2 yrs) and 7f winner, sister to Runnett: smart Italian horse: successful twice at 2 yrs (over 7.5f) and three times each at 3 yrs and 4 yrs between 1¼m and 1½m, mainly in minor events: better than ever at 5 yrs, winning 2 minor events, a handicap and a listed race (beat Khamaseen 1¾ lengths), all at Milan: respectable 3¼ lengths third of 5 to Assessor in St Leger Italiano at Turin: below form afterwards: stays 15f: acts on any going. *M. Ciciarelli, Italy* — 111

MY JAZZMYN 3 b.f. Chief Singer 131 – Azaiyma 58 (Corvaro (USA) 124) [1994 NR 1995 7m 8.1d Oct 10] first foal: dam placed at up to 1½m: tailed off in maiden and seller. *D. C. O'Brien* — –

MYJINKA 5 gr.m. Myjinski (USA) – Royal Bat 69 (Crowned Prince (USA) 128) [1994 28: a7g^{4} a7g 8g 11.9f 5m 6g^{6} 7m 7f^{2} 8d^{6} 7s^{4} a7g a7g a7g^{5} 1995 a6g* a8g a7g^{4} a6g^{3} a8g^{2} a6g* a8g 8f 8m 7m^{4} 6m 7.6m^{4} 10g a7g a6g* a7g^{2} Dec 14] modest handicapper: best on the all-weather, and won at Lingfield in January, February and November: effective at 6f, and stays 1m: acts on firm and dead ground and goes well on equitrack: usually blinkered: suitable mount for apprentice. *J. O'Donoghue* — 23 a56

MY KERRY DANCER (USA) 5 ch.g. Seattle Dancer (USA) 119 – Mumble Peg (General Assembly (USA)) [1994 NR 1995 10.9m 15f^{2} Jun 24] $10,000Y: ex-Irish gelding: third foal: half-brother to 2 winners, including 1¼m winner Halley (by Star de Naskra): dam unraced half-sister to high class Little Bonny and smart Noelino: ran 11 times at 3 yrs in Ireland (rated 84), winning minor event at Punchestown and handicap at Naas, both over 11f: won juvenile hurdle when still with P. Mullins but subsequently fractured a cannon bone: showed fair form for present stable in 2 runs over hurdles late in 1994: modest form at best on flat at 5 yrs: stays 15f: probably acts on any going. *J. J. O'Neill* — 58

MY KIND 2 ch.f. (Apr 19) Mon Tresor 113 – Kind of Shy 61 (Kind of Hush 118) [1995 6g* 6m^{2} 6m^{5} 6m^{2} 6f^{5} 6d 7d^{4} 8f a8.5g Oct 28] unfurnished filly: second foal: half-sister to 3-y-o Lady Pui (by Puissance), 5f winner at 2 yrs: dam, plater, stayed 1m: won seller at Thirsk in June: visored, creditable fourth in non-selling nursery at Brighton in September, easily best of last 5 starts: stays 7f (well beaten over 1m): acts on good to firm and dead ground: blinkered final outing: has been bandaged. *K. McAuliffe* — 59

MY LADY BRADY 3 b.f. Risk Me (FR) 127 – Miss Mischievous 66 (Star Appeal 133) [1994 67: 5m^{2} a5g^{2} 5g^{6} 6m a5g* 5.2m 1995 a5g 5m^{4} 5.1m^{4} a5g 5.1m Jun 2] leggy, lengthy filly: poor mover: poor form at best in 1995, trained first 3 starts — 46 by G. Oldroyd: likely to prove best at 5f: acts on good to firm ground and fibresand: races prominently. *M. Brittain*

MY LEARNED FRIEND 4 b. or br.g. Broken Hearted 124 – Circe 73 (Main Reef 126) [1994 70+: 8m 8g^2 9m* 8m 10.5g 1995 10m^3 10.5g* 10f* 10m^3 12m* 12g^6 12m Oct 21] workmanlike gelding: progressed into a fairly useful handicapper, winning at Haydock and Goodwood (both narrowly) in June and at Newbury (not clear run, squeezed through) in August: effective at 1¼m but better suited by 1½m: has raced only on a sound surface: held up. *A. Hide* 88

MY LEWICIA (IRE) 2 b.f. (Apr 12) Taufan (USA) 119 – Christine Daae 74 (Sadler's Wells (USA) 132) [1995 7g Sep 13] second foal: half-sister to 3-y-o To The Roof (by Thatching): dam, stayed 1¼m, half-sister to very useful 1981 2-y-o sprinter Travel On out of sister to Red Alert: 50/1, fourteenth of 19 to Shawanni, soon behind and never on terms, in maiden at Yarmouth: will improve. *P. W. Harris* – p

MY LIFETIME LADY (IRE) 4 ch.f. Indian Ridge 123 – Liffey Reef 77 (Main Reef 126) [1994 59d: 6d^5 6.1m 6.1f 8m 5m 5g^5 6m^6 7d 5g 5.1d 1995 a6g a8g^6 a8g a8g a10g^6 8m 9.2g May 5] smallish, leggy filly: poor performer at best in 1995: stays 6f: probably acts on any ground: blinkered (well beaten) third 4-y-o start: quite often bandaged behind: inconsistent. *K. T. Ivory* 36

MY LINDIANNE 8 gr.m. Alias Smith (USA) – Lindrick Passion (Silly Season 127) [1994 –: 10g 1995 8m May 21] plain mare: little form on flat. *J. Dooler* –

MY MARIAM 2 ch.f. (Mar 24) Salse (USA) 128 – Birch Creek (Carwhite 127) [1995 6m* 6g^4 7d 6d Oct 21] 17,000Y: sturdy filly: sixth foal: half-sister to 7f (at 2 yrs) and 1¼m winner Final Deed (by Final Straw) and 8.9f and 1½m winner Crackling (by Electric): dam French maiden placed in pattern company at 1m Italy: fair form: won maiden at Newmarket in August: respectable efforts in nurseries last 2 starts: will be suited by further than 7f. *C. R. Egerton* 79

MY MELODY PARKES 2 b.f. (Feb 12) Teenoso (USA) 135 – Summerhill Spruce 70 (Windjammer (USA)) [1995 5g* 5m^6 5m^3 6m^2 7g^3 6g^4 Sep 15] lengthy, useful-looking filly, shade unfurnished: fourth living foal: half-sister to winning sprinters Bella Parkes (by Tina's Pet) and useful 5-y-o Lucky Parkes (by Full Extent) and a winner abroad by Jupiter Island: dam 6f winner: won maiden at Newcastle in April: useful efforts when placed behind Blue Duster in Queen Mary Stakes at Ascot, Dance Sequence in Lowther Stakes at York then (1¼ lengths third) Priory Belle in Moyglare Stud Stakes at the Curragh: seemed to run below best in listed race at Ayr on final outing but set strong pace from unfavoured draw: stays 7f. *J. Berry* 102

MY MILLIE 2 ch.f. (Mar 26) Midyan (USA) 124 – Madam Millie 99 (Milford 119) [1995 5m^4 5g 7g Oct 9] 9,000Y: tall, lengthy, lightly-made filly: second reported foal: half-sister to 1½m winner Millie's Dream (by Petoski): dam sprinter: fourth of 8 to Clincher Club in maiden at Pontefract: no chance from bad draw in auction event at Sandown then mid-division in 7f maiden at Leicester, bumped when begining to weaken 2f out: tail flasher. *R. Boss* 55

MY MINNIE 5 b.m. Kind of Hush 118 – Miami Mouse (Miami Springs 121) [1994 58: 7.3s 8.3m 10.2m^3 10.2f^6 8.3f^5 8g 8.1g a8g^2 a7g a10g^5 1995 a10g^3 a10g^2 a12g^3 a10g^6 a9.4g^3 a11g* a9.4g* a12g Apr 26] sturdy, plain mare: fair handicapper: won at Southwell and Wolverhampton (made all in very good style), both in April: should stay 1½m: acts on good to firm and dead ground and on all-weather surfaces: blinkered (no improvement) twice as 4-y-o. *B. J. Meehan* 67

MY MOTHER'S LOCAL (USA) 2 b.f. (May 2) Local Talent (USA) 122 – My Mother's Eyes (FR) (Saint Cyrien (FR) 128) [1995 7m a7g a7g Dec 15] 6,600F, 5,000Y: leggy filly: second foal: sister to useful French 3-y-o 1m winner (stays 1¼m) Tarte Aux Pommes: dam maiden from good French family: well beaten in maidens at Doncaster and Lingfield (2). *K. O. Cunningham-Brown* –

MY MUM SAID 3 ch.f. Formidable (USA) 125 – Moorland Lady 74 (Swing Easy (USA) 126) [1994 66: 7m 7d 8s^4 1995 9.7m 12.5f May 8] lengthy filly: fair performer at 2 yrs: well beaten in 1995: stays 1m: blinkered (took little interest from halfway) final start: has joined P. Luckin. *Lady Herries* –

MY ROSSINI 6 b.g. Ardross 134 – My Tootsie 88 (Tap On Wood 130) [1994 56: a16.2g a12g^4 12.3m 16.5m^4 14.1m* 14.9m^6 14.1g 14.1m 14s* 1995 14s^3 Sep 30] workmanlike gelding: modest handicapper: ran creditably only 6-y-o start: stays 2m: 52

acts on good to firm and soft going: often makes the running: wears sliding bar bit: fairly useful hurdler. *P. J. Bevan*

MYRTLE 2 b.f. (Feb 28) Batshoof 122 – Greek Goddess 82 (Young Generation 129) [1995 6g 6.9g² 6g³ 7m³ 7.5m* 8g⁵ Sep 7] strong, compact filly: has a fluent, round action: third foal: half-sister to 1993 2-y-o 6f winner Grecian Garden (by Sharrood): dam should have stayed beyond 6f: won maiden at Beverley in August: much improved effort when just over 4 lengths fifth of 11 to Solar Crystal in May Hill Stakes at Doncaster 2 weeks later, staying on steadily: stays 1m. *R. Hannon* 96

MYRTLE QUEST 3 b.c. Rainbow Quest (USA) 134 – Wryneck 89 (Niniski (USA) 125) [1994 81p: 7m 8s⁴ 8.2g* 1995 8m⁶ 10.4m⁵ 8m 10g⁴ Jul 12] lengthy, good-topped gelding: unimpressive mover: fairly useful handicapper: stays 1¼m: acts on good to firm and soft ground: swished tail repeatedly in paddock (ran well) third 3-y-o start: stays in training. *R. Charlton* 86

MYSELF 3 ch.f. Nashwan (USA) 135 – Pushy 112 (Sharpen Up 127) [1994 108: 6g* 5m² 6m³ 7g² 6m⁵ 1995 7m* 8m 8m 7g⁴ 7d³ 7m Oct 15] smallish, angular, good-quartered filly: good walker: easy mover: smart performer: won Shadwell Stud Nell Gwyn Stakes at Newmarket (beat Epagris 2½ lengths) in April, but never threatened in 1000 Guineas and Coronation Stakes next 2 outings: third in steadily-run Supreme Stakes (didn't get best of runs, beaten ¾ length by Inzar) at Goodwood: tailed off in Prix de la Foret at Longchamp on final start: likely to stay beyond 1m: acts on good to firm ground and dead: flashes tail: wears bandages. *P. W. Chapple-Hyam* 110

MY SILVERSMITH (IRE) 4 b.f. Cyrano de Bergerac 120 – Golden Tears (Rheingold 137) [1994 –: 5m 8.1m⁶ 7g 1995 5g May 20] of no account. *P. Monteith* –

MYSTERIOUS TIMES 2 b.f. (Apr 2) Timeless Times (USA) 99 – Misty Rocket 75 (Roan Rocket 128) [1995 5m⁴ 5g a5g⁵ 6m 6m 7d⁶ 7.9m 8f Oct 16] 1,500Y: smallish, sturdy filly: fifth foal: dam won sellers at 1¼m and 1½m: signs of ability: trained by M. W. Easterby first 3 starts: blinkered penultimate start. *B. W. Murray* –

MYSTERY MATTHIAS 2 b.f. (Mar 11) Nicholas (USA) 111 – Devils Dirge 68 (Song 132) [1995 5m⁶ 5m⁶ 5g⁴ 6f⁵ 5g 7d⁶ a8g a8g⁵ Nov 14] workmanlike filly: first live foal: dam maiden who probably stayed 7f: modest maiden: ran too freely in blinkers final outing: will prove best at up to 7f. *Miss B. Sanders* 56 a51 +

MYSTIC DAWN 2 b.f. (Apr 10) Aragon 118 – Ahonita 90 (Ahonoora 122) [1995 5m 5g⁶ 6m 6d 8f Oct 18] fourth foal: half-sister to 1½m/1¾m winner Special Risk (by Simply Great): dam best at 5f (won at 2 yrs) and is out of a good 1¼m winner in Italy: modest form: trained by R. Boss on debut: probably stays 1m: may well be unsuited by a soft surface: carried head awkwardly third start. *S. Dow* 47

Shadwell Stud Nell Gwyn Stakes, Newmarket—
Myself (left) thoroughly upstages market leaders Epagris (right) and Red Carnival (centre)

MYSTIC HILL 4 b.g. Shirley Heights 130 – Nuryana 107 (Nureyev (USA) 131) [1994 90: 10.2g 10.4m* 12s* 12f^{4} 11.9m 12f^{3} 1995 10.1f^{3} 12m 12f^{3} 12m* 12d 10v Oct 7] rather leggy, useful-looking gelding: good walker and mover: fairly useful handicapper: won rated stakes at Kempton in August: effective at 1¼m to 1½m: acts on firm and soft ground: wears crossed noseband: held up and often set plenty to do: sold (R. Charlton to G. Harwood) 28,000 gns Newmarket Autumn Sales. *R. Charlton* — 91

MYSTIC KNIGHT 2 b.c. (Feb 6) Caerleon (USA) 132 – Nuryana 107 (Nureyev (USA) 131) [1995 7f^{6} 7.6d^{3} 8d* 8m* Oct 13] good sort: has scope: fourth foal: half-brother to fairly useful 4-y-o middle-distance winner Mystic Hill (by Shirley Heights) and 2 other winners, including 1991 2-y-o 8.1f winner Mystic Park (by Rainbow Quest): dam 1m winner out of half-sister to 1000 Guineas winner On The House: won maiden at Salisbury in September by 1¾ lengths from Decision Maker: followed up in 12-runner nursery at Newmarket in October, beating Magic Lake comfortably by a length, first 3 well clear: will stay middle distances: very much type to continue improving. *R. Charlton* — 93 p

MYSTIC LURE 3 b.f. Green Desert (USA) 127 – Splendid Girl (USA) (Golden Eagle (FR)) [1994 70: 5m^{2} 5f^{2} 6g^{2} 1995 7m^{4} 6m 7f^{4} Jul 29] sturdy filly: fair maiden: likely to prove best at up to 7f: has raced only on a sound surface: wears bandages behind: sold to race in USA. *E. A. L. Dunlop* — 70

MYSTIC MEMORY 6 b. or br.m. Ela-Mana-Mou 132 – Mountain Memory 109 (High Top 131) [1994 74: 12.4m 14.1m^{3} 15.1f* 12m^{2} 16.2g^{2} 15.8m^{2} 16.2m^{4} 14.6d^{3} 1995 17.1m Apr 25] quite good-topped mare: fair staying handicapper at 5 yrs: fit from hurdling, soundly beaten only outing in 1995. *Mrs M. Reveley* — –

MYSTIC TEMPO (USA) 2 ch.f. (Apr 25) El Gran Senor (USA) 136 – Doubling Time (USA) 117 (Timeless Moment (USA)) [1995 5f^{2} 6g* 6g^{3} 6f 6.1s^{5} a5g Nov 2] small filly: half-sister to several animals, easily best being useful 1m winner Timely (by Kings Lake): dam, suited by 1¼m, half-sister to Faraway Son and Liloy: won maiden at Pontefract in June: off course 3½ months after running poorly fourth start, creditable effort on return: better suited by 6f than 5f: possibly unsuited by very firm ground: sold 4,000 gns Newmarket December Sales, and has joined Dr J. D. Scargill. *P. W. Chapple-Hyam* — 76

MYSTICTICH 3 b.f. Germont – Bauhinia 70 (Sagaro 133) [1994 NR 1995 a8g a9.4g Nov 27] half-sister to several winners here and abroad, including fairly useful sprinter Sylvan Mistral (by Aragon): dam lightly raced: last in claimers at Southwell and Wolverhampton. *G. Barnett* — –

MYSTIC TIMES 2 b.f. (May 10) Timeless Times (USA) 99 – Chikala 81 (Pitskelly 122) [1995 5m^{4} 5g 6m^{5} 6f^{2} 6m 6m* 6.1d Sep 11] small, sparely-made filly: half-sister to 3-y-o 5f and 6f winner Brecongill Lad (by Clantime) and a winner in Italy by Uncle Pokey: dam 2-y-o 5f winner: won seller at Ripon in August: stays 6f: has been bandaged behind: sold 1,500 gns Doncaster November Sales: has joined Miss J. F. Craze. *Miss S. E. Hall* — 53

MYSTIQUE SMILE 2 ch.f. (Mar 21) Music Boy 124 – Jay Gee Ell 78 (Vaigly Great 127) [1995 5m^{3} 5m^{4} 5.1m* 5.5m 5.2g 5g^{4} 5g 5m Oct 13] 7,000Y: leggy, useful-looking filly: good mover: fourth foal: half-sister to 3-y-o 5f and 6f winner We're Joken (by Statoblest): dam 2-y-o 5f and 6f winner later suited by around 1¼m: won maiden at Chester in May by 4 lengths from Branston Danni: kept useful company next 2 starts but became disappointing, soundly beaten in nursery at Catterick final outing: has raced only at 5f: best form on good to firm ground: sold 5,000 gns Doncaster November Sales. *J. Berry* — 78 d

MYSTOSKI 3 b.f. Petoski 135 – Miss Adventure 69 (Adonijah 126) [1994 –: 7g a7g 1995 8f a12g 14.1m^{6} Aug 12] angular filly: poor maiden. *M. H. Tompkins* — 35

MYTTONS MISTAKE 2 b.g. (Feb 12) Rambo Dancer (CAN) 107 – Hi-Hunsley 82 (Swing Easy (USA) 126) [1995 7f* 5m* 6.1g^{4} 6m 6g 6g a7g^{3} Dec 12] 8,000Y: sixth foal: brother to 1994 2-y-o 5f winner Sly Dancer: dam sprinting sister to very useful sprinter Swinging Sam: won maiden at Ayr in June and minor event at Beverley (by a neck from Desert Tiger) in July: below best in nurseries last 4 starts: stays 7f: yet to race on a soft surface: blinkered (below best) penultimate start. *A. Bailey* — 79

MY WEST END GIRL 2 b.f. (May 26) Dunbeath (USA) 127 – Carnfield 42 – (Anfield 117) [1995 a6g Nov 20] first reported foal: dam maiden effective at up to 1m: 33/1, last of 14 in maiden at Southwell. *A. Streeter*

N

NAAWY 5 b.g. Reference Point 139 – Strike Home 82 (Be My Guest (USA) 126) 38 [1994 53d: 14.1d 15.8g^2 14.1m^2 17.2f^3 16g^3 16.2m^5 a14g 15.8g^3 14.1m 15.8g 18s 15.1g a14g 1995 14.1g 15.8g^2 16m^4 16m Jun 26] sturdy, lengthy gelding: bad mover: only poor maiden at best in 1995: sold (C. Smith to Miss S. Horner) 2,200 gns Doncaster August Sales: stays 17.1f: probably acts on any going: visored (out of form) last 2 starts at 4 yrs: sometimes wears bandages: is sometimes a front runner. *C. Smith*

NABHAAN (IRE) 2 b.c. (Apr 17) In The Wings 128 – Miss Gris (USA) 120 (Hail 74 + The Pirates (USA) 126) [1995 7f^6 7.5m^4 8g* 8g 8f Oct 18] big, strong, close-coupled colt: has scope: fourth foal: half-brother to fair 13.6f winner Elflaa (by Sure Blade), also successful over hurdles, and a winner in Italy by Wassl: dam won Italian 1000 Guineas and Oaks: won 5-runner maiden at Thirsk in September by 12 lengths from Arc of The Diver: no comparable form in nurseries: will stay at least 1¼m: coltish on debut. *D. Morley*

NABJELSEDR 5 b.g. Never So Bold 135 – Klewraye (Lord Gayle (USA) 124) 43 [1994 NR 1995 7d 7g 7g 8g Jun 3] leggy gelding: unimpressive mover: fair form (rated 76) for C. Benstead, lightly raced, in 1993: only poor at best on return: probably stays 1m: may be suited by a soft surface: sometimes bandaged behind. *A. G. Newcombe*

NADOR 2 ch.c. (Mar 20) Rainbow Quest (USA) 134 – Nadma (USA) 82 83 (Northern Dancer) [1995 7d* 7.3d Oct 19] angular colt: good walker: first foal: dam, 1¼m winner here and (at 4 yrs) in Italy, closely related to top-class American filly Sabin and half-sister to Fatah Flare: won maiden at Brighton by 3 lengths from Threesome, headway over 2f out, soon leading and never in danger last 1f: lost several lengths at start when last of 9 in Horris Hill Stakes at Newbury in October, weakening having got back into contention in steadily-run race: will stay 1¼m+. *D. R. Loder*

NADWATY (IRE) 3 b.f. Prince Sabo 123 – Faisalah (Gay Mecene (USA) 128) 59 d [1994 59: 5m^6 5d 6g^4 5g^3 6m 5m^2 6s 5.2g^2 a5g^3 a5g 1995 a6g^3 a6g^3 a6g a5g* 5g^3 a5g 5g^3 a5g 6g^5 6m a5g^5 5g 5f a6g Dec 1] workmanlike filly: modest performer on her day, blinkered first time, made all in seller (bought out of J. Bethell's stable 4,200 gns) at Southwell in March: mostly below form afterwards, including in blinkers: very best efforts at 5f: acts on fibresand, best turf form on a sound surface: usually front runner. *M. C. Chapman*

NAFTA 3 b.c. Music Boy 124 – Single Bid 68 (Auction Ring (USA) 123) [1994 54 63: 5v^6 5f 6m 6d 6g 6m^5 5m^2 a6g^3 1995 6.1g 7.1m^5 7g 6g 6m a7g Sep 16] sturdy, lengthy colt: modest maiden: below form last 4 starts, tailed off final one: probably stays 7.1f: acts on good to firm ground and fibresand: no improvement in blinkers: sold 500 gns Doncaster October Sales. *S. E. Kettlewell*

NAGNAGNAG (IRE) 3 b.f. Red Sunset 120 – Rubina Park 64 (Ashmore (FR) 103 125) [1994 89: 5v^2 5s* 5m 5.3f^2 6g* 6.1g^2 1995 7m 6m^5 6g 7m* 8d^2 8g^6 8g^3 7d 10d 8g^5 Oct 10] leggy, workmanlike filly: useful performer: won £17,800 handicap at Epsom in June: best efforts next 3 starts when placed in listed races and sixth in Group 2 event in France, beaten a head by Fairy Path on first occasion: below form afterwards: stays 1m: acts on any going: successful for apprentice: mulish to post final start. *S. Dow*

NAHLA 5 b.m. Wassl 125 – Bassita (Bustino 136) [1994 NR 1995 22.2m^5 Jun 23] – good-topped, workmanlike mare: third foal: dam unraced half-sister to top-class filly Pebbles: useful form in 3 NH Flat races in spring of 1994, highly impressive winner of Martell Champion race at Aintree: first run of any kind since, wearing crossed

Sir Clement Freud's "Nagnagnag"

noseband and backward, tailed off 6f out in Queen Alexandra Stakes. *Miss Jacqueline S. Doyle*

NAHRI (USA) 4 ch.g. Riverman (USA) 131 – Welden (USA) (Danzig (USA)) [1994 50: 13.4s 11.9s^6 14.1g 16.1d^5 1995 a16.2g^2 a16g^2 16.2m 16m 16d Sep 11] compact gelding: modest performer: stays 16.2f: much his best form on fibresand, acts on dead ground: fair winning hurdler. *J. Mackie* – a62

NAISSANT 2 b.f. (Mar 2) Shaadi (USA) 126 – Nophe (USA) 95 (Super Concorde (USA) 128) [1995 6m^4 5d^4 6m^6 6f^2 6m^5 6.1d^4 Sep 19] good-topped, quite attractive filly: has a roundish action: fifth foal: half-sister to 3-y-o Nuremberg (by Zalazl), 1½m winner in Sweden in 1995: dam, 5f winner at 2 yrs who didn't train on, out of half-sister to dam of Lianga: fair maiden: neck second of 7 to Silk Masque at Goodwood: respectable efforts in useful company on other occasions, but below form final start: stays 6f. *C. E. Brittain* 78

NAJEB (USA) 6 b.g. Chief's Crown (USA) – Modiste (USA) (Sir Ivor 135) [1994 –: a12g^3 a12g a16g 1995 16m^4 Jun 26] smallish gelding: of little account nowadays. *P. D. Evans* –

NAJIYA 2 b.f. (Jan 15) Nashwan (USA) 135 – The Perfect Life (IRE) 106 (Try My Best (USA) 130) [1995 6g^3 6f* 6m* 6d^3 Sep 26] well-made, attractive filly: fine mover: first foal: dam, winner at 5f (at 2 yrs) and 7f in France, sister to Last Tycoon and closely related to good French sprinter Astronef: won 5-runner maiden at Haydock and 3-runner minor event at Salisbury (very easily) in August: creditable 5½ lengths third of 5 to Blue Duster in Cheveley Park Stakes at Newmarket on final 100 p

Hamdan Al Maktoum's "Najiya"

start, tapped for foot 2f out then keeping on: will probably be suited by further than 6f: likely to make further improvement. *J. L. Dunlop*

NAJMAT ALSHEMAAL (IRE) 3 b.f. Dancing Brave (USA) 140 – Noretta (GER) (Cortez (GER)) [1994 71p: 8.2d² 1995 11.4m³ 10.2m² 12m³ 10m* 14.6m⁵ 10.9g⁶ Sep 16] angular, unfurnished filly: has a short action: useful form at best: comfortable winner of maiden at Goodwood in August: best effort when 3¼ lengths fifth of 8 to Noble Rose in steadily-run Park Hill Stakes at Doncaster, staying on: stayed 14.6f: acted on good to firm ground, shaped well on debut on dead: wore crossed noseband and had tongue tied down last 2 starts: stud. *Major W. R. Hern* 98

NAJM MUBEEN (IRE) 2 b.c. (Mar 3) Last Tycoon 131 – Ah Ya Zein (Artaius (USA) 129) [1995 7.6d* 7g Sep 29] 66,000Y: leggy, good-topped colt: half-brother to 2 winners in France by Shahrastani, including 8.5f and 1¼m winner Sharon Doll: dam French 1¼m winner: won maiden at Lingfield by 2½ lengths from Glenrazie, leading over 1f out and running on well: respectable seventh of 8 to Even Top in listed company at Newmarket 15 days later: likely to do better. *A. C. Stewart* 79 p

NAKED EMPEROR 2 b.g. (Feb 12) Dominion Royale 112 – Torville Gold (Aragon 118) [1995 6d a7g Nov 21] 5,000Y: sturdy gelding: second foal: half-brother to 3-y-o Garlande d'Or (by Belfort): dam no worthwhile form: well beaten in maidens at Newbury and Lingfield in the autumn. *M. J. Fetherston-Godley* –

NAKED WELCOME 3 ch.c. Most Welcome 131 – Stripanoora (Ahonoora 122) [1994 94: 6.1m⁶ 6f⁴ 6m³ 7.9d³ 8g* 7m 8m* 8s³ 10d 1995 8m⁴ 10.4m* 10f 8.9g³ 9g 12m* 12m⁴ Nov 4] good-bodied colt: carries condition: improved into a useful performer: won John Smith's Magnet Cup at York in July by a neck from Ringmaster 107 and competitive 10-runner rated stakes at Newmarket (looked in superb shape, comfortably best effort) in October by neck from Seckar Vale: in frame in listed races at York and Doncaster: stays 1½m: acts on good to firm and dead ground, probably on soft: best 2-y-o efforts in blinkers, but wore them only in Cambridgeshire (seemed to take little interest) at 3 yrs: has worn tongue strap, not at 3 yrs: held up (sometimes needs to be driven along early on) and has sharp turn of foot on his day: well able to win more races, but not one to trust implicitly. *M. J. Fetherston-Godley*

NAKHAL 2 b.c. (Mar 4) Puissance 110 – Rambadale 68 (Vaigly Great 127) [1995 6m^{6} 7.1d^{4} 7g Oct 23] 6,600F, IR 17,000Y: workmanlike colt: has scope: unimpressive mover: half-brother to 3-y-o Swallowdale (by Statoblest): dam 2-y-o 6f winner who stayed 1m: best efforts in maidens won by Charwelton at Goodwood and Lomberto at Sandown on first 2 starts: stays 7f. *D. J. G. Murray Smith* — 66

NAKITA 4 ch.f. Efisio 120 – Ra Ra (Lord Gayle (USA) 124) [1994 70d: 7m 6g^{3} 7m 7g^{6} 8g 6f 7g^{4} 6g a5g a6g 6g^{5} 6s* 6.9m a6g^{4} a7g^{3} 1995 7d^{3} a7g 6.9m^{6} 8f^{6} 8.3m 8g 7m 7m a7g 7m a7g Aug 4] small filly: has a quick action: modest at best in 1995: probably stays 1m: acts on firm and soft ground and on fibresand: visored/blinkered 4 times, running well only once: often bandaged: inconsistent: sold 3,000 gns Newmarket September Sales: sent to Belgium. *C. N. Allen* — 57 d

NAMELESS 2 ch.f. (Mar 20) Doc Marten 104 – Opuntia (Rousillon (USA) 133) [1995 a5g^{2} a5g^{3} a5g* a6g^{6} a6g^{2} 6m^{3} 5.2f^{2} a5g* 5.1f^{3} 5.3f^{5} 5g a5g Nov 2] 2,000Y: workmanlike filly: first foal: dam unraced: won twice in selling company on fibresand at Wolverhampton: long way below form last 3 starts: speedy and easily best at 5f: best turf form on firm going: blinkered final outing. *D. J. S. Cosgrove* — 57 a62

NAME OF OUR FATHER (USA) 2 b.g. (Apr 7) Northern Baby (CAN) 127 – Ten Hail Marys (USA) (Halo (USA)) [1995 7d^{4} 7.1d^{2} 7f Oct 23] leggy, close-coupled gelding: has a markedly round action: second foal: dam minor 2-y-o winner at up to 9f in USA: in frame in maidens at Salisbury and Haydock: sweating, poor effort on firm ground final start: should stay further than 7f: sold (J. Gosden to M. Fetherston-Godley) 12,000 gns Newmarket Autumn Sales and gelded. *J. H. M. Gosden* — 75

NAME THAT TUNE 3 ch.f. Fayruz 116 – Gandoorah 90 (Record Token 128) [1994 NR 1995 5d 5.1g 5.1m^{6} a5g 5.1m^{5} a6g Nov 20] 4,000Y: compact filly: half-sister to modest 1987 2-y-o 6f and 7f winner Axia (by Comedy Star) and a winner in Scandinavia: dam 2-y-o 5f winner out of half-sister to top-class sprinter Roman Warrior: poor sprint maiden. *C. J. Hill* — 40

John Smith's Magnet Cup (Handicap), York—from last to first for Naked Welcome; those caught close home are Ringmaster and Yoush

NAME THE TUNE 4 b.c. Chief Singer 131 – Try To Remember (Music Boy 124) [1994 76: a5g^{2} a6g^{6} 5m* 6d 5g^{4} 5d 6f^{3} 5m 5m^{3} 5m^{3} 5g^{5} 5f 5m^{3} 5g^{2} 5d* 5m 5m 5s 1995 5m^{4} 5m^{4} 5g^{3} 5m^{2} 5g^{2} 5g^{4} 5m^{4} 5m* 5m^{3} 5g* 5f 5m* 5.6m 6g 5s 5m^{5} a5g Nov 16] tall, strong colt: usually impresses in appearance: unimpressive mover: progressed steadily, and is a fairly useful handicapper: won Northern Rock Gosforth Park Cup at Newcastle and rated stakes at Ascot, both in July, and rated stakes at Sandown (well drawn) in August: effective at 5f (best form) and 6f: acts on firm and dead ground, not so good as yet on all-weather: blinkered (ran well) fifth 4-y-o start: usually bandaged: tough and consistent. *P. Howling* 94

NANNY DOON 3 ch.f. Dominion 123 – Sea Charm 70 (Julio Mariner 127) [1994 NR 1995 a8g a7g Jan 17] half-sister to fairly useful sprinter Profilic (by Ballacashtal) and 2 winners abroad: dam, third over 13f from 4 starts, is half-sister to high-class middle-distance stayer Mistigri and useful stayer Tanaka: well beaten in sellers. *M. Johnston* –

NANTON POINT (USA) 3 b.g. Darshaan 133 – Migiyas 87 (Kings Lake (USA) 133) [1994 49: 7.1m 7m 7m 1995 9g 11.6m 12d 14.1f* 15.4g* 14.1f* 16f* 14m^{2} 18.2g^{4} 13.9g 18m^{2} Oct 14] lengthy, robust gelding: progressed well into a fairly useful handicapper: won at Yarmouth and Folkestone (both easily) in June, and twice at Redcar (on consecutive days) in July: easily best effort when length second of 21 to Old Red in Cesarewitch at Newmarket: suited by good test of stamina: acts on firm ground: effective from front or held up: genuine: sure to win more races. *Lady Herries* 83 p

NAPIER STAR 2 b.f. (Apr 15) Inca Chief (USA) – America Star (Norwick (USA) 125) [1995 6.1d a6g^{5} a8g Dec 18] leggy, unfurnished filly: first foal: dam unraced: sire (by Mr Prospector) won from 5f to 7f: little worthwhile form in maidens. *Mrs N. Macauley* –

NAPOLEON'S LAW 3 b.g. Sharpo 132 – Test Case 90 (Busted 134) [1994 NR 1995 7g 8m 7m^{5} Jun 20] leggy, workmanlike gelding: third foal: dam lightly-raced 1m winner who probably stayed 1½m: signs of a little ability in maidens: hung badly left second start: sold 500 gns Newmarket July Sales. *R. Hannon* –

NAPOLEON'S RETURN 2 gr.c. (Mar 28) Daring March 116 – Miss Colenca (Petong 126) [1995 5m^{5} 5g^{4} 6m^{5} 5f^{2} 7m^{5} 6m^{5} 6d 5.3d^{4} 7f* 7f a8.5g^{6} Oct 28] 2,000Y: rather sparely-made colt: third foal: dam well beaten: modest form: won 28-runner claimer at Redcar in October on final outing for A. Foster: not discredited in nurseries after: seems to stay 8.5f but probably best at around 7f: acts on firm and dead ground: visored (below form) seventh start. *G. M. Moore* 58

NAPOLEON STAR (IRE) 4 ch.g. Mulhollande (USA) 107 – Lady Portobello (Porto Bello 118) [1994 74: a5g^{5} a7g^{3} a7g^{4} a7g^{3} a5g^{6} a8g^{5} 5v^{5} 5.1g^{4} 5.7m 5.7g^{2} 5.1f* 6f* 5.1f* 5m^{4} 5.1m^{4} 5m^{6} 5d 5.7g 7g 1995 6g^{3} 6m 5.1m^{5} 6g 6g^{4} 6m^{2} 5.7f^{5} 6m 7g^{4} 7.1d 7g 7g Oct 7] sparely-made gelding: fair handicapper: well beaten last 3 starts: effective at 5f to 7f: acts on firm ground and the all-weather, below form on a soft surface: blinkered (creditable effort at the time) eighth 3-y-o start. *M. S. Saunders* 74

NARBONNE 4 b.f. Rousillon (USA) 133 – Historical Fact 78 (Reform 132) [1994 59: 8d 8.2d^{3} 10g 8.2g 8m^{2} 8g^{4} 8.3f 8g* 8.2m^{5} 8s 1995 7m^{3} 8m 10g^{6} 8m^{2} 8m^{4} Jun 23] workmanlike filly: fluent mover: modest performer: best form at up to 1m: acts on good to firm and dead ground: races prominently: consistent at 4 yrs. *B. J. McMath* 60

NARDUS 2 ch.c. (Feb 7) Mujtahid (USA) 118 – Al Najah (USA) 96 (Topsider (USA)) [1995 7m^{6} 7g a6s^{3} Dec 17] lengthy, unfurnished colt: looked weak: fluent mover: second foal: half-brother to useful 4-y-o sprinter Tabook (by Cadeaux Genereux): dam 8.5f winner: modest form in maidens here: sold out of M. Stoute's stable 7,000 gns Newmarket Autumn Sales before finishing third in Sweden final start. *E. Henriksson, Sweden* 61 ?

NASEEM ALSAHAR 2 ch.f. (Mar 27) Nashwan (USA) 135 – El Fabulous (FR) 111 (Fabulous Dancer (USA) 124) [1995 8m^{2} Oct 20] good-topped filly: sixth foal: half-sister to 3 winners, including 5-y-o 10.1f and (in Dubai) 1½m winner Fabulous Mtoto (by Mtoto): dam French 1m (at 2 yrs) and 10.5f winner: 11/2 and gone in coat, 1¼ lengths second to easy winner Overruled in maiden at Doncaster, not much room 2f out then running on well to finish clear of remainder: will improve, and should be able to win a race. *Major W. R. Hern* 79 p

NASHAAT (USA) 7 b.g. El Gran Senor (USA) 136 – Absentia (USA) 108 (Raise A Cup (USA)) [1994 69, a73: a6g5 a8g a7g3 a8g2 a7g3 8.1g* 8g6 8f 8.1m 8.1g6 7v* 8g6 8d 1995 7.6m2 8m4 8g5 8g 8.5m 8d 7g* 7f* a7g* a8g6 Dec 1] stocky, good-topped gelding: fair handicapper: gave impression something amiss fourth and fifth outings: back to form to win seller at Leicester, claimer at Yarmouth (final start for N. Walker) and handicap at Southwell in the autumn: effective at 7f, and stays 8.5f: acts on the all-weather, firm and soft going: blinkered (ran creditably) at 5 yrs: has run well when sweating: held up last 4 starts. *M. C. Chapman* 74 + a78

NASHOTAH 3 ch.f. Nashwan (USA) 135 – Haiati (USA) 113 (Alydar (USA)) [1994 NR 1995 8g4 10g2 Jun 16] smallish filly: second foal: dam, 6f and 7f winner here and in USA, stayed 1¼m, from good family: fair form in maidens at Newbury (finishing best of all) in May and Sandown (beaten a neck) in June: should stay 1½m: may be capable of better: sold 26,000 gns Newmarket December Sales. *J. R. Fanshawe* 74

NASH TERRACE (IRE) 3 ch.c. Nashwan (USA) 135 – Gay Hellene 111 (Ela-Mana-Mou 132) [1994 86p: 8s* 1995 11g3 12g2 16.2m 9d5 10d2 11.9d3 Oct 11] sparely-made colt: useful form: good efforts when placed, including in listed race at Goodwood (to Revere) and minor event at Haydock (behind Sebastian) in the autumn: should prove better at 1½m than shorter: acts on soft ground, travelled well long way in 2m race only start on top-of-the-ground: sold 86,000 gns Newmarket Autumn Sales: sent to USA. *R. Charlton* 102

NASHWANAH 3 ch.f. Nashwan (USA) 135 – Sharpina (Sharpen Up 127) [1994 NR 1995 10.1g5 12.1m Jun 15] sister to 4-y-o 1¼m (and hurdles) winner Glamour Game and half-sister to several winners, including useful 5-y-o 7f and 1m winner Ertlon (by Shareef Dancer): dam never ran: around 10 lengths fifth of 10 in maiden at Newcastle, outpaced final 2f: tailed off at Chepstow 3 weeks later: sold 5,500 gns Newmarket December Sales. *H. Thomson Jones* 57

NASRUDIN (USA) 2 b.c. (May 27) Nureyev (USA) 131 – Sunshine O'My Life (USA) (Graustark) [1995 7d6 7f2 Oct 18] $107,000Y: eighth foal: closely related to Grade 3 8.5f winner in USA Dance O'My Life (by Sovereign Dancer) and half-brother to a minor winner in USA: dam winner at 6f/7f in USA from excellent family: 1¾ lengths second to ready winner Brighstone in maiden at Yarmouth, keeping on well: will stay 1m: will improve again. *D. R. Loder* 81 p

NATAL RIDGE 2 b.c. (Apr 20) Indian Ridge 123 – Song Grove 61 (Song 132) [1995 7f5 6m Nov 3] 22,000F, 21,000Y: quite attractive colt: half-brother to several winners, including useful sprinter Sir Harry Hardman (by Doulab) and 6f/9f performer Sir Arthur Hobbs (by Lyphard's Special): dam 4-y-o 5.8f winner in Ireland: modest form, taking keen hold, in late-season maidens. *D. Haydn Jones* 55

NATATARL (IRE) 2 ch.f. (Apr 7) Roi Danzig (USA) – Little Me (Connaught 130) [1995 6.1g2 6g 7.1s Oct 17] 8,200F, 4,000Y, 5,000 2-y-o: good-bodied filly: half-sister to 3-y-o 1½m winner Last Laugh (by Last Tycoon), 6f winner at 2 yrs, and Irish 1½m winner Blue Diana (by Bluebird): dam Irish middle-distance winner: second of 8 in seller at Chepstow: soundly beaten in maiden events at Warwick and Chepstow 4 months later: should stay beyond 6f. *M. C. Pipe* 49

NATIONAL GRID 3 b.g. Warning 136 – Current Raiser 108 (Filiberto (USA) 123) [1994 55p: 8m 1995 12m6 May 7] sparely-made gelding: has had 2 runs in maidens, bit backward only start in 1995. *R. J. R. Williams* –

NATIVE CHIEFTAN 6 b.g. Trojan Fen 118 – Habituee (Habitat 134) [1994 NR 1995 a13g Dec 6] close-coupled gelding: fair performer at 4 yrs then winning novice hurdler in 1993/4: no promise on return: probably stays 1¾m: acts on equitrack, best turf form on good going: tried blinkered and visored once each. *S. Dow* –

NATIVE SONG 2 b.f. (Apr 13) Hatim (USA) 121 – Ivors Melody 47 (Music Maestro 119) [1995 a8g6 Dec 18] first foal: dam stayed 9f: 10/1, around 11 lengths sixth of 9 to Apartments Abroad in maiden at Lingfield in December. *M. J. Haynes* –

NATURAL KEY 2 ch.f. (Apr 28) Safawan 118 – No Sharps Or Flats (USA) 67 (Sharpen Up 127) [1995 6g4 5f* 6.1m* 5m2 6g2 5m 5g 6g Sep 16] smallish filly: second foal: half-sister to Belgian 3-y-o Sharp Sabo (by Prince Sabo), winner at 7f/7.5f in 1995: dam, second over 6f at 2 yrs, out of half-sister to dam of Pebbles: won median auction maiden at Ripon in June and claimer at Chepstow (final start for Sir 69

Weatherbys Ireland Greenlands Stakes, the Curragh—
Nautical Pet (far side) narrowly turns the tables on Desert Style

Mark Prescott, claimed £10,000) in July: below form last 3 starts, including when running twice in 3 days at Ayr in seller (heavily-backed favourite) and nursery (blinkered): stays 6f: acts on firm ground. *D. Haydn Jones*

NATURAL PATH 4 b.f. Governor General 116 – Cuba Libre (Rum (USA)) [1994 49: 6.1d³ 5.9v 6m⁴ 6m⁶ 5m 6.1s 1995 7m Oct 30] quite attractive filly: poor maiden: tailed off only start in 1995: should stay 7f: acts on good to firm and dead ground. *Mrs V. A. Aconley* –

NAUTICAL JEWEL 3 b.g. Handsome Sailor 125 – Kopjes (Bay Express 132) [1994 58§: 6.1s 6.1m³ 6m⁵ 7f 7.3g 6g⁶ 7d 1995 a7g² 7m⁶ 8g a8g² 8m⁵ 8m³ 8.5g⁶ a12g² a11g 12s⁵ a14.8g Nov 11] plain, good-topped gelding: modest maiden handicapper: stays 1½m: acts on good to firm and soft ground, and on fibresand: visored (pulled hard) final 2-y-o start: sometimes sweats: held up: often apprentice ridden: hangs right, and not an easy ride. *M. D. I. Usher* 51 § a58 §

NAUTICAL PET (IRE) 3 b.c. Petorius 117 – Sea Mistress (Habitat 134) [1994 8d* 1995 7d² 6m* 7m 6m 6d⁴ 7d* Nov 12] IR 5,400Y: close-coupled colt: fourth foal: half-brother to 3 winners, including 4-y-o Roi de la Mer (1m seller, by Fairy King) and Irish 5-y-o Touching Moment (9f and 1¾m, by Pennine Walk): dam, unraced, from family of Pampapaul and Noble Patriarch: smart performer: narrow winner of maiden at the Curragh at 2 yrs: involved in close finishes with Desert Style at the Curragh in the spring, rather unlucky in Tetrarch Stakes then turning the tables in Weatherbys Ireland Greenlands Stakes: best efforts in the autumn, winning 16-runner listed event at Leopardstown in November by 4 lengths from Al Reet: effective at 6f and has won at 1m: yet to race on extremes of going. *D. K. Weld, Ireland* 113

NAVAL GAZER (IRE) 2 b.f. (May 10) Sadler's Wells (USA) 132 – Naval Light (USA) (Majestic Light (USA)) [1995 8g* Oct 1] 240,000 francs Y, resold 54,000Y: sister to German 4-y-o 9f winner Sadler's King, closely related to 9.7f seller winner Anguish (by El Gran Senor) and half-sister to a winner in Japan by Caerleon: dam, minor winner in USA at up to 9f, half-sister to American Grade 1 9f winner Polish Navy: favourite, won 7-runner maiden at Brighton comfortably by 1½ lengths from The Boozing Brief: sure to improve. *D. R. Loder* 75 p

NAVAL HUNTER (USA) 2 ch.c. (Mar 11) Jade Hunter (USA) – Navy Light (USA) (Polish Navy (USA)) [1995 7g 7g Oct 23] $30,000Y: first foal: dam unraced: sire (by Mr Prospector) best at 4 yrs when Grade 1 9f and 1¼m winner: towards rear in late-season maidens at Yarmouth and Lingfield. *P. W. Harris* 51

NAVIGATE (USA) 2 ch.c. (Mar 4) Diesis 133 – Libras Shiningstar (USA) 72 (Gleaming (USA)) [1995 5m 5m^{5} 6g^{2} 7.1g^{4} Jun 16] $75,000Y: quite attractive colt: closely related to useful 1986 2-y-o 6f winner but ungenuine 3-y-o Ghanayim (by Sharpen Up) and half-brother to several winners, including 8.2f and 10.1f winner Bright As Night (by Miswaki): dam, placed over 6f and 2m, half-sister to Ribero and Ribocco: fair form: short-headed by Depreciate in maiden at Goodwood: sweating, respectable fourth in similar event at Sandown week later: stays 7f. *R. Hannon* 79

NAWAASI 3 b.f. Green Desert (USA) 127 – Mountain Memory 109 (High Top 131) [1994 NR 1995 7m^{2} 7g* 8f^{3} 6m^{3} 6s 6.1s Oct 17] 26,000Y: good-topped filly: third foal: half-sister to 11.5f winner Rainbow Mountain (by Rainbow Quest) and 13.6f to 2m winner Mystic Memory (by Ela-Mana-Mou): dam, 6f (at 2 yrs) and 8.2f winner suited by 1¼m, is sister to Derby Italiano winner My Top: fair handicapper: won maiden at Yarmouth in June: stays 1m: acts on firm ground: sold 21,000 gns Newmarket December Sales. *H. Thomson Jones* 76

NAWAR (FR) 5 b.g. Kahyasi 130 – Nabita (FR) (Akarad (FR) 130) [1994 NR 1995 14.4m^{6} 13.3g^{6} 11.5g^{5} 20m 16.4m 20f^{5} Jul 26] well-made gelding: third foal: half-brother to high-class chaser Nakir (by Nikos) and a winner in France by Shardari: dam 13f winner in France: won 1¼m event in France for A. de Royer-Dupre, only outing on flat at 3 yrs: fair form at best over hurdles (difficult ride and not one to trust) and on flat here: stays 2½m. *J. R. Jenkins* 74

NDABA 4 b.g. Mtoto 134 – Lightning Legacy (USA) 78 (Super Concorde (USA) 128) [1994 NR 1995 a9.4g Nov 27] half-brother to 3 winners, notably useful 1¼m to 11f winner Black Monday (by Busted): dam, maiden, stayed 1m: poor form in NH Flat races: well beaten in Wolverhampton claimer. *N. A. Twiston-Davies* –

NEARLY HONEST 7 ch.m. Nearly A Hand 115 – Miss Saddler (St Paddy 133) [1994 39: 13.1g^{3} 16.4g^{4} a13g a16g 1995 a10g Jan 26] workmanlike mare: poor maiden on flat: stayed 2m: form only on good ground: dead. *R. J. Hodges* –

NEBRANGUS (IRE) 3 ch.g. Nashamaa 113 – Choral Park (Music Boy 124) [1994 –: 5s 5f 7m 6g 6g 6d^{6} 1995 8.3g^{6} 6.9m a8g 8m 7m^{6} 10m 10d Sep 18] small gelding: of little account: tried blinkered. *N. Bycroft* –

NEC PLUS ULTRA (FR) 4 b.c. Kendor (FR) 122 – Quintefolle (FR) (Luthier 126) [1994 114: 6d^{3} 8d^{4} 8g* 10s^{3} 7d^{2} 8g 8s^{2} 8d^{4} 8v^{3} 1995 8g^{5} 7m^{2} 7g^{4} 8.5d^{2} 8m* 8d* 6.5g 7s^{3} 8d^{3} 8g* 8g* Nov 12] good-topped colt: smart French performer: won listed race at Evry in June, Prix Messidor at Maisons-Laffitte (beat Bishop of Cashel a head) in July, listed race at Evry in October and Prix Perth at Saint-Cloud (beaten head by Neverneyev, but hampered and promoted) in November: effective at 7f to 1¼m: acts on heavy ground and good to firm. *A. de Royer Dupre, France* 115

NED AL SHEEBA 2 b.c. (Feb 22) Taufan (USA) 119 – Bold Polly 67 (Bold Lad (IRE) 133) [1995 a6g^{4} 6m^{3} 6m* 6m^{5} 6g 7g^{5} Oct 1] 20,000Y: close-coupled, rather sparely-made colt: half-brother to several winners here and abroad, including useful sprinter Viceroy (by Indian King): dam won twice at 5f: won maiden at Yarmouth in July by a length from Laafee: had valid excuses in nurseries last 3 starts: should stay 7f: sent to UAE: shouldn't be written off. *W. J. Haggas* 84 +

NED'S BONANZA 6 b.g. Green Ruby (USA) 104 – Miss Display 47 (Touch Paper 113) [1994 76: 5g 5m 5m 5f 5m^{4} 5.1m^{4} 5m^{3} 5g^{2} 5f^{6} 5g 5g* 5f 6m* 6m 6m^{6} 5g 5d 5g 1995 5g^{3} 5m^{4} 6m^{3} 5m 6g^{4} 5g^{3} 5f 5m* 5g^{6} 5g 6m* 6m^{6} 6m 6m^{6} 5g 5d Sep 27] workmanlike, good-topped gelding: fair sprint handicapper: gained narrow successes at Beverley and Thirsk (second year running) in July: acts on firm ground, probably unsuited by a soft surface: visored (ran well) sixth 5-y-o start. *M. Dods* 74

NED'S CONTESSA (IRE) 2 ch.f. (Jan 14) Persian Heights 129 – Beechwood (USA) (Blushing Groom (FR) 131) [1995 5s^{5} 5g 7m a7g 7.5m 7m^{5} 7.1f^{2} 7f^{3} 8m 7g^{3} Sep 16] 3,000Y: small filly: fifth foal: half-sister to 1993 2-y-o 7f winner Imposing Groom (by Posen): dam French 10.8f winner: plater: should stay at least 1m: acts on firm ground: often gets behind. *M. Dods* 48

NEEDHAM STAR (USA) 2 ch.f. (Apr 6) Mt Livermore (USA) – Passing Gull (USA) (Arctic Tern (USA) 126) [1995 6f^{4} 5.2g^{2} 7g 6f 7.3d^{3} Oct 21] $18,000F, 9,000Y: leggy, unfurnished filly: third foal: half-sister to a winner abroad by Clever Trick: dam maiden half-sister to dam of Danehill: useful errfforts when staying on 3½ lengths second of 17 to Blue Iris in Super Sprint at Newbury, then around 4 lengths 94 ?

eighth of 13 to Priory Belle in Moyglare Stud Stakes at the Curragh in September: not discredited in blinkers final start: will stay at least 1m: reportedly sold to race in USA. *P. A. Kelleway*

NEEDLE GUN (IRE) 5 b. or br.h. Sure Blade (USA) 130 – Lucayan Princess 111 (High Line 125) [1994 113: 9d^{3} 10f^{2} 10m 8m^{3} 10.5m 10.1g* 10s^{4} 1995 10m^{3} 12g^{6} 10m* 10.4m^{4} 10m^{5} 12f^{2} Dec 10] tall, leggy horse: shows knee action: smart performer: gained first pattern race win, after being in the frame many times, when beating Hushang a neck in 6-runner Meld Stakes at the Curragh in July: ran very well when 5¾ lengths fourth of 6 to Halling in Juddmonte International at York, 4 lengths fifth of 8 to Pentire in Champion Stakes at Leopardstown and neck second of 14 to Partipral in Hong Kong International Vase: effective at 1m and stays 1½m: acts on any going: genuine. *C. E. Brittain* — 119

NEEDLE KNOT (IRE) 2 b.g. (May 25) Don't Forget Me 127 – Needlewoman 73 (Moorestyle 137) [1995 5g 6m^{3} 6m^{6} 8f 8m^{5} Oct 28] IR 1,800F: lengthy gelding: poor mover: fifth foal: closely related to a winning sprinter in Europe by Ahonoora: dam, maiden best at 9f and 1¼m, half-sister to 2000 Guineas winner Mister Baileys: modest form, including in sellers: stays 1m: tends to wander off bridle: has been gelded. *M. Johnston* — 57

NEEDLE MATCH 2 ch.c. (Mar 23) Royal Academy (USA) 130 – Miss Tatting (USA) 89 (Miswaki (USA) 124) [1995 6m Oct 27] big, good-topped colt: has scope: second foal: dam 7f and 1m winner: 20/1 and bit backward, last of 8 in maiden at Newmarket. *C. F. Wall* — –p

NEEDWOOD EPIC 2 b.f. (Mar 22) Midyan (USA) 124 – Epure (Bellypha 130) [1995 6f^{5} 8.1m 8.2d^{6} Sep 11] big, good-topped filly: has plenty of scope: seventh foal: half-sister to French 3-y-o 1½m winner Eriza (by Distant Relative), useful 1990 — 53

Saeed Manana's "Needle Gun"

3-y-o stayer Pashto (by Persian Bold), and 3 other winners abroad: dam, 11.5f winner in France, is closely related to high-class French 1m and 11f winner Al Nasr: modest form in maidens: stays 1m: races keenly. *B. A. McMahon*

NEEDWOOD FANTASY 2 b.f. (Apr 13) Rolfe (USA) 77 – Needwood Nymph 45 (Bold Owl 101) [1995 5m^5 7.5d Sep 13] 400Y: leggy filly: fourth foal: dam, 1½m and 13f winner, probably stayed 2m: well beaten in maiden events at Beverley. *B. A. McMahon* –

NEEDWOOD LIMELIGHT 2 b.c. (Jun 4) Rolfe (USA) 77 – Lime Brook 56 (Rapid River 127) [1995 6g Sep 16] second foal: brother to 3-y-o Needwood Newt: dam best short of 7f: 25/1, never a factor in maiden at Catterick. *B. A. McMahon* –

NEEDWOOD NEWT 3 ch.f. Rolfe (USA) 77 – Lime Brook 56 (Rapid River 127) [1994 48: 5f a6g^6 a6g^5 6.1g a7g a6g^3 1995 a7g^4 a6g^5 a6g a6g^5 Feb 20] smallish filly: poor maiden plater: stays 6f: inconsistent: sold 750 gns Ascot July Sales. *B. A. McMahon* 43

NEED YOU BADLY 2 b.f. (Mar 7) Robellino (USA) 127 – Persian Tapestry 70 (Tap On Wood 130) [1995 5s^4 5f^4 6f Oct 23] IR 19,000Y: compact filly: fourth foal: half-sister to 3-y-o Stoneham Girl (by Nomination): dam 1¼m winner: modest form in maidens: bred to stay further than 6f. *S. P. C. Woods* 59

NEGATIVE EQUITY 3 ch.g. Be My Chief (USA) 122 – Rather Romantic (CAN) (Verbatim (USA)) [1994 60: 7m^6 7g 8.1g 1995 11.6m 12g^2 14.1g a12g 13.3f 10.1m^2 10m^5 Aug 16] plain gelding: modest maiden: effective at 1¼m and 1½m: has raced only on a sound surface on turf: visored/blinkered last 5 starts on turf: races prominently: inconsistent. *K. R. Burke* 51

NEITHER NOR 6 ch.m. Norwick (USA) 125 – Leap In Time (Dance In Time (CAN)) [1994 91: 8m 7d 7s 7s* 6m 7.3g 5g 7d* 6d^6 8g^4 1995 8g 7m 7.1m^4 8.5m* 7m^6 8f 8f^5 6.5f^5 8.5f^3 a8.5s* Dec 13] good-topped mare: shows knee action: easily best effort to win strongly-run listed event at Epsom in June on penultimate start for D. Wilson, late burst to catch Brave Revival: won claimer at Hollywood Park in December: effective at 6f to 8.5f: probably acts on any going: blinkered final start at 3 yrs, and all starts in USA: has run well when sweating and for claimer: held up here: raced on lasix and bute in USA. *S. Shulman, USA* 98

NELLIE NORTH 2 b.f. (Apr 30) Northern State (USA) 91 – Kimble Princess (Kala Shikari 125) [1995 5g^5 5g^2 5m^3 5.1m^3 5m* 5m^6 6m 6g^4 6d Oct 21] lengthy filly: second reported foal: dam ran twice at 2 yrs: modest form: made all under 7-lb claimer in median auction maiden at Windsor in July: ran well in face of very stiff task in Molecomb Stakes at Goodwood on sixth start: creditable eighth of 14 to Lunar Mist in nursery at Newbury on final outing: will prove best at 5f: best form on top-of-the-ground. *Mrs M. McCourt* 68

NELLYSSIA (FR) 3 b. or br.f. Always Fair (USA) 121 – Hecalene (FR) (Sir Gaylord) [1994 49p: 5.2m 7f 6.9m 1995 a8g 11.7h^5 14.1m^4 Jul 24] poor maiden plater: visored final 3-y-o start. *G. L. Moore* –

NEREUS 2 b.c. (May 10) Shareef Dancer (USA) 135 – Lady of The Sea 86 (Mill Reef (USA) 141) [1995 7m Aug 12] good sort: third foal: half-brother to 1994 2-y-o 5f winner Green Palm Tree (by Green Desert): dam 8.2f winner out of champion New Zealand mare La Mer: 12/1, but carrying plenty of condition, raced handily long way when eleventh of 22 to Silver Prey in maiden at Newbury: will improve. *B. W. Hills* 67 p

NERO KRIS 3 ch.c. Kris 135 – What A Pity 97 (Blakeney 126) [1994 7d^2 7.5v^6 1995 a10g 8m 8m^5 8.2d^5 8m 9.7g Oct 16] 33,000Y leggy colt: sixth foal: half-brother to 2 winners in Italy, notably Junk Bond (by Last Tycoon) who was also useful 1990 2-y-o 6f and 7f winner here: dam lightly-raced 7f winner from sprinting family: trained by L. d'Auria in Italy at 2 yrs, probably showing fairly useful form on debut: modest form at best here: stays 8.2f: probably acts on good to firm ground and dead: has worn tongue strap. *P. A. Kelleway* 63

NESSUN DORO 3 b.g. Hallgate 127 – Bamdoro 54 (Cavo Doro 124) [1994 –: 6s 1995 10m a8g^2 8.1m^6 10d 12.1d^4 a8.5g^5 Nov 13] compact gelding: fair maiden handicapper: stays 12.1f: acts on dead ground and fibresand: visored (below form over 8.5f) final 3-y-o start: inconsistent. *S. Mellor* 65

NEUWEST (USA) 3 b.c. Gone West (USA) – White Mischief 103 (Dance In Time (CAN)) [1994 80: 7s^2 8m^5 7g^2 1995 7g^3 8f* a8g^2 Nov 25] robust colt: poor walker: has a round action: off course over 11 months before reappearance: did not have to be at best to win maiden at Yarmouth in October, making all: sold out of H. Thomson Jones's stable 25,000 gns Newmarket Autumn Sales: good second in handicap at Lingfield in November: should stay beyond 1m: acts on good to firm (probably on firm) and soft ground, and on equitrack. *N. J. H. Walker* 80

NEVERENDING (USA) 3 ch.f. Sabona (USA) 94 – Play On And On (USA) (Stop The Music (USA)) [1994 79: 7m^3 7m^2 6.9m* 7m^2 7g^2 1995 7.5m^6 7.9g^5 7m 8f^2 7d* Sep 30] close-coupled, quite attractive filly: fairly useful handicapper: off course over 3 months, narrowly won at Goodwood in September, pushed along in rear 3f out: stays 1m: acts on firm and dead going: has worn bandage on near-fore and off-hind: nervous type: held up: sent to USA. *H. R. A. Cecil* 91

NEVER EXPLAIN (IRE) 3 b.f. Fairy King (USA) – Purchasepaperchase 104 (Young Generation 129) [1994 80: 6g^4 6m^3 7f 6.5g^4 7m 1995 7g 8g^5 10m* 10.3m Sep 6] big, good-topped filly: fair performer: 13/8 on, easy winner of 3-runner maiden at Ayr in August: stays 1¼m: acts on good to firm ground: blinkered last 2 starts as 2-y-o: pulled hard and carried head high on reappearance: found little final start at 3 yrs: not one to trust implicitly. *J. L. Dunlop* 80

NEVERNEYEV (USA) 5 b.h. Nureyev (USA) 131 – River Rose (FR) 116 (Riverman (USA) 131) [1994 117: 8d* 7d* 7g^3 8d 1995 5.5g^2 7m* 7g^5 7g^4 7m^5 8g^2 Nov 12] smart French horse: won listed event at Longchamp in May by a length from Nec Plus Ultra: rec 3 lb and beat him a head in Prix Perth at Saint-Cloud in November, but had caused interference and placed second: stays 1m: acts on good to firm ground and soft: front runner. *Mme C. Head, France* 112

NEVER SAY SO 3 ch.f. Prince Sabo 123 – So Rewarding (Never So Bold 135) [1994 48: 5m^2 5m^4 5g a6g 5g^4 a5g 1995 5m^3 5g^4 5d^5 6g 5d^6 6g Sep 22] small filly: poor maiden: failed to repeat form shown on reappearance: should stay 6f: acts on good to firm ground, well below form on fibresand. *C. Smith* 48

NEVER SO FIT 4 b.g. Never So Bold 135 – Darine 114 (Nonoalco (USA) 131) [1994 NR 1995 8d 9.2s^4 11.1f^4 10.1m Aug 17] 2,000Y: tall, workmanlike gelding: seventh foal: half-brother to several winners, including smart winner at up to 1¼m Penny Drops (by Sharpo): dam, middle-distance winner, improved greatly at 5 yrs when trained in France: modest maiden: tailed off last 3 starts: should stay 1¼m: blinkered (set very strong pace) on debut. *R. Bastiman* 57

NEVER SO RITE (IRE) 3 b.f. Nordico (USA) – Nephrite 106 (Godswalk (USA) 130) [1994 51: 5.2s^5 6g 6g^5 7m* 6g^6 6s^3 7.3v 1995 a8g^2 a10g^3 a8g^5 6.9g^3 8d^2 8m* 8f^2 7m^3 7f^3 8h^2 8.3m^3 8g a10g^3 a10g a10g^5 Dec 18] leggy filly: modest handicapper: in good form in the summer, winning at Brighton: stays 1m: acts on hard and soft ground and on equitrack: blinkered (below form) third 3-y-o start, visored (ran creditably) on eleventh. *D. W. P. Arbuthnot* 62 a52

NEVER SO TRUE 4 b.f. Never So Bold 135 – Cottage Pie 106 (Kalamoun 129) [1994 46: 8g 7.1g^5 7m^5 8.3f^3 a8.5g^3 a6g^2 7m^2 5.9h^4 a9.4g 8m 8.3g 1995 7.1g 8g 8.3g 10m^3 7g^6 11.1f^2 12.1m^5 13f^4 12.1m^3 11.1f* 9.2f^2 14.1m^4 12.4g^4 Aug 28] lengthy, rather sparely-made filly: poor handicapper: narrowly won maiden event at Hamilton in August, making all: stays 13f: acts on firm ground, dead and fibresand: tried visored/blinkered, no improvement: races prominently: carried head awkwardly final start. *Martyn Wane* 45

NEVER SUCH BLISS 3 b.f. Shavian 125 – Donna Bold 51 (Never So Bold 135) [1994 NR 1995 5.1g 5m^4 5m^2 6g 5m 6m^6 7m a6g^6 a7g Dec 2] small, compact filly: first foal: dam lightly raced at up to 7f: modest maiden: well below form last 4 starts: best efforts at 5f: has raced only on a sound surface on turf. *J. D. Bethell* 60 d

NEVER THINK TWICE 2 b.g. (Feb 9) Never So Bold 135 – Hope And Glory (USA) 87 (Well Decorated (USA)) [1995 5m^4 5m^3 6m^5 5g^6 5m 6m^2 6m^2 Sep 7] 11,000F: quite attractive gelding: fourth foal: half-brother to German 3-y-o 1m winner Hot Connection (by Unfuwain) and a winner in Spain: dam, 2-y-o 6f winner, only season to race, is daughter of half-sister to Legal Bid and Law Society: modest maiden: runner-up in seller penultimate start: stays 6f: bandaged, and ran as if something amiss, fifth outing. *K. T. Ivory* 64

NEVER TIME (IRE) 3 b.g. Simply Great (FR) 122 – Islet Time (Burslem 123) 43
[1994 57: 6g 6.1m 7.1d 6g^4 7s^4 8s 7g^4 a7g 1995 a6g^6 a8g 7g 6m 10.3m 10m 10g^3 8m 12m^3 11.9g^4 13.8g^6 11d 13.8f^3 a14g Nov 16] angular gelding: poor form at best in 1995: stays 13.8f: acts on firm and soft ground: has run poorly in visor and blinkers: takes a keen hold: went moodily to post eighth and ninth starts, early and ridden in spurs on tenth. *Mrs V. A. Aconley*

NEW ALBION (USA) 4 b. or br.g. Pleasant Colony (USA) – Grand Bonheur (USA) (Blushing Groom (FR) 131) [1994 74: 10m^6 8.1g^6 10.2m* 12g 1995 12m 10g Jun 12] big, good-topped gelding: has a markedly round action: fair performer: well below form for new stable in 1995: stays 10.2f: acts on good to firm ground: takes keen hold: decidedly edgy (finished last) final 3-y-o start: gelded. *N. J. Henderson* –

NEW BROOM (IRE) 3 b.f. Brush Aside (USA) 125 – Qurrat Al Ain (Wolver Hollow 126) [1994 NR 1995 12.3m^4 10.5g Sep 22] leggy filly: third live foal: dam winning 2m hurdler: no worthwhile form. *M. H. Easterby* –

NEWBURY COAT 5 b.g. Chilibang 120 – Deanta In Eirinn (Red Sunset 120) 66 d
[1994 NR 1995 a5g^3 5m a6g^5 a7g a5g a5g Dec 2] smallish, sturdy gelding: fair 5f performer: trained at 3 yrs by M. McCormack: had been running (and winning) in Jersey prior to third of 15 in claimer at Southwell: failed to repeat the form, sold out of B. Meehan's stable 575 gns Ascot September Sales after next start: acts on fibresand and on good to firm ground and soft: tried blinkered/visored. *B. Preece*

NEW CAPRICORN (USA) 5 ch.g. Green Forest (USA) 134 – Size Six (USA) 87
(Caerleon (USA) 132) [1994 100: 6s 7g* 8m^3 7g^2 7m* 7m^6 8s 7m^3 6d^3 8d 1995 7m 7m 7m 7m 8m Jul 2] sturdy, quite attractive gelding: only fairly useful at best in 1995: stays 8.1f: acts on soft ground and good to firm: normally held up/tracks leaders: hurdling with C. Parker. *M. A. Jarvis*

NEW CENTURY (USA) 3 gr.g. Manila (USA) – Casessa (USA) (Caro 133) 86
[1994 85: 7g^3 7.5f* 8.1g^2 7.6s^4 1995 10.5m^5 10m 7g 7.9m^6 7f Oct 24] big, good-bodied colt: fairly useful performer: off course nearly 5 months after second start, and sold out of H. Cecil's stable 23,000 gns Newmarket September Sales: worthwhile form for new stable only when fifth of 8 in rated stakes at York: stays 10.5f: acts on firm going, possibly unsuited by soft: strong-galloping type. *D. Nicholls*

NEWGATE BUBBLES 4 b.f. Hubbly Bubbly (USA) – Streets Ahead 67 (Ovid 95) [1994 –: 7.5m^6 12m 1995 10m 12m May 19] tall, leggy filly: no sign of ability. *B. W. Murray* –

NEWGATE HUSH 3 ch.f. Kind of Hush 118 – Mummys Colleen 75 (Mummy's Pet 125) [1994 NR 1995 13.8g 11d 11f a11g a14g^6 Dec 1] angular filly: half-sister to winning sprinter Jesters Pet (by Cawston's Clown) and a winner abroad: dam won twice over 5f: of little account. *B. W. Murray* –

NEWINGTON BUTTS (IRE) 5 br.m. Dowsing (USA) 124 – Cloud Nine 97 48
(Skymaster 126) [1994 49: 7m 6g^5 a6g^3 a7g^2 1995 a7g a6g a7g^3 a7g^4 6.9d a7g a6g^3 a5g^3 a5g Dec 6] small, close-coupled mare: poor maiden: trained until after fourth start by R. Akehurst: stays 7f: acts on good to firm and dead ground and on the all-weather: tried blinkered, no improvement: front runner. *K. McAuliffe*

NEW INN 4 b.g. Petoski 135 – Pitroyal 74 (Pitskelly 122) [1994 64, a74: 8g 11.1m 62
10m 13.8g^2 a11g* a14.8g* 13.6m^3 12.4d* a14.8g^2 a12g* a11g 1995 a12g a12g 16.2m 14.1g* 14.1m^4 12g^3 15.8g^5 12.3m 11.5g 18f Oct 16] workmanlike gelding: modest handicapper: won at Nottingham in April on fifth-last start for E. Weymes: well beaten for new stable: stays 14.8f: acts on good to firm ground, dead and fibresand: visored (well beaten) third 4-y-o start: races prominently: fair hurdler. *S. Gollings*

NEWLANDS CORNER 2 b.f. (Apr 28) Forzando 122 – Nice Lady 65 (Connaught 130) [1995 6d 7g 7g Oct 23] 5,200F: fifth foal: half-sister to winning sprinters Lady Sabo and Sabo Song (both by Prince Sabo) and a winner in Italy by Nordance: dam, lightly-raced maiden, second over 9.4f: no worthwhile form in maidens and a seller: has been bandaged. *J. Akehurst* –

NEWPORT KNIGHT 4 ch.g. Bairn (USA) 126 – Clara Barton (Youth (USA) 69
135) [1994 73: 10g^6 10m^3 10m^2 10.2f^3 12m^6 10.2g^6 9.7m 1995 10.2m^3 10.1m^6 11.5m* 12m^5 11.5s^3 Sep 28] lengthy, dipped-backed gelding: fair performer: won

(first time) handicap at Lingfield in August, leading approaching final 1f: stays 11.5f: acts on firm ground and soft: has carried head high. *R. Akehurst*

NEW REPUTATION 4 b.c. Law Society (USA) 130 – Reputation (Tower Walk 130) [1994 90+: 12g* 12f^4 13.9m^5 12g^2 12g^5 14.6g 13.3s^3 18m^3 1995 18.7m^4 16.5g^2 16.1g* 15.9m^4 14g* 18m Oct 14] tall, unfurnished colt: unimpressive mover: fairly useful handicapper: fourth in Chester Cup on reappearance: won minor events at Newmarket in July and Haydock (made most and rallied well) in September: pulled up after breaking down in Cesarewitch: stays very well: acts on firm ground and soft: blinkered final 3-y-o to second 4-y-o starts. *B. W. Hills* — 93

NEW TECHNIQUE (FR) 2 br.f. (Mar 23) Formidable (USA) 125 – Dolly Bea Sweet (USA) (Super Concorde (USA) 128) [1995 6m Jun 26] 2,800Y: small filly: third foal: dam won in USA at up to 9f: 40/1, tailed off in median auction maiden at Windsor. *K. McAuliffe* — –

NEZ CARRERA 4 ch.g. Aragon 118 – New Ribbons 79 (Ribero 126) [1994 47: 6g^3 7g 6m 8m 1995 a6g a7g Jan 6] leggy gelding: seems no longer of much account: sold 1,000 gns Ascot February Sales. *R. M. Whitaker* — –

NICKITOTO 3 gr.f. Mtoto 134 – Nicholas Grey 100 (Track Spare 125) [1994 NR 1995 10.5m 12m 12f^2 11.8g* 14.1m^2 Aug 23] leggy filly: closely related to 2 winners, notably very smart 9f to 1½m performer Terimon (by Bustino), and half-sister to several winners: dam 2-y-o 5f to 7f winner, second in Oaks d'Italia: fair handicapper: won minor event at Leicester in August: will probably be suited by further than 1¾m: yet to race on a soft surface: sold 18,000 gns Newmarket December Sales. *J. L. Dunlop* — 67

NICK THE BISCUIT 4 b.g. Nicholas Bill 125 – Maryland Cookie (USA) 101 (Bold Hour) [1994 73: 10s 8s^5 10g^4 a9.4g^2 10.5g^4 10m 8s 8.9d 1995 a9.4g a12g^2 Jan 18] useful-looking gelding: fair maiden: visored first time, neck second of 6 in Wolverhampton claimer: suited by middle distances nowadays: acts on fibresand, best turf efforts on good ground: has run creditably when sweating: joined R. Phillips. *M. D. I. Usher* — 61 +

NICKY'S FEELINGS 3 b.f. Feelings (FR) – Polly Potter (Pollerton 115) [1994 33: 9d 1995 13.1g^6 7.1m 11.1f^5 Jul 10] of little account. *T. Dyer* — –

NICOLOTTE 4 b.c. Night Shift (USA) – Nicoletta 81 (Busted 134) [1994 107+: 8d^4 1995 9m^4 10m^2 10d^3 8m* 8f^4 8g 8d* Oct 8] — 116

The reaction from a crowd of almost 40,000 people to the finish of the opening race at Royal Ascot wouldn't have given members of the Noise Abatement Society any cause for concern. Cheers were muted as 16/1-shot Nicolotte led home

Queen Anne Stakes, Royal Ascot—
surprises in the first race at the meeting as 16/1-shot Nicolotte quickens clear and 20/1-shot Nijo (left) beats favourite Soviet Line for second

20/1-shot Nijo in the seven-runner Queen Anne Stakes, a race which many had considered to be a match between Soviet Line and Sayyedati. Nicolotte was at last fulfilling the promise he'd shown as a two-year-old, having had few opportunities to do so after suffering a slab fracture of the bones across a hock when being prepared for the 1994 Two Thousand Guineas. The only cure for Nicolotte, who'd finished a close third to Grand Lodge in the previous year's Dewhurst Stakes, was rest, and it was a year before he was seen on a racecourse again. An encouraging run on his reappearance was followed by placings in two Group 3 events over a mile and a quarter at Sandown. Nicolotte ran well enough at the trip, but the return to a mile in the Queen Anne Stakes showed him in an even better light. He travelled well just behind the leaders and had the speed to take full advantage when a gap appeared two furlongs out, at which point Sayyedati was trapped on the rails behind the leader Soviet Line. Nicolotte quickly took command, and he ran on strongly to win by two lengths, with Nijo just coming out on top in the battle for the minor placings with Soviet Line, Young Ern and Sayyedati, who might have finished second with a clear run. Sayyedati easily turned the tables on Nicolotte in both the Sussex Stakes and Prix Jacques le Marois. Nicolotte, encountering firm ground for the first time, was unimpressive to post and didn't give his running at Goodwood, but ran respectably when seventh of nine at Deauville. An easier opportunity to win a Group 1 race came his way in October, in the Premio Vittorio di Capua at Milan, and he made the most of it, leading from two furlongs out and beating the only other British challenger Prince Arthur by one and three quarter lengths. It was Nicolotte's last race. In 1996 he will be standing at the Coolmore Stud at a fee of IR 5,000 guineas.

Nicolotte should make plenty of appeal to breeders. A rangy colt who very much takes the eye, he is from an excellent family. His dam Nicoletta, a lightly-raced

Mollers Racing's "Nicolotte"

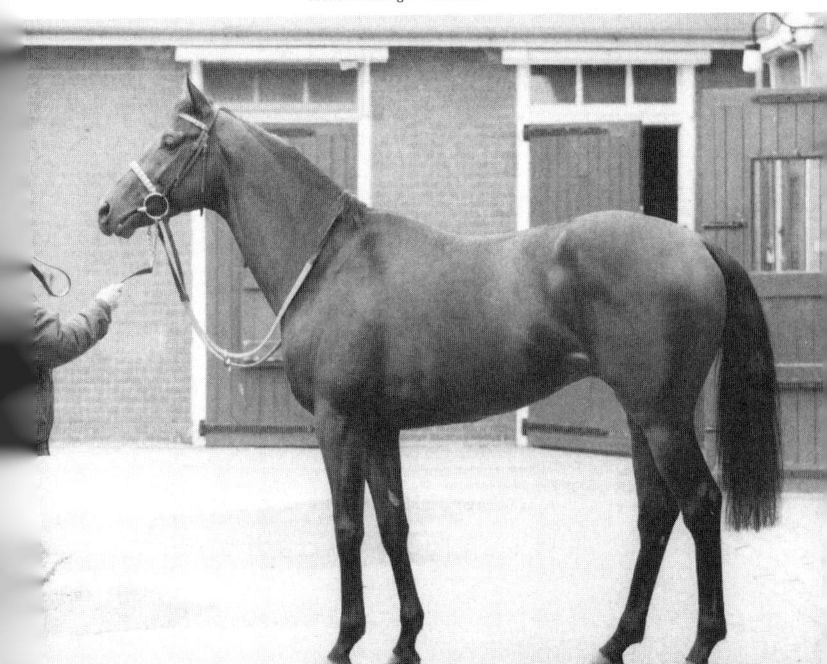

Nicolotte (b.c. 1991)	Night Shift (USA) (b 1980)	Northern Dancer (b 1961)	Nearctic
			Natalma
		Ciboulette (b 1961)	Chop Chop
			Windy Answer
	Nicoletta (b 1975)	Busted (b 1963)	Crepello
			Sans Le Sou
		Violetta III (b 1958)	Pinza
			Urshalim

nine-furlong winner, is a daughter of the 1961 Cambridgeshire dead-heater Violetta III and granddaughter of the very speedy Urshalim, a daughter of Horama. Violetta III produced ten winners in all, many of whom have had great success both on the racecourse and at stud: Favoletta, who won the Irish One Thousand Guineas, produced the flying two-year-old Amaranda and the One Thousand Guineas runner-up Favoridge; Furioso, second in the Oaks, bred the Derby and King George VI and Queen Elizabeth Diamond Stakes winner Teenoso plus the Sun Chariot winner Topsy, the dam of Derby runner-up Most Welcome; the Sun Chariot third Parthica is the dam of the Irish Oaks winner Give Thanks; Laughing Girl, fourth in the Oaks, has had the good-class middle-distance fillies Braiswick and Percy's Lass; and the fairly useful middle-distance performer Little Miss the high-class middle-distance stayer Old Country. Until Nicolotte, her seventh foal, came along Nicoletta herself hadn't met with much success at stud, the fairly useful seven-furlong to mile-and-a-half winner Nickle Plated (by Auction Ring) being the best of her three winners. Nicolotte's year-younger sister My Darlingdaughter showed little on her only outing, in a maiden at Sandown in September. Nicolotte acted on good to firm ground and soft. *G. Wragg*

NIGELSCHINAPALACE 6 b.g. Comrade In Arms 123 – Ergo 82 (Song 132) [1994 –: a12g a12g a8.5g 1995 a8.5g^4 a8.5g 8d a14g* a14.8g a16g Jun 8] leggy gelding: poor performer: won claimer at Southwell in April by 11 lengths: tailed off afterwards: stays 1¾m: tried blinkered at 3 yrs: usually bandaged. *Miss S. J. Wilton* 37

NIGEL'S LAD (IRE) 3 b.g. Dominion Royale 112 – Back To Earth (FR) (Vayrann 133) [1994 62: 7d 6d^2 a7g^5 a7g^3 1995 a8.5g^3 a10g* a8.5g^2 a10g* a10g^4 10d 10.5m^2 10g* 9.9m^3 9.2g* a9.4g^6 8g* 10g 8m 10m^5 9m^4 8m^2 10.5g^6 9.2g^2 10g* Sep 29] sturdy, close-coupled gelding: progressed steadily into a fairly useful handicapper: won at Lingfield (twice) in January, Nottingham (minor event) in April, at Hamilton and Newcastle in May and 20-runner event at Newmarket (best effort, led 1f out, stormed 4 lengths clear of Alkateb) in September: likely to prove best at up to around 1¼m: acts on all-weather surfaces, raced almost exclusively on good or good to firm ground at 3 yrs: tended to hang under pressure eighth and ninth 3-y-o starts: tough and genuine. *P. C. Haslam* 95

NIGGLE 3 b.f. Night Shift (USA) – Enchanted 116 (Song 132) [1994 NR 1995 8m^2 9g^5 Jun 3] big, robust filly: half-sister to several winners, including useful 11f and 11.7f winner Woodpecker (by Touching Wood): dam sprinter, best at 2 yrs: burly, beaten 1¼ lengths in Newmarket Challenge Whip: shaped as if worth trying over sprint distances in maiden at Kempton 4 weeks later: looked sort to do better. *H. Thomson Jones* 65

NIGHT ASSET 6 b.g. Night Shift (USA) – Fine Asset (Hot Spark 126) [1994 NR 1995 5m 6f^2 6m* 6g^3 6m Jun 26] strong, sprint type: carries condition: unimpressive mover: modest handicapper: won at Brighton in June: pulled up lame final start: stays 6f: acts on firm and dead ground: used to wear blinkers, not at 6 yrs: held up. *J. O'Donoghue* 59

NIGHT CITY 4 b.g. Kris 135 – Night Secret 86 (Nijinsky (CAN) 138) [1994 8v* 10g^5 1995 9m^4 8m 7g 8f 10.1m^2 10.3g^2 9g 8.1s* Oct 17] useful-looking gelding: first foal: dam, 1¼m winner, is half-sister to Royal Lodge winner Desert Secret from family of Seattle Slew: useful performer: won maiden at the Curragh at 3 yrs for J. Oxx: sold 16,000 gns Newmarket Autumn (1994) Sales and gelded: ran very well in rated stakes at Newbury and Royal Hunt Cup at Royal Ascot first 2 starts here: back almost to that form to win minor event at Chepstow in October, leading near finish to beat Decorated Hero a head: best form at up to 9f, should prove as effective at 1¼m: acts on good to firm and heavy ground: flashed tail fifth 4-y-o start: edgy sort, sometimes attended by 2 handlers and early to post. *Lady Herries* 103

Tote Festival Handicap, Ascot—Night Dance swoops late to deny market leaders Decorated Hero (far side) and Western Fame (No. 21); Fame Again is fourth

NIGHT DANCE 3 ch.c. Weldnaas (USA) 112 – Shift Over (USA) 62 (Night Shift (USA)) [1994 79: 7.1m* 7g4 1995 9m 8.1m 8g2 8m 7.1m* 8g3 8f 7m2 7d* 8s* 8m a9.4g Dec 2] good-topped colt: useful handicapper: won £8,800 event at Sandown in July, £52,900 Tote Festival Handicap at Ascot (beat Decorated Hero 1¼ lengths) in September and 22-runner £11,900 event at Ascot (travelled well, got perfect run up stand rail) in October: effective at 7f and 1m: acts on good to firm and soft ground, possibly not on firm: usually ridden for late challenge: finished behind on 4 occasions in 1995, and reportedly sometimes swallows his tongue. *G. Lewis* 99

NIGHT EDITION 5 b.g. Night Shift (USA) – New Chant (CAN) (New Providence) [1994 53, a–: 11g 13v 12.5d 11.7g 12s2 12d6 11.9f a12g 10s4 10d a12g a10g 1995 a10g2 a10g4 a10g4 a12g 12m a12g Nov 29] robust gelding: good mover: poor form at best in 1995: stays 1½m: acts on equitrack and soft going: inconsistent. *S. Dow* – a38

NIGHT EXCELLENCE 3 b.c. Night Shift (USA) – Briar Creek (Busted 134) [1994 –p: 7s 1995 a7g a7g Nov 10] compact colt: no form: sold out of B. Hills's stable after reappearance 4,500 gns Newmarket July Sales, resold 1,000 gns Ascot November Sales. *C. Weedon* –

NIGHT FANTASY (IRE) 7 br.m. King of Clubs 124 – Maria Renata (Jaazeiro (USA) 127) [1994 –: a8g 1995 a8g a10g6 Jan 28] has won several races in Jersey: no worthwhile form in claimers here: visored on reappearance: sold 725 gns (May), 1,350 (August) at Ascot Sales. *N. J. H. Walker* –

NIGHT FLARE (FR) 3 ch.c. Night Shift (USA) – Gold Flair 93 (Tap On Wood 130) [1994 NR 1995 8.1g4 10m 8.5m4 10g Sep 29] big, heavy-topped colt: second foal: half-brother to modest 1993 2-y-o 7f winner Duball Remy (by Roi Danzig): dam, maiden, stayed 1½m: broke out of stalls on intended debut in April: clearly best effort in maidens at Sandown on debut: stays 1m. *R. Hannon* 72

NIGHT HARMONY (IRE) 2 ch.c. (Mar 20) Digamist (USA) 110 – Quaver 86 (Song 132) [1995 6g 6d 5g4 Oct 16] 17,000Y: leggy colt: fifth foal: half-brother to useful 5f to 7f performer Night Melody, 1989 2-y-o 5f winner Key Shift (both by 53

Night Shift) and a winner in Denmark by Nordico: dam sprinter from good sprinting family: poor form in maidens: has worn bandages. *R. Hannon*

NIGHT HERO (USA) 3 ch.c. Mr Prospector (USA) – Lisaleen (USA) 97 (Northern Dancer) [1994 90p: 6m* 6d² 1995 7m⁴ 8.1m³ May 29] good-topped, attractive colt: has scope: fairly useful form: in frame in listed race at Newmarket (burly) and Whitsun Cup at Sandown (stayed on unable to land a blow, 2 lengths behind Dance Turn) in May: effective at 8.1f, may stay further: yet to race on extremes of going: sent to Dubai. *M. R. Stoute* — 93

NIGHT IN A MILLION 4 br.g. Night Shift (USA) – Ridalia 56 (Ridan (USA)) [1994 66: 10m 8.5g 7v⁴ 7d 7d* 7s 1995 a7g² 8m Jun 14] heavy-topped gelding: fair handicapper: good second of 15 at Southwell on reappearance but ran poorly at Kempton 6 days later: should stay 1m: acts on fibresand, best turf efforts on a soft surface: inconsistent: sold (Mrs J. Cecil to S. Woodman) 5,200 gns Newmarket July Sales. *Mrs J. Cecil* — 66

NIGHT OF GLASS 2 b.g. (Feb 2) Mazilier (USA) 107 – Donna Elvira 80 (Chief Singer 131) [1995 6m 6m 7g Oct 10] small, angular, unfurnished gelding: first foal: dam best efforts at 7f: well beaten in maiden events at Leicester (2) and Newmarket. *D. Morris* — –

NIGHT PARADE (USA) 2 b.c. (Feb 5) Rory's Jester (AUS) – Nocturnal Song (USA) (Northern Dancer) [1995 5m² 5.1m* 5m 6g 5m Jul 28] strong, deep-girthed colt: fine mover: first foal: dam unraced close relative of Carnegie out of Detroit: sire good Australian sprinter: won 5-runner maiden at Chester in May by 3 lengths from Repertory: failed to progress in pattern races: best form at 5f: had tongue tied down final start. *P. W. Chapple-Hyam* — 87

NIGHTSCENE (IRE) 3 b.f. Scenic 128 – Internet (Tender King 123) [1994 7g 1995 8m 10g 9g 8d⁴ 10m* Oct 7] IR 2,000F: good-topped filly: first foal: dam, winner in Italy, granddaughter of Castle Moon, dam of Moon Madness and Sheriff's Star: modest performer: trained at 2 yrs by T. Lacy, first 4 starts at 3 yrs by T. Mills: sent back to Ireland and won claimer at Down Royal in October (claimed IR £4,500 and joined Capt D. G. Swan): stays 1¼m: acts on good to firm ground, probably (though found less than seemed likely) on dead: tends to pull hard. *M. J. Grassick, Ireland* — 60 +

NIGHT SILENCE 2 ch.c. (Feb 4) Generous (IRE) 139 – Exclusive Life (USA) (Exclusive Native (USA)) [1995 7g 7f 7f⁶ Oct 23] workmanlike colt: fifth foal: half-brother to 3 winners, including 1½m winner Life At Sea (by Slip Anchor) and useful 1991 2-y-o 6f winner Fair Cop (by Al Nasr): dam sprint winner in USA: best effort in maidens when sixth of 11 to Dance On A Cloud at Leicester, running on from rear and not at all knocked about: slowly away on debut: will do better over 1m+: sent to Saudi Arabia. *Sir Mark Prescott* — 53 p

NIGHT TIME 3 b.c. Night Shift (USA) – Gathering Place (USA) (Hawaii) [1994 70: 5f⁴ 7.1m 7m⁶ 8g 7.3v 1995 7g² 12.1g 10m 10g³ 12m⁴ 10m⁴ 11.4d Sep 12] lengthy colt: modest maiden: jockey reported the horse had gurgled third outing: ran as if all was not well final outing: best form at up to 1¼m: well beaten on heavy going: hurdling with O. Sherwood before sold to join A. Streeter 700 gns Ascot December Sales. *R. Hannon* — 63

NIGHT WATCH (USA) 2 b.c. (Apr 1) Night Shift (USA) – Christchurch (FR) 88 (So Blessed 130) [1995 7.1m⁴ 7f⁴ 9m* 8.1d⁴ 8g* Sep 21] strong, compact colt: has a fluent, long stride: closely related to fairly useful 10.1f winner Duke's Lodge (by Shareef Dancer) and half-brother to numerous winners, including smart 6f to 10.5f winner Church Parade (by Queen's Hussar) and smart middle-distance stayer Castle Rising (by Blakeney): dam, 1½m winner, half-sister to Highclere, an excellent family: successful in maiden at Sandown in August and 3-runner minor event (made running, beat Dublin River easily by 4 lengths) at Pontefract in September: will stay at least 1¼m: possibly unsuited by good to soft ground: likely to improve further. *I. A. Balding* — 97 p

NIGHT WINK (USA) 3 ch.g. Rahy (USA) 115 – Lady In White 94 (Shareef Dancer (USA) 135) [1994 75: 6.1m 7.1d² 7g² 8.2g³ 1995 8m 10g 9m⁴ 8m² 8.5d 8g 7g* 7f³ 8f* 7m Oct 28] sturdy, lengthy gelding: carries condition: good mover: fairly useful performer: sold out of M. Stoute's stable 4,000 gns Newmarket July Sales after second start: won apprentice maiden at Leicester and handicap at Redcar (easily — 84

Sheikh Ahmed bin Saeed Al Maktoum's "Nijo"

best effort) in October: stays 1m: acts on firm and dead ground: well beaten only try in visor: tricky ride, tending to pull hard and wander: races prominently. *D. Nicholls*

NIJO 4 b.g. Top Ville 129 – Nibabu (FR) 101§ (Nishapour (FR) 125) [1994 108: 7g³ 8m 7g* 6m⁴ 7.3g⁵ 7m⁴ 7.9d* 8d* 1995 7g⁴ 8m² 7m⁵ 7.3m² 8g² Sep 7] tall, lengthy gelding: shows knee action: smart performer: 2 lengths second to Nicolotte in Queen Anne Stakes at Royal Ascot, and ¾-length second to both Harayir in Hungerford Stakes at Newbury and Bishop of Cashel in steadily-run Kiveton Park Stakes at Doncaster: stays 1m well: acts on good to firm and dead ground: blinkered (ran poorly) once as 3-y-o: sometimes sweating and edgy: sometimes flashes tail, carries head awkwardly and hangs markedly: usually held up. *D. R. Loder* 112

NIKITA'S STAR (IRE) 2 ch.c. (Feb 14) Soviet Lad (USA) 94 – Sally Chase 101 (Sallust 134) [1995 5m 7f⁴ 6f 7.6m⁵ 7.3d 8f³ 7.3d a8g Nov 10] 12,000Y: sturdy colt: half-brother to several winners, including 1994 2-y-o 7f and 1m winner Unanimous Vote (by Roi Danzig), smart 8.5f winner in USA in 1995, and useful 1m and 1¼m winner Super Sally (by Superlative): dam, sprinter, ran only at 2 yrs: fair maiden: will stay beyond 1m: acts on firm ground (seems unsuited by a soft surface and showed nothing on equitrack): visored fourth outing: blinkered last 3 starts. *D. J. G. Murray Smith* 68

NIKNAKS NEPHEW 3 br.g. Tragic Role (USA) – Bubulina 63 (Dunphy 124) [1994 NR 1995 12m 10g⁴ 10m 12f⁴ 12m 11.9g Sep 20] leggy, angular gelding: first foal: dam, middle-distance maiden, is half-sister to fairly useful middle-distance stayer Nikitas: fair maiden handicapper: trained first 2 outings by Miss A. J. Whitfield: well beaten last 2 starts: should stay further than 1½m: has raced only on a sound surface: blinkered final 3-y-o start. *D. J. S. ffrench Davis* 70

NILGIRI HILLS (IRE) 2 ch.c. (Apr 18) Indian Ridge 123 – Our Resolution (Caerleon (USA) 132) [1995 6m³ 5.9f² 6m³ 6d² 6m² Oct 4] 15,500Y: rather leggy, 84 p close-coupled colt: third foal: dam no sign of ability: fairly useful maiden: stayed on well when very good second of 14 to Dashing Blue in nursery at York on final start, first home of those towards stand side: bred to stay beyond 6f: acts on good to firm ground but gives impression will prove just as (if not more) effective back on an easy surface. *J. L. Dunlop*

NINA FROM PASADENA 2 ch.f. (May 6) Clantime 101 – Abalone (Abwah 118) [1995 5.1m^{6} 5g Jun 3] 4,000Y: small filly: sister to fair sprinter Echo Chamber and half-sister to 3 winners, all at up to 9f: dam unraced: well beaten in maiden auctions. *C. James* –

NINEACRES 4 b.g. Sayf El Arab (USA) 127 – Mayor 86 (Laxton 105) [1994 60: a5g^{2} a6g^{4} a6g^{5} 5m a5g^{4} 7.5g 5m^{2} 5f* 5d^{3} 5m^{2} 6f 5s 5.1s a5g^{5} a5g^{2} a6g^{2} a5g^{2} a5g* 1995 a6g a6g^{6} a5g^{3} a5g* a5g^{5} a6g 5g^{5} 5m 5m 5m^{3} a5g^{6} a6g Sep 16] angular, workmanlike gelding: modest handicapper: won at Lingfield (apprentices) in January: sold out of D. Nicholls' stable 1,000 gns Newmarket July Sales: stays 6f: acts on firm and soft ground and goes well on the all-weather: very best form in blinkers, visored (last 2 starts) for new stable. *C. A. Smith* 51 a61

NINE BARROW DOWN (IRE) 3 b.g. Danehill (USA) 126 – Rising Spirits 77 (Cure The Blues (USA)) [1994 75p: 7.1m^{3} 1995 10m 12m* 10g^{6} 12m 14m^{4} 14.8m^{5} Aug 25] leggy gelding: fluent mover: fairly useful form: got up close home in maiden at Thirsk in May: failed to progress, folding tamely last time: probably stays 1¾m: sometimes hangs and looks a hard ride: gelded: hurdling with Miss M. E. Rowland. *H. R. A. Cecil* 80 d

NINETTE (USA) 3 b.f. Alleged (USA) 138 – Stellaria (USA) 98 (Roberto (USA) 131) [1994 NR 1995 10f* 10m^{2} 10d^{3} 9m^{4} 9f* 9.5f Dec 10] smallish, robust filly: good mover: second foal: dam 2-y-o 5f and 6f winner: useful performer: won maiden at Ripon in July: good fourth to Restructure in listed race (sweating and edgy, stayed on again closing stages) at Newmarket final start for J. Gosden: raced on lasix, won allowance race at Hollywood Park in November, her better effort in USA: should stay beyond 1¼m: acts on firm ground, below best on dead. *R. Frankel, USA* 101

NINETY-FIVE 3 ch.f. Superpower 113 – Vanishing Trick 83 (Silly Season 127) [1994 64: 6m^{3} 5f^{2} 6f^{5} 5f^{4} 5g 5g^{2} 1995 5g^{2} 5m^{6} 5g^{2} 5g^{2} a5g^{4} 5g^{6} 5m Oct 4] good-topped filly: fair handicapper: best form at 5f: acts on fibresand and firm ground, yet to race on a soft surface: ran creditably only try in blinkers. *J. G. FitzGerald* 67

NINIA (USA) 3 ch.f. Affirmed (USA) – Lajna 88 (Be My Guest (USA) 126) [1994 63d: 6g^{2} 6m 7m 6s^{5} 6m 1995 a8g^{3} 8f* 8m^{2} 8m* 9f^{4} 8f* 7.5m* 8g* 8d 8.1s^{3} 8m Oct 14] leggy, close-coupled filly: fair handicapper: successful in 1995 at Carlisle in June, Newcastle in July, Redcar and Beverley in August and at Thirsk in September: should stay 9f: acts on firm ground, seemingly not on a soft surface: blinkered (below form) once at 2 yrs: effective from front or held up. *M. Johnston* 73

NINOTCHKA (USA) 2 b.f. (Mar 23) Nijinsky (CAN) 138 – Puget Sound 95 (High Top 131) [1995 7g^{5} Oct 23] $47,000Y: sixth foal: closely related to 7f winner Dagny Juel (by Danzig) and 1½m winner Middle Kingdom (by Northern Dancer): dam 7f and 1m winner out of half-sister to Nureyev: 10/1, 4½ lengths fifth of 14 to Jezyah in maiden at Lingfield, leading unfavoured stand-side group over 5f: will improve. *J. L. Dunlop* 66 p

NIRVANA PRINCE 6 ch.g. Celestial Storm (USA) 132 – Princess Sunshine (Busted 134) [1994 NR 1995 a12g^{2} Feb 8] third foal: dam, well beaten, out of half-sister to top-class performers Double Jump: won 2 NH Flat races in 1993: fairly useful hurdler who stays 21f: second of 10 in median auction maiden at Wolverhampton on flat debut: should stay beyond 1½m. *B. Preece* 53

NISYA 3 ch.f. Risk Me (FR) 127 – Lompoa (Lomond (USA) 128) [1994 NR 1995 5.1g a6g^{6} Apr 26] 1,000Y: sturdy, lengthy filly: first foal: dam ran twice: no worthwhile form in maidens. *Miss Gay Kelleway* –

NITA'S CHOICE 5 b.m. Valiyar 129 – What's The Matter 57 (High Top 131) [1994 NR 1995 10g 8g^{4} a8.5g 8m 10g^{6} Jul 20] lengthy, rather sparely-made mare: first foal: dam, maiden, stayed 1¼m: bad form at best on flat. *A. G. Newcombe* 23

NITE-OWL DANCER 3 b.f. Robellino (USA) 127 – Lady Tap 94 (Red Sunset 120) [1994 59: 7d 6s^{3} 7.1g^{6} 1995 a6g^{3} a7g^{2} a6g^{5} a7g^{3} 5m^{2} 6g^{4} 5d^{2} 5m^{2} 5f* 5m^{3} 5g 75 ?

Sep 8] workmanlike filly: thrived physically at 3 yrs: fair handicapper: second run in 2 days when winning 4-runner race at Redcar in August: appeared to excel herself from 13 lb out of handicap when third of 12 in £11,200 event at York 12 days later: only eleventh of 17 at Doncaster on final outing: best efforts at 5f, probably stays 7f: acts on fibresand and on firm and soft going. *J. A. Harris*

NITEOWL RAIDER (IRE) 2 ch.c. (Apr 19) Standaan (FR) 118 – Havana Moon (Ela-Mana-Mou 132) [1995 5m 5m³ 5f⁵ a8.5g Dec 2] IR 3,200F, 7,000 2-y-o: angular colt: brother to a winner in Macau: dam Irish 7f and 1m winner: poor maiden: stays 8.5f. *J. A. Harris* 49

NIVASHA 3 b.f. Shavian 125 – Rheinza 66 (Rheingold 137) [1994 43: 7m 7g 8d 1995 12f³ 14.1m⁶ 11.1f⁵ a9.4g³ 12s 12m a10g a7g⁴ a7g Dec 14] lengthy, workmanlike filly: poor mover: poor maiden: sold out of M. Bell's stable 2,300 gns Newmarket July Sales after fourth start: effective at 7f and stays 1½m: acts on firm and dead ground and the all-weather: sweating (ran creditably) on 3-y-o reappearance. *R. P. C. Hoad* 39

NIZAAL (USA) 4 ch.c. Diesis 133 – Shicklah (USA) 106 (The Minstrel (CAN) 135) [1994 83: 6s⁴ 7s* 8.1m 7g 7g 1995 a8g⁵ a12g⁵ a10g⁵ a10g 8.9g 8.2m 7m Nov 3] good-topped colt: has a powerful, markedly round action: fairly useful performer at 3 yrs for H. Thomson Jones: unplaced in 4 races in Dubai then sold 22,000 gns Newmarket July Sales: no form in handicaps on return: should stay at least 1m: acts on soft going, possibly not on top-of-the-ground. *D. Nicholls* 70 d

NKAPEN ROCKS (SPA) 2 b.g. (Mar 25) Risk Me (FR) 127 – Debutina Park 87 (Averof 123) [1995 5g⁵ a6g⁴ 6g Oct 3] 5,000Y: leggy, useful-looking colt: brother to a modest maiden and half-brother to winning sprinters Super Deb (by Superlative) and Avidal Park (by Horage): dam 2-y-o 6f winner: best effort in maiden events when seventh of 15 to Lay The Blame in auction race at Warwick final start: seems barely to stay 6f: modest effort on fibresand. *Capt. J. Wilson* 62

NO ANIMOSITY (IRE) 2 ch.c (Mar 29) Ajraas (USA) 88 – Arctic Ford (Fr) 85 (Arctic Tern (USA) 126) [1995 5s³ 6m⁴ 6g* 6m* 8d⁴ Oct 14] IR 4,300F: sixth living foal: brother to Irish 7f winner Barrichello and half-brother to 8.5f to 1¼m winner Cold Shower (by Kings Lake): dam 7f winner: won maiden in May and 29-runner £73,500 Tattersalls Breeders Stakes (leading 1f out and pulling 4 lengths clear of Troysend) in September, both at the Curragh: creditable fourth to Ahkaam in 5-runner Beresford Stakes there last time: should stay 1m: acts on good to firm ground. *A. P. O'Brien, Ireland* 98

NOBBY BARNES 6 b.g. Nordance (USA) – Loving Doll 72 (Godswalk (USA) 130) [1994 55, a57: a7g a8g 9.7s a10g² a7g⁶ a8g 8v 9.7s 8.5m⁶ 8.1g 9f* 6m⁴ 8f² 8.3m 8g⁶ 8.3m⁴ 8.1g² 8.2m⁵ 8g 7.9m⁶ 8.5g 10.3s⁵ 10.1d 1995 8f 8.3g⁴ 8f⁴ 8g 8g⁶ 8g³ 8.2m⁶ 10.1m⁴ 8.1m⁶ 9f³ 8.5m² 8.1m³ 9m⁶ 8.2m³ 7.9g⁴ 8.9g⁴ 8f a8g Nov 6] neat gelding: has a round action: poor handicapper: made frame on numerous occasions in 1995: stays 1¼m: acts on firm ground, soft and all-weather surfaces: sometimes bandaged: usually held up under Kim Tinkler. *Don Enrico Incisa* 47

NOBBY NORTH 3 b.g. Northern State (USA) 91 – One Degree 80 (Crooner 119) [1994 NR 1995 10m 10m⁴ 10m 12m 12m 11.9g Sep 20] rather unfurnished gelding: 66 d

Tattersalls Breeders Stakes, the Curragh—
Christy Roche chooses correctly from nine Aidan O'Brien runners as No Animosity wins by four lengths; the record-breaking trainer is also responsible for the second, fourth and fifth

sixth foal: brother to 4-y-o 1m winner (stays 1¼m) Waldo and half-brother to useful 1987 2-y-o 5f winner Pea Green (by Try My Best): dam 6f winner: fair maiden: below form after second start: should stay 1½m: visored (well beaten) final outing: usually races prominently: has joined G. Thorner. *Lord Huntingdon*

NOBLE BALLERINA (USA) 3 b.f. Green Dancer (USA) 132 – Noble Devorcee (USA) (Vaguely Noble 140) [1994 NR 1995 a12g⁴ a11g⁵ a7g a16g 15g 16.1g Oct 3] $6,000Y: first foal: dam unraced half-sister to 3 stakes winners, including Grade 2 6f winner at 5 yrs Rocky Marriage: no worthwhile form. *A. P. Jarvis* –

NOBLE CANONIRE 3 b.f. Gunner B 126 – Lucky Candy 61 (Lucky Wednesday 124) [1994 NR 1995 a7g a12g 10m 10d⁶ Sep 18] sturdy, plain filly: bad walker: fifth foal: half-sister to modest 1m winner Ace Girl (by Stanford): dam, form only at 2 yrs, is out of half-sister to Gunner B: no worthwhile form: wears crossed noseband: joined S.R. Bowring. *N. P. Littmoden* –

NOBLE COLOURS 2 b.g. (Mar 3) Distinctly North (USA) 115 – Kentucky Tears (USA) (Cougar (CHI)) [1995 6m a6g Jul 22] 22,000Y: fourth reported foal: half-brother to 1993 2-y-o 5f winner En-Cee-Tee (by Risk Me) and 1992 2-y-o 7f winner Kentucky Dreams (by Dreams To Reality): dam unraced: well beaten in median auction maiden at Redcar and maiden at Wolverhampton. *J. Berry* –

NOBLE KINGDOM 3 b.c. Pharly (FR) 130 – Certain Story (Known Fact (USA) 135) [1994 82: 7.1g 6g³ 6.1m³ 6m* 6d³ 6m 1995 7m² 7m⁴ May 5] lengthy colt: fairly useful handicapper: in frame at Newmarket both 3-y-o starts: stayed 7f: dead. *R. Akehurst* 86

NOBLELY (USA) 8 b.g. Lyphard (USA) 132 – Nonoalca (FR) 120 (Nonoalco (USA) 131) [1994 72: a10g* a10g³ 8.1g 10.2m² 10.2f⁴ 1995 a9.4g 10.2m³ Jun 15] angular gelding: fair handicapper: stays 1¼m well: acts on good to firm ground and equitrack: visored (tailed off) on reappearance: often bandaged: has worn crossed noseband. *N. J. H. Walker* 67

NOBLE NEPTUNE 3 b.g. Governor General 116 – Calibina 101 (Caliban 123) [1994 68: 6m 6m⁵ 5d² 6d 7v⁵ 1995 a7g⁴ 8m 8.3m⁵ 8m* 8.5m⁶ 8.1g 8m 10f⁶ Oct 24] smallish gelding: fair handicapper: won at Newmarket in July: probably stays 1¼m: acts on good to firm (probably on firm) and dead ground. *W. J. Musson* 65

NOBLE ROSE (IRE) 4 b.f. Caerleon (USA) 132 – Noble Lily (USA) (Vaguely Noble 140) [1994 113p: 10.2m² 11.9m* 12.5d² 1995 11.9m⁴ 11.9m 14.6m* 12.5s⁴ 109

Stones Bitter Park Hill Stakes, Doncaster—a pattern win for Noble Rose (centre); she justifies favouritism from Misbelief (left) and Saxon Maid

Sheikh Mohammed's "Noble Rose"

Sep 30] angular, quite attractive filly: reportedly took a long time to come to herself each year, and was never seen out before July: useful performer: back to near best when winning steadily-run Stones Bitter Park Hill Stakes at Doncaster in September, quickening on then holding Misbelief by ½ length: below form in Prix de Royallieu at Longchamp on final start: effective at 1½m and stayed 14.6f: acted on good to firm and dead ground, won maiden on soft: held up: genuine: stud. *L. M. Cumani*

NOBLE SOCIETY 7 b.g. Law Society (USA) 130 – Be Noble (Vaguely Noble 140) [1994 36§, a30§: 14.9s 11.9g^5 14.1d^5 a12g^3 a16g^2 16.4g^3 a16.2g^6 17.2g 1995 16d^4 Jun 15] angular gelding: poor and inconsistent staying maiden on flat: winning plater over hurdles. *K. G. Wingrove* — – §

NOBLE SPIRIT (IRE) 4 b.g. Cyrano de Bergerac 120 – Grecian Sky (African Sky 124) [1994 –: a6s^4 6g 5g a7g 1995 a6g 8g Jun 2] leggy gelding: of little account. *Mrs A. M. Naughton* — –

NOBLE SPRINTER (IRE) 3 b.c. The Noble Player (USA) 126 – Daybreaker (Thatching 131) [1994 61: 6g^3 7m* 7.1m^4 1995 8m 8.1d^2 8.1g^3 8.9g^3 8m^6 Oct 28] good-topped colt: fairly useful handicapper: will be suited by further than 9f: acts on good to firm and dead ground: blinkered (ran creditably) final 3-y-o start: often soon off bridle: consistent. *R. Hannon* — 85

NO CLICHES 2 ch.c. (Apr 12) Risk Me (FR) 127 – Always On A Sunday 101 (Star Appeal 133) [1995 6m^5 6m 6g^6 6m^6 8m* Sep 6] 39,000Y: lengthy, workmanlike colt: unimpressive mover: third foal: brother to 3-y-o Fishy Affair and another poor maiden: dam 1¼m winner: looking tremendously well, won 17-runner nursery at Doncaster on final start by ¾ length from Opera, idling in front: better suited by 1m than 6f: likely to improve further. *G. Lewis* — 83 p

NO COMEBACKS 7 b.m. Last Tycoon 131 – Dead End (Bold Lad (IRE) 133) [1994 63: 9.9s* 9.9d^3 10.3m^3 10m^3 10d^4 8.9f* 10g^3 8.5m^3 10.3g^5 10.3d 10s 9g 8g^4 10s 1995 10.5d 8.9m 12.3m* 15.9m^4 10g 10.9g^4 12.1g 10f 12m 12.1s^5 Nov 2] leggy mare: modest handicapper: broke a cannon bone final 6-y-o start: won at Chester in July: stays 1½m: acts on any going: below form in blinkers/visor: usually held up: sometimes carries head high: sold 6,200 gns Newmarket December Sales. *E. J. Alston* — 61

NOEPROB (USA) 5 b.m. Majestic Shore (USA) – Heat Haze (USA) (Jungle Savage (USA)) [1994 50: 6s 7m 8.3d* 8g 10.2m* 8.3m 9g 8g a7g 1995 6.9d 12.3d 8f^6 8m^4 8.2m^4 10m^4 8f* Jul 1] leggy, rather shallow-girthed mare: poor handicapper: won at Bath in July: stays 1¼m: acts on firm and dead ground: often sweating: suitable mount for apprentice. *R. J. Hodges* — 45

NO EXTRAS (IRE) 5 b.g. Efisio 120 – Parkland Rose (Sweet Candy (VEN)) [1994 96: 6v 7g^4 7d^2 5g^3 6m^3 7.6m^4 5m^4 7m^4 5g^4 6d 6g* 7g 6d 1995 7m 6m^2 6f 6f 5m 6m^6 7.3m^5 6m* 6g^4 6g^2 7d 5s^3 6d Oct 19] leggy, quite good-topped gelding: useful handicapper, better than ever in 1995: won £14,900 22-runner event at Goodwood in August: excellent efforts afterwards when neck second of 29 to Royale Figurine in Gold Cup at Ayr and length third of 24 to Coastal Bluff in £15,500 contest at Ascot, finishing strongly from well back on each occasion: effective at 5f to 7.6f: acts on good to firm and soft ground, ran poorly on fibresand: often hangs: has run creditably when sweating: held up: tough. *G. L. Moore* — 106

NO HIDING PLACE 2 ch.c. (May 15) Nabeel Dancer (USA) 120 – Blushing Pink (USA) (Blushing Groom (FR) 131) [1995 7m Aug 25] second foal: dam, placed at 7f to 1m in France, daughter of Ma Biche: 25/1, towards rear in 19-runner maiden at Newmarket won by Even Top: should improve. *B. Hanbury* — –p

NOIR ESPRIT 2 br.c. (May 4) Prince Daniel (USA) – Danse d'Esprit 54 (Lidhame 109) [1995 7.5m 7.5m^5 8.1g 8g 7d^6 Sep 27] rather leggy, workmanlike colt: first foal: dam 2-y-o 7f winner: seems only poor on balance of form: stays 7.5f. *J. M. Carr* — 47+

NOMADIC DANCER (IRE) 3 b.f. Nabeel Dancer (USA) 120 – Loveshine (USA) (Gallant Romeo (USA)) [1994 52: 5f^4 6f 6.1s^6 1995 a6g^4 a6g a6g^5 5.1m^2 7g 5.1m 6m 6f^5 5.1h^6 Aug 18] useful-looking filly: modest maiden at best: stays 6f: acts on firm ground and equitrack. *M. S. Saunders* — 51d

NOMOGRAM 4 b.g. Nomination 125 – Crosby Triangle 72 (Windjammer (USA)) [1994 –: 8g 7g 8g a8g 1995 a12g Jan 5] stocky gelding: little sign of ability: has joined L. Montague Hall. *G. Lewis* — –

NO MONKEY NUTS 2 ch.g. (Apr 1) Clantime 101 – Portvally (Import 127) [1995 5f* 5g^4 5m* 6m* 6m 6m^4 6.1d^2 5m^6 Nov 3] 5,400Y: strong, close-coupled gelding: half-brother to 1989 2-y-o 6f seller winner Stop High (by Crofthall): dam unraced: fair form: successful in median auction maiden at Hamilton in July and claimer at Beverley and valuable seller at York (by a length from White Emir, bought in 18,200 gns) in August: ran creditably last 3 starts: seems suited by 6f: acts on firm and dead ground: races prominently: sold 7,000 gns Doncaster November Sales. *J. Berry* — 80

NO MORE HASSLE (IRE) 2 ch.g. (Feb 24) Magical Wonder (USA) 125 – Friendly Ann (Artaius (USA) 129) [1995 7.5m 9g 10m 7m 8f Oct 31] 6,000Y: big, leggy gelding: half-brother to a winner over hurdles in Ireland: dam unraced half-sister to Annie Edge, the dam of Selkirk: no worthwhile form, including in a seller. *Mrs M. Reveley* — –

NONCONFORMIST (IRE) 2 ch.g. (Mar 7) Nashamaa 113 – Sperrin Mist 83 (Camden Town 125) [1995 7.5m^6 6m^5 Jul 27] IR 8,000Y: half-brother to several winners, including 2-y-o sprint winners Spark (by Flash of Steel) and Pastoral Jem (by Horage): dam 2-y-o 5f winner: poor form in sellers at Beverley (favourite) and Yarmouth (raced up unfavoured centre of track) in July: sold 1,800 gns Newmarket September Sales: sent to Germany. *M. R. Channon* — –

NON DIMENTICAR ME (IRE) 3 b.f. Don't Forget Me 127 – Amboselli 73 (Raga Navarro (ITY) 119) [1994 –: 6d 6s 1995 5g* 7m^4 7g^4 6g^2 6d Sep 18] leggy, sparely-made filly: modest performer: won median auction maiden at Leicester in — 63

July: stays 7f: well below form on a soft surface (saddle slipped only start on top-of-the-ground): sold 2,400 gns Newmarket Autumn Sales. *Sir Mark Prescott*

NONIOS (IRE) 4 b.g. Nashamaa 113 – Bosquet 59 (Queen's Hussar 124) [1994 86: 7d^3 a10g^5 8.1s 7d 7.1d 7m* 7f* 8m^2 7m 7g^4 7.3s 8g^6 8m 8m 1995 8.1m 12m^5 11m^6 Aug 27] good-topped gelding: fairly useful 7f/1m handicapper at best in 1994 for B. Meehan: no form on flat in 1995, but won novice hurdle in September. *G. M. Moore* –

NONONITO (FR) 4 b.c. Nikos 124 – Feuille d'Automne (FR) (Crystal Palace (FR) 132) [1994 112: 10s* 10d^5 10g^2 12v 10.5v* 1995 10v^5 10s^6 15.5v* 15.5d^2 12.5d^5 15g^2 15.5g^4 20s^3 12s Dec 3] leggy French colt: really good walker: smart performer: won Prix de Barbeville at Saint-Cloud by 1½ lengths from The Little Thief (gave 4 lb) in May: runner-up in small fields in Prix Vicomtesse Vigier at Longchamp (went down by ½ length to The Little Thief at levels) and Prix Kergorlay at Deauville (unable to get to grips with Peckinpah's Soul) in the summer: best effort when keeping-on third of 6 to Always Earnest in Prix du Cadran at Longchamp: below form in listed race at Toulouse in December: suited by a good test of stamina: acts on heavy going, yet to race on top-of-the-ground. *J. Lesbordes, France* 119

NON VINTAGE (IRE) 4 ch.g. Shy Groom (USA) – Great Alexandra (Runnett 125) [1994 77: 7.5d^6 10.4m^5 8f^3 8.1m 10m^6 8m 7g^3 10g^4 8.5f^2 18g* 10.4d^4 8.9d 8m 16.5d^4 1995 a12g^5 a11g^3 a11g 12.3f^5 11.6m^4 13.9m 18m^2 13.9g 10.1g 10d^3 14.6m^2 16.5m^4 Nov 4] lengthy, sparely-made gelding: just a modest handicapper in 1995: seems to stay 2¼m: probably acts on any ground on turf, below best on fibresand: tried blinkered: has an awkward head carriage and often hangs left: useful hurdler: unreliable. *M. C. Chapman* 62

NOON AIR 4 b.f. Dark Harmony – Pride of Ayr (Recoil) [1994 NR 1995 a14.8g^6 a8.5g Mar 8] second foal: dam ran once: tailed off in claimer and maiden. *R. Hollinshead* –

NOONDAY GUN (IRE) 3 b.c. Bluebird (USA) 125 – Soxoph 67 (Hotfoot 126) [1994 77: 7.1g^5 7f 8s^5 10s^2 8d 1995 11.8s^3 10m Apr 20] workmanlike colt: fair staying maiden: below form on reappearance: fractured off-hind in handicap at Newmarket 3 weeks later: acted well on soft ground: dead. *R. Hannon* 64

NOON (IRE) 2 b. or br.f. (May 6) Treasure Kay 114 – Tiempo 50 (King of Spain 121) [1995 6m^4 6m 5g Oct 16] second foal: half-sister to 3-y-o Time Is Money (by Sizzling Melody): dam sprint maiden: poor form in sellers and median auction maiden: seems likely to prove best at 5f or 6f: sold 1,600 gns Newmarket Autumn Sales. *M. H. Tompkins* 39

NOOR EL HOUDAH (IRE) 3 b.f. Fayruz 116 – Moira My Girl (Henbit (USA) 130) [1994 61: 5d 5d* 6s* 6g^4 6.1f^5 7m^2 7m^3 7.1m* 7.5f^6 6d* 7g^5 6d* 6g 1995 a7g 6s* 6m a6g^5 6m a6g^5 a7g 6.1d 6m Oct 2] close-coupled filly: modest performer: below form after winning seller at Leicester in March: stays 7f: acts on good to firm and soft ground, not at best on fibresand or equitrack: no improvement in visor. *J. Berry* 58 a49

NOOSA (IRE) 3 b.f. Petorius 117 – Miss Java 78 (Persian Bold 123) [1994 74: 5d^2 5s^2 5f 5g* 5g* 5m^2 5m* 1995 a6g 5m^2 6.1m^3 6.9m 6g Sep 1] sturdy filly: carried condition: had a quick action: modest form at best in 1995, claimed out of M. Johnston's stable £6,000 on third start: broke a hind leg at Haydock final outing: stayed 6f: acted on soft ground, but best form on good to firm. *D. Moffatt* 57

NO PATTERN 3 ch.c. Rock City 120 – Sunfleet 59 (Red Sunset 120) [1994 74: 6m^6 6d^4 8.5m^6 8g a6g* a8g a7g^2 a6g^4 1995 a8g* a8g^2 a8g^2 9m^4 10.2m^4 8m^5 11.5m* 11.6m^4 10g^3 12g^4 Oct 16] leggy colt: fairly useful handicapper: won at Lingfield in January and July: stays 11.6f: acts on good to firm ground and equitrack: seems effective visored or not: genuine. *G. L. Moore* 80 a86

NORDAN RAIDER 7 ch.m. Domynsky 110 – Vikris (Viking (USA)) [1994 76: 6d^2 6f a6g^6 6m 5g 6g^5 a6g^2 a6g^3 1995 a6g* 6g^6 a6g^3 7g^3 7g a6g Nov 11] strong, lengthy mare: impresses in appearance: fairly useful handicapper: won at Southwell in January: below form last 3 starts: suited by 6f: goes well on fibresand, best turf form with plenty of give in the ground: held up. *M. J. Camacho* 61 a81

NORDANSK 6 ch.g. Nordance (USA) – Free On Board 73 (Free State 125) [1994 NR 1995 10d Sep 27] workmanlike gelding: poor maiden handicapper at 4 yrs: fair hurdler since, but no promise on return to flat. *M. Madgwick* –

NORDESTA (IRE) 3 b.f. Nordico (USA) – Braconda 86 (So Blessed 130) [1994 72: 5d* 5m^5 5.3m^3 5d^5 6g 1995 7g 6g 5f^5 5m Jul 7] small, sparely-made filly: modest form at best in handicaps in 1995: should stay 6f: yet to race on soft ground, acts on any other. *M. R. Channon* 56

NORDIC BREEZE (IRE) 3 b. or br.g. Nordico (USA) – Baby Clair 79 (Gulf Pearl 117) [1994 55: 7s 1995 7g 7.1m 7g* 8f^2 7m^2 7.1g^3 8m^2 8m^2 8.1g Sep 22] leggy gelding: fairly useful handicapper: in good form in the summer, winning at Ayr in June: stays 1m well: acts on firm ground: visored (ran well) eighth 3-y-o start: has run creditably when sweating. *A. Bailey* 80

NORDIC CROWN (IRE) 4 b.f. Nordico (USA) – Fit The Halo (Dance In Time (CAN)) [1994 12g^3 8g 12g 10g* 1995 11.8m 10.3m^4 Jun 28] ex-Irish filly: fourth foal: dam 13f winner on flat in Ireland: lightly raced on flat for J. Bolger, winning claimer (rated 61) at Clonmel (claimed approx IR £7,000) in September 1994: blinkered/visored, won 4 times over hurdles in 1994/5 for new stable, but well beaten on return to flat: stays 1½m well. *M. C. Pipe* –

NORDIC DOLL (IRE) 3 ch.f. Royal Academy (USA) 130 – Maculatus (USA) (Sharpen Up 127) [1994 64: 6.1g^3 5g^6 8d 1995 7g* 8m^2 7g 7g^6 8m 8f^3 8f 7m^3 a8g a8g^2 a8g^6 Dec 15] rather leggy filly: fair performer: won maiden at Thirsk in April: stays 1m: acts on equitrack and firm ground, probably on dead: very edgy (ran poorly) seventh start, wandered and carried head awkwardly (short-headed) on second: none too consistent. *B. W. Hills* 71 a63

NORDIC MINE (IRE) 5 b.g. Nordico (USA) – Tower Belle (Tower Walk 130) [1994 NR 1995 10.5d^6 a14.8g* 12d^2 12g Oct 16] sturdy ex-Irish gelding: fourth foal: half-brother to 2 winners in Italy by My Dad Tom: dam unraced: modest handicapper: won amateurs maiden contest at Wolverhampton in August: needs good test at 1½m, and should stay 2m: acts on fibresand and any turf going: tried blinkered in Ireland. *P. J. Hobbs* 53

NORDICO PRINCESS 4 b.f. Nordico (USA) – Try Vickers (USA) 72 (Fuzzbuster (USA)) [1994 65: a8g^5 a6s^2 a6g^2 a5g^2 a6g* a5g^3 5v* 6.1m 5.3m^3 5.3g^3 5d^4 5m 5d a6g^6 a5g a5g* a5g^2 1995 a6g* a6g^5 a5g^2 a5g^2 5d* 5m* 5.1m^3 5m 5m 5d 5g 5.1m a6g a5g^4 a5g^6 Dec 6] smallish, sturdy filly: fair handicapper: successful at Lingfield (on all-weather) in January, Folkestone in March and again at Lingfield (on turf, subsequently left G. Oldroyd's stable) in April: effective at 5f and 6f: acts on any turf going and on all-weather surfaces: usually a front runner: game. *M. Brittain* 71

NORDIC SUN (IRE) 7 gr.g. Nordico (USA) – Cielsoleil (USA) (Conquistador Cielo (USA)) [1994 NR 1995 a12g^6 Dec 9] first foal: dam unraced: successful as 2-y-o in maiden and minor events and at 3 yrs in handicap (rated 94): did not run in 1992, rated 81 in 1993: sold 9,300 gns out of A. Martin's stable Doncaster September (1995) Sales: modest form when sixth of 11 in handicap at Wolverhampton on first start here: stays 17f: yet to race on firm going, acts on any other: one-time useful hurdler. *L. R. Lloyd-James* 61

NORDINEX (IRE) 3 b.g. Nordico (USA) – Debbie's Next (USA) 82 (Arctic Tern (USA) 126) [1994 68: 6g 6d^6 7s^4 a7g^4 1995 a8g* a8g^3 8m* 8m^3 8g* 8g^5 7m^3 8g^3 8m a8g a7g Dec 18] well-made gelding: good walker: made into a fairly useful handicapper, winning at Lingfield in January, Kempton in June and Newmarket in July: should stay beyond 1m: acts on good to firm ground and equitrack: blinkered (worst effort) second 2-y-o start: has run well for claimer: usually races prominently: consistent. *R. W. Armstrong* 81

NORDISK LEGEND 3 b.g. Colmore Row 111 – Nordic Rose (DEN) (Drumhead 122) [1994 NR 1995 6g^6 Sep 25] third reported foal in this country: dam behind all 3 starts at 2 yrs: 500/1, soundly beaten in minor event at Hamilton. *Mrs D. Thomson* –

NORD LYS (IRE) 4 b.g. Nordico (USA) – Beach Light 89 (Bustino 136) [1994 –: 8d 7g^5 10m 12.1m 12g 10.3s 1995 a12g a12g 7.1g 10m a12g Nov 27] small gelding: no worthwhile form: trained until after fourth 4-y-o start by R. Lee: tried blinkered and with tongue tied down. *B. J. Llewellyn* –

NORDMAN LASS 3 b.f. Risk Me (FR) 127 – Sundaysport Splash (Lord Gayle (USA) 124) [1994 59: 6m^5 5g^6 6s^3 6.1g 1995 7g 8.3m 6m 6g 6g 6m Jul 10] –

shallow-girthed filly: modest sprint maiden: soundly beaten in 1995. *Miss Jacqueline S. Doyle*

NORDOORA (IRE) 6 b.m. Fayruz 116 – African Cousin (Kampala 120) [1994 59, a–: 5d* 5v 5m 5m 1995 5g 5m Aug 13] angular, plain mare: modest sprint handicapper: no form in 1995: sold 500 gns Doncaster November Sales. *J. L. Harris* –

NORDROSS 7 b.m. Ardross 134 – Noreena (Nonoalco (USA) 131) [1994 –: a12g^3 a14.8g a12g^5 1995 a9.4g^6 a12g^6 a8.5g Jul 8] of little account on flat: tried blinkered and visored. *J. H. Peacock* –

NORFOLK GLORY 3 ch.g. Weldnaas (USA) 112 – Caviar Blini 80 (What A Guest 119) [1994 –: 7g 1995 a8g a7g 8f^6 8m 10f 8.5m^5 Jul 5] rather leggy gelding: no worthwhile form: tried in blinkers and tongue strap: looks temperamental. *D. J. G. Murray Smith* –

NORLING (IRE) 5 ch.g. Nashamaa 113 – Now Then (Sandford Lad 133) [1994 59: a8g 6m^3 6v^6 6g 6m 5m^5 6m 6m* 6f^2 5m^3 6f^2 6d 1995 6m 6m 6g 6m^6 6f^3 6f^6 6f* 6d 6g 6f Oct 23] sturdy gelding: modest handicapper: won at Salisbury (made all) in August: well beaten all 3 subsequent starts: best form at 6f to 7f: best on a sound surface (acts on firm ground): usually races prominently. *K. O. Cunningham-Brown* 56

NORMAN PRINCE (IRE) 3 b.c. Prince Rupert (FR) 121 – Norme (FR) (Dark Tiger) [1994 66: 6m 7g 7g^4 8m a7g^5 a8.5g a8g^2 a7g^3 1995 a9.4g^6 Apr 1] sparely-made colt: modest maiden at 2 yrs: tailed off in seller on only outing in 1995: sold 1,000 gns Ascot May Sales. *Mrs N. Macauley* –

NORNAX LAD (USA) 7 b.g. Northern Baby (CAN) 127 – Naxos (USA) (Big Spruce (USA)) [1994 68: a12g^4 a13g* 1995 17.2m 14g 8.1f 13f* 11.1f* 12.1f^2 Aug 14] close-coupled gelding: modest handicapper: successful twice in smallish fields at Hamilton in August: stays 1¾m: acts on equitrack, goes well on top-of-the-ground: blinkered last 4 starts. *Martyn Meade* 64

NORSONG 3 b.c. Northern State (USA) 91 – Winsong Melody (Music Maestro 119) [1994 58p: 5s 1995 7.3m 6m 6.9g^5 7.6m* 8.2m^4 8g 8.1d 7s Sep 28] rangy colt: modest handicapper: won at Lingfield in July: will prove best at up to 1m: acts on good to firm and soft ground. *R. Akehurst* 55

NORTH ARDAR 5 b.g. Ardar 87 – Langwaite (Seaepic (USA) 100) [1994 59: a8g^5 a8g^5 a7g^6 7d^5 7g 7m 7m^2 8.1f^2 9.2f^3 10m* 10.3m^5 10.5m^5 10.9g^2 10g^6 7.5f 10g^5 8f^3 1995 10.3g 9.9m^5 9m^5 9.9m^2 12m* 11.1m* 12m^2 12.3f^2 11.9m 12.1g^4 a12g Sep 30] close-coupled, angular gelding: fair handicapper: won at Thirsk in June and Edinburgh in July: stays 12.3f: acts on firm ground, soft and all-weather surfaces: has run well when sweating: held up. *Mrs M. Reveley* 65

NORTHERN BALLET (IRE) 2 b.f. (Apr 22) Sadler's Wells (USA) 132 – Miranisa (Habitat 134) [1995 6f Jun 29] 115,000Y: well-made filly: good walker: third foal: dam twice-raced close relative of Poule d'Essai des Pouliches winner Masarika: 12/1 from 6/1 and carrying condition, around 11 lengths seventh of 11 to Darling Flame in maiden at Newbury, green and not at all knocked about: moved well to post: looked sure to improve. *R. Hannon* – p

NORTHERN CELADON (IRE) 4 b.c. Classic Secret (USA) 91 – Exemplary 106 (Sovereign Lord 120) [1994 74: 7v* 7.5d^3 7s^5 7m 6.9m^5 7g 7.1d 8s 7d a8.5g* 1995 a9.4g^3 a9.4g a8g^4 a9.4g 8d* a8.5g^6 a8g^2 a7g a8.5g^5 a8.5g^3 a8.5g^2 a8g^3 a8.5g 8g* Oct 3] angular colt: has a quick action: fair performer: enterprisingly ridden (raced wide) to win claimer in April and minor event in October, both at Warwick: stays 1¼m: acts on fibresand, seems best with give in the ground (acts on heavy) when on turf: successful for apprentice: usually races prominently. *M. J. Heaton-Ellis* 74

NORTHERN CHARMER 3 br.g. Charmer 123 – Trading 74 (Forlorn River 124) [1994 –: 7.1s 7g 1995 7.1m 8.3g a9.4g^5 11.8f Oct 24] workmanlike, good-topped gelding: no worthwhile form: trained until after third start by M. Meagher. *E. J. Alston* –

NORTHERN CHIEF 5 b.g. Chief Singer 131 – Pacific Gull (USA) 67 (Storm Bird (CAN) 134) [1994 56: 7.5d 8g 8.5m 7.5g 10f 8m* 8f^4 8g 8.3g^5 8g^5 8.5g 7d 8m 1995 a9.4g a8.5g 10.8d 8m 8.2m 8m 7.5g 8.1f^4 8.1d Sep 2] leggy gelding: poor mover: poor handicapper at best in 1995, trained first 4 starts by R. Emery: effective 32 at 7f and 1m: acts on any going: has worn sliding bar-bit and tongue strap: inconsistent: sold 1,000 gns Doncaster October Sales. *Miss J. F. Craze*

NORTHERN CLAN 2 b.c. (Apr 16) Clantime 101 – Northern Line 92 (Camden Town 125) [1995 5m^4 5g^4 5m^5 7m 6f^5 7.5m 6d Sep 18] 5,000Y: workmanlike colt: has a round action: third foal: dam 2-y-o 5f winner: seemed to go backwards after finishing fourth of 12 in maiden auction at Haydock second start: doesn't stay 7.5f. *M. W. Easterby* — 57 d

NORTHERN FALCON 2 gr.f. (Mar 20) Polar Falcon (USA) 126 – Bishah (USA) 86 (Balzac (USA)) [1995 5m 7.5m^4 7g 7g 7.9m Oct 5] 9,000F, 3,400Y: well-grown, leggy filly: has scope: fifth foal: dam 11f winner out of half-sister to dam of Pawneese: poor form in varied company: bred to stay 1m+. *M. W. Easterby* — 48

NORTHERN FAN (IRE) 3 b.c. Lear Fan (USA) 130 – Easy Romance (USA) (Northern Jove (CAN)) [1994 57p: 7.1s a8g^3 1995 6.9g^5 8.3g^2 8.2d^2 8m Oct 2] good-topped colt: fair maiden: stays 1m: acts on dead going: sometimes bandaged: pulls hard. *A. C. Stewart* — 73

NORTHERN FLEET 2 b.c. (Apr 9) Slip Anchor 136 – Kamkova (USA) 62 (Northern Dancer) [1995 8m^4 Oct 27] quite good-topped colt: fifth foal: brother to Irish 4-y-o 9f winner Alongside: dam, placed at 11.7f and 15.5f, half-sister to top-class middle-distance performer Vanlandingham out of half-sister to champion 1980 American middle-distance 3-y-o Temperence Hill: 11/1 and better for race, around 3½ lengths fourth of 5 to Believe Me in slowly-run minor event at Newmarket, prominent until steadily outpaced from over 1f out: bred to require middle distances: may well do better. *G. Harwood* — 86 p

NORTHERN GREY 3 gr.g. Puissance 110 – Sharp Anne 74§ (Belfort (FR) 89) [1994 58: 5f^4 6.1g^3 5.1m^3 5g^6 1995 5d a5g^6 a6g^6 5.9f^3 5f^3 5.9h^2 5g^2 5d 6g a6g^4 a8g^4 a7g^4 Dec 19] leggy, close-coupled gelding: modest maiden handicapper: stays 1m: acts on hard ground and the all-weather: effective blinkered/visored or not: consistent. *J. Berry* — 52

NORTHERN HIGHLIGHT 4 ch.g. Pharly (FR) 130 – Unearthed 77 (Electric 126) [1994 62d: 10.2g^4 10.3m 11.8g^4 14.1m^3 12m 16g 12.3m^3 13.1g^4 14d^6 11.9s 1995 a11g^3 11.9d Sep 26] strong gelding: unimpressive mover: modest maiden: stays 1¾m: acts on good to firm and soft ground: has had tongue tied down: refused to race over hurdles in October. *T. P. McGovern* — 51

NORTHERN JUDGE 2 ch.g. (Apr 21) Highest Honor (FR) 124 – Nordica 99 (Northfields (USA)) [1995 6s 7f^4 Oct 18] 23,000Y: sturdy gelding: half-brother to 3-y-o Secret Spring (by Dowsing), very useful middle-distance filly (7f winner at 2 yrs) Sueboog (by Darshaan) and modest 7f winner Mindomica (by Dominion): dam won 3 times at 1m here then over 6f in Ireland: improved form when 5½ lengths fourth of 11 to Brighstone in maiden at Yarmouth, leading around 5f: stays 7f. *B. Hanbury* — 72

NORTHERN KINGDOM (USA) 6 b.g. Graustark – Wonder Mar (USA) (Fire Dancer (USA)) [1994 NR 1995 17.1m^4 12g 15.8g^3 18m^3 Jun 19] sturdy gelding: fair handicapper (rated 70) at 3 yrs: poor at best in 1995: stays 17.1f: acts on firm going, possibly not on a soft surface: visored (looked none too keen) once at 3 yrs: front runner: joined K. Bailey. *S. G. Norton* — 44

NORTHERN LAW 3 gr.c. Law Society (USA) 130 – Pharland (FR) (Bellypha 130) [1994 NR 1995 8g 12.3m 14g 14m^4 13.8m^2 15.8m* 16f* 16.1f 15.9d^6 Sep 20] 5,500Y: tall, rather leggy colt: third foal: half-brother to French 4-y-o 7f to 9f winner Lipharland (by Dance of Life): dam French 1¼m winner: fairly useful form: dictated pace when winning handicaps at Catterick (maiden event) and Thirsk (easily) in August: stays 2m: acts on firm and dead ground: sold only 3,500 gns Newmarket Autumn Sales. *B. W. Hills* — 82

NORTHERN MIRACLE (IRE) 2 b.f. (May 7) Distinctly North (USA) 115 – Danny's Miracle (Superlative 118) [1995 7m Nov 3] second foal: half-sister to 3-y-o Lordan Velvet (by Lord Americo), 11.5f winner in Norway in 1995: dam, unraced, out of 9f-winning half-sister to Coronation Stakes winner Chalon: 25/1, burly and green, tailed off in maiden at Doncaster. *C. F. Wall* — –

NORTHERN MOTTO 2 b.g. (Mar 13) Mtoto 134 – Soulful (FR) (Zino 127) [1995 7.1g 7.1s 7f Oct 31] 20,000Y: leggy gelding: first foal: dam won from 7.5f (at — 57

2 yrs) to 1½m in France: best effort in maidens (though again never a factor) when seventh of 14 to Carburton at Haydock on second start: slowly away and always behind on firm ground at Redcar on final outing: will be suited by middle distances. *Mrs J. R. Ramsden*

NORTHERN SAGA (IRE) 2 b.g. (Apr 30) Distinctly North (USA) 115 – Saga's Humour 61 (Bustino 136) [1995 5m^5 5m 6m^5 a6g^5 6d 7d Sep 26] 14,000 2-y-o: robust gelding: half-brother to several winners, including 3-y-o 1m (at 2 yrs) and 1¼m winner First Bite (by Be My Native) and fairly useful 1991 2-y-o 5f winner (better form at 6f/7f) Atmospheric Blues (by Double Schwartz): dam best at 6f: poor form, including in selling company: stays 6f: sold 500 gns Ascot October Sales. *Andrew Turnell* — 40

NORTHERN SKY 2 b.f. (Mar 5) North Col 116 – Emma Wright (Skyliner 117) [1995 7g 10g Oct 9] unfurnished filly: second reported foal: dam unraced: in rear in maiden at Warwick (pulled hard to post, slowly away) and seller at Leicester. *R. Dickin* — –

NORTHERN SOUL (USA) 2 b.c. (Mar 6) Tasso (USA) – Wajibird (USA) (Storm Bird (CAN) 134) [1995 7.9m^3 10m^2 8m^3 Nov 4] $12,000F, $10,200Y resold IR 18,000Y: strong, well-made colt: fifth foal: half-brother to 2 minor winners in USA by Strawberry Road: dam unraced: in frame in median auction maidens: improved effort (on seemingly-favoured stand side) when 3½ lengths third to impressive Shaamit at Doncaster on final outing: stays 1¼m. *M. Johnston* — 78

NORTHERN SPARK 7 b.g. Trojan Fen 118 – Heavenly Spark (Habitat 134) [1994 36: 6m 6g^3 1995 5.9m 5.9f^2 6.9m* 8m 7.5g^3 7f 7m 6g^4 7m* 8.1s^4 a6g^4 a7g^2 Dec 12] robust gelding: has a round action: modest handicapper: won at Carlisle in June and (after sold out of Martyn Wane's stable 2,000 gns Doncaster September Sales) at Newcastle (claimer) in October: effective at 6f, and stays 1m: acts on firm and soft going and on fibresand: blinkered (below form) once at 4 yrs. *Miss L. A. Perratt* — 52

NORTHERN SPRUCE (IRE) 3 ch.g. Astronef 116 – Perle's Fashion (Sallust 134) [1994 NR 1995 8.3m 8g 11.6g 10m 8.3g a12g Jul 13] 2,800Y: leggy gelding: eighth foal: half-brother to 3 winners, including poor stayer Cost Effective (by Burslem): dam Irish 9f to 1½m winner: little sign of ability. *Miss Jacqueline S. Doyle* — –

NORTHERN TRIAL (USA) 7 b.g. Far North (CAN) 120 – Make An Attempt (USA) (Nashua) [1994 NR 1995 a9.4g^5 a12g^6 Mar 29] sturdy gelding: modest 7f/1m performer on flat at 5 yrs: no worthwhile form on return: fair hurdler, winning in July: sold 4,200 gns Ascot September Sales. *K. R. Burke* — –

NORTHERN TROVE (USA) 3 b.c. Northern Jove (CAN) – Herbivorous (USA) (Northern Jove (CAN)) [1994 NR 1995 8m^3 8.1g^5 8f^3 7f^2 7m^2 7m^3 10f a8.5g 7m 10f a8g Nov 6] robust, sturdy colt: carries condition: seventh reported foal: half-brother to 2 minor winners in N. America: dam minor winner, placed in stakes races at 6f and 8.5f: fair maiden at best: long way below after fourth outing, and left G. M. Moore's stable after eighth: shapes like a 6f/7f performer: acts on firm ground: has had tongue tied down: blinkered (tailed off) final 3-y-o outing: one to be wary of. *Ronald Thompson* — 75 d

NORTHERN UNION (CAN) 4 b.c. Alwasmi (USA) 115 – Loving Cup (USA) (Big Spruce (USA)) [1994 80: 8v* 11.6g* 1995 12m 10g* 12g Jul 13] tall, close-coupled colt: fairly useful form: off course a year prior to reappearance: best effort to win handicap at Windsor in June, leading near finish: brought down in Ulster Harp Derby final start: effective at 1¼m, but likely to prove better over further and will stay beyond 1½m: acts on heavy going: sweating (successful) second 3-y-o start: looked capable of further improvement. *M. A. Jarvis* — 89 p

NORTH ESK (USA) 6 ch.g. Apalachee (USA) 137 – Six Dozen (USA) (What A Pleasure (USA)) [1994 65: 8g^6 8f^2 8f 8f^5 10m^3 8m^4 8f^3 8.5f* 6.9f^2 8m^2 10m 10.8s 10g 10.1g 8d 12s 1995 8m 7g 8.2m a8g a8g a7g a10g Dec 18] good-topped gelding: modest handicapper: effective at 7f to 1¼m: acts on firm ground, dead and equitrack, possibly not on very soft: often on edge: held up: has had tongue tied down. *C. A. Dwyer* — 55

NORTHGATE RAVER 4 ch.f. Absalom 128 – Real Party 68 (Realm 129) [1994 –: a5s 1995 a6g 5m 5m 5g Jul 18] sparely-made filly: no sign of ability. *Ronald Thompson* — –

NORTH REEF (IRE) 4 b.c. Danehill (USA) 126 – Loreef (Main Reef 126) 82
[1994 71: 7.1d^{2} 7g 7d 1995 a8g* a10g* 10f Jul 25] tall, lengthy, good-topped colt: won minor event in June and handicap (made all, eased) in July, both at Lingfield: sweating and rather edgy, below form in £35,300 handicap at Goodwood: stays 1¼m: acts on good to firm and dead ground and the all-weather. *Sir Mark Prescott*

NORTH STAR (IRE) 2 br.c. (Apr 5) Distinctly North (USA) 115 – King's Chase –
(King's Leap 111) [1995 6m 7f 7f Oct 23] IR 10,000F, 23,000Y: smallish, quite attractive colt: fluent mover: half-brother to several winners, including 1985 2-y-o 7f winner G G Magic (by Strong Gale), later winner at 1½m and 1¾m, and fair middle-distance winner Regal Lover (by Alzao): dam ran twice: well beaten in maiden events: sold 880 gns Doncaster November Sales: sent to Denmark. *R. Hannon*

NORTHWISE (IRE) 4 b.f. Northern Baby (CAN) 127 – Infinite Wisdom (USA) 43
(Sassafras (FR) 135) [1994 47: 8m^{3} 8m 8m 1995 9f 9f^{3} 9.9m Aug 24] quite good-topped filly: poor maiden handicapper: should be suited by further than 9f: acts on firm ground: sold 640 gns Doncaster September Sales. *W. W. Haigh*

NORWEGIAN BLUE (IRE) 2 b.c. (Mar 7) Mac's Imp (USA) 116 – Opening 84 +
Day (Day Is Done 115) [1995 6f^{4} 5m^{5} 6m^{5} 5g^{2} 5g^{4} 6s* Sep 28] IR 10,000F, 22,000Y: big, long-backed colt: unimpressive mover: fourth foal: half-brother to 6f winner Evanro (by Common Grounds) and Italian 3-y-o 6f winner Fire Conqueror (by Fayruz): dam Irish 1m winner: fairly useful form: ran well in listed race at Sandown and Richmond Stakes at Goodwood (sweating) on second and third starts: easy winner of maiden at Lingfield on final outing: stays 6f: acts on good to firm and soft ground. *A. P. Jarvis*

NOSE NO BOUNDS (IRE) 2 b.g. (Apr 24) Cyrano de Bergerac 120 – Damezao 69
(Alzao (USA) 117) [1995 6m^{3} 6f^{3} a7g^{2} a8.5d* 7.9m^{5} a8g^{6} Nov 10] 7,000Y: quite a75
good-topped gelding: has scope: third foal: half-brother to 1993 2-y-o 6f winner Salvezza (by Superpower): dam unraced: fair form at best: made hard work of winning slowly-run maiden at Wolverhampton (looked to have simple task) in September: soon off bit and never a factor in 2 nurseries: looks a thorough stayer. *M. Johnston*

NOSEY NATIVE 2 b.g. (Mar 23) Cyrano de Bergerac 120 – Native Flair 87 (Be 80
My Native (USA) 122) [1995 6m^{5} 7m^{2} 8.5s^{3} 8f* Oct 18] 14,500Y: unfurnished gelding: second foal: dam 1¼m and 12.3f winner: fair form: won 19-runner nursery at Yarmouth in October by neck from Prince of Florence, staying on strongly: better suited by 1m than less: acts on firm ground, raced on unfavoured side of track on soft. *J. Pearce*

NOSIRRAH 3 br.f. Rock City 120 – Miss Alkie 58 (Noalcoholic (FR) 128) [1994 48 d
57: 5m a5g^{3} 5d^{3} 6m 5m^{6} 6m^{4} 1995 7f 8g 10m 10g 10m 7m^{6} 7f Aug 2] compact filly: poor handicapper: well beaten last 5 starts: stays 1m: acts on firm and dead ground: below form in blinkers final 2-y-o outing. *C. A. Horgan*

NO SPEECHES (IRE) 4 b.g. Last Tycoon 131 – Wood Violet (USA) (Riverman 61
(USA) 131) [1994 59d: 7d a8.5g a7g a8g a10g^{4} 1995 10m 10m 10.8g 11.4g^{5} 12f a67
8m^{3} 10m^{5} 14m^{6} 10.8g 12s 8f^{2} a10g* a10g^{2} a12g^{2} a10g^{3} Dec 19] leggy gelding: fair handicapper: sold out of C. Cyzer's stable 8,800 gns Newmarket Autumn Sales after eleventh start: won amateurs event at Lingfield in November on first outing for new connections: stays 1½m: acts on firm ground, dead and goes well on equitrack. *S. Dow*

NOSTOI 2 b.f. (Mar 30) Rock City 120 – Norgabie 94 (Northfields (USA)) [1995 69
6h* 6m^{4} 7g^{3} 8h^{4} 8g^{5} 7g^{4} Oct 1] leggy filly: has a round action: first foal: dam sprinter: won median auction maiden at Newcastle in August: fair form in nurseries last 4 starts: stays 1m: acts on hard ground: blinkered (hung left) final outing: sold 7,800 gns Newmarket Autumn Sales. *Sir Mark Prescott*

NO SUBMISSION (USA) 9 b.h. Melyno 130 – Creeping Kate (USA) (Stop The –
Music (USA)) [1994 52, a73: a8g* a7g* a11g^{3} a7g* a7g* a7s a9.4g a8g^{3} a7g^{3} 8g^{6} 8d a73
8g^{5} 9m^{5} a8.5g^{6} a11g a8g a8g^{2} 8.9d^{4} 10s a8g^{6} a7g^{6} a8g^{2} 1995 a8g^{2} a8g a8g^{2} a7g* a7g^{2} a8g* a7g* a8g* a9.4g* a8.5g^{2} 8.3v^{5} 10g a8g^{3} a7g* 10m a11g^{5} a8.5g^{2} a7g^{3} a8.5g* a8.5g^{5} a11g^{4} a8.5g 10g a8g^{4} a11g Dec 1] tall, leggy horse: poor mover: no worthwhile form on turf in 1995, but still fair on the all-weather: successful at Southwell/Wolverhampton in 1995 in 4 claimers, 2 sellers and a handicap by July:

lost his form afterwards: best recent form at 7f to 9f: acts on any going: effective blinkered or not, well below form only try in visor: successful 13 times at Southwell: usually a front runner: tough. *D. W. Chapman*

NO SYMPATHY 2 ch.f. (May 4) Ron's Victory (USA) 129 – Ackcontent (USA) (Key To Content (USA)) [1995 5g^5 6m^5 5f^4 5g^4 a5g 6f^2 5.3f* 5m a5g^6 a6g^4 Dec 19] 5,000Y: third known foal: dam ran once at 2 yrs in North America: flattered (could be rated 60) when winning strongly-run nursery at Brighton in August: mostly poor form otherwise: stays 6f: acts on firm ground and equitrack, ran poorly on fibresand: visored (below form) third start. *G. L. Moore* 49

NOTE OF CAUTION (USA) 2 b.f. (Mar 31) Diesis 133 – Silver Dollar 106 (Shirley Heights 130) [1995 a8g^3 Dec 18] fifth foal: sister to modest 3-y-o maiden Silver Rondo and half-sister to 1m winner Money Spinner (by Teenoso): dam, 2-y-o 6f winner not quite so good at 1½m at 3 yrs, daughter of half-sister to Highclere: 5/1, over 2 lengths third of 9 to Apartments Abroad in maiden at Lingfield in December: should improve. *Lord Huntingdon* 58 p

NOT FOR SALE 4 b.f. Hotfoot 126 – Basic Bliss 72 (Tumble Wind (USA)) [1994 42: a8.5g a7g a8g^5 6.1d^4 8g 10g^5 10.8s 11.5g 1995 a12g^5 a8g Jun 16] lengthy filly: poor maiden: tried blinkered. *J. Wharton* –

NOTHING DOING (IRE) 6 b.g. Sarab 123 – Spoons (Orchestra 118) [1994 NR 1995 a12g^4 a12g^6 a13g a16g^2 a16g^5 a16.2g^3 a14.8g a12g* 12m^6 a12g 11.6m* 12m 12g 12m^2 Nov 6] sturdy gelding: has a round action: poor handicapper: won at Southwell in May and Windsor (seller) in July: stays 2m: acts on the all-weather and on any turf going: blinkered (tailed off) third 6-y-o start: found little (flashing tail) next time: rather temperamental and not one to trust implicitly. *W. J. Musson* 41

NOT IN DOUBT (USA) 6 b.h. Tom Rolfe – Trillionaire (USA) 111 (Vaguely Noble 140) [1994 88: 12m^5 14.1d^5 12m^2 12m^3 1995 14m 16.2m 16m May 21] close-coupled horse: disappointing staying handicapper: long way below form in 1995. *H. Candy* –

NOT QUITE GREY 2 gr.c. (Feb 12) Absalom 128 – Strawberry Song 87 (Final Straw 127) [1995 7.1m 7m^6 10m^3 8.1s^5 Nov 2] 11,500Y, 25,000 2-y-o: workmanlike colt: fourth foal: half-brother to 3-y-o Fragaria (by Be My Chief): dam 1¼m winner, daughter of half-sister to smart stayer Celtic Cone: unseated rider leaving stalls on debut: best effort when 1½ lengths third in median auction maiden at Nottingham in October: suited by a good test of stamina: well below form on soft ground. *K. McAuliffe* 70

NOT SO GENEROUS (IRE) 5 b.m. Fayruz 116 – Ribero's Overture 72 (Ribero 126) [1994 –, a59: a5g a5g^3 a5g 5.7g a5g a5g 1995 a5g Jan 12] leggy, close-coupled mare: modest sprinter: well beaten only 5-y-o start. *W. G. M. Turner* –

NOTTASH (IRE) 3 ch.f. Royal Academy (USA) 130 – Persian Polly 99 (Persian Bold 123) [1994 65p: 6m^6 1995 5.1g^3 6g^6 7.1m* 7g Sep 30] leggy, sparely-made filly: fair performer: won maiden at Sandown in August: stiff task when well beaten only subsequent outing: should stay 1m: has raced only on a sound surface. *J. R. Fanshawe* 74

NOT THE NADGER 4 b.g. Aragon 118 – Broken Accent (Busted 134) [1994 55: 8.2v 10d a7g 6s^2 1995 8d Apr 1] tall, useful-looking gelding: poor mover with a round action: worthwhile form only on final 3-y-o start when with M. Fetherston-Godley: should be suited by 7f+: acts on soft ground: sold 1,100 gns Doncaster October Sales. *P. D. Evans* –

NOTTONITEJOSEPHINE 2 ch.f. (Mar 20) Be My Chief (USA) 122 – Josephine Gibney (High Top 131) [1995 6g 5g 7g a7g Nov 10] 3,000F, 5,400Y: sparely-made, close-coupled filly: half-sister to 5f (at 2 yrs) to 1m winner Super One (by Superlative) and a winner in Belgium by Dowsing: dam 6f winner in Italy: behind in maiden events and seller: sold 700 gns Doncaster November Sales. *R. Boss* –

NOUFARI (FR) 4 b.g. Kahyasi 130 – Noufiyla 68 (Top Ville 129) [1994 75: 10.4g^3 13.4s^6 11.9s^4 12g^5 14.1d 12.4d a12g^3 a12g* a12g* a12g^5 1995 a14.8g* a12g* a12g* a12g^4 18g^2 14.9d 17.1m^2 18.7m 16.5g^3 20m^6 16.1m^4 16.1g^2 15.9m^3 Jul 30] quite good-topped gelding: fairly useful handicapper: successful 3 times at Wolverhampton early in 1995: successful at 1½m (soon chased along in rear last 2 80 a84 starts at trip), but is really a stayer and gets 2½m well: acts on good to firm ground and fibresand: comes from behind: consistent. *R. Hollinshead*

NOUVELLE CUISINE 7 b.m. Yawa 122 – Radigo 61 (Ragstone 128) [1994 54: a14g[5] 12m* 15.1m[2] 13.1g[2] 12m[2] 16m* 15d[5] 1995 12m[6] 15f[2dis] 12f[2] 15.1m[4] 14.1f Jul 12] plain mare: has a round action: modest performer: stays 2m well: acts on firm ground: tends to hang under pressure: lacks turn of foot. *G. M. Moore* 48

NOVOCENTO 5 b. or br.g. Nomination 125 – Top Stream 87 (Highland Melody 112) [1995 5m Apr 20] brother to fair maiden handicapper (probably stayed 1½m) Yimkin Bookra and half-brother to several winners, none better than fairly useful, including 6f and 7f winner Kedron (by Absalom): dam won 3 times over 1m at 2 yrs and seemed to stay 1½m: won 3 races over 5f in Vienna, Austria, at 4 yrs: unimpressive to post, soundly beaten on British debut in claimer at Ripon: subsequently gelded. *J. Dooler* –

NOYAN 5 ch.g. Northern Baby (CAN) 127 – Istiska (FR) (Irish River (FR) 131) [1994 –: 8s 9.2f 10m[5] 13m[4] 12s 12.4d 1995 13g* 13g* 16.1g[4] May 25] big, rangy gelding: rated 85d at 3 yrs: modest form at best in 1995: bandaged, won 2 handicaps at Hamilton in May: should prove suited by further than 13f: acts on firm and dead ground: tried in blinkers and visor at 3 yrs: held up: has joined D. Nicholls. *L. Lungo* 53

NUCLEAR EXPRESS 8 b.g. Martinmas 128 – Halka (Daring March 116) [1994 –: 7f a6g a7g 1995 6m 5.3f[6] Jul 24] leggy, workmanlike gelding: lightly raced and well beaten on flat since 1993: won 2-finisher novice chase in August. *J. M. Bradley* –

NUCLEAR JEWEL 2 b.f. (Jun 7) Superpower 113 – Emerald Gulf (IRE) (Wassl 125) [1995 6f 6m 5g Sep 14] 400Y: second foal: dam, bred to stay 1¼m, ran once: no worthwhile form: dead. *R. M. Whitaker* –

NUKUD (USA) 3 b.g. Topsider (USA) – Summer Silence (USA) (Stop The Music (USA)) [1994 NR 1995 7.1m Jul 7] small, robust gelding: fifth foal: brother to 4-y-o Ejtaaz, closely related to 9f winner Shaarid (by El Gran Senor) and half-brother to 5-y-o Saja (by Ferdinand): dam, 7f winner in USA, out of sister to Mill Reef: burly and blinkered, last of 13 in maiden at Haydock: sold (H. Thomson Jones to D. Nicholls) 3,000 gns Newmarket July Sales and gelded. *H. Thomson Jones* –

NUNNERY GROVE (IRE) 3 b.f. Waajib 121 – Manela Lady (Ela-Mana-Mou 132) [1994 49: 6.1s[5] 6g 7.1g 1995 8.2m[3] 8.2m[5] 8.3m 10g 8.3m Aug 26] leggy, angular, lightly-made filly: poor maiden handicapper: not certain to stay much beyond 1m: acts on good to firm ground: sold 500 gns Doncaster November Sales. *T. Thomson Jones* 42

NUNSHARPA 2 b.f. (Apr 4) Sharpo 132 – Missed Blessing 115 (So Blessed 130) [1995 6m Oct 13] tall, lengthy, unfurnished filly: ninth foal: half-sister to 5 winners, including smart 6f/7f performer Unblest (by Alzao) and 11.7f winner Lake Mission (by Blakeney): dam 6f and 1m winner: 20/1, tenth of 21 to Projection in maiden at Newmarket, midfield virtually throughout under hands and heels: will improve. *J. R. Fanshawe* 65 p

NURIVA (USA) 3 b.f. Woodman (USA) 126 – Mesmerize (Mill Reef (USA) 141) [1994 94: 6g[4] 6g* 6m 1995 8d 6m[3] 6g[3] Jul 15] big, lengthy filly: useful performer: best efforts when third in Cork And Orrery Stakes at Royal Ascot (3 lengths behind So Factual) and listed race at Newbury (beaten 1¼ lengths by Hard To Figure): should prove effective over 7f+: yet to race on extremes of going. *Saeed bin Suroor* 100

NUSHKA BABUSHKA 3 b.f. Nishapour (FR) 125 – Jessamine (Jalmood (USA) 126) [1994 –: 10g 1995 10.1m[6] 8.2m[6] 11.8g Oct 10] angular, unfurnished filly: no worthwhile form. *Bob Jones* –

NUTCRACKER 2 b.f. (Jun 3) Rambo Dancer (CAN) 107 – Fair Madame 88 (Monseigneur (USA) 127) [1995 6g[6] 7d[4] 7.9m a7g a7g Nov 16] angular filly: half-sister to 1m winner Fair Dare (by Daring March): dam 5f and 6f winner: modest maiden: no form in sellers last 2 starts: should stay 1m: blinkered final outing: sold 900 gns Doncaster November Sales: sent to Austria. *C. B. B. Booth* 53 ? a–

NUTHATCH (IRE) 3 b.f. Thatching 131 – New Edition 72 (Great Nephew 126) [1994 NR 1995 a6g[3] a7g[2] a7g[5] a7g a7g[3] a8g a7g 6f[4] 7.1m 6.9g 7d[6] Oct 19] fifth foal: half-sister to 7f winner Arabian King (by Sayf El Arab): dam, 2-y-o 5f winner, appeared to stay 7f: poor maiden handicapper: should stay 1m: acts on all-weather 36 surfaces and dead ground: tried visored: usually ridden by 7-lb claimer. *M. D. I. Usher*

NUVEEN (IRE) 4 br.g. Al Nasr (FR) 126 – Cactus Road (FR) (Iron Duke (FR) 122) [1994 –: 10g 8f 11.5g5 13.1g 1995 12.3d a7g 14.1f6 Jun 24] angular gelding: no form: tried in blinkers and visor. *Mrs J. Jordan* –

NWAAMIS (USA) 3 b.c. Dayjur (USA) 137 – Lady Cutlass (USA) (Cutlass (USA)) [1994 96P: 6d* 1995 8m3 8m5 8m May 21] tall, rangy, good sort: shows a powerful, rather rounded action: smart performer: very close third of 5 to Painter's Row in Craven Stakes then 5 lengths fifth of 11 to Pennekamp in 2000 Guineas, both at Newmarket: below best in Irish 2000 Guineas at the Curragh on only subsequent start: likely to prove best at up to 1m: yet to race on extremes of going: reportedly injured pelvis in summer but stays in training. *J. L. Dunlop* 117

NYALI BEACH (IRE) 3 b.f. Treasure Kay 114 – Gauloise Bleue (USA) (Lyphard's Wish (FR) 124) [1994 59: 6g4 6m 1995 a7g 7f2 7g6 8m5 7m a7g 8m4 9m Oct 27] leggy, lightly made filly: modest performer: sold out of B. Meehan's stable 1,300 gns Doncaster July Sales after sixth start: stays 7f: has raced only on a sound surface when on turf: usually races prominently: none too consistent: sold 1,200 gns Newmarket December Sales. *Dr J. D. Scargill* 51 d

O

OAKBURY (IRE) 3 ch.g. Common Grounds 118 – Doon Belle (Ardoon 124) [1994 72: 6g2 7.1m4 6g5 7m3 8.2d4 a7g5 1995 10.8m 8.3m 10f 10f2 10m2 11.8m3 10.3m3 Oct 21] angular, leggy gelding: has a round action: fair maiden claimer: stays 1½m: yet to race on soft ground, probably acts on any other: has been bandaged: claimed £7,000 by Miss L. Siddall final start. *R. Hannon* 71

OAKS STAR (USA) 4 b.g. Chief's Crown (USA) – Double Lock 104 (Home Guard (USA) 129) [1994 12d 7m 9.6m 1995 a10g Jan 5] lightly raced ex-Irish gelding: half-brother to several winners, including top-class miler Sure Blade (by Kris): dam 1¼m winner: best effort when blinkered on second start (rated 55) at 3 yrs for D. Weld: tailed off in Lingfield maiden on only start here. *P. F. I. Cole* –

OARE BUDGIE 2 ch.f. (Mar 29) Midyan (USA) 124 – Portvasco 90 (Sharpo 132) [1995 5g5 6.9g 6.1m5 5m3 6.1m Oct 26] close-coupled filly: fourth foal: sister to fairly useful 3-y-o 5.3f (at 2 yrs) and 6f winner (stays 1m) Midwich Cuckoo and half-sister to fair 6f to 7.1f winner Oare Sparrow (by Night Shift): dam 6f winner: modest maiden: stays 7f: visored (ran well) second start: sold 950 gns Doncaster November Sales. *P. T. Walwyn* 51

OARE SPARROW 5 b.m. Night Shift (USA) – Portvasco 90 (Sharpo 132) [1994 75: 6d2 6m2 6m2 6f6 6m6 6g* 5.1m3 6g* 7m 6d4 6g* 6.1g 1995 6f 6m 7m 6d* 6g* 7m Oct 28] good-bodied mare: fair handicapper: not seen out until August and ran well only when winning at Folkestone in September and October (minor event), racing towards favoured far side on both occasions: effective at 6f and stayed 1m at 3 yrs: acts on good to firm and dead ground: no improvement in a visor: tail swisher: usually races prominently. *P. T. Walwyn* 71

OATEY 2 ch.f. (Apr 23) Master Willie 129 – Oatfield 69 (Great Nephew 126) [1995 5m 6f 6m Nov 3] workmanlike filly: fluent mover: sister to 1991 2-y-o 6f winner High Sevens, closely related to several winners, including smart miler Barley Bill (by High Line), and half-sister to smart 3-y-o Munwar, winner up to 11.5f, and smart middle-distance stayer Hateel (both by Kalaglow): dam out of half-sister to High Line: under 7 lengths ninth of 18 to Wildwood Flower in maiden at Leicester in October on first run for 5 months, running on under considerate ride: never reached leaders in similar event won by Miss Riviera at Doncaster following month: remains capable of better, particularly over further than 6f. *Mrs J. R. Ramsden* 61 p

OBELOS (USA) 4 ch.c. Diesis 133 – Fair Sousanne 75 (Busted 134) [1994 NR 1995 10m* 10f May 1] workmanlike colt: brother to Lupe Stakes winner Gisarne: missed 1994 season due to a cracked pelvis: carrying condition, improved form to win 19-runner handicap at Pontefract in April, running on to lead entering last: favourite, finished lame there 12 days later: stays 1¼m. *Mrs J. Cecil* 70

OBERONS BOY (IRE) 2 b.g. (Mar 12) Fairy King (USA) – Bold Starlet (Precocious 126) [1995 5m^6 5m^2 6m^2 6m 6f^3 7f^6 6d^3 7d* 7s^3 8d^4 Oct 21] IR 20,000F, 19,000Y: useful-looking gelding: first foal: dam fairly useful Irish sprinter: fair performer: easy winner of (4-runner) minor event at Brighton in September: ran respectably afterwards in similar events won by Brandon Magic at Ascot and Henry The Fifth at Newbury: suited by 7f+: seems to act on any going: hung throughout fifth outing. *B. J. Meehan* 85

OBERON'S DART (IRE) 2 b.c. (Mar 2) Fairy King (USA) – Key Maneuver (USA) (Key To Content (USA)) [1995 7d^3 7g a6g^4 Nov 20] IR 20,000Y: fourth foal: half-brother to 4-y-o Thatchmaster (by Thatching), 7f and 8.2f winner Move Smartly (by Smarten) and a winner in USA: dam ran 4 times in North America: in frame in newcomers race at Milan and maiden (fourth of 14 to King's Harmony) at Southwell. *J. L. Dunlop* 62 +

OBLOMOV 2 b.c. (Mar 19) Most Welcome 131 – Flambera (FR) (Akarad (FR) 130) [1995 6m 6g 7.1m 7.1g* 8.1m^3 8d 8m 7m^2 a8g^2 Nov 10] 10,500Y: close-coupled colt: third foal: half-brother to French 4-y-o 1¼m/10.5f winner Yayoomel (by Roi Danzig) and very smart U.S. 3-y-o 8.5f winner Jumron (by Sharpo): dam 1¼m winner: made all in maiden at Sandown in July: easily best efforts when placed in minor event and nurseries: should stay 1¼m: acts on good to firm ground and equitrack: blinkered last 2 starts: strong-running galloper who seems best racing up with pace: sent to USA. *G. Lewis* 86

OBSESSIVE (USA) 2 b. or br.f. (Mar 4) Seeking The Gold (USA) – Secret Obsession (USA) 89 (Secretariat (USA)) [1995 6g^2 6g* 7g^2 Sep 30] quite attractive filly: third foal: closely related to a winner in USA by Woodman and half-sister to 7.2f winner Storm Nymph (by Storm Bird): dam 1¼m winner out of half-sister to Chris Evert: won maiden at Yarmouth in September: better form when 2½ lengths second to Ruznama in listed event at Newmarket on final start (sweating): will stay at least 1m: likely to improve again. *M. R. Stoute* 95 p

OBSIDIAN GREY 8 gr.g. Lyphard's Special (USA) 122 – Marcrest (On Your Mark 125) [1994 –: 7g 7m^5 6m 6g 6.1s 7g a7g a7g a6g a8g a7g 1995 a7g^5 7.1g 6m^6 6.9m* 7g^4 6.9f^2 7m 6.9m^4 6g 7.1m^5 5.9f Jun 28] sparely-made gelding: modest performer: won claimer at Carlisle in April: effective at 6f to 1m: acted on fibresand and any turf ground: visored (well beaten) once at 7 yrs: dead. *Miss L. C. Siddall* 53

OCCUPANDISTE (IRE) 2 b.f. (Jan 30) Kaldoun (FR) 122 – Only Seule (Lyphard (USA) 132) [1995 6m^4 7g 8g* 8f* Oct 22] first foal: dam, French 2-y-o 7.5f winner, is closely related to Irish 1000 Guineas winner Mehthaaf, from the brilliant Fall Aspen line: progressive French filly: won minor event at Chantilly in September and 5-runner Prix des Reservoirs at Longchamp (by 2 lengths from Raisonnable) in October, making all on both occasions: stays 1m: acts on firm ground: may well improve further. *Mme C. Head, France* 107 p

OCEAN GROVE (IRE) 2 b.f. (Jan 13) Fairy King (USA) – Leyete Gulf (IRE) (Slip Anchor 136) [1995 6g^6 7m^4 6.1d* 6d^4 Sep 27] lengthy, rather unfurnished filly: first foal: dam half-sister to very smart (stayed 1½m) Missionary Ridge out of 1000 Guineas third Shellshock, family of Dibidale and Tony Bin: won 20-runner maiden comfortably at Nottingham in September: creditable fourth of 10 to Brandon Magic in minor event at Salisbury 18 days later: will prove ideally suited by return to further than 6f: acts on good to firm and dead ground. *P. W. Chapple-Hyam* 84

OCEAN PARK 4 b.g. Dominion 123 – Chiming Melody 71 (Cure The Blues (USA)) [1994 60: 7.1m^5 7m 7m 7g^4 7m 6.9m^2 1995 a8g*^{dis} 8.5s 8.2m^3 10f^3 a9.4g^2 Nov 13] good-bodied gelding: good mover: fair performer: won maiden handicap at Southwell (subsequently disqualified for failing dope test) in June on first outing for new stable: best effort in handicap at Wolverhampton final start: stays 1¼m, at least under fast conditions: acts on fibresand and firm ground (shaped well on soft): blinkered (raced too freely) once as 3-y-o. *Lady Herries* 75

OCEAN STREAM (IRE) 2 b.c. (Mar 7) Waajib 121 – Kilboy Concorde (African Sky 124) [1995 6m^4 6g^4 6.1d^5 6g^2 6m^4 6m^2 a7g^5 Nov 21] 8,000Y, 15,000 2-y-o: compact, quite attractive colt: has a quick action: half-brother to 3-y-o 7f winner Lyford Law (by Contract Law), Irish 1m winner Father Phil (by Kampala) and 2 winners abroad: dam poor Irish maiden: fair maiden: stays 6f: disappointing on equitrack and when blinkered fifth start. *J. L. Eyre* 74

OCHOS RIOS (IRE) 4 br.g. Horage 124 – Morgiana (Godswalk (USA) 130) [1994 72, a59: 6d 7.5d⁴ 7m 7m 10m 6.9m 6m a6g⁵ a6g⁶ 6m 7d 7.1d* 7d 8.2d³ 7s a8g 1995 7.5m⁶ 8.3g 7.5g² 7.5m 7g⁵ 8.5d 7d⁵ 7g⁵ a7g³ a8g Dec 1] small gelding: good mover: just a modest handicapper at 4 yrs: stays 1m: acts on good to firm ground, heavy and fibresand: blinkered (below form) 4 times at 3 yrs: inconsistent. *B. S. Rothwell* 65 a61

O'CONNOR (IRE) 3 b.c. Ela-Mana-Mou 132 – Orillia (Red God 128§) [1994 8g* 9.5d* 1995 11g² 11s* 11s⁵ Jun 18] 3,000F: IR 26,000Y: seventh foal: brother to useful 1¼m winner Catherine Mary (second in 1½m Meld Stakes on third and final start) and half-brother to 2 winners: dam unraced daughter of smart French middle-distance filly Relicia: useful German colt: won maiden at Hoppegarten and listed event at Cologne at 2 yrs: successful in 1995 in Group 2 event at Munich by a head from subsequently demoted Dreamer, strong run to lead post: should stay 1½m: yet to race on top-of-the-ground. *A. Wohler, Germany* 105

OFFICE HOURS 3 b.g. Danehill (USA) 126 – Charmina (FR) (Nonoalco (USA) 131) [1994 54p: 6m 1995 8g⁴ 7m 7f³ 7m³ 10m⁴ 8m² 10.4g Aug 30] workmanlike gelding: fair maiden: jinked and unseated rider leaving stalls final start: stays 1m: has raced only on a sound surface. *C. A. Cyzer* 75

OFFICER 3 ch.c. General Holme (USA) 128 – Mode Classique (FR) (Top Ville 129) [1994 NR 1995 10m³ 12m Jul 11] good-bodied colt: third foal: dam French 1½m winner: third of 6 in maiden at Newmarket: broke a leg when favourite at Pontefract: would have stayed beyond 1¼m: dead. *H. R. A. Cecil* 76

OFF'N'AWAY (IRE) 3 ch.c. Be My Guest (USA) 126 – Irish Edition (USA) (Alleged (USA) 138) [1994 81p: 8g³ 7s* 1995 a10g³ 10m* a12f⁶ 8m³ 8g⁴ Jul 16] good-topped colt: smart performer: won minor event at Navan in May: bandaged, never able to land a blow and beaten 16½ lengths when sixth of 11 to Thunder Gulch in Belmont Stakes: best effort when staying-on 1½ lengths third of 7 to Darnay in Sea World International at the Curragh: successful at 1¼m, best effort at 1m: acts on good to firm ground, soft and dirt. *D. K. Weld, Ireland* 112

OFF THE AIR (IRE) 4 b.f. Taufan (USA) 119 – Milly Daydream (Hard Fought 125) [1994 54: 5v* a7g* a7g 8m⁴ a9.4g a9.4g* a14.8g a8.5g³ 10.2s a7g a9.4g 1995 a11g² a8.5g* a11g⁴ a9.4g⁴ a8.5g* a9.4g⁵ a9.4g a8g 10d 8.1d Oct 10] leggy filly: modest performer: won sellers at Wolverhampton in January and (third-last start for I. Campbell) February: well below form afterwards: effective at 8.5f, and stays 11f: acts on fibresand, good to firm ground and heavy: usually blinkered/visored. *B. J. Llewellyn* 51 d

OGGI 4 gr.c. Efisio 120 – Dolly Bevan 53 (Another Realm 118) [1994 –: 6.1d⁵ 1995 6g 5m 6g² 5.7f³ 6g* 6m a6g⁴ 6g⁵ 6s 6g Oct 7] angular colt: fair handicapper: won at Newbury in May: stays 6f well: acts on firm and dead ground and on fibresand: blinkered since fifth 4-y-o starts: usually has tongue tied down: inconsistent. *P. J. Makin* 71

OH DEARIE ME 3 b.f. Puissance 110 – Tyrian Princess 73 (Comedy Star (USA) 121) [1994 NR 1995 6.1g 8.2d Sep 19] 3,100Y: lightly-framed filly: third foal: dam 2-y-o 7f winner: looks of no account. *J. G. M. O'Shea* –

OH SO HANDY 7 b.g. Nearly A Hand 115 – Geordie Lass 58 (Bleep-Bleep 134) [1994 NR 1995 16d³ 17.2f³ 18.2m⁵ Jul 8] leggy gelding: poor staying maiden handicapper: blinkered last 2 starts: won novice chase in August. *R. Curtis* 38

OH WHATAKNIGHT 2 b.f. (May 4) Primo Dominie 121 – Carolside 108 (Music Maestro 119) [1995 5f⁴ 5g⁴ 5g* 5s⁶ Oct 7] 28,000Y: rather unfurnished filly: half-sister to several winners, including useful 1m to 9f winner Eton Lad (by Never So Bold): dam 2-y-o 5f winner who didn't progress: won 9-runner minor event at Ayr in September by ¾ length from Babsy Babe: well beaten in Cornwallis Stakes at Ascot final outing: will probably stay 6f: seems unsuited by very soft ground. *R. M. Whitaker* 85

OISIN AN OIR (IRE) 2 b.c. (Feb 6) Alzao (USA) 117 – Niamh Cinn Oir (IRE) (King of Clubs 124) [1995 6d a7g⁴ 7g 8g 10m Oct 2] leggy, unfurnished colt: poor mover: first foal: dam, Irish 1½m and 1¾m winner, half-sister to very smart Home On The Range, the dam of Reference Point: no worthwhile form in maidens: bred to be suited by further than 1m. *J. Berry* –

OKAVANGO (USA) 3 b.c. Riverman (USA) 131 – Baby Duck (USA) (Quack (USA)) [1994 80p: 7m^{2} 1995 10m^{6} 10m^{4} 10f* 10g^{5} 10g^{4} 9g Jun 17] angular, useful-looking colt: has scope: fair form: easily won 4-runner maiden at Brighton in May: runs as though will be well suited by further than 1¼m: acts on firm ground: visored since third 3-y-o start: front runner: sent to Dubai. *J. H. M. Gosden*

76

OKAY BABY (IRE) 3 b.f. Treasure Kay 114 – Miss Tuko (Good Times (ITY)) [1994 6v^{5} 6g^{5} 7s^{5} 7s 1995 a7g 12d 10g 8.3g^{3} 7m^{2} 8m 8g^{2} 8f^{2} 8.1f* 7m^{4} 7g 8f a7g Dec 2] sparely-made filly: third reported foal: half-sister to a winner in Norway: dam won in Norway: trained at 2 yrs by C. Collins in Ireland, best effort (rated 67) third start: modest form at best here, making all in claimer at Edinburgh in June: ran poorly last 3 starts: sold out of M. Tompkins' stable 4,400 gns Newmarket Autumn Sales before final one: stays 1m: acts on firm ground. *J. M. Bradley*

51

OLD COMRADES 8 ch.g. Music Boy 124 – Miss Candine 66 (King Emperor (USA)) [1994 55: a8g^{6} a7s* a7g^{6} a7g 7d^{3} 6f* 6g^{3} 6g^{3} 6g^{2} 6m a6g^{6} 8g a6g* 7g^{6} a6g^{5} 1995 6g^{4} 6m 6.1m^{4} a6g^{3} a6g^{3} Jul 13] workmanlike, good-quartered gelding: poor mover: modest handicapper: effective at 6f to 1m: acts on any going: blinkered (below form) final 6-y-o start: sold 2,000 gns Doncaster September Sales. *T. D. Barron*

50

OLD HAT (IRE) 2 b.c. (Apr 16) Thatching 131 – Crystal Fountain (Great Nephew 126) [1995 6s^{5} 6d Oct 19] leggy, unfurnished colt: brother to 1993 2-y-o 6.9f winner Summer Hail and half-brother to several winners, including 3-y-o 6f (at 2 yrs) and 10.1f winner Aqua Rigia (by Last Tycoon) and useful stayer High Fountain (by High Line): dam once-raced half-sister to Royal Palace: fifth of 11 to Midnight Blue in maiden at Ascot: disputed lead over 4f then eased when beaten in 20-runner maiden at Newbury 13 days later, finishing tenth behind Fly Tip: will improve again: sent to Saudi Arabia. *R. Hannon*

68 p

OLD HICKORY (IRE) 4 b.c. Alzao (USA) 117 – Fabled Lifestyle (Kings Lake (USA) 133) [1994 104: 7m 7.5g* 10.3m^{4} 10.4f* 10m^{3} 10f^{4} 10.4m^{3} 11.9d^{5} 1995 10m 10m^{4} 10.4g 10f^{4} 10m 10.4m Jul 15] strong, good-topped colt: shows a quick action: useful handicapper: fourth at Newmarket (to Burooj) in May and Ascot (to Salt Lake) in June: should prove suited by 1½m, respectable effort (tiring final 1f, flashing tail) on dead going when tried: goes well on top-of-the-ground: blinkered 4 of last 5 starts: occasional front runner: inconsistent at 4 yrs: sent to Saudi Arabia. *L. M. Cumani*

104

OLD HOOK (IRE) 4 b. or br.c. Digamist (USA) 110 – Day Dress (Ashmore (FR) 125) [1994 64: a5g a7g^{5} a8g a7g^{5} a7g* 5.5v^{6} a5g* a8.5g^{6} a6g 5m 7g^{5} 7g^{2} 6g* 7g^{6} a6.5g 1995 a6g a7.5g* 9g^{3} 9g 6g 6.5f^{3} 6f^{2} 6f^{2} 7f a7g* a7g^{4} a8g* Nov 25] neat Belgian-trained colt: fair handicapper: won at Boitsfort in March, Sterrebeek (apprentices) in October and Lingfield in November: stays 1m: acts on good to firm going and equitrack: not the most reliable. *Paul Smith, Belgium*

79

OLD IRISH 2 gr.c. (Feb 18) Old Vic 136 – Dunoof 92 (Shirley Heights 130) [1995 8.2m Oct 19] brother to 3-y-o 1¼m winner Mega Tid, closely related to fair middle-distance performer Folia (by Sadler's Wells) and half-brother to winners in Germany and France: dam, 2-y-o 7f winner, half-sister to high-class middle-distance stayer High Hawk, later dam of In The Wings: 14/1, slowly away and never better than midfield in 19-runner maiden at Nottingham: looks sort to do better in time. *L. M. Cumani*

– p

OLD MASTER (IRE) 4 b.g. Tate Gallery (USA) 117 – Nancy Drew (Sexton Blake 126) [1994 –: 8m 1995 10.2m 11.7h^{4} Aug 18] lengthy gelding: of little account. *R. J. Baker*

–

OLD PROVENCE 5 b.h. Rainbow Quest (USA) 134 – Orange Hill 75 (High Top 131) [1994 98+: 12g^{2} 1995 a12g* 12g^{5} a12g* a9.4g Dec 9] big, good-topped horse: has a high knee action: only modest form in 1995: won poor claimer at Wolverhampton (for I. Campbell) in June and seller at Wolverhampton in November: needs further than 9.4f, and should be suited by 1¾m: wears bandages. *R. Harris*

55

OLD RED (IRE) 5 ch.g. Ela-Mana-Mou 132 – Sea Port (Averof 123) [1994 74: a11g* 13.8d^{2} 12.4g^{5} 12.1f^{2} 13m^{4} 14.6m^{6} 13.1g^{2} 14.1g* 16m^{2} 18.2s^{3} 17.1s 16.5v^{3} 1995 17.5g^{4} 18m* 16.5m Nov 4] lengthy gelding: has a round action: had shaped well on belated return and was backed at long odds prior to winning 21-runner Tote Cesarewitch at Newmarket (well ridden by L. Charnock, last but one 6f out, weaved through to lead 1f out and beat Nanton Point a length) in October: stays very well:

74

acts on fibresand and any turf going: tends to pull hard and hang: early, alone and very quietly to post at Newmarket: consistent. *Mrs M. Reveley*

OLD ROUVEL (USA) 4 b.c. Riverman (USA) 131 – Marie de Russy (FR) (Sassafras (FR) 135) [1994 $14g^6$ 1995 a12g* $16.2m^2$ $16.2m^4$ $16.4m^2$ $20m^5$ $15.9m^5$ $18g^3$ $16g^4$ 16.5m* $16m^3$ Oct 27] tall colt: shows knee action: seventh foal: half-brother to very smart middle-distance stayer Top Sunrise (by Top Ville): dam, French 10.5f winner, is half-sister to smart pair Sakura Relko and Dom d'Albignac: ran once at 3 yrs for A. Fabre: won maiden at Lingfield in February and minor event at Doncaster (3 ran) in October: generally ran creditably in good company, including finishing third of 6 in Doncaster Cup and fourth of 8 (after none-too-clear a run) in Jockey Club Cup at Newmarket: suited by a thorough test of stamina: acts on good to firm ground: held up: hung right under pressure final start. *D. J. G. Murray Smith* — 107

OLD SCHOOL HOUSE 2 ch.c. (Mar 29) Polar Falcon (USA) 126 – Farewell Letter (USA) (Arts And Letters) [1995 6m 8g 10m 8f Oct 18] 7,600F, 30,000Y: quite attractive colt: half-brother to several winners, including very useful stayer Parting Moment (by The Minstrel) and 1992 2-y-o 6.9f winner Nico Mike (by Trempolino): dam very smart over middle distances: behind in maidens and a nursery, hinting at ability second start: struggling long way out on firm ground final start. *C. N. Allen* — –

OLD SWINFORD (IRE) 3 b. or br.f. Contract Law (USA) 108 – Rockalong Rosie (Martinmas 128) [1994 60p: $6g^6$ $6.1m^4$ $7g^5$ 1995 $8m^5$ $a9.4g^6$ $8m^5$ $8g^2$ $10m^3$ 8.2m 10m* $14m^2$ $14.9m^4$ $14g^6$ 14.1m* $17.2h^3$ $11.8m^4$ 15.4m 14d Sep 27] leggy filly: has a round action: modest performer: won claimer (only time blinkered) at Newmarket in June and selling handicap (bought in 4,000 gns) at Nottingham in July: below best afterwards: at least as effective at 1¾m as shorter: acts on hard ground, ran poorly only outing on the all-weather: has been bandaged behind: sold only 2,500 gns Newmarket Autumn Sales. *B. J. Meehan* — 58

OLEANA (IRE) 2 b.f. (Feb 6) Alzao (USA) 117 – Buraida 64 (Balidar 133) [1995 7g* $7.3d^5$ Oct 21] angular, unfurnished filly: first foal: dam, 6f winner, sister to smart sprinter Carol's Treasure: comfortable winner of 18-runner maiden at Leicester, leading going strongly over 2f out then green: raced keenly and ran below that form on softer ground when fifth of 9 to Sil Sila in listed event at Newbury 12 days later: wears bandage(s) behind: likely do better. *P. F. I. Cole* — 86 p

OLERON 3 b.f. Darshaan 133 – Orangerie (USA) (Gay Mecene (USA) 128) [1994 NR 1995 10m 8m 10g 10f $a12g^2$ $a11g^4$ $a12g^6$ $12.1g^6$ Sep 18] IR 9,000Y, — 42

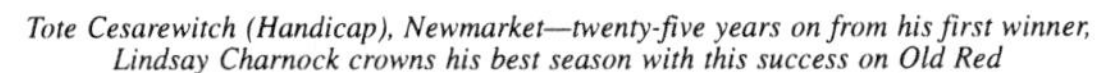

Tote Cesarewitch (Handicap), Newmarket—twenty-five years on from his first winner, Lindsay Charnock crowns his best season with this success on Old Red

15,000 2-y-o, resold 4,600 2-y-o: leggy, sparely-made filly: half-sister to 2 Italian winners, including Ogasawara (1m and 10.5f, by Doyoun): dam, lightly raced in France, is half-sister to outstanding Italian filly Orsa Maggiore: poor maiden handicapper: stays 1½m: broke blood vessel fourth intended start. *J. Norton*

OLIFANTSFONTEIN 7 b.g. Thatching 131 – Taplow (Tap On Wood 130) [1994 49: 5g 5g 5g 5m 5g 8.1f 5f^{6} 5g a5g a5g^{5} a6g^{4} a6g a6g 1995 a6g 5m 5m^{5} 6f^{6} 5m Aug 11] lengthy, angular gelding: poor on balance of form since 5 yrs: best at 5f: probably acts on any going: occasionally blinkered/visored. *D. Nicholls* — 46

OLIMPIA DUKAKIS (ITY) 3 ch.f. Isopach – Jaana (Cure The Blues (IRE)) [1994 106p: 7g* 7v* 8v* 1995 8m* 8m* 11g* 11d^{2} 8m* 10s* 10g^{2} 10m^{5} Nov 12] useful Italian filly with a fine record: successful in listed event at Milan, then 9-runner Premio Regina Elena (led entering last, beat Baaderah a length) and minor event at Rome, before length second of 11 to Valley of Gold in Oaks d'Italia at Milan (going on over 1f out but unable to quicken with winner final 150 yds), all in the spring: won 11-runner Premio Legnano at Milan in July by ½ length from Rosi Zambotti and valuable conditions event there in September: stays 11f: acts on good to firm ground and heavy: genuine and tremendously consistent. *G. Botti, Italy* — 108

OLIVER ROCK 2 b.c. (Feb 24) Shareef Dancer (USA) 135 – Short Rations (Lorenzaccio 130) [1995 7m 8m 8g Sep 29] compact colt: brother to a winner in France and half-brother to several winners: dam Italian 2-y-o 5f winner: seventh of 22 in maiden at Newbury on debut: well beaten afterwards: dead. *Major D. N. Chappell* — 79

OLIVIA VAL 5 b.m. Valiyar 129 – Traditional Miss 90 (Traditionalist (USA)) [1994 19: a8g 10.8m 7.1s 6m^{6} 7.1f^{4} 8.3m 8d 1995 a9.4g^{4} a8.5g^{5} a9.4g 8.1m Jul 2] angular mare: bad maiden: barely stays 9.4f: acts on fibresand and firm ground, no form on a soft surface: inconsistent. *A. G. Newcombe* — 22

OLIVIERO (FR) 2 b.c. (Apr 16) Vaguely Pleasant (FR) 113 – My Green Eyes (USA) (Big Spruce (USA)) [1995 6d^{2} 6.5s* 6.5s^{6} 9d^{5} 10g^{3} 6.5g^{5} Nov 7] 12,000 francs Y: sixth foal: half-brother to 4 minor winners in France: dam, placed, half-sister to very smart sprinter-miler (and broodmare) Polyponder: won minor event at Maisons-Laffitte in September: best effort when length third of 5 to Polaris Flight in Criterium de Saint-Cloud, setting steady pace: last of 5 in Criterium des 2 Ans at Evry, only subsequent start: stays 1¼m. *A. Mauchamp, France* — 110 ?

OMARA (USA) 2 b.f. (Apr 26) Storm Cat (USA) – Alamosa (Alydar (USA)) [1995 6m^{2} 5g^{5} Jun 5] $95,000Y: close-coupled filly: first foal: dam (unraced) from very good family: 1¾ lengths second of 9 to Paloma Bay in maiden at Newmarket, quickening clear and looking winner but caught 75 yds out: didn't improve at 5f in similar event at Leicester when fifth to Applaud and not seen out again: created quite a good impression at Newmarket, and looked worth another chance. *H. R. A. Cecil* — 77

ON A PEDESTAL (IRE) 3 b.f. Waajib 121 – Lady Lane (Tanfirion 110) [1994 50: 5m^{6} 5m 5h^{4} 7.5f 8m* 7g^{6} 1995 10d 12m* 12g^{4} 11.1f^{4} 10.5g 12m Oct 2] strong, close-coupled filly: modest handicapper: won at Carlisle in April, held up and leading 2f out: below form last 3 outings: stays 1½m: acts on good to firm ground and dead: inconsistent. *Mrs J. R. Ramsden* — 55

ONCE MORE FOR LUCK (IRE) 4 b.g. Petorius 117 – Mrs Lucky (Royal Match 117) [1994 79: 8g^{5} 10.5g^{2} 8m 7.1m^{3} 8m^{3} 7f^{6} 8d 8s 1995 6.9m^{4} 8g^{2} 8g 10f^{4} 10f^{4} 10.3f^{2} 10m^{2} 10.5m^{2} 12g^{2} 12g^{3} 11.9g 10.4m^{3} 12f* 10f Oct 24] sturdy gelding: fair handicapper: consistent on form in 1995, easy winner of claimer at Catterick in October: stays 1½m: acts on firm and dead ground: sometimes finds little and is not one to trust implicitly: won over hurdles in November. *Mrs M. Reveley* — 67

ONE DREAM 2 b.g. (Mar 16) Weldnaas (USA) 112 – Superb Lady 106 (Marcus Superbus 100) [1995 7m Nov 3] 7,200F, 8,000Y: close-coupled gelding: half-brother to winning sprinter Jacqui Joy (by Music Boy) and a winner in Macau: dam best at 5f: 12/1, always behind in 18-runner maiden at Doncaster. *B. Smart* — –

ONE FOR JEANNIE 3 b.f. Clantime 101 – Miss Henry 78 (Blue Cashmere 129) [1994 54: a6g^{2} a8.5g a6g^{3} 1995 a5g^{2} a7g^{2} a6g* a6g a5g* a6g^{4} 5.1m^{6} 5m 5g 6.1g^{2} 6f^{6} Jun 15] fair performer: won handicap at Lingfield in January and claimer at Wolverhampton in April: effective at 5f and 6f: acts on all-weather, has raced only on a sound surface on turf: effective visored or not. *A. Bailey* — 68

ONE FOR THE CHIEF 7 b.g. Chief Singer 131 – Action Belle (Auction Ring (USA) 123) [1994 NR 1995 21.6f May 1] sturdy gelding: of little account nowadays. *R. M. Whitaker* –

ONEFORTHEDITCH (USA) 2 gr.f. (Mar 11) With Approval (CAN) – Wee Dram (USA) (Nostrum (USA)) [1995 6g^2 Sep 30] $50,000Y: leggy filly: second reported foal: dam, winner of 9 races in USA, out of half-sister to dam of high-class 1m/1¼m performer and Oaks second All At Sea: sire high-class middle-distance performer: 7/1, length second of 17 to Polish Spring in maiden at Newmarket, finishing in good style after taking time to quicken: will be suited by at least 1m: sure to improve and win a race. *J. H. M. Gosden* 79 p

ONEFOURSEVEN 2 b.g. (Apr 29) Jumbo Hirt (USA) 90§ – Dominance (Dominion 123) [1995 7g 7m a7g Aug 19] 1,500Y, 3,500 2-y-o: leggy, unfurnished gelding: second foal: half-brother to 3-y-o Can She Can Can (by Sulaafah), 6f winner at 2 yrs: dam unraced daughter of Oaks and Irish Oaks winner Juliette Marny, a sister to St Leger winner Julio Mariner: never a factor in maiden auctions: blinkered last 2 starts. *S. R. Bowring* –

ONEINEVERYCOLOUR 3 ch.f. Midyan (USA) 124 – Matching Lines 72 (Thatching 131) [1994 58: 5g 5f 6.1s^4 5.1m* 5.1m* 5m^2 5.1m^3 5f^2 5m^2 5g^4 5m^5 5d a5g 1995 a5g^5 a5g 5.1g^6 5g 5g 6g a5g 5m 5f Jul 13] small filly: disappointing sprinter in 1995: acts on good to firm ground, probably on soft: active type: tends to hang left. *P. D. Evans* –

ONE LIFE TO LIVE (IRE) 2 gr.c. (Apr 10) Classic Music (USA) – Fine Flame (Le Prince 98) [1995 a7g^5 6m 6g a7g a7g Nov 24] IR 9,500Y, 11,000 2-y-o: half-brother to several winners, including sprinter Filicaia (by Sallust) and (at 1½m in Ireland) Fuego Del Amor (by Ahonoora): dam modest Irish maiden, placed twice at 2 yrs: looked modest maiden on debut but failed to reproduce that form (badly hampered final start): will be suited by 1m+. *A. Harrison* – a54 ?

ONE OFF THE RAIL (USA) 5 b.h. Rampage (USA) – Catty Queen (USA) (Tom Cat) [1994 48, a80: a10g a12g^4 a12g^2 a12g* a12g* 11.9d^6 12d^4 11.9f^6 a12g^2 10.1m^4 11.9g 1995 a9.4g a12g a12g^2 a12g a12g^3 a12g* 10g 11.9m* 12m^4 12f^4 14m 12m^4 11.9g a10g^5 a13g Nov 25] good-bodied horse: has a round action: handicapper, great deal better on all-weather than turf: won at Lingfield (claimer) in March and Brighton in June: stays 1½m: unproven on extremes of ground on turf: goes well on equitrack, below form all 3 times on fibresand (at Wolverhampton): tends to race prominently nowadays. *A. Moore* 44 a77

ONEOFTHEOLDONES 3 b.c. Deploy 131 – Waveguide 76 (Double Form 130) [1994 81: 7.1s^3 7d^3 7d^3 1995 10m^5 a8g* 11.9m 8.1g Sep 22] good-topped colt: has a round action: 5/4 on, easily best effort at 3 yrs when making all in median auction maiden at Southwell in June: should stay at least 1¼m: possibly unsuited by top-of-the-ground (best form, at 2 yrs, on a soft surface), acts on fibresand: pulled much too hard (for apprentice) third 3-y-o start. *S. G. Norton* 67

ONE POUND 2 b.g. (Apr 17) Shareef Dancer (USA) 135 – Beloved Visitor (USA) 83 (Miswaki (USA) 124) [1995 7m 7m 7.1d^6 Sep 13] good-topped gelding: shows knee action: first foal: dam Irish 2-y-o 6f winner: modest form in maidens: bred to stay at least 1m. *B. W. Hills* 59

ONE SHOT (IRE) 2 b.g. (Apr 20) Fayruz 116 – La Gravotte (FR) (Habitat 134) [1995 6.1m 6m^5 6m^3 6g Sep 1] 9,200Y: lengthy gelding: half-brother to Irish 8.5f winner Departure (by Gorytus) and winners abroad by Bellypha and Roi Danzig: dam lightly raced: modest form, including in seller: stays 6f. *W. R. Muir* 55

ONE VOICE (USA) 5 ch.h. Affirmed (USA) – Elk's Ellie (USA) (Vaguely Noble 140) [1994 89: 12g^3 16.2m 12m* a12g* 12h* 13.8g* 11.9f* 16.1m^3 14.6s^2 1995 14m^3 Aug 31] tall, angular horse: has a round action: fairly useful and genuine handicapper (mainly for Sir Mark Prescott) at 4 yrs: heavily bandaged, tailed off long way from home in 3-runner minor event at Salisbury on belated return: best short of 2m: probably acts on any going: races prominently. *K. Bishop* –

ONE WILD OAT 4 b.f. Shareef Dancer (USA) 135 – Short Rations (Lorenzaccio 130) [1994 60: 11.9g^6 10.2f^2 8.3m 9g 12g* 12.2g 12.5v^4 13g 12g a12g 1995 a12g Jan 5] leggy filly: good mover: modest performer: stays 1½m: acts on firm ground, probably on heavy: blinkered (finished last) only start in 1995. *C. F. Wall* –

ON FAIR STAGE (IRE) 2 b.f. (May 29) Sadler's Wells (USA) 132 – Fair Salinia 125 (Petingo 135) [1995 7m Oct 28] unfurnished filly: half-sister to several winners, including 3-y-o 1½m winner Crespo (by Kris), smart 7f (at 2 yrs) and 1m winner Perfect Circle (by Caerleon) and 1988 2-y-o 1m winner (later stayed 1¾m) Horn Dance (by Green Dancer): dam won Oaks and awarded Irish Oaks: 25/1 and very green in preliminaries, just under 8 lengths eighth of 19 to Awaamir in maiden at Newmarket, prominent until 2f out: should do better. *M. R. Stoute* **67 p**

ONLY ROYALE (IRE) 6 b.m. Caerleon (USA) 132 – Etoile de Paris 116 (Crowned Prince (USA) 128) [1994 121: 10s 12m 11.9m* 12g 12f^5 1995 12m* 12f^2 12d^3 Jul 2] **121**

Those who had summed up Only Royale as 'an autumn mare' were in for a shock when she lined up in the Madagans Jockey Club Stakes at Newmarket in early-May. Trainer Luca Cumani had changed Only Royale's routine—keeping her in training over the winter—and she reappeared in top form to account for her six rivals, notably the Breeders' Cup Turf winner Tikkanen. Held up as usual, but in a steadily-run race, Only Royale struck the front over a furlong out then held on bravely by a neck as Tikkanen rallied, the pair pulling two and a half lengths clear of Time Star and Sacrament. Only Royale had won as early as May earlier in her career, but that was in a maiden at Edinburgh way back in her three-year-old days. Between that and the Jockey Club Stakes there were wins in two handicaps at Newbury and a £9,300 contest and listed event at Milan later on at three years, the Prix Foy at Longchamp at four years and two runaway triumphs in the Yorkshire Oaks. There had also been two creditable but pretty luckless appearances in the Prix de l'Arc de Triomphe. Sadly, there was no attempt at third-time lucky, or at any other race in the autumn. The Coronation Cup was Only Royale's next target and she came within a head of winning it, Sunshack just coming out the better in a sprint finish, and she also made the places in the Grand Prix de Saint-Cloud three weeks later, two lengths behind Carnegie and Luso. The Rothmans International at Woodbine was mapped out for her in October, but just over two weeks beforehand it was announced that she would miss it with a bruised foot. In November, it was front page news that Cumani would once again be sent horses by the Aga Khan. Three days after that, it was reported that the trainer would be without one of his standard bearers in the Aga Khan's absence—Only Royale had been retired to her owner's stud in Kentucky. A good-topped mare, Only Royale was better at a mile and a half than shorter and should have stayed a mile and three quarters. A genuine performer, she acted on any going, was held up and had a good turn of foot. *L. M. Cumani*

Only Royale (IRE) (b.m. 1989)	Caerleon (USA) (b 1980)	Nijinsky (b 1967)	Northern Dancer
			Flaming Page
		Foreseer (b or br 1969)	Round Table
			Regal Gleam
	Etoile de Paris (b 1977)	Crowned Prince (ch 1969)	Raise A Native
			Gay Hostess
		Place d'Etoile (b 1967)	Kythnos
			Etoile de France

Madagans Jockey Club Stakes, Newmarket—Only Royale (right) wins in the spring! She just gets the better of Tikkanen

ONLY (USA) 2 ch.c. (Mar 19) Rahy (USA) 115 – Stay With Bruce (USA) (Grey Dawn II 132) [1995 a8g6 Dec 18] first foal: dam minor winner in USA at up to 9f, including at 2 yrs: 15/2, over 10 lengths sixth of 9 to Red Rusty in maiden at Lingfield, fading having been close up long way: will improve. *R. Hannon* 48 p

ON THE CARPET (IRE) 2 b.f. (May 25) Persian Bold 123 – Good Relations (Be My Guest (USA) 126) [1995 7d 8m 6d2 Nov 16] IR 3,000Y: well-made filly: half-sister to 2 winners, including 1m winner Tacoma Heights (by Taufan): dam, Irish 7f and 1½m winner, half-sister to Montekin: twelfth of 23 in median auction maiden at Doncaster in November, second start: also ran twice in Italy, second in minor event at Rome: should stay at least 1m. *J. L. Dunlop* 65 ?

ON THE HOME RUN 2 b.f. (May 22) Governor General 116 – In The Papers 87 (Aragon 118) [1995 6g Sep 2] second foal: half-sister to 3-y-o Most Welcome News (by Most Welcome): dam stayed 6f: 50/1 and very backward, slowly away and tailed off in maiden at Kempton. *J. R. Jenkins* –

ON THE OFF CHANCE 3 ch.g. French Gondolier (USA) 69 – Off And On (Touching Wood (USA) 127) [1994 NR 1995 10.5g Sep 22] smallish gelding: first reported foal: dam of little account: 100/1, in need of race and blinkered, tailed-off last of 16 in maiden at Haydock. *G. Holmes* –

ON THE WILDSIDE 2 ch.f. (Mar 23) Charmer 123 – No Control 82 (Bustino 136) [1995 7m 8m Oct 28] 2,000 2-y-o: leggy, unfurnished filly: fourth reported foal: dam 9f and 12.2f winner: slowly away and never dangerous in sellers at Newmarket: may do better over further. *M. R. Channon* –

ON Y VA (USA) 8 ch.m. Victorious (USA) – Golden Moony (Northfields (USA)) [1994 67, a53: a7g* a7g6 a7g6 7d* a7g4 7g 7m2 a7g3 7.1m4 a7g 7.6g 7g* a7g a7g6 1995 a7g a7g 7m a7g a7g6 Nov 24] sparely-made, angular mare: well beaten in 1995: effective at 7f to 1m: acts on any ground: usually ridden by 7-lb claimer Sarah Thompson: sold 3,000 gns Newmarket December Sales. *R. J. R. Williams* –

OOH AH CANTONA 4 b.g. Crofthall 110 – Chablisse 69 (Radetzky 123) [1994 73d: 7m5 7f 7.1m 7.9f 7f 8g 7g6 1995 8g 8m4 10f4 10.1m* 9.9m* 10.1m2 10f* 10.4g 10.3d Sep 9] leggy, angular gelding: fair handicapper: successful at Newcastle, Beverley (amateurs) and Redcar in the summer: running well when nearly falling at Doncaster on final start: stays 1¼m: acts on firm ground and dead. *J. L. Eyre* 71

OOZLEM (IRE) 6 b.g. Burslem 123 – Fingers (Lord Gayle (USA) 124) [1994 44: 8g4 8v 8f 8.3m2 8m* 8.3m5 9.7m 10m 8f* 8m4 8.2m 8m* 8d2 8s 8g 1995 a8g3 8m 8m 8g5 9m6 8.2m 9m 8f* 8g 8g6 9d 8f a8g4 Dec 15] workmanlike gelding: poor handicapper: left R. Flower's stable after seventh 6-y-o outing: won apprentice race at Salisbury in August on first start for new yard: flattered final one: effective at 1m and 1¼m: acts on any turf going: blinkered/visored nowadays: sometimes slowly away: tends to hang, and not one to trust implicitly. *Jamie Poulton* 44 a33

OPALETTE 2 b.f. (Jan 25) Sharrood (USA) 124 – Height of Folly 81 (Shirley Heights 130) [1995 7g6 Oct 9] sturdy, lengthy filly: has scope: fourth foal: half-sister to 4-y-o middle-distance performer Charity Crusader (by Rousillon), 7.5f and 8.1f winner at 2 yrs, and 1994 2-y-o 7.1f winner Opaline (by Salse): dam stayer: 10/1, just over 6 lengths sixth of 18 to Fairlight Down in maiden at Leicester, behind after slow start then running on well under hands and heels: sure to improve. *Lady Herries* 61 p

OPAQUE 3 b.g. Shirley Heights 130 – Opale 117 (Busted 134) [1994 NR 1995 12m 14g6 Jun 3] 50,000Y: tall, lengthy gelding: half-brother to 13.3f winner Pale Wine (by Rousillon) and 2 winners at up to 1m by Bellypha: dam won Irish St Leger at 4 yrs: easy in market, held up and never a threat in maidens at Newmarket in May and June: should stay well. *L. M. Cumani* –

OPENING CHORUS 2 ch.g. (Mar 14) Music Boy 124 – One Sharper (Dublin Taxi) [1995 5.1m5 5f6 5g* 5g 6m Oct 2] 7,400F, 12,500Y: compact gelding: half-brother to 5f winners Kimbolton Katie (by Aragon) and Kimbolton Korker (by Interrex): dam twice-raced half-sister to very smart miler General Vole: convincing winner of claimer at Newcastle (claimed out of Mrs J. R. Ramsden's stable £7,000) in August: creditable seventh of 17 in nursery at Redcar penultimate start: will stay 6f: may do better. *Mrs M. Reveley* 66

OPERA 2 ch.f. (Mar 29) Forzando 122 – Flattering (USA) (Nodouble (USA)) [1995 7m4 7m* 7f3 7m 8m2 8g* Sep 14] sturdy, attactive filly: second foal: half-sister 84 p to a 1½m winner in Scandinavia by Doulab: dam Irish 2-y-o 6f winner: won minor event at Lingfield in July and nursery at Yarmouth (very easily on favoured rail) in September: stays 1m: game: sold to race in USA. *W. Jarvis*

OPERA BUFF (IRE) 4 br.g. Rousillon (USA) 133 – Obertura (USA) 100 (Roberto (USA) 131) [1994 59: 14d^6 12m 12m^4 12m^2 1995 a12g^6 a12g^3 12g 14.1g 14.1f^3 13.1f^6 14d^2 14.1m* 15.1s^4 a12g* a12g* a13g* Nov 25] big, good-topped gelding: fairly useful performer: left M. Pipe after sixth 4-y-o start: ran well all outings for new stable, winning maiden at Nottingham in October and handicaps at Wolverhampton and Lingfield (2) in November: stays 15f, may well get 2m: acts on good to firm and soft ground and goes well on the all-weather: visored/blinkered fifth (looked reluctant) and sixth 4-y-o starts. *Miss Gay Kelleway* — 65 + a85 +

OPERA FAN (IRE) 3 b.g. Taufan (USA) 119 – Shannon Lady 67 (Monsanto (FR) 121) [1994 63: a6g 5d^5 6g^4 1995 a7g^4 a8g^3 8.2m^3 a8g 8f^4 8m^2 9.2f^4 6.9h^5 8g 8g Sep 29] leggy, sparely-made gelding: modest maiden handicapper: stays 1m: acts on hard and dead ground, respectable efforts at best on the all-weather: sold (Sir Mark Prescott to D. Cosgrove) 7,400 gns Newmarket Autumn Sales. *Sir Mark Prescott* — 60 d

OPERA LOVER (IRE) 3 b.f. Sadler's Wells (USA) 132 – Rensaler (USA) (Stop The Music (USA)) [1994 97: 7m 8.1g* 8g^4 7.3v 1995 8m 13.4m^4 14.6m 12d^5 Sep 24] sturdy, lengthy filly: has a quick action: useful performer: not disgraced when seventh in Park Hill Stakes at Doncaster third start: should be suited by around 1½m/1¾m: acts on good to firm ground, well below form on heavy. *M. R. Stoute* — 97

OPERATIC DANCER 4 b.g. Germont – Indian Dancer (Streak 119) [1994 NR 1995 8d 9.2s 6.9m 7m May 10] sturdy gelding: first reported foal: dam of no account: no worthwhile form. *R. M. McKellar* — –

OPTIONS OPEN 3 b.c. Then Again 126 – Zahiah 90 (So Blessed 130) [1994 105: 6g 5f^4 5.2m^3 6f* 7m* 7g 1995 7m^5 7m^5 Jul 1] sturdy, useful-looking colt: useful performer: sent to Dubai after 2-y-o career with R. Hannon: creditable fifth of 16 to Sergeyev in Jersey Stakes at Royal Ascot on return: shade disappointing in Van Geest Criterion Stakes at Newmarket 10 days later, weakening quickly from 2f out: stays 7f well: acts on firm ground, yet to race on a soft surface. *Saeed bin Suroor* — 102

OPUS ONE 4 b.f. Slip Anchor 136 – Rustle of Silk 67 (General Assembly (USA)) [1994 61: 10m^6 10m^3 14.1m* 16g^3 15.8m^3 16g 16m 1995 14.6g* 12f^2 15.8m^5 13f^3 a14.8g^6 Sep 16] leggy filly: modest handicapper: won at Doncaster (sweating and on toes) in July: stays 2m well: acts on firm ground, yet to race on a soft surface. *Miss S. E. Hall* — 63

ORANGE AND BLUE 2 br.f. (Mar 21) Prince Sabo 123 – Mazarine Blue 65 (Bellypha 130) [1995 5.1g* 5m^5 6g^5 6m 6m a7g^4 a6g a6g Dec 2] leggy filly: poor mover: has only one eye, and wears an eyecover: first foal: dam sprinting half-sister to very useful sprinter Rich Charlie: plater: won claimer at Nottingham in April: sold out of M. Jarvis' stable 1,500 gns Doncaster September Sales after fifth start: stays 7f: acts on fibresand, well below form last 2 starts on top-of-the-ground. *Miss J. F. Craze* — 50

ORANGE PLACE (IRE) 4 ch.g. Nordance (USA) – Little Red Hut (Habitat 134) [1994 94: 7v* 7d^6 7s 7m* 8m^4 8f 7g 1995 7m^6 6d a7g Nov 16] lengthy gelding: fairly useful front-running handicapper at 3 yrs for M. Bell: no promise on belated return: stays 1m: probably acts on any going. *T. J. Naughton* — –

ORCHARD GOLD 4 b.c. Glint of Gold 128 – On The Top (High Top 131) [1994 49: 10d 12.1s^4 10.5m 12.5m 10.2g 10m 8.1s^5 1995 6.9f 7g May 27] workmanlike colt: poor maiden: stiff tasks and well beaten over inadequate trips in 1995: stays 12.1f: below form on top-of-the-ground, acts on soft. *F. J. Yardley* — –

ORCHESTRA STALL 3 b.g. Old Vic 136 – Blue Brocade 91 (Reform 132) [1994 –p: 8m 1995 10s^3 Mar 30] good-topped gelding: unseated rider coming out on to course for maiden at Leicester on reappearance, but did not bolt when loose, and shaped quite well when third of 16 to Parthian Springs: subsequently gelded: will stay 1½m: looked capable of better: stays in training. *J. L. Dunlop* — 68 p

ORCHIDARMA 3 b.g. Reprimand 122 – My Fair Orchid 71 (Roan Rocket 128) [1994 64: 7g^5 7g^4 7.9d^3 7m^2 7s 1995 9m 10m^6 14g 10g^4 10m^5 8m^4 10m 10g Sep 23] leggy gelding: modest maiden: trained until after fifth 3-y-o start by R. Williams, next (sold 6,600 gns Newmarket July Sales afterwards) by R. Guest: no worthwhile — 61 d form in handicaps for new stable: stays 1¼m (far from certain to stay 1¾m): acts on good to firm ground, well beaten only outing on soft: effective blinkered/visored or not. *J. J. Quinn*

ORDAINED 2 b.f. (Apr 8) Mtoto 134 – In The Habit (USA) 88 (Lyphard (USA) 132) [1995 a7g Dec 9] third foal: dam 1¼m winner: sold out of M. Kauntze's stable 1,100 gns Newmarket Autumn Sales 1995: 40/1, slow-starting last of 7 in minor event at Wolverhampton. *T. T. Clement* –

ORIEL LAD 2 b.c. (Mar 6) Colmore Row 111 – Consistent Queen 55 (Queen's Hussar 124) [1995 5g 5m^4 5.2g^4 5.7f^2 5.9f* 5m^4 6m^2 6m^3 7m 7m^4 6m 6g^2 8g 7d* 7d^5 6m Oct 4] 4,100F, 7,600Y: sparely-made colt: half-brother to several winning platers, including (over 11.8f) Lifetimes Ambition (by Hotfoot): dam 1m seller winner: fair performer: won 3-runner maiden auction at Carlisle in July and 6-runner nursery at Chester in September: stays 7f: acts on firm and dead ground: trained by K. Burke first 3 outings: best in visor or blinkers: sometimes starts slowly: goes well for K. Fallon. *P. D. Evans* 75

ORIENTAL AIR (IRE) 4 b.f. Taufan (USA) 119 – More Candy 98 (Ballad Rock 122) [1994 55: 6g^3 6m 8.1f 6g^2 a6g 6m^3 5g* 6d^6 6g 5s^3 6.1s 1995 6m 5f^4 5m^5 5g^4 6m Jul 21] leggy filly: poor mover: modest handicapper: seemed to break down final start: should have stayed 7f: acted on fibresand and probably on any turf going: visored 4 times, running well twice: none too consistent: sold 21,000 gns, in foal to First Trump, Newmarket December Sales. *E. Weymes* 55

ORIENTAL SONG 6 ch.m. Battle Hymn 103 – Miss Kung Fu 70 (Caliban 123) [1994 –: 5.1m^6 6g 1995 a5g a5g^4 a7g Mar 1] workmanlike mare: no worthwhile form, including in blinkers. *K. S. Bridgwater* –

ORINOCO RIVER (USA) 2 ch.c. (May 15) El Gran Senor (USA) 136 – Miss Lilian 98 (Sandford Lad 133) [1995 8d 8m^6 Oct 12] lengthy colt: has scope: fifth foal: half-brother to 1992 Irish 2-y-o 6.5f winner One For Twenty Six (by Trempolino) and 2 minor winners in USA: dam Irish 7f winner at 3 yrs, won over 6f and 1m as 2-y-o: green, similar form in Newmarket maidens won by Helicon and Silver Dome, leading to around 3f out when one-paced sixth of 14 last time: looks the type to do better. *P. W. Chapple-Hyam* 75 p

ORIOLE 2 b.c. (May 2) Mazilier (USA) 107 – Odilese 82 (Mummy's Pet 125) [1995 5d 5m 5g^6 5g^2 6g^4 7m 5.9f^2 5g 6m* 6f^4 7.9g^6 7d 6f a7g Nov 16] 5,400Y: leggy, unfurnished colt: half-brother to 3-y-o Chase The Melody (by Sizzling Melody) and 5f winner Tutu Sixtysix (by Petong): dam 6f winner: modest performer: won nursery at Thirsk in July: well beaten all starts afterwards: best form at 6f: best form on a sound surface. *N. Tinkler* 56

ORSAY 3 b.c. Royal Academy (USA) 130 – Bellifontaine (FR) (Bellypha 130) [1994 59p: 8m 1995 8d* Apr 6] good-topped colt: won 10-runner maiden at Leicester on only 3-y-o outing by neck from Banadam, always prominent and staying on gamely: will be suited by further than 1m: looked sure to improve again. *W. R. Muir* 76 p

ORTHORHOMBUS 6 b.g. Aragon 118 – Honeybeta 105 (Habitat 134) [1994 80d: a6g 5d^2 6s^5 6d^6 6m 6g^5 6m 7g 5m^5 7f 6f 5.1g^4 6g a5g a8g^4 a6g 1995 a8g^2 a8g^5 a8g^2 a8.5g^5 a8g^5 a7g^6 a7g^2 a6g 6.9d* a7g^2 7.1g^4 7g 6m^6 8.5m 7m 6.9g 8.1f a7g Aug 4] strong, workmanlike gelding: modest handicapper nowadays: won at Folkestone in March: long way below form last 3 starts: stays 1m: acts on firm ground, soft and fibresand: has run creditably visored but usually blinkered: usually comes from behind: not one to rely on. *D. J. S. Cosgrove* 67 d

ORTOLAN 2 gr.c. (Apr 23) Prince Sabo 123 – Kala Rosa 79 (Kalaglow 132) [1995 5g^2 5m* 5.2g^3 Jul 15] 7,200F, 11,500Y: leggy, unfurnished colt: third foal: half-brother to 1993 2-y-o 6.1f winner Daily Star (by Music Boy): dam lightly-raced maiden, placed over 6f at 2 yrs: ridden by 7-lb claimer, won minor event at Salisbury in May by 5 lengths from Passion For Life: looking very well, third of 17 to Blue Iris in Super Sprint at Newbury (pulled hard to post) over 2 months later: will be better at 6f than 5f: looked open to further improvement. *R. Hannon* 95 p

OSCAR ROSE 2 b.g. (Mar 30) Aragon 118 – Mossy Rose 78 (King of Spain 121) [1995 5m^5 7m^4 6m 7.3m Aug 12] angular gelding: first foal: dam stayed 7f: fourth of 7 to Opera in minor event at Lingfield: well beaten afterwards in maiden there and nursery at Newbury (visored): stays 7f. *Lord Huntingdon* 62 ?

Oliver Lehane's "Oscar Schindler"

OSCAR SCHINDLER (IRE) 3 ch.c. Royal Academy (USA) 130 – Saraday (Northfields (USA)) [1994 96P: 7s* 1995 8g^{2} 8m^{6} 12m^{4} 10f^{4} 14g^{3} Sep 16] big, rangy, Irish-trained colt: smart performer: best efforts at the Curragh, when about 1½ lengths fourth of 13 to Winged Love in Irish Derby and around 3 lengths third of 7 to Strategic Choice in Irish St Leger, on both occasions held up behind strong pace, switched wide in straight then staying on: stays 1¾m well: acts on good to firm and soft ground, probably on firm: stays in training. *K. Prendergast, Ireland* 119

OSCAR THE SECOND (IRE) 5 b.g. Cyrano de Bergerac 120 – El Cerrito (Tribal Chief 125) [1994 40: a8g a7g a5g a6g^{6} 7d 6g^{3} 6g 6m^{2} 6.1m 6f 6f 6g 5g a6g 1995 6g 6.1m 5.9f^{5} 5.9f^{4} 6f Jul 29] lengthy, rather plain gelding: poor maiden handicapper: sold 950 gns Doncaster August Sales: stays 6f: best efforts on a sound surface: visored (tailed off) once at 3 yrs: inconsistent. *C. W. Fairhurst* 36 ?

OSCILIGHTS GIFT 3 b.f. Chauve Souris 108 – Oscilight 112 (Swing Easy (USA) 126) [1994 NR 1995 8d 7g 8f Oct 24] light-framed filly: ninth foal: half-sister to 7f and 1m winner Norfolk Breeze (by Blakeney) and fairly useful chaser Light Veneer (by Touching Wood): dam sprinter: well beaten in maidens and claimer. *P. Burgoyne* –

OSTIA 2 b.f. (Jan 17) Slip Anchor 136 – Sarsina 72 (Forli (ARG)) [1995 6g Sep 2] unfurnished filly: third foal: half-sister to 1994 2-y-o 6f winner Camicia (by Night Shift): dam lightly-raced half-sister to Carmelite House out of half-sister to dam of Kris and Diesis: 10/1 and bandaged off-hind, tailed off in maiden at Kempton, prominent until hampered at halfway and eased right up. *Mrs J. Cecil* –

OTTAVIO FARNESE 3 ch.g. Scottish Reel 123 – Sense of Pride (Welsh Pageant 132) [1994 NR 1995 10m^{6} 8.5m^{2} 10g* 12m Oct 21] 8,400Y: leggy gelding: 77

fifth foal: half-brother to 2 winners, including one (at up to middle distances) in Italy by Jupiter Island: dam Irish middle-distance winner: fair form: justified favouritism in maiden at Brighton in October: ran as if something amiss only subsequent outing: stays 1¼m well. *A. Hide*

OTTERBOURNE (IRE) 3 b.c. Royal Academy (USA) 130 – Marwell 133 (Habitat 134) [1994 77: 6m^4 6g^2 7m^5 1995 7m^3 7.1m^5 Jul 7] sturdy, good-topped colt: good mover: fairly useful performer: good third of 11 in handicap at Newmarket on reappearance: well below form in rated stakes at Haydock nearly 3 months later: stays 7f: has raced only on a sound surface: to join J. Noseda in USA. *J. H. M. Gosden* 82

OUBECK PRINCESS 3 b.f. Puissance 110 – Kalvee Dancer (Kalaglow 132) [1994 47: 5m^6 5f 5f 5s 5g 1995 5f 5.9f 6f 5.9h^4 Aug 21] leggy filly: poor maiden at 2 yrs: well beaten in 1995: sold 500 gns Doncaster September Sales. *E. Weymes* –

OUR ALBERT (IRE) 2 b.c. (May 14) Durgam (USA) – Power Girl 77 (Tyrant (USA)) [1995 6m 6.1m^5 7.5d Sep 13] 5,200Y, 15,000 2-y-o: stocky colt: has scope: half-brother to several winners here and abroad, including 2-y-o 5f winners Noble Power (by The Noble Player) and Powerful (by Tumble Wind): dam 5f and 6f winner: signs of a little ability in maiden events: seemed not to stay 7.5f. *J. A. Glover* –

OUR BAIRN 3 b.f. Bairn (USA) 126 – Bewitched 63 (African Sky 124) [1994 53: 6g 6m 6g 7s 9d* 1995 a9.4g 10.8g 12m Jul 25] small, sparely-made filly: only form when narrowly winning claimer at Newcastle in October 1994: left W. Bentley's stable after reappearance: has joined W. Barker. *R. Thompson* –

OUR BESSIE 4 b.f. Persian Bold 123 – Jamarj 113 (Tyrnavos 129) [1994 52: a7g^5 8d^6 6.9v^6 8.3d^3 7m 8.3f^6 9.7g^5 10m a8.5g^5 9.7d^2 11.5g^3 1995 a9.4g a12g a12g^5 12g^4 12.3f^3 12m^2 12.1m^2 12g a14.8g^3 Aug 11] lengthy filly: poor maiden handicapper: often contests ladies/amateur events: stays 14.8f: acts on fibresand and any turf going: visored (below form) fifth 3-y-o start. *D. Marks* 48 a33

OUR DOROTHY 3 b.f. Aragon 118 – Helewise 76 (Dance In Time (CAN)) [1994 NR 1995 a7g a8.5g Feb 4] 7,000Y: fourth foal: half-sister to 1992 5f winner George Roper (by Hotfoot): dam 2-y-o 1m winner: tailed off in maiden events: sold 800 gns Ascot May Sales. *C. N. Williams* –

OUR EDDIE 6 ch.g. Gabitat 119 – Ragusa Girl (Morston (FR) 125) [1994 51, a71: a10g^5 a12g^5 a12g^5 12m^3 a10g* a10g* a12g^2 a10g* 9f 11.5d a10g* a10g^4 1995 a10g^3 a10g a12g^4 a10g^6 Mar 25] leggy, sparely-made gelding: shows knee action: modest performer at best in 1995: probably stays 1½m: acts on equitrack: usually visored, tried blinkered at 3 yrs: none too consistent. *B. Gubby* – a63

OUR KRIS 3 b.c. Kris 135 – Our Reverie (USA) (J O Tobin (USA) 130) [1994 NR 1995 8m^5 11.4m 10m^6 14g 17.1m 14m* Oct 13] strong, workmanlike colt: has pronounced knee action: fourth foal: brother to very useful 1¼m and 1½m winner Peter Quince: dam, stakes winner at up to 11f, half-sister to Sharrood: fair performer: showed improvement to win handicap at Newmarket in October: should stay 2m: has raced only on a sound surface: none too consistent: sold (G. Harwood to N. Henderson) 20,000 gns Newmarket Autumn Sales: promising juvenile hurdler. *G. Harwood* 73

OUR LITTLE LADY 3 b.f. Queen's Soldier (USA) – Charlotte's Pearl (Monsanto (FR) 121) [1994 NR 1995 8.3m^6 10.1m^6 11.5m^4 a8.5g Oct 14] lengthy filly: first reported foal: dam never ran: signs of only a little ability: has joined J. Poulton. *J. E. Banks* –

OUR MAIN MAN 5 ch.g. Superlative 118 – Ophrys 90 (Nonoalco (USA) 131) [1994 NR 1995 12m 8g^5 13.1g^4 12m 11.1f* 10f^3 12.3m^5 11.9m 12.1g 8.9g 10f* a11g^3 a12g^4 a11g^6 Dec 1] £ood-topped gelding: fourth foal: half-brother to 7f winner Affordable (by Formidable): dam 2-y-o 7f winner from good family: won NH Flat race in 1993/4: modest form on flat, winning minor event at Edinburgh in July and handicap (50/1 after 4 below-form efforts) at Pontefract in October: stays 13f: acts on fibresand, goes well on firm going: visored (well beaten) eighth start: has been bandaged near-hind. *R. M. Whitaker* 61 a53

OUR MICA 5 gr.g. Belfort (FR) 89 – Aristata (Habitat 134) [1994 35: a7g a5g^6 5d a5g^5 a5g 5m a6g 1995 a6g a5g a5g 5.1g Jun 8] leggy gelding: poor sprinter: well beaten in 1995: carries head high and not an easy ride. *L. J. Barratt* –

OUR RAINBOW 3 b.f. Primitive Rising (USA) 113 – Cass Avon (Celtic Cone 116) [1994 –: 5m 5.9m 7.5m 7.5f 1995 9.9m^6 11.1f^3 12m^4 12m^5 10m Aug 12] poor maiden plater: will be suited by further than 1½m: has been bandaged. *Mrs S. M. Austin* — 36

OUR RITA 6 b.m. Hallgate 127 – Ma Pierrette 77 (Cawston's Clown 113) [1994 95: 8m* 7d 7d^2 7.6v* 8m 8d^3 7v^6 1995 8g^5 8.1m 9g 8d 9g 8m Oct 28] leggy, lengthy mare: bad mover: fairly useful performer: well below form in 1995 after reappearance: stays 1m: probably acts on any going: best held up. *Dr J. D. Scargill* — 95 d

OUR ROBERT 3 b.g. Faustus (USA) 118 – Duck Soup 55 (Decoy Boy 129) [1994 61: a6g^6 a6g a7g 8f^4 8s^2 7.9d^6 8s 1995 7g^4 8.3g^3 7.9g^3 8g 8.1g 8g Oct 9] sturdy, heavy-topped gelding: has a markedly round action: modest maiden: well below form last 3 starts: stays 8.3f: acts on any turf going (well beaten on fibresand). *J. G. FitzGerald* — 59

OUR SHADEE (USA) 5 b.g. Shadeed (USA) 135 – Nuppence 79 (Reform 132) [1994 55: 6g^6 6m a8g 8.3g 8f^4 7g* 7m^3 7g 6g^3 7g^2 7m^6 6g^2 7m 6g 7g 6m 7g a7g^4 a6g^4 a7g^3 a7g^4 a7g^5 1995 a7g^2 a6g* a6g^2 a6g* a6g^2 a6g 6m 6m^3 7g^5 6m^5 6f 6f^3 a7g 7g 6g^2 a7g^4 7f^6 a7g^4 a6g^6 a7g^3 a6g^5 Dec 18] lengthy gelding: modest handicapper: won twice at Lingfield in February, first race a minor event: best at 6f/7f: acts on firm and soft ground and goes well on equitrack: often blinkered in 1993, visored nowadays: often ridden by apprentice C. Scally: takes keen hold, and usually held up: tough. *K. T. Ivory* — 50 a61

OUR TOM 3 br.g. Petong 126 – Boa (Mandrake Major 122) [1994 52: a7g 6.1m a7g^5 6g 8s 8d a7g 1995 a7g* a7g^2 a6g a8.5g^2 a8.5g* a7g 10d^2 10g 8g 9m a9.4g a9.4g^4 Dec 9] good-topped gelding: fair handicapper: won at Wolverhampton in January and March: stays 1¼m: acts on dead ground and goes well on fibresand. *J. Wharton* — 57 a66

OUR TOM'S BOY 2 b.c. (May 7) Colmore Row 111 – Princess Silca Key 61 (Grundy 137) [1995 5g a5g^4 a6g 7d^3 7f^6 6.1m^4 6m^3 a6g^6 5.7h^5 Aug 8] 2,600Y: sparely-made colt: fourth foal: half-brother to fairly useful sprinter Silca-Cisa (by Hallgate): dam lightly-raced 7f winner: plater: stays 7f: blinkered 5 of last 6 starts: wears bandages: sold 1,800 gns Newmarket September Sales. *K. T. Ivory* — 47

OUR WORLEY (IRE) 2 b.f. (Apr 23) Mac's Imp (USA) 116 – Castleforbes (Thatching 131) [1995 5f^4 May 8] 5,000Y: quite good-topped filly, rather unfurnished: half-sister to 3-y-o Lorsanginner (by Contract Law), 1992 2-y-o sprint winner Hello Hobson's (by Fayruz), later one to avoid, and a winner (champion) in Czechoslovakia: dam a twin: 8/1, over 5 lengths fourth of 6 in maiden at Warwick: looked capable of better. *A. P. Jarvis* — 51

OUT OF THE BLUE 3 b.f. Lochnager 132 – Expletive 77 (Shiny Tenth 120) [1994 NR 1995 8.2d Sep 19] leggy, plain filly: first foal: dam 5f (at 2 yrs) to 1¼m winner: well beaten (took keen hold) in maiden at Nottingham. *M. W. Eckley* — –

OUT OF THE MIST 4 b.g. Damister (USA) 123 – Almitra (Targowice (USA) 130) [1994 –: 6m^6 7f 8f 7m 7m 7g 10d 1995 7m 8g 6g^5 6.1m a7g^5 Jul 3] tall, workmanlike gelding: no worthwhile form: tried blinkered/visored. *J. A. Pickering* — –

OUT ON A PROMISE (IRE) 3 b.c. Night Shift (USA) – Lovers' Parlour 83 (Beldale Flutter (USA) 130) [1994 79: 7g^3 7s^2 a7g* 1995 8d 8.1m^6 7.9g^6 8m^3 8g^3 7.1m 10m^2 10m^2 10.3m* 10m 10d^3 Oct 19] compact, quite attractive colt: fairly useful performer: won minor event at Doncaster in September, hanging left when challenging over 1f out but keeping on well: may well stay beyond 1¼m: acts on good to firm and soft ground: blinkered (respectable effort but pulled too hard) sixth 3-y-o start, sweating (ran well) eighth one: takes keen hold: sold (G. Wragg to N. Walker) 46,000 gns Newmarket Autumn Sales. *G. Wragg* — 86

OUTSET (IRE) 5 ch.g. Persian Bold 123 – It's Now Or Never 78 (High Line 125) [1994 –: 8m^5 12f 1995 14.6m^4 Nov 3] leggy gelding: fairly useful hurdler in 1993/4: first race of any sort for 14 months, showed modest form when fourth of 7 in minor event at Doncaster: stays 14.6f: takes keen hold. *M. D. Hammond* — 57

OUTSTAYED WELCOME 3 b.g. Be My Guest (USA) 126 – Between Time 75 (Elegant Air 119) [1994 51: 5v^2 5d^4 5f^5 7m^3 6m 1995 7g 8.2g 8m 10g 12.3f* 11.9m^2 12.1m^3 12.3f^3 14.1m* 14.1m^4 12d a12g^5 a13g^2 a13g^4 Dec 19] leggy gelding: modest handicapper: stepped up in trip and won ladies events at Ripon (made most) — 56 in June and Yarmouth (flashed tail) in August: will stay beyond 1¾m: acts on any going: blinkered last 2 starts in 1994: usually bandaged behind: usually races prominently. *M. J. Haynes*

OVERBROOK 3 b.f. Storm Cat (USA) – Spurned (USA) 91 (Robellino (USA) 127) [1994 92: 5.2m^{3} 5d^{6} 5.7g* 5m^{2} 6s^{5} 1995 6m^{4} 6m* 6g^{3} 6g^{4} 5g^{3} 5f^{4} Aug 9] lengthy, useful-looking filly: useful performer: won minor event at Kempton in May, and made the frame all 4 subsequent starts: stays 6f: acts on firm ground, below form on a soft surface: sold 52,000 gns Newmarket December Sales. *I. A. Balding* — 95

OVERBURY (IRE) 4 br.c. Caerleon (USA) 132 – Overcall (Bustino 136) [1994 111: 10s 12f^{2} 10.4f^{2} 12m^{2} 12g^{2} 9.5f* 1995 9m^{2} Apr 19] strong, close-coupled colt: smart performer: ran a fine first race of season when head second of 7 to Desert Shot in strongly-run Earl of Sefton Stakes at Newmarket, rallying bravely, pair 5 lengths clear: reportedly had operation to remove a bladder stone afterwards, and not seen out again: effective at 9f and stays 1½m: acts on firm ground, possibly unsuited by soft: genuine and consistent: sent to Dubai, but likely to return to Europe. *D. R. Loder* — 114

OVERPOWER 11 b.g. Try My Best (USA) 130 – Just A Shadow (Laser Light 118) [1994 58: 8.2f 8g* 10.1f^{6} 10m^{2} 8m^{6} 9.2g^{4} 9g^{3} 10f^{3} 10.1d^{3} 10d 8.2g 1995 10m 8g* 10m^{2} Jun 6] workmanlike gelding: carries condition: veteran handicapper, modest nowadays: won celebrity race at Newmarket in May for second year running: effective at 1m and 1¼m: best form on a sound surface (acts on firm going): blinkered and visored (below form) earlier in career: has found little in front, and suited by good gallop and waiting tactics. *M. H. Tompkins* — 54

OVERRULED (IRE) 2 b.f. (Feb 15) Last Tycoon 131 – Overcall (Bustino 136) [1995 7m 8m* Oct 20] sturdy, lengthy filly: good walker: has plenty of scope: fifth foal: half-sister to 3-y-o Sadly Sober (by Roi Danzig) and 2 winners, including smart Overbury (by Caerleon), winner from 7f (at 2 yrs) to 9.5f and effective at 1½m: dam Irish middle-distance stayer: impressive winner of 11-runner maiden at Doncaster in October, quickening several lengths clear of runner-up Naseem Alsahar and still on bridle before being eased considerably: will probably stay at least 1¼m: sure to improve further, and win more races. *D. R. Loder* — 91 p

OVERSMAN 2 b.c. (Mar 5) Keen 116 – Jamaican Punch (IRE) (Shareef Dancer (USA) 135) [1995 6m a7g^{3} 7f 7.9m a7g Nov 24] 28,000F: robust colt: has scope: first foal: dam ran twice: easily best effort when third of 9 in maiden at Southwell in July: badly hampered final start: stays 7f: acts on fibresand. *J. G. FitzGerald* — – / a71

OWDBETTS (IRE) 3 b.f. High Estate 127 – Nora Yo Ya (Ahonoora 122) [1994 69: 5.1m^{5} 7m^{5} a7g^{2} 6.9m* 7m^{5} 7.3v 1995 a8.5g^{6} 8.3m^{4} 9.7m^{5} 8.1m 7g* 7.6d 10f* 10.1m^{6} 7g 9.7s a9.4g^{5} a10g^{3} Dec 15] workmanlike filly: has a round action: modest performer: clear-cut winner in August of amateurs handicap at Leicester and claimer at Brighton: best form at around 7f, but stays 1¼m: acts on firm ground and fibresand, possibly not on a soft surface: has carried head awkwardly: takes keen hold: none too consistent. *G. L. Moore* — 60

OWINGTON 4 b.c. Green Desert (USA) 127 – Old Domesday Book 93 (High Top 131) [1994 123: 7s^{5} 6f* 6f* 6m* 6.5g^{5} 6g^{3} 1995 5m^{3} 5m^{3} 6g^{4} 6d^{3} a6s Oct 28] — 119

In 1994, Owington had been Europe's top sprinting three-year-old and won the Duke of York Stakes, the Cork And Orrery and the July Cup. In 1995, he rewarded win bets on him in just one race, the Breeders' Cup Sprint, but did that only because the race went to fellow outsider Desert Stormer who was coupled with him on the Pari-Mutuel in America. Owington himself came in about five lengths back in seventh. He was not at all discredited and finished ahead of the two other European challengers Hever Golf Rose (eighth) and Lake Coniston (twelfth), though he had produced nothing to match that pair's best during his season in Europe. Owington and Hever Golf Rose never actually met in European competition. Owington and Lake Coniston did so three times, first when Lake Coniston was still a hidden talent and came thirteenth in Owington's Cork And Orrery, most recently on both colts' final start in Europe, the Haydock Park Sprint Cup. In the 1994 running of that race, Owington had been a disappointing favourite, a contributory factor apparently being the deteriorating ground conditions. Rain had its say once more in the immediate run-up to the 1995 race, but Owington was allowed to take his chance, and again he came in third, this time putting up a much better display in being beaten two and a quarter lengths behind Cherokee Rose. It was not up to his best form at three years but it was as good as anything seen from him at four. Again he beat Lake Coniston. Lake Coniston's best, however, had left Owington six and three-quarter lengths behind when Owington came fourth of nine in his bid to win a second successive July Cup at Newmarket over seven weeks earlier. Owington had missed his intended start in between, the now-upgraded Prix Maurice de Gheest, because of slight lameness. The July Cup had been his first outing over six furlongs as a four-year-old. Both previous starts had been over five furlongs in May, in the Palace House Stakes at Newmarket and Temple Stakes at Sandown. Owington had never previously been tried over the minimum trip but had coped so well with any pace over further that he looked well worth a try. In the Palace House he emerged the best horse at the weights when one and a half lengths third to Mind Games, held up as ever, not getting the best of runs then making up his ground well until finding no extra in the last hundred yards. This was on a par with his form later on at Haydock. On his renewal with Mind Games in the Temple Stakes, however, Owington never got a look in.

Owington (b.c. 1991)	Green Desert (USA) (b 1983)	Danzig (b 1977)	Northern Dancer
			Pas de Nom
		Foreign Courier (b 1979)	Sir Ivor
			Courtly Dee
	Old Domesday Book (b 1983)	High Top (b 1969)	Derring-Do
			Camenae
		Broken Record (b 1973)	Busted
			Sam's Song

The leggy, attractive Owington has been retired to the New England Stud, Newmarket, where he will be available for £7,500 on October 1st terms. He has been partly syndicated and Lord Derby reportedly purchased a major share in him in a deal which valued Owington of £1.4 million. He will apparently have a book of sixty-five mares in his first season. Lord Derby's interest was understandable because Stanley Estate bred him; the dam Old Domesday Book (a fairly useful middle-distance winner) is from its most famous family of recent years as her grandam was a half-sister to Ouija, the ancestress of Teleprompter, Chatoyant, Ibn Bey and Roseate Tern. Old Domesday Book's fourth foal Great Inquest (by Shernazar) won a 7.3-furlong maiden at Newbury in May. Her fifth, Pink Cashmere (by Polar Falcon), was in training with David Loder but went to the December Sales unraced, making 21,000 guineas. *G. Wragg*

OXGANG (IRE) 2 b.c. (Feb 1) Taufan (USA) 119 – Casla (Lomond (USA) 128) [1995 7.5m a8g^{3} Nov 6] 15,000F: good-bodied colt: second foal: half-brother to 3-y-o 1m winner Strumming (by Ballad Rock): dam, Irish 1m winner, closely related to dam of Sueboog: much better effort in maidens (coltish on debut 3 months earlier) when staying-on third of 12 to Ground Game at Southwell. *J. G. FitzGerald* — 61

OZUBECK (USA) 3 b.f. Deputy Minister (CAN) – Whitethroat (Artaius (USA) 129) [1994 NR 1995 8.1m 10.5g 10.2d^{4} 8.2m 12.1s Nov 2] IR 28,000Y: tall filly: has a round action: fifth foal: half-sister to a winner in Trinidad: dam lightly-raced half-sister to Assert, Bikala and Eurobird: no worthwhile form. *B. Hanbury* — –

OZZIE JONES 4 b.g. Formidable (USA) 125 – Distant Relation (Great Nephew 126) [1994 50: 10d 12s^{4} 8m 12g 12m^{5} 12m* 11.8m^{3} 12m^{2} 12g 9.9f 18g^{4dis} 11.5m 18.2s^{6} 1995 a11g^{3} a12g^{4} a12g^{2} a12g^{5} a16g 12m May 12] good-topped gelding: poor handicapper: well below form last 3 starts: should stay beyond 1½m: acts on fibresand and good to firm ground, probably on soft: blinkered (well beaten) fifth 4-y-o start. *M. C. Chapman* — – a45

P

PAB'S CHOICE 4 ch.f. Telsmoss 91 – Dido 70 (Full of Hope 125) [1994 61: 7d* 6g^{3} 7m^{5} a6g* 6.1s 1995 a6g 6.1m 7.6m^{2} 7m 8.5m^{6} a7g a7g Nov 29] sparely-made filly: modest handicapper: stays 8.5f: acts on equitrack, dead ground (poorly drawn on soft) and good to firm: visored (ran creditably) final 4-y-o start: sweating (below form) on 4-y-o reappearance: inconsistent at 4 yrs. *M. McCormack* — 59

PACIFIC GIRL (IRE) 3 b.f. Emmson 125 – Power Girl 77 (Tyrant (USA)) [1994 61: 6m 5d^5 5.1m^5 5m^3 5m 5m 7m^3 6g 5.1g^5 5g 6.1d 1995 7.1m 6m a7g 5.7h^3 5m 5.1h^5 10.8f^4 10d 8m a7g^6 a8g a7g^6 Nov 29] sparely-made filly: disappointing maiden: should stay beyond 7f: acts on hard and dead ground: below form in blinkers: inconsistent. *B. Palling*
51 d

PACIFIC GROVE 2 b.f. (Feb 24) Persian Bold 123 – Dazzling Heights 99 (Shirley Heights 130) [1995 6m^6 5g^3 6m^4 7m^2 7.3m* 7f^4 8h* 7d* 7.3d^2 8g Nov 10] 19,000Y: sparely-made filly: second foal: half-sister to 3-y-o 10.2f and 11.4f winner Kimbridge Knight (by Night Shift): dam 7f (at 2 yrs) to 11f (in France) winner: won nurseries at Newbury, Bath and Newmarket, strong run closing stages to get up on line last 2 occasions: ran in listed races last 2 outings, very good second to Sil Sila at Newbury then last of 8 at Evry: will stay beyond 1m: acts on hard and dead ground: has run well for 7-lb claimer: genuine. *P. F. I. Cole*
89

PACIFIC OVERTURE 3 br.f. Southern Music 104 – Morning Miss 59 (Golden Dipper 119) [1994 NR 1995 7m 6m 8.1g^6 7m 8f 10.2m 8.1d Oct 10] small, sparely-made filly: half-sister to 5f and 1m seller winner Cobblers Hill (by Another Realm) and fair 1989 2-y-o 5.8f and 1m winner Conjurer (by Magic Mirror): dam lightly-raced 8.3f winner: no promise, tried blinkered and in selling company. *C. R. Barwell*
–

PACIFIC SPIRIT 5 b.m. Governor General 116 – Mossberry Fair 28 (Mossberry 97) [1994 –: a7g 8s 7d 1995 a6g^5 a6g^3 a8.5g 8g a7g^2 a9.4g a7g Sep 16] poor maiden handicapper: stays 1m: acts on fibresand, no form on turf: inconsistent. *M. Tate*
– a47

PADDYS CHERUB 3 b.f. Then Again 126 – Lady Stock 63 (Crofter (USA) 124) [1994 NR 1995 8.1g 7m 6.9g Oct 16] good-bodied filly: first foal: dam 7f winner who stayed 1¼m: no form in maidens and seller. *J. R. Arnold*
–

PADDY'S RETURN (IRE) 3 b.g. Kahyasi 130 – Bayazida (Bustino 136) [1994 7v 1995 10.2f^2 12m^3 Jun 14] ex-Irish gelding: sixth foal: half-brother to 5 winners, including useful stayer Irish Stamp (by Niniski): dam, placed in France, from family of Vaguely Noble: trained by K. Prendergast only 2-y-o start: fair form (well backed both times) placed in maidens at Bath and (off bridle some way out, wandering under pressure but staying on) Kempton: will stay further than 1½m: won twice over hurdles in the autumn, looking a likeable type. *F. Murphy*
72

PADDY'S RICE 4 ch.g. Hadeer 118 – Requiem (Song 132) [1994 52: 6v^6 5.7m 7m 6m* 6m^6 6f^5 6f 6m 6g 1995 6m^3 6g 6f* 6g^5 6f^2 6m^3 7m 7.6m^2 7m^6 7d Sep 14] sparely-made gelding: modest handicapper: won at Lingfield in May: stays 7.6f: acts on firm ground, raced on seemingly disadvantaged side only try at 4 yrs on a soft surface: usually held up. *L. J. Holt*
61

PADDY'S STORM 3 b.g. Celestial Storm (USA) 132 – Hot Tan (Hotfoot 126) [1994 NR 1995 10m 10g 11.9f^4 May 26] 950F, 4,800Y: second foal: dam little sign of ability: tailed-off last in maiden events. *R. M. Flower*
–

PADRE MIO (IRE) 7 b.g. The Parson 119 – Mwanamio (Sole Mio (USA)) [1994 NR 1995 8g Jul 22] good-topped gelding: second foal: dam Irish 1¼m winner also successful over hurdles: useful hurdler in 1993/4 for A. Mullins and went novice chasing here in 1994/5: 100/1, just over 15 lengths seventh of 14 in ladies race at Ascot on flat debut: will prove suited by further than 1m: changed hands 20,000 gns Ascot July Sales: won 'Fighting Fifth' Hurdle in November. *C. P. E. Brooks*
–

PAGEBOY 6 b.g. Tina's Pet 121 – Edwins' Princess 75 (Owen Dudley 121) [1994 80: a6g^2 a6g^3 a5g a6g^2 6f* 6f* 6f* 6d 6m 6f 5m^2 5g 6f 6m 1995 a6g* a6g^2 a6g^5 a5g a6g^6 a6g 5m 6m 5f 5g^3 6m^4 6m^3 6m^4 6f a6g 5g 6g^4 Sep 25] small, sturdy gelding: unimpressive mover: fair handicapper: comfortable winner at Lingfield in January: best form at up to 6f: acts on all-weather surfaces and firm ground: sometimes blinkered/visored, no improvement: usually a front runner: none too consistent. *P. C. Haslam*
67 a70

PAINTED DESERT 3 b.f. Green Desert (USA) 127 – Illusory 81 (Kings Lake (USA) 133) [1994 88: 5g^5 5.7f* 6f^2 1995 6g^5 5g^6 5f^5 5m^3 5m 5.6m Sep 6] good-bodied filly: fairly useful performer: best effort when third of 9 in rated stakes at Sandown: stays 6f: has raced only on a sound surface: usually races prominently. *R. Charlton*
89

Craven Stakes, Newmarket—
classic hopefuls Painter's Row (centre), Montjoy (far side) and Nwaamis

PAINTED HALL (USA) 3 br.g. Imperial Falcon (CAN) – Moon O'Gold (USA) (Slew O' Gold (USA)) [1994 NR 1995 10m 10m* 10g^{6} 11.9m^{4} Aug 4] $6,500F, IR 66,000Y: robust gelding: second foal: dam lightly raced: fair performer: won median auction maiden at Windsor in June: respectable efforts in handicaps afterwards: should stay 1½m. *J. A. R. Toller* — 73

PAINTER'S ROW (IRE) 3 b.c. Royal Academy (USA) 130 – Road To The Top 84 (Shirley Heights 130) [1994 112p: 7m* 7.3d* 1995 8m* 8m 10m 12f Jul 25] leggy, good sort: good mover: smart performer: won Craven Stakes (burly, led 2f out and battled on to beat Montjoy a neck) at Newmarket in April: ran right up to form when around 5 lengths eighth of 10 to Valanour in Grand Prix de Paris at Longchamp in June: dismounted in final 1f in Gordon Stakes at Goodwood, seemingly lame: stays 1¼m: acts on good to firm and dead ground: genuine. *P. W. Chapple-Hyam* — 112

PAINT IT BLACK 2 ch.c. (Mar 6) Double Schwartz 128 – Tableaux (FR) (Welsh Pageant 132) [1995 7f 7f^{3} 7m* 6d^{6} Sep 27] 5,600F, 34,000Y: tall colt: brother to a poor maiden and half-brother to 2 winners abroad, including French 8.7f winner Living Image (by Kenmare): dam French maiden: won median auction maiden at Epsom penultimate start comfortably by head from Laughing Buccaneer: creditable sixth of 10 in minor event at Salisbury 19 days later: will be ideally suited by return to further than 6f. *R. Hannon* — 75+

PAIR OF JACKS (IRE) 5 ch.g. Music Boy 124 – Lobbino 72 (Bustino 136) [1994 46d: a8g a7g a9.4g a7g^{6} 5m^{6} 6m 7.1m 7m 6d 6g 6m 10v^{6} 8g 1995 a8g a8g a10g^{6} a7g^{5} a8g a8g a8g^{2} a8g^{2} a8g^{4} a8g^{3} 6m^{6} 7m 7f 7g a7g Nov 8] strong, lengthy gelding: poor handicapper: stays 1m: best efforts on a sound surface or equitrack: tried blinkered and visored, no improvement: modest hurdler. *D. A. Wilson* — 37

PAKOL (IRE) 6 b.m. Martin John – Tamen John (African Sky 124) [1994 61d: 5g^{2} 6g^{2} 7g 6d a6g^{6} a6g^{5} 1995 6m^{3} 6f^{6} 8m 6g Aug 26] ex-Irish: seems a poor maiden plater here: stays 6.5f: best form on a sound surface (acts on hard going): inconsistent. *Mrs A. Swinbank* — 45

PALACEGATE CHIEF 2 b.g. (Apr 28) Inca Chief (USA) – Sports Post Lady (IRE) 72 (M Double M (USA)) [1995 5f^{5} Jul 31] 8,000F, IR 15,000Y: first foal: dam best at 5f: 3/1, well behind throughout when last of 5 in maiden auction at Carlisle. *J. Berry* — –

PALACEGATE EPISODE (IRE) 5 b.m. Drumalis 125 – Pasadena Lady (Captain James 123) [1994 111: 5g^5 5g^3 5m* 5.1g^3 5d^4 5d* 5d^2 5d* 1995 5g^5 5g^4 5m^3 5f^6 5m^6 5g* 5s^6 5d^2 Oct 15] leggy, lengthy mare: fluent mover: almost as good as ever in 1995, but not nearly so consistent: comfortable winner of listed Iduna/Nova-Flieger Preis at Cologne in September for third year running: ½-length second of 9 to Leap For Joy in Group 3 race at Milan final start: races at around 5f: acts on any ground: front runner: genuine. *J. Berry* — 107

PALACEGATE GOLD (IRE) 6 b.g. Sarab 123 – Habilite 94 (Habitat 134) [1994 54: 6d^3 5v* 6m^4 6m^5 7s^4 6.1s^3 6m 6m^3 6m^5 6m 5.7g^5 7v a6g a8g 1995 a7g a10g Dec 18] sturdy gelding: has a quick action: modest handicapper in 1994: well below form on belated return: stays 7f: probably acts on any going, including equitrack: occasionally wears blinkers (not since 1993), seems best without: usually held up. *R. J. Hodges* — –

PALACEGATE JACK (IRE) 4 gr.g. Neshad (USA) 108 – Pasadena Lady (Captain James 123) [1994 104: 5s^3 6g^3 5f 6m 5m^5 5m^3 5m 5m 5g 5s* 6s^6 1995 6g 5g 5g* 5f^2 5s^5 5m Oct 14] lengthy, workmanlike gelding: just a fairly useful performer at 4 yrs: won claimer at Catterick in June: ran as though something amiss final start: very best efforts over 5f: acts on any going: effective blinkered or not, visored (well beaten) 4-y-o reappearance: often hangs left: races prominently. *J. Berry* — 94 d

PALACEGATE JO (IRE) 4 b.f. Drumalis 125 – Welsh Rhyme (Welsh Term 126) [1994 65: a6g^6 a6g^2 a6g^4 a6g* a6s^4 a6g* a6g^3 a6g^6 a6g^2 a7g 8.3d^4 a9.4g* a8.5g* a9.4g a12g^2 a9.4g a9.4g a9.4g a8.5g^5 a9.4g^4 1995 a9.4g a11g^4 a11g^2 a11g* a12g* a11g^5 a12g^2 a11g^4 a11g^3 a14g^6 a12g^4 a12g* a12g a11g a12g a12g^3 a12g* a12g a12g^5 a9.4g^5 a9.4g a12g a7g Dec 2] leggy filly: fair handicapper who races almost exclusively on all-weather: won 2 handicaps and claimer (claimed out of R. Hollinshead's stable £8,000) by the end of May, and another handicap in July, all at Wolverhampton: well below form afterwards: stays 1½m: acts on all-weather surfaces, won on heavy at 2 yrs: effective from front or held up: inconsistent. *D. W. Chapman* — 67 d

PALACEGATE TOUCH 5 gr.g. Petong 126 – Dancing Chimes (London Bells (CAN) 109) [1994 89: 6d* 6m 6s^5 6d^3 6m 6.1m 6g 6m 6d 6d^4 6d 5d^2 1995 6d* 7m^5 6m 6m a6g^2 6.1m^4 6m 6f^5 6m^5 6g 5d^4 6f Oct 31] tall, good-topped gelding: fairly useful handicapper at best: won 23-runner contest at Ripon (for second consecutive year) on reappearance: reproduced that form only once (on all-weather), and well beaten last 3 starts: ideally suited by 6f: acts on fibresand, possibly unsuited by extremes of going on turf: visored or blinkered nowadays: usually makes running: tends to hang left and race with head high: goes well fresh: none too consistent. *J. Berry* — 94 d

PALACE GUARD 3 br.g. Daring March 116 – Royal Brush (King of Spain 121) [1994 NR 1995 10d 12v^5 Nov 19] tall gelding: first foal: dam showed signs of ability on only outing: tailed off in maiden at Newbury and minor event at Groenendaal, Belgium. *G. P. Enright* — –

PALACE RIVER (IRE) 7 b.m. Dragon Palace (USA) 96 – Rosebrook (Brother Birdbrook 74) [1994 NR 1995 7f 5.9h 11.9d Oct 11] plain mare: second reported foal: dam winning jumper: won Irish point in May 1994: 4,000 gns 6-y-o: soundly beaten here on flat: poor hurdler. *D. Moffatt* — –

PALAFAIRIA (FR) 3 br.f. Always Fair (USA) 121 – Palavera (FR) (Bikala 134) [1994 6m* 7d^4 6.5g 1995 8v^2 8d* 8g^3 8d^3 8g* Nov 10] first foal: dam, fairly useful French 1m winner, is sister to Prix du Jockey-Club winner Polytain: useful French filly: won minor event at Chantilly at 2 yrs: successful in 1995 in listed events at Evry in April and November: third in between in 4-runner Prix de Sandringham at Chantilly (2½ lengths behind Smolensk) in June and listed race at Maisons-Laffitte in September: stays 1m: acts on good to firm ground and heavy. *A. Fabre, France* — 106

PALAMON (USA) 2 ch.c. (Apr 5) Sanglamore (USA) 126 – Gantlette (Run The Gantlet (USA)) [1995 8d^6 Sep 26] 40,000Y: half-brother to several winners, including very useful middle-distance performer Run Don't Fly (by Lear Fan) and dam of Lancashire Oaks winner Pharian: dam French 2-y-o 1m winner: 12/1, 4½ lengths sixth of 20 to Helicon in maiden at Newmarket, racing keenly with leaders, — 76 p unable to quicken from 2f out: sure to do better, and should be able to win a race. *R. Charlton*

PALATIAL STYLE 8 b.g. Kampala 120 – Stylish Princess (Prince Tenderfoot (USA) 126) [1994 86+: 10f 1995 10m^5 10m 10.3d Sep 9] leggy, angular gelding: little worthwhile form in 1995: stays 1¼m: best form on a sound surface: bandaged at 8 yrs. *P. J. Makin* –

PALEY PRINCE (USA) 9 b.h. Tilt Up (USA) – Apalachee Princess (USA) (Apalachee (USA) 137) [1994 68d: 5.1m^6 5d 5g^5 5.1f* 5.1f^3 5m^6 5m 5.1m^6 5.1m^5 5m 5g^5 5m 5d^6 5d a5g a5g^4 1995 5.1m 5.1m 5g 5m^4 5f^6 5.7f^6 5.1h* 5g^3 5.1h^3 5.1h^6 5.1h^3 5m* 5m^5 Aug 30] strong-quartered, lengthy horse: still a fair handicapper: won apprentice races at Bath in July and Goodwood in August: stays 6f: acts on hard ground, dead and equitrack: effective in visor, not tried for some time: sometimes bandaged: inconsistent. *M. D. I. Usher* 67

PALLIUM (IRE) 7 b.g. Try My Best (USA) 130 – Jungle Gardenia (Nonoalco (USA) 131) [1994 69, a60: a5g^5 a5g^5 a5g a5g^3 a5g^5 5g 5g^4 5g 5v^6 5f^3 5m^5 5g^3 5.9m^5 5m^2 5m^2 5m^3 5f^2 5f^4 6g 5g 5d 5g 1995 5g 6g^5 7.5m 5m^2 5m* 5f 5m 5f* 5m^6 5m^4 5h^5 5g Sep 14] good-bodied gelding: unimpressive mover: modest handicapper: got up near finish in amateurs race at Edinburgh and seller at Ripon in July: best at 5f: acts on firm and dead ground and the all-weather: tried in visor/blinkers, no improvement: has hung: sometimes has tongue tied down: inconsistent. *Mrs A. M. Naughton* 63

PALO BLANCO 4 b.f. Precocious 126 – Linpac Mapleleaf 69 (Dominion 123) [1994 78: 5m* 5.1m^5 6m^5 5g^6 5g* 5g 6g^2 5m^3 1995 5m^4 6g^5 5d^6 6g^3 6d^3 Oct 11] rangy, workmanlike filly: fair handicapper: keeping-on third in competitive events at York and Haydock last 2 starts: stays 6f: acts on good to firm and dead going: usually edgy: consistent at 4 yrs. *T. D. Barron* 78

PALOMA BAY (IRE) 2 b.f. (Apr 6) Alzao (USA) 117 – Adventurine (Thatching 131) [1995 6m* 6m^2 6g Jul 11] 36,000Y: leggy, lengthy filly: has scope: good walker: has a quick action: fourth live foal: half-sister to 3-y-o Sandra Dee (by Be My Guest): dam, Irish sprinter, sister to very useful Irish sprinter Rustic Amber: won maiden at Newmarket in May: good 1¼ lengths second of 8 to World Premier in Chesham Stakes at Ascot in June: reportedly knocked herself coming out of stalls when taking virtually no part in Cherry Hinton Stakes at Newmarket in July. *M. Bell* 92

PAMPAS BREEZE (IRE) 3 b.f. Darshaan 133 – Pampas Miss (USA) (Pronto) [1994 NR 1995 10g 12m^2 12.3m^4 12s^4 12g^3 14.1m^2 a14g Nov 16] angular filly: unimpressive mover: half-sister to several winners, including very useful French 9f and 11f winner Samalex (by Ela-Mana-Mou): dam lightly-raced daughter of top-class American filly Bayou: fair maiden: best efforts at 1½m: sold 8,800 gns Newmarket December Sales. *W. Jarvis* 66

PAMPERED GUEST (IRE) 4 b.g. Be My Guest (USA) 126 – Miss Garuda 94 (Persian Bold 123) [1994 66: 10.3g 8f 10.1m^3 12m^4 14g^6 12g^4 11.5g^3 10m 11.9g 9.7m 1995 6g Apr 8] leggy, lengthy gelding: good mover: fair handicapper and hurdler: last in celebrity event over inadequate trip only start on flat at 4 yrs: stays 1¾m: acts on good to firm ground, yet to race on a soft surface: blinkered last 4 3-y-o starts. *K. C. Bailey* –

PANAMA HAT (IRE) 3 b.g. Thatching 131 – Lady Donna 92 (Dominion 123) [1994 –: 8m 1995 10m^3 a12g Jul 13] angular gelding: behind in maiden events: sold 600 gns Newmarket September Sales. *P. C. Haslam* –

PANCHELLITA (USA) 6 b.m. Pancho Villa (USA) – Counselor's Pride (USA) (Good Counsel (USA)) [1994 61: 8.3m 8f 6.9m* 7f^6 6.9g^2 6g^6 8.5m^5 7.6v^5 1995 a8g a7g a7g^6 a7g^4 a8g^3 a7g^5 8m 6f^4 7f 7m Jul 26] big, workmanlike mare: only a poor handicapper in 1995: stays 8.5f: acts on firm going (below form on a soft surface) and all-weather: tried in blinkers/visor, no improvement: normally a front runner. *G. L. Moore* 48

PANIKIN 7 gr.g. Red Sunset 120 – Haunting 79 (Lord Gayle (USA) 124) [1994 77: 6.1d 6f^5 7g 6g^5 8s 6s* 7m 1995 7s Mar 30] leggy, close-coupled gelding: fairly useful in 1991 and 1992: not so good, and inconsistent, afterwards: soon beaten on only 7-y-o start: ideally suited by 6f/7f: acted on firm and soft ground and the –

all-weather: blinkered (found little) final 5-y-o start: usually held up: sometimes bandaged: dead. *J. Wharton*

PANTHER (IRE) 5 ch.g. Primo Dominie 121 – High Profile (High Top 131) [1994 60, a51: a6g^3 a7g^5 a6g^3 a6g a6g 6v^4 5d^3 6d* 5d^5 7m 7.1f 6f^2 7g^3 6g a6g^3 a6g^5 1995 a6g* a6g^3 a6g^5 6s* a7g^3 6g 7g 6m 6f^3 6m^5 6g 7g^6 6g^5 7f^5 a6g a8g a7g^5 Nov 29] leggy gelding: modest handicapper: won at Wolverhampton (minor event) in January, Hamilton (made all) in April: below form last 7 starts: has form at 9f, raced mainly at sprint distances nowadays: acts on firm ground, soft and fibresand: visored 4 times in 1993/4, running well only on first occasion: tends to hang: inconsistent. *J. Hetherton* — 60 a58

PAOJIUNIC (IRE) 2 ch.c. (Mar 24) Mac's Imp (USA) 116 – Audenhove (GER) (Marduk (GER)) [1995 5g May 20] 24,000F, 31,000Y: half-brother to 1993 2-y-o 6f winner Rooftop Flyer (by Nordico) and several winners abroad: dam won in Germany: 11/4, last of 7 in maiden at Lingfield, weakened quickly last furlong. *L. M. Cumani* — – p

PAPAGOS (IRE) 4 b.g. Indian Forest (USA) 117 – Our Katy 68 (Dragonara Palace (USA) 115) [1994 –: 6s^4 6v^5 6f 5f a7g a8g a5g a7g 1995 a10g a6g^5 Jan 21] good-topped gelding: no form. *S. Dow* — –

PAPAHA (FR) 2 b.f. (Apr 2) Green Desert (USA) 127 – Turban 80 (Glint of Gold 128) [1995 6.1d^3 7d^4 7m^5 Oct 13] 31,000Y: compact filly: fourth foal: sister to fairly useful 1993 2-y-o 6.1f winner Tricorne and half-sister to 3-y-o 8.1f and 1½m winner Lovely Lyca and 1m/8.5f winner Barboukh (both by Night Shift): dam, 1¼m winner who stayed 1½m, half-sister to Old Vic: ran very well when fourth of 30 to Rio Duvida in valuable sales race at Newmarket in September, first home of those on stand side: respectable fifth of 8 to Bint Salsabil in Rockfel Stakes at Newmarket in October: will stay 1m: wore a bandage near-fore on debut: sure to win a race. *H. R. A. Cecil* — 91

PAPER CLOUD 3 b.f. Lugana Beach 116 – Sweet Enough 79 (Caerleon (USA) 132) [1994 70: 7.9d^4 8.2d^3 1995 10.3g^4 9m 11.6m 11.4g^5 10f^3 11.5g^3 11.9g^6 Sep 20] leggy filly: fair maiden handicapper: stays 11.5f: acts on good to firm ground and dead. *C. E. Brittain* — 66

PAPERING (IRE) 2 b.f. (Apr 5) Shaadi (USA) 126 – Wrapping 108§ (Kris 135) [1995 6g^5 7f* 7m^2 Aug 27] quite good-topped filly, slightly unfurnished: third foal: half-sister to 3-y-o 1m winner Cap And Gown (by Royal Academy): dam, placed in Oaks d'Italia and Lancashire Oaks but disappointing, sister to Royal Lodge winner Reach: progressive filly: won 6-runner maiden at Goodwood: beaten a head by Bint Shadayid in Prestige Stakes there following month, caught close home after leading 1f out: will stay 1m: will continue to progress. *L. M. Cumani* — 94 p

PAPER MAZE 2 b.f. (Apr 7) Mazilier (USA) 107 – Westonepaperchase (USA) 71 (Accipiter (USA)) [1995 a5g^3 5m^4 5f^4 a6g 6s^6 Sep 28] 1,000Y resold two 300Y: sixth foal: half-sister to two 2-y-o winners, including Paper Clip (1m, by Jalmood): dam ran once at 2 yrs: modest form first 2 starts, none afterwards: best form at 5f: sold (J. Harris to E. Owen jun) 1,500 gns Doncaster November Sales. *J. A. Harris* — 51

PARADISE NAVY 6 b.g. Slip Anchor 136 – Ivory Waltz (USA) (Sir Ivor 135) [1994 72: 18g* 16v^2 16.4d^6 1995 16m 14m^2 14m 17.2m^3 20m^5 16.2f^3 16.4m^2 18.7g^5 16.2m^5 17.2m^2 17.1m^4 16d^5 16.5m^2 a16g^4 Nov 20] close-coupled, quite attractive gelding: poor walker: fair handicapper: best efforts in 1995 when placed and when fifth in Ascot Stakes at Royal Ascot: stays 2½m: acts on any going: blinkered first 3 starts at 6 yrs. *C. R. Egerton* — 76

PARADISE WATERS 3 gr.f. Celestial Storm (USA) 132 – Gleaming Water 81 (Kalaglow 132) [1994 71p: 7f 7g 7g* 1995 10.2m^5 10f^3 11.8g^2 12m^2 12f^5 11.6m* 11.8g^2 11.4d^4 14g^4 11.8g Oct 9] unfurnished filly: modest handicapper: won at Windsor in July, battling back: probably stays 1¾m: acts on firm ground, below best on dead: tends to race prominently. *R. F. Johnson Houghton* — 62

PARELLIE 2 b.f. (Mar 4) Inca Chief (USA) – Parklands Belle 73 (Stanford 121§) [1995 a6g Dec 12] first foal: dam stayed 1m: 20/1, slow-starting last of 13 in seller at Wolverhampton. *C. J. Hill* — –

PARIS BABE 3 b.f. Teenoso (USA) 135 – Kala's Image 55 (Kala Shikari 125) [1994 66p: 5f^3 1995 6d^2 7m 6m^4 6g* 6g^3 6g* 6m^4 6m^5 6g* 6m 6g 6g Sep 29] — 94

smallish, workmanlike filly: fairly useful performer: won maiden at Lingfield in May and minor events at Yarmouth in June and Newmarket in July: may prove best at sprint distances: acts on good to firm and dead ground: usually held up: consistent. *D. Morris*

PARISH WALK (IRE) 4 ch.g. Pennine Walk 120 – Baby Caroline (Martin John) 47 [1994 –: 10g 11.8g^6 14g^6 14m 16.2g 1995 12.5g^6 10m 10m 12m 12.1m^4 13.1g* a16.2g Jul 21] sparely-made gelding: unimpressive mover: poor handicapper: 25/1, narrowly won 5-runner amateurs event at Ayr in July, making all: no comparable form: stays 13.1f: acts on good to firm ground. *K. W. Hogg, Isle of Man*

PARIS JOELLE (IRE) 2 b.f. (Mar 6) Fairy King (USA) – Gentle Freedom – (Wolver Hollow 126) [1995 6g May 20] 15,000Y: leggy, unfurnished filly: sister to 2 winners, including 1991 2-y-o 7f winner, Fairy Fable, and closely related to 1993 2-y-o 6f and 7f winner Amoret (by Jareer): dam unraced: 50/1, always behind in maiden at Newbury: unimpressive to post. *M. R. Channon*

PARKLIFE (IRE) 3 ch.g. Double Schwartz 128 – Silk Trade (Auction Ring 37 (USA) 123) [1994 –: a8.5g 1995 a9.4g^5 9m 6m^5 6.9f^5 Jun 29] compact gelding: poor maiden: best efforts in amateurs handicaps at Redcar and Carlisle (staying on) last 2 starts: likely to prove best at up to 1m: acts on firm ground. *P. C. Haslam*

PARK RIDGE 3 b.g. Indian Ridge 123 – Aspark (Sparkler 130) [1994 NR 1995 62 d 9g^6 8m 8.3m 10.2m Aug 28] 29,000Y: workmanlike gelding: fifth foal: half-brother to fairly useful 6f to 8.2f winner Amidst (by Midyan) and fair sprinter Arturian (by Vaigly Great): dam little form: failed by long way to repeat form shown on debut. *T. G. Mills*

PARKS PRIDE 4 b.f. Hubbly Bubbly (USA) – Valentine Song 63 (Pas de Seul – 133) [1994 –: 9v 12.1s 8f 10.8m 8.1m^6 9g 1995 16d Sep 11] leggy, sparely-made filly: no worthwhile form: tried visored. *Mrs L. A. Murphy*

PARLIAMENT PIECE 9 ch.g. Burslem 123 – Sallywell (Manado 130) [1994 77 77: 7m 7m^6 a8.5g^2 8g* 7g* 7g^6 8m* 8g^3 8m* 8g 1995 8g 8f* 7f^6 8m^5 7m* 8m^3 8.1g^6 7g 7f Oct 24] big, lengthy gelding: poor mover: fair performer nowadays: won claimers at Ayr and Newmarket (penultimate start for Mrs M. Reveley) in the summer: well beaten last 2 outings: suited by 7f/1m: acts on firm ground and dead: effective blinkered/visored or not: usually held up. *D. Nicholls*

PARME (USA) 4 b.c. Blushing Groom (FR) 131 – Petroleuse 104 (Habitat 134) 112 [1994 10.5g^5 8f^3 8g* 10.8g 11d^4 10d^3 10s^2 10d 1995 12g* 12d* 10d^2 10g* 12f Dec 10] seventh foal: half-brother to several winners, notably Peinture Bleue (at middle distances, by Alydar), graded stakes placed: dam, 6f (at 2 yrs) to 8.5f winner, half-sister to Pawneese: useful ex-French colt: unraced at 2 yrs, won minor event at Clairefontaine at 3 yrs: successful in 1995 in handicaps at Saint-Cloud and Longchamp in the spring, and Group 3 event in the provinces (final start for E. Lellouche, by ¾ length from Signoretto and Bulington) in October: towards rear, but beaten under 5 lengths and far from discredited, in Grade 1 Hollywood Turf Cup in USA final start: stays 1½m: probably acts on any going. *Jenine Sahadi, USA*

PARONOMASIA 3 b.g. Precocious 126 – The Crying Game 55 (Manor Farm – Boy 114) [1994 NR 1995 a6g a6g^4 a6g 7.6m 8g^6 Aug 26] fifth reported foal: dam, plater, stayed 1m: no worthwhile form: bred to stay 1m: visored (led over 5f, below form) final start. *M. Bell*

PARROT JUNGLE (IRE) 2 b.f. (Feb 13) High Estate 127 – Palm Dove (USA) 99 (Storm Bird (CAN) 134) [1995 7m^3 7f* 8h^2 7.1g^2 7m^2 7v^2 Nov 1] IR 45,000Y: useful-looking filly: has scope: half-sister to fair 1989 2-y-o 6f and 7f winner Long Island (by Law Society) and French 9.5f winner Love Dove (by Last Tycoon): dam twice-raced close relative of Nabeel Dancer and useful 2-y-o Anjiz: won 5-runner maiden at Redcar in August: demoted after first past post in 3-runner minor event at Haydock in September: improved again when ¾-length second, ducking right inside last, to Bint Salsabil in Rockfel Stakes at Newmarket: only fair second in listed race at Rome on final start: stays 1m: very nervy fourth start. *J. L. Dunlop*

PARSA (USA) 2 b.f. (Feb 20) Risen Star (USA) – Pallanza (USA) (Lyphard – p (USA) 132) [1995 7.1s 7m Nov 3] 20,000Y: big, good-topped filly: fifth foal: half-sister to useful French 3-y-o 1m winner Passionnee (by Woodman) and fairly useful winning French middle-distance stayer Partnership (by Shirley Heights): dam

French 1m winner out of top-class French mare Pistol Packer: refused to enter stalls in maiden on intended debut: slowly into stride and never a factor under considerate ride in similar events at Chepstow and Doncaster: looks capable of better. *J. L. Dunlop*

PARSIS (USA) 2 b.c. (Jan 24) Diesis 133 – Par Excellance (CAN) (L'Enjoleur (CAN)) [1995 6m^4 7m 7g^3 Oct 23] smallish, robust colt: half-brother to several winners, including Royal Lodge runner-up Khozaam (by Seattle Slew) and very useful 1986 2-y-o 6f winner Canadian Mill (by Mill Reef), later the dam of Hawajiss: dam won 9f Canadian Oaks: fourth to Charwelton in maiden at Goodwood: failed to progress, taking keen hold in maidens at Newmarket in August then Lingfield (steadied start, finished 9 lengths behind Ashjar who raced on favoured far side) in October: stays 7f. *Lady Herries* 68

PARTENAIRE 3 gr.g. Highest Honor (FR) 124 – Bint Secreto (USA) (Secreto (USA) 128) [1994 NR 1995 7m Apr 17] 56,000Y: leggy gelding: second foal: half-brother to French 11f winner Secrets Slip (by Slip Anchor): dam French maiden: 20/1 and bandaged, eleventh of 12 in maiden at Kempton. *K. McAuliffe* –

PARTHIAN SPRINGS 4 b.c. Sadler's Wells (USA) 132 – Princess Pati 124 (Top Ville 129) [1994 68p: 10g^4 10m^4 1995 10s* 12m* 12m* 13.9g^2 May 18] strong, lengthy colt: impresses in appearance: has an unimpressive, round action: most progressive performer: well-backed favourite, won 16-runner maiden at Leicester in March, 20-runner handicap at Newmarket in April and 11-runner £18,500 handicap at Newmarket in May: injured a knee when 1¼ lengths second of 7 to impressive Moonax (gave 5 lb) in Yorkshire Cup: stays 1¾m well and will stay 2m: acts on soft ground and good to firm: raced in touch first 3 starts at 4 yrs, made running final one: game and genuine: reportedly to attempt a comeback in 1996. *J. H. M. Gosden* 114

PARTIPRAL (USA) 6 b.h. Procida (USA) 129 – Partition (FR) (Top Ville 129) [1994 115: including 8s* 9.5v* 12s* 1995 9g* 10.5v^6 12g^3 12g 12.5d* 12.5g^5 12d 15.5f^4 12v* 12f* Dec 10] big, good-topped ex-Spanish-based horse (left M. Delcher after second 6-y-o start): smart performer: won minor event in Spain in April and slowly-run 5-runner Prix Maurice de Nieuil at Maisons-Laffitte (beat Tzar Rodney a short neck) in July: staying-on 8¼ lengths seventh of 16 to Lammtarra in Prix de l'Arc de Triomphe at Longchamp in October: easy winner of Group 3 event back in Spain (10/1 on) in November then gamely landed Hong Kong International Vase (just got up to beat Needle Gun a neck) in December: reportedly remains in Hong Kong to race: stays 2m: acts on any going: sometimes bandaged: genuine and consistent. *E. Lellouche, France* 120

PASH 3 b.f. Hallgate 127 – Pashmina 68 (Blue Cashmere 129) [1994 39: 5d 5m^6 6m^5 6m 7g 7.1m^2 7g a8g 1995 a8g 8.1d* 7g 8f^5 8.1g 8g 8.1f^6 8m 7m 8g 8.3g^3 8.1d^4 41

Ladbroke First Sunday Handicap, Newmarket—the last leg of Parthian Springs's early-season treble; he beats Blushing Flame (second right)

a10g Nov 14] small filly: poor form: 33/1, won selling handicap at Edinburgh in March: did not reproduce that form, leaving C. W. C. Elsey's stable after sixth start: should stay beyond 1m, very stiff task when tried: acts on dead ground: often visored, including when successful. *C. W. Fairhurst*

PASSAGE CREEPING (IRE) 2 b.f. (Apr 13) Persian Bold 123 – Tiptoe (Dance In Time (CAN)) [1995 7m Oct 28] IR 6,000Y: lengthy filly: has scope: eighth foal: half-sister to fairly useful Irish 6f winner Gentle Step (by Thatching) and winners in Ireland and USA by Melyno: dam unplaced in 4 starts at 2 yrs, is half-sister to Bedtime: 20/1, just over 8 lengths tenth of 19 to Awaamir in maiden at Newmarket, slowly away and in rear before making some late headway: will do better. *L. M. Cumani* 66 p

PASSING STRANGERS (USA) 2 b.c. (Mar 20) Lyphard (USA) 132 – The Way We Were (USA) (Avatar (USA)) [1995 7g 7d Sep 27] $250,000Y: ninth foal: half-brother to 4 winners in USA including a minor stakes winner: dam, won 2 minor events in USA, half-sister to Cacoethes and Grade 1 8.5f winner in USA, Fabulous Notion: similar form when tenth in maidens won by Shawanni at Yarmouth and Centre Stalls at Salisbury (took keen hold) 2 weeks later: unimpressive to post last time. *P. W. Harris* 68

PASSION FOR LIFE 2 br.g. (Mar 21) Charmer 123 – Party Game 70 (Red Alert 127) [1995 5s³ 5m* 5g* 5m² 5f⁴ Jun 9] 6,200Y: neat gelding: unimpressive mover: half-brother to 2 winning sprinters, including 7-y-o Very Dicey (by Tremblant), and a winner in Belgium: dam 6f winner who stayed 7f: made all in 16-runner maiden auction at Haydock and 3-runner minor event at Warwick in April: creditable efforts in minor events won by Ortolan at Salisbury and Prince Aslia at Epsom last 2 starts: speedy: hung badly right third outing: has been gelded. *G. Lewis* 82

PASSION SUNDAY 4 ch.g. Bairn (USA) 126 – Holy Day 82 (Sallust 134) [1994 52: a7g⁶ a7g⁵ 10.3g 10d 7.1g* 7g⁴ 8.1f⁵ 7g 6d 7m 6f 8.1m 1995 7.1m 8.3f⁵ 6f 8m 6g⁴ 7g 7d a9.4g Dec 9] leggy, close-coupled gelding: only poor form at best for new stable: stays 7f: acts on firm and good to soft ground, below form on fibresand: effective blinkered/visored or not. *L. R. Lloyd-James* 47 ?

PASS MARK 3 b.f. Never So Bold 135 – Selection Board 75 (Welsh Pageant 132) [1994 69: 7g² 7g⁵ 1995 7g⁴ 9f 10g² 10d³ 10d a12g 12m⁵ 12m Nov 6] unfurnished filly: fair maiden handicapper: stays 1½m: acts on good to firm and dead ground: has had tongue tied down. *J. R. Fanshawe* 65

PASTERNAK 2 b.c. (Jan 18) Soviet Star (USA) 128 – Princess Pati 124 (Top Ville 129) [1995 7f⁵ 7g 7m³ Nov 3] 30,000Y: big, good-topped colt: has plenty of scope: seventh foal: half-brother to smart 4-y-o middle-distance stayer Parthian Springs (by Sadler's Wells), 1½m winner Maxwelton Braes (by Lomond) and 1m to 12.5f winner Srivijaya (by Kris): dam won Irish Oaks: promising maiden who twice turned in very eye-catching performances, notably at Doncaster in November when 2¾ lengths third of 17 to Jackson Hill, travelling very smoothly 6f then running on well without rider resorting to whip: will stay beyond 7f: very much sort to do better at 3 yrs. *Sir Mark Prescott* 77 p

PATER NOSTER (USA) 6 b.h. Stately Don (USA) 122 – Sainera (USA) 89 (Stop The Music (USA)) [1994 111: 7.9d³ 8d* 8v* 1995 8g⁴ 8g³ Oct 6] leggy, quite attractive horse: has a round action: useful performer: has had only 14 starts altogether: again not seen out until the autumn, then respectable efforts in frame in listed races at Newmarket (bandaged, over 3 lengths fourth to Bin Rosie) and Saint-Cloud 8 days later: stays 1m: acts on good to firm and heavy going: front runner: genuine. *Mrs J. Cecil* 106

PATHAZE 2 b.f. (Apr 5) Totem (USA) 118 – Stilvella (Camden Town 125) [1995 5g³ 5g³ 5f* 5m 5m⁵ 5g 5g Sep 14] 400Y: workmanlike filly: second foal: dam twice-raced daughter of half-sister to top-class sprinter/broodmare Stilvi: won maiden auction at Ayr in June: below form in seller at Ayr final start: will stay 6f: acts on firm ground. *N. Bycroft* 61

PAT POINDESTRES 5 b.m. Interrex (CAN) – Glen Kella Manx 97 (Tickled Pink 114) [1994 33: a6g⁴ a5g a6g a5g 5s 8g a5g⁵ a6g² 1995 a6g² a5g a6g a6g a6g 5.3m a8g a5g Jul 22] small mare: poor sprinter: little form after reappearance: left R. O'Sullivan's stable after third start: acts on good to firm going and equitrack, well 36 d beaten on a soft surface and fibresand: blinkered (out of form) once at 4 yrs. *B. A. Pearce*

PATRIA (USA) 2 br.f. (Mar 14) Mr Prospector (USA) – Lypatia (FR) (Lyphard (USA) 132) [1995 7.6d* Sep 14] $275,000Y: tenth foal: sister to Middle Park winner and 2000 Guineas second Lycius and smart French 3-y-o 5f (at 2 yrs) to 7f winner Tereshkova, and half-sister to several winners, including Grade 2 9.5f and 1½m winner Abakir (by Riverman): dam won at 6.5f at 3 yrs in France and at 1m at 4 yrs in USA: weak 6/1-shot, won 12-runner maiden at Lingfield by ½ length from Crazy Chief, taking time to find stride then quickening really well close home to win going away: sure to improve. *M. R. Stoute* 76 p

PATRICE 4 b.g. Nordico (USA) – Broken Wide (Busted 134) [1994 –: 9g^6 8g 1995 a8.5g 13.1f^4 Jul 19] stocky gelding: poor maiden plater: stays 13.1f: acts on firm ground. *Mrs L. A. Murphy* 39

PATRINGTON BOY 2 b.c. (Mar 2) Sayf El Arab (USA) 127 – Gunnard 62 (Gunner B 126) [1995 5m^6 May 23] 2,000Y: half-brother to 3-y-o Hot Breeze and 11f winner Foot Soldier (both by Hotfoot) and 1½m seller winner Innovator (by Relkino): dam won 1m and 1¼m sellers: 20/1, no promise in seller at Beverley. *M. W. Easterby* –

PATRINGTON PARK 2 b.g. (May 1) Presidium 124 – Miss Skindles 58 (Taufan (USA) 119) [1995 5g^3 5m 5m^6 5m^3 6m^4 5.1m Aug 2] 1,800Y: short-backed gelding: looked weak: third foal: brother to 3-y-o Surgiva: dam 7f winner: modest maiden: rather disappointing after debut: will prove best at 5f: tends to sweat. *M. W. Easterby* 54 d

PATRIO (IRE) 2 b.f. (Apr 15) Polish Patriot (USA) 128 – Fleetwood Fancy (Taufan (USA) 119) [1995 6f 7f^5 a7g^5 Nov 11] 13,500F, 5,500Y: leggy filly: fifth reported foal: half-sister to 4 winners, including 3-y-o 11.6f winner Elly Fleetwood (by Elmaamul) and 1993 2-y-o 7.1f winner Western Fleet (by Westheimer): dam won at 5f at 2 yrs in Ireland and later at up to 9f in USA: modest form in maidens: stays 7f. *M. Johnston* 59

PATROCLUS 10 b.g. Tyrnavos 129 – Athenia Princess 80 (Athens Wood 126) [1994 42: a16g^6 21.6v* 16.1f^2 16g 18s 1995 16.1g Oct 3] workmanlike gelding: poor form: no promise only start in 1995: suited by thorough test of stamina: acts on any going: blinkered once earlier in career: often bandaged: modest hurdler. *J. Mackie* –

PAT'S CHOICE (IRE) 2 b.f. (Apr 14) Mac's Imp (USA) 116 – Guess Who 76 (Be My Guest (USA) 126) [1995 5m 5g 7.5m^2 7m 7.5m 7.5d Sep 13] 2,700Y: tall, unfurnished filly: half-sister to fairly useful middle-distance 5-y-o Hazard A Guess (by Digamist) and winners abroad by Henbit and Yashgan: dam, disqualified 10.4f winner, out of half-sister to Derby second Cavo Doro: plater: stays 7.5f: sold 1,400 gns Newmarket Autumn Sales: sent to Sweden. *M. H. Easterby* 44

PATS DELIGHT 3 ch.f. Crofthall 110 – Petroc Concert § (Tina's Pet 121) [1994 50: 5g a7g 6s a5g^2 a5g a5g a5g^4 1995 a5g^6 a5g^4 a6g^4 a5g a5g a5g^5 10m^5 Aug 14] leggy, unfurnished filly: poor sprint maiden: blinkered (tailed off) on 3-y-o reappearance. *S. Coathup* 44 d

PATS FOLLY 4 bl.f. Macmillion 110 – Cavo Varka 81 (Cavo Doro 124) [1994 –: 6s a12g 1995 10.2m a8.5g 10.8m 8h 10.8f Aug 28] leggy filly: of little account. *F. J. Yardley* –

PAT'S SPLENDOUR 4 b.f. Primitive Rising (USA) 113 – Northern Venture 80 (St Alphage 119) [1994 56: 7m 8.3f 8g 10g^2 11d 9.7m^5 9g 1995 10m 8.3m^4 8g 9d^4 12m^2 12m a12g a13g^3 Dec 6] angular filly: modest handicapper: stays 1½m: acts on good to firm ground and dead: inconsistent. *H. J. Collingridge* 49

PATSY GRIMES 5 b.m. Beveled (USA) – Blue Angel (Lord Gayle (USA) 124) [1994 71: a6g^3 a6g^5 5m^3 5.2g^5 5.1f^4 5m^4 5g^2 5d* 5d^6 1995 5d 6g 5g^3 6m* 6m^3 6m^2 6m 5m^2 6m 6.1d^5 a6g^6 a6g^3 Dec 18] leggy mare: fair handicapper: won minor event at Windsor in June: left L. J. Holt's stable after tenth start: effective at 5f and had form in 1993 over 1m: acts on any turf going and all-weather surfaces: effective blinkered (not tried in 1995) or not: often soon off bridle. *J. S. Moore* 71

PATTO (USA) 4 b.c. Dixieland Band (USA) – Pasampsi (USA) (Crow (FR) 134) [1994 99: a6g* 6v* 6.1d* 7g 1995 7.9g^6 6.1m* 6g^3 7d Sep 23] useful-looking colt: good walker: fluent mover: useful performer, but lightly raced: won £7,900 handicap 102

at Chester in June: very good third of 29 (beaten neck and head) to Royale Figurine in Ayr Gold Cup nearly 3 months later: reportedly suffered broken knee in £52,900 handicap at Ascot final start: suited by 6f/7f: acts on fibresand and on good to firm and heavy ground: reportedly likely to race again in 1996. *W. J. Haggas*

PAY HOMAGE 7 ch.g. Primo Dominie 121 – Embraceable Slew (USA) (Seattle Slew (USA)) [1994 100: 8m* 8m 7.9f^{4} 8.1d^{6} 8.5m 8.1m 8f 8.3m^{6} 8g^{5} 8s^{5} 8m 1995 8g 8m 9m* 8.5m 8f^{2} 8m 9m^{5} 9g 8.5s^{2} 7.9m 9d^{5} 8m Oct 28] angular, workmanlike gelding: just a fairly useful handicapper in 1995: won at Goodwood in May: well below form last 3 starts: suited by 1m/9f: best form on a sound surface, but comparable efforts at 7 yrs on firm and soft going: blinkered once at 2 yrs, visored once at 4 yrs: held up: none too consistent. *I. A. Balding* — 85

PC'S CRUISER (IRE) 3 b.g. Homo Sapien 121 – Ivy Holme (Silly Season 127) [1994 41: a5g 1995 a8g^{3} a7g^{3} a8g* a8g^{3} a6g* a7g a6g^{4} 7g 7g^{3} 7.5m^{5} 8m^{2} 7g a7g 8.2f 6g 7f 8.2m a11g Nov 6] sturdy gelding: modest handicapper: won at Southwell in January and February: very long way below form last 7 starts, leaving M. Chapman's stable after third of them: may well stay beyond 1m: acts on fibresand and good to firm ground: effective blinkered or not, out of form when tried in visor. *J. L. Eyre* — 53 d, a57 d

PEACE ENVOY 3 b.g. Warning 136 – Jubilee Trail 82 (Shareef Dancer (USA) 135) [1994 96p: 7m^{2} 7g* 1995 7g^{4} 7m* 8m* 8m 7.3g^{6} 7m^{3} 7m^{3} 8m Sep 1] strong, close-coupled gelding: shows a quick, unimpressive action: useful performer at best: won minor event at Newmarket and listed race (by 1¾ lengths from Ihtiram) at Kempton in the spring: back-to-form third in Beeswing Stakes at Newcastle and listed race at York: stays 1m: acts on good to firm going: blinkered (found little) fifth 3-y-o start: sometimes coltish: gelded after final start: sent to R. Frankel. *H. R. A. Cecil* — 106

PEACEFULL REPLY (USA) 5 b.h. Hold Your Peace (USA) – Drone Answer (USA) (Drone) [1994 59: 7.6g 6f 6.9f^{3} 7m 7d 6m 1995 7.1g 7g^{6} 7m 7g a7g 7d 7m a8g^{3} a9.4g Nov 27] close-coupled, good-topped horse: poor mover: just a poor handicapper nowadays: stays 1m: acts on firm ground and fibresand: tried blinkered, no improvement: inconsistent. *F. H. Lee* — 44

PEACHES POLLY 5 b.m. Slip Anchor 136 – Rostova 91 (Blakeney 126) [1994 72+: 10m^{4} 10m^{6} 10m 10m^{4} a10g 1995 10.8g^{6} 11.4g^{6} 10m^{6} Jun 30] lengthy mare: unimpressive mover: modest maiden on balance of form: stays 1½m: acts on firm and dead ground: has worn bandages: has run well when sweating: front runner last 2 starts: inconsistent: joined N. Wright. *G. Rimmer* — 65

PEARL ANNIVERSARY (IRE) 2 ch.g. (Mar 5) Priolo (USA) 127 – Tony Award (USA) (Kirtling 129) [1995 8.2m Oct 19] IR 6,000Y: leggy, lengthy, unfurnished gelding: poor walker: second foal: dam, minor sprint winner at 4 yrs in USA, half-sister to dam of Breeders' Cup Classic winner Skywalker: 40/1, showed up well 5f then faded into sixteenth of 19 to Dushyantor in maiden at Nottingham: likely to do better. *M. Johnston* — – p

PEARL DAWN (IRE) 5 b.m. Jareer (USA) 115 – Spy Girl (Tanfirion 110) [1994 6m 5g 6g* 5m^{2} 6m^{5} 5d^{3} 5d 6d^{5} 6v^{6} 6g 1995 a6g a6g^{4} a8.5g 5.1h^{4} 6m^{4} 6f^{2} 5.7h* 5.1h* 5f^{3} 5m^{3} 5g 5.3g^{3} 5m a5g^{5} Nov 10] sparely-made mare: half-sister to winning sprinter Terrific Star (by Wolverlife) and 3-y-o 5f (at 2 yrs) to 1½m winner Witney de Bergerac (by Cyrano de Bergerac): fairly useful handicapper (rated 81) in Ireland in 1994: fair here, and made all in 2 claimers at Bath in August, leaving N. T. Chance's stable after following start: stays 6f: acts on hard and dead ground, below form on the all-weather. *G. L. Moore* — 74, a–

PEARLS OF THOUGHT (IRE) 2 b.f. (Apr 10) Persian Bold 123 – Miss Loving 89 (Northfields (USA)) [1995 5m 6m^{5} 6.1m^{5} 7s 7f Oct 23] 4,800Y: half-sister to 3 sprint winners, best of them fairly useful Love Returned (by Taufan): dam 2-y-o 5f and 7f winner: modest maiden: best form at 6f: acts on good to firm ground: sweating last 2 starts: mulish at stalls on final outing: sold (P. Walwyn to J. Haldane) 950 gns Doncaster November Sales. *P. T. Walwyn* — 55

PEARL VENTURE 3 b.f. Salse (USA) 128 – Our Shirley 84 (Shirley Heights 130) [1994 84: 5m* 5m^{3} 6g^{4} 6m^{5} 6m^{5} 6s^{3} 1995 7m^{5} 10g^{3} 10.8g* 10m 10.2m^{3} 10g^{4} 10.1g^{6} 10.1g 8s Oct 6] lengthy, angular filly: good walker: fairly useful performer: won minor event at Warwick in June: generally faced stiff tasks afterwards: stays — 92

10.8f: probably acts on any going: blinkered (ran poorly) penultimate 3-y-o start. *S. P. C. Woods*

PEARLY RIVER 4 b.f. Elegant Air 119 – Mary Sunley 62 (Known Fact (USA) 67 135) [1994 72: 10m^5 10m a10g^6 1995 a8g a10g^6 a12g^3 a16g 11.5m 12f* Aug 15] smallish, workmanlike filly: has a short, quick action: fair handicapper: long way below form until winning at Folkestone in August, leading inside final 1f: stays 1½m, not 2m: acts on firm ground and equitrack. *Dr J. D. Scargill*

PEATSVILLE (IRE) 3 b.c. Ela-Mana-Mou 132 – Windy Cheyenne (USA) – (Tumble Wind (USA)) [1994 NR 1995 11m 8g 10.2f a14.8g Jun 10] big, useful-looking colt: half-brother to several winners, most of them successful at 2 yrs, including useful Keep Tapping (6f, by Tap On Wood): dam won 5 sprints in USA, including stakes at 2 yrs: no sign of ability. *M. R. Channon*

PECKINPAH'S SOUL (FR) 3 b.c. Zino 127 – Nashra (FR) (Brustolon 117) 113 [1994 7d 8g^6 8g* 7.5s* 9v* 1995 11m^4 12m^6 14m^3 15g^2 15g^2 15g* 15s^5 15.5f^6 Oct 22] rather leggy, attractive colt: second foal: dam 2-y-o 1¼m winner, also won over hurdles: smart performer: won minor events at Fontainebleau and Evry and listed event (by 5 lengths) at Evry at 2 yrs: placed 3 times in small fields in pattern races (events won by Swain and Affidavit) before winning 5-runner Prix Kergorlay at Deauville in August by 2½ lengths from Nononito, leading 1m out and not unduly pressed: well below form in Prix de Lutece (reportedly cast in box shortly before race, travelled as well as anything but quickly beaten in straight) and Prix Royal-Oak at Longchamp afterwards: stays 15f: acts on good to firm ground and heavy. *D. Smaga, France*

PEDALTOTHEMETAL (IRE) 3 b.f. Nordico (USA) – Full Choke 77 (Shirley 46 Heights 130) [1994 49: 7.8s 6.9m 7g a8g^6 1995 10g 11.6m 8f^4 8.3m^4 8.3g^5 10m^6 10.1m^6 10f 7.6m 8.1d^6 10g^4 9m^3 Oct 27] angular filly: poor maiden handicapper: stays 1¼m: acts on firm and dead ground: tried blinkered: has been bandaged behind: held up. *P. Mitchell*

PEDRAZA 3 ch.c. Belmez (USA) 131 – Polly's Pear (USA) (Sassafras (FR) 135) 101 [1994 63p: 8.2d 1995 12m^2 14g* 16.2m^3 16.1m Jul 1] sturdy colt: progressed well, into a useful stayer: won maiden at Newmarket in June: best effort when keeping-on 2¾ lengths third of 11 to Stelvio in Queen's Vase at Royal Ascot: would have stayed well: acted on good to firm ground: contracted laminitis: dead. *H. R. A. Cecil*

PEEP O DAY 4 b.f. Domynsky 110 – Betrothed (Aglojo 119) [1994 54p: 12g* – 1995 10.4m 13.8f^5 15.1s Nov 2] unfurnished filly: failed by long way to repeat debut winning form for Mrs M. Reveley. *J. L. Eyre*

PEGGOTTY 7 gr.m. Capricorn Line 111 – Silver Empress 63 (Octavo (USA) – 115) [1994 –: 6v 8g 6f 1995 7d Oct 19] leggy mare: of little account these days. *P. Hayward*

PEGGY ESS 2 b.f. (May 17) Seymour Hicks (FR) 125 – Daffodil 58 (Welsh – Pageant 132) [1995 7f 8.2d Sep 19] neat filly: poor mover: first reported foal: dam, maiden on flat, successful juvenile hurdler: last in maidens at Salisbury and Nottingham. *A. P. James*

PEGGY SPENCER 3 ch.f. Formidable (USA) 125 – Careful Dancer (Gorytus 68 (USA) 132) [1994 51p: 6s 1995 6g 5.1g^6 6m^3 7.1m 6g a6g^3 a6g* a7g* a6g^2 Dec 1] smallish, lengthy filly: fair performer: won handicap at Southwell and minor event at Lingfield (odds on), both in November: stays 7f: best form on the all-weather. *C. W. Thornton*

PEGS 4 b.f. Mandrake Major 122 – Siouxsie 90 (Warpath 113) [1994 60: 7.9d^3 8.2s – 5d 1995 7.1d 7m May 9] tall, angular filly: well beaten since debut: may need further than 7f. *C. W. Thornton*

PEKAY 2 b.c. (Mar 4) Puissance 110 – K-Sera 95 (Lord Gayle (USA) 124) [1995 71 5f^3 6g^3 5.1m^2 5g Sep 1] 38,000Y: leggy, angular colt: half-brother to several winners here and abroad, including smart German 5-y-o Kornado (by Superlative), successful from 5f (at 2 yrs) to 1½m: dam 2-y-o 7f winner: beaten under 2 lengths in maidens first 3 starts: first run for nearly 3 months when down the field in maiden at Haydock on final outing: will probably prove better suited by 6f than 5f: flashed tail third start. *J. Berry*

PELDER (IRE) 5 b.h. Be My Guest (USA) 126 – Sheer Audacity (Troy 137) 125
[1994 8v^2 8d^2 8g 8s* 8v 8v 1995 10s^2 10.5v* 9.3g^2 May 28]

Pelder reappeared briefly for a new trainer as a five-year-old to show himself a high-class horse, a better one than ever he looked in three seasons in Italy. He was transferred from Luciano d'Auria's stable to Paul Kelleway's at Newmarket after a somewhat disappointing year in 1994. He'd apparently had his problems, among them a bad sinus infection which required an operation. Pelder came to general notice when winning the Gran Criterium at Milan in 1992 from the British colt Right Win. The following year he won his first three races, notably the Premio Parioli, but was subsequently beaten by another British colt Alhijaz, unsuccessfully objecting, in the Premio Vittorio di Capua and finished a below-form seventh to yet another, Knifebox, in the Premio Roma.

Pelder's career as a five-year-old consisted of three runs at Longchamp for Kelleway, the last of them in May. He was being trained for the Arc when an old leg injury flared up in August. First time at Longchamp, Pelder came up against the strongest field he had ever faced, in the Prix d'Harcourt, and nearly pulled off a 76/1-upset, fighting back to run Freedom Cry to a neck. Next he was even more highly tried in the Prix Ganay, the first Group 1 race of the season and one that seemed up to the standard of recent runnings despite the absence of Carnegie, Tikkanen and the best of the German older horses. He was a revelation. Reopposed by five of the Harcourt field—Freedom Cry, Tuesday's Special, Millkom, Alderbrook and Marildo—alongside Hernando, Richard of York, Right Win and the Spanish-trained Partipral, Pelder moved very well on the heavy ground, held up. He cruised through to challenge over a furlong out and soon got well on top. Alderbrook, who had quickened into the lead at the distance, held on for second place from Richard of York and Freedom Cry, three lengths behind the winner. The ground in Paris had dried to good for the Prix d'Ispahan four weeks later. Pelder showed himself more than a mudlark by finishing a short-head second to Green Tune in the race, Group 1 again. He reproduced his Ganay form, and ran in a similar fashion, showing an excellent turn of foot, though this time he found one opponent with enough left to fight back going to the line.

Pelder (IRE) (b.h. 1990)	Be My Guest (USA) (ch 1974)	Northern Dancer (b 1961)	Nearctic
			Natalma
		What A Treat (b 1962)	Tudor Minstrel
			Rare Treat
	Sheer Audacity (b 1984)	Troy (b 1976)	Petingo
			La Milo
		Miss Upward (b 1964)	Alcide
			Aiming High

Pelder would have been an interesting runner in the Arc, on ground that would have suited him. He was untried beyond ten and a half furlongs but gave the impression he would have stayed further. On breeding he was worth a try. His dam Sheer Audacity, an Italian maiden, was bred to stay, being by Troy out of Miss Upward who won at a mile and a quarter and got at least a mile and a half. And Sheer Audacity is closely related to the 1973 Ribblesdale Stakes winner Miss Petard (by

Prix Ganay, Longchamp—Pelder's congratulations are well deserved; a good field of also-rans is led in by Alderbrook

Osvaldo Pedroni's "Pelder"

Petingo out of Miss Upward). On the other hand, another close relative, the useful Lucky Guest (by Be My Guest out of Sheer Audacity's sister Gay Fantasy) was campaigned during a long career as if thought best at up to a mile and a quarter. Other aspects of the pedigree were touched on in the commentary on Mister Baileys in *Racehorses of 1994*, as Pelder's third dam, the 1961 Coronation Stakes winner Aiming High, is half-sister to Mister Bailey's grandam Tender Annie. As for Sheer Audacity's producing record—she has yet to have a mile-and-a-half winner, but her fourth foal, the three-year-old of 1995, Sheer Danzig (by Roi Danzig), looks capable of putting that right. Her three-year-old of the previous year is the Italian one-mile winner El Rashid (by Jareer). Pelder has been retired to the Benham Stud, Newbury, at a fee of 3,000 guineas (October 1st). *P. A. Kelleway*

PELLEMAN 3 b.g. Distant Relative 128 – Lillemor (Connaught 130) [1994 69: 5f^4 6m 5g^3 5.2s^3 5m^4 1995 6g* 7m^3 6g 7.6m^4 6m^3 7m^5 7g 7f^2 8.2m Oct 26] rangy gelding: has scope: good mover: fair performer: won maiden at Thirsk in April: none too consistent in handicaps, best efforts when placed: stays 7f: appeared to act on any going at 2 yrs: has run well when sweating. *R. Boss* 75

PEMBRIDGE PLACE 4 b.g. Niniski (USA) 125 – Rose d'Amour (USA) (Lines of Power (USA)) [1994 84: 10.3m 12g^5 12g 12d^3 13.1d 1995 12m 12g^6 14g^6 13.3g^5 13.1g Sep 16] quite attractive gelding: fair handicapper: gelded after a disappointing season at 3 yrs, but failed to repeat even that form in 1995: should stay beyond 1½m: acts on heavy ground and good to firm: blinkered last 2 starts at 3 yrs, running well first occasion: sold (J. Dunlop to G. Johnson Houghton) 15,000 gns Newmarket Autumn Sales. *J. L. Dunlop* 72

PEMLEY 3 b.f. Superpower 113 – Redgrave Design 77 (Nebbiolo 125) [1994 58: 6g 5s^2 5s 1995 5g 7.5m 5m 6g 5f 5g^5 5d^4 6g Sep 25] small filly: bad form at best in 1995: easily best effort of soft ground: tried visored, no improvement: sold 1,200 gns Ascot November Sales. *R. M. Whitaker* 23

PENBOLA (IRE) 3 b.g. Pennine Walk 120 – Sciambola (Great Nephew 126) [1994 59: 5d 6f^{6} a7g^{6} 7.5m^{5} 7f 1995 9.9m 14d^{6} Jun 9] tall, lengthy, rather unfurnished gelding: unimpressive mover: modest form at best as 2-y-o: not knocked about in handicap at Beverley on reappearance, tailed off (over 1¾m) at Haydock around 6 weeks later: should stay at least 1m. *M. H. Easterby* –

PENCILLED IN 2 b.c. (Jan 11) Old Vic 136 – Graphite (USA) 80 (Mr Prospector (USA)) [1995 8.2m^{3} 8m Nov 4] quite attractive colt: fourth foal: half-brother to 3-y-o Montejurra (by Belmez) and 7f winner Clovis Point (by Kris): dam, 9f winner, out of smart sprinter Stellarette, a half-sister to champion Canadian filly and good broodmare Kamar: 4¼ lengths third of 11 to Dance Star in maiden at Nottingham: midfield in 23-runner median auction maiden at Doncaster following month: sent to Dubai. *P. W. Chapple-Hyam* 65

PENDINE 3 b.f. Pharly (FR) 130 – Springwell 73 (Miami Springs 121) [1994 45: 7m 8d a7g 1995 a10g 10g a8g May 11] little worthwhile form. *S. C. Williams* –

PENDING 3 b.g. Shareef Dancer (USA) 135 – Prelude 89 (Troy 137) [1994 74p: 8s 10s^{4} 1995 10g 12m May 7] lengthy, unfurnished gelding: mid-division in 23-runner maiden at Kempton on reappearance: pulled up lame at Salisbury 11 days later. *I. A. Balding* –

PENDLEY ROSE 2 ch.f. (Apr 1) Prince Sabo 123 – Rose Bouquet 78 (General Assembly (USA)) [1995 6m^{4} 6m^{5} a7g^{5} 7g^{6} 7s^{4} Sep 28] fourth foal: half-sister to ungenuine 4-y-o Rising Spray (by Waajib): dam, 2-y-o 6f winner who stayed 7f, out of smart filly (stayed 1m) Premier Rose: modest maiden: best effort after debut when second home on unfavoured stand side in nursery at Lingfield won by Warming Trends on final outing: stays 7f: acts on good to firm and soft ground. *P. W. Harris* 62 +

PENDOLINO (IRE) 4 b.g. Thatching 131 – Pendulina 102 (Prince Tenderfoot (USA) 126) [1994 7g 7g^{4} 6g^{3} 7g* 8g 7.5g 8g 1995 7.5m 8m 8.3g 10g^{5} 12.1m 12.1g 10.4m^{6} Oct 5] IR 38,000Y leggy gelding: half-brother to useful juveniles Sedulous and Tapolite (both by Tap On Wood): dam won 3 times at around 1m in Ireland from 3 starts: fair handicapper (rated 71) in Ireland for D. Weld, winning at Tralee but no form afterwards: sold 4,500 gns Newmarket Autumn Sales: only modest at best here: seems to stay 1¼m: no improvement in blinkers: inconsistent. *M. Brittain* 50

PENGAMON 3 b.c. Efisio 120 – Dolly Bevan 53 (Another Realm 118) [1994 92: 6f 6.1m* 6.1g* 6m^{6} 1995 7.5m^{3} 7g 8f^{4} 6g a8.5g a8g^{4} a7g Dec 18] smallish, strong, well-made colt: fairly useful handicapper: easily best effort as 3-y-o when in frame: stays 1m: has raced only on a sound surface on turf. *H. J. Collingridge* 88 d

PENMAR 3 b.g. Reprimand 122 – Latakia 80 (Morston (FR) 125) [1994 57+: 7f^{5} 6s^{5} 6s 8s 7.1g^{3} 1995 a7g^{3} a8.5g^{2} a7g^{2} 10.5s a8.5g^{3} 8.1s^{2} a7g Nov 24] good-topped gelding: modest maiden handicapper: stays 8.5f: acts on firm and soft ground and on fibresand: blinkered last 3 starts. *T. J. Etherington* 60

PENNEKAMP (USA) 3 b.c. Bering 136 – Coral Dance (FR) 111 (Green Dancer (USA) 132) [1994 123p: 6g* 7g* 7d* 7m* 1995 6.5g* 8m* 12f Jun 10] 130

Cancel that standing order for the annual Dick Francis novel, return those library tickets. Who needs fiction when racing can serve up dishes like the latest edition of the Two Thousand Guineas? The build-up, the race itself and its aftermath must have been gripping enough for even the most avid enthusiast of melodrama. Seldom can the running of a horse race have been accompanied by so much ballyhoo. Most of the attention centred on Celtic Swing, the winter favourite for both the Two Thousand Guineas and Derby after his brilliant twelve-length victory in the Racing Post Trophy as a two-year-old. The classic dreams entertained for Celtic Swing seemed a step closer to reality when he did everything asked of him in his Guineas trial, the Greenham Stakes at Newbury. The French-trained Pennekamp, unbeaten in four races as a two-year-old including the Dewhurst, was less convincing in his trial, the Prix Djebel over six and a half furlongs at Evry. Looking plenty fit enough, Pennekamp took a while to wear down relatively weak opposition in the Djebel, his rider having to resort to the whip before Pennekamp stretched clear for a decisive one-and-a-half length victory over Bene Erit. Though Pennekamp seemed sure to be better suited by the Guineas trip, Ladbrokes pushed him out in the Guineas betting after the Djebel and shortened Celtic Swing.

Prix Djebel, Evry—Pennekamp's season gets underway with a win over once-raced Bene Erit and the pacemaker Viva Nureyev

Celtic Swing started at 5/4 on for the Madagans Two Thousand Guineas with Pennekamp at 9/2 and Pennekamp's stable-companion the diminutive European Free Handicap winner Diffident third favourite at 6/1. All three were unbeaten, as was Painter's Row, the game winner of the Craven Stakes over the Guineas course and distance on his reappearance. Painter's Row and the Greenham runner-up Bahri (whom Carson preferred to the close Craven third Nwaamis) were the only others in the eleven-strong field to start at shorter than 25/1. The race produced a thrilling

Madagans Two Thousand Guineas Stakes, Newmarket—
the most eagerly awaited running of the race for years produces a thrilling duel as Jarnet unleashes a fine turn of foot from Pennekamp to cut down Celtic Swing (noseband) in the final furlong

spectacle, Celtic Swing being the first of the major contenders to make his move, quickening to lead over two furlongs out after being handy from the start. The confidently-ridden Pennekamp still had three lengths to make up with a furlong and a half to run but his rider Thierry Jarnet timed his finishing run to perfection, producing Pennekamp with a most impressive turn of foot to cut down Celtic Swing inside the final furlong. Celtic Swing rallied close home but Pennekamp held on by a head to record a memorable victory. Bahri finished two lengths behind Celtic Swing; fourth came the 50/1 outsider Pipe Major, two lengths behind Bahri, followed by Nwaamis, Diffident and Painter's Row. The timefigure recorded by Pennekamp—1.21 fast—provided confirmation that the Two Thousand Guineas represented top-class form. With the exception of Zafonic's 1.36 fast, the time *value* of Pennekamp's performance was the best achieved in the race since El Gran Senor's outstanding 1.54 fast in 1984. Though neither Pennekamp nor Celtic Swing ran again at a mile, Bahri went on to confirm himself one of the best around at the trip, winning the St James's Palace Stakes and the Queen Elizabeth II Stakes. The form-lines of some of those further back in the Guineas field can be used to pick holes but there's little doubt that Pennekamp fully deserves to be regarded as a good Guineas winner. His performance was certainly on a par with that of Zafonic, their Guineas-winning performances, judged on form, bettered only by Dancing Brave's in the last ten runnings of the race.

Sadly, like Zafonic, Pennekamp was seen out only once more as a three-year-old after winning the Guineas. Discussion and opinion about a rematch between him and Celtic Swing in the Derby dominated the racing news between Newmarket and Epsom, with Pennekamp (10/1 for the Derby early in the season) becoming a hot favourite when prevailing firm ground finally caused Celtic Swing to be switched to Chantilly. Pennekamp faltered and was off the bit in strides early in the straight at Epsom after travelling strongly in the middle of the field rounding Tattenham Corner. He beat only four home and was afterwards found to have sustained a hairline fracture to his off-fore. At first, his trainer Andre Fabre—who has the remarkable record of having sent out at least one Group 1 winner in Britain in each of the past eight seasons—seemed unsure about whether Pennekamp would race again. It has now been confirmed, however, that Pennekamp will be in training as a four-year-old when his first major target could be the newly-instituted Dubai World Cup, which will be the climax to the Dubaian season in late-March; the race, for four-year-olds and upwards over a mile and a quarter on sand, will be the world's richest race.

Pennekamp (USA) (b.c. 1992)	Bering (ch 1983)	Arctic Tern (ch 1973)	Sea Bird II
			Bubbling Beauty
		Beaune (ch 1974)	Lyphard
			Barbra
	Coral Dance (FR) (b 1978)	Green Dancer (b 1972)	Nijinsky
			Green Valley
		Carvinia (br 1970)	Diatome
			Coraline

The close-coupled, attractive Pennekamp is a good mover, though he was none too impressive in his slower paces before the Guineas. While Pennekamp's ability to stay the Derby trip couldn't be taken for granted, there were strong grounds, judged on pedigree, for believing he would do so. His sire Bering won the Prix du Jockey-Club and was an excellent second to Dancing Brave in a vintage Prix de l'Arc; and Pennekamp's dam Coral Dance, successful at up to a mile, had produced the high-class Nasr El Arab (by Al Nasr), a winner at up to around a mile and three quarters. Coral Dance has now bred four winners in all, including a full-brother to Nasr El Arab called Furiant, a minor winner for Fabre in France as a four-year-old who failed to add further to his successes on the sand in Dubai and fetched 26,000 guineas when sent up by Godolphin to the latest Tattersalls July Sales. Pennekamp's grandam Carvinia was successful twice at around a mile and a quarter in France, including in listed company, and is a half-sister to the high-class Carvin, placed in the Prix du Jockey-Club and the Prix Royal-Oak before finishing eighth in Sea Bird's Arc and being beaten a short head by Diatome in the Washington International. On the whole, this is not a particularly illustrious family, which, coupled with the fact that Bering's fortunes seemed in decline at the time, probably accounts for the fact that Pennekamp was picked up relatively cheaply as a yearling, costing 40,000 dollars at Keeneland's September Sale. Bering, now repatriated to France, also sired the latest Poule d'Essai des Pouliches winner Matiara. Pennekamp has yet to race on soft going, but, generally speaking, horses with a telling burst of speed are always likely to be favoured by top-of-the-ground and Pennekamp certainly looked in his element under the conditions on Guineas day. *A. Fabre, France*

PENNINE LAD (IRE) 5 ch.g. Pennine Walk 120 – Dominica (GER) (Zank) – [1994 52: a10g^4 12v^4 1995 a10g 11.8m^6 Aug 23] leggy gelding: modest maiden: never able to challenge (after 16-month absence) in handicap and claimer in 1995: effective at 1¼m to 1½m: best form on good ground and equitrack, well beaten on heavy: sold 550 gns Ascot October Sales. *B. Gubby*

PENNINE WIND (IRE) 3 b.g. Pennine Walk 120 – Wintina (Tumble Wind (USA)) 57 [1994 68: 5g a7g 7m 7f^2 7s^6 8.3g^2 1995 a10g^5 a10g^2 Feb 11] good-topped gelding: carries condition: fair maiden: probably stays 1¼m: acts on firm ground, probably on equitrack. *M. Johnston*

PENNY A DAY (IRE) 5 b.g. Supreme Leader 123 – Mursuma (Rarity 129) 102 [1994 100: 10m^6 10.5m^2 10g^2 11g* 10g^2 12g* 11.9s* 12s* 12v^2 1995 10m* 12m^6 10.4m 12d^5 11.9d^4 Oct 11] tall, good topped gelding: carries condition: poor mover: useful handicapper: won Zetland Gold Cup at Redcar in May by a head from Virtual Reality: respectable efforts at best afterwards, and those only in rated stakes at Newmarket and minor event at Haydock (beaten 15¾ lengths) last 2 starts: effective at 1¼m to 1½m: acts on good to firm ground and heavy: normally tracks the leaders: game: won both starts over hurdles in the autumn. *Mrs M. Reveley*

PENNYCAIRN 3 b.f. Last Tycoon 131 – Applecross 117 (Glint of Gold 128) 84 [1994 68: 7f^5 6.9m^5 8.2s^3 1995 10.2m^6 9.9m^5 8g^2 8m* 8.2m^2 8.1m^3 8.1d 8f Oct 12] angular, unfurnished filly: fairly useful handicapper: set pace when winning 4-runner maiden at Ripon in July: ran poorly last 2 starts: best efforts at 1m, but shaped as if stayed 1¼m: acts on firm and soft ground: races prominently: sold 18,500 gns Newmarket December Sales. *H. R. A. Cecil*

PENNY DIP 3 b.f. Cadeaux Genereux 131 – Penny Blessing 112 (So Blessed 130) 86 [1994 NR 1995 6m* 6g^5 6g^3 5.2m^2 6g Sep 9] rather unfurnished filly: half-sister to several winners, including 5f (at 2 yrs) to 7f winner Threepence (by Sharpo) and (at 9f and 1¼m) Tizzy (by Formidable): dam, best at 2 yrs when 5f winner, from family of Mummy's Pet: fairly useful form: won maiden at Lingfield in June: ran well when second in handicap at Newbury penultimate start, but a little disappointing at Goodwood 4 days later: effective at 5f and 6f: has raced only on a sound surface: sold 15,000 gns Newmarket December Sales. *R. F. Johnson Houghton*

PENNY DROPS 6 b.m. Sharpo 132 – Darine 114 (Nonoalco (USA) 131) [1994 108 111: 10v^5 8.1d* 8m 10d^6 10s 8v^3 1995 8g^6 10d* 8g* 8g* Oct 1] leggy mare: has a very round action: useful performer: won Group 3 Premio Ambrosiano at Milan in May by ¾ length from Zohar, 15-runner listed event at Cologne in September by a neck from Lara and listed race at Milan in October by a neck from Mandarina: effective at 1m to 1¼m: easily best efforts with give in the ground and acts on heavy: held up: tough and genuine: led out unsold at 100,000 gns Newmarket December Sales. *Lord Huntingdon*

PENNY GHENT 2 b.f. (Apr 29) Dominion 123 – On The Top (High Top 131) – [1995 6.1m^6 5d 6.1d Sep 19] 4,600F, 6,000Y: close-coupled, workmanlike filly: fifth foal: half-sister to 4-y-o Orchard Gold (by Glint of Gold) and 11.5f winner Top Rank (by Law Society): dam unraced half-sister to Double Schwartz: well beaten in maidens. *P. S. Felgate*

PENNY PARKES 2 ch.f. (Apr 19) Clantime 101 – Bonne Baiser 88 (Most Secret 57 119) [1995 5g* 5m^2 a5g^3 5m^2 May 9] 3,000Y: sparely-made filly: half-sister to 1989 2-y-o 6f and 7f winner J R Jones (by Blakeney): dam sprinter: plater: won at Doncaster in March: withdrawn lame later in May. *J. Berry*

PENNY RAMBLE (IRE) 4 b.f. Pennine Walk 120 – Celestial Melody (USA) – 75 (The Minstrel (CAN) 135) [1994 –: 8f^4 8f 10.3s 1995 a8g Feb 20] small, sturdy filly: seems of little account. *S. G. Norton*

PENNY'S WISHING 3 b.f. Clantime 101 – Lady Pennington 51 (Blue 60 d Cashmere 129) [1994 60: 5g 6v a5g^3 1995 a7g 6g^4 6m 6g 7.5m^4 6g* a7g 7m 6d 6m 7f 7f Oct 24] small, leggy filly: modest performer: won maiden at Catterick in June: well below form afterwards: stays 6f: acts on fibresand, probably on good to firm ground: sweating (well beaten) tenth 3-y-o start. *J. P. Leigh*

PENT-HOUSE BABY 3 ch.f. Risk Me (FR) 127 – Astral Suite 82 (On Your Mark 125) [1994 43: 5.1m6 6.1g6 5.1g 6s6 6.1g a8g5 a10g3 1995 a10g Jan 7] leggy filly: poor maiden: well beaten only start in 1995: sold 925 gns Ascot February Sales: stays 1¼m: blinkered (below form) twice at 2 yrs. *J. L. Spearing* –

PENTIRE 3 b.c. Be My Guest (USA) 126 – Gull Nook 120 (Mill Reef (USA) 141) [1994 103: 6m3 6g* 6m3 7m3 7m 1995 10m* 10.3m* 10m* 12f* 12g2 11.9m* 10m* Sep 9] 132

The winter favourite Celtic Swing wasn't the only notable absentee from the 1995 Derby field. Pentire was unbeaten in three of the traditional Derby trials—at Sandown, Chester and Goodwood—but, unfortunately, he had never been entered at Epsom. 'I just thought he would not be good enough,' said trainer Geoff Wragg. Pentire won only one of his five races as a two-year-old, when his form—which included a third in the Richmond Stakes—clearly endorsed his trainer's view, at the time, that he wouldn't reach classic standard. Pentire started at 25/1 when he reappeared in the eight-runner Thresher Classic Trial at Sandown in April. His success that day caused a radical reappraisal. Pentire quickened in the style of a smart performer in the making to win by a neck from Singspiel, proving well suited, as his pedigree suggested he would, by the step up to middle distances. A smooth success, carrying a penalty for his pattern-race victory in the Classic Trial, followed in the BNFL International Dee Stakes at Chester; and then, again conceding weight all round, Pentire scrambled home from Istidaad and Fahal in the Westminster Taxi Insurance Predominate Stakes at Goodwood. Pentire's trainer explained that he had no regrets about missing the Derby—'He is only a small horse and the race could have ruined him, we want to build up his confidence steadily'—but Pentire's victory in the so-called 'Ascot Derby', the King Edward VII Stakes, showed that he would have been a leading contender at Epsom. Pentire was most impressive, producing a fine turn of foot to beat the Prix du Jockey-Club fourth Classic Cliche with something in hand by two and a half lengths.

The King Edward VII Stakes was Pentire's first race over a mile and a half and it clearly represented his best performance so far (the Predominate runner-up Istidaad was beaten six and a half lengths into fifth). Next stop was the King George VI and Queen Elizabeth Diamond Stakes, also the target for the Derby winner Lammtarra. The Derby winner is usually an automatic favourite for the King

BNFL International Dee Stakes, Chester—Pentire from Sanoosea

King Edward VII Stakes, Royal Ascot—Pentire continues to progress through the ranks, completing his four-timer with breathtaking ease from Classic Cliche

George—or at least the shortest-priced in the field from his generation—but it was Pentire who was installed at the head of the ante-post market. On the day, however, Pentire drifted from 7/4 to 3/1, Lammtarra displacing him as favourite with the four-year-old Carnegie becoming second choice. Pentire went down to his only defeat of the season. Held up, he was switched wide to make smooth progress round the outside on the home turn, quickening into a narrow lead just after the two-furlong

Great Voltigeur Stakes, York—
it is virtually impossible to separate Pentire from Singspiel; Luso is third

marker, but he tired inside the last, began to edge right, and succumbed to Lammtarra's game rally. The margin between the pair was a neck and Dettori had to extract the last ounce out of Lammtarra to get him home. Pentire wasn't beaten again, though the evidence of the photo-finish camera was needed at the end of both his subsequent races. The judge took fifteen minutes to decide that Pentire had held on from Singspiel in the four-runner Great Voltigeur Stakes at York in August and the verdict was also a short head when Pentire was dropped in trip and got the better of the subsequent Arc and Breeders' Cup Turf runner-up Freedom Cry in the Guinness Champion Stakes the following month. Pentire's last-gasp victory at Leopardstown, where he was forced wide off the home turn and had plenty to do in the straight, crowned a remarkable season, the success of which could not have been envisaged back in April. His six victories yielded £291,202 and he looks sure to add to those earnings as a four-year-old when the newly-instituted Dubai World Cup, the King George and the Prix de l'Arc de Triomphe are said to be his main objectives.

Pentire (b.c. 1992)	Be My Guest (USA) (ch 1974)	Northern Dancer (b 1961)	Nearctic
			Natalma
		What A Treat (b 1962)	Tudor Minstrel
			Rare Treat
	Gull Nook (b 1983)	Mill Reef (b 1968)	Never Bend
			Milan Mill
		Bempton (b 1976)	Blakeney
			Hardiemma

The sturdy, attractive Pentire carries the colours of Mollers Racing which is financed from a trust fund set up by Eric Moller who wanted the well-known chocolate and gold colours associated with him and his brother to be carried on. Mr Moller died in 1988, since when the likes of Petardia, First Trump and Nicolotte have also kept the colours in the limelight. Pentire, who joined the Moller string as a yearling for 54,000 guineas, is by the champion sire of 1982 Be My Guest, who

Guinness Champion Stakes, Leopardstown—
a magnificent performance from Pentire who leads on the line after Freedom Cry had got first run

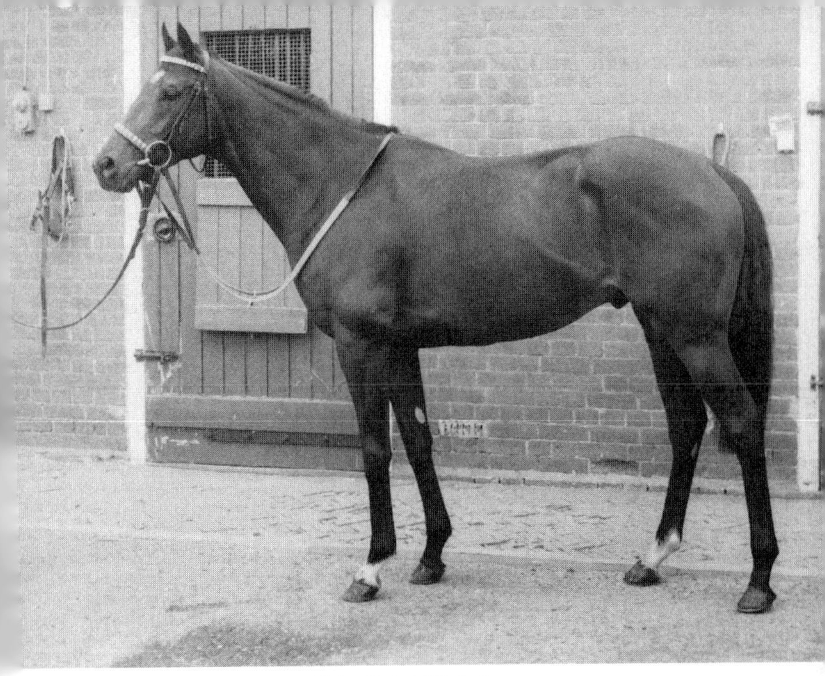

Mollers Racing's "Pentire"

enjoyed his best results for some time in the latest season. On the distaff side, Pentire comes from a family that has done well over the years for the Garrowby Stud of the Lords Halifax. Pentire is the second pattern winner bred by the Ribblesdale Stakes winner Gull Nook, following the smart middle-distance performer Spring (by Sadler's Wells, like Be My Guest a son of Northern Dancer). Pentire's grandam Bempton was a modest racemare, placed three times as a three-year-old, but, as a half-sister to Lord Halifax's Derby and Irish Derby winner Shirley Heights, she was always assured of a place at stud. She stepped into the shoes of her dam Hardiemma, who was sold by Garrowby Stud before Shirley Heights reached the racecourse, and has done very well, producing the useful middle-distance stayer Primrose Valley (third in the Galtres Stakes) and Gull Nook to coverings by Mill Reef, the sire of Shirley Heights. Bempton's next two foals after Gull Nook also won pattern races, Mr Pintips (by Kris) taking the Ormonde Stakes and Banket (by Mill Reef's son Glint of Gold) the Princess Royal. Generally speaking, this is a family of late-developers. Pentire is effective at a mile and a quarter to a mile and a half and acts on firm ground (he has yet to encounter a soft surface). He is held up in his races to make the most effective use of his very fine turn of foot. He is thoroughly genuine. *G. Wragg*

PENTRE FFYNNON (IRE) 3 ch.g. Ballad Rock 122 – One Better 77 (Nebbiolo 125) [1994 –: 6.1s 1995 5m* Jul 24] lengthy gelding: brother to smart sprinter Stack Rock: easily made all in 4-runner maiden at Newcastle in July: refused to enter stalls Aug 16: probably capable of better. *J. Berry* — 77 p

PEOPLE DIRECT 2 ch.f. (Feb 28) Ron's Victory (USA) 129 – Ayr Classic (Local Suitor (USA) 128) [1995 5.7m 6f^5 a6g^6 a7g^4 a8g* a8g^6 Dec 15] 4,000Y: sparely-made filly: first foal: dam 2-y-o 5f and 6f winner: modest form: swerved — 54 + a60 ?

stalls and unseated rider on debut: well backed, made all in seller at Southwell in December: stays 1m. *K. McAuliffe*

PEPITIST 4 b.g. Bold Owl 101 – Misoptimist 111 (Blakeney 126) [1994 51: 7m^6 8d 7g 8m 7g 8.1g 9m^4 12f^2 11.1g^3 10m^4 10m^3 9.9f^6 1995 13.6f Oct 12] sturdy gelding: modest maiden handicapper: tailed off for new stable on belated return: should stay beyond 1½m: acts on firm ground: modest winning hurdler. *M. D. Hammond* –

PEPPERS (IRE) 2 b.f. (Feb 26) Bluebird (USA) 125 – Pepilin (Coquelin (USA) 121) [1995 7g 7g^3 6f Oct 23] IR 5,000Y: angular, rather unfurnished filly: third foal: dam Irish 2-y-o 6f winner: fair form in 18-runner maidens at Leicester behind Oleana (led to 2f out then weakened noticeably inside last) and Wildwood Flower (one pace) 2 weeks later: stays 7f: ridden by 7-lb claimer last 2 starts: remains capable of better. *L. M. Cumani* 68 p

PERCY BRAITHWAITE (IRE) 3 b.g. Kahyasi 130 – Nasseem (FR) 118 (Zeddaan 130) [1994 87: 6m* 7f^3 7f* 7f 7g^6 7.9d 1995 10.5m 8.1m 10g^4 8.9m^2 8f^5 10.4m^6 8f Oct 12] leggy gelding: has scope: shows knee action: fairly useful handicapper: clearly best form at 3 yrs (in first-time blinkers) when neck second of 15 at York in June: should stay further than 9f: acts on firm ground, may be unsuited by a soft surface: blinkered since fourth 3-y-o start: forces pace: inconsistent: gelded. *M. Johnston* 85

PERCY PARK (USA) 2 br.g. (Feb 5) Rajab (USA) – Clayton's Miss (USA) (Distinctive (USA)) [1995 6m^3 6m^5 5.1m^6 8g 6f 7m Nov 4] $12,000F, IR 15,000Y: workmanlike gelding: half-brother to several minor winners in North America: dam won at up to 7f at 2 yrs: sire sprinter/miler: fair form first 2 starts: subsequently lost his way, absent 3 months prior to fourth outing (final one for M. Johnston stable): stays 6f. *M. W. Easterby* 69 d

PERCY PARROT 3 b.g. Lochnager 132 – Soltago 56 (Touching Wood (USA) 127) [1994 –: 6g 5s 6s 1995 8m 8.1d 7.1g a8.5g a8g Nov 20] workmanlike gelding: poor maiden: better at 1m than shorter: acts on dead ground: pulled hard and put head in air on 3-y-o reappearance: inconsistent. *R. M. Whitaker* 37

PERDITION (IRE) 5 b.m. Red Sunset 120 – Free Rein (Sagaro 133) [1994 56: 8d 8g 8m^4 8m* 7m^6 8g^6 8m 8m 10.3s^6 1995 a8g a11g 12m May 31] leggy mare: lost her form at 5 yrs: should stay beyond 1m: acts on firm and dead ground: tried blinkered/visored: sold 650 gns Ascot July Sales: sent to Cyprus. *K. R. Burke* –

PERFECT BERTIE (IRE) 3 b.g. Cyrano de Bergerac 120 – Perfect Chance 83 (Petorius 117) [1994 59p: 6m^5 6g 6g^6 7g^6 5s^3 1995 6.1g 7g^5 6m^5 7g 6m 8m 8.2m^3 11f^3 8.5g 10f 10m 10m^3 10m Aug 28] leggy gelding: modest maiden: claimed out of Mrs J. Ramsden's stable £3,500 fourth 3-y-o start: should stay 1½m: acts on firm and soft ground: visored (no improvement) last 2 starts: tends to hang left and carry head high: inconsistent: sold (G. Oldroyd to Mrs M. Kendall) 2,000 gns Doncaster October Sales. *G. R. Oldroyd* 52

PERFECT BRAVE 4 b.g. Indian Ridge 123 – Perfect Timing 107 (Comedy Star (USA) 121) [1994 61: 7v 5.7m 6v^4 6m^3 5.1m^2 5m^6 6d 5v^3 6g^6 5.1g a6g^2 1995 6m 5g^2 6m* 6m a5g^3 a7g Nov 21] leggy, workmanlike gelding: modest handicapper: won (first time) at Goodwood in June: stays 6f: acts on any ground: bandaged at 3 yrs: sold 1,600 gns Doncaster November Sales. *D. R. C. Elsworth* 64

PERFECT ENDING 4 b.g. Never So Bold 135 – Trinida (Jaazeiro (USA) 127) [1994 –: 8g 14g 1995 10.2f a14g^5 a13g^4 a14.8g Jul 17] good-topped gelding: poor maiden plater: stayed 13f: visored (tailed off) final start: dead. *C. A. Cyzer* 48

PERFECT GIFT 2 ch.f. (Jan 28) Generous (IRE) 139 – Knight's Baroness 116 (Rainbow Quest (USA) 134) [1995 7g 8.1m Aug 28] good-topped filly: unimpressive walker: second foal: very smart to high-class 3-y-o middle-distance performer Riyadian (by Polish Precedent): dam won Irish Oaks: last in maidens, pulling hard and soon off bridle last time: bred to be suited by middle distances. *P. F. I. Cole* –

PERFECT WORLD 3 b.c. Puissance 110 – More Or Less 64 (Morston (FR) 125) [1994 55: 5s^5 5m^5 a6g^4 5m^4 5.1g^4 6m 1995 6g^6 5.1g^5 7g a7g^6 a7g^3 Jun 10] leggy, angular colt: poor mover: modest maiden: stays 7f: acts on fibresand: inconsistent. *B. A. McMahon* 61

PERILOUS PLIGHT 4 ch.g. Siberian Express (USA) 125 – Loveskate (USA) 78 (Overskate (CAN)) [1994 62: 7v 8d 8d^6 7.8f^3 6g^2 7m* 6.5g 7.8s 9g^6 a7g 1995 a7g a8.5g^2 a8g^4 a8g* a8g* a8g^2 a8g* a7g* a8g^5 a7g^5 8g 7m^5 a8g^4 8m^5 7.1m 8f^2 8.3g^6 a7g^5 a8g^4 Nov 25] lengthy, angular gelding: fair performer on the all-weather: won claimer (awarded race), 2 handicaps and a minor event, all at Lingfield in January/February: stays 1m: acts on all-weather surfaces, best efforts on turf on a sound surface: tends to be awkward at stalls, and is blindfolded and put in last: patiently ridden. *W. R. Muir* 71 a76

PERIPATETIC 3 ch.f. Kris 135 – Sweet Mover (USA) 95 (Nijinsky (CAN) 138) [1994 –p: 7s 1995 11.9g^5 10m^2 Jun 23] big, unfurnished filly: very free to post before refusing to enter stalls on intended reappearance: best effort, allowed to dictate at steady pace, when second of 6 in maiden at Newmarket: wears a rope halter and blanket for stalls entry: sold 35,000 gns Newmarket December Sales. *M. R. Stoute* 72

PERPETUAL LIGHT 2 b.f. (Mar 19) Petoski 135 – Butosky 71 (Busted 134) [1995 7.5d^5 Sep 13] 3,000Y: half-sister to several winners, including Ebor runner-up Bush Hill (by Beldale Flutter) and 5-y-o 7f (at 2 yrs) to 10.3f winner Dutosky (by Doulab): dam middle-distance half-sister to very smart sprinter Crews Hill: 10/1, around 10 lengths fifth of 17 to Weet-A-Minute in maiden auction at Beverley, staying on under hands and heels: bred to stay very well: will improve. *J. J. Quinn* – p

PERRYSTON VIEW 3 b.c. Primo Dominie 121 – Eastern Ember 85 (Indian King (USA) 128) [1994 78p: 6g 6m 6g^6 6g* 6d^3 5s* 1995 5g* 5g* 6g* 6m 6g* 6f^3 6m^6 6g 6g Oct 7] lengthy, angular colt: fairly useful handicapper: won at Newcastle (hung left) and Catterick in April and at Newmarket in June (£23,400 Coral Sprint) and July: effective at 5f and 6f: probably acts on any going: visored since third 2-y-o start: usually races prominently. *P. Calver* 90

PERRYWINKLE WAY (IRE) 2 b.f. (Apr 13) Treasure Kay 114 – Miss Moat (Dike (USA)) [1995 6f 6m Nov 6] 6,500 2-y-o: smallish, deep-girthed filly: half-sister to several winners here and abroad, including 5f (at 2 yrs in Ireland) and 7f winner St Martha (by Double Schwartz): dam French 1m winner: behind in maidens. *Mrs A. L. M. King* –

PERSEPHONE 2 ch.f. (Mar 10) Lycius (USA) 124 – Elarrih (USA) (Sharpen Up 127) [1995 7g Sep 28] unfurnished filly: second foal: half-sister to 3-y-o Americus (by Old Vic): dam unraced: 33/1 and green, never a factor in maiden at Newmarket. *B. Hanbury* –

PERSIAN AFFAIR (IRE) 4 b.g. Persian Heights 129 – Lady Chesterfield (USA) (In Reality) [1994 77: a7g* a8g* a8g 7m* 8m 7.1g^6 7m 7m^3 8d^6 7g 1995 a7g a6g 8g 7m 6g^4 7f* 7m 8m^4 5f 7f 6f 7.1m 8.1m^5 7m^3 7m^5 7.1d 7g Sep 16] good-bodied gelding: fair handicapper: won at Brighton in May: stays 1m, at least when conditions aren't testing: acts on all-weather surfaces and firm ground, probably on dead: most inconsistent. *D. Haydn Jones* 72

PERSIAN BAILIWICK (IRE) 3 ch.f. Persian Heights 129 – A New Rose (IRE) (Saher 115) [1994 –: 5g 5.7f 7d 6g 6m 1995 10f 6f Aug 17] close-coupled filly: poor mover: no form: sold 900 gns Doncaster October Sales. *F. Jordan* –

PERSIAN BRAVE (IRE) 5 b.h. Persian Heights 129 – Commanche Belle 74 (Shirley Heights 130) [1994 114: 12m* 12s^2 13.4m^6 13.3m^2 11.8m^3 10.2s^3 12v* 1995 10m Apr 17] rangy horse: smart performer: weakened quickly in listed event at Kempton only start in 1995: should have stayed 1¾m: useful form on good to firm ground, but best effort on heavy: often a front runner: genuine: reported in September to have been retired after series of training set-backs: sold 6,800 gns Newmarket December Sales. *M. Bell* –

PERSIAN BUD (IRE) 7 b. or br.g. Persian Bold 123 – Awakening Rose (Le Levanstell 122) [1994 44, a30: a12g^3 a12g^3 a12g^6 12.3d* 10d^5 12d 12.5m^4 12m^5 12.1f^6 a16.2g 1995 a13g^6 a11g^6 a13g 12.3d^5 12.5g^2 9.7f 14.1m^5 Aug 12] well-made gelding: poor handicapper: stays 12.5f: acts on good to firm and soft ground: tried visored, no improvement: inconsistent. *J. R. Bosley* 40 a–

PERSIAN BUTTERFLY 3 b.f. Dancing Dissident (USA) 119 – Butterfly Kiss 69 (Beldale Flutter (USA) 130) [1994 NR 1995 7m^6 7m^5 Sep 5] 3,200F: IR 4,100Y: strong, good-bodied filly: third foal: half-sister to modest 9.2f and 11f winner Suivez (by Persian Bold): dam 1½m winner: 33/1 and short to post, sixth of 12 in maiden at 72

Newmarket, pulling hard in slowly-run race but running on quite well after wandering and running green into Dip: off course 4½ months, well below that form at Lingfield. *J. E. Banks*

PERSIAN CONQUEST (IRE) 3 b.c. Don't Forget Me 127 – Alaroos (IRE) (Persian Bold 123) [1994 58: 7s 7g a6g⁶ a7g⁶ 1995 a10g² a8g² a10g* a10g³ a10g⁵ a8g⁵ a10g² 12.5m a10g* 8m⁴ 11.6m² a12g* 10g⁴ 11.6m Jul 29] smallish, quite attractive colt: poor mover: fair performer, best on all-weather: won maiden in January and minor event in May, both at Lingfield, and minor event at Wolverhampton (rallying gamely) in July: stays 1½m: acts on all-weather surfaces, good to firm ground and probably on soft: blinkered since third 3-y-o start: normally front runner or races prominently: consistent on all-weather. *R. Ingram* 63 a74

PERSIAN DAWN 2 br.f. (Feb 21) Anshan 119 – Visible Form 99 (Formidable (USA) 125) [1995 7m Nov 3] 4,200F, 12,500Y: tall, leggy filly: half-sister to several winners, including 8.2f and 1¼m winner Living Image (by Taufan) and 1989 2-y-o 6f winner Azeb (by Young Generation): dam, 6f and 1¼m winner, out of half-sister to very smart stayer Raise You Ten: 20/1 and bandaged off-hind, slowly away and never a factor in 17-runner maiden at Doncaster. *Major D. N. Chappell* –

PERSIAN ELITE (IRE) 4 ch.g. Persian Heights 129 – Late Sally 101 (Sallust 134) [1994 80: 7.1d 7f⁵ 8.2m* 10m* 10m* 11.9d 10.5s 1995 12g 10.8g⁵ 10m⁴ 10.5m³ 10g* 10m⁵ 12g* 12d⁴ 13.9g Oct 7] strong, lengthy gelding: fairly useful handicapper: took time to come to himself, then won at Leicester (blinkered only time) in August and Kempton (gamely) in September: stays 1½m (beaten too far out to blame trip over 13.9f): acts on good to firm and dead ground: front runner. *P. F. I. Cole* 88

PERSIAN FAYRE 3 b.g. Persian Heights 129 – Dominion Fayre 49 (Dominion 123) [1994 68: 5s³ 5v⁴ 5m* 5m⁶ 6m⁴ 5m⁵ 8.3g⁴ 8s 1995 7g⁴ 8m* 8.3f 7f⁵ 8.1m³ 7g² 9.2f 7f⁶ 7.1m⁵ 7m Oct 20] sturdy gelding: fair handicapper: won minor event at Ayr in May: well below form 3 of last 4 starts: stays 1m: acts on firm ground. *J. Berry* 69

PERSIAN FLOWER 3 b.f. Persian Heights 129 – Edraianthus 78 (Windjammer (USA)) [1994 NR 1995 10.1m⁶ 10d⁵ a8.5g³ a12g a8g a9.4g⁶ Nov 27] 17,000Y, 10,000 2-y-o: lengthy filly: half-sister to fairly useful 6f and 7f performer Close To Reality (by Dreams To Reality): dam best form at 6f at 2 yrs: signs of ability in maidens at Newbury and Wolverhampton last 2 starts: seems to stay 9.4f: acts on fibresand: sold 2,000 gns Newmarket December Sales. *G. C. Bravery* –

PERSIAN HAZE (IRE) 6 ch.g. Bold Arrangement 127 – Crufty Wood (Sweet Revenge 129) [1994 –: a16g⁵ 1995 a11g Dec 1] smallish gelding: rated 65 at 2 yrs: soundly beaten in handicaps only starts in 1994 (for Miss B. Sanders) and 1995: ran well in visor once. *B. J. McMath* –

PERSIAN HERITAGE 4 ch.g. Persian Bold 123 – Middleham Jewel (Swing Easy (USA) 126) [1994 –: 7d 8.1m 8m 8.2m 1995 7g 10g May 30] leggy gelding: fair as 2-y-o: no longer of much account. *A. J. Chamberlain* –

PERSIAN LINNET 4 b.g. Persian Heights 129 – Swift Linnet (Wolver Hollow 126) [1994 48: 8.5g³ 12f² 15.1m⁴ 12m² 12m² 15.8g⁶ 13.8g⁴ 1995 12m⁶ 14.1m May 29] strong, lengthy gelding: tubed in 1995: maiden plater: stays 1½m, probably 15.1f: has raced only on a sound surface: sometimes has tongue tied down. *Mrs M. Reveley* –

PERSIAN SAINT (IRE) 4 b. or br.g. Persian Bold 123 – Santa Luciana (GER) (Luciano) [1994 –: 10.4f 1995 10m⁵ 10.2f 10m² 10m² 10m⁵ 11.7h* 13.3d Sep 16] tall, lengthy gelding: has a round action: fairly useful performer: won maiden at Bath in September, making all: sweating and edgy, behind in Autumn Cup at Newbury final start: needs further than 1¼m, and should stay beyond 11.7f: acts on hard ground: fractious (below form) second 4-y-o start: races prominently: won novice hurdle in October. *D. R. C. Elsworth* 86

PERSIAN SECRET (FR) 2 b.f. (Mar 5) Persian Heights 129 – Rahaam (USA) 91 (Secreto (USA) 128) [1995 6g* 6g* 6m² 7.1g⁴ 6m³ 7.3d Oct 21] neat, quite attractive filly: first foal: dam, 7f winner who stayed 1¼m, half-sister to Poule d'Essai des Poulains third Glory Forever: won median auction maiden at Ayr and 4-runner minor event at Pontefract (easily by 6 lengths) in June: beaten neck by Maid For The Hills in listed event at Newmarket: disappointing afterwards in listed races: 92

bred to be suited by further than 6f: may be unsuited by good to soft ground: sent to USA. *J. W. Watts*

PERSIANSKY (IRE) 5 b.g. Persian Bold 123 – Astra Adastra (Mount Hagen (FR) 127) [1994 –: 9.9s 8d 1995 12h3 Aug 16] lengthy, rather leggy gelding: fairly useful 3-y-o miler: well below best only outing at 5 yrs: probably acts on any going: temperamental sort. *W. T. Kemp* 31 +

PERSIAN SMOKE 4 b.f. Persian Bold 123 – Gauloise 93 (Welsh Pageant 132) [1994 39: 10.1g 11.7g 12d4 12g 1995 12g 12g 14m* 14g3 14.1m 16.4m5 14d 12m Oct 27] leggy filly: poor handicapper: ridden by 7-lb claimer, won at Lingfield in July, leading 6f out: seems to stay 16.4f: acts on good to firm ground: inconsistent. *A. Hide* 45

PERSIAN SOLDIER 8 b.g. Sandhurst Prince 128 – Persian Case (Upper Case (USA)) [1994 48: 12f3 12.3m 12f3 12f* 12f 1995 12g6 12m2 12.3m 11.9m4 12m4 Jul 21] workmanlike gelding: modest handicapper: pulled up on third start at 8 yrs: effective at 1½m to 1¾m: acts on firm going: visored (below form) once earlier in career: races prominently: one to treat with caution. *E. J. Alston* 49 §

PERSISTENT (IRE) 3 b.g. Nashamaa 113 – Reelin Elly (Pitskelly 122) [1994 59+, a70: 7m a7g4 a6g6 8g 8d a7g2 7.1g* 1995 9.9m a8g 15.8g Sep 16] leggy gelding: well beaten in 1995: dead. *M. H. Easterby* –

PERSONAL PRIDE (IRE) 4 br.g. Personal Flag (USA) – Terracotta Hut 99 (Habitat 134) [1994 –: 8s 10m a7g 1995 a9.4g Jan 4] sturdy gelding: seems of little account nowadays. *A. G. Foster* –

PERSONIMUS 5 b.g. Ballacashtal (CAN) – Sea Charm 70 (Julio Mariner 127) [1994 –, a40: 7g a8g6 10g a9.4g2 a10g6 8g a10g a12g 1995 a11g a8g 8f 11.1g 9m4 a8g3 a9.4g2 8.1m Jul 8] big, good-topped gelding: poor maiden handicapper: should stay 1¼m: acts on fibresand and good to firm ground: blinkered (hampered) final 3-y-o start: inconsistent. *Capt. J. Wilson* 38

PERSUASION 2 b.f. (May 28) Batshoof 122 – Primetta (Precocious 126) [1995 8g Oct 10] second live foal: half-sister to 4-y-o 1m winner Positivo (by Robellino): dam unraced daughter of half-sister to Molecomb winner Hatta: 14/1, backward and green, around 12 lengths seventh of 17 to Forest Buck in maiden at Leicester, in touch then keeping on: should do better. *Lord Huntingdon* – p

PERSUASIVE 8 b.m. Sharpo 132 – Queen's Eyot 79 (Grundy 137) [1994 NR 1995 12.1v5 14.1f2 14.1m3 13f4 14.1m4 Aug 27] lengthy, rather sparely-made mare: poor mover with a round action: seems just a modest handicapper nowadays: stays 1¾m: acts on any going: fairly useful hurdler. *Mrs M. Reveley* 50

PERTEMPS FLYER 4 b.g. Presidium 124 – Brilliant Future 58 (Welsh Saint 126) [1994 –, a61: 5m a8.5g3 a7g 8.2m 7g 5m 5s a5g a6g 1995 a10g6 a8g Dec 15] leggy gelding: modest maiden handicapper: well beaten late on in 1995, blinkered final start: better at 8.5f than shorter: acts on soft ground and on fibresand. *Simon Earle* –

PESCE D'APRILE 3 b.f. Mtoto 134 – Neatfoot 90 (Anfield 117) [1994 ?: 9v 8d* 1995 10m3 11d 11.8m6 9d 11d3 Oct 15] sturdy filly: fairly useful performer: faced stiff tasks most starts in 1995, creditable third of 5 in minor event at Milan final one: stays 11f: acts on good to firm and dead ground: sold 20,000 gns Newmarket Autumn Sales. *J. L. Dunlop* 92

PETAL'S JARRED 5 ro.m. Headin' Up – My Aisling 72 (John de Coombe 122) [1994 33: 7.1g* 8.5m 10g6 12g 10.4d 1995 a7g 7.1g 10m 11.1g 8f 8.1f 12m5 11.1f4 14.1f 12m Jul 20] lengthy mare: poor form: stays 1½m: acts on good to firm ground and heavy: visored since fifth 5-y-o start: inconsistent. *W. Storey* 27

PETE AFRIQUE (IRE) 4 b.c. Petorius 117 – Noir Afrique (African Sky 124) [1994 92?: 5g 5s* 5.1m4 6m 6d 5s 1995 6d 5m 6f 6g5 5m 5m Jul 19] sturdy colt: poor walker: fairly useful sprinter at best: has had numerous injury problems, and little worthwhile form in 1995: acts on good to firm and soft ground: often bandaged. *M. W. Easterby* –

PETER MONAMY 3 ch.g. Prince Sabo 123 – Revisit 86 (Busted 134) [1994 –p: 8.1g6 1995 a12g3 12.5m* 12.1m 11.8g Oct 10] good-bodied gelding: third living foal: dam stayer: won claimer (claimed out of P. Cole's stable £10,000) at Warwick in April: off course 4½ months, well below that form in similar events afterwards: 63

will probably stay beyond 12.5f: won selling hurdle in October: sold 3,200 gns Doncaster November Sales. *M. C. Pipe*

PETERREX 2 b.g. (May 25) Interrex (CAN) – Standard Rose 52 (Ile de Bourbon (USA) 133) [1995 7f3 5g 6m a7g Dec 14] sturdy gelding: first foal: dam stayed 2¼m on flat and 3m over hurdles: remote third of 10 in claimer at Salisbury: no form afterwards in sellers and claimer. *M. R. Channon* 48 d

PETER ROWLEY 4 gr.g. Absalom 128 – Tiszta Sharok 81 (Song 132) [1994 –: 7s 8m 6g 1995 6m 7.6m 8f 8g 8.3m Jun 19] small gelding: no worthwhile last 2 seasons: probably stays 1m: acts on firm ground, tailed off on soft. *R. Hannon* –

PETERS FOLLY 2 b.f. (Mar 19) King Among Kings 60 – Santo Star 55 (Monsanto (FR) 121) [1995 5f4 5g a5g5 6.1d 5g6 Sep 18] 500Y: small, lightly-made filly: fifth foal: sister to a winner in Austria: dam half-sister to Ebor winner Another Sam: poor form in sellers and nurseries: has worn bandages behind. *J. L. Eyre* 41 +

PETITE ANNIE 2 b.f. (Feb 13) Statoblest 120 – Kuwait Night 67 (Morston (FR) 125) [1995 5m6 5m3 5m6 5g2 a7g Nov 21] 12,000Y: smallish filly: sixth foal: sister to 3-y-o 5f and 6f winner Statius: dam, 1½m winner, sister to useful middle-distance stayer Mubarak of Kuwait out of half-sister to Dominion: placed in maiden at Lingfield and seller at Goodwood: off course 5 months before showing nothing final start: should be suited by further than 5f. *T. G. Mills* 64

PETITE BIJOU 4 b.f. Tina's Pet 121 – Highland Lassie 62 (Highland Melody 112) [1994 38: a7g4 a8g5 7v3 7d 10f3 10m 1995 a12g a12g Jan 23] small filly: poor maiden on flat: stays 1¼m: acts on any ground: poor winning hurdler. *R. Brotherton* –

PETITE-D-ARGENT 6 b.m. Noalto 120 – Honey To Spare 63 (Track Spare 125) [1994 NR 1995 7g 6g 6m 5g5 5g 6g Sep 25] compact mare: poor mover: only modest form at best for new stable on return after a spell at stud: effective at 5f and 7f: acts on good to firm and dead ground: ran well in visor at 2 yrs: tends to hang under pressure: inconsistent. *T. Dyer* 61

PETITE FANTASY 3 b.f. Mansooj 118 – Ride Bold (USA) (J O Tobin (USA) 130) [1994 6g4 5g* 5d2 6g3 5g2 6.3d5 5g4 1995 5g3 5g2 5m3 5g3 5m5 5m* 6m2 6m* 5m2 6g5 Sep 16] fourth foal: dam, out of sprint-winning half-sister to Jalmood, is unraced half-sister to smart 1¼m filly Vidor: smart Irish filly: successful in maiden at Navan at 2 yrs: showed considerable improvement to win good handicap at the Curragh, then landed listed race at Leopardstown, both in the summer: beaten a length by Bunty Boo in 10-runner Flying Five (went left from stalls, outpaced, still last 2f out, finished strongly) at Leopardstown in September: ideally needs a test of stamina at 5f, and stays 6f: raced only on a sound surface at 3 yrs, effective on dead ground at 2 yrs: blinkered since fifth 3-y-o start: consistent. *A. P. O'Brien, Ireland* 110

PETITE HERITIERE 2 b.f. (Apr 25) Last Tycoon 131 – Arianna Aldini (Habitat 134) [1995 7f 5m6 6g 7g Sep 12] 25,000Y: unfurnished filly: half-sister to several winners, including 5-y-o 6f to 1m winner Green's Bid and fairly useful miler Langtry Lady (by Pas de Seul): dam never ran: no worthwhile form in maidens and (visored, stiff task) nursery. *M. J. Ryan* –

PETITE JULIETTE 2 b.f. (Feb 6) Salse (USA) 128 – Cascade 39 (Shirley Heights 130) [1995 6g 7f a7g Nov 16] small, angular filly: second foal: dam (maiden) should have been suited by 1½m: modest form when eighth in maidens at Newmarket and Yarmouth: never a factor in seller at Southwell: bred to stay at least 1m: sold 500 gns Ascot December Sales. *W. Jarvis* 65 ?

PETITJEAN (IRE) 4 b.g. Last Tycoon 131 – Working Model 99 (Ile de Bourbon (USA) 133) [1994 –: 8.1g 1995 a12g a12g Dec 12] long-backed, workmanlike gelding: no form on flat since modest 2-y-o: fair hurdler. *D. Burchell* –

PETIT POINT (IRE) 2 b.f. (May 17) Petorius 117 – Minnie Tudor (Tudor Melody 129) [1995 6g4 6.1d Sep 19] IR 15,500Y: sturdy, close-coupled filly: closely related to 3-y-o Axeman (by Reprimand), useful 6f winner at 2 yrs, and half-sister to several winners, including fairly useful Bermuda Classic (by Double Form), 2-y-o 5f and 6f winner in Ireland and since dam of good Irish sprinter Tropical: dam won over 6f and 8.5f in Ireland: similar form in maidens won by Prima Volta at Kempton (slowly away) and Thracian at Nottingham (seventh of 23, given easy time when beaten) in September. *R. Hannon* 66

PETIT POUCET 3 b.c. Fairy King (USA) – City Ex (Ardross 134) [1994 7.5v^6 1995 8s* 8v* 8d^2 8d^3 7m 10f^3 8d^2 9f^4 Nov 26] good-bodied, attractive colt: second foal: half-brother to French 12.5f winner Bengale Lancer (by Sarhoob): dam French 1½m winner: smart performer: impressive winner of minor event at Evry and listed race at Saint-Cloud in March: in frame in Prix de Fontainebleau (1½ lengths behind Atticus), strongly-run Poule d'Essai des Poulains (never nearer, 2¼ lengths behind Vettori), Secretariat Stakes at Arlington, Prix du Rond-Point (stayed on never a real threat, 2 lengths behind Shaanxi) and Hollywood Derby, all races in France at Longchamp: effective at 1m and stays 1¼m: acts on heavy going and firm: consistent. *N. Clement, France*

115

PETOMI 3 ch.f. Presidium 124 – Missish (Mummy's Pet 125) [1994 75p: 6.9d* a6g* 7d* 1995 6m a7g^6 a6g^3 7m^2 a6g^4 6m^6 6d 6d^2 6.1d* Sep 19] close-coupled filly: fair performer: ran on consecutive days at Leicester and Nottingham (won 17-runner minor event) last 2 starts: stays 7f: acts on good to firm and dead going, goes well on fibresand: has run creditably when sweating: sold 6,200 gns Newmarket Autumn Sales: sent to Italy. *Sir Mark Prescott*

61
a67

PETONELLAJILL 5 br.m. Petong 126 – Crackerjill 37 (Sparkler 130) [1994 64: 7g 8.1g 10g^6 10.2f^5 10m 7f^4 8.3m 1995 8g a7g^5 Jul 8] leggy mare: good walker: modest performer: well beaten for new stable in 1995: seems best at up to 1m: acts on good to firm going: blinkered (no show) fifth 4-y-o start. *J. G. M. O'Shea*

–

PETOSIVA (IRE) 3 b. or br.c. Petorius 117 – Siva (FR) (Bellypha 130) [1994 8d 8g 1995 8d* 10v 10.3g^6 9s^6 Nov 22] IR 9,400Y: workmanlike colt: third foal: half-brother to a winner in Austria by Persian Bold: dam French 1m to 11.2f winner: won maiden at Saint-Cloud in April for P. Bary: off course over 4 months, always behind in minor event at Doncaster final start for J. Dunlop: stays 1m: sold 10,000 gns Newmarket Autumn Sales, returned to previous stable and finished sixth in claimer at Evry in November. *P. Bary, France*

80

PETOVA (IRE) 3 b.f. Petorius 117 – Kirsova (Absalom 128) [1994 –: 5m^6 5.7f 6f 1995 5g 6m 7.5m a6g Aug 4] small filly: no worthwhile form: sold 900 gns Doncaster August Sales. *M. J. Camacho*

–

PETRACO (IRE) 7 b.g. Petorius 117 – Merrie Moira (Bold Lad (IRE) 133) [1994 68: a6g^2 a6g^4 a6g a6g^6 6s^6 5.9v 5m^2 6d 5m 6g 1995 5d 5m^5 6f^3 5m^2 6g* 6m^2 6g^5 6m 6.1m 6f^2 5m* 6m 6m^6 6g 5g^4 6d^2 5f 6f^6 6m Oct 30] workmanlike gelding: has a quick action: fair handicapper: won at Leicester (seller) in June and Pontefract in August: suited by sprint distances: acts on the all-weather and any turf going: occasionally blinkered (not since 5 yrs), no improvement: usually races prominently: sometimes hangs. *N. A. Smith*

68

PETRA'S STAR 3 b.f. Rock City 120 – Meanieminymoe 66 (Star Appeal 133) [1994 61p: 6g 1995 8g 7g Jun 3] leggy filly: failed to repeat debut form: sold 7,000 gns Newmarket December Sales. *M. J. Heaton-Ellis*

–

PETREFUZ (IRE) 2 b.g. (Feb 4) Fayruz 116 – Fifth Quarter (Cure The Blues (USA)) [1995 6m 6f^4 5g 6d 8f Oct 12] 7,200Y: leggy, good-quartered gelding: good walker: half-brother to 2 winners abroad, including French 1¼m handicapper Mon Bugey (by Akarad): dam won at 1m and 1¼m in France: modest maiden: stays 1m: tends to hang left, and has looked a hard ride: taken early to post: sold 2,000 gns Newmarket Autumn Sales: sent to Austria. *E. Weymes*

58

PETRICO 3 b.c. Petong 126 – Balearica 90 (Bustino 136) [1994 NR 1995 7g a8.5g Nov 13] 6,200Y: brother to 2 winners, including Mahon G (7f to 1¼m) and half-brother to a winner: dam placed at up to 1m: tailed off in maidens. *J. Berry*

–

PETROS PRIDE 2 b.f. (Apr 1) Safawan 118 – Hala 57 (Persian Bold 123) [1995 6g 8d 7g Oct 23] compact filly: second foal: half-sister to 3-y-o Jhan Jeon (by Aragon): dam should have been suited by further than 7f: no promise on first 2 starts: raced on favoured far side and seemed to show improvement when over 5 lengths seventh of 13 to Tsarnista in maiden at Lingfield on final outing. *M. J. Bolton*

59 ?

PEUTETRE 3 ch.c. Niniski (USA) 125 – Marchinella 72 (Daring March 116) [1994 NR 1995 a8g* 8.1m^5 8f^3 10g 8.5m 10g^6 Sep 21] close-coupled, unfurnished colt: second foal: dam stayed 1m: won maiden at Lingfield in February: fairly useful form in minor events on turf next 2 starts: well below form afterwards: should stay

87

beyond 8.1f: sold (C. Brittain to F. Jordan) 8,000 gns Newmarket Autumn Sales. *C. E. Brittain*

PEVERIL PRINCESS 4 b.f. Town And Country 124 – Princess Siham 52 (Chabrias (FR) 103) [1994 –: 8m 8m 8g 10d 10d⁴ 10g⁴ 1995 8m 10g 12g 10d Sep 19] workmanlike filly: poor maiden. *G. B. Balding* –

PEWTER LASS 3 b.f. Dowsing (USA) 124 – Ragged Moon 72 (Raga Navarro (ITY) 119) [1994 56: 5.2s⁴ 6.1s 7m³ 7m 7.3g 1995 8.2g 12.5m 11.6m 12g⁴ 10.1g Sep 13] leggy, angular filly: no longer of much account. *M. Blanshard* –

PHANAN 9 ch.g. Pharly (FR) 130 – L'Ecossaise (Dancer's Image (USA)) [1994 NR 1995 11.5m⁶ 11.5s a14g a14g⁶ a12g a12g a10g Dec 15] leggy, workmanlike gelding: modest middle-distance handicapper (rated 68) at 4 yrs: bandaged, no promise on return. *R. E. Peacock* –

PHANTOM CREEK 2 b.f. (Feb 1) Mr Prospector (USA) – Danseur Fabuleux (USA) 106 (Northern Dancer) [1995 6g⁶ 6g Sep 30] tall, unfurnished, angular filly: sister to 1993 French 2-y-o 1m winner Columbus Day, closely related to 1992 French 2-y-o 7.5f winner Fortrose (by Forty Niner) and half-sister to 2 winners, notably outstanding juvenile Arazi (by Blushing Groom): dam (stayed 1½m) from top-class family: well backed, 4 lengths sixth of 8 to Applaud in Cherry Hinton Stakes (kept on again close home after seeming likely to drop away over 1f out), then fading seventh of 17 in maiden won by Polish Spring 2½ months later, both at Newmarket: pulled hard both starts, particularly second one, and needs to become more tractable if she's to realise her potential. *Saeed bin Suroor* 92 ?

PHANTOM DANCER (IRE) 2 b.g. (Mar 29) Distinctly North (USA) 115 – Angel of Music (Burslem 123) [1995 5m 5g⁴ 7m³ 7f⁴ 6s⁶ Sep 30] IR 3,700F, 6,400Y: second reported foal: dam never ran: plater: sixth of 24 in nursery at Haydock final start: stays 7f: carries head awkwardly: often slowly away: blinkered second start: sold 1,000 gns Doncaster October Sales. *J. Berry* 46

PHANTOM GOLD 3 b.f. Machiavellian (USA) 123 – Trying For Gold (USA) 103 (Northern Baby (CAN) 127) [1994 88p: 7g³ 8.1d* 1995 8m³ 10g⁶ 12m* 11.9m 12d* Oct 21] 110

The popularity of Festival occasions shows no signs of diminishing with the British public, who seem to like few things better than to indulge in their favourite pastimes against the backdrop of a summer's day. The long, hot summer of 1995 brought people out to the racecourses in their droves, with attendances standing up well overall. The crowd that flocked to Royal Ascot on Ladies Day was considerable—nearly 75,000 strong—prompting Ascot's racecourse director, Douglas Erskine-Crum, to comment: 'this is approaching our capacity, certainly our comfortable capacity'. In glorious weather, the assembled masses had plenty to

Ribblesdale Stakes, Royal Ascot—hats off! The Queen's Phantom Gold beats Tillandsia

Perpetual St Simon Stakes, Newbury—a characterful performance from Phantom Gold

celebrate, not least with the traditional raising of hats in recognition of that ever-popular event there, a winner in the Royal colours.

Phantom Gold's victory for the Queen in the opening Ribblesdale Stakes would have led to even more 'hats off', we suspect, had it been more widely expected. True, Phantom Gold had looked just the sort for the race at the end of her two-year-old career. Her grandam, Expansive, had won the race for the Queen in 1979, and the Ribblesdale was pinpointed for Phantom Gold in *Timeform Horses To Follow.* But, following a couple of defeats earlier in her second-season campaign, Phantom Gold looked to have it all to do, not only against the Oaks runner-up and short-priced favourite Dance A Dream, but also against two or three of the others in the seven-runner field for the Ribblesdale. Phantom Gold started joint-second favourite at 5/1, alongside the promising Lupe Stakes runner-up Tillàndsia. For a long way things went to plan for backers of the favourite, who was close to the steady pace set for the majority of the mile and a half trip by the outsider Musetta. But, as the race really took shape shortly after the home turn, it was Phantom Gold, who'd been tucked in just off the pace, who responded best. Ranging alongside the leader two furlongs out, she led soon after and ran on strongly to hold the late challenge of Tillandsia by a length and a quarter. Musetta kept on to finish third, a further two and a half lengths away, with Dance A Dream only fourth.

Success in the Ribblesdale has been by some way the career highlight of a number of the race's winners over the years, not least Expansive, for whom it was a final racecourse appearance. Not so for Phantom Gold, though. Following a poor run in the Yorkshire Oaks, in which she pulled too hard to do herself justice, she landed another major prize in the Perpetual St Simon Stakes at Newbury in October, assisted by the pace-making of her owner's other representative Whitechapel. Phantom Gold looked to have a bit to find again in a field of twelve and started third-best in the betting at 6/1. But, with her chief form rivals disappointing, she ran out a deserving winner, leading on the bit early in the home straight and keeping on despite hanging markedly left and flashing her tail under pressure. She reached the line with a length and a half to spare over the 20/1-shot Asterita (who, coincidentally, had finished second to Phantom Gold in a Sandown maiden when both were two-year-olds), with Whitechapel a game third, a further length and a quarter away.

Connections were reported to be unsure about plans for Phantom Gold's future following the St Simon. The temptation to retire the filly must be strong. Phantom Gold was not an outstanding Ribblesdale or St Simon winner, and future successes might not be easy for her to come by, added to which her wayward behaviour in the closing stages of the latter race hinted at more than a degree of temperament in her make-up. Phantom Gold seems sure to prove a valuable asset whenever it is that she is retired. The family has served the Queen well ever since Phantom Gold's great grandam Amicable was a rare acquisition at public auction for her as a yearling in 1961. Amicable won the Lingfield Oaks Trial and was runner-up in the Yorkshire Oaks before producing several useful or better winners, the pick of them the sisters Example (winner of the Park Hill Stakes, the Prix Jean de Chaudenay and the Prix de Royallieu) and Expansive. Expansive herself also had a fair amount of success at stud, with Phantom Gold's dam Trying For Gold one of the best of several winners. Trying For Gold's two wins came in relatively modest events at Salisbury and Wolverhampton, but they were achieved sufficiently impressively to mark her down as a useful filly. At stud, her first produce was the once-raced maiden Pandrop (by Sharrood); Phantom Gold is her second foal.

Phantom Gold (b.f. 1992)	Machiavellian (USA) (b 1987)	Mr Prospector (b 1970)	Raise A Native
			Gold Digger
		Coup de Folie (b 1982)	Halo
			Raise The Standard
	Trying For Gold (USA) (b 1986)	Northern Baby (b 1976)	Northern Dancer
			Two Rings
		Expansive (ch 1976)	Exbury
			Amicable

Phantom Gold is from the first crop of Machiavellian, the top-rated French two-year-old in 1989 and the runner-up in the Two Thousand Guineas the following year. Machiavellian has made a most promising start to his career at stud. His first crop also included the Dubai Poule d'Essai des Poulains winner Vettori and several other useful performers, while those of his second crop to have run have included the Prix d'Arenberg first-past-the-post and Prix Eclipse winner Titus Livius and the useful juveniles Don Micheletto and Laafee. A tall, leggy, light-bodied filly, Phantom Gold stays a mile and a half and acts on good to firm and dead going. *Lord Huntingdon*

PHANTOM HAZE 2 gr.g. (Apr 5) Absalom 128 – Caroline Lamb 74 (Hotfoot 126) [1995 6f^{6} 7m 6m 8m^{4} 8f^{6} Oct 31] 3,800Y: good-bodied gelding: has a round action: brother to 1992 2-y-o 6f winner Amerigue and winning jumper Master Lamb and half-brother to 11f winner Radio Caroline (by All Systems Go): dam won over 1m and over hurdles: modest maiden: creditable efforts in nurseries last 2 starts: will stay further than 1m: twice sweating and edgy. *Miss S. E. Hall* 60

PHARAMINEUX 9 ch.g. Pharly (FR) 130 – Miss Longchamp 94 (Northfields (USA)) [1994 74d: 14g* 12m* 12f^{5} 12d 11.8g a12g^{2} 1995 a12g^{3} a13g^{6} 11.9m* 11.9f^{6} 12m^{3} 14s 12g* 12m^{2} 12m* 14.8m^{3} 11.8m^{4} 12g 12d Oct 21] strong, workmanlike gelding: carries condition: unimpressive mover: fair form: won claimers at Brighton in April and Goodwood in June, and handicap at Newmarket (for second year running) in June: best at 1½m to 1¾m: suited by a sound surface on turf: blinkered once at 3 yrs: usually held up. *R. Akehurst* 68 a56

PHARAOH'S DANCER 8 b.g. Fairy King (USA) – Marie Louise 86 (King Emperor (USA)) [1994 70: 6v^{2} 6m^{3} 6m 6.1s^{2} a6g^{5} 6.1g 1995 a6g a6g 7d^{2} 7g^{5} 5.1d a7g^{6} a6g Nov 25] good-topped gelding: has round action: fair handicapper: well 70 a60 below form for new stable in 1995 except when second of 16 at Lingfield third start: stays 7f: acts on good to firm and heavy ground and on all-weather surfaces: blinkered (ran poorly) once at 6 yrs. *P. Burgoyne*

PHARAOH'S JOY 2 b.f. (May 9) Robellino (USA) 127 – Joyce's Best 58 (Tolomeo 127) [1995 6m^6 6.1f^3 6.1m* 7m^5 6d Sep 18] 7,000Y: leggy filly: third foal: half-sister to 1993 2-y-o 6f winner Sixpees (by Efisio): dam half-sister to Ormonde Stakes winner Zimbalon and Yorkshire Cup winner Band: overcame slipping saddle to win maiden auction at Nottingham in July: never dangerous in nurseries at Epsom and Leicester last 2 starts: should stay further than 6f: sweating freely and very edgy final start. *J. W. Payne* — 65

PHARAZINI 4 b.f. Pharly (FR) 130 – Arianna Aldini (Habitat 134) [1994 72§: 5.1f^5 8g 7g^2 7.1m 7d 1995 7m^6 8.5m 8g May 26] leggy, workmanlike filly: has twice refused to race (including final 4-y-o start) and is one to avoid. *M. J. Camacho* — §§

PHAR CLOSER 2 br.f. (May 27) Phardante (FR) 123 – Forever Together (Hawaiian Return (USA)) [1995 8g Sep 16] third foal: dam well beaten in juvenile hurdle: 200/1, tailed off in maiden at Ayr. *W. T. Kemp* — –

PHARLY DANCER 6 b.g. Pharly (FR) 130 – Martin-Lavell Mail (Dominion 123) [1994 –, a70: a13g^2 11.9s a14g* 1995 a12g* a12g* a12g* 12g 12g* 13.9g 12.1g a12g^2 a16g Nov 20] leggy, angular gelding: has suffered intermittently from knee problems: has a round action: fairly useful handicapper on all-weather at Southwell, winner 3 times in smallish fields prior to turf season: modest on turf, winning at Catterick in April: effective at 1½m and 1¾m: goes well on fibresand, used to act on dead ground: often wears crossed noseband and has tongue tied down: game front runner. *W. W. Haigh* — 57 a82

PHARLY REEF 3 b.g. Pharly (FR) 130 – Hay Reef 72 (Mill Reef (USA) 141) [1994 NR 1995 8g 9g^5 8m a8g 7g^6 a12g a8.5g Dec 12] 15,000Y: rather unfurnished gelding: brother to 7f winner Pressure and half-brother to several winners, including fairly useful Legendary Dancer (1½m, by Shareef Dancer): dam 1¼m winner: fifth of 14 in maiden at Lingfield in May, hampered and eased: no comparable form, sold out of I. Balding's stable 2,500 gns Ascot July Sales after fifth outing: should be suited by further than 9f: visored (no improvement) fourth start. *D. Burchell* — 62 d

PHARMACY 2 b.f. (Mar 21) Mtoto 134 – Anodyne 100 (Dominion 123) [1995 6m^2 5m^4 6m^2 6f* 6m 6m^3 Oct 4] leggy, quite attractive filly: good mover: third foal: half-sister to 3-y-o 6f winner Showery (by Rainbow Quest) and useful 1993 2-y-o 5f performer Stimulant (by Sharpo): dam, 6f winner, sister to very useful (at up to 1½m in USA) Domynsky: fair performer: easy winner of 5-runner maiden at Ayr in August: creditable third of 14 to Dashing Blue in nursery at York last time: stays 6f. *J. W. Watts* — 80

PHARR 3 b.f. Reference Point 139 – Pharian (USA) 114 (Diesis 133) [1994 NR 1995 10g Jun 6] first foal: dam won Cheshire Oaks and Lancashire Oaks: 25/1, soundly-beaten fifteenth of 16 in maiden at Pontefract: sold 5,500 gns (Newmarket July) and 3,200 gns (Doncaster October) at the Sales. *C. E. Brittain* — –

PHARSICAL 4 ch.f. Pharly (FR) 130 – Brown Velvet 68 (Mansingh (USA) 120) [1994 60: 8g 7f^3 7m^4 8.3m 7m* 7f^2 7f^3 6.9g 7m* 7d 6g^5 7.6v 1995 7g^3 6.1g^3 7m* 7m^3 6f 5.7f* 5.9f* 6g Jul 16] lengthy filly: reportedly in foal to Aragon: fairly useful performer: mostly in good form in 1995, successful in apprentice handicap at Brighton and minor events at Bath and Carlisle in the summer: effective at up to 7f: acted on firm going, seemingly not on heavy: usually early to post (tailed off after bolting fifth 4-y-o start): front runner. *M. R. Channon* — 80

PHASE ONE (IRE) 5 b.m. Horage 124 – Fayes Ben (Don 128) [1994 51: 8.2g a9.4g 8m^6 8g^5 7g^3 7.1s^6 8g^3 8.1g^5 1995 a8g 7g^6 8.2m 6.9f^2 6f 14.1m^5 8g* 8g^4 8d 8g Oct 9] good-bodied mare: poor mover: modest handicapper: won maiden contest at Newcastle in August: stays 1m: acts on firm ground, possibly not on soft: has had 3 runs (no form) on fibresand: most inconsistent. *J. L. Eyre* — 56 a–

PHILGUN 6 b.g. K-Battery 108 – Andalucia 57 (Rheingold 137) [1994 69: 16s^3 16d^6 18.7m 14g 12.4f 12.1m* 12.3m^5 13.1g* 13m^3 12g* 14.1m^2 12.1g^4 13.1d 14s 12g^3 12.4d a12g 1995 a12g^3 a12g a12g^6 a12g^3 Feb 13] leggy, close-coupled gelding: only modest form in 1995: effective at 1½m, and stays 2m: acts on any going: sometimes hangs head high: visored: races prominently: inconsistent. *C. W. C. Elsey* — – a59

PHILISTAR 2 ch.c. (Mar 25) Bairn (USA) 126 – Philgwyn 66 (Milford 119) [1995 6m5 6d 6d6 Sep 30] 16,000Y: fourth foal: half-brother to 3-y-o 7f (at 2 yrs) and 1m winner Prudent Pet (by Distant Relative) and 2 other winners, including useful 1m/1¼m performer Philidor (by Forzando): dam, maiden stayed 7f, half-sister to very smart sprinter Primo Dominie: modest form in maidens: should stay beyond 6f. *J. M. P. Eustace* 60 +

PHILMIST 3 b.f. Hard Fought 125 – Andalucia 57 (Rheingold 137) [1994 NR 1995 12m6 12.1g4 12.1g4 13.1g 11.1m5 15.1f a12g* a14g2 a16g5 a16g5 15g 13.6f a14g a14g3 Nov 16] leggy filly: half-sister to several winners, all at 7f+, including 9f to 1¾m winner Philgun (by K-Battery): dam won 1¼m seller: modest performer: trained by J. Hetherton until after sixth start: narrowly won handicap at Southwell in July: should prove suited by 2m+: acts on fibresand, probably on equitrack: tried blinkered. *C. W. C. Elsey* 58

PHILOSOPHER (IRE) 2 b.c. (Mar 8) Royal Academy (USA) 130 – Flyaway Bride (USA) 104 (Blushing Groom (FR) 131) [1995 7m Nov 3] 17,000Y: lengthy colt: half-brother to 3-y-o Dosses Dan (by Danehill), 1½m winner Handmaiden (by Shardari) and a winner in Italy by Kris: dam Irish sprinter, third in Moyglare Stud Stakes: 6/1 and green, didn't get best of breaks and never a serious threat in 18-runner maiden at Doncaster won by Wahiba Sands: will do better. *R. Hannon* – p

PHILS FORTUNE 3 ch.f. Kinglet 98 – Crimson Sol (Crimson Beau 124) [1994 NR 1995 a11g 11.8m Aug 23] second reported foal: dam poor novice hurdler: decidedly backward, tailed off in claimers: pulled up after looking reluctant on hurdling debut. *K. S. Bridgwater* –

PHIL'S TIME 4 b.g. Damister (USA) 123 – Coca (Levmoss 133) [1994 76: 12s3 12.5v2 12s2 12.5m2 14.1g 14g2 13.3g4 14g3 14.1m6 1995 14.9d4 16m 16.4m 20m 18.2m3 17.2f5 16.4m Aug 18] leggy gelding: only a modest maiden handicapper in 1995: stays 2¼m: acts on good to firm and heavy ground: usually visored or blinkered, not last 3 starts: not one to trust implicitly: sold 6,000 gns Newmarket Autumn Sales: sent to Germany. *T. G. Mills* 65 d

PHLIRTY 3 b.f. Pharly (FR) 130 – Aim To Please 102 (Gunner B 126) [1994 NR 1995 a8.5g 12d Oct 21] second foal: half-sister to useful 1m and 1¼m winner William Tell (by Chief Singer): dam middle-distance performer: tailed off in claimers. *R. F. Johnson Houghton* –

PHOENIX HOUSE 2 ch.c. (Apr 27) Formidable (USA) 125 – Ladysave (Stanford 121§) [1995 7f 6m* 5.2d 5.3d a7g Nov 10] workmanlike colt: fifth foal: half-brother to 2m winner Powersurge (by Electric): dam ran twice: well beaten except when winning seller (bought in 4,000 gns) at Lingfield in August, hanging left: stays 6f: visored second/third starts: sent to Saudi Arabia. *G. L. Moore* 56

PHYLIAN 4 b.f. Glint of Gold 128 – Phylae (Habitat 134) [1994 68: 11.1g* 14g 10f4 10m* 10m 12g 10m6 1995 8m 9.7g6 10g4 9.9g2 12f4 12f4 Aug 2] close-coupled filly: just a modest handicapper at best in 1995: stays 11.1f, probably not 1¾m: acts on firm and dead ground: blinkered (below form) final 4-y-o start. *S. C. Williams* 56

PICCOLO 4 b.c. Warning 136 – Woodwind (FR) 103 (Whistling Wind 123) [1994 112: 7d 8f 8m2 6f5 6f* 6m6 6g2 5m* 6g2 5g 7m6 1995 5m6 6d3 5f* 6g2 Jul 13] 121

It was bad news that Piccolo had fractured his near-hind joint on the gallops in July, particularly bad news for his owners who had just laid out £18,000 to supplement him into the Sussex Stakes. The colt's star seemed still to be rising, and if the Sussex wasn't the obvious race for him there were still plenty of good sprints to come. Then the good news: the injury wasn't life-threatening and Piccolo has been found a place at stud, the Lavington Stud in Sussex where he will start at £3,500 with the October 1st concession.

Piccolo progressed so well on the racecourse as a four-year-old that he was able to win the King's Stand Stakes at Royal Ascot under a Group 1 penalty he hadn't earned. Blue Siren had beaten him on merit in the Nunthorpe in 1994 but bumped him in doing so and positions were reversed by the stewards. Piccolo would have seemed up against it even unpenalized in the King's Stand. As it was, he started at 20/1 in a field of ten. Since the Nunthorpe he'd run five times without winning, generally giving a good account of himself but without much hint of the improvement that was to come. He'd apparently run well in both races in 1995 before Royal

King's Stand Stakes, Royal Ascot—Piccolo is very much on song, leaving Struggler and Mind Games (noseband) to battle it out for minor honours

Ascot, around four lengths sixth of fourteen to Mind Games under a maximum penalty in the Palace House Stakes at Newmarket, and just over a length third of eleven to the French colt Wessam Prince, unpenalized, in the Group 3 Benazet-Rennen at Baden-Baden. Piccolo was held by Mind Games and two more of the King's Stand Stakes field, Eveningperformance and Millstream, on Newmarket running. Mind Games had meanwhile won the Temple Stakes at Sandown in good style from Millstream and started odds on to prove himself the best five-furlong performer around. The King's Stand was run at a blistering pace on firm ground, a combination all-too-much for the trio of three-year-old Group 1 winners dropping back in distance, Fard, Hoh Magic and Eva Luna. On the other hand Piccolo, who has useful form at a mile, travelled well held up in the pack as Eveningperformance blazed away. Mind Games and Millstream were up with the leader going the better running towards the last furlong, but Piccolo and Struggler were going best. Piccolo came through strongly when shaken up and put under the whip, led inside the last and passed the post with his jockey punching the air, a length and a half in front of Struggler, two in front of third-placed Mind Games. The winning jockey was Richard Hughes, an Irishman who made a big impression in his first full season in Britain in 1995. Doing a minimum 8-5, he rode sixty-eight winners in Britain. Other big-race winners were Sergeyev (Jersey Stakes), Shikari's Son (Stewards' Cup), Posidonas (Gran Premio d'Italia), Cap Juluca (Cambridgeshire), Assessor (St Leger Italiano) and Prince of Andros (the first all-weather listed race winner).

Piccolo was able to confirm his improvement before injury intervened. Three weeks on from Royal Ascot he came out easily best of those chasing after Lake Coniston in the July Cup. Again he travelled well, kept in the rear to past halfway, and once he managed to squeeze through two furlongs out he ran on strongly without holding out hope of catching the four-length winner. These last two runs looked to give Piccolo a good chance of another Nunthorpe. By then, though, he was out of the reckoning.

Piccolo (b.c. 1991)	Warning (b 1985)	Known Fact (b 1977)	In Reality
			Tamerett
		Slightly Dangerous (b 1979)	Roberto
			Where You Lead
	Woodwind (FR) (ch 1973)	Whistling Wind (ch 1960)	Whistler
			Good As Gold
		Garden Green (b 1964)	Pinturischio
			Focal

It hasn't taken long for Warning to sire a colt good enough for stud. Piccolo was one of his first crop. The dam Woodwind had previously produced two well-above-average performers in the very useful miler Tahilla (by Moorestyle) and the useful six-furlong to one-mile filly Mummy's Favourite (by Mummy's Pet). Woodwind was useful herself, as a two-year-old over six furlongs, and is a half-sister to the Wokingham winner Le Johnstan. Piccolo in the end became pigeon-holed as a firm-ground sprinter. He was indeed particularly effective on firm and over five and six furlongs. However, if those considering using him as a stallion look more closely into his form they will find there was rather more to him than that. He got into the European Free Handicap as a two-year-old on his seven-furlong form, finished second in the German Two Thousand Guineas and was anything but disgraced on his two starts on good to soft. Compactly-built, he was a thoroughly genuine sort. *M. R. Channon*

PIE HATCH (IRE) 6 b.m. Huntingdale 132 – Small Is Beautiful (Condorcet (FR)) [1994 NR 1995 12f Jun 30] tall mare: modest handicapper (rated 50) at 4 yrs: well beaten on return: effective at 11.9f and probably stays 2m: acts on firm ground and equitrack: visored or blinkered nowadays: won novice hurdle in August. *R. J. O'Sullivan* –

PIERRE BLANCO (USA) 6 b.g. Sovereign Don (USA) – Kiss Off (USA) (Princely Native (USA)) [1994 NR 1995 a13g Feb 11] IR 17,000Y: second foal: half-brother to a winner in USA by Silent Screen: dam placed in USA: modest maiden (rated 57?) at 3 yrs for K. Prendergast in Ireland: tailed off in selling handicap at Lingfield on first flat start since: stays 1½m: tried blinkered, no improvement. *M. Bradstock* –

PIGALLE WONDER 7 br.g. Chief Singer 131 – Hi-Tech Girl 98 (Homeboy 114) [1994 33§, a43§: a8g6 a10g6 a8g a7g a10g5 a10g4 10m a7g 8.3f4 6.9g a10g a10g 1995 a8g5 a7g5 a8g6 a8g a12g4 12m a12g5 Dec 12] chunky gelding: unimpressive mover: poor handicapper: little worthwhile form in 1995: left R. O'Sullivan after sixth 7-y-o start: effective at 1m and 1¼m: acts on equitrack, best turf form on a sound surface: often blinkered: inconsistent. *N. M. Babbage* – §

PIGEON HOLE 2 b.f. (Apr 11) Green Desert (USA) 127 – Cubby Hole (Town And Country 124) [1995 5.2g May 19] neat filly: fifth foal: half-sister to 1993 1000 Guineas runner-up Niche (by Risk Me), fair 1991 2-y-o sprinter Holetown (by Prince Sabo) and 1m (at 2 yrs) and 1½m winner Alcove (by Faustus): dam half-sister to Little Wolf and Smuggler, family also of Sheikh Albadou: 9/2, around 12 lengths last of 7 in well-contested minor event at Newbury won by Marl, not knocked about when held: looked sure to do better. *R. Hannon* – p

PIKE CREEK (USA) 2 b.f. (May 2) Alwasmi (USA) 115 – Regal Heights (USA) (Forli (ARG)) [1995 8m4 Sep 5] $21,000Y: rangy filly: has scope: closely related to useful 6f (at 2 yrs) to 7.6f winner Moccasin Run (by Topsider) and several minor winners in North America: dam never ran: under 7 lengths fourth of 11 to Caribbean Quest in maiden at Leicester, staying on steadily under hands and heels: will do better. *I. A. Balding* 68 p

PILIB (IRE) 4 b.g. Salt Dome (USA) – Princess Elinor (Captain James 123) [1994 67d: 10d 8m6 10d 9.7d4 12m 1995 12g 15m6 Aug 5] angular gelding: has a round action: disappointing maiden: should stay 1½m: acts on dead ground: inconsistent: gelded. *J. Pearce* –

PILLOW TALK (IRE) 4 b.f. Taufan (USA) 119 – Concave (Connaught 130) [1994 56: 8d4 7m 6s6 7d3 7.1s 8m 8.5m* 8m4 10f3 8.5m3 7m a7g 1995 a9.4g2 a8g a8g5 a9.4g6 8.3m 9.7m2 10m 12m6 12f3 16.2m4 Aug 24] leggy, angular filly: modest performer at best: trained until after sixth start by K. Burke: below form afterwards: stays 9.7f: acts on fibresand and good to firm and dead ground: tried visored, no improvement. *S. W. Campion* 60 d

PILSUDSKI (IRE) 3 b.c. Polish Precedent (USA) 131 – Cocotte 111 (Troy 137) [1994 79: 8m6 8g 1995 9m2 12m 10g* 12f* 12d3 Sep 24] quite attractive colt: progressing physically: has a rather round action: useful and progressive performer: won H. E. Limited Duke of Cambridge Handicap at Newmarket and Tote Gold Trophy Stakes at Goodwood (held Rokeby Bowl by a neck) in July: carrying plenty of condition 2 months later, best effort when 1½ lengths third of 18 to Taufan's Melody in £46,800 event at Ascot, fair bit to do turning in, staying on strongly: stays 1½m well and will stay 1¾m: acts on firm ground and dead: bandaged behind/near-hind: held up: genuine: capable of better still and looks a good prospect for 1996. *M. R. Stoute* 104 p

PINATUBO 4 ch.g. Nicholas Bill 125 – Hi-Hunsley 82 (Swing Easy (USA) 126) [1994 40: 8.2f 6g 7m 6m 6f 8.2m6 8.1g 9s4 9.7d 8.1g4 1995 a8.5g Feb 4] small, leggy gelding: poor maiden plater: tailed off only start for new stable: stays 9f: acts on good to firm ground and soft: blinkered (well beaten) fifth 3-y-o outing. *M. C. Pipe* –

PINE ESSENCE (USA) 4 ch.f. Green Forest (USA) 134 – Paradise Coffee 81 (Sharpo 132) [1994 64: 8m^3 8.1s^4 7g^3 8.2d 1995 8m^4 8.3f 10f* 10f 10m* 12.1g 10.8g^5 10f 10f^6 a10g^5 a10g^6 Dec 18] lengthy filly: modest performer: won claimer at Redcar in June and seller at Pontefract (sweating and edgy, reluctant to jump off initially, then hung left across rivals, sold out of Mrs M. Reveley's stable 6,200 gns) in August: probably stays 1½m: possibly needs a sound surface: has been early to post. *J. L. Eyre* — 57 d

PINE NEEDLE 2 ch.f. (Mar 15) Kris 135 – Fanny's Cove 89 (Mill Reef (USA) 141) [1995 8m^5 8.2d* 8m^5 Oct 13] unfurnished filly: closely related to smart 1¼m and 11.9f winner Nibbs Point (by Sure Blade) and half-sister to several winners, including useful 1988 2-y-o 7f and 1m winner Prince Ibrahim (by Be My Guest): dam won at 1¼m on only start: won 11-runner maiden at Nottingham in September by a length from Ailesbury Hill, staying on very well: held up and never threatened when fifth of 12 to Mystic Knight in nursery at Newmarket following month: will be suited by a thorough test of stamina: acts on dead ground. *D. Morley* — 79

PINE RIDGE LAD (IRE) 5 gr.g. Taufan (USA) 119 – Rosserk (Roan Rocket 128) [1994 62, a67: 5d^4 6f 7m^2 7m 6.9m^6 a6g^2 7g 6g^2 7g 7g^4 a7g 8f^4 8.5g 8g 1995 a6g* a7g* a7g 6v 6d^6 7m^2 8.5m 7m 6g^3 6m 6.9f* 7f^3 7m^5 a7g^3 a8.5g^4 7g 8d^6 9f 8m 8f^2 8.1s^5 a8g* a9.4g^2 Dec 9] good-topped gelding: fair performer, best on all-weather: won 2 claimers at Southwell early in year, handicap at Carlisle in June and another claimer at Southwell in November: effective at 6f to 9.4f: goes well on the all-weather, and acts on any going on turf: visored twice as 4-y-o: often used to be blinkered, not at 5 yrs. *J. L. Eyre* — 58 a75

PING-PONG BALL 2 b.f. (Apr 21) Statoblest 120 – Desert Ditty 67 (Green Desert (USA) 127) [1995 5m Apr 17] 2,600Y: small filly: first foal: dam 6.1f winner out of useful 6f and 7f winner Royal Loft: 25/1 and bit backward, well behind from halfway in median auction maiden at Warwick. *T. R. Watson* — –

PINK BRIEF (IRE) 4 b.f. Ela-Mana-Mou 132 – Tumble Dale 88§ (Tumble Wind (USA)) [1994 71d: 10s 8.1g^2 8m^3 10g* 12g 7d a10g a10g a13g a16g a11g 1995 9.7d 10.8d^3 10m 10.8g Jun 7] leggy filly: modest performer: respectable effort for new stable in 1995 only when third of 15 in handicap at Warwick in April: stays 10.8f: acts on good to firm and dead ground, and on equitrack: blinkered (out of form) penultimate 3-y-o start: normally held up. *M. J. Ryan* — 63

PINKERTON POLKA 3 b.f. Shareef Dancer (USA) 135 – Holy Day 82 (Sallust 134) [1994 NR 1995 8g 7m 10d 8d 8m 8g 11.8f^4 12.1s Nov 2] 8,000Y, resold 8,500Y: strong filly: fifth living foal: half-sister to 2 winners, including 4-y-o 7f winner Passion Sunday (by Bairn): dam best at 2 yrs, when 5f winner: signs of only a little ability in varied company. *C. E. Brittain* — –

PINKERTON'S PAL 4 ch.g. Dominion 123 – White Domino 67 (Sharpen Up 127) [1994 105?: 6f^5 8.5m^2 7m 7f 7m 7g^6 9m^4 10g 1995 6m 7.9g^3 8.5m^5 7.1m^3 7.6m 8f Jul 27] smallish, close-coupled gelding: useful performer on his day: best efforts — 97

Tote Gold Trophy Stakes (Handicap), Goodwood—
a neck will separate them at the line as Pilsudski and Rokeby Bowl finish much the strongest

at 4 yrs when third in rated stakes at York and Haydock: stays 9f: acts on firm ground, yet to race on a soft surface: blinkered (ran badly) sixth 3-y-o outing: held up: inconsistent: has been gelded. *C. E. Brittain*

PINK PETAL 3 gr.f. Northern Game – Gratclo 65 (Belfort (FR) 89) [1994 –: a7g a8.5g a5g⁶ 1995 a8g a6g 10g⁶ 10.8m 8.1m a12g Jul 22] leggy filly: little worthwhile form: pulled hard fourth and fifth 3-y-o starts. *C. J. Hill* –

PINOCCHIO BOY (IRE) 2 b.c. (Apr 7) Soviet Lad (USA) 94 – Trust Sally 65 (Sallust 134) [1995 5m 5f 6m³ 6g³ 6.9f* 7.1m 8m a7g* 7g³ Sep 20] 6,000Y: neat colt: half-brother to several winners, including 6f winner Reasonable Kid (by Reasonable): dam won 5f seller: won sellers at Folkestone in August and Wolverhampton in September: better suited by 7f than shorter: sold 6,000 gns Newmarket Autumn Sales: sent to France. *B. J. Meehan* 55 a61

PINZON (USA) 3 ch.c. El Gran Senor (USA) 136 – Chalfont Place (USA) (Little Current (USA)) [1994 NR 1995 8g³ 7m² 7.3m³ 8.1g³ May 29] angular colt: closely related to 1988 2-y-o 5f winner Twain Harte (by Northern Jove) and half-brother to several minor winners: dam, winner at up to 9f in USA, is sister to high-class 7f/1m performer Chalon: started favourite when placed on all 4 starts in maidens, leading over 1f out until near finish at Chepstow final one: should stay beyond 8.1f: has raced only on a sound surface: sent to USA and has joined H. M. Tesher. *P. W. Chapple-Hyam* 80

PIONEER PRINCESS 3 b. or br.f. Prince Sabo 123 – Bloom of Youth (IRE) (Last Tycoon 131) [1994 47: 5d⁵ 5v⁶ 7g 1995 9.7m⁶ 10g 9.7g 8d 8.2m Jun 26] lengthy filly: poor maiden: well beaten after reappearance: stays 9.7f: blinkered (well beaten) fifth 3-y-o start: has worn dropped noseband: hurdling with P. J. Hobbs. *M. J. Ryan* 49 d

PIPE MAJOR (IRE) 3 b.c. Tirol 127 – Annsfield Lady (Red Sunset 120) [1994 101p: 6f* 6m⁴ 7g² 8g* 1995 8m⁴ 10.4g⁴ 7m* 7m⁴ Jul 24] 119

The title 'Best Horse in the North' is likely to remain in the Mark Johnston yard for the foreseeable future, but another Middleham-trained animal provided some opposition in 1995. Pat Haslam's three-year-old colt Pipe Major belied odds of 50/1 on his reappearance to finish fourth of eleven in the Two Thousand Guineas. He put up a really bold show as well, not creeping unnoticed into the frame late on like an also-ran, but travelling close to the pace and striking for home himself approaching the two-furlong marker. In the end, Pennekamp and Celtic Swing beat him by four lengths. Pipe Major's two-year-old form did not give him much of a chance, if any, in the Guineas, although he had looked a thoroughly likeable individual, winning a York maiden at 33/1 before making the frame in the Coventry

Van Geest Criterion Stakes, Newmarket—
a deserved pattern success for Pipe Major (rails) who pulls clear with Prince of India

Lord Scarsdale's "Pipe Major"

Stakes and Laurent-Perrier Champagne Stakes, finishing that year on a winning note with a most tenacious defeat of Chief Burundi in a minor event at Newmarket. Besides his courage, that last performance had indicated that he should stay beyond a mile. A step up in distance duly awaited him on his second start of 1995, in the Dante at York, but Pipe Major failed to reproduce his Guineas form in coming fourth of eight to Classic Cliche. Having made most of the running, it was clear that he would not win as soon as he was challenged over three furlongs out. It was nonetheless hard not to conclude that the trip had been too far. Pipe Major was dropped back to seven furlongs for his two remaining races. In the first of them, the Group 3 Van Geest Criterion Stakes at Newmarket, he was the clear pick on form. Presumably explaining the step down in class, Haslam reflected that 'It's a bit like owning a greyhound—sometimes you have to let them kill a rabbit' after Pipe Major had administered the coup de grace to Prince of India and six others. The greyhound proved less lethal and the rabbits more inbued with the spirit of self-preservation when Pipe Major turned up next in the Beeswing Stakes at Newcastle; racing away from the favoured stand rail did not help as he managed only fourth of seven.

Pipe Major (IRE) (b.c. 1992)	Tirol (br 1987)	Thatching (b 1975)	Thatch
			Abella
		Alpine Niece (b 1972)	Great Nephew
			Fragrant Morn
	Annsfield Lady (b 1985)	Red Sunset (b 1979)	Red God
			Centre Piece
		Petit Eclair (ch 1973)	Major Portion
			Cafe Au Lait

The good-topped colt Pipe Major impresses in appearance and has a powerful round action. He looks best at seven furlongs to a mile, won on firm ground on his debut and has yet to race on a soft surface. A game individual, he takes up a prominent position in his races. At 33,000 guineas, Pipe Major was the joint-sixth-highest-priced yearling from the first crop of Tirol whose encouraging start at stud is mentioned in connection with Miss Tahiti. Pipe Major comes from a solid winner-producing family. Third dam Cafe Au Lait had ten winners from fourteen foals of racing age, including the 1988 Prix Foy winner Beeshi and the 1985 and 1986 Magnet Cup winner Chaumiere. The latter took up a stud place in Bahrain. Cafe Au Lait and her daughter Petit Eclair were both fairly useful winners at two and three years for Doug Smith and stayed middle distances. Annsfield Lady registered a hat-trick of handicap wins (two at Dundalk, one at Ballinrobe) in less than four weeks for P. J. Finn, at between nine furlongs and a mile and a quarter. Pipe Major is her third foal, following Bitter's End (by Waajib), who won an Epsom maiden over seven furlongs, and Alfred The Bold (by Al Hareb) who was runner-up on one of his two runs in Ireland; the former has since won races in the US and the latter, renamed Wang Tak Supreme, has done so in Hong Kong. Annsfield Lady's fourth foal is Give Me A Ring (by Be My Guest) who has shown promise for Chris Thornton. He should win races in 1996, when Pipe Major too will again be in training. *P. C. Haslam*

PIPERS GLEN 3 ch.g. Domynsky 110 – Linanhot 46 (Hot Spark 126) [1994 55: 5.9m 6m 5.9f^3 7d^6 8g^5 1995 8g^5 8.1m 6.9f Jun 29] workmanlike gelding: disappointing maiden. *C. Parker* –

PIP'S DREAM 4 b.f. Glint of Gold 128 – Arabian Rose (USA) (Lyphard (USA) 132) [1994 –: 11.8s^3 10v^3 14.1m 8g 12g 12.1g 1995 a16g 12m 11.8m^2 9.7g^4 10f* 12m^3 a10g Dec 19] good-topped filly: poor handicapper: won maiden handicap at Salisbury in June: stays 1½m: acts on any going. *M. J. Ryan* 42

PIQUANT 8 b. or br.g. Sharpo 132 – Asnoura (MOR) (Asandre (FR)) [1994 76, a81: a8g^2 a9.4g 8m 8g 8f^3 8f^2 8.1m a8g* 1995 7.6m^5 8m^6 8m^3 9m^4 8.1m 8f* 8m^6 8f^4 Oct 24] small, stocky gelding: carries condition: fair handicapper: won at Bath in July: effective at 7f and 1m: acts on equitrack and any turf going: visored (below form) 3 times: effective held up or ridden from front: inconsistent. *Lord Huntingdon* 69 a–

PIRATES GOLD (IRE) 5 ch.g. Vaigly Great 127 – Hemline 77 (Sharpo 132) [1994 53: 8.3g^6 7f^4 6g 7d a7g a10g^5 1995 a7g a7g^4 a8g a7g^4 8m^5 7f^3 8m 7m^3 6m^4 6f^5 6f^3 6f^2 Jul 31] smallish gelding: modest handicapper: ran only at Lingfield and Brighton at 5 yrs: finds 6f a bare minimum, and probably stays 1¼m: acts on firm ground, dead and all-weather surfaces: sometimes gets behind: blinkered once (soundly beaten) at 4 yrs: inconsistent. *J. White* 51

PISTOL (IRE) 5 ch.g. Glenstal (USA) 118 – First Wind (Windjammer (USA)) [1994 64: 6m^6 6s 5.7g^3 7g 6m^5 7g^3 7.1m 10g^3 10m^4 9.7g* 11.5d^3 14.4g^5 11.9g^4 1995 8m 10.8m 8m^2 8m^4 10g 9.7m* 11.9m^5 10f Jun 23] workmanlike gelding: fair handicapper: won at Folkestone in May: effective at 1m and stays 11.5f: acts on good to firm and dead ground: blinkered (ran poorly on equitrack) once as 2-y-o: sometimes early to post: has been bandaged behind: not the easiest of rides and sometimes finds little: inconsistent. *C. A. Horgan* 65

PISTOL RIVER (IRE) 5 b.g. Simply Great (FR) 122 – Pampala (Bold Lad (IRE) 133) [1994 NR 1995 16.2d 18m Oct 14] small, angular gelding: useful performer (rated 99) at 3 yrs for R. Hannon, but one to treat with caution over hurdles in 1994/5: stayed on past beaten horses in £14,500 handicap at Ascot and Cesarewitch at Newmarket (mulish to post, ninth of 21 to Old Red) in 1995: stays 2¼m: best effort in 1995 on top-of-the-ground, but better in 1993 with give: visored (except reappearance) since penultimate 3-y-o start: often looks a hard ride. *N. J. H. Walker* 84

PISTOLS AT DAWN (USA) 5 b.g. Al Nasr (FR) 126 – Cannon Run (USA) (Cannonade (USA)) [1994 –: 13.3s 12g 11.6m^4 11.6m 12d 11.4d 1995 a12g* a12g^3 a16g^6 a12g* a12g^4 a12g^4 a12g^2 a12g* Dec 12] lengthy gelding: poor mover: fair handicapper: won in May, June (weak claimer) and December (gamely), all at Wolverhampton: suited by middle distances: acts on good to firm and soft ground and on fibresand: blinkered (below form) twice. *B. J. Meehan* 65

PITCROY 3 ch.f. Unfuwain (USA) 131 – Reuval 102 (Sharpen Up 127) [1994 72p: 7g^2 1995 10m* 11.5f^4 10m^6 10.1g^6 10g^4 10m^6 Oct 12] tall, leggy, workmanlike 99 filly: useful performer: won maiden at Sandown in April: easily best efforts when fourth in small fields for listed race at Lingfield (held up and tending to carry head high) and Sun Chariot Stakes at Newmarket (sweating and edgy, attended by 2 handlers in paddock) in September: has shown her form at 11.5f, but should prove at least as effective over shorter: yet to race on a soft surface. *J. R. Fanshawe*

PITTER PATTER 3 b.f. Shareef Dancer (USA) 135 – Rain Date (USA) (Blushing Groom (FR) 131) [1994 49: 7s^{6} 1995 10.1g 10.3g May 29] workmanlike filly: well beaten in maidens at Newcastle and Doncaster (mulish to post) for new stable: sold 3,000 gns Newmarket December Sales. *Mrs N. Macauley* –

PIVOTAL 2 ch.c. (Jan 19) Polar Falcon (USA) 126 – Fearless Revival 102 (Cozzene (USA)) [1995 6d 6m* 5m* Nov 6] strong, angular, good sort: second foal: half-brother to 3-y-o 1m winner Brave Revival (by Dancing Brave): dam, 2-y-o 6f and 7f who winner stayed 1¼m, daughter of very good Italian filly Stufida: impressive winner of maiden at Newcastle in October (stormed ahead well inside last 1f out to beat Domak Amaam 2½ lengths, pair clear) and minor event at Folkestone week later (easily, by 4 lengths from Smithereens): will stay 7f: very much one to follow as 3-y-o. *Sir Mark Prescott* 100 P

PLACID-WARRIOR 5 bl.h. Battle Hymn 103 – Full of Love (Full of Hope 125) [1994 NR 1995 a12g a14g Mar 3] second foal: dam, plater, won over hurdles: no sign of ability. *J. C. McConnochie* –

PLAIN SAILING (FR) 5 b.g. Slip Anchor 136 – Lassalia (Sallust 134) [1994 NR 1995 15.8g^{6} Jun 2] sturdy gelding: no worthwhile form on flat: sold 1,500 gns Doncaster July Sales, 1,150 gns Ascot August Sales: has worn tongue strap and blinkers. *Martyn Meade* –

PLATINI (IRE) 4 b.g. Gallic League 119 – Tardy (USA) (Tom Rolfe) [1994 NR 1995 10d 11.8m^{3} 11.6m 12d Sep 15] good-topped gelding: poor maiden: stays 11.8f: best effort on good ground: visored last 2 starts: modest winning hurdler. *G. B. Balding* 46

PLAUSILIUM 2 b.c. (Mar 20) Ilium 121 – Pause For Applause 57 (Rolfe (USA) 77) [1995 5.1m 7f^{4} a7g 6.9f Aug 15] strong, lengthy colt: poor mover: third foal: dam 1¼m and 1½m winner: well beaten in sellers and a claimer: blinkered on final start. *W. G. M. Turner* –

PLAYING TRICKS 4 b.f. Elegant Air 119 – Magic Kingdom 76 (Kings Lake (USA) 133) [1994 48d: a10g^{4} a8g^{6} a10g 10m^{6} 14.1m 10f 10m^{4} 8f 1995 a10g a14.8g^{5} Feb 4] sturdy filly: modest maiden at best: tailed off for new stable in 1995. *P. D. Evans* –

PLAYMAKER 2 b.g. (Mar 12) Primo Dominie 121 – Salacious (Sallust 134) [1995 5d* 5d^{5} 6f^{2} 6g^{3} 5m^{6} Oct 27] 35,000Y: workmanlike, rather unfurnished gelding: has scope: sixth living foal: half-brother to 1990 2-y-o 6f and 7f winner Highland Spirit (by Scottish Reel) and a winner in USA: dam Irish 7f and 9f winner: made all in 16-runner maiden at Ripon in April: best subsequent effort (after 3-month absence) when third of 13 to Lunar Mist in nursery at Haydock in September: stays 6f: best efforts on an easy surface (looked ill at ease on firm ground third start). *J. Berry* 78

PLEADING 2 b.c. (Apr 18) Never So Bold 135 – Ask Mama 83 (Mummy's Pet 125) [1995 6d 6d^{4} Oct 19] 9,400Y: good-topped colt: has scope: fifth foal: half-brother to 1992 2-y-o 7f winner Girl At The Gate (by Formidable): dam 1¼m winner: 1½ lengths fourth of 20, prominent throughout, to Fly Tip in maiden at Newbury: will improve again. *H. Candy* 77 p

PLEASANT MEMORIES 3 b.f. Danehill (USA) 126 – Julip 99 (Track Spare 125) [1994 NR 1995 a8g^{2} a9.4g^{3} 8g 8.3f* Aug 3] 19,000F: angular filly: half-sister to several winners, notably Belmont Stakes runner-up My Memoirs (by Don't Forget Me), also 6f and 7f winner at 2 yrs: dam, 2-y-o 7f winner who stayed 1¼m, from good family: modest performer: best effort when making all in 4-runner maiden handicap at Hamilton in August: stays 8.3f: acts on firm ground and the all-weather: slowly away first 2 starts: sold 5,500 gns Newmarket December Sales. *Lord Huntingdon* 63

PLEASANT SURPRISE 2 b.c. (Feb 6) Cadeaux Genereux 131 – Quiet Week-End 99 (Town And Country 124) [1995 6g^{6} 7.5g^{2} 7.5m^{2} 7.5m* 7d Sep 26] 84 p

68,000Y: leggy, quite attractive colt: second foal: half-brother to 3-y-o 1m winner Tranquillity (by Night Shift): dam, 2-y-o 6f and 7f winner later successful in USA, half-sister to Lemon Souffle: progressive colt: won maiden at Beverley in August: creditable effort when mid-division in 30-runner valuable sales race at Newmarket won by Rio Duvida final start: should progress again at 1m+. *M. Johnston*

PLEASE SUZANNE 2 b.f. (Apr 7) Cadeaux Genereux 131 – Aquaglow 84 (Caerleon (USA) 132) [1995 7m* 7d^2 6d^3 Sep 23] angular filly: third foal: half-sister to a winning sprinter in Italy by Kalaglow: dam 7f and 1m winner: won maiden at Lingfield in September: always close up and kept on well when second to Wild Rumour in minor event at Newbury and when third of 8 to Polska in Blue Seal Stakes at Ascot: will stay beyond 7f. *R. Hannon* — 93

PLEASURE BEACH 3 br.c. Pharly (FR) 130 – Teacher's Game 64 (Mummy's Game 120) [1994 ?, a71: 5m a5g 7m^5 a7g* 6g a6g^2 6m a7g^2 a7g^4 a7g^2 a6g^4 1995 a6g^3 Jan 12] good-bodied colt: bad mover: fair performer on the all-weather: effective at 6f, and should stay 1m: acts on the all-weather, little worthwhile form on turf: tried blinkered and visored: sold 7,200 gns Newmarket July Sales: sent to Macau. *W. A. O'Gorman* — – a67

PLEASURELAND (IRE) 2 ch.c. (Feb 21) Don't Forget Me 127 – Elminya (IRE) (Sure Blade (USA) 130) [1995 a7g^5 7d 6.9g Oct 16] 15,000Y: sturdy colt: first foal: dam unraced half-sister to very smart racemare Ruby Tiger (by Ahonoora): never-dangerous seventh to Centre Stalls in maiden at Salisbury on second outing: rather disappointing in maiden auction at Folkestone following month: will stay beyond 7f. *P. J. Makin* — 61

PLEASURE TIME 2 ch.c. (Apr 4) Clantime 101 – First Experience 58 (Le Johnstan 123) [1995 5g^4 5d^5 5m^3 5f* 5g^5 5g 5m^5 5m* 5m^2 5m^2 5m 5g Sep 28] 8,200Y: leggy, good-topped colt: fifth foal: dam, 5f winner, sister to smart 1982 2-y-o 5f winner Cat O'Nine Tails: won median auction maiden at Redcar in May and nursery at Haydock in August: speedy, and will prove best at 5f: acts on firm ground: blinkered last 6 outings: gave trouble in stalls final start. *C. Smith* — 72

PLEASURE TRICK (USA) 4 br.g. Clever Trick (USA) – Pleasure Garden (USA) (Foolish Pleasure (USA)) [1994 70: 7m^4 8m^4 8.1g^4 7.1m^2 7f* 7.6g^5 7m^6 7g* 7d 8.9d 7d 1995 8m 9f 8m* 8.5m^5 8g^4 Sep 2] good-quartered gelding: modest performer: won claimer at Pontefract in July: well below form otherwise in 1995: stays 1m: acts on firm ground, may be unsuited by a soft surface: usually races prominently: visored (ran creditably) once as 3-y-o: modest hurdler, twice successful in October. *N. Tinkler* — 62

PLEIN GAZ (FR) 2 b.c. (Apr 14) Lesotho (USA) 118 – Gazzara (USA) (Irish River (FR) 131) [1995 5g* 5d^6 5.5g* 6g* 6d^2 6d 6g* 7g^3 6g^5 7.5m 6s* 6g^6 6d^2 6d a7g^2 Dec 14] 35,000 francs Y: fourth foal: dam French maiden out of Oaks second Bonnie Isle: Belgian-trained colt: won 3 claimers (first of them in April) and 2 minor events in French Provinces when trained in France first 11 starts, claimed out of J. P. Totain's stable (150,011 francs) after seventh one and N. Clement's (87,999 francs) after final one: appeared to run well when sevenh of 9 in listed race at Evry on penultimate start: gives impression will prove best short of 7f: acts on soft ground fair effort on equitrack: front runner. *Andre Hermans, Belgium* — 82 ? a72

PLINTH 4 b.g. Dowsing (USA) 124 – Pedestal (High Line 125) [1994 53, a59: a10g^5 a10g* a10g^2 10.3g 12s^6 11.6g^3 10g^5 11.6m^3 10m 10s 1995 10m^5 10g* 9.7m^4 10m^2 10.2h^3 10.3g^4 10f^2 Aug 2] workmanlike gelding: modest handicapper: won at Lingfield in May: effective at 1¼m and 11.6f: acts on hard ground and equitrack: blinkered once, usually visored: often a front runner. *N. A. Graham* — 60

PLUCKY PET 3 br.f. Petong 126 – Lucky Flinders 77 (Free State 125) [1994 50?: 5m 6m 5d 7d 6m a6g 1995 a7g a8g a10g Feb 11] compact filly: poor maiden: well beaten in 1995: sold 1,000 gns Ascot February Sales. *C. J. Benstead* — –

PLUM DENNIS 4 b.g. Robellino (USA) 127 – Kaleidophone 73 (Kalaglow 132) [1994 39: 8.2g 10g 10.9g^4 15d^3 15s 1995 11.1g 14.1m a7g 10m Jul 11] leggy gelding: poor maiden: no form in 1995. *N. Bycroft* — –

PLUM FIRST 5 b.h. Nomination 125 – Plum Bold 83 (Be My Guest (USA) 126) [1994 61, a–: a6g 6m 7d 6g^4 8m 7.5m^6 6f 5f^4 6f^5 6m* 6f 6f^6 6f 6m^4 6f 5f^4 a6g a6g 6m^2 6g 6.1s 1995 a6g^4 6g^5 6d 6g^5 5m* 6g 6f* 7g 5f^3 5m 5.9f 6m^3 6m^6 6m^6 6m^4 — 64 a47

5m^2 6m 6m 6.1d Sep 19] lengthy, workmanlike horse: has a round action: modest performer: won apprentice race at Pontefract in April and minor event at Warwick in May: suited by sprint distances: acts on any turf ground, seemingly not at his best on the all-weather: often bandaged: effective visored/blinkered or not: tends to hang left. *L. R. Lloyd-James*

PODDINGTON 4 b.g. Crofthall 110 – Bold Gift 61 (Persian Bold 123) [1994 NR 1995 9m^3 Jul 15] sixth foal: half-brother to 2 winners, including 7f and 1m winner Mrs Gates (by Good Times): dam, ran only at 2 yrs, stayed 7f: 4 lengths third of 10 to Quandary in maiden at Lingfield, always prominent: looked likely to improve. *R. Akehurst* 78 p

POETIC DANCE (USA) 2 ch.c. (Mar 31) Seattle Dancer (USA) 119 – French Poem (USA) (Sharpen Up 127) [1995 7f 7d Sep 27] sturdy, lengthy colt: seventh foal: half-brother to 4 winners, including Fusion (by Lyphard's Wish) and French Senor (by El Gran Senor), 7f winners here: dam French 5f winner: behind in maidens at Doncaster and Salisbury: likely to do better. *J. L. Dunlop* – p

POETRY (IRE) 2 gr.f. (Feb 15) Treasure Kay 114 – Silver Heart (Yankee Gold 115) [1995 6.9g^3 Oct 16] IR 6,000Y: sister to a poor Irish maiden and half-sister to 2 winners, including useful Irish 1m to 1¼m winner Winning Heart (by Horage): dam Irish 7f to 9f winner: 33/1, beaten 2 short heads behind Ageeb in maiden auction at Folkestone, keeping on well: should improve. *M. H. Tompkins* 66 p

POINTER 3 b.c. Reference Point 139 – Greenhill Lass (Upper Case (USA)) [1994 –p: 7g 1995 10d Oct 19] tall colt: showed promise only 2-y-o start for P. Cole: sold approx £24,500 in Dubai in November 1994: resold only 1,300 gns Newmarket July (1995) Sales: soundly beaten in Newbury maiden. *Mrs P. N. Dutfield* –

POLAR CHAMP 2 b.g. (Feb 28) Polar Falcon (USA) 126 – Ceramic (USA) (Raja Baba (USA)) [1995 7m Aug 25] leggy gelding: fifth foal: half-brother to 1993 2-y-o 6f winner Little Beaut and 5f and 7f winner Sebosan (both by Prince Sabo) and a winner in Sweden: dam (ran once in Ireland) granddaughter of top-class 4.5f to 9f winner Furl Sail: 25/1, backward and green, last of 19 in maiden at Newmarket. *S. P. C. Woods* –

POLAR ECLIPSE 2 ch.c. (Feb 10) Polar Falcon (USA) 126 – Princess Zepoli 61 (Persepolis (FR) 127) [1995 7.1d* 10m^3 Oct 28] rangy, unfurnished colt: third foal: half-brother to 3-y-o Princess Sadie (by Shavian), 5f winner at 2 yrs: dam, stayed 9f, granddaughter of Roussalka: made all in 9-runner maiden at Haydock, beating Alessandra comfortably by 1¾ lengths, pair well clear: 5 lengths third of 6 to Gentilhomme in listed race at Newmarket later in month, racing keenly then keeping on at same pace: stays 1¼m: likely to improve further. *M. Johnston* 90 p

POLARIS FLIGHT (USA) 2 b.c. (Mar 4) Northern Flagship (USA) 96 – Anytimeatall (USA) (It's Freezing (USA) 122) [1995 5m* 5f^3 6g* 6m* 7g^2 10g* 8g^3 Nov 8] 112

Polaris Flight provided one of his stable's five Group 1 victories in 1995. Four of them were achieved on foreign soil—by Prince Arthur in the Premio Parioli, Spectrum in the Irish Two Thousand Guineas, Court of Honour in the Gran Premio del Jockey Club and Polaris Flight in the Criterium de Saint-Cloud. The victory of Polaris Flight went almost unnoticed as the same weekend's Breeders' Cup meeting at Belmont Park stole the headlines, but it secured for Peter Chapple-Hyam the distinction of being the British-based trainer who earned most prize-money abroad in 1995. According to figures produced by the International Racing Bureau, British-trained horses won a total of £7,319,400 on foreign soil, short of the record £8,613,467 earned in 1990 but £328,734 more than 1994, with Chapple-Hyam (£855,629) and Saeed bin Suroor (£804,539) leading the way. France took over from Italy as the happiest hunting ground for British challengers, Polaris Flight's Criterium de Saint-Cloud victory being one of thirty-eight British successes and ninety-four placed efforts in that country, which yielded a total of £2,903,928.

The last three races of Polaris Flight's season were all abroad but he received a good grounding at home before setting off on his travels. He looked a useful prospect when making a winning debut, backed down to odds on, in a maiden auction event at Leicester in June and was in the field for the Windsor Castle Stakes at Royal Ascot the following week. He ran well to finish third to Kuantan and Applaud, taking the eye as an individual and running as if he'd be suited by a step up to six furlongs.

Richmond Stakes, Goodwood—long-time leader Mubhij (right) is caught by Polaris Flight

Polaris Flight won both his remaining races in Britain, the listed Doncaster Bloodstock Sales Rose Bowl Stakes and the Group 2 Richmond Stakes, both over six. He upset the odds laid on Kahir Almaydan in a three-horse race at Newbury and more than confirmed the form with that horse when just getting the better of Mubhij at Goodwood with Kahir Almaydan in third (Kuantan was a well-beaten favourite). Polaris Flight was progressing well and was stepped up to Group 1 company in the National Stakes at the Curragh in mid-September when he was one of three British-trained challengers including the odds-on favourite Danehill Dancer. Peter Chapple-Hyam regarded Polaris Flight at the time as 'a little bit better than Woodborough', who had run Danehill Dancer to a neck in the Heinz 57 Phoenix Stakes the previous month. Polaris Flight went down by a length and a half to

Criterium de Saint-Cloud—in different colours,
Polaris Flight takes this Group 1 from Ragmar (No. 2) at the end of a slowly-run race

Danehill Dancer, staying on well after being slightly hampered approaching the final furlong. After missing the Grand Criterium, France's most prestigious two-year-old event, because of coughing, Polaris Flight was next seen out in the Criterium de Saint-Cloud over a mile and a quarter at the end of October. He started second favourite in a field of five to the Fabre-trained Quorum, but it was one of the outsiders, Ragmar, who proved the toughest nut to crack. Polaris Flight led from early in the straight and gamely held off Ragmar by a short head in a tight finish in which barely a length and a half separated Polaris Flight from Quorum in fifth. Polaris Flight ran his only disappointing race on his final start, in the Gran Criterium at Milan in November, when, starting long odds on, he could manage only third to home-trained Glory of Dancer and the Washington Singer third Line Dancer.

Polaris Flight (USA) (b.c. Mar 1, 1993)	Northern Flagship (USA) (b 1986)	Northern Dancer (b 1961)	Nearctic
			Natalma
		Native Partner (b 1966)	Raise A Native
			Dinner Partner
	Anytimeatall (USA) (b 1983)	It's Freezing (ch 1972)	TV Commercial
			Articana
		Vitesse (b 1969)	Bold Ruler
			Vit Reina

Polaris Flight, a strong, good sort with plenty of scope, cost 70,000 dollars as a foal, a sum which probably owed more to his looks than his pedigree. His sire Northern Flagship, a full brother to the top sprinter-miler Adjal, showed only fairly useful form in middle-distance maidens, looking one-paced, and was retired to stud in Kentucky at a fee of only 2,000 dollars. Polaris Flight's dam Anytimeatall (whose second reported foal he is) and his grandam Vitesse didn't reach the racecourse and the immediate family has produced only minor stakes winners at best in North America. Polaris Flight's great-grandam Vit Reina is Argentinian, winner of the important Gran Premio Carlos Pellegrini over fifteen furlongs in that country, as well as of another major race over the same trip in Uruguay, performances which led to her being imported into the States. Polaris Flight will stay a mile and a half and looks a likely type at this stage for the Derby Italiano, a race won by his stable with White Muzzle in 1993. Polaris Flight, who has worn bandages behind, has yet to race on a soft surface but acts on any other. *P. W. Chapple-Hyam*

POLAR LIGHTS (CAN) 2 b.c. (Apr 8) Trempolino (USA) 135 – Quickshine (USA) (The Minstrel (CAN) 135) [1995 7g^5 10g* Nov 20] 820,000 francs Y: second foal: half-brother to Irish 1¼m winner Swings 'N' Things (by Shernazar): dam Irish maiden placed over 7f/1m: French colt: won 13-runner minor event at Saint-Cloud by neck from Le Tourron in November: will stay beyond 1¼m: sure to improve again. *A. Fabre, France* — 109 p

POLAR PRINCE (IRE) 2 b.c. (Apr 23) Distinctly North (USA) 115 – Staff Approved 94 (Teenoso (USA) 135) [1995 7g^5 7m^5 7.1m^2 7.1g* 8m Oct 13] 20,000Y: robust, lengthy colt: has scope: good mover: second foal: dam, 1m winner at 2 yrs who should have stayed middle distances, daughter of Klairlone, placed in Irish 1000 Guineas and Irish Oaks: won 16-runner maiden at Haydock in September by 1¾ lengths from Stellar Line, racing keenly and keeping on gamely: held up (for first time) and never placed to challenge, hampered 2f out, when tenth of 12 in nursery at Newmarket in October: should be at least as effective at 1m as 7f: remains capable of better. *M. A. Jarvis* — 91 p

POLAR QUEEN 3 b.f. Polish Precedent (USA) 131 – Rain Date (Rainbow Quest (USA) 134) [1994 NR 1995 7f* 9d Sep 16] lengthy, deep-girthed filly: first foal: dam daughter of Roussalka, a half-sister to Oh So Sharp: weak 5/1-shot and green, made winning debut in 13-runner maiden at Salisbury in August, leading near finish: ran badly in well-contested minor event at Newbury over 5 weeks later, giving impression something amiss. *J. H. M. Gosden* — 76 +

POLAR REFRAIN 2 ch.f. (Mar 10) Polar Falcon (USA) 126 – Cut No Ice 97 (Great Nephew 126) [1995 5d^3 5s 5f Oct 14] 24,000Y: third foal: half-sister to useful 3-y-o sprinter Subzero (by Thatching): dam, stayed 1¼m, half-sister to useful middle-distance performer Gillson: third of 11 to Angel Chimes in maiden at Beverley, finishing well from off very strong pace: never a threat in similar events at Haydock (again slowly away) and Catterick last 2 starts: will be suited by 6f+. *Mrs J. R. Ramsden* — 54

POLAR SPIRIT 2 ch.f. (Apr 18) Polar Falcon (USA) 126 – Spirit of India (Indian King (USA) 128) [1995 7g 8m* a8.5g^2 Nov 13] 6,000F: lengthy filly: has scope: first live foal: dam unraced: fitted with rope halter, won seller at Newmarket in October: creditable second in Wolverhampton nursery final start: stays 1m: sold 5,000 gns Newmarket December Sales. *W. J. Haggas* — 60

POLHYMNIA 4 br.f. Chief Singer 131 – Six Ashes (Bruni 132) [1994 32: 8.2s 8.1g^6 1995 a5g 7f Oct 25] workmanlike filly: poor maiden plater: visored (most reluctant to post, tailed off) second 4-y-o start. *G. C. Bravery* — –

POLIGLOTE 3 b.c. Sadler's Wells (USA) 132 – Alexandrie (USA) 114 (Val de L'Orne (FR) 133) [1994 115p: 8g^3 8d* 9d* 10s* 1995 11m^3 12m^2 12g^2 10m^5 12d^2 12g Oct 15] — 121

A variety of riding tactics all failed to secure a victory in 1995 for the good-class but hard-pulling Poliglote. He finished runner-up three times, narrowly beaten on each. Poliglote had ended 1994 one of the top ten two-year-olds in Europe after winning the last three of his four starts, the last two of them being the Prix de Conde and Criterium de Saint-Cloud, in both of which he had made all the running. That was not supposed to happen at Saint-Cloud, but his pacemaker had swerved leaving the stalls and unseated its rider. When Poliglote did so well without him he became a leading candidate for the Prix du Jockey-Club the following June. He duly made it to that race but the pacemaker didn't. Poliglote was deprived of the service in surprising circumstances for a second time when a pacemaker was declared to run but had to be withdrawn because of an eleventh-hour injury. The whole race seemed to suffer for his absence because it was run at a slow pace. When the sprint commenced up the straight, Poliglote was in a very good position, disputing the lead, but he did not look to have arrived there by the desired route; drawn widest of all, Freddie Head had attempted to settle him towards the rear but had had to give up the plan before they had gone half a mile. Despite these inconveniences, Poliglote ran a fine race. Celtic Swing was at his quarters, travelling like the winner, turning for home, but Poliglote made it hard for the favourite, sticking to his guns to go down by only half a length and holding on for second by a head from Winged Love.

Poliglote had started at just over 8/1 for the Prix du Jockey-Club, officially ninth-favourite of eleven but in a betting market that had lost a good deal of its meaning after widespread coupling. He had had two starts on his way to Chantilly, the Noailles and Hocquart at Longchamp, and in these races at least he had a pacemaker who was able to do the job. It has to be said, however, that Poliglote did not look to benefit greatly from it. In the Noailles, he attempted to come from last of six and managed only third, it being reported that after the race 'there appeared to be some tension between the trainer and jockey'. In the Hocquart three weeks later, Poliglote raced in second, which did not noticeably help him to settle but did enable him to steal a march on the others early in the straight, only for Rifapour to collar him close home.

Poliglote had three more attempts to get off the mark for 1995 after the Prix du Jockey-Club. He was put back to a mile and a quarter and to making the running himself in the Grand Prix de Paris, but faded into fifth, clearly failing to reproduce his French Derby form. The Prix Niel nearly three months later saw a much better effort, albeit one registered in another slowly-run race, Poliglote leading from halfway until Housamix got to him on the post, Winged Love again in very close attendance back in third. No pacemaker was fielded for this race either, or for Poliglote's final appearance of the season, in the Rothmans International at Woodbine. An in-form Poliglote should have won the Rothmans but tactics did not appear to have much bearing on the result on this occasion—Poliglote was so far below his best that he finished a tailed-off last of fifteen.

Poliglote is owned and bred by Jacques Wertheimer, as was his dam the ten-and-a-half-furlong Prix Cleopatre winner Alexandrie, but the owner sold Alexandrie for 110,000 guineas at Tattersalls while Poliglote was still a foal. She was carrying a foal by Rainbow Quest at the time, a colt now called King Alex and in training with Roger Charlton. Five of Alexandrie's previous foals were winners over at least a mile and a quarter, two by Green Dancer and one each by Alleged, Bering and Alysheba. Easily the best of them was the first, Animatrice (by Alleged), who was third in 1988 Oaks. We do not have to go too far in this pedigree before finding a classic winner: second dam Apachee, herself very useful, is half-sister to Quest For

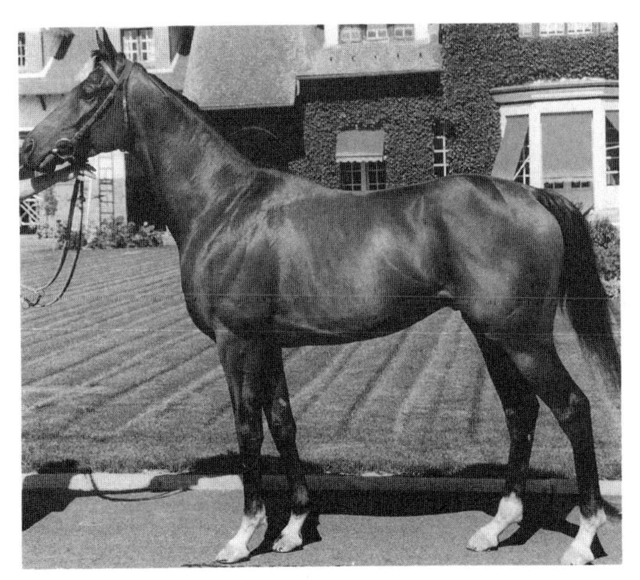

Mr J. Wertheimer's "Poliglote"

Fame's dam Aryenne. One of Alexandrie's half-sisters is Dance Indienne, the dam of Poliglote's ill-fated contemporary Indian Jones who broke a cannon bone when odds-on for the Grand Criterium.

Poliglote (b.c. 1992)	Sadler's Wells (USA) (b 1981)	Northern Dancer (b 1961)	Nearctic
			Natalma
		Fairy Bridge (b 1975)	Bold Reason
			Special
	Alexandrie (USA) (b or br 1980)	Val de L'Orne (b 1972)	Val de Loir
			Aglae
		Apachee (b 1975)	Sir Gaylord
			Americaine

Poliglote is medium-sized and rather sparely-made. He is better at a mile and a half than shorter, and indeed shapes as if he would stay even further than that, for all that he is such a hard puller. Yet to race on firm going, he acts on good to firm and soft. The tactics to be used with Poliglote were clearly a matter of debate in 1995, but by the season's close it appeared that the most effective were to ride him up with or close to the pace. He carries his head a little high, but is no push-over in a finish. *Mme C. Head, France*

POLISH BEAR (IRE) 2 ch.f. (Mar 13) Polish Patriot (USA) 128 – Camarat 69 (Ahonoora 122) [1995 5.1m^4 6m 5g^2 5g 6m^5 5.2d^2 6d^4 Oct 21] 11,000Y: leggy, workmanlike filly: first foal: dam, 9f winner, half-sister to Park Hill winner Trampship out of half-sister to Prix Vermeille winner Paulista: fair maiden: blinkered, much improved form when fourth in nursery at Newbury on final outing: better suited by 6f than 5f: best form on an easy surface: sold 7,500 gns Newmarket Autumn Sales: sent to Hungary. *B. J. Meehan* 77

POLISH CONSUL 4 ch.g. Polish Precedent (USA) 131 – Consolation 95 (Troy 137) [1994 68: 8.1s^{4} 7.9f^{6} 1995 16m^{6} 14d^{5} a12g^{5} 12d^{6} Sep 15] lengthy gelding: fair maiden handicapper: stays 2m: probably acts on any going: blinkered (reared stalls, withdrawn) once at 2 yrs: again troublesome at stalls on final start. *Major W. R. Hern* 68

POLISH LADY (IRE) 2 b.f. (May 3) Posen (USA) – Dame Ross 85 (Raga Navarro (ITY) 119) [1995 7m 7.1s Nov 2] IR 3,000F, IR 2,800Y: fourth foal: dam Irish 2-y-o 7f and 7.8f winner, stayed 1¼m: well beaten in maiden auction events at Catterick (very slowly away) and Edinburgh. *W. L. Barker* –

POLISH LEGION 2 b.c. (Jan 23) Polish Precedent (USA) 131 – Crystal Bright 75 (Bold Lad (IRE) 133) [1995 5.2m* Apr 21] strong, attractive colt: half-brother to several winners, including 1000 Guineas third Crystal Gazing (by El Gran Senor) and useful 1m/1¼m performer Wainwright (by Bering): dam, placed at 5f at 2 yrs and later at 1m: 7/1 from 3/1, won maiden at Newbury by a head from Caricature, never far away and running on well inside last, giving one flash of tail: bred to stay 1m: looked sure to improve. *J. H. M. Gosden* 88

POLISH SAGA 2 ch.f. (May 16) Polish Patriot (USA) 128 – Sagar 74 (Habitat 134) [1995 6f^{5} 5d 6g^{4} 6m 6f Oct 24] 8,200Y: half-sister to several winners, including useful 3-y-o 1m winner Tarawa (by Caerleon), French 1¼m winner Suruba (by Top Ville) and fairly useful 6f and 7f winner Be Warned (by Warning): dam 10.5f winner in France: improved effort in maidens when fourth of 9 to Last Second at Redcar: well beaten in nurseries last 2 starts: will stay further than 6f. *M. Dods* 59

POLISH SPRING (IRE) 2 ch.f. (Feb 12) Polish Precedent (USA) 131 – Diavolina (USA) (Lear Fan (USA) 130) [1995 6g* 6.1d^{4} 6m^{5} Oct 21] unfurnished filly: second foal: half-sister to 3-y-o Rozalina Lady (by Alzao): dam French 1¼m winner from family of Lyphard: very green beforehand when winning 17-runner maiden at Newmarket in September: failed to repeat that form in minor event at Chepstow (gave impression something amiss) and listed race at Doncaster: will stay 7f+: may be unsuited by a soft surface: reluctant to post and unseated rider last time. *B. W. Hills* 82 +

POLISH WIDOW 2 b.f. (Jan 21) Polish Precedent (USA) 131 – Widows Walk (Habitat 134) [1995 6m^{5} Oct 13] rangy filly: fourth foal: half-sister to 1¼m and 1½m winner Rainbow Walk (by Rainbow Quest) and 4-y-o 1¼m winner Sadler's Walk (by Sadler's Wells): dam once-raced daughter of 1000 Guineas winner On The House: 33/1, over 4 lengths fifth of 21 to Projection in maiden at Newmarket, niggled along throughout but staying on well: will do better, particularly over 7f+. *G. Wragg* 71 p

POLLEN COUNT (USA) 6 b.h. Diesis 133 – Apalachee Honey (USA) (Apalachee (USA) 137) [1994 117: 7v* 10v^{5} 7.3g* 8d* 10d^{3} 1995 8g^{4} 8d^{6} Oct 1] leggy, good-topped horse: has a powerful, round action: smart performer at 5 yrs for J. Gosden before being sent to Dubai: only useful form when fourth of 7 in Prix Quincey at Deauville and sixth of 7 to Shaanxi in Prix du Rond-Point at Longchamp in 1995, always prominent on each occasion: effective 7f to 1¼m: probably needs an easy surface: game and genuine. *Saeed bin Suroor* 108

POLLI PUI 3 b.f. Puissance 110 – Wing of Freedom (Troy 137) [1994 59: 5m 5d^{2} 5s^{2} 5d^{5} 5v^{6} a6g^{5} 1995 a6g 5d^{4} a6g^{6} 6g 8.2m a6g 7m a6g Nov 20] leggy filly: modest maiden: should stay at least 6f: acts on soft ground, well beaten on fibresand: inconsistent: has joined W. Brisbourne. *P. D. Evans* 59 d a–

POLLY GARTER 3 gr.f. Forzando 122 – Dawn Dance (USA) (Grey Dawn II 132) [1994 65: 5d 6m^{4} 5g^{2} 7m^{5} 7d a6g 1995 a6g^{4} a7g^{2} 6m^{4} 8f^{6} 7g^{2} 7m^{4} Jun 15] sparely-made filly: modest maiden: should have stayed further than 7f: acted on good to firm ground: sold 9,000 gns, in foal to Tirol, Newmarket December Sales. *R. Hannon* 51

POLLY GOLIGHTLY 2 ch.f. (May 8) Weldnaas (USA) 112 – Polly's Teahouse 68 (Shack (USA) 118) [1995 5.1m* 5.1f^{4} 6m^{5} 6m^{3} 7f^{5} 6f^{4} 6.5m 6d^{3} 5m* Nov 3] 2,800Y: smallish, leggy filly: fifth live foal: dam sprint maiden daughter of half-sister to 2000 Guineas winner Right Tack: won maiden auction at Bath in May and nursery at Doncaster (beat Music Gold by a short head) in November: seems just about to stay 7f but better form at shorter distances: acts on firm and dead ground: has run creditably for 7-lb claimer: keen sort: has swished tail but is game and genuine: blinkered last 2 starts. *B. Smart* 84

POLLY PARTICULAR 3 b.f. Beveled (USA) – Ballafort 73 (Ballacashtal (CAN)) [1994 84: 5d* 5g* 5g 5m^6 5.2g^5 5m^6 5s^6 1995 5g^6 5g 5m 5f Oct 14] tall, good-topped filly: modest handicapper: below form in 1995 after reappearance: raced only at 5f: acts on dead ground, probably on good to firm: has run creditably when sweating. *T. D. Barron*
77

POLLY PECULIAR 4 b.f. Squill (USA) 122 – Pretty Pollyanna (General Assembly (USA)) [1994 58: 10.3s a10g* a10g^3 1995 a11g a10g^4 8g* 8.1m^3 8g^6 7g^2 8g^3 9.7s* 10g^5 a9.4g Dec 9] leggy filly: fair performer: won amateurs handicap at Warwick in May and minor event at Folkestone in September: effective at 7f, and stays 1¼m: acts on good to firm ground, soft and equitrack. *B. Smart*
62
a–

POLO KIT (IRE) 4 b.g. Trempolino (USA) 135 – Nikitina 106 (Nijinsky (CAN) 138) [1994 82: 8m^6 9.9d^2 12.1s^3 14g* 16.4m^4 1995 14.9d 14m^4 16.4m^5 16m^4 May 21] quite attractive gelding: fairly useful handicapper: best at around 1¾m/2m: acts on soft going and good to firm: visored (ran creditably) final start: held up: sometimes sweating and rather edgy in preliminaries: sold (J. Fanshawe to R O' Sullivan) only 3,400 gns Newmarket July Sales. *J. R. Fanshawe*
82

POLONEZ PRIMA 8 ch.g. Thatching 131 – Taiga 69 (Northfields (USA)) [1994 69: 10f 7.3g 7m 7g 8s 7g 7g^3 7g^4 a8.5g^3 a8g^5 a9.4g^5 1995 a8g^4 8.5m 7m^5 8m^4 8g^4 8m^{3dis} 8.2m^4 6.9f^4 8f^5 8.3m Aug 7] good-bodied gelding: carries plenty of condition: fair handicapper: trained until after reappearance by J. Banks: seems suited by 7f/1m: acts on firm and dead ground and the all-weather: below best when sweating twice: good mount for apprentice: held up. *J. L. Spearing*
66

POLSKA (USA) 2 b.f. (Mar 28) Danzig (USA) – Aquaba (USA) (Damascus (USA)) [1995 6d* Sep 23] leggy, close-coupled filly: third foal: closely related to useful 5f winner Millstream (by Dayjur): dam, 7f to 9f winner in USA, including in Grade 3 event, granddaughter of Monade, also grandam of Sadeem: 7/4 favourite, made virtually all when winning 8-runner Blue Seal Stakes at Ascot by 1¼ lengths from Tarneem, running on strongly: will stay further than 6f: sure to go on to much better things. *D. R. Loder*
84 P

POLTARF (USA) 4 b.c. Alleged (USA) 138 – La Polonaise (USA) (Danzig (USA)) [1994 101: 12g 12f* 16.2m^4 15.9m 14d* 13.9d^3 1995 14.1g^3 16.2m^2 May 3] strong, good-bodied colt: shows knee action: very useful performer: sweating, very good head second of 9 to Double Trigger (gave 3 lb) in Sagaro Stakes at Ascot on final start, nosing ahead inside last, edging right under pressure and just losing out: stays well: acts on firm and dead ground: effective from front or held up. *H. R. A. Cecil*
111

POLY BY STAUFAN (IRE) 2 b.f. (Apr 18) Taufan (USA) 119 – Ana Gabriella (USA) (Master Derby (USA)) [1995 6m 6m 5.1h^6 5g 5.3d^2 5f^3 6f a5g a7g Nov 21] 7,000Y: lengthy, angular filly: sister to 3-y-o Ffynone, 6f winner at 2 yrs, and half-sister to several winners, including fairly useful sprinter Adwick Park (by Blazing Saddles): dam ran once: plater: best efforts at 5f but should stay further: acts on good to firm and dead ground, possibly not on fibresand. *M. R. Channon*
54 +
a–

POLYDAMAS 3 b.c. Last Tycoon 131 – Graecia Magna (USA) 109 (Private Account (USA)) [1994 77p: 8s^3 8.2d^2 1995 10g 11.4g^2 10.1m 10g^2 10m* 12m Oct 12] tall, rangy colt: fairly useful performer: justified favouritism in 18-runner maiden at Sandown in August: best efforts at around 1¼m: acts on good to firm ground, shaped well on soft: sometimes sweats and gets on edge: usually races prominently. *M. R. Stoute*
88

POLY LANE 3 b.g. Mazilier (USA) 107 – Another Lane 73 (Tina's Pet 121) [1994 63: 5g^4 5.1v* 5m* a6g^2 6m^3 6m^6 5m a6g 6d a6g^6 1995 a6g a8g^3 a8g^3 a8g* a9.4g^4 a8g^4 a8g^2 a7g Mar 1] neat gelding: modest performer: below form after winning selling handicap at Southwell in January: stays 1m well: acts on fibresand and probably on any turf going: blinkered since fourth 3-y-o start: sent to Macau. *W. R. Muir*
57

POLY LAUREON (IRE) 3 b.f. Fairy King (USA) – Laureon (Caerleon (USA) 132) [1994 63: 5m* 5d^2 5g^2 5g^3 5g^3 6g^5 6m 6m 6d 7.5g 7g^3 a5g* a6g^2 6.9s a6g^4 1995 a6g^2 a7g^3 a6g^6 a5g^4 a5g^2 6.1g a5g^5 6g a6g^3 a5g^6 5m^5 6.1g^5 5.9f^3 Jun 29] small, leggy filly: unimpressive mover: modest performer on the all weather: only poor on turf: stays 7f: goes well on fibresand and acts on firm and dead ground (below form on
47
a63

soft): sold (R. Hollinshead to J. Toller) 6,200 gns Newmarket July Sales. *R. Hollinshead*

POLY ROAD 3 b.f. Most Welcome 131 – Jump The Road (CAN) (Darby Creek Road (USA)) [1994 59: 8.2s^6 7s^6 7.1g a6g^4 a8g a8g* 1995 a8g^4 a8g* a8g^3 a9.4g^6 a11g^2 a12g* a9.4g* a10g 12d^6 10d^5 10.8m* 11.6m^{4dis} 12.5f^2 11.6m^3 9.9m May 23] small filly: bad mover: modest performer: won claimers at Southwell in January, Lingfield (apprentices) and Wolverhampton (2 days later) in March, and handicap at Warwick in April: finished lame final start: stayed 1½m: acted on good to firm and soft ground and on the all-weather: held up: tough: dead. *M. R. Channon* 59

POLY SCREEN 4 ch.g. Ballacashtal (CAN) – Scenic Villa (Top Ville 129) [1994 46: a10g^4 12s 12s^6 9.9m^2 10f 8.3d 10.2m^2 10f^4 11g^2 a12g 11.9g 1995 10d 14.1m Oct 26] workmanlike gelding: poor maiden handicapper: well beaten in 1995. *C. A. Smith* –

POLY STATIC (IRE) 2 b.f. (Mar 4) Statoblest 120 – Great Leighs 87 (Vaigly Great 127) [1995 5g^4 5d Apr 1] IR 4,200Y: fourth foal: half-sister to 1993 2-y-o 7f winner Rose Ciel (by Red Sunset) and fairly useful 5-y-o miler Embankment (by Tate Gallery): dam 1m winner: fourth of 8 in seller at Doncaster (flashed tail) then well beaten in maiden at Warwick. *M. R. Channon* 43

POMMARD (IRE) 2 b.c. (Feb 10) Darshaan 133 – Pont-Aven 113 (Try My Best (USA) 130) [1995 7.1g* Jun 16] lengthy, useful-looking colt: first foal: dam effective at up to 1m (second in Poule d'Essai des Pouliches): well-backed 7/4 favourite though green, won 11-runner maiden at Sandown readily by ¾ length from Detachment, switched over 1f out then running on well: impressive to post: will stay at least 1¼m+: looked sure to improve. *J. H. M. Gosden* 90 p

POMORIE (IRE) 4 b.f. Be My Guest (USA) 126 – Mpani 97 (Habitat 134) [1994 65§: 8m^3 10.2g* 12d^5 10g^5 14g^5 16g^6 1995 13g 14.9m^3 14.9m^3 16.2g Jul 21] sturdy, lengthy filly: has a quick action: fair handicapper: only creditable effort in 1995 on second start: stays 2m: blinkered last 3 starts at 3 yrs, going in snatches and finding little on final one: not one to trust: sold 7,500 gns Newmarket December Sales. *J. W. Payne* 67 §

PONTYNYSWEN 7 b.g. Ballacashtal (CAN) – Tropingay (Cawston's Clown 113) [1994 –: a12g a14.8g 1995 a12g* a12g Mar 8] neat gelding: fairly useful 2m jumper: lightly raced on flat, worthwhile form for long time only when winning weak amateurs handicap at Wolverhampton in February: stays 1½m: has raced only on the all-weather last 5 years on flat (probably acts on any going over jumps): tried visored (including when winning over fences), blinkered in 1995. *D. Burchell* 48

POOR PRINTER (IRE) 4 ch.f. Digamist (USA) 110 – No Reproach 74 (Northfields (USA)) [1994 –: a7g a8g 1995 7m 6m May 4] sparely-made filly: no form: sold 500 gns Newmarket July Sales: sent to Cyprus. *J. Akehurst* –

POPLAR BLUFF (IRE) 3 b.c. Dowsing (USA) 124 – Plume Bleu Pale (El Gran Senor (USA) 136) [1994 6.5s^4 1995 6s* 5.5g^3 5.5s^3 7d* 7g^3 7g^3 7s* 7m* 8s Oct 28] first foal: dam, French 1m winner, half-sister to William Hill Futurity runner-up Paradis Terrestre out of genuine sprinter Pixie Tower: smart performer: won minor event at Evry and listed race at Longchamp in the spring, and listed race (made all, swished tail) and 10-runner Prix de la Foret (soon travelling strongly behind fast pace, led over 1f out, gamely held Bin Ajwaad by a short neck) at Longchamp in the autumn: tailed off in Breeders' Cup Mile at Belmont on final start: stays 7f: acts on good to firm ground and soft: effective from front or held up. *A. Fabre, France* 117

POPPY CAREW (IRE) 3 b.f. Danehill (USA) 126 – Why So Silent (Mill Reef (USA) 141) [1994 100: 6.1g^5 7m^2 7g* 7g^2 8g^3 7g^3 1995 8m^2 10m^2 10f^5 10m* 10.1g* 10g^3 Sep 30] angular filly: has a fluent action: useful performer: won minor event at Ascot in August and listed race at Yarmouth (beat Jumilla by 1¼ lengths) in September: good effort, facing stiff task, when just over 3 lengths third to Warning Shadows in Sun Chariot Stakes at Newmarket on final start: effective at 1¼m, should stay 1½m: acts on firm ground, yet to race on a soft surface. *P. W. Harris* 107

POPPY MY LOVE 2 ch.f. (Feb 15) Clantime 101 – Yankeedoodledancer (Mashhor Dancer (USA)) [1995 5m 5g 5f^5 6m^5 a6g^5 5m^5 5g a5g^6 a8g Nov 24] 7,200Y: sturdy filly: first foal: dam of little account: of little account: trained by B. McMath first 3 starts. *R. Harris* –

POP TO STANS 6 b.g. Gold Crest (USA) 120 – Lady of Camelot (FR) (Bolkonski 134) [1994 –§, a59§: a8g* a8g^{3} a8.5g* a10g^{4} a8.5g a8.5g* a12g^{4} a9.4g^{3} a9.4g^{3} 8m a10g 8g a10g a8g 1995 a11g a8.5g^{6} a8g^{2} a8.5g a8g^{3} a10g^{3} a9.4g 8m^{3} a9.4g^{4} 8g* 10m^{2} 8m 9.7m 8.1g^{3} 8g 8h^{5} 11.7h^{3} 10.8f^{6} 10.1g 10g^{4} 8f^{6} 8f Oct 23] leggy, good-topped gelding: has a markedly round action: modest performer: won selling handicap at Pontefract in June: stays 1¼m: acts on any turf going and the all-weather: tried blinkered/visored: sometimes bandaged near-fore: held up: often ridden by 7-lb claimer: inconsistent, and not one to trust. *J. Pearce* — 54 d

PORT AUGUSTA (IRE) 3 b.c. Tirol 127 – Sweet Adelaide (USA) 98 (The Minstrel (CAN) 135) [1994 54: 7s 6s 1995 5d* Apr 1] quite attractive colt: 16/1 and in need of race, dead-heated with General Sir Peter in 17-runner maiden at Warwick, coming from well back: likely to prove at least as effective back at 6f/7f: looked capable of further improvement, but not seen out again. *B. W. Hills* — 66 p

PORTE BELLOCH 4 br.f. Belfort (FR) 89 – Keyanloch 57 (Lochnager 132) [1994 66d: 7v^{4} a8g 8g* 7m 8m^{6} 8g 7f 8.3m 10d 8g 1995 10m^{2} 11.7m^{4} 10m 10.8g Jun 12] sparely-made filly: poor handicapper: should prove best at around 1¼m: acts on good to firm ground: usually front runner. *C. T. Nash* — 45

PORTELET 3 b.f. Night Shift (USA) – Noirmant (Dominion 123) [1994 –: 6g a7g^{6} 1995 a8g^{3} a7g^{2} 6.1g^{2} a5g^{4} 5.1f 5.3f^{3} 5.3m^{2} 5m^{6} 6f^{2} 5g* 5g* 5g 5f^{3} 5m^{2} Nov 4] leggy filly: fairly useful handicapper: left R. Williams' stable after eighth 3-y-o start: much improved for new yard, making virtually all to win 16-runner race at Thirsk and 20-runner contest at Ayr in September: excellent second of 22 at Doncaster on final start, around 3 lengths clear of nearest pursuer on unfavoured stand side: best at sprint distances: acts on firm ground and equitrack: blinkered (finished last) fifth 3-y-o start: has hung under pressure. *R. Guest* — 81

PORTEND 3 b.g. Komaite (USA) – Token of Truth (Record Token 128) [1994 –: 6g 5f a7g^{5} 1995 a6g* a6g* a6g* a7g^{3} a6g* a6g^{3} a6g^{3} 5g* 5s* 5m^{5} Apr 29] sturdy, lengthy gelding: fairly useful handicapper: in fine form for new stable in first half of 1995, winning 4 times at Southwell in January/February and at Doncaster and Leicester within a week in March: effective at 5f to 7f: acts on soft ground, probably on good to firm, goes well on fibresand: usually claimer ridden. *S. R. Bowring* — 84

PORT HEDLAND 3 gr.f. Then Again 126 – Port Na Blath (On Your Mark 125) [1994 43: 6m 8.2s 7s 1995 a8.5g 10d 7g a7g Nov 2] tall leggy filly: tailed off in 1995: tried visored. *M. McCormack* — –

PORTITE SOPHIE 4 b.f. Doulab (USA) 115 – Impropriety (Law Society (USA) 130) [1994 38: 6d^{4} 6.1d^{5} 5d^{5} 7m 7.5m 6f^{6} 8m 7g^{3} a7g 7d^{3} 6m 7.1m^{6} 1995 — 42 a–

Prix de la Foret, Longchamp—Poplar Bluff beats Bin Ajwaad, Inzar and the course record

8.1d 11.1m³ 11.1f² 11.1f² 9.2f⁴ 10m⁶ a12g Sep 2] small, wiry filly: poor maiden handicapper: stays 11.1f: acts on firm and dead going: blinkered (well below form) twice in 1994. *M. Brittain*

PORTLAND WAY 3 b.g. Superpower 113 – Broadway Stomp (USA) 58 (Broadway Forli (USA)) [1994 –: 6.1s 7m 6.9m 1995 a8.5g⁶ 8.3m 8m⁶ 10.8f 7g Sep 9] good-topped gelding: of little account. *A. P. Jarvis* –

PORT LUCAYA 5 ch.h. Sharpo 132 – Sister Sophie (USA) (Effervescing (USA)) [1994 118: 10v 10s 8s* 9m 10g 8.5d² 8v* 10v⁶ 1995 7d⁶ 8v⁴ 8s 8.5f Aug 26] close-coupled horse: unimpressive mover: smart performer at 4 yrs: below his best in 3 pattern races and (at Arlington) quite valuable event in 1995: effective at 1m to 1¼m: best with give in the ground (acts on heavy): usually blinkered. *D. R. Loder* 103

PORTOLANO (FR) 4 b.g. Reference Point 139 – Kottna (USA) (Lyphard (USA) 132) [1994 67d: 12g³ 10s² 11.9m³ 10d 11.9d 10.8s 11.8d 12s a8g a10g 1995 a12g 14.1m 10m 10.8f Aug 28] smallish, well-made gelding: no form for a long time: sold out of C. Williams' stable 3,500 gns Doncaster February Sales after reappearance: tried visored. *W. Clay* –

PORTSCATHO (IRE) 3 b.g. Common Grounds 118 – Tweedling (USA) (Sir Ivor 135) [1994 NR 1995 12s 11.9d Oct 11] 31,000Y, 6,200 2-y-o: tall gelding: sixth foal: brother to Italian 1¼m winner Doonsday and half-brother to modest winners by Law Society (at up to 1m) and Mill Reef (at 11f): dam won at around 1m in USA: tailed off in maidens. *Miss Jacqueline S. Doyle* –

PORT SUNLIGHT (IRE) 7 ch.g. Tate Gallery (USA) 117 – Nana's Girl 109 (Tin Whistle 128) [1994 68, a58: a8.5g⁵ 9.7s² 10v⁴ 8s 9d⁶ 8m⁶ 8g 8.1g⁴ 10.5g³ 10m⁴ 9g³ 9d a12g a8.5g a8.5g 1995 a12g⁶ a12g² a12g⁵ a12g⁶ a11g 12.5g 11.1g a9.4g May 13] strong, workmanlike gelding: carries condition: has a quick action: fair handicapper at 6 yrs, disappointing in 1995: appears to stay 1½m: acts on good to firm and soft ground and on fibresand: tried blinkered and visored: normally held up. *P. D. Evans* – a46

PORTUGUESE LIL 2 ch.f. (Mar 17) Master Willie 129 – Sabonis (USA) 68 (The Minstrel (CAN) 135) [1995 7g⁵ 8m 8.1s⁶ Nov 2] 7,000Y: sturdy filly: second foal: dam 2-y-o 6f winner: fifth of 14 to Jo Mell in maiden at Ayr in September: behind in similar events at Doncaster and Edinburgh last 2 starts: should stay at least 1m. *D. Nicholls* 61

POSEN GOLD (IRE) 2 b.f. (Apr 24) Posen (USA) – Golden Sunlight (Ile de Bourbon (USA) 133) [1995 6m⁵ 7m³ a7g⁴ Nov 27] IR 5,700Y: angular filly: fifth foal: half-sister to 5f (at 2 yrs) to 7f winner Broctune Gold (by Superpower) and 2 winners abroad, including Lardner (by Dominion), winner at up to 9f in U.S.: dam unraced: in frame in maiden auctions at Yarmouth and Wolverhampton (below form) 4 months later: will stay middle distances. *P. A. Kelleway* 60

POSIDONAS 3 b.c. Slip Anchor 136 – Tamassos 67 (Dance In Time (CAN)) [1994 84p: 8d* 8s³ 1995 11g* 11s 12g* 12d* 12m⁵ Oct 15] 119

This colt must be one of the lesser-known Group 1 winners of 1995. We predict that he will have earned a higher profile in twelve months time. His one Group 1 victory so far came in the Gran Premio d'Italia at Milan in mid-September, a race that does not live up to its name; confined to three-year-old colts and fillies, it takes significantly less winning than Italy's four Group 1 races open to three-year-olds and older horses, and it is worth a lot less than the other two Gran Premios, del Jockey Club and di Milano. Posidonas was up against a four-strong home team in his Gran Premio that looked to contain nothing special (the 1994 Gran Criterium winner Golden Glenstal had made his reappearance just thirteen days earlier, and disappointed) while Peter Chapple-Hyam's Court of Honour and Dermot Weld's Humbel seemed exposed as smart colts but no better. That was the field of seven and Posidonas was an impressive winner, coming in three and a half lengths clear of Slicious with Court of Honour third. This win, added to those of Dashing Blade, Pigeon Voyageur, Masad, Right Win and Close Conflict, means that the Italians have failed to win their own 'Gran Premio' so far in the 'nineties. Twenty of their thirty-two pattern races in 1995 were won by horses trained abroad, and in order to keep a few more of these prizes at home from 1996, the Italian authorities have

Gran Premio d'Italia, Milan—the winner Posidonas (R. Hughes)

resorted to excluding foreign runners from a number of them which will consequently lose their pattern status.

Races on the Continent such as these have provided rich pickings over the years for Posidonas' trainer Paul Cole. That Posidonas would mount a successful raid so far from home must have been a surprise, however, to those who had read the reports on his first venture into pattern company, when only eighth of ten, beaten about twelve lengths, in a Group 2 at Munich in May. He was off the course nearly four months after that experience, one reporter stating that 'lightly-raced Posidonas travels badly and was knocked right back by a trip to Germany in May, otherwise he would be the ideal type for a Group race abroad.' One week after that appeared, Posidonas was lording it in Italy, presumably on this occasion armed with travel sweets. The Arc or Gran Premio del Jockey Club were mentioned as possible next ports of call, and in the end Posidonas did go to Longchamp, but for the Prix du Conseil de Paris a fortnight after the Arc. On good to firm ground, he finished a respectable fifth of eighth to De Quest, Slicious turning the tables by getting second.

On home soil in 1995, Posidonas had two starts and won them both, quite valuable conditions races at Newbury on Greenham day and Goodwood in early-September, in both of which he led in the final furlong and created a good impression against very useful opposition. At Goodwood, it was not until the final strides that he got up after being hemmed in behind leader Bal Harbour until just over one furlong out.

Posidonas (b.c. 1992)	Slip Anchor (b 1982)	Shirley Heights (b 1975)	Mill Reef
			Hardiemma
		Sayonara (b 1965)	Birkhahn
			Suleika
	Tamassos (ch 1984)	Dance In Time (b 1974)	Northern Dancer
			Allegro
		Salamina (ch 1978)	Welsh Pageant
			Femme Elite

Posidonas comes from a family that has carried the Christodoulou colours with distinction. The race with which they are both best-known, however, may still be the one in which those colours were deposited on the turf at Royal Ascot as Ile de Chypre (a half-brother to Posidonas' dam Tamassos) veered dramatically to his left when clear in the 1988 King George V Handicap. This incident created quite a stir at the time, but nothing compared to that twelve months later when a defendant in a cocaine-smuggling case claimed, ingeniously but disingenuously, that Ile de Chypre had been nobbled by a well-aimed 'sonic gun' concealed in a pair of binoculars. The incident did not do Ile de Chypre much harm as he improved into a high-class performer the following season and won the International Stakes. His dam, the useful five-furlong to one-mile winner Salamina, has since been represented by the useful middle-distance stayer and high-class hurdler Halkopous. Posidonas' dam Tamassos was not nearly so good, a modest mile-and-a-quarter winner, but all of her four foals that have lived to see the racecourse have now won: Continuity (by Celestial Storm) was a modest stayer; Porphyrios (by Mtoto) a fairly useful seven-furlong winner, and Rescue Time (by Mtoto) took a Tipperary maiden for two-year-olds over seven furlongs in the latest season.

Posidonas is a good-topped colt who shows knee action and whose best effort so far is on dead ground (he showed plenty of promise on soft as a two-year-old and was not disgraced on good to firm at Longchamp). Smart at a mile and a half, there is no doubt that he will stay further. Sire Slip Anchor is a strong influence for stamina. User Friendly remains clearly his best offspring, Posidonas disputing second spot with the ill-fated Dante second Weigh Anchor, and the aforementioned Slicious not far behind them. It would be no surprise to see Posidonas go a clear second at least in 1996; he may have a Group 1 penalty to carry but still appeals strongly as one who will win more pattern races. *P. F. I. Cole*

POSING (IRE) 3 b.f. Sadler's Wells (USA) 132 – Glancing 113 (Grundy 137) [1994 –p: 7d 1995 8m^3 10d^5 8m 10f^3 11m^4 10d^2 8d Sep 27] rather sparely-made filly: fair maiden: stays 1¼m: acts on firm and dead ground: effective visored or not: sold 38,000 gns Newmarket December Sales. *J. R. Fanshawe* 68

POSITIVE RESULT (IRE) 3 ch.f. Doulab (USA) 115 – Second Service (Red Regent 123) [1994 NR 1995 a5g 5.1m 5.1m Jun 2] leggy filly: fifth foal: half-sister to 5-y-o 1m winner Mary's Case (by Taufan): dam, unplaced, from family of Be My Chief and Shavian: no sign of ability. *R. J. Price* –

POSITIVO 4 br.g. Robellino (USA) 127 – Primetta (Precocious 126) [1994 69: a8g* 8g 8m^2 7.9f^4 9g^5 8.2m^3 8m 1995 9g 10m a10g^6 8.1m^2 Jul 2] leggy gelding: easy mover: fair performer: sold (Lord Huntingdon to Miss J. Caroe) 10,400 gns Ascot July Sales after final start: should stay 1¼m: acts on firm ground and fibresand: visored (below form) twice: looks an awkward ride. *Lord Huntingdon* 66

POSSESSIVE ARTISTE 2 b.f. (Mar 22) Shareef Dancer (USA) 135 – Possessive (Posse (USA) 130) [1995 6m^5 7m Aug 25] lengthy filly: has scope: fifth foal: sister to Irish and Italian Oaks winner Possessive Dancer and half-sister to 2 winners, including 3-y-o Desert Courier (by Green Desert), useful 6f winner at 2 yrs: dam (unraced) from good family: 7½ lengths fifth of 22 to Bosra Sham in maiden at Newbury, staying on well: no improvement when beaten similar distance behind Ruznama in similar event at Newmarket 2 weeks later: will stay middle distances: bandaged behind. *M. R. Stoute* 71

POSSIBILITY 4 b.f. Robellino (USA) 127 – Bentinck Hotel 74 (Red God 128§) [1994 53, a45: a6g^4 a7g^6 a7g^5 7m* 8g 6m 7g^3 6m^4 7f* 7f^5 6.9m a7g a7g^3 1995 a8g a8g a7g* a8g^3 a10g^5 Mar 16] workmanlike filly: poor mover: poor handicapper: got up close home at Lingfield in February: stays 1m: acts on good to firm ground, dead and equitrack: normally blinkered: wears bandages: effective from front or held up. *R. Ingram* – a45

POSTAGE STAMP 8 ch.g. The Noble Player (USA) 126 – Takealetter (Wolver Hollow 126) [1994 NR 1995 16g Jul 14] rangy, good-topped gelding: lightly raced and no form on flat since 1992: useful jumper. *F. Murphy* –

POSTED ABROAD (IRE) 3 b.g. Cyrano de Bergerac 120 – Postie (Sharpo 132) [1994 60p: a7g^3 a5g^3 1995 a6g* a6g^2 a7g* Feb 17] modest performer: won maiden at Wolverhampton in January and handicap at Southwell (took keen hold and hung) in February: stays 7f: acts on fibresand, yet to race on equitrack: sold (Sir Mark Prescott to J. Hellens) 8,000 gns Doncaster May Sales. *Sir Mark Prescott* 63

POTENZA 2 b.g. (Apr 14) Puissance 110 – Indivisible 56 (Remainder Man 126§) [1995 a6g a5g a6g Oct 14] first foal: dam stayed 1¼m: well beaten in maiden, seller and claimer at Wolverhampton. *R. Hollinshead* –

POURQUOIS PAS (IRE) 3 b.f. Nordico (USA) – Mystery Lady (USA) (Vaguely Noble 140) [1994 5s^2 7.5v^2 5v^3 6g 8v 5s^5 7.5d* 1995 7.5d^2 6d* 7.5g* 7.5g^3 8m^3 8m 8d^5 7.5g* 8g* 7.5g^2 10g* 10g* 10m Nov 12] sixth foal: half-sister to 2 winners, including fair 1¼m winner Conspicuous (by Alzao): dam ran twice: much-improved Italian filly: won sellers and minor event at Pisa around turn of year and minor events at Varese and Livorno and handicap at Turin in the summer: successful in listed race and Premio Lydia Tesio (beat Olimpia Dukakis ½ length), both at Rome in the autumn: last of 10 in Premio Roma final outing: stays 1¼m well: acts on good to firm ground and soft. *M. Gasparini, Italy* 109

POWER 4 b.g. Bustino 136 – Pushy 112 (Sharpen Up 127) [1994 62+: 10.3m^5 14.8m^6 1995 a12g* a12g^2 a12g 10.8m Apr 17] big, good-topped gelding: has a powerful, round action: fair performer: won maiden at Lingfield in February: disappointing in handicaps there and at Warwick last 2 starts (subsequently gelded): will stay beyond 1½m, stiff task in listed event when tried: best form on the all-weather. *C. E. Brittain* 76

POWER DEE 2 b.f. (Feb 3) Superpower 113 – Linn O'Dee 72 (King of Spain 121) [1995 5g^6 5m 5g^4 5m May 9] third foal: dam sprinter: little worthwhile form in sellers: blinkered final start. *M. W. Easterby* –

POWER DON 2 ch.c. (May 11) Superpower 113 – Donalee (Don 128) [1995 5g^3 5f^2 a7g^5 6m^3 5g^5 5.3d^3 Sep 26] 3,000Y, 3,000 2-y-o: lengthy colt: fourth foal: brother to 1994 2-y-o plater Toonalee: dam, twice-raced, placed at 8.5f: modest maiden plater: stays 6f: hung right fourth start: visored last 2 outings. *W. G. M. Turner* 56

POWER GAME 2 b.c. (Feb 23) Puissance 110 – Play The Game 70 (Mummy's Game 120) [1995 5g^3 6f^2 6f^5 5m^5 6m^3 6g 6g^3 6m^3 Oct 13] 16,000Y: tall colt: second foal: half-brother to 3-y-o I'm Playing (by Primo Dominie): dam 2-y-o 5f winner: modest maiden: stays 6f: has raced only on a sound surface. *J. Berry* 67

POWER MOUSE 3 ch.g. Hubbly Bubbly (USA) – Targuette (Targowice (USA) 130) [1994 NR 1995 5m Apr 27] plain, angular gelding: half-brother to 1984 2-y-o 5f winner Rocket Royale (by Roan Rocket), a winner in Belgium and 2 winners in Italy: dam poor plater: tailed off in maiden at Beverley: sold 925 gns Ascot July Sales. *H. J. Collingridge* –

POWER PRINCESS 2 b.f. (May 14) Superpower 113 – Hyde Princess 75 (Touch Paper 113) [1995 6m 5m^6 5d 5g 6s Sep 30] 2,200Y: deep-bodied filly: fourth foal: half-sister to 5f winner The Fed (by Clantime): dam sprinter: poor form: well beaten in selling nursery final outing. *R. M. Whitaker* 43

POWER SHARE 4 ch.g. Superpower 113 – Collegian 90 (Stanford 121§) [1994 –: 7.1s^4 7g 7.1g 7d 1995 a8g Mar 2] angular, unfurnished gelding: no form on flat: has joined R. Simpson. *Mrs A. Knight* –

POYLE JEZEBELLE 4 ch.f. Sharpo 132 – Hithermoor Lass 75 (Red Alert 127) [1994 –: 8.3m 7m 8m 1995 6.1m^6 7g^4 8g^4 8g^5 7g^5 6m* 6m 6f 6.1d^2 6d^4 5.1d 6f Oct 23] leggy, lengthy filly: modest handicapper: first success when winning at Lingfield in July: effective at 6f, stays 1m: acts on good to firm and dead ground: reluctant to post third 4-y-o start, and edgy and mulish at stalls next time. *M. Blanshard* 58

PRAGLIA (IRE) 3 b.f. Darshaan 133 – Nazanin 88 (Sharpo 132) [1994 64p: 8m 7s^3 1995 10g^6 11.4d 11.9g Sep 22] quite attractive filly: behind all starts in 1995, reluctant to race on final one: one to avoid. *J. L. Dunlop* – §

PRAGUE SPRING 3 b.f. Salse (USA) 128 – Wassl's Sister (Troy 137) [1994 61: 6m^5 6m^3 1995 10g^5 10m* 11.7h^3 Aug 8] sturdy filly: fair performer: trained by G. Rimmer on reappearance only: justified favouritism in maiden at Nottingham in July, making most: stays 11.7f: has raced only on a sound surface: sold (B. Hills to Lady Herries) 18,000 gns Newmarket Autumn Sales. *B. W. Hills* 66

PRAIRIE GROVE 5 b.g. Primo Dominie 121 – Fairy Fans (Petingo 135) [1994 –: 8m 10d 1995 a10g a16g Feb 14] leggy gelding: well beaten since fair performer at 3 yrs for R. Hannon: tried blinkered: joined Miss H. Knight. *J. S. King* –

PRANCING 2 br.f. (Feb 11) Prince Sabo 123 – Valika 75 (Valiyar 129) [1995 6f^2 5m* 6g^2 6f^5 Oct 12] 70,000Y: smallish, quite attractive filly: fourth foal: half-sister 97 to smart 1993 2-y-o 5f and 6f winner First Trump, later effective at 1m, and 5-y-o 6f and 7f (at 2 yrs) winner First Veil (both by Primo Dominie): dam, maiden placed from 1m to 1½m, half-sister to high-class sprinter Mr Brooks: had simple task in maiden at Beverley in August: good fifth of 26, around 3 lengths down on Blue Iris, in Redcar Two-Year-Old Trophy on final start: stays 6f: acts on firm ground. *D. R. Loder*

PRATIQUE (USA) 4 ch.f. Known Fact (USA) 135 – Scierpan (USA) 86 (Sharpen Up 127) [1994 60: 5m^3 5.1f^4 6m^2 5m 5g 5g 7g^2 1995 a7g Jan 20] small, compact filly: fair maiden at best: didn't progress at 3 yrs for J. Gosden, and soundly beaten only outing in 1995: sold 5,500 gns, in foal to Safawan, Newmarket December Sales. *P. Calver* –

PRECEDE 3 b.c. Polish Precedent (USA) 131 – Height of Passion (Shirley Heights 130) [1994 107p: 6g* 8d^2 7m^4 8v^2 1995 10m* 12m^3 May 28] rangy, rather angular colt: smart performer: 5-length winner of 4-runner minor event at Salisbury in May: good 2 lengths third of 12 to Luso in Derby Italiano on only subsequent outing: stays 1½m: acts on good to firm ground and heavy. *P. F. I. Cole* 110

PRECIOUS GIRL 2 ch.f. (Apr 30) Precious Metal 106 – Oh My Oh My (Ballacashtal (CAN)) [1995 5v* 5m^5 5g 6m^3 6g* 7d 5d^2 6.1m^6 7m^6 Nov 4] workmanlike filly: third live foal: dam poor sprint plater: won median auction maiden at Hamilton in March and nursery at Ayr in July: stays 6f: acts on good to firm and heavy ground: has sweated. *D. Moffatt* 71

PRECIOUS TIMES 3 b.c. Emarati (USA) 74 – Massawa (FR) (Tennyson (FR) 124) [1994 43: 5g 6g 6s a5g a5g^6 a6g 1995 a5g a5g^5 a5g a6g 5g May 5] neat colt: poor sprint maiden. *M. G. Meagher* –

PRECIOUS WONDER 6 b.g. Precocious 126 – B M Wonder (Junius (USA) 124) [1994 42: 6.9s 9.7v^6 7m 8v^5 8.1g 7g 9.7d^5 10.8s^3 8.1g^5 1995 10.8d 9.7g 8s^5 12g Oct 16] leggy, workmanlike gelding: poor performer: stays 10.8f: acts on good to firm and heavy going, below form on the all-weather: inconsistent. *P. Butler* –

PREDICTABLE 9 ch.g. Music Boy 124 – Piccadilly Etta 76 (Floribunda 136) [1994 –: a8g a8g 1995 a8g a16g Mar 2] lengthy, angular gelding: no form since 1993. *Mrs A. Knight* –

PREMAZING 3 ch.c. Precocious 126 – Amazing Journey (USA) (Spectacular Bid (USA)) [1994 –: 6s 7m 8d 1995 12g^6 12f^6 a16g 12g Sep 28] sturdy colt: no worthwhile form: tried visored: sold (J. Pearce to R. Stronge) 1,000 gns Newmarket Autumn Sales. *J. Pearce* –

PREMIER BLUES (FR) 5 b.m. Law Society (USA) 130 – Etoile d'Ocean (USA) (Northern Dancer) [1994 NR 1995 a12g a16g 12d^4 10m^5 11.6m 10m^5 10m^5 10.1g Sep 13] sparely-made mare: poor maiden plater: stays 1¾m: acts on good to firm and heavy ground and on equitrack: often blinkered: edgy sort. *R. J. R. Williams* 24

PREMIER DANCE 8 ch.g. Bairn (USA) 126 – Gigiolina (King Emperor (USA)) [1994 –, a57: a12g^3 a14.8g^2 a12g* a12g^2 a12g^5 a12g^5 a11g^4 11.6d a12g a12g* a12g^4 a14.8g^5 a12g^3 a12g^4 a12g^4 a11g a12g^2 a12g^3 1995 a14.8g* a12g^3 a12g^3 a12g^2 a14.8g a12g^6 a14.8g^3 a14.8g^3 14.9g^5 13f^5 a14.8g^2 a14.8g^2 a12g^6 a14.8g a14g^5 a13g^6 a12g* Dec 9] compact gelding: has quick action: modest handicapper on the all-weather: successful at Wolverhampton in January and December: poor on turf: stays 15f: effective with blinkers/visor, not tried in either since eighth 6-y-o start: sometimes carries head high. *D. Haydn Jones* 44 a64

PREMIER GENERATION (IRE) 2 b.c. (Mar 16) Cadeaux Genereux 131 – Bristle 96 (Thatch (USA) 136) [1995 8g 8.2m Oct 19] 8,000F, 10,000Y: good-topped colt: has a long stride: half-brother to several winners here and abroad, including 6f (at 2 yrs) to 1m winner Big Leap (by Auction Ring) and 7f winner Rakis (by Alzao): dam Irish 2-y-o 8.5f winner: never a significant factor in maidens: wore crossed noseband and unruly in stalls last time. *D. W. P. Arbuthnot* –

PREMIER LEAGUE (IRE) 5 gr.g. Don't Forget Me 127 – Kilmara (USA) 78 (Caro 133) [1994 –: 7.6m 10m^6 10m 1995 7m Jul 5] tall, good-bodied gelding: useful 1m/1¼m performer in the spring at 3 yrs before reportedly splitting a pastern: no worthwhile form since: sold 2,300 gns Ascot September Sales. *J. J. Bridger* –

PREMIER STAR 5 ch.g. Precocious 126 – Grove Star (Upper Case (USA)) [1994 48: a11g a8g 7g^5 8s^5 8.3d 8v^5 8m 9m 9.2g 8m 1995 a7g Jan 13] leggy gelding: –

poor maiden: tailed off in seller only 5-y-o start: sold 800 gns Ascot July Sales. *M. Dods*

PREMIUM GIFT 3 ch.f. Most Welcome 131 – Emerald Eagle 78 (Sandy Creek 123) [1994 –: 5m 1995 5m^6 5g^2 5g* 5m Aug 16] good-topped filly: modest form: won maiden at Doncaster in June: very stiff task when last of 12 in £11,200 handicap at York over 2 months later, soon outpaced: should stay at least 6f (dam won at up to 1m). *C. B. B. Booth* 63

PRENDS CA (IRE) 2 b.f. (Feb 2) Reprimand 122 – Cri de Coeur (USA) 82 (Lyphard (USA) 132) [1995 6m* 6m 7s* 7.3d^4 Oct 21] 8,400 2-y-o: smallish, unfurnished filly: sixth foal: half-sister to several middle-distance winners, including (in Dubai) Cap O'Rushes (by Rousillon): dam 2-y-o 9f winner: won maiden (under 7-lb claimer) at Goodwood in June and nursery at Ascot (first run for 3 months, came from off strong pace to beat Frezeliere) in October: respectable fourth of 9 to Sil Sila in listed race at Newbury on final start: better suited by 7f than 6f and will stay at least 1m: won on good to firm ground but best form on a soft surface. *R. Hannon* 85

PRENONAMOSS 7 b.g. Precocious 126 – Nonabella 82 (Nonoalco (USA) 131) [1994 74: 8m 8s 8g 8g^3 8m 8m 8s^3 8m 8d^3 10.1d 1995 10.3g^6 10m 10.8f 8m 9m a8g^6 a8.5g 8g* 8d 8g^2 Sep 29] lengthy, rather angular gelding: modest handicapper nowadays: plummeted in the weights prior to winning 21-runner race at Goodwood in September: effective at 1m, and stays 10.3f: has form on any going (well beaten last 3 tries on very firm): blinkered (below form) earlier in career, effective visored or not: often bandaged: held up. *D. W. P. Arbuthnot* 61

PRESENT ARMS (USA) 2 b.c. (Mar 29) Affirmed (USA) – Au Printemps (USA) (Dancing Champ (USA)) [1995 7d 8g^3 8.1s^3 Oct 17] $170,000Y: workmanlike colt: brother to 3-y-o 7f winner (better at 1½m) Bencher Q C and multiple stakes winner (also runner-up in Hollywood Derby) Charlie Barley, and half-brother to Breeders' Cup Juvenile winner Success Express (by Hold Your Peace): dam won 7 races: third in maidens won by Naval Gazer at Brighton and Latin Reign (faded quickly close home) at Chepstow in October: bred to stay beyond 1m. *P. F. I. Cole* 73 +

PRESENTING 3 br.c. Mtoto 134 – D'Azy 91 (Persian Bold 123) [1994 99p: 8g* 8m* 1995 10m* 10m* 10.4g^3 12f^3 12g^3 12f* 13.3m* 12g Oct 15] 120

Presenting won four times but still had a somewhat frustrating season, one reminiscent of the would-be boxing champ with a weak chin. This was particularly true, of course, of the challenges for two of the biggest prizes in his division that were

Westminster Taxi Insurance Gordon Stakes, Goodwood— Presenting is too strong for Don Corleone (right) and Istidaad

both effectively ended by a knockout. First, he was a late withdrawal from the Irish Derby field, ruled out at Cambridge airport when he panicked entering the plane and banged his head and withers. Three and a half months later, another blow to the head was the suggested explanation for his poor showing (fourteenth of fifteen) in the Rothmans International after a set-to with the starting stalls. After the first of these incidents, trainer John Gosden reported that Presenting had been 'very shaken', and after the second that 'he must have been seeing stars and probably did not know whether he was in Woodbine or Warwick.'

Had he lined up in either of these races fighting fit, Presenting would have had a major chance. He was clear second favourite to Celtic Swing for the Irish Derby and started 28/10 favourite for the Rothmans. His career record prior to the Irish Derby had been four wins, two losses. Undefeated on his first four starts, the first three had all tested him, meeting Bahri in a maiden at Doncaster then getting on top only in the closing stages in both a listed race at Ascot later on at two years and a well-contested minor event at Kempton on his reappearance. The fourth race, however, was a non-event, Presenting at 1/2 in the listed Newmarket Stakes and still managing to be mightily impressive as he stormed home clear by eleven lengths. That performance saw him start 11/8 favourite in the Dante, but it was at this point that a major weakness came to light and his title challenge met with its first set-back. The chink in Presenting's armour is a precise set of ground requirements. We do not hold with the maxim that 'a good horse acts on any going'—a horse that is high class only on top-of-the-ground must still be called high class—but the ability to act on any going is clearly a considerable asset. Presenting apparently does not have this ability, indeed his inability to act on a soft surface also reportedly extended to the good but rain-softened ground at York on which he finished four and a half lengths third to Classic Cliche. He had been allowed to participate only after prolonged deliberation, and, although the form of his performance did not look bad at all at that time, defeat appeared to convince connections that they had made a mistake, one that they would not make again. This naturally limited Presenting's opportunities, even in a drought year, and cast a repeated doubt on his participation. When ground conditions looked perfect in the Irish Derby, the airport incident intervened instead.

Before that though, there was the Derby at Epsom. The going had been a big issue here as well, with complaints that the course had been overwatered in an attempt to ensure the participation of Celtic Swing, but it was undoubtedly firm on the day and Presenting ran a fine race. Losing a prominent position starting down the hill, he put in some excellent work in the closing stages, but that was very much eclipsed by the even greater ground made up by Lammtarra. Presenting finished one-and-three-quarter lengths third of fifteen, and started favourite for all his remaining outings in 1995. Longest price was the 15/8 available in the Princess of Wales's Stakes at Newmarket not long after the Irish debacle; Presenting probably needed the run and managed only third having moved like the winner two furlongs out. After that, his campaign looked all geared towards the St Leger. The Westminster Taxi Insurance Gordon Stakes at Goodwood and Tripleprint Geoffrey

Tripleprint Geoffrey Freer Stakes, Newbury—top-of-the-ground, and Presenting wins again

Freer Stakes at Newbury were both run on top-of-the-ground and saw him put up impressive trials. At Goodwood, Presenting gamely saw off fellow St Leger aspirants Don Corleone, Istidaad, In Camera and Kalabo, while at Newbury eighteen days later he put three lengths between himself and Midnight Legend. But the St Leger went by without him. He had been the short-priced favourite for this as well (7/4 two days before the race) but try telling followers of Presenting that there was not enough rainfall in 1995. The rain put in another appearance just before the St Leger and Presenting was withdrawn. The elements were no more lenient at Milan for the Gran Premio d'Italia the following Saturday. The Woodbine disappointment came next and then, two weeks later, having received an invitation to the big Hong Kong race in December, it was announced that Presenting had sustained an injury to his near fore and would have to give up his quest for one of the sport's big prizes until 1996. Let's hope he gets another crack at one of them, with conditions in his favour. We don't wish to be writing again in a year's time that he 'coulda been a contender'.

Presenting (br.c. 1992)	Mtoto (b 1983)	Busted (b 1963)	Crepello
			Sans Le Sou
		Amazer (b 1967)	Mincio
			Alzara
	D'Azy (b 1984)	Persian Bold (br 1975)	Bold Lad
			Relkarunner
		Belle Viking (ch 1976)	Riverman
			Vallarta

Presenting's sire Mtoto was a top-class and thoroughly likeable performer over middle distances at both four and five years but not much has been heard of him at stud until his third crop, which Presenting heads with the Cambridgeshire winner Cap Juluca. Both should win good races at four. Presenting's dam D'Azy, was not seen out after her three-year-old season and won only at two, a Brighton minor event after finishing third in the Queen Mary. She was fairly useful and stayed a mile and a quarter. Her dam Belle Viking and grandam Vallarta both won in France, the former over a mile and a mile and a quarter, the latter at an extended mile and a half. Vallarta was half-sister to a high-class performer in Vitiges and a smart one in Virunga (the dam of Vacarme and Vin de France), while Belle Viking produced a smart colt, the middle-distance winner Sirk. D'Azy's only foal before Presenting was the useful but lightly-raced Azilian (by Top Ville), who shaped like a thorough stayer. Unlike Presenting, both Sirk and Azilian did contest the St Leger. Their finishing positions, however, were sixth of eight, beaten twelve and a half lengths, and last of nine, badly tailed off. We remain confident that had he been able to run in the race with suitable conditions, Presenting would have done much better than them and improved his already high standing. As it is, he is still rated the same as St Leger winner Classic Cliche. At a mile and a half, Presenting lacks something in turn of foot. Longer distances will suit him very well. A good-topped colt, he is a fluent mover, something he shares with his year-younger sister Introducing who, however, has much less in common with him in terms of physique; she has so far been placed in three maidens. *J. H. M. Gosden*

PRESENT 'N CORRECT 2 ch.g. (May 13) Cadeaux Genereux 131 – Emerald Eagle 78 (Sandy Creek 123) [1995 7.1d Oct 11] leggy gelding: fifth foal: half-brother to 3-y-o 5f winner Premium Gift (by Most Welcome) and 6f (at 2 yrs) and 7f winner Mummy's Emerald (by Mummy's Game): dam 6f to 1m winner: 25/1, tailed-off last in maiden at Haydock. *C. B. B. Booth* –

PRESENT SITUATION 4 ch.g. Cadeaux Genereux 131 – Storm Warning 117 (Tumble Wind (USA)) [1994 53, a68: a6g a6g^5 a7g^3 7m^3 7.1f^3 8.3f^4 8m^2 a8.5g* a8g* a7g^3 a8g* 1995 a7g^4 a7g* a7g^2 a6g 8.3m 7g^4 7d^5 a8g^2 a7g^2 a7g a7g^3 Dec 18] sparely-made gelding: unimpressive mover: fair handicapper on the all-weather: won at Lingfield (apprentices) in February: only modest on turf: stays 8.5f: acts on the all-weather and on firm and dead ground. *Lord Huntingdon* 57 a74

PRESIDENTIAL (FR) 4 b.g. Village Star (FR) 131 – Pokhara (FR) (Kashmir II 125) [1994 12g 11g 11g 1995 10.3g 12g 11.1g a12g Nov 2] half-brother to 3 winners (by Moulin, Trepan and Ginger Brink) at 1m+: dam French 11.5f winner: no worthwhile form: trained (until after third 4-y-o start) in France by A. Rossio and C. Mahe: blinkered, soon struggling in Lingfield claimer. *K. O. Cunningham-Brown* –

PRESS AGAIN 3 ch.f. Then Again 126 – Silver Empress 63 (Octavo (USA) 115) [1994 NR 1995 8m 8.3m Jun 26] unfurnished filly: fourth foal: dam maiden suited by 7f out of sister to smart Catherine Wheel: well beaten in maidens at Salisbury (pulled hard) and Windsor (difficult stalls) in June. *P. Hayward* –

PRESS THE BELL 5 b. or br.g. Belfort (FR) 89 – Northern Empress 80 (Northfields (USA)) [1994 81, a76: 5g 5.1m 5m^3 5.7m a5g^2 5.2m 5f 5.3f^4 5g^2 5.1s 5g 5v* a5g^3 a5g^3 a5g^3 1995 a5g^2 a5g^6 a5g^5 5.1m^6 Jul 4] lengthy gelding: had a quick action: fairly useful front-running 5f handicapper at his best, the winner of 6 races and rated 84 at 3 yrs: short-headed in claimer at Lingfield in January: disappointing afterwards, sold out of Jack Berry's stable only 6,800 gns Ascot April Sales before final start: acted on any surface: blinkered twice in 1994, finishing last: tended to swish tail and hang, but genuine in his prime: dead. *W. R. Muir* – a76

PRESTO BOY 3 b.g. Precocious 126 – Dingle Belle 72 (Dominion 123) [1994 50, a55: 5m^4 6.1g^2 5m 7.5f 7.1g 8m^2 7.5g^2 8.3g^5 a8.5g^2 1995 a8g^6 a8g^5 a7g^2 a6g 10m^3 11.9m^2 10m 12.5m^4 12m^6 11.9f^3 11.5m^3 11.9f^5 Aug 22] leggy gelding: modest maiden handicapper: stays 1½m: acts on firm ground and fibresand: effective blinkered/visored or not: sold 6,200 gns Newmarket September Sales. *M. Bell* 51 d

PRESTON GUILD (IRE) 5 b.g. Mazaad 106 – Dying Craft (Thatching 131) [1994 55, a53: 10v 12d^5 14.1f^5 10g^6 a12g^4 a14g 11.5g^2 11.5d^4 10s^2 a12g 1995 12.5g^3 12m^2 11.1g^3 14.1m 10.8g Oct 3] sturdy, compact gelding: modest handicapper: trained until after fourth start by A. Forbes: stays 1½m: acts on fibresand, good to firm ground and soft: sold to join Simon Earle after winning selling hurdle in October. *A. Streeter* 51

PRESUMING ED (IRE) 2 b.g. (May 12) Nordico (USA) – Top Knot (High Top 131) [1995 a8g a10g Nov 25] second foal: brother to 3-y-o Grandes Oreilles (stays 13f): dam, winning middle-distance stayer in Ireland, half-sister to useful stayer El Conquistador out of half-sister to Cesarewitch and Irish St Leger winner Mountain Lodge: behind in maidens at Lingfield in November. *N. J. H. Walker* –

PRETONIC 7 b.m. Precocious 126 – Northern Ballerina 52 (Dance In Time (CAN)) [1994 67d: a6g^4 a6g^5 a6g^4 a6g^3 a6g^4 a6g^2 a7g* 6s 6d^4 a6g^4 8.3g 7m a6g^2 a7g^3 a8g^4 a9.4g^3 a8g a6g^2 1995 a7g a6g^6 a7g^5 a8g^4 a7g^5 Apr 3] workmanlike mare: poor mover: poor performer: effective at 6f and shapes as if should stay 1m: acts on the all-weather and any going on turf: occasionally blinkered: has run well when sweating: inconsistent. *B. Palling* 41

PRETORIA DANCER 3 b.c. Dancing Brave (USA) 140 – Pretoria 100 (Habitat 134) [1994 NR 1995 10g 10g 10m^6 a11g^5 14g^4 14.1f* 13.6f^6 Oct 12] sturdy colt: third foal: brother to useful hurdler Aardwolf, and half-brother to useful 1993 middle-distance 3-y-o Nassma (by Sadler's Wells): dam 7f (at 2 yrs) and 1¼m winner: fair form: benefited from fine ride by L. Dettori when narrowly winning 7-runner handicap at Redcar in October, wandering after dictating pace: stays 14.1f well: acts on firm ground: blinkered last 2 starts: has joined C. Brooks. *J. H. M. Gosden* 73

PRETTY AVERAGE 5 b.m. Skyliner 117 – Marock Morley 59 (Most Secret 119) [1994 NR 1995 a5g 6f* 5f^3 Jul 31] stocky mare: poor sprinter: 20/1 from 50's on only second race under rules since 1992, won 18-runner ladies selling handicap at Thirsk in July, making all: subsequently under investigation for "flapping" (alleged to have won a 6f race earlier in month under the name Short And Sweet): acts on firm ground. *B. Richmond* 40

PRETTY CHIC 6 b.g. Kabour 80 – Boom Shanty 66 (Dragonara Palace (USA) 115) [1994 NR 1995 a6g^5 a5g a6g Aug 4] big, strong gelding: poor sprint maiden at 4 yrs: no worthwhile form on return: tried blinkered. *D. W. Chapman* –

PRETTY SCARCE 4 ch.f. Handsome Sailor 125 – Not Enough (Balinger 116) [1994 NR 1995 a8.5g a7g a9.4g Nov 27] third foal: dam novice hurdler: placed in Jersey in June: little sign of ability on the mainland: trained on reappearance by S. Sherwood. *B. Preece* –

PREVAIL (USA) 2 b.f. (May 1) Danzig (USA) – Primevere (USA) 91 (Irish River (FR) 131) [1995 8g^3 7.5d* 8f^3 Oct 22] sixth foal: closely related to high-class miler Priolo (by Sovereign Dancer): dam fairly useful 7f (at 2 yrs) and 1¼m winner in France: progressive French filly: won minor event at Maisons-Laffitte in Sep- 100 tember: 3½ lengths third of 5 to Occupandiste in Group 3 event at Longchamp last time: stays 1m: acts on firm ground and dead: may improve further. *P. Bary, France*

PRICKET (USA) 2 ch.f. (Feb 15) Diesis 133 – Cacti (USA) (Tom Rolfe) [1995 8.1m* Aug 25] leggy filly: has scope: sister to 2 winners, notably Diminuendo, and half-sister to several winners, one dam of smart 1m/1¼m performer Port Lucaya: dam minor winner at around 1m: long odds on, won 5-runner maiden at Sandown with something in hand by 2 lengths from Introducing, leading over 1f out and coming clear without being hard ridden: well regarded, and is sure to improve a good deal and win more races: sent to Dubai. *H. R. A. Cecil* — 85 P

PRICKWILLOW (USA) 3 b.f. Nureyev (USA) 131 – Braiswick 118 (King of Spain 121) [1994 NR 1995 7m 8m^2 10d^2 10.2m* Sep 25] first foal: dam very smart 1m to 11.3f winner from excellent family: fair form: 7/2 on, easy task to win maiden at Bath on final start: not certain to stay beyond 1¼m: yet to race on extremes of going: sent to Dubai. *J. H. M. Gosden* — 75

PRIDDY FAIR 2 b.f. (Jan 21) North Briton 67 – Rainbow Ring (Rainbow Quest (USA) 134) [1995 5g^6 6m^4 a6g 8m 7.5d 10g Oct 9] 900F, 2,200Y: good-topped filly: second foal: half-sister to 3-y-o Raindeer Quest (by Hadeer), 5f winner at 2 yrs: dam once-raced daughter of Lowther winner Circus Ring: poor maiden: well beaten in selling events on last 3 starts: best form at 6f, though still had every chance 2f out over 1¼m on final outing: always struggling on fibresand. *R. Boss* — 54 d

PRIDE OF BRIXTON 2 b.c. (Mar 21) Dominion 123 – Caviar Blini 80 (What A Guest 119) [1995 6g^3 6s^2 Sep 28] 8,800Y: useful-looking colt: third foal: half-brother to 3-y-o Norfolk Glory (by Weldnaas) and 6f (at 2 yrs) and 7f winner Norfolk Hero (by Elegant Air): dam, 2-y-o 5f winner, out of sister to top-class Deep Diver and half-sister to Irish 2000 Guineas winner King's Company: beaten 8 lengths by Apple Musashi in maiden at Lingfield but ran better than result suggests, eased when beaten: stays 6f: will improve again, and should win a race. *G. Lewis* — 83 p

PRIDE OF HAYLING (IRE) 4 ch.f. Bold Arrangement 127 – Malham Tarn (Riverman (USA) 131) [1994 –: 8m 8s 8g^6 1995 6f 5g^6 6f* 6f* 7m^4 6f 6d 6d a7g Oct 23] compact filly: modest performer: won selling handicap at Goodwood in June and minor event at Brighton in July: well below form last 4 starts: probably stays 7f: acts on firm ground. *P. R. Hedger* — 64 d

PRIDE OF KASHMIR 2 gr.g. (Feb 6) Petong 126 – Proper Madam 93 (Mummy's Pet 125) [1995 5m 5m 7.1g^4 8g 7f 6.9m^4 Nov 6] 20,000Y: good-topped gelding: unimpressive mover: half-brother to several winners, most at sprint distances, including 2 by Milford: dam sprinter: modest maiden: absent nearly 5 months after second start: best effort since debut when keeping-on fourth of 16 to Jerry Cutrona in nursery at Folkestone on final outing: stays 7f. *P. W. Harris* — 58

PRIDE OF MAY (IRE) 4 b.g. Law Society (USA) 130 – Aztec Princess (Indian King (USA) 128) [1994 72: 10s^6 11s 10m* 10.1m^6 10g^2 12m^4 12g 10m 16g 1995 a14.8g^3 a16g^2 18g 12m^4 14m^2 14m^4 11.8m^6 12g^6 14m^5 12.3m^2 12.3m^4 16.1h^5 a16g Sep 4] workmanlike gelding: fair handicapper: claimed out of R. Hannon's stable £10,000 tenth start: stays 2m: acts on good to firm ground and all-weather surfaces: best form in blinkers/visor: well suited by front-running tactics. *C. W. Fairhurst* — 67 d

PRIDE OF PENDLE 6 ro.m. Grey Desire 115 – Pendle's Secret 73 (Le Johnstan 123) [1994 73: 7g 8.5m 8.2m^5 8f^2 8f 8.5m^5 7.9f* 8f^6 8m 8m^3 8g* 8g^5 8g^3 8m 7.9m^3 8g^4 8s^4 7d^4 8m 8d 1995 8g 8g 8m* 7.6m 7m^5 10m^6 8.5m^5 8.9m* 10f 7.9m^5 8f^2 8f^2 8m^2 7.6m* 8m^6 8d 9g 8.9g 8m Oct 14] leggy, angular mare: fairly useful handicapper, remarkably consistent over the last 3 seasons: successful in 1995 at Thirsk (Hunt Cup) in May, York in June and Chester in August: stays 9f well: acts on any going: held up, and ideally suited by strongly-run race: splendidly tough and genuine, a credit to her trainer. *D. Nicholls* — 80

PRIDE OF WHALLEY (IRE) 2 b.f. (Mar 13) Fayruz 116 – Wilderness 88 (Martinmas 128) [1995 5g^6 a5g^4 5m^2 May 29] IR 5,500Y: workmanlike filly: half-sister to 4 winners, including 1986 2-y-o 5f winner Sameek (by Red Sunset): dam won over 7f: improved effort when 2½ lengths second of 12 to White Emir in maiden auction at Redcar under 7-lb claimer: has joined Martyn Wane. *J. Berry* — 61

PRIDWELL 5 b.g. Sadler's Wells (USA) 132 – Glowing With Pride 114 (Ile de Bourbon (USA) 133) [1994 NR 1995 18.7m May 10] quite good-topped gelding: — –

raced too freely and well beaten in Chester Cup on only 5-y-o flat outing: smart hurdler. *M. C. Pipe*

PRIMA COMINNA 3 ch.f. Unfuwain (USA) 131 – Cominna (Dominion 123) [1994 86p: 6m^3 6g* 7m 1995 6m^2 6m^3 7m^4 6g^3 5m 7m^2 7m^6 Jul 24] rather leggy, workmanlike filly: fairly useful handicapper: fast-finishing short-head second of 8 at Lingfield on penultimate start: stays 7f: has raced only on a sound surface: sold 17,000 gns Newmarket December Sales. *M. Bell* — 84

PRIMA SILK 4 b.f. Primo Dominie 121 – Silk St James (Pas de Seul 133) [1994 81: 6v^3 7d 6m 6f* 7g^2 7.1m^5 7m 7.5m^5 7f 7m^4 7g 7m 6g^6 5.7g 7m 1995 a7g^4 a7g a7g^2 7m^5 6.1g^6 6g* 5m* 6f^{3dis} 6m 6m 6m 5.7h 6.1d 6g 5.1d 6g^4 6f^4 5m a7g* Nov 24] angular filly: seldom impresses in appearance: fairly useful handicapper: won at Doncaster and Pontefract (minor event) in June and at Southwell in November: effective at 5f, and stays 7f: acts on fibresand and equitrack: best turf efforts on a sound surface, but probably acts on dead ground: no improvement in blinkers: sometimes wanders markedly. *M. J. Ryan* — 80

PRIMA VOLTA 2 b.f. (Jan 24) Primo Dominie 121 – Femme Formidable (Formidable (USA) 125) [1995 5m^4 6g* 7d 6m Oct 12] 7,500F, 23,000Y: angular filly: third foal: half-sister to 1994 2-y-o 6f winner Femme Savante (by Glenstal): dam poor maiden, stayed 1m: won 15-runner maiden at Kempton in September by neck from Obsessive: improved effort in face of stiff task in nursery at Newmarket last time: should stay 7f. *R. Hannon* — 80

PRIME CONNECTIONS 2 b.g. (Apr 18) Petoski 135 – Qualitair Princess (Bay Express 132) [1995 5f^5 a7g 7f 10g Oct 9] rather leggy gelding: fifth foal: dam won over hurdles: no form: blinkered last 2 starts, running very freely final outing: has worn bandages: sold 650 gns Doncaster November Sales: sent to Denmark. *M. P. Bielby* — –

PRIMELTA 2 b.f. (Feb 26) Primo Dominie 121 – Pounelta 91 (Tachypous 128) [1995 6g^6 6f 6.1d Sep 11] good-topped filly: sixth foal: closely related to 3-y-o 1m winner Anistop (by Nomination) and half-sister to 5f (at 2 yrs) to 7f winner Top Pet (by Petong) and untrustworthy 6f (at 2 yrs) and 7f winner Durneltor (by Hard Fought): dam, 2-y-o 7f winner who probably stayed 1½m, half-sister to Dead Certain: sixth of 10 to Agnella in maiden at Folkestone: poor form afterwards in similar events at Newbury and (2½ months later) Nottingham. *R. Akehurst* — 55

PRIME MATCH (IRE) 3 ch.c. Primo Dominie 121 – Last Blessing 73 (Final Straw 127) [1994 77: 7f^6 a6g^2 6g^2 6g^4 1995 6m 6m* 6m 6m^6 6m a6g 5d Sep 18] strong, lengthy colt: fair performer: won maiden at Redcar in May: well beaten in handicaps afterwards, including in blinkers: stays 6f: acts on fibresand and on good to firm ground: sold 4,000 gns Newmarket Autumn Sales: sent to Denmark. *P. W. Harris* — 77 d

PRIME PARTNER 2 b.g. (Apr 11) Formidable (USA) 125 – Baileys By Name 66 (Nomination 125) [1995 6g 5g^6 6m^2 6f^5 6f 6.1s 6d Oct 21] 10,000F, 13,000Y: strong gelding: first foal: dam 2-y-o 6f winner: best effort when second in maiden at Lingfield in July: failed to show his form in nurseries, tailed off when blinkered at Newbury on final outing: stays 6f: acts on good to firm ground. *W. R. Muir* — 63

PRIME PROPERTY (IRE) 3 b.f. Tirol 127 – Busker (Bustino 136) [1994 60: 8f 6s^6 7s 1995 a6g 7.5m 7g 6g 10m 12m a12g 7m 6m^2 6m* 7d^6 7f Oct 3] lengthy, angular filly: poor mover: poor handicapper: trained reappearance only by G. Kelly: led dying strides at Pontefract in August: best effort at sprint distances: acts on good to firm and soft ground: blinkered last 6 starts: has run well when sweating. *M. W. Easterby* — 40

PRIME SECRET 2 ch.c. (May 8) Primo Dominie 121 – Secret Freedom (USA) 87 (Secreto (USA) 128) [1995 6m 6.1m Aug 21] 4,800Y: small colt: first foal: dam, 6f winner at 2 yrs, half-sister to Gimcrack winner Full Extent: soundly beaten in minor event at Windsor and maiden auction (slowly away) at Nottingham. *B. J. Meehan* — –

PRIM LASS 4 b.f. Reprimand 122 – Vague Lass 85 (Vaigly Great 127) [1994 65d: 8m^3 7d^6 7g 8.2d a7g a10g^6 1995 8.2m 7g^3 7m a8g Jul 13] tall filly: poor maiden at best in 1995: worth a try at sprint distances: may be temperamental. *J. Hetherton* — 49

PRIMO LAD 2 b.c. (Feb 15) Primo Dominie 121 – Zinzi (Song 132) [1995 5f⁶ May 1] well-grown, leggy colt: brother to 5f winner El Arz and useful sprinter Sarcita and half-brother to a winner in Hong Kong by Midyan: dam Irish 5f winner at 4 yrs: 10/1, soon tailed off in 6-runner maiden at Pontefract (rider reported horse was lame): moved poorly to post. *W. G. M. Turner* –

PRIMO LARA 3 ch.c. Primo Dominie 121 – Clara Barton (Youth (USA) 135) [1994 55: 7g⁶ a8g⁵ 1995 8m² 8m⁴ 8d⁶ 8.5m⁵ 8m³ 7g³ 7f⁴ Oct 14] strong, lengthy colt: fair maiden: should stay beyond 1m: acts on good to firm ground, probably on dead. *P. W. Harris* 70

PRIMO PANACHE 3 ch.f. Primo Dominie 121 – Royal Agnes 71 (Royal Palace 131) [1994 –: 5m 7m 9d 1995 12m May 20] tall, leggy filly: no form. *M. P. Bielby* –

PRIMROSE PATH 2 b.f. (Feb 15) Shaadi (USA) 126 – Crimson Conquest (USA) 85 (Diesis 133) [1995 6g 6.9f³ 8.2d⁶ Sep 19] quite attractive filly: first foal: dam 2-y-o 6f winner, stayed 1¼m: third of 7 to Expensive Taste in maiden at Folkestone in August: carrying condition, only sixth of 11 in similar event at Nottingham following month: should stay 1m. *C. E. Brittain* 65

PRIMULA BAIRN 5 b.m. Bairn (USA) 126 – Miss Primula 81 (Dominion 123) [1994 64: 5g 5g 5m 5m⁶ 5m⁴ 5g⁶ 5f 5g² 5g 5.1d 5g² 5v⁴ a5g⁴ a6g a6g a5s² 1995 a5g⁵ a5g* a5g* a6g³ a5g³ a5g* 5g a5g a6g a5g⁵ 5g 5.1d 5g Sep 21] workmanlike mare: not a fluent mover: modest performer: won seller in January and claimers in February and April (claimed out of Mrs J. Ramsden's stable £5,000), all at Wolverhampton: ran poorly (twice for J. Mackie) after: best form at 5f: acts on fibresand, ideally suited by give in the ground on turf (acts on heavy): usually visored or blinkered: usually races prominently: sold 2,800 gns Doncaster October Sales. *D. Nicholls* 64

PRINCE ARTHUR (IRE) 3 b.c. Fairy King (USA) – Daniela Samuel (USA) (No Robbery) [1994 101p: 6d² 1995 7m² 8g* 8m⁵ 8g⁶ 8d² Oct 8] smart performer: won Premio Parioli at Rome in April by 1½ lengths from Thomire despite hanging: 116

Mr M. Tabor's "Prince Arthur"

best efforts when sixth of 9 to Miss Satamixa in Prix Jacques le Marois at Deauville in August and when second of 11 to Nicolotte in Premio Vittorio di Capua at Milan in October: likely to stay beyond 1m: yet to race on extremes of going. *P. W. Chapple-Hyam*

PRINCE ASLIA 2 b.c. (Feb 15) Aragon 118 – Aslia 74 (Henbit (USA) 130) [1995 5m^3 5m* 5f* 5m 5m^2 5g^2 5d 6f Oct 12] tall, close-coupled colt: has scope: first foal: dam, placed over 7f at 2 yrs but tailed off as 3-y-o, is out of half-sister to smart sprinting 2-y-o Kingscote, dam of very smart colt Rainbow Corner: won median auction maiden at Beverley in May and £9,300 event at Epsom in June: runner-up in minor event at Ripon and listed race at Deauville in August: creditable eighth of 26 to Blue Iris in Redcar Two-Year-Old Trophy on final outing: speedy and ideally suited by 5f: seems to need a sound surface: active sort (sweating penultimate start) who sometimes takes strong hold to post. *M. Johnston* — 98

PRINCE BELFORT 7 b.g. Belfort (FR) 89 – Princess Sharpenup 63 (Lochnager 132) [1994 66: 6g^2 5m 7g* 5f^2 7f 7.1m^3 7.6g^4 8f 7g^4 8f 7g^4 7m 5g^5 5d^3 6g* 5g 1995 a5g 7.1g 5m* 5m^3 5m^6 6m Jul 28] leggy, workmanlike gelding: fair performer: best effort when winning apprentice handicap at Ripon in April: broke down in handicap at Thirsk in July: effective at 5f to 7f: acted on firm and dead ground and on equitrack: effective visored/blinkered or not: usually held up: dead. *J. L. Eyre* — 67

PRINCE DANZIG (IRE) 4 ch.g. Roi Danzig (USA) – Veldt (High Top 131) [1994 58, a71: a8g^3 a10g^4 a10g* 10.3g 11.4s^4 11.6g 10s 11.9f 10f^4 10f* 10.1m 9.7d 1995 a12g* a10g^2 a10g^3 a12g^6 a12g* a10g^3 11.9f^3 10g^4 11.9m^2 17.2m^4 11.9f* 11.9f^2 11.7h^2 11.5m^5 11.9g^2 11.9g^4 a10g^4 Nov 21] close-coupled gelding: good mover: fairly useful performer on the all-weather, successful in claimer in January and handicap in March, both at Lingfield: fair handicapper on turf: got up close home at Brighton in July: stays 1½m: acts on equitrack and on any turf going: occasionally blinkered or visored (not in 1995), better form without. *D. J. G. Murray Smith* — 67, a83

PRINCE EQUINAME 3 gr.g. Dominion 123 – Moments Peace (Adonijah 126) [1994 NR 1995 10m 12.1g^3 10.5g^4 12g a11g^6 12g 11.1g Sep 25] 13,500Y, 20,000Y: smallish gelding: first foal: dam Irish 7f winner: modest maiden: should stay 1½m: headstrong: inconsistent. *D. Eddy* — 64 d

PRINCE KINSKY 2 ch.c. (Feb 6) Master Willie 129 – Princess Lieven (Royal Palace 131) [1995 7m 8m Oct 12] angular colt: seventh living foal: half-brother to fairly useful but unreliable sprinter Anonymous (by Night Shift) and 11.5f winner Beau Ideal (by Brigadier Gerard): dam unraced daughter of sister to Brigadier Gerard: shaped well in maidens won by Silver Prey at Newbury and Silver Dome at Newmarket, running on steadily from rear not knocked about: sweating and took good hold last time: sold 36,000 gns Newmarket Autumn Sales: likely to do better. *Lord Huntingdon* — 73 p

PRINCELY AFFAIR 2 b.g. (Apr 3) Prince Sabo 123 – Shillay (Lomond (USA) 128) [1995 6.1d 5s 5f Oct 14] 9,000F, 12,000Y: good-bodied gelding: fourth foal: dam French 1¼m and 11f winner: no worthwhile form in maidens at Nottingham, Lingfield and Catterick: gelded after final start. *M. Bell* — –

PRINCELY GAIT 4 b.g. Darshaan 133 – Roussalka 123 (Habitat 134) [1994 70: 8g 10g a12g^2 a12g^4 a13g* a16g* a10g 1995 a13g^3 a12g* a16g* a16g^4 Nov 14] big, good-topped gelding: shows plenty of knee action: fair handicapper: successful 4 — 76

T. G. I. Friday's Gordon Richards Stakes, Sandown—Prince of Andros is clear of Nicolotte (right) and Ionio

times at Lingfield (never elsewhere), including twice in February: effective at 1½m, and stays 2m: acts on equitrack: held up. *C. A. Cyzer*

PRINCELY HUSH (IRE) 3 b.c. Prince Sabo 123 – So Kind 90 (Kind of Hush 118) [1994 109: 5s* 5v* 5d* 5f^4 6d^4 6s* 6g^2 5s^2 1995 6g May 18] strong, good-topped colt: has a round action: useful form at 2 yrs: last of 7, soon outpaced, in Duke of York Stakes on only 3-y-o start: stays 6f: best form on an easy surface (goes well on soft ground). *M. Bell* –

PRINCELY SOUND 2 b.c. (Apr 12) Prince Sabo 123 – Sound of The Sea 91 (Windjammer (USA)) [1995 5m^4 5m^2 6m Jul 29] 32,000Y: well-grown, useful-looking colt: half-brother to 3-y-o Endless Wave (by Indian Ridge), 5f winner at 2 yrs, and 1991 Irish 2-y-o 5f and 6f winner Cu Na Mara (by Never So Bold): dam 5f and 6f winner: made most and kept on well when beaten a neck in maiden at Windsor in May: needed race only subsequent run: should stay 6f. *M. Bell* 69

PRINCELY SWORD (USA) 2 ch.g. (Feb 12) Sanglamore (USA) 126 – Princess of Man 104 (Green God 128) [1995 9m Aug 30] big, rangy gelding: closely related to 3-y-o 1½m winner Royal Scimitar, 6f (at 2 yrs) to 11.5f winner Ausherra (both useful performers by Diesis) and 6f (at 2 yrs) and 1¼m winner Alderney Prince (by Trempolino), and half-brother to several winners: dam won Musidora Stakes: 12/1, led around 5f, eased when beaten, when last of 8 in maiden at Sandown won by Night Watch: sold 4,400 gns Newmarket Autumn Sales. *P. F. I. Cole* –

PRINCE MIKE (IRE) 2 b. or br.c. (Mar 31) Anita's Prince 126 – Kiss The Bride (Sweet Revenge 129) [1995 5f Jul 29] IR 3,500F, IR 8,200Y, 8,000 2-y-o: leggy colt: good walker: brother to fair 6f/7f performer Princely Favour and a winner in Italy: dam Irish sprinter: 9/1, well beaten in maiden at Thirsk. *J. Berry* –

PRINCE OF ANDROS (USA) 5 b.h. Al Nasr (FR) 126 – Her Radiance (USA) (Halo (USA)) [1994 111: 10s^2 13.4m^4 10m^2 12m^3 10g 1995 10m* 10m* 10m^2 10m 10f 12d 10m^4 a9.4g* Dec 2] 116

All-weather racing had a mixed reception when it was introduced in October 1989, criticism having led to the start being postponed from January. Bland programmes contested by poor horses were the order of the day and the betting market, on course and off course, was weak. But the all-weather has moved up-market since those early days, with more of the top jockeys and leading trainers now among the regulars. Wolverhampton, the newest of Britain's three all-weather tracks, staged the first listed event on an all-weather track in the latest season, the Bass Wulfrun Stakes with £50,000 added. Despite being staged in early-December, the race attracted a smart field under the floodlights, including a smattering of 1995 pattern and listed winners, and provided a clear indication that, given the prize-

Bass Wulfrun Stakes, Wolverhampton—the first all-weather listed race goes to Prince of Andros

Lucayan Stud's "Prince of Andros"

Prince of Andros (USA) (b.c. 1990)	Al Nasr (FR) (b 1978)	Lyphard (b 1969)	Northern Dancer
			Goofed
		Caretta (b 1973)	Caro
			Klainia
	Her Radiance (USA) (b 1985)	Halo (b or br 1969)	Hail To Reason
			Cosmah
		Rissa (b 1976)	Nijinsky
			Kittiwake

money, the winter all-weather programme could support more races of such quality. The winner of the Wulfrun Stakes, Prince of Andros, had twice been successful in pattern company earlier in the season, and was one of three intended runners for the David Loder stable. Another of them, Nijo, who had been runner-up in three pattern races during 1995, had to be withdrawn after breaking out of the stalls, but Loder's remaining representative, the useful handicapper Verzen, completed a 1, 2 for the stable, going down by three quarters of length. Prince of Andros conceded weight all round in the Wulfrun Stakes, carrying a 6 lb penalty for his victory in the Group 2 Tattersalls Gold Cup at the Curragh in May when he just held the renewed challenge of Just Happy. That victory followed a two-length success for Prince of Andros over Nicolotte in the Group 3 T. G. I. Friday's Gordon Richards Stakes at Sandown in April on his first run for nine months following an operation on a near-hind joint. Prince of Andros spent most of the rest of the season in very good company, taking in races such as the Coral-Eclipse, the Arlington Million and the Premio Roma, all Group 1 events. His only other placing, however, came in the Gallinule Stakes at the Curragh in June when he went down by half a length to the odds-on Shemaran in a four-runner race.

The tall, lengthy Prince of Andros is by the well-bred Prix d'Ispahan winner Al Nasr who started his stud career at Spendthrift Farm, Kentucky, before being repatriated to France at the end of 1990. Surprisingly, Al Nasr failed to prove popular with French breeders and now stands in Germany. Prince of Andros is one of Al Nasr's last American-foaled pattern winners, the vast majority of which made their names in Europe, though Pennekamp's half-brother Nasr El Arab won good races on both sides of the Atlantic. Her Radiance, the dam of Prince of Andros, won a maiden race over a mile and a half in Ireland; Prince of Andros is her first foal and only winner to date. Further details of the pedigree were given in *Racehorses of 1993*. Prince of Andros is effective at a mile and a quarter to a mile and a half. He acts on good to firm and soft going as well as on fibresand, and is game and genuine. *D. R. Loder*

PRINCE OF FLORENCE (IRE) 2 ch.c. (Feb 26) Bluebird (USA) 125 – Seme de Lys (USA) 61 (Slew O' Gold (USA)) [1995 5m^4 5m^3 7m^5 6f^2 7m^2 7g 7d^2 8f^2 Oct 18] IR 22,000Y: leggy, quite attractive colt, on small side: first foal: dam maiden (stayed 1m) daughter of half-sister to Exceller: fair maiden: second in nurseries on 3 occasions, best effort at Yarmouth in October on final start: will stay beyond 1m: seems suited by a sound surface: sold 31,000 gns Newmarket Autumn Sales. *L. M. Cumani* — 85

PRINCE OF INDIA 3 b.c. Night Shift (USA) – Indian Queen 115 (Electric 126) [1994 99: 6m* 6g* 7d^5 7m 1995 10m 7.3m^3 8.5m^5 7m^2 9g^6 7m^3 7d^5 8d Dec 2] deep-bodied colt: good mover: useful performer: best effort when ½-length second of 8 to Pipe Major in Van Geest Criterion Stakes at Newmarket in July, staying on really well, pair clear: effective at 7f, and should stay 1m: yet to race on extremes of going: inconsistent. *Lord Huntingdon* — 109

PRINCE OF MY HEART 2 ch.c. (Mar 27) Prince Daniel (USA) – Blue Room 70 (Gorytus (USA) 132) [1995 6m 7m 8.1m^3 7.1g^3 7.9m* 8f^6 Oct 16] rangy colt: has scope: second foal: brother to poor 1994 2-y-o Lady of the Realm: dam, effective at 7f and 1m, granddaughter of very smart Joking Apart: won median auction event at York in October by 1¾ lengths from Iamus: last of 6 in listed race at Pontefract 12 days later, close up until short of room 1f out and eased: better suited by 1m than less. *B. W. Hills* — 87

PRINCE OF SPADES 3 ch.g. Shavian 125 – Diamond Princess 69 (Horage 124) [1994 –: 7g 7g 1995 8m^5 10m* 10g 10f* 8f 8d^6 10f Oct 16] workmanlike, good-quartered gelding: unimpressive mover: modest performer: led closing stages to win seller at Ripon and handicap at Brighton in July: well beaten last 3 starts: not bred to be suited by much further than 1¼m: acts on firm going: sold 10,000 gns Newmarket Autumn Sales. *C. A. Cyzer* — 63

PRINCE PALACIO 5 ch.g. Legend of France (USA) 124 – Thatchville 65 (Thatch (USA) 136) [1994 NR 1995 a12g Jan 7] strong, good-bodied gelding: poor maiden: finished lame only 5-y-o start: stayed 1¾m: acted on good to firm going and fibresand: dead. *D. Burchell* — –

PRINCE PELLINORE 3 b.g. Prince Sabo 123 – Pellinora (USA) (King Pellinore (USA) 127) [1994 47: 5f^4 6.1s 6g 5g 1995 8.2g a7g a8g 8f 6m 5.3f^4 8h^4 7f 6.9g Oct 16] smallish gelding: poor maiden handicapper: stays 1m: acts on hard ground: bolted to post on reappearance, final outing for M. Bell: trained next 4 starts by John Berry: usually races prominently: sold 1,800 gns Newmarket Autumn Sales: sent to Sweden. *C. A. Dwyer* — 41

PRINCE RODNEY 6 gr.g. King of Spain 121 – Dancing Diana 82 (Raga Navarro (ITY) 119) [1994 –: 8s 8.5m 7m 8.3m a7g a7g^5 1995 a6g 8.3m a7g May 11] rather sparely-made gelding: no longer of any account. *C. J. Drewe* — –

PRINCE RUDOLF (IRE) 3 b.g. Cyrano de Bergerac 120 – Princess Raisa (Indian King (USA) 128) [1994 59: 5d^6 5s 5d 5.3g* 5g^6 5.1m^4 5.1m^4 6m^5 5.3f^3 6m^4 6g* 6g 7m^5 6m a7g a6g a6g 1995 a5g^3 a6g^2 a6g^4 a7g^3 a7g^3 a6g^5 a5g^4 6s a6g 6g 5.3m^3 6.1m 5m 7m^3 8f^4 8m^3 Aug 3] workmanlike gelding: poor handicapper: left N. Littmoden's stable after reappearance: stays 1m: acts on the all-weather and firm ground, probably on soft: has worn blinkers/visor since tenth 2-y-o start: inconsistent. *Mrs N. Macauley* — 53 d

PRINCERULLAH 4 gr.g. Prince Des Coeurs (USA) – Chevrullah (Grisaille 115) [1994 –: 12.1f a12g 8.1g 10g 1995 a13g Jan 10] smallish, workmanlike gelding: of little account. *C. D. Broad* — –

PRINCE'S FEATHER (IRE) 3 ch.f. Cadeaux Genereux 131 – Amaranthus (Shirley Heights 130) [1994 77: 6g^{3} 6d^{2} 6g 1995 8g^{5} 7m^{5} 7f 9.7f^{6} Aug 11] lengthy filly: fair maiden handicapper: easily best effort in 1995 on second start: sold out of D. Morley's stable 11,000 gns Newmarket July Sales after next outing: stays 7f: very best effort on only outing on a soft surface: tried blinkered. *K. R. Burke* 68

PRINCE SONGLINE 5 b.g. Prince Sabo 123 – Question Mark 83 (High Line 125) [1994 54: a7g^{4} 8.3m^{2} 9.7m* 9.9m 8m 8.2m 8g 1995 8.1g May 22] good-bodied gelding: modest handicapper at 4 yrs for R. Boss: well beaten in seller only start in 1995. *Mrs A. Swinbank* –

PRINCESS BRIANA 2 b.f. (Mar 12) Daring March 116 – Jersey Maid 82 (On Your Mark 125) [1995 5h 7d 6m Oct 13] third live foal: half-sister to poor miler Mai Pen Rai (by All Systems Go): dam, 2-y-o 5f winner, stayed 7f: soundly beaten in seller and maiden events. *D. Moffatt* –

PRINCESS DANIELLE 3 b.f. Prince Daniel (USA) – Bells of St Martin 89 (Martinmas 128) [1994 57: 6m^{6} 5m^{4} 6m 6m 6g 1995 7.3g 7g^{3} 8.2m* 8m^{5} 8.2m^{3} 10d* 9m Oct 27] leggy filly: easy mover: modest handicapper: won at Nottingham in June and Salisbury (favoured by racing on far side) in September: stays 1¼m: acts on good to firm going and dead: genuine. *C. C. Elsey* 58

PRINCESSE ABIGAIL 4 b.f. Esprit du Nord (USA) 126 – Princesse Vali (FR) (Val de L'Orne (FR) 133) [1994 –: 8.1g 10m 10g 8.3m 1995 12m 17.2m 16.4g 10m Jun 17] lengthy filly: no worthwhile form: tried blinkered. *R. M. Flower* –

PRINCESS EFISIO 2 b.f. (Apr 16) Efisio 120 – Cutlass Princess (USA) 41 (Cutlass (USA)) [1995 5.1m^{5} 6m^{6} Jul 8] smallish, rather dipped-back filly: second foal: half-sister to 3-y-o Bretton Princess (by Handsome Sailor): dam poor maiden: bit backward, well beaten maidens at Chester (slowly away) and Haydock (hung badly left halfway). *B. A. McMahon* –

PRINCESS GAY (IRE) 3 b.f. Fairy King (USA) – Tripoli 70 (Great Heron (USA) 127) [1994 NR 1995 5.1g Apr 4] IR 10,000Y: ninth living foal: sister to 2 winners, including 1990 Irish 2-y-o 6f winner Fairy Folk, and half-sister to 4 winners: dam lightly-raced maiden: backward and bandaged near-hind, down the field in maiden at Nottingham: sold 1,400 gns Newmarket July Sales. *M. Bell* –

PRINCESS IN BLUE (IRE) 3 b.f. Bluebird (USA) 125 – Parkeen Princess (He Loves Me 120) [1994 –: 6g 5m 6m a5g a7g^{4} a6g a6g 1995 a6g Jan 24] leggy, unfurnished filly: bad maiden: probably stays 7f: tried blinkered. *C. J. Hill* –

PRINCESS KAMINA 3 b.f. Nomination 125 – Danaka (FR) (Val de Loir 133) [1994 –: 5g 7m 7s 7d 1995 a8g a11g Feb 17] quite good-topped filly: no worthwhile form in varied company: tried visored. *M. J. Camacho* –

PRINCESS MAXINE (IRE) 6 b.m. Horage 124 – Sallywell (Manado 130) [1994 68: 8.3d^{5} 6.9v* 8.3m^{3} 7m^{5} 6.9f* 8h* 8.1g 1995 8.3v 6g^{6} 8g^{5} 8m 9g 8f 6.9f^{2} 7.5g^{4} 8.1f^{2} 8f^{4} 8.1m^{4} 8.3f 6g 6g^{3} 7.1s 7g^{6} Oct 10] leggy mare: fair handicapper at best: well below form last 7 starts: effective at 6f and stays 1m well: acts on any going on turf, respectable effort on fibresand: has run well for amateur/7-lb claimer. *J. J. O'Neill* 66 d

PRINCESS OBERON (IRE) 5 b. or br.m. Fairy King (USA) – Flash of Gold 78 (Pardao 120) [1994 85: 6f 5d 5m* 5.7f^{4} 5f* 5f* 6g 5.2g^{4} 5g 5.6g^{3} 6m^{4} 5m 1995 5g 5g* 6m^{4} 5m^{6} 5m^{2} 6g^{4} 5m Aug 19] leggy mare: in foal to Selkirk: fairly useful handicapper: won at Newmarket in June: won only at around 5f, but stayed 6f: acted on firm ground. *M. Bell* 91

PRINCESS PAMGADDY 2 gr.f. (Apr 13) Petong 126 – Edwins' Princess 75 (Owen Dudley 121) [1995 5m^{3} 5g^{5} 5g 5g^{6} 7.1g* 8.3g^{6} 7f^{4} 7m Oct 12] 9,200Y: leggy filly: fifth foal: half-sister to 3-y-o 11.1f winner Royal Expression (by Sylvan Express), 5f and 6f winner Pageboy (by Tina's Pet) and a winner in Sweden by Chilibang: dam disappointing 2-y-o 5f winner who stayed 1m: well below early-season form when winning poor claimer at Edinburgh in September: stays 7.1f: sold 3,500 gns Doncaster November Sales. *J. Berry* 58 d

PRINCESS RENATA (IRE) 2 ch.f. (Feb 26) Maelstrom Lake 118 – Sajanjal (Dance In Time (CAN)) [1995 a5g 5m^{6} 5g^{6} 6m^{6} Jul 27] 3,500Y, 5,500 2-y-o: half-sister to 3-y-o 5f winner Bajan Frontier (by Imperial Frontier), 1m winner Sirtelimar (by Montelimar) and 3 winners in USA: dam unraced half-sister to useful –

Irish 7f to 1¼m winner Toca Madera: signs of ability in maiden auctions (for D. Thom) and a Yarmouth seller (raced on unfavoured part of track). *R. Harris*

PRINCESS SADIE 3 ch.f. Shavian 125 – Princess Zepoli 61 (Persepolis (FR) 127) [1994 86: 5m^5 5f* 5m^2 6.1g^5 6d 5d* 5s^3 5m 5s 1995 5.1f^3 5m^5 6m^5 5m 5m Nov 4] lengthy, useful-looking filly: fairly useful handicapper: good third on reappearance (penultimate outing for M. Channon) but ran poorly afterwards: bred to stay at least 7f, but looks a sprinter: acts on any going: sometimes restless in stalls. *M. Johnston* — 80 d

PRINCESS SHERA (IRE) 4 b.f. Prince Rupert (FR) 121 – Crown Coral (Main Reef 126) [1994 44: a8.5g^6 5d 10d^4 11.1g^5 12s^2 10m a12g^5 8.3g^2 11.1g^6 a7g 1995 a8.5g 9.2m 7f^6 10m Aug 22] neat filly: poor maiden: no form in 1995: headstrong and temperamental: sold 550 gns Doncaster October Sales: one to leave alone. *E. J. Alston* — – §

PRINCETHORPE 8 b.g. Ring Bidder 88 – Sparkling Jenny (Sparkler 130) [1994 NR 1995 a8.5g a7g a12g Oct 28] first foal: dam moderate staying hurdler: no promise in claimers at Wolverhampton: won selling hurdle in November. *B. R. Cambidge* — –

PRINCE ZIZIM 2 b.c. (May 1) Shareef Dancer (USA) 135 – Possessive Lady 62 (Dara Monarch 128) [1995 6m 8g^4 Oct 1] 10,500F: quite attractive colt: first foal: dam, 1m winner, half-sister to Irish Oaks winner Possessive Dancer (by Shareef Dancer): better effort in maidens when 6 lengths fourth of 7 to Naval Gazer at Brighton: will be suited by middle distances: joined R. Spicer. *C. A. Dwyer* — 60 p

PRINCIPAL BOY (IRE) 2 br.g. (Feb 12) Cyrano de Bergerac 120 – Shenley Lass (Prince Tenderfoot (USA) 126) [1995 6m^5 7m^4 8.1g 6g^5 7d 5m 5s^6 a5g Dec 1] IR 4,500F, 8,000Y: compact gelding: has a round action: third foal: brother to 1992 2-y-o 1¼m seller winner Trepidation: dam Irish maiden: poor maiden on balance of form: probably stays 7f: blinkered last 2 outings. *T. J. Etherington* — 42 +

PRINTERS QUILL 3 b.g. Squill (USA) 122 – On Impulse 63 (Jellaby 124) [1994 NR 1995 10d 10.2m^3 10d Oct 19] leggy gelding: first reported living foal: dam best at around 1m also in frame over hurdles: no worthwhile form in maidens. *Major D. N. Chappell* — –

PRIOLO PRIMA 2 b.c. (Feb 1) Priolo (USA) 127 – Jungle Rose 90 (Shirley Heights 130) [1995 6g^2 Sep 21] 48,000Y: third foal: half-brother to 1994 2-y-o 5.9f winner Jungle Patrol (by Night Shift), and 1m to 10.5f/hurdles winner Desert Fighter (by Green Desert): dam lightly-raced 1¼m winner out of Lowther winner Prickle: 5/1 and green, 2½ lengths second of 11 to Sketchbook in maiden at Pontefract, always close up and leading from 2f out until last: moved fluently to post: will stay 1m: sure to improve, and win races. *Sir Mark Prescott* — 90 p

PRIORY BELLE (IRE) 2 ch.f. (Apr 10) Priolo (USA) 127 – Ingabelle 108 (Taufan (USA) 119) [1995 6f* 7m^2 7g* Sep 10] — 103 p

The reputation of the Moyglare Stud Stakes, the only Group 1 race in Ireland restricted to two-year-old fillies, has enjoyed a mini-revival in the last few years when the race has fallen to the likes of the One Thousand Guineas winner Sayyedati and the high-class two-year-old Lemon Souffle. Whether its latest winner Priory Belle will come to be remembered as one of its better winners only time will tell, but the renewal she won by three quarters of a length and half a length from Tamnia and My Melody Parkes, the first eight home covered by only four lengths, doesn't look to be an outstanding one. Indeed, the subsequent performance in the Prix Marcel Boussac of the fourth horse Dance Design, denied a clear run at the Curragh until much too late, suggests that Priory Belle was rather fortunate to win the Moyglare at all. Priory Belle had few supporters beforehand, sent off at 16/1 after two runs which yielded a three-quarter-length victory in a five-runner minor event at Fairyhouse and a length-and-a-half defeat at the hands of Dance Design, who was conceding 3 lb, in the listed Debutante Stakes at Leopardstown. Most of the money at the Curragh was for Zelzelah, who was representing the connections of the 1994 Moyglare winner Belle Genius, and running for the first time since trouncing Axford in the Donnington Castle Stakes at Newbury in July. There were two other British challengers, Rouge Rancon, an impressive winner of a maiden at Newmarket in July on her only start, and Tamnia, who'd won the listed Milcars Star Stakes and had then gone on to finish fourth in the Prix du Calvados; Dance Design, on a hat-trick, started co-second favourite behind Zelzelah. The Moyglare was a muddling race with several fillies finding trouble, but it made for an exciting finish from a furlong out where the 20/1-shot Ceirseach finally gave way to the hard-ridden Rouge Rancon. No sooner had Rouge Rancon taken up the running, however, than Priory Belle, her tail flashing repeatedly, went on only to find her lead threatened immediately by Tamnia on one side and by the Lowther runner-up My Melody Parkes and Dance Design on the other. A flashing tail is often interpreted as a sign of irresolution or unsatisfactory temperament but that certainly couldn't be levelled at Priory Belle on this occasion; pressed hard, she had every opportunity to shirk the issue, but she kept on gamely to provide the Irish with their first victory in the Moyglare since Capricciosa in 1990. Both Rouge Rancon and Zelzelah ran disappointingly, particularly the latter whose trainer was reportedly confident beforehand that she would head the market for the One Thousand Guineas after the contest, and neither achieved much of note subsequently in the Fillies' Mile. Although mentioned as a possible for the Marcel Boussac, Priory Belle wasn't seen out again. She should stay a mile, and seems likely to be trained for the Irish One Thousand Guineas.

Priory Belle (IRE) (ch.f. Apr 10, 1993)	Priolo (USA) (b 1987)	Sovereign Dancer (b 1975)	Northern Dancer Bold Princess
		Primevere (br 1982)	Irish River Spring Is Sprung
	Ingabelle (b 1984)	Taufan (b 1977)	Stop The Music Stolen Date
		Bodelle (ch 1975)	Falcon Shade

Priory Belle was bred by her owners the Ballylinch Stud, for whom she is a first Group 1 winner. She is also the first pattern winner for her sire Priolo, one of the best milers of 1990 when he won the Prix Jean Prat and Prix Jacques le Marois before finishing an excellent third to Royal Academy in the Breeders' Cup Mile. Priory Belle's dam Ingabelle was a useful sprinter in the Ireland. Both her first and last appearances were winning ones, the latter in the Group 3 Phoenix Sprint Stakes, but she managed to win only one of her twenty-one races in between, the listed Mill Ridge Stakes. She is the dam of three winners besides Priory Belle, her fourth foal, the best of the others being the smart Irish three-year-old seven-furlong winner Wild Bluebell (by Bluebird), successful in the Group 3 Concorde Stakes at Tipperary in October. Ingabelle is a daughter of the versatile Irish middle-distance winner

Moyglare Stud Stakes, the Curragh—Priory Belle takes it from Tamnia (No. 12) inside the final furlong

Bodelle, who was useful over hurdles too, and a granddaughter of a mare, Shade, who won at up to thirteen furlongs. There's plenty of stamina in the pedigree—Priory Belle's fourth dam Summer Tan was an out-and-out stayer—but one of Bodelle's half-sisters Synchronise is the grandam of the 1988 Gimcrack winner Sharp N' Early. *J. S. Bolger, Ireland*

PRIVATE AUDIENCE (USA) 2 b.c. (Apr 8) Private Account (USA) – Monroe (USA) 102 (Sir Ivor 135) [1995 7.9g^6 Oct 7] close-coupled, good-topped colt: half-brother to numerous winners here and abroad, 4 at least useful, notably French miler Masterclass (by The Minstrel) and French 1¼m/10.5f winner Diese (by Diesis): dam useful Irish sprinter, is sister to Malinowski and half-sister to dam of Try My Best and El Gran Senor: 10/3, well-beaten sixth of 8 to Committal in maiden at York, slowly away and never dangerous: moved fluently to post: capable of better. *H. R. A. Cecil* – p

PRIVATE FIXTURE (IRE) 4 ch.g. The Noble Player (USA) 126 – Pennyala (Skyliner 117) [1994 71: 8m^3 8g^2 7.1d 7d 8s 8d^4 a8.5g 1995 a8g^4 8m 8g^6 a8.5g a7g Dec 12] quite good-topped gelding: fair miler at best at 3 yrs: long way below form in 1995. *D. Marks* –

PRIVATE LINE (USA) 3 ch.f. Private Account (USA) – Miss Summer (Luthier 126) [1994 69p: 7s* a8.5f* 1995 7g^3 8f* 8.1m* 8g a8.5f* Dec 14] tall, leggy, close-coupled filly: useful form: won minor event at Kempton (made most) in June, listed race at Sandown (penultimate start for H. Cecil) in August and allowance event in USA in December: should stay further than 8.5f: acts on firm and soft ground. *R. Frankel, USA* 105

PRIVATE SONG (USA) 2 b.c. (Feb 15) Private Account (USA) – Queen of Song (USA) (His Majesty (USA)) [1995 7m^2 Nov 3] strong, lengthy colt: has plenty of scope: half-brother to 3-y-o 10.2f winner Easy Listening (by Easy Goer) and several winners in North America, one in stakes by Northern Dancer: dam, twice graded winner over 8.5f at 5 yrs, sister to smart 6f to 9f winner Cormorant: 8/1, promising ½-length second of 18 to Wahiba Sands in maiden at Doncaster, very green beforehand and taking time to get hang of things once racing, but running on in good style final 150 yds: will be well suited by middle distances: sure to improve, and win a race. *R. Charlton* 78 p

PRIVILEGED 2 ch.g. (Feb 12) Efisio 120 – Prejudice 83 (Young Generation 129) [1995 5m^6 6f* Jul 31] compact gelding: third foal: brother to fair 7f to (in Italy) 10.5f winner Al Moulouki and half-brother to fairly useful 6f/1m performer Hob Green (by Move Off): dam maiden suited by 1m: well-backed co-favourite after eye-catching debut, won maiden at Ripon by a length from Vasetto, slowly into stride again but good headway halfway: subsequently gelded: looked sure to improve again: sent to Hong Kong. *Mrs J. R. Ramsden* 78 p

PRIVITY (USA) 3 b.f. Private Account (USA) – Sylph (USA) 110 (Alleged (USA) 138) [1994 106: 6.5g* 6.5g^2 8v^2 1995 8d^3 10.5g^3 12g^3 12m* 12d 12s^5 10f 12f^4 Dec 10] smart French filly: won 6-runner Prix de Malleret at Longchamp in June by 2 lengths from Ultra Finesse: best efforts when around 2½ lengths eighth of 10 to Carling in Prix Vermeille at Longchamp (when still with P. Bary) next start and when 3¼ lengths fourth of 14 to Royal Chariot in Hollywood Turf Cup: stays 1½m, may well get further: acts on any going. *R. Frankel, USA* 114

PRIZEFIGHTER 4 b.g. Rambo Dancer (CAN) 107 – Jaisalmer 97 (Castle Keep 121) [1994 74: 7m^6 8.1f* 7g 8.1g* 8.3m^6 8.2m^6 8f^2 8.1m* 8.2g^2 8g* 8m^4 8.2m 8.2m^3 8m 8g 9g 1995 7m 8f 8.1m^6 8.5m^6 8.1m* 8m 8.9g a8g* Dec 6] neat gelding: fair handicapper: left S. Gollings' stable after reappearance: won at Sandown (apprentices) in August and Lingfield (all-weather debut) in December: stays 8.2f: acts on equitrack, best efforts on a sound surface (acts on firm going): makes running/races prominently. *J. L. Eyre* 70

PRIZE GIVING 2 ch.c. (Feb 14) Most Welcome 131 – Glowing With Pride 114 (Ile de Bourbon (USA) 133) [1995 6g^6 7f^2 7m^3 7f* Oct 18] strong, lengthy colt: seventh foal: half-brother to several winners, including 10.5f to 17.2f winner Inchcailloch (by Lomond) and useful 6f to 7.3f winner Everglades (by Green Desert): dam 7f and 10.5f winner: fair form in maidens: won 11-runner event at Yarmouth on 82 final outing by a neck from Unreal City, setting steady pace then all out to hold on with head rather high: will stay at least 1¼m: sweating penultimate outing. *G. Wragg*

PRIZE PUPIL (IRE) 3 b.c. Royal Academy (USA) 130 – Bestow 76 (Shirley Heights 130) [1994 65p: 7g^6 1995 8m^2 8.3m^5 10g* 10m^3 11.9g 10g Sep 29] lengthy colt: fluent mover: fair performer: won maiden at Ascot in July: stays 1¼m well, may well get 1½m: has raced only on a sound surface: hung and carried head awkwardly on reappearance: has run well when sweating. *C. F. Wall* 76

PROFIT RELEASE (IRE) 4 b.f. Dowsing (USA) 124 – Going Digital (USA) (Northern Baby (CAN) 127) [1994 8g 7d^3 6d 7v 1995 a7g a8g^3 a10g^4 a8g^2 a7g^3 a8g^3 a8g* a7g 8s 8m^2 6.9m^2 8m 6.9f* 8.1g^3 7g^6 6m^2 6m^3 7f^6 7g^4 6f* Jul 7] ex-Irish filly: fourth foal: half-sister to 3 winners, including Irish 7f/1m winner Strategic Timing (by Chief Singer): dam showed little: fair performer (rated 78) at 3 yrs: sold out of D. Weld's stable 4,400 gns Newmarket December Sales: modest form here: won seller at Lingfield in February, claimer at Carlisle (flashed tail) in May and handicap at Hamilton in July: effective at 6f to 1m: acts on firm and dead ground and the all-weather: blinkered once in Ireland and last 9 starts: usually races prominently: tough. *M. Johnston* 65 a59

PROGRESSION 4 b.c. Reprimand 122 – Mainmast 63 (Bustino 136) [1995 9g^3 12m 10m 10.1g^4 12g^3 a12g^5 12f* 11.9m* 12m^2 14.6m^6 12d Sep 24] rather leggy colt: has a round action: fair performer: trained in 1993 by P. Cole: won 4 races in 1994 (between 7f and 13f) in Eastern Europe, notably the Czech Derby: clear-cut winner of handicaps at Goodwood in July and York (15-runner £15,700 event, beat Jameel Asmar by 2½ lengths) in August: best form at up to 1½m: acts on firm ground: blinkered last 5 starts: held up: joined C. Murray. *P. C. Haslam* 77

PROJECTION (USA) 2 b.c. (Feb 11) Topsider (USA) – Image of Reality (USA) (In Reality) [1995 6m* Oct 13] good-topped, attractive colt: eighth foal: closely related to 2 winners by El Gran Senor, notably Toussaud, smart performer at up to 7f here later Grade 1 9f winner in USA, and half-brother to several winners here and in North America, including 1993 2-y-o 7f winner Rameau (by Zilzal): dam smart winner at up to 9f in North America: 4/1, won 21-runner maiden at Newmarket by a short head from Mutadarra, pushed along some way out then doing very well to come 4 lengths clear last 200 yds: moved unimpressively to post: sure to improve, and looks a useful prospect. *B. W. Hills* 89 p

PROLIFIC LADY (IRE) 3 b.f. Nabeel Dancer (USA) 120 – Aljood 111 (Kris 135) [1994 NR 1995 7g^4 6.9g^4 6m* 6m 6m^2 6.1g 5f^6 6f^2 6m^5 6f^2 5.3f^3 6g Sep 12] lengthy filly: second foal: half-sister to 6f (including at 2 yrs) and 1m winner Desert Invader (by Lead On Time): dam, maiden who stayed 1m, finished fourth in Prix Marcel Boussac: bought out of M. Stoute's stable 400 gns Doncaster November (1994) Sales: fair performer: won median auction maiden at Folkestone in April on final outing for G. Oldroyd: probably needs a stiff 5f, but unlikely to stay beyond 7f: has raced only on a sound surface: blinkered/visored last 6 starts: usually races prominently: sold 4,500 gns Newmarket Autumn Sales: sent to Sweden. *M. Brittain* 73

PROMISE FULFILLED (USA) 4 b.f. Bet Twice (USA) – Kind Prospect (USA) (Mr Prospector (USA)) [1994 85: 6g^2 7d 6m^6 7.1g 8m 1995 a9.4g 8g 7.6m 8.5m^4 7g^4 8m 10g 7.1s Sep 30] sturdy filly: unimpressive mover: fair handicapper at best in 1995, trained until after sixth start by S. Norton: stays 8.5f: has won on dead going, but best efforts on a sound surface: tried blinkered/visored: sold 4,800 gns Newmarket December Sales. *A. Bailey* 76 d

PROMITTO 5 ch.m. Roaring Riva 103 – I Don't Mind 97 (Swing Easy (USA) 126) [1994 NR 1995 8f^5 10m Jul 3] big mare: poor maiden: well beaten in 1995: sold 3,200 gns Doncaster October Sales. *M. D. Hammond* –

PROMPTLY (IRE) 2 b.f. (Jan 10) Lead On Time (USA) 123 – Ghariba 112 (Final Straw 127) [1995 6m^2 Aug 26] leggy filly: third foal: half-sister to 1992 2-y-o 7f winner Hawayah (by Shareef Dancer) and Italian 3-y-o 5f and 7f winner Reinaldo (by Green Desert): dam, Nell Gwyn winner, half-sister to Braashee, a good family: 7/1, strong-finishing neck second to My Mariam in 14-runner maiden at Newmarket in August, running green then keeping on well after being checked and switched when not clear run 1f out: will stay 7f: looked sure to improve, and win a race. *M. R. Stoute* 80 p

PROPER BLUE (USA) 2 b.c. (Mar 19) Proper Reality (USA) – Blinking (USA) 88 p
(Tom Rolfe) [1995 6m^4 6m^3 7m^3 7f^2 7f* Aug 22] $12,000Y: stocky colt: third foal: half-brother to a winner in North America by Cox's Ridge: dam, from family of Bakharoff and Emperor Jones, won at up to 1¼m: sire very smart Grade 1 1m and 9f winner: fairly useful form: improved effort to win strongly-run 7-runner nursery at Brighton last time by short head from General Rose, staying on really well: will be at least as effective at 1m: has worn crossed noseband. *T. G. Mills*

PROPHETS HONOUR 3 ch.g. Deploy 131 – Cat's Claw (USA) (Sharpen Up 80
127) [1994 NR 1995 8m^4 10m 10m^4 10g^4 13.4d^4 14.1f^3 Oct 12] 17,500Y: workmanlike gelding: unimpressive mover: first foal: dam never ran: fairly useful maiden: trained until after fifth start by C. Cyzer: probably stays 14.1f: acts on firm and dead ground: progressive juvenile hurdler, completing hat-trick in December. *P. C. Haslam*

PROPOLIS POWER (IRE) 2 ch.g. (May 20) Simply Great (FR) 122 – Now –
Then (Sandford Lad 133) [1995 5m 5m^5 6m 7.5m Jul 8] 6,200F, 9,400Y: brother to ungenuine 1994 2-y-o Kennedy's Gold and half-brother to winning sprinter Norling (by Nashamaa) and 1½m winner Salubrious (by Sallust): dam placed in Ireland from 7f to 1¼m: no form in median auction maiden and sellers: sweating third start. *M. W. Easterby*

PROPOSING (IRE) 3 b.c. Rainbow Quest (USA) 134 – La Romance (USA) 98 p
(Lyphard (USA) 132) [1994 NR 1995 a10g* a10g^2 Apr 7] good-topped colt: fifth foal: half-brother to French middle-distance winner Amal (by Top Ville) and fair 1989 2-y-o 6f winner New Romantic (by Miswaki): dam French 1¼m winner out of half-sister to Green Dancer: won maiden at Lingfield in March in comfortable fashion: improved a good deal on that when second of 7 to Maralinga in £8,100 event there week later, soon bustled along in rear then staying on resolutely: will stay at least 1½m: looked likely to improve again. *J. H. M. Gosden*

PROSARCH (IRE) 2 ch.f. (Apr 30) Archway (IRE) 115 – Biddy Mulligan –
(Ballad Rock 122) [1995 5g 6g Oct 3] IR 10,000Y: sturdy filly: fourth foal: closely related to a winner in Italy by Thatching and half-sister to Irish 5f winner Miss Potter (by Dancing Dissident): dam, placed at up to 1m, half-sister to high-class sprinter The Blues: no chance from bad draw on debut: signs of ability in maiden auction following month: sold 1,050 gns Doncaster November Sales: may do better. *R. F. Johnson Houghton*

PROSEQUENDO (USA) 8 b.g. Robellino (USA) 127 – Allegedly (USA) (Sir –
Ivor 135) [1994 –: a13g^4 a13g 1995 a16g 14.1f 14d Sep 14] tall, quite good-topped gelding: has quick action: little form since 6 yrs: left M. Dixon's stable after reappearance. *G. L. Moore*

PROSPECTOR'S COVE 2 b.g. (May 11) Dowsing (USA) 124 – Pearl Cove 63 77 p
(Town And Country 124) [1995 7.1s* Nov 2] 5,000Y: sixth foal: half-brother to German 3-y-o 7f winner Magical Rock (by Rock City), 7f winner St Louis Lady (by Absalom) and 1¼m winner Beldonayr (by Rabdan): dam lightly raced: 6/1, won 14-runner maiden auction at Edinburgh by 3 lengths from Scenicris, never far away and running on strongly despite giving flash of tail: subsequently gelded: will stay beyond 7f: will improve. *J. Pearce*

PROSPERO 2 b.g. (Feb 14) Petong 126 – Pennies To Pounds 80 (Ile de Bourbon – p
(USA) 133) [1995 8m Oct 12] strong, lengthy gelding: half-brother to 2 winners by Song, including 7f winner Platinum Disc, and to 1992 2-y-o 6f winner Midwinter Dream (by Midyan): dam 8.5f winner out of sprinting half-sister to Mummy's Pet: 50/1, burly and green, always towards rear in maiden at Newmarket won by Silver Dome: sold 13,500 gns Newmarket Autumn Sales: probably capable of better. *I. A. Balding*

PROTEKTOR (GER) 6 b.h. Acatenango (GER) 127 – Prioritat (Frontal (FR) 116
122) [1994 116: 12s^3 16v^3 11g^4 12g 12d^3 12s^4 20s^2 14.5v^4 1995 12s^2 16v^6 11m^5 12m^5 12g^6 12g^3 12s^4 Oct 22] smart German horse: ran well, though no match for Monsun, when 1¾ lengths second of 9 in Group 2 Gerling Preis at Cologne: best effort in 1995 (as the year before) when third in strongly-run Europa-Preis at Cologne, never nearer and 4½ lengths behind Solon: effective at 1½m and stays well: acts on good to firm and heavy ground. *A. Lowe, Germany*

PROTON 5 b.g. Sure Blade (USA) 130 – Banket 120 (Glint of Gold 128) [1994 79: 8g 10m 11.5g* 12g^2 10v^2 11.5d* 12s^3 12v^3 1995 10m 12m^5 12m^3 12m 12f^2 12m^2 12m* 13.3d 12m Nov 4] strong, quite attractive gelding: fairly useful handicapper: won £10,400 amateurs race at Epsom in August: well beaten in Autumn Cup at Newbury and November Handicap at Doncaster afterwards: should stay beyond 1½m: acts on any going: visored (well beaten) once at 3 yrs: races prominently. *R. Akehurst* — 85

PROUD BRIGADIER (IRE) 7 b.g. Auction Ring (USA) 123 – Naughty One Gerard (Brigadier Gerard 144) [1994 68: 9.7v^4 7m 10g 7.1m^6 7m* 7.5f^6 1995 8g Oct 3] lengthy, sparely-made gelding: fair handicapper at 6 yrs: bandaged on first run for nearly 14 months, no promise in minor event at Warwick. *P. Burgoyne* — –

PROUD DESTINY 3 b.f. Green Desert (USA) 127 – Pumpona (USA) (Sharpen Up 127) [1994 NR 1995 7m 8m^2 8.5d^2 7.1m* 8.3m^4 7f^3 7m^2 7.1d^6 Sep 2] leggy filly: third foal: closely related to 4-y-o 7f winner Canary Falcon (by Polish Precedent): dam, unraced, from speedy family: fairly useful performer: comfortably won maiden at Chepstow in July: creditable efforts in handicaps next 3 starts: effective at 7f to 8.5f: acts on firm and dead ground: usually races prominently: consistent: sold 8,200 gns Doncaster October Sales. *M. R. Stoute* — 83

PROUD IMAGE 3 b.g. Zalazl (USA) 120 – Fleur de Foret (USA) 61§ (Green Forest (USA) 134) [1994 NR 1995 8g 8f^2 10m 8m^5 a8g 8f^4 7.1m^4 8.5g^5 8m* 7.6d* 7m^3 7m Aug 26] small gelding: second foal: dam, sprint maiden, became ungenuine at 3 yrs: fair performer: successful in seller at Ripon and handicap at Lingfield in July: stays 1m: acts on firm and dead ground: visored 3 times, including for both victories. *A. P. Jarvis* — 70

PROUD MONK 2 gr.c. (Mar 16) Aragon 118 – Silent Sister 78 (Kind of Hush 118) [1995 6m^4 6.1m^6 5.7h^3 6f^5 5g^6 7d^3 7g^3 7.3d* 7m^3 a7g Nov 16] strong, lengthy colt: has scope: first foal: dam stayed 1m: won 19-runner nursery at Newbury in October: showed little on fibresand final outing: stays 7.3f: acts on good to firm ground and good to soft. *G. L. Moore* — 77

PROVENCE 8 ch.g. Rousillon (USA) 133 – Premier Rose 117 (Sharp Edge 123) [1994 80: 16s^4 16.2m^4 16.1m^5 20f 18.2s^5 1995 14m 16.1g May 25] rangy gelding: good mover: fairly useful handicapper at 7 yrs for P. Harris: winning hurdler for new stable, but well below form on return to flat: stays well: acts on firm and soft ground: well below form visored and blinkered: sold 1,050 gns Doncaster September Sales. *L. Lungo* — –

PRUDENT PET 3 b.f. Distant Relative 128 – Philgwyn 66 (Milford 119) [1994 63: 5.9m 7m^4 7g^5 7g 7g* 8s^6 7d 1995 7.5m a7g^5 8.3f 9f^2 8m* a8g* 10g 10.5d 8.2m a9.4g Nov 13] leggy, useful-looking filly: good walker: modest handicapper: won at Pontefract in July and Southwell (amateurs) in September: soundly beaten afterwards: probably best at up to 1m: acts on soft ground, firm and fibresand. *C. W. Fairhurst* — 65

PRUDENT PRINCESS 3 b.f. Puissance 110 – Princess Story 64 (Prince de Galles 125) [1994 NR 1995 7m^4 6m^5 6f^3 a7g^4 7g^3 a8.5g^6 Nov 13] 4,200Y: angular filly: half-sister to several winners, including 6f winner Aquarian Prince (by Mansingh) and 1¼m and 1½m winner Kiki Star (by Some Hand): dam won sellers at around 1m: modest maiden: should stay 1m: yet to race on a soft surface. *A. Hide* — 63

PRUSSIA 4 b.c. Roi Danzig (USA) – Vagrant Maid (USA) 85 (Honest Pleasure (USA)) [1994 59: 9f 10m* 10g^2 10.2g 10d 1995 10d 14s 14.1m Oct 26] heavy-bodied colt: modest handicapper: off course a year and no promise for new stable in 1995: should prove well suited by further than 1¼m: flashes tail. *W. Clay* — –

PRUSSIAN BLUE (USA) 3 b.c. Polish Navy (USA) – Lit'l Rose (USA) (Mr Prospector (USA)) [1994 78p: 8g^6 1995 10m^3 12m* 12m Jun 22] leggy colt: fairly useful form: narrowly landed the odds in 3-runner minor event at Beverley in May, making all: stiff task, below form in King George V Stakes at Royal Ascot: stays 1½m: usually races prominently: stays in training. *H. R. A. Cecil* — 91

PRUSSIAN FLAG 3 b.c. Infantry 122 – What A Present (Pharly (FR) 130) [1994 97: 5g^3 6m^3 6g* 7g* 7.3d 1995 8f^4 7.6m 8f 8.2m Oct 19] close-coupled colt: deteriorated badly in 1995, beating only one rival of 41: sold only 1,800 gns Newmarket Autumn Sales. *R. Hannon* — –

PUBLIC ACCLAIM 2 ch.f. (Feb 7) Weldnaas (USA) 112 – Sure Victory (IRE) 75 (Stalker 121) [1995 6.1g a7g Jul 17] 1,300Y: first foal: dam 6f to 1m winner: behind in sellers at Chepstow and Wolverhampton: sold 525 gns Ascot August Sales. *M. Blanshard* –

PUBLIC OFFERING 2 b.f. (Mar 14) Warrshan (USA) 117 – Money Supply (Brigadier Gerard 144) [1995 7g 6s Sep 28] 4,000F, 1,800Y: half-sister to several winners, including 5-y-o 7f to 1½m winner Credit Squeeze (by Superlative) and middle-distance performer Classic Account (by Pharly): dam unraced sister to smart Irish 1m winner Senior Citizen: bit backward, behind in claimers. *M. Blanshard* –

PUBLIC REPROOF 2 b.g. (Feb 8) Reprimand 122 – Zelda (USA) (Sharpen Up 127) [1995 7m Nov 3] 7,800Y: first living foal: dam once-raced half-sister to Moorestyle: 33/1, always behind in 18-runner maiden at Doncaster. *P. C. Haslam* –

PUFFY 8 ch.g. Wolverlife 115 – Eskaroon (Artaius (USA) 129) [1994 38, a44: 10d 8g^{4} a8g a8g 1995 a11g^{3} a8g^{3} a9.4g a8g^{3} 8.1d^{6} 10m^{6} 8m 8g^{4} a8g* a8g^{5} a8g^{4} Jul 13] leggy, rather sparely-made gelding: poor mover: poor handicapper: won seller at Southwell in June: stays 1¼m: acts on fibresand and any turf going: usually blinkered/visored: often slowly away. *M. Dods* 38 a49

PULGA CIRCO 2 b.f. (Feb 14) Tina's Pet 121 – Pulga (Blakeney 126) [1995 a6g a6g^{3} a7g^{5} a7g^{2} 8m a7g^{4} 10g a8.5g a8.5g Oct 28] good-bodied filly: first foal: dam unraced: plater: ran poorly last 2 starts: appears to stay 1¼m: best effort on fibresand. *B. A. McMahon* 40 a50

PULMICORT 5 b.g. Red Sunset 120 – Finesse 87 (Miralgo 130) [1994 NR 1995 11.6m 11.6g 11.4g Jun 16] workmanlike gelding: half-brother to several winners, including very useful sprinter Princess Seal and Irish 1½m winner South Meadow (both by Prince Tenderfoot): dam won over 1½m: fair handicapper in Ireland at 3 yrs (rated 72) for M. Halford: poor novice hurdler here in 1994/5 for Miss Merrita Jones: well beaten in handicaps (visored and blinkered) and claimer on return to flat: stays 11f: acts on good to firm ground and soft: effective in blinkers in Ireland. *P. Burgoyne* –

PUMICE 3 ch.f. Salse (USA) 128 – Horseshoe Reef 88 (Mill Reef (USA) 141) [1994 77p: 6g^{5} 6g^{3} 1995 6g 8m* 11.9m^{6} 10.3m^{5} 10.5d 14.1m Oct 26] useful-looking filly: has a quick action: fair performer: won maiden at Pontefract in August: failed to progress: probably stays 1¾m: acts on good to firm ground, well beaten on dead: sold 19,000 gns Newmarket December Sales. *L. M. Cumani* 75

PUNCH 3 b.g. Reprimand 122 – Cartooness (USA) 60 (Achieved 125) [1994 55?: 5d 5s 6f 8g 8.3g 8g^{5} 1995 10m^{5} 11.1f^{3} 14.1f^{3} 12.3m^{4} 14.1h* 14.1m^{4} 15g 12.1g Sep 24] tall, strong gelding: modest handicapper: won maiden event at Carlisle in August: stays 1¾m: acts on hard ground: blinkered since fifth 3-y-o start: sold 3,800 gns Newmarket Autumn Sales. *N. Tinkler* 57

PUNKAH (USA) 2 b.c. (Mar 8) Lear Fan (USA) 130 – Gentle Persuasion 95 (Bustino 136) [1995 7d^{5} 6d Oct 19] well-made colt: fifth foal: half-brother to smart 5f to 7f winner Sharp Prod (by Sharpo) and 1991 2-y-o 5f winner Prompting (by Primo Dominie): dam 2-y-o 6f winner later suited by 1m: shaped well when just under 6 lengths fifth of 13 to Centre Stalls in maiden at Salisbury, prominent until one pace over 1f out: well beaten in 20-runner maiden at Newbury in October. *Lord Huntingdon* 70

PURBECK CENTENARY 5 b.g. Lidhame 109 – Double Stitch 74 (Wolver Hollow 126) [1994 54d: a6g^{4} 5s^{5} 5d^{5} 5g 5.1f a5g a5g a6g^{6} 1995 a6g^{2} a6g^{3} a6g^{2} a6g 5m 5.1m 5g 5m 6f^{3} Jun 30] leggy gelding: poor mover: modest handicapper: shows plenty of pace on turf, but has won over 7f on equitrack: acts on firm and dead ground, best form on equitrack: usually front runner: sold 3,800 gns Newmarket July Sales. *P. Howling* 45 a51

PURE GRAIN 3 b.f. Polish Precedent (USA) 131 – Mill Line 71 (Mill Reef (USA) 141) [1994 103p: 6m^{2} 7m* 6m^{3} 7g* 8g^{4} 1995 10.4m* 12m^{3} 12g* 11.9m* 12d^{5} 12f Nov 26] 121

Fortune doesn't necessarily favour the brave. A change of plan which saw Pure Grain sent on from the Prix de l'Arc de Triomphe to Tokyo for the Japan Cup rather than into winter quarters had almost disastrous consequences. After finishing tenth of fourteen to Lando in Tokyo, Pure Grain was found to be lame on her off-hind. The source of lameness was diagnosed as a potentially life-threatening compound

Tattersalls Musidora Stakes, York—Pure Grain beats Caramba

spiral fracture of the lower cannon-bone. Though the bulletins eventually turned more optimistic and she was fit enough to be flown back to Britain in January, there seems little chance now that she will be able to race as a four-year-old.

Pure Grain came out best of the fillies in the Arc, running a good race to finish fifth of sixteen to Lammtarra, just under seven lengths behind the winner. That was her first race against the colts. Against her own age and sex she had been beaten only once in four previous starts during the season, when third to Moonshell in the Oaks, and she had won the Kildangan Stud Irish Oaks by six lengths, a good margin in any classic. But to begin at the beginning: Pure Grain, who progressed really well as a two-year-old until only fourth to Aqaarid in the Fillies' Mile at Ascot, made her reappearance as a three-year-old in the Tattersalls Musidora Stakes at York in May. There were excuses for her reverse in the Fillies' Mile—she had pulled hard in a slowly-run affair—and she started at even money in a field of five at York. She looked a long odds-on shot when going ahead three furlongs out but in the end seemed to have to call on her greater experience to prevail by a length from Caramba. Pure Grain's Epsom odds shortened as a result, but she was still third favourite

Kildangan Stud Irish Oaks, the Curragh—
it's six lengths back to Russian Snows (centre) and another four to third-placed Valley of Gold (right)

Aston Upthorpe Yorkshire Oaks, York—things are far less clear cut up against 33/1-shot Magical Retreat

behind Aqaarid and Moonshell, and remained so up to the day. Caramba's jockey was impressed with the Musidora winner, saying 'whatever beats Pure Grain will win the Oaks'. He was nearly right, and would have been spot on except for a greatly improved run from Pure Grain's long-priced stable-companion, the Cheshire Oaks winner Dance A Dream who came between her and Moonshell, holding Pure Grain's sustained challenge by three quarters of a length. Having been in contention from three furlongs out without quite threatening to get her head in front, Pure Grain finished just over two lengths behind the winner, reportedly losing her near-fore shoe in running.

Moonshell had a set-back after Epsom; as a result she was missing from the line-up for the Irish Oaks. Dance A Dream had in the meantime had a set-back of a different kind at Royal Ascot, managing only fourth in the Ribblesdale. But the Oaks fourth Musetta and fifth Asterita accompanied Pure Grain to Ireland where they came up against an interesting collection of opponents. Three were particularly interesting—Larrocha and Valley of Gold who both started shorter than Pure Grain, and Russian Snows. Larrocha and Russian Snows were lightly-raced, classically-bred fillies of great potential; the more-experienced Fabre-trained Valley of Gold had won the Oaks d'Italia last time out. Pure Grain left her Epsom form well behind, powering home six lengths clear of runner-up Russian Snows and ten clear of Valley of Gold who just pipped Musetta and Larrocha for third. It was certainly a powerful display from the winner, one that could be seen coming on the home turn where Pure Grain was moving easily, close up in third behind the front-running Musetta and Larrocha as most of the rest struggled to keep up in a truly-run race. When a gap appeared between the first two in the straight, Pure Grain was through and gone. Russian Snows never came close, although she ran on well on the outside from some way back.

None of Michael Stoute's four previous Irish Oaks winners went on to tackle the Prix de l'Arc de Triomphe. The one of the four he perhaps regarded the highest, Unite, went on to contest the King George VI and Queen Elizabeth Diamond Stakes, then into retirement. Dead-heater Melodist went for the Geoffrey Freer Stakes. Fair Salinia and Colorspin were both sent on for the Yorkshire Oaks, and so was Pure Grain. Like Fair Salinia, Pure Grain won it, but at 11/10 against she was made to work the harder, hindering herself by racing freely again in a steadily-run event. Having moved easily to the front three furlongs out, she couldn't shake off the in-foal

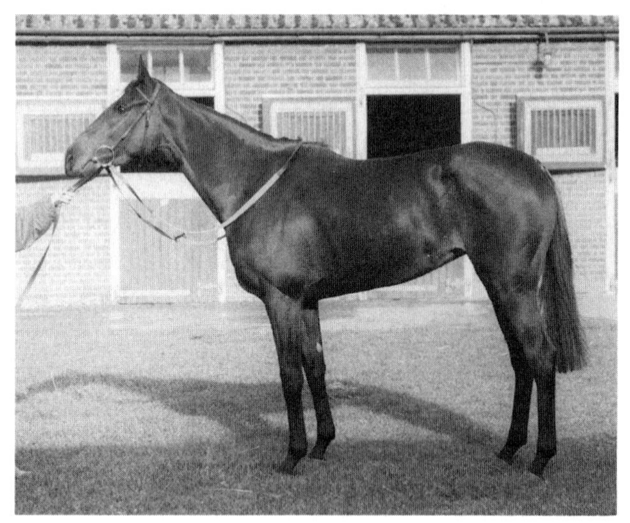

Mr R. Barnett's "Pure Grain"

five-year-old Magical Retreat, a 33/1-shot who showed as much improvement as could possibly be expected of one in her condition—running in-foal mares in hope of improvement is in vogue at present—and Pure Grain had to be driven out to prevail by a head.

Pure Grain (b.f. 1992)	Polish Precedent (USA) (b 1986)	Danzig (b 1977)	Northern Dancer
			Pas de Nom
		Past Example (ch 1976)	Buckpasser
			Bold Example
	Mill Line (b 1985)	Mill Reef (b 1968)	Never Bend
			Milan Mill
		Quay Line (b 1976)	High Line
			Dark Finale

While fortune did not smile on Pure Grain's venture to Japan, her owner-breeder will have little else to regret if she comes through to the paddocks, and he must bless the day when no-one bid the 300,000-franc reserve he put on her at the Deauville Yearling Sales in 1993. The dam's second foal found a buyer at 31,000 guineas at the Newmarket October Yearling Sales in 1994; the third, a brother to Pure Grain, has been retained and put into training with Michael Stoute. That second foal is Sir Mark Prescott's Serious Trust (by Alzao), a modest performer to date but one who should be suited by a much stiffer test of stamina than he has faced thus far. Stamina is a strong point of the family, and all three dams on the bottom line won over at least a mile and a half, Pure Grain's dam Mill Line and grandam, the 1979 Park Hill Stakes winner Quay Line, both being successful over further. Quay Line has not produced anything so good as herself, but one of her foals is the useful middle-distance filly Known Line, dam of the promising Story Line who won at Ascot in September.

Pure Grain's sire is turning out to be a stronger influence for stamina than might have been anticipated, and there is little doubt that she would have got further than a mile and a half as a four-year-old. Pure Grain, a smallish, rather sparely-made filly, a good walker and fluent galloper with a powerful, round action, acted on good to firm and soft going. She was game, genuine and consistent. *M. R. Stoute*

PURPLE FLING 4 ch.g. Music Boy 124 – Divine Fling (Imperial Fling (USA) 116) [1994 76: 5s³ a6g⁴ a5g⁶ 5.9f* 5.1f⁴ 6d 6.1g 7d 5v 1995 a5g⁵ 6g⁵ 5g² 5m² a6g* 5.7f² 5g 6f* 6.9f* a6g 7g Sep 9] strong gelding: fair performer: always well there when winning minor events at Southwell, Doncaster and Carlisle in the summer: stays 7f: acts on firm and soft ground and on fibresand: game: sold (Sir Mark Prescott to L. G. Cottrell) 14,000 gns Newmarket Autumn Sales. *Sir Mark Prescott* 76

PURPLE MEMORIES 2 b.c. (May 24) Don't Forget Me 127 – Tyrian Belle 77 (Enchantment 115) [1995 5g* 6f³ Jul 27] compact colt: second foal: half-brother to 3-y-o Twice Purple (by Then Again): dam sprinter: won 4-runner median auction maiden at Ayr by 1¼ lengths from Domino Flyer: had poor run when 2 lengths third of 4 in minor event at Doncaster 12 days later, but didn't find much off bridle when clear: stays 6f. *M. Johnston* 65

PURPLE SPLASH 5 b.g. Ahonoora 122 – Quay Line 117 (High Line 125) [1994 82: 16.4d 18.7m⁶ 13.9d² 16d 16.5v 1995 14.9d³ 14g* 16g 16g³ 13.3d⁶ 16d³ Oct 19] smallish, good-topped gelding: has a scratchy action: fairly useful handicapper: won at Haydock in June: very good third of 11 (clear of remainder) at Newbury on final start: suited by test of stamina: has form on good to firm ground, goes well on an easy surface (acts on heavy): visored/blinkered since final 4-y-o start: bandaged (ran poorly) third 5-y-o start. *P. J. Makin* 85

PURSUANCE (IRE) 3 b.c. Glenstal (USA) 118 – Pocket (Tumble Wind (USA)) [1994 56: 5m⁵ a6g³ 5m a6g 6s⁶ 7.1g⁴ a5g⁴ 1995 a5g³ a6g⁴ a6g⁵ a5g* a5g⁴ 5f 5.1d a6g* a6g³ a5g 7m Oct 20] sturdy, good-bodied colt: has a round action: fair handicapper on the all-weather: won at Wolverhampton in June (maiden event after 4½-month absence) and September: seems only modest on turf: effective at 5f to 7f: acts on good to firm and soft ground and goes well on fibresand: visored/blinkered last 9 starts: usually forces pace: often ridden by 7-lb claimer J. Edmunds. *J. Balding* – a66

PURSUIT OF GLORY 4 b.f. Shirley Heights 130 – Propensity 93 (Habitat 134) [1994 82: 8s 10m⁵ 10.4f 10g* 10g⁶ 10.3g* 12g 12m 1995 10f 10m* 10f 10m 12m Sep 6] leggy, sparely-made filly: in foal to Green Desert: fairly useful handicapper: easily best effort in 1995 to win at Newmarket in July: effective at 1¼m, probably at 1½m: acted on good to firm going. *C. A. Cyzer* 82

PUSEY STREET BOY 8 ch.g. Vaigly Great 127 – Pusey Street 96 (Native Bazaar 122) [1994 59, a46: a8.5g³ a7g² a7g⁴ 7m⁵ 8g 7v⁶ 8d⁶ 7.1s² 6.9m⁴ a8.5g² 8.3f 10g⁵ 7g* 8.1g 7d² 8d 7s⁵ 7.1g² 7d 1995 7g⁴ 7f⁵ 8g 7.1m 8m² 7m 7g⁵ 8d 7g 8f⁵ Oct 23] lengthy, dipped-backed gelding: tubed: modest handicapper: none too consistent in 1995: best efforts at 7f/1m: acts on any going: visored twice in 1994, running creditably first occasion: has worn bandages. *J. R. Bosley* 57 d a–

PUSHKA FAIR 4 b.g. Salse (USA) 128 – Orient 106 (Bay Express 132) [1994 NR 1995 a7g Dec 19] third foal: half-brother to Irish 5f winner Arcade (by Rousillon) and 7f winner Lamsonetti (by Never So Bold): dam sprinter: 20/1, last of 10 in maiden at Lingfield. *T. R. Watson* –

PUT OFF 2 b.f. (Jan 12) Hadeer 118 – Dame Margot (USA) (Northern Dancer) [1995 6g 7g Aug 7] smallish, strong filly: half-sister to several winners abroad: dam unraced: well beaten in maidens: unruly in paddock, mounted on track and free to post last time: has joined N. C. Wright. *B. W. Hills* –

PYRAMUS (USA) 4 b.c. Danzig (USA) – Royal Honoree (USA) (Round Table) [1994 75: 8.3m³ 6m⁵ 8.3m⁴ 8.3m⁵ 7g⁵ 7g⁴ 6g³ 6g⁶ 6d⁵ 7d* 7g⁶ 1995 6m 6g 7f* 7g* 7m* 7.6m Jul 30] strong-quartered colt: unimpressive mover: fair performer: successful in the summer in smallish fields for apprentice handicap at Goodwood and minor event and handicap at Catterick: effective at 6f to 8.3f: acted on firm and dead ground: blinkered 4 times, twice running well: sometimes bandaged: twice ran well on consecutive days and when sweating: suitable mount for claimer: sometimes bandaged: to stand £1,000 (1st Oct) Boxalland Stud, West Sussex. *Mrs L. Piggott* 78

PYTCHLEY NIGHT 8 b.g. Red Sunset 120 – Lili Bengam (Welsh Saint 126) [1994 –, a71+: a7g² a7g* 1995 a7g³ May 15] lengthy, quite good-topped gelding: very lightly raced last 2 seasons, and well below form in claimer only 8-y-o start: best – a51 at 7f/1m: acts on firm going (none too consistent on turf) and all-weather surfaces, unsuited by dead ground. *D. Morris*

Q

QAFFAL (USA) 5 b.g. Seattle Dancer (USA) 119 – Samalex 110 (Ela-Mana-Mou 132) [1994 NR 1995 16.4g Jun 7] finely-made, rather attractive gelding: has been hobdayed: modest handicapper (rated 62) at 3 yrs for D. Morley: tailed off on return to flat: stays 1¾m: acts on firm and dead ground: blinkered final 3-y-o start: pulled up lame in claiming hurdle Aug 18. *R. T. Phillips* –

Q FACTOR 3 br.f. Tragic Role (USA) – Dominiana (Dominion 123) [1994 75: 5s^3 5s^3 a6g^2 a7g 6m^2 6g^3 8g^6 7.6v^3 6v^5 6v* a7g^3 1995 6.1m^3 7m 6m^4 6f^4 7f 6g 6.1s^6 7m a8.5g a7g Nov 16] leggy filly: has a quick action: fair handicapper: effective at 6f, and almost certainly stays 1m: acts on any ground: visored (ran well) fifth 2-y-o start: often bandaged behind: none too consistent. *D. Haydn Jones* 73

QUADRANT 6 b.g. Shirley Heights 130 – Sextant 98 (Star Appeal 133) [1994 NR 1995 a13g a12g^6 a16g Mar 29] good-bodied gelding: fair 3-y-o, but seems no longer of much account. *A. Moore* –

QUAKERS FIELD 2 b.c. (Apr 10) Anshan 119 – Nosey 96 (Nebbiolo 125) [1995 5g 6m* 7d^2 7g* 7.3d^6 Oct 19] 8,800F, 13,000Y: workmanlike colt: has a round action: fifth foal: half-brother to 3-y-o Lloc (by Absalom), 5f winner at 2 yrs: dam Irish 2-y-o 5f and 6f winner: won 6-runner maiden at Kempton in August and well-contested auction event at Goodwood in September (by a head from Astuti): well placed throughout when under 2 lengths sixth of 9 to Tumbleweed Ridge in steadily-run Horris Hill Stakes at Newbury in October: will stay 1m: acts on good to firm and dead ground. *G. L. Moore* 96

QUALITAIR PRIDE 3 b.f. Siberian Express (USA) 125 – Qualitairess 49 (Kampala 120) [1994 59: 5g^3 5m^2 6m^3 5d^6 6m 7s^4 7d 1995 7g 6g a8.5g^6 10m 9.9m Aug 24] tall, leggy filly: modest maiden: no worthwhile form in 1995: bred to stay 1m, but 7f on soft ground seemed to stretch her stamina at 2 yrs: acts on good to firm ground and soft: blinkered (out of form) last 2 starts. *J. F. Bottomley* –

QUALITAIR RIDGE 3 ch.f. Indian Ridge 123 – Comtec Princess 73 (Gulf Pearl 117) [1994 –: 6f^5 7g 6m 7f a7g^5 a7g 1995 a7g a9.4g Feb 8] leggy, unfurnished filly: little worthwhile form: visored at 3 yrs. *J. F. Bottomley* –

QUALITY (IRE) 2 b.c. (Mar 26) Rock City 120 – Queens Welcome 60 (Northfields (USA)) [1995 6m^4 a7g^4 6.1d^2 6g^6 6.9s^5 8f* 8f 7m* 7m a8g* a8g^2 a8g^4 Nov 30] 6,200Y: leggy, quite attractive colt: sixth foal: half-brother to 3-y-o Aragonce (by Aragon) and half-sister to 7f winner Susanna's Secret (by Superlative): dam, ran only at 2 yrs, is half-sister to high-class 1973 2-y-o sprinter The Blues: fairly useful performer: successful late on in maiden at Redcar and nurseries at Newcastle and Lingfield: stays 1m: acts on firm and good to soft ground, and on all-weather: blinkered/visored last 5 starts: sold to go abroad. *W. A. O'Gorman* 82 a87

QUANDARY (USA) 4 b.f. Blushing Groom (FR) 131 – Lost Virtue (USA) (Cloudy Dawn (USA)) [1994 –: 8g 1995 10g^2 10.3m 9f^2 9m* 10.1g*^{dis} 10v* 10m* Oct 27] leggy, sparely-made filly: first past the post in maiden at Lingfield in July, handicap at Yarmouth (disqualified for jockey's irresponsible riding) in September, 104

James Seymour Stakes, Newmarket—Quandary leaves for the paddocks at the top of her form

then rated stakes at Ascot and 4-runner listed race at Newmarket (odds on, made all in convincing style, by 6 lengths from Jagellon) in October: stayed 1¼m well and should have got further: acted on good to firm and heavy ground: stud. *H. R. A. Cecil*

QUANGO 3 b.g. Charmer 123 – Quaranta 83 (Hotfoot 126) [1994 NR 1995 a8g* 8m⁴ 7m² 10.4m* 10.4m Jul 15] 4,500Y: half-brother to several winners, including 9f (Cambridgeshire) and 1½m winner Quinlan Terry (by Welsh Pageant): dam, 2-y-o 5f winner, half-sister to smart 5f to 7f performer Quy: useful performer: won median auction maiden at Southwell in May and 4-runner listed rated stakes handicap at York (by neck from Ela-Aristokrati) in June: ran as if something amiss in Magnet Cup at York only subsequent start: stays 10.4f well: has raced only on good to firm ground and fibresand. *J. G. FitzGerald* 95

QUEENBIRD 4 b. or br.f. Warning 136 – Song Test (USA) (The Minstrel (CAN) 135) [1994 90: 7g³ 7g³ 6m 7g⁵ 1995 7m 6m 7m 6.1m 7g 7.1d 8g 7g 10f a9.4g Nov 13] workmanlike filly: just a fair handicapper at best in 1995: very long way below form last 5 starts: stays 7f: acts on good to firm and dead ground, probably on soft: blinkered (out of form) eighth 4-y-o start: often wears dropped noseband: not one to trust implicitly. *M. J. Ryan* 71 d

QUEEN EMMA (IRE) 2 b.f. (Apr 25) Mac's Imp (USA) 116 – Hinari Disk Deck 75 (Indian King (USA) 128) [1995 5.7m 5.7m 6f Oct 23] IR 2,600Y: leggy filly: second reported foal: dam 2-y-o 5f winner: poor form in maidens at Bath (2, absent 4 months in between) and Leicester. *J. S. Moore* –

QUEENFISHER 3 b. or br.f. Scottish Reel 123 – Mavahra 93 (Mummy's Pet 125) [1994 101: 5.1m* 6s⁴ 5g 7.1g³ 7f³ 7d³ 6g³ 1995 8m 7f⁴ 8f⁴ 7.3g⁵ 7f 7.1m* 7g Sep 7] leggy, useful-looking filly: fairly useful performer on balance of form, flattered by around 8½ lengths eleventh of 14 in 1000 Guineas at Newmarket on reappearance: disappointed on several occasions, but won weakly-contested 3-runner minor event at Chepstow in August: takes keen hold, and likely to prove best at up to 7f: acts on firm and dead ground: blinkered (ran poorly) fifth 3-y-o start: sweating and edgy (well beaten) final start. *R. Hannon* 91

Daniel Prenn Rated Stakes (Handicap), York—
lightly-raced Quango (left) shows plenty of ability in accounting for Ela-Aristokrati

QUEEN OF SHANNON (IRE) 7 b.m. Nordico (USA) – Raj Kumari (Vitiges (FR) 132) [1994 53: 7.6v 5.1g 6g a8g^6 a10g^2 a13g^3 1995 a10g a11g Jan 16] quite good-topped, angular mare: reportedly has had 3 wind operations: modest performer nowadays: no form in 1995: may prove suited by 1½m: acts on any going: tried visored/blinkered, no improvement: inconsistent. *B. J. Meehan* –

QUEENS CHECK 2 b.f. (Apr 30) Komaite (USA) – Ski Baby (Petoski 135) [1995 5d 6g^5 5f^6 5s* Nov 2] first foal: dam never ran: blinkered and had favoured stand rail when showing improved form to win maiden at Edinburgh in November by ½ length: races keenly, and likely to prove best at sprint distances. *Miss J. F. Craze* 60 ?

QUEENS CONSUL (IRE) 5 gr.m. Kalaglow 132 – Queens Connection (Bay Express 132) [1994 80, a53+: a11g a7g^3 a8g* a8g 7m 7.5m^4 8f^6 8m^4 a7g^5 8m a9.4g^3 8.5m* 8.2g* 8.2m* 8g^2 7.9m 8.9d 8g^3 1995 a8g^5 a8g^6 a8g^5 8g 9.9m^6 8g^2 8m^2 a8g 8m^2 7m 10m 8.5m 8m* 8m^3 8.5m^2 8f Jul 27] tall, leggy mare: only modest form on the all-weather, but fairly useful handicapper on turf: won at Thirsk in June: best at up to 8.5f: acts on firm and soft ground and on fibresand: successful over hurdles in November: game front runner. *B. S. Rothwell* 84 a63

QUEENS CONTRACTOR 5 b.g. Formidable (USA) 125 – Salazie 87 (Ile de Bourbon (USA) 133) [1994 49: 11.9d a9.4g^6 9m^4 a12g* a12g 1995 12m 12g 11.5m^5 10f* 10m 12m Aug 27] lengthy gelding: poor handicapper: easily best effort when winning 4-runner apprentice race at Lingfield in June: stays 1½m: best form on a sound surface (acts on firm ground) or fibresand: seems best in blinkers: front runner: sold 1,200 gns Ascot December Sales. *S. Mellor* 45

QUEENS FANCY 2 ch.f. (May 7) Infantry 122 – Sagareina (Sagaro 133) [1995 a7g Nov 21] third reported foal: dam little worthwhile form: 16/1, slowly into stride and always behind in 10-runner maiden at Lingfield. *S. Dow* –

QUEEN'S INSIGNIA (USA) 2 b.f. (Mar 1) Gold Crest (USA) 120 – Years (USA) (Secretariat (USA)) [1995 5m^5 6m^4 6m* 8d* 8f Oct 18] 6,800Y: tall filly: first foal: dam, unraced, out of sister to 1987 champion American older mare North Sider: won seller at Windsor in June and nursery (by 3 lengths from Goodwood Rocket) at Goodwood 3½ months later: bandaged behind, disappointing in nursery final start: stays 1m: may be unsuited by very firm ground. *P. F. I. Cole* 68

QUEEN'S MUSIC (USA) 2 ch.f. (Mar 27) Dixieland Band (USA) – Sticky Habit 79 (Habitat 134) [1995 5.2g^5 5m 6m^6 6.9f 8h^6 10d Sep 19] $200,000Y: angular filly: half-sister to several winners, including useful 1992 2-y-o 6f winner Splendent (by Shadeed) and very useful 6f to 8.5f winner Aim For The Top (by Irish River): dam from good family, won at 1m and 1¼m: modest maiden: stays 1¼m: blinkered (ran respectably) penultimate outing: sold 36,000 gns Newmarket December Sales. *P. F. I. Cole* 57

QUEEN'S RANSOM (IRE) 3 b.f. Last Tycoon 131 – Never So Fair 65 (Never So Bold 135) [1994 70p: 5g^2 7.1g* 1995 8s^6 8.1d a8g Nov 2] rather leggy, unfurnished filly: fair form at 2 yrs: last of 6 in listed race then no promise in handicaps: should stay 1m: sold 11,000 gns Newmarket December Sales. *P. W. Chapple-Hyam* –

QUEENS STROLLER (IRE) 4 b.f. Pennine Walk 120 – Mount Isa (Miami Springs 121) [1994 61, a69: a8g^3 a8g^5 a7g* a8g^3 8s^6 a7g^2 8.3d 7.1d a7g^6 9f 10.2m^5 10d^6 8g^2 8.2d^2 a8.5g^4 a8.5g^2 1995 a9.4g* 9.7d* 10d 10g^6 9.2g 8g 8.1g^4 10f^2 10.2m 10.1g 12d 12m a9.4g^4 Nov 27] leggy, lightly-made filly: fair handicapper: narrow winner at Wolverhampton (amateurs) and Folkestone in March: below form last 5 starts, claimed by T. Wall £5,000 final start: stays 1¼m: acts on any turf going and on fibresand: usually held up: suitable mount for an inexperienced rider: inconsistent. *C. C. Elsey* 59 a70

QUEENS THEATRE 3 ch.f. Old Vic 136 – Hello Cuddles 99 (He Loves Me 120) [1994 NR 1995 8g 11.4m^4 Aug 30] 10,000Y: big, lengthy filly: half-sister to 4-y-o Mutiara (by Never So Bold) and 6.9f and 1m winner Inderaputeri and sprint winner Samson-Agonistes (both by Bold Fort): dam sprinter: off course over 4 months, 7 lengths fourth of 13 to Fire On Ice in maiden at Sandown, staying on very well from rear under hands and heels: should stay at least 1½m: looked sure to improve again. *B. W. Hills* 68 p

QUEST AGAIN 4 ch.g. Then Again 126 – Eagle's Quest 62 (Legal Eagle 126) [1994 67: 8g^4 10d^2 10.2g^2 12.1g 1995 10m 11.9m^2 11.6m* 12m^4 14.4m 14d 12d 70

14.1m^3 12m^4 Nov 6] leggy, angular, plain gelding: not a good walker: easy mover: fair handicapper: won at Windsor in July: found little next start: stays 14.1f: acts on dead going and good to firm: inconsistent. *D. W. P. Arbuthnot*

QUESTIONAIRE 2 b.f. (Mar 26) Northern State (USA) 91 – Broken Melody (Busted 134) [1995 7.6d 6s Sep 28] rather sparely-made filly: half-sister to several winners here and abroad, including 8.3f and 9.2f winner Bold Melody (by Never So Bold): dam unraced half-sister to smart middle-distance filly Sing Softly: well beaten in maidens at Lingfield in September: sold 850 gns Ascot October Sales. *R. Akehurst* –

QUESTION ALI 3 b.f. Petoski 135 – Wild Lover (USA) (Lyphard (USA) 132) [1994 83d: 6m* 6m^2 6.1g^2 6.1m* 6g 6g^5 6.5g 6d^4 1995 5m^6 6m^6 7g 7d 7f Oct 3] sturdy filly: fairly useful performer at 2 yrs: soundly beaten in 1995, bandaged when down the field on final start: bred to stay at least 1m, but races keenly. *J. Berry* –

QUESTRILL 3 ch.f. Rainbow Quest (USA) 134 – Krill (Kris 135) [1994 74p: 8m^4 1995 10d Oct 19] unfurnished filly: second foal: dam French 1¼m winner: ran as though something amiss (virtually pulled up) only 3-y-o start. *J. H. M. Gosden* –

QUICK MILLION 4 b.f. Thowra (FR) – Miss Quick (Longleat (USA) 109) [1994 61: 7g a7g a8g^3 1995 a12g^3 a8g a8g^5 14d a12g Dec 18] workmanlike filly: poor maiden on most form: sold out of B. Meehan's stable 1,500 gns Ascot April Sales after third start: will probably stay 1¼m: acts on equitrack. *J. W. Mullins* 40

QUICK THINKER (IRE) 3 ch.g. Carmelite House (USA) 118 – Snap Decision 77 (Bay Express 132) [1994 48: 6g 7f 6.1m^6 a6g^6 5m^4 5f 5f^3 5m^6 5m^2 5m^5 a6g 1995 5g 6g^6 Jun 3] leggy gelding: poor maiden: seems to stay 7f: usually blinkered. *W. S. Cunningham* –

QUIET AMUSEMENT (USA) 4 ch.f. Regal And Royal (USA) – My Little Guest (Be My Guest (USA) 126) [1994 60: 7f 10m 10m 10m^3 1995 a13g Dec 14] rangy filly: modest maiden at 3 yrs: sold 8,800 gns Newmarket December (1994) Sales: modest winning (August) hurdler: resold only 850 gns Newmarket Autumn (1995) Sales before reappearance, when tailed off. *T. T. Clement* –

QUIET MISSION 4 ch.c. Hubbly Bubbly (USA) – Woodlands Arabella VII (Pedigree Unknown) [1994 –: 8f 7g^6 8m 7d a6g a8.5g 1995 a7g a8g 7g 9.2g May 4] leggy colt: of no account. *J. L. Eyre* –

QUIET MOMENTS (IRE) 2 b.g. (Apr 18) Ron's Victory (USA) 129 – Saint Cynthia (Welsh Saint 126) [1995 6m 6m 6.1d 6.1s Oct 17] 5,200F, 4,500Y: tall, leggy gelding: looked weak: half-brother to 3-y-o Aconorace (by Midyan) and to several winners, notably fairly useful Saint Caligula (at 6f and 7f, by Petorius): dam won over 1¾m and over hurdles in Ireland: behind in maiden events and a nursery: gelded after final start. *P. G. Murphy* –

QUILLING 3 ch.g. Thatching 131 – Quillotern (USA) (Arctic Tern (USA) 126) [1994 69: 7.1m 7m 7.6v^5 8m 1995 10f^4 6g^5 7m^5 6m^4 7.5g^5 6m^2 6f^4 5d^3 7f* 6d 7f* 7m^2 7m Nov 3] rangy gelding: fairly useful handicapper for new stable in 1994: won 27-runner race and 15-runner contest, both at Redcar in October: effective at 6f, probably stays 1m: acts on firm ground, possibly not on dead: visored 3 times, running well on first 2 occasions: sometimes gives trouble in preliminaries, and broke out of stalls and withdrawn on ninth intending 3-y-o outing: makes running/races prominently. *M. Dods* 84

QUILLON ROSE 3 ch.f. Sure Blade (USA) 130 – Grey Walls 86 (Habitat 134) [1994 –: 6g 8.1d 1995 10m 8.1d^6 7m^6 7g* 7.6m* 7m^4 8g Sep 29] good-topped filly: has scope: modest handicapper: won at Ayr and Lingfield (apprentices) in the summer: best form at around 7f, should prove at least as effective over further: acts on good to firm ground: sold 11,000 gns Newmarket Autumn Sales. *C. F. Wall* 52

QUILLWORK (USA) 3 b.f. Val de L'Orne (FR) 133 – Quaff (USA) 115 (Raise A Cup (USA)) [1994 68: 8m^6 8g^5 7.9d 1995 14.1f a12g^3 10g^4 10d^3 Oct 19] sparely-made filly: good walker: fair maiden: will prove ideally suited by further than 1¼m: acts on good to firm and good to soft ground. *Mrs J. Cecil* 65

QUINNTESSA 2 ch.f. (Mar 5) Risk Me (FR) 127 – Nannie Annie 60 (Persian Bold 123) [1995 6g a5g a6g^2 a6g Dec 12] 6,600F, 2,600Y: compact filly: third live foal: sister to 3-y-o Brandon Express, 1m winner in Sweden in 1995: dam thrice raced at 2 yrs, is out of 2m-winning sister to top Australian winner Raffindale: second 51 in seller at Wolverhampton in December, only form: should stay beyond 6f. *B. Palling*

QUINTA BOY 2 b.g. (Apr 3) Puissance 110 – Figment 75 (Posse (USA) 130) [1995 5g^6 5f Jul 12] 5,000Y, 14,000 2-y-o: first foal: dam sprinting half-sister to Windsor Castle winner Prince Reymo: showed plenty of speed in maiden auctions, weakening very quickly when headed: looks a short-runner. *J. Berry* –

QUINTUS DECIMUS 3 b.g. Nordico (USA) – Lemon Balm (High Top 131) [1994 80p: 8s 7s* 1995 6m 8.1m^5 7.9g^3 8.1m^5 7d 8s^4 10d Oct 19] smallish, useful-looking gelding: fairly useful handicapper: off course over 3 months and not at best after third 3-y-o start: should stay 1¼m: acts on good to firm ground and soft: takes keen hold: hung markedly left second 3-y-o start. *Lord Huntingdon* 80

QUINWOOD (USA) 3 ch.f. Woodman (USA) 126 – Qirmazi (USA) 113 (Riverman (USA) 131) [1994 59p: 7g^6 1995 7g^6 8d* Jun 15] sparely-made, lengthy filly: has an unimpressive, round action: fairly useful performer: easily best effort to win maiden at Yarmouth in June by head from Bonne Etoile, getting up close home having looked held 2f out: will stay beyond 1m: acts on dead ground: looked capable of better still. *J. H. M. Gosden* 87 p

QUINZII MARTIN 7 b.g. Song 132 – Quaranta 83 (Hotfoot 126) [1994 –, a54: a7g^2 a7g* a8.5g^3 a6g^6 a7g^3 a7g^5 a7g^5 a7g^6 a7g a7g a7g a8.5g a7g a7g^3 1995 a7g a7g* a8g a7g^2 a7g* a7g^3 a7g a8.5g a7g a9.4g^3 a8g 7m^6 a7g^6 a7g a7g a7g a7g a9.4g a7g^2 Dec 15] strong, good-bodied gelding: has a quick action: modest handicapper at best: yet to win on turf, but successful 8 times on the all-weather, including at Southwell in January and February: effective from 6f to 11f: acts on all-weather surfaces: sometimes blinkered/visored. *D. Haydn Jones* – a61 d

QUIVIRA 4 ch.f. Rainbow Quest (USA) 134 – Nobly Born (USA) (The Minstrel (CAN) 135) [1994 56: 8m 9v 8.1g 11.6m* 12m^3 1995 12g^6 11.6m^2 10f* 10f^3 10g* 9f^3 10f 12.3m^2 12g^2 10.1g 8.9g 10.3m^3 Nov 3] leggy, lengthy filly: fairly useful performer: won minor events at Ripon in June and Windsor in July: should prove best at 1¼m+: acts on firm ground: tried visored: tends to sweat and get on edge: genuine. *T. T. Clement* 81

QUIZ TIME 3 b.f. Efisio 120 – Explosiva (USA) 88§ (Explodent (USA)) [1994 87: 5f^2 5m* 5.2m 5f* 5.2g^2 5m^5 5.1g^6 1995 5.1m^2 5m^3 5m^2 5m^5 5.6m 5d Sep 23] small, good-topped filly: has a round action: fairly useful handicapper: raced at around 5f but may well stay 6f: acts on firm going. *Sir Mark Prescott* 90

Criterium du Fonds Europeen de l'Elevage, Deauville—Rabican's profitable trip to France, beating Mayoumbe

R

RAAH ALGHARB (USA) 3 b.c. Gone West (USA) – Pharlette (FR) (Pharly (FR) 130) [1994 106: 5.1f^3 6m^2 5m^2 6m* 5m* 6m^4 5g* 6m^5 5m^3 1995 5m 6g^6 5m^4 5f 7.3m 5g Sep 28] compact, good-bodied colt: useful performer: faced stiff tasks in pattern races first 5 starts, running creditably on 3 occasions, including when fourth to Mind Games in Temple Stakes at Sandown: soon off bridle when last in listed race at Newmarket final start: effective at 5f, probably stays 7.3f: has raced only on a sound surface: usually taken to post early: needs strong handling: none too reliable: sent to Dubai. *M. R. Stoute* — 102

RAAHIN (USA) 10 ch.g. Super Concorde (USA) 128 – Bonnie Hope (USA) (Nijinsky (CAN) 138) [1994 NR 1995 16.4m Apr 28] lengthy gelding: unimpressive mover: modest handicapper in 1990: fair hurdler in 1994/5: tailed off on return to flat: best at up to 2m: acts on any going: visored once. *S. Woodman* — –

RAASED 3 b.c. Unfuwain (USA) 131 – Sajjaya (USA) 97 (Blushing Groom (FR) 131) [1994 73p: 7m^4 7.1g^2 1995 10m* 12g^3 10.1m Jun 9] well-made colt: has been hobdayed: easy winner of median auction maiden at Brighton in April: stiff task, last in handicap at Epsom in June: stays 1¼m: has raced only on a sound surface: has looked headstrong and shown signs of temperament: front runner: sold (J. Dunlop to F. Watson) only 1,200 gns Newmarket Autumn Sales. *J. L. Dunlop* — 85

RAAYAAT (USA) 3 b. or br.c. Phone Trick (USA) – Badge of Courage (USA) (Well Decorated (USA)) [1994 NR 1995 8m 6m 7.5m^6 a8g^3 7.1m^4 9f a8.5f^2 a7f a8.5d^4 Dec 3] $70,000Y: good-topped colt: has scope: sixth foal: half-brother to 2 winners, notably useful 7f (at 2 yrs) and 1¼m winner True Hero (by The Minstrel): dam well bred but unraced: modest performer: sold out of A. Stewart's stable 10,000 gns Newmarket July Sales after fifth start: stays 8.5f: blinkered 5 of last 6 starts. *E. R. Freeman, USA* — 56

RABICAN (IRE) 2 b.c. (Apr 5) Distinctly North (USA) 115 – Kaysama (FR) (Kenmare (FR) 125) [1995 6m^2 6m* 6m 6m* 6.5g* 6m^4 6.5g Oct 17] IR 18,000F, 16,000Y: leggy, lengthy, rather unfurnished colt: half-brother to 5f winner Kinaana (by Posse) and useful Irish 1m/1¼m performer Kayfa (by Shernazar): dam winning French sprinter: fairly useful performer: won median auction maiden at Redcar in June, valuable nursery at Newmarket (last early on in strongly-run race) in July and valuable listed race at Deauville in August: well beaten in pattern event at Deauville on final start: will probably stay 7f: acts on good to firm ground, yet to race on a soft surface. *G. C. Bravery* — 95 +

RACING BRENDA 4 b.f. Faustus (USA) 118 – Icecapped 91 (Caerleon (USA) 132) [1994 57, a72: 6g^4 6m^3 a7g* a9.4g^4 a9.4g^2 10g a8.5g^2 10s^6 8s 1995 10.3m 8m^5 7.5g^3 6m^6 7g^6 8.2m* 9m 8.5d^2 8g Oct 9] sturdy filly: fair handicapper on the all-weather at 3 yrs: modest on turf: won at Nottingham in August: probably needs further than 7f nowadays (stays 1¼m): acts on fibresand, good to firm and soft ground. *B. A. McMahon* — 60 a–

RACING HAWK (USA) 3 ch.c. Silver Hawk (USA) 123 – Lorn Lady (Lorenzaccio 130) [1994 NR 1995 11.5m^5 a12g^2 14s Sep 28] rather leggy colt: brother to 2 winners in France, notably Prix de Diane winner Lady In Silver, and half-brother to several winners: dam Irish 8.5f winner from very good family: looks a modest staying maiden: well beaten on soft ground: sold 6,000 gns Newmarket December Sales. *H. R. A. Cecil* — 58

RACING TELEGRAPH 5 b.g. Claude Monet (USA) 121 – Near Enough (English Prince 129) [1994 –: 7.3s^6 6m^5 6.1m a6g^5 7v^6 6g 1995 7.1m a8g 8.1g 7m^3 7g^3 7d^4 7m a7g^6 Dec 14] tall, angular gelding: has had wind operation: only poor at best in 1995: sold out of J. Pearce's stable 8,000 gns Ascot July Sales after fourth start: stays 7f: acts on good to firm and dead ground: races freely. *J. W. Payne* — 45

RACING WINGS (FR) 3 ch.f. In The Wings 128 – Racing Home (FR) 89 (Dom Racine (FR) 121) [1994 NR 1995 12f^4 11g Aug 14] angular filly: second foal: half-sister to 4-y-o staying handicapper Sheltered Cove (by Bold Arrangement): dam won at 6f and 7f at 2 yrs and is out of half-sister to dam of Pebbles: 20/1 and bit backward, little promise in 4-runner maiden at Kempton: behind in minor event at Clairefontaine in August. *K. O. Cunningham-Brown* — –

RAD 5 b.g. Valiyar 129 – Phlox 101 (Floriana 106) [1994 61: a7g* a7g^2 a7g a7g a7g 6.9g 7m^5 7m^5 a7g^2 a7g a8g^4 a7g^2 a7g^2 1995 a8g a8g^5 a8g* a8g a8g a8g a8g 6.9f^4 8.1g 8f^5 8h^3 10m^4 8f 8f Oct 23] workmanlike gelding: modest handicapper: won apprentice race at Southwell in February: stays 1m: acts on hard ground and the all-weather: blinkered (finished last) once at 4 yrs: often finds little: inconsistent and needs treating with caution. *S. P. C. Woods* — 61 d

RADEVORE 2 ch.c. (Feb 5) Generous (IRE) 139 – Bloudan (USA) (Damascus (USA)) [1995 8m* 8s^3 9s^3 Nov 22] tall, leggy colt: third foal: half-brother to 1992 2-y-o 6f winner Felucca (by Green Desert): dam unraced daughter of Chain Store, dam of Al Bahathri: won newcomers race from Loup Solitaire at Longchamp in September: 4 lengths third of 6 to Le Triton in Prix La Rochette at Longchamp (niggled along some way out, made headway only late on) then 2¼ lengths third of 6 to Spinning World in steadily-run Prix Saint-Roman at Evry: will stay 1½m: acts on good to firm ground and soft. *A. Fabre, France* — 102

RADIANCE (IRE) 3 b.f. Thatching 131 – Dazzlingly Radiant 81 (Try My Best (USA) 130) [1994 54: 5.2m 7.1g 1995 7.1m 8.3m 7m Aug 25] workmanlike filly: little worthwhile form at 3 yrs: not bred to be suited by much further than 7f: blinkered final 3-y-o start: stays 1,500 gns Newmarket Autumn Sales. *R. Hannon* — –

RADIANT STAR 2 b.c. (Feb 5) Rainbow Quest (USA) 134 – Miss Kuta Beach 91 (Bold Lad (IRE) 133) [1995 7m Nov 3] lengthy colt: half-brother to several winners, including 1993 2-y-o 7f winner Miss Rinjani (by Shirley Heights): dam, 6f and 1¼m winner, half-sister to very useful 1m and 9f winner Bali Dancer: 5/1 from 7/2, slow-starting eighth of 17, beaten around 11 lengths, to Jackson Hill in maiden at Doncaster, fading 1f out, not knocked about: sure to improve. *G. Wragg* — 62 p

RADIO CAROLINE 7 b.g. All Systems Go 119 – Caroline Lamb 74 (Hotfoot 126) [1994 NR 1995 10.8g a8.5g 7g a8.5g Jun 24] close-coupled gelding: no form for long time. *M. Tate* — –

RADMORE BRANDY 2 b.f. (Mar 12) Derrylin 115 – Emerin 85 (King Emperor (USA)) [1995 7m Oct 30] 840F: smallish, angular filly: sister to a poor performer and half-sister to several winners on flat and over hurdles, including 1988 2-y-o 5f winner Katherine's Emerald (by Aragon): dam 6f winner: 50/1, slow-starting ninth of 14, in maiden at Newcastle: has joined N. Littmoden. *S. G. Norton* — –

RAED 2 b.c. (Apr 2) Nashwan (USA) 135 – Awayed (USA) 108 (Sir Ivor 135) [1995 6m^2 6d Sep 27] sturdy, well-made colt: has scope: second foal: closely related to 3-y-o Daffaq (by Unfuwain): dam Irish 1m to 9.2f winner from good family: extremely green, ¾-length second of 7 to Charwelton in maiden at Goodwood, losing place at halfway and taking long time to get hang of things: disappointing favourite in similar event at Folkestone 2 months later: bred to be suited by further than 6f. *P. T. Walwyn* — 79 +

RAFFLES ROOSTER 3 ch.g. Galetto (FR) 118 – Singapore Girl (FR) 117 (Lyphard (USA) 132) [1994 NR 1995 9.8g 10g^3 13.5s^3 12g^2 13.5d^2 10.5d^6 12.5g 12d 15g^4 12g^2 a7g^3 Dec 19] 260,000 francs Y: half-brother to very smart French 4-y-o middle-distance performer Gunboat Diplomacy (by Dominion) and several minor winners in France (3 of them by Gay Mecene) from 7f to 1½m: dam smart performer at up to 1¾m: fair form in France for J. Pease: 25/1, first run here when 8½ lengths third of 9 to Samwar in maiden at Lingfield, staying on from rear over inadequate trip: stays 15f: acts on soft ground: blinkered (well beaten) eighth French start. *A. G. Newcombe* — 77

RAFTER-J 4 b. or br.g. Petoski 135 – Coming Out (Fair Season 120) [1994 65?: 7g 7m^6 10m 8.3f^3 8.3m 7.1d^3 8s 1995 a8g 7m 8.3m^5 8g* 8m 8f 10f Oct 31] lengthy gelding: modest performer nowadays: sold out of Miss J. Doyle's stable 2,700 gns Ascot February Sales after reappearance: won claimer at Pontefract in May: well beaten in handicaps afterwards: may prove best at up to around 1m: acts on firm and dead ground: inconsistent. *J. A. Harris* — 57

RAFTERS 6 b.g. Celestial Storm (USA) 132 – Echoing 93 (Formidable (USA) 125) [1994 65: 8s^5 10g 8d 1995 10.5g Sep 23] tall gelding: poor mover: fair maiden, lightly raced: bandaged, showed little only start in 1995: probably stays 1½m: acts on heavy going, probably on firm: fair hurdler. *J. M. Bradley* — –

RAGAZZO (IRE) 5 b.g. Runnett 125 – Redecorate (USA) (Hatchet Man (USA)) [1994 47: 7m^3 7g^2 8.3m 8.3m^2 8f^5 7d 7m^2 8g 8m a7g a8g a8.5g^3 1995 a5g^5 a7g* a7g^5 — 39 a51

a7g² a7g a8g 6.9d 8.3m 7m 7f 5.9f⁴ 7.1m 8.3m⁶ 6g 7f⁴ 9.2f⁶ 6g Sep 23] angular gelding: has a round action: modest handicapper on the all-weather: won (for first time) at Lingfield in January: poor on turf: left K. Cunningham-Brown's stable after tenth start: effective at 6f, had seemed suited by 1¼m at 3 yrs: acts on firm ground and all-weather surfaces: effective blinkered or not: inconsistent. *J. S. Wainwright*

RAGMAR (FR) 2 ch.f. (Mar 26) Tropular – Reggae (FR) (New Chapter 106) [1995 8g² 10g² Oct 29] sixth foal, all by Tropular: sister to 3 winners, including (at up to 11f) Rasmussen: dam French 10.5f winner, also successful over jumps: runner-up in newcomers event at Deauville (for B. Vanheeghe, behind Le Triton) and Criterium de Saint-Cloud (finished strongly, short head behind Polaris Flight) nearly 3 months later: will be suited by further than 1¼m: may well improve further. *P. Bary, France* 112 p

RAGSAK JAMEEL (USA) 2 b.g. (Jan 14) Northern Baby (CAN) 127 – Dream Play (USA) (Blushing Groom (FR) 131) [1995 7m Nov 3] sturdy gelding: eighth foal: brother to fairly useful Irish 1¼m winner Salmon River and half-brother to 2 winners including Party Cited (by Alleged), very useful 1m/1¼m winner here and later Grade 1-placed in USA: dam, winner at up to 9f at 2 yrs, is half-sister to very useful American colt Irish Fighter: 8/1 from 12/1, around 8 lengths seventh of 18 to Wahiba Sands in maiden at Doncaster, staying on without threatening: moved fluently to post: should do better. *Major W. R. Hern* 59 p

RAGTIME SONG 6 b.g. Dunbeath (USA) 127 – Kelowna (USA) (Master Derby (USA)) [1994 –, a49: a13g⁴ a16g⁴ a16g³ a16.2g 14.4m⁵ 11.9m⁶ 11.5d 12m a16g a16g 1995 a16g a12g⁴ a16g⁶ a16g 11.9m 11.9m⁶ a16g 11.9m 11.6g Jun 12] good-bodied gelding: seems no longer of much account: sold 600 gns Ascot July Sales. *A. Moore* –

RAHEEN (USA) 2 b.c. (Mar 18) Danzig (USA) – Belle de Jour (USA) (Speak John) [1995 6g² 6f³ 6m⁴ Aug 17] rather leggy, useful-looking colt: brother to 1991 2-y-o 6f winner Jode and half-brother to several winners, including 3-y-o 8.2f winner Crown of Sheba (by Alysheba) and Kentucky Derby winner Spend A Buck (by Buckaroo): dam won 6f claiming race: beaten around a length in maidens won by Danehill Dancer at Newmarket, Woodborough at Goodwood and Desert Boy at York: sure to win a race. *M. R. Stoute* 93

RAHY ZOMAN (USA) 3 b.c. Rahy (USA) 115 – Micki Bracken (USA) (Baldski (USA)) [1994 86: 7m² 7.1s² 1995 9m* 10g³ 10m² 10g⁵ 12f Jul 26] workmanlike colt: fairly useful performer: won maiden at Goodwood in May, hanging then leading entering final 1f: good efforts in handicaps next 3 starts: moved poorly to post and finished last final start: stays 1¼m: acts on good to firm and soft ground: sold 12,500 gns Newmarket Autumn Sales: sent to Italy. *J. R. Fanshawe* 89

RAINBOW DANCER (FR) 4 b.c. Rainbow Quest (USA) 134 – Ramanouche (FR) 122 (Riverman (USA) 131) [1994 114: 10v* 10.5v* 10m⁶ 12d 12g⁴ 10.5v³ 12g* 1995 12s³ 12g⁵ 12d* 12m³ 15g² 14d Dec 1] smart French colt: won minor event at Maisons-Laffitte in September: in frame (for second year running) in Prix du Conseil de Paris, running on 4 lengths third to De Quest in 1995: seems to stay 15f: acts on heavy going and good to firm. *P. Bary, France* 111

RAINBOWS RHAPSODY 4 b.f. Handsome Sailor 125 – Rainbow Trout 76 (Comedy Star (USA) 121) [1994 47, a40: a8g 10d² 8d⁴ 10d a9.4g a7g² a7g³ 7d 8.2d 1995 a7g⁵ a8g³ 7.1d⁶ a7g 7g Sep 16] leggy filly: unimpressive mover: poor maiden handicapper: stays 1¼m: probably acts on soft ground: inconsistent. *M. J. Camacho* – a44

RAINBOW TIARA 3 ch.f. Night Shift (USA) – Loreef (Main Reef 126) [1994 –: 6g 1995 7g May 24] compact filly: last in maidens at Newmarket and (tongue tied down, bit backward) Salisbury: sold only 1,000 gns Newmarket July Sales: sent to Australia. *M. R. Stoute* –

RAINBOW WALK (IRE) 5 ch.g. Rainbow Quest (USA) 134 – Widows Walk (Habitat 134) [1994 92: a10g* 8m⁴ 8d³ a12g* 11.9f³ 15m⁶ 10m 1995 a9.4g a9.4g⁶ a12g 8g Mar 25] lengthy gelding: fairly useful performer at 4 yrs, but has completely lost his way. *J. G. M. O'Shea* –

RAINCHECK 4 b.g. Mtoto 134 – Lashing (USA) 98 (Storm Bird (CAN) 134) [1994 NR 1995 9f⁶ 9m 9d⁵ 12f Aug 11] third foal: half-brother to 7f to 1¼m winner Straw Thatch (by Thatching): dam 6f (at 2 yrs) to 1m winner: well beaten in maidens. *Mark Campion* –

RAIN CLOUD 2 ch.f. (May 18) Totem (USA) 118 – Cool Number 74 (Swing Easy (USA) 126) [1995 7.1d a8g Nov 6] medium-sized filly: second foal: half-sister to useful German 3-y-o sprinter Property Man (by Clantime): dam 13.8f winner: soundly beaten in maidens at Haydock and Southwell: unimpressive to post and bandaged behind on debut. *W. W. Haigh* –

RAINDEER QUEST 3 ch.f. Hadeer 118 – Rainbow Ring (Rainbow Quest (USA) 134) [1994 53: 5s^3 5f* 7m^6 6.1d^5 8s 1995 11.1g^6 6d Sep 18] sturdy, angular filly: has knee action: modest form at 2 yrs: tailed off in 1995, looking headstrong. *C. Smith* –

RAINELLE 3 ch.f. Rainbow Quest (USA) 134 – Dame Ashfield 90 (Grundy 137) [1994 NR 1995 10m 12m^3 11.9g^6 11.4m 11.4d Sep 12] 62,000Y: lengthy filly with scope: sixth foal: half-sister to 2m winner Rosina Mae and fair 2-y-o 6f and 7f winner Dame Rousara (both by Rousillon): dam 1½m winner out of Park Hill winner African Dancer: no worthwhile form, including in handicap: sold 6,000 gns Newmarket December Sales. *C. E. Brittain* –

RAINFEST (FR) 4 ch.f. Rainbow Quest (USA) 134 – Rockfest (USA) 104 (Stage Door Johnny) [1994 84p: 10m* 10.1m 1995 10g^6 12m^5 14g^3 Sep 22] lengthy, good-topped filly: has a round action: fairly useful form: towards rear in 1995, undoubtedly disappointing (notwithstanding trip) in minor event at Haydock final start: unlikely to stay beyond 1½m: reported to have leg problems twice at 3 yrs: edged left and looked very unco-ordinated second 4-y-o start: sold 22,000 gns Newmarket December Sales. *R. Charlton* 81

RAIN WARRIOR 5 br.g. Lidhame 109 – Rainbow Star (Star Appeal 133) [1994 NR 1995 11.6g Jun 12] fourth foal: dam no worthwhile form: tailed off in NH Flat race in January: well beaten in Windsor claimer in June: sold 675 gns Ascot October Sales. *Miss A. J. Whitfield* –

RAINY DAY SONG 2 br.f. (Jun 4) Persian Bold 123 – Sawaki 71 (Song 132) [1995 6f Oct 23] second foal: dam, suited by 7f, out of half-sister to Music Maestro: 16/1, bandaged behind and green, around 6½ lengths eighth of 18 to Wildwood Flower in maiden at Leicester, slowly away then running on from 2f out: should improve. *Miss Gay Kelleway* 61 p

RAINY DAY WOMAN 3 ch.f. Sure Blade (USA) 130 – Hocus 88 (High Top 131) [1994 –: 5m 1995 a12g^6 a8.5g^4 Apr 15] smallish, compact filly: best effort when fourth of 11 in seller at Wolverhampton, leading halfway until over 2f out. *Dr J. D. Scargill* 40

RAISA POINT 4 ch.f. Raised Socially (USA) – To The Point 96 (Sharpen Up 127) [1994 –: 5.1g 5f 1995 5.1m^4 5m 5g^5 5.1h^3 6m 6f Aug 15] leggy filly: poor handicapper: no form last 2 starts: should stay 6f: acts on hard ground: blinkered (well beaten) once at 3 yrs: races prominently. *W. R. Muir* 55 d

RAISE A PRINCE (FR) 2 b.c. (Jan 31) Machiavellian (USA) 123 – Enfant d'Amour (USA) (Lyphard (USA) 132) [1995 7g^5 Sep 28] 400,000 francs F, 90,000Y: half-brother to 3 winners in France, including useful 1990 2-y-o 5f to 7f winner Love Shack (by Persepolis): dam unraced: 25/1 and carrying plenty of condition, shaped well when just under 5 lengths fifth of 23 to Astor Place in maiden at Newmarket, chasing leaders throughout and staying on: moved short to post: sure to improve. *R. W. Armstrong* 85 p

RAISE THE STAKES 3 ch.c. Forzando 122 – Timely Raise (USA) (Raise A Man (USA)) [1994 72: 7g 7.1d^4 6d 7m^5 1995 8.5m^5 8.3m^2 8.3m^2 9f^3 8m^2 8m^2 7m^2 8.5m^3 8g^4 8m Oct 2] sturdy, lengthy colt: impresses in appearance: fair maiden, runner-up on 5 occasions: stays 9f: acts on firm ground: takes keen hold: best efforts racing up with pace: sold 28,000 gns Newmarket Autumn Sales: sent to Malaysia. *I. A. Balding* 78

RAISONNABLE 2 b.f. (Feb 28) Common Grounds 118 – Salvora (USA) (Spectacular Bid (USA)) [1995 8g^5 8g* 8d^3 8f^2 9s^5 Dec 5] seventh foal: sister to French 3-y-o 1m winner Spenderella and half-sister to 4 winners, notably Grade 1 1¼m Yellow Ribbon winner Aube Indienne (by Bluebird): useful French filly: won minor event at Deauville in August: 3½ lengths third of 11 to Shake The Yoke in Prix d'Aumale then 2 lengths second of 5 to Occupandiste in Prix des Reservoirs, both at 103

Longchamp in the autumn: below form in listed event at Evry final start: should stay beyond 1m: acts on firm ground and dead. *D. Sepulchre, France*

RAKIS (IRE) 5 b. or br.g. Alzao (USA) 117 – Bristle 96 (Thatch (USA) 136) [1994 a7g* a6g a8g a7g^2 a7g^2 1995 7.1m a7g^5 7g a7g* Dec 12] good-topped gelding: quite useful form (rated 84) on his day in 1993 for C. J. Benstead: trained by S. Seemar in UAE, winning handicap in January 1994 but not seen out in 1994/5 season: bought 1,200 gns Newmarket July 1995 Sales: easily best effort for new connections when making all at Wolverhampton in December: best up to 1m: acts on good to firm and soft ground and on fibresand: effective in blinkers in 1993: usually races prominently: bandaged nowadays. *M. Brittain* — 70 +

RAMBLING BEAR 2 ch.c. (Apr 18) Sharrood (USA) 124 – Supreme Rose 95 (Frimley Park 109) [1995 5.2g^2 5m* 5m^2 6g* 5d^4 Sep 9] workmanlike colt: third foal: half-brother to fairly useful 3-y-o sprinter Bajan Rose (by Dashing Blade): dam sprinter: useful colt: won maiden at Windsor in July and Bonusprint Sirenia Stakes at Kempton (by short head from Eastern Prophets, making all) in September: creditable fourth of 8 to Cayman Kai in Flying Childers Stakes at Doncaster on final outing: effective at 5f or 6f: unseated rider on way to post at Kempton (taken down steadily at York, early at Doncaster): races keenly. *M. Blanshard* — 101

RAMBO DELIGHT 2 b.c. (Mar 13) Rambo Dancer (CAN) 107 – Light The Way 72 (Nicholas Bill 125) [1995 5.1m* 6f^4 5m* 5m^4 Jul 27] strong, useful-looking colt: fourth foal: dam won 8.2f seller: won maiden at Nottingham in June and nursery at York in July: sweating and on toes, good fourth of 12 to Admiral Jones in nursery at Goodwood on final outing: bred to stay beyond 5f but is a keen sort: looked ill-at-ease on very firm ground second outing: tends to hang. *J. L. Eyre* — 78

RAMBOLD 4 b.f. Rambo Dancer (CAN) 107 – Boldie 81 (Bold Lad (IRE) 133) [1994 72: 6s 6g^4 6f^4 6m* 7.1m 6m 7f 6d^2 6g 6.1g a6g^6 a7g^5 1995 a6g^5 6g 6m 6m^2 6m 6m 6.1d a6g 6f Oct 23] angular filly: sold out of T. M. Jones's stable 6,200 gns Ascot April Sales after reappearance and just a modest handicapper for new connections: stays 6f: acts on firm and dead ground: sometimes sweats: usually races prominently. *N. E. Berry* — 67 d

RAMBOLLINA 4 b.f. Rambo Dancer (CAN) 107 – Midriff 62 (Busted 134) [1994 52: 7m 5m 8m 5g^6 8f a7g a12g^6 8.5g^4 8s 1995 a8g^4 a8g a11g Mar 20] tall, angular filly: poor maiden: easily best effort at 8.5f: blinkered (well below form) second 4-y-o start: inconsistent. *M. W. Easterby* — – a36

RAMBORETTE 3 b.f. Rambo Dancer (CAN) 107 – Petiller 37 (Monsanto (FR) 121) [1994 60: 5m 5f^6 6g^5 6g^6 5m* 1995 6g^6 6g^6 5m^6 5m^6 5f 5f^3 5g^3 5f 5m^4 5m^3 5.9h^2 5m^6 5g Sep 14] modest sprint handicapper: has raced only on a sound surface (acts on hard ground): tried visored, no improvement: inconsistent: sold 1,000 gns Doncaster October Sales. *Denys Smith* — 50

RAMBO'S HALL 10 b.g. Crofthall 110 – Murton Crags 81 (No Argument 107) [1994 NR 1995 7g^6 7m 10m^5 8d^5 9g 10d a8g^5 Dec 1] workmanlike gelding: only fairly useful at best on return: effective at 1m to 10.5f: best efforts on an easy surface: held up. *J. A. Glover* — 87

RAMBO'S RUMTIME 3 b.f. Rambo Dancer (CAN) 107 – Errol Emerald 60 (Dom Racine (FR) 121) [1994 NR 1995 5.9f 7f 7f^5 Aug 17] 1,200Y: fifth foal: half-sister to 1991 2-y-o 5f winner Jiggerak (by Belfort): dam, 1¼m to 1½m winner, often gave trouble at start: well beaten, including in claimers: sold 1,000 gns Doncaster September Sales. *F. Watson* — –

RAMBO WALTZER 3 b.g. Rambo Dancer (CAN) 107 – Vindictive Lady (USA) (Foolish Pleasure (USA)) [1994 ?, a79: 5g^3 5d^6 a7g* a6g* 7s 8d 7v 1995 10.3g 7.5m^5 10g^5 9f^6 8m^4 a7g a8.5g^3 a8.5g^4 Nov 11] smallish, sturdy gelding: fairly useful on the all-weather, modest at best on turf: stays 1¼m: acts on fibresand, no form 4 outings on a soft surface: visored (below form) fifth 3-y-o start: joined D. Nicholls. *S. G. Norton* — 51 a80

RAMBRINO 3 b.g. Robellino (USA) 127 – Ballerine (USA) (Lyphard's Wish (FR) 124) [1994 98: 6f* 6m^6 7f^4 6m 1995 7g^5 10.3m^4 7m 10.3g^5 Sep 8] tall gelding, somewhat unfurnished: useful performer: creditable 12¼ lengths fifth of 9 to Celtic Swing in Greenham Stakes at Newbury and 4½ lengths fourth of 5 to Pentire in listed race at Chester: well beaten in Jersey Stakes (blinkered) at Royal Ascot and (after — 98 being gelded) minor event at Doncaster 2½ months later: has form at 10.3f, should prove best at up to 1m: yet to race on a soft surface: front runner last 2 starts: sent to race in Barbados. *P. W. Chapple-Hyam*

RAMOOZ (USA) 2 b.c. (Mar 6) Rambo Dancer (CAN) 107 – My Shafy 92 (Rousillon (USA) 133) [1995 6m^2 6.1m^2 7m^2 7.9g* 7.3d* 8v^4 Oct 7] rangy, useful-looking colt: first foal: dam 1m winner out of smart French middle-distance mare Lys River: useful form: won nurseries at York in August and Newbury (particularly impressive, beat Sava Dancer by 5 lengths despite being eased): looked very well but rather disappointing when only fourth of 5 to Beauchamp King in listed race at Ascot on final outing: stays 1m: acts on good to firm and dead ground, possibly unsuited by heavy: blinkered (best effort at the time) third outing. *B. Hanbury* — 102

RAMSDENS (IRE) 3 b.g. Danehill (USA) 126 – To The Limit (Junius (USA) 124) [1994 55p: 6s 1995 7f^3 7g 7s 9m^2 12m Nov 6] lengthy, good-topped gelding: fair maiden: made most when neck second of 19 in apprentice handicap at Newmarket: stays 9f: acts on firm ground, below form on soft. *W. J. Haggas* — 72

RAMSEY HOPE 2 b.c. (Feb 16) Timeless Times (USA) 99 – Marfen (Lochnager 132) [1995 5g 5d^2 5m^4 5m^4 5m^4 6g^2 6f* 6m^4 6m^4 5g^2 7m^3 5m^3 6m* 6d 6g 6m Oct 4] 9,000Y: compact colt: progressed well physically: first foal: dam unraced: made all in maiden auction at Hamilton in June and minor event at Ripon in August: fair efforts in nurseries at Ayr and York last 2 starts: best at 6f: acts on firm and dead ground: tough, reliable and genuine. *C. W. Fairhurst* — 80

RANDOM 4 ch.f. Beveled (USA) – Martian Melody 62 (Enchantment 115) [1994 65: a5g^3 a5g^5 a5g* a6g 5.1g* 5.1g^3 5.3f^2 5.1f^2 5m^4 5.1g^5 a5g a5g^6 1995 a5g^5 a5g^4 5.1g^5 5.1m 5g^5 5m a5g^3 6m^2 6f^4 5.7h^5 6g a7g^6 a6g^5 Nov 25] sparely-made filly: modest performer: effective at 5f and 6f, may well stay further: acts on firm ground, dead and equitrack: inconsistent. *C. James* — 56 a60

RANGER SLOANE 3 ch.g. Gunner B 126 – Lucky Amy (Lucky Wednesday 124) [1994 49: 10g 8.2d a5g 1995 a12g^2 a12g 11.9g 10g Sep 21] leggy gelding: poor maiden: no form after reappearance: has been gelded: stays 1½m: blinkered (well beaten) second 3-y-o start. *G. Fierro* — 43

RANKAIDADE 4 b.f. Governor General 116 – Keep Cool (FR) 42 (Northern Treat (USA)) [1994 60, a–: 5m 6d 5.1m^5 6g 6f^6 5m^5 6.1s^4 a5g a5g 1995 6d 5m 5m^6 6g 6m 5g 7m Oct 20] strong filly: no worthwhile form in 1995: stays 6f: acts on soft going, possibly not on top-of-the-ground: well beaten both starts on fibresand. *Don Enrico Incisa* — –

RANOSH (USA) 3 ch.f. Rahy (USA) 115 – Knoosh (USA) 113 (Storm Bird (CAN) 134) [1994 NR 1995 8.1g^5 10m^3 9m^3 10m^2 8d Sep 15] strong, deep-girthed filly: unimpressive mover: second foal: dam won from 7f (at 2 yrs) to 1½m: fair maiden: beaten 2 short heads at Redcar third start: stays 1¼m: acts on good to firm ground, disappointing on dead: bandaged. *E. A. L. Dunlop* — 79

RAPID LINER 2 b.c. (Mar 12) Skyliner 117 – Stellaris (Star Appeal 133) [1995 5m^5 6m^6 5m 7m^4 6m Oct 2] 4,200F, 8,600Y: leggy, lengthy colt: has a round action: brother to 2 winners, including 6f (at 2 yrs) and 1m winner Blue Radiance, and half-brother to one-time fairly useful 6f/1m performer Ashdren (by Lochnager): dam lightly raced: modest performer ran as though something amiss third start: off course around 2 months prior to both subsequent outings: will stay beyond 7f. *A. Harrison* — 60 +

RAPID MOVER 8 ch.g. Final Straw 127 – Larive 80 (Blakeney 126) [1994 –: a12g 11.1d 11.1f^6 9.2f 11.1m 13m^5 12.1g 1995 11.1s^6 Apr 12] workmanlike gelding: no worthwhile form on flat for long time: modest jumper. *D. A. Nolan* — –

RAPIER POINT (IRE) 4 gr.g. Cyrano de Bergerac 120 – Renzola (Dragonara Palace (USA) 115) [1994 70, a54+: a6g^3 a5g^3 a7g^4 6g* 6f 1995 a6g a6g^6 a6g 6g 8g 7m^4 6g^6 a5g 6.1d Sep 19] compact gelding: modest performer: needs further than 5f and should stay 7f: acts on good to firm and heavy ground and on fibresand: below form when tried in visor/blinkers: has been bandaged: sold (P. Haslam to C. Murray) 2,400 gns Newmarket Autumn Sales. *P. C. Haslam* — 63 d a51 d

RAPPORTEUR (USA) 9 b.g. His Majesty (USA) – Sweet Rapport (USA) (Round Table) [1994 –, a75: a12g^4 a12g* a10g^6 a12g* 1995 a12g a12g 10.3g^5 11.8d^4 14.1g^6 13g 11.5m Jun 24] leggy, angular gelding: gained all 19 of his wins at — 57

Lingfield (a record there), 14 times on the equitrack, achieving a career-high rating of 92 in 1991: underwent knee surgery for cartilage deterioration in the summer of 1994 and was clearly not himself in 1995: peak form at 1¼m (at which trip he has the equal-best time on equitrack) and stayed 1½m: acted on good to firm and heavy going, best on equitrack: often bandaged: won for amateur and apprentice, but went best for W. Newnes, to whose home he has been retired: splendidly tough and genuine in his prime. *C. C. Elsey*

RASAS (IRE) 3 b. or br.c. Lead On Time (USA) 123 – Hufoof 90 (Known Fact (USA) 135) [1994 72p: 5.7g 5s^{2} 6g^{2} 1995 6g^{5} 5.1m^{5} 6g* 6m* 6m* Jul 30] tall, useful-looking colt: progressed after each run in 1995, making into a useful handicapper: successful at Newcastle in May and at Ripon and Lingfield in July: stays 6f well: acts on good to firm and soft ground: looked open to further improvement. *H. Thomson Jones* 97 p

RASAYEL (USA) 5 b.m. Bering 136 – Reham 67 (Mill Reef (USA) 141) [1994 56: a12g^{5} a12g a12g^{7} a12g^{4} a12g 12.3d a12g 1995 a16.2g a12g^{6} 10m^{3} 10.8f^{2} 13.1f* 12g^{6} 13f^{6} 11.1m^{2} 10m^{6} 12.3m^{3} 10.3m^{3} 10.4g* 10g^{6} 10.5g Sep 23] big, leggy mare: has a round action: modest handicapper: won at Bath in May and at York (apprentices, back to form) in August: effective at around 1¼m, and stays 14.1f: acts on firm and dead ground, and on fibresand: blinkered (out of form) final 4-y-o start: sometimes pulls hard: usually held up at 5 yrs: inconsistent. *P. D. Evans* 56

RASH GIFT 2 ch.f. (Mar 5) Cadeaux Genereux 131 – Nettle 106 (Kris 135) [1995 7g^{2} Jul 28] fourth foal: half-sister to 3-y-o 1m winner Stinging Reply (by Belmez): dam, 2-y-o 6f and 7.3f winner, appeared to stay 1½m: 3/1, beaten a head by Subterfuge in steadily-run 4-runner maiden at Newmarket, keeping on gamely when headed: looked likely to improve. *Lord Huntingdon* 78 p

RASMI (CAN) 4 ch.c. Riverman (USA) 131 – Snow Blossom (CAN) (The Minstrel (CAN) 135) [1994 65: 7.5m^{2} 1995 7m^{5} 6.9m^{5} 8g^{6} 10.2m^{5} 7m 7g a13g Nov 25] good-topped colt: reportedly had wind operation after 3-y-o start: fair maiden: sold out of A. Stewart's stable 7,000 gns Newmarket July Sales after fourth start: well beaten for new connections: stays 1m: has raced only on a sound surface. *P. Howling* 71 d

RATICOSA 3 b.f. Hallgate 127 – Rose Meadow 45 (Mummy's Game 120) [1994 –: 5m^{6} 5g 6.1m 6.1m 7m 1995 6.1g 12.4g^{6} Apr 17] sparely-made filly: of little account: visored at 3 yrs. *Don Enrico Incisa* –

RATTLE 2 b.g. (Apr 18) Mazilier (USA) 107 – Snake Song 94 (Mansingh (USA) 120) [1995 5f^{3} 5g^{4} 6g a7g^{5} 6s^{4} 8f Oct 16] 4,600Y, 4,400 2-y-o: small gelding: third foal: half-brother to 3-y-o Hornpipe (by Handsome Sailor): dam sprinter: modest form at best: stays 6f: showed little on fibresand. *J. J. O'Neill* 52

RAVEN'S ROOST (IRE) 4 b.g. Taufan (USA) 119 – Al Zumurrud 80 (Be My Guest (USA) 126) [1994 58: 11.6m^{5} 10m^{4} 10m^{3} 10.2g 8.1d^{6} 1995 10m 8.3g 8f Jun 28] leggy, lengthy gelding: refused to race final 4-y-o start and is one to avoid: sold 2,600 gns Ascot July Sales. *Major D. N. Chappell* §§

RAVE-ON-HADLEY (IRE) 5 b.g. Commanche Run 133 – Fleet Fact (Known Fact (USA) 135) [1994 –, a56: a10g* a12g^{5} a10g^{5} a9.4g a9.4g^{5} a10g^{6} 9.2f^{5} a9.4g^{2} a9.4g^{6} 8.3g^{4} a10g^{5} a10g a8g 1995 a9.4g 10.3g 8m Apr 29] lengthy gelding: sold out of A. Bailey's stable 750 gns Doncaster February Sales before reappearance: well beaten for new stable: should stay beyond 1¼m: acts on the all-weather, no form on turf: inconsistent. *S. W. Campion* §§ –

RAWI 2 ch.c. (Jan 29) Forzando 122 – Finally (Final Straw 127) [1995 5g 6m 6m 6g^{6} 6g^{6} 8g a7g^{4} a7g a6g a7g Dec 12] 20,000F, 26,000Y: workmanlike colt: second reported foal: dam poor daughter of William Hill Gold Cup winner Boswellia: modest maiden: sold out of C. J. Benstead's stable 8,000 gns Newmarket Autumn Sales after sixth start: well beaten last 3 outings: stays 7f: blinkered (no form) eighth outing. *W. R. Muir* 64

RAWYA (USA) 4 ch.f. Woodman (USA) 126 – Dance It (USA) (Believe It (USA)) [1994 76: 8d 7d 8d a8g^{2} 1995 a10g^{2} a10g^{2} Jan 24] useful-looking filly: fluent mover: fair form: second in 2 handicaps at Lingfield in January: stays 1¼m: acts on equitrack, has raced only on dead ground on turf. *B. W. Hills* 78

RAYNER (IRE) 2 b.g. (Mar 22) Lycius (USA) 124 – Rosati (USA) (Caro 133) [1995 7.1g⁶ 7g⁵ Oct 23] rangy, attractive gelding: second foal: half-brother to useful Irish 3-y-o 1¼m winner Rosillo (by Mtoto): dam Irish 2-y-o 7f, winner stayed 1¼m: absent over 3 months, under 5 lengths fifth of 9 to Alhawa in maiden at Lingfield, second home of those on favoured far side: will stay further than 7f: very slowly away on debut: gelded after final start: will improve again: sent to Dubai. *P. W. Chapple-Hyam* 62 p

RAY OF HOPE 3 b.f. Rainbow Quest (USA) 134 – Widows Walk (Habitat 134) [1994 53: 7g 7g 1995 10s 9.7m Apr 25] lengthy, good-topped filly: modest form as 2-y-o: soundly beaten in 1995: should be suited by further than 7f. *G. Wragg* –

RAZANA (IRE) 3 b.f. Kahyasi 130 – Raysiya (Cure The Blues (USA)) [1994 NR 1995 10.2m* 10.2m⁶ Jul 20] IR 26,000Y: first foal: dam, fairly useful Irish 1¼m and 1½m winner, is half-sister to smart Irish middle-distance stayer Rayseka: narrowly won maiden at Chepstow in July: not disgraced when sixth of 7 in listed race there 16 days later: would have stayed 1½m: stud. *J. H. M. Gosden* 71 +

R DRAGON 3 ch.f. Insan (USA) 119 – Hyde Princess 75 (Touch Paper 113) [1994 –: 5g 5.1m 6s⁶ 6g 6m 1995 7m 8.3m 7g May 18] plain filly: no worthwhile form: tried visored. *M. Madgwick* –

REACH FOR GLORY 6 b.g. Reach 122 – Carlton Glory (Blakeney 126) [1994 45: 15.8g⁵ 13.1f² 1995 15.8g* a14g³ Jun 16] small gelding: poor performer: won steadily-run seller at Catterick in June: stays 15.8f: acts on any turf going and on fibresand: tried visored/blinkered, no improvement: has run in snatches, and tends to hang right: winning selling hurdler. *W. G. M. Turner* 41

REACT 2 b.f. (Jan 24) Reprimand 122 – Shehana (USA) 86 (The Minstrel (CAN) 135) [1995 6m² 6g* 6m³ 7m⁵ 7d Sep 26] rangy, good-quartered, useful-looking filly: has scope: second living foal: half-sister to 1½m winner Legion of Honour (by Ahonoora): dam 2-y-o 9f winner, apparently stayed 1½m: easy winner of maiden at Yarmouth in June: creditable third to Maid For The Hills in listed race at Newmarket (more settled in preliminaries) in July and fifth to Bin Shadayid in Prestige Stakes at Goodwood on penultimate outing: likely to prove best short of 7f. *W. Jarvis* 86 +

READYPOWER 3 b.g. Newski (USA) – Bay Runner (Bay Express 132) [1994 –: 8d 1995 10g Sep 29] strong, plain gelding: first foal: dam tailed off on only start: tailed off in seller and maiden. *J. J. Bridger* –

READYSPEX 5 b.g. Kala Shikari 125 – Set To Work (Workboy 123) [1994 NR 1995 7.5d 8f⁶ 10.3g 14.1f 7f Jul 27] plain, leggy gelding: half-brother to 2 winners: dam never ran: no sign of ability: tried blinkered: sold 800 gns Ascot July Sales. *R. D. E. Woodhouse* –

READY TEDDY (IRE) 2 b.f. (Mar 31) Fayruz 116 – Racey Naskra (USA) 75 (Star de Naskra (USA)) [1995 5f⁵ 5g 6g Sep 24] 4,800Y: second foal: half-sister to Swedish 3-y-o 6f winner Overtaker (by Contract Law): dam 7.5f winner: signs of ability in auction events and a seller. *Miss L. A. Perratt* –

REAGANESQUE (USA) 3 b.g. Nijinsky (CAN) 138 – Basoof (USA) 83 (Believe It (USA)) [1994 NR 1995 10g 10m⁵ 10m⁵ 10d 13.6f Oct 12] lengthy –

Royal Hunt Cup (Handicap), Royal Ascot—
Realities and Darnay have mastered third-placed Indian Fly and sixth-placed Moving Arrow

gelding: has scope: fifth foal: half-brother to French 1993 2-y-o 7f winner Melting Gold (by Cadeaux Genereux): dam 1m winner: little worthwhile form: gelded after third start: should stay 1½m: best watched: has joined P. Murphy. *E. A. L. Dunlop*

REAL GEM 2 b.f. (Mar 1) Formidable (USA) 125 – Emerald Ring 74 (Auction Ring (USA) 123) [1995 6.1m^{3} a6g^{6} 7g^{5} 7g Sep 29] sparely-made filly: second foal: sister to 4-y-o Forbidden Gem: dam sprinter: third of 11 in maiden auction at Nottingham: failed to repeat that form, sweating and well beaten in seller at Goodwood final start: best effort at 6f: slowly away first 2 starts. *P. J. Makin* — 62 d

REALITIES (USA) 5 ch.h. Cozzene (USA) – Alquizar (USA) (Star de Naskra (USA)) [1994 105: 10d 7g* 8m^{4} 8f^{2} 10m 8m* 7g^{2} 1995 8g 7m 7m 7m^{2} 8m* 10m^{4} 8f^{2} 8m^{3} 8m^{2} 8g^{5} Sep 28] strong, good-quartered horse: fluent mover: progressed again, and is a smart performer: won Royal Hunt Cup at Royal Ascot and short-headed by Khayrapour in Schweppes Golden Mile at Goodwood: stepped up from handicaps last 3 outings, notably 1¾ lengths third of 6 to Harayir in Celebration Mile at Goodwood: effective from 7f to 1¼m: acts on firm and dead going: usually held up: has run well when sweating: tough, consistent and thoroughly genuine: sold to join T. Amoss in USA, where he should add considerably to his earnings. *G. Harwood* — 112

REALLY A DREAM (IRE) 2 br.f. (Mar 8) Last Tycoon 131 – Ancestry (Persepolis (FR) 127) [1995 7m^{4} Oct 28] rather leggy filly: fourth foal: half-sister to fairly useful 3-y-o 5f and 6f winner Christmas Kiss (by Taufan), 7f winner Mistress Gwyn (by Night Shift) and 6f to 1¼m winner Devilry (by Faustus): dam never ran: 11/4 and green beforehand, shaped well when 4½ lengths fourth of 19 to Awaamir in maiden at Newmarket, prominent throughout and staying on when short of room over 1f out: moved well to post: sure to do better, and should win a race. *M. R. Stoute* — 74 p

REAL MADRID 4 b.g. Dreams To Reality (USA) 113 – Spanish Princess (King of Spain 121) [1994 –, a60: 7s 8.5s 7m 10m^{5} 10.8m 16.4m 10g^{6} 8g 7g^{5} a8g* 1995 — 34

Roy Taiano's "Realities"

8.3m 8g 7.6m^{5} 7.6d 8g 7d a9.3g^{4} 9.3v* a10g^{3} Dec 18] good-bodied gelding: poor performer: ran twice in Belgium in the autumn, winning handicap at Groenendaal in November: stays 1¼m: best turf efforts with give in the ground: sometimes blinkered/visored. *G. P. Enright*

REALMS OF GLORY (IRE) 2 b.c. (Mar 31) Reprimand 122 – Wasaif (IRE) 79 (Lomond (USA) 128) [1995 5.7m^{6} 7g Oct 10] 20,000 2-y-o: lengthy colt: first foal: dam 6.9f winner who stayed 1m: similar form (beaten around 10 lengths) in maidens won by Celandine at Bath and Gold Disc at Leicester 15 days later: bandaged behind last time. *P. Mitchell* 56 p

REAL POPCORN (IRE) 4 ch.f. Jareer (USA) 115 – Avidal Park 68 (Horage 124) [1994 52: a9.4g 12m* 11.9g 1995 a16g Mar 2] sparely-made filly: modest form at best: wore hood and visor, saddle slipped only start in 1995: stays 1½m: best efforts on good to firm ground: edgy sort: front runner: hurdling with W. Jenks. *K. McAuliffe* –

REBECCAS SECRET (IRE) 4 ch.g. Classic Secret (USA) 91 – Cordon 89 (Morston (FR) 125) [1994 51p: 13.1m^{2} 1995 12.1d^{4} 12.3f Jun 21] smallish, workmanlike gelding: modest maiden, lightly raced: well beaten (as if something amiss) in ladies handicap at Ripon final start: will stay beyond 13.1f. *R. F. Fisher* 55

REBEL COUNTY (IRE) 2 b.f. (Apr 12) Maelstrom Lake 118 – Haven Bridge 88 (Connaught 130) [1995 5m^{5} 6.1m^{4} 5m^{2} 5m^{2} 6m* 6s^{2} 7f Oct 23] IR 1,000Y, 4,000 2-y-o: big, workmanlike filly: half-sister to 6f (at 2 yrs) and 7f winner Sharphaven (by Sharpo) and 2 winners abroad: dam 6f winner at 2 yrs: won maiden at Lingfield in September: pulled hard and never a threat in nursery last time: best form at 6f: acts on good to firm and soft ground. *D. J. S. Cosgrove* 68

RECALL TO MIND 2 b.g. (Feb 22) Don't Forget Me 127 – Northern Notion (USA) (Northern Baby (CAN) 127) [1995 6m 7.5m 8.5m^{4} 8f Oct 12] close-coupled, leggy gelding: second living foal: dam, poor French maiden, half-sister to very smart French middle-distance stayer Balompie: fourth of 7 to Belana at Beverley in August, only worthwhile form: will stay beyond 8.5f. *M. H. Easterby* 66 ?

RECESSIONS OVER 4 b.g. Komaite (USA) – Lucky Councillor (Lucky Wednesday 124) [1994 NR 1995 a6g Dec 12] second foal: dam never ran: 50/1, signs of a little ability in claimer at Wolverhampton. *N. P. Littmoden* –

RECLAIMED 2 ch.f. (Apr 4) Tina's Pet 121 – Far Claim (USA) 35 (Far North (CAN) 120) [1995 5g 6m^{6} 6m^{6} Aug 12] 2,100Y, 2,000 2-y-o: second foal: half-sister to 3-y-o 5f (at 2yrs) to 1m winner Media Express (by Sayf El Arab): dam, plater, suited by 6f: soundly beaten in auction events and seller at Lingfield. *J. S. Moore* –

RECLUSE 4 b.g. Last Tycoon 131 – Nomadic Pleasure 91 (Habitat 134) [1994 61§: 8d 10.2g^{4} 13.4m^{5} 10.8m^{3} 11.9f* 13.6m^{5} 1995 14m 12g Sep 2] well-made gelding: ran as if something amiss only start for Lady Herries and again 2 weeks later: probably stays 13.6f: acts on firm and dead ground: blinkered fourth 3-y-o outing to 4-y-o reappearance: sometimes looks reluctant, and not one to rely on: won over hurdles in September: sold (M. Hammond to Miss L. Perratt) 6,000 gns Doncaster October Sales. *M. D. Hammond* – §

RECORD LOVER (IRE) 5 b.g. Alzao (USA) 117 – Spun Gold 106 (Thatch (USA) 136) [1994 –: a11g 13.9f 12g 12.3m 14.6f^{5} 14.1g^{6} 1995 10.5d 18m^{4} 16.2f 14.1m 10m^{6} 12m 18m^{4} 16m 14s 18f^{4} Oct 16] leggy, close-coupled gelding: modest hurdler: poor at best on flat since 1993: stays 2m: acts on firm ground and all-weather surfaces, probably on soft: most inconsistent. *M. C. Chapman* 45 d

RECOVERY LAD (IRE) 3 b.g. Prince Rupert (FR) 121 – Hill of Tara (Royal Palace 131) [1994 6d 1995 a8g^{6} a9.4g^{3} a11g^{3} 12.5m^{2} a12g 14.1m^{6} 13.8g^{2} 16d^{2} 14m Jul 7] IR 5,300Y: small gelding: half-brother to several winners: dam ran twice: trained by P. Molloy in Ireland at 2 yrs: modest form here: stays 2m: acts on fibresand and good to firm ground: visored (no improvement) last 2 starts: hangs markedly under pressure and not one to trust. *K. R. Burke* 56 § a47 §

RED ACUISLE (IRE) 2 br.c. (Apr 19) Soviet Lad (USA) 94 – Scottish Gaelic (USA) (Highland Park (USA)) [1995 5m^{3} 5f^{2} 5m 6m^{5} 5m^{6} 6d^{5} 6s a8.5g^{2} a6g^{2} a7g^{2} a6g^{6} a7g Dec 14] IR 15,000Y: first foal: dam Irish 2-y-o 7.9f winner: modest maiden: trained first 8 outings by M. Bell: stays 8.5f: acts on firm and dead ground and on all-weather surfaces: visored (well beaten) seventh start: joined J. Berry. *G. Lewis* 61

RED ADMIRAL 5 ch.g. Formidable (USA) 125 – Dancing Meg (USA) 113 (Marshua's Dancer (USA)) [1994 68: a6g^3 a6g* a6g^5 6m^3 6.1m 5.3f^2 5m* 5.2g a6g a6g* a6g 1995 a6g^3 a5g 6g 5m 6g* 6m^5 6f^3 6f^2 5.2m^5 6m^4 6f* 5m^5 Aug 14] heavy-topped, workmanlike gelding: fair handicapper: won at Yarmouth (made all) in June and Folkestone in August: effective at 5f and 6f: acts on firm ground and the all-weather: has run creditably when sweating: successful for 7-lb claimer: usually bandaged behind: races prominently: none too consistent: joined C. Murray. *P. C. Haslam* — 64 a69

RED AZALEA 3 b.f. Shirley Heights 130 – Cerise Bouquet 75 (Mummy's Pet 125) [1994 95p: 7m* 8g^5 1995 10m* 10.2m^4 10.1g 10.1g Sep 12] good-topped filly: useful performer: sweating, easy winner of minor event at Windsor in June: contested listed races afterwards, easily best attempt (led over 7f, would have run creditably but for being badly hampered over 1f out) in rated stakes at Newcastle penultimate start: should stay 1½m: has raced only on a sound surface: blinkered (well beaten) final 3-y-o start: has wandered and swished tail. *Sir Mark Prescott* — 95

RED BEACON 8 b.g. Red Sunset 120 – Mount of Light 61 (Sparkler 130) [1994 NR 1995 12g^6 14.1f^6 Jun 28] no longer of much account. *J. L. Goulding* — –

RED BISHOP (USA) 7 b. or br.h. Silver Hawk (USA) 123 – La Rouquine (Silly Season 127) [1994 121: a10g* a11g^2 a12g^2 12m^6 10g* 10d^2 12g^3 11s^2 12g* 1995 11d* 14f* 10m^3 Jul 8] — 121

Not a conventional career, this one's. Once firmly based in Britain, Red Bishop raced in Italy as a four-year-old, and in France, the UAE, Hong Kong and North America at six and seven, finishing second in the Gran Premio del Jockey Club e Coppa d'Oro in Italy, and winning in each of the other countries. Added to that, he won for four different trainers. Red Bishop was trained by John Gosden until the end of his five-year-old season, winning five races, most notably the 1993 Brigadier Gerard Stakes at Sandown, and finishing placed in another six pattern events. After being sent to Dubai for the winter of 1993/4, where he won once and was twice narrowly second to Cezanne when under the care of Hilal Ibrahim, Red Bishop was returned to Europe and soon joined John Hammond in France. He won a minor event at Deauville and ran well in pattern events in France and America before showing improved form to win the Hong Kong International Vase in December by two and a quarter lengths from Urgent Request before returning once again to Dubai.

Hilal Ibrahim was again down as trainer when Red Bishop reappeared, back at Sha Tin, for the valuable Queen Elizabeth II Cup in April. Red Bishop won easily, quickening clear two furlongs out and eased to beat Volochine by two and a quarter lengths with the rest of the fourteen-strong field three and a half lengths and further behind. Saeed bin Suroor had taken over by the time Red Bishop was flown halfway round the world about three weeks later, to California. The Grade 1 San Juan Capistrano Invitational Handicap at Santa Anita is the longest graded stakes event in the USA these days at 'about a mile and three quarters' on turf, and has a roll of honour including Cougar II, Exceller, John Henry and, more recently, Nasr El Arab, Kotashaan and Bien Bien. The 1995 renewal was a little below standard, notwithstanding the presence of the very smart Sandpit. Red Bishop quickened away from Sandpit early in the straight and held the late challenge of Special Price by a head. Sadly, Red Bishop's British summer amounted only to the Eclipse Stakes at Sandown in July. Dropping back considerably in trip, he was outpaced when the slow tempo increased and eventually finished three and a quarter lengths third of eight to Halling, staying on well to pull four lengths clear of the remainder. Plans to run in the King George VI And Queen Elizabeth Diamond Stakes were shelved after a 'joint-related problem', and that was that.

Red Bishop, who cost 100,000 dollars as a yearling, is the sixth foal out of La Rouquine, the previous five amounting to four runners and three relatively minor winners. Since Red Bishop, the dam has produced two more winners, notably the smart American four-year-old Pennine Ridge (by Cure The Blues), successful in Grade 2 and Grade 3 races at a mile to nine furlongs. Barren in 1993, she has a yearling filly by Sheikh Albadou. La Rouquine was a miler, winning two races in France, and another in America where she also finished third in the Grade 3 Orchid Handicap; she was the best of the once-raced Wether Fell's offspring. Further back in the pedigree, West Shaw won over six furlongs at two (easily her best season), three and four before producing five winners, including Marisela, who was runner-up to

Waterloo in the Cheveley Park Stakes and One Thousand Guineas, and Golden City, later the grandam of Indian Ridge. Silver Hawk, placed in the Derby and Irish Derby of 1982, is a good sire. However, it was not easy to establish him in Kentucky, and support for him was dwindling when horses such as million-dollar earners Hawkster and Silver Ending, Prix de Diane winner Lady In Silver and graded stakes winners Dansil, Silver Medallion and Silver Lane turned things around in 1988 and 1989. More recently, Grade 1-winning two-year-old Zoonaqua, Yorkshire Oaks winner Magnificent Star, the Robins-owned trio Silver Wisp, Silver Wizard and Silver Wedge and, in 1995, Secretariat Stakes winner Hawk Attack, Dubai-based Karoo Lark and Derby-fourth Fahal have all joined Red Bishop in keeping Silver Hawk prominent among active stallions. He stood for 40,000 dollars in 1995 and his twenty-five yearlings sold at the sales in America later in the year averaged over 160,000 dollars. The good-topped Red Bishop has now been retired to stud himself, to Margaux Farm in Midway, Kentucky, at 4,000 dollars (live foal, Nov 1). He well earned his chance. He was a very smart, genuine and consistent racehorse, with a turn of foot, who was effective at a mile and a quarter to around a mile and three quarters, and acted on firm and soft ground as well as sand. It speaks volumes that his last four races, contested on three different continents, marked the pinnacle of his career. *Saeed bin Suroor*

Red Bishop (USA) (b. or br.h. 1988)	Silver Hawk (USA) (b 1979)	Roberto (b 1969)	Hail To Reason
			Bramalee
		Gris Vitesse (gr 1966)	Amerigo
			Matchiche II
	La Rouquine (b 1976)	Silly Season (b 1962)	Tom Fool
			Double Deal
		Wether Fell (b 1968)	Klairon
			West Shaw

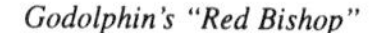

Godolphin's "Red Bishop"

REDBROOK LADY 2 ch.f. (Apr 6) Clantime 101 – Silently Yours (USA) 53 (Silent Screen (USA)) [1995 5f 5m^{5} 6.1d 5g a5g Sep 30] sturdy filly: half-sister to 3-y-o Fiveaday (by Komaite) and 5f winner Tommy Tempest (by Northern Tempest): dam 5f winner: poor maiden: well beaten in selling nursery final start. *S. G. Norton* — 43

RED BUSTAAN 3 b.c. Aragon 118 – Red Rose Garden 87 (Electric 126) [1994 77p: 7m 8.3g* 8s^{2} 1995 10g^{5} 11.6m^{2} 14g* 16.4m^{4} 14f^{3} 16.2m^{2} 16.1g^{3} 16.2d Sep 23] tall, sturdy colt: good mover: fairly useful handicapper: won 4-runner rated stakes at Haydock (led over 1f out, idled) in May: in frame at Sandown, Goodwood (blinkered, moved short to post), Beverley and Newcastle (£13,700 event, ¾ length behind Star Rage) in the summer: will stay beyond 2m: fair form (and best effort at the time) on soft going, best efforts on a sound surface and acts on firm: a lazy sort, and rather one paced: game and most consistent: to join C. Hayes in Australia. *A. C. Stewart* — 86

RED CARNIVAL (USA) 3 b.f. Mr Prospector (USA) – Seaside Attraction (USA) (Seattle Slew (USA)) [1994 101P: 5g* 6m* 1995 7m^{3} 8g^{2} 7m^{3} Oct 12] strong, lengthy filly: has plenty of scope: sister to 1995 leading US 2-y-o filly Golden Attraction: useful performer: 3 lengths third of 8 to Myself in steadily-run Nell Gwyn Stakes at Newmarket (operated afterwards on injured near-fore) in April: had little luck in running when keeping-on 2 lengths second of 12 to Bin Rosie in listed race there next start: best form when 2 lengths third of 8 to Harayir in Challenge Stakes there (sweating and woolly in coat) 2 weeks later: stays 1m: has raced only on good or good to firm ground: carries head awkwardly and high under pressure. *M. R. Stoute* — 109

RED CHANNEL (IRE) 5 b.g. Import 127 – Winscarlet North (Garland Knight 92) [1994 NR 1995 a7g^{6} Dec 19] sixth foal: dam unraced: no sign of ability in novice hurdles: 33/1, 11¾ lengths sixth of 10 to Bubble Wings in maiden at Lingfield, never dangerous. *T. Casey* — –

RED DRAGON 3 b.g. Caerleon (USA) 132 – Soemba 86 (General Assembly (USA)) [1994 NR 1995 10m 10d 10g 8m 9m Aug 18] compact, robust gelding: fifth foal: half-brother to 4 winners, including useful 7f and 1m winner Sumonda (by Lomond) and 4-y-o 9.4f to 2m winner Lalindi (by Cadeaux Genereux): dam 9f winner from good family: little worthwhile form, including in claimer final start: has been fitted with tongue strap: inconsistent. *G. Wragg* — –

RED FIVE 4 b.g. Clantime 101 – Miami Dolphin 85 (Derrylin 115) [1994 58: 7d^{3} 6g^{6} 7g^{4} 5s^{2} 6.1s 6s 1995 a6g 6s^{6} 6s 7m a7g Nov 13] sturdy, plain gelding: still a maiden, well below form in 1995: trained first 2 starts at 3 yrs only by Jack Berry: stays 6f: acts on soft ground. *D. Moffatt* — –

RED HASSETT (IRE) 3 b.c. Red Sunset 120 – Rekolette (Relko 136) [1994 49: a5g^{6} 5m 5g 6g 5s 5g^{4} 6d 6d^{4} a5g 1995 a8g Jan 16] compact colt: poor maiden: tried blinkered: sent to Belgium. *P. A. Blockley* — –

RED HOT RISK 3 b.g. Risk Me (FR) 127 – Hot Sunday Sport 42 (Star Appeal 133) [1994 57§: 5v^{6} 5g* 6f^{5} a5g 5m^{3} 7m 5g^{2} 5m 5s a6g 1995 5m 7g 7m 10m 8m Jun 19] compact gelding: well beaten in 1995: should stay beyond 5f: best form on an easy surface: often visored: inconsistent, temperamental and best left alone: sold (M. Dods to S. Campion) 550 gns Doncaster October Sales. *M. Dods* — – §

RED INDIAN 9 ch.g. Be My Native (USA) 122 – Martialette (Welsh Saint 126) [1994 40, a49: a11g^{5} 10g^{4} a11g^{2} a11g^{2} 11g^{3} a12g^{2} 10.8s^{6} 1995 a12g* a11g^{5} a12g^{4} a12g^{3} 10m 9.9d^{5} a11g^{4} Jun 22] tall, lengthy gelding: carries condition: unimpressive mover: poor performer: won seller at Southwell in February: suited by middle distances: acts on any going, including on fibresand: held up/tracks leaders. *W. W. Haigh* — 36 a52

RED LIGHT 3 b.g. Reprimand 122 – Trull (Lomond (USA) 128) [1994 82: 5d 7g^{4} 7s* 7v 1995 8.1m^{6} 10g^{6} 8s^{5} 12d^{6} Oct 21] sparely-made gelding: fair handicapper at best: should be suited by further than 1m (shapes as if stays 1½m): acts on soft ground: visored (below form) third 3-y-o start: put head in air and hung badly left second 3-y-o start: sold (Lord Huntingdon to S. Sherwood) 14,500 gns Ascot October Sales. *Lord Huntingdon* — 71

RED MARCH HARE 4 b.f. Daring March 116 – Happy Harriet (Red Sunset 120) [1994 34: 7d^{4} 8d 7.5m 7m^{3} 10g^{5} 8m 1995 a8g Jan 6] angular filly: poor maiden: — –

no chance in claimer only start (for new stable) in 1995: stays 1¼m but may prove ideally suited by around 1m: acts on dead ground, well beaten on firm and heavy. *D. Moffatt*

RED MISTY (IRE) 2 b.f. (Feb 17) Red Sunset 120 – Decoy Duck 67 (Decoy Boy 129) [1995 6f 5.1f6 6f2 6m6 7.5d6 6s 7m Oct 12] 8,500Y: workmanlike filly: half-sister to 4-y-o 11.1f winner Missus Murhill (by Mon Tresor), 7f winner in Ireland at 2 yrs, 1½m winner Portofino (by Coquelin) and 7f (at 2 yrs) to 1m winner Drumdonna (by Drumalis): dam, 2-y-o 6f winner, only season to race: ran for Mrs M. McCourt on debut: second of 5 in median auction maiden at Brighton in August, apparently easily best effort: probably stays 7.5f: sent to Norway. *M. R. Channon* 57 d

RED MORNING 3 b.f. Warning 136 – Beautiful Dawn (USA) (Grey Dawn II 132) [1994 NR 1995 8g 9g 10g 8g 10m 9m4 Aug 18] 6,000F, 23,000Y: workmanlike filly: half-sister to 7f winner Point House (by Diesis), 10.2f winner Beau Rou and 4-y-o German 7f and 1m winner Beautiful Fighter (both by Rousillon): dam minor 6f stakes winner at 5 yrs: failed to confirm promise of debut, well beaten in claimer final start: stays 1¼m: sold 2,300 gns Newmarket Autumn Sales. *D. R. C. Elsworth* 61 d

RED NOSE (IRE) 2 b.g. (Jan 23) Cyrano de Bergerac 120 – Crimson Glen 70 (Glenstal (USA) 118) [1995 5m5 5m5 7m 6m3 6f2 6m4 6g2 7m5 Oct 21] 21,000Y: workmanlike gelding: poor walker: second foal: half-brother to 3-y-o 1½m winner Court Joker (by Fools Holme): dam Irish 7f and 9f winner: fair form: visored, good efforts last 2 starts in maiden at Catterick and nursery at Doncaster: stays 7f but likely to prove more effective at 6f: front runner last 2 starts: sold 8,200 gns Newmarket Autumn Sales: sent to Singapore. *M. H. Tompkins* 74

RED NYMPH 2 b.f. (Mar 13) Sharpo 132 – Red Gloves 83 (Red God 128§) [1995 6m3 6m* 6m4 7d Sep 26] tall, unfurnished filly: sister to 3-y-o Mo Stopher and fairly useful 6f and 1m winner Takdeer, and half-sister to 2 winners at up to 7f: dam placed at 6f and 7f at 2 yrs, later won in Norway: much improved effort to win minor event at Windsor in August by 7 lengths from High Priority: below that form afterwards in listed race at Ripon and valuable sales race at Newmarket: stays 6f. *W. Jarvis* 91 ?

RED O'REILLY 3 ch.g. Hubbly Bubbly (USA) – Name The Game 66 (Fair Season 120) [1994 NR 1995 6g a6g 6.1g 6.1m5 8g a8g Jun 8] workmanlike gelding: second foal: half-brother to 4-y-o 1m winner Calder King (by Rakaposhi King): dam maiden sprint plater: poor maiden plater: tried visored/blinkered: inconsistent. *Mrs N. Macauley* 47

RED OWA LADY (IRE) 3 b.f. Jareer (USA) 115 – The Woman In Red 68 (Red Regent 123) [1994 –: 6g 6g6 1995 a8g a9.4g Feb 8] leggy, close-coupled filly: of little account. *C. J. Hill* –

RED PHANTOM (IRE) 3 ch.g. Kefaah (USA) 124 – Highland Culture (Lomond (USA) 128) [1994 7d 8g 1995 a7g4 a12g3 a12g* a9.4g* Aug 5] IR 4,500Y: ex-Irish gelding: second foal: dam unraced: trained by M. Robinson at 2 yrs: much improved form to win maiden claimer at Southwell and claimer (came from behind in strongly-run race) at Wolverhampton in the summer: stays 1½m. *S. Mellor* 71

RED RAJA 2 b.c. (Apr 10) Persian Heights 129 – Jenny Splendid 101 (John Splendid 116) [1995 7f 7g 6m 7.3d Oct 21] 14,000Y: workmanlike colt: half-brother to 4 winners (one abroad), including 1984 2-y-o 5f winner Shelley Marie (by Gunner B) and sprinter Shari Louise (by Radetzky): dam won from 5f to 7f: behind in maidens at Newmarket (2) and nursery at Newbury: often slowly away, particularly on debut when pulled up after 100 yds. *P. Mitchell* –

RED RITA (IRE) 4 ch.f. Kefaah (USA) 124 – Katie Roche (Sallust 134) [1994 97§: 7g4 8m 6d2 6m2 7.1m2 6f 7m3 1995 7f4 6m 6m* 7m3 7m5 6m6 7g Sep 30] workmanlike filly: unimpressive mover: only fair form at best in 1995 for new stable: made all in 6-runner median auction event at Folkestone in July: well beaten last 2 starts: effective at 6f to 1m: acts on firm and dead ground: sometimes reluctant to post: not one to trust implicitly. *W. R. Muir* 79

RED RIVER ROSE (IRE) 3 b.f. Red Sunset 120 – Salonniere (FR) 88 (Bikala 134) [1994 51: 5v 5.1g 6g5 7m a6g* 6.1d a8.5g a8.5g 1995 8.2g a8g4 7m3 8m 8.2m 7.5m 7m Aug 25] workmanlike filly: poor plater: stays 1m: acts on fibresand: blinkered since second 3-y-o start: often wears tongue strap: inconsistent: sold 2,300 gns Newmarket September Sales. *N. P. Littmoden* 40 a51

RED RIVER VALLEY 2 br.g. (Jan 30) Belfort (FR) 89 – Play For Time (Comedy Star (USA) 121) [1995 5g2 5g* 6f3 6f3 5g2 6f* 6f2 6g 6f6 Oct 12] 2,800Y: leggy gelding: fourth foal: half-brother to a winner abroad by Sulaafah: dam never ran: won maiden auction at Hamilton in May and nursery at Redcar in August: ran well when sixth of 26 to Blue Iris in Redcar Two-Year-Old Trophy in October on final start: stays 6f: acts on firm ground: sent to Malaysia. *Denys Smith* 86

RED ROBBO (CAN) 2 b.c. (Apr 29) Red Ransom (USA) – Aunt Jobiska (USA) (What Luck (USA)) [1995 7g* 8d5 Oct 21] well-made colt: has plenty of scope: eighth foal: half-brother to several minor winners in North America: dam ran 4 times: won maiden at York in August by short head from Sasuru, niggled along at halfway then improving to lead inside last, tending to idle close home: odds on, last of 5 in minor event at Newbury nearly 2 months later, every chance 2f out but soon beaten: should stay at least 1m: seems unsuited by soft surface. *H. R. A. Cecil* 92

RED RUSTY (USA) 2 ch.g. (Apr 5) The Carpenter (USA) – Super Sisters (AUS) (Call Report (USA)) [1995 a8g a8.5g7 a8g* Dec 18] fourth foal: brother to a winner in USA at up to 7f: dam, Australian maiden, half-sister to a Grade 2 winner there: sire Grade 2 winner at up to 8.5f at 2 yrs in USA: made all in maiden at Lingfield in December, beating Sahhar by 2 lengths: will stay beyond 8.5f. *D. Morris* 69

RED SIMBA 2 ch.g. (Feb 22) Absalom 128 – Plie 75 (Superlative 118) [1995 5v3 5.1g4 a6g3 a7g4 a7g* a7g5 6.1m 6m a6g a6g a6g3 a6s2 Dec 17] 5,800Y: small, stocky gelding: second foal: half-brother to a winner abroad by Sayf El Arab: dam, 2-y-o 5.8f winner, stayed 1m: plater: won at Wolverhampton in July: sold out of J. Berry's stable 1,000 gns Newmarket Autumn Sales after tenth start: placed both outings in Sweden: stays 7f. *B. Nilsson, Sweden* 47 a55

RED SKY DELIGHT (IRE) 2 b.f. (Apr 11) Skyliner 117 – Blazing Sunset 55 (Blazing Saddles (AUS)) [1995 5d 5m 6f6 5g 6f 6g Oct 16] 450Y: leggy filly: first foal: dam sprinter: seems of little account. *P. Butler* –

RED SLANEY (IRE) 4 ch.g. Mazaad 106 – Carrick Slaney (Red God 128§) [1994 51: 7s 7.6m 6.9g4 8d 7d 1995 7m 6g Jun 5] angular, workmanlike gelding: modest maiden at best: well beaten in sellers in 1995: stays 7f: blinkered (looked reluctant) on 4-y-o reappearance: not one to trust. *R. Akehurst* – §

RED SPECTACLE (IRE) 3 b.g. Red Sunset 120 – Buz Kashi 123 (Bold Lad (IRE) 133) [1994 52: 5g5 6g a6g3 8s a6g 1995 a8g6 a9.4g* a8g a9.4g6 10g 10m 12.1m3 9.2m2 11.1f2 11.1f4 12m 12h* 14.1m* Aug 23] quite good-topped gelding: modest handicapper: won apprentice contest at Wolverhampton in January and made all at Carlisle and Redcar within 3 days in August: stays 1¾m: acts on hard going and fibresand, possibly unsuited by soft ground: has run well for amateur/apprentice. *P. C. Haslam* 62

REDSTELLA (USA) 6 ch.h. Theatrical 128 – Orange Squash 78 (Red God 128§) [1994 NR 1995 10.5g5 11.9m4 Jun 16] big, good-topped horse: fairly useful performer (rated 87) at 4 yrs: burly, only fair form in handicaps at Haydock (tended to hang) and York (6 days later) on return: stays 1½m: acts on good to firm and heavy going: visored (ran creditably) twice: held up. *R. M. Whitaker* 68

RED STREAM (USA) 2 b.f. (Apr 10) Red Ransom (USA) – Beetwentysix (USA) (Buckaroo (USA)) [1995 5g* 5d5 6.1m2 6.5m3 7d2 Sep 20] $47,000F, 95,000Y: leggy, close-coupled filly: has a fluent, rounded action: sister to a winner in USA, closely related to a winner by Silver Hawk and half-sister to a winner by Green Forest: dam, 9f and 1¼m winner in France, from family of Lear Fan (by Roberto): won maiden at Doncaster in May: good efforts last 3 starts in minor event and nurseries: stays 7f: acts on good to firm and dead ground: visored last 2 outings: sold only 4,500 gns Newmarket Autumn Sales. *M. R. Stoute* 80

RED TIE AFFAIR (USA) 2 b.c. (Apr 16) Miswaki (USA) 124 – Quiet Rendezvous (USA) (Nureyev (USA) 131) [1995 8g Oct 10] $80,000Y: sturdy colt: fifth foal: brother to useful 4-y-o 6f (at 2 yrs) to 1¼m winner Knave's Ash: dam ran once: 25/1, always behind in 17-runner maiden at Leicester. *M. Bell* –

RED TIME 2 br.g. (Feb 27) Timeless Times (USA) 99 – Crimson Dawn (Manado 130) [1995 6.1g5 5g5 Jun 12] 2,500Y: rather leggy gelding: fourth foal: dam, maiden, probably stayed 6f: never a factor in seller at Chepstow (swerved badly left start) and 39 maiden auction at Pontefract (still green, hampered late on) 2 weeks later: may prove suited by further than 5f. *M. S. Saunders*

RED VALERIAN 4 b.g. Robellino (USA) 127 – Fleur Rouge 71 (Pharly (FR) 130) [1994 77: 8m^5 7.5g^5 7f^2 7g 7m^2 7m* 7m^3 8m* 7g 8g 8s 8m a8g^4 a8g* a7g^2 1995 a7g* a8g^2 a8g^2 a8g^6 8g 10.8d^2 10m 10f^4 10.3m^2 10.3g^3 8.3m^3 Jul 24] close-coupled gelding: fairly useful handicapper: best form on the all-weather and won 16-runner Ladbroke All-Weather Trophy Final at Lingfield in January: effective at 1m and stays 10.8f: acts on equitrack, firm ground and dead: visored (below form) once at 2 yrs, blinkered since sixth 3-y-o start: sometimes bandaged off-hind: held up: hurdling (winner twice in September) with J. O'Shea. *K. McAuliffe*

76 a89

RED WHIRLWIND 5 b.g. Shadeed (USA) 135 – Red Red Rose (USA) 90 (Blushing Groom (FR) 131) [1994 51, a57: 10.1g 7.2g^4 7m a8.5g^2 8s^6 a8g^6 a9.4g a8g^4 a9.4g^2 a10g 1995 a12g a16g^2 a16.2g^2 15.4g^6 a14.8g^2 Apr 29] tall, good-topped gelding: modest maiden handicapper: left B. McMath's stable after reappearance: suited by around 2m: acts on good to firm going and all-weather surfaces: blinkered (well beaten) third 4-y-o start. *R. J. O'Sullivan*

48 + a60

REED MY LIPS (IRE) 4 br.g. Thatching 131 – Taunsa 85 (Nishapour (FR) 125) [1994 –: a8g^5 a9.4g a8.5g^6 9.9d 12.5m a9.4g a14.8g 1995 10.3g 8m 8f 6.9f^6 8.1g^3 8g 7g^2 8f 7.1m^3 7.5g^5 7f 8.1d 7.1g^5 10.5s Oct 1] angular gelding: poor performer nowadays: stays 1m: acts on good to firm and dead ground: tried visored and blinkered, no improvement: sometimes wears near-side pricker/bandages. *B. P. J. Baugh*

38

REEFA'S MILL (IRE) 3 b.g. Astronef 116 – Pharly's Myth (Pharly (FR) 130) [1994 79: 6g^2 6m 7f^3 8.1g^3 7g 1995 8.3m 8.5m^2 7m^5 9m^2 10g^5 Oct 1] lengthy gelding: fair maiden: ran as if something amiss final outing: likely to prove suited by middle distances: has raced only on a sound surface: inconsistent. *J. W. Hills*

71

REEF RAIDER 2 gr.c. (Mar 26) Siberian Express (USA) 125 – Superior Quality 67 (Star Appeal 133) [1995 6g 6m 6m 8.3g 10m 8.2m Oct 26] 4,000F, 13,000 2-y-o: workmanlike colt: half-brother to a useful winner in Belgium by Ile de Bourbon: dam unraced: always behind in maiden events and a nursery: blinkered last 2 starts: wears a severe bridle. *N. Tinkler*

–

REELING 9 br.m. Relkino 131 – Mother Brown 103 (Candy Cane 125) [1994 NR 1995 a9.4g 18.2m Jul 8] big, lengthy mare: probably of little account. *Paddy Farrell*

– §

REEM DUBAI (IRE) 3 ch.f. Nashwan (USA) 135 – Gesedeh 117 (Ela-Mana-Mou 132) [1994 NR 1995 12m^5 12.3m^3 11.4m^5 17.1m Oct 2] long-backed filly: has a long stride: fourth foal: dam, suited by 1¼m, half-sister to Ardross out of half-sister to Arctique Royale: modest maiden: should have stayed beyond 1½m: stud. *J. H. M. Gosden*

63

REGAL AURA (IRE) 5 ch.g. Glow (USA) – Dignified Air (FR) 70 (Wolver Hollow 126) [1994 –: 12.3m 15.8f^5 15.8m^6 12g 1995 11.5s 12s Oct 6] big, workmanlike gelding: no worthwhile form since 2 yrs: tried blinkered and visored. *D. C. O'Brien*

–

REGAL CHIMES 6 gr.g. Another Realm 118 – London Cries (FR) (Bellman (FR) 123) [1994 99: 6m 6m 5f^4 5m^3 5f 1995 6g 5m 5.2m Apr 21] leggy gelding: useful performer: below form in 1995, running respectably only in listed race at Beverley second start: stays 6f: best on top-of-the-ground: has won when sweating and edgy: usually front runner: inconsistent: sold only 5,000 gns Newmarket Autumn Sales and gelded. *B. A. McMahon*

91

REGAL EAGLE 2 b.c. (May 2) Shirley Heights 130 – On The Tiles (Thatch (USA) 136) [1995 7m Aug 11] angular colt: fifth foal: closely related to Prix Saint-Alary winner Air de Rien (by Elegant Air) and half-brother to useful though unreliable 3-y-o Stiletto Blade (by Dashing Blade), 7f winner at 2 yrs, and 8.1f winner Singer On The Roof (by Chief Singer): dam, from family of Blushing Groom, won 1¼m maiden in Ireland from 3 starts: 12/1 and burly, tailed-off last of 8 in listed race at Newbury. *I. A. Balding*

–

REGAL FANFARE (IRE) 3 b.f. Taufan (USA) 119 – Tender Time (Tender King 123) [1994 94: 6.1m^2 6m* 6.1g* 6s^5 6g^3 1995 8m 7f^5 8f 7m^2 7f^5 10m^6 11.9g Sep 20] smallish filly: fairly useful form at 2 yrs: disappointing in 1995: should stay

69

1¼m: acts on good to firm ground, possibly not on soft: blinkered (no improvement) twice at 3 yrs: one to treat with caution. *J. W. Hills*

REGAL PORTRAIT (IRE) 3 b.f. Royal Academy (USA) 130 – Regal Beauty (USA) (Princely Native (USA)) [1994 NR 1995 8.1g^6 10.3m^6 Nov 3] lengthy, unfurnished filly: fifth foal: half-sister to 3 winners, all at least very useful, including Racing Post Trophy and King George winner King's Theatre (by Sadler's Wells) and high-class 1988 2-y-o High Estate (by Shirley Heights): dam ran twice: promising sixth of 15 in maiden at Sandown in July, but well-beaten sixth of 7 in minor event at Doncaster over 3 months later: sold 100,000 gns Newmarket December Sales. *H. R. A. Cecil* 57

REGAL PURSUIT (IRE) 4 b.f. Roi Danzig (USA) – Pursue 78 (Auction Ring (USA) 123) [1994 61: 10m^3 12g 14m 11.5g 13.1g^3 14d 1995 a10g^2 a13g^3 a12g^6 a12g^2 a12g^5 a16g^4 17.2m 13.1f 12.5g^4 Jun 17] lengthy filly: unimpressive mover: modest maiden at best: well below form (on turf) last 3 starts: stays 13.1f: acts on good to firm ground and equitrack: tried visored, blinkered and in hood: normally held up: races with head in air: sold 4,500 gns Ascot July Sales. *C. A. Horgan* 57 d

REGAL RAMBLER (CAN) 4 ch.g. Regal Classic (CAN) – Rushing Rachel (USA) (Breezing On (USA)) [1994 54d: a8.5g^2 a8.5g^4 a9.4g^3 a8s^6 10.3m a9.4g a9.4g a7g 1995 a16.2g a8g^6 a12g^6 Feb 18] good-bodied gelding: disappointing maiden: stays 8.5f: acts on fibresand (has shown little ability on turf): blinkered last 2 starts. *L. J. Barratt* –

REGGAE BEAT 10 b.g. Be My Native (USA) 122 – Invery Lady 65 (Sharpen Up 127) [1994 NR 1995 a16.2g^4 Jan 18] leggy, lightly-made gelding: winning hurdler/chaser: close fourth in handicap at Wolverhampton, first run on flat since 1993: stays 2m: acts on fibresand. *I. Campbell* 49

REGIMENT (IRE) 2 gr.c. (May 18) Shaadi (USA) 126 – Rossaldene 79 (Mummy's Pet 125) [1995 6g* 7.1m^2 Jul 7] IR 12,000Y: quite attractive colt: has a fluent action: half-brother to several winners, including 7f (at 2 yrs) to 8.3f winner Green's Ferneley (by Taufan) and fairly useful 1985 2-y-o 5f winner Lammastide (by Martinmas): dam 2-y-o 5f winner: won maiden auction at Windsor in June by 1½ lengths from Essentialselection: beaten 1¼ lengths by Honest Guest, having looked to be going marginally better over 1f out, in minor event at Sandown following month: will probably prove better back over shorter than 7f. *R. Hannon* 87

REIGNING ROYAL 4 ch.f. Tina's Pet 121 – Regency Brighton (Royal Palace 131) [1994 NR 1995 a8g 12.1m Jul 20] lengthy, leggy filly: seems of no account. *D. Burchell* –

REIMEI 6 b.g. Top Ville 129 – Brilliant Reay 74 (Ribero 126) [1994 67: 12v^3 10d 11.9m 11.8g* 11.4g^2 11.4m* 1995 12s^3 12m Nov 4] tall, angular gelding: fair handicapper: ran well at Ascot (first run for 15 months) but never able to challenge in November Handicap at Doncaster: effective at 11.4f, will be suited by 1¾m+: acts on good to firm ground and soft. *R. Akehurst* 71

REINALDO (FR) 3 b.c. Green Desert (USA) 127 – Ghariba 112 (Final Straw 127) [1994 NR 1995 6d* 7m* 5f^2 5d^2 5s^4 5m^3 5g^2 7g^4 5m* 6d* 5d^3 6g^4 6d^5 Dec 10] second foal: half-brother to 1992 2-y-o 7f winner Hawayah (by Shareef Dancer): dam, Nell Gwyn winner, half-sister to smart middle-distance stayer Braashee, a good family: progressed into useful Italian colt, winning maiden and 3 minor events at Milan: 1¾ lengths third of 9 to Leap For Joy in Group 3 event there in October: has won at 7f, best as a sprinter: acts on firm ground and dead. *G. Botti, Italy* 108

REINHARDT (IRE) 2 b.g. (Jan 24) Bluebird (USA) 125 – Rhein Bridge 107 (Rheingold 137) [1995 7f^3 7m^2 6m 7g^2 10.2m^3 Sep 25] IR 23,000Y: strong, lengthy gelding: has scope: good mover: half-brother to Gold Cup and Irish St Leger runner-up Tyrone Bridge (by Kings Lake), 1992 Irish 2-y-o 6f winner Just Speculation (by Ahonoora) and a bumpers winner: dam won Lancashire Oaks: useful form (could be rated 92) when caught on post by Silver Prey in 22-runner maiden at Newbury in August on second start: failed to repeat that form, again off bridle throughout (had shaped as though he'd improve for test of stamina) and hung left at Bath final one: subsequently gelded: may do better in blinkers. *P. W. Chapple-Hyam* 84 +

REITERATE 2 b.f. (Mar 11) Then Again 126 – Indubitable 87 (Sharpo 132) [1995 7d^5 Sep 15] smallish, workmanlike filly: first foal: dam stayed 1¾m: 33/1 and – p in need of race, 10 lengths fifth of 10 to Wild Rumour in minor event at Newbury, never a factor from halfway: showed a poor action: should improve. *G. B. Balding*

REJECTS REPLY 5 b.g. Balliol 125 – Fair Dino 48 (Thatch (USA) 136) [1994 NR 1995 a12g 12.3d² 13g a16g⁶ 12g a13g a14.8g⁶ Aug 11] leggy, plain gelding: poor maiden plater: probably stays 2m: acts on dead ground, probably on equitrack: blinkered (no form) penultimate 5-y-o start: hung badly left for lady amateur: inconsistent: sold (W. Musson to M. Lloyd) 1,850 gns Ascot September Sales. *W. J. Musson* 37 a32

RELATIVELY CLEVER (USA) 2 gr.c. (Apr 23) Clever Trick (USA) – Cousin Jen (USA) (Age Quod Agis (USA) 116) [1995 6m⁴ 5f⁴ 6m Jul 20] $35,000Y: compact colt: third foal: half-brother to a winner in USA by Marfa: dam minor stakes winner in USA: fourth of 8 to Shontaine in maiden at Doncaster: very weak in market and never dangerous in similar events subsequent starts: sold 7,800 gns Newmarket Autumn Sales. *Mrs J. R. Ramsden* 62

RELENTLESS (IRE) 3 b.c. Fayruz 116 – Scotch Rocket 60 (Roan Rocket 128) [1994 53: 6.1s⁶ 5s 1995 6d 7g Oct 9] workmanlike colt: modest maiden on balance of form, flattered by seventh of 19 in claimer at Leicester (burly) on 3-y-o reappearance: stays 6f. *B. A. McMahon* 53

RELENTLESS PURSUIT (IRE) 7 b.g. Thatching 131 – Daring Way (USA) 78 (Alydar (USA)) [1994 61: 5f⁵ 5m⁶ 6g 6g⁶ 1995 5m Aug 30] quite attractive gelding: carries condition: modest handicapper: well beaten only start in 1995: effective at 5f to 7f: seems to need a sound surface: blinkered (well beaten) once earlier in career. *P. W. Chapple-Hyam* –

RELIABLE EDIE 2 ch.f. (Mar 25) Hadeer 118 – Ever Welcome 58 (Be My Guest (USA) 126) [1995 5m⁶ May 23] 2,700F: leggy, sparely-made filly: third living foal: half-sister to 1m winner Exotic Forest (by Dominion): dam 4-y-o 1¼m winner: 33/1 and moved poorly to post, slowly away and soon well behind in 7-runner maiden at Goodwood. *J. Ffitch-Heyes* –

REMAADI SUN 3 gr.g. Cadeaux Genereux 131 – Catch The Sun (Kalaglow 132) [1994 NR 1995 10m 10g 10m⁴ 9m a8g a8g³ a9.4g Dec 9] 105,000Y: lengthy colt: carries condition: has a round action: third foal: half-brother to smart stayer Tioman Island (by Midyan) and a 9f winner in Italy by Lead On Time: dam unraced: no worthwhile form: sold out of J. Gosden's stable 3,400 gns Newmarket Autumn Sales after fourth outing. *M. D. I. Usher* –

REMEMBER THIS (IRE) 5 b.g. Don't Forget Me 127 – Regal Twin (USA) 77 (Majestic Prince (USA)) [1994 –: 8m a12g a7g 1995 a8g⁶ a13g⁵ a12g⁶ a16g a12g⁵ 11.9m⁵ 9m 11.5m 11.9f⁴ a14.8g Aug 11] heavy-topped gelding: no worthwhile form. *C. A. Cyzer* –

REMONTANT (IRE) 3 ch.f. Al Hareb (USA) 123 – Red Red Rose (USA) 90 (Blushing Groom (FR) 131) [1994 47?: 5v⁴ 5d 5g 8.2s 7g 1995 a7g³ 14.1m⁵ a14.8g a12g⁵ 14.1f 12g² 12m³ 12m³ 14.1h⁴ 11d³ 14.1m⁶ a12g Oct 28] close-coupled filly: unimpressive mover: poor maiden plater: stays 1¼m: acts on good to firm and dead ground and on fibresand: has looked unenthusiastic. *R. Hollinshead* 40

RENNYHOLME 4 ch.g. Rich Charlie 117 – Jacqui Joy 63 (Music Boy 124) [1994 –: a6g a5g 5g 5g 5f 5m 1995 5m 7g 10g a6g a5g⁶ Dec 6] leggy, close-coupled gelding: of little account: sold out of M. Ellerby's stable 820 gns Doncaster August Sales after third start. *J. Hetherton* –

RENOWN 3 b.g. Soviet Star (USA) 128 – Starlet 119 (Teenoso (USA) 135) [1994 56p: 7s⁶ 8.2d 1995 a8g⁴ a7g* a8.5g² a8g⁵ a10g* Dec 19] small, angular gelding: second foal: half-brother to 1¼m winner Success Story (by Sharrood): dam best at middle distances as 4-y-o: fair performer: won maiden at Lingfield in February and handicap there in December: stays 1¼m: acts on the all-weather: races prominently. *Lord Huntingdon* 72

REPATRIATE (AUS) 2 ch.f. (Jan 11) Rory's Jester (AUS) – Turkish Trousers (Kings Lake (USA) 133) [1995 5.2g³ 5.2m⁵ 5d² 5s* 6m 5m Nov 3] workmanlike filly: third foal: half-sister to a winner in Australasia by Sackford: dam (never ran) out of half-sister to Irish 1000 Guineas winner Arctique Royale and very smart middle-distance filly Racquette, the family of Ardross: fair form: comfortable winner of maiden at Haydock in September: not discredited in nurseries after: will prove best 75 +

at sprint distances: best form on soft ground: ran poorly in blinkers in listed race second outing: sold 6,000 gns Newmarket December Sales. *P. W. Chapple-Hyam*

REPERTORY 2 b.c. (May 4) Anshan 119 – Susie's Baby (Balidar 133) [1995 5m² 5.1m² 5g* May 18] 19,000Y: well-grown colt: half-brother to 6f winner Brockton Dancer (by Fairy King) and 3 other sprint winners: dam lightly raced: heavily backed when runner-up to Whicksey Perry in minor event at Lingfield and Night Parade in maiden at Chester first 2 starts: never off bridle to win maiden at Salisbury on final outing: will probably stay 6f: said by trainer to have had a muscle problem after final start: looked sure to do better. *M. R. Channon* 84

REPLOY 2 gr.f. (Apr 24) Deploy 131 – Nelly Do Da 78 (Derring-Do 131) [1995 7.1s⁴ a8g⁶ Nov 8] half-sister to 3-y-o Mamlouk (by Distant Relative) and several winners, including stayers Retouch (by Touching Wood) and Jonsalan (by Robellino): dam 2-y-o 5.8f winner, half-sister to Further Flight: 14/1, about 4 lengths fourth of 19 to Ski For Gold in maiden at Chepstow, easily best of those held up: showed little in similar event at Lingfield: will be suited by thorough test of stamina. *Lord Huntingdon* 66

REPONIST 3 b.f. Reprimand 122 – Dragonist 82 (Dragonara Palace (USA) 115) [1994 54: 6m 6d 6g⁴ 7s⁴ a6g a6g⁴ a8.5g³ a7g 1995 a7g⁶ a8g⁶ Jan 30] close-coupled filly: modest maiden: well below form in 1995: sold 2,000 gns Doncaster February Sales: best efforts at 6f: acts on soft ground and fibresand: usually blinkered or visored. *M. J. Camacho* –

REPORTED (IRE) 6 ch.h. Heraldiste (USA) 121 – Peach Melba 96 (So Blessed 130) [1994 76: a9.4g⁶ 10v a7g⁴ 7g 8d⁵ 1995 a9.4g* 8g³ a9.4g* 10.8g³ 12.3m⁴ a12g⁶ Jul 3] good-topped, workmanlike horse: has a round action: fair performer nowadays: won claimer in May then seller in June, both at Wolverhampton: not so good on turf: stays 10.8f: acts on any going, including fibresand. *B. Preece* 59 a70

REPREHEND 4 br.g. Reprimand 122 – Lake Ormond (Kings Lake (USA) 133) [1994 100: 6g⁴ 7f* 8f 7g² 8.1g² 1995 7.6g⁴ 7m 9f³ 8.3m* 8f 7m² Oct 20] leggy, close-coupled gelding: only fair form in 1995: contested claimers last 4 starts, winning at Windsor in July: probably stays 9f: acts on firm ground, yet to race on a soft surface: sold only 600 gns Newmarket Autumn Sales: sent to Italy. *R. Hannon* 78

REQUESTED 8 b.g. Rainbow Quest (USA) 134 – Melody Hour 105 (Sing Sing 134) [1994 –§: 14g 12v 16.5v 1995 11.8d 16m 14.1m³ 14m* 14s² 14g² 16.4m⁵ 14d 16.2s 16m 14.1m⁶ 16.4m Nov 6] leggy, sparely-made gelding: poor mover: modest handicapper: won at Newmarket in May: well below form last 5 starts: stays 2½m: acts on any going: rarely blinkered, had been successful in them earlier in career: one to treat with caution. *P. Burgoyne* 60 d

RESOLUTE BAY 9 b.g. Crofthall 110 – Spinner 59 (Blue Cashmere 129) [1994 53§: 8.1g⁴ 7m³ 7m* 8g³ 7s 7f 8f⁶ 7.5m³ 7.6g 8m 8g 8f 1995 8m 8g³ 8f 7.6m³ 8m* 8.1f⁶ 8m 9.2f³ 8m⁶ 8g 10g 8.2m Oct 19] lengthy gelding: has a rather round action: poor handicapper at best nowadays: won apprentice event at Thirsk in July: stays 9.2f: probably acts on any going: effective visored/blinkered or not: has been bandaged near-hind: lazy and unreliable. *R. M. Whitaker* 45 §

RESOUNDER (USA) 2 b.c. (Apr 13) Explodent (USA) – Rub Al Khali (USA) (Mr Prospector (USA)) [1995 6g 6m* 6f² 6d⁴ 6g⁵ 6g* 6m² Oct 21] $125,000Y: useful-looking colt: good mover: fourth foal: half-brother to minor winners in USA by Cozzene and Local Talent: dam unraced daughter of half-sister to multiple Grade 1 winner Versailles Treaty: useful colt: won maiden at Newbury in June and listed race at York (by 2 lengths from Warning Time) in October: good efforts in Mill Reef Stakes at Newbury, Middle Park Stakes at Newmarket and listed race (final start, ¾ length second to Thrilling Day) at Doncaster: bred to stay beyond 6f: held up for turn of foot last 2 starts: genuine. *J. H. M. Gosden* 102

RESPECTABLE JONES 9 ch.g. Tina's Pet 121 – Jonesee 64 (Dublin Taxi) [1994 –, a66: a7g a6g* a8g* a6g⁶ a7g a8g³ a8g⁴ a7g³ a7g⁵ a10g a10g 8d 7g 7m 6.9v 7m⁵ a7g⁴ a8g⁵ 1995 a7g² a6g a6g⁴ a7g³ a8g 8.2g⁶ 6m 7m⁵ 8m⁵ 7g 5.9f* 7g a7g⁴ a7g Dec 12] leggy, lengthy gelding: modest performer nowadays, generally on the downgrade: won seller at Carlisle in June: effective at 6f to 1m: used to act on any turf going: effective visored/blinkered or not: usually held up. *R. Hollinshead* 42 a52

RESPECT A SECRET 3 ch.f. Respect 95 – Pendle's Secret 73 (Le Johnstan 123) [1994 NR 1995 7.1m 5m⁴ 8f⁴ 6g 6g Sep 25] half-sister to fair 6-y-o 6f to 8.9f –

winner Pride of Pendle (by Grey Desire) and 1986 2-y-o 8.2f winner Rivers Secret (by Young Man): dam 1¼m winner: no worthwhile form. *S. E. Kettlewell*

RESTIV STAR (FR) 3 b.f. Soviet Star (USA) 128 – Restiver (FR) 116 (River River (FR) 117) [1994 NR 1995 10v* 10s² 10d³ 10d³ 10.5d² Nov 17] second foal: closely related to French 1m winner Risantaya (by Nureyev): dam, Group 3 1m winner at 2 yrs who stayed 10.5f, is half-sister to Prix de Diane winner Resless Kara: useful French filly: won minor event at Saint-Cloud in May: placed on all starts afterwards, best effort when length second of 13 to Marie de Ken in Prix Fille de l'Air at Evry: stays 10.5f: has raced only on a soft surface. *A. Fabre, France* 108

RESTRAINT 5 b.m. Bustino 136 – Queens Message 93 (Town Crier 119) [1994 NR 1995 12.3f 6.9f Jun 29] workmanlike mare: of little account. *J. J. Birkett* –

RESTRUCTURE (IRE) 3 b.c. Danehill (USA) 126 – Twine (Thatching 131) [1994 NR 1995 8.3m 8g² 8m* 8m 8m* 10.4m³ 9m* Oct 13] deep-bodied, attractive colt: impresses in appearance: half-brother to several winners, including very smart 6-y-o Alderbrook (by Ardross) and very useful 6f (at 2 yrs) and 1¼m winner Native Twine (by Be My Native): dam unraced: made into a smart performer, winning maiden at Kempton in May, rated stakes at Newmarket (by short head from Bin Rosie) in July and 8-runner listed race at Newmarket in October: moved poorly to post but showed plenty of improvement when beating Lap of Luxury a short head final start, leading over 1f out and battling on well: stays 10.4f: has raced almost exclusively on good to firm going: game: a most progressive colt, and probably capable of better still. *Mrs J. Cecil* 112 p

RETENDER (USA) 6 br.g. Storm Bird (CAN) 134 – Dandy Bury (FR) (Exbury 138) [1994 70: 10.1g² 12.4g* 14d⁶ 13.9f³ 11.1f² 12d 12m⁴ 12.4f* 13.3m³ 11.9m³ 16.1m⁵ 12m⁴ 1995 9.9m³ 12m 12m a12g³ a10g⁵ Dec 15] useful-looking gelding: fair handicapper: sold out of Mrs J. Ramsden's stable only 2,000 gns Newmarket July Sales after second start: clear signs of retaining ability afterwards: finds 1¼m a minimum and stays 16.1f: needs a sound surface (acts well on firm ground): has a turn of foot and is usually held up. *J. Pearce* 68 a60

RET FREM (IRE) 2 b.g. (Mar 26) Posen (USA) – New Light 78 (Reform 132) [1995 7m 7f 6m Oct 27] IR 26,000F, IR 32,000Y: well-made gelding: half-brother to 54 p

Baring International Darley Stakes, Newmarket—Alderbrook's half-brother Restructure (right) grabs his own slice of glory with a short-head victory over Lap of Luxury

several winners here and abroad, including high-class miler Then Again (by Jaazeiro): dam, from family of Sun Princess and Saddlers' Hall, won at 1¼m: modest form in maiden events: looks a good sort, and may well be capable of better. *M. A. Jarvis*

RETURN TO BRIGHTON 3 b.f. Then Again 126 – Regency Brighton (Royal Palace 131) [1994 NR 1995 8m 8m 8.1g May 29] rather leggy filly: fifth reported foal: half-sister to 7f seller winner Royal Resort (by King of Spain): dam showed little on flat: tailed off in maidens. *P. C. Clarke* –

REVERAND THICKNESS 4 b.g. Prince Sabo 123 – Wollow Maid 73 (Wollow 132) [1994 67: 5.1v 7m^2 5m^2 7m^2 6m^2 7g^3 7m 1995 a6g^3 7.1d* a7g* 7g^3 7g^4 6m 8m^3 7.9g^6 9g^4 10d 9g 8m^5 Oct 12] lengthy, angular gelding: fair handicapper: won at Edinburgh (maiden event) in March and Wolverhampton in April: stays 9f: acts on good to firm and dead ground and on fibresand: blinkered (no improvement) last 2 starts: sometimes wanders under pressure, and suited by strong handling: consistent. *S. C. Williams* 78

REVERE (IRE) 5 b.h. Dancing Brave (USA) 140 – Bint Pasha (USA) 126 (Affirmed (USA)) [1994 108: 10v^6 10d^3 13.4m^5 11.5v^2 10m* 10f* 10g* 11.5s* 11d^4 1995 10f* 10g^3 10.5f^6 10d* 12d Oct 21] deep-bodied horse: carries condition: powerful galloper: smart performer: made all in listed races at Kempton in June and Goodwood (beat Nash Terrace 1½ lengths easing down) in September: tried in pattern races on his other 3 starts at 5 yrs, running creditably only when 3½ lengths third of 7 to Baron Ferdinand in Scottish Classic at Ayr: favourite, ran as if something amiss in St Simon Stakes at Newbury: effective at 1¼m and stays 11.5f: acts on any going: sometimes wears tongue strap: often a front runner: reluctant to enter stalls (ran poorly) third 5-y-o start: usually bandaged: game. *P. F. I. Cole* 112

REVEUSE DE JOUR (IRE) 2 b.f. (Mar 22) Sadler's Wells (USA) 132 – Magic of Life (USA) 118 (Seattle Slew (USA)) [1995 7g Sep 28] smallish, attractive filly: good mover: fourth foal: half-sister to 3-y-o 1¼m winner Mountains of Mist (by Shirley Heights), and useful French middle-distance performer From Beyond and 10.7f winner Circle of Chalk (both by Kris): dam 5f to 1m winner from excellent family: 16/1, never dangerous and not knocked about towards rear in 23-runner maiden at Newmarket won by Astor Place: will do better. *R. Charlton* – p

RHUMBA DANCER 2 b.f. (Feb 27) Aragon 118 – Battle of Flowers 63 (Shernazar 131) [1995 5d 5m 5.7f* 6m^2 6m^4 7.3d^3 7s^3 8m^3 Oct 13] 8,200Y: rangy filly: has scope: second foal: dam stayed 1¼m: fairly useful form: won maiden auction at Bath in July: ran well afterwards, particularly in nursery at Newmarket on final outing: better suited by 7f/1m than 6f: acts on firm and soft ground: sent to Trinidad. *R. Hannon* 86

RHYTHMIC BALL 2 ch.f. (Feb 5) Classic Music (USA) – Chrisanthy 81 (So Blessed 130) [1995 a6g^6 6g^5 6g Sep 24] 8,800Y: closely related to 7f (at 2 yrs) to 1¼m winner Satis Dancer (by Mashhor Dancer) and half-sister to 2 winners, including 7f (at 2 yrs) to 1¼m winner Ivan The Terrible (by Siberian Express): dam 2-y-o 5f winner failed to train on: only form in maidens when fifth of 10 to The Man at Catterick in September: likely to stay beyond 6f. *T. R. Watson* 56

RHYTHMIC DANCER 7 b.g. Music Boy 124 – Stepping Gaily 79 (Gay Fandango (USA) 132) [1994 –, a78: a5g^3 a5g^5 a5g^5 1995 5g 5g^3 5.1m^5 5m 5m^2 5.7h^4 5f* a5g* 5g* Sep 29] leggy, close-coupled gelding: fair performer: successful in big fields in claimers at Warwick in August and Southwell (claimed out of J. Spearing's stable £3,000) in September then in handicap at Goodwood 25 days later: suited by sprint distances: acts on firm and dead going and goes well on the all-weather: headstrong: has run well when sweating: often rears in stalls. *A. Streeter* 73

RIBOT'S SECRET (IRE) 2 b.f. (Mar 9) Danehill (USA) 126 – Glim (USA) (Damascus (USA)) [1995 5g* 6m^3 6g^2 6m 6.3m^4 7d^4 Oct 7] IR 8,500Y: workmanlike filly: fluent mover: fourth reported foal: half-sister to 7f winner Owner's Dream (by Northern Baby): dam unraced half-sister to Glow: fairly useful Irish performer: dead-heated in maiden at Tipperary in May: placed behind Flame of Athens in Railway Stakes at the Curragh and Blue Duster in Princess Margaret Stakes at Ascot in July: back to best when 1¾ lengths fourth of 7 to Last Second in CL Weld Park Stakes at the Curragh final outing: stays 7f: yet to race on extremes of going: visored/blinkered (ran creditably) third and fourth starts: sent to USA. *A. P. O'Brien, Ireland* 92

RICANA 3 ch.f. Rich Charlie 117 – Woolcana 71 (Some Hand 119) [1994 50: 5g^{5} 5d 6f^{5} 6f a7g^{4} 5m^{4} a5g 5m^{5} 5m 7.1m^{4} 6s 7.1g^{2} 1995 11.1d^{4} 8.1g^{3} 8.3s^{2} 8.3g 8.1g 6g^{4} 8.1m 7.1m^{3} 8.1m^{3} 7.1m 7.1f^{3} 8.3f^{4} 12.1s Nov 2] sparely-made filly: poor maiden: stays 8.3f: acts on firm ground: blinkered (finished last) tenth 3-y-o start: sometimes gives trouble in stalls: often sweats. *W. T. Kemp* 40

RICHARD HOUSE LAD 2 b.c. (Feb 7) Warrshan (USA) 117 – Sirenivo (USA) 113 (Sir Ivor 135) [1995 5.1g 5m 7g^{6} a7g^{6} 8.2m^{6} a8.5g a7g a8g Nov 14] 4,600F, IR 6,600Y: smallish, quite attractive colt: closely related to fairly useful 1985 2-y-o 7f winner Sunley Sinner (by Try My Best) and half-brother to several winners, including 14.7f winner Sirundy (by Grundy): dam very useful at around 1¼m: modest maiden: trained first 4 starts by C. Smith: will be suited by 1¼m+: acts on good to firm ground, poor form all starts on all-weather. *R. Hollinshead* 59 a48

RICHARD OF YORK 5 b.h. Rainbow Quest (USA) 134 – Triple First 117 (High Top 131) [1994 123: 12g* 10s^{5} 12d* 12g 1995 10.5v^{3} 12.5g^{3} 10g^{4} 12d^{2} 11d^{4} 10m Nov 12] smallish, ex-French horse: has reportedly suffered from foot problems throughout his career: rather disappointing in 1995, showing only smart form: 4½ lengths third of 10 to Pelder in Prix Ganay at Longchamp (best 5-y-o effort, final start for A. Fabre) on reappearance: off course 3½ months afterwards: blinkered last 3 starts, finishing in frame in Cumberland Lodge Stakes at Ascot (no match for Riyadian, clear of remainder) and Blandford Stakes at the Curragh (evens, quickly beaten 2f out) but well beaten in Premio Roma: better at 1½m than shorter and should stay further: acts on heavy going, possibly not on top-of-the-ground. *J. H. M. Gosden* 117

RICHELIEU (IRE) 3 ch.c. Kris 135 – Madame Dubois 121 (Legend of France (USA) 124) [1994 NR 1995 10.2m^{2} 11.9d* Oct 11] angular colt: first foal: dam won Park Hill: off course over 3 months after being short-headed on debut: 6/1, won 19-runner maiden at Haydock in October by neck from Taklif, waited with going well, leading 1f out and finding extra when challenged close home: will stay beyond 11.9f: open to further improvement: sold (H. Cecil to P. Webber) 25,000 gns Newmarket Autumn Sales. *H. R. A. Cecil* 88 p

RICH GLOW 4 b.g. Rich Charlie 117 – Mayglow (Sparkling Boy 110) [1994 43: 5g 6m a5g 6m 5g^{2} 5m^{2} 5m^{4} 5g^{6} 5m 5s^{4} 1995 5d 5m 5.9m^{2} 5m* 5g^{3} 5g* 6m 5f* 5m^{5} 6m 5m^{2} 5g^{2} 5m^{4} 5f^{5} 6m 6m^{2} 6g 6g 5d 5m Oct 4] leggy, angular gelding: fair handicapper: without a win before successful 3 times at Ayr in May/June: held his form for most of season: effective at 5f and 6f: acts on firm and soft ground: effective blinkered or not, not tried since 4-y-o reappearance: has worn tongue strap: usually held up. *N. Bycroft* 70

RICOCHET (IRE) 2 b.g. (Apr 28) West China 107 – Waajib's Song (IRE) (Waajib 121) [1995 a7g a7g a7g Nov 6] IR 2,100Y: first foal: dam unraced: no sign of ability in all-weather maiden auction and sellers: visored then blinkered last 2 starts. *S. G. Norton* –

RIDGEWOOD BEN 4 b.c. Indian Ridge 123 – Ben's Pearl (Tap On Wood 130) [1994 113: 7v* 7v^{2} 8v^{3} 5g^{2} 6v^{5} 7g^{4} 1995 7d^{2} 8.1m^{2} 8m^{5} 7f^{4} Oct 1] rangy, good sort: smart Irish performer: good second in Gladness Stakes (length behind Bin Ajwaad) at the Curragh and Sandown Mile (short of room before running on well, 1¾ lengths behind Missed Flight) in April: respectable efforts when fifth of 7 in Sea World International at the Curragh in July and fourth of 7 in Group 3 event at Tipperary in October: effective at 5f, and a testing 1m stretched his stamina: acted on good to firm ground and heavy: blinkered second and fourth 4-y-o starts: normally held up: retired to Irish National Stud, fee IR £2,500 (Oct 1). *J. Oxx, Ireland* 113

RIDGEWOOD PEARL 3 ch.f. Indian Ridge 123 – Ben's Pearl (Tap On Wood 130) [1994 105p: 6d^{3} 7v* 1995 7d* 8g* 8m* 8m* 8d^{2} 8s* Oct 28] 125

If religion had felt the need for further advertisement in these increasingly secular days, the services of Sean and Anne Coughlan and their superb filly Ridgewood Pearl were heaven-sent. The Irish three-year-old was the best of her sex in Europe and had all the spoils to prove it, winning five of her six starts in 1995 (taking her overall total to six from eight) including Group or Grade 1 events in four different countries. Her exuberant owners were naturally unstinting in their praise of her—and they also found cause to thank the power of prayer, Lourdes water, the Papal colours of yellow and white, visits to cathedrals and the St Christopher sewn into their jockey's skullcap. The nearest thing that racing has come to omnipotence,

Airlie/Coolmore Irish One Thousand Guineas, the Curragh—
on home soil, Ridgewood Pearl powers clear of Warning Shadows (second right),
Khaytada (second left) and eventual fifth-placed Harayir

the Godolphin team, earnt a case of champagne from them when their security personnel heard Ridgewood Pearl cast in her box late at night on the eve of the Breeders' Cup and got her to her feet again before she sustained an injury. This scare might well have not come to light, of course, had Ridgewood Pearl made the line-up for the Breeders' Cup Mile only to be yet another European also-ran. As it was, the Coughlans could afford champagne in abundance when Ridgewood Pearl took the prize back to Ireland. Drawn on the inside, she took a strong hold and was tracking the leaders Fourstars Allstar and Poplar Bluff after a couple of furlongs, the American five-year-old Fastness upsides her. A furlong out Fastness was still upsides her but nothing else was within hailing distance and Ridgewood Pearl was always going to win; she drew clear in the last hundred yards, having two lengths to spare over Fastness at the line and another seven over third-placed Sayyedati. Ridgewood Pearl's drinking supply pre-race, incidentally, was where her owner's slipping in of the Lourdes water played its part.

The Breeders' Cup Mile field was, of course, a strong one, and here is exactly who Ridgewood Pearl beat: from Europe there were the winners of the 1995 Prix de

Coronation Stakes, Royal Ascot—
in Britain, Ridgewood Pearl is impressive again, comfortably seeing off Smolensk (right) and Harayir

Emirats Prix du Moulin de Longchamp—Shaanxi and six others are beaten in France

la Foret (Poplar Bluff), Lockinge Stakes (Soviet Line), Haydock Park Sprint Cup (Cherokee Rose), Prix du Rond-Point (Shaanxi) and Sussex Stakes (Sayyedati); and from the United States, going into the race, there were two 1995 Grade 1 winners (Fastness and Earl of Barking), three Grade 2 winners (The Vid, Fourstars Allstar and Savinio) and two Grade 3 winners (Dove Hunt and Mighty Forum). One who did not take Ridgewood Pearl on was the top British-trained three-year-old filly at a mile, Harayir, who picked up an injury in training the day before. The two had met before, however, and, on one occasion, also failed to meet. The failure came in the One Thousand Guineas at Newmarket back in May, Harayir's finest hour, for which Ridgewood Pearl was declared at the five-day stage but did not travel after the ground turned good to firm; it had been reported shortly before that she had an ankle problem and would be kept away from anything firmer than good. She was not greatly missed if the 25/1 available with British bookmakers was anything to go by, but when she lined up against Harayir in the Airlie/Coolmore Irish One Thousand Guineas on good ground at the Curragh three weeks later Ridgewood Pearl was a 9/4-shot, second favourite. This more positive assessment was much more in keeping with Ridgewood Pearl's record. Odds on for a listed event on her debut the previous September, she failed to get a clear run and was beaten, but in her two other races Ridgewood Pearl made no mistake—the Group 3 C.L. Weld Park Stakes at the Curragh fifteen days later fell to her by four and a half lengths, the listed Athasi Stakes at the same course on her reappearance by seven. On form, as well as potential, she was the pick of the six-strong Irish team for their Guineas, the only one who looked of remotely comparable merit being her stable-companion Khaytada. In the race, Ridgewood Pearl proved a class apart from the foreign challenge as well. Four lengths was the winning margin after she had gone to the front two furlongs out, Khaytada just failing to hold off Clive Brittain's Warning Shadows for second, the French-trained Ghostly in fourth and Harayir's short-lived effort to stay with Ridgewood Pearl resulting in only fifth. The only remaining foreign runner, Mick Channon's Fleet Hill, was sixth.

Ireland's two other Irish One Thousand winners in the last decade were Trusted Partner in 1988 and Kooyonga in 1991, the former a failure after her classic win, the latter a conspicuous success. For her post-Guineas campaign, Ridgewood Pearl followed the Kooyonga route by going to the Coronation Stakes at Royal Ascot. Sean Coughlan had first come to Britain thirty-eight years earlier in less auspicious but now famous circumstances, 'with a packet of cigarettes in one pocket and nothing in the other', and had a spell as a London bus conductor. He has had rather more to declare at customs since then. Making his fortune in the building and civil engineering business, his first horse was a winner (and David Elsworth's first as a trainer, at Exeter in 1979) in Fortune Cookie, and Ridgewood Pearl was bidding to take his record at Royal Ascot to three runners, three winners, following the Jersey Stakes and King's Stand exploits of her sire Indian Ridge. Ridgewood Pearl extended the sequence in grand style. The change in ground conditions (Ridgewood Pearl's participation had been in some doubt) appeared to explain a spectacular disregard for the Curragh form in which Ridgewood Pearl started at 9/2 and Harayir at 15/8. The French fillies Macoumba and Smolensk were next in the betting at 6/1. Turning for home, Ridgewood Pearl was in close company with the pacesetting Mamlakah, Harayir and a hard-pulling Macoumba, but there was no doubt about the winner as soon as she went on approaching the two-furlong marker, and she had two lengths to spare at the line, Smolensk and Harayir emerging best among the chasers. The winning time broke Shadeed's track record. A word about Ridgewood Pearl's physical appearance in the Coronation: she made a very strong impression on our representative, both in terms of physique—strong, lengthy and most imposing—and with her condition, looking as well as any horse he'd seen previously in the season. Almost as striking is her powerful action, and it was this that apparently explained her next target, the Emirats Prix du Moulin de Longchamp as opposed to the Sussex Stakes on the gradients at Goodwood.

Clearly the best filly of her age in either Britain or Ireland, Ridgewood Pearl now took on her elders and the best of the French. She may have missed the Jacques le Marois, but among her seven opponents at Longchamp were the Marois first, second, third and fifth in Miss Satamixa, Sayyedati, Shaanxi and Green Tune. Smolensk was there again, and the field was completed by Missed Flight and Darnay. Against this sterner opposition, Ridgewood Pearl could not win with the same authority she had shown earlier in the season, but win she did. As usual racing close to the leader, she overhauled Smolensk in the final furlong then held on by three quarters of a length from Shaanxi with the same distance back to Missed Flight in third. One obvious target remained for Ridgewood Pearl before the Breeders' Cup, another visit to Ascot for the Queen Elizabeth II Stakes in which she started 13/8 on in a six-runner field. Her final start in Europe, this was her first and only defeat of the season, falling victim to the only obvious danger, Bahri, and to the tactics employed by Bahri's jockey, Willie Carson, who took his mount to race alone on the less testing ground under the trees. It was far less testing judged by the way in which Bahri stormed clear by six lengths, but Ridgewood Pearl was not at her best anyway; that

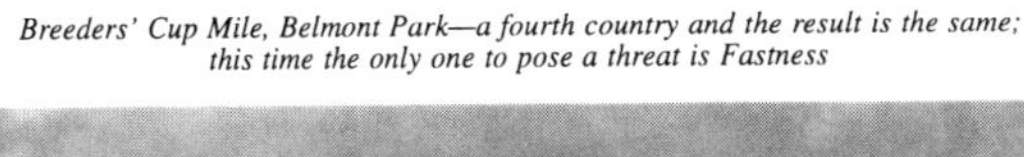

Breeders' Cup Mile, Belmont Park—a fourth country and the result is the same; this time the only one to pose a threat is Fastness

Mrs Anne Coughlan's "Ridgewood Pearl"

powerful action went to pieces after she had got to Bahri's quarters entering the straight. The Breeders' Cup, however, was still to come. The Queen Elizabeth was a rare reverse not only for Ridgewood Pearl but also for trainer John Oxx, and for jockey John Murtagh who rode Ridgewood Pearl throughout her career except when Christy Roche was on board for her debut and in the Irish Guineas. Both Oxx and Murtagh were clear-cut winners of their divisions in Ireland judged on races won, ninety-nine by Oxx and eighty-six by Murtagh, and Oxx was similarly well in front in the trainers' championship decided on prize money. Each was winning his title for the first time, Murtagh doing so after suffering serious weight problems since he was champion apprentice in 1989. Timarida, Shemaran and Russian Snows were others from the Oxx stable who had to be taken very seriously in pattern races.

Ridgewood Pearl (ch.f. 1992)	Indian Ridge (ch 1985)	Ahonoora (ch 1975)	Lorenzaccio
			Helen Nichols
		Hillbron (ch 1975)	Swing Easy
			Golden City
	Ben's Pearl (b 1985)	Tap On Wood (ch 1976)	Sallust
			Cat O'Mountaine
		Joshua's Daughter (b 1973)	Joshua
			Legal Love

Back to Ridgewood Pearl's owners. It is very hard to think that their enthusiasm did not play a major part in Ridgewood Pearl's beating Lammtarra to the Cartier Award as Horse Of The Year, a decision influenced as well, of course, by the timely nature of her Breeders' Cup win just before the voting. The Coughlans are also in the rare position of not just owning and breeding an outstanding racehorse, but of having raced both the parents as well. Indian Ridge was not quite so good as

Ridgewood Pearl despite registering those two victories at Royal Ascot. A hard puller, he did not stay a mile, his one attempt at the trip coming when he too disappointed in the Queen Elizabeth II Stakes. He began his stud duties in 1990 at the Campbell Stud near Bury St Edmunds, fee 5,000 guineas, and, although he was by no means unpopular, that sum had fallen to £3,000 for his third and fourth seasons. Switched to the Irish National Stud (who had stood his sire Ahonoora with such success) in 1994, the fee doubled and the number of mares covered increased by nearly two thirds to 108. In 1996, having also had such as Cheyenne Spirit, Definite Article, Fumo di Londra, Indian Fly, Island Magic, Maid For The Hills, Moving Arrow, Tumbleweed Ridge and Vindaloo to represent him, Indian Ridge will be standing at IR 20,000 guineas. A success story. Going into the latest season, the best form shown by any offspring of Indian Ridge was that of Ridgewood Pearl's year-older brother Ridgewood Ben. Winner and runner-up in the last two editions of the Gladness Stakes, he was also placed in the Irish Two Thousand Guineas, Flying Five and Sandown Mile, and will now be joining his sire at the Irish National Stud. Sadly, those are the only two foals out of the short-lived mare Ben's Pearl. Trained by Oxx, Ben's Pearl won a seven-furlong Curragh maiden as a two-year-old and the one-mile Irish Cambridgeshire at the same course as a three-year-old, and is a sister to the useful 1986 two-year-old On Tap. Their dam Joshua's Daughter passed through the sale ring for 880 guineas and 470 guineas before her racing career and could not have been worth much more after it—she was runner-up three times over middle distances, showing modest form—but she is out of a useful winner, the sprinter Legal Love who showed easily her best form as a two-year-old. The Coughlans reportedly ignored advice to have Joshua's Daughter put down before she ever produced Ben's Pearl. Their reward has been huge. Ridgewood Pearl was a high-class miler with an almost unblemished record. Often bandaged, she never raced on firm ground but acted on any other. She was thoroughly genuine. Her stud career is likely to begin with a visit to Rainbow Quest. *J. Oxx, Ireland*

RIFAPOUR (IRE) 3 b.c. Shahrastani (USA) 135 – Rifada 103 (Ela-Mana-Mou 132) [1994 NR 1995 10.5v* 10.5g* 12m* 12g 11g³ 10s³ 12s⁴ 12f Dec 10] smart French colt: second foal: dam, genuine 1½m winner, would have stayed 1¾m: progressed really well in the spring, winning newcomers race and minor event at Saint-Cloud, then 9-runner Prix Hocquart (did well, plenty to do entering straight and quickening well to beat Poliglote by a neck) at Longchamp: in frame in Furstenberg-Rennen at Baden-Baden (¾ length behind Solon), slowly-run Prix du Prince d'Orange at Longchamp (final start for A. de Royer Dupre, outpaced by Tamure and Spectrum) and Turf Classic Invitational at Belmont (8 lengths behind Turk Passer), but below form in Hollywood Turf Cup: will stay beyond 1½m: acts on good to firm and soft ground, won newcomers event on heavy: consistent: stays in training. *R. Rash, USA* — 114

RIFIFI 2 ch.c. (Feb 5) Aragon 118 – Bundled Up (USA) (Sharpen Up 127) [1995 7g⁵ 6.9g Oct 16] 10,000Y: small, sturdy colt: second foal: half-brother to 3-y-o Midnight Spell (by Night Shift): dam, won over 9.7f at 2 yrs in France, daughter of good 1973 2-y-o Bundler: fifth of 12 to Gold Disc in maiden at Leicester, staying on steadily after being slowly away and bumped at start: faded noticeably last 100 yds when eighth of 13 in maiden auction at Folkestone 6 days later: sold 3,800 gns Newmarket Autumn Sales. *J. L. Dunlop* — 66

RIGHTACRES LAD 4 ch.g. Librate 91 – Sue Clare 51 (Busted 134) [1994 –: 10.8m 10.1d 8.1g 1995 10.8f Aug 28] plain, lengthy gelding: of little account. *J. M. Bradley* — –

RIGHTEOUS GENT 2 b.g. (May 20) Superpower 113 – Golden 69 (Don 128) [1995 7.1m⁶ 6.1d 8m⁶ a7g a8g⁵ a7g⁴ Dec 14] rangy, unfurnished gelding: first foal: dam stayed 2m: appeared to show plenty of improvement when fourth of 12 in claimer at Lingfield final start: stays 7f: blinkered 3 of last 4 outings. *K. McAuliffe* — 43 a59 ?

RIGHT WIN (IRE) 5 br.h. Law Society (USA) 130 – Popular Win 103 (Lorenzaccio 130) [1994 119: 12s* 13.3m* 10s* 12f 12d⁴ 1995 12g⁴ 10.5v 12g 13.3m⁵ 12s³ 12d Oct 15] lengthy, workmanlike horse: smart performer: not quite so good as at 4 yrs: in frame only in John Porter Stakes at Newbury in April and when 8½ lengths third of 10 to Germany in Grosser Preis von Baden: needs testing conditions at 1¼m and will stay 1¾m: has form on good to firm ground (sustained — 112 leg injury on firm) but is very well suited by a soft surface: blinkered last 3 starts: usually held up: genuine: to go hurdling. *R. Hannon*

RINGMASTER (IRE) 4 b.g. Taufan (USA) 119 – Salustrina (Sallust 134) [1994 92: 6g 6s* 7f⁴ 6g 6g⁶ 8m³ 8.1g³ 10.5g² 10d* 10g* 9g 1995 10.4g 12d⁶ 10m⁶ 10.4m² 10f 10m³ 10d 12d Sep 24] lengthy gelding: fairly useful handicapper: not the most consistent, and clearly best efforts of 1995 when neck second of 16 to Naked Welcome in steadily-run Magnet Cup at York in July and joint-third in rated stakes at Newmarket in August: effective at 1¼m to 1½m: acts on any going: usually held up. *M. H. Tompkins* 92

RING OF VISION (IRE) 3 br.g. Scenic 128 – Circus Lady (High Top 131) [1994 52p: 9d 10s 7d 7d 1995 8g 10m* 10m⁵ Jun 12] sturdy gelding: good walker: modest form: easily best effort in 1995 when winning 15-runner handicap at Redcar in May, leading 1f out: will be well suited by further than 1¼m. *Mrs M. Reveley* 52

RING THE CHIEF 3 b.g. Chief Singer 131 – Lomond Ring (Lomond (USA) 128) [1994 47: 5.1m 6m 6m⁶ 1995 8f a6g² 6.1m a6g² a5g³ a6g a7g⁶ a6g Nov 30] leggy, workmanlike gelding: has a round action: modest maiden handicapper: well below form last 3 starts, sold out of R. Akehurst's stable 6,400 gns Newmarket September Sales after penultimate one: should stay beyond 6f: acts on fibresand, has raced only on top-of-the-ground (poor form) on turf. *M. D. I. Usher* 57

RINUS MAGIC 2 ch.c. (Jun 3) Timeless Times (USA) 99 – Callace 51 (Royal Palace 131) [1995 7.1s Oct 1] 1,200 2-y-o: lengthy colt: fourth foal: dam, maiden, stayed 1m: 33/1, green and backward, slowly away and tailed off in maiden at Haydock: showed a round action. *E. J. Alston* –

RINUS MANOR (IRE) 4 b.g. Ballad Rock 122 – Never Never Land (Habitat 134) [1994 50d: 7.1g a7g² 6g a7g⁴ a5g⁵ 5m⁴ 6g a8.5g 5.1g 1995 a6g 6g⁶ 7g⁵ 8g 6d⁶ Sep 18] sturdy gelding: only poor on balance of form: left D. McCain's stable after third 4-y-o outing: should stay 1m: acts on fibresand and dead ground: inconsistent. *E. J. Alston* 48 ?

RIO DUVIDA 2 ch.c. (Feb 25) Salse (USA) 128 – Fluctuate 87 (Sharpen Up 127) [1995 6g* 6f* 6g⁴ 7g² 7d* Sep 26] 107

Rio Duvida seems greatly flattered by fourth place in the International Classification for Two-Year-Olds. If the BHB ratings are to be believed, Rio Duvida showed a higher level of form in his first season than the Prix de la Salamandre winner Lord of Men, the Grand Criterium winner Loup Solitaire and the Racing Post Trophy winner Beauchamp King. In awarding Rio Duvida a mark just 7 lb below that given to the champion two-year-old Alhaarth, the handicappers have taken the view that Alhaarth achieved virtually no more in the Dewhurst than he had in the Champagne Stakes at Doncaster in September when he conceded 4 lb to Rio Duvida

Tattersalls Houghton Sales Conditions Stakes, Newmarket—
a £100,000 bonus goes to the connections of Rio Duvida as the favourite beats Mezzogiorno

and beat him readily by half a length; Rio Duvida is then considered to have reproduced his Champagne form in beating Mezzogiorno and Honest Guest by a length and two lengths in the Tattersalls Houghton Sales Conditions Stakes at Newmarket in October. Alhaarth is rightly given top billing in the International Classifications after his impressive defeat of Group 1 winners Danehill Dancer and Tagula in the Dewhurst, but that form is well in advance of what was needed to account for the hard-ridden Rio Duvida in a Champagne Stakes which was run at a crawl for the first five furlongs. Indeed, the official view asks us to believe a line of form through Alhaarth which suggests that Rio Duvida improved past Tagula who, two months earlier in the July Stakes at Newmarket, had had Rio Duvida back in fourth and in the interim had gone on to win the well-contested Prix Morny in convincing fashion. Rio Duvida has yet to score in pattern company. His most important success came in the Houghton Sales Stakes, a race restricted to graduates of the 1994 Houghton Yearling Sales, in which he started a short-priced favourite in the absence of any top opposition and won as comfortably as his form entitled him to. Rio Duvida's other victories came in June, in a maiden at Yarmouth and a minor event at Newbury. His fourth place in the July Stakes was a useful performance but was more remarkable for the fact that it was the first time in twenty-four races since the start of the season that a Loder-trained two-year-old had failed to reach the first three: the previous twenty-three had resulted in sixteen wins at an astonishing strike-rate of nearly 70%. It would have been asking the impossible of Loder to keep up that strike-rate, but at the end of the season the figures for the two-year-olds were still impressive: twenty-nine wins from sixty-six runs at a success rate of 44%.

The leggy Rio Duvida, a 36,000-guinea yearling, is a half-brother to three winners, including Prince Hannibal (by High Top) and Dodgy Dancer (by Shareef Dancer) over middle distances. His dam, Fluctuate, a winner over five furlongs as a two-year-old, is a half-sister to the dam of the smart middle-distance colt Midnight Legend out of the mile-and-a-quarter winner Hay Reef. The dam of several winners,

Lady Harrison's "Rio Duvida"

Rio Duvida (ch.c. Feb 25, 1993)	Salse (USA) (b 1985)	Topsider (b 1974)	Northern Dancer
			Drumtop
		Carnival Princess (ch 1974)	Prince John
			Carnival Queen
	Fluctuate (b 1981)	Sharpen Up (ch 1969)	Atan
			Rocchetta
		Hay Reef (b 1976)	Mill Reef
			Haymaking

Hay Reef is a daughter of the Coronation Stakes and Nassau Stakes winner Haymaking and is therefore closely related to the Irish Two Thousand Guineas winner Wassl. Rio Duvida acts on firm and dead ground, and will probably stay beyond a mile. Prince Hannibal and Fluctuate's other winner Suhail Dancer (by Shareef Dancer) both had quirks of temperament, but though Rio Duvida carried his head rather high in the July Stakes he seems game and genuine. *D. R. Loder*

RIPARIUS (USA) 4 b.g. Riverman (USA) 131 – Sweet Simone (FR) (Green Dancer (USA) 132) [1994 79: 11s^4 10.2g^4 12g^6 13.3g^3 12g^3 12m^3 10g 12m^3 11.5g* 1995 12m^5 12d* 12m 11.8g^5 12m^3 11.9g 16.2s Oct 6] rangy, workmanlike gelding: fairly useful handicapper: made all at Beverley in June: suited by 1½m, did not stay 16.2f: acts on soft going and good to firm: seems effective whether blinkered (usually is) or not: sometimes looks none too keen, hangs, and looks a difficult ride: has been gelded. *H. Candy*
81

RIPSNORTER (IRE) 6 ch.g. Rousillon (USA) 133 – Formulate 119 (Reform 132) [1994 59, a52: a8g a8g^3 a8.5g^5 10d 8d* 8m^2 8g^5 a8g^2 a9.4g 1995 10g 8g a8g^6 a8g a8g a10g Dec 15] big, strong gelding: carries plenty of condition: poor mover: below form in 1995, looking less than resolute second start, final one for J. Bennett: seems best at up to 1m: acts on good to firm ground, dead and all-weather surfaces. *K. Bishop*
–
a47

RISALAH 2 b.f. (Mar 4) Marju (IRE) 127 – Alsaaybah (USA) 73 (Diesis 133) [1995 6g^6 May 24] rather unfurnished filly: first foal: dam ran twice, winning at 7f at 2 yrs: 11/4, around 11 lengths sixth of 11 to Like A Hawk in maiden at Salisbury, eased off when held: moved poorly to post: sold 3,000 gns Newmarket December Sales. *J. L. Dunlop*
–

RISE UP SINGING 7 ch.g. Noalto 120 – Incarnadine 67 (Hot Spark 126) [1994 69: 7g 7m* 7g 7m 7m 7g^4 8f 7m 7d 7g 1995 7m^2 8g 6m^3 7g Aug 31] strong, lengthy gelding: unimpressive mover: only a modest handicapper at best nowadays: reportedly fractured pelvis final 6-y-o start: creditable efforts in 1994 when placed at Newmarket where he has gained 7 of his 8 victories: ideally suited by 7f to 1m: acts on any going, except apparently heavy: best in blinkers: often sweats: usually races up with pace: none too consistent. *W. J. Musson*
62

RISING DOUGH (IRE) 3 br.g. Dowsing (USA) 124 – Shortning Bread 83 (Blakeney 126) [1994 80: 7m 6.9m^6 7g^2 7m 7.3g^3 8g^2 7.6v^6 8g 1995 10m^2 8m^2 9m* 7.6m^5 8f* 8.5m^4 Aug 28] good-bodied, workmanlike gelding: fair performer: made all in 4-runner median auction maiden (7/4 on) at Lingfield and 2-runner minor event (beat below-form Veuve Hoornaert) at Brighton in the summer: stays 1¼m: acts on firm ground, seems unsuited by heavy: visored (below form) final 2-y-o outing: should prove suited by strong handling: forces pace. *G. L. Moore*
76

RISING RIVER 3 b.f. Warning 136 – Double River (USA) (Irish River (FR) 131) [1994 NR 1995 7m 7m^4 8m^5 Jun 16] rather leggy filly: third foal: half-sister to 4-y-o 7f and 9.2f winner Twin Creeks (by Alzao) and 5f and 6f winner So Intrepid (by Never So Bold): dam, French 6f and 7f winner, half-sister to Digression: no sign of ability. *S. Woodman*
–

RISING SPRAY 4 ch.g. Waajib 121 – Rose Bouquet 78 (General Assembly (USA)) [1994 72§: 9m 10m^5 10g^2 10.1g^4 10.1d 1995 12m 12m 12g 10g^6 8.3g^3 7f 8g 7d 8m^3 9d^3 10g Oct 10] quite good-topped gelding: has a quick action: disappointing maiden: stays 1¼m: acts on good to firm ground and dead: quite often slowly away: has looked temperamental, and not one to trust. *C. A. Horgan*
55 §

RISING STREAM 2 b.f. (Mar 5) Pharly (FR) 130 – River's Rising (FR) 88 (Mendez (FR) 128) [1995 7g a6g^5 a6g^4 a6g Dec 6] third foal: half-sister to 3-y-o Jigadee Creek (by Sharpo) and Italian 4-y-o 7.5f winner The Potato (by Entitled):
42

dam 1m winner: best effort fourth in seller at Wolverhampton: bred to stay beyond 6f: has looked headstrong: sold 1,100 gns Ascot December Sales. *Sir Mark Prescott*

RISK A MILLION 3 ch.f. Risk Me (FR) 127 – Romana 72 (Roman Warrior 132) [1994 –: 9.7s 1995 10m 11.9f^3 May 26] tall, plain filly: fourth foal: behind in maidens. *J. R. Jenkins* –

RISKIE THINGS 4 ch.f. Risk Me (FR) 127 – Foolish Things (Song 132) [1994 58: a6g^6 a5g* a5g^4 a6g* a5g^4 a6g^2 a5g 1995 a6g 6f 6.9g 5m^6 6m 5m a5g Dec 19] close-coupled filly: poor handicapper nowadays: stays 6f: acts on any turf going and on equitrack: tried visored, not in 1995. *J. S. Moore* 49

RISKING 2 b.f. (Mar 26) Risk Me (FR) 127 – Dark Kristal (IRE) 66 (Gorytus (USA) 132) [1995 a6g Sep 2] 13,500Y: first foal: dam (stayed 7f) half-sister to dam of Risky (by Risk Me): 7/1, well beaten in maiden auction at Wolverhampton. *G. Lewis* –

RISK MASTER 6 b.g. Risk Me (FR) 127 – Trigamy 112 (Tribal Chief 125) [1994 94: 8.1d^3 8m 8.1d^2 7.3g 9v 1995 8g 8m^3 9m 9d Oct 21] lengthy, dipped-backed gelding: fairly useful 1m-to-1¼m performer: no worthwhile form in varied company in 1995: yet to show his best on top-of-the-ground, acts on soft: held up. *C. A. Horgan* –

RISKY 4 b.f. Risk Me (FR) 127 – Dona Krista 84 (King of Spain 121) [1994 105: 7.3s^3 6m^2 5g^5 1995 5g 5.1g^5 5.2d^6 Sep 15] sturdy, good sort: unimpressive mover: useful performer on her day: best of 3 runs in 1995 when close fifth of 8 in £15,500 event at Chester: bandaged in front, soundly beaten on final start: probably best at up to 6f: went well on soft ground (sometimes withdrawn on top-of-the-ground): sold 95,000 gns Newmarket December Sales. *R. Hannon* 92

RISKY ROMEO 3 b.g. Charmer 123 – Chances Are (He Loves Me 120) [1994 70, a97+: 5m 5d^4 a6g^4 6m^4 7d 6g 8g^3 a8g* a8g* 1995 7g^4 8d 8.2g 7.6m^4 8m 10m 7.1g^4 10g^5 8.3m 8f* 8d 7f 8.2m a8.5g a8g^5 a8g^6 Dec 14] leggy, workmanlike gelding: only fair at best in 1995, winning handicap at Warwick in August: stays 1m: acts on equitrack, on firm going and probably on dead: tends to sweat: takes keen hold, and usually held up: sometimes slowly away: none too consistent. *G. C. Bravery* 68

RISKY ROSE 3 b.f. Risk Me (FR) 127 – Moharabuiee 60 (Pas de Seul 133) [1994 49: 5g 6g 5m^6 6m 6m^5 8m^6 a7g a6g^6 a8g^6 a7g^5 1995 a8g^6 a8g^4 a8g^5 10g^5 12f* 9.9m^4 13.8g* 12m^5 13.1f 12m^3 12h^4 Aug 16] neat filly: poor performer: won seller at Pontefract in May and claimer at Catterick in June: stays 13.8f: acts on firm ground and the all-weather: yet to race on a soft surface. *R. Hollinshead* 44

RISKY ROYAL 3 ch.g. Risk Me (FR) 127 – Royal Clover 63 (Mansingh (USA) 120) [1994 60: 6m^3 5m^4 6m 5d^3 5s 5m^4 5.2g a5g^6 1995 5.1d 7m a6g Nov 8] leggy, sparely-made gelding: well below form in 1995: best form at 5f: acts on good to firm and dead ground and on fibresand. *T. J. Naughton* –

RISKY TU 4 ch.f. Risk Me (FR) 127 – Sarah Gillian (USA) (Zen (USA)) [1994 –, a62: a8g^2 a10g^6 a12g^3 12.3d a12g^5 11.1f^5 a8g* a8g^3 a12g* 11.9m 1995 a11g a16g^2 a16g^3 a16g^3 12g^3 a12g^5 12g a14g a12g a14g^3 a11g^2 a12g^4 Dec 18] tall, leggy filly: modest handicapper at best: effective at 1m at 3 yrs and stays 2m: acts on the all-weather and soft ground: none too consistent. *P. A. Kelleway* 54 d a61 d

RISTON LADY (IRE) 5 b.m. Salt Dome (USA) – Trompe d'Oeil 75 (Longleat (USA) 109) [1994 61d: 5g 5g 5m 5f a5g 6m 5m^4 5m^6 5g 5s 5.1s^6 a5g 1995 a5g Dec 2] small mare: fairly useful 5f handicapper (rated 81) at 3 yrs: on the downgrade, tailed off only start in 1995. *B. S. Rothwell* –

RITA'S JOY 4 ch.f. Jalmood (USA) 126 – Cash Limit 62 (High Top 131) [1994 36: 12m^3 12m^5 1995 a13g Jan 10] unfurnished filly: poor middle-distance maiden: acts on firm going, dead and fibresand. *W. G. M. Turner* –

RITA'S SOFA 4 b.f. Sulaafah (USA) 119 – Rainbow Springs 82 (Silly Season 127) [1994 –: 8.1g 8s 10.2g 1995 10.2m Jun 17] small filly: no sign of ability. *Mrs A. E. Jermy* –

RIVA-DEVA 3 b.g. Roaring Riva 103 – Hilly's Daughter (Hillandale 125) [1994 –: 6m a6g a7g 1995 12g a14.8g Sep 16] close-coupled gelding: of no account: trained until after reappearance by S. Coathup. *B. Preece* –

RIVAL BID (USA) 7 b.g. Cannonade (USA) – Love Triangle (USA) (Nodouble (USA)) [1994 71: 10.8m^2 10.8d^5 10.3m^2 10.1g^3 10f^3 11.5g 8.9m* 10d^3 1995 10m 71 a55

10g^{6} 10m^{4} 9m^{5} 10.3f^{5} 9m^{2} 12m a8g^{5} 10.1g^{3} 10d^{2} 10.8g* 10g^{4} 10f* a11g^{6} a10g^{4} Dec 18] workmanlike, close-coupled gelding: fair handicapper: trained until after sixth 7-y-o start by M. Jarvis: won at Warwick (claimer) and Leicester in October: effective at 9f and stays 1½m: acts on firm ground and dead, has only modest form on the all-weather: has run creditably for amateur: has worn net muzzle: often sweating: usually held up, and is suited by a good gallop: tough. *Mrs N. Macauley*

RIVAL QUEEN (IRE) 3 ch.f. Royal Academy (USA) 130 – Maria Stuarda (Royal And Regal (USA)) [1994 73p: 7g^{4} 1995 8f^{5} 10d^{4} Oct 19] angular filly: fair form only 2-y-o start: disappointing in 1995: may prove best at up to 1m: sold 2,000 gns Newmarket December Sales. *H. R. A. Cecil* –

RIVA ROCK 5 b.g. Roaring Riva 103 – Kivulini (Hotfoot 126) [1994 NR 1995 9.7m^{6} a8g 9.7g^{6} 11.9f^{2} Jul 20] sturdy, lengthy gelding: poor maiden handicapper: stays 11.9f: acts on firm ground: won two 3-runner races over hurdles in August. *T. P. McGovern* 31

RIVA'S BOOK (USA) 4 b.c. Mari's Book (USA) – Riva's Revenge (USA) (Riva Ridge (USA)) [1994 59: 8.3d 6.9v* 8.3f* 11.1m^{4} 8m^{5} 10g^{4} 8.5m 1995 a12g Feb 15] compact colt: modest performer: ran as if something amiss (for new stable) only 4-y-o start. *S. Coathup* –

RIVERBANK RED 4 ch.f. Lighter 111 – Gypsy Louise (Ascendant 96) [1994 NR 1995 12.1g May 29] first foal: dam unraced: beaten over 20 lengths in Chepstow maiden: has joined T. Caldwell. *P. C. Clarke* –

RIVER BOARD 5 b.g. Dominion 123 – Miss Thames 105 (Tower Walk 130) [1994 98: 7.5m* 7g^{2} 8m^{4} 7.9m 9g 7m 8d 1995 8.5m^{2} 8m Jun 21] strong, good-topped gelding: useful performer: creditable second of 5 in rated stakes at Beverley on reappearance, drifting left: well beaten in Royal Hunt Cup at Royal Ascot on only subsequent outing: effective at 7f to 9f (may well stay 1¼m): acts on good to firm ground: possibly best forcing pace. *W. J. Haggas* 94

RIVER DIVINE (USA) 2 ch.f. (Jan 8) Irish River (FR) 131 – Etoile d'Amore (USA) 81 (The Minstrel (CAN) 135) [1995 7m Oct 30] lengthy, rather unfurnished filly: half-sister to 3-y-o 7f winner Moonlight Saunter (by Woodman) and 2 other winners, including 7f (at 2 yrs) and 8.5f winner Hadaad (by Mr Prospector): dam twice-raced 7f winner out of high-class sprinter Gurkhas Band: 9/4 but green, beginning to stay on when badly hampered 2f out in maiden at Newcastle won by Shemozzle, eventually finishing around 13 lengths down in eighth (would probably have finished fourth and rated accordingly): sure to do better. *M. R. Stoute* 59 p

RIVER GARNOCK 3 br.c. Dowsing (USA) 124 – Duboff 120 (So Blessed 130) [1994 82p: 6f* 6m^{6} 1995 6g 5f Jun 14] strong, good-bodied colt: fairly useful form at 2 yrs: well beaten in handicaps at Newmarket and Hamilton in 1995. *J. Berry* –

RIVER ISLAND (USA) 7 b.g. Spend A Buck (USA) – Promising Risk (USA) (Exclusive Native (USA)) [1994 NR 1995 12.1g^{5} May 29] quite attractive gelding: fairly useful performer early on at 3 yrs for P. Cole: very lightly raced on flat and no form since. *J. A. B. Old* –

RIVER KEEN (IRE) 3 ch.c. Keen 116 – Immediate Impact (Caerleon (USA) 132) [1994 82p: 7.1d^{3} 7g^{3} 1995 8d^{4} 7m 9g^{6} 10g* 9f 10.1g 12s^{5} 12.1s a10g* a12g* Dec 2] tall, leggy, sparely-made colt: useful handicapper on the all-weather, fairly useful on turf: won at Ascot (sweating) in July, Lingfield in November and Wolverhampton (by 10 lengths) in December: stays 1½m: possibly unsuited by top-of-the-ground, acts on soft and goes well on the all-weather: effective blinkered or not: inconsistent. *R. W. Armstrong* 82 a102

RIVER MAY 3 b.f. Sulaafah (USA) 119 – Five Diamonds (FR) (Sir Gaylord) [1994 NR 1995 8.3m 7f 10m 8m Sep 25] smallish filly: half-sister to several winners abroad, including prolific winning miler Fly North (by Arctic Tern): dam never ran: no worthwhile form. *Andrew Turnell* –

RIVER NORTH (IRE) 5 ch.g. Lomond (USA) 128 – Petillante (USA) (Riverman (USA) 131) [1994 122: 11.8m^{2} 12g* 10m^{2} 12g* 12d^{2} 1995 12g Apr 22] sturdy gelding: impresses in appearance: has a quick action: very smart performer in 1994: well below form, reportedly pulled muscles, in John Porter Stakes at Newbury on only 5-y-o start: ideally suited by 1½m+: acts on dead going and good to firm: held up (idles in front) and has good turn of foot: reportedly suffers from leg 105 +

problems, and wears bandages: sometimes wanders and hangs under pressure, but is tough and genuine. *Lady Herries*

RIVER TERN 2 b.c. (Mar 20) Puissance 110 – Millaine 69 (Formidable (USA) 125) [1995 6m 5f3 6d4 Sep 27] tall, leggy colt: has scope: fourth foal: half-brother to 1991 2-y-o 5f winner Tenacity (by Primo Dominie), fairly useful sprinter Amber Mill (by Doulab) and a winner in Italy: dam stayed 1½m: only modest form in maidens but twice shaped with promise, on debut and then on final start (after 3½-month absence) when 12 lengths fourth of 11, keen early on, to impressive Meldorf at Newcastle: stays 6f: looks sort to do better. *J. Berry* 58 p

RIVER WYE (IRE) 3 b.g. Jareer (USA) 115 – Sun Gift (Guillaume Tell (USA) 121) [1994 –: 5m 1995 8g5 10m 8m5 8m 10d a7g a8g5 Nov 20] tall gelding: poor maiden: bred to stay 1¼m, but looks headstrong. *J. M. Carr* 49

RIVIERE ROUGE 2 ch.f. (Feb 5) Forzando 122 – Furry Dance (USA) (Nureyev (USA) 131) [1995 6g 5m a6g a7g Nov 21] 3,000Y: small filly: first foal: dam once-raced daughter of middle-distance winner Kenanga, a half-sister to Ribblesdale winner Strigida out of Ribblesdale winner Catalpa: no form, including in claimer. *S. G. Knight* –

RIYADIAN 3 ch.c. Polish Precedent (USA) 131 – Knight's Baroness 116 (Rainbow Quest (USA) 134) [1994 NR 1995 10m3 10g* 11.5f2 12f 10.3g* 12d* 10m2 Oct 14] 122

The 1990 Irish Oaks winner Knight's Baroness came up with a classic runner at the first attempt with Riyadian. Seventh of fifteen was the best the colt could manage in his classic, the Derby, but that was less than two months after his racecourse debut and Riyadian has looked increasingly the part since, in the process showing a higher level of form than Knight's Baroness ever did. The Derby was Riyadian's fourth race. The first two were Kempton maidens in which he lost out to Minds Music and Istidaad on the first occasion then nine days later beat Quandary and Kutta. The Lingfield Derby Trial followed hot on their heels and, 8/1 co-fourth favourite of seven, he booked his place at Epsom by giving the odds-on Munwar a mighty scare and going down by only a head. Four weeks later, Riyadian had every chance rounding Tattenham Corner before finishing the Derby in the same position that he'd been sent off in the betting.

A hock injury sustained while cast in his box meant that his next three months were decidedly less active. The St Leger was mentioned in August as a possible target but although he did appear at the St Leger meeting it was in a £7,275 conditions stakes rather than the final classic. This is where Riyadian began to make up for lost time: a slide in the betting (from 4/5 to 11/8 favourite) proved most misleading and he bolted up from Night City. Fifteen days later, facing much stiffer opposition in the Cumberland Lodge Stakes at Ascot, he bolted up again. In betting order, the field was Riyadian; the tremendously progressive Royal Ascot and York handicap winner Medaille Militaire; the previous year's Cumberland Lodge and Prix Foy winners Prince of Andros and Richard of York; September Stakes first and third Burooj and Wayne County; and outsiders Fire On Ice and Silver Wedge. Prince of Andros trailed in lame and Riyadian ran right away from the rest in the final one and a half furlongs; he had taken the lead on the bridle and was then pushed out by Richard Quinn who

Cumberland Lodge Stakes, Ascot—Riyadian is most impressive; Richard of York gave battle in vain

looked round about seventy-five yards out, found that the race was all over and dropped his hands. Riyadian still finished five lengths up on Richard of York with Burooj four lengths further back back in third. Like stable-mates Strategic Choice and Posidonas, Riyadian now had to be considered for the Arc. In the event, only Strategic Choice appeared in the Arc field. The other two would have had to have been supplemented at a cost of 400,000 francs, and Riyadian's connections opted for the £20,000 alternative into the Champion Stakes field thirteen days later. There was a much greater chance of getting some money back at Newmarket—there were seven opponents instead of sixteen for a start—and Riyadian returned a £46,480 profit by coming in an excellent second. Once more, he challenged smoothly approaching the two-furlong marker, but, although staying on gamely, this time he was soon put in his place by Spectrum who beat him by two lengths.

Riyadian (ch.c. 1992)	Polish Precedent (USA) (b 1986)	Danzig (b 1977)	Northern Dancer
			Pas de Nom
		Past Example (ch 1976)	Buckpasser
			Bold Example
	Knight's Baroness (b 1987)	Rainbow Quest (b 1981)	Blushing Groom
			I Will Follow
		Knight's Beauty (b 1977)	True Knight
			Broadway Beauty

Riyadian could easily develop into a serious contender for the Arc in 1996. He shapes as if a mile and a half will suit him better than a mile and a quarter, even though his sire, the top-class Polish Precedent, was a miler. Polish Precedent is a close relation to an even better miler, his contemporary Zilzal, and it was that colt who proved the only horse capable of beating Polish Precedent as a three-year-old, bringing a run of seven victories to an end in the Queen Elizabeth II Stakes. Polish Precedent never raced beyond a mile but plenty of his progeny seem to have relished the opportunity, including Pure Grain, Her Ladyship, Bobinski, Precede, Pilsudski, Red Route and Waiting. It was stamina and courage that won the day for Knight's Baroness when she caught dual Italian classic winner Atoll in the final strides of the Irish Oaks. She also won a maiden at two years and made the frame in all of her five other starts, including the May Hill, Lingfield Oaks Trial, Oaks and Park Hill. Since Riyadian, Knight's Baroness has been covered three times by Generous and once (in 1994) by Generous' sire Caerleon, a sequence that got off to an unpromising start when Perfect Gift finished last in two maiden races in the summer. Knight's Baroness is the only winner out of her short-lived dam Knight's Beauty and Knight's Beauty looks to be clearly the best of her sire's progeny, the winner of twelve races in all including three minor stakes races (from six and a half to eight and a half furlongs) as a four-year-old. Thirteen years after Knight's Beauty, Broadway Beauty produced the Royal Lodge runner-up and Predominate Stakes winner Geisway.

The medium-sized, lengthy Riyadian should add significantly to the family record in 1996. Not at all the best of movers (he has a short action), he twice showed smart form on firm ground before putting up those high-class efforts on dead and good to firm in the autumn. The Champion Stakes is Riyadian's best form to date, but a return to a mile and a half should suit him ideally. He got on his toes and was then keen to post before the Cumberland Lodge. *P. F. I. Cole*

ROADSWEEPER (FR) 3 b.g. Bold Arrangement 127 – Sweeperette (High Line 125) [1994 NR 1995 a10g a12g^4 12.5m^6 12g 10g^5 11.6g^3 13.5g* 10g 12d Sep 11] leggy gelding: first reported foal: dam never ran: modest performer: claimed 120,000 francs out of K. Cunningham-Brown's stable after dead-heating for claimer at Deauville in August: stays 13.5f: best efforts on good ground: no improvement in blinkers/visor. *L. Auriemma, France* 55

ROAR ON TOUR 6 b.g. Dunbeath (USA) 127 – Tickled Trout 70 (Red Alert 127) [1994 50: 8m a7g* a7g^6 8g* a8g^2 a8.5g^2 1995 a8g* a8g* a8g^4 a8g* a8g* a8g^3 a8g 8.3v Mar 31] good-bodied gelding: fair handicapper on the all-weather: won 4 times at Southwell (including an amateurs event) early in year: well below form there and at Hamilton (reportedly suffered back injury) last 2 starts: best efforts at up 8.5f: acts on good to firm and soft ground, and goes well on fibresand: effective blinkered or not: not tried in visor since 1992: tough. *Mrs M. Reveley* – a69

ROBAMASET (IRE) 2 b.c. (Mar 20) Caerleon (USA) 132 – Smageta (High Top 131) [1995 7m^5 7.5s 8m^4 Oct 12] robust, lengthy colt: has plenty of scope: tenth foal: 77 p half-brother to several winners here and abroad, including 10.6f winner Regordes (by Commanche Run) and 7.5f winner Ratafia (by Rousillon): dam Group 3 1m winner in Italy at 2 yrs later third in Italian 1000 Guineas and Oaks: behind in quite valuable race at Milan on second start: easily better effort in maidens here when just over 4 lengths fourth of 14 to Silver Dome at Newmarket, keeping on: will be suited by middle distances: may well be unsuited by soft ground: upset in stalls final start: will improve further. *L. M. Cumani*

ROBATY'S LAW (IRE) 3 b.g. Be My Native (USA) 122 – River Low (IRE) (Lafontaine (USA) 117) [1994 –: 5d 1995 a6g^{6} 8.3g 5g 5g May 24] leggy gelding: no worthwhile form: sold out of M. Heaton-Ellis' stable 1,250 gns Doncaster March Sales after reappearance: sold 720 gns Doncaster September Sales. *P. Monteith* –

ROBELLINA 3 b.g. Faustus (USA) 118 – Express Edition 58 (Comedy Star (USA) 121) [1994 –: 6f 7.1m 1995 11.1d^{6} 11d Sep 22] leggy gelding: of no account on flat. *M. Dods* –

ROBELLION 4 b.g. Robellino (USA) 127 – Tickled Trout 70 (Red Alert 127) [1994 74: 6m 6g 5m 5.1f 5g^{3} 5.7g^{2} 5d 5m 7m 7s 1995 7m 7f^{4} 6g^{3} 5.7m^{2} 5.7f^{4} 5m^{5} 5.2g^{2} 5.1m* 5m 5.2m^{4} 5m 5m^{2} 5.1d 5g 5m 6.1s 6f a5g a6g a7g^{4} Dec 15] sturdy, workmanlike gelding: fair handicapper: justified favouritism at Chepstow in July: below form last 5 starts: effective at 5f to 7f: acts on firm ground, below form all 4 outings on a soft surface: effective visored or not. *D. W. P. Arbuthnot* 74

ROBERTY LEA 7 b.g. Alleging (USA) 120 – Rosy Lee (FR) (Le Haar 126) [1994 70: 12g 10m^{4} 13.9m^{5} 14.6g 13.1d^{6} 14s^{2} 16g 12v 1995 18g^{3} 17.1m* 17.1m 18m Oct 14] close-coupled gelding: fair handicapper: won at Pontefract in April: stays well: acts on good to firm and soft ground: blinkered (below form) once at 3 yrs: tends to sweat and get on edge. *Mrs M. Reveley* 67

ROBINGO (IRE) 6 b.g. Bob Back (USA) 124 – Mill's Girl (Le Levanstell 122) [1994 NR 1995 14g 16.4m Jul 8] close-coupled gelding: progressed into a useful stayer (rated 102) for M. Pipe as 4-y-o: bandaged, well below form on return to flat: withdrawn on veterinary advice in August. *Mrs L. A. Murphy* –

ROBIN ISLAND 3 b.g. Robellino (USA) 127 – Irish Isle 67 (Realm 129) [1994 68: 6g^{4} 6.1s 1995 7.6m^{4} 8.2m 10.1g^{6} 8m Jun 23] close-coupled, quite attractive gelding: appeared to show fair form on debut, but failed to confirm it: tried blinkered: sold (R. Hannon to P. Hedger) 3,100 gns Ascot July Sales. *R. Hannon* –

ROBINS (IRE) 3 b.c. Scenic 128 – Roman Walk 80 (Petorius 117) [1994 8d^{2} 1995 8.5g* 9g* 10g^{3} 8s* 8g^{3} 8m^{6} 9g* 7.5s* 8d Oct 8] first foal: dam 2-y-o 6f winner: useful Italian colt: won maiden at Naples, minor event at Rome and listed event at Rome by the end of April: best effort when around 1½ lengths third of 14 to Prince Arthur in Premio Parioli at Rome in May, always thereabouts: off course over 3 months, won minor event at Naples and quite valuable race at Milan (beat Thomire by ¾ length), both in September: well beaten in Group 1 event final start: stays 9f: acts on soft ground. *A. Colella, Italy* 106

ROBO MAGIC (USA) 3 b.g. Tejano (USA) – Bubble Magic (USA) (Clever Trick (USA)) [1994 58, a69: 6g^{6} 7m 7.1m 6d^{3} 6g 7g^{5} 6s a6g^{2} a6g* a6g 1995 a7g^{3} a7g a6g* a7g^{5} 7g 7g^{4} 6m^{4} 6.1m 6m 6m* 6m 7d a7g^{4} a6g a5g^{2} a6g* Dec 18] neat gelding: fair performer on the all-weather, modest on turf: won seller in February (left A. Moore's stable after next start) and handicaps in August and December, all at Lingfield: effective at 6f and 7f: acts on good to firm and dead ground (below form on soft) and goes well on equitrack: blinkered (ran creditably) twice. *L. Montague Hall* 58 a75

ROBSERA (IRE) 4 b.g. Robellino (USA) 127 – Que Sera 91 (Music Boy 124) [1994 84: 8s 8s 9m* 10m 8.5m* 8m 8f* 8.3f* 8.1g 8.3m^{2} 10g 8m 1995 8g 7m 8m 8.5m 8m a8.5g^{4} 8f^{5} 8.3m 8g 8.2m^{4} Oct 19] strong gelding: just a fair handicapper in 1995: best at up to 9f: acts on firm and dead going (respectable effort on heavy): tried blinkered: sold (G. Lewis to J. Quinn) 7,000 gns Newmarket Autumn Sales. *G. Lewis* 72

ROC DE FER (IRE) 2 br.g. (Apr 2) Polar Falcon (USA) 126 – Miss Blitz 83 (Formidable (USA) 125) [1995 6.1m 6.1m Oct 26] 44,000Y: lengthy gelding: second living foal: half-brother to fair 4-y-o 6f and 7f winner Berge (by Most Welcome): dam, 6f winner who stayed 7f, daughter of half-sister to Mummy's Pet: signs of – p ability in maiden and minor event (good speed 4f then hung left) at Nottingham: looks sort to do better. *W. A. O'Gorman*

ROCKCRACKER (IRE) 3 ch.g. Ballad Rock 122 – Forest Blaze (USA) 82 (Green Forest (USA) 134) [1994 67: 5g^6 6.1m^3 5.7f* 6.1m^5 6m^2 6m 1995 a6g^4 a7g 6.1g^5 6m 5.1m a7g Dec 15] neat, strong gelding: modest performer: off course 6 months after third 3-y-o start, and below form afterwards: better at 6f than 5f: has raced only on a sound surface on turf: tried blinkered: sold out of R. Charlton's stable 4,000 gns Newmarket Autumn Sales before final outing. *G. G. Margarson* 64 a56

ROCK DAISY 2 b. or br.f. (Feb 18) Rock City 120 – New Pastures (Formidable (USA) 125) [1995 6d Oct 19] rather unfurnished filly: third foal: dam unraced: 33/1, bit backward and green, always behind in 20-runner maiden at Newbury. *B. J. Meehan* –

ROCKETEER (IRE) 4 ch.c. Bluebird (USA) 125 – Chive (St Chad 120) [1994 59+, a98: a6g* a5g* a5g^3 a7g* a6g^5 6f^4 7f 7m^6 7.1m a7g^2 a6g^3 a6g a6g* 1995 a7g* a8.5g a6g^6 a7g 6.1m* 6m^3 6m* 6m^3 7m 7m Sep 5] stocky colt: unimpressive mover: useful handicapper on the all-weather, successful at Wolverhampton in January: fair on turf, and won at Chepstow (celebrity event, after 4-month absence) and Thirsk (plenty to do 2f out) in July: effective at 5f to 7f: acts on the all-weather and firm ground, seems unsuited by heavy: usually blinkered: sold 26,000 gns Newmarket Autumn Sales. *W. R. Muir* 76 a98

ROCKET GROUNDS (IRE) 2 b.f. (Apr 16) Common Grounds 118 – Ginosa 62 (Kalamoun 129) [1995 6g a7g a6g Dec 2] IR 3,300Y: neat filly: half-sister to 1988 2-y-o 5f winner Generousity Gem (by Burslem) and a winner in Scandinavia by Taufan: dam placed over 1½m: little worthwhile form in maiden auction and sellers. *J. J. Quinn* –

ROCKFIELD LADY (IRE) 3 b.f. Dancing Dissident (USA) 119 – Come True (FR) (Nasram II 125) [1994 –: 5.1g 6m a9.4g^5 1995 a7g a7g Jan 17] no form: tried visored: has joined B. Llewellyn. *I. Campbell* –

ROCKFORCE 3 ch.g. Rock City 120 – Sleepline Princess 86 (Royal Palace 131) [1994 73: 7.1m 7f 8s 7g^3 6m^5 1995 9m* 8m* 10g 9f* 10m^5 Aug 11] good-topped gelding: fairly useful handicapper: successful at Kempton in April and at Salisbury and Ripon in July: will prove best at up to 1¼m: acts on firm ground: has run well when sweating. *M. R. Channon* 87

ROCK FOUNDATION 3 b.g. Rock City 120 – Runelia (Runnett 125) [1994 70p: 7m a7g^4 a7g* 1995 8m^5 8.3g 8m 8.3f* 8.3f* Aug 3] sturdy gelding: fair performer: won seller and claimer (2/1 on, easily, claimed £6,000) at Hamilton in the summer: stays 8.3f: acts on fibresand and firm ground: joined G. M. Moore. *P. C. Haslam* 66

ROCK GROUP 3 b.g. Rock City 120 – Norska 67 (Northfields (USA)) [1994 61?: 7g 7m 7s 1995 11.8g 12m^3 Jul 29] tall, unfurnished gelding: modest maiden: stays 1½m: acts on good to firm going (poor effort only outing on soft). *J. Pearce* 61

ROCK OYSTER 3 b.g. Ballad Rock 122 – Bombshell 76 (Le Levanstell 122) [1994 59: 7g 7m 1995 8g 8.2m 8.3m 10m^3 11.6m 10f 8m^6 8f a9.4g Nov 13] rangy gelding: poor maiden handicapper: stays 1¼m: raced mainly on top-of-the-ground: hung left after losing lead third 3-y-o start: tried blinkered: inconsistent. *B. J. Meehan* 53

ROCK RAMBLER 3 ch.g. Rock City 120 – Moonwalker (Night Shift (USA)) [1994 NR 1995 7g 8.5d^6 8.2d Sep 19] 8,000Y: small gelding: bad mover: first foal: dam unraced: well beaten in claimer and maidens. *Lady Herries* –

ROCK SCENE (IRE) 3 b.c. Scenic 128 – Rockeater 94 (Roan Rocket 128) [1994 NR 1995 a8g^5 a8.5g^4 a9.4g^5 Aug 5] 2,600F, 8,000Y: half-brother to 2 winners, including fair 5f (at 2 yrs) to 1¼m winner Black Sophie (by Moorestyle), and to dam of Italian 1000 Guineas winner Arranvanna: dam stayed 11f: modest maiden: stays 8.5f. *R. Hollinshead* 64

ROCK SHARP 2 b.c. (May 14) Rock City 120 – Keen Melody (USA) 60 (Sharpen Up 127) [1995 6.1f 6.1m^3 7m* 7m* 7d^4 Sep 20] 7,500Y: compact colt: has a fluent, round action: second foal: dam stayed 1m: won maiden auction at Thirsk and nursery at Ascot in August: creditable fourth in nursery at Chester final start: stays 7f: acts on good to firm and dead ground: upset in stalls at Thirsk: sold 13,000 gns Newmarket Autumn Sales. *R. Hannon* 74

ROCKSTINE (IRE) 4 b.f. Ballad Rock 122 – Huldine 93 (Cure The Blues (USA)) [1994 47+, a61: a8g^2 a10g^2 a8g^2 11.6g^6 8g^4 9.7g 10.1m^3 9g a10g^4 8.5m^5 9g^3 10g 10.1m^4 a10g* a9.4g^2 a8.5g* a10g a12g^6 1995 a9.4g^3 a10g^3 a8g^3 a8g^3 a10g a10g 8m^2 a8g^3 9.7s a12g Sep 30] leggy filly: unimpressive mover: modest handicapper, better on all-weather surfaces than turf: best form at up to 1¼m: acts on good to firm ground: tried blinkered/visored: sometimes takes plenty of driving: sold 2,000 gns Doncaster October Sales. *P. Mitchell* — 45 a57

ROCK SYMPHONY 5 ch.g. Ballad Rock 122 – Shamasiya (FR) (Vayrann 133) [1994 96: 6d^5 6m^2 6m^4 7m^5 7m^3 6g* 6m 6m^6 5g^3 6d 5m 1995 6m 6f^4 6f 6m^6 6f* 6m 6m 5m Oct 14] strong gelding: fairly useful handicapper: justified favouritism in rated stakes at Ripon in July: effective at stiff 5f to 7f: acts on firm and dead ground: blinkered (very edgy, below form) final 3-y-o start: held up. *W. J. Haggas* — 93

ROCK THE BARNEY (IRE) 6 ch.h. Coquelin (USA) 121 – Lady Loire 94 (Wolverlife 115) [1994 54: 10v^5 10g 9.7s^3 10g* 8.1g^2 10.2m^4 10g^2 10m 10s 10d 10.1d^4 1995 10d 10m^3 10g^5 11.4g* 12f* 11.4m 12f^3 11.9m 12g 12m^5 Nov 6] smallish horse: unimpressive mover: modest handicapper: won at Sandown and Kempton in June: stays 1½m: acts on any going: blinkered once at 3 yrs: best held up. *P. Burgoyne* — 59

ROCKUSA 3 b.f. Rock City 120 – Miss Derby (USA) (Master Derby (USA)) [1994 52: 6m^5 7d 1995 9g 10g a8.5g^4 8d^3 7g^5 9m Oct 27] neat filly: poor and inconsistent maiden: trained until after third 3-y-o start by Lady Herries: stays 8.5f. *P. R. Hedger* — 41

ROCKVILLE PIKE (IRE) 3 b.g. Glenstal (USA) 118 – Sound Pet (Runnett 125) [1994 78: 5d* 5g^4 5m 1995 6m 6g^4 6f^4 a6g Dec 18] compact, sprint type: fairly useful performer: best effort when close fourth of 7 in rated stakes at Newmarket on second start, staying on well: tailed off on subsequent outings: probably better at 6f than 5f: below form all 3 outings on top-of-the-ground. *S. Dow* — 83

ROCKY BAY 6 ch.m. Bold Owl 101 – Overseas 48 (Sea Hawk II 131) [1994 40: a12g^2 a12g^2 8.1g a12g 1995 a12g^4 a12g Apr 13] neat mare: poor middle-distance performer: well beaten in 1995. *B. J. Llewellyn* — –

ROCKY FORUM 3 ch.f. Deploy 131 – Beau's Delight (USA) (Lypheor 118) [1994 NR 1995 a10g^5 a8g^4 a10g^6 12d^2 11.6m^6 11.4g^4 14d* 13.3f^6 a12g^2 a16g* Aug 5] unfurnished filly: second foal: half-sister to 4-y-o 11.9f and 13f seller winner Glow Forum (by Kalaglow): dam, should have stayed at least 1m, is out of half-sister to smart French 1¼m winner/top-class US performer Sangue: modest handicapper: won at Haydock in June and Lingfield (steadily-run race by 9 lengths) in August: stays 2m: acts on equitrack and dead ground, possibly unsuited by firm. *G. L. Moore* — 64

ROCKY MELODY 3 b.g. Music Boy 124 – Summer Posy 93 (Posse (USA) 130) [1994 –: 6g 7s 1995 a7g Nov 14] sturdy, rather plain gelding: no worthwhile form. *P. C. Ritchens* — –

ROCKY OASIS (USA) 2 b.c. (Apr 17) Gulch (USA) – Knoosh (USA) 113 (Storm Bird (CAN) 134) [1995 7g^3 Sep 7] third foal: half-brother to 3-y-o Ranosh (by Rahy): dam won from 7f (at 2 yrs) to 1½m: 13/2 and burly, 4¾ lengths third of 8 to comfortable winner Mawwal in minor event at Doncaster, making good headway from rear 2f out and keeping on not knocked about: has plenty of scope, and is sure to improve and win a race. *M. R. Stoute* — 84 p

ROCKY'S METEOR 2 b.c. (Apr 19) Emarati (USA) 74 – Hoop La (Final Straw 127) [1995 6m^2 a6g Sep 2] 6,000F, 6,000Y: first foal: dam, lightly-raced maiden, half-sister to smart 6f (at 2 yrs) and 7f winner Mojave out of smart but temperamental middle-distance filly Out of Shot: slow-starting second of 7 to easy winner Missile Toe in maiden auction at Newcastle: in rear in similar event at Wolverhampton 6 weeks later: will probably stay beyond 6f. *R. A. Fahey* — 61

ROCKY TWO 4 b.c. Cree Song 99 – Holloway Wonder 93 (Swing Easy (USA) 126) [1994 64: 5m 5d^3 5v^2 5.1g^2 5.1g^2 5d^2 5m^5 a5g^5 6m^4 a5g^2 5m 5m^2 5.1g^6 a5g^3 6g a5g a5g^6 a5g a5g^5 1995 a5g^2 5d^6 a5g^5 a5g a6g 5m 6m^5 6g 5m^3 5f^5 5m^6 5.1d 5.3g a5g^3 a5g^5 a5g Dec 6] leggy colt: has a quick action: modest handicapper: none too consistent in 1995: stays 6f, very best form at 5f: acts on the all-weather and any turf ground: usually wears blinkers/visor, but effective without: usually races prominently. *P. Howling* — 60

ROCKY WATERS (USA) 6 b. or br.g. Rocky Marriage (USA) 95 – Running Melody 86 (Rheingold 137) [1994 85: a8g^{4} a6g^{2} 6f^{6} a6g 7m^{6} 7d a6g* a6g 1995 a6g^{3} a7g^{2} a7g^{3} a6g^{2} a6g^{5} 7m a7g^{4} 7g 6m 6m 7.1m 5g Sep 12] leggy, lightly-made gelding: has a roundish action: fair handicapper: trained until after seventh 6-y-o start by G. L. Moore: bandaged behind, well below form for new connections: stays 7f: acts on all-weather surfaces and on firm ground, probably on soft: tends to sweat: sometimes takes strong hold. *P. Burgoyne* — 64 a75

ROCQUAINE BAY 8 b.m. Morston (FR) 125 – Queen's Royale 80 (Tobrouk (FR)) [1994 47: 10.8m 12g^{2} 11.9f^{5} 12m* 11.5g^{5} 11.9m^{3} 12.1g 1995 12m^{4} 12g 12m^{4} 12f^{5} 14m^{5} 12m* 12f* 11.9f^{3} Aug 23] good-topped mare: poor handicapper: won at Epsom (for second year running) in July and Salisbury in August: should stay beyond 1½m: best on a sound surface: held up. *M. J. Bolton* — 46

RODERICK HUDSON 3 b.c. Elmaamul (USA) 125 – Moviegoer 104 (Pharly (FR) 130) [1994 –p: 7m 1995 7m^{6} 7f^{2} 7m^{2} 7m* 7.1m^{5} 7f Jul 28] angular, quite attractive colt: fairly useful performer: won apprentice maiden at Newbury in June: likely to stay beyond 7f: has raced only on top-of-the-ground: has worn crossed noseband. *J. A. R. Toller* — 86

ROGER THE BUTLER (IRE) 5 ch.h. Ahonoora 122 – Indian Jubilee 81 (Indian King (USA) 128) [1994 104: 6v* 6m^{6} 6m* 6v 6m* 6f^{2} 5m 6m 6m 5g^{5} 5m^{4} 6m 1995 6m^{4} 6g* 6m 6m 6m Aug 13] strong, lengthy horse: unimpressive mover: useful performer: won listed race at Lingfield in June by 1¼ lengths from Fard, making all: well below form afterwards: best at up to 6f: successful on heavy ground but very best efforts on a sound surface and acts on firm: blinkered (raced too freely) once at 3 yrs: occasionally bandaged: often a front runner: game: sold only 10,000 gns Newmarket December Sales. *M. Bell* — 104

ROI DE LA MER (IRE) 4 b.c. Fairy King (USA) – Sea Mistress (Habitat 134) [1994 73: 9m 8.3m^{4} 8.3m 8.9d^{2} 10d 1995 8g 10d 10m 10.8f^{4} 8g 9m 8.3g^{3} 8.1g* 10m 8g^{6} 8d^{5} 8.2m^{5} Oct 19] leggy, angular colt: fair handicapper: won selling event at Sandown in July: best form at 1m/9f: acts on good to firm ground (probably on firm) and dead: visored (below form) twice. *J. Akehurst* — 70

ROISIN CLOVER 4 ch.f. Faustus (USA) 118 – Valiyen (Valiyar 129) [1994 67: 8m 9.7g^{2} 11.9f* 10g 10m^{6} 11.6m^{2} 12m* 12g 12d^{4} 11.5d 1995 12g* 12m^{3} 12f^{2} 12m 12m^{4} 10d Sep 13] leggy, lengthy filly: fair handicapper: won at Kempton in April: stays 1½m: acts on firm and dead going: held up. *S. Dow* — 69

ROKA 3 br.f. Rock City 120 – Kalandariya 78 (Kris 135) [1994 NR 1995 7m 6g 7g Jun 3] 17,500Y: close-coupled filly: fourth reported foal: dam best form at 1m: modest maiden: best effort at 6f, should stay further. *R. Hannon* — 58

ROKEBY BOWL 3 b.c. Salse (USA) 128 – Rose Bowl (USA) 131 (Habitat 134) [1994 74p: 6f^{2} 1995 6g^{4} 6.9g 7.5m^{2} 7.9g 10g* 9g* 10.3m^{2} 10.4m^{4} 12f^{2} 11.9g^{2} 12d 10v^{5} Oct 7] small, quite attractive colt: useful handicapper: won at Pontefract and Sandown in June: best efforts when second in £37,300 race at Goodwood (beaten neck by Pilsudski after twice meeting trouble in running) and rated stakes at York on ninth and tenth starts: stays 1½m well: acts on firm ground, below form on a soft surface: held up: genuine and consistent. *I. A. Balding* — 101

ROLL A DOLLAR 9 b.g. Spin of A Coin 88 – Handy Dancer 87 (Green God 128) [1994 NR 1995 12g 13.3d Sep 16] big, rangy gelding: useful performer (rated 103) at 7 yrs: bandaged, well beaten in handicaps in 1995. *D. R. C. Elsworth* — –

ROLLING (IRE) 3 gr.f. Last Tycoon 131 – Faakirah (Dragonara Palace (USA) 115) [1994 69: 5.1g^{2} 5.1m^{2} 5.7g^{2} 5g^{2} 5.2g^{6} 1995 6g^{3} 5.1f 6g 7f^{5} 6m 8s^{3} 6d^{2} Nov 7] leggy, light-framed filly: fair maiden: sold out of B. Hills's stable 9,800 gns Ascot July Sales after fourth start: good efforts afterwards when in frame: stays 1m: acts on good to firm and soft ground. *A. P. O'Brien, Ireland* — 68

ROLLING SETTLEMENT (IRE) 3 b.f. Contract Law (USA) 108 – Ellaline (Corvaro (USA) 124) [1994 NR 1995 7g 8f Oct 24] sparely-made filly: third foal: half-sister to modest Irish 13f winner Mobile Miss (by Classic Secret): dam, Irish 7f winner, out of smart Smelter: no sign of ability. *J. A. Harris* — –

ROLLING THE BONES (USA) 6 b.g. Green Dancer (USA) 132 – Davelle's Bid (USA) (Bold Bidder) [1994 38: 16.2s 14.1d 14.1d^{6} 16.2m* 16.1f^{4} 16.5m^{6} 18m^{4} 16.2g a16.2g 1995 16.2m^{2} 15.4m* 16.2m* a16g^{4} 16.4g 14.1f Oct 3] lengthy gelding: — 43 poor handicapper: won at Folkestone in April and Beverley (for second year running) in May: stays 17.5f: acts on firm and dead going, below form on the all-weather: blinkered/visored once each, below form: drifted badly right on 6-y-o reappearance: normally held up: won over hurdles in October. *P. S. Felgate*

ROLLING WATERS 5 b.g. Robellino (USA) 127 – Idle Waters 116 (Mill Reef (USA) 141) [1994 –, a53: a9.4g^3 a9.4g^3 10m^5 9g a10g^2 a10g^2 a10g^2 a12g* a12g 1995 a9.4g* a12g 10g a12g^2 10.8g a12g^5 a14.8g* a10g^3 a10g^2 a16g^4 a10g^6 a14.8g^5 a12g Sep 30] smallish, round-barrelled gelding: fair handicapper on the all-weather: won at Wolverhampton in April and July: stays 14.8f: goes well on all-weather surfaces, no worthwhile form on turf: inconsistent: sold (J. Toller to P. Eccles) 5,500 gns Newmarket Autumn Sales. *J. A. R. Toller* – a65

ROMALITO 5 b.g. Robellino (USA) 127 – Princess Zita 90 (Manado 130) [1994 61: 14g^5 14.4g^2 16.4m 16m^3 16d 16.2g 18m 1995 a16g^3 16m 14.9g 16.5g 14.1f* 14g^5 14g^5 16m^6 16m^5 16d 17.2m^5 16.1g Oct 3] good-topped gelding: has a markedly round action: poor handicapper: won (first time) selling race at Nottingham in July: stays 17.2f: acts on firm ground and dead: blinkered/visored once each, below form. *M. Blanshard* 43

ROMAN GOLD (IRE) 2 b.c. (Feb 6) Petorius 117 – Saffron (FR) (Fabulous Dancer (USA) 124) [1995 7f^5 6g 7f^4 6f^6 7m^4 8m^3 8.5s^2 a8g* a8g* Nov 20] IR 19,000Y: close-coupled colt: first living foal: dam French 12.5f winner: best form on equitrack in November when clear-cut winner of maiden at Lingfield and nursery at Southwell: will stay beyond 1m: probably acts on any turf going, yet to race on fibresand. *R. Hannon* 94

ROMAN REEL (USA) 4 ch.g. Sword Dance – Our Mimi (USA) (Believe It (USA)) [1994 70: 7d^4 8d^5 7m 7.6g^4 10m* 10.1m^3 12d^5 9g^5 9.7m^4 8.2d 1995 a8g^6 a9.4g a10g* a10g a10g^4 9.7g^3 8m 10m^4 8.1m* 10.1m^5 8f^2 a10g 9f^3 8f a10g Nov 2] lengthy, good-quartered gelding: good mover: fair handicapper: won at Lingfield in February and Chepstow (ladies race) in July: effective at 1m and should stay beyond 1¼m: acts on firm going and goes well on the all-weather, below form all starts on dead ground: effective from front or held up. *G. L. Moore* 71 a62

ROMANSH 6 b.g. Shernazar 131 – Romara 105 (Bold Lad (IRE) 133) [1994 –: 10m 8f 1995 8.3m 10m 10f Aug 23] tall, angular gelding: fair middle-distance handicapper for G. Wragg at 3 yrs: no worthwhile form since. *B. J. Meehan* –

ROMANTIC FOLLY 3 b.f. Thowra (FR) – Beaver Skin Hunter (Ballacashtal (CAN)) [1994 43: 6m 6g 6f 6.9m 7d 1995 10.8m Apr 17] sturdy filly: poor maiden: well beaten in blinkers final 2-y-o start: has joined K. Burke. *B. J. Meehan* –

ROMANZOF 3 ch.c. Kris 135 – Russian Countess (USA) 104 (Nureyev (USA) 131) [1994 84p: 7.1s^2 1995 8.5m* 10m^4 7g^2 7m* 8.1m^2 Aug 9] close-coupled, rather lightly-made colt: fluent mover: useful performer: won maiden at Beverley in April and rated stakes at Yarmouth (made all) in July: good second to Shemaq in minor event at Sandown following month: has form at 1¼m, but may prove best at 7f/1m: wears a crossed noseband: got loose going to post after reins broke in June, and taken down early last 2 starts: races prominently. *H. R. A. Cecil* 108

ROMIOS (IRE) 3 ch.c. Common Grounds 118 – Domino's Nurse 104 (Dom Racine (FR) 121) [1994 86: 5v* 6f^4 6m^3 7.3s^5 7s* 7.3v 7v 1995 10.4m^3 10m 10.5g* 10g 10v^2 Oct 7] sturdy, workmanlike colt: fairly useful handicapper: won rated stakes at Haydock in June: stays 10.5f well: acts on good to firm and heavy going: effective blinkered at 2 yrs, did not wear them at 3 yrs: sometimes bandaged near-fore: tends to pull hard and is a tricky ride: none too consistent and not one to trust implicitly. *P. F. I. Cole* 91

RON'S GEM 2 b.g. (Mar 15) Ron's Victory (USA) 129 – Crystal Gael 79 (Sparkler 130) [1995 5g^6 5f^6 Jul 13] 6,400Y: angular gelding: half-brother to 3-y-o Euro Singer (by Chief Singer) and several minor winners: dam 2-y-o 1m winner: well beaten in maidens in the summer: withdrawn after getting loose at start of seller at Southwell in November. *W. W. Haigh* –

RON'S SECRET 3 br.f. Efisio 120 – Primrose Bank 91 (Charlottown 127) [1994 62p: 6g^2 1995 7m^5 8m^3 8f* 8m^4 9f* 10m^3 10m 8.1d^4 8.1s* 8g^3 8m Oct 28] neat filly: has a round action: fairly useful handicapper: successful twice at Goodwood in the 92 summer and in 3-runner race at Haydock in October: stays 1¼m: acts on firm and soft going. *J. W. Payne*

ROODMAS (IRE) 4 b.f. Sharrood (USA) 124 – Taustaff 80 (Taufan (USA) 119) [1994 –: 8m^{6} 10m 12.1g 1995 a8g Jan 6] leggy filly: of little account: sold 620 gns Doncaster February Sales. *J. Parkes* –

ROOD MUSIC 4 ro.g. Sharrood (USA) 124 – Rose Music 86 (Luthier 126) [1994 59: 7.1g^{5} 7g^{4} 8g^{5} 6m^{4} 8.3g 7.1d 1995 8g 8.1m* 10.1f 7m 8.1g 9f 8.1s^{6} a8g* a9.4g^{2} a8g* Dec 1] lengthy, workmanlike gelding: modest handicapper on turf, game winner at Haydock in August: better on the all-weather, and won at Southwell in November and December: stays 9.4f: acts on good to firm ground and goes particularly well on fibresand: best efforts ridden prominently. *M. G. Meagher* 60 a78

ROOKERY GIRL 3 b.f. Pharly (FR) 130 – Persian Grey (Persepolis (FR) 127) [1994 NR 1995 a8g 7d 7g 7.3g 7m Jun 14] angular filly: first foal: dam unraced half-sister to fair sprinters Chain Shot and The Kings Daughter: modest maiden: likely to prove suited by 1m+. *D. Morris* 55

RORY 4 b.g. Dowsing (USA) 124 – Crymlyn 68 (Welsh Pageant 132) [1994 86: 7m^{3} 8g^{3} 8g* 8m^{2} 8g* 8d 9g* 8g^{2} 1995 9.9m^{4} 10m 9m^{5} 8g 8g^{5} 8.9g^{6} 8f^{6} Oct 24] leggy gelding: fairly useful handicapper: ideally suited by further than 1m (yet to race beyond 1¼m): acts on firm and dead ground: held up. *Mrs J. Cecil* 82

RORY JOHN 7 ch.g. Country Classic – Rasimareem (Golden Mallard 103) [1994 NR 1995 a7g a12g^{6} Feb 17] first foal: dam poor maiden: no sign of ability. *S. W. Campion* –

ROSA BONHEUR 3 b.f. Absalom 128 – Masirah 62 (Dunphy 124) [1994 60: 6g^{3} 5.9m^{4} 6.1m^{4} 8m 8d 6.9m^{3} 1995 6.1g 8m^{5} 7m^{2} 6m^{2} 6g* 6m^{5} 7m^{3} 6.1d 6m Oct 2] neat filly: modest performer: won claimer at Salisbury in July: best form at up to 7f (stiff tasks at 1m): acts on good to firm ground: often bandaged behind: usually races prominently. *M. A. Jarvis* 54

ROSCOMMON JOE (IRE) 5 b.g. Simply Great (FR) 122 – Kilvarnet 78 (Furry Glen 121) [1994 NR 1995 9.2g 10.9m 14.1f^{5} Jun 28] rangy gelding: little form on flat and has refused to race. *J. J. O'Neill* – §

ROSCOMMON LAD (IRE) 3 b.g. Groom Dancer (USA) 128 – Preoccupy (Habitat 134) [1994 –: 7s 10s 1995 10.3g 10.3m 10g 10m^{4} 12m^{3} Jul 28] workmanlike gelding: no form in maidens: tried visored: sold 700 gns Doncaster September Sales and gelded. *R. Hollinshead* –

ROSEATE LODGE 9 b.g. Habitat 134 – Elegant Tern (USA) 102 (Sea Bird II 145) [1994 66d: a8.5g a12g a10g^{5} 9.7v^{5} 8.3g* 10g^{5} 7g 7.1s 9.2g 8.3m^{3} 8g 9.7d^{6} 1995 a8g^{5} 7d* 6m^{4} 8.3m^{2} 8m^{2} 8g^{4} 8m^{5} 8.9m 8m^{5} 8.1d 7g 8g^{3} 7d 8g Sep 29] compact, workmanlike gelding: modest performer: won seller at Leicester in April: claimed out of K. Burke's stable £4,000 sixth start: below form afterwards: effective at 6f, and stays 1¼m: acts on any going: tried blinkered: bandaged: held up: sold 2,000 gns Doncaster October Sales. *N. Bycroft* 62 d

ROSEBERRY AVENUE (IRE) 2 b.c. (Mar 12) Sadler's Wells (USA) 132 – Lady's Bridge (USA) 81 (Sir Ivor 135) [1995 7g 10g^{6} 8f^{5} Oct 24] IR 58,000Y: good-topped colt: has scope: fifth foal: brother to fairly useful 8.5f to 11.7f winner Grand Master: dam 11f and 14.7f winner: fair form, though never on terms, in minor event won by Flyfisher and maiden won by Lady Carla at Leicester in October last 2 starts: will be suited by good test of stamina. *Lady Herries* 76 p

ROSEBERRY RAY (IRE) 3 b.c. High Estate 127 – Rained Off 83 (Welsh Pageant 132) [1994 –: 6m 1995 8.1g 8m^{3} 8.3f* 10.1g 8m Oct 2] sturdy colt: fairly useful form when justifying favouritism in handicap at Hamilton in August: disappointed in similar events at Yarmouth and Pontefract (blinkered) afterwards: should be suited by further than 1m: acts on firm going: sold 13,000 gns Newmarket Autumn Sales: sent to Malaysia. *G. Wragg* 81

ROSEBERRY TOPPING 6 gr.g. Nicholas Bill 125 – Habitab (Sovereign Path 125) [1994 63: a11g^{3} 10s^{3} 8d^{3} 8.3s 10m^{5} 10g^{2} 11g^{2} 9.9f^{4} 8s^{5} 10g^{2} 1995 a11g^{3} Dec 1] big, workmanlike gelding: modest maiden handicapper: stays 11f: probably acts on any going: usually edgy beforehand: rather headstrong, and sometimes finds little. *Mrs M. Reveley* 59

ROSEBUD 3 b.f. Indian Ridge 123 – Tiszta Sharok 81 (Song 132) [1994 67: 6g 5.2m² 5.3f² 5.2s⁴ 1995 6m* 7.3g³ 6g⁶ 8f* 8f* a8.5f³ 8.5d Oct 27] tall, leggy filly: fairly useful performer: won maiden at Pontefract in April (third-last start for R. Hannon) and allowance races at Del Mar in July and September: bandaged, below form afterwards: stays 1m: acts on firm going: raced on bute (first 2 starts only) and lasix in USA. *J. C. Servis, USA* — 80 +

ROSE CHIME (IRE) 3 b. or br.f. Tirol 127 – Repicado Rose (USA) (Repicado (CHI)) [1994 58: 5.2s³ 5d⁶ 5m⁶ 6.1f* a6g⁶ 7.1m* 7m 7.1m* 8g a8.5g 1995 a8.5g⁵ a7g⁵ a8g⁴ 9.2g⁶ 8g 7f⁵ a12g⁴ 11.1f⁶ a8g Nov 16] leggy, lengthy filly: poor form at best in 1995, leaving M. Johnston after fourth start: probably stays 1m: acts on good to firm and soft ground and fibresand. *J. L. Harris* — 45 a37

ROSE OF CADENCE 3 gr.f. Chief Singer 131 – Couleur de Rose (Kalaglow 132) [1994 61: 6m 6.1g² 7m 1995 8g⁴ Jun 10] big, lengthy filly: good mover: modest maiden: respectable effort in seller at Newmarket only start in 1995: probably stays 1m: has joined C. Egerton. *P. F. I. Cole* — 46 +

ROSE OF GLENN 4 b.f. Crofthall 110 – May Kells (Artaius (USA) 129) [1994 52: 12.5m 12f* a12g² 13.8g* 14.1m² a16g 13.8g* a12g³ a12g* a16g⁴ a13g⁶ a14g⁶ 1995 a16g³ a12g⁴ a16g³ a14g a14g⁴ 17.2f* 17.2f⁶ 16m 11.7h² 16d³ 14d a12g⁶ 16.4m a14g a14g* a13g⁶ Dec 19] leggy, sparely-made filly: modest performer: won selling handicap at Bath in July and claimer at Southwell in December: stays 17.2f: acts on hard ground, soft and all-weather surfaces: visored (below form) once at 2 yrs. *B. Palling* — 55 a51

ROSE OF SIBERIA (USA) 2 gr.f. (Apr 3) Siberian Express (USA) 125 – Exuberine (FR) 82 (Be My Guest (USA) 126) [1995 5g⁴ 7m⁵ 6.1m² 6m⁶ 10d⁴ 10m* Oct 19] 42,000Y: workmanlike filly: sister to Italian 1000 Guineas winner Ancestral Dancer and half-sister to 3 winners, including fairly useful 1993 2-y-o 7.5f winner Michelle Hicks (by Ballad Rock): dam 1m winner: fair form: won median auction maiden at Nottingham in October: stays 1¼m well: acts on good to firm and dead ground. *M. Bell* — 68

ROSES IN THE SNOW (IRE) 2 gr.f. (Mar 26) Be My Guest (USA) 126 – Desert Bluebell 83 (Kalaglow 132) [1995 5m² 5m⁴ 6m² 6g⁶ 5m² 6m² 7d 7f² Oct 24] 18,000Y: leggy, close-coupled filly: fluent mover: third foal: dam maiden who stayed 13.6f, daughter of Park Hill winner Idle Waters, dam of useful staying filly Shining Water: fairly useful maiden: creditable efforts in valuable sales race at Newmarket and minor event at Redcar (odds on, head second of 5 to La Volta) last 2 starts: will stay 1m: acts on firm and dead ground: consistent. *J. W. Hills* — 82

ROSE TINT (IRE) 2 b.f. (Apr 17) Salse (USA) 128 – Sally Rose 92 (Sallust 134) [1995 5.2g⁶ Jul 14] rather unfurnished filly: half-sister to several winners, including 3-y-o 1¼m winner Rosy Hue (by Shaadi) and 1¾m winner Mountain Bloom (by Shirley Heights): dam won 3 times from 1m to 10.2f: 12/1, 11 lengths sixth of 7 to Marjaana in maiden at Newbury, slowly into stride and never a factor: looked sure to improve. *Lord Huntingdon* — – p

ROSEVEAR (IRE) 3 b.f. Contract Law (USA) 108 – Caimanite 62 (Tap On Wood 130) [1994 48: 6g 7m⁶ 7d 8g 1995 a7g a8.5g⁴ 8.3g a8.5g³ a12g⁴ a12g Nov 13] leggy, workmanlike filly: has knee action: poor maiden handicapper: should stay beyond 8.5f: acts on fibresand and good to firm ground, well beaten on dead: tailed off in visor. *S. Mellor* — 49

ROSIE SWEETHEART (IRE) 3 b.f. Sadler's Wells (USA) 132 – Passamaquoddy (USA) (Drone) [1994 57p: 7d 1995 12m⁴ 12.1m⁴ 12.3m³ Jul 10] sturdy, attractive filly: fair maiden: stays 1½m: acts on good to firm ground: tends to hang and carry head awkwardly. *H. R. A. Cecil* — 71

ROSINA'S FOLLY 4 b.f. Tina's Pet 121 – Rosie Dickins 59 (Blue Cashmere 129) [1994 –: 6m 7g 6f 7g⁶ a7g a5s 1995 a7g² a7g⁵ a7g⁶ a11g a7g a8g 7d 8m 7m⁶ 10m⁶ 10g⁵ 8f a7g Jul 21] leggy filly: modest maiden, clearly best effort in 1995 on reappearance: may be best at up to 1¼m: acts on fibresand: blinkered (well beaten) fifth 4-y-o start: sent to Pakistan. *J. L. Harris* — 56 d

ROSSCOYNE 5 b.m. Ardross 134 – Banking Coyne 76 (Deep Diver 134) [1994 –: 12d 10d 14.4g⁶ 11.6m 11.6f 1995 11.9m a16g May 27] compact mare: no worthwhile form since 1993: has joined K. Morgan. *J. Ffitch-Heyes* — –

ROSSEL (USA) 2 b.c. (May 6) Blushing John (USA) 120 – Northern Aspen (USA) 120 (Northern Dancer) [1995 7g 8f^5 Oct 25] rangy colt: third foal (all by Blushing John): dam, winner at up to 1¼m, closely related to very smart French 1m to 10.5f winner Elle Seule (dam of Mehthaaf) and half-sister to 4 Grade 1/Group 1 winners, including July Cup winner Hamas and Preakness Stakes winner Timber Country: similar form in maidens won by Astor Place at Newmarket and Bright Water at Yarmouth: looks sort to do better in time. *M. R. Stoute* 65 p

ROSSINI BLUE 4 ch.g. Music Boy 124 – Miss Rossi (Artaius (USA) 129) [1994 69: 6f^4 6f 5.1f^2 6f^4 1995 a6g a7g a5g^4 5m^2 7m 7.6m^3 7m 7g a7g 7f 6m^6 7g^3 6m* 6m 6m 6d^3 7g^3 7d^2 7g 6d 7m^4 Oct 20] lengthy, angular gelding: fair handicapper: claimed out of R. Hannon's stable £6,000 on reappearance, out of A. Bailey's stable £4,000 twelfth start: won maiden event at Ripon in July on first outing for new connections: effective at 6f to 7.6f: probably acts on any ground: no improvement in blinkers: sometimes carries head awkwardly: sold 5,600 gns Newmarket Autumn Sales: sent to Italy. *Mrs J. R. Ramsden* 75 a61

ROSTAQ 2 b.c. (Feb 22) Keen 116 – American Beauty 74 (Mill Reef (USA) 141) [1995 7g^3 7m^2 Aug 7] 8,500Y: angular colt: half-brother to several winners, including smart French 7f to 9f winner Stephany's Dream (by Reform) and 1½m winner Candane (by Danehill): dam, second twice over 1¼m, daughter of Oaks second West Side Story: similar form when placed in maiden auctions at Leicester and Thirsk: will stay 1¼m. *D. J. G. Murray Smith* 68

ROSY HUE (IRE) 3 b.f. Shaadi (USA) 126 – Sally Rose 92 (Sallust 134) [1994 63p: 7d 1995 9g^3 10.4m^3 8.1d^3 10g* 10.5d Oct 11] tall filly: fair form: made all in maiden at Goodwood in September, holding on by short head: pulled hard and didn't see race out in handicap at Haydock on only subsequent start: stays 1¼m: acts on dead going, disappointing only start on top-of-the-ground: sold 18,000 gns Newmarket December Sales. *R. Charlton* 74

ROSY LYDGATE 4 br.f. Last Tycoon 131 – Sing Softly 112 (Luthier 126) [1994 53: 10.2g 9.9g^4 9m 7g^6 7g^6 7.1s^5 8g 1995 a8g Jan 6] leggy, lightly-made filly: modest maiden: well beaten only 4-y-o start: should stay beyond 1¼m. *S. E. Kettlewell* –

ROTHERFIELD PARK (IRE) 3 b.f. High Estate 127 – Alriyaah 73 (Shareef Dancer (USA) 135) [1994 66d: 5g^4 5g^{*dis} 6m 6g 5d 6v a5g* a5g^4 a6g^5 a6g^3 1995 a6g^5 a6g a6g^4 6m a5g 5m 5d 6m a6g Nov 20] neat filly: poor handicapper at best in 1995: stays 6f: acts on the all-weather: inconsistent. *C. Smith* 40

ROTHLEY IMP (IRE) 2 b.f. (Apr 19) Mac's Imp (USA) 116 – Valediction 71 (Town Crier 119) [1995 5m 6g 7g^5 7m^6 6m^2 5m^2 6d Sep 18] 10,000 2-y-o: tall, leggy filly: has scope: half-sister to 1½m winner Fairy Wisher (by Fairy King) and 1987 Irish 2-y-o 6f winner Classic Dilemma (by Sandhurst Prince): dam none-too-genuine middle-distance maiden: modest maiden: second in sellers at Leicester in August: stays 6f: rather headstrong early in career. *J. Wharton* 55

ROUFONTAINE 4 gr.f. Rousillon (USA) 133 – Bellifontaine (FR) (Bellypha 130) [1994 NR 1995 10m^2 10g 10m^5 10.2m^5 12m^5 12f^4 Aug 9] workmanlike filly: fourth foal: half-sister to 2 winners by Law Society, notably useful 1½m winner Close Friend: dam French 1m winner: won NH Flat race over 13f at Market Rasen in March: fair form on flat: unlikely to stay much beyond 1½m: tried blinkered: sometimes finds little: not one to rely on. *W. R. Muir* 72 §

ROUGE RANCON (USA) 2 b.f. (Mar 21) Red Ransom (USA) – Lady O'Lyph (Lyphard (USA) 132) [1995 6g* 7g^5 8d^4 Sep 24] $22,000F, $45,000Y: tall, good-topped filly: has plenty of scope: fourth foal: half-sister to a minor winner in USA by Pancho Villa: dam unraced: heavily-backed favourite, won maiden at Newmarket in promising fashion by 2½ lengths: didn't really make improvement expected, 2 lengths fifth to Priory Belle in Moyglare Stud Stakes at the Curragh in September then 11 lengths fourth of 6, taking very keen hold, to Bosra Sham in Fillies' Mile at Ascot: will stay 1m: bandaged near-hind on debut. *P. F. I. Cole* 98

ROUSHAN 2 ch.c. (Feb 3) Anshan 119 – Fleur Rouge 71 (Pharly (FR) 130) [1995 6g Sep 8] 18,000Y: leggy colt: fourth living foal: half-brother to fair 4-y-o 7f/1m performer Red Valerian (by Robellino) and fair middle-distance stayer Addicted To Love (by Touching Wood): dam, 2-y-o 6f winner, well beaten at 3 yrs: 10/1, chased leaders over 4f when tenth of 15 in maiden at Goodwood: will stay beyond 6f: should improve: has joined J. O'Shea. *K. McAuliffe* – p

ROUSITTO 7 ch.g. Rousillon (USA) 133 – Helenetta 97 (Troy 137) [1994 44, a56: a11g^4 a12g^5 a12g^2 a12g^2 a14g a12g* a14g^3 a12g^3 12.4g^6 a12g^3 12m^4 a14.8g* 12g^3 16.5m a12g a12g a12g^4 1995 a11g* a12g^3 a11g^2 a12g^5 a12g^4 a14g^6 a12g^2 Dec 12] sparely-made gelding: modest performer: won seller at Southwell in January: effective at 1¼m, and stays 14.8f (unlikely to be suited by any further): goes well on the all-weather and used to act on any turf going: sometimes looks none too keen: usually held up. *R. Hollinshead* – a63

ROUSSI (USA) 3 b.c. Nureyev (USA) 131 – Iva Reputation (USA) (Sir Ivor 135) [1994 NR 1995 10g^3 11.9d 10d^4 Oct 19] good-bodied colt: closely related to smart 4-y-o 7f to 13.4f winner Zilzal Zamaan (by Zilzal) and half-brother to several winners, including prolific Canadian stakes winner Triple Wow (by Coastal): dam never ran: seems just a fair maiden: should stay beyond 1¼m: sold (M. Stoute to D. Nicholls) 10,000 gns Newmarket Autumn Sales. *M. R. Stoute* 69

ROVING MINSTREL 4 ch.c. Cree Song 99 – Klairove 74 (Averof 123) [1994 85: a6g^4 5.1v* 5g^3 5.1m^6 5g^2 6f 5m^2 6m^5 6m^2 5f 5m 6g* 7.1d^2 6d^4 1995 8g* 8g 7m 7.9g 7m^2 8g^4 7.6m 8d^2 9g Sep 30] good-topped colt: fairly useful handicapper: won 23-runner £46,300 William Hill Lincoln at Doncaster in March by short head from Moving Arrow: good efforts afterwards when in frame: stays 1m: twice below form on very firm ground, acts on any other, including fibresand: races close up: game and genuine. *B. A. McMahon* 92

ROWHOME 2 b.g. (Jun 4) Colmore Row 111 – Stride Home 78 (Absalom 128) [1995 5.1g^6 a6g^4 7f a7g^4 a7g^6 Jul 17] small, light-framed gelding: first foal: dam stayed 1½m: seems of little account. *M. R. Channon* –

ROWLANDSONS CHARM (IRE) 2 b.f. (Apr 27) Fayruz 116 – Magic Gold (Sallust 134) [1995 5g^3 6m 5m 5m 6m^3 5g 6.9s 6.9g a7g^6 a7g^2 a7g^3 Dec 14] 5,400 2-y-o: sturdy, workmanlike filly: carries condition: fourth foal: dam Irish 1¼m 60 a64

William Hill Lincoln Handicap, Doncaster—Roving Minstrel's one win of 1995 is a big one; at 33/1, he just holds on from No. 9 Moving Arrow

winner: modest maiden: will stay 1m: acts on good to firm ground (no form on soft) and equitrack: visored last 4 starts. *G. L. Moore*

ROWLANDSONS LINKS 2 b.c. (Apr 23) Picea 99 – Charlotte Piaf (Morston (FR) 125) [1995 7.6d 7g Sep 29] 400Y: small, light-framed colt: third foal: dam unraced: well beaten in maiden at Lingfield and seller at Goodwood: sold 600 gns Newmarket Autumn Sales: sent to Holland. *B. J. Meehan* –

ROWLANDSONS SILVER (FR) 3 b.g. Reprimand 122 – African Dash 76 (African Sky 124) [1994 62: 6m 6g^6 6d^3 a8g^5 7g 8d a6g^4 a7g^5 1995 a7g^5 a7g^5 a10g^5 a10g 8.5m^6 Jul 26] leggy, unfurnished gelding: inconsistent maiden: stays 1m: below form visored and blinkered. *D. J. G. Murray Smith* –

ROWLANDSONS STUD (IRE) 2 b. or br.c. (Mar 25) Distinctly North (USA) 115 – Be My Million (Taufan (USA) 119) [1995 6m^5 6m a6g a5g^4 Dec 18] IR 2,400F: first foal: dam poor Irish maiden: form only in maiden and claimer on Lingfield equitrack last 2 starts: will probably stay 7f. *G. L. Moore* – a58 +

ROXANE (IRE) 2 b.f. (Mar 28) Cyrano de Bergerac 120 – Janet Oliphant 49 (Red Sunset 120) [1995 a7g Nov 27] IR 6,000Y, 4,200 2-y-o: first foal: dam, Irish 1m winner, half-sister to high-class middle-distance performer Amyndas: tailed off in maiden auction at Wolverhampton, pulling hard. *A. Bailey* –

ROXANIAN (IRE) 4 b.g. Cyrano de Bergerac 120 – Sassanian (Sassafras (FR) 135) [1994 89d: 6f^2 6m 6g^4 7m 6d 6d 5g 1995 5g Sep 12] sturdy, attractive gelding: fairly useful handicapper on his day at 3 yrs: sold out of M. Heaton-Ellis' yard only 2,400 gns Newmarket July Sales and showed nothing on only start in 1995: stays 6f: acts on firm ground, well beaten on heavy: usually makes running: often taken last to post: tends to wander: unreliable: has joined Gerard Cully in Ireland. *M. Johnston* –

ROXY RIVER 6 ch.m. Ardross 134 – Royal Yacht (USA) 65 (Riverman (USA) 131) [1994 38: 13f* 14.1f^4 12.3m^4 1995 12m 16.2g^3 15.1f Jul 28] leggy mare: worthwhile form on flat only when winning handicap at Hamilton in May 1994: may stay 2m: acts on firm ground: won handicap hurdle in August. *J. L. Spearing* –

ROYAL ABJAR (USA) 4 ch.c. Gone West (USA) – Encorelle (FR) (Arctic Tern (USA) 126) [1994 121: 8g* 7.7d* 8m* 8m^6 8m^{*dis} 8g* 8g^3 1995 8.5v* 8m^2 Jul 9] big, good-topped colt: very smart performer, but seen out only twice in 1995: won minor event at Dusseldorf in June: neck second of 16 to Kill The Crab (who rec. 13 lb more than w.f.a) in Group 2 event at Hoppegarten, caught close home: raced only at around 1m, should have been effective over shorter: acted on good to firm and heavy ground: usually held up, and had good turn of foot: tended to get on toes and sweat: retired to Gestut Brummerhof for 9,000 DM. *A. Wohler, Germany* 118

ROYAL ACCLAIM 10 ch.g. Tender King 123 – Glimmer 58 (Hot Spark 126) [1994 –§, a46§: a8.5g^4 a8.5g^2 a8.5g^2 a9.4g^4 a8g a8g a8.5g 1995 a8.5g^5 a8.5g^4 a11g^5 a8g^5 a9.4g^3 a8g^5 10.3g 9.7g 10g a9.4g Aug 19] sturdy gelding: carries condition: poor handicapper: stays 11f: acts on all-weather surfaces, probably on any turf going: tried blinkered, nearly always visored: ridden by apprentice/amateur in 1995: often gets behind: none too resolute. *J. M. Bradley* – § a46 §

ROYAL ADDICTION (IRE) 3 b.g. Prince Rupert (FR) 121 – Opium Queen 82 (King's Troop 118) [1994 NR 1995 a8g a8g 12m Jul 5] seventh foal: half-brother to a 5f winner in Ireland by Miami Springs and a winner at up to 1¼m in Hong Kong by Skyliner: dam 1m winner: no sign of ability: trained first 2 starts by P. Blockley: sold 1,200 gns Doncaster August Sales. *Mrs M. Reveley* –

ROYAL APPLAUSE 2 b.c. (Feb 24) Waajib 121 – Flying Melody (Auction Ring (USA) 123) [1995 5.2g* 6m* 6m* 6g* Sep 28] 123 p

Will he stay a mile? The unbeaten Royal Applause's run in the Middle Park Stakes on the last of his four starts as a two-year-old was the best seen in the race for a long time, form that, if reproduced, would give him a chance second only to Alhaarth in the Two Thousand Guineas. But afterwards his trainer was quoted as saying: 'Walter believes Royal Applause will get further than six furlongs next year, but I would have to be very hesistant about that and he could even be kept to six furlongs in 1996 .... personally I wouldn't back him for the Guineas. I would have to be very reserved about him getting a mile'. Walter Swinburn's opinion will be based to some extent on the strength of his mount's finish both at Newmarket and at Royal Ascot in the Coventry Stakes. On the other hand Royal Applause has speed to

Coventry Stakes, Royal Ascot—Royal Applause makes all from Russian Revival (spotted cap), South Salem (left), Tagula and eight other previous winners

burn—he got the better of Kahir Almaydan by halfway in the Middle Park—and his speedy half-sister Lyric Fantasy didn't quite last home in the One Thousand Guineas. Our view is that Royal Applause has an outside chance of staying, therefore it would be a shame not to run him in the Guineas; the sprint championship can wait. It is also our view that he will prove a better sprinter than miler and could well be the next champion. A well-made colt, he looks sure to train on, and do better than his half-sister did.

Royal Applause was one of twelve winners in a field of thirteen for the Coventry Stakes, following a convincing debut in a Newbury maiden at the end of

Scottish Equitable Gimcrack Stakes, York—a scare for odds-on backers as Royal Applause has just a head to spare over Tumbleweed Ridge (centre); Take A Left is third

May. The field at Ascot split in to two, Royal Applause and seven others including joint-favourite Russian Revival on the far side; the rest, including the other joint-favourite Allied Forces, on the stand side. Royal Applause led the race throughout and responded very strongly in the last furlong to fend off Russian Revival and South Salem by two lengths. Tagula led the other group home, in fourth overall. Next time out Royal Applause collected another prestigious two-year-old race, the Scottish Equitable Gimcrack Stakes at York in August, and yet he was sent off only second favourite, to the odds on Kahir Almaydan, in the Middle Park. This was to some extent because he made hard work of it in the end at York. Uncharacteristically a little on edge in the stalls there, he broke well and led the small field after two furlongs; he was travelling on the bridle just after halfway but found himself fully stretched from the distance by Tumbleweed Ridge, who never quite managed to head him.

The photo at York went Royal Applause's way by a head. In contrast Kahir Almaydan won his last race before Newmarket, the Mill Reef Stakes, by six lengths; the one before that by nine, on both occasions allowed to bowl along in front. As usual the Middle Park attracted few runners. Completing the smallest field since 1987—as small a field as there had been since 1971—were Woodborough, Lucky Lionel and Resounder. Woodborough had been running consistently well in pattern races in Ireland and France; Lucky Lionel had won the Norfolk Stakes and the Prix Robert Papin; Resounder had looked clear second-best to Kahir Almaydan in the Mill Reef until tiring in the last fifty yards. The race got under way as anticipated with Kahir Almaydan jumping out quickly and attempting to dominate. But there was a surprise in store: Swinburn sent Royal Applause up to take him on. Upsides, Royal Applause looked much the better horse. Having won that battle by halfway, he wasn't seriously challenged again and he stormed clear when shaken up, cracked with the whip, a furlong and a half out. At the line he had four lengths to spare over Woodborough who finished better than Kahir Almaydan. Royal Applause became the first to achieve the Coventry Stakes, Gimcrack and Middle Park treble since Crocket in 1962, and only the second in all. Crocket topped the Free Handicap in his day. Through Woodborough, a case can be made for Royal Applause to have had top weight in 1995, but the style of Alhaarth's victory in the Dewhurst is enough to sway it.

Royal Applause (b.c. Feb 24, 1993)	Waajib (b 1983)	Try My Best (b 1975)	Northern Dancer
			Sex Appeal
		Coryana (b 1976)	Sassafras
			Rosolini
	Flying Melody (b 1979)	Auction Ring (b 1972)	Bold Bidder
			Hooplah
		Whispering Star (ch 1963)	Sound Track
			Peggy West

A case can be argued from the pedigree that Royal Applause ought to get a mile—if he takes after his sire, the now-exported Waajib, or his year-older half-brother Lucayan Cay (by Al Hareb). But Flying Melody's other winning offspring, Mere Melody (by Dunphy), Flying Monarch (by Tender King) and, above all, Lyric Fantasy (by Tate Gallery) were sprinters. And the three mares on the bottom line of

Middle Park Stakes, Newmarket—
Royal Applause storms clear from Woodborough (left) and Kahir Almaydan (right)

the pedigree were all best over five or six furlongs; one of them, Peggy West, was a half-sister to the tip-top sprinter Pappa Fourway. Further details of the family can be found in Lyric Fantasy's entry in *Racehorses of 1992*. As a result of Lyric Fantasy's performances that year—she won the Nunthorpe Stakes, Queen Mary Stakes and National Stakes—the Gainsborough Stud bought the mare Flying Melody privately, carrying, as it turned out, Royal Applause. There is a colt by Sadler's Wells coming along who could give the breeding pundits a headache so far as stamina potential is concerned, although by then more should be known about Royal Applause. *B. W. Hills*

ROYAL BALLERINA (IRE) 5 b.m. Sadler's Wells (USA) 132 – Fremanche 111 (FR) (Jim French (USA)) [1994 111: 12s* 11.5v* 12m 12f^5 10g^2 10.5m^5 11d* 12.5d^4 11d* 12g^5 1995 12g^5 10g^4 12m^4 11.9m^4 12s 9d* 12d^2 Oct 15] big, lengthy, attractive mare: smart performer: pulled up in Germany (jockey reported she gurgled) fifth start: back to form when winning listed event at the Curragh then staying-on short-head second of 8 to Court of Honour in Gran Premio del Jockey Club Italiano at Milan, both in October: effective at 9f (at least on a soft surface) and would probably have stayed 1¾m: acted on good to firm ground and heavy: blinkered twice, including penultimate start: game: visits Kris. *M. Kauntze, Ireland*

ROYAL CANASKA 2 ch.c. (Mar 28) Royal Academy (USA) 130 – North 81 p Telstar 104 (Sallust 134) [1995 7f^3 Oct 25] 30,000Y: compact colt: fifth foal: half-brother to 3-y-o The Aspecto Girl (by Alzao) and 7f winner Canaska Star (by Doyoun): dam Irish 6f (at 2 yrs) and 9f winner: 4/1, length third of 10 to Mawjud in maiden at Yarmouth, taking good hold in prominent position, challenging over 1f out and no extra towards finish: will stay further than 7f: sure to improve and win a race. *D. R. Loder*

ROYAL CARLTON (IRE) 3 b.g. Mulhollande (USA) 107 – Saintly Angel 87 – (So Blessed 130) [1994 5d 5d^6 8d^3 6g^6 5g^3 6d 1995 6f^6 5.2g 5m 5d 7m Oct 28] IR 20,000Y: half-brother to several winners, including useful 1983 sprinting 2-y-o African Abandon (by African Sky) and fair 7f and 1m performer Britannia Bell (by Pitskelly): dam lightly-raced 2-y-o 5f winner: modest maiden (rated 62) at 2 yrs for D. K. Weld: little worthwhile form in handicaps here: stays 1m: acts on dead going, probably on good to firm. *R. Akehurst*

ROYAL CEILIDH (IRE) 2 b.f. (Apr 11) Prince Rupert (FR) 121 – Isa (Dance 74 In Time (CAN)) [1995 5g* 5d^6 6m^3 7m^5 8g 7f* Oct 14] 10,000 2-y-o: big, strong, lengthy filly: has a quick action: half-sister to several winners, including prolific 1988 2-y-o sprint winner Time To Go Home (by Day Is Done), listed winner at 3 yrs in Germany, and fair sprinter Fairy Fay (by Fayruz): dam never ran: fair form: won maiden at Newcastle in May and nursery at Catterick in October: stays 7f: races keenly. *Denys Smith*

ROYAL CIRCLE 3 b.f. Sadler's Wells (USA) 132 – Queen Midas 119 (Glint of 95 Gold 128) [1994 NR 1995 11m^2 10g* 13.3m^6 12d^4 12v^4 12m^5 Nov 4] big, lengthy filly: powerful mover: third foal: dam 1½m winner out of half-sister to Owen Dudley and Abwah: useful performer: won maiden at Newmarket in July: creditable efforts in pattern/listed races in 3 of 4 subsequent starts: probably stays 13.3f: acts on good to firm ground, probably on heavy: stays in training. *R. Charlton*

ROYAL CIRCUS 6 b.g. Kris 135 – Circus Ring 122 (High Top 131) [1994 42, 40 a37: 14.1d^5 12.1g^2 a14.8g 12.1f* 12d* 11.1m^6 15.1f 12.1f* 12.1m^4 a13g a13g^5 1995 a16g a13g* a12g^2 a12g^4 a13g^4 a13g* a12g a13g^2 12g 13f^2 13f 12.1m^5 11.1f Jul 7] workmanlike gelding: trained by J. O'Shea for flat campaign, by P. Hiatt most NH runs: poor handicapper: won at Lingfield in January and (amateurs event) February: effective at 1½m and 1¾m: acts on firm and dead ground and equitrack: game front runner. *J. G. M. O'Shea*

ROYAL CITIZEN (IRE) 6 b.g. Caerleon (USA) 132 – Taking Steps 100 (Gay – Fandango (USA) 132) [1994 61: a12g* a11g^3 a12g^2 a12g^3 a11g 10g^5 10g^2 10g 10g a65 8.3f^4 1995 a12g^2 a11g^2 a12g^5 a14.8g* a14.8g* a14g^2 a16.2g^5 14.1m May 2] sturdy gelding: fair performer: won 2 claimers at Wolverhampton in February: stays 14.8f: acts on fibresand, suited by a sound surface on turf: effective blinkered/visored or not (no headgear in 1995): normally held up. *J. F. Bottomley*

ROYAL COLLEGE (IRE) 3 b.c. Sadler's Wells (USA) 132 – Lady Capulet – (USA) 116 (Sir Ivor 135) [1994 72p: 7g^5 1995 10.2m 10f^3 May 11] rather leggy colt:

shaped well only 2-y-o start, but well below form in 1995: bred to stay 1¼m: sold 13,000 gns Newmarket July Sales: sent to Bahrain. *P. F. I. Cole*

ROYAL COMEDIAN 6 gr.m. Jester 119 – Royal Huntress (Royal Avenue 123) [1994 47: 7g a8g 7m 7.6g* 7g 7g 7.1s^4 1995 a6g 7m* a7g 7m^3 7.6m^4 7m 8g^5 7g 7.1s 8f Oct 24] leggy mare: poor handicapper: won amateurs race at Ayr in May: well below form last 5 starts: stays 7.6f: acts on good to firm and soft going, no worthwhile form on fibresand: takes good hold: none too consistent. *B. W. Murray* — 47 d a–

ROYAL DANCER 3 ch.f. Dancing Dissident (USA) 119 – Aquarula 88 (Dominion 123) [1994 39: 7s 6m 5s^6 a5g^6 a5g 1995 a7g Nov 2] small filly: poor sprint maiden. *R. J. Weaver* — –

ROYAL DIVERSION (IRE) 2 b.f. (Mar 11) Marju (IRE) 127 – Royal Recreation (USA) (His Majesty (USA)) [1995 6s^6 7g^2 Oct 23] 20,000Y: unfurnished filly: first foal: dam Irish maiden, stayed 2m: better effort in Lingfield maidens (slowly away on debut) when 2 lengths second of 13, keeping on well, to comfortable winner Tsarnista, first home on unfavoured stand side: will improve again, particularly at 1m+. *J. L. Dunlop* — 73 p

ROYAL DOME (IRE) 3 b.g. Salt Dome (USA) – Brook's Dilemma 80 (Known Fact (USA) 135) [1994 –: 5m^6 1995 7.1g^3 a6g^5 6g 5f^2 5f^4 5.1m* 5h^2 5g* 5g^2 5m* Oct 4] good-quartered gelding: made into a fair handicapper, winning at Nottingham in August, Pontefract in September and York (22-runner race, drifted markedly left but held Chadwell Hall by a head) in October: easily best form at 5f: has raced only on a sound surface on turf: visored (ran creditably) fifth 3-y-o start: may well do better still in 1996. *Martyn Wane* — 75 p

ROYALE FIGURINE (IRE) 4 ch.f. Dominion Royale 112 – Cree's Figurine 63 (Creetown 123) [1994 93: 5s^5 5.1m* 6m 6f 5m 5m 5.6g 5.2s^4 5g 5m^2 5s 1995 5.2m* 5.1m^6 5g^3 6f 5g^4 6m^2 6g* 6m* 5f^2 6m^3 Nov 4] quite attractive filly: useful handicapper: better than ever in 1995, winning rated stakes at Newbury in April, 29-runner Ladbroke (Ayr) Gold Cup (beat No Extras a neck) in September and 12-runner listed race at Newmarket (in good style by 1¼ lengths from Hello Mister) in October: effective at 5f and 6f: acts on firm and soft ground: usually held up: genuine. *M. J. Fetherston-Godley* — 106

ROYAL EXPOSE (USA) 2 ch.c. (Mar 24) Unzipped (USA) – Royal Tasha (USA) (Northern Prospect (USA)) [1995 8g Sep 8] $27,000Y: strong, workmanlike — – p

Ladbroke (Ayr) Gold Cup (Handicap)—Royale Figurine narrowly from No Extras (right) and Patto (obscured)

colt: fifth foal: closely related to 3 winners in USA by Naked Sky, notably smart 1994 2-y-o Sea Emperor, winner at up to 8.5f: dam minor stakes winner in USA at 2 and 3 yrs: sire (by Naked Sky) useful sprinting juvenile: 20/1, burly and green, slowly away and always behind in 17-runner maiden at Doncaster: looks capable of better. *R. Hannon*

ROYAL EXPRESSION 3 b.g. Sylvan Express 117 – Edwins' Princess 75 (Owen Dudley 121) [1994 60: 5s^6 6f^6 7f^5 7m^3 8g 8s 7g^2 1995 11.1g^3 12g^4 11.1f* 12.3m^2 10.9g^5 Jul 15] tall, leggy gelding: has a round action: modest performer: made all in maiden at Hamilton in June: stays 12.3f, should stay 1¾m: blinkered (ran well) final 2-y-o start: won juvenile hurdle in August. *Mrs M. Reveley* 58

ROYAL HILL 4 b.g. Danehill (USA) 126 – Royal Caprice (USA) (Swaps) [1994 84: a7g* 8.1s^3 8g^3 7.1g^4 8s 8m^2 1995 8g^5 8g 7m^2 8m 8f* 8f a9f^6 8d^3 Dec 16] tall, leggy gelding: fairly useful handicapper: better than ever in 4 top races here in 1995, notably when staying on neck second of 25 to Jawaal (pair clear) in Victoria Cup at Ascot on penultimate start for Lord Huntingdon: racing on lasix and bute, won allowance race at Del Mar in August: stays 1m: acts on firm and soft ground: held up/ tracks leaders. *R. B. Hess, USA* 90

ROYAL JADE 2 b.f. (Mar 16) Last Tycoon 131 – Imperial Jade 105 (Lochnager 132) [1995 6f^3 Aug 5] sturdy, good-quartered filly: has scope: sixth foal: sister to 6f winner Taalif and half-sister to several winners, including 3-y-o 7f winner Hawaash (by Royal Academy) and useful 4-y-o 5f to 7f performer Averti (by Warning): dam sprinting sister to smart sprinter Reesh: 5/1, 2¾ lengths third of 5 to Najiya in maiden at Haydock, keeping on well under hands and heels: sure to improve. *B. W. Hills* 82 p

ROYAL MARK (IRE) 2 b.c. (Mar 29) Fairy King (USA) – Take Your Mark (USA) (Round Table) [1995 6m^3 7g* 7m* 7m^2 7d Sep 26] good-topped colt: progressed well physically: closely related to several winners, notably 2000 Guineas second Charmer (by Be My Guest), later winner at up to 13.3f, and half-brother to 3-y-o Callonescy (by Royal Academy) and several winners: dam lightly-raced half-sister to dam of Irish St Leger winner Leading Counsel: progressive form: won maiden at Ayr in July and nursery at Newmarket in August: unlucky second in nursery at Ascot on penultimate start then ran well (though never dangerous) when mid-division in 30-runner valuable sales race at Newmarket month later: will stay 1m. *J. W. Watts* 84

ROYAL ODDSOX 2 ch.c. (Feb 8) Dominion Royale 112 – Kevin's Pet (Petorius 117) [1995 a7g Sep 4] first reported living foal: dam no sign of ability: 33/1, showed nothing in maiden at Southwell. *N. P. Littmoden* –

ROYAL PHILOSOPHER 3 b.c. Faustus (USA) 118 – Princess Lucy 42 (Local Suitor (USA) 128) [1994 105: 6m 7.5g^3 8.2d^4 8s* 8v^5 1995 8m^3 8.5m 8g^2 9d Sep 16] big, strong colt: useful performer: 3¾ lengths third to Peace Envoy in listed event at Kempton on reappearance: below form afterwards: stays 1m: acts on heavy and good to firm ground: takes keen hold, and seems suited by front-running tactics. *K. McAuliffe* 99

ROYAL PRINT (IRE) 6 ch.g. Kings Lake (USA) 133 – Reprint 99 (Kampala 120) [1994 44: a16.2g^2 a16.2g^4 a14g 12.5m^5 1995 a16.2g Jan 7] sturdy gelding: poor staying maiden on flat. *W. R. Muir* –

ROYAL RABBIT 3 b.g. Prince Daniel (USA) – Lirchur 35 (Lir 82) [1994 47: 5d 6d 7m a8.5g^6 1995 a10g^6 12g* 12m^4 a14.8g^5 a12g 14d^3 11.6m 11.9f^2 13.8g^4 Sep 16] close-coupled gelding: modest performer: won claiming handicap at Salisbury in May: seems to stay 13.8f: acts on firm ground: visored (no improvement) final 2-y-o start: has joined C. Nash. *G. L. Moore* 50

ROYAL RAPPORT 2 ch.g. (Feb 1) Rich Charlie 117 – Miss Camellia 70 (Sonnen Gold 121) [1995 5m 5m^5 6g 7.5d 6g Sep 22] 7,200F, 8,200Y: compact gelding: second foal: half-brother to a poor animal: dam won from 1m (at 2 yrs) to 13.8f: modest form in maidens second and third starts: well beaten in blinkers and visor last 2 outings. *B. A. McMahon* 55 +

ROYAL REBUKE 3 br.f. Reprimand 122 – Noble Lustre (USA) 71 (Lyphard's Wish (FR) 124) [1994 71: 6g^2 6m^5 7s^6 6.9m^5 6.1d^2 1995 7m* 7g^3 8f^2 7.6m^4 8f^5 8.5f^2 8.5f^2 8f* 8g* Dec 16] leggy, useful-looking filly: useful handicapper: won £14,600 event at Newmarket in May: creditable efforts all 4 subsequent starts for R. Charlton: 95 +

took well to racing in USA, winning allowance race and $53,000 event at Fair Grounds in December: effective at 7f and stays 8.5f: acts on firm ground: raced on lasix last 3 starts: genuine and consistent. *T. Amoss, USA*

ROYAL RIGGER **35** 2 gr.f. (May 22) Reprimand 122 – Overdraft (Bustino 136) [1995 5g^{5} 5g a5g^{3} 10d Sep 19] 1,000Y: neat filly: has a round action: third foal: half-sister to 3-y-o Cranbrook Kate (by Damister) and Irish 1½m winner Musical Banker (by Music Boy): dam barely stayed 1¾m: poor form in varied company: very slowly away and looked bit reluctant after 4½-month absence last time. *C. Smith*

ROYAL ROMANCE **– §** 2 b.f. (Apr 2) Crowning Honors (CAN) – Bali Sunset 67 (Balidar 133) [1995 7m 7m Jul 28] leggy filly: second foal: half-sister to 3-y-o Sunshine Belle (by Belfort): dam sprinter: withdrawn after proving very unruly in preliminaries before seller at Catterick in July: slowly away when last of 14 in similar event there later in month then swerved and unseated rider leaving stalls at Thirsk: evidently very temperamental. *G. M. Moore*

ROYAL SCIMITAR (USA) **97** 3 ch.c. Diesis 133 – Princess of Man 104 (Green God 128) [1994 101: 8m^{3} 8m^{3} 10d^{2} 1995 12f^{2} 12m* 12.3m^{6} 12m 11.8m^{3} 11.9m^{4} 12m 12d Nov 19] close-coupled, lightly-made colt: good walker and mover: useful performer: landed the odds in maiden at Carlisle in April: ran at least respectably (including in Chester Vase and Derby Italiano) afterwards, except (blinkered first time) final start: will stay 1¾m: acts on firm and dead ground: bandaged behind in 1995: lacks turn of foot and may prove suited by forcing tactics: game and consistent. *P. F. I. Cole*

ROYAL SOLO (IRE) **113** 3 b.c. Sadler's Wells (USA) 132 – Sharp Castan 101 (Sharpen Up 127) [1994 NR 1995 7m^{5} 10.3m* 10g* 10g^{4} 12.5g Aug 27] 215,000Y: rangy colt: ninth foal: half-brother to 7 winners, including Dewhurst winner Dashing Blade (by Elegant Air), later successful over 1½m, and useful 1985 2-y-o 7f winner Navarzato (by Dominion), later 6f to 1m winner in France: dam best at 2 yrs, when 5f winner and placed in Hoover Fillies' Mile: smart performer: won maiden at Chester in May and Prix Eugene Adam at Saint-Cloud (always close up, led near finish and beat Montjoy a neck) in July: good fourth to Montjoy (rec 4 lb) in Prix Guillaume d'Ornano at Deauville following month: should stay 12.5f: has raced only on a sound surface: sold to USA. *P. W. Chapple-Hyam*

ROYAL SOVEREIGN (IRE) **–** 3 b.f. Royal Academy (USA) 130 – Adjarida (Red God 128§) [1994 NR 1995 6g May 20] 160,000 francs Y: half-sister to several winners including useful 7f winner Adjanada (by Nishapour) and useful German 6-y-o 5f (listed race) to 7f winner Adjmal (by Dancing Brave): dam, useful 1m to 1¼m winner in France, is half-sister to dam of Blushing Groom: always behind in maiden at Lingfield: dead. *G. L. Moore*

ROYAL UPRISING (IRE) **–** 3 b.f. Red Sunset 120 – Wilderness 88 (Martinmas 128) [1994 48: 5g^{5} 6f^{6} 6m 1995 a6g a7g^{5} a8g^{5} Mar 4] leggy, unfurnished filly: poor maiden: best run on debut. *G. L. Moore*

ROYAL YORK **75** 3 b.f. Bustino 136 – Rustle of Silk 67 (General Assembly (USA)) [1994 68: 8d^{3} 7.9d^{5} 1995 10.1g^{6} 10m* 12.3m* 14f^{2} 11.9m 15g Sep 14] tall, leggy filly: fair handicapper: won at Redcar in June and Ripon (edged right) in July: probably better at 1¾m than shorter: acts on firm going. *Miss S. E. Hall*

ROY BOY **72** 3 b.g. Emarati (USA) 74 – Starky's Pet (Mummy's Pet 125) [1994 71p: 7g^{6} 6g^{5} 7d^{5} 1995 7g^{5} 8.5m^{6} 6g^{2} 5m^{3} 6m^{4} 6g Jun 7] rangy, good-topped gelding: good mover: fair maiden: stays 7f: acts on good to firm and dead ground: below form only try in blinkers: sometimes carries head awkwardly under pressure. *Mrs M. Reveley*

ROYRACE **–** 3 b.g. Wace (USA) 82 – Royal Tycoon (Tycoon II) [1994 –: 7.1s 8d 1995 13.4d 11.8g 14.1m Oct 19] tall gelding: soundly beaten in varied company. *W. M. Brisbourne*

ROZALINA LADY **–** 3 b.f. Alzao (USA) 117 – Diavolina (USA) (Lear Fan (USA) 130) [1994 –: 7f 1995 8m 9g 8d 10f 8m 10m Aug 21] smallish, good-bodied filly: little sign of ability: tried blinkered. *N. A. Graham*

ROZEL BAY **49** 2 ch.f. (Apr 6) Beveled (USA) – Salinas 65 (Bay Express 132) [1995 5g^{5} a7g^{2} a7g a8.5g^{5} a8.5g Oct 28] 1,000Y resold 575Y: fourth foal: sister to 3-y-o Cinders Chance: dam maiden who stayed 6f: second of 11 to Bumblefoot in maiden auction at Wolverhampton in August: well beaten in sellers there afterwards: stays 7f: blinkered on debut and final start. *J. L. Spearing*

RUBADUB 4 b.f. Kalaglow 132 – Ravens Peak (High Top 131) [1994 NR 1995 8f 10.2f 10m^5 12.5g^5 10.8m 11.1m^5 7.1m 10f Jul 24] tall, sparely-made filly: third foal: dam lightly raced: poor maiden at best: bred to stay 1½m: tried visored: pulls hard. *J. M. Bradley* 41 d

RUBISLAW 3 ch.g. Dunbeath (USA) 127 – Larnem 43 (Meldrum 112) [1994 –: 7m 7.5g 7s 9d 1995 a8g 14.1f^5 14.1m 8m 9.2m^4 10m Jul 24] angular, close-coupled gelding: poor maiden: sold (C. Fairhurst to Mrs K. Lamb) 2,000 gns Doncaster August Sales: bred to be suited by 1¼m+: visored since fourth 3-y-o start. *C. W. Fairhurst* 31

RUBY ESTATE (IRE) 4 b.f. High Estate 127 – Tuesday Morning (Sadler's Wells (USA) 132) [1994 63: 10m^2 a9.4g^5 8.5g^2 11m^6 a8.5g* a8g^2 a8g^2 8.2m^2 8.3g^2 1995 8m 10g Jul 28] tall filly: modest performer at 3 yrs: well beaten for new stable in 1995: effective at 1m to 1¼m: acts on good to firm going and fibresand. *A. P. James* –

RUBY HEIGHTS 4 b.f. Shirley Heights 130 – Hence (USA) (Mr Prospector (USA)) [1994 63d: 10d^3 12f^3 14d^5 10.1m^2 a10g^2 10m^3 10m 10m a8.5g 12g 1995 10f^3 9.7g^2 10m^5 9.9m* 12m^5 10d^3 12m^4 Oct 27] rangy filly: modest handicapper: received quiet ride when winning apprentice maiden event at Beverley in August: probably stays 1½m: acts on firm ground, dead and equitrack: tried visored, blinkered and tongue tied at 3 yrs: tends to find little under pressure. *R. Hannon* 56

RUBYLEE 3 ch.f. Persian Bold 123 – Miss Merlin 79 (Manacle 123) [1994 59: 5.2s^2 5.1g^5 5m^6 7.5m^2 6m 7d 1995 a7g^6 10m 10f 8.3m Jul 10] leggy filly: modest form in maidens at 2 yrs: below form in 1995, edgy in visor on final start: stays 7.5f: sometimes sweats: sold 5,000 gns Doncaster November Sales. *K. McAuliffe* –

RUBY ROCK 3 b.f. Rock City 120 – Resonation (CAN) (Coastal (USA)) [1994 NR 1995 7.9m^4 10.3g^5 7f 8g 13.8g Sep 16] 1,000Y: leggy filly: second foal: dam won 3 races in North America: no sign of ability: tried visored. *B. W. Murray* –

RUBY TWO SHOES 2 b.f. (Feb 20) Revlow 108 – Miss Burgundy (Gambling Debt 98) [1995 8d 8.1s Oct 17] smallish filly: third reported foal (all by Revlow): dam poor novice hurdler: always behind in maidens. *B. R. Millman* –

RUBY VENTURE 3 br.f. Ballad Rock 122 – Sherkraine 98 (Shergar 140) [1994 49p: 6g^3 1995 10m 10.5m^6 12.1g^6 May 29] good-topped filly: modest maiden: stays 1¼m: has raced only on a sound surface. *S. P. C. Woods* 56

RUDDIGORE 3 ch.c. Old Vic 136 – Sea Saga 91 (Dara Monarch 128) [1994 67: 7m 7m 8g 1995 10m 11.7m^5 12.5m 10f^4 11.9f^5 10d 8g 8f Oct 23] smallish, sturdy colt: poor maiden on balance of form: left R. Hannon's stable after fifth 3-y-o start: blinkered, tailed off on final one: stays 12.5f: acts on firm ground: sometimes sweats. *K. R. Burke* 46

RUG 3 ch.c. Persian Bold 123 – Golden Form (Formidable (USA) 125) [1994 NR 1995 7m^6 7m* 9f 8f 8.5f^2 8f^3 a9f^5 9f 9f 8f^3 8.5g^5 Dec 17] workmanlike colt: has a quick action: fifth foal: half-brother to winners abroad by Nijinsky and Baillamont: dam 9f winner in Ireland: won maiden at Thirsk in May on final start for G. Wragg: placed in 4 allowance events in USA and far from disgraced in Grade 3 event eighth start: will stay at least 1¼m: blinkered 7 of last 8 starts: best efforts in USA with lasix. *M. A. Mollica, USA* 98

RUMBA RHYTHM (CAN) 2 ch.f. (Feb 4) Thorn Dance (USA) 107 – Skoblikova (USA) (Phone Trick (USA)) [1995 5m^5 6g^4 5m^4 Jun 16] $26,000Y: unfurnished filly: good mover: first foal: dam sprint claimer winner: fourth of 11 to Amazing Bay in maiden at Newbury in May: never a serious threat in similar event won by Warning Time at Sandown following month: appears to need further than 5f. *J. W. Hills* 70

RUMI 4 ch.f. Nishapour (FR) 125 – Seldom (Rarity 129) [1994 80: 10g 11.9g^2 12.1m* 10g 10.1d* 12m 11.8g 1995 14m 11.7m May 2] lengthy, angular filly: fairly useful form at 3 yrs for A. Stewart: behind in handicaps in 1995: should stay beyond 1½m: acts on good to firm ground and dead. *C. R. Egerton* –

RUMPELSTILTSKIN 3 ch.c. Sharpo 132 – Ouija 104 (Silly Season 127) [1994 NR 1995 7m 8m 8.1g May 29] 2,500F: good-topped colt: half-brother to several –

winners, notably Teleprompter (by Welsh Pageant) and Chatoyant (by Rainbow Quest): dam best at 1m: well beaten in maidens. *Martyn Meade*

RUMPIPUMPY 2 b.f. (Apr 30) Shirley Heights 130 – Wanton 106 (Kris 135) 80 +
[1995 6f^5 7m^2 8.1m^4 7d^2 8.5f* Dec 10] lengthy, rather unfurnished filly: fifth foal: half-sister to 1994 2-y-o 5f winner Magongo (by Be My Chief) and 1991 2-y-o 6f winner Wilde Rufo (by Sharrood), later successful in USA: dam sprinter best at 2 yrs: short-headed in nursery at Newmarket on final start for Lord Huntingdon: racing on Lasix and bute, won maiden at Hollywood Park in December: stays 8.5f. *Kathy Walsh, USA*

RUMPUS (IRE) 5 b.m. Kahyasi 130 – Helietta 78 (Tyrnavos 129) [1994 49: 10g^6 –
12g^{4dis} 16.2m 10m 1995 17.2m 13.1f May 22] leggy, lengthy mare: shows traces of stringhalt: disappointing maiden: should stay beyond 1½m: acts on good to firm ground and dead. *Mrs L. A. Murphy*

RUN-DO-RUN 3 b.f. Gabitat 119 – Do-Run-Do (Palm Track 122) [1994 64: 6g^4 §§
6s 1995 7f 8.3m^6 10f 8g 8.2m 12m Nov 6] leggy, lengthy filly: modest maiden: refused or reluctant to race last 3 starts: thorough jade. *H. J. Collingridge*

RUNFORACTION (IRE) 3 b.f. Contract Law (USA) 108 – Prissy Miss 68 –
(Free State 125) [1994 41, a53: 5g^6 5d^4 5g^5 a5g^2 a6g^4 5m^4 7.5g^6 a6g* a6g^5 a6g^2 6g a43
a6g a8g^3 1995 a8g^4 a8g^4 a8g a8g^3 a11g^6 a11g a8g 12.3f 12m Jul 3] small, sparely-made filly: poor performer: best form at up to 1m: acts on fibresand: inconsistent. *B. S. Rothwell*

RUN HIGH 12 b.g. Thatch (USA) 136 – Fleet Noble (USA) (Vaguely Noble 140) –
[1994 46: a12g^3 13f^4 12s 14g^3 1995 14g a13g 14.1f^5 Jul 8] strong gelding: veteran handicapper, poor at best on flat nowadays: needs at least 1½m, and stays 2m: acts on any going. *P. Mitchell*

RUNIC SYMBOL 4 b.g. Warning 136 – Pagan Deity 88 (Brigadier Gerard 144) 42 d
[1994 51d: 8.2d^6 11.6g 10d^3 11.7m^6 10m^6 10.2f^3 10g 12m^5 10.5g 8d^4 8s^2 8d^5 1995 8m^3 8f^5 8g^4 8.1m 7.6d^3 8.1m^6 10.2m^6 8g Sep 13] leggy, angular gelding: poor maiden handicapper: well below form last 5 starts: effective at 1m, and probably stays 11.6f: acts on firm and soft ground: tried blinkered: normally comes from behind. *M. Blanshard*

RUNNING GREEN 4 b.g. Green Desert (USA) 127 – Smeralda (GER) 63
(Dschingis Khan) [1994 NR 1995 9.2s^3 Apr 12] half-brother to several winners, notably useful middle-distance stayer Lille Hammer (by Sadler's Wells) and Group winner Soto-Grande (by Kaiseradler): dam won 3 times in Germany, and is half-sister to Preis der Diana winner Slenderella: no sign of ability in 5 runs over hurdles, but (33/1) showed modest form when third of 13 in claimer at Hamilton on flat debut, always well there: will stay 1¼m: may improve. *T. Dyer*

RUNRIG (IRE) 5 b.m. Jalmood (USA) 126 – Bluethroat 95 (Ballymore 123) 42
[1994 NR 1995 8.3g 7m 8.3f^3 11.1m^2 11.1f^5 11.1m^5 13f^6 9.2m 8g^5 Aug 26] leggy mare: poor maiden handicapper: stays 11f: acts on firm and dead going: sometimes carries head high: visored (ran well) once at 3 yrs: none too consistent: won novice hurdle in September. *Miss L. A. Perratt*

RUNS IN THE FAMILY 3 b.f. Distant Relative 128 – Stoneydale 83 (Tickled 57
Pink 114) [1994 64: 5m 7m 5g 5d 6s* 5s^2 6.1g^2 6.1d^4 1995 6.1g^5 6.1m 5.7f 6g^6 a6g a43
a6g^4 a7g 5g^3 5g 5.1d Oct 10] sturdy, useful-looking filly: modest handicapper: stays 6f: probably needs an easy surface, and acts well on soft ground: tried blinkered: none too consistent. *P. G. Murphy*

RUPERT'S PRINCESS (IRE) 3 b.f. Prince Rupert (FR) 121 – Llanelli (Welsh 52
Saint 126) [1994 63: 5s* 5d^2 5g^2 5g^2 6s^2 6g^4 5d 6.1d 5s 6.1g^4 6.1d 1995 6s^6 a5g^6 6.1g^4 a6g^2 6g May 26] lengthy filly: poor mover: modest performer: should stay 7f: acts on fibresand and soft going, yet to race on top-of-the-ground: blinkered last 2 starts. *M. J. Heaton-Ellis*

RUPIANA (IRE) 3 b.f. Prince Rupert (FR) 121 – Webbiana (African Sky 124) –
[1994 79: 7m* 7m 7g 7d^4 7v 1995 8m 7.3g 8m Jun 2] lengthy filly: deteriorated at 2 yrs, and soundly beaten in 1995. *J. R. Arnold*

RUSHAWAY 4 b.g. Robellino (USA) 127 – Brush Away (Ahonoora 122) [1994 59
59: 8s 10g^3 1995 10s^6 10m 10g^5 May 24] good-topped gelding: modest middle-distance maiden: has joined Miss C. Johnsey. *R. Hannon*

RUSHCUTTER BAY 2 br.c. (Apr 1) Mon Tresor 113 – Llwy Bren (Lidhame 109) [1995 a5g^4 5g* 6m^3 6m^6 Aug 26] 450Y: neat colt: first foal: dam unraced: won maiden auction at Windsor in July: improved again when third of 8 to Red Nymph in minor event there a month later then not discredited when sixth of 15 to Creative Account in valuable nursery at Newmarket (visored) final outing: stays 6f: acts on good to firm going: slowly away on debut: wore bandages first 2 starts: races prominently. *T. T. Clement* 80

RUSHEN RAIDER 3 br.g. Reprimand 122 – Travel Storm 77 (Lord Gayle (USA) 124) [1994 58: 6m^6 5.9m^6 7m 1995 7.5m 7m* 7g^6 8.1d^5 10m^6 10f* 9.9m^5 10f^5 Aug 17] leggy gelding: modest performer: won seller at Thirsk in May and claimer at Redcar in August: stays 1¼m: acts on firm and dead ground. *K. W. Hogg, Isle of Man* 62

RUSK 2 b.c. (Apr 19) Pharly (FR) 130 – Springwell 73 (Miami Springs 121) [1995 7.9g^4 Oct 7] 8,000Y, 16,000 2-y-o: unfurnished, useful-looking colt: has a round action: fifth foal: brother to 3-y-o Pendine and half-brother to 1½m winner Marros Mill (by Glint of Gold) and a winner in Sweden by Primo Dominie: dam 10.2f winner: 33/1, around 6½ lengths fourth of 8 to comfortable winner Committal in maiden at York, held up and green but staying on well: will improve. *J. Pearce* 73 p

RUSSIAN HEROINE 3 b.f. Domynsky 110 – Actress 73 (Known Fact (USA) 135) [1994 79: 5d^6 5m^2 5s* 5g* 6m^6 5f* 5m^6 5d 5s 5g 1995 a5g^5 a6g^3 a6g a5g^2 6s^3 a6g^4 6g^2 6m 5g^3 a6g^3 6m 7g* 7g 7.1m* 7.1f* 7m* 7g* 7m^3 7.5g^4 7f 7m^4 7m 7g 6m Oct 2] small, sturdy filly: fair performer: in fine form in the summer, successful in minor event at Catterick, claimer at Chepstow and handicaps at Edinburgh, Chester and Catterick: stays 7.5f: acts on fibresand and any turf going: usually races prominently: tends to hang left: sold 10,000 gns Newmarket Autumn Sales. *M. Johnston* 75

RUSSIAN MAID 3 ch.f. Cadeaux Genereux 131 – Tsar Maiden (USA) 60 (Nijinsky (CAN) 138) [1994 NR 1995 7d^4 7m* 8.1m^2 7g^4 6g Sep 29] leggy filly: first foal: dam, lightly-raced middle-distance maiden, is half-sister to high-class miler Golden Opinion and daughter of Musidora winner Optimistic Lass: fairly useful form: won maiden at Thirsk in July: good efforts in handicaps next 2 starts: unsuited by step down to 6f on final one: stays 1m: acts on good to firm ground: has run well when sweating: bandaged behind: sent to Dubai. *J. R. Fanshawe* 85

RUSSIAN MUSIC 2 b.g. (Mar 17) Forzando 122 – Sunfleet 59 (Red Sunset 120) [1995 6m^3 6g^3 Aug 31] 27,000F, 27,000Y: smallish, good-quartered gelding: fourth foal: half-brother to 3-y-o No Pattern (by Rock City), winner from 6f (at 2 yrs) to 11.5f, and 1993 2-y-o 5f winner Nera (by Robellino): dam maiden, seemed suited by 1¼m: similar form when third in maidens at York won by Desert Boy (not clear run) and Leonine 2 weeks later: will stay 1m: sure to win a race. *P. C. Haslam* 91 +

RUSSIAN RASCAL (IRE) 2 b.g. (Mar 4) Soviet Lad (USA) 94 – Anglo Irish (Busted 134) [1995 5m 6g* 6m^3 6m^3 7.5m^2 8g Sep 21] IR 9,000F, IR 5,500Y: half-brother to a winner (including of listed 1½m event, by Flash of Steel) in Belgium: dam never ran: won claimer at Newcastle in May: best effort in nurseries when second of 10 at Beverley penultimate start: pulled up (broke blood vessel) final outing: better suited by 7.5f than shorter. *M. H. Easterby* 64

RUSSIAN REVIVAL (USA) 2 ch.c. (May 3) Nureyev (USA) 131 – Memories (USA) (Hail The Pirates (USA) 126) [1995 6m* 6m^2 6g^4 Aug 20] $200,000Y: angular colt: fine mover: third foal: brother to 3-y-o Melmoth: dam won Grade 2 9f event at 4 yrs: won maiden at Newbury in May: 2 lengths second of 13 to Royal Applause in Coventry Stakes at Ascot following month (reportedly returned home with a temperature) then respectable 2¾ lengths fourth of 8 (made running) to Tagula in Prix Morny at Deauville in August: will be suited by further than 6f: joined Godolphin and wintered in Dubai: a useful colt who's almost certainly capable of winning a good race. *P. W. Chapple-Hyam* 108 p

RUSSIAN SNOWS (IRE) 3 b.f. Sadler's Wells (USA) 132 – Arctique Royale 114 (Royal And Regal (USA)) [1994 NR 1995 10m* 10g^2 12g^2 10f^2 12g* 12.5s* Sep 30] 113 p

Russian Snows quickly developed into a very useful middle-distance filly in 1995, having been unraced at two, and the style of her win on her final start, in the Group 2 Prix de Royallieu on the first day of the Arc meeting at Lonchamp, promised

Prix de Royallieu, Longchamp—Russian Snows has shot past Daraydala (noseband) and Genovefa

better to come. She looks the type to progress from three to four and with the likely benefit from a winter in Dubai she could be a much more prominent name in 1996. Russian Snows ran six times for John Oxx in her first season, following a debut win in a maiden at Roscommon with three seconds at the Curragh in smart company. She went down narrowly in the Pretty Polly Stakes (a neck behind Flagbird) and the Royal Whip Stakes (beaten half a length by Shemaran) and in between finished a six-length runner-up to Pure Grain in the Irish Oaks. She won the listed Ardilaun House Hotel Oyster Stakes at Galway in September at odds on, but was unimpressive in doing so, beating Ballykett Nancy by only a head with the weights in her favour. After the race her trainer, as he had been after the Royal Whip, was reported to say that the filly would be seen to better advantage given softer ground. So it proved at Longchamp, where she revelled in the very soft conditions, showing a telling turn of foot to come from second last over a furlong out, switched round the field, to lead towards the finish and win going away. The form doesn't look out of the ordinary by Group 2 standards—the three-length runner-up Daraydala ran twice subsequently, finishing last when favourite for the Prix du Conseil de Paris and third, confirming her Royallieu form, in the Prix Fille de l'Air at Evry; the third Genovefa is no more than useful and the one-paced fourth Noble Rose, the Park Hill winner, was below her best—but it was the style of Russian Snows's win which impressed.

Russian Snows comes from an excellent family. Her dam Arctique Royale won the 1981 Irish One Thousand Guineas and has produced six winners, the best of them Russian Snows's brother Modhish, a very smart French middle-distance colt, who won the Grand Prix de Deauville and the Prix Jean de Chaudenay. Her half-sister Truly Special (by Caerleon) won the ten-and-a-half-furlong Prix de Royaumont and has bred a Royaumont winner in Truly A Dream, who was also successful in the E. P. Taylor Stakes. Arctique Royale is half-sister to three other successful broodmares. The first, Le Melody, is the dam of Ardross and Larrocha, the latter another winter migrant to Dubai in 1995, and this branch of the family is dealt with on the comment

Sheikh Mohammed's "Russian Snows"

Russian Snows (IRE) (b.f. 1992)	Sadler's Wells (USA) (b 1981)	Northern Dancer (b 1961)	Nearctic
			Natalma
		Fairy Bridge (b 1975)	Bold Reason
			Special
	Arctique Royale (b 1978)	Royal And Regal (b or br 1970)	Vaguely Noble
			Native Street
		Arctic Melody (b 1962)	Arctic Slave
			Bell Bird

on her. The second, Racquette, runner up in the Irish Oaks, is the dam of four useful-or-better winners, the best of them the smart mile-and-a-quarter performer Splendid Moment. The third, Nilie, produced the Princess of Wales's Stakes winner and useful hurdler Pollerton and Mona Curragh, the dam of Castletown. That may not be a familiar name to European racegoers but Castletown is one of the outstanding New Zealand racehorses of recent years. He's a stayer, and while his record of six wins over six seasons in Group 1 company may not sound that impressive, it should be remembered that many of the races he ran in were ultra-competitive handicaps where he was conceding weight. The mere fact that he ran in forty Group 1 races in Australia and New Zealand illustrates the difference in emphasis between European and Australasian racing. The good-topped Russian Snows stays twelve and a half furlongs well and is likely to stay further. She looks well suited by soft going and, given such conditions, will be an interesting prospect in 1996. *J. Oxx, Ireland*

RUSTAVI (IRE) 4 b.g. Entitled 126 – Sweet Tones (Lord Gayle (USA) 124) – [1994 7.8m^3 12g^3 8g^2 8.5g^4 10s^2 10d^2 12g* 12g^2 12d^4 1995 17.2m Sep 25] fifth foal:

half-brother to fairly useful Nordic Tones (at up to 1¼m, by Nordico): dam, ran twice, second over 1½m in Ireland: fairly useful and consistent performer (rated 82) for J. Bolger at 3 yrs, winning maiden at Downpatrick: tailed off on British debut: stays 1½m: acts on good to firm ground and soft. *R. Curtis*

RUSTIC LEAGUE (IRE) 4 b.g. Gallic League 119 – Walnut Lass (Tap On Wood 130) [1994 –: a7g a6g a7g 1995 a7g a7g³ a6g⁴ a6g 5d³ a6g 5.3m 10g a7g Jun 22] poor maiden handicapper: sold out of T. J. Naughton's stable 1,550 gns Ascot May Sales after seventh 4-y-o start: effective at 5f, stays 7f: acts on fibresand and dead ground. *D. Burchell* 38

RUSTIC SONG (IRE) 2 b.f. (Mar 10) Fayruz 116 – Red Note (Rusticaro (FR) 124) [1995 5m 5m³ a6g 5g² 5g 6.1m Oct 26] 14,500Y: close-coupled, angular filly: third foal: sister to 3-y-o Sound The Trumpet, 5f winner at 2 yrs, and half-sister to a winner in Hungary: dam unraced: modest form: placed in maiden at Beverley in August and nursery (second of 17 to Swynford Dream) at Redcar following month: below form in nurseries last 2 starts: should stay 6f. *J. Wharton* 53

RUTHY'S ROMANCE 4 b.f. Then Again 126 – What's The Matter 57 (High Top 131) [1994 –: 7.1s 1995 8.3m May 15] lengthy filly: no sign of ability: threw rider at start and withdrawn May 30. *A. G. Newcombe* –

RUWY 2 b.f. (Mar 14) Soviet Star (USA) 128 – Psylla 96 (Beldale Flutter (USA) 130) [1995 7g³ Oct 23] sixth foal: sister to a poor maiden and half-sister to 3 1¼m winners, including 3-y-o Akayid (by Old Vic) and Kabayil (by Dancing Brave): dam 9f and 1¼m winner out of half-sister to Kris and Diesis: 14/1, 2¾ lengths third of 13 to comfortable winner Tsarnista in maiden at Lingfield, chasing leaders after starting slowly (had given trouble in stalls) then keeping on in good style: sure to improve. *C. J. Benstead* 68 p

RUZNAMA (USA) 2 ch.f. (Apr 20) Forty Niner (USA) – Last Feather (USA) 120 (Vaguely Noble 140) [1995 6m 7m* 8g³ 7g* Sep 30] 105 p

Ruznama's progression into a useful two-year-old was a much more low-key process than that of Sheikh Hamdan Al Maktoum's other two-year-old fillies Bint Salsabil and Bint Shadayid, leading fancies for the classics even before their racecourse debuts, but by the end of the season there was little to choose on form

Mary Reveley Racing Club Oh So Sharp Stakes, Newmarket—Ruznama and Obsessive

between the three of them and Ruznama, a close-coupled, deep-girthed filly, has the scope to progress with the others at three. Faced with a choice between Bint Salsabil and Ruznama in the May Hill Stakes, Carson chose Ruznama, or as the Press saw it, 'rejected' or 'deserted' Bint Salsabil, and Ruznama was sent off the 3/1 favourite. Ruznama had shaped well on her debut, staying on under a considerate ride when seventh to the odds-on Bosra Sham in a maiden at Newbury a month before the May Hill. Ruznama had been Carson's preference then, too, over the well-bred Hern-trained newcomer Min Elreeh. Two weeks later, again partnered by Carson, she justified support from 6/1 to 7/2 by winning an eighteen-runner maiden at Newmarket from another of her owner's filles Ta Rib, joining the leaders in the Dip and winning by a length in a time that took nearly half a second off the two-year-old course record. Ruznama faced some proven performers in listed and pattern company at Doncaster the following month and while she again showed plenty of improvement, it was only enough to see her into third place behind Solar Crystal and Like A Hawk. She was beaten only two lengths though, closing on the leading pair after needing to be pushed along three furlongs out, and ran a much better race than Bint Salsabil back in eighth. Ruznama faced a much easier task on her final start in the listed Mary Reveley Racing Club Oh So Sharp Stakes at Newmarket at the end of September. The return to seven furlongs proved no problem as she moved easily into the lead two furlongs out and needed only to be pushed out to beat the Yarmouth maiden winner Obsessive two and a half lengths, with three lengths back to the Prestige Stakes third Fag End.

Ruznama's sire the game and consistent Forty Niner established himself as champion American two-year-old colt by winning the one-mile Champagne Stakes; he gained the most important of his eleven successes in the ten-furlong Travers Stakes. He made a promising start at stud, gaining the top freshman sire award in 1992 and finished seventeenth on the General Sires list (and second-best sire of

Hamdan Al Maktoum's "Ruznama"

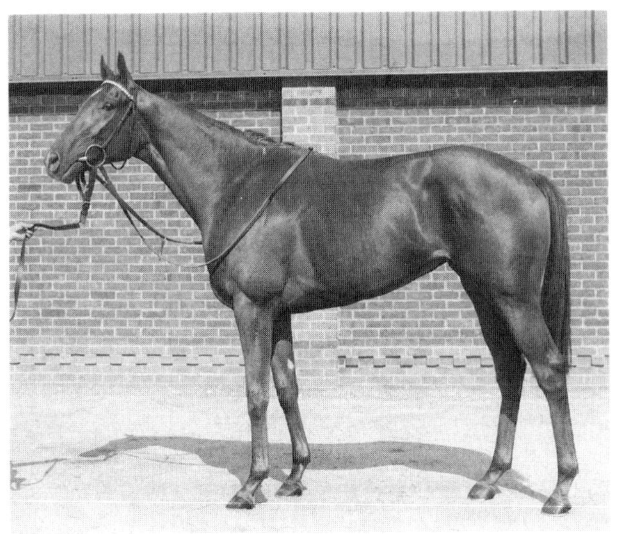

	Forty Niner (USA) (ch 1985)	Mr Prospector (b 1970)	Raise A Native Gold Digger
Ruznama (USA) (ch.f. Apr 20, 1993)		File (ch 1976)	Tom Rolfe Continue
	Last Feather (USA) (b 1979)	Vaguely Noble (b 1965)	Vienna Noble Lassie
		Quill (ch 1956)	Princequillo Quick Touch

two-year-olds) in 1995. He has had a small number of runners in Europe, the best of them so far being the smart middle-distance colt Luhuk and Takkatamm, fourth in the 1994 Dewhurst Stakes. Ruznama's dam Last Feather was, like her, trained by Barry Hills. She won the Musidora Stakes before running third to Time Charter in the Oaks. As her name suggests Last Feather was the last foal of Quill, a mare who enjoyed great success on the track and at stud in a career spanning more then twenty years. Quill was champion juvenile filly in the USA in 1958 and won fourteen of her twenty-six starts, while at stud she produced, among others, First Feather, dam of Run The Gantlet; champion Canadian grass horse One For All; and Irish St Leger winner Caucasus who was also later a top performer on turf in the USA. She is also the great-grandam of Vettori. Ruznama is the first return on the 1.7 million dollars paid for Last Feather at the 1989 Keeneland November Sale. By then she had foaled three winners—the Irish ten-furlong winner Limber Dancer (by Nijinsky), the useful French two-year-old nine-furlong winner Phar Feather (by Lyphard) and the one mile winner Contessa (by Blushing Groom). Her other winner, Eqtesaad (by Danzig), ran only twice for Sheikh Hamdan without success but won three times at up to ten furlongs on the all-weather early in 1995 as a four-year-old. Ruznama, a good mover who has yet to race on a soft surface, is far from certain to stay as far as her dam but she should make up into a smart filly at around ten furlongs. *B. W. Hills*

RYE HILL QUEEN (IRE) 5 b.m. Wassl 125 – Jendeal (Troy 137) [1994 13g5 13m4 16m6 18g 16g 1995 a16g May 15] half-sister to a juvenile winner by Rousillon: dam unraced half-sister to smart sprinter Tarib: winning hurdler and poor form (rated 48) on flat for A. P. O'Brien (sold IR 2,200 Tattersalls August Sales) in Ireland at 4 yrs: tailed off on only run on flat here: stays 1¾m: acts on any going: tried blinkered. *R. A. Fahey* –

RYMER'S RASCAL 3 b.g. Rymer 121 – City Sound 63 (On Your Mark 125) [1994 64: 5m 5m6 7m5 6m3 6g4 5m4 5m2 6d6 5m4 6s4 6s* 1995 6m 6.1m5 8m 6g2 6g3 6f 5g 6s a6g Oct 14] sturdy gelding: fair handicapper: well beaten last 3 starts: stays 6f: acts on good to firm and soft ground, ran poorly on firm. *E. J. Alston* 67

S

SAAFI (IRE) 4 b.c. Primo Dominie 121 – Baby's Smile 68 (Shirley Heights 130) [1994 56: 8v 12.1s4 11.7m3 1995 12g 11.6m 14f 14f5 Aug 17] strong colt: carries condition: modest maiden: no form in 1995: should stay beyond 12.1f: acts on good to firm and soft going. *R. J. Baker* –

SAAHI (USA) 6 b.g. Lyphard (USA) 132 – Dumtadumtadum (USA) (Grey Dawn II 132) [1994 NR 1995 12g a16.2g5 12g Jun 9] compact gelding: fairly useful performer at his best at 4 yrs, and as hurdler in 1993/4: bandaged, tailed off on return to flat: stays 1m: used to act on soft ground and went particularly well on equitrack: tried blinkered/visored, no form. *C. Weedon* –

SAATCHMO 3 b.g. Forzando 122 – Into The Fire 74 (Dominion 123) [1994 –: 6g 1995 6.1g3 7g5 5.1f a8.5g 8d Sep 22] sturdy, lengthy gelding: modest maiden: should stay beyond 7f. *J. L. Spearing* 57

SABAAH ELFULL 2 ch.f. (Jan 30) Kris 135 – Putupon 89 (Mummy's Pet 125) [1995 6m 7.5d3 Sep 13] 90,000Y: lengthy, unfurnished filly: has plenty of scope: seventh foal: closely related to smart French sprinter Pole Position (by Sharpo) and half-sister to 5f winner Putout (by Dowsing): dam, 2-y-o 5f winner, sister to Precocious and half-sister to Jupiter Island: eleventh of 22 to Bosra Sham in maiden at Newbury in August, making good progress when badly checked inside final 1f: 75+

heavily-backed favourite, 2½ lengths third of 12 to Wavey in similar event at Beverley following month, hampered over 1f out but finding only one pace: stays 7.5f. *A. C. Stewart*

SABELLA 4 ch.f. Prince Sabo 123 – Pour Moi 73 (Bay Express 132) [1994 63: 7m^3 7g 1995 a7g a5g a7g Sep 16] seemed of little account at 4 yrs for new stable. *R. Harris* –

SABICAS 3 b.c. High Kicker (USA) – Spanish Estates 65 (Firestreak 125) [1994 52: 7f 8g a7g^3 1995 a10g a9.4g^6 Jan 21] workmanlike colt: bad maiden: tried blinkered, no improvement. *S. C. Williams* –

SABOT 2 b.c. (May 11) Polar Falcon (USA) 126 – Power Take Off 109 (Aragon 118) [1995 6m^6 6d^2 6m^4 Oct 13] 39,000Y: tall, angular colt: has scope: first foal: dam 1m/1¼m performer, half-sister to very useful sprinter Governor General: ½-length second of 8 to King of The East in minor event at Doncaster in September, not getting clear run then coming through well: edgy, below that form when fourth of 21 to Projection in maiden at Newmarket in October: will stay 7f: best form on a soft surface. *B. W. Hills* 86

SACHA STAR 5 b.m. Green Ruby (USA) 104 – Rymerstar (Rymer 121) [1994 NR 1995 11.7f^6 Jul 1] second foal: dam placed in NH Flat races and over hurdles: no sign of ability over jumps: 50/1, never-dangerous sixth of 8 in maiden at Bath: sold 1,100 gns Ascot August Sales. *B. Palling* –

SACHO (IRE) 2 b.c. (May 4) Sadler's Wells (USA) 132 – Oh So Sharp 131 (Kris 135) [1995 8m^2 Oct 12] lengthy, good sort, shade unfurnished: good walker: seventh foal: closely related to very useful Shaima (by Shareef Dancer), 7.3f and 8.9f winner here and successful at 1½m in USA, and half-brother to several winners, including useful 3-y-o 7f and 8.3f winner Felitza (by Soviet Star) and smart French filly Rosefinch (by Blushing Groom), successful in Prix Saint-Alary: dam won 1000 Guineas, Oaks and St Leger and is half-sister to Roussalka: 4/1, very much caught the eye when 1½ lengths second of 14 to Silver Dome in maiden at Newmarket, travelling strongly in mid-division then finishing best of all pushed out with hands and heels: will be well suited by middle distances: has a great deal of potential, and is sure to win races. *J. H. M. Gosden* 89 P

SACRAMENT 4 b.c. Shirley Heights 130 – Blessed Event 117 (Kings Lake (USA) 133) [1994 118: 8m^4 10m* 8.5g* 11.9m* 11.9m* 14.6g^4 10m 1995 12m^4 May 5] tall colt: smart performer: had run of 7-runner Jockey Club Stakes at Newmarket on reappearance, setting steady pace and unable to quicken from under 3f out, beaten 3¼ lengths by Only Royale: effective at 1½m and should stay 1¾m+ (never travelling well in St Leger when tried): has raced only on a sound surface: tracked the lead when successful at 3 yrs. *M. R. Stoute* 116

SACRAMENTO (IRE) 2 b.c. (Apr 18) Distinctly North (USA) 115 – Cool Gales 85 (Lord Gayle (USA) 124) [1995 5f* 5g* 5.5g 7g^2 6m 5s Oct 7] IR 7,500F, IR 17,000Y: sparely-made colt: fifth reported foal: half-brother to Irish 9f winner Scotsman's Bay (by Double Schwartz): dam, maiden, probably stayed 1½m: Belgian colt: won newcomers event and listed race at Ostend in July: eighth of 29 in valuable sales race at the Curragh penultimate start then last of 7 in Cornwallis Stakes at Ascot month later: looks a sprinter: wears blinkers. *B. Tevels, Belgium* 88

SACRED MIRROR (IRE) 4 b.f. Shaadi (USA) 126 – Heavenly Abode (FR) (Habitat 134) [1994 63: 8m^4 9.7d^3 8.2s^2 8s 8g a8g^5 1995 a8g a8g^5 a12g 9.7d^5 11.7m^5 May 2] good-bodied filly: modest maiden: best efforts at 4 yrs on last 2 starts: stays 11.7f: acts on good to firm and soft ground, probably on equitrack. *C. E. Brittain* 52

SADARAH (USA) 3 b.c. Dixieland Band (USA) – Chriso (USA) (Highland Blade (USA)) [1994 NR 1995 6.5v^5 8m 7.8f 9.6g 8f Oct 18] $13,500F: $55,000Y: workmanlike ex-Irish colt: fourth foal: brother to a minor American winner: dam, lightly-raced maiden: best effort in Ireland when seventh of 16 at Dundalk on third start: sold out of K. Prendergast's stable 1,200 gns Newmarket July Sales: no encouragement on first start here. *C. Smith* 71 d

SADDLEHOME (USA) 6 b.g. Aragon 118 – Kesarini (USA) 87 (Singh (USA)) [1994 78: a5g* a5g* 5g* 5g^2 5f* 5m 5f 6m 5d* a5g 1995 a5g* 6d^2 5g^6 6m 5g^2 6f* 6m 5.1m^6 Aug 19] leggy, short-backed gelding: fairly useful handicapper: better than ever at 6 yrs, and won at Wolverhampton (unbeaten in 3 outings there) in March and 83 a86

Epsom in June: stays 6f: acts on fibresand and any turf going: visored (below form) once at 3 yrs: held up. *T. D. Barron*

SADLER'S IMAGE (IRE) 4 b.c. Sadler's Wells (USA) 132 – Exclusive Order (USA) 120 (Exclusive Native (USA)) [1994 112: 10d* 12.3m^3 11.9f* 12m 13.4g* 12m* 12v^4 1995 13.3g^2 May 20] rangy colt: impressed good deal in appearance: good walker: smart performer: respectable ¾-length second of 6 to Escarpment in listed event at Newbury on only start at 4 yrs: stayed 13.4f: very best form on a sound surface (acted on firm), respectable effort on heavy: reportedly suffered twisted gut later in May: dead. *M. R. Stoute* 108

SADLER'S PEARL 3 b.f. Thowra (FR) – Queens Pearl (Queen's Hussar 124) [1994 NR 1995 7m 8g 8m 10m a14.8g^6 a16g 11.5m 12m^6 a16.2g Jul 21] plain, sturdy filly: sixth reported foal: half-sister to winning sprinters Queen's Tickle and Albert Henry (both by Tickled Pink): dam of little account: poor maiden: no form last 4 starts, blinkered in amateur riders handicaps last 3: stays 1½m. *B. J. Meehan* 49 d

SADLER'S REALM 2 b.c. (Apr 10) Sadler's Wells (USA) 132 – Rensaler (USA) (Stop The Music (USA)) [1995 8.2m^6 Oct 26] 110,000Y: attractive colt: brother to useful 3-y-o Opera Lover, 8.1f winner at 2 yrs, closely related to 1989 2-y-o 6f winner Jovial (by Northern Jove), later very smart graded winner at up to 1¼m in USA, and half-brother to several winners, including 1m winner Convivial (by Nordance): dam 1m winner in USA: weak 6/1-shot, needed race when around 5 lengths sixth of 11 to Dance Star in maiden at Nottingham, travelling quite well for nearly 6f then fading: unimpressive to post: sure to do better. *M. R. Stoute* 63 p

SADLER'S WALK 4 b.g. Sadler's Wells (USA) 132 – Widows Walk (Habitat 134) [1994 71: 10d 10m* 10.1d 1995 10d^4 10m^5 10.3m^2 10f^3 10f* 10f^4 10d 10.4m^2 Oct 4] good-bodied colt: impresses in appearance: has a quick action: fairly useful handicapper: won at Kempton in July: good efforts in frame at Goodwood (William Hill Cup) and York afterwards: suited by at least 1¼m: acts on firm going, not at his best on a soft surface: usually held up. *G. Wragg* 82

SADLY SOBER (IRE) 3 b.f. Roi Danzig (USA) – Overcall (Bustino 136) [1994 70: 6g^4 6m^2 1995 10m^4 10.5d a6g^2 a8g^6 a7g^5 Dec 2] sturdy filly: fair maiden: needs further than 6f, stays 1¼m well: acts on good to firm ground and equitrack: blinkered last 3 starts: sold 26,000 gns Newmarket December Sales. *P. F. I. Cole* 66

SAFECRACKER 2 ch.c. (Feb 12) Sayf El Arab (USA) 127 – My Polished Corner (IRE) 53 (Tate Gallery (USA) 117) [1995 7.1m 7.6d Sep 14] 10,000F, 950Y: lengthy colt: first foal: dam stayed 11f: never-dangerous seventh of 12 in median auction maiden at Sandown in August: tailed off in maiden at Lingfield following month. *J. W. Hills* –

SAFE SECRET 4 b.f. Seclude (USA) – Safe Passage (Charlottown 127) [1994 50: 12d^2 12g a12g 1995 11.8m 11.6m 8.3g 8m 7.1m 8h Aug 8] leggy filly: poor handicapper: sold out of J. Pearce's stable 3,800 gns Doncaster March Sales before reappearance: seems to stay 1½m: best effort on dead ground on debut at 3 yrs, has raced only on a sound surface since: inconsistent: awarded selling hurdle in November. *R. Brotherton* 33

SAFETY FACTOR (USA) 4 b.c. Known Fact (USA) 135 – Sookera (USA) 117 (Roberto (USA) 131) [1994 –: 6m 1995 6m^6 6g^3 Jul 27] was a steadily-improving maiden, third of 10 at Salisbury final start: should have stayed 7f: dead. *G. Harwood* 82

SAFEY ANA (USA) 4 b.g. Dixieland Band (USA) – Whatsoraire (USA) (Mr Prospector (USA)) [1994 80?: 8d 12m^5 10g^2 10.1d^3 10g 10m 8m 1995 8d^6 8m^5 10m 8m^3 7m* 6m 7g* 7.6m^5 7m^6 7g^3 7.3d 7g Sep 30] good-bodied gelding: poor mover: fair handicapper: won at Redcar (maiden) in May and Newbury in July: effective at 7f, and stays 1¼m: acts on good to firm and dead ground: effective blinkered or not: sometimes rears stalls: wears bandages. *B. Hanbury* 77

SAFIO 2 ch.c. (Feb 12) Efisio 120 – Marcroft 91 (Crofthall 110) [1995 5g* 6g^6 6g^3 5f 5m^5 6m 5.2d Sep 16] workmanlike colt: first foal: dam best at 7f to 1m: won minor event at Thirsk in April: never a factor when third of 6 to South Salem in similar event at Doncaster and eighth of 14 behind Kuantan in Windsor Castle Stakes at Ascot, best subsequent efforts: outpaced in nurseries last 2 starts: stays 6f: bandaged near-hind penultimate outing. *C. Smith* 79 ?

SAFWAN 3 b.c. Primo Dominie 121 – French Plait (Thatching 131) [1994 NR 1995 8d Sep 15] 10,000F, 35,000Y: strong colt: half-brother to modest 7f/1m performer Rural Lad (by Town And Country): dam, out of a 2m winner, seemingly of little account: soundly beaten in 19-runner maiden at Newbury. *Miss Gay Kelleway*
–

SAGAR PRIDE (IRE) 2 br.f. (Apr 26) Jareer (USA) 115 – Sagar Island (USA) 75 (Sagace (FR) 135) [1995 5g^{2} 5g* 5g^{2} 5m Jun 21] sparely-made filly: second foal: half-sister to a winner in Italy by Shardari: dam, lightly-raced maiden, should have stayed 1½m, out of sister to top-class Irish River: won maiden at Milan in May: best effort when head second to Nashcash in listed race at the Curragh following start: lost prominent early position then kept on towards finish when eighth of 12 behind Blue Duster in Queen Mary Stakes at Ascot on final outing: will be suited by further than 5f: looked likely to improve further. *J. G. Burns, Ireland*
94

SAGASAN 4 b.g. Rousillon (USA) 133 – Scholastika (GER) (Alpenkonig (GER)) [1994 60, a67: 7m 10m^{5} a9.4g a12g^{2} a12g* a12g^{6} 12.1g^{3} 12s^{6} 1995 a11g a12g^{2} a12g a12g^{4} 11.6m Jun 5] smallish gelding: modest performer: form in 1995 only when second in claimer at Southwell: stays at least 1½m: acts on fibresand and on heavy ground, may be unsuited by top-of-the-ground: occasional front runner: has been gelded: sold 4,700 gns Newmarket Autumn Sales: sent to Germany. *W. R. Muir*
–
a59

SAGEBRUSH ROLLER 7 br.g. Sharpo 132 – Sunita (Owen Dudley 121) [1994 90: 6m* 6s^{4} 8s^{4} 7.6m^{2} 8g^{4} 7f^{4} 7m 7m^{2} 7.6g 7s^{3} 7g* 7m^{2} 1995 6g 7m^{3} 7.6m 7g 7m^{6} 7g^{4} 7g^{2} 7g 7g 7m Nov 3] rangy gelding: fairly useful handicapper: effective at 6f to 1m: probably acts on any going: visored (below form) once at 4 yrs: sometimes hangs under pressure, and best held up. *J. W. Watts*
87

SAGITTA'S REEL (HOL) 4 b.f. Scottish Reel 123 – Sagitta's Choice 51 (Welsh Pageant 132) [1994 NR 1995 10f^{2} 9.7m a9.5g^{5} a9.3g^{2} a9g Dec 17] Dutch-bred filly: runner-up in minor events at Ostend in August and Sterrebeek in November: 16/1, well-beaten seventh of 8 in maiden at Folkestone on second outing: probably stays 1¼m: acts on all-weather. *Mrs J. Reynaert, Belgium*
27

SAHHAR 2 ch.c. (Apr 7) Sayf El Arab (USA) 127 – Native Magic 97 (Be My Native (USA) 122) [1995 6m a10g^{3} a8g^{2} Dec 18] small colt: first foal: dam stayer: progressive form: second of 9 to Red Rusty in maiden at Lingfield: stays 1¼m. *R. W. Armstrong*
65

SAHIL (IRE) 3 b.c. Taufan (USA) 119 – Bouffant (High Top 131) [1994 57p: 7m 1995 10m^{4} 9.9m* 10g Jun 3] good-topped colt: has a round action: fairly useful form: narrowly won median auction maiden at Beverley in May, making virtually all: tailed-off last in handicap at Lingfield 3 weeks later: stays 1¼m: acts on good to firm ground: sold 16,000 gns Newmarket July Sales: sent to Macau. *D. Morley*
81

SAIBOT (USA) 6 ch.g. Riverman (USA) 131 – Arabev (USA) (Damascus (USA)) [1994 6.3s^{3} 8.5g* 9g 8m 8d* 10s^{3} 10v^{6} 1995 9m^{4} 10.1f^{6} 9.6g 9m Jul 22] $160,000F: big, lengthy gelding: third foal: dam unraced half-sister to Grade 3-placed Spectacular Bev: useful Irish handicapper: won maiden (over 1½m) at 3 yrs, handicaps (9f and 1¼m) at 4yrs then valuable handicap at Galway and Irish Cambridgeshire at the Curragh at 5 yrs: ran well when fourth of 7 in listed race at Leopardstown on reappearance: respectable efforts at best afterwards, including at Epsom on second start: stays 1½m, but generally races at shorter nowadays: seems to act on good to firm ground, though had previously seemed suited by some give and acts on soft: blinkered final outing and on 4 of last 5 starts at 5 yrs. *D. K. Weld, Ireland*
95

SAIFAN 6 ch.g. Beveled (USA) – Superfrost 49 (Tickled Pink 114) [1994 75d: 8.1d^{6} 8m 8.1g 8m 8m 8s 8m 8d 1995 7s 8m^{2} 8m 8g^{3} 8m* 8g^{6} 8m^{2} 8f^{4} 7m* 8d 8m 8f 8m Oct 28] tall, close-coupled, angular gelding: has a round action: fair handicapper: won at Yarmouth in July and Leicester in August: effective at 7f and 1m: probably acts on any going: almost always blinkered or visored: held up. *D. Morris*
79

SAILORMAITE 4 ch.g. Komaite (USA) – Marina Plata (Julio Mariner 127) [1994 80p: a11g a8g^{3} a7g^{3} 8m a6g* 6.1m a6g* a7g^{2} 5m^{3} a7g* a8g* 8.5g* 7.1d 8s 8.2g 6g* 1995 6g^{2} 6d^{4} 6m 6d* a6g* 5g^{2} 5.6m 6g a6g^{4} a7g^{2} Nov 16] tall, leggy gelding: made into a useful handicapper: won at Haydock and Wolverhampton in June: short-head second of 8 in £15,400 rated stakes at Ascot next start: best effort at Southwell final one: successful at 8.5f, but best at up to 7f: acts on fibresand and soft going, probably unsuited by top-of-the-ground: blinkered (well beaten) on debut:
87
a96

Phil Bull Trophy, Pontefract—easy for Salaman

often mounted on track and taken down early: rather a difficult ride (carries head high, tends to idle, unseated jockey to post eighth start): tough. *S. R. Bowring*

SAILORS MOON 3 ch.f. Indian Ridge 123 – Premiere Moon 80 (Bold Owl 101) 38
[1994 –: 6m 8.2s 5d 1995 a7g^{6} 10g 8m Apr 20] small filly: has a quick action: poor maiden plater: stays 7f. *H. J. Collingridge*

SAILS LEGEND 4 b.c. Hotfoot 126 – Miss Polly Peck (March Past 124) [1994 –
–: 10m 12s 1995 16.4m 16m 12s 16.1g Oct 3] smallish, workmanlike colt: no worthwhile form on flat since 2 yrs: probably a stayer. *Mrs M. E. Long*

SAINT AMIGO 3 gr.c. Presidium 124 – Little Token (Shack (USA) 118) [1994 52 ?
56: 5g^{3} 6f^{5} 5f 5m^{3} 6g 6g^{5} 7g^{3} 7d* 6g^{5} 7s^{6} 7d^{3} a7g^{3} 1995 8f 8.2m 8f 5.9f^{6} 7m 6g 6m 8.2m 7m a11g a6g Nov 30] small colt: modest performer: mostly disappointing in 1995: stays 1m: acts on fibresand and on good to firm and soft ground: tried in blinkers/visor, no improvement. *J. L. Eyre*

SAINT CIEL (USA) 7 b.h. Skywalker (USA) – Holy Tobin (USA) (J O Tobin –
(USA) 130) [1994 53d: 10.8s^{3} 10v 10v 10.5g^{3} 10.2m 10s^{3} 10.4d^{5} 10d 1995 10d Sep 19] leggy, quite attractive horse: has a round action: modest handicapper at best nowadays: stays 1½m: acts on any going: twice below form in blinkers at 3 yrs: sometimes has tongue tied down: held up: fair hurdler: inconsistent. *F. Jordan*

SAINT EXPRESS 5 ch.g. Clantime 101 – Redgrave Design 77 (Nebbiolo 125) 109
[1994 91: 6v^{4} 5.2s 5.1m 5f^{6} 5d^{5} 5m^{3} 5m* 6f^{2} 6d 5s^{6} 1995 5g^{2} 5m* 5m^{2} 5f^{3} 6m^{4} 5m 5d^{3} 6m Oct 14] lengthy, sparely-made gelding: has a quick action: better than ever at 5 yrs, and is a useful performer: won handicap at York (for second year running) in June: in frame in listed race at Sandown (¾ length second to Bunty Boo), King George Stakes at Goodwood (close third to Hever Golf Rose) and listed race at Newmarket (to Cheyenne Spirit) next 3 starts: below form afterwards: stays 6f, but may be ideally suited by 5f: acts on soft going, best efforts on top-of-the-ground: genuine. *Mrs M. Reveley*

SAINT ROSALINA 2 b.f. (Mar 5) Common Grounds 118 – Saint Systems 68 49
(Uncle Pokey 116) [1995 7m^{3} a6g^{2} 6.1m^{2} 6.1s a6g Nov 8] leggy filly: blind in near eye and wears an eyecover: first foal: dam sprinter: placed in claimer and sellers in the summer: no form afterwards: stays 7f: may be unsuited by soft ground. *C. J. Hill*

SAKEEN 2 ch.c. (Feb 27) Keen 116 – Santa's Queen (USA) (Sovereign Dancer ?
(USA)) [1995 7f^{5} 8f^{4} 6d^{5} a7.5g^{6} 9s a8g Nov 8] 3,700F, 1,800Y: first foal: dam unraced: poor form in Belgium: visored, tailed off in maiden at Lingfield final start. *Paul Smith, Belgium*

SAKHAROV 6 b.g. Bay Express 132 – Supreme Kingdom 85 (Take A Reef 127) 59
[1994 58: 6m^{6} a7g^{6} 7m^{4} 7f 5.9m* a6g^{4} 6.9g* 7m^{6} 7.1g^{5} 8d 8g 1995 a6g^{2} a6g^{6} 5.9m 6f^{3} 8.3f^{2} 6.9f^{3} 8m^{2} Jul 10] leggy gelding: modest handicapper: narrowly beaten last 4 starts: stays 8.2f: acts on firm and dead ground and on fibresand: held up: consistent. *M. Johnston*

SAKTI (AUS) 2 b.f. (Mar 11) Kenmare (FR) 125 – Sakala (NZ) (Gold And Ivory (USA) 128) [1995 5m⁴ 6m⁶ 7g⁶ 8g³ 7.5d⁶ 7.5g³ 7.5m⁵ 7d³ Nov 24] first foal: dam Australian sprinter: 4/1, fourth of 6 to Arvzees in seller at Folkestone: went to France and finished third in claimers and a weak minor event: stays 1m. *Mme A. Bollack-Badel, France* — 64 ?

SAKURA (IRE) 4 ch.f. Dominion 123 – Ariadne 79 (Bustino 136) [1994 35: 7m⁶ 8g a6g⁵ 9.2f 15.8g 1995 15.8m⁶ Aug 11] plain filly: poor maiden at best on flat here: broke leg over hurdles: dead. *M. D. Hammond* — –

SALAMANDER KING 3 b.g. Distant Relative 128 – Spirit of The Wind (USA) (Little Current (USA)) [1994 NR 1995 8g May 19] lengthy gelding: fourth known foal: half-brother to 1m winner Moon Mistress (by Storm Cat) and 11f winner North Wind (by Lomond): dam unraced half-sister to Grade 1 1¼m winner Dawn's Curtsey: 6/1 and bit backward, nineteenth of 21 in maiden at Newbury, slowly away and always behind: moved poorly to post: joined Lady Herries and gelded. *P. W. Chapple-Hyam* — –

SALAMAN (FR) 3 b.g. Saumarez 132 – Merry Sharp (Sharpen Up 127) [1994 75p: 7g⁵ 7s³ 1995 10s 12.3m³ 12m⁵ 14.9m* 16.2m* 18.7g* 20f³ 18m* 18m Oct 14] sturdy, lengthy gelding: progressive handicapper: successful in small fields at Warwick in June, at Beverley and Chester in July and (after good third in Goodwood Stakes) in extremely slowly-run Phil Bull Trophy at Pontefract (9/1 on) in August: eleventh in Cesarewitch final start, eased when beaten: will prove best with an out-and-out test of stamina: gelded and stays in training: capable of better still. *J. L. Dunlop* — 89 p

SALBUS 5 b.g. Salse (USA) 128 – Busca (USA) 49 (Mr Prospector (USA)) [1994 –, a78: 9.7s 7d 8m 8g 8.3m 7m a9.4g⁵ 1995 a12g² a12g* a12g⁵ a9.4g⁴ a12g Mar 4] lengthy, good-bodied gelding: carries condition: modest performer: landed odds in claimer at Wolverhampton in January: stays 1½m: acts on all-weather surfaces: tried visored (below form) and blinkered (including when successful): inconsistent. *F. J. Yardley* — – a62

SALDUBA 3 b.f. Fijar Tango (FR) 127 – Silver Ore (FR) 94 (Silver Hawk (USA) 123) [1994 –: 7g 9d 1995 10g⁵ 8.1m 7g⁶ 8.3f⁴ 8.3g⁵ Sep 24] small, leggy filly: no worthwhile form: bred to stay 1¼m. *T. Dyer* — –

SALEEL (IRE) 3 b.c. Salse (USA) 128 – Kentfield (Busted 134) [1994 NR 1995 10m 10m⁴ 9.9m² 12m* 13.9m* 14.6m² 18m⁵ 16m⁴ Oct 27] IR 80,000Y: lengthy, robust colt: carries plenty of condition: unimpressive mover: first foal: dam once-raced half-sister to very useful Irish sprinter Puissance: useful performer: won 3-runner maiden at Pontefract and 5-runner rated stakes at York (got the better of last — 101

Stakis Casinos Melrose Rated Stakes (Handicap), York—
hard work for the judge as Saleel (left) and Grey Shot have a terrific battle

2f battle with Grey Shot by a short head) in the summer: best effort when neck second of 6 to Grey Shot in £12,900 handicap at Doncaster in September: stays 2m, appeared not truly to stay 2¼m in Cesarewitch: has raced only on good to firm ground: sent to Dubai. *A. C. Stewart*

SALFRILL (IRE) 3 b.f. Salt Dome (USA) – Frill (Henbit (USA) 130) [1994 –: 7m 1995 10.8g4 11.6g Jun 12] no worthwhile form, in claimers at 3 yrs. *Mrs P. Sly* –

SALILIAN TWILIGHT 2 b.f. (Apr 3) Bairn (USA) 126 – Salilia 93 (Nishapour (FR) 125) [1995 5m6 6f5 Aug 2] 500Y: leggy, angular filly: not a good walker: seventh foal: half-sister to 1993 2-y-o 5f winner Nsx (by Roi Danzig), French 9.5f and 1½m winner Sakara (by Lashkari) and a winner in Sweden: dam 9f and 1¼m winner: no worthwhile form in maiden auction (very slowly away) at Beverley and seller at Brighton: sold 700 gns Newmarket September Sales: sent to Cyprus. *J. Pearce* –

SALINGER 7 b.g. Rousillon (USA) 133 – Scholastika (GER) (Alpenkonig (GER)) [1994 NR 1995 a8g4 a8g 14.1g 14.1m6 12m* 11m* 10.4g Aug 31] workmanlike gelding: poor handicapper on flat: won (first time) amateur contests at Catterick and Redcar in August: seems best at up to 1½m: acts on soft ground, good to firm and fibresand. *J. Parkes* 46

SALLYOREALLY (IRE) 4 b.f. Common Grounds 118 – Prosapia (USA) (Our Native (USA)) [1994 57: 10v4 9s4 7f4 7g 1995 10m 12g 12.4g 10g 10f 10.1m5 8m 15.8m6 15.1g6 12f 8f Oct 24] leggy, lengthy filly: looked only poor at best for new stable in 1995: probably stays 1½m: acts on firm ground and soft. *W. Storey* –

SALLY SLADE 3 b.f. Dowsing (USA) 124 – Single Gal 97 (Mansingh (USA) 120) [1994 78: 5m4 6m6 6f5 6m 5.3m* 6m 5d2 5s* 7m 1995 a5g5 6m 5m* 5.1m 6g2 5f Jun 24] unfurnished filly: fair handicapper: won at Windsor in May: stays 6f: acts on good to firm and soft ground: edged left penultimate 3-y-o start: inconsistent. *C. A. Cyzer* 80

SALLY STATE 2 b.f. (May 1) Northern State (USA) 91 – Cadenza 52 (Radetzky 123) [1995 6f4 6m 8.2d Sep 19] sturdy, angular filly: third live foal: dam, non-thoroughbred probably stayed 1½m, half-sister to Vocalist, very useful winner at up to 9f here and in USA: burly, well beaten in varied company, including selling. *Mrs M. McCourt* –

SALLY'S TWINS 2 b.f. (May 9) Dowsing (USA) 124 – Bird of Love 82 (Ela-Mana-Mou 132) [1995 7.6d 8d6 10g Oct 9] 5,000Y, 5,000 2-y-o: good-topped filly: third foal: dam twice-raced half-sister to very useful middle-distance stayer Water Boatman out of half-sister to high-class stayer Sea Anchor: modest form in maidens and a minor event: seems to stay 1¼m. *J. S. Moore* 59

SALLY WELD 3 ch.f. Weldnaas (USA) 112 – Sallytude (Tudor Music 131) [1994 65: 5g 5.7f5 6f* 6m 5.1g6 6g 6g 6v a5g3 a7g 1995 6m4 5.1f 6g 6f5 6m6 7f* 7m 7d 7g5 a7g a7g4 Dec 14] compact filly: modest handicapper: won at Brighton in August: stays 7f: acts on firm ground and equitrack, well below form on a soft surface: usually races prominently. *C. J. Benstead* 60

SALMIS 2 b.f. (Apr 15) Salse (USA) 128 – Misguided 106 (Homing 130) [1995 6.9s* 8.1d2 Oct 11] 4,200Y: angular filly: half-sister to useful 5-y-o middle-distance stayer Misbelief (by Shirley Heights), German 3-y-o 6.5f winner May Be Best (by Night Shift) and fairly useful 1987 2-y-o 5f and 7f winner Kajar (by Persian Bold): dam sprinting half-sister to smart 6f and 1m winner Missed Blessing: won 11-runner maiden auction at Folkestone in September by 1¼ lengths from Missile: beaten ¾ length by comfortable winner Inchrory in 4-runner minor event at Haydock following month: will probably stay beyond 1m: likely to improve again. *J. R. Fanshawe* 84 p

SALMON LADDER (USA) 3 b.c. Bering 136 – Ballerina Princess (USA) (Mr Prospector (USA)) [1994 90p: 8d3 7.9d* 1995 10.4g6 12f 12d5 Oct 21] good-topped colt: has scope: useful form: sixth of 8 in Dante Stakes at York (wore dropped noseband and bandaged near-hind) and tenth of 15 in Derby at Epsom (never in the hunt) first 2 starts at 3 yrs: reportedly had wind operation afterwards: looked well but ran as if in need of race when nearly 11 lengths fifth of 12 to Phantom Gold in St Simon Stakes at Newbury over 4 months later, no extra after promising effort over 2f out: should stay 1½m. *P. F. I. Cole* 101

SALSIAN 2 b.f. (Mar 8) Salse (USA) 128 – Phylae (Habitat 134) [1995 8g 8.2m Oct 26] lengthy, dipped-backed filly: third foal: half-sister to 3-y-o Bad News (by Pharly) and middle-distance winner Phylian (by Glint of Gold): dam poor maiden from family of Upper Nile and champion US grass filly De La Rose: signs of ability in maidens at Leicester (nearest finish after being slowly away) and Nottingham (always behind), both in October: bandaged near hind: will stay middle distances: likely to do better. *S. C. Williams* – p

SALSKA 4 b.f. Salse (USA) 128 – Anzeige (GER) (Soderini 123) [1994 67d: 6g^5 7f 7m^4 10.5g 7.1d^4 8s 8d^5 8.2d^5 a8g a12g a9.4g^5 1995 a9.4g 10m 8.1m^4 10m 10m 10m^2 11m^3 10m^6 10m 10d^5 14g* 16m Oct 19] strong, lengthy filly: modest handicapper: trained by P. Bevan (reappearance) then A. Forbes first 4 starts at 4 yrs: won 20-runner maiden handicap at Haydock in September: much better suited by 1¾m than 1¼m and should get further: acts on good to firm ground, probably on dead: tried visored, no improvement. *A. Streeter* 51

SALTANDO (IRE) 4 b.g. Salt Dome (USA) – Ange de Feu (Double Form 130) [1994 NR 1995 6g 6m 8.2m^4 8m 7m^3 8g^4 10d 8g^3 8s^3 8m 10f 12m a8g* a11g^4 Dec 1] angular gelding: third reported foal: dam never ran: modest handicapper: won minor event at Southwell in November: should prove fully effective at 11f (respectable effort final start): acts on good to firm and soft going, and on fibresand. *Pat Mitchell* 55

SALTIS (IRE) 3 ch.g. Salt Dome (USA) – Mrs Tittlemouse (Nonoalco (USA) 131) [1994 57: 6m 7m^4 7.5g^3 6s^3 6m^3 1995 8.3m a8g^4 7.1m^4 8m^4 7m 7m 7s^4 7m a7g a10g Dec 15] angular gelding: modest maiden handicapper: stays 1m: acts on good to firm ground, soft and equitrack: takes keen hold: often bandaged behind: inconsistent. *D. W. P. Arbuthnot* 56

SALT LAKE 4 b.c. Mtoto 134 – Bluebook (USA) 120 (Secretariat (USA)) [1994 87: 8.2m* 7d^4 10m 1995 8g^6 9m^2 10f* 10m^2 10.5f 10m^4 10.9g^3 9f Nov 25] well-made colt: impresses in appearance: fluent mover: useful performer: won £18,600 handicap at Ascot in June: ran very well when second of 17 to Yoush in £45,900 handicap at Sandown and 3 lengths fourth of 9 to Desert Shot in Winter Hill Stakes at Windsor: below best in Doonside Cup at Ayr (final start for P. Chapple-Hyam) and Grade 3 event in USA last 2 starts: useful form at 1¼m and should be at least as effective over 1½m: acts on firm and dead ground: made running second to fourth starts at 4 yrs: edgy (ran as if something amiss) fifth 4-y-o start: genuine. *J. Servis, USA* 106

SALTY GIRL (IRE) 2 b.f. (Feb 16) Scenic 128 – Sodium's Niece (Northfields (USA)) [1995 6g^5 7f^3 8g^4 7.1s^2 6.9g^6 Oct 16] IR 9,500F, 13,000Y: sturdy filly: half-sister to Italian 3-y-o 9f winner Shariba (by Bluebird) and fair 6f (at 2 yrs) and 9f winner Danzarin (by Kings Lake): dam, lightly raced, placed over 8.5f at 2 yrs in Ireland: fair maiden: ran poorly in maiden auction at Folkestone on final outing: will be suited by middle distances. *B. W. Hills* 70

SALTZ (IRE) 3 b.g. Salt Dome (USA) – Heather Hut (Shack (USA) 118) [1994 72: 5.1m^3 5m^4 6f^6 6m^2 5m^5 6g^5 5d^3 6g 1995 a5g^5 a5g 6g 5g^5 7.1m^5 6m 8m^2 8.2m* 8f Aug 28] compact gelding: modest handicapper: won at Nottingham in August: stays 8.2f: acts on good to firm ground and (best 2-y-o efforts) dead. *P. T. Dalton* 58

SALUTATION (IRE) 4 b.g. Salt Dome (USA) – Salvationist (Mill Reef (USA) 141) [1994 –: a8.5g a11g a11g 1995 a11g Mar 20] no worthwhile form: tried visored. *T. Kersey* –

SALUTING WALTER (USA) 7 b.g. Verbatim (USA) – Stage Hour (USA) (Stage Director (USA)) [1994 39: a9.4g a10g a8.5g 8.2m 6.1m a7g^4 10m 1995 a10g Nov 25] leggy, good-topped gelding: just a poor performer in 1994 for P. D. Evans: stiff task, no immediate promise in seller at Lingfield on belated return: stays 1¼m: acts on fibresand and on good to firm and dead ground: visored (no form) on 6-y-o reappearance: inconsistent. *R. Akehurst* –

SALVATORE GIULIANO 5 ch.g. Superlative 118 – Bonny Bright Eyes 58 (Rarity 129) [1994 NR 1995 10f^6 14f^6 a10g^3 8.5s 8m^5 a12g Oct 23] strong, compact gelding: poor form at best: stays 1¼m: acts on good to firm and dead ground and on equitrack: blinkered (no form) once at 3 yrs: inconsistent. *A. G. Foster* 42

SAMAH 5 ch.g. Pennine Walk 120 – Ghanayim (USA) 107 (Sharpen Up 127) [1994 74: 7v^6 6v^3 5.1m 6m 7s^6 7m 8m* 8f^4 7d^3 7s^3 1995 8g^5 8m 8m 8.9m 8g* 7g* 7g 80

H & K Commissions Handicap, Newmarket—
20/1 has become 7/2 as Samah (noseband) short heads Deevee to win the race for a second year running

8g 6g 7d 7g* 7g Oct 7] deep-bodied gelding: fairly useful handicapper: justified heavy support at Newmarket (for second year running) in July then won at York (sweating) in August and Newmarket in September: effective at 6f to 1m: acts on any going: best held up: usually early to post: reportedly to race in USA. *D. Nicholls*

SAMAKA HARA (IRE) 3 b.g. Taufan (USA) 119 – Aunt Hester (IRE) 68 (Caerleon (USA) 132) [1994 55?: 5d 5g⁴ 6s 6g 6m* 6g 7.5g 7m 1995 7.1g⁶ a8g⁶ 8.3g* 9.2g⁵ 8.1g⁴ a8g² 8.5g³ 11.1f² 10.4g 10g Sep 23] rather unfurnished gelding: modest performer on turf, poor on all-weather: won claimer at Hamilton in May: stays 11.1f: acts on firm ground and fibresand: wears a severe noseband. *W. S. Cunningham* — 54, a40

SAMANA CAY 3 ch.f. Pharly (FR) 130 – Brown's Cay 71 (Formidable (USA) 125) [1994 52: 7m 7m⁴ 6.9m* 8m 7.5g⁵ 10s 7s a8g⁵ 1995 a6g⁴ a7g² a8g⁴ a8g³ a8g³ 10m⁴ 12g⁵ 6.9f⁵ 8.3f³ 8m Aug 7] small, stocky filly: has knee action: poor performer: should stay beyond 1m: acts on good to firm ground and fibresand, well below form on soft: tried blinkered and visored: sold (D. Nicholls to P. Felgate) 1,200 gns Doncaster October Sales. *D. Nicholls* — 40, a48

SAMARA (IRE) 2 ch.f. (Apr 21) Polish Patriot (USA) 128 – Smeralda (GER) (Dschingis Khan) [1995 6d 6s 6f² Oct 23] 58,000Y: good-topped filly: has plenty of scope: has a fluent, round action: half-sister to several winners here and abroad, including Soto Grande (by Kaiseradler), winner of German 2,000 Guineas, and useful 3-y-o 7.5f (at 2 yrs) and 1¼m winner in Italy Steady Ready Go (by Night Shift) and smart middle-distance stayer Lille Hammer (by Sadler's Wells): dam winner in Germany and is half-sister to German Oaks winner Slenderella and to dam of high-class middle-distance 3-y-o Solon: 3½ lengths second of 18 to Wildwood Flower in maiden at Leicester on final start, staying on well: will stay 7f+: will improve again. *J. L. Dunlop* — 69 p

SAMARA SONG 2 ch.c. (May 9) Savahra Sound 111 – Hosting (Thatching 131) [1995 6m 8.1m 6d Sep 27] lengthy, unfurnished colt: first reported foal: dam unraced: well beaten in minor events and a maiden. *R. J. Baker* –

SAMBA SHARPLY 4 b.g. Rambo Dancer (CAN) 107 – Sharper Still (Sharpen Up 127) [1994 80: 8.2d* 9m* 10m^3 8m^5 8d^2 8s* 1995 8m 8.1g^2 8f^2 8m^5 7m^3 8d 8.2m* 8m Oct 28] compact gelding: fairly useful handicapper: won at Nottingham in October, staying on strongly to lead close home: not discredited over 7f, but really wants further and stays 1¼m: acts on firm and soft ground: sweating (below form) final 4-y-o start: genuine. *A. Hide* 84

SAM COLES (USA) 2 br.f. (May 4) Pirate Army (USA) 118 – Ancora (GER) (Cortez (GER)) [1995 5m 5.3m* 5m May 1] $5,500F, 2,100Y: small filly: half-sister to several winners in North America: dam won in Germany: dead-heated in 7-runner maiden auction at Brighton: dead. *B. J. Meehan* 56

SAMIM (USA) 2 b.c. (May 27) Nureyev (USA) 131 – Histoire (FR) (Riverman (USA) 131) [1995 7m^6 7g^3 8.5m^3 7d* 7.9m^4 Oct 5] small, attractive colt: eighth foal: brother to smart 7f (at 2 yrs) to 1¼m winner Oumaldaaya and half-brother to several winners, notably Derby winner Erhaab (by Chief's Crown): dam French 10.5f winner: much improved effort when winning 15-runner nursery at Redcar in September: creditable fourth to Weet-A-Minute in similar event at York 13 days later, soon off bit and making only a little headway when short of room over 1f out: stays 1m: acts on good to firm ground but better suited by a soft surface: probably capable of better. *J. L. Dunlop* 84 p

SAMRAAN (USA) 2 br.c. (Jan 11) Green Dancer (USA) 132 – Sedra 116 (Nebbiolo 125) [1995 7m^4 Oct 14] angular, unfurnished colt: looked weak: half-brother to several winners, including useful 6f (at 2 yrs) and 7f winner Star Talent (by Local Talent) and Irish 7f and 1m winner Topper Up (by Sharpen Up): dam 6f (at 2 yrs) to 1¼m winner: 4/1, 8½ lengths fourth of 5 to Babinda in minor event at Newmarket, very green for much of way but getting hang of things close home: will improve. *J. L. Dunlop* 68 p

SAMSOLOM 7 b.g. Absalom 128 – Norfolk Serenade 83 (Blakeney 126) [1994 80: a6g^2 a6g^2 a6g 6f 6m^3 6m 6m 6m^5 6m^5 6f 6g 6m 1995 6d 6g 6m 6f^4 6m^4 6d^6 6f* 6m^3 6m^2 6m 6m* 6f^2 6m 6m^4 6g 7f^6 7f Oct 25] strong, good-quartered gelding: has round action: fair handicapper: won at Goodwood and Yarmouth in the summer: stays 6f, probably 7f: has won on dead ground, but easily best form on a sound surface (acts on firm) or the all-weather: tried blinkered/visored, not since 4 yrs: usually held up: taken down early (below form nonetheless) last 4 starts. *P. Howling* 76

SAMSON-AGONISTES 9 b.g. Bold Fort 100 – Hello Cuddles 99 (He Loves Me 120) [1994 63, a78: a5g* a5g^2 a5g^2 a5g^2 a5g* a5g^4 6s a5g^2 a6g^3 5m 6m^3 5m a5g 5m a5g^3 a6g^4 1995 a5g^6 a5g^3 a5g^2 a5g a6g a5g^3 a6g Mar 16] leggy gelding: poor mover: a front-running sprinter in his prime, who won 14 and was in the frame in a further 25 of his 78 starts, reaching his peak (rated 83) in 1992: just a fair performer and none too consistent at end of career: probably acted on any surface, except very soft: visored (well beaten) twice: collapsed and died from a heart attack after returning from exercise April 15. *P. D. Evans* – a69

SAMSONESQUE 4 ch.f. Unfuwain (USA) 131 – Fatal Distraction (Formidable (USA) 125) [1994 NR 1995 8d^4 9.9m^3 10.9m^6 10m a8g^2 10g^5 a10s^3 a12g* Nov 28] sturdy, plain filly: off course over 17 months prior to reappearance: fair handicapper: sold out of J. Fanshawe's stable 2,500 gns Newmarket July Sales after fourth start: won at Taby in November: stays 1½m: acts on good to firm ground and dead, and on dirt: visored (well below form) final start here. *M. Khan, Sweden* 66

SAMSUNG LOVELYLADY (IRE) 3 b.f. Petorius 117 – Kentucky Wildcat 64 (Be My Guest (USA) 126) [1994 NR 1995 5.1g 7g 5m^6 5g 5m^4 a5g 6m Jul 22] IR 13,500Y: lengthy filly: third foal: half-sister to 1993 2-y-o sprint winner (7f and 1m winner in France in 1995) Randonneur (by Red Sunset) and fair 5f and 6f winner Two Moves In Front (by Ballad Rock): dam, maiden, stayed 2m: poor maiden: looks a sprinter: acts on good to firm ground: no improvement in visor: inconsistent. *E. Weymes* 47

SAMUEL SCOTT 2 b.g. (Feb 18) Shareef Dancer (USA) 135 – Revisit 86 (Busted 134) [1995 6m Jul 22] quite attractive gelding: fourth living foal: half-brother to 3-y-o 12.5f winner Peter Monamy (by Prince Sabo): dam stayer: 14/1 – p and unimpressive to post, slowly away when ninth of 10 to Akalim in maiden at Newmarket: bred to need middle distances: looked likely to improve. *M. Bell*

SAMWAR 3 b.g. Warning 136 – Samaza (USA) 90 (Arctic Tern (USA) 126) [1994 78: 5f^{2} 6g^{5} 1995 7m^{4} 6m^{4} 6g^{6} a7g* Dec 19] leggy gelding: fair performer: sold out of B. Hills's stable 9,000 gns Newmarket July Sales and gelded: off course 7 months and heavily-backed favourite, impressive 6-length winner of maiden at Lingfield in December: will stay 1m: has raced only on a sound surface on turf: may do better. *Miss Gay Kelleway* 78 +

SANDABAR 2 b.c. (Apr 21) Green Desert (USA) 127 – Children's Corner (FR) 106 (Top Ville 129) [1995 7f Aug 17] useful-looking colt: half-brother to smart 1992 French 2-y-o 1m winner Kindergarten (by Trempolino) and a winner in France by Akarad: dam French 1m (at 2 yrs) and 9f winner: 3/1, over 10 lengths seventh of 15 to Alzanti in maiden at Salisbury, taking good hold after slow start and never a serious factor: will improve. *M. R. Stoute* 60 p

SANDBLASTER 2 ch.f. (Feb 10) Most Welcome 131 – Honeychurch (USA) 93 (Bering 136) [1995 5m 5g 7m 5f 6f^{4} Oct 24] 1,800Y: sparely-made filly: first foal: dam won over 10.5f: never a factor in maiden events for Miss J. Craze first 3 starts: tenderly handled in maiden at Catterick before showing improved form when fourth of 20 to Times of Times in nursery at Redcar 10 days later: capable of better still, particularly over further than 6f. *Mrs J. R. Ramsden* 47 p

SANDICLIFFE (USA) 2 b.f. (Feb 8) Imp Society (USA) – Sad Song (USA) (Roberto (USA) 131) [1995 7g Oct 9] 18,500Y: workmanlike filly: seventh foal: half-sister to 2 minor stakes winners in USA: dam unraced: 10/1, green and in need of race, never a factor when twelfth of 18 to Fairlight Down in maiden at Leicester. *B. W. Hills* –

SANDMOOR CHAMBRAY 4 ch.g. Most Welcome 131 – Valadon 72 (High Line 125) [1994 70: 9.9d^{5} 7.5m* 7.9f 10.5g^{5} 8m^{3} 8m^{2} 8.5g^{3} 1995 8g 7.5m* 8m 8m^{2} 8.1g^{4} 8m^{6} 8d 7d Sep 22] lengthy gelding: fair handicapper: won at Beverley in April: well below form at Doncaster (bit backward after 2-month absence and no blinkers) and Redcar last 2 starts: best form at around 1m: acts on good to firm and dead ground: best form in blinkers: possibly suited by strong handling: front runner/races prominently: game. *M. H. Easterby* 75

SANDMOOR DENIM 8 b.g. Red Sunset 120 – Holernzaye 93 (Sallust 134) [1994 75: 7.5d 9.9d 8.5m^{2} a7g^{5} 7m^{2} a8g^{5} 7d a7g^{4} 8g* 7s^{2} a7g^{4} a8.5g* a8g* a9.4g^{4} 1995 a8g^{3} a7g^{6} a8g 7s* a8.5g^{5} 8m a8g^{2} a8.5g 8.5d 8g a8.5g^{3} a8g^{2} a7g^{5} Nov 24] close-coupled gelding: carries condition: fair handicapper: won at Leicester in March: effective at 7f to 8.5f: acts on firm and soft ground and on all-weather surfaces: blinkered (below form) earlier in career: bandaged since sixth 7-y-o start: usually held up: often ridden by 7-lb claimer: tough. *S. R. Bowring* 72 a69

SANDMOOR VELVET 3 b.f. Primo Dominie 121 – Rectitude 99 (Runnymede 123) [1994 64d: 5m^{3} 5g 5m^{2} 6m^{5} 5f 5m^{3} 6g^{4} 6g 7g 1995 5m^{4} 6g^{4} 5f 5m 5m Aug 13] leggy filly: poor maiden handicapper: soundly beaten last 3 starts: stays 6f: acts on good to firm ground: has worn bandages: inconsistent: sold 550 gns Doncaster September Sales. *M. H. Easterby* 47

SANDPIPER 2 b.f. (May 7) Green Desert (USA) 127 – Sojourn 87 (Be My Guest (USA) 126) [1995 7d Sep 27] 10,000Y: neat filly: sixth reported foal: half-sister to fair stayer Arctic Guest (by Arctic Tern) and to 3-y-o 7f and 1m winner Distant Princess (by Distant Relative): dam 2-y-o 7f winner later successful in USA: 33/1 and better for race, tailed off after slow start in maiden at Salisbury: unimpressive and green to post. *K. O. Cunningham-Brown* –

SANDRA DEE (IRE) 3 ch.f. Be My Guest (USA) 126 – Adventurine (Thatching 131) [1994 60: 5.7g 6g^{3} a9.4g^{3} 1995 a7g^{2} a8g^{3} a7g^{5} a7g a7g^{6} 6.9m 5.3m^{5} 7m^{5} 7f a7g a10g 7g Oct 9] leggy filly: modest maiden, best form on all-weather: possibly best at up to 7f: acts on equitrack: most inconsistent. *B. A. Pearce* 60 d

SAND REEF 4 b.c. Reference Point 139 – Reine d'Egypte (USA) 114 (Val de L'Orne (FR) 133) [1994 117: 8s* 12g^{4} 10g* 10m^{3} 10d^{3} 10g* 10v* 1995 10m^{2} 12g^{2} 10m^{4} 10d^{2} 10d^{2} Dec 2] smart French performer: in frame in listed event at Longchamp, slowly-run Prix Jean de Chaudenay at Saint-Cloud (¾ length behind Sunshack), La Coupe at Evry, and, after nearly 5 months off, listed races at 113

Fontainebleau (beaten 1½ lengths by Suave Tern) and Saint-Cloud (neck second to Admise): effective at 1¼m and 1½m: acts on good to firm ground and heavy: races prominently. *Mme C. Head, France*

SAND STAR 3 b.f. Lugana Beach 116 – Overseas 48 (Sea Hawk II 131) [1994 NR 1995 a7g a6g^{4} a8.5g^{2} a7g* a8g^{6} a7g^{2} a6g a8.5g a7g^{3} a7g* a7g^{2} Dec 18] half-sister to several winners, including 1½m to 2m winner Atlantic Way (by Bold Owl): dam poor maiden: fair performer: won median auction maiden at Lingfield in February and handicap at Wolverhampton in December: stays 7f: has raced only on the all-weather: usually races prominently. *D. Haydn Jones* — 75

SANDY FLOSS (IRE) 2 b.c. (May 5) Green Desert (USA) 127 – Mill On The Floss 117 (Mill Reef (USA) 141) [1995 7f^{4} Jun 28] good-topped, attractive colt: good walker: easy mover: brother to temperamental 3-y-o Desert Harvest and middle-distance winner Hatta's Mill and half-brother to several winners, including useful middle-distance filly Milly Ha Ha (by Dancing Brave): dam 7f (at 2 yrs) and 1½m winner from very good family: 4/1 and carrying condition, over 11 lengths fourth of 7 to Canons Park in maiden at Kempton, always in same place and not knocked about: looks sort to do better. *H. R. A. Cecil* — – p

SANMARTINO (IRE) 3 b.c. Salse (USA) 128 – Oscura (USA) 82 (Caro 133) [1994 NR 1995 10m^{4} 10.3m^{2} 10.5g* 12f^{5} 13.9m* 15s^{4} Sep 30] sturdy colt: good mover: sixth foal: half-brother to several winners, notably very smart middle-distance performer Urgent Request (by Rainbow Quest): dam, 1m winner, half-sister to champion grass horse Johnny D: progressed into a useful performer: won maiden at Haydock (idling) in May and 21-runner £98,000 Tote Ebor Handicap at York (by short head from Midyan Blue, challenging wide and leading 1f out) in August: creditable 7½ lengths fourth of 7 to Grey Shot in Prix de Lutece at Longchamp final start: should stay 2m: acts on good to firm ground and soft. *B. W. Hills* — 102

SANOOSEA (USA) 3 b.c. Storm Bird (CAN) 134 – Nobiliare (USA) (Vaguely Noble 140) [1994 NR 1995 7g^{3} 7.1m* 8.1m^{2} 10.3m^{2} 11.8f^{5} Oct 23] good-topped colt: carries condition: brother to top-class 1¼m filly Indian Skimmer, and half-brother to 2 winners, including useful 8.5f winner Ajzem (by Blushing Groom): dam, unraced, out of half-sister to Champion US filly Dark Mirage: made hard work of landing odds in maiden at Haydock in April, making most: useful form when second in falsely-run races to Spectrum in minor event at Sandown and Pentire in listed race — 105

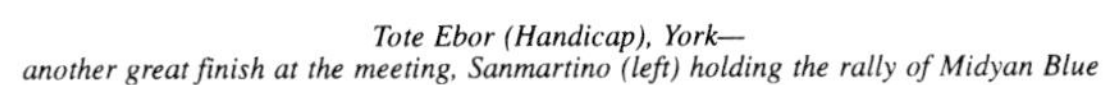

Tote Ebor (Handicap), York—
another great finish at the meeting, Sanmartino (left) holding the rally of Midyan Blue

at Chester (beaten 1¼ lengths) later in the spring: off course 5½ months, looking really well and favourite, well below form in minor event at Leicester: stays 10.3f: yet to race on a soft surface. *M. R. Stoute*

SAN PIETRA (IRE) 3 b.f. Caerleon (USA) 132 – La Koumia (FR) 119 (Kaldoun (FR) 122) [1994 NR 1995 10m 10.4m* 10g 12f Jul 26] tall, unfurnished filly: third known foal: half-sister to 7f winner La Kermesse (by Storm Bird): dam 5.5f (at 2 yrs) to 1¼m winner in France, later Grade 1 winner in USA: won 3-runner maiden at York in June, leading over 1f out: below that form in handicaps at Newbury and Goodwood (stiffish task in £37,300 event) afterwards: stays 10.4f: sold 51,000 gns Newmarket December Sales. *P. W. Chapple-Hyam* — 74

SANTA FAN (IRE) 3 b.f. Taufan (USA) 119 – Les Saintes (Kris 135) [1994 72: 6g 6.1m* 6g^5 1995 8m 8m^4 10.2m^3 10g^5 10g^4 a5.5f* Dec 2] tall filly: fair handicapper: looked reluctant when asked for effort fourth and fifth starts here, claimed out of P. Cole's stable £15,000 on fifth: racing on lasix and bute, won allowance race at Remington Park in December: effective at 5½f and appeared to stay 1¼m here: yet to race on a soft surface. *G. Blasi, USA* — 72

SANTANA LADY (IRE) 6 b.m. Blakeney 126 – Santalina (Relko 136) [1994 71: a12g* 12m^5 11.6m* 11.5d 10m 1995 a11g^6 12f^6 16g^3 11.6m^6 12.3m^3 Aug 19] rather leggy mare: just a modest handicapper at 6 yrs: stays 2m: acts on good to firm ground, dead and equitrack: often front runner: sold 5,400 gns Newmarket December Sales. *M. J. Heaton-Ellis* — 61

SANTELLA BOY (USA) 3 b.g. Turkoman (USA) – Dream Creek (USA) (The Minstrel (CAN) 135) [1994 74?: 6s^4 6f 7d 8g 1995 9g 11.6m 12m^2 11.5m^2 14m^3 16m^3 12f^2 13.1h^3 11.9d 9.7g^5 Oct 16] tall, leggy gelding: modest maiden handicapper: stays 2m: acts on hard ground (probably not on dead) and equitrack: visored last 3 starts: sometimes sweating and edgy: often a front runner: sold (G. Harwood to C.J. Mann) 15,000 gns Newmarket Autumn Sales. *G. Harwood* — 63

SANTILLANA (USA) 2 ch.c. (May 13) El Gran Senor (USA) 136 – Galway (FR) (Irish River (FR) 131) [1995 7g^3 8.1s* Nov 2] $155,000Y: fifth foal: brother to a winner in USA and half-brother to 2 winners, including fairly useful Irish 6f (at 2 yrs) to 1m winner Mine Dancer (by Mr Prospector): dam, 1m winner in France at 2 yrs, later 8.5f stakes winner in USA: third of 23 to Astor Place in maiden at Newmarket: won similar event at Edinburgh in November by 1¾ lengths, challenging on bridle 3f out and having something in hand: will stay beyond 1m: probably remains capable of improvement. *J. H. M. Gosden* — 87 p

SAPISTON 2 b.c. (Apr 26) Waajib 121 – Camera Girl (Kalaglow 132) [1995 8d^3 Sep 26] 19,000Y: leggy, attractive colt: second foal: half-brother to lightly-raced Irish maiden Instamatic (by Night Shift), useful at 1m: dam unraced granddaughter of 1000 Guineas second Photo Flash: 12/1, always-prominent 1¾ lengths third of 20 to Helicon in maiden at Newmarket: will probably stay beyond 1m: sure to improve, and win a race. *D. R. Loder* — 90 p

SAPPHIRE SON (IRE) 3 ch.g. Maelstrom Lake 118 – Gluhwein (Ballymoss 136) [1994 57: 5d 6g 6f 6g* 6g^2 7g* 8m 6.9s 1995 a7g 7f^3 7g^2 7.1m^3 7g^6 7m 7g a7g 7g Sep 12] sparely-made gelding: modest performer: below form in claimers and sellers last 5 starts: stays 7f: acts on firm ground: effective with or without visor: front runner/races prominently. *C. N. Williams* — 60 d

SARACEN PRINCE (USA) 3 ch.g. War (USA) – My Gallant Duchess (USA) (My Gallant (USA)) [1994 58: 6f^5 6f^2 7.1g 7m a8g 10s 7m 1995 a8.5g* a8g Nov 6] good-topped gelding: first start for over a year, won maiden at Wolverhampton in October: disappointing favourite in Southwell handicap 9 days later: stays 8.5f: acts on firm ground and fibresand: blinkered twice at 2 yrs: sold (P. Kelleway to H. Alexander) 4,400 gns Doncaster November Sales. *P. A. Kelleway* — 58

SARAH'S GUEST (IRE) 2 ch.f. (Feb 9) Be My Guest (USA) 126 – Lady Bennington (Hot Grove 128) [1995 7m 7d 7s^4 7m 7m^4 7d 9m* Oct 4] 22,000Y: lengthy filly: half-sister to 3-y-o Kennet Lad (by Persian Bold), winner in Slovakia in 1995, and a useful 1m to 1¼m performer in Italy by Mister Majestic: dam well behind in 3 races on flat: fairly useful Irish filly: not discredited in valuable sales race at Newmarket penultimate start: improved form to win nursery at Dundalk following month: stays 9f: acts on good to firm ground. *Victor Bowens, Ireland* — 80

SARASI 3 ch.g. Midyan (USA) 124 – Early Call 102 (Kind of Hush 118) [1994 63: 6f 6d 7m^2 7.5g^6 7m^2 1995 a7g* a8g^4 a9.4g^5 a8g^4 7.9g a8g^6 a7g a9.4g* Dec 9] angular gelding: fair handicapper: won at Lingfield in January: gelded and left P. Cole's stable after fourth start: won seller at Wolverhampton in December, making all: stays at least 9.4f (dam won at up to 11.5f): acts on all-weather and good to firm ground: visored (below form) penultimate 3-y-o start. *M. J. Camacho*
73

SARASONIA 4 b.f. Dunbeath (USA) 127 – La Graciosa (Comedy Star (USA) 121) [1994 –: a8g^3 a7g 1995 6m 7f 6.9f^6 6g a10g a6g Nov 30] angular filly: probably of little account nowadays. *J. W. Payne*
–

SARASOTA STORM 3 b.g. Petoski 135 – Challanging 95 (Mill Reef (USA) 141) [1994 73p: 7g^3 7g^6 1995 11.1d* 12m 14g^4 8m 8m^6 8m 10m Sep 5] workmanlike gelding: fair performer at best: made hard work of landing odds in median auction maiden at Edinburgh in March: effective at 1m and stays 11.1f: acts on good to firm and dead going. *M. Bell*
67 d

SARAWAT 7 b.g. Slip Anchor 136 – Eljazzi 92 (Artaius (USA) 129) [1994 83: 12d^6 12m 16.1f^5 1995 9.9m 16m 13.9g 14g May 27] smallish, workmanlike gelding: has been hobdayed: has a round action: fairly useful handicapper for R. Akehurst at 6 yrs: no form in 1995, finding little last 2 starts: stays 2m: acts on soft going and firm. *D. Nicholls*
–

SARAZAR (USA) 6 ch.g. Shahrastani (USA) 135 – Sarshara 93 (Habitat 134) [1994 52: 16.4g^5 17.2m^3 18f^2 17.2f* 17.2m^5 1995 17.2m 17.2m 16.2f 17.2f^4 a16g^6 14.1m Aug 12] lengthy gelding: poor handicapper: stays 2¼m: acts on firm and soft ground: tried blinkered, no improvement: sold 1,600 gns Newmarket Autumn Sales. *R. Akehurst*
40

SARI MARAIS 3 ch.f. Most Welcome 131 – Willowbank 66 (Gay Fandango (USA) 132) [1994 NR 1995 8f Jun 27] second foal: dam winning middle-distance stayer: 20/1, always behind in maiden at Yarmouth: dead. *Mrs J. Cecil*
–

SARIYAA 4 b.f. Persian Bold 123 – Bedouin Veil (USA) (Shareef Dancer (USA) 135) [1994 70: 8m^3 10m* 13.3g 12.3m^2 11.5m^4 1995 12g^5 9.9g^5 12m^3 13f^5 12g 12d^3 a12g^5 Sep 30] plain, angular filly: only a modest handicapper at 4 yrs: effective at 1¼m, and stays 13.3f: acts on good to firm and soft ground, and on fibresand: has tongue tied down: takes keen hold, usually front runner at 4 yrs: sold 13,500 gns Newmarket December Sales. *M. Brittain*
59

SARMATIAN (USA) 4 br.g. Northern Flagship (USA) 96 – Tracy L (USA) (Bold Favorite (USA)) [1994 64: 8v 9m^4 8.3d^6 8.1g^2 8m^5 8.2m^2 7m 8m* 10m 8d 8s^4 8d 1995 8.3v^2 7m^3 7g 8.3f^2 8.3m^3 8.3f* Aug 9] leggy gelding: fair handicapper: creditable efforts on 5 of his 6 starts at 4 yrs, gaining deserved success at Hamilton in August: effective at 7f, and should stay further than 9f: acts on any ground. *M. D. Hammond*
70

SASEEDO (USA) 5 ch.g. Afleet (CAN) – Barbara's Moment (USA) (Super Moment (USA)) [1994 90, a–: 6m 6v^3 7d^6 6m^3 6m^6 7g^3 6m^5 a6g 7m 7m^4 7d^6 7m 8d 1995 7m 6m* 7m 6m^6 6f 7g 6g^6 7.3d 5d^5 7g^4 5s^6 5m 6f* a7g^4 Nov 24] close-coupled gelding: unimpressive mover: fairly useful handicapper: won 21-runner race at Newmarket in May and 5-runner minor event at Yarmouth in October: stays 7f: acts on any ground on turf, and probably also on the all-weather: equipped with rope halter and blanket for stalls entry: often slowly away: held up. *W. A. O'Gorman*
90
a79

SASSETTA (IRE) 2 ch.f. (Apr 14) Soviet Lad (USA) 94 – Sun Gift (Guillaume Tell (USA) 121) [1995 6.1m 7f^5 7g 7d 7f Oct 3] 4,000Y: sparely-made filly: half-sister to 3-y-o River Wye (by Jareer) and several winners here and abroad, including 1½m winner Golden Gunner (by Mazaad) and 7.1f (at 3 yrs) and 15f winner Gymcrak Cyrano (by Cyrano de Bergerac): dam unraced: little worthwhile form. *N. Tinkler*
–

SASSIVER (USA) 5 b.g. Riverman (USA) 131 – Sassabunda 108 (Sassafras (FR) 135) [1994 45: 9.9s 12g 12g 14.1m a12g^5 14.1m a12g^3 a16g^5 14d 14s a14.8g a14g* a14g a16.2g^3 1995 a16.2g^4 a16g^3 a16.2g a14.8g^4 a16.2g a16g May 15] strong gelding: poor performer: sold out of R. Hollinshead's stable 6,200 gns Doncaster February Sales and gelded: tailed off both runs on flat for new stable: stays 2m: acts on soft going and fibresand: modest hurdler (acts on top-of-ground), winner in November. *P. A. Kelleway*
45

SASSY STREET (IRE) 2 b.g. (Apr 26) Danehill (USA) 126 – Sassy Lane (Sassafras (FR) 135) [1995 a7g Nov 21] IR 8,800F, 6,000Y: half-brother to winners abroad by Silent Cal and Persian Heights: dam French 1¼m and 1½m winner: 20/1, slowly away and always towards rear in 11-runner maiden at Lingfield in November: probably capable of better. *R. F. Johnson Houghton* — p

SASTRUGI (IRE) 3 br.c. Bluebird (USA) 125 – Royal Wolff (Prince Tenderfoot (USA) 126) [1994 NR 1995 8g^6 8m^5 a9.4g^6 11.8m a12g Sep 2] IR 2,600F, 13,500Y: angular colt: sixth foal: half-brother to 3 modest winners at up to 7f: dam Irish sprinter: no worthwhile form on flat: blinkered/visored last 4 starts. *S. P. C. Woods* —

SASURU 2 b.c. (May 4) Most Welcome 131 – Sassalya (Sassafras (FR) 135) [1995 6m^2 7g^2 8d^3 Sep 15] lengthy, good-bodied colt: brother to 1993 2-y-o 6f winner Tzu'mu and half-brother to several winners, including useful 3-y-o Baltic Raider (by Polish Precedent), 7f winner at 2 yrs, useful stayer Chauvre Souris (by Beldale Flutter) and smart 7f performer Sally Rous (by Rousillon): dam useful Irish 7f and 1¼m winner: narrowly beaten in maidens at Yarmouth and York (short-headed by Red Robbo) before finishing 2¼ lengths third of 8 to Mick's Love in well-contested minor event at Newbury: stays 1m: will improve again, and is sure to win a race. *G. Wragg* 95 p

SATELLITE STAR (IRE) 2 b.f. (Apr 3) Red Sunset 120 – Coffee Bean (Doulab (USA) 115) [1995 5m^5 5.3m* 5m^3 5.2g^2 6g^3 6f* 6m 7.3d 5g Sep 28] 5,000Y: sturdy, close-coupled filly: second foal: sister to 3-y-o 1m seller winner Java Red: dam poor Irish maiden: fair performer, successful in maiden auction at Brighton in April and minor event at Hamilton in June: below form afterwards in nurseries: stays 6f: acts on firm ground, possibly unsuited by a soft surface: sold 6,200 gns Newmarket Autumn Sales: sent to Austria. *M. R. Channon* 69

SATERNE LADY 3 b.f. Deploy 131 – Alghabrah 70 (Lomond (USA) 128) [1994 56: 6m 6d^3 6s a10g^2 1995 11.7h^4 10d 8m Sep 25] robust, leggy filly: modest maiden at 2 yrs: well beaten on return: should stay 1½m: acts on dead ground and equitrack: sold 1,100 gns Newmarket Autumn Sales. *P. F. I. Cole* —

SATIN SECRET (IRE) 2 ch.f. (May 7) Thatching 131 – Silky (USA) 112 (Nijinsky (CAN) 138) [1995 6g^6 7m Aug 25] lengthy, good-topped filly: fluent mover: half-sister to several winners, including 3-y-o 1½m winner Silktail (by Jalmood) and good middle-distance performer Kirtling (by Grundy): dam, second in Irish 1000 Guineas, half-sister to Benson & Hedges Gold Cup winner Moulton and John Porter winner Freefoot: towards rear in maidens at Pontefract and Newmarket (led briefly over 2f out) 2½ months later: may do better: sent to Dubai. *J. M. P. Eustace* 51 +

SATURIBA (USA) 2 b.c. (Apr 15) Fighting Fit (USA) – My Popsicle (USA) (Raja Baba (USA)) [1995 5v 6f^6 5m 6g 8f^6 Oct 16] $15,000F, 13,000Y: tall, useful-looking colt: half-brother to several winners abroad: dam maiden in USA: sire graded winner at 6f and 9f: modest maiden: sixth of 18 in nursery at Pontefract last time, in clear lead until weakening and headed 1f out: should stay 1m ridden with more restraint: sold 5,600 gns Doncaster October Sales, and joined J. A. Harris. *M. Johnston* 51 ?

SAUCY MAID (IRE) 4 ch.f. Sure Blade (USA) 130 – Gay Milly (FR) 74 (Mill Reef (USA) 141) [1994 69: 10g^3 1995 10g 11.7f^4 10m 8m^2 8g Sep 14] workmanlike filly: modest maiden handicapper: stays 1¼m: sweating (ran well) penultimate 4-y-o start: sold 8,000 gns Newmarket December Sales. *Major D. N. Chappell* 59

SAVA RIVER (IRE) 2 ch.c. (Apr 26) Lycius (USA) 124 – Slava (USA) (Diesis 133) [1995 6m^3 6.1m* 7.6m^2 7.3d^2 8.3g^3 Sep 24] close-coupled, quite attractive colt: first foal: dam French 11f winner out of close relative of Soviet Star: fairly useful form: won maiden at Nottingham in August: good second to easy winners Lord of Men in minor event at Lingfield and Ramooz in nursery at Newbury then creditable last of 3 in minor event at Hamilton: best form at around 7f: acts on good to firm and dead ground: sent to Dubai. *M. R. Stoute* 91

SAV-ED 6 b.h. Today And Tomorrow 78 – Ole Flo 80 (Frimley Park 109) [1994 –: 5s 8.1s 7d^6 6g^6 6f 1995 a8g a6g a6g Jan 27] rather sparely-made horse: no worthwhile form: tried blinkered. *A. P. Jarvis* —

SAWA-ID 2 b. or br.c. (Feb 24) Anshan 119 – Bermuda Lily 78 (Dunbeath (USA) 127) [1995 8m Nov 4] 14,000F, 45,000Y: rangy colt: second foal: half-brother to — p

Sheikh Mohammed's "Saxon Maid"

3-y-o Dee-Lady (by Deploy), 5f winner at 2 yrs (stays 1¼m): dam 2-y-o 5f winner: 14/1 and backward, chased leaders on stand side long way and not knocked about when eleventh of 23 to impressive Shaamit in median auction maiden at Doncaster: will do better. *J. H. M. Gosden*

SAXON HEIR (IRE) 3 b.g. Anita's Prince 126 – Royal Accord (King of Spain 121) [1994 51: 5.3g* 5d6 5g5 5f6 6m a6g 6g 7.1g a6g6 a7g4 a8.5g a8.5g a6g a5g a6g6 1995 a8.5g5 a7g a5g 7m Jun 6] leggy, sparely-made gelding: no form in 1995: sold out of M. Usher's stable 750 gns Ascot February Sales after third start: stays 7f: usually visored or blinkered: carries head high. *John Berry* –

SAXON KING (IRE) 5 ch.g. Ahonoora 122 – My Therape 112 (Jimmy Reppin 131) [1994 50: 7v 5d 7d 6s 5.7g 6m2 5f5 5m3 6f3 6f4 6f5 7d 5m4 a7g2 a8g a6g2 1995 a6g4 6.1g 5g3 5m6 Jun 16] strong, lengthy gelding: poor maiden handicapper: claimed £5,000 final start: effective at 5f and stays 7f, possibly not 1m: acts on firm ground and the all-weather: wears bandages: visored (not disgraced) eighth 4-y-o start. *M. D. I. Usher* 50

SAXON MAGIC 5 ch.m. Faustus (USA) 118 – Wessex Kingdom 68 (Vaigly Great 127) [1994 34: a8g a8g 8.2g6 8m6 a7g2 a7g5 9.7g3 10m5 9.7d4 12m 12s 1995 a8g 9.7g Jul 5] leggy, lengthy mare: unimpressive mover: poor maiden handicapper: should stay 1½m: acts on fibresand, good to firm going and dead: tried blinkered/ visored, no improvement: often ridden by 7-lb claimer: modest hurdler, winner in September. *J. A. Bennett* –

SAXON MAID 4 b.f. Sadler's Wells (USA) 132 – Britannia's Rule 108 (Blakeney 126) [1994 104p: 10.3m 10m5 12m4 12.3g* 12m2 12m* 12m4 12v* 1995 14m4 12m3 108

12m* 13.9m* 16f⁶ 13.9m 14.6m³ 12d² 12v² 14g⁴ Nov 26] compact filly: useful performer: won 5-runner listed races at Newmarket and York (rated stakes) in July, both from Magical Retreat: in frame last 4 starts, running creditably in Park Hill Stakes (third to Noble Rose) at Doncaster, listed race at Ascot and Princess Royal Stakes (second of 5 to Labibeh) at Ascot, but below best in Group 3 event at Rome: effective at 1½m and should have stayed 2m: acted on good to firm ground and heavy: stud. *L. M. Cumani*

SAYEH (IRE) 3 b.c. Fools Holme (USA) – Piffle 87 (Shirley Heights 130) [1994 96p: 6g* 8s² 1995 8g³ 10.4g⁵ 10.4m³ 10.1m* 10.1m* 10d Sep 30] big, deep-girthed colt: has a round action: useful form at his best: disappointing and beginning to look temperamental until making all in minor event at Yarmouth in August and rated stakes at Epsom (best effort, beat Warning Order by a neck) in September: stays 1¼m: yet to race on firm going, acts on any other: pulls hard, and now wears special bridle: sent to Dubai. *H. Thomson Jones* 98

SAYITAGAIN 3 b.c. Bering 136 – Casey 119 (Caerleon (USA) 132) [1994 NR 1995 8d⁶ 10g Apr 26] 38,000Y: lengthy, rather unfurnished colt: has scope: third foal: half-brother to 1992 7f winner Fortensky (by Blushing Groom): dam won Park Hill: sixth of 10 in maiden at Leicester then towards rear in 23-runner maiden at Kempton in April: should be well suited by further than 1m: sold only 700 gns Ascot July Sales. *T. G. Mills* 68

SAYYED ALRAQS (USA) 3 b.c. Seattle Dancer (USA) 119 – Glamorous Siren (USA) (Raise A Native) [1994 NR 1995 10m 9.9m⁴ 12.1g² 11.1f* 10m⁶ 11.8g Jul 19] $47,000Y: leggy colt: half-brother to 2 winners in USA: dam won 3 races: fair form: won 2-runner maiden at Hamilton in June by 10 lengths: stayed 1½m: raced only on a sound surface: dead. *M. A. Jarvis* 67

SAYYEDATI 5 b.m. Shadeed (USA) 135 – Dubian 120 (High Line 125) [1994 121: 7f³ 8f 8f⁴ 8g² 8g⁵ 8g 1995 7g² 8m⁵ 8f* 8g² 8m⁴ 8s³ Oct 28] 122

The unconventional policy of keeping the good-class mare Sayyedati in training after a largely fruitless four-year-old campaign was ultimately well rewarded with a win in the Sussex Stakes at Goodwood and creditable efforts in three of the top international races over a mile, all of which took her career earnings to over £850,000. Such an outcome was hard to predict as she went to post at Goodwood following two runs earlier in the season that had failed to suggest she was back to her best. Her most recent effort, in the Queen Anne Stakes at Royal Ascot where she was a well-supported second favourite to Soviet Line, had been disappointing for all that she found difficulty getting a run, and her fifth-of-seven placing that day behind the

Sussex Stakes, Goodwood—Sayyedati and Brett Doyle pounce on Bahri (left); Darnay chases them

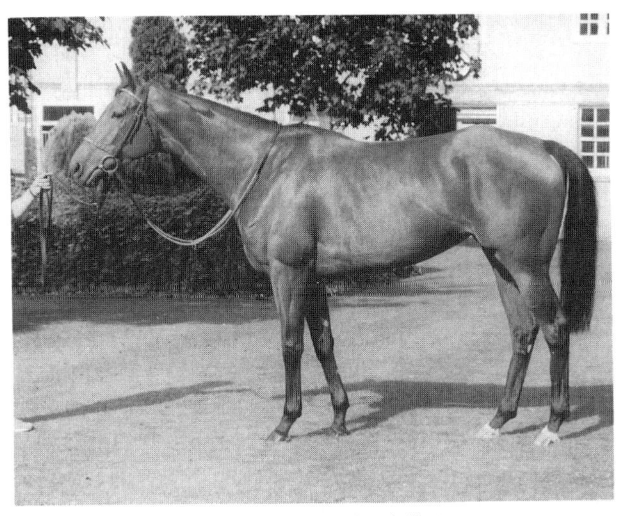

Mohammed Obaida's "Sayyedati"

outsider Nicolotte left her plenty to prove at Goodwood. Nicolotte and Soviet Line, the latter third at Ascot and now 5 lb better off with the other pair, reopposed in the Sussex, joined by Darnay, recent winner of a Group 2 race at the Curragh; however, all seemed likely to find the three-year-old Bahri, impressive winner of the St James's Palace Stakes at Royal Ascot, hard to beat. Bahri's pacemaker Sulb, who completed the field of six, ensured a strong pace which suited not only Bahri but also Sayyedati who moved through smoothly from the rear two furlongs out and challenged the favourite entering the final furlong, getting the better of a fine tussle with Bahri by a neck with Darnay three and a half lengths back in third. She comprehensively reversed Ascot placings with a wayward Soviet Line, and with Nicolotte who may have found the ground too firm.

Sayyedati (b.m. 1990)	Shadeed (USA) (b 1982)	Nijinsky (b 1967)	Northern Dancer
			Flaming Page
		Continual (b or br 1976)	Damascus
			Continuation
	Dubian (b 1982)	High Line (ch 1966)	High Hat
			Time Call
		Melodina (br 1968)	Tudor Melody
			Rose of Medina

The Sussex Stakes was Sayyedati's fifth Group 1 win. She'd won the Moyglare Stud Stakes and the Cheveley Park Stakes in showing herself the best two-year-old filly of 1992, and the One Thousand Guineas and Prix Jacques le Marois in a good three-year-old campaign (when she was also second in the Sussex Stakes behind Bigstone). She had put up her best performance as a four-year-old when second to East of The Moon in the Jacques le Marois and her third attempt at the race, after the Sussex, was as a good a performance as any she has given though she was unable to hold the late challenge of Miss Satamixa. Sayyedati ran up against the top Irish filly Ridgewood Pearl on her final two starts, finishing fourth, beaten a length and a half or so, in the Prix du Moulin de Longchamp in September, and third, beaten two lengths and seven, in the Breeders' Cup Mile at Belmont in October. Sayyedati was retired after the Mile and is reportedly to visit Gulch in 1996.

It was somewhat surprising, on breeding at least, that Sayyedati was never raced beyond a mile given that her dam Dubian stayed a mile and a half well. Dubian was a smart filly, who ran her best race when third behind Oh So Sharp and Triptych in the Oaks, a race run on soft ground. Dubian was also third in the Irish Oaks and gained pattern-race wins in Ireland and Italy as a four-year-old. Her dam Melodina and grandam Rose of Medina also showed smart form and stayed a mile and a half well. Melodina bred eight winners, notably the triple champion hurdler See You Then. Sayyedati is Dubian's second foal. Her first Shihama, also by Shadeed, won over six furlongs at two years from three starts. Her third, Tigwa (by Cadeaux Genereux), showed fair form in maiden company in 1994. Dubian's fifth foal North Cyclone (by Gulch) was in training with Clive Brittain in the latest season as was Shihama's first foal Gulf Tycoon. Sayyedati is a rangy, attractive mare and a fluent mover. She probably acted on any going, though her two runs on very soft ground (the Moyglare Stud and the Breeders' Cup Mile) weren't among her best. She was a game and genuine mare with a fine turn of foot which she used to good effect in her long career. *C. E. Brittain*

SCALE THE SUMMIT 3 b.c. Distant Relative 128 – Top Heights (High Top 131) [1994 49p: 6g a6g 6g 1995 a9.4g^{3} a8g^{4} a12g a12g^{5} Jul 13] lengthy colt: has scope: good walker: poor maiden handicapper: stays 9.4f, not 1½m: acts on fibresand: sent to Spain. *Sir Mark Prescott* — 44

SCALP 'EM (IRE) 7 b.g. Commanche Run 133 – Supremely Royal (Crowned Prince (USA) 128) [1994 33, a50: 14.1f^{3} 15.1m^{4} 16m^{2} 14.9m 15.1m 18s^{5} a12g^{3} a16g^{6} a14g^{2} a13g* a16.2g a12g* 1995 a13g^{2} a14.8g^{2} a12g^{2} a12g^{2} a14.8g a14.8g^{6} 12m^{3} 13g^{4} a12g a14g^{2} 16m^{2} 14.1f^{5} a16.2g^{3} Jul 21] rangy gelding: has round action: modest handicapper at best: stays 2m: acts on firm ground (probably on soft) and the all-weather, stiff task on heavy: sold 1,300 gns Doncaster October Sales. *P. D. Evans* — 42 a55

SCARABEN 7 b.g. Dunbeath (USA) 127 – Varushka 74 (Sharpen Up 127) [1994 55: 9.2d^{2} 8v^{3} 7v* 8d^{2} 8g 8.9d^{6} 10.1d^{5} 8.1g 1995 8.3v* 9.2f^{3} 8m* 8m* 8m* 8g* 8d^{2} 8g* 8m Oct 14] big, strong, lengthy gelding: has a quick action: injected over winter with anti-arthritis serum: went from strength to strength in handicaps in 1995: won at Hamilton in March, at Redcar, Newmarket and Newcastle (twice) in the summer, and £22,300 contest at Ayr in September: effective at 7f (under testing conditions) and stays 1¼m: acts on any ground: held up: genuine. *S. E. Kettlewell* — 76

SCARLET PLUME 2 b.f. (Feb 8) Warning 136 – Circus Plume 124 (High Top 131) [1995 6m^{2} 7m^{3} 8.1d* 8d* Oct 15] angular filly: has a quick action: fifth foal: half-sister to several winners, including middle-distance performer Circus Colours (by Rainbow Quest): dam, 7f winner at 2 yrs, won Oaks: made all in maiden at Sandown in September and 11-runner Group 3 Premio Dormello at Milan (comfortably, by 2½ lengths from Beauty Dancer) in October: will stay beyond 1m: should improve further. *J. L. Dunlop* — 100 p

SCATHEBURY 2 b.g. (May 22) Aragon 118 – Lady Bequick 81 (Sharpen Up 127) [1995 5m^{2} 5m^{4} a6g^{2} a6g^{2} 6m a7g^{6} a6g* 6m 7.9m^{2} 8f Oct 18] 20,000Y: smallish, compact gelding: brother to smart 6f (at 2 yrs) and 1m winner Cloud of Dust and half-brother to several winners, including useful sprinters Joytotheworld (by Young Generation) and 3-y-o Crowded Avenue (by Sizzling Melody): dam 2-y-o 5f winner: won maiden at Wolverhampton in July: stays 1m: acts on good to firm ground, best form on fibresand: poor effort in blinkers sixth start and visored next 2 outings: carries head awkwardly and doesn't always look genuine: inconsistent: has been gelded. *S. P. C. Woods* — 60 § a69 §

SCBOO 6 b.g. Full Extent (USA) 113 – Maygo 57 (Maystreak 118) [1994 NR 1995 8f 8.3m a7g Nov 10] tall, lengthy, angular gelding: fifth reported foal: dam 2-y-o 5f winner, also won over hurdles: of no account. *R. E. Peacock* — –

SCENIC AIR 2 ch.f. (Feb 19) Hadeer 118 – Shark Song 103 (Song 132) [1995 7m 7m^{6} Jul 15] 3,600Y: half-sister to several winners, including fair 1¾m winner Hidden (by Secreto): dam, won from 5f to 9f, including in USA, sister to very smart sprinter Prince Sabo: behind in auction events at Catterick and Warwick in July. *E. Weymes* — –

SCENIC DANCER 7 b.g. Shareef Dancer (USA) 135 – Bridestones 92 (Jan Ekels 122) [1994 52: 11.9m^{5} 11.6d* 12d^{4} 12.3m 10.1g* 11.6m^{3} 12g 11.5m^{6} 12s — 50

11.5g 1995 10g^3 11.6m^3 10.1d^4 11.6g^3 12.1m 12g 11.5m^4 16.2m 11.5g* 11.8g^4 12m Nov 6] small, stocky gelding: modest handicapper on his day: back to form and won very strongly-run ladies event at Yarmouth in September: effective at 1¼m to 1¾m: acts on firm and dead ground, looked all at sea on soft: tried blinkered and visored, no improvement: often slowly away. *A. Hide*

SCENIC HEIGHTS (IRE) 3 b.c. Scenic 128 – Evangola (Persian Bold 123) [1994 85p: 6s* 1995 8.1m^4 7.3d Sep 15] close-coupled colt: fair performer: burly, coltish and facing stiff task, tailed off in 4-runner minor event at Sandown on belated return: well backed, short of room final 2½f (after travelling strongly) and allowed to coast home in handicap at Newbury 5 weeks later: should stay 1m: sent to Australia. *R. W. Armstrong* –

SCENICRIS (IRE) 2 b.f. (Apr 18) Scenic 128 – Princesse Smile 99 (Balidar 133) [1995 5g 5m^3 7g^5 7m^2 7f^2 7d^5 6g^3 7m^3 7.1s^2 a7g^3 a7g Dec 6] IR 5,000F, IR 2,300Y: workmanlike filly: half-sister to several winners in France, including 1983 2-y-o 7f winner Island Smile (by Ile de Bourbon) and 7f (at 2 yrs) and 1½m winner Shy Gremlin (by Home Guard): dam 7f to 9f winner in Italy, is sister to Bolkonski: fair maiden: should stay beyond 7f: acts on firm and soft ground: usually comes from well off pace. *R. Hollinshead* 66 a53

SCENT OF POWER 5 b.g. Fairy King (USA) – Agreloui 59 (Tower Walk 130) [1994 44: 5g 6d 6m^6 8g 8.3m a7g^4 a6g^2 1995 a6g 7.1d^4 a7g 7m 8.2m* 8g Jun 6] good-topped gelding: unimpressive mover: poor performer nowadays: won apprentice maiden handicap at Nottingham in May: stays 8.2f: acts on good to firm going and fibresand: blinkered (no improvement) twice at 4 yrs. *Martyn Wane* 38

SCHARNHORST 3 b.g. Tacheron 52 – Stardyn (Star Appeal 133) [1994 59: 7g 6g^6 7s^5 6.9s^6 1995 5d a7g 7m* 7.1m* 7m^2 8f^3 7f 7.1d 7d 7d a8g a10g Nov 8] sturdy, useful-looking gelding: fair handicapper: won at Salisbury (apprentices) and Sandown (made all) in May: ran poorly for 5 starts before pulling up lame final one: should stay 1m: acts on firm ground, probably on soft. *S. Dow* 75 d

SCHOOL BOY 2 b.c. (Feb 20) Aragon 118 – Grovehurst (Homing 130) [1995 7g 6d^2 6f Oct 12] 12,000F, 18,000Y: useful-looking colt: third foal: brother to fairly useful 5-y-o sprinter Aragrove: dam ran once: 2 lengths equal-second of 9 to Sylva Paradise in maiden at Folkestone: had stiff task in Redcar Two-Year-Old Trophy on final outing (took good hold to post): almost certainly a sprinter: acts on soft ground. *C. N. Allen* 74

SCHOOL CLOCK 2 b.c. (Mar 28) Puissance 110 – Village Idol 74 (Blakeney 126) [1995 6g Sep 13] 5,200F: half-brother to several winners here and abroad, including 7f seller winner Sporting Idol (by Mummy's Game): dam stayed 1½m: 50/1, around 14 lengths eighth of 10 to Obsessive, behind throughout, in maiden at Yarmouth: sent to Hungary. *C. N. Allen* –

SCHOOL OF SCIENCE 5 b.g. Then Again 126 – Girl's Brigade (Brigadier Gerard 144) [1994 36: 11.1m^3 12m^5 1995 11f Oct 24] workmanlike gelding: probably no longer of much account. *R. M. McKellar* –

SCISSOR RIDGE 3 ch.g. Indian Ridge 123 – Golden Scissors 76 (Kalaglow 132) [1994 63: 5s^5 5d^2 7.1g^5 7m^6 a7g* 7f^4 7g 7g 6d^5 7.3v 1995 a7g^6 a8g^4 a7g^4 6s a8g^6 7g 8m 7f^4 a6g^3 7g 6d 6.9g^6 7m^2 a7g a10g a7g^5 a7g^2 a7g* Dec 14] sparely-made gelding: modest handicapper: won at Lingfield in December: stays 7f: acts on firm and dead ground and the all-weather: blinkered (finished last) sixth 3-y-o start: takes keen hold: inconsistent. *J. J. Bridger* 47 a59

SCOFFERA 5 b.m. Scottish Reel 123 – Single Bid 68 (Auction Ring (USA) 123) [1994 39: 8g 8m^6 8g^6 8.2m 8m^6 8m 8m^6 8f 7g^5 10.4d 8.2g 1995 a8g a8g^5 a8g^6 Feb 10] good-topped mare: has a round action: poor performer: stays 1¼m: acts on fibresand and firm and dead ground: blinkered (tailed off) once at 3 yrs: finished unsound over hurdles Mar 21. *N. Tinkler* – a31

SCORCHED AIR 5 b.m. Elegant Air 119 – Misfire 56 (Gunner B 126) [1994 69d: 12g 11.9m 12m^2 12m 12.3g 11.9f^3 a14.8g^4 12m^3 11.8g^2 1995 a14.8g 12d 10d Sep 19] workmanlike mare: no worthwhile form at 5 yrs for new stable: stays 1½m: acts on good to firm and soft going: modest hurdler, winner in October. *J. G. M. O'Shea* –

SCORED AGAIN 5 b.g. Music Boy 124 – Thorner Lane 86 (Tina's Pet 121) 62
[1994 62: 5.1g 5m 6f 5f^6 5m 5.1f^4 5s 5.1d^4 5.1s* 5d^4 5m^5 a5g* a6g^3 a6g 1995 a5g^6 a5g* a5g* a5g^4 a5g^5 a5g^2 Apr 13] lengthy gelding: modest handicapper: successful at Wolverhampton in January and February: best at 5f: acts on good to firm and soft ground and on fibresand: usually ridden by claimer Amanda Sanders. *M. J. Heaton-Ellis*

SCORPIUS 5 b.h. Soviet Star (USA) 128 – Sally Brown 120 (Posse (USA) 130) 68 d
[1994 a12g^6 a11g^3 a12g^3 a12g^6 a10g^3 a9g^3 a10g* a8g^3 a10g* 1995 a9g^2 a8g^2 a12g^6 a10g a10g 7m^5 7m 11.5g 9.7s Sep 27] leggy, angular horse: successful twice in Dubai at 4 yrs for K. McLaughlin: sold 16,000 gns Newmarket July (1995) Sales: form on return only on first start back: stays 1½m: acts on good to firm ground and sand: blinkered (well backed, apparently choked) final 5-y-o start: has been bandaged: sold 1,300 gns Doncaster November Sales. *C. N. Williams*

SCOTONI 9 ch.g. Final Straw 127 – Damiya (FR) (Direct Flight) [1994 NR 1995 –
12m Aug 27] close-coupled, rather sparely-made gelding: fair chaser: modest staying handicapper (rated 57, went well on equitrack) on flat at 7 yrs, but never a factor in NH jockeys race on return: blinkered once at 4 yrs. *R. J. O'Sullivan*

SCOTSKY (IRE) 3 b.c. Astronef 116 – Lady Heather (Manado 130) [1994 88: 89
6f^3 6m 6m* 7s* 7.5v^4 1995 7f^5 8m 7d Sep 23] useful-looking colt: fairly useful form: good fifth of 6 in minor event at Salisbury on reappearance: respectable effort next time: very stiff task, slowly away and always behind in £52,900 handicap at Ascot final one: stays 1m: acts on firm and soft ground: sold only 10,000 gns Newmarket Autumn Sales. *J. L. Dunlop*

SCOTS LAW 8 b.g. Law Society (USA) 130 – Tweedling (USA) (Sir Ivor 135) –
[1994 –, a44: a8g^4 a6g a8g a8g^2 6d 8.3m a8.5g 6g 1995 a7g a6g a7g a8g a8g Mar 16] leggy, quite attractive gelding: seems of little account nowadays. *J. E. Long*

SCOTTISH BAMBI 7 ch.g. Scottish Reel 123 – Bambolona 108 (Bustino 136) –
[1994 74: 10g 10d^3 12m^5 8m^2 10.2f 1995 10m 10m^6 10.8g^5 10.8g Jun 17] rangy, workmanlike gelding: has a round action: off course 10 months, no worthwhile form in 1995: effective at 1m and 1¼m: acts on firm and dead ground: normally held up: joined P. R. Webber. *R. Hannon*

SCOTTISH PARK 6 ch.m. Scottish Reel 123 – Moss Agate (Alias Smith 47 d
(USA)) [1994 54: a8.5g* a8g^3 a8g a8.5g 8m a8g^2 8s* 8m 7s^3 7.6g a8g 7.1s 10s a8g a7g a8g a8g^4 1995 a10g* a9.4g a10g^6 10d a9.4g 10g a8g^6 a11g 8m^3 8.5d^6 9m 8f 8m Jul 10] sturdy, lengthy mare: poor handicapper: won at Lingfield in January: stays 1¼m: acts on good to firm and soft ground and the all-weather: tried visored/ blinkered, below form: difficult ride: inconsistent: joined J. L. Harris. *R. W. Emery*

SCUD MISSILE (IRE) 4 b. or gr.g. Persian Heights 129 – Desert Bluebell 83 –
(Kalaglow 132) [1994 58: 9.7m^3 12g^5 14m^6 16.4g 13.1g 11.9g^4 1995 12m May 31] close-coupled gelding: has been hobdayed: modest maiden handicapper: below form only start for new stable: stays 1½m: acts on good to firm ground: inconsistent: won handicap hurdle in June. *G. F. Johnson Houghton*

SCYLLA 3 b.f. Rock City 120 – Hearten (Hittite Glory 125) [1994 50: 6m 8g a8g –
1995 a9.4g 9.9m 8m 8f^6 12m Jul 3] leggy, workmanlike filly: poor maiden: well beaten in 1995: sold 2,200 gns Newmarket September Sales. *P. C. Haslam*

SEA-AYR (IRE) 5 ch.m. Magical Wonder (USA) 125 – Kunuz (Ela-Mana-Mou 51
132) [1994 54: a8.5g^6 7d^3 8d^3 6.9s^6 8.1g^3 8m* 8f 7.5m* 7.5m* 8.5m^4 8m 7g 1995 7.5m^2 8m 7.5g 7g^2 7.5g Jul 17] small mare: has a round action: modest handicapper: stays 8.5f: acts on good to firm and soft ground: sometimes hangs (has worn near-side pricker): bandaged: usually claimer ridden: inconsistent at 5 yrs. *Mrs S. M. Austin*

SEA DANE 2 b.c. (Feb 14) Danehill (USA) 126 – Shimmering Sea 89 (Slip 94 +
Anchor 136) [1995 6m* 6m^6 6m* 7g^4 6d Sep 27] 6,000Y: sturdy, close-coupled colt: not the best of walkers: has a powerful, round action: first foal: dam, 2-y-o 5f and 7f winner, stayed 1m, half-sister to top-class middle-distance performer Petoski: fairly useful colt: won maiden at Goodwood in May and minor event (by 2 lengths from Line Dancer) at Pontefract in July: off course 2 months then below form in minor events, running poorly on soft surface: should be at least as effective at 7f as 6f: acts on good to firm ground. *P. W. Harris*

SEA DANZIG 2 ch.g. (Feb 27) Roi Danzig (USA) – Tosara 84 (Main Reef 126) [1995 7f 6m^4 6m^6 Nov 3] big, plain gelding: fourth foal: half-brother to 1m winner Dibloom (by Nomination): dam, 1¼m winner, half-sister to smart French stayer Chawn: still in need of race, around 4½ lengths fourth of 8 to Farhana in maiden at Newmarket in October: not far below that form when sixth of 20 to Miss Riviera in similar event at Doncaster following month: should stay 7f: slowly away on debut. *P. Howling* — 64

SEA-DEER 6 ch.g. Hadeer 118 – Hi-Tech Girl 98 (Homeboy 114) [1994 94: 5g^5 6d* 5.1m* 5f^3 5m* 5m* 5g 5g^2 1995 6g 6m 5m^5 6f 5.2g^4 6g Jul 28] strong, deep-girthed gelding: fairly useful handicapper: below best last 3 starts: effective at 5f and 6f: acts on any going: sometimes bandaged: held up: genuine: sold (L. J. Holt to D. Chapman) only 7,500 gns Newmarket Autumn Sales. *L. J. Holt* — 90

SEA DEVIL 9 gr.g. Absalom 128 – Miss Poinciana 78 (Averof 123) [1994 51+, a77: a6g* a6g* 6v^6 a6g* 6.9s^5 5.9v^6 a6g a6g^6 1995 a6g^2 a6g^2 a6g^2 a6g^2 a6g* a7g* a6g^2 7d^4 a6g^7 a6g* May 11] lengthy, heavy-topped gelding: carries plenty of condition: unimpressive mover: fair performer on the all-weather, only modest on turf nowadays: won sellers at Southwell in February and May, and at Wolverhampton in March: stays 7f, at least when conditions aren't testing: acts on fibresand and any turf going: visored (well below form) third 8-y-o start: sometimes hangs right: tough. *M. J. Camacho* — 56 a71

SEAFORD STAR (IRE) 2 ch.g. (Apr 13) Waajib 121 – Frensham Manor (Le Johnstan 123) [1995 5.7f^5 6.1m^2 5f^4 6f^6 7m 7s Sep 28] 6,200Y, 7,400 2-y-o: rather leggy gelding: third foal: half-brother to 3-y-o Kellaire Girl (by Gallic League): dam poor sister to smart 1982 2-y-o 5f winner Cat O'Nine Tails: modest form on second and third starts in maiden auction events: stays 6f: possibly unsuited by soft ground: sold 6,000 gns Doncaster October Sales: sent to Denmark. *M. R. Channon* — 65

SEA FREEDOM 4 b.c. Slip Anchor 136 – Rostova 91 (Blakeney 126) [1994 84p: 8m^4 12m^3 1995 10g 12g 13.3g 16.1g^2 16.4m^6 14f^3 14.4m^2 16g^4 16.2d 16.2s^4 18m 14.1m^5 Oct 26] strong, workmanlike colt: has a quick action: reportedly had knee operation after final 3-y-o start: fair maiden handicapper: thorough stayer: consistent on form, but has run rather in snatches and is not one to trust implicitly. *G. B. Balding* — 73

SEA GOD 4 ch.g. Rainbow Quest (USA) 134 – Sea Pageant (Welsh Pageant 132) [1994 –: 10s 10g 10g 1995 8f a11g a6g^5 Nov 24] tall, angular gelding: poor form: sold out of B. Hills's stable 1,400 gns Newmarket July Sales before reappearance: should stay beyond 6f: acts on fibresand. *M. C. Chapman* — 44

SEALED WITH A KISS 5 ch.m. High Line 125 – The Crying Game 55 (Manor Farm Boy 114) [1994 48: a11g 10s^4 12v^4 1995 13g May 4] angular, plain mare: poor maiden: tailed off only start at 5 yrs: stays 1½m. *M. Bell* — –

SEA OF BLUE 2 b.f. (Feb 14) Superlative 118 – Persian Joy 45 (Persian Bold 123) [1995 5m 6m a5g Jul 13] leggy filly: second foal: dam (poor maiden) stayed 1¼m: never a factor in claimer and sellers: apprentice ridden first 2 starts: sold 1,200 gns Doncaster September Sales. *M. W. Easterby* — –

SEASIDE MINSTREL 7 ch.g. Song 132 – Blackpool Belle 70 (The Brianstan 128) [1994 62: 5.1d 6m^5 8v 5.9v^2 8g 7.1s 6m 6m 7.5m 5g^5 6f^5 5m* 5m 5d* 5g* 5m^6 6d 5.7g^3 5.2s 5d* 5m 5m a5g 1995 5.1m 5.7f^4 5g May 27] leggy gelding: modest handicapper: below form in 1995: probably best at sprint distances: acts on any turf going (below form on fibresand): tried once in visor, usually blinkered nowadays: suitable mount for inexperienced rider. *D. L. Williams* — 53

SEASONAL SPLENDOUR (IRE) 5 b.m. Prince Rupert (FR) 121 – Snoozy Time 65 (Cavo Doro 124) [1994 87: 12v^6 12d^5 12d^3 13.9f 8g^2 12m^4 12m* 11.8m* 12g^2 12m* 14.6d^2 1995 12f* 11.9m^4 12m^6 12m 16d*^{dis} 16d Oct 19] workmanlike mare: fairly useful handicapper: won rated stakes at Salisbury in June and at Goodwood (on merit, but disqualified after interference) in September: stays 2m: probably acts on any going: blinkered (below form) twice as 3-y-o: best held up: won maiden hurdle in December. *M. C. Pipe* — 92

SEA SPOUSE 4 ch.g. Jalmood (USA) 126 – Bambolona 108 (Bustino 136) [1994 –: 10g a12g a7g 1995 a8g a12g* a12g a12g 10g 8.3g^2 8.3m 8g 8.1d 8.2m a9.4g^3 Dec 9] workmanlike gelding: poor performer: won apprentice seller at Southwell in — 44

April: effective at 8.3f to 1½m: acts on fibresand: races prominently: inconsistent. *M. Blanshard*

SEA SPRAY (IRE) 2 b.f. (Jan 26) Royal Academy (USA) 130 – Sailor's Mate 114 (Shirley Heights 130) [1995 7m* 8d Oct 1] lengthy filly: fourth foal: half-sister to 3-y-o Lavender (by Kris) and French 1½m winner Cutlass (by Sure Blade): dam 1½m winner, half-sister to dam of Yorkshire Oaks winner Hellenic: impressive winner of 5-runner minor event at Kempton in September, beating Kirov Lady 4 lengths: soon off bridle when tenth of 11 in Prix Marcel Boussac at Longchamp month later: will be suited by middle distances: looked very promising on debut and remains capable of better. *P. W. Chapple-Hyam* 88 p

SEA THUNDER 3 ro.f. Salse (USA) 128 – Money Moon (Auction Ring (USA) 123) [1994 6.5g⁴ 5.5g³ 7d³ 1995 7m² 6g² 6m³ 6g* 6m⁵ 6g 7d³ 6d Oct 11] quite good-topped ex-French filly: poor mover: third foal: half-sister to French 7.3f to 1¼m winner Money Melody (by Sharrood): dam French maiden: trained by J. Hammond as 2-y-o, third in Prix d'Arenberg at Maisons-Laffitte second start: fairly useful form in Britain: won maiden at Salisbury in July: stays 7f: yet to race on extremes of going. *I. A. Balding* 83

SEATTLE ALLEY (USA) 2 b.c. (Feb 25) Seattle Dancer (USA) 119 – Alyanaabi (USA) 74 (Roberto (USA) 131) [1995 7g 6d⁶ 7g 7f Oct 23] $47,000F, $65,000Y: good-topped colt: easy mover: first reported foal: dam 1¼m winner: seemed to be given extremely tender ride when sixth of 11 in maiden at Newcastle (running subject of stewards enquiry): not unduly knocked about in maiden and nursery at Leicester last 2 starts: will stay middle distances: takes keen hold: almost certainly capable of better. *Mrs J. R. Ramsden* 60 p

SEATTLE SPECIAL (USA) 2 b. or br.f. (Jan 26) Nureyev (USA) 131 – O' Slewmova (USA) (Seattle Slew (USA)) [1995 6.5m³ 6.5d* 6.5g³ 6.5g³ Nov 7] $475,000F: second foal: dam lightly-raced sister to Prix de la Foret winner Septieme Ciel, an excellent family: useful French filly: won minor event at Maisons-Laffitte in September: 2 lengths third of 9 to Titus Livius in Prix Eclipse at Deauville then 1¼ lengths third of 5 to same horse in Criterium des 2 Ans at Evry last 2 starts: should stay 7f: front runner. *Mme C. Head, France* 103

SEA VICTOR 3 b.g. Slip Anchor 136 – Victoriana (USA) (Storm Bird (CAN) 134) [1994 –: 7g 1995 10.3g* 12g⁴ 10.1m 8.1m 14g 10m⁶ 11.5g³ 15.1g³ 11.8g³ 15.8m* 18f² 16m* 16.5m³ a16g² a12g² Dec 2] sturdy, good-topped gelding: fairly useful performer: won maiden at Doncaster in March: sold out of J. Gosden's stable 12,000 gns Newmarket July Sales after fourth start: had 4 outings in space of 10 days in October, winning handicaps at Catterick and Nottingham: stays very well: has raced only on a sound surface (acts on firm going) or all-weather: has had tongue tied down: game: tough. *J. L. Harris* 84

SEBASTIAN 3 b.c. Sadler's Wells (USA) 132 – Sandy Island 110 (Mill Reef (USA) 141) [1994 NR 1995 12f* 12m² 12g* 11.9d* Oct 11] 116 p

An ante-post gamble on Sebastian was a feature of the run-up to the 216th Derby: having been 40/1 in the spring, he stood as low as 9/2 once Celtic Swing was switched to Chantilly. The gamble went astray in an unfortunate manner when the colt came off the gallops 'sore across his back' on the Wednesday of race week and did not recover in time for Epsom. In fact it was October before he raced again. Sebastian's public form did not entitle him to be a 9/2-shot, or anything like that, for the Derby. He had never contested a pattern or listed event. In essence he was a progressive, very well-bred individual, the subject of increasingly enthusiastic work reports, from a top-class stable. We thought he looked more of a Leger type in his three starts before Epsom, particularly on the second one, when beaten a length by Tamure in a slowly-run race at Newmarket, and in the third, when landing the odds by ten lengths from Nash Terrace in a race at Salisbury in which a stable-companion ensured a good gallop. First time up, in April, he had overcome obvious inexperience to win a Newmarket maiden. Sebastian made a pleasing return to the track at Haydock in the autumn, in what was his third conditions race in a row contested by a small field. He had done well physically in the interim, looked very well, and won by four lengths from the useful six-year-old Mack The Knife, leading throughout and staying on stoutly when shaken up two furlongs from home, getting right on top in the closing stages. At that, he was put away to wait for another year, after talk that he might go on to Newbury for the St Simon Stakes.

Sebastian (b.c. 1992)	Sadler's Wells (USA) (b 1981)	Northern Dancer (b 1961)	Nearctic
			Natalma
		Fairy Bridge (b 1975)	Bold Reason
			Special
	Sandy Island (b 1981)	Mill Reef (b 1968)	Never Bend
			Milan Mill
		Sayonara (b 1965)	Birkhahn
			Suleika

It is to be hoped that Sebastian will finally be able to put in a full season in 1996. Reportedly he was held up as a two-year-old by a split pastern (a pulled muscle in the rib cage seems to have been the problem before the Derby). He is very much the type to make a good four-year-old. Whether he will be fully effective in top company over middle distances remains to be seen; if he proves not to be, he has a future over further, being certain to stay well. Sebastian's dam Sandy Island was a lightly-raced staying type of some note. She won the Lancashire Oaks on her final appearance, having previously won the Pretty Polly Stakes and been placed in the Musidora and the Ribblesdale. Easily the best of her three earlier foals to reach the racecourse, Sardegna (by Pharly), also won the Pretty Polly and reached a place in the Musidora. Sandy Island's two-year-old of 1995, Subterfuge (by Machiavellian), won over seven furlongs at Newmarket on her only start to date. Importing the German mare Sayonara for stud purposes in the late-'seventies continues to pay dividends, then, for Lord Howard de Walden. It paid its biggest dividend a while ago, of course, when Sandy Island's three-parts brother Slip Anchor seized the opportunity denied to Sebastian at Epsom. *H. R. A. Cecil*

SECKAR VALE (USA) 3 ch.g. Elmaamul (USA) 125 – Both Sides Now (USA) (Topsider (USA)) [1994 87: 7s* 8s 6d^2 1995 9m 8m 10.3m^4 10d 12d* 12m^2 12f^5 8d^6 Dec 16] strong, lengthy gelding: useful form: left J. Hanson's stable and gelded after second 3-y-o start: really caught the eye after 4-month absence next time, and (after disappointing at Newbury) won rated stakes at Newmarket in September: moved unimpressively to post but best effort when rallying neck second of 10 to Naked Welcome in competitive rated stakes at Newmarket: subsequently sold out of B. Hills's stable 40,000 gns Newmarket Autumn Sales: creditable fifth on first of 2 runs in allowance races at Hollywood Park: suited by middle distances: acts on soft ground and good to firm: refused to enter stalls third intended 3-y-o start: takes keen hold. *S. Shulman, USA* — 96

SECOND CELLO 3 ch.f. Music Boy 124 – Tufty Lady 91 (Riboboy (USA) 124) [1994 59: 6m^3 6m^3 6.1m 6d 6.1d 6g^3 7m 1995 7g^3 7g^6 6g^6 7f* 7m^2 6g 6m^5 Oct 2] small, light-framed filly: has a quick action: fair performer: narrowly won maiden at Salisbury in June: stays 7f: acts on firm ground, below form both outings on a soft surface: sold 4,000 gns Newmarket Autumn Sales. *D. Morris* — 69

SECOND CHANCE (IRE) 5 ch.g. Digamist (USA) 110 – Flash Donna (USA) 70 (Well Decorated (USA)) [1994 88: 6.9s 7g^5 7.6g^2 7v 6.9g^5 7f^2 9g* 9d^3 8.1d 9v* 1995 a9.4g^6 a8g^2 8g 7f^6 8.5m^4 8f* 10f^4 8f^6 8.3m^5 10.1m 9g^3 8d^2 9d^4 Oct 21] sparely-made gelding: poor mover: fairly useful handicapper: won at Goodwood in June: stays 9.4f: acts on any going: wore visor (which slipped) once at 2 yrs: often a front runner: sold 21,000 gns Newmarket Autumn Sales: sent to USA. *P. Mitchell* — 88

SECOND COLOURS (USA) 5 b. or br.g. Timeless Moment (USA) – Ruffled Silk (USA) (Our Hero (USA)) [1994 55+, a75: a6g* a7g* a7g^4 a7g^2 a8.5g* 6g 7.1m^6 1995 a7g^3 a8.5g* 7.5m a8.5g^2 a8g 7g^5 8.2m* 8.3f^5 10m^5 8f* 9.2f* 8g^2 9f^5 8.5m* a8.5g* 8.9g* 8g^6 a9.4g^3 a8g^2 Dec 15] strong, compact gelding: carries condition: fairly useful performer: won seller at Wolverhampton in March and held his form well in the summer, winning handicap at Nottingham, minor event at Carlisle and claimers at Hamilton, Beverley, Wolverhampton and York: best effort in claimer at Lingfield (beaten a head) final start: stays 9.2f: acts on firm ground, dead and goes well on the all-weather: visored (ran well) once at 2 yrs: successful when sweating. *Mrs M. Reveley* — 69 a81

SECONDS AWAY 4 b.g. Hard Fought 125 – Keep Mum 63 (Mummy's Pet 125) [1994 NR 1995 6s 8.1m^4 8f 7.1m^4 8g 8.3f^4 7f 6g^3 Sep 25] small gelding: maiden, — 41 d rated 58 at 2 yrs: trained until after reappearance by A. Harrison: effective at 6f, and stays 1m: acts on good to firm ground: tried blinkered/visored. *J. S. Goldie*

SECOND TIME LUCKY (IRE) 2 b.c. (Mar 7) Digamist (USA) 110 – Sallymiss (Tanfirion 110) [1995 5g^{4} 6m^{2} 5g^{6} 6g* 7.3d^{2} Oct 21] IR 7,000Y: smallish, angular colt: fourth foal: half-brother to Irish 3-y-o 1m winner Scene One (by Scenic): dam Irish 5f winner: fair form: won maiden auction at Warwick in October by 2 lengths from Sorbie Tower, one of only 2 to race stand side in straight: very good second of 19 to Proud Monk in nursery at Newbury later in month: much better suited by 6f/7f than 5f: sent to France. *Lord Huntingdon* — 77

SECRET ALY (CAN) 5 b.g. Secreto (USA) 128 – Bouffant (USA) (Alydar (USA)) [1994 78: a8g^{3} 7s^{4} 8.1d^{5} 7.6m 10m 8.9f^{3} 10m 8.3f 8m^{2} 7.9m^{5} 10.3d 9g 8.9d 10d 8d a8g^{3} a7g* a8.5g* 1995 a7g a10g^{3} a10g* a10g^{2} 10m^{4} 10m 8.1g* 10f 8g 8f* 7.6m 9g 9g 8.9g 8f* a8g^{4} Dec 1] good-bodied gelding: usually impresses in appearance: fairly useful handicapper: won at Lingfield in February, Sandown in June, Goodwood (£8,000 race) in July and Leicester in October: effective at 1m (best form) to 1¼m: acts on the all-weather and goes well on firm going: usually races prominently, but went well from off pace last 2 starts. *C. E. Brittain* — 86, a90

SECRET ASSIGNMENT (USA) 5 ch.g. Naevus (USA) – Swedish Ivy (USA) (Northjet 136) [1994 44: a7g a12g^{6} a6g^{3} 5v a6g^{4} a6g^{4} a7g a7g 1995 a8g a7g a6g a10g^{6} 15.4m 17.2m 16.1g^{4} 16m 16.4m Nov 6] lengthy gelding: no worthwhile form in 1995: sold out of C. Cyzer's stable 850 gns Ascot April Sales after fourth start. *R. Curtis* — –

SECRET BALLAD (IRE) 3 b.c. Classic Secret (USA) 91 – Bally 74 (Balidar 133) [1994 62: 5d 7.1m 7.1m 6f^{3} 6m^{6} 1995 8.3m^{4} 10m Jul 24] compact colt: modest form: stayed 8.3f: dead. *J. Akehurst* — 61

SECRET COMMANDER 2 ch.g. (Mar 10) Ron's Victory (USA) 129 – Louise 71 (Royal Palace 131) [1995 5m May 1] 7,200Y: strong, close-coupled gelding: half-brother to several winners, including 5f to 1m winner Kummel King (by Absalom) and 7f winner Acapulco (by Music Boy): dam 1½m winner: 16/1 and very backward, always tailed off in maiden at Windsor. *T. J. Naughton* — –

SECRET MISS 3 ch.f. Beveled (USA) – Zamindara (Crofter (USA) 124) [1994 53p: 6d 1995 5d 5.1g 6.1m^{5} 6m 5g^{2} 6g 5m^{6} 5g 6m^{6} 5.1m 6g 5d* 5g a6g^{5} a7g a6g Nov 20] leggy, sparely-made filly: modest handicapper: won maiden event at Lingfield in September by 6 lengths, racing towards favoured far rail: well below form afterwards: best efforts on a soft surface: sweating (ran respectably) seventh start: tried blinkered/visored, no improvement: none too consistent. *A. P. Jarvis* — 55, a–

SECRET PLEASURE (IRE) 2 ch.f. (May 28) Classic Secret (USA) 91 – Abbessingh (Mansingh (USA) 120) [1995 6g^{5} 5g^{4} 7.6d^{3} 8d 6m Oct 12] 8,200 2-y-o: smallish, workmanlike filly: third foal: half-sister to 1993 French 2-y-o 7f winner Fasil (by Diamond Prospect): dam French maiden half-sister to useful sprinter Roaring Riva: fair maiden: ran well third start, after 3-month break: will prove best short of 1m: acts on dead ground. *R. Hannon* — 66

SECRET QUEST 3 b.f. Rainbow Quest (USA) 134 – Secret Dancer (FR) 70 (Fabulous Dancer (USA) 124) [1994 8s^{2} 8d^{2} 1995 10s* 10m* 9.3v* 10d^{3} 10g^{3} Aug 5] second foal: half-sister to French 1¼m winner Sideslip (by Last Fandango): dam, maiden, stayed 1¼m but often looked none too keen: useful performer: won 2 minor events then Prix Vanteaux (made all, by 2½ lengths from Marble Falls) at Longchamp in the spring: third of 5 in Prix Saint-Alary there (4 lengths behind Muncie) and Prix de Psyche at Deauville (respectable effort behind Angel In My Heart on return from 2½ month break) afterwards: should stay beyond 1¼m: acts on good to firm ground and heavy. *P. Bary, France* — 108

SECRET SERENADE 4 b.g. Classic Secret (USA) 91 – Norfolk Serenade 83 (Blakeney 126) [1994 77: 8g^{2} 8.5g^{4} 10m^{6} 12.4f^{2} 12m^{2} 14.1m^{4} 14.6g 15s^{3} 14.1g^{2} 14.6d 16.5v 1995 a14.8g^{4} a16.2g* 14.9d^{5} 18.7g Jul 15] smallish, sturdy gelding: good mover: fair handicapper: won at Wolverhampton in January: stays 2m: probably acts on any ground: visored (below form) once at 2 yrs: sold (C. Fairhurst to R. Juckes) only 500 gns Ascot October Sales. *C. W. Fairhurst* — –, a77

SECRET SERVICE (IRE) 3 b.g. Classic Secret (USA) 91 – Mystery Bid (Auction Ring (USA) 123) [1994 73: 6m^{6} 7g^{5} 7g^{5} 7d^{3} 8d^{2} 8.3g^{2} 7.9d^{5} 1995 10d 8g — 78

12m* 12m^{3} Nov 4] compact, attractive gelding: not seen out until September, then won 18-runner apprentice handicap at Pontefract in October: sold out of J. Hanson's stable 27,000 gns Doncaster October Sales: 25/1, very good staying-on third of 18 to Snow Princess in November Handicap at Doncaster when back with 2-y-o stable: should stay beyond 1½m: acts on good to firm ground and dead. *C. W. Thornton*

SECRET SPRING (FR) 3 b.c. Dowsing (USA) 124 – Nordica 99 (Northfields (USA)) [1994 NR 1995 a8g^{2} 6.9g^{3} 8m^{2} 10g^{3} 8d^{5} 10d Oct 19] 16,000Y: leggy colt: fifth foal: half-brother to 2 winners, notably very useful winner at around 7f (probably stayed 1½m) Sueboog (by Darshaan): dam 6f and 1m winner: fairly useful maiden: has shown his form at 1¼m, but may well prove best over shorter: acts on good to firm ground and on equitrack: sold (R. Charlton to P. Hedger) 20,000 gns Newmarket Autumn Sales. *R. Charlton* — 81

SECRET VOUCHER 2 b.c. (Apr 29) Vouchsafe 91 – Welsh Secret 85 (Welsh Captain 113) [1995 5.1m^{6} 5f^{3} 5m^{5} 5m* 5g^{3} Sep 23] 2,500Y: smallish, unfurnished colt: poor mover: first foal: dam sprinter: fair performer: made all in maiden auction at Ripon in August: creditable third of 17 to Swynford Dream in nursery at Redcar almost month later: speedy, and likely to prove best at 5f. *B. A. McMahon* — 68

SEDBERGH (USA) 2 b.c. (Apr 27) Northern Flagship (USA) 96 – Crumbaugh Pike (USA) (Within Hail (USA)) [1995 6m a7g^{2} 8.1g^{6} 7d^{3} Sep 27] $10,000F, IR 8,000Y: workmanlike colt: half-brother to winners in USA by Nain Bleu and Doonesbury: dam winner of 3 race in USA at up to 7f: modest maiden: should stay at least 1m: looks one paced. *Mrs M. Reveley* — 61

SEDVICTA 3 b.g. Primitive Rising (USA) 113 – Annes Gift (Ballymoss 136) [1994 57p: 7m 6g 7g 8s 1995 12.3d 11.1g^{2} 14.1m May 30] good-topped gelding: has plenty of scope: has a quick action: modest form: will stay long distances. *Mrs M. Reveley* — 53

SEEKING DESTINY (IRE) 2 b.g. (Mar 26) Two Timing (USA) 124 – Heads We Called (IRE) (Bluebird (USA) 125) [1995 5g 6m 5s 7f a8g Nov 20] 10,000F, 15,000Y: first foal: dam unraced sister to Blues Traveller: sold out of Mrs M. McCourt's stable 600 gns Newmarket September Sales after second outing: showed ability last 2 starts, from 16 lb out of handicap at Southwell on final one: takes keen hold, and may well prove best short of 1m. *M. C. Chapman* — – a47 +

SEEKING FORTUNE (USA) 2 b.f. (May 25) Seeking The Gold (USA) – Gabfest (USA) (Tom Rolfe) [1995 7g^{6} Sep 28] $42,000Y: half-sister to several winners in USA, including minor stakes winner: dam stakes-placed winner at up to 1½m in USA: 10/1, just under 7 lengths sixth of 23 to Astor Place in maiden at Newmarket, improving from mid-division over 2f out then one pace: sure to do better. *J. R. Fanshawe* — 75 p

SEENTHELIGHT 3 ch.f. Rich Charlie 117 – Ackabarrow 97 (Laser Light 118) [1994 61: 5g^{4} 5g* 6m^{4} 5m* 6g^{6} 5m 5s^{5} 1995 a6g 6s 8.3g 6g 6m^{4} 7g 5.9f Jul 31] workmanlike filly: only poor plater at best in 1995: stays 6f: acts on good to firm ground: tried visored, no improvement. *D. Moffatt* — 39

SEE YOU AGAIN 3 b.c. Then Again 126 – Down The Valley 73 (Kampala 120) [1994 43p: a7g^{4} 1995 a10g^{6} 10f^{5} 7f^{6} 8h^{5} 7f^{2} 7g 7g a8.5g Nov 13] disappointing maiden: stays 1¼m: acts on firm ground: sold out of R. Hannon's stable 1,100 gns Newmarket Autumn Sales after final turf start. *M. Brittain* — 54

SEGALA (IRE) 4 b.c. Petorius 117 – Cerosia (Pitskelly 122) [1994 78: 9g^{2} a7g^{4} 8.3f* 8s^{5} 8g* 1995 a8.5g^{3} 9g 9.2g^{4} Sep 24] quite good-topped colt: fair handicapper: stays 9.2f: acts on fibresand and any turf going: sold (Sir Mark Prescott to J. J. O'Neill) 12,500 gns Newmarket Autumn Sales. *Sir Mark Prescott* — 74

SEGOVIA 3 b.f. Groom Dancer (USA) 128 – Sedova (USA) (Nijinsky (CAN) 138) [1994 NR 1995 10m* 12m^{5} 11.9m^{2} Aug 17] good-topped, attractive filly: has plenty of scope: second foal: half-sister to fairly useful 4-y-o 1¼m winner Sue's Artiste (by Damister): dam French middle-distance winner: 5/4 favourite, narrowly won 8-runner maiden at Ripon in May: useful form, beaten 9 lengths, when fifth of 7 to Phantom Gold in Ribblesdale Stakes at Royal Ascot and second of 4 to Larrocha in listed race at York: 1½m stretches her stamina: has raced only on good to firm ground: may well be capable of better. *H. R. A. Cecil* — 95 p

SEIGNEURIAL 3 b.g. Primo Dominie 121 – Spinner 59 (Blue Cashmere 129) [1994 91: 5m6 5d* 5g* 5m4 5.2m 5m5 5s3 5g6 1995 5g 5s 5m 6f2 5m Nov 4] lengthy, workmanlike gelding: good mover: fairly useful performer: effective at 5f and 6f: acts on firm and soft ground: sweating (reared stalls and virtually took no part) on 3-y-o reappearance. *G. Harwood* 85

SEIRENES 2 b.f. (Mar 2) Formidable (USA) 125 – Seriema 72 (Petingo 135) [1995 6d4 Sep 23] sturdy, lengthy filly: half-sister to several winners, including very smart 1¼m and 1½m winner Infamy (by Shirley Heights): dam, best at 1m, half-sister to good staying filly High Hawk (dam of In The Wings): 20/1, 2½ lengths fourth of 8 to Polska in Blue Seal Stakes at Ascot, staying on: looked green and in need of run, and should improve. *P. T. Walwyn* 78 p

SEIZE THE DAY (IRE) 7 b.g. Lomond (USA) 128 – Cheerful Heart (Petingo 135) [1994 NR 1995 14.1g2 15.4m 14m* 14g6 May 27] good-topped, attractive gelding: unimpressive mover: ran only once at 4 yrs to 6 yrs: modest form nowadays: won handicap at Haydock in May: should stay 2m (visored when well beaten over 15.4f): acts on good to firm going. *C. D. Broad* 60

SEJAAL (IRE) 3 b.c. Persian Heights 129 – Cremets 94 (Mummy's Pet 125) [1994 NR 1995 8g 8f3 8.3m3 8h* 7.6d Sep 14] 35,000Y: rangy, attractive colt: half-brother to multiple Italian winner at up to 15f My Irish (by Assert): dam 6f and 7f winner, is sister to Runnett: fair form in maidens and very comfortably landed odds of 6/1 on in 3-runner race at Bath in August: stays 1m: acts on hard ground, seemingly not on a soft surface: takes strong hold: sold 28,000 gns Newmarket Autumn Sales. *J. L. Dunlop* 71

SELECT FEW 2 b.c. (Mar 23) Alzao (USA) 117 – Elect (USA) 113 (Vaguely Noble 140) [1995 7m 8.2d5 8g* Sep 29] big, rangy colt: has scope: closely-related to a 6.5f to 1¼m winner in France by Lyphard and half-brother to several winners, including Grade 3 8.5f winner Aquaba (by Damascus), later the dam of Millstream: dam 1¼m to 12.3f winner from excellent family: won 13-runner maiden at Goodwood readily by 3 lengths from Ashanti Dancer, running on well: will stay middle distances: very much type to go on progressing. *L. M. Cumani* 84 p

SELF EXPRESSION 7 b.g. Homing 130 – Subtlety (Grundy 137) [1994 62: 8m 8g* 8d 8d 8f5 9.9g3 8.1g5 8m* 9.9g2 9.9m5 8g 8g 8g4 8m6 8g6 10s 8g6 8.1g 1995 a8g2 8.2g 8g 8m6 a8g4 8g 8g2 8.5d3 8g 9.9m2 9.9m6 Jul 25] leggy gelding: poor mover: modest handicapper: effective at 1m and 1¼m: acts on firm and dead ground and on fibresand, below form on very soft: tried blinkered/visored at 4 yrs, no improvement: effective from front or held up: carries head high and tends to hang, but has run well for inexperienced claimer. *Mrs J. R. Ramsden* 58 a62

SELF RELIANCE 3 b.f. Never So Bold 135 – Tahilla 112 (Moorestyle 137) [1994 NR 1995 7d5 a6g3 8f3 8m4 7m* 7m4 7f a8.5g4 Aug 11] tall, leggy filly: has a short action: fourth foal: sister to fair winning sprinter Pluck: dam suited by 1m: fair performer: won maiden handicap at Brighton in June: should stay beyond 1m: acts on firm ground, ran poorly (hanging right) on fibresand: sold 16,000 gns Newmarket December Sales. *M. Bell* 72 a59

SELF STYLED (IRE) 3 b.g. Taufan (USA) 119 – Swinging Gold 80 (Swing Easy (USA) 126) [1994 NR 1995 7m6 7f5 5m5 5f Aug 25] lengthy gelding: tubed: fourth foal: half-brother to 2 winners: dam sprinter: form only in claimer at Redcar on second start: dead. *T. D. Barron* 50

SELHURSTPARK FLYER (IRE) 4 b.g. Northiam (USA) – Wisdom To Know (Bay Express 132) [1994 105: 7d3 7.1g3 6v6 6f 6m3 6m 7m 6m 6d 6g2 5s5 1995 6m 6m 7m4 6m 7m 7m 6g 6d 5m Nov 4] leggy, workmanlike gelding: just a fairly useful handicapper at 4 yrs, best efforts on third and seventh (Ayr Silver Cup, first of those on far side) starts: stays 7f: acts on firm and dead ground, well beaten on soft and heavy: below form when tried in blinkers/visor in 1994: usually races prominently: inconsistent. *J. Berry* 84 d

SELMESTON (IRE) 3 b.g. Double Schwartz 128 – Baracuda (FR) (Zeddaan 130) [1994 NR 1995 8g a6g a6g Dec 12] 3,000F, 15,000Y: brother to 6f winner Prince of The Sea and half-brother to a winner in France: dam French maiden: of little account: sold out of A. Stewart's stable 700 gns Ascot June Sales after debut. *P. S. Felgate* –

SEMI SERIOUS 3 b.g. Midyan (USA) 124 – Modica 89 (Persian Bold 123) [1994 NR 1995 a8g^4 a10g a6g 7f 7m Oct 30] 25,000Y: good-bodied gelding: third foal: half-brother to French 1½m winner English Invader (by Rainbow Quest): dam Irish 1m and 1¼m winner: sold out of W. Jarvis' stable 1,700 gns Doncaster March Sales after second start: of little account since debut: resold 650 gns Doncaster November Sales. *D. W. Chapman* –

SEMPER (IRE) 2 b.c. (Apr 19) Soviet Lad (USA) 94 – Classic Dilemma (Sandhurst Prince 128) [1995 7f* 7m^3 7m^4 Jul 29] IR 10,500F, 19,000Y: sparely-made colt: unimpressive mover: second reported foal: half-brother to a winner in Hong Kong: dam Irish 2-y-o 6f winner from 3 starts: won maiden at Milan in June by 3 lengths: bandaged near hind, never a factor in minor events at York (third of 4 to Fag End) and Newmarket following month: will stay 1m. *L. M. Cumani* 83

SENAAN 3 b.c. Faustus (USA) 118 – Frighten The Life (Kings Lake (USA) 133) [1994 –: 5f 1995 8.3m 7f 8.3m 8.2m 6.9g Jul 5] strong, lengthy colt: seems of little account: visored (virtually bolted) penultimate 3-y-o start: sold 3,200 gns Newmarket July Sales: sent to Italy. *T. Thomson Jones* –

SENEBROVA 4 b.f. Warning 136 – Stemegna (Dance In Time (CAN)) [1994 8g* 8g^4 8g 8d^5 8d^2 7.5g^4 8v^4 1995 8m^3 8m* 8g^4 8g^3 8m^3 8m* 8s* 8g^3 8d^5 8g* Nov 8] half-sister to 3 winners, notably Leopoldo di Lorena (at up to 11f, in Italy, by Bustino): dam unraced: useful performer, who races mainly at Milan: won maiden there (at 3 yrs) and minor event in April and (after 1¾ lengths third of 11 to Olimpia Dukakis in Premio Legnano) minor race and quite valuable event in September: gained first pattern success in Group 3 event (beat Lara by ½ length) in November: stays 1m: acts on good to firm and soft ground, probably on heavy. *V. Valiani, Italy* 104

SENORITA DINERO (USA) 3 ch.f. Ferdinand (USA) – Martha's Fastmoney (USA) (Fast (USA)) [1994 65p: 7s^3 1995 10g* 12g^3 10.1f* 10.2m* 10.5m^2 9.9m^4 Aug 10] tall, lengthy filly: fairly useful performer: successful in maiden at Salisbury in May and handicaps at Yarmouth in June and Chepstow in July: effective at 1¼m and 1½m: acts on firm ground, shaped well on soft on debut: very edgy (disappointing effort) final start. *M. R. Stoute* 88

SENSE OF PRIORITY 6 ch.g. Primo Dominie 121 – Sense of Pride (Welsh Pageant 132) [1994 64: 7m a7g^4 7g^2 a6g^6 a7g^4 a7g^3 1995 a7g a6g^3 a6g^4 a6g^3 6f 5g^6 6m 5.9f^4 6m* a6g* 6m^5 7m^5 7f^5 a7g Aug 11] leggy, workmanlike gelding: fair performer: left M. H. Easterby's stable after sixth start: won seller at Catterick and claimer at Wolverhampton in July: best at up to 7f: acts on the all-weather, suited by a sound surface (acts on hard ground) on turf: visored twice at 4 yrs. *D. Nicholls* 59 a68

SENSO (IRE) 4 b.g. Persian Heights 129 – Flosshilde (Rheingold 137) [1994 76: 10g^2 9s^5 10s^4 1995 10g^4 Jul 15] fair form at best in Italy at 3 yrs for J. Dunlop: poor novice hurdler: tailed-off last of 4 in maiden on only run on flat here. *J. S. Wainwright* –

SEPOY (IRE) 2 ch.c. (Mar 14) Common Grounds 118 – Song of The Glens (Horage 124) [1995 5g 5m^2 5g^5 6g* Sep 24] 15,000Y: leggy, lengthy colt: third foal: half-brother to 1993 2-y-o 7f winner Syabas (by Northiam): dam maiden daughter of half-sister to 2000 Guineas winner Right Tack: progressive colt: 8-length winner of median auction maiden at Hamilton in September: will stay 7f: wears bandages: sold 44,000 gns Doncaster October Sales: likely to remain on the upgrade: sent to France. *C. W. Thornton* 82 p

SERAPHIC 4 b.f. Slip Anchor 136 – Cephira (FR) (Abdos 134) [1994 63: 10d^4 8g^3 10.1g 1995 a8.5g a12g 6m 10m 15.1m^6 Jul 4] leggy, close-coupled filly: no form for new stable at 4 yrs: sold 700 gns Doncaster October Sales. *B. R. Cambidge* –

SERENDIPITY (FR) 2 b.c. (Feb 22) Mtoto 134 – Bint Damascus (USA) (Damascus (USA)) [1995 7f^5 8m^5 Nov 4] 11,000Y: lengthy, good-quartered colt: has scope: third living foal: dam, placed once in USA, closely related to Grade 1 9f Hollywood Oaks winner Moment To Buy: fifth of 8 to Mark of Esteem in maiden at Goodwood, staying on without being given hard race: caught eye when around 4 lengths fifth of 23 to Shaamit in median auction maiden at Doncaster over 3 months later, making strong late headway and giving impression might have troubled winner had run begun sooner: will be well suited by middle distances: sure to improve further, and win a race or two. *J. L. Dunlop* 85 p

SEREN QUEST 5 b.m. Rainbow Quest (USA) 134 – Serenesse (Habat 127) [1994 79: 9s 10g 10m 1995 11.7m^2 12g^6 May 19] leggy mare: fair handicapper: 77

looking as though outing would do her good, second of 11 in handicap at Bath but failed to progress as anticipated when sixth of 11 at Newbury later in May: suited by middle distances: acts on any going. *R. Akehurst*

SERGEYEV (IRE) 3 ch.c. Mulhollande (USA) 107 – Escape Path (Wolver Hollow 126) [1994 91: 6m^3 6m^2 5m* 5m^3 6d^6 1995 7m* 6m* 6g* 7m* 6g 7m Jul 24] useful-looking colt: smart performer: justified favouritism in minor event at Brighton, £8,000 contests at Kempton and Newbury (all easily) and 16-runner Jersey Stakes at Royal Ascot (with something in hand, by 1¼ lengths from Shahid), all by mid-June: well below best last 2 starts in July Cup (took very strong hold to post) at Newmarket and Beeswing Stakes at Newcastle: effective at 6f and 7f: acts on good to firm ground, disappointing only start on dead: pulls hard, and is held up for a late run. *R. Hannon* — 112

SERGIO (IRE) 3 ch.g. Doubletour (USA) – Shygate (Shy Groom (USA)) [1994 NR 1995 a8g a8g a8.5g^5 a11g 12f May 1] IR 3,000Y: first foal: dam modest Irish 1½m winner: no worthwhile form: has joined J. Leigh. *M. C. Chapman* — –

SERIF (USA) 2 b.c. (Apr 22) Diesis 133 – Ribbon (USA) (His Majesty (USA)) [1995 6d a7g^3 a7g^3 6d Sep 18] angular, unfurnished colt: brother to fairly useful 1992 2-y-o 6f winner Ribbonwood and half-brother to several winners here and in USA, including dual classic winner Risen Star (by Secretariat): dam prolific winner from 6f to 11f in USA: best effort in maidens first 3 starts when third of 11 to Double Diamond at Wolverhampton: well beaten in nursery at Leicester final outing: should stay further than 7f: acts on fibresand: well bred, but seems only modest: sent to Dubai. *J. H. M. Gosden* — 60 a68

SERIOUS 5 b.g. Shadeed (USA) 135 – Azallya (FR) (Habitat 134) [1994 93: 6g^6 6m^5 6m 7m 6m 7m 8m^6 7m 1995 7m 9m^6 7.3g 8m 10.5g^2 10v 8m^2 Oct 28] lengthy, good-topped gelding: normally impresses in appearance: fairly useful handicapper: second at Haydock (tending to carry head high) and Newmarket (running on strongly in 30-runner £24,100 race) in the autumn: stays 10.5f: acts on good to firm and dead going, no form (though stiff task) on heavy: visored (well beaten) third 4-y-o start: has run creditably when sweating: has had tongue tied down: won novice hurdle in December. *Lady Herries* — 89

SERIOUS FACT 3 b.g. Aragon 118 – Plain Tree 71 (Wolver Hollow 126) [1994 –: a6g 6v a7g 1995 5m a6g^5 Nov 30] workmanlike gelding: poor sprint maiden. *Sir Mark Prescott* — 41

Jersey Stakes, Royal Ascot—jockey find of the year Richard Hughes produces Sergeyev to beat Shahid (left), First Island (out of picture) and Inzar

SERIOUS HURRY 7 ch.g. Forzando 122 – Lady Bequick 81 (Sharpen Up 127) [1994 54: a5g^{4} a5g^{5} a6g^{5} 1995 5d 5g 5g^{3} 5g 5g 5f 5m^{2} 5f 5g 5f 5f* 5h^{4} 5h* 5m^{2} 6g 5f Oct 14] strong, heavy-topped gelding: has a quick action: modest handicapper: made all in apprentice races at Hamilton and Carlisle in August: soundly beaten last 2 starts: best at around 5f: acts on hard ground and equitrack, seems unsuited by a soft surface: blinkered (seemed sharpened up after 2½ years without headgear) last 6 starts: usually forces pace: none too consistent. *R. M. McKellar* 56

SERIOUS OPTION (IRE) 4 b.g. Reprimand 122 – Top Bloom (Thatch (USA) 136) [1994 85: 7v^{2} 7f 7.1g^{4} 7.1m 7g^{5} 1995 7s 6m 7g 8.1g^{4} 7.6m 8.3m^{4} 11.5m^{3} Aug 12] sturdy, well-made gelding: only fair at best in 1995, and below even that last 4 starts: probably stays 1m: probably acts on any going: tried blinkered, no improvement. *P. F. I. Cole* 69 d

SERIOUS TRUST 2 b.c. (Mar 6) Alzao (USA) 117 – Mill Line 71 (Mill Reef (USA) 141) [1995 7.5m^{5} 7.5m 7m^{5} 7g 7f Oct 14] 31,000Y: good-topped colt: has scope: second living foal: half-brother to Irish and Yorkshire Oaks winner Pure Grain (by Polish Precedent): dam 14.6f winner out of Park Hill winner Quay Line: modest maiden: tailed off in nursery at Catterick final start: likely to need good test of stamina. *Sir Mark Prescott* 52

SET TABLE (USA) 6 gr.g. Caro 133 – Room For The Sauce (USA) (Sauce Boat (USA)) [1994 76: 8m^{2} 8s 1995 8g^{2} 7m^{6} 7m^{3} May 9] leggy, workmanlike gelding: fair handicapper, lightly raced: creditable efforts in 1995, second (again) in £15,900 William Hill Spring Mile at Doncaster on reappearance: effective at 7f and stays 1¼m: best on a sound surface: effective visored/blinkered or not: races prominently. *J. H. M. Gosden* 74

SET THE FASHION 6 br.g. Green Desert (USA) 127 – Prelude 89 (Troy 137) [1994 80, a69: a7g^{3} 7m^{2} a8.5g^{3} 7m^{2} 8m^{3} 8f 8s 7g^{4} 8m 8d 1995 8m 8m 8d 7m a7g* a8g* a7g Nov 8] good-topped gelding: has a round action: fair performer: won minor event (final outing for Lord Huntingdon, sold 10,000 gns Newmarket Autumn Sales) and handicap at Lingfield in the autumn: best form at up to 1m: acts on all-weather surfaces and probably on any turf going: wears visor: normally held up. *D. L. Williams* – a76

SEVEN CROWNS (USA) 2 b.c. (Jan 23) Chief's Crown (USA) – Ivory Dance (USA) (Sir Ivor 135) [1995 6m^{6} 7.1g^{4} 8f^{5} 9m^{6} Aug 30] $60,000Y: stocky colt: unimpressive mover: first foal: dam won 5 races and was second in Canadian Oaks: trained by T. Mills on debut: modest form in maidens: never-dangerous sixth of 8 to Night Watch at Sandown final start: will stay further than 9f. *R. Hannon* 65

SEVEN KISSES (IRE) 2 b.f. (Mar 5) Kefaah (USA) 124 – Avidal Park 68 (Horage 124) [1995 5g Mar 24] 4,000F, 4,000Y: third living foal: half-sister to 1½m winner Real Popcorn and Italian 3-y-o 7.5f (at 2 yrs) to 11f winner Rosso Fiorentino (both by Jareer): dam 2-y-o 5f winner: 8/1, green and always long way behind in seller at Doncaster. *B. A. McMahon* –

SEVENTEENS LUCKY 3 gr.g. Touch of Grey 90 – Westminster Waltz (Dance In Time (CAN)) [1994 69: 7s 7g^{5} 6g^{2} 6.1d 1995 6m 7g^{2} 7m^{2} 8m 7.5g^{3} 7f^{2} 7m^{4} 7f^{6} 8m^{3} 8.9g* 10d a10g^{4} Dec 15] close-coupled gelding: fair handicapper: came from midfield to lead over 1f out and gamely won 25-runner £11,600 contest at York in October: probably stays 1¼m: acts on firm going (probably on equitrack), below form on a soft surface: visored (no improvement, setting pace) sixth 3-y-o start. *Bob Jones* 76

SEVERN GALE 5 br.m. Strong Gale 116 – Miss Apex 57 (Wolverlife 115) [1994 NR 1995 a8.5g^{4} a12g a7g^{6} Feb 22] first foal: dam won over 7.2f and 1m, and over hurdles: winning hurdler in 1994/5: never-nearer fourth on debut, easily best effort in maidens at Wolverhampton: should be suited by further than 8.5f: blinkered final start: joined F. Jordan. *K. White* 45

SEYOUF (USA) 3 ch.c. Woodman (USA) 126 – Lady In Silver (USA) 127 (Silver Hawk (USA) 123) [1994 NR 1995 8g Jun 7] $200,000Y: first foal: dam, won Prix de Diane, from excellent family: 5/1, always behind (refused to settle early on) in maiden at Yarmouth: sent to Dubai. *J. H. M. Gosden* –

SHAAMIT (IRE) 2 b.c. (Feb 11) Mtoto 134 – Shomoose (Habitat 134) [1995 8d^{4} 8m* Nov 4] big, rangy colt: has plenty of scope: third foal: dam unraced, out of useful 90 p

Epithet (stayed 1½m well): well-backed favourite, won 23-runner median auction maiden at Doncaster in November impressively by 3½ lengths from Classy Chief, having plenty to do 3f out but responding well when ridden and powering clear from 1f out: will stay beyond 1m: will be able to hold his own in stronger company, and is one to follow. *W. J. Haggas*

SHAANXI (USA) 3 ch.f. Zilzal (USA) 137 – Rich And Riotous (USA) (Empery (USA) 128) [1994 8s* 8d* 1995 8v* $8d^2$ $8d^3$ $10.5m^6$ $8g^2$ $8g^3$ $8m^2$ 8d* 8s 9f Dec 10] 122

Shaanxi was a standing dish in the top French mile races of 1995. Her first three career starts had been victories: a newcomers race in October as a two-year-old by four lengths, a listed contest the following month by a neck and another listed race in March by four lengths, all of them at Saint-Cloud. It was after this most encouraging start that Shaanxi switched from the ownership of Anthony Holmes to Teruya Yoshida. In 1993 and 1994, the Yoshida-owned filly Ski Paradise regularly kept company with the best in a similar campaign, as a three-year-old winning two of her seven starts and finishing runner-up in all the rest. Shaanxi did not do quite so well as that, indeed it was October before she won again, but there was little to criticise as she stepped up to pattern company and was placed in five of her next six outings. The exception was the Prix de Diane, in which she probably failed to stay but was beaten only about a length and three quarters and showed form as good as anything seen from her previously; in a muddling affair, she was hampered before quickening into second a furlong out before finishing in sixth. All of Shaanxi's other races in Europe were at a mile. In the Prix de la Grotte and Poule d'Essai des Pouliches, she made the places with Matiara and Carling, splitting the pair when beaten a neck on the first occasion then going down by two lengths and a neck, set plenty to do and meeting interference in the pack, on the second. Those were before the Diane. After it, half a length denied her victory against Smolensk in the Prix d'Astarte, two and a half lengths against Miss Satamixa and Sayyedati in the Jacques le Marois, and three quarters of a length against Ridgewood Pearl in the Moulin. With less taxing opposition in the Group 2 Prix du Rond-Point at Longchamp on Arc day, Shaanxi found a gap a furlong out and employed her turn of foot to winning effect, not at all hard pressed to account for Petit Poucet and Nec Plus Ultra by two lengths and a neck. It was a fitting way to end her European season. She was well below form in two races abroad after that, the Breeders' Cup Mile at Belmont Park and the Hong Kong International Cup at Sha Tin.

Shaanxi now looks extremely well bought at 36,000 dollars at the Keeneland September Yearling Sale. She is the eighth foal and sixth winner out of Rich And Riotous, the best of the rest being the first foal Kraemer (by Lyphard) who took a seven-and-a-half-furlong race in France as a two-year-old, three races (one a listed stakes) in the US as a three-year-old and was placed in two graded stakes events at around nine furlongs. Rich And Riotous herself won a one-mile minor event at

Prix du Rond-Point, Longchamp—Shaanxi is much too good for Petit Poucet, Nec Plus Ultra and Atticus

Maisons-Laffitte on the last of ten starts. Her dam Carnauba has not been a great success at stud, but her early years were pretty newsworthy. A 20,000-dollar purchase as a yearling, she won eight races, including the Fred Darling Stakes and Oaks d'Italia, and was the champion filly of her age in Italy. Her value had risen to 300,000 dollars one week after her final three-year-old start, at least that was the opinion of the kidnappers who took her from her Milan stable and then attempted to exact a ransom. Some four months afterwards she was found in 'very poor condition' at a slaughterhouse, apparently on the verge of being worth just her carcase value, before rejoining the high life at the stud of her owner Nelson Bunker Hunt. At the Bunker Hunt Dispersal Sale in 1988, Carnauba did not appear to be too high on anybody's list of targets and fetched 35,000 dollars, since when she has produced two more winners (taking her total to five), including her first in a stakes race. A half-sister to Carnauba is Carnival Princess, the dam of Salse. Shaanxi's sire Zilzal has been re-imported from Kentucky to Lanwades Stud, Newmarket, where he will be standing at £10,000 (live foal) in 1996. The live foal concession is an important reassurance given Zilzal's considerable early fertility problems, but he has reportedly been operating with an 80% success rate in recent seasons. The 1989 Timeform Horse of the Year's first two crops together totalled just thirty-nine foals and Shaanxi is the best of them, followed by the Ormonde Stakes winner Zilzal Zamaan and useful performers such as Star of Zilzal and Monaassabaat. The 1995 two-year-old and yearling half-brothers to Lammtarra are among the larger number of Zilzal's representatives that will be coming through from now on.

Shaanxi (USA) (ch.f. 1992)	Zilzal (USA) (ch 1986)	Nureyev (b 1977)	Northern Dancer
			Special
		French Charmer (ch 1978)	Le Fabuleux
			Bold Example
	Rich And Riotous (USA) (b 1978)	Empery (b 1973)	Vaguely Noble
			Pamplona II
		Carnauba (b 1972)	Noholme II
			Carnival Queen

The strong, attractive Shaanxi has smart form in a steadily-run race over an extended mile and a quarter, but is better at a mile. Below form on her only start on firm ground, in Hong Kong, and yet to show her best (though twice a winner) on soft going, she acts on good to firm and dead. She wears a crossed noseband and is held up. Consistency and a turn of foot should ensure that Shaanxi wins more good races if she remains in training. *E. Lellouche, France*

SHAARID (USA) 7 b.g. El Gran Senor (USA) 136 – Summer Silence (USA) (Stop The Music (USA)) [1994 –: 11.7g 1995 9.7g^4 10m^3 May 12] smallish gelding: showed himself still capable of fair form in amateurs handicaps in the spring: should be well suited by further than 1¼m: fair jumper, winner of novice hurdle in October and handicap chase in December. *I. A. Balding* — 68

SHABANAZ 10 b.g. Imperial Fling (USA) 116 – Claironcita 97 (Don Carlos) [1994 68: 10d 10g^5 10s^3 10.2s^4 10m^2 10.4f 12m^4 10g* a12g^3 a10g^3 a11g* a10g* a13g^3 a11g 1995 12m^4 10m 12m^2 9.7m* 10m* 11.6g^2 a11g^2 10f 12.1m^4 11.6m* 9m^3 10.8f* 11f* a12g^6 a10g^3 Nov 25] rangy, angular gelding: good mover: modest performer: had a fine season in claimers and sellers, winning at Folkestone, Brighton, Windsor, Warwick and Redcar between May and October: effective at 9.7f, and stays 13f: acts on fibresand and probably on any turf going: visored (well below form) once at 7 yrs: has run well in blinkers, not tried for long time: held up: slowly away last 2 starts: suitable mount for a claimer. *W. R. Muir* — 62, a57

SHADES OF JADE 7 gr.m. General Wade 93 – Gellifawr 80 (Saulingo 122) [1994 40: 5v 5.1g 5s* 5s* 5g 5f 5m a5g^5 5f 5m 1995 5.1m 6f 5m 5m 5g 5g Jun 9] rangy mare: has a very round action: poor handicapper: well beaten in 1995: best at 5f: acts on good to firm ground and soft: blinkered (well beaten) last 2 starts at 6 yrs. *J. J. Bridger* — –

SHADIRWAN (IRE) 4 b.c. Kahyasi 130 – Shademah 88 (Thatch (USA) 136) [1994 12d^3 12d^3 12g^3 14g* 16v 1995 16m^2 16m* 20m^4 16.1m 16g 16.2d 18m Oct 14] small ex-Irish colt: sixth foal: half-brother to 3 winners, notably dual Derby winner Shahrastani (by Nijinsky): dam, 7f and 8.2f winner, is half-sister to Shakapour and Sharannpour: won maiden at Tralee at 3 yrs for J. Oxx and steadily-run handicap at Thirsk in May: good fourth of 27 to Harlestone Brook in — 83

Ascot Stakes at Royal Ascot: disappointing afterwards: stays 2½m: acts on good to firm and heavy ground: blinkered (out of form) final 4-y-o start. *R. Akehurst*

SHADOW JURY 5 ch.g. Doulab (USA) 115 – Texita 65 (Young Generation 129) [1994 66, a60: a6g a7g a6g^{2} 5d 5f^{2} 5f^{4} 5m^{3} 5m 5g 5m^{3} 6g^{5} 5m a6g a5g^{6} a6g 1995 a6g^{4} a6g^{3} a6g^{3} a6g* a5g^{5} a6g 6g^{6} 5m^{3} 5m* 5f* 5m^{3} 5m^{2} 5m* 5g* a5g* 6.1m^{5} 6m^{2} 5m^{2} 5f 5h^{6} a6g^{6} 5m 5g 5d 5d 5m^{6} 5m^{6} a5g^{3} a7g a5g^{3} Dec 14] rather leggy gelding: has a quick action: fair handicapper: won at Southwell in February, Redcar in May, Hamilton in June and Haydock, Ayr and Southwell in July: effective at 5f and 6f: acts on the all-weather and probably on any turf ground: effective blinkered (most starts in 1995)/visored or not: usually races prominently: tough. *D. W. Chapman* 80 a75

SHADOW LEADER 4 br.g. Tragic Role (USA) – Hush It Up (Tina's Pet 121) [1994 74: 8m^{3} 10.3m^{3} 10m^{2} 12f 10g^{5} 12m^{5} 13.3s 12d* 18m 12v^{3} 12.4d^{2} 1995 12g^{2} 12m^{2} 12g^{5} 14m^{4} 12g 12m^{3} 11.9m^{3} 13.9m^{6} 11.9d^{3} 13.3d Sep 16] sturdy gelding: fairly useful handicapper: third in Bessborough Stakes at Royal Ascot (final outing for Miss A. Whitfield), and Old Newton Cup and rated stakes at Haydock: lack-lustre effort in Autumn Cup at Newbury final start: best at around 1½m and 1¾m: acts on any going: held up/tracks leaders. *D. J. S. ffrench Davis* 86

SHADY DEED (USA) 3 ch.f. Shadeed (USA) 135 – Sum Sharp Lady (USA) (Sharpen Up 127) [1994 80: 6g^{5} 6m^{2} 6m^{5} 6.5g 7m 1995 6g 10g^{5} 10.1f^{5} 10f^{5} 8f^{2} 8h* 7m^{3} 8f^{6} 8d^{3} a10g Nov 21] lengthy filly: fair performer: won maiden handicap at Bath in August: stays 1¼m: acts on hard going: blinkered/visored fifth to ninth 3-y-o starts: front runner: none too consistent. *J. W. Hills* 67

SHADY GIRL (IRE) 2 b.f. (Jun 5) Shaadi (USA) 126 – Octavia Girl 104 (Octavo (USA) 115) [1995 6.1d 6d 7f^{5} Oct 12] leggy, quite good-topped, attractive filly: half-sister to several winners, including 3-y-o Eight Sharp (by Sure Blade), 7f winner at 2 yrs, 7f and 1m winner Festival Mood (by Jalmood) and 1992 2-y-o 5f winner Touch Silver (by Local Suitor): dam 2-y-o 6f winner, later stayed 1m: modest form in maidens and in Blue Seal Stakes at Ascot (seventh of 8 to Polska) in between: should stay 1m. *B. W. Hills* 67

SHADY LINK (IRE) 2 b.c. (Feb 17) Mujtahid (USA) 118 – Lady In Green (Shareef Dancer (USA) 135) [1995 7g Sep 13] second foal: half-brother to 3-y-o Green Seed (by Lead On Time), 6f winner at 2 yrs: dam unraced: 16/1, around 8½ lengths ninth of 19 to Shawanni in maiden at Yarmouth, eased when beaten: sold 20,000 gns Newmarket Autumn Sales, to S. Shulman in USA. *M. R. Stoute* 72 p

SHAFFIC (FR) 8 b.g. Auction Ring (USA) 123 – Tavella (FR) 98 (Petingo 135) [1994 –: a16s^{5} 1995 a16g^{3} Jan 2] rather angular, leggy gelding: fair handicapper (rated 78) in 1990: ran only 7 times on flat afterwards: stayed 2m: acted on good to firm and heavy ground: suffers from arthritis and retired. *Mrs M. Reveley* –

SHAFFISHAYES 3 ch.g. Clantime 101 – Mischievous Miss 73 (Niniski (USA) 125) [1994 NR 1995 7.1g* 8m^{3} 7m 7d Sep 22] 5,400Y: lengthy, unfurnished gelding: third foal: dam suited by 1¾m to 2m: overcame greenness to win steadily-run 4-runner median auction maiden at Edinburgh in April: stays 1m: acts on good to firm ground, shaped quite well on dead: may do better. *Mrs M. Reveley* 63 +

SHAFIR (IRE) 2 b.f. (Apr 8) Shaadi (USA) 126 – Cheese Soup (USA) (Spectacular Bid (USA)) [1995 5g^{3} 5g^{4} 5g* 5g 5f^{5} Oct 14] IR 5,000Y, 9,400 2-y-o: leggy filly: fifth reported foal: half-sister to useful 3-y-o 1m winner A La Carte (by Caerleon) and a winner in North America by Chief's Crown: dam unraced: won maiden auction at Catterick in June by 3½ lengths: absent 3½ months then behind in minor events at Ayr and Catterick: will be at least as effective at 6f as 5f: nearly unseated rider leaving stalls on second outing, slowly away when winning: wears a tongue strap: sold 5,000 gns Doncaster November Sales. *J. Berry* 68

SHAFT OF LIGHT 3 gr.g. Sharrood (USA) 124 – Reflection 111 (Mill Reef (USA) 141) [1994 NR 1995 a10g^{2} a9.4g^{2} a11g* a10g* 12m* 13.3g^{2} 14f^{2} 13.9m^{3} Aug 15] tall gelding: has scope: has a roundish action: sixth foal: brother to 7f (at 2 yrs) to 1¼m winner Empire Pool and half-brother to 2 winners (one of them ungenuine) by Clever Trick: dam, 2-y-o 5f to 7f winner, proved disappointing: progressed with virtually every start and is a fairly useful performer: won median auction maiden at Southwell and handicap at Lingfield early in year and amateurs handicap at Salisbury in July: ran well in handicaps last 3 starts: will be very well suited by further than 1¾m: acts on firm ground and both all-weather surfaces: 90

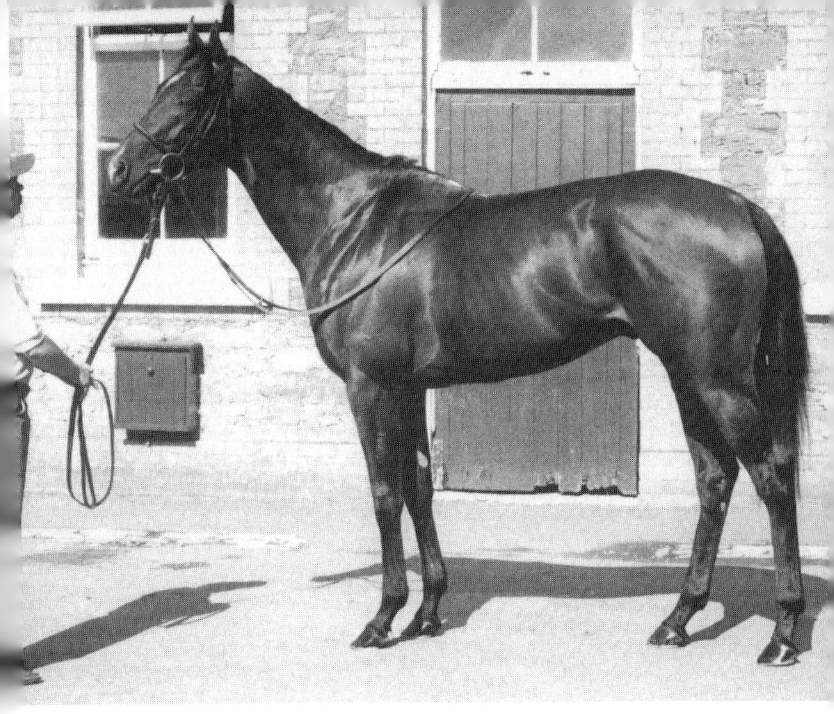

Hamdan Al Maktoum's "Shahid"

blinkered last 2 starts on all-weather: resolute galloper, well suited by forcing tactics: genuine. *Lord Huntingdon*

SHAHA 2 b.c. (Apr 8) Polish Precedent (USA) 131 – Height of Passion (Shirley Heights 130) [1995 6g^6 8.1m^6 Aug 28] 38,000F, 90,000Y: useful-looking colt: unimpressive walker: brother to smart 3-y-o middle-distance colt Precede, 6f winner at 2 yrs, and half-brother to several winners, including smart middle-distance stayer Warm Feeling (by Kalaglow): dam ran 3 times: sixth in maidens won by Tagula at Newmarket and Ski Academy at Chepstow 3 months later: may do better. *R. Hannon* 65 +

SHAHID 3 b.c. Green Desert (USA) 127 – Roussalka 123 (Habitat 134) [1994 80: 7m 7m^2 8g 7g^2 1995 7g* 7.5m* 7f* 7m* 7m^2 7m* 8m^5 8g^5 7d 7m^5 Oct 12] strong, well-made colt: smart performer: won handicaps at Newcastle, Beverley (rated stakes), Lingfield (rated stakes) and Goodwood (£11,500 event) in the spring: second to Sergeyev in Jersey Stakes at Royal Ascot before winning 7-runner Beeswing Stakes at Newcastle (tracked pace on favoured stand rail, quickened to beat Mistle Cat a length) in July: below form in Supreme Stakes at Goodwood and Challenge Stakes at Newmarket last 2 starts: has shown his form at 1m, but only in steadily-run race: acts on firm going, below form only run on a soft surface: takes keen hold, and held up: genuine: sent to Dubai. *J. L. Dunlop* 111

SHAHRANI 3 b.c. Lear Fan (USA) 130 – Windmill Princess 55 (Gorytus (USA) 132) [1994 –: 6f 6.1s 1995 8m^5 10g 11.8f Oct 24] lengthy colt: has scope: off course over 4 months after fifth of 11 in maiden at Bath: well beaten afterwards: should prove suited by further than 1m: has joined B. Meehan. *M. C. Pipe* 64 ?

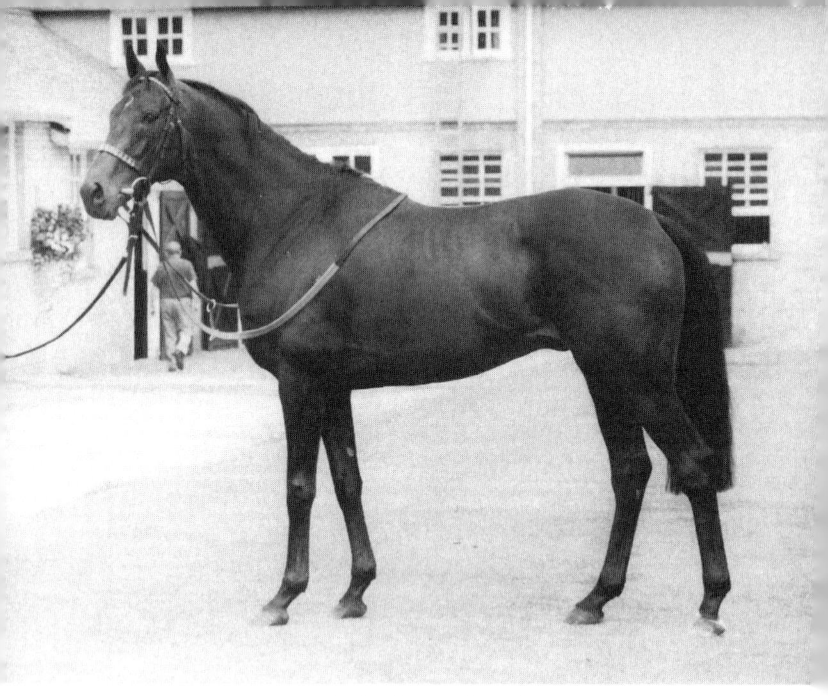

Mrs C. E. Brittain's "Shambo"

SHAKE THE YOKE 2 b.f. (Apr 1) Caerleon (USA) 132 – Bermuda Classic 98 (Double Form 130) [1995 7g^4 6.5g 8d* 8d^2 Oct 1] 400,000 francs Y: smallish filly: keen walker: fourth foal: half-sister to very smart sprinter Tropical (by Green Desert): dam, Irish 2-y-o 5f and 6f winner, stayed 1m: very useful French filly: won Prix d'Aumale at Longchamp in September by 2 lengths from Miss Tahiti, leading over 2f out: favourite, 2 lengths second of 11 to Miss Tahiti in Prix Marcel Boussac there 17 days later: will probably stay beyond 1m. *E. Lellouche, France* 110

SHAKIRI 6 b.m. Sizzling Melody 117 – Aspark (Sparkler 130) [1994 –: 7.1m 1995 5g May 11] leggy, angular mare: of little account. *R. M. McKellar* –

SHAKIYR (FR) 4 gr.g. Lashkari 128 – Shakamiyn (Nishapour (FR) 125) [1994 –p: 11.8g^4 1995 a11g* a12g^6 a12g* a12g* a14.8g^4 12.3m^2 12g 11.9g 13.9g 12m a12g^2 Dec 9] workmanlike gelding: fair performer: won median auction maiden at Southwell in January and handicaps at Wolverhampton in February and April: will stay 2m: acts on good to firm ground and fibresand: held up. *R. Hollinshead* 64 a69

SHAMAKA 4 b.f. Kris 135 – Sharka 97 (Shareef Dancer (USA) 135) [1994 53: 10d^5 12g 10d^6 1995 a12g a8g Jan 23] small, sparely-made filly: modest performer: well beaten in 1995: reportedly in foal to Deploy. *J. A. Glover* –

SHAMAND (USA) 2 br.g. (Feb 10) Minshaanshu Amad (USA) 91§ – Rose And Betty (USA) (Dare To Command) [1995 7f 7.1g 7m 10d Sep 19] 9,400Y: robust gelding: sixth foal: half-brother to 3 minor winners in USA: dam won 14 races in USA, including minor stakes at 6f and 8.3f at 5 yrs: always behind in maidens and a nursery (very stiff task). *B. J. Meehan* –

SHAMANIC 3 b.c. Fairy King (USA) – Annie Albright (USA) (Verbatim (USA)) 97
[1994 97: 5g* 5.1m* 6m^2 5f^2 5.5g 5f^6 1995 6m* 6g 6m 7.3g 7f^6 5m 6m^2 6g^6 6m Nov 4] smallish, useful-looking colt: useful performer: sweating, gamely won minor event at Salisbury in May: stiff task, appeared to run creditably in listed race at Doncaster final start, wandering under pressure: probably stays 7f: has raced only on a sound surface: none too consistent. *R. Hannon*

SHAMBO 8 b.h. Lafontaine (USA) 117 – Lucky Appeal 36 (Star Appeal 133) 113
[1994 111: 12s 16.2d^4 13.4m* 13.9f^4 12g^3 12m 16f 13.3g^3 15d^4 12v^5 1995 12g^3 13.4m^2 13.9g^3 May 18] strong, attractive horse: unimpressive mover: smart performer who has held his form remarkably well over the last 5 seasons: ran well on all 3 starts in 1995, placed in John Porter Stakes at Newbury, Ormonde Stakes (1¼ lengths second of 4 to Zilzal Zamaan in bid for unprecedented hat-trick) at Chester and Yorkshire Cup (staying on well, 1½ lengths behind Moonax), all within a month: effective at 1½m and stays 2m: has useful form on soft ground, but better form on firm and dead: held up. *C. E. Brittain*

SHAMEKH 3 b.g. In The Wings 128 – Troyanos (Troy 137) [1994 64: 7g 7m 1995 10m 14.1m 12g 14.1g 11.6m Jun 26] close-coupled gelding: modest maiden handicapper: probably stays 1¾m: blinkered and bandaged (refused to race) final 3-y-o outing. *J. E. Banks* – §

SHAMOKIN 3 b.c. Green Desert (USA) 127 – Shajan (Kris 135) [1994 NR 1995 8m Oct 2] first foal: dam unraced daughter of High Hawk, dam also of In The Wings: 50/1, burly and green, last of 18 in maiden at Pontefract. *F. Watson* –

SHAMROCK DANCER (IRE) 5 b.m. Dance of Life (USA) – Practical 95 (Ballymore 123) [1994 NR 1995 11.9m Jun 6] workmanlike mare: bad maiden. *R. J. Baker* –

SHAMROCK FAIR (IRE) 3 ch.f. Shavian 125 – Fair Country 89 (Town And Country 124) [1994 77: 7f^2 7m* 7g^4 1995 6g^4 8f^5 Jun 23] compact filly: good mover: fair form at 2 yrs: below best in 1995: should stay at least 1m. *Lord Huntingdon* 65

SHAMSHADAL (IRE) 5 b.g. Darshaan 133 – Shabarana (FR) (Nishapour (FR) 125) [1994 –: 12v^5 12m 14d 1995 14.1m 18.2m Jul 4] rangy gelding: no worthwhile form on flat here: modest hurdler. *J. R. Jenkins* –

SHAMWARI (USA) 4 ch.f. Shahrastani (USA) 135 – Exotic Treat (USA) (Vaguely Noble 140) [1994 63: 10.2g^2 10g 13.1g^2 11.6m 16g^2 14d^4 17.2g a13g 1995 a16.2g a12g^2 a12g^4 a12g^2 Feb 27] sparely-made filly: modest maiden: stays 2m: acts on fibresand: tried blinkered, no improvement. *J. W. Hills* – a53

SHANDINE (USA) 3 b.c. Riverman (USA) 131 – Proflare (USA) 101 (Mr Prospector (USA)) [1994 96: 5g^2 6s* 6s^2 6g* 6.1g* 8d^5 1995 8.1g 7m Jun 15] leggy colt: useful performer at 2 yrs: well beaten at Haydock (left standing as stalls opened for £17,700 handicap) and rated stakes at Newbury (pulling hard) in 1995: should stay 1m: acts on soft ground: sold only 7,500 gns Newmarket Autumn Sales: sent to Malaysia. *R. Charlton* –

SHANGHAI LIL 3 b.f. Petong 126 – Toccata (USA) (Mr Leader (USA)) [1994 47: 5d 5m 6m 6g 7g 10g a7g^6 1995 a6g* a6g 7m 6f 8m 8.3m Jul 29] smallish filly: poor performer: won maiden handicap at Wolverhampton in April: well below that form afterwards: should stay 7f: acts on fibresand and on good to firm and dead ground: tried blinkered, below form. *M. J. Fetherston-Godley* – a42

SHANGHAI VENTURE (USA) 4 br.g. Unfuwain (USA) 131 – Intrepid Lady (USA) (Bold Ruler) [1994 82: 7d^6 10m* 10s^4 12d 10m 8f 8.2m^2 8g^3 10m 1995 8.1m^6 8.5m 9m 10.8g^3 6.9f^5 a8.5g^4 a8.5g^3 a9.4g* 10d Sep 14] big, lengthy gelding: has a rather round action: fair handicapper: won at Wolverhampton in September: stays 1¼m: acts on fibresand and good to firm and soft ground: virtually refused to race second 4-y-o start: has found little, and not one to rely on: sent to Macau. *S. P. C. Woods* 76 § a78 §

SHANIKO (IRE) 2 b.c. (Feb 9) Shaadi (USA) 126 – Homely Touch 84 (Touching Wood (USA) 127) [1995 5f^6 6g* 5m^5 6d^4 6f Oct 12] quite attractive colt: not the best of walkers: has a quick action: third foal: brother to 3-y-o Shashi, 5f winner at 2 yrs: dam, fair but disappointing maiden who would have stayed 1¼m, granddaughter of Full Dress II: made all in maiden at Newbury in July: similar form afterwards in Molecomb Stakes at Goodwood, minor event at Doncaster and Redcar 88

Two-Year-Old Trophy (thirteenth of 26 behind Blue Iris): stays 6f: bandaged last time: sent to Dubai. *P. W. Chapple-Hyam*

SHANOORA (IRE) 2 gr.f. (Apr 30) Don't Forget Me 127 – Shalara (Dancer's Image (USA)) [1995 5d^5 a5g* a6g^5 6.1g^3 8m 7.5d 8g a8.5g^6 a7g^6 a7g^4 a7g^5 a6g Dec 2] 5,500Y: lengthy filly: half-sister to several winners, including (at 1m and 9f in France) useful Shayzari (by Nishapour) and (at 6f in Ireland) Majesterium (by Red Regent): dam unraced half-sister to very useful miler Shasavaan: plater: won at Southwell in April: sold out of B. Palling's stable 1,900 gns Doncaster November Sales before final outing: shaped as if 6f was too short final start: acts on all-weather surfaces: effective visored/blinkered: takes keen hold. *Mrs N. Macauley* — 53

SHANSI (IRE) 4 b.g. Shaadi (USA) 126 – Chic Belle (USA) (Mr Prospector (USA)) [1994 45: 8s 7.1s 8m 10.8m a12g^4 a9.4g^3 a9.4g^2 9g a9.4g^2 a8.5g^3 a8g^3 a8g 1995 a10g* a8g^3 a10g^5 a10g a8g a9.4g a9.4g^4 a10g 10.3m Aug 18] good-topped gelding: poor form on the all-weather: won handicap at Lingfield in January: effective over 1m and stays 1¼m: visored/blinkered nowadays: often bandaged: sold 5,000 gns Newmarket September Sales. *M. D. I. Usher* — – a45

SHANUKE (IRE) 3 b.f. Contract Law (USA) 108 – Auntie Ponny (Last Fandango 125) [1994 56: 6s 7g 8d 9.7s 1995 10m^4 a12g 8m 12g^4 16.1g Jun 12] angular filly: disappointing maiden: reported by jockey to have gurgled badly second 3-y-o start: best run at 9.7f on soft ground: sold (J. S. Moore to Mrs L. Richards) 4,000 gns Ascot July Sales. *J. S. Moore* — –

SHARAAR (USA) 5 ch.h. Bering 136 – Trasimeno (Kings Lake (USA) 133) [1994 79: 9s* 10s^6 10.5g 10.2s^3 10.4d a12g 1995 10d 10g Apr 24] leggy horse: poor mover: well beaten for new stable in 1995: stays 1¼m: acts on soft going, last of 3 on good to firm: blinkered in 1995: none too reliable: sold 1,600 gns Ascot June Sales: sent to Italy. *J. L. Spearing* — –

SHARAF (IRE) 2 b.c. (Jan 28) Sadler's Wells (USA) 132 – Marie de Flandre (FR) 109 (Crystal Palace (FR) 132) [1995 8g 9g^5 8.1s^2 Oct 17] 230,000Y: lengthy, unfurnished colt: unimpressive walker: seventh foal: closely related to French middle-distance winner Flanders Moss (by Shareef Dancer) and half-brother to 2 winners, including fairly useful 1¼m winner Count of Flanders (by Green Desert): dam, French 1¼m and 10.5f winner, half-sister to high-class French mare Sakura Reiko: progressive form in maidens: ½-length second of 10 to Latin Reign at Chepstow on final outing: looks a thorough stayer: acts on soft ground: likely to improve further. *J. L. Dunlop* — 83 p

SHARAZI (USA) 4 ch.c. Shahrastani (USA) 135 – Rio Rita (USA) (Secretariat (USA)) [1994 NR 1995 12g 12m^5 16.1g^5 14.8m^6 10m^6 12m 12s^4 a14g Nov 16] $13,500Y: workmanlike colt: sixth foal: half-brother to 4 minor winners in USA: dam fairly useful winner at up to 7f in USA: fair maiden: will stay extreme distances: has raced only on a sound surface on turf: blinkered since fifth 4-y-o start: inconsistent. *D. J. S. Cosgrove* — 74 d

SHAREDA (IRE) 2 ch.f. (Mar 31) Anshan 119 – Mawaal Habeebee (Northfields (USA)) [1995 7g 7f Oct 18] rangy filly: has scope: fourth foal: dam unraced half-sister to smart sprinter Chapel Cottage: always behind in maidens at Leicester (mulish preliminaries) and Yarmouth: stud. *W. J. Haggas* — –

SHARED (IRE) 3 b. or br.g. Doyoun 124 – Fenjaan 77 (Trojan Fen 118) [1994 NR 1995 7g a9.4g 14f 10g 8d^5 8f Oct 24] well-made gelding: second foal: dam miler: no worthwhile form: sold out of W. Haggas' stable 1,350 gns Ascot May Sales and gelded after second (blinkered) start: resold 1,200 gns Ascot December Sales. *M. Madgwick* — –

SHARED RISK 3 ch.g. Risk Me (FR) 127 – Late Idea 78 (Tumble Wind (USA)) [1994 58: a5g^4 a6g* a6g^5 7d a7g 1995 a6g a7g^2 8f a8g a12g^4 a12g^2 a11g^2 a16g 10d a12g Sep 30] tall, leggy gelding: modest performer: stays 1½m: acts on fibresand: tried blinkered, no improvement: takes keen hold: most inconsistent: sold 1,000 gns Newmarket Autumn Sales. *S. G. Norton* — – a59

SHAREOFTHEACTION 4 gr.g. Sharrood (USA) 124 – Action Belle (Auction Ring (USA) 123) [1994 63, a67: a7g* a8g^3 a5g^4 7g^4 8d^6 a6g* 6m^4 6g^4 a6g^5 7m^4 7.1m^6 10g^4 1995 13.1g^2 a16g 14.1m a9.4g a9.4g a8g Nov 6] sparely-made gelding: no worthwhile form at 4 yrs, jockey reporting horse choked second start: should stay — 45 beyond 1m: acts on all-weather surfaces and good to firm ground, ran poorly on dead: has often worn blinkers/visor/eyeshield on all-weather. *Mrs A. M. Naughton*

SHARE THE SECRET 3 b.g. Dowsing (USA) 124 – Baino Fit (USA) (Fit To Fight (USA)) [1994 –: 7g 6m 7s 1995 10m5 12m 11.1g 10m 8m 8.2m Jun 26] compact gelding: little promise: blinkered third 3-y-o start: usually bandaged. *B. Hanbury* –

SHARKASHKA (IRE) 5 ch.m. Shardari 134 – Kashka (USA) (The Minstrel (CAN) 135) [1994 NR 1995 16m6 12d 12.3f 9.9g Jul 17] angular mare: third foal: half-sister to an Irish middle-distance (and hurdles) winner by Darshaan: dam French 1½m winner: fairly useful performer (rated 84) in Ireland in 1993 for J. Oxx, winner at 1½m, raced mainly on good ground: sold 20,000 gns Newmarket Doncaster (1993) Sales: behind in handicaps in 1995. *M. H. Easterby* –

SHARMOOR 3 b.f. Shardari 134 – Linpac North Moor 69 (Moorestyle 137) [1994 –: 5m 6g 8.2s 9d 10s 1995 14.1m 10g Jun 12] lightly-made filly: of no account. *Miss L. C. Siddall* –

SHARP AT SIX (IRE) 5 ch.g. Sure Blade (USA) 130 – Sixpenny (English Prince 129) [1994 NR 1995 10.9g Sep 14] seventh foal: half-brother to 2 winners, notably useful 1m/1¼m handicapper Cumbrian Challenge (by Be My Native): dam unraced: poor maiden (rated 43) for M. Kauntze at 2 yrs (subsequently sold IR 1,100 gns) and D. Weld at 3 yrs in Ireland: well beaten only start here: stays 1¼m: tried blinkered: modest hurdler. *T. Dyer* –

SHARP CONQUEST 4 ch.c. Sharpo 132 – Likeness 101 (Young Generation 129) [1994 70: 7s4 8.3m2 8.3m 8g 1995 a8.5g* a9.4g a8g 8g 6g3 6g Apr 21] useful-looking colt: fair form at best: won maiden at Wolverhampton in January: failed to repeat the form, running creditably only in celebrity event at Aintree penultimate start: probably better at around 1m than shorter: easily best form on good to firm ground or fibresand: blinkered/visored last 3 starts: sent to Sweden. *W. R. Muir* 66

SHARP CONSUL (IRE) 3 br.c. Exactly Sharp (USA) 121 – Alicia Markova 64 (Habat 127) [1994 5s 5d 1995 8g 7.1g6 8.3m3 7m 7.3d 7s* 8f Oct 24] IR 4,600Y: rangy ex-Irish colt: has scope: half-brother to several winners, mainly modest: dam ran 3 times at 2 yrs: trained by A. Leahy at 2 yrs: fair form here: won 16-runner handicap at Lingfield in September, needing all of trip to get up: seems to need testing conditions when at 7f: best effort on soft ground. *H. Candy* 73

SHARPENING 4 ch.f. Sharpo 132 – False Lift 75 (Grundy 137) [1994 55: 8s3 8v 6m 8m2 a8g3 8d5 a7g* 8g5 a8g5 1995 a8g6 a7g Feb 11] strong filly: modest performer: visored, well beaten in 1995: stays 1m: acts on good to firm and soft ground and on fibresand: covered by Pursuit of Love, and sent to France. *Lord Huntingdon* –

SHARP FALCON (IRE) 4 gr.f. Shaadi (USA) 126 – Honey Buzzard (Sea Hawk II 131) [1994 74+: 8.2d2 9.9g5 10m* 10m4 8.2g3 10g3 12.3m4 10d* 10.5s6 10d3 12.4d3 10.3s2 1995 10d5 12m3 10m6 12m2 12.5g* 12m4 12d 12s3 a11g Dec 1] leggy filly: fair handicapper: landed odds in 3-runner race at Warwick in June: stays 1½m: yet to race on firm going, probably acts on any other on turf, but well beaten on all-weather debut: occasionally tracks pace, normally held up: most consistent. *J. Wharton* 76

SHARP GAZELLE 5 ch.m. Beveled (USA) – Shadha 57 (Shirley Heights 130) [1994 49: 7f 8m3 8f 9.7m5 10f a8g3 a8.5g2 1995 a8g5 a8.5g3 a8g a8g 11.9m 10.2m3 9.7f 9.7m5 10f Aug 2] leggy mare: has a round action: poor handicapper: stays 10.2f: acts on firm going and fibresand, probably not on a soft surface: no form on equitrack: inconsistent. *B. Smart* 41

SHARP HOLLY (IRE) 3 b.f. Exactly Sharp (USA) 121 – Children's Hour (Mummy's Pet 125) [1994 45: 6.1m a7g3 a7g4 6m 5s 1995 a7g4 a6g2 a6g3 6d4 a6g5 a6g6 5.1m3 6f4 5m 5g5 6d 7g a6g Nov 8] smallish filly: modest maiden: well below form last 4 starts: stays 7f: acts on fibresand and on firm and soft ground: no improvement in visor: usually held up. *J. A. Bennett* 50

SHARPICAL 3 b.g. Sharpo 132 – Magical Spirit 70 (Top Ville 129) [1994 NR 1995 6.9g 8.5m3 8m4 8m 9m* 10m2 8g2 8g3 Sep 8] 17,000Y: leggy, angular gelding: first foal: dam placed over middle distances: fair performer: won claimer at Sandown 74 (claimed out of J. Fanshawe's stable for £8,000) in August: good efforts, including in handicaps, afterwards: stays 1¼m: has raced only on a sound surface: reportedly lost a shoe when tailed off fourth start, and is most consistent. *B. J. Meehan*

SHARP IMP 5 b.g. Sharpo 132 – Implore 71 (Ile de Bourbon (USA) 133) [1994 53
39, a50: a8g^5 a10g^6 a10g^5 a7g^2 a8g^6 a7g^4 7m* 7.6m^6 8.3f 6.9g^6 a7g^2 a6g^2 a7g^3 a7g^2 a7g^2 1995 a7g^2 a7g^3 7g 7m 7f^6 6f* 7m^5 6m^3 6.9f^4 6f* 7f^2 7.1m^5 a6g^2 a5g^2 a7g^4 Dec 14] workmanlike gelding: modest handicapper: won at Brighton in July and Folkestone (minor event) in August: ran well on form when in frame afterwards, but tended to hang in behind winner penultimate start: effective at 5f to 7f: acts on the all-weather, best turf efforts on a sound surface: nearly always blinkered: normally races prominently. *R. M. Flower*

SHARP MONTY 2 b.g. (Apr 4) Mon Tresor 113 – Sharp Anne 74§ (Belfort (FR) 66
89) [1995 5d 5m^3 5g^5 6g^4 5.9f^3 7m^2 6.1m Aug 21] 5,000Y: good-topped gelding: second foal: half-brother to 3-y-o Northern Grey (by Puissance): dam unreliable sprinter: fair maiden: poor effort final start, first for 7 weeks: stays 7f: acts on firm ground. *R. Hollinshead*

SHARP NIGHT 2 ch.g. (Apr 18) Sharpo 132 – Midnight Owl (FR) (Ardross 134) 47
[1995 5m 5.1m^6 7.1d 7g Sep 20] 11,000Y: leggy gelding: second foal: dam lightly raced: poor form: gelded and absent over 4 months after second start: pulled hard third outing. *M. S. Saunders*

SHARP 'N' SHADY 2 b.f. (Apr 16) Sharpo 132 – Shadiliya 90 (Red Alert 127) –
[1995 6f 6m a6g Nov 20] 15,000F, IR 48,000Y: heavy-topped filly: sister to fairly useful 3-y-o 5f and 6f winner Twice As Sharp and half-sister to several winners, including 1989 2-y-o 7f winner Tears of Happiness (by Rousillon): dam, 7f winner at 2 yrs, is closely related to very useful 5f to 1m winner Shasavaan: poor form in maidens. *C. F. Wall*

SHARP 'N SMART 3 ch.c. Weldnaas (USA) 112 – Scottish Lady (Dunbeath 77
(USA) 127) [1994 65: 6.1m 5f^4 6g^3 6s^2 1995 6.9d^2 a6g^2 6.9m 6f* 6m 6f^4 7.6d* 7g 8s a8g^4 Nov 29] workmanlike colt: fair performer: has 3 performances which are far better than anything else he's achieved, notably winning median auction maiden at Folkestone in June and minor event at Lingfield in September: stays 1m: acts on firm ground and equitrack, best effort on dead: races prominently: inconsistent. *B. Smart*

SHARP N' SMOOTH 8 ch.g. Sharpo 132 – Winning Look 71 (Relko 136) 53
[1994 54, a–: 8d 8m 7m 9.2f 8.1g a8.5g 7.1m* 7.1m* 8g^4 8.1m^3 a8g 7d 8f^6 8.1g 1995 a7g 12.1d^6 7.1g^2 8g 7g 8.1g^5 8g^3 9.2f Jun 14] close-coupled gelding: poor mover: modest handicapper: best form at up to 1m: acted on good to firm and soft ground: effective blinkered or not: dead. *W. T. Kemp*

SHARP PEARL 2 ch.c. (Mar 21) Sharpo 132 – Silent Pearl (USA) (Silent Screen 73
(USA)) [1995 6m 6d^5 6s^4 6d Oct 21] 20,000F, 55,000Y: good-topped, quite attractive colt: half-brother to 3 winners here and abroad, including July Stakes winner Always Valiant (by Valiyar), later successful at 1¼m: dam winner twice in USA at up to 7f: 5½ lengths fifth of 8 to King of The East in minor event at Doncaster: ran poorly in maiden at Lingfield later in month then had stiff task when down the field in nursery at Newbury: has raced only at 6f: acts on dead ground. *R. Charlton*

SHARP POINT (IRE) 3 ch.f. Royal Academy (USA) 130 – Nice Point (Sharpen 105
Up 127) [1994 102: 6g* 6g^2 6g^2 7d^6 7m^3 1995 7g^3 5g^4 5m^4 5m* 5m^4 5m^4 5.5f a8f^4 Dec 28] good-topped filly: useful performer: won listed race at Tipperary in July by ½ length from Dairine's Delight: ran well when 4 lengths fourth of 8 to So Factual in Nunthorpe Stakes at York and when just over a length fourth of 10 to Bunty Boo in Flying Five at Leopardstown on final start for D. Weld: best at up to 6f: acts on good to firm ground: blinkered (except at Tipperary) since third 3-y-o start. *D. W. Lukas, USA*

SHARP PROD (USA) 5 ch.h. Sharpo 132 – Gentle Persuasion 95 (Bustino 136) 106
[1994 110: 8m^6 7d^4 6g* 6.5m^2 6d 6d^4 1995 6g^2 6s 5.2d^3 6d 6.5d^2 7d^6 6d* Nov 24] rather leggy horse: unimpressive mover: useful performer: good second in Cammidge Trophy at Doncaster (beaten neck by Montendre) and listed race at Munich (1¼ lengths behind Macanal): blinkered, narrowly won listed race at Evry in November, beating Branston Abby a nose: very best form at up to 7f: acts on any going: usually races prominently: none too consistent: sold 36,000 gns Newmarket December Sales, probably to Germany. *Lord Huntingdon*

SHARP PROSPECT 5 ch.h. Sharpo 132 – Sabatina (USA) 95 (Verbatim (USA)) [1994 80: 6s 8g^2 8d 8.1g 8f^2 8s* 10.5d 8m 1995 8g* 8g Apr 22] big, strong horse: fairly useful handicapper: better than ever for new stable when winning £15,900 23-runner William Hill Spring Mile at Doncaster by 3 lengths from Set Table: reportedly chipped a knee in Newbury Spring Cup: stays 1m: acts on firm and soft ground: normally held up. *R. Akehurst* — 83

SHARP REBUFF 4 b.c. Reprimand 122 – Kukri (Kris 135) [1994 68: 8m 8.3d 7g* 1995 7s^3 7.1g^2 8.3g^2 7m^2 8g* 7g^5 7.3d^3 8s a7g Nov 16] lengthy colt: good walker: poor mover: fair handicapper: won at Warwick in June: probably best at 7f/1m: acts on good to firm and soft ground, below form only start on fibresand: occasional front runner, normally chases pace. *P. J. Makin* — 77

SHARP REVIEW (IRE) 7 b.g. Sharpen Up 127 – Pleasant Review (USA) (The Minstrel (CAN) 135) [1994 95: 7g 8m^3 8g^3 9g^6 8.5g 7g 7d^6 1995 8g 8g^4 9f* 9m^3 8m^4 8m Oct 28] robust ex-Irish gelding: carries condition: useful performer: won minor event at Dundalk in July: sold out of D. Weld's stable only 10,000 gns Doncaster October Sales: poorly drawn, last of 30 in £24,100 handicap at Newmarket on first run for new stable: stays 9f: acts on any going: blinkered (well beaten) final 6-y-o start. *J. R. Jenkins* — 95

SHARP SENSATION 5 ch.g. Crofthall 110 – Pink Sensation 69 (Sagaro 133) [1994 46d: a11g* a11g a11g 12d 12.3d 12g 11.1m^4 11.1m 16m^6 1995 a11g a14.8g^6 a12g^5 a11g 15.1f^3 15.1f^4 Jul 28] leggy, workmanlike gelding: poor performer: left D. Nicholls' stable after fourth outing: stays 1½m: acts on fibresand: raced freely and carried head high in blinkers final 4-y-o start: modest winning hurdler. *W. L. Barker* — 39

SHARP SHUFFLE (IRE) 2 ch.c. (Apr 26) Exactly Sharp (USA) 121 – Style (Homing 130) [1995 5.3m^5 6m 7m^2 10m^5 8m^2 Oct 28] IR 800F, IR 4,000Y: smallish colt: unimpressive mover: third foal: dam unraced: narrowly beaten in sellers at Newmarket in October: stays 1¼m: sweating third start. *R. Hannon* — 65

SHARP SPRING 4 ch.g. Beveled (USA) – Sea Farer Lake 74 (Gairloch 122) [1994 45: a7g^4 a9.4g a8g^2 7m 8.5m^4 1995 10.2m^6 8.1g 7f^4 8h Aug 8] leggy gelding: poor maiden: stays 1m: acts on firm ground (yet to race on a soft surface) and equitrack: pulls hard. *J. White* — 36

SHARP STOCK 2 b.c. (Apr 29) Tina's Pet 121 – Mrewa (Runnymede 123) [1995 5g^2 5g^4 Oct 23] 22,000Y: sixth foal: brother to sprinters Stocktina and Ashtina, the latter useful at best: dam twice-raced maiden: similar form in frame in median auction maiden at Folkestone and minor event at Lingfield: will stay 6f. *B. J. Meehan* — 70

SHARP THRILL 4 ch.g. Squill (USA) 122 – Brightelmstone 105 (Prince Regent (FR) 129) [1994 –: 10d^6 8m 10m^4 8m 8.1g a9.4g^6 1995 a12g^2 a11g a12g^6 12m^5 a12g^3 Nov 27] close-coupled gelding: poor maiden: stays 1½m: best effort (at 2 yrs) on dead ground: effective visored or not: inconsistent. *B. Smart* — 38 a45

SHARTEL 3 b.g. Sharpo 132 – Hinari Televideo 97 (Caerleon (USA) 132) [1994 –: 6g 6d 1995 a6g a6g^5 a6g 5d 7g Jun 9] no sign of ability: tried blinkered: sold 600 gns Doncaster July Sales. *M. Johnston* — –

SHASHI (IRE) 3 br.f. Shaadi (USA) 126 – Homely Touch 84 (Touching Wood (USA) 127) [1994 71: 6.1g 6m 5.2g^3 5f^2 5m* 6d 1995 5m^2 5.3f^2 6g^5 5m^3 5m^3 5m^3 5.1h 5g Sep 28] smallish filly: fair handicapper: in good form in the summer, but down the field last 2 starts: best form at 5f, probably as effective at 6f: acts on firm ground: blinkered (ran creditably) sixth 3-y-o start: sold 11,000 gns Newmarket December Sales. *D. Morley* — 79

SHAWAHIN 3 b.c. Nashwan (USA) 135 – Bempton 57 (Blakeney 126) [1994 57p: 8m 1995 12f 12m* 14f 13.9g Aug 30] angular, unfurnished colt: 16/1, squeezed out approaching halfway, but stayed on well to win maiden at Pontefract in July by 6 lengths: tailed off all other starts in 1995, badly hampered final one: should be suited by further than 1½m: sold 19,000 gns Newmarket Autumn Sales. *J. L. Dunlop* — 77

SHAWANNI 2 gr.f. (Apr 5) Shareef Dancer (USA) 135 – Negligent 118 (Ahonoora 122) [1995 7g* 8d^5 Sep 24] small, well-made filly: first foal: dam, winner of Rockfel Stakes at 2 yrs and third in 1000 Guineas, half-sister to smart stayer Ala Hounak: impressive 1¼-length winner from Hal's Pal in 19-runner maiden at Yarmouth, showing a good turn of foot to lead well inside final 1f after being last early on: became very agitated before running poorly in Fillies' Mile at Ascot (took — 95 p very keen hold) 11 days later: created a very favourable impression at Yarmouth, and is well worth another chance: sent to Dubai. *B. W. Hills*

SHAW HOUSE 2 ch.f. (May 7) Shavian 125 – Spinelle 88§ (Great Nephew 126) 56 [1995 6m^3 6m^5 Aug 16] 4,200F: lengthy filly: fourth foal: half-sister to untrustworthy 7f winner Sweet Jaffa (by Never So Bold): dam, 1½m winner, disappointing daughter of Jacinth: showed modest ability in median auction maidens: dead. *D. W. P. Arbuthnot*

SHAYIM (USA) 3 b. or br.c. Storm Cat (USA) – Bundler (USA) (Raise A Native) 82 [1994 88p: 7g^2 1995 7.5m* 6g^5 8.5m^2 10m 8.1g Sep 22] compact colt: fairly useful form: won maiden at Beverley in May and good second of 5 to Hakika in handicap there in July: needs further than 6f, but possibly does not stay 1¼m: yet to race on a soft surface: blinkered (well beaten) final start: sold 22,000 gns Newmarket Autumn Sales. *R. W. Armstrong*

SHAYNES DOMAIN 4 b.g. Dominion 123 – Glen Na Smole 86 (Ballymore 48 123) [1994 40, a48: 6d 6.1d 6g 7d^4 8.1g 8.3m a7g* 7d 9g 1995 a7g 9g 7m^4 8f 7g^2 7m 7f 8f a7g Dec 14] lengthy gelding: carries condition: poor handicapper: stays 7f: acts on fibresand and on good to firm and dead ground: effective blinkered or not: inconsistent. *R. M. Flower*

SHAZANNI (IRE) 3 gr.f. Durgam (USA) – Donna Katrina (Kings Lake (USA) 47 133) [1994 NR 1995 a6g^5 7m 5m 10m 7m 8h^3 10f^2 8f^4 Aug 28] rather leggy filly: first foal: dam half-sister to very useful sprinter Rocket Alert: poor maiden on balance: trained by J. FitzGerald first 5 starts: probably flattered in steadily-run races last 2 starts: unlikely to stay beyond 1¼m. *M. R. Channon*

SHEAMA (USA) 3 ch.f. Miswaki (USA) 124 – Perl (USA) (Graustark) [1994 60: 65 6f^6 7g^4 1995 8g^4 8m* 10.3g^5 8.1m^4 8f^5 8m 8g Sep 20] rather unfurnished filly: fair performer: won maiden at Thirsk in May: long way below form last 2 starts: stays 10.3f: has raced only on a sound surface: tried blinkered, no improvement. *W. Jarvis*

SHEATH KEFAAH 2 ch.c. (Jun 1) Kefaah (USA) 124 – Wasslaweyeh (USA) 66 56 (Damascus (USA)) [1995 7m 7m Oct 12] sparely-made colt: sixth foal: half-brother to 3 winners by Sharpo, two at 7f/1m and Slmaat at up to 1½m: dam stayed 1¼m: eighth of 11 in maiden at Leicester then mid-division in 27-runner seller at Newmarket: will be suited by 1m+: sold 6,000 gns Newmarket Autumn Sales. *W. J. Haggas*

SHEDANSAR (IRE) 3 b.g. In The Wings 128 – Evening Kiss (Kris 135) [1994 – –: 7s 1995 8.3m a8g Dec 15] workmanlike, angular gelding: behind in maidens (for M. Dixon) and claimer. *G. L. Moore*

SHEECKY 4 b.g. Green Ruby (USA) 104 – Beth of Houndhill (Filiberto (USA) – 123) [1994 –: a11g a11g 14.1g 1995 a11g Nov 20] leggy, workmanlike gelding: always behind on flat: won 5-runner selling hurdle Dec 6. *B. A. McMahon*

SHEEMORE (IRE) 2 b.g. (Mar 19) Don't Forget Me 127 – Curie Abu (Crofter – (USA) 124) [1995 6m 7g 6g a10g Nov 25] 11,000F, 10,000Y: big, lengthy, workmanlike gelding: has scope: has a round action: fourth foal: half-brother to 3-y-o 8.5f winner Equity's Darling (by Law Society) and Irish 9f and 1¼m winner Solas Abu (by Red Sunset): dam, Irish 7f winner at 4 yrs, is half-sister to very useful Irish mare Noora Abu (best at up to 1¼m): signs of ability in maiden events: has swished tail. *J. D. Bethell*

SHEER DANZIG (IRE) 3 b.c. Roi Danzig (USA) – Sheer Audacity (Troy 137) 91 [1994 74p: 7s^3 1995 a8g* 10m^3 7.9g 8m 7.1m 8m* 7.9g^2 8g^5 10.4m* 10d Oct 19] tall, rangy colt with scope: impresses in appearance: fairly useful handicapper: won at Southwell (maiden) in March, Newmarket in July and York (leading over 1f out and forging clear) in October: much better at around 1¼m than 1m, and should stay further: best form on a sound surface, acts on fibresand. *R. W. Armstrong*

SHEFOOG 3 ch.f. Kefaah (USA) 124 – Masarrah 91 (Formidable (USA) 125) 90 [1994 83p: 6m^2 7d* 1995 8m^5 8m 7m^6 7.1g^3 7.1m^2 7.3d^5 6g 7f* Oct 23] tall, good-topped filly: fairly useful performer: won minor event at Leicester in October, leading over 3f out: stayed 1m: acted on firm and dead ground: sometimes mulish to post: tail swisher: consistent: stud. *R. W. Armstrong*

SHEILANA (IRE) 2 b.f. (Mar 13) Bluebird (USA) 125 – Shadia (USA) 53 69 (Naskra (USA)) [1995 6m 6.1m^3 6m^5 6.1d^2 6g Sep 30] IR 8,000F, IR 32,000Y:

smallish filly: third foal: half-sister to 5-y-o Thatched (by Thatching), winner at around 1m, and a middle-distance winner in Italy by Roi Danzig: dam, lightly-raced maiden placed over 5f at 2 yrs, half-sister to dams of Paean, Shavian and Be My Chief: best effort when 3 lengths second of 22 to Antonias Melody in nursery at Nottingham in September: didn't repeat that form in similar event at Newmarket next time: will be suited by 7f+. *T. G. Mills*

SHEILAS DREAM 2 b.f. (Mar 27) Inca Chief (USA) – Windlass (Persian Bold 123) [1995 7g Oct 23] second foal: half-sister to 3-y-o Baroque Lady (by Squill): dam unraced granddaughter of half-sister to Blakeney and Morston: 50/1, no promise in maiden at Lingfield. *R. Simpson* –

SHEILA'S SECRET (IRE) 5 b.m. Bluebird (USA) 125 – Exemplary 106 (Sovereign Lord 120) [1994 97: 6s 5.2s 6m^4 6s 6g 6m 5m^2 5.2m^5 5m^3 5g* 5d* 5m^2 5.2s^6 1995 6m May 16] sturdy, good-topped mare: has a quick action: useful handicapper: no encouragement when last in rated stakes at York only start in 1995: effective at 5f and 6f: acts on firm and dead ground, not on soft: blinkered once (ran creditably) at 2 yrs: usually bandaged behind: genuine. *T. G. Mills* –

SHELTER 8 b.g. Teenoso (USA) 135 – Safe House 81§ (Lyphard (USA) 132) [1994 NR 1995 10m 9.7f^6 Jun 30] robust gelding: probably no longer of much account. *John Berry* –

SHELTERED COVE (IRE) 4 ch.g. Bold Arrangement 127 – Racing Home (FR) 89 (Dom Racine (FR) 121) [1994 59: 10d 11.8g^3 14.1m^6 14.1m^2 14m^4 11.6m^4 17.2m* 16.4m^2 16d^2 15.4d^6 12g 16.2m^6 1995 a12g^5 a16g* a16g^2 a16g 16m 16.4m 17.2m May 13] angular gelding: modest handicapper: won at Lingfield in February: well below form on return to turf: stays 17.1f: acts on good to firm ground, dead and equitrack (well below form only outing on fibresand): visored (no improvement) fifth 3-y-o start: bandaged since fourth 4-y-o start: wore pricker near side sixth 4-y-o start: not normally a front runner: inconsistent. *K. O. Cunningham-Brown* – a57

SHEMAQ (USA) 3 b.f. Blushing John (USA) 120 – Geraldine's Store (USA) (Exclusive Native (USA)) [1994 80p: 7d* 1995 7.9m^2 8.1m* 10.1g^5 8g 8g* Oct 10] tall, lengthy, attractive filly: won minor events at Sandown (made virtually all) in August and Leicester (led 1½f out, idled and driven out) in October: best form at around 1m, shaped as though further would have suited: acted on good to firm and dead ground: tail flasher: visits Dayjur. *H. Thomson Jones* 98

SHEMARAN (IRE) 3 b.c. Kahyasi 130 – Sherzana (Great Nephew 126) [1994 8d^2 1995 8s* 10m^2 10g^2 10m* 8m 10f* 9f^5 Nov 5] rangy colt: second foal: half-brother to winning Irish hurdler Sheregori (by Darshaan): dam unraced sister to Shergar: very smart performer: won maiden in April, slowly-run 4-runner Gallinule Stakes (by ½ length from Prince of Andros, dashed clear 2f out and holding on) in June and 5-runner Royal Whip (improved form on final start for J. Oxx, led inside last and beat Russian Snows, who rec. 8lb, ½ length) in August, all at the Curragh: below form in Grade 3 event at Santa Anita final start: quite stoutly bred, but shapes as if will prove best at up to 1¼m: acts on firm ground, won maiden on soft: held up: very edgy (ran as if something amiss, reportedly coughing) fifth 3-y-o start. *R. Rash, USA* 120

SHEMOZZLE (IRE) 2 b.f. (Apr 25) Shirley Heights 130 – Reactress (USA) (Sharpen Up 127) [1995 7m* 7m* Oct 30] leggy filly: fourth foal: half-sister to 7f (at 2 yrs) and 1m winner Realize (by Al Nasr): dam 6f winner at 2 yrs later fourth in Grade 3 8.5f events: won 3-runner private sweepstakes at Newmarket and 14-runner maiden at Newcastle (by 1¼ lengths from Abir, pair 5 lengths clear, keeping on well despite flashing tail) in October: will be well suited by 1¼m+: bandaged behind at Newcastle: may improve further. *J. H. M. Gosden* 71 p

SHENANGO (IRE) 2 b.g. (Apr 13) Shernazar 131 – Pipina (USA) 81 (Sir Gaylord) [1995 a8g^2 Dec 18] closely related to winning stayer Pipitina (by Bustino) and very useful 1¼m to 1½m winner Pipsted (by Busted) and half-brother to several winners, including useful 7f to 1m winner Night Out Perhaps (by Cure The Blues): dam, 10.5f winner, half-sister to Amaranda and Favoridge: 13/8 favourite, beaten a head by Apartments Abroad in maiden at Lingfield, tending to run in snatches and hanging left late on: will stay beyond 1m: should improve. *G. Wragg* 65 p

SHEN YANG (USA) 3 ch.g. Fighting Fit (USA) – Our Mimi (USA) (Believe It (USA)) [1994 84: 6g^2 7g^2 6.1d^6 1995 a7g^2 6g 6.9m* 7m 7m^4 7.1m^5 6m^4 7m^4 Aug 5] 74

leggy gelding: fair performer: won maiden at Folkestone in May: stayed 7f: acted on good to firm ground and equitrack: inconsistent: dead. *G. L. Moore*

SHEPHERD MARKET (IRE) 4 b.g. Common Grounds 118 – Dame Solitaire (CAN) (Halo (USA)) [1994 73d: a7g^{4} 6d^{6} 7m^{4} 6m 6m 7f 7.1d^{6} 6g 9.7m 1995 a10g a8g a8g 6.9d^{3} 7m^{2} 7m^{2} 8m 7m^{2} 7.3g* 7g^{3} 8.5m^{3} 7g 7m 7.1m 7g 7g 6d^{6} 7.1d^{3} 6f Oct 23] leggy gelding: fair handicapper: in good form in the spring, and won at Newbury in May: ran well next 2 starts: lost his way afterwards: stays 8.5f: acts on good to firm and dead ground and on equitrack: visored (out of form) once as 3-y-o: takes keen hold and usually races prominently: sold only 600 gns Newmarket Autumn Sales: sent to Italy. *D. A. Wilson* — 68 d

SHEPHERDS DEAN (IRE) 2 b.f. (Apr 8) Tirol 127 – Royal Episode (Royal Match 117) [1995 5m a7g a7g Nov 27] IR 1,100F, 3,200Y: leggy, sparely-made filly: second reported foal: dam Irish 6f and 7f winner: no worthwhile form in maiden events and seller, but showed signs of ability (front rank long way) final start. *P. C. Haslam* — –

SHEPHERDS REST (IRE) 3 b.g. Accordion – Mandy's Last (Krayyan 117) [1994 NR 1995 10m 10m 10.2f 10.8g^{4} 12f 12.1m^{5} a12g^{5} Jul 22] IR 1,000F, IR 450Y, 1,500 2-y-o: good-topped gelding: third foal: dam ran once at 3 yrs in Ireland: poor maiden: stays 10.8f: apparently easily best effort only start on an easy surface: ridden by 7-lb claimer last 5 starts: pulls hard. *S. Mellor* — 44 ?

SHEPPARD'S CROSS 4 b.f. Soviet Star (USA) 128 – Cutlers Corner 111 (Sharpen Up 127) [1994 85: 7d* 7f^{5} 8.1s^{4} 7d^{2} 7s* 8m 8d 1995 8g^{6} 7m* 8g 7m^{5} 6f 7g Sep 29] big, strong filly: fairly useful handicapper: won in good style at Lingfield in April: off course 3 months, shaped as if retaining her ability in rated stakes at Newmarket final start: best form at 7f, should prove effective at 6f: acts on good to firm and soft ground, possibly not on firm. *P. T. Walwyn* — 88

SHERAKA (IRE) 2 b.f. (Apr 22) Doyoun 124 – Sherzana (Great Nephew 126) [1995 6g* 8d^{2} Oct 14] third foal: half-sister to 2 winners, notably very smart Irish 3-y-o 1m to 1¼m winner Shemaran (by Kahyasi): dam unraced sister to Shergar: won maiden at the Curragh in July: much better form when head second of 5 to Ahkaam in Beresford Stakes there 3 months later: may stay beyond 1m: should improve further. *J. Oxx, Ireland* — 100 p

SHERAZ (IRE) 3 b.c. Persian Bold 123 – Miss Siddons (Cure The Blues (USA)) [1994 72: 6g^{4} 7g 7s 1995 8.3m 10.1m^{2} 10m^{3} Sep 5] strong, attractive colt: fluent mover: fairly useful maiden: better suited by 1¼m than shorter: sold (G. Wragg to N. Tinkler) 12,000 gns Newmarket Autumn Sales. *G. Wragg* — 80

SHERBLU 4 ch.g. Cigar 68 – Glyn Blue (Fine Blue 103) [1994 39§: 12v 8.2m^{5} 8.3m 7m 1995 a6g^{5} a8g^{4} a8g^{5} a8g^{2} a7g^{5} a7g 8m Jun 2] strong gelding: poor maiden: stays 1m: acts on equitrack, ran poorly at Wolverhampton on fibresand: effective blinkered/visored or not: often taken down early: inconsistent. *J. Ffitch-Heyes* — 49

SHERIFF 4 b.g. Midyan (USA) 124 – Daisy Warwick (USA) 91 (Ribot 142) [1994 72: 8m^{3} 8g^{3} 10.1m 10m^{5} 12m 11.8d 1995 12f 11.9m^{3} Jul 7] small gelding: bad mover: fair handicapper at best at 3 yrs: long way below form in 1995: should stay 1½m: acts on good to firm and dead ground: blinkered (favourite for claimer, below form) final 4-y-o start: winner of 3 races over hurdles (fair form) in the autumn. *J. W. Hills* — 47 +

SHERMAN (IRE) 4 b.c. Caerleon (USA) 132 – Aghsan 78 (Lord Gayle (USA) 124) [1994 98: 10m^{3} 12m^{5} 10.4f 10s^{4} 10m* 9v^{2} 1995 10m^{6} 10.4g* 10.1f 10.4m 10.4m Aug 16] robust colt: usually looks well: has a fluent, rather round action: useful handicapper: won rated stakes at York in May, leading 2f out: ran respectably afterwards only in mid-division in Magnet Cup at York: effective over 9f with very testing conditions and should stay 1½m: disappointed twice on firm ground, acts on any other: blinkered since penultimate 3-y-o start: held up/tracks leaders. *H. Thomson Jones* — 100

SHERMOOD 2 b.f. (Apr 14) Shere Khan – Jalebird Blues (Jalmood (USA) 126) [1995 a7g 7f Aug 28] 700Y: neat filly: first foal: dam unraced: seventh in maiden auctions at Wolverhampton and Warwick, ridden by 7-lb claimer and finishing well behind Just Millie last time: will be suited by further than 7f: probably capable of going close in a seller. *M. Bell* — 42 +

SHERNADEED (FR) 2 b.f. (Mar 9) Shernazar 131 – A Kiss In Deed (USA) (Shadeed (USA) 135) [1995 7f^6 7g^3 7g^5 Aug 26] smallish, good-topped filly: has scope: second foal: dam unraced: still burly, third of 9 to Baltic Dream in median auction maiden at Leicester in August, making much of running: tailed off in maiden at Newcastle later in month, eased right up when beaten: sold 2,400 gns Newmarket December Sales. *M. Johnston* — 66

SHEROOT 3 b.c. Cigar 68 – Act of Treason 80 (Absalom 128) [1994 NR 1995 7g 6g 11d 7m 7m Oct 30] dipped-backed colt: fourth foal: dam, best at 2 yrs, stayed 1¼m: of little account. *D. Moffatt* — –

SHERQY (IRE) 3 br.c. Persian Bold 123 – Turkish Treasure (USA) 111 (Sir Ivor 135) [1994 80: 6g^4 6g 7m^4 7f^6 8g^2 7.9d^4 8g^2 8m^3 1995 9m^3 10g^3 10f^2 10m^2 10.1m* 9.9m 12g^4 Sep 16] medium-sized, quite attractive colt: has been hobdayed: has a fluent action: fairly useful performer: placed on numerous occasions before winning 3-runner maiden at Newcastle (made all) in July: folded tamely over 2f out penultimate start: probably stays 1½m: acts on firm and dead ground: sold (J. Dunlop to S. Kettlewell) only 8,500 gns Newmarket Autumn Sales. *J. L. Dunlop* — 85

SHERRINGTON 3 b.f. Thatching 131 – Pertinent (Persepolis (FR) 127) [1994 NR 1995 12m 10m 8.1m^5 8g Sep 2] lengthy filly second foal: dam Irish 1¼m winner: form in maidens only when 11½ lengths fifth of 10 at Sandown, putting head in air but running on under tender handling: should stay beyond 8.1f: sold 1,500 gns Newmarket Autumn Sales. *A. C. Stewart* — 56

SHE SAID NO 3 ch.f. Beveled (USA) – She Said Yes (Local Suitor (USA) 128) [1994 NR 1995 6m 7g 6g^5 a8.5g^2 a10g* Jul 22] 7,400Y: angular filly: first foal: dam unraced half-sister to Sharpo (by Sharpen Up): modest form: won maiden handicap at Lingfield in July: stays 1¼m. *Lord Huntingdon* — 56

SHE'S A MADAM 4 b.f. Kabour 80 – Mrs Buzby 71 (Abwah 118) [1994 –: 6.1d^4 a10g 1995 a5g^4 Apr 1] sturdy filly: of little account. *L. R. Lloyd-James* — –

SHE'S DYNAMITE (IRE) 3 b.f. Danehill (USA) 126 – Flaxen Hair (Thatch (USA) 136) [1994 84p: 5m* 5f 5s* 1995 6g^2 7m^6 7g 7d Sep 23] sturdy filly: has a round action: fairly useful form: ran well when second of 6 in minor event at Newmarket on reappearance and when 11 lengths seventh of 12 to Branston Abby in listed race at Doncaster third start: stays 7f: won maiden (modest form) on good to firm ground, but easily best form with give, and acts on soft. *W. Jarvis* — 87

SHE'S MY LOVE 2 ch.f. (May 11) Most Welcome 131 – Stripanoora (Ahonoora 122) [1995 6.1f* 7m^3 8m^4 7g Sep 29] 6,000Y, 20,000 2-y-o: lengthy, unfurnished filly: third foal: sister to useful 3-y-o 1m (at 2 yrs) to 1½m winner Naked Welcome: dam (maiden) stayed 1m: won maiden auction at Nottingham in July: third of 4 in minor event at Yarmouth then fourth of 7, pulling hard early on, in nursery at Newmarket: modest effort on final outing: stays 1m: has pulled hard. *J. E. Banks* — 76

SHE'S SIMPLY GREAT (IRE) 2 b.f. (Feb 26) Simply Great (FR) 122 – Petrine (IRE) (Petorius 117) [1995 6m^4 6f^4 8.3g Sep 25] 6,600 2-y-o: smallish filly: first foal: dam ran 4 times in Ireland: poor form in maidens: should stay 1m. *J. J. O'Neill* — –

SHIFT AGAIN (IRE) 3 b.f. Siberian Express (USA) 125 – Pushkinia (FR) 95 (Pharly (FR) 130) [1994 –: 7d 1995 7g^5 7m^3 8m* 8m^5 9.9m 7.5m^6 8.5s 10.5d^4 12.1s^3 Oct 17] tall, leggy filly: fair form: won maiden at Brighton in June: inconsistent afterwards: stays 12.1f: acts on good to firm and soft ground: tends to carry head high: sold (W. Jarvis to S. Sherwood) 10,500 gns Newmarket Autumn Sales. *W. Jarvis* — 68

SHIFTING MOON 3 b.g. Night Shift (USA) – Moonscape 87 (Ribero 126) [1994 78: 6m^2 6m 7.1d^4 7m 8d 1995 8m 7.6m^5 8m 7.9m^3 8.1m* 8f^2 8f^2 Jul 29] stocky gelding: poor mover: fairly useful handicapper: went well with forcing tactics last 3 starts, winning at Chepstow in July: claimed by F. Jordan £12,000 final start: should stay beyond 8.1f: acts on firm and dead ground: visored (below form) fourth 3-y-o start, blinkered since: won juvenile hurdle in August, but looked reluctant in October. *I. A. Balding* — 86

SHIKARI'S SON 8 br.g. Kala Shikari 125 – Have Form (Haveroid 122) [1994 92: 7d 7f 7s 8f* 6m^2 6m* 6f 5.3f* 7g^2 6g^2 6d 7d 6d 1995 6m* 7m 7.6m^5 7m^4 6f^3 6f 7m^2 7g^5 6m* 7.3m 7m 6g Sep 16] tall, leggy gelding: useful handicapper: won — 99

Vodac Stewards' Cup (Handicap), Goodwood—
40/1, ridden at 4lb overweight, slowly away and last two furlongs out,
erstwhile Brighton specialist Shikari's Son (No. 12) surprises Top Banana (far rail) and Jayannpee (noseband)

claimer at Brighton (improved his record number of wins there to 9) in April and 27-runner £50,500 Vodac Stewards' Cup at Goodwood (40/1, weaved his way through to lead near finish having been last 2f out) in July: still travelling well enough and beginning to take closer order when hampered and falling under 2f out in Ayr Gold Cup final outing: effective at 5f and probably stays 1m: acts on hard and dead ground: goes well on sharp tracks: usually held up. *J. White*

SHINEROLLA 3 b.g. Thatching 131 – Primrolla 64 (Relko 136) [1994 55: 7d 6d^4 a6g^5 1995 5g^3 5s^4 7g^2 8m^2 8f* 7.9g^2 8g* 10g^2 8.3f^4 8g 8d 8m* 8m^3 Oct 14] tall, leggy gelding: fairly useful handicapper: won at Pontefract in May (twice) and October: good third of 23 to Stone Ridge in £29,600 event at Newmarket, making up plenty of ground to lead stands side group final 1f: effective at 1m to 1¼m: acts on firm and soft ground: held up: sold (Mrs. J. Ramsden to C. Parker) 40,000 gns Newmarket Autumn Sales. *Mrs J. R. Ramsden* 88

SHINING CANDLE (USA) 3 b.f. Bering 136 – Reham 67 (Mill Reef (USA) 141) [1994 56: 7g 8d 1995 7m May 10] close-coupled filly: failed to repeat debut form: bred to stay middle distances: sold 2,200 gns Newmarket September Sales: sent to Belgium. *B. Hanbury* –

SHINING CLOUD 2 ch.f. (Feb 23) Indian Ridge 123 – Hardiheroine 76 (Sandhurst Prince 128) [1995 5.7m^3 5m^2 Jun 16] lengthy filly: has scope: first foal: dam should have stayed beyond 1m: fair form in maidens at Bath and Sandown: will be better suited by 6f+. *L. G. Cottrell* 73

SHINING DANCER 3 b.f. Rainbow Quest (USA) 134 – Strike Home 82 (Be My Guest (USA) 126) [1994 –p: 7g 1995 9g^6 13.8m^5 10g 12s a12g a16g^6 Nov 30] angular filly: has a markedly round action: bandaged, stayed on late when sixth of 12 in maiden at Kempton in June, penultimate outing for M. Stoute: well beaten afterwards: should be suited by further than 9f: has had problems going to post, virtually bolting second 3-y-o outing. *S. Dow* 61 d

SHINING EDGE 3 ch.g. Beveled (USA) – Lustrous 73 (Golden Act (USA)) [1994 71§: 5v^3 6f^3 7g^2 7f^4 7g^3 a7g^2 7f^3 8s 1995 8.5m 8m 10m^3 10g^5 9f 8.5m^3 8.5g^2 9f^6 9m 8d^2 8m^5 Oct 2] rangy, workmanlike gelding: has a markedly round action: modest maiden handicapper on flat: seems to stay 1¼m: acts on firm and dead ground: visored final 2-y-o start: won on hurdling debut in October: unreliable. *M. H. Easterby* 58 §

SHINING EXAMPLE 3 ch.g. Hadeer 118 – Kick The Habit 94 (Habitat 134) [1994 69: 7g 7.9d^4 6d^2 1995 8m 7.1m^5 8.5d^3 a11g^2 10.5s^2 9m* Oct 27] strong, workmanlike gelding: fair handicapper: won 19-runner apprentice race at Newmarket in October, smooth progress 3f out and leading inside last: stays 11f: acts on fibresand and good to firm and soft ground: consistent. *P. J. Makin*

75

SHINING HIGH 3 b.f. Shirley Heights 130 – Padelia (Thatching 131) [1994 76p: 7g^4 8m^4 8.2s^2 1995 10g 12m^3 16.4m* 16.1m^2 16.1g 18m Oct 14] big, rangy filly: had plenty of scope: fairly useful handicapper: won at Sandown (made all, by 5 lengths) in July: tailed off in £13,700 event at Newcastle and Cesarewitch at Newmarket (headed 3f out) last 2 starts: should have stayed beyond 2m: acted on good to firm ground and soft: was sometimes unruly at start: stud. *J. L. Dunlop*

90

SHINING MOLLY (FR) 2 b.f. (Mar 26) Shining Steel (FR) 123 – Molly Martine (FR) (Lou Piguet (FR) 126) [1995 4.9g* 4.8g* 5.5d* 5.5g* 5m^2 5.5g^2 6g^5 5.5g^3 Sep 5] 65,000 francs Y: fourth foal: half-sister to French 9f winner Highest Martine (by Highest Honor): dam, ran 4 times, is half-sister to good broodmare Miss Manon: useful performer: successful in newcomers claimer and a minor event in the provinces and then a minor event and a listed race at Evry for M. Pimbonnet: second in Prix du Bois at Chantilly and Prix Robert Papin (best effort, narrowly beaten by Lucky Lionel) at Maisons-Laffitte next 2 starts: respectable efforts in Prix Morny at Deauville and Prix d'Arenberg at Chantilly afterwards: a sprinter: acts on good to firm ground and dead. *P. Bary, France*

103

SHIP OF THE LINE 5 ch.h. High Line 125 – Corvette (AUS) (Biarritz 115) [1994 66: 10.1g 10m 8.2s^3 8g 1995 a8.5g^3 a9.4g^6 Feb 4] sparely-made horse: modest maiden: should be suited by further than 8.5f. *J. R. Fanshawe*

–
a52

SHIP'S DANCER 2 b.f. (May 9) Shareef Dancer (USA) 135 – Sunderland (Dancer's Image (USA)) [1995 7m 8.2d 8g Oct 10] quite attractive filly: half-sister to several winners, including 7f winner Ships Lantern (by Kalaglow) and fair 1986 2-y-o 7f winner Sannox Bay (by Shirley Heights): dam 2-y-o 5f and 6f winner in Ireland: ran green then stayed on well into eleventh of 18 behind Ruznama in maiden at Newmarket: considerately handled throughout and never dangerous in similar events at Nottingham and Leicester last 2 starts: will do better over middle distances. *J. L. Dunlop*

62 p

SHIRLATY 2 b.f. (Apr 8) Shirley Heights 130 – Jameelaty (USA) 96 (Nureyev (USA) 131) [1995 6g 7g Oct 23] lengthy filly: first foal: dam, 2-y-o 6f winner who stayed 1m, out of sister to versatile graded stakes performer (stayed 1½m) Bounding Basque: last in maidens at Newmarket (backward, unimpressive to post and eased right up closing stages) and Lingfield: sold 1,100 gns Doncaster November Sales. *E. A. L. Dunlop*

–

SHIRLEY'S TRAIN (USA) 6 br.g. Malinowski (USA) 123 – Tiger Trap (USA) 80 (Al Hattab (USA)) [1994 NR 1995 12m^4 Jul 6] leggy, attractive gelding: fourth of 10 in amateurs handicap on first run on flat since 4 yrs: probably effective at 1½m: acts on good to firm ground and fibresand: visored (out of form) once at 3 yrs: fair jumper. *P. J. Hobbs*

–

SHIRLEY SUE 2 b.f. (Mar 22) Shirley Heights 130 – Dame Ashfield 90 (Grundy 137) [1995 7g 8m a8g^4 Nov 14] sturdy filly: half-sister to 3-y-o Rainelle (by Rainbow Quest) and several winners, including stayer Rosina Mae and fair 2-y-o 6f and 7f winner Dame Rousara (both by Rousillon): dam 1½m winner out of Cheshire Oaks and Park Hill winner African Dancer: never a threat in late-season maidens, upset in stalls on debut: will be very well suited by middle distances. *M. Johnston*

56

SHOCK-A-LOT (IRE) 2 ch.c. (Mar 18) Fayruz 116 – Vote Barolo (Nebbiolo 125) [1995 6f^4 6m^4 6m^6 7m^4 7.3d Sep 15] 7,400Y: seventh foal: half-brother to Irish 1989 2-y-o 7f winner Manuale Del Utente (by Montekin): dam ran twice at 2 yrs: modest form: stays 7f: may well be unsuited by a soft surface: taken down early last 2 starts: sold 4,500 gns Newmarket Autumn Sales. *G. Lewis*

62

SHONARA'S WAY 4 b.f. Slip Anchor 136 – Favorable Exchange (USA) (Exceller (USA) 129) [1994 99?: 9v^4 12.1s* 14.8m^3 14.8m* 14.6g^6 14d^3 1995 14.8m^2 13.3d 16d^2 18m 16m^5 Oct 27] big, leggy filly: shows knee action: useful handicapper: stays 2m: acts on good to firm and soft ground: inconsistent. *R. Charlton*

96

SHONTAINE 2 b.g. (Apr 10) Pharly (FR) 130 – Hinari Televideo 97 (Caerleon (USA) 132) [1995 6d^{3} 6m* 6m 6m* 7m 6m^{2} 6g 7f Oct 14] smallish, strong gelding: second foal: half-brother to 3-y-o Shartel (by Sharpo): dam sprinter: made most when winning maiden at Doncaster and nursery at Newcastle in July: good second in nursery at Redcar in August: stays 7f. *M. Johnston* — 79

SHOODAH (IRE) 4 ch.g. Common Grounds 118 – Tunguska 76 (Busted 134) [1994 NR 1995 8.3m 8.1g a8g a10g Dec 18] close-coupled gelding: eighth foal: half-sister to 1m winner Trooping (by Auction Ring): dam 1¼m winner who stayed 1½m: well beaten. *P. Hayward* — –

SHOOFK 4 ch.g. Dunbeath (USA) 127 – River Reem (USA) (Irish River (FR) 131) [1994 72: 8s^{5} 9m 10m^{3} 8.2m^{3} 8g^{4} 9f^{2} 10g 8s 10g 9.7m^{6} 10d 1995 9.7d 9.7g^{6} 10.8m^{4} 12.5g Apr 27] plain, good-topped gelding: just a modest handicapper at 4 yrs: acts on firm going, probably on soft: sometimes sweats and gets on edge: hard puller: has been taken down early: has been gelded: fairly useful hurdler. *S. Dow* — 58

SHOOTER 3 b.c. Salse (USA) 128 – Debbie Harry (USA) 70 (Alleged (USA) 138) [1994 70: 5f^{6} 7m^{4} a7g^{2} 1995 10m 10.1m^{4} a8.5g^{6} 10.1g^{4} Sep 13] strong, lengthy, good-quartered colt: unimpressive mover: only modest at best in 1995: should stay middle distances: acts on good to firm ground and (though looked reluctant last time) fibresand: one to treat with caution: sold 5,500 gns Newmarket Autumn Sales: sent to Spain. *P. F. I. Cole* — 53

SHOOTING LIGHT (IRE) 2 b.c. (Apr 6) Shernazar 131 – Church Light 88 (Caerleon (USA) 132) [1995 8m Nov 4] lengthy colt: third foal: half-brother to Irish 11f winner Day Light (by Doyoun) and Italian 3-y-o 6f and 9f winner Noryema (by Nordico): dam effective at 1m and 1¼m: 16/1 and backward, slowly away when well beaten in 23-runner median auction maiden at Doncaster. *M. A. Jarvis* — –

SHOOT THE MINSTREL 2 ch.c. (May 15) Brotherly (USA) 80 – Shoot To Win (FR) (Rabdan 129) [1995 a8.5g Dec 9] fifth foal: half-brother to 6-y-o 5f winner Little Saboteur (by Prince Sabo): dam French 7.5f winner: tailed off in maiden at Wolverhampton. *J. A. Pickering* — –

SHOT AT LOVE (IRE) 4 br.f. Last Tycoon 131 – Cooliney Dancer (Dancer's Image (USA)) [1994 79: 8g* 8m^{4} 8m^{4} 7g 8s^{6} 1995 8.1m 9f^{5} 8.1f^{6} Aug 5] angular, workmanlike filly: has a quick action: fair performer: stiff tasks in handicaps as 4-y-o, running creditably first 2 starts: stays 9f: acts on firm ground, probably on soft. *C. A. Cyzer* — 79

SHOTLEY AGAIN 5 b.g. Then Again 126 – Sweet Candice 71 (African Sky 124) [1994 41, a33: a6g a8g 6.1v 7g* 8.3d^{6} 7.1f 6.9m a7g^{3} 7g 8m 1995 6g 5.9m 7m^{5} a8g 7g May 27] tall, angular gelding: no longer of much account. *N. Bycroft* — –

SHOT THE SHERIFF 3 b.c. Warning 136 – Dearest 63 (Alzao (USA) 117) [1994 62p: 6s a7g^{3} a6g* 1995 8.2g 7m 10m 6.9g Oct 16] lengthy colt: no worthwhile form in 1995: should prove suited by further than 6f: blinkered (made most) final 3-y-o start: sold 1,500 gns Newmarket Autumn Sales: sent to Spain. *P. F. I. Cole* — –

SHOWERY 3 b.f. Rainbow Quest (USA) 134 – Anodyne 100 (Dominion 123) [1994 53: 6m^{6} 7.1d 1995 5m^{2} 7g^{2} 6g* 6m^{3} 6m^{4} 6m^{2} 6s Oct 1] small, sturdy filly: fair handicapper: won apprentice race at Haydock in May by 5 lengths: worth another try at 7f: acts on good to firm ground, ran poorly both starts on a soft surface: sold 17,000 gns Newmarket December Sales. *J. W. Watts* — 76

SHOW FAITH (IRE) 5 ch.g. Exhibitioner 111 – Keep The Faith 86 (Furry Glen 121) [1994 90: 8m 8m^{5} 8.1d^{4} 8m 10m^{5} 8f 10.3d 9g 8g 1995 10d^{3} 10m 8.1m^{3} 8.1g^{3} 8m 8g* 10f 10m 10d^{3} 9g^{4} 9d Oct 21] good-topped gelding: fairly useful handicapper: won at Newbury in July: good fourth in Cambridgeshire at Newmarket penultimate start: effective at 1m to 1¼m: acts on good to firm ground and soft: blinkered (well beaten) last 2 starts in 1994: normally held up: has sometimes looked temperamental. *R. Hannon* — 90

SHOW FLAIR (IRE) 3 ch.g. Exhibitioner 111 – Tudor Loom (Sallust 134) [1994 –: 6g 7.9d^{6} 1995 7.1m 7.5g^{6} Jul 18] workmanlike gelding: has a round action: little sign of ability: blinkered final start. *J. S. Wainwright* — –

SHREWD ALIBI 4 gr.g. Sharrood (USA) 124 – Alsiba 68 (Northfields (USA)) [1994 NR 1995 12m^{6} 12.1g^{6} 16.1g^{3} 20m 18.2m^{5} Jul 4] leggy gelding: has a round — 72 action: off course over 20 months prior to reappearance: fair maiden handicapper: probably stays 2½m. *I. A. Balding*

SHREWD IDEA 5 b.h. Alleged (USA) 138 – Domludge (USA) (Lyphard (USA) 132) [1994 113: 10v^4 13.4m^2 11v^3 12.1f* 12m 10f 12v 12s 1995 11g^3 12.5s^2 12m^4 14g* 10.5g* 15.5f^2 12f Dec 10] lengthy horse: unimpressive walker: smart performer: ran in Spain for J. de Salas first 4 starts in 1995: won minor events at San Sebastian and Saint-Cloud: ran well when 2½ lengths second of 7 to Sunshack in Prix Royal Oak at Longchamp in October on final start for C. Laffon-Parias: creditable eighth of 14, beaten around 4 lengths, in Hollywood Turf Cup in December: stays 15.5f: acts on any going. *Randy Bradshaw, USA* 115

SHROPSHIRE BLUE 5 gr.m. Risk Me (FR) 127 – Six Ashes (Bruni 132) [1994 NR 1995 7.1g 6.9m 6g 9.2f^4 Jun 14] leggy mare: of no account. *D. A. Nolan* –

SHU GAA (IRE) 2 ch.g. (Feb 3) Salse (USA) 128 – River Reem (USA) (Irish River (FR) 131) [1995 7.5m^6 8d Sep 27] sturdy, deep-bodied gelding: has scope: fourth living foal: half-brother to 4-y-o Shoofk (by Dunbeath), 1m winner at 2 yrs, and a winner in Belgium: dam, unraced, from family of Irish 1000 Guineas winner Katies: trained by Mrs L. Piggott on debut: still carrying plenty of condition, just over 6 lengths eighth of 18 to Mystic Knight in maiden at Salisbury, staying on well never dangerous: will stay beyond 1m: will improve again. *W. J. Haggas* 70 p

SHUJAN (USA) 6 b.h. Diesis 133 – Linda's Magic (USA) 114 (Far North (CAN) 120) [1994 83: 12d 13.3s 14m^4 16d^2 16.5v* 1995 18.7m May 10] good-topped horse: impresses in appearance: shows knee action: fairly useful handicapper: useful handicap hurdler in 1994/5: slowly away and never got into Chester Cup only run on flat at 6 yrs: will stay 2¼m: acts on heavy going and fibresand, probably not ideally suited by top-of-the-ground: lion-hearted front runner. *R. Akehurst* –

SHUTTLECOCK 4 ch.g. Pharly (FR) 130 – Upper Sister (Upper Case (USA)) [1994 42, a65: a7g^3 a8.5g^3 a7g^2 a8.5g^3 a10g^4 10g a8.5g* a9.4g^2 10m 9.7m^5 12.1g 9g a7g a8.5g a9.4g 1995 a8g* a8g* a8.5g a8g^3 a8g^5 a8g^6 a8g 10m^6 12.4g^5 14.9g 10m^4 8.2m^3 7.6m a7g^5 Jul 22] angular gelding: fair performer at best on all-weather, poor on turf: won 2 claimers at Southwell in January, former on final start for N. Littmoden: below form last 2 starts: effective at 1m and seems to stay 12.4f: acts on good to firm ground, dead and all-weather surfaces: visored (ran poorly) once at 2 yrs: has had tongue tied down: races prominently. *Mrs N. Macauley* 43 a66

SHUTTLINGSLOW 4 b.f. Celestial Storm (USA) 132 – Sharanella (Shareef Dancer (USA) 135) [1994 52: a10g 12.5m 10m^5 12m^2 12m^5 a12g^2 a12g^5 12.1m^3 1995 a10g a14g 11d* 12m 13g^4 Jul 13] workmanlike filly: modest performer: sold out of N. Gaselee's stable 8,200 gns Ascot June Sales: won at Gelsenkirchen in June, next start: should stay further than 1½m: acts on good to firm ground, soft and fibresand. *C. von der Recke, Germany* 49

SHY PADDY (IRE) 3 b.g. Shy Groom (USA) – Griqualand (Connaught 130) [1994 66: 7g 9.7s^6 a10g a9.4g* 1995 a10g a8.5g^3 14.1m a14.8g 10m Jul 24] workmanlike gelding: modest performer at best at 2 yrs: well beaten in 1995: stays 9.4f: acts on soft ground and fibresand: blinkered (tailed off) third 3-y-o start. *K. O. Cunningham-Brown* –

SIAN WYN 5 ch.m. Hotfoot 126 – Curzon House 73 (Green God 128) [1994 NR 1995 a9.4g^3 12g Jun 10] workmanlike mare: poor maiden: stays 9.4f: acts on fibresand, probably on heavy ground: modest hurdler, winner in July. *K. R. Burke* 25

SIBBERTOFT (IRE) 2 b.f. (Mar 22) Shaadi (USA) 126 – Rossnagran (Ardross 134) [1995 6m^2 7m^2 Jul 21] IR 19,000Y: tall, leggy filly: third reported living foal: dam unraced: beaten a length or so when second to Kilvine in median auction maiden at Leicester and Matiya in maiden at Newmarket month later: stays 7f: likely to do better. *P. F. I. Cole* 81 p

SIBERIAN HENRY 2 b.g. (Apr 2) Siberian Express (USA) 125 – Semperflorens (Don 128) [1995 10m Oct 2] useful-looking gelding: fourth living foal: half-brother to 1¼m winner Sweet Revival (by Claude Monet): dam ran 3 times at 2 yrs: 50/1 and burly, well-beaten eighth of 14 in maiden at Pontefract *B. Smart* –

SIBERIAN MYSTIC 2 gr.f. (Mar 24) Siberian Express (USA) 125 – Mystic Crystal (IRE) 85 (Caerleon (USA) 132) [1995 5g 5.1m^6 6g 7f Jun 24] 5,800Y: lengthy filly: poor walker: has scope: first foal: dam, 7f winner at 2 yrs, placed over 43 +

1m at 3 yrs: poor form in maidens first 3 starts: gambled on and ridden by 7-lb claimer, well beaten in seller at Redcar on final outing: should stay at least 1m. *P. G. Murphy*

SICARIAN 3 b.c. Kris 135 – Sharka 97 (Shareef Dancer (USA) 135) [1994 NR 1995 10g 10.5g Sep 22] big, leggy colt: has a round action: second foal: dam 1m (at 2 yrs) and 8.5f winner and not beaten far in 11.3f Cheshire Oaks: beaten over 10 lengths when seventh in maidens at Goodwood and Haydock in September: sold 21,000 gns Newmarket Autumn Sales. *M. J. Heaton-Ellis* –

SIDE BAR 5 b.g. Mummy's Game 120 – Joli's Girl 79 (Mansingh (USA) 120) [1994 31§: 12m 14.1m 14.1m a12g^{3} a12g^{3} a14g^{5} 14.1d 12s^{4} 1995 a13g* a13g a16g 9.7m May 31] lengthy gelding: has a round action: poor handicapper: made all (able to dominate, third last start for M. Ryan) in selling handicap at Lingfield in February: no form afterwards: stays 1¾m: acts on good to firm ground, heavy and both all-weather surfaces: usually blinkered: none too keen. *K. G. Wingrove* 34 §

SIEGE PERILOUS (IRE) 2 b.c. (Feb 3) Taufan (USA) 119 – Carado 82 (Manado 130) [1995 8.2d 7.1g 10m Oct 2] 36,000Y: rangy, unfurnished colt: fourth foal: half-brother to 6f winner In The Game (by Mummy's Game): dam 8.2f winner later successful over hurdles: poor form in maidens. *Bob Jones* –

SIEVE OF TIME (USA) 4 b.g. Arctic Tern (USA) 126 – Got A Cold (USA) (Drone) [1994 88: 8m^{3} 10d* 12.3m^{5} 10.4f 10g^{3} 10.9d^{4} 10m a9.4g^{4} 1995 a9.4g^{3} Feb 1] tall, leggy gelding: fairly useful form: creditable third in handicap at Wolverhampton, held up: subsequently gelded: stays 1½m: below form (helped set too strong a pace) on firm ground: usually makes the running. *C. E. Brittain* 87

SIGAMA (USA) 9 ch.g. Stop The Music (USA) – Lady Speedwell (USA) (Secretariat (USA)) [1994 57d: 5g 5g 5m 5f^{6} 5g 5g 5m 1995 a5g* a5g^{6} 5d^{4} a5g^{2} 5m^{4} 5m^{6} 5m^{4} 5g^{4} 5g^{4} 5m 5m 5m Jul 19] sturdy, dipped-backed gelding: modest performer nowadays: made all in claimer at Wolverhampton in February: 5f specialist: acts on fibresand, ideally suited by top-of-the-ground when on turf: blinkered (out of form) last 2 starts in 1994: front runner: consistent at 9 yrs. *D. Nicholls* 55 a64

SIGER WATER 2 ch.f. (Jun 8) Rakaposhi King 119 – Kates Fling (USA) (Quiet Fling (USA) 124) [1995 5g Apr 17] second foal: dam winning hurdler: 20/1, showed nothing in maiden at Newcastle: sold 500 gns Doncaster October Sales. *R. F. Fisher* –

SIGHT'N SOUND 4 b.f. Chief Singer 131 – Optaria 83 (Song 132) [1994 63: 9s^{2} 8g^{3} 10.2f^{5} 10g^{3} 9.7g^{4} 13.1g* 12s^{5} 1995 16m 12m May 4] big, good-topped filly: modest performer: never a threat in handicaps for new stable in 1995: stays 13.1f: acts on soft ground, below form on top-of-the-ground. *D. R. C. Elsworth* –

SIGNATURE 3 b.f. Sadler's Wells (USA) 132 – Riverstreak (USA) (Irish River (FR) 131) [1994 NR 1995 11.7f^{3} Jul 1] fourth foal: closely related to 1m winner Fluvial (by Lomond): dam French 1m winner: 7/4 favourite, 8½ lengths third of 8 to Woodcrest in maiden at Bath, leading 4f out to over 2f out: looked sure to improve: sold 10,000 gns Newmarket December Sales. *H. R. A. Cecil* 62 p

SIGN FROM HEAVEN 2 b.c. (Feb 18) Keen 116 – Sarah's Love (Caerleon (USA) 132) [1995 6m 8d Sep 26] compact colt: third foal: dam, ran once at 2 yrs, closely related to very useful stayer Sudden Victory out of Princess Royal winner Shebeen: backward, poor form in maidens at Newmarket: trained by G. Rimmer on debut: sent to Spain. *N. C. Wright* –

SIGNORETTO (FR) 8 b.h. Mille Balles (FR) 124 – Sardagnola (FR) (Bon Mot III 132) [1994 8s^{5} 8s 7v 8m 8.5d^{2} 8g^{5} 8g 8g 8d^{2} 8.3g* 9.3g^{4} 10g^{6} 10v^{6} 8s^{4} 1995 8.5s^{2} 8.5d^{3} 8g* 8g^{4} 8g* 8g^{2} 8g* 8s* 8d^{5} 10g^{2} Oct 25] late-blooming French horse: had a record of 4 wins (1m to 9.3f) from 68 starts between 2 yrs and 7 yrs: claimed to join present stable 132,000 francs on 8-y-o reappearance and showed himself better than ever: successful in good handicaps at Saint-Cloud and Deauville (twice) in the summer then landed listed race at Chantilly in September: career-best efforts to be never-nearer 3¾ lengths fifth of 7 to Shaanxi in Prix du Rond-Point at Longchamp (soon off bridle, never a threat) and ¾-length second of 12 to Parme in Group 3 event in the provinces: effective at 1m to 1¼m: acts on heavy ground: tried blinkered earlier in career: effective from front or held up. *D. Smaga, France* 110

SIGNS 3 ch.f. Risk Me (FR) 127 – Sunday Sport Star 96 (Star Appeal 133) [1994 88: 5.1m^{2} 5g* 5m 6m 1995 7.3m 5m 6m^{5} 7f^{2} 6m^{5} 7g^{4} 7f 8.3m Aug 26] lengthy filly: 91

fairly useful performer: stays 7f: yet to race on a soft surface: rather headstrong, and usually a front runner: inconsistent: sold 24,000 gns Newmarket December Sales. *R. Hannon*

SIGNS R US (IRE) 2 b.g. (Mar 9) Al Hareb (USA) 123 – O La Bamba (IRE) (Commanche Run 133) [1995 6m 5m 7m Oct 12] IR 4,000Y, 6,800 2-y-o: small gelding: first foal: dam unraced half-sister to very smart 1m to 11f performer Commodore Blake: well beaten in maiden events and seller. *Dr J. D. Scargill* –

SIHAFI (USA) 2 ch.c. (Mar 28) Elmaamul (USA) 125 – Kit's Double (USA) (Spring Double) [1995 6m 6m^2 Oct 4] leggy, useful-looking colt: half-brother to several winners, including fairly useful 1m winner Sindeed (by Northern Baby): dam won from 6f to 9f in USA, including in minor stakes: wearing net muzzle, 5 lengths second of 6 to Victoria Regia in maiden at York, free early on then staying on well not knocked about: will improve again. *E. A. L. Dunlop* 77 p

SIKOSARKI (USA) 2 ch.f. (Mar 23) Inishpour 88 – Miss Sarcastic (USA) (Vitriolic (USA)) [1995 6g^6 7f a8.5g Oct 14] tenth reported foal: half-sister to 4 minor winners in USA: dam minor winner: soundly beaten in claimer at Hamilton (for W. S. Cunningham) in May and sellers at Thirsk (for G. M. Moore) in August and Wolverhampton in October. *Ronald Thompson* –

SILCA BLANKA (IRE) 3 b.c. Law Society (USA) 130 – Reality 88 (Known Fact (USA) 135) [1994 99: 5d* 6m* 6m 6g^4 6d^4 8g^5 6g 1995 7m 8m 6g^5 7f* 7m 8m^2 Jul 30] quite attractive colt: useful performer: won minor event at Epsom in June: ran well when neck second to A Magicman (Mr Martini third) in Group 3 race at Cologne following month: effective at 6f to 1m: acts on firm and dead ground. *M. R. Channon* 104

SILENCE IN COURT (IRE) 4 b.c. Law Society (USA) 130 – Fair Flutter (Beldale Flutter (USA) 130) [1994 98p: 12.3d^2 12.3d* 12v^4 14.1g* 12.3m^4 14f* 14.8m* 18g 16.1g* 1995 16.2m^3 16.2m^3 May 3] rangy colt: has scope: has progressed into a useful performer: around 2 lengths third of 9 to Double Trigger in Sagaro Stakes at Ascot final start: should stay 2½m: acts on firm and dead ground, never travelling well on heavy: often reluctant at stalls: tracks leaders/held up: genuine. *B. A. McMahon* 108

SILENT EXPRESSION 5 gr.m. Siberian Express (USA) 125 – Silent Sun 90 (Blakeney 126) [1994 73, a79: 8.3g^2 7g^4 8g 8f^5 8f 8g^2 8m 7f^3 8.3m^3 7d 8.5m 8s a7g* a6g* a5g^2 1995 a6g* a8g 7m* 6g^4 5.7m* 6.1m^3 6m 6m^5 7m* 7g Sep 7] rangy mare: unimpressive mover: fairly useful handicapper: won at Lingfield in January, Goodwood in May, Bath in June and Salisbury (always going well, quickened to lead inside final 1f) in August: very stiff task and tailed off in listed event at Doncaster final start: best at up to 7f: acts on equitrack, suited by a sound surface on turf: visored (no improvement) eighth to twelfth 4-y-o starts: usually races prominently. *B. J. Meehan* 88

SILENT GUEST (IRE) 2 b.g. (Feb 7) Don't Forget Me 127 – Guest House (What A Guest 119) [1995 6g^6 7.1d^5 7m 6.9m a7g Nov 24] IR 5,800F, IR 16,500Y: good-topped gelding: third living foal: half-brother to a winner in Sweden by Runnett: dam Irish 1½m winner: modest form in maidens and nurseries, very slowly away fourth start: will be well suited by 1m+. *Sir Mark Prescott* 57

SILENTLY 3 b.c. Slip Anchor 136 – Land of Ivory (USA) 109 (The Minstrel (CAN) 135) [1994 69: 7f 7g^3 8d 1995 10d* 10g 10m^4 11.4g 10m^2 10m* 10.2h* 11.9f^5 12m^4 10m^6 10g^3 10.4m^5 Oct 4] good-topped colt: fairly useful handicapper on his day: won at Ripon in April and at Pontefract and Bath in July: stays 1¼m: acts on dead ground and hard: has an awkward head carriage: tail swisher and sometimes looks none too genuine: not one to trust: sold 23,000 gns Newmarket Autumn Sales. *I. A. Balding* 83 §

SILENT SKY 3 b.f. Then Again 126 – Summer Sky 75 (Skyliner 117) [1994 –: 7m a8g 6.1s a8.5g a6g 1995 5.1m 8.1m Jun 15] leggy filly: no worthwhile form. *C. J. Hill* –

SILENT SOPRANO 2 b.f. (Apr 22) Kind of Hush 118 – Musical Note 44 (Sharpo 132) [1995 5g^2 5g^4 6g^6 5m^4 5f^5 7.1f^4 8f^2 7.1m* 8m 7.1g Sep 18] 1,200F, 3,700Y: leggy, lengthy filly: first foal: dam won 1¼m seller and stayed 1½m: modest performer: won nursery at Edinburgh in August: stays 1m: has raced only on a sound surface: sold 2,400 gns Doncaster October Sales. *Denys Smith* 49

SILENT SOVEREIGN 6 ch.g. Kind of Hush 118 – Regency Brighton (Royal Palace 131) [1994 NR 1995 12.1g May 29] fourth reported foal: half-brother to 7f seller winner Royal Resort (by King of Spain): dam showed little: probably of little account. *P. C. Clarke* –

SILENT SYSTEM (IRE) 2 gr.c. (Mar 12) Petong 126 – Light Thatch (Thatch (USA) 136) [1995 a6g a8.5g Dec 9] 42,000F, 40,000Y: half-brother to 1988 2-y-o 5f winner Before The Crash (by Stanford) and winners in Hong Kong and Spain: dam temperamental half-sister to dam of very smart sprinter Paris House: well beaten in maidens at Southwell and Wolverhampton. *J. G. FitzGerald* –

SILENT WARRIOR (IRE) 3 b.c. Nashwan (USA) 135 – Idyllic (USA) (Foolish Pleasure (USA)) [1994 9d* 10s^6 1995 10.5g* 10g^5 9g* 10g^3 Aug 15] sixth foal: related to 5 winners (3 by Sadler's Wells) notably Dewhurst dead-heater Scenic: dam, unraced, from excellent family of Noblesse, Rainbow Quest, Warning and Commander In Chief: won newcomers race at Longchamp at 2 yrs: successful in 1995 in valuable conditions event at Saint-Cloud in June and Prix Daphnis at Evry (10/9 on, beat Sharpest Image by 1½ lengths) in July: creditable third of 7 to Montjoy in Prix Guillaume d'Ornano at Deauville final start: effective at 9f and would have stayed 1½m: sold 250,000 gns Newmarket December Sales: reportedly to stand at stud in Ireland in 1996 before export to Australia. *J. E. Hammond, France* 111

SILHOUETTE (IRE) 2 gr.f. (Feb 1) Standaan (FR) 118 – Frill (Henbit (USA) 130) [1995 7m 6g 5.3d^6 5g Oct 16] 7,000F, 8,200Y: leggy filly: third foal: sister to French 6f and 7f (at 2 yrs) winner Lady Frill and half-sister to 3-y-o Salfrill (by Salt Dome): dam, Irish 1½m winner, half-sister to high-class miler Pitcairn and to dam of Assessor: poor form in maidens and seller: bred to stay 6f+: hung and carried head awkwardly on debut. *D. R. C. Elsworth* 36

SILK COTTAGE 3 b.g. Superpower 113 – Flute Royale 74 (Horage 124) [1994 66: 5g^2 5s^6 5m^2 5m^2 5.3m 5g^5 5s^4 5g^6 1995 5m 5f 5d 5g^5 5d^5 5m^4 a5g^2 5.1m 5m^5 a6g Nov 6] sturdy, good-quartered gelding: fair maiden handicapper: best form at around 5f: acts on good to firm and soft ground and on fibresand: no improvement in blinkers/visor: often hangs markedly left: usually races prominently. *R. M. Whitaker* 67

SILK MASQUE (USA) 2 b.f. (Jan 26) Woodman (USA) 126 – Silk Slippers (USA) 104 (Nureyev (USA) 131) [1995 6f* Jul 25] tall, unfurnished filly: good walker: first reported foal: dam won Hoover Fillies' Mile: evens favourite, won 7-runner maiden at Goodwood by neck from Naissant, held up going well then green when asked for effort and only getting on top towards finish: will stay 7f: looked sure to improve. *P. W. Chapple-Hyam* 85 p

SILKS AND STUDS 3 b.g. Danehill (USA) 126 – Gild The Lily 83 (Ile de Bourbon (USA) 133) [1994 –: 7.1s^6 7d 1995 8m 8.3m 11.7m^6 10.8g Oct 3] sturdy, lengthy gelding: has a round action: no worthwhile form, signs of a little ability on reappearance: blinkered final 3-y-o start. *J. White* –

SILKTAIL (IRE) 3 b.f. Jalmood (USA) 126 – Silky (USA) 112 (Nijinsky (CAN) 138) [1994 50: 7.1s 6d^3 a7g a8g 1995 6.9d 8.2g^4 11.6m^3 10m a9.4g^6 12g 10f^2 12m* 11.9m* 11.9m 10m^5 11.9g^3 12.1s a13g^6 Dec 6] lengthy, attractive filly: fair handicapper: impressive winner at Newmarket (final outing for John Berry) and Haydock (by 7 lengths) in the summer: should stay beyond 1½m: probably acts on firm and dead ground, no worthwhile form on all-weather: none too consistent. *C. A. Dwyer* 74 a–

SIL SILA (IRE) 2 b.f. (Feb 18) Marju (IRE) 127 – Porto Alegre (Habitat 134) [1995 7g* 7.3d* Oct 21] leggy filly: good walker: seventh living foal: half-sister to useful 1988 2-y-o 5f and 6f winner Frequent Flyer (by Night Shift), later winner at up to 9f in USA, and a winner in Belgium: dam won in Germany: long-priced winner of maiden at Warwick and Newgate Stud Radley Stakes (beat Pacific Grove 3½ lengths) at Newbury in October: will stay 1m: clearly a useful filly at least on an easy surface. *B. Smart* 97

SILVER ACADEMY (IRE) 3 gr.g. Standaan (FR) 118 – Right Cash (Right Tack 131) [1994 –: 6.1d 1995 6m 7g 5g^5 6.1m^6 5.1m^4 Jul 8] neat gelding: well beaten in varied company: tried visored and blinkered: dead. *Miss Gay Kelleway* –

SILVER BIRD (IRE) 3 b.f. Vision (USA) – Caralia 77 (Caracolero (USA) 131) [1994 –: 7s 6.9m 8d 1995 11.8g May 30] sparely-made filly: seems of little account. *M. J. Ryan* –

SILVER BORDER 2 ch.c. (Jan 21) Kris 135 – Silver Fling (USA) 120 (The Minstrel (CAN) 135) [1995 5m^3 Jul 1] big, strong, lengthy colt: third foal: brother to modest 1994 3-y-o Sundin and half-brother to 3-y-o Silver Sting (by Nashwan): dam sprinting sister to good 6f/7f performer Silverdip and close relative of smart 5f and 1½m winner Imperial Fling: well-backed 15/8-shot, 2½ lengths third of 6 to Atraf in maiden at Newcastle, soon niggled along but keeping on well: looked sure to improve, particularly at 6f: to USA. *I. A. Balding* — 77 p

SILVER BRIEF 4 gr.g. Sulaafah (USA) 119 – Briefing (Rusticaro (FR) 124) [1994 –: 10m 6f 11.6f^5 1995 a10g Jan 12] compact gelding: of little account. *D. J. S. ffrench Davis* — –

SILVERDALE COUNT 3 b.g. Nomination 125 – Its My Turn 80 (Palm Track 122) [1994 –: 6m 6g 6m^6 8.3g 1995 12.3m 15.8m^5 13.1f* Aug 17] leggy, lengthy, unfurnished gelding: little form in maidens and handicaps: won poor 4-runner seller at Ayr in August: should stay beyond 13.1f. *K. W. Hogg, Isle of Man* — 47

SILVERDALE FOX 8 ch.g. Sweet Monday 122 – Its My Turn 80 (Palm Track 122) [1994 NR 1995 11.1g^5 Sep 25] angular, plain gelding: probably no longer of much account on flat: won selling hurdle in November. *K. W. Hogg, Isle of Man* — –

SILVERDALE KNIGHT 2 b.c. (Apr 7) Nomination 125 – Its My Turn 80 (Palm Track 122) [1995 5m 5.1m^3 6g^3 5f* 5d^6 6m^6 6g^4 7m* 7h 7.5m^6 8f^4 7g 8.3g 6m Oct 2] 6,000Y: workmanlike colt: sixth foal: brother to 3-y-o 13f seller winner Silverdale Count and half-brother to fair 1989 2-y-o 6f winner Silverdale Fox (by Sweet Monday): dam miler: won median auction maiden at Hamilton in June and nursery at Catterick in July: below form afterwards in nurseries: stays 7f: acts on firm ground: sometimes sweats: usually races prominently (held up last time). *K. W. Hogg, Isle of Man* — 65

SILVER DOME (USA) 2 b. or br.c. (Feb 24) Silver Hawk (USA) 123 – Pink Topaze (FR) (Djakao (FR) 124) [1995 8m* Oct 12] — 90 P

The powerful Cecil stable introduced a number of promising two-year-olds in maiden company at the back-end. Dushyantor, a half-brother to Warning, Deploy and Commander In Chief, won at Nottingham and Tenby's brother Bright Water was successful at Yarmouth, while Lady Carla, who made a winning debut at Leicester, looks a possible Oaks type. The first two are among the stable's Derby hopes, as is Silver Dome who looked a fine prospect when overcoming greenness to land the odds in the EBF Chesterton Maiden over a mile at Newmarket in October. Silver Dome shaped like a horse who'll be seen to best advantage over middle distances as a three-year-old. Pat Eddery had to push him along to take the lead three furlongs out and he stayed on up the hill to hold off another highly-regarded newcomer, the Gosden-trained Sacho, by a length and a half. Silver Dome seemed to idle in front and is sure to improve a good deal with the experience behind him. Watch out for him in the Derby trials!

Silver Dome (USA) (b. or br.c. Feb 24, 1993)	Silver Hawk (USA) (b 1979)	Roberto (b 1969)	Hail To Reason
			Bramalea
		Gris Vitesse (gr 1966)	Amerigo
			Matchiche II
	Pink Topaze (FR) (b 1976)	Djakao (b 1966)	Tanerko
			Diagonale
		Pink Silk (ch 1957)	Spy Song
			Bayrose

The tall, close-coupled Silver Dome is by the very well bred 1982 Derby third Silver Hawk whose career as a stallion has taken a turn for the better in the 'nineties. Silver Dome is the eighth reported foal out of Pink Topaze, a filly who showed ability, without reaching a place, from six starts in varied company in France. Easily the best so far of her offspring is Fast Topaze (by Far North), winner of the Poule d'Essai des Poulains and the Prix Lupin in a career that spanned only five races, all in pattern company. Fast Topaze was beaten only once, when conceding 15 lb more than weight-for-age to the high-class Fitnah in the Prix du Prince d'Orange on his final outing. Fast Topaze gave the impression that he'd have been suited by a mile and a half (he missed both the Prix du Jockey-Club and the Prix de l'Arc because of injury). Another of Pink Topaze's winning offspring, Peak Value (by Blushing Groom), won over a mile and showed very useful form at up to a mile and a quarter. Pink Topaze herself is a half-sister to the top-class sprinter Amber Rama, the Poule d'Essai des Poulains winner Blue Tom and the Prix du Jockey-Club runner-up Timmy My Boy. *H. R. A. Cecil*

SILVER GROOM (IRE) 5 gr.g. Shy Groom (USA) – Rustic Lawn (Rusticaro (FR) 124) [1994 69: 8.3m6 7.6g2 7.9m2 8s 7d 1995 10m 10f* 10m 10m3 10d5 9g 10d4 Oct 19] smallish, angular gelding: fairly useful handicapper: ridden by 5-lb claimer, impressive winner of 14-runner £35,300 William Hill Cup at Goodwood in July by 2½ lengths from Hunters of Brora: creditable third of 14 in £27,900 contest at Goodwood in August: ran respectable races in big fields last 3 starts: stays 1¼m well: successful on soft ground at 3 yrs (modest form), and goes very well on firm: won handicap hurdle in November. *R. Akehurst* — 80

SILVER HARROW 2 ch.c. (Mar 12) Belmez (USA) 131 – Dancing Diana 82 (Raga Navarro (ITY) 119) [1995 6g2 6.1m4 7g4 7m3 6f3 6m6 6g3 Oct 16] 12,000Y: workmanlike colt: fourth foal: half-brother to 3 winners, including 7f and 1m winner Prince Rodney (by Don't Forget Me): dam 5f (at 2 yrs) to 1m winner: capable of fair form but looks to have lost his way and has shown signs of temperament: stays 7f: has raced only on a sound surface: blinkered fifth outing: sold 4,500 gns Newmarket Autumn Sales: one to treat with caution: joined A. Newcombe. *Sir Mark Prescott* — 74 d

SILVER HUNTER (USA) 4 b.g. Silver Hawk (USA) 123 – Martha Queen (USA) (Nijinsky (CAN) 138) [1994 75: 11s3 10g2 11.9m3 10m* 1995 12m 10m 11.1g 12m 12m 14.4m5 16d 12g Oct 16] big, close-coupled gelding: carries condition: reportedly broke blood vessel final start (June) at 3 yrs: only modest at best in handicaps in 1995 for new stable: stays 14.4f, may stay 2m: acts on soft ground and firm: visored and tongue tied down since sixth 4-y-o start: strong-galloping type who may well be best with forcing tactics. *G. C. Bravery* — 62

SILVER PREY (USA) 2 b.c. (Mar 9) Silver Hawk (USA) 123 – Truly My Style (USA) (Mount Hagen (FR) 127) [1995 7g3 7m* Aug 12] tall, unfurnished colt: first foal: dam stakes winner at 1m in USA: won 22-runner maiden at Newbury in August by a short head from Reinhardt, challenging strongly from over 1f out: will stay 1¼m: will improve again: sent to Dubai. *E. A. L. Dunlop* — 92 p

SILVER RONDO (USA) 3 b.f. Diesis 133 – Silver Dollar 106 (Shirley Heights 130) [1994 NR 1995 a7g6 a10g3 10g 10f3 a12g3 11.1f3 Aug 3] angular, light-framed filly: fourth foal: half-sister to 1m winner Money Spinner (by Teenoso): dam, 2-y-o 6f winner below best at 1½m at 3 yrs, is out of half-sister to Highclere: modest maiden handicapper: stays 1½m: acts on both all-weather surfaces and firm ground: flashed tail and looked none too keen fourth start. *Lord Huntingdon* — 51

SILVER SAMURAI 6 b.g. Alleging (USA) 120 – Be My Lady (Be My Guest (USA) 126) [1994 NR 1995 a11g 9.9m a12g Apr 26] smallish gelding: has a quick action: fairly useful performer (rated 83) at 4 yrs: well beaten in handicaps in 1995: used to be best at 1¼m and act on any going: blinkered (respectable effort) once as 4-y-o. *Mrs V. A. Aconley* — –

SILVER SINGER 3 gr.f. Pharly (FR) 130 – Bustling Nelly 94 (Bustino 136) [1994 NR 1995 9.7m4 10.5g4 11.9d a10g2 a10g a14.8g2 Nov 27] 21,000Y: small, angular filly: has a round action: half-sister to several winners, including 1½m — 65 a56

William Hill Cup (Handicap), Goodwood—apprentice Matthew Henry has an armchair ride on Silver Groom

winner Passion And Mirth (by Known Fact): dam middle-distance half-sister to Further Flight (by Pharly): modest maiden handicapper: probably stays 14.8f: acts on good to firm ground and all-weather: sold 9,000 gns Doncaster November Sales. *D. R. Loder*

SILVER SLEEVE (IRE) 3 b.g. Taufan (USA) 119 – Sable Coated (Caerleon (USA) 132) [1994 66?: 6g 7m 7m^4 7m 8s 8g 1995 10d Oct 19] lengthy gelding: modest maiden at best: bit backward, behind at Newbury on belated return: sold (J. Toller to M. Hammond) 7,000 gns Newmarket Autumn Sales. *J. A. R. Toller* –

SILVER STING 3 ch.c. Nashwan (USA) 135 – Silver Fling (USA) 120 (The Minstrel (CAN) 135) [1994 –p: 10d 1995 7g^2 7m^3 6m^2 May 7] lengthy colt: fair maiden: placed on all starts, but found little closing stages, making most at Salisbury on final start: stays 7f: has had tongue tied down: sent to USA. *I. A. Balding* 75

SILVER TZAR 3 gr.g. Dominion 123 – Altaia (FR) 90 (Sicyos (USA) 126) [1994 81p: 6m 7g^5 6.9m* 1995 7m 7m 6m 6f^5 Jul 24] lengthy gelding: progressive form in maiden auctions at 2 yrs: wearing net muzzle, long way below form in handicaps on return: stays 7f: has raced only on a sound surface: sometimes early to post. *W. J. Haggas* –

SILVER WEDGE (USA) 4 ch.g. Silver Hawk (USA) 123 – Wedge Musical (What A Guest 119) [1994 105: a10g^3 12m* 16.2m* 16f 1995 16d^3 12d^6 Sep 23] useful-looking gelding: good mover: useful performer for G. Lewis at 3 yrs: one of the best juvenile hurdlers in 1994/5 for D. Nicholson: bandaged off-fore, sweating and on toes, better effort on return when 12½ lengths sixth of 8 to Riyadian in Cumberland Lodge Stakes at Ascot, headed just before turn: suited by test of stamina: probably acts on any going: blinkered or visored since final 2-y-o start: suited by strong handling: genuine: front runner: joined O. Sherwood, and won Grade 1 staying hurdle in December. *Lord Huntingdon* 99

SILVER WELCOME 2 ch.g. (Apr 3) Most Welcome 131 – Silver Ore (FR) 94 (Silver Hawk (USA) 123) [1995 5.9f^3 5m^4 6h^2 5h^2 7g* 7d^6 8g 7f^5 8m Oct 28] 3,100Y: sturdy gelding: second foal: half-brother to 3-y-o Salduba (by Fijar Tango): dam 6f (at 2 yrs) and 1m winner: won 15-runner auction event at Thirsk in September: ran poorly in seller at Newmarket final start: bred to stay beyond 7f: acts on hard ground: tends to carry head high: pulled hard sixth start: races prominently. *M. H. Easterby* 65 d

SILVER WILL 5 gr.g. Skyliner 117 – Silver Cygnet 71 (My Swanee 122) [1994 –: 6m^6 6f 1995 6g Apr 26] angular gelding: no worthwhile form. *W. L. Barker* –

SILVER WING (USA) 2 b.f. (May 4) Silver Hawk (USA) 123 – Cojinx (USA) (Crafty Prospector (USA)) [1995 7m^5 9g^4 7.9g^2 Oct 7] $145,000Y: angular filly: has a fluent, round action: second foal: dam useful stakes winner in USA, third in Grade 1 7f event: progressive form in maidens at Newmarket, Redcar, and York, keeping-on second to comfortable winner Committal last time: has been bandaged near-hind/behind: stays 9f. *M. Bell* 73

SILVICOLOUS (USA) 3 ch.c. Woodman (USA) 126 – Golden Oriole (USA) (Northern Dancer) [1994 53p: 7.5g^5 1995 7.1m^2 8m^4 8g* Jun 3] small colt: has a rather round action: fairly useful performer: claimer ridden, won 6-runner maiden at Ayr in June, leading going well 3f out and staying on determinedly: will stay beyond 1m: has raced only on a sound surface: sent to USA. *P. W. Chapple-Hyam* 81

S'IL VOUS PLAIT (GER) 3 b.f. Dashing Blade 117 – Silver Form 65 (Formidable (USA) 125) [1994 6g^5 6.5s^3 5.5s^2 1995 7s* 8s* 8g^2 11g^6 8m^2 8s^3 8g Sep 24] useful German-bred filly: dam, out of high-class 2-y-o, maiden who stayed 7f: won maiden at Hanover in March and listed event at Dusseldorf in April: best effort when ¾-length second of 16 to Tryphosa in Arag Preis at Dusseldorf (leading 2f out to inside last): below from afterwards, including in 11f Preis der Diana: stays 1m: acts on soft ground. *A. Wohler, Germany* 108

SIMAFAR (IRE) 4 b.g. Kahyasi 130 – Sidama (FR) (Top Ville 129) [1994 12d^4 13m* 12g^2 16v^5 16v 1995 14m 14s^6 20m 16g 16.2d Sep 23] sparely-made gelding: third foal: half-brother to 2 winning stayers in Ireland, notably Irish Cesarewitch winner Sinntara (by Lashkari): dam French middle-distance winner: fairly useful (rated 87) and consistent handicapper in Ireland at 3 yrs for J. Oxx, winner of 4-runner maiden at Wexford: stepped up in trip and ran very well when around 9 lengths seventh of 27 to Harlestone Brook in Ascot Stakes at Royal Ascot: off course 73 ?

nearly 3 months, soundly beaten afterwards: stays 2½m: acts on good to firm ground and heavy: won over hurdles in October. *N. A. Graham*

SIMAND 3 b.f. Reprimand 122 – Emmylou (Arctic Tern (USA) 126) [1994 59: 6m^6 7m^6 5.9f* 7f^3 6m^6 6d 8d^4 7v^4 1995 7g 8g^6 8.1g 10g^2 a11g 8m^4 8m* 6.9f* 8h^4 8g a7g Dec 2] leggy, sparely-made filly: good walker: modest performer: won selling handicap at Thirsk and claimer at Carlisle in July: left E. Weymes's stable before final start: effective at 7f and 1¼m: acts on any turf going: looked reluctant sixth 3-y-o start. *G. M. Moore* — 59 a–

SIMON HAROLD 2 b.c. (Mar 11) Mazilier (USA) 107 – Alison Rose 58 (Jaazeiro (USA) 127) [1995 a5g^4 May 4] 5,000Y: brother to a poor maiden and half-brother to 3 winners, including 1m winner Turbo Rose (by Taufan): dam, lightly raced at 2 yrs, out of half-sister to Runnett: 9/2, signs of ability when fourth of 5 in maiden auction at Wolverhampton: looked capable of better. *W. R. Muir* — – p

SIMPLY (IRE) 6 b.g. Simply Great (FR) 122 – Be A Dancer (Be Friendly 130) [1994 38: 14m^4 14.9m^3 16.4g 1995 15.4m Apr 25] small gelding: poor performer at best nowadays: well beaten for new stable only start in 1995: stays at least 14.9f: acts on good to firm and dead ground: effective blinkered at 3 yrs: fair hurdler. *T. P. McGovern* — –

SIMPLY MISS CHIEF (IRE) 2 b.f. (Apr 29) Mac's Imp (USA) 116 – Wolverhants 79 (Wolver Hollow 126) [1995 5.1h^4 5g 6g a5g a6g Nov 13] IR 3,800Y, 5,800 2-y-o: light-framed, leggy filly: half-sister to numerous winners, best of them useful 6f (at 2 yrs) and 8.5f winner Sylva Honda (by Adonijah): dam second over 6f on both starts, is half-sister to dam of very smart middle-distance winner King's Island: poor maiden: showed little in seller final outing. *D. W. P. Arbuthnot* — –

SIMPLY SILLY (IRE) 2 b.f. (Mar 19) Simply Great (FR) 122 – Zany (Junius (USA) 124) [1995 6m^4 7g 6m 6g^4 6d 6f Oct 16] 3,100 2-y-o: fourth foal: half-sister to fairly useful 1992 5f winner Zany Zanna (by Petorius): dam Irish 9.5f and 1¼m winner at 2 yrs: trained by R. Thompson first 2 starts: worthwhile form only when fourth of 10 in maiden at Catterick in September: stays 6f: swerved stalls on debut. *W. L. Barker* — 57 ?

SIMPLY SIMON 3 b.c. Today And Tomorrow 78 – Hamrahi (Final Straw 127) [1994 –: 6d 6g a8g 1995 6s 10g^6 a8g 8.3m 7g 6f Jun 30] workmanlike colt: well beaten, including in seller: tried visored: sold 600 gns Ascot July Sales. *K. R. Burke* — –

SIMPOSA (IRE) 3 b.g. Simply Great (FR) 122 – Mariposa (Cure The Blues (USA)) [1994 7m 1995 a10g^4 a8g a12g 11d^4 11.8g 8f Oct 24] sparely-made ex-Irish gelding: first foal: dam fair Irish 1½m winner: trained on debut by D. Gillespie, next 3 starts by J. Banks: modest form on debut here, nothing worthwhile afterwards: sold 500 gns Doncaster November Sales. *E. J. Alston* — 53 d

SINCLAIR LAD (IRE) 7 ch.g. Muscatite 122 – Kitty Frisk 64 (Prince Tenderfoot (USA) 126) [1994 50: 14.1v* 9.7v^3 12d 10g 14.1m 11.6m 8m^4 10m^2 10g 1995 10m 11.6m 10m^3 10m^6 10m 10.8m^5 Jul 15] leggy, quite good-topped gelding: poor mover: poor performer: stays 1¾m: acts on any ground on turf and on equitrack: visored once at 3 yrs, usually blinkered nowadays: hung left under pressure on 7-y-o reappearance: has been gelded. *R. J. Hodges* — 41

SING AND DANCE 2 b.f. (Apr 22) Rambo Dancer (CAN) 107 – Musical Princess 66 (Cavo Doro 124) [1995 7d 7m Oct 30] workmanlike filly: seventh foal: half-sister to 8.9f to 10.3f winner Drummer Hicks (by Seymour Hicks) and 1m to 1½m winner Oh Danny Boy (by Rabdan): dam won 4 times, at 1½m and 2m, at 5 yrs: burly, green and slowly away, down the field in maidens at Newcastle in the autumn. *E. Weymes* — –

SINGING PATRIARCH (IRE) 2 b.c. (Apr 11) Marju (IRE) 127 – Busker (Bustino 136) [1995 6m 7m^2 6g^2 7d 6m* 5m^3 Nov 6] 31,000F, 22,000Y: rather leggy, useful-looking colt: fourth foal: half-brother to 3-y-o 6f winner Prime Property (by Tirol) and winners in Germany and Italy: dam twice-raced (at 2 yrs) half-sister to very useful 8.5f to 2m winner Arden: fairly useful form when ninth of 30 to Rio Duvida in valuable sales race at Newmarket: didn't need to show that form when winning maiden at Catterick in October after giving impression possibly not at ease on track: bred to stay beyond 7f, but takes keen hold: likely to do better: sent to USA. *J. L. Dunlop* — 88 p

SINGING ROCK (IRE) 3 ch.f. Ballad Rock 122 – Swift Pursuit 57 (Posse (USA) 130) [1994 67: 5m^4 5m^4 5m^5 5m* 6m 5d^3 7m 6.1g^3 1995 7m^6 6m 7.1m^6 8.3g 6.9g^6 6f^6 Jul 20] useful-looking filly: modest handicapper: should stay 1m: acts on good to firm and dead ground: blinkered (well beaten) final start: inconsistent. *R. Hannon* 62

SINGOALLA (IRE) 2 b.f. (Apr 20) Alwuhush (USA) 121 – Broadway Gal (USA) (Foolish Pleasure (USA)) [1995 6m^3 6m^2 7m^2 6.9s^3 Sep 27] 5,000Y: leggy filly: second foal: dam third once from 4 starts in North America: fair maiden: will stay at least 1¼m: acts on good to firm ground and soft: looks one paced: sent to Sweden. *J. L. Dunlop* 69

SINGSPIEL (IRE) 3 b.c. In The Wings 128 – Glorious Song (CAN) (Halo (USA)) [1994 108p: 7m^5 7s* 7m^2 1995 10m^2 12.3m^4 10m^2 10m^2 11.9m^2 12g* Sep 8] 121

A little more could have gone a long way in Singspiel's three-year-old season. One judiciously-spread length would have won him the Thresher Classic Trial, Grand Prix de Paris, Eclipse Stakes and the Great Voltigeur. As it was, Singspiel had just the single victory in 1995, in the listed O & K Troy Stakes at Doncaster. As a two-year-old, he had won a maiden at Chester and was then second in a conditions stakes at Ascot, beaten eight lengths by Celtic Swing. Singspiel gave some of the stars an awful lot more to think about in 1995. Pentire met him twice, the neck margin between them in the Thresher Classic Trial at Sandown in April representing a stroll in the park in comparison with their memorable encounter in the Great Voltigeur at York in August; having led over two furlongs out and been headed entering the last, Singspiel's final rally at York meant that it was another fifteen minutes before the judge was able to give his verdict against him and to the 5/4-on favourite. Singspiel had three starts between his two meetings with Pentire. Fourth in the Chester Vase was well below his best, but two necks were all that prevented him from being a dual Group 1 winner in the summer. Singspiel finished strongly in both the Grand Prix de Paris and Eclipse but, coming from off the pace first time then always prominent on the second, it was not quite enough to beat either Valanour or Halling. Given performances of this calibre, Singspiel made hard work of landing the odds when faced by just two opponents in the Troy Stakes in September. In a slowly-run race on good ground (easier than he had encountered earlier in the year), he beat the useful Jumairah Sun by two and a half lengths, trainer Michael Stoute stating afterwards that 'he never gives himself an easy race, even at home.' All of the top middle-

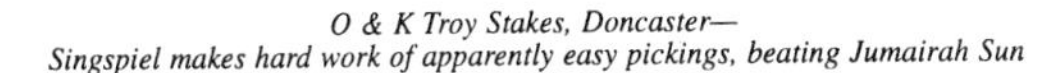

O & K Troy Stakes, Doncaster—
Singspiel makes hard work of apparently easy pickings, beating Jumairah Sun

distance contests were possible targets in the autumn, but these were hard races that Singspiel in the end did not contest.

Singspiel (IRE) (b.c. 1992)	In The Wings (b 1986)	Sadler's Wells (b 1981)	Northern Dancer
			Fairy Bridge
		High Hawk (b 1980)	Shirley Heights
			Sunbittern
	Glorious Song (CAN) (b 1976)	Halo (b or br 1969)	Hail To Reason
			Cosmah
		Ballade (b 1972)	Herbager
			Miss Swapsco

Singspiel comes from a famous family, but one whose chief triumphs have been abroad. The best of his dam's five previous winners were Rahy (by Blushing Groom), a smart two-year-old who never won a European pattern race but took the Grade 2 Bel Air Handicap at Hollywood Park as a four-year-old, and Rakeen (by Northern Dancer) who won two minor events in Britain and two pattern contests in South Africa. Rahy has made a bigger name for himself as a sire, with such as the top American 1995 three-year-old filly Serena's Song and Cherry Hinton winner Applaud. One step back in Singspiel's pedigree there are two North American champions. His dam Glorious Song was Canadian Horse of the Year and Champion Older Mare in both Canada and the USA during a four-season, seventeen-win career; she passed the million-dollar barrier, the first Canadian racehorse to do so, thanks to a 7,500-dollar fourth place in the December of her five-year-old season, the last of thirty-four starts. Two years later, Glorious Song's brother Devil's Bag had five races and won them by an aggregate of twenty-seven lengths, topping the Experimental Free Handicap by 5 lb. Injury cut short his three-year-old career, and he retired with a total of one defeat in nine starts. Singspiel's sire In The Wings has two representatives from his first crop in the top twenty middle-distance three-year-olds, the other being Irish Derby winner Winged Love who will be at stud in Germany in 1996.

Sheikh Mohammed's "Singspiel"

The quite attractive, good-topped Singspiel, a good walker, has an assured stud place already but will campaign on for what would be some most deserved success in pattern races. Effective at a mile and a quarter and a mile and a half, he won on soft going as a two-year-old but all of his fine efforts of 1995 were on good to firm. *M. R. Stoute*

SING UP 3 b.g. Sizzling Melody 117 – Hellene (Dominion 123) [1994 61: 6g^2 6m^4 6.1d^4 1995 7.3d 8m^6 10d a8g^6 a7g Dec 14] sturdy gelding: modest maiden: stays 7f: acts on equitrack and good to firm ground. *M. McCormack* 47

SING WITH THE BAND 4 b.f. Chief Singer 131 – Ra Ra Girl 77 (Shack (USA) 118) [1994 –: 6m 5.1m^6 7f^6 6m 5m 6.1s 1995 5m^3 a6g^2 5m a5g* a5g^6 a5g^4 a5g* 5m^5 a6g^3 5g^2 5.1d a6g^2 a6g^3 Dec 12] strong, compact filly: fair handicapper: best form on the all-weather and won at Southwell in May and June: effective at 5f and 6f: acts on good to firm ground (possibly not on dead) and on fibresand: usually races prominently. *B. A. McMahon* 62 a74

SINKING SUN 2 gr.f. (Jan 26) Danehill (USA) 126 – Oscura (USA) 82 (Caro 133) [1995 8m^5 Oct 20] heavy-topped filly: seventh foal: half-sister to several winners, including useful 3-y-o 10.5f and 13.9f (Ebor) winner Sanmartino (by Salse) and very smart middle-distance performer Urgent Request (by Rainbow Quest): dam, 1m winner, half-sister to champion grass horse Johnny D: 10/1 and green, over 6 lengths fifth of 11 to easy winner Overruled in maiden at Doncaster, keeping on never a threat: wore blinkers: will improve. *B. W. Hills* 68 p

SIR ARTHUR HOBBS 8 b.g. Lyphard's Special (USA) 122 – Song Grove 61 (Song 132) [1994 68d: 6.9s 9.2d 8.3m* 8g^2 9.2g* 10g^3 8.3g* 8m 8.3m* 8.5f^4 8.3f^2 8.9m^3 9.7d 8.2g 1995 8.3f^4 10m^6 9.2f^2 8.1m^2 8.3f^5 Aug 9] strong gelding: unimpressive mover: modest performer: stays 9.2f, possibly not 1¼m: acts on firm ground, dead and fibresand: tried blinkered (refused to enter stalls) and visored, not for long time: genuine. *J. L. Eyre* 62

SIR DICKIE COX (IRE) 4 b.g. Nordico (USA) – Arthur's Daughter 77 (Artaius (USA) 129) [1994 –: 14g^6 10.3m 11.1m 1995 16.2m 13g 12m^6 May 9] workmanlike, lengthy gelding: no form: sold (F. Lee to J. Birkett) 1,050 gns Doncaster September Sales. *F. H. Lee* –

SIRIUS (IRE) 3 br.g. Skyliner 117 – Shantung Lassie (FR) (Shantung 132) [1994 –: 6g 6.9d 1995 10m 16.4m Nov 6] compact gelding: of little account. *C. Weedon* –

SIR JOEY (USA) 6 ch.g. Honest Pleasure (USA) – Sougoli (Realm 129) [1994 92: 5.2s 5.1g^3 5.1m 5d 6s 6m 5.1f^2 6f* 5m^6 6m 5.6g 6d 5m^3 6.1g^3 1995 5.2m^6 5m 6m^3 5g^6 6m^3 6f 5.1m* 6m^5 6m 5m^5 6g 5s 6.1s Oct 17] lengthy, workmanlike gelding: has been hobdayed: fairly useful handicapper: won at Chepstow (has a good record there) in July and ran well when fifth of 27 to Shikari's Son in Stewards' Cup at Goodwood: below form afterwards, poorly drawn on several occasions: effective at 5f and 6f: acts on any going: successful for apprentice: held up, and sometimes finds little. *P. G. Murphy* 92

SIR KING (GER) 3 b.c. Konigsstuhl (GER) – Shirbella 85 (Shirley Heights 130) [1994 8.5d 8s^2 1995 10s* 10.5m^5 10.2g^4 11s^3 12m^4 11g^6 14s 12s^2 Oct 22] smart German colt: third reported foal: dam 1m winner: won maiden at Gelsenkirchen in April: around 2¾ lengths fourth of 18 to All My Dreams in Deutsches Derby at Hamburg fifth start: well below form next 2 starts, best effort when ½-length second of 12 to Caballo in Group 3 event at Dusseldorf final one: stays 1½m: acts on good to firm ground and soft. *R. Suerland, Germany* 111

SIR NORMAN HOLT (IRE) 6 b.g. Ela-Mana-Mou 132 – Ploy 87 (Posse (USA) 130) [1994 61, a72: a7g^3 a7g^3 a7g* a8g* a8g a8g* 8d 8m^2 8s^6 8m^3 a10g^5 a7g 1995 8m 9.7g a12g^2 a10g^6 Dec 15] good-topped gelding: modest handicapper: seems to stay 1½m: acts on firm ground and equitrack, not on a soft surface: tried visored, usually blinkered nowadays: effective from front or held up. *R. J. O'Sullivan* – a63

SIR OLIVER (IRE) 6 b.g. Auction Ring (USA) 123 – Eurorose (Busted 134) [1994 47: 5.7g^6 6v^5 5g^6 6m^3 6m 5m^4 6d^3 7f 7m 1995 a10g a8g a7g Dec 14] good-topped gelding: poor handicapper: tailed off for new stable in 1995. *B. A. Pearce* –

SIR SILVER SOX (USA) 3 gr.c. Corwyn Bay 115 – Sox In The Box (USA) (Cresta Rider (USA) 124) [1994 89: 5s^2 5v^3 6g* 6m 1995 7d^6 7.5g^6 6m^2 6m* 6m^5 6g 107

Sep 16] leggy colt: useful handicapper: won IR £22,750 event at the Curragh in July by ½ length from Ailleacht, leading well inside final 1f: ran creditably at Leopardstown next time, poorly (reluctant stalls) in Ayr Gold Cup final one: best efforts at 6f: acts on good to firm and dead ground: blinkered/visored since fourth 3-y-o start. *T. Stack, Ireland*

SIR TASKER 7 b.h. Lidhame 109 – Susie's Baby (Balidar 133) [1994 67: a5g^{3} a5g^{6} a5g^{2} a5g a5g^{2} a6g 5g* 5m^{4} 5f^{5} 5m^{2} 5m^{5} 5f 5f 5g 5g^{3} 5g 5.1d 5.1g a5g a5g 1995 a5g* a5g a5g^{5} a6g* a6g^{5} a6g* a6g* 6.1g 5m 5m^{5} 5g 6m 5m^{2} 5f^{2} 5m 6f^{2} 6m* 6d a5g^{4} 6g a7g^{6} 5f 6m a6g^{6} a5g a6g^{4} a6g Dec 18] compact, quite attractive horse: fairly useful handicapper on the all-weather: successful once at Wolverhampton (claimer) and 3 times at Lingfield (including a career-best effort in AWT Sprint Series Final) early in year: only modest on turf, but won apprentice contest at Newmarket in August: effective at 5f and an easy 6f: acts on firm and dead ground and the all-weather: has won in visor and without: often front runner: tough. *J. L. Harris* — 60 a84

SIR THOMAS BEECHAM 5 b.g. Daring March 116 – Balinese 86 (Balidar 133) [1994 64: a13g^{2} a16g^{6} a16g^{3} 14g 16.5m^{5} 16.1m* 15.4d 16g a13g a16g^{6} 1995 a13g^{2} 14.9d 15.4m a13g Dec 19] leggy gelding: modest handicapper: well beaten on turf in 1995: stays 2m: acts on good to firm ground and equitrack: sometimes bandaged behind: held up/tracks leaders. *S. Dow* — – a64

SIS GARDEN 2 b.f. (May 25) Damister (USA) 123 – Miss Nanna 56§ (Vayrann 133) [1995 7g 7m^{4} a8g^{6} Nov 6] unfurnished filly: fourth foal: half-sister to 3-y-o Cumbrian Minstrel (by Efisio), 5f winner at 2 yrs: dam temperamental sprint maiden: modest form in maidens at Newcastle and Southwell last 2 starts: stays 1m. *M. H. Easterby* — 52

SISKA (USA) 3 ch.f. Diesis 133 – Kind Hope (USA) (Chieftain II) [1994 NR 1995 8m Jun 13] leggy, rather unfurnished filly: sixth foal: half-sister to Kindled (by Mummy's Pet), modest winner from 6f (here) to middle distances (in Belgium) in 1990: dam unraced half-sister to Known Fact: bought out of B. Hills's stable 16,000 gns Newmarket December (1994) Sales: 12/1 and unruly in stalls, twelfth of 13 in maiden at Salisbury, pulling hard and hanging left throughout. *J. L. Dunlop* — –

SISON (IRE) 5 b.g. Vacarme (USA) 121 – Silent Sail (Aglojo 119) [1994 59: 5g a5g a5g^{5} 1995 a6g a5g^{3} a5g a5g^{4} 5.1g^{3} 5.1m 5m 6d^{3} 5m^{4} Jun 24] sturdy, angular gelding: modest handicapper: effective at 5f, and should stay beyond 6f: acts on good to firm and dead ground and all-weather surfaces: blinkered (ran creditably) sixth 5-y-o start: usually bandaged behind. *K. G. Wingrove* — 59 a62

SISTAR ACT 2 b.f. (Apr 25) Salse (USA) 128 – Unsuitable (Local Suitor (USA) 128) [1995 6g^{4} 6m Aug 11] 7,600F, 13,000Y: well-made filly: good walker: third foal: half-sister to Italian 3-y-o 5f winner Lady Unsuitable (by Warrshan): dam unraced daughter of half-sister to good milers Final Straw and Achieved: green, last of 4 in maiden at Ascot then in rear in 22-runner maiden at Newbury. *M. R. Channon* — –

SISTER KIT (IRE) 2 b.f. (Apr 23) Glacial Storm (USA) 127 – Good Holidays 60 (Good Times (ITY)) [1995 8.2d 8d^{4} 8g Oct 10] robust filly: first foal: dam stayed 7f: fourth of 12 to White Sea in median auction at Salisbury, best effort: will be suited by midde distances: wears bandages: mulish at stalls on debut. *B. Palling* — 59

SIX CLERKS (IRE) 2 b.g. (Mar 16) Shadeed (USA) 135 – Skidmore Girl (USA) (Vaguely Noble 140) [1995 7g 6m^{4} 6m^{3} 7.9m a8g^{5} a8g^{2} Dec 15] 17,000F, 12,000Y: tall, lengthy colt: first foal: dam lightly-raced daughter of high-class French 7f/1m performer Sanedtki: fair maidens good second in nursery at Lingfield final start: will stay beyond 1m. *J. G. FitzGerald* — 68

SIX FOR LUCK 3 b.g. Handsome Sailor 125 – Fire Sprite 83 (Mummy's Game 120) [1994 68: 5g* 5m 5.2m 1995 6m^{2} 6.1m^{4} 6f 6g^{5} 5m Oct 30] leggy, lengthy gelding: good mover: disappointing sprinter: trained until after third 3-y-o start by J. Berry: has raced only on a sound surface: blinkered (looked reluctant) second 3-y-o start: usually bandaged behind: carries head high: one to treat with caution. *D. A. Nolan* — 57 §

SIZZLING 3 b.g. Sizzling Melody 117 – Oriental Splendour 85 (Runnett 125) [1994 –: 5.2s^{5} 5s^{6} 1995 5.1g^{6} 5.1f* 5m^{5} 6m 6m^{4} 6m^{3} 5m^{4} 5g^{6} 6f* Oct 23] smallish, sturdy gelding: fair performer: won minor event at Bath in May and handicap at — 65

Leicester (rallied, by a head) in October: stays 6f: acts on firm ground: consistent. *R. Hannon*

SIZZLING ROMP 3 b.f. Sizzling Melody 117 – Its A Romp (Hotfoot 126) – [1994 59: 5d 5s^4 5g 5m^2 6m 1995 a6g 5g 5g a5g 5.2m^6 Aug 3] sturdy filly: disappointing maiden: should stay 6f: acts on good to firm ground. *D. T. Thom*

SIZZLING SERENADE 2 gr.f. (Mar 31) Sizzling Melody 117 – Trynova 66 – (Tyrnavos 129) [1995 5d 7f a6g Dec 2] 420F, 450Y: strong, close-coupled filly: fourth foal: dam 2-y-o 7f and 8.2f winner out of half-sister to Music Maestro: no form, including in seller. *S. G. Norton*

SIZZLING SYMPHONY 2 b.c. (Apr 6) Sizzling Melody 117 – Polly Worth 55 66 (Wolver Hollow 126) [1995 5g 6m 7f* 7m^4 Jul 20] 4,700Y: tall, lengthy colt: has scope: sixth foal: half-brother to 7f winner Aragona (by Aragon) and 1993 2-y-o 5f and 6f winner Culsyth Flyer (by Nomination): dam maiden, stayed 1m: dropped in class, much improved effort to win seller at Redcar in June: creditable fourth in non-selling nursery at Catterick on final outing: will stay 1m. *R. A. Fahey*

SKEDADDLE 3 b.f. Formidable (USA) 125 – Norfolk Serenade 83 (Blakeney 57 126) [1994 NR 1995 7g^4 7m 8.5d^4 8m^4 9.9m^4 a12g 10m 13.8g^3 a14g^2 a13g^5 Dec 19] 3,000F, 14,500Y: lengthy filly: half-sister to fairly useful sprinter Samsolom (by Absalom) and 4-y-o 6f (at 2 yrs) to 2m winner Secret Serenade (by Classic Secret): dam 11.7f winner: modest maiden at best: sold out of J. FitzGerald's stable 3,800 gns Doncaster October Sales after eighth start: should stay beyond 1¼m: acts on good to firm and dead ground: inconsistent. *Ronald Thompson*

SKELTON COUNTESS (IRE) 2 ch.f. (Apr 28) Imperial Frontier (USA) 112 – 54 Running Brook (Run The Gantlet (USA)) [1995 5m 5g 5.1m 5g^4 6m^3 a5g^6 5m^3 Jul 3] IR 2,300Y: leggy filly: half-sister to several winners, including French 9f and 1¼m winner Bright Stream (by Cure The Blues): dam, Irish 2-y-o 7f winner, half-sister to dam of Niniski: modest maiden: will stay further than 6f: ran poorly on fibresand: active sort, but more settled on later starts. *R. Hollinshead*

SKELTON PRINCESS (IRE) 4 b.f. Carmelite House (USA) 118 – Fariha – (Mummy's Pet 125) [1994 32: a9.4g^6 a8.5g^2 a8.5g^5 a11g^5 a9.4g^4 a8g a7g a12g 1995 a9.4g Jun 24] leggy, lengthy filly: poor maiden: sold out of R. Hollinshead's stable 1,700 gns Doncaster February (1995) Sales: well beaten over hurdles in April for D. McCain and again in handicap (blinkered) at Wolverhampton on return to flat: probably stays 11f: sold 1,200 gns Ascot July Sales. *P. D. Evans*

SKETCHBOOK 2 ch.g. (Mar 6) Sharpo 132 – Cape Chestnut 87 (Bustino 136) 98 p [1995 6m 6m^5 5g^4 6g* 7.3d^4 Oct 19] 22,000Y: strong gelding: has a round action: half-brother to several winners, including useful 1987 2-y-o 6f winner Moogie (by Young Generation) and useful 7f (at 2 yrs) and 1¼m winner Dazzling Heights (by Shirley Heights): dam 1m winner: won maiden at Pontefract in September by 2½ lengths from Priolo Prima: progressed again when fourth to Tumbleweed Ridge in Horris Hill Stakes at Newbury, pulling hard early on then running on when getting clear run: stays 7f: acts on dead ground: taken early to post: sold 60,000 gns Newmarket Autumn Sales: should continue on the upgrade. *G. Lewis*

SKI ACADEMY (IRE) 2 b.c. (Feb 14) Royal Academy (USA) 130 – Cochineal 96 p (USA) 52 (Vaguely Noble 140) [1995 8.1m* 8g^3 7d Sep 26] 41,000Y: tall, rather unfurnished colt: first foal: dam stayed at least 11.7f: won maiden at Chepstow in August then much better form when 2 lengths third of 5 to Bonarelli in listed race at Goodwood following month: soundly beaten in valuable sales race at Newmarket last time: will do better over 1¼m+. *P. W. Chapple-Hyam*

SKI CHALET 3 b.f. Petoski 135 – Silver Lodge (Homing 130) [1994 NR 1995 – a12g Jul 13] first foal: dam well beaten on only outing: beaten over 30 lengths in Southwell claimer. *A. Hide*

SKIDDAW SAMBA 6 b.m. Viking (USA) – Gavea (African Sky 124) [1994 NR 38 + 1995 12m^4 12m Jul 20] second foal: dam twice-raced half-sister to very smart 1m to 1¼m winner Cataldi: fair form in 3 NH Flat races then won only start over hurdles in 1993/4 season: favourite, fourth of 9 in claimer at Catterick, pulling hard early on, weakening over 1f out: very stiff task and well beaten in similar event there 2 weeks later. *Mrs M. Reveley*

SKI FOR GOLD 2 b.f. (Apr 16) Shirley Heights 130 – Quest (USA) 90§ (The Minstrel (CAN) 135) [1995 7m^4 8g^6 7.1s* Oct 17] 82,000Y: quite attractive filly: good mover: half-sister to 4 winners, including 1¼m Grade 1 winner Bequest (by Sharpen Up) and useful miler Fitzcarraldo (by Riverman): dam, 9f and 1¼m winner, is sister to high-class French 2-y-o Treizieme and half-sister to Gold Cup second Eastern Mystic: won 19-runner maiden at Chepstow in October by a head from Lothlorien: will be well suited by middle distances: acts on soft ground: capable of more improvement. *J. L. Dunlop* — 76 p

SKILLINGTON (USA) 2 b.c. (Mar 19) Danzig (USA) – Annie Edge 118 (Nebbiolo 125) [1995 7g^2 7m^6 8m^3 8g^2 Sep 8] good-topped colt: has plenty of scope: has round action: half-brother to several winners, notably top-class miler Selkirk (by Sharpen Up): dam 5f and 7f, winner later won at up to 11f in USA: fairly useful form in maidens at Ascot (2), Newbury and Doncaster, making much of running and rallying when head second of 17 to Heron Island at Doncaster: stays 1m: sure to win a maiden. *I. A. Balding* — 92

SKIPMAN (IRE) 2 b.g. (Feb 20) Posen (USA) – Near Miracle (Be My Guest (USA) 126) [1995 a8.5g^6 Dec 9] IR 8,400Y resold 13,500Y: fourth foal: half-brother to 3 winners abroad by Bob Back: dam won at 7f in Ireland: beaten around 18 lengths when sixth of 13 in maiden at Wolverhampton. *N. A. Smith* — –

SKIPTAMALOO 4 b.f. Northern State (USA) 91 – Pronetta (USA) (Mr Prospector (USA)) [1994 32§: 10d 8m 7m a8g^6 a7g 7f^5 5.9h 6f^6 6g^5 5m 5g^4 6s 1995 5m 6g 6g 6f 7m 5m 6g^2 6m 6f 5g 5d^5 Sep 13] leggy filly: poor sprint maiden: best form on an easy surface: tried visored and blinkered. *Don Enrico Incisa* — 32

SKIP TO SOMERFIELD 3 ch.f. Shavian 125 – St Isadora (Lyphard (USA) 132) [1994 79: 6g* 6m^2 1995 8f 6m Jul 11] unfurnished filly: fair form at 2 yrs: no worthwhile form in minor event and handicap in 1995. *K. McAuliffe* — –

SKOLERN 11 b.g. Lochnager 132 – Piethorne 86 (Fine Blade (USA) 121) [1994 –: 8m a7g 1995 12.3d Apr 5] rather leggy, good-topped gelding: modest hurdler: no form on flat for long time. *A. Harrison* — –

SKRAM 2 b.c. (Mar 9) Rambo Dancer (CAN) 107 – Skarberg (FR) (Noir Et Or 125) [1995 7.1m 6.1d 7g Oct 3] 2,000F: lengthy, unfurnished colt: third reported foal: brother to 3-y-o Le Bal: dam won at 1¼m in France: poor form in varied maiden company: wore crossed noseband last 2 starts. *R. Dickin* — –

SKY DIVER 4 b.g. Salse (USA) 128 – Sutosky 78 (Great Nephew 126) [1994 –: 7.1s^6 6m^5 8.5g^6 8.3m a10g a8.5g 1995 7g 10.8m 7.1m^4 Jul 2] tall, close-coupled gelding: modest maiden: no worthwhile form since 1993. *B. J. Llewellyn* — –

SKY DOME (IRE) 2 ch.c. (Feb 2) Bluebird (USA) 125 – God Speed Her (Pas de Seul 133) [1995 5m^6 5m* 5d^4 Jun 8] IR 15,000F, IR 32,000Y: leggy colt: second foal: dam, Irish maiden, half-sister to smart middle-distance performer Noble Patriarch: won maiden at Carlisle in April: remote fourth of 6 in £7,900 event at Beverley 6 weeks later, soon outpaced in disadvantaged centre of track: will stay beyond 5f. *M. H. Tompkins* — 73

SKY GIRL 3 b.f. Statoblest 120 – Alpine Sunset (Auction Ring (USA) 123) [1994 NR 1995 7m^4 6g^4 Sep 2] 5,200F: 20,000Y: lengthy filly: third foal: half-sister to useful 5f to 6f winner Afif (by Midyan) and modest 5f to 1m winner Alpine Johnny (by Salse): dam unraced half-sister to Cyrano de Bergerac: modest maiden: stays 7f: pulled hard on debut. *C. B. B. Booth* — 59

SKY MUSIC 4 ch.f. Absalom 128 – On The Record 72 (Record Token 128) [1994 78: 7m* 7.1m^5 6g* 6m* 6g 1995 6m^5 7g^2 7m^4 Jul 24] good-quartered filly: fairly useful handicapper: good head second of 19 to Cadeaux Tryst in Bunbury Cup at Newmarket second start: effective at 6f and 7f: acts on good to firm ground: suitable mount for an apprentice: sometimes bandaged. *Miss S. E. Hall* — 85

SLANEY PROJECT (IRE) 3 b.g. Project Manager 111 – Sundrive (Status Seeker) [1994 6m^6 7m^4 7.8s^3 6.5g^2 7.8g 1995 9v* 10m^2 10s* 10m 10m 11.9g 14s 11.8g Oct 9] workmanlike gelding: not a good walker: seventh foal: half-brother to prolific winner at up to 1m Cool Enough (by Welsh Captain): dam poor Irish maiden: fair performer: trained until after third 3-y-o start by J. Bolger, successful in handicaps at Tipperary in March and the Curragh (made most) in April: below his — 76 d best in 5 handicaps here: probably stays 11.9f: acts on good to firm ground and heavy. *W. R. Muir*

SLAPY DAM 3 b.g. Deploy 131 – Key To The River (USA) (Irish River (FR) 131) [1994 57p: 7d 7g 1995 a8g^{5} a8g^{5} 10g^{2} 11.1g* 14.6m 11.6m 10m 10m^{3} 10.5m^{4} 10d^{4} 12s* 11.8g* 12.1s^{6} Oct 17] close-coupled gelding: fair handicapper: won at Edinburgh in April on third-last outing for Mrs J. Ramsden: in fine form in the autumn, winning at Folkestone (by 7 lengths) and Leicester: met plenty of trouble in running when beaten favourite on final start: will stay further than 1½m (out of form when tried): acts on good to firm and soft ground, probably on fibresand. *J. Mackie* 67

SLASHER JACK (IRE) 4 b.g. Alzao (USA) 117 – Sherkraine 98 (Shergar 140) [1994 89: 11.1g* 12.3m^{4} 12m* 11.9m^{5} 11.9f* 13.9m^{5} 11.9g^{6} 14.1g^{5} 12s^{6} 1995 12g 9.9m 12g^{6} 11.9m* 14g^{5} 11.9m^{2} 10m^{3} 11.9m^{3} Jul 14] leggy gelding: has a markedly round action: fairly useful handicapper: won at Haydock in May: effective at 1¼m to 1¾m: acts on firm ground, below best on a soft surface: blinkered (ran well) last 2 starts: best form on galloping tracks. *S. G. Norton* 84

SLEEP STANDING (IRE) 2 b.f. (May 1) Standaan (FR) 118 – Sleeping Car (Scorpio (FR) 127) [1995 a5g Jul 13] 5,800Y, 2,000 2-y-o: sixth foal: sister to Irish 7f winner Track Twenty Nine and 3-y-o Fred Said Right: dam unraced: 12/1, soundly beaten in seller at Southwell. *A. Harrison* –

SLEEPTITE (FR) 5 gr.g. Double Bed (FR) 121 – Rajan Grey (Absalom 128) [1994 56: a8g^{3} a10g a8g^{3} a10g^{5} a16g^{2} a16g^{5} a12g^{4} a10g^{2} a14.8g* a14g 1995 a13g* a12g^{2} a16g^{2} a14.8g^{3} 16.2m a12g^{3} a12g^{4} Sep 30] workmanlike gelding: poor mover: modest handicapper: won seller at Lingfield in February: effective at 1½m and stays 2m: best efforts on a sound surface or the all-weather: often ridden by claimer: held up in 1995. *W. G. M. Turner* – a65

SLEEPY BOY 2 br.g. (Apr 21) Zero Watt (USA) 107 – Furnace Lass VII (Damsire Unregistered) [1995 7f^{4} Oct 24] first known foal: dam, non-thoroughbred, never ran: 200/1, well-beaten fourth of 5 in minor event at Redcar. *W. Storey* –

SLICIOUS 3 b.c. Slip Anchor 136 – Precious Jade 72 (Northfields (USA)) [1994 8s^{3} 8v* 1995 8d^{2} 10f^{5} 12s* 12g* 12d^{2} 12m^{2} 10m* Nov 12] 41,000Y: half-brother to several winners, smart miler (won Group 1 event in Italy) Just A Flutter (by Beldale Flutter) easily the best of them: dam stayed 1m: progressive Italian colt: successful in maiden at Milan at 2 yrs and minor event at Milan and listed race at Turin in June: runner-up in Gran Premio d'Italia (no match for 3½ length winner Posidonas) at Milan and Prix du Conseil de Paris (running on, 2 lengths behind De Quest) at Longchamp: won 10-runner Premio Roma in November by 1½ lengths from Hollywood Dream, leading inside last: stays 1½m: acts on heavy ground and good to firm. *V. Caruso, Italy* 118

SLIP A COIN 4 b.f. Slip Anchor 136 – Luck Penny 87 (Bustino 136) [1994 52+: 10m 8.3m a12g^{4} 8.1d^{5} 1995 a7g^{3} a8g a8.5g^{2} a7g^{4} a9.4g* a9.4g^{2} a9.4g a9.4g a9.4g Sep 30] leggy filly: modest performer: made all in seller (sold out of R. Hollinshead's stable 5,400 gns) at Wolverhampton in February: left I. Campbell's stable after eighth start: stays 9.4f: acts on firm ground, dead and fibresand: takes keen hold and races prominently. *D. Burchell* 62

SLIPARIS 2 b.f. (Feb 12) Slip Anchor 136 – Parisian Express (FR) 48 (Siberian Express (USA) 125) [1995 8d Sep 27] 5,500Y: unfurnished filly: first foal: dam, 1m winner, granddaughter of Oaks winner Pia, also grandam of Chief Singer: 33/1, green and unimpressive to post, tailed off in maiden at Salisbury after leading to halfway. *K. O. Cunningham-Brown* –

SLIVOVITZ 5 b.g. Petoski 135 – Hiding 84 (So Blessed 130) [1994 68: 6m* 5g 6s 6m* 6.1g^{2} 6m^{3} 6m* 6d 6s^{5} 6.1g 1995 6m 6g 6m 6m 6f 6m 5f^{3} 6m^{3} a7g^{5} a6g Nov 30] rangy gelding: modest handicapper at best in 1995: suited by sprint distances: acts on equitrack and good to firm ground, probably on a soft surface: usually blinkered or visored, has won without either: successful for apprentice: usually a front runner. *M. J. Heaton-Ellis* 59

SLMAAT 4 ch.f. Sharpo 132 – Wasslaweyeh (USA) 66 (Damascus (USA)) [1994 76+: a7g* a7g 7m^{4} 8.2m^{4} 10m^{4} 8.1d^{5} 10.5s* 10d^{4} a12g* 1995 a11g* a11g^{3} a12g 11.8d^{2} 11.8m^{4} 12.3m 12g 12m 12.1s Nov 2] sparely-made filly: fair handicapper: won at Southwell in January: below form last 3 starts, left in stalls (reportedly 75 became stuck) at Edinburgh on final one: stays 1½m well: acts on fibresand and good to firm ground, looks well suited by a soft surface: has run well for 7-lb claimer: has joined D. Nicholls. *Mrs M. Reveley*

SLOE BRANDY 5 b.m. Hotfoot 126 – Emblazon 91 (Wolver Hollow 126) [1994 NR 1995 a12g Jul 13] shallow-girthed mare: poor form (rated 44) at 3 yrs for Sir Mark Prescott: no threat in handicap at Southwell on return: has joined O. Brennan. *A. P. Jarvis* –

SLYBIRD 3 b.f. Precocious 126 – Demerger 61 (Dominion 123) [1994 NR 1995 a7g a10g a6g⁶ Feb 14] 1,250Y: third foal: half-sister to 1993 2-y-o 5f winner Bev's Folly (by Chilibang): dam best at 2 yrs, is half-sister to dam of Tenby: no sign of ability. *M. J. Ryan* –

SLY'S FANCY 2 gr.f. (Apr 29) Rambo Dancer (CAN) 107 – Fancy Flight (FR) 74 (Arctic Tern (USA) 126) [1995 5g Sep 14] 6,300Y: half-sister to useful 1994 2-y-o 5f and 6f winner Sumoquinn (by Then Again), 1¼m seller winner Barley Cake (by Midyan) and a winner in Sweden by Prince Sabo: dam 1¼m winner: 33/1, mid-division in 18-runner seller at Ayr after showing up 3f: gave trouble at stalls: sold 550 gns Doncaster November Sales: sent to Denmark. *J. Berry* –

SLYTLY BEVELED 3 ch.c. Beveled (USA) – Bright Sunlight (Alzao (USA) 117) [1994 55, a64: 7.1g 6.1m⁵ 7.1g 6m⁵ a7g 7m⁶ 10g a8g⁴ a7g* 1995 a8g a7g⁴ a7g a9.4g⁴ a7g⁶ 8.3g* 9.2g⁴ 8m⁵ 8.2m⁶ 8m Aug 27] small colt: has a round action: modest performer: won claimer at Hamilton in May, hanging badly left: best efforts short of 1¼m: acts on good to firm ground and the all-weather: blinkered last 7 starts: sold 2,100 gns Newmarket September Sales. *N. P. Littmoden* 62 ? a41

SMART DEBUTANTE (IRE) 6 b.m. Glenstal (USA) 118 – Cecily (Prince Regent (FR) 129) [1994 NR 1995 a12g Jan 4] half-sister to several winners, including 7f and 1m winner Lady Lacey (by Kampala) and 1m and 9f winner Xylophone (by Tap On Wood): dam Irish 11.2f winner: modest maiden (rated 59) in Ireland for M. O'Toole in 1992: winning selling hurdler in 1993/4: tailed off in claimer at Wolverhampton first outing on flat since. *Miss S. J. Wilton* –

SMARTER CHARTER 2 br.c. (Mar 8) Master Willie 129 – Irene's Charter 72 (Persian Bold 123) [1995 6.1d 5s Sep 30] 15,500Y: tall, leggy colt: has scope: third foal: brother to 3-y-o 7f winner Master Charter: dam, probably best short of 1½m, won 4 races: never a factor in maidens at Nottingham and Haydock, better effort on debut when not knocked about to finish tenth of 19 after slow start from poor draw: will do better, particularly over 7f+. *Mrs J. R. Ramsden* – p

SMART FAMILY (USA) 4 ch.g. Homebuilder (USA) – Enceinte (USA) (Forli (ARG)) [1994 74: 8s 8g³ 7m³ 8m 1995 10.5m² Aug 4] useful-looking gelding: fair performer at 3 yrs: below-form short-head second of 5 in steadily-run claimer at Haydock only start in 1995: should have been suited by further than 1m: acted on good to firm ground and fibresand: pulled up lame over hurdles in August: dead. *M. C. Pipe* 58

SMART GENERATION 4 b.g. Cadeaux Genereux 131 – Gull Nook 120 (Mill Reef (USA) 141) [1994 78: 8.1g* 8.1m⁶ 10.3g³ 10g⁴ 12m 1995 10g* 12m 9g 10v⁴ 9d* Oct 21] workmanlike, good-topped gelding: good walker: found to have irregular heartbeat final 3-y-o start: made into a fairly useful handicapper in 1995, winning 16-runner race in May and rated stakes in October (beat Wilcuma a short head), both at Newbury: stays 1¼m well: acts on heavy going: visored (ran creditably) penultimate 3-y-o outing: sold 46,000 gns Newmarket Autumn Sales. *Lord Huntingdon* 94

SMART GUEST 3 ch.g. Be My Guest (USA) 126 – Konbola 91 (Superlative 118) [1994 96: 6g³ 6s⁶ 6m² 6m* 6m³ 7m⁵ 6.3d* 7m 1995 7m 8m* 7f⁴ 8m 7.1m Jul 7] sturdy, lengthy gelding: unimpressive mover: fairly useful performer: landed the odds in claimer at Newmarket (claimed out of M. Bell's stable £16,000) in May: soundly beaten in competitive handicaps last 2 starts: stays 1m: acts on firm and dead ground: takes keen hold. *J. A. Harris* 90

SMART TEACHER (USA) 5 b. or br.h. Smarten (USA) – Finality (USA) (In Reality) [1994 53: 8.5m* 7.5g³ 8.3m⁴ 8.3m⁶ 7s 1995 a10g⁶ a8g 8.3m 7.5m Jul 7] big, useful-looking horse: fluent mover: modest performer in 1994 for P. Harris: well beaten at 5 yrs, including visored and in sellers: stays 8.5f: best form on a sound –

surface and acts on firm ground (ran poorly on soft final 4-y-o start): headstrong, and usually makes running: one to treat with caution: sold 1,400 gns Ascot July Sales. *K. R. Burke*

SMILE FOREVER (USA) 2 b.f. (Mar 27) Sunshine Forever (USA) – Awenita (Rarity 129) [1995 6.9f² 8.2d⁵ 7m Oct 28] $57,000Y: sturdy filly: closely related to smart middle-distance winner Fly Away Soon (by Lear Fan) and a winner in North America by Darby Creek Road and half-brother to a winner in USA: dam unraced: ½-length second of 7 to Expensive Taste in maiden at Folkestone: failed to progress (took good hold) in similar events at Nottingham and Newmarket: bred to stay further than 1m but is headstrong. *P. F. I. Cole* 69

SMILEY FACE 3 b.g. Colmore Row 111 – Count On Me 77 (No Mercy 126) [1994 47: 5.1f³ 5.1m⁶ 6m 6m 1995 5.1m May 2] sparely-made gelding: poor maiden. *R. J. Hodges* –

SMILING BESS 2 b.f. (Mar 30) Salse (USA) 128 – Wanda 74 (Taufan (USA) 119) [1995 6.1d 5s Sep 30] first reported foal: dam sprinter: well beaten in maidens at Nottingham and Haydock. *K. R. Burke* –

SMILING THRU 3 b.g. Reference Point 139 – Ever Genial 117 (Brigadier Gerard 144) [1994 –: 8g 8d 1995 12.5m Apr 17] angular gelding: behind in maidens and claimer. *H. R. A. Cecil* –

SMILIN N WISHIN (USA) 2 b.f. (Feb 3) Lyphard's Wish (FR) 124 – Smilin Michele (USA) (Sharpen Up 127) [1995 8.1s² Oct 17] $30,000 2-y-o: fourth foal: dam unraced half-sister to Smiling And Dancin (by Lyphard's Wish), winner of Grade 3 events at around 1m: 5/1 from 5/2, ¾-length second of 11 to comfortable winner Classic Eagle in maiden at Chepstow, chasing leaders and staying on well: will improve. *P. W. Chapple-Hyam* 79 p

SMITHEREENS 2 ch.f. (Mar 4) Primo Dominie 121 – Splintering 80 (Sharpo 132) [1995 6g 5m² Nov 6] good-topped, quick-actioned filly with scope: third foal: half-sister to 3-y-o 5f and 6f winner Midnight Break (by Night Shift): dam sprinter: 4 lengths second of 9, clear, to Pivotal in minor event at Folkestone in November: speedy: may improve again. *P. T. Walwyn* 74

SMOCKING 5 ch.m. Night Shift (USA) – Sue Grundy 104 (Grundy 137) [1994 39: a12g² a14g a12g 1995 12m² 10f⁵ 11.5g⁴ 12m 12m a13g a12g a10g⁴ Dec 18] angular, plain mare: poor maiden handicapper: stays at least 1½m: acts on good to firm ground and equitrack: blinkered once at 3 yrs: sold 1,700 gns Ascot December Sales. *J. Pearce* 35

SMOLENSK (IRE) 3 b.g. Ela-Mana-Mou 132 – Merry Twinkle (Martinmas 128) [1994 –: 7g⁵ 1995 7.1m 10.2m⁵ 8m⁶ a7g⁴ a8.5g³ 8.1m⁴ Jul 3] tall, workmanlike gelding: modest maiden: stays 1¼m: acts on fibresand and good to firm ground: lacks pace. *J. Berry* 61

SMOLENSK (USA) 3 b.f. Danzig (USA) – Blush With Pride (USA) (Blushing Groom (FR) 131) [1994 6.5g* 1995 6.5g² 8d⁴ 8g* 8m² 8g* 8g 8m⁵ Sep 3] 118

Prix d'Astarte, Deauville—leading French fillies Smolensk (left) and Shaanxi are separated by half a length

Mme Paul de Moussac's "Smolensk"

good-topped, attractive filly: seventh foal: closely related to an allowance winner (at around 1m) by Nijinsky and half-sister to 2 minor winners by Devil's Bag: dam, won Kentucky Oaks, is half-sister to Gielgud and Malinowski: won newcomers event at Craon at 2 yrs: smart performer: 4 lengths fourth of 16 to Matiara in Poule d'Essai des Pouliches (hampered early in straight) at Longchamp before winning Prix de Sandringham (2/1 on) at Chantilly, then 2 lengths second of 10 to Ridgewood Pearl in Coronation Stakes at Royal Ascot before landing Prix d'Astarte (by ½ length from Shaanxi) at Deauville: ran very well when 2½ lengths fifth of 8 to Ridgewood Pearl in Prix du Moulin de Longchamp final start: stays 1m: acts on good to firm ground, probably on dead, yet to race on extremes. *A. Fabre, France*

SMOOTH HOUND 4 b.g. Petong 126 – Ocean Hound 53 (Main Reef 126) [1994 NR 1995 10.2m 8f Jul 1] neat gelding: modest maiden (rated 60) at 2 yrs for B. Hills: blinkered, well beaten on return to flat. *M. C. Pipe* –

SMUGGLER'S POINT (USA) 5 b.g. Lyphard (USA) 132 – Smuggly (USA) 121 (Caro 133) [1994 67: 13.3s 14g 16.2m^5 11.4m^4 14g^5 1995 14.1g 15.4m Sep 7] sturdy gelding: fair staying handicapper: well below form in 1995: has joined R. O'Sullivan. *J. J. Bridger* –

SMUGGLING 4 b.c. Slip Anchor 136 – Strigida 120 (Habitat 134) [1994 61+: 14.1m* 13.9d^4 1995 14.9d^2 16.4m* 16m* 20m^3 Jun 20] big, rangy, angular colt: trained by H. Cecil at 3 yrs: improved into a fairly useful handicapper in 1995, winning at Sandown and Newbury (made all) in May: not seen out after good third of 27 to Harlestone Brook in Ascot Stakes: stays 2½m: yet to race on extremes of going: races prominently: genuine. *R. Akehurst* 87

SNAKE PLISSKEN (IRE) 4 ch.g. Reasonable (FR) 119 – Shalie (Windjammer (USA)) [1994 44: a8g4 a7g4 7m6 8.1g 8.3m 1995 8.1m4 a8.5g5 8g a7g5 a10g6 Dec 18] poor handicapper: should stay beyond 1m: acts on all-weather surfaces and good to firm ground: sometimes wears tongue strap. *D. Haydn Jones* 46

SNICKERSNEE 7 b.g. Kris 135 – Cat Girl (USA) (Grey Dawn II 132) [1994 NR 1995 a16.2g Jul 21] big, rangy gelding: no worthwhile form on flat since 3 yrs. *Paddy Farrell* –

SNIPE HALL 4 b.f. Crofthall 110 – Geopelia 109 (Raffingora 130) [1994 NR 1995 5m 5g4 6m6 6m May 16] leggy, good-quartered filly: fairly useful sprinter: reportedly returned lame on final 4-y-o start: effective at 5f and 6f: acts on firm and soft going, possibly not on heavy: sometimes very edgy: bandaged behind in 1995. *T. R. Watson* 88

SNITCH 2 ch.g. (May 7) Blow The Whistle 72 – Whispering Sea 52 (Bustino 136) [1995 a5g6 5m5 5g 5m5 5g2 5m 5m a6g a5g a5g Dec 1] lengthy, sparely-made gelding: second foal: brother to a poor maiden: dam ran twice: front-running plater: barely stays 5f: no form on fibresand: visored/blinkered last 7 starts. *C. Smith* 49 a–

SNOW DOMINO (IRE) 2 ch.g. (May 6) Habyom – Magic Picture (Deep Diver 134) [1995 7f a8g5 a8.5g Dec 2] strong gelding: half-brother to fair 7f/1m performer Highland Magic (by Stalker): dam Irish sprint maiden: well beaten in claimer and maidens. *J. M. Jefferson*

SNOW DREAM 5 b.m. Siberian Express (USA) 125 – National Dress 64 (Welsh Pageant 132) [1994 –: 9.7s 1995 a12g a12g5 15.4g4 13g a16g5 14.9g* 15.8g* 16.5g6 14.6g Jul 1] lengthy mare: poor handicapper: won at Warwick (first time) in May and Catterick (hung badly right) in June: ran as if something amiss final start: stays 2m: sold 1,700 gns Doncaster November Sales. *M. J. Ryan* 46

SNOW FALCON 2 b.g. (Feb 14) Polar Falcon (USA) 126 – Cameroun 106 (African Sky 124) [1995 7m3 7f6 6m6 7.3d Sep 15] 19,000Y: unfurnished gelding: half-brother to 7f/8.5f winner Eternal Flame (by Primo Dominie) and Italian 7.5f winner Pelican Island (by Damister): dam 2-y-o 5f winner: third of 9 to Swift Fandango in maiden at Newmarket in July: rather disappointing afterwards in nursery at Newbury final start. *M. Bell* 76

SNOW FOOT 3 b.f. Formidable (USA) 125 – Able Mabel 77 (Absalom 128) [1994 47: 6m 6m a6g6 1995 6g a5g Jun 30] strong, good-bodied filly: poor maiden: broke down final start: stayed 6f: dead. *P. C. Haslam* –

SNOWING 4 gr.f. Tate Gallery (USA) 117 – Biding 97 (Habat 127) [1994 81: 5m* 5g 5m* 6d 5d3 5m6 5d 1995 5g2 5g 5g2 5m 5g 5g6 5m4 5m4 5m3 5g6 Oct 28] angular filly: fairly useful handicapper: mostly creditable efforts in 1995, including third of 12 to Croft Pool in rated stakes at Newmarket on penultimate start, always well there: best form at 5f: acts on good to firm and dead ground: sold 15,000 gns Newmarket December Sales. *T. Stack, Ireland* 88

SNOWPOLES 2 b.f. (Mar 19) High Estate 127 – Bronzewing 103 (Beldale Flutter (USA) 130) [1995 7.6d Sep 14] 4,000Y: fourth foal: half-sister to 3-y-o Snowy Petrel (by Petorius) and 2m winner Sun Grebe (by Arctic Tern): dam 6f and 1m winner: 25/1, over 7 lengths seventh of 12 to Patria in maiden at Lingfield, leading 5f: should improve. *Mrs J. Cecil* 57 p

SNOW PRINCESS (IRE) 3 b.f. Ela-Mana-Mou 132 – Karelia (USA) 111 (Sir Ivor 135) [1994 60p: 7.1g6 1995 10m 10.5g6 10.5s* 12.1s* 12m* 12m* Nov 4] leggy 87 p

Tote Credit November Handicap, Doncaster—a four-timer for Snow Princess; she and Dato Star are clear

filly: progressed extremely well in second half of 1995, winning minor event at Haydock and handicaps at Chepstow and Newmarket in October, and 18-runner £24,800 Tote Credit November Handicap (favourite, quickened on 2f out and beat Dato Star 1½ lengths) at Doncaster: much better at 1½m than shorter and will stay at least 1¾m: acts on good to firm and soft ground: idled in front at Doncaster: open to further improvement and should make a useful performer in 1996. *Lord Huntingdon*

SNOW QUEEN (USA) 3 b.f. Gone West (USA) – Lady Ice (CAN) (Vice Regent (CAN)) [1994 NR 1995 8g Jun 3] $150,000Y: sixth foal: closely related to 3 winners in USA by Fappiano, including Surging, Grade 2 winner at around 7f: dam, listed winner, was runner-up in Canadian Oaks: backward and edgy, well-beaten eighth of 12 to Bin Rosie in maiden at Newmarket: sent to Japan. *J. H. M. Gosden* –

SNOWTOWN (IRE) 3 b.f. Alzao (USA) 117 – Golden Bough (USA) (Graustark) [1994 102: 7f* 7d^5 8g^6 8g^3 1995 11.4m^4 10m 10m^5 12d^3 12v^5 10d^2 Oct 29] rangy filly: has a fluent, round action: useful performer: inconsistent in 1995, best effort when third in listed race at Ascot in September: stayed 1½m: best efforts on good to soft ground (well beaten on heavy): front runner last 3 starts: stud. *P. W. Chapple-Hyam* 103

SNOW VALLEY 3 b.c. Shirley Heights 130 – Mountain Lodge 120 (Blakeney 126) [1994 62p: 8m 1995 10m 12m^3 12.3m^6 11.6m^6 14m^2 14s Sep 28] rangy colt: good walker: fair maiden: well beaten on soft ground: lacks turn of foot, and looks out-and-out stayer: sent to Dubai. *L. M. Cumani* 79

SNOWY PETREL (IRE) 3 b.c. Petorius 117 – Bronzewing 103 (Beldale Flutter (USA) 130) [1994 81: 7m^5 7m^2 7.5g 1995 9m 9m 8m^3 10m^4 11.8g^4 12m^{wo} 12.3m^4 16g 12g^2 12.1d^5 14.6m Oct 20] rangy colt: good mover, with a long stride: fairly useful handicapper: walked over in minor event at Thirsk in August: ran well most other 3-y-o starts: stays 1½m (refused to settle over 2m): acts on good to firm ground and dead: often a front runner: sold (J. Dunlop to K. Bailey) 22,000 gns Newmarket Autumn Sales. *J. L. Dunlop* 80

SOAKING 5 b.g. Dowsing (USA) 124 – Moaning Low 85 (Burglar 128) [1994 69: 7m^2 7.6g 8f 8.3m^6 7f* 7g 7g a7g^2 a8g^3 a7g* a8g a7g a7g^6 1995 a7g^2 7g 7m^5 a8g^6 7.1m a8g^5 7.1m* 7f^2 7m^2 8.3m 7m 7.1d^5 8d Sep 27] strong, useful-looking gelding: fair performer: made most to win seller at Chepstow in July on final outing for G. L. Moore: stays 1m: acts on firm and soft ground and on equitrack: none too consistent. *P. Burgoyne* 67

SO AMAZING 3 b.f. Hallgate 127 – Jussoli (Don 128) [1994 58: 5g^4 6m^4 5m^4 6s^3 1995 10m^6 7g^4 8m^4 5.9h^3 7m^6 Oct 20] strong, good-topped filly: good walker: modest maiden handicapper: headstrong, and likely to prove best at up to 1m: acts on good to firm and soft ground, seemingly not on hard: tends to wander under pressure: wears bandages. *Miss S. E. Hall* 61

SOBA GUEST (IRE) 6 ch.g. Be My Guest (USA) 126 – Brazilian Princess 66 (Absalom 128) [1994 –§, a60d: a6g^2 a5g^4 a6g^5 a6g^6 a6g^4 6s^5 6g 6d^6 a6g a7g^4 1995 a6g a7g^6 a9.4g^6 a7g^4 a7g 12.5g 16m Jun 26] close-coupled gelding: poor sprinter: acts on the all-weather (no form on turf since 1992): sometimes visored/blinkered: inconsistent and not one to trust: sold 1,450 gns Ascot October Sales. *R. T. Juckes* – §

SOBA UP 5 ch.m. Persian Heights 129 – Soba 127 (Most Secret 119) [1994 59d: 11.1f^2 10g 12.3m 10.3g 12f 10d^4 10.5d^2 10.4d 10d^5 10.1d^3 12.1g^2 1995 12g^3 9.2g^3 9.9m^6 12d 12.1m* 11.1f* 12.3m* 11.1m^2 12.1f* 12.3m* 12m^2 12.3m^2 13.4m^3 13.9g 14.1m 12.1s^4 Nov 2] big, lengthy, workmanlike mare: fair handicapper: had a good season, successful 3 times at Edinburgh and twice at Chester in the summer: yet to win on any other course: stays 13.4f well: acts on firm and soft going: blinkered (below form) fourth 5-y-o start: tough and genuine. *T. J. Etherington* 74

SOBELOVED 3 gr.g. Beveled (USA) – Miss Solo (Runnymede 123) [1994 46: 5m 6m 5g 6m 1995 6.9d^3 8.3g 8g 8.3m 8.1m^2 8.2m 8.1m^5 7.6m^4 7f^4 8h 7d Oct 19] leggy, sparely-made gelding: modest maiden: left M. Channon after seventh 3-y-o start: stays 1m: acts on good to firm and dead ground: none too consistent. *N. E. Berry* 50

SOBERING THOUGHTS 9 ch.g. Be My Guest (USA) 126 – Soba 127 (Most Secret 119) [1994 69: 5f 6g 6m 6m^4 6f^3 6.1g 6m^3 7d 7g^3 6g 7g 1995 7g^4 6f^6 6m^4 5.9f^4 6m Jun 13] big, plain gelding: modest handicapper: stays 7f: best form on a sound 64 surface: usually blinkered at 6 yrs, not since: suitable mount for an apprentice: usually races up with pace. *J. L. Eyre*

SOCIAL REGISTER 3 ch.c. Unfuwain (USA) 131 – Bluebook (USA) 120 (Secretariat (USA)) [1994 46: 7g 6.1s^5 1995 7.1m 8.2m 8g 6g^5 Jul 1] good-bodied colt: poor maiden: should have stayed 7f: acted on soft ground: blinkered (ran well) final start: dead. *H. Thomson Jones* 41

SOCIETY GIRL 2 b.f. (Apr 17) Shavian 125 – Sirene Bleu Marine (USA) (Secreto (USA) 128) [1995 6g 6m* 7g* 7m^2 7m^3 6g^3 6.5m 7m^6 Oct 30] workmanlike filly: has a fluent, round action: second foal: half-sister to 3-y-o Boost (by Superpower): dam never ran: easy winner of sellers at Thirsk in June and Newmarket (retained for 20,000 gns) in July: placed in nurseries and claimer afterwards: stays 7f: sometimes bandaged. *C. W. Thornton* 73 ?

SOCIETY MAGIC (USA) 2 b.g. (Mar 6) Imp Society (USA) – Lady Kirtling (USA) (Kirtling 129) [1995 7.9m^5 8.1s^6 Oct 17] 13,500F: big gelding: has scope: has a round action: fourth foal: half-brother to winners in USA by Far North and Irish Tower (2): dam unraced: fifth of 13 to Prince of My Heart in median auction maiden at York, fading noticeably closing stages: well beaten on soft ground in maiden at Chepstow 13 days later. *I. A. Balding* 63

SOCIETY SUE (IRE) 2 b.f. (Mar 28) Mac's Imp (USA) 116 – Ivory Wisdom (USA) (Sir Ivor 135) [1995 7m 5m 5f^5 6h^4 5h^2 Aug 21] 1,700 2-y-o: leggy filly: fourth reported foal: dam never ran: modest form: runner-up in seller final start: stays 6f: acts on hard ground: slowly away first 2 starts: withdrawn after thoroughly obstinate display final appearance: clearly temperamental. *Ronald Thompson* 50 §

SODA POPINSKI (USA) 7 b.g. Sir Ivor 135 – Four Runs (USA) (Reviewer (USA)) [1994 NR 1995 a8g a14.8g Jul 17] quite attractive gelding: poor maiden on flat: winning hurdler. *J. L. Harris* –

SO DISCREET (USA) 7 b.g. Secreto (USA) 128 – I'll Be Around (USA) (Isgala) [1994 NR 1995 a13g^2 a13g^6 a16g^6 Feb 16] smallish, round-barrelled gelding: fair jumper: poor form at best on flat in 1995: sold 1,000 gns Doncaster July Sales: stays 13f well: acts on equitrack and has form on any turf going. *J. White* 42

SO FACTUAL (USA) 5 br.h. Known Fact (USA) 135 – Sookera (USA) 117 (Roberto (USA) 131) [1994 117: a6g^2 a5g* a7g* a7g* 6f^2 1995 6g^2 6m* 6g 5m* 6f^3 Dec 17] 120

The lightly-raced five-year-old So Factual had a busier and more successful season in Britain than he had had in any of the previous three. He won two races, including the Nunthorpe Stakes at York in August with a career-best effort. That was his fourth run in Britain, three more than he'd managed here in 1994 (though he ran four times in the United Arab Emirates very early in the year) and one more than in either 1992 or 1993 (when he won the Free Handicap). The Nunthorpe is a Group 1

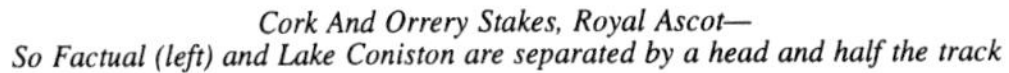

Cork And Orrery Stakes, Royal Ascot—
So Factual (left) and Lake Coniston are separated by a head and half the track

contest, the only one over five furlongs in Britain since the demotion of the King's Stand Stakes, but the latest field hardly looked up to Group 1 standard and it required no more than a smart performance for So Factual to win. His success was clear cut: he travelled well through the race, held up as usual, quickened to lead over a furlong out and was well on top at the line. He beat the outsider Ya Malak, running the race of his life, a length and a half, with Hever Golf Rose, the subsequent Prix de l'Abbaye winner who wasn't at her best, the same distance away third. Another runner below form was the odds-on Mind Games who faded into sixth after taking time to recover from a slow start.

Earlier in the season, So Factual had run three times against Lake Coniston. He ran second to him, no match, in the Duke of York Stakes at York on his reappearance and seventh of nine, reportedly unsuited by rain-softened ground, in the July Cup at Newmarket, a much stronger race than the Nunthorpe though both have the same status officially. In between, So Factual got the better of Lake Coniston by a head in the Cork And Orrery Stakes at Royal Ascot where the pair fought out the finish after racing wide apart. There's no doubt overall though which is the better. After York, So Factual was due to run in the Haydock Park Sprint but was withdrawn on the day of the race due to the ground. He wasn't seen again in Britain but ran in mid-December in the Sprinters Stakes at Nakayama in Japan where he finished third to two local runners, Hishi Akebono and Biko Pegasus. In doing so he earned over £156,000, virtually half as much again as his two wins in Britain were worth. So Factual went to Dubai from Japan, to spend his third winter there.

So Factual (USA) (br.h. 1990)	Known Fact (USA) (b 1977)	In Reality (b 1964)	Intentionally
			My Dear Girl
		Tamerett (b or br 1962)	Tim Tam
			Mixed Marriage
	Sookera (USA) (br 1975)	Roberto (b 1969)	Hail To Reason
			Bramalea
		Irule (gr 1968)	Young Emperor
			Iaround

The strong, attractive So Factual is the best offspring so far produced by Sookera who won the 1977 Cheveley Park Stakes on her final racecourse appearance. Her previous winners include the lightly-raced maiden winners Kerali (by High Line) and Krameria (by Kris), Field Dancer (by Northfields) who was very useful at around a mile and raced rather more often than most of her relatives, and Soothfast (by Riverman) who won on the flat in France before showing fairly useful form over hurdles from a few starts. Further back in So Factual's pedigree there are mostly minor winners, though the grandam Irule is a half-sister to I'm A Pleasure, a filly who was rated only 5 lb behind the best of her age at two years. So Factual, a fluent mover, was more settled in 1995 than previously. He stays seven furlongs but

Nunthorpe Stakes, York—So Factual asserts from Ya Malak and Hever Golf Rose

Godolphin's "So Factual"

his best form is over sprint distances on a sound surface, his very best on top-of-the-ground. *Saeed bin Suroor*

SO INTREPID (IRE) 5 ch.h. Never So Bold 135 – Double River (USA) (Irish River (FR) 131) [1994 83d: 6s* 6m 7f^4 7.3g 6g 6g 6d a7g^5 a6g^5 1995 a6g a6g^4 6g^6 6m 6g^6 5g* 6g^2 5g* 5.7f 5g^3 5m* 6f^4 5.1m 6m 6g^6 5g Sep 23] tall, close-coupled horse: fair performer: won seller at Newcastle in May, minor event at Warwick in June and handicap at Newcastle in July: effective at 5f and 6f: acts on firm and soft ground: has run well when sweating. *J. M. Bradley* — 78 a–

SOLANO (IRE) 3 ch.g. Aragon 118 – Hard To Stop 77 (Hard Fought 125) [1994 50: 5.1m 5m 6d 7m a6g 1995 a7.5g^6 7.5d^5 6m Apr 25] compact gelding: blind in near eye: unimpressive mover: poor maiden: well beaten in 1995, including median auction event at Folkestone. *Alex Vanderhaeghen, Belgium* — –

SOLAR CRYSTAL (IRE) 2 b.f. (May 7) Alzao (USA) 117 – Crystal Spray 75 (Beldale Flutter (USA) 130) [1995 6m* 6m^4 7.1g^2 8g* 8d^3 Oct 1] — 110

It was fitting that Henry Cecil should gain the three-hundredth pattern-race win of his career in the May Hill Stakes, a race the trainer has now won nine times, beginning with Formulate in 1978. Since the race gained Group 3 status in 1981, Bright Crocus, Ever Genial, Laluche, Intimate Guest, Tessla, Rafha, Midnight Air and, in the latest season, Solar Crystal, have contributed to the triple century by winning the May Hill. Solar Crystal was not her stable's first choice for the May Hill, but when Bosra Sham bruised a foot she was allowed to take her chance. Her starting price of 15/2, longer than any of Cecil's previous winners, seemed to reflect her status as understudy. Solar Crystal had shown progressive form in her three starts prior to the May Hill. After easily winning a maiden on her debut at Leicester in May over six furlongs, she reached the frame in listed races at Newmarket and Sandown in July, on the latter occasion ridden more aggressively and seeing out the seven furlongs well to be beaten one and a quarter lengths by Tamnia with the promise of further improvement to come over a mile. Favourite for the eleven-strong contest at Doncaster was Ruznama, winner of a Newmarket maiden on her previous start and the preferred ride of Willie Carson over unbeaten second-favourite and winner of the Sweet Solera Stakes Bint Salsabil. Next in the betting came Prix du Calvados runner-up Like A Hawk and Lowther-third Sweet Robin, with Solar Crystal sharing joint-fifth spot with Staffin. Partnered as usual by Willie Ryan, Solar Crystal was again ridden to make the most of her stamina and had her rivals in trouble fully three furlongs out. Keeping up the gallop really well, Solar Crystal had one and a quarter lengths to spare at the line over Like A Hawk who had chased her throughout, with Ruznama staying on for third a further three quarters of a length back. Ruznama won a listed race at Newmarket next time out and Bint Salsabil the Rockfel Stakes.

Most of Cecil's May Hill winners that ran again in their first season had the Fillies' Mile as their next target but, with Bosra Sham fully recovered, Solar Crystal became the first of her stable's May Hill winners to go to Longchamp for the Prix Marcel Boussac. It seemed virtually certain that she would have to improve again to figure in the shake-up. Unlikely to do so in a typically-run French race, with a steady pace to the home turn and a rush in the straight, Ryan repeated the tactics which had worked so well at Doncaster, setting a strong gallop on the soft surface that Solar Crystal was encountering for the first time. Although soon tackled by the favourite Shake The Yoke in the straight, Solar Crystal fought back bravely on the rails to be beaten a head by that filly, both succumbing to the late challenge of Miss Tahiti who won by two lengths.

Solar Crystal (IRE) (b.f. May 7, 1993)	Alzao (USA) (b 1980)	Lyphard (b 1969)	Northern Dancer
			Goofed
		Lady Rebecca (b 1971)	Sir Ivor
			Pocahontas II
	Crystal Spray (b 1986)	Beldale Flutter (b 1978)	Accipiter
			Flitter Flutter
		Crystal Fountain (b 1977)	Great Nephew
			Crystal Palace

Although Solar Crystal's sire Alzao won his only pattern race as a four-year-old over one and a half miles on heavy ground and has a middle-distance pedigree, he's far from being a sire of late-developers, or indeed, purely middle-distance performers. Sussex Stakes winner Second Set is his best produce to date and he has had plenty of success with two-year-olds, particularly fillies. Alzao's first Group 1 winners in Britain were the Cheveley Park winners Pass The Peace and Capricciosa.

May Hill Stakes, Doncaster—Solar Crystal extends Henry Cecil's outstanding record in the race with a game success over Like A Hawk

Owner Michael Poland has had plenty of success in recent years. His colours have been carried to victory in the last two runnings of the Isle of Wight Grand National and, even more notably, on the Flat by such as Midnight Air (the 1991 May Hill winner), King's Theatre (whom he owned in partnership with Sheikh Mohammed) and Solar Crystal's half-sister State Crystal (by High Estate) who won the Lancashire Oaks and was third in the Yorkshire Oaks and Prix Vermeille. State Crystal, another frequent front-runner, is the first foal out of Crystal Spray. Solar Crystal is the second to live, and the third is a 1995 filly by Brief Truce. Much of Mr Poland's success as a breeder (he was listed with four broodmares in 1995) comes from remnants of the Childwick Bury Stud. King's Theatre's dam came from that source, as did the useful stayer High Fountain (a half-sister to Crystal Spray) whose first foal Brighstone won both his starts in 1995. Crystal Spray herself provided strictly limited returns on the racecourse, winning a mile-and-three-quarter maiden at Down Royal as a four-year-old, but fetched 500,000 guineas when sold in foal to Sadler's Wells at the latest Tattersalls' December Sales. Solar Crystal's grandam Crystal Fountain was well beaten on her only start, but that mattered little at Mr Joel's bloodstock dispersal in 1986 in which she made 380,000 guineas—she was a half-sister to the Two Thousand Guineas and Derby winner Royal Palace and to Glass Slipper, the dam of St Leger winner Light Cavalry and One Thousand Guineas winner Fairy Footsteps. These Joel classic winners descended from another, the 1944 One Thousand Guineas winner Picture Play who is also the ancestress of recent Oaks winners User Friendly and Moonshell.

Solar Crystal improved with every race in her first season and there is good reason to think that she will do well as a three-year-old, particularly when campaigned over middle distances. She should add further to her trainer's pattern-race tally. A neat filly who is an easy mover, Solar Crystal has shown herself thoroughly genuine. *H. R. A. Cecil*

SOLAR FLIGHT 3 b.c. Soviet Star (USA) 128 – Fanciful (FR) (Gay Mecene (USA) 128) [1994 NR 1995 8m* 10m4 7m* 8f5 8g Sep 28] quite attractive colt: unimpressive mover: third foal: dam, French 1m winner, half-sister to Lowther winner Kingscote out of sprinter/miler Bold Fantasy: useful form: won newcomers race at Newmarket in April and minor event (clearly best effort) at Yarmouth in July: well below form last 2 starts: will prove best at up to 1m: has raced only on a sound surface: takes good hold, and often taken alone to post: sent to UAE. *B. W. Hills* — 100

SOLAR ONE (FR) 3 b.c. Alleged (USA) 138 – Nouvelle Lune (FR) (Be My Guest (USA) 126) [1994 115p: 8d* 10s2 1995 11m2 10.5d2 May 14] leggy, close-coupled French colt: smart performer: second in strongly-run 6-runner Prix Noailles (bandaged, short neck behind Walk On Mix) and 6-runner Prix Lupin (on toes, set steady pace and beaten a length by Flemensfirth), both at Longchamp: subsequently joined A. Spanu: will be suited by 1½m+: acts on good to firm ground and soft: missed Prix du Jockey-Club due to a bout of coughing. *J. E. Pease, France* — 115

SOLATIUM (IRE) 3 b.g. Rainbow Quest (USA) 134 – Consolation 95 (Troy 137) [1994 51p: 7s 1995 12f 10.4m5 14.1m Oct 19] lengthy, good-topped gelding: modest maiden: sold out of J. Gosden's stable 10,500 gns Newmarket July Sales (and gelded) after reappearance: unimpressive to post, hung on turn and tenderly handled at York on penultimate start: should be well suited by 1½m+. *M. C. Pipe* — –

SOLAZZI (FR) 3 b.f. Saint Cyrien (FR) 128 – Sunclad (FR) (Tennyson (FR) 124) [1994 NR 1995 10m Jun 5] 2,700Y: workmanlike filly: has a round action: sixth reported foal: half-sister to French 11.5f winner Zinzio (by Zino) and Irish 7f winner Suntan (by Sicyos): dam French 1¼m winner: 50/1, towards rear in maiden at Windsor. *L. G. Cottrell* — –

SOLDIER COVE (USA) 5 ch.g. Manila (USA) – Secret Form 120 (Formidable (USA) 125) [1994 NR 1995 5g4 10.1s5 10.4m 6f Oct 23] sparely-made gelding: first foal: dam won Prix de l'Opera and stayed 10.5f: trained at 2 and 3 yrs in France by F. Boutin, winning 1m newcomers event at Maisons-Laffitte: went to Dubai but did not race: sold 2,500 gns Newmarket July (1995) Sales: apparently best effort here when staying-on fourth of 13 in 5f claimer at Sandown (racing toward favoured far side): well beaten last 2 starts: should prove effective at middle distances. *Martyn Meade* — 57 ?

SOLDIER MAK 2 ch.g. (Apr 6) Infantry 122 – Truly Blest 75 (So Blessed 130) [1995 6m 7g 8f 6.9m Nov 6] 5,000Y: workmanlike gelding: ninth live foal: — 62 half-brother to winners abroad by Pas de Seul and General Holme: dam 9f winner in Ireland, is half-sister to Cry of Truth: best effort in maiden events (though never placed to challenge) when remote seventh of 13 to Bright Water at Yarmouth in October on third start: bred to need a good test of stamina. *A. Hide*

SOLDIER'S LEAP (FR) 3 b.c. Warning 136 – Thalestria (FR) 91 (Mill Reef (USA) 141) [1994 73: 7m^6 7g 8s 7m a8g* a7g^2 a8g^4 1995 a10g a8g^3 a9.4g* a8g* a10g^4 10m^6 8d^5 8d^4 10g^3 12f^4 8g^2 10g^4 8.5g^5 10.5g 8d 8m^2 8g* 10g 8s^4 Dec 5] workmanlike colt: fair performer: wide-margin winner of claimer at Wolverhampton and handicap at Lingfield in February (claimed out of C. Brittain's stable 151,200 francs at Deauville on eleventh start): claimed out of S. Wattel's stable 128,888 francs at Longchamp 5 starts later: won handicap at Compiegne later in October on first outing for new connections: stays 1¼m: acts on all-weather surfaces, probably on firm and soft ground: usually blinkered/visored: often a front runner. *C. Lerner, France* 79

SOLIANNA 3 ch.f. Beveled (USA) – Reclusive (Sunley Builds 102) [1994 64: 6.1s^4 6d^4 6d^3 5m^3 1995 a7g^3 a7g^3 a7g^6 6m 7f^4 7m* a6g^2 5.1f^3 6g^5 6f^6 Aug 9] tall, leggy filly: modest performer: won median auction maiden at Catterick in July: stays 7f, but at least as effective at sprint distances: acts on firm and soft ground and on fibresand: usually races prominently. *M. R. Channon* 59

SOLID ILLUSION (USA) 4 b.c. Cozzene (USA) – Polly's Harde (FR) (Lyphard (USA) 132) [1994 117: 10.5v^4 10.5v^4 10.5m^2 10.5g^2 12d^2 10d^2 1995 12s^2 12g^2 12d^6 10g Aug 19] smart French-trained colt: second in listed event at Longchamp and Grand Prix d'Evry (just failed, head behind Tot Ou Tard) first 2 outings in 1995: well below form afterwards: effective at 1¼m and 1½m: acted on good to firm ground and dead: blinkered last 4 starts at 3 yrs: bandaged: had turn of foot: stud in France. *P. H. Demercastel, France* 117

SOLIDOUN (FR) 4 gr.c. Kaldoun (FR) 122 – Solidarite (FR) (Far North (CAN) 120) [1994 8s^2 8g^2 8g^3 8g^6 7g^5 8.5d^2 8s^4 8v* 8v 1995 8s^6 8s* 8g 7m^6 10g^3 10m^3 8d 10g^2 11d 8g Oct 6] fourth foal: brother to La Kaldoun, winner of 11 races at up to 13.5f in France and second in Group 3 company in USA, and half-brother to French 6f to 9f winner by Sicyos: dam won over 6.5f in France: smart French colt: unraced at 2 yrs: won minor event at Maisons-Laffitte at 3 yrs and listed race at Longchamp (by 3 lengths from Scandinavian) in March: best effort when just over a length third of 6 to Marildo in La Coupe at Evry sixth start: stays 1¼m: acts on good to firm ground and heavy: rather inconsistent. *E. Lellouche, France* 113

SOLOMON'S DANCER (USA) 5 b. or br.g. Al Nasr (FR) 126 – Infinite Wisdom (USA) (Sassafras (FR) 135) [1994 79: 8.5g 10m 10m^4 10.3f^3 12f^2 12.4f* 14m* 13.9m 14.6g 14.1g^3 14.6d 1995 16m^5 14m^6 12d 14m^6 12f^2 Jul 29] good-topped gelding: carries condition: has a round action: fair handicapper: well below form after reappearance: probably stays 2m: acts on firm ground, has run respectably on dead: sometimes reluctant at stalls, and refused to enter them when favourite in August: won over hurdles in December. *W. W. Haigh* 75 d

SOLON (GER) 3 b.c. Local Suitor (USA) 128 – Scilla (GER) (Alpenkonig (GER)) [1994 6g 6g* 7g* 7s* 1995 7.5g^2 8g 12g* 10g* 12g* 11g* 12g* Sep 24] German-bred colt: third foal: dam unraced sister to useful miler Slenderhagen and leading filly (won Preis der Diana) Slenderella: progressed into a high-class performer: won maiden at Hassloch, minor event at Dresden and quite valuable race at Cologne at 2 yrs: disappointing in Mehl-Mulhens-Rennen in May, but subsequently won Swiss Derby at Frauenfeld, Ammerschlager Frankfurt-Pokal (by 2 lengths from Silent Lake), valuable event at Hanover, Furstenberg-Rennen (by ¾ length from Jural) at Baden-Baden and EMS-Kurierpost-Europa-Preis at Cologne: showed considerable improvement on each of last 2 starts, leading 2f out and running on strongly to beat Sternkoenig 2½ lengths for first Group 1 success at Cologne: stays 1½m: has already won 3 pattern races, and sure to win plenty more in 1996. *H. Jentzsch, Germany* 123

SOLO PRIZE 3 b.g. Chief Singer 131 – Raffle 82 (Balidar 133) [1994 73: 5.2s^3 5s* 5.1m^2 5.1g^4 6m 6.1g^3 5m^4 5f^5 6d 6d^3 6d^2 6v a6g 1995 5m 6.1m 6g 6g 6f a6g Dec 1] stocky gelding: has a round action: failed to progress at 2 yrs, and modest form at best in handicaps in 1995 (reluctant to race final start): stays 6f: acts on soft and good to firm ground (hampered on heavy): tried blinkered. *P. Howling* 62 d

SOLOR DANCER 3 b.g. Rambo Dancer (CAN) 107 – Just Super 33 (Star Appeal 133) [1994 –: 7s 1995 a8.5g^{5} a11g 14.1g 12.4g 10m May 10] angular gelding: no sign of ability: tried visored. *C. B. B. Booth* –

SOLO SYMPHONY (IRE) 2 ch.f. (Mar 27) Fayruz 116 – Keen Note 69 (Sharpo 132) [1995 5d^{3} Apr 1] 24,000Y: quite attractive filly: third foal: half-sister to 3-y-o Kim Tate (by Contract Law) and a winner in Italy: dam won in Belgium at 4 yrs: favourite, over 3 lengths third of 13 to Miss Bigwig in maiden at Warwick, leading over 1f out until swerving and hitting rail inside last: looked sure to improve. *P. W. Chapple-Hyam* 67

SOLVA MIST 2 gr.f. (Feb 21) Sharrood (USA) 124 – Irish Ditty 58 (Derrylin 115) [1995 5m^{6} 5m^{3} 6f^{4} 6g^{3} 5g^{5} 6m^{4} 5m a6g Jul 21] 3,500Y: lengthy filly: second reported foal: dam stayed 1¼m and won over hurdles: plater: stays 6f: best run on good ground (soundly beaten on fibresand): sold 1,550 gns Ascot July Sales. *L. J. Holt* 45

SOMBREFFE 3 b.f. Polish Precedent (USA) 131 – Somfas (USA) (What A Pleasure (USA)) [1994 NR 1995 7g^{5} 6f^{2} a7g^{2} a7g* a6g^{4} Dec 1] rather leggy, good-quartered filly: closely related to very useful 1988 2-y-o 6f winner Russian Bond and very useful sprinter Snaadee and half-sister to several winners, including useful 7f winner Adbass (by Northern Dancer): dam, from excellent family, won at up to 7f: fair performer: landed the odds in maiden at Lingfield in November: stays 7f: acts on firm ground and the all-weather: visored (ran creditably) final start: sold 130,000 gns Newmarket December Sales. *D. R. Loder* 71

SOME HORSE (IRE) 2 ch.c. (Mar 30) Astronef 116 – Daniela Lepida (ITY) (El-Muleta) [1995 5g^{2} a6g 5g* 6d* 7.6d^{4} 7m^{4} Oct 21] IR 4,600Y: tall, rather unfurnished colt: sixth reported foal: dam winner in Italy at 8.5f: won maiden at Haydock and nursery at Doncaster in September: good fourth of 11 in nursery at Doncaster final start: stays 7f: acts on good to firm and dead ground: well beaten on fibresand: may have been unsuited by track at Chester fifth start. *M. G. Meagher* 93

SOMER SOLO 2 b.f. (Mar 31) Prince Daniel (USA) – Shift Over (USA) 62 (Night Shift (USA)) [1995 7g 6.9f^{6} 7m^{3} 8d 8f Oct 25] close-coupled filly: second foal: half-sister to useful 3-y-o 7f and 1m winner Night Dance (by Weldnaas): dam, third at 6f at 2 yrs, daughter of sister to top-class middle-distance filly April Run: modest maiden: should stay 1m. *P. Mitchell* 54

SOMERTON BOY (IRE) 5 b.h. Thatching 131 – Bonnie Bess 95 (Ardoon 124) [1994 71: 6f^{3} 7m* 7f^{3} 7m^{5} 8g 7d 1995 8m 8g* 7g^{6} 7g* 7g^{2} 7d 7g 7m^{6} a7g Nov 16] quite attractive horse: fairly useful handicapper: won at Newcastle in May and Ayr in July: stays 1m: acts on any going: blinkered twice (in Ireland) early in career. *P. Calver* 83

SOMETHING SPEEDY (IRE) 3 b.f. Sayf El Arab (USA) 127 – Fabulous Pet (Somethingfabulous (USA)) [1994 53: 6g a7g^{4} a7g a6g 6s 6d a8.5g^{5} a8g a8.5g* 1995 a9.4g^{5} a11g a12g^{4} a14.8g Jun 10] sturdy filly: bad mover: poor performer: stays 1½m: acts on fibresand: twice blinkered at 2 yrs, no improvement. *P. J. Bevan* 42

SOMMERSBY (IRE) 4 b.g. Vision (USA) – Echoing 93 (Formidable (USA) 125) [1994 –: 7g 10.1d a13g 1995 10m^{4} a12g^{2} a12g* a12g^{2} a12g^{3} a12g^{6} a12g^{3} a12g* 11.9m a12g a12g Nov 13] sturdy, angular gelding: fair handicapper on the all-weather: won at Wolverhampton in May (final start for A. Stewart) and September: modest at best on turf: stays 1½m well: acts on good to firm ground and fibresand: sometimes bandaged: has gone early to post. *Mrs N. Macauley* 51 a71

SONDERISE 6 br.g. Mummy's Game 120 – Demderise 80 (Vaigly Great 127) [1994 58d: 5g^{3} 6s 5m 5d^{6} 5m 7f 6g 5d 5d 6s 1995 5d^{2} 5g^{4} 6g 5m 5m 5g May 27] lengthy gelding: modest sprint handicapper: well below form last 4 starts (reportedly bled from nose on final one): best on an easy surface (acts on heavy going): tried blinkered/visored: inconsistent. *N. Tinkler* 50

SONDOS 2 b.f. (Mar 22) Dowsing (USA) 124 – Krameria 72 (Kris 135) [1995 6m^{3} 6m^{4} Aug 26] 8,200Y: third foal: half-sister to 4-y-o Daring Gift (by Never So Bold): dam 2-y-o 5f winner out of Cheveley Park winner Sookera, also dam of So Factual: ½-length third of 16 to Kiss Me Again in median auction maiden at Windsor, better effort: will be suited by at least 7f. *J. W. Hills* 63

SONEETO 9 b.g. Teenoso (USA) 135 – Flying Bid 71 (Auction Ring (USA) 123) [1994 NR 1995 a12g^{6} a12g a12g Jan 26] tall, close-coupled gelding: of little account on flat: dead. *D. R. Laing* – §

SONG OF TARA (IRE) 3 b.c. Sadler's Wells (USA) 132 – Flame of Tara 124 (Artaius (USA) 129) [1994 NR 1995 12.1g* 12d* 12d^4 Sep 10] IR 1,500,000Y: seventh foal: brother to 3 winners, including triple classic winner Salsabil, and half-brother to 3 winners, notably high-class Marju (by Last Tycoon): dam, high-class, won at up to 1½m: trained at 2 yrs by M. V. O'Brien, but suffered a viral infection and did not run: won maiden at Chepstow (very easily) in May and listed race at Maisons-Laffitte in July: challenged entering straight in slowly-run Prix Niel at Longchamp in September, but soon outpaced and beaten around 3 lengths by Housamix: stays 1½m: yet to race on top-of-the-ground: may improve further. *P. W. Chapple-Hyam* 116

SONG OF YEARS (IRE) 4 b.f. Shareef Dancer (USA) 135 – Seattle Serenade (USA) 82 (Seattle Slew (USA)) [1994 NR 1995 a8g^2 a8g^3 12g^6 10f^2 8.3f^3 12g^4 10m 9.7s Sep 27] small, round-barrelled filly: rated 89 at 2 yrs but reportedly suffered fracture of off-hind tibia in 1994: modest maiden handicapper at best in 1995: stays 1½m: acts on firm ground: has run with tongue tied down: usually sweats up: sometimes hangs and goes in snatches: races prominently: sold 3,200 gns Newmarket Autumn Sales. *J. W. Hills* 58

SONGSHEET 2 b.f. (Feb 10) Dominion 123 – Songstead 92 (Song 132) [1995 5m^2 5g^2 5m^5 Nov 6] 9,200Y: lengthy filly: third foal: half-sister to 3-y-o Arasong (by Aragon) and 4-y-o Tenor (by Music Boy), both fair winning sprinters: dam 6f winner, is out of half-sister to smart sprinter Crews Hill: fair form when second in maiden at York and minor event (beaten 3½ lengths by Tadeo) at Lingfield: slowly away and never able to challenge in minor event at Folkestone final start: will stay 6f. *R. Guest* 74

SONG SONG BLUE (IRE) 2 b. or br.g. (Apr 28) Ballad Rock 122 – Bluethroat 95 (Ballymore 123) [1995 6m 9g Sep 23] IR 6,200Y, 4,200 2-y-o: close-coupled gelding: seventh living foal: half-brother to 1989 2-y-o 6f and 1m winner Simply Blue (by Simply Great): dam successful over 6f and 8.2f here at 2 yrs and at 1½m at 3 yrs in Ireland: well beaten in seller at Haydock and maiden at Redcar 2½ months later. *N. Tinkler* –

SONIC BOY 3 b.c. Celestial Storm (USA) 132 – Sharanella (Shareef Dancer (USA) 135) [1994 98: 5f^2 5s* 5g^6 6f^4 5.5g^4 6m^2 7.1g^2 7g^2 6g 1995 7m^6 8m* 10.4g^3 8.1g* 8.5m^4 8d^6 10.5f^3 10m 8.9g^2 Aug 31] strong, workmanlike colt: useful performer: won minor event at Doncaster and Tote Credit Silver Bowl Handicap at Haydock in May: best effort afterwards when third of 8 to Fahal in Rose of Lancaster Stakes at Haydock: may well stay beyond 10.5f: acts on firm and soft going: active sort: front runner: tough and genuine: sent to USA. *R. F. Johnson Houghton* 109

SONIC MAIL 2 b.g. (Apr 13) Keen 116 – Martin-Lavell Mail (Dominion 123) [1995 5m^5 5g^2 5.1m* 5m^3 5f^4 Aug 17] 8,400Y: leggy colt: half-brother to fair middle-distance stayer Pharly Dancer (by Pharly) and a winner abroad by Petorius: 77

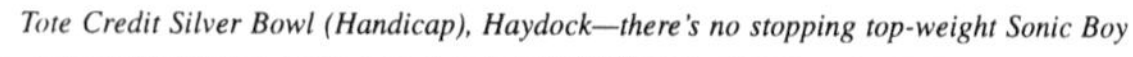

Tote Credit Silver Bowl (Handicap), Haydock—there's no stopping top-weight Sonic Boy

dam unraced: won maiden auction at Bath in May: good third to First Fiddler in minor event at Windsor in June, easily better subsequent effort: speedy: acts on good to firm ground. *K. McAuliffe*

SONNY PLACE 4 br.g. Glebe Place (USA) 101 – Out To Lunch (Anax 120) [1994 NR 1995 11.8m 11.8g Oct 10] third foal: dam of little account: tailed off in Leicester claimers. *J. L. Harris* –

SON OF ANSHAN 2 b.g. (Mar 23) Anshan 119 – Anhaar (Ela-Mana-Mou 132) [1995 7.1d Oct 11] 10,000F, 6,000Y: second foal: dam half-sister to very speedy 1985 2-y-o Nashia: refused to enter stalls on intended debut in September: 40/1 and bit backward, well-beaten seventh of 9 in maiden at Haydock: bandaged behind. *Mrs A. Swinbank* –

SON OF SHARP SHOT (IRE) 5 b. or br.h. Sharp Shot 82 – Gay Fantasy (Troy 137) [1994 78: 10d 10d^{3} 10.2s 10.8m^{4} 10.2f^{5} 10g^{6} 8.3m* 8g^{4} 8d^{6} 10g* 10d* 1995 10.8m* 10.3m* 12m* 12m* 12f^{4} 13.9m^{4} 12d 12m^{5} Oct 12] leggy, quite attractive horse: impresses in appearance: good mover: useful handicapper, vastly improved: successful at Warwick in April, at Chester (£10,500 event) and Goodwood in May and in 20-runner Bessborough Stakes (caught Zaralaska close home) at Royal Ascot: good fourth afterwards in valuable rated stakes at Goodwood and Ebor (4 lengths behind Sanmartino) at York: stays 13.9f but at least as effective over shorter: has won on soft going, best form on top-of-the-ground: usually held up in rear, suited by a good gallop and is a tricky ride (well handled by Pat and Paul Eddery): tail swisher, but genuine: stays in training. *J. L. Dunlop* 105

SONYA MARIE 2 b.f. (Apr 6) Green Ruby (USA) 104 – Susie Hall (Gold Rod 129) [1995 5m 7.5m^{4} 6f 6s Sep 30] workmanlike filly: sister to a poor plater and half-sister to several winners, including milers Golden Game (by Mummy's Game) and Foolish Ways (by Comedy Star): dam unraced half-sister to top 1970 2-y-o filly Cawston's Pride: little worthwhile form: trained by G. Kelly first 2 starts. *J. G. FitzGerald* –

SOOJAMA (IRE) 5 b.g. Mansooj 118 – Pyjama Game 56 (Cavo Doro 124) [1994 36: 14.9s^{3} 16.1g^{6} 12v^{4} 14.9d^{3} 1995 15.4g* 15.4m^{2} 14.1m^{5} 17.2m^{5} 16.4g* 16.1g^{2} 14.1m^{4} 16.2f 16.1g^{2} 12g^{2} a14g Nov 6] rather leggy gelding: poor handicapper: won at Folkestone in April and June: effective at 1½m and stays well: acts on good to firm and soft ground, well beaten on fibresand: blinkered last 3 starts at 3 yrs. *R. M. Flower* 48

SOOTY (IRE) 3 br.f. Caerleon (USA) 132 – Aghsan 78 (Lord Gayle (USA) 124) [1994 62: 6g^{5} 5g 1995 6m 8.2m 5m 6f a7g Nov 2] small, strong-quartered filly: no worthwhile form since debut at 2 yrs: sold 80,000 gns Newmarket December Sales. *H. Thomson Jones* –

Bessborough Stakes (Handicap), Royal Ascot—
the much-improved Son of Sharp Shot (white cap) beats gambled-on Zaralaska (white face)

SOOTY TERN 8 br.h. Wassl 125 – High Tern 93 (High Line 125) [1994 71: 8s a9.4g 8m 8.3s* 8v 8g^{2} 8.3m^{2} 8.1m* 10.5m^{6} 8f^{4} 8f* 8g 8m 8s 8d 1995 a8.5g^{4} 9g^{5} 8m^{6} 7.6m^{6} 8g 8g* 8m* a8g 8f^{5} 8.1m^{4} 8.3m* 8m^{5} 8m^{5} 7.6m^{2} 7.6m a7g^{2} 8g 8d Sep 16] compact horse: fair handicapper: won at Kempton (apprentices), Brighton and Hamilton in the summer: best at around 1m: acts on any going (won on both all-weather surfaces in 1992): usually races prominently: often ridden by apprentice: tough and genuine. *J. M. Bradley* — 78 a56

SOPHISM (USA) 6 b.g. Al Nasr (FR) 126 – Over The Waves (Main Reef 126) [1994 52: 14d^{3} 1995 12g^{6} 17.2m^{5} 16m Oct 19] close-coupled gelding: fairly useful jumper: poor at best on flat in 1995: stays 2m: acts on good to firm and dead ground. *M. C. Pipe* — 48 ?

SORBIE TOWER (IRE) 2 b.c. (Apr 1) Soviet Lad (USA) 94 – Nozet (Nishapour (FR) 125) [1995 7d 6g^{2} Oct 3] 15,000F, 13,000Y: tall, useful-looking colt: has scope: half-brother to 1992 2-y-o 6f winner Penang Star (by Jareer) and a winner in Belgium by Al Hareb: dam French 9f winner: last of 8 in minor event at Ascot: better effort when 2 lengths second of 14 to Second Time Lucky in maiden auction at Warwick 9 days later, first home of main body of field on far side: will stay 1m: sure to improve further. *Miss Gay Kelleway* — 67 p

SORISKY 3 ch.g. Risk Me (FR) 127 – Minabella (Dance In Time (CAN)) [1994 44: 5m 7.1g 7m 5.3f^{4} 7m^{6} a8g 1995 11.6m 10m 8g 8.3m a12g^{6} Dec 18] tall gelding: well beaten in 1995: unlikely to stay middle distances: tried visored. *B. Gubby* — –

SO SELECT 2 ch.f. (May 6) Northern State (USA) 91 – Zamindara (Crofter (USA) 124) [1995 5m 6g 5g 6g Oct 16] sparely-made filly: sixth foal: half-sister to 3 winning sprinters, including 3-y-o Secret Miss and Another Jade (both by Beveled): dam, poor maiden, stayed 1m: well beaten, including in sellers. *A. P. Jarvis* — –

SOTOBOY (IRE) 3 b.c. Danehill (USA) 126 – Fire Flash 74 (Bustino 136) [1994 94p: 6g* 6m* 7.1g^{4} 1995 8m 10m^{3} 7m 8m^{3} 8m 7m^{5} 7g 8.5s 8m^{6} Oct 12] small, well-made colt: fairly useful performer: below form in 1995 after fourth start: will prove best at up to 1¼m: acts on good to firm ground, never dangerous only start on a soft surface: takes good hold: early to post. *P. W. Harris* — 90

SOTTISES (IRE) 4 b.f. Northern State (USA) 91 – Doppio 62 (Dublin Taxi) [1994 NR 1995 12m 9.9m 7g May 8] rangy filly: no worthwhile form: tried blinkered. *P. T. Dalton* — –

SOUL OF HONOUR (FR) 2 b.g. (Feb 23) Highest Honor (FR) 124 – Wink Beauty (USA) (Shahrastani (USA) 135) [1995 5.1m^{4} 5.1m^{4} 5m 6m^{2} 7m^{6} 6d^{6} 8g^{4} Sep 21] 13,000Y: angular gelding: first foal: dam unraced: fair maiden: never able to challenge in nurseries last 3 starts, not looking easiest of rides on final outing: stays 1m: may do better in blinkers: sent to Macau. *Mrs J. R. Ramsden* — 69

SOUL RISK 2 ch.c. (Feb 3) Risk Me (FR) 127 – Farras 86 (Song 132) [1995 5g 6m 5g Sep 12] 14,000F, IR 10,000Y: smallish colt: fourth foal: brother to 3-y-o 6f winner Tiheros and temperamental 1993 2-y-o Risky Affair: dam 6f (at 2 yrs) and 7.6f winner: behind in maiden auctions: sold 1,000 gns Newmarket Autumn Sales. *J. A. R. Toller* — –

SOUND CHECK 2 b.f. (Feb 24) Formidable (USA) 125 – Imperatrice (USA) (Kings Lake (USA) 133) [1995 5m 5m 6g^{4} 6g^{3} 7g^{2} 7m* 8m 8h Sep 4] 4,200Y: smallish filly: unimpressive mover: fourth foal: dam ran once in France: won maiden auction at Warwick in August: needs further than 5f and stays 7f: acts on good to firm ground: twice ran as if something amiss, including penultimate outing. *B. J. Meehan* — 62

SOUND THE TRUMPET (IRE) 3 b.g. Fayruz 116 – Red Note (Rusticaro (FR) 124) [1994 80: 5g* 5d^{3} 6f^{3} 5m^{2} 5g^{3} 5m^{2} 5d^{6} 5.2s^{5} 1995 5.1m^{6} 6f^{6} 5f^{6} a5g 5g a6g Oct 28] rangy gelding: modest performer at best in 1995, sold out of Mrs J. Ramsden's stable 4,400 gns Doncaster August Sales after second start: best form at 5f: seems suited by a sound surface: usually blinkered or visored: inconsistent: has joined R. Spicer. *A. Streeter* — 52

SOUND TRICK (USA) 3 b.f. Phone Trick (USA) – Lettre d'Amour (USA) (Caro 133) [1994 56: 7g 1995 10m 8g^{5} a8.5g^{6} 7g^{5} 10d 7f a6g^{6} a7g Nov 29] leggy filly: modest maiden at best: soundly beaten most starts in 1995: stays 1m: tried visored: sometimes carries head high. *G. C. Bravery* — –

SOUPERFICIAL 4 gr.g. Petong 126 – Duck Soup 55 (Decoy Boy 129) [1994 52: 6d 5m 6f³ 5m* a5g⁴ 5m⁶ 5m⁶ 6g 7m 6g² 5d⁴ 6g 1995 a6g⁵ a6g* a6g* a6g³ 7g² a6g a7g* 7g 6m² 6.9f⁴ 6m* 6m⁶ 6m a6g² 6d a6g 8g Oct 9] sturdy gelding: fair handicapper: won at Southwell in March, at Wolverhampton in April and May and at Pontefract in July: effective at 6f and 7f: acts on firm and dead ground and on fibresand: usually visored: held up. *J. A. Glover* 69 a71

SOUPREME 3 ch.f. Northern State (USA) 91 – Soupcon 73 (King of Spain 121) [1994 NR 1995 10f⁴ 12m⁵ Oct 13] first foal: dam 2-y-o 6f winner, later stayed 1m: 20/1 and apprentice ridden, close fourth of 6 in slowly-run claimer at Redcar, staying on well: soon tailed off in apprentice maiden at Catterick over 2 months later. *Mrs M. Reveley* 55

SOURCE OF LIGHT 6 b.g. Rainbow Quest (USA) 134 – De Stael (USA) 93 (Nijinsky (CAN) 138) [1994 107: 10.3m* 12m 10g⁵ 1995 12m⁴ 12m⁶ 11.9m 12f³ 13.4m* 14m* 16g⁶ Sep 30] leggy, good-topped gelding: good mover: useful performer: easily won 4-runner listed rated stakes at Chester (by 1¼ lengths from Labibeh) and 3 runner minor event at Salisbury in August: well below form under forceful ride when tried at 2m in Jockey Club Cup at Newmarket on final start: effective at 1¼m and stays 1¾m: acts on any going: effective from front or held up: carried head high under pressure (ran creditably) fourth 6-y-o start. *R. Charlton* 106

SOUTHAMPTON 5 b.g. Ballacashtal (CAN) – Petingo Gold 69 (Pitskelly 122) [1994 36: 9.7s⁵ 11.9d⁴ a12g 11.7g 1995 11.8d 16.4m³ 14g Sep 23] plain gelding: fair hurdler, winner in October and November: poor maiden on flat: stays well: acts on good to firm ground: below form blinkered/visored. *G. B. Balding* 38

SOUTH EASTERN FRED 4 b.c. Primo Dominie 121 – Soheir 74 (Track Spare 125) [1994 56+, a71: 6v² 7m 6g 8.3m* 7g 8.3f² 8g³ 8m⁴ 8m a8g a10g* a10g* 1995 a10g* a9.4g* 10m⁴ 8.5m⁴ 8g⁵ 10m⁴ 8.3m 8m⁶ 7d 10f a10g² a8g Dec 14] tall, workmanlike colt: poor mover: fairly useful handicapper on the all-weather, successful at Lingfield and Wolverhampton in January: modest form at best on turf: stays 1¼m: acts on the all-weather, probably acts on any going on turf: sometimes bandaged. *H. J. Collingridge* 61 a87

SOUTHERN DOMINION 3 ch.g. Dominion 123 – Southern Sky 89 (Comedy Star (USA) 121) [1994 57: 5g 6m 5.2s³ 6g 5f⁶ 6g a5g⁶ a6g⁵ a6g³ a5g⁵ 1995 a5g⁵ 5.1m* 5.1f² a5g 5.1m³ 5m 5f² a5g* a5g⁴ 5f⁵ 5m⁴ 6f⁴ 7.1m⁴ 5g 6g² 5g a5g³ a6g* a6g³ a5g⁵ a6g² Dec 18] small gelding: trained until after seventh 3-y-o start by W. G. M. Turner: fair performer: won seller at Bath (made all) in May and handicaps at Wolverhampton (awarded race after Ashkernazy failed dope test) in July and Lingfield in November: effective at 5f, and stays 7f: acts on the all-weather, ideally suited by a sound surface on turf: blinkered 4 times at 2 yrs: races prominently. *M. Johnston* 65 a62

SOUTHERN MEMORIES (IRE) 5 b.g. Don't Forget Me 127 – Our Pet 64 (Mummy's Pet 125) [1994 –: 6d⁶ 7g 7m 8.3g 6g 8.1g 7g 7g 1995 8m* 7g Oct 10] lengthy, good-bodied gelding: modest handicapper at best nowadays: won amateurs race at Goodwood (made all) in August: best at up to 1m: acts on good to firm ground and dead: blinkered (below form) once at 3 yrs: races prominently. *W. J. Musson* 58

SOUTHERN POWER (IRE) 4 b.g. Midyan (USA) 124 – Tap The Line (Tap On Wood 130) [1994 76: 7d 8m 7f 7m 8m 8g⁴ 10.3g² 10m 1995 9.9m² 10.8m³ 12g⁴ 12.4g² 9.9m³ May 13] leggy, good-topped gelding: good mover: fairly useful handicapper: stays 12.4f: acts on any going: bandaged near-hind in 1995: sometimes edges left: held up/tracks pace: has rejoined D. Loder. *Mrs M. Reveley* 82

SOUTHERN RIDGE 4 b.g. Indian Ridge 123 – Southern Sky 89 (Comedy Star (USA) 121) [1994 –: 8s 8g 6g 7.1g 7m a7g 1995 6m 6m 8.3m Aug 7] neat gelding: fairly useful performer at 2 yrs: no worthwhile form since: has joined R. Baker. *C. A. Horgan* –

SOUTH FOREST (IRE) 4 b.g. Pennine Walk 120 – Route Royale (Roi Soleil 125) [1994 57+: 5.1v³ 5d² 5d³ 1995 a6g² a7g⁴ 5d⁶ a6g* a8g 6.1d Sep 19] fair performer: neck second of 13 in median auction maiden at Southwell on reappearance: well below that form afterwards, including when landing the odds in maiden claimer at Southwell in April: should stay beyond 6f: acts on fibresand, has raced only on a soft surface on turf: blinkered (well beaten) final start: usually claimer ridden: has been bandaged and worn crossed noseband. *S. R. Bowring* 60 a68

SOUTH PAGODA (IRE) 2 b.c. (Apr 29) Distinctly North (USA) 115 – Lamya 73 (Hittite Glory 125) [1995 6m^4 6m 6.9g Oct 16] IR 10,000Y: half-brother to winning sprinter Murray's Mazda (by M Double M) and a winner in Belgium: dam won 3 races in Sweden: modest form: reportedly lame after finishing towards rear in valuable restricted race at the Curragh on second outing: sold 6,000 gns Newmarket Autumn Sales: has joined D. Nicholls. *P. W. Chapple-Hyam* — 64

SOUTH ROCK 3 b.f. Rock City 120 – South Shore 102 (Caerleon (USA) 132) [1994 73p: 6d 6s^2 6g^2 1995 6g^6 6m^6 8.2f* 9.9g^6 8m 7.1d* 7.1d^2 7.1g* 6m^5 7g* Oct 23] leggy filly: made into a useful handicapper in 1995, winning at Nottingham in July and twice at Haydock in September: best efforts in listed races last 2 starts, narrowly winning at Evry in October: stays 1m, best efforts forcing pace over 6f/7f: acts on firm and soft ground: genuine. *J. A. Glover* — 102

SOUTH SALEM (USA) 2 b.c. (Feb 6) Salem Drive (USA) – Azzurrina (Knightly Manner (USA)) [1995 5m* 6g* 6m^3 Jun 20] strong, good-bodied colt: carries condition: has scope: half-brother to several winners here and abroad, including useful Irish middle-distance stayer Too Phar (by Pharly): dam very good winner in Italy from 7f (at 2 yrs) to 1¼m: sire (half-brother to St Jovite) very smart from around 1m to 1½m: created very favourable impression when winning median auction maiden at Leicester in April and minor event at Doncaster in May: looked in excellent shape when very good third, beaten just over 2 lengths, to Royal Applause in Coventry Stakes at Ascot final outing: bred to stay at least 1m: looked a really progressive sort but not seen out after Royal Ascot. *D. R. Loder* — 107 p

SOUTH SANDS 9 ch.g. Sayf El Arab (USA) 127 – Collegian 90 (Stanford 121§) [1994 NR 1995 a16g^5 a16g^4 Feb 16] sparely-made gelding: poor stayer nowadays: tried blinkered. *A. M. Forte* — 32

SOUTH SEA BUBBLE (IRE) 3 b.f. Bustino 136 – Night At Sea 107 (Night Shift (USA)) [1994 NR 1995 10g^6 10m^3 Oct 26] lengthy filly: first foal: dam sprinter: unimpressive to post and still not fully fit, fair form when staying-on third of 9 to Main Offender in minor event at Nottingham: likely to be suited by further than 1¼m: should improve again. *L. M. Cumani* — 71 p

SOUTH SOUND (IRE) 3 b.c. Petorius 117 – Randolina (Wolver Hollow 126) [1994 63: 6f 6f^2 5d 6g 1995 6.1g 6m 6.1g 7g 8m^3 8f^5 8.1g 8h^6 a8s^6 Dec 10] strong colt: modest maiden handicapper: should stay beyond 1m: acts on firm and dead ground: tried blinkered: sold out of R. Hannon's stable 4,400 gns Newmarket Autumn Sales before final start. *M. Khan, Sweden* — 59

SOVEREIGN PAGE (USA) 6 ch.g. Caro 133 – Tashinsky (USA) (Nijinsky (CAN) 138) [1994 83: 8v 10d 10f^3 10m^3 10.2f^2 10m^4 10.1m* 10.5g^6 10m^3 10.1m^4 10.1g^6 1995 10m^2 10.3m^4 10m^3 May 21] tall, rather leggy gelding: good mover: fairly useful handicapper: ideally suited by around 1¼m: best on a sound surface (acts on firm going): blinkered (no improvement) twice at 3 yrs: bandaged nowadays: held up/tracks leaders: consistent. *B. Hanbury* — 82

SOVEREIGN PRINCE (IRE) 2 b.c. (Apr 15) Bluebird (USA) 125 – Everything Nice 107 (Sovereign Path 125) [1995 8d a8g^6 a8.5g a6g Dec 19] IR 30,000Y: quite good-topped colt: has scope: brother to 3-y-o Early Peace and half-brother to several winners, including Irish 1000 Guineas winner Nicer (by Pennine Walk): dam won from 5f (at 2 yrs) to 10.5f: signs of ability in nursery final start: will stay 1¼m: has worn bandage off-hind. *N. A. Callaghan* — –

SOVEREIGN'S CROWN (USA) 2 br.c. (Mar 7) Chief's Crown (USA) – Beau Prospector (USA) (Mr Prospector (USA)) [1995 6g^3 6d* 7g^3 6f Oct 12] $110,000Y: useful-looking colt: second foal: dam unraced: won 25-runner maiden at Newbury in September: good efforts after when 2 lengths third of 8 to Even Top in listed race at Newmarket and ninth to Blue Iris in Redcar Two-Year-Old Trophy: will be better suited by 1m+: remains capable of better: sent to USA. *J. H. M. Gosden* — 99 p

SOVEREIGNS PARADE 3 ch.g. Chromite (USA) – Queen's Visit (Top Command (USA)) [1994 NR 1995 7g 7m^2 8.3m 8f 8m^4 8g^2 10d^4 9.7g Oct 16] 13,500Y: strong gelding: fifth foal: half-brother to 5f winner Bryan Robson (by Topsider): dam, maiden suited by 1¼m, half-sister to very smart 1984 2-y-o stayer Khozaam: sire (by Mr Prospector) won over 5.5f and is brother to Woodman: fair performer: trained first 4 starts by L. J. Holt: stays 1¼m well: acts on dead ground, — 66 well beaten on firm: sold (J. Banks to N. Henderson) 21,000 gns Newmarket Autumn Sales: made winning hurdling debut in December. *J. E. Banks*

SOVIET BRIDE (IRE) 3 b.f. Soviet Star (USA) 128 – Nihad 76 (Alleged (USA) 138) [1994 57: 7m 8f^5 6g 1995 8.2g^5 8g^5 10f* 10.1m* 10f^2 12f^2 10m^4 11.9g^4 11.8g^4 12.1s Oct 17] lengthy filly: fair handicapper: left E. Dunlop's stable after second 3-y-o start: won at Brighton and Epsom (apprentices) in July: stays 1½m well: acts on firm ground, well beaten only run on soft: sometimes bandaged behind: takes keen hold, and races prominently. *S. Dow* — 72

SOVIET KING (IRE) 2 b.c. (Mar 29) Soviet Lad (USA) 94 – Finessing (Indian King (USA) 128) [1995 8g^3 10.2m^6 10m Oct 19] IR 3,800F, IR 4,400Y: angular colt: fourth foal: half-brother to 11f winner Sir Edward Henry (by Taufan): dam ran several times in Ireland: in need of run and bandaged, third of 6 to Dreamhill in maiden at Goodwood: well beaten both starts at 1¼m, racing too freely final outing: has been bandaged behind. *P. Mitchell* — 61 ?

SOVIET LINE (IRE) 5 b.g. Soviet Star (USA) 128 – Shore Line 107 (High Line 125) [1994 122: 8m^2 7.9f* 8.5m^6 8m^6 8m^2 10m^4 8g* 8g* 7m* 7m^2 7g* 1995 8m* 8m^3 8f^5 8d^3 7m^2 8s^6 Oct 28] — 121

The upgrading of the Juddmonte Lockinge Stakes to Group 1 status in the latest season wasn't quite the success it might have been. Of the five runners who took part, only the middle-distance performer Muhtarram had won in the category, and the turnout emphasised the shortage of top-class older milers in training in 1995. Nevertheless, the horses who contested the race, run in May at Newbury's first Sunday meeting, were good enough to meet the requirements necessary to enable the Lockinge to remain a Group 1 event: that is, over a three-year period the first four horses home must achieve an average rating of 115 in the International Classifications. Apart from Muhtarram the field included Missed Flight and Mutakddim, first and third respectively in the Sandown Mile the previous month, Young Ern, who'd

Juddmonte Lockinge Stakes, Newbury—an impressive start to the season from Soviet Line

Maktoum Al Maktoum's "Soviet Line"

won a listed race at Leicester on his seasonal reappearance, and Soviet Line. The last-named had made great strides in 1994, winning the Hong Kong International Bowl on his final start. Unlike Muhtarram, Soviet Line was well forward for his first outing of the season, and he went off favourite at 2/1. He gave his supporters few anxious moments in what turned out to be a tactical race. With no recognised front runner in the field, Swinburn took the initiative on Soviet Line and dictated the pace, increasing the tempo from halfway. Soviet Line, running on strongly, was well in command going into the final furlong and won by two lengths from Young Ern, with Missed Flight a further two and a half lengths back in third. As a result of this win Soviet Line had to carry a 5 lb penalty in the Queen Anne Stakes at Royal Ascot a month later, and in finishing third to Nicolotte, beaten two lengths, he performed creditably. It was disconcerting, however, that Soviet Line should be mulish going to post, though he did run his race out well enough. That wasn't the case on his next start, though. Soviet Line was moved down a place after finishing fourth to Sayyedati in the Sussex Stakes at Goodwood, having hung badly left when asked for his effort over two out, taking Nicolotte with him, and ending up towards the stand rail. However, any thoughts that Soviet Line might be going the wrong way were dispelled when he finished runner-up, for the second year in succession, in the Challenge Stakes at Newmarket. Back on top-of-the-ground after finishing a remote third on softish going in the Queen Elizabeth II Stakes at Ascot, Soviet Line returned to his best and went down by only half a length to Harayir at Newmarket, tracking the winner from the start and doing nothing wrong under pressure. As in the previous season Soviet Line raced abroad after the Challenge Stakes. One of two British-trained challengers for the Breeders' Cup Mile at Belmont, Soviet Line, encountering soft ground for the first time, wasn't disgraced in finishing sixth to Ridgewood Pearl.

He didn't get the clearest of runs for much of the race, but made headway in the straight and was just over a length behind third-placed Sayyedati at the line.

Soviet Line (IRE) (b.g. 1990)	Soviet Star (USA) (b 1984)	Nureyev (b 1977)	Northern Dancer
			Special
		Veruschka (b 1967)	Venture VII
			Marie d'Anjou
	Shore Line (b 1980)	High Line (ch 1966)	High Hat
			Time Call
		Dark Finale (b 1965)	Javelot
			Peeky

Soviet Line is the fifth foal of the 1983 Oaks fourth Shore Line, a sister to several talented performers including the Park Hill Stakes winner, Pure Grain's grandam Quay Line. While Soviet Line is most effective at seven furlongs and a mile, Shore Line's other winning produce, namely Ahwak (Shareef Dancer), South Shore (by Caerleon) and Mamdooh (by Green Desert), the last two both useful, were best over middle-distances. Shore Line's latest foal to reach the racecourse is the three-year-old Soviet Shore, a full brother to Soviet Line who showed promise when third over a mile at two years, his only start to date. Soviet Line, a compact gelding, has shown his best form on a sound surface, and he acts on firm. *M. R. Stoute*

SOVIET SAKTI (IRE) 2 b.c. (Jan 16) Soviet Lad (USA) 94 – Hill's Realm (USA) 68 (Key To The Kingdom (USA)) [1995 6.1f 6.1m^{6} 7m 6m 5g 10d 8f Oct 18] IR 6,500Y: workmanlike colt: unimpressive mover: half-brother to several winners, including fair 1m (at 2 yrs) and 11.8f winner Home From The Hill (by Jareer) and fairly useful 1990 2-y-o 9f winner All The King's Men (by Alzao): dam stayed 6f: poor form: tailed off in nursery at Yarmouth final start: likely to prove best short of 1¼m: blinkered/visored twice. *P. Mitchell* — 49 +

SOVIET STYLE (AUS) 2 b.g. (Feb 4) Rory's Jester (AUS) – Kitty Russe 68 (Nureyev (USA) 131) [1995 5g^{3} 5m* 5m* 5g^{3} 5g Sep 14] lengthy gelding: first foal: dam second twice (at up to 1½m) from 3 starts, daughter of Lowther Stakes winner Kittyhawk and half-sister to Nomadic Way: sire good Australian sprinter: useful performer: won minor events at Lingfield and Ripon in August: good third of 4 to Branston Jewel in similar event at York in August: below form in listed race at Ayr on final start: speedy: sold only 7,500 gns Newmarket Autumn Sales. *P. W. Chapple-Hyam* — 97 +

SOVIET UNION 3 b.g. Soviet Star (USA) 128 – Chalon 125 (Habitat 134) [1994 NR 1995 a7g Jul 3] seventh living foal: half-brother to high-class French 7f (at 2 yrs) to 10.5f winner Creator (by Mill Reef): dam, suited by 1m, out of very speedy Areola: soon tailed off in claimer at Wolverhampton. *J. J. Bridger* — –

SOVITAKA (IRE) 2 br.f. (Feb 15) Soviet Lad (USA) 94 – Pitaka (Pitskelly 122) [1995 5f^{5} 6g^{3} 7m^{5} a7g^{6} 7.5m* 7m 7m^{6} 7.5d 8g Sep 21] 2,600Y: rather leggy filly: half-sister to several winners here and abroad, including fair sprinter Wanda (by Taufan): dam never ran: plater: made all at Beverley in June: below form afterwards, blinkered final start: stays 7.5f: sold 3,200 gns Newmarket Autumn Sales. *M. H. Easterby* — 48

SOZZLED 4 gr.g. Absalom 128 – The High Dancer (High Line 125) [1994 68: 7m^{3} 7g* 7f 10m 7d 7m a9.4g 1995 a10g Feb 2] sturdy gelding: fair handicapper: well beaten only 4-y-o start: stays 7f: possibly unsuited by firm going: tried blinkered/visored: won novice hurdle in August for M. Pipe. *A. Barrow* — –

SPAIN LANE (USA) 4 b.f. Seeking The Gold (USA) – Regent's Walk (CAN) (Vice Regent (CAN)) [1994 115: 6d* 5g* 6.5g^{6} 6g^{3} 6d* 5g^{3} 1995 5g^{2} 5g^{5} Jun 1] tall, robust filly: very useful performer: better effort in 1995 when 1½ lengths second of 7 to Struggler (rec 9 lb more than w.f.a.) in Prix de Saint-Georges at Longchamp in May: effective at 5f to 7f: acts on dead going, yet to race on top-of-the-ground. *A. Fabre, France* — 111

SPA LANE 2 ch.g. (Mar 31) Presidium 124 – Sleekit 78 (Blakeney 126) [1995 7.1m 6g 8g 6f Oct 24] brother to 3-y-o Braydon Forest and half-brother to several winners, including 1¼m winner Kitty Clare (by Milford) and 1m winner Clipper One (by Dreams To Reality): dam 1½m winner: poor form in maiden events: unseated rider penultimate start. *C. J. Drewe* — –

SPANDREL 3 ch.f. Pharly (FR) 130 – Oxslip 106 (Owen Dudley 121) [1994 NR 1995 7f Aug 10] smallish filly: sister to useful sprinter Top Banana and half-sister to 4 winners, all at 1m+, including quite useful 1¼m and 1¾m winner Sixslip (by Diesis): dam, 7f to 13f winner, is half-sister to very useful stayer Kambalda: slowly away and never a threat in maiden at Salisbury: moved poorly to post: may do better. *H. Candy* –

SPANIARDS CLOSE 7 b.g. King of Spain 121 – Avon Belle 75 (Balidar 133) [1994 96: 5d^3 5g^4 5s 6v 1995 5.2m a5g* 5g* 5d* 6d^2 Oct 19] lengthy, workmanlike gelding: useful performer: successful in claimers at Southwell and Sandown and (best effort for over 2 years) 13-runner £15,600 rated stakes at Ascot, all in September: stays 6f: acts on fibresand: best turf efforts on good and dead ground, possibly unsuited by soft: visored (tailed off) final start at 5 yrs: held up. *P. J. Makin* 101

SPANISH GIRL (USA) 3 b.f. Alwuhush (USA) 121 – Nat's Pleasure (USA) (Mr Prospector (USA)) [1994 56: a7g^5 6.9m a8g^4 1995 a8g Jan 30] sparely-made filly: modest 2-y-o form: refused to race only start in 1995: blinkered (ran well) once: sold 1,350 gns Ascot February Sales: one to have reservations about. *P. A. Kelleway* – §

SPANISH LUCK 2 b.f. (Feb 28) Mazilier (USA) 107 – Spanish Heart 86 (King of Spain 121) [1995 6.1g^4 5.1m^6 7m* 7f 7f 7.1m^6 6m^6 6s a6g Nov 13] small, dipped-backed filly: second foal: dam effective from 7f to 9f: poor performer: won claimer at Warwick in July: needs at least 7f: acts on good to firm ground: blinkered last 4 outings. *J. W. Hills* 47

SPANISH STEPS (IRE) 3 b.g. Danehill (USA) 126 – Belle Enfant 87 (Beldale Flutter (USA) 130) [1994 59: 5m 6m^6 6m 7.9d 1995 8m^3 12m 8g^5 8g^3 May 25] tall gelding: shows knee action: modest maiden handicapper: should be suited by further than 1m (never placed to challenge over 1½m): yet to race on extremes of going: tried blinkered. *M. W. Easterby* 62 d

SPANISH STRIPPER (USA) 4 b.g. El Gran Senor (USA) 136 – Gourmet Dinner (USA) (Raise A Cup (USA)) [1994 –: 7g^6 1995 a7g a7g^4 a8.5g^2 a7g a7g^3 a8g^5 a8g a8g a11g 7g^4 10f 8m^6 a8g 6m* 6.9g 5m^3 7m 7m^3 7.5m^5 7f Oct 25] good-topped gelding: fair handicapper on turf: won amateurs race at Redcar in May: effective at stiff 5f, and may prove best at up to 7f: acts on good to firm ground and (only poor form) fibresand: has run well when sweating: none too consistent. *M. C. Chapman* 69 a48

SPANISH VERDICT 8 b.g. King of Spain 121 – Counsel's Verdict (Firestreak 125) [1994 74: 7d^4 8s^3 8m* 7f 8m 7m 8m^4 8m^4 8.1m* 8f^5 8g 8g^6 8f^6 8s^6 8.9d 8.1g 1995 7.1g^6 8g^3 8m^2 8m 8.1g 8m^2 8f^2 8.1f^3 8.3m^5 8m^2 8f* 9m^5 8h^2 8m* 8g 9f 8f 8f Oct 24] sturdy, good-quartered gelding: impresses in appearance: has a round action: fair handicapper: made all at Carlisle (apprentice race, fifth course win) in July and Ripon in August: effective at 7f, probably at 1¼m: has some form on soft going, but goes particularly well (11 of his 12 wins) on top-of-the-ground: sometimes visored early in career: often claimer ridden: usually races prominently: tough and genuine. *Denys Smith* 74

SPANKING ROGER 2 ch.c. (Feb 4) Unfuwain (USA) 131 – Hi-Tech Girl 98 (Homeboy 114) [1995 7m 8g^5 8.5v* 8d^2 Dec 2] strong, heavy-topped colt: fourth foal: half-brother to fairly useful 6-y-o sprinter Sea-Deer (by Hadeer) and 1m/1¼m performer Pigalle Wonder (by Ballad Rock): dam 2-y-o 5f winner suited by 6f: still backward when around 12 lengths fifth of 17 to Heron Island in maiden at Doncaster: sold out of B. Hills's stable 14,000 gns Newmarket Autumn Sales: subsequently won in Belgium. *R. Crepon, Belgium* 71

SPARA TIR 3 b.g. Dowsing (USA) 124 – Jetelle (USA) (Northjet 136) [1994 59: 6g 7m 7m^5 7g^3 6g 1995 7g^5 6g^3 6m^3 6g^6 Jul 1] well-made gelding: has a round action: modest maiden handicapper: best form at 6f, should stay 1m: has raced only on a sound surface. *Bob Jones* 57

SPARKLING ROBERTA 4 b.f. Kind of Hush 118 – Hitesca 110 (Tesco Boy 121) [1994 48, a–: 9.7v^4 12.5m 12s^3 12d 14.1m^3 a14.8g^4 10g^4 11.5m^2 8g* 8g^6 9g^5 a10g 1995 a8.5g^3 10m^3 10.1g^5 8.3m a9.4g^2 a12g^5 9.7s 11.9m a10g^4 a7g^6 Dec 2] small filly: shows knee action: poor handicapper: effective at 1m, and stays 1¾m: acts on good to firm and soft ground and on fibresand: tried visored. *M. D. I. Usher* 43 a39

SPARROWHAWK (IRE) 3 b.f. Doyoun 124 – Sparrow's Air (USA) 105 (Assert 134) [1994 73p: 6m 7.3v 1995 10.4m^4 8.1g^2 7f^2 10.2h* 10f 10.3m^6 14g 77

11.8g^5 11.8f^6 a10g Nov 21] tall filly: fair performer: won 3-runner maiden at Bath in July, making all: tailed off last 2 starts, looking rather mulish on first of them: stays 11.8f: seems to act on any going: inconsistent: sold 17,500 gns Newmarket December Sales. *B. W. Hills*

SPARTAN HEARTBEAT 2 b.c. (Feb 28) Shareef Dancer (USA) 135 – Helen's Dream (Troy 137) [1995 8f 8m Nov 4] 15,000Y: good-bodied colt: brother to a 9f to 1¼m winner in Italy and half-brother to fairly useful 1¼m winner Helens Dreamgirl (by Caerleon): dam, unraced, from family of Gorytus: backward, behind in maidens at Leicester (slowly away) and Doncaster in autumn. *C. E. Brittain* –

SPECIAL BEAT 3 b.f. Bustino 136 – Special Guest 67 (Be My Guest (USA) 126) [1994 NR 1995 10.1m^5 10m^4 8.3m^5 13.1h^5 11.4d Sep 12] unfurnished filly: has a round action: fifth foal: half-sister to useful 7f winner Cragganmore (by Faustus) and 2-y-o 5f winners Special One (by Aragon) and Northern Host (by Petorius): dam 2-y-o 7f winner who stayed 9f: modest maiden: stays 13.1f: acts on hard ground, ran badly on dead. *P. F. I. Cole* 61

SPECIAL DAWN (IRE) 5 ch.g. Be My Guest (USA) 126 – Dawn Star 94 (High Line 125) [1994 80: 11.9d^4 12g^4 9.9m* 10d* 1995 10m* 10m 10g* 10m* 9g 10d 10v Oct 7] lengthy, sparely-made gelding: good mover: useful handicapper: has reportedly been difficult to train: won Westminster-Motor Taxi Insurance Rosebery Handicap at Kempton (by neck from Blushing Flame) in April, and gained further successes at Sandown in June and Newmarket (best effort, awarded race on disqualification of Ball Gown) in July: below form last 3 starts, off bridle long way from home at Ascot on final one: stays 1½m, best form at 1¼m: acts on good to firm and heavy going: held up. *J. L. Dunlop* 96

SPECIALIZE 3 b.g. Faustus (USA) 118 – Scholastika (GER) (Alpenkonig (GER)) [1994 58?: 7m a7g 7g 8s 1995 10.8m 8f 10m 10f Jul 8] good-bodied gelding: poor maiden: should stay at least 1¼m: acts on firm ground. *K. R. Burke* 48 ?

SPECIAL-K 3 br.f. Treasure Kay 114 – Lissi Gori (FR) (Bolkonski 134) [1994 63: 5m^6 5f^5 5g^5 6m* 5f^3 7m 6g^5 1995 6m^2 6f^3 5.9f^2 7f* 7.5g* 8f^6 7m^6 7.5m^3 8m* Aug 29] leggy filly: fair performer: won claimers at Redcar and Beverley in July and at Ripon in August: stays 1m: acts on firm ground: consistent. *E. Weymes* 65

SPECIAL RISK (IRE) 5 br.g. Simply Great (FR) 122 – Ahonita 90 (Ahonoora 122) [1994 52: a10g a13g* a12g^2 a12g^2 11.9d* 12v^2 11.8d^3 12m^2 12m^2 14g* 15.4d 14.1d* 1995 14.1g Apr 24] small, leggy gelding: poor handicapper: well beaten only 5-y-o start: should stay 2m: acts on good to firm ground, heavy and all-weather surfaces: tried blinkered earlier in career. *R. Akehurst* –

SPECTACLE JIM 6 b.g. Mummy's Game 120 – Welsh Blossom 100 (Welsh Saint 126) [1994 53: 6v 5m 6m 6m 6m^5 6m^3 6f^4 5m^2 6f 5m^6 8m^6 6m^5 7d a8g^4 a7g^3 a7g^5 1995 a6g^3 6m^6 6m 6m^3 8.3m 6m 6f^2 8s 6g 7m a5g^2 a5g^6 Nov 30] leggy gelding: modest handicapper: effective at 5f, and stays 8.3f: acts on equitrack and on firm and soft ground: usually blinkered/visored: wears dropped noseband: usually held up: inconsistent. *J. O'Donoghue* 53

SPECTRUM (IRE) 3 b.c. Rainbow Quest (USA) 134 – River Dancer 118 (Irish River (FR) 131) [1994 105P: 8v* 1995 8.1m* 8m* 12f 10s^2 10m* Oct 14] 126

The decision to keep Spectrum in training as a four-year-old—he is to be retired to Coolmore at the end of 1996—will surely pay off. Though he already has two Group 1 victories to his name, he has had only six races and is just the lightly-raced, progressive type one would expect to continue to train on. Those two Group 1 victories came at either end of a three-year-old campaign in which injuries sustained in the Derby prevented Spectrum from playing an even bigger part in the season. Spectrum was off the course for three months after returning from Epsom 'very stiff and sore in front, and with a slight muscular problem in his back'. He'd gone to Epsom still unbeaten, following up an impressive victory in a minor event at Newbury on his only start at two with successes in a similar contest at Sandown on his reappearance and in the First National Building Society Irish Two Thousand Guineas. Spectrum's victory at the Curragh in May confirmed the highly favourable impression created by his earlier victories. He took the big step up in class in his stride, winning a somewhat unsatisfactory race—the tempo was slow for a classic until well into the straight—in good style by a length and a short head from Adjareli

First National Building Society Irish Two Thousand Guineas, the Curragh—Spectrum (light colours) is too strong for Adjareli (white face) and Bahri

and the English Guineas third Bahri. Spectrum's trainer Peter Chapple-Hyam, saddling his third Irish Two Thousand Guineas winner in four years, said after the race that he regarded Spectrum every bit as highly as his two previous winners Rodrigo de Triano and Turtle Island. Spectrum's odds for the Derby shortened dramatically, Ladbrokes, for example, making him 3/1 second favourite behind Pennekamp immediately after the race. Spectrum, one of five unbeaten colts and one of three Group 1 winners in the Derby field, started at 5/1 second favourite on the day but ran no sort of race, never out of the rear division and looking ill-at-ease coming down the hill.

Spectrum's recovery seemed to go well at first and there was talk of his returning in time for the Sussex Stakes at Goodwood or the Juddmonte International at York. But, in the event, his comeback was delayed until mid-September when he ran the Derby second Tamure, who had also been off the course since Epsom, to a neck, conceding 7 lb, in the falsely-run Prix du Prince d'Orange at Longchamp. The pair met again the following month in the Dubai Champion Stakes at Newmarket where Spectrum comfortably turned the tables at level weights. In a fairly open-looking Champion, Spectrum showed conclusively that he had suffered no lasting ill-effects from his injuries, winning a truly-run race in good style by two lengths

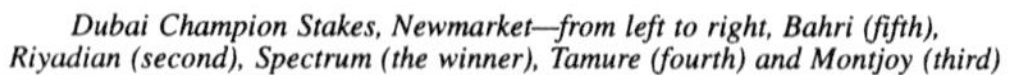

Dubai Champion Stakes, Newmarket—from left to right, Bahri (fifth), Riyadian (second), Spectrum (the winner), Tamure (fourth) and Montjoy (third)

Lord Weinstock and The Hon Simon Weinstock's "Spectrum"

from the Cumberland Lodge winner Riyadian with the 25/1-shot Montjoy a head away third, Tamure fourth and the favourite Bahri fifth in a field of eight. Spectrum travelled well throughout and looked the winner from the Dip, quickening impressively when finally sent about his business after being waited with.

Spectrum (IRE) (b.c. 1992)	Rainbow Quest (USA) (b 1981)	Blushing Groom (ch 1974)	Red God
			Runaway Bride
		I Will Follow (b 1975)	Herbager
			Where You Lead
	River Dancer (b 1983)	Irish River (ch 1976)	Riverman
			Irish Star
		Dancing Shadow (b 1977)	Dancer's Image
			Sunny Valley

Spectrum is a rangy, attractive colt with plenty of scope; he is a good walker and has a quick action in his faster paces. Spectrum is a rarity among the leading progeny of Rainbow Quest in that he has won a pattern race over a trip as short as a mile after the age of two; most of Rainbow Quest's pattern-race winners have made their mark at a mile and a half or further. Spectrum's dam River Dancer, however, won over five furlongs as a two-year-old and over a mile, the longest distance she attempted, as a three-year-old when she was third in the Poule d'Essai des Pouliches. River Dancer has bred two other winners who didn't stay so far as their pedigrees suggested, the mile and a quarter Beverley maiden winner Snow Plough (by Niniski), whose career was curtailed by injury, and the fair sprinter Ballet Shoes (by Ela-Mana-Mou). Staying types predominate further back with Spectrum's grandam the smart mile to mile and a quarter winner Dancing Shadow being a half-sister to Oaks and St Leger winner Sun Princess and to Coronation Cup winner and St Leger runner-up Saddlers' Hall. Their dam Sunny Valley was a useful winner at up to a mile and a half by the French Derby winner Val de Loir out of the staying Sunland, a half-sister to the 1960 Park Hill winner Sunny Cove. Spectrum is effective at a mile and should stay a mile and a half, which will give his connections a wide variety of races to aim at in the next season. He has a fine turn of foot and has won on going ranging from heavy to good to firm, his only poor run being on firm in the Derby. Though he tends to flash his tail in the preliminaries and has given trouble at the stalls, Spectrum has never shown the slightest sign of temperament once racing. *P. W. Chapple-Hyam*

SPEEDSTER 3 ch.c. Exactly Sharp (USA) 121 – Flushing Meadow 103 (Raise A Native) [1994 8.3g* 1995 8.3s* 8v^{4} 10g* 11s 12m 10g Jul 30] 8,200F: fifth foal: half-brother to 3 winners including (at up to 10.5f in France) Caupe Davis (by No Pass No Sale): dam, French 7f (at 2 yrs) and 1m winner, is half-sister to 3 pattern race winners: useful German colt: easily won maiden at 2 yrs and minor event in March, both at Neuss, then landed Group 3 event at Frankfurt in April by ¾ length from Rivero, leading 1½f out but veering badly right inside last: seventh of 18 in Deutsches Derby in Hamburg, only respectable effort afterwards: stays 1¼m, respectable effort at 1½m: acts on soft ground, respectable effort on good to firm. *B. Schutz, Germany* — 101

SPEED TO LEAD (IRE) 3 b.f. Darshaan 133 – Instant Desire (USA) 86 (Northern Dancer) [1994 75p: 8d^{3} 1995 11.5m^{2} 11.8f^{3} Oct 23] leggy filly: fairly useful maiden, lightly raced: will be suited by further than 11.8f: acts on firm and dead ground: hung left on reappearance. *H. R. A. Cecil* — 84

SPEEDYBIRD (IRE) 3 b.f. Danehill (USA) 126 – Mille Fleurs (USA) 100 (Jacinto) [1994 NR 1995 a10g^{4} a7g 8d^{6} 7g* Apr 27] 15,500Y: smallish, angular filly: half-sister to several winners, including useful stayer Crusader Castle (by The Minstrel) and 1¼m performer In The Picture (by Tate Gallery): dam, 7.6f winner, is half-sister to Mill Reef: fair form: best effort when making all in maiden at Warwick in April, quickening clear from 2f out: not seen out afterwards: should stay 1m. *B. J. Meehan* — 71

SPEEDY CLASSIC (USA) 6 br.g. Storm Cat (USA) – Shadows Lengthen 73 (Star Appeal 133) [1994 67: a6g* a7g^{2} a6g^{3} a6g^{5} a6g a7g 5.3g^{2} 5.1g 5m 6m* 6m^{3} 5.1m* 5.3f^{2} 5m^{5} 5d 5.1d a5g* a6g* a6g^{3} 1995 a6g^{2} a6g^{3} a5g^{4} a6g^{4} 6m 5m^{6} a6g^{4} a5g^{2} a5g^{2} a6g^{4} Dec 18] workmanlike gelding: has round action: fair handicapper: consistent on the all-weather: effective at 5f to 7f: acts on all-weather surfaces and good to firm ground: often used to be blinkered, not since mid-1994: sweating profusely (ran poorly) eighth 5-y-o start: has given trouble at stalls and sometimes taken down early. *M. J. Heaton-Ellis* — 68

SPEEDY SNAPPER 4 ch.g. Hotfoot 126 – Pearling 72 (Ribero 126) [1994 –: 10d^{4} 8s 10.2g 12s^{6} 1995 a11g a14g Apr 11] lengthy, angular gelding: seems of little account: tried blinkered: sold 500 gns Ascot October Sales. *P. D. Cundell* — –

SPEEDY SNAPS PRIDE 3 gr.g. Hallgate 127 – Pineapple's Pride (John de Coombe 122) [1994 –: 6s 7m 6s 1995 a7g^{3} a8.5g 6s^{5} a7g^{3} a6g^{3} a7g^{3} 8.3g a6g^{5} 7g^{3} 7m^{2} 7m 8m^{4} Sep 25] plain, sparely-made gelding: poor maiden handicapper: stays 1m: acts on fibresand and on good to firm and soft going: blinkered final start at 2 yrs. *P. D. Cundell* — 46, a38

SPENCER'S REVENGE 6 ch.g. Bay Express 132 – Armour of Light (Hot Spark 126) [1994 65, a73: 6.5d^{5} 8g a8.5g^{2} 7.9m 7.3s^{4} 8d^{3} 8d a8g^{3} a8g^{2} 1995 a7g* a7g* a7g* a7g^{2} a7g^{3} a8g 7g* a7g* 7f* 7f^{2} a8g* Dec 15] sturdy gelding: poor mover: fairly useful performer: had a very good 1995, winning seller and minor event at Lingfield in January, claimer at Wolverhampton in February, amateurs handicap at Salisbury (final outing for Lord Huntingdon) in May, claimer at Wolverhampton in September, handicap at Yarmouth in October and claimer at Lingfield in December: effective at 7f and 1m: acts on firm ground and all-weather surfaces, probably on dead (well beaten on heavy): tried visored, no improvement: held up nowadays. *M. J. Ryan* — 81

SPENDER 6 b. or br.g. Last Tycoon 131 – Lady Hester (Native Prince) [1994 65, a77: a5g a6g* a6g* a6g* a6g^{2} 5.3g* 5m* 5m^{3} 5.1s^{5} 5d 5.1g a5g a6g^{2} a6g^{6} 1995 a6g^{3} a6g^{2} a5g* a6g^{4} a5g^{3} a6g^{6} a5g* 5m^{3} 5m^{2} 5g 5.1h* 5.2m 5m^{6} 5.1d 5f Oct 14] small, — 76, a83 well-made gelding: fairly useful sprint handicapper: better than ever in 1995, winning on the all-weather at Lingfield in January and March and on turf at Bath (first run for 2½ months) in August: effective at 5f and 6f: acts on the all-weather and on hard and soft ground: tough and genuine. *P. W. Harris*

SPHINX LEVELV (IRE) 2 ch.c. (Mar 9) Digamist (USA) 110 – Fantoccini (Taufan (USA) 119) [1995 6g a6g^4 a7g^6 6.1m^3 7.1m 6d a7g Nov 6] IR 5,200Y: smallish colt: third foal: half-brother to 1993 2-y-o 5f winner Monticino (by Dominion): dam Irish maiden: plater: probably stays 7f: modest effort on fibresand: visored final start: looks none too easy a ride. *A. P. Jarvis* — 52 a45

SPICE AND SUGAR 5 ch.m. Chilibang 120 – Pretty Miss (So Blessed 130) [1994 52, a36: a8.5g^6 a12g^2 a12g^6 a12g 10d^4 10g^3 12g* 8d 10.5g a12g^5 11.8m a14.8g 14s 1995 a14.8g May 13] lengthy mare: poor performer: tailed off only 5-y-o start. *B. R. Cambidge* — –

SPILLO 2 b.c. (Apr 26) Midyan (USA) 124 – Myth 89 (Troy 137) [1995 7g 8d 7.1d^3 Oct 11] 8,400Y: leggy, useful-looking colt: good mover: fifth foal: half-brother to 3 winners, notably smart winner at up to 1¾m Midnight Legend (by Night Shift): dam middle-distance winner, is out of close relation to Wassl: best effort in maidens when 5½ lengths eighth of 20 to Helicon at Newmarket penultimate start, travelling strongly in rear then running on under little more than firm hands and heels: disappointing behind Polar Eclipse at Haydock 15 days later: will stay further than 1m: likely to do better. *L. M. Cumani* — 80 p

SPINNING MOUSE 2 b.f. (May 3) Bustino 136 – Minute Waltz (Sadler's Wells (USA) 132) [1995 8.2m 8m a7g Nov 21] quite good-topped filly: third foal: half-sister to 3-y-o 1m winner Daunt (by Darshaan) and 1¼m winner Changing Partners (by Rainbow Quest): dam (unraced) out of smart half-sister to Welsh Pageant: signs of ability in late-season maidens: bred to stay well. *D. Morley* — –

SPINNING WORLD (USA) 2 ch.c. (Mar 5) Nureyev (USA) 131 – Imperfect Circle (USA) 111 (Riverman (USA) 131) [1995 8m* 9s* Nov 22] first foal: dam, runner-up in Cheveley Park and winner at 6f and 7f, is half-sister to very smart Chimes of Freedom from very good family: successful in newcomers event at Longchamp in October and steadily-run 7-runner Prix Saint-Roman at Evry (led 2f out, beat Luna Wells a short neck) in November: will probably stay 1¼m: acts on good to firm ground and soft: an interesting prospect. *J. E. Pease, France* — 106 p

SPIRAL FLYER (IRE) 2 b. or br.f. (Apr 11) Contract Law (USA) 108 – Souveniers (Relko 136) [1995 6m 6g 7g Oct 9] IR 1,800F, 4,000Y: good-topped filly: half-sister to several winners, including 1994 2-y-o 5f winner Nazute (by Cyrano de Bergerac) and fairly useful 6-y-o 7f/1m winner Whatever's Right (by Doulab): dam, showed ability at 3 yrs in Ireland, out of Princess Royal winner Aloft: well beaten in maiden events at Kempton, Brighton and Leicester. *M. D. I. Usher* — –

SPIRITO LIBRO (USA) 2 b.f. (Feb 3) Lear Fan (USA) 130 – Teeming Shore (USA) 110 (L'Emigrant (USA) 129) [1995 6m^4 6f^4 7f^3 5m* 6m* 7g 7s 7m Oct 12] IR 19,000Y: smallish filly: second foal: dam best at 5f: won seller at Edinburgh in August and claimer (claimed out of Sir Mark Prescott's stable £7,000) at Folkestone in September: below form afterwards: really needs further than 5f, and stays 7f: seem unsuited by soft ground. *C. N. Allen* — 62

SPIRITUELLE 3 b.f. Distant Relative 128 – Haunting 79 (Lord Gayle (USA) 124) [1994 69: 5g 5.7f^6 7m^6 7d^3 7g 7s 1995 7g 7.5m^6 12.1m^5 8g Sep 15] leggy, sparely-made filly: no worthwhile form in 1995, soundly beaten after leaving M. McCormack's stable after second start: should stay 1m: acts on dead ground: tried blinkered: sold 3,600 gns Doncaster October Sales. *J. J. O'Neill* — –

SPITFIRE BRIDGE (IRE) 3 b.g. Cyrano de Bergerac 120 – Maria Renata (Jaazeiro (USA) 127) [1994 56: 6m 7g 7.1d a7g^3 8g 1995 a8g^3 a12g^5 10m^3 a10g^4 8.3m^6 10.2m* 10d 10.8g^3 a10g* a10g* a12g^6 a10g^5 Dec 6] compact gelding: fair all-weather performer, modest on turf: won seller at Bath in June and minor event and handicap at Lingfield in November: stays 10.2f: acts on good to firm and dead ground and on equitrack (well beaten on fibresand): blinkered twice (ran well first occasion) at 2 yrs. *M. McCormack* — 50 a69

SPLASH OF SALT (IRE) 5 b.m. Salt Dome (USA) – Indian Splash 94 (Prince Tenderfoot (USA) 126) [1994 63: a7g 6m 5d^3 5g^2 5m* 5m^4 5m 5m 6.1s 5d 1995 a6g — 43

a6g^4 a6g a6g^6 a6g^4 a6g^6 6m 5m 7m 6f 5m^4 Jul 12] good-topped, quite attractive mare: has a quick action: poor form at best in 1995: effective at 5f, and stays 7f: acts on all-weather surfaces and on good to firm ground: effective blinkered or not: sold 4,200 gns Newmarket July Sales: sent to Bahrain. *T. J. Naughton*

SPLICING 2 ch.f. (Apr 1) Sharpo 132 – Soluce 98 (Junius (USA) 124) [1995 5g^2 5f^4 6m^3 6.5m Sep 6] sparely-made filly: fifth living foal: sister to useful sprinter Splice, closely related to fairly useful miler Alfujairah (by Diesis) and half-sister to a 1m winner in Ireland by Slip Anchor: dam Irish 7f winner: placed in maiden at Warwick in June and minor event at Ripon in August: stays 6f: below form on very firm ground: hung left last 2 starts: sold 12,500 gns Newmarket Autumn Sales. *J. R. Fanshawe* 69

SPLINTERCAT (USA) 3 ch.f. Storm Cat (USA) – My Cherie Amour (USA) (Sham (USA)) [1994 NR 1995 7.1m^4 7.6m^3 7m* 7m^2 7.1g^4 Sep 23] $80,000Y: lengthy, rather unfurnished filly: second foal: dam winner from 9f to 1½m in France: fair performer: won maiden at Chester in August by 5 lengths: creditable efforts in handicaps last 2 starts: should stay at least 1m: wandered second start: sent to Dubai. *J. H. M. Gosden* 75

SPLINTER (IRE) 2 b.c. (May 5) Warning 136 – Sharpthorne (USA) 91 (Sharpen Up 127) [1995 5.1f* Jul 19] first foal: dam, 6f winner, daughter of Queen Mary and Flying Childers winner Abeer: odds on, won maiden at Bath by 1½ lengths from Dramatic Entry, leading on bridle 1f out but hanging right: looked sure to improve. *R. Charlton* 81 p

SPORTING FANTASY 2 b.g. (Feb 15) Primo Dominie 121 – Runelia (Runnett 125) [1995 5m 5g 5g^3 5f^2 5m* 5g 5f^4 a5g a6g Dec 12] 6,000F, 13,500Y: smallish, robust gelding: third reported foal: half-brother to 3-y-o 7f (at 2 yrs) and 8.3f winner Rock Foundation (by Rock City): dam half-sister to very useful sprinter Touch Paper: won 4-runner seller at Edinburgh (bought out of M. Channon's stable 6,000 gns) in July: well below form afterwards: should stay 6f: below form on very firm ground/ fibresand. *J. Balding* 61 d

SPORTING RISK 3 b.g. Risk Me (FR) 127 – Sunday Sport's Pet (Mummy's Pet 125) [1994 55p: 6d 6s^4 1995 7g 8g 8.3m 8f^3 8.5g 8m^4 a8.5g^5 8m 8g Sep 14] leggy gelding: modest maiden handicapper: stays 1m: acts on firm ground: blinkered (below form) once: sold (P. Harris to P. Webber) 8,400 gns Newmarket Autumn Sales. *P. W. Harris* 52

SPORTING SPIRIT 5 br.g. Dunbeath (USA) 127 – Silent Plea 43 (Star Appeal 133) [1994 41: a13g a11g* a12g a12g 1995 12.3f 9.9m Jul 8] lengthy gelding: poor handicapper at best: no promise (without usual blinkers) in 1995: stays 11f: acts on fibresand. *G. P. Kelly* –

SPORTS VIEW 6 b.g. Mashhor Dancer (USA) – Persian Express (Persian Bold 123) [1994 NR 1995 15.4g Apr 10] compact gelding: fair hurdler: poor form at best on flat since 1992. *R. J. Hodges* –

SPOT PRIZE (USA) 4 ch.f. Seattle Dancer (USA) 119 – Lucky Brook (USA) (What Luck (USA)) [1994 108: 8d^5 10.4m^2 12s^4 12f^4 12m^6 11.9m^4 10.2g^4 1995 11.7m^3 10g^5 10.1f^3 11.9m^4 Jun 17] sturdy, lengthy filly: fairly useful form at best in 1995 for new stable: stays 1½m: acts on any going: bandaged behind first 6 starts at 3 yrs: needs treating with caution. *I. A. Balding* 89

SPOTTED EAGLE 2 ch.g. (Apr 13) Risk Me (FR) 127 – Egnoussa 76 (Swing Easy (USA) 126) [1995 5.2g^5 May 31] 7,000Y: good-bodied gelding: has a quick action: brother to 2-y-o 5f winners Prince Manki (in 1992) and Dimes (in 1994) and half-brother to 2 winners, including 6f winner Fiorini (by Formidable): dam, 7f winner, half-sister to very smart Devon Ditty: 9/1 and bit backward, never a factor when around 10 lengths last of 5 to Royal Applause in maiden at Newbury: looked likely to do better. *R. Hannon* 60

SPOUT 3 b.f. Salse (USA) 128 – Arderelle (FR) 80 (Pharly (FR) 130) [1994 103p: 7m* 8g^2 1995 8m 10g* 10m^3 12d* 12v^3 Oct 7] quite attractive filly: good walker: easy mover: smart performer: won listed events at Newbury (sweating) in May and Ascot (after operation to correct sinus infection, beat Saxon Maid 1¾ lengths) in September: favourite, well-beaten third of 5 in Princess Royal Stakes at Ascot final 110 start: will stay 1¾m: acts on good to firm ground and good to soft, probably not on heavy: wears blanket for stalls entry: stays in training. *R. Charlton*

SPREAD THE WORD 3 b.f. Deploy 131 – Apply 87 (Kings Lake (USA) 133) [1994 NR 1995 9g 12m 10g^{3} 10d 11.5s^{2} 12g Oct 16] lengthy filly: fifth foal: half-sister to Belgian 4-y-o 11f and 1½m winner Appro (by Rousillon) and 1½m winner Administer (by Damister): dam 1¼m and 1½m winner out of very useful middle-distance filly Alia: fair maiden: will stay 1¾m: acts on soft ground. *L. G. Cottrell* 69

SPRING CAMPAIGN (IRE) 2 b.c. (Apr 5) Sayaarr (USA) – March The Second (Millfontaine 114) [1995 7.1m^{5} 7.9m^{4} 10m^{4} Oct 19] IR 6,200F, IR 6,000Y, 10,500 2-y-o: big angular colt: first foal: dam never ran: sire (closely related to Maroof) won at 1¾m in France: fair form in median auction maidens: will stay at least 1½m: lacks a turn of foot. *M. C. Pipe* 70

SPRING LOADED 4 b.g. Last Tycoon 131 – Time For Romance (Cure The Blues (USA)) [1994 61d: 8.3d* 10.3f 10m^{4} 9.2f^{2} 10m^{3} 10m* 13.1g* 10.9g^{4} a14.8g a9.4g a12g a12g^{2} a8.5g a13g 1995 a12g a12g Feb 15] leggy, short-backed gelding: tailed off in 1995. *J. G. M. O'Shea* –

SPRING SILHOUETTE 2 b.f. (Mar 12) Kind of Hush 118 – Hasland 40 (Aragon 118) [1995 5m^{5} 5g 6m 6f 7m 5f a8g Nov 24] sparely-made filly: third foal: sister to 2 poor maidens: dam won 5f seller at 2 yrs: well beaten, including in sellers: visored last 3 starts. *Mrs V. A. Aconley* –

SPRINGTIME AFFAIR 4 br.f. Danzig Connection (USA) – Springtime Sugar (USA) (Halo (USA)) [1994 46: 8m 10g 14g 10d 13.8g^{2} a12g 16.4s^{2} 1995 a12g 11.8m 16.1g Oct 3] smallish, sturdy filly: poor maiden: trained by J. W. Mullins for second 4-y-o start only: stays 2m: best form in the mud: won selling hurdle in November. *Mrs N. Macauley* –

SPUMANTE 3 ch.g. Executive Man 119 – Midler (Comedy Star (USA) 121) [1994 56: a7g^{3} 7m^{3} 1995 8.3m 8.2f^{2} 8.2m^{6} 7f 8.2m a7g Dec 19] rangy gelding: fair maiden: likely to stay 1¼m: acts on firm ground and fibresand: has run well when sweating: inconsistent: left R. Champion before final start. *M. P. Muggeridge* 65 d

SQUANDAMANIA 2 b.c. (Feb 16) Ela-Mana-Mou 132 – Garden Pink (FR) (Bellypha 130) [1995 8m Nov 4] 47,000Y: leggy, angular colt: second foal: dam, French 8.2f and 10.5f winner, half-sister to smart French 1¼m performer Pink out of half-sister to top-class Green Dancer: 12/1, down the field in 23-runner median auction maiden at Doncaster: likely to do better. *P. F. I. Cole* – p

SQUIRE CORRIE 3 b.g. Distant Relative 128 – Fast Car (FR) (Carwhite 127) [1994 67: 5m^{4} 7.1g^{6} 7m 6m^{2} 6g^{6} 6m^{3} 6g 1995 6m 5m 6f^{3} 8m 6m^{2} 6g 5g* 5f^{3} a5g^{4} Nov 2] leggy, angular gelding: unimpressive mover: fair handicapper: left L. J. Holt's stable after fourth 3-y-o start: gained first success in 18-runner race at Newmarket (made all) in September: sold out of J. Banks' stable 13,500 gns Newmarket Autumn Sales after next outing: effective at 5f (best form) and 6f: acts on equitrack, has raced only on sound surface on turf: tends to sweat. *G. Harwood* 73

SQUIRES MOUNT 3 b.f. Sharpo 132 – Plaything 69 (High Top 131) [1994 NR 1995 5.1g Apr 4] 11,000Y: lengthy filly: first foal: dam lightly-raced 1m winner: backward, never dangerous in maiden at Nottingham: sold 1,200 gns Newmarket September Sales. *M. Bell* –

ST ADELE (USA) 2 b.f. (May 26) Pleasant Colony (USA) – Northern Sunset (Northfields (USA)) [1995 8f Oct 25] leggy filly: sister to top-class middle-distance performer St Jovite and half-sister to several very smart winners, including 1995 Breeders' Cup second L'Carriere (by Carr De Naskra), winner at up to 1¼m: dam Irish 6f and 7f winner also successful over hurdles: 11/1, never-dangerous tenth of 13 to Bright Water in maiden at Yarmouth: should be capable of better over middle distances. *D. R. Loder* – p

STAFFIN 2 b.f. (Apr 10) Salse (USA) 128 – Fetlar (Pharly (FR) 130) [1995 6m^{3} 7g* 7m^{2} 7.1m^{2} 8g 8.5f* a8d^{5} Dec 30] angular filly: second foal: half-sister to useful 3-y-o Be Mindful (by Warning), 6f and 7f winner at 2 yrs who stay 1¼m: dam unraced half-sister to Jersey Stakes winner Ardkinglass: won maiden at Doncaster in July: good second to Bint Salsabil in listed race at Newmarket and Alhaarth in Solario Stakes at Sandown then creditable seventh in May Hill Stakes at Doncaster 93 (sweating and edgy) on final start for J. Fanshawe: off course 3 months and racing on bute, won allowance event at Hollywood Park in December: well-beaten fifth in $84,000-stakes at Bay Meadows later in month: stays at least 8.5f. *D. Vienna, USA*

STAGE STRUCK (IRE) 3 b.f. Sadler's Wells (USA) 132 – Sun Princess 130 (English Prince 129) [1994 50p: 7d 1995 10m^{3} 12.1m* 10.2m 10f 12m^{2} 10m Aug 27] lengthy filly: fairly useful performer: won maiden at Chepstow in June: stays 1½m: acts on good to firm ground: sometimes bandaged near-hind: found little fourth 3-y-o start. *M. R. Stoute* — 83

STALLED (IRE) 5 b.g. Glenstal (USA) 118 – Chauffeuse 76 (Gay Fandango (USA) 132) [1994 63: a8.5g 8g^{5} 9m^{6} 9.7m 9.2g^{3} 12g^{3} 11.5g^{5} 10.2g^{2} 10s^{3} 12g* 11.5d^{2} 12m^{6} a10g^{6} a16g* a16g* 1995 12g 16m 16.4m a16g 11.8m^{5} 12g^{3} 11.5m* 12m^{3} a16.2g^{4} a14g^{6} a10g a14g* a12g^{4} a12g* Dec 18] sturdy gelding: modest handicapper: won amateurs races at Lingfield in June, Southwell in November and Lingfield in December: stays 2m well: acts on good to firm ground, soft and the all-weather: visored (well below form) once at 3 yrs: sometimes hangs: held up. *P. T. Walwyn* — 57

STAMSHAW 6 ch.m. Noalto 120 – Saint Motunde 84 (Tyrant (USA)) [1994 41d: a7g a7g a7g^{2} a6g^{3} a6g^{3} 5s^{5} 5v 5d a6g^{6} 6d 5m^{5} 5.9m^{6} 1995 11f Oct 24] workmanlike mare: poor maiden: well beaten only 6-y-o start. *W. Storey* — –

STANDOWN 2 b.g. (Mar 30) Reprimand 122 – Ashdown (Pharly (FR) 130) [1995 5m* 5.1m^{3} 5g^{2} 5m 5g* 5g^{4} 6m^{6} 6m^{4} 7m Oct 30] 6,200F, 8,500Y: compact gelding: third reported foal: half-brother to 3-y-o Logie (by Prince Sabo): dam thrice-raced granddaughter of Irish 1000 Guineas winner Favoletta, a very useful family: won claimers at Thirsk in May and Sandown in September: stays 6f: has raced only on a sound surface. *J. Berry* — 69

STAND TALL 3 b.g. Unfuwain (USA) 131 – Antilla 87 (Averof 123) [1994 NR 1995 7g 7.1m^{6} 8m 10g 7g 6d 5g 6m^{4} a7g^{2} a6g* Nov 30] 7,400Y: tall, quite good-topped gelding: ninth foal: half-brother to 7f winner Sympathy (by Precocious) and 1986 2-y-o 6f winner Uniformity (by Formidable): dam, 2-y-o 5f winner, is half-sister to very smart John French and daughter of half-sister to Derrylin: modest handicapper: won at Lingfield in November: effective at 6f to 1m: acts on good to firm ground and the all-weather: usually races prominently. *C. W. Thornton* — 59

STAND YOUR GROUND 2 b.c. (Apr 26) Common Grounds 118 – Proserpina (FR) (Shafaraz (FR) 124) [1995 6m^{6} 6s Sep 28] 5,600F, 9,600Y: lengthy colt: fourth foal: dam French maiden: behind in maiden and claimer at Lingfield: sold 1,050 gns Doncaster November Sales: sent to Austria. *G. L. Moore* — –

STAR AND GARTER 2 ch.f. (Apr 24) Soviet Star (USA) 128 – On Show 92 (Welsh Pageant 132) [1995 5m^{3} 6g^{3} 6.1d^{6} 7f^{4} Oct 12] leggy, close-coupled filly: half-sister to useful 3-y-o 7f and 1¼m winner Wild Rice (by Green Desert) and several other winners, including smart milers Inchmurrin (by Lomond) and Guest Artiste (by Be My Guest) and smart 1989 2-y-o 6f winner Welney (by Habitat): dam 1¼m winner out of Park Hill winner African Dancer: fair form in maidens: will stay beyond 7f: acts on firm ground, badly drawn on dead. *G. Wragg* — 75

STAR ANISE 3 ch.f. Prince Daniel (USA) – Elmajarrah (CAN) 77 (Caro 133) [1994 NR 1995 7m^{5} 8.5m Sep 6] first foal: dam maiden (possibly didn't stay 11.5f) out of half-sister to Siberian Express: soundly beaten in Epsom maidens. *M. R. Channon* — –

STARFIDA 2 b.f. (Jan 8) Soviet Star (USA) 128 – Stufida (Bustino 136) [1995 6g Sep 30] 5,000 2-y-o: small, angular filly: sixth foal: half-sister to 3 winners here and abroad, including 1989 2-y-o 6f and 7f winner Fearless Revival (by Cozzene) and 1992 2-y-o 7f winner Abtaal (by Green Desert): dam very good Italian filly, winner of 1¼m Group 3 event: 33/1, behind throughout in maiden won by Polish Spring at Newmarket. *C. A. Dwyer* — –

STAR FIGHTER 3 gr.c. Siberian Express (USA) 125 – Eezepeeze 88 (Alzao (USA) 117) [1994 62, a67: 6m^{3} 7f^{3} a7g 7m^{5} 7m a8g a8g^{5} a10g* a8g^{3} 1995 a10g^{4} a10g^{4} a10g* a10g a8.5g^{5} 12.5m^{4} a8g 12g^{4} 12d^{6} 14.1g^{6} 8m a10g^{6} Nov 2] quite good-topped colt: unimpressive mover: modest performer: well below form after winning claimer at Lingfield in February: left W. O'Gorman after eleventh start: unlikely to stay beyond 1¾m: acts on firm ground and equitrack (below form on fibresand): tried blinkered and visored: held up. *M. J. Haynes* — 47, a62

STAR INFORMATION 3 ch.f. Mazilier (USA) 107 – Mary Miller 71 (Sharpo 132) [1994 –: 5.1g 7s 6g 1995 a7g^4 a7g a10g a6g Feb 10] smallish filly: little sign of ability. *J. S. Moore* –

STARLIGHT FLYER 8 b.g. In Fijar (USA) 121 – Nareen (USA) (The Minstrel (CAN) 135) [1994 –: 9.7v 8.1d 10g 8d 9m a9.4g^4 9g a9.4g 7d 10s 11.5d 1995 9.7g 11.9m 10m a8.5g^4 10m 8m^5 7g a14g Nov 24] good-bodied gelding: no longer of any account. *J. E. Long* –

STAR MANAGER (USA) 5 b.g. Lyphard (USA) 132 – Angel Clare (FR) (Mill Reef (USA) 141) [1994 82: 8s 8m 10m 8.1g* 8m 8m 8s^4 8m 1995 8g* 8m 7.9m^4 10f 10d 8s^6 8f^3 Oct 24] close-coupled gelding: fluent mover: fairly useful handicapper on his day: produced late burst to win 20-runner Ladbroke Spring Cup at Newbury in April: stays 1m well (not beaten by trip when tried at 1¼m): acts on any going: held up and takes good hold (has worn crossed noseband): below form 4 times when sweating and/or edgy. *P. F. I. Cole* 83

STARMANIAC (USA) 2 b.c. (Feb 3) Septieme Ciel (USA) 123 – Silver Lane (USA) 115 (Silver Hawk (USA) 123) [1995 7g* 7g^2 8s^5 6.5g^2 6.5g^2 Nov 7] first foal: dam, 5.5f (at 2 yrs) to 1m (Prix de la Grotte) winner and third in Irish Oaks, is sister to high-class middle-distance colt Hawkster: useful French colt: won newcomers event at Maisons-Laffitte in July: best efforts when beaten a nose in Prix Eclipse at Deauville (running on well) and a short neck in Criterium des 2 Ans at Evry (led briefly close home), behind Titus Livius both times: should prove as effective at 1m as shorter. *C. Laffon-Parias, France* 107

STAR OF GOLD 3 b.g. Night Shift (USA) – Sure Gold 100 (Glint of Gold 128) [1994 70: 6m 6m^2 6m* 7m 1995 6m 6m 7.5m^6 8.2m^2 8.2f^3 8f^4 8.3m^3 7m* 7.1m^6 7f 7d Oct 19] small, sturdy gelding: good mover: fair performer: won minor event at Leicester in August: stays 8.3f: acts on firm ground: usually races prominently. *C. R. Egerton* 65

STAROFGREATINTENT (USA) 3 ch.c. Lomond (USA) 128 – Soliciting (USA) (Sassafras (FR) 135) [1994 –: a6g 1995 10g 8g Jun 3] lengthy colt: no worthwhile form: sent to USA. *J. M. P. Eustace* –

STAR OF PERSIA (IRE) 3 gr.c. Persian Bold 123 – Caranina (USA) 85 (Caro 133) [1994 74: a8g^5 8g^5 1995 10g^5 10.3g* 10g 10m* 10m* Aug 26] close-coupled colt: useful performer: won maiden at Doncaster in July and 2 handicaps (latter a rated stakes by 3 lengths) at Newmarket in August: effective at 1¼m and will probably get further: yet to race on a soft surface: takes good hold: sweated up (below form) third 3-y-o start. *P. W. Harris* 96

STAR OF RING (IRE) 2 b.c. (Apr 10) Taufan (USA) 119 – Karine (Habitat 134) [1995 7.1g^6 7.1g^5 Jul 19] 40,000Y: good-bodied colt: half-brother to Irish 1m 71

Ladbrokes Spring Cup (Handicap), Newbury—
it looks like being a very tight finish until Star Manager (near side) produces an amazing late burst

winner Uptothehilt (by Kris), later winner in USA, and 2 winners abroad: dam lightly-raced half-sister to Earl of Sefton winner Heaven Knows: carrying plenty of condition, sixth of 11 to Pommard in maiden at Sandown: well-backed 5/1-shot, disappointing fifth of 8 in similar event there following month: likely to stay 1m. *M. J. Heaton-Ellis*

STAR OF THE GLEN 9 b.g. Glenstal (USA) 118 – Bamstar 70 (Relko 136) 23
[1994 NR 1995 14.1f^4 14.9m^6 Jul 15] angular, lengthy gelding: poor at best nowadays: sold 600 gns Doncaster November Sales. *S. Coathup*

STAR OF ZILZAL (USA) 3 b.g. Zilzal (USA) 137 – Tell Me Sumthing (USA) 101
(Summing (USA)) [1994 85p: 7m^3 7g* 1995 7g* 8m 7m^6 7m 8m^4 8m* 10m^3 Oct 27] tall, lengthy gelding: useful performer: won minor events at Leicester in May and Bath (beat Desert Green ½ length) in September: ran in pattern or listed races otherwise in 1995, giving impression 1¼m stretched his stamina on final start: may prove best at around 1m: acts on good to firm ground: has run creditably when sweating: held up. *M. R. Stoute*

STAR PERFORMER (IRE) 4 b.g. Petorius 117 – Whitstar 93 (Whitstead 125) 49
[1994 49+: 9.9f 7m^6 7d 7d 8.1g 1995 a7g 7m^4 9f^6 7m^5 8g 8d Sep 22] sturdy, good-bodied gelding: modest handicapper at best last 2 seasons: stays 9f: best form (at 2 yrs) with give in the ground: sometimes unruly at stalls. *Mrs M. Reveley*

STAR PLAYER 9 ch.g. Simply Great (FR) 122 – Star Girl (Sovereign Gleam 50 §
117) [1994 82§: 16.2s^2 14m^5 18.7m 16.5m^3 20m 18.7g* 15.9m 14m^4 14g^4 14.6g^5 15.9s^3 16.2m^2 18m^5 16.5v 1995 18.7m 16m 20m 16.2d 16.2s 16m^5 Oct 19] close-coupled gelding: fairly useful in 1994 and did well over hurdles in 1994/5: well below form at 9 yrs: stays 2½m: probably acts on any going, except firm: blinkered (below form) once at 7 yrs: best held up: lacks resolution and not one to rely on. *R. J. Baker*

STAR QUEST 8 b.h. Rainbow Quest (USA) 134 – Sarah Siddons (FR) 122 (Le 42
Levanstell 122) [1994 69d: 18g^4 16s 16m^6 16s 20m 16.1m 16m 15.9g a16g a16g^2 a16.2g 1995 a16g^5 Jan 3] lengthy horse: poor handicapper at best nowadays: stays at least 2¼m: acts on equitrack, good to firm and dead ground, possibly not soft: tried visored and blinkered: inconsistent. *J. R. Jenkins*

STAR RAGE (IRE) 5 b.g. Horage 124 – Star Bound (Crowned Prince (USA) 84
128) [1994 81: 8d^4 9.2d^2 12.1g* 12m* a11g* 16m^2 11.1f^3 a12g* 16.5m* 18m^2 12m^3 16.2m^3 14.6f^2 16.1f* 15.1m* 16m^2 16.2m* 16.2m 17.2m^2 16.2f* 15.9g^2 14.1m^3 16d^4 14.1d^3 14m^6 18m 16.5v^6 a12g^2 1995 12d^5 13.9m 20m 16.1m 14m^5 16.1h* 16.2m* 16m^5 13.9m 14.1m^2 16.1g* 13.9g 15.9d^4 17.2m^4 14.1f^4 13.9g^3 18m Oct 14] angular gelding: fairly useful handicapper: typically busy in 1995: won in August at Newcastle twice (including £13,700 event) and Beverley: stays 17.2f: acts on hard and dead ground and on fibresand (below form only start on heavy): normally held up: fairly useful form over hurdles for J. L. Harris, successful twice in November: game, genuine and outstandingly tough. *M. Johnston*

STARRY EYED 3 b.f. Warning 136 – Star of The Future (USA) 100 (El Gran 84 p
Senor (USA) 136) [1994 NR 1995 7m* 8g^6 7m^2 Nov 3] sturdy, lengthy filly: first foal: dam, 7f (at 2 yrs) and 8.2f winner stayed 1¼m, out of half-sister to very smart 6f to 1¼m performer Beau's Eagle: fairly useful form: won maiden at Ascot in August, and ran very well when 1½ lengths second of 21 to Charlie Sillett in handicap at Doncaster on final start: will prove best at up to 1m: possibly capable of better: sold 19,000 gns Newmarket December Sales: sent to France. *J. H. M. Gosden*

STARSPORT (IRE) 4 ch.g. Salt Dome (USA) – Ivory Smooth (USA) (Sir Ivor –
135) [1994 55: a8g 6v^3 7m^2 6m^6 6.9s^5 7.1s^3 7f^2 7m 1995 6m 6.9m 8m Jun 1] tall gelding: modest maiden: well below form in 1995: has joined P. Eccles. *D. J. S. ffrench Davis*

STAR TALENT (USA) 4 b.c. Local Talent (USA) 122 – Sedra 116 (Nebbiolo 105
125) [1994 100: 7d 7f^5 6m 7d^4 1995 7m* 7m^5 6m May 4] robust colt: has been hobdayed: impresses in appearance: useful performer at best: returned to best when winning strongly-run minor event at Warwick on reappearance by 1½ lengths from Cool Jazz: disappointing in listed race and minor event afterwards: effective at 6f and 7f: acts on firm and dead ground: found little final 3-y-o start: sold (D. Elsworth to Miss G. Kelleway) only 5,000 gns Newmarket Autumn Sales. *D. R. C. Elsworth*

STAR TULIP 3 b.f. Night Shift (USA) – Silk Petal 105 (Petorius 117) [1994 89: 5.2s^{2} 6m^{3} 6g^{3} 6g^{2} 6m* 6d* 7m 6.1g^{2} 6v 1995 6m^{4} 6m 6g* 6g Jul 15] smallish, strong filly: had a quick action: useful handicapper: reportedly in season when well beaten on second 3-y-o start: best effort to win listed rated stakes at Haydock later in May: tailed-off last of 10 in listed race at Newbury on only subsequent outing: stayed 6f: acted on good to firm and dead ground: stud. *J. L. Dunlop* 99

STAR WITNESS (IRE) 3 b.c. Contract Law (USA) 108 – Star Heading 74 (Upper Case (USA)) [1994 75: 5g^{2} 5.1f 6s^{2} 7m* 7f^{5} 7.9d^{2} 7d 7g^{3} 7s 8m a8g 1995 a8g^{5} Jan 17] strong, compact colt: fair form at best for R. Hannon at 2 yrs: well beaten only start in 1995: sent to Czech Republic. *J. S. Moore* –

STASH THE CASH (IRE) 4 b.g. Persian Bold 123 – Noble Girl (Be Friendly 130) [1994 94: 8s* 8.1s* 10.3m 8g 8g 9v 1995 9.2s^{2} Apr 12] quite good-topped gelding: fairly useful at best at 3 yrs for R. Hannon: just fair form when second of 13 in claimer at Hamilton only 4-y-o start: stays 9.2f: acts on soft ground. *T. Dyer* 70 +

STATAJACK (IRE) 7 b.g. King of Clubs 124 – Statira 103 (Skymaster 126) [1994 89: 12v^{3} 12d^{3} 12d^{6} 14f^{4} 10s* 10.1m 12.5f^{2} 10m* 12m* 12g^{2} 12m^{5} 13.3s^{6} 12m^{3} 1995 12m 10m^{3} 10m^{4} May 27] leggy, sparely-made gelding: fairly useful handicapper: effective at 1¼m and 1½m: acts on any ground: best form in blinkers: sometimes carries head high and runs in snatches: suited by strong handling and well ridden by T. Quinn: held up. *D. R. C. Elsworth* 90

STATE APPROVAL 2 b.c. (Mar 23) Pharly (FR) 130 – Tabeeba (Diesis 133) [1995 a6g^{2} 6m a7g^{2} 8g 8g 8m^{3} Oct 28] 3,100F, 5,400Y: small colt: third foal: half-brother to 3-y-o Elsie's Bar (by Primo Dominie) and a winner in Denmark by Reprimand: dam never ran: modest performer: best efforts when placed in sellers: will be well suited by 1¼m+: stays 1m: acts on fibresand and good to firm ground. *A. P. Jarvis* 61

STATE LAW 3 b.g. Law Society (USA) 130 – Miss Zadig 102 (Thatch (USA) 136) [1994 82: 7f 7g^{3} 7.6v^{3} 8d^{5} 8m^{6} 1995 9m^{3} 10m* 10f^{2} 10f^{4} 10m 12g^{2} 10g^{3} Sep 29] strong, good sort: easy mover: fairly useful performer: very easy winner of maiden at Brighton in June: in frame in handicaps on 4 of his 5 starts afterwards: stays 1½m: acts on firm ground: sold 50,000 gns Newmarket Autumn Sales. *G. Harwood* 94

STATELY 2 ch.f. (Mar 7) Be My Chief (USA) 122 – Lady Barrister (Law Society (USA) 130) [1995 6m^{3} 6m a7g 8m 7g* 8g^{3} 8f Oct 18] sturdy filly: third foal: half-sister to 2 winners, notably 3-y-o Edipo Re (by Slip Anchor), 1m Italian listed winner at 2 yrs: dam unraced out of sister to Irish 2000 Guineas winner Kings Lake and half-sister to top-class middle-distance performer Salmon Leap: won nursery at Catterick in September: ran well when third in similar event at Warwick in October but well beaten when blinkered on final start: will stay beyond 1m: usually bandaged behind: sold 15,000 gns Newmarket Autumn Sales. *Sir Mark Prescott* 57

STATELY DANCER 2 b.f. (Feb 18) Be My Guest (USA) 126 – Wild Pavane (Dancing Brave (USA) 140) [1995 6m 6f^{3} Oct 23] first foal: dam (unraced) out of half-sister to On The House (by Be My Guest): 5 lengths third of 18 to Wildwood Flower in maiden at Leicester, always prominent and keeping on gamely: will improve again, particularly over 7f+. *G. Wragg* 65 p

STATELY HOME (IRE) 4 b. or br.g. Fools Holme (USA) – Water Splash (USA) 85 (Little Current (USA)) [1994 9s^{4} 13s^{2} 12g 12d^{5} 8.5g^{4} 14g 1995 8.5m 10.2m^{4} 12f^{3} 12g* 14.9m^{2} 16.2g Jul 21] leggy, angular gelding: fair maiden (rated 71) in Ireland at 3 yrs for N. Meade: sold IR 4,000 gns Goffs October (1994) Sales: modest form in handicaps here, winning at Folkestone in July: stays 15f: acts on soft ground, probably on firm: sold (B. R. Millman to P. Bowen) 900 gns Ascot September Sales. *B. R. Millman* 58

STATE OF CAUTION 2 b.c. (Feb 14) Reprimand 122 – Hithermoor Lass 75 (Red Alert 127) [1995 7g 7g^{5} Oct 10] 17,000F, 37,000Y: useful-looking colt: good walker: half-brother to several winners, including smart sprinter Poyle George (by Sharpo) and 1990 2-y-o 7f winner Eastern Magic (by Faustus): dam placed from 5f to 7f: under 9 lengths fifth of 14 to Don Micheletto in maiden at Leicester, ridden along behind early on then improving to have every chance before fading: will improve again. *J. L. Dunlop* 76 p

STATE THEATRE (IRE) 2 b.c. (May 17) Sadler's Wells (USA) 132 – Fruition 89 (Rheingold 137) [1995 8d Sep 26] IR 150,000Y: brother to Breeders' Cup Turf 70 p winner Northern Spur, closely related to high-class stayer Kneller (by Lomond) and a listed winner in Germany, and half-brother to smart stayer Great Marquess (by Touching Wood): dam middle-distance half-sister to high-class Flame of Tara, dam of Salsabil (by Sadler's Wells): 4/1, 7½ lengths ninth of 20 to Helicon in maiden at Newmarket, one paced when pushed along from 3f out: looked rather weak: will be well suited by middle distances: sure to improve. *P. W. Chapple-Hyam*

STATE VISITOR 2 b.c. (Jan 28) Be My Guest (USA) 126 – Totham 84 (Shernazar 131) [1995 6m May 21] 18,000Y: lengthy, useful-looking colt: first foal: dam, 1½m winner, granddaughter of Full Dress II: 25/1 and bit backward, ran green, hung left and always behind in maiden at Newbury: unimpressive to post: looked sort to do better. *R. Hannon* –

STATIC LOVE 2 b.f. (Apr 20) Statoblest 120 – Run For Love 70 (Runnett 125) [1995 5m a5g^6 7f Oct 18] good-topped filly: has scope: fourth foal: half-sister to 1992 2-y-o 5f winner Tom Piper (by Music Boy): dam, best at 2 yrs, seemed of little account as 3-y-o: well beaten in sellers (left S. C. Williams' yard after second start) and maiden. *T. T. Clement* –

STATISTICIAN 3 b.g. Statoblest 120 – Sharp Lady 70 (Sharpen Up 127) [1994 NR 1995 7m^4 8m 6m^3 6f^2 6g* Jul 6] tall gelding: half-brother to several winners, including 5f and 1m winner Good N Sharp (by Mummy's Pet) and middle-distance winner Prime Painter (by Robellino): dam won five 6f races: fair performer: won handicap at Catterick in July, making all: will prove best at up to 7f: has raced only on a sound surface: races prominently. *John Berry* 72

STATIUS 3 ch.g. Statoblest 120 – Kuwait Night 67 (Morston (FR) 125) [1994 NR 1995 a6g^4 6g a6g^3 7g^3 6g^2 6m^2 6m^2 7m^6 6f* 6m^2 6m^4 6g 6g 5f* Oct 16] 5,000F, 23,000Y: robust, quite attractive gelding: fifth foal: dam, 1½m winner, sister to useful middle-distance stayer Mubarak of Kuwait out of half-sister to Dominion: bought out of M. Stoute's stable 2,000 gns Newmarket Autumn (1994) Sales: fairly useful handicapper: held his form really well, winning at Thirsk in July and Pontefract in October: best at sprint distances: has raced only on a sound surface on turf: tough and reliable: sold 27,000 gns Newmarket Autumn Sales: sent to Malaysia. *T. D. Barron* 86

STATOMIST 3 ch.f. Statoblest 120 – Misty Arch (Starch Reduced 112) [1994 59: 5s 5g^6 5s^4 5s 1995 5g a5g 5m 7.5m 5m a5g 5.1d Sep 11] leggy filly: modest maiden: no form in 1995, trained first 6 starts by G. Fierro. *R. Harris* –

STATOYORK 2 b.c. (Mar 2) Statoblest 120 – Ultimate Dream 74 (Kafu 120) [1995 6f^5 7m^6 Aug 25] 12,500F, 31,000Y: strong, attractive colt: third foal: dam 5f winner at 2 yrs: similar form in maidens won by Woodborough at Goodwood and Even Top at Newmarket (where travelled smoothly long way): likely to prove best at short of 7f: will improve. *B. W. Hills* 76 p

STEADFAST ELITE (IRE) 4 b.f. Glenstal (USA) 118 – Etching 109 (Auction Ring (USA) 123) [1994 47: 6d^6 5.9s 8.2m 5.9m^2 5g^4 5g 6g 8.3g^5 5s 5d 1995 8f 10.9g Sep 14] workmanlike filly: poor and inconsistent performer: bandaged, well beaten in 1995: won selling hurdle afterwards. *J. J. O'Neill* –

STEADY READY GO (IRE) 3 b.c. Night Shift (USA) – Smeralda (GER) (Dschingis Khan) [1994 ?: 7.5v* 1995 10f^4 8m^2 10m* Jun 17] tall colt: useful performer: second of 5 in £8,800 event at Thirsk (edged left) on only British outing: won minor event at Milan in June: may well stay 1½m: probably acts on any going: sold (L. Cumani to Jamie Poulton) only 4,500 gns Newmarket Autumn Sales. *L. M. Cumani* 103

STEADY RISK 4 ch.g. Risk Me (FR) 127 – Greenstead Lass (Double-U-Jay 120) [1994 –: a6g a5g 5g 1995 7m 6m 7.5m Aug 24] leggy gelding: of no account. *Mrs A. M. Naughton* –

STEAL 'EM 2 b.f. (May 25) Efisio 120 – Eastern Ember 85 (Indian King (USA) 128) [1995 6d 6.1m^5 7m 7.1g^4 Sep 23] 8,200Y: workmanlike filly: third foal: half-sister to fairly useful 3-y-o sprinter Perryston View (by Primo Dominie) and 6f winner Champagne Ateaster (by Hubbly Bubbly): dam stayed 1m: modest maiden: probably stays 7f: withdrawn injured at start second intended outing and gave plenty of trouble at stalls next time. *A. Bailey* 53 +

STEALTH ATTACK (IRE) 2 b.c. (May 5) Fayruz 116 – Adivara 58 (Tyrnavos 129) [1995 5g 5.1m^4 5.1g^2 5.1m^5 5m^4 6s Sep 30] 7,700Y: leggy colt, looked on weak 63 ?

side: fourth foal: brother to a poor maiden and half-brother to Italian 3-y-o 7f winner Mister Time (by Gallic League): dam 1¼m winner: modest form when second of 5 to Whittle Rock in maiden at Chester third start: off course 2 months after next outing and ran poorly both starts afterwards, in selling nursery last time: bred to stay 6f: sold 5,000 gns Doncaster November Sales: sent to Sweden. *J. Berry*

STEAMROLLER STANLY 2 b.g. (Mar 28) Shirley Heights 130 – Miss Demure 106 (Shy Groom (USA)) [1995 6d a8g³ Nov 8] second foal: half-brother to 3-y-o Missel (by Storm Bird), useful 6f winner at 2 yrs: dam won Lowther Stakes: went right at stalls and well behind throughout on debut: 6½ lengths third of 11 to Roman Gold in maiden at Lingfield 6 weeks later: will be well suited by further than 1m: likely to improve again. *C. A. Cyzer* — 70 p

STEEPHOLME 3 ch.f. Fools Holme (USA) – Shalati (FR) (High Line 125) [1994 NR 1995 7g 8g 7.1m 6.9g a12g Oct 28] third reported foal: sister to 10.8f winner Shalholme, and half-sister to a 1m winner in Norway by Northern State: dam French 1m winner: signs of ability, but no worthwhile form: sold 500 gns Ascot October Sales. *R. R. Millman* — –

STELLAR LINE (USA) 2 ch.c. (Mar 16) Zilzal (USA) 137 – Stellaria (USA) 98 (Roberto (USA) 131) [1995 6m 7.1d⁴ 7.1g² Sep 23] close-coupled colt: third foal: half-brother to useful 3-y-o 1¼m winner Ninette (by Alleged): dam 2-y-o 5f and 6f winner: progressive form in maidens: mulish at stalls but settled better than previously when 1¾ lengths second of 16 to Polar Prince at Haydock, drawing clear with winner over 2f out and held only inside last: stays 7f. *B. W. Hills* — 87

STELVIO 3 b.c. Shirley Heights 130 – Beveridge (USA) 86 (Spectacular Bid (USA)) [1994 83P: 8.2d* 1995 11g⁴ 13.9m* 16.2m* Jun 21] tall, close-coupled colt: good mover: useful performer: won minor event at York (by 5 lengths) in May and 11-runner Queen's Vase at Royal Ascot (not clear run turning for home, ran on strongly to beat Double Eclipse by a neck) in June: not seen out afterwards, and sold only 2,000 gns Newmarket December Sales: stays 16.2f well: acts on good to firm and dead ground: wears a rope halter: held up: game and genuine. *H. R. A. Cecil* — 106

STEP ALOFT 3 b.f. Shirley Heights 130 – Pas de Deux 80 (Nijinsky (CAN) 138) [1994 NR 1995 8.3m 12.1g⁴ 10m² 12s² 10.4m² 12m² Oct 21] angular filly: has a quick action: half-sister to several winners, notably smart middle-distance performer Starlet (by Teenoso) and middle-distance stayer Insular (by Moulton): dam 1¼m — 83

Queen's Vase, Royal Ascot—Stelvio (right) inches ahead of Double Eclipse

winner out of very smart Example: fairly useful form: neck second of 19 in handicap at Doncaster on final start, improving to lead 2f out (looked sure to win) but tying up and caught on line: will prove best at up to 1½m: best form on good to firm ground, respectable effort on soft. *Lord Huntingdon*

STEPHANENTSE 5 gr.m. Another Realm 118 – Stephandre 94 (Derring-Do 131) [1994 31: 13m^5 13m^6 12s^3 10.1d 1995 a16g^6 Jan 30] leggy, sparely-made mare: poor middle-distance maiden. *E. J. Alston* –

STEPHENSONS ROCKET 4 ch.g. Music Boy 124 – Martian Princess 90 (Cure The Blues (USA)) [1994 79: 5g^5 5g* 5.1m^3 5.1m^2 5d* 5.1g^4 5f* 5m* 5m 5g 5g 1995 5g 5g 5m 7g 7g Oct 7] good-topped gelding: impresses in appearance: shows knee action: fair handicapper: below form in 1995, off course nearly 4 months after third start: suited by 5f: acts on firm and dead ground: sometimes bandaged behind. *J. Berry* 70

STEP ON DEGAS 2 b.f. (May 8) Superpower 113 – Vivid Impression (Cure The Blues (USA)) [1995 5m^5 5g 6m^3 6m^2 Sep 5] 2,800Y: rather leggy filly: fourth foal: half-sister to Irish 1m winner Puppet Theatre (by Theatrical) and Irish 3-y-o 11.9f winner White Claret (by Alzao): dam won in Ireland as 2-y-o at 6f and later at 1¼m: shaped well when placed in maiden events won by Lady Thiang at Windsor (from outside draw) and Rebel County at Lingfield (after setting too strong a pace): stays 6f: may be capable of better. *S. Dow* 60 +

STEREO DANCER 2 b.c. (Apr 4) Groom Dancer (USA) 128 – Trystero (Shareef Dancer (USA) 135) [1995 6f Aug 25] second foal: half-brother to smart 3-y-o 6f (at 2 yrs) and 7f winner Cadeaux Tryst (by Cadeaux Genereux): dam unraced, from good family: 10/1, last of 8 in maiden at Thirsk, racing well away from stand rail and dropping away from 2f out. *E. A. L. Dunlop* –

STERLING FELLOW 2 b.c. (Apr 24) Pharly (FR) 130 – Favorable Exchange (USA) (Exceller (USA) 129) [1995 7.6d 7g^5 a10g^2 Nov 25] 11,000Y: sixth living foal: brother to 1989 2-y-o 5f and 6f winner Nobody's Sweetheart and half-brother to 3 winners, including 3-y-o stayer Unchanged (by Unfuwain) and useful middle-distance stayer Shonara's Way (by Slip Anchor): dam French 1¼m to 1½m winner: progressive maiden: made most when beaten head by Thorntoun Estate at Lingfield: will stay beyond 1¼m. *R. Hannon* 64

STERNKOENIG (IRE) 5 gr.h. Kalaglow 132 – Sternwappen (GER) (Sternwacht (GER)) [1994 122: 12m^5 11v^4 11g^2 12m* 1995 9.5g* 11d* 12g^2 12d^3 14g* Nov 26] very smart German-trained horse: off course 13 months, easy winner of minor event at Cologne in August: showed himself almost as good as ever when winning 8-runner Premio Federico Tesio at Milan by 2¼ lengths from Caballo, leading under 2f out: ran well when 2½ lengths second of 10 to Solon in strongly-run Europa-Preis at Cologne and unlucky when head-third of 8 to Court of Honour in Gran Premio del Jockey Club Italiano at Milan: won 11-runner Premio Roma Vecchia by a nose from Asterita, coming from last to lead 150 yards out then holding on: stayed 1¾m: acted on any going: genuine and consistent: has been retired to Gestut Rottgen. *H. Blume, Germany* 120

STEVIE'S WONDER (IRE) 5 ch.g. Don't Forget Me 127 – Azurai 80 (Dance In Time (CAN)) [1994 61, a54: a10g^6 7.6g 10g^6 8d 10v* 10d* 10g a12g^3 1995 a12g* a12g* a12g^2 a12g^2 11.8m 12g^5 11.8g* 12m^4 11.6m a11g* a14.8g^4 12d 14d* a12g^2 a12g^4 a11g Dec 1] sturdy gelding: fair performer: won apprentice claimer at Lingfield (final start for T. Mills) and handicap at Southwell in January, handicap at Leicester in June, claimer at Southwell in August and handicap at Salisbury in September: stays 1¾m: acts on any going, including all-weather surfaces: blinkered (below form) once at 2 yrs, visored last 4 starts: wears a tongue strap: has won for 7-lb claimer: front runner/races close up: genuine. *M. J. Ryan* 63 a72

STICKS AND STONES (IRE) 3 b.g. Waajib 121 – Maiacourt (Malacate (USA) 131) [1994 78p: 7f 7.1m^4 7g* 1995 7.9g 7g 10.5g^4 8f^4 Jun 23] strong, attractive gelding: impresses in appearance: good mover: fair handicapper: ran creditably all starts in 1995, blinkered on final one: stays 10.5f: acts on firm going. *Mrs J. Cecil* 78

STICKS MCKENZIE 2 ch.c. (Mar 15) Hadeer 118 – Tithing (USA) (Nureyev (USA) 131) [1995 6g 6m^5 7m^5 8g 8g Oct 3] well-made colt: good mover: fifth foal: brother to 3-y-o Tenpenny and useful 1¼m (in USA) and 1½m (in France) winner 62

Sans Ecocide: dam placed 4 times from 6 starts in USA: modest form: below best last 2 starts: best effort at 6f: sold 8,500 gns Newmarket Autumn Sales: sent to France. *B. W. Hills*

STIFFELIO (IRE) 3 ch.c. Be My Guest (USA) 126 – Ivor's Honey (Sir Ivor 135) [1994 90: 7m 8s^2 8m 10g* 1995 11g^5 12.3m^5 10.1f^2 12f^3 11.9m^4 10.5f^5 10m* 12s Sep 27] rather leggy, attractive colt: has a short action: useful performer: won minor event at Windsor in August, outbattling Golden Ball, on final outing for R. Hannon: eighth of 11 in Grade 3 race at Belmont following month: stays 1½m: acts on firm and soft ground. *W. E. Walden, USA* — 103

STILETTO BLADE 3 b.c. Dashing Blade 117 – On The Tiles (Thatch (USA) 136) [1994 110p: 7g* 8g^2 7m^5 1995 8m^3 8.1m^3 8m^3 10.4g 8f^5 8.5f^3 a9f^5 9f^2 10f* 9f^3 Dec 30] rangy, good sort: useful form as 2-y-o: went wrong way temperamentally in the spring, wearing net muzzle in preliminaries and taken down early in listed race at Kempton (hung right), minor events at Sandown (sweating) and Doncaster (mulish) and Dante Stakes at York (last of 8, final race for I. Balding): raced on lasix and bute in USA, running consistently and winning allowance event at Hollywood Park in December: stays 1¼m: raced only on a sound surface. *H. Stokes, USA* — 97 §

STILL HERE (IRE) 2 b.g. (May 8) Astronef 116 – Covey's Quick Step (Godswalk (USA) 130) [1995 a6g a7g^4 a6g^5 a7g^3 6s Sep 30] IR 4,600F, 3,000 2-y-o: third foal: half-brother to 3-y-o Cup Magic (by Magical Strike), 1m winner in Hungary: dam Irish maiden: modest form in maiden auction events second and third starts: well beaten in selling nursery last time: stays 7f: acts on fibresand. *M. J. Heaton-Ellis* — 55

STINGING REPLY 3 ch.f. Belmez (USA) 131 – Nettle 106 (Kris 135) [1994 59: 7s^4 7.1g 1995 8g* 8m 9g^5 10.2m^2 10g^6 8h^3 Aug 3] sparely-made filly: has a round action: fair performer: made all in maiden at Warwick in April: may prove best at up to 1¼m: acts on good to firm ground, probably on soft: sold (I. Balding to Lord Huntingdon) 7,000 gns Newmarket December Sales. *I. A. Balding* — 75

STIPPLE 4 ch.f. Blushing Scribe (USA) 107 – April 107 (Silly Season 127) [1994 50: 6m^5 5.9m 7g 1995 a10g a8g^5 6f 9.7m May 31] small, sparely-made filly: well beaten for new stable in 1995: should stay at least 1m. *S. Woodman* — –

ST KITTS 4 b.f. Tragic Role (USA) – T Catty (USA) 62 (Sensitive Prince (USA)) [1994 43: 9.9m* 12f^{4dis} 13.8d^2 12m^5 16.2f^2 16d 1995 16.4m^6 Nov 6] angular, workmanlike filly: poor performer: stays 2m: acts on firm and dead ground. *W. G. M. Turner* — –

ST LOUIS LADY 4 gr.f. Absalom 128 – Pearl Cove 63 (Town And Country 124) [1994 51+: 7d^2 8.3d^4 7d* 1995 7m 7m^3 7.1m Aug 30] tall filly: modest handicapper: effective at 7f, and should stay beyond 1m: acts on good to firm and dead going: often blinkered. *W. Jarvis* — 59

ST MAWES (FR) 2 ch.c. (Feb 10) Shahrastani (USA) 135 – Exemina (USA) (Slip Anchor 136) [1995 7g 7f* Aug 9] 320,000 francs Y: good-bodied, attractive colt: first foal: dam, French middle-distance winner, daughter of smart French mare El Fabulous: favourite, unimpressive to post and still backward, won 9-runner maiden at Salisbury by 1¼ lengths from Proper Blue, taking good hold in rear before improving to lead inside final 1f: will be suited by middle distances: will improve again. *J. L. Dunlop* — 89 p

STOLEAMARCH 2 br.c. (Apr 28) Daring March 116 – Pennine Star (IRE) 68 (Pennine Walk 120) [1995 5g^6 6g^6 7m Jun 13] rather leggy colt: first foal: dam effective from 1¼m to 1½m: little worthwhile form in varied company, including selling. *Mrs M. Reveley* — –

STOLEN KISS (IRE) 3 b. or br.f. Taufan (USA) 119 – Sweet Goodbye (Petorius 117) [1994 68: 5g^3 5s 5.1m 5f^4 5m^3 6d^4 5d^5 5s 1995 6m^4 6m^5 6g^4 5g^2 6g^2 5m* 5f^5 5m^2 5.1m^5 5m^5 5g^2 6g^3 5d 5s Oct 7] big, workmanlike filly: poor mover: fair handicapper: looked reluctant fourth and fifth 3-y-o starts, but did little wrong afterwards, winning at Beverley in June and holding her form well: effective at 5f and 6f: acts on firm and good to soft ground, seems unsuited by soft: usually blinkered/visored. *M. W. Easterby* — 76

STOLEN MELODY 3 b.f. Robellino (USA) 127 – Song of Hope 103 (Chief Singer 131) [1994 74p: 6m^6 6d^2 6m* 1995 8.5s 7g 7m^5 7f Oct 18] sturdy, lengthy — 69

filly: poor mover: fair handicapper: probably stays 7f: acts on firm and dead ground. *S. Dow*

STOLEN MUSIC (IRE) 2 b.f. (May 11) Taufan (USA) 119 – Causa Sua (Try My Best (USA) 130) [1995 7g Oct 9] IR 8,800Y: workmanlike filly: third foal: dam Irish 7f and 1¼m winner: 50/1 and better for race, slowly away and never a threat in maiden at Leicester: will do better. *Major D. N. Chappell* – p

STONE CROSS (IRE) 3 b.g. Pennine Walk 120 – Micro Mover (Artaius (USA) 129) [1994 NR 1995 11.1d^2 12g^5 Apr 21] IR 2,000F, IR 6,600Y: leggy gelding: half-brother to several winners here and abroad, including 1989 2-y-o 6f winner Ela-Yemou (by Dara Monarch): dam won at 10.5f in France: modest form in maidens: likely to benefit from a thorough test of stamina. *R. F. Fisher* 60

STONEHAM GIRL 3 b.f. Nomination 125 – Persian Tapestry 70 (Tap On Wood 130) [1994 33: 5s^6 5v^2 5d 6s^6 6g^5 7m 9.7s 1995 12d 10m 10g Oct 1] workmanlike filly: poor plater. *P. Butler* –

STONE RIDGE (IRE) 3 b.c. Indian Ridge 123 – Cut In Stone (USA) 72 (Assert 134) [1994 82p: 7g^3 7g^2 1995 10m 8m* 9m^6 7.1m 8m^5 8.1m^5 8d 8m* 8m Oct 28] useful-looking colt: fairly useful handicapper: won maiden at Brighton in April and 23-runner £29,600 Rothmans Royals North South Challenge Series Final (led 3f out, held on really well by neck from Mo-Addab) at Newmarket in October: probably stays 9f: best form on a sound surface: blinkered (probably unsuited by conditions) seventh 3-y-o start: tends to carry head high: sold 37,000 gns Doncaster November Sales. *R. Hannon* 91

STONEY END (USA) 2 b.c. (May 8) High Brite (USA) – Cranareen (USA) (Nice Dancer (CAN)) [1995 6m Jul 22] $35,000Y: strong colt: ninth foal: closely related to a minor stakes winner by Best Turn and half-brother to several minor winners in USA: dam minor 1m stakes winner: sire smart 6f to 9f winner at 2 to 5 yrs: 3/1 and in need of race, eighth of 10 to Akalim in maiden at Newmarket, travelling well until checked when beginning effort 2f out: looked sure to do better. *M. R. Channon* – p

STONEY VALLEY 5 b.g. Caerleon (USA) 132 – Startino 111 (Bustino 136) [1994 86d: 8s 10.4f^5 10.1m 12m 10m^6 1995 16m 16.4m 14m 14s May 30] rangy, angular gelding: has a quick action: fair handicapper at best in 1995: rated on his 71

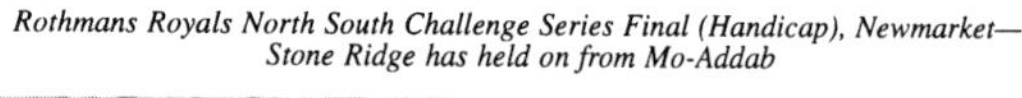

Rothmans Royals North South Challenge Series Final (Handicap), Newmarket— Stone Ridge has held on from Mo-Addab

form at 2m: acts as good to firm ground (probably on firm) and dead: fair hurdler, winner in August and September. *J. R. Jenkins*

STOOP TO CONQUER 2 b.g. (Feb 4) Machiavellian (USA) 123 – Chesnut Tree (USA) 97 (Shadeed (USA) 135) [1995 7g 7m^5 Jul 30] rangy gelding: has a round action: first foal: dam, 1½m winner, daughter of Ribblesdale winner Expansive: never dangerous in maidens won by Alhaarth at Newmarket and Bonarelli at Chester (blinkered) in July. *R. Charlton* — 69 ?

STOPPES BROW 3 b.g. Primo Dominie 121 – So Bold (Never So Bold 135) [1994 60, a83: 5s^4 5f^3 5d 5m 6g a5g* a5g* a6g^2 1995 a5g* a6g* a6g^3 a6g* 6m 5m 6m^6 6f^4 7f^4 7m* 7g^4 7g^3 6g^2 a6g Nov 11] strong, lengthy gelding: poor mover: made into a fairly useful handicapper on the all-weather in the winter, winning 3 times at Lingfield after turn of year: not so good on turf, but won at Goodwood in August in good style: stays 7f: acts on firm going and the all-weather: effective visored or not: successful for 7-lb claimer: usually held up: consistent. *G. L. Moore* — 72, a89

STOP PLAY (IRE) 2 b.f. (Feb 9) Distinctly North (USA) 115 – Church Mountain 83 (Furry Glen 121) [1995 5m^5 5g^5 5.2g* 6m 5m^3 6m^2 6d^5 6.1m 7m^5 Nov 4] 12,500F: good-topped filly: has scope: half-sister to several winners, including 3-y-o 1½m winner Vaugrenier (by Scenic) and 1985 2-y-o 6f winner Mac's Flyer (by Godswalk): dam 2-y-o 6f winner: fair form: won maiden at Yarmouth in July: mostly respectable efforts in nurseries after: should stay further than 6f: raced freely in visor final start. *M. H. Tompkins* — 78

STOPROVERITATE 6 ch.m. Scorpio (FR) 127 – Luscinia 73 (Sing Sing 134) [1994 54: a8g^5 8.3v 9d^2 8.3s^4 10g 10.4d 10s 8g^5 1995 10.3g 9.9m 12.4g^2 a12g^4 Jul 22] workmanlike mare: poor handicapper: stays 12.4f: acts on good to firm ground, heavy and fibresand: visored once at 3 yrs. *Mrs M. Reveley* — 48

STORITHS (IRE) 5 b.h. Double Schwartz 128 – Atlantic Dream (USA) (Muscovite (USA) 105) [1994 105: 6m^2 6m 7.1g^3 6f^3 7m 7f^4 7m^5 8g^3 7s^3 1995 7m^3 7.1m^2 7.9g^4 7.1g^5 6m^6 7f^3 7m^4 8f^2 Dec 31] leggy horse: very useful performer on his day: best efforts in listed rated stakes at Haydock (beaten head by Moccasin Run) and York second and third 5-y-o starts: sold out of J. Watts's stable 22,000 gns Newmarket Autumn Sales after penultimate start: ½-length second in claimer in USA final one: stays 1m: acts on firm and soft ground: sometimes drifts right: probably effective blinkered or not: wears bandages: often soon off bridle: not one to rely on. *S. Shulman, USA* — 110 d

STORMAWAY (ITY) 3 ch.c. Glenstal (USA) 118 – Smurfiusa (USA) (Sharpen Up 127) [1994 NR 1995 10m 10g 10d^6 11f^4 15.4g^5 14m 11g 8m 14g Nov 26] 12,000 (approx) Y: leggy, quite attractive colt: half-brother to smart 1¼m/1½m performer Usaidit (by Commanche Run): dam won in Italy: little worthwhile form: trained first 6 starts by T. Mills. *P. Martometti, Italy* — –

STORM BIDDER 4 b.g. Gabitat 119 – Queen's Bidder 84 (Auction Ring (USA) 123) [1994 39: a7g^4 a8g^5 8d 10.8m^5 9.7m 7f^4 8.3m a7g 1995 a12g a8g 8g 5m Jun 16] lengthy gelding: poor maiden: no worthwhile form in 1995. *B. Gubby* — –

STORM BID (USA) 3 b. or br.c. Storm Cat (USA) – Slam Bid (USA) (Forli (ARG)) [1994 NR 1995 7g^2 7g* 6g^4 Jun 14] $220,000Y: lengthy colt: poor mover: fourth reported foal: half-brother to 3 winners, including useful 7f (Prix Imprudence) winner Cydalia (by Cresta Rider): dam lightly-raced French 1m winner out of half-sister to dam of L'Emigrant and Salpinx: fairly useful form: very unruly in preliminaries prior to debut: won maiden at Salisbury in May by 5 lengths: early to post, ran well in minor event at Yarmouth on final start: should stay 1m: races prominently. *E. A. L. Dunlop* — 89

STORM FLASH 3 b.f. Green Desert (USA) 127 – Storm Warning 117 (Tumble Wind (USA)) [1994 65: 6m^3 a6g^4 a7g 1995 8.2m Oct 26] sparely-made filly: fair maiden: well beaten in handicap at Nottingham (after 10-month absence) on only 3-y-o start. *Lord Huntingdon* — –

STORM LEADER 4 br.g. Squill (USA) 122 – African Dash 76 (African Sky 124) [1994 –: 10d 8.3m 8.2m 9m 10g 8f 8.5m 1995 8.1m Jun 19] sparely-made gelding: seems of little account nowadays. *M. Brittain* — –

STORMLESS 4 b.g. Silly Prices 110 – Phyl's Pet (Aberdeen 109) [1994 –: 10g 6g 11.9s 1995 11.1g^6 12.1g 12.1g^3 11.9m^6 Oct 5] tall gelding: poor maiden handicapper: stays 1½m: tends to wander under pressure. *P. Monteith* — 40

STORM TROOPER (USA) 2 b.c. (Feb 17) Diesis 133 – Stormette (USA) (Assert 134) [1995 7f[5] 7g[2] 8.2d* 8v[2] Oct 7] IR 67,000Y: leggy, unfurnished colt: has a round action: fourth reported foal: brother to May Hill and Musidora winner Marillette: dam, Irish 1½m winner, half-sister to Storm Bird out of Canadian Oaks winner and very good broodmare South Ocean: most progressive colt: won 20-runner maiden at Nottingham in good style by 6 lengths from Dark Waters: very good 1¼ lengths second of 5, keeping on resolutely, to Beauchamp King in listed race at Ascot on final outing: will stay middle distances: acts on heavy ground: sure to win more races. *H. R. A. Cecil* — 104 p

STORM WIND (IRE) 2 ch.c. (May 22) Digamist (USA) 110 – Hilton Gateway (Hello Gorgeous (USA) 128) [1995 7.1g 7g Oct 3] close-coupled colt: third reported foal: dam (unraced) from family of Mesopotamia: 50/1 and backward, well beaten in maidens at Haydock and Warwick. *K. R. Burke* — –

STORY LINE 2 ch.f. (Feb 16) In The Wings 128 – Known Line 100 (Known Fact (USA) 135) [1995 7d* Sep 24] 15,000Y: sturdy, good-bodied filly: fourth foal: half-sister to 8.5f winner Party Line (by Never So Bold): dam, 8.2f winner at 2 yrs better at 1½m, half-sister to dam of Pure Grain out of Park Hill winner Quay Line: 16/1 from 8/1, burly and very green, won 8-runner minor event at Ascot by 1¾ lengths from Double Leaf, racing midfield after sluggish start, making headway 2f out then knuckling down in good style: will be suited by middle distances: sure to do better. *B. W. Hills* — 93 p

STOTFOLD BOY (IRE) 2 b.c. (Mar 21) Cyrano de Bergerac 120 – Princess Biddy 86 (Sun Prince 128) [1995 5.1m 5g Jul 18] IR 5,600F, IR 11,000Y: small, attractive colt: poor walker and mover: half-brother to several winners, including 1986 2-y-o 6f winner Hydraulic Power (by Northfields) and 6f winner Fawley's Girl (by He Loves Me): dam, stayed 7f, half-sister to Double Jump and Sunyboy: behind in maiden auctions at Nottingham (very slowly away and raced on unfavoured part of track) and Beverley. *R. Hollinshead* — –

STRAIGHT THINKING (USA) 2 ch.c. (Feb 7) Bering 136 – Sharp Perception (USA) (Sharpen Up 127) [1995 6g[4] a8g[5] Dec 18] 18,000Y: strong, angular colt: a twin: first foal: dam, winner at around 1m in North America, from good family: last of 4 to Tamhid in maiden at Ascot in July: late progress when about 5 lengths fifth of 9 to Apartments Abroad in similar event at Lingfield in December: will be suited by further than 1m. *P. F. I. Cole* — 54

STRATEGIC CHOICE (USA) 4 b.c. Alleged (USA) 138 – Danlu (USA) (Danzig (USA)) [1994 113: 8s[2] 10g* 12d[5] 11.9m 12m[2] 12v[2] 1995 12g* 12f[3] 12g[3] 12s 14g* 12d Oct 1] — 122

In winning the Irish St Leger, Martyn Arbib's Strategic Choice succeeded at the first attempt where the same owner's admirable and enduring Snurge had failed twice. Snurge came a neck second in 1992 but only sixth of eight in 1993. Also in

Lanes End John Porter Stakes, Newbury—Strategic Choice (white nose) moves easily upsides Broadway Flyer

Jefferson Smurfit Memorial Irish St Leger, the Curragh—another narrow victory, but this time Strategic Choice (left) is all out in the end to beat Moonax; Oscar Schindler gets third

both of those renewals was Vintage Crop who was back again for the latest running with what punters reckoned was an outstanding chance—now eight years old and bidding for a unique treble in the race, he started favourite at 11/10. Two more in the seven-runner field who had classic form already were Moonax, bidding for unprecedented British, French and Irish St Leger victories, and Oscar Schindler, a close fourth in the Irish Derby. As in Snurge's battle with Mashaallah three years earlier, the race was resolved in an exciting head-to-head. Moonax tracked Zilzal Zamaan and Vintage Crop into the straight and had just about mastered them two furlongs out, Oscar Schindler and long-shot Double On threatening to get into the argument as well, but what really caught the eye was an extremely confident-looking Richard Quinn making his challenge through the centre on Strategic Choice. They looked set for a clear-cut win at that stage, but over the final furlong Quinn at his cheekiest became Quinn at almost his strongest as Moonax provided stern resistance to go down by just a head. The pair finished three lengths clear of Oscar Schindler, Vintage Crop back in fourth.

Strategic Choice was another who had earlier classic form; the previous June, with just two runs in maidens to his name, he had come fifth of fifteen in the Prix du Jockey-Club. His progress after that was hindered by a heel infection, but he went close in the St Simon Stakes at Newbury in the autumn and returned to that course in fine form for the Lanes End John Porter Stakes on his reappearance in April. Capping an excellent afternoon for owner, trainer and jockey, Strategic Choice shadowed Broadway Flyer and Linney Head up the straight, was still travelling smoothly as Linney Head dropped away, and then had to be pushed out firmly to get his neck in front of Broadway Flyer in the last hundred yards. All of Strategic Choice's appearances after that were in Group 1 events. Lando and Broadway Flyer beat him in the Gran Premio di Milano, Lammtarra and Pentire in the King George. He put up a particularly bold display in the latter, racing in second for most of the way and holding his own with the two three-year-olds for nearly all the straight. Strategic Choice's two other races in 1995, however, were disappointments. Last of nine finishers on very soft ground in the Grosser Preis von Baden preceded his Irish St Leger triumph; fourteenth of sixteen in the Arc de Triomphe followed it fifteen days later.

Strategic Choice is a big, strong colt with a long, easy stride. His four very smart efforts in 1995, and career-best form, were all on a sound surface, the two disappointing ones on softer ground, but his 1994 St Simon Stakes second obviously suggests that he acts on any going. Effective at a mile and a half ridden close to the pace, as he usually is, Strategic Choice stays a mile and three quarters well. He is sometimes bandaged.

Strategic Choice (USA) (b.c. 1991)	Alleged (USA) (b 1974)	Hoist The Flag (b 1968)	Tom Rolfe
			Wavy Navy
		Princess Pout (b 1966)	Prince John
			Determined Lady
	Danlu (USA) (b 1985)	Danzig (b 1977)	Northern Dancer
			Pas de Nom
		Lulu Mon Amour (b 1980)	Tom Rolfe
			Sister Shu

Always Earnest, Flemensfirth, Muhtarram and Strategic Choice are the latest in the long list of good winners by the dual Arc winner Alleged. Strategic Choice's dam Danlu and grandam Lulu Mon Amour both won a race at around a mile at two and three years. Danlu did so for the Jim Bolger stable and she is a sister to two noteworthy European winners, the smart sprinter Nicholas, a Group 2 winner in Germany but probably at least as well known for providing Lester Piggott with his first winner back from retirement, and the useful filly Arbusha who stayed a mile and a half. The different distance requirements are not too surprising given the contrasting influences of sires Danzig (also sire and grandsire respectively of Lulu Mon Amour's smart half-brothers Nordance and Shudanz) and Tom Rolfe (who also figures in the top half of Strategic Choice's pedigree). Third dam Sister Shu was a sister to the outstanding racemare Shuvee. Mr Arbib got his rewarding part of this family after Danlu was sold for 110,000 dollars at Keeneland in 1989. She was then reported in foal to Conquistador Cielo, but Strategic Choice is her first living foal. He is followed by the maiden Suvalu (by Woodman), who has now been sold, by the promising 1995 two-year-old Swift Fandango (by Lear Fan), and by a yearling colt by Gone West. A standard-bearer as successful as Snurge is a lot to ask for. In money terms, Strategic Choice still has about one million pounds to go, but in all other respects he is doing pretty well. *P. F. I. Cole*

STRATEGIC PLOY 2 b.f. (Feb 21) Deploy 131 – Wryneck 89 (Niniski (USA) 125) [1995 7d^5 7f 7f Oct 31] 7,000F, 12,000Y: well-made filly: seventh foal: half-sister to 3-y-o Myrtle Quest (by Rainbow Quest), 8.2f winner at 2 yrs, and 3 winners here and abroad by Sharpo, including 7f to 1m winner Wrybill and 1¼m and 10.8f winner Fox Sparrow: dam won over 7f at 2 yrs on only start: never placed to challenge in maidens at Newcastle (fifth of 11 to Insatiable, on a soft surface and best effort) and Redcar (2) following month: will do better at 3 yrs, particularly over 1m+. *Mrs J. R. Ramsden* – p

STRATH KITTEN 4 ch.f. Scottish Reel 123 – Elemis (USA) 70 (Sir Ivor 135) [1994 36: 8g 10.2m^6 10m 8m 8f^5 7f 1995 a16g May 27] small, sparely-made filly: poor maiden: soundly beaten in 2m selling handicap at Lingfield only 4-y-o start: may prove best at up to 1¼m: acts on good to firm ground: tried blinkered. *W. J. Musson* –

STRATHTORE DREAM (IRE) 4 b. or br.f. Jareer (USA) 115 – Beyond Words (Ballad Rock 122) [1994 NR 1995 7.1d 6s 6g 8g 5g 7.1g 6g Sep 25] leggy filly: well beaten in Scottish handicaps in 1995. *Miss L. A. Perratt* –

STRAT'S LEGACY 8 b.g. Chukaroo 103 – State Romance 67 (Free State 125) [1994 47, a57: a13g^5 a12g^4 a12g^4 a16g^6 11.7g^6 10g^3 11.9f^4 12.1f* 12m^6 10m^6 12g^2 a12g^6 a16g^2 a12g^5 a16g^4 1995 a13g 11.5m^4 12.1m* 12g^6 12.1m^5 12d^4 12g a12g^4 a12g^4 a16g^5 Dec 15] small, light-framed gelding: modest handicapper: won amateurs race at Chepstow in July: best over 1½m+ (stays 2m): acts on the all-weather and on firm and dead ground: often bandaged behind: blinkered once. *D. W. P. Arbuthnot* 48

STRAW THATCH 6 b.g. Thatching 131 – Lashing (USA) 98 (Storm Bird (CAN) 134) [1994 47: 10g 8.3m 7d 8m 10.1d a8g a12g^5 1995 10g* 10g^4 9.9d 10.1m^2 10m 12.4g^6 10.1g 10g 11.8g Oct 10] strong, workmanlike gelding: modest handicapper: won at Pontefract in May: sold out of Mrs J. Ramsden's stable 3,400 gns Doncaster August Sales after fourth start: no worthwhile form afterwards: stays 50 d

1¼m: probably acts on any going: has worn bandages: tried blinkered: swishes tail. *R. Bastiman*

STRAY REIN 3 gr.f. Lochnager 132 – Olibanum 61 (Frankincense 120) [1994 NR 1995 8m^5 11d Sep 22] 6,000Y: angular, good-topped filly: sister to 1993 2-y-o 5f winner Fort Erie and half-sister to 4 winners here and abroad, including winning sprinters Capeability Pound (by Balboa) and Blochairn Skolar (by Most Secret): dam plater: burly, tailed off in maiden and seller. *J. J. Quinn*
–

STREAKY HAWK (USA) 3 b.g. Hawkster (USA) – Veroom Maid (USA) (Distinctive (USA)) [1994 80p: 8s^4 1995 11m 10f^3 a14.8g a11g^4 12d 14g a12g^5 Dec 18] strong, lengthy gelding: disappointing maiden: sold out of P. Cole's stable 11,000 gns Newmarket Autumn Sales after sixth start: should stay at least 1¼m. *J. Pearce*
58 d

STREETE DANCER (IRE) 2 b.f. (Mar 21) Alzao (USA) 117 – Dwell (USA) 96 (Habitat 134) [1995 6.9g^3 7f^4 Jul 27] 29,000Y: third foal: sister to a winning sprinter in Hong Kong and half-sister to King Leon (by Caerleon), useful Irish 2-y-o 1m and 8.5f winner in 1994: dam effective at 6f, won at 1m: in frame in maidens at Folkestone and Goodwood in July: dead. *P. F. I. Cole*
66

STREET LADY 5 b.m. Street Kafu – Lonely Dawn (USA) 63 (Plenty Old (USA)) [1994 –: 10s 8d 7d 5f 1995 7.1g a6g Jun 2] big, workmanlike mare: more sign of temperament than ability: sold 1,300 gns Doncaster September Sales, 575 gns Ascot December. *A. Bailey*
–

STREETWISE SID 3 b.g. Presidium 124 – New Street (USA) 53 (Our Native (USA)) [1994 47: 5.1f 6g 6.1m 5g^5 5d 5m 1995 7f Jun 23] leggy gelding: poor maiden: sold (T. M. Jones to D. Williams) 900 gns Ascot July Sales: withdrawn on intended debut for new stable later in month. *T. M. Jones*
–

STRICTLY PERSONAL (USA) 5 b. or br.g. Secreto (USA) 128 – Tash (USA) (Never Bend) [1994 –: a10g 1995 a12g^3 14.1m 11.9m^6 11.9m Oct 5] good-bodied gelding: only form on flat since 1993 when third in claimer at Wolverhampton in January (final start for K. Burke): burly, tongue tied and most reluctant to leave paddock final outing: stays 1½m: one to treat with caution. *M. A. Barnes*
–
a62

STRIFFOLINO 3 b.g. Robellino (USA) 127 – Tizona (Pharly (FR) 130) [1994 68p: 6g 7f* 1995 9f* 10.1m^5 8f^3 8m^5 7m 8g^4 Sep 15] leggy, lengthy, dipped-backed gelding: good mover: fair handicapper: won at Redcar in June: stays 9f: has raced only on a sound surface: sold (T. D. Barron to A. Barrow) 7,000 gns Newmarket Autumn Sales. *T. D. Barron*
74

STRIKE-A-POSE 5 ch.m. Blushing Scribe (USA) 107 – My Bushbaby 100 (Hul A Hul 124) [1994 38: a8.5g^5 a8g 10.8m 8.1g 1995 16m^6 Jun 26] tall, leggy, sparely-made mare: poor form at best nowadays, and well beaten only 5-y-o start. *B. J. Llewellyn*
–

STRIP CARTOON (IRE) 7 ch.g. Tate Gallery (USA) 117 – Reveal (Pitskelly 122) [1994 51: a6g a7s a6g 1995 6d Sep 18] smallish, workmanlike gelding: modest handicapper: very tough at 5 yrs, but not seen from February 1994 until soundly beaten 19 months later. *S. R. Bowring*
–

STROLLING MINSTREL (IRE) 4 b.g. Fayruz 116 – Airy Queen (USA) (Sadair) [1994 –: 8m 12m 1995 a12g Jan 16] sturdy gelding: of little account: dead. *B. S. Rothwell*
–

STRONZ (IRE) 2 b.c. (May 2) Classic Music (USA) – Carnival Fugue 58 (High Top 131) [1995 6g^3 6f^5 6m^{3dis} 7m^4 6d^5 7m Oct 12] 9,400Y: good-bodied colt: half-brother to several winners, including 6f winner Party Games (by Red Alert) and fairly useful 1¼m winner Honey Line (by High Line): dam poor maiden: modest maiden: pulled up in seller at Newmarket final outing: stays 7f: acts on firm ground, raced towards unfavoured middle of track on soft. *R. Akehurst*
62

STRUGGLER 3 b.c. Night Shift (USA) – Dreamawhile 85 (Known Fact (USA) 135) [1994 6m* 6s^3 1995 5.5g* 5g* 5g^3 5f^2 5f Jul 25] small, strong, good-bodied colt: first foal: dam, 3-y-o 7f winner (not tried beyond 1m), is half-sister to Derby Italiano winner My Top, out of 2m winner: smart performer: won minor event and third in listed race at 2 yrs: successful in 1995 in listed event at Evry and Prix de Saint-Georges (by 1½ lengths from Spain Lane) at Longchamp in the spring: ran well when ¾-length third to Millyant in Prix du Gros-Chene at Chantilly and 1½ lengths second of 10 to Piccolo in King's Stand Stakes at Royal Ascot (moved poorly to post)
111

in June: always outpaced over sharper 5f when favourite for King George Stakes at Goodwood final start: stays 6f: acts on firm ground: held up: sold to join D. Loder 140,000 gns Newmarket December Sales. *C. Laffon-Parias, France*

STRUMMING (IRE) 3 ch.f. Ballad Rock 122 – Casla (Lomond (USA) 128) [1994 67p: 7d^4 1995 8m* 8.1d^5 Sep 13] lengthy, quite attractive filly: fair form: bandaged behind, narrowly won 5-runner maiden at Ripon in August: stays 1m: acts on good to firm and dead ground: sent to G. Jones in USA. *J. H. M. Gosden* — 75

STRUTTING (IRE) 3 b.f. Ela-Mana-Mou 132 – Taking Steps 100 (Gay Fandango (USA) 132) [1994 85p: 7f^4 7g* 1995 8m^6 10g^3 12m^6 10.1g 10d^6 10.2d* 8m 10.3m^2 Nov 3] quite attractive filly: has a quick action: useful performer: best efforts when third in listed event at Newbury and sixth in Ribblesdale Stakes at Royal Ascot second and third 3-y-o starts: won 4-runner minor event at Chepstow in October by 8 lengths: needs further than 1m (stays 1½m): acts on good to firm and dead ground. *R. Hannon* — 95

STUDIO THIRTY 3 gr.g. Rock City 120 – Chepstow Vale (USA) 97 (Key To The Mint (USA)) [1994 –: 5d 6s 6d 1995 a9.4g 7.5m 10g a8.5g^4 8g a9.4g* a9.4g a9.4g^6 10.3m^6 a12g a10g^6 a10g* a10g^3 a8.5g^6 Dec 12] leggy gelding: modest handicapper: won at Wolverhampton (maiden event) in June on fourth last outing for R. Hollinshead, and at Lingfield in November: stays 1¼m well: acts on the all-weather: effective visored or not. *D. Morris* — – a56

STUFFED 3 ch.g. Clantime 101 – Puff Pastry 78 (Reform 132) [1994 63?: 5d 5s 6f* 6f^6 6m 5g 7g 1995 5g^2 6m^2 5m 5f^2 6m^2 Oct 30] workmanlike gelding: modest handicapper: best efforts on last 2 starts: stays 6f: acts on firm ground. *M. W. Easterby* — 64

STUNNING PROSPECT (USA) 2 b.c. (Apr 17) Gold Seam (USA) 124 – Stunning Native (USA) (Our Native (USA)) [1995 8m a8g Nov 14] $23,000F, 16,500Y: leggy colt: half-brother to several winners, including by Giboulee and Stalwart in minor stakes: dam won 3 races in North America and was second in 9f Monmouth Oaks: no form in maiden events at Doncaster and Lingfield (blinkered, tailed off) 10 days later: sold 950 gns Ascot December Sales. *P. F. I. Cole* — –

ST VALERY 3 b.f. Statoblest 120 – Fleur du Val (Valiyar 129) [1994 NR 1995 6g^3 Jun 6] 5,500Y: second foal: dam unraced half-sister to Superpower: shaped well when always-prominent third of 7 in apprentice maiden at Pontefract in June: looked sure to do better. *C. R. Egerton* — 69 p

STYLISH INTERVAL 3 ch.g. Interrex (CAN) – Super Style (Artaius (USA) 129) [1994 66: 6m a7g^3 a8g^6 a8.5g 1995 10.2m^6 8g 10g 8h Sep 4] leggy, quite good-topped gelding: modest maiden: long way below form in 1995 after reappearance: probably stays 1¼m: sold (R. Hodges to N. Waggott) 2,000 gns Ascot September Sales. *R. J. Hodges* — 60

STYLISH WAYS (IRE) 3 b.g. Thatching 131 – Style of Life (USA) (The Minstrel (CAN) 135) [1994 83: 6m^4 6.1s* 6g^3 1995 6g* 6m^3 7m^3 7m^5 6m Oct 14] compact, quite attractive gelding: fluent mover: useful performer: won minor event at Leicester in May: good efforts at York (third of 15 in £39,000 handicap) and Newmarket (third of 8 to Pipe Major in Van Geest Criterion Stakes) next 2 starts: stays 7f: acts on good to firm and soft ground: keen sort: sold 30,000 gns Newmarket Autumn Sales and gelded. *G. Wragg* — 98

SUALTACH (IRE) 2 b.c. (Apr 9) Marju (IRE) 127 – Astra Adastra (Mount Hagen (FR) 127) [1995 5.1m^3 6g^4 6.1m^2 6.1m* 6m 7g^4 6m Oct 21] IR 21,000Y: strong, lengthy colt: has plenty of scope: half-brother to several winners, including useful 3-y-o 1¼m winner Yoush (by Dominion), 1½m winner Baraz (by Busted) and (at 5f to 1m) Precious Air (by Precocious): dam, Irish 2-y-o 5f winner, half-sister to Ballad Rock: fair form at best: had heavily favoured stand rail when making all in maiden at Nottingham in June: finished distressed in minor event at Pontefract in July and gave impression something still amiss last 2 starts: will stay beyond 6f: has raced only on a sound surface. *R. Hollinshead* — 78

SUAVE TERN (USA) 4 b.c. Arctic Tern (USA) 126 – Suavite (USA) (Alleged (USA) 138) [1994 114: 10g* 10d 12s^2 12d^2 10.5v^2 1995 10v^6 10s 12g^6 12g^3 12d^6 10d* 12f Dec 10] smart French colt: inconsistent in 1995: around 1½ lengths third of 9 to Tot Ou Tard in Grand Prix d'Evry (off course 3½ months afterwards) in June: won listed race at Fontainebleau in November by 1½ lengths from Sand Reef: stays — 114

1½m: acts on heavy going, possibly not on top-of-the-ground. *J. E. Hammond, France*

SUBFUSK 2 b.f. (Mar 27) Lugana Beach 116 – Hush It Up (Tina's Pet 121) [1995 a6g* 6m5 6g 5m3 a6g* 7d 6.1d a5g Nov 2] smallish filly: poor mover: third live foal: half-sister to fairly useful 4-y-o 1½m winner Shadow Leader (by Tragic Role): dam poor maiden: comfortable winner of sellers at Wolverhampton in May and June: off course 3 months after second win and failed to recapture early-season form: stays 6f: acts on good to firm ground and fibresand: tends to hang left. *W. G. M. Turner* 56 a60

SUBTERFUGE 2 br.f. (Mar 18) Machiavellian (USA) 123 – Sandy Island 110 (Mill Reef (USA) 141) [1995 7g* Jul 28] seventh foal: half-sister to smart 3-y-o 1½m winner Sebastian (by Sadler's Wells) and 7f (at 2 yrs) and 1¼m winner Sardegna (by Pharly): dam, winner of Pretty Polly Stakes and Lancashire Oaks, is closely related to Slip Anchor: odds-on, won 4-runner maiden at Newmarket by a head from Rash Gift, running green then improving to lead inside last: will stay middle distances: looked sure to improve. *H. R. A. Cecil* 78 p

SUBTLE ONE (IRE) 2 b.f. (Apr 3) Polish Patriot (USA) 128 – Subtle Change (IRE) 102 (Law Society (USA) 130) [1995 6m4 7g 7g 10g Oct 9] close-coupled filly: first foal: dam 8.5f winner here at 2 yrs later successful at 1¾m and 2m in Ireland: little worthwhile form in claiming/selling company: bred to stay further than 6f. *G. L. Moore* –

SUBYA 3 b.f. Night Shift (USA) – Ashshama (USA) 84 (Arctic Tern (USA) 126) [1994 94: 5m 5f* 6g* 7f2 7.1g* 7m6 7v5 7m2 1995 8m* 8g4 10m* 10g 10f6 10.1g Sep 12] sturdy, compact filly: very good mover: useful performer: won listed races at Kempton (from Poppy Carew) in April and Goodwood (from Tillandsia) in May: below form in Pretty Polly Stakes at the Curragh, Nassau Stakes at Goodwood and listed race at Yarmouth last 3 starts: may well have stayed 1½m: best form on a sound surface: tail flasher: rather a flighty sort (tended to get on toes): held up: stud. *J. L. Dunlop* 107

SUBZERO 3 b.c. Thatching 131 – Cut No Ice 97 (Great Nephew 126) [1994 91: 5f2 6f2 5g3 5m4 5f* 6g4 7d3 1995 6g3 6g2 7f3 6.1d* Oct 10] good-bodied colt: has a sharp action: useful performer: off course 13 months prior to reappearance: won minor event at Chepstow in October in good style: should stay beyond 6f: successful on firm ground, best effort on dead: bandaged all round last 2 starts: sold 25,000 gns Newmarket Autumn Sales. *M. R. Stoute* 96

SUDDEN SPIN 5 b.g. Doulab (USA) 115 – Lightning Legacy (USA) 78 (Super Concorde (USA) 128) [1994 53: 7.5m5 7.5g 10f 12m 6.1s 1995 a11g* a12g3 10g6 12g4 a11g* a12g3 12m4 a9.4g2 a12g6 10g3 a9.4g* a9.4g3 Nov 13] leggy, good-topped gelding: fair all-weather performer: won amateurs handicap in January and claimer in June, both at Southwell, and handicap at Wolverhampton (gambled on) in September: stays 1½m: has form on good to firm and soft ground, goes well on fibresand: often used to be visored, but not tried in 1995. *S. G. Norton* 40 + a66

SUEDORO 5 b.m. Hard Fought 125 – Bamdoro 54 (Cavo Doro 124) [1994 –: 8.5d 8m 10g 1995 8g 6g5 9.9m 6.9m 6f* 5.9f6 6f4 6g 6f* 6f4 6f* 7g 6g Sep 25] angular mare: modest handicapper: left G. Kelly's stable after third 5-y-o start: does much of her racing at Hamilton, and won there in June (dead heat), July and August: best form at 6f: acts on firm ground. *R. M. McKellar* 51

SUE ME (IRE) 3 b. or br.g. Contract Law (USA) 108 – Pink Fondant (Northfields (USA)) [1994 75: 5m6 6m4 a6g3 5.3g2 6d* 6m 6v3 6.1d5 1995 a7g2 5m 6m5 6g 6d2 6g 6d 6.1s a6g Nov 6] quite attractive gelding: fair handicapper: will stay beyond 6f: acts on good to firm and heavy ground, not at best on fibresand: goes well fresh. *W. R. Muir* 75 a64

SUE'S ARTISTE 4 b.f. Damister (USA) 123 – Sedova (USA) (Nijinsky (CAN) 138) [1994 91: 8m2 8g2 10g5 10d* 10g* 10.1m3 10.3d 1995 12g 10m6 10m 8m 7.9m3 10f 10.3d* 9g6 10.3m* 10.5d Nov 17] leggy filly: fairly useful performer: in very good form in the autumn, winning 25-runner handicap and 7-runner minor event at Doncaster: stiff task (in Group 3 event) at Evry final start: ideally needs 9f+ nowadays, and should stay 1½m: acts on good to firm and dead ground: edgy type: sold 33,000 gns Newmarket December Sales. *B. W. Hills* 92

SUE'S RETURN 3 b.f. Beveled (USA) – Return To Tara (Homing 130) [1994 79: 6m 6f2 6g 6d* 7m3 7m 1995 7m 8.1g2 10g6 8.1m5 9f2 7.9m 10m 8d 9g 7f3 Oct 91

12] angular filly: fairly useful handicapper: stays 9f: acts on firm and dead ground: panicked in stalls fourth intended 3-y-o start. *A. P. Jarvis*

SUGAR MILL 5 b.g. Slip Anchor 136 – Great Tom 99 (Great Nephew 126) [1994 NR 1995 10m^{3} 10m 10m 11.9m^{3} 14g^{2} 14.6m* 16.5m Nov 4] tall, angular gelding: has round action: eighth foal: half-brother to two winners, notably fair 1½m and 1¾m winner Five Farthings (by Busted): dam 2-y-o 6f winner: won NH Flat race at Doncaster in March: fair handicapper: game winner at Doncaster in October: ran as if something amiss there on final start: will stay beyond 14.6f: acts on good to firm ground. *Mrs M. Reveley* — 70

SUILE MOR 3 b.f. Satin Wood 117 – Ra Ra (Lord Gayle (USA) 124) [1994 65: 5.1g 7m* 7m^{5} 7m^{3} 8g^{5} 6.9s 1995 8g 8m^{6} 10.2m^{3} 10.8m^{2} 10m^{4} 10.2h^{3} 10.8f^{5} Aug 28] unfurnished filly: modest handicapper: stays 10.8f: acts on good to firm, well beaten on soft going: tail swisher: may be temperamental. *B. R. Millman* — 56

SUITOR 2 b.c. (Feb 4) Groom Dancer (USA) 128 – Meliora 73 (Crowned Prince (USA) 128) [1995 8m 8f Oct 25] big, rangy colt: has plenty of scope: half-brother to several winners, notably good-class stayer Weld (by Kalaglow): dam 7f winner: signs of ability in late-season maidens at Newmarket and Yarmouth: will do better again given good test of stamina. *W. Jarvis* — – p

SUIVEZ 5 b.g. Persian Bold 123 – Butterfly Kiss 69 (Beldale Flutter (USA) 130) [1994 58: a8g 12g 10d^{4} 9.2f 9.2f* 8.3m^{4} 10m^{2} 10m^{5} 10m^{2} 10g 1995 a14.8g^{6} a9.4g^{4} a11g^{3} a11g* a11g* a11g^{5} Apr 3] sturdy gelding: modest handicapper: won twice at Southwell within a week in February: well beaten on final start (trainer reported the horse might have had a recurrence of a trapped nerve behind the saddle): effective at around 1¼m and stays 1½m: acts on firm ground, dead and fibresand: game. *Mrs N. Macauley* — 58

SUIVEZ LA (USA) 3 ch.f. Trempolino (USA) 135 – Arisen (USA) (Mr Prospector (USA)) [1994 8g^{6} 1995 8d^{2} 8m^{3} 10g* 10g^{3} 10m^{2} 12d^{3} 10.5g^{2} Oct 29] $42,000F: $120,000Y: related to several winners, notably 1989 Beresford Stakes winner Victory Piper (by Nijinsky): dam, minor stakes winner at around 1m, half-sister to smart middle-distance performer Pair of Deuces: useful French filly: won minor event at Longchamp in July: best effort when 2½ lengths second of 7 to Tamise in Prix de Flore at Saint-Cloud last time: seems to stay 1½m: yet to race on extremes of going. *J-C. Cunnington, France* — 108

SUJUD (IRE) 3 b. or br.f. Shaadi (USA) 126 – Sit Elnaas (USA) 82 (Sir Ivor 135) [1994 NR 1995 7m^{6} 8m 9.7m^{5} 11.9d 14.1m^{2} Oct 19] leggy, narrow filly: third foal: dam, winning stayer and second in Cesarewitch, is granddaughter of Juliette Marny: modest maiden at best: stays 1¾m: sold (H. Thomson Jones to Mrs J. Ramsden) 4,000 gns Newmarket Autumn Sales. *H. Thomson Jones* — 58

SULB (USA) 3 b.c. El Gran Senor (USA) 136 – Stricly (ARG) (Dancing Moss 113) [1994 NR 1995 7g* 8f* 8f^{6} 7.9m Aug 17] 70,000Y: good-topped colt: second foal: half-brother to 14.9f winner Teddy's Play (by Theatrical): dam stakes winner in Argentina: useful performer: held up when justifying favouritism in maiden at Kempton in April and minor event at Newbury in June: acted as pacemaker in Sussex Stakes (bandaged behind) at Goodwood next start: ran poorly in £23,600 handicap at York on final one: should stay 1¼m: acts on firm ground: sent to Dubai. *A. C. Stewart* — 95

SUL FOSSO 3 b.g. Skyliner 117 – Sveltissima 48 (Dunphy 124) [1994 –: 5g 6f 6s 1995 7.1d^{5} 8.3s^{3} 8.3g May 4] tall, narrow gelding: poor maiden: probably stays 8.3f: acts on soft ground: sold (J. Berry to Mrs S. Smith) 2,100 gns Doncaster October Sales. *J. Berry* — 33

SULLAMELL 4 b.g. Sulaafah (USA) 119 – Melody Lane 69 (Horage 124) [1994 NR 1995 a7g Jan 26] big, good-topped gelding: very lightly raced and little sign of ability: has joined J. King. *R. J. Hodges* — –

SULTAN'S SON 9 b.g. Kings Lake (USA) 133 – Get Ahead 58 (Silly Season 127) [1994 –: a16.2g 1995 a14.8g Apr 29] strong, good-bodied gelding: no form on flat since 4 yrs. *K. S. Bridgwater* — –

SUMMERHILL SPECIAL (IRE) 4 b.f. Roi Danzig (USA) – Special Thanks (Kampala 120) [1994 9v^{3} 9d 9f^{3} 9.6m^{5} 9g^{2} 8g 10d^{2} 10g 10g^{5} 10v 10d 1995 10d Oct 19] IR 5,200Y: sturdy ex-Irish filly: third foal: half-sister to Italian 6-y-o middle-distance performer Imco Classic (by Bob Back): dam Irish 7f winner: won — –

auction event at Bellewstown at 2 yrs when trained by P. Beirne: fairly useful handicapper (rated 80) in 1994 for M. Kauntze: sold IR 10,000 gns Goffs October (1994) Sales: won maiden hurdle in March for current trainer, but never a threat on return to flat: stays 1¼m: acts on any ground. *Mrs P. N. Dutfield*

SUMMER RETREAT (USA) 3 b.f. Gone West (USA) – Devon Diva (USA) (The Minstrel (CAN) 135) [1994 NR 1995 6g 7m^3 7.1m^2 7.1d* 8.1g^5 Sep 22] compact filly: sister to smart sprinter Western Approach, closely related to 7f winner Daki (by Miswaki) and half-sister to smart 7f and 1m winner Tinner's Way (by Secretariat), last-named Grade 1 winner at 1¼m in USA: dam, 9f winner at 4 yrs in USA, out of Devon Ditty: fair form: won minor event at Sandown in September, and ran well in handicap at Haydock on only subsequent outing: will prove best at up to 1m: bandaged behind first 2 starts: sent to USA. *J. H. M. Gosden* 78

SUMMERTOWN (USA) 3 ch.f. Diesis 133 – Solar (CAN) 109 (Halo (USA)) [1994 66p: 6g^3 1995 7m^2 7.1m^4 Jul 8] good-topped filly: fair maiden: bred to stay beyond 7f: flighty in paddock on debut, and sweating and edgy on reappearance. *J. H. M. Gosden* 68

SUMMER VILLA 3 b.f. Nomination 125 – Maravilla 73 (Mandrake Major 122) [1994 –: 5m^5 a6g a6g 6s 1995 a8g^3 a8g* a8.5g* a10g 8f 8m^2 8.1f^3 7m^4 8m a7g Dec 2] neat filly: modest performer: won maiden handicap at Southwell and seller at Wolverhampton (2 days later) in February: stays 8.5f: acts on firm ground and goes well on fibresand. *P. C. Haslam* 43 a52

SUMMIT 4 b.g. Salse (USA) 128 – Reltop 72 (High Top 131) [1994 104: 8s^3 10g* 12d* 16.2m^3 14.8m^2 16f 14g^4 1995 11.8m^5 Jun 17] good-topped gelding: useful performer at 3 yrs for R. Hannon: well beaten in listed event at Leicester on return: stays 16.2f: acts on firm and soft ground: keen sort. *Mrs J. Pitman* –

SUN CIRCUS 3 b.f. Statoblest 120 – Carmen Maria (Bold Lad (IRE) 133) [1994 NR 1995 8.2d 7g 10d^6 Oct 19] 800F, 3,000Y: useful-looking filly: eighth reported foal: half-sister to Irish 5f and 6f winner My Precious Daisy (by Sharpo): dam ran once: behind in maidens. *J. L. Spearing* –

SUNDAY MAELSTROM (IRE) 2 b.f. (Apr 8) Distinctly North (USA) 115 – Make Your Mark (On Your Mark 125) [1995 5g 6g 5f^5 Jul 10] IR 6,000Y: unfurnished filly: half-sister to several winners, including 6f to 1m winner Bronze Cross (by Rontino): dam ran 3 times at 2 yrs in Ireland: little worthwhile form in maidens: hung badly left final 2f on debut: has joined T. Dyer. *J. Berry* –

SUNDAY MAIL TOO (IRE) 3 b.f. Fayruz 116 – Slick Chick 89 (Shiny Tenth 120) [1994 53: 5d* 5m^5 5m^3 5f^3 5m^2 6s 1995 5d^6 6s 5g 6g 5g^6 5g 5f 7.1m^4 7.1f^5 5m 5m^6 6f^5 6m^6 5g 6f^6 5.9f^5 5f^6 5m 6g Sep 25] sparely-made filly: poor handicapper at best in 1995: should stay 7f: below form on soft ground, acts on any other: tried visored/blinkered: sometimes hangs. *Miss L. A. Perratt* 40

SUNDAY NEWS'N'ECHO (USA) 4 b.f. Trempolino (USA) 135 – Icy Pop (USA) (Icecapade (USA)) [1994 78d: 8d 10.5g* 11.5d^6 10.5g^6 8m^6 8.1m 8m^2 9g^2 8.9m 8g^4 10.3s^3 12.1g a14g^4 1995 a11g 10.9m 12.4g* 14g^2 14.1g^2 12g 11.9m 15.1s Nov 2] leggy filly: modest handicapper: won at Newcastle in May: stays 1¾m well: acts on heavy going, probably on good to firm: often used to be blinkered, not since tenth 3-y-o start. *W. Storey* 62 d

SUNDERLAND ECHO 6 br.g. Daring March 116 – Incarnadine 67 (Hot Spark 126) [1994 80: 11.8g^4 12.3m^2 12.4f^2 11.9f^5 12.3m^3 11.9g* 13.9m 1995 12g 11.8m 12.4g^4 12.4m^4 12.3m 11.9g 11.9s^3 12d^4 Oct 21] good-bodied, workmanlike gelding: fair handicapper: below form after third 6-y-o start: best form at around 1½m: acts on any going: inconsistent. *Mrs M. Reveley* 72 d

SUN DREAMER 6 ch.m. Dreams To Reality (USA) 113 – Erica Alba (Yukon Eric (CAN)) [1994 NR 1995 10.2m Sep 25] half-sister to 3 winning jumpers: dam never ran: well behind in NH Flat race and Bath maiden. *J. L. Spearing* –

SUNDRIES 5 ch.g. Kabour 80 – Tolly's Best 58 (Hittite Glory 125) [1994 NR 1995 a5g 5d 7g Sep 23] fourth foal (all by Kabour): dam poor sprint maiden: tailed off in claimer (for J. A. Harris) and maidens: sold 950 gns Doncaster November Sales. *D. W. Chapman* –

SUNGAI MAS (USA) 3 ch.c. Lomond (USA) 128 – Slow March 105 (Queen's Hussar 124) [1994 NR 1995 10m 10m 8.2d 15.8m^6 Oct 13] $22,000Y: sparely-made –

colt: unimpressive mover: ninth reported foal: closely related to a minor winner in USA by Nureyev and half-brother to 3 winners, including 1986 2-y-o 6f winner Misk (by Miswaki) and 1½m winner Silent Journey (by Gregorian): dam 6f to 1¼m winner in Ireland and stakes placed in USA: well beaten in maidens and handicap. *S. P. C. Woods*

SUNLEY SECURE 2 b.g. (Feb 14) Warrshan (USA) 117 – Brown Velvet 68 (Mansingh (USA) 120) [1995 7.1d^2 8.3g^5 Sep 25] workmanlike gelding: has scope: eighth foal: brother to 3-y-o Godmersham Park and half-brother to several winners at up to 1m, including 4-y-o 6f/7f winner Pharsical (by Pharly): dam (possibly short runner) half-sister to smart Stumped, the dam of Sonic Lady: 3½ lengths second of 9 to Lomberto in maiden at Sandown: only fifth of 10 in median auction maiden at Hamilton 12 days later: seems not to stay 1m. *M. R. Channon* — 71

SUN MARK (IRE) 4 ch.g. Red Sunset 120 – Vivungi (USA) (Exbury 138) [1994 7s 9s 7s^4 8g^5 8.5g 6.5g^2 7g^2 6d 8g^6 7.5g 9d^2 8d^3 9s^6 1995 8m 9.9d^3 9.9m^6 Jun 14] IR 1,800Y: close-coupled gelding: half-brother to several winners, including fairly useful 1m (at 2 yrs) to 9f winner Nail Don (by Don) and Norwegian St Leger winner Timbylin (by Hatim): dam placed at around 7f in France and Ireland: fair maiden handicapper (rated 70) in Ireland for T. Kinane at 3 yrs: modest form at best here: stays 1¼m: acts on dead ground: normally blinkered at 3 yrs: visored (below form) final 4-y-o start. *Mrs S. M. Austin* — 61

SUN OF SPRING 5 b.g. Green Desert (USA) 127 – Unsuspected 95 (Above Suspicion 127) [1994 a10g^3 a12g* a12g^4 1995 14.8m 18m Oct 14] sturdy gelding: fairly useful performer at 3 yrs (rated 93) for M. Stoute: won minor event in Dubai in 1994 for H. Ibrahim: sold 31,000 gns Newmarket July (1995) Sales: well beaten in handicaps at Newmarket on return: stays 1¾m well (seemed not to stay 2¼m in Cesarewitch): acts on firm going. *J. White* — –

SUNOMA VALLEY 3 ch.g. Hubbly Bubbly (USA) – Empress Valley (Gay Fandango (USA) 132) [1994 NR 1995 8g 9m 10.4g^5 14g Sep 23] 1,000Y, 3,600 2-y-o: big, rangy, unfurnished gelding: looks weak: sixth foal: half-brother to 3 winners abroad, including Persian Valley (by Persian Bold) at up to 9.5f in Ireland: dam never ran: no worthwhile form. *J. M. P. Eustace* — –

SUNRISE SONG (FR) 4 gr.f. General Holme (USA) 128 – Marissiya (Nishapour (FR) 125) [1994 112: 10s^2 12v* 10.5v^4 10.5d^5 12s^2 12d 10d 12g^3 12.5d^3 10.5s^3 10.5v 1995 12m^6 10.5s^4 12g^4 13.5g* 12.5g^3 12d 15.5f^3 10d Nov 18] leggy, plain filly: smart French performer: won 7-runner Prix de Pomone at Deauville in August by ¾ length from Fanjica: easily best runs afterwards when creditable third in Grand Prix de Deauville (2¼ lengths behind Swain) and Prix Royal Oak (2¾ lengths behind Sunshack) at Longchamp: stays 15.5f: acts on any going. *F. Doumen, France* — 112

SUNRISE SPECIAL (IRE) 2 b.c. (May 12) Petorius 117 – Break of Day (On Your Mark 125) [1995 6f 6f 5m 7d a8.5g^5 Oct 28] IR 8,200Y: rangy, useful-looking colt: closely related to 7f and 1m winner Bath (by Runnett) and half-brother to 3 winners, 2 in Hong Kong: dam never ran: poor form in maiden events and nurseries (final one a seller): may prove best short of 8.5f: blinkered final outing: sold to join C. J. Hill 650 gns Ascot October Sales. *G. Lewis* — –

SUNSET HARBOUR (IRE) 2 br.f. (Jan 29) Prince Sabo 123 – City Link Pet 79 (Tina's Pet 121) [1995 5f^6 5.2g^5 5g^5 6m^4 5.1h^3 5.2d Sep 16] 5,800Y: first foal: dam 5f winner: modest maiden: stays 6f: acts on hard ground. *D. A. Wilson* — 53

SUNSET REIGNS (IRE) 2 b.f. (Mar 24) Taufan (USA) 119 – More Candy 98 (Ballad Rock 122) [1995 5d^2 5s^2 6g^4 5g^5 5.8m* 5g* 5g^3 6m* 6m^5 5f* 6.3m^5 Sep 2] IR 14,000Y: sister to 5f winner Oriental Air and half-sister to 2 winners, notably Choice Lot (5f in Ireland, by Auction Ring): dam Irish 6f winner: useful form: successful in maiden at Navan, minor event at Tipperary, listed race at Leopardstown and nursery at the Curragh, all in the summer: outsider of 5, but rather disappointing nonetheless, in Anglesey Stakes at the Curragh final start: effective at 5f and 6f: acts on firm ground. *A. P. O'Brien, Ireland* — 99

SUNSHACK 4 b.c. Rainbow Quest (USA) 134 – Suntrap (USA) 112 (Roberto (USA) 131) [1994 120: 12g^3 12m 12d^3 12g* 1995 12v^4 12g* 12f* 12d^5 15.5f* Oct 22] — 122

What a difference a year makes! For Sunshack, one of those who finished down the back in the Derby in 1994, it was a different story altogether twelve months

Vodafone Coronation Cup, Epsom—from left to right,
Only Royale (second), Sunshack (the winner), Tikkanen (fourth), Carnegie (fifth) and Time Star (third)

later when he was returned to Epsom on Derby Day for the Vodafone Coronation Cup. Among the explanations put forward for Sunshack's always-behind nineteenth of twenty-five in Erhaab's Derby had been that he had possibly been unsuited by the good to firm going, the firmest going he had encountered. Four further runs under his belt in the interim had confirmed Sunshack as a much better horse than his first outing in Britain suggested, but had done nothing to dispel doubts about his ability to run up to his best on top-of-the-ground; all of them had been on an easy surface. With the ground riding probably even firmer than the official good to firm for the Coronation Cup, there were many willing to oppose him on this alone. There were other reasons to think that Sunshack had his work cut out, too. Despite a number of smart efforts to his name, Sunshack still looked to have improvement to make in terms of form to see off the likes of his stable-companion, the 1994 Prix de l'Arc de Triomphe winner Carnegie, the Jockey Club Stakes, Prix Foy and dual Yorkshire Oaks winner Only Royale and the Jockey Club Stakes runner-up and 1994 Breeders' Cup Turf winner Tikkanen. Sunshack started fourth favourite at 10/1 behind that trio

Prix Royal-Oak, Longchamp—
Sunshack has flown as Shrewd Idea and Sunrise Song (grey) fight it out for second

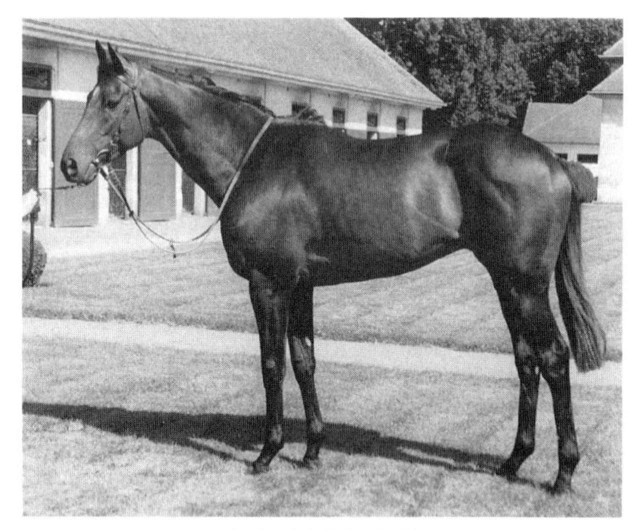

Mr K. Abdulla's "Sunshack"

in a field of seven, with Tikkanen shading favouritism at 5/2 over the other two at 11/4. One thing that Sunshack did have in his favour was that he'd already had two races in the latest season (Carnegie was making his reappearance, Only Royale and Tikkanen had had one race each) and he seemed sure to be at the very top of his form. Following a less than auspicuous fourth of six to Tot Ou Tard on heavy going in the Prix d'Hedouville at Longchamp in April, Sunshack had returned to winning ways in the Prix Jean de Chaudenay at Saint-Cloud in May, gamely getting the better of Sand Reef by three quarters of a length.

The lack of a confirmed front-runner in the Coronation Cup resulted in a slow pace in the early stages, particularly so in the first quarter of a mile where all of the runners were pulling for their head. The rank outsider Ionio was the first definite leader, passed after four furlongs by the Jockey Club Stakes third Time Star. By halfway the pace was a sound one, and Sunshack, who'd been settled in mid-division on the rails, was struggling to hold his place. Rounding Tattenham Corner he had a fair bit to do, but into the straight he found a good run up the rails and quickened to dispute second behind the two-length leader Time Star. Maintaining his run under strong pressure, Sunshack got to the front just over a furlong out, hard pressed all the time now by Only Royale. Throughout the final furlong it was nip-and-tuck between the pair, but at the line Sunshack had a head to spare over Only Royale, with Time Star a length back in third and the never-dangerous Tikkanen a further two lengths back in fourth. Carnegie never got out of mid-division, finishing fifth. With the exception of Time Star, all the principals from the Coronation Cup crossed swords again in the Grand Prix de Saint-Cloud at the beginning of July. In what was another muddling race, this time run on good to soft going, it was Carnegie who came out on top, whereas Sunshack could finish only fifth, nearly eight lengths off the winner.

Sunshack wasn't seen out again for nearly four months. The Prix Royal-Oak at Longchamp seemed to provide him with a fine chance of victory following the late-withdrawal of Always Earnest, as well as giving him his first opportunity to race beyond a mile and a half. His rivals were an unexceptional lot by Group 1 standards, and it was left to Shrewd Idea, who'd raced mainly in Spain earlier in the year, and Sunrise Song to chase him home. Sunshack settled the issue with a fine turn of foot over a furlong out, having been tucked in behind the leaders, reaching the post two and a half lengths to the good. This was Sunshack's final race of the season. Plans to run him in the Japan Cup in late-November had to be shelved when a leg injury was discovered just a few days before the race. A recurrence of a splint problem which had caused him to miss the Arc was diagnosed. We're glad to be able to report that Sunshack remains in training, with the top mile-and-a-half races, including the Coronation Cup, again on his agenda. At this juncture, he cannot be rated a good winner of the race, but is still relatively lightly raced and may be open to improvement. He seems sure to be placed to win more good contests.

Sunshack (b.c. 1991)	Rainbow Quest (USA) (b 1981)	Blushing Groom (ch 1974)	Red God
			Runaway Bride
		I Will Follow (b 1975)	Herbager
			Where You Lead
	Suntrap (USA) (b 1985)	Roberto (b 1969)	Hail To Reason
			Bramalea
		Sunny Bay (b 1975)	Northern Bay
			Staunch Lady

It scarely needs saying that Sunshack should prove a valuable prospect as a stallion when the time comes. Like his sire Rainbow Quest, Sunshack has now won good races at two (the Criterium de Saint-Cloud) , three (the Prix du Conseil de Paris) and four. He still has some way to go to measure up fully to Rainbow Quest on the racecourse, though, and it would be expecting a lot of him indeed to equal Rainbow Quest as a stallion. Rainbow Quest has been a conspicuous success at stud, with a host of good winners to his name, the majority of them showing their best form from three years onwards over middle distances and upwards. Rainbow Quest was responsible for a Derby winner and an Arc winner in 1990 with Quest For Fame and Saumarez respectively, while his other good winners in the latest season included Spectrum, winner of the Irish Two Thousand Guineas and the Dubai Champion Stakes, and Urgent Request, who landed the Santa Anita Handicap.

Sunshack is a second foal and a full-brother to the very smart performer Raintrap. Raintrap won the Prix Royal-Oak two years before Sunshack, as a three-year-old, and went on to success the following year in the Rothmans International over a mile and a half at Woodbine. Sunshack has a year-younger sister, Hunt The Sun, placed three times over a mile and a quarter in France in the latest season, and a two-years-younger half-brother by Generous, the unraced Setting Sun. Sunshack's dam Suntrap was a very useful performer, a winner over six and seven furlongs as a juvenile and an excellent third in the Prix d'Aumale over a mile. She is a half-sister to several winners, including the useful middle-distance colt Jalaajel and the very useful middle-distance stayer (winner of the German St Leger) Non Partisan. *A. Fabre, France*

SUNSHINE BELLE 3 b.f. Belfort (FR) 89 – Bali Sunset 67 (Balidar 133) [1994 39: 5f a5g^4 6g 5s 1995 5m a5g^6 5g^3 5g 5m^2 5f 5m Jul 3] modest maiden: should have stayed 6f: acted on good to firm ground, probably on fibresand: blinkered (hit rail, rider unseated) final start: dead. *G. M. Moore* — 50

SUPAMOVA (USA) 2 b.f. (Feb 22) Seattle Slew (USA) – Maximova (FR) 121 (Green Dancer (USA) 132) [1995 7d^3 6d^5 Sep 26] 380,000Y: useful-looking filly: sister to very smart 7f to 9f performer in France and USA Septieme Ciel and half-sister to several winners, including French 3-y-o Macoumba (by Mr Prospector), winner of Prix Marcel Boussac at 2 yrs: dam good class at up 1m: 2 lengths third of 10 to Wild Rumour in minor event at Newbury, leading after 2f until 2f out: faced very stiff task in 5-runner Cheveley Park Stakes at Newmarket 11 days later and did well to finish just 10 lengths last behind Blue Duster: will do better. *P. F. I. Cole* — 88 p

SUPAROY 2 b.g. (Feb 3) Midyan (USA) 124 – Champ d'Avril 89 (Northfields (USA)) [1995 6m^5 8f^3 8g 10d a10g a8g^4 Dec 18] 30,000F, 24,000Y: neat gelding: half-brother to several winners, including smart sprinter Superpower (by Superlative): dam 5f winner (seemed to stay 7f) out of half-sister to Music Boy: broke out of stalls on intended debut in July: modest form at best, seemed to go — 62 d backwards after third start: stays 1m: best form on firm ground: has sweated up. *T. G. Mills*

SUPER ASSIGNATION (IRE) 4 ch.f. Bold Arrangement 127 – Sabrine (Mount Hagen (FR) 127) [1994 58: 12s^4 10g a8g 1995 a13g^4 a13g^6 17.2m May 13] angular filly: soundly beaten after debut: sold out of D. Elsworth's stable 850 gns Ascot February Sales after second 4-y-o start. *Miss Gay Kelleway* –

SUPER BARON 2 b.c. (May 12) Emarati (USA) 74 – Carmen Maria (Bold Lad (IRE) 133) [1995 8d 7m Oct 12] 5,000F, 5,400Y: 13,500 2-y-o: workmanlike colt: ninth reported foal: half-brother to 3-y-o Sun Circus (by Statoblest) and Irish 5f and 6f winner My Precious Daisy (by Sharpo): dam ran once: well beaten in maiden at Salisbury (virtually pulled up) and seller at Newmarket: sold 500 gns Doncaster November Sales. *R. Hannon* –

SUPER BENZ 9 ch.g. Hello Gorgeous (USA) 128 – Investiture 62 (Welsh Pageant 132) [1994 62, a67: a6g^4 a6g* a6g^2 a6g^5 a7g 7g 6m^4 7.1f^2 7g^2 6f^4 7g 6m 5g 7d^6 8g 7.1g a7g a6g^2 a7g^4 1995 a7g* a7g^4 a7g^3 a8g^3 a6g^6 a7g^3 7m* 7m^2 7h^2 6m 7g 7f^3 7m^3 a7g a7g^4 Dec 18] leggy, lengthy gelding: fair performer: has won at least one race in each of the last 8 seasons: successful in 1995 in claimers at Southwell in January and Catterick in July: left F. O'Mahony's stable after fourteenth outing: effective at 6f to 1m: acts on hard ground, dead and all-weather surfaces: tried blinkered and visored, but no improvement: successful for apprentice: sometimes bandaged: tough. *J. L. Eyre* 65

SUPERBIT 3 b.c. Superpower 113 – On A Bit 66 (Mummy's Pet 125) [1994 52: 5m 5m 5f^4 6g a6g^4 1995 a5g^5 a5g^3 a6g^2 a6g^3 a5g 5d a5g 5.1m a6g 5.1m* 5g^3 5g 5.1f^4 5.1m^6 5m 5f 6d a7g^4 a6g^6 a5g^3 Dec 2] small, good-bodied colt: poor mover: modest performer: 33/1, won 17-runner claimer at Bath (uncompetitive affair as 10 stalls opened slowly) in June: stays 6f: acts on firm and dead ground and on fibresand: blinkered (finished last) fifth 3-y-o start: sometimes looks none too keen: inconsistent. *B. A. McMahon* 52

SUPERCOOL 4 ch.g. Superlative 118 – Florentynna Bay 61 (Aragon 118) [1994 61: 7g^4 7g^4 a8.5g^2 1995 a8g a8.5g^4 8d a7g a9.4g Nov 13] strong gelding: modest maiden: stays 8.5f: acts on fibresand: sold out of B. McMahon's stable 600 gns Newmarket Autumn Sales after third 4-y-o start: inconsistent. *D. W. Chapman* 56 d

SUPERFLEX 3 b.f. Jupiter Island 126 – Off The Mark (On Your Mark 125) [1994 NR 1995 8d 7g Apr 26] 500F: sturdy filly: half-sister to several winners, including 1983 2-y-o 5f and 6f winner Redhouse Charm (by Swing Easy) and 1½m winner On Your Bridge (by Scottish Rifle): dam won over 1m in France: well beaten in maidens. *D. Morris* –

SUPERFRILLS 2 b.f. (Apr 20) Superpower 113 – Pod's Daughter (IRE) 43 (Tender King 123) [1995 5f 5m 5f^3 5f^6 5g^3 5g a5g 5f Oct 24] 1,000Y: small filly: first foal: dam 2-y-o 5f winner: poor maiden: refused to enter stalls on debut: has raced only at 5f. *Miss L. C. Siddall* 48

SUPERGAL 2 b.f. (Mar 14) Superpower 113 – Spinney Hill (Dominion 123) [1995 5s^6 5m^6 5m^6 May 9] workmanlike filly: fourth foal: half-sister to Belgian 3-y-o 1¼m winner Butterfly Knife (by Dashing Blade): dam poor close relative of prolific winner Misty Halo: well beaten in median auction maidens at Hamilton and Thirsk (bit slipped though mouth, hung badly left) and seller at Doncaster (looked slightly ungenerous). *M. W. Easterby* –

SUPER GIFT (IRE) 2 b.f. Darshaan 133 – Speciality Package (USA) (Blushing Groom (FR) 131) [1995 7m^2 8g* 8g* 7d^2 Oct 7] fourth foal: dam fourth in 6f listed event on only start, out of half-sister to Taufan: useful Irish filly: won minor event at Tralee in August and nursery at Listowel in September: ran well when head second of 7 to Last Second in C.L. Weld Park Stakes at the Curragh final start: will stay middle distances: yet to race on extremes of going. *D. K. Weld, Ireland* 96

SUPERGOLD (IRE) 2 ch.c. (Mar 7) Keen 116 – Superflash (Superlative 118) [1995 a8.5g Dec 2] 18,000Y: third foal: half-brother to a winner in Hungary by Niniski: dam unraced daughter of 1000 Guineas second Photo Flash, a half-sister to Welsh Pageant: 10/1, well-beaten eighth of 9 in maiden at Wolverhampton. *W. A. O'Gorman* –

SUPER HEIGHTS 7 b.g. Superlative 118 – Shadha 57 (Shirley Heights 130) 39 § [1994 44§: a13g a8.5g* a8.5g^{4} a12g* a8.5g 1995 a16g a9.4g^{6} a8.5g^{4} a12g^{5} Apr 13] useful-looking gelding: poor performer: stays 1½m: acts on all-weather surfaces: tried blinkered/visored: often gets behind: has proved unreliable. *D. L. Williams*

SUPER HIGH 3 b.c. Superlative 118 – Nell of The North (USA) (Canadian Gil 65 (CAN)) [1994 69: 6f 6g 7s 6s 1995 7g^{6} a8g* a8.5g* 8m 8g^{5} 7d 9.7s^{2} 9.7g^{4} 8.2m^{3} a75 8.1s Nov 2] big, good-topped colt: has a round action: fair handicapper, successful at Southwell in May and Wolverhampton in June: stays 9.7f: acts on good to firm and soft ground and goes well on fibresand: has had tongue tied down: often early to post. *P. Howling*

SUPERIOR FORCE 2 ch.g. (Feb 20) Superlative 118 – Gleeful 72 (Sayf El 63 Arab (USA) 127) [1995 6s^{4} 6.9g Oct 16] 15,000Y: smallish, workmanlike colt: second reported foal: half-brother to 1993 2-y-o 5f winner Dockyard Dora (by Fijar Tango): dam 2-y-o 5f winner out of sister to smart miler Saher: modest form in maiden events at Lingfield and Folkestone (faded after racing prominently): wore a tongue strap on debut. *Miss B. Sanders*

SUPERLAO (BEL) 3 b.f. Bacalao (USA) – Princess of Import (Import 127) 57 [1994 a5g^{5} a5g 5g^{2} 5f* 7g^{5} 5g* a6g^{2} a6.5g* 6d^{2} a5g^{2} a5g* 1995 a5g^{4} a5g^{2} 7.5d a5g^{6} 5f 5f* 5f^{4} a5g a8g Dec 15] Belgian-trained filly: winner 4 times in her native land as 2-y-o: modest form in frame in 2 claimers at Lingfield (first runs in Britain) early in 1995: won handicap at Ostend in July: stays 6.5f: acts on firm ground and dirt. *Andre Hermans, Belgium*

SUPERLATIVEMAXIMUS (IRE) 7 ch.g. Superlative 118 – Samra (Welsh – Saint 126) [1994 –, a67: a6g^{2} a6g^{3} a6g^{2} a6g a5g 5v^{5} 1995 5m a5g a6g Aug 4] strong, heavy-topped gelding: one-time fair handicapper: no form in 1995: stayed 6f: acted on fibresand: often bandaged: dead. *J. A. Bennett*

SUPER LOOK 3 b.f. Superlative 118 – False Look (USA) (Alleged (USA) 138) – [1994 NR 1995 5g^{6} 5g a7g Jul 3] 6,500Y: compact filly: first foal: dam unraced: no sign of ability: sold 750 gns Ascot July Sales. *T. J. Etherington*

SUPERLUMINAL 4 b.g. Unfuwain (USA) 131 – Branitska (Mummy's Pet 125) 77 [1994 71+: 8f 8m^{4} 11.5g^{5} 10d* 10s^{2} 1995 10d^{2} 10m^{4} 10g^{2} May 24] sparely-made gelding: fair handicapper: stays 1¼m, but races freely and should prove as effective at 1m: acts on soft ground and good to firm: bandaged behind as 3-y-o. *G. Rimmer*

SUPERMICK 4 ch.g. Faustus (USA) 118 – Lardana 65 (Burglar 128) [1994 46: – a7g^{2} a7g^{4} a8g^{4} 9.7v^{5} 8.3g 1995 10g 7m 7m Sep 1] angular gelding: poor maiden: gambled on in selling handicap at Newmarket on second 4-y-o start: stays 1m, possibly not 1¼m: acts on all-weather surfaces: tried visored and blinkered: rejoined 3-y-o trainer W. Muir, and won selling hurdle in November. *P. J. McBride*

SUPERMISTER 2 br.g. (Apr 14) Damister (USA) 123 – Superfina (USA) 51 (Fluorescent Light (USA)) [1995 7m^{5} 7.5m 6m^{5} 8g^{4} Sep 2] 4,800F, 7,400Y: workmanlike gelding: has a quick action: fifth foal: dam unraced: modest form: ran well in blinkers third outing: may well prove best at around 6f. *M. H. Easterby*

SUPEROO 9 b.g. Superlative 118 – Shirleen (Daring Display (USA) 129) [1994 75 70: 7g* 7m 7f^{3} 7m^{3} 7.5f^{2} 8g^{2} 8m 1995 7m 8.5m^{3} 8g^{3} 7.5m 7m* 8.5m 8d 7f a7g a7g* a7g* a7g Dec 18] big, workmanlike gelding: fair handicapper: won at Thirsk (ladies race) in June and twice at Lingfield (first in a claimer) in November: effective at 7f to 8.5f: acts on firm going and equitrack: blinkered 4 times (including when successful) at 7 yrs. *Mrs P. Sly*

SUPER PARK 3 b.c. Superpower 113 – Everingham Park 54 (Record Token 128) 69 [1994 96: 6m^{6} 6m^{5} 5g^{3} 6g^{4} 6d* 1995 6f^{4} 5m 6g 5.1d 5d 5f 7f Oct 24] strong, lengthy colt: fair handicapper at best in 1995: stays 6f: acts on dead ground: no improvement in blinkers: inconsistent: sold 5,200 gns Doncaster November Sales. *M. H. Easterby*

SUPERPRIDE 3 b.g. Superpower 113 – Lindrake's Pride (Mandrake Major 122) 69 [1994 60p: 5m^{3} 5m^{2} 6d* 1995 5g 5m^{2} 5g^{3} 6m 6d 7f 5m Nov 4] good-bodied gelding: fair handicapper: left T. D. Barron's stable after third 3-y-o start: well beaten last 3 outings: stays 6f: acts on good to firm and dead ground. *Mrs M. Reveley*

SUPER ROCKY 6 b.g. Clantime 101 – Starproof 46 (Comedy Star (USA) 121) 78 [1994 66, a62: 5m* 5f^{3} 5f a5g^{3} 5m 5g 5.1g^{6} 5s a5g^{3} a5g^{5} a5g 1995 a5g 5g* 5g^{6} 5.2m^{2} a67 + 5m* 5f* 5m* 5m 5d 5f^{5} a5g* Dec 19] good-topped gelding: fair handicapper: had a very good season, winning at Doncaster in May, Folkestone and Edinburgh in July, Beverley in August and Lingfield in December: speedy, and best at 5f: acts on firm going and equitrack: tends to hang left: wears bandages: tried visored earlier in career: successful for apprentice: has run well when sweating. *R. Bastiman*

SUPER SERENADE 6 b.g. Beldale Flutter (USA) 130 – Super Melody 72 (Song 132) [1994 54+, a–: 8d 7.1s^5 8.3m 7g^6 7m^5 8m 1995 6m 8.3m^3 7.1m 8.3m 8.3m^5 8f^2 8m^4 Aug 31] angular gelding: modest handicapper: should stay further than 8.3f: acts on firm ground, soft and equitrack: sometimes sweats: suitable mount for inexperienced rider. *G. B. Balding* — 54

SUPER SHARP (NZ) 7 ch.g. Brilliant Invader (AUS) – Aspen Annie (NZ) (Amalgam (USA) 114) [1994 NR 1995 10s Mar 30] big New Zealand-bred gelding: won NH Flat race in 1993: modest hurdler/chaser: last of 16 in maiden at Leicester on debut on flat. *H. Oliver* — –

SUPER SONATA 3 b.f. Interrex (CAN) – Super Lady (Averof 123) [1994 65: 5g^5 5.3m^2 5g^5 5g 5g* a5g 1995 a5g 5m^6 5m^3 5m a5g Sep 4] small filly: modest performer at best in 1995: sold out of M. Tompkins' stable 1,800 gns Doncaster March Sales before reappearance: should stay 6f: races prominently: tried visored/blinkered. *P. D. Evans* — 52 a–

SUPERTOP 7 b. or br.g. High Top 131 – Myth 89 (Troy 137) [1994 64: 9.9m 10g^2 10.1m* 10f 10g 9.9m 10g^5 1995 11.1g^6 12m Oct 13] leggy, workmanlike gelding: has a round action: modest handicapper: should stay 1½m: acts on firm and dead ground, below form only start on equitrack: won 2 novice chases in the autumn. *L. Lungo* — 54

SUPREME COMMANDER (FR) 2 b.c. (Mar 11) Saumarez 132 – Autocratic (Tyrant) [1995 9d* 9s* Dec 5] 1,650,000 francs Y: half-brother to several winners, including useful Irish filly Majestic Role (by Theatrical), second in Prix de la Salamandre and later stayed 1½m, and smart Irish 1m/1¼m (stayed 1½m) Fair of The Furze (by Ela-Mana-Mou), later the dam of White Muzzle: dam fairly useful Irish 2-y-o 5f winner: French colt: won 17-runner minor event then 9-runner listed race (beat Le Tourron by ½ length), both at Evry: will stay 1½m: sure to improve. *A. Fabre, France* — 110 p

SUPREME DESIRE 7 gr.m. Grey Desire 115 – Fire Mountain 87 (Dragonara Palace (USA) 115) [1994 39: 5f^6 5m^4 5m* 5.1g a5g 6.1s 5d 5.1g 1995 5m 5g 5m 5m 6.1m 7.5m Jul 7] angular mare: poor handicapper: no worthwhile form since winning in July 1994. *G. R. Oldroyd* — –

SUPREME POWER 2 ch.c. (Mar 7) Superpower 113 – Spinner 59 (Blue Cashmere 129) [1995 5m^6 5m 5m* 5m^4 5d^4 6f 6d a8g^5 a6g^6 a7g^6 Dec 14] 17,000Y: robust colt: half-brother to several winners, including one-time fairly useful 5f to 1m performer Resolute Bay (by Crofthall) and 3-y-o sprinter Seigneurial (by Primo Dominie): dam sprinter: won median auction at Sandown in August: not so good late in year on Lingfield equitrack: takes keen hold and looks a sprinter: usually blinkered. *W. R. Muir* — 74 a66

SUPREME SCHOLAR 2 b.f. (Apr 5) Superpower 113 – Double Decree 69 (Sayf El Arab (USA) 127) [1995 5m 6g Jun 5] 2,200Y: sparely-made filly: first foal: dam 6f winner: well beaten in maiden auction at Redcar and seller at Thirsk. *B. W. Murray* — –

SUPREME STAR (USA) 4 b.g. Gulch (USA) – Just A Game 108 (Tarboosh (USA)) [1994 58: 10v 10m 14.1m^2 14.1m 12.5f a12g^3 a12g^5 11.6f* 15.4d 10d 1995 11.6m 12.5g* 12f^3 14g* 14f^2 14m* 12m^2 16g^2 16.2d^3 16.2s^6 16m^2 16.5m a16g^3 a16g^3 Nov 29] lightly-made, quite attractive gelding: fair handicapper: won at Warwick (seller), Salisbury and Sandown in the summer: stays well: acts on firm and dead ground, has only modest form on the all-weather: tried blinkered/visored: genuine and consistent. *P. R. Hedger* — 75 a59

SUPREME THOUGHT 3 b.f. Emarati (USA) 74 – Who's That Girl (Skyliner 117) [1994 68p: 6d^5 1995 7g^2 6m^5 5.1f^5 5d^5 5g Sep 29] tall filly: fair maiden at best: stays 7f. *L. G. Cottrell* — 66 d

SUPREME (USA) 3 b.f. Lomond (USA) 128 – Suprematie (FR) (Gay Mecene (USA) 128) [1994 NR 1995 8m 9m^5 7g 12.1g Sep 24] neat filly: fourth reported foal: half-sister to French provincial 8.7f to 9.5f winner Suprelly (by Bellypha) and a — –

winner in USA by Secretariat: dam French 1m (at 2 yrs) and 10.5f winner: trained for debut by I. Balding: no worthwhile form. *M. D. Hammond*

SURANOM (IRE) 3 b.c. Alzao (USA) 117 – Gracieuse Majeste (FR) (Saint Cyrien (FR) 128) [1994 NR 1995 8v* 8m^{2} 10d* 11d^{2} Nov 5] 40,000Y: second foal: dam, won at 6.5f at 2 yrs in France, from good French family: has raced only at Milan, easy winner of maiden in May and handicap in September: stays 11f: acts on good to firm and heavy ground: stays in training. *L. M. Cumani* 99

SURCOAT 8 b.g. Bustino 136 – Mullet 75 (Star Appeal 133) [1994 NR 1995 a16g 17.2m Jun 2] small, sturdy gelding: fair hurdler: has run only 5 times on flat since 1990, and tailed off in 1995. *R. J. Baker* –

SURE CARE 4 ch.f. Caerleon (USA) 132 – Sure Gold 100 (Glint of Gold 128) [1994 –: 8.2s 1995 10.2f^{4} 12.3m* 10f 8.3m 12f a14.8g Nov 27] sturdy, lengthy filly: modest performer: well beaten after winning claimer at Chester (dictated steady pace, claimed out of C. Egerton's stable £11,000) in July: trained next 3 starts by B. Meehan: stays 12.3f: acts on firm ground. *M. J. Ryan* 62

SURE PRIDE (USA) 7 b.g. Bates Motel (USA) – Coquelicot (CAN) (L'Enjoleur (CAN)) [1994 44: a16g^{2} 1995 a16g^{5} 16.4g a16g^{5} Jun 17] big gelding: modest jumper: lightly raced on flat and poor form at best: stays 2m: acts on equitrack. *A. Moore* –

SURE TO WIN (IRE) 6 ch.g. Sure Blade (USA) 130 – Mahabba (USA) 74 (Elocutionist (USA)) [1994 –: a9.4g a8.5g 10d 1995 a8g 10g Apr 24] lengthy gelding: no form for a long time. *J. M. Carr* –

SURGIVA 3 b.f. Presidium 124 – Miss Skindles 58 (Taufan (USA) 119) [1994 –: 6f 1995 10m 8m 8f 7.1m 8.1m^{6} Jul 4] leggy filly: no worthwhile form: tried blinkered: sold 525 gns Ascot July Sales. *J. R. Arnold* –

SURPRISE GUEST (IRE) 4 ch.g. Be My Guest (USA) 126 – Olderfleet 59 (Steel Heart 128) [1994 73: a7g^{3} a7g^{4} a10g^{3} a9.4g* a10g* a10g* a10g^{2} 10.3g* 10.5s^{4} 12.3d^{2} 12s* 13.1m^{3} 11.4g 11.6m* 10m 12f^{6} 12.3m^{6} 12m 10.4d 10d 1995 a10g^{4} a12g^{2} a13g^{4} 12m a14.8g 12f 14.1m 14.9m^{4} a12g Sep 30] good-bodied gelding: has a quick action: won 6 races at 3 yrs: disappointing in 1995, leaving M. Johnston's stable after third outing: suited by around 1½m: acts on firm ground, soft and all-weather surfaces: tried blinkered: has looked reluctant and no longer one to trust: sold 1,100 gns Ascot November Sales. *A. P. James* 66 d

SURPRISE MISSION 3 ch.g. Clantime 101 – Indigo 86 (Primo Dominie 121) [1994 NR 1995 5m 5m 5g* 5.1m* 5f^{3} Jun 24] leggy gelding: first foal: dam sprint-bred 2-y-o 5f winner: progressive form: won median auction maiden at Doncaster in May and handicap at Nottingham (readily) in June: third of 7 in handicap at Ayr, tying up having looked sure to win over 1f out: reportedly put away because of the firm ground: speedy, and will prove best at 5f: has raced only on a sound surface: still lightly raced, and may well make a fairly useful handicapper in 1996. *R. M. Whitaker* 74 p

SURREY DANCER 7 b.g. Shareef Dancer (USA) 135 – Juliette Marny 123 (Blakeney 126) [1994 75: a12g^{4} 10.3g 10v* 10v^{2} 10g^{2} 10.1m 11d^{5} 11.9s 1995 12g^{3} 10.4m Oct 4] leggy gelding: usually impresses in appearance: poor mover: useful hurdler: fair handicapper on flat: below form in 1995: suited by middle distances: probably acts on any going, very best efforts with some give: occasionally blinkered, not since 1993: has won for amateur/apprentice: usually held up, and suited by good gallop. *Mrs M. Reveley* 60 +

SURTEES 2 b.c. (May 14) Easy Goer (USA) – In Full Cry (USA) (Seattle Slew (USA)) [1995 6m^{6} 6m^{2} 6f^{3} 6g^{2} a7f^{6} Nov 25] well-made, attractive colt: first foal: dam, winner twice in USA and Grade 2-placed at 6f at 2 yrs, half-sister to Posse: fair form in 4 maidens for R. Charlton here: prominent long way in similar event at Aqueduct final start: will eventually prove suited by further than 6f. *W. Badgett, jnr, USA* 76

SUSAN-H 3 ch.f. Clantime 101 – Just A Spark (Sparkler 130) [1994 –: 5f 6m 1995 6m Jul 5] sturdy, plain filly: of no account. *Miss J. F. Craze* –

SUSELJA (IRE) 4 b.f. Mon Tresor 113 – Stifen (Burslem 123) [1994 –: 7m 8m 6s 1995 8d 12m^{5} a14g Nov 6] close-coupled, good-topped filly: poor maiden handicapper: stays 1½m: acts on good to firm ground. *J. M. Jefferson* 37

SUSHI BAR (IRE) 4 gr.g. Petorius 117 – Sashi Woo (Rusticaro (FR) 124) [1994 52: 7m 9.9d4 8g a10g4 1995 9.9m a11g2 14.1f* Jun 28] big, rather leggy gelding: modest performer: won maiden at Carlisle in June: stays 1¾m: acts on the all-weather and firm ground. *Mrs M. Reveley* 65

SUVALU (USA) 3 b.c. Woodman (USA) 126 – Danlu (USA) (Danzig (USA)) [1994 73: 7m4 6g 1995 8m3 10m 10m5 10.1m4 Aug 28] tall, close-coupled colt: fair maiden: stays 1¼m: takes keen hold, and held up in 1995: sold (P. Cole to M. Meagher) 6,000 gns Newmarket Autumn Sales. *P. F. I. Cole* 75

SVELTANA 3 b.f. Soviet Star (USA) 128 – Sally Brown 120 (Posse (USA) 130) [1994 NR 1995 7m* 8g4 10g Sep 29] angular, unfurnished filly: shows knee action: fifth living foal: sister to fair 11.5f winner Scorpius and half-sister to useful 1m and 1¼m winner Anne Bonny (by Ajdal): dam won Ribblesdale Stakes and Yorkshire Oaks, and is half-sister to Untold and Shoot Clear: fairly useful form: won maiden at Yarmouth in July: well beaten in handicap at Newmarket on final start: should be suited by further than 1m. *J. R. Fanshawe* 82

SWAIN (IRE) 3 b.c. Nashwan (USA) 135 – Love Smitten (CAN) (Key To The Mint (USA)) [1994 NR 1995 14v* 14g* 14m* 12.5g* 12.5g* 12d3 Oct 1] 128

Barring a dead-heat, one unbeaten record had to go in the Arc. Just the one did go, that of the French three-year-old Swain who lacked the turn of foot to halt Lammtarra's all-conquering progress but nevertheless excelled himself in third, within three lengths of the winner. Swain was positioned perfectly for a move early in the straight, having tracked the strong pace from the start; he managed to close to around a length at one stage, and he stayed on to the finish.

On this running, Swain would have won the St Leger. Immediately after his three-quarter-length defeat of Zilzal Zamaan in the Grand Prix de Deauville Lancel in August there was said to be a strong possibility of his going on to Doncaster; he was even quoted as second favourite, but in the end he waited for the Arc while his owner's Affidavit represented Fabre. Swain started at odds on in a nine-runner field for the Grand Prix, a Group 2 race, following a run of four victories which gradually revealed him as a high-class colt in the making. He had an unconventional introduction for such a colt, in that, unraced at two, he was put in over a mile and three quarters in testing conditions for his debut. In fact, his first three races were at that

Grand Prix de Deauville Lancel—Swain's fifth start and fifth victory; Zilzal Zamaan gives him most to do

distance, all at Saint-Cloud, the first of them in early-May. Evidently Swain was regarded very much a stayer to begin with, and the chances are that in the spring he did not rate very highly as a potential Arc candidate in his talent-packed yard which eventually fielded three major contenders for the race in himself, Carnegie and Freedom Cry. However, once Swain had progressed from minor company to land the odds from Madaiyn in the Group 3 Prix du Lys on his third outing he was dropped in distance to around a mile and a half. He has not been over further since. The Grand Prix marked his second appearance at the month-long Deauville meeting; before that, on his first attempt at a mile and a half, he ran in the listed Prix de Reux. On both these occasions he looked to need a test. Richard of York reluctantly set the pace to Swain in the Reux. Swain took over a furlong and a half out, then held the once-raced Lord of Appeal's late effort by a neck. Broadway Flyer set a strong gallop until just over two out in the Grand Prix, giving way to Zilzal Zamaan. Having been fourth of nine into the straight, Swain took time to make ground and had to be driven to challenge; he headed Zilzal Zamaan inside the last and stayed on.

Swain (IRE) (b.c. 1992)	Nashwan (USA) (ch 1986)	Blushing Groom (ch 1974)	Red God
			Runaway Bride
		Height of Fashion (b 1979)	Bustino
			Highclere
	Love Smitten (CAN) (b 1981)	Key To The Mint (b 1969)	Graustark
			Key Bridge
		Square Angel (b 1970)	Quadrangle
			Nangela

Swain remains in training. Presumably he will be aimed at the top middle-distance races, even though a longer trip might well suit him better. He was well served by the strong gallop and quite testing ground in the Arc. With that in mind, providing a pacemaker on a regular basis would seem a sensible precaution to take. Third place in the Arc makes Swain the highest achiever so far in his sire Nashwan's first two crops. His dam Love Smitten was a high achiever herself, a late-developer as well. Foaled in Canada, she was raced in the States where she won nine of her seventeen starts. Her most important victories came as a five-year-old in the Grade 1 Apple Blossom Handicap at Oaklawn and the Grade 2 Santa Maria Handicap at Santa Anita, both over eight and a half furlongs. In three seasons' racing she won at six furlongs to nine furlongs and ran second over a mile and a quarter once, in the Grade 1 Santa Barbara Handicap at Santa Anita. Love Smitten's sister Kamar and their dam Square Angel both made their mark in Canadian racing: both were Oaks winners and champion three-year-old fillies there. Both have left their mark at stud, too. Kamar is the dam of at least seven winners, among them the multiple Grade 1 winner Gorgeous, the Kentucky Oaks winner Seaside Attraction and the 1,500,000-dollar yearling Hiaam, a very useful filly who took the Princess Margaret Stakes at Ascot in 1986. The third dam Nangela won a minor stakes as a two-year-old. Swain is Love Smitten's third live foal and second winner, following the year-older filly Starstruck (by Soviet Star), successful over nine furlongs in the French Provinces.

Swain very much took the eye in the paddock at Longchamp: he is a robust, attractive colt. He lobbed down to the start with a fluent, if somewhat round, action. He races as if he possesses a good, even temperament, and would seem a safe bet to train on well. *A. Fabre, France*

SWALLOWDALE 3 ch.f. Statoblest 120 – Rambadale 68 (Vaigly Great 127) [1994 56?: 5d 5m^4 5.1g^5 5d 5g 1995 a5g 5m Jun 24] lengthy, sparely-made filly: modest maiden: no worthwhile form in 1995: has joined G. Margarson. *C. F. Wall* –

SWALLOW RIDGE (IRE) 6 ch.m. Martin John – Sheil-Na-Gig 63 (Ridan (USA)) [1994 33: a7g a10g a7g^4 1995 a8g^6 a7g^3 a8g^2 a8g^2 a8g Mar 31] plain, lengthy mare: poor maiden handicapper: sold 575 gns Ascot July Sales: stays 1m: form only on equitrack: edgy, hung left and well below form only try in blinkers. *R. J. O'Sullivan* 33

SWALLOWS DREAM (IRE) 4 ch.g. Bluebird (USA) 125 – Gay Fantasy (Troy 137) [1994 82: 8m^6 7d* 7g^4 10.3f* 11.4m^2 12.3m^2 1995 11.9m^2 12g^2 14g^4 12f^3 12g^3 12g 12s 10d Oct 19] quite attractive gelding: fairly useful handicapper: well below form last 3 starts, blinkered on 2 of them: barely stays 14f: successful on dead, goes well on top-of-the-ground: normally held up. *J. L. Dunlop* 88

SWAN AT WHALLEY 3 b.g. Statoblest 120 – My Precious Daisy (Sharpo 132) [1994 67p: 5g 5f^5 5.1g* 1995 a5g 5g^4 5g 5.1m^4 5m^4 5f^4 5g 5m Oct 4] compact gelding: fair sprint handicapper: below form after second 3-y-o outing, penultimate start for Jack Berry: has raced only on a sound surface on turf: tailed off in visor: usually a front runner. *Martyn Wane* — 71 d

SWANDALE FLYER 3 ch.g. Weldnaas (USA) 112 – Misfire 56 (Gunner B 126) [1994 70: 7g 7d^4 1995 9m 8g 8.1m^5 10.5g 10.5s Sep 30] big, workmanlike gelding: no worthwhile form in 1995: should stay beyond 1m: acts on dead ground. *N. Bycroft* — –

SWAN FLYER 4 b.f. Hadeer 118 – Fly The Coop (Kris 135) [1994 –: 8g 10m 14d 1995 10m 9.7m^6 12g 10.1m^6 11.6m Jul 17] plain filly: no worthwhile form in varied company: sold 825 gns Ascot October Sales. *J. J. Sheehan* — –

SWANGROVE (IRE) 2 b.f. (Mar 30) Classic Music (USA) – Nishapours Baby (Nishapour (FR) 125) [1995 a6g May 13] third reported foal: half-sister to 9f winner Malibu Magic and a winner in Macau (both by Be My Native): dam ran twice: 33/1, tailed off in seller at Wolverhampton: sold 600 gns Doncaster July Sales. *Martyn Meade* — –

SWAYNES LAD 3 b.g. Sulaafah (USA) 119 – Swaynes Lady 76 (St Alphage 119) [1994 NR 1995 10m 10g Sep 9] leggy, dipped-backed gelding: ninth living foal: half-brother to modest 1982 2-y-o 6f winner Leadenhall Lad (by Comedy Star) and a winning jumper: dam 2-y-o 5f winner: looks of no account. *C. P. Wildman* — –

SWEET ALLEGIANCE 5 b.m. Alleging (USA) 120 – Child of Grace 100 (King's Leap 111) [1994 NR 1995 8.3m 7.1m^4 7m^6 7g 8g 7d a8g Nov 20] leggy mare: half-sister to poor 1½m winner Amazing Silks (by Furry Glen), also successful over hurdles: dam useful Irish 2-y-o 6f winner: modest maiden: apparently best effort second start: should stay 1¼m. *Jamie Poulton* — 59 ?

SWEET AMORET 2 b.f. (Feb 18) Forzando 122 – Primrose Way 59 (Young Generation 129) [1995 6g 6m 7.5d Sep 13] 3,600Y: workmanlike filly: poor mover: fifth foal: dam middle-distance maiden: never a factor in maidens, pulling hard final outing: sweating and edgy, withdrawn third intended outing after giving trouble in preliminaries: has joined P. Howling. *R. C. Spicer* — –

SWEET CAROLINE 4 br.f. Squill (USA) 122 – Think Ahead 104 (Sharpen Up 127) [1994 –: 8m 12g 11.5g 8.1d a10g^6 a13g 1995 a13g a10g^3 a13g^5 a12g a13g Feb 2] leggy, unfurnished filly: no worthwhile form: tried blinkered. *Pat Mitchell* — –

SWEET CHEAP PET 3 b.f. Petong 126 – Westonepaperchase (USA) 71 (Accipiter (USA)) [1994 51: 5d^4 5g a5g* 5m^3 6f* 6f^3 a7g^2 a7g^3 6.1g^3 a6g^4 7.1m^2 8m^3 7.5g 8.3g^6 8s^6 1995 a8g a6g a7g^3 a8.5g^6 5.9m 8.3g 6f 5m 8m 12m Jul 3] angular, close-coupled filly: poor performer: left Jack Berry's stable after fourth start, and well beaten afterwards: stays 1m: acts on firm ground and fibresand: effective visored or not, no improvement in blinkers. *J. J. O'Neill* — 49 d

SWEET DISORDER (IRE) 5 br.m. Never So Bold 135 – Mists of Avalon (USA) 76 (Nureyev (USA) 131) [1995 11.9m a9.4g a12g Dec 9] leggy, sparely-made mare: modest maiden (rated 58) at 3 yrs for G. Pritchard-Gordon: won three races at 1½m to 1¾m in Jersey in 1994 and two 1½m handicaps there in the spring: no form on return to mainland, trained for reappearance by D. Gandolfo. *B. J. Meehan* — –

SWEET GLOW (FR) 8 b.g. Crystal Glitters (USA) 127 – Very Sweet (Bellypha 130) [1994 81: 14.1d^6 11.7m 14g 20m* 16.1f 20f 1995 20m 16d Oct 19] leggy, narrow gelding: very good staying hurdler at best: never a threat in Ascot Stakes (bidding for repeat win) and handicap at Newbury in 1995. *M. C. Pipe* — –

SWEETLITTLEMYSTERY 4 ch.f. Gabitat 119 – Bildara (Balidar 133) [1994 35: a6g a9.4g^6 a7g 9g^5 10m 7.1m 8.1m^3 7.1m 1995 8f 10g 8g Jul 28] angular filly: no form in 1995. *E. J. Alston* — –

SWEET MAGIC 4 ch.g. Sweet Monday 122 – Charm Bird 60 (Daring March 116) [1994 75p: 6d 6m 6g 5g* 5f^2 1995 5m^2 6m^3 5m^2 5m* 5.2m^6 Aug 12] lengthy, plain gelding: tends to look dull in coat: fairly useful handicapper: held fast-finishing Princess Oberon by a short head at Newmarket in July: rare poor effort on final start: speedy, and best at 5f: acts on firm ground: usually races prominently: has joined P. Howling. *L. J. Holt* — 87

SWEET MATE 3 ch.g. Komaite (USA) – Be My Sweet 78 (Galivanter 131) [1994 36: 5f 6g 6m a5g 1995 a7g a8g^3 a8g^6 a6g* a6g^4 8g^6 a8g^6 7.5m 6.1m^5 6m^2 5f — 48 a60

5m^5 6d^5 7f^4 7m a6g^2 a6g^3 a7g^6 Dec 12] workmanlike gelding: has a round action: modest handicapper: won at Southwell in May: effective at 6f, and stays 1m: acts on firm and dead ground and goes well on fibresand: usually wears adapted (one-eyed) blinkers: has run well when sweating: somewhat wayward, but successful for apprentice. *S. R. Bowring*

SWEET MIGNONETTE 7 b.m. Tina's Pet 121 – Ixia 91 (I Say 125) [1994 80: 8m^4 9f^6 10g* 8g^6 10.1m* 8g 10s^4 9g^6 8m 10.1d 1995 10.3g 10.4g^5 10d^4 10g* 10.4m^4 Oct 4] lengthy, workmanlike mare: fair performer: won apprentice event at Pontefract in September by 6 lengths: effective at 1m to 1¼m: acts on firm and dead ground, possibly not on soft: tends to idle in front and is held up: ran as if something amiss over hurdles in October. *Mrs M. Reveley* — 76

SWEET NATURE (IRE) 2 b.f. (Mar 11) Classic Secret (USA) 91 – So Kind 90 (Kind of Hush 118) [1995 5.2g^2 5g a6g* 6m Oct 12] 17,000Y: sturdy filly: third foal: half-sister to 3-y-o Princely Hush (by Prince Sabo), useful 5f and 6f (Mill Reef Stakes) winner at 2 yrs: dam 6f winner, probably stayed 7f: comfortable winner of median auction maiden at Wolverhampton in September: gave impression something amiss in nursery at Newmarket 12 days later: stays 6f: acts on fibresand. *W. Jarvis* — 70 +

SWEETNESS HERSELF 2 ch.f. (Apr 29) Unfuwain (USA) 131 – No Sugar Baby (FR) (Crystal Glitters (USA) 127) [1995 8.2d^3 7g^4 Oct 3] 21,000Y: tall, rather leggy filly: second foal: half-sister to a winner in Germany by Law Society: dam French maiden: similar form in frame in maidens won by Storm Trooper at Nottingham and Sil Sila at Warwick 3 weeks later: will stay at least 1¼m. *M. J. Ryan* — 74

SWEET PAVLOVA (USA) 3 b.f. Zilzal (USA) 137 – Meringue Pie (USA) (Silent Screen (USA)) [1994 71p: 6m^3 7m^3 1995 6m^6 8f 10.2m^2 11.5f^2 10.2h* 12m Sep 7] leggy, lengthy filly: fair performer: justified favouritism in maiden handicap at Bath in August, making all: tailed off in minor event at Folkestone on only subsequent start: suited by middle distances: has raced only on top-of-the-ground: sold 36,000 gns Newmarket December Sales. *P. F. I. Cole* — 71

SWEET ROBIN (IRE) 2 b.f. (Apr 13) Mujtahid (USA) 118 – La Romance (USA) (Lyphard (USA) 132) [1995 5m* 5m 6m^2 5g^2 6m^3 8g^4 Sep 7] leggy, lengthy filly: sixth foal: half-sister to 3-y-o 1¼m winner Proposing (by Rainbow Quest), French middle-distance winner Amal (by Top Ville) and 1989 2-y-o 6f winner New Romantic (by Miswaki): dam French 1¼m winner out of half-sister to Green Dancer: won maiden at Thirsk in May: in frame in 2 pattern events in Ireland, Lowther Stakes at York and May Hill Stakes (had to switch over 1f out and finished well into fourth behind Solar Crystal) at Doncaster: stays 1m: takes a long time to find her stride and may benefit from forcing tactics. *M. Johnston* — 103

SWEET ROMEO 5 ch.g. Local Suitor (USA) 128 – Ladoucette 102 (Bustino 136) [1994 a8g^4 a8.5g a8.5g a10g a9.3g a8.5g a8.5g a9.3g a9.3g a9.3g a8.5g 1995 a12g^5 11f^3 11g^2 13.5f^2 11f^5 13.5g* a13.5g^3 12.5g^3 a13.5g* a12g* a13g Dec 14] close-coupled gelding: modest performer for M. Johnston at 3 yrs: based in Belgium since, performing much better in 1995 than in 1994 and winning handicaps at Ostend and Sterrebeek (2): eleventh of 14 in apprentice handicap at Lingfield on final 5-y-o start: stays 1¾m: acts on firm, dead ground and all-weather. *Alex Vanderhaeghen, Belgium* — 58 a63

SWEET SUPPOSIN (IRE) 4 b.c. Posen (USA) – Go Honey Go (General Assembly (USA)) [1994 75: 7m 8g 8g^6 8g^6 10g 12s 11d a8g* a10g^2 1995 a8g^3 a11g^5 a8g^2 a7g* a7g* a7g^3 a6g^3 6m 6.9m^3 6.9g a8.5g* a7g* 7.6m a7g* 8g a7g a8g a9.4g* a8g^2 Dec 15] leggy colt: fairly useful performer on the all-weather: won claimers at Lingfield (2) in February, Wolverhampton (3, claimed out of K. McAuliffe's stable £9,000 after middle one) in the summer, and Wolverhampton in November: seems only modest on turf: needs further than 6f (stays 1¼m): best turf efforts on good ground: often held up: usually blinkered/visored. *C. A. Dwyer* — 61 a90

SWEET TIMES 2 ch.f. (Apr 3) Riverman (USA) 131 – Affection Affirmed (USA) (Affirmed (USA)) [1995 7g 7g^6 Oct 23] unfurnished filly: fourth foal: sister to 7f winner River Deep, smart performer on his day, and half-sister to useful 3-y-o middle-distance performer Dreamer (by Zilzal), 5.1f and 8.1f winner at 2 yrs: dam, 1m to 9f winner, half-sister to dam of Zoman (by Affirmed): modest form in maidens won by Sil Sila at Warwick and Jezyah at Lingfield, not given hard race either time: should stay beyond 7f: likely to do better. *P. F. I. Cole* — 60 p

SWEET TRENTINO (IRE) 4 b.g. High Estate 127 – Sweet Adelaide (USA) 98 (The Minstrel (CAN) 135) [1994 69: 8m 7v 6.9v 7d 10.2g 8.3d² 7.5m² 8.1f⁴ 9.7g 8m* 8m* 8m² 8m² 8m⁴ 8m⁵ 8d⁴ 1995 a9.4g 8g 10.5d 12.3m⁶ 10.2m⁴ 8g a9.4g Aug 19] compact gelding: fair performer at 3 yrs: showed little in 1995, leaving C. Smith's stable after reappearance. *M. Tate* –

SWEET WATER (IRE) 3 b.f. Fayruz 116 – Stamina 78 (Star Appeal 133) [1994 56: 5.7f a5g⁵ 5.3m³ 5d 1995 6g⁶ 7m Jun 19] leggy filly: modest maiden: no worthwhile form in handicaps in 1995: should be suited by further than 5f. *D. J. S. Cosgrove* –

SWEET WHISPER 4 gr.f. Petong 126 – Softly Spoken 87 (Mummy's Pet 125) [1994 63d: 6g² 5.1g⁶ 6g a6g 6f a6g⁵ 6m 6.9g 6m 1995 a6g⁵ a6g² a6g⁵ a6g⁶ Mar 4] leggy filly: has a quick action: poor performer nowadays: stays 6f: acts on firm ground, dead and equitrack: blinkered 3 times, usually visored. *K. McAuliffe* 47

SWEET WILHELMINA 2 b.f. (Apr 9) Indian Ridge 123 – Henpot (IRE) 68 (Alzao (USA) 117) [1995 7g a7g* a8g* Nov 30] 9,200F, 9,200Y: first foal: dam 1¼m winner at 4 yrs: won maiden at Wolverhampton and nursery (with plenty in hand, always travelling smoothly) at Lingfield late in year: will stay beyond 1m: acts on all-weather surfaces: will improve again. *Lord Huntingdon* 83 p

SWIFT FANDANGO (USA) 2 b.c. (Feb 17) Lear Fan (USA) 130 – Danlu (USA) (Danzig (USA)) [1995 7m* 7m² Jul 15] tall, good-topped colt: slightly unfurnished: has plenty of scope: powerful mover with a long, rounded stride: third reported foal: half-brother to 3-y-o Suvalu (by Woodman) and smart middle-distance performer Strategic Choice (by Alleged): dam, probably stayed 1¼m in Ireland, is sister to smart 6f/7f performer Nicholas out of half-sister to Nordance: convincing winner from House Of Riches in maiden at Newmarket in July, always travelling strongly: heavily-backed favourite, never travelling with particular fluency when second of 4 to Fag End in minor event at York 2 weeks later, tending to hang in behind winner: will stay 1m: worth another chance to confirm good impression created on debut. *P. F. I. Cole* 90 p

SWIFT MAIDEN 2 gr.f. (Mar 28) Sharrood (USA) 124 – Gunner Girl 85 (Gunner B 126) [1995 6m⁶ 8.1m³ 8d³ 7.3d 7m Nov 4] sturdy filly: sixth live foal: half-sister to 1993 2-y-o 6f winner Bold Alex (by Full Extent): dam 7f to 1¼m winner: modest maiden: stiff tasks in nurseries last 2 starts: will stay at least 1¼m: acts on good to firm and dead ground. *Mrs L. A. Murphy* 62 +

SWIFT MOVE 3 ch.f. Move Off 112 – Phyl's Pet (Aberdeen 109) [1994 NR 1995 11.1g Sep 25] eighth reported foal: half-sister to fair 7f to 11f winner Invertiel (by Sparkling Boy): dam well behind all starts: 100/1, tailed off in claimer. *P. Monteith* –

SWIFT NICK NEVISON 4 b.g. Grey Desire 115 – Bunnyloch 49§ (Lochnager 132) [1994 41: 5.1g a5g⁴ 5m 5d 5.2m⁶ 5s a5g³ a5g⁴ 1995 a5g 5d 5f 6f⁵ 9.5d⁴ a6g a5g⁶ Nov 11] tall, angular gelding: poor sprinter: acts on the all-weather and dead ground: sold to Belgium 1,500 gns Newmarket July Sales after second 4-y-o start. *K. T. Ivory* 23

SWIFTY NIFTY (IRE) 2 b.f. (Feb 1) Runnett 125 – Swift Verdict 89 (My Swallow 134) [1995 5m 5m 5g 5s⁵ 5f Oct 14] IR 8,000Y: sparely-made filly: sister to useful 1991 2-y-o 5f winner Nifty Fifty and half-sister to several winners abroad: dam Irish 1¼m winner: poor maiden. *J. Berry* –

SWINGALONG GIRL 2 ch.f. (Feb 18) Weldnaas (USA) 112 – Singalong Lass 63 (Bold Lad (IRE) 133) [1995 6s 6f 7g Oct 23] 3,200F, 2,000Y: workmanlike filly: half-brother to 5f winner Don't Run Me Over (by Kafu) and a good winner in Germany at around 1m by Elegant Air: dam placed at 1m and 9.4f at 3 yrs: soundly beaten in claimer and maiden events: unruly in paddock first 2 outings: wears bandages. *T. M. Jones* –

SWINGING SIXTIES (IRE) 4 b.g. Fairy King (USA) – La Bella Fontana (Lafontaine (USA) 117) [1994 54: 7d 8m 8.5s 10m 8.5m³ 8.5m⁵ 8f³ 7.2g 7g² 1995 7.1m 7.6m 8g* 8g⁴ Oct 9] tall, lengthy gelding: modest handicapper: improved form to win 22-runner contest at Goodwood in September: good fourth in minor event at Leicester on only subsequent start: should stay 1¼m: acts on firm ground, probably on soft: tried blinkered/visored, better form without: none too consistent. *G. L. Moore* 64

SWINGING TICH 6 b.m. Swing Easy (USA) 126 – Little Tich (Great Nephew 126) [1994 46: a7g^2 a8g^3 a7g^4 a6g^5 a6g* a6g 7m 6.1s^5 6s^4 7d a6g 1995 a6g^6 a6g^3 a6g^2 a6g a6g a7g 8m^6 a8g 10.8m 9.7s Sep 27] leggy mare: poor performer: sold privately out of B. McMahon's stable 2,000 gns Doncaster March Sales after fifth 6-y-o outing: well beaten last 3 starts, leaving A. Forbes after second of them: stays 1m: acts on firm and soft going and on fibresand: blinkered (well beaten) once at 4 yrs: tends to be slowly away. *I. Campbell*
47

SWING MANIA (IRE) 2 b.f. (Apr 5) Polish Patriot (USA) 128 – Exclusive Melody (CAN) (Commemorate (USA)) [1995 6g^5 6m^3 a5g^3 a6g^4 a6g 7.1g^5 7f Oct 3] leggy, close-coupled filly: unimpressive mover: second foal: dam unraced half-sister to dam of high-class French middle-distance colt Dancehall: plater: will stay beyond 7f: acts on fibresand: blinkered fifth outing (below form): sold 4,500 gns Newmarket Autumn Sales. *S. G. Norton*
47

SWISH 2 b.g. (Feb 14) Primo Dominie 121 – Honey Pot 111 (Hotfoot 126) [1995 6g 6d 8.5m 8g^5 8.2d 7d Sep 22] 18,000Y: good-topped gelding: has scope: half-brother to several winners, including useful 1987 2-y-o Ship of Fools (by Windjammer) and useful 4-y-o 7.1f (at 2 yrs) and 8.1f winner (stays 10.5f) Girl From Ipanema (by Salse): dam sprinting 2-y-o: no worthwhile form in maidens and a nursery: active sort who races keenly: sold 1,400 gns Newmarket Autumn Sales: sent to Norway. *N. Tinkler*
–

SWISS BANK 3 b.f. Robellino (USA) 127 – Granny's Bank 88 (Music Boy 124) [1994 55p: 6s^2 1995 7f^5 8d^4 Sep 26] leggy filly: fair maiden: best effort on reappearance: carried head high final start: should stay 1m: sold 800 gns Newmarket December Sales: sent to Sweden. *Lord Huntingdon*
70

SWISS MOUNTAIN 5 b. or br.m. Formidable (USA) 125 – Helvetique (FR) (Val de Loir 133) [1994 NR 1995 12d 10.8m^3 Jul 7] lengthy mare: has a round action: poor maiden: will stay further than 10.8f: acts on good to firm and heavy going: no improvement blinkered/visored. *P. J. Bevan*
25

SWISS VALLEY LADY 2 b.f. (Apr 24) Tout Ensemble – Jokers High (USA) (Vaguely Noble 140) [1995 5g^2 a5g* 5g^2 5m^2 5g^4 May 25] small filly: half-sister to 7f winner Blue Room (by Gorytus): dam unraced daughter of Joking Apart, very smart at up to 1m: won seller at Wolverhampton in April: best effort when fourth of 8 in minor event at Newcastle final start: had fine early pace: dead. *W. G. M. Turner*
68

SWIVEL 3 ch.f. Salse (USA) 128 – Spin Turn (Homing 130) [1994 60p: 7g^3 1995 10m 11.9g^3 12g^5 14.1f^2 14.1m^2 16.4m^2 15g Sep 14] leggy, useful-looking filly: fair maiden handicapper: looks a thorough stayer: acts on firm ground: sweating and edgy (ran badly) final start: has joined D. Nicholson. *J. R. Fanshawe*
73

SWORDKING (IRE) 6 ch.g. Kris 135 – Reine Mathilde (USA) 123 (Vaguely Noble 140) [1994 40, a56: a12g^3 a16.2g^3 a14g 12g a16.2g^3 a12g^6 14.1d* 12g 12.3m^5 a14.8g* a14.8g* a14g^2 a14.8g^4 16.1m^4 a14.8g^3 a12g a14.8g a14g^2 a14g 1995 a14g^5 a14.8g a16.2g a14g^4 14.1g* 14.1g 14.1m a14.8g^2 14.1g^6 14.1m^5 a14.8g^4 a14.8g^3 a14g Aug 4] stocky gelding: modest handicapper: won at Nottingham in April: stays 16.2f: acts on fibresand, best turf form on good/dead ground: effective visored or not: inconsistent. *J. L. Harris*
47

SWORD MASTER 6 b.g. Sayf El Arab (USA) 127 – Swordlestown Miss (USA) (Apalachee (USA) 137) [1994 NR 1995 14m Apr 18] workmanlike gelding: fairly useful staying handicapper (rated 77, a86) in 1993, winning 4 races: well below form only 6-y-o start: pulled up lame over hurdles in June. *Bob Jones*
63 +

SWYNFORD DREAM 2 b.g. (Feb 26) Statoblest 120 – Qualitair Dream 80 (Dreams To Reality (USA) 113) [1995 5.1m^5 5g* 5g* 5g^2 5m* 5m Oct 27] workmanlike gelding: first foal: dam, 6f winner at 2 yrs, later stayed 1m: progressive form when making all in well-contested seller at Ayr and nurseries at Redcar and Catterick in the autumn: well below form in nursery at Newmarket final start: speedy: yet to race on a soft surface. *J. F. Bottomley*
85

SWYNFORD FLYER 6 b.m. Valiyar 129 – Qualitairess 49 (Kampala 120) [1994 34, a53: a12g^2 a11g^6 a8g a9.4g* a11g^3 a10g a11g a8g^5 a9.4g^5 a8.5g 10m^6 11.6f* 11.6m^6 10.8m^2 a12g^4 a8g* 10s 8g a9.4g a11g 1995 a9.4g a9.4g^2 a11g^4 a12g a9.4g a9.4g 10m a8g 8f^4 8m^6 11.6m 8.3m 10m^4 7m 8.2m a8g a10g^2 a10g a10g^4 Dec
32
a43

19] plain, good-topped mare: poor handicapper at best in 1995: stays 11.6f: acts on firm ground and fibresand: blinkered (well beaten) once: inconsistent. *J. A. Harris*

SYCAMORE LODGE (IRE) 4 ch.g. Thatching 131 – Bell Tower 98 (Lyphard's Wish (FR) 124) [1994 6v 9s^5 8s^3 7d^2 8s^4 7m^4 7g^3 a8g^3 6.5g^3 7s^5 8d^3 8g 1995 7g^3 8m^6 7g^2 7g^2 8.9m^6 8f^2 10f^2 10.1m^4 10m^5 Aug 19] 13,000 2-y-o: lengthy ex-Irish gelding: shows a quick action: second foal: half-brother to Irish 6f winner Markievicz (by Doyoun): dam (won 3 times in Ireland) stayed 1m: fair maiden handicapper: sold out of D. Weld's stable 10,000 gns Newmarket Autumn (1994) Sales: stays 1¼m: acts on firm and soft ground: effective blinkered, tried here only on eighth 4-y-o start: has flashed tail: consistent: sold (P. Calver to Mrs J. Ramsden) 6,800 gns Doncaster November Sales. *P. Calver* 74

SYLVAN CELEBRATION 4 b.f. Sylvan Express 117 – Footstool 61 (Artaius (USA) 129) [1994 –: a7g a8g^6 8d^5 a6g^3 7.1g 1995 11.1g 13g 11.1g^6 9.2m 8.3f^5 11.1f^5 13.1f^4 Aug 17] tall filly: no worthwhile form: has joined J. Goldie. *Miss L. A. Perratt* –

SYLVANDRA 3 b.f. Mazilier (USA) 107 – Pattis Pet (Mummy's Pet 125) [1994 81: 5d^5 5m 6g^2 6.1m^2 6m 5s^6 5.7g* 6.1g* 7.3v^5 1995 8m 6m^6 6m^4 7g 8.1m^6 7m^5 7g^2 7f^6 8g 6.1d 6m^4 7d 7m Nov 3] small filly: fair handicapper: below form last 5 starts: stays 1m: acts on any ground: visored final outing: sold 5,400 gns Newmarket December Sales. *P. G. Murphy* 69

SYLVAN POINT 4 b.c. Reference Point 139 – Sovereign Dona 117 (Sovereign Path 125) [1994 9.5g^5 9g^3 10g^4 10.5g* 9.5g* 11g* 9g* 9.5d^5 1995 10s^2 10g* 10g* 10g^4 10g^5 10g^2 10d^2 10d^3 Oct 29] IR 46,000Y: half-brother to several winners, including smart Irish middle-distance stayer Foresee (by Vision) and Breeders' Cup Mile fourth Royal Touch (by Tap On Wood): dam, half-sister to good milers Don and American Prince, won 1¼m Prix de Psyche: smart German colt: unraced at 2 yrs and not highly tried at 3 yrs, winning minor events at Hanover, Cologne (2) and Baden-Baden: successful twice in 1995 at Frankfurt, including in quite valuable event in June: contested pattern races afterwards, improved form when head second of 9 to Hushang in Group 2 race at Frankfurt and (after changing hands for 160,000 DM) ½-length second of 14 to Concepcion in Group 3 event at Hoppegarten: stays 11f, should get 1½m: best efforts on good or dead ground: nearly always blinkered. *H. Remmert, Germany* 114

SYLVAN PRINCESS 2 b.f. (Apr 13) Sylvan Express 117 – Ela-Yianni-Mou 73 (Anfield 117) [1995 7.1m 10m Oct 2] rather unfurnished filly: second known foal: half-sister to 4-y-o 1½m winner Achilles Heel (by Superlative): dam sprinter: well beaten in maiden events at Sandown (very slowly away) and Pontefract: bandaged behind last time. *C. N. Allen* –

SYLVAN STARLIGHT 5 b. or br.m. Sylvan Express 117 – Kakisa 81 (Forlorn River 124) [1994 –: 6g 8.1g 1995 10.2m Aug 28] lengthy mare: no form on flat since 1993. *J. M. Bradley* –

SYLVA PARADISE (IRE) 2 b.c. (Feb 12) Dancing Dissident (USA) 119 – Brentsville (USA) (Arctic Tern (USA) 126) [1995 6m^6 5.2g^6 6m^4 6d* Sep 27] 12,500Y: smallish, lengthy colt: first foal: dam Irish 2-y-o 6f winner: ran a good race when sixth of 17 to Blue Iris in Super Sprint at Newbury in July: won 9-runner maiden at Folkestone in September comfortably by 2 lengths from School Boy: will stay 7f: best form on an easy surface. *C. E. Brittain* 79

SYLVELLA 2 b.f. (Feb 6) Lear Fan (USA) 130 – Suprematie (FR) (Gay Mecene (USA) 128) [1995 6g 7m Oct 28] 30,000Y: leggy filly: fifth foal: half-sister to 3-y-o Supreme (by Lomond), a winner at up to 9.5f in France by Bellypha and one in USA by Secretariat: dam French 1m (at 2 yrs) and 10.5f winner: never dangerous in autumn maidens at Newmarket won by Polish Spring and Awaamir. *M. A. Jarvis* –

SYRIAN QUEEN 3 b.f. Slip Anchor 136 – Rimosa's Pet 109 (Petingo 135) [1994 NR 1995 10g^2 10g^3 10m* 10g Oct 1] 74,000F, IR 230,000Y: sturdy filly: ninth living foal: sister to 4-y-o 1m winner On The Tide and half-sister to several winners, including smart sprinter Kerrera (by Diesis), very smart sprinter/miler Rock City (by Ballad Rock) and useful 8.5f to 11f winner Peto (by Petoski): dam 6f to 10.5f winner: off course 3 months, made all in maiden at Leicester in September: very stiff task and beat only one in 9-runner Group 2 event at Rome on final start: should have stayed 1½m: blinkered last 2 starts: stud. *H. R. A. Cecil* 82+

SZLOTO 2 ch.c. (Mar 26) Polish Patriot (USA) 128 – Swinging Gold 80 (Swing Easy (USA) 126) [1995 5f^5 6f^5 7g 7d Sep 27] good-topped colt: fifth living foal: half-brother to 3-y-o Self Styled (by Taufan), 1990 2-y-o 5f winner Spinechiller (by Grey Ghost) and 6f to 1m winner So So (by Then Again): dam sprinter: modest form in maidens, twice shaping well: will prove best short of 7f. *T. D. Barron* 57 +

T

TAAHHUB (IRE) 5 b.g. Nordico (USA) – Undiscovered (Tap On Wood 130) [1994 NR 1995 a12g^4 a10g 8m^4 10.8g^4 12.3m Jun 28] big gelding: disappointing maiden on flat, for N. Twiston-Davies on reappearance, then R. O'Sullivan next 2 starts: stays 1½m: blinkered once at 3 yrs: winner of 2 novice hurdles. *R. J. Price* 47

TABARD GARDEN 3 ch.f. Scottish Reel 123 – Wigeon 80 (Divine Gift 127) [1994 42: 5m^5 a5g 7m 6g 6g^6 9d^3 a8g 1995 7.5m 10m Jun 12] lengthy filly: poor maiden: well beaten in 1995: may well stay further than 9f: acts on good to firm and dead ground. *D. Nicholls* –

TABDEEL 3 b.c. Warrshan (USA) 117 – Tartique Twist (USA) 78 (Arctic Tern (USA) 126) [1994 NR 1995 10m^6 10m 16.2m* 17.5g Sep 15] 14,000F, IR 32,000Y: quite attractive colt: second foal: dam 1¾m and 2m winner: improved effort stepped up in distance to win steadily-run 4-runner maiden at Beverley in August, leading inside final 1f: well beaten in handicap at Ayr afterwards: stays 16.2f: acts on good to firm ground: sent to Dubai. *A. C. Stewart* 74

TABLETS OF STONE (IRE) 2 b.g. (Apr 28) Contract Law (USA) 108 – Remember Mulvilla (Ballad Rock 122) [1995 6m 6f 8.2m 8f a10g Nov 25] IR 5,400F, 13,000Y: compact gelding: half-brother to winning sprinter Comet Whirlpool (by Waajib) and a winner in Italy: dam Irish 2-y-o 6f winner: no worthwhile form in maidens and a nursery. *J. R. Bosley* –

TABOOK (IRE) 4 b.c. Cadeaux Genereux 131 – Al Najah (USA) 96 (Topsider (USA)) [1994 102: 6f* 6g* 6f 6m^3 5m^6 6g 1995 7f^5 6m^3 6g^6 5.6m 7g 6d^6 Oct 19] sturdy, lengthy colt: good mover: only fairly useful performer at 4 yrs: seems suited by around 6f: acts on firm going and dead: usually races prominently: inconsistent: sold 22,000 gns Newmarket Autumn Sales to Malaysia. *E. A. L. Dunlop* 91

TABRIZ 2 b.f. (May 15) Persian Heights 129 – Faisalah (Gay Mecene (USA) 128) [1995 5m^3 7m^3 6m^3 7m^2 7d^6 8m^6 7.1s^4 Nov 2] angular, leggy filly: fourth foal: half-sister to 3-y-o 5f winner Nadwaty (by Prince Sabo): dam unraced: fair maiden: stays 1m: may not be suited by very soft ground. *J. D. Bethell* 74

TACHYCARDIA 3 ch.f. Weldnaas (USA) 112 – Gold Ducat 74 (Young Generation 129) [1994 56: 5d 6s 6m^3 5g^4 6m* 6m 6g^3 6g^3 6.1d 7m^2 a8.5g* 6.9s 1995 a8g^4 a10g a8g^5 a6g a6g a6g a7g^5 5m^3 5.3m* 6g 5m^2 6f^6 5.3f^3 6m 5g Sep 29] rather sparely-made filly: modest handicapper: made all at Brighton in June: effective at 5f, and stays 8.5f: acts firm ground and fibresand (below form on a soft surface and equitrack): has run well for 7-lb claimer: none too consistent. *R. J. O'Sullivan* 50 a44

TADELLAL (IRE) 4 ch.f. Glint of Gold 128 – Meissarah (USA) (Silver Hawk (USA) 123) [1994 NR 1995 12g^5 7f^5 10m 11.5m^5 a10g 10g a10g* a10g* 10.2m^3 a14.8g^5 a12g^4 a10g^2 a12g^5 a12g^4 Nov 29] big, workmanlike filly: reportedly broke blood vessel on intended 3-y-o reappearance: modest performer: trained by M. Dixon first 3 starts at 4 yrs: ridden by claimer J. Wilkinson, won seller (sold out of B. Pearce's stable 5,100 gns) and handicap at Lingfield in August: stays 1½m: acts on equitrack and firm ground. *W. G. M. Turner* 59 a64

TADEO 2 ch.c. (Feb 23) Primo Dominie 121 – Royal Passion 78 (Ahonoora 122) [1995 5m^4 5f^2 5f* 5.1f^2 5f^2 5f^5 5m^6 6.1m^3 5g^2 5m^5 5g^3 6g^4 5g* Oct 23] lengthy, good-topped colt: first foal: dam, winner 3 times at around 1¼m, stayed 1½m: fairly useful performer: successful in maiden at Carlisle in May and (after creditable efforts in listed races at Ayr and York) minor event at Lingfield (beat Songsheet readily by 3½ lengths) in October: stays 6f, but best form at 5f: acts on firm ground: left M. Channon's stable after seventh start: tough. *M. Johnston* 92

TADJONI 3 b.c. Mtoto 134 – Nobly Born (USA) (The Minstrel (CAN) 135) [1994 NR 1995 10m 10.2m May 2] unfurnished colt: fifth foal: brother to a winner in Belgium and half-brother to 1¼m and 11.5f winner Quivira (by Rainbow Quest): dam ran once: eighth of 21 in maiden at Kempton on debut: broke leg 15 days later: dead. *I. A. Balding* –

TAEL OF SILVER 3 b.f. Today And Tomorrow 78 – Schula 81 (Kala Shikari 125) [1994 46p: a6g^3 1995 a6g^6 a7g^5 a7g^6 6.1g* 6.1m 6m 6m^6 5m* 6g^2 6g^3 6f^6 a6g 6.1d^3 6g 5.1m Oct 19] leggy filly: fair performer on turf, modest on all-weather: won seller at Nottingham in April and handicap at Warwick in June: stays 6f: acts on good to firm and dead ground and on fibresand: blinkered (well below best) final start. *K. R. Burke* 69 a57

TAFAHHUS 3 b.g. Green Desert (USA) 127 – Mileeha (USA) 97 (Blushing Groom (FR) 131) [1994 59: 6g 6.1s 6g 1995 6.1g^4 6m* 7f^5 6f* 6m^3 6g 6f* 6m* 6g^5 6m 5m^6 a6g a6g a6g Dec 18] close-coupled, attractive gelding: has a quick action: fairly useful handicapper: progressed well while winning at Brighton in April (minor event) and May, and at Lingfield in June and Epsom in July: well beaten last 6 starts, sold out of R. Armstrong's stable 8,000 gns Newmarket Autumn Sales and gelded after third of them: stays 6f: acts on firm ground. *M. J. Polglase* 84 d

TAFFETA SILK (USA) 4 b.f. Clever Trick (USA) – Silk Sari (USA) 101 (Raja Baba (USA)) [1994 66: 6g^3 7.1m^2 8g^3 8.1m^3 5g* 6g^3 6.1s^4 5m^5 6m 1995 5g^5 6g^4 6m^5 6f^3 6m^3 a6g Oct 14] good-topped filly: fair handicapper: successful at 5f and stays 1m: acts on good to firm and soft ground, well beaten (after 3 months off) only start on all-weather: races prominently: consistent: sold 5,000 gns Newmarket Autumn Sales. *W. Jarvis* 70

TAFIA (IRE) 4 ch.f. Pharly (FR) 130 – Tafila 101 (Adonijah 126) [1994 84: 8.5m^4 10g^5 10m 1995 8f^4 10.1m^5 10d a12g a9.3g^4 Nov 12] leggy, close-coupled filly: no worthwhile form here in 1995: sold 1,600 gns Newmarket Autumn Sales after fourth start: fourth of 7 in minor event at Sterrebeek final outing. *J. Pearce* –

TAGATAY 2 b.g. (Mar 13) Nomination 125 – Salala 83 (Connaught 130) [1995 a8g a6g Nov 20] fifth foal: brother to 7f winner My Nominee and a winning sprinter in Sweden by Ballacashtal: dam, 7f winner, half-sister to Beau Sher: slowly into stride and always behind in maidens at Southwell. *M. J. Camacho* –

TAGULA (IRE) 2 b.c. (Mar 3) Taufan (USA) 119 – Twin Island (IRE) (Standaan (FR) 118) [1995 6m^5 6g* 6m^4 6g* 6g* 7m^3 Oct 13] 116

The July Stakes and Prix Morny winner Tagula failed to advance his Two Thousand Guineas claims in the Dewhurst Stakes at Newmarket in October. At the line he was four lengths behind the ready winner Alhaarth, in third place of four, a

SBJ Group July Stakes, Newmarket—Tagula shades Take A Left (obscured) and World Premier

Prix Morny Piaget, Deauville—Tagula and Walter Swinburn again come out on top; then With Fascination, Barricade and Russian Revival

length and a half also behind Danehill Dancer with whom he had been neck and neck a furlong out. Tagula, who was tackling seven furlongs for the first time, reportedly underwent a rushed preparation for the Dewhurst after missing the Middle Park with a slight injury and may not have been at his best, but it's near impossible to see his reversing the form with the first two over a mile in the Guineas. Tagula, a good-topped colt, looks the sort to hold his own as a three-year-old, though, and he should make a very smart performer at up to seven furlongs.

The first of Tagula's pattern victories came in the July Stakes at Newmarket, and followed an excellent fourth in the Coventry at Royal Ascot, where he beat those on his side easily enough but couldn't overcome the advantage held by those led home by Royal Applause on the far side. Given a more favourable draw at Ascot Tagula would probably have run Russian Revival close for second. He had previously finished over seven lengths fifth behind the same horse in a Newbury maiden in May, then trounced Tumbleweed Ridge by five lengths in a similar event at Newmarket two weeks later. Available at 14/1 that day, he started at 7/2 on his return visit for the SBJ Group July Stakes, second favourite in an unusually-large field (nine ran, the most since 1981) behind the unbeaten Rio Duvida from the all-conquering Loder yard. The seven other runners included the Norfolk winner Lucky Lionel and the Chesham winner World Premier but none could go with Tagula once Swinburn sent him three lengths clear with less than two furlongs to run. The Coventry seventh Take A Left and World Premier managed to whittle that advantage down to a neck and three quarters of a length on the climb to the line, but neither ever looked like winning and if anything were slightly flattered. Tagula produced an improved performance ridden with greater restraint in the Prix Morny Piaget at Deauville in August. With a furlong and a half to run he was travelling well in behind as the Prix de Cabourg winner With Fascination, still moving smoothly herself, took up the running from the eventual fourth Russian Revival, but once Tagula was switched to the outside he quickly made up the deficit, went a length up with half a furlong to run and wasn't hard pressed to maintain that advantage over With Fascination despite Swinburn losing his whip in the closing stages. It was a very useful performance, the best needed to win the race since Arazi in 1991, with those behind including World Premier and the Prix Robert Papin one-two-three Lucky Lionel, Shining Molly and Barricade. Ridden in a similar manner, Tagula ran very nearly as well in the Dewhurst, but Alhaarth proved to be in a different league.

The quite good-topped Tagula went through the sale-ring twice before being put into training, initially for 11,000 guineas as a foal in Ireland then for 32,000 guineas as a yearling at the Doncaster St Leger Sales. A first Group 1 winner for the smart sprinter Taufan in his eleventh crop of racing age, Tagula is the first foal of a once-raced mare Twin Island. The dam is a half-sister to the C. L. Weld Park Stakes winner Jolly Saint and a useful mare in Italy, Camille Bloch, who won three listed

Robert & Elizabeth Hitchins' "Tagula"

Tagula (IRE) (b.c. Mar 3, 1993)	Taufan (USA) (b 1977)	Stop The Music (b 1970)	Hail To Reason
			Bebopper
		Stolen Date (b 1970)	Sadair
			Stolen Hour
	Twin Island (IRE) (ch 1989)	Standaan (gr 1976)	Zeddaan
			Castania
		Jolly Widow (ch 1974)	Busted
			Veuve Joyeuse

races from a mile to a mile and a quarter. Tagula's second dam Jolly Widow never ran and third dam Veuve Joyeuse was a maiden. Jolly Saint is the dam of the smart American miler Da Hoss, while Jolly Widow is a half-sister to a mare Crufty Wood who threw the well-known sprinter, Our Fan, when covered by Taufan: Our Fan won eleven races in all and ran fourth in listed company in Italy, from where the family originates. *I. A. Balding*

TAHYA (USA) 2 ch.f. (Feb 2) Elmaamul (USA) 125 – Tatwij (USA) 94 (Topsider (USA)) [1995 5m $5s^5$ 5f $a7g^3$ Dec 15] lengthy, unfurnished filly: unimpressive mover: second foal: half-sister to 3-y-o 6f winner Masafah (by Cadeaux Genereux): dam, 2-y-o 5f winner who probably stayed 1m, half-sister to Tejano, second-best 2-y-o of 1987 in USA: modest maiden: sold out of H. Thomson Jones' stable 5,000 gns Newmarket Autumn Sales after third start: will be suited by further than 7f. *C. C. Elsey* 52

TAIPAN (IRE) 3 b.c. Last Tycoon 131 – Alidiva 105 (Chief Singer 131) [1994 82p: 8.2d 7s* 1995 10m $10.4m^4$ $10.5g^2$ 12m Jun 22] leggy, unfurnished colt: good walker: has a roundish action: fairly useful performer: in frame in rated stakes at York (never going that well) and Haydock (best effort, led over 2f out to near line) before respectable ninth of 20 (eased once held) in strongly-run King George V Stakes at Royal Ascot: stays 10.5f: acts on good to firm and soft ground: has run well when sweating: stays in training. *J. L. Dunlop* 91

TAJANNUB (USA) 3 ch.f. Dixieland Band (USA) – Empress Jackie (USA) (Mount Hagen (FR) 127) [1994 102: 6m* 6m* 7g³ 6m 1995 6m⁴ 5m 6g⁶ 6f 6m* 7m* Aug 26] leggy filly: useful performer: won 5-runner listed event at York (made all, gamely held Epagris a short head) in July and rated stakes at Goodwood (tracked pace, got up close home to beat Moccasin Run) in August: may well have stayed 1m: raced only on a sound surface: visits Zafonic. *R. W. Armstrong* — 104

TAJAR (USA) 3 b.g. Slew O' Gold (USA) – Mashaarif (USA) (Mr Prospector (USA)) [1994 77: 7g³ 8g² 7g 1995 10m 12m⁶ 7g 8.5g⁴ 9.9m³ 10d 9.7s⁵ Sep 27] lengthy gelding: has a scratchy action: modest maiden: stays 1¼m: acts on good to firm ground, possibly not on a soft surface: usually sweating: has looked none too keen: stays in training. *D. Morley* — 62

TAKADOU (IRE) 4 br.c. Double Schwartz 128 – Taka (Blakeney 126) [1994 86: 7m 7f 6s³ 5m 5m 5.1g³ 6g 5g³dis 6g 5g 5d³ 5m* 5s 6d⁴ 5d* 1995 5g⁴ 5m 5m 6f⁶ 5m 5.1d⁵ 5d* 5s³ 5s 5m² 5m 6m Nov 4] big, lengthy colt: impresses in appearance: fairly useful performer: more consistent in the autumn, and won 5-runner minor event at Newcastle in September: creditable efforts in handicaps and listed race (stiff task) last 3 starts: effective at 5f to 7f: acts on good to firm and soft going: effective blinkered or not, last tried on ninth 3-y-o start: has run well when sweating: held up, and often gets behind. *Miss L. C. Siddall* — 92

TAKAPUNA (IRE) 2 ch.f. (Apr 26) Be My Native (USA) 122 – Tenoria 82 (Mansingh (USA) 120) [1995 5m⁴ 5.1g³ 6m* 7.5m⁵ 7f⁵ 7d a6g a8g² a7g Dec 14] IR 1,650F, IR 4,400Y: sparely-made filly: half-sister to 3 winners, including (at 1½m) Hataal (by Hatim) and Welsh Tenor (by Welsh Saint): dam 7f (at 2 yrs) and 10.6f winner: won claimer at Goodwood (claimed out of R. Hannon's stable £8,000) in May: easily best of last 4 starts when second in seller at Southwell: bred to stay beyond 1m. *T. J. Naughton* — 51 + a46

TAKE A LEFT 2 b.c. (Mar 26) Formidable (USA) 125 – Casamurrae 87 (Be My Guest (USA) 126) [1995 6g 5m* 5d³ 6m 6g² 6m³ 7g³ Sep 8] 19,500Y: strong, lengthy colt: has scope: good walker: second foal: dam, 1m and 1½m winner who stayed 16.5f, out of half-sister to On The House: useful colt: won maiden at Ripon in May: best efforts when beaten a neck by Tagula in July Stakes at Newmarket and just under 2 lengths when third to Royal Applause in Gimcrack Stakes at York: rather disappointing last of 3 to Alhaarth in Laurent-Perrier Champagne Stakes at Doncaster final outing: should be suited by further than 6f: sold 160,000 gns Newmarket Autumn Sales to join J. Noseda in USA. *Mrs J. R. Ramsden* — 103

TAKEAPULL 3 ch.g. Clantime 101 – Dayana (Burglar 128) [1994 53: 5m 5m² 5m 1995 5m 5d⁶ a8g Jun 16] close-coupled gelding: a plater: well beaten in 1995: sold 900 gns Doncaster July Sales: blinkered final 2-y-o start. *J. Balding* — –

Sport On 5 Rated Stakes (Handicap), Goodwood—
Croft Valley (rails) is about to be passed by, from left to right, Tajannub, Moccasin Run and Behaviour

TAKE A RIGHT 3 b.g. Skyliner 117 – Miss Colenca (Petong 126) [1994 NR 1995 10.1m^{3} Jul 24] 4,200Y: second foal: dam well beaten: 66/1, distanced in 3-runner maiden. *N. Chamberlain* –

TAKE LIBERTIES 3 b.f. Warning 136 – Libertine 114 (Hello Gorgeous (USA) 128) [1994 6m* 7g^{2} 7g^{3} 8d^{4} 1995 6.5g^{3} 8d 10s^{2} 9g^{2} 10g^{2} 10g^{3} 10g Oct 15] leggy, angular filly: third foal: half-sister to French 1994 3-y-o 1m winner Amandine (by Darshaan): dam 5.5f (at 2 yrs) and 1m winner also third in Pouliches and stayed 1¼m: useful French filly: won minor event at Evry and fourth in Prix d'Aumale at Longchamp at 2 yrs: runner-up in pattern company in 9f Prix Chloe at Evry (beaten head by Garden Rose) and Prix de Psyche at Deauville (4 lengths behind Angel In My Heart) in the summer: far from disgraced when around 7½ lengths ninth of 13 to Timarida in E. P. Taylor Stakes at Woodbine final start: stays 1¼m: acts on good to firm ground and dead: consistent. *A. Fabre, France* 110

TAKE NOTE (IRE) 2 b.c. (Feb 19) Don't Forget Me 127 – Verthumna (Indian King (USA) 128) [1995 7f^{6} 7.1m a7g^{4} Dec 15] 11,000Y: good-topped colt: half-brother to several winners abroad: dam maiden, ran only at 2 yrs in Ireland: first run for nearly 4 months when fourth of 9 to Accountancy Jewel at Lingfield, best effort in maiden events. *N. A. Graham* 50

TAKESHI (IRE) 3 b.f. Cadeaux Genereux 131 – Taplow (Tap On Wood 130) [1994 67: 6m^{6} 7m^{4} 7.6v 7g 1995 7g^{2} 8m^{2} 7m 7g^{2} 7.1m^{2} 6.9f^{5} 7m^{6} 7m 8g^{6} a7g^{2} a7g^{6} a8g Dec 6] compact filly: modest maiden handicapper: sold out of E. Dunlop's stable 7,200 gns Newmarket Autumn Sales after ninth 3-y-o start: ran well next 2 starts: effective at 7f and 1m: acts on good to firm ground and equitrack: well beaten only outing on heavy: blinkered (no improvement) ninth 3-y-o start. *W. R. Muir* 65

TAKE TWO 7 b.g. Jupiter Island 126 – Dancing Daughter 79 (Dance In Time (CAN)) [1994 –: 8.3g^{6} 1995 10m^{6} a10g Dec 15] workmanlike gelding: fair 4-y-o, but nowhere near that form nowadays: should stay 1¼m: acts on good to firm ground: blinkered twice in 1991: prolific winning jumper. *J. White* –

TAKHLID (USA) 4 b.c. Nureyev (USA) 131 – Savonnerie (USA) 108 (Irish River (FR) 131) [1994 NR 1995 7g^{3} 6g^{3} 7.1g^{2} 8m^{3} 7m^{5} 7f* 8.5s* Sep 19] $750,000Y: strong, compact colt: third foal: dam very useful 1986 2-y-o later successful in US: fairly useful performer: just best in driving finishes last 2 starts in handicap at Brighton and rated stakes (made all) at Epsom: stays 8.5f: acts on firm ground and soft: carries head high, but game: sent to Dubai. *H. Thomson Jones* 83

TAKLIF (IRE) 3 b.g. Sadler's Wells (USA) 132 – Porphyrine (FR) (Habitat 134) [1994 92p: 7m^{5} 7.3d 1995 11m^{6} 11.9m^{4} 13.3d^{3} 14s^{2} 11.9d^{2} 14g^{3} Oct 23] robust, quite attractive gelding: good walker: fairly useful form: best effort when third of 23 to Whitechapel in £15,400 handicap at Newbury in September: second in big fields of maidens at Lingfield and Haydock next 2 starts, but disappointing favourite final one: stays 1¾m: seems suited by a soft surface: sold 32,000 gns Newmarket Autumn Sales: joined M. P. O'Brien in Ireland. *B. W. Hills* 87

TALENTED TING (IRE) 6 ch.g. Hatim (USA) 121 – An Tig Gaelige (Thatch (USA) 136) [1994 74: 8s 9.9s 8g 8.3s 8g^{4} 8.5g^{2} 8.3m* 8.9f^{4} 8f 8m 8.3g^{3} 9.9m^{6} 8.3g* 8s 10d^{6} 1995 8.2g a8.5g 8m 10.3m 10m 9.2f* 8.3f* 8.3f^{5} 8.1m^{6} 10m 8.3m^{2} 8.3f^{3} 8.3f^{2} a9.4g 8h^{4} 9.2g a10g^{6} a13g^{4} Dec 14] strong, lengthy gelding: good walker: fair handicapper: won twice at Hamilton (7 successes there overall) in June: had seemed best at up to 1¼m, not discredited over 13f last time: acts on all-weather surfaces and firm ground, seems unsuited by soft: effective with or without visor, blinkered (raced too freely) once as 5-y-o: has won for apprentice: usually races prominently. *P. C. Haslam* 74 a58

TALK BACK (IRE) 3 b.g. Bob Back (USA) 124 – Summit Talk (Head For Heights 125) [1994 7v 1995 10m* 10m Jul 10] IR 50,000Y: rather leggy gelding: second foal: dam, fair Irish 7.5f winner, out of very useful French 9f to 10.5f winner Prattle On: 25/1, won 13-runner maiden at Naas in May for G. Cusack: well beaten in minor event at Windsor over 2 months later. *Miss H. C. Knight* 82

TALLULAH BELLE 2 b.f. (Apr 19) Crowning Honors (CAN) – Fine A Leau (USA) 51 (Youth (USA) 135) [1995 6.1m a6g^{2} a7g^{6} 5g a6g^{5} 6f Oct 24] fourth foal: sister to Italian 3-y-o 1m winner Charlie Firpo: dam sprinter: best efforts at Wolverhampton, second in seller and good fifth of 12 in median auction maiden (ridden by 7-lb claimer): no comparable form on turf: should stay 7f. *N. P. Littmoden* 37 a55

TALOS (IRE) 7 b.g. Taufan (USA) 119 – Jovial Josie (USA) (Sea Bird II 145) [1994 NR 1995 11.9s 16m 15.1s Nov 2] leggy gelding: rated 65 at best for B. Hills at 5 yrs: of little account in 1995. *D. Moffatt* –

TAMANDU 5 b.m. Petoski 135 – Gohar (USA) (Barachois (CAN)) [1994 NR 1995 a12g4 Nov 2] half-sister to 2 minor winners in Canada and 2 winners over jumps: dam, 5f winner at 2 yrs, is half-sister to good North American performer Par Excellence, dam of very smart 1984 2-y-o stayer Khozaam: poor form in NH Flat races: 50/1, 12½ lengths fourth of 12 to Elementary in claimer at Lingfield: shapes like a stayer. *C. James* 40

TAMARIND COVE 2 ch.g. (Feb 4) Safawan 118 – Sayf As Houses (Sayf El Arab (USA) 127) [1995 a7g Jul 22] 9,600F, IR 6,500Y: third foal: half-brother to 2 winners abroad: dam unraced: 10/1, slow-starting last of 8 in seller at Wolverhampton: sold 600 gns Newmarket September Sales. *B. J. Meehan* –

TAMARPOUR (USA) 8 b.g. Sir Ivor 135 – Tarsila (High Top 131) [1994 NR 1995 14m 14.9g3 17.2m4 20m 18.2m* 20f6 16m Aug 2] strong, lengthy gelding: modest handicapper on return from nearly 3 years off: won at Chepstow in July: stays 2½m: acts on good to firm ground: has run well when sweating and on edge: blinkered/visored (also tried at 5 yrs) last 4 starts: held up: has gone in snatches, and looked reluctant to race final start. *M. C. Pipe* 62

TAMAYAZ (CAN) 3 b.c. Gone West (USA) – Minstrelsy (USA) (The Minstrel (CAN) 135) [1994 85p: 7m4 7.1m* 1995 8f* 8g4 Aug 13] tall, good-topped colt: weak in betting on return from UAE but in fine shape, most impressive winner of 5-runner £13,400 event at Goodwood on reappearance by 4 lengths (value 8) from First Island, readily going clear: favourite, ran well when 4 lengths fourth of 9 to Miss Satamixa in Prix Jacques le Marois at Deauville 15 days later: stays 1m: acts on firm going: made the running at 3 yrs: still in training with Goldolphin, and should win a pattern race. *Saeed bin Suroor* 119

TAMHID (USA) 2 b.c. (Feb 23) Gulch (USA) – Futuh (USA) 95 (Diesis 133) [1995 6g* 6m5 6d2 6f* Oct 18] strong, compact colt: first foal: dam 2-y-o 6f winner: won maiden at Ascot in July and (after good efforts in Gimcrack Stakes at York and minor event at Salisbury) minor event (made all, beat Farhana 1¾ lengths) at Yarmouth in October: should stay beyond 6f: acts on firm and dead ground: unruly stalls at Salisbury. *H. Thomson Jones* 94

TAMISE (USA) 3 b.f. Time For A Change (USA) – Tanapa (FR) (Luthier 126) [1994 NR 1995 8v* 8d2 10.5g* 10.5m 10d* 10.5g* 10f Nov 12] seventh foal: half-sister to 6 winners, including graded stakes-placed Luthier's Launch (by Relaunch), middle-distance filly Quiriretta (by Ardross) and useful French colt Tabac (by Storm Cat): dam, minor French 2-y-o 7.5f winner later successful in Italy, is half-sister to high-class French juvenile Big John: smart French filly: won newcomers event and listed race at Saint-Cloud in the spring, and listed race at Longchamp then 7-runner Prix de Flore (by 2½ lengths from Suivez La) at Saint-Cloud in October: well beaten in Yellow Ribbon Invitational at Santa Anita final start: stays 10.5f: acts on heavy ground: seemed to be acting as pacemaker (for Muncie) fourth start. *A. Fabre, France* 113

Vodapage Conditions Stakes, Goodwood—
a tantalising glimpse of Tamayaz's abilities as he slams the useful First Island

TAMNIA 2 br.f. (Feb 10) Green Desert (USA) 127 – Tanouma (USA) 114 (Miswaki (USA) 124) [1995 6m² 6m* 7.1g* 7g⁴ 7g² 7d⁵ Sep 26] smallish, well-made filly: fifth foal: half-sister to 3-y-o Maysann (by Shirley Heights) and 3 winners, notably smart 4-y-o stayer Khamaseen (by Slip Anchor) and smart middle-distance stayer Azzilfi (by Ardross): dam, 6f (at 2 yrs) and 7f winner who stayed 1m, out of very speedy French 2-y-o Diffusion: won maiden at Haydock in July and listed event at Sandown (ran on well to beat Solar Crystal by 1¼ lengths) in August: best efforts afterwards when fourth to Blushing Gleam in Prix du Calvados at Deauville and second to Priory Belle in Moyglare Stud Stakes at the Curragh: will be at least as effective at 1m as 7f. *J. L. Dunlop* 101

TAMURE (IRE) 3 b.c. Sadler's Wells (USA) 132 – Three Tails 121 (Blakeney 126) [1994 NR 1995 11m* 12m* 10.4g* 12f² 10s* 10m⁴ 12s⁴ Oct 28] 125

For the second year in a row a horse carrying the maroon and white silks of Sheikh Mohammed was collared close home in the Derby after looking likely to win. Like King's Theatre with Erhaab the year before, Tamure couldn't hold the very strong late challenge of Lammtarra after being produced with a well-timed run to lead inside the final furlong. Sheikh Mohammed has now had eighteen runners in the Derby (the favourite Pennekamp also carried his colours in 1995) and none of the others have reached the frame. Tamure was unraced at two and followed a similar path to Epsom to the 1993 winner Commander In Chief, completing a three-race Derby preparation when maintaining his unbeaten record in the Glasgow Stakes over an extended mile and a quarter at York's May meeting. Tamure had followed up a success in a Newbury maiden with a hard-fought victory over another promising colt Sebastian over a mile and a half at Newmarket on Two Thousand Guineas day, and he started a short-priced favourite at York. Tamure won despite his rider being forced to switch him over two furlongs out; forging ahead at the distance, Tamure kept on to hold off Minds Music by a neck, giving the strong impression he'd be all the better for a return to a mile and a half. Tamure was one of five unbeaten colts in the Derby line-up and, starting fourth favourite at 9/1, confirmed himself a most progressive type, going down by a length to Lammtarra, and finishing three quarters of a length in front of his third-placed stable-companion Presenting. Tamure's progress came to a halt for a time after Epsom. He wasn't seen out again for over three months, his trainer reporting that he had jarred himself on the firm ground in the Derby. Tamure resumed winning ways in the slowly-run Prix du Prince d'Orange on soft going at Longchamp in mid-September, receiving 7 lb from Spectrum (who was also having his first race since the Derby) and beating him by a neck in a sprint finish. After such an encouraging return, Tamure sweated up profusely and was a shade disappointing—back on a firm surface—in the Dubai Champion Stakes in which he kept on for

Prix du Prince d'Orange, Longchamp—
the sprint for home is won by Tamure, from Spectrum (pale cap) and Rifapour

Sheikh Mohammed's "Tamure"

fourth behind Spectrum, the pair meeting at levels this time. Tamure's season ended on a higher note, however, when he finished a very good fourth (running on lasix for the first time) to the ex-French Northern Spur, Freedom Cry and Carnegie in the Breeders' Cup Turf at Belmont Park at the end of October. In testing conditions, Tamure stayed on well to pip Hernando as European-trained runners filled four of the first five places.

Tamure (IRE) (b.c. 1992)	Sadler's Wells (USA) (b 1981)	Northern Dancer (b 1961)	Nearctic
			Natalma
		Fairy Bridge (b 1975)	Bold Reason
			Special
	Three Tails (b 1984)	Blakeney (b 1966)	Hethersett
			Windmill Girl
		Triple First (b 1974)	High Top
			Field Mouse

The Breeders' Cup Turf was another fine advertisement for the Coolmore stallion Sadler's Wells, sire of Northern Spur and Carnegie, as well as of Tamure. Tamure is the third foal of the Lancashire Oaks winner Three Tails, a daughter of the smart Triple First, winner of the Musidora, the Nassau and the Sun Chariot Stakes. Three Tails, a half-sister to the One Thousand Guineas and Oaks-placed Maysoon, had foals by Topsider and Secreto before Tamure, easily the better being the Secreto filly Threemilestone, a fair staying maiden. Her two-year-old Triple Leap, a full brother to Tamure, was in training with Gosden in 1995 but didn't reach the racecourse. The lengthy, rather unfurnished Tamure stays a mile and a half well and it's over that trip (or further) that he should do best as a four-year-old. He has shown his form on soft and firm going, though there was a suspicion in the Champion

Stakes, on his first outing on a firm surface since the Derby, that he didn't fully extend himself. *J. H. M. Gosden*

TANAH MERAH (IRE) 4 b.g. Alzao (USA) 117 – Lady's Bridge (USA) 81 (Sir Ivor 135) [1994 63: 8d^2 a9.4g 11.6g^2 11.9g^5 1995 a8.5g a7g a11g 12.1v^2 11.1s^3 16m 10.5d 16.5m^3 Oct 20] workmanlike gelding: disappointing maiden: no form last 3 starts: stays 12.1f: acts on heavy ground, no form in 4 tries on fibresand: blinkered (poor effort) once as 2-y-o: unreliable. *E. J. Alston* 58

TANAMI 3 br.f. Green Desert (USA) 127 – Propensity 93 (Habitat 134) [1994 111: 5f* 5g^2 5m^4 5m 6s* 6m^2 7m^4 1995 6g^4 6m^6 7m^3 Jul 16] small, lightly-made filly: unable to recapture her 2-y-o form, seeming only useful: best effort at 3 yrs when staying-on third of 5 to Felitza in minor event at Yarmouth: stayed 7f: acted on any going: stud. *D. R. Loder* 98

TANCRED MISCHIEF 4 b.f. Northern State (USA) 91 – Mischievous Miss 73 (Niniski (USA) 125) [1994 –: 10m 12f 12f^6 11.1f 1995 8m 12m^4 12m^4 15.8m^3 Aug 11] small, lengthy filly: has a round action: poor maiden handicapper: stays 15.8f, at least in slowly-run race: acts on good to firm ground: won novice handicap hurdle in August. *W. L. Barker* 31

TANIYAR (FR) 3 b.g. Glenstal (USA) 118 – Taeesha (Mill Reef (USA) 141) [1994 NR 1995 a8g^4 Nov 21] fourth foal: half-brother to French 11.5f winner Telhara (by Natroun): dam unraced half-sister to Top Ville: 9/1, over 15 lengths fourth of 10 to Easy Choice in maiden at Lingfield, never a threat: will stay further than 1m: may do better. *R. Hollinshead* –

TANNERRUN (IRE) 3 b.f. Runnett 125 – Six Penny Express (Bay Express 132) [1994 65: 5m* 5g 6m^5 5g 1995 5g 7g 6f Jun 15] leggy, lengthy filly: looked of little account in 1995. *J. Berry* –

TANSEEQ 4 b.g. Green Desert (USA) 127 – Kawkeb (USA) 72 (Vaguely Noble 140) [1994 73: 8m^5 10m^4 8m* 8.2m^4 8d^3 10g 1995 8g 9g 8f^5 May 15] big, good-bodied gelding: only a modest handicapper at 4 yrs: should stay 1¼m: acts on good to firm and dead ground: blinkered (raced too freely) final 4-y-o start: usually races prominently: sold (H. Thomson Jones to M. Meagher) 14,500 gns Newmarket July Sales, and gelded: won over hurdles in December. *H. Thomson Jones* 59

TAPATCH (IRE) 7 b.g. Thatching 131 – Knees Up (USA) (Dancing Champ (USA)) [1994 57: 12.3m 11g^5 10m^4 10m^4 10.3s 1995 a10g^3 Feb 21] compact gelding: probably just a modest performer nowadays: suited by middle distances: acts on firm going, possibly not soft: sweating at 6 yrs: fair hurdler but disappointing at start of 1995/6 season. *J. S. Wainwright* 57

TAPESTRY ROSE 4 ch.f. Arrasas (USA) 100 – Sharelle 67 (Relko 136) [1994 NR 1995 9.7m 12s Sep 27] third known foal: dam maiden: tailed-off last in maidens. *Jamie Poulton* –

TAPINTIME (USA) 2 b.c. (Apr 8) Timeless Moment (USA) – Dancinmyway (USA) (Far North (CAN) 120) [1995 5m^4 7m^5 7m 7g^4 8d^5 8f^5 Oct 12] $21,000F, $32,000Y: angular colt: has a short, round action: first foal: dam ran 4 times in North America: modest maiden: stays 1m: acts on good to firm (possibly not on firm) and dead ground: has worn severe bridle: sold 10,000 gns Newmarket Autumn Sales: sent to Switzerland. *P. F. I. Cole* 68

TAPIS ROUGE (IRE) 6 ch.g. Irish River (FR) 131 – Marie Noelle (FR) 114 (Brigadier Gerard 144) [1994 –: 10.3g^5 10m 12g 13.9m 8.5g 1995 a9.4g a14.8g^6 a12g Jan 18] tall, angular gelding: disappointing since 4 yrs, and one to leave alone. *T. H. Caldwell* –

TAP ON TOOTSIE 3 b.f. Faustus (USA) 118 – My Tootsie 88 (Tap On Wood 130) [1994 NR 1995 8d^5 8.3m 10m 12s a14.8g^3 a13g Dec 14] 1,200Y: good-topped filly: has a round action: sixth foal: half-sister to fair winning stayers My Rossini and My Chiara (both by Ardross): dam won from 7f to 1¼m: signs of only a little ability. *I. Campbell* –

TAPPEN LADY (IRE) 3 ch.f. Doulab (USA) 115 – Tappen Zee (Sandhurst Prince 128) [1994 46: 6f^6 6.1g^4 6f^2 6m 6m^3 7m^3 a7g 6m^5 6g^3 6g 6m 5m 1995 a6g a8g Feb 20] smallish filly: has a round action: plater: well beaten in 1995: sold 650 gns –

Doncaster March Sales: stays 7f: tried visored/blinkered, no improvement. *J. S. Wainwright*

TAPPETO 3 b.g. Liboi (USA) 76 – Persian Carpet (FR) (Kalamoun 129) [1994 NR 1995 10.2m⁴ 9m⁴ 10m³ 10m* 10.5g 12.1d⁶ Oct 10] workmanlike gelding: fifth reported living foal: dam won 6 times in France, at 1¼m and 10.5f: fair performer: won handicap at Nottingham in August, going on in good style over 2f out: stays 12.1f: acts on dead ground, impressive on good to firm. *H. Candy* 78

TAPPING FEET 3 b.f. Dominion 123 – Vitry 48 (Vitiges (FR) 132) [1994 54: a6g⁴ a5g⁴ a7g³ 1995 a8.5g a8g⁴ a7g a7g 6g 10.2m 13.1f Jul 19] sturdy filly: well beaten in 1995, sold out of Sir Mark Prescott's stable 775 gns Ascot February Sales after third start: visored (out of form) sixth 3-y-o start. *D. M. Hyde* –

TARA COLLEEN (IRE) 3 b.f. Petorius 117 – Peace Mission (Dunbeath (USA) 127) [1994 56: 5m 5d 5m 5m 6g 6.1d 5.7g³ 6s⁴ 7.3v a8g⁴ a7g* 1995 a8g⁵ 7.3g 7.1m 8.3m 8.2m 6m 6m a7g Aug 5] neat filly: little worthwhile form in 1995: stays 1m: acts on good to firm ground and equitrack: usually headstrong to post (has worn net muzzle) and has shown signs of temperament: sold 950 gns Ascot August Sales. *C. A. Horgan* 40

TARAWA (IRE) 3 br.g. Caerleon (USA) 132 – Sagar 74 (Habitat 134) [1994 NR 1995 7.3m 8d* 8s³ 8m* 8m* a9.4g³ Dec 2] tall, workmanlike gelding: has a round action: seventh foal: brother to winning hurdler Chummy's Saga and half-brother to several winners, including middle-distance performers Kaleidos (by Rainbow Quest) and Suruba (by Top Ville): dam 10.5f winner in France: quickly made into a useful performer in the autumn: won maiden at Newbury, 20-runner handicap (short to post) at Newmarket and 30-runner £24,100 Ladbroke Autumn Handicap (led over 2f out, beat Serious 1¼ lengths) again at Newmarket: good 2¼ lengths third of 12 to Prince of Andros in listed race at Wolverhampton last time: stays 9.4f: acts on good to firm and soft ground, and on fibresand. *N. A. Callaghan* 103

TARF (USA) 2 ch.f. (Jan 22) Diesis 133 – Tadwin 109 (Never So Bold 135) [1995 5g² 5d³ 5.1m² 5f² 5f* 5g Sep 14] neat filly: second foal: half-sister to useful 3-y-o 5f and 6f winner Iltimas (by Dayjur): dam sprinting half-sister to Reesh: fairly useful sprinting filly: won minor event at Salisbury in August by 3½ lengths from Cross The Border: wasn't well drawn then met trouble in running when eighth of 13 behind Westcourt Magic in listed race at Ayr the following month: will probably stay 6f: acts on firm and dead ground. *P. T. Walwyn* 92

TARHHIB 3 br.f. Danzig (USA) – Cancan Madame (USA) (Mr Prospector (USA)) [1994 NR 1995 7m* 7m³ 6g May 19] useful-looking filly: has a fluent, round action: sixth foal: half-sister to French 11f winner Can Do Madame (by Trempolino) and high-class French middle-distance performer Dancehall (by Assert): dam won at 9f in USA: heavily-backed favourite, narrowly won 19-runner maiden at Newbury in April: looked likely winner when sent on over 1f out when close third of 7 to Peace 95

Ladbroke Autumn Handicap, Newmarket—the progressive Tarawa leads home a field of thirty

Envoy in minor event at Newmarket 2 weeks later: 5/4 favourite and sweating, below form in minor event at Newbury last time: stayed 7f: raced only on a sound surface: visits Nashwan. *J. H. M. Gosden*

TARIAN (USA) 3 b.c. Lyphard (USA) 132 – Chain Fern (USA) (Blushing Groom (FR) 131) [1994 NR 1995 10m Oct 26] 5,500 3-y-o: smallish colt: third foal: half-brother to fairly useful 1m winner (stayed 11.4f) Woodwardia (by El Gran Senor): dam unraced sister to Al Bahathri: bit backward and green, showed nil in minor event at Nottingham. *G. B. Balding* –

TA RIB (USA) 2 ch.f. (Apr 23) Mr Prospector (USA) – Madame Secretary (USA) (Secretariat (USA)) [1995 7m² 7d³ Sep 24] good-topped filly: has scope: has a quick action: half-sister to 3 winners, including 3-y-o 7f winner, Itab (by Dayjur) and useful sprinter/miler Tabdea (by Topsider): dam, won at up to 9f, half-sister to Stewards' Cup winner Green Ruby and useful stayer Zero Watt: length second to Ruznama in 18-runner maiden at Newmarket, giving impression would have given winner close race had her run started sooner: over 3 lengths third of 8 to Story Line in minor event at Ascot following month, travelling strongly long way but bumped by runner-up and unlucky not to finish second: may prove best on a sound surface: sure to improve, and win a race. *E. A. L. Dunlop* 89 p

TARJUMAAN (USA) 4 b. or br.g. Private Account (USA) – Etoile d'Amore (USA) 81 (The Minstrel (CAN) 135) [1994 NR 1995 a7g a10g a10g⁶ 8m Apr 24] lengthy gelding: fifth foal: half-brother to 2 winners, including useful French Bint Lariaaf (1m, by Diesis): dam twice-raced 7f winner: sold out of A. Scott's stable 6,200 gns Newmarket July (1994) Sales: well beaten in 1995: joined John Berry. *R. J. O'Sullivan* –

TARNEEM (USA) 2 b.f. (Mar 27) Zilzal (USA) 137 – Willowy Mood (USA) (Will Win (USA)) [1995 6g⁵ 6d² 7m² Oct 20] workmanlike filly: third foal: dam won 14 races in USA, including Grade 3 1m event at 2 yrs: fairly useful form: runner-up last 2 starts in Blue Seal Stakes at Ascot and 21-runner maiden (beaten a length by Germano) at Doncaster: will stay 1m: tended to edge off bridle last 2 starts: sure to win a race. *M. R. Stoute* 82

TARN LANE (IRE) 3 b.f. Fools Holme (USA) – Amber Lightning 61 (On Your Mark 125) [1994 55: 5d 5m⁵ 5f 5m⁶ 5g² 5g² 6g 5d⁵ 5m⁵ 1995 6m a5g Jul 22] small, sparely-made filly: modest maiden at 2 yrs: no promise on return. *J. Pearce* –

TARO CARD (IRE) 4 b.g. Lancastrian 126 – More Chat (Torenaga) [1994 NR 1995 8m⁵ Apr 19] angular gelding: third foal: dam placed in NH Flat race: behind in 2 NH Flat races then a minor event. *R. D. E. Woodhouse* –

TAROUCCA (IRE) 3 b.f. Tirol 127 – Glendora (Glenstal (USA) 118) [1994 63p: 6g 6d⁵ 1995 8.2d Sep 19] rather leggy, unfurnished filly: modest form at 2 yrs: well beaten in maiden at Nottingham only start at 3 yrs: should stay 1m: keen sort: sold 1,500 gns Newmarket Autumn Sales. *C. E. Brittain* –

TAROUDANT 8 b.g. Pharly (FR) 130 – Melbourne Miss (Chaparral (FR) 128) [1994 80: 16d³ 18.7m⁴ 16.2f 15.9g* 15.9s⁶ 18m a14.8g* 1995 a16.2g⁵ a16g⁴ a14.8g⁵ Mar 18] rangy gelding: carries condition: usually impresses in appearance: has long stride: useful hurdler: fair handicapper on flat: suited by good test of stamina: acts on firm going and fibresand, probably unsuited by a soft surface: game: joined R. Woodhouse. *Mrs M. Reveley* 67

TARRY 2 b.f. (Jan 15) Salse (USA) 128 – Waitingformargaret 78 (Kris 135) [1995 6m 6m 7m* 8m⁶ 8m 7g 8f² 8f³ Oct 31] small filly: second foal: half-sister to 3-y-o 6f (at 2 yrs) and 7f winner Linger (by Sharrood): dam, 2-y-o 5f winner, out of useful sprinter Princess Seal: won seller (sold out of Lord Huntingdon's stable 6,500 gns) at Newmarket in August: good efforts in nurseries at Pontefract (blinkered) and Redcar (visored, unlucky loser after poor run) last 2 starts: will stay beyond 1m. *C. N. Williams* 62

TARSID 3 ch.c. Indian Forest (USA) 117 – Small Fee 75 (Blue Cashmere 129) [1994 NR 1995 a5g 8.3s Apr 12] 400Y: first foal: dam stayed 7f: last in sellers. *S. Coathup* –

TART 2 b.f. (Apr 30) Tragic Role (USA) – Fee 111 (Mandamus 120) [1995 7m a8g² a8.5g* Dec 2] workmanlike filly: half-sister to several winners here and in France, including middle-distance performer Gold Blade (by Rousillon): dam French 1¼m 68 +

winner (stayed 1½m) from good family: progressive filly: won 9-runner maiden at Wolverhampton in December by 3½ lengths from Bath Knight, running on well: will stay beyond 8.5f: acts on all-weather surfaces. *R. F. Johnson Houghton*

TART AND A HALF 3 b.f. Distant Relative 128 – Vaigrant Wind 75 (Vaigly Great 127) [1994 81: 5g^6 6m^4 5m^3 5.3f* 5g 5m^2 5m 1995 5m 5.1m^4 5.1m^2 5.3f^4 6g 5f 5m^3 7m^4 8g 5m^4 5m^3 5m^3 Aug 31] rather leggy filly: fairly useful handicapper: creditable efforts when in frame: effective at 5f, stays 7f: has raced only on a sound surface: best recent efforts in blinkers: usually races prominently. *B. J. Meehan*
81

TARTAN DANCER 6 b.g. Ballacashtal (CAN) – Waltzing Willow (Swing Easy (USA) 126) [1994 NR 1995 8.3g Jul 3] workmanlike gelding: probably of little account. *R. P. C. Hoad*
–

TARTAN EXPRESS (IRE) 2 b.g. (May 8) New Express 95 – Running Feud (Prince Tenderfoot (USA) 126) [1995 6m^5 a7g^6 6m 7f a8g Dec 18] 3,450Y, resold 2,400Y, 1,200 2-y-o: sturdy gelding: bad mover: fourth foal: half-brother to Irish 4-y-o 1¾m winner Baby Elegance (by Persian Heights): dam ran 3 times in Ireland at 2 yrs: soundly beaten, blinkered in seller third start. *B. A. Pearce*
–

TARTAN GEM (IRE) 4 ch.c. Lomond (USA) 128 – Red Jade 82 (Red God 128§) [1994 77: 8g a9.4g* 10m^5 10g^2 10.1m^4 1995 9g 10d a9.4g^2 Dec 9] lengthy, dipped-backed colt: unimpressive mover: fair handicapper: sold out of J. Toller's stable 4,500 gns Newmarket Autumn Sales after second start: only modest form when second in seller at Wolverhampton on final one: stays 1¼m: acts on fibresand and good to firm ground. *M. Brittain*
54 +

TARTE AUX POMMES (FR) 2 gr.f. (May 4) Noblequest (FR) 124 – Battle Lady (Persepolis (FR) 127) [1995 5.5s* 5.5g^2 6m* 6d^6 8d^6 Oct 1] third foal: half-sister to French 3-y-o 5.5f (at 2 yrs) to 11f winner I Hope So (by Fill My Hopes): dam unraced half-sister to useful middle-distance horse Battle On: first past the post in minor events at Evry and Chantilly (hampered runner-up, demoted) in the spring and in Group 3 event at Milan (by 5¼ lengths from Last Hero) in June: ran creditably when 7 lengths sixth of 11 to Miss Tahiti in Prix Marcel Boussac at Longchamp final start, never dangerous: stays 1m: acts on good to firm and soft ground. *J. Bertran de Balanda, France*
100

TARTHOOTH (IRE) 4 ch.c. Bob Back (USA) 124 – Zoly (USA) (Val de L'Orne (FR) 133) [1994 71p: 10d 8m 11.6g 12.5m^3 13.1f* 14.1g* 16.4g 16s^2 1995 16m^5 17.2m^4 16.5g* 20m 14.9m^2 16.2g Jul 21] big, strong colt: shows knee action: fair handicapper: favourite, won at Doncaster in June, leading well over 2f out and staying on: stays 17.2f: probably acts on any going: likely to prove suited by strong handling: hurdling with A. Moore in Ireland. *C. J. Benstead*
72

TASCILLA (GER) 3 b.f. Kamiros 108 – Tawinja (GER) (Windwurf (GER)) [1994 NR 1995 10.5v* 11g^2 11g^2 11m^5 12m^3 10g^4 12d^3 14s^2 10.5d^6 Nov 17] third foal: half-sister to 9.5f winner Tamira (by Konigsstuhl): dam 10.5f and 11f winner also third in Preis der Diana: useful German filly: won maiden at Neuss in April: best efforts when 3 lengths second of 15 to Centaine in Preis der Diana (ran on unable to catch winner) at Mulheim in June and when staying-on 1¾ lengths second of 13 to First Hello in German St Leger at Dortmund: stays 1¾m: acts on heavy ground. *H. Remmert, Germany*
104

TASDIK 2 ch.f. (Jan 23) Unfuwain (USA) 131 – Stay Sharpe (USA) (Sharpen Up 127) [1995 7g^3 8.2m^2 Oct 26] good-topped filly: third foal: half-sister to fairly useful sprinter Ishtiyak and fair 7f and 1¼m winner Fawz (both by Green Desert): dam unraced: fair form in maidens at Leicester (third of 18 to Fairlight Down) and Nottingham flashed tail when 1¾ lengths second of 10 to Censor) in October: will stay beyond 1m. *R. W. Armstrong*
75

TASHJIR (USA) 2 ch.f. (Feb 19) Slew O' Gold (USA) – Mashaarif (USA) (Mr Prospector (USA)) [1995 7g 7g 8.2m Oct 26] lengthy, unfurnished filly: poor mover: second foal: sister to 3-y-o Tajar: dam unraced daughter of Larida, dam also of Magic of Life and half-sister to Miss Oceana: no worthwhile form in maidens. *D. Morley*
–

TASLIYA (USA) 2 ch.f. (Mar 26) Gulch (USA) – Aghani (USA) (Blushing Groom (FR) 131) [1995 6g 6.1m 6m 7m^3 Oct 30] quite attractive filly: good mover: third foal: half-sister to 3-y-o Karayib, 7f winner at 2 yrs, and Irish 7f winner Hamseh (both by Danzig): dam, ran 4 times, half-sister to Prix de L'Abbaye winner Polonia
86 p

and high-class American middle-distance stayer Peat Moss: ran well when 5½ lengths third of 8 to Quality in nursery at Newcastle on final start, making eye-catching late progress (has been rated as finishing equal-second): will stay 1m: capable of improving again, and should win a race. *J. L. Dunlop*

TASSAGH BRIDGE (IRE) 5 b.m. Double Schwartz 128 – Kasarose (Owen Dudley 121) [1994 –: a7g a10g⁶ 8.1g a6g⁵ a7g 1995 a7g Jan 6] short-backed mare: no sign of ability: tried blinkered. *R. Ingram* –

TATIKA 5 ch.g. Tate Gallery (USA) 117 – Independentia 68 (Home Guard (USA) 129) [1994 77p: 7.5g³ 1995 a8.5g² 7.5m³ 6m² 7m⁴ 7g 7f 6m⁶ a8.5g a8g³ a7g⁵ Dec 18] lengthy gelding: fair maiden handicapper: finds 6f a bare minimum, and stays 8.5f: acts on all-weather and good to firm ground: blinkered (below form) twice. *G. Wragg* 75

TATJANA 4 ch.f. Soviet Star (USA) 128 – Dancing Crystal 76 (Kris 135) [1994 62§: 8m⁵ 8g⁴ 8.2m 1995 8f Jul 19] rangy filly: modest form, only on debut: off course nearly 13 months, well below form in handicap at Bath for new stable: temperamental: sold 3,000 gns in foal to Distant Relative Newmarket December Sales. *Major D. N. Chappell* – §

TAUFAN BLU (IRE) 6 b.m. Taufan (USA) 119 – Engage (Whistling Wind 123) [1994 –§: 6g⁵ 7.1g⁶ 6m 8m 10s 6g⁵ 1995 a7g Feb 24] tall, leggy mare: most disappointing since 4 yrs, becoming reluctant. *F. J. O'Mahony* – §

TAUFAN BOY 2 b.c. (Feb 28) Taufan (USA) 119 – Lydia Maria 70 (Dancing Brave (USA) 140) [1995 7.1m³ 7f³ a7g* 7d 7f Oct 14] quite attractive colt: has a round action: first foal: dam (placed at 1m and 10.2f) daughter of high-class middle-distance performer Connaught Bridge: fair form: won maiden at Southwell in September: ran creditably in nursery penultimate start: will stay beyond 7f. *P. W. Harris* 79

TAUFAN'S MELODY 4 b.g. Taufan (USA) 119 – Glorious Fate (Northfields (USA)) [1994 96: 9m* 10.3g² 10m⁴ 1995 10m² 10.4g⁵ 12m 10g² 10.4m² 12d* 12g* 12d* 12d³ Nov 19] rather leggy, good-topped gelding: smart performer: improved 111

Tote Sunday Special Handicap, Ascot—
the step back up in trip suits Taufan's Melody who holds Better Offer (checked cap) and Pilsudski

form to win £46,800 Tote Sunday Special Handicap at Ascot (by 1¼ lengths from Better Offer, close up, leading under 2f out and holding on bravely) and listed races at Lyon Parilly and Nantes (beat leading Swedish mare Cinnamon) in the autumn: stays 1½m well and gives impression will stay 1¾m: acts on good to firm ground and good to soft: consistent. *Lady Herries*

TAUREAN FIRE 2 ch.g. (Apr 29) Tina's Pet 121 – Golden Decoy 73 (Decoy Boy 129) [1995 5m 6f^5 6m 5g 6f Oct 24] unfurnished gelding: brother to winning sprinter For Real and half-brother to 1993 2-y-o 5f to 6.1f winner Dangerous Shadow (by Absalom): dam 7f winner: plater: best effort second start: ridden by 7-lb claimer last two. *Mrs M. Reveley* — 41

TAUTEN (IRE) 5 br.m. Taufan (USA) 119 – Pitaka (Pitskelly 122) [1994 –: 11.6d 1995 8f 12m Nov 6] leggy mare: seems no longer of much account. *P. Burgoyne* — –

TAWAADED (IRE) 2 ch.f. (Feb 6) Nashwan (USA) 135 – Thaidah (CAN) 105 (Vice Regent (CAN)) [1995 6s Oct 6] rangy filly: third foal: dam, 5f (at 2 yrs) to 7f winner, half-sister to top-class American filly Glorious Song and champion 1983 2-y-o Devil's Bag: 16/1 and green, never-dangerous seventh of 11, beaten around 11 lengths, to Midnight Blue in maiden at Ascot: looks type to do better. *P. T. Walwyn* — – p

TAWAFEK (USA) 2 br.c. (May 4) Silver Hawk (USA) 123 – Tippy Tippy Toe (USA) 60 (Nureyev (USA) 131) [1995 8g 8f^3 Oct 24] $50,000Y: robust colt: second reported foal: dam lightly-raced close relative of Grade 3 11f winner Gallant Archer: still carrying some condition and green, much better effort in maidens at Leicester when 7½ lengths third of 12 to Lady Carla, staying on under hands and heels: slowly away on debut: will improve again. *D. Morley* — 76 p

TAWAFIJ (USA) 6 ch.g. Diesis 133 – Dancing Brownie (USA) (Nijinsky (CAN) 138) [1994 81: 6m 7g^4 8s^6 8m 7m 7m* 7f^6 7m^3 7m^4 7m^2 7m^3 7g 1995 7s 7m 7g^2 7m* 7g^5 7m^5 7m^5 7.9m 7g 8g Sep 15] good-topped, attractive gelding: fairly useful handicapper: awarded £11,600 contest at Newcastle in July: ran creditably next 3 starts: below form afterwards: stays 1m: probably acts on any going: tried visored, no improvement: held up for turn of foot: tough. *T. Dyer* — 87

TAWKIL (USA) 2 b.c. (Feb 20) Riverman (USA) 131 – Lyphette (FR) (Lyphard (USA) 132) [1995 7f^2 7m* Aug 18] $260,000Y: robust, attractive colt: has a quick action: eighth foal: half-brother to several winners in North America, including Grade 1 1¼m Travers Stakes winner Thunder Rumble (by Thunder Puddles): dam French 1m winner: second to Mark of Esteem in maiden at Goodwood: made all in 5-runner maiden at Chester following month, beating Hidden Oasis by 1¼ lengths, pair clear: will stay at least 1¼m: will improve again. *B. W. Hills* — 99 p

TAYLORD 3 ch.g. Cadeaux Genereux 131 – Figini 74 (Glint of Gold 128) [1994 60: 5s 5m^4 a6g^2 1995 6g^5 5d 6f^3 5m^6 5f 5.2g 5d Sep 14] compact gelding: fair maiden at best, but mostly disappointing: has been gelded: needs further than 5f, and should stay beyond 6f: acts on firm ground: visored (finished last) final 3-y-o start: usually races prominently. *R. Hannon* — 66 d

TAZAMISHA 6 b.m. Blakeney 126 – Ardverikie (Red Alert 127) [1994 NR 1995 17.2h^4 Jul 10] quite attractive filly: of little account. *Mrs J. G. Retter* — –

TE AMO (IRE) 3 b.c. Waajib 121 – Avebury Ring (Auction Ring (USA) 123) [1994 75: 7m^4 7g 7m^2 7d* 8v^4 1995 8.1m 7m^5 7m^2 8m^6 8.5s^3 10g 9d Oct 21] small, good-bodied colt: shows a quick action: fairly useful performer: below form in handicaps last 2 outings: at least as effective at 8.5f as 7f: acts on good to firm and heavy ground: blinkered final 3-y-o start. *R. Akehurst* — 83

TECHNOLOGICAL RISK 4 ch.g. Risk Me (FR) 127 – Technology (FR) 82 (Top Ville 129) [1994 –: a7g a9.4g^6 a8.5g 1995 a7g Jul 8] angular gelding: no worthwhile form: dead. *D. Burchell* — –

TEDBURROW 3 b.g. Dowsing (USA) 124 – Gwiffina 87 (Welsh Saint 126) [1994 62: 5m 5m* 5m^5 5f^6 5m 1995 6g^3 6m 5f* 5m* 5g* 6f* 5m^6 7g^6 6g Sep 16] leggy, workmanlike gelding: fairly useful handicapper: won at Ayr, Sandown (twice) and Doncaster in midsummer: unfavourably drawn in Ayr Silver Cup final start, and far from disgraced in finishing mid-division after travelling well 4f: may prove ideally suited by 6f: has raced only on a sound surface: successful when sweating: will win more races. *Mrs A. M. Naughton* — 85 +

TEE-EMM 5 b.g. Lidhame 109 – Tower Glades 90 (Tower Walk 130) [1994 45, a63: a5g^6 a5g^3 a5g* a5g*^{dis} a5g^3 a5g^5 a5g^3 5m 5m^4 5m^5 5.3f^4 5.1g^4 5m^4 5g^3 5g^2 5m a5g^4 a5g^2 a5g* a5g^4 a5g^6 1995 a5g^4 a5g^3 a5g^3 5m 5m^6 5m 5m^6 5m* 5m 5m 5.2m^4 5m^4 5m a5g^3 a5g^4 a5g^3 a5g^5 Dec 6] good-topped, plain gelding: carries condition: modest handicapper on the all-weather, poor on turf: won at Lingfield in June: best form at 5f: acts on all-weather surfaces and on firm and dead ground: usually front runner. *P. Howling* — 42 a59

TEEJAY'N'AITCH (IRE) 3 b.g. Maelstrom Lake 118 – Middle Verde (USA) (Sham (USA)) [1994 49: 5d^6 5f 6m 1995 8m^6 11.1g^6 8g^4 6f^2 7f 7g^3 7m 9.2f^6 6f^5 8g 7g 7.1g^6 7d^3 7f Oct 3] leggy gelding: good mover: modest maiden handicapper: effective at 6f, probably at 1m: acts on firm and dead ground: visored (no improvement) ninth 3-y-o start: inconsistent. *J. S. Goldie* — 52 d

TEEN JAY 5 b.h. Teenoso (USA) 135 – Spoilt Again 91 (Mummy's Pet 125) [1994 67+: 11.9d 1995 10.3g^3 12g^5 12.3m^3 10.3f^3 11.5g 10d a12g^4 Oct 14] lengthy horse: shows round action: fair form at best: claimed out of S. Sherwood's stable £10,000 third 5-y-o start: effective at 10.3f and 1½m: acts on firm and dead going: visored/blinkered third to sixth 5-y-o starts: has run well when sweating: inconsistent: fairly useful hurdler, now with R. Stronge. *M. J. Ryan* — 73

TEE TEE TOO (IRE) 3 ch.g. Hatim (USA) 121 – Scottish Welcome (Be My Guest (USA) 126) [1994 75: 7g a6g^2 a6g^2 6g^4 a6g* 6g a6g^4 a7g^2 1995 a6g^2 a7g^5 a6g^5 7g 6d^4 6m 5g^2 5g 5g^4 6m 8.1f^3 7m^6 6f 6f^3 6m Aug 12] stocky gelding: fair handicapper at best in 1995: moved poorly to post, finished last at Ripon final start: effective at 5f, probably at 1m: best efforts on dead ground or on fibresand: blinkered (ran poorly) once at 3 yrs: takes keen hold and usually races prominently: has joined A. Harrison. *P. C. Haslam* — 75 d

TEETOTALLER (IRE) 4 gr.g. Taufan (USA) 119 – Mainly Dry (The Brianstan 128) [1994 66: 6v^2 7d 6g^4 1995 6g* 6m 6g 6d^3 Jun 9] leggy, lengthy gelding: shows knee action: fair handicapper: won at Kempton on reappearance: back-to-form staying-on third of 13 at Haydock final start: should stay beyond 6f: best efforts on an easy surface, and acts on heavy going. *G. B. Balding* — 72

TELEPHUS 6 b.g. Efisio 120 – Mrs Bizz (Status Seeker) [1994 46, a51: a12g^6 9.9g 10g a10g^6 10m^3 10.4d^2 10m^4 10m a12g^2 a12g a14g^6 a12g* a12g^4 a13g^6 1995 a12g a12g 10m a12g a12g a13g Dec 14] compact gelding: modest handicapper: no form in 1995: stays 1½m: acts on the all-weather and on good to firm and dead ground: blinkered (well beaten) twice: often gets behind: inconsistent. *B. J. McMath* — –

TELMO (IRE) 3 b.c. Alleged (USA) 138 – Chilly Welcome (General Assembly (USA)) [1994 NR 1995 14d 10.4m^6 14.1m Oct 19] 15,000F, IR 24,000Y: close-coupled colt: half-brother to 4 winners, including Absolutely Fact (1m to 1¼m, by Known Fact): dam Irish 12.8f winner: well beaten in maidens: sold out of H. Cecil's stable 5,800 gns Newmarket September Sales after debut: resold 700 gns Newmarket Autumn Sales. *C. F. Wall* — –

TELOPEA 4 b.f. Teenoso (USA) 135 – Orlaith 68 (Final Straw 127) [1994 80: 8s^5 10.1m^3 10m^3 10.1d* 10.2s 1995 10g 10.8g^6 8m 8.1m Jul 8] sturdy, lengthy filly: fair handicapper, disappointing in 1995: should stay 1½m: acts on good to firm and soft ground: often a front runner. *H. Candy* — 72 d

TEMORA (IRE) 3 b.f. Ela-Mana-Mou 132 – Romara 105 (Bold Lad (IRE) 133) [1994 NR 1995 10f^2 10m* 10.1g Sep 12] sister to smart 6f and 1½m winner Ela Romara and half-sister to several winners, including Bustara (6f at 2 yrs, by Busted) and Halstead (1m and 1¼m, by Bustino): dam 6f and 1m winner: much improved when winning 7-runner maiden at Pontefract by 5 lengths, comfortably making all: failed by long way to repeat form in listed race at Yarmouth 2 months later: will stay 1½m: has joined J. Noseda in USA. *H. R. A. Cecil* — 90

TEMPERING 9 b.g. Kris 135 – Mixed Applause (USA) 101 (Nijinsky (CAN) 138) [1994 –, a64: a12g* a11g^4 a11g^4 a11g* a12g^2 a12g a14g^4 a14g^6 a8g^2 a12g a11g a12g 10.1d a14g a11g^2 a11g 1995 a11g* a11g^3 a11g^6 a11g^2 a11g^4 a12g a11g a11g^5 Dec 1] strong, good-bodied gelding: game and genuine front runner on the fibresand at Southwell: still capable of modest form, and won amateurs handicap (20th course success) in January: effective at 11f to 1¾m: suited by fibresand (below form on equitrack): acts (though only poor form) on any turf going: no improvement in blinkers: often sweats. *D. W. Chapman* — – a58

TEMPTING (IRE) 3 b.f. Waajib 121 – Balela (African Sky 124) [1994 –p: 8d6 1995 10m 8m5 May 13] good-topped filly: 20/1, best effort in maidens when fifth of 12 at Bath, one-paced from 3f out: will stay beyond 1m: sold (R. Hannon to J. Norton) 2,300 gns Newmarket September Sales. *R. Hannon* 62

TEMPTRESS 2 br.f. (May 9) Kalaglow 132 – Circe 73 (Main Reef 126) [1995 6m3 7.5d 6.9s Sep 27] 4,700Y: third foal: half-sister to 3-y-o 1m seller winner Miss Zanzibar (by Kefaah) and 9f to 1½m winner My Learned Friend (by Broken Hearted): dam 1m winner (stayed 1¼m) from very good family: well beaten in varied company: visored final start. *P. T. Walwyn* –

TENNYSON BAY 3 b.g. Allazzaz – Richards Folly 59 (Hotfoot 126) [1994 –: 7.1m 6g 1995 6.9g 12m May 4] of no account. *R. M. Flower* –

TENOR 4 b.g. Music Boy 124 – Songstead 92 (Song 132) [1994 53: 6m 7m 5g3 5d 1995 a7g6 a6g6 a6g a6g a5g* a5g* a5g3 5g2 5g* 5m 5m6 5m6 5g4 5g5 5g 5m 5g 5g 5d 5m Oct 4] strong, lengthy gelding: fair handicapper: won at Lingfield (twice) in February and Thirsk in April: held his form fairly well next 7 starts: below form afterwards: suited by 5f: acts on equitrack and good to firm ground: blinkered (no improvement) sixteenth 4-y-o start: best held up for a turn of foot: genuine. *D. Nicholls* 69

TENORIO 3 b.c. Law Society (USA) 130 – One Life (USA) (L'Emigrant (USA) 129) [1994 82p: 7m 7.5g* 8.1s4 1995 11.8m* 16.2m 11.9m* 12g3 Sep 8] tall, good-topped colt: useful form: won minor event at Leicester in June, making most, and rated stakes at York in July, leading final 1f: set slow pace when last of 3 to Singspiel in listed race at Doncaster final start: should stay beyond 1½m (edgy, second run in 5 days when below form over 2m at Royal Ascot): acts on soft ground and good to firm: tends to carry head high, but is genuine. *D. R. Loder* 102

TEN PAST SIX 3 ch.c. Kris 135 – Tashinsky (USA) (Nijinsky (CAN) 138) [1994 84p: 7m4 7d2 1995 7.1m* 10.4g 8m2 9d Sep 16] lengthy, angular, good-quartered colt: won maiden at Haydock in May: best effort when 11½ lengths seventh of 8 to Classic Cliche in Dante Stakes at York: found little 3f out and tailed off final start: better at 10.4f than shorter: acts on good to firm and dead ground: sold (B. Hills to Martyn Wane) only 10,000 gns Newmarket Autumn Sales. *B. W. Hills* 98

TENPENNY 3 ch.f. Hadeer 118 – Tithing (USA) (Nureyev (USA) 131) [1994 –: 7g 1995 11.8s6 Mar 30] compact filly: well behind in maidens: sold 4,000 gns Newmarket July Sales. *G. Rimmer* –

TEOFILO STEPHENSON (IRE) 2 b.c. (Feb 18) Taufan (USA) 119 – Crufty Wood (Sweet Revenge 129) [1995 7f 5g3 7.5g3 7.5g6 7.5d3 6g 7.5g 7.5g Dec 10] IR 6,000Y: brother to winning sprinter Our Fan, closely related to a winner in Italy and half-brother to 1991 2-y-o 10.5f winner Persian Haze (by Bold Arrangement): dam unraced: placed in claimers at Milan: ran for Mark Campion on debut: stays 7.5f. *V. Bignani, Italy* ?

TEOROMA 5 ch.h. Teofane – Poppy Kelly (Netherkelly 112) [1994 22+: a12g a12g3 1995 a16g3 16.5g a13g5 18.2m6 Jul 8] close-coupled, workmanlike horse: poor maiden handicapper: suited by 2m+: acts on equitrack: held up. *Dr J. D. Scargill* 28

TERDAD (USA) 2 ch.c. (Mar 23) Lomond (USA) 128 – Istiska (FR) (Irish River (FR) 131) [1995 7g5 8d5 Sep 15] sturdy, lengthy colt: has scope: closely related to fairly useful 1992 2-y-o 7f winner Noyan (by Northern Baby), later modest winner at 13f, and a winner in France by Cresta Rider and half-brother to 3 winners, including smart 1991 American 2-y-o Zurich (by Private Account): dam French maiden: fifth to Red Robbo in maiden at York: eased a length close home when 5 lengths fifth of 8 to Mick's Love in well-contested minor event at Newbury following month: will stay at least 1m: sure to win a race. *M. R. Stoute* 88

TERESHKOVA (USA) 3 b.f. Mr Prospector (USA) – Lypatia (FR) (Lyphard (USA) 132) [1994 104: 5g* 5m2 5.5g2 6d* 6d3 7d2 1995 6.5g4 8d 7g* 6d2 Sep 11] smart French filly: tenth of 16 to Matiara in Poule d'Essai des Pouliches at Longchamp in May: off course 3½ months, comfortably won conditions event at Deauville in August: showed improvement when keeping-on neck second of 9 to Hever Golf Rose in Prix de Seine-Et-Oise at Chantilly in September: useful form at 1m, best effort at 6f: acts on good to firm ground and dead: joined Godolphin and sent to Dubai. *A. Fabre, France* 113

TERMON 2 b.f. (Apr 26) Puissance 110 – Alipura 74 (Anfield 117) [1995 5g^6 6f^3 6m^5 6g^5 6g^4 7d 6g^2 7m^4 Oct 30] 9,200Y: quite good-topped filly: third foal: half-sister to 1993 2-y-o 6.5f winner Rajmapata (by Robellino): dam 7f and 1m winner: modest maiden: stays 7f: acts on firm ground, showed little on dead. *Miss L. A. Perratt* 58

TERTIUM (IRE) 3 b.g. Nordico (USA) – Nouniya (Vayrann 133) [1994 NR 1995 8m^2 8m* 10.3g^6 8m 7.3d 8f^6 Oct 12] strong, good-bodied gelding: third foal: half-brother to 1¼m and 1½m winner Halham Tarn (by Pennine Walk) and German 4-y-o 1m and 1¼m winner Ninjo (by Vision): dam poor maiden: fairly useful form at best: won maiden at Kempton in May: disappointing afterwards: races very keenly and may prove best at around 1m: sold (P. Chapple-Hyam to Martyn Wane) 10,000 gns Newmarket Autumn Sales and gelded. *P. W. Chapple-Hyam* 82

TERVEL (USA) 4 b.g. Chief's Crown (USA) – Eurobird 118 (Ela-Mana-Mou 132) [1994 11m 12g 13m 1995 a12g^4 Feb 9] ex-French gelding: second foal: half-brother to useful Irish 7f (at 2 yrs) to 1¼m winner Eurostorm (by Storm Bird): dam, very useful Irish middle-distance stayer, is half-sister to Prix du Jockey Club winners Assert and Bikala: little worthwhile form at 3 yrs for J. Hammond: bought 8,000 gns Ascot December (1994) Sales: headed inside final 1f when fourth of 11 in maiden at Lingfield: smart juvenile hurdler in 1994/5: will stay beyond 1½m: joined E. O'Grady. *J. Pearce* 63

TESSAJOE 3 ch.g. Clantime 101 – Busted Love (Busted 134) [1994 –: 6m 6g 7.5g 1995 10d^6 12.3m* 12.3m^5 12m* 10.9g* 12.3m* 12g^5 10.5s^4 12m Oct 21] workmanlike gelding: fair handicapper: won at Ripon in April and at Catterick, Ayr and Ripon in July: involved in scrimmaging final start: effective at 10.5f, will stay 1¾m: acts on good to firm ground and soft: consistent. *M. J. Camacho* 74

TETHYS (USA) 4 b.f. Topsider (USA) – Tide (USA) (Coastal (USA)) [1994 96: 10m^6 10m^2 12m^3 14m^3 12m* 13.9m* 14d^2 16g^3 1995 16.5g^6 11.9m* 16.1m 13.9m^5 13.9m 11.9d^4 12g^5 14.1g^3 13.9m^3 16m 12.1s^6 a12g* Nov 30] leggy filly: fairly useful at her best: won 4-runner lady amateurs rated stakes at York in June and amateurs event at Lingfield in November: effective at 1½m to 2m: acts on good to firm and 94

Queen Mother's Cup (Ladies Rated Stakes) (Handicap), York—
Tethys (Diana Jones up) from Slasher Jack

dead ground, and on equitrack: tried blinkered/visored when out of form: front runner: inconsistent: sold 40,000 gns Newmarket December Sales. *J. L. Eyre*

TEXANNE (BEL) 4 b.f. Efisio 120 – Texan Rose (FR) (Margouillat (FR) 133) [1994 5.5v^{2} a8.5g^{2} 8g* a9.3g^{3} 7f* 8g* a8.5g^{4} 7.5m^{3} 1995 7.5v* 8d a9.3g^{4} 8v* 7f 7.3g 8f^{4} a8.5g^{5} a9.3g 8v^{5} Nov 18] compact filly: little form here at 2 yrs: much better in Belgium, winning 3 races at 3 yrs and a handicap at Groenendaal in March and a major race there in June: unruly leaving paddock and refused to race in well-contested minor event at Newbury in June: best at up to around 1m: seems to act on any going. *Paul Smith, Belgium* — 66 §

TEXAS COWGIRL (IRE) 5 ch.m. Salt Dome (USA) – Cloven Dancer (USA) 86 (Hurok (USA)) [1994 a6g^{4} a5g^{2} a6g^{4} a6g* 5f^{3} a6g* 5g^{2} a5g^{2} a6g* a6g* a5g^{6} 1995 5d^{5} a5g^{3} 6g 5m^{2} 5f 5f^{3} 6m^{5} 5f^{3} a7.5g a6g* a5g 5v^{6} Nov 19] workmanlike mare: poor form: won handicap at Sterrebeek in October: ran creditably in 3 races here: effective at 5f and 6f: acts on good to firm and soft ground and on dirt: blinkered (ran poorly) once at 3 yrs. *H. Vanderdussen, Belgium* — 47

TEXAS TRAMP 2 gr.f. (Apr 22) Formidable (USA) 125 – Katy Lou 48 (Nishapour (FR) 125) [1995 7g 6.9g Oct 16] 3,200Y: leggy filly: first reported foal: dam winning hurdler, probably stayed 1¼m on flat: well beaten in well-contested auction event at Goodwood and maiden auction (sweating) at Folkestone: sold 750 gns Ascot October Sales. *Major D. N. Chappell* — –

THABIT (USA) 4 b.c. Alleged (USA) 138 – Close Comfort (USA) (Far North (CAN) 120) [1994 85: 10s* 10s 8f^{2} 10.4f 1995 8.1m^{4} 8g^{6} 8.3m 7d Sep 22] well-made colt: fairly useful handicapper: good fourth of 8 in Whitsun Cup at Sandown on reappearance: below form afterwards: effective at 1m and 1¼m: acts on firm and soft going: takes strong hold and often makes running: sold only 4,500 gns Newmarket Autumn Sales: sent to Sweden. *P. T. Walwyn* — 84 d

THAI MORNING 2 gr.c. (Jan 27) Petong 126 – Bath 76 (Runnett 125) [1995 5g 5.1g^{3} 6g^{6} 6.1f 5m* 5g^{4} 5m^{4} Oct 27] 12,000Y: compact, sturdy colt: has a fluent action: second foal: dam suited by 7f/1m: won maiden at Folkestone in September: similar form after when fourth in nurseries: should stay 6f. *P. W. Harris* — 70

THALEROS 5 b.g. Green Desert (USA) 127 – Graecia Magna (USA) 109 (Private Account (USA)) [1994 67: 10.1g^{4} 9.9s^{6} 12.4m^{3} 1995 a12g* a12g^{3} a12g^{3} a12g a12g 16.2m 12.4g^{6} 11.9m^{5} 14.1f^{2} 10.1m 12m* 10m^{5} 12m^{3} 10m^{5} 9m^{2} 10m* 10.1f 10m 9.2g^{5} 8.9g Oct 7] big, strong, lengthy gelding: fair performer: won maiden at Southwell in January, claimer at Catterick in July and handicap at Ripon in August: below form in handicaps last 4 starts: stays 1½m: acts on fibresand (ran poorly only outing on equitrack) and firm ground, probably on soft: blinkered (mulish, tailed off) tenth 5-y-o start: often a front runner: not one to trust implicitly. *G. M. Moore* — 60 a66

THALJANAH (IRE) 3 ch.c. In The Wings 128 – Dawn Is Breaking (Import 127) [1994 79: 6f 7m^{3} 7.5f^{3} 7m^{2} 8g^{4} 8g 1995 8d 9.9m^{5dis} 12.3m* 12m* 12m^{4} 14g* 14m^{2} 14.8m^{3} Aug 25] workmanlike colt: progressed into a fairly useful handicapper: won at Ripon in May, Beverley (led 2f out) in June and Sandown (made all) in July: stays 1¾m well: acts on good to firm ground: sometimes bandaged behind: edgy sort, sometimes sweating and on toes: genuine and consistent: sold 25,000 gns Newmarket Autumn Sales. *A. C. Stewart* — 92

THAMES SIDE 4 gr.g. Beveled (USA) – Free Range 78 (Birdbrook 110) [1994 –: 7d 8.3m 8.5m^{6} 1995 a8g^{4} a10g^{2} 11.9m 8.3m^{3} 9.7m^{4} 10m^{3} 10m 7f^{2} 10f^{2} 10m^{2} 9m^{4} 10d 8m* 10g^{2dis} 10f^{5} Oct 24] tall gelding: modest performer: suited by strong pace when winning 17-runner apprentice maiden handicap at Bath in September, staying on very well to lead inside final 1f having been last of all over 2f out: should stay beyond 1¼m: acts on equitrack and firm ground: visored (well beaten on softish ground) twelfth 4-y-o start. *M. Madgwick* — 65

THARWA (IRE) 3 b.f. Last Tycoon 131 – Victory Kingdom (CAN) (Viceregal (CAN)) [1994 63: 5d^{3} 5s^{3} 5m^{4} 6m 6m 5d^{4} 5.2g* 5g^{3} 1995 6.1g 5m^{3} 5m^{3} 6g^{4} 6d* 5.2f^{2} 5.2m^{3} 6m* 6m 7m Aug 26] sturdy, lengthy filly: modest handicapper: narrowly won at Yarmouth in June and July: well below form at Newmarket last 2 starts: effective at 5f and 6f: acts on firm and soft ground: blinkered (well below form) fourth 3-y-o start: has wandered and flashed tail: bandaged at 3 yrs: usually races prominently. *N. A. Callaghan* — 63

THATCHED (IRE) 5 b.g. Thatching 131 – Shadia (USA) 53 (Naskra (USA)) 62
[1994 47: 8g^{6} 7.1g^{2} 7.1g^{2} 7.1f^{3} 9m^{3} 8.1m* 7m^{5} 9g^{5} 8f^{3} 8m* 8.1m^{6} 8g 8g^{4} 8f^{5} 8g 1995 9.9m^{6} 8g* 8m^{3} 8.5m^{6} 9m^{6} 8g^{5} 8f^{3} 8.1m* 8m^{4} 8f^{4} 8.3f^{4} 8h* 8g^{2} 9.2g 8.9g 8f^{4} 8f^{5} Oct 24] tall, leggy gelding: has a quick action: fair handicapper: won at Newcastle in April, Edinburgh in July and Carlisle in August: effective at 1m, and stays 1¼m: acts on hard going: sometimes blinkered (ran creditably) at 3 yrs: effective with or without a visor, not tried at 5 yrs: suitable mount for apprentice: tough and genuine. *R. E. Barr*

THATCHERELLA 4 br.f. Thatching 131 – Ella Mon Amour 65 (Ela-Mana-Mou 132) 80 d
[1994 67: 6.1m 6g 6m^{4} 5m* 5g^{2} 5f^{4} 5m 5m 5.1g 1995 6m* 6g^{3} 6.1g* 6f^{2} 5m 6m^{5} 6m 6g 5.3g^{5} 5f 7m Oct 28] smallish, good-bodied filly: fairly useful handicapper: better than ever in first half of 1995 for new connections, winning at Salisbury and Chepstow in May: well below form last 6 starts: effective at 5f and 6f: acts on firm ground: successful when sweating: generally raced prominently at 4 yrs. *Major D. N. Chappell*

THATCHER'S ERA (IRE) 3 ch.f. Never So Bold 135 – Prima Domina (FR) 89 (Dominion 123) 57
[1994 57: 7g^{6} 1995 8m^{3} 8f^{2} 10f 10.5s 8g^{5} Oct 9] workmanlike filly: modest maiden: should stay 1¼m: acts on firm ground. *T. D. Barron*

THATCHMASTER (IRE) 4 b.g. Thatching 131 – Key Maneuver (USA) (Key To Content (USA)) 54
[1994 –: 8.3m 7g 8s^{6} 1995 10.8f 7g 8m^{4} 8g 10m 10m 8g^{4} 8g Sep 29] tall gelding: modest handicapper: stays 1m: acts on good to firm ground: headstrong: inconsistent. *C. A. Horgan*

THAT MAN AGAIN 3 ch.g. Prince Sabo 123 – Milne's Way 83 (The Noble Player (USA) 126) 105
[1994 88: 6m 5.7f^{4} 5m 5m^{3} 5.3m* 6g^{6} 5s^{2} 5m 5g* 5g^{2} 5s^{4} 1995 5g^{5} a5g^{6} 5m^{4} 6m^{5} 6g^{5} 5f^{3} 5m* 5.1f* 5f* 5m^{4} 5d 5m^{3} Oct 21] smallish, compact gelding: took time to come to himself, then progressed into a useful handicapper: won at Sandown and Bath in July and £10,800 contest at Haydock in August: going in coat but best effort when length third of 10 to Croft Pool in rated stakes at Doncaster last time: best at 5f: probably acts on any going on turf, below form only run on the all-weather: usually blinkered: has won for claimer: usually races prominently: genuine. *G. Lewis*

THAT OLD FEELING (IRE) 3 b.c. Waajib 121 – Swift Reply (He Loves Me 120) 94
[1994 81p: 7g^{6} 8.5m* 1995 8.1m^{4} 8m^{4} 8g^{6} 10m^{2} 8m^{6} 10.1s^{2} 10m Oct 12] quite

Coral Handicap, Haydock—That Man Again (near side) and Lepine are always in the front rank

good-topped colt: fairly useful performer: stays 1¼m: acts on good to firm ground: sweating (tailed off) final 3-y-o start: sold (R. Hannon to J. White) 26,000 gns Newmarket Autumn Sales. *R. Hannon*

THE ASPECTO GIRL (IRE) 3 b.f. Alzao (USA) 117 – North Telstar 104 (Sallust 134) [1994 53: 6.1m 5g^4 6f^6 6d 8d 1995 a7g^6 a8g Mar 25] good-topped filly: modest maiden at 2 yrs: well beaten in 1995: sold 2,900 gns Doncaster March Sales. *M. Johnston* –

THEATRE MAGIC 2 b.g. (Mar 14) Sayf El Arab (USA) 127 – Miss Orient (Damister (USA) 123) [1995 5f^4 5.1m^3 5f^6 5m 7.5d a7g* Nov 24] 4,700F, 6,800Y: close-coupled gelding: unimpressive mover: first foal: dam ran once: poor form before sold out of T. Etherington's stable 2,500 gns Doncaster September Sales and gelded: much improved on first run for new connections, doing well to win nursery at Southwell by a neck after slow start: stays 7f: acts on fibresand: blinkered or visored last 3 outings. *S. R. Bowring* 50 a66

THEA (USA) 2 br.f. (Mar 9) Marju (IRE) 127 – Switched On 84 (Known Fact (USA) 135) [1995 8m^6 Nov 4] 7,500Y: lengthy, heavy-bodied filly: third foal: dam 9f winner: 33/1 and burly, 4 lengths sixth of 23 to Shaamit in median auction maiden at Doncaster, quickening ahead on far side 3f out but caught inside last and finishing third in her group: will improve. *J. R. Fanshawe* 76 p

THE BANSHEE (FR) 3 b.c. Shernazar 131 – Strident Note 89 (The Minstrel (CAN) 135) [1994 53p: 7s^5 1995 10m^6 Apr 25] lengthy, quite attractive colt: never-dangerous sixth of 10 in maiden at Pontefract only start at 3 yrs: sent to Dubai. *J. M. P. Eustace* –

THE BARNSLEY BELLE (IRE) 2 b.f. (Apr 10) Distinctly North (USA) 115 – La Tanque (USA) (Last Raise (USA)) [1995 a6g 6g a6g^6 7m^5 6f a5g Dec 1] IR 1,200Y, 4,200 2-y-o: fourth foal: dam Irish 5f winner: modest maiden: sprint-bred, but seems to need further than 5f. *S. G. Norton* – a54

THE BLACK DUBH (IRE) 2 b.g. (May 5) Classic Secret (USA) 91 – Coral Cave 79 (Ashmore (FR) 125) [1995 6m^4 7m 5h^4 Aug 21] IR 4,700Y: half-brother to fair handicapper Diaco (by Indian King), best around 1m, and 2 winners abroad: dam, 2-y-o 5f winner, half-sister to high-class miler Saintly Song: showed some ability when fourth of 5 in claimer at Pontefract on debut: well beaten in sellers afterwards. *J. J. Quinn* –

THE BOOZING BRIEF (USA) 2 b.g. (Apr 14) Turkoman (USA) – Evening Silk (USA) (Damascus (USA)) [1995 8g^2 7f^5 Oct 18] $60,000Y: tall gelding: fifth foal: half-brother to a Grade 3 8.5f winner in USA by Dixieland Band: dam minor sprint winner at 4 yrs in USA: second of 7 to Naval Gazer in maiden at Brighton: carried head rather high and never threatened in similar event at Yarmouth nearly 3 weeks later: subsequently gelded: will stay beyond 1m. *M. A. Jarvis* 69

THE BUTTERWICK KID 2 ch.g. (Apr 21) Interrex (CAN) – Ville Air 85 (Town Crier 119) [1995 6m^2 5g* 7d 6m Oct 2] 1,500Y: workmanlike gelding: fourth foal: dam won over 6f at 2 yrs on only start: won claimer at Beverley in July: well beaten afterwards in nurseries: needs a good test at 5f (should stay 7f). *R. A. Fahey* 61

THE CAPE DOCTOR (IRE) 3 b.g. Distant Relative 128 – Yldizlar 77 (Star Appeal 133) [1994 64: 6m^6 a6g^4 a7g^3 1995 a8g^3 a9.4g^6 6.1g 8.2m 10g 7m^4 a9.4g Aug 5] quite attractive gelding: modest maiden at best: left B. Hills's stable after reappearance: no comparable form afterwards: should stay 1¼m: acts on good to firm ground and equitrack: blinkered last 2 starts: sometimes bandaged: has had tongue tied. *A. G. Foster* 64 d

THE CHAIRMAN (IRE) 4 b.g. Last Tycoon 131 – Bhama (FR) (Habitat 134) [1994 66§: 8g^5 10m^4 11.9f^2 a10g^2 13.1f^2 16g^4 1995 a11g 14.9g 12g 11.6m 8f Aug 17] big, leggy gelding: no longer of much account. *F. Jordan* – §

THE CLAN 2 b.f. (Mar 28) Clantime 101 – Scottish Tina (Scottish Reel 123) [1995 6f 6m^6 Jul 14] first foal: dam no form: behind in sellers at Lingfield. *A. Moore* –

THE COTTONWOOL KID 3 b.g. Blakeney 126 – Relatively Smart 76 (Great Nephew 126) [1994 49: 5v^3 5d 7f a7g 1995 11.1f a11g 13.4m^5 a14.8g^3 a16g Nov 20] close-coupled gelding: no worthwhile form at 3 yrs. *T. H. Caldwell* –

THE COUNTRY DANCER 5 br.m. Mashhor Dancer (USA) – Slip The Ferret 109 (Klairon 131) [1994 –: a12g^6 1995 a8g a16g a8g a10g Feb 28] leggy mare: of no account. *K. T. Ivory* –

THE DEACONESS 4 b.f. Minster Son 130 – Haddon Anna (Dragonara Palace (USA) 115) [1994 NR 1995 10d 8.2d 8.2m Oct 19] close-coupled filly: no worthwhile form. *Mrs A. L. M. King* –

THE DILETTANTI (USA) 2 br.c. (Jan 17) Red Ransom (USA) – Rich Thought (USA) (Rich Cream (USA)) [1995 7d Sep 27] $40,000Y: stocky colt: first foal: dam minor winner at up to 9f at 4 yrs in USA: 11/2 and bit backward, well-beaten eighth of 12 to Final Stab in maiden at Salisbury, chasing leaders until 2f out: should do better. *J. A. R. Toller* – p

THE FED 5 ch.g. Clantime 101 – Hyde Princess 75 (Touch Paper 113) [1994 64: 5g^6 5f 5m^4 5m^4 5m^6 5m^3 5g^3 5g^3 5.1g* 5.2g^2 5m^3 5m* 5g^2 5g 5.1d* 5d 5g 1995 5d 5m 5m 5f^4 5f^3 5m 5m 5f^4 5.1m^3 5m 5.1d^4 5d 5f 5.1m 6m Oct 30] small, strong gelding: modest handicapper: well beaten last 4 starts: best at 5f: acts on firm and dead ground: often visored (best efforts in 1995 when wearing one): usually races prominently: inconsistent. *R. M. Whitaker* 59 d

THE FLYING FIDDLE 3 ch.f. Northern State (USA) 91 – Miss Flossa (FR) (Big John (FR) 125) [1994 NR 1995 8d 8f 10.1m^3 8g Jul 28] sparely-made filly: third foal: half-sister to useful stayer The Flying Phantom (by Sharrood): dam French maiden: well beaten in maidens and (visored) sellers: sold (M. Tompkins to S. Cole) 875 gns Ascot September Sales. *M. H. Tompkins* 24

THE FLYING PHANTOM 4 gr.g. Sharrood (USA) 124 – Miss Flossa (FR) (Big John (FR) 125) [1994 96: 8s^6 12g^2 12.3m^4 12m 9g^2 8f^6 10f^2 10m^3 11.9d^4 10.9s^2 12m^2 13.9d* 12v 1995 14.1g^5 18.7m^3 16.4m^4 20m^6 16.1m 13.9m^3 16m^2 15.5g^6 Sep 6] leggy gelding: useful performer: ran very well when third in Chester Cup and when fourth of 7 to Double Trigger in Henry II Stakes at Sandown (headed over 2f out) in May: just respectable efforts at best afterwards: suited by a good test of stamina: acts on firm and soft going: sometimes a front runner. *M. H. Tompkins* 97

THE FRENCH FRIAR (IRE) 4 b.g. Carmelite House (USA) 118 – Netweight (FR) (Pampabird 124) [1994 79p: 10g^6 10.4g 10d^4 10g^2 10d* 8d^5 1995 10g 12g^3 10m 10.4m 10m^6 Aug 13] tall, workmanlike gelding: showed fair form, including in valuable handicaps, despite it later coming to light that he had been suffering from the onset of cancer: stayed 1½m: acted on good to soft going, probably on good to firm: dead. *G. B. Balding* 78

THE FRISKY FARMER 2 b.g. (May 7) Emarati (USA) 74 – Farceuse (Comedy Star (USA) 121) [1995 5m* 5g^2 6g^2 7m 6m^2 6m a5g Nov 25] leggy gelding: fourth foal: dam seemed of little account: won seller at Beverley in April: little form in nurseries last 2 starts, sweating first occasion, when rider lost irons: stays 6f: flashed tail fifth start: gelded off course over 3 months before final one. *W. G. M. Turner* 73

THE FROG LADY (IRE) 4 ch.f. Al Hareb (USA) 123 – Lady Bettina (Bustino 136) [1994 52: 7s 8g 10f^2 12g^2 11.9m^3 11.9g^3 16.1s^3 16.1d 1995 a12g^4 a14.8g Aug 11] modest maiden: no form in 1995: stays 1½m well: acts on firm ground. *D. W. P. Arbuthnot* –

THE FROG PRINCESS 2 ch.f. (Apr 2) Crowning Honors (CAN) – Sally Tadpole 44 (Jester 119) [1995 7g 7g Sep 29] angular, sparely-made filly: first foal: dam ran 3 times, placed over 5f at 2 yrs: well beaten in claimer at Brighton (slowly away and swerved at stalls) and seller at Goodwood. *K. McAuliffe* –

THE FULLBANGLADESH 2 ch.f. (Jun 16) Hubbly Bubbly (USA) – Oakhurst § (Mandrake Major 122) [1995 7m^6 a7g^2 a8.5g Dec 2] leggy, lengthy filly: first reported foal: dam temperamental: poor maiden: second of 15 in seller at Southwell in November, best effort: stays 7f. *J. L. Eyre* 48

THE HAPPY FOX (IRE) 3 ch.c. Ballad Rock 122 – Amanzi 94 (African Sky 124) [1994 81: 5.1m^2 5.1f^5 5g^2 6f^4 5.1m^4 a5g* 5f 5m^4 5m^5 5s^5 6g 1995 5.1m^3 5g^4 5f 5m^5 5.1m^6 5f^2 5m* 6m 6g^4 5m^4 Oct 21] strong, lengthy colt: fairly useful performer: won 5-runner claimer at Pontefract in August, leading on bit entering final 1f: 5 lb out of handicap and claimer ridden, excelled himself when always-prominent fourth of 10 to Croft Pool in rated stakes at Doncaster last time: stays 6f: acts on firm ground 89 (below form on soft in visor penultimate 2-y-o start) and fibresand: effective blinkered or not: tends to hang left: none too consistent. *B. A. McMahon*

THE HAPPY LOON (IRE) 4 b.g. Mazaad 106 – Skimmer 86 (Skymaster 126) [1994 63: 8.2v^2 8.3d* 8m 8.1g 8d^2 8f 8g^4 8g^5 8d 1995 a8g 8.3v^4 7m 8g 7g^5 7.5g 7.1m^6 6g^3 7m^5 6g^6 Sep 25] sturdy gelding: modest handicapper: effective at 6f to 8.3f: acts on good to firm and heavy ground (well beaten after 7-month break only start on all-weather): races prominently: inconsistent: sent to Denmark. *Denys Smith* 58

THEHILLSAREALIVE (IRE) 3 b.g. Tirol 127 – Hillbrow 100 (Swing Easy (USA) 126) [1994 NR 1995 7m^6 6g 5f 5g Sep 12] IR 15,000Y: lengthy gelding: has a round action: closely-related to good-class 5f to 7f winner Indian Ridge (by Ahonoora) and half-brother to 3 winners: dam 2-y-o 6f winner: 40/1, easily best effort when ninth of 16 in claimer at Warwick third start: should stay at least 6f: sold only 1,000 gns Newmarket Autumn Sales. *D. R. C. Elsworth* 50

THE IMPS (IRE) 2 b.g. (Mar 2) Mac's Imp (USA) 116 – Claire's Thatch (Thatch (USA) 136) [1995 5m 6g 5.1m^2 5.2f* 5g^3 7g^6 a5g^4 a6g^4 6s^3 a6s* Dec 17] IR 10,000Y: workmanlike, unfurnished gelding: fourth foal: half-brother to German 3-y-o 1m winner Catanese (by Contract Law): dam Irish 1½m winner: won seller at Yarmouth in June: sold out of B. Hills's stable 3,200 gns Newmarket Autumn Sales before winning in Sweden next start: stays 6f: acts on any surface: usually taken early to post: blinkered (ran creditably) penultimate start here. *M. Khan, Sweden* 59 a55+

THE INSTITUTE BOY 5 b.g. Fairy King (USA) – To Oneiro 69 (Absalom 128) [1994 57: a5g^6 5g^2 5m 5m 5m 5.9m a5g 5g 6s 5.1g a5g^2 5d 1995 a6g^2 a5g^2 a6g^6 a5g a6g 6g 5f^5 a5g^2 a5g^4 5m^3 a5g^6 5m^4 5f^5 5g a5g 5m^6 5h 5f^4 5.1d Sep 11] smallish, strong gelding: poor mover: modest performer: effective at 5f and 6f: goes well on the all-weather, acts on firm and dead ground: effective in blinkers/visor or not. *Miss J. F. Craze* 46 a56

THE JOLLY BARMAID (IRE) 2 b.f. (Apr 20) Don't Forget Me 127 – Gay Broad 78 (Gay Fandango (USA) 132) [1995 6.1d 6g Oct 3] IR 7,000Y: lengthy, rather unfurnished filly: half-sister to 1989 2-y-o 6f winner Indian Chief (by Indian King) and winners in France and Hong Kong: dam won over 7f at 3 yrs: signs of ability when tenth of 23 to Thracian in maiden at Nottingham: tailed off in maiden auction at Warwick 2 weeks later. *P. Calver* –

THE JOTTER 3 b.f. Night Shift (USA) – Note Book 94 (Mummy's Pet 125) [1994 99: 5d^4 5s* 5.2m^2 6m^4 6g^2 7m^2 7m^2 7g^4 6.5g* 1995 6d^3 7m 6m^5 6g 6g^4 6g^6 Sep 29] compact, attractive filly: fluent mover: fairly useful handicapper: best efforts as 3-y-o on last 2 starts: effective at 6f and 7f: acts on soft and good to firm ground. *W. Jarvis* 93

THE KASTARBIDS (IRE) 2 b.g. (Apr 10) Red Sunset 120 – All Alright (Alzao (USA) 117) [1995 a6g 7g 7g^2 7m 6.9f^5 8.1m Aug 25] IR 4,200F, IR 5,000Y, 6,200 2-y-o: leggy gelding: third foal: brother to Italian 4-y-o 6f and 8.5f winner My Luca: dam Irish maiden stayed 1¼m: plater: well beaten last 3 starts: should stay 1m: visored last 4 starts: one to have reservations about: sent to Sweden. *D. Morris* 48

THE KINGS RANSOM 3 b.g. Cadeaux Genereux 131 – The Kings Daughter 79 (Indian King (USA) 128) [1994 44p: 5g 5g 5s 1995 5d 6.1g^3 6g^3 5.9f* 6.9m^5 6m* 5m^3 5g^2 5m* Jul 28] good-quartered gelding: won at Carlisle in May and at Pontefract in June and (much his best effort, by 5 lengths, storming clear final 1f) July: stays 6f: acts on firm ground: visored since fourth 3-y-o start: held up and has turn of foot: was progressing well, but sold 20,000 gns Newmarket September Sales: sent to Macau. *Mrs J. R. Ramsden* 84

THE LEAF SWEEPER 4 b.f. Tinoco 80 – Queen's Royale 80 (Tobrouk (FR)) [1994 –: 10m 11.5g 1995 a12g a8g Feb 25] leggy filly: of no account. *M. J. Bolton* –

THE LEGIONS PRIDE 2 b.c. (Apr 26) Rambo Dancer (CAN) 107 – Immaculate Girl 67 (Habat 127) [1995 6m 6m^4 7g 7.3m^5 7m^5 8d Sep 30] 5,000Y: leggy colt: has scope: half-brother to 1992 2-y-o 6f winner Tee Gee Jay (by Northern Tempest) and a winner in Italy: dam, maiden, should have stayed 1½m: modest maiden: should stay beyond 7f: acts on good to firm ground. *J. W. Hills* 58

THE LITTLE FERRET 5 ch.g. Scottish Reel 123 – Third Movement 75 (Music Boy 124) [1994 69: 7s 8d 6s^2 6s 6m 6.9m^3 7f* 7.6g 7m* 7m^3 8g 1995 a8g^5 a7g^2 a8g a7g^2 a8g 8m a8g^2 7f^6 7f^5 a10g^4 a10g 7f^6 a8g a10g^2 a10g^6 a8g Dec 15] leggy 63 d gelding: modest handicapper on his day: left G. L. Moore's stable after eighth start: seems to stay 1¼m: acts on soft and good to firm ground and on equitrack: none too consistent. *A. Moore*

THE LITTLE THIEF (FR) 4 b.c. Ela-Mana-Mou 132 – Oui Papa (FR) (Riverman (USA) 131) [1994 112: 10s^{3} 10g^{4} 12g^{6} 10g^{5} 13.5d^{2} 12s^{3} 15d* 1995 15.5s^{3} 15.5v^{2} 15.5d* 20m Jun 22] leggy, close-coupled colt: smart performer: runner-up to Nononito (rec 4 lb) in Prix de Barbeville at Saint-Cloud then reversed placings at levels in Prix Vicomtesse Vigier (by ½ length, pair 5 lengths clear of Epaphos) at Longchamp in the spring: pulled up with fractured off-hind fetlock in Gold Cup at Royal Ascot: effective at around 15f and would probably have proved well suited by an extreme test of stamina: acted on heavy ground: dead. *E. Danel, France*
117

THE LONE DANCER 4 b.g. Mashhor Dancer (USA) – Solo Vacation (Pas de Seul 133) [1994 74: 10.3g^{2} 11.1f* 12g^{6} 10m^{2} 10.2f^{3} 1995 10f 10m May 15] good-topped gelding: carries condition: fair performer: off course 10 months (gelded) and not right in coat, shaped well under 5-lb claimer in handicap at Pontefract on first run for new stable: well-backed favourite, disappointing in minor event at Windsor 2 weeks later: should stay beyond 1¼m: acts on firm ground. *K. McAuliffe*
71

THE MAN 2 b.c. (Apr 17) Marju (IRE) 127 – Mirkan Honey 83 (Ballymore 123) [1995 6f 6m^{3} 6m^{2} 6g* 7.6d^{3} 6d^{3} 5s^{3} 6g^{2} Nov 8] lengthy colt: has scope: unimpressive walker: half-brother to several winners, including useful 3-y-o Fleet Hill (by Warrshan), 6f and 7f winner at 2 yrs, and useful 5f and 6f winner Lee Artiste (by Tate Gallery): dam Irish 4-y-o 2m winner: won maiden at Catterick in September: fairly useful form afterwards when third in Cornwallis Stakes (outpaced before finishing 7½ lengths behind Mubhij) at Ascot and second in listed race at Milan: probably stays 7.6f: acts on good to firm and soft ground: sold 46,000 gns Doncaster November Sales. *M. R. Channon*
90

THE MERRY MONK 4 ch.g. Balidar 133 – Floret 49 (Monsanto (FR) 121) [1994 NR 1995 8d Apr 1] leggy, lengthy gelding: first foal: dam, maiden, stayed 1½m: 25/1 and green, soon pushed along in claimer at Warwick: has joined H. Sawyer. *C. N. Allen*
–

THE MESTRAL 3 br.f. Formidable (USA) 125 – Lariston Gale 81 (Pas de Seul 133) [1994 48§: 5d 6g 6g^{4} 5m 6d 6m 5d 1995 6.1g^{6} 6g 6m^{2} 5f^{4} 6m 7m^{4} 8.2m^{4} 8.3m^{2} 8m^{2} 7f a7g a8.5g^{5} a7g^{5} Dec 14] small, compact filly: has a round action: poor handicapper: stays 8.3f: acts on good to firm ground, below best on all-weather: tried blinkered/visored, no improvement: tail swisher. *M. J. Ryan*
48

THEM TIMES (IRE) 6 b.m. Petorius 117 – Atropine (Beldale Flutter (USA) 130) [1994 –: a9.4g 8s^{6} 10d 8m^{6} 8.2f 10g 10m 10.8f 1995 10m 10m 10.8m 7m 6m Aug 23] sturdy mare: no worthwhile form. *F. Jordan*
–

THE NOBLE OAK (IRE) 7 ch.g. The Noble Player (USA) 126 – Sea Palace (Huntercombe 133) [1994 59, a57: a5g^{4} a5g 5.1g 5g^{4} 5m^{2} a5g^{4} 5.1m^{5} 5m 5m a5g 1995 5.3m 5g 5g^{6} 5g 6m 5.1h^{2} 5.1m 5m^{4} 5m 6f 5m^{6} 5m Aug 31] small, strong gelding: modest handicapper: below form last 4 starts: best at around 5f: acts on hard and dead ground and on equitrack: tried blinkered/visored, no improvement: usually races prominently: inconsistent. *M. J. Bolton*
51 d a–

THENORTHERNPLAYBOY (IRE) 2 gr.c. (May 26) Distinctly North (USA) 115 – Monetary Wish (Wishing Star 117) [1995 6.1m Oct 26] sparely-made colt: sixth reported foal: half-brother to Irish 6f winner God's Express (by Godswalk): dam successful Irish sprinter: 25/1 and in need of race, always behind in maiden at Nottingham: sold (B. McMahon to B. Preece) 2,300 gns Doncaster November Sales. *B. A. McMahon*
–

THE OIL BARON 9 gr.g. Absalom 128 – Ruby's Chance 71 (Charlottesville 135) [1994 NR 1995 12g 11.6m 14d^{4} 11.6m Aug 7] leggy gelding: no longer of much account. *R. P. C. Hoad*
–

THE OLD CHAPEL 6 b.g. Lomond (USA) 128 – Chapel Cottage 117 (Homing 130) [1994 64, a70: 6m 6s^{2} 6s^{3} 6f 7g 6g a7g^{2} a6g^{2} a6g^{2} a6g^{4} a6g^{5} 6d 6d^{3} 6s^{4} 6.1g a6g^{4} 1995 a6g^{2} 6d^{3} 6m^{4} 6m* a6g* 6m^{6} 6d Jun 9] leggy, good-topped gelding: bad mover: fair handicapper: successful at Leicester in April and Wolverhampton in May: bit below form afterwards: stays 7f, best form at 6f: acts on good to firm and
66 a74

soft ground and goes well on fibresand: usually blinkered nowadays, below form (in Ayr Silver Cup) only try in visor: has run creditably for apprentice: front runner: game. *B. A. McMahon*

THE POWER OF ONE 6 b.g. Bellypha 130 – Biding 97 (Habat 127) [1994 –: a10g 1995 a9.4g Feb 1] lengthy, rather dipped-backed gelding: probably no longer of much account. *R. W. Emery* –

THE PREMIER EXPRES 5 gr.g. Siberian Express (USA) 125 – Home And Away (Home Guard (USA) 129) [1994 –: a7g a11g 11g 12g 10d 11.1g 10.8s 1995 12g 12.1v³ 12.1s* 11.1g May 5] lengthy gelding: modest handicapper: won at Hamilton (apprentice) in April: stays 12.1f: acts on good to firm and heavy ground: blinkered once (below form) in 1993: fair hurdler. *F. J. O'Mahony* 53

THE PUZZLER (IRE) 4 br.g. Sharpo 132 – Enigma 87 (Ahonoora 122) [1994 105: 5d² 5v² 6d² 5g 6.3g 5m 7g⁵ 7d⁵ 6v* 6d 1995 5g⁵ 6m* 6m 5m 7g³ 6m 6m 7g⁶ 7f 6d 7d⁶ Nov 12] leggy, useful-looking gelding: bad mover: useful performer on his day: won handicap (under 10-0) at Leopardstown in May: second run in 24 hours and ran well when under a length third of 8 to Desert Style in Ballycorus Stakes at Leopardstown: below form afterwards, running badly on 3 occasions: stays 7f: acts on good to firm and heavy going: has gone lame while racing on several occasions and, hence, cannot be relied upon. *M. Kauntze, Ireland* 109 §

THE REAL WHIZZBANG (IRE) 4 b. or br.c. New Express 95 – Gail's Crystal (Crofter (USA) 124) [1994 –: 5g 5m 5.2m⁵ a6g 1995 a7g a6g⁵ a7g a6g³ a6g⁴ a6g a5g* a5g³ a6g 5.1g⁵ a5g³ a6g 5.1d a5g Dec 2] smallish, strong colt: modest handicapper: won at Wolverhampton in May: best at 5f: acts on fibresand: best recent form in blinkers: often claimer ridden: usually forces pace. *P. S. Felgate* 35 + a51

THERHEA (IRE) 2 b.c. (Mar 30) Pennine Walk 120 – Arab Art (Artaius (USA) 129) [1995 5g³ 5m³ 6f⁴ 7m⁵ 6m 7.3d⁶ 5.7m² 6f Oct 12] IR 13,500Y: good-bodied colt: brother to smart 5-y-o 5.7f (at 2 yrs) to 8.5f winner Mr Martini and half-brother to 3 winners: dam Irish maiden: fair maiden: ran good races in big fields in sales race at the Curragh on fifth start and Redcar Two-Year-Old Trophy (blinkered) on final one: stays 7f: sold 12,500 gns Newmarket Autumn Sales. *B. R. Millman* 73 +

THE RIGHT TIME 10 b.g. King of Spain 121 – Noddy Time 97 (Gratitude 130) [1994 –§: 5f 5g 5m 1995 7g 5g 6g⁶ Jun 5] robust gelding: no longer of much account. *J. Parkes* – §

THE SCYTHIAN 3 ch.g. Komaite (USA) – City To City 55 (Windjammer (USA)) [1994 59: 5.3f* 6g⁶ 5.2g 1995 6m* 6.1m 6m* 6f² 6m³ 5g⁴ Jul 20] stocky, deep-girthed gelding: fair handicapper: won at Ripon in April and May, making virtually all: stays 6f: acts on firm ground: races prominently: consistent. *Bob Jones* 74

THE STAGER (IRE) 3 b.c. Danehill (USA) 126 – Wedgewood Blue (USA) 87 (Sir Ivor 135) [1994 67: 8d⁵ 7m 7m⁶ 1995 7.5m* 7.5m⁴ 9m⁴ 8m 8m⁶ 8.1m⁴ 7m⁶ 12f 7f⁴ 7m² Aug 27] tall, lengthy colt: has scope: good mover, with a long stride: fair handicapper: won at Beverley in April, leading final 1f: returned to near best at Goodwood last time, making most: stays 9f: acts on good to firm ground: blinkered last 2 starts: takes good hold. *J. R. Jenkins* 74

THE SWAN 2 ch.f. (Mar 28) Old Vic 136 – El Vino (Habitat 134) [1995 7.6d⁴ 8d 8.2m Oct 19] leggy, rather unfurnished filly: fourth foal: half-sister to a winner in Hungary by Petoski: dam ran twice: similar form in maidens at Lingfield (fourth of 12 to Patria) and Salisbury (ninth of 18 to Mystic Knight) on first 2 starts, running on from rear not knocked about: never better than mid-division on good to firm ground in similar event at Nottingham on final outing: remains capable of better, particularly over 1¼m+. *J. L. Dunlop* 65 p

THE WAD 2 b.g. (Apr 7) Emarati (USA) 74 – Fair Melys (FR) 81 (Welsh Pageant 132) [1995 6m 7.5m 7m 5m 7.5d² 7.9m 7f⁶ Oct 14] 4,200Y: good-topped, leggy gelding: unimpressive mover: ninth live foal: half-brother to 3-y-o Ketchican (by Joligeneration): dam, 7f and 1m winner, half-sister to high-class middle-distance winner Pelerin: modest form in nurseries last 3 starts: stays 1m, but races keenly and likely to prove best at shorter: acts on firm and dead ground: trained first 5 outings by M. W. Easterby. *D. Nicholls* 56

THICK AS THIEVES 3 b.c. Shavian 125 – Vivienda 93 (Known Fact (USA) 135) [1994 75: 5.1d² 5m² 6f* 6.1g* 6m⁴ 5m* 6g 5f* 5.3m² 6d² 5g 1995 5m⁵ 5m⁴ 6m 59 d

6g 5g 6m a5g a6g a5g^4 Dec 19] strong, workmanlike colt: fair performer at 2 yrs: well below that form in 1995: stays 6f: acts on firm and dead ground. *Ronald Thompson*

THINK OF ENGLAND 3 ch.f. Night Shift (USA) – Final Thought (Final Straw 127) [1994 –: 5.2s^6 6m 7m^5 1995 a10g Jul 22] sturdy filly: well beaten all starts: blinkered final 2-y-o outing. *S. Dow* –

THISONESFORALICE 7 b.g. Lochnager 132 – Bamdoro 54 (Cavo Doro 124) [1994 38: 9m 8.1m^3 8.1f^4 7d^2 10g^5 8g^3 8.1m* 8.1m^5 a9.4g 1995 9.2g 8.3g 11.1f^2 12.1m^2 9.2m 12.1m^2 10.9g Sep 14] leggy gelding: poor handicapper: trained until after second 7-y-o start by A. Harrison: found little sixth start: stays 12.1f: acts on good to firm and soft ground: visored (well beaten) once as 4-y-o. *J. S. Goldie* 40

THOMAS CROWN (IRE) 3 ch.c. Last Tycoon 131 – Upward Trend 112 (Salmon Leap (USA) 131) [1994 64p: 7g 7f 1995 8g 8g May 18] quite good-topped colt: has a quick action: modest maiden at 2 yrs: well beaten for new stable in 1995: should stay 1m. *N. J. H. Walker* –

THOMIRE 3 ch.c. Be My Chief (USA) 122 – Timarete (ITY) (Green Dancer (USA) 132) [1994 7m^2 7.5g^3 7.5d* 7v^3 8v^4 1995 7.5g* 8s^4 8g^2 12m 8f* 8d 7.5s^2 7d Nov 4] third foal: half-brother to Italian winners by Local Suitor (at 7f to 8.5f) and Sure Blade (at 1¼m): dam, placed in listed events at 1½m, is half-sister to Italian Derby winner Tisserand: useful Italian colt: won minor event at Merano then in frame in good company at 2 yrs: won minor event at Rome in March: improved form when 1½ lengths second of 14 to Prince Arthur in Premio Parioli at Rome in April: won listed event at Milan in July: may yet stay beyond 1m (found little and well beaten in Derby Italiano when tried): acts on any going: inconsistent. *P. Mazzoni, Italy* 106

THORDIS 2 b.g. (May 1) Mazilier (USA) 107 – Doppio 62 (Dublin Taxi) [1995 6.1d^5 a6g^2 6f* Oct 24] quite good-topped gelding: sixth foal: half-brother to 6f winner Wandering Stranger and 1990 2-y-o 5f winner Garth Gold (both by Petong): dam 2-y-o 5f winner: progressive form: won 19-runner median auction maiden at Leicester by 1½ lengths from Blue Suede Hoofs: stays 6f: acts on firm and dead ground and on fibresand. *P. J. Makin* 77

THORNIWAMA 4 b.f. Hadeer 118 – Hidden Asset (Hello Gorgeous (USA) 128) [1994 33: 6d 6g 5m^5 7d 6.9m a6g^6 a7g a7g^3 a8g 1995 a10g^4 a13g^6 a10g^5 a8g^3 a12g a8g Feb 25] leggy filly: poor maiden: stays 1¼m: acts on equitrack: blinkered (no improvement) last 3 starts. *J. J. Bridger* 41 ?

THORNTOUN ESTATE (IRE) 2 b.g. (Apr 23) Durgam (USA) – Furry Friend (USA) (Bold Bidder) [1995 a8.5d^5 8.3g^4 10g^4 a8.5g^3 a10g* Nov 25] sixth reported foal: half-brother to 1990 2-y-o 6f winner Russian Mink (by L'Emigrant): dam lightly raced: in frame in sellers before winning 14-runner median auction maiden at Lingfield in November: will stay beyond 1¼m: acts on equitrack. *M. Johnston* 64

THORNTOUN JEWEL (IRE) 2 b.f. (Feb 9) Durgam (USA) – Blue Bouquet (Cure The Blues (USA)) [1995 5g^5 5g^2 6g* 6m^6 7m^3 7h^5 6.1d 7g 6s Sep 30] smallish filly: third foal: half-sister to Irish 6f/7f winner Queen of All Birds (by Bluebird): dam Irish maiden: won claimer at Hamilton in May (claimed out of M. Johnston's stable £5,000): below form last 4 starts, final one a seller: will stay 1m: sweating and edgy, reared stalls seventh start: early to post (very slowly away) next time. *J. Balding* 50

THORNY BISHOP 4 b.g. Belfort (FR) 89 – Hill of Fare (Brigadier Gerard 144) [1994 75d: a7g^2 a7g^2 a6g* a6g* a7g^3 a6g* a6g 6s^5 6f a6g^6 5g a6g 1995 a6g^6 a6g^5 a6g^5 Feb 14] big, lengthy gelding: has completely lost his way. *J. J. Bridger* –

THOUSLA ROCK (IRE) 6 ch.g. Thatching 131 – Resooka (Godswalk (USA) 130) [1994 110: 6m 5.6m^4 5g^4 6d^5 6g^3 5d^3 6d* 1995 6g Jul 15] big, good-topped gelding: had leg problems at 2 and 3 yrs: useful performer: well beaten in listed race at Newbury only start in 1995: effective at 5f to 7f: acted on soft going and good to firm: has been retired. *P. W. Chapple-Hyam* –

THRACIAN 2 b.f. (May 1) Green Desert (USA) 127 – Triple First 117 (High Top 131) [1995 6f^6 6.1d* 7m* 7.3d Oct 21] well-made filly: half-sister to several winners, including smart 5-y-o middle-distance horse Richard of York (by Rainbow Quest), Oaks third Three Tails (by Blakeney) and 1000 Guineas and Oaks-placed Maysoon (by Shergar): dam won from 5f to 1¼m: won 23-runner maiden at Nottingham in 92 p

September and 2-runner minor event at York (beat eased-up Dimakya by 5 lengths) in October: heavily-backed favourite, only seventh of 9 in listed race at Newbury later in October: will stay further than 7f: worth another chance. *J. L. Dunlop*

THREE ARCH BRIDGE 3 ch.f. Sayf El Arab (USA) 127 – Alanood 85 (Northfields (USA)) [1994 54: 5g^3 5s 5d^2 6f* 7m 8g^6 1995 a7g^2 a7g^2 a7g a8g^4 a7g^3 a7g* 8f 8g^2 9.2g^3 7.5m^2 8m 7g^4 8d^3 7f^2 8.3f* 8.5g a9.4g^2 9.2f* 8.2m^2 8.3f^6 8h^3 8m^6 8.5d* 8d 8m^6 Oct 2] quite good-topped filly: fair handicapper: won at Southwell in April, Hamilton (twice, minor event first occasion) in July and Beverley in September: stays 9.2f: acts on all-weather surfaces, hard ground and dead: blinkered since sixth 3-y-o start: usually races prominently: tough. *M. Johnston* 68

THREE HILLS 2 b.c. (Jan 28) Danehill (USA) 126 – Three Stars 93 (Star Appeal 133) [1995 7d^5 8m^3 Oct 12] strong, deep-bodied colt: has scope: fifth live foal: half-brother to Irish Oaks winner Bolas (by Unfuwain) and French 1½m winner Star of Dance (by Sadler's Wells): dam 1½m winner from staying family: 1¾ lengths third of 14 to Silver Dome at Newmarket, taking good hold before improving to challenge over 1f out and only caught for second near line: will stay beyond 1m: will improve again. *B. W. Hills* 82 p

THREE OF HEARTS 4 b.f. Governor General 116 – Friendly Miss (Be Friendly 130) [1994 62, a49: a6s^3 a6g^6 5.1v^4 a5g* 5v* 5.1g^5 a5g 6.1s 5m^2 5.1g 1995 a6g Jan 13] leggy, good-topped filly: poor mover: modest performer: well beaten only start in 1995: best efforts at 5f: acts on heavy ground, good to firm and fibresand: has given trouble stalls. *Mrs N. Macauley* –

THREESOCKS 2 ch.f. (Apr 5) Weldnaas (USA) 112 – Jeethgaya (USA) 61 (Critique (USA) 126) [1995 a7g^6 8.1m^5 8.1d^6 Sep 12] rather sparely-made filly: first foal: dam maiden placed from 1m to 1¼m: apparently best form when fifth of 9 to Waterland in steadily-run maiden at Chepstow, prominent until entering final 1f and flashing tail when hit with whip: never threatened in similar event at Sandown following month. *B. Smart* 62 ?

THREESOME (USA) 2 ch.f. (Feb 28) Seattle Dancer (USA) 119 – Triode (USA) 105 (Sharpen Up 127) [1995 7m^3 7m^5 7d^2 Sep 26] lengthy, angular filly: good mover: second foal: half-sister to a winner in Germany by Storm Bird: dam 1m winner from the family of smart middle-distance filly Trillionaire: fair form in maidens: will be better suited by 1m+. *L. M. Cumani* 79

THREE STOPS (USA) 3 b.c. Nureyev (USA) 131 – Smart Angle (USA) (Quadrangle) [1994 81p: 7g^5 7d^2 1995 5m* 6g 7f^2 8g 7g Sep 30] strong, lengthy colt: has plenty of scope: has a quick action: made rather hard work of landing the odds in maiden event at Beverley in May: best effort when ½-length second of 16 to Easy Dollar in £19,800 handicap at Goodwood, challenging final 1f then finding little: well beaten afterwards: will prove best at up to 7f: acts on firm and dead ground: visored (weakened tamely) final 3-y-o start: looks none too hearty and isn't one to trust implicitly: sent to Dubai. *M. R. Stoute* 86

THREE WEEKS 2 ch.g. (Apr 6) Formidable (USA) 125 – Zilda (FR) 46§ (Zino 127) [1995 7.1d 7.1d Sep 13] 12,500Y: lengthy, rather unfurnished gelding: unimpressive mover: fourth foal: brother to a poor maiden and half-brother to 1993 2-y-o 1¼m winner Stradishall (by Squill): dam (stayed 1½m) was ungenuine: backward, well beaten in maidens at Haydock (unruly in paddock) and Sandown. *W. R. Muir* –

THREE WILD DAYS 3 b.g. Nishapour (FR) 125 – Golden Curd (FR) 70 (Nice Havrais (USA) 124) [1994 NR 1995 10.5g 11.9d Oct 11] lengthy, workmanlike gelding: has plenty of scope: has a markedly round action: second foal: brother to 4-y-o Silver Shred, 17f NH Flat race winner in 1994/5: dam 14.7f winner: no form in maidens at Haydock, but fared best of those to come stand side last time and was not unduly knocked about: likely to need test of stamina: sort to improve steadily. *T. P. Tate* – p

THRESHFIELD (USA) 9 b.g. Northern Prospect (USA) – French Cutie (USA) (Vaguely Noble 140) [1994 50: 8f* 9.7m^4 8g^2 1995 7.1m 7m^5 8.3m 10m* 10d 8f Oct 18] tall, good-topped gelding: just a modest performer nowadays: gamely made all in selling handicap at Nottingham in August: no comparable form in 1995: stays 1¼m: probably acts on any going: sometimes bandaged: takes keen hold and has worn crossed noseband. *B. J. Curley* 53

THRILLING DAY 2 b.f. (Mar 18) Groom Dancer (USA) 128 – Pushoff (USA) 78 (Sauce Boat (USA)) [1995 6m^3 6m^2 6m* 6m^4 6g* 7m^6 6m* Oct 21] small, close-coupled filly: lacks scope: fourth foal: half-sister to unreliable Irish 7f winner Champagne 'N Roses (by Chief Singer): dam, 5f winner, half-sister to 1995 Nell Gwyn Stakes winner Myself, out of Queen Mary and Cornwallis winner Pushy: useful filly: won maiden at Thirsk in July and listed races at the Curragh in September and Doncaster (improved effort, quickened smartly to beat Resounder ¾ length) in October: not discredited in 7f Rockfel Stakes but suited by 6f: tail flasher. *N. A. Graham* 100

THROWER 4 b.g. Thowra (FR) – Atlantic Line (Capricorn Line 111) [1994 –: 7g 10d 14.6s^5 1995 11.8m^4 14.1m 10.8g^2 12.3m^5 11.4m 10m 10.5m 14g^3 14d^3 Sep 27] sparely-made gelding: poor maiden handicapper: trained until after seventh start by W. Brisbourne: stays 1¾m: acts on good to firm ground and dead. *P. D. Evans* 48

THRUSHWOOD 3 b.f. Move Off 112 – Spring Garden 54 (Silly Prices 110) [1994 NR 1995 7g 10m May 10] fourth foal: dam poor maiden: 100/1, soundly beaten. *N. Chamberlain* –

THUNDERHEART 4 b.c. Celestial Storm (USA) 132 – Lorelene (FR) 97 (Lorenzaccio 130) [1994 82: 11.6g 11.1f^4 12m^5 14.1m^3 16.2m* 15.4m^3 16.2m^2 17.2m^3 16.2f^2 16.4g^4 16g^4 16s 15.8g* 18s^2 1995 14m^2 18.7m 16m^3 14s^5 16.2f^2 14.6g^6 16.1g^3 16m 16.5m Nov 4] deep-bodied colt: fairly useful handicapper at best: sold out of L. Cumani's stable 23,000 gns Newmarket Autumn Sales after penultimate start: pulled up lame final outing: will prove best granted thorough test of stamina: acts on firm ground and soft: normally held up: joined Mrs D. Thomson. *J. J. O'Neill* 80 d

THUNDEROUS 4 b.g. Green Desert (USA) 127 – Mixed Applause (USA) 101 (Nijinsky (CAN) 138) [1994 –: 7d 8.1g 10d 1995 a10g Dec 6] lengthy, well-made gelding: well bred but no worthwhile form: tried blinkered. *J. J. Bridger* –

THUNDER RIVER (IRE) 5 ch.g. Thatching 131 – In For More (Don 128) [1994 64+: 8f 8g 8g 8m^6 7d^6 1995 7f 7f 7g 7g* 8d 7d 7m^6 Oct 28] lengthy gelding: poor mover: fair handicapper: made all in 19-runner apprentice race at Yarmouth in September: respectable efforts afterwards: stays 7f: acts on firm and dead going: visored (not penultimate outing) since fourth 5-y-o start: usually races prominently. *M. J. Heaton-Ellis* 67

THWAAB 3 b.g. Dominion 123 – Velvet Habit 89 (Habitat 134) [1994 –: 5m 5f 6g 6s 1995 7.1f^5 7m^3 7g^6 7.1g 7m^4 a8g^6 Nov 20] strong, good-bodied gelding: poor maiden: bred to be best at up to 1m. *F. Watson* 43

TIAMA (IRE) 2 b.f. (Feb 13) Last Tycoon 131 – Soyata (Bustino 136) [1995 7m^5 6s 7g Oct 9] 11,500F, 13,000Y: small filly: half-sister to fairly useful miler Hesell Street (by Dancing Dissident) and a middle-distance winner in Germany by Ela-Mana-Mou: dam unraced: poor form in maidens at Lingfield (2) and Leicester: jockey reported horse unsuited by soft ground second start: bred to stay further than 7f. *S. Dow* 50

TIBETAN 3 b.g. Reference Point 139 – Winter Queen 60 (Welsh Pageant 132) [1994 NR 1995 10g^5 10g^4 14d^4 16g^2 14g^2 Oct 23] good-topped gelding: seventh living foal: closely related to very useful 1m and 1¼m winner Main Objective (by Main Reef) and half-brother to smart stayer Safety In Numbers (by Slip Anchor): dam 4-y-o Irish 13f winner: fair maiden: consistent but showed unsatisfactory temperament second and third starts: stays 2m: tends to hang left: not one to trust implicitly: promising hurdler. *Lady Herries* 76 §

TICKA TICKA TIMING 2 b.c. (Feb 13) Timeless Times (USA) 99 – Belltina 41 (Belfort (FR) 89) [1995 6g 7m 7f 6m^6 a6g* 6f^6 a6g 6s a7g^3 Nov 6] small colt: first foal: dam, plater, stayed 7f: plater: won at Southwell in July: stays 7f: easily best efforts on fibresand: blinkered then visored second and third starts: inconsistent. *B. W. Murray* – a59

TICKERTY'S GIFT 5 b.g. Formidable (USA) 125 – Handy Dancer 87 (Green God 128) [1994 63, a–: 12d 10g 10d^5 12g^5 11.5m* 11.4m^5 12g a10g a16g 1995 12m Nov 6] good-topped gelding: impresses in appearance: just a modest performer at 4 yrs: no promise on belated return: stays 1½m: acts on dead ground and good to firm, –

probably not on soft: effective blinkered or not, visored (below form) last 3 starts at 4 yrs. *G. L. Moore*

TIDAL REACH (USA) 3 b.f. Kris S (USA) – Davie Lady (USA) (Bold And Brave) [1994 68p: 6f^5 6m^5 a8g* 8s^3 1995 10.5m 7.6m 10.3g^6 a9.4g^4 Jul 21] unfurnished filly: has scope: modest handicapper: stays 10.5f: acts on fibresand, soft ground and good to firm: sold 3,400 gns Newmarket December Sales. *A. Bailey* 62

TIDDY OGGIE 4 b.g. Nomination 125 – Careless Whisper (USA) (Broadway Forli (USA)) [1994 54+: a7g* 1995 a7g^5 a7g 6.1g 7f^3 8g 7m Jun 17] lengthy gelding: modest performer: only poor form at best in 1995: stays 1m: acts on firm ground: blinkered (no improvement) final 4-y-o start: inconsistent. *N. A. Graham* 44

TIGANA 3 b.f. Lugana Beach 116 – Tina's Beauty 41 (Tina's Pet 121) [1994 –: 6g 6m 10g 6d a7g a7g 1995 11.6m 7.6m^5 Aug 12] leggy filly: of little account. *Mrs L. C. Jewell* –

TIGER SHOOT 8 b.g. Indian King (USA) 128 – Grand Occasion 63 (Great Nephew 126) [1994 59, a69: 11.6d^3 a11g* a12g* a14g^2 a12g^3 11.6m^2 12m 16g^6 14.1d^5 1995 a11g^4 a13g^5 a12g^6 May 11] close-coupled, workmanlike gelding: fair handicapper: off course over 3 months, never placed to challenge nor knocked about at any stage at Southwell (trainer fined, jockey suspended and horse banned for 30 days as a result) final start, running on from last to finish sixth of 15: effective at 11f to 2m: acts on good to firm ground, soft and fibresand: has run creditably in a visor, not tried since 5 yrs: usually has tongue tied down: has run well when sweating: goes well with forcing tactics. *D. T. Thom* – a61 +

TIGERSONG (USA) 5 b.g. Seattle Song (USA) 130 – Tovalop (USA) (Northern Dancer) [1994 NR 1995 16m 14.1m Oct 26] workmanlike gelding: half-brother to 2 winners, notably smart miler Torrey Canyon (by Gone West): dam won 3 races at up to 1m: fairly useful (rated 90) but lightly raced (won maiden over 1½m at Leopardstown) at 2 and 3 yrs in Ireland for D. K. Weld: backward, tailed off in handicaps at Nottingham here: stays 1½m. *Miss M. K. Milligan* –

TIHEROS 3 ch.g. Risk Me (FR) 127 – Farras 86 (Song 132) [1994 73: 5v 5f^3 6g^4 6m^6 7s 6v a6g 1995 6d* 5d 6f 5.1m 5f^5 6g 6g Oct 16] quite good-topped gelding: only modest at best in 1995: won median auction maiden at Folkestone in March: trained until after fifth start by R. Hannon: tailed off afterwards: stays 6f: well below form 3 outings on very soft ground at 2 yrs: tried blinkered. *Jamie Poulton* 61 d

TIKKANEN (USA) 4 gr.c. Cozzene (USA) – Reiko (FR) (Targowice (USA) 130) [1994 130: 10.5v^3 10.5m* 10.5g^3 12d^4 12g^5 11g^2 12s^4 12f* 12f* 1995 12m^2 12f^4 12d^4 11f 12s^6 12f Dec 10] tall, handsome colt: won 1994 Breeders' Cup Turf: rather disappointing as 4-y-o: shaped well when neck second of 7 to Only Royale in steadily-run Jockey Club Stakes at Newmarket on reappearance but regressed gradually in Group 1/Grade 1 races, leaving J. Pease's stable after third start: should stay further than 1½m: smart form on dead going (below form on soft), but easily best efforts on top-of-the-ground: held up, and suited by a strongly-run race. *C. Clement, USA* 124 d

TILAAL (USA) 3 ch.c. Gulch (USA) – Eye Drop (USA) 96 (Irish River (FR) 131) [1994 NR 1995 10m^3 10g^4 10.3g^3 11.9m^6 8m^3 8m^4 10d Sep 22] strong, rangy colt: sixth foal: half-brother to 1992 Irish 2-y-o 7f winner Tbaareeh (by Chief's Crown) and useful 1½m (in France at 3 yrs) to 2m winner Latahaab (by Lyphard): dam 6f winner at 2 yrs (only season to race) out of Pushy: eye-catching third of 11 in maiden at Ripon on debut: failed to progress, looking ungenuine: stays 1¼m: visored (tailed off) final start: takes a good hold: best treated with caution: sold 16,000 gns Newmarket Autumn Sales. *E. A. L. Dunlop* 77 §

TILER (IRE) 3 br.g. Ballad Rock 122 – Fair Siobahn (Petingo 135) [1994 94p: a6g^5 7m* 7d* 7m^6 6g^6 6g 1995 7g^2 7m 7m^5 7g 8f 6m* 7m^2 6m 6g 7d 6f^3 Oct 31] tall, lengthy gelding: fairly useful handicapper: well drawn, won £15,000 20-runner race at York in August: stays 7f: acts on firm and dead ground: tends to wander under pressure: races prominently: inconsistent. *M. Johnston* 86

TILLANDSIA (IRE) 3 b.f. Unfuwain (USA) 131 – Till You (USA) (Exclusive Native (USA)) [1994 NR 1995 8.5m^2 10.5m* 10m^2 12m^2 12m^3 10g^2 10.1g^5 Sep 12] rangy, attractive filly: fifth reported foal: half-sister to a winner in Germany by Irish River: dam, 6f to 1m winner in USA, is half-sister to J O Tobin and Mysterious: 107

useful performer: odds on, won maiden at Haydock in May: second in Lupe Stakes at Goodwood, Ribblesdale Stakes (beaten 1¼ lengths by Phantom Gold) at Royal Ascot and valuable listed race (beaten head by Balanka) at Deauville: below form in listed race at Yarmouth final start: stays 1½m: has raced only on good or good to firm ground: usually front runner: to join J. Noseda in USA. *D. R. Loder*

TILLY OWL 4 b.f. Formidable (USA) 125 – Tilly Tavi 74 (Welsh Pageant 132) [1994 44: 10m 12.3f 11.1m 10m a11g⁶ 10g a7g* 1995 a8g a8g a7g² a7g* a8.5g⁵ a12g a7g³ Dec 2] small, angular filly: poor handicapper on her day: won at Wolverhampton in February: should stay 1m: acts on fibresand. *J. A. Harris* 47

TILLY TUPGILL 2 ch.f. (Mar 3) Domynsky 110 – Sarsta Grai 57 (Blakeney 126) [1995 7m a7g Aug 4] first foal: dam 1m (at 2 yrs) and 1½m winner, probably stayed 2m: well beaten in sellers. *M. D. Hammond* –

TILTHAMS 3 br.g. Prince Sabo 123 – Sparklingsovereign 53 (Sparkler 130) [1994 –: 5.1m 6m 5m 1995 8.2m 7g 10m May 27] angular gelding: no worthwhile form. *D. A. Wilson* –

TILTY (USA) 5 b.g. Linkage (USA) – En Tiempo (USA) (Bold Hour) [1994 63§: 14g 14g 20m 16.1m 17.2f³ 20f 1995 a16.2g 16m 14.1m Oct 26] rangy, good sort: modest staying handicapper: no worthwhile form in 1995, trained reappearance only by A. Forbes: acts on firm and dead ground: often blinkered or visored: needs plenty of driving: untrustworthy. *A. Streeter* – §

TIMARIDA (IRE) 3 gr.f. Kalaglow 132 – Triumphant 90 (Track Spare 125) [1994 NR 1995 7v* 7g* 8.5s* 8m* 8f³ 8g* 9.3d* 10g* Oct 15] 124

John Oxx's yard at the Curragh housed 1995's best filly or mare at a mile, in Ridgewood Pearl. No surprise there, but in another box at Currabeg stables he had a three-year-old who showed arguably the year's best form by a European-trained female over middle distances. This particular filly will not be well known in Britain, never having raced here, and although seen out on six occasions in Ireland and a winner on five of those, it is a fair bet that the title of top middle-distance filly accorded to Timarida will be something of a surprise to racegoers over there as well. Timarida has never raced over middle distances in her own country. It was October before she did so anywhere, and on the other side of the Atlantic that she registered her best effort.

On those six starts in Ireland, from mid-March (the first day of the season) until mid-September, Timarida did not look much better than useful on form. Her first four starts were winning ones, in a minor event at Leopardstown, an IR £16,250 handicap at the Curragh three and a half months later, and an IR £15,500 handicap at Galway and a listed race at Leopardstown in the space of a week at the start of August. Her margins of victory were two lengths, a neck, three lengths and four lengths. Things were not at all clear-cut, however, when Timarida stepped up to pattern races, in the Desmond Stakes at the Curragh. Starting 5/4 favourite, she was involved in a three-way photo-finish and one of those rare stewards' inquiries in

Sunset & Vine Prix de l'Opera, Longchamp—Timarida is in unstoppable form

H. H. Aga Khan's "Timarida"

which the third horse gets promoted to first. There were only five runners but three of them got in each other's way before Ivory Frontier passed the post in front of Timarida and Mr Martini, Timarida having every chance and edging right under left-handed driving. Three weeks later at the same course in the Trusted Partner Matron Stakes it was close again between her and the Newmarket-trained pair Lap of Luxury and Warning Shadows, but this time Timarida emerged on top and the principals gave each other a wider berth.

In both of those Group 3 contests, Timarida had come through to dispute the lead at the two-furlong marker but had not been able to put daylight between herself and her rivals. Steps up in class and distance on her two remaining starts saw her challenges turn into runaway triumphs, the Sunset & Vine Prix de L'Opera at Longchamp on Arc day falling to her by two and a half lengths and the E. P. Taylor Stakes at Woodbine by three and a half. Timarida claimed some notable scalps. A ten-runner field in the Opera included the previous year's Opera and E. P. Taylor first-past-the-posts in Erin Bird and Truly A Dream, and the Norwegian and German classic winners Kill The Crab and Tryphosa, the last-named being one of four in the field who had run in the Prix de Diane. In the end, it was the Prix de Psyche winner Angel In My Heart who gave Timarida most to do, but that wasn't much. A fortnight later in Canada, Poule d'Essai des Pouliches winner Matiara, Truly A Dream, Take Liberties and Warning Shadows joined a group of smart North American fillies in opposition to Timarida. The Irish three-year-old again came home alone. Matiara's poor luck in running made Timarida's task easier, but there is no getting away from the fact that this was a very good performance.

Timarida's sire Kalaglow died in Germany in 1994 and her dam Triumphant made a less than triumphant appearance in the sale-ring at Goffs the same year, fetching just IR 5,200 guineas. Jeune, Munwar and Sternkoenig were other notable winners for Kalaglow around the world in 1995. Triumphant's earlier producing record was a respectable one—four winners from seven previous foals, including the fairly useful pair Double Entendre (by Dominion) and Timiniya (by Kahyasi)—but she was kept in the Aga Khan's broodmare band for less than eight years, having entered it when the Aga Khan purchased mares from the Cleaboy Stud stock developed by Major Lionel Holliday. Triumphant did all her racing at around seven furlongs or a mile, showing fairly useful form and winning once, and she is a daughter of Pugnacity, a smart filly over sprint distances at two years and over five furlongs and a mile at three. Pugnacity was rather disappointing on the racecourse as a four-year-old but plenty more has been heard of her at stud; she produced seven winners from eight foals of racing age, including the top-class middle-distance performer Relkino.

Timarida (IRE) (gr.f. 1992)	Kalaglow (gr 1978)	Kalamoun (gr 1970)	Zeddaan
			Khairunissa
		Rossiter (ch 1970)	Pall Mall
			Sonia
	Triumphant (b 1977)	Track Spare (b 1963)	Sound Track
			Rosy Myth
		Pugnacity (b 1962)	Pampered King
			Ballynulta

Timarida's emergence as a middle-distance performer comes as no surprise given the influence of Kalaglow, and the dam had shown that she could produce a horse with stamina when the aforementioned Timiniya, also trained by Oxx, finished fourth in the 1994 Irish Cesarewitch. Timarida stays in training and deserves to get a chance at a mile and a half. A big, workmanlike filly who is sometimes bandaged, Timarida raced on going that ranged from firm to heavy in her appearances at up to a mile, showing that she probably acts on any. She looks certain to win more good races at middle distances and it would not take much more improvement to see her land one of the very best. *J. Oxx, Ireland*

TIME AGAIN 5 b.g. Then Again 126 – Vaula 49 (Henbit (USA) 130) [1994 NR 1995 8g 9.2g Sep 24] rangy gelding: rated 85 in 1993 for L. Cumani: soundly beaten in 1995. *T. Dyer* –

TIME ALLOWED 2 b.f. (Apr 2) Sadler's Wells (USA) 132 – Time Charter 131 (Saritamer (USA) 130) [1995 7m Aug 12] rather unfurnished filly: fifth foal: half-sister to smart stayer Zinaad and useful 1988 2-y-o 7f winner By Charter (both by Shirley Heights): dam top-class middle-distance performer (also second in 1000 Guineas) out of sister to Nicholas Bill and Centroline: 20/1, down the field behind Silver Prey in maiden at Newbury: likely to do better. *M. R. Stoute* – p

TIME CLASH 2 b.f. (Mar 27) Timeless Times (USA) 99 – Ash Amour 54 (Hotfoot 126) [1995 a5g^{6} 6f^{4} 6.1m^{5} 6g* 7.3d 7g 6.1s a7g a6g* a6g^{2} Dec 19] 1,400F, 1,500Y: sparely-made filly: first foal: dam 1¼m winner who stayed 1½m: won selling nursery at Leicester in August and nursery at Lingfield in December: well below form in between: should stay beyond 6f: may well be unsuited by a soft surface. *B. Palling* 63 a67

TIME FOR ACTION (IRE) 3 b.g. Alzao (USA) 117 – Beyond Words (Ballad Rock 122) [1994 76: 6m 7.1g^{3} 8.3g* 8d^{4} 1995 12.3m 12g^{4} 12m 11.9m^{2} 10m^{4} 12m Nov 4] small gelding: fairly useful handicapper: needs further than 1¼m (should stay beyond 1½m): acts on good to firm and dead ground. *M. H. Tompkins* 90

TIME FOR A GLASS 2 b.f. (Apr 23) Timeless Times (USA) 99 – Marie Zephyr 75 (Treboro (USA) 114) [1995 5f^{5} 7g^{4} Aug 26] second reported foal: dam maiden who stayed 13f: well beaten in claimer at Edinburgh and maiden at Newcastle: withdrawn on vet's advice at start of maiden at Ayr in September. *W. T. Kemp* –

TIME FOR TEA (IRE) 2 ch.f. (Apr 28) Imperial Frontier (USA) 112 – Glowing Embers 107 (Nebbiolo 125) [1995 5m 6m^{2} 6f^{4} 6f^{3} 5.2f^{3} a5g^{2} a6g^{5} Nov 14] 5,200Y: sturdy filly: fifth foal: closely related to fairly useful 1m and 1¼m winner Valley of Fire (by Dancing Brave): dam, 7f and 1¼m winner, half-sister to Kalaglow: fair maiden: bred to stay further than 6f: has raced only on top-of-the-ground and equitrack. *C. A. Cyzer* 73

TIME IS MONEY (IRE) 3 br.g. Sizzling Melody 117 – Tiempo 50 (King of Spain 121) [1994 52: 6m 5m 5.3m^3 6v 6s^6 1995 6.9m^6 6g^6 6g^6 5m^5 5g 5.2m^3 6g a5g 5.1m Oct 19] workmanlike gelding: modest maiden handicapper: well below form last 3 starts: stays 6f: acts on good to firm ground, not disgraced on soft: visored (met trouble in running) fifth 3-y-o start. *M. H. Tompkins* 54

TIME LEADER 3 ch.c. Lead On Time (USA) 123 – Green Leaf (USA) 97 (Alydar (USA)) [1994 65p: 6.1d^3 1995 7m 10m 8m^4 8m Jul 1] quite attractive colt: shows a quick action: fair maiden: visored, tailed-off last of 9 in Newmarket claimer on final start, dropping himself out when ridden 3f out: should stay 1¼m: one to treat with caution: sold (M. Stoute to R. Dickin) 4,000 gns Newmarket July Sales. *M. R. Stoute* 67 §

TIMELESS 3 b.f. Royal Academy (USA) 130 – Glory of Hera 99 (Formidable (USA) 125) [1994 NR 1995 11.4m^6 10g^5 8f^3 Oct 18] 39,000Y: long-backed, attractive filly: fifth live foal: half-sister to 4-y-o 1½m winner Neptunalia (by Slip Anchor) and French middle-distance winner Savonarole (by Shirley Heights): dam fairly useful sprinter as 2-y-o: modest form in maidens: probably stays 11.4f: sold 6,000 gns Newmarket December Sales. *H. R. A. Cecil* 58

TIMELY EXAMPLE (USA) 4 ch.c. Timeless Moment (USA) – Dearest Mongo (USA) (Mongo) [1994 66: 7g^2 8.5m^3 8m^5 10.3m^3 10g^4 1995 a7g Feb 18] workmanlike colt: fair maiden: well beaten only outing in 1995. *B. R. Cambidge* –

TIME OF NIGHT (USA) 2 gr. or ro.f. (May 1) Night Shift (USA) – Tihama (USA) (Sassafras (FR) 135) [1995 7m^5 8.1m^4 6.1d^6 6d^3 Sep 27] $23,000F, 17,500Y: leggy, unfurnished filly: has a quick action: half-sister to 2 winners in North America: dam won in North America: fair maiden: gave strong impression last 2 starts finds 6f much too sharp, and will stay further than 1m. *R. Guest* 65

TIMES OF TIMES (IRE) 2 b.f. (Mar 10) Distinctly North (USA) 115 – Lady Fandet (Gay Fandango (USA) 132) [1995 a5g^6 6m* a6g^3 6.1m* 6f* 6m^3 6f* 6m^2 7g* 7g^6 6f* 5m^6 a6g Nov 14] 2,500Y, 3,600 2-y-o: rather leggy filly: half-sister to 3-y-o Jilly Jaffa Cake (by Waajib) and leading bumpers winner Rhythm Section (by Where To Dance): dam, lightly raced, from family of Circus Plume: fair performer: won maiden auction at Folkestone, sellers at Nottingham and Folkestone, nursery at Warwick, claimer at Brighton (claimed out of D. Cosgrove's stable £10,000) and nursery at Redcar: suited by 6f/7f: acts on firm ground, below form on all-weather: tended to hang right throughout penultimate start. *M. J. Ryan* 78 a50

TIME STAR (USA) 4 b.c. Manila (USA) – Valdemosa (ARG) (Ringaro (USA)) [1994 114: 10d* 10s^3 12m* 1995 12m^3 12f^3 12f^6 12g Jul 11] tall, lengthy colt: good walker: powerful mover: smart performer: operated on in January for stomach problem: best efforts when third of 7 in slowly-run races for Jockey Club Stakes (2¾ lengths behind Only Royale) at Newmarket and Coronation Cup (made much of running, just over a length behind Sunshack) at Epsom: disappointing in Hardwicke Stakes at Royal Ascot and Princess of Wales's Stakes at Newmarket afterwards: probably better at 1½m than shorter: acts on soft ground and firm: often awkward in preliminaries first 2 seasons: usually races prominently: sent to USA. *P. F. I. Cole* 119

TIME TO FLY 2 b.c. (Apr 15) Timeless Times (USA) 99 – Dauntless Flight (Golden Mallard 103) [1995 5m^5 5f 6h^3 5m^5 5h^3 5m 6f^2 Oct 24] good-topped colt: fourth reported foal: half-brother to 6f winner Dauntless Fort (by Belfort): dam unraced: modest maiden: stays 6f: acts on hard ground: consistent. *B. W. Murray* 59

TIME TO TANGO 2 b.f. (May 3) Timeless Times (USA) 99 – Tangalooma 56 (Hotfoot 126) [1995 5f^5 5f^2 Oct 24] fourth foal: half-sister to Italian 4-y-o Sparrow (by Belfort), successful from 6f (at 2 yrs) to 1¼m: dam (maiden on flat stayed 1½m) won over hurdles: similar form in maiden events at Catterick and Redcar, keeping on strongly to be beaten head by Mister Joel in median auction contest last time: will stay 6f: will improve. *G. M. Moore* 57 p

TIMSON 2 ch.g. (May 22) Timeless Times (USA) 99 – Pickwood Sue 74 (Right Boy 137) [1995 5m a6g^4 a6g a7g a6g Jul 22] half-brother to several winners, including sprinters by Workboy (2) and Morston: dam 5f winner: plater. *J. P. Leigh* –

TINA KATERINA 2 ch.f. (Apr 26) Executive Man 119 – Tria Romantica (Another Realm 118) [1995 6.1d 7g a6g a8.5g^2 Nov 27] 3,000 2-y-o: plain, good-topped filly: fourth foal: sister to Italian 5f to 7.5f winner Executive Passione: 42

dam Italian maiden: neck second of 4 in nursery at Wolverhampton: needs further than 6f (stays 8.5f): acts on fibresand. *R. Champion*

TINA'S CHARM (IRE) 6 b.m. Hatim (USA) 121 – Tinas Image (He Loves Me 120) [1994 41: 10m 10.5m 8.3m 8s^4 10.8s^4 1995 a10g 10.3g Mar 24] angular, shallow-girthed mare: poor mover: poor maiden on flat: should stay 1¼m: probably acts on any turf going: tried in blinkers in 1993: won selling hurdle in April *J. S. Moore* –

TINASHAAN (IRE) 3 b.f. Darshaan 133 – Catina 102 (Nureyev (USA) 131) [1994 NR 1995 7m^2 8m^2 10.3g^2 11.5m* 12m^2 12g* 12d Sep 24] workmanlike filly: third foal: half-sister to a German middle-distance winner by Mtoto: dam, Irish 2-y-o 6f winner suited by 1m, is half-sister to Premio Regina Elena winner Rosananti and good English and German performer Claddagh: useful performer: won 7-runner maiden at Yarmouth in July and minor event at Kempton (3-runner race, had little more than an exercise canter) in September: 2½ lengths second to Hagwah in listed race at Newmarket in between: stays 1½m: acts on good to firm ground, possibly not on good to soft: wears blanket for stalls entry. *J. R. Fanshawe* 100

TINA'S RIDGE 2 ch.c. (Apr 19) Indian Ridge 123 – Polly's Pear (USA) (Sassafras (FR) 135) [1995 6f^2 6m* Aug 28] angular colt: sixth foal: half-brother to useful 3-y-o 1¾m winner Pedraza (by Belmez) and several other winners: dam never ran: won maiden at Epsom, finishing strongly: would have been suited by 7f+: looked sure to do better: dead. *R. Hannon* 86

TINKER AMELIA 3 b.f. Damister (USA) 123 – Miss Primula 81 (Dominion 123) [1994 53: 7s a6g^5 1995 a6g a6g^2 a6g^5 a6g^6 7g 5m^2 7m^3 6m^4 5m 6g^4 5m 6d Nov 7] modest maiden: sold out of W. Muir's stable 2,000 gns Doncaster March Sales after fourth 3-y-o start: better form afterwards in Ireland: stays 6f: acts on good to firm ground and equitrack (below form all 3 starts on fibresand). *J. G. McDonnell, Ireland* 64

TINKER OSMASTON 4 br.f. Dunbeath (USA) 127 – Miss Primula 81 (Dominion 123) [1994 64: 6m 6f 6m 6g^4 6f^2 6m 5m^2 5m^4 6m^5 5m^3 6.1g 1995 5.1m 5m 5.7f* 6.1g^5 6m^2 5.7m^3 6f^6 5.1m^4 6g 5g^4 5.1d* 6.1s^2 5.1m 5m Nov 4] workmanlike filly: fair handicapper: won at Bath in May and Chepstow in October: stays 6f: acts on firm ground, goes particularly well on a soft surface: effective blinkered at 3 yrs (not tried in 1995): usually held up. *M. S. Saunders* 79

TINKLERS FOLLY 3 ch.g. Bairn (USA) 126 – Lucky Straw 57 (Tumble Wind (USA)) [1994 47: 7g^3 8f^6 7s 7s 1995 7g 8g^4 8.1g 7.1m^2 7.1f^2 10f^4 8.1f* 8m^3 8.3f^4 7.1m^3 8d Sep 22] strong, sturdy gelding: poor handicapper: won at Edinburgh in July: best form at up to 1m: acts on firm ground, no form on a soft surface: usually races prominently. *Denys Smith* 48

TIN MAN 2 b.c. (Apr 3) Tina's Pet 121 – April Flower (Parva Stella) [1995 5.1f^5 5m^6 5.1m 6m^6 Aug 14] smallish, leggy colt: second foal: dam selling hurdler: poor form: tailed off in seller last time: sold 450 gns Doncaster September Sales. *B. A. McMahon* –

TINO TERE 6 ch.g. Clantime 101 – Blueit (FR) 101 (Bold Lad (IRE) 133) [1994 70: 5m^6 5f^2 5m^3 5.1g 5g 5g^6 1995 5g^6 5g 5f Jun 21] sturdy gelding: good walker: modest handicapper at best in 1995: stays an easy 6f: acts on firm ground, dead and all-weather surfaces: blinkered (well below form) once at 3 yrs and on final 5-y-o outing: front runner. *J. Balding* 59

TINTARA (IRE) 2 b.f. (May 9) Caerleon (USA) 132 – Justsayno (USA) (Dr Blum (USA)) [1995 7g 7m a8g^3 Nov 14] tall, leggy filly: has plenty of scope: fourth foal: half-sister to Italian 3-y-o 9f and 1½m winner Spus (by Alzao): dam, 5f winner at 2 yrs, later smart at around 1m, second in Grade 1 7f Matron Stakes: tenderly handled when mid-division in 2 large fields of maidens on turf: well-backed favourite, respectable third of 8 in maiden at Lingfield: should be suited by 1¼m+: will probably do better. *B. W. Hills* 63 p

TINY ASTRO 2 b.g. (May 1) Superpower 113 – Moonwalker (Night Shift (USA)) [1995 5g^6 Apr 10] 1,000Y: second foal: half-brother to 3-y-o Rock Rambler (by Rock City): dam unraced: 33/1, last of 6 in maiden auction at Edinburgh. *M. H. Easterby* –

TIP THE DOVE 6 br.m. Riberetto 107 – Nimble Dove 62 (Starch Reduced 112) [1994 NR 1995 a10g^{6} 10s 16.2m Apr 15] plain mare: third foal: half-sister to a winning hurdler: dam soft-ground stayer who also won over hurdles: fair NH Flat race winner in 1993/4: modest form at best in novice hurdles in 1994/5: tailed off on flat. *R. J. Price* –

TIRA HEIGHTS (USA) 3 gr.g. Bering 136 – Tira (FR) (Bellypha 130) [1994 83+: 7g^{6} 7m^{5} 8s* 7.3d 1995 10m 12g^{5} 13.3d 10g Sep 29] rather leggy, close-coupled gelding: fairly useful winner at 2 yrs: soundly beaten in 1995: should prove very well suited by 1¼m+: acts on soft ground: sold (R. Armstrong to J. J. O'Neill) 10,000 gns Doncaster November Sales. *R. W. Armstrong* –

TIRLIE (IRE) 3 b.g. Tirol 127 – Lisa's Favourite (Gorytus (USA) 132) [1994 –: 6d 7g 1995 8d Apr 6] big, good-topped gelding: no worthwhile form. *J. W. Payne* –

TIROLEAN GOLD 3 b.f. Tirol 127 – Pale Gold (FR) (New Chapter 106) [1994 NR 1995 8f^{4} Jun 22] 7,500Y: angular filly: half-sister to several winners, including (at 1¼m) fairly useful My Tony (by Be My Guest) and 7f winner Desert Nomad (by Green Desert): dam minor French 6.5f and 11.5f winner: 26 lengths last of 4 in maiden at Ripon: sold 580 gns Doncaster September Sales. *M. H. Easterby* –

TIROLETTE (IRE) 3 b.f. Tirol 127 – Etage (Ile de Bourbon (USA) 133) [1994 60: 7g 7m 7m 6s^{4} 6g 8m 1995 10.3m 10g^{3} 10.1d* 11.5f^{5} 12m* 11.9g 12m Oct 27] tall, leggy filly: modest handicapper: won apprentice races at Yarmouth (gamely) in June and Ascot (after 8-week break) in August: stays 1½m: acts on good to firm and dead ground: carried head awkwardly second 3-y-o start, blinkered afterwards: not one to trust implicitly. *R. J. R. Williams* 64

TIROLLAC (IRE) 3 br.f. Tirol 127 – Lago Real (Kings Lake (USA) 133) [1994 –: 6m 6d^{5} 6d 7d^{6} 6m 1995 10m 8.1m^{4} 8f^{3} 8m^{4} 7g 8d Sep 26] lengthy, unfurnished filly: poor mover: poor maiden: probably stays 1¼m: acts on firm ground: tried blinkered/visored at 2 yrs: has run creditably for amateur: sold 650 gns Ascot October Sales. *L. G. Cottrell* 38

TIROLS TYRANT (IRE) 2 b.g. (Feb 12) Tirol 127 – Justitia (Dunbeath (USA) 127) [1995 7m Aug 25] 15,500Y: smallish, leggy gelding: second foal: half-brother to Belgian 3-y-o 5f (at 2 yrs) to 7f winner Justinianus (by Try My Best): dam won 6 races at 3 yrs in Belgium: 50/1 and green, around 9 lengths eighth of 19 to Even Top in steadily-run maiden at Newmarket, close up over 5f: should improve. *Mrs A. Swinbank* 67 p

TISH 3 b.f. Kabour 80 – Boldera 69 (Persian Bold 123) [1994 37: 5m 6g^{3} 6g 10g 1995 a5g^{6} 6s 5m^{6} 6.1g a6g^{6} a8g May 11] small, leggy filly: poor plater: appeared not to stay 1¼m at 2 yrs, and ran creditably over 5f on reappearance: acts on fibresand: below form in blinkers. *A. Smith* 33

TISSUE OF LIES (USA) 2 b. or br.c. (Mar 28) Ascot Knight (CAN) 130 – Choral Group (CAN) (Lord Durham (CAN)) [1995 9g^{6} 10m^{5} a8g^{2} Nov 14] $18,000F: 4,400Y: rangy colt: has scope: half-brother to several winners here and in USA, including useful 1m winner Balakirev (by Nijinsky) and fairly useful 10.1f winner Choir Master (by Assert): dam joint top-rated Canadian filly at 2 yrs in 1981: progressive form in maidens: seemed not quite to stay 1¼m: can improve again. *M. Johnston* 79 p

TITANIA'S DANCE (IRE) 4 br.f. Fairy King (USA) – Camden Dancer (Camden Town 125) [1994 NR 1995 a8g a8g Feb 2] quite good-topped filly: lightly raced and no form since 1993: sold 3,500 gns Ascot February Sales. *M. Bell* –

TITANIUM HONDA (IRE) 4 gr.g. Doulab (USA) 115 – Cumbrian Melody 83 (Petong 126) [1994 –: 5s 6g a7g^{6} a6g a7g a7g 1995 a7g^{6} a8g^{4} a8g^{4} a8g^{5} a6g^{2} a8g^{5} a7g* a7g a7g 7g 6g a8g^{3} 7f a6g^{6} 8h 7g Sep 12] sturdy gelding: poor handicapper on the all-weather, successful in maiden event at Southwell in April: no worthwhile form on turf: effective at 6f, and stays 1m: acts on the all-weather: tried blinkered, no improvement: sold 3,000 gns Newmarket Autumn Sales. *C. E. Brittain* – a50

TITUS LIVIUS (FR) 2 ch.c. (Feb 28) Machiavellian (USA) 123 – Party Doll 108 (Be My Guest (USA) 126) [1995 6g^{3} 5.5g*^{dis} 7s^{4} 6.5g* 6.5g* Nov 7] 113 +

From a two-year-old string of just twenty-five, Chantilly trainer Jonathan Pease sent out three individual pattern winners in Prix de Cabourg winner With Fascination (also runner-up in the Prix Morny and Prix de la Salamandre), Prix

Criterium des 2 Ans, Evry—left to right, Titus Livius beats Starmaniac and Seattle Special again

Saint-Roman winner Spinning World and Titus Livius, first past the post in three such events in the autumn. The last-named pair, owned by Stavros Niarchos, were part of the batch transferred to Pease's stable after the death of Francois Boutin early in the year. Over the years Boutin introduced several good Niarchos two-year-olds in the Prix Yacowlef, a listed event for newcomers at the beginning of Deauville's August meeting, among them Titus Livius' sire Machiavellian. Titus Livius could not emulate his sire by winning, and finished just over a length third of four after making most. Nonetheless, he was stepped up to pattern company in the Prix d'Arenberg at Chantilly at the beginning of September and duly showed considerable improvement. Third favourite behind Shining Molly, who had been beaten a nose in the Prix Robert Papin, and the unbeaten filly Branston Jewel, who had looked a useful sprinter in the making when winning at York, he came from off the pace to lead over a furlong out, then sprinted clear to win by four lengths from the outsider Ella Nico. Ultimately though, Titus Livius' impressive performance earned him little more than prestige. Over two months later he was disqualified and placed last for returning a positive post-race urine sample. The offending substance was dembrexine, the active ingredient of a cough medicine.

Titus Livius' next appearance was in the Prix de la Salamandre at Longchamp, a race Niarchos and Boutin had dominated, winning six runnings between 1983 and 1993. The colt did not live up to expectations. With Fascination came out best of the French runners in second, splitting the British pair Lord of Men and Woodborough, Titus Livius beaten a total of four lengths in fourth. Looking rather warm and taking a good hold, Titus Livius was unable to quicken when a gap opened in the straight, seeming barely to get the trip. A month later, back at Deauville, Titus Livius was made favourite for the six-and-a-half-furlong Prix Eclipse. Again he faced a couple of British challengers in Apple Musashi, winner of his previous start at Lingfield by eight lengths, and Rabican, a course-and-distance winner of a valuable listed race in August. In the end it was Starmaniac who gave Titus Livius the most to do once he got a run, but Titus Livius just held on, with Seattle Special third. The first three clashed again on the same terms in the Criterium des 2 Ans (formerly the seven-furlong Criterium de Maisons-Laffitte) and filled the same three places, this time Titus Livius winning by a short neck, having had plenty to do a furlong out.

Unbeaten as a two-year-old (he won the Prix Morny as well and topped the Free Handicap) Machiavellian showed very smart form at three but had an unfortunate time of it, meeting trouble in both the Guineas and the Irish Guineas. He was retired after an inconclusive return to sprinting in the Prix Maurice de Gheest. He has made a most promising start at Dalham Hall, with Poule d'Essai des Poulains winner Vettori and Ribblesdale and St Simon Stakes winner Phantom Gold among his first crop. Also owned by Niarchos and trained by Boutin, Titus Livius' dam Party Doll was a useful two-year-old, winning three times at up to six furlongs (including listed races at Bordeaux and Deauville), and fourth in the one-mile Prix d'Aumale. After a winning reappearance in a one-mile listed race, she failed to stay the ten and a half furlongs of the Prix Penelope. Titus Livius is Party Doll's second foal, after the unraced Baillamont filly Party Bloom. The next dam Midnight Lady ran twice for Peter Walwyn as a two-year-old, winning a Nottingham maiden and finishing fifth in the May Hill Stakes. Party Doll is the best of her seven winning progeny to date; she also produced the useful 1986 French two-year-old Microcosme (by Golden Fleece). Like her daughter and granddaughter, Mia Pola was a successful two-year-old and a smart one at that, winning the Prix la Rochette. She was a half-sister to the top French two-year-old of 1964 Grey Dawn and the 1966 Poule d'Essai des Pouliches winner Right Away. This is the same family as Alhaarth, who shares an ancestress with Titus Livius in Mia Pola's grandam Ampola.

Titus Livius (FR) (ch.c. Feb 28, 1993)	Machiavellian (USA) (b 1987)	Mr Prospector (b 1970)	Raise A Native
			Gold Digger
		Coup de Folie (b 1982)	Halo
			Raise The Standard
	Party Doll (ch 1986)	Be My Guest (ch 1974)	Northern Dancer
			What A Treat
		Midnight Lady (b 1975)	Mill Reef
			Mia Pola

The chances are that Titus Livius' three-year-old campaign will set out on a similar path to those of his sire and dam. He is reportedly to reappear in the Prix Djebel in the spring, when a good performance would no doubt see him contesting one of the Guineas. However, on his Salamandre running he will be well worth opposing at a mile. *J. E. Pease, France*

T'NIEL 4 ch.f. Librate 91 – Classy Colleen (St Paddy 133) [1994 –: 10.3m 8m 7g a8.5g^6 1995 a9.4g 7m 10m Aug 21] lightly-made filly: no worthwhile form. *G. Fierro* –

TOASTED 3 b.f. Statoblest 120 – Load Line (High Line 125) [1994 61: 6g^6 6g^4 1995 5g 7.1m^2 Jul 2] smallish filly: modest maiden: looked awkward ride final start: should be suited by further than 6f. *W. Jarvis* 53

TOAT CHIEFTAIN 3 b.g. Puissance 110 – Tribal Lady 80 (Absalom 128) [1994 –: 7g 1995 8g 9m 15.4g 14d a10g^4 a11g^6 a10g Nov 25] stocky gelding: modest maiden at best: sold out of G. Harwood's stable 600 gns Newmarket Autumn Sales after fourth 3-y-o start: inconsistent. *D. Morris* 51

TOBAGO BOY 3 b.g. Colmore Row 111 – Perfect Double 43 (Double Form 130) [1994 –: 6g 7s 7d 1995 7g 8.1g 10m 11.1f Jun 15] no worthwhile form: tried visored. *M. G. Meagher* –

TOCCO JEWEL 5 br.m. Reesh 117 – Blackpool Belle 70 (The Brianstan 128) [1994 38: a10g^3 8m 8d 10g 10.1m^5 10m 10d a11g 1995 11.1g 10m 10m 8g 9.7m^6 11.6m Aug 7] smallish mare: poor plater: stays 1¼m: best effort on soft ground: tried blinkered. *M. J. Ryan* 22

TODAY'S FANCY 7 b.g. Today And Tomorrow 78 – Fancy Pages 67 (Touch Paper 113) [1994 NR 1995 a10g Sep 5] tall, leggy gelding: of little account nowadays. *D. C. O'Brien* –

TODAY TONITE 3 b.f. Adbass (USA) 102 – Meet Again (Lomond (USA) 128) [1994 54: 6g 6d 6v a6g 1995 8g^4 8.1m 8m 10.1m* 11.6m^3 11.9f^3 Aug 22] small filly: poor performer: won seller at Yarmouth in July: stays 1½m: acts on firm ground: best effort at 2 yrs on equitrack. *J. Pearce* 42

TODD (USA) 4 b.g. Theatrical 128 – Boldara (USA) (Alydar (USA)) [1994 8g 8.5g^6 10m^2 8g^4 12g 10d 1995 10m 12m a10g^6 a12g Nov 29] fourth foal: closely related to French 2-y-o 6f winner Miss Heidi (by Nureyev) and half-brother to 2 winners in USA by Nijinsky: dam, stakes winner in USA (best at around 1m), is half-sister to high-class (at up to 1½m) Nasty And Bold: fair maiden (rated 73) at 3 yrs in Ireland for D. Weld, though failed to repeat form shown on third start: sold 13,000 gns Newmarket Autumn (1994) Sales: well beaten here: stays 1¼m: acts on good to firm ground: blinkered (finished last) final 3-y-o start. *P. Mitchell* –

TOE TAPPIN MUSIC (USA) 2 b.g. (Apr 4) Show Dancer (USA) – Miss Garrett (USA) (Speak John) [1995 5m^6 6.1d 5g Oct 16] $5,200F, $7,500Y: good-topped gelding: eighth foal: half-brother to several minor winners in USA: dam ran 4 times in USA: sire high class at 1m/9f at 5 yrs: signs of ability in maiden events at Sandown, Nottingham and (blinkered) Folkestone. *Martyn Meade* –

TOFFEE 2 ch.f. (Feb 9) Midyan (USA) 124 – Vaula 49 (Henbit (USA) 130) [1995 6g^5 7.5m^2 7m 7d Sep 26] 16,000Y: unfurnished filly: has a quick action: fifth foal: sister to 1991 French 2-y-o 5f winner Amizour and half-sister to 7f winner Time Again (by Then Again): dam won over middle distances at 4 yrs: absent nearly 2½ months, easily best effort when second to easy winner Myrtle in maiden at Beverley: will be well suited by middle distances: will stay 1m+. *J. R. Fanshawe* 66 +

TOKANDA 11 ch.g. Record Token 128 – Andalucia 57 (Rheingold 137) [1994 NR 1995 a13g^5 a13g Feb 2] workmanlike gelding: of little account on flat nowadays: tried blinkered and visored: ungenuine pointer and bad steeplechaser. *F. J. Yardley* –

TOLENT (IRE) 3 b.f. Taufan (USA) 119 – Green Bonnet (FR) (Green Dancer (USA) 132) [1994 47: 6g^4 5.1m^5 7f^6 7m 1995 6.9d a8g 6.5h 6g a9.3g a7.5g 7.5g^5 9f 11g^3 12f^5 10f 8f Aug 20] good-topped Belgian-trained filly: poor maiden: tailed off at Folkestone on reappearance only 3-y-o start in Britain: stays 11f. *H. Vanderdussen, Belgium* 22

TOLLS CHOICE (IRE) 6 ch.g. Sun Valley 103 – Creativity (Creative Plan (USA)) [1994 60: 10d^5 9.9d 8f* 8.5m 9.9m 8.5g^5 8.1d 8g 8d a8g 1995 7.5m^4 8m 8m 8.5m^4 8f* 8g^4 8m^6 8.5d^4 8f^4 7m^6 7.5m^5 8d Sep 22] leggy, angular gelding: modest handicapper: won ladies race at Redcar in May: best at around 1m: probably acts on any ground: effective blinkered or not: best 6-y-o efforts when held up. *M. W. Easterby* 56

TOMAL 3 b.g. King Among Kings 60 – Jacinda (Thatching 131) [1994 57: 5f 5g* 5.3f^6 5.1g^4 5g^6 6g^5 6.1d 1995 5m 6m 5m a5g^6 7f^5 6.9f^2 8f^3 8g 8.5s^6 7f^5 6.9g^5 7f a7g Dec 14] small gelding: modest handicapper: stays 8.5f: acts on firm ground, probably on soft: well beaten in blinkers: sometimes bandaged behind: withdrawn after giving trouble in preliminaries once in November. *R. Ingram* 54

TOMBA LA BOMBA (USA) 2 b. or br.c. (Apr 16) Green Dancer (USA) 132 – Easter Mary (USA) (Lord Avie (USA)) [1995 8d Sep 26] $60,000Y: fourth foal: half-brother to 2 minor winners in USA: dam, minor 8.5f stakes winner in USA, third in Grade 2 6f event at 2 yrs: 33/1, in need of race and very green, always behind in 20-runner maiden at Newmarket. *P. A. Kelleway* –

TOM MORGAN 4 b.g. Faustus (USA) 118 – Pirate Maid (Auction Ring (USA) 123) [1994 83: 6v^6 8d 8m* 7d^4 6.9g^6 6m* 6g^4 7.6g* 7f 6g^4 7m* 1995 7.3g 7g^5 7.3d 7g Sep 30] lengthy, good-topped gelding: fairly useful handicapper: ran creditably in 1995 only on second start: stays 7.6f: acts on heavy going and good to firm: won in first-time visor at 2 yrs, has worn one only once since: often forces pace. *P. T. Walwyn* 83

TOMMY COOPER 4 br.c. Macmillion 110 – My Charade 79 (Cawston's Clown 113) [1994 52: 11.4s^6 14.1m^2 16.2m^4 16g^4 14.1g 1995 14.1m^6 14.9m^5 18.2m^2 16m^2 16.4m^6 16d 17.2m^6 Sep 25] leggy colt: poor maiden handicapper: thorough stayer: acts on good to firm and dead ground: tried visored: often sweats: wears crossed noseband: sometimes bandaged behind: may prove best with strong handling. *Mrs Barbara Waring* 46

TOMMYKNOCKER (IRE) 3 ch.g. Woodman (USA) 126 – Repercutionist (USA) 111 (Beaudelaire (USA) 125) [1994 49d: 5m 6g^6 6m 7g^5 7m 8g^6 10s^4 8m 1995 12d^5 14.1g^5 14.1m 16m^4 Jul 22] leggy, angular gelding: disappointing maiden: stays at least 1¼m: acts on good to firm ground, probably on soft: tried blinkered: looked none too keen over hurdles in December. *J. R. Jenkins* 39 d

TOMMY TEMPEST 6 ch.g. Northern Tempest (USA) 120 – Silently Yours (USA) 53 (Silent Screen (USA)) [1994 –, a43: a5g a5g a5g a7g a6g 5d a5g* 5m^6 a5g^2 5.1s a5g^4 a5g a5g 1995 a5g a5g a5g a5g^3 a5g^4 a5g 5g a5g^6 a6g a5g a5g* a5g^6 5.1h^2 5.1m 5m^6 5.7h a5g Nov 30] angular gelding: poor 5f performer: left A. Bailey's stable after fifth 6-y-o start: 25/1, made all in 5-runner claimer at Lingfield in July: acts on any ground, including the all-weather: often blinkered/visored: often sweating and on toes: races prominently: none too consistent. *R. E. Peacock* 40 a43

TOM SWIFT (IRE) 2 b.c. (May 28) Law Society (USA) 130 – Debbie's Next (USA) 82 (Arctic Tern (USA) 126) [1995 7f 7m Nov 3] IR 2,300Y, 2,800 2-y-o: small, good-topped colt: third foal: brother to French 4-y-o 1½m winner Debbie's Law and half-brother to fairly useful 3-y-o 1m winner Nordinex (by Nordico): dam maiden, stayed 1m: behind in maiden events in the autumn. *R. C. Spicer*
–

TONDRES (USA) 4 br.g. Chief's Crown (USA) – Icing 112 (Prince Tenderfoot (USA) 126) [1994 77: 8m^4 7s 7m 12m 10f^2 8.1m 10.1d 10g 10.1g^2 1995 a10g^6 a13g^4 a10g 10m^4 12f 11.4m 13.3g 10m 16.4m Aug 18] big, good-bodied gelding: has a free, round action: fair maiden handicapper: below form at 4 yrs after fourth start: effective at 1¼m, probably stays 13f: best form on a sound surface (acts on firm): tried in visor/blinkers: none too consistent. *R. Ingram*
72 d

TONKA 3 b.c. Mazilier (USA) 107 – Royal Meeting 44 (Dara Monarch 128) [1994 66: 6.1s^3 7m 7g 7s* 7d 7.3v a8g a8.5g^2 1995 a8g^5 a9.4g 12.5m^3 9.9m* 12.3m^5 12g^5 10m 10.2h^5 10m^6 10m^5 11.4d^2 9.7s^3 9.7g^6 12m Nov 6] small colt: has a quick action: fair performer at best: won claimer at Beverley in April: claimed out of D. Murray-Smith's stable £10,000 sixth start: stays 12.3f: acts on good to firm and soft ground, below form on the all-weather: visored (ran poorly) second 3-y-o start. *P. J. Makin*
71 d

TONNERRE 3 b.c. Unfuwain (USA) 131 – Supper Time 71 (Shantung 132) [1994 –: 8g 1995 12g^4 14d* 16.2m^4 13.1g 11.9s^5 Oct 1] rather leggy, plain colt: fair form to win maiden at Haydock in June: failed to reproduce it in handicaps: should stay further than 1¾m: acts on dead ground: sold 14,000 gns Doncaster November Sales. *C. W. Fairhurst*
79

TONTO 2 b.c. (Apr 17) Nomination 125 – Brigado 87 (Brigadier Gerard 144) [1995 8.1s Nov 2] 8,000Y: half-brother to several winners, including 3-y-o 7f and 1m winner Ism (by Petong) and 1½m winner Vado Via (by Ardross): dam 2-y-o 1m winner: 66/1, slowly away and tailed off in maiden at Edinburgh. *C. W. Thornton*
–

TONY'S DELIGHT (IRE) 7 b.g. Krayyan 117 – Tinas Image (He Loves Me 120) [1994 NR 1995 a9.4g May 13] first foal: dam showed little ability: fairly useful handicapper (rated 82) at 3 and 4 yrs in Ireland for K. Prendergast, winning 3 times at 9f and once at 8.5f: lightly-raced novice hurdler: well beaten (close up 7f) in Wolverhampton claimer on return to flat. *C. R. Egerton*
–

TONY'S FEN 6 b.h. Trojan Fen 118 – Ladyfish 79 (Pampapaul 121) [1994 8s^4 8v 8d^2 10s^3 11m^3 11g 16s 12g^3 12g 14d^5 14g^6 16v^6 11g^4 16g^3 9s^2 16v^5 1995 10m^6 10m* 13.3g^4 12f^4 12.4m* 10.3d 10d^6 Sep 16] neat ex-Irish horse: half-brother to several winners, none better than fairly useful: dam, 1m winner, is half-sister to Carroll House: successful on 5 occasions in Ireland, twice at 1½m at 3 yrs, then twice at 1m (including Irish Lincoln) and once at 1¼m at 4 yrs: sold out of K. Prendergast's stable 30,000 gns Newmarket December (1994) Sales: fairly useful form here, winning minor event at Windsor in May and handicap at Newcastle in July: has shown his form at 1m to 2m: acts on any going: bandaged last 2 starts: impressive winner over hurdles in September, not seen out again. *D. R. C. Elsworth*
79

TONYS GIFT 3 b.f. Midyan (USA) 124 – Harmonical (USA) 70 (Lyphard's Wish (FR) 124) [1994 5m^3 5m^2 6g^5 5g^6 1995 6m^4 5g 6f^2 6m^3 6g^3 7m* 7g 8g^3 8f* Oct 24] 1,800F: sparely-made ex-Irish filly: third foal: half-sister to useful sprinter Straight Arrow (by Indian Ridge): dam 11f winner: fair performer: trained by K. Prendergast at 2 yrs: well-backed winner of maiden at Epsom in August and claimer at Leicester in October, claimed by M. Pipe for £10,000 after latter: stays 1m: has raced only on a sound surface: has run well when sweating. *R. Hannon*
69

TONY'S MIST 5 b.g. Digamist (USA) 110 – Tinas Image (He Loves Me 120) [1994 –: a7g^4 8d 1995 10.8m 10.8f 10.2m 10.8m^2 9.9m^6 Jul 8] close-coupled gelding: rated 77 at 3 yrs for R. Hannon: modest at best in 1995: seems to stay 10.8f: acts on good to firm ground, used to go well on a soft surface: blinkered (below best) once at 2 yrs. *J. M. Bradley*
55

TOO HASTY 2 b.c. (Feb 17) Dunbeath (USA) 127 – Suggia (Alzao (USA) 117) [1995 6m^4 7m^2 7m* 7m 7g^6 6g^4 7f Oct 14] smallish, sturdy colt: second live foal: dam lightly raced and well beaten: fair form: comfortable winner of median auction maiden at Catterick in July: mostly creditable efforts in nurseries afterwards: stays 7f. *M. H. Easterby*
77

T O O MAMMA'S (IRE) 4 ch.f. Classic Secret (USA) 91 – Bohemian Rhapsody 86 (On Your Mark 125) [1994 50: 6s a5g^5 5.9v^6 a8g^2 8.3f^2 8.3m^5 a9.4g* 9.2g^5 11g* 11.1m* 11.1g^5 8m^5 10.8m a12g^5 10g a10g 1995 a8g a11g^5 a12g a9.4g^2 a9.4g^4 a8.5g^4 Mar 18] small, sparely-made filly: poor performer: stays 11f: acts on firm ground and fibresand: has run well when sweating: effective visored or not: modest winning hurdler for J. K. Oliver. *J. Berry* — 47

TOPAGLOW (IRE) 2 ch.g. (Mar 30) Topanoora 118 – River Glow (River Knight (FR) 118) [1995 5m 5m 6m a7g 8.1s Oct 17] IR 4,200Y, 5,200 2-y-o: small gelding: first reported foal: dam won from 7f to 1¾m in Ireland and stayed 2m: poor form in maiden events and a seller. *P. T. Dalton* — 46

TOPANGA 3 b.g. Dancing Brave (USA) 140 – Trampship 110 (High Line 125) [1994 NR 1995 12m^4 14.1f^3 Jun 27] sturdy, compact gelding: fourth foal: brother to French Provincial 1½m to 15f winner Vagrancy and half-brother to fairly useful 1½m winner Trammel (by Shirley Heights) and 10.2f winner Touring (by Sadler's Wells): dam (from good family) won Park Hill: fair form in maidens at Kempton (coltish and green) and Yarmouth (no extra final 1f) in June: probably stays 14.1f: sold (H. Cecil to J. Bennett) 11,000 gns Newmarket Autumn Sales and gelded. *H. R. A. Cecil* — 71

TOP BANANA 4 ch.g. Pharly (FR) 130 – Oxslip 106 (Owen Dudley 121) [1994 75p: 6g 8.3m 7m^5 6m^5 7m^2 1995 7m^3 8m 6g* 5.2f* 5.2g* 6m^2 6m^3 6g Sep 16] close-coupled, workmanlike gelding: continued his improvement in 1995, winning minor event at Warwick (easily) in June and handicaps at Newbury in June and (best effort) July: in frame in Stewards' Cup at Goodwood and Great St Wilfrid at Ripon, heavily backed on each occasion: wasn't well drawn and not entirely disgraced when fourteenth of 29 to Royale Figurine in Ayr Gold Cup on final start: effective at 5f, and stays 7f: has raced only on a sound surface. *H. Candy* — 94

TOP CAT (FR) 2 ch.f. (Mar 22) Be My Chief (USA) 122 – Pussy Foot 83 (Red Sunset 120) [1995 5g^2 5m^2 6.1m* 5d* 5m 5.2m^6 6.5m 5g 5s^5 Oct 1] 5,800Y: attractive, good-bodied filly: has scope: second foal: half-sister to 3-y-o Chief's Lady (by Reprimand): dam top-of-the-ground 5f performer from family of 3 Ribblesdale winners: fairly useful form when winning maiden at Nottingham in May and £9,000 event at Beverley in June: ran bit better than ninth-of-12 position suggests in Queen Mary Stakes at Royal Ascot but well below form afterwards: stays 6f: acts on good to firm and dead ground (well beaten on soft last time): blinkered penultimate outing: one to treat with caution: sold 10,500 gns Newmarket December Sales. *E. Weymes* — 85 d

TOP CEES 5 b.g. Shirley Heights 130 – Sing Softly 112 (Luthier) [1994 84: 13.9m^5 13.3m^6 12m 10.5d^4 12m 1995 12g^6 14m^5 18.7m* 20m 14.6m^4 18m^3 Oct 14] close-coupled gelding: has a round action: fairly useful handicapper: ran a most — 86

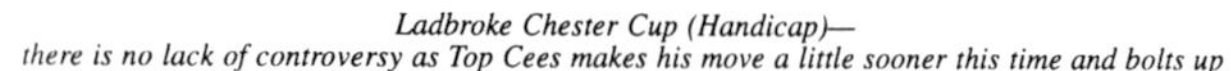

Ladbroke Chester Cup (Handicap)—
there is no lack of controversy as Top Cees makes his move a little sooner this time and bolts up

eye-catching race at Newmarket on second 5-y-o start, and confirmed the strong impression made there by winning 18-runner Ladbroke Chester Cup in May by 5 lengths from Harlestone Brook, leading over 1f out and storming clear: gelded and off course 2½ months after next start: ran very well when strong-finishing third of 21 to Old Red in Cesarewitch at Newmarket on final one: suited by a thorough test of stamina: acts on good to firm ground, probably on dead: usually held up. *Mrs J. R. Ramsden*

TOP FELLA (USA) 3 b. or br.g. Horatius (USA) – Annapurna (USA) (Blade (USA)) [1994 61: 6f 6m^{3} 6.1m 6g^{3} 8s 8m 1995 a8g^{3} a8g^{6} a8g^{3} a11g a8g^{3} 10.3m^{4} 12m a8g* 10f a7g^{3} 8m^{3} a10g a11g Sep 4] leggy, rather sparely-made gelding: has a round action: modest handicapper: awarded maiden contest at Southwell in June: effective at 7f, and stays 10.3f (not 1½m): acts on good to firm ground and the all-weather: effective blinkered/visored or not: has worn severe bridle: joined P. Dennis. *W. A. O'Gorman* 54

TOP GUIDE (USA) 4 ch.g. Diesis 133 – Raahia (CAN) 91 (Vice Regent (CAN)) [1994 81+: 8m* 8d^{5} 1995 7m 8m 8.1g^{6} 8m Aug 27] angular gelding: fair handicapper: upset in stalls and virtually pulled up on final outing: will be suited by further than 1m: acts on good to firm and dead ground: bandaged in 1995. *E. A. L. Dunlop* 78

TOPICAL (USA) 2 b.c. (Feb 21) Topsider (USA) – Meteoric 102 (High Line 125) [1995 7g Sep 29] workmanlike colt: sixth foal: half-brother to French 1¼m winner From Afar (by Riverman): dam sprinting daughter of game sprinter Metair: 11/1 and blinkered, last of 18 in seller at Goodwood, slowly away and behind throughout: sent to Denmark. *G. Harwood* –

TOP LADY (IRE) 3 b.f. Shirley Heights 130 – Happy Kin (USA) (Bold Hitter (USA)) [1994 61p: 7s 8d 1995 10.2m^{3} 12.3m^{2} 12.3m^{2} 14.1m^{3} 12.3m^{2} 12m^{2} 12s* 11.9g 14.1f* Oct 12] lengthy, rather angular filly: unimpressive mover: fairly useful performer: demoted winner (drifted right) of handicap at Epsom in September, but won maiden there later in month and handicap at Redcar (made all) in October: stays 1¾m: acts on firm ground and soft: visored (below form) fourth 3-y-o start: races prominently: game. *M. R. Stoute* 83

TOP OF THE STACK 2 b.c. (Mar 17) Thatching 131 – Prima Domina (FR) 89 (Dominion 123) [1995 7.1m 6m^{6} 6.1d Sep 11] 58,000F, 46,000Y: sturdy, compact colt: fourth foal: half-brother to 6f (at 2 yrs) and 1¾m winner Primo Figlio (by Assert): dam sprinting sister to Primo Dominie: fair maiden: dead. *R. Hannon* 66 +

TOP PEARL 3 ch.f. Superlative 118 – Believe The Chick (USA) (Believe It (USA)) [1994 69: 5m^{3} 5g* 5m 5g^{4} 5s 1995 a5g 5m 7g May 20] small filly: fair form at 2 yrs: tailed off in handicaps in 1995: tried blinkered. *N. A. Graham* –

TOP PET (IRE) 5 br.g. Petong 126 – Pounelta 91 (Tachypous 128) [1994 73: 7g^{3} 7m^{4} 7m* 7g 7.1g^{5} 7m^{3} 7m^{4} 7f^{4} 7m^{3} 7g 7m 7d^{2} 1995 7m 7f^{6} 8.1g^{5} 6.9g^{4} 7.1m^{4} 11.5m^{3} 12m^{5} 10m^{3} 10m^{4} 7g 7g 8g Sep 29] leggy gelding: just a modest handicapper in 1995: stays 1¼m: acts on firm and dead ground, well below best on heavy: often needs plenty of driving, and worth a try in blinkers/visor: not one to trust implicitly. *R. Akehurst* 60 d

TOP PRIZE 7 b.g. High Top 131 – Raffle 82 (Balidar 133) [1994 31, a38: a16.2g^{5} 12.3d^{5} 16.2m^{2} 16g 14.1m^{4} 18m 13m^{6} 14.9m 16.2f^{4} 14.1m^{4} 14.1m* 16g a16g* 17.5s 1995 a16g^{6} a14g 16.2m^{4} 14.1m* 16.2m* 15.4m 17.5g 17.1m Oct 2] leggy, lengthy gelding: poor handicapper: won sellers at Nottingham and Beverley (by 8 lengths) in August: stays well: acts on firm ground and on fibresand: visored since fourth 7-y-o start: lazy and suited by strong handling. *M. Brittain* 44

TO PROVE A POINT 3 b.g. Weldnaas (USA) 112 – Run Little Lady (USA) 81 (J O Tobin (USA) 130) [1994 –: 5g 5v a7g 1995 5.9m 8.3g 10m^{5} 10m^{5} 10m Jun 13] small gelding: poor maiden: stays 1¼m: acts on good to firm ground: tried blinkered. *J. J. O'Neill* 34

TOP ROYAL 6 br.g. High Top 131 – Maria Isabella (FR) (Young Generation 129) [1994 NR 1995 11.5m^{5} 14.4m Sep 1] good-bodied gelding: tough and consistent handicapper (rated 85) in 1992 for J. Dunlop: no form on return. *J. Pearce* –

TOP SHIEL 7 b.h. Top Ville 129 – Gelder Shiel (Grundy 137) [1994 70, a73: a12s* a12g* a12g^{3} 10v a12g^{2} 10s^{2} 10d^{6} 10g a11g* a8g* 10d^{2} 10m^{4} 10.3s 1995 a11g^{3} –

a11g Jan 20] big, strong, lengthy horse: fair performer: ran as if something amiss towards end of career: stayed 1½m: possibly best with give in the ground on turf, acted on fibresand: tried visored: dead. *K. R. Burke*

TOP SHOP 3 ch.f. Nashwan (USA) 135 – Select Sale (Auction Ring (USA) 123) [1994 NR 1995 10.5m^{2} 11.9g* May 26] quite good-topped filly: fifth living foal: half-sister to 4-y-o Hello Ireland (by Reference Point), 7f winner at 2 yrs, and 2 middle-distance winners by Shirley Heights: dam unraced daughter of half-sister to Abwah and Owen Dudley: similar form in Haydock maidens in May, landing the odds in 6-runner race on second start: stays 1½m: sent to USA. *H. R. A. Cecil* — 75 p

TOP SHOW (IRE) 4 b.g. Digamist (USA) 110 – Acquire 105 (Burglar 128) [1994 –: 6g 6g 1995 a6g^{6} 6f^{4} 7m May 29] angular gelding: lightly raced and only modest form since fair and consistent (rated 72) at 2 yrs: stays 7f: best form on a sound surface. *K. W. Hogg, Isle of Man* — 55

TOP SKIPPER (IRE) 3 b.g. Nordico (USA) – Scarlet Slipper (Gay Mecene (USA) 128) [1994 NR 1995 8g^{6} 8g^{6} 8f^{5} 8g 10d 7.1g 8f Oct 18] IR 9,000F, IR 10,000Y: close-coupled gelding: half-brother to 2 winners, including modest Shimmering Scarlet (7f on flat, and staying hurdles, by Glint of Gold): dam French 1m winner: fair maiden: well below form last 4 starts, including in blinkers and selling company: should stay beyond 1m: sold (B. Hanbury to Martyn Wane) 1,600 gns Newmarket Autumn Sales. *B. Hanbury* — 67 d

TOP SPIN 6 b.g. Niniski (USA) 125 – Spin (High Top 131) [1994 –: 18.7m 18m 1995 16m Apr 17] small, leggy gelding: useful hurdler: no form on flat since 4-y-o: taking no interest in Queen's Prize at Kempton in April: needs treating with caution. *J. R. Jenkins* — – §

TOP TYCOON (IRE) 4 b. or br.g. Last Tycoon 131 – Pounelta 91 (Tachypous 128) [1994 52d: 7v^{4} 8g^{4} 8m 8m 11.8g 7m^{5} 8g a7g 1995 7f 5g 6g Jun 3] leggy, workmanlike gelding: modest maiden at best in 1994: no promise in 1995. *J. J. Bridger* — –

TORAJA 3 b.g. Petoski 135 – Helvetique (FR) (Val de Loir 133) [1994 NR 1995 12.4g^{2} 12.1g^{2} 14d^{3} 17.2h* 16.2m^{5} 16.2m^{6} Aug 9] 1,000F, 9,000Y: workmanlike gelding: half-brother to several winners, including smart stayer Harly (by Pharly): dam won twice at around 1¼m in France: fair performer: made all in 4-runner maiden handicap at Bath in July: disappointing afterwards: very much a stayer: sold 4,000 gns Newmarket Autumn Sales. *J. L. Dunlop* — 79

TORCH DANCER (IRE) 4 b.c. Sadler's Wells (USA) 132 – River Dancer 118 (Irish River (FR) 131) [1994 NR 1995 8f^{6} May 8] half-brother to 5f winner Ballet Shoes (by Ela-Mana-Mou), 1¼m winner Snow Plough (by Niniski) and high-class 3-y-o Spectrum (by Rainbow Quest): dam French 5f (at 2 yrs) and 1m winner from family of Sun Princess and Saddlers' Hall (by Sadler's Wells): very early to post, sixth of 7 in maiden at Warwick, missing break and hanging off bridle in closing stages: sold 3,400 gns Newmarket December Sales. *M. R. Stoute* — –

TORCH OCHRE (USA) 2 b.c. (Mar 12) Seattle Dancer (USA) 119 – Paris Jewel (USA) (Well Decorated (USA)) [1995 7g 8d Sep 15] IR 30,000Y: quite attractive colt: first reported foal: dam won 4 times in USA: tailed-off last of 8 in minor events at Doncaster and Newbury: sold 3,600 gns Newmarket Autumn Sales: sent to Norway. *B. W. Hills* — –

TORCH VERT (IRE) 3 b.g. Law Society (USA) 130 – Arctic Winter (CAN) (Briartic (CAN)) [1994 68p: 8m 1995 12f^{6} 13.9m 12m* 15g^{2} 14f^{5} 14.6m^{5} 13.1g* 18m^{6} Oct 14] compact, attractive gelding: fairly useful performer on his day: made all in maiden at Beverley in June and handicap at Ayr (well backed) in September: led 3f out to 2f out before fading in Cesarewitch at Newmarket on final start: may prove best at up to 2m: acts on good to firm ground, yet to race on a soft surface: sold (B. Hills to N. Walker) 46,000 gns Newmarket Autumn Sales. *B. W. Hills* — 87

TORREGLIA (IRE) 3 ch.f. Elmaamul (USA) 125 – Dance Machine 111 (Green Dancer (USA) 132) [1994 NR 1995 10g 12.1m^{6} 11.7f^{2} 16.2g^{2} 16m^{4} 16.2m^{2} 14g Sep 23] leggy, light-bodied, plain filly: fifth foal: closely related to tip-top 4-y-o Halling (by Diesis) and half-sister to 2 winners in France at 1m by Bering: dam 7f and 1¼m winner: fair maiden: stays 16.2f well: has raced only on a sound surface: has wandered under pressure. *J. L. Dunlop* — 67

TORRENTIAL (USA) 3 b.c. Gulch (USA) – Killaloe (USA) (Dr Fager) [1994 NR 1995 7g* 9d* 10m^5 9g* 10m^4 9.5g^2 Jul 23] 117

Torrential had a lot going for him right from the start. A very well-bred colt, a grand looker and a horse stabled with one of the very best trainers in the business, it is not all that surprising that in a short space of time he's proved himself a well-above-average perfomer on the racecourse too. Unraced at two years, Torrential had six races within four months during the first part of the 1995 season. His reputation preceded him to Doncaster in March for his debut, and he started a short-priced favourite in a twelve-runner maiden, creating a very good impression in quickening after a slow start to beat Silver Sting by one and a half lengths. Torrential, as expected, showed considerably better form on his next start when following up at 7/4-on by three and a half lengths from Heathyards Rock in a seven-runner conditions event at Ripon in April, again showing a smart turn of foot and having plenty left in him at the finish. A hiccup then occurred when Torrential could finish only fifth in the Thresher Classic Trial at Sandown, though it transpired that he'd sustained an injury during the race. Torrential had not originally been entered for the Derby, and his early-June target proved to be the Prix Jean Prat, over only nine furlongs, at Chantilly. Even making due allowance for the circumstances of Torrential's sole defeat, we suspect that the horse's connections would have been more hopeful than confident in his ability to cope with the big step up to Group 1 class. But he coped with it admirably. In a particularly slowly-run race, he showed the best turn of speed to come out best in a blanket finish with Annus Mirabilis, Labeeb and the unlucky Bobinski. Torrential went on to confirm himself a smart performer in his two remaining races, without adding to his haul of three victories. He was beaten little more than two lengths by Valanour in the Grand Prix de Paris at Longchamp later in June and rounded off with a second (beaten one and a quarter lengths) to the French-trained Gold And Steel in an un-American finish to the American Derby at Arlington in July. Giving the winner 6 lb, Torrential ran right up to his previous best in the American Derby, but the fact that he cut a stifle leaving the stalls and wasn't seen out again suggests that he could possibly have run even better. He was sent to Dubai for the winter.

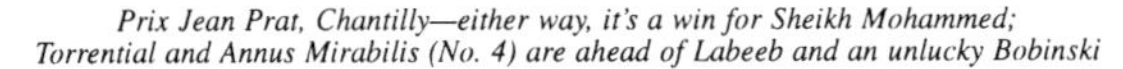
Prix Jean Prat, Chantilly—either way, it's a win for Sheikh Mohammed; Torrential and Annus Mirabilis (No. 4) are ahead of Labeeb and an unlucky Bobinski

Sheikh Mohammed's "Torrential"

Torrential (USA) (b.c. 1992)	Gulch (USA) (b 1984)	Mr Prospector (b 1970)	Raise A Native
			Gold Digger
		Jameela (b or br 1976)	Rambunctious
			Asbury Mary
	Killaloe (USA) (b 1970)	Dr Fager (b 1964)	Rough'n Tumble
			Aspidistra
		Grand Splendor (b 1962)	Correlation
			Cequillo

It is interesting and possibly significant that Torrential should already have turned up in competition in the USA, for his appeal as a potential stallion could be even greater over there in due course. His dam, the winner of four minor races in that country, has produced numerous other winners, including four in stakes company. Two of those, Fappiano and Portroe, are by Mr Prospector and therefore close relatives to Torrential. Fappiano is a particularly important close relative for Torrential to have. A good performer, the winner of stakes events from six to nine furlongs, including the Grade 1 Metropolitan Handicap, Fappiano went on to prove himself a top-class sire, leading the juvenile sire rankings in 1985 and 1989 and being second overall in 1990, the year of his death. His best runners included Tasso, the champion US two-year-old of 1985, Unbridled, the champion US three-year-old of 1990, and the ex-British Man O'War Stakes winner Defensive Play. Torrential's grandam Grand Splendor bred several other winners besides Killaloe, among them Gonfalon, the dam of the high-class performer and successful sire Ogygian. Torrential's sire Gulch, a top-class performer from two to four years, winner of the Metropolitan Handicap twice and of the Breeders' Cup Sprint, has made a fine start at stud, particularly in his native country. In Britain he was also represented in the latest season by the One Thousand Guineas winner Harayir, among others. No surprise, therefore, that Torrential, a big, good-bodied, attractive individual, commanded considerable interest when offered for sale at the Keeneland July Yearling Sale. Indeed, at 375,000 dollars, Torrential was the most expensive yearling by his sire in 1993.

Already the winner in Europe of a Group 1 race, admittedly a rather substandard one, Torrential would be worth a pretty penny if he could win at a similar level in the USA. If he does, it's likely that it'll be at nine or ten furlongs; he's not sure to stay further. He has yet to race on extremes of going. *J. H. M. Gosden*

TORREY PINES (IRE) 3 b.g. Red Sunset 120 – Yukon Baby (USA) (Northern Dancer) [1994 –: a8g a8g 1995 a10g a8.5g^3 a8g 10m 10.5m^3 12.1m^4 Aug 28] good-topped gelding: poor maiden: stays 12.1f: acts on good to firm ground: unruly stalls (below form) fourth 3-y-o start: joined M. Bell. *D. Haydn Jones* 46

TOSHIBA TALK (IRE) 3 ch.g. Horage 124 – Court Ballet (Barrons Court) [1994 48: 5.9m 5m^5 5.9f^6 1995 10.3g 8.3v^3 10f* 10m^6 10m 10.4g 12d Sep 15] leggy gelding: has a quick action: modest performer: below form after winning handicap at Redcar in May: stays 1¼m: acts on firm ground. *B. Ellison* 52

TOSKANO 3 b.g. Salse (USA) 128 – Kukri (Kris 135) [1994 58: 8m 8.2d 1995 10g^5 9d^4 10m^3 11.5s Sep 28] big, quite attractive gelding: fair maiden: sold out of I. Balding's stable 12,000 gns Doncaster September Sales after third 3-y-o start: stays 1¼m: best effort on good to firm ground: sometimes carries head high. *D. L. Williams* 63

TOTAL ALOOF 2 b.f. (Feb 5) Groom Dancer (USA) 128 – Bashoosh (USA) (Danzig (USA)) [1995 6.1m 5f^2 Aug 5] IR 3,500Y: first foal: dam, ran 4 times over middle distances, daughter of Yorkshire Oaks winner Condessa: bandaged behind, beaten short head by Crissem in 10-runner maiden auction at Haydock, chasing leaders and staying on strongly: bred to stay at least 1m: will do better again. *Mrs L. Piggott* 60 p

TOTALITY 4 b.f. Dancing Brave (USA) 140 – Slightly Dangerous (USA) 122 (Roberto (USA) 131) [1994 85p: 12m^2 14.1g* 1995 11.8m^2 11.9m^2 13.5g^6 14.6m^4 Sep 6] sturdy filly: useful performer: second in Lancashire Oaks at Haydock (niggled along good way out, stuck on determinedly, 1¼ lengths behind Fanjica) in July on second start: keeping-on fourth of 8 to Noble Rose in Park Hill Stakes at Doncaster on final outing: effective at around 1½m and should have stayed 2m: acted on good to firm ground: stud. *H. R. A. Cecil* 103

TOTAL JOY (IRE) 4 gr.g. Persian Bold 123 – Caranina (USA) 85 (Caro 133) [1994 67: 10.2g^6 10g^6 10m^6 10m^2 10m* 10.1m 11.4d 1995 10d 10.8m 12.5g* 11.9f^5 13.3g^6 14.4m^5 11.5m 12g^6 11.9f^3 Jul 20] tall, good-topped gelding: fair handicapper: won amateurs event at Warwick in April: below form last 5 outings: stays 12.5f: acts on good to firm ground, well beaten on good to soft: blinkered (out of form) twice: sometimes a front runner: wears dropped noseband: has joined C. Mann. *P. F. I. Cole* 67

TOTALLY DIFFERENT 2 b.c. (Feb 2) Totem (USA) 118 – Bold Difference 66 (Bold Owl 101) [1995 7f 7m Nov 3] small, angular colt: second foal: dam won from 6f (at 2 yrs) to 1¼m: well beaten in seller at Redcar in June (for John Berry) and maiden at Doncaster in November. *G. R. Oldroyd* –

TOTAL RACH (IRE) 3 b.f. Nordico (USA) – Miss Kelly (Pitskelly 122) [1994 66: 7m 7m 7m^2 6.9d^2 6.9m^4 1995 8.2g 9m 10f 8g^5 10.8g 8g^6 8f* a10g a10g^3 a12g a10g* Dec 18] close-coupled filly: modest handicapper: sold out of Mrs L. Piggott's stable 2,400 gns Newmarket July Sales after reappearance: won at Yarmouth (seller) in October and Lingfield in December: stays 1¼m well: acts on firm and dead ground and on equitrack: blinkered since sixth 3-y-o start: wears bandages. *R. Ingram* 59

TOTAL STRANGER 3 b.g. Puissance 110 – Jaisalmer 97 (Castle Keep 121) [1994 73: 6.1m 5m^4 6g^5 6.1m 5m^2 5m* 5m^2 5d^4 1995 5s^2 5.1m* 5m^3 5g 5.1m^4 5f 5.1m Aug 19] leggy, angular gelding: fair handicapper: made all at Chester in May: well below form last 2 starts: speedy, and best form at 5f: acts on good to firm ground and soft: usually races prominently: visored (ran well) final 2-y-o start: moved poorly to post (and well below form) fourth 3-y-o start: genuine: sent to Macau. *Mrs L. Piggott* 76

TO THE ROOF (IRE) 3 b.g. Thatching 131 – Christine Daae 74 (Sadler's Wells (USA) 132) [1994 61p: 7g 6s 1995 7m 6f^{2} a6g^{3} 6m^{3} 6g^{6} 5.1d^{2} Oct 10] lengthy, good-bodied gelding: carries condition: fair maiden handicapper: stays 6f: acts on firm and dead ground and on fibresand: looked none too keen second 3-y-o start. *P. W. Harris* 70

TO THE WHIRE 2 br.f. (Feb 6) Rock City 120 – Free Dance (FR) (Green Dancer (USA) 132) [1995 5m^{4} 5m* 6m^{3} 6f^{4} 5m a6g^{5} Nov 29] 6,200F, 6,600Y: leggy, rather unfurnished filly: half-sister to several winners over middle distances plus, notably smart Free Fact (by Known Fact): dam French 8.5f and 9f winner: fair form in first half of year, winning maiden at Lingfield in May: off course nearly 5 months before disappointing last 2 starts: stays 6f: acts on good to firm ground. *G. L. Moore* 73

TOT OU TARD (IRE) 5 b.h. Robellino (USA) 127 – She's My Lovely (Sharpo 132) [1994 8s^{3} 12m 10g^{6} 10.6g^{2} 12.5g* 1995 10g^{6} 11g^{3} 13s^{5} 15.5s^{5} 15.5s 12m* 12v* 12g* 12d 12d^{3} 12d 15.5f 12f Dec 10] sturdy horse: third foal: half-brother to German 5f to 8.7f winner Achilleus (by Formidable): dam unraced half-sister to very smart sprinter-miler Comrade In Arms (by Brigadier Gerard) out of high-class sprinter-miler Girl Friend: smart French horse: unraced at 2 yrs: won minor event and listed race at Evry at 3 yrs and minor event in the provinces in 1994: joined S. Wattel, successful in 1995 in listed event and 6-runner Prix d'Hedouville (by 4 lengths from Grioun) at Longchamp in April and Grand Prix d'Evry (held Solid Illusion by a head) in June: worthwhile form afterwards only when 3 lengths third of 4 to Carnegie in slowly-run Prix Foy at Longchamp: back with former trainer last 2 starts: best at up to 1½m: acts on good to firm ground and heavy. *J. Foresi, France* 116

TOUCH ABOVE 9 b.g. Touching Wood (USA) 127 – B A Poundstretcher 82 (Laser Light 118) [1994 52: 8d 9.9m 9.9g^{5} 11.1m^{3} 10m* 11.1m^{3} 12m^{6} 9.9m^{2} 10g^{5} 1995 8.5m 9m^{3} 9.9d^{4} 11.1m^{6} 10m 9.9m^{5} 10m^{3} 10.1f^{5} Aug 26] sturdy gelding: carries condition: good mover: modest handicapper: stays 1½m: acts on soft ground, but goes very well on a sound surface: has won when sweating, and for 7-lb claimer: used to be held up and well suited by strongly-run race, but often raced prominently in 1995: successful 8 times at Beverley: tough. *T. D. Barron* 52

TOUCH A MILLION (USA) 3 b.c. Mr Prospector (USA) – Magic Gleam (USA) 122 (Danzig (USA)) [1994 67p: 6s^{6} 1995 7.1g^{2} 8m* 8g^{5} Jul 13] sturdy colt: fair form: justified favouritism in 4-runner maiden at Newcastle in July: should stay beyond 1m: acts on good to firm ground. *E. A. L. Dunlop* 78

TOUCHING TIMES 7 b.g. Touching Wood (USA) 127 – Pagan Deity 88 (Brigadier Gerard 144) [1994 –: 16g 16.4g 16d 1995 15.4m Sep 7] angular, sparely-made gelding: no longer of much account. *J. J. Bridger* –

TOUCH OF FANTASY 2 b.f. (Mar 31) Never So Bold 135 – Brera (IRE) 45 (Tate Gallery (USA) 117) [1995 5m^{6} 5g^{3} 5.1m^{5} a5g^{4} a5g^{3} 5m a5g^{4} a5g^{5} a5g Nov 25] 400Y: smallish, sparely-made filly: first foal: dam, poor maiden, should have stayed 7f: plater: ran for John Berry first 6 starts: likely to prove best at 5f: acts on fibresand, best turf run on good ground. *C. A. Dwyer* 43

TOUCH OF SNOW 2 b.f. (Mar 31) Touch of Grey 90 – Snow Huntress 80 (Shirley Heights 130) [1995 6f^{5} a7g 6.9g Oct 16] 480Y: second foal: sister to 4-y-o Wendals Touch: dam 1¼m and 1½m winner: well beaten in sellers and a maiden auction. *J. A. Bennett* –

TOUJOURS RIVIERA 5 ch.g. Rainbow Quest (USA) 134 – Miss Beaulieu 106 (Northfields (USA)) [1994 88: 10g 7g^{3} 6.9g* 7f 8.5m^{4} 8f^{3} 8.3f^{5} 8.1m* 7.9m 8m* 8m* 8d 1995 9m 8m* 8f 8m^{4} 8.3m^{6} 8d^{4} 8s 9m a8g^{3} Dec 14] rangy gelding: fairly useful handicapper: won at Yarmouth in July: narrowly-beaten fourth of 18 to Mo-Addab in £28,900 contest at Ascot on sixth start: effective at 7f and stays 1¼m: acts on firm and dead going, and ran well on equitrack debut last time: often a front runner. *J. Pearce* 91

TOUR LEADER (NZ) 6 ch.g. Nassipour (USA) 95 – Colleen (NZ) (Karayar) [1994 NR 1995 14d 17.1m Oct 2] sturdy, workmanlike gelding: modest maiden on flat, well beaten in 1995: fair hurdler, winner in November and December. *R. H. Buckler* –

TOUT DE VAL 6 b.m. Tout Ensemble – Julie Emma (Farm Walk 111) [1994 33: 7g^{5} 8m^{5} 7.1m^{4} 10f^{4} 8m 8m 8.1g^{3} 1995 8f^{5} 8g 10m^{3} a13g 9.7m 10f^{4} 10.2h^{2} 10.2m 31

Aug 28] strong mare: poor maiden handicapper: stays 1¼m: acts on hard going: tends to hang and carry head high. *K. Bishop*

TOVARICH 4 b.g. Soviet Star (USA) 128 – Pretty Lucky 68 (Shirley Heights 130) [1994 66: 6f² 6m 7g 12d⁶ 1995 a7g⁵ a8g⁶ a8g 9.9m 8m* 8f³ 8g a8g⁴ a12g² 13.3g⁶ a11g³ a12g* a12g² a12g Oct 14] strong gelding: fair handicapper: won ladies race at Ripon (third-last start for D. Nicholls) in April and seller at Wolverhampton (sold out of G. Lewis' stable 10,200 gns) in September: stays 1½m: acts on firm ground and fibresand: effective blinkered or not. *Ronald Thompson* 62 a66

TOWER GREEN 4 b.g. Aragon 118 – Pilley Green 100 (Porto Bello 118) [1994 85?: 7s² 8.1m 7.9d⁴ 7d⁶ 1995 7.6d 7d Oct 19] sturdy, well-made gelding: has been tubed: fairly useful performer: none too reliable, and no form in 1995. *Lady Herries* –

TOY PRINCESS (USA) 3 b.f. Arctic Tern (USA) 126 – Princess Toy (Prince Tenderfoot (USA) 126) [1994 69: 7m 8g³ 7m 1995 a12g² a8g³ 10d³ 12.5m* 14.6m⁵ 14.1m⁴ 14.1m² Aug 3] tall filly: unimpressive mover: fair performer: won minor event at Warwick in April: stays 14.6f: acts on good to firm and dead going and the all-weather: races prominently: consistent. *C. E. Brittain* 69

TRACEABILITY 2 b.g. (Apr 17) Puissance 110 – Miss Petella (Dunphy 124) [1995 5m 7m* 7m⁴ 7m 7.1f* 7f* 8m* Aug 25] 6,000F, 6,600Y: tall, lengthy gelding: has scope: shows knee action: third foal: half-brother to 3-y-o Dovedon Lad (by Statoblest): dam half-sister to 1000 Guineas second Meis-El-Reem: won sellers at Redcar and Edinburgh and claimer at Salisbury (claimed out of J. Berry's stable for £8,000) and nursery at Newmarket, all in the summer: stays 1m: has raced only on top-of-the-ground. *S. C. Williams* 72

TRACI'S CASTLE (IRE) 2 b.f. (Apr 27) Ajraas (USA) 88 – Mia Gigi (Hard Fought 125) [1995 6g Sep 20] 1,000 2-y-o: third foal: half-sister to 3-y-o Small Hiccup (by Common Grounds), winner in Denmark in 1995: dam Irish maiden: 16/1, in rear in 16-runner maiden at Brighton, never a factor after slow start. *R. Akehurst* –

TRADE WIND 4 br.g. Rambo Dancer (CAN) 107 – Cadasi 68 (Persian Bold 123) [1994 79: 8s⁶ 8m⁴ 10g² 10g⁴ 12f 10.2f* 12f⁵ 10.1m⁶ 10g⁵ 12m 14m 1995 12g 10m* 12g 12g⁴ 10m* 11.6m⁵ 10d 12s⁵ Oct 6] big, lengthy gelding: impresses in appearance: good mover: fair performer: won claimer at Goodwood in May and handicap at Windsor in July: below form last 3 starts: stays 1½m: acts on firm ground, shaped well on a soft surface on one occasion but yet to show his best form on it: blinkered (all but one start) since win at 3 yrs: held up: hung right fourth 4-y-o start: won novice hurdle in November, before sold 7,400 gns Doncaster November Sales. *D. R. C. Elsworth* 75

TRAFALGAR LADY (USA) 2 b.f. (May 15) Fairy King (USA) – Tremulous (USA) 102 (Gregorian (USA) 124) [1995 6d* 6.1d² Oct 10] neat filly: closely related to 1990 Irish 2-y-o 7f winner Rinka Das (by Nureyev), later successful in USA, and Irish 1¼m winner Great Cabaret (by The Minstrel), and half-sister to 1½m winner Glidingonby (by Alzao): dam, 1¼m and 1½m winner (stayed 1¾m) and later successful in USA, half-sister to pattern winners Seismic Wave and Missionary Ridge: won maiden at Goodwood in September: improved form when ½-length second to Chalamont in 7-runner minor event at Chepstow following month: will stay 7f: refused to enter stalls on intended debut and wore blanket for stalls entry at Chepstow: will improve further. *R. Charlton* 86 p

TRAGIC HERO 3 b.g. Tragic Role (USA) – Pink Mex (Tickled Pink 114) [1994 58: 7g⁵ 7s 1995 9g⁴ 8.5d⁵ 10f 8g⁶ 8.3m² 8h* 10m* 8g Oct 9] compact gelding: modest performer: won seller at Bath (made most, sold out of I. Balding's stable 9,100 gns) and claiming handicap at Goodwood, both in August: stays 1¼m well: acts on hard ground: blinkered (well below form) fourth 3-y-o start. *M. C. Pipe* 63

TRAIKEY (IRE) 3 b.c. Scenic 128 – Swordlestown Miss (USA) (Apalachee (USA) 137) [1994 96p: 8g* 1995 10.3g³ May 27] big, lengthy, good sort: a most fluent mover: impressive winner on only 2-y-o start: missed Craven Stakes on intended return after contracting a viral infection: looked in magnificent shape on reappearance in £8,400 event at Doncaster in May and ran well when close third to Don Corleone and Minds Music: subsequently discovered to have damaged sesamoid in near-hind, then damaged a foot in the autumn: will probably stay 1½m: looked sure to progress again. *J. E. Banks* 105 p

TRAIL OF TEARS 5 ch.g. Kings Lake (USA) 133 – Spring Water (USA) (Effervescing (USA)) [1994 –: a7g a8g 8.9m 12g 1995 a11g^{4} a11g 12.3d Apr 5] tall gelding: no worthwhile form: tried blinkered: headstrong. *W. W. Haigh* –

TRAINGLOT 8 ch.g. Dominion 123 – Mary Green 81 (Sahib 114) [1994 79+: 14.4m^{3} 1995 14g Sep 22] compact gelding: very useful performer (rated 110) on flat as 4-y-o: very lightly raced since, well beaten only start in 1995. *J. G. FitzGerald* –

TRANQUILLITY 3 b.f. Night Shift (USA) – Quiet Week-End 99 (Town And Country 124) [1994 65p: 6g 7g^{2} 1995 8m^{3} 8m* 9g 8g^{6} 7f^{5} 8.9g Oct 7] lengthy, angular filly: has a quick action: fair performer: won maiden at Bath in June: stays 1m: yet to race on a soft surface. *Lord Huntingdon* 70

TRANSOM (USA) 4 b. or br.g. Private Account (USA) – Trestle (USA) (Tom Rolfe) [1994 97p: 10g^{3} 10m* 12.3m* 14f^{3} 13.9m^{3} 14m^{2} 16.2m* 18m 1995 16.2m May 3] strong, good-topped gelding: grand sort with plenty of scope: progressive handicapper at 3 yrs: burly, eased once held when seventh of 9 in Sagaro Stakes at Ascot on only 4-y-o start: subsequently gelded: stays 2m well: acts on firm and dead ground: held up/tracks leaders. *G. Harwood* –

TRANS SIBERIA 4 gr.g. Siberian Express (USA) 125 – Olivian 79 (Hotfoot 126) [1994 91p: 10v^{2} 10m^{2} 12d^{2} 14m^{3} 14m* 14.6s* 1995 14m 14m^{2} 16.5g* 13.9m^{6} 16.1m^{2} Jul 1] tall, leggy gelding: fairly useful handicapper: narrow winner of rated stakes at Doncaster in May: good second of 17 to Bold Gait in Northumberland Plate at Newcastle on final start: will stay extreme distances: acts on good to firm and soft ground and the all-weather: normally races prominently: thoroughly game and genuine. *S. P. C. Woods* 87

TRAPEZE 4 br.g. Shirley Heights 130 – Fiesta Fun 105 (Welsh Pageant 132) [1994 11m^{2} 1995 12g a9.4g 10.2f May 22] rangy ex-French gelding: half-brother to several winners, notably Arc winner Saumarez (by Rainbow Quest): dam 1m and 1¼m winner: neck second in newcomers race at Longchamp only 3-y-o start for A. Fabre: sold 6,800 gns Newmarket Autumn (1994) Sales, then 3,100 gns Ascot December (1994) Sales: well beaten in 1995, including in blinkers. *C. L. Popham* –

TRAPPER NORMAN 3 b.g. Mazilier (USA) 107 – Free Skip 68 (Free State 125) [1994 NR 1995 a7g Dec 19] first foal: dam thorough stayer: well beaten in maiden at Lingfield. *R. Ingram* –

TRAUMA (IRE) 3 b.f. Broken Hearted 124 – Remoosh (Glint of Gold 128) [1994 NR 1995 10.3g a7g^{6} Apr 3] long-backed filly: has scope: fourth foal: sister to 1993 2-y-o 7f winner Footsteps and half-sister to 2 winners by Dominion, including 1991 2-y-o 6f winner Paradise Way: dam poor half-sister to high-class 1985 2-y-o Nomination: well beaten in maidens: sold 700 gns Ascot May Sales. *W. Jarvis* –

TRAVEL OUT 3 b.f. Presidium 124 – Travel Bye 62 (Miller's Mate 116) [1994 –: 6g 1995 a7g a6g a6g^{5} Feb 10] no worthwhile form. *Mrs M. Reveley* –

TRAZL (IRE) 3 b.f. Zalazl (USA) 120 – Triple Reef (Mill Reef (USA) 141) [1994 62p: 7g^{6} 7d^{6} 1995 10m 8m^{3} 10.2m^{3} 13.1f* 14m* 14.9m* 17.2h^{3} 14.1m^{3} 14.1g* 14.1f^{2} Oct 12] small, leggy, close-coupled filly: fairly useful performer: won median auction maiden (made all) at Ayr, minor event at Salisbury and handicap at Warwick, all in the summer, and another handicap at Redcar in September: best short of 17f: acts on hard ground. *J. L. Dunlop* 88

TREASURE KEAY 3 b. or br.f. Treasure Kay 114 – Doppio 62 (Dublin Taxi) [1994 46: 6d^{5} 6s 1995 8m 6g 7f Jun 29] leggy, quite good-topped filly: poor maiden: tailed off as though something amiss final start. *P. J. Makin* –

TREGARON (USA) 4 b.c. Lyphard (USA) 132 – Klarifi 91 (Habitat 134) [1994 66p: 8.2s^{6} 8g^{4} 1995 8d^{5} 8m^{3} 8.1g 7.9m^{6} 8g Sep 15] useful-looking colt: fair maiden handicapper: well beaten last 3 starts: should stay beyond 1m: acts on good to firm ground, probably on dead. *P. Calver* 77 d

TREMENDISTO 5 b.g. Petoski 135 – Misty Halo 93 (High Top 131) [1994 55, a52: 11.9m^{3} 10g 15.8g^{2} 14d^{5} 16g^{5} a14.8g a14g^{4} a14g^{2} a16.2g^{2} 1995 10.5d^{5} a14.8g^{6} 12.1g^{2} a12g^{3} 12m^{4} 15.1s^{2} a14.8g^{4} a14g Nov 24] plain, strong gelding: shows a round action: modest maiden handicapper: effective at 1½m to 2m: acts on good to firm and soft ground and on fibresand: usually races up with pace. *Capt. J. Wilson* 55 a51

TREMOLANTE 4 b.f. Governor General 116 – Glimmer 58 (Hot Spark 126) [1994 –: 7g 8d a7g 1995 a9.4g^{5} a8g^{6} a8g^{3} a9.4g^{4} a11g^{6} 10m May 26] poor maiden – a36

handicapper: should stay 1¼m: acts on fibresand, yet to show her form on turf. *Capt. J. Wilson*

TREMPLIN (USA) 3 gr.c. Trempolino (USA) 135 – Stresa (Mill Reef (USA) 141) [1994 8v3 1995 10s* 10m 10g3 12g5 10d3 10.8s Oct 28] rather leggy, short-necked colt: half-brother to several winners, notably Arlington Million winner Mill Native (by Exclusive Native) and high-class 1m and 9f winner French Stress (by Sham): dam French 1¼m winner: useful form: narrowly won minor event at Longchamp in April, leading close home: seventh of 8 to Pentire in Classic Trial at Sandown later in month, tending to hang and unable to challenge: third in listed races at Longchamp and Maisons-Laffitte afterwards: stays 1¼m: acts on heavy ground. *A. Fabre, France* 104

TRES HEUREUX (GER) 5 b.h. Konigsstuhl (GER) – Tres Magnifique (GER) (Gay Fandango (USA) 132) [1994 9v3 7g4 6s6 7s* 8.5d5 10d4 8.5v2 8d* 8s2 8v3 1995 8s* 8s2 8s4 8.5v3 7g 8.5s3 10v* Oct 8] first reported foal: dam, 2-y-o 7f winner, placed twice in Group events at 3 yrs: useful German horse: successful on 5 occasions in minor events at 7f/1m, gained easily most important win in Group 2 race at Dusseldorf (beat Devil River Peek by ¾ length) in October: stays 1¼m: goes well on heavy ground. *Frau E. Mader, Germany* 108

TRIA KEMATA 2 b.c. (Mar 22) Kris 135 – Third Watch 114 (Slip Anchor 136) [1995 7g3 7f6 7g2 7d* 7g3 Oct 7] good sort: first foal: dam, winner at 7f at 2 yrs and of Ribblesdale Stakes, half-sister to Oaks-placed Three Tails and Maysoon, latter also placed in 1000 Guineas: won minor event at Leicester in September: ¾-length third of 4 to Believe Me in minor event at York 19 days later, keeping on well once headed: bred to stay beyond 7f but takes a good hold: acts on good to soft ground: sometimes sweating (particularly so when below form second start). *J. L. Dunlop* 95

TRIARIUS (USA) 5 b.h. Trempolino (USA) 135 – Nobile Decretum (USA) (Noble Decree (USA) 127) [1994 12v2 12g2 10.5m2 10d* 10g* 10s2 1995 8.9g* 10g* 9.8s3 9f Dec 10] sturdy, attractive horse: fluent mover: eleventh reported foal: closely related to fairly useful middle-distance performer Sharp Noble (by Sharpen Up) and half-brother to 2 winners and the dam of smart French filly Bint Alnasr: dam unplaced in 5 races: very smart performer: unbeaten in 3 starts at 3 yrs, including listed race at Deauville, and landed the odds in 2 minor events at 4 yrs when still with A. Fabre: successful in 1995 in 4-runner listed race at York and 6-runner Westminster Taxi Insurance Select Stakes (cruised up to challenge, ran on strongly, despite drifting right, to beat Fahal by 1½ lengths) at Goodwood: not disgraced when 3½ lengths third of 7 to Flemensfirth in Prix Dollar at Longchamp next start: well beaten in Hong Kong International Cup final one: effective at 9f, stays 1½m: acts on heavy going. *Saeed bin Suroor* 115

TRIBAL PEACE (IRE) 3 ch.g. Red Sunset 120 – Mirabiliary (USA) 74 (Crow (FR) 134) [1994 64: 6d 7.6v 10g2 8d2 1995 a10g* a10g2 10.5m4 9m 9m2 10m 10d 9d* 9.7g 9d6 a8g a10g2 Dec 15] small gelding: fair performer: won median auction 74

Westminster Taxi Insurance Select Stakes, Goodwood—
the now-familiar Godolphin colours in their now-familiar position; Triarius beats Fahal and Wayne County

maiden at Lingfield in February and apprentice handicap at Goodwood in September: should stay beyond 1¼m: acts on good to firm and dead ground and the all-weather. *B. Gubby*

TRIBLE PET 2 b.f. (Mar 22) Petong 126 – Fire Sprite 83 (Mummy's Game 120) 48 [1995 5g^4 5g^4 5f^6 a5g^2 5m^5 5m a6g^6 Sep 14] 4,800Y: sparely-made filly: third foal: half-sister to ungenuine 3-y-o Six For Luck (by Handsome Sailor), 5f winner at 2 yrs: dam 2-y-o 5f winner: plater: creditable effort in blinkers penultimate start: best form at 5f: acts on fibresand (never a factor on equitrack final outing). *B. Gubby*

TRICKLEDOWN 2 b.f. (Feb 14) Dowsing (USA) 124 – Pillowing 69 (Good 58 d Times (ITY)) [1995 5m^5 6m^4 6g 6g a6g^2 a5g Dec 1] 1,800F, 6,200Y: rather leggy a46 filly: third live foal: half-sister to 4-y-o 7f and 1m winner Greatest (by Superlative) and 8.5f winner Hugging (by Beveled): dam sprinter out of half-sister to Blushing Groom: in frame in maiden at Ripon (lost form afterwards) in May and seller at Wolverhampton in November: left C. Fairhurst after fourth intended start: stays 6f: gave trouble before start on 3 occasions: clearly temperamental. *Martyn Wane*

TRILBY 2 b.f. (Feb 11) In The Wings 128 – Fur Hat (Habitat 134) [1995 8m^4 Oct 71 p 20] rangy filly: has scope: fifth foal: half-sister to 3-y-o 1½m to 16.5f winner Merit (by Rainbow Quest), 1¼m winner Wild Sable (by Kris) and a winner abroad by Mtoto: dam unraced half-sister to Teenoso: 6/1, 5 lengths fourth of 11 to easy winner Overruled in maiden at Doncaster, very green and soon chased along in rear then staying on well: will stay 1¼m: will improve. *P. F. I. Cole*

TRIMMING (IRE) 3 b.f. Thatching 131 – Tatouma (USA) 79 (The Minstrel 85 (CAN) 135) [1994 89p: 7g^2 7d* 1995 7m Apr 18] sturdy, lengthy filly: edgy, bandaged behind and wearing plaster on off hock, well-held seventh of 8 in Nell Gwyn Stakes at Newmarket on only 3-y-o outing, edging left off bridle: would have stayed 1m: dead. *J. H. M. Gosden*

TRINA 4 b.f. Malaspina 118 – Tremmin 67 (Horage 124) [1994 –: 6s 6d 7.1s 7f 37 1995 5m 5m 5g 5.9f^2 5.9f 7.1m^3 6m 8.3m^3 8m 11.6m^6 8f Aug 17] sturdy, plain filly: poor maiden handicapper: unseated apprentice rider in stalls and tailed off on final outing: stays 8.3f (appeared not to stay 11.6f): acts on firm ground. *D. L. Williams*

TRIOMING 9 b.g. Homing 130 – Third Generation 58 (Decoy Boy 129) [1994 45 48, a53: a5g^4 a5g^2 a5g^4 a5g^4 5g 5.1g^5 5d 5.1f^2 5.1m 5.7m^4 a5g a5g a7g a6g 1995 5m^6 a– 5.7h a7g Nov 13] compact gelding: unimpressive mover: poor handicapper: suited by 5f and a sound surface (acts on firm ground and fibresand): below form visored and blinkered: inconsistent. *A. P. Jones*

TRIPLE (FR) 3 b.f. General Holme (USA) 128 – Triemma (IRE) (M Double M – (USA)) [1994 NR 1995 a8g Dec 15] first foal: dam poor maiden (raced only at 2 yrs) from German family: tailed off in Lingfield claimer. *Lord Huntingdon*

TRIPLE JOY 4 b.f. Most Welcome 131 – Triple Reef (Mill Reef (USA) 141) 104 [1994 84p: 7g^2 8g a6g* a6g* a7g* 1995 a7g^3 a6g* 6m^2 6g^3 6m^3 Jul 1] lengthy, strong-quartered filly: in foal to Nashwan: useful performer: impressive winner of handicap at Lingfield in February: creditable efforts in listed company all 3 subsequent starts, on final one when ½ length behind Branston Abby at Newcastle: effective at 6f, and should have stayed 1m: acted on good to firm and dead ground and the all-weather: raced prominently. *Sir Mark Prescott*

TRIPLE TIE (USA) 4 ch.f. The Minstrel (CAN) 135 – Tea And Roses (USA) 54 d (Fleet Nasrullah) [1994 79: 12g^5 12m^5 11.9g^3 14d* 12d^6 12.1g 1995 16m 11.8m 10m 10f^6 12m^6 11.8m^5 14s 12.1d Oct 10] sparely-made filly: has a very round action: fair form at 3 yrs for P. Chapple-Hyam: modest at best in 1995: stays 1¾m: acts on dead ground: tends to sweat. *M. Blanshard*

TRIPLE TRICKS (IRE) 3 ch.f. Royal Academy (USA) 130 – Tricky Note 97 69 (Song 132) [1994 70: 6.1s^2 6m^4 1995 7g^4 6g 8.2m^3 8.1m^2 8.1m 7g Sep 13] leggy, unfurnished filly: fair maiden handicapper: stays 8.2f: acts on good to firm and soft ground. *W. J. Haggas*

TRIQUETTI (IRE) 3 b.c. Royal Academy (USA) 130 – Marie Noelle (FR) 114 97 (Brigadier Gerard 144) [1994 NR 1995 8m^2 9g* 11.8m^2 10f 10.1m^5 Sep 6] lengthy colt: half-brother to several winners, including Prix Marcel Boussac winner Mary Linoa (by L'Emigrant) and useful middle-distance performer Tapis Rouge (by Irish River): dam French 2-y-o 7.5f winner who later won 3 races at up to 1¼m in USA:

useful performer: won maiden at Lingfield in May: best effort when ¾-length second to Tenorio in minor event at Leicester in June: better at 1½m than shorter: has raced only on a sound surface: sent to Dubai. *L. M. Cumani*

TRISTAN'S COMET 8 br.g. Sayf El Arab (USA) 127 – Gleneagle 91 (Swing Easy (USA) 126) [1994 33: a12g^4 a12g 1995 a12g^4 16.2m Apr 7] leggy gelding: poor performer, very lightly raced on flat in recent seasons: stays 1½m: acts on fibresand. *J. L. Harris* – a49

TROJAN RISK 2 ch.c. (Mar 20) Risk Me (FR) 127 – Troyes 81 (Troy 137) [1995 7m^4 7.6d^4 6.9s^4 6.9g^2 a6g^4 Oct 28] 5,000Y: sturdy, good-bodied colt: fourth foal: half-brother to 9f winner Tromond (by Lomond): dam, 1½m winner, half-sister to Yorkshire Oaks winner Hellenic: fair maiden: needs further than 6f and will stay beyond 1m: may well be unsuited by very soft ground. *G. Lewis* 73

TROOPING (IRE) 6 b.g. Auction Ring (USA) 123 – Tunguska 76 (Busted 134) [1994 –: 10d 1995 8.3g^5 9.9m May 13] good-bodied gelding: has a round action: fair handicapper at 4 yrs for G. Harwood: modest at best in 1995: may well prove suited by 9f+: acts on firm and dead ground: blinkered twice (ran well first occasion) as 4-y-o. *M. G. Meagher* 57

TROPICAL BEACH 2 b.g. (Apr 9) Lugana Beach 116 – Hitravelscene (Mansingh (USA) 120) [1995 5g* 5g^4 5d 6f Oct 24] 3,000Y: leggy gelding: half-brother to winning sprinter B Grade (by Lucky Wednesday): dam poor plater: won maiden auction at Edinburgh in April: off course 6 months before finishing down the field in nurseries in October: slowly away first 3 starts: gelded after final one. *J. Berry* 56

TROPICAL DANCE (USA) 2 ch.f. (Jan 25) Thorn Dance (USA) 107 – Missuma (USA) (Procida (USA) 129) [1995 5m 5m^3 5m* 5m^5 6g* 6m* 7m^5 6.1m* 6g^5 Sep 2] $57,000Y: workmanlike filly: first foal: dam unraced half-sister to Belmont Stakes winner Summing: fairly useful filly: made all in maiden at York in May and minor events in the summer at Windsor (2) and Chester: unable to dominate when well beaten in listed race at Kempton last time: best form at 6f: has raced only on a sound surface: awkward stalls last 2 starts: sold 25,000 gns Newmarket December Sales. *Mrs J. Cecil* 93

TROPICAL JUNGLE (USA) 5 b.g. Majestic Shore (USA) – Diamond Oyster 72 (Formidable (USA) 125) [1994 NR 1995 a10g^3 a10g a10g* 12m^2 10m* 10g^2 10.2m^2 10.8m^3 a10g^2 a10g^2 Sep 5] lengthy, sparely-made gelding: has a round action: modest performer: won sellers at Lingfield (awarded race) in March and Ripon in April: stays 1½m: acts on any turf going and on equitrack: blinkered since third 5-y-o start. *P. J. Makin* 55 a60

TROUBADOUR SONG 3 b.g. King of Clubs 124 – Silver Singing (USA) 96 (Topsider (USA)) [1994 NR 1995 8.3m^6 8m^2 10m^4 8.5d 8m Sep 25] close-coupled gelding: first foal: dam sprinter: fair maiden: looked none too keen third start, and soundly beaten afterwards, including in blinkers: should stay beyond 1m: sold (I. Balding to W. Haigh) 3,200 gns Newmarket Autumn Sales. *I. A. Balding* 77

TRUANCY 2 b.c. (May 12) Polar Falcon (USA) 126 – Zalfa (Luthier 126) [1995 6g 6.1m* 7g^6 6g^5 Oct 7] 19,000Y: smallish, useful-looking colt: half-brother to 3-y-o 8.3f winner Alerting (by Warning) and a winner in Italy by Fast Topaze: dam French 1m to 12.5f winner: made all in maiden at Nottingham in June: absent 3 months, good effort when sixth of 8 to Even Top in listed race at Newmarket: not discredited when last of 5 in similar event at York 8 days later: bred to stay 1m. *M. Bell* 84 +

TRUE BALLAD 3 ch.g. Ballad Rock 122 – Ajuga (USA) 102 (The Minstrel (CAN) 135) [1994 NR 1995 6s 6d 7g^4 5m^5 7.8f^5 8m Oct 2] ex-Irish gelding: third foal: half-brother to 1992 2-y-o 8.2f winner Ajanta (by Rousillon): dam, 6f and 7f winner, out of Cairn Rouge: fair maiden: sold out of C. Collins' stable 1,400 gns Newmarket July (1995) Sales after fifth start: pulled up and dismounted in Pontefract handicap on British debut: stays 1m: acts on firm and dead ground. *T. Dyer* 65

TRUE BIRD (IRE) 3 b.f. In The Wings 128 – I Want My Say (USA) (Tilt Up (USA)) [1994 NR 1995 12g^2 10.4g^6 13.1g^{4dis} 14g 15.8m^2 Oct 13] 9,000Y: close-coupled, angular filly: third foal: dam once-raced half-sister to Irish Oaks winner Regal Exception and St Leger runner-up Esprit du Nord: fair maiden: stays 15.8f: has raced only on a sound surface. *J. D. Bethell* 63

TRULY A DREAM (IRE) 4 b.f. Darshaan 133 – Truly Special 116 (Caerleon (USA) 132) [1994 116: 9v² 10.5g⁴ 12s* 10.5g⁶ 10g² 12d⁴ 12g 10f* a9f⁵ 12f⁵ 1995 10v 10s 10.5s³ 12g 13.5g⁵ 9.3d 10g 10.5g⁵ Oct 29] smart French filly: creditable efforts in 1995 only when around a neck third of 8 to Hollywood Dream in slowly-run Prix Corrida (finishing well having been held up) at Evry in April and about 7 lengths eighth of 13 in E. P. Taylor Stakes at Woodbine in October: stays 1½m: acts on any going: inconsistent. *R. Collet, France* 111

TRULY MADLY DEEPLY 3 b.f. Most Welcome 131 – Council Rock 74 (General Assembly (USA)) [1994 NR 1995 7.3m a8g a11g a6g a5g 7m Aug 5] 1,800Y: third foal: half-sister to 4-y-o Rockabye Baileys (by Midyan): dam, maiden, suited by 1¼m, daughter of Nassau Stakes winner Dancing Rocks: no worthwhile form: trained first 3 starts by Mrs J. Ramsden. *J. A. Harris* –

TRUMBLE 3 b.g. Tragic Role (USA) – Sideloader Special 66 (Song 132) [1994 56: 5s 5m 6f⁵ 6m⁵ 7m⁵ 6d⁵ 6s⁵ 6g 1995 8g⁴ 7g 8m² 8.2m 8m⁴ 12m² 12h² 12.4g* 13.8g⁵ 11f⁵ Oct 31] small, quite attractive gelding: modest performer: won seller at Newcastle in August: probably stays 1¾m: acts on hard and soft ground: often a front runner. *C. W. Thornton* 53

TRUTH 2 b.f. (Feb 3) Prince Sabo 123 – Pursuit of Truth (USA) 69 (Irish River (FR) 131) [1995 6f a6g⁵ a7g* Nov 21] unfurnished filly: has scope: first foal: dam, 2-y-o 7f winner on only start, out of half-sister to Sun Princess: 6/1, won 10-runner maiden at Lingfield by a head, clear, from Autobabble, quickening clear on home turn then just holding on: stays 7f: acts on equitrack: will improve further. *Sir Mark Prescott* 66 p

TRUTHFUL IMAGE 6 b.m. Reesh 117 – Token of Truth (Record Token 128) [1994 –: 6s 5.1m 5.7m 6m 1995 6d 6m Apr 17] good-topped mare: fairly useful sprint handicapper (rated 90) at 4 yrs for M. Ryan: no worthwhile form since. *R. J. Hodges* –

TRY AGAIN JANE 5 ch.m. Alias Smith (USA) – Jane Again (Spartan General 109) [1994 –: 10.3s 1995 a8g⁶ Feb 17] sparely-made mare: no sign of ability: tried visored. *D. Eddy* –

TRY-HAITAI (IRE) 4 ch.g. Colmore Row 111 – Grain of Sand (Sandford Lad 133) [1994 NR 1995 6g 7m³ 6m 8m 7.1d a7g Nov 10] sparely-made gelding: fourth reported foal: half-brother to fairly useful 1m to 1¼m winner Knowth (by Exhibitioner): dam dual Irish 6f winner: signs of a little ability, but no form: sold 500 gns Ascot December Sales. *R. Akehurst* –

TRY OMNIPOTENT 3 b.g. Nomination 125 – Try G'S (Hotfoot 126) [1994 NR 1995 8g⁵ 10.2m⁵ 10m 11.6m⁵ 11.5m⁶ 13.8g² 12s Sep 27] 2,900 2-y-o: leggy gelding: third foal: half-brother to a winner in Italy: dam unraced: poor form: virtually pulled up on final start: likely to stay well: sold 1,000 gns Newmarket Autumn Sales. *C. N. Allen* 47

TRYPH 3 b.f. Pharly (FR) 130 – Troja (Troy 137) [1994 52: 7m 7.1d 1995 8.1g Jun 10] rather leggy filly: form only on debut: tailed off (bandaged behind) only 3-y-o start. *J. Berry* –

TRYPHOSA (IRE) 3 b.f. Be My Guest (USA) 126 – Thekla (GER) (Prince Ippi (GER)) [1994 6g² 6g* 7d* 8v³ 1995 8s² 8g* 10.5m³ 10m 10g³ 9.3d Oct 1] strong, lengthy filly: half-sister to multiple German pattern race winner from 1m to 11f, including in Group 1 event, Turfkonig (by Anfield), and another winner: dam won in Germany: successful at 2 yrs in maiden at Frankfurt and listed race at Baden-Baden then third in Preis der Winterkonigin: led inside last when winning 16-runner Arag Preis at Dusseldorf in May by ¾ length from S'il Vous Plait: comfortably best effort when running-on length third of 12 to Carling in Prix de Diane Hermes at Chantilly: below form in good races afterwards, including the Eclipse: should stay 1½m: acts on good to firm and heavy. *A. Wohler, Germany* 116

TRYST (IRE) 4 b.c. Thatching 131 – Finalist 78 (Star Appeal 133) [1994 71d: 7v* 8.5m* 7g 8g⁶ 7g 8d 8m 1995 a8.5g Oct 14] good-bodied colt: fair performer: off course a year, well beaten only 4-y-o outing: stays 8.5f: acts on good to firm and heavy ground. *Dr J. D. Scargill* –

TRY TO PLEASE (IRE) 3 br.g. Try My Best (USA) 130 – Amiga Irlande (Whistling Deer 117) [1994 86: 5m⁴ 5.2m 6f⁴ 6m* 6d³ 5m* 6g 1995 5m 6f³ 6m 6m⁶ a6g Aug 19] medium-sized, lengthy gelding: has a round action: fairly useful 81 d handicapper: trained until after reappearance by M. Heaton-Ellis: well below form last 3 starts: stays 6f: acts on firm and dead ground. *E. A. L. Dunlop*

TSARNISTA 2 b.f. (Mar 14) Soviet Star (USA) 128 – Princess Genista 108 (Ile de Bourbon (USA) 133) [1995 6m^4 7m 6g^2 7g* 8m^6 Nov 3] leggy, sparely-made filly: fourth foal: sister to useful 7f and 1m winner Sovinista and half-sister to 1m (at 2 yrs) and 1½m winner Tomos (by Sure Blade): dam, 1m (at 2 yrs) and 8.5f winner who stayed 15f, out of half-sister to Old Country: fair form: unextended 2-length winner of 13-runner maiden at Lingfield in October then always last of 6 in slowly-run minor event at Doncaster in November: should be as effective at 1m as less. *J. L. Dunlop* 80

TSARSKAYA (USA) 2 ch.f. (Apr 9) Elmaamul (USA) 125 – Wyandra (So Blessed 130) [1995 6g^5 Sep 13] ninth reported foal: closely related to useful 1988 2-y-o 6f winner Stone Flake (by Diesis) who later stayed 1m and half-sister to 3 winners in USA, including a stakes winner by Best Turn: dam unraced daughter of smart middle-distance staying filly Outback: 20/1, around 10 lengths fifth of 10 to Obsessive in maiden at Yarmouth, green to halfway then running on well: will improve. *Mrs J. Cecil* 68 p

TSHUSICK 4 b.f. Dancing Brave (USA) 140 – Infanta Real 108 (Formidable (USA) 125) [1994 81: 7f* 8m^5 7.1d 7.1s^2 6d^3 1995 6d 6g May 20] angular filly: poor mover: fair handicapper: disappointing finishing effort final start: effective at 6f to 1m: acts on any ground: bandaged behind last 4 outings. *J. R. Fanshawe* 74

TTYFRAN 5 b.g. Petong 126 – So It Goes 73 (Free State 125) [1994 –: a12g^5 10.5g 1995 12m 14.1g Apr 17] smallish, stocky gelding: fair middle-distance performer in 1993: well beaten since: refused to race (blinkered) over hurdles in April. *B. P. J. Baugh* –

TUCAN (USA) 3 ch.c. Storm Bird (CAN) 134 – Tuca Tuca (USA) (Miswaki (USA) 124) [1994 73: 6.1m 8g^4 8.2d^5 1995 10g Apr 17] good-topped colt: good mover: fair maiden: well beaten in handicap only 3-y-o start: should stay 1¼m: sent to France. *H. R. A. Cecil* –

TUDOR FLIGHT 4 b.f. Forzando 122 – Tudor Pilgrim 58 (Welsh Pageant 132) [1994 68d: 10.3m^2 10m^3 10g^3 10m 10g 10.1d^4 11.9g^6 10s a8.5g^5 a8g a10g 1995 a10g Dec 18] leggy filly: one-time fair maiden handicapper, but has lost his way: should stay beyond 1¼m: acts on good to firm ground: visored sixth 3-y-o start. *A. G. Newcombe* –

TUDOR ISLAND 6 b.g. Jupiter Island 126 – Catherine Howard 68 (Tower Walk 130) [1994 79: 12m^5 14g* 14m^6 14.8m^3 14.6g^2 13.3s^2 14m* 16d^5 1995 14m* 12m 16.4m^3 14g^2 13.9m 14.6m^3 13.9g* 14.6m Oct 20] tall gelding: fairly useful handicapper: won at Newmarket in April and York (bravely under strong ride from L. Dettori) in October: stays 16.4f: acts on good to firm ground, soft and equitrack: blinkered (easily best effort at the time) once at 3 yrs: sweating (never dangerous in Ebor) fifth 6-y-o start: sometimes hangs, but is genuine. *C. E. Brittain* 86

TUESDAY'S SPECIAL (USA) 5 b.h. Irish River (FR) 131 – Cielo's Love (USA) (Conquistador Cielo (USA)) [1994 10v* 10v* 10v^3 10m* 10g^4 10.5v^5 1995 10v* 10v* 10s^3 10.5v 10g^6 11f^5 12s Oct 7] $100,000F: second foal: dam, sprint maiden winner in USA, is half-sister to high-class 2-y-o Local Suitor: smart French horse: won handicap at 3 yrs then (after being sold out of J. Hammond's stable 180,000 francs) 3 handicaps at 4 yrs: successful in 1995 in 17-runner minor event and 14-runner Prix Exbury (beat En Cascade a length), both at Saint-Cloud in March: ran very well when never-nearer third of 10 to stable-companion Freedom Cry in Prix d'Harcourt at Longchamp and (first start after leaving A. Fabre) when 3 lengths fifth of 12 to Millkom in Man o'War Stakes at Belmont in September: tailed off as if something amiss final start: should stay beyond 11f: acts on firm ground and heavy: held up. *C. Clement, USA* 114

TUIGAMALA 4 b.g. Welsh Captain 113 – Nelliellamay (Super Splash (USA) 106) [1994 37: 8.3g 8.3g 6.9s 6f 8f^6 8.3m 6.9m^6 9g 1995 9g 7m 7f* 8.1m 8f a10g a7g* a7g Dec 12] good-topped gelding: modest performer: won maiden at Brighton in August and minor event at Lingfield (easily best effort) in November: stays 9f: acts on firm going and equitrack: inconsistent. *R. Ingram* 46 a62

TUKANO (CAN) 4 ch.g. Halo (USA) – Northern Prancer (USA) (Northern Dancer) [1994 80: 10.3m^6 10.4f 12.1s^4 14g^3 14g 16g 11.7g^4 12s* 16.2m^3 14m^3 1995 65

14g 16.2f 14.1m5 16.1g5 Jul 12] tall gelding: fair form at best in 1995: stays 2m: probably acts on any going. *J. R. Jenkins*

TULU 4 ch.f. Nicholas Bill 125 – Falcrello 51 (Falcon 131) [1994 81: 8.2v* 10d* 11.9g2 10s2 11.9d 10.5s4 10.1d 1995 10g* 10.5g6 Sep 23] sturdy filly: fairly useful handicapper: tends to go well after lay-off, and (though looking burly) got up close home to win at Ayr in September: lack-lustre effort 8 days later: stays 1½m: acts on heavy going, yet to race on top-of-the-ground: held up and has turn of foot. *Mrs J. R. Ramsden* 78

TUMBLEWEED RIDGE 2 ch.c. (Mar 7) Indian Ridge 123 – Billie Blue 63 (Ballad Rock 122) [1995 6g2 5f4 5m* 6m2 7g2 7.3d* Oct 19] 106

The Horris Hill winner Tumbleweed Ridge looks set to provide up-and-coming trainer Brian Meehan—forty-seven winners and over £220,000 in win prize money in 1995—with his first runner in a classic in the 1996 Two Thousand Guineas. The colt is widely available at 33/1 at the time of writing and those odds look a fair reflection of his chance. The easy winner of a Lingfield maiden in July after promising efforts behind Tagula in a similar event at Newmarket and Kuantan in the Windsor Castle at Ascot, where he was first home on the disadvantageous stand side, Tumbleweed Ridge came within a head of pulling off a first pattern win for his trainer two months before the Horris Hill in the Gimcrack at York. Tumbleweed Ridge isn't quite so smart as the Gimcrack result might suggest—Royal Applause was below par—and he had his limitations exposed by the subsequent Racing Post Trophy runner-up Even Top in the Somerville Tattersall Stakes over seven furlongs at Newmarket in September. Favourite there after Royal Applause's triumph in the Middle Park the previous day, Tumbleweed Ridge looked all over the winner a furlong out but found himself outstayed on the climb to the line and went down by a length and a half. Meehan reported afterwards that his colt had not been fully fit. It nonetheless seemed plausible that Tumbleweed Ridge would find trouble staying the extra sixty yards in the Horris Hill, but the steady pace set by the front-running Busy Flight put the emphasis firmly on finishing speed and Tumbleweed Ridge took full advantage to win by half a length from Busy Flight. It wasn't a high-quality Horris Hill, however, Tumbleweed Ridge having easily the best form beforehand, and with little more than three lengths covering the first eight the form looks well below classic standard.

A 15,000-guinea foal and 29,000-guinea yearling, Tumbleweed Ridge is by Indian Ridge out of the once-raced Ballad Rock mare Billie Blue whose only

Vodafone Horris Hill Stakes, Newbury—
up front, from left to right, Tumbleweed Ridge, Brandon Magic and Busy Flight

Tumbleweed Ridge (ch.c. Mar 7, 1993)	Indian Ridge (ch 1985)	Ahonoora (ch 1975)	Lorenzaccio Helen Nichols
		Hillbrow (ch 1975)	Swing Easy Golden City
	Billie Blue (b 1986)	Ballad Rock (ch 1974)	Bold Lad True Rocket
		Blue Nose (b 1977)	Windjammer Hill Slipper

previous foal Billie Grey (by Chilibang) won over seven furlongs as a two-year-old in 1993. The dam Billie Blue, second over seven furlongs on that one run, is a daughter of the speedy Blue Nose, who won twice as a two-year-old in Ireland at around six furlongs, and a granddaughter of the mile-and-a-half winner Hill Slipper, herself a half-sister to the Irish One Thousand Guineas runner-up Lovely Kate. Tumbleweed Ridge will be doing very well if he makes the frame in the Two Thousand Guineas, particularly as a mile seems likely to stretch his stamina. A lengthy colt who acts on firm and dead ground, he may well prove ideally suited by sprint distances. *B. J. Meehan*

TU OPES 4 ch.g. Most Welcome 131 – Axiana (FR) (Akarad (FR) 130) [1994 76: 6g 7m* 8m* 8m 8m^3 8g 7g^5 8m 8d a8.5g a8.5g a8g 1995 a9.4g^6 a8g^6 a10g^2 a9.4g^2 a11g^2 a9.4g^2 10m 11.1g^4 8g^6 10f^3 12f^2 14.1m* 16f^2 14g^3 15.9m^5 Jul 30] compact gelding: fair handicapper: gained a deserved success at Yarmouth in July: stays 2m: acts on dead ground, firm and all-weather surfaces: visored (ran creditably) ninth 4-y-o start: genuine and consistent. *J. L. Harris* 77 a73

TURBO NORTH 2 b.g. (May 2) Nordico (USA) – Turbo Rose 81 (Taufan (USA) 119) [1995 5m 6m 5d Sep 13] 8,800Y: leggy gelding: fourth foal: half-brother to 2-y-o 6f winners Co Pilot (by Petorius) and (in Ireland) Quick Blush (by Fools Holme): dam miler: always towards rear in maiden events at Redcar (2) and Beverley. *M. Dods* –

TURFMANS VISION 5 b.g. Vision (USA) – Persian Alexandra (Persian Bold 123) [1994 NR 1995 a12g^4 a16g a14g a11g^3 12.3d a14g^6 a14.8g^5 15.8g Jun 2] leggy gelding: no worthwhile form on flat in 1995, pulled up (reportedly lame) final start: stays 1¾m: blinkered third to sixth 5-y-o starts. *R. Hollinshead* –

TURIA 2 b.f. (Mar 1) Slip Anchor 136 – Tura (Northfields (USA)) [1995 7g Oct 9] 24,000F, 20,000Y: smallish, sturdy filly: half-sister to 4 winners, including German 3-y-o 1m listed winner Tristano (by Colmore Row) and fairly useful 6f winner Young Turpin (by Young Generation): dam 7f winner in Ireland: 16/1, slowly away and never really a factor in maiden at Leicester. *Major D. N. Chappell* –

TURNER PRIZE (IRE) 5 b.h. Tate Gallery (USA) 117 – Pansoverina (Sovereign Path 125) [1994 NR 1995 a14g Aug 4] IR 10,000F, 100,000 francs Y: sixth living foal: half-brother to Irish 1¼m winner Lady Grafton (by Junius): dam, Irish 11f winner, is half-sister to Pampapaul: fair maiden (rated 76, stayed 13f) at 3 yrs in Ireland for T. Stack: modest hurdler in 1994/5, winner on a soft surface over 2½m to 3m: behind on flat reappearance: sold (M. Ryan to K. Wingrove) 500 gns Doncaster November Sales. *M. J. Ryan* –

TURNPOLE (IRE) 4 br.g. Satco (FR) 112 – Mountain Chase (Mount Hagen (FR) 127) [1994 NR 1995 10m^5 10m 10.1g^5 12.4m^2 11f* 12m^2 Oct 2] strong gelding: fifth foal: half-brother to 3 winners, notably useful 7f to 9f performer Amazing Feat (by Petorius): dam never ran: fair performer: narrowly won handicap at Redcar in August: will stay beyond 1½m: acts on firm ground, yet to race on a soft surface: has run well when sweating: won 2 novice hurdles in November in impressive style. *Mrs M. Reveley* 72

TURQUOISE SEA (USA) 3 b.f. Shirley Heights 130 – Aminata 98 (Glenstal (USA) 118) [1994 65p: 7.9d 7d 1995 10m 12g^2 13.3f^5 17.5g* 17.2m 16.2s 16d Oct 19] lengthy filly: unimpressive mover: fairly useful handicapper: clearly best effort when winning at Ayr in September: a thorough stayer: seems to need give in the ground: sold 22,000 gns Newmarket December Sales. *J. L. Dunlop* 82

TURRET 4 b.f. Shirley Heights 130 – Moogie 103 (Young Generation 129) [1994 77: 11.9g^5 12.3f^3 12m^5 17.2m^3 15.9g^5 1995 17.2m Jun 2] lengthy, rather plain filly: fair staying maiden: tailed off only 4-y-o start. *R. Brotherton* –

TURRILL HOUSE 3 b.f. Charmer 123 – Megabucks (Buckskin (FR) 133) [1994 NR 1995 a9.4g a9.4g⁴ 10g Jun 17] leggy, sparely-made filly: first foal: dam Irish middle-distance winner: no sign of ability. *W. J. Musson* –

TURTLE POWER 5 ch.g. May Be This Time 74 – Miss Chianti (Royben 125) [1994 NR 1995 a9.4g a16g Mar 2] sparely-made gelding: seems of little account: tried blinkered. *A. P. James* – §

TUSCAN DAWN 5 ch.g. Clantime 101 – Excavator Lady 65 (Most Secret 119) [1994 94: 5.1m² 5d³ 5m² 5f⁴ 5f 5m 5g⁴ 5m² 5.2s 5m 1995 5.1m⁵ 5g 5f 5m 5m 5m⁶ 5.1m Aug 19] leggy, lengthy gelding: unimpressive mover: fairly useful handicapper: disappointing in 1995: speedy, and best at 5f: acts on any going: usually makes running: sometimes ruins chance by rearing in stalls (usually put in last), and not a reliable betting proposition. *J. Berry* 81 d

TUSCANIA 5 ch.m. Faustus (USA) 118 – The Shrew 92 (Relko 136) [1994 –: 10d 12g a12g⁶ a14g 16.2m⁶ 1995 a12g⁴ a12g³ a16g⁵ 16m Jun 26] angular, workmanlike mare: poor staying maiden: sold 650 gns Doncaster October Sales. *J. Wharton* 30

TUTU SIXTYSIX 4 br.f. Petong 126 – Odilese 82 (Mummy's Pet 125) [1994 56: 5d 6d 6d² 6m 6g 7f 5m* 6f⁴ 5f* 5m³ 6m⁵ 5f⁵ 6m 5.1d 1995 6f 5m⁵ 6m 6g 6m 5.9f⁵ 5m 5g 6f² 5m 6m Aug 22] leggy, sparely-made filly: poor sprint handicapper: acts on firm ground, dead and equitrack: blinkered (ran well) once at 2 yrs: best form in visor: comes from off pace and often meets trouble in running: usually ridden by Kim Tinkler. *Don Enrico Incisa* 43

TWICE AS SHARP 3 ch.c. Sharpo 132 – Shadiliya 90 (Red Alert 127) [1994 99?: 5g² 5s² 5g⁶ 6g⁵ 6g³ 1995 6m² 6g* 6g³ 7.1m 6g 5d* 5s Oct 7] well-grown colt: fairly useful performer: made all in maiden at Pontefract in May and handicap at Newcastle (seemed suited by step back to 5f) in September: last of 24 in £15,500 handicap at Ascot on final start: effective at 5f (best form) and 6f: acts on good to firm and soft ground: usually a front runner. *P. W. Harris* 87

TWICE IN BUNDORAN (IRE) 4 ch.f. Bold Arrangement 127 – Asturiana (Julio Mariner 127) [1994 55: 6g⁴ 5g⁶ 5.1g 7m 6m 5.1f⁵ 1995 a6g a6g a8g a6g³ 8d 6.1g 6g 6.1m³ 5g* 5m² 5m⁵ 5m⁵ 5m 6.1d 5d 5d 7f Oct 14] lengthy filly: modest handicapper: won at Newcastle in May: effective at 5f and 6f: acts on good to firm and dead ground and on equitrack: blinkered (well beaten) once at 3 yrs: races prominently. *P. S. Felgate* 57

TWICE KNIGHTLY 4 b.g. Double Bed (FR) 121 – Charter Belle 60 (Runnymede 123) [1994 61: 10m⁴ 10g 1995 7.6m⁵ 12m May 31] leggy, angular gelding: only form when fourth of 6 in steadily-run claimer at Kempton in August 1994: sold 4,200 gns Doncaster July (1995) Sales. *J. R. Jenkins* –

TWICE PURPLE (IRE) 3 b.g. Then Again 126 – Tyrian Belle 77 (Enchantment 115) [1994 –: 8g 1995 8g 7g 7m⁶ 8.1d⁴ 8g⁶ Oct 9] tall, good-topped gelding: modest maiden: stays 1m: acts on good to firm and dead ground. *B. J. Meehan* 62

TWICE REMOVED 2 b.f. (May 4) Distant Relative 128 – Nigel's Dream (Pyjama Hunt 126) [1995 6m Jun 16] 11,000Y: fifth reported foal: half-sister to 1992 2-y-o 6f winner Ten To Six (by Night Shift) and a winner in Italy by Kalaglow: dam ran once here then sent to Belgium: 33/1, hampered stalls and soon behind in maiden at Goodwood: may do better. *S. Dow* –

TWICE THE GROOM (IRE) 5 b.g. Digamist (USA) 110 – Monaco Lady 83 (Manado 130) [1994 73: 8d 10g* 9.2f* 8g² 9m 10m 12m 1995 12.3m³ 11.9s Oct 1] tall, rather leggy gelding: bad mover: modest handicapper: stays 1¼m: acts on firm going. *R. Lee* 60

TWICE TWO (IRE) 2 ch.f. (Mar 8) Double Schwartz 128 – Ever So 78 (Mummy's Pet 125) [1995 5.2f Jun 27] half-sister to several winners here and abroad, including modest sprinter Ever So Artistic (by Claude Monet): dam 2-y-o 6f winner: 8/1, always well behind in seller at Yarmouth: sold 1,200 gns Newmarket July Sales: sent to Norway. *M. H. Tompkins* –

TWILIGHT HOUR (USA) 3 b.f. Majestic Light (USA) – If Winter Comes (USA) (Dancing Champ (USA)) [1994 66p: 7d³ 1995 10g² 10m⁴ 12.3m² 14g Sep 23] leggy, unfurnished filly: unimpressive mover: fair maiden: stays 12.3f: yet to race on extremes of going: sold 6,200 gns Newmarket December Sales. *B. W. Hills* 70

TWILIGHT PATROL 3 b.f. Robellino (USA) 127 – Warning Light (High Top 131) [1994 85p: 6m^2 6m* 6d 7m 7d* 1995 8.1m 7f^3 8.1g^6 8m* 8g^2 7f^4 8.1m^6 7m* 7g Sep 7] leggy filly: useful handicapper: won at Newmarket in July and August: effective at 7f and 1m: acts on firm ground and good to soft: often bandaged near-fore: held up: suitable mount for a claimer: consistent. *R. Hannon* 96

TWILIGHT SLEEP (USA) 3 b.c. Shadeed (USA) 135 – Sleeping Beauty 87 (Mill Reef (USA) 141) [1994 83p: 6g^6 7m^3 7g* 1995 8g^6 10m 14m Jun 13] strong, compact colt: good mover: fairly useful performer: pulled up on final start: should prove suited by further than 1m: has raced only on a sound surface. *Lord Huntingdon* 83

TWIN CREEKS 4 b.g. Alzao (USA) 117 – Double River (USA) (Irish River (FR) 131) [1994 61: 8m^5 8.2f 7.5g 6m 7m^3 8.1d 8g^3 1995 a8g^6 a7g* a7g^6 7.6m 6.9m 7.5m 6.9f^3 8.1m^5 9.2m* 8m 7d Sep 27] compact gelding: modest performer: won maiden at Southwell in February and amateurs handicap at Hamilton in July: stays 9f: acts on fibresand and firm ground, well beaten on a soft surface: takes keen hold: none too consistent. *M. D. Hammond* 56 a61

TWO CHALK 3 b.g. Mazilier (USA) 107 – Feast-Rite (Reform 132) [1994 48: 5m 6.1m a6g^3 6m 6m a5g a7g a6g a7g^4 1995 a6g^6 a6g Feb 1] small gelding: poor sprint maiden: visored (below form) 4 of last 6 starts: has worn tongue strap/been bandaged behind. *P. D. Evans* –

TWO FOUR SPORTS (IRE) 2 b.g. (Mar 21) Red Sunset 120 – Golden Empress (Cavo Doro 124) [1995 7d 7g Oct 10] IR 2,350F, IR 2,000Y, 3,800 2-y-o: half-brother to 4 winners here and abroad, including fairly useful 1990 2-y-o 6f winner Soweto (by Kafu), later minor stakes winner in USA: dam lightly-raced granddaughter of 1000 Guineas winner Belle of All: burly, soundly beaten in maidens at Newcastle and Leicester: moved poorly to post last time: sold 500 gns Doncaster November Sales. *J. A. Harris* –

TWO MOVES IN FRONT (IRE) 5 ch.g. Ballad Rock 122 – Kentucky Wildcat 64 (Be My Guest (USA) 126) [1994 83: 6v 6d 5g* 5m^4 5m^4 6m* 5g* 6f 6f 6g 6d 5m 5d 1995 6g 6f^5 6g 7g 6g 5f 5f Oct 16] strong, workmanlike gelding: fair handicapper: well below form after second 5-y-o start: effective at 5f and 6f: acts on any ground: tried blinkered, no improvement: sold 2,100 gns Doncaster November Sales: sent to Sweden. *J. Berry* 72 d

TWO O'CLOCK JUMP (IRE) 3 b.c. Be My Guest (USA) 126 – Magic Spell (FR) (Dancer's Image (USA)) [1994 83: 6m^2 6g^3 6d^4 6g* 6d^2 1995 8m* 10m^6 8g^4 8g^4 8g^3 8g* Aug 26] leggy, quite good-topped colt: useful performer: won 10-runner listed race at Kempton in April and 7-runner Prix Quincey at Deauville (led near finish, beat Bishop of Cashel a head) in August: stays 1m, possibly not 1¼m: acts on good to firm ground: blinkered (ran well) last 2 starts at 2 yrs: sold to South Africa 180,000 gns Newmarket December Sales. *R. Hannon* 108

TWO SOCKS 2 ch.g. (Apr 10) Phountzi (USA) 104 – Mrs Feathers 57 (Pyjama Hunt 126) [1995 5.2m 6m 6g 6m a7g^4 a7g^3 a8.5d^2 7.6d^5 6.9g a8g Nov 6] 2,200F, 7,200Y: leggy, unfurnished gelding: half-brother to fairly useful 1988 2-y-o 5f to 8.5f winner (later successful in USA) Nightstalker (by Night Shift): dam, maiden, ran 5 times at 2 yrs: modest form: twice in frame in sellers: stays 8.5f: best efforts on fibresand: blinkered (below form) fourth start. *M. McCormack* 49 a60

TWO TIMER 2 ch.c. (Mar 21) Clantime 101 – Two's Up (Double Jump 131) [1995 5h^4 6g a6g a7g Nov 24] 3,000Y: half-brother to 1m to 1½m winner Burcroft (by Crofthall) and 10.5f seller winner Bob Double (by Import): dam never ran: poor form in maiden events and nursery. *M. Johnston* 39

TWO WAY STRETCH 3 b.f. Prince Daniel (USA) – Playtex 72 (Be Friendly 130) [1994 41: 6m 6m^6 7g^5 1995 a8g a11g^4 a10g a12g^5 7g^5 10m May 29] small filly: poor maiden: stays 1½m: acts on fibresand, twice well below form on equitrack: best turf efforts on good ground. *G. L. Moore* 39

TYKEYVOR (IRE) 5 b.g. Last Tycoon 131 – Ivoronica 89 (Targowice (USA) 130) [1994 89d: 10s^3 7.9f 8.5g^6 7g 10.4f 8s 12m 1995 8.3m^5 10g* 8.9m^3 10m* 10d 9g 12m^5 Oct 21] lengthy, quite good-topped gelding: fairly useful performer: won minor event at Salisbury (by 6 lengths) in May and handicap at Sandown (despite carrying head awkwardly) in August: ideally needs further than 9f, and stays 1½m: 81

acts on firm ground, no form on a soft surface: visored twice, running well first occasion: usually bandaged. *Lady Herries*

TYMEERA 2 b.f. (Feb 28) Timeless Times (USA) 99 – Dear Glenda 66 (Gold Song 112) [1995 a5g^3 a5g^4 5f* 5.1m* 5g^6 Sep 13] 2,000Y: neat filly: unimpressive mover: third living foal: half-sister to 5f winner Jade City (by Belfort): dam sprinter: won seller at Folkestone in June and claimer at Nottingham (hung left from half-way) in August: bandaged, disappointing in Sandown claimer final start: speedy. *B. Palling* — 62

TYPHOON EIGHT (IRE) 3 b.c. High Estate 127 – Dance Date (IRE) (Sadler's Wells (USA) 132) [1994 96: 7m 7.3d^6 1995 11m 10.2f^6 11.4m^5 12g^4 16.2d Sep 23] smallish, sturdy colt: poor mover: fair maiden at best in 1995: ran in snatches and tailed off in handicap at Ascot on final start: should prove suited by further than 1½m: best form with give in the ground. *B. W. Hills* — 78

TYRELESS (IRE) 3 ch.f. Milk of The Barley 115 – Sigwell's Gold 62 (Sonnen Gold 121) [1994 –: 6.1s 6.9m 7m 7m 1995 a7g^5 a8g^5 a8.5g^4 a8g Jan 30] leggy filly: poor maiden: stays 8.5f: acts on fibresand. *A. P. Jarvis* — 38

TYRIAN PURPLE (IRE) 7 b.h. Wassl 125 – Sabrine (Mount Hagen (FR) 127) [1994 65: 6m^4 a7g a6g^3 a6g^2 a7g 5m^2 a5g* a5g a6g^5 a5g a5g 1995 a5g^4 a7g^4 a6g^4 a6g* a6g* a6g^2 a6g a5g^3 6m 6m 5m^3 5.3f* 6f^3 a5g 6d a7g Dec 15] leggy, angular horse: fair performer, best on the all-weather: made all in claimer and seller at Lingfield in February and in handicap at Brighton in July: effective at 5f and 6f, won over 1m in 1992: acts on firm and dead ground and all-weather surfaces: usually blinkered: good mount for claimer: has worn tongue strap: often a front runner. *T. J. Naughton* — 61 a70

TYRONE FLYER 6 b.g. Celestial Storm (USA) 132 – Dance A Jig (Dance In Time (CAN)) [1994 56: 5d^3 7m 6m 7m^2 5d* 5s^5 5m 6f^3 1995 a7g a8g a11g a7g 7g a6g^4 a6g^2 a7g^2 7g^6 6g a7g a7g^4 7m a7g^5 6g 5.1m Oct 19] strong, workmanlike gelding: modest performer: left P. McEntee after fourth 6-y-o start, G. Fierro after twelfth and R. Harris after fourteenth: stays 7f: acts on fibresand and probably on any turf going: no improvement in blinkers: occasionally bandaged: takes good hold and usually forces pace: sold 1,700 gns Newmarket Autumn Sales: sent to Italy. *C. N. Allen* — 56

TZAR RODNEY (FR) 3 b.c. Assert 134 – Laquifan (USA) (Lear Fan (USA) 130) [1994 7g^3 8g* 8g* 8.3v^2 9v^3 1995 10s^2 8.5s* 10s^2 10.5v* 10.5v* 10.5s^2 10.5d^4 10d* 10g 12.5d^2 12.5g Aug 27] second foal: dam 7f (at 2 yrs) and 6.5f winner in France: useful French colt: won minor events at Clairefontaine and Compiegne at 2 yrs: successful in 1995 in minor events at Cagnes-sur-Mer and Saint-Cloud, listed event at Saint-Cloud and 4-runner Prix la Force at Chantilly (by a nose from Copent Garden), all by the end of May: best form when short-neck second of 5 to Partipal in slowly-run Prix Maurice de Nieuil at Maisons-Laffitte and when close seventh of 9 in Grand Prix de Deauville: stays 12.5f: acts on heavy ground: effective from front or held up: sent to USA. *G. Doleuze, France* — 109

U

UCKERBY LAD 4 b.g. Tobin Lad (USA) 124 – Chomolonga (High Top 131) [1994 –: a8.5g 1995 a11g^2 a12g a12g^5 a12g a8g^3 a8g a8g Mar 20] leggy, workmanlike gelding: poor maiden plater: sold (N. Littmoden to A. Dunn) 1,500 gns Ascot July Sales: stays 11f: acts on fibresand: twice blinkered (no improvement): inconsistent: resold 1,300 gns Ascot October Sales. *N. P. Littmoden* — 42

ULTIMATE WARRIOR 5 b.g. Master Willie 129 – Fighting Lady 104 (Chebs Lad 120) [1994 75: 7.6v^3 12.1s 10g 10.5m 1995 a10g a8g* a8g 10m^3 a10g^3 a10g^5 a14.8g Sep 16] lengthy, angular gelding: fair performer: easily won maiden at Lingfield in February: stays 1¼m: acts on heavy and good to firm ground and on equitrack. *C. A. Cyzer* — 71 a62

ULTRA BARLEY 2 ch.g. (Mar 9) Beveled (USA) – Chapter One (Hello Gorgeous (USA) 128) [1995 6m^5 a6g* 6f* 6m^4 6f^3 6g a6g* a7g* Dec 14] 3,000Y, 5,800 2-y-o: workmanlike gelding: second foal: dam poor maiden: fair form: com- — 68+ a79 fortable winner of seller at Wolverhampton and claimer at Hamilton in August, and of claimers at Wolverhampton in October and Lingfield in December: stays 7f: acts on firm ground, best form on fibresand. *P. C. Haslam*

ULTRA BEET 3 b.g. Puissance 110 – Cassiar 84 (Connaught 130) [1994 57: 5m 5m^3 5m^3 1995 a5g^4 a5g* a5g* a5g* a5g* a5g* 5g 5g^5 a5g^2 6.1g^3 6f* 5m^6 5g a5g a5g Dec 14] compact gelding: fairly useful performer on all-weather: won minor event at Lingfield, claimers at Wolverhampton (2) and Lingfield and handicap at Lingfield, all by March 1: fair on turf, winner of handicap at Hamilton in June: disappointing returned to all-weather: effective at 5f and 6f: acts on firm ground and goes well on the all-weather: visored (winner first time, below form next day) twice at 3 yrs: races prominently. *P. C. Haslam* — 75 a84

ULTRA FINESSE (USA) 3 b.f. Rahy (USA) 115 – Suavite (USA) (Alleged (USA) 138) [1994 7d 1995 10g* 10.5g^4 12g* 12m^2 12.5g^3 12d^6 Sep 27] $135,000Y: fifth foal: half-sister to 3 middle-distance winners, notably top-class Suave Dancer (by Green Dancer) and smart Suave Tern (by Arctic Tern): dam stakes-placed winner in USA: useful French filly: won minor events at Evry in April and Saint-Cloud in May: 2 lengths second to Privity in Prix de Malleret at Longchamp next start: stays 12.5f: acts on good to firm ground, possibly not on dead. *Mme C. Head, France* — 107

ULTRA POWER 2 ch.g. (Apr 19) Sharpo 132 – Scottish Legend (Legend of France (USA) 124) [1995 5f^4 5g^5 5g Sep 14] smallish, good-bodied gelding: second foal: half-brother to 3-y-o Flamboro (by Handsome Sailor), 6f and 7f winner at 2 yrs: dam unraced half-sister to Stewards' Cup winner Rotherfield Greys: poor form in claimers and seller: tail swisher. *P. C. Haslam* — 47

UMBERSTON (IRE) 2 b.c. (Feb 25) Nabeel Dancer (USA) 120 – Pivotal Walk (IRE) (Pennine Walk 120) [1995 7m 8g 10m Oct 19] IR 21,000Y: useful-looking colt: first foal: dam Irish 1¼m winner, stayed 2m: modest form in maidens at Newmarket and Yarmouth and median auction maiden at Nottingham: will stay beyond 1¼m. *L. M. Cumani* — 52 +

UNCHANGED 3 b.f. Unfuwain (USA) 131 – Favorable Exchange (USA) (Exceller (USA) 129) [1994 54: 7m 8.1g 8.1d 1995 12m^2 11.9f^4 15.4m* 15.9d* 17.1m^2 Oct 2] good-topped filly: not seen out until July: fair handicapper: won at Folkestone (led over 5f out) and Chester (settled, led well inside last) in September: very much a stayer: acts on good to firm ground and dead, yet to race on soft: may improve further. *C. E. Brittain* — 78

UNCHARTED WATERS 4 b.f. Celestial Storm (USA) 132 – Try The Duchess 99 (Try My Best (USA) 130) [1994 68: 8g^5 10g* 10.2g^5 12g a10g^6 a12g 1995 a10g a14.8g 11.7m^3 11.9f^2 13.1f^6 11.9m^6 12m^5 11.4m^5 14g 12m 9.7s^4 12.1d Oct 10] lengthy, angular filly: fair handicapper: below form after fourth start: stays 11.7f: acts on firm going, below form on the all-weather: blinkered (out of form) eighth 4-y-o start: occasionally makes the running: sometimes looks lazy. *C. A. Cyzer* — 68

UNCLE DOUG 4 b.g. Common Grounds 118 – Taqa 85 (Blakeney 126) [1994 54: 8v^5 12g 10m^3 12f 12.1m^4 12.1g^2 16.1d* 1995 16m^2 13.9g^4 16m^3 20m 15.8g Sep 16] close-coupled, quite attractive gelding: progressed into a fairly useful winning hurdler in 1994/5: modest handicapper: demoted after narrow winner at Ripon (hung both ways under pressure) in April: has form at 2½m, but at least as effective at 1¾m/2m: acts on good to firm ground (below form on firm) and dead: best held up but (sometimes hangs, looked reluctant once at 3 yrs) is not an easy ride. *Mrs M. Reveley* — 57

UNCLE GEORGE 2 ch.g. (Apr 5) Anshan 119 – Son Et Lumiere (Rainbow Quest (USA) 134) [1995 5.1g^5 6m 6m* 8g^6 6g Sep 30] 10,000Y: lengthy gelding: good walker: second foal: half-brother to Irish 3-y-o 7.8f winner Ansal Boy (by Robellino): dam lightly-raced maiden: won maiden at Yarmouth in August: beaten some way out in nurseries at Yarmouth and Newmarket following month: subsequently gelded: should stay further than 6f. *M. H. Tompkins* — 73

UNCLE OSWALD 4 ch.g. Nashwan (USA) 135 – Riviere Bleue (Riverman (USA) 131) [1994 87: 12m^5 12s 1995 12g 10m^5 8m^5 8m^6 10g^2 12m 10.2m^2 10m^5 Aug 7] close-coupled, sturdy gelding: fairly useful handicapper: generally ran creditably in 1995, leading inside last when narrowly-beaten second at both Windsor and Chepstow: effective at strongly-run 1m, but appeared not to stay 1½m in strongly-run race at Royal Ascot sixth 4-y-o start: acts on good to firm ground. *R. Hannon* — 86

UNCONDITIONAL LOVE (IRE) 2 b.f. (Feb 11) Polish Patriot (USA) 128 – Thatcherite (Final Straw 127) [1995 5d² 5m* 5m* 5.2g³ 5m⁴ 5m Jul 7] IR 5,800Y: sturdy, lengthy, good sort: thrived physically, and has plenty of scope: good walker and powerful mover: fourth foal: closely related to Italian 3-y-o 7.5f and 1m winner Casque Bleu (by Roi Danzig) and half-sister to 4-y-o 1¼m and 11.1f winner Bajan (by Taufan): dam unraced half-sister to Kampala: fairly useful filly: wide-margin winner of maiden auction at Beverley and well-contested minor event at Ascot in spring: creditable fourth of 12 from low draw to Blue Duster in Queen Mary Stakes at Ascot penultimate outing, best subsequent effort: gave impression something amiss on final start: bred to stay 6f: active type who tends to swish tail: wandered closing stages both starts at Ascot. *M. Johnston* 93

UNDAWATERSCUBADIVA 3 ch.g. Keen 116 – Northern Scene 78 (Habitat 134) [1994 NR 1995 8g 7g 6.1m 5g 6d Sep 18] 1,200F: leggy, sparely-made gelding: half-brother to several winners, including fairly useful 6f (at 2 yrs) and 7f winner Rocton North (by Ballad Rock): dam Irish 2-y-o 5f winner: looked well out of his depth, except possibly in claimer on final outing. *M. P. Bielby* –

UNFORESEEN 3 ch.c. Unfuwain (USA) 131 – Eversince (USA) (Foolish Pleasure (USA)) [1994 67p: a7g⁶ 7g⁶ 6d⁴ 6m² 1995 a8.5g a9.4g a12g Nov 21] rangy colt: off course 14 months and well beaten on return; sold 5,200 gns Ascot December Sales. *Sir Mark Prescott* –

UNFORGIVING MINUTE 6 b.g. Bellypha 130 – Kindjal 84 (Kris 135) [1994 –: 10m 12v 1995 10m 10.4m 10.3d⁵ 10d⁵ 12s Oct 6] quite attractive gelding: has a round action: fairly useful handicapper: failed to repeat form shown in steadily-run Magnet Cup at York second 6-y-o start, running particularly poorly at Ascot last time: effective at 1¼m to 1½m: acts on good to firm and heavy ground. *P. W. Harris* 82

UNFUWAANAH 3 ch.f. Unfuwain (USA) 131 – Jeema 102 (Thatch (USA) 136) [1994 NR 1995 7m⁴ 7f 5.2g* 5g Sep 28] lengthy filly: fifth foal: half-sister to useful middle-distance maiden Trebly (by Top Ville) and a 7f winner in Italy by Green Desert: dam, best at 2 yrs, won 3 times at 5f: easily best effort in maidens when winning at Yarmouth in September, travelling strongly before bursting through to lead close home: well-beaten favourite in handicap final start: looks a sprinter: has raced only on a sound surface. *H. Thomson Jones* 74

UNIHOC BALL 2 ch.f. (Feb 27) Indian Ridge 123 – Soon To Be 84 (Hot Spark 126) [1995 6m Jul 2] 7,500F, 12,000Y: sturdy filly: third reported foal: dam (6f and 7f winner) from family of Oaks-placed Suni and Media Luna: 33/1 and in need of run, ran green and always behind, hanging, in maiden at Doncaster: unruly stalls. *T. R. Watson* –

UNISON 4 gr.g. Merdon Melody 98 – Bri-Ette 53 (Brittany) [1994 –: 9m 8.3d 7g 6m 6m⁵ 6f⁵ 8g 1995 a6g a7g⁴ a8.5g Jun 30] lengthy gelding: no longer of much account. *C. R. Barwell* –

UNITED FORCE (IRE) 3 b.g. High Estate 127 – Exuberine (FR) 82 (Be My Guest (USA) 126) [1994 71p: 6m⁴ 1995 11m 10g² 10g² 16.2m 10m³ 10.4g Aug 30] rangy, attractive gelding: fairly useful maiden: broke leg at York: should have stayed beyond 1¼m (tailed off in Queens Vase): front runner: dead. *P. W. Chapple-Hyam* 85

UNITED FRONT 3 br.g. Be My Chief (USA) 122 – Julia Flyte 91 (Drone) [1994 NR 1995 10.2m² 10f* 10g 11.8g 16d Oct 19] 16,500F, 40,000Y: tall, good-topped gelding: good mover: half-brother to 2 winners, notably useful 1½m winner Alphard (by Kalaglow): dam 2-y-o 6f winner: 11/4 on, won 8-runner maiden at Redcar in May, making all: tailed off afterwards, sold out of H. Cecil's stable 26,000 gns Newmarket July Sales after next start, looking less than keen final one: lazy sort, should stay beyond 1¼m. *R. J. O'Sullivan* 79

U-NO-HARRY (IRE) 2 b.c. (May 29) Mansooj 118 – Lady Roberta (USA) (Roberto (USA) 131) [1995 5m a5g² a5g² a6g 6m* 7m⁴ 5f³ 5g* 6.1m² 5.7h⁴ 5m 5m³ 5m³ 6d 6g² 6m 5m⁵ Oct 27] IR 3,400Y: sturdy colt: poor mover: usually looks well: half-brother to several winners here and in North America, including 5f and 6f winner Continental Carl (by Two Punch): dam leading 3-y-o filly in Canada in 1980 when successful at up to 9f: won claimer at Leicester in May and seller at Catterick in July: mostly creditable efforts afterwards in nurseries: stays 6f: acts on hard ground and fibresand: ran poorly in blinkers fourth start: has sweated: tough and genuine. *R. Hollinshead* 67

UN PARFUM DE FEMME (IRE) 4 b.c. Mill Native (USA) 124 – Hail To You (USA) (Kirtling 129) [1994 73: 8s 10.8v 10.1f 10f^2 10.8m* 12m* 12g^2 11.8m^2 12m^2 12g^2 12d* 12g 1995 10.8d^6 10.8m^6 11.8m^5 13.3g 12m^6 11.5m^2 14g^2 14f^5 Aug 10] sparely-made colt: has a round action: fair handicapper: stays 1¾m: acts on firm and soft ground: sometimes pulls hard: consistent: sold 15,000 gns Newmarket September Sales: sent to Saudi Arabia. *J. Pearce* 69

UNPREJUDICE 4 b.g. North Briton 67 – Interviewme (USA) (Olden Times) [1994 70: 7m* 7m 8m 8m 1995 8m^6 7g 10.3g^2 10.8g^6 10.4m 10f^3 10f Oct 31] small, lengthy gelding: fair handicapper: sold out of G. Rimmer's stable 5,000 gns Newmarket July Sales after fourth start: stays 10.3f: has raced only on a sound surface: bandaged first four 4-y-o starts. *M. D. Hammond* 69

UNREAL CITY (IRE) 2 b.c. (Mar 25) Rock City 120 – Tolmi 122 (Great Nephew 126) [1995 7f^2 Oct 18] sturdy, good-bodied colt: ninth foal: half-brother to useful 4-y-o middle-distance performer Double Dagger (by Reference Point), 1m winner Nile Delta (by Green Desert) and a winner abroad by Niniski: dam 1000 Guineas second out of outstanding broodmare Stilvi: 3/1 from 5/2, bit backward and green, beaten a neck by Prize Giving 11-runner maiden at Yarmouth, well placed throughout and staying on well: sure to do better. *H. R. A. Cecil* 78 p

UNSOLD 2 b.c. (Apr 2) Green Desert (USA) 127 – Shoot Clear 111 (Bay Express 132) [1995 6g^2 6m^4 6g 6g^4 Sep 30] IR 24,000Y: small, sturdy colt: half-brother to several winners, including useful middle-distance performer Shoot Ahead (by Shirley Heights) and 1990 2-y-o 7f winner Dance Ahead (by Shareef Dancer): dam, 5f to 7f winner at 2 yrs and fourth in 1000 Guineas, half-sister to Yorkshire Oaks winners Sally Brown and Untold: second of 8 to Rio Duvida in maiden at Yarmouth: off course 2½ months afterwards and proved disappointing until fourth to King of Peru in nursery at Newmarket on final outing: will stay beyond 6f: sold 21,000 gns Newmarket Autumn Sales: sent to USA. *J. R. Fanshawe* 77 +

UNSPOKEN PRAYER 2 br.f. (May 4) Inca Chief (USA) – Dancing Doll (USA) (Buckfinder (USA)) [1995 6.1d 6s a6g a7g^6 Dec 12] leggy filly: first foal: dam unraced half-sister to Grade 1 9f runner-up Burnt Hills: well beaten in maidens and nursery. *J. R. Arnold* –

UONI 2 ch.f. (Mar 22) Minster Son 130 – Maid of Essex 66 (Bustino 136) [1995 5m a7g^3 a8.5g^3 Dec 2] lengthy, unfurnished filly: first foal: dam best at 1¼m to 1½m: third in maidens at Lingfield and Wolverhampton late on, her first run since May: will stay beyond 8.5f. *C. E. Brittain* 51

UPEX LE GOLD TOO 3 ch.g. Precocious 126 – Restless Star (Star Appeal 133) [1994 46: a6g 7f 6g 9d^5 a7g^6 1995 7g 10m^4 9.9m 6g 8.1m^4 8f 12.1m^6 7m* 8m^5 7g^6 Sep 13] neat gelding: has a round action: poor handicapper: sold out of Mrs A. Swinbank's stable 1,900 gns Doncaster May Sales after third 3-y-o start: won apprentice maiden event at Thirsk in July: effective at 7f, stays 9f: acts on dead ground and good to firm. *L. R. Lloyd-James* 38

UP IN FLAMES (IRE) 4 br.c. Nashamaa 113 – Bella Lucia (Camden Town 125) [1994 66: 8s 9m 8g 7f^3 7.6g^2 1995 7.5m 8g^5 8.1g* 8.5m* 8m^3 10f Jul 25] leggy colt: made into a fairly useful handicapper, winning at Haydock in May and Epsom (£14,300 contest) in June: well beaten in £35,300 event at Goodwood on final start: seemed likely to stay beyond 8.5f: acts on soft and good to firm going (probably on firm), below form on fibresand. *M. D. Hammond* 85

UPLIFT 2 ch.f. (Feb 4) Bustino 136 – Relatively Easy 70 (Relkino 131) [1995 7g 7g 8m Oct 20] angular filly: second foal: half-sister to 5f and 1m winner (at 2 yrs) Beats Working (by Aragon), later stayed 1½m: dam middle-distance stayer also won over jumps: always in rear in maidens in October. *Sir Mark Prescott* –

UPPANCE 7 b.m. Kabour 80 – Final Cast 50 (Saulingo 122) [1994 32: 5m^4 5m^4 5m 5m^5 5m^3 5s 7.1m 6g 1995 5d 5.9m 5m 5m 5g^6 5f^6 6m 5f 5m Aug 24] workmanlike, angular mare: poor mover: poor maiden handicapper: best at 5f: acts on firm and dead ground: effective blinkered or not: inconsistent. *D. A. Nolan* 30

UPPER MOUNT CLAIR 5 b.m. Ela-Mana-Mou 132 – Sun Street 73 (Ile de Bourbon (USA) 133) [1994 –: 10d^5 13.1g 14.6m a13g 1995 a14.8g a16g^5 a13g^4 a16g^3 a16g 18g* 16m 17.1m 14.1g* 20m 18.7g^3 20f^2 16.1f^4 18.2g^2 a16g^5 Nov 8] smallish, leggy mare: fair performer: won handicap at Doncaster (40/1) in March and 64 a54 minor event at Yarmouth in June: suited by a test of stamina: blinkered (no improvement) first 3 starts at 5 yrs: inconsistent. *C. E. Brittain*

UPPER TORRISH 3 b.f. Sharrood (USA) 124 – Upper Caen (High Top 131) [1994 NR 1995 12m^5 May 20] unfurnished filly: fourth live foal: sister to useful 1991 German 2-y-o Kilphedir and half-sister to 6f to 8.3f winner Arndilly (by Robellino): dam unraced sister to very useful miler Miner's Lamp: backward and green, fifth of 7 in maiden at Thirsk, running on steadily: not seen out again: sold 4,000 gns Newmarket July Sales. *B. Hanbury* 64

URANIA 3 b.f. Most Welcome 131 – Aonia 97 (Mummy's Pet 125) [1994 NR 1995 8.1m 8f^2 9.7m^3 10g^2 Oct 1] angular filly: second foal: dam, 2-y-o 5f winner, is half-sister to Forzando: fair maiden: may well stay beyond 1¼m: seems to lack turn of foot. *M. A. Jarvis* 66

URGENT SWIFT 2 ch.c. (May 2) Beveled (USA) – Good Natured § (Troy 137) [1995 6g^5 7f^4 7.1m 7f^2 7m 7.9m 6.9g^5 Oct 16] 4,200Y: unfurnished colt: fifth foal: half-brother to German 6.5f and 1m winner Roman (by Robellino): dam temperamental: fair maiden: will stay 1m: acts on firm ground. *A. P. Jarvis* 65

UTMOST ZEAL (USA) 2 b.c. (Feb 13) Cozzene (USA) – Zealous Lady (USA) (Highland Blade (USA)) [1995 7f^5 Aug 9] $65,000Y: unfurnished colt: second foal: half-brother to a 2-y-o winner in North America by Northern Prospect: dam 6f winner in USA from the family of Raintrap and Sunshack: 20/1, 4 lengths fifth of 10 to Villeggiatura in maiden at Salisbury, always well placed: likely to stay further than 7f: will improve. *P. W. Harris* 72 p

UTRILLO (USA) 6 b.g. Dahar (USA) 125 – Waltz Me Sue (USA) (Olden Times) [1994 NR 1995 10m Jul 10] compact, good sort: impressively won 11.5f maiden handicap at Yarmouth (rated 53+) at 4 yrs: burly and sweating, well beaten in handicap at Windsor after almost 2-year absence. *B. J. Curley* –

UTR (USA) 3 ch.f. Mr Prospector (USA) – Hasbah 111 (Kris 135) [1994 –p: 6m 1995 6m 6m 5g Sep 21] leggy, attractive filly: no form: edgy type, reluctant to go down second 3-y-o start: pulls hard: probably temperamentally unsatisfactory. *H. Thomson Jones* –

V

VADE RETRO SATANAS (FR) 3 b.g. Holst (USA) 119 – Praise Be Given (Kings Lake (USA) 133) [1994 45: 5f 5g 6g^4 a8.5g^5 1995 a8g a8g 10.3g Mar 23] smallish, angular gelding: poor form: well beaten in 1995: sold 1,150 gns Doncaster March Sales. *B. S. Rothwell* –

VADLAMIXA (FR) 3 gr.f. Linamix (FR) 127 – Vadlava (FR) (Bikala 134) [1994 6m^3 6g^3 7g^3 7d^2 8g* 1995 8d 8d 10.5m 8g* 9.3d^5 10d^6 Nov 18] leggy, sparely-made filly: fourth foal: half-sister to 2 winners, notably useful 4-y-o 1¼m and 1½m winner Vadlawys (by Always Fair): dam French 9f (at 2 yrs) winner: smart French filly: won minor event at Evry in 1994 and listed event (narrowly) at Deauville in August: good fifth, beaten 3 lengths by Timarida, in Prix de l'Opera at Longchamp in October, much better effort afterwards: had earlier finished seventh in Poule d'Essai des Pouliches at Longchamp (hampered before keeping on well) and tenth in Prix de Diane at Chantilly: stays 10.5f: acts on good to firm ground and dead, yet to race on extremes. *A. Fabre, France* 114

VAGUELY GAY (USA) 3 b.c. Bering 136 – Solveig (FR) (Gay Mecene (USA) 128) [1994 NR 1995 10v* 10d^4 10m* 10g^3 10g^6 Aug 15] second foal: brother to French 8.5f winner Solving: dam French 7f (at 2 yrs) and 10.5f winner: won newcomers event at Saint-Cloud in April and listed event at Longchamp (by a length from East of Heaven) in June: ran well when under ½-length third of 7 to Royal Solo in steadily-run Prix Eugene Adam at Saint-Cloud, never nearer: may well stay beyond 1¼m: acts on good to firm ground and heavy. *Mme C. Head, France* 112

VAGUE SPIRIT 2 ch.c. (Apr 18) Vague Shot 108 – Dawn Vigil VII (Pedigree Unknown) [1995 7m 7m 8.5s Sep 19] neat colt: first known foal: dam unraced: never a factor in maidens. *C. E. Brittain* –

VAIGLY SUNTHYME 5 ch.g. Vaigly Great 127 – Red Roses (FR) (Roi Dagobert 128) [1994 –: 12g 13d 12g 12g^5 1995 a14g 13g 13f^5 Jun 5] rather leggy gelding: no longer of any account: dead. *J. M. Carr* –

VAIN PRINCE 8 b.g. Sandhurst Prince 128 – Vain Deb 66 (Gay Fandango (USA) 132) [1994 51?: 16.1g 16.2s 14.1d 15.1f^4 14.6m^4 13.6g 15.1m^2 15.1m* 14.1g^4 14.1d^6 16m^5 1995 16.2m^2 16m^5 14.1m* 14.1m 15.1f* 15.1m* 16.2g^4 13f* 16f^3 Aug 25] rangy gelding: modest handicapper: won at Redcar in May and at Edinburgh (twice) and Hamilton in the summer: stays 2m: acts on any going: effective blinkered or not: fair hurdler, ran out Nov 4. *N. Tinkler* 58

VALANOUR (IRE) 3 b.c. Lomond (USA) 128 – Vearia (Mill Reef (USA) 141) [1994 NR 1995 8g* 9.3m* 9g^6 10m* 10m^6 Sep 9] 122

Remarkably for such a huge and successful breeding operation as the Aga Khan's, Valanour's win in the Grand Prix de Paris was the first by one of his colts in a French Group 1 race since Natroun, to whom Valanour is related (they are both grandsons of the mare Val Divine), took the Prix du Jockey-Club in 1987. Valanour faced a competitive field for the Grand Prix de Paris and was one of seven out of the ten runners to have competed in a Group 1 contest last time out. Valanour had already met three of his rivals in the Prix Jean Prat three weeks earlier, where, in a very muddling race on easier going, he had finished sixth in a bunched finish behind Torrential, Bobinski (fourth) and Leeds (fifth). A very different result was expected this time with Valanour starting at 63/10 ahead of both Bobinski and Leeds (the 52/1 outsider) in the betting. Poliglote and Diamond Mix, the first two in the betting, were coming back in distance after finishing second and sixth respectively in the Prix du Jockey-Club. There was a three-strong British challenge, Painter's Row and Singspiel joining Torrential. Positioned in mid-division early on, Valanour avoided an incident towards the rear in the back straight which saw Bobinski effectively put out of the race as he was knocked into the rails. Valanour took over from Poliglote in the lead once into the straight and never looked like being troubled by his nearest challenger Diamond Mix. Singspiel finished best of all, running Valanour to a neck, Diamond Mix half a length away in third with one and a half lengths and the same back to Torrential and Poliglote.

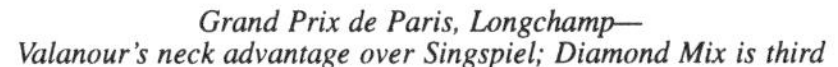

Grand Prix de Paris, Longchamp—
Valanour's neck advantage over Singspiel; Diamond Mix is third

The Grand Prix was only Valanour's fourth race. Unraced at two, he had made a winning debut in a newcomers race at Saint-Cloud in April and followed up in the Group 3 Prix de Guiche at Longchamp, again in good style. Those efforts saw him start evens favourite for the Prix Jean Prat at Chantilly on the day of the Jockey-Club. Connections attributed Valanour's defeat to the ground which, while officially good, was described by his jockey as sticky after some heavy showers. Valanour never confirmed the good impression he made in the Grand Prix de Paris. There were ambitious plans for him against older horses for the second half of the season. With the end of the Aga Khan's boycott of British racing, the Sussex Stakes was on the agenda and Valanour was installed as second favourite in the ante-post lists but a high temperature in the days leading up to the race ruled him out. The Arlington Million was mentioned as another possible target but when he did reappear, Valanour failed to do himself justice, trailing home sixth in the Guinness Champion Stakes at Leopardstown in September.

Valanour (IRE) (b.c. 1992)	Lomond (USA) (b 1980)	Northern Dancer (b 1961)	Nearctic
			Natalma
		My Charmer (ch 1969)	Poker
			Fair Charmer
	Vearia (b 1985)	Mill Reef (b 1968)	Never Bend
			Milan Mill
		Val Divine (b 1971)	Val de Loir
			Pola Bella

Valanour's pedigree will no doubt ensure him a place at stud in due course. His sire, the Two Thousand Guineas winner Lomond, had had more success at stud with his fillies, among them top-class miler Marling, Prix Marcel Boussac winner Ashayer and Irish St Leger winner Dark Lomond. Valanour's dam Vearia won two races over ten furlongs, including a listed event at Maisons-Laffitte. Valanour is her second foal and first winner after the Alleged colt Veadari. Her next foal is a filly by Kahyasi called Vereva. Vearia is one of numerous winners out of Val Divine, the most notable of them being the Champion Stakes winner Vayrann, Queen Anne Stakes winner Valiyar and Oak Tree Invitational winner Yashgan. Val Divine, who won over ten and a half furlongs, is a daughter of the Poule d'Essai des Pouliches winner Pola Bella, herself out of the One Thousand Guineas and Oaks winner Bella Paola.

Valanour is a strong, sturdy colt and with just five races behind him there may be further improvement to come. He carried his head awkwardly at Leopardstown and tended to carry it a little high when winning the Grand Prix de Paris but he is genuine. Valanour stays ten furlongs, seems well suited by top-of-the-ground and has a good turn of foot. *A. de Royer Dupre, France*

VALES ALES 2 b.g. (May 5) Dominion Royale 112 – Keep Mum 63 (Mummy's Pet 125) [1995 5v^{6} 5g^{5} 5m^{4} 5f^{3} 8.3g Sep 25] fourth foal: half-sister to 3-y-o Hutchies Lady (by Efisio) and 5-y-o 1¼m and 11f winner Keep Battling (by Hard Fought): dam sprint maiden best at 2 yrs: little worthwhile form. *R. M. McKellar* –

VALETTA 4 b.f. Faustus (USA) 118 – Mrewa (Runnymede 123) [1994 NR 1995 7g^{6} 7m^{4} 8.2m^{5} 7m Aug 16] angular filly: easily best of siblings is veteran sprinter Ashtina (by Tina's Pet), useful at his best: dam twice-raced maiden: well beaten in maidens, weakening after around 5f: joined Miss Gay Kelleway: may do better at sprint distances. *B. J. Meehan* –

VALIANT MAN 4 br.g. Valiyar 129 – Redcross Miss 64 (Tower Walk 130) [1994 63d: a6g^{3} a6g^{5} 8g 8g 7g^{2} 7m^{5} 7m 8s 8.2d a8g a8g^{5} 1995 a8g^{6} Jan 6] leggy, lengthy gelding: modest performer: stays 1m: acts on any turf going and fibresand: tried blinkered, no improvement: none too consistent: joined Miss J. Bower. *J. Hetherton* 53

VALIANT TOSKI 4 b.c. Petoski 135 – Corvelle (Reliance II 137) [1994 –: 10v 10g 11.1m^{3} 10m a12g 11.5g 15.8g 1995 12.5g^{3} a13g^{2} 11.9f* Jul 20] sturdy, close-coupled colt: has pronounced knee action: modest performer: comfortably won selling handicap at Brighton in July: stays 13f: acts on firm ground and equitrack: visored (well beaten) once at 3 yrs: blinkered (made running, best efforts) last 2 starts. *M. C. Pipe* 50

VALINCO 4 b.f. Malaspina 118 – Sagareina (Sagaro 133) [1994 –: 9g 7g 1995 9g 9.7g 12m 10m Jun 26] strong, workmanlike filly: no worthwhile form: reluctant to post third 4-y-o start: sold 620 gns Ascot August Sales. *S. Dow* –

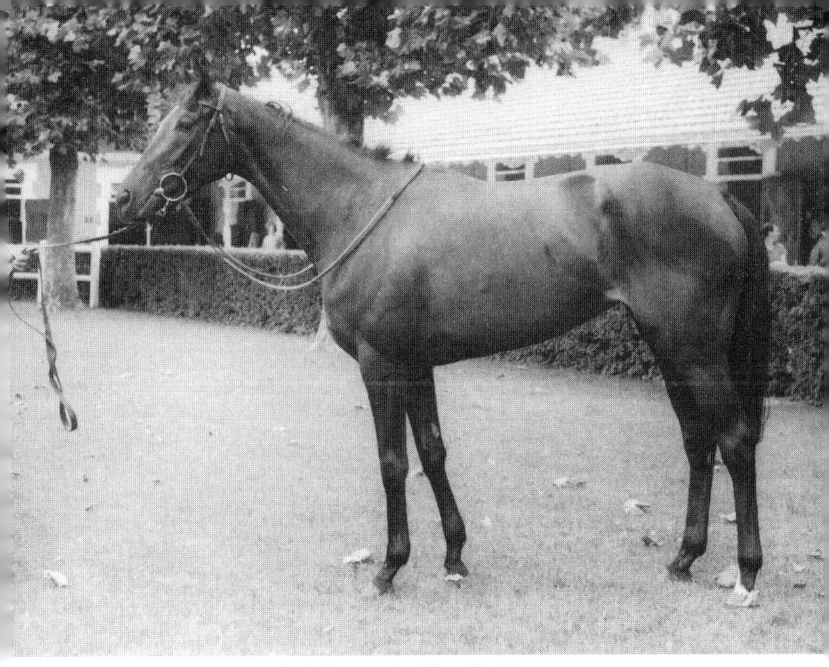

Sheikh Mohammed's "Valley of Gold"

VALISE 2 b.f. (Mar 29) Salse (USA) 128 – Secret Valentine 71 (Wollow 132) [1995 5f^4 5f^3 6g Sep 14] 4,200Y: fifth foal: half-sister to useful 4-y-o 7f and 1m winner Billy Bushwacker (by Most Welcome) and fair sprinter Gondo (by Mansingh): dam 6f to 1m winner: modest form in maiden auctions: should prove effective at 6f+. *Mrs M. Reveley* — 52

VALJESS 2 b.f. (Mar 1) Today And Tomorrow 78 – Emmer Green 64 (Music Boy 124) [1995 6s Oct 6] second foal: dam best at 5f: 50/1, tailed off in maiden at Ascot. *D. C. O'Brien* — –

VALLEY OF GOLD (FR) 3 b.f. Shirley Heights 130 – Lustre (USA) 90 (Halo (USA)) [1994 NR 1995 10s* 10.5s* 10.5g^3 10.5g* 11d* 12g^3 12d^2 Sep 10] third foal: dam, 2-y-o 6f winner who stayed 9f, is half-sister to smart middle-distance filly Whitehaven and daughter of Kentucky Oaks winner White Star Line: smart performer: successful in minor event at Evry and listed event at Longchamp in March then 5-runner Prix Cleopatre at Saint-Cloud (beat Loretta Gianni by 1½ lengths) and 11-runner Oaks d'Italia at Milan (led inside last and beat Olimpia Dukakis by a length) in May: placed in Irish Oaks at the Curragh (but beaten 10 lengths by impressive Pure Grain) and 10-runner Prix Vermeille at Longchamp (best effort, ran on well to take second near line, length behind Carling) afterwards: stays 1½m: acts on soft going, yet to race on top-of-the-ground: consistent: joined Godolphin and sent to Dubai. *A. Fabre, France* — 117

VALLEY OF TIME (FR) 7 br.m. In Fijar (USA) 121 – Vallee Sarthoise (FR) (Val de Loir 133) [1994 –: a6g 6v 5m^5 6g 9.2g 1995 6f 5f 8.1m 6.9f^4 7.1f^6 8.3f^6 Jul 29] sturdy mare: seems of little account nowadays. *D. A. Nolan* — –

VANBOROUGH LAD 6 b.g. Precocious 126 – Lustrous 73 (Golden Act (USA)) [1994 58: 8.3d 8g* 8.3m^4 8f^4 8.1g^3 7f^5 7d 8g 8d 1995 7m^3 8.3g^5 8f* 8g 8.3m^2 8.1m^4 — 56

7.1m⁵ 8.3m⁴ 8g Sep 8] strong, lengthy gelding: poor mover: modest handicapper nowadays: won at Bath in May: effective at 7f, and stays 11.6f: acts on any going: visored (below form) once at 2 yrs. *M. J. Bolton*

VANESSA ROSE 4 ro.f. Simply Great (FR) 122 – Phoenix Rose 85 (Frankincense 120) [1994 58: a8.5g 7m 7d 10.3m 10m^4 7.6g^3 7g 7g* 5s 6s 7d^5 a6g 1995 6g Apr 26] leggy filly: just a modest performer in 1994: well beaten only start in 1995: stays 7.6f: best efforts on good ground: tried blinkered: tended to sweat and get on edge: dead. *A. Bailey* –

VAN GURP 2 ch.c. (May 18) Generous (IRE) 139 – Atlantic Flyer (USA) 98 (Storm Bird (CAN) 134) [1995 7.1d^3 7d Sep 24] strong colt, on small side: fluent mover: first foal: dam should have stayed beyond 1m: 3½ lengths third of 11 to Kings Witness in maiden at Haydock, staying on strongly final 2f: well backed but took keen hold in minor event at Ascot 3 weeks later, dropping away to finish well-beaten seventh of 8: bred to stay at least 1m: evidently well regarded: worth another chance. *B. A. McMahon* 81

VANISHING POINT 2 ch.c. (Mar 16) Rock City 120 – Lady River (FR) (Sir Gaylord) [1995 5g 6m^2 5g 7f* 7.5m^4 7f^3 8g* 8g 8f^4 Oct 18] 10,000Y: angular colt: has a round action: half-brother to 3-y-o Campaspe (by Dominion) and numerous winners in France, including middle-distance performers Satin River (by Satingo) and Tonaccio (by Fabulous Dancer), former also winner at nearly 2½m: dam showed a little ability in France: made all or most of running when successful in nurseries at Goodwood in July and Pontefract (beat Warbrook a length) in September: good fourth of 19 to Nosey Native in similar event at Yarmouth final start: suited by 7f/1m: sold 23,000 gns Newmarket Autumn Sales: sent to Switzerland. *G. Lewis* 84

VANOLA 3 b.f. Salse (USA) 128 – Salilia 93 (Nishapour (FR) 125) [1994 –: 7m 1995 11.9m^5 14.1f 12f^6 16.4f^6 16d 14s Sep 28] lengthy filly: of no account. *P. Howling* –

VANROY 11 b.g. Formidable (USA) 125 – Princess Tavi (Sea Hawk II 131) [1994 56: 8.3g^4 8.3d^2 8.3m^3 8.3m* 8.3m^2 11.6f^4 8g^5 a10g^4 a10g 1995 8.3m 8.3g^6 Jun 12] sturdy gelding: carries plenty of condition: veteran handicapper: stays 1¼m: acts on firm ground, dead (not very soft) and all-weather surfaces: normally visored, has run well without: sometimes bandaged behind: held up. *J. R. Jenkins* 54

VAPORIZE 3 ch.g. Handsome Sailor 125 – Belle Appeal (Teenoso (USA) 135) [1994 NR 1995 6m 8f 7m 16.2m^6 Jul 20] strong, lengthy gelding: first live foal: dam unraced: well beaten. *D. M. Hyde* –

VARNISHING DAY (IRE) 3 b.c. Royal Academy (USA) 130 – Red Letter Day 100 (Crepello 136) [1994 87: 7g* 7g^5 1995 7f^3 Jun 28] rather leggy, useful-looking colt: good mover: ran well when 1½ lengths third of 4 to Moon King in strongly-run minor event at Salisbury in June: may stay 1m, unlikely to get further: reported by trainer to have suffered from back problems, pulled muscles and a suspected hairline fracture of the pelvis: sold only 3,000 gns Newmarket Autumn Sales. *P. W. Chapple-Hyam* 91

VARSAVIA (USA) 4 br.f. Nureyev (USA) 131 – Header Card (USA) (Quack (USA)) [1994 84: a7g* 7.8g* 7m^4 8g* 1995 8m Jun 21] leggy, unfurnished filly: in foal to Zafonic: fairly useful performer: facing very stiff task, ran as if something amiss and virtually pulled up in Royal Hunt Cup at Royal Ascot only start in 1995: stayed 1m. *Lord Huntingdon* –

VARVARKA 3 b.f. Soviet Star (USA) 128 – Helen Street 123 (Troy 137) [1994 NR 1995 8m* 8f 8f^4 10.1g Aug 28] lengthy filly: sixth foal: sister to French 1m and 1½m winner Sovetsky and half-sister to useful 8.3f to 11.6f winner Grecian Slipper (by Sadler's Wells): dam won from 6f to 1½m (Irish Oaks): fair form: won maiden at Carlisle in June: should have stayed further than 1m: dead. *J. W. Watts* 79

VASETTO 2 b.g. (Mar 7) Midyan (USA) 124 – Canna (Caerleon (USA) 132) [1995 7f^4 6f^2 8f^2 7m^3 Sep 6] IR 17,000Y: sturdy colt: second foal: half-brother to 3-y-o Anchorena (by Slip Anchor): dam unraced half-sister to Oaks d'Italia and E P Taylor Stakes winner Ivor's Image: fair form in maidens: needs further than 6f, and stays 1m: sold 15,500 gns Newmarket Autumn Sales: sent to Malaysia. *Sir Mark Prescott* 72

VASILIEV 7 b.g. Sadler's Wells (USA) 132 – Poquito Queen (CAN) 113 (Explodent (USA)) [1994 –§: 17.1s 1995 14.1g Apr 24] big gelding: fair hurdler (often reluctant) at best nowadays: looked one to leave alone on return to flat. *S. Gollings*

– §

VASLAV NIJINSKY 3 b.c. Hadeer 118 – Pacific Gull (USA) 67 (Storm Bird (CAN) 134) [1994 NR 1995 a11g a8g^{2} a8g^{6} a7g 7g 8f* a8.5g^{4} Nov 26] second foal: half-brother to 7f/1m winner Northern Chief (by Chief Singer): dam 8.5f winner: modest maiden here for G. Rimmer: stays 1m: acts on firm going: blinkered (pulled hard, no form) fourth start: sold 3,000 gns Newmarket July Sales and won minor event at Ostend following month on first start for new connections. *F. Wouters, Belgium*

57

VAUGRENIER (IRE) 3 b.c. Scenic 128 – Church Mountain 83 (Furry Glen 121) [1994 84p: 8m^{5} 8g^{5} 1995 12f 10m^{3} 11.9f* 12m^{4} 12m^{2} 12f^{6} 12.1s 11f^{3} Oct 31] strong, good-bodied, attractive colt: fairly useful form: easily made all in poor 4-runner maiden at Brighton in May: stays 1½m: acts on firm ground, well beaten on soft. *R. Hannon*

84

VAVONA 3 ch.f. Ballad Rock 122 – Savahra 82 (Free State 125) [1994 60p: 6s 6g^{3} 1995 6m 6g^{6} 6m^{5} 6m Jul 17] strong filly: modest maiden handicapper: likely to prove well suited by 7f+: acts on good to firm and soft ground. *L. J. Holt*

56

VAX NEW WAY 2 gr.c. (May 1) Siberian Express (USA) 125 – Misty Arch (Starch Reduced 112) [1995 5g^{6} a6g* 5g^{5} 6m^{5} 6.1s 6.1m^{3} Oct 26] 8,200Y, 12,500 2-y-o: sparely-made colt: sixth live foal: half-brother to 3-y-o Statomist (by Statoblest) and 2 modest winners, including Priscilla Rose (1m, by Rambo Dancer): dam ran twice: won maiden auction at Wolverhampton in September: mainly creditable efforts afterwards in nurseries: stays 6f: acts on fibresand and good to firm ground, well beaten on soft: raced keenly in blinkers final start. *J. L. Spearing*

67

VAYELLO 4 b.g. Mtoto 134 – Khalkeva (FR) (Vayrann 133) [1994 52d: a8g^{5} a10g^{5} a10g^{3} 10.3m 12.3d^{5dis} 12.3d^{4} 14.6f* 14.1f^{5} 14.1m^{5} 14.1m^{6} 14m^{3} 13.8g^{5} 16.2f 15.1m^{4} 1995 12d a14g Jun 16] small, sturdy gelding: wayward and one to leave well alone: sold 1,000 gns Ascot July Sales. *C. Smith*

§§

VEESEY 2 b.f. (May 31) Rock City 120 – Travel On 111 (Tachypous 128) [1995 5m^{4} 5.1m 5.2g 5.2d^{5} 5g 6g^{3} 5f Oct 24] 10,500F, 6,600Y: sturdy, good-quartered filly: progressed well physically: seventh live foal: half-sister to 2 winners abroad: dam won Cherry Hinton Stakes: modest maiden: better form at 6f than 5f. *John Berry*

57

VEILED DANCER (IRE) 2 b.f. (Jan 29) Shareef Dancer (USA) 135 – Fatal Distraction (Formidable (USA) 125) [1995 7f 8.1d^{3} Sep 12] useful-looking filly: third foal: closely related to Samsonesque (by Unfuwain), 1½m winner in Sweden in 1995: dam unraced half-sister to smart middle-distance stayer Casey: 8 lengths third of 7 to stable-companion Scarlet Plume in maiden at Sandown, one pace last 2f: will improve again. *J. L. Dunlop*

69 p

VELOCE (IRE) 7 b.g. Kafu 120 – Joanns Goddess (Godswalk (USA) 130) [1994 73, a–: a8.5g 8m 7.6m 7g^{4} 8.1g^{5} 8.1g^{3} 7f 8f 7f^{5} 7.1m 7.6g^{3} 7m^{3} 8g* 8.3m 8.1g 8.1m* 7.6g 8g a9.4g 1995 a7g a7g a7g^{5} a7g^{5} a7g^{3} a7g^{5} a8g^{6} 6g 7.5m^{5} 8m^{4} 7m 7.6m 7m* 7m* 10.3g^{3} 7.1g* 7m 7g^{6} 7g 8g^{2} 8.1m 10.3m^{5} 7.6m Aug 19] lengthy, robust gelding: fair performer on turf, nowhere near that on the all-weather: won sellers at Thirsk and Redcar in May and handicap at Sandown in June: below form last 5 starts: effective of 6f to 10.3f: effective in blinkers/visor or without: sometimes bandaged: best held up: tough. *A. Bailey*

73
a49

VELVET JONES 2 b. or gr.g. (Apr 17) Sharrood (USA) 124 – Cradle of Love (USA) 87 (Roberto (USA) 131) [1995 6m 5m^{2} a6g^{2} 6m^{6} 8.1m^{2} 8m^{3} 7g^{4} 7d 10g^{6} a8g Nov 10] angular gelding: first foal: dam 9f winner: plater: left P. Cole after seventh outing: seemed to run well first start for new connections but below form last 3 outings: should stay beyond 1m. *G. F. H. Charles-Jones*

55

VENA (IRE) 3 b.f. Danehill (USA) 126 – Massawippi (Be My Native (USA) 122) [1994 92p: 6g 6s^{5} 7m^{5} 1995 7m^{5} 8m^{5} 9g* 10f^{4} 10g^{4} 9f* 10f^{3} 10.1g^{2} 9g Sep 30] leggy filly: generally progressive and is a useful performer: won maiden at Kempton in June and handicap at Goodwood in July: very good efforts placed in listed contests won by Ellie Ardensky at Salisbury and Bonne Etoile (caught post) at Newcastle:

97

down the field in Cambridgeshire (gone in her coat) final start: stays 1¼m: acts on firm ground. *J. L. Dunlop*

VENDETTA 2 b.f. (Apr 21) Belmez (USA) 131 – Storm Warning 117 (Tumble Wind (USA)) [1995 6m Jun 15] useful-looking filly: has scope: sixth foal: half-sister to 4-y-o 7f to 8.5f winner Present Situation (by Cadeaux Genereux) and 3-y-o Storm Flash (by Green Desert): dam sprinter: 14/1 and bit backward, slowly away, green and always behind, not knocked about, in maiden at Newbury: looked sort to do better. *I. A. Balding* – p

VENGAN 3 ch.f. Efisio 120 – La Crima 63 (Runnymede 123) [1994 50: a5g^{5} 5.1m a5g^{5} 6m 5.1g^{5} 6m^{5} a6g^{6} 1995 6m a5g a5g a6g^{5} Jul 17] workmanlike filly: seems no longer of much account: sold 750 gns Ascot August Sales. *D. Haydn Jones* –

VENICE BEACH 3 b.g. Shirley Heights 130 – Bold And Beautiful 105 (Bold Lad (IRE) 133) [1994 –p: 7m 1995 7.9m^{2} 8m^{4} 10m^{2} 10d^{4dis} Oct 19] lengthy gelding: has scope: fair maiden: best efforts (making most) when second at York and Ayr: saddle slipped (and lost weight cloth) final start: stays 1¼m: takes good hold, and goes early to post: sold (B. Hills to C. Brooks) 22,000 gns Newmarket Autumn Sales. *B. W. Hills* 73

VENI VIDI VICI (IRE) 2 b.c. (Mar 24) Fayruz 116 – Divine Apsara (Godswalk (USA) 130) [1995 7g^{5} 6f Oct 12] IR 9,200F, 20,000Y: stocky colt: half-brother to 1989 2-y-o 5f winner Burslem Beau (by Burslem) and a winner in Macau: dam Irish 5f to 1m winner: late progress when fifth of 17 to Ali-Royal in maiden at Warwick: last of 26 in Redcar Two-Year-Old Trophy 9 days later: capable of better. *M. J. Heaton-Ellis* 68 p

VENTURE CAPITALIST 6 ch.g. Never So Bold 135 – Brave Advance (USA) 98 (Bold Laddie (USA)) [1994 95: 7d 6m* 6f^{6} 7m 6g 6d 6d 1995 6g^{6} 5m^{4} 6g* 7.1m^{4} 112

Paul Caddick and MacGay Sprint Trophy Rated Stakes (Handicap), York—
another notable success for trainer David Nicholls
and his wife, jockey Alex Greaves,
as Venture Capitalist (left) short-heads Branston Abby

6m* 7.6g^5 6f^4 6m^4 7m^6 6g^2 5.6m 6g Sep 16] lengthy, deep-girthed gelding: unimpressive mover: progressed into a smart performer for new connections in 1995: won minor event at Thirsk in April and rated stakes at York in May: best efforts when fourth of 30 to Astrac in the Wokingham at Royal Ascot and length second of 12 to Branston Abby in rated stakes at York: first home on unfavoured near side when seventh of 22 to Hello Mister in Portland Handicap at Doncaster: again poorly drawn in Ayr Gold Cup final start: effective at stiff 5f to 7f: acts on firm and dead ground: effective blinkered or not: best coming with late challenge off strong pace (has a fine record in the big traditional sprint handicaps) and well ridden by Alex Greaves: tough and genuine. *D. Nicholls*

VENTURE FOURTH 6 b.g. Hotfoot 126 – Four Lawns 77 (Forlorn River 124) [1994 27, a39: a7g^2 a7g a7g^4 a8.5g a7g^6 a11g 10v^5 11.1f^2 11.1f^4 13g 12.1g^5 12.3g^6 12f^5 14.1m 11.8g^5 a11g^4 a12g 1995 a7g^5 a11g a8g 12.3d 6.9m^6 11.1g 9.2f^4 12m 8.3f Jul 29] leggy gelding: poor maiden handicapper at best: stays 1½m: acts on firm ground and fibresand: tried blinkered/visored, but no improvement: inconsistent. *E. J. Alston* –

VERA'S FIRST (IRE) 2 b.f. (Feb 26) Exodal (USA) – Shades of Vera 76 (Precocious 126) [1995 5m 6g^5 5f^2 6.9g^6 6f^3 6f^3 6m^2 6m^4 6.1s^4 6.1m^5 a7g* a7g^2 a6g Dec 2] leggy, workmanlike filly: first foal: dam 6f winner: fair performer: very game winner of seller at Lingfield in November: stays 7f: acts on firm and soft ground, best all-weather form on equitrack: blinkered last 6 starts: has been bandaged. *G. Lewis* 69 a64

VERDE LUNA 3 b.g. Green Desert (USA) 127 – Mamaluna (USA) 114 (Roberto (USA) 131) [1994 NR 1995 8.3m 7.5m^2 8g^2 10m 8m 7m^4 8.2m^3 8g 8g 7s Sep 28] quite good-topped gelding: first foal: dam won Nassau Stakes: fair maiden handicapper: stays 1m: acts on good to firm ground (poorly drawn and visored first time when well beaten on soft): inconsistent: sold (M. Tompkins to D. Arbuthnot) 9,200 gns Newmarket Autumn Sales. *M. H. Tompkins* 71

VERONICA FRANCO 2 b.f. (Apr 20) Darshaan 133 – Maiden Eileen (Stradavinsky 121) [1995 7m Oct 20] 16,000Y: leggy, unfurnished filly: sister to French 3-y-o 1¼m winner Maidenhair and half-sister to 1988 2-y-o 6f winner Nazanin and a winner in Italy (both by Sharpo): dam Irish 7f to 1¼m winner: 16/1 and green, always behind in maiden at Doncaster. *J. L. Dunlop* –

VERRO (USA) 8 ch.g. Irish River (FR) 131 – Royal Rafale (USA) (Reneged) [1994 –§: a13g 10d 9d 8.3s 9m a14g a13g a12g 11.5d a12g 1995 a12g a13g^3 14.1f a16.2g Jul 21] robust, good-quartered gelding: bad performer nowadays: stays 13f: acts on all-weather and heavy ground: tried blinkered/visored: none too keen and not one to rely on. *K. Bishop* 18 §

VERULAM (IRE) 2 b. or br.c. (Feb 2) Marju (IRE) 127 – Hot Curry (USA) (Sharpen Up 127) [1995 7m 8.1m^4 7.5d 8.1s Oct 17] IR 13,000Y: lengthy, unfurnished colt with scope: third foal: half-brother to 3-y-o 11.5f winner Marchant Ming (by Persian Bold): dam 1m winner in USA: easily best effort in maidens when fourth of 8 to Ski Academy at Chepstow in August: stays 1m: seems unsuited by soft ground: sold 12,000 gns Newmarket Autumn Sales. *J. A. R. Toller* 71 ?

VERY DICEY 7 b.g. Tremblant 112 – Party Game 70 (Red Alert 127) [1994 80: a5g^6 a6g^5 a5g* a5g a5g* a5g* a6g^5 a5g* 5d* 5f^3 a5g^2 5m^6 5m 5m^2 5.1m* 5f^4 5m^2 a5g^3 5d^5 a5g* a6g a5s^4 1995 a5g* a5g^6 a5g^2 a5g^3 a5g^2 a5g Apr 1] strong, workmanlike gelding: a fairly useful sprinter who won 13 and was in frame in a further 33 of his 80 starts: successful at least once in each of his 6 seasons, in a claimer at Wolverhampton in January: broke down final start: effective at 5f and an easy 6f: acted on firm and dead ground, and on the all-weather: tried blinkered (ran creditably) and visored earlier in career: good ride for apprentice/amateur: used to race up with pace: tough and genuine: dead. *J. Berry* 75

VERZEN (IRE) 3 ch.c. Salse (USA) 128 – Virelai 72 (Kris 135) [1994 86: 7m^2 8g^3 1995 7m* 8m 7m* 7d 7.9m^3 a9.4g^2 Dec 2] lengthy, workmanlike colt: useful performer: won minor event at Redcar in May and £18,600 handicap at Newmarket (led close home, after edging left) in August: improved form when ¾-length second of 12 to Prince of Andros in listed race at Wolverhampton in December: effective at 7f and stays 9.4f: acts on good to firm ground and fibresand, below form (never going 99 a106

New Zealand Handicap, Newmarket—an excellent shot of Verzen (No. 7), Hi Nod and Celestial Key

well) only run on a soft surface: visored (ran well) fifth 3-y-o start: tends to carry head awkwardly. *D. R. Loder*

VESHCA LADY (IRE) 2 b.f. (Feb 11) Contract Law (USA) 108 – Genzyme Gene 38 (Riboboy (USA) 124) [1995 5m 5m^3 5m* a6g 5m^4 7f^6 7.1m^2 7m^3 7h^3 7m* 7.1m^3 7f 7f Oct 14] 3,800Y: leggy filly: half-sister to 1992 2-y-o 5f winner Make It Happen (by Fayruz) and several winners abroad: dam, plater, stayed 1¼m: won sellers at Beverley in May and Catterick in August: stays 7f: acts on hard ground, ran poorly on fibresand. *E. Weymes* 54

VETTORI (IRE) 3 b.c. Machiavellian (USA) 123 – Air Distingue (USA) 120 (Sir Ivor 135) [1994 93p: 8s^4 8m* 1995 8d* 12f^6 8m^3 Jun 20] 119

The latest Dubai Poule d'Essai des Poulains, won narrowly by the ex-Cecil-trained colt Vettori from Atticus, was a weak renewal of that classic, as had seemed probable at the time with only two of the eight runners pattern-race winners. The

Dubai Poule d'Essai des Poulains, Longchamp—
Vettori and Atticus have had the race to themselves all the way up the straight

Maktoum Al Maktoum/Godolphin's "Vettori"

principals had the Poulains between them the whole of the way up the straight after Atticus, one of those pattern winners, had set such a gallop that the pacemaker could never get to the front. Vettori, who was having his first run of the season, his first outside maidens and only his third in all, lay handy and knuckled down to his work when brought to challenge. Atticus fought back strongly after being edged out of the lead halfway up the straight but Vettori saw the mile out very well.

In view of his limited experience it was reasonable to anticipate more improvement from Vettori in his next race—a really significant amount, even. However, on breeding, he seemed far from certain to be as effective over the mile and a half of the Derby, the race chosen for him, and he started at 20/1, the longer-priced of the Saeed bin Suroor horses. He was never really a factor at Epsom, and although he stayed on steadily into sixth place behind his stable-companion Lammtarra he was beaten six lengths. Vettori soon improved on his Epsom form back at a mile in the St James's Palace Stakes at Royal Ascot, confirming Longchamp running with Atticus into the bargain. He just lost the battle for second with Charnwood Forest, four lengths behind the very impressive Bahri, keeping on gamely having caught a bump at halfway. He was not seen out again, and has now been retired to Haras de Fresnay-Le-Buffard in Normandy at a covering fee of 40,000 francs (about £5,250, with the October 1st concession).

Royal Ascot provided evidence that Vettori's sire Machiavellian is capable of getting a good-class mile-and-a-half winner, when Phantom Gold took the Ribblesdale Stakes. Vettori and Phantom Gold are from the Two Thousand Guineas runner-up's first crop. Machiavellian himself never raced beyond a mile and gave the impression, that that might be his limit. Vettori's dam Air Distingue ran her best race when third in the ten-and-a-half-furlong Prix de Diane for Dick Hern's stable. She won two races in France for Francois Boutin as a two-year-old, including the one-mile Prix d'Aumale; later she had two seasons in the United States, during which she won at eight and a half furlongs at Hollywood Park. Air Distingue's record as a broodmare has been improved considerably by Vettori. Three of her five previous foals—Decided Air (by Sure Blade), Lodestar (by Rainbow Quest) and Livonian (by Kris)—won at nine furlongs or a mile and a quarter. The French filly Decided Air was easily the pick, and was allowed to take her chance in the Diane, cutting little ice. Vettori's great-grandam Quill made her mark on the track and left her mark at stud. She was champion two-year-filly in the States in 1958, trained on very well and three seasons on retired the winner of fourteen races. Her offspring include the Irish St Leger winner Caucasus (later one of the best turf performers of his time in the USA), the Canadian champion One For All, the Oaks third Last Feather (dam of Ruznama) and Run The Gantlet's dam First Feather. Vettori's grandam Euryanthe, a sister to Caucasus, never ran.

Vettori (IRE) (b.c. 1992)	Machiavellian (USA) (b 1987)	Mr Prospector (b 1970)	Raise A Native
			Gold Digger
		Coup de Folie (b 1982)	Halo
			Raise The Standard
	Air Distingue (USA) (b 1980)	Sir Ivor (b 1965)	Sir Gaylord
			Attica
		Euryanthe (ch 1975)	Nijinsky
			Quill

Vettori is a well-made, attractive colt, and a good mover. He stayed a mile well and would almost certainly have been just as effective at a mile and a quarter had he been given the opportunity. He acted on good to firm and good to soft going. *Saeed bin Suroor*

VEUVE HOORNAERT (IRE) 3 gr.f. Standaan (FR) 118 – Hazy Lady (Habitat 134) [1994 88: 5.7f^{2} 5.7f* 5.2m^{4} 6f^{3} 6d^{2} 5g^{2} 1995 6m^{6} 6g^{4} 6g^{6} 8f^{2} 6g Sep 12] tall, unfurnished filly: fairly useful performer: stays 6f: acts on firm and dead ground: sold 26,000 gns Newmarket December Sales: none too consistent. *R. Hannon* 86

VEZELAY (USA) 3 b.f. Diesis 133 – Vexation (USA) (Vice Regent (CAN)) [1994 NR 1995 8m 9g 7g a7g Jul 21] $85,000Y: lengthy, angular filly: sixth foal: half-sister to 3 winners, notably very useful 6f to 1m performer Robellation (by Robellino): dam unraced half-sister to smart 1m to 1¼m performer Baronet: no worthwhile form: should stay at least 1m: sold 7,000 gns Newmarket December Sales. *J. H. M. Gosden* –

VIARDOT (IRE) 6 b.g. Sadler's Wells (USA) 132 – Vive La Reine (Vienna 127) [1994 83+: a12g 11.8s^{2} 12.4m^{4} 13.9f^{6} 1995 12.3m^{5} 12g Sep 28] big, rangy gelding: carries condition: has a quick action: fairly useful handicapper at 5 yrs: off course 14 months, below form in claimers as 6-y-o: stays 1¾m: acts on firm ground, very best effort on soft: sometimes looks none too keen and may well benefit from blinkers/visor: won claiming hurdle in November. *Mrs M. Reveley* –

VIATICUM (IRE) 3 gr.f. Scenic 128 – Pete's Money (USA) (Caucasus (USA) 127) [1994 6g^{5} 6m* 6d 6d* 7s^{4} 1995 6m 8m 8g 7f^{5} 9d^{4} 10d* 8m^{4} 10g Oct 30] IR 9,200Y: eighth foal: half-sister to several winners, including fairly useful 6f/7f performer Corrin Hill and Irish 1m winner Moneybroker (both by Petorius): dam unraced: smart Irish performer: won auction race at the Curragh and listed race at Leopardstown at 2 yrs and competitive listed race at the Curragh (beat Magic Feeling a length) in October: pulled up final start, and reported afterwards to be coughing: stays 1¼m: acts on good to firm ground and dead: blinkered since third 3-y-o start. *N. Meade, Ireland* 110

VIBRO (IRE) 3 b.c. Sharp Victor (USA) 114 – Binnissima (USA) (Tilt Up (USA)) [1994 50: 5s 6g 5g^{6} a7g 1995 a5g Jan 3] poor form in maidens: sold 875 gns Ascot April Sales. *G. C. Bravery* –

VICENZA 3 ch.f. Old Vic 136 – Ela Romara 124 (Ela-Mana-Mou 132) [1994 NR 1995 10m Oct 26] unfurnished filly: second foal: closely related to smart middle-distance colt Foyer (by Sadler's Wells): dam won Lowther and Nassau –

Stakes: bit backward, showed nothing in minor event at Nottingham: sold 10,500 gns Newmarket December Sales. *G. Wragg*

VICEROY RULER 4 gr.g. Faustus (USA) 118 – Viceroy Princess 65 (Godswalk (USA) 130) [1994 –: 8.2m 9.7m 8.1m 8.3f 1995 12.5m Jun 26] workmanlike gelding: poor mover: fair hurdler, winner in December: no form on flat since modest maiden at 2 yrs: tried visored. *J. R. Jenkins* —

VICTIM OF LOVE 2 b.f. (Apr 19) Damister (USA) 123 – Tantalizing Song (CAN) (The Minstrel (CAN) 135) [1995 7m a8g^4 a7g* a7g^2 Dec 9] 9,000Y: angular filly: seventh foal: sister to 3-y-o Dance Motion and 3 winners, including 8.5f winner Miss Fascination, and half-sister to a winner in USA: dam ran 5 times in North America: progressive filly: sweating, won maiden auction at Wolverhampton in November: good second, beaten a head, to Le Sport in minor event there following month: should stay 1m: acts on fibresand, probably on equitrack. *R. Charlton* 75

VICTORIA DAY 3 b.f. Reference Point 139 – Victoress (USA) (Conquistador Cielo (USA)) [1994 NR 1995 12m 13.4m^4 12.3m^5 15g Sep 14] third foal: half-sister to 4-y-o Pyrrhic Victory (by Groom Dancer) and fairly useful 1¼m winner Fermoy (by Irish River): dam, lightly-raced French 11f winner, is half-sister to Awaasif (dam of Snow Bride, herself dam of Lammtarra) and several other good winners: no form: sold 13,000 gns Newmarket Sales. *J. W. Watts* —

VICTORIA HALL 5 b.m. Hallgate 127 – Thorganby Victory 82 (Burglar 128) [1994 59: 5m^5 5f^5 a6g a7g 1995 a8g a6g a6g Feb 18] good-bodied mare: modest sprint maiden: well below form in 1995, including in visor and blinkers: sold 875 gns Ascot April Sales. *W. G. M. Turner* —

VICTORIA PRINCESS 8 b.m. King of Spain 121 – Renira 60 (Relkino 131) [1994 –: a8g 1995 a7g 6m Apr 6] compact, workmanlike mare: no longer of much account. *M. Madgwick* —

VICTORIA REGIA (IRE) 2 b.f. (Apr 13) Lomond (USA) 128 – Will of Victory 102 (Dancer's Image (USA)) [1995 6m 7m^3 7.1d^3 6m* Oct 4] angular filly: unimpressive mover: half-sister to several winners, including French 1989 2-y-o 6.5f winner Victory Chorus (by Seattle Song) and French middle-distance stayer Vengador (by Bob Back): dam, 2-y-o 6f winner, half-sister to Prix Vermeille winner Walensee: won 6-runner maiden at York by 5 lengths (eased close home and could have been 8) from Sihafi: stays 7f but looked speedy at York and may prove suited by 6f: bandaged off-hind last 2 starts: sent to USA. *R. Charlton* 90+

VICTORIA SIOUX 2 ch.f. (Apr 1) Ron's Victory (USA) 129 – Blues Indigo 103 (Music Boy 124) [1995 5m^6 6.1m^4 6m^5 6.1d Sep 11] 16,000Y: useful-looking filly: second foal: half-sister to 3-y-o 5f winner Blue Sioux (by Indian Ridge): dam sprinter: modest maiden: poor effort in nursery at Nottingham final outing. *J. Wharton* 54

VICTORIA'S SECRET (IRE) 3 b.f. Law Society (USA) 130 – Organdy 84 (Blakeney 126) [1994 70: 6g^3 5d 6g 7d^5 7m 7.1g^3 1995 8m 10f 10g^2 12f^3 13.1h 9.7g Oct 16] leggy filly: fair maiden handicapper: stays 1½m: acts on firm and dead ground: edgy (mounted on track) second 3-y-o start: best efforts in 1995 in blinkers. *D. R. C. Elsworth* 65

VICTORIA VENTURE 2 b.f. (Mar 23) Ron's Victory (USA) 129 – Leafy Garland (USA) (Lypheor 118) [1995 5m^6 6m^6 6.1m^4 a7g^3 7.1m a7g* a7g^3 7m^5 8m a7g^2 a8.5g Oct 14] lengthy, rather leggy filly: third foal: dam unraced daughter of smart middle-distance filly Trillionaire: plater: won at Wolverhampton in July: stays 7f: acts on fibresand and good to firm ground: sold 2,000 gns Newmarket Autumn Sales. *S. P. C. Woods* 54

VICTOR LASZLO 3 b.g. Ilium 121 – Report 'em (USA) 51 (Staff Writer (USA)) [1994 NR 1995 10g^3 12.3m^5 13.8g a14g Nov 16] workmanlike gelding: fourth foal: half-brother to 7f winner Chance Report (by Beldale Flutter): dam, maiden, form only at 6f: little promise, including in selling company: sold 4,500 gns Doncaster November Sales. *J. D. Bethell* —

VICTORY COMMANDER 2 b.g. (Apr 30) Efisio 120 – Gay Hostess (FR) (Direct Flight) [1995 6g 5m 7.1m Aug 30] 10,000Y: sturdy gelding: poor mover: brother to 3-y-o Dally Boy and half-brother to 3 winners here and in France, —

Edmundson Electrical Handicap, Lingfield—
Vindaloo's third win in four days is a record-equalling one

including 6f and 7f winner Clare Kerry Lass (by Alleging): dam French 7f (at 2 yrs) and 1¼m winner: well beaten in maiden events. *T. J. Naughton*

VICTORY TEAM (IRE) 3 b.g. Danehill (USA) 126 – Hogan's Sister (USA) (Speak John) [1994 NR 1995 7m 8.3m⁴ 8.1g 8m³ 8g 12s⁶ Sep 27] 52,000F, 74,000Y: strong, good-bodied gelding: good mover: half-brother to several winners, notably top-class 6f/7f performer Salieri (by Accipter): dam unraced: fair maiden: well beaten last 2 starts: rather headstrong, and not sure to stay beyond 1m: sometimes has tongue tied down: sold (J. Fanshawe to G. Balding) 13,000 gns Newmarket Autumn Sales. *J. R. Fanshawe* — 69

VIEW FROM ABOVE 9 b.m. Dara Monarch 128 – Organdy 84 (Blakeney 126) [1994 76: a10g* a10g* a12g a10g* 12g⁴ 12m³ 12m 12.5f³ a11g 1995 a10g a12g⁵ a12g a13g⁶ Feb 16] strong mare: fair handicapper: soundly beaten last 2 starts: effective from 1¼m to 1¾m: acts on firm ground and all-weather surfaces: sometimes wears tongue strap. *N. J. H. Walker* — 69

VILAYET 2 ch.c. (Apr 22) Machiavellian (USA) 123 – Vilikaia (USA) 125 (Nureyev (USA) 131) [1995 7m* 8.1m⁴ Aug 18] well-made, attractive colt: seventh foal: half-brother to 5f to 1m winner Villeroi (by Kris): dam, effective from 5f to 1m, half-sister to good filly (at up to 1m) Maximova and daughter of half-sister to 2000 Guineas winner Nonoalco: won 6-runner maiden at York by ½ length from Moody's Cat, leading 1f out then green: didn't make anticipated improvement when fourth of 5 to Bonarelli in minor event at Sandown following month, tending to edge right: has joined Mme C. Head. *H. R. A. Cecil* — 90 +

VILLAGE KING (IRE) 2 b.c. (Mar 23) Roi Danzig (USA) – Honorine (USA) (Blushing Groom (FR) 131) [1995 8m 8m Nov 4] 25,000Y: strong, sturdy colt: eighth foal: half-brother to several winners here and abroad, including Italian 1m winner (including in Group 3 at 2 yrs) Foolish Heart (by Fools Holme) and fairly useful 9f and 1¼m winner Lord Bertie (by Roberto): dam placed at 1m in France: similar form when seventh in maiden events won by Silver Dome at Newmarket and Shaamit at Doncaster following month: will stay beyond 1m. *R. Hannon* — 74

VILLAGE NATIVE (FR) 2 ch.c. (Apr 8) Village Star (FR) 131 – Zedative (FR) 74 (Zeddaan 130) [1995 7g 5m^2 5g^3 6g^5 7f^5 6m* a6g Nov 14] 10,000Y: lengthy, angular colt: sixth reported foal: half-brother to Irish 7f winner Satrap (by Persian Bold): dam barely stayed 5f: fair form: made all in median auction maiden at Folkestone in November: gives impression will prove best at sprint distances: acts on firm going: blinkered third start: very keen type (upset in stalls and had to be withdrawn from Molecomb Stakes on third intended outing). *K. O. Cunningham-Brown* — 72

VILLAGE OPERA 2 gr.f. (Jan 29) Rock City 120 – Lucky Song 91 (Lucky Wednesday 124) [1995 5m 5m 8g Sep 16] 8,000Y: half-sister to 1991 2-y-o 6f and 7f winner X My Heart (by Aragon) and fair 1990 2-y-o 5f and 6f winner Level Xing (by Stanford): dam 5f and 7f winner: well beaten in maidens at Carlisle (very slowly away), Ripon and (after 3½ month absence) Ayr. *G. M. Moore* — –

VILLEGGIATURA 2 b.c. (Mar 15) Machiavellian (USA) 123 – Hug Me 96 (Shareef Dancer (USA) 135) [1995 6m^2 7g 7f* 7g^4 Aug 28] strong, workmanlike colt: fourth foal: half-brother to fairly useful 3-y-o 12.1f and 1¾m winner Embracing and French 11.5f and 13f winner General Yaasi (both by Reference Point): dam 7f and 12.2f winner out of half-sister to Clever Trick: fairly useful form: won maiden at Salisbury in August: ran well when fourth of 7 to Double Diamond in nursery at Newcastle final start: should stay further than 7f: acts on firm ground: edgy second start. *B. W. Hills* — 84

VINDALOO 3 ch.g. Indian Ridge 123 – Lovely Lagoon 68 (Mill Reef (USA) 141) [1994 45: 5.9m 7.5m 8f 7.1m^6 10g^6 9d^4 6.9s^5 1995 a8g^2 a10g^5 a8.5g^4 a10g^4 7.1g* 7g^5 8g* 8.1g^6 8g* 10.1g* 10m* 10.8g* 10m^4 10f* 10.1m^3 12.4m^2 12f* 11.8g* a9.4g* a12g* 14f^4 9.9m 11.9m^3 a7g^3 10m^2 11.9g^4 10.1g^4 10g^2 9.2g^3 10g Sep 29] robust, close-coupled gelding: trained by M. Johnston until after fourth 3-y-o start: showed dramatic improvement for new stable, making into a fairly useful handicapper and winning at Edinburgh (selling event), Newcastle, Leicester (claimer), Yarmouth, Nottingham (minor event), Warwick, Redcar, Carlisle, Leicester (awarded race), Wolverhampton and Lingfield, last 3 successes in 4 days: equalled the twentieth-century record for number of handicap wins in a season (9): made frame on 8 of his 10 subsequent starts, but finished lame (struck into himself) at Newmarket on final one: successful at 7f, but best form from 9f to 1¾m: acts on any going: has won for apprentice: sometimes hangs under pressure: most genuine and consistent, and outstandingly tough. *J. L. Harris* — 91

VIN ST KOOLA 3 b.g. Vin St Benet 109 – Nikoola Eve 69 (Roscoe Blake 120) [1994 75+: 6.1m 7g^5 10s^3 8g^5 10d^6 1995 a10g* a10g^6 10m^3 12g 8g 10m 10d 12m Oct 2] leggy gelding: fair performer: won maiden at Lingfield in March: mostly disappointing afterwards, leaving H. Collingridge's stable (and gelded) after fifth outing: should stay 1½m: acts on soft ground and equitrack. *M. C. Chapman* — 75 d

VINTAGE CROP 8 ch.g. Rousillon (USA) 133 – Overplay 107 (Bustino 136) [1994 121: 14g* 20f^2 14g^2 14d* 14d* 16g 1995 12g* 20m^4 14m* 14m* 14g^4 16s^3 — 120

Anheuser Busch Curragh Cup—Vintage Crop concedes years and weight to Capias and Mohaajir (right)

Nov 7] big, lengthy gelding: easy mover: very smart Irish performer: won minor event at Leopardstown (by 6 lengths) in June, 7-runner Anheuser Busch Curragh Cup (by ½ length from Capias, having looked unlikely to win turning for home) in July and 3-runner listed race at Leopardstown (by 12 lengths) in August: attempting third successive Irish St Leger when bit-below-form fourth of 7 to Strategic Choice at the Curragh in September: set plenty to do when good third of 21 to Doriemus in Melbourne Cup at Flemington on final outing: very best form at 1¾m to 2m: acts on firm ground and soft: very game and genuine. *D. K. Weld, Ireland*

VINTAGE RED 5 b.g. Sulaafah (USA) 119 – Armonit 81 (Town Crier 119) [1994 NR 1995 a8g Dec 15] compact gelding: of little account. *N. A. Twiston-Davies* –

VINTAGE TAITTINGER (IRE) 3 b.g. Nordico (USA) – Kalonji (Red Alert 127) [1994 –: 5m a6g 1995 5d a12g* 11.1g^{5} a14.8g^{3} a12g^{2} a12g Jun 24] small, plain gelding: poor handicapper: won at Wolverhampton in April: stays 14.8f: acts on fibresand: sold (M. Bell to T. Dyer) 6,500 gns Newmarket Autumn Sales. *M. Bell* 34 + a47

VIRIDIS (USA) 2 b.f. (May 4) Green Dancer 77 – Vachti (FR) 114 (Crystal Palace (FR) 132) [1995 8.2m^{4} Oct 26] workmanlike filly: seventh foal: half-sister to several winners, including 1¼m winner White Lodge (by Lyphard) and 1½m and 13f winner Vishnu (by Storm Bird): dam French 1¼m and 10.5f winner who stayed 1½m: 4/1 from 5/4 and better for race, shaped quite well when staying-on 4¾ lengths fourth of 11 to Dance Star in maiden at Nottingham: will be well suited by middle distances: sure to improve. *H. R. A. Cecil* 59 p

VIRKON VENTURE (IRE) 7 b.g. Auction Ring (USA) 123 – Madame Fair (Monseigneur (USA) 127) [1994 60: 10v^{4} 10d^{6} 10v^{3} 12d* 13s* 11.8d^{5} 11.9d 12g 12s 1995 12.1v^{4} Mar 31] lengthy, angular gelding: modest performer: stays 1½m: best efforts with give in the ground: sometimes bandaged: fair hurdler. *M. H. Tompkins* 50 +

VIRTUAL REALITY 4 b.g. Diamond Shoal 130 – Warning Bell 88 (Bustino 136) [1994 81: 10d 10.3f^{3} 10m* 10m^{2} 10m* 10m^{2} 12f 12d 10.3d 1995 10g^{2} 10m^{2} 10f^{5} 10.4m^{6} 10m 10.1g^{3} 9g 10d Oct 19] quite good-topped gelding: fairly useful handicapper: ran well in competitive handicaps first 4 starts, finishing second (beaten head by Penny A Day) in Zetland Gold Cup at Redcar and close sixth in Magnet Cup at York: well below form last 2 outings: stays 1¼m: acts on firm ground, seems unsuited by soft surface: visored (ran creditably) once: held up and has turn of foot. *A. Hide* 83

VISHNU (USA) 5 b.g. Storm Bird (CAN) 134 – Vachti (FR) 114 (Crystal Palace (FR) 132) [1994 77, a87: a13g* a12g^{2} 18g 12.4g^{2} 12g^{6} 13.9f 13.9d a11g 1995 a14.8g a12g^{6} a16g a16g 17.1m Apr 25] strong gelding: fairly useful at best: well beaten in 1995. *J. L. Eyre* –

VISUAL ILLUSION (IRE) 3 b.f. Hatim (USA) 121 – Trompe d'Oeil 75 (Longleat (USA) 109) [1994 NR 1995 a8g a8g a8.5g^{6} Jan 27] IR 3,500Y: second foal: half-sister to winning sprinter Riston Lady (by Salt Dome): dam won here at 1m at 2 yrs and at 9.9f at 3 yrs in Ireland: no sign of ability: sold (B. Rothwell to G. Oldroyd) 800 gns Doncaster May Sales. *B. S. Rothwell* –

VITAL EVIDENCE 2 br.f. (Mar 11) Today And Tomorrow 78 – Vital Witness (Garda's Revenge (USA) 119) [1995 a6g^{5} 6m^{4} Aug 12] first reported foal: dam, ran once on flat at 2 yrs, poor novice over hurdles: 11/2 from 12/1, better effort in sellers when keeping-on fourth (beaten just under a length) of 8 to Phoenix House at Lingfield. *D. C. O'Brien* 49

VITUS 3 b.c. Dancing Brave (USA) 140 – Sancta 106 (So Blessed 130) [1994 NR 1995 11m Apr 21] lengthy, rather unfurnished colt: ninth foal: half-brother to several winners, including very useful 7f (at 2 yrs) and 1¼m winner Carmelite House (by Diesis), very useful middle-distance performer Wolsey (by Our Native) and useful stayer Saint Keyne (by Sadler's Wells): dam (useful at 1¼m) is daughter of Soft Angels: green, shaped quite well when just over 10 lengths seventh of 15 to Tamure in maiden at Newbury, keeping on steadily: likely to stay well: looked sure to do better: stays in training. *H. R. A. Cecil* 82 p

VIYAPARI (IRE) 3 b.c. Last Tycoon 131 – Rowa 83 (Great Nephew 126) [1994 90p: 7m^{3} 1995 8d^{2} 7m 8.3m^{5} 7.9g^{2} 10d Sep 27] heavy-bodied colt: carries condition: shows a quick action: disappointing maiden: should be well suited by middle distances: sent to Dubai. *L. M. Cumani* 80 d

VIZARD (IRE) 3 ch.g. Old Vic 136 – Impudent Miss 105 (Persian Bold 123) 67
[1994 72: 7m^5 7m^4 8.1g 8g^3 7m 1995 12.5m^4 11.6m 11.6m 14.1m^2 14.1g^4 18.2m Jul 8] compact gelding: fair maiden handicapper: should stay beyond 1¾m: blinkered at 3 yrs: sold (M. Heaton-Ellis to T. Wall) 2,400 gns Newmarket Autumn Sales. *M. J. Heaton-Ellis*

VLAANDEREN (IRE) 3 b.f. In The Wings 128 – Marie de Flandre (FR) 109 77
(Crystal Palace (FR) 132) [1994 NR 1995 10d 14.1f^6 11.3d^2 8g^2 8.3g^2 10d* Nov 18] 85,000F: angular filly: sixth foal: half-sister to French 1¼m and 11f winner Flanders Moss (by Shareef Dancer), 1¼m winner Count Flanders (by Green Desert) and a winner in Italy: dam, French 1¼m and 10.5f winner, half-sister to Sakura Reiko and dam of good French stayer Top Sunrise: signs of ability in maidens at Sandown and Yarmouth for M. Stoute: won apprentice race at Fontainebleau in November: stays 11.3f: acts on dead ground: sold 39,000 gns Newmarket December Sales. *H. Pantall, France*

VLADIVOSTOK 5 gr.g. Siberian Express (USA) 125 – Tsungani 64 (Cure The 48
Blues (USA)) [1994 –: a6g 5.1g a7g 8m 1995 11.6m 8f a6g^3 a6g^7 a6g^4 Nov 30] leggy gelding: poor performer: sold out of R. Lee's stable 1,400 gns Ascot July Sales after reappearance: best efforts at 6f: acts on firm ground and the all-weather. *B. De Haan*

VOCAL COMMAND 3 b.g. Chief Singer 131 – To Oneiro 69 (Absalom 128) –
[1994 61: 5m 5v^3 5d^4 a6g* a6g a7g* 8.3g^3 8g 1995 a5g a8g a8g Nov 16] leggy gelding: modest form at 2 yrs for G. Lewis: well beaten in 1995, not seen out until October. *W. W. Haigh*

VOILA PREMIERE (IRE) 3 b.c. Roi Danzig (USA) – Salustrina (Sallust 134) 68
[1994 53: 6d 6s 7g 1995 6.1g 6.1g 8.3g* 9g^2 10.5g^5 Sep 1] compact colt: impresses in appearance: fair performer: well-backed winner of maiden at Hamilton in May: good efforts both subsequent starts, visored on first of them: stays 10.5f: yet to race on top-of-the-ground. *M. H. Tompkins*

VOLARE 2 b.f. (Feb 4) Prince Sabo 123 – Nazmiah 73 (Free State 125) [1995 5g^3 60
Jun 12] first foal: dam stayed 1½m: slow-starting 7 lengths third of 9 to Baize in maiden at Warwick: looked sure to improve, particularly over further than 5f: has joined B. Meehan. *M. C. Pipe*

VOLA VIA (USA) 2 b. or br.g. (Mar 17) Known Fact (USA) 135 – Pinking 86
Shears (USA) (Sharpen Up 127) [1995 6g 5m^4 6.1m^5 5.7h* 6g^4 7.3m^3 7m^2 7.3d 7d Sep 26] $52,000Y, resold 40,000Y: quite good-topped gelding: third foal: half-brother to a minor sprint winner in USA by Proud Truth: dam won in USA at around 6f: won maiden at Bath in July: ran well when tenth of 30 to Rio Duvida in valuable sales race at Newmarket last time: subsequently gelded: stays 7.3f: acts on hard and dead ground. *I. A. Balding*

VOLOCHINE (IRE) 4 ch.c. Soviet Star (USA) 128 – Harmless Albatross 115 117
(Pas de Seul 133) [1994 121: 7m 6d^2 6g^2 6f 7.5s* 8g^3 10s* 10d^2 9.8d^2 12f^3 12f 9g^3 1995 10v 11d^2 10s^5 10d* 10g^4 9.8s^2 12g 9f^5 Dec 10] good-bodied colt: only a smart performer in 1995: runner-up to Red Bishop in very valuable event at Sha Tin in April: won listed race in the provinces in May: ½-length second of 7 to Flemensfirth in Prix Dollar at Longchamp (plenty to do on turn then running on strongly) in October: below form afterwards: stays 1½m: acts on any going: held up and has turn of foot. *R. Collet, France*

VOLUNTEER (IRE) 3 b.g. Midyan (USA) 124 – Sistabelle (Bellypha 130) 66
[1994 NR 1995 10.2m^4 10m 10d 10d^4 a13g Dec 6] 10,000Y: smallish, sturdy gelding: easy mover: fifth foal: half-brother to smart 5f (at 2 yrs) to 1m winner Torch Rouge (by Warning): dam unraced sister to Bella Colora (dam of Stagecraft) and Colorspin (dam of Opera House): fair maiden: sold out of H. Cecil's stable 7,500 gns Newmarket July Sales after second start: should stay beyond 1¼m: won novice hurdle in October. *R. J. O'Sullivan*

W

WACKY (IRE) 4 b. or br.f. Petorius 117 – Zany (Junius (USA) 124) [1994 –: 6d –
7.5m 6m 6g 7g a6g 6s 1995 7m Aug 1] smallish, sturdy filly: most disappointing since 2 yrs: tried blinkered. *D. Nicholls*

WADADA 4 b. or br.g. Adbass (USA) 102 – No Rejection (Mummy's Pet 125) [1994 –: a6g 8m a8g^{4} 8d 1995 12g 7d Apr 6] small gelding: no sign of ability on flat: blinkered last 2 starts: sold (S. Campion to D. Burchell) 900 gns Doncaster May Sales. *S. W. Campion* –

WADERS DREAM (IRE) 6 b.g. Doulab (USA) 115 – Sea Mistress (Habitat 134) [1994 47: a6g^{5} a7g a6g a7g 6s 7m^{5} 6.1m^{6} 6g^{3} 6g^{5} 7g 6f^{3} 8m 6g 6m^{5} 5m^{4} 6g 6m^{6} 1995 a7g a6g a6g a6g^{5} a6g^{5} 7f 5g^{6} 6g 7m 6f^{3} 6f^{3} 6m^{6} 6g 7f Oct 25] leggy gelding: poor handicapper: stays 7f: acts on firm ground: blinkered or visored: inconsistent. *Pat Mitchell* 48 a31

WAFT (USA) 2 ch.f. (Feb 15) Topsider (USA) – Gliding By (USA) (Tom Rolfe) [1995 a7g^{6} Nov 21] $210,000F: closely related to 2 winners, including useful middle-distance performer Song of Sixpence (by The Minstrel), and half-sister to several winners, including useful performer at up to 1½m Clare Bridge (by Little Current): dam 6f winner on only start, is closely related to top-class Key To The Mint and half-sister to top American horse Fort Marcy: very weak in market and visored, slowly into stride and never a threat when about 11 lengths sixth of 11 in maiden at Lingfield: sold 46,000 gns Newmarket December Sales. *J. H. M. Gosden* – p

WAHEM (IRE) 5 b.g. Lomond (USA) 128 – Pro Patria 86 (Petingo 135) [1994 –: 10m 7m 9.7m 10g 1995 a10g a10g a8.5g 10f^{2} a10g^{2} a10g Dec 18] small, sturdy gelding: good mover: best efforts since fair 3-y-o when second at Redcar and Lingfield: probably best at up to 1¼m: best efforts on a sound surface: tried blinkered, no improvement: inconsistent. *C. E. Brittain* 43

WAHIBA SANDS 2 b.g. (Mar 11) Pharly (FR) 130 – Lovely Noor (USA) (Fappiano (USA)) [1995 7m* Nov 3] 7,800Y: big, good-topped gelding: has plenty of scope: third foal: half-brother to useful 3-y-o 1m and 10.4f winner Medaille Militaire (by Highest Honor): dam, winner at around 1m in USA, granddaughter of Glass Slipper, dam of Fairy Footsteps and Light Cavalry: 6/1 from 9/2 and green, won 18-runner maiden at Doncaster by ½ length from Private Song, held up after slowish start, leading over 1f out and running on well under hand riding: sure to improve. *J. L. Dunlop* 79 p

WAIKIKI BEACH (USA) 4 ch.g. Fighting Fit (USA) – Running Melody 86 (Rheingold 137) [1994 100: 6g 6m^{6} 6g^{2} 7.1f* 7.5m^{4} 7m^{2} 8g* 7m 1995 7m 8.1m 7m 7m 7m 7.6d^{3} 7g a8g a8g^{5} Nov 25] lengthy gelding: useful performer at 3 yrs: most disappointing in 1995: stays 1m: acts on firm ground: tried visored, no improvement. *G. L. Moore* 65

WAINWRIGHT (USA) 6 ch.h. Bering 136 – Crystal Bright 75 (Bold Lad (IRE) 133) [1994 106: 8m^{3} 10d^{2} 10f* 10.4f^{2} 10m* 10m* 10m^{6} 10m^{4} 1995 10.3m 10.5f Aug 5] strong, attractive horse: useful handicapper: broke near-fore in Group 3 event at Haydock in August: better at 1¼m than 1m: acted on firm and dead ground, ran poorly on heavy: superbly consistent: dead. *J. H. M. Gosden* –

WAITING 4 b.c. Polish Precedent (USA) 131 – Just You Wait (Nonoalco (USA) 131) [1994 102: 10.3m^{2} 12m 11.9s^{3} 10m^{5} 1995 10m^{2} 11.5g* 12m^{2} 12m^{3} 12.1m^{2} Jul 13] tall, rather leggy colt: useful performer: won steadily-run minor event at Lingfield in June: placed in steadily-run rated stakes at Epsom and truly-run listed race at Newmarket (1¾ lengths third to Saxon Maid) next 2 starts: beaten length by Edbaysaan in match at Chepstow final start, cruising up to challenge under 3f out but no extra final 1f: stays 1½m well and may do even better over further: acts on good to firm ground and soft. *P. F. I. Cole* 107

WAITINGFORWALNUTS (IRE) 2 b.f. (Feb 8) Fayruz 116 – Centre Travel (Godswalk (USA) 130) [1995 a5g a5g a7g 5m Aug 23] IR 2,100Y: sturdy filly: carries condition: half-sister to 5-y-o 7f winner Different Times (by Cyrano de Bergerac) and a winner in Italy: dam unplaced: behind in sellers. *C. A. Smith* –

WAKEEL (USA) 3 b.g. Gulch (USA) – Raahia (CAN) 91 (Vice Regent (CAN)) [1994 88: 6f^{3} 7g^{2} 7m* 8d^{6} 8g^{6} 1995 10.3g^{5} 11.8m^{5} 10m^{5} 8.3m^{2} 10.1m^{6} 10d 9g 8m Oct 28] tall, attractive gelding: fairly useful performer: left E. Dunlop after third 3-y-o start: improved effort when second in rated stakes at Windsor (for 7-lb claimer) next time: failed to repeat that form, and gelded after final start: probably best at around 1m: acts on firm ground and dead: visored (sweating and edgy, ran creditably but looked none too keen) final 2-y-o start. *S. Dow* 93

WAKING (CAN) 4 ch.g. Rahy (USA) 115 – Dreamsend (USA) (Herbager 136) [1994 65: 9m^5 12g^5 8.1g 12g^6 10g^5 10.3g 12s 1995 14g Sep 23] strong, lengthy gelding: good walker: fair maiden when trained at 3 yrs by D. Elsworth: burly and 25/1, well beaten in maiden handicap at Haydock only start in 1995: stays 1½m: blinkered (no form) last 2 starts at 3 yrs. *J. G. FitzGerald* –

WALDO 4 ch.g. Northern State (USA) 91 – One Degree 80 (Crooner 119) [1994 67: 10s 10g 10d^5 a7g^3 8f* 8.3f* a10g^3 8g^4 9d^5 10m a7g^4 a9.4g^2 1995 a7g a10g^3 a8g 7f a9.4g^6 8.3m^2 8f^3 a10g^3 8.5s^3 9d^5 8m Oct 12] leggy gelding: fair handicapper: stays 1¼m: acts on firm and soft ground and the all-weather: visored: consistent: sold 13,000 gns Newmarket Autumn Sales. *Lord Huntingdon* 68

WALI (USA) 5 b.g. Lomond (USA) 128 – Magic Slipper 97 (Habitat 134) [1994 70, a74: 7d* 6.9s* 6.9v^2 a7g* 7g^3 a7g 7f 7g^3 7m^6 6.9h^3 1995 9.2s 6.9m a7g May 15] sturdy gelding: unimpressive mover: fair performer at 4 yrs: no form in claimers for new stable: effective at 7f and 1m: acts on soft going, seemingly not top-of-the-ground: usually has tongue tied down. *V. Thompson* –

WALK IN THE WILD 3 b.f. Bold Owl 101 – Tripolitaine (FR) (Nonoalco (USA) 131) [1994 NR 1995 8g a8.5g Nov 13] half-sister to several winners, including fairly useful sprinter Walk In The Park (by Valiyar) and 1989 2-y-o 5f winner Western Music (by Music Boy): dam won twice at around 11f in France: always behind in claimer and maiden. *A. Bailey* –

WALK ON MIX (FR) 3 gr.c. Linamix (FR) 127 – Walk On Air 91 (Cure The Blues (USA)) [1994 110p: 8d^2 7g* 8d^2 1995 11m* 12g 12m^4 Oct 15] rangy, rather sparely-made colt: smart performer: won strongly-run 6-runner Prix Noailles at Longchamp in April by short neck from Solar One, leading 2f out and staying on well: below form in steadily-run Prix du Jockey-Club at Chantilly in June: ran well when 4¼ lengths fourth of 8 to De Quest in Prix du Conseil de Paris at Longchamp 4 months later: stays 1½m: acts on good to firm ground and dead, yet to race on extremes: stays in training. *A. Fabre, France* 117

WALK THE BEAT 5 b.g. Interrex (CAN) – Plaits 93 (Thatching 131) [1994 69: 5.1d^2 5.1m 6m 5d^6 6.1g a6g* a6g^2 1995 a5g^2 a6g^4 a7g^2 a6g^6 a7g^6 a6g* 7.6m a7g 5f^3 6f^2 6m^2 5f^4 5.1d Oct 10] strong gelding: impresses in appearance: has a round action: fair performer: first run since leaving R. Simpson's stable, won strongly-run claimer at Wolverhampton in May: effective at 5f and 6f: acts on firm and dead going and on fibresand: blinkered/visored once each, and below best: sometimes bandaged: usually held up. *Martyn Meade* 67

WALNUT BURL (IRE) 5 b.h. Taufan (USA) 119 – Hay Knot (Main Reef 126) [1994 60: 6s 6d^4 6d 7m^2 7f* 6m* 7m^3 7g^2 7m^5 7m^2 7g 1995 7m^4 7f^2 7m 7m^5 7f 6f^4 6f* 7f^4 7g^6 7g Oct 1] rather leggy horse: modest handicapper: often appears at Brighton: won 5-runner race there in August: effective at 6f and 7f: acts on firm and soft ground: visored twice, most recently for first 4-y-o success: has had tongue tied down: held up. *L. J. Holt* 62

WALSHAM WHISPER (IRE) 4 b.f. Taufan (USA) 119 – Papsie's Pet (Busted 134) [1994 82: 7d^4 8v 7m* 8f^4 8m^2 8g^6 10g^4 10m^2 9.9f^2 10.1d^3 10m 10m^2 12s^4 1995 9.9m 12m 14m May 7] leggy, workmanlike filly: shaped as though coming to hand for new stable first 2 starts in 1995, but tailed off final one: stays 1½m: acts on firm and dead going, ran poorly on heavy: visored (ran well) 3 times at 3 yrs: sold 500 gns Doncaster November Sales. *J. Wharton* –

WANDERING MINSTREL (IRE) 3 ch.c. Ballad Rock 122 – Priddy Blue (Blue Cashmere 129) [1994 65: 6m^5 6m 6m^5 1995 8m^6 7g^2 8.3m^2 7m 7m^4 7m 7.1g 8g Oct 9] useful-looking colt: modest performer: ran poorly 3 of last 4 starts: effective at 7f and 1m: has raced only on a sound surface: blinkered (found little) final start: sold 7,000 gns Newmarket Autumn Sales: sent to Norway. *J. M. P. Eustace* 64

WANDERING STAR (USA) 2 b.f. (Apr 16) Red Ransom (USA) – Beautiful Bedouin (USA) (His Majesty (USA)) [1995 6g Jul 12] $37,000Y resold 35,000Y: sturdy filly: closely related to 1½m winner Badawi (by Script Ohio): dam unraced half-sister to Silver Hawk (by Roberto): 33/1 and in need of race, around 11 lengths ninth of 14 to Rouge Rancon in maiden at Newmarket, never threatening leaders: looked sure to improve. *J. R. Fanshawe* –p

WANNAPLANTATREE 4 b.f. Niniski (USA) 125 – Cataclysmic 78 (Ela-Mana-Mou 132) [1994 72: 14d^2 12m^5 12m^4 14.1g^4 14m^5 14.1d 1995 a12g^6 62

14.9d 17.2m 14.4m² 14m⁴ 14.9m³ a14g⁵ 14.1m* 14g⁴ Sep 22] sparely-made filly: modest performer: trained first 3 starts at 4 yrs by G. Yardley: led well inside last and stayed on strongly to win 4-runner handicap at Nottingham in August: will stay beyond 14.1f: acts on good to firm and dead ground: visored (below form) sixth 4-y-o start: inconsistent. *N. M. Babbage*

WARBROOK 2 b.c. (Feb 18) Warrshan (USA) 117 – Bracey Brook (Gay Fandango (USA) 132) [1995 6.1m⁵ 7.1m 7.1m³ 8g² 10m* 8f² Oct 16] rather leggy, quite attractive colt: shows plenty of knee action: fifth foal: closely related to 13f bumpers winner Brook Dance (by Mashhor Dancer) and a winner in Italy by Glenstal and a half-brother to a winner abroad by Robellino: dam poor Irish maiden: improved form at Pontefract last 3 starts: beat Benatom 1¾ lengths in maiden then 2½ lengths second of 6 to Weet-A-Minute in listed race: well suited by test of stamina: genuine. *I. A. Balding* 87

WARDARA 3 ch.f. Sharpo 132 – Ward One 68 (Mr Fluorocarbon 126) [1994 86p: 5g 6g² 6g² 6s 6m* 6v* 6s⁶ 1995 6m 7m 7d⁵ 6g a7g Dec 15] strong, stocky filly: not seen out until August and failed by long way to recapture her 2-y-o form: left Miss G. Kelleway after fourth start: probably stays 7f: acts on good to firm and heavy ground: usually visored/blinkered. *C. A. Dwyer* 62

WARHURST (IRE) 4 b.g. Nordance (USA) – Pourboire 47 (Star Appeal 133) [1994 67d: 10.3g³ 12.5v⁵ 10m 10m 10m⁴ 8g⁶ 1995 a8g a7g⁴ a8g a9.4g³ Feb 18] angular gelding: only poor form at best for new connections in 1995: stays 10.3f well: acts on fibresand: inconsistent. *D. Nicholls* 46

WARLUSKEE 3 b.f. Dancing Brave (USA) 140 – Walesiana (GER) (Star Appeal 133) [1994 60p: 7.9d⁶ 8d 1995 a12g* 14.6m 14.8m Aug 25] leggy, angular filly: put up easily best effort when winning maiden at Southwell in March by 6 lengths: tailed off as if something amiss in handicaps at Doncaster 2 months later and Newmarket 3½ months after that: stays 1½m: sold 13,000 gns Newmarket December Sales. *M. Johnston* – a78

WARM HEARTED (USA) 3 ch.g. Known Fact (USA) 135 – Lovin' Lass (USA) (Cutlass (USA)) [1994 NR 1995 5.1m a7g a7g⁴ Dec 19] sparely-made gelding: half-brother to several winners, including fair 1¾m winner Demonstrable (by Alleged) and useful 7f winner Paddle Steamer (by Riverman): dam stakes-placed winner at 6f and 7f in USA: reared and unseated rider leaving stalls on debut: best effort when fourth of 10 at Lingfield final start. *R. Ingram* 60

WARMING TRENDS 2 b.g. (Feb 18) Warning 136 – Sunny Davis (USA) 71 (Alydar (USA)) [1995 6m 6f 6m 6d* 7d* 7s* Sep 28] 21,000Y: angular gelding: has reportedly been hobdayed: poor walker: has a quick action: first foal: dam, 2-y-o 7f winner, out of sister to Larida (dam of Magic of Life) and half-sister to Miss Oceana: much improved form in September, winning nurseries at Leicester, Brighton and Lingfield (one of only 3 who raced on heavily-favoured far side but still won impressively by 8 lengths): will stay 1m: acts on soft ground: progressing well. *Sir Mark Prescott* 86 p

WARM SPELL 5 b.g. Northern State (USA) 91 – Warm Wind 84 (Tumble Wind (USA)) [1994 79: 16v 14f 12s⁴ 12m⁴ 12m 11.5d 12d 13.3s* 12m³ 12.1g² 12v² 12v⁴ 1995 a13g* 10.2m² 13.3g 12m 12m⁵ 13.3d⁵ 11.9g Oct 1] good-quartered gelding: has a round action: fair handicapper: won apprentice race at Lingfield in February: had interrupted 1995 campaign and rather inconsistent: effective at 1¼m to 1¾m: acts on good to firm ground and equitrack, revels in the mud: normally held up in touch. *G. L. Moore* 77

WARNING ORDER 3 b.c. Warrshan (USA) 117 – Bell Toll 87 (High Line 125) [1994 86: 7m⁵ 8.1g* 8d² 10g³ 1995 10m³ 12m² 12f² 10m* 10f 12m⁴ 10m³ 10.1m² 10.1s* 12g³ 10m² 10d³ 9.5s Dec 13] useful-looking colt: progressed gradually throughout 1995, into a useful performer: won minor events at Windsor (narrowly) in July and Epsom (easily) in September: ran well afterwards in listed event and minor race at Newmarket (best effort when length second to Bal Harbour, hanging right and run out of it close home): sold out of J.Dunlop's stable 60,000 gns Newmarket Autumn Sales and finished third in minor event at Evry on first of 2 starts for new connections: effective at 1¼m to 1½m: acts on firm ground and soft: blinkered (best effort at the time, but looked none too keen) seventh 3-y-o start: consistent on form, but not one to place maximum faith in. *G. Henrot, France* 107

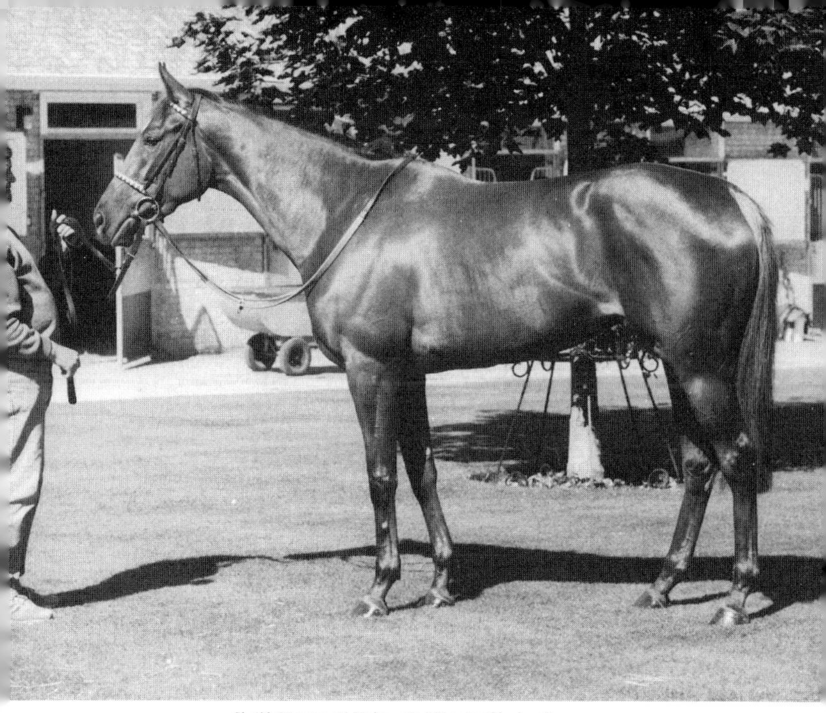

Sheikh Marwan Al Maktoum's "Warning Shadows"

WARNING REEF 2 b.c. (Feb 8) Warning 136 – Horseshoe Reef 88 (Mill Reef (USA) 141) [1995 7.1g⁵ 7f² 7g 7.3m⁴ Aug 12] 16,500Y: rangy colt: second foal: half-brother to 3-y-o 1m winner (probably stays 1¾m) Pumice (by Salse): dam, 1¼m winner, daughter of smart mare Miss Toshiba: fair form: ran well when fourth of 12 to Pacific Grove in nursery at Newbury on final outing: will stay at least 1¼m. *M. R. Channon* 76

WARNING SHADOWS (IRE) 3 ch.f. Cadeaux Genereux 131 – Silent Movie (Shirley Heights 130) [1994 NR 1995 7m* 7m² 8g² 8m⁴ 8g⁵ 10f² 10g² 11.1g⁴ 8g³ 10g* 10g Oct 15] strong, lengthy filly: carries condition: sixth foal: half-sister to 1¼m winner Pearly Mist (by Persian Heights) and 7f winner Runun (by Sharpo): dam poor half-sister to very smart 7f to 1¼m performer Noalto: smart performer: won maiden in April and Sun Chariot Stakes (gamely by a head from Flagbird) in September, both at Newmarket: in frame most other outings, notably Irish 1000 Guineas at the Curragh, Coronation Stakes at Royal Ascot (behind Ridgewood Pearl both times, beaten 4 lengths and 5 lengths respectively) and Nassau Stakes (½-length second to Caramba) at Goodwood: stiffish task and ran creditably when about 7 lengths seventh of 13 to Timarida in E. P. Taylor Stakes at Woodbine final start: best at up to 1¼m: acted on firm going: game: stud. *C. E. Brittain* 113

WARNING SHOT 3 b.g. Dowsing (USA) 124 – Warning Bell 88 (Bustino 136) [1994 72p: 5d* 1995 7m⁶ 7g⁴ 7.1g 7f 6f a6g 8.1d 7.1d⁶ 5.1m Oct 19] big, workmanlike gelding: has a round action: capable of fair form but generally most disappointing: should be suited by further than 7f: sometimes sweating. *Martyn Meade* 79 d

WARNING STAR 3 b.f. Warning 136 – Blade of Grass 78 (Kris 135) [1994 96: 5m* 5m* 6m^6 6m^3 5g^4 6m 1995 5m* 5g 7m 5m^3 6g^2 5m^5 6m Oct 14] smallish, leggy filly: has a quick action: useful performer: won 5-runner minor event at Haydock in May: best effort when 1½ lengths second of 10 to Missed Flight in Prix de Meautry at Deauville in August: ran poorly in listed race at Newmarket final start: effective at 5f and should stay 7f: yet to race on a soft surface. *B. W. Hills* 104

WARNING TIME 2 b.c. (Apr 28) Warning 136 – Ballad Island 83 (Ballad Rock 122) [1995 5m* 7g^6 6g* 6d^3 6g^2 Oct 7] strong, workmanlike colt: half-brother to several winners at up to 7f, including useful Savoyard (by Sayf El Arab) and fairly useful Hong Kong Girl (by Petong): dam 7f/1m performer: useful colt: won maiden at Sandown in June and 5-runner minor event at Salisbury in July: good efforts last 2 starts in Mill Reef Stakes at Newbury and listed race (hung right) at York (2 lengths second of 5 to Resounder), though hung badly right inside final 1f last time: will prove best at 5f or 6f: acts on good to firm and dead ground. *B. J. Meehan* 96

WARREN KNIGHT 2 b.c. (May 3) Weldnaas (USA) 112 – Trigamy 112 (Tribal Chief 125) [1995 6s Oct 6] good-quartered colt: half-brother to 3-y-o Bella Coola (by Northern State) and several winners, including 7f winner Mango Manila (by Martinmas) and fairly useful 6-y-o 1m/1¼m performer Risk Master (by Risk Me): dam 5f performer: 40/1, never-dangerous ninth of 11 in maiden at Ascot. *C. A. Horgan* –

WAR REQUIEM (IRE) 5 b.h. Don't Forget Me 127 – Ladiz (Persian Bold 123) [1994 –: 8g 8.1g a10g^6 1995 a10g a10g^5 10d Sep 13] strong, good-quartered horse: seems no longer of much account. *Miss Gay Kelleway* –

WARRGEM 3 b.f. Warrshan (USA) 117 – Flying Flynn 64 (Vaigly Great 127) [1994 NR 1995 10.1g 12m 16m Jun 13] workmanlike filly: fourth foal: dam 1m winner at 2 yrs: yet to beat a horse. *B. Ellison* –

Stephen Crown's "Warning Star"

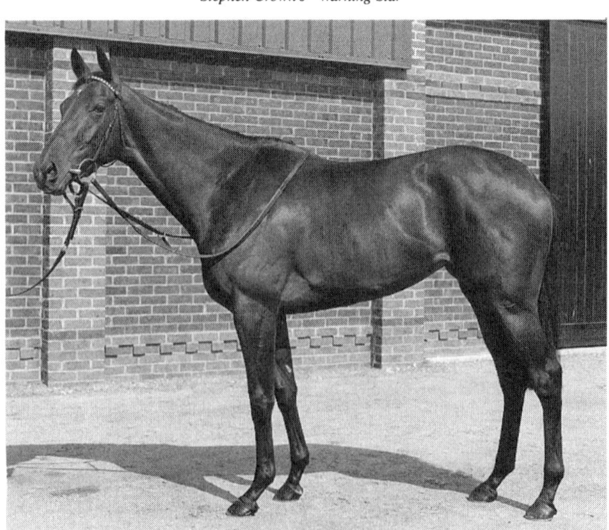

WARRIOR LADY (IRE) 3 ch.f. Al Hareb (USA) 123 – Lady Bettina (Bustino 136) [1994 40: 7m 6g 7m a5g 1995 a8g^{2} a7g^{5} a8g^{6} a10g 12m a14.8g a12g^{5} Jun 22] leggy filly: poor maiden plater: stays 1m: acts on fibresand: sent to Kuwait. *P. J. McBride* 43 d

WAR SHANTY 2 b.f. (Jan 28) Warrshan (USA) 117 – Daring Ditty (Daring March 116) [1995 8m Nov 4] fourth foal: half-sister to middle-distance winner Sparky's Song (by Electric) and useful 4-y-o sprinter Brave Edge (by Beveled): dam twice-raced daughter of useful sprinter Dawn Ditty: 33/1 and backward, tailed off in median auction maiden at Doncaster: bandaged near-hind. *J. R. Arnold* –

WARWICK MIST (IRE) 3 ch.f. Digamist (USA) 110 – Flash Donna (USA) 70 (Well Decorated (USA)) [1994 –: 7d 6d a6g 1995 a8g^{4} a8g^{2} a7g Dec 2] leggy, unfurnished filly: has scope: poor maiden: stays 1m: acts on fibresand. *P. C. Haslam* 35

WARWICK WARRIOR (IRE) 4 b.g. Reasonable (FR) 119 – Almost Heaven (Corvaro (USA) 124) [1994 68: a6g* 6f 6m^{6} a6g^{3} 5m* 5g* 5.1g^{2} 6f* a5g a6g* 6g a5g^{7} a7g 1995 a6g^{5} a5g^{6} a6g* a6g^{2} a6g^{6} 6m 6g Apr 26] sturdy gelding: fair handicapper: won at Southwell in January: below form last 3 starts: stayed 6f well: acted on firm ground and went well on all-weather surfaces: blinkered (below form) final start: was not an easy ride, and well handled by J. Weaver: sometimes slowly away: dead. *Mrs L. Piggott* – a74

WASBLEST 3 b.f. Statoblest 120 – Safety First (Wassl 125) [1994 59: a6g^{6} a6g^{4} a5g* 1995 a5g^{3} a5g^{2} a5g^{2} a5g 5m^{2} 5f^{4} 5m^{2} 5m^{2} 5f^{4} Jul 10] workmanlike filly: modest handicapper: best at 5f: acts on the all-weather and firm ground: blinkered (ran to form) final 3-y-o start: races prominently: tough and consistent: sold 700 gns Doncaster November Sales. *M. Johnston* 56

WASHINGTON REEF (USA) 2 b.g. (Apr 2) Seattle Dancer (USA) 119 – Broken Wave 103 (Bustino 136) [1995 8d 8g Oct 10] strong, attractive gelding: has a fluent, round action: third live foal: dam, 1¼m to 15f winner, here and in France, out of Oaks third Britannia's Rule, herself daughter of half-sister to Vaguely Noble: very green and not knocked about towards rear in maiden at Salisbury won by Mystic Knight: tailed off in maiden at Leicester 13 days later as though something amiss: bandaged in front and went keenly to post last time. *J. H. M. Gosden* –

WASSL'S GUEST (IRE) 4 b.f. Be My Guest (USA) 126 – Wassl's Sister (Troy 137) [1994 NR 1995 12m 12m May 19] 1,800 3-y-o: smallish, lengthy filly: half-sister to 6.9f and 1m winner Waseela (by Ahonoora): dam, maiden suited by 1½m, is half-sister to Wassl: no show in maiden and claimer. *R. F. Marvin* –

WASSL'S NANNY (IRE) 6 b.m. Wassl 125 – Granny's Bank 88 (Music Boy 124) [1994 –: 9v a12g 1995 a8g 8.1d^{5} 8m Apr 19] still a maiden: stays 1m: acts on dead ground: tailed off both runs on fibresand: visored final 5-y-o start. *B. Ellison* –

WASSL STREET (IRE) 3 b.c. Dancing Brave (USA) 140 – One Way Street 119 (Habitat 134) [1994 NR 1995 10g 11.4m 14s Sep 28] good-bodied colt: half-brother to 4 winners, notably smart Red Route (stayed 14.8f, by Polish Precedent) and fair Usk The Way (suited by test of stamina, by Caerleon): dam won Princess Royal Stakes: signs of a little ability in maidens first 2 starts, tailed off last time: probably a stayer: visored/blinkered last 2 outings: sold 4,400 gns Newmarket Autumn Sales. *J. H. M. Gosden* –

WATCH ME GO (IRE) 6 b.g. On Your Mark 125 – Nighty Night (Sassafras (FR)) [1994 36, a39: a8g^{4} a8.5g 7d 9.9d^{4} 8.5m 9.2f^{6} 9m^{4} 8m 11.1f^{3} 12.3m 1995 7.5m^{6} a10g* a10g^{2} Dec 18] quite attractive gelding: modest handicapper: off course 14 months prior to reappearance: narrowly won selling handicap at Lingfield in September on second start for new stable: stays 11f: acts on firm ground, dead and all-weather surfaces: tried visored at 4 yrs, but no improvement: headstrong on occasions: inconsistent. *Bob Jones* 33 + a50

WATCH ME (IRE) 2 b.f. (Jan 29) Green Desert (USA) 127 – Fenny Rough 114 (Home Guard (USA) 129) [1995 6g^{2} 5g^{4} 6m Aug 11] 125,000Y: well-made filly: half-sister to winners abroad by Icecapade and Sharpen Up: dam 5f to 7f winner later successful in USA: second to Amazing Bay in maiden at Newbury: failed to progress in similar events at Leicester and Newbury: may do better. *R. Hannon* 78

WATCH MY LIPS 3 b.g. Vin St Benet 109 – Manor Farm Toots 70 (Royalty 130) [1994 NR 1995 8m 10m 8g^{6} 7m 10.1g Sep 13] sparely-made gelding: fifth foal: 44

dam 12f and 13f winner suited by test of stamina: poor form: probably stays 1¼m: has raced only on a sound surface: inconsistent: won juvenile hurdle in October. *M. H. Tompkins*

WATCH THE CLOCK 3 b.f. Mtoto 134 – Brilliant Timing (USA) (The Minstrel (CAN) 135) [1994 93: 6.1m* 7.5g* 7.1g^4 7m^3 8g 1995 10m^4 10.4g^2 10.8g^5 Jun 17] leggy filly: lacks scope: fairly useful performer: good efforts in listed race at Newmarket and minor event at York first 2 starts, ran as if something amiss final one: may well prove best at up to 1¼m: yet to race on a soft surface: took a strong hold at 3 yrs. *D. R. Loder* — 93

WATER BEBE (IRE) 3 b.f. Persian Bold 123 – Bebe Altesse (GER) (Alpenkonig (GER)) [1994 58: 7m^2 5.9f 7m* 6g^6 7g 7m 7g 7v a7g^3 a6g^3 a7g 1995 a8g^2 a8.5g^4 a7g* a7g Jan 17] close-coupled filly: modest form: won seller at Southwell in January: broke a leg next start: likely to have stayed beyond 8.5f: acted on good to firm ground and all-weather surfaces, well beaten on heavy: tail swisher. *G. C. Bravery* — 60

WATER CHESTNUT 2 ch.g. (Mar 30) Most Welcome 131 – Water Pageant 58 (Welsh Pageant 132) [1995 a8g Nov 6] 4,800F, 2,200Y: half-brother to several winners, including 1991 2-y-o 6f winner Baileys By Name (by Nomination) and middle-distance stayer Sanchi Steeple (by Niniski): dam middle-distance maiden: 50/1 and ridden by 7-lb claimer, always behind in maiden at Southwell. *Mrs N. Macauley* — –

WATER DIVINER 5 b.g. Dowsing (USA) 124 – Prudence 68 (Grundy 137) [1994 –: a7g 11.6m^5 13.8g 1995 10.1g Sep 13] leggy gelding: of little account nowadays. *K. G. Wingrove* — –

WATER HAZARD (IRE) 3 b.c. Maelstrom Lake 118 – Simply Inch (Simply Great (FR) 122) [1994 45: 6m 6m 7m 7m a8g a6g 1995 a7g* a8g^3 a8g^4 a7g* a7g^5 8m 7g 8g a8g^5 a10g^2 7g 8f^3 a10g^4 11.9f* 10f^3 10g^2 a12g a12g Dec 18] compact colt: modest handicapper: won at Lingfield (twice) early on and apprentice selling race at Brighton (led over 5f out) in August: stays 1½m: acts on firm ground and equitrack: held up. *S. Dow* — 53 a57

WATERLAND (USA) 2 ch.f. (Feb 11) Explodent (USA) – Water Angel (USA) (Halo (USA)) [1995 7f^5 8.1m* 8h^3 Sep 4] angular filly: first foal: dam unraced daughter of sister to Canadian Oaks winner Northernette and Storm Bird, an excellent family: won maiden at Chepstow in August: led over 6f then eased right up when beaten in minor event at Bath following month: stays 1m: sold 10,500 gns Newmarket December Sales. *R. Charlton* — 72

WATERLOO BELLE 4 ch.f. Kind of Hush 118 – Afrabela 76 (African Sky 124) [1994 NR 1995 a16g 10.8m 11.5g^5 Jul 18] second foal: dam 6f winner: seems of little account: tried blinkered. *Mrs N. Macauley* — –

WATERLORD (IRE) 5 b.g. Bob Back (USA) 124 – Ringtail 102 (Auction Ring (USA) 123) [1994 62: a7g a10g 7d^2 7.5d^4 8d* 8m^2 7.1f^5 8g 8.5g^4 8m 10m 1995 a7g 7.5m 8m 8m 7m^4 8.3g 10g 8.2m Oct 19] small, sturdy gelding: carries condition: only poor form at best in 1995: stays 8.5f: probably acts on any going, including equitrack: blinkered (below form) once at 3 yrs: sometimes has tongue tied down. *D. Nicholls* — 40

WATER MUSIC MELODY 2 b.f. (Mar 11) Sizzling Melody 117 – Raintree Venture (Good Times (ITY)) [1995 5.1f 5.7h^3 Aug 3] 3,700F: fifth foal: half-sister to 3-y-o Istiwa (by Statoblest) and to a winner in Italy: dam poor daughter of half-sister to smart middle-distance filly Seventh Bride, dam of Oaks winner Polygamy: poor form in maiden and seller at Bath. *Martyn Meade* — 38

WATHBAT MTOTO 3 b.f. Mtoto 134 – Alwathba (USA) 100 (Lyphard (USA) 132) [1994 NR 1995 10g^4 10f* 10g 10m* 11.9m^2 10.1g^4 Aug 28] quite attractive filly: first foal: dam 2-y-o 6f winner suited by 1m, is sister to smart 7f performer Dreams To Reality from good family: won maiden at Brighton in May and 4-runner handicap at Pontefract (under 7-lb claimer) in July: good efforts in frame in handicaps at Haydock and Newcastle (listed rated stakes) in August: stayed 11.9f: stud. *L. M. Cumani* — 88

WATHEEQAH (USA) 4 b.f. Topsider (USA) – Reyah 83 (Young Generation 129) [1994 60: 5d 6d 8f 8f 5m* 6g^3 a6g a8g 1995 a6g Jan 2] quite good-topped filly: — –

modest performer in 1994: well beaten on the all-weather all outings for new stable: probably a sprinter: acts on good to firm ground: blinkered since fifth start. *M. Brittain*

WAVE HILL 6 b.g. Sizzling Melody 117 – Trikymia 68 (Final Straw 127) [1994 74: a7g^2 a8g^6 a8g^4 8f 7.1d 9g^6 8.2g^2 7d^4 a8g a7g^2 a8g^6 a8g^6 1995 8f 8.3m^6 Aug 7] close-coupled gelding: usually looks very well: good mover: fair handicapper: not knocked about in 1995: stays 8.2f: acts on firm ground, dead and equitrack: usually blinkered or visored, not in 1995: usually wears crossed noseband: fair jumper, winner over fences in October: inconsistent. *P. R. Hedger* –

WAVERLEY STAR 10 br.g. Pitskelly 122 – Quelle Blague (Red God 128§) [1994 –: 5d 5m 5.1g 7d a6g^6 a7g^4 1995 a6g^4 a6g^2 a6g a6g^6 a6g a6g^6 a8g 6m^3 6m 6m 5g^5 6f 6f a5g Sep 4] big, workmanlike gelding: poor mover: poor performer: trained until after ninth 10-y-o start by K. Cunningham-Brown: stays 6f: acts on firm and dead ground and the all-weather: no improvement in blinkers/visor: inconsistent. *J. S. Wainwright* 42 d

WAVEY 2 b.f. (Mar 4) Kris 135 – Throw Away Line (USA) (Assert 134) [1995 7.5d* 7d^4 7m Oct 13] 50,000F: good-bodied, lengthy filly: has a powerful, round action: fourth foal: dam, minor winner in USA, half-sister to very good animals Go For Wand and Dance Spell: made virtually all to win maiden at Beverley in September: hampered over 1f out and eased right off in Rockfel Stakes at Newmarket in October, final start: will stay 1¼m+: sent to France. *J. H. M. Gosden* 82

WAVIAN 3 b.c. Warning 136 – Vian (USA) (Far Out East (USA)) [1994 100: 5.1f^2 5m* 6m^2 6m^4 5m^2 5m* 5g^5 1995 5m^2 5m 6g 6m^5 5m^2 6m^4 Sep 6] neat, attractive colt: has a quick action: useful performer: creditable second of 6 (to Mind Games) in listed race at Haydock and in minor event at Lingfield (taken down early, didn't look entirely resolute): well-below-form fourth of 6 in similar event at Epsom 2 weeks later: stays 6f: has raced only on a sound surface: blinkered last 2 starts: sold 25,000 gns Newmarket Autumn Sales. *R. Charlton* 96

WAYFARERS WAY (USA) 4 ch.g. Manastash Ridge (USA) – Miss Daytona (USA) (Nashua) [1994 79d: 8g 9g^5 8.1m 10f 10d 1995 8.1g^4 7f 10m^2 9m^6 Aug 26] strong gelding: fair performer nowadays: stays 1¼m: acts on good to firm and dead ground: joined N. Henderson. *R. Hannon* 68

WAYNE COUNTY (IRE) 5 b.h. Sadler's Wells (USA) 132 – Detroit (FR) 131 (Riverman (USA) 131) [1994 72+: a11g^2 10s* 12g* 11.8s^4 13.9f^5 10s^4 12m 10m 1995 9.9m* 12m^5 12g 12m 12m^4 10d^4 11.8m^6 12m* 11.1g^3 10g^3 12d^4 Sep 23] good-topped horse: impresses in appearance: improved into a smart performer: won handicap at Beverley in April: first run since leaving G. Fierro's stable, made nearly all (new tactics) to win well-contested 5-runner minor event at Newbury in August: third in smallish fields in September Stakes at Kempton and Select Stakes (headed 1½f out, stuck on well, 1¾ lengths behind Triarius) at Goodwood: effective at 1¼m and probably stays 1¾m: has won on soft ground, but easily best efforts on a sound surface: probably effective visored/blinkered or not: often coltish: sometimes sweats. *R. Akehurst* 110

WAYPOINT 2 b.f. (Mar 19) Cadeaux Genereux 131 – Princess Athena 119 (Ahonoora 122) [1995 7.1d^6 Oct 11] lengthy, unfurnished filly: looks weak: third foal: dam best at 5f: 8/1 and green, remote sixth of 9 to Polar Eclipse in maiden at Haydock, never better than mid-division: should do better. *R. Charlton* – p

WEATHER BREAK 4 b.c. Mtoto 134 – Favourite Girl 82 (Mummy's Pet 125) [1994 84: 8s 8.1g^5 8.3m* 8d 1995 7m 8.5d^5 7.1g 6.9f^2 7g 8.5f 8.5f a5f* a6f a7f Dec 2] sparely-made colt: good mover: just a fair performer at 4 yrs: left H. Candy after fifth start: form in USA only when winning allowance race (racing on lasix first time) at Philadelphia Park: won over 8.3f at 3 yrs, but seems best as a sprinter: acts on good to firm ground and dirt: blinkered last 4 starts: headstrong, and wore a net muzzle as 3-y-o: inconsistent. *J. A. Nazareth, jnr, USA* 76

WEAVER BIRD 5 b.m. Master Willie 129 – Sweet Snow (USA) (Lyphard (USA) 132) [1994 81: 8m* 8m^5 8m 7.1d 8m^4 1995 8m^6 8m^2 8f* 8f 8f^3 8.3m* 9g 8m Oct 28] leggy, angular mare: has a round action: fairly useful handicapper, better than ever: won at Salisbury in June and Windsor (rated stakes) in August: effective at 1m to 1¼m: acts on firm and (at 3 yrs) soft ground: often wears bandages: usually held up: sold 20,000 gns Newmarket December Sales. *H. Candy* 92

WEAVER GEORGE (IRE) 5 b.g. Flash of Steel 120 – Nephrite 106 (Godswalk (USA) 130) [1994 NR 1995 13g4 14.1m4 May 29] leggy gelding: shows knee action: fair hurdler, but poor maiden on flat: stays 14.1f: acts on any going: blinkered (no improvement) twice. *J. A. Hellens* 31

WEB OF INTRIGUE 3 ch.f. Machiavellian (USA) 123 – Catawba 98 (Mill Reef (USA) 141) [1994 66: 7.2g5 7m4 7.1g 1995 8g Apr 27] rather leggy, unfurnished filly: fair form as 2-y-o: respectable seventh of 14 in maiden at Warwick only start in 1995: bred to stay beyond 1m: yet to race on a soft surface: sold 23,000 gns Newmarket December Sales. *H. R. A. Cecil* 59

WEDDING GIFT 2 b.f. (Apr 26) Always Fair (USA) 121 – Such Style 80 (Sassafras (FR) 135) [1995 6m6 7g* 7.5g4 8g2 7g3 8d4 8d 8g* Nov 10] 100,000 francs Y: leggy filly: ninth foal: half-sister to several minor winners, including Chehana (by Posse), fourth in Grade 2 event at 1¼m at 4 yrs: dam, placed over 1½m on only start, is half-sister to Prix Hocquart winner Regency and Oaks-third Britannia's Rule out of a half-sister to Vaguely Noble: won maiden at Compiegne in July and listed race at Evry in November: useful form in Prix du Calvados at Deauville, Prix d'Aumale and Prix Marcel Boussac (held up, 8 lengths seventh of 11 to Miss Tahiti) at Longchamp: stays 1m: yet to race on extremes of going. *P. H. Demercastel, France* 101

WEE HOPE (USA) 2 b.c. (May 20) Housebuster (USA) – Tell Me Sumthing (USA) (Summing (USA)) [1995 6m6 6.1d2 6g3 Sep 21] $160,000Y: leggy colt: fourth foal: half-brother to useful 3-y-o 7f and 1m winner Star of Zilzal (by Zilzal) and useful German 4-y-o 7f winner Star Carnival (by Nashwan): dam won at up to 7f, half-sister to Green Forest: sire top-class sprinter who stayed 1m: showed good speed long way but tended to hang closing stages when placed in maidens won by Keepers Dawn at Nottingham and Brandon Magic at Pontefract: stays 6f. *M. R. Stoute* 82

WEET-A-MINUTE (IRE) 2 ro.c. (Mar 6) Nabeel Dancer (USA) 120 – Ludovica (Bustino 136) [1995 7f5 7m3 8.1g3 7.5d* 7.9m* 8f* 10m2 Oct 28] 6,400Y, 22,000 2-y-o: lengthy colt: good walker: sixth foal: closely related to Italian 3-y-o 1¼m and 10.5f winner Ombre Rosse (by Jareer) and half-brother to 1990 2-y-o 6f winner Where's Carol (by Anfield): dam unraced daughter of Ebor second Lorelene: 95

Tote Silver Tankard Stakes, Pontefract—
the Reg Hollinshead-trained Weet-A-Minute continues on his impressive progress

won auction event at Beverley, nursery at York and listed race at Pontefract (beat Warbrook 2½ lengths) in the autumn: ran creditably when 5 lengths second of 6 to Gentilhomme in listed race at Newmarket on final outing: stays 1¼m: acts on firm and good to soft ground. *R. Hollinshead*

WEE TINKERBELL 2 ch.f. (Apr 7) Timeless Times (USA) 99 – Kiveton Komet 71 (Precocious 126) [1995 5g^{3} 5g^{6} 6f^{4} Jun 14] 2,700F, 2,000Y: first foal: dam sprinter: modest form when in frame in maiden auctions at Edinburgh and Hamilton: stays 6f. *Miss L. A. Perratt* 51

WEETMAN'S WEIGH (IRE) 2 b.c. (Apr 19) Archway (IRE) 115 – Indian Sand (Indian King (USA) 128) [1995 a5g^{3} a6g^{5} 6m^{2} a6g^{2} 6.1m^{4} 5f* 6m^{6} 6m^{2} 6m Oct 12] IR 5,500Y: useful-looking colt: second foal: dam very poor Irish maiden: fair performer: won 5-runner maiden auction at Carlisle in July: best effort in nurseries when head second of 18 at Pontefract penultimate start: stays 6f: acts on firm ground and fibresand. *R. Hollinshead* 66

WELCOME LU 2 ch.f. (Apr 13) Most Welcome 131 – Odile (Green Dancer (USA) 132) [1995 6f 6f Oct 24] sturdy, strong-quartered filly: seventh foal: sister to Italian 3-y-o 7f and 7.5f winner Green Most and half-sister to 2 winners by Mummy's Pet, including fair 1m winner Odilex: dam once-raced granddaughter of 1000 Guineas winner Waterloo: backward, always well behind in maiden events at Redcar and Leicester. *P. S. Felgate* –

WELCOME ROYALE (IRE) 2 ch.g. (Mar 27) Be My Guest (USA) 126 – Kirsova (Absalom 128) [1995 6m^{5} 7m^{4} 7.5m 8g^{6} 8d^{3} 8f^{4} Oct 12] 15,500F, 15,000Y: strong, heavy-topped gelding: unimpressive mover: half-brother to 3-y-o Petova (by Petorius) and several winners, including 9f and 14.8f winner La Ballerine and 7.6f winner Ler Cru (both by Lafontaine): dam lightly raced: fair maiden: will stay beyond 1m: acts on firm and dead ground. *M. H. Tompkins* 68

WELL AND TRULY 8 b.m. Rousillon (USA) 133 – Altana 71 (Grundy 137) [1994 –, a53: a12g^{4} a14.8g^{6} a13g^{3} a16s^{3} a14g^{4} a12g^{2} a14.8g^{3} a16.2g* 17.1d a14.8g^{2} a14.8g^{3} a16g^{4} a12g^{6} a16.2g^{5} 1995 a16.2g* a16.2g^{3} a16g a16g^{6} Feb 17] leggy, light-framed mare: modest handicapper: won at Wolverhampton in January: well below form at Southwell last 2 starts: stays 16.2f: acts well on fibresand, well beaten only outing on turf in 1994: covered by Tragic Role. *B. A. McMahon* – a58

WELL ARRANGED (IRE) 4 ch.c. Bold Arrangement 127 – Eurynome (Be My Guest (USA) 126) [1994 84: 8m 10m 10g^{5} 12m^{2} 12g^{3} 14s* 1995 16m 13.9g 14g 12f 16.1g Oct 3] lengthy ex-Irish colt: fairly useful form at 3 yrs: very long way below form in 1995, though did not encounter a soft surface: stays 1¾m: acts well on soft ground. *R. Akehurst* –

WELL BELOVED 4 b.c. Sadler's Wells (USA) 132 – Sancta 106 (So Blessed 130) [1994 86: 10d 12g^{4} 14g^{2} 14.1m* 16.2m^{2} 14f^{5} 16g* 18.2s* 16.1g^{2} 1995 14m^{3} 18.7m May 10] big, useful-looking colt: fairly useful handicapper: no headgear, set plenty to do when length third of 16 to Tudor Island in strongly-run handicap at Newmarket on reappearance: favourite but seemed unsuited by track in Chester Cup, lacking pace: suited by good test of stamina: acted on soft going, possibly unsuited by firm: visored/blinkered 5 of last 7 starts: has been retired. *H. R. A. Cecil* 84

WELL DRAWN 2 b.c. (Apr 21) Dowsing (USA) 124 – Classic Design (Busted 134) [1995 7m a8g^{3} Dec 18] 29,000Y: rangy, quite attractive colt: fourth foal: half-brother to smart 4-y-o sprinter Eveningperformance (by Night Shift): dam unraced half-sister to Tirol: well-backed 9/4 shot on first run for nearly 4 months, 2 lengths third of 9 to Red Rusty in maiden at Lingfield, keeping on strongly: will be well suited by 1¼m+: likely to improve again. *H. Candy* 65 p

WELLSIAN (USA) 3 b.c. Sadler's Wells (USA) 132 – My Darling One (USA) (Exclusive Native (USA)) [1994 69p: 7m 7g 7d^{6} 1995 10.1f^{4} 8g 10.3f^{4} 12.3m* 11.4m^{2} Aug 25] sturdy, lengthy, good sort: has plenty of scope: has a quick action: fair performer: won handicap at Ripon in August, held up and leading final 1f: effective at 1¼m to 1½m: acts on firm ground: type to make a better 4-y-o: sent to Dubai. *L. M. Cumani* 77 p

WELL SUITED 5 b.g. Elegant Air 119 – Gay Appeal 76 (Star Appeal 133) [1994 –: 10d 10m a13g a8g a8g 1995 a11g^{5} Jan 6] lengthy gelding: soundly beaten since –

fair 3-y-o maiden: stays 1¼m: acts on good to firm going: blinkered (below form) once at 3 yrs: joined R. O'Sullivan. *B. J. McMath*

WELLS WHISPER (FR) 3 b.f. Sadler's Wells (USA) 132 – Whakilyric (USA) 113 (Miswaki (USA) 124) [1994 NR 1995 10m4 11.4m 8f3 10g3 12.3m4 10.1m3 Aug 10] 880,000Y: leggy, quite attractive filly: sister to very smart 1m to 1¼m performer Johann Quatz and smart 1¼m to 13.5f winner Walter Willy, and half-sister to high-class middle-distance horse Hernando (by Niniski): dam (won at up to 7f) probably stayed 1m: fair maiden handicapper: should stay beyond 1¼m but below form (at Chester) when tried: has raced only on a sound surface: blinkered (no improvement) third 3-y-o start: sent to Germany. *G. Wragg* 71

WELLSY LAD (USA) 8 ch.g. El Baba (USA) – Iwishiknew (USA) (Damascus (USA)) [1994 –: a6g 1995 a6g a7g5 a6g4 a6g2 8.1d2 a6g a6g a8g a7g2 a8.5g3 a7g6 a7g* a8g2 Jun 22] leggy, angular gelding: poor handicapper nowadays: won at Southwell in June: stays 8.5f: acts on fibresand, best with give in the ground when on turf: effective blinkered/visored or not: sometimes refuses to enter stalls. *D. W. Chapman* 47

WELSH COLUMN 9 b.m. Welsh Captain 113 – Bally's Step (Ballynockan 112) [1994 NR 1995 a8.5g 8.1m6 Jul 4] angular mare: no longer of much account. *M. W. Eckley* –

WELSH HERITAGE (IRE) 5 b.m. Slip Anchor 136 – Mohibbah (USA) 86 (Conquistador Cielo (USA)) [1994 –: a9.4g6 a8.5g 8g 1995 a7g a7g5 Feb 1] unfurnished mare: poor maiden: soundly beaten in 1995: sold 900 gns Ascot July Sales. *R. J. Price* –

WELSH LIBERTY (IRE) 6 b.h. Caerleon (USA) 132 – Bernica (FR) 114 (Caro 133) [1994 8s* 8.5s 8d3 8.5g4 10m5 9g* 8g* 8g* 10d 10d 8d3 1995 8g2 8d5 8m5 8g2 8m5 8m 8g* 10g3 8.5g3 8g2 10g2 8m* Nov 12] half-brother to several winners, none better than smart 1985 French 2-y-o 6f winner Excalibur's Lake (by Nureyev): dam, from very good family, won 3 times at around 1m in France: smart Italian horse: successful twice at Naples at 4 yrs and 4 times at Rome at 5 yrs: winner at Rome in 1995 of minor event in September and 11-runner Premio Ribot (around 55/1, easily best effort to lead post and short head Lake Storm) in November: has form at up to 1¼m, best efforts at 1m: acts on good to firm and soft ground. *D. Ducci, Italy* 113

WELSHMAN 9 ch.g. Final Straw 127 – Joie de Galles 72 (Welsh Pageant 132) [1994 78: 16s6 18.7m3 16s 16.1f 18.7g 15.9m2 17.2m4 15.9g6 16.1m 15.9s 1995 18.7m 18.7g6 15.9m2 16.1f 15.9d Sep 20] close-coupled, workmanlike gelding: carries condition: has deteriorated considerably, showing only modest form (even at Chester, where he has a fine record) at best in 1995: stays very well: acts on any going: suited by racing up with pace: fair hurdler. *M. Blanshard* 59

WELSH MELODY 2 b.f. (Mar 9) Merdon Melody 98 – Young Whip (Bold Owl 101) [1995 6.1m a6g* a6g a7g6 6s a8.5g a6g5 a7g3 Nov 24] third foal: sister to temperamental 3-y-o 7f/7.5f winner Mountgate: dam unraced: won seller at Wolverhampton in July: visored/blinkered, back to form last 2 starts: stays 7f: best form on fibresand. *K. R. Burke* – a47

WELSH MILL (IRE) 6 b.g. Caerleon (USA) 132 – Gay Milly (FR) 74 (Mill Reef (USA) 141) [1994 84d: 13.9f 12m 13.9m 16.1f 11.9f 1995 11.9g 11.9m Oct 5] close-coupled, attractive gelding: disappointing since fairly useful 4-y-o: backward and no worthwhile form in 1995: stays 1¾m: probably acts on any ground. *Mrs M. Reveley* –

WELSH MIST 4 b.f. Damister (USA) 123 – Welwyn 92 (Welsh Saint 126) [1994 100: 6m 6.1d2 5f* 5m3 6f* 5m5 6m 5g 1995 5m 6m6 6m3 6m5 5m 6m3 5f5 7m5 6g 5.6m Sep 6] workmanlike filly: useful performer: best efforts on sixth and seventh outings when head third of 5 to Tajannub in listed race at York and when fifth of 11 to Hever Golf Rose in King George Stakes at Goodwood: just fairly useful form on other starts: stays 6f: acts on firm ground, possibly unsuited by a soft surface: has run creditably when sweating and edgy. *R. Boss* 102

WELSH MOUNTAIN 2 b.c. (Apr 9) Welsh Captain 113 – Miss Nelski 84 (Most Secret 119) [1995 5m5 5m2 5g3 5m* 6m 5m2 5g3 Aug 26] 22,000Y: good-bodied colt: has scope: ninth foal: brother to winning sprinter Ski Captain (fairly useful at best) and a winner abroad: dam 5f winner who stayed 7f: won nursery at Folkestone in 74

July: twice ran creditably in nurseries afterwards: speedy, and best at 5f: acts on good to firm ground. *M. J. Heaton-Ellis*

WELSH OWL 2 ch.f. (Apr 26) Bold Owl 101 – Thabeh 57 (Shareef Dancer (USA) 135) [1995 7f a7g 6f^{6} Aug 11] smallish filly: second foal: dam poor maiden: little promise in claimer and 2 sellers: sold 500 gns Ascot November Sales. *K. R. Burke* –

WELSH WIZZARD 3 b.g. Robellino (USA) 127 – My Greatest Star 93 (Great Nephew 126) [1994 NR 1995 a8g^{5} a8g^{6} Feb 13] 8,400Y: second foal: dam shaped well sole outing at 2 yrs but modest maiden (barely stayed 1¼m) afterwards: well beaten in maiden and seller: sold 1,000 gns Ascot May Sales. *C. N. Williams* –

WELTON ARSENAL 3 b.g. Statoblest 120 – Miller's Gait 74§ (Mill Reef (USA) 141) [1994 91: 6s^{6} 6g 7g^{3} 7m^{2} 7f^{3} 6f* 6g^{3} 6m^{4} 1995 8g^{5} 6m^{2} 5.1m^{4} 7.6m 7g^{4} 6g^{2} 6g 6m Jun 17] sturdy gelding: useful handicapper: best effort in valuable event at York on fifth start, but found little after travelling best of all 2f out: well beaten last 2 starts: effective at 6f to 1m: acts on firm ground: a tricky ride, and not one to trust implicitly. *M. R. Channon* 101

WELVILLE 2 b.c. (Mar 28) Most Welcome 131 – Miss Top Ville (FR) (Top Ville 129) [1995 5m 5m^{2} 6g* Sep 8] tall, unfurnished colt: fourth foal: brother to fairly useful 4-y-o 1m winner Wilcuma and half-brother to 3-y-o Eurolink Shadow (by Be My Guest) and a winner in Germany by Petong: dam French middle-distance winner: absent 4 months, won 15-runner maiden at Goodwood by 1½ lengths from Brandon Magic, making all and running on strongly: will improve again, particularly at 7f+. *P. J. Makin* 87 p

WENDALS TOUCH 4 gr.f. Touch of Grey 90 – Snow Huntress 80 (Shirley Heights 130) [1994 NR 1995 6m^{6} 6d 8d a7g Nov 10] first foal: dam 1¼m and 1½m winner: well beaten in maidens and claimers. *R. M. Flower* –

WENDY'S WAY 3 b.f. Merdon Melody 98 – Piccadilly Rose 63 (Reform 132) [1994 53: 5d 5s^{2} a5g* 5m^{5} 6m a5g 6m^{3} 7.5g^{6} 7.1m^{3} 1995 a7g a7g^{6} a7g Jan 27] compact filly: modest performer at 2 yrs: well below form in 1995: sold 1,500 gns Doncaster March Sales: stays 7f: acts on good to firm ground: blinkered (finished last) once at 2 yrs: covered by Cyrano de Bergerac. *J. Berry* –

WENTBRIDGE LAD (IRE) 5 b.g. Coquelin (USA) 121 – Cathryn's Song (Prince Tenderfoot (USA) 126) [1994 52, a80: 8s a12g a8.5g^{2} a7g* 8.2m^{4} 8m^{3} a9.4g* 8m^{3} a9.4g* 7m^{5} 8.1g^{6} 10.8s^{3} 10d a8.5g* a7g 1995 10.8d^{5} 9.9m^{4} 8f^{3} a9.4g^{2} 8f^{2} 8g^{2} 9.2f^{5} a7g* 7.1m^{3} a6g^{5} 8f a7g^{2} a8.5g^{5} a8.5g* 7.6m* 10m^{3} 8.1m^{3} 8m^{5} 7.6m^{4} 8m^{5} 10.3d^{3} 8.1g 8d^{5} 11.9s^{6} 10.4m 8.9g 12m a8.5g Nov 11] lengthy, rather leggy gelding: fair handicapper: won 2 claimers at Wolverhampton (6 wins there) and £8,900 event at Chester in midsummer: below form 6 of last 7 starts: effective at 7f to 1¼m: acts on soft and firm ground and goes well on fibresand: often wears blinkers/visor, but effective without: bandaged on the all-weather at 5 yrs: has run well for amateur: normally held up: carries head high: tough. *P. D. Evans* 68 a80

WE'RE JOKEN 3 b.f. Statoblest 120 – Jay Gee Ell 78 (Vaigly Great 127) [1994 62: 5d^{3} 5v* 5g 6g* 6f^{4} 6m 6f^{2} 6g^{4} 1995 a7g^{6} 7.1g 6g* 6.1m a6g* 6g* 6.1g^{4} 6f^{5} 6g a6g a6g Nov 20] leggy filly: modest handicapper: won at Catterick (apprentices), Wolverhampton and Catterick by June: well beaten last 4 starts: stays 6f well: acts on fibresand and heavy ground, has hung badly right on firm: wears bandages behind: races prominently: sold 3,100 gns Doncaster November Sales. *J. Berry* 55 a50

WESSAM PRINCE 4 b.c. Soviet Star (USA) 128 – Clare Bridge (USA) 107 (Little Current (USA)) [1994 113: 8d^{3} 8g^{4} 7m^{3} 7d^{6} 7.5s^{3} 6g^{4} 5d^{3} 6d^{2} 5s^{5} 1995 5.5s* 6d* 6m^{4} 6g^{3} 6.5g^{3} 6d^{3} 6d^{5} 7m Oct 15] good-topped, attractive French colt: smart performer: won listed race at Evry in April and Group 3 event at Baden-Baden (by ½ length from Glenlivet) in May: in frame next 4 starts, including in Prix Maurice de Gheest at Deauville (creditable third behind Cherokee Rose) in August: creditable fifth of 15 to Cool Jazz in Diadem Stakes at Ascot then below form in Prix de la Foret last 2 starts: effective at 5f to 1m: useful form on good to firm ground, best with some give: blinkered sixth to final 3-y-o starts. *C. Laffon-Parias, France* 113

WESSHAUN 5 b.m. Shaunicken – Wessex Flyer (Pony Express 85) [1994 31: 10g a9.4g 5.1f a7g 1995 a8g Jun 16] leggy, plain mare: poor maiden plater: blinkered (pulled hard) second 4-y-o start: joined A. Sims. *W. G. M. Turner* –

WEST AUSTRIA (IRE) 2 b.c. (Jan 24) Tirol 127 – Labwa (USA) (Lyphard (USA) 132) [1995 6d^6 6m Aug 19] tall, leggy colt: has scope: poor walker: sixth foal: closely related to a winner in Germany by Thatching and half-brother to useful 3-y-o 6f winner Baaderah (by Cadeaux Genereux): dam unraced: sixth of 15 to Miss Waterline in maiden at Haydock in June: slowly away when well-beaten last of 7 in minor event at Ripon 2½ months later: looks a slow learner: sent to Dubai. *J. Berry* 58+

WESTCOAST 4 b.g. Handsome Sailor 125 – Pichon (Formidable (USA) 125) [1994 NR 1995 8d a9.4g Apr 13] smallish, sturdy gelding: rated 56 on easily best effort at 2 yrs for G. M. Moore: backward, tailed off in 1995: stays 6f: acts on dead ground: blinkered (below form) twice at 2 yrs. *M. Tate* –

WESTCOURT MAGIC 2 b.c. (Jan 27) Emarati (USA) 74 – Magic Milly 60 (Simply Great (FR) 122) [1995 5m 5f 7.5g 5m* 5m* 5m* 6f* 5g^2 5g* 5s^2 Oct 7] 5,800F: sturdy colt: second foal: half-brother to 4-y-o Folly Finnesse (by Joligeneration), successful from 6f (at 2 yrs) to 10.8f: dam 2-y-o 1m winner: vastly improved colt: made all in seller at Newcastle and nurseries at Beverley, Sandown and Thirsk in the summer before winning Timeform Harry Rosebery Trophy at Ayr (by length from Kunucu) in September: creditable second to Mubhij in Cornwallis Stakes at Ascot on final outing: stays 6f: seems to act on any going: sweating and very on toes at start eighth outing: taken early to post. *M. W. Easterby* 99

WESTCOURT PRINCESS 3 b.f. Emarati (USA) 74 – Petrol 73 (Troy 137) [1994 55: 5m^2 5f a7g^5 a6g^2 6m^3 6d 6s a7g 1995 a7g a6g^4 6m 10m 9f^4 9.9m* 8.5g 9.9m^2 10m* 10.4g^4 10.5s 8.9g Oct 7] workmanlike filly: modest handicapper: won at Beverley in July and Ripon in August: below form last 3 starts: better form at around 1¼m than 1m: acts on firm ground and fibresand, seemingly not on a soft surface: tried blinkered, no improvement: has worn sliding bar bit: takes good hold: usually front runner. *M. W. Easterby* 59

WESTERN COUNTRY 3 ch.g. Beveled (USA) – Country Singer (Town And Country 124) [1994 NR 1995 8m 10.2f May 22] workmanlike gelding: second reported foal: dam lightly-raced novice hurdler: tailed off in maidens: subsequently gelded. *S. Mellor* –

Timeform Harry Rosebery Trophy, Ayr—seller, nurseries and now a listed race; Westcourt Magic (left) keeps on winning

WESTERN FAME (USA) 3 b.c. Gone West (USA) – Fariedah (USA) 96 (Topsider (USA)) [1994 67p: 7m 1995 8g 8m 7m* 8g³ 7g* 7d³ 7m² 8m Oct 28] strong, angular colt: progressed into a useful handicapper: won at Leicester in June and Newcastle (£11,100 event) in August: excellent seventh of 30 (held when checked final 1f) in £24,100 event at Newmarket final start: effective at 7f and 1m: acts on good to firm ground and dead, yet to race on extremes: held up: consistent: sent to USA. *J. L. Dunlop* 97

WESTERN FLEET (USA) 4 ch.g. Westheimer (USA) – Fleetwood Fancy (Taufan (USA) 119) [1994 64d: 10s⁵ 10.2s 11.6m⁶ 11.5m⁵ 10f³ 10d 1995 a12g Apr 4] small, angular gelding: disappointing since 3-y-o reappearance, for new stable in 1995: should stay beyond 1¼m: acts on soft ground (probably on good to firm), ran poorly on fibresand. *J. H. Peacock* –

WESTERN GENERAL 4 ch.g. Cadeaux Genereux 131 – Patsy Western 81 (Precocious 126) [1994 81: 6g 7d⁴ 8.5s⁶ 8m² 8.1s* 8s² 10.1g 1995 8m* 8.5m 8m 10.5g³ 8m 10.4m² 10.3m⁴ Oct 21] quite attractive gelding: fairly useful handicapper: won at Pontefract in April: effective at 1m to 10.5f: acts on good to firm and soft ground: tried blinkered, at least as effective without: inconsistent, but often runs well fresh: has joined Miss K. Milligan. *Miss S. E. Hall* 83

WESTERN HORIZON (USA) 3 ch.f. Gone West (USA) – Norette (Northfields (USA)) [1994 58: 6m 6g 7d 1995 6.9d⁴ a8g⁴ 9.7m⁵ 9.9m 14.1g 12.1f⁴ 10f⁵ 12f⁴ 13.1h² 13.4d 14s⁶ 13.6f³ a12g Oct 23] smallish filly: unimpressive mover: poor maiden nowadays: will stay beyond 1¾m: acts on hard and dead ground, seemingly not on equitrack: blinkered (not discredited) eleventh 3-y-o start. *C. E. Brittain* 49

WESTERN PLAYBOY 3 b.g. Law Society (USA) 130 – Reine d'Beaute 97 (Caerleon (USA) 132) [1994 NR 1995 10m Apr 17] 17,000Y: tall, lengthy gelding: first foal: dam, 4-y-o 1m and and 9f winner only starts, from very good family: 20/1, burly and green, beaten about 12 lengths when fourteenth of 25 in maiden at Kempton, pulling hard: subsequently gelded: looked sure to do better. *R. Hannon* – p

WESTERN PLOY 3 b.f. Deploy 131 – Westerlake (Blakeney 126) [1994 –: 7g 8d 1995 a7g Jan 9] workmanlike filly: no sign of ability. *J. L. Harris* –

WESTERN REEL (USA) 3 b.f. Gone West (USA) – River Jig (USA) 98 (Irish River (FR) 131) [1994 83: 6m² 6g² 6.1g³ 8m² 7.9d² 1995 8.2m 8m* 8f³ 10f⁴ 10g 10.1g⁴ Sep 12] leggy, quite good-topped filly: fluent mover: won maiden at Salisbury in June: fairly useful form on 3 of last 4 starts, and somewhat flattered by bare form of fourth in steadily-run Nassau Stakes at Goodwood (could be rated 106): stays 1¼m: acts on firm and dead ground: sometimes edgy, and has failed to settle: usually wears crossed noseband: held up. *P. F. I. Cole* 95 +

WESTERN SAL 3 b.f. Salse (USA) 128 – Patsy Western 81 (Precocious 126) [1994 NR 1995 7g³ 7.1m² 8.3m³ 10m* 10d Sep 26] close-coupled filly: has a fluent, round action: second foal: half-sister to 4-y-o 1m winner Western General (by Cadeaux Genereux): dam twice-raced 6f winner, is half-sister to Mr Fluorocarbon and Western Jewel: fair form in maidens, winning at Leicester in August: ran badly final start: should prove better at 1¼m than shorter: acts on good to firm ground. *W. Jarvis* 75

WESTERN VALLEY 5 ch.m. Valiyar 129 – Another Western 58 (Good Times (ITY)) [1994 27: 7s 6m 7g 6f 6.1s a7g a12g⁵ a13g 1995 10m 7g 7g Sep 13] lengthy mare: poor performer: effective at 7f, and seems to stay 1½m: acts on soft ground: visored (well beaten) twice: bandaged at 5 yrs *C. P. Wildman* –

WESTERN VENTURE (IRE) 2 ch.c. (Feb 26) Two Timing (USA) 124 – Star Gazing (IRE) (Caerleon (USA) 132) [1995 6m³ 5g³ 5f* 5m Sep 7] 4,400Y: quite attractive colt: has a quick action: first foal: dam never ran: fair form: fortunate winner of 6-runner maiden at Folkestone in August, well held when leader's saddle slipped: stiffish task when last of 13 in nursery there following month: probably stays 6f. *J. W. Payne* 67

WEST FARM BOY 3 b.g. Full Extent (USA) 113 – La Melodie 77 (Silly Season 127) [1994 38: 6g 7g 7.1m 1995 5.9f 8m 5.9f Jul 31] leggy, angular gelding: poor performer: well behind in sellers for new stable in 1995: blinkered last 2 starts: sold 750 gns Doncaster September Sales. *J. J. O'Neill* –

WESTFIELD 3 b.g. Lyphento (USA) 108 – Wessex Flyer (Pony Express 85) [1994 NR 1995 a11g Nov 20] third reported foal: dam had extremely bad reputation in points: 20/1, tailed off in seller at Southwell. *W. G. M. Turner* –

WESTFIELD MOVES (IRE) 7 b.h. Montelimar (USA) 122 – Rathcoffey Daisy (Pampapaul 121) [1994 56, a53: a14g^5 a13g^4 a11g* a11g* 10v^6 9.9d^2 9.2s^3 10g 10m a11g a11g 1995 a11g Jan 16] leggy, lengthy horse: modest handicapper: no form only start in 1995: suited by middle distances: acts on any going: effective in visor, not tried for some time: has won for apprentice and when sweating: rather lazy, but game. *H. J. Collingridge* –

WEST HUMBLE 2 ch.f. (Mar 13) Pharly (FR) 130 – Humble Pie 92 (Known Fact (USA) 135) [1995 7g^3 Oct 3] 22,000Y: medium-sized filly: fourth foal: half-sister to smart 3-y-o sprinter Leap For Joy (by Sharpo) and 6f winner Waffle On (by Chief Singer): dam 2-y-o 6f winner from sprinting family: 20/1 and bit backward, 1¾ lengths third of 17 to Sil Sila in maiden at Warwick, racing keenly after hampered at start then keeping on well though green: will stay beyond 7f: sure to do better. *Lady Herries* 81 p

WESTMINSTER (IRE) 3 ch.g. Nashamaa 113 – Our Galadrial (Salmon Leap (USA) 131) [1994 72d: 7g^5 7m 7s 8s 1995 12.3m^2 12.1g* 12m^4 10g^5 Jul 3] angular gelding: disappointing at 2 yrs and subsequently gelded: narrowly won median auction maiden at Hamilton in May: ran well next start: seemed unsuited by drop in trip at Windsor last time: may well stay beyond 12.1f: acts on good to firm ground: visored (ran well) second and third 3-y-o starts: held up. *M. H. Tompkins* 65

WET PATCH (IRE) 3 b. or br.g. Common Grounds 118 – Disco Girl (FR) (Green Dancer (USA) 132) [1994 65: 7g 7.1d 7g 1995 9.7m 10g^2 8.3g^4 11.6m^4 10g^2 10m^4 10m* 10m^5 9m a10g* Dec 18] sturdy, good-bodied gelding: has a round action: fair handicapper: won at Kempton (apprentices) in August and Lingfield in December: really needs at least 1¼m, and stays 11.6f: acts on good to firm ground and equitrack: sweating (ran well) fifth 3-y-o start: usually held up. *R. Hannon* 68

WHACKFORD SQUEERS 3 ch.g. Komaite (USA) – Manhunt 70 (Posse (USA) 130) [1994 NR 1995 a8g* a8g^5 8m Jul 1] 3,000Y: second foal: brother to winning hurdler Mokaite, modest 7f winner at 2 yrs: dam, maiden, probably stayed 7f: fair form at best: won median auction maiden at Lingfield in January by 5 lengths: failed to repeat that form: sold (C. Cyzer to D. Nicholls) 6,000 gns Ascot October Sales. *C. A. Cyzer* 66

WHALLEY ABBEY 2 ch.f. (Feb 23) Mon Tresor 113 – Last Note (Welsh Pageant 132) [1995 5m^5 6.1m 6m^2 8d Sep 27] 4,000Y: compact filly: third foal: dam fourth over 1½m on only start: visored, best effort in auction events at Lingfield penultimate start: should have stayed further than 6f: dead. *G. L. Moore* 57

WHARFEDALE MUSIC 4 ch.f. Grey Desire 115 – Flute Royale 74 (Horage 124) [1994 42: 6g^2 8.3d 8m 10g 1995 10.2m 10.8m^3 a10g^5 Aug 5] good-topped filly: poor maiden: stays 10.8f: acts on good to soft and good to firm ground and on equitrack: blinkered (no form) third 3-y-o start. *M. C. Pipe* 33

WHAT A NIGHTMARE (IRE) 3 gr.g. Petorius 117 – Mysterious Lady (Melyno 130) [1994 51, a65: 5g 6g^5 a7g^2 7m a7g* a6g^4 7g^3 8g 7g^4 8s^3 a8.5g* 1995 a9.4g^4 a9.4g^3 a7g* a6g a8g^4 a7g^6 a7g^2 a7g* a7g^2 a7g* 7.6m* 7m* 7m^3 7d a7g^3 a7g a7g Dec 15] sparely-made gelding: shows a markedly round action: fair handicapper: won at Southwell (claimer, promoted) in March, and at Southwell, Wolverhampton, Chester (apprentices) and Catterick in the summer: sold out of J. Glover's stable 7,500 gns Doncaster November Sales before final start: effective at 7f, stays 9.4f: acts on good to firm and soft ground and on fibresand: nearly always visored/ blinkered nowadays: sometimes sweats: takes good hold and goes well with forcing tactics. *P. Howling* 66 a70

WHATEVER'S RIGHT (IRE) 6 b.g. Doulab (USA) 115 – Souveniers (Relko 136) [1994 63: a8g* a8g^6 8.2f^4 8g^6 8.2m* 8f^6 7.6m* 7.6g^3 8.2m^4 7m* 7.1d 1995 8m a8g* 8m^5 7g* 7m^3 7f^3 7m^2 7.1m^3 7m^4 7g a7g^3 a8g^2 Dec 6] workmanlike gelding: fair handicapper: won at Lingfield in May and Warwick (minor event) in June: best form at 7f/1m: acts on equitrack, firm and dead ground: blinkered (well beaten) final 4-y-o start: occasionally bandaged: makes running/races close up: genuine and consistent. *M. D. I. Usher* 75 a68

WHAT FUN 2 b.c. (Mar 31) Petong 126 – State Romance 67 (Free State 125) [1995 5m^{3} 5.1m* 6m 7s^{4} 6f 6m^{6} Oct 21] 6,200F: neat colt: half-brother to 3 winners by Chuckaroo, including Stewards' Cup winner Very Adjacent and middle-distance performer Strat's Legacy: dam won at 7f and 1m: won minor event at Chester in May then creditable ninth of 13 in Coventry Stakes at Ascot in June: failed to repeat that form after 3½ month break: will prove best at sprint distances: sold 16,000 gns Newmarket Autumn Sales: sent to Sweden. *R. Hannon* 84

WHAT JIM WANTS (IRE) 2 b.g. (Mar 9) Magical Strike (USA) 114 – Sally Gone (IRE) (Last Tycoon 131) [1995 a7g 5g 7f 7.1d^{6} 10m 7.1s Nov 2] IR 3,000Y: smallish gelding: poor mover: shows knee action: first foal: dam never ran: seems of little account. *J. J. O'Neill* –

WHATONE BELL 5 b.g. Presidium 124 – Betbellof 65 (Averof 123) [1994 –: 6m a10g 1995 a12g^{4} a7g a7g a8g Feb 25] angular gelding: of no account. *P. Hayward* –

WHAT'S SECRETO (USA) 3 gr.g. Secreto (USA) 128 – What A Shack (USA) (Al Hattab (USA)) [1994 NR 1995 12m 10d 12g 12d a12g^{3} a16g Nov 8] $15,000F, $50,000Y: strong, plain gelding: poor walker: tenth foal: half-brother to 9 minor winners in USA: dam 6f winner: modest maiden at best: stays 1½m: acts on equitrack: best in visor: wandered markedly fourth start and may be none too genuine: sold (P. Kelleway to H. Alexander) 3,200 gns Doncaster November Sales. *P. A. Kelleway* 57

WHAT'S THE VERDICT (IRE) 3 b.g. Law Society (USA) 130 – Cecina 100 (Welsh Saint 126) [1994 75: 8g^{6} 8g^{4} 8d^{4} a8g* 1995 a10g^{3} 12.3m^{5} 10.8g^{2} 10g* Jun 3] tall gelding: fair performer: won claimer at Ayr in June by 6 lengths despite carrying head awkwardly, making most: stays 1¼m: acts on good to firm and dead ground and all-weather surfaces: sometimes early to post: takes keen hold, and probably best allowed to stride on. *M. Johnston* 73

WHERE'S MARGARET 2 b.f. (Mar 20) Jareer (USA) 115 – Dancing Chimes (London Bells (CAN) 109) [1995 6m 5m^{2} 6m^{2} 5g^{2} 5m 5m^{5} a6g* 7s^{6} 6m^{6} Oct 12] 5,000Y: tall, angular filly: has scope: fourth foal: half-sister to 1994 2-y-o 5f winner Sunday Mail Lass (by Colmore Row) and useful 6f and 7f winner Palacegate Touch (by Petong): dam unraced: modest form: won seller at Lingfield in September: stays 6f (soundly beaten over 7f on soft ground): acts on good to firm ground and equitrack: blinkered last 3 starts: has been slowly away: sometimes finds little off bridle: sold 18,000 gns Newmarket Autumn Sales. *G. Lewis* 62 a65 +

WHICKSEY PERRY 2 b.g. (Feb 25) Presidium 124 – Phamilla (IRE) (Bellypha 130) [1995 5d* 5m* 5m* 5d^{3} 5m^{6} 5g 5d Oct 11] 3,400Y, resold 3,000Y: leggy, lengthy gelding: has a quick action: second foal: brother to 3-y-o 6f winner Das Island: dam never ran: successful in maiden auction at Edinburgh and minor events at Lingfield and Windsor early in season: ran creditably in listed race at Sandown and Norfolk Stakes at Ascot next 2 starts then off course 3 months and below form on return: speedy: acts on good to firm and good to soft ground. *J. Berry* 83

WHISPERING DAWN 2 b.f. (Apr 18) Then Again 126 – Summer Sky 75 (Skyliner 117) [1995 5g^{4} 6g 6.1g* 6g^{4} 8m 8g* 10d Sep 19] 5,200Y: tall, leggy filly: has a round action: fourth foal: sister to 3-y-o Silent Sky and half-sister to fair sprint winner Lord Sky (by Emarati): dam 2-y-o 5f winner: fair form: won seller at Chepstow in May and nursery at Ayr in September: second start in 5 days, lost several lengths at start and faded 2f out in nursery at Nottingham final outing: stays 1m: races keenly: reared stalls 2 of last 3 starts. *M. R. Channon* 66

WHISPERING LOCH (IRE) 4 ch.c. Lomond (USA) 128 – Why So Silent (Mill Reef (USA) 141) [1994 –: 10.1g 10v 1995 8m^{4} 8.2m 8m 11.6m^{5} Jul 17] smallish, good-bodied colt: poor mover: poor performer: broke down final start: stayed 1m: best effort on soft ground, at 2 yrs: tried blinkered: dead. *J. Akehurst* 42

WHITECHAPEL (USA) 7 b.g. Arctic Tern (USA) 126 – Christchurch (FR) 88 (So Blessed 130) [1994 92: 12g^{4} 14.6g^{3} 12g* 16.2m^{4} 12v 1995 12g^{4} 12m 13.9m 13.3d* 12d^{4} 12m^{3} 12d^{3} 12m Nov 4] big, lengthy gelding: useful handicapper: won 23-runner Tote Autumn Cup at Newbury in September: in frame next 3 starts in £46,800 event (for fourth year running) at Ascot, rated stakes at Newmarket and St Simon Stakes (25/1, appeared to run really well and could be rated 103 when 2¾ lengths third of 12 to Phantom Gold) at Newbury: only ninth in November Handicap 94 +

Tote Autumn Cup (Handicap), Newbury—Whitechapel stays on resolutely from Arctic Thunder (left)

at Doncaster final start: effective at 1½m to 2m: acts on fibresand, good to firm ground and soft: sometimes makes the running: game. *Lord Huntingdon*

WHITE EMIR 2 b.g. (Jan 31) Emarati (USA) 74 – White African (Carwhite 127) [1995 5g 5m* 5m² 5g⁶ 6m² 5g* 5.2d 6m³ Oct 12] 2,200F, 4,000Y: good-quartered gelding: progressed well physically: second foal: dam unraced: won maiden auction at Redcar in May and (after being claimed out of Mrs J. Ramsden's stable £10,000 after fifth outing) nursery at Sandown in September: sweating, good third of 18 to Lunar Mist in nursery at Newmarket last time: stays 6f: acts on good to firm ground: twice ran poorly (flashing tail and finding little) when having second race in quick succession: nervy sort. *B. J. Meehan* 86

WHITE ENSIGN (IRE) 2 b.c. (Apr 18) Imperial Frontier (USA) 112 – Markon (On Your Mark 125) [1995 6g 7m³ 6f² Jul 12] IR 19,000F, 8,500Y, 9,600 2-y-o: good-topped colt: half-brother to several winners here and abroad, including useful 1984 Irish 2-y-o 7f winner Stramar (by Orchestra) and 7f to 1m winner One To Mark (by He Loves Me): dam unraced daughter of half-sister to Humble Duty: around a length third of 12 to Lac Dessert in median auction maiden at Thirsk, best effort: stays 7f: sold 6,800 gns Newmarket Autumn Sales. *R. Hannon* 75

WHITE FLASH 4 b.f. Sure Blade (USA) 130 – Princess Matilda 110 (Habitat 134) [1994 –: 10s 11s⁶ 10.2g⁵ 10s⁴ 12s 1995 10m 8.3g⁴ 8.1g 8h⁴ 10m⁴ Aug 14] tall, rather leggy filly: poor maiden: should stay further than 8.3f: acts on hard ground, probably on soft: tried blinkered: covered by Lugana Beach. *D. R. C. Elsworth* 39

WHITEGATESPRINCESS (IRE) 4 b.f. Valiyar 129 – Whitegates Lady (Le Coq d'Or 101) [1994 NR 1995 12f 7f Aug 4] fifth foal: dam winning 2½m hurdler: well beaten in NH Flat races for J. H. Johnson: no promise in sellers on flat: tried visored. *B. Ellison* –

WHITE HEAT 3 b.f. Last Tycoon 131 – Sweeping 104 (Indian King (USA) 128) [1994 67p: 7s⁴ 1995 8m⁵ 8.3m 10m 8g 8g Oct 9] leggy filly: fair maiden: well beaten in 1995 after reappearance: will prove best at up to 1m: best effort on soft ground: visored last 2 starts: sold 1,400 gns Newmarket Doncaster Sales. *M. J. Heaton-Ellis* 57 d

WHITE KNOWLE 5 b.m. Governor General 116 – Teresa Way 66 (Great White Way (USA)) [1994 NR 1995 8m 7m May 19] sturdy mare: half-sister to fair 7f –

performer Brizlincote and quite useful sprinter Master Cawston (by Cawston's Clown): dam placed over 5f at 2 yrs: no worthwhile form: sold 850 gns Ascot July Sales. *P. T. Dalton*

WHITE LADY 4 ch.f. Risk Me (FR) 127 – Cassiar 84 (Connaught 130) [1994 63d: 7d³ 7m² 6f³ 5.2m* a6g a6g a8g 1995 a11g Nov 20] strong filly: modest at best in 1994: soundly beaten on belated reappearance. *B. J. Llewellyn* –

WHITELOCK QUEST 7 b.g. Rainbow Quest (USA) 134 – Sagar 74 (Habitat 134) [1994 –: a13g a10g⁵ a10g 8s 11.1f 9m 1995 a8g* a8g a8.5g* May 13] poor handicapper: won apprentice races at Southwell (33/1, first form on debut for new stable) in March and Wolverhampton in May: well beaten in between: should stay beyond 1m: acts on fibresand: tried blinkered in 1994. *N. E. Berry* 40

WHITE PALACE 3 b.f. Shirley Heights 130 – Blonde Prospect (USA) (Mr Prospector (USA)) [1994 56p: 7g 1995 8.2m* 10g 10f⁶ Jun 24] leggy, unfurnished filly: fairly useful form: won maiden at Nottingham in May: stiff tasks, unplaced in listed event at Newbury and slowly run handicap at Redcar (last of 6) afterwards: should stay beyond 1m: has raced only on a sound surface. *J. R. Fanshawe* 80

WHITE PLAINS (IRE) 2 b.c. (Mar 25) Nordico (USA) – Flying Diva 100 (Chief Singer 131) [1995 7g 6m⁵ 6m* Nov 6] good-bodied colt: second foal: half-brother to fairly useful but disappointing 3-y-o Cypress Avenue (by Law Society): dam, 2-y-o 6f and 7f winner who stayed 1m, out of sister to Flying Water: won median auction maiden at Folkestone late in year: will prove very well suited by 7f+: likely to improve again. *M. Bell* 72 p

WHITE SEA (IRE) 2 ch.f. (Apr 29) Soviet Lad (USA) 94 – Bilander 78 (High Line 125) [1995 7g² 7m⁴ 7.1m³ 8d* 7.3d Oct 21] IR 15,000Y: leggy, sparely-made filly: lacks scope: third foal: half-sister to useful 4-y-o sprinter Humbert's Landing (by Cyrano de Bergerac): dam, stayed 1½m, from staying family: fair form: game winner of median auction event at Salisbury in September: ran very well in face of stiffish task when ninth of 19 in nursery at Newbury following month: will stay beyond 1m. *P. F. I. Cole* 76

WHITE SETTLER 2 b.c. (Mar 4) Polish Patriot (USA) 128 – Oasis (Valiyar 129) [1995 7m⁵ 6m³ 6g Sep 13] sturdy colt: first foal: dam, winner twice over hurdles, half-sister to smart 1991 2-y-o Magic Ring: modest form in maidens. *R. Hannon* 62 +

WHITE SORREL 4 ro.c. Chilibang 120 – Midnight Imperial (Night Shift (USA)) [1994 60: 5g 6f⁶ 5g⁵ 1995 a6g* a6g* 6g 6m⁵ 5.1g² 5m 6m³ a6g 6g a6g a7g Nov 24] stocky colt: fairly useful handicapper, best efforts on the all-weather: trained first 3 starts in 1995 by J. L. Eyre, winning at Southwell in February and Wolverhampton (in very good style) in March: rather disappointing afterwards: stays 6f: goes well on fibresand, has raced only on a sound surface on turf: no improvement in blinkers. *A. Harrison* 69 a87

WHITE WHISPERS 2 gr.f. (Mar 10) Absalom 128 – Love Talk 69 (Hotfoot 126) [1995 5m⁵ 6g 7f* 7.1m⁵ 6g⁴ 7m⁶ 7.1m⁴ 6m² 6.5m⁴ 6g⁶ 6d⁵ Sep 27] lengthy, quite attractive filly: first foal: dam, stayed 1¼m, half-sister to smart sprinter Dead Certain (by Absalom): claimed out of B. Hills's stable £6,000 after winning claimer at Salisbury in June easing down by 10 lengths: highly tried afterwards, appearing to run excellent race when fourth of 17 behind My Branch in Doncaster nursery in September: below that form last 2 starts, helping force pace: stays 7f: acts on firm ground: sometimes sweating: sold 36,000 gns Newmarket Autumn Sales. *B. J. Meehan* 87 ?

WHITE WILLOW 6 br.g. Touching Wood (USA) 127 – Dimant Blanche (USA) 77 (Gummo (USA) 117) [1994 69, a84: a14g* a12g³ 12.4g 12g 14g 13s⁶ 16m³ 15.8g 16s 13.9d² 14.1d³ 1995 16.2m³ 16m⁴ 14g Jun 10] sturdy gelding: impresses in appearance: fair handicapper: iron broke and unseated rider after 4f final 6-y-o outing: stays 16.2f: acts on any going: best form in 1994 on the all-weather: no improvement in blinkers/visor: moody and not easiest of rides. *Mrs M. Reveley* 70 a–

WHITLEY GRANGE BOY 2 b.g. (May 18) Hubbly Bubbly (USA) – Choir (High Top 131) [1995 8g 7.9g⁵ a8g³ a5g Nov 24] big, leggy gelding: eighth foal: brother to 3-y-o 7f winner Cashmere Lady and half-brother to several winners, including fairly useful miler Celestial Choir (by Celestial Storm) and 8.5f to 10.2f 65 winner Choral Sundown (by Night Shift): dam behind in 4 races: third of 13 in maiden at Southwell in November: needs much further than 5f. *J. L. Eyre*

WHITTINGHAM GIRL 3 b.f. Primo Dominie 121 – Snub (Steel Heart 128) [1994 57: 6s 6g a6g a5g^5 a5g* 1995 a6g^3 a6g* a6g* a6g^6 a6g^4 a6g Mar 4] good-topped filly: modest performer: won sellers at Southwell in January and Wolverhampton in February: below form last 3 starts, and sold 4,200 gns Doncaster March Sales: stays 6f: acts on fibresand: races up with pace: covered by Fayruz. *J. Berry* — 58

WHITTLE ROCK 2 b.f. (Jan 25) Rock City 120 – Lurking 69 (Formidable (USA) 125) [1995 5g 5d^3 5m^5 5g^2 5.1g* 5m 6.1m^3 6.1m^3 5g^4 5s^2 Oct 1] 11,000F, 14,500Y: lengthy filly: has scope: second foal: half-sister to ungenuine 3-y-o Benten (by Sharrood): dam 6f winner who stayed 7f: won maiden at Chester in June: creditable efforts last 4 starts, including in listed company: stays 6f: acts on good to firm and soft ground: has been slowly away: mounted on track last time. *E. J. Alston* — 74

WHITTLE WOODS GIRL 4 b.f. Emarati (USA) 74 – Flitteriss Park 62§ (Beldale Flutter (USA) 130) [1994 80p: a6g a8.5g a6g^3 a6g^3 6g* 6d* 6.1m* 7.1d 6m^2 6f* 6m^3 6m^3 6d^3 6m* 6d^5 1995 6d 6m a6g Apr 26] lengthy filly: fairly useful handicapper: well below form in 1995: stays 6f: acts on good to firm and dead ground, has only modest form on fibresand: genuine: covered by Common Grounds. *E. J. Alston* — –

WHO'S TEF (IRE) 7 b.g. Muscatite 122 – Eternal Optimist (Relko 136) [1994 NR 1995 9.9m 10m^6 Aug 19] rather leggy, close-coupled gelding: modest handicapper (rated 57) at 5 yrs: well beaten in 1995. *M. H. Easterby* — –

WHO'S THE BEST (IRE) 5 b.g. Wassl 125 – Rip Roaring (Royal And Regal (USA)) [1994 –: 10m 12g 12v 12s 1995 a12g^3 a11g^2 a12g^2 a16g* a16g^5 a16.2g^6 15.4m^5 a16g^3 17.2m a16g^3 a14g* a14.8g a14g^3 a16g* 17.5g a14g a16g a14g Dec 1] close-coupled gelding: modest handicapper on the all-weather: won at Southwell in February, June (claimer) and September: soundly beaten afterwards, breaking leg final start: no worthwhile form on turf in 1995: effective at 1½m and stayed 2m: acted on fibresand: blinkered (below form) once as 2-y-o: held up: dead. *A. P. Jarvis* — – a55

WHOTHEHELLISHARRY 2 ch.g. (Mar 25) Rich Charlie 117 – Ballagarrow Girl 66 (North Stoke 130) [1995 5f 8.5m^5 8.1g a8g^4 Nov 6] 1,300F, 10,000 2-y-o: quite good-topped gelding: half-brother to 1990 2-y-o 5f winner Northern Nation (by Nomination) and a winner abroad by Prince Tenderfoot: dam, suited by 1¼m, half-sister to smart 6f and 7f winner The Quiet Bidder: poor form in maiden events. *J. Berry* — –

WICKLOW BOY (IRE) 4 b.g. Roi Danzig (USA) – Pickety Place 83 (Prince Tenderfoot (USA) 126) [1994 44: 7m 11.4d 8s 8m a12g^6 a16g a12g^4 1995 a16g^6 a12g^3 a12g a13g Feb 16] sturdy gelding: poor maiden: stays 1½m: acts on good to firm ground and the all-weather: tried blinkered/visored and with tongue tied down: has joined R. Weaver. *T. T. Clement* — 36

WICK POUND 9 b.g. Niniski (USA) 125 – Hors Serie (USA) 103 (Vaguely Noble 140) [1994 –: a16g 1995 12d Sep 15] small, lightly-made gelding: no longer of any account. *J. A. B. Old* — –

WIGBERTO (IRE) 3 ch.c. Old Vic 136 – Royal Loft 105 (Homing 130) [1994 88: 5m^3 a7g* 7g^2 7g^5 6g^3 7d^4 7m 1995 7d 8.1s^3 a7g Nov 16] compact colt: fairly useful at 2 yrs for D. Loder: stiff task, only form in 1995 when allowed a clear early lead and possibly flattered in 6-runner minor event won by Night City at Chepstow on second start: sold out of Major D. Chappell's stable 16,000 gns Newmarket Autumn Sales before final outing: stays 1m: acts on good to firm and soft ground and on fibresand. *J. L. Eyre* — 96 ?

WIGHT 2 gr.f. (Feb 24) Sharrood (USA) 124 – Wrangbrook (Shirley Heights 130) [1995 7d* 7m^3 Oct 14] 6,000Y: angular, unfurnished filly: has a roundish action: fourth live foal: half-sister to useful 1991 6f and 7f winner Punch N'Run (by Forzando), 1m winner in Italy in 1995: dam little form: won newcomers race at Milan in September by 4¼ lengths: 7 lengths third of 5 to Babinda in minor event at Newmarket following month: bred to stay middle distances. *R. Hannon* — 78 +

WIJARA (IRE) 3 b.c. Waajib 121 – Nawara 75 (Welsh Pageant 132) [1994 91p: 7.1d* 7g* 1995 9m^5 10m^5 10d^4 9d* 9m^3 Oct 13] sturdy, quite attractive colt: — 108 powerful galloper with a rather round action: useful performer: won well-contested minor event at Newbury (made all in determined style, by 3 lengths from Clan Ben) in September: just over a length third of 8 to Restructure in listed race at Newmarket only subsequent start: stays 1¼m: acts on good to firm and dead ground: races prominently. *R. Hannon*

WILAWANDER 2 ch.c. (Apr 4) Nashwan (USA) 135 – Wilayif (USA) 75 (Danzig (USA)) [1995 7g^5 7m^2 7d^4 Sep 18] good-quartered, quite attractive colt: fluent mover: first foal: dam, 7f winner, from top-class North American family: fairly useful form: second to Lord of Men in Newmarket maiden in August then (favourite) 2¼ lengths fourth of 8 to Tria Kemata in minor event at Leicester in September: will stay 1m: sure to win a race. *B. W. Hills* 89

WILCUMA 4 b.g. Most Welcome 131 – Miss Top Ville (FR) (Top Ville 129) [1994 88p: 8m^4 10g^3 12m 10m^4 8m* 8d* 8.1d* 8m^6 1995 8.1m^5 9m^3 8g^4 8m 9g^6 8.1g* 9g 9d^2 Oct 21] sturdy, useful-looking gelding: fairly useful handicapper: won 18-runner race at Haydock in September: very good short-head second of 12 to Smart Generation in rated stakes at Newbury on final outing, just failing: effective at 1m to 1¼m: acts on good to firm ground and dead: usually held up: has run well when sweating. *P. J. Makin* 94

WILD ADVENTURE 6 b. or br.g. Kabour 80 – Magic Mover (Julio Mariner 127) [1994 –: 9g 7g a6g^3 1995 a6g a7g 7m 11.1g May 20] robust, workmanlike gelding: no worthwhile form on flat. *D. W. Chapman* –

WILD BLUEBELL 3 b.f. Bluebird (USA) 125 – Ingabelle 108 (Taufan (USA) 119) [1994 97p: 7m* 7g^2 7g* 6d^5 6g* 1995 8m^2 8m^3 6m^2 8g^5 7f* Oct 1] pedigree details in Racehorses of 1994, but also sister to Irish 7f and 1m winner Bellissi: smart performer: much improved to win 7-runner Coolmore Stud Home of Champions Concorde Stakes at Tipperary in October by a short head from Wizard King, leading post: stays 1m: acts on firm ground: consistent: sent to USA. *J. S. Bolger, Ireland* 111

WILDFIRE (SWI) 4 br.g. Beldale Flutter (USA) 130 – Little White Star (Mill Reef (USA) 141) [1994 67: 8m 8m 10d^5 12.1s* 13.3g 12d^6 11.8g 12v^5 12s 1995 12g 12.1g^3 12m 14m a14g^4 a11g* a13g^3 Dec 14] sturdy gelding: has a quick action: modest handicapper: worthwhile form in 1995 only on the all-weather, winning at Southwell in December: stays 13f: acts on soft ground and all-weather surfaces. *R. Akehurst* 59

WILD HUMOUR (IRE) 2 b.f. (Apr 1) Fayruz 116 – Nous 76 (Le Johnstan 123) [1995 5.2g 5m^5 5g 6.1d 5d Oct 11] IR 5,000F, 11,000Y: strong filly: unimpressive mover: half-sister to 4 winners, including Irish 11f winner and leading juvenile hurdler Autumn Gorse (by Salmon Leap): dam sprinter: modest maiden: well beaten in nursery final start: may be unsuited by a soft surface. *W. R. Muir* 60

WILD PALM 3 b.c. Darshaan 133 – Tarasova (USA) (Green Forest (USA) 134) [1994 NR 1995 8.3m^4 10m^5 8.2d* 8g^6 Oct 3] sturdy, useful-looking colt: unimpressive mover: first foal: dam twice-raced half-sister to top-class French middle-distance colt Le Marmot: fair form: won maiden at Nottingham in September: not at all discredited in minor event at Warwick only subsequent outing: should prove well suited by further than 1m: acts on good to firm ground and dead: has worn severe noseband/citation bridle all starts: probably capable of better. *W. A. O'Gorman* 74 p

WILD PROSPECT 7 b.g. Homing 130 – Cappuccilli 111 (Lorenzaccio 130) [1994 44: 8.2m 8.2m^5 7d* 7.1m^4 7.5m^6 7g 8.1m 7g^6 a7g 1995 8m 8g Jun 5] smallish, good-quartered gelding: tailed off in 1995. *B. S. Rothwell* –

WILD RICE 3 b.c. Green Desert (USA) 127 – On Show 92 (Welsh Pageant 132) [1994 NR 1995 a7g* a10g* 7m^3 7f* 7m* 7d Sep 23] good-bodied colt: half-brother to several winners, including very useful milers Inchmurrin (by Lomond) and Guest Artiste (by Be My Guest): dam 1¼m winner out of Park Hill winner African Dancer: fairly useful performer: won maiden and minor event at Lingfield in February and handicaps at Kempton (impressively) and Chester (found less than seemed likely but got up by a head) in August: never going well in 27-runner £52,900 handicap at Ascot (on good to soft ground) on final start: effective at 7f and stays 1¼m: acts on firm ground and equitrack: wears bandages. *G. Wragg* 92

WILD RITA 3 ch.f. Risk Me (FR) 127 – Ma Pierrette 77 (Cawston's Clown 113) [1994 NR 1995 8f^2 8m^3 8m^3 10g 11.9g* 11.9g^5 10.5d^3 12.1s^4 Oct 17] leggy, lengthy 74

filly: half-sister to several winners, notably 5f to 1m (Lincoln) winner Our Rita (by Hallgate): dam won from 5f to 1¼m: fair performer: easily won minor event at Brighton in September: good efforts in handicaps next 2 starts: stays 1½m well: acts on firm and dead ground, probably on soft. *W. R. Muir*

WILD ROSE OF YORK 4 gr.f. Unfuwain (USA) 131 – Chepstow Vale (USA) 97 (Key To The Mint (USA)) [1994 57, a64: a9.4g^{3} 8d* 8.3d 8m 8.2g^{6} a12g^{5} a12g* 15.1m^{4} 1995 10.9g 11.1f^{3} 13.1f^{2} 15.1m^{2} Aug 24] rangy filly: has a round action: poor at best in 1995: stays 1½m, probably not 15f: acts on fibresand and dead ground (well beaten on heavy): sometimes pulls hard: modest hurdler, winner in September, October and November. *P. Monteith* — 39

WILD RUMOUR (IRE) 2 b.f. (Apr 8) Sadler's Wells (USA) 132 – Gossiping (USA) (Chati (USA)) [1995 7d* Sep 15] rangy, attractive filly, rather unfurnished: has scope: fifth reported foal: closely related to useful 1991 2-y-o Musicale (by The Minstrel) who should have been well suited by 1m, and half-sister to 1989 2-y-o 8.2f winner Idle Chat (by Assert): dam, 6f winner in USA, is half-sister to Committed: 11/4 favourite, won 10-runner minor event at Newbury by ½ length from Please Suzanne, leading 2f out and running on well: will stay 1¼m: sure to improve, and is potentially useful. *P. W. Chapple-Hyam* — 89 p

WILD STRAWBERRY 6 ro.m. Ballacashtal (CAN) – Pts Fairway (Runnymede 123) [1994 67: 10m* 12m 1995 a16g^{4} 16m 16.4m^{4} 12m^{4} 13.1f^{2} 12f^{2} 14.4m* 16.2f^{4} 14m^{2} 14m^{6} 11.9g^{3} 18m Oct 14] tall, workmanlike mare: fair handicapper: made all in minor event at Kempton in June: stays 16.4f: acts on firm ground and equitrack: out of form when tried in visor at 3 yrs: races prominently: genuine and most consistent: won handicap hurdle in September. *Miss B. Sanders* — 64

WILDWOOD FLOWER 2 b.f. (Mar 28) Distant Relative 128 – Tolstoya (Northfields (USA)) [1995 6g 5s^{6} 6.1d^{3} 6f* Oct 23] sturdy, lengthy filly: half-sister to 3-y-o Calling Jamaica (by Elmaamul), 1¼m seller winner at 2 yrs, 1990 2-y-o 5f and 6f winner Lear Leader (by Lear Fan) and a winner in USA by Arctic Tern: dam Irish 2-y-o 5f winner: progressive form: won 18-runner maiden at Leicester in October by 3½ lengths from Samara: bred to stay at least 1m: acts on firm (best effort) and dead ground: will progress again. *R. Hannon* — 81 p

WILFULL LAD (IRE) 2 b.g. (Apr 30) Distinctly North (USA) 115 – Lisa's Music (Abwah 118) [1995 7g 5f* 5m 6m 8h^{5} Sep 4] IR 4,600F, IR 5,200Y: workmanlike gelding: half-brother to several animals, no winners: dam won twice in Belgium: won maiden auction at Hamilton in July: stiff tasks in nurseries after: may prove best at up to 7f. *Martyn Meade* — 64

WILLIE CONQUER 3 ch.c. Master Willie 129 – Maryland Cookie (USA) 101 (Bold Hour) [1994 71p: 8d^{4} 8m 1995 7m^{3} 8m^{5} 7g Sep 30] lengthy, good-bodied colt: has a quick action: fairly useful handicapper, very lightly raced: off course 5 months after second 3-y-o start, and far from disgraced in big field on return: may well prove suited by further than 1m: remains capable of better. *R. Akehurst* — 80 p

WILLIE RUSHTON 2 ch.f. (Mar 6) Master Willie 129 – Amberush 41 (No Rush) [1995 5f 7g^{4} 7f^{3} 7.1m^{2} 8m^{4} 10g* Oct 9] lengthy filly: sixth reported foal: half-sister to a winner over hurdles by Lir: dam plater who stayed 1½m and also won over hurdles: progressive form in selling company: won 19-runner contest at Leicester by 5 lengths: well suited by a good test of stamina: races keenly: has been bandaged behind: taken down early last 3 starts. *G. L. Moore* — 63

WILLISA 2 ch.f. (Feb 23) Polar Falcon (USA) 126 – Ghassanah 73 (Pas de Seul 133) [1995 5m^{6} 6m^{3} 6f^{4} 6g 6g 7.3d Oct 21] 14,000Y: tall, unfurnished filly: third foal: half-sister to fairly useful 1994 2-y-o 7f and 7.6f winner Amin (by Last Tycoon) and useful 4-y-o sprinter Alzianah (by Alzao): dam, lightly-raced 7f winner, half-sister to Italian Derby winner Don Orazio: fair maiden: respectable efforts in nurseries last 3 starts: should prove suited by further than 6f. *J. D. Bethell* — 67

WILLOW DALE (IRE) 2 b.f. (Apr 26) Danehill (USA) 126 – Miss Willow Bend (USA) (Willow Hour (USA)) [1995 6g 5g^{4} 5f* 6m* 6.5m^{6} 5.2d* 6d 7m Oct 13] 20,000 2-y-o: close-coupled filly: second foal: half-sister to Danish-trained 3-y-o 1m winner Young Lucius (by Bluebird): dam won twice in USA at up to 7f: successful in maiden at Salisbury in June and nurseries at Kempton and Newbury in September: seventh of 8, not discredited, in Rockfel Stakes at Newmarket final outing: seems to stay 7f: acts on firm and dead ground: sometimes flashes tail. *D. R. C. Elsworth* — 80

WILLSHE GAN 5 b.m. Precocious 126 – Quisissanno 76 (Be My Guest (USA) 126) [1994 66d: 8g^4 8m 7g^2 8f 7f 7.1m 6m 6g^6 6g a5g 7g 6g 1995 8g^6 7m* 7f^2 7g^2 6m^4 6f^5 7f^4 6m Jul 19] good-topped mare: modest handicapper: narrowly won at Thirsk in May: effective at 6f to 1m: acted on firm and dead ground: tried blinkered/visored once each, no improvement: raced prominently: formerly unreliable, consistent in 1995: broke pelvis final start: dead. *Denys Smith* 56

WINAGINS (IRE) 4 b.f. Roi Danzig (USA) – Mallee (Malinowski (USA) 123) [1994 –: 12.1s 12.1m^5 8.1f^5 11.1g 1995 a8g a16g Jan 13] bad maiden. *T. R. Watson* –

WINDI IMP (IRE) 2 b.f. (Mar 17) Mac's Imp (USA) 116 – Windini (Windjammer (USA)) [1995 5m 5.1m^3 5m^4 6f 6m^6 5m 5.3f^6 Aug 23] IR 9,000Y: angular filly: fourth foal: half-sister to 3-y-o Curie Express, 5f winner at 2 yrs, and 2 other winning sprinters (all by Fayruz): dam unraced: modest maiden on balance of form: had favoured rail second outing (could be rated 54) and seems flattered by that form: best form at 5f: blinkered last 2 starts: withdrawn after trying to break out of stalls once: sold 1,200 gns Doncaster September Sales: sent to Holland. *B. J. Meehan* 47+

WIND IN HER HAIR (IRE) 4 b.f. Alzao (USA) 117 – Burghclere 86 (Busted 134) [1994 111: 10m* 10m* 12s^2 12s^4 10f^5 14.6g^4 1995 10g^3 12f^5 12m^2 12g* 11.9m^3 Aug 16] sturdy filly: in foal to Arazi: smart performer: below form first 3 4-y-o starts but better than ever on last 2, winning Group 1 Aral-Pokal at Gelsenkirchen in August (by 2 lengths from Lecroix) and about 2 lengths third of 8 to Pure Grain in Yorkshire Oaks at York 10 days later: stays 1½m: acts on soft going and good to firm. *J. W. Hills* 114

WINDMACHINE (SWE) 4 b.f. River Scape (USA) 93 – Miami Flyer (Miami Springs 121) [1994 a6g^2 a6g^2 a6g* 6s* 5d* 1995 6m 5m 5g 5f 5m 6g* 5s* 5f^5 Oct 22] big, lengthy Swedish-bred filly: unraced at 2 yrs: won 4 of her 7 races in Norway, Sweden and Germany in 1994 (rated 112), including listed race at Dortmund: well beaten in Britain at 4 yrs (trained by B. Olsen first start, next 4 by R. Harris) but won in Sweden and Germany (listed race at Dortmund) after returning to Scandinavia: 106

Aral-Pokal, Gelsenkirchen-Horst—a Group 1 for Wind In Her Hair; Lecroix (centre) finishes a clear second

short-neck second (demoted to fifth) to Millyant in Prix du Petit Couvert at Longchamp final start: best form at 5f: acts on firm and soft ground: blinkered fourth 4-y-o start: bandaged in front: forces pace. *M. Khan, Sweden*

WINDOW DISPLAY 4 gr.g. Chilibang 120 – Stubble 93 (Balidar 133) [1994 50: a5g^{6} a5g^{6} a6g^{4} a7g^{3} a6g^{4} a6g^{4} 7m a7g 1995 a7g^{6} Jul 8] tall gelding: modest performer: ran as though needing race only 4-y-o start. *Mrs N. Macauley* –

WINDRUSH BOY 5 br.g. Dowsing (USA) 124 – Bridge Street Lady 93 (Decoy Boy 129) [1994 61: 5g 5m* 5m 5.7g 1995 5m^{6} 6f 5m^{4} 5g 5g^{2} 5m^{5} 5m^{2} 5.1m^{3} 5m^{5} 5m* 5m 5.3g a5g a5g^{5} Nov 30] lengthy, leggy gelding: fair handicapper: won at Leicester in August: best form at 5f: acts on good to firm going, below form on equitrack: successful when sweating: suitable mount for an inexperienced rider. *J. R. Bosley* 66

WINDRUSH LADY 5 ch.m. Risk Me (FR) 127 – Pusey Street 96 (Native Bazaar 122) [1994 85: 8m 10d* 10m 1995 12g 10m 10g 10.5g^{6} 10g^{4} 10.3d 11.9g Sep 22] tall, angular mare: fair at best on balance of form in 1995: better at 1¼m than shorter: acted on good to firm and dead ground: dead. *M. McCormack* 69

WINDSWEPT (IRE) 2 b.f. (Mar 26) Taufan (USA) 119 – Sutica 91 (Don 128) [1995 5.2m^{3} 5f* 6m^{4} 6m^{6} 5f^{5} 6.5m^{5} 6g Sep 30] IR 10,500Y: leggy filly: good mover: third foal: dam Irish 2-y-o 6f winner later won over hurdles: won maiden at Warwick in May: generally ran creditably afterwards: stays 6.5f: had tongue tied down fourth outing. *D. J. S. ffrench Davis* 68

WINDYEDGE (USA) 2 ch.c. (Apr 28) Woodman (USA) 126 – Abeesh (USA) 77 (Nijinsky (CAN) 138) [1995 7m Oct 20] closely related to fairly useful 1990 Irish 2-y-o 6f winner Beloved Visitor (by Miswaki) and half-brother to 3-y-o Almuhimm (by Diesis) and several winners, including 1m and 1¼m winner Desert Conqueror (by Rahy): dam lightly-raced middle-distance maiden: 25/1, steadied at stalls, pulled hard then ran on into mid-field in 21-runner maiden at Doncaster won by Germano: will do better. *B. W. Hills* – p

WINGED LOVE (IRE) 3 b.c. In The Wings 128 – J'Ai Deux Amours (FR) (Top Ville 129) [1994 8g* 9d 1995 10v^{2} 10.5g^{2} 10.5v* 12g^{3} 12m* 12g^{4} 12d^{3} Sep 10] 121

The Irish Derby's position in the calendar—four weeks after the Prix du Jockey-Club and three after the Derby in the latest season—has helped to enhance its prestige over the years. The race attracted the winners from both Epsom and

Budweiser Irish Derby, the Curragh—
a storming finish between Winged Love (near side) and Definite Article, Celtic Swing only eighth

Chantilly on four occasions in its twelve runnings between 1983 and 1994. There were high hopes of another such meeting in the latest season when Derby winner Lammtarra and Prix du Jockey-Club winner Celtic Swing were both announced as likely runners a week or so before the race. A training set-back eventually ruled out Lammtarra, however, and Celtic Swing's participation was in doubt for a while as a continuing spell of very hot, dry weather led to speculation that there would be similar conditions at the Curragh to those which had caused Celtic Swing's connections to bypass Epsom. Celtic Swing eventually took his chance, starting 5/4 favourite in a field of thirteen from which the Derby third Presenting was another late absentee after injuring himself while being loaded for the journey. In a rare twist, following all the pre-race anticipation, the finish of the Budweiser Irish Derby was fought out by two colts who had not originally held an entry for the race. There had been talk for some time of the connections of Irish-trained Definite Article paying the IR £60,000 supplementary entry fee but the decision to supplement the Prix du Jockey-Club third Winged Love, originally aimed at the German Derby, was more of a surprise (Classic Cliche was also supplemented as a substitute for Lammtarra). The late-developing Winged Love stayed on very strongly to all but snatch second in the Prix du Jockey-Club, improving markedly on the form he had shown when winning a three-runner listed event at Longchamp on his previous start. The Prix du Jockey-Club trip—the race was his first at a mile and a half—certainly suited Winged Love and his stamina again stood him in good stead at the Curragh. Ridden closer to the pace than he had been at Chantilly, Winged Love took the lead two furlongs out and then rallied gamely after being headed by Definite Article about a furlong out to regain the lead again in the shadow of the post. Winged Love's Irish Derby victory confirmed him as a strong-galloping, staying type who might well show further improvement when conditions placed the emphasis even more firmly on stamina. Definite Article's short-head defeat was his first in four races but with Annus Mirabilis and Oscar Schindler fairly close in third and fourth and the maiden Dimancher only four lengths away in sixth the race looked substandard overall. Celtic Swing, beaten in strides early in the straight, was subsequently found to have damaged his near-fore knee, an injury which kept him off the course for the rest of the season.

Winged Love's Irish Derby victory—the first, incidentally, in a major European Derby for his trainer—came on the day that Carnegie won the Grand Prix de Saint-Cloud for the same connections. Both horses ran next in the King George VI and Queen Elizabeth Diamond Stakes at Ascot, Winged Love doing the better in finishing fourth, beaten a little under two lengths by the winner Lammtarra. That Winged Love was a horse with more stamina than speed was evident again as he stayed on strongly in the closing stages after being off the bit with plenty to do approaching the home turn. Winged Love would have been a prime candidate for the St Leger had he been aimed at the race but he had his final race in start Prix Niel, one of the traditional Arc trials, in which he was beaten less than half a length when third to Housamix and the Prix du Jockey-Club runner-up Poliglote, just outpaced at the end of a falsely-run race.

Winged Love (IRE) (b.c. 1992)	In The Wings (b 1986)	Sadler's Wells (b 1981)	Northern Dancer
			Fairy Bridge
		High Hawk (b 1980)	Shirley Heights
			Sunbittern
	J'Ai Deux Amours (FR) (b 1986)	Top Ville (b 1976)	High Top
			Sega Ville
		Pollenka (br 1973)	Reliance II
			Polana

The tall, rangy Winged Love who has a rather round action, is from the first crop of the very well-bred In The Wings, winner of the Coronation Cup, the Grand Prix de Saint-Cloud and the Breeders' Cup Turf as a four-year-old. Winged Love is the second foal of the staying-bred J'ai Deux Amours, a winner over a mile in France and joint-third in a blanket finish to the 1989 Prix de l'Opera (which is run over an extended nine furlongs). Winged Love's grandam Pollenka was also placed in the Prix de l'Opera, putting up a good effort to finish a clear second in the 1976 edition; she won at up to ten and a half furlongs and would probably have stayed a mile and a half. Winged Love's character as a racehorse turned out very much in line with his pedigree in which there are many more influences for stamina than speed. Unfortunately, it's akin to the kiss of death these days for a stallion to be thought of as a stayer, and Winged Love will be starting his stud career in Germany; he has been

Sheikh Mohammed's "Winged Love"

leased to Gestut Karlshof at Frankfurt where he will stand at a fee of DM 15,000 (about £6,725) in 1996. The genuine Winged Love acted on good to firm ground, and although he had previously won on heavy it was said that the ground and had turned against him when he was an absentee from the Arc. *A. Fabre, France*

WINGED PRINCE 2 b.g. (Mar 14) Prince Daniel (USA) – Phyl (Ballad Rock 122) [1995 6.1m 7f 7m 8m Sep 6] 3,800Y: rangy, rather unfurnished gelding: third foal: half-brother to 1993 2-y-o 6f winner Lady Phyl (by Northiam), later winner in Holland at up to 1¼m: dam never ran: never dangerous in maidens or in 17-runner nursery (had stiff task) at Doncaster. *B. J. Meehan* –

WINGNUT (IRE) 2 ch.f. (Feb 27) Digamist (USA) 110 – Royal Cloak (Hardicanute 130) [1995 5m 5f^5 a6g 5.1m^3 a5g^3 5g* 5m^3 5g 6f^2 5.3f^5 5d^3 a5g a6g^4 Nov 8] IR 3,200F, 5,200Y: unfurnished filly: half-sister to several winners, including 1988 Irish 2-y-o 7f winner Coat of Arms (by Tumble Wind) and middle-distance stayer Cosmic Dancer (by Horage): dam placed at 7f in Ireland as 2-y-o: modest performer: won seller at Folkestone in July: stays 6f: acts on firm ground and dead, only poor form on all-weather: has worn bandage near-hind: not particularly consistent: joined J. Bridger. *G. Lewis* 61 a43

WINGS COVE 5 b.g. Elegant Air 119 – Bel Esprit (Sagaro 133) [1994 81: 16.4d^3 16.5m^4 13.9m^3 14m^2 13.9m 13.9m 14.1d 1995 14.1g^5 14m^3 May 7] good-bodied gelding: fair handicapper: stays 2m: acts on good to firm and dead ground: visored (ran poorly) final 4-y-o start: held up/tracks leaders. *Lady Herries* 77

WINGS OF DESIRE (IRE) 3 b.c. Grey Desire 115 – Minizen Lass 82 (Hittite Glory 125) [1994 59d: 5.7f 5m^5 5.1g^5 5m 6d^6 a7g a6g 1995 a7g^4 a6g Jan 23] leggy, lengthy colt: poor sprint maiden: tried blinkered. *R. Champion* 38

WINGS OF FREEDOM (IRE) 7 b.g. Fairy King (USA) – Wingau (FR) 70 (Hard To Beat 132) [1994 NR 1995 21.6f May 1] rangy gelding: well beaten on flat since modest 3-y-o: fair winning hurdler, suffered fatal fall in June. *J. R. Jenkins* –

WINNING WONDER 3 b.f. Charmer 123 – Salchow 116 (Niniski (USA) 125) [1994 –: 6g^{5} 1995 a6g^{6} Jan 25] workmanlike filly: no sign of ability: sold (C. Brittain to Miss Jacqueline Doyle) 1,550 gns Ascot August Sales. *C. E. Brittain* –

WINN'S PRIDE (IRE) 4 b.g. Indian Ridge 123 – Blue Bell Girl (Blakeney 126) [1994 61d: a8.5g 10.5s^{3} 12.3d 12.3d 8.3d* 10d^{2} 11.8g 10m 10m^{5} 10.5g 10.5s 8.2d^{4} 1995 a12g a11g^{3} a12g^{3} a12g^{5} a12g a12g a12g a14.8g 12m^{6} Oct 2] tall gelding: carries condition: poor handicapper at best in 1995: stays 11f: acts on good to firm and soft ground and on fibresand: inconsistent. *R. Hollinshead* 48 d

WINSOME WOOSTER 4 ch.f. Primo Dominie 121 – Bertrade 75 (Homeboy 114) [1994 70: 6g 5.7m^{3} 5.2g^{3} 5m^{5} 5m^{5} 5.1f^{5} 6f 5m 5g 5d 5.7g* 5m 6.1g 1995 5.1m^{3} 5.1m^{2} 6g^{4} 5.7m 6f 6m^{4} 6m^{2} 6m 5.7h^{4} 7m^{3} 7.1d 7m^{5} 7m^{4} Nov 3] plain, close-coupled filly: fair handicapper: stays 7f: acts on hard and dead ground: often unruly at stalls: usually held up. *P. G. Murphy* 70

WINSTON 2 b.g. (Feb 23) Safawan 118 – Lady Leman 74 (Pitskelly 122) [1995 6m^{6} 7g Jul 19] 15,000F, 6,000Y: sturdy gelding: fourth foal: half-brother to Irish 3-y-o 9f winner Points Pass (by Primo Dominie): dam 2-y-o 5.3f winner later suited by 1m: never dangerous in maiden events. *J. D. Bethell* –

WINTERBOTTOM 3 gr.c. Reference Point 139 – Snowing (USA) (Icecapade (USA)) [1994 57: a7g^{4} a7g a5g 1995 a6g a10g a8g Feb 13] modest maiden: soundly beaten in 1995: tried visored. *I. Campbell* –

WINTER GEM 6 b.m. Hasty Word 84 – Masami (King Log 115) [1994 NR 1995 a12g^{6} Feb 20] half-sister to winning hurdler Mashum (by Humdoleila): dam ran once at 2 yrs: well beaten in claimer at Southwell. *R. T. Juckes* –

WINTER QUARTERS (USA) 2 ch.c. (Mar 13) El Gran Senor (USA) 136 – Refill 88 (Mill Reef (USA) 141) [1995 6m^{5} 6m^{3} 7f* 7g* 7g^{2} 8s^{2} a8.5s^{6} Oct 28] sturdy colt: brother to useful 3-y-o (stays 1¼m) Jumilla, 6f winner at 2 yrs, and half-brother to 2 winners, including 7f to 1¼m winner Shaffaaf (by Shadeed): dam (placed over 6f here) won at up to 11f in USA: useful performer: won maiden at Kempton and listed race at Baden-Baden in August: close second to Manninamix in Prix des Chenes at Chantilly on last start for I. Balding: respectable sixth of 14 to Unbridled's Song in Breeders' Cup Juvenile at Belmont: will stay beyond 1m: acts on any going. *R. Frankel, USA* 105 +

WINTER ROMANCE 2 ch.c. (Apr 28) Cadeaux Genereux 131 – Island Wedding (USA) 89 (Blushing Groom (FR) 131) [1995 7g 7d^{3} 7g^{2} Oct 10] good-topped, attractive colt: good mover: second foal: half-brother to 3-y-o Dream Wedding (by Soviet Star): dam, 7f and 8.5f winner, out of sister to Storm Bird: progressive colt: very much caught the eye on second start when would have gone close to winning had run begun sooner: much improved form when ½-length second of 14, 4 lengths clear, to Don Micheletto in maiden at Leicester on final outing: will stay 1m: sure to win a race or two. *E. A. L. Dunlop* 93 p

WINTERS COTTAGE (IRE) 7 ch.g. Sandalay 86 – Hilltown Yvonne (Avocat) [1994 NR 1995 12m^{5} Jul 11] first reported foal: dam seemingly never ran: modest novice hurdler: never a threat in maiden at Pontefract. *P. D. Evans* –

WINTER SCOUT (USA) 7 ch.g. It's Freezing (USA) 122 – His Squaw (USA) (Tom Rolfe) [1994 56: 6m^{3} 8.3m 5.9m* a8g 7g 6m* 8g 1995 7m^{3} 7m^{5} 6m^{4} 6g* 7g^{5} Sep 12] strong, good-bodied gelding: poor mover: modest performer: second favourite, raced alone on favoured stand rail when winning apprentice claimer at Newcastle in August: stays 7f well: acts on good to firm ground (best Irish form with some give), stiffish task on fibresand: tried blinkered in Ireland. *Mrs M. Reveley* 63

WIRE ACT (USA) 2 gr.g. (Apr 22) Gate Dancer (USA) – Giovanelli (USA) (Monteverdi 129) [1995 7f 8.1g^{4} 8g 7s a6g^{3} 8f Oct 12] $6,000Y: workmanlike, good-bodied gelding: unimpressive mover: third foal: brother to a minor winner in USA: dam ran 3 times in USA: modest maiden: stays 1m: best form on fibresand and on an easy surface on turf (never travelling fluently on firm). *Martyn Meade* 63

WISAM 2 b.c. (May 7) Shaadi (USA) 126 – Moon Drop 103 (Dominion 123) [1995 5m* 6m 6m^{4} Jul 27] tall colt: has scope: easy mover: fourth foal: half-brother 100 p to useful 3-y-o 5f (at 2 yrs) and 7f winner Moon King (by Cadeaux Genereux) and 1992 2-y-o 6f winner Mithl Al Hawa (by Salse): dam sprinter: won maiden at Goodwood in May: disadvantaged by racing on stand side in Coventry Stakes at Ascot: ran well when around 3 lengths fourth of 6, eased slightly, to Polaris Flight in Richmond Stakes at Goodwood: stays 6f: got geed up then taken to post steadily final outing: looked sure to improve further. *R. Hannon*

WISDOM 3 b.c. Insan (USA) 119 – Emaline (FR) 105 (Empery (USA) 128) [1994 –p: 6m 1995 a8.5g² a11g³ a10g³ a11g* Feb 24] quite attractive colt: modest performer: bought by K. Morgan 8,200 gns after making all in seller at Southwell in February: will stay at least 1½m: acts on the all-weather: blinkered last 2 starts: won juvenile hurdle in November. *P. F. I. Cole* 58

WISE BRAVE 3 ch.g. Be My Chief (USA) 122 – Fair And Wise 75 (High Line 125) [1994 NR 1995 8d 10d Oct 19] 6,600Y: smallish, compact gelding: fifth foal: half-brother to 3 winners, including fairly useful 1992 2-y-o 7.1f winner Surprise Surprise (by Robellino) and 1¼m winner Musical Note (by Sharpo): dam suited by 1¾m: always behind in maidens at Newbury. *H. Candy* –

WISHING (USA) 4 b.c. Lyphard's Wish (FR) 124 – Vivre Libre (USA) (Honest Pleasure (USA)) [1994 96: 11s² 10m* 11.5d³ 12m 10.4m 11.9g 10g 12m 1995 12m* 12m 14m² 12m⁵ 13.9m* 12f⁵ 13.9m 11.9d Sep 2] good-topped, attractive colt: carries condition: good mover: useful handicapper: won at Kempton in April and York (rated stakes) in June: tailed off last 2 starts: better suited by 1¾m than shorter and will stay further: acts on firm ground and dead (in need of race when below form on soft): runs some poor races: useful but unreliable hurdler, winner in September. *R. Akehurst* 100

WITCHFINDER (USA) 3 b.c. Diesis 133 – Colonial Witch (USA) (Pleasant Colony (USA)) [1994 74p: 8.2d⁴ 1995 10.5g⁵ Sep 22] big, rangy, good sort: has a long, round stride: fair maiden: still green and unimpressive to post only 3-y-o start: sent to Dubai. *J. H. M. Gosden* 69 +

WITCH OF FIFE (USA) 2 b.f. (Jan 28) Lear Fan (USA) 130 – Fife (IRE) 95 (Lomond (USA) 128) [1995 6m* 7m³ 8g 7.1g* Sep 23] small, lengthy filly: first foal: dam, 1m who winner stayed 1½m, half-sister to very useful stayer El Conquistador out of half-sister to Irish St Leger winner Mountain Lodge: won maiden at Newmarket in July and 3-runner minor event (awarded race) at Haydock in September: creditable effort behind Bint Salsabil in listed race at Newmarket second start: bred to stay 1m+. *B. W. Hills* 91

WITH FASCINATION (USA) 2 b. or br.f. (Mar 6) Dayjur (USA) 137 – Fran's Valentine (USA) (Saros 120) [1995 6d² 6.5g* 6g* 6g² 7s² 5d Oct 1] small French filly: fourth foal: half-sister to minor US winner (including at 1½m) He's A Valentine (by Risen Star): dam, top-class American filly from 2 to 5 yrs, stayed 1¼m: smart performer: won minor event at Evry in July and 5-runner Prix de Cabourg at Deauville (beat Kistena by 3 lengths) in August: travelled smoothly long way when length second to Tagula in Prix Morny at Deauville and to Lord of Men in Prix de la Salamandre at Longchamp: always outpaced in Prix de l'Abbaye de Longchamp final start: stays 7f: acts on soft ground: races prominently. *J. E. Pease, France* 111

WITH GUSTO 8 b.g. Taufan (USA) 119 – Finesse 87 (Miralgo 130) [1994 NR 1995 a12g Feb 3] good-topped gelding: no longer of any account. *J. J. Bridger* –

WITH INTENT 3 b.g. Governor General 116 – Don't Loiter (Town And Country 124) [1994 NR 1995 6m 7g⁶ 6f⁵ 8g 7m 7m Sep 1] sturdy gelding: third foal: half-brother to 4-y-o Arafel (by Northern State) and 7.1f winner Feather Face (by Tina's Pet): dam poor maiden: modest maiden: failed to progress from debut. *C. James* 52 d

WITHOUT A FLAG (USA) 5 ch.g. Stately Don (USA) 122 – Northerly Cheer (USA) (Northjet 136) [1994 62: 11.4d² 12g³ 1995 12m Apr 15] smallish, sturdy gelding: modest middle-distance handicapper: no promise only 5-y-o start: modest hurdler, winner in May. *J. White* –

WITH THE FAIRIES 3 b.f. Fairy King (USA) – Upper Circle (Shirley Heights 130) [1994 77p: 5d⁴ 5m² 7g* 1995 7m⁵ 6g 6g⁶ 7g 8g⁴ Sep 10] lengthy filly: useful performer: best effort when fourth of 9 to Timarida in Matron Stakes at the Curragh on final start: stays 1m: acts on good to firm and dead ground. *R. Hannon* 99

WITNEY-DE-BERGERAC (IRE) 3 b.g. Cyrano de Bergerac 120 – Spy Girl (Tanfirion 110) [1994 61: 5v 5d^5 5v^4 5.1m* 6g^6 6m 5m a6g^6 a7g a8g^5 1995 a8g^3 a8g^5 a10g^4 a10g^3 a10g 8f^4 8.3m 11.6m^3 12d* 16.2d 12d a12g Nov 10] close-coupled gelding: fair performer: best effort when winning very strongly-run ladies handicap at Newbury in September, coming from well off pace: stays 1½m well: acts on firm and dead ground and on equitrack: visored (well beaten) once as 2-y-o: held up. *J. S. Moore*
67 a61

WIZARD KING 4 b.c. Shaadi (USA) 126 – Broomstick Cottage (Habitat 134) [1994 108+: 8.2v^3 7d* 8d^2 7g* 8m* 7g* 8g^3 7g* 7g 1995 7.6m^2 8g^3 8f* 7m 7g* 7f^2 8d^3 Dec 2] tall, lengthy colt: poor mover: smart performer: better than ever in 1995, and won listed races at Fairyhouse in August and the Curragh (by a length from Burden of Proof) in September: short-head second of 7 to Wild Bluebell in Group 3 event at Tipperary then respectable third in listed event at Saint-Cloud afterwards: effective at 7f and 1m: acts on firm going, probably also on heavy: genuine. *Sir Mark Prescott*
114

WIZZARD STAR 3 ch.f. Prince Sabo 123 – Wizzard Art 71 (Wolver Hollow 126) [1994 NR 1995 8.3m Jun 26] sparely-made filly: third reported foal: half-sister to 1½m winner Baby Wizard (by Scottish Reel): dam won from 7f to 1¼m: well beaten in maiden at Windsor: sold 500 gns Ascot December Sales. *M. J. Haynes*

WIZZY LIZZY (IRE) 4 ch.f. Waajib 121 – Ladiz (Persian Bold 123) [1994 –: 9.7d 12s 1995 10g 13.1f^3 11.6m 17.2f^4 17.2h^3 13.1f^5 Jul 19] leggy filly: modest winning hurdler: poor maiden plater on flat: stays 17.2f: acts on firm ground. *D. R. C. Elsworth*
47

WOLF CLEUGH (IRE) 2 b.f. (Apr 13) Last Tycoon 131 – Santa Roseanna 111 (Caracol (FR)) [1995 7m Oct 28] 12,000F, 10,000Y: smallish, lengthy filly: sister to Irish 3-y-o Glamour Model, 7f winner at 2 yrs, and half-sister to several winners in Ireland, including smart 6f winner King's College (by Golden Fleece) and 1m (at 2 yrs) and 1½m winner Stadler (by Sadler's Wells): dam won from 7f to 9f in Ireland and stayed 1½m: 50/1 and backward, just under 9 lengths eleventh of 19 to Awaamir in maiden at Newmarket, never able to get on terms: will do better in due course. *A. Hide*
65 p

WOLLBOLL 5 b.g. Layal 94 – Top of The Barley (Oats 126) [1994 40: 9.2d^5 11.6d 12g 12.5m^4 14.9m^2 14.9m a14g^2 a16g^6 1995 a10g^5 Feb 28] leggy gelding: poor staying maiden: won over hurdles in Jersey in June. *P. J. Makin*
–

WOLLSTONECRAFT (IRE) 2 b.f. (May 4) Danehill (USA) 126 – Ivory Thread (USA) (Sir Ivor 135) [1995 5m^3 May 29] lengthy, quite attractive filly: fourth reported foal: half-sister to Irish 3-y-o Credit Crunch (by Caerleon): dam won at 1¾m at 4 yrs in Ireland: 9/1, around 4 lengths third of 9 to Blue Duster in maiden at Sandown, leading 3f then keeping on at same pace: looked sure to improve, and win a race. *J. H. M. Gosden*
85

WOLVER MURPHY (IRE) 3 b.f. Persian Heights 129 – Wolverstar 100 (Wolverlife 115) [1994 NR 1995 6m 7m 6m 6g a7g Dec 12] ex-Irish filly: first foal: dam useful Irish sprinter: no worthwhile form, trained first 4 starts by V. Kennedy. *K. McAuliffe*
–

WONDERFUL DAY 4 b.f. Niniski (USA) 125 – Zipperti Do 70 (Precocious 126) [1994 69p: 8f 8m^6 7f^5 10m^4 9.7d^5 9.7m* 1995 9.9m* 12.4g^3 12d^2 12.4m^4 10f Oct 24] leggy, sparely-made filly: fair handicapper: won at Beverley in April: left S. Williams after fourth start: stays 1½m: acts on good to firm ground and dead. *T. T. Clement*
71

WOODBOROUGH (USA) 2 ch.c. (Feb 21) Woodman (USA) 126 – Performing Arts 104 (The Minstrel (CAN) 135) [1995 5.2m 6f* 6m^2 6.3m* 7s^3 6g^2 Sep 28]
110

Woodborough went lame when all the rage in the betting to make a winning debut in the Beckhampton Maiden Stakes at Newbury in April, a race won by his stable the previous two years with Turtle Island and General Monash. Fortunately he came right in time for Goodwood in July and was able to run regularly afterwards and fulfil his engagements in the Prix de la Salamandre and the Middle Park Stakes on his last two starts, in which he did enough to confirm himself a very useful youngster, somewhere in between the standard of Turtle Island and General Monash at the same age. Ironically it was the promising winner of the Newbury maiden, Polish Legion, who wasn't seen out again.

Woodborough justified heavy market support at the second attempt when he returned to account for two other well-regarded colts, Bijou d'Inde and Raheen, getting up late on after showing inexperience, at Goodwood. Maidens out of the way, he was sent on a pattern-race campaign, starting with the Group 1 Heinz 57 Phoenix Stakes at Leopardstown. Turtle Island had won the 1993 running from another subsequent Guineas winner Las Meninas; General Monash injured himself when unplaced favourite in 1994. The favourite Danehill Dancer won the latest renewal, by a neck from Woodborough who was worn down only near the finish after travelling strongly towards the front from the start. Woodborough met with a similar fate in his two other Group 1 races—placed, running well—and will need abnormal improvement to make much of an impact in top company at three, though there is some compensation for those defeats in that he goes into 1996 free of the millstone Group 1 penalty. His one win after Goodwood came in the Group 3 Anglesey Stakes at the Curragh in the first of three runs in September, when a reproduction of his Phoenix Stakes form was enough to see off all four home-trained contenders led by maiden-race winner Lidanna; he made all. Reportedly, Woodborough's trainer thought he didn't quite get home when stepped up to seven furlongs on soft ground in the Salamandre. It looked that way but the horse was probably beaten by a better one in Lord of Men who had a length to spare over the Prix Morny runner-up With Fascination, Woodborough two lengths further back in third. He was certainly beaten by a better one in the Middle Park. Royal Applause won that by four lengths. Woodborough was physically thriving on his racing but couldn't get in a blow, staying on strongly under pressure past Kahir Almaydan for second place, having been niggled along from an early stage.

Woodborough (USA) (ch.c. Feb 21, 1993)	Woodman (USA) (ch 1983)	Mr Prospector (b 1970)	Raise A Native
			Gold Digger
		Playmate (ch 1975)	Buckpasser
			Intriguing
	Performing Arts (ch 1987)	The Minstrel (ch 1974)	Northern Dancer
			Fleur
		Noble Mark (ch 1971)	On Your Mark
			Noble Joan

Woodborough will probably stay a mile as a three-year-old. His dam Performing Arts ran her best race when finishing third to In The Groove in the Irish One Thousand Guineas; she showed form as a two-year-old over five furlongs and six furlongs, winning at both distances. Performing Arts is one of numerous winners, some at middle distances, out of the good sprinter Noble Mark, and is the best of the mare's produce apart from The Noble Player. A full brother to Performing Arts, The Noble Player was placed in the Royal Lodge Stakes and the Grand Criterium in 1982. He beat Diesis in the Heron Stakes at Kempton as a three-year-old, and later showed smart form at up to a mile and a quarter in the USA. Woodborough is the first foal of his dam and is a strong colt with scope. He appears to act on any going. *P. W. Chapple-Hyam*

WOODBURY LAD (USA) 2 ch.c. (Mar 24) Woodman (USA) 126 – Habibti 136 (Habitat 134) [1995 6.5g 5g Sep 1] strong, lengthy colt: good mover: sixth living foal: half-brother to Irish 3-y-o Desert Lily (by Green Desert), 5f winner at 2 yrs: dam outstanding sprinter, also third in 1000 Guineas: 8½ lengths seventh of 9 behind Rabican in valuable listed race at Deauville in August: seemed to find step down to 5f against him when eighth of 18 in maiden at Haydock following month: worth another chance at 6f+. *W. R. Muir* 73 p

WOODCREST 3 b.f. Niniski (USA) 125 – Cryptomeria 86 (Crepello 136) [1994 NR 1995 10g³ 10g 11.7f* 12g 11.6m* 13.1g⁵ Sep 16] angular filly: sister to 4-y-o NH Flat race winner Agistment and half-sister to several winners, including fair miler Poterium (by Persian Bold): dam middle-distance filly: fairly useful performer: won maiden at Bath and handicap at Windsor in the summer: may well prove suited by further than 1½m: has raced only on a sound surface. *H. Candy* 82

WOODLANDS ELECTRIC 5 b.g. Rich Charlie 117 – Hallowed (Wolver Hollow 126) [1994 –: 6m 7f 1995 a5g a6g 7m⁶ 7.6m⁶ 6m 5d a6g Nov 27] neat gelding: no worthwhile form: probably a sprinter: tried visored. *P. A. Pritchard* –

WOODLANDS ENERGY 4 b.f. Risk Me (FR) 127 – Hallowed (Wolver Hollow 126) [1994 NR 1995 8m^5 8.3m 10m 10d 10.8g Oct 3] workmanlike filly: second foal: dam winning selling hurdler/novice chaser: no worthwhile form. *P. A. Pritchard* –

WOODLANDS LAD TOO 3 b.c. Risk Me (FR) 127 – Hallowed (Wolver Hollow 126) [1994 NR 1995 8m^3 10d 10.2m Sep 25] leggy colt: third foal: brother to 4-y-o Woodlands Energy: dam winning selling hurdler/novice chaser: well beaten in maidens. *P. A. Pritchard* –

WOOD MAGIC 2 b.g. (Mar 22) Shaadi (USA) 126 – Majenica (USA) (Majestic Light (USA)) [1995 7f^4 a7g* 7.6d* Sep 20] good-quartered, attractive gelding: first foal: dam twice-raced sister to Prix de Diane winner Lacovia out of half-sister to Miswaki: very easy winner of poor maiden at Southwell in September: favourite, beat Henry The Fifth 2½ lengths in 5-runner minor event at Chester later in month, taking time to find stride then staying on well: will stay beyond 1m: early and steadily to post at Chester: likely to improve further. *D. R. Loder* 96 p

WOODMANS LADY 3 b.f. Midyan (USA) 124 – Diva Madonna 85 (Chief Singer 131) [1994 NR 1995 11.8g 14.1m Oct 19] lengthy, plain filly: first foal: dam 1½m winner: backward, no form in claimer and maiden. *J. J. Sheehan* –

WOODRISING 3 b.f. Nomination 125 – Bodham 88 (Bustino 136) [1994 59: 6m 7d 1995 6d^3 8.1g^2 a7g 8m^2 10g^3 10.8m^5 10g* 12m 10.1m* 10m* Aug 14] smallish filly: modest performer: showed an improved attitude in the summer and won claimers at Sandown (claimed out of Lady Herries' stable £4,000), Yarmouth and Leicester (claimed £6,000), making all on each occasion: should stay further than 1¼m: acts on good to firm going and dead: blinkered fourth and sixth (looked reluctant) 3-y-o starts: seems suited by forcing tactics: won twice over hurdles in September for C. Egerton, but ran as if something amiss in October. *G. Lewis* 64

WOOLAW GIRL 7 br.m. Sayf El Arab (USA) 127 – Pacific Princess 82 (Dom Racine (FR) 121) [1994 NR 1995 5m 8g Aug 26] small, sturdy mare: has run in pony races under the name of Lively Lady, winning once: tailed off all 4 starts on flat under rules. *J. S. Haldane* –

WOOLVERSTONE HALL (IRE) 3 b.f. Roi Danzig (USA) – Silver Mantle 70 (Bustino 136) [1994 69d: 6f^3 6d^5 6d a8g 1995 a6g a6g^4 6f a10g^5 a7g^5 a7g Dec 14] compact filly: poor maiden at best in 1995. *D. J. G. Murray Smith* 42

WORDSMITH (IRE) 5 b.g. Cyrano de Bergerac 120 – Cordon 89 (Morston (FR) 125) [1994 53: a12g^5 8d^2 10d^2 8v 1995 a12g 8.1g 8g a11g 8m^6 10m^2 10.1g Sep 13] compact, good-quartered gelding: poor performer at best nowadays: effective at strongly-run 1m and stays 1½m: best form on ground no softer than dead: sometimes carries head high and finds little: won twice over hurdles in October. *J. L. Harris* 46

WORDS OF WISDOM (IRE) 5 b.g. Petorius 117 – Never So Lovely 87 (Realm 129) [1994 58§: 7m 10s 8.3d 6.1s^5 6m 7g 7f^3 8.3m 6f 7m^5 7m 7g a7g* a7g^4 a5g^3 a7g a6g^5 1995 a7g* a8g* a7g^4 a7g^5 a8g^6 8m a7g^2 6m^4 7m 6m^5 a7g a8g^3 a8g^3 6m a10g^6 a7g Aug 11] workmanlike gelding: poor handicapper on turf, modest on the all-weather: won apprentice races in January and February, both at Lingfield: best form at 7f/1m, may stay further: acts on any going: tried blinkered/visored early at 4 yrs: sold 1,600 gns Newmarket Autumn Sales: sent to Spain. *C. A. Cyzer* 46 a63

WORKINGFORPEANUTS (IRE) 5 ch.m. Entitled 126 – Tracy's Sundown (Red Sunset 120) [1994 39d: a9.4g^2 a12g 7.1g 7m 10g 12.5m 1995 12g Jun 10] close-coupled mare: seems of little account nowadays. *C. A. Smith* –

WORLD EXPRESS (IRE) 5 b.g. Jareer (USA) 115 – Eight Mile Rock 76 (Dominion 123) [1994 68: 12d 10m 10.2s* 10g 10.2g 10.2s* 12g^5 10d^5 12.1g^5 12v 1995 a12g Jul 8] rather leggy gelding: fair handicapper: tailed off only 5-y-o start. *B. R. Millman* –

WORLDNEWS EXTRA (USA) 3 ch.c. Elmaamul (USA) 125 – Wrap It Up (Mount Hagen (FR) 127) [1994 NR 1995 a10g^2 10m* 6g^5 12f^4 8.5m^4 Jul 5] IR 70,000Y: leggy, unfurnished colt: good mover: closely related to very useful 6f (at 2 yrs) winner Pure Genius (by Diesis): dam thrice-raced half-sister to Gift Wrapped, smart winner at up to 1½m and dam of Royal Lodge winner Reach: fair performer: made all to win maiden at Pontefract in April: below form afterwards: should be 76 suited by further than 1¼m: bandaged: sold 18,000 gns Newmarket July Sales: sent to Macau. *P. F. I. Cole*

WORLD PREMIER 2 b.c. (Mar 4) Shareef Dancer (USA) 135 – Abuzz 101 (Absalom 128) [1995 5g* 5m^2 6g^5 6f^2 6m* 6g^3 6g^6 Aug 20] compact, good-quartered colt: third foal: half-brother to 3-y-o Agoer (by Hadeer): dam won at 5f (at 2 yrs) and 7.3f: useful performer: won Brocklesby Stakes at Doncaster in March and Chesham Stakes (by 1¼ lengths from Paloma Bay) at Royal Ascot: excellent third of 9 to Tagula in July Stakes at Newmarket but only sixth of 8 behind same colt in Prix Morny at Deauville (reported to have returned with colic) on final outing: bred to stay at least 1m: acts on firm ground: tends to sweat. *C. E. Brittain* 103

WORLD TRAVELLER 4 ch.g. Most Welcome 131 – Prudence 68 (Grundy 137) [1994 61, a75: a8g^2 a6g^2 a7g^6 a8g^4 7m 7m^5 8m^5 10m 6m^4 a8g a7g^3 a7g* 1995 a7g^5 a7g a7g^5 a8g 8.1g 7g 8m^4 10g Jul 28] stocky, gelding: fair handicapper on the all-weather, modest on turf: effective at 6f to 1m: acts on good to firm and dead ground: wore hood (ran well) once as 2-y-o: best efforts in blinkers, visored (soundly beaten) twice: sold 5,200 gns Newmarket September Sales. *W. A. O'Gorman* 51 a70

WORLDWIDE ELSIE (USA) 2 b.f. (Mar 2) Java Gold (USA) – Tender Camilla 115 (Prince Tenderfoot (USA) 126) [1995 5g^6 5m^3 a6g* 6m 7f 7f* 6.9m^2 a8.5g* Nov 13] IR 10,000Y: tall, useful-looking filly: half-sister to several winners, including Grade 3 1¼m handicap winner Noble Damsel (by Vaguely Noble) and fairly useful sprinter Gentle Hero (by Hero's Honor): dam, smart 2-y-o sprinter, seemed to stay 1¼m, half-sister to smart stayer Bonne Noel: sire stayed 1½m: won maiden at Wolverhampton in June and nurseries at Leicester in October and Wolverhampton (by 12 lengths) in November: better at around 1m than shorter: acts on fibresand and firm ground. *R. Harris* 76 a90

WOT-IF-WE (IRE) 3 b.c. Alzao (USA) 117 – Awatef (Ela-Mana-Mou 132) [1994 80: 6s* 6f^6 7m 8.1d^3 8d^3 1995 12g* 13.9m^6 16.2m^4 15g^4 15g^4 14m^2 16g Sep 30] sturdy colt: useful performer: won minor event at Catterick in April: fourth to Stelvio in Queen's Vase at Royal Ascot and 2 French pattern races won by Affidavit in the summer: beaten 2 lengths by sole rival Jellaby Askhir in listed race at Goodwood on penultimate outing: will stay beyond 2m: probably acts on any going: sold 75,000 gns Newmarket Autumn Sales: sent to Malaysia. *T. G. Mills* 100

WOTTASHAMBLES 4 b. or br.g. Arrasas (USA) 100 – Manawa 81 (Mandamus 120) [1994 44: 6d 10s^4 11.7m 10m 10m 10d 11.9g^6 12s^2 a13g* a13g^3 1995 a12g^2 a13g^6 a16g^6 a16g a12g^4 12f^4 12.1m* 12m 14f^3 14.4m^4 12m^2 12m a12g Oct 23] leggy gelding: has a round action: poor handicapper: trained by G. Lewis until after fifth 4-y-o start: won apprentice race at Chepstow in July: stays 1¾m, worth another try at 2m: acts on firm and soft ground and equitrack: blinkered (below form) once. *L. Montague Hall* 48 a43

WRAYS (USA) 2 b.f. (May 1) Known Fact (USA) 135 – Sunshine Law (USA) (Tisab (USA)) [1995 5g^2 5m^4 5g 6s^4 7f Oct 3] $20,000F, 4,200Y: robust filly: ninth foal: sister to Miss Bondi, 2-y-o sprint winner races in USA, and half-sister to 3 other winners in USA: dam unraced: beaten a neck in maiden auction at Beverley on debut: disappointing afterwards, though had poor draw third start and may not have been suited by soft ground on fourth: should stay beyond 5f: sold 2,500 gns Doncaster October Sales: sent to Denmark. *M. Johnston* 60 d

WRITTEN AGREEMENT 7 ch.g. Stanford 121§ – Covenant 75 (Good Bond 122) [1994 –: a10g^5 17.2f^6 12.1f 16.5m^6 a14g 1995 a12g a12g a13g^6 a16g Feb 6] sparely-made gelding: bad maiden: tried visored. *R. E. Peacock* –

WURLITZER (USA) 3 ch.c. Riverman (USA) 131 – Wedge Musical (What A Guest 119) [1994 NR 1995 10m^6 10g^5 13.1g^2 13.3f 16.1g^4 Jul 12] $150,000Y: tall, rangy colt: shows traces of stringhalt: second foal: half-brother to useful 4-y-o Silver Wedge (by Silver Hawk), winner from 7.1f (at 2 yrs) to 16.2f (Queen's Vase): dam won at 6.5f at 2 yrs in France and at 1m at 4 yrs in USA: fair maiden: may prove best at around 1¾m: best efforts on good ground, yet to race on a soft surface: wears crossed noseband. *J. H. M. Gosden* 71

WYCHWOOD-PALACE 3 ch.f. Presidium 124 – Cardinal Palace 85 (Royal Palace 131) [1994 62: 8.2s^5 10g^4 9.7s^4 1995 8.3g 8f May 22] progressive form in 2-y-o maiden events: ran as if something amiss in 1995: dead. *H. J. Collingridge* –

WYCHWOOD SANDY 4 b.g. Mansingh (USA) 120 – Do-Run-Do (Palm Track 122) [1994 –: 6f 6s 6f 5m 5m 1995 5d 6f Oct 23] angular gelding: of little account. *H. J. Collingridge* –

WYDALE 2 b.c. (Apr 27) Rich Charlie 117 – Julia Mawe (Dominion 123) [1995 5g 5g 5g Jun 12] 550F, 400Y: small, plain colt: fourth foal: dam unraced half-sister to useful sprinter Our Dynasty: soundly beaten in maiden auctions. *M. W. Ellerby* –

WYEDEAN 2 ch.c. (Mar 2) Faustus (USA) 118 – Coleford (USA) (Secreto (USA) 128) [1995 a6g Oct 28] first foal: dam unraced daughter of close relative of 3 good winners by Nijinsky, including Irish St Leger winner Mashaallah: 20/1, well beaten in median auction maiden at Wolverhampton. *W. R. Muir* –

X

XENOPHON OF CUNAXA (IRE) 2 b.g. (Mar 1) Cyrano de Bergerac 120 – Annais Nin (Dominion 123) [1995 6f^5 5.7h* 6m Sep 2] IR 13,000Y: tall gelding: sixth foal: half-brother to Irish 1m winner Winston Murphy (by Don) and a winner in Italy by Nordico: dam unraced: won 4-runner median auction maiden at Bath in August comfortably by 4 lengths from Meg's Memory: dead-heated for ninth in 29-runner valuable restricted race at the Curragh 15 days later: will stay 6f+: acts on hard ground: will improve further. *M. J. Fetherston-Godley* 83 p

Y

YAAKUM 6 b.g. Glint of Gold 128 – Nawadder 73 (Kris 135) [1994 50: a14g a16g* 18g 1995 16.5g 15.8g 13.1g^3 Jul 16] robust gelding: below form for new stable in 1995: stays 2m: acts on good to firm ground, soft and equitrack: effective in a visor, blinkered (out of form at the time) once at 3 yrs: won novice chase in July. *S. E. Kettlewell* –

YAA WALE 3 br.c. Persian Bold 123 – Starr Danias (USA) (Sensitive Prince (USA)) [1994 64p: 5g^4 6s 1995 5m 7.1m* 7.1m* 7f 8.1m 8g^2 Sep 20] smallish, sturdy colt: fairly useful handicapper: won 2 races at Chepstow in July, first a maiden event and second most impressively: good head second of 12 at Brighton final start: will prove best at up to 1m: acts on good to firm ground: usually wears bandages. *J. H. M. Gosden* 81

YACHT 3 b.g. Warning 136 – Bireme 127 (Grundy 137) [1994 73p: 6m^5 7.1m^3 a7g* 8m 1995 10m 10g Jun 12] tall gelding: tailed off in handicaps in 1995: should be suited by 1m+: has been bandaged near-hind: blinkered/visored since final 2-y-o start: sold (B. Hills to C. Mann) 4,800 gns Newmarket July Sales: modest but irresolute hurdler. *B. W. Hills* –

YAHMI (IRE) 5 b.g. Law Society (USA) 130 – Hogan's Sister (USA) (Speak John) [1994 –: 11.7g 1995 12.1g 11.5s Sep 28] useful-looking gelding: well beaten on flat since fairly useful 3-y-o maiden: staying hurdler. *J. A. B. Old* –

YA MALAK 4 b.g. Fairy King (USA) – La Tuerta 96 (Hot Spark 126) [1994 102: 5g^2 5g* 5m 5g^2 5.1m* 5.1g* 5m 5d^2 5.2s^5 5g^5 1995 5g^3 5f^2 5g* 5m^2 5.1g^6 5g^4 5m^2 5m^6 Sep 6] good-topped gelding: good mover: progressed into a smart performer: won listed race at Kempton in June by 2 lengths from Eveningperformance: good efforts in frame in 2 French listed races and Nunthorpe Stakes (1½ lengths second of 8 to So Factual) at York: races at around 5f: acts on good to firm and dead ground: has run well when sweating: usually races prominently. *J. W. Payne* 116

YA MARHABA 2 b.g. (Feb 4) Efisio 120 – Ichnusa 83 (Bay Express 132) [1995 5d 5s a5g Nov 24] workmanlike gelding: has a round action: third foal: brother to 4-y-o 6f winner Maid O'Cannie and 6f and 1m winner Sartigila: dam 7f winner who appeared to stay 9f: behind in maidens, twice slowly away. *J. W. Payne* –

YAMUNA (USA) 2 b.f. (Jan 26) Forty Niner (USA) – Nimble Feet (USA) 82 (Danzig (USA)) [1995 6g^5 May 20] good-quartered filly: fourth foal: half-sister to very smart 3-y-o Eltish (by Cox's Ridge), useful 4-y-o sprinter Forest Gazelle (by 67 p

Green Forest) and a winner in France at 1¼m by Majestic Light: dam, 2-y-o 5f winner who stayed 6f, sister to Contredance, a good 2-y-o in USA: odds on, just under 5 lengths fifth of 11 to Amazing Bay in maiden at Newbury, slowly away and pushed along 2f out but not making much progress until late on: wore blanket for stalls entry: needed experience badly, and looked sure to improve. *H. R. A. Cecil*

YARN (IRE) 3 b.f. Don't Forget Me 127 – Domiciliate (Kings Lake (USA) 133) [1994 51p: 7d 1995 8m* 11.4m² 10m³ 10m 10g Jul 12] sturdy filly: won maiden at Salisbury in May: useful form when ¾-length second of 7 to Dance A Dream in Cheshire Oaks and 2¼ lengths third of 9 to Subya in steadily-run Lupe Stakes at Goodwood in May: tailed off both starts afterwards, and said by trainer to have broken blood vessels: stays 11.4f: sold 17,000 gns Newmarket December Sales. *M. R. Channon* 99

YAROB (IRE) 2 ch.c. (May 19) Unfuwain (USA) 131 – Azyaa 101 (Kris 135) [1995 6m* 7m² 6d Sep 9] good-topped colt: fifth foal: half-brother to 3-y-o 1m winner Mukhatab and useful 7f winner Ihtiraz (both by Soviet Star) and 10.5f winner Shafi (by Reference Point): dam, 7.5f winner, is granddaughter of Milly Moss, dam of Mill On The Floss: comfortably made all in maiden at Lingfield in July: ran well when 1¾ lengths second of 8 to Mons in listed race at Newbury 12 days later: became worked up in preliminaries and raced too keenly when well beaten in minor event at Doncaster on final outing: stays 7f. *H. Thomson Jones* 97

YARROW (IRE) 3 b.c. Danehill (USA) 126 – Alyara (USA) (Alydar (USA)) [1994 NR 1995 10d³ 10.4m² 10.3g² 10d 10d Oct 19] lengthy, deep-girthed colt: has scope: second foal: dam, French 10.7f winner, is half-sister to smart middle-distance performer Tralos: fair form on second and third starts in maidens at York (hung right) in June and Doncaster (hung left) in July: well beaten (after near 3-month absence) on return: stays 10.4f: yet to race on extremes of going: sold 14,000 gns Newmarket Autumn Sales: sent to Malaysia. *J. H. M. Gosden* 78

YAVERLAND (IRE) 3 b.c. Astronef 116 – Lautreamont (Auction Ring (USA) 123) [1994 53: 7.6v⁵ 7g 7s⁶ 1995 8.2d 8m Oct 2] big, strong colt: has a round action: modest maiden: will stay beyond 1m: acts on good to soft going, edged left under pressure only start on top-of-the-ground. *C. A. Dwyer* 59

YEAST 3 b.g. Salse (USA) 128 – Orient 106 (Bay Express 132) [1994 NR 1995 6g⁶ 7m³ 7g² Sep 23] 16,500Y: fourth foal: half brother to Irish 5f winner Arcade (by Rousillon) and 7f winner Lamsonetti (by Never So Bold): dam sprinter: progressive form in maidens: beaten a neck at Redcar last time, always thereabouts and keeping on well: not stoutly bred, but shapes as if will stay 1m: should win a race. *W. J. Haggas* 80 p

YEATH (IRE) 3 ch.c. Exhibitioner 111 – Grain of Sand (Sandford Lad 133) [1994 NR 1995 7.1g 8.3m⁶ 8.3m 8.1m 10d Sep 14] rather leggy colt: fifth reported foal: brother to fairly useful 1m to 1¼m winner Knowth: dam dual Irish 6f winner: modest maiden handicapper: soundly beaten final start, quickly beaten 3f out: should stay beyond 1m: looks one paced. *R. Akehurst* 57

YELLOW DRAGON (IRE) 2 b.g. (Mar 12) Kefaah (USA) 124 – Veldt (High Top 131) [1995 5g 8.5s⁶ 10g³ Oct 9] IR 7,200F, IR 10,000Y: unfurnished gelding: third foal: half-brother to 1994 2-y-o 7.3f and 1m winner Rowlandsons Rocks (by Magical Strike) and 4-y-o 1m to 1½m winner Prince Danzig (by Roi Danzig): dam never ran: off course long time after debut: staying-on third in seller at Leicester final start: looks likely to be suited by a thorough test of stamina: sold 2,100 gns Doncaster October Sales. *Miss Gay Kelleway* 55

YENGEMA 4 b.f. Petoski 135 – Bundu (FR) 88 (Habitat 134) [1994 –: 8.2v a8g a8g 8.5g⁵ 8.2m 8.3g³ 8s 8s 1995 16.4g 10.1m Jul 27] angular filly: seemed of little account at 4 yrs: tried visored/blinkered. *R. C. Spicer* –

YEOMAN OLIVER 2 b.g. (Mar 1) Precocious 126 – Impala Lass 81 (Kampala 120) [1995 a5g⁶ a6g⁶ Dec 12] third foal: half-brother to 3-y-o Young Benson (by Zalazl) and 6f winner I'm Your Lady (by Risk Me): dam 5f performer: signs of ability in maiden at Southwell and seller at Wolverhampton: likely to do better. *B. A. McMahon* – p

YET AGAIN 3 ch.g. Weldnaas (USA) 112 – Brightelmstone 105 (Prince Regent (FR) 129) [1994 NR 1995 a10g⁶ 10m² 8.5d⁵ 11.9m* 12g 10.1g 8d Sep 27] 10,000F: 61

compact, good-bodied gelding: half-brother to several winners, including 6f (at 2 yrs) to 1½m winner Golden Torque (by Taufan): dam useful at up to 7f: modest performer: cosily won 4-runner maiden event at Brighton in June, leading final 1f: well beaten afterwards: stays 1½m: acts on good to firm ground, hung right both starts on dead. *B. Hanbury*

YET MORE ROSES 4 b.g. Gallic League 119 – Ominous 91 (Dominion 123) [1994 70: 8s⁶ 8m 5.3m⁵ 6m* 5m² 5.1f³ 5m 6g 1995 6m⁴ 6m⁴ 5f³ 5g 5.1h⁶ a6g⁴ a6g Sep 2] lengthy gelding: fair handicapper: well below form final start: stays 6f: acts on firm and dead ground: visored (weakened quickly after showing blistering early speed) fourth start: bandaged: often early to post: sold only 3,800 gns Newmarket Autumn Sales. *Lady Herries* 73 a64

YEZZA (IRE) 2 b.f. (Apr 21) Distinctly North (USA) 115 – Small Paradise (Habat 127) [1995 6m⁵ Nov 3] rangy filly: has scope: half-sister to Irish 7f winners Lipnik (by Tanfirion) and Spalato (by Sagaro), latter as 2-y-o: dam, of no account, half-sister to dam of smart Domynsky and Petrullo: 25/1, over 8 lengths fifth of 20 to Miss Riviera in maiden at Doncaster, soon in touch then keeping on same pace: will improve. *A. P. Jarvis* 61 p

YO KIRI-B 4 b.f. Night Shift (USA) – Briar Creek (Busted 134) [1994 62d: 8.3g⁴ 8g⁵ 10.3m³ 10m 9m² 10.1g⁵ 10m⁶ 9.7d⁶ 8s⁴ 9g 1995 a10g⁵ 9.7g³ 8m⁶ 8m⁵ 9.7m* 9m⁵ 10f a10g⁴ a8g⁶ a7g³ Nov 29] good-quartered filly: modest performer: won selling handicap at Folkestone in July, running on strongly (flashed tail) to lead close home: mostly below form afterwards: appears to stay 10.3f: acts on good to firm ground and soft: visored (below form) final 4-y-o start: inconsistent: has shown signs of temperament and not one to trust implicitly. *J. Ffitch-Heyes* 58 a54

YO-MATE 4 b.c. Komaite (USA) – Silent Sun 90 (Blakeney 126) [1994 –: 12d⁵ 1995 12m⁵ a14.8g⁴ 14d Jul 30] little sign of ability. *J. Ffitch-Heyes* –

YOSIF (IRE) 3 b.c. High Estate 127 – Respectfully (USA) (The Minstrel (CAN) 135) [1994 NR 1995 8g 7.3m 10d 7.1g⁵ 8m Jul 6] IR 18,500Y, resold 42,000Y: rangy colt: has scope: half-brother to several winners in Ireland and USA, including Irish 7f to 8.5f winner Robertolomy (by Roberto) and fairly useful Irish 2m winner Limbo Lady (by Theatrical): dam ran once in France: modest maiden: probably stays 1¼m: blinkered (no improvement) penultimate 3-y-o start: has looked awkward ride. *R. Hannon* 52

YOUCANSTOPLOOKING (IRE) 4 ch.g. Krayyan 117 – Juju 78 (Dragonara Palace (USA) 115) [1994 –: 7v 7d 6d 6m a8g 1995 a7g a6g⁶ Jan 21] leggy gelding: no worthwhile form. *S. Dow* –

YOUDONTSAY 3 ch.f. Most Welcome 131 – Fabulous Luba (Luthier 126) [1994 57: 6m⁴ 6f² 6.9m 6g⁴ 5d³ 6g⁶ 5.2g 1995 5m² 6m* 5.1f⁴ 6g⁴ 6m* 6f² 5g⁵ 7d² 5s 7m Oct 14] workmanlike filly: fairly useful handicapper: successful in large fields at Windsor in May and June: best effort when short-headed at Goodwood on eighth start but failed to repeat that form: effective at 5f to 7f: acts on firm and dead ground: genuine. *R. Curtis* 85

YOUGO 3 b.g. Good Times (ITY) – Young Wilkie (Callernish) [1994 NR 1995 16.2m³ 13.4d³ 14s 15.8m⁴ a16g⁵ a13g³ a13g Dec 6] big, workmanlike gelding: has a round action: second foal: brother to modest 1½m winner Magic Times: dam made frame both starts over hurdles: fair maiden handicapper: stays 13f: acts on good to firm and dead ground, and on equitrack: front runner. *M. Johnston* 74

YOUGOA 2 ch.f. (Apr 30) Mon Tresor 113 – Our Mable (Posse (USA) 130) [1995 5g 6m⁵ 6f² 6m 5g 5g⁵ Sep 18] 700F: lengthy, good-topped filly: half-sister to a winner abroad by Superlative: dam seemed to stay 11f: poor form: stays 6f: ran creditably in blinkers final start. *M. W. Easterby* 44

YOUNG BEN (IRE) 3 ch.g. Fayruz 116 – Jive (Ahonoora 122) [1994 NR 1995 6m⁶ 7.5m⁵ 7m 5g 6d a6g Nov 24] IR 450Y: smallish gelding: first foal: dam placed over 5f at 3 yrs in Ireland: no worthwhile form. *J. S. Wainwright* –

YOUNG BENSON 3 b.c. Zalazl (USA) 120 – Impala Lass 81 (Kampala 120) [1994 48: 6s⁶ 6s 1995 7.1m⁵ 7.5m³ 7.5d⁵ 7m 7.1m² 7m³ 8m⁴ 8.2m⁵ 8f³ 7g 8.2m a6g a7g Dec 12] angular, workmanlike colt: fair maiden: below form after seventh 3-y-o start: stays 1m: acts on good to firm and dead ground. *B. A. McMahon* 71 d

Mr M. F. Kentish's "Young Ern"

YOUNG BUSTER (IRE) 7 b.h. Teenoso (USA) 135 – Bustara 92 (Busted 134) [1994 117: 10v 10m* 10m² 10m³ 10m* 11.1d⁴ 10m³ 1995 10m³ 10f² 10g⁴ 10.5f² 10m⁶ 10g⁶ Sep 9] rather angular, quite attractive horse: has a quick action: smart performer: in frame in 1995 in 2 listed events at Kempton, Scottish Classic at Ayr (well below form) and Rose of Lancaster Stakes (beaten 2½ lengths by Fahal) at Haydock: effective at 1¼m and 1½m: acts on firm and dead ground, possibly not on heavy: blinkered twice at 4 yrs, running well first occasion: effective from front or held up. *G. Wragg* 111

YOUNG BUTT 2 ch.c. (Mar 30) Bold Owl 101 – Cymbal 80 (Ribero 126) [1995 5m 6m 7.1g 6f a7g³ a6g⁶ 7g⁴ 10g² a8.5g* Oct 28] 2,600F: leggy colt: half-brother to several winners, including 1¼m winner Beau Mirage (by Homing) and 1992 2-y-o 1m winner Precussion (by Dominion): dam middle-distance half-sister to smart performers Band and Zimbalon: plater: won nursery at Wolverhampton in October: suited by a good test of stamina: acts on fibresand: sometimes wears bandages. *J. Ffitch-Heyes* 60

YOUNG CLIFFORD (USA) 4 b. or br.g. Lear Fan (USA) 130 – Smile For Awhile (USA) (Norcliffe (CAN)) [1994 67: 11.9m⁴ 14d⁴ 1995 12.1g 14.9m⁶ 18.2m Jul 8] strong gelding: shows knee action: disappointing maiden: pulled up lame when favourite for novice hurdle in August. *F. Jordan* –

YOUNG DALESMAN 2 br.g. (Apr 12) Teenoso (USA) 135 – Fabulous Molly (Whitstead 125) [1995 9g 8g 8.2m Oct 26] unfurnished gelding: second reported foal: dam showed some promise on NH debut: behind in maidens at Redcar (carried head awkwardly), Leicester and Nottingham: subsequently gelded: bandaged behind last time: rather headstrong. *A. Streeter* –

YOUNG DUKE (IRE) 7 gr.g. Double Schwartz 128 – Princess Pamela 70 (Dragonara Palace (USA) 115) [1994 68: a7g a8g^5 a8g^2 8m 7m^6 7g^4 7.1m* 7m^3 7m^4 1995 8m^2 Jun 26] leggy gelding: fair handicapper: neck second of 9 at Warwick only 7-y-o start: stays 1m well: acts on firm ground, soft and equitrack: effective in blinkers or visor, has worn neither since 1992: sometimes carries head awkwardly and wanders under pressure. *Mrs S. D. Williams* — 70

YOUNGER DAYS (IRE) 4 b.g. My Generation 111 – Schlarigna (Kings Lake (USA) 133) [1994 41: 8.3m 7g 7d 5s^6 1995 5g 6m a5g a5g^5 5g^6 6m Jul 22] smallish ex-Irish gelding: little worthwhile form. *Martyn Wane* — –

YOUNG ERN 5 b.h. Efisio 120 – Stardyn (Star Appeal 133) [1994 117: 7.9f^3 7d* 7m^2 7f^2 7.3g* 7m^4 7g^{4dis} 7g^4 1995 7m* 8m^2 8.5m^6 8m^4 6.5g^2 7s^2 6d^2 7m 7f Dec 10] good-topped horse: has a round action: smart performer: impressive winner of listed race at Leicester in April: in frame on 5 occasions afterwards, short-head second to Cherokee Rose in Prix Maurice de Gheest at Deauville in August on fifth outing and to Cool Jazz in Diadem Stakes at Ascot in September on seventh: rare poor efforts in Prix de la Foret at Longchamp and Hong Kong International Bowl last 2 starts: effective at 6f to 1m: probably acts on any going: held up: genuine and consistent. *S. Dow* — 120

YOUNG FREDERICK (IRE) 2 ch.g. (Feb 23) Polish Patriot (USA) 128 – Notre Histoire (Habitat 134) [1995 6.9g a6g a7g^5 Dec 14] IR 9,200Y: second foal: dam French 7f winner: best effort never-dangerous fifth of 12 in claimer at Lingfield final start: will stay 1m. *K. R. Burke* — 55

YOUNG FREEMAN (USA) 6 b.h. Nijinsky (CAN) 138 – Committed (USA) 128 (Hagley (USA)) [1994 76: 8d 7.6g^5 10m* 10.2f^2 9d 1995 a10g* a10g^2 a10g* Mar 25] big, rangy horse: impresses in appearance: has a markedly round action: back to best 3-y-o form in 1995: put up 2 most impressive displays under top weight to win handicaps at Lingfield in February and (£10,500 event, by 7 lengths) March: suited by around 1¼m: acts on firm and dead going and on equitrack: tried blinkered (no improvement) at 4 yrs: best as a front runner. *D. R. Loder* — 101

YOUNG MAZAAD (IRE) 2 b.c. (Mar 2) Mazaad 106 – Lucky Charm (IRE) (Pennine Walk 120) [1995 6g 8g Sep 29] IR 2,000F: workmanlike colt: first foal: dam never ran: soundly beaten in maidens. *R. Curtis* — –

YOUNG SAFFY 2 ch.g. (Apr 23) Safawan 118 – Miss Pisces 86 (Salmon Leap (USA) 131) [1995 8.1g 8.2d 7.1d Oct 11] rather leggy gelding: has a round action: third foal: dam 7f winner stayed 1m: always behind in maiden events. *Mrs M. Reveley* — –

YOUNG SENSATION 3 ch.g. Arrasas (USA) 100 – Jianna 60 (Godswalk (USA) 130) [1994 –: 6m 7m 1995 6m a8.5g 5m May 25] plain, angular gelding: no form. *B. A. Pearce* — –

YOUNG STEVEN 4 b.g. Singing Steven 116 – Adoration (FR) 60 (Dancer's Image (USA)) [1994 –: 11.1g^6 1995 10m^4 10.1g 13g 14.1m Jun 1] leggy, angular gelding: seems of no account. *W. T. Kemp* — –

YOUNG VIC 3 b.f. Old Vic 136 – Loralane 86 (Habitat 134) [1994 NR 1995 10g Jun 6] half-sister to several winners, including 4-y-o 1m winner Red October (by Soviet Star) and useful milers Nuryana (by Nureyev) and Diggers Rest (by Mr Prospector): dam, 7f winner, is half-sister to On The House: tenth of 16 in maiden at Pontefract, slowly away, short of room in straight: sent to USA. *G. Wragg* — – p

YOUR MOST WELCOME 4 b.f. Most Welcome 131 – Blues Player 70 (Jaazeiro (USA) 127) [1994 NR 1995 10m^3 11.4m 8.2d^6 Sep 19] good-bodied filly: third foal: half-sister to a winner in Italy by Superlative: dam 2m winner: trained by P. Burgoyne, fourth in NH Flat race in July: no worthwhile form in maidens: should stay beyond 1m: bandaged near-hind last 2 starts. *D. J. S. ffrench Davis* — –

YOUSH (IRE) 3 ch.c. Dominion 123 – Astra Adastra (Mount Hagen (FR) 127) [1994 77: 7.1d^6 8d^2 7.1s^3 1995 a8g^3 a10g 8m^3 10m* 10.1m* 10m* 10.4m^3 9d^3 9g Sep 30] leggy colt: unimpressive mover: useful performer: won median auction maiden at Windsor in May, handicap at Epsom in June and £45,900 Royal Hong Kong Jockey Club Trophy Handicap at Sandown (in fine style by 4 lengths, bursting into lead over 1f out) in July: good placed efforts afterwards in Magnet Cup at York in July and well-contested minor event at Newbury (didn't travel with usual fluency — 104

Royal Hong Kong Jockey Club Trophy (Handicap), Sandown—
Yoush sprints past Salt Lake (rails) to land this valuable prize

on softer ground but kept on dourly behind Wijara) in September: favourite, rare poor effort in Cambridgeshire at Newmarket on final start: useful form at 1¼m and should stay further: acts on good to firm and dead ground: takes keen hold: has good turn of foot: sometimes sweats and gets on edge: sent to Dubai. *M. A. Jarvis*

YOXALL LODGE 5 b.h. Aragon 118 – Opal Fancy 83 (Kibenka 119) [1994 62: 7s* 8d 8s⁴ 9.7s⁶ 1995 7.5m 8m 9.2g 7g³ 8.1g² a8g⁴ Aug 4] big, lengthy horse: modest handicapper: stays 1m well: acts on heavy ground: makes running/races prominently. *H. J. Collingridge* — 63

YUBRALEE (USA) 3 ch.c. Zilzal (USA) 137 – Kentucky Lill (USA) (Raise A Native) [1994 67p: 7d⁴ 1995 7g⁵ 7m 10.2m 8.1g* 8.2m³ 10.8g⁵ 8.1d Oct 10] lengthy, quite attractive colt: good mover: fair performer: won claimer at Sandown (claimed out of M. Stoute's stable £10,000) in May: best at around 1m: acts on good to firm and dead ground: won selling hurdles in October and November. *M. C. Pipe* — 72

YUPPY GIRL (IRE) 2 ch.f. (Feb 24) Salt Dome (USA) – Sloane Ranger 84 (Sharpen Up 127) [1995 6m⁶ 6.1m² 7m⁵ 7g² 7.5d⁴ 6g⁴ 6f⁴ Oct 16] IR 2,600Y: sparely-made filly: half-sister to 2 winners, including 6f to 1m winner Liffey Reef (by Main Reef): dam won at up to 1m: modest form in auction events: nearest finish after having plenty to do last 3 starts: will stay beyond 7.5f: has been bandaged off-hind: not easiest of rides. *Capt. J. Wilson* — 61

Z

ZAAHEYAH (USA) 5 ch.m. Irish River (FR) 131 – Shoag (USA) (Affirmed (USA)) [1994 48d: 9.9d 13s² 13f⁵ 12.1g 12g 14s 1995 a12g a16g⁴ a14.8g² a14.8g⁴ a14g 13v* 12.1s² 13g⁵ 13g⁶ May 11] sturdy, lengthy mare: unimpressive mover: poor form: won (first time) handicap at Hamilton in March: stays at least 14.8f: acts on heavy going: visored (no improvement) first 2 outings at 5 yrs: one paced, and races prominently: sold 5,800 gns Doncaster May Sales, 6,500 gns Newmarket July Sales. *M. D. Hammond* — 45 a39

ZAALEFF (USA) 3 ch.c. Zilzal (USA) 137 – Continual (USA) (Damascus (USA)) [1994 NR 1995 7.1g 8.3m Jul 10] rangy, rather unfurnished colt: half-brother to Shadeed (by Nijinsky) and 9f winner Basoof (by Believe It): dam, successful at 6f and 7f, is sister to Tuerta, dam of Swale: 7 lengths seventh of 10 in steadily-run maiden at Sandown: again weak in betting, below that form in similar event at Windsor: sold 2,600 gns Newmarket Autumn Sales. *M. R. Stoute* — 63

ZACAROON 4 b.f. Last Tycoon 131 – Samaza (USA) 90 (Arctic Tern (USA) 126) [1994 70+: a9.4g* 5g 10g 8d³ 8s 8m 1995 a10g⁵ a8g³ a8g³ a10g² 10.3m² 10g³ 10g* 10m² 10g⁵ 10g⁴ a8.5g⁴ 10f⁵ a10g a10g Dec 18] lengthy filly: fair performer: won apprentice handicap at Sandown in July: below form last 5 starts, sold out of Lord Huntingdon's stable 8,200 gns Newmarket Autumn Sales after third of them: — 69 a64 should stay beyond 1¼m: acts on all-weather surfaces, good to firm and dead ground: visored (ran well) third 4-y-o start: usually held up. *J. Ffitch-Heyes*

ZADOK 3 ch.g. Exodal (USA) – Glenfinlass (Lomond (USA) 128) [1994 NR 1995 11.8g 14g^6 a10g a16g Nov 30] first foal: dam unraced sister to 10.5f to 17.2f winner Inchcailloch: no worthwhile form. *R. T. Phillips* –

ZAFORUM 2 b.c. (Mar 30) Deploy 131 – Beau's Delight (USA) (Lypheor 118) [1995 9m^5 8.1d^5 10g^5 10m^4 9s Dec 5] strong colt: has a round action: third foal: brother to 3-y-o 1¾m and 2m winner Rocky Forum and half-brother to 11.9f and 13f seller winner Glow Forum (by Kalaglow): dam, should have stayed at least 1m, out of half-sister to smart French 1¼m winner Sangue: fairly useful form: possibly shade flattered by bare form when towards rear in listed races at Newmarket and Evry last 2 starts: requires thorough test of stamina. *L. Montague Hall* 89 ?

ZAHID (USA) 4 ch.g. Storm Cat (USA) – Time An' Care (USA) (Twin Time (USA)) [1994 60: 7.1m 5m^3 7.1m 9m^4 7m^5 1995 10.3g 15.4g 14m^4 12.5m^5 9.7g^4 9.7m^3 9m^4 10m^6 8m^4 Aug 23] good-topped, attractive gelding: impresses in appearance: modest maiden: trained first 3 starts at 4 yrs by Bob Jones: probably stays 12.5f: has raced only on a sound surface: blinkered (ran well) seventh start, visored (well below form, third run in 11 days) final one at 4 yrs. *K. R. Burke* 50

ZAHRAN (IRE) 4 b.c. Groom Dancer (USA) 128 – Welsh Berry (USA) (Sir Ivor 135) [1994 77: 8s^3 7.5g* 8m^5 a8.5g^3 1995 a8.5g^4 a8.5g^6 a8g a8g^2 a9.4g^4 a8g^4 a8g* a8.5g 7g a8g 8m 8g^2 10.2m a8.5g^6 8f^2 8m^3 8.1g 8m^4 9.2f* 10m^6 a10g^4 10.1g^6 Sep 13] strong, good-topped colt: unimpressive mover: just a modest handicapper at 4 yrs: won at Lingfield in March and Hamilton (seller) in August: stays 1¼m: acts on firm and soft ground and goes well on all-weather surfaces: sometimes wears bandages. *J. M. Bradley* 60 d

ZAHWA 3 ch.f. Cadeaux Genereux 131 – Peace Girl 98 (Dominion 123) [1994 60p: 7d 1995 6m^6 7.1m^3 7.1d^3 7f Oct 18] unfurnished filly: unimpressive mover: fair maiden: stays 7f: acts on good to firm ground (looked past her best, well beaten on firm) and good to soft: sold 5,000 gns Newmarket December Sales. *R. W. Armstrong* 72

ZAJKO (USA) 5 b.g. Nureyev (USA) 131 – Hope For All (USA) (Secretariat (USA)) [1994 73: 10.5g^4 8m* 8.3m^3 10f^4 7.9m* 8s 1995 8m 8m* 10f 8d 7g 8f^2 Oct 24] good-topped gelding: fairly useful handicapper: won 25-runner event at Newbury in May: favourite, best effort when head second of 13 at Leicester final start, leading 2f out until close home: best at 1m: acts on firm ground, possibly not on a soft surface: visored (ran poorly) once at 2 yrs: best held up behind sound pace. *Lady Herries* 83

ZALAMENT 3 b.f. Zalazl (USA) 120 – Key To Enchantment (Key To Content (USA)) [1994 65p: 7m 8d^6 1995 11m 10.5g^5 10g 12m^3 14m^5 12s 11.9m a12g a7g Dec 19] leggy, angular filly: modest maiden at best: should stay further than 1½m: visored (tailed off) seventh 3-y-o start, and subsequently left A. Jarvis' stable: inconsistent. *N. P. Littmoden* 57 d

ZALOTTI (IRE) 2 ch.f. (Feb 12) Polish Patriot (USA) 128 – Honest Penny (USA) (Honest Pleasure (USA)) [1995 5g* Jun 3] IR 17,000Y: half-sister to several winners here and abroad, including 7f to 12.5f winner Return To Romance (by Trojan Fen) and fair 1991 2-y-o 6f winner Penny Orchid (by Taufan): dam placed over 5f at 2 yrs in Ireland: well-backed 4/1-shot, won 6-runner maiden at Ayr impressively by 3 lengths: reportedly sustained a fracture of off-hind cannon bone: looked promising. *T. J. Etherington* 84

ZAMALEK (USA) 3 b.g. Northern Baby (CAN) 127 – Chellingoua (USA) (Sharpen Up 127) [1994 89p: 7m^5 7g* 8.1s^2 1995 8g^4 10.4m^4 8m^5 Jul 2] sturdy, good sort: fairly useful performer: looked none too keen when last of 5 in maiden event at Doncaster final start: best form at up to around 1m: acts on soft ground, respectable effort on good to firm: blinkered (calm only on second occasion) last 2 starts: may well have unsatisfactory temperament: sold (H. Cecil to G. L. Moore) 7,800 gns Newmarket September Sales and gelded. *H. R. A. Cecil* 85

ZAMHAREER (USA) 4 b.g. Lear Fan (USA) 130 – Awenita (Rarity 129) [1994 60: 10d 10m^5 11.6d^2 11.4g^3 14.1m 12g 11.9d^2 16.1d^4 1995 12.1s^5 15.8g 14g^6 14s^5 Sep 30] rather leggy gelding: poor maiden handicapper on flat at 4 yrs: needs further than 1½m nowadays: may well be suited by give in the ground. *W. Storey* 48

ZANZARA (IRE) 4 ch.f. Efisio 120 – Slick Chick 89 (Shiny Tenth 120) [1994 –: 6.1d 7m 7.1s 1995 a7g3 a8g6 a8g 10m 8f a8g5 10g 10m4 a12g 13.8m* 17.1m2 a16g 13.8f* 15.1s Nov 2] smallish, strong filly: modest performer: won seller at Catterick in August and steadily-run minor event at Catterick (settled well, stayed on under strong pressure to lead inside last) in October: appears to stay 17.1f: acts on fibresand and firm ground: visored (no form) final 3-y-o start: consistent. *Mrs V. A. Aconley* — 54

ZARALASKA 4 ch.g. Shernazar 131 – Eskimo Spring (USA) (Riverman (USA) 131) [1994 72p: 8m6 7g5 1995 8d 10f2 12g* 12m2 Jun 21] sturdy, quite attractive gelding: has a quick action: most progressive form: impressive winner of handicap at Newbury in May: gambled on, neck second of 20 to Son of Sharp Shot in Bessborough Stakes at Royal Ascot, quickening on entering last but, despite staying on, collared close home: very well suited by 1½m, and should stay 1¾m: looked sure to progress further and win more races: stays in training. *L. M. Cumani* — 98 p

ZATOPEK 3 b. or br.c. Reprimand 122 – Executive Lady 59 (Night Shift (USA)) [1994 55: 6f 1995 7f5 9g 8g4 7d Oct 19] sturdy colt: has quick action: modest maiden handicapper: stays 1m: acts on firm ground, poorly drawn on dead: sold 6,000 gns Newmarket Autumn Sales. *R. Hannon* — 61

ZDENKA 2 b.f. (Jan 13) Dominion 123 – Short And Sharp 88 (Sharpen Up 127) [1995 6f 7m2 7m2 7f5 6.9s2 8g6 Oct 3] 4,800Y: leggy filly: unimpressive mover: sister to 7f winner Step High and half-sister to 3-y-o Drumochter (by Prince Sabo) and 2 winners in Italy: dam placed at 6f and 7f at 2 yrs, only season to race: improved effort when beaten a length in maiden auction at Folkestone: stays 1m: acts on good to firm ground but well suited by soft. *M. Blanshard* — 67

ZEB (IRE) 3 b.c. Cyrano de Bergerac 120 – Bap's Miracle (Track Spare 125) [1994 93: 6g2 6m2 6m6 6g 1995 7.1m* 8m 6g5 6g3 6m Jun 17] tall, workmanlike colt: useful performer: won maiden at Haydock in April: best efforts when tenth of 11 (disputing lead 5f) in 2000 Guineas at Newmarket, fifth of 7 to Lake Coniston in Duke of York Stakes and third of 9 (visored) to Star Tulip in listed rated stakes at Haydock: effective at 6f, and probably stays 1m: has raced only on a sound surface: sent to Hong Kong. *B. A. McMahon* — 98

ZEETARO 4 b.g. Taufan (USA) 119 – Gem Bracelet (USA) 68 (Sir Ivor 135) [1994 98d: 8m2 10.3m4 10m5 10g2 10m3 10.2g5 10d 1995 10.2h2 9.7f* 10m4 10m4 10d3 10d* Sep 22] sturdy, compact gelding: usually impresses in appearance: fluent mover: fairly useful handicapper: not so good as at 3 yrs, but ran consistently and won at Folkestone (maiden event) in August and Redcar in September: stays 10.3f: probably acts on hard and dead going: visored last 3 starts at 4 yrs, blinkered final one as 3-y-o: has sometimes looked none too keen. *Major W. R. Hern* — 83

ZELAYA (IRE) 2 b.f. (Mar 26) Shaadi (USA) 126 – Zizania 77 (Ahonoora 122) [1995 6g May 20] good-topped filly: second foal: half-sister to 3-y-o Zitziana (by Salse): dam 1m winner out of sister to Bolkonski: 33/1 and carrying condition, around 7 lengths eighth of 11 to Amazing Bay in maiden at Newbury, slowly into stride and never able to challenge: looked sure to improve. *C. E. Brittain* — 62 p

ZELDA ZONK 3 b.f. Law Society (USA) 130 – Massive Powder (Caerleon (USA) 132) [1994 NR 1995 7.3m 8m5 8d3 7d 8m4 7m3 Oct 28] sturdy filly: second foal: dam out of half-sister to Alydar's Best: fair maiden handicapper: should stay beyond 1m: acts on good to firm and dead ground: has been bandaged behind. *B. J. Meehan* — 67

ZELIBA 3 br.f. Doyoun 124 – Zia (USA) 88 (Shareef Dancer (USA) 135) [1994 –: 7g 6s 1995 a7g a7g6 7f Aug 2] small, leggy filly: no worthwhile form. *C. E. Brittain* — –

ZELZELAH (USA) 2 b.f. (Feb 14) Timeless Moment (USA) – Allevition (USA) (Alleged (USA) 138) [1995 7g* 7g 8d6 Sep 24] $22,000Y: long-backed, rather unfurnished filly: fifth foal: dam winner at around 1m in USA from 2 starts: sire very smart at up to 1m: won £8,100 event at Newbury in excellent style by 3 lengths from Axford, showing really smart turn of foot to settle issue 2f out: failed to repeat that form in Moyglare Stud Stakes at the Curragh and Fillies' Mile (tailed-off last of 6) at Ascot: should stay 1m: looked a good prospect at Newbury. *P. A. Kelleway* — 96

ZERMATT (IRE) 5 b.h. Sadler's Wells (USA) 132 – Chamonis (USA) 101 (Affirmed (USA)) [1994 78: 7v4 10d4 8.3g3 10m 8.1s* 10m4 8.1m2 8m 12g 10g2 8s 9g 8m 1995 10m 10.1f 8m* 8f2 8.1m3 8m4 8m 10m5 8.3m 10.5g5 9d Sep 30] tall, — 74

strong horse: unimpressive mover: fair handicapper: won at Bath in June: effective at 1m and 1¼m: acts on firm and soft ground. *M. D. I. Usher*

ZESTI 3 br.g. Charmer 123 – Lutine Royal 46 (Formidable (USA) 125) [1994 –: a7g^6 1995 a8.5g^3 a8g a8.5g 8.3g 8.2m Jun 26] poor maiden: best effort at 8.5f on fibresand. *T. T. Clement* — 43

ZIDAC 3 b. or br.c. Statoblest 120 – Sule Skerry 78 (Scottish Rifle 127) [1994 –p: 7.1s^5 1995 10g^4 10m^5 9m^4 10m^4 10g 12.1s Oct 17] tall colt: fair maiden: well beaten (after 3½-month absence) last 2 starts: likely to prove best at up to 1¼m: acts on good to firm ground: races prominently. *P. J. Makin* — 75

ZIFTA (USA) 4 ch.f. Zilzal (USA) 137 – Shoalih (USA) 83 (Alydar (USA)) [1994 73: 6f^6 5.1f* 6f^5 6m^2 6m 1995 6m 7.1m 7f* 7m 7.6m 7m Jul 24] smallish, sturdy filly: fairly useful performer: well-backed winner (made all) of 5-runner handicap at Redcar in May: should stay 1m: acts on firm and dead ground: takes keen hold, usually taken down alone. *S. C. Williams* — 82

ZIGGY'S DANCER (USA) 4 b.c. Ziggy's Boy (USA) – My Shy Dancer (USA) (Northjet 136) [1994 69: 7.1g^5 7.1m^6 7m^3 7g^3 7m^4 7m^2 7.9d^2 10d^6 8m 8g^2 7g a8.5g^4 1995 a9.4g a7g^3 a7g* a7g^2 a6g* 6g 5.9m* 6m^2 5f* 6m 6f 6.1m^2 6m^4 5.1g* 5g^6 6g 5m 5s^6 6g 5m^5 5m^6 a5g* Dec 14] lengthy colt: poor mover: useful performer: won handicaps at Wolverhampton in February (maiden event) and March and Carlisle in April, minor event at Beverley in May, £15,500 contest at Chester in July and another handicap at Lingfield in December: best form at sprint distances: acts on firm and dead ground and the all weather. *E. J. Alston* — 97

ZILAYAH (USA) 3 ch.f. Zilzal (USA) 137 – Welsh Garden 123 (Welsh Saint 126) [1994 79p: 6g 6d^3 7g* 1995 7m 7.1m May 29] unfurnished filly: progressive form at 2 yrs: well beaten in handicaps in 1995. *M. R. Stoute* — –

ZILZAL ZAMAAN (USA) 4 b. or br.c. Zilzal (USA) 137 – Iva Reputation (USA) (Sir Ivor 135) [1994 109: 7d* 8f^4 7.9f^3 10m* 10.3m^2 10m^2 12v* 1995 12g — 113

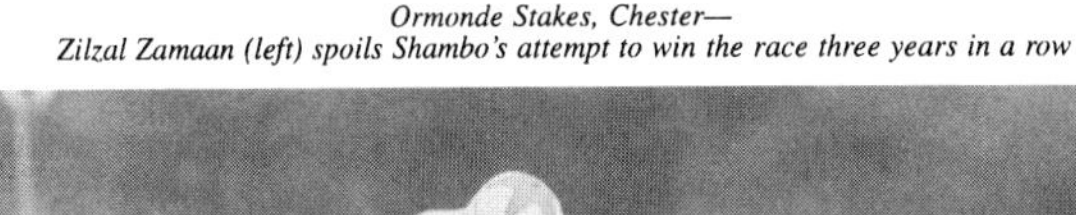

Ormonde Stakes, Chester—
Zilzal Zamaan (left) spoils Shambo's attempt to win the race three years in a row

13.4m* 12f4 12.5g2 14g 12d5 Oct 15] close-coupled colt: carries condition: smart performer: best 4-y-o efforts when winning 4-runner Ormonde Stakes at Chester (by 1½ lengths from Shambo) in May and when ¾-length second of 9 to Swain in Grand Prix de Deauville in August: stays 13.4f (well beaten in Irish St Leger fifth start): similar form on good to firm ground and (won impressively) heavy: normally held up: often bandaged. *M. R. Stoute*

ZINBAQ 9 ch.h. Ahonoora 122 – Zaiyundeen (FR) (Exbury 138) [1994 36, a47: a7g* 6.9s 6m5 a8g* 8.5m 7g 7m a7g 6.9g5 7d 7d 7d a8g a7g3 a7g 1995 a8g4 a8g5 a8g5 a8g a8g5 8m6 7f 6.9g3 6.9f Aug 11] quite attractive horse: carries condition: unimpressive mover: poor handicapper: may well stay beyond 1m: acts on any going, including equitrack: none too consistent. *C. J. Benstead* 33

ZINE LANE 3 ch.g. Minster Son 130 – Pine (Supreme Sovereign 119) [1994 65: 7.6v6 7d6 1995 6.9g 10m6 12s6 12.1s Oct 17] lengthy, unfurnished gelding: fair maiden: no worthwhile form in 1995: should prove suited by further than 1¼m. *Major W. R. Hern* –

ZINGIBAR 3 b.g. Caerleon (USA) 132 – Duende 75 (High Top 131) [1994 75: 6g3 7m* 7g5 1995 10m 10.2m6 8m 8.2m4 10m 8.1d4 Sep 2] strong, good-topped gelding: has a round action: fair performer on his day: effective at 8.2f, should stay further: acts on good to firm ground and dead: tried blinkered: sold (B. Hills to J. Bradley) 3,800 gns Newmarket Autumn Sales. *B. W. Hills* 67

ZIRO (IRE) 3 b.g. Alzao (USA) 117 – Nazeera (FR) (Lashkari 128) [1994 NR 1995 10.2f 14d6 10.2m6 Jul 4] smallish, leggy gelding: first foal: dam, French 11.5f winner, closely related to Prix du Jockey-Club winner Natroun: bandaged, well beaten in maidens: tried visored. *P. D. Evans* –

ZITZIANA (IRE) 3 ch.f. Salse (USA) 128 – Zizania 77 (Ahonoora 122) [1994 –p: 7d 1995 8.2m 7g Jun 14] unfurnished filly: well beaten in maidens: sold 3,000 gns Newmarket July Sales. *C. E. Brittain* –

Mana Al Maktoum's "Zilzal Zamaan"

ZONK 5 ch.g. Nishapour (FR) 125 – Liberty Tree 96 (Dominion 123) [1994 44: a11g^{4} 10m^{3} 11.9f* 11.6f^{2} 13.1f* 1995 a13g Feb 2] sturdy gelding: poor handicapper in 1994 for J. Pearce: soundly beaten on only flat outing for new connections. *R. G. Frost* –

ZUHAIR 2 ch.c. (Feb 25) Mujtahid (USA) 118 – Ghzaalh (USA) 87 (Northern Dancer) [1995 6m^{3} 6m* 6g^{5} Jul 12] well-made colt: second foal: half-brother to 3-y-o Mihriz (by Machiavellian), 6f winner at 2 yrs: dam, placed at 10.4f from 2 starts, out of Irish Oaks winner Give Thanks and close relative of dam of Harayir: long odds on, won 5-runner maiden at Newmarket in June: around 2 lengths fifth of 9 to Tagula in July Stakes there following month, never far away and keeping on: will be suited by further: looked sure to improve further. *Major W. R. Hern* 97 p

ZUIENA (USA) 3 ch.f. Sunshine Forever (USA) – Hattab Voladora (USA) (Dewan (USA)) [1994 66p: 8.1g^{4} 1995 10.5m^{4} 12m^{4} 12m^{6} 17.2h^{2} 16.2g* 16.4f^{2} 15.4m^{6} Sep 7] big, lengthy filly: fair performer: won maiden at Beverley in July: blinkered, good efforts in handicaps both subsequent starts: stays 17.2f: acts on hard ground, yet to race on a soft surface: sold 36,000 gns Newmarket Autumn Sales. *P. F. I. Cole* 70

ZUNO FLYER (USA) 3 br.g. Lyphard (USA) 132 – Triple Tipple (USA) 111 (Raise A Cup (USA)) [1994 NR 1995 6.9g 8m^{6} 6m 10g 11.7m 7m 12s 7f a7g Nov 10] 86,000Y: stocky gelding: fourth foal: half-brother to useful 1m winner Triode (by Sharpen Up): dam 7f to 1m winner: no worthwhile form: tried blinkered. *G. Lewis* –

ZUNO NOELYN 4 b.f. Most Welcome 131 – Artist's Glory (Rarity 129) [1994 61: 6v 8m* 8.5s 8f^{4} 8m^{4} 10m^{5} 9f 8.5m^{3} 8d 9s^{5} 8m 8g 12g^{6} a12g^{4} 1995 a10g* a10g^{3} a12g^{5} a10g^{2} a10g 10f* Jul 24] good-topped filly: won handicap at Lingfield in January on first start for new stable and claimer at Brighton (broke down badly on pulling up) in July: best at up to 1¼m: acted on firm ground and equitrack, not on a soft surface: blinkered (ran poorly) seventh 3-y-o start: dead. *R. Akehurst* 59

ZUNO PRINCESS (IRE) 2 br.f. (Apr 24) Distinctly North (USA) 115 – Flash Donna (USA) 70 (Well Decorated (USA)) [1995 5d 5g 5.1h^{4} 5m a8.5g Oct 14] 4,000Y: good-bodied filly: sixth foal: half-sister to 3-y-o Warwick Mist and fairly useful 5f (at 2 yrs) to 9f winner Second Chance (both by Digamist) and a winner by Cyrano de Bergerac in Scandinavia: dam best at 2 yrs: well beaten in maidens and sellers: blinkered final outing: sold (G. Lewis to J. O'Donoghue) 600 gns Ascot November Sales. *G. Lewis* –

ZUSHA 4 b.f. Kind of Hush 118 – Zamandra 39 (Foggy Bell 108) [1994 NR 1995 10m 14.1f Jun 24] leggy, angular filly: half-sister to a fairly useful NH Flat race winner by Morston: dam poor on flat, but fair hurdler: tailed-off last in maidens. *S. G. Norton* –

ZYGO (USA) 3 b.c. Diesis 133 – La Papagena (Habitat 134) [1994 69p: 6s^{6} 1995 8m^{4} May 9] lengthy, useful-looking colt: unimpressive mover, fair maiden: looked sort to do better, but seen out only once each season. *W. Jarvis* 72 p

PROMISING HORSES

All the horses in *Racehorses of 1995* thought capable of noteworthy improvement are listed below under the trainers for whom they last ran.

R. AKEHURST
Express Routing 3 b.c 62p
Willie Conquer 3 ch.c 80p
Bimsey (IRE) 5 b.h 84p
Poddington 4 b.g 78p

R. ALLAN
High Pyrenees 3 b.c 72p

C. N. ALLEN
Firm Contract (IRE) 3 b.c 56p

R. W. ARMSTRONG
Alwarqa 2 b.f —p
Antiguan Jane 2 b.f 56p
Formidable Partner 2 b.c 70p
Murheb 2 b.g 87p
Mutadarra (IRE) 2 ch.c 89p
Raise A Prince (FR) 2 b.c 85p
Kutta 3 b.c 101p
Mufarej (USA) 3 ch.c 82p

G. B. BALDING
Indian Nectar 2 b.f —p
Reiterate 2 b.f —p

I. A. BALDING
Agile 2 b.c 72p
Crystal Warrior 2 b.f 55p
Dashing Blue 2 ch.c 96p
Dramatic Moment 2 b.f 55p
High Cut 2 b.f 84p
Night Watch (USA) 2 b.c 97p
Pike Creek (USA) 2 b.f 68p
Prospero 2 b.g —p
Silver Border 2 ch.c 77p
Vendetta 2 b.f —p

J. E. BANKS
Magic Heights 2 gr.c 57p
Traikey (IRE) 3 b.c 105p

T. D. BARRON
Frontman (IRE) 2 ch.c 67p
Coastal Bluff 3 gr.g 97p
Dana Point (IRE) 3 br.g 65p

P. BARY, FRANCE
Eternity Range (USA) 2 b.c 111p
Ragmar (FR) 2 ch.f 112p

M. BELL
A Likely Tale (USA) 2 b.c 78p
Calypso Run 2 ch.f —p
Go With The Wind 2 b.c —p
Green Bopper (USA) 2 b.c 71p
Hamlet (IRE) 2 b.c 78p
Samuel Scott 2 b.g —p
White Plains (IRE) 2 b.c 72p

C. J. BENSTEAD
Alhawa (USA) 2 ch.c 76p
Ruwy 2 b.f 68p
Akayid 3 b.f 79p

J. BERRY
Lilburne (IRE) 2 b.g —p
River Tern 2 b.c 58p
Pentre Ffynnon (IRE) 3 ch.g 77p

J. S. BOLGER, IRELAND
Priory Belle (IRE) 2 ch.f 103p

R. BOSS
Apicella 2 ch.c 60p
Billaddie 2 b.g 55p

G. BOTTI, ITALY
Brave Indigo 2 b.c 100p

S. R. BOWRING
Maiteamia 2 ch.g 45p

C. E. BRITTAIN
Babinda 2 b.c 92p
Hippy 2 b.f 68p
Zelaya (IRE) 2 b.f 62p
Bay of Islands 3 b.g 79p

F. BROGI, ITALY
Glory of Dancer 2 b.c 105p

P. CALVER
Escobar (IRE) 2 br.c —p
Gilling Dancer (IRE) 2 b.c 58p

M. J. CAMACHO
Adler (IRE) 2 b.g —p
Kingdom Princess 2 br.f —p

H. CANDY
Age of Reality (USA) 2 b.f 63p
Beauchamp Kate 2 b.f 61p
Generosa 2 b.f 80p
Mourne Mountains 2 b.c —p
Pleading 2 b.c 77p
Well Drawn 2 b.c 65p

J. M. CARR
Killmessan-Town (IRE) 2 ch.g —p

H. R. A. CECIL
Ali-Royal (IRE) 2 b.c 87p
Annecy (USA) 2 b.f 73p
Benatom (USA) 2 gr.c 82p
Bosra Sham (USA) 2 ch.f 115p
Brighstone 2 ch.c 95p
Bright Water 2 b.c 95p
Caxton Star 2 ch.c 77P
Censor 2 b.c 84p
Degree 2 b.f 81p

Dushyantor (USA) 2 b.c 92P
Flaming June (USA) 2 ch.f 69p
Forest Buck (USA) 2 ch.c 87p
Glen Parker (IRE) 2 ch.c 79p
Green Charter 2 b.f 77p
Helicon (IRE) 2 b.c 96P
Lady Carla 2 b.f 90p
Mark of Esteem (IRE) 2 b.c 105p
Pricket (USA) 2 ch.f 85P
Private Audience (USA) 2 b.c —p
Sandy Floss (IRE) 2 b.c —p
Silver Dome (USA) 2 b.c 90P
Storm Trooper (USA) 2 b.c 104p
Subterfuge 2 br.f 78p
Unreal City (IRE) 2 b.c 78p
Viridis (USA) 2 b.f 59p
Yamuna (USA) 2 b.f 67p
Aldevonie 3 b.f 75p
Bequeath 3 ch.c 89p
Charnwood Forest (IRE) 3 b.c 116p
Coburg 3 ch.c 85p
Dacha (IRE) 3 b.c 83p
Felitza (IRE) 3 b.f 100p
General Assembly (IRE) 3 b.c 92p
Lost Lagoon (USA) 3 ch.c 83p
Montejurra 3 b.c 96p
Richelieu (IRE) 3 ch.c 88p
Sebastian 3 b.c 116p
Segovia 3 b.f 95p
Signature 3 b.f 62p
Top Shop 3 ch.f 75p
Vitus 3 b.c 82p

MRS J. CECIL
Dragon's Back (IRE) 2 ch.c 63p
Fly Fishing (USA) 2 ch.c 74p
Snowpoles 2 b.f 57p
Tsarskaya (USA) 2 ch.f 68p
Restructure (IRE) 3 b.c 112p

M. R. CHANNON
Mental Pressure 2 ch.g 75p
Mironov 2 b.c 79p
Stoney End (USA) 2 b.c —p

MAJOR D. N. CHAPPELL
Classic Look (IRE) 2 b.f —p
Dwingeloo (IRE) 2 b.f 83p
Stolen Music (IRE) 2 b.f —p

P. W. CHAPPLE-HYAM
Alpine Twist (USA) 2 b.f 68p
Astor Place (IRE) 2 b.c 106p
Backdrop (IRE) 2 b.c 74p
Desert Boy (IRE) 2 br.c 100p
Elite Force (IRE) 2 b.g 82p
Heron Island (IRE) 2 b.c 99p
Inner Circle (USA) 2 ch.f 76p
Legal Right (USA) 2 b.c 91p
Lothlorien (USA) 2 ch.f 76p
Meribel (IRE) 2 b.f 65p
Musick House (IRE) 2 b.c 96p
Orinoco River (USA) 2 ch.c 75p
Rayner (IRE) 2 b.g 62p
Russian Revival (USA) 2 ch.c 108p
Sea Spray (IRE) 2 b.f 88p
Silk Masque (USA) 2 b.f 85p
Ski Academy (IRE) 2 b.c 96p
Smilin N Wishin (USA) 2 b.f 79p
State Theatre (IRE) 2 b.c 70p
Wild Rumour (IRE) 2 b.f 89p

R. CHARLTON
High Note 2 b.f 70p
Jackson Hill 2 b.c 85p
Mystic Knight 2 b.c 93p
Palamon (USA) 2 ch.c 76p
Private Song (USA) 2 b.c 78p
Reveuse de Jour (IRE) 2 b.f —p
Splinter (IRE) 2 b.c 81p
Trafalgar Lady (USA) 2 b.f 86p
Waypoint 2 b.f —p
Cap Juluca (IRE) 3 b.c 117p
Easy Listening (USA) 3 b.g 79p

P. F. I. COLE
Chalk Dust (USA) 2 b.f 80p
Corporal Nym (USA) 2 gr.c 85p
El Opera (IRE) 2 b.f 71p
Fairlight Down (USA) 2 b.f 80p
Filmore West 2 b.c 65p
Gentilhomme 2 ch.c 100p
Infamous (USA) 2 ch.c 68p
Leonine (IRE) 2 gr.c 99p
Ma Belle Poule 2 b.f 73p
Oleana (IRE) 2 b.f 86p
Sibbertoft (IRE) 2 b.f 81p
Squandamania 2 b.c —p
Supamova (USA) 2 b.f 88p
Sweet Times 2 ch.f 60p
Swift Fandango (USA) 2 b.c 90p
Trilby 2 b.f 71p
Forever Roses 3 b.f 70p
Merit (IRE) 3 b.c 74p
Monarch 3 b.c 92p

L. M. CUMANI
Coldstream 2 b.c 90P
Ela-Yie-Mou (IRE) 2 ch.c 63p
Flamands (IRE) 2 b.f —p
Frequent 2 ch.c 78p
Funky 2 ch.f 69p
Galaka 2 b.f —p
House of Riches 2 b.c 80p
Humourless 2 ch.c 77p
Old Irish 2 gr.c —p
Paojiunic (IRE) 2 ch.c —p
Papering (IRE) 2 b.f 94p
Passage Creeping (IRE) 2 b.f 66p
Peppers (IRE) 2 b.f 68p
Robamaset (IRE) 2 b.c 77p
Select Few 2 b.c 84p
Spillo 2 b.c 80p
Lucky Di (USA) 3 b.c 103p
South Sea Bubble (IRE) 3 b.f 71p
Wellsian (USA) 3 b.c 77p
Zaralaska 4 ch.g 98p

C. A. CYZER
Bowled Over 2 b.g 67p
Steamroller Stanly 2 b.g 70p

S. DOW
Elegantissima 2 b.f 57p

E. A. L. DUNLOP
Dawawin (USA) 2 b.f 81p
Jamrat Jumairah (IRE) 2 b.f 77p
Minoletti 2 b.g 70p
Sihafi (USA) 2 ch.c 77p
Silver Prey (USA) 2 b.c 92p
Ta Rib (USA) 2 ch.f 89p
Winter Romance 2 ch.c 93p
Mubariz (IRE) 3 b.c 75p

J. L. DUNLOP
Alicia (IRE) 2 b.f —p
Beauchamp King 2 gr.c 114p
Bint Salsabil (USA) 2 ch.f 104p
Bint Shadayid (USA) 2 gr.f 105p
Della Casa (IRE) 2 ch.f 58p
Elshabiba (USA) 2 b.c 93p
Insiyabi (USA) 2 b.c 81p
Lady Joshua (IRE) 2 ch.f 88p
Liberatrice (FR) 2 b.f —p
Masehaab (IRE) 2 b.c 91p
Minnisam 2 ch.c —p
Najiya 2 b.f 100p
Nilgiri Hills (IRE) 2 ch.c 84p
Ninotchka (USA) 2 b.f 66p
Parsa (USA) 2 b.f —p
Poetic Dance (USA) 2 ch.c —p
Royal Diversion (IRE) 2 b.f 73p
Samara (IRE) 2 ch.f 69p
Samim (USA) 2 b.c 84p
Samraan (USA) 2 br.c 68p
Scarlet Plume 2 b.f 100p
Serendipity (FR) 2 b.c 85p
Sharaf (IRE) 2 b.c 83p
Ship's Dancer 2 b.f 62p
Singing Patriarch (IRE) 2 b.c 88p
Ski For Gold 2 b.f 76p
State of Caution 2 b.c 76p
St Mawes (FR) 2 ch.c 89p
Tasliya (USA) 2 ch.f 86p
The Swan 2 ch.f 65p
Thracian 2 b.f 92p
Veiled Dancer (IRE) 2 b.f 69p
Wahiba Sands 2 b.g 79p
Orchestra Stall 3 b.g 68p
Salaman (FR) 3 b.c 89p

C. A. DWYER
Prince Zizim 2 b.c 60p

C. R. EGERTON
St Valery 3 b.f 69p

D. R. C. ELSWORTH
Magic Galop (USA) 2 b.c —p

J. M. P. EUSTACE
Magic Mail 2 b.c 71p

J. L. EYRE
Cashmere Lady 3 b.f 75p

A. FABRE, FRANCE
Anziyan (USA) 2 b.c 96p
Loup Solitaire (USA) 2 b.c 113p
Manninamix 2 gr.c 113p
Martiniquais (IRE) 2 ch.c 100p
Miss Tahiti (IRE) 2 b.f 114p
Polar Lights (CAN) 2 b.c 109p
Supreme Commander (FR) 2 b.c 110p
Bobinski 3 br.c 115p
De Quest 3 b.c 120p

J. R. FANSHAWE
Alisura 2 br.f —p
Major Quality 2 b.c 75p
Milford Sound 2 b.c —p
Nunsharpa 2 b.f 65p
Salmis 2 b.f 84p
Seeking Fortune (USA) 2 b.f 75p
Thea (USA) 2 br.f 76p
Wandering Star (USA) 2 b.f —p
Almond Rock 3 b.g 88p
Crespo (IRE) 3 b.c 81p

P. S. FELGATE
Double Splendour (IRE) 5 b.g 74p

M. J. FETHERSTON-GODLEY
Xenophon of Cunaxa (IRE) 2 b.g 83p

J. A. GLOVER
Carburton 2 b.c 91p

J. H. M. GOSDEN
Aerleon Jane 2 ch.f 85p
Annaba (IRE) 2 ch.f 75p
Apple Musashi 2 b.c 101p
Arctiid (USA) 2 b.c 61p
Attarikh (IRE) 2 b.c —p
Awaamir 2 b.f 85p
Badri (USA) 2 b.c —p
Catumbella (USA) 2 ch.f 69p
Dancing Debut 2 b.f 58p
Danesman (IRE) 2 b.c 96p
Daydreamer (USA) 2 b.c —p
Domak Amaam (IRE) 2 b.c 77p
Elashath (USA) 2 b.c —p
Herodian (USA) 2 b.c 81p
Intidab (USA) 2 b.c 90p
Keiko 2 ch.f 69p
Kerry Ring 2 b.f 82P
L'Ami Louis (USA) 2 ch.c 93p
Liefling (USA) 2 b.f —p
Lituus (USA) 2 gr.c —p
Lord of Men 2 ch.c 116p
Misky Bay 2 b.c 61p
Muhandis 2 b.c 67p
Oneforthediteh (USA) 2 gr.f 79p
Pommard (IRE) 2 b.c 90p
Sacho (IRE) 2 b.c 89P
Santillana (USA) 2 ch.c 87p
Sawa-Id 2 b.c —p
Shemozzle (IRE) 2 b.f 71p

Sovereign's Crown (USA) 2 br.c 99p
Waft (USA) 2 ch.f —p
Allemande (IRE) 3 b.c 104p
As You Like It (USA) 3 b.g 77p
Bakers' Gate (USA) 3 b.c 79p
Bibliotheque (USA) 3 ch.f 79p
Daunt 3 b.c 90p
Joyful (IRE) 3 b.f 71p
Melmoth (USA) 3 b.c 68p
Merry Festival (USA) 3 b.f 82p
Miswaki Belle (USA) 3 b.f 73p
Motakabber (IRE) 3 b.c 92P
Proposing (IRE) 3 b.c 98p
Quinwood (USA) 3 ch.f 87p
Starry Eyed 3 b.f 84p

N. A. GRAHAM
Conwy 2 ch.f —p
Fursan (USA) 2 b.c 65p

M. J. GRASSICK, IRELAND
Flame of Athens (IRE) 2 b.c 98p

R. GUEST
My Emma 2 b.f 63p

W. J. HAGGAS
Crimson Rosella 2 b.f —p
Kings Witness (USA) 2 b.c 98p
Missile 2 b.g 83p
Shaamit (IRE) 2 b.c 90p
Shu Gaa (IRE) 2 ch.g 70p
Hand Craft (IRE) 3 b.g 85p
Yeast 3 b.g 80p

B. HANBURY
Caribbean Quest 2 b.f 85p
Jarah (USA) 2 b.c 98p
No Hiding Place 2 ch.c —p
Hugwity 3 ch.c 73p

D. HANLEY, IRELAND
Lidanna 2 b.f 103p

R. HANNON
Catch The Lights 2 b.f 81p
Charlie Chang (IRE) 2 b.c 82p
Clouds Hill (FR) 2 b.c 84p
Dazzling Star 2 gr.f 50p
Flint And Steel 2 b.g 58p
Flying Pennant (IRE) 2 ch.c 59p
Future's Trader 2 b.c —p
Honorable Estate (IRE) 2 b.f 72p
Lomberto 2 b.c 100p
Lonely Leader (IRE) 2 ch.c 86p
Love Bateta (IRE) 2 b.f 60p
Lovely Morning 2 b.f —p
Major Dundee (IRE) 2 b.c 74p
Northern Ballet (IRE) 2 b.f —p
Old Hat (IRE) 2 b.c 68p
Only (USA) 2 ch.c 48p
Ortolan 2 gr.c 95p
Philosopher (IRE) 2 b.c —p
Pigeon Hole 2 b.f —p
Royal Expose (USA) 2 ch.c —p
Wildwood Flower 2 b.f 81p
Wisam 2 b.c 100p
Western Playboy 3 b.g —p

P. W. HARRIS
Arctic Fancy (USA) 2 ch.c 79p
Dreamhill (USA) 2 b.c 70p
Final Stab (IRE) 2 b.c 84p
Fourdaned (IRE) 2 b.c 81p
Melt The Clouds (CAN) 2 ch.c 73p
My Lewicia (IRE) 2 b.f —p
Utmost Zeal (USA) 2 b.c 72p
Delta Soleil (USA) 3 b.c 96p

G. HARWOOD
Hoofprints (IRE) 2 b.c 61p
Northern Fleet 2 b.c 86p

MME C. HEAD, FRANCE
Occupandiste (IRE) 2 b.f 107p

M. J. HEATON-ELLIS
Arterxerxes 2 b.c 63p
Happy Taipan (IRE) 2 b.g 58p
Veni Vidi Vici (IRE) 2 b.c 68p

MAJOR W. R. HERN
Alhaarth (IRE) 2 b.c 126p
Min Alhawa (USA) 2 b.f 87p
Min Elreeh (USA) 2 b.f 68p
Mukhlles (USA) 2 b.c 69p
Naseem Alsahar 2 ch.f 79p
Ragsak Jameel (USA) 2 b.g 59p
Zuhair 2 ch.c 97p

LADY HERRIES
Aethra (USA) 2 ch.f 89p
Fancy Heights 2 b.f 59p
Harbour Dues 2 b.c 65p
Kitty Kitty Cancan 2 b.f —p
Medieval Lady 2 ch.f 78p
Opalette 2 b.f 61p
Roseberry Avenue (IRE) 2 b.c 76p
West Humble 2 ch.f 81p
Moon Magic 3 b.f 62p
Nanton Point (USA) 3 b.g 83p
Elfland (IRE) 4 b.g 89p

A. HIDE
Wolf Cleugh (IRE) 2 b.f 65p
Melody Wheel 3 b.f 60p

B. W. HILLS
Busy Flight 2 b.c 100p
Fly Tip (IRE) 2 b.f 79p
Gold Disc (USA) 2 ch.c 81p
Light Reflections 2 b.c —p
Moody's Cat (IRE) 2 b.f 93p
Nereus 2 b.c 67p
Projection (USA) 2 b.c 89p
Royal Applause 2 b.c 123p
Royal Jade 2 b.f 82p
Ruznama (USA) 2 ch.f 105p
Shawanni 2 gr.f 95p
Sinking Sun 2 gr.f 68p

Statoyork 2 b.c 76p
Story Line 2 ch.f 93p
Tawkil (USA) 2 b.c 99p
Three Hills 2 b.c 82p
Tintara (IRE) 2 b.f 63p
Windyedge (USA) 2 ch.c —p
Charlie Sillett 3 ch.c 87p
Port Augusta (IRE) 3 b.c 66p
Queens Theatre 3 ch.f 68p

J. W. HILLS
Al Abraq (IRE) 2 b.c 89p
Bright Eclipse (USA) 2 br.c —p
Divina Luna 2 b.f —p
Iberian Dancer (CAN) 2 b.f 70p
Mohannad (IRE) 2 b.c 68p

R. HOLLINSHEAD
Lachesis 2 ch.f 55p

G. HOLMES
Gymcrak Gem (IRE) 2 b.f 57p

C. A. HORGAN
Country Thatch 2 b.c 56p

R. F. JOHNSON HOUGHTON
Sassy Street (IRE) 2 b.g —p

LORD HUNTINGDON
Arabian Story 2 gr.c 78p
Doctor Green (FR) 2 b.c —p
Hurtleberry (IRE) 2 b.f 68p
Idle Fancy 2 b.f —p
In The Band 2 b.f 64p
Mongol Warrior (USA) 2 b.c 79p
Note of Caution (USA) 2 b.f 58p
Persuasion 2 b.f —p
Prince Kinsky 2 ch.c 73p
Rash Gift 2 ch.f 78p
Rose Tint (IRE) 2 b.f —p
Sweet Wilhelmina 2 b.f 83p
Beyond Doubt 3 ch.f 82p
Clear Attraction (USA) 3 b.f —p
Snow Princess (IRE) 3 b.f 87p

A. P. JARVIS
Mattimeo (IRE) 2 b.g 66p
Yezza (IRE) 2 b.f 61p

M. A. JARVIS
Blue Iris 2 b.f 104p
Dance Star 2 b.f 75p
Lakeline Legend (IRE) 2 ch.c 77p
Polar Prince (IRE) 2 b.c 91p
Ret Frem (IRE) 2 b.g 54p
Northern Union (CAN) 4 b.c 89p

W. JARVIS
Capstone 2 b.f —p
Farhana 2 b.f 79p
Fog City 2 b.c 71+ a83p
Lay The Blame 2 b.c 90p
Line Dancer 2 b.c 101p
Midnight Blue 2 br.f 83p
Opera 2 ch.f 84p
Suitor 2 b.c —p
Zygo (USA) 3 b.c 72p

J. M. JEFFERSON
Dato Star (IRE) 4 br.g 95p

M. JOHNSTON
Balios (IRE) 2 b.c 56p
Beacontree 2 ch.c —p
Bijou d'Inde 2 ch.c 106p
Chauvelin (IRE) 2 ch.c 57p
Desert Frolic (IRE) 2 b.f 62p
Desert Tiger 2 br.f 90p
Disc of Gold (USA) 2 ch.f —p
Freedom Flame 2 b.f 79p
Marcomir (USA) 2 b.c 76p
Mick's Love (IRE) 2 b.c 102p
Pearl Anniversary (IRE) 2 ch.g —p
Pleasant Surprise 2 b.c 84p
Polar Eclipse 2 ch.c 90p
Tissue of Lies (USA) 2 b.c 79p
Mr Oscar 3 b.g 95p

BOB JONES
Le Teteu (FR) 2 b.c —p

MISS GAY KELLEWAY
Rainy Day Song 2 br.f 61p
Sorbie Tower (IRE) 2 b.c 67p

G. LEWIS
Alakhluki 2 b.f 57p
Civil Liberty 2 b.c 87p
Master Lynx (USA) 2 b.c —p
No Cliches 2 ch.c 83p
Pride of Brixton 2 b.c 83p
Sketchbook 2 ch.g 98p

D. R. LODER
Applaud (USA) 2 ch.f 105p
Blue Duster (USA) 2 b.f 116p
Cornish Snow (USA) 2 br.c 70p
Ground Game 2 b.f 67p
Hal's Pal 2 br.c 89p
Maid For The Hills 2 b.f 101p
Meldorf 2 ch.c 93p
Mountain Holly 2 b.f 69p
Nasrudin (USA) 2 b.c 81p
Naval Gazer (IRE) 2 b.f 75p
Overruled (IRE) 2 b.f 91p
Polska (USA) 2 b.f 84P
Royal Canaska 2 ch.c 81p
Sapiston 2 b.c 90p
South Salem (USA) 2 b.c 107p
St Adele (USA) 2 b.f —p
Wood Magic 2 b.g 96p
Bonne Etoile 3 b.f 94p
Grand du Lac (USA) 3 ch.c 83p

J. MACKIE
Ciracusa (IRE) 3 b.g —p

P. J. MAKIN
Maristax 2 b.f 74p
Welville 2 b.c 87p
Crowded Avenue 3 b.g 101p

K. MCAULIFFE
Accountancy Jewel (IRE) 2 b.f 71p
Roushan 2 ch.c —p

B. A. MCMAHON
Yeoman Oliver 2 b.g —p

B. J. MCMATH
Docklands Limo 2 b.c 54p

T. G. MILLS
Lady Isabell 2 b.f 58p
Proper Blue (USA) 2 b.c 88p

P. MITCHELL
Realms of Glory (IRE) 2 b.c 56p

G. M. MOORE
Time To Tango 2 b.f 57p

D. MORLEY
Giddy 2 b.f —p
Tawafek (USA) 2 br.c 76p
Celeric 3 b.g 100p

W. R. MUIR
Simon Harold 2 b.c —p
Woodbury Lad (USA) 2 ch.c 73p
Orsay 3 b.c 76p

C. MURRAY
Happy Traveller (IRE) 2 b.c 54p

D. J. G. MURRAY SMITH
Jelali (IRE) 2 b.c 68p

W. J. MUSSON
Dauphin (IRE) 2 b.g —p
Broughtons Champ 3 b.g —p

CHARLES O'BRIEN, IRELAND
Golden Orb (IRE) 3 ch.g 111p

W. A. O'GORMAN
Arctic Zipper (USA) 2 gr.g 78p
Roc de Fer (IRE) 2 br.g —p
Wild Palm 3 b.c 74p

F. J. O'MAHONY
Magic Mill (IRE) 2 b.c 82p

G. R. OLDROYD
Mybotye 2 br.c 69p

J. OXX, IRELAND
Aylesbury (IRE) 2 ch.c 99p
Deynawari (IRE) 2 b.c 103p
Sheraka (IRE) 2 b.f 100p
Russian Snows (IRE) 3 b.f 113p

J. PEARCE
Athenry 2 gr.c 87p
Prospector's Cove 2 b.g 77p
Rusk 2 b.c 73p

J. E. PEASE, FRANCE
Spinning World (USA) 2 ch.c 106p
Contare 1 b.f 108p

MRS L. PIGGOTT
Total Aloof 2 b.f 60p

SIR MARK PRESCOTT
Circus Star 2 b.c 65P
Creeking 2 b.f 59p
Farmost 2 ch.g 74p
Frog 2 b.f —p
Last Second (IRE) 2 gr.f 97P
Music Theatre 2 b.c 75p
Night Silence 2 ch.c 53p
Pasternak 2 b.c 77p
Pivotal 2 ch.c 100P
Priolo Prima 2 b.c 90p
Truth 2 b.f 66p
Warming Trends 2 b.g 86p

J. J. QUINN
Bashtheboards 2 b.g —p
Bowlers Boy 2 ch.g —p
Perpetual Light 2 b.f —p

MRS J. R. RAMSDEN
Alpine Joker 2 b.g —p
Ancestral Jane 2 b.f 77p
Appeal Again (IRE) 2 br.g —p
Fairywings 2 b.f 61p
Hawksley Hill (IRE) 2 ch.c —p
Known Secret (USA) 2 ch.c —p
Lawn Order 2 b.f 51p
Oatey 2 ch.f 61p
Privileged 2 ch.g 78p
Sandblaster 2 ch.f 47p
Seattle Alley (USA) 2 b.c 60p
Smarter Charter 2 br.c —p
Strategic Ploy 2 b.f —p

P. RAU, GERMANY
Lavirco (GER) 2 br.c 107p

H. REMMERT, GERMANY
Massada 2 b.f 106p
All My Dreams (IRE) 3 b.c 116p

MRS M. REVELEY
Duo Master 2 b.c 78p
Angus-G 3 br.g 67p
Barton Heights 3 b.g 57p

J-C. ROUGET, FRANCE
Cliptomania (USA) 2 b.c 105p

A. DE ROYER-DUPRE, FRANCE
Ashkalani (IRE) 2 ch.c 111p

DR J. D. SCARGILL
Juba 3 b.f 59p

D. SELVARATNAM
Aswaat (IRE) 3 b.c 69p

D. SEPULCHRE, FRANCE
Luna Wells (IRE) 2 b.f 103p

A. C. STEWART
Ameer Alfayaafi (IRE) 2 b.g —p
Angaar (IRE) 2 b.c 77P

Budby 2 ch.f 64P
Dabka Dancer 2 b.c 89p
Divine 2 b.f 60p
Fahim 2 b.c 74P
Iceni (IRE) 2 b.f —p
Kamari (USA) 2 ch.c 71p
Najm Mubeen (IRE) 2 b.c 79p
Debutante Days 3 ch.f 72p
Fakih (USA) 3 b.c 79p
Hadeyya Ramzeyah 3 b.g 80p

M. R. STOUTE
Bathilde (IRE) 2 ch.f 72p
Bonarelli (IRE) 2 b.c 100p
Cerdan (USA) 2 ch.c 74p
Clerkenwell (USA) 2 b.c 75p
Dance On A Cloud (USA) 2 b.f 76p
Dark Waters (IRE) 2 b.c 82p
Double Leaf 2 b.c 97p
Eastern Paradise 2 b.c 79p
Fort de France (USA) 2 b.c —p
Hidden Oasis 2 b.c 96p
Insatiable (IRE) 2 b.c 93p
Kass Alhawa 2 b.c 76p
Marigliano (USA) 2 b.c 75p
Menoo Hal Batal (USA) 2 b.c 75p
Obsessive (USA) 2 b.f 95p
On Fair Stage (IRE) 2 b.f 67p
Patria (USA) 2 br.f 76p
Promptly (IRE) 2 b.f 80p
Really A Dream (IRE) 2 br.f 74p
River Divine (USA) 2 ch.f 59p
Rocky Oasis (USA) 2 b.c 84p
Rossel (USA) 2 b.c 65p
Sadler's Realm 2 b.c 63p
Sandabar 2 b.c 60p
Shady Link (IRE) 2 b.c 72p
Time Allowed 2 b.f —p
Election Day (IRE) 3 b.c —p
Fujiyama Crest (IRE) 3 b.g 92p
Harbour Island 3 b.c 89p
Pilsudski (IRE) 3 b.c 104p

SAEED BIN SUROOR
Deceive 3 b.f 100p

MRS A. SWINBANK
Tirols Tyrant (IRE) 2 b.g 67p

T. P. TATE
Three Wild Days 3 b.g —p

H. THOMSON JONES
Abir 2 ch.f 68p
Alsahib (USA) 2 b.c 74p
Asmahaan (USA) 2 br.f 65p
Mawjud 2 b.c 84p
Mutamanni (USA) 2 b.c 84p
Rasas (IRE) 3 b.c 97p

C. W. THORNTON
Give Me A Ring (IRE) 2 b.c 66p
Mustang 2 ch.c 62p
Sepoy (IRE) 2 ch.c 82p
Me Cherokee 3 br.f —p

J. A. R. TOLLER
Illuminate 2 b.c 70p
The Dilettanti (USA) 2 br.c —p

M. H. TOMPKINS
Air Wing 2 ch.c 83p
Belmarita (IRE) 2 ch.f —p
Poetry (IRE) 2 gr.f 66p

M. D. I. USHER
Etterby Park (USA) 2 b.g —p

C. F. WALL
Lady Thiang 2 gr.f 70p
Needle Match 2 ch.c —p

P. T. WALWYN
Mua-Tab 2 ch.f 76p
Seirenes 2 b.f 78p
Tawaaded (IRE) 2 ch.f —p

MARTYN WANE
Royal Dome (IRE) 3 b.g 75p

MRS BARBARA WARING
Absolutelystunning 2 br.f —p

J. W. WATTS
Ladykirk 2 b.f 78p

D. K. WELD, IRELAND
Ahkaam (USA) 2 ch.c 102p
Force of Will (USA) 2 ch.c 108p

R. M. WHITAKER
Surprise Mission 3 ch.g 74p

S. C. WILLIAMS
Classic Beauty (IRE) 2 b.f 63p
Classic Eagle 2 b.c 89p
Salsian 2 b.f —p

S. P. C. WOODS
Halebid 2 b.c 69p
Another Time 3 ch.g 79p
Bubble Wings (FR) 3 b.f 71p

G. WRAGG
Anthelia 2 b.f 100p
Charlotte Corday 2 b.f 63p
Don Micheletto 2 b.c 94P
Germano 2 b.c 89P
Henry Island (IRE) 2 ch.c —p
Mezzogiorno 2 b.f 96p
Miss Riviera 2 b.f 84P
Polish Widow 2 b.f 71p
Radiant Star 2 b.c 62p
Sasuru 2 b.c 95p
Shenango (IRE) 2 b.g 65p
Stately Dancer 2 b.f 65p
Alusha 3 b.f 88p
Young Vic 3 b.f —p

M. ZILBER, FRANCE
Danefair 3 b.f 109p

THE TIMEFORM IRISH HANDICAP

Here are listed the Timeform Ratings for every horse that ran on the flat in Ireland, plus a few who were trained there and ran abroad, during the 1995 season. † indicates that the horse appears in commentary or essay form in *Racehorses of 1995*.

Two-Year-Olds

–	Academy House
71p	Accountancy Jewel†
75	Adamant
83	Adjalabad
102p	Ahkaam†
68p	Alaska
77	Al Bashak
–	Allamanda
–	All The One
110	Almaty†
–	Al Shabak
77	Although
77	Alum
94	Amaretto Bay†
–	Amazenus
–	Amazing Sail
–	Amidancing
69p	Analisa
75p	Annagh Belle
–	Another Crab
58	Antithesis
90	Anwaar
64	Apache Park
84	Apache Twist
95+	April The Eighth†
76	Arabian Ransom
84	Archobello
82	Archway Belle
–	Arcus
67	Aristocratique
–	Artique Fish
90	Ashbal
–	Ashford Bridge
74	Ashiions
94	Asmara
–	Astrellino
–	Aughaloora Lass
72	Aughamore
95	Axford†
99p	Aylesbury†
76	Azura
–	Bailenagun
62	Barton Cottage
–	Bellfan
106p	Bijou d'Inde†
–	Bint Shaadi
–	Blending Element
80p	Blue Bit
82	Bluemas
76	Blues Project
–	Bonny
40	Brazen Miss
–	Brickey Beech
83	Brighton Road
65	Broken Rites
72	By Charlie Allen
78	Caca Milis
–	Caer Melyn
–	Cake Contract
–	Calm Beauty
78	Canadian Dream
73p	Canadian Patriot
65	Canadian Project
76	Capellino
77	Carransprawn
–	Cascatelle Bleue
79	Cashel Princess
103	Catch A Glimpse†
73	Catwalk Queen
76	Caudillo
94	Ceirseach†
–	Cento
–	Cheerful Knight
75	Chere Amie
–	Child of Fortune
84p	Chuffed
74	Chuiphoga
–	Cimarosa
–	Ckr Racing
77	Classic Express
90	Classic Fountain
82p	Clear Blue Water
85	Cloudburst
58	Cois Na Farraige
–	Common Affair
92	Common Spirit
41	Comrade Chinnery†
71	Confectioner
68p	Cooraclare
–	Copelands
77p	Cordial Knight
70	Corn Abbey
84p	Cossack Count
79	Countryweave
79p	Courier
79+	Crocodile Shoes†
–	Cross The Sky
–	Crowfort Boy
83	Cuddles
82	Daddy's Hat
57	Daedalin
–	Dame Pique
92	Dance Clear
107	Dance Design†
70	Dance Twister
72	Dancing Bluebell
117	Danehill Dancer†
86	Dathuil
66	Davenport Weekend
71p	Debs Affair
108	Deed of Love†
–	Desert Gift
75	Desert Mountain
60	Deviock
103p	Deynawari†
68	Diamond Project
66	Dieci Anno
–	Dillon's Taxi
–	Dissident Lady
82p	Dissident Prince
83	Don't Dwell
–	Double Impression
88?	Double Oscar†
83	Double Seeker
63p	Dragon's Back†
83	Dr Beat
74	Dreams And Schemes
–	Dream Tycoon
–	Dubai Dolly
76	Dunemer
81	Dunmurry Lass
77	Dunrally Fort
75	Durrah Green
–	Earhart
69p	Easy Definition
–	Emmal
–	Epigram
58	Erin Oileain Acla
75	Erne Project
64	Errant Earl
94	Errazuriz
–	Euro Parade
81p	Ever Bubbly
74	Evriza
78p	Factice
59	Fairly Sharp
–	Fairy Lake
–	Falcon's Fire
75	Fallens
64	Family Project
65	Fast Feather
80	Fast Princess
46	Feelin' Looser
82p	Finest Hour
98p	Flame of Athens†
88	Flaming Feather
–	Flower Show
102+	Flying Squaw†
108p	Force of Will†
78p	French Ballerina
–	Fridolin
82	Friendly Bird
60	Fun Fashion

76p	Gaelic Symphony
–	Gail Gordon
86p	General Allgood
74	Genuine John
72	Gisbella
46	Glenrol
73	Global Walk
63	Golden Reproach
–	Gold Wind
77	Greenhue
–	Green Patriot
76	Grief
77p	Hakone
102	Harghar†
84p	Harveys Point
–p	Health And Wealth
60	Heather's Folly
68	Hello John
79p	Helsingor
65	Henry Otis
80p	Highly Motivated
93	High Target†
88	Hint of Humour
65	Hint-Of-Romance
80p	Hi Plains Drifter
84	His Excellence†
66	Holy Blossom
68	Honeyschoice
76	Honni By
60	Hypnotic Rhythm
87	Iacchus
92	Identify
82	Ilanga
–	Illusions Tom
84	Imagine The Chat
75	In Generosity
70	Inner Peace
–	Jackie John
82	Jalber
80p	Joking Rebuff
72	Jubilee Scholar
70	Kayaliyna
82+	Keal Ryan
80p	Key Change
84	Key To A Million†
68	Khambani
85	Khasib
78	Kilbaha
72	Killary
67	King of Peace
87p	Kingsandvagabonds
76	Kiribati
–	Koko Nor
–	Krasika
58	Krystallos
–	Kurajus
78p	Kuwait Bay
92	Lacinia
–	Lady Goodbye
88p	Lady Joshua†
–	Lady Patrice
78	Lady's Dream
50	Lancaster House
97P	Last Second†
73	Latest Fling
60	Lavender Bloom†
80	Leaving Home
–	Lessons In Love
56+	Lia Fail†
77	Libarchie
103p	Lidanna†
94p	Liprandi
–	Live Comment
81P	Lone Eagle
95	Long Beach
–	Loren Lodge
73	Love Bird†
61	Love Heart
–	Lower The Tone
58	Lucky One
84p	Luna Spectrum
56	Lyrical Look
64	Ma-Ani
80p	Machalini
58	Madame Bergerac
87	Magarah
–	Magical Ivor
74	Magic Combination
–	Maiden Mist
56	Maid To Move
75	Major Crisis
70	Major Hamill
64	Mam'selle Bergerac†
64	Manon du Source
–	Marchaway
63	Marino Street†
–	Marlonette
–	Master Angler
–	Masterly
74p	Matsuri
–	Mayhaps
66	Maytpleasethecourt
71	Megascene
–	Mentelle
90p	Merawang
68	Mind Me Brody
84	Minzal Legend
–	Miss Cyrano
–	Miss Elona
66	Miss Jarmag
60	Miss Margate
85	Misterio
–	Mister Munnelly
95	Mitch
–	Moatfield Girl
–	More In Hope
68	More Risk
72	Mukhif
102	My Melody Parkes†
84	Nakayama Express
–	Nashalong
97	Nashcash
–	Native Eclipse
57	Naxia
94?	Needham Start†
67	New Rain
83	Night Spell
98	No Animosity†
–	Nonamesleft
66	Nord Vente
–	Northern Brook
–	Northern Diamond
67	North of What
–	Nymph In The Ski
66	Oakmont
48	Ody Morody
–	Oh Doe
–	Oh So Reckless
78	One More Spin
–	Onyourown
–	Orange Grouse
88	Orange Walk
67	Orions Treasure
–	Other Options
71	Pancasari
89	Panga
75	Park Petard
92p	Party Poll
–	Peace Dividend
–	Peace Offering
82p	Peace Prize
77	Peace Trail
66	Pebbledash
50	Pecan
–	Pegus Junior
73	Pegwood
85	Penka
–	Perfect Fit
59	Persian Dream
82	Petasus
80	Petticoat Rose
44	Picard
73	Pink Perignon
69+	Pippa Passes
58	Playprint
112	Polaris Flight†
78	Polygueza
–	Power Moves
–	Praise of Peace
83p	Predappio
67	Prelude To Fame
74	Premier Code
76p	Primo Secundus
68	Prince Montelimar
–	Princess Lil
77	Princess Tycoon
–	Princess Zaana
86	Priolina
103p	Priory Belle†
63	Pro Active
–	Promising Routt
86p	Pro Trader
82p	Proud Titania
54	Prove The Point
83	Qualtron
73p	Queenly
53	Queens Counsel
68	Quill Project
55	Quote Unquote
96	Rainbow Blues
85p	Raiyoun
73	Real Guest

93 Red Robin
– Red Rose Walk
77 Red Tonic
79p Reem Fever
65d Reg's Double
84+ Reinhardt†
52 Rekondo
69 Renata's Prince
86p Rescue Time
74p Rhum Dancer
92 Ribot's Secret†
60 Rince Abhann
63 Rita's Killaloe
98 Rithab
– Rivercare
– River of Dreams
67 River Rock
65 Rizzoli
79 Rockcorry Rose
76+ Roi Estate
98 Rouge Rancon†
81 Royal South
– Run Forrest Run
– Run To The Ace
77 Ryazana
88 Sacramento†
88 Safflower
94 Sagar Pride†
80 Sarah's Guest†
68 Sauganash Song
56 Sausalito Girl
65p Sea Idol
73p Sea Leopard
– Secret Hope
73p Secret Magic
– Seiche Raoi
71 Set The Mousetrap
– Shargan
74 Sharpnkeen
– Sharp Outlook
93 Sheffield
100p Sheraka†
74 Sholam
57 Short Shift
– Should I Stay
75 Shunaire
– Sigma Comms
74 Silks of The Field
– Sir Big John
70p Sir Oracle
83p Slayjay
76 Sliabh Bawn
83 Slide By
79p Slightly Simple
92 Slightly Speedy
– Smeraldina
61 Sofyaan
88p Sommar
77 Sonic Tour
64 South Pagoda†
– Souvenier
49+ Soviet Sakti†
– Soviet Town
– Spanish Craft
72 Squire's Occasion
65 Stilly Night
– Stone Head
80p Sun Ballet
– Sunset Alley
99 Sunset Reigns†
96 Super Gift†
76 Suposenitdid
44 Sweet Ciseaux
103 Sweet Robin†
– Sweet September
– Take A Seat
– Tally-Ho-Major
77 Tamani
101 Tamnia†
66p Tarakhel
84p Tarwara
83p Tasdid
– Tazi
62 Teer On Eer
53 The Gent
73+ Therhea†
– The Toddy Tapper
74 Three Rivers
100 Thrilling Day†
53 Tijuana Tango
76 Tikashar
60 Tilbrook
62 Timidjar
68 Tiralle
67 Tirano
86 Tirol Hope
57 Titania's Palace
– Toblino
83 Tossup
80p Touch Judge
– Touchy Subject
93 Tout A Coup
– Travel North
72p Treasure
88 Troysend
66p Truth Or Dare
68 Twosing
72 Typhoon Lad
84 Vanishing Frontier
79 Vice President
86 Vincitore
93p Vivo
85 Wedding Gallery
62 Welsh Project
62 Welsh Thatcher
84p Western Seas
58 Windy Project
66p Wing Partner
80 Winsome Magic
110 Woodborough†
– Wooden Dance
83 Woodren
– Worth Avenue
51 Xavier
83p Xenophon of Cunaxa†
93p Zafzala
83 Zalzie
85 Zampa
86 Zebra Stripes
96 Zelzelah†
56 Zolba

Three-Year-Olds

83 Abbey Player
87p Abbey Street
– Abigail Rose
– Acra Free
– Adalya
118 Adjareli†
– Adrians Dream
59 Against The Clock
107 Ailleacht
87p Akilara
83 Alexanders Way
73 Alina
105 Alisidora
– Alkarlian
– All Apologies
74d Almus
56 Alpine Chime
– Alpine Mist
68 Alpine Villa
– Alva Clare
56 Alzeam
81 Amahsan
74 Amandari
83 American Heat
102 America's Cup
73 Amlah
83 Amontillado
92 Anazara
80 Ancaty
99 Anemone Garden
76 Angel From Heaven
– Anita's Galaxy
120 Annus Mirabilis†
– Another Perk
72 Ansal Boy
58 Antiplano
81 Any Dream
100p Approvance
– Arboe Lady
– Archie
96 Archive Footage
– Arctic Glade
83 Argideen Vale
57 Arif
– Artya
103 Asterita†
– Astro Ruler
69 Ath Cheannaithe
– Auld Scall
64 Auntie Maureen
67 Back For Good
125 Bahri†
60 Bakema
– Ballad of Eire
– Ballinahaun
70 Balmyra
82 Banariya
83 Barbara Cadabra
60 Basil Street

– Battle Rage
87 Bawader†
96 Beating The Buzz
53 Beau Cyrano
82 Belle de Cadix
– Belvoir Belle
72 Be My Folly
62 Benbradagh Glow
72 Ben Bruff
79d Bermuda Dance
– Berry Sharp
– Birdhill
57 Bird In My Hand
93 Black N Brilliant
83 Blitzer
90+ Blue Kestrel
102 Bluffing
– Bold Bequest
76 Bolivar
– Boristova
58 Bourdonner
62 Break For Tee
– Breaktime Treat
67 Bright Lake
57 Bright Project
76 Bronica
84 Brown Reef
61 Brushetta
96 Bukhari
113 Burden of Proof†
64 Caradene
84 Caraiyma
63 Carmel Honeymoon
– Carmenoura
? Carnauba Sword
71 Carraig Topaig
– Carriglegan Beauty
47 Cashflow Crisis
68d Castle Blake
96 Catch The Blues
79 Ceide Dancer
77 Ceili Queen
107 Celladonia
95 Celtic Lore
129 Celtic Swing†
– Centinela
95 Chance For Peace
104 Charillus
68 Chef d'Equipe
107 Cheyenne Spirit†
74 Ckr Sport
120 Classic Cliche†
73 Classic Silk
59 Clonageera
– Clontubrid
– Club Coupe
– Common Lady
– Composin
– Comtesse Miesque
58d Cora-B
– Coral Cottage
118 Court of Honour†
– Crumpet
81 Crystal Bird
60d Cuban Nights†
– Cuckooland
– Cuirassier
– Cultural Icon
106 Damancher
97 Damani
83 Damemill
97 Danaa Minni
78 Danalia
85 Dance Academy
72 Dancing Clodagh
– Dancing Poser
– Dannevang
107 Daraydan†
106 Daryabad
42 Dash To The Phone
64 Da Silva
121 Definite Article†
77 Delightful Chime
77 Dellsboy
75 Desert Haze
79 Desert Lily
121 Desert Style†
57+ Deymiar
58 Difficult Times
61 Digadust
65 Don't Get Caught†
54 Don't Loose Faith
– Don't Rocket
51d Doo Han†
65 Doth Protest
88 Double Colour
115 Double Eclipse†
107 Double Quick†
– Dragonara Lad
36 Dromalane†
57 Dublin Treasure
72d Dulwich Gate
– Dunlewy
– Dunmore Flash
– Dunmore Jenny
87 Earp
72 Easter Heroine
69 Elas Image
– Elle Meme
– Eloquent Way
81 Embellished
– Emmsons Pride
– Ervedya
99 Eva Luna†
– Faheen's Boy
75 Fahs
66 Fair Lane Lady
– Fairy Court
– Fanadiyr
76 Fassan
71 Festival Project
106 Fill The Bill†
66 Final Project
– First Strike
– Flagship Ahoy
75 Flame of Sion
81 Flaunt
99 Fleet Hill†
87 Fleet Petite†
– Floral Emblem
82 Flow Back
49 Forest Lady
– Forest Princess
– Forever Famous
66 For Example
– Formezza
– Framley Garth†
85 Fraser Carey
104 Free To Speak
84 French Project
70 Galloping Guns
57 Garraun Native
75 Garter Royale
– Gay Nineties
98 Gazalani
58 General Jimbo
– Genuine Leader
78 Ghassak
110 Ghostly†
– Gifted Dancer
78 Glamour Model
76 Glasderrymore
79 Glenista
– Glen of Imaal
63? Glounthaune
67 Go Indigo
111p Golden Orb†
48 Grand Crack
74 Greenspan†
73 Guest Performance
70 Haido'hart†
119 Harayir†
– Harry's Express
109 Hasainiya
– Hatalee
40 Hazy Empress
– Hazy Princess
83 Heart of Oak
82 Heavens Gable
– Hibba
69 High In The Clouds
80 Hill of Snow
84 Hill Society
62 Holders Hill
63 Home Port
116 Humbel†
65 Icy Project
61 Ilandra
– Imperial Destiny
112 I'm Supposin†
76 Inaka
82 Inchacooley
73? Indian Outlaw
89 Irish Academy
– Irish Victory
90+ Isla Del Rey
– Jackson's Panther
81 Jack Yeats
– Jahid
84 Jane Digby
62 Jarvey
– Jennyflex

–	Jewel of The Night
107	Johansson
–	Johns Conquerer
–	Johns Tough Lady
95	Journey of Hope
–	Juggling Act
73	Julmat John
79	Just An Illusion
–	Justasec
57	Justice System
96	Just Little
71	Kabrika
102	Kadamann
–	Kafayef
84	Kalyani
67	Kashana
86	Kates Choice
76	Katiymann
64	Katsuko
99	Kayaara
76	Keep Bobbin Up
–	Keep The Pace
79	Kerry Project
103	Khayrawani
111	Khaytada†
–	Khozabad
66	King Puck
77	King's Flagship
79	Kinnincha
65	Kippanour
83	Kookabb
–	Laced Memories
79	Lady Arpel
53	Lady Be Lucky
–	Lady Blayney
–	Lady Bourbon
84	Lady of Dreams
75	Lady Rushmore
66	Lago Lago
–	La Maya
79	Lannkala
–	Laridissa
116	Larrocha†
93+	Lasting Peace
54?	Laura's Own
60	Legal Drama
68	Le Mistral
87	Lenni Lenape
73	Lessons Lass
65	Life Is Precious
84	Life Support
73	Lililo
83	Lilting Air
56	Lingering Melody
74	Lithe Spirit
77d	Live Project†
98	Logstown
–	Loma Linda
85	Looks Good
102	Louis' Queen†
64?	Love Me Please
95d	Loveyoumillions†
86	Loving Contract
67	Lucky Fan
–	Mack Trans
–	Madame Mornay
74	Madeira Man
77	Maelalong
84	Magical Fun
76	Magical Lady
61	Magic Gesture
–	Maiden Bold
105	Manashar
69	Manetti
68	Mannagar
49	Mannoori
–	Marandas Girl
90	Maraniza
88	Marqueta
64	Mary Ellen Best
77	Meaghers
64	Media Miss
110	Mediation†
81	Mendeluci
72	Menoo Who
–	Merry Shiels
72	Metastasio
–	Middleofthenight
71d	Millie's Return
107	Millstream†
65	Mindless Miss
89	Mining Project
94	Mini Project
63d	Minnesota Fats
–	Minor Saint
83	Minstrelina
66	Mirmande
–	Miss April
61	Mister
102	Mister Chippy
–	Mixed Pint
66	Money Mile
51?	Montegna
73	Moon Over Awir†
88	Moscow At Night
–	Mountain Hop
87	Moy Water
71	Mr Buster
–	Mrs Ting
70p	Muffle
80	Muhybh
–	Multipit
72	Multy
–	Mumtaz Queen
107	Munif†
113	Munwar†
107	Musetta†
72d	Mushtari
58	My Blue
–	My Hector
–	Mystic Shadow
78	Nadedge
100p	Nafasiyr
32	Native Cailin
–	Native Gale
–	Native Valentine
113	Nautical Pet†
55	Navan Royal
99	Nayil
87	Nazzareno
72	Nellie's Away
52	New Chapter
37	Niall's Pet
60+	Nightscene†
82	Noels Choice
67	Nominee
–	Nordic Spree
–	Nostalga Rose
59	Notluckytochange
117	Nwaamis†
112	Off'n'away†
91	Oh'cecilia
78	Ormond Jenny
119	Oscar Schindler†
76	Otani
68	Our Call
105	Park Charger
85	Park Cottage
–	Parliament Poise
–	Party Chatter
–	Paulas Choice
84	Peace Process
64	Peirseach
132	Pentire†
83	Perils of Joy
69	Permit Me
69	Persian Danser
72	Persian Mystic
110	Petite Fantasy†
73	Piccanin
89	Pickens
66	Pickerel
82	Pier House
–	Pluckstown
60	Pocket Book
92	Points Pass
50	Poison Ivy
75+	Powder River Grey
80	Pozzoli
–	Premier Event
78	Premier Project
–	Pre Ordained
116	Prince Arthur†
105	Private Line†
81	Probity
86	Propaganda Coup
54	Prophits Pride
101	Propitious
81	Prosaic Star
121	Pure Grain†
–	Queen of Life
73	Queen's Flagship
81	Quiet Counsel
106	Radomsko
102?	Raghida
75	Ralitsa
–	Rathcoffey Dee
101	Rawy
62	Ray River
66	Red Adair
74	Relic Image
–	Re Roi

70 Rescinding Motion
125 Ridgewood Pearl†
81 Rigobertha
87 River Project
56 River Run
92+ Riyama
74 Rockny
87 Rockwood
57 Rodalia
77 Roi Croft
68 Rolling†
51 Roman Fever
53 Roscolvin
– Rosie's Guest
100 Rosillo
86+ Royal Canal
– Royal Gardenia
98+ Royal Premiere
75 Royal Recluse
96 Royal Regatta
41 Runabout
113p Russian Snows†
56 Saborinie
71 Sacred Blossom
71d Sadarah†
65 Salvador
88 Samanid
69 Samina
– Sandra's Pride
77 Sandrine
70 San Michel
95 Sannkaya
76 Saving Bond
71 Sawaaleff
69 Scene One
– Scorpio Boy
44 Sea of Dreams
– Secret Dreamworld
64 Seismic
91 Selatan
58 September Tide
– Sergeant Bill
81 Sesaro
84 Shades of Summer
– Shadowglow
61 Shanid
92 Sharatan
– Sharply Paddy
105 Sharp Point†
– Sharp Poser
84 Shasneeha
77 Shaunies Lady
57 Shayrdia
41 Shazam
– She'll Be Good
– Shelly Baby
120 Shemaran†
– Sheramie
67 Shinkoh Rose
98 Shirdari
71 Shortening Sail
75 Silly View
85 Silvian Bliss
107 Sir Silver Sox†
77 Sir True Blue
67 Skirteen
76d Slaney Project†
39 Slightly Special
85 Smarts Castle
57 Snoozeandyoulose
85 Soaring High
82 Soft Spot
56 So Natural
102 Soreze
69 Sounds Perfect
– Spanky
66 Special Ritual
126 Spectrum†
65 Speed Board
– Squire Danagher
67 Star Club
50d Stitching
106 Storm Ashore
69d Storm Damage
78 Stormy Reply
85 Street View
83 Striesen
– Stylish Trip
107 Subya†
68 Suga Hawk
83 Summer Trysting
73 Susquehanna
65 Swift Cert
84 Swings'n'things
89 Taajreh
80 Tabbassam
100p Taglioni
94 Taibhseach
83d Talina's Law
82 Talk Back†
– Tanavalla
54 Tandridge
102 Tarajan
– Tarandale
87 Tassov
– Teacher Preacher
95 Tea Service
80 Theatreworld
70 Theatrical Wings
75 The Bould Vic
– The Plotter
– Theprincess Manhar
– The South Pole Inn
44 The Squire
93p Tidjani
73 Tiffany Victoria
124 Timarida†
59d Tinbretto
64 Tinker Amelia†
82 Tirols Result
75 Toast The Spreece
– Toledana
– Tom's Merc
101 Tom Tom
72 Trade Dispute
62 Transparent
60 Trench Warfare
77 Trouville Lass
65 True Ballad†
50? Trumped
53d Tuva
108 Two O'Clock Jump†
70p Tycoon Aly
– Unbearable
– Unboxable
105 Union Decree
59? Upper Club
78 Vail Star
122 Valanour†
117 Valley of Gold†
84 Venusia
110 Viaticum†
72 Viking Dream
– Vintners Venture
99p Vinza
69 Violets Wild
– Vistula
– Vivace Maid
71 Voronova
92 Wafir
54 Wanstead
113 Warning Shadows†
73 Wesperada
79 Wey Bridge
69 White Claret
– White Satin
71 White's Island
– Wicken Wonder
111 Wild Bluebell†
121 Winged Love†
77 Winger
– Wissywis
99 With The Fairies†
– Wolver Murphy†
64? Woodland Orchid
78 Wood Leopard
71 Wood Sorrel
96 Wray
96 Yavana's Pace
101 Zabadi
81 Zalara
– Zambrano
87 Zanella

Older Horses

65d Absolute Ruler†
101 Acumen
65 Adjalisa
– Adventurous Scribe
61 Aegean Fanfare
74 Aine's Pet
109 Akhiyar†
46 Alberta Rose
51 Allabomba
– Allaracket
71 All At Night
– Allatrim
96 Allegan
73? All The Vowels
113 Al Mohaajir†
58 Alongside
92 Al Reet
– Alshou

102	Alzianah†
88	Andante
67	An Gabh Dubh
44	Angareb
63	Annadot
–	Annagoes
–	Anna Sophia
69	Annella
62	Another Flyer
35	Another Monk†
92	Another Sky-Lark
90	Antiquity
55	Anusha
–	Anvil Spark
56	Aphrike
92	Arctic Park
58	Arctic Weather
50	Ardee Flo Jo
48	Ardlea House
50	Ashby Hill
71	Assert Star
55	Asta Madera
–	Athy Spirit
45	Aurliano
51	Avalin
70	Aventuriere
77	Avoid The Rush
46	Baby Elegance
–	Back Door Johnny
50	Back To Black
61	Bailiwick Frontier
57+	Bajan Queen
57	Ballinasloe Lad
40	Ballyhook
110	Ballykett Nancy†
89	Ballykett Prince
–	Ballyloop
73p	Balyara
69	Bamapour
–	Banagher Belle
75	Bank Statement
–	Bart Owen
105	Baydur†
76	Beakstown
–	Beau Beauchamp
–	Beaumont House
75	Bellissi
63	Belmartin
–	Be My Hope
68	Bene Merenti
57	Best Before Dawn
56	Betterbebob
63d	Better Folly
54	Better Style
–	Bhavnagar
73	Billy Buzz
115	Bin Ajwaad†
54	Bird's Wing
63	Bizana
–	Black Dale
–	Black Piper
67	Black Queen
40	Blacktrench Lady
56	Blake's Fable
67	Blaze of Honour
93	Blazing Spectacle
82	Bless Me Sister
–	Bluebell Maid
67d	Blues Composer
–	Boardwalker
78	Bob Barnes
–	Bold Encounter
36	Bold Not Beat
54	Bolero Dancer
85	Bolino Star
–	Bo Mullen
82	Boro Eight
–	Boston View
–	Botanic Treasure
55	Bothsidesnow
50	Blackloon Boy
92	Brave Fountain
74	Brave Raider
67	Brazen Angel
–	Brer Fox
79	Brief Reunion
26	Brookville Star
78	Bubbly Prospect
–	Buck The Tide
110	Bunty Boo†
58	Butches Boy
–	Butternut
–	Cangerac
110	Capias†
–	Carmelite Church
–	Carmel's Blush
–	Castleconner
–	Castlesheila
–	Cedar Court
60	Celibate
56	Celticcaro
74	Cen Fath
81	Champagne Hurley
74	Chips Are Down
66	Chuck's Treasure
46d	Ciara Cane
–	Circin Rua
75	Clahada Rose
–	Clancy Nossel
36	Clanfluther
68d	Clanlucky
–	Classical Affair
88	Classic Match
–	Clear Ability
69	Clear Bid
–	Clear Crack
63§	Clear Look†
54	Clodaghs Fancy
–	Cnoc An Riog
45	Cnocma†
54d	Coast Is Clear
80+	Cockney Lad
–	Commander John
48	Command 'n Control
63	Commodity Market
–	Common Sound
–	Cons Princess
57	Coolowen Flash
–	Cormac Lady
–	Cossack Princess
–	Cotton Call
–	Craigary
50d	Creevagh Lass
–	Cregmore Boy
62	Crimson City
84	Cross Question
51	Crucial Move
54	Cullenstown Lady
66	Cult Hero
81	Currency Basket
–	Cyrano's Song
58	Dahlia's Best
109	Dairine's Delight†
–	Dakarna
–	Dalkey Island
–	Damers Duke
115	Dance Turn†
–	Dancing Seer
111	Dancing Sunset†
45	Dancing Vision
59	Darcy's Thatcher
44	Dark Swan
117	Darnay†
64	Dashing Rose
–	Dearmistershatter
47	Derryad
70	Desert Calm
99	Devil's Holiday
105	Diamond Class
–	Diamond Cluster
88	Diamond Display
100	Diligent Dodger
–	Dinka
–	Divinity Run
64	Dona Delle Rose
–	Done Instantly
–	Dont Bug Me
74	Don't Care
35	Do-Tell-Me
72	Double Flutter
110	Double On†
41	Double Strike
–	Drumaaler
–	Drumcairn
60	Duharra
61	Eastern Custom
–	Eastern Fox
–	Ela Koru Mou
63	Ela's Gold
74+	El Caid
58d	El Cyrano
53	Elle A Ted
–	Elle Carvoeiro
–	Elupa
–	Emarrceeveess
–	Enqelaab
–	Entitled Lady
113	Environment Friend†
106	Escarpment†
–	Estradeb
80	Euphoric
–	Ever So Bold

–	Exhibition Prince
70	Fabriano
–	Fairy Music
–	Fairy Strike
83	Fairy Water
45	Fame And Fantasy
62	Fancy Boots
64	Father Hayes
79	Faydini
–	Feathered Gale
–	Ferrycarrig Hotel
32	Fill My Glass
–	Fill The Sack
56	Final Reminder
73	Five Point Five
119	Flagbird†
–	Flagship Royal
–	Flash of Speed
79	Fleeting Vision
–	Flicker of Hope
–	Fohenagh Star
63?	Fontenoy
84	Force Seven
–	Fornido
–	Fotolights
112	Fraam†
132	Freedom Cry†
48	Freedom's Flame
76	Friends of Gerald
–	Further Notice
79	Gaily Running
78	Gale Toi
70d	Gallic Victory†
68	Gallopen Garry
72	Galyph
66	Garaiyba
–	Genevieve Fleur
–	George Ashford
50	Gerrydardis
97	Ger's Royale
–	Geva Witch
90	Glacial Arctic
64	Glad You Asked Me
51	Glance Card
–	Glenshane Pass
67	Glowing Lines
–	Golden Horizion
78	Gospel Singer
77	Graceful Resign
–	Grand Tour
55	Granny Bowly
–	Grecian Lady†
–	Halton
93	Hamseh
62	Haunting Angle
41	Hawaian Tasca
–	Heathfield
87	Heist
59?	Helen Belle
62	Helen's Quay
38	Hello Excuse Me
–	Henry Arklow
125	Hernando†
–	Higher Ground
70	Hi Handsome
–	Hilton Heights
81	Holiway Star
85	House Music
49	Huncheon Chance
73	Huraymila
114	Hushang†
–	Iada
44§	Icy Hot
85	Ideal Plan
73	Idiots Venture
111	Idris†
89	If You Say Yes
96	Imperial Bailiwick†
73	Imposing Time
–	Inauguration
–	Indiana Gold
38	Innovative
–	Instant Joy
–	Irelands Gale
–	Irish Wedding
–	Island Rock
59	Island Vision
–	Isle of Pines
109	Ivory Frontier†
–	Ivory Reef
94	Jakdul
69?	Jazzy Refrain
72	Jenbro
–	Jenzsoph
49	Jingling Silver
75	Jomacoon
45	Josh's Ben
47	Joyful Music
70	Jumped Bail
77	Jupiter Jimmy
–p	Justaway
118	Just Happy†
80	Kakashda
–	Karawara
63	Kelly's Pearl
53	Kentucky Baby
48	Kephren
–	Kept Lady
–	Kerryhead Girl
54	Kess
110	Khamaseen†
81	Kharasar
99	Kilconnel
56	Kilmood Lass
–	Kilspindie
98	Kiltimony
70	Kimanicky
79	King Sancho
81+	King Wah Glory
–	Knight of Vision
57?	Ko Samui
94	Krayyalei
37	Kuda Chantik
86	Kurdistan†
–	La Berta
79	Ladies Gallery
63	Lady Noble
100	Lake Kariba
107	Lap of Luxury†
–	La Veine
–	Leading Time
71	Legal Aim
72	Leggagh Lady
–	Leopardess
58	Less Hassle
59	Let It Ride
–	Lignumvitae
–	Limaheights
79	Limbo Lady
–	Little Buck
78	Little Joe
81	Lock's Heath
–	Look Nonchalant
38	Lord Barnard†
75	Lord Bentley
?	Loshian
66	Loughmogue
–§	Lough N Uisce
77	Louises Fancy
40	Love And Porter
54	Lowlack
66	Ludden Lady
64+	Luzarches
–	Lyric Player
–	Mabes Town
68	Mabsoot
84	Macgillycuddy
80	Madaraka
44	Magic Don
108	Magic Feeling
–	Magic Royale
–	Magnificent Oak
–	Magnum Star
–	Mahhy
57	Maid of Glenduragh
67	Main Refrain
59	Majestic John
58	Majestic Mind
94	Majestic Role†
81?	Make An Effort
75d	Make That Call
61	Mangans Hill
75	Man of Arran
37d	Marian Year
66	Martin Tom
69?	Maryjo
65	Masai Warrior
60	Mascot
–	Master Adam
–	Master Joey
36	Master Work
–	Matchless Prince
45	Mazuma
–	McKellar†
46	Megan's Dream
84	Meglio Che Posso
49?	Mejeve
63	Mercy Bien
84	Metroella
–	Micks Delight
65	Midushi
38	Millenium Lass

–	Millers Mill
114	Millyant†
67	Miltonfield
70	Minatina
55	Miss Gatsby
83	Miss Kristin
77	Miss Merenti
91	Miss Potter
98	Miss Provider
105	Mistertopogigo†
111	Mistle Cat†
79	Model Show
108	Mohaajir†
–	Moments To Care
80	Monica's Choice
99+	Montelado
122	Moonax†
85	Moonbi Range
53	Moorefield Girl
57	More Justice
–	Morloch
48	Morning Nurse
53	Morning Sarge
55	Mountain Bloom
51	Moussahim
116	Mr Martini†
49	Mrs Barton
96	Mubadir
–	Muir Station
57	Muscovy Duck
78d	Musical Sunset
77	Mutamanni
–	My Ambassador
59	My Gossip
28	My Hall Door
84	Mystery Tune
67	Mystical City
64	Mystic Ring
77	My Trelawny
69	My Trivet
73	Nabeel
45	Na Huibheachu
–	Nancys Wood
53	Nannaka
–	Native Island
76	Native Joy
62	Native Portrait
64	Near Gale
119	Needle Gun†
80	Never Back Down
58	Never Told
52	New Legislation
58	New Rochelle
–	Neykari
–	Nice And Simple
112	Nijo†
–	Niord
–	Nishaya
–	Niyampour
84	Noble Choice
–	Noble Shoon
71	No Compromise
–	No Diamond
68	No Dunce
–	No News
63	Nordic Air
97	Nordic Brief
81	Nordic Flavour
–	Nordic Halo
50	Nordic King
105	Nordic Oak
–	Nordic Queen
–	Nordic Race
47	Nordic Saint
59	Nordic Sensation
59	Nordic Thorn
–	Nordic Waters
59	Noreaster
–	North Caramel
68	Northern Bars
54	Northern Fancy
?	Northern Hide
67	Northern Slope
89p	Northern Union†
66	No Tag
–	Nuit Des Temps
–	Oak Court
–	Oakland Bridge
52	Oakler
–	Oaks Pride
64+	Oh So Grumpy
–	Old Archives
–	Omey Island
93	One False Move
71	One Man Band
68	Open Market
82	Opulent
–	Orbis
66	Osvaldo
90	Out In The Sun
–	Owenbwee
99	Ozette
107	Palacegate Episode†
74	Paliapour
–	Parcacurry Pete
67	Parskint
85	Penndara
76	Pennine Tune
100	Persian Creek
–	Persian Halo
102?	Peruke
–	Phardanaire
66	Phardy
–	Pharella
–	Plough The Lea
–	Pokono Trail
82	Political Domain
65	Porte Des Iles
–	Porterstown Boy
103	Port Lucaya†
–	Port Noble
64	Port Queen
–	Power Steering
–	Practician
61	Prate Box
–	Pre-Eminent
116	Prince of Andros†
54	Printout
–	Pristine Gale
72+	Private Encore
75	Ptarmigan Lodge
88	Quintiliani
–	Radical Action
–	Raloo
–	Rates Relief
40	Rathnally Star
67	Reasilvia
–	Red Remedy
80	Regal Domain
38	Regal Pretender
–	Respondtochallange
76	Return Again
112	Richard of York†
113	Ridgewood Ben†
–	Rin Awa
–	Rising Waters
–	Rocklands Cottage
53	Rock Pool
85	Rogerdor
104	Roger The Butler†
–	Rolands Girl
67	Roman Forum
93	Rondelli
–	Ros Castle
96	Rosie's Mac
48	Roundwood Rose
111	Royal Ballerina†
72	Royal Crimson
–	Royal Insignia
64	Royal Rosy
75	Royal Thimble
79	Rupert Belle
–	Rupestrian
60	Rustic-Ort
–	Rutabaga
66	Rye Fontaine
95	Saibot†
–	Saint Hilda
–	Salamiste
–	Salience
–	Salmon Eile
76	Salmon River
–	Samaria
64	Sambara
64	Sand Or Stone
49	Script
–	Sea Fisher
–	Sea Gale
54	Secret War
69	Seek The Faith
–	Sender Victorious
38	Sensitive King
55	Serrana Bank
51	Shahnaad
80	Shaihar
77	Shanamara
73	Shanrue
95	Sharp Review†
30	Sheslookinatme
57	Shindarar
–	Shinora
53	Shirwan

63	Shoof Althahab
37	Showboat Melody
–	Sign of Peace
–	Silver Sharp
–	Silver Wisp
37	Sir Alwah
82	Skipo
–	Skittin
65	Slaney Glow
53	Slightly Shy
65	Smoggy Spray
88	Snowing†
–	Solar Attraction
–	Songs of Innocence
61	Soralena
44	Southern Rule
–	Sovereign Choice
86	Sovetsky
67	Space Trucker
75	Sparkly Girl
35	Spinning A Yarn
76	Square Deal
–	Stapleford Lass
102	State Crystal
79	State Princess
61	Steel Mirror
–	Stevie Be
58d	Strangford Lough
122	Strategic Choice†
49	Strawberry Belle
66	Strawtaldi
–	Stretch
81	Subarashii
–	Subtle Touch
59	Suite City Lass
61d	Sundance Madera
–	Super Flame
57	Super Midge
–	Super Shannen
–	Super Trig
–	Supervene
–	Sweetest Thing
90	Sweet Nasha
–	Sweet Realm
19	Swift Pal
57	Swinford Swinger
57	Switched
–	Tabu Lady
61	Taganini
72	Taidja
–	Takahashi
85	Take No Chances
–	Tales of Hearsay
–	Tanhoney
–	Tannoor
65	Templeroan Prince
27	Tender Lass
20	Teresian Girl
44	Texas Friday
52	Thatch And Gold
71	The Augustinian
70	The Barracuda
90	The Bower
74	The Carrig Rua
–	The Keegster
41	The Lad
–	The Lady's Knight
61	The Mardyke
–	The Odd Time
109§	The Puzzler†
57	This Is My Life
76	Three Musketeers
–	Three Stepstoheven
76	Tiger Bittern
32	Time Is Up
77	Timiniya
87	Timourid
55	Tinco Paleno
50d	Tinerana Memories
–	Tirmizi
–	Titled Dancer
–	Toddy Mark
81	Tomos
–	Top Hen
–	Top State
63§	Touching Moment
109	Tourandot
51	Tranquil Beauty
76+	Treble Bob
–	Trickana
89	Trigger Happy John
–	Trolly Dolly
100p	Tropical Lake
67	Trufit
–	Tryfirion
–	Tullerolli
94	Two Shonas
46	Tymoole
26	Ultra Magic
–	Unabashed
71	Up She Flew
–	Up The Junction
50	Urban Dancing
–	Valamir
35	Veritable Gallery
–	Very Little
73	Vicar Street
120	Vintage Crop†
52	Vistage
–	Viva Vita
43	Von Carty
–	Wadablast
59	Waqar
–	Warthill Whispers
61	Waterloo Ball
–	Waterloo Lady
38	Wee Dougal
–	Welcome Express
–	Welsh Royal
–	Wesbest
–	Whatt Ya Doin
–	Wherewilitall End
–	White Wine
54	Wicklow Way
–	Wild Impulse
–	Winged Knight
–	Wings of Boa
–	Winning Willie
95	Winter Belle
–	Without Equal
114	Wizard King†
–	Wollongong
73	Woody
–	Yellow Princess
79	Zabargar
–	Zalewska
63d	Zara's Birthday
–	Zara Zareen
–	Zavaleta
–	Zebba
66	Zico
97	Ziggy's Dancer†
113	Zilzal Zamaan†
63	Zoe Baird

SELECTED BIG RACES 1995

Prize money for racing abroad has been converted to £ sterling at the exchange rate current at the time of the race. The figures are correct to the nearest £.

LONGCHAMP Sunday, Apr 2 SOFT

1	**Prix d'Harcourt (Gr 2) (4yo+) £37,879**		1¼m	
	FREEDOM CRY *AFabre,France* 4-8-11 OPeslier	12/5cp		1
	PELDER (IRE) *PAKelleway,GB* 5-8-11 LDettori	76/1	nk	2
	TUESDAY'S SPECIAL (USA) *AFabre,France* 5-8-11 TJarnet	12/5cp	1½	3
	Green Tune (USA) *MmeCHead,France* 4-9-4 ODoleuze	66/10	½	4
	Millkom *J-CRouget,France* 4-9-4 JDubosc	7/5f	sn	5
	Nononito (FR) *JLesbordes,France* 4-8-11 GMosse	72/10	1½	6
	Alderbrook *MrsJCecil,GB* 6-9-1 PaulEddery	59/10	sh	7
	Suave Tern (USA) *JEHammond,France* 4-8-11 JReid	18/1	4	8
	Marildo (FR) *DSmaga,France* 8-9-4 (b) GGuignard	10/1	1	9
	Truly A Dream (IRE) *RCollet,France* 4-8-11 WMongil	23/1	1	10

Mr Daniel Wildenstein 10ran 2m12.10

NEWBURY Saturday, Apr 22 GOOD

2	**Tripleprint Greenham Stks (A) (Gr 3) (3yo c+g) £21,840**		7f	
	CELTIC SWING *LadyHerries* 3-9-0 KDarley (7)	4/9f		1
	BAHRI (USA) *JLDunlop* 3-9-0 WCarson (5)	14/1	1¼	2
	MOON KING (IRE) *RHannon* 3-9-0 WRSwinburn (9)	16/1	9	3
	Peace Envoy *HRACecil* 3-9-0 PatEddery (2)	9/1	½	4
	Rambrino *PWChapple-Hyam* 3-9-0 JReid (1)	16/1	1½	5
	Henry Koehler *CEBrittain* 3-9-0 MRimmer (6)	100/1	2½	6
	Knight Commander (USA) *RHannon* 3-9-0 LDettori (4)	33/1	3½	7
	Bishop of Cashel *JRFanshawe* 3-9-0 DHarrison (8)	12/1	5	8
	Art of War *RCharlton* 3-9-0 JWeaver (3)	12/1	7	9

Mr P. D. Savill 9ran 1m24.31

LONGCHAMP Sunday, Apr 30 HEAVY

3		**Prix Ganay (Gr 1) (4yo+ c+f) £63,775**		1¼m110y	
	1	PELDER (IRE) *PAKelleway,GB* 5-9-2 LDettori	13/1		1
	1	ALDERBROOK *MrsJCecil,GB* 6-9-2 PaulEddery	36/1	3	2
		RICHARD OF YORK *AFabre,France* 5-9-2 SGuillot	21/10cp	1½	3
	1	Freedom Cry *AFabre,France* 4-9-2 OPeslier	21/10cp	¾	4
		Hernando (FR) *JEHammond,France* 5-9-2 CAsmussen	6/4f	¾	5
		Partipral (USA) *MDelcher-Sanchez,Spain* 6-9-2 GMosse	94/10	½	6
	1	Tuesday's Special (USA) *AFabre,France* 5-9-2 TJarnet	11/2	1½	7
		Right Win (IRE) *RHannon,GB* 5-9-2 PatEddery	18/1	8	8
	1	Marildo (FR) *DSmaga,France* 8-9-2 GGuignard	16/1	3	9
	1	Millkom *J-CRouget,France* 4-9-2 JDubosc	29/10	5	10

Mr Osvaldo Pedroni 10ran 2m20.70

SAINT-CLOUD Monday, May 1 HEAVY

4		**Prix du Muguet (Gr 2) (4yo+) £37,975**		1m	
	1	GREEN TUNE (USA) *MmeCHead,France* 4-9-4 ODoleuze	6/5cpf		1
		BIN AJWAAD (IRE) *BHanbury,GB* 5-8-11 PatEddery	34/10	3	2
		KALDOUNEVEES (FR) *JEHammond,France* 4-8-11 CAsmussen	3/1	3	3
		Port Lucaya *DRLoder,GB* 5-9-4 JWeaver	24/1	5	4
		Moonlight Dance (USA) *AFabre,France* 4-9-1 OPeslier	11/1	hd	5
		Scandinavian (FR) *NPelat,France* 4-8-11 GGuignard	12/1	4	6
		Dernier Empereur (USA) *AFabre,France* 5-9-4 SGuillot	64/10	4	7
		Simply Tricky (USA) *MmeCHead,France* 4-8-11 RLibert	6/5cpf	1½	8

Mr J. Wertheimer 8ran 1m48.10

NEWMARKET Friday, May 5 GOOD to FIRM (Rowley Mile Course)

5	**Madagans Jockey Club Stks (A) (Gr 2) (4yo+) £32,589**		1½m	
	ONLY ROYALE (IRE) *LMCumani* 6-8-11 LDettori (5)	4/1		1

	TIKKANEN (USA) *JEPease,France* 4-9-0 CAsmussen (3)	2/1f	nk	2
	TIME STAR (USA) *PFICole* 4-9-0 TQuinn (7)	7/1	2½	3
	Sacrament *MRStoute* 4-8-12 WRSwinburn (6)	7/2	½	4
	Alriffa *RHannon* 4-8-9 (b) PatEddery (2)	13/2	1¾	5
	Garden of Heaven (USA) *CEBrittain* 6-8-9 MJKinane (1)	25/1	4	6
	Wayne County (IRE) *GFierro* 5-8-9 (v) MWigham (4)	100/1	½	7

Mr Frank Stronach 7ran 2m31.26

NEWMARKET Saturday, May 6 GOOD to FIRM (Rowley Mile Course)

6 Madagans 2000 Guineas Stks (A) (Gr 1) (3yo c+f) £117,912 — 1m

	PENNEKAMP (USA) *AFabre,France* 3-9-0 TJarnet (11)	9/2		1
2	CELTIC SWING *LadyHerries* 3-9-0 KDarley (7)	4/5f	hd	2
2	BAHRI (USA) *JLDunlop* 3-9-0 WCarson (1)	14/1	2	3
	Pipe Major (IRE) *PCHaslam* 3-9-0 JWeaver (8)	50/1	2	4
	Nwaamis (USA) *JLDunlop* 3-9-0 RHills (5)	40/1	¾	5
	Diffident (FR) *AFabre,France* 3-9-0 MJKinane (4)	6/1	3	6
	Painter's Row (IRE) *PWChapple-Hyam* 3-9-0 JReid (9)	14/1	2½	7
	Chilly Billy *MrsJRRamsden* 3-9-0 KFallon (6)	33/1	½	8
	Silca Blanka (IRE) *MRChannon* 3-9-0 RHughes (2)	200/1	3½	9
	Zeb (IRE) *BAMcMahon* 3-9-0 TIves (3)	100/1	1¼	10
	Green Perfume (USA) *PFICole* 3-9-0 TQuinn (10)	25/1	3½	11

Sheikh Mohammed 11ran 1m35.16

NEWMARKET Sunday, May 7 GOOD to FIRM (Rowley Mile Course)

7 Madagans 1000 Guineas Stks (A) (Gr 1) (3yo f) £110,791 — 1m

	HARAYIR (USA) *MajorWRHern* 3-9-0 RHills (2)	5/1		1
	AQAARID (USA) *JLDunlop* 3-9-0 WCarson (13)	3/1f	1½	2
	MOONSHELL (IRE) *SaeedbinSuroor* 3-9-0 LDettori (6)	5/1	¾	3
	Hoh Magic *MBell* 3-9-0 MHills (15)	16/1	2	4
	Epagris *HRACecil* 3-9-0 WRyan (1)	8/1	½	5
	Macoumba (USA) *MmeCHead,France* 3-9-0 FHead (10)	13/2	1½	6
	Gay Gallanta (USA) *MRStoute* 3-9-0 WRSwinburn (11)	10/1	sh	7
	Myself *PWChapple-Hyam* 3-9-0 JReid (14)	8/1	1	8
	Bring On The Choir *RBoss* 3-9-0 KDarley (4)	150/1	sh	9
	Autumn Affair *CEBrittain* 3-9-0 BDoyle (9)	40/1	¾	10
	Queenfisher *RHannon* 3-9-0 BRouse (3)	150/1	½	11
	Menas Gold *SDow* 3-9-0 TQuinn (5)	200/1	nk	12
	Fleet Hill (IRE) *MRChannon* 3-9-0 RHughes (12)	100/1	1½	13
	All Time Great *LMCumani* 3-9-0 JWeaver (7)	40/1	4	14

Mr Hamdan Al Maktoum 14ran 1m36.72

LONGCHAMP Sunday, May 14 GOOD to SOFT

8 Dubai Poule d'Essai Des Pouliches (Gr 1) (3yo f) £127,551 — 1m

	MATIARA (USA) *MmeCHead,France* 3-9-2 FHead	26/10f		1
	CARLING (FR) *MmePatBarbe,France* 3-9-2 TThulliez	96/10	ns	2
	SHAANXI (USA) *ELellouche,France* 3-9-2 OPeslier	37/10	2	3
	Smolensk (USA) *AFabre,France* 3-9-2 TJarnet	51/10	2	4
	Collecta (FR) *JEHammond,France* 3-9-2 ESaint-Martin	45/1	nk	5
	Ghostly (IRE) *PBary,France* 3-9-2 DBoeuf	23/1	1½	6
	Vadlamixa (FR) *AFabre,France* 3-9-2 SGuillot	35/1	½	7
7	Hoh Magic *MBell,GB* 3-9-2 MFenton	10/1	1½	8
	Tirolling (IRE) *JForesi,France* 3-9-2 FSanchez	80/1	sn	9
	Tereshkova (USA) *AFabre,France* 3-9-2 TGillet	58/10cp	¾	10
	Fairy Path (USA) *DSmaga,France* 3-9-2 PatEddery	29/1	nk	11
	Deceive *SaeedbinSuroor,GB* 3-9-2 LDettori	58/10cp	¾	12
	Piquetnol (USA) *JEHammond,France* 3-9-2 CAsmussen	83/10	¾	13
	Nuriva (USA) *SaeedbinSuroor,GB* 3-9-2 MJKinane	58/10cp	¾	14
	Take Liberties *AFabre,France* 3-9-2 PaulEddery	45/1	¾	15
	Chrysalu *NClement,France* 3-9-2 GMosse	42/1	2½	16

Ecurie Aland 16ran 1m42.40

9 Dubai Poule d'Essai Des Poulains (Gr 1) (3yo c) £127,551 — 1m

	VETTORI (IRE) *SaeedbinSuroor,GB* 3-9-2 LDettori	9/2cp		1
	ATTICUS (USA) *MmeCHead,France* 3-9-2 ODoleuze	6/4cpf	sn	2
	PETIT POUCET *NClement,France* 3-9-2 CAsmussen	36/10	2	3
	Lyphard's Honor (FR) *AFabre,France* 3-9-2 TJarnet	21/10	2½	4

Bene Erit (USA) *CLaffon-Parias,France* 3-9-2 FHead 14/1 4 5
General Monash (USA) *PWChapple-Hyam,GB* 3-9-2 JReid 10/1 sn 6
Viva Nureyev (USA) *AFabre,France* 3-9-2 SGuillot 9/2cp 10 7
Sea Gone (USA) *MmeCHead,France* 3-9-2 RLibert 6/4cp 6 8

Maktoum Al Maktoum / Godolphin 8ran 1m40.40

YORK Thursday, May 18 GOOD

10 Yorkshire Cup (A) (Gr 2) (4yo+) £51,963 1m5f194y

MOONAX (IRE) *SaeedbinSuroor* 4-9-0 PatEddery (1) 11/4f 1
PARTHIAN SPRINGS *JHMGosden* 4-8-9 LDettori (6) 7/2 1¼ 2
SHAMBO *CEBrittain* 8-8-9 BDoyle (3) 8/1 nk 3
Double Trigger (IRE) *MJohnston* 4-8-9 JWeaver (4) 3/1 nk 4
Further Flight *BWHills* 9-8-9 MHills (8) 12/1 3½ 5
Bold Gait *JRFanshawe* 4-8-9 DHarrison (2) 6/1 1¼ 6
Golden Ball (IRE) *MRStoute* 4-8-9 WRSwinburn (7) 10/1 2 7

Godolphin 7ran 2m58.89

11 Duke of York Stks (A) (Gr 3) (3yo+) £22,242 6f

LAKE CONISTON (IRE) *GLewis* 4-9-4 PatEddery (4) 8/11f 1
SO FACTUAL (USA) *SaeedbinSuroor* 5-9-0 LDettori (2) 7/2 3 2
BRANSTON ABBY (IRE) *MJohnston* 6-8-11 JWeaver (7) 12/1 3½ 3
6 Chilly Billy *MrsJRRamsden* 3-8-10 KFallon (5) 13/2 sh 4
6 Zeb (IRE) *BAMcMahon* 3-8-4 JFortune (1) 33/1 2 5
Raah Algharb (USA) *MRStoute* 3-8-10 WRSwinburn (6) 14/1 6 6
Princely Hush (IRE) *MBell* 3-8-10 MFenton (3) 14/1 3½ 7

Highclere Thoroughbred Racing Ltd 7ran 1m11.52

NEWBURY Sunday, May 21 GOOD to FIRM

12 Juddmonte Lockinge Stks (A) (Gr 1) (4yo+) £70,210 1m

SOVIET LINE (IRE) *MRStoute* 5-9-0 WRSwinburn (4) 2/1f 1
YOUNG ERN *SDow* 5-9-0 TQuinn (5) 7/2 2 2
MISSED FLIGHT *CFWall* 5-9-0 GDuffield (3) 3/1 2½ 3
Mutakddim (USA) *JHMGosden* 4-9-0 GHind (2) 14/1 ½ 4
Muhtarram (USA) *JHMGosden* 6-9-0 RHills (1) 3/1 5 5

Maktoum Al Maktoum 5ran 1m36.96

CURRAGH Sunday, May 21 GOOD to FIRM

13 First National Building Society Irish 2,000 Guineas (Gr 1) (3yo c+f) 1m
£133,367

SPECTRUM (IRE) *PWChapple-Hyam,GB* 3-9-0 JReid (6) 10/3 1
ADJARELI (IRE) *JOxx,Ireland* 3-9-0 JPMurtagh (2) 9/1 1 2
6 BAHRI (USA) *JLDunlop,GB* 3-9-0 WCarson (8) 11/8f sh 3
Burden of Proof (IRE) *CharlesO'Brien,Ireland* 3-9-0 CRoche (7) 12/1 4½ 4
Prince Arthur (IRE) *PWChapple-Hyam,GB* 3-9-0 PatEddery (5) 8/1 ½ 5
Oscar Schindler (IRE) *KPrendergast,Ireland* 3-9-0 WJSupple (4) 16/1 sh 6
6 Nwaamis (USA) *JLDunlop,GB* 3-9-0 MJKinane (9) 13/2 hd 7
Celladonia (IRE) *JSBolger,Ireland* 3-9-0 KJManning (3) 50/1 1½ 8
I'm Supposin (IRE) *KPrendergast,Ireland* 3-9-0 SCraine (1) 100/1 10 9

Lord Weinstock & The Hon Simon Weinstock 9ran 1m40.30

CURRAGH Saturday, May 27 GOOD

14 Airlie/Coolmore Irish 1,000 Guineas (Gr 1) (3yo f) £87,306 1m

RIDGEWOOD PEARL *JOxx,Ireland* 3-9-0 CRoche (2) 9/4 1
WARNING SHADOWS (IRE) *CEBrittain,GB* 3-9-0 MJKinane (4) 9/1 4 2
KHAYTADA (IRE) *JOxx,Ireland* 3-9-0 JPMurtagh (1) 8/1 1 3
8 Ghostly (IRE) *PBary,France* 3-9-0 CAsmussen (6) 14/1 1½ 4
7 Harayir (USA) *MajorWRHern,GB* 3-9-0 WCarson (8) 11/10f 1½ 5
7 Fleet Hill (IRE) *MRChannon,GB* 3-9-0 CRutter (5) 20/1 3 6
Mediation (IRE) *JOxx,Ireland* 3-9-0 PVGilson (7) 16/1 1½ 7
Park Charger *APO'Brien,Ireland* 3-9-0 SCraine (10) 25/1 1 8
Taibhseach (USA) *JSBolger,Ireland* 3-9-0 JAHeffernan (3) 50/1 ¾ 9
Ailleacht (USA) *JSBolger,Ireland* 3-9-0 KJManning (9) 50/1 10 10

Mrs Anne Coughlan 10ran 1m43.90

BADEN-BADEN Sunday, May 28 SOFT

15 **Grosser Preis Der Wirtschaft (Gr 2) (4yo+) £72,399** 1m3f

3	FREEDOM CRY *AFabre,France* 4-9-4 SGuillot	43/10	1
3	ALDERBROOK *MrsJCecil,GB* 6-9-6 PaulEddery		¾ 2
	LANDO (GER) *HJentzsch,Germany* 5-9-6 ATylicki		½ 3
	Aratikos (GER) *HBlume,Germany* 4-9-0 OSchick		1¼ 4
	Kornado *ALowe,Germany* 5-9-4 MRimmer		1½ 5
	Monsun (GER) *HJentzsch,Germany* 5-9-6 PSchiergen		9 6
	Bad Bertrich (IRE) *ALowe,Germany* 4-9-4 AHelfenbein		8 7
	Embarcadero (GER) *HJentzsch,Germany* 7-9-0 SEccles		12 8
	Theophanu (USA) *HRemmert,Germany* 4-8-12 KWoodburn		48 9

Mr Daniel Wildenstein 9ran 2m22.17

LONGCHAMP Sunday, May 28 GOOD

16 **Prix d'Ispahan (Gr 1) (4yo+ c+f) £64,267** 1m1f55y

4	GREEN TUNE (USA) *MmeCHead,France* 4-9-2 ODoleuze	8/5cpf	1
3	PELDER (IRE) *PAKelleway,GB* 5-9-2 PatEddery	19/10	sh 2
3	MARILDO (FR) *DSmaga,France* 8-9-2 (b) GGuignard	18/1	2½ 3
	Thames (FR) *LAudon,France* 4-9-2 FHead	24/1	2 4
	Agathe (USA) *AFabre,France* 4-8-13 OPeslier	89/10	ns 5
	Flagbird (USA) *SaeedbinSuroor,GB* 4-8-13 CAsmussen	84/10	½ 6
4	Dernier Empereur (USA) *AFabre,France* 5-9-2 TJarnet	64/10	½ 7
4	Simply Tricky (USA) *MmeCHead,France* 4-9-2 NGuesdon	8/5cpf	6 8
	Del Deya (IRE) *JHMGosden,GB* 5-8-13 LDettori	79/10	10 9

Mr J. Wertheimer 9ran 1m53.70

SANDOWN Monday, May 29 GOOD to FIRM

17 **Tripleprint Temple Stks (A) (Gr 2) (3yo+) £38,075** 5f6y

	MIND GAMES *JBerry* 3-8-8 JCarroll (2)	10/11f	1
	MILLSTREAM (USA) *MJohnston* 3-8-5 MJKinane (1)	7/1	3 2
	OWINGTON *GWragg* 4-9-10 PaulEddery (3)	13/8	2½ 3
11	Raah Algharb (USA) *MRStoute* 3-8-12 WRSwinburn (5)	25/1	1 4
	El Yasaf (IRE) *GFierro* 7-9-3 LDettori (4)	16/1	½ 5

Mr Rob Hughes 5ran 1m00.10

CHANTILLY Sunday, Jun 4 GOOD

18 **Les Emirats Arabes Unis Prix du Jockey-Club (Gr 1) (3yo c+f) £318,877** 1½m

6	CELTIC SWING *LadyHerries,GB* 3-9-2 KDarley	1/1f	1
	POLIGLOTE *MmeCHead,France* 3-9-2 FHead	81/10	½ 2
	WINGED LOVE (IRE) *AFabre,France* 3-9-2 OPeslier	5/1cp	sh 3
	Classic Cliche (IRE) *SaeedbinSuroor,GB* 3-9-2 WRSwinburn	5/1cp	2 4
	Flemensfirth (USA) *JHMGosden,GB* 3-9-2 LDettori	5/1cp	sh 5
	Diamond Mix (IRE) *AFabre,France* 3-9-2 TJarnet	38/10cp	2 6
	Affidavit (USA) *AFabre,France* 3-9-2 MJKinane	5/1cp	½ 7
	Rifapour (IRE) *AdeRoyerDupre,France* 3-9-2 GMosse	28/10	3 8
	Walk On Mix (FR) *AFabre,France* 3-9-2 SGuillot	38/10cp	4 9
	Indian Light *JLDunlop,GB* 3-9-2 PatEddery	52/1	1 10
	Commoner (USA) *RHannon,GB* 3-9-2 JReid	117/1	½ 11

Mr P. D. Savill 11ran 2m32.80

EPSOM DOWNS Friday, Jun 9 Round course: GOOD to FIRM
Straight course: FIRM

19 **Vodafone Oaks (A) (Gr 1) (3yo f) £147,800** 1½m10y

7	MOONSHELL (IRE) *SaeedbinSuroor* 3-9-0 LDettori (9)	3/1	1
	DANCE A DREAM *MRStoute* 3-9-0 WRSwinburn (10)	14/1	1¼ 2
	PURE GRAIN *MRStoute* 3-9-0 JReid (8)	7/2	¾ 3
	Musetta (IRE) *CEBrittain* 3-9-0 MRoberts (7)	33/1	3½ 4
	Asterita *RHannon* 3-9-0 PatEddery (6)	20/1	2½ 5
7	Aqaarid (USA) *JLDunlop* 3-9-0 WCarson (1)	6/4f	1¾ 6
	Bint Zamayem (IRE) *BWHills* 3-9-0 MHills (2)	25/1	13 7
	Kshessinskaya *CEBrittain* 3-9-0 KDarley (5)	33/1	5 8
	Last Spin *JRJenkins* 3-9-0 TQuinn (3)	200/1	3½ 9
	Bunting *JHMGosden* 3-9-0 (v) MJKinane (4)	25/1	4 10

Maktoum Al Maktoum / Godolphin 10ran 2m35.44

EPSOM DOWNS Saturday, Jun 10 FIRM

20 Vodafone Coronation Cup (A) (Gr 1) (4yo+) £92,520 1½m10y

	SUNSHACK *AFabre,France* 4-9-0 PatEddery (2)	10/1		1
5	ONLY ROYALE (IRE) *LMCumani* 6-8-11 LDettori (7)	11/4	hd	2
5	TIME STAR (USA) *PFICole* 4-9-0 TQuinn (5)	11/1	1	3
5	Tikkanen (USA) *JEPease,France* 4-9-0 CAsmussen (3)	5/2f	2	4
	Carnegie (IRE) *AFabre,France* 4-9-0 TJarnet (1)	11/4	1½	5
	Ionio (USA) *CEBrittain* 4-9-0 MRoberts (6)	33/1	7	6
	Environment Friend *GRimmer* 7-9-0 MJKinane (4)	16/1	1½	7

Mr K. Abdulla 7ran 2m35.85

21 Vodafone Derby Stks (A) (Gr 1) (3yo c+f) £504,500 1½m10y

	LAMMTARRA (USA) *SaeedbinSuroor* 3-9-0 WRSwinburn (7)	14/1		1
	TAMURE (IRE) *JHMGosden* 3-9-0 LDettori (13)	9/1	1	2
	PRESENTING *JHMGosden* 3-9-0 CAsmussen (2)	12/1	¾	3
	Fahal (USA) *DMorley* 3-9-0 RHills (12)	50/1	1¼	4
	Court of Honour (IRE) *PWChapple-Hyam* 3-9-0 BThomson (15)	66/1	sh	5
9	Vettori (IRE) *SaeedbinSuroor* 3-9-0 RCochrane (9)	20/1	3	6
	Riyadian *PFICole* 3-9-0 TQuinn (8)	16/1	hd	7
	Humbel (USA) *DKWeld,Ireland* 3-9-0 MJKinane (6)	25/1	nk	8
	Munwar *PTWalwyn* 3-9-0 WCarson (3)	8/1	7	9
	Salmon Ladder (USA) *PFICole* 3-9-0 KDarley (1)	50/1	6	10
6	Pennekamp (USA) *AFabre,France* 3-9-0 TJarnet (5)	11/8f	1	11
	Korambi *CEBrittain* 3-9-0 MRoberts (14)	150/1	11	12
13	Spectrum (IRE) *PWChapple-Hyam* 3-9-0 JReid (4)	5/1	nk	13
	Daffaq *PTWalwyn* 3-9-0 BRouse (11)	500/1	nk	14
	Maralinga (IRE) *MBell* 3-9-0 MFenton (10)	200/1	20	15

Mr Saeed Maktoum Al Maktoum 15ran 2m32.31

CHANTILLY Sunday, Jun 11 GOOD to FIRM

22 Prix de Diane Hermes (Gr 1) (3yo f) £177,891 1¼m110y

8	CARLING (FR) *MmePatBarbe,France* 3-9-2 TThulliez	7/2		1
8	MATIARA (USA) *MmeCHead,France* 3-9-2 FHead	5/1	nk	2
	TRYPHOSA (IRE) *AWohler,Germany* 3-9-2 ABoschert	24/1	¾	3
	Balanka (IRE) *AdeRoyerDupre,France* 3-9-2 GMosse	16/1	sh	4
	Muncie (IRE) *AFabre,France* 3-9-2 OPeslier	6/5cpf	hd	5
8	Shaanxi (USA) *ELellouche,France* 3-9-2 LDettori	9/1	sn	6
	Caramba *RHannon,GB* 3-9-2 PatEddery	10/1	½	7
	Garden Rose (IRE) *PBary,France* 3-9-2 DBoeuf	27/1	sn	8
	Loretta Gianni (FR) *DSmaga,France* 3-9-2 GGuignard	35/1	nk	9
8	Vadlamixa (FR) *AFabre,France* 3-9-2 TJarnet	14/1	2	10
	Tamise (USA) *AFabre,France* 3-9-2 SGuillot	6/5cpf	2½	11
	Tibersen (FR) *RCaget,France* 3-9-2 ODoleuze	70/1	2	12

Ecurie Delbart 12ran 2m07.70

MILAN Sunday, Jun 18 FIRM

23 Gran Premio di Milano (Gr 1) (3yo+ c+f) £126,539 1½m

15	LANDO (GER) *HJentzsch,Germany* 5-9-7 MRoberts	3/5cpf		1
	BROADWAY FLYER (USA) *JWHills,GB* 4-9-7 MHills	43/10	2¼	2
	STRATEGIC CHOICE (USA) *PFICole,GB* 4-9-7 TQuinn	29/10	¾	3
	Scribano *GBotti,Italy* 5-9-7 EBotti	11/1	9½	4
	Linney Head (USA) *JHMGosden,GB* 4-9-7 LDettori	68/10	¾	5
15	Embarcadero (GER) *HJentzsch,Germany* 7-9-7 ATylicki	3/5cpf	22	6
	Guado d'Annibale (IRE) *ARenzoni,Italy* 6-9-7 JacquelineFreda	28/1	7	7

Gestut Haus Ittlingen 7ran 2m24.80

ASCOT Tuesday, Jun 20 GOOD to FIRM

24 Queen Anne Stks (A) (Gr 2) (3yo+) £51,030 1m (Str.)

	NICOLOTTE *GWragg* 4-9-2 MHills (2)	16/1		1
	NIJO *DRLoder* 4-9-2 MJKinane (3)	20/1	2	2
12	SOVIET LINE (IRE) *MRStoute* 5-9-7 WRSwinburn (5)	13/8f	sh	3
12	Young Ern *SDow* 5-9-2 TQuinn (7)	15/2	hd	4
	Sayyedati *CEBrittain* 5-8-13 LDettori (1)	2/1	½	5
	Dance Turn *RWArmstrong* 4-9-2 JReid (4)	50/1	3	6

2	Peace Envoy *HRACecil* 3-8-6 PatEddery (6)	6/1	8	7

Mollers Racing 7ran 1m40.28

25 Prince of Wales's Stks (A) (Gr 2) (3yo+) £57,852 1¼m

12	MUHTARRAM (USA) *JHMGosden* 6-9-8 WCarson (5)	5/1		1
	ELTISH (USA) *HRACecil* 3-8-8 PatEddery (3)	4/1	sh	2
	NEEDLE GUN (IRE) *CEBrittain* 5-9-3 MJKinane (6)	33/1	1½	3
	Just Happy (USA) *MRStoute* 4-9-6 WRSwinburn (4)	13/2	2	4
	Balanchine (USA) *SaeedbinSuroor* 4-9-5 LDettori (2)	4/5f	3½	5
20	Ionio (USA) *CEBrittain* 4-9-3 (v) MRoberts (1)	33/1	¾	6

Mr Hamdan Al Maktoum 6ran 2m04.94

26 St James's Palace Stks (A) (Gr 1) (3yo c+f) £124,056 1m (Rnd)

13	BAHRI (USA) *JLDunlop* 3-9-0 WCarson (7)	11/4f		1
	CHARNWOOD FOREST (IRE) *HRACecil* 3-9-0 JReid (6)	6/1	4	2
21	VETTORI (IRE) *SaeedbinSuroor* 3-9-0 MJKinane (2)	6/1	hd	3
9	Atticus (USA) *MmeCHead,France* 3-9-0 ODoleuze (3)	10/1	1	4
	Annus Mirabilis (FR) *MRStoute* 3-9-0 PatEddery (9)	6/1	nk	5
18	Flemensfirth (USA) *JHMGosden* 3-9-0 LDettori (1)	12/1	2½	6
13	Adjareli (IRE) *JOxx,Ireland* 3-9-0 JMurtagh (8)	5/1	¾	7
	Star of Zilzal (USA) *MRStoute* 3-9-0 WRSwinburn (4)	8/1	5	8
	Muhab (USA) *PTWalwyn* 3-9-0 RHills (5)	66/1	3	9

Mr Hamdan Al Maktoum 9ran 1m40.15

ASCOT Wednesday, Jun 21 GOOD to FIRM

27 Coronation Stks (A) (Gr 1) (3yo f) £119,133 1m (Rnd)

14	RIDGEWOOD PEARL *JOxx,Ireland* 3-9-0 JMurtagh (8)	9/2		1
8	SMOLENSK (USA) *AFabre,France* 3-9-0 TJarnet (7)	6/1	2	2
14	HARAYIR (USA) *MajorWRHern* 3-9-0 WCarson (9)	15/8f	1¾	3
14	Warning Shadows (IRE) *CEBrittain* 3-9-0 MJKinane (10)	14/1	1¼	4
7	Gay Gallanta (USA) *MRStoute* 3-9-0 (v) WRSwinburn (6)	12/1	6	5
	A La Carte (IRE) *JLDunlop* 3-9-0 PatEddery (5)	16/1	1¼	6
7	Myself *PWChapple-Hyam* 3-9-0 JReid (4)	12/1	½	7
	Mamlakah (IRE) *HThomsonJones* 3-9-0 RHills (3)	25/1	nk	8
	Brief Glimpse (IRE) *MajorDNChappell* 3-9-0 BThomson (1)	33/1	3½	9
7	Macoumba (USA) *MmeCHead,France* 3-9-0 FHead (2)	6/1	20	10

Mrs Anne Coughlan 10ran 1m38.58

ASCOT Thursday, Jun 22 GOOD to FIRM

28 Gold Cup (A) (Gr 1) (4yo+) £111,750 2½m

10	DOUBLE TRIGGER (IRE) *MJohnston* 4-9-0 JWeaver (6)	9/4		1
10	MOONAX (IRE) *BWHills* 4-9-0 PatEddery (5)	13/8f	5	2
	ADMIRAL'S WELL (IRE) *RAkehurst* 5-9-2 TQuinn (3)	25/1	hd	3
	Vintage Crop *DKWeld,Ireland* 8-9-2 MJKinane (1)	3/1	2	4
	Old Rouvel (USA) *DJGMurraySmith* 4-9-0 LDettori (7)	14/1	8	5
	The Flying Phantom *MHTompkins* 4-9-0 PRobinson (2)	40/1	7	6
	The Little Thief (FR) *EDanel,France* 4-9-0 AJunk (4)	11/1		pu

Mr R. W. Huggins 7ran 4m20.25

29 Cork And Orrery Stks (A) (Gr 3) (3yo+) £33,350 6f

11	SO FACTUAL (USA) *SaeedbinSuroor* 5-8-13 LDettori (9)	9/2		1
11	LAKE CONISTON (IRE) *GLewis* 4-9-3 PatEddery (4)	8/11f	hd	2
8	NURIVA (USA) *SaeedbinSuroor* 3-8-2 GCarter (3)	33/1	3	3
	Wessam Prince *CLaffon-Parias,France* 4-9-3 WRSwinburn (6)	10/1	2½	4
	Welsh Mist *RBoss* 4-8-10 WRyan (2)	40/1	¾	5
	Tanami *DRLoder* 3-8-2 WCarson (8)	8/1	1¼	6
	Adjmal (IRE) *PLautner,Germany* 6-8-13 ABond (5)	66/1	sh	7
	Cheyenne Spirit *BHanbury* 3-8-2 MRoberts (10)	25/1	3	8
	Shamanic *RHannon* 3-8-5 KDarley (7)	50/1	9	9
	Roger The Butler (IRE) *MBell* 5-8-13 MFenton (13)	14/1	4	10
	Selhurstpark Flyer (IRE) *JBerry* 4-8-13 (es) JCarroll (1)	66/1	1	11

Godolphin 11ran 1m12.99

ASCOT Friday, Jun 23 FIRM

30 King's Stand Stks (A) (Gr 2) (3yo+) £61,354 5f

	PICCOLO *MRChannon* 4-9-6 RHughes (7)	20/1		1

	STRUGGLER *CLaffon-Parias,France* 3-8-10 WRSwinburn (3)	14/1	1½ 2
17	MIND GAMES *JBerry* 3-8-10 JCarroll (6)	8/11f	½ 3
17	Millstream (USA) *MJohnston* 3-8-7 MJKinane (8)	11/1	1¾ 4
	Fard (IRE) *DMorley* 3-8-13 (b) WCarson (2)	10/1	1½ 5
	Eveningperformance *HCandy* 4-9-0 WNewnes (5)	20/1	nk 6
	Millyant *RGuest* 5-9-0 CAsmussen (1)	12/1	3 7
8	Hoh Magic *MBell* 3-8-10 MHills (4)	8/1	hd 8
	Mistertopogigo (IRE) *WSCunningham* 5-9-3 (b) JMurtagh (9)	20/1	5 9
	Eva Luna (IRE) *JSBolger,Ireland* 3-8-10 KJManning (10)	10/1	7 10

John White and Partners 10ran 59.67secs

31 King Edward VII Stks (A) (Gr 2) (3yo c+g) £62,832 1½m

	PENTIRE *GWragg* 3-8-8 MHills (4)	4/1	1
18	CLASSIC CLICHE (IRE) *SaeedbinSuroor* 3-8-11 LDettori (2)	2/1f	2½ 2
	KALABO (USA) *HRACecil* 3-8-8 MJKinane (5)	7/1	1¼ 3
	Don Corleone *RCharlton* 3-8-8 DHarrison (8)	11/2	1¼ 4
	Istidaad (USA) *ACStewart* 3-8-8 WCarson (7)	8/1	1½ 5
	In Camera (IRE) *MRStoute* 3-8-8 WRSwinburn (6)	10/1	20 6
	Inquisitor (USA) *JHMGosden* 3-8-8 PatEddery (3)	10/1	6 7
	Murajja (USA) *PTWalwyn* 3-8-8 RHills (1)	20/1	3 8

Mollers Racing 8ran 2m28.75

LONGCHAMP Sunday, Jun 25 GOOD to FIRM

32 Grand Prix de Paris (Gr 1) (3yo c+f) £151,707 1¼m

	VALANOUR (IRE) *AdeRoyerDupre,France* 3-9-2 GMosse	63/10	1
	SINGSPIEL (IRE) *MRStoute,GB* 3-9-2 MJKinane	41/10cp	nk 2
18	DIAMOND MIX (IRE) *AFabre,France* 3-9-2 TJarnet	4/1	½ 3
	Torrential (USA) *JHMGosden,GB* 3-9-2 LDettori	41/10cp	1½ 4
18	Poliglote *MmeCHead,France* 3-9-2 FHead	13/10f	1½ 5
	Gold And Steel (FR) *J-CRouget,France* 3-9-2 JDubosc	11/2	sh 6
	Dancing Beggar (USA) *AFabre,France* 3-9-2 OPeslier	41/10cp	ns 7
6	Painter's Row (IRE) *PWChapple-Hyam,GB* 3-9-2 JReid	23/1	1 8
	Leeds (IRE) *HVandePoele,France* 3-9-2 ESaint-Martin	52/1	½ 9
	Bobinski *AFabre,France* 3-9-2 SGuillot	86/10	dist 10

H.H. Aga Khan 10ran 2m02.20

CURRAGH Sunday, Jul 2 GOOD to FIRM

33 Budweiser Irish Derby (Gr 1) (3yo c+f) £345,255 1½m

18	WINGED LOVE (IRE) *AFabre,France* 3-9-0 OPeslier	5/1	1
	DEFINITE ARTICLE *DKWeld,Ireland* 3-9-0 MJKinane	5/1	sh 2
26	ANNUS MIRABILIS (FR) *MRStoute,GB* 3-9-0 WRSwinburn	9/1	¾ 3
13	Oscar Schindler (IRE) *KPrendergast,Ireland* 3-9-0 CRoche	33/1	¾ 4
31	Classic Cliche (IRE) *SaeedbinSuroor,GB* 3-9-0 LDettori	8/1	2 5
	Damancher *PatrickMullins,Ireland* 3-9-0 RHughes	200/1	½ 6
13	I'm Supposin (IRE) *KPrendergast,Ireland* 3-9-0 WJSupple	400/1	3 7
18	Celtic Swing *LadyHerries,GB* 3-9-0 KDarley	5/4f	nk 8
21	Court of Honour (IRE) *PWChapple-Hyam,GB* 3-9-0 JReid	16/1	1 9
	Double Eclipse (IRE) *MJohnston,GB* 3-9-0 JWeaver	33/1	½ 10
21	Humbel (USA) *DKWeld,Ireland* 3-9-0 PShanahan	25/1	11 11
21	Munwar *PTWalwyn,GB* 3-9-0 WCarson	9/1	2½ 12
	Daraydan (IRE) *JOxx,Ireland* 3-9-0 (b) PVGilson	200/1	dist 13

Sheikh Mohammed 13ran 2m30.10

SAINT-CLOUD Sunday, Jul 2 GOOD to SOFT

34 Grand Prix de Saint-Cloud (Gr 1) (3yo+) £154,044 1½m

20	CARNEGIE (IRE) *AFabre,France* 4-9-8 TJarnet	19/10	1
	LUSO *CEBrittain,GB* 3-8-9 RCochrane		sn 2
20	ONLY ROYALE (IRE) *LMCumani,GB* 6-9-5 GMosse		2 3
20	Tikkanen (USA) *JEPease,France* 4-9-8 CAsmussen		2½ 4
20	Sunshack *AFabre,France* 4-9-8 PatEddery		3 5
	Solid Illusion (USA) *PHDemercastel,France* 4-9-8 DBoeuf		8 6
	Tot Ou Tard (IRE) *SWattel,France* 5-9-8 ESaint-Martin		2 7
	Citizen Darnet (USA) *JEPease,France* 4-9-8 WMessina		4 8

Sheikh Mohammed 8ran 2m35.20

SANDOWN Saturday, Jul 8 GOOD to FIRM

35	**Coral-Eclipse Stks (A) (Gr 1) (3yo+) £154,560**		1¼m7y
	HALLING (USA) *SaeedbinSuroor* 4-9-7 WRSwinburn (3)	7/1	1
32	SINGSPIEL (IRE) *MRStoute* 3-8-10 MJKinane (1)	9/2	nk 2
	RED BISHOP (USA) *SaeedbinSuroor* 7-9-7 LDettori (7)	4/1	3 3
20	Environment Friend *CEBrittain* 7-9-7 BDoyle (8)	25/1	4 4
25	Eltish (USA) *HRACecil* 3-8-10 PatEddery (6)	10/3f	hd 5
25	Muhtarram (USA) *JHMGosden* 6-9-7 WCarson (4)	4/1	2 6
	Prince of Andros (USA) *DRLoder* 5-9-7 KDarley (5)	9/1	2½ 7
22	Tryphosa (IRE) *AWohler,Germany* 3-8-7 AndreasBoschert (2)	16/1	5 8

Godolphin 8ran 2m05.32

NEWMARKET Tuesday, Jul 11 GOOD (July Course)

36	**Princess of Wales's Stks (A) (Gr 2) (3yo+) £35,576**		1½m
	BEAUCHAMP HERO *JLDunlop* 5-9-5 JReid (6)	8/1	1
31	ISTIDAAD (USA) *ACStewart* 3-8-3 WCarson (8)	12/1	1 2
21	PRESENTING *JHMGosden* 3-8-3 LDettori (2)	15/8f	½ 3
	Bal Harbour *HRACecil* 4-9-2 PatEddery (4)	8/1	2½ 4
31	In Camera (IRE) *MRStoute* 3-8-3 MRoberts (7)	5/1	1¾ 5
25	Needle Gun (IRE) *CEBrittain* 5-9-2 MJKinane (9)	8/1	2 6
3	Right Win (IRE) *RHannon* 5-9-5 RHughes (5)	33/1	10 7
20	Time Star (USA) *PFICole* 4-9-7 TQuinn (1)	14/1	1 8
	Midnight Legend *LMCumani* 4-9-2 JWeaver (3)	8/1	8 9

Mr E. Penser 9ran 2m28.83

NEWMARKET Thursday, Jul 13 GOOD (July Course)

37	**July Cup (A) (Gr 1) (3yo+) £85,774**		6f
29	LAKE CONISTON (IRE) *GLewis* 4-9-6 PatEddery (9)	13/8f	1
30	PICCOLO *MRChannon* 4-9-6 RHughes (6)	7/1	4 2
30	HOH MAGIC *MBell* 3-8-10 WRSwinburn (4)	20/1	2½ 3
17	Owington *GWragg* 4-9-6 PaulEddery (2)	4/1	nk 4
30	Fard (IRE) *DMorley* 3-8-13 WCarson (5)	12/1	¾ 5
30	Millstream (USA) *MJohnston* 3-8-10 DHolland (3)	33/1	¾ 6
29	So Factual (USA) *SaeedbinSuroor* 5-9-6 RCochrane (8)	10/1	2 7
	Sergeyev (IRE) *RHannon* 3-8-13 TQuinn (1)	5/1	1¼ 8
	Heart Lake *SaeedbinSuroor* 4-9-6 LDettori (7)	15/2	10 9

Highclere Thoroughbred Racing Ltd 9ran 1m12.42

CURRAGH Sunday, Jul 16 GOOD

38	**Kildangan Stud Irish Oaks (Gr 1) (3yo f) £116,186**		1½m
19	PURE GRAIN *MRStoute,GB* 3-9-0 JReid	9/2	1
	RUSSIAN SNOWS (IRE) *JOxx,Ireland* 3-9-0 MJKinane	13/2	6 2
	VALLEY OF GOLD (FR) *AFabre,France* 3-9-0 LDettori	4/1	4 3
19	Musetta (IRE) *CEBrittain,GB* 3-9-0 MRoberts	14/1	nk 4
	Larrocha (IRE) *LMCumani,GB* 3-9-0 WRSwinburn	9/4f	sh 5
19	Asterita *RHannon,GB* 3-9-0 JWeaver	16/1	1 6
	Bluffing (IRE) *JSBolger,Ireland* 3-9-0 KJManning	50/1	25 7
	Riyama (IRE) *JOxx,Ireland* 3-9-0 JPMurtagh	14/1	½ 8
	Crystal Bird (IRE) *MJGrassick,Ireland* 3-9-0 PVGilson	200/1	2 9
	Alisidora (IRE) *CharlesO'Brien,Ireland* 3-9-0 CRoche	10/1	sh 10

Mr R. Barnett 10ran 2m33.60

ASCOT Saturday, Jul 22 GOOD

39	**King George VI And Queen Elizabeth Diamond Stks (A) (Gr 1) (3yo+)** £278,760		1½m
21	LAMMTARRA (USA) *SaeedbinSuroor* 3-8-9 LDettori (3)	9/4f	1
31	PENTIRE *GWragg* 3-8-9 MHills (1)	3/1	nk 2
23	STRATEGIC CHOICE (USA) *PFICole* 4-9-7 TQuinn (7)	25/1	1½ 3
33	Winged Love (IRE) *AFabre,France* 3-8-9 OPeslier (5)	9/2	hd 4
23	Broadway Flyer (USA) *JWHills* 4-9-7 RHills (2)	12/1	hd 5
34	Carnegie (IRE) *AFabre,France* 4-9-7 TJarnet (6)	11/4	1¼ 6
35	Environment Friend *CEBrittain* 7-9-7 BDoyle (4)	50/1	4 7

Mr Saeed Maktoum Al Maktoum 7ran 2m31.01

DUSSELDORF Sunday, Jul 23 GOOD to FIRM

40 Preis Der Privatbankiers Merck, Finck & Co (Gr 1) (3yo+) £108,108 1½m

23	LANDO (GER) *HJentzsch,Germany* 5-9-7 PSchiergen	6/10		1
	LAROCHE (GER) *HJentzsch,Germany* 4-9-7 (b) ATylicki		2½	2
15	KORNADO *ALowe,Germany* 5-9-7 GBocskai		3	3
	Manzoni (GER) *AWohler,Germany* 3-8-6 ABoschert		½	4
	Protektor (GER) *ALowe,Germany* 6-9-7 MLarsen		2	5
	Flying Dream *BSchutz,Germany* 4-9-3 ASuborics		nk	6
15	Aratikos (GER) *HBlume,Germany* 4-9-7 OSchick		14	7
15	Bad Bertrich (IRE) *ALowe,Germany* 4-9-7 AHelfenbein		6	8

Gestut Haus Ittlingen 8ran 2m26.60

GOODWOOD Wednesday, Jul 26 FIRM

41 Sussex Stks (A) (Gr 1) (3yo+) £111,220 1m

Order as they passed the post

24	SAYYEDATI *CEBrittain* 5-9-1 BDoyle (4)	11/2		1
26	BAHRI (USA) *JLDunlop* 3-8-13 WCarson (5)	1/1f	nk	2
	DARNAY *SaeedbinSuroor* 4-9-7 LDettori (6)	9/1	3½	3
24	Soviet Line (IRE) *MRStoute* 5-9-7 WRSwinburn (3)	5/1	3½	4
24	Nicolotte *GWragg* 4-9-7 MHills (2)	7/1	sh	5
	Sulb (USA) *ACStewart* 3-8-13 RHills (1)	50/1	6	6

Soviet Line was demoted a place for interference

Mr Mohamed Obaida 6ran 1m36.17

GOODWOOD Thursday, Jul 27 Straight course: GOOD to FIRM
Round course: FIRM

42 Tiffany Goodwood Cup (A) (Gr 2) (3yo+) £36,080 2m

28	DOUBLE TRIGGER (IRE) *MJohnston* 4-9-5 JWeaver (7)	2/1f		1
33	DOUBLE ECLIPSE (IRE) *MJohnston* 3-7-12 TWilliams (6)	15/2	nk	2
	KHAMASEEN *JLDunlop* 4-9-0 JReid (8)	25/1	4	3
10	Bold Gait *JRFanshawe* 4-9-0 WRSwinburn (1)	10/3	2½	4
28	Admiral's Well (IRE) *RAkehurst* 5-9-0 TQuinn (3)	12/1	sh	5
	Saxon Maid *LMCumani* 4-8-11 LDettori (2)	6/1	2	6
	Cuff Link (IRE) *MajorWRHern* 5-9-0 PaulEddery (5)	20/1	1	7
	Juyush (USA) *BWHills* 3-7-12 WCarson (9)	14/1	2½	8
10	Further Flight *BWHills* 9-9-0 MHills (4)	20/1	3	9

Mr R. W. Huggins 9ran 3m25.86

DEAUVILLE Sunday, Aug 6 GOOD

43 Prix Maurice de Gheest (Gr 1) (3yo+) £65,445 6f110y

	CHEROKEE ROSE (IRE) *JEHammond,France* 4-8-12 CAsmussen	17/10f		1
24	YOUNG ERN *SDow,GB* 5-9-1 TQuinn	12/1	sh	2
29	WESSAM PRINCE *CLaffon-Parias,France* 4-9-1 WRSwinburn	13/1	3	3
6	Diffident (FR) *AFabre,France* 3-8-11 TJarnet	21/10	¾	4
37	Hoh Magic *MBell,GB* 3-8-8 MHills	13/1	hd	5
	Lavinia Fontana (IRE) *JLDunlop,GB* 6-8-12 MKinane	16/1	1½	6
26	Atticus (USA) *MmeCHead,France* 3-8-11 ODoleuze	33/10	sn	7
37	Fard (IRE) *DMorley,GB* 3-8-11 (b) WCarson	11/1	1	8
	Nec Plus Ultra (FR) *AdeRoyerDupre,France* 4-9-1 GMosse	89/10	5	9
9	General Monash (USA) *PWChapple-Hyam,GB* 3-8-11 BThomson	29/10	½	10

Sheikh Mohammed 10ran 1m16.50

DEAUVILLE Sunday, Aug 13 GOOD

44 Prix du Haras de Fresnay-Le-Buffard Jacques Le Marois (Gr 1) (3yo+ c+f) £129,533 1m

	MISS SATAMIXA (FR) *AFabre,France* 3-8-8 SGuillot	217/10		1
41	SAYYEDATI *CEBrittain,GB* 5-9-1 BDoyle	42/10	1	2
22	SHAANXI (USA) *ELellouche,France* 3-8-8 DBoeuf	12/1	1½	3
	Tamayaz (CAN) *SaeedbinSuroor,GB* 3-8-11 CAsmussen	28/10f	1½	4
16	Green Tune (USA) *MmeCHead,France* 4-9-4 ODoleuze	52/10	hd	5
13	Prince Arthur (IRE) *PWChapple-Hyam,GB* 3-8-11 BThomson	36/1	1½	6
41	Nicolotte *GWragg,GB* 4-9-4 MHills	12/1	1	7
27	Smolensk (USA) *AFabre,France* 3-8-8 TJarnet	47/10	1	8

22	Carling (FR) *MmePatBarbe,France* 3-8-8 TThulliez	51/10	6	9

Mr J. L. Lagardere 9ran 1m35.70

LEOPARDSTOWN Sunday, Aug 13 GOOD to FIRM

45 Heinz 57 Phoenix Stks (Gr 1) (2yo c+f) £100,000 6f

	DANEHILL DANCER (IRE) *NACallaghan,GB* 2-9-0 PatEddery	2/1f		1
	WOODBOROUGH (USA) *PWChapple-Hyam,GB* 2-9-0 JReid	11/2	nk	2
	CATCH A GLIMPSE (USA) *DKWeld,Ireland* 2-8-11 MJKinane	25/1	1½	3
	Flying Squaw *MRChannon,GB* 2-8-11 RHughes	8/1	¾	4
	Sunset Reigns (IRE) *APO'Brien,Ireland* 2-8-11 CRoche	5/1	3½	5
	April The Eighth *BWHills,GB* 2-9-0 WCarson	6/1	sh	6
	Rockcorry Rose (IRE) *KPrendergast,Ireland* 2-8-11 WJSupple	40/1	nk	7
	Ribot's Secret (IRE) *APO'Brien,Ireland* 2-8-11 (b) PVGilson	8/1	sh	8
	Deed of Love (USA) *JSBolger,Ireland* 2-9-0 (b) KJManning	7/1	5½	9
	Nymph In The Ski (IRE) *WilliamJFitzpatrick,Ireland* 2-8-11 PShanahan	500/1	15	10

Mr M. Tabor 10ran 1m14.60

46 Phoenix Sprint Stks (Gr 3) (3yo+) £16,582 6f

	DESERT STYLE (IRE) *JSBolger,Ireland* 3-9-3 KJManning	4/1		1
	PETITE FANTASY *APO'Brien,Ireland* 3-8-7 (b) JFEgan	5/1	2½	2
29	CHEYENNE SPIRIT *BHanbury,GB* 3-8-7 WRyan	5/1	1½	3
	Peruke (IRE) *NMeade,Ireland* 4-8-12 (b) RHughes	25/1	hd	4
14	Mediation (IRE) *JOxx,Ireland* 3-8-7 PatEddery	8/1	¾	5
	Bunty Boo *RHannon,GB* 6-8-12 JReid	9/1	hd	6
	Nautical Pet (IRE) *DKWeld,Ireland* 3-9-0 MJKinane	11/4f	1½	7
	America's Cup (IRE) *CharlesO'Brien,Ireland* 3-8-10 CRoche	8/1	1½	8
29	Roger The Butler (IRE) *MBell,GB* 5-9-1 MFenton	10/1	7	9

Maktoum Al Maktoum 9ran 1m14.00

YORK Tuesday, Aug 15 GOOD to FIRM

47 Juddmonte International Stks (A) (Gr 1) (3yo+) £161,720 1¼m85y

35	HALLING (USA) *SaeedbinSuroor* 4-9-6 WRSwinburn (2)	9/4f		1
41	BAHRI (USA) *JLDunlop* 3-8-11 WCarson (4)	11/4	3½	2
33	ANNUS MIRABILIS (FR) *MRStoute* 3-8-11 MJKinane (3)	10/3	1¾	3
36	Needle Gun (IRE) *CEBrittain* 5-9-6 RCochrane (1)	16/1	½	4
35	Eltish (USA) *HRACecil* 3-8-11 PatEddery (6)	7/2	3½	5
	Ela-Aristokrati (IRE) *MRStoute* 3-8-11 MHills (5)	33/1	nk	6

Godolphin 6ran 2m06.42

48 Great Voltigeur Stks (A) (Gr 2) (3yo c+g) £49,737 1m3f195y

39	PENTIRE *GWragg* 3-8-12 MHills (1)	4/5f		1
35	SINGSPIEL (IRE) *MRStoute* 3-8-9 MJKinane (3)	5/2	sh	2
34	LUSO *CEBrittain* 3-9-0 RCochrane (4)	5/1	3½	3
	Ihtiram (IRE) *JLDunlop* 3-8-9 WCarson (2)	11/1	4	4

Mollers Racing 4ran 2m29.86

YORK Wednesday, Aug 16 GOOD to FIRM

49 Aston Upthorpe Yorkshire Oaks (A) (Gr 1) (3yo+ f+m) £82,731 1m3f195y

38	PURE GRAIN *MRStoute* 3-8-8 JReid (2)	11/10f		1
	MAGICAL RETREAT (USA) *CACyzer* 5-9-4 DBiggs (6)	33/1	hd	2
	WIND IN HER HAIR (IRE) *JWHills* 4-9-4 RHills (4)	7/1	2	3
	Royal Ballerina (IRE) *MKauntze,Ireland* 5-9-4 WJO'Connor (1)	14/1	1¼	4
	La Confederation *DRLoder* 4-9-4 MJKinane (3)	7/1	hd	5
19	Dance A Dream *MRStoute* 3-8-8 WRSwinburn (7)	7/1	½	6
	Noble Rose (IRE) *LMCumani* 4-9-4 JWeaver (8)	9/1	2	7
	Phantom Gold *LordHuntingdon* 3-8-8 PatEddery (5)	7/1	7	8

Mr R. Barnett 8ran 2m28.68

50 Scottish Equitable Gimcrack Stks (A) (Gr 2) (2yo c+g) £70,144 6f

	ROYAL APPLAUSE *BWHills* 2-9-0 WRSwinburn (1)	4/6f		1
	TUMBLEWEED RIDGE *BJMeehan* 2-8-11 BDoyle (2)	8/1	hd	2
	TAKE A LEFT *MrsJRRamsden* 2-8-11 KFallon (4)	4/1	1¾	3
	Gothenberg (IRE) *MJohnston* 2-8-11 DHolland (3)	11/1	2½	4
	Tamhid (USA) *HThomsonJones* 2-8-11 RHills (5)	5/1	2½	5

Maktoum Al Maktoum 5ran 1m11.42

YORK Thursday, Aug 17 GOOD to FIRM

51 Nunthorpe Stks (A) (Gr 1) (2yo+) £72,030 5f

37	SO FACTUAL (USA) *SaeedbinSuroor* 5-9-6 LDettori (5)	9/2		1
	YA MALAK *JWPayne* 4-9-6 BThomson (8)	20/1	1½	2
	HEVER GOLF ROSE *TJNaughton* 4-9-3 JWeaver (1)	4/1	1½	3
	Sharp Point (IRE) *DKWeld,Ireland* 3-9-0 (b) MJKinane (6)	16/1	1	4
30	Millyant *RGuest* 5-9-3 CAsmussen (4)	12/1	sh	5
30	Mind Games *JBerry* 3-9-3 JCarroll (3)	10/11f	nk	6
37	Millstream (USA) *MJohnston* 3-9-0 DHolland (2)	11/1	3	7
30	Mistertopogigo (IRE) *WSCunningham* 5-9-6 MRoberts (7)	25/1	1½	8

Godolphin 8ran 57.47secs

CURRAGH Saturday, Aug 19 FIRM

52 Royal Whip Stks (Gr 3) (3yo+) £16,582 1¼m

	SHEMARAN (IRE) *JOxx,Ireland* 3-8-13 JPMurtagh	5/1		1
38	RUSSIAN SNOWS (IRE) *JOxx,Ireland* 3-8-5 CRoche	11/10f	½	2
	AL MOHAAJIR (USA) *JSBolger,Ireland* 4-9-1 KJManning	5/1	½	3
33	Oscar Schindler (IRE) *KPrendergast,Ireland* 3-8-7 WJSupple	7/2	1½	4
33	Humbel (USA) *DKWeld,Ireland* 3-8-10 PShanahan	8/1	1½	5

H.H. Aga Khan 5ran 2m02.90

DEAUVILLE Saturday, Aug 19 GOOD

53 Prix Gontaut-Biron (Gr 3) (4yo+) £28,277 1¼m

3	HERNANDO (FR) *JEHammond,France* 5-8-9 CAsmussen	13/10cpf		1
15	FREEDOM CRY *AFabre,France* 4-9-4 OPeslier	4/1	1½	2
3	MILLKOM *J-CRouget,France* 4-8-9 JDubosc	13/2	1	3
	Volochine (IRE) *RCollet,France* 4-8-11 ESaint-Martin	12/1	¾	4
	Erin Bird (FR) *PWChapple-Hyam,GB* 4-8-8 BThomson	73/10	sh	5
3	Tuesday's Special (USA) *AFabre,France* 5-9-1 TJarnet	13/1	2½	6
16	Marildo (FR) *DSmaga,France* 8-9-4 (b) GGuignard	68/10	2	7
34	Solid Illusion (USA) *PHDemercastel,France* 4-8-11 SGuillot	81/10	1	8
	Agent Cooper (FR) *JEHammond,France* 6-8-9 GDubroeucq	13/10cpf	20	9

Mr S. S. Niarchos 9ran 2m07.30

DEAUVILLE Sunday, Aug 20 GOOD

54 Prix Morny Piaget (Gr 1) (2yo c+f) £102,827 6f

	TAGULA (IRE) *IABalding,GB* 2-9-0 WRSwinburn	87/10		1
	WITH FASCINATION (USA) *JEPease,France* 2-8-11 CAsmussen	18/10f	1	2
	BARRICADE (USA) *AFabre,France* 2-9-0 TJarnet	42/10	¾	3
	Russian Revival (USA) *PWChapple-Hyam,GB* 2-9-0 BThomson	26/10	1	4
	Shining Molly (FR) *PBary,France* 2-8-11 OPeslier	51/10	3	5
	World Premier *CEBrittain,GB* 2-9-0 BDoyle	22/1	sh	6
	Lucky Lionel (USA) *RHannon,GB* 2-9-0 JReid	14/1	2	7
	Sangria (USA) *JFellows,France* 2-8-11 GGuignard	13/1	6	8

Robert & Elizabeth Hitchins 8ran 1m11.60

GOODWOOD Saturday, Aug 26 GOOD to FIRM

55 Tripleprint Celebration Mile (A) (Gr 2) (3yo+) £35,388 1m

27	HARAYIR (USA) *MajorWRHern* 3-8-12 WCarson (3)	5/4f		1
41	DARNAY *SaeedbinSuroor* 4-9-4 JReid (4)	9/1	½	2
	REALITIES (USA) *GHarwood* 5-9-1 PaulEddery (2)	9/1	1¼	3
	Emperor Jones (USA) *SaeedbinSuroor* 5-9-4 LDettori (6)	7/2	1¾	4
	Shahid *JLDunlop* 3-8-9 RHills (5)	4/1	5	5
24	Dance Turn *RWArmstrong* 4-9-1 (v) MRoberts (1)	16/1	7	6

Mr Hamdan Al Maktoum 6ran 1m36.73

HAYDOCK Saturday, Sep 2 GOOD to SOFT

56 Haydock Park Sprint Cup (A) (Gr 1) (3yo+) £72,160 6f

43	CHEROKEE ROSE (IRE) *JEHammond,France* 4-8-11 CAsmussen (4).	5/1		1
11	BRANSTON ABBY (IRE) *MJohnston* 6-8-11 DHolland (3)	14/1	1½	2
37	OWINGTON *GWragg* 4-9-0 PaulEddery (2)	11/1	¾	3
37	Lake Coniston (IRE) *GLewis* 4-9-0 PatEddery (7)	1/3f	2½	4
51	Mind Games *JBerry* 3-8-11 JCarroll (5)	20/1	8	5

43	Lavinia Fontana (IRE) *JLDunlop* 6-8-11 LDettori (6)	10/1	5	6

Sheikh Mohammed 6ran 1m13.74

BADEN-BADEN Sunday, Sep 3 SOFT

57 Grosser Preis Von Baden (Gr 1) (3yo+) £142,544 1½m

	GERMANY (USA) *BSchutz,Germany* 4-9-6 LDettori	37/10		1
	LECROIX (GER) *MHofer,Germany* 3-8-9 ATylicki	71/10	5	2
36	RIGHT WIN (IRE) *RHannon,GB* 5-9-6 (b) MRoberts	38/1	3½	3
40	Kornado *ALowe,Germany* 5-9-6 GBocskai	27/1	1½	4
36	Beauchamp Hero *JLDunlop,GB* 5-9-6 JReid	85/10	nk	5
	Oxalagu (GER) *BSchutz,Germany* 3-8-11 THellier	23/1	5	6
40	Lando (GER) *HJentzsch,Germany* 5-9-6 PSchiergen	6/5f	10	7
	Concepcion (GER) *HJentzsch,Germany* 5-9-6 SEccles	38/1		8
39	Strategic Choice (USA) *PFICole,GB* 4-9-6 TQuinn	39/10		9
49	Royal Ballerina (IRE) *MKauntze,Ireland* 5-9-2 WJO'Connor	30/1		pu

Mr Jaber Abdullah 10ran 2m37.72

LONGCHAMP Sunday, Sep 3 GOOD to FIRM

58 Emirates Prix du Moulin de Longchamp (Gr 1) (3yo+ c+f) £114,649 1m

27	RIDGEWOOD PEARL *JOxx,Ireland* 3-8-8 JPMurtagh	13/10f		1
44	SHAANXI (USA) *ELellouche,France* 3-8-8 DBoeuf	12/1	¾	2
12	MISSED FLIGHT *CFWall,GB* 5-9-2 GDuffield	79/10	¾	3
44	Sayyedati *CEBrittain,GB* 5-8-13 BDoyle	52/10	ns	4
44	Smolensk (USA) *AFabre,France* 3-8-8 TJarnet	81/10	¾	5
44	Miss Satamixa (FR) *AFabre,France* 3-8-8 SGuillot	41/10	½	6
44	Green Tune (USA) *MmeCHead,France* 4-9-2 ODoleuze	62/10	2½	7
55	Darnay *SaeedbinSuroor,GB* 4-9-2 WRSwinburn	16/1	8	8

Mrs Anne Coughlan 8ran 1m36.90

DONCASTER Thursday, Sep 7 GOOD

59 East Coast Doncaster Cup (A) (Gr 3) (3yo+) £21,020 2¼m

42	DOUBLE TRIGGER (IRE) *MJohnston* 4-9-7 JWeaver (6)	4/11f		1
42	FURTHER FLIGHT *BWHills* 9-9-3 MHills (3)	11/1	3	2
28	OLD ROUVEL (USA) *DJGMurraySmith* 4-9-0 MJKinane (1)	25/1	1½	3
42	Admiral's Well (IRE) *RAkehurst* 5-9-0 TQuinn (4)	10/1	1	4
42	Cuff Link (IRE) *MajorWRHern* 5-9-0 PaulEddery (5)	10/1	12	5
	Escarpment (USA) *PWChapple-Hyam* 4-9-0 LDettori (2)	14/1	½	6

Mr R. W. Huggins 6ran 3m58.74

DONCASTER Friday, Sep 8 GOOD

60 Laurent-Perrier Champagne Stks (A) (Gr 2) (2yo c+g) £45,622 7f

	ALHAARTH (IRE) *MajorWRHern* 2-9-0 WCarson (1)	2/5f		1
	RIO DUVIDA *DRLoder* 2-8-10 PatEddery (2)	11/2	½	2
50	TAKE A LEFT *MrsJRRamsden* 2-8-10 KFallon (3)	7/2	5	3

Mr Hamdan Al Maktoum 3ran 1m31.57

DONCASTER Saturday, Sep 9 GOOD to SOFT

61 Pertemps St Leger Stks (A) (Gr 1) (3yo c+f) £166,802 1¾m132y

33	CLASSIC CLICHE (IRE) *SaeedbinSuroor* 3-9-0 LDettori (7)	10/3f		1
	MINDS MUSIC (USA) *HRACecil* 3-9-0 WRyan (10)	12/1	3½	2
36	ISTIDAAD (USA) *ACStewart* 3-9-0 WCarson (8)	11/1	2½	3
36	In Camera (IRE) *MRStoute* 3-9-0 (v) KDarley (4)	33/1	½	4
18	Affidavit (USA) *AFabre,France* 3-9-0 WRSwinburn (9)	4/1	2½	5
	Anchor Clever *PAKelleway* 3-9-0 RHughes (3)	16/1	hd	6
31	Kalabo (USA) *HRACecil* 3-9-0 PatEddery (1)	11/2	½	7
48	Luso *CEBrittain* 3-9-0 RCochrane (6)	5/1	sh	8
	Jellaby Askhir *RAkehurst* 3-9-0 JReid (2)	25/1	2½	9
	Jural *MJohnston* 3-8-11 JWeaver (5)	7/1	1¾	10

Godolphin 10ran 3m09.74

LEOPARDSTOWN Saturday, Sep 9 GOOD to FIRM

62 Guinness Champion Stks (Gr 1) (3yo+ c+f) £89,082 1¼m

48	PENTIRE *GWragg,GB* 3-8-11 MHills (3)	9/4f		1

53 FREEDOM CRY *AFabre,France* 4-9-4 OPeslier (7) 9/1 sh 2
16 FLAGBIRD (USA) *SaeedbinSuroor,GB* 4-9-1 JPMurtagh (2) 8/1 2 3
33 Definite Article *DKWeld,Ireland* 3-8-11 (b) MJKinane (8) 6/1 ½ 4
47 Needle Gun (IRE) *CEBrittain,GB* 5-9-4 BDoyle (5) 20/1 1½ 5
32 Valanour (IRE) *AdeRoyerDupre,France* 3-8-11 GMosse (6) 6/1 10 6
53 Hernando (FR) *JEHammond,France* 5-9-4 CAsmussen (1) 5/2 sh 7
Kayaara (IRE) *NoelFurlong,Ireland* 3-8-11 PShanahan (4) 50/1 dist 8
Mollers Racing 8ran 2m04.40

LONGCHAMP Sunday, Sep 10 GOOD to SOFT

63 Prix Vermeille (Gr 1) (3yo f) £102,040 1½m

44 CARLING (FR) *MmePatBarbe,France* 3-9-2 TThulliez (1) 66/10 1
38 VALLEY OF GOLD (FR) *AFabre,France* 3-9-2 TJarnet (7) 26/10cp 1 2
38 LARROCHA (IRE) *LMCumani,GB* 3-9-2 LDettori (4) 26/10cp sn 3
22 Matiara (USA) *MmeCHead,France* 3-9-2 FHead (3) 41/10 sn 4
22 Muncie (IRE) *AFabre,France* 3-9-2 OPeslier (10) 44/10 sh 5
Dance Partner (JPN) *MmePatBarbe,France* 3-9-2 YTake (2) 23/10f ¾ 6
Fanjica (IRE) *JLDunlop,GB* 3-9-2 PatEddery (5) 29/1 sh 7
Privity (USA) *PBary,France* 3-9-2 DBoeuf (6) 14/1 sn 8
38 Musetta (IRE) *CEBrittain,GB* 3-9-2 BDoyle (9) 72/1 6 9
22 Caramba *RHannon,GB* 3-9-2 MRoberts (8) 13/1 hd 10
Ecurie Delbart 10ran 2m32.80

64 Prix Foy (Gr 3) (4yo+ c+f) £28,061 1½m

39 CARNEGIE (IRE) *AFabre,France* 4-9-2 TJarnet (1) 1/10cpf 1
25 BALANCHINE (USA) *SaeedbinSuroor,GB* 4-8-13 LDettori (4) 1/10cpf sh 2
34 TOT OU TARD (IRE) *SWattel,France* 5-9-2 ESaint-Martin (2) 67/10 3 3
Zillion (FR) *JEHammond,France* 4-9-2 GDubroeucq (3) 1/10cpf 20 4
Sheikh Mohammed 4ran 2m35.60

65 Prix Niel (Gr 2) (3yo c+f) £51,020 1½m

HOUSAMIX (FR) *AFabre,France* 3-9-2 TJarnet (2) 38/10 1
32 POLIGLOTE *MmeCHead,France* 3-9-2 FHead (4) 18/10 hd 2
39 WINGED LOVE (IRE) *AFabre,France* 3-9-2 OPeslier (1) 11/10f nk 3
Song of Tara (IRE) *PWChapple-Hyam,GB* 3-9-2 JReid (3) 29/10 2½ 4
Mr J. L. Lagardere 4ran 2m36.10

BELMONT PARK Saturday, Sep 16 FIRM

66 Man O'War Stks (Gr 1) (3yo+) £154,839 1m3f

53 MILLKOM *J-CRouget,France* 4-9-0 GStevens 83/10 1
4 KALDOUNEVEES (FR) *JEHammond,France* 4-9-0 CAsmussen 28/10 1¼ 2
SIGNAL TAP (USA) *FSSchulhofer,USA* 4-9-0 JSantos 136/10 1 3
Boyce (USA) *JForbes,USA* 4-9-0 JulieKrone 50/1 nk 4
53 Tuesday's Special (USA) *CClement,USA* 5-9-0 CNakatani 162/10 ½ 5
Flag Down (CAN) *CClement,USA* 5-9-0 JVelasquez 6/1cp 1 6
King's Theatre (IRE) *WMott,USA* 4-9-0 JDBailey 58/10 1¾ 7
34 Tikkanen (USA) *CClement,USA* 4-9-0 MSmith 24/10f 2 8
Warning Glance (USA) *CHadry,USA* 4-9-0 KDesormeaux 22/1 3½ 9
Manilaman (USA) *WHoward,USA* 4-9-0 RRomero 37/1 1½ 10
Yokohama (USA) *WMott,USA* 4-9-0 PDay 6/1cp ¾ 11
Potomac View (USA) *JForbes,USA* 5-9-0 EMaple 123/1 hd 12
Mr Gary A. Tanaka 12ran 2m12.80

CURRAGH Saturday, Sep 16 GOOD

67 National Stks (Gr 1) (2yo c+f) £60,306 7f

45 DANEHILL DANCER (IRE) *NACallaghan,GB* 2-9-0 PatEddery (7) 4/5f 1
POLARIS FLIGHT (USA) *PWChapple-Hyam,GB* 2-9-0 WRSwinburn (3) 2/1 1½ 2
FORCE OF WILL (USA) *DKWeld,Ireland* 2-9-0 MJKinane (5) 13/2 ¾ 3
45 Deed of Love (USA) *JSBolger,Ireland* 2-9-0 JAHeffernan (2) 16/1 sh 4
Harghar (USA) *JOxx,Ireland* 2-9-0 JPMurtagh (1) 8/1 2½ 5
Roi Estate (IRE) *DHanley,Ireland* 2-9-0 WJSupple (6) 66/1 2 6
Double Oscar (IRE) *MJohnston,GB* 2-9-0 JWeaver (4) 16/1 4½ 7
Mr M. Tabor 7ran 1m24.10

68 Jefferson Smurfit Memorial Irish St Leger (Gr 1) (3yo+) £90,612 1¾m

57 STRATEGIC CHOICE (USA) *PFICole,GB* 4-9-8 TQuinn (1) 6/1 1

28 MOONAX (IRE) *BWHills,GB* 4-9-8 PatEddery (5) .... 9/4 hd 2
52 OSCAR SCHINDLER (IRE) *KPrendergast,Ireland* 3-8-12 WJSupple (2) 10/1 3 3
28 Vintage Crop *DKWeld,Ireland* 8-9-8 MJKinane (7) 11/10f 2 4
Double On (IRE) *PJFlynn,Ireland* 4-9-5 MichaelDuffy (4) .... 40/1 ¾ 5
Johansson (USA) *JOxx,Ireland* 3-8-12 JPMurtagh (6) 33/1 4½ 6
Zilzal Zamaan (USA) *MRStoute,GB* 4-9-8 WRSwinburn (3) .... 10/1 nk 7

Mr M. Arbib 7ran 3m00.90

LONGCHAMP Sunday, Sep 17 SOFT

69 Prix de La Salamandre (Gr 1) (2yo c+f) £50,761 7f

LORD OF MEN *JHMGosden,GB* 2-8-11 LDettori 6/1 1
54 WITH FASCINATION (USA) *JEPease,France* 2-8-8 OPeslier 39/10 1 2
45 WOODBOROUGH (USA) *PWChapple-Hyam,GB* 2-8-11 JReid 5/2 2 3
Titus Livius (FR) *JEPease,France* 2-8-11 CAsmussen 34/10 1 4
54 Barricade (USA) *AFabre,France* 2-8-11 TJarnet 19/10f 2 5
Restless Carl (IRE) *AFabre,France* 2-8-11 GMosse .... 16/1 sh 6
Star Finch (FR) *PBourgoin,France* 2-8-11 RO'Brien 52/1 15 7

Sheikh Mohammed 7ran 1m27.00

70 Prix du Prince d'Orange (Gr 3) (3yo) £27,918 1¼m

21 TAMURE (IRE) *JHMGosden,GB* 3-8-11 LDettori 7/10f 1
21 SPECTRUM (IRE) *PWChapple-Hyam,GB* 3-9-4 JReid .... 43/10 nk 2
18 RIFAPOUR (IRE) *AdeRoyerDupre,France* 3-9-2 GMosse 31/10 1½ 3
Philanthrop (FR) *JEPease,France* 3-8-11 CAsmussen .... 44/10 ¾ 4
Parfait Glace (FR) *JEHammond,France* 3-8-11 FSanchez 13/1 2 5

Sheikh Mohammed 5ran 2m25.90

ASCOT Saturday, Sep 23 GOOD to SOFT

71 Royal Lodge Stks (A) (Gr 2) (2yo c+g) £63,730 1m (Rnd)

MONS *LMCumani* 2-8-11 LDettori (6) 7/2 1
MORE ROYAL (USA) *IABalding* 2-8-11 WRSwinburn (5) 6/1 5 2
JACK JENNINGS *BAMcMahon* 2-8-11 JReid (7) .... 66/1 nk 3
Hammerstein *MRStoute* 2-8-11 MJKinane (1) 8/1 4 4
Bijou d'Inde *MJohnston* 2-9-0 JWeaver (2) .... 5/2 nk 5
Acharne *CEBrittain* 2-8-11 BDoyle (4) 50/1 2 6
Mawwal (USA) *RWArmstrong* 2-8-11 WCarson (8) 2/1f 3 7
Oblomov *GLewis* 2-8-11 PaulEddery (3) 66/1 10 8

Mrs E. H. Vestey 8ran 1m42.74

72 Queen Elizabeth II Stks (A) (Gr 1) (3yo+) £194,760 1m (Rnd)

47 BAHRI (USA) *JLDunlop* 3-8-11 WCarson (1) 5/2 1
58 RIDGEWOOD PEARL *JOxx,Ireland* 3-8-8 JMurtagh (5) 8/13f 6 2
41 SOVIET LINE (IRE) *MRStoute* 5-9-1 WRSwinburn (3) 13/2 5 3
2 Bishop of Cashel *JRFanshawe* 3-8-11 LDettori (6) 14/1 1 4
Mr Martini (IRE) *CEBrittain* 5-9-1 BDoyle (4) 40/1 15 5
26 Muhab (USA) *PTWalwyn* 3-8-11 RHills (2) 100/1 20 6

Mr Hamdan Al Maktoum 6ran 1m40.54

ASCOT Sunday, Sep 24 GOOD to SOFT

73 Diadem Stks (A) (Gr 3) (3yo+) £40,560 6f

COOL JAZZ *CEBrittain* 4-9-0 CNakatani (1) 33/1 1
43 YOUNG ERN *SDow* 5-9-0 TQuinn (15) .... 7/2f sh 2
56 BRANSTON ABBY (IRE) *MJohnston* 6-8-11 MRoberts (6) .... 6/1 sh 3
55 Harayir (USA) *MajorWRHern* 3-9-0 WCarson (13) .... 6/1 ¾ 4
43 Wessam Prince *CLaffon-Parias,France* 4-9-0 FHead (8) .... 14/1 nk 5
Montendre *MMcCormack* 8-9-0 RCochrane (2) .... 20/1 nk 6
46 Desert Style (IRE) *JSBolger,Ireland* 3-8-11 WRSwinburn (12) 5/1 3 7
Double Blue *MJohnston* 6-9-0 JWeaver (4) .... 20/1 nk 8
Hello Mister *JO'Donoghue* 4-9-0 PMcCabe (16) 33/1 1½ 9
Foxhound (USA) *SaeedbinSuroor* 4-9-0 MJKinane (10) 8/1 2½ 10
Carranita (IRE) *BPalling* 5-8-11 TSprake (9) 16/1 3 11
Sharp Prod (USA) *LordHuntingdon* 5-9-0 DHarrison (5) 25/1 2 12
Easy Dollar *BGubby* 3-8-11 (b) PaulEddery (14) .... 40/1 nk 13
Hill Hopper (IRE) *JHMGosden* 4-8-11 PatEddery (7) 16/1 2½ 14

Katya (IRE) *MRChannon* 3-8-8 RHughes (3) 66/1 nk 15
Mr Saeed Manana 15ran 1m18.56

74 **Fillies' Mile (A) (Gr 1) (2yo f) £90,495** 1m (Rnd)
BOSRA SHAM (USA) *HRACecil* 2-8-10 PatEddery (5) 10/11f 1
BINT SHADAYID (USA) *JLDunlop* 2-8-10 WCarson (1) 5/1 3½ 2
MATIYA (IRE) *BHanbury* 2-8-10 RHills (4) 20/1 3½ 3
Rouge Rancon (USA) *PFICole* 2-8-10 TQuinn (2) 10/1 4 4
Shawanni *BWHills* 2-8-10 MJKinane (3) 5/2 ½ 5
Zelzelah (USA) *PAKelleway* 2-8-10 PaulEddery (6) 16/1 9 6
Mr Wafic Said 6ran 1m43.13

COLOGNE Sunday, Sep 24 GOOD
75 **Ems-Kurierpost-Europa-Preis (Gr 1) (3yo+) £129,870** 1½m
SOLON (GER) *HJentzsch,Germany* 3-8-10 PSchiergen 33/10 1
STERNKOENIG (IRE) *HBlume,Germany* 5-9-6 OSchick 2½ 2
40 PROTEKTOR (GER) *ALowe,Germany* 6-9-6 THellier 2 3
57 Germany (USA) *BSchutz,Germany* 4-9-6 LDettori 2 4
57 Kornado *ALowe,Germany* 5-9-6 GBocskai 2 5
39 Broadway Flyer (USA) *JWHills,GB* 4-9-6 (b) MHills ¾ 6
Almaz (SU) *AMSavujev,Czechoslovakia* 3-8-10 ATschugujewez 4½ 7
Caballo (GER) *HJentzsch,Germany* 4-9-6 LHammer-Hansen 2½ 8
40 Laroche (GER) *HJentzsch,Germany* 4-9-6 (b) ATylicki nk 9
57 Beauchamp Hero *JLDunlop,GB* 5-9-6 JReid 6 10
Gestut Schlenderhan 10ran 2m27.06

NEWMARKET Tuesday, Sep 26 GOOD to SOFT (Rowley Mile Course)
76 **Shadwell Stud Cheveley Park Stks (A) (Gr 1) (2yo f) £84,680** 6f
BLUE DUSTER (USA) *DRLoder* 2-8-11 MJKinane (5) 4/5f 1
MY BRANCH *BWHills* 2-8-11 MHills (3) 10/3 2½ 2
NAJIYA *JLDunlop* 2-8-11 WCarson (1) 7/1 3 3
Dance Sequence (USA) *MRStoute* 2-8-11 WRSwinburn (4) 7/1 ½ 4
Supamova (USA) *PFICole* 2-8-11 TQuinn (2) 12/1 4 5
Sheikh Mohammed 5ran 1m12.78

NEWMARKET Thursday, Sep 28 GOOD (Rowley Mile Course)
77 **Middle Park Stks (A) (Gr 1) (2yo c) £72,929** 6f
50 ROYAL APPLAUSE *BWHills* 2-8-11 WRSwinburn (5) 3/1 1
69 WOODBOROUGH (USA) *PWChapple-Hyam* 2-8-11 JReid (2) 11/2 4 2
KAHIR ALMAYDAN (IRE) *JLDunlop* 2-8-11 WCarson (1) 8/11f 1¾ 3
54 Lucky Lionel (USA) *RHannon* 2-8-11 PatEddery (4) 9/1 2 4
Resounder (USA) *JHMGosden* 2-8-11 LDettori (3) 25/1 1¼ 5
Maktoum Al Maktoum 5ran 1m11.14

NEWMARKET Saturday, Sep 30 GOOD (Rowley Mile Course)
78 **Jockey Club Cup (A) (Gr 3) (3yo+) £22,995** 2m
59 FURTHER FLIGHT *BWHills* 9-9-3 MHills (3) 5/2 1
ASSESSOR (IRE) *RHannon* 6-9-0 RHughes (1) 14/1 2½ 2
42 DOUBLE ECLIPSE (IRE) *MJohnston* 3-8-2 TWilliams (7) 6/4f nk 3
59 Old Rouvel (USA) *DJGMurraySmith* 4-9-0 MRoberts (8) 16/1 1 4
59 Cuff Link (IRE) *MajorWRHern* 5-9-0 PaulEddery (2) 14/1 hd 5
Source of Light *RCharlton* 6-9-0 CNakatani (5) 9/2 10 6
Wot-If-We (IRE) *TGMills* 3-8-2 GCarter (4) 33/1 8 7
19 Kshessinskaya *CEBrittain* 3-7-13 JFEgan (6) 40/1 20 8
Mr S. Wingfield Digby 8ran 3m28.14

LONGCHAMP Saturday, Sep 30 SOFT
79 **Prix Dollar (Gr 2) (3yo+) £38,610** 1m1f165y
26 FLEMENSFIRTH (USA) *JHMGosden,GB* 3-9-2 LDettori 3/5cpf 1
53 VOLOCHINE (IRE) *RCollet,France* 4-9-0 TJarnet 34/10 ½ 2
TRIARIUS (USA) *SaeedbinSuroor,GB* 5-9-0 MJKinane 3/5cpf 3 3
Madrileno (IRE) *RMartin,Spain* 3-8-10 J-LMartinez 11/1 ½ 4
53 Marildo (FR) *DSmaga,France* 8-9-0 (b) GGuignard 81/10 hd 5
25 Just Happy (USA) *MRStoute,GB* 4-9-0 WRSwinburn 3/5cpf sn 6

	Vetheuil (USA) *AFabre,France* 3-8-10 OPeslier	38/10	10 7
	Sheikh Mohammed 7ran 2m07.80		
80	**Prix du Cadran (Gr 1) (4yo+)** £64,350		2½m
	ALWAYS EARNEST (USA) *MmeMBollack-Badel,France* 7-9-2 (b) ABadel	17/2	1
68	MOONAX (IRE) *BWHills,GB* 4-9-2 PatEddery	21/10	sh 2
1	NONONITO (FR) *JLesbordes,France* 4-9-2 GMosse	12/1	2½ 3
59	Double Trigger (IRE) *MJohnston,GB* 4-9-2 JWeaver	1/2f	3 4
59	Admiral's Well (IRE) *RAkehurst,GB* 5-9-2 LDettori	14/1	8 5
	Epaphos (GER) *PBary,France* 5-9-2 DBoeuf	12/1	20 6
	Mme M. Bollack-Badel 6ran 4m36.50		
	LONGCHAMP Sunday, Oct 1 GOOD to SOFT		
81	**Prix de L'Abbaye de Longchamp (Gr 1) (2yo+ c+f)** £64,350		5f
51	HEVER GOLF ROSE *TJNaughton,GB* 4-9-8 JWeaver	31/10	1
56	CHEROKEE ROSE (IRE) *JEHammond,France* 4-9-8 CAsmussen	4/5cpf	2½ 2
30	EVENINGPERFORMANCE *HCandy,GB* 4-9-8 WNewnes	24/1	nk 3
	Easy Option (IRE) *SaeedbinSuroor,GB* 3-9-8 LDettori	4/5cpf	sn 4
56	Lavinia Fontana (IRE) *JLDunlop,GB* 6-9-8 CNakatani		1 5
51	Millyant *RGuest,GB* 5-9-8 MRoberts		hd 6
73	Cool Jazz *CEBrittain,GB* 4-9-11 MJKinane		sn 7
56	Mind Games *JBerry,GB* 3-9-11 WCarson		1½ 8
46	Bunty Boo *RHannon,GB* 6-9-8 MHills		2 9
69	With Fascination (USA) *JEPease,France* 2-8-4 OPeslier		4 10
	Bruttina *MmePatBarbe,France* 3-9-8 (b) TThulliez		4 11
	Late Parade (IRE) *ASpanu,France* 4-9-11 JReid		6 12
	Mr M. P. Hanson 12ran 57.70secs		
82	**Prix Marcel Boussac Criterium Des Pouliches (Gr 1) (2yo f)** £102,960		1m
	MISS TAHITI (IRE) *AFabre,France* 2-8-11 OPeslier	106/10	1
	SHAKE THE YOKE *ELellouche,France* 2-8-11 DBoeuf	29/10f	2 2
	SOLAR CRYSTAL (IRE) *HRACecil,GB* 2-8-11 WRyan	58/10	hd 3
	Dance Design (IRE) *DKWeld,Ireland* 2-8-11 MJKinane	76/10	1½ 4
	Blushing Gleam *MmeCHead,France* 2-8-11 ODoleuze	71/10	3 5
	Tarte Aux Pommes (FR) *JBertrandeBalanda,France* 2-8-11 CAsmussen	21/1	½ 6
	Wedding Gift *PHDemercastel,France* 2-8-11 TJarnet	29/1	1 7
	Clever Dorothy (USA) *DSepulchre,France* 2-8-11 ESaint-Martin	44/1	1½ 8
	Moody's Cat (IRE) *BWHills,GB* 2-8-11 MHills	26/1	3 9
	Sea Spray (IRE) *PWChapple-Hyam,GB* 2-8-11 JReid	39/10	½ 10
	Caribbean Quest *BHanbury,GB* 2-8-11 WRSwinburn	38/10	2½ 11
	Mr Daniel Wildenstein 11ran 1m40.20		
83	**Forte Prix de L'Arc de Triomphe (Gr 1) (3yo+ c+f)** £514,801		1½m
39	LAMMTARRA (USA) *SaeedbinSuroor,GB* 3-8-11 LDettori	21/10f	1
62	FREEDOM CRY *AFabre,France* 4-9-5 OPeslier	64/10cp	¾ 2
	SWAIN (IRE) *AFabre,France* 3-8-11 MJKinane	22/10cp	2 3
57	Lando (GER) *HJentzsch,Germany* 5-9-5 MRoberts	24/1	1½ 4
49	Pure Grain *MRStoute,GB* 3-8-8 JReid	87/10	2½ 5
64	Carnegie (IRE) *AFabre,France* 4-9-5 TJarnet	22/10cp	½ 6
3	Partipral (USA) *ELellouche,France* 6-9-5 GGuignard	67/1	1 7
	Gunboat Diplomacy (FR) *ELellouche,France* 4-9-5 DBoeuf	64/10cp	1 8
63	Carling (FR) *MmePatBarbe,France* 3-8-8 TThulliez	54/10	8 9
64	Balanchine (USA) *SaeedbinSuroor,GB* 4-9-2 WRSwinburn	22/10cp	sn 10
	El Tenor (FR) *ASpanu,France* 3-8-11 SCoerette	58/1	2 11
64	Tot Ou Tard (IRE) *SWattel,France* 5-9-5 ESaint-Martin	33/1	3 12
61	Luso *CEBrittain,GB* 3-8-11 (b) CAsmussen	22/1	3 13
68	Strategic Choice (USA) *PFICole,GB* 4-9-5 TQuinn	21/1	2½ 14
	El Sembrador (ARG) *JoseLuisPalacios,Argentina* 4-9-4 GESena	23/1	½ 15
	Sunrise Song (FR) *FDoumen,France* 4-9-2 GMosse	43/1	5 16
	Mr Saeed Maktoum Al Maktoum 16ran 2m31.80		
84	**Sunset & Vine Prix de L'Opera (Gr 2) (3yo+ f+m)** £51,480		1m1f55y
	TIMARIDA (IRE) *JOxx,Ireland* 3-8-9 JPMurtagh	5/2cpf	1
	ANGEL IN MY HEART (FR) *JEHammond,France* 3-8-9 CAsmussen	67/10	2½ 2

22	BALANKA (IRE) *AdeRoyerDupre,France* 3-8-9 GMosse	5/2cpf	nk 3
22	Garden Rose (IRE) *PBary,France* 3-8-9 DBoeuf	58/10	¾ 4
22	Vadlamixa (FR) *AFabre,France* 3-8-9 TJarnet	66/10	nk 5
53	Erin Bird (FR) *MmePatBarbe,France* 4-8-12 TThulliez	108/10	½ 6
	Marie de Ken (FR) *AdeRoyer-Dupre,France* 3-8-9 OPeslier	27/10	2 7
35	Tryphosa (IRE) *AWohler,Germany* 3-8-11 ABoschert	88/10	sn 8
1	Truly A Dream (IRE) *RCollet,France* 4-8-12 ESaint-Martin	37/1	1½ 9
	Kill The Crab (IRE) *WNeuroth,Norway* 3-8-11 MLarsen	20/1	1½ 10
	Coco Passion (FR) *JEHammond,France* 3-8-9 WRSwinburn	17/1	1 11

H.H. Aga Khan 11ran 1m55.70

NEWMARKET Thursday, Oct 12 GOOD to FIRM (Rowley Mile Course)

85 Challenge Stks (A) (Gr 2) (3yo+) £35,721 7f

73	HARAYIR (USA) *MajorWRHern* 3-8-12 WCarson (8)	13/8f	1
72	SOVIET LINE (IRE) *MRStoute* 5-9-4 WRSwinburn (6)	7/1	½ 2
	RED CARNIVAL (USA) *MRStoute* 3-8-8 JReid (5)	3/1	1½ 3
	Mistle Cat (USA) *SPCWoods* 5-9-0 WWoods (4)	25/1	½ 4
55	Shahid *JLDunlop* 3-8-11 RCochrane (1)	16/1	5 5
7	Autumn Affair *CEBrittain* 3-8-8 DHarrison (2)	40/1	nk 6
55	Emperor Jones (USA) *SaeedbinSuroor* 5-9-0 PatEddery (3)	6/1	nk 7
81	Cool Jazz *CEBrittain* 4-9-0 KDarley (7)	10/1	2 8

Mr Hamdan Al Maktoum 8ran 1m23.79

NEWMARKET Friday, Oct 13 GOOD to FIRM (Rowley Mile Course)

86 Generous Dewhurst Stks (A) (Gr 1) (2yo c+f) £82,390 7f

60	ALHAARTH (IRE) *MajorWRHern* 2-9-0 WCarson (1)	4/7f	1
67	DANEHILL DANCER (IRE) *NACallaghan* 2-9-0 PatEddery (3)	2/1	2½ 2
54	TAGULA (IRE) *IABalding* 2-9-0 WRSwinburn (4)	13/2	1½ 3
	Albaha (USA) *RWArmstrong* 2-9-0 RHills (2)	100/1	25 4

Mr Hamdan Al Maktoum 4ran 1m24.64

NEWMARKET Saturday, Oct 14 GOOD to FIRM (Rowley Mile Course)

87 Dubai Champion Stks (A) (Gr 1) (3yo+) £179,250 1¼m

70	SPECTRUM (IRE) *PWChapple-Hyam* 3-8-10 JReid (1)	5/1	1
21	RIYADIAN *PFICole* 3-8-10 TQuinn (4)	7/2	2 2
	MONTJOY (USA) *PFICole* 3-8-10 PatEddery (6)	25/1	hd 3
70	Tamure (IRE) *JHMGosden* 3-8-10 WRSwinburn (8)	11/4	1½ 4
72	Bahri (USA) *JLDunlop* 3-8-10 WCarson (3)	5/2f	sh 5
21	Fahal (USA) *DMorley* 3-8-10 RHills (7)	10/1	6 6
75	Germany (USA) *BrunoSchutz,Germany* 4-9-2 JWeaver (5)	25/1	1¾ 7
39	Environment Friend *CEBrittain* 7-9-2 MRoberts (2)	66/1	15 8

Lord Weinstock & The Hon Simon Weinstock 8ran 2m02.55

LONGCHAMP Sunday, Oct 15 GOOD to FIRM

88 Prix du Conseil de Paris (Gr 2) (3yo+) £37,831 1½m

	DE QUEST *AFabre,France* 3-8-9 TJarnet (1)	31/10	1
	SLICIOUS *VCaruso,Italy* 3-8-9 CAsmussen (4)	97/10	2 2
	RAINBOW DANCER (FR) *PBary,France* 4-9-2 DBoeuf (5)	12/1	2 3
18	Walk On Mix (FR) *AFabre,France* 3-9-0 SGuillot (3)	47/10	sn 4
	Posidonas *PFICole,GB* 3-9-2 TQuinn (7)	33/10	2½ 5
	Capias (USA) *JHMGosden,GB* 4-9-2 (b) MJKinane (2)	62/10	sh 6
83	El Tenor (FR) *ASpanu,France* 3-8-9 ESaint-Martin (6)	17/1	1½ 7
	Daraydala (IRE) *AdeRoyerDupre,France* 3-8-6 GMosse (8)	28/10f	3 8

Mr K. Abdulla 8ran 2m27.40

89 Grand Criterium (Gr 1) (2yo c+f) £126,103 1m

	LOUP SOLITAIRE (USA) *AFabre,France* 2-8-11 OPeslier (4)	10/1	1
	MANNINAMIX *AFabre,France* 2-8-11 TJarnet (2)	11/10f	sh 2
	ETERNITY RANGE (USA) *PBary,France* 2-8-11 DBoeuf (5)	78/10	1 3
	Le Triton (USA) *MmeCHead,France* 2-8-11 WRSwinburn (3)	29/10	ns 4
	Astor Place (IRE) *PWChapple-Hyam,GB* 2-8-11 JReid (1)	15/2	2 5
	Committal (IRE) *JHMGosden,GB* 2-8-11 MJKinane (7)	73/10	sh 6
	Dark Nile (USA) *MmeCHead,France* 2-8-11 PatEddery (6)	82/10	nk 7

Mr Daniel Wildenstein 7ran 1m37.60

90 Prix de La Foret (Gr 1) (3yo+ c+f) £63,051 7f

	POPLAR BLUFF (IRE) *AFabre,France* 3-9-0 OPeslier (5)	4/1	1
4	BIN AJWAAD (IRE) *BHanbury,GB* 5-9-2 PatEddery (7)	12/1	sn 2
	INZAR (USA) *PFICole,GB* 3-9-0 TQuinn (1)	49/10	1½ 3
12	Mutakddim (USA) *JHMGosden,GB* 4-9-2 WCarson (4)	13/1	sh 4
	Neverneyev (USA) *MmeCHead,France* 5-9-2 ODoleuze (3)	88/10	1 5
	Anabaa (USA) *MmeCHead,France* 3-9-0 DBoeuf (2)	15/1	1½ 6
73	Wessam Prince *CLaffon-Parias,France* 4-9-2 WRSwinburn (6)	13/1	1½ 7
73	Branston Abby (IRE) *MJohnston,GB* 6-8-13 MRoberts (10)	19/1	1½ 8
27	Myself *PWChapple-Hyam,GB* 3-8-11 TJarnet (8)	10/1	ns 9
73	Young Ern *SDow,GB* 5-9-2 MJKinane (9)	8/5f	1½ 10

Mr Daniel Wildenstein 10ran 1m18.40

WOODBINE Sunday, Oct 15 GOOD

91 E. P. Taylor Stks (Gr 2) (3yo+ f+m) £101,486 1¼m

84	TIMARIDA (IRE) *JOxx,Ireland* 3-8-5 LDettori	11/2	1
63	MATIARA (USA) *MmeCHead,France* 3-8-5 FHead	6/4f	3½ 2
	BOLD RURITANA (CAN) *MrsBMinshall,USA* 5-8-11 PDay	9/1	½ 3
	Alice Springs (USA) *JSheppard,USA* 5-8-11 JulieKrone	56/10	ns 4
	Northern Emerald (USA) *WMott,USA* 5-8-11 RPerez	9/1	2¾ 5
	Morgana (USA) *GJones,USA* 4-8-11 GStevens	12/1	ns 6
27	Warning Shadows (IRE) *CEBrittain,GB* 3-8-5 CNakatani	16/1	nk 7
84	Truly A Dream (IRE) *RCollet,France* 4-8-11 JBailey	27/1	hd 8
8	Take Liberties *AFabre,France* 3-8-5 DPenna	33/1	nk 9
	Danish (IRE) *CClement,USA* 4-8-11 JSantos	13/1	1¼ 10
	Hey Hazel (CAN) *RAttfield,Canada* 5-8-11 RLandry	38/1	2¾ 11
	My Marchesa (USA) *DVella,Canada* 5-8-11 TKabel	66/1	1½ 12
	Overcharger (USA) *AMullen,USA* 3-8-5 JMcAleney	86/1	6 13

H.H. Aga Khan 13ran 2m03.60

DONCASTER Saturday, Oct 21 GOOD to FIRM

92 Racing Post Trophy (A) (Gr 1) (2yo c+f) £87,737 1m (Rnd)

	BEAUCHAMP KING *JLDunlop* 2-9-0 JReid (3)	11/4	1
	EVEN TOP (IRE) *MHTompkins* 2-9-0 PRobinson (4)	3/1	1¼ 2
71	MONS *LMCumani* 2-9-0 PatEddery (1)	4/5f	nk 3
	Iamus *PTWalwyn* 2-9-0 WRSwinburn (2)	33/1	2 4

Mr E. Penser 4ran 1m38.89

LONGCHAMP Sunday, Oct 22 FIRM

93 Prix Royal Oak (Gr 1) (3yo+) £51,151 1m7f110y

34	SUNSHACK *AFabre,France* 4-9-4 TJarnet	9/10f	1
	SHREWD IDEA *CLaffon-Parias,France* 5-9-4 ODoleuze	29/1	2½ 2
83	SUNRISE SONG (FR) *FDoumen,France* 4-9-1 GMosse	13/1	sn 3
83	Partipral (USA) *ELellouche,France* 6-9-4 OPeslier	36/10	1½ 4
78	Assessor (IRE) *RHannon,GB* 6-9-4 RHughes	7/2	2 5
	Peckinpah's Soul (FR) *DSmaga,France* 3-8-9 FHead	62/10	8 6
83	Tot Ou Tard (IRE) *JForesi,France* 5-9-4 ESaint-Martin	14/1	6 7

Mr K. Abdulla 7ran 3m16.20

BELMONT PARK Saturday, Oct 28 Dirt course: MUDDY
Turf course: SOFT

94 Breeders' Cup Sprint (Gr 1) (3yo+) £329,114 6f

	DESERT STORMER (USA) *FrankLyons,USA* 5-8-11 KDesormeaux	14/1cp	1
	MR GREELEY (USA) *NZito,USA* 3-8-11 JulieKrone	31/1	nk 2
	LIT DE JUSTICE (USA) *JenineSahadi,USA* 5-9-0 (b) CNakatani	14/1cp	2 3
	Not Surprising (USA) *JudsonVanWorp,USA* 5-9-0 RDavis	3/1f	nk 4
	Friendly Lover (USA) *JPierce,USA* 7-9-0 (b) RWilson	14/1	2 5
	Our Emblem (USA) *CRMcGaugheyIII,USA* 4-9-0 PDay	19/2	hd 6
56	Owington *GWragg,GB* 4-9-0 (v) LDettori	14/1cp	nk 7
81	Hever Golf Rose *TJNaughton,GB* 4-8-11 JWeaver	12/1	1 8
	Golden Gear (USA) *PNHickey,USA* 4-9-0 CPerret	15/2	2 9
	You And I (USA) *RFrankel,USA* 4-9-0 JChavez	3/1	hd 10
	Track Gal (USA) *JSadler,USA* 4-8-11 CMcCarron	7/1	10 11
56	Lake Coniston (IRE) *GLewis,GB* 4-9-0 PatEddery	14/1	8 12

	Da Hoss (USA) *MWDickinson,USA* 3-8-11 JBailey	21/2	1 13

Joanne Nor 13ran 1m09.14

95	**Breeders' Cup Mile (Gr 1) (3yo+) £329,114**		1m
72	RIDGEWOOD PEARL *JOxx,Ireland* 3-8-7 JPMurtagh	2/1f	1
	FASTNESS (IRE) *JenineSahadi,USA* 5-9-0 GStevens	6/1	2 2
58	SAYYEDATI *CEBrittain,GB* 5-8-11 CNakatani	16/1	7 3
	Dove Hunt (USA) *NHoward,USA* 4-9-0 PDay	11/1	ns 4
	Savinio (USA) *WGreenman,USA* 5-9-0 CMcCarron	11/1cp	nk 5
85	Soviet Line (IRE) *MRStoute,GB* 5-9-0 WRSwinburn	35/1	1 6
	Fourstars Allstar (USA) *LO'Brien,USA* 7-9-0 JSantos	11/1cp	5 7
81	Cherokee Rose (IRE) *JEHammond,France* 4-8-11 CAsmussen	4/1	½ 8
	Mighty Forum *MHennig,USA* 4-9-0 EDelahoussaye	16/1	½ 9
	Earl of Barking (IRE) *RCross,USA* 5-9-0 LDettori	11/1	½ 10
58	Shaanxi (USA) *ELellouche,France* 3-8-7 DBoeuf	12/1	¾ 11
	The Vid (USA) *MartinWolfson,USA* 5-9-0 JBailey	6/1	1½ 12
90	Poplar Bluff (IRE) *AFabre,France* 3-8-10 OPeslier	11/1	20 13

Mrs Anne Coughlan 13ran 1m43.65

96	**Breeders' Cup Turf (Gr 1) (3yo+) £658,228**		1½m
	NORTHERN SPUR (IRE) *RMcAnally,USA* 4-9-0 CMcCarron	3/1	1
83	FREEDOM CRY *AFabre,France* 4-9-0 OPeslier	4/1	nk 2
83	CARNEGIE (IRE) *AFabre,France* 4-9-0 TJarnet	3/1cpf	1½ 3
87	Tamure (IRE) *JHMGosden,GB* 3-8-9 LDettori	3/1cpf	2½ 4
62	Hernando (FR) *JEHammond,France* 5-9-0 CAsmussen	5/1	nk 5
	Awad (USA) *DDonk,USA* 5-9-0 (b) EMaple	8/1	6¾ 6
91	Alice Springs (USA) *JSheppard,USA* 5-8-11 JulieKrone	43/1	3½ 7
	Flitch (USA) *WilliamBadgettJr,USA* 3-8-9 (b) MSmith	15/1	1 8
	Turk Passer (USA) *FSSchulhofer,USA* 5-9-0 JVelasquez	17/1	5 9
	Celtic Arms (FR) *RRash,USA* 4-9-0 GStevens	19/1	nk 10
66	Signal Tap (USA) *FSSchulhofer,USA* 4-9-0 JSantos	25/1	4 11
83	Lando (GER) *HJentzsch,Germany* 5-9-0 MRoberts	23/1	3 12
	Talloires (USA) *RMandella,USA* 5-9-0 (b) KDesormeaux	30/1	nk 13

Mr Charles Cella 13ran 2m42.07

97	**Breeders' Cup Classic (Gr 1) (3yo+) £987,342**		1¼m
	CIGAR (USA) *WMott,USA* 5-9-0 JBailey	7/10f	1
	L'CARRIERE (USA) *HaroldJamesBond,USA* 4-9-0 (b) JChavez	51/1	2½ 2
	UNACCOUNTED FOR (USA) *FSSchulhofer,USA* 4-9-0 (b) PDay	11/2	1 3
	Soul of The Matter (USA) *RMandella,USA* 4-9-0 KDesormeaux	11/1	¾ 4
	Star Standard (USA) *NZito,USA* 3-8-9 CMcCarron	54/1	6 5
	Peaks And Valleys (USA) *JDay,Canada* 3-8-9 JulieKrone	15/1	1¾ 6
	Tinners Way (USA) *RFrankel,USA* 5-9-0 EDelahoussaye	19/1	2 7
	Concern (USA) *RSmall,USA* 4-9-0 (b) MSmith	19/1	¾ 8
	French Deputy (USA) *NDrysdale,USA* 3-8-9 GStevens	14/1	4 9
	Jed Forest (USA) *ACallejas,USA* 4-9-0 RDouglas	116/1	3 10
47	Halling (USA) *SaeedbinSuroor,GB* 4-9-0 WRSwinburn	8/1	26 11

Mr Allen E. Paulson 11ran 1m59.58

SAINT-CLOUD Sunday, Oct 29 GOOD

98	**Criterium de Saint-Cloud (Gr 1) (2yo c+f) £51,613**		1¼m
67	POLARIS FLIGHT (USA) *PWChapple-Hyam,GB* 2-9-0 JReid	21/10	1
	RAGMAR (FR) *PBary,France* 2-9-0 DBoeuf	88/10	sh 2
	OLIVIERO (FR) *AMauchamp,France* 2-9-0 (b) ABadel	17/1	1 3
	Go Between (FR) *ASpanu,France* 2-9-0 ESaint-Martin	23/10	ns 4
	Quorum *AFabre,France* 2-9-0 TJarnet	2/1f	nk 5

Mr Richard S. Kaster 5ran 2m13.70

EVRY Tuesday, Nov 7 GOOD

99	**Criterium Des 2 Ans (Gr 2) (2yo c+f) £45,278**		6f110y
69	TITUS LIVIUS (FR) *JEPease,France* 2-9-2 CAsmussen	9/10f	1
	STARMANIAC (USA) *CLaffon-Parias,France* 2-8-11 GMosse	16/10	sn 2
	SEATTLE SPECIAL (USA) *MmeCHead,France* 2-8-8 ODoleuze	5/1	1 3
	Jasminola (FR) *NClement,France* 2-8-8 (b) OPeslier	13/1	3 4
98	Oliviero (FR) *AMauchamp,France* 2-8-11 (b) ABadel	85/10	½ 5

Mr S. S. Niarchos 5ran 1m19.07

TOKYO Sunday, Nov 26 FIRM

100	**Japan Cup (Gr 1) (3yo+) £1,083,805**		1½m
96	LANDO (GER) *HJentzsch,Germany* 5-9-0 MRoberts	135/10	1
	HISHI AMAZON (USA) *TNakano,Japan* 4-8-10 ENakadate		1½ 2
96	HERNANDO (FR) *JEHammond,France* 5-9-0 CAsmussen		nk 3
	Taiki Blizzard (USA) *KFujisawa,Japan* 4-9-0 YOkabe		ns 4
96	Awad (USA) *DDonk,USA* 5-9-0 (b) EMaple		1¼ 5
	Narita Brian (JPN) *MOkubo,Japan* 4-9-0 YTake		1¾ 6
	Royce And Royce (JPN) *YMatsuyama,Japan* 5-9-0 NYokoyama		½ 7
	Sandpit (BRZ) *RMandella,USA* 6-9-0 CNakatani		2½ 8
	Danewin (AUS) *RThomsen,Australia* 4-9-0 CKTse		ns 9
83	Pure Grain *MRStoute,GB* 3-8-5 JReid		½ 10
83	Carling (FR) *MmePatBarbe,France* 3-8-5 TThulliez		¾ 11
	Matikanetannhauser (JPN) *YIto,Japan* 6-9-0 YShibata		½ 12
	Nice Nature (JPN) *YMatsunaga,Japan* 7-9-0 MMatsunaga		nk 13
	Stony Bay (NZ) *MsGWaterhouse,Australia* 4-9-0 RSDye		hd 14

Gestut Haus Ittlingen 14ran 2m24.60

ERRATA & ADDENDA

'Racehorses of 1994'

Above The Cut (USA)	brother to fair 1993 2-y-o Placitana and half-brother to 2 fair ...
Bigstone (Ire)	P113, line 6: Missed Flight was 2nd, Neverneyev 3rd
Danbys Gorse	second foal
Diffident (Fr)	is a bay; he is half-brother to two French 1m winners by Groom Dancer; he won a minor race at Evry in June on debut (6m*); his dam's best rating was 117
Double Quick (Ire)	nursery at Newmarket not Nottingham
Green Land (Bel)	dam French 2-y-o 7f and 7.5f winner
Jalmaid	third foal
Our Rita	third to Nijo in *listed* event at Newmarket *penultimate* start
Puck's Castle	third to Double Eclipse in *listed race* at Newmarket
Silver Wedge (USA)	visored Goodwood Cup only
Smart Alec	P898 Ahead is sister to Criquette
Torch Vert (Ire)	dam won at 2yrs in Germany

INDEX TO SELECTED BIG RACES

THE TIMEFORM 'TOP HORSES ABROAD'

Here are listed the Timeform Ratings for the top two-year-olds, three-year-olds and older horses of 1995 in France, Germany, Ireland, Italy, other European countries and North America. Horses who are not rated high enough to be included in the main lists but who finished in the first three in a European pattern race during the season are included below the cut-off line. Fillies and mares are denoted by (f), * denotes the horse was trained for only a part of the season in the country concerned.

FRANCE

Two-Year-Olds

114p	Miss Tahiti (f)
113p	Loup Solitaire
113p	Manninamix
113+	Titus Livius
112p	Ragmar
111p	Ashkalani
111p	Eternity Range
111	Barricade
111	Go Between
111	Le Triton
111	With Fascination (f)
110p	Supreme Commander
110	Battle Dore
110	Shake The Yoke (f)
110?	Oliviero
109p	Polar Lights
109	Le Tourron
109	Quorum
108p	Contare
107p	Occupandiste (f)
107	Starmaniac
106p	Spinning World
106	Esquive (f)
106	Grenadier
105p	Cliptomania
105	Andrea's Shadow (f)
105	Dark Nile
105	L'Africain Bleu

104	Blushing Gleam (f)
103p	Luna Wells (f)
103	Mayoumbe
103	Raisonnable (f)
103	Seattle Special (f)
103	Shining Molly (f)
102	Radevore
101	Gaitero
101	Wedding Gift (f)
100p	Martiniquais
100	Prevail (f)
98+	Media Nox (f)
96p	Anziyan
96	Ella Nico (f)
94+	Kistena (f)

Three-Year-Olds

130	Pennekamp
128	Swain
123	Miss Satamixa (f)
122	Housamix
122	Shaanxi (f)
122	Valanour
121	Poliglote
121	Winged Love
120p	De Quest
120	Diamond Mix
119	Affidavit
119	Angel In My Heart (f)
119	Carling (f)
119	Diffident
119	*Labeeb
119	Matiara (f)
118	Atticus
118	Smolensk (USA) (f)
117	Poplar Bluff
117	Valley of Gold (f)
117	Walk On Mix
116	Balanka (f)
116	Muncie (f)
115p	Bobinski
115	*Dance Partner (f)
115	Garden Rose (f)
115	Petit Poucet
115	Solar One
115	*The Key Rainbow
114	Dancing Beggar
114	*Gold And Steel
114	*Privity (f)
114	Rifapour
114	Vadlamixa (f)
113	Peckinpah's Soul
113	Tamise (f)
113	Tereshkova (f)
112	East of Heaven
112	Vaguely Gay
111	Macoumba (f)
111	Rainbow Dancer
111	Silent Warrior
111	Struggler
110	Angel Falls
110	Bashaayeash
110	Collecta (f)
110	*Dirca (f)
110	Fairy Path (f)
110	Ghostly (f)
110	Madaiyn
110	Marie de Ken (f)
110	Senneville
110	Take Liberties (f)
109p	Danefair (f)
109	Amato
109	*Beau Temps
109	Homme d'Honneur
109	Kassani
109	Kirdoun
109	Lord of Appeal
109	Lyphard's Honor
109	*Tabor
109	Tzar Rodney
108	*Bene Erit
108	Daraydala (f)
108	Hexane (f)
108	Irish Wings
108	Le Silencieux
108	Linoise (f)
108	Philanthrop
108	*Pinfloron
108	Pont Audemer (f)
108	Restiv Star (f)
108	Rio Verde
108	Secret Quest (f)
108	Shannjar
108	Sharpest Image
108	Suivez La (f)
108	Super Gascon
107	Baba Thong
107	Copent Garden
107	El Tenor
107	Faru
107	Genofeva (f)
107	Highest Cafe
107	Loretta Gianni (f)
107	Marble Falls (f)
107	Parfait Glace
107	Perche No
107	Periple
107	Redwood Falls (f)
107	Suresnes
107	Ultra Finesse (f)

106	Bulington
106	Farenvaros
106	Palafairia (f)
105	Bruttina (f)
105	Enquiry (f)
104	Denver County
104	Syvanie (f)

103 *Nimble Mind (f)

Older Horses

132 Freedom Cry
129 Carnegie
125 Green Tune
125 Hernando
124d *Tikkanen
122 Cherokee Rose (f)
122 Sunshack
121 Millkom
120 Always Earnest
120 Gunboat Diplomacy
120 Marildo
120 *Partipral
119 Nononito
118 Kaldounevees
117 *Richard of York
117 Solid Illusion
117 Thames
117 The Little Thief
117 Volochine
116 Tot Ou Tard
115 Dernier Empereur
115 Nec Plus Ultra
115 Shrewd Idea
115 *Windsharp (f)
114 Agathe (f)
114 Suave Tern
114 *Tuesday's Special
113 Sand Reef
113 Solidoun
113 Wessam Prince
112 Neverneyev
112 *Parme
112 *Sans Ecocide
112 Sunrise Song (f)
111 Danseur Landais
111 *Erin Bird (f)
111 Matarun
111 Pibarnon
111 Rainbow Dancer
111 Spain Lane (f)
111 Truly A Dream (f)
111 *Walter Willy
110 Signoretto
109 Fanion de Fete
109 *Smart Wise
109 West Man
109 Zillion
108 Captain Haddock
108 Epaphos
108 Scandinavian
108 Scribe
108 Way West
107 Abrek
107 Alamtara
107 *Allez Les Trois (f)
107 Bybus
107 *Electric Society (f)
107 Grioun (f)
107 Kanuni
107 Lac Ladoga
107 Napoli (f)
107 Northern Spy

---

106 L'Ile Tudy (f)
106 Tellurium
105 *En Cascade
104 Ballet Prince
103 Michel Georges

GERMANY

Two-Year-Olds

107p Lavirco
106p Massada (f)
103 Barlovento
102 Wind of Chance
101 Roseate Wood (f)
101 Topastino
100 Dulcero
100 Happy Boy
100 Likoto
99 Midday Girl (f)
99 Song of Peace (f)
98 Catoki
98 Savage (f)
98 Sir Warren
98 Surako
97 Fairlight (f)
96 Accento
96 Guilestro
96 Ocean Sea
96 Wonder of Dashing
95 Decamerone
95 Salista (f)
94p Bon Jovi
94 Henning's Boy
94 Peppito
93 Masai Mara (f)
93 My Happy Guest
93 Top Express

Three-Year-Olds

123 Solon
116p All My Dreams
116 Tryphosa (f)
113 Macanal
112 Lecroix
112 Manzoni
112 Masterplayer
111 Artan
111 First Hello
111 Sir King
110 A Magicman
109 Centaine (f)
108 Chato
108 Ladoni
108 Prairie Shadow
108 S'Il Vous Plait (f)
107 Tristano

---

106 Devil River Peek
105 Alpha City (f)
105 Moltaire
105 O'Connor
105 Siberian Grey
105 Sinyar
104 Oxalagu
104 Tascilla (f)
103 Anna Domani (f)
103 Kalimnos
103 Lara (f)
102 Chadayed
102 Desidera (f)
102 Matula
101 Secret Energy (f)
101 Speedster
100 Lost Love (f)
100 Rivero
96 Music Palace

Older Horses

128 Lando
123 Germany
120 Sternkoenig
119 Monsun
118 Laroche
118 Royal Abjar
116 Protektor
115 Caballo
115 Concepcion
115 Hollywood Dream (f)
114 Sylvan Point
113 Kornado
111 Aratikos
111 Erminius
111 Hondero
109 Bad Bertrich
108 Flamingo Paradise
108 Prince Firebird
108 Tres Hereux
107 Dream For Future
107 No Dancer
107 Perfect Vintage
107 Silent Lake
107 Upper Heights

---

104 Fabriano
104 Flying Dream (f)
104 Munaaji
104 Zohar
103 Purple Rain (f)
98 Telasco
97 Ostwahl (f)
96 Ibiano

IRELAND

Two-Year-Olds

110 Almaty
108p Force of Will
108 Deed of Love
107 Dance Design (f)
103p Deynawari
103p Lidanna (f)
103p Priory Belle (f)

103 Catch A Glimpse (f)
102p Ahkaam
102 Harghar
100p Sheraka (f)
99p Aylesbury
99 Sunset Reigns (f)
98p Flame of Athens
98 No Animosity
98 Rithab (f)
97 Nashcash
96 Rainbow Blues
96 Super Gift (f)
95 Long Beach
95 Mitch
94 Asmara (f)
94 Ceirseach (f)
94 Errazuriz (f)
94 Liprandi
94 Sagar Pride (f)
93p Vivo
93p Zafzala (f)
93 High Target
93 Red Robin
93 Sheffield (f)
93 Tout A Coup (f)
92p Party Poll
92 Common Spirit
92 Dance Clear (f)
92 Identify (f)
92 Ribot's Secret (f)
92 Slightly Speedy
90p Merawang
90 Anwaar (f)
90 Ashbal
90 Classic Fountain
90 Lacinia (f)

Three-Year-Olds

125 Ridgewood Pearl (f)
124 Timarida (f)
121 Definite Article
121 Desert Style
120 *Shemaran
119 Oscar Schindler
118 Adjareli
116 Humbel
113p Russian Snows (f)
113 Burden of Proof
113 Nautical Pet
112 I'm Supposin
112 Off'N'Away
111p Golden Orb
111 Khaytada (f)
111 Wild Bluebell (f)
110 Mediation (f)
110 Petite Fantasy (f)
110 Viaticum (f)
109 Hasainiya (f)
107 Ailleacht (f)
107 Celladonia
107 *Daraydan
107 Johansson
107 Munif

107 Sir Silver Sox
106 Damancher
106 Daryabad
106 Fill The Bill
106 Radomsko
106 Storm Ashore
105 Alisidora (f)
105 Manashar
105 Park Charger (f)
105 Sharp Point (f)
105 Union Decree
104 Charillus
104 Free To Speak
103 Khayrawani
102 America's Cup
102 Bluffing (f)
102 Kadamann
102 Mister Chippy
102 Soreze (f)
102 Tarajan
102? Raghida (f)
101 Propitious (f)
101 Rawy
101 Tom Tom
101 Zabadi
100p Nafasiyr
100p Taglioni
100 Rosillo

---

99 Kayaara

Older Horses

120 Vintage Crop
114 Hushang
113 Al Mohaajir
113 Ridgewood Ben
111 Dancing Sunset (f)
111 Idris
111 Royal Ballerina (f)
110 Ballykett Nancy (f)
110 Double On (f)
109 Akhiyar
109 Dairine's Delight (f)
109 Ivory Frontier
109 Tourandot
109§ The Puzzler
108 Magic Feeling (f)
108 Mohaajir
105 Baydur
105 Diamond Class
105 Nordic Oak
102 State Crystal (f)
102? Peruke
101 Acumen (f)
100 Diligent Dodger
100 Lake Kariba
100 Persian Creek

ITALY

Two-Year-Olds

105p Glory of Dancer
100 Brave Indigo
100 Kafhar
98 Konic
97 Blu Taxidoo
97 Monkey Trouble
96 Bog Wild (f)
96 Coral Reef
96 Tuareg Blu
95 Beauty Dancer (f)
95 Blu Tuama (f)
94 Armando Carpio
93 Dancer Mitral
93 Nerina Vergottini (f)
93 Sergesto
92 Anticolano
92+ Germignaga (f)
92 Infiel (f)
92 Power Pach
92 Secret Lear
92 Sharp Reproach
91 Alabastro
91 Attimo Fuggente
91 Last Hero
91 Robereva (f)
91 Sooki Sooki (f)
91 Try My Segnor
90 Blu Meltemi (f)
90 Cohiba Lanceros
90 Golden Agos
90 Karla Wyller (f)
90 Lawrence Durrel
90 Pappa Reale (f)
90 Toto Le Moko

Three-Year-Olds

118 Slicious
109 Pourquois Pas (f)
109 Tarhelm
108 Ice And Glacial
108 Olimpia Dukakis (f)
108 Oxford Line
108 Reinaldo
108 Seattle John

---

106 Robins
106 Thomire
104 De Puntillas (f)
104 Rosi Zambotti (f)
103 Red Paper
94 Love Secret (f)

Older Horses

114 Beat of Drums
113 Lake Storm
113 Les Boyer
113 Morigi
113 Welsh Liberty
111 Firing Line
111 Lear White
111 My Irish
110 Scribano
109 Guado d'Annibale
109d Fred Bongusto
108 Imprevedibile

107 Puerto Escondido
107 Ravier
107 Sabi Groom
107 Sotabrasciet

---

104 New Herald
104 Senebrova (f)
103 Golden Bechett
103 Sugarland Express
102 Ashoka

OTHER EUROPEAN COUNTRIES

Three-Year-Olds

114 Val d'Arbois
110 Almaz
108 Madrileno
108 Trois Temps

---

106 Kill The Crab (f)

Older Horses

116 King Cobra
110 Glenlivet
107 *Alexandrovich
107 Toba

NORTH AMERICA

European-trained horses who showed or reproduced their best form in North America are included in this list

† commentary in *Racehorses of 1995*

Two-Year-Olds

123p Unbridled's Song
122 Cobra King
122 Hennessy
121p Maria's Mon
119p Ide
119? Matty G
118 My Flag (f)
117 Cara Rafaela (f)
116 Future Quest
116 Golden Attraction (f)
116 Louis Quatorze
115 Advancing Star (f)
115 Editor's Note
114 Honour And Glory
114? Crafty But Sweet (f)
113 Antespend (f)
113 Birr (f)
113 Flat Fleet Feet (f)
112 Diligence
112 Exetera
112 Gomtuu
112 Odyle
112 Othello
112 Tipically Irish (f)
112? La Rosa (f)
111 Appealing Skier
111 Batroyale (f)
111 Cavonnier
111 Seeker's Reward
111 Ticket To Houston (f)
111 Top Secret (f)
111 Western Dreamer (f)
111? Crown Attorney
110 Devil's Honor
110 Gold Fever
110 Pareja (f)
110 Sealaunch
110 Silken Cat (f)
110 Wheatly Special (f)
110? J J's Dream (f)
109 Bright Launch
109 Feather Box
109 Gastronomical (f)
109 Ocean View (f)
109 Old Chapel
109 Seacliff
108 Blazing Hot (f)
108 Firm Dancer
108 Gold Sunrise (f)
108 Kristy Krunch
108 Northernprospector
108 Raw Gold (f)
108 Skip Away
108 Tropicool

DIRT

Three-Year-Olds

129 Thunder Gulch
124 Timber Country
123 Serena's Song (f)
123? Oliver's Twist
122 Afternoon Deelites
122 Larry The Legend
122 Mr Greeley
122 Peaks And Valleys
121 Jumron
121 Tejano Run
120 †Eltish
120 Pyramid Peak
120 Talkin Man
119 Chaposa Springs (f)
119 Star Standard
119 Urbane (f)
119 Wild Syn
118 French Deputy
118 Golden Bri (f)
118 Suave Prospect
117 Flying Chevron
117 Gal In A Ruckus (f)
117 Kiridashi
117 Malthus
117 Pretty Discreet (f)
116 Cat's Cradle (f)
116 †Citadeed
116 Knockadoon
116 Lord Carson
116 Regal Discovery
116 Scotzanna (f)
115 Ft Stockton
115 Tethra

Older Horses

135 Cigar
131 Holy Bull
130 Inside Information (f)
128 Silver Goblin
127 Concern
126 Devil His Due
125 Heavenly Prize (f)
125 L'Carriere
124 Unaccounted For
123 Best Pal
123 Not Surprising
123 Soul of The Matter
122 Cherokee Run
122 Desert Stormer (f)
122 Dramatic Gold
122 Sky Beauty (f)
122 Tinners Way
122 Tossofthecoin
121 Dare And Go
120 Hollywood Wildcat (f)
120 Lit de Justice
120 Paseana (f)
120 Queens Court Queen (f)
120 Twist Afleet (f)
119 Educated Risk (f)
119 Lakeway (f)
119 Siphon
119 Track Gal (f)
119 Wekiva Springs
118 Birdonthewire
118 Blumin Affair
118 Calipha (f)
118 Classy Mirage (f)
118 Pirate's Revenge (f)
118 You And I
117 Borodislew (f)
117 Chimes Band
117 Del Mar Dennis
117 Friendly Lover
117 Jade Flush (f)
117 Lite The Fuse
117 Schossberg
117 Urgent Request
116 Basqueian
116 Fit To Lead (f)
116 Forest Gazelle
116 Key Contender
116 Lykatill Hil
116 Mariah's Storm (f)
116 Rapan Boy
115 Alphabet Soup
115 College Town
115 Dusty Screen
115 Halo America (f)
115 Lucky Forever
115 Mr Shawklit
115 Yourmissinthepoint

TURF

Three-Year-Olds

125 †Ridgewood Pearl (f)
125 †Tamure
124 †Timarida (f)
120 Mecke
120 Perfect Arc (f)
119 †Angel In My Heart (f)
119 Hawk Attack
119 †Labeeb
119 †Matiara (f)
118 †Helmsman
117 †Torrential
117 Unanimous Vote
116 Auriette (f)
116 †Balanka (f)
116 Dowty
116 Sleep Easy (f)
115 Da Hoss
115 Diplomatic Jet
115 †Fanjica (f)
115 The Key Rainbow

Older Horses

133 Northern Spur
132 †Freedom Cry
129 †Carnegie
126 Fastness
125 †Hernando
124 Awad
123 Sandpit
122 Possibly Perfect (f)
121 Fourstars Allstar
121 Lassigny
121 †Millkom
121 †Red Bishop
121 Royal Chariot
121 Turk Passer
120 Duda (f)
120 Talloires
119 Alpride (f)
119 Blues Traveller
119 Earl of Barking
119 Exchange (f)
119 Finder's Fortune
119 The Vid
118 Alice Springs (f)
118 Bold Ruritana (f)
118 Celtic Arms
118 Dove Hunt
118 †Kaldounevees
118 Kiri's Clown
118 Megan's Interco
118 Mighty Forum
118 Misil
118 River Flyer
118 Romarin
118 Special Price
118 Ventiquattrofogli
118 Wandesta (f)
117 Danish (f)
117 Interim (f)
117 †La Confederation (f)
117 Savinio
117 Silver Wizard
117 Star of Manila
117 Unfinished Symph
117 Vaudeville
116 Alywow (f)
116 Debutant Trick
116 Hasten To Add
116 Irish Linnet (f)
116 Northern Emerald (f)
116 Pride of Summer
116 Signal Tap
116 Slew of Damascus
116 Yenda (f)
115 Boyce
115 Dumaani
115 Fly Cry
115 Windsharp (f)

NORTH AMERICAN REVIEW **Cigar**. The five-year-old one-time failure on turf put up a season the like of which had not been seen in America since 1980. He won all ten of his races—eight of them Grade 1 events—on six courses, in six states and in every calendar month from January to October with the exception of August. If not quite so breathtaking as Spectacular Bid fifteen years earlier, he nonetheless disposed of all challengers, effective from the front or held up, and never looked in serious danger of defeat. Perhaps the pick of his races on form was when giving 8 lb and a three-and-a-half-length beating to Tinners Way and Tossofthecoin in the Hollywood Gold Cup, but it is worth noting that in his three races in New York afterwards, all at weight-for-age, he gave the impression he was just doing enough to win. If more improvement is to be wrought from Cigar, it may have to come from increasingly stern weight assignments. In 1995 Cigar contested six handicaps and never had to carry more than nine stone; backers were so unconcerned about his weight concessions that in the last five he was sent off at odds on, winning by between two and a quarter and seven and a half lengths. Notwithstanding that racetracks will be competing to attract Cigar (there is no centralised handicapping in America and the days when outstanding champions like Forego were assigned and carried huge burdens are a fading memory), things will surely be made harder for him in 1996. Perhaps his very best form is yet to come. Either way, European racegoers may find it hard to believe that, after all his accomplishments, Cigar will still be around in 1996—as a six-year-old! Connections have made the 'racehorses are meant to race' decision which is arrived at far more often in America than Britain. The general attitude to defeat of a top-class horse (it doesn't necessarily detract from his accomplishments) is one of many excellent aspects of racing in America. One of the worst—certainly to foreigners who are perhaps in the dark as to some of the facts—was a challenger for news space with Cigar in 1995, which, like him, can be summed up in one five-letter word: **Lasix**.

New York State had held out against the use of race-day 'medication' for a long time after it had become legal in every other major racing state. But, after a year in

America's Horse of the Year Cigar records his twelfth win in a row in the Breeders' Cup Classic

which New York had voted in a new governor, and new chairmen had been appointed to the New York State Racing and Wagering Board and the New York Racing Association, it capitulated. Lasix (which helps prevent horses bleeding) was allowed from September 1st amidst justifications like 'rules (in America) should be uniform', though there are still considerable differences between states as to how much can be administered and when, and the leniency of the rules restricting which horses qualify as being in need of medication. In an article in *The Sporting Life*, Alan Shuback brought to task new NYSRWB chairman Dr Jerry Bilinski's 'hope that a rule change ... will provide more of a level playing field and help attract quality horses', Shuback stating that if the chairman meant that bleeders which are denied race-day medication are running at a disadvantage, didn't it follow that once such horses are allowed medication, horses which do not bleed, that is healthy horses, will necessarily be punished for being healthy? It is easy to sympathise with Shuback, while, at the same time, understand that the suppression of infirmity and pain (the pain killer butazolidin, or 'bute', is allowed in many states, though not New York) is a help in keeping races filled with entries when you have centralised racing (meetings can last several months) and nine races a day six days a week. Americans who do not want to allow medication in the graded stakes—the races which sort out the equine hierarchy and whose runners will breed the next generation—would face monumental legal battles to get things changed. However, are horses which 'bleed' or which are unsound, likely to pass these traits on to their offspring? This is an important question facing the purchasers of American bloodstock, particularly if the horse in question is due to race outside the States. In an article in *Thoroughbred Times* George Williams quoted leading trainer 'Shug' McGaughey as saying 'I would prefer to breed to a horse that raced lasix-free just in case it is hereditary'. George Williams himself wrote, 'In twenty years, North American-bred horses might not be able to compete with horses from countries with long term no-medication policies.' On the other hand, just as blinkers have been sweepingly generalised as 'the rogue's badge', so all horses which run on medication aren't necessarily infirm. Hall of Fame trainer Woody Stephens said 'I think nine-tenths of trainers using all available medication don't know whether the horses need it or don't need it, so they just give it to them anyway.' Even Eclipse Award-winning trainer Bill Mott was quoted in 1995 as saying that 'he (Cigar) does not necessarily need lasix ... But it's a precaution against bleeding. We might as well use it if it's available.' It will not be available at the Dubai World Cup in March, but it would be foolish to believe that as a result Cigar's chances of proving himself still the best horse around are necessarily diminished.

Many horses chased Cigar during 1995. How close they got is largely reflected by their ratings, the notable exception being **Holy Bull**. The 1994 Horse of the Year gave weight and a comfortable beating to smart sprinter Birdonthewire over seven furlongs on his reappearance, but sadly broke down in the Donn Handicap, while racing alongside Cigar, and was retired to stud. **Silver Goblin** did marginally best of the rest, going down by two and a half lengths to the champion in the Oaklawn Handicap (9f) before injuring himself on his next outing. **Devil His Due** showed the same form as in 1994, beaten just over two lengths in the Pimlico Special (9.5f), as did **Concern** (winner of the nine-furlong Californian) who finished behind Cigar on four occasions. **L'Carriere** and **Unaccounted For** (Whitney Handicap over 9f) made great strides in the second half of the year and filled the places in the Breeders' Cup Classic. Further behind that day, **Soul of The Matter** and **Tinners Way** (1¼m Pacific Classic again) had greater success in their base state of California; they had a particularly fine set-to in the Grade 2 Goodwood Handicap. Seven-year-old **Best Pal** continued to pile up the dollars and failed by only a head to give 6 lb to **Urgent Request** in the Santa Anita Handicap (1¼m), with **Dare And Go** back in third. Dare And Go improved a little in 1995 and had previously taken advantage of a 6 lb weight concession to beat **Dramatic Gold** in the Strub Stakes (1¼m). The sprinters were not particularly distinguished, narrowly the best being the tough gelding **Not Surprising,** although the 1994 Breeders' Cup Sprint winner **Cherokee Run** had an impressive win early on before injury intervened, and the 1995 renewal was won by a filly, **Desert Stormer**, who saved her best effort for her last.

Among the rest of the older females there was a marked changing of the guard. **Paseana** (who was rated at 128 in 1992) fully deserved her retirement, aged eight, no longer quite the force of old, while **Queens Court Queen** retired aged six after putting up her best efforts at the end of her career by beating her illustrious stable companion. **Hollywood Wildcat** was injured after an impressive winning reappearance, but reigning champion **Sky Beauty** was ushered to the paddocks after suffering crushing defeats behind the McGaughey fillies **Heavenly Prize** and **Inside Information**, both from the renowned Phipps family breeding operation. By the time of the Breeders' Cup Distaff each filly had run sixteen times in her career, Heavenly Prize winning nine times, Inside Information thirteen, and neither had ever finished out of the first three. Heavenly Prize seemed to have grabbed most of the headlines with eight Grade 1 victories, including two at Saratoga back in the summer by eleven lengths and eight and a half lengths. However, Inside Information's record bore the closest inspection too, the winner of five Grade 1 races, two of them by eleven lengths. Beforehand it was clear that Heavenly Prize would have been suited by the Distaff being run at a mile and a quarter (at which trip no horse had ever got within seven lengths of her) rather than nine furlongs, and it seemed, on limited evidence, that Inside Information would probably be the better suited by the muddy track; but few could have predicted what was about to happen. Leading before halfway, Inside Information quickened on the sweeping turn and kept increasing her advantage until she crossed the line thirteen and a half lengths clear. Heavenly Prize—as far behind the winner after about two furlongs as she was at the finish—ran on to take second with the remainder (including **Mariah's Storm**, who is rated on the balance of her form and not on one seemingly-excellent defeat of Serena's Song) strung out behind, only **Twist Afleet** (later winner of 1m Top Flight Handicap) missing from a good field. It was a stunning performance, and the news that both Phipps fillies will be at stud in 1996 will be of particular comfort to the owners of good three-year-olds.

The classic generation was dominated by horses from the D. Wayne Lukas stable. **Serena's Song** won nine races—six of them Grade 1 events—and although well beaten in the Kentucky Derby she did beat the colts twice, including in the nine-furlong Haskell Invitational Handicap, and (after being allowed to set a slow pace) held off Heavenly Prize by three quarters of a length in the Beldame (8.5f). **Urbane** (8.5f Ashland), **Golden Bri** (1¼m Coaching Club American Oaks over an apparently non-staying Serena's Song), **Pretty Discreet** (1¼m Alabama in terrible conditions) and **Chaposa Springs** (7f Test) had their moments, but Serena's Song comfortably takes the palm. **Thunder Gulch** and **Timber Country** took the triple crown events between them. Thunder Gulch struck the first blow, winning the Kentucky Derby by two and a quarter lengths from **Jumron** (**Tejano Run** beaten three lengths in fourth) before Timber Country, who had finished third after none too clear a run in Kentucky, won the Preakness narrowly from **Oliver's Twist** (who never ran to anything like the same form before or afterwards) and Thunder Gulch. Timber Country injured himself and was retired to stud in Japan, but Thunder Gulch went on to win four more races, including the Belmont (1½m) and the Travers (1¼m, easily from **Pyramid Peak**), before suffering an injury behind Cigar in the Woodward. He was a really tough and genuine colt. Of the others rated 120 or more, **Afternoon Deelites** and **Larry The Legend** also failed to complete a full season due to injury. Larry the Legend (bought for just 2,500 dollars) beat Afternoon Deelites and Jumron a head and a neck in the Santa Anita Derby (9f), but while he failed to return, Afternoon Deelites made a promising come-back by winning the Malibu (7f) in December. **Mr Greeley** did not race beyond a mile and showed improved form when beaten a neck in the Breeders' Cup Sprint (6f) before being retired. **Peaks And Valleys** progressed steadily and won the Molsen Export Million and the Meadowlands Cup over nine furlongs, before disappointing somewhat in the Breeders' Cup Classic. **Mecke** won the Super Derby (1¼m) impressively before running two good races back on turf, while **Talkin Man** won the Grade 2 Wood Memorial (9f) impressively, but the latter was retired after failing in two classics. It will be interesting to see how the very lightly raced **French Deputy** gets on in 1996; he won the Grade 2 Jerome Handicap (1m) by four lengths from Mr Greeley after a long layoff, but was beaten in an allowance event next time out.

The two-year-old divisions both lacked a clear leader, though Eclipse Award winner **Golden Attraction** (a sister to Red Carnival) did win three Grade 1 races leading up to the Breeders' Cup Juvenile Fillies (8.5f); however, none was by so much as a length, and at Belmont two of her previous victims, **Cara Rafaela** (who later beat **Advancing Star** a head in the 8.5 furlong Hollywood Starlet) and **My Flag** turned the tables on her. My Flag produced a strong finish to snatch the spoils close home but it remains to be seen whether this very well bred filly (by Easy Goer out of Personal Ensign), who looks to be crying out for middle distances, will be hampered by the relative scarcity of opportunities at a mile and a quarter plus for three-year-old fillies. The form among the fillies is not outstanding and, with the leaders having been highly tried, there is scope for some new names to emerge as 1996 progresses.

Among the colts, the early leader was **Hennessy**, whose spectacular run of wins included the Hopeful (6f, by 3¼ lengths from **Louis Quatorze**) at Saratoga. Third that day, **Maria's Mon**, earned the Eclipse Award by winning the Futurity (7f, by 2¾ lengths from Louis Quatorze) and the Champagne (1m) at Belmont, but was subsequently injured and is not expected to return until at least June. Maiden winner **Unbridled's Song** disappointed in the Champagne (setting far too strong a pace) but he settled much better and beat Hennessy by a neck after a fine duel in the Breeders' Cup Juvenile (8.5f)—the pair four lengths clear of **Editor's Note.** Late in the year **Cobra King** confirmed his mid-season promise by beating Hennessy half a length in a Grade 3 event over seven furlongs while **Matty G** (twice a disappointment previously in stakes) ran away with what was an admittedly unsatisfactory Hollywood Futurity (8.5f). **Ide** reportedly suffered breathing problems early on, but won his last five races, giving 3 lb and beating Editor's Note by three quarters of a length in a Grade 3 event over 8.5 furlongs at Churchill Downs in November. At this early stage, Ide, Unbridled's Song and Cobra King look the best prospects for the triple crown races, though their form is not yet at the level required to win a classic.

With the retirement of Paradise Creek and Lure (now at Coolmore Stud in Ireland after a fertility-hit year at Claiborne) there was room at the top for new stars on the turf. Touted in *Racehorses of 1994* as a potential champion stayer in Europe, **Northern Spur** was sent to the USA where he did not reappear until August, breaking a blood vessel on his second start. Lasix was administered for his last two starts and he won the Oak Tree Invitational from **Sandpit** (9.5f Caesar's International Handicap) before improving considerably again to beat Freedom Cry a neck in the Breeders' Cup Turf. Northern Spur remains in training and should win more good races. A word of caution, though: conditions for the Breeders' Cup Turf were extremely testing (Arlington Million winner **Awad**, for one, failed to give his running) and probably brought out the very best in him—such conditions are seldom seen in America. **Fastness** had a very good year, winning the Eddie Read Handicap (9f) at Del Mar, finishing clear of the remainder when 2 lengths second to Ridgewood Pearl in the Breeders' Cup Mile, then breaking a course record over nine furlongs in the Grade 2 Citation Handicap. The 1994 Prix du Jockey-Club winner **Celtic Arms** raced without great success in 1995, but another ex-French colt, **Lassigny**, improved in the autumn, winning the Rothmans International (1½m). **Royal Chariot's** best effort came with a narrow win over **Talloires** in the Hollywood Turf Cup (1½m) in December, while **Turk Passer** took advantage of being allowed to set a slow pace when upsetting Hernando in the Turf Classic (1½m), easily his best effort. Of the fillies, **Duda** came out best in a bunched finish to the Matriarch Stakes (1¼m) in November, but by then the best turf mare had retired. **Possibly Perfect** ended a fine career by winning all but one of her races (3 Grade 1 events) in 1995, though her best effort was possibly when failing by a length and three quarters to give 9 lb to ex-Italian **Alpride** in the Beverly Hills Handicap (9f). The three-year-old colts on turf were a comparatively poor lot, smart ex-French colt **Labeeb** beating **Helmsman** in the Hollywood Derby (9f). Among the fillies, though, **Perfect Arc** was indeed perfect, winning all seven of her races culminating in the Queen Elizabeth II Challenge Cup (9f). She will race on at four and should prove a tough nut for her elders, and for the European imports that stay in training. 1996 will provide the answers. 1995's achievements are now in the form-book, however, and the best of them belonged to a horse called Cigar.

With the traffic in horses between Europe and America, and the growing internationalism of racing, there is a demand for a reliable measure of racing merit. Timeform Ratings are available for all 'black-type' performers in the northern hemisphere. The Timeform Race Card for the Breeders' Cup at Belmont was very well received by on-line subscribers to Bloodstock Research Information Services, Inc, in Kentucky and we hope to continue to provide information to North American customers about the best horses. We are always pleased to have comments from American and other overseas subscribers.

INTERNATIONAL CLASSIFICATIONS

The International Classifications were published on 11th January, 1996. The leading horses are shown (* trained exclusively outside Europe).

TWO-YEAR-OLDS

126 Alhaarth
124 Royal Applause
120 Danehill Dancer
119 Blue Duster
119 Rio Duvida
118 Lord of Men
118 Loup Solitaire
117 Manninamix
117 Miss Tahiti
117 Tagula
116 Almaty
116 Woodborough
115 Beauchamp King
115 Eternity Range
115 Kahir Almaydan
115 Le Triton
115 Mons
114 Bosra Sham
114 Shake The Yoke
113 Allied Forces
113 Ashkalani
113 Barricade
113 Bint Salsabil
113 Cayman Kai
113 Even Top
113 Mawwal
113 Occupandiste
113 Spinning World
113 Tumbleweed Ridge
113 With Fascination
112 Lucky Lionel
112 Mezzogiorno
112 My Branch
112 Polaris Flight
112 Russian Revival
112 Solar Crystal
112 South Salem
112 Storm Trooper
112 Titus Livius
112 Winter Quarters
112 World Premier
111 Astor Place
111 Cliptomania
111 Committal
111 Glory of Dancer
111 Mubhij
111 Ragmar
110 Applaud
110 Bijou d'Inde
110 Dance Design
110 Dance Sequence
110 Dark Nile
110 Deed of Love
110 Force of Will
110 Go Between
110 Like A Hawk
110 Mick's Love
110 Oliviero
110 Priory Belle
110 Take A Left
109 Battle Dore
109 Blue Iris
109 Blushing Gleam
109 Busy Flight
109 Contare
109 Darling Flame
109 Heron Island
109 Kings Witness
109 Luna Wells
109 Mayoumbe
109 More Royal
109 Quorum
109 Radevore
109 Raisonnable
109 Restless Carl
109 Ruznama
109 Sovereign's Crown
109 Trivellino
108 Brandon Magic
108 Brave Indigo
108 Gaitero
108 Honest Guest
108 Iamus
108 Inchrory
108 Lavirco
108 Mark of Esteem
108 Martiniquais
108 My Melody Parkes
108 Parrot Jungle
108 Resounder
108 Shining Molly
108 Sweet Robin
108 Wedding Gift
108 Yarob
107 Bint Shadayid
107 Brighstone
107 Jack Jennings
107 Kafhar
107 Kuantan
107 Latin Reign
107 Line Dancer
107 Lomberto
107 Papaha
107 Prevail
107 Rupert
107 Starmaniac
107 Tamnia
107 Wood Magic
106 Al Abraq
106 Bahamian Knight
106 Catch A Glimpse
106 Coldstream
106 Danesman
106 Dismissed
106 Double Leaf
106 Flying Squaw
106 Lidanna
106 Maid For The Hills
106 Media Nox
106 Myrtle
106 Najiya
106 Quakers Field
106 Red Robbo
106 Sasuru
106 Scarlet Plume
106 Sketchbook
106 Warning Time
106 Zuhair

THREE-YEAR-OLDS

130 Lammtarra
129 Bahri
126 Pentire
126 Ridgewood Pearl
126 Serena's Song*
126 Thunder Gulch*
125 Pennekamp
125 Swain
125 Timber Country*
124 Celtic Swing
124 Perfect Arc*
124 Spectrum
123 Timarida
122 Luso
122 Peaks And Valleys*
122 Singspiel
122 Tamure
122 Urbane*
121 Larry The Legend*
121 Miss Satamixa
121 Poliglote
121 Tejano Run*
121 Valanour
121 Winged Love
120 Afternoon Deelites*
120 Definite Article
120 Desert Style
120 Eltish
120 Flemensfirth
120 Gal In A Ruckus*
120 Golden Bri*
120 Jumron*
120 Riyadian
120 Shaanxi
120 Star Standard*
119 Annus Mirabilis
119 Cat's Cradle*

119 Classic Cliche
119 Diamond Mix
119 Labeeb
119 Mecke*
119 Mind Games
119 Montjoy
119 Mr Greeley*
119 Presenting
119 Pyramid Peak*
119 Solon
118 Country Cat*
118 Harayir
118 Helmsman
118 Moonshell
118 Pure Grain
118 Shemaran
118 Slicious
117 Adjareli
117 Affidavit
117 Angel In My Heart
117 Carling
117 Charnwood Forest
117 Court of Honour
117 Fahal
117 Matiara
117 Oliver's Twist*
117 Oscar Schindler
117 Smolensk (USA)
117 Vettori
116 All My Dreams
116 Atticus
116 Bail Out Becky*
116 Chaposa Springs*
116 Dance A Dream
116 Diplomatic Jet*
116 Housamix
116 Miss Union Avenue*
116 Pineing Patty*
116 Pipe Major
116 Poplar Bluff
116 Posidonas
116 Suave Prospect*
116 Talkin Man*
116 Tamayaz
116 Torrential
116 Unanimous Vote*
115 Aqaarid
115 Auriette*
115 Balanka
115 Citadeed
115 Hawk Attack*
115 Hoolie*
115 Kathie's Colleen*
115 Larrocha
115 Sleep Easy*
115 Valley of Gold

FOUR-YEAR-OLDS AND UPWARDS

132 Cigar*
129 Inside Information*
129 Northern Spur*
128 Freedom Cry
128 Halling
128 Heavenly Prize*
127 Holy Bull*
127 Lake Coniston
126 Carnegie
126 Silver Goblin*
125 Fastness*
125 Lando
125 L'Carriere*
124 Concern*
124 Possibly Perfect*
123 Muhtarram
123 Unaccounted For*
122 Awad*
122 Cherokee Run*
122 Green Tune
122 Missed Flight
122 Sky Beauty*
122 Soul of The Matter*
121 Germany
121 Hernando
121 Mariah's Storm*
121 Millkom
121 Pelder
121 Piccolo
121 Romarin*
121 Sandpit*
121 Strategic Choice
121 Tinners Way*
120 Best Pal*
120 Broadway Flyer
120 Devil His Due*
120 Lassigny*
120 Not Surprising*
120 Queens Court Queen*
120 Sayyedati
120 Soviet Line
120 Sunshack
119 Double Trigger
119 Dramatic Gold*
119 Duda*
119 Educated Risk*
119 Hever Golf Rose
119 Irish Linnet*
119 Monsun
119 Moonax
119 Our Emblem*
119 Paseana*
119 The Vid*
119 Vintage Crop
119 You And I*
119 Young Ern
118 Alderbrook
118 Alice Springs*
118 Alpride*
118 Bold Ruritana*
118 Cherokee Rose
118 Dove Hunt*
118 Flagbird
118 Lakeway*
118 Lite The Fuse*
118 Needle Gun
118 Pirate's Revenge*
118 Red Bishop
118 Schossberg*
118 Special Price*
118 Unfinished Symph*
117 Borodislew*
117 Danish*
117 Desert Stormer*
117 Golden Gear*
117 Halo America*
117 Jade Flush*
117 Kaldounevees
117 Laroche
117 Partipral
117 So Factual
117 Time Star
116 Beauchamp Hero
116 Boyce*
116 Caress*
116 Classy Mirage*
116 Cox Orange*
116 Dare And Go*
116 Darnay
116 Exchange*
116 Hasten To Add*
116 Interim*
116 Lit de Justice*
116 Marildo
116 Market Booster*
116 Northern Emerald*
116 Onceinabluemamoon*
116 Only Royale
116 Royal Chariot*
116 Signal Tap*
116 Silver Wizard*
116 Tossofthecoin*
116 Turk Passer*
116 Wandesta*
115 Bin Ajwaad
115 Celtic Arms*
115 Del Mar Dennis*
115 Desert Shot
115 Flag Down*
115 Friendly Lover*
115 Gunboat Diplomacy
115 Hollywood Wildcat*
115 Just Happy
115 La Confederation
115 Misil*
115 Nec Plus Ultra
115 Soviet Problem*
115 Tikkanen
115 Tuesday's Special
115 Twist Afleet*
115 Weekend Madness*
115 Wekiva Springs*
115 Windsharp

JOHN CROFTS

Racing & Stud Photography

European Horse-Racing Photo and Press Agency

P.O. Box 79, Newmarket CB8 8EA, Suffolk, England

England

France

Ireland

Germany

Conformation portraits

Racing Scenes

Our colour and black & white photo library of big race finishes, cantering and conformation portraits of important winners and comprehensive file of racing personality portraits goes back to 1980.

For all your press and advertising features

Tel. England : 0385 320320

Tel. France : 44 51 20 42

Fax France : 44 51 20 53

INDEX TO PHOTOGRAPHS

PORTRAITS & SNAPSHOTS

Desert Shot	5 b.g Green Desert Out of Shot (Shirley Heights)	*John Crofts*	277
Desert Style	3 b.c Green Desert Organza (High Top)	*Peter Mooney*	278
Didina	3 ch.f Nashwan Didicoy (Danzig)	*W. W. Rouch & Co*	282
Diffident	3 b.c Nureyev Shy Princess (Irish River)	*John Crofts*	285
Double Eclipse	3 b.c Ela-Mana-Mou Solac (Gay Lussac)	*Alec Russell*	299
Double Trigger	4 ch.c Ela-Mana-Mou Solac (Gay Lussac)	*John Crofts*	304
Fahal	3 b.c Silver Hawk By Land By Sea (Sauce Boat)	*John Crofts*	339
Fanjica	3 b.f Law Society Florie (Gay Mecene)	*John Crofts*	344
Flame of Athens	2 b.c Royal Academy Flame of Tara (Artaius)	*Caroline Norris*	356
Flemensfirth	3 b.c Alleged Etheldreda (Diesis)	*John Crofts*	360
Green Tune	4 ch.c Green Dancer Soundings (Mr Prospector)	*Bertrand*	405
Grey Shot	3 gr.g Sharrood Optaria (Song)	*John Crofts*	407
Halling	4 ch.c Diesis Dance Machine (Green Dancer)	*John Crofts*	415
Harayir	3 b.f Gulch Saffaanh (Shareef Dancer)	*John Crofts*	421
Hernando	5 b.h Niniski Whakilyric (Miswaki)	*John Crofts*	433
Hever Golf Rose	4 b.f Efisio Sweet Rosina (Sweet Revenge)	*John Crofts*	437
Humbel	3 b.c Theatrical Claxton's Slew (Seattle Slew)	*Peter Mooney*	451
Istidaad	3 b.c Chief's Crown Mazzei Mood (Roberto)	*Clare Williams*	469
Kahir Almaydan	2 b.c Distinctly North Kilfenora (Tribal Chief)	*Rex Coleman*	487
Kaldounevees	4 gr.c Kaldoun Safaroa (Satingo)	*John Crofts*	489
Kayvee	6 gr.g Kaldoun Secret Life (Elocutionist)	*Rex Coleman*	493
Lake Coniston	4 b.c Bluebird Persian Polly (Persian Bold)	*John Crofts*	519
Lammtarra	3 ch.c Nijinsky Snow Bride (Blushing Groom)	*John Crofts*	526
Larrocha	3 b.f Sadler's Wells Le Melody (Levmoss)	*John Crofts*	533
Lavinia Fontana	6 ch.m Sharpo Belle Origine (Exclusive Native)	*John Crofts*	537
Lord of Men	2 ch.c Groom Dancer Upper Strata (Shirley Heights)	*John Crofts*	555
Loup Solitaire	2 b.c Lear Fan Louveterie (Nureyev)	*Bertrand*	559
Luso	3 b.c Salse Lucayan Princess (High Line)	*John Crofts*	567
Mark of Esteem	2 b.c Darshaan Homage (Ajdal)	*Laurie Morton*	585
Matiara	3 b.f Bering Most Precious (Nureyev)	*John Crofts*	592
Millyant	5 ch.m Primo Dominie Jubilee Song (Song)	*Clare Williams*	609

Horse	Details	Artist	Page
Missed Flight	5 b.h Dominion Loveskate (Overskate)	*John Crofts*	617
Miss Tahiti	2 b.f Tirol Mini Luthe (Luthier)	*Bertrand*	623
Mons	2 b.c Deploy Morina (Lyphard)	*John Crofts*	632
Mr Martini	5 b.h Pennine Walk Arab Art (Artaius)	*John Crofts*	646
Muncie	3 b.f Sadler's Wells Martingale (Luthier)	*John Crofts*	654
Musetta	3 b.f Cadeaux Genereux Monaiya (Shareef Dancer)	*John Crofts*	656
Nagnagnag	3 b.f Red Sunset Rubina Park (Ashmore)	*John Crofts*	667
Najiya	2 b.f Nashwan The Perfect Life (Try My Best)	*Rex Coleman*	668
Needle Gun	5 b.h Sure Blade Lucayan Princess (High Line)	*John Crofts*	675
Nicolette	4 b.c Night Shift Nicoletta (Busted)	*John Crofts*	679
Nijo	4 b.g Top Ville Nibabu (Nishapour)	*John Crofts*	683
Noble Rose	4 b.f Caerleon Noble Lily (Vaguely Noble)	*John Crofts*	687
Oscar Schindler	3 ch.c Royal Academy Saraday (Northfields)	*Caroline Norris*	708
Pelder	5 b.h Be My Guest Sheer Audacity (Troy)	*John Crofts*	725
Pentire	3 b.c Be My Guest Gull Nook (Mill Reef)	*John Crofts*	733
Pipe Major	3 b.c Tirol Annsfield Lady (Red Sunset)	*Alec Russell*	749
Poliglote	3 b.c Sadler's Wells Alexandrie (Val de L'Orne)	*Bertrand*	757
Prince Arthur	3 b.c Fairy King Daniela Samuel (No Robbery)	*John Crofts*	773
Prince of Andros	5 b.h Al Nasr Her Radiance (Halo)	*John Crofts*	776
Pure Grain	3 b.f Polish Precedent Mill Line (Mill Reef)	*John Crofts*	788
Realities	5 ch.h Cozzene Alquizar (Star de Naskra)	*Rex Coleman*	803
Red Bishop	7 b.h Silver Hawk La Rouquine (Silly Season)	*John Crofts*	806
Ridgewood Pearl	3 ch.f Indian Ridge Ben's Pearl (Tap On Wood)	*John Crofts*	820
Rio Duvida	2 ch.c Salse Fluctuate (Sharpen Up)	*John Crofts*	823
Russian Snows	3 b.f Sadler's Wells Arctique Royale (Royal And Regal)	*Caroline Norris*	849
Ruznama	2 ch.f Forty Niner Last Feather (Vaguely Noble)	*Fiona Vigors*	851
Saxon Maid	4 b.f Sadler's Wells Britannia's Rule (Blakeney)	*John Crofts*	867
Sayyedati	5 b.m Shadeed Dubian (High Line)	*John Crofts*	869
Shahid	3 b.c Green Desert Roussalka (Habitat)	*Rex Coleman*	885
Shambo	8 b.h Lafontaine Lucky Appeal (Star Appeal)	*John Crofts*	886
Singspiel	3 b.c In The Wings Glorious Song (Halo)	*John Crofts*	908

Smolensk (USA)	3 b.f Danzig Blush With Pride (Blushing Groom)	*John Crofts*	916
So Factual	5 br.h Known Fact Sookera (Roberto)	*John Crofts*	921
Soviet Line	5 b.g Soviet Star Shore Line (High Line)	*John Crofts*	932
Spectrum	3 b.c Rainbow Quest River Dancer (Irish River)	*John Crofts*	937
Sunshack	4 b.c Rainbow Quest Suntrap (Roberto)	*Bertrand*	962
Tagula	2 b.c Taufan Twin Island (Standaan)	*John Crofts*	978
Tamure	3 b.c Sadler's Wells Three Tails (Blakeney)	*John Crofts*	983
Timarida	3 gr.f Kalaglow Triumphant (Track Spare)	*Caroline Norris*	1005
Torrential	3 b.c Gulch Killaloe (Dr Fager)	*John Crofts*	1018
Valley of Gold	3 b.f Shirley Heights Lustre (Halo)	*John Crofts*	1039
Vettori	3 b.c Machiavellian Air Distingue (Sir Ivor)	*John Crofts*	1045
Warning Shadows	3 ch.f Cadeaux Genereux Silent Movie (Shirley Heights)	*John Crofts*	1055
Warning Star	3 b.f Warning Blade of Grass (Kris)	*Fiona Vigors*	1056
Winged Love	3 b.c In The Wings J'Ai Deux Amours (Top Ville)	*Bertrand*	1076
Young Ern	5 b.h Efisio Stardyn (Star Appeal)	*John Crofts*	1086
Zilzal Zamaan	4 b.c Zilzal Iva Reputation (Sir Ivor)	*John Crofts*	1092

RACE PHOTOGRAPHS

Race and Meeting	*Copyright*	*Page*
Advanced Micro Devices Sprint Stakes (Sandown)	*John Crofts*	161
Airlie/Coolmore Irish One Thousand Guineas (the Curragh)	*Caroline Norris*	817
Anglo African Holdings Autumn Stakes (Ascot)	*George Selwyn*	108
Anheuser Busch Curragh Cup (the Curragh)	*John Crofts*	1049
Aral-Pokal (Gelsenkirchen)	*Frank Nolting*	1073
Ascot Stakes (Handicap) (Royal Ascot)	*George Selwyn*	423
Asko Appliances Zetland Stakes (Newmarket)	*John Crofts*	384
Aston Upthorpe Yorkshire Oaks (York)	*George Selwyn*	787
Baring International Darley Stakes (Newmarket)	*John Crofts*	814
Bass Wulfrun Stakes (Wolverhampton)	*Les Hurley Photography*	775
Bessborough Stakes (Handicap) (Royal Ascot)	*John Crofts*	927
BNFL International Dee Stakes (Chester)	*Alec Russell*	730
Bonusprint Mill Reef Stakes (Newbury)	*Ed Byrne*	487
Bonusprint September Stakes (Kempton)	*W. Everitt*	162
Bradford & Bingley Rated Stakes (Handicap) (York)	*John Crofts*	171
Breeders' Cup Mile (Belmont Park)	*George Selwyn*	819
Britannia Stakes (Handicap) (Royal Ascot)	*John Crofts*	596
Budweiser Irish Derby (the Curragh)	*John Crofts*	1075
Challenge Stakes (Newmarket)	*John Crofts*	420
Charterhouse Conditions Stakes (Sandown)	*John Crofts*	143
Child & Co. Superlative Stakes (Newmarket)	*John Crofts*	44
Computer Timeform Nursery Handicap (Pontefract)	*Alec Russell*	279
Coral-Eclipse Stakes (Sandown)	*George Selwyn*	413
Coral Handicap (Haydock)	*Alec Russell*	994
Coral Sprint Trophy (Handicap) (York)	*Alec Russell*	297

Standing at Woodland Stud

INCHINOR

chesnut 1990 by AHONOORA - INCHMURRIN by Lomond

A Leading 7-8F Performer by AHONOORA

WON Hungerford Stakes **Gr.3**, 7f
WON Criterion Stakes **Gr.3**, 7f **TRACK RECORD**
WON Greenham Stakes **Gr.3**, 7f
WON Personnel Selection Stakes, 7f by 2 lengths
WON EBF Park Lodge Stakes, 6f on his debut
2nd Dewhurst Stakes **Gr.1**, 7f to Champion 2yo **ZAFONIC**
3rd Sussex Stakes **Gr.1**, 8f to **BIGSTONE** and **SAYYEDATI**

Fee: £3,000 October 1st NFNF

First Yearlings 1996

Woodland Stud, Snailwell Road, Newmarket, Suffolk.
Telephone: Newmarket 01638 - 663081. Fax: 01638 - 663036.

Enquiries to:

LONDON THOROUGHBRED SERVICES LTD.,
Biddlesgate Farm, Nr Cranborne, Dorset BH21 5RS.
Telephone: 01725 - 517711. Fax: 01725 - 517833.

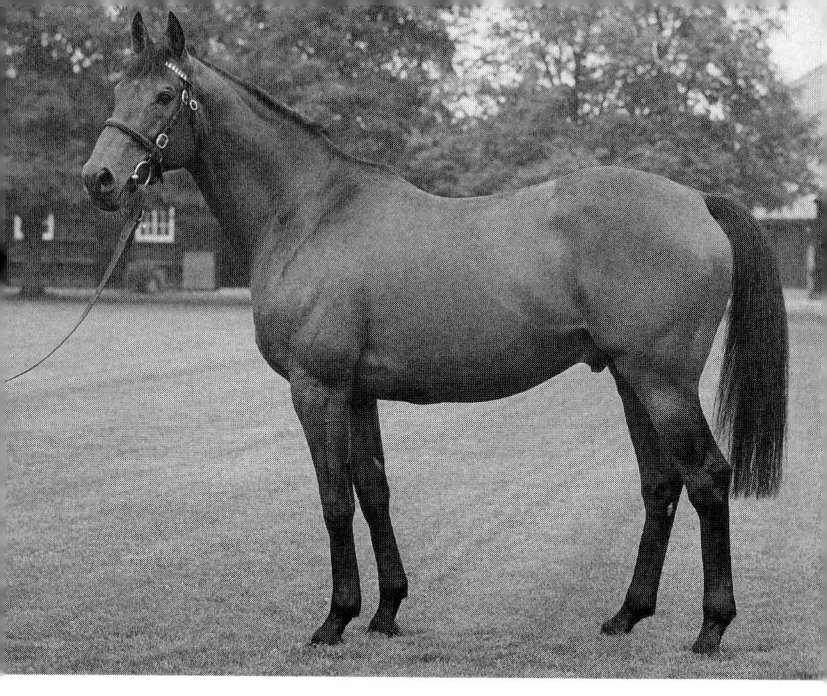

Standing at Barleythorpe Stud

OLD VIC

bay 1986 by SADLER'S WELLS - COCKADE by Derring-Do

Champion European 3yo in 1989

58% Winners to Runners from his First Crop

Fee: £3,500 October 1st NFNF

Standing at Barleythorpe Stud, Oakham, Leicestershire LE15 7EE.

Enquiries to:
LONDON THOROUGHBRED SERVICES LTD.,
Biddlesgate Farm, Nr Cranborne, Dorset BH21 5RS.
Telephone: 01725 - 517711. Fax: 01725 - 517833.

Standing at Plantation Stud

SLIP ANCHOR

bay 1982 by SHIRLEY HEIGHTS - SAYONARA by Birkhahn

Champion European 3-year-old in 1985

Champion British Based Sire in 1992

Sire of 6 individual Group/Stakes Winners in 1995

Fertility average to date over 90%

Fee: £8,000 October 1st NFNF

Leslie Harrison, Plantation Stud, Exning, Newmarket, Suffolk CB8 7LJ.
Telephone: 01638 - 577341. Fax: 01638 - 578474.

Enquiries to:

LONDON THOROUGHBRED SERVICES LTD.,
Biddlesgate Farm, Nr Cranborne, Dorset BH21 5RS.
Telephone: 01725 - 517711. Fax: 01725 - 517833.

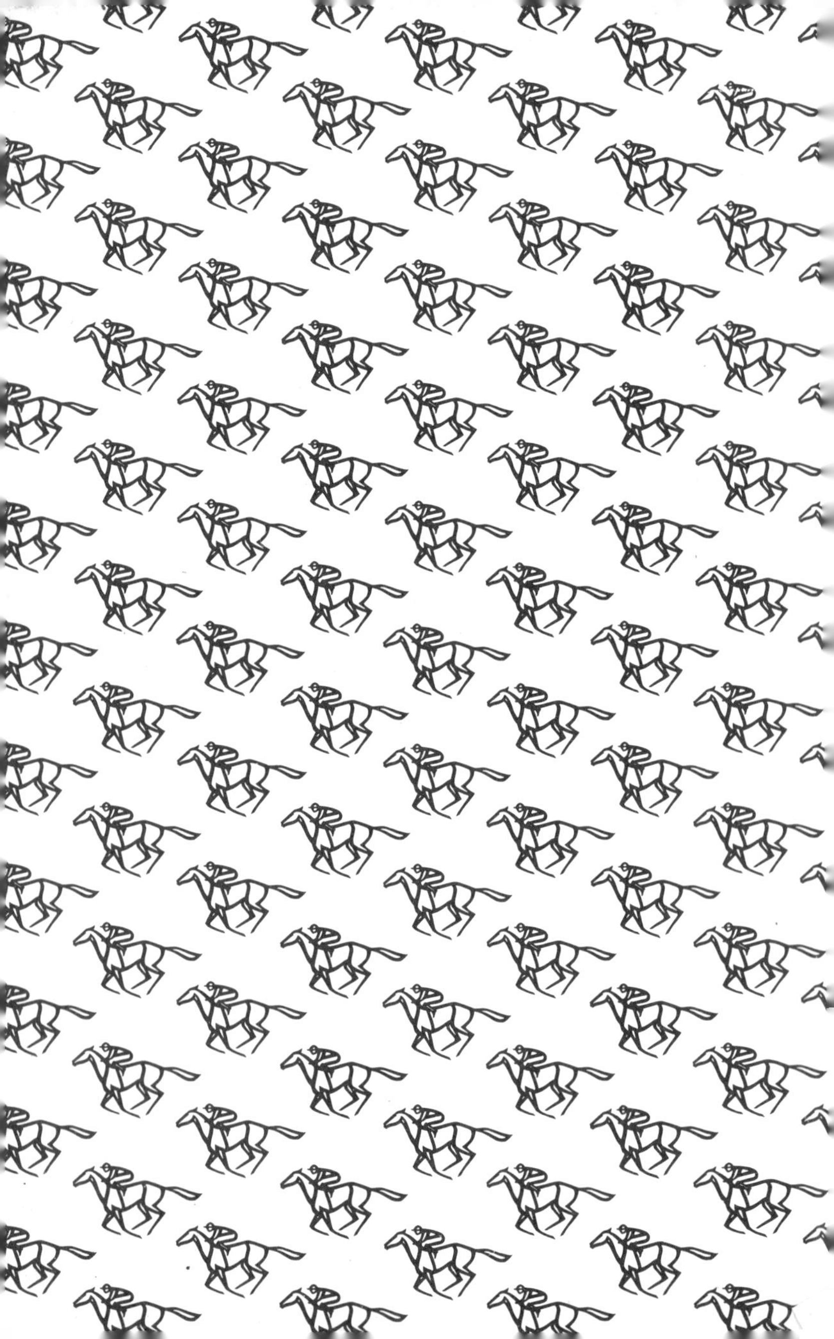